ENCYCLOPEDIA OF WORLD ART

Vol. XIII
SHAMANISM – TERROR AND THE MALIGN

ENCICLOPEDIA
UNIVERSALE
DELL'ARTE

Sotto gli auspici della Fondazione Giorgio Cini

ISTITUTO PER LA COLLABORAZIONE CULTURALE
VENEZIA-ROMA

ENCYCLOPEDIA
OF
WORLD ART

McGRAW-HILL BOOK COMPANY

NEW YORK, TORONTO, LONDON

ENCYCLOPEDIA OF WORLD ART: VOLUME XIII

Paper for plates and text supplied by Cartiere Burgo, Turin — Engraving by Zincotipia Altimani,
Milan — Black-and-white and color plates printed by Tipocolor, Florence — Text printed
by "L'Impronta," Florence — Binding by Stabilimento Stianti, San Casciano Val di Pesa,
Florence — Book cloth supplied by G. Pasini e C., Milan

Printed in Italy

Library of Congress Catalog Card Number 59-13433
19470

INTERNATIONAL COUNCIL OF SCHOLARS

ABBREVIATIONS

Museums, Galleries, Libraries, and Other Institutions

Antikensamml.	— Antikensammlungen
Antiq.	— Antiquarium
Bib. Nat.	— Bibliothèque Nationale
Bib. Naz.	— Biblioteca Nazionale
Brera	— Pinacoteca di Brera
Br. Mus.	— British Museum
Cab. Méd.	— Cabinet des Médailles (Paris, Bibliothèque Nationale)
Cleve. Mus.	— Cleveland Museum
Conserv.	— Palazzo dei Conservatori
Gall. Arte Mod.	— Galleria d'Arte Moderna
IsMEO	— Istituto Italiano per il Medio ed Estremo Oriente
Kunstgewerbemus.	— Kunstgewerbemuseum
Kunsthist. Mus.	— Kunsthistorisches Museum
Louvre	— Musée du Louvre
Medagl.	— Medagliere
Met. Mus.	— Metropolitan Museum
Mus. Ant.	— Museo di Antichità
Mus. Arch.	— Museo Archeologico
Mus. B. A.	— Musée des Beaux-Arts
Mus. Cap.	— Musei Capitolini, Capitoline Museums
Mus. Civ.	— Museo Civico
Mus. Com.	— Museo Comunale
Mus. Etn.	— Museo Etnologico
Mus. Naz.	— Museo Nazionale
Nat. Gall.	— National Gallery
Öst. Gal.	— Österreichische Galerie
Pin. Naz.	— Pinacoteca Nazionale
Prado	— Museo del Prado
Rijksmus.	— Rijksmuseum
Samml.	— Sammlung
Staat. Mus.	— Staatliche Museen
Staatsbib.	— Staatsbibliothek
Städt. Mus.	— Städtisches Museum
Tate Gall.	— Tate Gallery
Uffizi	— Uffizi Gallery
Vat. Mus.	— Vatican Museums
Vict. and Alb.	— Victoria and Albert Museum
Villa Giulia	— Museo di Villa Giulia

Reviews and Miscellanies

AAE	— Archivio per la Antropologia e la Etnologia, Florence
AAnz	— Archäologischer Anzeiger, Berlin
AAs	— Artibus Asiae, Ascona, Switzerland
AAV	— Archivo de Arte Valenciano, Valencia
AB	— Art Bulletin, New York
AbhAkMünchen	— Abhandlungen der Bayerischen Akademie der Wissenschaften, Munich
AbhPreussAk	— Abhandlungen der preussischen Akademie der Wissenschaften, Berlin; after 1945, Abhandlungen der Deutschen Akademie der Wissenschaften zu Berlin, Berlin
ABIA	— Annual Bibliography of Indian Archaeology, Leiden
ABMAB	— Anales y Boletín de los Museos de Arte de Barcelona
ABME	— Ἀρχεῖον τῶν Βυζαντινῶν Μνημείων τῆς Ἑλλάδος, Athens

AC	— Archeologia Classica, Rome
ACCV	— Anales del Centro de Cultura Valenciana, Valencia
ActaA	— Acta Archaeologica, Copenhagen
ActaO	— Acta Orientalia, Leiden, The Hague
AD	— Antike Denkmäler, Deutsches Archäologisches Institut, Berlin, Leipzig
AE	— Arte Español, Madrid
AEA	— Archivo Español de Arqueología, Madrid
AEAA	— Archivo Español de Arte y Arqueología, Madrid
AEArte	— Archivio Español de Arte, Madrid
AErt	— Archaeologiai Értesitö, Budapest
AfA	— Archiv für Anthropologie, Brunswick
AfO	— Archiv für Orientforschung, Berlin
AfrIt	— Africa Italiana, Bergamo
AGS	— American Guide Series, U.S. Federal Writers' Project, Works Progress Administration, Washington, D.C., 1935-41
AIEC	— Anuari de l'Institut d'Estudies Catalans, Barcelona
AIEG	— Anales del Instituto de Estudios Gerundenses, Gerona
AJA	— American Journal of Archaeology, Baltimore
AM	— Mitteilungen des deutschen archäologischen Instituts, Athenische Abteilung, Athens, Stuttgart
AmA	— American Anthropologist, Menasha, Wis.
AmAnt	— American Antiquity, Menasha, Wis.
AN	— Art News, New York
AnnInst	— Annali dell'Instituto di Corrispondenza Archeologica, Rome
AnnSAntEg	— Annales du Service des Antiquités de l'Egypte, Cairo
AntC	— L'Antiquité Classique, Louvain
AntJ	— The Antiquaries Journal, London
AnzAlt	— Anzeiger für die Altertumswissenschaft, Innsbruck, Vienna
AnzÖAk	— Anzeiger der Österreichischen Akademie der Wissenschaften, Vienna
APAmM	— Anthropological Papers of the American Museum of Natural History, New York
AQ	— Art Quarterly, Detroit
ArndtBr	— P. Arndt, F. Bruckmann, Griechische und römische Porträts, Munich, 1891 ff.
ARSI	— Annual Report of the Smithsonian Institution, Bureau of Ethnology, Washington, D.C.
ArtiFig	— Arti Figurative, Rome
ASAtene	— Annuario della Scuola Archeologica Italiana di Atene, Bergamo
ASI	— Archivio Storico Italiano, Florence
ASWI	— Archaeological Survey of Western India, Hyderabad
AttiCongrStAMed	— Atti dei Congressi di Studi dell'Arte dell'Alto Medioevo
AttiDeSPa	— Atti e Memorie della Deputazione di Storia Patria
AttiPontAcc	— Atti della Pontificia Accademia Romana di Archeologia, Rome
Atti3StArch	— Atti del III Convegno Nazionale di Storia dell'Architettura, Rome, 1938
Atti5StArch	— Atti del V Convegno Nazionale di Storia dell'Architettura, Florence, 1957

AZ — Archäologische Zeitung, Berlin

BA — Baessler Archiv, Leipzig, Berlin

BABsch — Bulletin van de Vereeniging tot bevordering der kennis van de antieke Beschaving, The Hague

BAC — Bulletin du Comité des Travaux Historiques et Scientifiques, Section d'Archéologie, Paris

BAcBelg — Bulletin de l'Académie Royale de Belgique, Cl. des Lettres, Brussels

BACr — Bollettino di Archeologia Cristiana, Rome

BAEB — Bureau of American Ethnology, Bulletins, Washington, D.C.

BAER — Bureau of American Ethnology, Reports, Washington, D.C.

BAFr — Bulletin de la Société Nationale des Antiquaires de France, Paris

BAmSOR — Bulletin of the American Schools of Oriental Research, South Hadley, Mass.

BArte — Bollettino d'Arte del Ministero della Pubblica Istruzione, Rome

BAT — Boletín Arqueológico Tarragona

BBMP — Boletín de la Biblioteca Menéndez Pelayo, Santander

BByzI — The Bulletin of the Byzantine Institute, Paris

BCH — Bulletin de Correspondance Hellénique, Paris

BCom — Bullettino della Commissione Archeologica Comunale, Rome

BCPMB — Boletín de la Comision Provincial de Monumentos de Burgos

BCPML — Boletín de la Comision Provincial de Monumentos de Lugo

BCPMO — Boletín de la Comision Provincial de Monumentos de Orense

Beazley, ABV — J. D. Beazley, Attic Black-figure Vase-painters, Oxford, 1956

Beazley, ARV — J. D. Beazley, Attic Red-figure Vase-painters, Oxford, 1942

Beazley, EVP — J. D. Beazley, Etruscan Vase-painting, Oxford, 1947

Beazley, VA — J. D. Beazley, Attic Red-figured Vases in American Museums, Cambridge, 1918

Beazley, VRS — J. D. Beazley, Attische Vasenmaler des rotfigurigen Stils, Tübingen, 1925

BEFEO — Bulletin de l'Ecole Française d'Extrême-Orient, Hanoi, Saigon, Paris

BerlNZ — Berliner Numismatische Zeitschrift, Berlin

Bernoulli, GI — J. J. Bernoulli, Griechische Ikonographie, Munich, 1901

Bernoulli, RI — J. J. Bernoulli, Römische Ikonographie, I, Stuttgart, 1882; II, 1, Berlin, Stuttgart, 1886; II, 2, Stuttgart, Berlin, Leipzig, 1891; II, 3, Stuttgart, Berlin, Leipzig, 1894

BHAcRoum — Bulletin Historique, Académie Roumaine, Bucharest

BICR — Bollettino dell'Istituto Centrale del Restauro, Rome

BIE — Bulletin de l'Institut de l'Egypte, Cairo

BIFAN — Bulletin de l'Institut Français d'Afrique Noire, Dakar

BIFAO — Bulletin de l'Institut Français d'Archéologie Orientale, Cairo

BIFG — Boletín de la Institución Fernán González, Burgos

BInst — Bullettino dell'Instituto di Corrispondenza Archeologica, Rome

BJ — Bonner Jahrbücher, Bonn, Darmstadt

BM — Burlington Magazine, London

BMBeyrouth — Bulletin du Musée de Beyrouth, Beirut

BMC — British Museum, Catalogue of Greek Coins, London

BMCEmp — H. Mattingly, Coins of the Roman Empire in the British Museum, London

BMFA — Museum of Fine Arts, Bulletin, Boston

BMFEA — Museum of Far-Eastern Antiquities, Bulletin, Stockholm

BMImp — Bullettino del Museo dell'Impero, Rome

BMMA — Bulletin of the Metropolitan Museum of Art, New York

BMN — Boletín Monumentos Navarra

BMQ — The British Museum Quarterly, London

BNedOud — Bulletin van de Koninklijke Nederlandse Oudheidkundige Bond, Leiden

BPI — Bullettino di Paletnologia Italiana, Rome

BRA — Boletín de la Real Academia de Ciencias, Bellas Letras y Nobles Artes de Córdoba, Córdoba

BRABASF — Boletín de la Real Academia de Bellas Artes de San Fernando, Madrid

BRABLB — Boletín de la Real Academia de Buenas Letras de Barcelona

BRAH — Boletín de la Real Academia de la Historia, Madrid

BrBr — H. Brunn, F. Bruckmann, Denkmäler griechischer und römischer Skulptur, Munich

Brunn, GGK — H. Brunn, Geschichte der griechischen Künstler, 2d ed., Stuttgart, 1889

Brunn, GK — H. Brunn, Griechische Kunstgeschichte, Munich, I, 1893; II, 1897

BSA — Annual of the British School at Athens, London

BSCC — Boletín de la Sociedad Castellonense de Cultura, Castellón de la Plana

BSCE — Boletín de la Sociedad Castellana de Excursiones, Valladolid

BSEAAV — Boletín del Seminario de Estudios de Arte y Arqueología, Universidad de Valladolid

BSEE — Boletín de la Sociedad Española de Excursiones, Madrid

BSEI — Bulletin de la Société des Etudes Indochinoises, Saigon

BSOAS — Bulletin of the School of Oriental and African Studies, London

BSPF — Bulletin de la Société Préhistorique Française, Paris

BSR — Papers of the British School at Rome, London

Cabrol-Leclercq — F. Cabrol, H. Leclercq, Dictionnaire d'archéologie chrétienne et de liturgie, Paris, 1907

CAF — Congrès Archéologique de France, Paris, 1841–1935

CahA — Cahiers Archéologiques, Fin de l'Antiquité et Moyen-Age, Paris

CahArt — Cahiers d'art, Paris

CAJ — Central Asiatic Journal, Wiesbaden

CAUG — Cuadernos de Arte de la Universidad de Granada

CEFEO — Cahiers de l'Ecole Française d'Extrême-Orient, Paris

CEG — Cuadernos de Estudios Gallegos, Santiago de Compostela

CIE — Corpus Inscriptionum Etruscarum, Lipsiae

CIG — Corpus Inscriptionum Graecarum, Berolini

CIL — Corpus Inscriptionum Latinarum, Berolini

CIS — Corpus Inscriptionum Semiticarum, Parisiis

Coh — H. Cohen, Description historique des Monnaies frappées sous l'Empire Romain, Paris

Collignon, SG — M. Collignon, Histoire de la sculpture grecque, Paris, I, 1892; II, 1897

Comm — Commentari, Florence, Rome

Cr — La Critica, Bari

CRAI — Comptes Rendus de l'Académie des Inscriptions et Belles-Lettres, Paris

CrArte — La Critica d'Arte, Florence

CVA — Corpus Vasorum Antiquorum

DA — N. Daremberg, N. Saglio, Dictionnaire des antiquités grecques et romaines, Paris, 1877–1912

Dehio, I-V — G. Dehio, Handbuch der deutschen Kunstdenkmäler, Berlin, I, Mitteldeutschland, 1927; II, Nordostdeutschland, 1926; III, Süddeutschland, 1933; IV, Südwestdeutschland, 1933; V, Nordwestdeutschland, 1928

Dehio, DtK — G. Dehio, Geschichte der deutschen Kunst, 8 vols., Berlin, 1930–34

Dehio-VonBezold — G. Dehio, G. von Bezold, Die kirchliche Baukunst des Abendlandes, Stuttgart, 1892–1901

DissPontAcc — Dissertazioni della Pontificia Accademia Romana di Archeologia, Rome

EA — Photographische Einzelaufnahmen, Munich, 1893 ff.

EAA — Enciclopedia dell'Arte Antica, Rome, I, 1958; II, 1959; III, 1960; IV, 1961

EArt — Eastern Art, London

EB — Encyclopaedia Britannica

'ΕΕΒΣ — Ἐπετερὶς Ἑταιρεία Βυζαντινῶν Σπουδῶν Athens

'Εφημ — Ἀρχαιολογικὴ Ἐφημερίς, Athens

EI	— Enciclopedia Italiana, Rome, 1929 ff.
EphDR	— Ephemeris Dacoromana, Rome
'Εργον	— Τὸ 'ἐργον τῆς ἀρχαιολογικῆς ἑταιρείας, ed. A. K. Orlandos, Athens
ES	— Estudios Segovianos, Segovia
ESA	— Eurasia Septentrionalis Antiqua, Helsinki
Espér	— E. Espérandieu, R. Lantier, Recueil général des Bas-Reliefs de la Gaule Romaine, Paris
EUC	— Estudis Universitaris Catalans, Barcelona
FA	— Fasti Archaeologici, Florence
FD	— Fouilles de Delphes, Paris
Friedländer	— Max Friedländer, Altniederländische Malerei, Berlin, 1924–37
Furtwängler, AG	— A. Furtwängler, Antiken Gemmen, Leipzig, Berlin, 1900
Furtwängler, BG	— A. Furtwängler, Beschreibung der Glyptothek König Ludwig I zu München, Munich, 1900
Furtwängler, KlSchr	— A. Furtwängler, Kleine Schriften, Munich, 1912
Furtwängler, MP	— A. Furtwängler, Masterpieces of Greek Sculpture, London, 1895
Furtwängler, MW	— A. Furtwängler, Meisterwerke der griechischen Plastik, Leipzig, Berlin, 1893
Furtwängler Reichhold	— A. Furtwängler, K. Reichhold, Griechische Vasenmalerei, Munich
FWP	— U.S. Federal Writers' Project, Works Progress Administration, Washington, D.C., 1935–1941
GBA	— Gazette des Beaux-Arts, Paris
GJ	— The Geographical Journal, London
HA	— Handbuch der Archäologie im Rahmen des Handbuchs der Altertumswissenschaft . . . , herausgegeben von Walter Otto, Munich, 1939–53
HABS	— Historic American Buildings Survey, U.S. Library of Congress, Washington, D.C.
HBr	— P. Herrmann, F. Bruckmann, Denkmäler der Malerei des Altertums, Munich, 1907
Helbig-Amelung	— W. Helbig, W. Amelung, E. Reisch, F. Weege, Führer durch die öffentlichen Sammlungen klassischer Altertümer in Rom, Leipzig, 1912–13
HIPBC	— A Handbook for Travellers in India, Pakistan, Burma and Ceylon, London, 1955
HJAS	— Harvard Journal of Asiatic Studies, Cambridge, Mass.
Hoppin, Bf	— J. C. Hoppin, A Handbook of Greek Black-figured Vases with a Chapter on the Red-figured Southern Italian Vases, Paris, 1924
Hoppin, Rf	— J. C. Hoppin, A Handbook of Attic Red-figured Vases Signed by or Attributed to the Various Masters of the Sixth and Fifth Centuries B.C., Cambridge, 1919
HSAI	— J. H. Steward, ed., Handbook of South American Indians, 6 vols., Bureau of American Ethnology, Bull. 143, Washington, D.C., 1946–50
IAE	— Internationales Archiv für Ethnographie, Leiden
IBAI	— Bulletin de l'Institut Archéologique Bulgare, Sofia
IFAN	— Institut Français Afrique Noire, Dakar
IG	— Inscriptiones Graecae, Berolini
ILN	— Illustrated London News, London
IPEK	— Ipek, Jahrbuch für prähistorische und ethnographische Kunst, Berlin
ITTM	— Instituto Tello Tellez de Meneses, Palencia
JA	— Journal Asiatique, Paris
JAF	— Journal of American Folklore, Lancaster, Pa.
JAOS	— Journal of the American Oriental Society, Baltimore
JAS	— Journal of the African Society, London
JBORS	— Journal of the Bihar and Orissa Research Society, Patna, India
JdI	— Jahrbuch des deutschen archäologischen Instituts, Berlin
JEA	— Journal of Egyptian Archaeology, London
JhbKhSammlWien	— Jahrbuch der kunsthistorischen Sammlungen in Wien, Vienna
JhbPreussKSamml	— Jahrbuch der preussischen Kunstsammlungen, Berlin
JHS	— Journal of Hellenic Studies, London
JIAI	— Journal of Indian Art and Industry, London

JIAN	— Journal International d'Archéologie Numismatique, Athens
JISOA	— Journal of the India Society of Oriental Art, Calcutta
JNES	— Journal of Near Eastern Studies, Chicago
JPS	— Journal of the Polynesian Society, Wellington, New Zealand
JRAI	— Journal of the Royal Anthropological Institute of Great Britain and Ireland, London
JRAS	— Journal of the Royal Asiatic Society, London
JRS	— Journal of Roman Studies, London
JS	— Journal des Savants, Paris
JSA	— Journal de la Société des Africanistes, Paris
JSAH	— Journal of the Society of Architectural Historians, Charlottesville, Va.
JSAm	— Journal de la Société des Américanistes, Paris
JSO	— Journal de la Société des Océanistes, Paris
KbNed	— Kunstreisboek voor Nederland, Amsterdam, 1960
Klein, GrK	— W. Klein, Geschichte der griechischen Kunst, Leipzig, 1904–07
KS	— Communications on the Reports and Field Research of the Institute of Material Culture, Moscow, Leningrad
Lippold, GP	— G. Lippold, Die griechische Plastik (W. Otto, Handbuch der Archäologie, II, 1), Munich, 1950
Löwy, IGB	— E. Löwy, Inschriften griechischer Bildhauer, Leipzig, 1885
MAAccIt	— Monumenti Antichi dell'Accademia d'Italia, Milan
MAARome	— Memoirs of the American Academy in Rome, Rome, New York
MAF	— Mémoires de la Société Nationale des Antiquaires de France, Paris
MAGWien	— Mitteilungen der anthropologischen Gesellschaft in Wien, Vienna
Mâle, I	— E. Mâle, L'art religieux du XII° siècle en France, Paris, 1928
Mâle, II	— E. Mâle, L'art religieux du XIII° siècle en France, Paris, 1925
Mâle, III	— E. Mâle, L'art religieux de la fin du moyen-âge en France, Paris, 1925
Mâle, IV	— E. Mâle, L'art religieux après le Concile de Trente, Paris, 1932
MALinc	— Monumenti Antichi dell'Accademia dei Lincei, Milan, Rome
Mattingly-Sydenham	— H. Mattingly, E. Sydenham, C. H. V. Sutherland, The Roman Imperial Coinage, London
MdI	— Mitteilungen des deutschen archäologischen Instituts, Munich
MdIK	— Mitteilungen des deutschen Instituts für ägyptische Altertumskunde in Kairo, Wiesbaden
Mél	— Mélanges d'Archéologie et d'Histoire (Ecole Française de Rome), Paris
Mem. Junta Sup. Exc.	— Memoria de la Junta Superior de Excavaciones y Antigüedades, Madrid
MemLinc	— Memorie dell'Accademia dei Lincei, Rome
MGH	— Monumenta Germaniae Historica, Berlin
MIA	— Material and Research in Archaeology of the U.S.S.R., Moscow, Leningrad
Michel	— A. Michel, Histoire de l'art depuis les premiers temps chrétiens jusqu'à nos jours, Paris, 1905–29
MInst	— Monumenti dell'Instituto di Corrispondenza Archeologica, Rome
MLJ	— Modern Language Journal, St. Louis, Mo.
MnbKw	— Monatsberichte über Kunstwissenschaft
MPA	— Monumenti della pittura antica scoperti in Italia, Rome
MPiot	— Fondation Eugène Piot, Monuments et Mémoires, Paris
MPontAcc	— Memorie della Pontificia Accademia Romana di Archeologia, Rome
NBACr	— Nuovo Bullettino di Archeologia Cristiana, Rome
NChr	— Numismatic Chronicle and Journal of the Royal Numismatic Society, London
NedKhJb	— Nederlandsch Kunsthistorisch Jaarboek, 1945ff.
NedMon	— De Nederlandse Monumenten van Geschiedenis en Kunst, 1911 ff.
NIFAN	— Notes de l'Institut Français d'Afrique Noire, Dakar

NSc	— Notizie degli Scavi di Antichità, Rome
OAZ	— Ostasiatische Zeitschrift, Vienna
OIP	— Oriental Institute Publications, Chicago
ÖJh	— Jahreshefte des Österreichischen archäologischen Instituts, Vienna
ÖKT	— Österreichische Kunsttopographie, Vienna
OMLeiden	— Oudheidkundige Mededeelingen van het Rijksmuseum van Oudheten te Leiden, Leiden
OpA	— Opuscola Archaeologica, Lund
OTNE	— Old Time New England; the Bulletin of the Society for the Preservation of New England Antiquities, Boston, Massachusetts, I, 1910
OudJb	— Oudheidkundig Jaarboek, Leiden
Overbeck, SQ	— J. Overbeck, Die antiken Schriftquellen zur Geschichte der bildenden Künste bei den Griechen, Leipzig, 1868; reprint, Hildesheim, 1958
Oxy. Pap.	— The Oxyrhynchus Papyri, by B. P. Grenfell, A. S. Hunt, H. I. Bell, et al., eds., London, 1898 ff.
ΠΑΕ	— Πρακτικά τῆς ἐν Ἀθήναις Ἀρχαιολογικῆς Ἑταιρίας, Athens
PEQ	— Palestine Exploration Quarterly, London
Perrot-Chipiez	— G. Perrot, C. Chipiez, Histoire de l'art dans l'Antiquité, Paris, I, 1882; II, 1884; III, 1885; IV, 1887; V, 1890; VI, 1894; VII, 1898; VIII, 1903; IX, 1911
Pfuhl	— E. Pfuhl, Malerei und Zeichnung der Griechen, Munich, 1923
PG	— J. P. Migne, Patrologiae cursus completus, Series Graeca, 162 vols., with Latin trans., Paris, 1857–66.
Picard	— C. Picard, Manuel d'Archéologie, La Sculpture, Paris, I, 1935; II, 1939; III, 1948; IV, 1, 1954
PL	— J. P. Migne, Patrologiae cursus completus, Series Latina, 221 vols., Paris, 1844–64
PM	— B. Porter and R. L. B. Moss, Topographical Bibliography of Ancient Egyptian Hieroglyphic Texts, Reliefs and Paintings, 7 vols., Oxford, 1927–51, 2d ed., 1960 ff.
Porter	— A. Kingsley Porter, Romanesque Sculpture of the Pilgrimage Roads, Boston, 1923
Post	— Charles Post, A History of Spanish Painting, 10 vols., Cambridge, Mass., 1930 ff.
ProcPrSoc	— Proceedings of the Prehistoric Society, Cambridge
PSI	— Pubblicazioni della Società Italiana per la ricerca dei papiri greci e latini in Egitto, Florence, 1912 ff.
RA	— Revue Archéologique, Paris
RAA	— Revue des Arts Asiatiques, Paris
RAAB	— Revista de la Asociacion Artístico-Arqueológica Barcelonesa, Barcelona
RABM	— Revista de Archivos, Bibliotecas y Museos, Madrid
RACr	— Rivista di Archeologia Cristiana, Rome
RArte	— Rivista d'Arte, Florence
RArts	— Revue des arts, Paris
RBib	— Revue Biblique, Paris
RCHS	— Records of the Columbia Historical Society, Washington, D.C., I, 1897
RE	— A. Pauly, G. Wissowa, Real-Encyclopädie der classischen Altertumswissenschaft, Stuttgart, 1894 ff.
REA	— Revue des Etudes Anciennes, Bordeaux
REByz	— Revue des Etudes Byzantines, Paris
REE	— Revista des Estudios Extremesios, Badajoz
REG	— Revue des Etudes Grecques, Paris
Reinach, RP	— S. Reinach, Répertoire des Peintures Grecques et Romaines, Paris, 1922
Reinach, RR	— S. Reinach, Répertoire des Reliefs Grecs et Romains, Paris, I, 1909; II and III, 1912
Reinach, RS	— S. Reinach, Répertoire de la Statuaire Grecque et Romaine, Paris, I, 1897; II, 1, 1897; II, 2, 1898; III, 1904; IV, 1910
Reinach, RV	— S. Reinach, Répertoire des Vases peints, grecs et étrusques, Paris, I, 1899; II, 1900
REL	— Revue des Etudes Latines, Paris
RendAccIt	— Rendiconti della R. Accademia d'Italia, Rome
RendLinc	— Rendiconti dell'Accademia dei Lincei, Rome
RendNapoli	— Rendiconti dell'Accademia di Archeologia di Napoli, Naples
RendPontAcc	— Rendiconti della Pontificia Accademia Romana di Archeologia, Rome
RepfKw	— Repertorium für Kunstwissenschaft, Berlin, Stuttgart
REthn	— Revue d'Ethnographie, Paris
RhMus	— Rheinisches Museum für Philologie, Frankfort on the Main
RIASA	— Rivista dell'Istituto Nazionale d'Archeologia e Storia dell'Arte, Rome
RIE	— Revista de Ideas Estéticas, Madrid
RIN	— Rivista Italiana di Numismatica, Rome
RlDKg	— Reallexicon zur deutschen Kunstgeschichte, Stuttgart, 1937 ff.
RLV	— M. Ebert, Real-Lexicon der Vorgeschichte, Berlin, 1924–32
RM	— Mitteilungen des deutschen archäologischen Instituts, Römische Abteilung, Berlin
RN	— Revue Numismatique, Paris
RNA	— Revista Nacional de Arquitectura, Madrid
Robert, SR	— C. Robert, Die antiken Sarkophag-Reliefs, Berlin, 1890 ff.
Roscher	— W. H. Roscher, Ausführliches Lexikon der griechischen und römischen Mythologie, Leipzig, 1884–86; 1924–37
RQ	— Römische Quartalschrift, Freiburg
RScPr	— Rivista di Scienze Preistoriche, Florence
RSLig	— Rivista di Studi Liguri, Bordighera, Italy
RSO	— Rivista degli Studi Orientali, Rome
Rumpf, MZ	— A. Rumpf, Malerei und Zeichnung (W. Otto, Handbuch der Archäologie, IV, 1), Munich, 1953
RUO	— Revista de la Universidad de Oviedo
SA	— Soviet Archaeology, Moscow, Leningrad
SAA	— Seminario de Arte Aragonés, Zaragoza
SbBerlin	— Sitzungsberichte der preussischen Akademie der Wissenschaften, Berlin
SbHeidelberg	— Sitzungsberichte der Akademie der Wissenschaften zu Heidelberg, Heidelberg
SbMünchen	— Sitzungsberichte der bayerischen Akademie der Wissenschaften zu München, Munich
SbWien	— Sitzungsberichte der Akademie der Wissenschaften in Wien, Vienna
Schlosser	— J. Schlosser, La letteratura artistica, Florence, 1956
Scranton, Greek Walls	— R. L. Scranton, Greek Walls, Cambridge, Mass., 1941
SEtr	— Studi Etruschi, Florence
SNR	— Sudan Notes and Records, Khartoum
SPA	— A Survey of Persian Art, ed. A. U. Pope and P. Ackerman, Oxford, 1938
SymbOsl	— Symbolae Osloenses, Oslo
Tebtunis	— The Tebtunis Papyri, B. P. Grenfell, A. S. Hunt, et al., eds., London, 1902 ff.
ThB	— U. Thieme, F. Becker, Künstler Lexikon, Leipzig, 1907–50
TitAM	— Tituli Asiae Minoris, Vindobonae, 1901–44
TNR	— Tanganyika Notes and Records, Dar-es-Salaam
Toesca, Md	— P. Toesca, Il Medioevo, 2 vols., Turin, 1927
Toesca, Tr	— P. Toesca, Il Trecento, Turin, 1951
TP	— T'oung Pao, Leiden
UCalPAAE	— University of California, Publications in American Archaeology and Ethnology, Berkeley
USMB	— United States National Museum, Bulletin, Washington, D.C.
Van Marle	— R. van Marle, The Development of the Italian Schools of Painting, The Hague, 1923–38
Vasari	— G. Vasari, Vite, ed. Milanesi, Florence, 1878 ff. (Am. ed., trans. E. H. and E. W. Blashfield and A. A. Hopkins, 4 vols., New York, 1913)
Venturi	— A. Venturi, Storia dell'Arte Italiana, Milan, 1901 ff.
VFPA	— Viking Fund Publications in Anthropology, New York
Vollmer	— H. Vollmer, Allgemeines Lexikon der bildenden Künstler des XX. Jahrhunderts, Leipzig, 1953
Warburg	— Journal of the Warburg and Courtauld Institutes, London
Weickert, Archaische Architektur	— C. Weickert, Typen der archaischen Architektur in Griechenland und Kleinasien, Augsburg, 1929
Wpr	— Winckelmannsprogramm, Berlin
WürzbJ	— Würzburger Jahrbücher für die Altertumswissenschaft, Würzburg
WVDOG	— Wissenschaftliche Veröffentlichungen der Deutschen Orient-Gesellschaft, Leipzig, Berlin

ZäS	— Zeitschrift für ägyptische Sprache und Altertumskunde, Berlin, Leipzig
ZfAssyr	— Zeitschrift für Assyriologie, Strasbourg
ZfbK	— Zeitschrift für bildende Kunst, Leipzig
ZfE	— Zeitschrift für Ethnologie, Berlin
ZfKg	— Zeitschrift für Kunstgeschichte, Munich
ZfKw	— Zeitschrift für Kunstwissenschaft, Munich
ZfN	— Zeitschrift für Numismatik, Berlin
ZMG	— Zeitschrift der deutschen morgenländischen Gesellschaft, Leipzig
ZSAKg	— Zeitschrift für schweizerische Archäologie und Kunstgeschichte, Basel

Languages and Ethnological Descriptions

Alb.	— Albanian
Am.	— American
Ang.	— Anglice, Anglicized
Ar.	— Arabic
Arm.	— Armenian
AS.	— Anglo-Saxon
Bab.	— Babylonian
Br.	— British
Bulg.	— Bulgarian
Chin.	— Chinese
D.	— Dutch
Dan.	— Danish
Eg.	— Egyptian
Eng.	— English
Finn.	— Finnish
Fr.	— French
Ger.	— German
Gr.	— Greek
Heb.	— Hebrew
Hung.	–– Hungarian
It.	— Italian
Jap.	— Japanese
Jav.	— Javanese
Lat.	— Latin
Mod. Gr.	— Modern Greek
Nor.	— Norwegian
Per.	— Persian
Pol.	— Polish
Port.	— Portuguese
Rum.	— Rumanian
Rus.	— Russian
Skr.	— Sanskrit
Sp.	— Spanish
Swed.	— Swedish
Yugo.	— Yugoslav

Other Abbreviations (Standard abbreviations in common usage are omitted.)

Abh.	— Abhandlungen
Acad.	— Academy, Académie
Acc.	— Accademia
Adm.	— Administration
Ak.	— Akademie
Allg.	— Allgemein
Alm.	— Almanacco
Amm.	— Amministrazione
Ann.	— Annals, Annali, Annuario, Annual, etc.
Ant.	— Antiquity, Antico, Antiquaire, etc.
Anthr.	— Anthropology, etc.
Antr.	— Antropologia, etc.
Anz.	— Anzeiger
Arch.	— Architecture, Architettura, Architettonico, etc.
Archaeol.	— Archaeology, etc.
Archeol.	— Archeologia, Archéologie
Arqueol.	— Arqueología, etc.
attrib.	— attributed
Aufl.	— Auflage
Aufn.	— Aufnahme
B.	— Bulletin, Bollettino, etc.
b.	— born
Belg.	— Belgian, Belga, etc.
Berl.	— Berlin, Berliner
Bern.	— Berner
Bib.	— Bible, Biblical, Bibliothèque, etc.
Bibliog.	— Bibliography, etc.
Bur.	— Bureau
Byz.	— Byzantine

C.	— Corpus
ca.	— circa
Cah.	— Cahiers
Cal.	— Calendar
Cap.	— Capital, Capitolium
Cat.	— Catalogue, Catalogo, etc.
Cath.	— Cathedral
Chr.	— Chronicle, Chronik
Civ.	— Civiltà, Civilization, etc.
cod.	— codex
col., cols.	— column, columns
Coll.	— Collection, Collana, Collationes, Collectanea, Collezione, etc.
Com.	— Comunale
Comm.	— Commentaries, Commentari, Communications, etc.
Cong.	— Congress, Congresso, etc.
Cr.	— Critica
Cron.	— Cronaca
Cuad.	— Cuadernos
Cult.	— Culture, Cultura, etc.
D.	— Deutsch
d.	— died
Diss.	— Dissertation, Dissertazione
Doc.	— Documents, etc.
E.	— Encyclopedia, etc.
Eccl.	— Ecclesiastic, Ecclesia, etc.
Ep.	— Epigraphy
Esp.	— España, Español
Est.	— Estudios
Et.	— Etudes
Ethn.	— Ethnology, Ethnography, Ethnographie, etc.
Etn.	— Etnico, Etnografia, etc.
Etnol.	— Etnologia
Eur.	— Europe, Europa, etc.
ext.	— extract
f.	— für
fasc.	— fascicle
Fil.	— Filologia
Filos.	— Filosofia, Filosofico
fol.	— folio
Forsch.	— Forschung, Forschungen
Gal.	— Galerie
Gall.	— Gallery, Galleria
Geog.	— Geography, Geografia, Geographical, etc.
Giorn.	— Giornale
H.	— History, Histoire, etc.
hl.	— heilig, heilige
Holl.	— Hollandisch, etc.
Hum.	— Humanity, Humana, etc.
Ill.	— Illustration, Illustrato, Illustrazione, etc.
Ind.	— Index, Indice, Indicatore, etc.
Inf.	— Information, Informazione, etc.
Inst.	— Institute, Institut, Instituto, etc.
Int.	— International, etc.
Ist.	— Istituto
J.	— Journal
Jb.	— Jaarboek
Jhb.	— Jahrbuch
Jhrh.	— Jahreshefte
K.	— Kunst
Kat.	— Katalog
Kchr.	— Kunstchronik
Kg.	— Kunstgeschichte
K.K.	— Kaiserlich und Königlich
Kunsthist.	— Kunsthistorische
Kw.	— Kunstwissenschaft
Lett.	— Letteratura, Lettere
Lib.	— Library
ling.	— linguistica, lingua, etc.
Lit.	— Literary, Literarische, Littéraire, etc.
Mag.	— Magazine
Med.	— Medieval, Medievale, etc.
Meded.	— Mededeelingen
Mél.	— Mélanges
Mém.	— Mémoire
Mem.	— Memorie, Memoirs
Min.	— Minerva
Misc.	— Miscellany, Miscellanea, etc.
Mit.	— Mitteilungen
Mnb.	— Monatsberichte
Mnbl.	— Monatsblätter
Mnh.	— Monatshefte

Mod.	— Modern, Moderno, etc.
Mon.	— Monuments, Monumento
Münch.	— München, Münchner
Mus.	— Museum, Museo, Musée, Museen, etc.
Muz.	— Muzeum
N.	— New, Notizia, etc.
Nac.	— Nacional
Nachr.	— Nachrichten
Nat.	— National, etc.
Naz.	— Nazionale
Notit. dign.	— Notitia Dignitatum
N.S.	— new series
O.	— Oriental, Orient, etc.
Ö.	— Österreichische
obv.	— obverse
öffentl.	— öffentlich
Op.	— Opuscolo
Pap.	— Papers, Papyrus
Per.	— Periodical, Periodico
Pin.	— Pinacoteca, Pinakothek
Pr.	— Prehistory, Preistoria, Preystori, Préhistoire
Proc.	— Proceedings
Pub.	— Publication, Publicación
Pubbl.	— Pubblicazione
Q.	— Quarterly, Quaderno
Quel.	— Quellen
R.	— Rivista
r	— recto
r.	— reigned
Racc.	— Raccolta
Rass.	— Rassegna
Rec.	— Recueil
Recens.	— Recensione
Rech.	— Recherches
Rel.	— Relazione
Rend.	— Rendiconti
Rép.	— Répertoire
Rep.	— Report, Repertorio, Repertorium
Rev.	— Review, Revue, etc.
Rl.	— Reallexikon
Rom.	— Roman, Romano, Romanico, etc.
rv.	— reverse
S.	— San, Santo, Santa (saint)
S.	— Studi, Studies, etc.
Samml.	— Sammlung, Sammlungen
Sc.	— Science, Scienza, Scientific, etc.
Schr.	— Schriften
Schw.	— Schweitzer
Script.	— Scriptorium
Sitzb.	— Sitzungsberichte
s.l.	— in its place
Soc.	— Social, Society, Società, Sociale, etc.
Spec.	— Speculum
SS.	— Saints, Sante, Santi, Santissima
St.	— Saint
Sta	— Santa (holy)
Ste	— Sainte
Sto	— Santo (holy)
Sup.	— Supplement, Supplemento
s.v.	— under the word
Tech.	— Technical, Technology, etc.
Tecn.	— Tecnica, Tecnico
Tr.	— Transactions
trans.	— translator, translated, etc.
Trav.	— Travaux
Treas.	— Treasury
u.	— und
Um.	— Umanesimo
Univ.	— University, Università, Université, etc.
Urb.	— Urban, Urbanistica
v	— verso
Vat.	— Vatican
Verh.	— Verhandlungen, Verhandelingen
Verz.	— Verzeichnis
Vf.	— Verfasser
Wien.	— Wiener
Yb.	— Yearbook
Z.	— Zeitschrift, Zeitung, etc.

NOTES ON THE ENGLISH EDITION

Standards of Translation. Contributors to the Encyclopedia, drawn from the outstanding authorities of over 35 different countries, have written in many languages — Italian, Spanish, French, German, Russian, etc. To ensure faithful translation of the author's thought, all articles have been translated into English from the original language, checked for the accuracy of technical terms and accepted English forms of nomenclature by English and American art historians, and correlated with the final editorial work of the Italian edition for uniformity and coherence of the over-all presentation. Naturally the McGraw-Hill Book Company assumes full responsibility for the accuracy and completeness of all translations. Those articles written in English appear in the words and style of the authors, within the bounds of editorial attention to consistency and stylistic and organizational unity of the work as a whole. Article titles are in most cases parallel to those in the Italian edition, though occasionally they have been simplified, as *Dravidian Art* for *Dravidiche Correnti e Tradizioni.*

New Features. Although generally the English-language edition corresponds to the Italian version, a small number of purely editorial changes have been made in the interest of clear English-language alphabetization and occasional deletions or amplifications solely in the interest of clarity. Three major differences between the two editions do exist, however:

A considerable number of cross-references have been added in many places where it was felt that relating the subject under consideration to other pertinent articles would be of value to the reader.

A more extensive article on the Art of the Americas was projected for Volume One of the English edition with an entirely new text and many plates in black and white and color. This article was designed to give the completest possible coverage within the existing space of some 100,000 words to a subject which, because of its interest to the English-speaking public, was entrusted to a group of well-known American scholars, each expert in his respective area.

Some 300 separate short biographies have been added to the English edition to provide ready access to data on the lives, works, and critical acceptance of certain artists identified with schools, movements, and broad categories of historical development that are treated in the longer monographic articles. These articles are unillustrated, but works of the artists are represented in the plates accompanying the longer articles.

Bibliographies. The bibliographies of the original Italian edition have been amplified at times to include titles of special interest to the English-speaking world and English-language editions of works originally published in other languages.

In undertaking these adaptations of the Italian text and preparing original material for the English edition, the publisher has been aided by the generous advice and, in many cases, collaboration of the members of the Editorial Advisory Committee.

CONTRIBUTORS TO VOLUME XIII

Santiago ALCOLEA, Instituto Amatller de Arte Hispánico, Barcelona

Bianca Maria ALFIERI, University of Rome

Giulio Carlo ARGAN, University of Rome

Anthony J. ARKELL, Reader in Egyptian Archaeology, University of London

Bernard ASHMOLE, Emeritus Professor, Oxford University

Rosario ASSUNTO, University of Urbino

Umberto BALDINI, Director, Soprintendenza alle Gallerie di Firenze

Joan T. BASTABLE, Closter, N.J.

Alessandro BAUSANI, Istituto Orientale, Naples; University of Rome

Gunnar BEREFELT, University of Stockholm

Stefano BOTTARI, University of Bologna

Theodore M. BROWN, University of Louisville, Ky.

Arnaldo BRUSCHI, Rome

Herman BURSSENS, University of Ghent, Belgium

Mario BUSSAGLI, University of Rome

Antonino BUTTITTA, University of Palermo

Michelangelo CAGIANO DE AZEVEDO, Università Cattolica del Sacro Cuore, Milan

Piero M. CAPPONI, Rome

Enrico CASTELNUOVO, Accademia Albertina, Turin

Ernesta CERULLI, University of Rome

Paul COLLART, Director, Swiss Institute, Rome

Gemma CORTESE DI DOMENICO, Rome

Daria DE BERNARDI, Politecnico, Turin

S. Lane FAISON, Jr., Williams College, Williamstown, Mass.

Oreste FERRARI, Rome

Mercedes FERRERO VIALE, Turin

Silvio FERRI, University of Pisa

Pierre FRANCASTEL, Director of Studies, Ecole Pratique des Hautes Etudes, Paris

Antonio FROVA, Soprintendenza alle Antichità dell'Emilia e della Romagna, Parma

Francesco GABRIELI, University of Rome

Giovanni GARBINI, University of Rome

Gherardo GNOLI, Rome

Hermann GOETZ, University of Heidelberg

Lloyd GOODRICH, Director, Whitney Museum of American Art, New York City

Alexander B. GRISWOLD, Breezewood Foundation, Monkton, Md.

José GUDIOL, University of Barcelona; Director, Instituto Amatller de Arte Hispánico

Madeleine HALLADE, Musée Guimet, Paris

Louis HAMBIS, Ecole Pratique des Hautes Etudes, Paris

Dora HEINZ, Österreichisches Museum für Angewandte Kunst, Vienna

Julius S. HELD, Barnard College, Columbia University, New York City

Robert L. HERBERT, Yale University, New Haven, Conn.

Ferdinand HERRMANN, Heidelberg

Henry-Russell HITCHCOCK, Smith College, Northampton, Mass.

Josef P. HODIN, formerly, Director of Studies, Institute of Contemporary Arts, London

Henry R. HOPE, Indiana University, Bloomington

Sergei Vassilevich IVANOV, Leningrad

Ulla JOHANSEN, Museum für Völkerkunde, Hamburg

Willibald KIRFEL, University of Bonn

Oliver W. LARKIN, Emeritus Professor of Art, Smith College, Northampton, Mass.

Victor LASAREFF, Presidium of the Academy of Sciences of the U.S.S.R., Moscow

Jean LAUDE

James B. LYNCH, Jr., Department of Art, University of Maryland, College Park

Arthur McCOMB, Boston, Mass.

Fernanda de' MAFFEI, University of Rome

Paolo MATTHIAE, Rome

† Alfred MÉTRAUX, Ecole Pratique des Hautes Etudes, Paris

Robin MIDDLETON, Technical Editor, Architectural Design Magazine, London

Paolo MORA, Rome

Francesco NEGRI ARNOLDI, Rome

David O'CONNOR, London

Henri PAUWELS, Ghent

Michele PIRONE, Istituto Universitario della Somalia, Mogadishu

Luciano PONTUALE, Rome

Antonio PRIORI, Rome

Svetozar RADOJČIĆ, University of Belgrade

Adolf REINLE, Basel

Goffredo ROSATI, Rome

Margaretta M. SALINGER, Metropolitan Museum of Art, New York City

Marcello SALVATORI, Rome

Willy SCHULZ-WEIDER, Frankfurt am Main

E. Margaret SHAW, South African Museum, Capetown

Calambur SIVARAMAMURTI, Director, National Museum, New Delhi

Dorothy STROUD, Sir John Soane's Museum, London

Giorgio TORRACA

† Martin WEINBERGER, Institute of Fine Arts, New York University

Hellmut WILHELM, University of Washington, Seattle

ACKNOWLEDGMENTS

The Institute for Cultural Collaboration and the publishers express their thanks to the collectors and to the directors of the museums and galleries listed below for permission to reproduce works in their collections and for photographs supplied.

The Institute also acknowledges the kind permission of H. M. Queen Elizabeth II to reproduce works belonging to the Crown.

AMMAN, Jordan, Archaeological Museum
AMSTERDAM, Rijksmuseum
ANGERS, France, Musée des Tapisseries
ANTWERP, Musée Royal des Beaux-Arts
ATHENS, Museum of the Agora
ATHENS, National Museum
AYELET-HASHACHAR, Israel, Hazor Museum

BAGHDAD, Iraq Museum
BANGKOK, National Museum
BARCELONA, Museo Arqueológico
BARCELONA, Museo de Arte de Cataluña
BASEL, Historisches Museum
BASEL, Kunstmuseum
BASEL, Schweizerisches Museum für Volkskunde
BEIRUT, National Museum
BELÉM, Brazil, Museu Paraense Emilio Goeldi
BERGAMO, Italy, Galleria dell'Accademia Carrara
BERLIN, Museum für Völkerkunde
BERLIN, Staatliche Museen
BOSTON, Museum of Fine Arts
BRUSSELS, Musée Royaux d'Art et d'Histoire
BRUSSELS, Musées Royaux des Beaux-Arts
BUDAPEST, National Museum
BUFFALO, N.Y., Albright-Knox Art Gallery

CAIRO, Egyptian Museum
CAMAIORE, Italy, Museo d'Arte Sacra
CAMBRIDGE, England, University Museum of Archaeology and Ethnology
CAMBRIDGE, Mass., Fogg Art Museum
CHICAGO, Art Institute, J. Winterbotham Coll.
COPENHAGEN, Nationalmuseet
COPENHAGEN, Ny Carlsberg Glyptotek

DIJON, France, Musée des Beaux-Arts
DRESDEN, Albertinum, Skulpturensammlung
DRESDEN, Gemäldegalerie

FLORENCE, Accademia
FLORENCE, Biblioteca Laurenziana
FLORENCE, Coll. Corsini
FLORENCE, Museo Archeologico
FLORENCE, Museo Nazionale
FLORENCE, Museo Nazionale di Antropologia e Etnologia
FLORENCE, Uffizi
FRANKFORT ON THE MAIN, Museum für Kunsthandwerk
FRANKFORT ON THE MAIN, Städelsches Kunstinstitut

GÖTEBORG, Sweden, Etnografiska Museet
GRANADA, Spain, Museo Provincial

HAMBURG, Museum für Völkerkunde
HELSINKI, Kansallismuseo
HERAKLION, Crete, Archaeological Museum
HUESCA, Spain, Museo Provincial

ISTANBUL, Archaeological Museums

JERUSALEM, Jordan, Palestine Archaeological Museum

KHABAROVSK, U.S.S.R., Museum
KLAGENFURT, Austria, Diocesan Museum
KOBLENZ, Germany, Staatsarchiv
KOLAROVGRAD, Bulgaria, Archaeological Museum
KRAKÓW, Poland, National Museum

LA SERENA, Chile, Museo Arqueológico
LENINGRAD, Ethnographical Museum of the Peoples of the U.S.S.R.
LENINGRAD, The Hermitage
LENINGRAD, Russian Museum
LENINGRAD, State Library
LISBON, Museu Nacional de Arte Antiga
LONDON, British Museum
LONDON, National Gallery
LONDON, Roland Penrose Coll.
LONDON, Tate Gallery
LONDON, Victoria and Albert Museum
LONDON, Wallace Coll.
LÜBECK, Germany, Museum für Völkerkunde
LUGANO, Switzerland, Thyssen-Bornemisza Coll.
LYONS, University, Laboratoire de Géologie

MADRID, Prado
MEXICO CITY, Museo Nacional de Historia
MILAN, Brera
MILAN, Cathedral Treasury
MILAN, Galleria d'Arte Moderna
MILAN, Museo Poldi Pezzoli
MODENA, Italy, Biblioteca Estense
MODENA, Italy, Galleria Estense
MONKTON, Md., Breezewood Foundation Coll.
MOSCOW, Historical Museum
MOSCOW, Korin Coll.
MOSCOW, The Kremlin, Hall of Arms
MOSCOW, Tretyakov Gallery

MUNICH, Alte Pinakothek
MUNICH, Bayerische Staatsbibliothek
MUNICH, Bayerisches Nationalmuseum
MUNICH, Residenzmuseum

NAPLES, Museo di Capodimonte
NAPLES, Museo Nazionale
NAPLES, Museo Nazionale di S. Martino
NEW CANAAN, Conn., James Thrall Soby Coll.
NEW DELHI, National Museum of India
NEW YORK, Brooklyn Museum
NEW YORK, Metropolitan Museum
NEW YORK, Museum of Modern Art
NÜRNBERG, Germany, Germanisches National-Museum

PADUA, Italy, Museo Civico
PARIS, Cabinet des Médailles
PARIS, Coll. Daniel Cordier
PARIS, Coll. H. Kamer
PARIS, Louvre
PARIS, Mobilier National
PARIS, Musée d'Art Moderne
PARIS, Musée des Arts Décoratifs
PARIS, Musée Cernuschi
PARIS, Musée de Cluny
PARIS, Musée Guimet
PARIS, Musée de l'Homme
PERUGIA, Italy, Museo dell'Opera del Duomo
PHILADELPHIA, University Museum
PIALI, Greece, Museum
PRAGUE, Náprestek Museum
PRAGUE, National Museum

OXFORD, England, Ashmolean Museum
OXFORD, England, Pitt Rivers Museum

RAJSHAHI, Pakistan, Varendra, Research Society Museum
ROME, Coll. Albonetti
ROME, Calcografia Nazionale
ROME, Galleria Borghese
ROME, Galleria Colonna
ROME, Galleria Doria Pamphili
ROME, Galleria Nazionale
ROME, Galleria Spada
ROME, Lateran Museums
ROME, Museo delle Arti e delle Tradizioni Popolari
ROME, Museo Nazionale d'Arte Orientale
ROME, Museo Nazionale Romano
ROME, Museo di Palazzo Venezia
ROME, Museo Pigorini
ROME, Museo di Villa Giulia
ROME, Palazzo dei Conservatori
ROME, Coll. Taliani De Marchio
ROME, Coll. Torlonia
ROME, Vatican Library
ROME, Vatican Museums
ROTTERDAM, Museum Boymans-van Beuningen

SAINT-GERMAIN-EN-LAYE, France, Musée des Antiquités Nationales
ST. LOUIS, City Art Museum
SALAMANCA, Spain, Museo Diocesano
SALEM, Mass., Peabody Museum
SALTWOOD CASTLE, Kent, England, Sir Kenneth Clark Coll.
SAN GIMIGNANO, Italy, Museo di Arte Sacra
SANTA FE, N. Mex., Museum of Navajo Ceremonial Art
SANTINIKETAN, India, Visva-Bharati Rabindra-Sadana
SÃO PAULO, Brazil, Museu Paulista
SARAGOSSA, Spain, Cathedral, Museo de Tapices
SARAGOSSA, Spain, Museo Provincial
SEATTLE, Thomas Burke Memorial Washington State Museum
SEOUL, National Museum of Korea
SIENA, Italy, Archivio di Stato
SOLSONA, Spain, Museo Diocesano
SORRENTO, Italy, Museo Correale di Terranova
STOCKHOLM, Nationalmuseum
STOCKHOLM, Östasiatiska Museet
STOCKHOLM, Statens Etnografiska Museum
STOCKHOLM, Statens Historiska Museum
STRASBOURG, Musée des Beaux-Arts
STUTTGART, Staatsgalerie
STUTTGART, Württembergisches Landesmuseum
SYRACUSE, Sicily, Museo Archeologico

TARANTO, Italy, Museo Nazionale
TEHERAN, Archaeological Museum
TEOTIHAUCÁN, Mexico, Museum
TERVUEREN, Belgium, Musée Royal de l'Afrique Centrale
TOKYO, K. Magoshi Coll.
TOKYO, Shiobara Coll.
TRIVANDRUM, India, Sri Chitra Art Gallery
TURIN, Coll. G. Agnelli
TURIN, Biblioteca Nazionale
TURIN, Museo Civico
TURIN, Museo Egizio
TURIN, Palazzo Reale

VALLADOLID, Spain, Museo Nacional de Escultura
VALLETTA, Malta, National Museum
VENICE, Doges' Palace
VENICE, Galleria Internazionale d'Arte Moderna
VENICE, Museo Correr
VENICE, Museo Marciano
VICH, Spain, Museo Episcopal
VIENNA, Kunsthistorisches Museum
VIENNA, Museum für Völkerkunde
VIENNA, Nationalbibliothek
VIENNA, Österreichisches Museum für Angewandte Kunst

WASHINGTON, D.C., Corcoran Gallery of Art, W. A. Clark Coll.
WASHINGTON, D.C., Freer Gallery of Art
WASHINGTON, D.C., National Gallery
WASHINGTON, D.C., National Gallery, Chester Dale Coll.
WINDSOR, England, Royal Colls.

ZURICH, Coll. E. Leuzinger
ZURICH, Schweizerisches Landesmuseum

PHOTOGRAPHIC CREDITS

The numbers refer to the plates. Those within parentheses indicate the sequence of subjects in composite plate pages. Italic numbers refer to photographs owned by the Institute for Cultural Collaboration.

A.C.L., Brussels: 196 (1); 239 (2); 249 (2); 251 (2); 401; 408 (1); 412 (1, 2)
AERO-PHOTO, Paris: 254 (3)
AGENZIA FOTOGRAFICA INDUSTRIALE, Venice: 325 (1)
ALINARI, Florence: 33; 35 (1, 2); 36 (1); 107 (5); 109; 112 (1); 113 (1); 195 (1); 216 (2); 220 (4); 221 (2); 222 (3); 225 (3, 4); 226 (1, 4); 227 (1, 3, 4); 232 (1, 2); 233 (4, 6, 8); 234 (3); 235 (4); 237 (1-3); 238 (1, 2); 239 (1, 3); 240 (2); 242 (3); 244 (4, 5); 246 (4); 248 (2); 249 (1, 3); 251 (1); 252 (3); 254 (1); 258 (1); 259 (1); 261 (1); 264 (1, 2, 4); 265 (3, 4); 270 (2, 3); 271 (1); 281 (2); 282; 283 (1-3); 284 (2, 3); 289 (2); 290; 335 (4); 336; 338 (1, 3); 339 (1); 341 (6); 342 (2); 344 (1); 345 (2); 347 (3); 351 (2); 352 (3); 372 (2, 3); 373 (3); 397; 404 (1, 2); 439 (3); 448 (1); 468; 470
ANDERSON, Rome: 112 (2); 195 (2); 219 (3); 220 (2); 221 (1); 230 (5); 238 (6); 240 (1); 247 (1); 252 (4); 255 (3, 4); 256 (3, 4); 268 (1); 270 (1); 273 (2); 280; 289 (1); 337 (1); 340 (1); 344 (2); 345 (3); 352 (1, 2); 354 (2, 3); 355 (2, 3); 370 (2)
ANDREWS, Wayne, New York: 247 (4)
ARTE E COLORE, Milan: 360 (1); 406; 413
ARTIA PRAGA: 466 (1, 2)

BAYERISCHE VERWALTUNG DER STAATLICHE SCHLÖSSER, GÄRTEN U. SEEN, Munich: 258 (2); 421 (1)
BECCARIA, Turin: 412 (3)
BENEVOLO, Rome: 218 (4); 260 (3)
BERTONI, Marcello, Florence: 469
BILDARCHIV FOTO MARBURG, Marburg, Germany: 41 (2); 73 (1, 2); 74 (1, 2); 217 (4); 218 (1); 223 (3); 225 (1); 226 (3); 233 (1); 237 (4); 246 (3); 255 (2); 257 (1); 266 (1); 278 (2, 3); 391
BÖHM, Osvaldo, Venice: 292 (1)
BONARDI, Francesca, Rome: 459
BOVIS, Marcel, Paris: 235 (3)
BROGI, Florence: 223 (4); 238 (4); 241 (1); 264 (3); 343 (3)
BROMPTON STUDIO, London: 317
BRUNEL, Lugano, Switzerland: 197 (1)

CAISSE NATIONALE DES MONUMENTS HISTORIQUES, Paris: 77, 78 (1, 2); 79 (1, 2); 80 (1-3); 147 (2); 208 (3); 216 (1, 4); 219 (1); 228 (2); 230 (3); 231 (1); 243 (3); 245 (5); 281 (1); 337 (3); 340 (2); 345 (1); 360 (2); 363 (4); 398 (1); 410
CENTRAL INSTITUTE FOR THE PROTECTION OF CULTURAL WORKS, Skoplje, Yugoslavia: 53 (1)
CHUZEVILLE, M., Paris: 361
COUNTRY LIFE, London: 292 (2); 294; 296
CREA, Rome: 125

DABAC, Tošo, Zagreb, Yugoslavia: 49 (1); 53 (2); 54 (1); 75 (1, 2)
DE ANTONIS, Rome: 41 (1); 93; 94; 97; 100 (2); 103 (3); 104 (1-3); 200; 203; 204; 217 (2); 223 (1); 285; 288; 304 (2); 306 (4); 308; 315; 318; 394; 404; 414 (1-4); 457 (1)
DE GASPERI, P., Rome: 215 (2)
DENIC, Kosta, Belgrade: 47 (1, 2); 48 (1-3); 49 (2); 50; 51 (1-3); 52; 53 (3); 54 (3); 55 (1-3)
DEPARTMENT OF ARCHAEOLOGY, GOVERNMENT OF INDIA, New Delhi: 231 (4); 236 (4); 243 (1); 253 (2); 272 (2); 333 (1-3)
DEUTSCHE FOTOTHEK, Dresden: 110 (2); 206 (2)

DEUTSCHES ARCHÄOLOGISCHES INSTITUT, Rome: 216 (3); 338 (2)
DEWSBURY: 253 (1)

ENTE PER LE VILLE VENETE, Venice: 247 (3)

FESL, Anton, Vienna: 424 (1); 428
FIDES FOTO, Rome: 215 (1)
FINISHERS, Sheffield: 228 (3)
FLEMING, R. B., & Co., London: 145; 379
FOTO ALBERTO LUISA, Brescia, Italy: 275 (1)
FOTO CELERE, Turin: 219 (3); 247 (2)
FOTOCINETECNICA, Rome: 257 (3)
FOTOLABOR LTDA, São Paulo, Brazil: 101; 102 (1)
FOTOTECA ASAC BIENNALE, Venice: 322 (2)
FOTOTECA UNIONE, Rome: 217 (1); 224 (3, 4); 248 (3); 250 (2); 262 (1); 269; 339 (2)
FREEMAN, London: 425; 432
FREQUIN, A., The Hague: 198 (1); 202 (1)

GABINETTO FOTOGRAFICO NAZIONALE, Rome: 201 (1); 205 (4); 211 (3); 235 (2); 250 (3); 271 (2); 274; 279 (2); 286 (1); 339 (3); 346 (1); 407 (1); 458 (1)
GALERIE STADLER, Paris: 326
GHERARDI & FIORELLI, Rome: 266 (4, 5)
GIRAUDON, Paris: 1; 31 (2); 100 (1); 110 (3); 181; 196 (3); 208 (2); 211 (2); 212 (2); 236 (3); 241 (2); 251 (3); 301; 303; 304 (1, 3); 310 (1); 327; 335 (1); 342 (4); 346 (2); 354 (1); 363 (7, 8); 365 (1); 369 (2); 393; 439 (1)
GRASSI, Siena, Italy: 347 (2)
GRISWOLD, Monkton, Md.: 17 (1, 2); 18

HERVÉ, Lucien, Neuilly-sur-Seine, France: 229 (2)
HIRMER VERLAG, Munich: 41 (3); 107 (4); 108 (1); 110 (1); 220 (1); 230 (2, 4); 233 (2, 5); 242 (1, 2); 248 (1); 254 (4); 255 (1); 267; 273 (1); 292 (3); 293; 297; 341 (3, 4); 362; 365 (4)
HURAULT, Saint-Germain-en-Laye, France: 191

ISTITUTO CENTRALE DEL RESTAURO, Rome: 450 (1-4)
ISTITUTO GEOGRAFICO DE AGOSTINI, Novara, Italy: 135; 136

JAMMES, André, Paris: 262 (2)
JIMENEZ, J.: 240 (3)

KEMPTER, Munich: 156; 199; 202 (2); 208 (1)
KERSTING, A. F., London: 255 (4); 260 (4)
KIDDER SMITH, G. E., New York: 264 (5)
KONSTANTINIDIS, Athens: 261 (3)

LEHMANN, Henri, Paris: 253 (3); 332 (2)
LISSONI, Osvaldo, Milan: 278 (1)
LOTZE, Verona, Italy: 234 (2)

MANSELL, W. F., London: 230 (1); 370 (1)
MARIANI, Enrico, Como, Italy: 39; 40; 221 (4); 225 (2); 255 (3)
MARQUES, Lisbon: 126
MAS, Barcelona: 54 (2); 117; 118 (1, 2); 119 (1-3); 121 (1); 122 (1, 2); 123 (1-3); 124 (2, 3); 127 (1-4); 128 (1, 2); 129 (1-4); 131 (1-3); 132 (1, 2); 133; 134 (1-3); 137 (1-3); 138; 140;

CONTENTS - VOLUME XIII

SHAMANISM. Certain characteristic religious concepts and practices known as shamanism exist among the so-called "primitive" races in many parts of the world. The spiritual roots of shamanism go back to the oldest form of social organization, the hunting culture, with its animistic conception of reality. Shamanism finds its most complete expression among the hunting tribes of Siberia, the North American Indians, the Eskimos of the Old and New Worlds, and the Lapps of northern Europe (see ESKIMO CULTURES; NORTH AMERICAN CULTURES; SIBERIAN CULTURES). Although related to a wide variety of possession cults and healing techniques of medicine men, shamanism is to be distinguished from these phenomena. Its special characteristics are described below as they appear in arctic and subarctic cultures.

Shamanists view the world as populated with beings, powers, and spirits — some friendly, some neutral, others hostile. These spirits inhabit an other-worldly realm, leading an existence not unlike that of human beings on earth. They are able to incarnate themselves at will in men and animals, thus rendering their hosts "possessed." The spirits may also take temporary abode in certain inanimate objects.

Certain men — shamans (PL. 1) — are "called" to make contact with the world of the spirits, frequently by way of unusual personal experiences such as dreams or hallucinations; these generally occur during puberty. Shamans cannot choose to evade their destined roles. They undergo an apprenticeship of several years with an experienced practitioner who instructs them in the appropriate techniques. On completion of this training, public trials decide whether the apprentices will be accepted by the community.

Shamans function as priests, soothsayers, exorcisers, healers, poets, singers, and leaders of important enterprises such as hunting and war. Psychologically they differ from others in their exaggerated instability. Whereas ordinary men may become possessed by the spirits against their will, shamans assume the ecstatic state deliberately. By exerting all their mental and physical powers, aided by songs, dances, narcotics, drums, and other instruments, they are able to summon their auxiliary or protective spirits whenever the sick or needy require. The number of auxiliary spirits that the shaman can voluntarily incarnate in himself, over which he is then lord and master, is the basis of his power and prestige. So long as he does not abuse this power, an authorized shaman enjoys a highly respected social position.

It is believed that all animate and inanimate objects have a soul — an indwelling life force or vital essence. Among the Eskimos this essence is viewed as the "owner" or "proprietor" of the object in question. The concept of the soul is particularly significant in healing the sick, one of the shaman's most important duties. Frequently the illnesses treated are due to psychic disturbances, which in northern regions affect not only single individuals but also entire groups (mass psychoses, the "arctic hysteria" in northern Siberia). The commonest method of treatment is for the shaman, in a state of alienation or trance, to recapture the stolen soul of the sick man before it reaches the other world, from which it can never return. Should the patient die, the shaman escorts the soul into the hereafter. While in a trance the shaman describes to the hearers gathered about him his experiences and the dangers he must overcome during his journey to heaven or to hell — his "voyage of the soul." He wanders through lands never before seen by mortal eye and wrestles with spirits in the shape of animals or with the spirit of some evil shaman, a master of black magic. In order to be equal to this dangerous task the shaman either makes use of his auxiliary spirit, which he conjures up by magic spells, or changes into an animal spirit by putting on an animal disguise or a mask. The identification of man's nature with that of the animals, the interchangeability of the two forms of existence, is a characteristic phenomenon of the spiritualism of hunting cultures, and one to which the origin of shamanistic beliefs is attributed.

As pure hunting cultures gradually adopted a pastoral-nomadic way of life, or settled into an agricultural economy, or were influenced and transformed by more advanced cultures, shamanism experienced fresh impulses and new formative ideas. This process is particularly apparent in Central Asia, where the shamanism of the Tungus, Altaic, and Turkic peoples shows strong influences of plant manism and later of Buddhism, Manichaeanism, Nestorianism, Eastern Orthodox Christianity, and Islam. Bon, the ancient Tibetan religion, was originally shamanistic, but was quite early modified by the more evolved religions of Buddhism from India and Mazdaism and Manichaeanism from Iran, particularly in western Tibet and neighboring Himalayan regions. Indicative of outside influence on Tungusic shamanism is the derivation of the Tungusic word *samān* (Skr., *śramaṇa*, a Buddhist ascetic; perhaps ultimately from Pali, *samana*, beggar monk).

Although as a distinct world concept and a system of religious practices shamanism has given a particular stamp to the cultures of its adherents, particularly in the Asiatic and North American zones, the images and symbols of shamanist ecstasy are found in some degree in all religions: for example, the initiatory trial symbolically comprising the suffering, death, and resurrection of the neophyte; and the tree symbol (*axis mundi*), which in shamanism is the home of the souls or a connection between the three cosmic planes, permitting ascent to the various heavens or descent to the world beyond the tomb. Shamanism has inspired its own sphere of iconographical depictions. It has also created some categories of liturgical objects and added to others, although its contributions are much less than those of more evolved religions. Whether shamanism originated in northern or southern Asia is a problem still awaiting irrefutable scientific proof.

Among the equipment necessary for the shaman to fulfill his function successfully are a costume symbolizing an animal form (the most extensive gear including a headdress, skirt, necklet, belt, leggings, boots, and various adornments), the instruments of ecstasy (drums, rattles, tambourines, small bells), a rod or staff, among certain tribes a mask, and in isolated cases simple images or statues of auxiliary spirits (PLS. 2–4). These are the objects that are of interest as shamanistic art. From the esthetic standpoint, most products of this genre cannot compare to achievements in the religious art of other primitive peoples.

Shamanistic art is not concerned with realistic representation but seeks the symbol or sign, its subject matter drawn from myth and magic. Suggestion and allusion are sufficient to evoke a particular concept. Of primary importance is the spiritual power concealed within the objects. The shamanistic artist gives this power no adequate formal expression, nor has he any need to do so, since the meaning of his work lies in its function rather than its beauty. To the Western viewer a shamanistic object may appear crude, primitive, misshapen, artless; to the shamanist it is an intimation of a higher reality, a transcendental world accessible only by mystical experience and magicoreligious techniques.

In many parts of Siberia, where the shaman costume serves as a symbol for an animal disguise or metamorphosis, the animal represented is usually capable of great speed (stag, reindeer, bird) or bears characteristics that render it suitable as a messenger, mediator, or mount for the journey to nether or heavenly regions (marine animal, beaver, diving bird or other bird). Renderings of skeletal parts of such animals in iron, or more rarely copper, are sewn onto the costume in correct anatomical order to provide its animal character. The custom of adorning the shaman costume with a great number of ornaments in sheet iron (northern Siberia), cloth, or materials such as feathers and shells (southern Siberia) is widely diffused and is not restricted to animal costumes. These ornaments consist of small bells, metal disks symbolizing earth and heaven, representations of mythical animals (resembling eagles, swans, bears, dogs, etc.), parts of the human body, and representations of particular spirits (PL. 2). Metal objects of this sort go back as far as the Siberian Bronze and Iron ages. They are always works of great simplicity and depict abstract geometrical images (moon, sun, earth, hands, ribs). Their symbolic meaning is so familiar to the shamanists that even where representation would not be difficult (e.g., hands) the craftsmen still dispense with all realism. Although the animal and human figures are highly stylized, the shamanistic artists have emphasized the essential features of the animal representations by omitting details and adopting the greatest economy of form. This can be seen in the slender streamlined shape of the diving bird, the long neck of the swan, the heavy squat shape of the bear, the taut body of a dog whose sharp-pointed, forward-reaching legs suggest hurried movement, the eagle whose wings stretched parallel to its body give the illusion of flight (Nioradze, 1925). The sheet-metal figurines representing the shamans' souls or their auxiliary spirits are considerably more clumsy, being restricted to the essential bodily characteristics. Very rare are the round polished copper disks (mirrors) that were at one time sewn onto the costume or attached to a leather belt (e.g., Gold and Tungus shamans) or hung as pectorals from a string. Their purpose was to grant magical protection and the possibility of yet deeper immersion into the spirit world. Central Asian (Chinese-Manchurian) influences are unmistakable in this context, as some of the mirrors were decorated with pictures of twelve animals, possibly representing the zodiac.

Little is known about the uses of the shamans' staves, occasionally associated with the shaman tree. The staves are made of wood or iron, the top end sometimes in the form of a trident (Yenisei area, Siberia). A crosspiece in the center serves as a seat for the conjured spirits. It is reported that the female shamans of the Araucanians in south Chile use holy ladders furnished with human faces whose significance is unknown. Among the Buryat of the Baikal region in Siberia, a staff shaped like a horse's head at the tip and a hoof at the bottom clearly symbolizes a mount that the shaman rides on his journey into the world of the spirits. Some ceremonial staffs (medicine men's "wands") of the South American Indians exhibit a dual motif of bird and quadruped that is intended to signify the animal alter ego of the shaman.

Masks (q.v.) are among the high points of shamanistic art. Here, too, the best examples are found among the Hyperborean tribes, who are the shamanists par excellence. The masks have many purposes: they prevent the shaman from being recognized and pursued by hostile spirits, assist him in penetrating or changing into the auxiliary spirit, preserve the necessary distance between the shaman and his profane audience, and facilitate his concentration on the meeting with the spirits.

Masks are very rare in Siberia. Among the Buryat they used to be made of leather, wood, or metal; they were painted and sometimes had beards. Birch-bark masks with hair applied for eyebrows and beards were used in some Tartar tribes (e.g., Altaic Turks). The carved-wood Eskimo masks, so strangely flat and lacking the plasticity of masks of other peoples, evidently derive from these leather or birch-bark examples. Mask making represents only a small sector of the prolific and highly skilled art of carving practiced by the Eskimos, who were strongly influenced by the American Indians of the north and northwest.

In mask making, the creative imagination is concerned mainly with representing mythical beings; it has, therefore, great scope. Animal masks are not intended to represent any particular species but rather the lord, protector, or proprietor of that species — a concept that also characterizes animal masks in Eskimo cultures and in primitive North and South American tribes. Only the most essential features are indicated by affixing attributes or ornaments. In Alaska the shaman masks follow a certain pattern: the centerpiece, or mask proper, usually suggests a face representing the lord of an animal species. In the double-faced masks, which also appear, the shaman's own spirit is also represented. Other masks emphasize this duality by making half the face human and the other half animal. Among the technical refinements of the mask makers of the Kwakiutl Indians (northwest coast of the American continent) are double masks in which the face can be divided into four parts by pulling strings; the parts are then swung sideways to reveal a second face. The masks of northwest America (X, PL. 357) have an austere symmetry and monumental majesty, stylized under the influence of flat ornamental art. They are worn by members of celebrated secret societies, which may be considered "organized shamanism" (Krickeberg, 1956).

Characteristic of the Eskimo masks of Alaska are the one or two concentric wooden rings running round the edge of the centerpiece, symbolic of the terrestrial and spiritual worlds (PL. 4). On the outer edge of the mask are fixed attachments in confusing abundance: body parts of the animal auxiliary spirits broken up in an almost cubist manner (V, PL. 6), suggesting, as does cubism, a destruction of objective reality in favor of an underlying truth. These appendages may also represent animals over which the Lord of the Animals (the moon spirit in Alaska) holds sway. Also attached to the outer edge of the mask are images of little boats, tools, weapons, and so forth, which assist the shaman on his journey into the other world.

In order to draw the sickness demons from the bodies of his patients, the shaman uses certain sucking instruments known as "soul catchers." They are made of bone or ivory, often inlaid with mother-of-pearl, and have an animal head carved at each end (PL. 3). The soul catchers of the northwest coast are good examples of a symmetrical ornamental art depicting stylized animals. Among the Haida and Tsimshian the soul catchers represent a mythical snake which, if seen or touched by man, causes sickness or death.

The drums used by the shaman are less significant for their form, which reveals little noteworthy craftsmanship, than for the paintings decorating their surfaces. Secular scenes depicting events that befell the ancestors of certain families appear on the Kuskokwim Eskimo drums of Alaska. The round drums of the Altaic tribes, the Yenisei, and particularly the north European Lapps bear complete representations of their spiritual universe, although the wealth of figures and symbols has for the most part now been adequately deciphered (IV, PL. 262; IX, PL. 156). The Lapps depict a complete encyclopedia of their beliefs with interesting archaic Norse and Christian intrusions into the shamanistic ideology. Their painting is linear, seldom naturalistic, yet never reduced to mere sign or ornament.

Figures and symbols also decorate the drums of the North American shamans; however, these Indians generally use rattles instead of drums. In the rattle designs a mythical bird (possibly the raven as the god of creation, or the thunderbird) plays an important role (PL. 3). Shaman rattles of this area are a lovingly worked minor art, subjecting well-observed natural forms to a restraint intended to heighten the magical reality.

BIBLIOG. H. von Lankenau, Die Schamanen und das Schamanenwesen, Globus, XXII, 1872, pp. 278-83; F. W. Radloff, Aus Sibirien, 2 vols., Leipzig, 1884; F. W. Radloff, Das Schamanentum und sein Kultus, Leipzig, 1885; G. A. Wilken, Het Shamanisme bij de volken van den Indischen Archipel, Bijdragen tot de Taal-, Land- en Volkekunde van Nederlandsch Indië, 5th Ser., II, 1887, pp. 427-97; F. Boas, The Use of Masks and Head-Ornaments on the North West Coast of America, IAE, III, 1890, pp. 7-15; W. J. Hoffman, Pictography and Shamanistic Rites of the Ojibwa, Ama I, 1898, pp. 209-29; W. Sieroszewski, Du chamanisme d'après les croyances des Yakoutes, Rev. de l'h. des religions, XLVI, 1902, pp. 204-33, 299-338; A. Byhan, Die Polarvölker, Leipzig, 1909; J. Stadling, Shamanismen i norra Asien, Stockholm, 1912; M. A. Czaplicka, Aboriginal Siberia, Oxford, 1914; F. G. Speck, Penobscot Shamanism, Mem. Am. Anthr. Assoc., VI, 1919, pp. 239-98; I. Lublinski, Der Medizinmann bei den Naturvölkern Südamerikas, ZfE, LII-LIII, 1920-21, pp. 234-63; U. Harva, The Shaman Costume and Its Significance (Ann. Univ. Fennicae Aboensis, I, 2), Turku, 1922; L. Adam, Nordwestamerikanische Indianerkunst (Orbis Pictus, 17), Berlin, 1923; A. Byhan, Nord-, Mittel- und Westasien, in G. Buschan, Illustrierte Völkerkunde, 2d ed., II, Stuttgart, 1923, pp. 273-420; E. von Sydow, Die Kunst der Naturvölker und der Vorzeit, Berlin, 1923; T. Lehtisalo, Entwurf einer Mythologie der Jurak-Samojeden (Mém. Soc. finno-ougrienne, LIII), Helsinki, 1924; E. M. Loeb, The Shaman of Niue, AmA, XXVI, 1924, pp. 393-402; G. Nioradze, Der Schamanismus bei den sibirischen Völkern, Stuttgart, 1925; E. Vatter, Religiöse Plastik der Naturvölker, Frankfurt am Main, 1926; K. F. Karjalainen, Die Religion der Jugra-Völker, 1-3 (FF. Communications, 65), Helsinki, 1927; W. Krickeberg, Das Kunstgewerbe der Eskimo und nordamerikanischen Indianer, in H. T. Bossert, Geschichte des Kunstgewerbes, II, Berlin, 1929, pp. 154-294; E. M. Leob, Shaman and Seer, AmA, XXXI, 1929, pp. 60-84; J. W. Layard, Shamanism, JRAI, LX, 1930, pp. 525-50; M. Gusinde, Der Medizinmann bei den südamerikanischen Indianern, MAGWien, LXII, 1932, pp. 286-94; K. Donner, Sibirien: Folk och Forntid, Helsinki, 1933; E. J. Lindgren, The Shaman Dress of the Dagurs, Solons and Numinches in North West Manchuria, Geografiska Ann., I, 1935, pp. 365-78; S. Shirokogorov, Psychomental Complex of the Tungus, London, 1935; F. de Laguna, Indian Masks from the Lower Yukon, AmA, XXXVIII, 1936, pp. 569-85; E. D. Harvey, Shamanism in China, in G. P. Murdock, ed., Studies in the Science of Society, New Haven, 1937, pp. 247-66; U. Harva, Die religiösen Vorstellungen der altaischen Völker, FF Communications, 125, Helsinki, 1938, pp. 499-525; E. Manker, Die lappische Zaubertrommel (Acta Lapponica, I, VI), 2 vols., Stockholm, 1938-50; W. Z. Park, Shamanism in Western North America (Northwestern Univ. S. in the Social Sciences, II), Chicago, 1938; K. Breysig, Völker ewiger Urzeit, 2 vols., Berlin, 1939; W. Krickeberg, Amerika, in H. A. Bernatzik, Die grosse Völkerkunde, III, Leipzig, 1939, pp. 18-258; Å. Ohlmarks, Studien zum Problem des Schamanismus, Lund, Copenhagen, 1939; O. Zerries, Eine seltene südamerikanishe Rassel, Paideuma, I, 1940, pp. 279-83; P. Wirz, Exorzismus und Heilkunde auf Ceylon, Bern, 1941 (Eng. trans., Leiden, 1954); A. Métraux, Le chamanisme araucan, Rev. Inst. de Antr. de la Univ. Nacional de Tucumán, II, 1942, pp. 309-62; A. Métraux, Le chamanisme chez les Indiens de l'Amérique du Sud tropicale, Acta Americana, II, 3-4, 1944, pp. 197-219, 320-41; E. Emsheimer, Schamanentrommel und Trommelbaum, Ethnos, IV, 1946, pp. 166-81; L. Adam, Primitive Art, 2d ed., Harmondsworth, 1949; A. Métraux, Religion and Shamanism HSAI, V, 1949, pp. 559-99; M. Bouteiller, Chamanisme et guérison magique, Paris, 1950; R. B. Inverarity, Art of the Northwest Coast Indians, Berkeley, Los Angeles, 1950; E. Manker, Menschen und Götter in Lappland, Zürich, 1950; M. Eliade, Le chamanisme et les techniques archaïques de l'extase, Paris, 1951; H. Himmelheber, Eskimokünstler, 2d ed., Eisenach, 1953; O. Zerries, Kürbisrassel und Kopfgeister in Südamerika, Paideuma, V, 1953, pp. 323-39; W. Müller, Die blaue Hütte, Wiesbaden, 1954; O. Zerries, Wild- und Buschgeister in Südamerika, Wiesbaden, 1954; W. Müller, Weltbild und Kult der Kwakiutl-Indianer, Wiesbaden, 1955; A. Theile, Die Kunst der Naturvölker, Hamburg, 1955; W. Krickeberg, Die Völker Amerikas ausserhalb der Hochkulturen, Stuttgart, 1956, pp. 229-56; W. Müller, Die Religionen der Waldlandindianer Nordamerikas, Berlin, 1956; H. Findeisen, Schamanentum, Stuttgart, 1957; F. A. Wagner, Indonesia: The Art of an Island Group (trans. A. E. Keep), New York, 1959; W. Müller, Die Religionen der Indianervölker Nordamerikas, Stuttgart, 1961; O. Zerries, Die Religionen der Naturvölker Südamerikas und Westindiens, Stuttgart, 1961; B. P. Groslier, The Art of Indochina (trans. G. Lawrence), New York, 1962.

Willy SCHULZ-WEIDNER

Illustrations: PLS. 1-4.

SHAW, RICHARD NORMAN.

SHAW, RICHARD NORMAN. English architect (b. Edinburgh, May 7, 1831; d. London, Nov. 17, 1912). Shaw was the most successful, the most typical, and the most influential English architect of his generation, although not the most original. Yet it is not possible to define his architecture at all clearly because of the many divergent manners he developed successfully, none of which he ever completely abandoned. His last and most conspicuous work, the Piccadilly Hotel in London of 1905-08, is, for example, even more characteristic of the Edwardian "baroque" of the beginning of the 20th century than his church at Bingley, Yorkshire, of 1866-68 is of the high Victorian Gothic. The intervening late Victorian period in English architecture can hardly be described except in terms of his various manners.

Coming to London at an early age, he worked first with William Burn (1789-1870), a very successful builder of early Victorian country houses. Shaw also studied at the Royal Academy, winning the Academy's Silver Medal in 1853 and Gold Medal in 1854. About 1858 he succeeded Philip Webb (1831-1915) as the principal assistant of G. E. Street (1824-81), leaving Street in 1862 to begin practice with W. E. Nesfield (1835-88).

Shaw's independent work began with the designing of the church at Bingley and of Glen Andred near Withyham in Sussex (1866-67), a country house that initiated the influential mode of domestic architecture that can be called "Shavian manorial." Loose functional plans, rambling masses, usually covered with red tiles, tall fluted chimneys, and extensive areas of mullioned windows characterize this mode, toward which Nesfield and George Devey (1820-86) had paved the way. This manner he never entirely gave up for his country houses. In the early 1870s, beginning with New Zealand Chambers, an office block of 1872-73, and Lowther Lodge, a freestanding mansion of 1873-74, both in London, he took over the leadership of a new movement called the "Queen Anne." Echoing up to a point the domestic architecture of about 1700, this developed from relative freedom of handling toward a quite formal 18th-century revival. That in turn led to a more monumental and academic mode initiated in the 1890s and pursued by Shaw to the end of his life.

OTHER PRINCIPAL WORKS. 1868: English church, Lyons, France. - 1868-69: Leyswood, Sussex. - 1870: Cragside, Northumberland. - 1870: Preen Manor, Shropshire. - 1873: Hopedene, Surrey. - 1875: Shaw's own house, London. - 1875-76: Cheyne House, London. - 1876: Old Swan House, London. - 1876 ff.: Bedford Park, London. - 1877: St. Margaret's, Ilkley, Yorkshire. - 1877: Adcote, Shropshire. - 1879: Albert Hall Mansions, London. - 1882: Alliance Assurance Offices, London. - 1886: All Saints, Leek, Staffordshire. - 1887: 170 Queen's Gate, London. - 1887-90: New Scotland Yard, London. - 1889: Holy Trinity, Latimer Road, London. - 1889-90: Bryanston, Dorset. - 1891: Chesters, Northumberland. - 1896: White Star Offices, Liverpool. - 1902: Gaiety Block, London.

BIBLIOG. R. Blomfield, Richard Norman Shaw, London, 1940; H.-R. Hitchcock, Modern Architecture: Nineteenth and Twentieth Centuries, 2d ed., Harmondsworth, 1963, Chap. 12; N. Pevsner, Richard Norman Shaw, in P. Ferriday, ed., Victorian Architecture, London, 1963.

Henry-Russell HITCHCOCK

SHINTOISM.

SHINTOISM. Originally an aniconic religion (see IMAGES AND ICONOCLASM) whose places of worship were simple enclosures in the open, Shinto, the ancient native cult of Japan, began to evolve an iconography of its own and to modify its traditional architecture after the middle of the 6th century, when the introduction of Buddhism from China, via Korea, brought to the scene a force that both influenced and competed with the indigenous faith. Shinto architecture in its beginnings revived and developed the primitive Japanese rural dwelling; a very early adaptation that became traditional is the torii, or detached portal, a local modification, as the name indicates, of the Indian torana (see BUDDHIST PRIMITIVE SCHOOLS; INDIAN ART; JAPANESE ART).

SUMMARY. Sources and early history (6). Sculpture and painting (7). Architecture (8).

SOURCES AND EARLY HISTORY. In the current practice of Shinto — the traditional customs and rituals, the pilgrimages to shrines, and the popular festivals — there survive, despite modifications and adaptations, elements of its essential form as a polytheistic nature cult, pervaded by sentiments of the beneficence of nature and of loving recognition of its gifts, in contrast to the sense of fear typically animating primitive religions. Thus in very ancient times the people of Japan gave evidence of that sensitivity to the beauties of creation which is a basic ingredient of the Japanese temperament and which has permeated all Japanese art and literature.

The name Shinto (Jap., *Shintō*) is not of great antiquity.

It is said to have been coined when the need was felt for a term to distinguish the native religion from the newly arriving Buddhism. The two characters comprising the word are usually translated " the Way, or Teaching, of the Gods." "Shinto" is the Chinese reading of the characters; the Japanese is "Kami-no-michi." But the word *kami*, commonly rendered as " god" or "spirit," is in fact almost untranslatable. It has been characterized as applying to "anything whatsoever which was outside of the ordinary, which possessed power or which was awe-inspiring." Thus in its earliest forms there seem to have been, in this rudimentary polytheism, elements of animism and an absence of any doctrinal or moral system. However, theological and philosophic elements have entered into its later forms, largely as a result of the influence of Buddhism and Confucianism (qq.v.).

The written sources relating to Shinto are few and do not go back to its beginnings; but they are sufficient to establish the outlines of the religion in its primitive form and to indicate the loosely organized character of its mythology: the *Kojiki* ("Records of Ancient Matters"), compiled A.D. 712; the *Nihongi*, or *Nihon-shoki* ("Chronicles of Japan"), of 720; the *Kogoshūi* ("Collected Fragments of Old Stories"), by Imibe no Hironari, 806–809; the *Kujiki* ("Annals of Ancient Events"), written during the lifetime of Prince Shōtoku (572–621) but known only in a revision dating from the 9th century; and the *Engishiki* ("Ceremonial Code of the Engi Period"), of 927. The mythology of Shinto as revealed in these sources is highly complex. The characteristics of the *yao yorozu no kami-tachi* — the "eight million *kami*" of the early myths — shift and fluctuate, and their powers are not clearly defined; nor is there a consistent pattern in regard to their dwelling places. Early Shinto partook in full measure of the confusion that necessarily characterizes an emerging mythology as the various phases of the deification of natural forces progress at differing rates. Moreover, the character of its pantheon reflects the fact that it probably grew out of an aggregate of cults rather than a single cult; thus not only animistic, shamanistic, fertility, and nature deities but ancestors, rulers, and heroes could claim a place.

It was precisely the nebulousness of the Shinto pantheon that, in early times, precluded the possibility of the birth of art forms such as sculpture and painting that would have represented, either through symbols or in the realistic form of the idol, at least the most exalted divinities: Amaterasu Omikami the great august deity who illumines the sky, that is, the goddess of the sun; Tsuki-yomi-no-Mikoto, the divine master of moonlit nights, that is, the god of the moon; and the violent, swift, and impetuous Susa-no-o-no-Mikoto, the storm god.

Traditional Shinto, with its two distinct aspects — the simple popular beliefs and rituals and the elaborate and organized official cult, closely connected to the political system — was profoundly affected by the influx of Chinese culture in the 6th century: the worship of ancestors and then of national heroes appeared, and the Confucian morality and Buddhist metaphysics drew the Japanese into philosophical reflection and theological speculation. So great was the impact of Buddhism, in particular, with its overwhelming spiritual and material resources, as to bring about the syncretic adaptation of Shinto known as Ryōbu ("Two Aspects") Shinto, based on the *honji-suijaku* concept of the Shingon sect. According to this doctrine, which emerged in the Nara period (645–793) but reached its highest development in the Kamakura period (1185–1333), the various *kami* of Shinto could be identified with Buddhist deities, who, having abandoned their original state (*honji*), had appeared in Japan as *kami*.

SCULPTURE AND PAINTING. It was in line with the evolution of Ryōbu Shinto that there appeared in the Heian period (794–1185) the first fleeting traces of a Shinto sculpture; these are limited to a group of images from the end of the 9th century, preserved in the shrine of Hachiman connected with the temple of Yakushi, in Nara, which represent the war god Hachiman as a Buddhist priest, the empress Jingo as a divinity (Paine and Soper, 1955, pl. 30A), and another female divinity called Nakatsuhime. Though graceful and polychromed, these statues lack the spiritual depth that characterizes the best Buddhist works. The appearance of a Shinto sculpture (PL. 10; VIII, PLS. 271, 273, 295) indicates, as has been suggested, that the adherents of Shinto felt the need of an iconography vis-à-vis the Buddhists, but it may safely be said that Shinto has not made a significant contribution in the fields of sculpture and painting. In painting, it was Ryōbu Shinto that brought about, in the Kamakura period, the appearance of the kind of Shintoist paintings known as *suijaku-ga*.

One category of these paintings, *suika-ga*, depicts as scenic subjects the dwelling places of local Shinto deities. Stylistically there is nothing particularly unusual about such paintings, for they are similar to the Yamato-e (q.v.), with emphasis on the landscape rather than on religious significance. Among the most beautiful of these *suika-ga* is the one in Tokyo (VIII, PL. 299) representing the Nachi Waterfall, a pure landscape painted in veneration of this natural phenomenon as the abode of a divinity. A second group of *suijaku-ga* achieves the same end by means of a symbol, as in the case of the sacred deer representing the Kasuga Shrine at Nara (Paine and Soper, 1955, pl. 55B).

ARCHITECTURE. A naturalistic religion par excellence, Shinto did not originally have any shrine buildings; its rites were conducted in the open, centering on the sacred space reserved to the deity; the rice-straw rope (*shime-nawa*) still used to designate such areas goes back at least as far as the *Kojiki* and the *Nihongi*. The *himorogi*, also of great antiquity, is thought to have been a sort of primitive altar set up in space set aside for religious ceremonies (*shiki*) and probably included a branch of sakaki (*Cleyera japonica* or *Cleyera ochnacea*), the evergreen tree sacred to Shinto, at its center. From the *shime-nawa* hung the *shide* (in modern usage, strips of pure white paper) denoting the sacred character of the place (see DEVOTIONAL OBJECTS AND IMAGES). The first shrines were built to provide an enclosed place in which to keep the *mitama-shiro* (substitute for the *mitama*, or august jewel that represented the spirit of the *kami*); this symbol, also called *shintai*, was a material token (mirror, stone, saber, tablet with the name of the divinity written on it) in which the divinity, invisible, was believed to reside in order to come into contact with the faithful. Pre-Buddhist Shinto architecture is generally extremely simple, notably different from that of the Buddhist temple (*tera*); in effect it imitates the ancient indigenous thatched hut. The Shinto shrine (*miya*, or *yashiro*) is constructed entirely of rough timber, generally hinoki cypress (*Chamaecyparis obtusa*), and usually comprises two free-standing structures, the *honden*, or sanctuary, closed to laymen, where the *mitama-shiro* is kept, and the *haiden*, or hall for the worshipers, the two often being connected by a raised covered passageway (*ai-no-ma*). In the case of major shrines, other structures stand beside these two edifices, and the whole complex is encircled by one or more fences (*tamagaki*).

A striking characteristic of Shinto shrines has already been mentioned: the torii, a wooden gateway placed at the entrance to the complex, generically derived from the Indian torana. There is no reference to the torii in the *Kojiki* or the *Nihongi*, and its symbolic significance in the context of Shintoism is

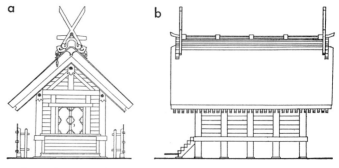

Osaka, Sumiyoshi Shrine: (*a*) Front elevation; (*b*) side elevation (*from Ponsonby-Fane, 1942*).

not clearly understood. The design of the sacred gateway is of the utmost simplicity, utilizing two vertical cylindrical elements, supporting a rectangular crossbeam joining them and extending beyond the upper ends, and another horizontal beam below this, which terminates against the poles.

The architectural type (tenchi gongen) of the original Shinto shrine can be observed, virtually unaltered, in the structure of the Great Shrine of Ise (PLS. 5, 6). The archetype of Shinto sanctuaries, it has been rebuilt every twenty years since the time of the emperor Temmu (r. 672–86). In its modern state it does not differ greatly from its ancient form, described in manuscripts of the Nara period such as the Kō-dai-jingū gishiki-chō ("Documents on the Rituals of the Great Shrine of Ise") of the year 804. The fences around the sanctuary probably retain the original design, and the structure preserves the basic elements of the style known as shimmei-zukuri: the supporting pillars of the ridgepole (munamochi-bashira); the logs (katsuogi) placed across the ridgepole as billets; and the two bargeboards (chigi) projecting obliquely skyward above the ridge (iraka-ōi), with the characteristic "wind holes" (kaze-kiri). It is a structure of extraordinary beauty and solemnity, a true architectural monument.

Another structural style of Shinto shrine is known as taisha-zukuri; this is best exemplified by the Great Shrine of Izumo, dedicated to the god Okuni-nushi, or Okuni-nushi-no-Mikoto (PL. 9). The present reconstruction (1744), unlike that of the Great Shrine of Ise, is not entirely faithful to the original design. Only the ancient plan has remained unchanged. The bargeboards are no longer extended in the original way, hence the chigi are merely ornamental; the roof gable is slightly curved.

With the diffusion and entrenchment of Buddhism, Shinto architecture yielded to its influence, and the primitive types began to display elements of the continental style (PLS. 7, 8). This stylistic alteration of structure was strongly accelerated by the spread of Ryōbu Shinto. Shrines began to be painted and to be built with upcurving roofs, the eaves of which were supported by a system of brackets (tō-kyō). It became common to use two-story portals in place of the traditional torii, and passageways replaced fences. Within the enclosure of the Shinto shrines were erected pagodas, Buddha halls, and other Buddhist structures. The most important types of Buddhist-influenced shrines that appeared during the Heian period are designated by the names nagare, Kasuga, Hachiman, Hie, and gongen.

The nagare type, which remained the most popular form of Shinto shrine up to the Edo (or Tokugawa) period (1615–1867), is represented by the main sanctuary of the Kamo Shrine of Kyoto, which has a rectangular plan, with the entrance on the long side, parallel to the ridgepole. The roof is gabled, and the curved front portion has an exaggerated forward projection that affords shelter for the faithful (a type of overhang known as gohai, "place for worship"). The Kasuga type of shrine, so named after the Kasuga Shrine of Nara, has a gabled roof of cypress bark, the ridge surmounted by two rows of curved crossed poles (oki-chigi) that are far removed from the primitive straight examples; the wooden parts of the shrine are painted with cinnabar. The Hachiman type, which derives its name from the earliest shrine dedicated to this god, the Usa Shrine in Oita prefecture, would seem to have a different origin; it is characterized by two adjacent structures with gabled roofs, one building in front of the other, with the entrances on the side parallel to the ridgepoles. The roofs of the two buildings are joined and have a common drainage trough at the line of junction. This design is evidently of Buddhist inspiration, for it is found in the "twin halls" (sō-dō) of Buddhist temples. The Hie type, seen in the principal edifice of the Hie Shrine in Shiga prefecture, is covered with a gabled roof that, viewed from the front, resembles a canopy (irimoya). The gongen type, exemplified by the Kitano Shrine of Kyoto, is probably a derivative of the Usa Shrine, in which the two structures are separated by a passageway covered by a roof.

In the Kamakura period changes took place that notably transformed the earlier styles, making the Shinto shrine more similar to Buddhist models. As early as the end of the Heian period the system of brackets and the bracket with arm in the form of a boat, the so-called "boat bracket" (funa-hijiki) — typically Shintoist — had been replaced by brackets of a more complex sort, the "three cubes on an arm" type (mitsu-to); these were universally adopted by the larger shrines during and after the Kamakura period. The gables, too, with their bargeboards in the shape of bottles (taihei-zuka), reveal Buddhist influence.

The primitive worship of mountain and forest had brought the Japanese to look upon the tree, the waterfall, or other natural phenomenon as the principal component of the Shinto sanctuary; the shrine itself was intended only as a place of repose for the divine spirit and hence was constructed on a very small scale. Some tiny shrines (ko-miya) dating from the Muromachi period (1334–1573), such as the Fusaji of Kyoto and the Enjōji of Nara, had façades measuring less than 6 ft. in height. But gradually the example of the great Buddhist temples prevailed, and much larger dimensions became usual in the latter part of the Muromachi period.

In general, as has been indicated, the many thousands of Shinto shrines that dot the Japanese islands no longer present the primitive features of simplicity and linearity characteristic of the traditional indigenous architecture, in which the curved line is nonexistent; rather, they are to be identified with the architecture of Buddhism as it came to Japan from China. The purest style of ancient Japanese architecture is to be seen only in the Great Shrine of Ise and, in part, in the Great Shrine of Izumo.

BIBLIOG. Imperial Japanese Commission to the Panama-Pacific International Exposition, Japanese Temples and Their Treasures, Tokyo, 1915; K. A. Florenz, Die historischen Quellen der Shinto-religion aus dem altjapanischen und chinesischen übersetzt und erklärt, Göttingen, Leipzig, 1919; J. M. Martin, Le Shintoïsme, 2 vols., Hong Kong, 1924–27; K. Hattori, Nihon Ko-Kenchiku-shi (History of Old Japanese Architecture), Kyoto, 1926–28; G. B. Sansom, Japan: A Short Cultural History, London, 1931 (2d ed., New York, 1955); S. Kiyowara, Shinto-shi (History of Shintoism), Tokyo, 1932; A. Akiyama, Shinto and Its Architecture, Kyoto, 1936; A. L. Sadler, A Short History of Japanese Architecture, London, 1941 (2d ed., Tokyo, Rutland, Vt., 1963); T. Fukuyama, Jinja Kozushu (A Collection of Old Shrine Plans), Tokyo, 1942; N. Miyaji, Shinto Ronpo (On Shinto), Tokyo, 1942; R. A. B. Ponsonby-Fane, Studies in Shinto and Shrines, Kyoto, 1942 (2d ed., 1953); I. Oba, Shinto Kokogaku Ronpo (On Shinto and Archaeology), Tokyo, 1943; K. Yanagida, Shinto to Minzokugaku (Shinto and Ethnology), Tokyo, 1943; T. Harada, Nihon Kodai Shukyo (Religion in Early Japan), Tokyo, 1948; M. Muccioli, Lo Shintoismo: religione nazionale del Giappone, Milan, 1948; G. Kato, A Bibliography of Shinto in Western Languages from the Oldest Times till 1952, Tokyo, 1953; Pageant of Japanese Art, VI: Architecture and Garden, Tokyo, 1954; R. T. Paine and A. Soper, The Art and Architecture of Japan, Harmondsworth, 1955; N. Kawazoe, Tami to Kami no Sumai (Dwellings of the People and the Gods), Tokyo, 1960; T. Fukuyama and K. Kikutake, Nihon no Yashiro — Sumiyoshi (Japan's Shrines — Sumiyoshi), Tokyo, 1962; T. Fukuyama and Y. Kojiro, Nihon no Yashiro — Izumo (Japan's Shrines — Izumo), Tokyo, 1962; Y. Futagawa, The Roots of Japanese Architecture, New York, 1963; J. M. Richards, An Architectural Journey in Japan, London, 1963; R. A. B. Ponsonby-Fane, Visiting Famous Shrines in Japan, Kyoto, 1964; F. H. Ross, Shinto: The Way of Japan, Boston, 1965; K. Tange and N. Kawazoe, Ise: Prototype of Japanese Architecture, Cambridge, Mass., 1965 (bibliog.).

Antonio PRIORI

Illustrations: PLS. 5–10; 1 fig. in text.

SIAM: See THAILAND.

SIAMESE ART. At its beginnings the culture of Siam (see THAILAND), which was chiefly inspired by Buddhism (q.v.), was quite distinct from that of Cambodia (see KHMER ART), although the origin of both cultures was connected with the immigration of Indian settlers into the Indochinese peninsula (see INDIA, FARTHER). Siamese art deserves to be considered independently, both for its undoubted esthetic value and for its historical significance, insofar as it marks the point of farthest diffusion of several important Indian cultures (see ANDHRA; GUPTA, SCHOOL OF; PALA-SENA SCHOOLS), whose influence spread in varying degrees over a large part of Asia.

SUMMARY. Introduction (col. 11). Dvāravatī (col. 12): *Architecture; Sculpture.* Lopburi (col. 14). Sukhodaya (col. 14): *Archi-*

tecture; *Sculpture; Pictorial art.* Northern Siam (col. 17): *Architecture; Sculpture; Painting.* Ayudhyā (col. 18): *Architecture; Sculpture; Painting.* Bangkok (col. 19): *Architecture; Sculpture; Painting.*

INTRODUCTION. For fourteen centuries the artists of Siam have chiefly devoted themselves to the service of Theravāda Buddhism. The most serious of their works are "reminders of the Doctrine," and a large portion of the rest are connected, directly or indirectly, with religion.

Orthodoxy recognizes several sorts of reminders. "Reminders by association" (*paribhogacetiya*) may not be accessible to everyone: for instance the places in India where the Great Events of the Buddha's career occurred, the Bo tree that sheltered him at the moment of Enlightenment, the footprints he left on riverbank and mountaintop, and the stupas built by the faithful to contain his bodily relics. "Indicative reminders" (*uddesikacetiya*) are objects which, though neutral in themselves, the general opinion may regard as substitutes for reminders by association: pictures or bas-reliefs depicting the Great Events, trees grown from cuttings of the original Bo tree or one of its descendants, copies of the footprints, and copies of stupas that contained relics; such things as these can be made available anywhere. Images of the Buddha are also indicative reminders. They are always copies of older images, being theoretically reproduced, at however many removes, from legendary original likenesses such as those made by artists who knew the Buddha during his life. Their "supernatural anatomy" therefore recalls the aniconic symbols that preceded the invention of the Buddhist icon, especially symbols of flame and sun (see IMAGES AND ICONOCLASM). In devising this anatomy, fire worshipers who had been converted to Buddhism took a leading part; they naturally emphasized the fiery energy (*teja*) of the Sage and conceived of him in terms of such symbols.

As a rule an indicative reminder owes its power to the fact that it is a copy of a reminder by association. Yet it is not a copy in the Western sense: like the young Bo tree, it is supposed to *be* like the original but need not *look* like it. The great artists of India, and doubtless those of Farther India as well, did not work in the presence of the model: they studied it while they worshiped it, forming in their minds an indelible memory-picture of its essential qualities. Then, having left it, they rendered the memory-picture in the chosen material. A few famous models in India or Ceylon established the types of stupas and images that became current in Siam. Usually the intermediary that gave form to the artist's memory-picture was a small portable replica of the faraway original, such as a miniature shrine or a statuette; and the final copy would be reenlarged to the desired scale. This in turn would inspire an endless series of imitations. In the process, although certain essential features of the model would be preserved, the appearance would inevitably be altered.

In sculpture, for instance, the features the copy had to preserve correspond approximately to what may be called the iconography. For Buddha images this involves three things: anatomy, costume, and posture. There is little latitude for choice. The anatomy may vary, within limits, for the form of supernatural details. The dress is the garb of a Buddhist monk, either draped over both shoulders in the "covering" mode or else leaving the right shoulder bare in the "open" mode; it is always rendered as if reduced to transparency by the incandescence of the Sage's limbs; occasionally princely attire is superimposed or substituted. Four postures are permissible: walking, standing, sitting, and reclining; there are fewer than a dozen usual gestures of the hand. Whatever combination of these characteristics the model exhibits is likely to be duplicated in the copy, although if the model is badly eroded or parts of it have been broken off, some improvisation may be necessary.

DVĀRAVATĪ. The earliest school of art in Siam (6th–11th cent., or if we include its offshoots, 6th–13th cent.) has been given the name Dvāravatī, after a kingdom that lay in the lower valley of the Mè Nâm (Menam) near the Gulf. The Tai, who predominate in Thailand today, had not yet arrived; the people of Dvāravatī, or at least the upper classes, were Mòn. They were converted to the Theravāda at an early date by missionaries from India or Ceylon.

Architecture. Nothing survives of Dvāravatī architecture except foundations and fragments in the region where the kingdom was centered and one or two monuments at Lampûn (Lamphun), the little kingdom in northern Siam that was

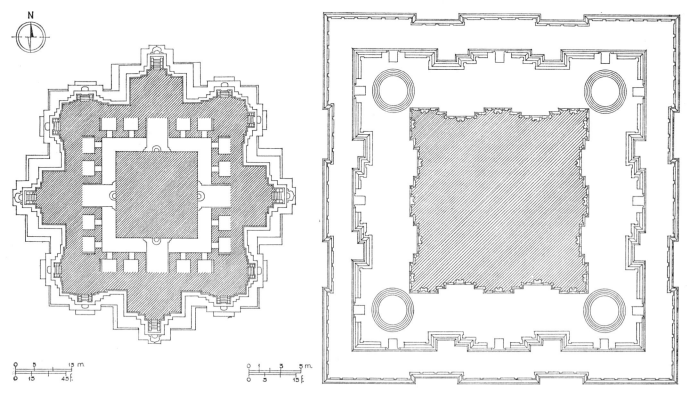

Monuments of the Dvāravatī school on the outskirts of Nagara Paṭhama. *Left*: Wat Braḥ Meru, reconstructed plan. *Right*: Wat Braḥ Padona, plan (*from Dupont, 1959*).

a cultural offshoot of Dvāravatī (FIGS. 11, 13; Le May, 1938, figs. 108, 109; Dupont, 1959, passim). Stereobates were made of brick or laterite, and brick was the principal material for monuments; the trim was generally of stucco. In addition to the solid monuments, certain remains indicate that the monastic architecture included square shrines (mandapas) and oblong assembly halls (viharas).

(PL. 12; Dupont, 1959, figs. 172–84, 197–202, 207–18, 308–11, 508–16; Bowie, 1960, fig. 28).

LOPBURÎ (LOP BURI). After Dvāravatī lost its independence to the Khmer (ca. A.D. 1000) there was a long interlude in which the official art echoed the styles of Angkor (see CAMBODIA; KHMER ART; Bowie, 1960, figs. 39–61). But although the con-

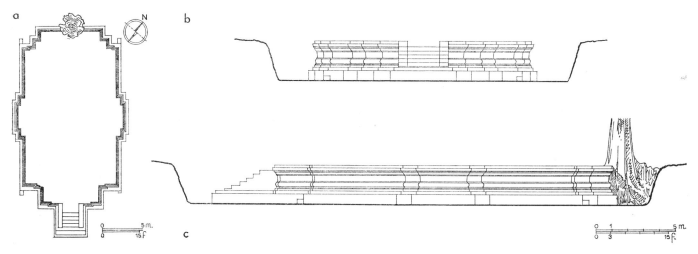

Pong Dük, base of the San Chao vihara: (a) Plan; (b) view from southeast side; (c) view from northeast side (from Dupont, 1959).

Sculpture. At the outset, the school of Dvāravatī must have had Indian masters, but their work has disappeared. The Mòn sculptors owe much to Indian example, especially to the late Gupta style of the cave temples, but they did not take over the conventions of any one Indian school wholesale. Their finest productions are stone, bronze, and terra-cotta images of the Buddha, which are full of simple dignity, youthful but timeless, lacking neither in grace nor in finish (PL. 11).

Among standing figures a single type is overwhelmingly predominant: the robe is worn in the covering mode, and both hands are raised to shoulder level with the thumb and forefinger joined in the gesture of exposition, or *vitarka* (Dupont, 1959, figs. 373, 397, 404, 425–27, 432–51; Bowie, 1960, figs. 9, 12). This type seems to be an adaptation of a type occasionally seen at Ajanta (e.g., in Cave XXVI; Dupont, 1959, fig. 334; Bowie, 1960, fig. 8), in which the right hand performs the gesture of dispelling fear (*abhaya*), and the left hand grasps a corner of the robe. Though the position of the hands is nearly the same in both cases, their function is different, as if the Dvāravatī type had been first established when a Mòn artist, copying an imported model whose fingers were broken, improvised a reconstruction.

Much more rarely the standing figure imitates another occasional Gupta type: the robe in the covering mode, the right hand performing the gesture of bestowing favors (*varada*), the left hand grasping a corner of the robe (PL. 12; Dupont, 1959, figs. 339, 392; Bowie, 1960, fig. 10). Here the original iconography is faithfully reproduced. It is curious that among Dvāravatī cult images in stone there are no copies of the type which predominates in the Indian cave temples and which is like the one just described except that the robe is in the open mode (cf. the principal figures in VII, PL. 454; Bowie, 1960, fig. 74). In small reliefs and bronzes, however, it appears occasionally. Images in the seated position generally follow Gupta models, but with certain adaptations and also with occasional echoes of other schools such as those of Amaravati and Ceylon (VII, PL. 445; Bowie, 1960, figs. 14–17, 21).

In contrast to the Buddha images, whose beauty lies in their subtle renderings of a stereotyped theme, the incidental figures in relief scenes are alive with delightful invention (Bowie, 1960, figs. 17, 18). Some of the finest are in stucco, ranging in mood from the graceful and the sublime to sheer comedy

querors were predominantly followers of the Hindu religions, most of the educated population of Siam seem to have remained faithful to the Theravāda; hence the great number of Buddha images ascribed to the Lopburî school, which combines the Dvāravatī and the Khmer traditions in varying proportions (Bowie, 1960, figs. 57, 58).

SUKHODAYA (SUKHOTHAI). Tai emigrants, drifting in from their old homelands in China in search of richer lands and freedom from Chinese domination, formed settlements inside the borders of the Khmer empire. Probably the movement was very gradual, so imperceptible at first that it is useless to try to date its beginning. At an unknown date, perhaps about 1220, the Tai settlements in the region of Sukhodaya in central Siam renounced their allegiance to the Khmer and formed an independent kingdom. It grew rapidly, and by the end of the century it included nearly the whole of Siam.

Under the influence of their Mòn neighbors, the Tai became staunch adherents of the Theravāda. Later they established religious relations with Ceylon, which was then considered to be the fountainhead of the purest Doctrine. The profound originality of Tai art, as developed at Sukhodaya, lies not in the invention of new forms, which would have been meaningless, but in the harmonious rearrangement of those already in existence.

Architecture. For monuments the Tai, like the Mòn, preferred brick, or brick over a core of laterite, with stucco trim. The *prāṅg* is a free imitation of the Khmer tower, or *prāsāda* (Le May, 1938, fig. 95; Bowie, 1960, fig. 66). There are several different types of stupa, each, it may be supposed, an imitation of some famous monument in Siam (Bowie, 1960, figs. 62, 65, 69). One type has an octagonal base, doubtless inspired by a Mòn model (Le May, 1938, fig. 97). Some of the bell-shaped stupas are plain and small, while others are huge and elaborate; several, copied from the Mahāthūpa at Anuradhapura in Ceylon, are supported on the backs of masonry elephants (PL. 16; Bowie, 1960, fig. 64). The most characteristic form of Sukhodaya *cetiya* is vaguely reminiscent of a minaret (PL. 19; Bowie, 1960, fig. 65): it seems to be a copy, enlarged to a monumental scale, of some small bronze miniature shrine of the sort produced at Negapatam in India.

While the importation of small models can determine type, even though rather imprecisely, the importation of craftsmen can have a very marked effect on style. An inscription indicates that craftsmen from Ceylon helped to rebuild the Great Relic Monastery at Sukhodaya in the 14th century, and some of its pediments strongly recall Singhalese art (PLS. 16, 19; Bowie, 1960, fig. 85; Le May, 1938, fig. 136).

The precinct of a monastery included various sorts of structure besides stupas. The mandapa, built to house a Footprint or a cult image, was a hollow cube with a pyramidal roof (Bowie, 1960, fig. 4). The assembly hall (vihara), like the almost identical ordination hall (uposathagāra), was a long nave, usually with stuccoed brick walls and a tiled roof; sometimes the nave was flanked by a pair of side aisles, or even two or three pairs, separated by the rows of columns that supported the roof (Le May, 1938, fig. 135).

Sculpture. The Sukhodaya sculptors were modelers rather than carvers, preferring bronze for *ronde-bosse* and stucco for reliefs. Their first masters in the art of image making were doubtless the Mòn and Khmer, especially the Khmer sculptors of the post-Bayon school. Singhalese artists, arriving after the Sukhodaya plastic style was established, helped to refine and perfect it. Possibly technicians from southern India also taught at Sukhodaya: the three-dimensional quality and the fluency of Tai bronzes suggest their example.

It is not known when the school of Sukhodaya sculpture started, but there is positive evidence that it was producing in quantity before the close of the 13th century. It continued well into the 16th century and perhaps longer. Its output, which ranges in quality from folk art to the most accomplished masterpieces, includes thousands of life-size or larger images and innumerable statuettes. Out of this enormous mass of sculpture, about half a dozen images bear 15th-century dates (PL. 13, right; Bowie, 1960, figs. 75, 82; Griswold, 1956, figs. 1–6). A chronological framework for the rest can be established by postulating a preclassic style, assignable to the 13th century, a high classic dating mainly from the 14th, and a postclassic found in the 15th and 16th centuries. This is a purely arbitrary division, the usefulness of which remains to be tested.

The most astonishing invention of Sukhodaya sculpture, and the glory of Siamese art, is the representation *en ronde bosse* of the walking Buddha — or, to be more precise, the Buddha who has just come to a pause in walking. The finest example is a bronze statue somewhat more than life-size now in the Monastery of the Fifth King (Peñcamapabitra) in Bangkok (Bowie, 1960, fig. 72; Griswold, 1953, figs. 4, 5). Dating from about the mid-14th century, it displays all the most remarkable qualities of the high classic style. The anatomy, with its seemingly arbitrary proportions and its auspicious marks, typifies the physical and mental development of the Yogi and especially his fiery energy. From the protuberance of the skull (ushnīsha) there springs a jet of flame (in this case a restoration, and not quite the right shape). The distended ear lobes are the mark of a prince who wore heavy earrings before becoming a monk. Several features correspond more especially to those curious descriptions of the Buddha's person given in the Pali commentaries composed in medieval Ceylon: the shoulders are broad, the chest full, and the arms very long; the soles of the feet are flat and the heels projecting. Other features are based on the stereotyped similes used in Sanskrit poetry to describe gods and heroes, or (what amounts to the same thing) on comparisons with familiar objects prescribed in the Indian art manuals as guides to anatomical form. The legs are "like the legs of a deer," and the thighs are "like the stems of banana trees." The arms are smooth and rounded "like the trunk of an elephant"; the hands are "like lotus flowers just beginning to open," with the fingertips turning backward like petals. The shape of the head is "like an egg"; and the chin, with its incised oval line, is "like a mango stone"; the nose is "like a parrot's beak" and the eyebrows are "like drawn bows." The curls of the hair are "like the stings of scorpions." At the same time, without making any attempt at realism, the artist has put something of the Tai physiognomy into the inflection

of the eyelids and lips, the slim hands and tapering fingers; and the vigorous abdominal muscles recall the prolonged breathing exercises that precede the Buddhist practice of mental concentration and meditative trance (samadhi, dhyana).

To visualize the fiery being whom he has here portrayed in bronze, the artist himself may well have used this practice, or at least the initial stages of it, concurrently with his study of the model. The routine often begins with concentrating the gaze on an object (kasina), such as the flame of a lamp; and as subject and object merge, the nature of the object affects the nature of the vision. The modeling of the figure has a trancelike quality. The material is knowingly used, but not to give the illusion of flesh and drapery. The surfaces of the bronze flicker, the silhouette leaps like a fire. The robe is worn in the open mode, and the cloth that falls from the extended forearm assumes an undulating silhouette, as if still rippling from the movement of walking. The left hand is raised in the gesture of exposition, the right arm swings naturally at the side. The left leg supports the weight of the body, while the raising of the right heel not only makes its supernatural projection more conspicuous but also shows beyond all possibility of doubt that the walking posture is intended.

Whereas most Buddha images, being designed to be seen mainly from the front, are not particularly interesting when looked at from the side or the back, this statue looks superb from any angle, and best of all when seen, as circumambulators would see it, from every angle in succession. It would be vain to seek as its prototype a walking Buddha *en ronde bosse*: there was no such thing until Sukhodaya invented it; or rather, there was none that was sharply distinguished from a Buddha standing still, though earlier styles had sometimes produced statuettes that could be interpreted either way, with both feet firmly planted on the ground. In the earlier styles even figures in basrelief where the context indicates that walking is to be understood very rarely have the heel raised. Yet by all the rules this bronze must be a copy of an earlier image. The model for the first of the series was doubtless a stucco high relief in the Sukhodaya preclassic style (PL. 13). While the intermediary that transmitted to it the iconography of its ultimate prototype can only be surmised (a small figure in a Dvāravatī relief?), there can be no doubt that the ultimate prototype was one of the standard late Gupta figures in the Indian cave temples, with the robe in the open mode, the left hand raised to shoulder level, and the right hand down (VII, PL. 454). The function of the hands, however, is reinterpreted: the left, instead of grasping the robe, performs the gesture; the right, instead of performing the gesture, is at leisure. Yet the bronze, though separated by eight centuries from its prototype, carries the spirit of the late Gupta model to its logical conclusion.

The walking Buddhas all wear the robe in the open mode, but sometimes the hand position is reversed: the right hand may be raised to perform the gesture, either dispelling fear (abhaya) or exposition (vitarka), while the left arm swings at the side. A fine example, cast in 1426 at the order of the Prince of Nân, is of postclassic style (PL. 13). This model evidently springs from a different prototype, originating in north Indian Gupta art. (For three other images cast for the Prince of Nân in the same year, see Griswold, 1956.)

Bronze images of the Buddha standing still are rare in the high classic period, but frequent in the postclassic (PL. 14; Griswold, 1953, figs. 33, 34; Griswold, 1956, fig. 4; Bowie, 1960, fig. 75). In contrast to the walking figures, they always wear the robe in the covering mode. Like the walking figures, they can perform a gesture with either hand; but unlike them, they can also perform it with both or not at all.

The vast majority of Sukhodaya images are in the seated posture (PL. 14). They wear the robe in the open mode. As in Singhalese and Khmer art, the legs are folded, one lying on top of the other (vīrāsana). With few exceptions the right hand is in the position of calling the earth to witness (bhūmi-sparśa). The theme is too common in earlier sculpture to make it possible to point to a specific prototype, but not common enough to explain its overwhelming predominance at Sukhodaya. The explanation doubtless lies in the reputation of some particular statue that occupied a place of high honor in the capital. At their best, the seated figures in the high classic style have the same plastic qualities as the walking images; and although the interest of momentarily arrested motion is absent, they have the same nervous energy. In their own way they are just as flamelike.

Reclining figures are rare. The finest example is in the Monastery of the Excellent Abode in Bangkok (PL. 14).

A Buddhist monarch, by tradition, is the protector of all religions, not merely his own. The kings of Sukhodaya had subjects of Hindu faith; and in particular they had Brahman advisers on secular matters. For use in their ceremonies they provided them with splendid bronze images of Hindu deities (PL. 15).

The Sukhodaya sculptors were skillful workers in stucco as well as in bronze. They inherited the technique from Dvāravatī and refined it under the tutelage of Singhalese craftsmen. The stucco detail of the brick monuments is animated and delightful. Some of the stucco reliefs representing episodes from the Buddha's life are profoundly moving works of art (PL. 19). A particularly fine one, in spite of the damage it has suffered, is the *Descent from Heaven* on the wall of a ruined mandapa outside the ramparts of old Sukhodaya (Bowie, 1960, fig. 86). The Buddha, accompanied by the gods Indra and Brahmā and their followers, descends a miraculously created ladder to the earth, while the gods remaining in heaven — filled with piety as a result of listening to him while he preached for three months to his mother — look on from a sort of gallery above. The relief was polychromed and partly gilded; the deep red of the Sage's robe has faded to a soft rose, and a few flecks of gold on the *parure* of the gods still catch the light.

Pictorial art. Except for a few obscure fragments, no Sukhodaya painting has survived; but there are a few clues as to what it was like. Apart from the stucco reliefs, which give an idea of both pictorial composition and color, there are a number of drawings incised on stone or bronze tablets. Some of them depict Jatakas (Le May, 1938, fig. 139; Bowie, 1960, fig. 68), some the Buddha's footprints (Griswold, 1953, fig. 20).

NORTHERN SIAM. From the late 13th to the mid-16th century, northern Siam was the seat of the independent Tai kingdom of Lân Nâ. It inherited the Mòn traditions of Lampûn; in the 14th and 15th centuries its religion and art were strongly influenced by Sukhodaya, and the period from the latter part of the 15th to the mid-16th century was its golden age of art and letters.

Architecture. The oldest Tai monument still standing in Lân Nâ dates from about the year 1300 (Le May, 1938, fig. 106). Making allowance for the extensive restorations, it hardly differs in design or in style from the Mòn monuments of Lampûn (Le May, 1938, figs. 108, 109).

The great masterpiece is the Seven Spires Monastery (Wat Jet Yòt), begun in 1455 (PL. 20; Bowie, 1960, fig. 97; for a complete description, see Hutchinson, 1951). Probably it was intended as an act of merit in connection with the 2000th anniversary of the Buddha's death (1456/57). Officially named Mahābodhārāma, it is a copy on a smaller scale of the Mahābodhi temple at Bodhgaya in India (VII, PL. 133); apparently the founder, like his fellow monarch the King of Pegu, sent a mission of architects to India to get the plans. As at Bodhgaya, the main structure is a cube, supporting a large central obelisk with a lesser obelisk at each corner. On the walls are stucco reliefs of great elegance, clearly inspired by the example of Sukhodaya: celestial beings float among flowers, pressing their palms together in the gesture of respect. Nominally they are the gods that came to applaud the Buddha's victory over evil; in fact, as they are dressed in the ceremonial costume of the court of Lân Nâ, they are doubtless idealized portraits of the founder and his family.

Sculpture. At the outset, Lân Nâ followed the example of Lampûn (Le May, 1938, fig. 109). In the second half of the

14th century it began to follow the example of Sukhodaya. In the second half of the 15th century its sculptors, trained in the Sukhodaya tradition, made bronze Buddha images in imitation of several different models (Griswold, *Dated Buddha Images of Northern Siam*, 1957). The most striking are the lion type, based on an Indian model, the Śākyasimha at Bodhgaya. Doubtless the intermediary that introduced the Śākyasimha to Lân Nâ was a replica of it made in the Pala period, obtained by the same mission that got the plans of the Mahābodhi temple. The lion-type images have the robe in the open mode and sit with crossed legs (*vajrāsana*), the right hand calling the earth to witness. More numerous are the mixed-type images, which more or less continue the Sukhodaya tradition.

The lion type dates from about 1470 to 1565, with a revival in the late 19th and 20th centuries; the mixed types began a little earlier and have continued without interruption to the present time. There is ample evidence to support this chronology (Griswold, *Dated Buddha Images of Northern Siam*, 1957); but a contrary opinion, strongly held in Bangkok, maintains that the most beautiful of the lion type belong to the "early Chieng Sèn" school and date from somewhere between the 9th and 12th centuries, while only the poorer examples (i.e., those bearing dated inscriptions) are attributable to the 15th and 16th centuries (Mom Chao Chand and Khien Yimsiri, 1957). Bangkok opinion dates the mixed types from the 14th to the 16th century. The name Chieng Sèn, which Bangkok gives both types, is a misnomer (except for a relatively small number of images actually found at Chieng Sèn and dating from the 15th to the 18th century).

Painting. Northern Siam contains some pleasant murals of the 19th and 20th centuries, to some extent inspired by Burmese example. The great majority of the older paintings have perished. One exception, now in the Bangkok Museum, is a painting on cloth (ca. 16th cent.) representing the Descent from Heaven.

AYUDHYĀ. In 1350 the Prince of Û Tòng founded Ayudhyā, which became the strongest and most prosperous kingdom of the southeast-Asia peninsula. About 1430 its armies invaded Cambodia and captured Angkor but retired soon after. Sukhodaya, which had already been reduced to vassalage, was incorporated into the kingdom a few years later. The rulers of Ayudhyā thought of themselves as the inheritors of both the Tai tradition of Sukhodaya and the Khmer tradition of Angkor (see KHMER ART). Though they were Theravāda Buddhists and gave generously to religion, they also honored the Brahmans and took over the Hindu ceremonial of the Angkor court.

Architecture. Two traditions, the Khmer and the Tai, gradually merged, perhaps at first as a result of the exponents of each copying the models of the other (Le May, 1938, figs. 192–95). The most characteristic and splendid form of monument is the *prăng*. It preserves the old concept of the Khmer temple-mountain, stylized and modified. One of the finest examples is Wat Rājapūraṇa, founded in 1424 (Bowie, 1960, figs. 117, 118). The bell-shaped stupas perpetuate the traditions of Sukhodaya and Ceylon (Le May, 1938, fig. 190). Another form of stupa is bell-shaped in outline but square in plan, with deeply recessed angles.

Sculpture. The so-called "Û Tòng bronzes" mostly date from the beginning of the Ayudhyā period. One group, which resemble Dvāravatī bronzes, may be pre-Ayudhyā. A second, in which the Khmer physiognomy is imitated, perhaps date from 1350 to 1425. A third, with more oval faces, may date from between 1400 and 1475. The last group were produced in enormous quantity: the bronze casters developed great dexterity in making the metal go as far as possible, often using so little wax in preparing for the casting that the metal is no more than a paper-thin skin over the baked-clay core.

A large group of stone Buddhas have much the same plastic qualities as the Û Tòng bronzes (Le May, 1938, figs. 186–89). In an article written several years ago the present author attributed them to the 17th century (Luang Boribal Buribhand and Griswold, 1951), but it now seems likely that they run from the late 14th to the 17th century. Some of them would therefore be contemporary with the second and third Û Tòng groups.

About the middle of the 15th century the Û Tòng style began to merge into the Ayudhyā national style. At the beginning it produced some excellent work, for example the splendid series of Jataka figures cast in 1458 (Bowie, 1960, fig. 127). The national style lasted more than 300 years and ended in decadence. Mass production was its downfall; the image makers seemingly forgot how to use the sort of memory-picture that could give life to "copying," and became content with mere imitation. Some of their best works are figures of the Buddha wearing royal attire; but it is the attire, rather than the Buddha, that is significant.

Painting. The most important surviving examples are some recently discovered murals in a crypt in Wat Rājapūraṇa Ayudhyā, dating from the first half of the 15th century. They depict 24 Past Buddhas, scenes of worship and monastic ceremony, and moral tales. There are also some fine 18th-century murals at Bejrapuri.

BANGKOK. Ayudhyā was destroyed in a war against the Burmese in 1767. Instead of rebuilding it, the Siamese founded a new capital at Bangkok.

Architecture. The builders of Bangkok wanted to make it as much like the old capital as possible. An immense amount of building had to be done, but there was no need to introduce new architectural forms, as monasteries and palaces reproduced the remembered glories of the past. After a time, however, Chinese architecture became popular; and a little later, imitations of European buildings began to appear, often modified into an easygoing *chinoiserie*. The intrusion was at first pleasant enough, and even the late Victorian domestic architecture in Bangkok is comfortable and picturesque. But in the present century the epidemic of unsightly adaptations of Western and Chinese styles has got out of control.

The Siamese monumental style, as manifested in the first hundred years of the Bangkok period, is a marvel of grace and fantasy (PLS. 17, 18). Architectural forms grew more exuberant without losing anything of their elegant coherency. Often, to catch the light and enchant the eye, the surfaces of wall and stupa are faced with porcelain tiles or inlaid with bits of chinaware in floral patterns.

One of the most impressive monuments in the world is the Paṭhamacetiya at Nagara Paṭhama (Nakhon Pathom), which is over 375 ft. high and is covered with brilliantly glazed orange-yellow tiles (PL. 17). Completed in the early years of the 20th century, it encases an older monument, which is itself probably composed of several successive encasements, the innermost core dating perhaps from the Dvāravatī period or even earlier.

Sculpture. The Bangkok sculptors excelled in miniature figures and reliefs. Scenes from the Buddha's life, evocations of hell, episodes from the Indian epics, and figures of the Hindu gods riding their chosen animals — such subjects are composed with *brio* and executed with assurance (Bowie, 1960, figs. 145–48; Griswold, *A Warning to Evildoers*, 1957, pp. 18–28).

The Bangkok period produced countless mediocre Buddha images but few noteworthy ones. The tradition was already in decline before the end of the Ayudhyā period, and in the early days of Bangkok the need to restore the glories of the past, which gave such an impetus to architecture, had the opposite effect on image making; it was far more pressing to rescue and restore the old images that lay neglected in the ruined cities than to make new ones. For some time the supply of large statues was more than sufficient; and when at length the demand for new works revived, it was too late: competence could be regained, but not inspiration.

Painting. The same forces that stimulated architecture stimulated painting (Bowie, 1960, figs. 154–63). The pictorial

tradition of Ayudhyā continued almost without a break in Bangkok in the late 18th and early 19th centuries. From the murals on monastery walls to the miniatures in manuscripts, this art preserves an ancient tradition related to Ajanta, Sigiriya, and Pagan. The old legends are placed in the immediate scene, rendered timeless by the happy anachronisms. A Bangkok palace is heaven, where the gods in the garb of Tai princes respectfully entertain visiting monks; the Siamese countryside is a wonderland of hermits, fabulous animals, and quite ordinary people; huge dragons calmly survey steamboats, and the Buddha's father lives in a palace guarded by rifle-bearing sentries.

BIBLIOG. G. Coedès, Les collections archéologiques du Musée National de Bangkok, Paris, 1928; E. S. Le May, A Concise History of Buddhist Art in Siam, Cambridge, 1938; Luang Boribal Buribhand and A. B. Griswold, Sculpture of Peninsular Siam in the Ayuthya Period, J. of the Siam Soc., XXXVIII/2, 1951, pp. 1–60; E. W. Hutchinson, The Seven Spires, J. of the Siam Soc., XXXIX/1, 1951, pp. 1–68; A. B. Griswold, The Buddhas of Sukhodaya, Arch. Chinese Art Soc. of Am., VII, 1953, pp. 5–41; G. Coedès, L'art siamois de l'époque de Sukhodaya (XIIIᵉ–XIVᵉ siècles), circonstances de son évolution, Arts asiatiques, I, 1954, pp. 281–302; A. B. Griswold, L'époque de Sukhodaya, Arts asiatiques, I, 1954, pp. 303–08; Luang Boribal Buribhand, Excavations at the Chapel Royal at Ayudhya, J. of the Siam Soc., XLIII/2, 1955, pp. 137–38; Dhani Nivat, The Reconstruction of Rāma I of the Chakri Dynasty, J. of the Siam Soc., XLIII/2, 1955, pp. 212–247; A. B. Griswold, New Evidence for the Dating of Sukhodaya Art, AAs, XIX, 3/4, 1956, pp. 240–50; C. N. Spinks, Siam and the Pottery Trade of Asia, J. of the Siam Soc., XLIV/2, 1956, pp. 61–111; Mom Chao Chand and Khien Yimsiri, Thai Monumental Bronzes, Bangkok, 1957; A. B. Griswold, Dated Buddha Images of Northern Siam, Ascona, 1957 (rev. by J. A. Pope, Ars Orientalis, IV, 1961, pp. 446–52); A. B. Griswold, A Warning to Evildoers, AAs, XX/1, 1957; K. G. Heider, New Archaeological Discoveries in Kanchanaburi, J. of the Siam Soc., XLV/1, 1957, pp. 61–70; H. G. Quaritch Wales, An Early Buddhist Civilization in Eastern Siam, J. of the Siam Soc., XLV/1, 1957, pp. 42–60; Silpa Birasri, The Origin and Evolution of Thai Murals, Bangkok, 1959; P. Dupont, L'archéologie mône de Dvāravatī, 2 vols., Paris, 1959; T. C. Bowie ed., The Arts of Thailand, Bloomington, Ind., 1960 (cat.); A. B. Griswold, Five Chieng Sen Bronzes of the 18th Century, Arts Asiatiques, VII, 1960, pp. 3–24, 101–20, 199–204; A. B. Griswold, Notes on Siamese Art, AAs, XXIII, 1960, pp. 5–14; R. S. Le May, A Gold Lacquer Cabinet from Siam, O. Art, N.S., VII, 1961, pp. 135–37; Dhani Nivat, A Gilt Lacquer Screen in the Audience Hall of Dusit, AAs, XXIV, 1961, pp. 275–82; H. R. van Heekeren, A Preliminary Note on the Excavation of the Sai-Yok Rock Shelter, J. of the Siam Soc., XLIX/2, 1961, pp. 99–108; E. Nielsen, The Thai-Danish Pre-Historic Expedition 1960–1961, J. of the Siam Soc., XLIX/1, 1961, pp. 47–55; M. C. Subhadradis Diskul, A Dated Crowned Buddha Image from Thailand, AAs, XXIV, 1961, pp. 409–12; Kraisri Nimmānahéminda, An Inscribed Statuette from Northern Siam, AAs, XXV, 1962, pp. 163–66; M. C. Subhadradis Diskul, Guide to the Ayudhya National Museum Chao Sam Praya, Bangkok, 1962; J. J. Boeles, The King of Śri Dvāravatī and his Regalia, J. of the Siam Soc., LII/1, 1964, pp. 99–114; S. J. O'Connoer, Jr., An Early Brahmanical Sculpture at Sonkhlā, J. of the Siam Soc., LII/2, 1964, pp. 163–69; R. and L. Sharp, Some Archeological Sites in North Thailand, J. of the Siam Soc., LII/2, 1964, pp. 223–39; P. Sørensen, Ban Kao, J. of the Siam Soc., LII/1, 1964, pp. 75–97; M. C. Subhadradis Diskul, Guide to the Ram Khamhaeng National Museum, Sukhothai, Bangkok, 1964; M. C. Subhadradis Diskul, G. Coedès, and J. Boisselier, Trésors de l'art de Thaïlande, Paris, 1964 (cat.); J. Boisselier, Récentes recherches archéologiques en Thailande, Arts asiatiques, XII, 1965, pp. 125–73; A. B. Griswold, Imported Images and the Nature of Copying in the Art of Siam, Essays offered to G. H. Luce . . . , Ascona, 1965; J. Boisselier, Rapport préliminaire d'une mission en Thailande, Arts asiatiques, XII, 1966; C. Chongkol, H. Woodward, Jr., et al., U-Thong National Museum, Suphanburi, Bangkok, 1966; M. C. Subhadradis Diskul, Hindu Gods at Sukhodaya, AAs, 1967.

Alexander B. GRISWOLD

NOTE: For the transcription of Siamese names there are numerous different systems, but few authors follow any one of them consistently. In this article those which are borrowed directly from Sanskrit or Pali are written in the standard fashion for those languages, while names of Tai origin are given according to the author's phonetic system (see A. B. Griswold, Afterthoughts on the Romanization of Siamese, *J. of the Siam Soc.*, XLVIII/1, 1965; Bowie, 1960, p. 27), with parenthetical variants for place names representing other forms in common use.

Illustrations: PLS. 11–20; 2 figs. in text.

SIBERIAN CULTURES. The artistic production of the native populations of Siberia, which extends across northern Asia between the Ural Mountains and the Pacific Ocean, has been influenced by the neighboring civilizations of Asia and to a lesser extent by the cultures of Europe from prehistoric times to the era of Russian penetration. Some original characteristics have also developed; these are particularly noticeable along the northeastern edge of the area, which has remained relatively primitive even up to the present time and whose artistic production bears some similarity to that of certain North American culture areas. Contemporary Siberian art is more modest in quality and intention than it formerly was, consisting mainly in the ornamentation of clothing, furnishings, and domestic articles. In many cases the arrival of the Russian resulted in the introduction of new processes, styles, and motifs and either spurred a decisive evolution or caused the complete neglect of traditional techniques. The Ainu of the Japanese archipelago are also discussed here because their art shows numerous affinities with that of the natives of the extreme eastern Siberian regions and the northwest coast of North America. (See also CHINESE ART; ESKIMO CULTURES; JAPAN; JAPANESE ART; MONGOLIAN ART; NORTH AMERICAN CULTURES; STEPPE CULTURES; TURKIC ART.)

SUMMARY. Derivation and development of Siberian art (col. 21): *General considerations; Cultural classification; Chronological development.* Peoples of the east and south (col. 32): *The Yakuts; The Buryats; The Tuvintsy; The Altaitsy; The Khakasy.* Peoples of the north and farthest east (col. 37): *The Ob Ugrians; The Nentsy; The Evenki; The peoples of the lower Amur and Sakhalin; The Chukchi, Asian Eskimos, and Koryaks.* The Ainu of Japan (col. 41).

DERIVATION AND DEVELOPMENT OF SIBERIAN ART. *General considerations.* The art of Siberia gives an initial impression of uniformity. This is due not only to the homogeneity of materials used (fur, leather, wood, and bone), which are sewn, carved, fused, or painted, but also to the scarcity of modern ceramics and the total absence of architecture or figural monumental sculpture. These general characteristics can be explained by the limitations of fairly similar geographic conditions. The great majority of the population lives in the taiga — the swampy, coniferous forest lands between tundra and steppe. The northern Samoyeds (Nentsy and others; see below), Dolgans, certain Yakut groups, Yukagiry, Koryaks, and Chukchi — all of whom occupy the arctic tundra — have nomadic cultures and thus have not developed any pottery or architecture. The coastal strip along the Pacific, on the other hand, permits a more sedentary life due to fishing and whale hunting. Upon closer examination of Siberian art, variations in style and content become apparent. Each artistic region (see below) belongs to a different ethnic group (FIG. 29), which in the course of its history assimilated various influences.

Paleolithic finds ("Venus" representations and birdlike figures from Malta and Buret in the Angara River valley; VIII, PL. 235) are as yet too scarce to clarify exact stylistic zones for the period or to indicate the precise movements of external influences. The conditions in which the objects were found help to explain their meaning: in the large collective huts the female statuettes were placed on the same side as all other objects belonging to the women; the representations of birds always appeared in the part of the lodgings reserved for men. Very possibly these figures represented the protecting spirits of women and men respectively.

The great cultural currents that animated and characterized the Neolithic period form a clearer picture. The finds in western Siberia, for example, reveal influences from eastern Europe and, even more clearly, stylistic affinities with the production of eastern Siberia. Early Siberian art reached its highest point in the valleys of the central Yenisei, the Angara, and the Lena rivers and in the region around Lake Baikal. Single anthropomorphic figures have been found, as well as numerous representations of elk carved from antlers or engraved in rock. The carvings contain no detail and in the rock representations are limited to simple contour. These techniques enabled Stone Age artists to create pictures of a dynamic and surprising esthetic quality, indicating an attentive observation of animals. Why the neolithic craftsmen represented particular animals is difficult to determine; certainly there must have been some religious meaning, as Okladnikov (1950–55) asserts. The stone ichthyomorphic representations, according to Ivanov (1952), functioned merely as bait.

The extreme eastern end of Siberia, which is geographically detached from the internal regions and is turned toward maritime life and traffic, developed independently from the rest of Siberia since most ancient times. Paleolithic finds there reveal a definite relationship with southeastern Asia. Even during the Neolithic period great migratory movements occurred from south to north as far as the Kamchatka Peninsula; these movements may be seen in relationship to the penetration of the present-day Chukchi, Koryaks, and Itelmeny. As archaeological discoveries prove, the extreme north also received cultural impulses from Alaska, the northwest coast of North America, and continental Siberia during the Neolithic period.

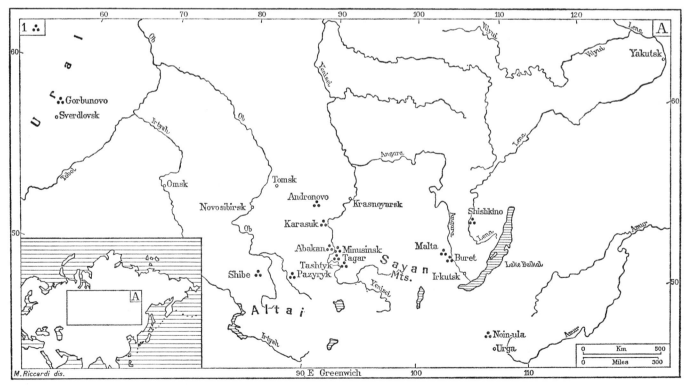

Distribution of the principal centers of archaeological interest in the area of the Siberian cultures. The extent of the area is shown on the inset map. *Key:* (1) Archaeological centers.

In the remaining regions of Siberia the present populations appeared no earlier than the beginning of the metal age. Archaeological material permits detection of cultural diffusion northward from the steppe borders and from the transition zone of forest steppe between steppe and taiga. These strong cultural influences were linked with the commercial traffic and the migratory movements of more southern peoples. It is now definitely established that the Ob Ugrians (Khanty and Mansi), who today live along the middle course of the Ob River and beside its tributaries, and who with the Samoyed-speaking peoples form a stylistic region of Siberia (see below), forged ahead from the steppe in the north of present-day Kazakhstan to the taiga; specialists do not agree, however, as to the date and course of this migration. The original habitat of the Samoyeds was at the foot of the Sayan Mountains — farther south than today; they moved north when the breeding of reindeer enabled them to lead a more nomadic life. It is also likely that the Evenki (Tungus) part of the present-day population of the Lake Baikal region occupied this territory only from the Bronze Age onward, having come from the southeast; precise information regarding their more ancient past is lacking. Southern and southeastern influences in this area can nonetheless be established about 1700 B.C., at the time of the first appearance of metal. These influences did not cause any substantial cultural transformation; the region as a whole presents a picture of independent and continuous development. The art of the early metal age was chiefly concerned with portrayals of shamanist spirits and the representation of anthropomorphic figures and human faces having a religious function; this is shown by the conditions in which the artifacts were found (see SHAMANISM).

The Pacific coastal region, after the spread of metallurgy from China, absorbed influences that came mainly from the south, just as the far north received new developments by way of Neo-Eskimo culture. The isolation of the coastal areas from the inland regions eventually ended because the breeding of reindeer caused the Evenki to spread to the zone of the Amur River and to central Siberia.

The fame of prehistoric Siberian art rests mainly on the masterpieces of the so-called "Scythian animal style" found in southern Siberia in the Minusinsk Basin bordering the Yenisei and in the kurgans, or barrows, of the Altai area. The style at first produced little figures carved on dagger hilts and the monumental stone steles of the Karasuk period (1200–700 B.C.). The peak of artistic production was reached by the nomadic Scythian warriors only between 700 B.C. and A.D. 100 during the Tagar and Pazyryk periods (named after the most famous archaeological centers of the region) and during the following period of Hunnish domination (see ASIATIC PROTOHISTORY; PLS. 186–189; II, FIG. 31; X, PL. 136). The best of this work appears in the representation of wild animals. Minute observation of nature produced an organic and dynamic quality of design, a perfection of proportion, and a refined sense of form apparent in the scenes within a frame (e.g., a rectangular ornamental slab or a semicircular horse's bit). The Scythian artists during their most flourishing period succeeded in fully rendering the characteristics of the animal with only a few strokes and, without diminishing the harmony of the whole, sometimes accentuated typical traits such as antlers or hindquarters. A strong trend toward ornamentation is especially noticeable in the treatment of the horns and hoofs. In later works, especially those of the kurgan of Noin-ula constructed by the Huns, the Scythian tendency toward pure ornamentation became so strong that the clarity of design was marred. This was particularly true in needlework and the textile arts, where Chinese stylistic influences, too, are most evident (PL. 190).

It would be erroneous to view the Scythian animal style in Siberia as limited to a small area. Owing to the mobility of the nomads and their far-reaching commercial exchanges the Altaitsy and more northerly ethnic groups came into contact with peoples living much farther to the west. Steppe culture was so homogeneous that the name Scythian has been applied to all its members, although the term was introduced by the Greeks to designate only the western steppe nomads around the Black Sea (see GRECO-BOSPORAN AND SCYTHIAN ART; STEPPE CUL-

TURES). Although the prototypes of the Scythian animal style in the Black Sea region were the ancient theriomorphic representations of western Asia, the style emerges as a completely new artistic tendency. Nothing is known of the reasons for representing certain animals; religious beliefs most likely had a strong influence. Scenes depicting griffins, lions, various felines, and wild beasts with horns are frequent. While the zoomorphic figures of the Yenisei area are identical with those of western Asia, the Scythians of the Altai regions and the bearers of the Tagar culture in the Minusinsk area were not mere slavish imitators. Particularly significant is the frequent application of the principle of *pars pro toto* in the kurgans of the Altai, where as a rule only the head of the animal — sometimes of two animals — was represented. Fights between beasts were also shown, and in the most varied ways. At Pazyryk abstract and phytomorphic ornamentation makes its appearance; rosettes, little palms, and interwoven undulating lines that can be traced back to Persian models are found beside more simple spirals that are clearly an abstraction of the curved lines of ram's horns.

In the periods following that of the Huns, which are better known to us from a historical point of view, Turkic peoples and later Mongols held supremacy in southern Siberia. Phytomorphic ornamentation became predominant in forms which denote Iranian-Hellenistic influences and, at the same time, closer ties with Chinese art (see MONGOLIAN ART; TURKIC ART). Ornamentation — at least that of the Kirghiz, who dominated this territory toward the middle of the 9th century (although their bases were actually along the Yenisei in the region of present-day Minusinsk) — led to the creation of an independent style manifested mainly in the decoration of ornamental plaques and metal recipients; however, human figures were frequently depicted.

The various cultural influences on Siberia throughout its history — including northern China in the east and Iran and Asia Minor in the west — have been active until present times. They are particularly apparent in ornamentation, whose motifs can be traced back in many forms — to the neolithic, for example, among the Ob Ugrians. By the early 2d millennium of our era the embroidery of the Ob Ugrians showed affinities to Russian and Tatar art. Among the Yakuts and the peoples of southern Siberia, phytomorphic motifs are still predominant today (FIG. 31) and have been replaced only partially by later Russian or Mongol-Chinese forms. Modern Siberian populations are still attached to the ancient artistic traditions because of religious influences and the need to create decorative and pleasantly shaped objects of common use (see below). Although the European trend toward giving the artist greater individual liberty has been felt since the Revolution of 1917, it has been checked by the artistic norms of the state, which demand a "social realism" rooted in the visual arts of the 19th century. Insofar as one can judge from the outside, artists of the minor republics appear to lack an appreciation of their own value. Examination of their modern production readily indicates that their artistic possibilities are far from exhausted (see UNION OF SOVIET SOCIALIST REPUBLICS: MODERN MOVEMENTS).

During the 19th century, prior to the substantial increase of craftsmanship and the arts under the Soviet regime, it is rather doubtful whether there were Siberian artists in the modern sense of the term — that is, individuals fully conscious of their own profession. The ornamentation of cloth, leather, skins, and bark was a role assigned to women, among whom there naturally emerged particularly skillful workers who could assist others without neglecting their domestic duties. But there were no professional artisans (with rare exceptions) even in the crafts traditionally performed by men, such as the ornamentation of wood and bone objects. One such exception appeared on the coastal strip of the northern Pacific, which saw a great flourishing of sculpture in bone, walrus tusk, and mammoth ivory. This area had established contact with the Russians, and a genuine art industry grew up among the groups living on the borders of the inland territories, especially among the commercially gifted Yakuts. The roots of this industry reach back to the pre-Russian period, when there were professional artisans who could work metal, most notably among the Buryats, Yakuts, Tuvintsy, and the peoples of the Altai and neighboring regions. Ironmongers were generally wandering craftsmen and occupied a special social position. Since iron was considered an element that spirits particularly feared, the ironmonger, who could shape the metal as he pleased, was thought to possess special powers. In most cases the profession was hereditary.

Even before the introduction of the Russian political directives that accomplished so much for the artisan classes, a more complex political organization existed among the Mongolian and Turkic-speaking peoples. Groupings among these peoples, unlike those in the north, were no longer determined solely by kinship or common property; larger units had emerged, based partly on the bellicose attitude prevalent among cattle breeders and nomad horsemen. Among the Yakuts in the 19th century, for example, one *ulus* (people, sovereign region) was composed of about 1,100 individuals, although it was divided, of course, into smaller sections. Leaders and other important persons who required more ceremonial objects than others kept the best artisans in their employ for long periods of time, thus strongly stimulating craftsmanship.

The nature of Siberian art cannot be fully appreciated without an understanding of the animistic beliefs that characterize religion in this area. It was generally believed — independent of Christian influences — that not only men and beasts but also certain plants (e.g., beautiful trees) and even objects of common use possess a soul. According to many peoples, particularly those of southern Siberia, one must bury the dead with a multitude of broken or damaged objects so that the souls of these objects may follow the soul of the dead man, who, having become an unrecognizable image to himself, may need unrecognizable objects in the other world. Life in the other world was commonly thought to resemble that on earth, although the dead undergo certain changes; in many Siberian religions the dead were held to be tiny. In western Siberia it was believed that they move upside down with their feet pointing toward the world of the living. According to all north Asian religions, man possesses two or more souls lodged in various parts of the body; these control the respective bodily functions. Still another soul, the "free" soul, provokes dreams and visions when the host is at rest. The free soul can abandon the body and live its own life as an insect, a bird, or a tiny image of its owner, who meanwhile follows the soul in a trance or dream. Frequently this soul was thought to be the shadow. The Khanty (Ostyaks) placed a representation of it in the shape of a bird on the front of seat cradles on a level with the child's head; this prevented the child's soul, which could easily be lost, from leaving its body in the daytime while the child was seated in his cradle. After the death of its owner the free soul went in search of the world of the dead. In the case of particularly important persons such as shamans, who were mediators between the world of men and the world of spirits, this search did not occur immediately because shamans' souls attempted to remain among the living. The Siberians greatly feared lingering souls and held them responsible for many wicked actions.

Protection against persecution by the spirits of the dead was sought through numerous ritual practices and by forcing the spirit into a specially prepared image, often with the help of the shamans (PL. 3). Thus the 19th-century Yakuts made straw dolls into which they lured the spirit after extracting it by noise and flattery from the body of an ailing patient whom the spirit was trying to carry away; the doll was disposed of afterward. A doll or image of this sort was made as soon as it was learned that a member of the group had died without burial or had died young before tiring of life. Food offerings were brought to obtain advance protection from the unquiet soul and to secure supernatural aid in case of eventual need.

All the Siberian peoples possessed figures representing the house and fire spirits, whose benevolence they sought. These spirits are part of an ancient religious tradition of Siberia and the steppelands to the south (as Guillaume Rubruquis in his *Itinerarium* had observed among the 13th-century Mongols). Representations of the lords of the forest beasts, the protector spirits of a mountain or forest, or a particularly important species

of hunt animal were painted on tree trunks or carved on branches, as among the Yakuts. Images of anthropomorphic and zoomorphic spirits to which the shamans had recourse during their visions are particularly abundant. These were hung on the shaman's costume or in his tent. Executed to his order and according to his personal ideas, the images possessed a peculiarly individual character even though traditional concepts were of great importance in their creation. The animal species considered most desirable as shamans' assistants varied from people to people and included wild beasts, horses, serpents, and, most importantly, birds because of their capacity to fly and sometimes dive into water. With a bird assistant the shaman in trance obtained the impression that he was flying in the heavens or descending into the underworld.

The peoples of southern Siberia were the first in that land to attempt a representation of the cosmos and its inhabitants, both men and spirits. During the first quarter of the 20th century, in the Altai region and the territories immediately to the north, the shamans still possessed drums on whose skins were represented all the parts of the universe their owners had presumably visited (IV, PL. 262). A line was drawn across the middle of this map, separating the supernatural world from that of man and the lower spirits. Among the lower spirits were included toads and serpents; in the higher category were birds, the sun, and the moon. On some of the drums the dividing line indicated the actual ground of the earthly world. Frequently the drum surface was divided vertically by a design of an axis or "tree of the world." Other lines marked off the borders between the various regions of the cosmos, all of which were accessible to the shaman. The power attributed to such images can be clarified through an example among the Buryats: When one man wanted to harm another, on a rag he drew a picture of his enemy with his head downward and then hid the rag somewhere in the victim's house. The house was then supposed to become unpeaceful and the victim to be pursued by bad luck. Similar practices, depending to a certain extent on sympathetic magic, are found among other Siberian peoples.

Beauty of representation had no religious importance in Siberia; even when the figures were placed on the shaman's costume they were never intended to give esthetic pleasure as were abstract ornaments. Pictures of the spirits — whether painted, carved, sewn, or smelted — had to possess the potentiality of "animation" as well as the traditionally recognized characteristics of such figures. Any attempt to vary these characteristics for esthetic reasons would risk deforming the figure and hence endanger control over it.

From the time when contact with Russian culture and the Russian Orthodox and Lamaistic missions became closer (possibly even before), there has been an evident tendency among all Siberian peoples to liberate visual art from religious implications. This tendency was most highly developed in the Pacific coastal zone. In the extreme north the carving of anthropomorphic and zoomorphic figures for pure esthetic pleasure was widespread since relatively ancient times; farther south, theriomorphic themes (e.g., birds, butterflies, fish, dragons) converted into ornamental spiral motifs were noted by the most ancient European travelers. Many of the Evenki (Tungus), who reached the coast in more recent times, appropriated this ornamentation and used it with mastery in the decoration of clothing and objects of common use. In western Siberia, among the Ob Ugrians (Khanty and Mansi), the same process of breaking down the composition can be seen in the theriomorphic motifs, mostly reindeer and birds, which assume intricate and very decorative angular shapes. In southern Siberia, Chinese and Lamaistic influences, with their highly developed graphic art, transformed the anthropomorphic and zoomorphic figures into playthings. In central Siberia as well, highly stylized figures used by children in their games have been in existence for centuries.

Ulla JOHANSEN

Attributed to the Neolithic period are numerous pieces of ornamented pottery, elk figures carved of bone (PL. 21), small human figurines of bone, stone fish presumably used as weights or fishing lures (PL. 21), and colored cliff drawings representing animals, mostly elk (Lake Baikal region). From the transition period between the Neolithic and metal ages come the remarkably expressive wooden figures of birds, elks, snakes, and stylized representations of human beings (Gorbunovo peat bog, Urals Area; PL. 22).

The art of the Bronze and Iron ages is considerably richer and more diversified. At this time ceramic ornamentation became more elaborate, as evidenced by the pottery decoration of the Andronovo culture (Minusinsk Basin). In contrast to the earlier decorative designs of the Afanasievo period, Andronovo decoration contains many intricately combined geometric motifs such as meanders, hooks, and hachured triangles, which are most often arranged in bands. To the same period belong two bone plaques from Abakan, each with an engraving of women whose loose hair covers their shoulders. The style of these works makes it possible to assign to the Andronovo period several stone sculptures from the Minusinsk steppe formerly attributed to the more recent Karasuk period. These stone figures of human beings are the oldest examples of such sculpture in Siberia. The Karasuk stage of the Bronze Age produced small bronze sculptures realistically depicting wild sheep, elk, and oxen; they were used as decoration for knife handles. Many cliff drawings also date to the Bronze Age. Particularly interesting are the dark-crimson drawings from Shishkino, which show figures of deer, people seated in boats, and anthropomorphic representations of fantastic beings. Despite an over-all realistic rendering, the animals are shown in a somewhat sketchy manner and the human figures are extremely simplified.

The period between the 7th century B.C. and the 1st century of our era is marked by a development in the art of the early nomads from the Altai region, made widely known by the excavations of the kurgans at Shibe and Pazyryk. These excavations have brought to light some exceptionally valuable artistic finds, including carved-bone figures, silver belt plaques, patterned rugs, fur mosaics, samples of needlework, embroidery in black glass beads, leather appliqué work, polychrome ornaments, and small wooden sculptures in the round representing real and fantastic animals (PLS. 23, 24; see ASIA, CENTRAL; GOLD- AND SILVERWORK). Many of the wooden and leather images are covered with gold leaf. All these items have survived owing to the special construction of the kurgan mounds and the frozen condition of the tombs.

Remains from the Tashtyk culture in Khakass (2d/1st cent. B.C. – 1st/2d cent. of our era) include painted terra-cotta portrait masks (PL. 25), wooden statuettes of human figures, bronze figurines of horses, and wooden figures of rams covered with gold. Equally interesting are the art objects of the Huns (1st cent. B.C. – 1st cent. of our era) found in Transbaikalia and Tuva. Particularly noteworthy are silk fragments richly patterned with curvilinear geometric and plant designs as well as bronze pieces, including figurines of horses, heads of yaks, and gilded, figured plaques from a coffin.

Among the works of art produced by the Altaic Turks under the Turkish khanate (6th – 8th cent. of our era) are stone figures of human beings, an engraved bone facing on the pommel of a saddle showing wild animals and a man on horseback, bone and horn objects (whip handles, clasps, buckles) with incised animal figures or motifs of circles and spirals, and bronze and silver bridle pieces displaying engraved plant motifs, butterflies, and bees.

Very distinctive in character is the figural art produced by the Khakasy (Yenisei Kirghiz) from the 9th to the 11th century, when this people was crushed by the Khitans. The Khakasy had many craftsmen — potters, jewelers, wood carvers, and stonecutters. They made clay vessels (known as Kirghiz vases) with impressed or scratched geometric designs, bronze and copper ornaments and belts, iron stirrups and bits inlaid with gold and silver, silver and gold ware decorated with chased plant patterns and medallions showing figures of birds, and many other articles. The stonecutters' cliff carvings represent scenes of hunts and battles and are highly interesting,

yielding information about warriors' clothing, weapons, the use of camels for riding, and so forth.

Of great significance are the numerous cliff drawings of the early part of the second millennium ascribed to the Kurykan Turks. Discovered in the Kachug region of the Irkutsk province, these realistic and well-executed drawings resemble those of the Kirghiz; they represent hunting and battle scenes, figures of horses and warriors, and episodes from nomadic wanderings.

As new archaeological finds come to light it becomes increasingly clear that many present-day Siberian peoples are perpetuating a culture inherited directly from ancient tribes. The ornamental art of the peoples of the lower Amur is related to Far Eastern ornamental art of neolithic times; the artistic culture of the modern Eskimos, at the northeastern extremity of Asia, has many features in common with ancient Eskimo culture. A particularly close bond exists between the contemporary art of the Yakuts, Altaitsy, Khakasy, Tuvintsy, and Buryats and the art of the ancient Turkic peoples of Siberia, especially those in the Lake Baikal region (see ASIATIC PROTO-HISTORY).

Cultural classification. In pre-Revolutionary times the population of Siberia was divided into two large groups: the stock-raising and partly agricultural peoples of the east and south; and the hunters, fishermen, and reindeer breeders of the north and farthest east. Differences between the two groups in natural environment and way of life left an unmistakable imprint on their respective cultures and were reflected in their art.

The classification of Siberian art cultures by Schneider (1929) and Findeisen (1930) remains fundamentally valid. On the whole, it can be expressed as follows:

I Peoples of the east and south
    A. Yakuts, Altaitsy, reindeer-breeding Tuvintsy, Tofalary (Karagasy), Khakasy, Shortsy, and western Buryats
    B. Eastern (Transbaikalian) Buryats and stock-raising Tuvintsy
II Peoples of the north and farthest east
    A. Extreme northeastern Asia: Chukchi, Asian Eskimos, Koryaks, and Itelmeny
    B. Evenki (Tungus), Eveny (Lamuty), Dolgans, and Yukagiry
    C. Lower Amur and Sakhalin: Nanaitsy (Golds), Ulchi, Orochs, Udegeitsy, Oroks, and Nivkhi (Gilyaks)
    D. 1. Ob Ugrians: Khanty (Ostyaks) and Masi (Voguly)
        2. Samoyed-speaking peoples: Nentsy (Samoyeds), Entsy (Yenisei Samoyeds), Nganasany (Tavgiitsy), Selkupy (Ostyako-Samoyeds), Kety

In category I*A* a highly developed decorative art was characterized by intricate curvilinear embroidery patterns (spirals, palmettes, parallel wavy lines, cruciform rosettes), by wood carving developed to a high level (particularly among the Yakuts), and by numerous metal objects such as personal ornaments and harness gear. Sculpture in wood and metal was less developed. Among the Khakasy, Altaitsy, and Shortsy, designs painted on leather appear mostly on shaman drums and tambourines. In Yakutsk and in southern Siberia the wealthy were adorned with costly materials (e.g., silks, colored broadcloth, velveteen, gold and silver objects) and used an abundance of ornaments on their garments and horse harnesses. Several of these peoples are discussed at greater length below.

In category I*B* the art of the eastern Buryats and the stock-raising Tuvintsy was influenced to a considerable extent by Mongolian, Tibetan, and Chinese art and therefore differs markedly from the craft production of the previous category. Embroidery was less well developed and was supplanted by the use of colored fabrics and Chinese silk for clothing and by large quantities of silver ornaments among the wealthier Buryat and Tuvinian families. Furniture, such as small tables and chests, was decorated with vivid colors and was a prominent feature of the household. Under the influence of Lamaism wooden statuettes representing Lamaistic deities and pictures of religious subjects brightly painted on paper or fabric penetrated into the culture of these peoples. Very effective were the painted wooden masks used for religious festivals (PL. 26).

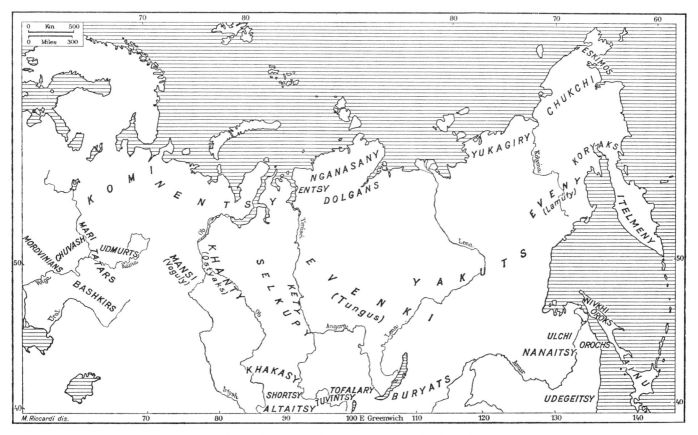

Distribution of the main ethnic groups within the Siberian culture area.

Many of these articles were made by lamas. The ornaments of this category show a prevalence of intricate motifs and figures, which can be seen in plaitwork and designs using lotus leaves, occasionally dragons, pairs of fish, and Far Eastern symbols such as the "knot of good fortune." Also of interest are the cast copper or bronze chess figurines; these figurines were sometimes carved in wood and occasionally painted. In contrast to the religious sculpture, chess pieces were realistic in style. (See below, *The Buryats* and *The Tuvintsy*).

The first category of Group II consists of cultures in the extreme northeastern region of Asia. These will be discussed at length in a following section.

The art of the Evenki (see below), Eveny (PL. 32), Dolgans, and Yukagiry constitutes category IIB. It is characterized by a widespread use of reindeer fur and colored beads, skilled wood and bone carving, engraving on iron, and small iron sculpture predominantly religious in nature (as were most of the larger wooden animal and human figures). The forged-iron figures of people and animals appear stylized and static. Some small animal images, skillfully cut from birch bark, were used as toys. Designs painted on leather by the peoples in this category were frequently bordered by a braid of white reindeer hair.

The artistic work of the peoples around the lower Amur River and in Sakhalin constitutes a third category of Siberian art from the north and extreme east (PLS. 27, 30–32). It will be discussed at length in a later section.

In the fourth category of northern and easternmost Siberian art, ornament usually presents rectilinear, wide, ribbon patterns, at times rather intricate in arrangement, with characteristic projections and angles and occasional depictions of deer; more rarely are there stylized representations of birds. Among the southern Khanty and Mansi there was a wide diffusion of colored wool embroidery on linen, using designs of birds and trees side by side with geometric patterns. Birch bark (PL. 31) and reindeer fur were widely used, the first for food vessels, the second for various types of clothing, for example, footwear and headdresses; wood carvings and engravings on bone or

metal were more scarce. The ancient sculpture was mostly intended for religious purposes and presented a schematic appearance. While the decorative arts of the Kety may be included with that of the peoples in category IID, their wood and iron sculpture shows a marked affinity with that of the Evenki.

Chronological development. Three major periods can be distinguished in the development of Siberian art: the pre-Russian stage, the period of integration of the Siberian peoples into the Russian state, and the Soviet period. As has been noted, the earliest cultures and arts of the Siberian peoples have not yet been sufficiently investigated. They may be judged to some extent, however, by products of the 17th and 18th centuries, which retain many features characteristic of earlier periods; occasionally these features can also be found in examples of 19th-century art. In the pre-Russian stage the peoples of northern Siberia did not utilize colored yarns and cloth, silver thread, artificial dyes, cotton fabrics, or glass beads and certain other types of necklaces. Only a limited number of coloring agents were used, mostly of mineral origin, and garments were made of fur and leather rather than textiles. These were sewn with animal sinew, reindeer hair, seal hair (dyed or natural), or, in the case of the Yakuts, horsehair. Embroidery colors were originally softer and more subdued; lack of color was compensated for by a discriminate choice of materials and diversity of decorative stitches.

The peoples of the lower Amur, under the influence of China, began earlier than the northerners to embroider with colored thread, to create fabric appliqués, and to use silver for decoration on iron objects, such as spearheads and knife handles. Many Chinese products found their way to the cultures of this area, including brightly colored fabrics, silk thread, and copper coins and shells used as clothing decoration. The Buryats, Tuvintsy, and to some extent the southern Altaitsy obtained from Mongolia the Chinese silks, gold thread, colored cord, decorated furniture, pieces of silver and finished silver articles (jewelry), and art objects connected with Lamaism.

Various forms of art connected with shamanism were widely developed during the pre-Russian period: wooden sculptures representing the shamans' auxiliary spirits, drawings on shaman drums and tambourines, and images painted on garments and on ritual objects. The peoples along the Amur made figures of the spirits in wood, peat, and grass. In Yakutsk, leather appliqué work and embroidery with white reindeer hair on suède (PL. 28) were used on a large scale, judging from surviving 17th- and 18th-century articles.

Following the incorporation of the Siberian peoples within the Russian nation Siberian art underwent certain transformations. As has been noted, the spread of Christianity resulted in a decline of drawing and sculpture connected with shamanism. These art forms also tended to disappear in the regions penetrated by Lamaism. At the same time, the color schemes of embroideries and appliqués became more vivid and richer owing to the introduction of glass beads, industrial threads, and textiles; motifs borrowed from Russian art appeared in ornaments (Yakutsk). The Yakuts began to make decorated furniture and various household objects according to Russian models. Gradually the animist-inspired fear of representing human beings in decoration lessened, and genre scenes, even caricatures, made their appearance in Yakut and Khakas art (wood carvings and engravings on metal). Plant motifs also became prominent.

Many nationalities increased the production of their handicrafts in order to sell them. Local arts were affected by the availability of Russian-made tools (e.g., gouges, gimlets, chisels), particularly those used for work on iron and silver. In the 18th century large amounts of copper, and in the 19th, cheap silver, were brought into Yakutsk from European Russia.

In Soviet times the outlying backward areas of Siberia have been transformed into industrial-agrarian autonomous republics and provinces. The arts of the Siberian peoples underwent significant changes. New techniques were added, production was facilitated and expanded, and different forms of art, especially printing and stage decoration, emerged. Most importantly, the conditions of artistic endeavor were altered: many talented craftsmen were organized into artels and received help in obtaining necessary tools and materials; they were also provided with an outlet for their handicrafts. Regional and provincial art shows, along with exhibits representing painters throughout an entire republic, helped foment creative activity and developed the artistic standards of folk art. Artists entered exhibitions outside the U.S.S.R. and received the constant interest and support of Soviet public agencies. Contemporary themes were treated in painting and sculpture.

The manufacture of bone articles and jewelry has been greatly expanded in the Chukotski Peninsula, Yakutsk, and

Buryat, as has the manufacture of wall rugs among the Nanaitsy and fur articles among the Koryaks. Decorative patterns throughout Siberia have acquired considerable variety owing to the incorporation of new motifs and compositions. The walrus-tusk engravings of the Asian Eskimos and the sedentary Chukchi present a great diversity of subjects, including historical compositions and episodes from daily life.

PEOPLES OF THE EAST AND SOUTH. Before the Revolution the chief occupation of the Yakuts and other southern Siberian peoples was raising horses, cattle, and sheep, and that of the Buryats and Tuvintsy raising camels. The products derived from stock raising and related activities such as hunting provided materials for the home production of various articles of leather, fur, felt, and bone. In forest zones many essential articles were made of wood. The handiwork of these peoples clearly indicates the existence of class distinctions. Homes of the feudal nobility were filled with large quantities of silver and silver-plated iron objects, brocaded silks and velveteens, and art objects made to order or purchased from merchants. The common people were limited to inexpensive materials, and most of their decorative articles were of their own making.

The Yakuts. The earliest artistic expression of the Yakuts took the form of decoration and handicrafts, of which embroidery, wood and metal engraving, and the manufacture of articles of leather, fur, and birch bark reached a high level of development. The ancient embroideries were executed with reindeer hair or sinew on leather (clothing, saddlebags, and quivers). The Yakuts painted designs on leather, mostly in brown. Leather garments and quivers of the 17th and 18th centuries were frequently decorated with beadwork or appliqués of fine leather pieces bordered with colored thread. Patterned carpets sewn together from bits of light- and dark-colored fur, as well as various items of handiwork in black, white, and brown horsehair, were common in Yakut households.

In the 19th century fur decoration was partially replaced by the use of Russian colored thread and cloth (PL. 28); hair decoration was almost wholly replaced. Embroidery was frequently supplemented by the addition of iron plaques with stamped decoration (horse trappings). Engraving on silver came into greater use in the 19th century as silver articles displaced the brass ones that had been characteristic of the 17th and 18th centuries. Engraving appeared on women's ornaments, on the metal parts of saddles, and elsewhere. There were many carved wooden articles: hitching posts, food vessels, boxes, and chests; some were first painted black. Birch-bark boxes were frequently stitched with black horsehair and sometimes decorated

Decorative motifs of the Yakuts (*from Johansen, 1954*).

with openwork backed with colored foil. Decoration on birch-bark snuffboxes was incised with the tip of a knife. Until recently, ancient clay vessels decorated with designs stamped on with wooden dies remained in use, along with commercially manufactured ware.

Yakut ornamentation (FIG. 31) exhibits older patterns, mainly of rectilinear geometrical motifs (zigzags, crisscrossed squares, etc.), as well as more recent and sophisticated curvilinear figures (spirals, plant tendrils, palmette- and lyrelike figures); the latter group of motifs resembles the ornament of the Turkic-speaking peoples of southern Siberia and Central Asia. The ornamentation employed by the wealthier Yakuts in former times was particularly lavish: generous use was made of gold and silver thread, colored cloth, and silver or, occasionally, gold decorations.

Wood sculpture was only slightly developed. Toys have been found representing cows and saddled horses; hitching posts, sometimes decorated with a wooden horse's head, are similar to the heads carved on some early Yakut grave markers. In the 19th century the Yakuts carved and painted many small wooden statuettes, for sale at bazaars, representing their people in national costume.

Some small sculpture of fossilized mammoth bone was developed mainly from the 17th to the 19th century and was produced for commercial purposes. The pieces included miniature furniture and dishes, occasionally models of buildings, and figurines of people and animals, sometimes in groups (PL. 29). The figurines were fairly simplified and movement was insufficiently shown; however, they often reveal a sense of humor. Carved frames, combs, little boxes, and other objects richly decorated with openwork or with scenes from Yakut life were also made for sale.

During the Soviet period the decorative and applied arts of the Yakuts, particularly their bone carving, continued to develop. Bear hunts, dog teams, tethered horses, and various other subjects drawn from Yakut life appear in many carvings. Contemporary bone sculpture is characterized by well-emphasized movement, the finish of the compositions, and a variety of poses in the human and animal figures. Bas-relief carving is developing, as is jewelry, wood carving, and easel painting.

A completely new form of the graphic arts for the Yakuts is easel painting. Lacking traditions of their own in this field, they have learned from the Russians. Many new painters, whose work is realistic in style, emerged in the years following World War II. Yakut paintings have been exhibited on numerous occasions in Yakutsk and were presented at an exhibition in Moscow in 1957.

The Buryats. The artistic activity of the Buryats has found expression in colored-cloth appliqué work, embroidery, ornamental quilted felts, wood carving, wood painting, artistic metalwork, and the manufacture of wool stockings in a patterned knit. Appliqués were used on ancient quivers and arrow cases, tobacco pouches, saddle blankets, footwear, mittens, and other types of clothing. Carved decoration, often painted, appeared on wooden chests and other furniture.

As has been noted earlier, crafts produced by the eastern Buryats exhibit a predominance of Sino-Mongolian motifs, while the ornamentation of the western Buryats shows affinities to work of the Yakuts and the Altaitsy, with whom the western Buryats are culturally related. Significant inroads in Buryat art were made by Lamaistic religious painting (17th–20th cent.), which is distinguished by its brilliant colors and subject matter. Discernible in this type of painting are devices adapted from the Mongolo-Tibetan tradition, with its fine lines and accomplished technique and composition. Black and red were the colors most frequently used by the Buryats on antique objects; polychrome, which made a later appearance, shows the influence of Russian painting among the western Buryats and of Sino-Mongolian art among the eastern Buryats (with an occasional appearance of gilding). The colors are bright: red with green and yellow, blue with yellow, blue with green.

Ornamentation on ancient wooden articles was of a geometric type (circles, stripes); more recent objects bear many plant and floral motifs, as well as plaitwork and eastern Asiatic symbols. Simple geometric patterns appeared on knitted stockings and quilted felts, and curvilinear designs (spirals, "horns," wavy lines) were used in cloth appliqué and on some metal articles. Among the western Buryats rosettes often appear in silver-inlay work on iron in such items as horse trappings and belt plaques; in the area of the eastern Buryats stamped silverwork (jewelry, small boxes, dishes) shows intricate plant designs and various Chinese symbols. The art of the wealthy Buryats in former times was marked by great splendor and the use of costly materials.

During the Soviet era new developments in the figural arts appeared in the Buryat area: sculpture, easel painting, horsehair lacework, needlework on various themes, much original silverwork, and stage decoration. Wood carving broke away from traditional incised methods as Buryat carvers attempted bas-relief. Elegant jewelry work is greatly prized in the Buryat area and beyond its confines and silver is often used in combination with horn, stone, wood, or coral; gilding is sometimes employed. Techniques include stamping and filigree work. Ornamentation is varied, including plaiting, "knots," "hearts," "wheels," stylized lotuses, pairs of fish, Soviet emblems, cloudlike motifs, and dragon heads.

The Tuvintsy. The Tuvintsy had a well-developed traditional art of small wooden, stone, and metal sculpture; embroidery was used in moderation on clothing, sometimes on headdresses and footwear. Many Tuvinian craftsmen made objects for sale, including jewelry, wood carvings, stone sculpture, and paintings on wood. Although the art of feudal Tuva shows borrowing in subjects and techniques from Mongolian, Tibetan, and Chinese cultures, the work of the broad masses of the people was unostentatious and restricted to an artistic handling of inexpensive materials.

The particular economy existing in different regions of Tuva played an important role in the development of the figural arts. As has been noted, the people of the eastern forest zone had been reindeer breeders and hunters from earliest times; in the western part of Tuva, which is chiefly steppe, the people raised cattle, horses, and, to a lesser extent, camels. Substantial differences appear in every area of the respective cultures of the eastern and western Tuvintsy. Among the reindeer breeders, shaman costumes were embroidered with white reindeer hair. The ornamentation consisted of parallel lines, circles, zigzags, and spirals. Sculpture and painting were almost nonexistent. Wood carving appeared chiefly on reindeer saddles, drum and tambourine handles, and drumsticks. Decorative patterns consisted of the simplest geometric figures.

The art of the western Tuvintsy was considerably richer and more varied in the choice of materials and forms; the most commonly produced articles were of wood, leather, stone, metal, and quilted felt, the last with geometric designs. Repoussé work on leather flagons, horses' feedbags, and saddlecloths presents a variety of patterns. This type of decoration is obtained by first carving the design deeply on a board and then transferring it to the leather, where it becomes a relief pattern. Designs on leather articles consist of palmettes, rosettes, plant tendrils, and various geometrical motifs (meanders, lozenges, crossed circles, "waves," and spirals); a few motifs and symbols borrowed from Sino-Mongolian art also appear. Curvilinear designs based on plant motifs are similar to those of the Buryats, Mongolians, and Kirghiz. Leather pieces may be dyed dark brown, dark red, bright green, or yellow.

The patterns that appear in western Tuvinian wood carving are of two kinds: traditional geometric figures, which suggest the designs of the Altaitsy and reindeer-breeding Tuvintsy; and more intricate forms similar to those of Sino-Mongolian ornamentation. The former are found on cradles, chests, door bolts, small ewerlike pails, mortars used for pounding millet, and other small articles; some of these objects are painted red. Patterns of the second type are found on low tables, on door bolts, on small boxes for storing chess pieces, and sometimes along with geometric decoration on mortars. In former times the handles on ritual spoons were also covered with finely executed carving.

The ornament on all these objects is predominantly curvilinear and includes spirals, rosettes, elements of plant origin, various symbols, and designs similar to Chinese conventionalized clouds or lotus leaves. A luxuriant and sumptuous ornamentation strongly resembling the Mongolian is executed in vivid colors, occasionally with gold leaf, and appears on wooden cupboards, tables, and coffers. Although painted articles were at one time acquired primarily by affluent Tuvintsy, today they may be found in the homes of working people. Blue, green, red, and black are the colors used in painted designs on wood.

Wooden sculpture is of considerable interest and includes children's toys, chess pieces, small decorative statuettes, and animal figurines formerly placed for ritual purposes inside the *obo* (a special construction for sacrificial offerings). The work of Tuvinian carvers is distinguished by painstaking finish and a love for the craft, which is evidenced equally in small figurines of people and in larger representations of animals; both types of sculpture are often painted. Movement is well rendered in the animals, and their proportions are in most cases correct. The Tuvintsy were particularly good at carving horses, which they endowed with much expression. Their prominent muscles, powerful limbs, thick manes, and strongly arched necks often bring to mind the steeds described in folk tales.

The characteristics of Tuvinian wood sculpture hold true, to a large extent, for agalmatolite, or soapstone, carvings, which are also executed with a knife. The small works made of these materials are as expressive and diversified in subject matter as the wood sculpture and frequently depict the people in their national costume, sometimes holding an object. All this sculpture shows a remote resemblance to the ancient Chinese sculptural arts of the Han and T'ang periods.

The Tuvintsy are masters in the art of casting small copper chess pieces in the shape of animals, people, and carriages. Occasionally these were also cast in bronze. The chess figurines present considerable interest from the artistic point of view: set on a stand, they show fine workmanship, well-expressed movement, and correct proportions. The animals are shown in rather contorted attitudes, and the over-all execution is painstaking. Particularly well rendered are horses and camels, with which the stock-raising Tuvintsy are thoroughly familiar.

Metal parts of harnesses are often made of silver and decorated with incised or relief ornament of spirals and tendrils (PL. 32). Occasionally one finds a plaque showing animals of the 12-year zodiac cycle, a time-measuring system common in many parts of eastern and Central Asia (q.v.; see also ASTRONOMY AND ASTROLOGY). All these articles are characterized by fine craftsmanship and resemble Mongolian work in style.

The Altaitsy. The decorative arts of the southern Altaitsy are varied; their ornamental patterns are most often geometric. Embroidery is found on women's attire, tobacco pouches, cushions, and parts of horses' saddles. Patterns include rosettes, figure-eight designs, rams' horns, and cruciform figures ending in paired scrolls, which recall motifs of Kazakh and Kirghiz ornamentation. Gold braids, brocade, galloon tapes, and strips of colored fabrics and black plush are also sewn together in consecutive rows to form a wide and variegated band that is used to trim saddles, side seams on cushions, and the hems of wearing apparel.

Decoration on leather articles such as flagons, tobacco pouches, shot bags, purses, and horse trappings is more varied. Flattened oval high-necked containers made of leather are covered with repoussé work in designs consisting of spirals, circles, cruciform figures, and plant and hornlike motifs; in the midst of these designs there occasionally appear small figures of horses, Siberian mountain goats, and Siberian stags. The ornament is nearly invisible on the dark, almost black background of the leather. On leather purses the repoussé work is frequently combined with figured copper plaques. Tobacco pouches and horse trappings are also decorated with appliqué work of leather strips, crossed circles, arcs, and paired scrolls. Leather openwork is sometimes lined with colored fabric, usually red, which harmonizes well with the dark-brown or black hide. In pre-Revolutionary times, the Altaitsy used to decorate the leather of shaman drums and tambourines with red-and-white designs representing Siberian stags, trees, the sun and stars, and sometimes human beings. These extremely simplified outline figures were drawn with the finger or the tip of a sharpened stick dipped in paint.

On wooden articles — milk pails, door bolts, mortars, platters, and chests — the incised carving consists of meanders, networks, zigzags, circles, squares, tau- and gamma-shaped figures, and other simple geometric designs. Also carved on some pails are small figures of Siberian stags and sometimes hunting scenes or trees. Pokerwork figures are found more rarely on such objects; linear in style, they recall the figures painted or carved on southern Siberian cliffs. More detailed workmanship appears in relief carvings on ancient Altaic wooden calendars with signs of the 12-year zodiac cycle. The calendar figures include wild and domestic animals and a fantastic dragon, most of which are represented realistically. Relief carving also appears on beds and other household objects of the Telengity, a group of southern Altaitsy in the Chulym River Basin. This type of work can be seen not only in ornamentation but also in figures of goats, horses, bears, and other animals. Wooden door bolts were sometimes fashioned in the shape of birds.

Although sculpture in the round was not much developed among the Altaitsy, their toy wooden horses are noteworthy. Before the Revolution small figures representing ancestor spirits were carved in wood and sometimes colored brick red. Drum and tambourine handles were made in human shape with one or two heads, with round copper plaques set in to mark the eyes and elongated plaques representing the beard and mustache.

The Altaitsy also carved small bone plaques for inlays on wooden scabbards. The plaques were covered with simple engraving composed of stripes as well as circlets with a central dot, sometimes grouped to form rosettes. These circlets were also used to decorate bone powder horns and buttons. Various metal objects such as tobacco pipes, stirrups, harness pieces, and the copper facing on flints were incised or stamped with designs consisting of minute rosettes, circles, zigzags, scrolls, and meanders.

The Kumandintsy, a group of northern Altaitsy inhabiting the middle course of the Biya River, used various patterns on articles of knitted wool such as belts, mittens, and stockings. The patterns differ radically from those of the southern Altaitsy but show an affinity to the embroidery of the southern Khanty and to the weaving and embroidery patterns of peoples in the European part of the Soviet Union.

The Khakasy. Khakas folk art is characterized by the decoration of wearing apparel and of smaller objects such as tobacco-pouches and pipes. Although before the Revolution there was much color drawing on shaman drums and tambourines, the most widespread form of Khakas decorative art was embroidery. A wide range of thread colors was used: various shades of red, pink, yellow, orange, lilac, and blue. Like the Nanaitsy and other peoples of the lower Amur River, Khakas women used stencils made by cutting out a sheet of paper that had been folded over once or twice. The stencil was basted to the cloth, the symmetrical design then traced with a needle, and the pattern finally removed. Clothes embroidered by the Khakasy were made of black velveteen or, among the wealthier, velvet. A black background is preferred even today; embroidered in bright colors, the fabric looks rich and festive. Most of the patterns are clearly plant motifs, but there are also cruciform figures ending in paired spirals, wavy lines, and so on. They are all fairly large, and the majority are curvilinear. Khakas embroidery motifs are in many ways akin to those of the Yakuts and Kazakhs.

In former times the Kiziltsy, a subgroup of the Khakasy, made wall carpets of white felt with a quilted geometric design. Usually the design appeared in the border, but on some carpets it also covered the central field. The design included plant patterns, figure-eight forms, cruciform figures with arrow-tipped ends, and so on. Some of these figures suggest the ornamental motifs on Kazakh and Kirghiz felt rugs.

There was little artistic wood carving among the Khakasy.

Chests and boxes were decorated with combinations of trihedrons (borders and rosettes), diagonally intersected squares, and other motifs. Animal figures, such as goats and horses, as well as trees, buildings, and people were occasionally carved on the earlier chests. This carving was always in low relief, with the figures generally represented schematically or only in contour. Painting on wood was rare; some appears on furniture, on which the designs include rosettes.

Saddlecloths were decorated with needlework, leather appliqué, and shells and mother-of-pearl disks sewn onto the leather or cloth. Among the older items of feminine jewelry, some pectorals are almost completely covered with beadwork and mother-of-pearl disks and buttons. The Khakasy also did tin inlay work on wood (e.g., tobacco pipes) with strictly geometric motifs.

PEOPLES OF THE NORTH AND FARTHEST EAST. In the pre-Revolutionary period the chief materials used by the northern peoples for the production of household articles were hides of deer and wild animals, fishskins, wood, bone, horn, and sinew. A sharp division of labor existed. The men made and decorated articles of wood, bone, and imported iron. The women treated animal hides, fishskins, and birch bark; wove mats and sacks of grass; and ornamented clothing, household utensils, fur rugs, cradles, and other objects.

The decorative arts of the peoples of the north and extreme east were characterized by fine workmanship and achieved a considerable degree of development. There were also some forms of art connected with religious practices: designs on shaman drums and tambourines (Evenki) and on shaman costumes (Nanaitsy), wooden figures of spirits in animal and anthropomorphic representation (peoples of the lower Amur, Evenki, Koryaks, Nentsy), and iron figurines of the shamans' spirit-helpers (Evenki, Kety, Selkupy). After the Revolution, as the old cults died out and the production of ritual art ceased almost entirely, many forms of the decorative and applied arts made new advances. New art forms arose, including water color, oil and gouache painting, clay sculpture, colored pencil drawing, and book illustration.

The Ob Ugrians. The decorative arts of the Khanty (Ostyaks) and Mansi (Voguly), who constitute the Ob Ugrians, are represented mainly by the ornamentation found on wearing apparel made of fur, fabric, and in part of fishskin and suède (the early footwear) and on objects made of birch bark and more rarely wood. The northern groups of Ob Ugrians evolved a rectilinear, geometric type of ornamentation on fur and birch bark. The ornamentation was fairly large, two-tone, and strictly symmetrical, marked by abrupt changes in line direction and a tendency toward an equal division of decorated and undecorated surfaces (FIG. 39). Typical motifs were meanders, triangles, squares, stripes, cruciform rosettes, broken lines with offshoots, and similar motifs named after the local fauna and flora (e.g., "horns of a young deer," "pike's teeth," "fir cone"). Occasional birch-bark objects bore designs representing deer, birds, or horses, incised with the point of a knife. Carved designs also appeared on small wooden boxes, cutting boards, and little paddles used to remove snow. The most common motifs in carving were triangles, zigzags, and diagonally intersected squares.

The southern groups of Khanty and Mansi embroidered in colored thread (usually in red and blue) on nettle cloth, which adorned women's blouses and occasionally men's clothing. Patterns included "horns," starlike rosettes, jagged-edged lozenges, stylized trees with figures of birds in heraldic arrangement on the sides of the pattern, and a number of other geometric motifs held in common with the northern Khanty and Mansi. The birds, trees, and many of the geometric figures closely resemble analogous motifs of the Volga Basin peoples (Mari, Mordvinians, Chuvash, and Bashkirs). Another typical feature of Ob Ugrian art consisted of cast-tin figures sewn onto clothing.

Before the Revolution the Ob Ugrians carved wooden figures of an archaic appearance representing various spirits in human or animal form. More expressive are the animal and human figures of carved wood that were used as toys. Dolls were also fashioned from bits of fur and fabric, their fur clothing copied from the national costume; features were not indicated. During the Soviet period many young people have come to practice easel painting, sculpture, and pencil and ink drawing.

The Nentsy. The ornamentation of the Nentsy (Samoyeds) shows a close relationship with that of the northern Khanty (see outline above), but the patterns are less diversified. Winter clothes were decorated with designs of light- and dark-colored reindeer skins, and summer clothes with pieces of red, green, and yellow cloth. Leather belts worn by the women in early periods had openwork buckles of cast copper, sometimes with figures representing a reindeer or a bird in the middle of the buckle. The wooden sculpture produced before the Revolution was usually anthropomorphic and was characterized by extreme simplification: many figures were mere sticks with a few incisions to indicate the face; arms and legs were usually absent (PL. 26).

The Evenki. The arts of the Evenki (Tungus) differ according to the region they inhabit: in the Yenisei Basin they have for the most part preserved the old traditions; in Yakutsk they have been influenced by the art of the Yakuts; and in the regions of the Stanovoi and Yablonovoi mountains they show some borrowings from the art of the lower Amur peoples. Evenki beadwork was more extensively developed in the west; in the east there was greater development of embroidery in colored thread and dyed reindeer hair and of appliqué work using bits of fur and strips of cloth and leather. Ornamentation was geometric, the main motifs being stripes, squares, rectangles, chevrons, zigzags, and arcs with dart or trefoil motifs at the point of junction. Decoration appeared on clothing, reindeer harnesses, and various wood and bone articles (PL. 31).

Small silhouette figures of animals, mostly northern reindeer, were cut from birch bark and were used as toys; they were sharply realistic. Wooden sculpture was common chiefly among the Evenki of the Yenisei. The anthropomorphic and zoomorphic representations of spirits were conventionalized and simplified to the extreme. In early times small iron sculpture also appeared, mostly zoomorphic representations of the shaman spirit-helpers. Images of these spirits, usually stylized, were reproduced in color on shamans' costumes, drums, tambourines, and other accessories.

The art of the Dolgans parallels that of the Evenki, except that the former were fond of decorating their clothing with numerous strips of cloth, mostly in pale colors.

During the 1930s easel painting, drawing, clay sculpture, and book illustration made their first appearance among the Evenki.

The peoples of the lower Amur and Sakhalin. The decorative art of these peoples, including the Nanaitsy (Golds), Ulchi, Orochs, Oroks, Niukhi (Gilyaks), and Udegeitsy, is vivid in color, rich in form, and finely executed. Their ornament is generally curvilinear in intricate patterns, with a predominance of spirals and ribbons. Stylized figures of birds, fish, butterflies, reptiles, and dragons also occur, especially among the Nanaitsy and Ulchi (PL. 32), and are prominently displayed side by side with geometric designs. From the standpoint of composition the ornamentation of this area is more complex than that of the Evenki or the Paleo-Asians.

The proximity to China and the presence of many Chinese articles in Amur households as recently as the early 1900s left an imprint on the work of craftsmen of the Amur region. Chinese articles acquired by affluent Nanaitsy and Ulchi on visits to Sanhsing in the first half of the 19th century included rugs, coffers, cupboards, copper coins, and silks. Colored Chinese silk thread of brilliant colors, dyed calico, and India ink, as well as individual motifs of east Asian ornamentation (e.g., figures of dragons and bats), also found their way from China into the Amur region.

Techniques of textile ornamentation were extremely varied. Needleworkers used over twenty different types of stitches in decorating clothing, footwear, and other articles for everyday use. On occasion, white deer hair or elk hair was used in embroidery on suède; clothing, cushions, and carpets were sometimes adorned with appliqué work of fishskin or colored fabrics. In the past, fishskin was used extensively for clothing and footwear. Such garments were generally decorated with red and blue painted designs and with shells and Chinese copper coins sewn to the hems. Patterns cut from birch bark, fishskin, or paper were often used in ornamentation (FIG. 39). Peculiar to the Nanaitsy and Udegeitsy was the application of ancient designs painted in color on leather or white fabric (shamans' garments, cloth pieces used as a type of icon).

Decoration of birch-bark vessels was well developed and was executed in various ways: with appliqué work or with incised, repoussé, or painted designs. In wood and bone carving geometric shapes predominate (spirals and ribbon interlace). Carved work was also painted, usually in black and red. Houses

trenched animist concepts in the lower Amur region, has gradually lost ground and is no longer produced today.

The cultures in this area were adept in the highly developed art of inlaying iron with silver and copper. Artistic objects of metal were rare and greatly prized, and particular value was attached to iron spearheads and knife handles covered with silver and copper insets. Ornamentation on such objects included small animal figures set in the midst of a geometric pattern. Many well-to-do Nanaitsy and Ulchi wore small silver talismans around their necks. These were in the shape of anthropomorphic figures representing the spirits of heaven. Udegei shamans at one time attached tin or iron figures of snakes and lizards to their clothing.

In the 1920s and 1930s water-color painting and pencil drawing appeared.

1

2

3

Examples of Siberian decorative art: (1) Decorative motifs of the Nanai paper cutout; (2) strip of Koryak decorated hide for clothing; (3) Khant incised-bark cradle.

built on the Russian model, which have gradually displaced the traditional indigenous dwellings, exhibit carving of a mixed character, consisting of both local and Russian elements. Carved wooden vessels have sharply decreased as a result of the penetration into the Amur region of Chinese clay and porcelain ware and, later, Russian metal dishes. Household articles (chests, boxes, tools, various implements) formerly exhibited carving, as did storage houses and architectural elements of winter dwellings (e.g., posts, pediment boards, doors).

Before the Revolution the Nanaitsy, Ulchi, and Nivkhi produced large quantities of wooden animal sculpture of a religious nature, usually made to order for a shaman and used for the treatment of illness. The more common figures were bears, panthers, tigers, wild boars, turtles, and frogs; birds and fish were less frequent. Wooden anthropomorphic figures of spirits measured up to about 3 ft. in height or even, among the Udegeitsy, exceeded life size (PL. 26). There were also many miniature figurines executed with an adze or a knife and usually archaic in style. Despite this extremely conventionalized treatment, every animal can be easily recognized by some typical feature: the tiger by his round head and short ears, the wild boar by his flat snout, and so on. The Nivkhi often carved realistic figures of bears on ceremonial ware (dippers and spoons) used for the bear festival. More painstaking was the treatment of figures by the Udegeitsy, whose painted wooden tigers, birds, and snakes were particularly expressive. Anthropomorphic spirits were characterized by severity; disproportionately large heads were frequently covered with hair that was glued on, bodies were wrapped in pieces of leather and fur, and various objects such as spears, bows, and arrows were placed in the hands. Household sculptures were very infrequent among the peoples of the Amur. Wooden, cloth, or birch-bark dolls have been found in their homes, and birch-bark or paper cutouts of reindeer, elk, bears, and other animals were used as toys. The religious sculpture, which at one time mirrored strongly en-

The Chukchi, Asian Eskimos, and Koryaks. Marine hunting and reindeer breeding provide these peoples with the basic materials used in their crafts: for sculpture, the hard and beautiful walrus tusk; for embroidery, reindeer fur and sinew and light and dark sealskin. As recently as the early 1900s extensive use was still made of sinew thread, reindeer hair, fur and hides of land and sea mammals, and other local materials for the decoration of clothing and household utensils.

The finely executed ornamentation of this group of peoples bears considerable resemblance to that of the Eskimos of the Old Bering Sea culture. Both bone engravings and sculpture show a close kinship with the work of the American Eskimos (see ESKIMO CULTURES; IVORY AND BONE CARVING). Designs are marked by small and extremely simple figures such as stripes, squares, lozenges, and triangles organized in strictly geometric patterns (FIG. 39); curvilinear figures include circles, semicircles, and concentric circles. On Koryak woven-grass articles, ornamentation is entirely geometric. Decoration was applied to clothing, headdresses, belts, purses, and fur and leather rugs made for sale. Leather quivers and bow facings were at one time ornamented with particular lavishness. Koryak fur decoration often included small animal figures and occasionally human forms or simple compositions depicting reindeer and hunting scenes. Embroidery techniques varied greatly.

Small sculptures of walrus bone (PL. 30) reflect the extremely diversified local fauna in this area. Among the many wonderfully eloquent and animated figures carved by the northerners are whales, polar bears, seals, walruses, northern reindeer, and dogs, some of these formerly used as amulets. At the present time sculptured figures are made for sale or to order for various individuals or institutions. The carvers also produce bone zoomorphic chess pieces, inkstands, letter openers, matchboxes, scale models of schooners, and other minor articles decorated with engraving or with small animal figures in relief (VIII, PL. 249).

Bone engraving has received a strong impetus in recent years, with decorative patterns resembling those used in embroidery. Walrus tusks, whole or sawed into pieces, are covered on both sides with scrimshaw engraving, sometimes colored, depicting many small but complex compositions of preponderantly maritime hunting scenes, although genre scenes from the life of the reindeer breeders are not infrequent. Subjects for these compositions include reindeer teams hauling sleds, shopping at cooperative stores, dogs pulling skiers, domestic occupations, ancient and modern dwellings of the Chukchi and Eskimos, and scenes of schools, villages, and festivities. Men and animals are portrayed realistically (PL. 29). The old minute engravings of human figures, which were extremely simplified and executed as outline drawings or as silhouettes, usually rubbed with black, have been replaced by larger figures in which the details of face, body, and clothing are indicated. Large collections of contemporary Chukchi and Eskimo bone carving exist in many museums of the U.S.S.R. including the State Museum of Ethnography of the Peoples of the U.S.S.R., the Museum of Anthropology and Ethnography of the U.S.S.R. Academy of Sciences, and the Museum of Khabarovsk.

Wood carving is not highly developed among these peoples. Designs on wood appear among the Chukchi and Eskimo. Some pottery has been produced by the Eskimos.

Sergei Vassilevich IVANOV

THE AINU OF JAPAN. The Ainu, aborigines of the Japanese archipelago, are today reduced to no more than a few dozen individuals of pure blood who live on the island of Hokkaido. Until relatively recent times they also occupied parts of the Kuril Islands and Sakhalin. If the numerous prehistoric finds are correctly attributed, the Ainu were very early diffused throughout the Japanese archipelago. The pertinent prehistoric material includes pottery (figurines and mat- and cord-impressed pots; II, PL. 16), bone ornaments, and stone objects (probably phallic) in the shape of clubs with geometrically engraved knobs, mainly from the period known as Jōmon (see ASIATIC PROTOHISTORY; CERAMICS; JAPAN). Between the 10th and 5th centuries B.C. Mongolian invaders of various tribes began to push into the southern part of present-day Japan, gradually limiting the habitat of the Ainu and forcing them to move increasingly farther north.

The cultural affinities of the Ainu with the natives of Siberia are numerous, especially in the recent past. It is obvious, however, that in both groups close contact with more civilized peoples caused profound changes in traditional culture and greatly influenced contemporary artistic production. Modern Ainu art work is limited to ornamentation (mostly geometric) on wood, furnishings, cloth (FIG. 41), and plaitwork. In cloth and plaitwork ornamentation, cultural links with peoples of the Siberian mainland and the ornamental styles of cultures from the northwest coast of North America are apparent (see NORTH AMERICAN CULTURES). Geometric tattoos on the forearm and back, which repeat motifs appearing on cloth, plaitwork, wood sculptures, and elsewhere, are similar to tattoos found among the Chukchi, Evenki, Nanaitsy, and the American and Asian Eskimos. The tradition of feminine tattoos around the mouth prolongs, without interruption, a very ancient practice, judging by the neolithic evidence that has survived.

In the absence of freestanding wooden statues (few zoomorphic sculptures in the round appear on utensils) there arose a splendid art of ornamental engraving, particularly applied to libation sticks (mustache lifters), spoons, trays, wooden plates, knife scabbards, and small shovel-shaped stirring paddles (PL. 31). The libation sticks are unique to Ainu culture. All these objects are decorated with motifs that can be reduced to five main types: (1) heads with pseudo horns, (2) single, double, or treble commas, (3) fish, (4) eyes, and (5) snakes. The first motif, which also appears in the art of the Nivkhi, may not represent a horned animal but rather a stylization of the head and ears of a bear, which was the object of a religious cult among both these peoples. The comma motif shows affinities with the Chinese yin and yang signs and with a Japanese ornamental motif; it may also symbolize lightning. The fish theme, which is sometimes rendered naturalistically but more often schematically or even symbolically, is very probably connected with the predominant fishing trade. The eye reveals affinities with a similar motif found on the northwest coast of North America. The snake is often a simple geometric motif (spiral, zigzag, double undulating line) rather than an actual snake. These same motifs are found on cloth, plaitwork, and tattoo patterns, giving the artistic production of the Ainu a decidedly ornamental character.

* *

BIBLIOG. *Archaeology*: A. O. Heikel, Antiquités de la Sibérie occidentale, Helsinki, 1894; G. von Merhart, Bronzezeit am Jenissei, Vienna, 1926; S. A. Teploukhov, Drevnie pogrebeniia v Minusinskom krae (Ancient Tombs in the Region of Minusinsk), Materialy po etnografii, III, 2, 1927, pp. 57–112; E. R. Shneider, M. P. Griaznov, Drevnie izvaianiia Minusinskikh stepei (Ancient Sculpture of the Minusinsk Steppe), Materialy po etnografii, IV, 2, 1929, pp. 63–92; H. Appelgren-Kivalo, ed., Alt-Altaische Kunstdenkmäler, Helsinki, 1931; M. M. Gerasimov, Raskopki paleoliticheskoi stoianki v sele Mal'te (Excavations of Paleolithic Dwellings in the Village of Malta), Izvestiia Gosudarstvennoi Akad. Istorii Material'noi Kultury, CXVIII, Moscow, Leningrad, 1935; V. P. Levashova, Iz dalekogo proshlogo iuzhnoi chasti Krasnoiarskogo kraia (From the Far-off Past of the Southern Krasnoyarsk Region), Krasnoyarsk, 1939; D. N. Eding, Reznaia skul'ptura Urala (Intaglio in the Urals), Moscow, 1940; S. I. Rudenko, Drevniaia kul'tura Beringova moria i eskimosskaia problema (The Ancient Culture of the Bering Sea and the Eskimo Problem), Moscow, Leningrad, 1947 (Eng. trans., P. Tolstoy, Toronto, 1961; review by I. Paulson, Ethnos, XVI, 1951, pp. 136–39); M. P. Griaznov, Minusinskie kamennye baby v sviazi s nekotorymi novymi materialami (Stone Idols of Minusinsk in Relation to Some New Material), SA, XII, 1950, pp. 128–56; A. P. Okladnikov, Neolit i bronzovyi vek Pribaikal'ia (The Neolithic and Bronze Age in the Baikal Region), MIA, XVIII, 1950, XLIII, 1950; V. N. Chernetsov et al., Po sledam drevnikh kul'tur (On the Trail of Ancient Cultures), Moscow, 1951; K. Jettmar, The Altai before the Turks, BEFEA, XXIII, 1951, pp. 135–223; S. V. Kiselev, Drevniaia istoriia iuzhnoi Sibiri (Ancient History of Southern Siberia), Moscow, 1951; L. A. Evtiukhova, Kamennye izvaianiia iuzhnoi Sibiri i Mongolii (Stone Sculpture of Southern Siberia and Mongolia), MIA, XXIV, 1952; V. N. Chernetsov, V. I. Moshinskaia and I. A. Talitskaia, Drevniaia istoriia Nizhnego Priob'ia (Ancient History of the Lower Ob Region), MIA, XXXV, 1953, pp. 7–71; S. I. Rudenko, Kul'tura naseleniia Gornogo Altaia v skifskoe vremia (The Culture of the Population of the Altai Upland Plain in Scythian Times), Moscow, Leningrad, 1953; V. N. Chernetsov, Nizhnee Priob'e v I tysiacheletii nashei ery (The Lower Ob Region in the 1st Millennium A.D.), MIA, LVIII, 1957, pp. 136–245; A. D. Grach, Petroglify Tuvy (Petroglyphs of Tuva), Sbornik Muz. Antr. i Etn. Akad. Nauk SSSR, XVII, 1957, pp. 385–428, XVIII, 1958, pp. 339–84; T. Talbot Rice, The Scythians, London, 1957; M. P. Griaznov, Drevnee iskusstvo Altaia (Ancient Art of the Altai), Leningrad, 1958; A. P. Okladnikov, V. D. Zaporozhskaia, Lenskie pisanitsy (Lena Inscriptions), Moscow, Leningrad, 1959; J. Wiesner, Eurasische Kunst in Steppenraum und Waldgebiet, in Illustrierte Welt-Kunstgeschichte, I, Zurich, 1959, pp. 199–232; S. I. Rudenko, Kul'tura naseleniia tsentral'nogo Altaia v skifskoe vremia (The Culture of the Population of the Central Altai in Scythian Times), Moscow, 1960.

Modern production. a. General works: M. A. Czaplicka, Aboriginal Siberia, Oxford, 1914; A. Byhan and E. Krohn, Das Kunstgewerbe der Völker Nord-, Mittel- und Vorderasiens, in H. T. Bossert, Geschichte des Kunstgewerbes aller Zeiten und Völker, II, Berlin, 1929, pp. 1–50; H. Findeisen, Die Kunstkriese Nordasiens, Berlin, 1930; E. R. Shneider, Iskusstvo narodnostei Sibiri (Folk Art of Siberia), Leningrad, 1930; L. J. Shternberg, Ornament iz olen'ego volosa i igol dikobraza (Ornament from Reindeer Hair and Porcupine Quills), Sovetskaia etn., 3–4, 1931, pp. 103–21; U. Harva, Die religiösen Vorstellungen der altaischen Völker, Folklore Fellows Comm., 125, Helsinki, 1938; A. Leroi-Gourhan, Documents pour l'art comparé de l'Eurasie septentrionale, Paris, 1943; K. Donner, La Sibérie, Paris, 1946; S. V. Ivanov, Ornament narodov Sibiri kak istoricheskii istochnik (Ornament of the Siberian Peoples as a Historical Source), Kratkie soobshcheniia Inst. etn. Akad. Nauk SSSR, XV, 1952, pp. 8–18; S. V. Ivanov, Materialy po izobrazitel'nomu iskusstvu narodov Sibiri XIX – nachala XX veka (Materials on the Art of the Siberian Peoples from the 19th to the Beginning of the 20th Century), Trudy Inst. etn. Akad. Nauk SSSR, N.S., XXII, Moscow, Leningrad, 1954; G. Turner, Hair Embroidery in Siberia

Ainu decorative motifs embroidered on belts from the Kuril Islands (*from Montandon, 1929*).

and North America, Oxford, 1955; B. Brodskii et al., Iskusstvo narodov Sibiri (Art of the Siberian Peoples), Narodnoe dekorativnoe iskusstvo RSFSR, Moscow, 1957, pp. 207–38; F. I. Paulson, Die primitiven Seelenvorstellungen der nordeurasiatischen Völker, Ethn. Mus. of Sweden, Monograph Ser., 5, Stockholm, 1958; I. Paulson, Å. Hultkrantz, and K. Jettmar, Die Religionen Nordeurasiens und der amerikanischen Arktis, Stuttgart, 1962.

b. Stock-raising peoples of the south and west: W. Jochelson, Kumiss Festivals of the Yakut and the Decoration of Kumiss Vessels, Boas Anniversary Vol., New York, 1906, pp. 257–71; B. E. Petri, Ornament Kurdinskikh buriat (Ornament of the Kurdish Buryats), Sbornik Muz. antr. i etn. Akad. Nauk SSSR, V, 1917–25, pp. 215–52; P. P. Khoroshikh, Ornament severnykh buriat: Uzory na shitykh rabotakh (Ornament of the Northern Buryats: Patterns in Embroidered Work), Buriatovedcheskii sbornik, III–IV, 1927, pp. 83–89; I. M. Miagkov, Iskusstvo Tannu-Tuvy (Art of Tannu-Tuva), Sbornik materialy po izucheniiu Sibiri, III, Tomsk, 1931, pp. 283–315; W. Jochelson, The Yakut, APAmM, XXXIII, 2, 1933, pp. 33–225; M. M. Nosov, Stilevye priznaki iakutskogo uzora (Stylistic Indications of Yakut Patterns), Sbornik materialov po etnografii iakutov, Yakutsk, 1948, pp. 107–16; E. D. Prokof'eva, Ornament sel'kupov (Ornament of the Selkupy), Kratkie soobshcheniia Inst. etn. Akad. Nauk SSSR, X, 1950; U. Johansen, Die Ornamentik der Jakuten, Hamburg, 1954; S. I. Vainshtein, Sovremennoe kamnerezoe iskusstvo tuvintsev (Contemporary Art of Stone Carving among the Tuvintsy), Sovetskaia etn., 3, 1954, pp. 31–37; L. I. Iakunina, Iakutskaia reznaia kost' (Bone Carving among the Yakuts), Yakutsk, 1957; P. P. Khoroshikh, Ornament na sherstiianykh i volosianykh izdeliiakh Pribaikal'skikh buriat (Ornament of Woolen and Horsehair Articles among the Baikal Buryats), Zapiski buriat-mongol'skogo nauchno-issledovatel'skogo inst. kul'tury, XXII, Ulan-Ude, 1957; A. V. Tumahani, Buriatskii narodnyi uzor (Buriat Folk Designs), Zapiski buriat-mongol'skogo nauchno-issledovatel'skogo inst. kul'tury, XXV, Ulan-Ude, 1958.

c. Peoples of the far north: U. T. Sirelius, Ornamente auf Birkenrinde und Fell bei den Ostjaken und Wogulen, Helsinki, 1904; Izdeliia Ostiakov Tobol'skoi gub. (Ostyak Products from the Province of Tobolsk), Ezhegodnik Tobol'skogo Muz., XIX, Tobolsk, 1911; Z. Batky, ed., Ostjakische Stickereien (Ethn. Samml. des Ungarischen Nationalmuseums, IV), Budapest, 1921; S. I. Rudenko, Graficheskoe iskusstvo ostiakov i vogulov (Graphic Art of the Ostyaks and Voguly), Materialy po etn., IV, 2, 1929, pp. 13–39; S. M. Shirokogoroff, Psychomental Complex of the Tungus, London, 1935; V. N. Chernetsov, Ornament lentochnogo tipa u obskikh ugrov (Ribbon Ornament of the Ugrians of the Ob), Sovetskaia etn., I, 1948, pp. 139–52; T. Vahter, Ornamentik der Ob-Ugrier, Soc. Finno-Ougrienne, Trav. ethn., IX, Helsinki, 1953.

d. Peoples of the lower Amur River: B. Laufer, The Decorative Art of the Amur Tribes, Mem. Am. Mus. of Natural H., VII, 1902, pp. 1–86; S. V. Ivanov, Medved' v religioznom i dekorativnom iskusstve narodnostei Amura (The Bear in the Religious and Decorative Art of the Amur Peoples), Sbornik pamiati V. G. Bogoraza, Leningrad, 1937, pp. 1–45; S. V. Ivanov, Arkhitekturnyi ornament narodov Nizhnego Amur (Architectural Ornament among the Lower Amur Peoples), Sbornik Muz. antr. i etn. Akad. Nauk SSSR, XV, 1953, pp. 243–90; I. A. Lopatin, Animal Style among the Tungus on the Amur, Anthropos, LVI, 1961, pp. 856–68.

e. Peoples of the extreme northeast: H. Hildebrand, Beiträge zur Kenntnis der Kunst der niederen Naturvölker, in A. E. von Nordenskiöld, Studien und Forschungen, Leipzig, 1885, pp. 289–386; V. G. Bogoraz, Ocherk material'nogo byta olennykh chukchiei (Essay on the Economic Culture of the Reindeer Chukchi), Sbornik Muz. antr. i etn. Akad. Nauk, II, St. Petersburg, 1901; W. Jochelson, The Koryak, Leiden, New York, 1908; W. Jochelson, The Yukaghir and the Yukaghirized Tungus, Leiden, New York, 1926; V. V. Antropova, Starinnye kamchadal'skie sani (Ancient Sledges of Kamchadal), Sbornik Muz. antr. i etn. Akad. Nauk SSSR, X, 1949, pp. 47–92; V.V. Antropova, Sovremennaia chukotskaia i eskimosskaia reznaia kost' (Contemporary Chukchi and Eskimo Bone Carving), Sbornik Muz. antr. i etn. Akad. Nauk SSSR, XV, 1953, pp. 5–122.

f. The Ainu: G. Montandon, La civilisation Ainou et les cultures arctiques, Paris, 1937; W. Koppers, Künstlicher Zahnschliff am Bären im Altpaläolithikum und bei den Ainu auf Sachalin, Quartär, I, 1938, pp. 97–103; F. Maraini, Gli iku-bashui degli Ainu, Tokyo, 1942; R. T. Paine, Jr., An Ainu Clay Figure, BMFA, XLV, 1947, pp. 14–17; M. O. Baba, "Ikunishi" of the Saghalien Ainu, JRAI, LXXIX, 1951, pp. 27–35; A. Slawik, Die Wallburgen der Ainu, in J. Haebel, ed., Die Wiener Schule der Völkerkunde, Vienna, 1956, pp. 372–99; T. Obayashi, On the Origin of the "Inau" Cult-sticks of the Ainu, Jap. J. of Ethn., XXIV, 1960, pp. 277–306 (in Jap.: Eng. summary); M. Gusinde and C. Sano, An Annotated Bibliography of Ainu Studies by Japanese Scholars, Nagoya, 1962.   * *

Illustrations: PLS. 21–32; 5 figs. in text.

SIERRA LEONE. Since 1961 Sierra Leone has been an independent member of the British Commonwealth. The country is bounded on the north and east by Guinea, on the south by Liberia, and on the west by the Atlantic Ocean. The culture of Sierra Leone has numerous features in common with that of Guinea and of Liberia (qq.v.). Its artistic production forms a part of the civilization of the Gulf of Guinea (see GUINEAN CULTURES). Knowledge of this area is still incomplete, especially for the northern section of the country.

Among the peoples of Sierra Leone the Mende (Mendi) and the Kissi (Ghizi, Gissi, Kisi) are the leaders in artistic production. The work of the Sherbro, Bulom, Krim, Vai (Vei), Limba, Koranko, and Temne is less important artistically.

Anthropomorphic steatite figurines have been found in Mende country about 35 miles from the coast and in Kissi and Sherbro country. The Kissi call this stone statuary *pomdo* or *pombo*; the Mende, *nomori* or *nomoli*. Rütimeyer (1901) was the first to study the figurines, and declared that they were all produced in Mende country between the Sewa and Kittam rivers several centuries ago and were the work of neolithic people who came from the Red Sea coast and had distant affinities with the Egyptians and Ethiopians. More recently, scholars (Joyce, 1905, 1909; Neel, 1913; Paulme, 1942; Jeremine, 1945; Brown, 1948) have reached different conclusions, but although they have disagreed in regard to certain details, they all maintained that the steatite figurines were the product of African peoples, considering the obviously Negroid physical characteristics of most of the figurines and the fact that their original function was

Sierra Leone, distribution of the principal tribal groups with artistic production. Key: (1) Modern political boundaries.

funerary. Thus the sculpture found in the fields, which the present-day natives associate with the fertility of the fields and the fecundity of women (a belief especially held by the Mende and Kissi rice cultivators), was probably brought there at a later time. Person (1961) has suggested that, in view of the area throughout which the figurines were dispersed in Kissi and Sherbro country, it is very likely that they were at one time a characteristic element of the "forest" civilization of West Africa, which still survives, in some forms, in the Kissi and Sherbro cultures. This civilization was destroyed in the 16th century by the invasion of the Toma, who knew only wood sculpture. Today the *nomori* and *pomdo* are closely connected with religion; the natives believe they are charged with great spiritual power, which must be propitiated by offerings of boiled rice. Although it is not possible to speak of a stylistic unity in the steatite figurines, they have some features in common, particularly the large size of the head, another reason to think they are Negro-African in origin.

In the Mende area, where the finds have been most abundant, the statuettes have the following characteristics: large head with low forehead, hooked nose, big froglike eyes, and thick lips. Most of the figurines represent men, almost always circumcised, in various attitudes. Sometimes brass or iron armbands have been discovered in the funeral mounds with the *nomori*; if both types of objects could be proved to belong to the same period, the metal trinkets would be useful in approximately dating the figurines.

The Kissi *pomdo* are of less esthetic value. They are found in a greater variety of types (Neel counted seven), and always represent the human figure, sometimes full length and naturalistic, sometimes phallic-shaped, and occasionally bust length. The Kissi identify these figurines with their ancestors; they wrap them in cotton and keep them on the altars. The figurines found in Sherbro country have prominent navels and hypertrophic genitals. The rare steatite statuettes found among the Temne are kept in forges and in meeting places. Figurines in granite and sandstone and steatite statuettes representing animals are very rare.

A recent theory propounded by Fagg (1959) holds that at least part of the ivories known as Afro-Portuguese, which have been attributed to the Benin civilization for a long time, are rather the work of the natives of Sierra Leone, as the similarity between the style of the ivories and of the *nomori* figurines demonstrates. If this should be confirmed, ivory work would then represent the most notable artistic production of Sierra Leone.

Contemporary wood sculpture is of considerable interest, especially from the Mende area. The Mende make anthropomorphic figurines representing their ancestors; masks associated with secret societies for men and women; ceremonial staffs for the secret societies, which are decorated with figures carved in the same style as Liberian statues; carved drums, used by the Ngufui sect, as well as spoons and combs with handles decorated in fine geometric inlays; and, in the eastern Mende area, anthropomorphic figurines carved in wood and painted to represent forest spirits. The dance masks are worn with a costume that covers the entire body; the dancers perform on stilts. The masks are either naturalistic, with rounded forms, or geometric, with rectangular volumes. Sometimes the two styles are fused.

The Mende figurines and the large head masks of the secret female society, the Bundu, depict spiral-necked women. In these masks, as well as those of another female society, the Sande, which is widespread among the Krim and Vai, the mouth is always represented in the act of whistling. The headdresses are helmet-shaped and very elaborately decorated.

Other masks have two or four faces. The Sierra Leone masks are usually painted black or white.

The masks used by the secret male society, the Poro, have no particular regional features that might be an aid in attributing them to one tribe or another. They are always face masks, and are sometimes topped with horns or with female figurines in the style of the statuettes. The dancers wear long cloaks that completely envelop the body.

Masks that may or may not be connected with the secret societies are found among the Temne (hat masks), the Susu (face masks, with broad brows and very thin noses), and the Vai. The Vai masks are a cruder version of the Mende masks; they are used in initiation rites, in the worship of the dead, and generally for all festivals (VII, PL. 120). The wood statuary produced by these tribes is not of high quality.

The anthropomorphic figurines of terra cotta made by the Mende, Temne, and Bulom and the pottery produced by the women are of little esthetic value.

Contacts with the West have not given rise to new styles or new artistic activity in Sierra Leone, and the ancient tribal arts, such as the goldwork of the Limba and Koranko, have declined. The modern cities are architecturally uninteresting. Freetown, the capital, founded in 1788, is Victorian in appearance; the churches of St. George and St. Patrick, some of the mosques, and the original home of Fourah Bay College (erected 1843) are noteworthy. On the island of Bance are remains of some farms and British fortifications of the 17th century.

BIBLIOG. T. J. Alldridge, The Sherbro and Its Hinterland, London, 1901; L. Rütimeyer, Über westafrikanische Steinidole, IAE, XIV, 1901, pp. 195–215; T. A. Joyce, Steatite Figures from West Africa in the British Museum, Man, V, 1905, pp. 97–100; L. Rütimeyer, Weitere Mitteilungen über westafrikanische Steinidole, IAE, XVIII, 1908, pp. 167–78; T. A. Joyce, Steatite Figures from Sierra Leone, Man, IX, 1909, pp. 65–68; H. Neel, Statuettes en pierre et en argile de l'Afrique Occidentale, L'Anthropologie, XXIV, 1913, pp. 419–43; M. Delafosse, Au sujet des statuettes en pierre du Kissi, Rev. d'ethnographie et de sociologie, V, 1914, pp. 143–44; N. W. Thomas, Anthropological Report on Sierra Leone, 3 vols., London, 1916; W. Addison, Steatite Figures from Moyamba District, Central Province, Sierra Leone, Man, XXIII, 1923, pp. 176–77; R. Eberl-Elber, Westafrikas letztes Rätsel, Salzburg, 1936; H. U. Hall, The Sherbro of Sierra Leone, Philadelphia, 1938; D. Paulme, Deux statuettes en pierre de Guinée Française, B. Soc. d'Anthr., III, 1942, pp. 38–43; E. Jeremine, Etude des statuettes kissiennes au point de vue minéralogique et petrographique, JSA, XV, 1945, pp. 3–14; S. Brown, The Nomoli of Mende Country, Africa, XVIII, 1948, pp. 18–20; M. McCulloch, The Peoples of Sierra Leone Protectorate, London, 1950; K. L. Little, The Mende of Sierra Leone, London, 1951; H. Lavachery, Statuaire de l'Afrique noire, Brussels, 1954; R. Lewis, Sierra Leone: A Modern Portrait, London, 1954; W. Fagg, Afro-Portuguese Ivories, London, 1959; R. Mauny, Masques mende de la société Bundu (Sierra Leone), NIFAN, LXXXI, 1959, pp. 8–13; G. P. Murdock: Africa: Its Peoples and Their Culture History, New York, London, 1959; L. Proudfoot, Mosque-building and Tribal Separatism in Freetown, East Africa, XXIX, 1959, pp. 405–16; Y. Person, Les Kissi et leurs statuettes de pierre dans le cadre de l'histoire ouest-africaine, BIFAN, XXIII, 1961, pp. 1–60.

Ernesta CERULLI

Illustration: 1 fig. in text.

SIGNAC, PAUL. Painter and theorist of the pointillist, or neoimpressionist, movement (b. Paris, 1863; d. Paris, 1935). The son of well-to-do parents, and a gay and stimulating conversationalist, his natural self-confidence and intellectuality assured his position as the chief propagandist of the group that formed around Georges Seurat (q.v.) in the 1880s; upon Seurat's death in 1891 he assumed its leadership.

After mastering impressionist technique under the inspiration of Monet and Armand Guillaumin, Signac became a cofounder of the Salon des Indépendants and organizer of its annual nonjury exhibitions, the first of which opened in May, 1884, and included works by 400 artists. His friendship with Seurat began at this time, and although he was by no means the latter's artistic equal, he persuaded him to alter *Une Baignade* (*The Bathers*; VII, PLS. 436, 437) by eliminating brownish tones and adding small dots of high-intensity color. Signac exhibited his work in all nine exhibitions of the Indépendants between 1884 and 1893 (only Charles Angrand and Henri Edmond Cross were equally faithful) and continued as president of the society until his death.

It was Signac who introduced Pissarro (q.v.) to Seurat in 1885, with the result that Pissarro joined the new group and radically altered his own style until, about five years later, he became restive with a "technique that ties me down and prevents me from producing with spontaneity of sensation." Pissarro wrote these words to his son Lucien, a minor figure in pointillism, with whom Signac maintained a long and close association.

As an artist, Signac showed two distinct tendencies. On the one hand his paintings are debilitated by an excess of theory, lacking the observation and warmth that enliven even the most austere works of Seurat. This was particularly true after 1900, when Signac replaced the small round dots of pointillism with larger squarish spots that give his paintings, despite their brilliant color, the chilling effect of Roman stone mosaics. Many of these later paintings represent harbor views, especially in the neighborhood of Saint-Tropez, where he bought a house in 1893 (cf. VII, PL. 438). On the other hand, Signac's pencil and water-color sketches have the verve and spontaneity that most of his paintings lack. They closely resemble the watercolors of the Dutch artist Johan Barthold Jongkind (1819–91), a forerunner of impressionism, who worked primarily in France; Signac collected these sketches avidly and in 1927 published many of them in an excellent monograph that he wrote on Jongkind.

Signac's other publications reveal his theoretical interests. *D'Eugène Delacroix au néo-impressionistes* (Paris, 1899) was extremely influential among younger artists, including Henri Matisse and André Derain (qq.v.). An article, "Les besoins individuels de la peinture," appeared in *L'Encyclopédie française* (XVI, ch. 2).

See also EUROPEAN MODERN MOVEMENTS; FAUVISM; IMPRESSIONISM.

BIBLIOG. J. Rewald, Post-Impressionism: From Van Gogh to Gauguin, New York, 1956; P. Signac, Fragments du journal, Arts de France, 17–18, 1947, pp. 75–84; J. Rewald, ed., Extraits du journal inédit de Paul Signac 1894–1895, 1897–1900, GBA, XXXVI, 1949, pp. 97–128, XXXIX, 1952, pp. 298–304, XLII, 1953, pp. 27–57.

S. Lane FAISON, Jr.

SIGNORELLI, LUCA. Painter, born between 1445 and 1450 in Cortona, where he died Oct. 16, 1523. The first picture signed by Signorelli is a processional standard painted for the Church of S. Maria del Mercato in Fabriano; on one side (inscribed "Opus Luce Cortonensis") was a Flagellation (PL. 33) and on the other a Madonna and Child with seraphim. These two small panels, now disjoined (Milan, Brera), were long considered to be the first paintings by Signorelli, probably done between 1470 and 1475. But Salmi (*Luca Signorelli*, 1953) convincingly places them later than 1480, when there is documentary evidence to show that the master worked on the Sacristy of St. John within the Sanctuary of the Holy House of Loreto (angels, Evangelists, Doctors of the Church, Christ and the Apostles, Doubting Thomas, Conversion of St. Paul; PL. 35).

The two small panels are thus more logically related to what are probably Signorelli's earliest works (some of whose dates, however, are problematic): the fresco of St. Paul (part of a larger composition perhaps echoed in a painting in the parish church of Micciano, near Anghiari), commissioned in 1474 for the municipal tower of Città di Castello (Città di Castello, Pin. Comunale); the *Annunciation* of Casa da Monte, now in the Church of S. Francesco at Arezzo (which Longhi, 1951, disagreeing with Salmi's 1916 attribution, ascribes instead to Bartolomeo della Gatta); a *Madonna and Child* in Boston (Mus. of Fine Arts) and another in Oxford (Ashmolean Mus.); and the Villamarina Madonna in Venice (Cini Coll.; Berenson, 1926).

These last three works, obviously influenced by Piero della Francesca (the one in the Cini Collection in particular is perhaps even ascribable to him), raise the question of the young Signorelli's connection with Piero, noted as early as Luca Pacioli's *Summa de Arithmetica* (Venice, 1494) and then in Vasari's *Lives*. It has been thought, because of this connection, that Signorelli may have collaborated on Piero's polyptych painted for the Church of S. Agostino at Sansepolcro (1454–69; see PIERO DELLA FRANCESCA) and especially on two of the panels, namely, the St. Michael in London (Nat. Gall.; Cavalcaselle, 1898) and the St. Augustine in Lisbon (Mus. Nac. de Arte Antiga; Salmi, *Luca Signorelli*, 1953). Their association, however, should be placed no earlier than the seventh decade of the century if one accepts 1445–50 as Signorelli's birth date, instead of 1441 as given by Vasari, and relates it to the earliest mention (in the year 1470) of his paintings in Cortona, now lost.

Although his connection with Piero della Francesca was initially a decisive factor, it was certainly not the only influence that acted upon the creative genius of Signorelli, who, understandably interested in the dramatic fervor of Pollaiuolo (q.v.), was soon to turn to the Florentine environment. But the texture of the drawing — so sharp and clear in the Florentine painter — in the Cortonese is absorbed into thick, solid color that gives the figures a compactness, a massive unity, and a touch of primitiveness corresponding to the manly vigor Signorelli expresses with such genuine immediacy.

In 1482 he worked on the *Testament and Death of Moses* fresco in the Sistine Chapel with Bartolomeo della Gatta and an Umbrian painter.

The S. Onofrio altarpiece from the Cathedral of Perugia (PLS. 34, 38), executed in 1484 (Vasari), indicates that Signorelli was in touch with the Florentine circle of Donatello and Pollaiuolo (Cruttwell, 1899) and perhaps also shows the influence of the Florentine group of Leonardo da Vinci and Lorenzo di Credi; the slight Flemish echoes, in the wake of Hugo van der Goes, have been changed into deeply sonorous tones. This is one of Signorelli's most beautiful works prior to the *Realm of Pan* (III, PL. 392), executed about 1488 for Lorenzo the Magnificent (Vasari) and destroyed in 1945. Here classicism is a state of mind, that is, a balanced completeness of existence attained by the contemplation of all that is eternal and fascinating on earth, from physical beauty to intellectual elevation; the whole is a far cry from the subtle pathos and delicate shadows of Botticelli's refinement. It is a powerful exaltation of the virile Herculean beauty of the nudes which Signorelli was to place in the backgrounds of his paintings and to which he was to return insistently in Orvieto.

A *Holy Family* (Rome, Coll. Pallavicini) and a fresco of the Nativity (Arezzo, Pin.), dated 1487, must have been done after the Perugia altarpiece and indicate Signorelli's adjustment to the Florentine figural tondo, which also appears as a decorative motif in the signed *Circumcision*, executed for the Church of S. Francesco in Volterra (London, Nat. Gall.). It also characterizes other works of his: a *Madonna and Child* in the Uffizi, a *Holy Family* in the Pitti, and a later *Madonna and Child with Saints* in the Corsini Collection (all, Florence), a *Madonna* in Munich (Alte Pin.), a *Madonna and Child with Saints* in Castel di Poggio near Florence (Coll. Baduel), a *Holy Family* in the Uffizi (XII, PL. 34), a *Visitation* in Berlin (Mus. Dahlem), and a *Madonna and Child with Saints* in London (Vincent Korda Coll.).

Another sure date in Signorelli's artistic activity is 1491. It appears in two paintings in Volterra (Pin. Comunale): a *Madonna*

and Child with Saints done for the Church of S. Agostino and an *Annunciation* done for the Cathedral. Also in Volterra is a fresco of St. Jerome, dated 1490–91 (Palazzo dei Priori); here the conception has become broader and more monumental.

An *Adoration of the Magi* (Louvre) and a *Nativity* (Naples, Mus. di Capodimonte), painted for the Church of S. Agostino at Città di Castello, are from 1493–94. From 1494 there is the gonfalon of Urbino (Palazzo Ducale) with the Crucifixion on one side and the Descent of the Holy Ghost on the other; from 1496, the *Nativity* done for the Church of S. Francesco in Città di Castello (London, Nat. Gall.); and from 1498, the *Martyrdom of St. Sebastian* (Città di Castello, Pin. Comunale).

In the same period Signorelli, after having completed his *Portrait of a Jurist* (Berlin, Mus. Dahlem), executed portraits of Niccolò Vitelli (Birmingham, England, Barber Inst. of Fine Arts), Camillo and Vitellozzo Vitelli (Settignano, near Florence, Berenson Foundation), and an unknown young man (Philadelphia, Mus. of Art, Johnson Coll.).

The next work is Signorelli's first great fresco cycle in the large cloister of the Abbey of Monte Oliveto Maggiore, near Siena: ten scenes from the life of St. Benedict painted 1497–98, which are precursors of the Orvieto cycle. They reveal an unevenness of quality and inventiveness, partly due to the fairly important contribution of assistants. Where the master's active participation is greater, as in the story of the two monks lodged outside the monastery (PL. 35), the composition is solemn and imbued with warmly intimate humanity in spite of the presence of motifs already utilized elsewhere. There is also a greater emphasis on the bizarre, which comes perhaps from a deliberately stressed Nordic influence.

Belonging to the same period but of much higher quality are the fragments (Berlin, Mus. Dahlem) of the Bichi Chapel altarpiece from S. Agostino in Siena. Borenius (1913), in an attempt to reconstruct the barbarously dismembered work, associated with them two small panels in Toledo, Ohio (Mus. of Art), another in Dublin (Nat. Gall.), a *Martyrdom of St. Catherine* (Williamstown, Mass., Clark Art Inst.), and a *Lament for the Dead Christ* (formerly Pollockshaws, Scotland, Maxwell Coll.).

On Apr. 5, 1499, Signorelli received his first assignment to work on the vaults of the Chapel of S. Brizio in Orvieto Cathedral, in order to complete what Angelico (q.v.) and Benozzo Gozzoli had begun in 1447, since only two of the eight compartments had been finished. On Apr. 27 of the following year he was commissioned to decorate the walls as well. Here he painted the appearance of the Antichrist and the Last Judgment, with the Resurrection of the Body (PL. 36), the Damned (IV, PL. 179; VII, PL. 380), the Blessed (PL. 37), the Arrival in Paradise, and Hell; and, at the base, figures of famous men as well as illustrations of ancient poems and of the *Divine Comedy*. This Last Judgment amplifies the traditional iconography, typical examples of which are Nardo di Cione's frescoes in the Strozzi Chapel of S. Maria Novella in Florence (IV, PL. 465) or, better, Angelico's *Last Judgment* depicting the Resurrection of the Body, Paradise, and Hell (I, PL. 261). Precise directions for this amplification were given Signorelli by the theologians of the Cathedral of Orvieto, based on episodes from the Apocalypse and the Gospels of Mark and Matthew, including the appearance of the Antichrist, rarely treated in Italian art; according to Chastel (1952), its inclusion can be explained as a specific reference to Savonarola. The subject matter is largely drawn from Jacopo da Voragine's *Golden Legend*, numerous editions of which had been published in Latin and the vernacular; other sources are the revelations of the Swedish saint, Bridget, printed in 1492 in Lübeck, and the apocryphal Gospels. There is no need to seek the source of Signorelli's iconography in German engravings and in sacred plays (Dussler, 1927), since many parts of the scenes repeat and develop ideas already used elsewhere by him or by other artists (e.g., architecture that evokes Perugino's settings; decoration and motifs in the style of Pintoricchio).

The Last Judgment follows the *Dies irae*. As for the other themes, no new sources are required to explain their treatment. The idea of linking Dante and famous personages (PL. 36) in an attempt to absorb classical culture into Christian civilization might have been suggested by some theologian inspired less probably by the series of Famous Men in Federico da Montefeltro's *studiolo* in the Ducal Palace of Urbino (Dussler, 1927) than by the intellectual atmosphere of Florence, where love of the classics and the cult of Dante held sway in the late 15th century (Salmi, *Luca Signorelli*, 1953).

Other painters collaborated with Signorelli on the frescoes of Orvieto, and in some places their work can be detected. But in the painting of the vaults it is not possible to make accurate attributions — despite the attempts of Venturi (1913) and Dussler (1927) — except for the Doctors, where Salmi *Luca Signorelli*, 1953) sees the brush of Girolamo Genga and perhaps of Francesco Signorelli, the master's nephew; nor is it possible to identify the contributions of Mariotto and Francesco, sons of the sculptor Urbano da Cortona and students in Cortona, whose names appear on the employment contract. Carli (1946) again suggests Girolamo Genga as the author of the two episodes on the right of the back wall, which seem to be related to the frescoes formerly in the Palazzo del Magnifico in Siena. The same painter also worked on the Arrival in Paradise and on other parts of the chapel.

The entire cycle (for which Signorelli received the last payment in December, 1504) was probably already completed before the end of 1502, that is, when the decision was made to replace the colored windowpanes with white ones so that the paintings would have better light.

The Chapel of S. Brizio remains a great product of the early Renaissance. There is something archaic in its spatial values and in the occasional lack of integration between the various figures; but man has been released from hedonistic aims and is represented in his moral seriousness, exalted in his virile power, full of vigor and profound intensity.

The Lament for the Dead Christ, formerly in the Church of S. Margherita, Cortona (now, Mus. Diocesano), bore the date 1502, according to Vasari; it is another example of the scene in three episodes, of which Signorelli was so fond. At about this time his work increasingly reveals the brush of assistants, whom he had to call on to cope with his numerous commissions. Frequently he utilized earlier cartoons or compositional motifs. Nevertheless, there are truly distinguished paintings of this period, such as the *Crucifixion* in the Uffizi and the altarpiece of Arcevia (1503; Brera). The frescoes in the Church of S. Crescentino at Morra (near Città di Castello) are less carefully executed. The *Communion of the Apostles* (1512) in Cortona (Mus. Diocesano) reveals increasingly intense contacts with Pintoricchio (q.v.) and the Umbrian painters.

Other works with verified dates are the *Madonna and Child with Saints* in S. Domenico, Cortona, and the *Madonna* of Montone (London, Nat. Gall.), both 1515; the *Deposition* in Sta Croce, Umbertide, 1516–17; the altarpiece of Paciano (Perugia, Gall. Naz. dell'Umbria), 1517; the *Assumption* from the parish church of Cortona (Cortona, Mus. Diocesano) and the Gamurrini altarpiece for S. Girolamo of Arezzo (Arezzo, Pin.), both 1520; the *Immaculate Conception* for the former Gesù in Cortona (Mus. Diocesano), 1521; and the *Coronation of the Virgin* in the Church of S. Martino at Foiano della Chiana.

Among Signorelli's numerous collaborators of this period were Tommaso Bernabei, nicknamed "il Papacello," and, of lesser importance, Francesco Signorelli, the painter's nephew. Bartolomeo della Gatta, who perhaps had been associated with him only in the work on the Sistine Chapel, the Griselda Master, and Girolamo Genga, who had worked with Signorelli in the first decade of the century, had by then become figures of his past.

Umberto BALDINI

BIBLIOG. G. Vasari, Le vite . . . , 1st ed., Florence, 1550 (ed. G. Milanese, III, Florence, 1878, pp. 683–96); R. Borghini, Il Riposo, Florence, 1584; C. Crispolti, Perugia augusta, Perugia, 1648; D. M. Manni, Vita di Luca Signorelli, in Raccolta milanese, 1756; F. Baldinucci, Le vite dei professori del disegno da Cimabue in qua . . . , II, Turin, 1770, pp. 165–72; L. Pungileoni, Elogio storico di Giovanni Santi, Urbino, 1822; G. Mancini, Memorie di alcuni artefici del disegno, Perugia, 1832; A. Ricci, Memorie storiche delle arti e degli artisti della Marca d'Ancona, Macerata, 1834; M. Gualandi, Memorie originali italiane risguardanti le belle arti, V, Bologna, 1845; G. F. Waagen, Ueber Leben, Wirken und Werke der Maler

Andrea Mantegna und Luca Signorelli, in Historisches Taschenbuch von Raumer, Leipzig, 1850, pp. 471–594; R. Vischer, Luca Signorelli und die italienische Renaissance, Leipzig, 1879; G. Morelli, Italian Masters in German Galleries: A Critical Essay on the Italian Pictures in the Galleries of Munich, Dresden, Berlin, trans. L. M. Richter, London, 1883; L. Fumi, Il Duomo d'Orvieto e i suoi restauri, Rome, 1891; A. Anselmi, Istrumenti di allogazione e di quietanza della tavola di Luca Signorelli figurante il Battesimo nella chiesa di San Medardo di Arcevia, Arch. storico dell'arte, V, 1892, pp. 196–97; A. Anselmi, Il ritrovamento della tavola dipinta in Arcevia da Luca Signorelli, Arch. storico dell'arte, V, 1892, pp. 202–08; C. von Fabriczy, Ein wiederaufgefundener Signorelli, RepfKw, XV, 1892, p. 553; G. Frizzoni, La Pinacoteca di Brera e il suo nuovo catalogo, Arch. storico dell'arte, V, 1892, pp. 400–06; P. Fontana, Di una tavoletta di Luca Signorelli della Pinacoteca di Brera, Arch. storico dell'arte, 2d ser., II, 1896, pp. 269–76; M. Cruttwell, Luca Signorelli, London, 1899 (3d ed., 1907); H. Makowsky, Ein männliches Bildnis von Luca Signorelli in der Berliner Galerie, ZfbK, N.S., XI, 1900, pp. 117–20; E. Jacobsen, Italienische Gemälde im Louvre, RepfKw, XXV, 1902, p. 279; B. Berenson, The Drawings of the Florentine Painters, 2 vols., London, 1903 (rev. ed., 3 vols., Chicago, 1938); C. von Fabriczy, Mitteilungen über neue Forschungen: Signorellis Pansbild in der Berliner Galerie, RepfKw, XXVI, 1903, p. 261; G. Mancini, La vita di Luca Signorelli, Florence, 1903; P. Schubring, Florenz, I, Die Gemälde-Galerien der Uffizien und des Palazzo Pitti, Stuttgart, 1907; W. Kallab, Vasaristudien, ed. J. von Schlosser (Quellenschr. f. Kg. u. Kunsttechnik, N.S. XV), 1908, pp. 40, 224; B. Berenson, The Central Italian Painters of the Renaissance, 2d ed., London, 1909; R. Fry, The Umbrian Painters at the Burlington Fine Arts Club, 1909–10, pp. 267–74; A. Venturi, Luca Signorelli, Il Perugino e Pier d'Antonio Dei a Loreto, L'Arte, XIV, 1911, pp. 290–307; A. Venturi, Paramenti istoriati su disegno di Justus di Gand e di Luca Signorelli, L'Arte, XV, 1912, pp. 299–304; T. Borenius, The Reconstruction of a Polyptych by Signorelli, BM, XXIV, 1913, pp. 32–36; H. F. Cook, A Catalogue of the Paintings . . . in the Collection of Sir F. Cook, London, 1913; Venturi, VII, 2, 1913, pp. 298–407; J. A. Crowe and G. B. Cavalcaselle, A History of Painting in Italy, Umbria, Florence and Siena From the Second to the Sixteenth Century, 2d ed., V, London, 1914, pp. 82–121; C. Gamba, La Ca' d'Oro e la collezione Franchetti, BArte, X, 1916, pp. 321–34; A. Venturi, L'atmosfera artistica umbra all'arrivo di Raffaello a Perugia, L'Arte, XXI, 1918, pp. 93–108; A. Venturi, Affreschi inediti di Luca Signorelli, L'Arte, XXII, 1919, pp. 9–12; A. Chiappelli, Un nuovo tondo di Luca Signorelli, Rass. d'Arte, XX, 1920, p. 74; R. Fry, A Tondo by Luca Signorelli, BM, XXXVIII, 1921, pp. 105–06; M. Salmi, Catalogo della Pinacoteca Comunale di Arezzo, Città di Castello, 1921; R. Fry, A Signorelli Republished, BM, XL, 1922, p. 134; A. Venturi, Luca Signorelli, Florence, 1923; M. Salmi, Luca Signorelli, Florence, 1924; A. Venturi, La quadreria di Ludwig Mond nella Galleria Nazionale di Londra, L'Arte, XXVII, 1924, p. 205; L. Dussler, An Unpublished Signorelli in an English Private Collection, BM, XLVII, 1925, p. 3; A. Venturi, Per Luca Signorelli, L'Arte, XXVIII, 1925, pp. 220–23; B. Berenson, An Early Signorelli in Boston, Art in America, XIV, 1926–27, p. 111; T. Borenius, The Benson Collection, Apollo, VI, 1927, pp. 65–70; L. Dussler, Signorelli: Des Meisters Gemälde, Stuttgart, 1927; L. Dussler, Ein unbekanntes Altarwerk des L. Signorelli, Pantheon, III, 1929, pp. 212–14; B. Berenson, Italian Painters of the Renaissance, Oxford, 1930, London, 1952; T. Borenius, Pictures from American Collections at Burlington House, Apollo, XI, 1930, pp. 153–67; W. Heil, Eine Predella des Luca Signorelli, Der Cicerone, XXII, 1930, pp. 272–75; L. Serra, Il Palazzo Ducale e la Galleria Nazionale di Urbino, Rome, 1930; A. E. Popham, Italian Drawings Exhibited at the Royal Academy . . . 1930, London, 1931; L. Venturi, Pitture italiane in America, Milan, 1931; B. Berenson, Les dessins de Signorelli, GBA, VII, 1932, pp. 173–210; B. Berenson, Italian Pictures of the Renaissance, Oxford, 1932; B. Berenson, Nouveaux dessins de Signorelli, GBA, X, 1933, pp. 279–93; L. Dussler, ThB, XXXI, 1937, s.v.; R. van Marle, The Development of the Italian Schools of Painting, XVI, The Hague, 1937, pp. 1–145; O. Morisani, Predelle del Signorelli, L'Arte, XLV, 1942, p. 25; E. Carli, Luca Signorelli, gli affreschi nel Duomo di Orvieto, Bergamo, 1946; A. Minto, Il sarcofago romano del Duomo di Cortona, RArte, XXVI, 1950, pp. 1–22; A. E. Popham and P. Pouncey, Italian Drawings in the Department of Prints and Drawings in the British Museum, the Fourteenth and Fifteenth Centuries, 2 vols., London, 1950, pp. 145–54; M. Salmi, Luca Signorelli a Morra, RArte, XXVI, 1950, pp. 131–47; R. Longhi, La mostra di Arezzo, Paragone, II, 15, 1951, pp. 50–63; Paintings and Sculpture from the Kress Collection, U. S. National Gallery of Art, Washington, 1951; A. Chastel, L'Apocalypse en 1500: la fresque de L'Antéchrist à la chapelle Saint-Brice à Orvieto, Humanisme et Renaissance, XIV, 1952, pp. 124–40; Mostra di Luca Signorelli, Cortona, (cat.), ed. M. Moriondo, Florence, 1953; M. Salmi, Chiosa Signorelliana, Comm, IV, 1953, pp. 107–18; M. Salmi, Luca Signorelli, Novara, 1953; P. Rotondi, Un'ipotesi sui rapporti tra Luca Signorelli e Ercole Roberti, in Studies in the History of Art Dedicated to W. E. Suida, London, 1959, pp. 110–15; A. Martindale, Luca Signorelli and the Drawings Connected with the Orvieto Frescoes, BM, CIII, 1961, pp. 216–20; Sterling and Francine Clark Art Institute, Luca Signorelli: The Martyrdom of St. Catherine and the Bichi Altar, Williamstown, Mass., 1961; W. Welliner, Signorelli's "Court of Pan," AQ, XXIV, 1961, pp. 334–45.

* *

Illustrations: PLS. 33–38.

SIGNS AND SYMBOLS. See SYMBOLISM AND ALLEGORY.

SILVERWORK. See GOLD-AND SILVERWORK; METALWORK.

SINĀN. Generally considered the greatest Turkish architect, Sinān was active through the second and third quarters of the 16th century during the reigns of Süleyman (Ar., Sulaymān) the Magnificent and his son Selim II. He is commonly known as Koca Mimar Sinān ("the great architect Sinān"), to avoid confusion with two other architects who, according to recent studies, bore the same name. The first, Atīk Sinān, designed the Mosque of Mehmet the Conqueror; the other, Sinān of Balikesir, was active during the reign of Selim I and was responsible for some of the monuments formerly attributed to the great Sinān.

Koca Mimar Sinān was born on Apr. 15, 1489, in a village near Kayseri, in Anatolia. It is generally accepted by modern scholars that Sinān's parents were not Turkish, but Greek Christians. The name of his father is not known. His grandfather, who seems to have been a builder, used to take young Sinān with him on business trips, enabling Sinān to become familiar with the Seljuk monuments (see SELJUK ART) of Kayseri and the surrounding countryside. In 1502 he was sent to study in Istanbul, and the following year he entered military training as a janizary. During the expeditions against Belgrade (1521) and Rhodes (1522) he so distinguished himself that he was appointed chief of artillery. Subsequently he took part in the expedition of Hayrüddin Barbarossa and Lufti Paşa against Corfu and also visited some Italian cities. He later became a chief constable (*subashi*).

In 1534, in the course of a campaign against Persia, Sinān revealed his extraordinary engineering talents for the first time by building a bridge of boats across Lake Van so cleverly that the leaders of the expedition were amazed. Later, while taking part in an invasion of Walachia, Sinān threw a bridge across the Danube and erected thoroughly professional military fortifications. After these successes he devoted himself exclusively to architecture and during the following forty years built an immense number of monuments in every part of the Ottoman Empire, from Bosnia to Mecca. His biographers attribute about 360 structures to him, but many of these no longer exist. Some of Sinān's disciples — and he had many — also became outstanding architects: Davut Ağa, Ahmet Ağa, Kemaleddin, and Yusuf. Yusuf, Sinān's favorite pupil, achieved great fame at the Moghul court; he constructed for Akbar some of the most beautiful palaces of Delhi, Agra, and Lahore.

The most famous works of Sinān are the Şehzade and Süleymaniye mosques in Istanbul and the Selimiye Mosque in Edirne, which he himself called examples of his artistic parabola: the first an apprentice work, the second a mature work, and the third a masterwork. Sinān's contemporary and biographer, Mustafa Sāī, a celebrated painter, writes that in addition to these, Sinān built 79 mosques as well as 34 palaces, 33 public baths, 50 chapels, 19 turbehs (Turk., *türbe*, "funerary monument"), 55 schools, 16 refectories for the poor, 7 madrasahs (Turk., *medrese*), about a dozen hostelries, and numerous granaries, fountains, aqueducts, and hospitals. Sinān died at an advanced age on July 17 of either 1578 or 1588 — the latter date according to the studies of Ahmet Refik, based on the testimony of Mustafa Sāī. He asked to be buried in the garden of his house, behind the Mosque of Süleyman, his best-loved work and certainly one if his masterpieces.

Sinān has often been accused of lack of originality, of constantly using the plan of Hagia Sophia in Istanbul as his source of inspiration in the construction of his mosques; but even though he cannot be called an innovator in the strict sense of the word, he cannot be considered a mere follower of the Byzantine school. In studying the plans of Christian churches he became convinced that they were poorly adapted to the needs of Islamic worship, which requires spacious halls for common prayer. To this end he made an attentive study of various planimetric solutions that might satisfy both functional and esthetic requirements. His chief problems were those of space and of the dome. To achieve spaciousness and light for his interiors he not infrequently neglected the exterior effect. His most important mosques fall into six types: (1) the square hall, covered by a simple dome (Haseki Hurrem Cami); (2) the square hall under one central dome with two half domes along the main axis of the building (Süleymaniye Cami, Kılıç Ali Paşa Cami); (3) the square hall covered by a central dome and four half domes set along the two axes (Şehzade Cami); (4) the oblong hall with central dome on a square base (Mihrimah Cami near the Edirne Gate, Ibrahim Paşa Cami, Zal Mahmut Paşa Cami, Bāli Paşa Cami); (5) the oblong hall with central dome on hexagonal base (Ahmet Paşa Cami, Sokullu Mehmet Paşa Cami); and (6) the oblong hall with central dome on octagonal base (Rüstem Paşa Cami, Selimiye Cami at Edirne, Azap Kapı Cami). All these, except the Selimiye, are situated in Istanbul or its immediate neighborhood.

The first of these mosques was constructed by Sinān in 1539 (A.H. 946) but was enlarged during the course of the 17th century. Originally it had the form of a single square hall (although today it has two) with a dome resting on pendentives and with a portico comprising five bays in front. The year of construction of the Mihrimah Cami — which was founded by the daughter of Süleyman the Magnificent after her marriage to Rüstem Paşa — is unknown, but it appears to have been after 1539 and may be estimated as about 1547. In this mosque Sinān adopted the oblong plan for the prayer hall and covered it with a beautiful central dome, harmonious but not excessively large, rising to a height of over 120 ft. and dominating the surrounding buildings and the towers of the Edirne Gate. The turquoise tones of the interior walls augment the sense of light and spaciousness. The Mihrimah suffered much damage from earthquakes but was carefully restored at the beginning of the 20th century.

The Mosque of Rüstem Paşa is perhaps of the same period as the Mihrimah, for it repeats the same general plan in smaller dimensions. The prayer hall is oblong and has a central dome on an octagonal base, supported by pendentives on octagonal pillars.

For the first of his more important works, the Şehzade Cami (Mosque of Shah Zade or Mosque of the Princes; PL. 39, FIG. 53), finished in 1548, Sinān again adopted the square plan for the prayer hall, with the central dome supported by four pendentives placed on octagonal pillars and with four half domes. Compared to those of the Beyazıt Cami of Istanbul (1501–05), these half domes are more convex and are, moreover, enlarged by two hemispherical niches each. Outside, at the corners of the square where the half domes meet, Sinān set cylindrical turrets, which support the thrust of the great internal arches and also lighten the exterior effect. Thus the whole assumed the form of a sloping pyramid. The plan of the Şehzade, something quite new for Istanbul, had had precedents at Maraş and in Elbistan, where for the first time, in the Ulu Cami (Great Mosque), the innovation of joining dome and half dome by means of diagonal buttresses was tried.

The Mosque of Bāli Paşa was heavily damaged by fire in 1917 and left to fall into ruin. Its construction seems to date from the middle of the 16th century: it had an oblong plan and proportions similar to those of the Mosque of Ibrahim Paşa at Silivri Kapı, built in 1551, with slight variations in the squinches of the dome. Also built in 1551 (A.H. 958) was the Zal Mahmut Paşa Cami, in Eyüp, with the same plan as the two preceding examples and a dome on a square base, without openings. On the three sides corresponding to the north, south, and west faces of the dome there are arcades of five bays supported by small columns. The arcades in turn support galleries with vaulted ceilings.

For the construction of the Süleymaniye (PL. 40; VIII, PL. 161; X, PLS. 444, 445), to which he dedicated himself from 1550 to 1557, Sinān was inspired by the plan of Hagia Sophia, but he introduced all the modifications and improvements necessary for Moslem worship, which he had been working out in his previous buildings. He designed a square plan for the prayer hall with an aisle rendered symmetrical at the extremities by means of two half domes linked to the corners by arched recesses. Over the central square he placed a beautiful dome nearly 175 ft. high, resting on four powerful rectangular pillars and pierced by 32 openings; the two side aisles are covered by five domes each, all of different diameters. He eliminated the upper galleries of the Christian church and the apse in the center of

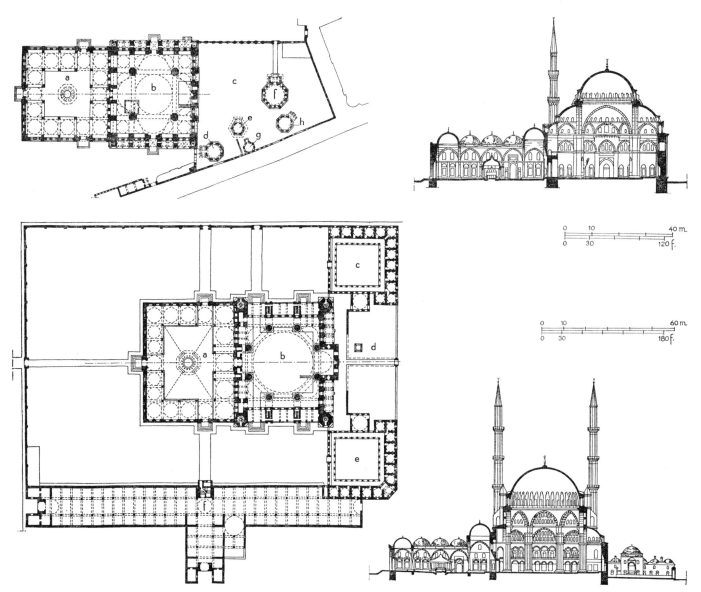

Above: Istanbul, Mosque of Şehzade (Shah Zade), plan and section. (a) Courtyard; (b) mosque; (c) garden; (d) Türbe of Ibrahim Paşa; (e) Türbe of Şehzade Mahmut; (f) Türbe of Şehzad Mehmet; (g) Türbe of the Sheik ul-Islam, Bostani Sade; (h) Türbe of Rüstem Paşa. *Below*: Edirne, Mosque of Şelim, plan and section. (a) Courtyard; (b) mosque; (c) madrasah; (d) cemetery; (e) hospital; (f) bazaar (from *C. Gurlitt, Die Baukunst Konstantinopols, Berlin, 1912*).

the south half dome, since it had no functional value in a mosque. This functional suppression of the apse, however, forced the architect to unite the two lateral exedras with an arch closed by a wall, and this is the only real weakness of the work. Sinān was also successful in avoiding the tiresome junction of several domes halfway up the height of the aisle, by covering the joins as far as possible with a series of stalactites, while the four large arches supporting the central dome strongly accentuate its effect in relation to the smaller domes. The windows are well placed to flood the vast hall with light. In the interior the limited use of arabesque decoration is highly effective. On the lateral façades are two-storied arcaded galleries corresponding to the internal galleries. The upper ones on the outside are covered by a sloping roof that, besides providing shelter, serves to break up the monotony of the façade. Four doors lead into the prayer hall, one at each end of the lateral façades, and there is a principal door in the center of the axis that connects the interior to a vast rectangular courtyard surrounded by porticoes. At the four corners of the court are graceful minarets, which noticeably accentuate the elegance of the mosque and give to the whole a sense of harmony and balance.

In the Mosque of Ahmet Paşa, built in 1555 for the Grand Vizier of Süleyman the Magnificent, Sinān traced a hexagonal plan inscribed in a rectangle. The central dome, pierced by

18 openings, is supported by six ancient columns with honeycomb capitals and surrounded by four small half domes, which also have numerous openings. The interior is richly decorated with polychrome ceramic tiles and splendid wood paneling painted with red flowers and gilded arabesques on a blue ground — the best example of painted decoration of the period in Istanbul. Recent restoration has perhaps overaccentuated the already vivid coloring of the building. The Sokullu Mehmet Paşa Cami, built in 1572 for the Grand Vizier of the same name, has the same plan as the Mosque of Ahmet Paşa — a hexagon inscribed in a rectangle — but the dome and the four half domes cover the whole hall without interruption. Both the wall containing the mihrab and the pendentives of the large dome are covered with polychrome ceramics, and the same decoration is repeated under the portico — seven bays covered by small domes — and around the windows, but it appears to have been added at a later date.

In the Azap Kapı Cami, built in 1577 on the north bank of the Golden Horn, Sinān combined features of two earlier mosques: the Rüstem Paşa and the Şehzade. The prayer hall, which is oblong, is covered by a dome supported by squinches set at a 45-degree angle and buttressed by four half domes placed along the axes; the east half dome covers an apse containing the mihrab. Curiously enough, the minaret stands apart from the mosque to the northwest and is linked to the body of the building by an arcade that passes over the street.

Sinān achieved the greatest spatial effect and exterior perfection with the Mosque of Selim in Edirne (FIG. 53; X, PLS. 446, 447). He worked on it from 1568 to 1574, for Selim II (son of Süleyman the Magnificent), who commissioned the building to commemorate the conquest of Cyprus. In this work of his maturity Sinān succeeded in solving all the technical and esthetic problems he had faced in his previous work; in spite of undeniable defects in the interior, the Selimiye has the most evocative exterior of all the Turkish mosques. Constructed on a hill in Edirne, the former capital of the Ottoman Empire, its great mass dominates the city with magnificent effect. The central dome, more than 100 ft. in diameter, rests with admirable grace on the elegant buttresses of the base (the first instance of this was in the Şehzade Cami). The four splendid minarets help to make the whole the most graceful building in Turkey. The central part of the prayer hall is octagonal — a plan Sinān had already tried out in other mosques, particularly the Rüstem Paşa. The central dome, which rests on eight large pillars between which open the same number of exedras (all semicircular with the exception of the two lateral ones and that over the entrance, which are rectangular), is united to the octagon by means of a well-designed play of stalactite corbels, which wonderfully resolve the transition from the circle of the dome to the polygon of the base. All this is inserted into a rectangular perimeter that affords a spacious, completely uncluttered area for the faithful at prayer. The mihrab is in a small rectangular vaulted room set against the qibla wall. The mihrab, the mimbar, and the window head are decorated with tiles of extraordinarily delicate design and refinement of color. The adjacent rectangular courtyard, which is wider than it is long, is surrounded by porticoes and has a large pavilion in the center. In the interior, the most noticeable defect of the Selimiye is apparent in the too obvious contrast between the splendid central dome and the smaller elements that surround it. Lacking the half domes that flank the central domes in other buildings, the transition from large to small is not gradual here but, rather, abruptly stressed. But it cannot be denied that in this way the power of the great mass of the dome is brought out to an extraordinary degree. Even though he fell short of perfection in the Selimiye, Sinān created a new and harmonious structure that may well be considered his masterpiece.

The Kılıç Ali Paşa Cami (1580) is clearly inferior to the Selimiye. Built for the admiral whose name it bears, it originally stood on the seashore, although today it stands a few hundred yards back. Its square plan, with central dome and two half domes along the principal axis, is well balanced, but many details make it more like a church than a mosque. In this more than in any other building of Sinān's, the influence of Hagia Sophia is strongly felt. The mihrab is inserted in an apse at the end of the central aisle, which is flanked by raised galleries covered by arcades. The entrance porch, with its flattened arch, is surmounted by a triangular pediment on which a long inscription is painted. The portico in front of the mosque is of much more recent date.

Among Sinān's best constructions are numerous turbehs, such as those of Şehzade Mehmet and Hüsrev Paşa. The latter, built in 1545, is the type of Turkish mausoleum found in Azerbaijan: it has an octagonal plan, with a ribbed dome placed on a high drum. The corners are softened by graceful columns and, in the upper part, by elegant stalactite friezes. The windows, on two levels, are rectangular, decorated with broken arches and framed by moldings. The Türbe of Şehzade Mehmet, built in 1548 in the courtyard of the mosque of the same name, also has an octagonal plan. The walls are decorated in inlay work of colored stone and are reminiscent of the Mameluke architecture of Cairo (see MAMELUKE ART), while the dome, in fluted sections, goes back to the oldest Turkish structures. Four large windows on each side lighten the whole structure and add to the charm of the exterior. The Türbe of Süleyman the Magnificent (1566) is a little masterpiece. The body of the building is surrounded by a portico covered by a sloping roof and supported by columns. To add to the effect of both the interior and the exterior, the turbeh is covered by two domes of different curvatures, one inside the other. The exterior one has a massive cornice at the base, while the interior one rests on eight arches, which in turn rest on splendid porphyry columns with honeycomb capitals. The triple windows are each completed by a pointed arch. The interior decoration, too, of which Sinān was sparing in this sort of monument, is of refined elegance. Almost as if to emphasize the splendor of the Sultan's turbeh, Sinān put alongside it in 1573 that of the favorite, Roxelane (Hurrem Sultan), built in a simple and unadorned style, though by no means without elegance.

BIBLIOG. M. Agha Oglu, Herkunft und Tod Sinans, O. Literaturzeitung, XXIX, 1926, cols. 858–65; A. Gabriel, Les Mosquées de Constantinople, Syria, VII, 1926, pp. 353–419; H. Glück, Neues zur Sinan-Forschung, O. Literaturzeitung, XXIX, 1926, cols. 854–58; F. Babinger, E. of Islam, s.v. Sinan, IV, 1927, pp. 428–32; M. A. Charles, Hagia Sophia and the Great Imperial Mosques, AB, XII, 1930, pp. 321–44; A. Refik, Türk mimarları (Turkish Architects), Istanbul, 1937; S. Corbett, Sinan: Architect in Chief to Suleiman the Magnificent, Arch. Rev., CXIII, 1953, pp. 291–97; E. Diez, Der Baumeister Sinan und sein Werk, Atlantis, XXV, 1953, pp. 183–86; E. Egli, Sinan: Der Baumeister osmanischer Glanzzeit, Zürich, Stuttgart, 1954; B. Ünsal, Turkish Islamic Architecture in Seljuk and Ottoman Times, 1071–1923, London, 1959; S. K. Yetkin, L'architecture turque en Turquie, Paris, 1962.

Bianca Maria ALFIERI

Illustrations: PLS. 39–40; 1 fig. in text.

SIQUEIROS, DAVID ALFARO. Mexican painter (b. Chihuahua, 1898). He, Orozco, and Rivera (qq.v.) comprise the "Big Three" of the Mexican mural movement. Like the other two, Siqueiros studied at the Academia de San Carlos, where he whetted his appetite for political agitation in student strikes. Subsequently he implemented his leftist beliefs as a soldier, labor leader, teacher, and writer. Siqueiros' militant commitment to Marxism has deeply affected his art. Not even direct contact with the European avant-garde (1919–22) has diverted him from his lifelong goal of art for the masses; despite his many easel pictures, he has long favored public murals as the best means to this end.

In the initial phase of the mural movement (National Preparatory School 1922–24) only one fresco — Siqueiros' monumental *Burial of a Worker* — transcended the general output of inflated easel paintings of idealized themes. At the same time, conceiving mural painting as a proletarian activity, he herded his colleagues into the unionlike Syndicate of Technical Workers, Painters, and Sculptors. In 1932 he furthered this process of "proletarianization" by organizing painting teams that sprayed frescoes on outdoor concrete (Los Angeles, Plaza Art Center; no longer extant). The following year Siqueiros began to substitute silicates for pigments and curved for flat surfaces.

The latter innovations foreshadowed his preeminence as a technical experimenter. Banishing or concealing those architectural divisions which have given an episodic character to most murals since the baroque, Siqueiros effected a continuous flow of forms and space above and around the spectator. Concave armatures, sprayed with transparent films of lacquer, dissolve static architectural planes into a pervasive spatial geometry, while the thrusts and counterthrusts of simplified images, extraordinarily foreshortened, create a "kinetic" perspective (I, PL. 145). Plastic values are sometimes enhanced by sculptural relief; and effects borrowed from cinematography often add to these spatial dynamics.

MAJOR WORKS. *a. Murals:* Portrait of the Bourgeoisie, 1939, Casa del Sindicato Mexicano de Electrecistas, Mexico City. - *Death to the Invader,* 1941–42, Escuela México, Chillán, Chile. - *New Democracy,* 1944–45, Palacio de Bellas Artes, Mexico City. - *Song to Life and Health,* 1952–54, Social Security Hospital No. 1, Mexico City. - *People Go to the University, the University Goes to the People,* 1952–56, University City, Mexico City. *b. Easel paintings:* Proletarian Mother, 1930, Mexico City, Coll. of Inés Amor. - *Our Present Image,* 1947, Mexico City, Inst. Nac. de Bellas Artes.

BIBLIOG. B. S. Myers, Mexican Painting in Our Time, New York, 1956; A. Reed, The Mexican Muralists, New York, 1960; R. Tibol, Siqueiros, Mexico City, 1961.

James B. LYNCH, Jr.

SISLEY, ALFRED. French painter of British parentage (b. Paris, Oct. 30, 1839; d. Moret-sur-Loing, Seine-et-Marne, Jan. 29, 1899). After serving a halfhearted commercial apprenticeship in London, during which he spent much time studying the work of Turner and Constable (qq.v.), he returned to Paris in 1862 and enrolled at the Ecole Nationale des Beaux-Arts as a student in the atelier of Charles Gleyre. There he met Monet, Renoir (qq.v.), and Jean-Frédéric Bazille and thus began a lifelong association with the group that came to be known as the impressionists.

With the exception of two summer trips to England in middle life, Sisley spent his entire career in France. Owing, however, to the pervasive influence of English painting on French impressionism (q.v.) as a whole (stimulated by the extended London sojourn of Monet and Pissarro during the war years of 1870–71) and to Sisley's own heritage, his work has a notably English character. It frequently recalls that of the early romantic British landscapist Richard Parkes Bonington (q.v.) who also painted chiefly in France. Both artists prefer low horizons, overarching skies, a curving diagonal entry into a deep picture space, and effects of atmospheric transparency. In the works of both the touch is deft and aqueous. Sisley experienced fewer tensions in early life than most of his colleagues. His father was a successful merchant who supported his son's artistic ambitions after Alfred's early ventures into business proved fruitless. In the first years of the impressionists' poverty-wracked conflict with the Academy and officialdom, Sisley shared with his friends his relative good fortune. But in the aftermath of the Franco-Prussian War his father was ruined, and Sisley found himself penniless, with a small family to support and with no hope of the official success on which public recognition depended. Although in the 1870s and early 1880s he took a vigorous part in the impressionist movement, participating in four of its eight group exhibitions, and produced his finest work, his creative gift went into decline as he tried to emulate the more aggressive art of Claude Monet. His spirit was eventually broken, and he moved to Moret, near Fontainebleau, where he lived in solitude and died forgotten.

Flood at Port-Marly (VII, PL. 423) is generally considered Sisley's masterpiece, but *L'Île de la Grande Jatte* (VII, PL. 422; the locale later to be celebrated by Seurat), *Snow at Louveciennes* (VII, PL. 421), and *Road at Louveciennes* (IX, PL. 24) also show him at his elegant and charming best. In some ways he was the purest of all the impressionists; his paintings demonstrate none of Pissarro's Millet-oriented love of peasants at work, Renoir's Bohemian abandon, or Monet's elemental power. Sisley was the pure nature poet whose work sings of subtle and transient nuances, of water and skies and reflections. Like other great minor masters, he was supreme within his own restricted range.

BIBLIOG. G. Geffroy, Sisley, Paris, 1923, new ed. 1927; P. Francastel, Manet, Sisley, Pissarro, Paris, 1939; J. Rewald, The History of Impressionism, New York, 1946, 2d ed. 1961; H. E. Bates, French Painters, V: Pissarro and Sisley, Apollo, 1952, pp. 176–180; François Daulte, Découverte de Sisley, Connaissance des arts, LX, 1957, pp. 46–53.

S. Lane FAISON, Jr.

SKOPAS. Skopas (Σκόπας) of Paros was one of the leading Greek sculptors of the 4th century B.C. He may have been a son of the sculptor Aristandros of Paros, who worked with Polykleitos of Argos (q.v.) on a memorial for the battle of Aigospotamoi (405 B.C.); this parentage is that suggested by the fact that some centuries later (ca. 100 B.C.) another Parian sculptor named Skopas had a son Aristandros (in Greek families a grandfather's name was commonly given to a grandson).

Although the dates of Skopas cannot be precisely determined, his active life seems to have covered about fifty years in the middle of the 4th century B.C. That he was famous by mid-century is proved by his selection as one of the four principal sculptors of the Mausoleum at Halikarnassos, the tomb of Maussollos (Mausolus), satrap of Caria (d. 353 B.C.). His work on the Temple of Athena Alea at Tegea may perhaps have been earlier but is probably later than this. The old temple was burned down in 395; and rebuilding is not likely to have begun until after the end of the Corinthian War (387), possibly not until the quiet period that succeeded the battle of Mantineia (362). A date between 360 and 330 is suggested by the architectural style, and one after 350 B.C. by a relief found at Tegea showing Idrieus and Ada, the successors of Mausollos, worshiping the Carian Zeus Stratios. The best explanation for such a subject in such a setting is that a sculptor who had worked on the Mausoleum under Skopas later came to work for him at Tegea.

His association with the Temple of Artemis at Ephesos, even if it were certain, would provide only a *terminus post quem*, for the archaic temple there was probably destroyed in 356, but the new temple replacing it was still unfinished in 334. The date for Skopas given by Pliny (*Historia naturalis*, XXXIV, 49), namely, the 90th Olympiad (420–416 B.C.), is clearly erroneous; elsewhere (*ibid.*, XXXVI, 25) he implies that Skopas was contemporaneous with Praxiteles (q.v.) and his son the younger Kephisodotos — that is, of the middle and later 4th century — and (XXXVI, 30) that he worked with Bryaxis, Timotheos, and Leochares, who were also active in the middle of the 4th century.

Any judgment on the style of Skopas must rest on the sculptures of the Temple of Athena Alea at Tegea (PL. 41; III, PL. 378), of which, according to Pausanias he was also the architect (see XI, FIG. 169). The sculptural remains (distributed between the local museum and the Nat. Mus., Athens) are fragmentary, but the style is both original and fairly homogeneous; it is reasonable to suppose that they were executed under his supervision and partly by him. They are carved not, as is usually stated, in the local marble from Dolliana near Tegea that was used for the structure of the temple, but of Parian marble. The subject of the east pediments, described in some detail by Pausanias (*Description of Greece*, VIII, xlv, 5), was the hunt of the Calydonian boar, that of the west pediment the fight between Achilles and Telephos in the plain of the Kaïkos. From the east pediment a male head and thigh, fragments of female drapery, and the head of the boar survive; there is also a female torso in a short tunic, which, if it belongs to this pediment, may be Atalante. From the west pediment come two helmeted heads and a head in a lionskin cap, presumably Herakles (PL. 41). Many smaller fragments cannot be attributed with certainty. The peculiarities of the style, more marked in some of the heads than in others, are the massiveness of the main forms and the depth and boldness of the detail. The short, round eyes are set deeply in the head and closely ovehung by the eyebrows, the general effect corresponding to the expression of men in anger or violent action. The carving of the nude shows the same massive boldness; and it is perhaps not fanciful to detect the same mind at work in the design of the Corinthian capitals of the temple, which are exceptionally heavy and bold. In ancient opinion Skopas was the sculptor of passion; this is confirmed by the remains from Tegea.

The problem of his style has been confused by the discovery in these excavations of a female head of fine late-4th-century style (XI, PL. 78) that was at first believed to fit the female torso in short tunic mentioned above. But it is now certain that the head does not belong to the torso and almost certain that it does not belong to the pedimental sculptures — it is even possible that the torso itself does not belong to them. For the Temple of Athena Alea at Tegea Skopas also made statues of Asklepios and Hygieia that stood one on each side of the cult image (Pausanias, *Description of Greece*, VIII, xlvii, 1). The belief of some archaeologists that this Hygieia is reproduced in the Hygieia once in the Hope Collection (now Los Angeles, County Mus.) is unsupported by evidence of any kind and indeed is contradicted by the style (Attic, of the generation before Praxiteles) of the Hope Hygieia and its replicas.

Another major undertaking by Skopas was the marine group extravagantly praised by Pliny (*Historia naturalis*, XXXVI, 25). Since both Achilles and Thetis, as well as Poseidon, were represented, the scene may have been Thetis with the arms of Achilles. They were accompanied by a host of sea creatures. Perhaps carved for a Temple of Poseidon in Bithynia, this group was later carried off to Rome and set up in the temple built by Cnaeus Domitius in the Circus Flaminius. A Nereid of less than life size found at Ostia (Mus. Ostiense) may be considered a copy from a figure in this group because of its style: the torso is massive, the head thrown back sharply, the expression of the face charged with emotion. The torso of a Triton in East Berlin (Pergamon Mus.), a Triton in the Vatican, and other surviving statues of sea creatures seem to have been inspired by, if not directly copied from, figures in this group; and it is possible that the frieze of marine creatures on the so-called "altar of Cn. Domitius Ahenobarbus" also reflects the same work (VII, PL. 210).

That Skopas was employed on the Mausoleum of Halikarnassos is attested by both Pliny (*Historia naturalis*, XXXVI, 30 and Vitruvius, pref., 12); according to Pliny, he and three other famous sculptors, Bryaxis, Timotheos, and Leochares, decorated with sculptures in relief (*caelavere*) the four sides of the building, Skopas being allotted the east side; according to Vitruvius, his fellow artists were Leochares, Bryaxis, Praxiteles, and perhaps Timotheos, and each was allotted one side "ad ornandum et probandum."

The remains of three friezes were discovered on the site of the Mausoleum of Halikarnassos and are now in the British Museum: one of chariot racing, one of a centauromachy, and a third, the best preserved, of an Amazonomachy (PL. 41; III, PL. 377). No slab of any of these friezes has been assigned with certainty either to its position in the structure as an architectural element or to a particular side of the building: attributions of them to individual sculptors must therefore rest on stylistic criteria alone.

Of the Amazonomachy 17 slabs survive more or less complete, although most are defaced, and numerous attempts have been made to attribute particular slabs to Skopas; but none is convincing. This is not surprising, since even if Pliny's statement is true, it cannot be supposed that a single sculptor both designed and executed with his own hand all the reliefs on the side of the building allotted to him; he must have employed numerous assistants, who may have imported into the work some of their own style in carrying out his design. Moreover, four sculptors working in close proximity for months, perhaps even years, may well have affected one another's style. If a greater proportion of the sculptures had survived, it would have been easier to detect both differences of design and differences of execution and so to make a more reasoned classification. The slabs that have been most generally accepted as by Skopas are the series of four (Br. Mus., nos. 1013–16) found near the northeast corner of the building in Charles T. Newton's excavations on the site in 1856. This attribution rests mainly on the resemblance of the standing Amazon on slab 1014 (III, PL. 377) to the statuette in Dresden (PL. 43) commonly believed to be a copy of the maenad of Skopas. The resemblance is superficial: it is true that this Amazon wears a short chiton that reveals the body in a similar way and is more stocky than some others on the rest of the frieze, but neither the build of the other figures on these four slabs, who are lithe rather than muscular, nor the facial expressions, which are calm and unemotional, resemble closely the sculpture from Tegea, which must always be regarded as the touchstone for the style of Skopas.

Another building with which the name of Skopas has been associated is the 4th-century Temple of Artemis at Ephesos, where, according to Pliny, 36 of the columns were carved with reliefs, one of them by Skopas. Surviving remains show that the sculpture was on the lower part of the columns, as it had been in the archaic structure (VII, FIG. 83), and this had led to an ingenious emendation in Pliny's text (without support from the Mss.). of *una a Scopa* ("one by Skopas") to *imo scapo* ("on the bottom drum").

Even if we accept Pliny's statement without emendation, there is no reason to suppose that the one column that has survived in a better state of preservation than any of the others (Br. Mus., no. 1206) is that by Skopas. It is the work of an eclectic sculptor, who reproduced, in relief, statuary types of various schools; his scene (probably the return from Hades of Alkestis or Persephone) is pervaded with a gentle melancholy quite at variance, even granted the difference of subject, with the stormy passion of the sculpture at Tegea. One of the figures, probably Thanatos (Death), has something of the intensity of Skopas's work in the features, but nevertheless it is closer to the feeling of 4th-century Attic grave reliefs; although it must be admitted that even among these there are occasional imitations, notably in the stele of Aristonautes (III, PL. 369), of the style inferred from Tegea to be that of Skopas. To compare the drum of column 1206 with any particular slab of the Mausoleum and to deduce that Skopas carved both is to argue from the unknown to the unknown; whereas comparison with the sculpture from Tegea shows that column 1214 has a stronger claim than 1206 to be by Skopas.

Single statues by Skopas may now be considered. Of work executed on the mainland of Greece, the bronze Aphrodite Pandemos mentioned by Pausanias (*Description of Greece*, VI, XXV, 1) in a precinct of Aphrodite at Elis appears on Roman coins of that city, but only the main outlines of the composition are visible, and nothing of the style can be inferred from them. At Gortys in Arcadia he records (VIII, XXVIII, 1) a marble group of Asklepios and Hygieia, in which the Asklepios was beardless; at Argos there was a marble Hekate, and in the gymnasium at Sikyon a marble Herakles. This last may be the original of which the Lansdowne Herakles (Malibu, Calif., J. Paul Getty Mus.) and its numerous fragmentary replicas (including a bronze head from Herculaneum; Naples, Mus. Naz.) are copies, but the attribution rests on style alone: there is no external evidence for it. In Athens, in the shrine of the Erinyes near the Areopagos, Skopas made two marble Erinyes, of mild aspect, flanking one by Kalamis (q.v.) that must have been about a century older. At Megara he made statues of Love, Longing, and Desire (Aphrodite, Himeros, and Pothos); of these, the Pothos may be preserved in the numerous replicas of a youth leaning forward on a thyrsos and looking upward, with a goose at his feet (PL. 42). This might, however, reproduce the Pothos of Samothrace, where Skopas also made a statue of him with Aphrodite. Of the two statues in Thebes, Athena Pronaia in the Ismeneion and Artemis Eukleia in her own temple, again the only evidence is the passing mention by ancient writers.

Outside mainland Greece Skopas was especially active in Asia Minor, making an Apollo Smintheos for Troas, Leto and Ortygia for Ephesos, Dionysos and Athena for Knidos, and perhaps Ares and Aphrodite for Pergamon.

Of statues recorded in antiquity as being by Skopas, but of which the location is unknown, that of a maenad was the most famous to judge from epigrams and from a long rhetorical account by Callistratus (*Statuae*, 2); but these give no information about the place or purpose of its dedication. A statuette in Dresden (PL. 43), thought to be a reduced copy of this statue, has tense muscular limbs and a wild convulsive expression; it is not incompatible with the style of the Tegean sculptures, and it has a close general similarity to the Nereid from Ostia. Pliny mentions an Apollo on the Palatine in Rome (possibly carried off from Rhamnous in Attica) and a seated Hestia (Lat., Vesta), flanked by two candelabra, in the Gardens of Servilius near Rome; Propertius mentions an Apollo (perhaps the same statue) between Leto and Artemis: this may be reproduced on a base from Sorrento (Mus. Correale di Terranova). An Apollo playing the lyre (Apollo Kitharoidos) of different type on coins of Nero is also thought to be inspired by a statue by Skopas: it has something of the tensity of pose that is seen in the Dresden maenad and the Nereid from Ostia. A Hermes pillar is also mentioned in an epigram of the Greek Anthology.

Of existing statues ascribed to Skopas on grounds of style, although not mentioned by ancient writers, the one of Meleager is the most important. This has survived in several copies (PL. 44), and a head in the Villa Medici in Rome has even been claimed as the original from which they derive. It is certainly of high quality and resembles the heads from Tegea. In addition, it might be considered likely that Skopas, having represented the hunt of the Calydonian boar on the pediment there, was afterward moved to make a separate figure of the protagonist.

A head in Magdeburg (Kulturhistorisches Mus.), recently claimed as the copy of a masterpiece by Skopas, seems to be the work rather of one of the pupils of Polykleitos, a slightly older contemporary of Skopas, perhaps Naukydes of Argos (see PELOPONNESIAN ART, col. 145). There was uncertainty in ancient times about the authorship of a group of Niobe and her children, some critics ascribing it to Skopas, some to Praxiteles. This uncertainty is intelligible when the surviving copies (e.g., in the Uffizi) of figures from this group are studied, for they seem to incorporate elements from the style of both sculptors. The most likely explanation is that the group was by neither but rather by a younger contemporary or a sculptor of the next generation; an original work by this same artist can be recognized in the head from the south slope of the Acropolis in Athens (Nat. Mus.).

It is impossible to establish with precision the achievement of a sculptor of whose original work nothing certain remains, but the general impression left by probable copies is that of a forceful personality, original in ideas, vigorous in execution, and excelling in representations of passion and violent action. It appears that he solved some of the problems of expressing emotion in sculpture by his handling of the forms and postures of face and body and thus made a major contribution to certain phases of Hellenistic art (q.v., col. 322–323); but that he was famous throughout antiquity is certain, and it is therefore also likely that his influence on the whole subsequent development of sculpture was substantial.

SOURCES: Overbeck, SQ, 1169–89.

BIBLIOG. *Comprehensive accounts*: L. Urlichs, Skopas–Leben und Werke, Greifswald, 1863; G. Bandinelli, EI, s.v.; M. Bieber, ThB, sv.; G. Lippold, RE, s.v.; G. M. A. Richter, The Sculpture and Sculptors of the Greeks, New Haven, 1950, pp. 11, 267–74; P. E. Arias, Skopas, Rome, 1952 (cites all relevant passages from ancient authors, has critical bibliography and illustrations).

Style and attributions: L. von Sybel, Skopas, ZfbK, XXVI, N.S. II, 1891, p. 249 f., 291 f.; A. Furtwängler, Meisterwerke der griechischen Plastik, Kunstgeschichtliche Untersuchungen, Leipzig, Berlin, 1893, pp. 515–29; J. Overbeck, Geschichte des griechischen Plastik, Leipzig, 1892–94, II, pp. 10–23, 62–80; M. Collignon, Scopas et Praxitèle, Paris, 1907; W. Amelung, Saggio sull'arte del IV sec. a. C., Ausonia, III, 1908, pp. 91–235; G. Cultrera, Una statue di Eracle. Contributo alla storia della scultura greca nel IV sec. a. C., MemLinc, 1910, pp. 192–214, 217–70; E. A. Gardner, Six Greek Sculptors, London, 1911, pp. 177–209, pls. I and LI–LXV; E. Loewy, Die griechische Plastik, Leipzig, 1911, pp. 57–70, 81–97; H. Bulle, Der schöne Mensch im Altertum. Eine Geschichte des Körperideals bei den Ägyptern, Orientalen und Griechen, Munich, Leipzig, 1912, pp. 261, 442, 479, 502, 532; A. Neugebauer, Studien über Skopas, Leipzig, 1913; C. Picard, La sculpture antique de Phidias à l'époque byzantine, Paris, 1926, pp. 78–108; G. Rodenwaldt, Die Kunst der Antike, Berlin, 1927, p. 50, pls. 399–405; A. Della Seta, Il nudo nell'arte, Milan, 1930, pp. 283–307; A. Della Seta, I monumenti dell'antichità classica, I, Grecia, Naples, 1931, pp. xi-xiii, 86–88; A. Rumpf, Griechische und römische Kunst, Florence, 1936, pp. 105–08; H. K. Süsserott, Griechische Plastik des 4. Jahrhunderts vor Christus. Untersuchungen zur Zeitbestimmung, Frankfurt am Main, 1938, pp. 147, 149, 159, 161, 165, 185, 187; L. Curtius, Die klassische Kunst Griechenlands, Potsdam, 1938, p. 381 ff., 406 ff.; P. J. Riis, Om den skopasiske Stil, Festskrift til Frederik Poulsen, Copenhagen, 1941, pp. 15–23; J. Charbonneaux, La sculpture grecque classique, Paris, 1945, II, pp. 81–94; P. Mingazzini, Scopas minore, ArtiFig, II, 3–4, 1946, pp. 137–48; Picard, III, 2, pp. 633–780; H. Bulle, Skopas und die Persönlichkeitsfrage in der griechischen Plastik, ÖJh, 1948, pp. 1–42; Lippold, GP, pp. 249–57; H. Koch, Die angebliche Skopas-Säule vom jüngeren Artemision, Theoria (f. W. H. Schuhhardt), Baden-Baden, 1950, p. 123; M. Bieber, The Sculpture of the Hellenistic Age, New York, 1955, index, s.v.; E. Bielefeld, Ein skopasisches Meisterwerk, JdI, LXXIV, 1959, pp. 158–63.

Individual groups and statues. a. Tegea: P. Cavvadias, Sculture di Scopa al Museo di Tegea, BInst, 1880, pp. 199–203; G. Treu, Werke des Skopas in Museum zu Piali (Tegea), AZ, XXXVIII, 1880, pp. 98–100; A. Milchhöfer, Zu den Skulpturen von Tegea, AZ, XXXVIII, 1880, pp. 190–91; G. Treu, Fragmente aus den tegeatischen Giebelgruppen des Skopas, AM, VI, 1881, pp. 393–423; G. Treu, Köpfe und Fragmente zu den tegeatischen Giebelgrupper des Skopas, Berliner Philologische Wochenschrift, II, 1882, col. 505–06; G. Treu, Köpfe aus den Giebelgruppen des Tempels der Athena Alaea zu Tegea, AD, I, 3, 1888, pl. 35, pp. 21–22; G. Mendel, Fouilles de Tégée, BCH, 25, 1901, p. 241 ff., especially p. 259 ff., pl. VI; E. Thiersch; Zum Problem des Tempels von Tegea, JdI, XXVIII, 1913, p. 266 ff.; JHS XXXVI, 1916, p. 65; C. Dugas et al. Le sanctuaire d'Aléa Athéna à Tégée au IVᵉ siècle, Paris, 1924; E. Pfuhl, Bemerkungen zur Kunst des vierten Jahrhunderts, JdI, XLIII, 1928, pp. 27–53; C. Picard, Remarques sur les sculptures monumentales au sanctuaire d'Aléa Athéna à Tégée, REG, XLVI, 1933, pp. 381, 422; XLVII, 1934, pp. 385–420, XLVIII, 1935, pp. 475–504. *b. Mausoleum at Halikarnassos*: C. T. Newton, A History of the Discoveries at Halicarnassus, Cnidus and Branchidae, 1862–63, II, 1, pp. 100, 239–42, 247–60; H. Brunn, Studien über den Amazonfries des Mausoleums, SbMüchen, 1882, II, p. 114 ff.; P. Wolters and J. Sieveking, Der Amazonenfries des Mausoleums, JdI, XXIV, 1909, p. 171 ff., 181 ff.; A. Neugebauer,

Neue Beiträge zur Kenntnis und Beurteilung des Mausoleumssculptur, und ihrer Künstler, Kunstchronik, XXII, 1923, III, p. 437 ff.; E. Pfuhl, Bemerkungen zur Kunst des vierte Jahrhunderts, JdI, XLIII, 1928, pp. 24–53; K. A. Neugebauer, Das Maussolleion von Halikarnass und sein bildnerischer Schmuck, Neue Jbb. f. antike und deutsche Bildung, V, 1942, pp. 49–73; E. Buschor, Maussollos und Alexander, Munich, 1950, pp. 55, 65, 111; G. Donnay, L'amazonomachie du Mausolée d'Halicarnasse, AntC, XXVI, 1957, pp. 383–403. *c. Marine group*: H. Brunn, Der Poseidonfries in der Glyptothek zu München, SbMünchen, I, 1876, p. 342 ff.; F. Spiro, Hochzeitszug des Poseidon, in Spiro und Wentzel, Göttingen, 1890, pp. lix-lxiii; A. Furtwängler, Der Münchner Poseidonfries und der Neptuntempel des Domitius, Intermessi, 1896, pp. 33–48; J. Sieveking, Der sogenannte Altar des Domitius Ahenobarbus, ÖJh, XIII, 1910, pp. 95–101; J. Sieveking, (JdI) AAnz 26, 1911, p. 168; A. von Domaszewski, Die Triumphstrasse auf dem Marsfelde, Abh. zur römischen Religion, 1919, p. 230 ff.; W. Klein, Vom antiken Rokoko, Vienna, 1921, p. 112; K. A. Neugebauer, Die Berliner Tritonstatue, JdI, LVI, 1941, pp. 179–200; F. Castagnoli, Il problema della "Ara di Domizio Enobarbo," ArtiFig, I, 4, 1945, pp. 181–96; O. Jahn, Über ein Marmorrelief der Glyptothek in München, Berichte der sächsischen Gesellschaft der Wissenschaften, Munich VI, 1854, pp. 160–94, pls. III-VIII. *d. Aphrodite Pandemos*: R. Weil, Die Aphrodite Pandemos des Skopas, Historische und philologische Aufsätze f. Curtius, Berlin, 1884, pp. 134–35, pl. III, 8; M. Böhm, Aphrodite auf dem Bock, JdI, IV, 1889, p. 208 ff.; M. Collignon, Aphrodite Pandemos: Relief de miroir en bronze et disque en marbre, MPiot, I, 1894, pp. 143–50. *e. Hygieia*: L. Curtius, Über einen weiblichen Kopf in Rom, JdI, XIX, 1904, p. 55 ff., figs. 1–9; K. A. Neugebauer, (JdI) AAnz, 49, 1934, pp. 254–56. *f. Heracles*: B. Graef, Herakles des Skopas und Verwandtes, RM, IV, 1889, pp. 189–226, pls. VIII-IX. *g. Pothos*: A. Furtwängler, Der Pothos des Skopas, SbMünchen, 1901, pp. 783–86; F. Eichler, Ein antiker Marmortorso in Wiener Privatbesitz, Belvedere, XII-XIII, 1938, p. 132; A. M. Colini, Scoperta di un gruppo di statue sulla pendice del Cispio, Capitolium, 1940, pp. 871–75; G. Becatti, Il Pothos di Cispa, Le Arti, III, 1941, pp. 401–12; H. Bulle, Zum Pothos des Skopas, JdI, LVI, 1941, pp. 121–50; W. Müller, Zum Pothos des Skopas, JdI, LVIII, 1943, pp. 154–82; K. Lehmann, Samothrace, New York, 1960, p. 23. *h. Maenad*: G. Treu, Zur Mänade des Skopas, Mél. Perrot, 1903, pp. 317–24; J. Six, Die Mänaden des Skopas, JdI, XXXIII, 1918, pp. 38, 48, fig. 4. *i. Apollo*: H. Heydemann, Due monumenti dell'Italia Meridionale, RM, 1889, pp. 307–11; W. Amelung, Bemerkungen zur sorrentiner Basis, RM, 1900, p. 198; P. Gardner, Two Heads of Apollo, JHS, XXIII, 1903. p. 177 ff.; L. Savignoni, Apollo Pythios, Ausonia, II, 1907, p. 16 ff., pls. VI-VII; G. Lippold, Kopien und Umbildungen griechischer Statuen, Munich, 1923, pp. 50, 51, 55, 227, 230; G. R. Rizzo, La base di Augusto (Sorrento, Mus. Correale di Terranova), BCom, LX, 1932, p. 1 ff. *j. Meleager*: F. Poulsen and K. Rhomaios, Erster vorläufiger Bericht über die dänisch-griechischen Ausgrabungen von Kalydon, Copenhagen, 1927, pp. 57–60; E. Buschor, Varianten (IV Meleager), Walther Amelung zum sechzigsten Geburtstag, Berlin, 1928, p. 56; G. Becatti, Attikà: Saggio sulla scultura attica dell'ellenismo, RIASA, VII, 1940, pp. 62–66. *k. Niobids and Acropolis head*: L. Julius, Weiblicher Kopf in Athen, AM, I, 1876, p. 269 ff., pls. 13–14; E. Buschor and J. Sieveking, Niobiden, MJhb, VII, 1912, pp. 111–46; G. Lippold, Zur Florentiner Niobidengruppe, MJhb, VIII, 1913, pp. 243–54; F. Studniczka, Der Frauenkopf vom Südabhang der Burg in Athen, Leipziger Winckelmannsblatt, 1913–15; E. Buschor, Die Oxforder Niobe, MJhb, IX, 1914–15, pp. 191–206; G. Rodenwaldt, Zu den Niobiden, RM, XXXIV, 1919, p. 53 ff.

Bernard ASHMOLE

Illustrations: PLS. 41–44.

SLAVIC ART. The Slavic peoples, who penetrated south-central Europe in successive waves of settlement beginning with the 6th and 7th centuries, became divided into three main groups: the western Slavs (Poles, Kashubes, Czechs, Slovaks, Lusatians), the southern Slavs (Bulgarians, Macedonians, Croats, Serbs, Slovenes), and the eastern Slavs (Russians, Ukrainians, White Russians). From the standpoint of artistic development the western Slavs followed the trends of European art history; the southern and eastern Slavs, on the contrary, were chiefly influenced by Byzantine art (q.v.), which they reworked and adapted to their own ancient traditions. The present discussion is divided into three sections dealing with the Bulgarian, the Serbian, and the Russian centers of Slavic art from the 10th to the 18th century. This subdivision is based on the need to stress those particular stylistic differences which, while occurring within the framework of a common background and approach, distinguished the art of the various Slavic groups for whom the medieval period persisted until the 18th century.

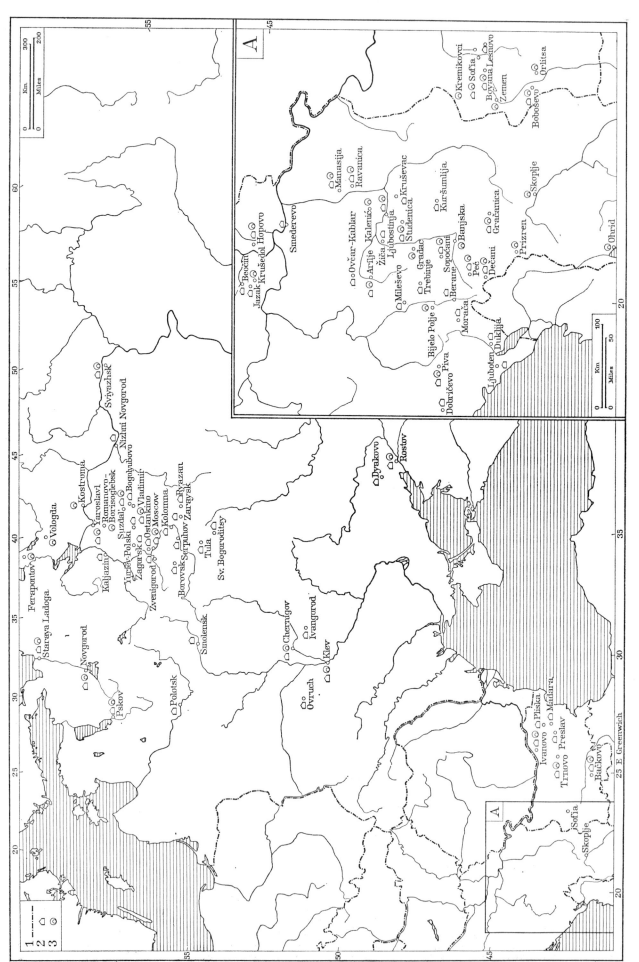

Principal centers of architecture and fresco painting of the Slavic peoples of Bulgaria, Yugoslavia, and Russia between the 8th and 18th centuries. *Key:* (1) Modern national boundaries; (2) architecture; (3) fresco painting.

The Morava school (col. 80): *Architecture; Painting and minor arts.* The post-Byzantine period (1495–1690) (col. 81): *Architecture; Painting and minor arts.* III. Russia (col. 83). Kievan Russia (col. 83): *Architecture; Painting, sculpture, and minor arts.* The principality of Vladimir-Suzdal (col. 87): *Architecture and sculpture; Painting and minor arts.* Novgorod (col. 89): *Architecture; Painting and minor arts.* Pskov. (col. 92): *Architecture; Painting.* The principality of Moscow (col. 93): *Architecture; Painting.* The centralized state of Russia (ca. 1450–17th cent.) (col. 95): *Architecture; Painting; Sculpture; Minor arts.* The closing phase of early Russian art (col. 100): *Architecture; Painting; Sculpture; Minor arts.*

GENERAL INTRODUCTION. The forebears of the Slavs, a people belonging to the Indo-European ethnic group, were already settled in the vast territory stretching from the Elbe in the west to the left bank of the Dnieper in the east in the 2d millennium B.C. In the 6th and 7th centuries of our era Slavic tribes from the east began to push vigorously southward and finally came to rest in the Balkan Peninsula. Actively involved in the great transmigration of peoples, the early Slavs later divided into three main branches: the eastern Slavs, the western Slavs, and the southern Slavs (see above).

Although the first Slavic states were already taking form between the 7th and 10th centuries (the principality of Samo in Bohemia, the first Bulgarian kingdom, the state of Great Moravia, the ancient Polish state, the Croatian kingdom, Kievan Rus), the historical evolution of the Slavs suffered grave setbacks, and its rate of progress was considerably slower than that of medieval Western Europe. The intensive struggle waged by the southern Slavs against Byzantine expansion and by the western Slavs against Germanic expansion, the continual inroads made by the peoples of the steppe, the devastating Tatar invasion, and, lastly, the subjugation of the Balkans by the Turks — all these circumstances created adverse conditions for the development of a Slavic culture and not infrequently led to a break in cultural traditions. In this respect Western Europe was in an incomparably better situation since the states that had sprung up on its soil were relatively stable and had not experienced those cataclysms which were to accompany the Slavs for such a long period of their history.

The diverse paths followed by Bulgarian, Serbian, and early Russian art on the one hand and Croatian, Czech, and Polish art on the other were determined not only by geographical, social, and economic factors but also by a difference in religious outlook. When the Slavs were converted to Christianity during the course of the 9th and 10th centuries, the Bulgarians, Serbs, and Russians adopted the forms of the Eastern Church, while the Croats, Czechs, and Poles accepted those promulgated by the Western Church. For this reason Bulgarians, Serbs, and Russians looked for inspiration to Byzantium, which exercised a profound influence on their cultures, distinguished as a whole by unmistakable common traits and heritage. Both in architecture and painting these peoples accepted Byzantine traditions, which in the process of development acquired a national flavor, thus giving valid grounds to speak of three national schools: the Bulgarian, the Serbian, and the early Russian. Even though the Serbs and Russians assimilated single elements of Romanesque architecture and sculpture [as in Serbian churches of the end of the 12th and the beginning of the 13th century in Raška (Rashka, Rascia) and Zeta, and in churches of the 12th century in the principalities of Galicia and Vladimir-Suzdal], the world of Romanesque art was by and large alien to them or at least very remote. The history of art in Czechoslovakia and Poland was quite different. Here Romanesque architecture and sculpture, closely bound up with Western liturgy, won a predominating position. A similar situation can be seen in Dalmatia, which was part of the Croatian kingdom. Among the western Slavs, the Romanesque style was succeeded by the Gothic, exemplified in Czechoslovakia and Poland by many fine buildings. For the southern Slavs (except the Croats) and the eastern Slavs the Gothic style was meaningless. The theories of scholars who claim to discern Gothic influence in Russian tent-roofed (*shater*) architecture of the 16th century have turned out to be groundless, as no reliable evidence has been found to support them.

Although the cultural influence of Byzantium on the southern and eastern Slavs was profound and long-lasting, it should nevertheless not be overestimated. As the archaeological and ethnographic research of the last decades has shown, the Slavs had long possessed ancient artistic traditions of their own, based on a rich variety of crafts. They had their own mythology, their pagan temples decorated with images of gods, their rites, their style of dress, their decorative art, and their favorite ornamental motifs. Surrounded by vast areas of forest, the early Slavs built exclusively in wood, which was to remain the most common material at their disposal even after the advent of stone architecture. The Arabian geographer al-Mas'ūdī, who lived in the 10th century, extolled the Slavic temples for their beauty; brilliantly colored, these shrines glowed in the light of the rising sun. Bishop Thietmar of Merseburg records around 1020 that in the sacred wood of the Lutitians (Lusitians) in Retra (Mecklenburg) stood a temple hewn of wood with its outer walls decorated with "wondrous carved images of gods and goddesses." The author of the *Life of Otto of Bamberg* (1124–29), in his description of the main *kontina* (sacred building) of the Slavs in Stettin, draws a picture which involuntarily calls to mind the decoration of the 12th-century churches of Vladimir-Suzdal: both the exterior and the interior walls of the *kontina* were covered with carvings of people, birds, and animals represented "so faithfully and naturally that they seemed to live and breathe. ... The colors of the images on the exterior walls could not be dimmed by rain or snow, nor be rubbed off — such was the art of the painters." Finally, the Danish chronicler Saxo Grammaticus (12th cent.), describing the exterior of the *kontina* in Arkona on the island of Rügen, defines it as an *opus elegantissimum* and tells us that it "glittered with bas-reliefs of various figures, skillfully executed, but hideously and crudely colored." Usually these temples contained statues of gods carved of wood and decorated with gold and silver. The Triglav idol in Stettin had a silver mustache, and the idol in Wolin was covered with gold. Polish archaeologists have found wooden and stone idols in the territory once occupied by the Poles and the Mazovians. All these facts leave no room for doubt that the traditions of early Slavic wooden architecture were deeply rooted and could not have failed to influence stone architecture, which began to be extensively used after the conversion of the Slavs to Christianity. This influence is particularly telling in the churches of Kievan Rus with their open galleries girdling the main building, their abundance of domes, and their characteristic soaring pyramidal design and numerous mutually independent spatial units. The traditions of popular wooden architecture persisted obstinately even in later times, combining in different ways with those of stone architecture according to successive stages of development. A complicated process of reciprocal influence was involved that was far from being as one-sided as it appeared to early researchers, who reduced everything to the influence of wood on stone architecture. Examples of early Slavic architecture have survived in a particularly pure form in the wooden churches of the 16th–18th centuries in northern Russia and the Transcarpathian Ukraine. But there are echoes of it in stone architecture as well, many forms of which were inspired by wooden prototypes. It is in any case impossible to understand the development of stone architecture among the southern and eastern Slavs without taking into account that it had been preceded for centuries, and accompanied for as many more, by superb masterpieces of wooden architecture, built in the material beloved by the Slavs and intimately connected with the life of the people.

A controversial question to this day is the origin of the early stone churches of circular form which a number of scholars have considered typical of early Slavic Christian architecture. Such round churches with five or six apses have been discovered in Split (Church of the Holy Trinity, 9th cent.) and Zadar (Church of St. Ursula, 9th cent.). This church form could have passed from the southern Slavs to the western Slavs together with Orthodox Christianity as first preached by Constantine (St. Cyril; 827–69) and Methodius. Variants of the round church were common throughout Czech, Moravian, and Slovakian territories and, beyond their borders, also in Poland (Church of St. Mary on the Wawel in Kraków and others). During the 9th and 10th centuries round churches were built in the Czech territory in the strongholds of Prince Borivoj (Lévy Hradec) and of his son Spytihněv (Budeč), as well as in Prague (Church of St. Vitus, 926–29), and in the Castle of Znojmo in Moravia (end of 9th cent.), and in other places. A number of similar buildings, dating, however, from the 12th century, have survived in Prague (the round chapel of the Church of the Holy Cross, St. Martin in the castle of Vyšehrad, the Chapel of St. Longinus). Recent excavations in Staré Město (now Uherské Hradiště), where once stood Velehrad, capital of the Great Moravian state, have clearly shown that until the Romanesque-type basilica penetrated into Moravia small rectangular churches in stone, surmounted by a dome and undeniably harking back to the Byzantine domed cruciform plan, were built there in the 9th century. It is well known that the latter plan formed the basis of all stone architecture among the southern and eastern Slavs. Among the western Slavs, however, it did not develop but was supplanted by the Romanesque basilica, which was deliberately propagated by the Catholic clergy as more suitable to the Latin Rite.

While painting among the southern and eastern Slavs remained for a long time under strong Byzantine influence, the same cannot be said of their sculpture, which they used far more widely to decorate their churches than the Byzantines did, a fact determined mainly by pre-Christian tradition. As is well known, the pagan Slavs liked to decorate their temples with statues of gods and carved reliefs, so they were accustomed to sculpture as an art form. Wood and stone were the most common materials employed (e.g., the Zbruch idol). Centuries of working in wood had led the Slavs to evolve certain established techniques, so that when the forms and motifs of Romanesque sculpture began to seep through from Western Europe they transformed them according to the familiar idiom of wood carving, hence the flattening of volumes, the substitution, in relief, of rounded contours by straight ones perpendicular to the carved area, and the evident preference for bas-relief rather than high relief. Ancient Slavic wood carving and embroidery, of which only a very few fragments have survived, were the two art forms that contributed the greatest number of figural and ornamental motifs during the period of the conversion of the Slavs to Christianity. These provided a source of extraordinary variety from which medieval artists freely drew decorative motifs, including some that in pagan times were intended to be mythological images of an anthropomorphic character (e.g., the highly stylized image of the "Great Goddess"). The Church made every effort to stem this infiltration of pagan elements into Christian art, but it was not successful. Thus the traditions of ancient Slavic art were no less evident in medieval Slavic sculpture than they were in medieval Slavic architecture. In this connection Slavic painting occupied a place apart since its esthetic canons and its strictly regulated iconography were established on the basis of the new Christian conception of the world and, thus, painting did not have behind it the great traditions possessed by architecture and wood carving. This is one of the reasons for the more "Byzantine" character of early Slavic painting, which often decorates churches that even the most unpracticed eye could not mistake for Byzantine.

The first flowering of southern Slavic art occurred in Bulgaria in the 9th and 10th centuries when the first Bulgarian kingdom was at the height of its power: monumental stone architecture (Pliska, Preslav), goldsmiths' work (the treasure of Nagy-Szent-Miklós), and painted ceramics (Patleina and Preslav) reached a high degree of excellence. Undoubtedly, it was during this period that sculpture of a proto-Romanesque type began to appear in Bulgaria, but its further development was interrupted by the Byzantine invasion. In the 11th and 12th centuries Macedonia, then under Byzantine sway, was the center of the greatest building activity. After the end of the 12th century the center of activity shifted to Serbia, where Stephen Nemanya's powerful state of Raška was being created. At that time Serbia, which had been fortunate enough to escape the domination of the Mongols, was the most advanced Slavic country. It had its own original contribution to make, not only in the sphere of architecture, where the creative reelaboration of Byzantine

and Romanesque traditions led to entirely new artistic solutions, but also in the sphere of fresco painting. In the 14th century Serbian and Bulgarian art had their last flowering. The defeat of Kosovo (1389) and the fall of Trnovo (1393), capital of the Bulgarian state, marked the beginning of the Turkish subjugation of the Balkans, which had a fatal effect on the development of southern Slavic culture, and led to a long period of stagnation.

The historical destiny of Russia was different. Its artistic evolution began somewhat later than that of the southern Slavs — at the end of the 10th and the beginning of the 11th century (Kievan Rus). By the second half of the 12th century Novgorod and the powerful principality of Vladimir-Suzdal, where many stone churches could be distinguished for the rich relief decoration of their walls, attained a pre-eminent position in the sphere of the arts. The Tatar invasion of the 13th century struck a terrible blow to early Russian culture and brought about the interruption of artistic traditions for a long period. The two free republics of northern Russia, Novgorod and Pskov, which had preserved their independence, were in a better position. The greatest period of early Russian art (14th and 15th cent.) is connected with these two cities and with Moscow, which had risen swiftly during the 14th century. In the 16th and 17th centuries Moscow led the field; it was here and in the provincial centers of Rostov, Yaroslavl, Vologda, and Kostroma, among others, that the most important works of architecture and painting were created. During the 17th century the crisis in early Russian art, invaded as it was by a flood of Western motifs and forms, became more and more clearly marked. The process reached its logical conclusion by the end of the 17th and the beginning of the 18th century when Peter the Great resolutely opened a window onto Europe at St. Petersburg and the traditions of early Russian art gradually ceased to hold sway with the rise of new trends; thus began the modern era in the history of Russian art (see UNION OF SOVIET SOCIALIST REPUBLICS: MODERN MOVEMENTS).

Victor LASAREFF

I. BULGARIA. The ancient Bulgarian kingdom founded in A.D. 680 gradually increased in size until it stretched well beyond the frontiers of present-day Bulgaria, extending far into the Balkan Peninsula and almost reaching and subjugating Constantinople. After the fall of the first Bulgarian kingdom (972), western Bulgaria (Macedonia, southern Albania, and northwestern Bulgaria) maintained its autonomy for another 50 years.

The function of Macedonia in preserving the older Christian culture and serving as a source for the revival of archaic forms in the 14th century was to prove very important.

The development of the arts in Bulgaria was characterized by complex and often contradictory factors; many questions still remain unanswered in a country in which the artistic monuments, numerous but often defaced or even half-destroyed by the long Turkish occupation, began to be studied and classified in the early years of the 20th century. Knowledge of prehistoric and classical cultures in Bulgarian territory has been increased extensively by the continual discovery of religious buildings dating from a period prior to the advent of the Bulgarians in the very places that were to become the earliest centers of Bulgarian culture. Examples of these are Momina Krepost in Trnovo, where materials of the 5th and 6th centuries have been unearthed, and Deli Duska outside the walls of Preslav, where there is a basilica of the same period. The fact that a homogeneous artistic culture existed in the heart of the Balkan Peninsula is worthy of note, but it is not yet clear how this ancient culture was linked with the proto-Bulgarian culture that was superimposed upon it from the 8th century onward, with its Iranian traditions, its imposing fortifications and stone palaces evidencing cultures that had been centered in the courts of the khans, its rock reliefs of Sassanian flavor, and its goldsmiths' work, sculpture, and painted ceramic ornamentation.

With the conversion of the Bulgarians to Christianity (865) and the absorption of the Slavic element the links with the Christian culture and with neighboring Constantinople became more evident. After the fine Thraco-Hellenistic and Romano-

Christian painted tombs of the region and the extraordinary paintings of the church in Perushtitsa (7th cent.; a rare specimen of preiconoclastic art) frescoes did not appear again until the 11th and 12th centuries, when the civilization of Constantinople was at its height. The frescoes of Bačkovo are from this period. In Thrace the style of painting was like that of Byzantium, with its typical abstractions, preponderantly decorative character, and eclecticism of themes. By the 13th century Trnovo and Boyana displayed a little-known aspect of Byzantine fresco art, not decorative but akin to easel painting, whose realism was a development of Byzantine artistic tradition of the 11th and 12th centuries. A similar quest for realism was characteristic of Italian and French art in the 13th century, but Bulgaria remained more faithful to Byzantine esthetic principles. The Boyana paintings — the art of a princely court — are "primitive" masterpieces (PL. 46). The 13th-century works were more "European" than those of the 14th and 15th centuries, which tended toward a pronounced Eastern elaboration of form. There followed a movement of archaic revival and of folk art. The traditions of Romano-Christianity, nurtured on a Thraco-Hellenistic ground, with barbarian influences and the unique and magnificent proto-Bulgarian culture, enabled Bulgaria, poised between East and West, to affirm its forceful personality in the world of the Byzantine Empire.

The first Bulgarian kingdom (7th–10th cent.). In the first Bulgarian kingdom, founded in a region that had previously enjoyed a flourishing civilization, large blocks began to be used in construction, especially in the centers of Pliska (the capital) and Madara; bricks were used only for arches, windows, and portals. This type of building, completely different from that of contemporary Byzantium, is related to the Hellenistic-Roman architecture of the Black Sea coast and Scythia Minor (Dobruja) and shows Sassanian influences (see SASSANIAN ART). At Pliska (anc. Aboba), besides the more ancient palace of Krum (r. 802–14) with its checkerboard walls, a "little palace" consisting of two chambers surrounded by a corridor, and a basilican-type "great palace" with a nave and two side aisles and apses were built; in Madara a building of the same type as the "little palace" and in Preslav fortified walls and a palace were constructed. Sculpture was influenced by Turkish art, while the rock relief of Madara (8th–9th cent.; PL. 45) shows Iranian influence, which can also be discerned in the treasure of Nagy-Szent-Miklós (Vienna, Kunsthist. Mus.; V, PL. 96).

The conversion of the Bulgarians to Christianity led to their first contacts with Byzantine art. The capital was moved from Pliska to Preslav (until 972), which became a thriving art center, reaching the peak of its development in the 10th century under Simeon (893–927). In architectural and particularly in interior decoration the many churches that were founded have a character that differentiates them from Byzantine models. Two basilicas, in different styles, have survived in Pliska: a large one outside the walls, and the palatine church. The two types of basilica — Hellenistic and Byzantine — are fused in the first; three semicircular apses characterize the second. Two churches in Preslav (Avradaka and Bial Briag) are quite free from Byzantine influence in their architectural decoration, which, austere as it is, seems to have traits in common with some of the most ancient churches of Pliska.

The so-called "Church of Gold" in Preslav, dating from the 9th century (PL. 45; FIG. 70) and excavated in 1927–28, is a monument of the greatest importance. It consists of a rotunda with eight exedras, a square atrium, a narthex, and an inner peribolos. The complex ground plan and structures of this remarkable church represent a synthesis of more ancient Roman and Byzantine structural elements and forms adopted to meet the practical requirements of the new religion. The rich, somewhat complicated style of decoration, found also in other recently discovered churches and developed along the entire Black Sea coast, harks back to local traditions.

Characteristic of all Bulgarian churches of the 8th, 9th, and 11th centuries is the reversion to archaic forms. While domed churches were being built in Constantinople, the predominating type of church in Bulgaria was the basilica with a nave and side

aisles, three apses, and a narthex, similar in some respects to the basilicas of Asia Minor and showing preference for polychrome decoration.

In large-scale secular architecture (e.g., the palace and fortified walls in Preslav), the practice of using large blocks continued; in other buildings smaller blocks or slabs were used, while bricks made their appearance in arches and domes. The flat sculptured-stone decoration of the cornices, which reproduced Greco-Roman motifs and close-set honeycomb patterns in the Eastern manner, was the main feature distinguishing the architecture of Preslav from contemporaneous Byzantine architecture.

The monasteries became art centers. Typical among these was the Monastery of Patleina, in Preslav, where there remain

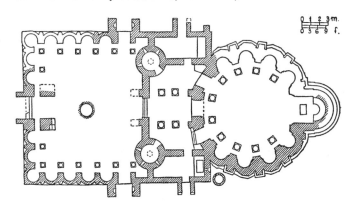

Preslav (Bulgaria), "Church of Gold," 9th century, plan.

kilns for the firing of glazed pottery, which must have been produced in large quantities at the time, as evidenced by the many artisans' workshops and kilns discovered in Preslav. Cups, dishes, and decorative tiles, often enameled in color on an ivory-white ground, were mounted in walls (e.g., the Church of Gold, Preslav), set in floors, or used to make frames and small pilasters. The Cyrillic or Glagolitic letters of the Bulgarian alphabet on these ceramics indicate that they were produced for the Bulgarians themselves. Preslav seems to have been the major center of this ceramic production at the end of the 9th and the beginning of the 10th century.

During the reign of Peter (d. 969), Byzantine influences grew stronger, as can be observed in the upper church of Ciupkata (Preslav), a complex type, built on a cruciform plan with a dome, arches, and pilasters. In Preslav the great literary evolution of the 10th century was accompanied by a vast production of manuscripts, which, owing to the destruction by the Turks, are known only through 11th-century Russian copies and even later Bulgarian ones. On the basis of Byzantine and Greco-Oriental originals the Bulgarian artists created a new style characterized by a revival of geometric letters, with the addition of human hands, ears, eyes, animal heads, and so on, and later by the complete transformation of the elegant, flower-decorated Byzantine letters into an original Bulgarian version with interlacing patterns and fantastic animals. During the 10th century the Bogomile sect had a negative influence on art; following the precepts of the iconoclasts, they condemned sacred images and objects of worship and even denied the need for churches.

The Byzantine domination (972–1186). In the more than two centuries that Bulgaria was under the dominion of Byzantium the building of monasteries in Thrace and Macedonia received new impetus. Not only monastic rules but also architectural projects and prototypes for decoration originated in Constantinople. Churches became smaller and were generally of two types: the first with a single vaulted nave, with or without a dome, and the second with a cruciform plan and a dome. Also typical was the two-storied church (in Bačkovo; Church of Ivan Assen, near Stanimaka; in Boyana, near Sofia), with the lower story serving as a crypt and having a west door and the upper story housing the church proper and having an external flight of steps on the south side. The decoration of the façade became more elaborate, and painting acquired great importance, as can be seen at Bačkovo, Boyana, and the old metropolis of Mesembria.

The restoration of the Bulgarian state: the school of Trnovo. A new era began with the restoration of the Bulgarian state, which became independent in 1186 under the Assen dynasty. Trnovo was the capital of art and letters, the center of a creative movement that spread abroad as far as Russia and Siberia. Wall painting developed greatly, and churches were entirely decorated with tempera frescoes. The art of the 13th century turned unhesitatingly to the Byzantium of the Macedonian and Comnenian dynasties for its inspiration, and Constantinopolitan originals were reproduced, perhaps by Greek artists who had fled the city, then occupied by the crusaders.

The masterpiece of the school of Trnovo is the Church of St. Panteleimon in Boyana, which was founded in 1259, according to the inscription in the narthex. Its frescoes were painted over more ancient ones; those representing Christ Evergetes and Christ of the Chalke are copies of two images venerated in Constantinople. Characteristics of these works are the realistic detail (the Last Supper), the spirituality of the faces and the individuality of the two expressions (the donors; PL. 46), the humanity and gentleness of feeling, and the depiction of local costumes. Though conforming to the Byzantine tradition, the artists rose above the level of merely copying Constantinopolitan models and imparted new shades of expression to the faces. Some Western elements are discernible, and an echo of classical sculpture can be seen in the calm rhythm of the composition; the drapery is imbued with the Byzantine idealism of the 11th and 12th centuries. The frescoes of the Boyana master and other similar works represent a Byzantine trend with a realistic flavor, free from the intensity and stylization of later works and significant for the artistic development of the Slavic countries. The surviving fragments of the Church of the Forty Martyrs in Trnovo (built by Ivan Assen in 1230) can be seen to derive from miniatures of the 12th century, which carried on the traditions of the Constantinople workshops. These paintings are permeated with archaic feeling and have no architectural backgrounds; the tempera technique allowed for a rich variety of color. Little is left of the paintings decorating the 18 chapels of Trapesitsa (Trapesica) in Trnovo. The 13th- and 14th-century school of Trnovo acted as a link etwbeen Byzantine and late Balkan art.

The 14th and 15th centuries. Culture in the 14th century was more refined. It was the period of Ivan Alexander, an active builder, of the Hesychast monasteries, and of Theodosius and other Bulgarian disciples of Gregory, who having studied Greek and being familiar with Constantinople left a marked Byzantine imprint on this Trnovo-centered culture. Under the artistic supremacy of Byzantium local schools grew up in the Orthodox countries and Slavic states.

Toward the end of the 13th and the beginning of the 14th century architecture diminished in scale, and new elaborate forms were evolved, in which the importance of detail, the regular alternation of stone and brick, and the decorative effects of color and design (including interlaced patterns in brick) were the distinguishing features. The exterior decoration of churches became very elaborate, as for example in Trnovo and in Mesembria (St. John of the Harbor; PL. 46). Rose windows and green and yellow slabs adorned the exterior of St. Demetrius in Trnovo; a decorative effect was obtained by the use of shallow niches to break the monotony of the large flat surfaces.

In painting monumentality of form was abandoned in favor of richness and an exaggeratedly dramatic and rhetorical expressionism. Many works of this period have been lost; those that survive can be divided into different categories. The first of these, covering works influenced by the art of Constantinople, is remarkable for refined and careful workmanship, presupposing a high standard of artistic culture in which the role of Byzantium was preponderant. The frescoes of this group are at times manneristic and rhetorical, but also highly decorative, with refined figures. The number of personages, accessories, and architectural details increased, and the painters expressed themselves with a rich variety of means and sophisticated techniques. An example of this type is the frescoes in the grotto church at Ivanovo, near Ruse (Turk., Ruschuk), which show affinities with those of the Church of the Chora (Kariye Camii) in Constantinople (see BYZANTINE ART); there is a similar grotto church near Ivanovo — the Gospodev Dol.

The second group belongs to the archaic tradition and is chiefly represented by the frescoes of the church in Zemen. It differs markedly from the first group, reflecting another artistic conception not unrelated to preiconoclastic art, of which it preserved the iconographic type, the ornamental motifs, and even the style. This was a folk art, in sharp contrast with works in the Byzantine tradition. In the Zemen church the scenes are represented in continuous bands as in preiconoclastic frescoes, which they resemble also in subject matter and style. The colors used are red, yellow, and brown; the figures are awkward in their attitudes but lively and expressive, and the faces are flat and outlined; the drapery is often simplified and geometric, and the rocky hills are stylized. The distortion of line, the odd proportions of the bodies, the lack of balance, and the taste for the anecdotal are all typical of folk art. The criterion of composition is also clearly opposed to that of Byzantine art. The church of Ljutibrod in western Bulgaria, which can be ascribed to the second half of the 14th century, also belongs to this group.

The third category occupies an intermediate position and represents the fusion of the first two currents: the portrait of Ivan Alexander (1344–63) in the narthex of the funerary chapel in Bačkovo has a flattened oval face, sharply outlined, which is schematized and inexpressive; the costume, a faithful copy of Greek models, is somewhat careless in execution. The frescoes of St. John of the Harbor in Mesembria (the portrait of the old donor being particularly interesting) belong to the same group. Like that of Bačkovo, this church has affinities with Zemen.

The following works must be considered separately: firstly, the frescoes of the church in Berenda, faithful to the Byzantine esthetic concept and harmonious in composition but also comprising archaic elements typical of the more ancient Christian painting, are provincial works lacking in unity and belonging to another age; secondly, the frescoes with the Pantocrator and 22 prophets in the dome of the Church of St. George in Sofia depict figures transfigured by ecstasy, their heads thrown back, their garments agitated and wind-blown; and finally, the frescoes of SS. Peter and Paul in Trnovo (a domed cruciform church) repeat the formulas of the flowery Byzantine style of the 14th century in a heavy and oversimplified manner and represent a late example of Balkan mannerism, on the one hand preserving the Byzantine style and on the other remaining faithful to the motifs of ancient Hellenistic art.

The small single-aisle chapels built in the 15th century under Turkish rule, which from the outside cannot be distinguished from the most humble secular buildings, were decorated with paintings in the older tradition, although executed with greater technical skill. Byzantine stylistic and iconographic formulas were presented under new guises. Some painters harked back to the archaic style; others combined elements typical of preiconoclastic art with those typical of the style of Comnenian Byzantium while remaining within the Byzantine tradition. The folk paintings in the church of Kalotino (end of 15th cent.) show affinities with Zemen (round, flat heads with large eyes); the small church of Dragalevchi (1476), near Sofia, is decorated with paintings of the same period. With their heavy outlining, almost complete absence of modeling, and extremely limited color range (red, ocher, yellow), the Dragalevchi paintings represent a very weak interpretation of Byzantine formulas. The church of the Monastery of St. Demetrius in Boboševo on the banks of the Strma (Strymon), built in 1488 with a single aisle and without a narthex, follows the decorative scheme of the Balkan churches (Berenda and Dragalevchi), having scenes in two registers with stylized flat and monotonous figures in tones of olive gray and ocher gray.

Traces of Western influence, which was steadily increasing, are not lacking. Orlitsa, near Rila, has frescoes (1491) in a pleasanter and livelier style, but they are also more superficial and less expressive. In Kremikovci the paintings in the chapel of the Monastery of St. George (1503?) show an attempt, due to Western influence, at rendering spatial depth (the oblique position of the furniture). The influence of the Renaissance was by now widespread and was evident not only in the style of execution but also in the costumes of the characters depicted. The monastery church of Poganovo, which the Bulgarians ceded with Caribrod to the Serbs in 1918, followed models of the Italian Renaissance and abandoned Byzantine traditions, thus bearing witness to the attempt to cast off medieval esthetic principles. This marked a turning point in the history of painting in Bulgaria, but, in contrast to what had occurred at Boyana in the 13th century, no new trends appeared. In some respects similar to Balkan works of art of the 15th century, the new style merely reflected, without originality of expression, results achieved in Italy long before, even though it gave rise to a number of iconographic motifs that were later to become common in the art of Mount Athos.

In the villages tradition was followed by humble artisans. In icon painting, however, a higher standard was sometimes achieved as can be seen in the important collections of the 14th century and later in the Archaeological Museum and the Archaeological Museum of the Holy Synod, both in Sofia, and in churches throughout Bulgaria. In some of these icons a style strongly influenced by the art of the last period of the empire predominates; others, reflecting local styles or belonging to the period of Turkish domination, absorbed Arab motifs. Folk art produced icons with crude figures in awkward attitudes, but with a decorative stylization that is often highly expressive. The icon of the Hodegetria (Virgin and Child, with the faces painted over) in the Archaeological Museum of Sofia, which is inscribed by a relative of Tsar Alexander, who donated it to the monastery of Mesembria, belongs to the 14th century. The icon from Poganovo with the Virgin and John the Evangelist on one side and the visions of Ezekiel and Habakkuk on the other is also of the 14th century; the Eleousa icon of Mesembria is another example of this rare type (both, Sofia, Arch. Mus.).

Among the illuminated manuscripts the following are worthy of note: the 13th-century Gospel of Pope Dobreyko (Sofia, State Lib., Cod. 307; Belgrade, Nat. Lib., Cod. 214), whose naïve realism is characteristic of folk art; the Bulgarian translation of the Chronicle of Constantine Manasses of 1345 (Rome, Vat. Lib., Cod. slav. 2); the Gospel of Tsar Ivan Alexander (1356; Br. Mus., Add. 39627); and the 14th-century Bulgarian Psalter in Moscow. All of these belong to the courtly tradition and are faithful to Byzantine models.

Antonio FROVA

II. SERBIA. During their stormy history the Serbs were often forced to shift the center of their political power; hence the geographic frontiers of medieval Serbian art were constantly changing. From the southeastern coast of the Adriatic Sea the nucleus of the medieval Serbian state moved across the central region of Raška (Rascia) toward Macedonia; later, under pressure from the Turks, it was pushed to the north, where, after the fall of Smederevo (1459), Serbia lost its independence. Serbian art, however, though suppressed and almost hidden in the inaccessible mountain regions of the Balkans and in the distant borderlands of devastated Hungary, survived in the monasteries until the end of the 17th century. This is why at the time of the Renaissance and, later, during the baroque period, medieval art forms were still in use among the Serbs. Only from the middle of the 18th century, through the powerful influence of Illuminism, did Serbian art begin to develop within the sphere of Western European culture.

The history of early Serbian art can be divided into three phases according to periods. The first, from the 10th to the end of the 12th century, gravitated toward the Mediterranean civilization of the West, and its chief propagators were the members of the Benedictine Order. The second and most important phase, from the 13th century to 1459, was entirely oriented toward Byzantium. The third, from 1459 to the end of the 17th century (the period of Turkish domination), can be defined as a separate branch of post-Byzantine art.

THE SCHOOL OF DIOCLEA. Serbian art originated on the Adriatic coast in Dioclea, the first Serbian medieval state. Architecture and sculpture in stone did not differ greatly from those of neighboring Croatia. The small churches, with their complex ground plans and stone vaults, have rarely survived in their original form; but the basilican-type buildings are in an even worse condition owing to restorations carried out in the 13th and 14th centuries. Hardly anything is left of the Benedictine Basilica of SS. Sergius and Bacchus in Boyana, used in the 11th and 12th centuries as the mausoleum of the princes of Dioclea; the church of the Benedictine Monastery of St. Peter in Trebinje is in a better state of preservation; only insignificant fragments remain of the Monastery of the Virgin in Krajina and of the ancient cathedral of Kotor (Cattaro). In the sculptured decoration of these churches interlace patterns are repeated to the point of monotony, but, in contrast with Croatia, floral and zoomorphic motifs — the result of Near Eastern influences that arrived by way of Durrës and Apulia — are plentiful.

The relatively well-preserved small Church of St. Michael in Stonsko Pole (Field of Tin), with its interior decoration based on the alternation of pilasters and niches, contains 11th-century frescoes inspired by prototypes from France and from Cassino. Particularly interesting is the figure holding a model of the church, the first in a series of portraits of Serbian kings and a frequent theme in mural painting. The miniatures of the Gospel of Prince Miroslav (end of 12th cent.; Belgrade, Nat. Mus.) offer invaluable evidence of the transitional forms of a civilization that was gradually drawing nearer to that of Byzantium.

THE SCHOOL OF RAŠKA TO THE TIME OF KING MILUTIN. In the second half of the 12th century Raška became the political center of the Serbian territory. Stephen Nemanya (Nemanja), founder of the Nemanyich dynasty, took up arms against Byzantium and concluded the war victoriously (ca. 1180). After Nemanya's abdication and death his sons, taking advantage of the fall of Constantinople (1204), laid the foundations of the strongest Serbian state of the Middle Ages (1216–1371). In the new kingdom, which also had an autocephalous church, medieval Serbian literature and art began to take shape during the first half of the 13th century.

Architecture and sculpture. The first buildings on a large scale date from the time of Stephen Nemanya (1170–96); Byzantine and Romanesque elements of the late 12th century can be observed, together with some traces of Armenian influence. Around 1170 the fusion of Byzantine and Romanesque forms took place, giving rise to the architectural style of the school of Raška (St. Nicholas in Kursumlija; Djurdjevi Stupovi near Raš).

The Church of the Virgin in the monastery of Studenica was built between the end of the 12th and the beginning of the 13th century (PL. 47; FIG. 75). In this church the blending of heterogeneous elements led to the original unity of style that marked the foundation of the school of Raška, which for over a century remained faithful to its basic principles. The churches of this school were simple in form: a vaulted nave with a dome supported by pillars, as in 12th-century Armenian prototypes, and a spacious semicircular apse. The bema was usually tripartite owing to the addition of the prothesis and diaconicon, and the area under the dome ran from north to south, extending into considerably lower wings similar to transepts. The finest churches had three doors. A large, rather complex narthex with two bell towers and an open porch surmounted by a chapel was often added to the north façade. More ancient traditions are clearly discernible in this style of architecture. In the regions bordering on Byzantium churches were built of brick and were very similar to 12th-century Byzantine edifices. Those in a more sophisticated style were constructed of stone; the finest had marble façades with richly decorated windows and doors and were Romanesque in form.

From the second half of the 12th century the construction of principal churches proceeded at a quickening pace: the Church of St. Nicholas in Kursumlija, Djurdjevi Stupovi near Raš, and the Church of the Virgin at Studenica; between 1207 and 1220, the monastery church of Žiča; toward 1235, the monastery church of Mileševa (PL. 48; FIG. 75); about 1250, the Church of the Holy Apostles in Peć; in the same period, Djurdjevi Stupovi near Berane (now Ivangrad); in 1252, the monastery church of Morača; about 1262, the Church of the Trinity at Sopoćani (PL. 47); toward 1280, the monastery church of Gradac; and in 1295, the monastery church of Arilje. Up to the end of the 13th century the tendency to create a single, spacious, well-lighted area gained ground. During the second half of the century smaller, lower wings were often added to the north and south sides of the main architectural body. In the last decades of the 13th century the central area of the church became smaller, and a marked trend toward vertical lines became apparent, which even later, in the 14th century, was to reappear whenever there was a weakening of Byzantine influence.

In medieval Serbia sculpture was used only for architectural purposes. The most important sculptural group of the 12th century was that of the portal and windows of the Church of the Virgin in Studenica. The Virgin Enthroned with the Child and two angels over the main door displays a successful synthesis of Byzantine and Romanesque elements. The surprising maturity of the Romanesque forms in the reliefs of the church (1190–96; PL. 49) contradicts the frequently advanced hypothesis of the Dalmatian origin of their authors; there are, instead, historical grounds for believing that their prototypes were French. In addition, certain generic similarities between the relief of the tympanum and the altar frontal of the Tempietto of Civi-

dale (see GOLD- AND SILVERWORK; ROMANESQUE ART) allow for the possibility of Venetian influences.

Although the Serbian sculptures of the 13th century were executed by foreign artists, the Studenica works undoubtedly had a decisive effect on the development of medieval Serbian sculpture; in stone churches, up to the middle of the 14th century, sculptors invariably turned to Studenica for inspiration, while only a few Gothic elements were incorporated. The motifs of Studenica were repeated in the churches of Mileševa (1235), Banjska (1314), and Dečani (1325–37; PL. 49) and in the Church of the Holy Archangels near Prizren (ca. 1343). In the latter, the extremely elaborate decoration of the mausoleum of Tsar Stephen Dushan (Dušan), of which only a few fragments remain, is a chaotic jumble of Romanesque, Gothic, and Byzantine elements.

Painting and minor arts. Fresco painting followed a different course. From 1170, when the first frescoes appeared in the churches of Stephen Nemanya, the basic principles of medieval Serbian painting were established for more than 500 years. In the first churches founded by the Nemanyich dynasty the oldest frescoes followed the style of late Byzantine painting of the Comnenian period; the masterpiece in this style is the wall decoration in the Church of St. Panteleimon in the village of Nerezi, near Skoplje. The Nerezi frescoes (PL. 52), dating from 1164, are by Greek artists, as are those (ca. 1180) of Djurdjevi Stupovi near Raš, of which there are fragments in the National Museum in Belgrade. The latter are, however, more austere and akin to the frescoes of Mount Athos, Vatopedi, and Ravdhoukha. In the earliest frescoes of the Church of the Virgin in Studenica (late 12th cent.) the decorative style of the late

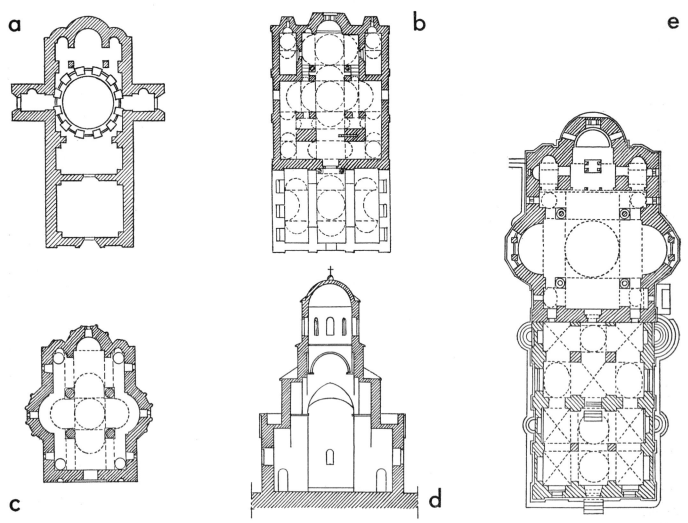

Serbian churches, 12th–14th centuries: (*a*) Studenica, church of the monastery, plan; (*b*) Gračanica, church, plan; (*c*) Ravanica, church, plan; (*d*) Mileševa, church of the monastery, cross section; (*e*) Mount Athos, Chilandari monastery, Church of the Virgin, plan.

Comnenian period gave way to a broader conception, free of calligraphic details, with a gold background in place of the traditional blue one. This marked the inauguration of a new style that flourished in Serbia throughout the first half of the 13th century, culminating after 1250 in the Church of the Trinity in Sopočani (PL. 53; II, PL. 462). In the monastery church of Mileševa (ca. 1235; PL. 53) the difference between paintings with a gold background and those with a blue one was clearly established. In the former type the solemn, luminous atmosphere and the rich coloring were based on late classical mosaics. In the latter type (in the narthex) the monastic character and the realistic conception of the work are strongly in evidence; the portraits of the first Nemanyich kings are particularly noteworthy. The frescoes of the patriarchal Church of the Holy Apostles in Peć, executed in 1250, differ considerably from the rest of 13th-century Serbian painting.

The trends of the style that culminated in Mileševa were continued in the frescoes at Morača (1252), though here the style was already very close to the monumental style of the chief artists of the Sopočani monastery. The church and chapels of this monastery house the most impressive complex of Serbian painting of the 13th century. In the church the frescoes decorating the bema are the finest expression of the style that was already firmly established in the frescoes with a gold background in the Church of the Virgin at Studenica. In these, Hellenistic traditions reappeared not only in the subject matter but also in the free, rapid, and lively painting technique.

In the narthex of the church of Sopočani this great style was already beginning to be eclipsed, while the frescoes of the prothesis, the Chapel of St. Nicholas, and the north and south chapels of the narthex (1262–1314), which are different in style and quality, reveal the hesitancy of a period of transition during which, around 1280, the first traces of the late Palaeologian style began to appear (II, PL. 462).

The frescoes in the church of Gradac illustrate the rapid abandonment of the style of Sopočani. In the sanctuary (ca. 1270) the artists revealed their naïve eclecticism, at times copying the calligraphic draftsmanship of the late Comnenian painters and at other times imitating the artists of Sopočani. In the heavily damaged scenes from the life of the Virgin (ca. 1290) in the narthex there appeared a new style that is also found in the frescoes of St. Clement in Ohrid. The frescoes in Arilje (1296), recently restored and of inferior quality, belong to the same trend. The painting of the late 13th century once more acquired a clearly defined character.

Though few in number, the Serbian icons of the late 12th and of the 13th century have the same artistic features as the frescoes of the same period. The most ancient is the mosaic icon of the Hodegetria in the Serbian monastery of Chilandari (Mount Athos), but this is the work of foreign artists; the *Holy Face* of Laon (early 13th cent.; see III, col. 597), which had already arrived in France during the Middle Ages, is most likely the work of a Serbian master. The 13th-century Serbian icons of Chilandari followed the stylistic development of contemporaneous mural painting. Important in the history of the Serbian icon are the fresco copies of several particularly famous, probably miraculous icons, from which it appears that their authors were subject to far more varied external influences than can be found in the frescoes. Italian influences can be observed in the fresco icons of Prizren (1270); there are traces of Western influence in the late-13th-century icon representing SS. Peter and Paul (Rome, Vat. Mus.). The icon of St. Panteleimon in Chilandari, which belongs stylistically to Palaeologian renaissance art, is of the same period.

Thirteenth-century Serbian miniature painting had its own peculiar history, since it remained archaic in tone and adhered to ancient prototypes. The Evangelistary of Prince Vukan (early 13th cent.), written in Raš and now in Leningrad, clearly shows the capabilities of the first Serbian scriptoriums. In its miniatures there is a blending of the calligraphic style of the late Comnenian period (in its provincial Macedonian variant) with 11th-century elements deriving from Montecassino. The ornamentation of the initials, on the other hand, marks a return to the primitive and vividly colored forms of the teratological

style of the early Middle Ages. The most important Serbian codex of the 13th century, the Evangelistary of Prizren, was destroyed by fire in 1941. Serbian manuscripts from the 13th century, like those of Bulgaria and Russia, formed part of Slavonic and Cyrillic literature; in their ornamentation a chaotic unevenness of quality prevailed. They can be distinguished from other 13th-century Slavic manuscripts by their use of Romanesque prototypes.

Local written sources indicate that handicrafts in medieval Serbia were of high quality. The biography of King Dragutin mentions that a goldsmiths' workshop was active at his court; though there are extant some metal objects, jewels, and vessels, no outstanding example of the work of Serbian goldsmiths has survived.

FROM THE REIGN OF MILUTIN TO THE END OF THE NEMANYICH DYNASTY. From the time of King Milutin (d. 1321) to the death of Tsar Stephen Uroš V (1371) Serbian art, as a result of new economic prosperity, spread over a larger geographical area than ever before. During the last years of the 13th century Serbia became the strongest state in the Balkan peninsula, widening its borders beyond Macedonia as far as Epirus and Thessaly. Though political conflicts between Serbia and Byzantium increased in intensity, the influence of Greek culture became predominant.

Architecture and sculpture. During the first 20 years of the 14th century King Milutin began a new style of architecture that was to continue without a break until the middle of the 15th century; it is first clearly expressed in the Church of Bogorodica Ljeviška (PL. 48) in Prizren. This five-domed building, built by the architect Nicholas on the prototype of early-14th-century Byzantine churches and on the foundations of an earlier Byzantine basilica with a nave and two side aisles, was to serve as a model for later churches, such as St. George at Staro Nagoričino (1313) and those in Gračanica (1321; FIG. 75) and Matejić (1356). All these churches belong to the inscribed-cross type, with the east arm of the cross considerably longer than the others. As a result the central dome was shifted to the west, while the four smaller domes rested on the terminals of the cross; the asymmetry of this ground plan was corrected by the addition of a very large narthex. The façades (that of the Church of Bogorodica Ljeviška in Prizren is particularly noteworthy) consisted of alternating courses of stone and brick laid with great precision. Arches, tympanums, windows, crenelated copings, and the apse were entirely of brick. The simplest churches (St. Nikita near Skoplje, 1307; St. Nicholas in Ljuboten, 1337; and the Church of the Archangel Michael in Lesnovo, 1341) have the same plan but only one dome and far more modest façades.

The churches that served as princely mausoleums comprise a separate category: they were the work of architects from the Adriatic coast who tried to conform with the compulsory model of the Church of the Virgin at Studenica. The only surviving one is the Church of the Saviour of the Dečani Monastery (1327–35; PL. 48), the most important medieval building in the continental zone of the Balkans. Built with five aisles, a dome, and a narthex, it is a bold mixture of Byzantine, Romanesque, and Gothic forms. The façades are of marble, and the pattern of alternating pale-yellow and violet-gray courses created a vivid polychrome effect similar to that of the two-toned façades of 13th- and 14th-century Italian cathedrals.

Serbian architecture of the first half of the 14th century can be divided into three categories. In the first the architects were inspired by Byzantine models and over a period of about 20 years evolved new forms characterized by an increasing use of stepped roofs and domes. The novelty of this style is particularly evident in the façades of the Church of the Virgin at the monastery of Gračanica. The second category includes the large marble buildings linked both to the traditional architecture of Raška and to the monumental stone architecture that flourished at the end of the 13th century in the regions between Ragusa (Dubrovnik) and Scutari. The third somewhat limited group comprises the simple traditional churches in Raška without side aisles and with only one dome, such as the Bela Crkva (White Church; ca. 1335) in the village of Karan.

In this period of extensive building activity local traditions were the most important factors in determining the style of a church, as is particularly apparent in the large Church of the Virgin that Milutin had built at Chilandari on Mount Athos at the beginning of the 14th century. The ground plan (FIG. 75), typical of Mount Athos churches, was introduced into Serbian architecture only in the last quarter of the 14th century.

The richest evidence of Serbian sculpture of this period, although fragmentary, is provided by the Church of the Holy Archangels near Prizren, where the tombstones of members of the dynasty bear sculptured recumbent figures of the deceased.

Painting and minor arts. A variety of trends can be observed in the mural painting of the period. During the first two decades of the 14th century King Milutin's artists predominated: Astrapas, who painted the frescoes in the Church of Bogorodica Ljeviška in Prizren (1307–09) and a considerable part of the frescoes at Žiča (1313–16); and Michael and Eutychios, two artists who worked together in the Church of St. Nikita near Skoplje (ca. 1307) and in St. George in Staro Nagoričino (1317; PL. 61). Anonymous masters patronized by Milutin worked at Studenica (1314), Gračanica (1321), and in the Church of St. Peter in Bijelo Polje. Cycles of frescoes, often covering more than ten parallel horizontal rows, gradually filled the interiors of the new churches, and the themes increased in variety. In the 13th century frescoes appeared only in the narthex, but at the beginning of the 14th century they were extended to the bema, becoming one of the most valuable sources of medieval Christian iconography. Their quality, however, is noticeably uneven. The frescoes of King Milutin's churches in the territory of old Raška are, in style and quality, nearest to the art of the Palaeologian epoch in Byzantium (see II, cols. 814–819).

After King Milutin's death fresco painting underwent a transitional phase until about 1375. King Stephen Dečanski (1321–31) summoned Greek painters from the Adriatic coast to Serbia. Greek painters also worked in Dečani, where the largest complex of early Serbian painting, consisting of more than 20 cycles executed over a period of 10 years (1340–50), has been preserved (PLS. 54, 61). The expressiveness and pictorial qualities of these works vary; the artists often approached Western art in their choice of subject matter, iconographic detail, and ornamentation, but on the whole they kept within the limits of Byzantine Orthodox art. Until about 1370 the minor Macedonian artists continued to paint in the style of the early 14th century, recalling with their revival of archaism the first phase of the refined Palaeologian style and somewhat hesitantly introducing a degree of spontaneity in the more realistic rendering of the faces. Outstanding as a portraitist is the anonymous fresco painter of the Church of St. Nicholas in Psača (ca. 1370). More provincial in character are the frescoes of the monastery of Lesnovo (Church of the Archangel Michael, ca. 1341–46; PL. 55), executed by three or more painters who successfully fused elements of ancient Macedonian painting with the style of the Palaeologian school.

Icons were produced in exceptionally large quantity during the last phase of this period. A heavily damaged icon in the Serbian monastery of Chilandari, representing the Purification of the Virgin (the maidens accompanying the Virgin are very similar to the young female figures in Prizren Cathedral), can be numbered among the masterpieces of the 14th century. The icons of the iconostasis at Dečani afford the best opportunity for evaluating the style of the Greek masters. There is a marked difference between the Greek painters of Kotor (Cattaro) and the artists trained in the Byzantine school. The Dečani icons (ca. 1340), painted by Kotor artists, with their brilliant colors, crude features, and lively figures, have a note of realism that contrasts sharply with the style of the famous miraculous icon of the Virgin Tricheirousa in Chilandari (painted on both sides), whose smooth forms, predominant olive gray tones, and immobile posture are typical of Constantinopolitan painting. The high quality of reliquary icons is represented by the perfectly preserved specimen that belonged to Thomas Pre-

ljubović (PL. 55). Of the Serbian icons donated during the Middle Ages to famous foreign churches the great 14th-century icon of St. Nicholas offered by King Stephen Dečanski to the Church of St. Nicholas in Bari still survives.

Serbian miniature painting permanently adopted Byzantine forms only in the 14th century. The portraits of the Evangelists with muses, or personifications of wisdom (early 14th century), inspired by Evangelistary No. 69 of the Serbian Academy of Sciences in Belgrade, reflect the style of Milutin's school. Refined Byzantine decorations adorn the Gospel of the voivode Nicholas Stanjević in Chilandari. The richly decorated Serbian Evangelistary of 1355 in London (Br. Mus., Ms. 154) contains a dedicatory portrait of a bishop in realistic style, similar to the bishops' portraits of Lesnovo. The images of the Evangelists in Evangelistary No. 9 in Chilandari (1360), with their particularly refined colors, are rare examples.

Among the objects of precious metals a large quantity of gilded-silver seals and silver jewelry has been preserved; examples of ecclesiastical gold embroidery and wooden furniture have survived in perfect condition.

THE MORAVA SCHOOL. *Architecture.* After suffering tragic defeats at the hands of the Turks in the 14th century the Serbs retreated northward to the Morava Valley, where an art of high standard and exceptional vitality, characterized by a unity of style in every field, came into being. Serbian architecture revived the forms created in the 13th century and, after 1370, evolved a style that became known as the Morava school. Single elements were borrowed from the architecture of the early 14th century: the technique of construction was the same; the triapsidal ground plan was derived from Mount Athos; and the five-domed church continued to predominate. But the general conception of the building changed considerably, and stone sculpture was used for decoration as was the custom of the school of Raška. Façades were elaborately articulated and a pictorial effect was achieved by the sharp contrasts between projecting and receding surfaces. Sculptural decoration in low relief was used for portals, windows, *rosaces*, and arcades. Motifs of floral garlands and brightly colored fantastic animals were inspired by Armenian art (q.v.), illumination, and the ornamental sculpture of 13th-century secular buildings.

The five-domed church of the monastery of Ravanica, the most ancient surviving monument of the Morava school, was built about 1375 (PLS. 50, 51). Also belonging to the late 14th century are the narthex of the Church of the Virgin at Chilandari, the Church of St. Stephen (or Lazarica) at Kruševac, and the monastery church of Ljubostinja; all of these were built by the same group of architects, among whom only Rade Borović is known by name. The church of the monastery of Kalenić, with sculptural decoration that is particularly well preserved (PL. 51), dates from the beginning of the 15th century. The church and fortifications of the monastery of Manasija (1407–18; PL. 51) constitute the last example of large-scale sacred buildings of the Morava school and of medieval Serbian architecture.

During the last years of political independence, building activity in Serbia assumed an entirely new character. Just before the final catastrophe many fortifications were built, particularly in the environs of the larger cities; Novo Brdo, Kosovo, and Smederevo on the Danube (now in ruins) are the most famous. The fortress of Smederevo, capital of Djurdje (George) Brancović, the last great monarch of medieval Serbian history, is one of the finest monuments of military architecture of a Byzantine type.

Painting and minor arts. The Morava school of painting developed in the same atmosphere of fruitful activity that grew more and more intense as the Turkish menace increased. Konstantin, the first outstanding artist of this school, executed the Ravanica frescoes about 1375, considerably reducing the number of cycles (as other painters were to do later). The new themes included the figure of Christ, scenes of his miracles and the Passion, and processions of saints, among which the warrior saints acquired increasing prominence. Once again the style received its impetus from the refined early-14th-century painting of Constantinople. The frescoes of the narthex at Kalenić are the finest copies of the mosaics of the Church of the Chora (Kariye Camii) in Constantinople. This is a nostalgic style that shows vitality only in its colors; it later passed into Russia with emigrant painters. The Ravanica and Kalenić frescoes, both of the same style, are suited to the interiors of medium-sized buildings and are therefore intimate in scale. The frescoes of Manasija (PLS. 54, 62) are in a large church and have a solemn monumentality. The work of the metropolitan Jovan and his collaborators occupies a special place. This painter came from the outskirts of Prilep and in 1389 worked at the Monastery of St. Andrew, on the Traska River near Skoplje; a little later his brother Macarius painted in Ljubostinja. These artists drew inspiration from 13th-century painting.

Late in the 14th century icon painting gradually increased in importance as a result of the development of the iconostasis (PL. 55), to which was added a second row of icons, the so-called "ordo," representing the Deësis between archangels and Apostles. The oldest of these (ca. 1380) are preserved at Chilandari. Among the icons of the monastic school, one of Christ painted by the metropolitan Jovan (1382) and two of the Virgin by Macarius (ca. 1420) are particularly noteworthy.

The medieval Serbian miniature reached its apogee with the Morava school. The Serbian Psalter of Munich (1370–90; Bayerische Staatsbibl., Cod. slav. 4) contains the richest collection of 14th-century miniatures — illustrations of the Old Testament (including the Psalms), the New Testament, and the hymn to the Virgin (the Acathistus) and several other hymns. Theories on the Eastern origin of these miniatures have turned out to be unfounded. The painters of this codex, though working during the period of the Morava school, conformed to earlier prototypes dating from before the mid-14th century, and only a few details, particularly the slender proportions of the figures, betray the influence of the new style. The style of the Morava school is recognizable in the figures of the Evangelists in the Serbian Evangelistary of 1428 in Leningrad (State Lib., Ms. 591) executed by Radoslav, who closely imitated fresco painters. In other codices of the period only ornamentation was used, especially in the initials (e.g., Vienna Nationalbib., Cod. slav. 32, 1372). Late in the 14th century illustrated romances of chivalry, mostly of Western origin, began to appear, but their illustrations show no Western influences.

The artistic handicrafts of the Morava school are known through the reliquaries, crosses, and cups, almost exclusively of silver, which the Serbian nobility donated to the monasteries of Mount Athos. The chief centers of metalwork and the goldsmith's art were to be found in mining regions, among which Novo Brdo was one of the most important. The embroideries of the time were of fine quality. Particularly famous is one in the Chilandari monastery; worked in gold and representing the figures of Christ, angels, and fathers of the church, it was executed in 1399 by Princess Euphemia (Jefimija), who was a nun.

The first Serbian books, printed in 1494 in Montenegro, were accompanied by excellent illustrations representing a synthesis of Renaissance and Byzantine elements. The Serbian monks, who had been trained in the Venetian printing houses of the 15th century, thoroughly mastered the craft.

THE POST-BYZANTINE PERIOD (1495–1690). *Architecture.* After the fall of Smederevo and the collapse of the political independence of Montenegro the opportunities for cultural development were reduced to a minimum, but the many noble families who still lived within the Serbian territory endeavored to keep art alive. The architecture of this period can be divided into three groups: Serbian churches that were intended as a prolongation of the monumental art of the Serbian monarchs; small monastic communities that remained faithful to their own style, in addition to developing qualities notably superior to those of rural art; and rural art itself, which was gradually reverting to its folk origins.

The large Serbian churches, among which Papraća (early 17th century), Čačak (1528), and Hopovo (1576) were out-

standing, continued the traditions of the Morava school, mainly imitating models from Mount Athos. Some architects returned to the traditions of 13th-century Serbia. The churches of the small monasteries (the Holy Trinity and others in the Ovčar-Kablar gorge; those at Dobričevo and Dabrilovna in Herzegovina and Tronoša) adhered strictly to the style of the Raška school. The small country churches, many of which were built by architects from Ragusa, were grouped around more important monastic or urban centers (Dečani, Studenica, Peć, Prizren, and Niš). They were extremely modest in size, built of stone, with one aisle, an arched roof, and a semicircular apse.

The finest works under the Turkish domination were created between 1590 and 1660, culminating during the tenure of the patriarch Pajsije (1614–47). The last monasteries on the Fru-

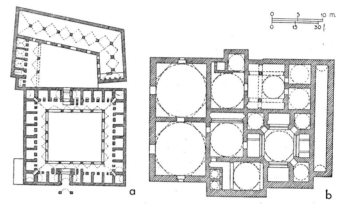

Skoplje (Yugoslavia): (*a*) Kursumli-han (caravanserai), 15th century, plan; (*b*) Hammam of Daut Pasha, 15th century, plan (*from W. Molé, 1962*).

ška Gora were built at the end of the 16th and the beginning of the 17th century; the monasteries in the Ovčar-Kablar gorge were built during the same period. The most important monument of the end of the 16th century is the church of the monastery of Piva, once surrounded by massive walls, together with the residential buildings of the metropolitan Savatije and monks' cells.

Painting and minor arts. Mural painting can also be divided into three stylistic phases. An academic style of the highest quality was cultivated by the artists of Mount Athos and their pupils; it is well known in its Serbian variant from the frescoes of Molivo-Klisija (1536). The desire to stimulate fresco painting became particularly strong after the restoration of the patriarchate in 1557. As early as 1561 the patriarch Macarius restored many of the paintings in the churches of Peć; in 1571 the narthex of Gračanica and that of St. Nicholas Dabarski were enriched by new frescoes. The paintings in St. Nicholas reveal that a distinct school of painting had grown up under the patronage of the patriarchate; during the last decades of the 16th century the famous icon painter Longin came from this school. During this time Serbian fresco painting, detached from that of Mount Athos, developed its own themes and style, which were most clearly expressed in the frescoes in the church of the monastery of Orahovica in Slavonia (1594).

Extensive fresco cycles appeared in the more important new buildings. From 1604 to 1606, paintings were executed in Piva, in 1608 in the church of Hopovo, and in 1621 the finest Serbian frescoes of the Turkish period were completed in the large refectory of Chilandari. Although from the artistic point of view these frescoes do not represent a homogeneous whole (in Piva, they were the work of humble local masters; in Hopovo, of Greek artists from Mount Athos; and in Chilandari, of the Serbian Djordje Mitrofanovič), all were inspired by local literature and were very skillfully adapted to the spaces and surfaces provided by the architecture. The high standard of mid-17th-century fresco painting was maintained in the frescoes of the narthex of Hopovo (1654). Those of the Church of St. Nicholas in Chilandari, painted 10 years later, show marked signs of decadence.

In the 16th and 17th centuries icon painting became the principle form of painting among the Serbs. From the end of the 16th century the chief decoration of Serbian churches was the high, two-tiered wooden iconostasis with a large cross at the center of the architrave. Gilded carved icons with large crosses painted at the top appeared in Serbian monasteries, first in Mileševa; the iconostasis of Dečani was completed in 1594 and that of Morača between 1596 and 1607. All these icons are older than those of Mount Athos and have a close affinity with the painted crosses of Dalmatia. Longino and Djordje Mitrofanovič, who may be considered the two finest Serbian icon painters of the period, were also outstanding painters of iconostases.

The same Serbian masters who executed icons and frescoes were also painters of miniatures. From the works signed by the icon painter Andrija Raičević, who was active at the end of the 17th century, it is evident that the best artists of his generation were able to paint frescoes, icons, and miniatures with equal ability. Among Serbian manuscripts of the period examples of fine miniatures are to be found in the evangelistaries of the priest Jovan of Kratovo (five copies produced between 1558 and 1583); their decoration has a distinctly Eastern flavor and is remarkable for its enamellike brilliant colors. The Serbian copy of Cosmas Indicopleustes, with miniatures by Andrija Raičević (1649), was strongly influenced by a Russian copy dating from the first decades of the 16th century. The last Serbian manuscripts of value were produced at Chilandari about 1660; the finest is that of the Acts of the Apostles preserved in the monastery (Ms. 107).

In the same centers that produced illuminated manuscripts artistic wood and metal objects were also made. Wood carving was particularly developed in the monasteries, metalwork mainly in secular workshops. Carving gradually fell more and more under Western influence. Baroque forms made their first appearance in gilded wood carvings; in wooden objects that were not gilded (lecterns, chairs, doors, and decorative testers) the traditional style — a mixture of Byzantine and Moslem elements — predominated even during the 16th and 17th centuries. Furniture in this style, with elegant proportions and surfaces richly decorated with inlays of multicolored wood, bone, and mother of pearl, was made in Chilandari and many other monasteries. The metal most widely used was silver, and censers, candlesticks, book covers, and reliquaries were made. Among the 17th-century goldsmiths Konde Vuk was outstanding. The art of gold- and silver-thread embroidery passed from the court workshops to the monasteries. Nearly all the minor arts maintained a high standard until the end of the 16th century. Later, Russian and Wallachian gifts from the workshops of the tsar and the boyars, with their variety of materials and technically more perfect workmanship, caused the almost complete disappearance of local goldsmiths and carvers.

By the end of the 17th century all techniques and arts in the Serbian territory subject to the Turks had reverted to the primitive forms of rural craftsmanship. The Serbian population that had retreated to the north adapted quickly to a more advanced culture and, in its new environment in Hungarian territory, succeeded by the middle of the 18th century in laying the foundations of its secular art in the modern era.

Svetozar Radojčić

III. Russia. Early Russian art, ranging over a period of seven centuries, began to take form after the conversion of the eastern Slavs to Christianity (989) and developed up to the age of Peter the Great (1696–1725), when the esthetic values of the Middle Ages underwent a radical reassessment. The first flowering of early Russian art was connected with the political rise of Kiev, the center of a powerful Russian state.

Kievan Russia. *Architecture.* The technique of building in stone was introduced into Kievan Russia from Byzantium (see BYZANTINE ART), from which Vladimir the Great (r. 980–1015) called the builders who erected the first stone church — the Church of the Blessed Mother of God (990–96), better known as the Church of the Tithe (or Desyatinnaya Church) because

Vladimir donated a tenth of his income for its upkeep. Archaeological examination of its foundations has shown that the church was originally a domed cruciform building with nave and side aisles, six piers, three apses, and a small west porch. The church was richly decorated on the inside with marble, slate, mosaics, and frescoes. It had several domes (the exact number has not been ascertained), and the walls were constructed of a mixture of stone and brick, with the courses "immersed" in mortar, a technique typical of Byzantine *opus mixtum.* Not later than 1039 two spacious open galleries with massive cruciform piers were built on the south and north sides. These low galleries gave the profile of the church a tiered effect rarely found in Byzantine architecture.

Church building in stone soon spread throughout Russia. Previously, only about 40 churches were known to belong to the period of the 10th to 13th century, but as a result of archaeological excavations the number has risen to 150 (fewer than 69, however, have survived above ground). The greatest number of stone churches was built in Kiev. Vladimir's son, Yaroslav the Wise (1019–54), wanted Kiev to become a worthy rival of Constantinople. It was no coincidence that a number of buildings in Kiev bore the same names as celebrated Constantinople monuments (the Golden Gate, St. Sophia, etc.). The largest of the Kiev churches was the Cathedral of St. Sophia, founded in 1037; the central part was completed in 1046 (II, PL. 452; XII, PL. 128). The church was designed to be used for services officiated by the metropolitan and as a burial place for princes. Unfortunately, as is the case with the majority of early Russian churches, it has lost its original character as a result of numerous alterations. However, careful study of the building has made reconstruction possible (FIG. 84). It was a vast cruciform church with nave and four side aisles, five apses, and thirteen domes and was originally encircled on the south, north, and west sides of the interior by a one-story gallery, the flat roof of which was used as an ambulatory. Evidently the galleries were raised for enlargement at the beginning of the 12th century. During the same period the building was encircled on three sides by a new, wider one-story gallery supported by powerful flying buttresses; a tower was added at the southwest corner (the northwest tower was built later); only in the late 12th or early 13th century was the outer gallery also raised. The original façades, as in all other buildings of this period, were not stuccoed; alternating courses of roughhewn stone and brick were "immersed" in mortar that contained traces of finely ground brick (*tsemyanka*) and acquired a rosy color. This technique of *opus mixtum* gave the surface of the wall a rough, uneven character resulting in unusual and picturesque effects. There is no doubt that, together with the Kievan builders, Greek architects also took part in the building of St. Sophia. But the latter had to allow for local taste, which had been formed on the basis of the ancient traditions of wooden architecture. Owing to its pyramidal form, its numerous domes, its open galleries, towers, and massive cruciform piers, St. Sophia did not closely resemble contemporaneous Byzantine churches.

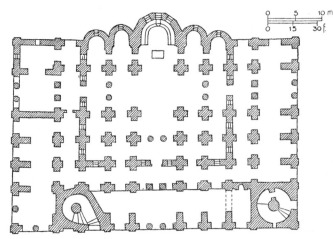

Kiev, Cathedral of St. Sophia, 1037 to beginning of 12th century, plan.

Its imposing bulk bore the archaic stamp typical of all architectural monuments belonging to the early stages of historical development.

The construction of stone churches was also widespread in Chernigov, where Yaroslav's brother Mstislav, prince of Chernigov and Tmutarakan, founded the Cathedral of the Transfiguration (completed under Yaroslav ca. 1036). This large cruciform church (almost completely destroyed in World War II) had eight piers, a massive tower, and five domes. In the southwest corner there was a small baptistery, and in the 11th century funerary chapels for burial of members of the prince's family were added to the east corners. The roofing followed the line of the zakomari (arched wall sections) that retraced the inner structure of the vaults, and the outside walls were decorated with niches. The Cathedral of St. Michael in the Vydubetski Monastery (1070–88) in Kiev and the Church of SS. Boris and Gleb in Vyshgorod (consecrated in 1115; no longer extant) were also eight-piered with a tower and porches. Both these buildings were remarkable for their somewhat unusual elongated shape, which, however, does not justify their being considered basilican-type churches. Domed cruciform churches with nave and side aisles and six piers were more common, such as the Cathedral of the Dormition in the Pecherski Monastery (1073–77; consecrated 1089; destroyed 1941), the church of the Monastery of St. Michael (founded 1108; completed before 1113; extant until the 1930s), both in Kiev, and the Church of Our Saviour in Berestovo (early 12th cent.). The chief decoration on their austere façades consisted of decorative niches and smooth engaged pilasters that led directly into the semicircular arches of the zakomari. [N. B. The Russian term sobor is commonly rendered as "cathedral." However, it may be used in reference to a church (tserkov) of size or importance and need not imply the seat of a bishop. See also A. Graybar, "Cathédrales multiples et groupement d'eglises en Russie," Rev. des Et. Slaves, XX, 1942, pp. 91–120.]

A new phase in the development of Kievan architecture began in the first third of the 12th century: the tower with stairs leading to the choir gallery was replaced by a narrow passage in the thickness of the west or north wall, and the special annex that served as a baptistery was no longer built separately but inside the main church, where it occupied one of the side wings. The old system of decorating the façades with many-stepped niches, faced with meanders and crosses in brick, began to die out; rows of ornamental arches and small niches served as the only decoration. The technique of masonry also changed fundamentally: the opus mixtum consisting of alternating courses of brick and stone was replaced by so-called "even layered" masonry intended for plastering. A transitional method between the opus mixtum and the new technique was used in the all-brick construction of the Church of Our Saviour in Berestovo, where every other course was embedded in the wall and smoothed over with mortar. In "even layered" masonry plaster of a pinkish color was applied very thinly and left with a rough finish. Sometimes the surface of the plaster was marked with smooth white strips to simulate courses of stone blocks laid in the usual manner (the Cathedral of the Dormition in the Eletski Monastery at Chernigov). Typical examples of Kievan religious architecture of the second half of the 12th century are the church of the St. Cyril Monastery near Kiev (built between 1146 and 1171) and the Cathedral of the Annunciation (1186), the Cathedral of the Dormition of the Eletski Monastery, and the Church of SS. Boris and Gleb (end of 12th cent.; PL. 56), all in Chernigov.

Along with such six-piered churches, four-piered ones were also built and became predominant toward the end of the century when buildings became smaller and often had only one dome. One of these four-piered, single-dome churches is the remarkable Church of Paraskeva-Pyatnitsa (Good Friday) in Chernigov (PL. 57). Recently restored with great skill, it is striking for the boldness and modernity of its architectural design. The ground plan of the building is quite common: four piers, three apses, one dome, and a stairway inside the west wall leading to the gallery. But the construction of its roof bears no relation to the architecture of an earlier period, and it has certain affinities only with the Cathedral of St. Sophia in Polotsk. The semicircular vaulting over the side aisles joins the quadrant vaults of the corner areas in such a way as to create a trilobed effect at the summit of the façades. Since the wall arches are considerably higher than the vaults over the crossing, the drum, which rests on a square pedestal, is pushed upward. Externally, this construction presents itself in a tier of zakomari and above this in yet another tier of purely decorative kokoshniki (superimposed arches or gables resembling the headdresses worn by Russian women). The building has an extraordinarily dynamic character: the vertical lines of the engaged columns seem to be caught up by the trilobed roofing and soar upward toward the dome through the zakomari, the kokoshniki, and the half columns of the drum. This reworking of the domed cruciform plan bears no resemblance to its squat, cubic prototype. Many concepts of later Russian architecture were anticipated in this church.

During the 11th century and early in the 12th the architecture of Kiev played a decisive part in the formation of all local schools. Its traditions were widely used in Volynia, Galich, Polotsk, Smolensk, Ryazan, Vladimir, Suzdal, and Novgorod. Particularly interesting was the original work of the architect Ioann (John) in his Cathedral of the Spaso-Evfrosinievski Monastery in Polotsk (prior to 1159) and of an unknown master in the Church of the Archangel Michael in Smolensk (1191–94). These vertically elongated buildings have a close affinity with tower-shaped churches, in particular with the Church of Paraskeva-Pyatnitsa in Chernigov; they represent one of the most original indigenous trends in 12th-century architecture, which was in many respects to determine the development of Moscow architecture.

Painting, sculpture, and minor arts. The most ancient churches of Kiev were decorated with mosaics, usually in combination with frescoes. The iconographic scheme originated in the art of Constantinople of the 9th and 10th centuries. The Virgin Orans, the Communion of the Apostles, and a procession of saints were generally depicted in the apse, the Pantocrator in the dome, gospel scenes representing the cycle of religious feasts on the vaults and walls, and half-length figures of the Forty Martyrs of Sebaste on the transverse arches. Only a few fragments representing heads have survived from the frescoes of the Church of the Tithe; the heavy brushwork and harsh shading are typically archaic in character. There are also many archaic features in the mosaics of St. Sophia, which are remarkable for their color; they were executed between 1043 and 1046, as were the frescoes of the central crossing (PL. 64). The stocky figures in frontal poses, their large heads, features, and heavy extremities and the slow rhythm of the movement — all these elements find their closest stylistic analogy in the mosaics of Hosios Loukas in Phocis (Greece). Evidently the Greek guild of mosaic craftsmen that worked in St. Sophia in Kiev consisted of no less than eight men, including artists from both the metropolis and the provinces, and these visiting Greek artists were undoubtedly assisted by local masters. Thus there came into being the Russo-Byzantine workshop that was responsible for the entire fresco decoration of the church (completed in the 1060s; with scenes from the life of the Virgin, the archangel Michael, the Apostle Peter, and St. George as well as the Gospel cycle). Particularly interesting was the group portrait of Prince Yaroslav's family on the west side of the central crossing: Yaroslav, his wife Irina, and their children were shown approaching Christ, seated in the center, to whom the prince was offering a model of the church he had built (only the figures of four daughters and two sons have survived). The frescoes of secular content (scenes representing the Constantinople Hippodrome, court life, and the hunt) that decorate both towers were executed only in the second or third decade of the 12th century. Most probably they were painted by order of the Grecophile Vladimir Monomakh, the grand prince of Kiev (1113–25).

A surviving mosaic masterpiece of the period in the territory of Kiev is a group from the Monastery of St. Michael (ca. 1108; later transferred to St. Sophia; PL. 65). These mosaics are also the result of the joint efforts of visiting Greek and local artists. The theme of the Communion of the Apostles appears in a freer and more lively version than that in St. Sophia (the mosaic representing St. Demetrius of Salonika, which belonged to the same group, is in the Tretyakov Gallery in Moscow). Shades of emerald green predominate among the brilliant colors and create, in combination with gold, an especially vibrant palette.

In Kievan Russia fresco painting gradually replaced mosaics, and by the 12th century the latter were no longer found. The surviving frescoes of the early 12th century (Church of St. Michael in Oster) and of the second half of the 12th century (church of the Monastery of St. Cyril; baptisteries of St. Sophia in Kiev and the Cathedral of the Dormition in Chernigov) are very fragmentary but seem to be characterized by solidity of form and linear accentuation.

Sculpture played an important part in the interior decoration of the churches of Kiev and Chernigov. Altar gates were decorated with slabs covered with rich ornamental carving of Byzantine type; the same ornamental motifs appeared on marble sarcophagi (e.g., sarcophagus in the Church of the Tithe and that of Prince Yaroslav in St. Sophia) and on the slate parapets of galleries. The technique used indicates the work of craftsmen skilled in stone carving. Later reliefs on slate, dating from the 11th century and different in style (Hercules wrestling with the lion, Cybele in her chariot, St. George, St. Theodore Stratelates, SS. Nestor and Demetrius) were found in the Pecherski Monastery and the Monastery of St. Michael; they are now conserved in the Church of Our Saviour in Berestovo and in the Tretyakov Gallery in Moscow. These reliefs had once decorated the façades of buildings. The centuries-old techniques of wood carving are clearly evident in all of them and point to the work of local craftsmen. The Kiev reliefs can be considered a preparatory step toward the extremely rich sculptural decoration of the 12th-century churches of Vladimir-Suzdal.

The minor arts reached a high level in this period. Among the treasures unearthed in the area there are many precious objects decorated with cloisonné enamels (PL. 70), pearls, and filigree. The casting of copper and the working and chasing of silver, copper, and gold were also widespread. Patterns and figures on silver were usually executed in the niello technique. Books written on parchment were decorated with initials of a zoomorphic character and with illuminated miniatures (the Gospels of Ostromir, PL. 73; the Svyatoslav Miscellany, 1073, Moscow, Historical Mus., Fol. Perg. no. 161; the Yuriev Gospel, 1120–28, Moscow, Historical Mus., Fol. Perg. no. 1003). The miniatures sewn into the Egbert Psalter, or Codex Gertrudianus (1078–87; Cividale del Friuli, Italy, Mus. Arch.), hold a special place; one of these miniatures (fol. 5v) is a group portrait of Prince Yaropolk's family before the Apostle Peter, while another (fol. 10v) represents the crowning of Yaropolk and his wife Irina by Christ. The style of the miniatures, combining Byzantine and Romanesque features, suggests that they were executed in the West.

THE PRINCIPALITY OF VLADIMIR-SUZDAL. *Architecture and sculpture*. The principality of Vladimir-Suzdal was Russia's second center for the convergence of national talent. The princes Andrei Bogolyubski (1157–74) and Vsevolod Bolshoe Gnezdo ("Big Nest"; 1176–1212) were active builders, employing not only local but also Western masters who familiarized the Russians with advanced forms of Romanesque architecture and sculpture. At first the architecture of Vladimir-Suzdal was closely related to that of Kiev (Cathedral of the Dormition in Rostov, Cathedral of the Nativity in Suzdal; both founded by Vladimir Monomakh in the late 11th and the early 12th century), but it gradually acquired its own personality. The building activity (1152–57) of Yuri Dolgoruki represents a transitional phase. He founded the Church of SS. Boris and Gleb in Kideksha, near Suzdal, and the Cathedral of the Transfiguration of Our Lord in Pereyaslavl-Zaleski — both small buildings of cruciform type with four piers, three apses, one dome, and a gallery on the west end. The walls are divided into three sections by flat pilasters, which are surmounted by *zakomari* that correspond to the semicircular vaults of the roof. The walls, faced with blocks of "white stone" (a local limestone), present an even surface and are decorated only with simple arches and equally unpretentious perspective portals.

A new phase in the development of Vladimir-Suzdal architecture was initiated by the building of the Cathedral of the Dormition in Vladimir (1158–61), the castle in Bogolyubovo (1158–65), and the Church of the Virgin of the Intercession (Pokrov; 1165) on the Nerl River, all of which were founded by Andrei Bogolyubski. Damaged by fire in 1185, the Cathedral of the Dormition was radically altered between 1185 and 1189 when buildings were added to it on all four sides and it was converted from a three-aisled church into a five-aisled one. Nevertheless, the original appearance of the Cathedral can be reconstructed. The façades, faced with white stone, were marked off by complicated pilasters surmounted by half columns that were crowned with leafy capitals; half way up the wall ran a frieze of colonnettes and arches; the shafts of these columns were gilded, and saints, peacocks, and ornamental motifs were painted in fresco in the niches; and the *zakomari* were topped by openwork ornaments of gilded copper in the form of birds or cups. But the chief novelty in the treatment of the façades, on which the whiteness of the stone alternates with gilding and the variegated colors of the frescoes, was the use of sculptured stone representing scenes with figures and masks of women and lions. This practice, alien to the Byzantine tradition of Kiev, is typical of Romanesque art and had been introduced into Vladimir by stonemasons from the West, possibly emigrants from Galicia-Volynia.

Reliefs in stone were even more widely employed on the façades of the Church of the Virgin of the Intercession, a splendid example of early Russian architecture, exceptionally graceful in its proportions, and beautifully set in the surrounding landscape. The half columns placed against the pilasters and leading directly into the semicircular arches of the *zakomari*, and the columned frieze accentuate the soaring movement of every line in the building. The reliefs decorating the three divisions of the façade create an effect of a composition set within a vault. Although the figures and masks are arranged in rows one above another there is no interruption in the vertical lines, which give lightness and grace to the entire building. The iconography of the reliefs is inspired by the 97th, 148th, and 150th psalms; King David, represented three times, appears surrounded by lions and birds. The lateral sections show griffins clawing at hinds, and below them there is a frieze of female masks. The technique of wood carving native to the Russian people is clearly discernible in the manner of working the stone (the figures of David and the lions). The griffins and the consoles decorated with birds, animals, and masks are more Romanesque in character. Evidently the craftsmen consisted of local people cooperating with foreign artists. Subsequently, the latter yielded entirely to the craftsmen of Vladimir, who radically altered the techniques of sculpturing in stone by introducing the techniques of wood carving. This can be clearly seen in the reliefs of the Cathedral of St. Demetrius (1193–97; PL. 57), which are remarkable for the flatness of their carving. They cover the entire upper part of the wall like a patterned carpet, and below there is a frieze of columns and arches, also filled with reliefs. One of the main themes again is King David offering praise to his Creator, with animals and birds symbolizing the natural universe.

In contrast to Western Europe, where high relief gradually increased in depth until it approached sculpture in the round, relief in Russia developed in the opposite direction. Under the influence of wood carving it lost its three-dimensional character and acquired the characteristics of two-dimensional art. A further stage in its development can be seen in such churches as the Cathedral of the Nativity of the Virgin in Suzdal (1222–25) and the Cathedral of St. George in Yuriev-Polski (1230–34). The walls of the Cathedral of St. George are entirely covered with a rich plant pattern that enmeshes the façade of the church and its porches like a fine cobweb. Above, there was a frieze of arches and columns with figures of saints and the Deësis; the four center *zakomari* were decorated with scenes from the Old Testament and the gospels, as well as with a theme often represented on ancient Russian amulets — the seven noble youths of Ephesus. Unfortunately, the original order of the reliefs was altered when the church was restored in the 15th century, and much remains unclear in the decorative scheme, the general character of which recalls precious icon covers and richly fashioned bookbindings.

Painting and minor arts. The churches of Vladimir-Suzdal were decorated with frescoes, some of which have been preserved. As the original façade of the Cathedral of the Dormition shows, frescoes decorated not only church interiors but their exteriors as well (figures of saints between the gilded columns of the decorative arcades). Vsevolod Bolshoe Gnezdo, who had spent his youth in Constantinople, invited artists from that city to paint the Cathedral of St. Demetrius. In the frescoes of the two west vaults the free and confident brushwork reveals the hand of a major artist. He was undoubtedly assisted by local masters, whose work can be recognized without difficulty (heavier forms, accentuated linear elements, Slavic faces; PL. 67). Fragments of frescoes have also survived in the Cathedral of the Dormition in Vladimir (ca. 1189), the Church of SS. Boris and Gleb in Kideksha (1180s), and in the diaconicon of Suzdal Cathedral (1233).

Easel painting was also widespread. A considerable number of superb icons of the late 12th and the early 13th century can be attributed to the school of Vladimir-Suzdal (two Deëses with half-length figures and a St. Demetrius of Salonika, both in the Tretyakov Gallery, Moscow; the icon of the Maksimov Virgin). Stylistically these icons, with their somber colors, are still close to their Byzantine prototypes. Yaroslavl also had its own school, which in the 13th century executed icons of outstanding quality that owe their beauty to their bright, cheerful colors, the variety of feelings they express, and their lavish ornamentation. Local characteristics are so clearly in evidence that they neutralize the legacy of Byzantium.

Derivation from the culture of Kiev is particularly noticeable in the minor arts of Vladimir-Suzdal. Local craftsmen created cloisonné enamels and gilded and engraved designs on silver. They were also familiar with the niello technique. Parchment manuscripts were copiously illustrated with miniatures. Particularly interesting are the copper gates of Suzdal Cathedral (1220–30), with gospel scenes and various other episodes executed in an unusual kind of engraving with gold foil. The design was etched through the varnish covering the copper plate, after which the areas cleared of varnish were corroded with acid and gilded. This technique, introduced into Russia from Byzantium, was also common in later periods for the decoration of church gates.

The invasion of the Tatars put a sudden end to the brilliant flowering of ancient Russian art. From 1223 the Tatars began the systematic destruction and looting of Russian towns; only Novgorod and Pskov, which were situated in the north, did not fall prey to the Tatars and became the guardians of the great artistic traditions that they were subsequently to transmit to Moscow.

NOVGOROD. *Architecture.* Because of extensive overseas trade and highly developed crafts the merchants and artisans of Novgorod represented a formidable political force; this helps to explain the democratic, simple nature of Novgorod art. The first large stone building was the Cathedral of St. Sophia (1045–50; PL. 56), which replaced a cathedral of the same name (an oak structure with 13 domes) built at the end of the 10th century. As has now been established, the five-aisled stone Cathedral, similar in plan to St. Sophia in Kiev, was surrounded at a very early period by open galleries supported by massive buttresses and roofed by three center vaults running on an axis perpendicular to the main body of the church. At the beginning of the 12th century three large churches with nave and side aisles were built in Novgorod; the Cathedral of St. Nicholas Dvorishchenski (1113), the Cathedral of the Nativity of the Virgin at the St. Anthony Monastery (1117), and the Cathedral of St. George at the Yuriev Monastery (1119), the latter built by Master Peter. Each of the last two buildings had a tower with

stairs. Remarkable for their size and austere monumentality, these cathedrals had smooth walls marked off by flat pilasters, and their only ornament consisted of niches and small rows of decorative arches, on the drums. The masonry technique was similar to that used in Scandinavian architecture: the walls were built of one type of stone, roughly hewn on the visible surface and set in the façades with a pink mortar (*tsemyanka*). The arches, vaults, and drums were built of almost square bricks laid in uniform strata.

After 1135, when the classes represented by the *veche* (popular assembly) became more powerful, the princes no longer built in Novgorod itself. From then on, architects were patronized by boyars, rich merchants, and craft guilds and the buildings became smaller and acquired a more intimate character. The domed cruciform church was simplified, becoming almost square in ground plan, with four square piers, three apses, and one dome. The technique of masonry also changed: courses of stone alternated with irregular courses of brick. Façades were covered with pink mortar, which was applied so thinly that it did not conceal the irregularities of the masonry. Typical examples of this new type of architecture were the Church of St. George in Staraya Ladoga (ca. 1165), the Church of the Annunciation in Arkazha (1179), and the Church of SS. Peter and Paul on Sinichy Hill (1185–92). It is significant that when Prince Yaroslav Vladimirovich built the Church of the Saviour in Nereditsa (near Novgorod, 1198) he also followed the architectural tradition of the second half of the 12th century. Destroyed during World War II and again rebuilt, this church is an expression of the marked austerity and terseness of 12th-century Novgorod architecture.

From the end of the 13th century and throughout the 14th and 15th centuries the square church with four piers, one apse, and one dome predominated in Novgorod. Among the more important churches built in Novgorod during the 14th and 15th centuries are St. Theodore Stratelates (1360–62; PL. 58), the Church of the Saviour (1374), St. John the Evangelist in Radokovitsi (1384), and SS. Peter and Paul in Kozhevniki (1406). As a rule, these were comparatively small, intimate buildings whose charm lay in their spare silhouette, their compactness, and their modest exterior decoration.

The Novgorod kremlin (citadel), first mentioned as a fortress in 1044, was surrounded at a much later date (between 1331 and 1400) by stone walls that replaced the original wooden ones. The development of firearms in the late 14th and the early 15th century led to the need for a partial reconstruction of the kremlin; a more radical reconstruction (1484–90) was undertaken by Moscow after its union with Novgorod. During this period the twelve kremlin towers (nine have survived) were erected or modernized. The Novgorod kremlin also enclosed the archbishop's court, with its stone edifices built at the time of Archbishop Euphemius (1429–58): the Granovitaya Palace (1433), with its large hall with Gothic ribbed vaulting; the archbishop's palace; and the clock tower, at that time surmounted by a tent roof. Together with the Cathedral of St. Sophia, these buildings represent the architectural image of the Novgorod kremlin to this day.

Painting and minor arts. The first flowering of Novgorod painting occurred in the 12th century. From the 11th century only one fresco fragment, representing Constantine and Helen, has survived in the Cathedral of St. Sophia (PL. 64). The Cathedral style of painting indicates the hand of a local artist. The Cathedral of St. Sophia had no other wall paintings until 1108, when its decoration with frescoes was begun. The iconographic scheme derived from the Kiev tradition; only single figures of saints and five figures of prophets in the dome have survived. The heavy, statuesque forms retain many archaic elements of the art of the 11th century and have many features in common with the Mstislav Gospel (Moscow, Historical Mus., Patr. 1203), whose miniatures were executed in Novgorod between 1103 and 1117. Two other groups of frescoes in the Cathedral of St. Nicholas Dvorishchenski (1100–20) and the Cathedral of the Nativity of the Virgin in the St. Anthony Monastery (1125) show the variety of artistic trends existing in the city at the time. The first of these groups clearly displays its derivation from the artistic tradition of Kiev, whereas the second reveals Romanesque features introduced from the West. The finest works of the Novgorod school of painting were created in the second half of the 12th century, when its characteristics became crystallized into a distinct style, as seen in the frescoes of the Church of St. George in Staraya Ladoga (ca. 1167; PL. 66), in the Church of the Annunciation in Arkazha (1189), and in the Church of the Saviour in Nereditsa (1199; destroyed). In the highly refined frescoes of Staraya Ladoga linear stylization of the type used in the Nerezi frescoes in Yugoslavia is very apparent. The Arkazha and Nereditsa frescoes show a broader and freer manner of painting with heavy massive forms that are peculiar to the Novgorod school.

Easel painting also flourished in Novgorod in the 12th century; traditional Byzantine elements were more prevalent than in the frescoes. Among the strongly Byzantine icons are those depicting an archangel (PL. 66), the head of Christ (the "Image Not Made with Hands"), the Annunciation, a full-length St. George, the Dormition, and St. Nicholas Thaumaturgus (last five, Moscow, Tretyakov Gall.). These works, usually somewhat somber in color and of extremely delicate draftsmanship, undoubtedly reflect the tastes of the princely courts. Besides this Grecophile trend there existed another more original current in which local characteristics prevailed over alien Byzantine ones; the colors were lighter and more joyous in tone, the forms flatter, the linear element more accentuated, and faces based on the traditional Greek canon were more and more frequently succeeded by the national type. These differences are easily traceable in such 13th-century works as the icon with St. John Climacus flanked by SS. George and Blaise and another with scenes from the life of St. George (both, Leningrad, Russian Mus.).

The Novgorod school of painting reached the apex of its development in the second half of the 14th century and in the 15th. Greek artists working in the city familiarized local painters with the most advanced forms of the Palaeologian school of art, which underwent an original transmutation. Subject matter became more varied, with new themes either connected with the liturgy or else inspired by apocryphal sources or by the cult of local saints; the once heavy, immobile figures became slender, well proportioned, and assumed bold, free attitudes; the architectural backgrounds, which often included realistic forms, became more complex; and the palette glowed with brilliant colors, dominated by fiery vermilion. The earliest Novgorod paintings in this style are the frescoes of the Church of St. Michael in the Skovorodski Monastery near Novgorod (ca. 1360; destroyed during World War II). The Russian facial types, the range of intense colors transferred from easel painting and alien to the Byzantine style, and the miniaturist technique indicate the work of local artists. When the famous painter Theophanes the Greek (ca. 1330–ca. 1410) came to Novgorod from Constantinople in the 1370s, his extraordinary skill made such an impression that many of the Russian artists became his pupils and followers. Theophanes himself decorated the Church of Our Saviour of the Transfiguration (1378; PL. 68; II, PL. 464). These frescoes, remarkable for their psychological insight and their bold painting technique, are similar to the paintings in the Church of St. Theodore Stratelates and the Church of the Dormition in Volotovo Pole (PL. 68). The last-mentioned frescoes, however, were the work not of Theophanes but of his Novgorod followers. Later paintings of the Novgorod school reveal a different, more linear style.

During the 15th century wall painting tended to decline and the leading role was taken over by icon painting, the best examples of which are conserved in the Tretyakov Gallery in Moscow (PL. 71), the Russian Museum in Leningrad, and the Museum of History and Art in Novgorod. The colors acquired a great purity, and forms became simplified and more geometrical — that is, flat rather than three-dimensional, with the chief accent placed on silhouette. The typical Novgorod saint made his appearance: a sturdy, somewhat squat figure with sloping shoulders, a round head with small features, and a characteristic beaked nose. A freshness distinguishes these Novgorod

icons, which are painted lightly and freely, as seen in those with the Prophet Elijah and St. George in Moscow (Tretyakov Gall.) and in the Four-part Icon in Leningrad (Mus. of History and Art). During the second half of the 15th century the style of icon painting became more refined and akin to miniatures. In the representation of faces, drapery, and landscape there appeared that repetition of devices that was subsequently to become part of the canonized system of icon painting. But even in this period masterpieces such as the *Praying Citizens of Novgorod*, the *Battle between Suzdal and Novgorod* (Leningrad, Mus. of History and Art), and the *SS. Florus and Laurus* (PL. 69) were created. Toward the end of the 15th century Novgorod icon painting began to lose its former fantasy, brightness, and freshness, and new elements appeared — most notably a preference for more complex themes and greater formality (the two-sided tablets from the Cathedral of St. Sophia). In following this trend Novgorod easel painting entered a critical phase, and during the 16th century nothing was produced comparable to the level of the preceding century.

Novgorod was an important center for crafts and had long been famous for its artistic wares. Books were richly decorated with miniatures and initials in the teratological style which, during the 13th and 14th centuries, spread from the city throughout Russia. The decoration of church plate reached a high standard as evidenced by the silver tabernacles and craters (12th cent.) and a panagiarion (1436) by Master Ivan, all in the Novgorod Cathedral of St. Sophia (IX, PL. 173). The technique of gold foil as practiced in Kiev was also well known to the craftsmen of Novgorod (the St. Basil gates executed in 1336 for the Cathedral of St. Sophia; now preserved in Aleksandrov). Large stone sculpture had no part in the decoration of Novgorod churches, but smaller carved objects (small icons, amulets, carved wooden crosses, etc.) were very common. From the artistic point of view the craft of embroidery attained the highest standard of excellence in the 15th century. The charm of these works lies in the beauty of their colors, the simplicity of their composition, and the fine feeling for fabric. Figures and objects seem to float on the cloth; they are embroidered either in colored thread (the procession of saints in the Tretyakov Gall., Moscow; the Khutinski cloth in Novgorod) or only in gold and silver thread (the cloth of Prince Vasili Vasilevich, 1452, in the Russian Museum in Leningrad and that of Prince Dmitri Shemyaka in the Museum of Novgorod). Traditional Byzantine models underwent a completely original transformation.

PSKOV. *Architecture*. Like Novgorod, Pskov was a free republic in which the artisan class was strong. Among the monuments of early Russian architecture the churches of Pskov are the most austere. They are massive and ponderous, with powerful walls built of local limestone, and have numerous chapels, galleries, and porches; embellishments are reduced to a minimum (pilasters marking off the walls, rampant arches, decorative cornices on the apses and drums). Examples of this type are the Cathedral of the Saviour of the Mirozhski Monastery (ca. 1156), the substantially rebuilt Cathedral of the Ivanovski Monastery (first half of the 13th cent.), the Cathedral of the Snetogorski Monastery (1311), the Church of St. Basil the Great (1413), the Church of SS. Cosmos and Damian "s Primostya" (1463), the Church of the Dormition in Melětovo (1463; FIG. 93), and others of the 16th century with more complex ground plans (e.g., the Church of St. Nicholas "na Usokhe"; 1535). The prevailing type of building was the four-piered, single-domed square church, to which were gradually added numerous chapels, porches, flights of steps, and bell towers; the latter, which were attached directly to one of the walls of the church, consisted of thick stone piers pierced by one or more arched openings in which the bells were suspended. In the larger churches stepped vaults were most widely used (FIG. 93), and in the smaller ones, lowered wall arches. The roofs consisted of either sixteen or eight gables. On the interior the walls and stepped vaults were in most cases simply whitewashed, and against this unpretentious background the colors of the iconostasis glowed all the more brightly. Some merchants' houses in Pskov that have survived from the 17th century are distinguished by the same architectural simplicity.

Painting. Only three groups of Pskov frescoes have survived: in the Cathedral of the Saviour at the Mirozhski Monastery (before 1156), executed by local painters with the assistance of Greek artists; in the Cathedral of the Snetogorski Monastery (1313; PL. 68), remarkable for the harsh expressiveness of the images; and in the Church of the Dormition in Melëtovo (1465), a continuation of the best traditions of 14th-century painting. Restoration work of the last few decades has clearly shown that Pskov had an independent and individual school of icon

mental frieze. The roof design is particularly interesting. The use of stepped vaults necessarily involved the introduction of a base beneath the drum. To conceal this a new row of *zakomari*, facing the corners of the church, was built above the four center *zakomari* that surmounted the walls. This mode of building, anticipated in many respects by the architect of the Church of Paraskeva-Pyatnitsa in Chernigov, continued to evolve during the 16th and 17th centuries.

Painting. In the 14th century the Moscow school of painting became crystallized. At first it was only one of many local schools, but by the middle of the 15th century it began to

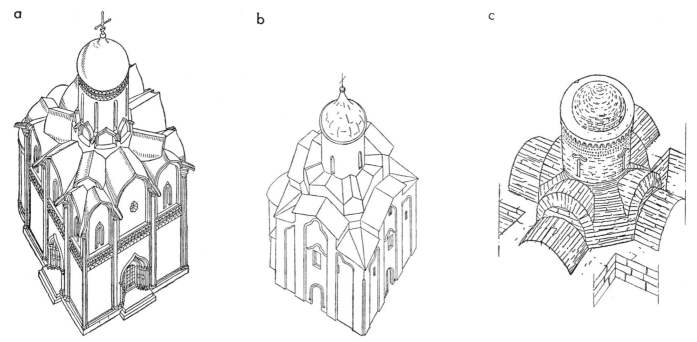

a   b   c

Russian churches, 15th and 16th centuries: (*a*) Zvenigorod, Cathedral of the Dormition, ca. 1400, axonometric projection (*reconstruction by P. Maksimov*); (*b*) Melëtovo, Church of the Dormition, 1463, axonometric projection (*reconstruction by I. Abramëv*); (*c*) Pskov, characteristic construction of stepped vaults, axonometric detail.

painting. The finest Pskov icons belong to the period from the 13th to the 15th century (*St. Nicholas*, the *Prophet Elijah*, the *Virgin's Assembly*, the *Descent into Hell*; all in Moscow, Tretyakov Gall.). Peculiar to the school are the representation of peasant types, the patriarchal feeling, and the naïveté of expression. Dark greens and orange reds, hues derived from local minerals, predominate among the thick, somber colors. The Pskov school of icon painting gradually lost its independent significance after the final annexation of Pskov by Moscow in 1510.

THE PRINCIPALITY OF MOSCOW. *Architecture.* With the swift political rise of Moscow in the 14th century building activity began on a large scale, and the first stone edifices, still submerged in the mass of wooden houses, churches, and fortifications, were erected. At first, Moscow followed the architectural traditions of Vladimir-Suzdal, and white stone (a particular type of limestone), which was later to be replaced by brick, remained the basic building material until the middle of the 15th century. Several churches of the first third of the 15th century have survived (the Cathedral of the Dormition in Zvenigorod, ca. 1400, FIG. 93; the Cathedral of the Nativity of the Savvino-Storozhevski Monastery, also in Zvenigorod, early 15th century; the Trinity Cathedral of the Trinity-Sergius Monastery near Moscow, 1422–23; and the Cathedral of Our Saviour of the Andronikov Monastery, ca. 1427). All these churches, though varying in size, are unmistakably similar in type, with four piers, three apses, and one dome. The façades are divided into three parts by pilasters or pilaster strips and decorated with perspective portals and sometimes by an orna-

play a leading role. Early examples of Moscow painting (the Siiski Gospel miniatures, 1339, Leningrad, Lib. of the Acad. of Sciences; the icons of St. Nicholas and SS. Boris and Gleb, Moscow, Tretyakov Gall.) are still archaic in tone. Muscovites evidently became acquainted with the novelties of Palaeologian art in 1344, when the metropolitan Theognostus, a Greek from Constantinople, invited Byzantine painters to decorate the Church of the Nativity, which was attached to his residence in the Moscow Kremlin. The chronicles state that in 1344 and 1345 Russian masters were also active painting the Cathedral of the Archangel Michael, the Church of the Saviour in the Wood (Spas na Boru), and the Church of St. John Climacus. All these artists, whose work has vanished without leaving a trace, undoubtedly prepared the ground for the brilliant flowering of Moscow painting in the late 14th and the early 15th century, which owed not a little to Theophanes the Greek. The only surviving works of Theophanes are the Deësis in the Cathedral of the Annunciation (1405), remarkable for the beauty of its colors and the harmony of its composition, and two richly illustrated manuscripts from his studio — the Koshka Gospel of 1392 and the Khitrovo Gospel of the late 14th century (Moscow, Lenin Lib., mss. 8654 and 8657). There is no doubt that Theophanes the Greek influenced the greatest painter of ancient Russia — Andrei Rublëv (XII, PL. 338). In Rublëv's works (the icons in the Cathedral of the Annunciation in Moscow and in the Trinity Cathedral in Zagorsk, and the frescoes and iconostasis of the Cathedral of the Dormition in Vladimir) the esthetic ideals of the Moscow school of painting reached their fullest expression (PL. 72).

The names of Theophanes and Rublëv are linked with the

Moscow, Kremlin. *Left*: Planimetric outline with the principal monuments: (*a*) Church of the Nativity; (*b*) Granovitaya Palata (Palace of Facets); (*c*) Church of the Saviour "na Boru"; (*d*) Cathedral of the Dormition and Church of the Ordination; (*e*) Cathedral of the Archangel Michael; (*f*) bell tower of Ivan the Great; (*g*) Cathedral of the Annunciation. *Right*: Historical development: (1) 13th century; (2) first half of the 14th century; (3) second half of the 14th century; (4) 15th and 16th centuries (*from W. Sas-Zalozieoky, Die byzantinische Baukunst in den Balkanländern . . . , Munich, 1955*).

evolution of the classical form of the tall Russian iconostasis, in which the height of the tiered icons was increased to 6 or 9 ft. and their number greatly multiplied; they were at first arranged in four rows (the local saints, the Deësis, the cycle of religious festivals, and the prophets) and later in five or more rows (the patriarchs, the Apostles, the Passion, etc.). Rublëv's school also brought forth a number of talented artists in the sphere of the applied arts, particularly in embroidery, which attained a high artistic level (PL. 70).

THE CENTRALIZED STATE OF RUSSIA (CA. 1450–17th CENT.). *Architecture*. Under Grand Duke Ivan III (r. 1462–1505) and Vasili (Basil) III (r. 1505–33) the small principality of Moscow became a powerful centralized state. Ivan III called to Moscow the most gifted architects from various Russian cities and invited Lombard and Venetian artists from Italy in order to transform the Kremlin into a residence worthy of the tsar of Russia (see RENAISSANCE). Marco Ruffo and the Milanese Pietro Solari, who was both an architect and an engineer, rebuilt and extended the fortifications of the Kremlin (PL. 60); the Bolognese Aristotele Fioravanti built the Cathedral of the Dormition (1474–79; PL. 58). Between 1484 and 1489 architects from Pskov radically reconstructed the Cathedral of the Annunciation, and during the same period (1487–89) Ruffo and Solari built the Granovitaya Palata (Palace of Facets). In 1499 the Milanese architect Aloisio da Carcano replaced the old wooden palace with a new one of stone. Between 1505 and 1509 another Italian, Aloisio (Alevisio Novi) from Venice, rebuilt the Cathedral of the Archangel Michael (PL. 58). Transported to the soil of Moscow, the forms and building techniques of Italian Renaissance architecture underwent many substantial changes. The Moscow Kremlin, situated on a hill shaped like an irregular triangle, retained its free and picturesque ground plan, which had nothing in common with the strictly geometrical plans of the Italian *castelli*. In the building of the Kremlin churches the Italian architects had to make allowances for local architectural traditions, at least in respect to ground plan and façade decoration. They chose the solution of incorporating single elements of North Italian Renaissance ornamentation into the traditional scheme of Russian 16th-century architecture; however, Italian building techniques (the combination of brick with white stone, thicker mortar, iron rafters, and the use of compasses, of set squares, and of a variety of lifting devices) were widely used by Russian architects.

Wood remained the favorite building material in Russia even after the coming of the Italian architects. Unfortunately not a single wooden building erected before the late 14th century has survived. Already in the 10th and 11th centuries wooden churches were remarkable for their variety [small churches of simple rectangular shape with pitched roofs, tower-shaped churches with tent-shaped (*shater*) roofs, churches with complex ground plans and many domes, similar to St. Sophia in Novgorod (PL. 56) and others]. Later, the ground plans and general designs of wooden churches became increasingly complex; spaces delimited by four and eight sides placed one above the other accentuated the upward movement, the number of domes increased, and barrel vaulting and roofing was widely used (FIG. 95). The best examples of 16th- and 17th-century wooden architecture survive in northern Russia.

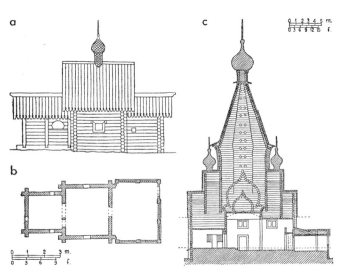

Russian wooden churches: (*a, b*) Olonets, Muromski Monastery, St. Lazarus, end of 14th century, reconstruction of elevation and ground plan; (*c*) Una, St. Clement, 1501, axial section.

During the 16th century the rapid rise of the centralized state gradually caused local schools of architecture to lose importance, and Moscow resolutely set the style. The most original form of 16th-century stone architecture was the church with a *shater* (tent or pyramid) roof, which can be traced back to the models of wooden architecture. The long series of these churches was initiated with the Church of the Ascension near Kolomenskoe (1530–32), built by Vasili III to celebrate the birth of his son, who became Ivan the Terrible. The Church of St. John the Baptist in Dyakovo (1553–54) consists of five octagonal towers topped by helmet-shaped domes. The Cathedral of St. Basil the Blessed in Moscow (1554–60; PL. 59) unites as many as nine tower-shaped churches, the central one topped by a *shater* roof. Given such a design, the interior space was inevitably divided into small cell-like units that were practically sealed off from each other. Enormous possibilities were opened up for exterior decoration and ornamentation, and brightly colored angular pediments, machicolations, *kokoshniki*, rosettes, and little panels appear in the most unexpected combinations, always with an eye to purely decorative values.

Sixteenth-century architecture also included monumental five-domed cathedrals, such as those of Rostov Veliki, Kalyazin (1521–23), the Novodevichi Monastery in Moscow (1524), Vologda (1568–70), and the Trinity-Sergius Monastery (1554–85). Small single-domed churches with several rows of *kokoshnik* gables were also built (Cathedral of the Donskoi Monastery in Moscow, 1593). Finally, town dwellers living on the same street or in the same neighborhood commissioned architects to build small churches with unpretentious façades and intimate interiors, such as the Church of the Conception of St. Anne in Zaryade, Moscow (1478–93), and the Church of St. Nicholas in Myasniki (mid-16th cent.). In the monasteries a special place was occupied by the refectories, which were often richly decorated, as exemplified by the refectory of the Trinity Monastery in Kalyazin (1525–30).

The building of fortifications was the most common form of construction in the 16th century. Under the threat of invasion by the Germans and Swedes, the systems of fortification in the territories of Novgorod and Pskov (Ladoga, Yam, and Orekhov) were radically altered and in the case of Ivangorod completed with a fortress. Strong towers were erected along the perimeter of the walls. Towns were also fortified, and many of them owe their architectural image entirely to these new constructions (Nizhni Novgorod, Kolomna, Serpukhov, Tula, Zaraisk, Sviyazhsk, Smolensk, and others). A number of monasteries were turned into auxiliary forts and surrounded by strong walls with rectangular and round towers [the Simonov Monastery in Moscow, the Trinity-Sergius Monastery in Zagorsk, the Pafnutiev-Borovski Monastery, the Kirillovski Monastery on Lake Siversk, the Solovetski Monastery on the Beloe Ozero (White Lake), and others].

Painting. In the second half of the 15th century the Moscow school of painting produced an outstanding artist, Dionysius (ca. 1440 – ca. 1505), who worked in the Cathedral of the Dormition in Moscow (1481) and in various monasteries. Only the paintings in the Pokhvalski Chapel of the Cathedral of the Dormition and those in the Church of the Virgin in the Therapont Monastery (1500–02) have survived. Usually Dionysius did not work alone, but with his entire studio, to which his sons Theodosius and Vladimir also belonged. The many fine icons produced in Dionysius' studio maintain for the most part the splendor of Rublëv's art. However, new elements also appeared in Dionysius' work: the faces of his saints were psychologically less expressive than those by earlier masters; his palette was less brilliant, and a fondness for the purely decorative emerged. Dionysius and the artists of his circle were interested in a more secular interpretation of the religious image, loved everything that was graceful and delicate, and set the highest value on decorative principles. At the same time their work reveals an increasing conformity and more standardized forms.

After the death of Dionysius painting declined. The state and church rigidly regulated the subject matter of icons and frescoes; complex and obscure symbolic images multiplied, didactic tendencies became exaggerated, the narration of sacred events lost its vividness, and colors that had once been as bright as precious stones grew dim and lost their splendor. These changes can be clearly seen in the frescoes of the Cathedral of the Annunciation in Moscow (1508), the Cathedral of the Dormition of the Sviyazhski Monastery (1561), and the Cathedral of the Spasski Monastery in Yaroslavl (1564), as well as in the chief easel paintings of the Moscow school (*The Vision of St. Eulogius* in the Russian Mus., Leningrad; *The Church Militant* in the Tretyakov Gall., Moscow; the famous four-part icon in the Cathedral of the Annunciation in Moscow, and many others). Icons of a similar style were also created in Novgorod (PL. 69), Pskov, and Yaroslavl.

Richly illustrated manuscripts executed at the court of Macarius, metropolitan of the Novgorod eparchy from 1526 to 1542, were widely diffused (the *Life of Nifont*, the *Christian Topography* by Cosmas Indicopleustes; Moscow, Historical Mus., mss. 340 and Patr. 987). Moscow manuscripts included the Gospel of Theodosius (1507; Leningrad, State Lib., Pogodinski ms. 133) and a collection of illuminated chronicles. Realistic elements that undermined the traditional schemes of icon painting made their way into miniature art, particularly when secular subjects were represented. Paper, which had supplanted parchment, contributed to bringing the miniature nearer to engraving. [The first printed Russian books (1550s and 1560s) were produced by an anonymous Moscow printing press and by the press of Ivan Fëdorov, whose activity in the capital encountered the opposition of conservative circles, forcing him to move to Lvov, where he died in 1583.]

At the end of the 16th and the beginning of the 17th century a new trend emerged in Moscow icon painting that produced many works of high quality. These have been attributed to the "Stroganov school," which reflected the tastes of the Stroganovs, rich patrons of the arts and possessors of vast

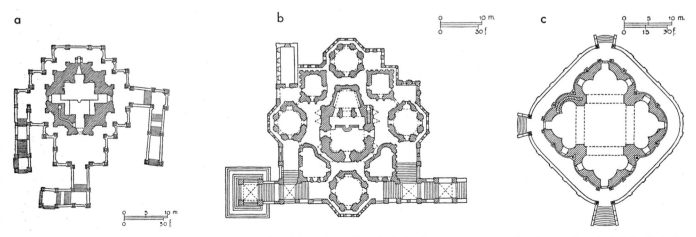

Russian churches, 16th and 17th centuries, ground plans: (*a*) Kolomenskoe, Church of the Ascension, 1530–32; (*b*) Moscow, Cathedral of St. Basil the Blessed, 1554–60; (*c*) Ubory, Church of the Saviour, 1694–97.

estates in the north of the country. Actually the Stroganovs were not the only patrons of the Moscow artists who were members of the tsar's icon-painting workshop (Procopi Chirin, Istoma Savvin, Nazari Savvin). The icons of this school were usually small in size and characterized by the painstaking draftsmanship typical of miniature painting (XI, PL. 361). Their muted color range with predominating golden-brown shades also included an abundant use of gold and silver, applied in gossamer lines that harmonized with the unearthly, elongated fragility of the figures and the fairy-tale quality of the landscapes. In the virtuoso calligraphy of the "Stroganov icons," the painters' fascination with formal skill, which often obscured the religious content of the icon, is clearly evident. In many respects this was an anticipation of the growth of the secular tendencies that were to be so typical of Russian 17th-century art.

Sculpture. In the 16th century wood continued to be the chief material for sculpture. Statues, which were regarded with extreme hostility by the Orthodox clergy, were rare. Nor did high relief, introduced in the 1460s by V. D. Ermolin, become widespread. Bas-relief prevailed with many-figured compositions similar in style to the contemporary icons (the tsar's throne in the Moscow Cathedral of the Dormition, 1551; the shrine of Zosima Solovetski, 1566, now in the Tretyakov Gall., Moscow). "Holy doors" were often decorated with carving in fine patterns and complex ornamentation. The artist's talent for sculpture was best expressed in the minor sculptural arts: small icons, folding traveling icons, and cross-framed images of the Virgin, carved of wood, stone, or bone (the Kilikievski cross in Vologda; an evangelist carved of bone, PL. 73; and others). Among wood carvers, Master Ambrose (Amvrosi, ca. 1430–ca. 1494), who worked in the Trinity Monastery, enjoyed particular fame. His small folding icons and crosses were carved of various kinds of wood in a remarkably free manner, so that the surface of the relief seemed soft and almost vibrant. In later wooden articles this freedom of execution was unfortunately lost and was replaced by a more pedestrian style of carving.

Minor arts. The 16th and 17th centuries marked the high point of early Russian minor arts. Life at court, which had become increasingly ceremonious, with a magnificence that astounded all foreigners, demanded a setting of corresponding pomp and luxury. At the end of the 15th century a special building for the safekeeping of valuables was erected — the so-called "Kazënni dvor." The Hall of Arms, or Armory Palace (Oruzheinaya Palata), for the production and custody of valuable weapons was established in the 16th century (not later than 1547). Soon afterward the Hall of Silver was attached to it, and somewhat later the Hall of Gold was added. Craftsmen from every corner of Russia and from Eastern and Western countries were employed in the Kremlin workshops. Superb objects of gold and silver were executed (covers for icons and books, church vessels, censers, tabernacles, thrones, ewers, loving cups, etc.). Niello, pale-blue enamels, precious stones (sapphires, emeralds, rubies), and the most delicate filigree were used to decorate them. Highly qualified craftsmen also worked in Novgorod, Pskov, Solvychegodsk, Vologda, and other towns, creating everyday articles that were simpler but nevertheless had a charm of their own.

Embroidery still flourished, with the best examples dating from the late 14th and the 15th century. They are characterized by restrained composition, economy of design, fine fabrics, and a purity and intensity of color achieved by the use of silk thread (the *pelena* of ca. 1389, PL. 70; the cloth of the Princess Agrafena Constantinovna, 1409–25, Moscow, Historical Mus.; and the veil bearing the portrait of Sergei Radonezhski in the museum at Zagorsk, near Moscow). Many exquisite embroideries were also created at the end of the 15th and the beginning of the 16th century (especially the cloths of 1498 and 1499 that are linked with the name of Sophia Palaeologus, the wife of Ivan the Great). Later, the simple satin stitching was gradually replaced by embroidery with heavy gold and silver thread. Pieces of patterned material, pearls, and precious stones began to be sewn onto the fabric; the soft silk threads became stiff when combined with metallic ones and could no longer be made to pass through the cloth; they had to be stretched in rows on the surface of the material and tacked down with small stitches in colored silk thread, making the cloth heavy and less supple. Compositions with single full-length figures became common, as well as those with a large image in the center and smaller roundels surrounding it. Cloths with the traditional representation of the Entombment were still produced in large numbers. The best embroideries of the mid-16th century came from the workshops of Tsaritsa Anastasia Romanovna and Princess Ephrosenia Staritskaya (wife of the pretender to the throne Andrei Staritski). At the end of the 16th and the beginning of the 17th century the chief commissioners of embroidered cloths were Boris Godunov and the Stroganov family. The distinguishing features of the "Godunov school" of embroidery were an ostentatious richness, an abundance of pearls and precious stones, and a great complexity of design. The works produced by the "Stroganov school" were less pretentious and more restrained in style. Pearls were rarely employed, simple stitching predominated, and color, including gold, was provided by multicolored silk thread.

THE CLOSING PHASE OF EARLY RUSSIAN ART. *Architecture.* The 17th century was a closing phase in the history of early Russian art, and the premises of the new secular culture that took definitive shape after the reforms of Peter the Great began to be established. There was an advance in the economic status of merchants and craftsmen, who more and more frequently became the clients of architects and painters, leading inevitably to a more realistic and secular trend in art, particularly in architecture. But conservative public authorities continued to wield great power in the centralized state and succeeded in holding back overdue reforms. The patriarch Nikon (1605–81), for example, took a firm stand against the secularization of architecture and demanded a return to the former severity of church buildings. By the end of the 17th century, however, the secularization of architecture had prevailed.

After the expulsion of the Swedes and Poles building activity began on a large scale. The names of famous architects (Bazhen Ogurtsov, Osip and Dmitri Startsev, Averki Mokeiev, Pavel Potekhin, Yakov Bukhvostov, and others) appear in written records. An improved building technique made it possible to build churches and palaces more rapidly. Brick had already acquired standard measurements by the end of the 16th century; shaped brick, iron clamps, and glass were also in use. Apart from Moscow, which set the tone, Yaroslavl, Rostov, Ryazan, and Suzdal also had schools of their own.

The characteristics of 17th-century architecture emerged clearly between 1625 and 1650. Architectural design lost the severity typical of earlier church building. Chapels of various shapes and sizes were added to the north and south of the main body of the church; a low refectory was attached to the west wall, the entrance to which usually led through a high, *shater*-crowned bell tower. Little porches, covered galleries, and access stairs completed these annexes, whose varied roofs made the silhouette of the church seem even more fanciful. The interior was usually divided into self-contained cell-like chambers covered by barrel or domical vaulting. In view of such a complex compartmentalization of interior space, the architect's interest was concentrated more on the adornment of the façades. These were of red brick, decorated with ornamental motifs of white stone and colored tiles mounted in the wall. Frescoes were often added to increase the polychrome effect.

The most interesting architectural designs of the period were realized in Moscow. Such churches as the Nativity of the Virgin in Putinki (1649–52), the Trinity in Nikitniki (1628–53), St. Nicholas on the Bersenevka (1656), the Trinity in Ostankino (PL. 60), and St. Nicholas in Khamovniki (1679) offer an extremely varied selection of decorative motifs in the most unexpected combinations. A great deal of building work was carried out in the Kremlin, where superstructures were added to most of the towers (PL. 60). At the same time, old palaces were enlarged and new ones were built: the Terem Palace (1635–36), the Palace of the Patriarchs (1643–55), and the Land

Office (1683). At Kolomenskoe, near Moscow, a group of wooden buildings was erected for the tsar's summer residence (1667–81; destroyed in 1768). Of the brick residences built in Moscow hardly anything remains.

The constructions sponsored by the patriarch Nikon occupy a special place in 17th-century architecture. In his struggle against the secular powers the patriarch endeavored to outdo the tsar in the scope of his building activity. At the same time he was oriented toward the most traditional types of 16th-century architecture (e.g., the five-domed cathedral). Between 1656 and 1658, Averki Mokeiev built the Iverski Monastery in Valdai to the patriarch's order, and a little later (1660) the Monastery of the Cross on the Island Kii. But the most important of Nikon's works was the magnificent Cathedral in the Monastery of the New Jerusalem (mid-17th cent.; destroyed during World War II), which Nikon intended to be a copy of the Church of the Holy Sepulcher in Jerusalem. In the hands of the Russian architects, however, the prototype underwent such substantial alterations that ultimately the Cathedral had much in common with the most richly ornamented churches of the 17th century.

Much building was carried out in other cities. In Rostov the metropolitan Jonah Sysoevich erected a magnificent residence for himself (known as the Rostov Kremlin), which is one of the most interesting and well-preserved architectural ensembles of the 17th century. In Yaroslavl the local merchants built a series of fine churches, often surpassing those of Moscow in size (St. Elias the Prophet, 1647–50; St. John Chrysostom in Korovniki, 1649–54; St. Nicholas Mokry, 1665–72; St. John the Baptist in Tolchkovo, 1671–88; and others). The building of monasteries also received a new impetus (the Monastery of SS. Boris and Gleb near Rostov, the Iosifo-Volokolamsk Monastery, the Spasski Monastery in Suzdal, the "new town" of the Kirillo-Belozerski Monastery, and others). Some of the towers and refectories of these monasteries are among the masterpieces of early Russian architecture.

The last flowering of medieval Russian architecture occurred at the end of the 17th century with the phase that has been somewhat inaccurately designated "Moscow baroque." This term is purely conventional, since the decorative motifs of baroque art, brought to Russia via the Ukraine and White Russia, underwent such radical reworking that they acquired a quite different meaning from the one Western masters had given them. Even at this stage Russian architects considered an order not as the expression of a specific structural logic, dictated by the mutual relations of supporting and supported parts, but as an element of decoration, part and parcel of the *uzorechie*, or ornateness, which they valued so highly.

The architects of the end of the 17th century strove to create more spacious designs; ground plans provided for a freer treatment of interior space, which became larger and full of light. As before, the chief emphasis was placed on the exterior of the building and its superabundant decoration. Portals, window frames, half columns, columns, pilasters, rosettes, conchs, and purely decorative motifs were usually executed in white stone, which was sharply set off by the pinkish-red background of the brick walls. All these façade decorations achieved a variety never seen before and were combined in a most unexpected and capricious manner. Classic examples of this style are the Church of the Intercession (Pokros) at Fili (1690–93); the churches of the Saviour at Ubory (1694–97; PL. 60) and the Trinity at Troitskoe-Lykovo (end of 17th cent.), both of which were built by Yakov Bukhvostov; and the bell tower (1689) and the refectory (1686–92) of the Novodevichi Monastery in Moscow. Although such famous 18th-century architects as Prince D. V. Ukhtomski, Bartolomeo Rastrelli (1700–71), and Vasili Ivanovich Bazhenov (1737–99) at times drew inspiration from this architecture, on the whole it represented to them an outdated phase. In their estimation the "Moscow baroque" was indistinguishable from the image of pre-Petrovian Russia and the *uzorechie* that was favored by early Russian masters.

Painting. The transitional character of 17th-century art emerged most clearly in painting, where the rapid rise of realistic tendencies undermined the traditional iconographic system. All 17th-century painting was marked by this conflict and compromise, and one cannot search for the perfection of artistic achievement that distinguished the work of Theophanes the Greek, Rublëv, or Dionysius. Nevertheless, this style of painting is of great interest as a purely historical phase.

In the frescoes of the first half of the 17th century (the Cathedral of the Dormition in Moscow, 1642–43, and the Kniaginin Monastery in Vladimir, 1647–48) the increasing complexity of the iconographic content and the intensification of the moralistic, didactic elements are immediately apparent. The frescoes, usually executed by several artists' guilds numbering from 15 to 30 artists each, suffered from a breakdown of the decorative style and lacked monumentality. In easel painting the traditions of the "Stroganov school" were maintained, though they gradually declined and lost their refinement. The high iconostasis, made up of many icons, continued to be made. The colors became more muted, with oranges and pinks predominating in conjunction with warm olive greens.

By the middle of the 17th century the building of churches became so widespread that the activity of the tsar's workshops, which employed painters, miniaturists, and many other artists, had to be expanded. An independent icon workshop had already existed in the Kremlin, with its separate building, the Hall of Icon Painting (first mentioned in 1621). In the 1640s it was merged with the Hall of Arms, which thereafter became an extremely important artistic center — in a sense, a forerunner of the Academy of Fine Arts. The Hall of Arms was most active from the 1650s to the 1670s, when it was headed by the enlightened Khitrovo. Artists came to the Hall of Arms not only from Moscow but also from the provinces (Kostroma, Yaroslavl, Vologda, Pakov, Novgorod, Nizhni Novgorod, etc.) and from other countries (Johann Detterson and Daniel Vuchters from Holland, Stefan Loputski from Poland, the German Peter Engels, and others).

The central figure among these painters was Simon Ushakov (1626–86). In his work he introduced many new features, such as the chiaroscuro modeling of faces, a greater use of portraiture in icons, and architectural backgrounds rendered according to the laws of perspective (PL. 69) — all inspired by Western engravings and paintings. His icons, with their pale, smoky tones, were painted with unusual care, but this did not save them from oversweetness and an undisguised incursion of eclecticism. Ushakov was unable to arrive at an organic synthesis of the old and the new, and he lacked the authority to make a clean break with the centuries-old traditions of icon painting. Nevertheless, his work provoked the harsh opposition of the zealots of tradition (including the famous archpriest Avvakum). Deploring the loss of spiritual values in icon painting, they called on painters to work according to old "models" and resolutely condemned everything marked by the new spirit, which they naïvely qualified as "nemetchina," or "Germanicism." However, they failed to halt the growth of realistic trends, all the more so because realism had been given a well-developed theoretical grounding in the treatises of Ushakov and the icon painter Josif Vladimirov (active 1642–64).

During the last third of the 17th century realistic elements became especially widespread in icons and frescoes. Their chief sources were Western European engravings and, above all, the richly illustrated *Theatrum Biblicum* by J. Piscator (1674). From this book Russian artists borrowed figures, realistic details, and architectural backgrounds (PL. 73) and introduced them into their own compositions, even though they were still based on the old two-dimensional principle. While for Renaissance artists the new realism was the fruit of a lengthy and intensive study of nature, for Russian painters of the 17th century it was a marginal and alien phenomenon. The distinguishing features of late-17th-century painting were its lack of stylistic unity and its many contradictory tendencies.

Outstanding among Moscow wall paintings are the frescoes in the Cathedral of the Archangel Michael (1652–66), which was the burial place of the princes and tsars of the Moscow principality. Hence the lowest tier of the iconostasis consists of their portraits, while the deeds of their patron, the Archangel

Michael, appear on the south and north walls. The frescoes in the Church of the Trinity in Nikitniki (1652–53), commissioned by a wealthy merchant family, are different in style. They are rich in entertaining genre details, particularly in the scenes from the lives of the Apostles. The number of episodes represented is so great that the spectator immediately loses his bearings, involuntarily passing from the particular to the general, and views the whole composition as a gigantic colored carpet entirely covering the walls and vaulting. This "carpet" concept is even more strikingly adopted in a group of Yaroslavl frescoes, all of which overflow with shrewdly observed realistic details that must have made a strong impression on the rich merchants who commissioned them. But as a general rule the compositions were overladen and congested, ornamental interweaving lines were present everywhere, buildings and interiors depicted according to the laws of perspective alternated in the most arbitrary fashion with two-dimensional forms, and color schemes were based on the repetition of patches of pale blues, golden yellows, and pinks. In the 1670s Yaroslavl masters, together with those of Kostroma and Vologda, painted the frescoes of the churches belonging to the Rostov Kremlin. Between the 1670s and 1690s large-scale fresco cycles were also executed in Romanovo-Borisoglebsk (Cathedral of the Resurrection), Kostroma (Ipatevski Monastery), Vologda (Cathedral of St. Sophia), and in a number of other provincial towns. These frescoes, varying in style from the freer to the more severe, have in common their craftsmanlike technique. They were produced by numerous painters' guilds for whom the illustrative aspect was more important than the artistic one.

The easel painting of the last third of the 17th century is far more interesting. The icons of the Moscow school by Nikita Pavlovets (d. 1677) and Fëdor Zubov (d. 1689) are remarkable for their unusual delicacy of design and a jeweler's care in the elaboration of decorative detail. A considerable number of fine icons were painted by Yaroslavl artists, who liked to surround the large central figure of the saint with episodes from his life, which were depicted in roundels or in picturesque disorder against the landscape and architectural scenery of the background. So much was new and diverting in these miniature scenes that these icons began to resemble secular pictures. This process is still more evident in portraits (the so-called "parsuny"), which to a great extent maintained the traditional icon composition, but also anticipated 18th-century portrait painting. The influence of realism was just as strong in 17th-century miniatures and engravings.

Sculpture. Similar changes can be traced in 17th-century sculpture. Wood remained the chief material, but carving became richer, more rounded, and frequently approached the depth of high relief. In ornamentation Western baroque motifs imported from the Ukraine and White Russia were widely used and skillfully worked into the traditional ancient Russian patterns. Wood carvers and carpenters came to work in Moscow in a Hall of Carving and Carpentry that was directed by the painters of the Hall of Arms. The larger monasteries also had their own workshops, in which carved ciboria, imperial and patriarchal thrones, doors, icon cases, small images, crosses, and traveling icons were made. Wood carving was also widely used in residential building for door casings, window frames, cornices, pillars for porches and balconies, and gate posts. In the carved many-tiered iconostasis Russian wood carvers achieved the highest perfection. In the icons of the second half of the 17th century the size of the figures, arrayed in sumptuous garments lined with gold, was increased, and backgrounds in true perspective with realistic landscapes and buildings made their appearance. The flat wood strips that had been used to support the row of icons in iconostases from the 15th to the middle of the 17th century were no longer sufficient for the purpose and were replaced by lavishly carved supports that provided a fitting frame for the new-style icons. Twisted columns were entwined with vines bearing luxuriant foliage and bunches of grapes; icon frames were decorated with large, heavy volutes and the most intricate patterns of interwoven flowers, leaves, fruit, and berries, which were often designed

with openwork so that this rich ornamentation made an effect when viewed against the light. As carving was usually covered with a thick layer of gold it often gave the impression of being cast in metal. Iconostases of this style were created in large numbers during the last third of the 17th century (in the Smolensk Cathedral of the Novodevichi Monastery in Moscow, 1683–85; the Church of the Transfiguration of the same monastery, 1688; the Cathedral of the Donskoi Monastery in Moscow, 1693–99; and many others).

Toward the end of the 17th and the beginning of the 18th century the tendency toward high relief and sculpture in the round became increasingly marked. Wooden tomb covers were decorated with statues of the deceased almost fully in the round; crucifixes and figures of saints and holy elders (*startsy*) were sculptured in wood. Particularly interesting is the wooden sculpture of the Perm region, where the traditions of pagan sculpture were still firmly rooted. Statues were usually colored. Although the canons of icon painting were respected in the design of the figures, the faces are remarkable for their lifelike quality and the expression of peasant strength.

The aspiration of Russian artists toward sculpture in the round, which they had shunned for centuries under ecclesiastical pressure, can be discerned also in metal objects. The figure of the Tsarevich Dmitri on the silver lid of his tomb in the Cathedral of the Archangel Michael in Moscow (1630) is in low relief, but the head is practically in the round. In a fine silver icon of the Annunciation, the upper parts of the figures are almost freestanding and are even attached separately to the background (PL. 73). These same tendencies are also evident in cast-copper objects (chandeliers, masks, and lions' heads).

Minor arts. This period marks the highest achievement in the field of the early Russian minor arts. The chief centers for the execution of objects made of gold, silver, and precious stones continued to be the silver and gold workshops in the Moscow Kremlin. The patriarchal court also had its hall of gold. The larger monasteries possessed their own workshops and employed qualified craftsmen. In addition, many fine silver articles were made in Novgorod, Pskov, Yaroslavl, Nizhni Novgorod, Vologda, Solvychegodsk, Veliki Ustyug, and other provincial towns. At the beginning of the 17th century plant and flower motifs were still highly stylized, but by the second half of the century they had become richer and more realistic in character. Among the decorative motifs single flowers and fruit and bunches of flowers, fruit, and berries appeared more and more frequently. The extensive use of precious stones and enamel gave the coloring of both liturgical and secular objects a brightness and splendor previously unknown.

The most perfect objects were produced in the tsar's workshops, in which visiting artists were also employed (for the most part Greek jewelers from Constantinople). Here precious icon covers, massive bookbindings, ewers, loving cups (PL. 73), goblets, cups, and glasses were made and decorated with rich carving or niello. Images of people, animals, birds, sibyls, and Biblical scenes, which closely resembled illustrated manuscripts, appeared on silver vessels during the second half of the 17th century; decoration was executed in higher relief; and gold and silver articles were studded with precious stones, at times in entire bands and patterns. These stones were chiefly emeralds, rubies, almandines, and diamonds of Greek cut, replacing the sapphires preferred by the 16th century. Enamel, predominantly emerald green in color, was also widely employed. In the last quarter of the 17th century, painting on the enamel decorating the metal plaques on icon covers and crosses first appeared in Russia. One of the most extraordinary samples of 17th-century applied art is the full-dress apparel of Tsar Michael Fëdorovich, consisting of the tsar's crown, scepter, orb, bow sheath, and quiver. Executed by foreign and Russian artists in 1627–28, it was intended for triumphal public processions and receptions. The combination of gold, precious stones, and enamel created a fairy-tale splendor that enhanced the magnificence and pomp of the tsar's attire.

In the 17th century embroidery developed in the same

direction as icon painting, which was gradually obscured by sumptuous gold and silver frames (*rizy*). In embroidery, colored silks of soft shades were replaced by heavy gold and silver threads that entirely covered backgrounds and garments. Only faces and hands were embroidered in silk thread. The decorative motifs and the figures were outlined with pearls, a technique that added even greater weight to the already heavy cloth. The finest embroideries were produced by the tsarina's workshop, in which more than 80 embroideresses worked from cartoons prepared by designers in the gold and silver workshops. The large gold-embroidered chalice veils and altar cloths executed in workshops founded by the Stroganovs were also famous. Relief embroidery was attained in many of these works by the insertion of precious stones. A special place was occupied by decorative embroidery in which the human figure was completely excluded. Here, too, pearls were abundantly used, and gold and silver disks decorated with plant or geometric decoration in niello, relief, or enamel were applied to the cloth. By the end of the century embroidery had acquired even higher relief, becoming similar to chased metal, and thus lost its special quality and a large part of its esthetic appeal.

Although religious art continued to exist in Russia in the 18th and 19th centuries it had started to decline before the time of Peter the Great. It became the art of pale and lifeless epigoni, who later merged with the artists of the academic school. The leading role passed to secular art. At the beginning of the 18th century, when this transition was completed, early Russian artistic culture came to a close.

Victor LASAREFF

Other centers of Slavic art cannot be discussed at length but are treated in the articles pertaining to the various geographical areas (CZECHOSLOVAKIA; POLAND; UNION OF SOVIET SOCIALIST REPUBLICS; and YUGOSLAVIA). Needless to say the art of the regions bordering on Slavic countries (especially Greece and Romania) were influenced by Slavic and Byzantine currents (PL. 74); on the other hand, many Slavic areas received some artistic orientation from Western European countries (PL. 76; see also BAROQUE ART; GOTHIC ART; RENAISSANCE; ROMANESQUE ART).

* *

BIBLIOG. *General*: A. Gilferding, Istoriya baltiiskikh slavyan (History of the Baltic Slavs), 3 vols., Moscow, 1855; L. Niederle, Slovanské starožitnosti (Slavic Antiquity), 4 vols., Prague, 1906–25; V. Gorodcov, Dakosarmatskie religioznye elementy v russkom narodnom tvorchestve (Religious Daco-Sarmatian Elements in Russian Folk Art), Trudy Gosudarstvennogo Istoricheskogo Museya, I, 1926, pp. 7–36; J. Strzygowski, Die altslavische Kunst, Augsburg, 1929; R. Popov, Kultura i zhivot na predistoricheskiia chovek v Balgariya, II, Metalna epokha (Culture and Life of Prehistoric Man in Bulgaria, II, Age of Metal), Sofia, 1930; R. J. Šafařík, Slovanské starožitnosti (Slavic Antiquity), Prague, 1937; A. Artsikhovskii, Vyedenie v archeologiyu (Introduction to Archaeology), Moscow, 1947; N. N. Voronin, M. K. Karger, and M. A. Tikhanova, eds., Istoriya kultury drevnei Rusi (History of Culture of Ancient Russia), 2 vols., Moscow, Leningrad, 1948–51; J. Kostrzewski, Kultura prapolska (Pre-Polish Culture), 2d ed., Poznán, 1949; M. Garašanin and G. Kovačević, Pregled materijalne kulture Južnih Slovena (Material Culture of the Southern Slavs), Belgrade, 1950; J. Korošec, Uvod v materijalno kulturo Slovenskov zgodnjega srednjega veka (Introduction to the Material Culture of the Slavs in the High Middle Ages), Ljubljana, 1952; I. Grabar, V. Lasareff, and V. Kemenov, eds., Istoriya russkogo iskusstva (History of Russian Art), I, Moscow, 1953, pp. 39–91; L. Niederle, Rukovět slovanskych starožitnosti (Manual of Slavic Antiquity), Prague, 1953; P. Tretyakov, Vostochno-slavyanskie plemena (Eastern Slavic Tribes), Moscow, 1953; J. Kostrzewski, Wielkopolska w pradziejach (Great Poland in Prehistory), 3d ed., Warsaw, 1955; W. Sas-Zaloziecky, Die byzantinische Baukunst in den Balkanländern, Munich, 1955; P. N. Tretyakov and A. A. Mongait, eds., Ocherki istorii SSSR: Pervobytno-obshchinnyi stroi i drevneishie gosudarstva na territorii SSSR (Outline History of the USSR: The Earliest Communes and the Oldest States in the Territory of the USSR), Moscow, 1956; N. Mavrodinov, Starobalgarskoto iskustvo (Ancient Bulgarian Art), Sofia, 1959; J. Neustupný, Pravěk Československa (Prehistory of Czechoslovakia), Prague, 1960; W. Molé, Sztuka Slowian południowych (Art of the Southern Slavs), Wrocław, 1962; O. Bihalji-Merin, Primitive Artists of Yugoslavia, New York, Toronto, London, 1964.

Bulgaria. K. Mijatev, Bǎlgarskoto jzkustvo prez IX i X vek (Bulgarian Art from the 9th to the 10th Century), in Bǎlgarija v 1000 godini, pp. 139–82; B. Filov, Early Bulgarian Art, Bern, 1919; V. Ivanova, Eglises et monastères en pays bulgare (IV–XII siècle), Godinšk na Narodnija Muzei, 1926, pp. 429–582; A. Grabar, La peinture religieuse en Bulgarie, Paris, 1928; N. Mavrodinov, L'église à nef unique et l'église cruciforme en pays bulgare jusqu'à la fin du XIVᵉ siècle, Sofia, 1931; B. Filov, Geschichte der altbulga-
rischen Kunst, Berlin, 1932; K. Mijatev, L'église ronde de Preslav, Sofia, 1932; B. Filov, Geschichte der neueren bulgarischen Kunst, Berlin, 1933; I. Akrabova, La céramique decorative de Touzlalak à Patleina, Sofia, 1949, pp. 101–28; Istoria na Bǎlgarija (History of Bulgaria), I, Sofia, 1954; I. Akrabova, Un atelier de céramique peinte au sud de l'église ronde à Preslav, B. de l'Inst. Archéologique Bulgare, XX, 1955, pp. 485–510 (in Bulgarian); N. Mavrodinov, Bizantiskata architektura (Byzantine Architecture), Sofia, 1955; Madarskijat Konnik (The Knight of Madara), Sofia, 1956; S. Georgieva and V. Velkov, Bibliografija na bǎlgarskata arheologija 1879–1955 (Bibliography of Bulgarian Archaeology), Sofia, 1957; V. Mavrodinova, Veliki Preslav (The Great Preslav), Archeologicheski otkritia v Bǎlgarija, 1957, pp. 161–95.

Serbia. *a. General*: M. Kašanin, L'art yougoslave dès origines à nos jours, Belgrade, 1939; V. Petković, Pregled crkvenih spomenika kroz povesnicu srpskog naroda (Religious Monuments in the History of the Serbian People), Srpska Akademija Nauka, special no., CLVII, 1950.
b. Architecture: V. Petković, Spasova crkva u Žiči (Church of the Ascension in Žiča), Belgrade, 1911; G. Millet, L'ancient art serbe. Les églises, Paris, 1919; V. Petković, Ravanica, Belgrade, 1922; L. Mirković and Ž. Tatić, Markov manastir (Monastery of Marko), Belgrade, 1925; L. Mirković, Ž. Tatić, Manastir Kalenić (Monastery of Kalenić), Belgrade, 1926; N. L. Okunev, Stolpy sv. Georgia (Church of St. George), Seminarium Kondakovianum, I, 1927, pp. 225–46; R. Grujić, Otkopavanje sv. Arhandjela kod Prizrena (Discovery of the Church of the Holy Archangels near Prizren), Glasnik Skopskog naučnog društva, III, 1, 1928, pp. 239–74; S. Stanojević, L. Mirković, and D. Bošković, Manastir Manasija (Monastery of Manasija), Belgrade, 1928; M. Vasić, Žiča i Lazarica (Žiča and Lazarica), Belgrade, 1928; A. Deroko, Nemanjina crkva sv. Bogorodice u Bistrici (The Nemanja Church of Our Virgin in Bistrica), Glasnik Skopskog naučnog društva, V, 2, 1929, pp. 305–08; Ž. Tatić, Tragom velike prošlosti (In the Traces of a Great Past), Belgrade, 1929; G. Bošković, Staro Nagoričino et Gračanica, L'art byzantin chez les Slaves, I, 1, Paris, 1930, pp. 195–212; A. Derocco, Les deux églises des environs de Ras, L'art byzantin chez les Slaves, I, 1, Paris, 1930, pp. 130–46; G. Millet, Études sur les églises de Rascie, L'art byzantin chez les Slaves, I, 1, Paris, 1930, pp. 147–94; A. Deroko, Banjska, Starinar, III, 6, 1931, pp. 107–09; D. Bošković, Beleške s putovanja (Travel Notes), Starinar, III, 7, 1932, pp. 88–126 (Our Lady of Ljeviška in Lesnovo); A. Deroko, Morača, Starinar, III, 7, 1932, pp. 9–14; A. Deroko, Matejča, Starinar, III, 8–9, 1933–34, pp. 84–90; D. Bošković, Osiguranje i restauracija crkve manastira sv. Patrijaršije u Peći (Consolidation and Restoration of the Church of the St. Patricia Monastery in Peć), Starinar, III, 8–9, 1933–34, pp. 91–165; V. Petković and D. Bošković, Manastir Dečani (Monastery of Dečani), in D. Bošković, Arhitektura i skulptura (Architecture and Sculpture), I, Belgrade, 1941; A. Deroko, Srednjevekovni gradovi u Srbij, Crnoj Gori i Makedoniji (Medieval Cities in Serbia, Montenegro, and Macedonia), Belgrade, 1950; D. Bošković and S. Nenadović, Gradac, Belgrade, 1951; A. Deroko, Monumentalna i dekorativna arhitektura u srednjevekovnoj Srbiji (Monumental and Decorative Architecture in Medieval Serbia), Belgrade, 1953; D. Bošković, Arhitektura srednjeg veka (Architecture of the Middle Ages), Belgrade, 1957, pp. 128–47, 273–306; R. F. Hoddinott, Early Byzantine Churches in Macedonia and Southern Serbia: A Study of the Origins and Initial Development of Early Christian Art, London, 1963.
c. Sculpture: M. Kašanin, Srpska srednjevekovna skulptura (Medieval Serbian Sculpture), Umetnički pregled, I, Belgrade, 1937, pp. 11–14; D. Bošković, La sculpture de Dečani et la question du développement de cycles iconographiques dans la sculpture médiévale de l'Italie Méridionale et de l'Occident, Atti del V Congr. Internazionale di Studi Bizantini, II, 1940, pp. 37–47.
d. Painting: V. Petković, Spasova crkva u Žiči (Church of the Ascension in Žiča), Belgrade, 1911; V. Petković, Ravanica, Belgrade, 1922; V. Petković, Crkveni kalendar u starom živopisu srpskom (The Ecclesiastical Calendar in Ancient Serbian Painting), Starinar, III, 1, 1922, pp. 3–18; V. Petković, Manastir Studenica (Monastery of Studenica), Belgrade, 1924; L. Mirković, Ž. Tatić, Markov manastir (Monastery of Marko), Belgrade, 1925; V. Petković and Ž. Tatić, Manastir Kalenić (Monastery of Kalenić), Belgrade, 1926; V. Petković, Živopis crkve sv. Bogorodice u Patrijaršiji pećkoj (Frescoes in the Church of the Virgin in the Patriarchate of Peć), Izvestia na bǎlgarski arheologičeski Inst., IV, Sofia, 1926–27, pp. 145–71; N. L. Okunev, Stolpy sv. Georgia (Church of St. George), Seminarium Kondakovianum, I, 1927, pp. 225–46; S. Stanojević, L. Mirković, and D. Bošković, Manastir Manasija (Monastery of Manasija), Belgrade, 1928; M. Kašanin, Bela Crkva Karanska (The White Church of Karan), Starinar, III, 4, 1928, pp. 115–221; V. Petković, La peinture serbe du Moyen âge, 2 vols., 1930–34; N. L. Okunev, Monumenta artis Serbicae, 4 vols., Prague, 1928–32; N. L. Okunev, Crkva sv. Djordja u Starom Nagoričinu (Church of St. George in Old Nagoričino), Glasnik Skopskog naučnog društva, V, 1929, pp. 87–120; N. L. Okunev, Sostav rospisi hrama v Sopočanah (Condition of the Frescoes in the Church of Sopočani), Byzantinoslavica, I, 1929, pp. 119–50; F. Mesesnel, Živopis crkve sv. Nikite u Skopskoj Crnoj Gori (Frescoes in the Church of St. Nikita in Serbian Montenegro), Godišnjak Skopskog Filozofskog fakulteta, I, 1930, pp. 139–54; N. L. Okunev, Crkva sv. Bogorodice Mateič (Church of the Virgin in Mateič), Glasnik Skopskog naučnog društva, VII–VIII, 1930, pp. 89–113; L. Mirković, Rudenica, Prilozi za književnost, jezik, istoriju i folklor, XI, 1931, pp. 83–112; V. Petković, Srpsko slikarstvo srednjeg veka (Serbian Painting in the Middle Ages), Bratsvo, XXV, 1931, pp. 56–59; V. Petković and P. Popović, Staro Nagoričino, Psača, Kalenić, Belgrade, 1933; D. Mano-Zisi, Nova Pavlica, Starinar, III, 8–9, 1933–34, pp. 193–206; S. Radojčić, Portreti srpskih vladara u srednjem veku (Portraits of Serbian Sovereigns in the Middle Ages), Skoplje, 1934; N. L. Okunev, Arilje, Seminarium Kondakovianum, VIII, 1936, pp. 221–58; S. Radojčić, Gračanica, Hrišćansko delo, IV, 1938; N. L. Okunev, Mileševo, Byzantinoslavica, VII, 1938, pp. 33–107; N. L. Okunev, Monastir Morača v Černogorii (Monastery of Morača in Montenegro), Byzantinoslavica, VIII, 1939–46, pp. 109–44; V. Petković and D. Bošković, Manastir Dečani, in V. Petković, Živopis

(Painting), II, Belgrade, 1941; S. Radojčić, Uloga antike u starom srpskom slikarstvu (The Role of Antiquity in Old Serbian Painting), Glasnik Zemaljskog muzeja u Sarajevu, N.S., I, 1946, pp. 39–50; G. Millet and A. Frolow, La peinture du Moyen âge en Yougoslavie (Serbie, Macedoine, et Montenegro), 2 vols., Paris, 1954–57; S. Radojčić, Majstori starog srpskog slikarstva (Masters of Ancient Serbian Painting), Srpska Akademija Nauka, Arheološki inst., special no., CCXXXV, 3, 1955; D. Talbot Rice and S. Radojčić, Yugoslavia, Medieval Frescoes, Paris, 1955.

e. Icons: M. Alpatov, Eine serbische Ikone des Propheten Elias und Johannes des Theologen, Belvedere, 1928, pp. 115–18; L. Mirković, Starine fruškogorskikh manastira (The Fruška Gora Monastery in Ancient Times), Belgrade, 1931; S. Stanojević, Beleške o nekim starim ikonama (Notes on Some Old Icons), Belgrade, 1931; L. Mirković, Starine Stare crkve u Sarajevu (The Old Church of Sarajevo in Ancient Times), Spomenik Srpska Akademija Nauka, LXXXIII, 1936; D. Bošković, Ikona Dečanskog u Bariju (Icon of Dečani in Bari), Starinar, III, 12, 1937, pp. 55–58; L. Mirković, Crkvene starine is Dečana, Peći, Cetinja, i Praskvice (Churches of Dečani, Peč, Cetinje, and Praskvica in Ancient Times), Godišnjak Museja Južne Srbije, I, 1937, pp. 97–148; W. F. Volbach, Die Ikonen der Apostelfürsten in St. Peter zu Rom, Orientalia Christiana Periodica, VII, 3–4, 1941, pp. 480–97; M. Ćorović-Ljubinković, Nekoliko ohridskikh ikona is XIII i XIV veka (Some 13th- and 14th-century Icons from Ochrida), Jugoslavija, V, 1952, pp. 81–87; S. Radojčić, Die serbische Ikonenmalerei vom 12. Jahrhundert bis zum Jahre 1459, Jhb. der Österreichischen byzantinischen Gesellschaft, V, 1956, pp. 61–83; S. Radojčić, Icones de Serbie et de la Macédonie, Zagreb, 1963.

f. Miniatures: Die Miniaturen des serbischen Psalters . . . , Denkschriften der Königlichen Ak. der Wissenschaft in Wien, Philosophische-historische Klasse, LII, 1906, pp. 1–139; A. Grabar, Recherches sur les influences orientales dans l'art balkanique, Strasbourg, 1928; S. Radojčić, Stare srpske minijature (Old Serbian Miniatures), Belgrade, 1950; S. Radojčić, Umetnički spomenici manastira Hilandara (Artistic Works in the Chilandari Monastery), Zbornik radova, Srpska Vizantološki inst., Akademija Nauka, XLIV, 3, 1955, pp. 163–95.

g. Minor arts: L. Mirković, Crkveni umetnički vez (Artistic Church Embroidery), Belgrade, 1940; M. Purković, Dj. Mano-Zisi, Srpski srednjevekovni nakit i ukras (Medieval Serbian Jewelry and Ornaments), Umetnički pregled, I, 1941, pp. 15–22; M. Ćorović-Ljubinković and D. Mano-Zisi, Osvrti na primenjenu umetnost u Srbiji kroz vekove (Serbian Minor Arts Across the Centuries), Belgrade, 1951; Umetnička obrada metala naroda Jugoslavije (Artistic Metalware of the Yugoslav People), I–II, Belgrade, 1956 (cat.).

Russia. a. General: I. Tolstoy and N. Kondakov, Russkie drevnosti v pamyatnikakh iskusstva (Russian Antiquities in Monuments of Art), 6 vols., St. Petersburg, 1889–99; A. Novitskii, Istoriya russkogo iskusstva s drevneishikh vremen (History of Russian Art from the Earliest Times), I, Moscow, 1903; F. Buslaev, O narodnosti v drevnerusskoi literature i iskusstve (Folk Elements in Early Russian Literature and Art), Sochineniya F. I. Buslaeva (Works of F. I. Buslaev), II, St. Petersburg, 1910, pp. 63–99; I. Grabar, Istoriya russkogo iskussta (History of Russian Art), I, II, VI, Moscow, 1910–15; A. Eliasberg, Russische Kunst, Munich, 1915; V. Nikolskii, Istoriya russkogo iskusstva (History of Russian Art), I, Moscow, 1915; L. Réau, L'art russe dès origines à Pierre le Grand, Paris, 1921 (new ed., 1945); F. Halle, L'art de la vielle Russie, Paris, 1922; V. Nikolskii, Istoriya russkogo iskusstva (History of Russian Art), Berlin, 1923; N. Sychev, Iskusstvo srednevekovoi Rusi (Art of Medieval Russia), Leningrad, 1929; D. Ainalov, Geschichte der russischen Monumentalkunst der vormoskovitischen Zeit, Berlin, Leipzig, 1932; M. Alpatov, N. Brunov, Geschichte der altrussischen Kunst, Augsburg, 1932; D. Ainalov, Geschichte der russischen Monumentalkunst zur Zeit des Grossfürstentums Moskau, Berlin, Leipzig, 1933; A. Nekrasov, Drevnerusskoe izobrazitelnoe iskusstvo (Ancient Russian Figurative Art), Moscow, 1937; F. Nemitz, Die Kunst Russlands, Berlin, 1940; G. Bunt, Russian Art from Scyths to Soviets, London, New York, 1946; N. N. Voronin, M. K. Karger, and M. A. Tikhanova, eds., Istoriya kultury drevnei Rusi: Domongolskii period, I. Materialnaya kultura (History of Culture of Ancient Russia: Premongolian Period, I. Material Culture), N. N. Voronin and M. K. Karger, eds., II. Obshchestvennii stroi i dukhovnaya kultura (Social Structure and Spiritual Culture), Moscow, Leningrad, 1948–51; T. Talbot Rice, Russian Art, West Drayton, England, 1949; I. E. Grabar, V. N. Lasareff, and V. S. Kemenov, eds., Istoriya russkogo iskusstva (History of Russian Art), 4 vols., Moscow, 1953–59 (detailed bibliog.); G. Hamilton, The Art and Architecture of Russia, Harmondsworth, 1954; A. Alpatov, Vseobshchaya istoriya iskusstv (History of World Art), III, Moscow, 1955.

b. Theory of art: Rozysk po delu Viskovatogo (Inquiry into the Viskovati Question), Chteniya v obshchestve istorii i drevnostei rossiiskikh, II, 1858, pp. 1–42; S. Ushakov, Slovo k lyubotshchatelnomu ikonnogo pisaniya (On the Painting of Icons), Vestnik obshchestva drevnerusskogo iskusstva pri moskovskom publichnom museye (B. of the Soc. of Ancient Art at the Moscow Public Mus.), I–III, 1874, pp. 22–24; F. Buslaev, Russkaya estetika XVII veka (Russian Esthetics of the 17th Century), Sochineniya F. I. Buslaeva (Works of F. I. Buslaev), II, St. Petersburg, 1910, pp. 423–34; A. Nikolskii, Slovo k lyubotshchatelem ikonnogo pisaniya (On the Painting of Icons), Vestnik arkheologii i istorii, XX, 1911, pp. 65–70; Protopop Avvakum, Kniga besed (Essays), Leningrad, 1927, pp. 281–88; N. Andreyev, O dele dyaka Viskovatogo (The Question of Deacon Viskovati), Seminarium Kondakovianum, V, 1932, pp. 219–41; G. Ostrogorsky, Les décisions du Stoglav au sujet de la peinture d'images et les principes de l'iconographie byzantine, Orient et Byzance, IV, 1933; N. Andreyev, Inok Zinovii ob ikonopochitanii i ikonopisanii (The Monk Zenobius on the Cult and Painting of Icons), Seminarium Kondakovianum, VIII, 1936, pp. 259–78; I. Vladimirov, Traktat ob ikonopisanii (Treatise on the Painting of Icons), Mastera iskusstva ob iskusstve (Masters of Art on Art), IV, Moscow, Leningrad, 1937, pp. 19–26; Y. Dmitriev, Teoriya iskusstva i vzglyady na iskusstvo v pismennosti drevnei Rusi (Theories of Art and Opinions on Art in Early Russian Literature), Trudy otdela drevnerusskoi literatury Instituta russkoi literatury Akademii Nauk SSSR, IX, 1953, pp. 97–116; Y. Dmitriev, O tvorchestve drevnerusskogo khudozhnika (Work of the Ancient Russian Painter), Trudy otdela drevnerusskoi literatury Instituta russkoi literatury Akademii Nauk SSSR, XIV, 1958, pp. 551–56.

c. Architecture: V. Suslov, Materialy k istorii drevnei novgorodskopskovskoi arkhitektury (Materials on the History of Early Novgorod and Pskov Architecture), St. Petersburg, 1888; A. Pavlinov, Istoriya russkoi arkhitektury (History of Russian Architecture), Moscow, 1894; V. Suslov, Pamyatniki drevnogo russkogo zodchestva (Monuments of Ancient Russian Architecture), 7 vols., St. Petersburg, 1895–1901; I. Zabelin, Cherty samobytnosti v drevnerusskom zodchestve (Original Traits in Ancient Russian Architecture), Moscow, 1900; A. Potapov, Ocherk drevnei russkoi grazhdanskoi arkhitektury (Early Russian Civic Architecture), 2 vols., Moscow, 1902–03; K. Romanov, Georgievskii sobor v Jureve-Polskom (Cathedral of St. George in Yurev-Polski), Izvestiya arkheologicheskoi komisii, XXXVI, 1910, pp. 70–93; M. Krasovskii, Ocherk istorii moskovskogo perioda drevnerusskogo tserkovnogo zodchestva (Historical Material on the Moscow Period in Early Russian Church Architecture), Moscow, 1911; N. Sobolev, Russkii zodchii XV veka V. D. Ermolin (The 15th-century Russian Architect V. D. Ermolin), Staraya Moskva (Old Moscow), II, Moscow, 1914, pp. 16–23; B. Eding, Moskovskaya arkhitektura do kontsa XVII veka (Moscow Architecture to the End of the 17th Century), Moscow, 1915; N. Petrov, Chernigovskoe zodchestvo XI–XII vekov (Chernigov Architecture in the 11th–12th Century), Chernigov, 1915; I. Rylskii, Grazhdanskoe zodchestvo v Pskove (Civic Architecture in Pskov), Trudy moskovskogo arkheologicheskogo obshchestva, VI, 1915, pp. 35–53; M. Krasovskii, Kurs istorii russkoi arkhitektury, I. Derevyannoe zodchestvo (On the History of Russian Architecture, I. Wooden Architecture), Petrograd, 1916; N. Brounoff, Un type nouveau d'église dans la Russie du nord-ouest au XIIe siècle, Årsbok der Vatenskaps-Societaten i Lund, 1925, pp. 3–38; K. Romanov, Pskov, Novgorod i Moskva v ikh culturno-khudozhestvennykh vzaimootnosheniyakh (Pskov, Novgorod, and Moscow and Their Cultural and Artistic Relationships), Izvestiya Gosudarstvennoi Akademii istorii materialnoi kultury, IV, 1925, pp. 209–41; R. Mischnitzer, Orientalische Einflüsse in der russischen Architektur, Osteuropa, I, 1925–26; Barokko v Rossii (The Baroque in Russia), Moscow, 1926; N. Brunoff, Due cattedrali del Kremlino costruite da italiani, Arch. e arti decorative, VI, 1926, pp. 97–100; K. Romanov, K voprosu o vliyanii vzaimootnoshenii mezhdu stroitelyami i zakazchikami na formy zodchestva v Novgorode v XV–XVI vekakh (The Question of the Infl uence of the Relationship Between Builders and Officials on Novgorod Architecture of the 15th–16th Century), Izobrazitelnoe iskusstovo, I, Leningrad, 1927, pp. 29–58; N. Brunov, Belaruskaya arkhitektura XI–XII st. (Byelorussian Architecture of the 11th–12th Century), Minsk, 1928, pp. 247–307; N. Brunov, K voprosu o ranne-moskovskom zodchestve (The Question of Early Moscow Architecture), Trudy sektsii arkheologii RANION, IV, 1928, pp. 93–106; N. Ernst, Bakhchisaraiskii khanskii dvorets i arkhitektor velikogo knyazya Ivana III Friyazin Aleviz Novi (Palace of the Bakhchisarai Khan and the Architect of the Grand Duke Ivan III — Alevisio Novi), Simferopol, 1928; G. Korzukhina, Ryazan v slozhenii arkhitekturnikh form XII–XIII vekov (Ryazan in the Formation of Architectural Forms of the 12th–13th Century), Sbornik aspirantov GAIMK, Leningrad, 1929, pp. 69–82; A. Nekrasov, Vozniknovenie moskovskogo iskusstva (Origins of Moscow Art), I, Moscow, 1929, pp. 9–104; A. Speranskii, Ocherki po istorii prikaza kamennykh del Moskovskogo gosudarstva (Essays on the History of Construction in Stone in the State of Moscow), Moscow, 1930; A. Nekrasov, Problema proizkhozhdeniya drevnerusskikh stolpoobraznykh khramov (Problem of the Origin of the Early Russian Pier Churches), Trudy kabineta istorii materialnoi kultury moskovskogo universiteta, Moscow, 1930, pp. 17–50; N. Voronin, Ocherki po istorii russkogo zodchestva XVI–XVII vekov (Essays on the History of Russian 16th–17th-century Architecture), Leningrad, 1934; V. Snerigev, Aristotel Fioravanti i perestroika moskovskogo Kremlya (Aristotele Fioravanti and the Construction of the Moscow Kremlin), Moscow, 1935; S. Cross and K. Conant, The Earliest Mediaeval Churches of Kiev, Speculum, X, 1936, pp. 477–99; A. Nekrasov, Ocherki po istorii drevnerusskogo zodchestva XI–XVII veka (Essays on Early Russian Architecture of the 11th–17th Century), Moscow, 1936; A. Filippov, Drevnerusskie izrazy (Early Russian Majolica), I, Moscow, 1938; Russkaya arkhitektura (Russian Architecture), Moscow, 1940; M. Rzyanin, Pokrov na Nerli (Church of the Intercession on the River Nerl), Moscow, 1941; S. Zabello, V. Ivanov, and P. Maksimov, Russkoe derevyannoe zodchestvo (Russian Wooden Architecture), Moscow, 1942; N. Brunov, Moskovskii Kreml (Moscow Kremlin), Moscow, 1944; Y. Pasternak, Starii Galich (Old Galič), Kraków, Lwów, 1944; N. Voronin, Pamyatniki vladimiro-suzdalskogo zodchestva XI–XII vekov (Architectural Monuments of Vladimir-Suzdal in the 11th–12th Century), Moscow, Leningrad, 1945; N. Voronin, Tverskoe zodchestvo XIII–XIV vekov (Tver Architecture of the 13th–14th Century), Izvestya otdeleniya istorii i filosofii Akademii Nauk SSSR, V, 1945, pp. 373–86; Arkhitekturnye pamyatniki Moskvy XV–XVII vekov (Architectural Monuments of 15th–17th-century Moscow), Moscow, 1947; Arkhitektura Sofiiskogo sobora v Novgorode: Noveishie issledovaniya (Architecture of the Cathedral of St. Sophia in Novgorod: Recent Findings), Soobshcheniya instituta istorii i teorii arkhitektury Akademii Arkhitektury SSSR, VII, 1947; M. Karger, K voprosu ob ubranstve interera v russkom zodchestve domongolskogo perioda (Question of Interior Decoration in Russian Architecture of the Premongol Period), Trudy Vserossiiskoi Akademii Khudozhestv, I, 1947, pp. 15–50; P. Baranovskii, Sobor Pyatnitskogo monastyrya v Chernigove (Cathedral of the Pyatnitski Monastery in Chernigov), in Pamyatniki iskusstva razrushennye nemetskimi zakhvatchikami v Rossii (Monuments of Art Destroyed by the German Invaders in Russia), Moscow, Leningrad, 1948, pp. 13–34; P. Maksimov, K kharakteristike moskovskogo zodchestva XIV–XV vekov (Characteristics of Moscow 14th–15th-century Architecture), MIA, XII, 1949, pp. 209–16; P. Rapoport, Russkoe shatrovoe zodchestvo kontsa XVI veka (Russian

Tent-roofed Architecture at the End of the 16th Century), MIA, XII, 1949, pp. 238–301; M. Karger, Arkheologicheskie issledovaniya drevnogo Kieva: Otchety i materialy (Archaeological Findings in Old Kiev), Kiev, 1950; M. Karger, Pamyatniki pereyaslavskogo zodchestva XI–XII vekov v svete arkheologicheskikh issledovanii (Monuments of 11th–12th-century Pereyaslavl Architecture in the Light of Archaeological Findings), SA, XV, 1951, pp. 44–63; N. Voronin, U istokov russkogo natsionalnogo zodchestva (Origins of Russian National Culture), Ezhegodnik instituta istorii iskusstv Akademii Nauk SSSR, 1952, pp. 257–316; N. Brunov, Mastera drevnerusskogo zodchestva (Masters of Early Russian Architecture), Moscow, 1953; L. Tverskoi, Russkoe gradostroitelstvo do kontsa XVII veka (Russian Town Planning to the End of the 17th Century), Leningrad, Moscow, 1953; O. Powstenko, The Cathedral of St. Sophia of Kiev, New York, 1954; A. Voyce, The Moscow Kremlin: Its History, Architecture and Art Treasures, Los Angeles, 1954; L. Kirillova, Voprosy kompozitsii v russkoi arkhitekture XVI–XIX vekov (Problems of Structure in Russian 16th–19th-century Architecture), Moscow, 1955; M. Ilin, Bukhvostov, Moscow, 1956; Istoriya russkoi arkhitektura (History of Russian Architecture), 2d ed., Moscow, 1956; A Voyce, National Elements in Russian Architecture, J. of the Soc. of Architectural Historians, XVI, 2, 1957, pp. 6–16; M. Karger, Drevnii Kiev (Ancient Kiev), 2 vols., Moscow, 1958–61; V. Lasareff, Le opere di Pietro Antonio Solari in Russia ed i rapporti artistici italo-russi nel tardo Quattrocento: Arti ed artisti dei laghi lombardi, Como, 1959, pp. 423–40; P. Maksimov, Zarubezhnye svyazi v arkhitekture Novgoroda i Pskova XI–nachala XVI vekov (Foreign Links in Novgorod and Pskov Architecture from the 11th to the Beginning of the 16th Century), Arkhitekturnoe nasledstvo, XII, 1960, pp. 23–44; B. Ognev, Nekotorye problemy rannemoskovskogo zodchestva (Some Problems of Early Moscow Architecture), Arkhitekturnoe nasledstvo, XII, 1960, pp. 45–62; K. Afanasev, Postroenie arkhitekturnoi formy drevnerusskimi zodchimi (Creation of Architectural Form by Early Russian Builders), Moscow, 1961; N. Voronin, Zodchestvo severovostochnoi Rusi XII–XV vekov (Architecture of Northeast Russia from the 12th to the 15th Century), 2 vols., Moscow, 1961–62.

d. Painting: N. Kondakov, O freskakh lestnits Kievo-Sofiiskogo sobora (Frescoes of the Stairs in St. Sophia in Kiev), Zapiski russkogo arkheologicheskogo abshchestva, III, 1888, pp. 287–306; D. Ainalov and E. Redin, Kievo-Sofiiskii sobor (Cathedral of St. Sophia in Kiev), Zapicki russkogo arkheologicheskogo obshchestva, IV, 1890, pp. 231–381; F. Buslaev, Dlya istorii russkoi zhivopisi XVI veka (Toward the History of Russian 16th-century Painting), in Sochineniya F. I. Buslaeva (Works of F. I. Buslaev), II, St. Petersburg, 1910, pp. 286–344; N. Pokrovskii, Ocherki pamyatnikov khristianskogo iskusstva i ikonografii (Review of Christian Art and Iconography), St. Petersburg, 1910; V. Georgievskii, Freski Ferapontova monastyrya (Frescoes of the Ferapontov Monastery), St. Petersburg, 1911; N. Okunev, Vnov otkrytaya rospis tserkvi Sv. Fedora Stratilata v Novgorode (The Recently Discovered Frescoes in the Church of St. Theodore Stratelates in Novgorod), Izvestiya arkheologicheskoi komissii, XXXIX, 1911, pp. 88–101; N. Pervukhin, Tserkov Ioanna Predtechi v Yaroslavle (Church of St. John the Baptist in Yaroslavl), Moscow, 1913; N. Okunev, Kreshchalnya Sofiiskogo sobora v Kieve (Baptistery of St. Sophia in Kiev), Zapiski otdeleniya russkoi i slavyanskoi arkheologii russkogo arkheologicheskogo obshchestva, X, 1915, pp. 113–37; N. Pervukhin, Tserkov Ili Proroka v Yaroslavle (Church of the Prophet Elijah in Yaroslavl), Moscow, 1915; D. Ainalov, Freskovaya rospis khrama Uspeniya v Sviyazhskom monastyre (Frescoes of the Church of the Dormition in the Sviyazhski Monastery), Moscow, 1916; N. Pervukhin, Tserkov Bogoyavleniya v Yaroslavle (Church of the Apparition of God in Yaroslavl), Yaroslavl, 1916; D. Gordeyev, O novgorodskikh fedorovskikh freskakh (Frescoes of the Church of St. Theodore in Novgorod), Vizantiiskii vremennik, XXII, 1917, pp. 281–96; A. Grabar, Freski Apostolskogo pridela Kievo-Sofiiskogo sobora (Frescoes of the Chapel of the Apostle in St. Sophia in Kiev), Zapiski otdeleniya russkoi i slavyanskoi arkheologii russkogo arkheologicheskogo obshchestva, XII, 1918, pp. 98–106; V. Myasoedov, Freski severnogo pritvora Sofii Kievskoi (Frescoes of the Northern Atrium in St. Sophia in Kiev), Zapiski otdeleniya russkoi i slavyanskoi arkheologii russkogo arkheologicheskogo obshchestva, XII, 1918, pp. 1–6; N. Sychev, Zabytye fragmenty ńovgorodskikh fresko XII veka (Forgotten Fragments of 12th-century Novgorod Frescoes), Zapiski otdeleniya russkoi i slavyanskoi arkheologii russkogo arkheologicheskogo obshchestva, XII, 1918, pp. 116–31; I. Evdokimov, Vologodskie stennye rospisi (Murals of Vologda), Vologda, 1922; I. Grabar, Feofan Grek (Theophanes the Greek), Kazan, 1922; V. Myasoedov, Freski Spasa Nereditsy (Frescoes in the Church of Our Saviour in Nereditsa), Leningrad, 1925; D. Ainalov, Die Mosaiken des Michaelklosters in Kiev, Belvedere, Oct., 1926, pp. 201–16; I. Grabar, Die Freskomalerei der Dimitrij Kathedrale in Wladimir, Berlin, 1926; N. Sychev, Drevneishii fragment russkoi zhivopisi (The Earliest Fragment of Russian Painting), Seminarium Kondakovianum, II, 1928, pp. 91–104; M. Artamonov, Odin iz stilei monumentalnoi zhivopisi XII–XIII vekov (One of the Styles of 12th–13th-century Painting), Sbornik po delam aspirantov GAIMK, I, 1929, pp. 51–68; V. Nechaev, Nutrovye palaty v russkoi zhivopisi XVII veka (Interiors in Russian 17th-century Painting), in Russkoe iskusstvo XVII veka, Leningrad, 1929, pp. 27–62; E. Sochavets-Fedorovich, Yaroslavskie stenopisi i bibliya Piskatora (Murals in Yaroslavl and the Piscator Bible), in Russkoe iskusstvo XVII veka (Russian 17th-century Art), Leningrad, 1929, pp. 85–108; A. Anisimov, La peinture russe du XIVe siècle, GBA, 1930, pp. 158–77 (Theophanes the Greek); P. Schweinfurth, Geschichte der russischen Malerei im Mittelalter, The Hague, 1930; I. Nadejena, The Pskov School of Painting, AB, XXI, 1931, pp. 183–91; A. Grabar, Les fresques des escaliers à St. Sophie de Kiev et l'iconographie impériale byzantine, Seminarium Kondakovianum, VII, 1935, pp. 103–17; N. Porfiridov, Zhivopis Volotova (Painting of Volotov), Novgorodskii istoricheskii sbornik, VII, 1940, pp. 55–65; A. Varganov, Freski XI-XII vekov v Suzdalskom sobore (11th–13th-century Frescoes in the Cathedral of Suzdal), KS, V, 1940, pp. 39–40; B. Mikhailovski and B. Purishev, Ocherki istorii drevnerusskoi monumentalnoi zhivopisi so vtoroi poloviny XIV veka do nachala XVIII veka (Essays on the History of Early Russian Painting from the Second Half of the 14th Century to the Beginning of the 18th Century), Moscow, Lenigrad, 1941; E. Ovchinnikova, Stenopis tserkvi "Troitsy v Nikitnikakh" v Moskve serediny XVII v. (Murals in the Church of the Trinity "v Nikitniki" in Moscow in the mid-17th Century), Trudy Gosudarstvennogo Istoricheskogo Muzeya, XIII, 1941, pp. 147–66; S. Cross, The Mosaic Eucharist of St. Michael's (Kiev), Am. Slavic and East European Rev., VI, 1947, pp. 56–61; V. Lasareff, Iskusstvo Novgoroda (Art of Novgorod), Moscow, 1947; M. Alpatov, Freski khramov Uspeniya na Volotovom Pole (Frescoes of the Church of the Dormition in Volotovo Pole), in Pamyatniki iskusstva razrushennye nemetskimi zakhvatchikami v Rossii (Monuments of Art Destroyed by the German Invaders in Russia), Moscow, Leningrad, 1948, pp. 103–48; V. Lasareff, Rospisi Skovorodskogo monastyrya v Novgorode (Frescoes of the Skovorodski Monastery in Novgorod), in Pamyatniki iskusstva razrushennye nemetskimi zakhvatchikami v Rossii, Moscow, Leningrad, 1948, pp. 77–101; Y. Dmitriev, Stennye rospisi Novgoroda, ikh restavratsiya i issledovanie: Raboty 1945–48 gg (Murals in Novgorod, Their Restoration and Investigation: The Work of 1945–48), in Praktika restavratsionnykh rabot (Practice of Restoration), Moscow, 1950, pp. 134–72; Y. Dmitriev, Melëtovskie freski i ikh znachenie dlya istorii drevnerusskoi literatury (Frescoes of Melëtovo and Their Significance in the History of Early Russian Literature), Trudy otdela drevnerusskoi literatury Instituta russkoi literatury Akedemii Nauk SSSR, VIII, 1951, pp. 403–12; N. Sychev, Predpolagaemoe izobrazhenie zheny Yuriya Dolgorukogo (The Presumed Image of Yuri Dolgoruki's Wife), Soobshcheniya Instituta istorii iskusstv Akademii Nauk SSSR, I, 1951, pp. 51–62; P. Schweinfurth, Die Fresken der Erlöserkirche von Neredica bei Novgorod: Ihre Stellung in der Kunstgeschichte Russlands, Munich, 1953; G. Galassi, Musaici di Kiew a San Michele, Arte russa, Felix Ravenna, XIX, 1956, pp. 5–30; V. Lasareff, La méthode de la collaboration des maîtres byzantins et russes, Classica ed Mediaevalia, rev. danoise de philologie et d'h., XVII, 1956, pp. 82–90; V. Lasareff, Snetogorskie rospisi (Frescoes of the Snetogorski Monastery), Soobshcheniya Instituta istorii iskusstv Akademii Nauk SSSR, VIII, 1957, pp. 78–112; V. Lasareff, Kovalevskaya rospis i problema yuzhnoslavyanskikh svyazei v russkoi zhivopisi XIV veka (Painting in the Church of Our Saviour "na Kovaleve" and the Question of South Slavic Ties with Russian 14th-century Painting), Ezhegodnik Instituta istorii iskusstv Akademii Nauk SSSR, 1957–58, pp. 233–78; V. Bryusova, Izuchenie i restavratsiya fresko Rostovskogo Kremlya (Investigation and Restoration of the Frescoes in the Rostov Kremlin), Materialy po izucheniyu i restavrastii pamyatnikov arkhitektury Yaroslavskoi oblasti, I. Rostov Velikii (Materials on the Study and Restoration of Architectural Monuments of the Province of Yaroslavl, I. Rostov Veliki), Yaroslavl, 1958, pp. 95–110; N. Sychev, K istorii rospisi Dmitrievskogo sobora vo Vladimire (History of the Paintings in the Cathedral of St. Dmitri in Vladimir), Pamyatniki kultury (Monuments of Culture), I, Moscow, 1959, pp. 143–76; N. Kresalnii, Sofiiskii zapovednik v Kieve (Museum of St. Sophia in Kiev), Kiev, 1960; V. Lasareff, Freski Staroi Ladogi (Frescoes of Staraya Ladoga), Moscow, 1960; V. Lasareff, Mosaiki Sofii Kievskoi (Mosaics of St. Sophia in Kiev), Moscow, 1960.

e. Icons: G. Filimonov, Simon Ushakov i sovremennaya emu epokha russkoi ikonopisi (Simon Ushakov and his Period of Russian Icon Painting), Sbornik na 1873 god, Izdannyi obshchestvom drevnerusskogo iskusstva pri moskovskom publichnom muzee, Moscow, 1873, pp. 1–104; V. Uspenskii, Ocherki po istorii ikonopisaniya (Essays on the History of Icon Painting), St. Petersburg, 1899; D. Trenev, Ikonostas Smolenskogo sobora moskovskogo Novodevichego monastyrya (Iconostasis of the Smolensk Cathedral in the Novodevichi Monastery in Moscow), Moscow, 1902; N. Likhachev, Kratkoe opisanie ikon sobraniya P. M. Tretyakova (Brief Description of the Tretyakov Icon Collection), Moscow, 1905; N. Likhachev, Materialy dlya istorii russkogo ikonopisaniya (Materials on the History of Russian Icon Painting), I–II, St. Petersburg, 1906; A. Uspenskii, Tsarskie ikonopistsy i zhivopistsy XVII veka (17th-century Court Painters and Icon Painters), I–IV, Moscow, 1910–16; V. Georgievskii, Ikony Ivana Groznogo (Icons of Ivan the Terrible), Starye gody, Nov., 1911, pp. 3–20; N. Shchekotov, Nekotorye cherty stilya russkikh ikon XV veka (Some Characteristics of the Style of 15th-century Russian Icons), Starye gody, Apr., 1913, pp. 38–42; Vystavka drevnerusskogo iskusstva ustroennaya v 1913 godu (Exhibit of Early Russian Art in 1913), Moscow, 1913; P. Muratov, Drevnerusskaya ikonopis v sobranii I. S. Ostroukhova (The Painting of Early Russian Icons in the Ostroukhov Collection), Moscow, 1914; Russkaya ikona (Russian Icon), Sbornik, I–III, St. Petersburg, 1914; A. Anisimov and P. Muratov, Novgorodskaya ikona Sv. Fedora Stratilata (The Novgorod Icon of St. Theodore Stratelates), Moscow, 1918; Y. Olsufiev, Opis ikon Troitse-Sergievoi Lavry (Inventory of the Icons in the Trinity-Sergius Monastery), Sergiev, 1920; A. Vvedenskii, Zametki po istorii truda na Rusi v 16–17 vv., II. Stroganovskie ikonniki (Notes on the History of Labor in 16th–17th-century Russia, II. The Painters of the Stroganov Icons), Arkhiv istorii truda v Rossii, III, 1922; N. Sychev, Vystavka proizvedenii iskusstva "Stroganovskoi shkoly" (Exhibit of the Art Works of the "Stroganov School"), Petrograd, 1923; V. Bogusevich, Severnye pamyatniki drevnerusskoi zhivopisi (Northern Examples of Early Russian Painting), Vologda, 1924; O. Wulff, Denkmäler der Ikonenmalerei, Hellerau bei Dresden, 1925; I. Grabar, Andrei Rublëv, Voprosy restavratsii, I, 1926, pp. 7–112; N. Kondakov, The Russian Icon, Oxford, 1927; P. Mouratov, Les icones russes, Paris, 1927; A. Anisimov, Domongolskii period drevnerusskoi zhivopisi (Pre-mongolian Period of Early Russian Painting), Voprosy restavratsii, II, 1928, pp. 102–80; M. Karger, Iz istorii zapadnykh vliyanii v drevnerusskoi zhivopisi (The History of Western Influences on Early Russian Painting), Materialy po russkomu iskusstvu (Materials on Russian Art), I, Leningrad, 1928, pp. 66–77; G. Zhidkov, Moskovskaya zhivopis serediny XIV veka (Muscovite Painting in the Mid-14th Century), Moscow, 1928; N. Kondakov, Russkaya ikona (The Russian Icon), 3 vols., Prague, 1928–34; V. Bogusevich, Severnye pamyatniki drevnerusskoi stankovoi zhivopisi (Northern Examples of Early Russian Easel Painting), Vologda, 1929; I. Grabar, Die Malerschule des alten Pskov, ZfbK, 1929–30, pp. 3–9; Masterpieces of Russian Painting, London, 1930; Y. Olsufiew,

The Development of Russian Icon Painting from the Twelfth to the Nineteenth Century, AB, 1930, pp. 347–73; P. Schweinfurth, Geschichte der russischen Malerei im Mittelalter, The Hague, 1930; D. Talbot Rice, Beginnings of Russian Icon Painting, Oxford, 1938; A. Grabar, L'expansion de la peinture russe aux XVIe et XVIIe siècles, Ann. de l'Inst. Kondakov, Belgrade, 1940, pp. 92–95; N. Scheffer, Symbolism of the Russian Icon, GBA, XXV, 1944, pp. 77–94; A. Leonov, Simon Ushakov, Moscow, 1945; N. Scheffer, Days of the Week in Russian Religious Art, GBA, XXVIII, 1945, pp. 321–34; V. Lasareff, O metode raboty v Rublevskoi masterskoi (Method of Work in the Rublëv Workshop), Doklady i soobshcheniya filologicheskogo fakulteta moskovskogo universiteta, I, 1946, pp. 60–64; V. Lasareff, La scuola di Vladimir-Susdal: due nuovi esemplari della pittura da cavalletto russa dal XII al XIII secolo, Arte veneta, X, 1946, pp. 9–18; N. Scheffer, Historic Battles on Russian Icons, GBA, XXIX, 1946, pp. 193–206; V. Lasareff, Iskusstvo Novgoroda (Art of Novgorod), Moscow, 1947; D. Talbot Rice, Russian Icons, London, New York, 1947; V. Antonova, Novootkrytye proizvedeniya Dionisiya v Gosudarstvennoi Tretyakovskoi galeree (Newly Discovered Works of Dionysius in the Tretyakov Gallery), Moscow, 1952; V. Lasareff, K voprosu o "grecheskoi manere" italo-grecheskoi i italo-kritskoi shkolakh zhivopisi (The Problem of the "Greek Manner" in the Italo-Greek and Italo-Cretan Schools of Painting), Ezhegodnik Instituta istorii iskusstv Akademii Nauk SSSR, 1952, pp. 152–200; L. Ouspensky and W. Lossky, Der Sinn der Ikonen, Bern, Olten, 1952; P. Schweinfurth, Russian Icons, Oxford, 1953; H. Rothemund, Ikonenkunst, Ein Handbuch, Munich, 1954; E. Ovchinnikova, Portret v russkom iskusstve XVII veka (The Portrait in Russian 17th-century Art), Moscow, 1955; H. Kjellin, Ryska Ikoner i Svensk och Norsk ägo, Stockholm, 1956; N. Mneva, Drevnerusskaya zhivopis Nizhnego Novgoroda (The Early Russian Painting of Nizhni Novgorod), Gosudarstvennaya Tretyakovskaya gallereya, Materialy i issledovaniya (Tretyakov State Gallery, Materials and Investigations), Moscow, 1958, pp. 28–36; A. Svirin, Drevnerusskaya zhivopis v Tretyakovskoi galleree (Early Russian Painting in the Tretyakov Gallery), Moscow, 1958; USSR: Early Russian Icons, pref. I. Grabar, text V. Lasareff and O. Demus, UNESCO World Art Ser., New York, 1958; V. Lasareff, Andrei Rublëv, Moscow, 1960; L. Ouspensky, Essai sur la théologie de l'icône dans l'église orthodoxe, Paris, 1960; V. Lasareff, Feofan Grek i ego Shkola (Theophanes the Greek and his School), Moscow, 1961; M. Alpatov, Andrei Rublëv, Milan, 1962; W. Weidlé, Les icônes byzantines et russes, Milan, 1962.

f. Miniatures and illumination: I. Butovskii, Istoriya russkogo ornamenta s X do XVI stoletya po drevnim rukopisyam (History of Russian Illumination from the 10th to the 16th Century in Ancient Manuscripts), 2 vols., Moscow, 1870; F. Buslaev, Svod izobrazhenii litsevykh Apokalipsisov po rukopisyam s XVI veka do XIX (Inventory of the Illustrations of the Apocalypse in 16th–19th-century Manuscripts), Moscow, 1884; S. Stasov, Slavyanskii i vostochnii ornament po rukopisyam drevnogo i novogo vremeni (Slavic and Eastern Illumination in Manuscripts of Old and Modern Times), St. Petersburg, 1887; V. Stasos, Miniatyury nekotorykh rukopisei visantiinskikh, bolgarskikh, russkikh, dzhagataiskikh i persidskikh (The Miniatures in Some Byzantine, Bulgarian, Russian, Dzhagatay, and Persian Manuscripts), St. Petersburg, 1904; D. Ainalov, Ocherki i zametki po istorii drevnerusskogo iskusstva, IV. Miniatyury "skazaniya" o sv. Borise i Glebe Silvestrovskogo sbornika (Essays and Notes on the History of Early Russian Art, IV. The Miniatures of the "Legend" of SS. Boris and Gleb in the Silvestrovskii Collection), Izvestiya otdeleniya russkogo yazika i slovesnosti Akademii Nauk, III, 1910, pp. 1–128; A. Nekrasov, Ocherki po istorii slavyanskogo ornamenta (Essays on the History of Slavic Illumination), St. Petersburg, 1913; E. Redin, Khristianskaya topografiya Kozmy Indikoplova po grecheskim i russkim spiskam (The Christian Topography of Cosmas Indicopleustes According to Greek and Russian Copies), Moscow, 1916; Y. Olsufev, Opis litsevykh izobrazhenii i ornamenta knig riznicy Troice-Sergevoi lavry (Inventory of the Figures and Illumination of the Books in the Trinity-Sergius Monastery), Sergiev, 1921; V. Shchepkin, Miniatyura v russkom iskusstve dotatarskogo perioda (Miniatures of Russian Art of the Pre-Tatar Period), Slavia, 1928, pp. 742–57; N. Born, Das Tiergeflecht in der nordrussischen Buchmalerei, Seminarium Kondakovianum, V, 1932, pp. 63–95, VI, 1933, pp. 89–108; V. Vladimirov and G. Georgievskii, Drevnerusskaya miniatyura (Old Russian Miniatures), Moscow, Leningrad, 1933; A. Artsikhovkii, Drevnerusskie miniatyury kak istoricheskii istochnik (Old Russian Miniatures as a Historical Source), Moscow, 1944; A. Svirin, Drevnerusskaya miniatyura (Old Russian Miniatures), Moscow, 1950.

g. Engraving: Ivan Fedorov, Pervopechatnik: Dokumenty, pisma (Ivan Fedorov, the First Printer: Documents, Letters), Moscow, Leningrad, 1935; A. Zernova, Nachalo knigopechataniya v Moskve i na Ukraine (The Beginning of Printing in Moscow and in the Ukraine), Moscow, 1941; A. Zernova, Staropechatnye knigi kak istoricheskie pamyatniki russkoi kultury (Early Printed Books as Historical Documents of Russian Culture), Moscow, 1943; A. Sidorov, Drevnerusskaya knizhnaya gravyura (Early Russian Book Engravings), Moscow, 1951; A. Zernova, Ornamentika knig moskovskoi pechati (Illuminations in Books Printed in Moscow), Moscow, 1953; U istokov russkogo knigopechataniya (Origins of Russian Book Printing), Moscow, 1959.

h. Sculpture. A Bobrinskii, Narodnye russkie derevyannye izdelya (Russian Wooden Folk Sculpture), Moscow, 1911–14; N. Sobolev, Reznye izobrazheniya v moskovskikh tserkvakh (Carved Figures in Moscow Churches), Staraya Moskva (Old Moscow), II, Moscow, 1914, pp. 87–107; A. Bobrinskii, Reznoi kamen v Rossii, I. Sobory Vladimiro-Suzdalskoi oblasti XII–XIII stoletya (Stone Carving in Russia, I. The Cathedrals of the Vladimir-Suzdal Region in the 12th–13th Century), Moscow, 1916; L. Maculevich, Khronologiya relefov Dmitrievskogo sobora vo Vladimire-Zalesskom (Chronology of Reliefs in the Cathedral of St. Dmitri in Vladimir-Zalesski), Ezhegodnik rossiiskogo instituta istorii iskusstv, I, 1922, pp. 253–99; N. Malitskii, Pozdnie relefi Dmitrievskogo sobora v gorode Vladimire (Late Reliefs in the Cathedral of St. Dmitri in the City of Vladimir), Trudy vladimirskogo nauchnogo obshchestva po izucheniiu mestnogo kraya, V, 1923, pp. 3–46; A. Nekrasov, Relefni portreti XI stoletiya (Relief Portraits of the 11th Century), Naukovii zbirnik Ukrainskoi akademii nauk, XX, 1925, pp. 16–40; P. Florenskii, Y. Olsufev, Amvrosii troitskii rezchik XV veka (The 15th-century Carver Ambrose of the Trinity Monastery), Sergiev, 1927; A. Anisimov, Avtoportret russkogo skulptora Avraam (The Self-portrait of the Russian Sculptor Avraam), Izvestiya Akademii Nauk SSSR otdelenie gumanitarnykh nauk, III, 1928, pp. 173–84; K. Romanov, K voprosu o tekhnike vypolneniya relefov sobora Georgiya v g. Yureve-Polskom (The Technique of Executing the Reliefs in the Cathedral of St. George in Yurev-Polski), Seminarium Kondakovianum, II, 1928, pp. 149–60; F. Halle, Die Bauplastik von Wladimir-Suzdal, Russische Romanik, Berlin, Vienna, Zurich, 1929; M. Makarenko, Skulptura i rizbyarstvo Kiivskoi Rusi pered mongolskikh chasiv (Sculpture and Carving in Kievan Russia Before the Mongol Period), Kiivskii zbirniki istorii i arkheologii, pobutu i mistetstva, I, 1931, pp. 27–96; K. Romanov, Vnov otkrytye relefy suzdalskogo sobora (Newly Discovered Reliefs in the Cathedral of Suzdal), Soobshcheniya Gosudarstvennoi akademii istorii materialnogo kultury, III, 1931, pp. 16–21; K. Romanov, La collonade du pourtour de la cathédrale de Saint-Georges à Yurev-Polski, Rec. Uspenskii, II, Paris, 1932, pp. 54–67; N. Sobolev, Russkaya narodnaya rezba po derevu (Russian Folk Carving in Wood), Moscow, Leningrad, 1934; N. Kholostenko, Neizvestnye pamyatniki monumentalnoi skulptury drevnei Rusi (Unknown Monumental Sculptures in Ancient Russia), Iskusstvo, III, 1951, pp. 84–91; V. Lasareff and N. Mneva, Pamyatnik novgorodskoi derevyannoi rezby XIV veka: Lyudogoshchenskii krest (An Example of 14th-century Novgorod Wood Carving: The Lyudogoshchenski Cross), Soobshcheniya Instituta istorii iskusstv Akademii Nauk SSSR, IV–V, 1954, pp. 145–66.

i. Minor arts: I. Zabelin, Istoricheskoe obozrenie finiftyanogo i tseninnogo dela v Rossii (Historical Survey of Enamel and Goldsmith Ware in Russia), Moscow, 1853; I. Zabelin, O metallicheskom proizvodstve v Rossii do kontsa XVII veka (Russian Metalware to the End of the 17th Century), Zapiski imperatorskogo russkogo arkheologicheskogo obshchesta, V, 1853, pp. 1–136; N. Kondakov, Russkie klady (Russian Treasures), St. Petersburg, 1896; V. Trutovskii, Boyarin i oruzhnichii Bogdan Matveevich Khitrovo i moskovskaya Oruzheinaya palata (The Boyar and Armorer Bogdan Matveevich Khitrovo and the Armory Palace in Moscow), Starye gody, July–Sept., 1909, pp. 345–83; P. Simoni, Sobranie izobrazhenii okladov na russkikh bogosluzhebnykh knigakh XII–XVIII stoletii, I. Drevneishie tserkovnye oklady XII–XIV stoletii (Collection of Covers on 12th–18th-century Russian Liturgical Books, I: The Oldest Covers of the 12th–14th Century), St. Petersburg, 1910; N. Pokrovskii, Drevnaya riznitsa novgorodskogo Sofiiskogo sobora (The Old Sacristy of the Cathedral of St. Sophia in Novgorod), Trudy XV arkheologicheskogo sezda v Novgorode, I, 1914; V. Nikolskii, Drevne-russkoe dekorativnoe iskusstvo (Early Russian Decorative Art), Petrograd, 1923; A. Nekrasov, Ocherki dekorativnogo iskusstva drevnei Rusi (Compendium of Decorative Art of Ancient Russia), Moscow, 1924; Sbornik Oruzheinoi Palaty (Collection of the Armory Palace), Moscow, 1925; M. Alpatoff, Die früh-moskauer Reliefplastik, Belvedere, LI–LII, 1926, pp. 237–56; Y. Olsufev, Opis drevnego tserkovnogo serebra byvshei Troitse Sergievoi Lavry (Inventory of Old Church Silver in the Former Trinity-Sergius Monastery), Sergiev Posad, 1926; E. Jones, Old Silver of Europe and America, London, 1928, pp. 292–300; V. Troitskii, Slovar moskovskikh masterov zolotogo, serebryanogo i almaznogo dela XVII veka (Dictionary of Moscow Jewelers [Gold, Silver, Diamonds] of the 17th Century), Leningrad, 1930; A. Gushchin, Pamyatniki khudozhestvennogo remesla drevnei Rusi (Artistic Handicrafts of Ancient Russia), Moscow, Leningrad, 1936; T. Goldberg and M. Postnikova-Loseva, Kleimenie zolotykh i serebryanykh izedelii XVII–nachala XVIII veka (The Chasing of Gold- and Silverware in the 17th–18th Century), Trudy Gvsudarstvennogo Istoricheskogo Museya, XIII, 1941, pp. 5–82; I. Troitskii, Organizatsiia zolotogo i serbryanogo dela v Moskve v XVII veke (Gold- and Silverware in 17th-century Moscow), Istoricheskie zapiski, XII, 1941, pp. 96–127; E. Medvedeva, O datirovke vrat Suzdalskogo sobora (On the Dating of the Gates of the Suzdal Cathedral), KS, XI, 1945, pp. 106–11; B. Rybakov, Remeslo drevnei Rusi (Handicrafts of Ancient Russia), Moscow, 1948; N. Sobolev, Russkii ornament (Russian Ornament), Moscow, 1948; M. Rabinovich, Moskovskaya keramika (Moscow Ceramics), MIA, XII, 1949, pp. 57–105; V. Lasareff, Vasilevskie vrata 1336 goda (The Vasilevski Gates of 1336), SA, XVIII, 1953, pp. 386–442; M. Postnikova-Loseva, Russkie zolotye i serbryanye kovshi (Russian Gold and Silver Bailing Scoops), Moscow, 1953; Gosudarstvennaya Oruzheinaya palata moskovskogo Kremlya (The State Armory Palace of the Moscow Kremlin), Moscow, 1954; N. Voronov and I. Sakharov, O datirovke i rapsrostranenii nekotorykh vidov moskovskikh izraztsov (Dating and Diffusion of Several Types of Moscow Majolica), MIA, XLIV, 1955, pp. 67–115; N. Platonova and M. Postnikova-Loseva, Russkoe khudozhestvennoe serebro XV–XIX v. (Artistic Russian Silver of the 15th–19th Century), Moscow, 1959; M. Postnikova-Loseva, Serebryanoe delo v Yaroslavle XVII–XIX vekov (Silverware in Yaroslavl in the 17th–19th Century), Kraevedcheskie zapiski, IV, 1960, pp. 97–152; N. Levinson, Mastera khudozhniki Moskvy XVII veka (Artists of Moscow in the 17th Century), Moscow, 1961; M. Postnikova-Loseva, Mastera serebryanogo dela (Masters of Artistic Silverware), Kaluga, 1961; Russkoe dekorativnoe iskusstvo (Russian Decorative Arts), Moscow, 1962.

j. Embroidery: V. Georgievskii, Drevnerusskoe shite v riznitse Troitse-Sergievoi lavry (Old Russian Embroideries in the Sacristy of the Trinity-Sergius Monastery), Svetilnik, XI–XII, 1914, pp. 3–26; N. Shchekotov, Drevnerusskoe shite (Old Russian Embroidery), I, Sofia, 1914, pp. 5–32; T. Aleksandrova-Dolnik, Shite moskovskoi masterskoi XVI veka (Embroidery of Moscow Artists of the 16th Century), Voprosy restavratsii, I, 1926, pp. 125–36; N. Shabelskaya, Materialy i tekhnicheskie priemy v drevnerusskom shite (Materials and Technical Devices in Old Russian Embroidery), Voprosy restavratsii, I, 1926, pp. 113–25; A. Svirin, Opis tkanei XIV–XVII vekov byvshei Troitse-Sergievoi Lavry (Inventory of 14th–17th-century Textiles from the Former Trinity-Sergius Monastery), Sergiev, 1926; N. Knats, K voprosu o tekhnike drevnerusskogo zolotogo shitya v svyazi s predmetami shitya riznitsy solovetskogo monastyrya (The Technique of Old Russian Embroidery in Gold in Relation to the Embroidered Objects in the Solovetski Monastery), Izobrazitelnoe iskusstvo (Figurative Art), Leningrad, 1927, pp. 84–112; E. Georgievskaya-Druzhinina, Sergievskaya lavra XVII veka (The 17th-century Sergievski Monastery), in Russkoe iskusstvo XVII veka (Russian Art of the 17th Century), Leningrad, 1929, pp. 133–57; E. Georgievskaya-Druzhinina, Stroganovskoe shite v XVII veke (Embroidery of the Stroganov School in the 17th Century), in Russkoe iskusstvo XVII veka, Leningrad, 1929, pp. 109–32; E. Kalinina, Tekhnika drevnerusskogo shitya i nekotorye sposoby vypolneniya khudozhestvennykh zadach (Technique of Old Russian Embroidery and Some Methods of Solving the Artistic Problems), in Russkoe iskusstvo XVII veka, Leningrad, 1929, pp. 133–57; N. Sobolev, Ocherki po istorii ukrasheniya tkaney (Essays on the History of Decorating Textiles), Moscow, 1934; M. Levinson-Nechaeva, Zoloto–serebryanoe kruzhevo XVII veka (17th-century Gold and Silver Lace), Trudy Gosudarstvennogo Istoricheskogo muzeya, XIII, 1941, pp. 167–90; V. Faleyeva, Russkaya narodnaya vyshivka (Russian Folk Embroidery), Leningrad, 1949; M. Levinson-Nechaeva, Odezhda i tkani XVI–XVII vekov (Sixteenth- and Seventeenth-century Clothing and Textiles), Gosudarstvennaya Oruzheinaya Palata moskovskogo Kremlya, Moscow, 1954, pp. 307–86; M. Shchepkina, Izobrazhenie russkikh istoricheskikh lits v shite XV veka (Representation of Russian Historical Personages in 15th-century Embroidery), Moscow, 1954; A Svirin, Drevnerusskoi shite (Early Russian Embroidery), Moscow, 1963.

Illustrations: PLS. 45–76; 9 figs. in text.

SLOAN, JOHN. American painter and etcher (b. Lock Haven, Pa., Aug. 2, 1871; d. Hanover, N.H., Sept. 7, 1951). With little instruction, he began his career at sixteen in commercial art, then became a newspaper artist for the *Philadelphia Inquirer*, 1892–95, and the *Philadelphia Press*, 1895–1903. He studied briefly at the Pennsylvania Academy in 1892–93, but the strongest influence came from Robert Henri (see I, col. 298 ff.), leader of the group of young Philadelphia realists who were in revolt against the academic idealism of established American art. With Henri's encouragement Sloan began to paint seriously in 1897. In 1901 he married Anna Marie Wall, and in 1904 he moved to New York, where for some years he supported himself chiefly by magazine illustration. But his creative work was in painting and etching the teeming life of New York City, with its infinite variety of human incident. Based on direct observation and a fresh eye, his work was marked by a rich sense of character, humor, and a strong graphic quality. In style it belonged in the naturalistic tradition of Velázquez, Goya, Hogarth, and Daumier.

Together with Henri and Arthur B. Davies, Sloan led the struggle against academic control of the art world. He was the chief organizer of "The Eight" exhibition (1908) and of the Exhibition of Independent Artists (1910); he was president of the Society of Independent Artists (1918–44). In politics a Socialist, he acted as art editor (1912–16) of the radical magazine *The Masses*, which published the most trenchant pictorial commentary of the time. From 1916 to 1937 he was an active and popular teacher, mostly in the Art Students League of New York. His teaching experience resulted in *The Gist of Art*, produced in collaboration with Helen Farr, who became his second wife in 1944.

In his late fifties Sloan completely transformed his art, in subjects, style, and technique. Abandoning contemporary genre, he concentrated on the figure, especially the female nude. His chief aim became the realization of sculptural form, using a complex technique of underpainting, glazing, and linework (I, PL. 113).

The largest groups of his works are in the Whitney Museum of American Art, New York, and the Delaware Art Center in Wilmington.

BIBLIOG. J. Sloan (with Helen Farr), The Gist of Art, New York, 1939; L. Goodrich, John Sloan, New York, 1952; Van Wyck Brooks, John Sloan, 1955; B. St. John (ed.), John Sloan's New York Scene, New York, 1965.

Lloyd GOODRICH

SLUTER, CLAUS (also KLAAS; CLAUX DE CELOISTRE, DE CELESTRE). Dutch-Burgundian sculptor (native of Haarlem) of the late 14th century, in the service of Philip the Bold, Duke of Burgundy. Sluter's place of origin, which was long a subject of controversy, was definitely established with the discovery of his name in the lists of the *Steenbickeleren* (the masons' and

stonecutters' guild) of Brussels, where he appears as Claes de Slutere van Herlam. These lists give only a few scattered dates, but by deduction this entry, and therefore Sluter's probable arrival in Brussels, can be dated about 1379–80. Although this document is the only direct reference to Sluter's stay in Brussels, the diphthongization of his name revealed by later documents in Dijon (Klaas, Claes, becoming Claux, Claus; Sluter becoming Celoistre, Celestre) gives the impression that Sluter stayed in Brussels for some time.

From Mar. 1, 1385, Sluter was in Dijon. He worked there in the workshop of Jean (Hennequin) de Marville, who had been commissioned by Philip the Bold to make the sculptures for the Chartreuse of Champmol, which was founded by the Duke himself. The accounts of the ducal workshop in Dijon are relatively well preserved, and it is therefore possible to follow Sluter's career there in some detail. From the time of his arrival he occupied a position of primary importance among Jean de Marville's collaborators and received the highest salary of any assistant. After Marville's death in 1389, Philip the Bold put Sluter in charge of the workshop. Sluter kept few of Marville's assistants, who were for the most part from Flanders; instead he chose Brabantines, most of whom are mentioned in the lists of the *Steenbickeleren* in Brussels. This may be a further indication of Sluter's prolonged stay in Brussels, where he was able to establish connections with his future assistants. The name of Claus de Werve, Sluter's nephew and successor, who also came from Haarlem, appears for the first time in Dijon in 1396; he helped his uncle until the latter's death.

The Dijon accounts mention several journeys undertaken by Sluter. In 1392 he went to Paris to buy alabaster, and in 1393 he was sent with Jean de Beaumetz to Mehun-sur-Yèvre to inspect some work that André Beauneveu (q.v.) had done for Jean de France, Duke of Berry, the brother of the Duke of Burgundy. Then, in 1395, Sluter undertook a rather long journey in the Low Countries, to Dinant and Malines, partly for the purpose of buying marble. It also seems that his return to Brabant allowed him to reestablish contact with his former Brussels companions, for it was in the following year that a new group of Brabantine sculptors joined Sluter's workshop.

No doubt Sluter, who had been seriously ill in 1399, felt his strength failing, for on Apr. 7, 1404, he made a contract with the Abbey of St-Etienne in Dijon, where he was to receive board and lodging. However, he seems to have remained just as active, and it is not certain that after this agreement he did, in fact, leave the lodgings that the Duke had put at his disposal. Having probably remained a bachelor, he was perhaps merely trying to free himself from daily cares or to ensure a place of refuge for his old age. On Jan. 31, 1406, an inventory was drawn up at "l'ostel de feu Sluter" (the lodgings of the late Sluter). The sculptor therefore died before this date, probably only shortly before, but in any case after Sept. 24, 1405.

The accounts of the ducal workshop, although incomplete, reveal that a large number of works came out of Sluter's studio. Unfortunately, most of them are not extant. Among the works that have disappeared are sculptures for the Chapel of the Angels at the Chartreuse of Champmol; for the Ste-Chapelle in Dijon (among other things, a sundial with the figure of an angel, 1395); and for Germolle Castle (statues of the Duke and Duchess surrounded by a flock of sheep; a statue of the Virgin). However, three remarkable compositions whose history can be traced still exist, at least in part: the portal of the Chartreuse of Champmol (PLS. 77, 78; V, PL. 387); the Calvary (the so-called "Well of Moses"; PLS. 79, 80) in the cloister of the same Chartreuse; and the tomb of Philip the Bold (PL. 80), formerly in the Chartreuse chapel and now in the Musée des Beaux-Arts, Dijon.

The first references to the construction of the portal for the Chartreuse of Champmol date from 1385–86, the time when the stonework was started. In 1386 the detailed plan of the architectural layout had already been supplied by Drouet de Dammartin, the architect whom Philip the Bold had commissioned to construct the Chartreuse. At about the same time, the sculptures were planned and the general iconography of the doorway was established under Jean de Marville. Work, however, hardly progressed. Only one canopy was in position at Marville's death in 1389; four others were in storage at the Chartreuse.

When Sluter was put in charge of the workshop, he immediately speeded up operations and even made some changes in the architectural part of the doorway. The canopy of the *trumeau*, which was already in position, had to be replaced because it was broken, and Sluter took advantage of this fact to make a much more ornate substitute, which was finished in 1400. The statue of the Virgin and Child was already installed in 1391, and a payment dated Aug. 6, 1391, refers to the transporting of the statues of St. John the Baptist and St. Catherine. These last two are therefore roughly contemporary with that of the Virgin and Child. The statue representing the Duchess was transported in the course of 1393, and although there is no document to confirm the fact, it is likely that the statue of the Duke was executed at about the same time. When the buildings and church of the Chartreuse were demolished after their sale in 1791, the doorway and its sculptures escaped this demolition and are still extant, although somewhat mutilated.

The sculptural composition of the doorway is relatively simple: the Virgin with the Child on her left arm is placed against the central *trumeau*, while on either side, on wide corbels, kneel the Duke and Duchess, presented to the Virgin by St. John the Baptist and St. Catherine, respectively. The canopy of the *trumeau*, which has disappeared, was decorated with angels bearing the instruments of the Passion. Under the statues of the Duke and Duchess there is a shield-bearer; each corbel bearing a patron saint has two figures of prophets reading a manuscript (V, PL. 387). The base supporting the statue of the Virgin bears the initials of the Duke and Duchess: P and M (Philip and Margaret).

In some respects the portal is still strongly dominated by tradition, especially in the arrangement of the figures. Sluter probably adopted the plan made by his predecessor, Jean de Marville, who was merely applying a scheme of composition already in widespread use in the 14th century. Bound by this heritage, he nevertheless re-created this formula and gave it a completely new meaning. The traditional Gothic sway of the Virgin has been accentuated and cleverly exploited by Sluter; seeing the Child's terror at the sight of the instruments of the Passion carried by the angels in the canopy above His head, the Virgin has thrown back her arm in a violent, convulsive gesture. In this way the artist introduced two new elements into sculpture: movement and the expression of emotion. A sense of movement is also to be found in the two patron saints, who have come forward and are about to kneel. As for the style, there is a distinct difference between the statue of the Virgin and that of St. John the Baptist on the one hand and the Duke and Duchess on the other. It should be emphasized that these last two statues are slightly later and that, being portraits, they are less dependent on tradition than the statues of the saints. Thus Sluter's realism is already fully apparent in the faces of the Duke and Duchess. Finally, all the statues are completely detached from the surrounding architecture, this being the culminating point in a long evolution that goes back to the Romanesque period.

The Calvary (also called "Well of Moses" or "Well of the Prophets"; PLS. 79, 80) is the only surviving work whose plan and execution are known to be entirely by Sluter. The sculptor had already been at the head of the ducal workshop for several years when Philip the Bold commissioned him, in 1395, to do a "grande croix" to decorate the well in the middle of the main cloister of the Chartreuse of Champmol. Sluter immediately set to work, and in the same year he had already sent to Asnières for blocks of stone for this work. The completion of the central pillar of the monument made it possible to put the cross in position at the end of 1398. Meanwhile, Sluter was busying himself with the sculptural part, and as early as June 30, 1399, a commission was able to go to the Chartreuse to inspect the work. It is not certain, however, that at this juncture all the figures of the Calvary proper — the Christ, the Virgin, St. John,

and St. Mary Magdalen — were already in place, as has been supposed. Some entries in the accounts for 1400 and 1401 seem evidence to the contrary. The six angels at the angles of the cornice (PL. 80) were fixed to the pillar in 1400–01. The six large statues of the prophets (PL. 79) came last. Three of them, those of David, Moses, and Jeremiah, were transported to the Chartreuse and put in position before July, 1402. The blocks of stone for the last three statues, those of Zechariah, Daniel, and Isaiah, arrived from Asnières in November, 1402. The exact date of their installation is not known. Work was certainly finished before Sluter's death and even probably before July, 1404, since the agreement that Duke John the Fearless concluded with Sluter at this time makes no mention of the Calvary.

The polychromy of the composition, of which only a few traces remain, was entrusted to Herman of Cologne for the gilding and to Jean Malouel for the rest.

The monument consisted of a hexagonal base placed in the middle of a well and topped by a cross and statues of the Virgin, St. John, and St. Mary Magdalen. Of the upper part, the Calvary proper, only a few fragments have survived, of which the most important is the torso of the Christ (V, PL. 320; Dijon, Archaeol. Mus.). The base, decorated with six large figures of Old Testament characters (Moses, Isaiah, Daniel, Zechariah, Jeremiah, David) and with six angels with wings spread holding up the cornice, is well preserved. In 1842 the statue of Isaiah fell into the well; the head and left arm broke off. The statue was put back in position by the Dijon sculptor Pierre Darbois, and the restoration of the whole monument was entrusted to the sculptor François Jouffroy.

The position in the middle of a well shows clearly that the Calvary was conceived as a *fons vitae*, and it is even highly probable that the idea for it came from the writings of the Carthusian monk Ludolph of Saxony. The six Old Testament figures carry scrolls with texts referring to the death of Christ. The arrangement of these figures has been carefully studied; each one presents a well-defined character. Two of the figures, placed one on either side, balance each other: Moses, on his descent from Mount Sinai, angered by the sight of the Jews worshiping the golden calf, and Zechariah, old and despondent, rejected by his people. The four others are grouped two by two: David and Jeremiah meditating on the death of Christ, and the young Daniel discussing the advent of the Messiah with Isaiah. These six statues are highly individualized, and the realism reveals itself not only in the faces but just as much in the treatment of the medium. The architecture of the monument is, as it were, drowned by the sculpture, for which it merely serves as a support.

The few surviving fragments of the upper part can give only a vague idea of this part of the composition. The torso in the Archaeological Museum, Dijon, shows Christ just after His death, with bowed head and a large wound in His side. This fragment expresses, above all, the Saviour's submission in the face of sacrifice.

It seems evident that the very founding of the Champmol Chartreuse by Philip the Bold was linked with the idea of erecting a funerary monument in the church of this monastery, but is was only in 1381 that the Duke commissioned his sculptor, Jean de Marville, to start work on the monument. At first progress was slow, and by 1384 nothing had yet been accomplished. It was only in about 1387, undoubtedly after the Duke's visit to the Dijon workshop, that the sculptor set to work seriously. At Marville's death in 1389 the architectural part was nearly finished.

When Sluter was put in charge of the workshop he seems to have been too busy with other commissions to work on the tomb. Philippe van Erein completed a few more architectural details, and in 1392 a large block of alabaster for the recumbent figure was ordered, but the work still made very slow progress. At the Duke's death on Apr. 27, 1404, the architectural parts were transferred to the church at Champmol; the large slab of black Dinant marble on which the figure was to rest was also there. At this point Duke John the Fearless concluded an agreement with Sluter whereby the tomb was to be completed within four years for a lump sum. This contract indicates that only two of the mourners had been completed and that they were to serve as a model for the others. After this date there are no more documents that throw light on the progress of the work, and it is impossible to establish what stage the tomb had reached when, after Sluter's death, John the Fearless commissioned Claus de Werve to finish the monument. It was completed at the end of 1410. Meanwhile Jean Malouel had polychromed it.

The tomb remained nearly intact until the French Revolution. At the time of the confiscation of the Chartreuse of Champmol the tomb was removed, as well as that of John the Fearless, on which the mourners are in large part rather faithful copies of those of Philip the Bold's tomb. After many vicissitudes the two tombs were reconstituted in the Archaeological Museum of Dijon. This work was carried out by the sculptor Jean Baptiste Moreau. The restoration of Philip the Bold's tomb, which was completed in 1824, was a considerable work: several mourners had been removed (about ten statuettes for the two tombs), the architecture had been damaged in several places, the little angels that decorated it had disappeared, and the recumbent figure had been badly defaced. At the time of the restoration the figure was largely recarved and completely polychromed, and it has become impossible to distinguish which parts are original. Furthermore, the mourners of the two tombs, that of Philip the Bold and that of John the Fearless, had been mixed up and reinstalled at random around the tombs. Only in 1932, thanks to François Gilquin's drawings showing the tomb in 1736, was it possible to restore the mourners to their original places and reestablish the unity of the funeral procession that runs all around the monument. Among the mourners of Philip the Bold's tomb, numbered from 1 to 40, only the first figure (a choirboy carrying the stoup and sprinkler, known from a copy on John the Fearless's tomb) and the group of two choirboys who followed directly behind are lost. The few other missing mourners have been found: No. 17 in the Perret-Carnot Collection in Saint-Loup-de-la-Salle and Nos. 18, 35, and 38 in the Cleveland Museum of Art.

Philip the Bold's tomb represents the climax of Sluter's art. As has already been shown, at Jean de Marville's death the architectural part of the tomb was well advanced. The general plan of the monument, with an openwork gallery all around instead of juxtaposed niches, therefore goes back to Marville, but the figural part can be considered Sluter's work. It is true that the sculptor died 18 months after the contract with John the Fearless, but it appears that he worked quickly, and at this time he was engaged only on the tomb. Even though the completion of the monument dragged on until the end of 1410, it is clear that Claus de Werve merely followed faithfully the plans already drawn by his uncle. An authentic work by Claus de Werve, the reredos in Bessey-les-Cîteaux, gives abundant proof that this rather mediocre artist cannot have been the creator of the lifelike mourners' procession that surrounds the tomb.

Unfortunately, it is no longer possible to judge how far the recumbent figure of the tomb is still authentic: it was too extensively restored in the 19th century. Appreciation of the artistic merit of this monument must therefore be confined to the figures of the mourners (PL. 80), which are well preserved. At the head of the procession walk the choirboys, followed by the clergy; then come the 30 mourners, all wearing full, hooded mourners' cloaks. Some of the figures advance alone, others are arranged in groups of two or three. This procession, like the Calvary, shows certain distinctive features of Sluter's art at its height and reveals the same careful integration of all the elements in a unified composition. Each figure occupies a well-defined place, expressing in some cases poignant grief and in others deep resignation. The human emotions find varied expression and emphasize the distinct character of each mourner. Although many mourners are completely covered by their robes, with a mere gesture, an attitude, a movement, the sculptor succeeds in conveying the thoughts, the feelings, the spiritual attitude of each of his figures. Completely realistic in expression, they are equally so in the treatment of the subject matter. Far more than in his earlier works, Sluter has stripped his mourners of all unnecessary detail and given to their modeling a rare monumental quality.

A question that is often raised is that of Sluter's training and activities before his arrival in Dijon. The confusion about his place of origin, the retrospective attribution of influences, and the misinterpretation of certain documents have given rise to hypotheses of scant validity: a Westphalian apprenticeship, Tournai as the place of origin of Sluter's style, the influence of André Beauneveu, etc. The same is true of the attribution of certain sculptures to Sluter, most of which are strongly influenced by his style but are not by the hand of the master. The first composition that is undoubtedly Sluter's, the Champmol portal, clearly shows traces of the mannered Gothic tradition, and a marked evolution is discernible in his works. Sluter's stay in Brussels toward 1380, a stay that certainly covered a considerable period of time, suggests this milieu as the probable starting point of his career and as the possible location of his works prior to the Dijon sculptures. The figures of prophets from the porch of the Brussels Town Hall (Brussels, Mus. Communal) have been mentioned in this connection. They probably date from about 1380 and show a striking resemblance to the corbel figures of the Champmol portal. The question arises whether they are by Sluter himself or whether they merely reveal the first signs of that new art which found full expression in Sluter's work. The present state of knowledge does not afford an answer to the question; too little is known about the part that Sluter played in Brussels.

The diffusion of Sluter's influence, however, is easier to follow. There are few traces of it in the Low Countries (with the exception of the Apostles of the Church of St-Martin in Halle, which date from about 1409, and a few tombs from Ghent). But his influence is evident in Burgundian sculpture of the first half of the 15th century, and it also spread to such centers as Souvigny, Bourges, and Lyons; to Geneva, where some of Sluter's assistants later worked (Jan van Prindale, Willem Smout); and especially to Spain — Navarre (Pamplona), Catalonia (Poblet), Mallorca (Palma), and Castile (Tordesillas).

BIBLIOG. A. Kleinclausz, Claus Sluter et la sculpture bourguignonne au XVe siècle, Paris, 1905; H. Drouot, L'atelier de Dijon et l'exécution du tombeau de Philippe le Hardi, Rev. belge d'archéol. et d'h. de l'art, II, 1932, pp. 11–39; D. Roggen, Klaas Sluter: Karakter en leven, Maandblad voor oude en jonge kunst, III, 1932, pp. 2–10; D. Roggen, Les origines de Klaas Sluter, Ann. de Bourgogne, IV, 1932, pp. 293–302; G. Toescher, Claus Sluter und die burgundische Plastik um die Wende des XIV. Jahrhunderts, Freiburg im Breisgau, 1932; H. David and A. Liebreich, Le Calvaire de Champmol, B. mon., XCII, 1933, pp. 419–67; J. Duverger, De brusselsche steenbickerelen . . . met een aanhangsel over Klaas Sluter, Ghent, 1933; D. Roggen, André Beauneveu en de "visite" van Klaas Sluter te Mehun sur Yèvre, Gentsche Bijdragen, II, 1935, pp. 114–26; D. Roggen, De "Fons vitae" van Klaas Sluter te Dijon, Rev. belge d'archéol. et d'h. de l'art, V, 1935, pp. 107–18; D. Roggen, Is Klaas Sluter van Duitse afkomst?, Gentsche Bijdragen, II, 1935, pp. 103–13; D. Roggen, De plorants van Klaas Sluter te Dijon, Gentsche Bijdragen, II, 1935, pp. 127–74; P. Rolland, Dijon, Bruxelles et Tournai (le mouvement préslutérien), Rev. belge d'archéol. et d'h. de l'art, V, 1935, pp. 335–43; E. Andrieu, Le cadran solaire de Claus Sluter à Dijon, Mém. Commission des ant. du département de la Côte d'Or, XXI, 1936–39, pp. 400–04; E. Andrieu, Introduction à la symbolique du Puits de Moïse, Mem. Soc. éduenne, XLVIII, 1936, pp. 114–15; H. David, Encore Sluter, Rev. belge d'archéol. et d'h. de l'art, VI, 1936, pp. 193–201; H. David, Mehun-sur-Yèvre et Germolles, Ann. de Bourgogne, VIII, 1936, pp. 31–34; H. David, A propos de la destruction du Calvaire du Puits de Moïse, Mém. Commission des ant. du département de la Côte d'Or, XXI, 1936–39, pp. 79–80; H. Drouot, Sluter en Belgique, Ann. de Bourgogne, VIII, 1936, pp. 278–87; H. Drouot, La visite de Claus Sluter à André Beauneveu, Rev. du Nord, XXII, 1936, pp. 169–74; M. Laurent, Claes Sluter et la sculpture brabançonne, Ann. XXXe Cong. de la Fédération archéol. et historique de Belgique, Brussels, 1936, pp. 257–70; A. Liebreich, Claus Sluter, Brussels, 1936 (bibliog.); A. Liebreich, Recherches sur Claus Sluter, Brussels, 1936; D. Roggen, Les chefs d'oeuvre de Klaas Sluter, I: Les pleurants de Klaas Sluter à Dijon, Antwerp, 1936; D. Roggen, De Kalvarieberg te Champmol, Gentsche Bijdragen, III, 1936, pp. 31–85; D. Roggen, Klaas Sluter n'est pas allemand, Ann. XXXe Cong. de la Fédération archéol. et historique de Belgique, Brussels, 1936, pp. 61–72; H. David, De nieuw et encore Sluter, Rev. belge d'archéol. et d'h. de l'art, VII, 1937, pp. 193–98; M. Devigne, Le milieu franco-flamand de Paris, Oud-Holland, LIV, 1937, pp. 115–30; M. Durand, Les pleurants du Tombeau de Philippe le Hardi, Aesculape, XXVII, 1937, pp. 122–29; A. Liebreich, De nouveau Sluter, Rev. belge d'archéol. et d'h. de l'art, VII, 1937, pp. 53–56; D. Roggen, De portaalsculpturen van Champmol, Gentsche Bijdragen, IV, 1937, pp. 107–50; D. Roggen, De rekeningen betreffende het atelier van Klaas Sluter, Gentsche Bijdragen, IV, 1937, pp. 151–71; E. Gavella, A propos du lieu de naissance de Claus

Sluter, B. Commission historique du Nord, XXXV, 1938, pp. 11-12, 16; H. David, Au pays de Claus Sluter, Ann. de Bourgogne, XI, 1939, pp. 187-204; H. Drouot, Autour de la Pastorale de Claus Sluter, Ann. de Bourgogne, XIV, 1942, pp. 7-24; P. Quarré, Les mains de Philippe le Hardi, duc de Bourgogne, sur son tombeau et au portail de la Chartreuse de Champmol, BAFr, 1942, pp. 267-81; A. Carlier, Visite de Claus Sluter à André Beauneveu de Valenciennes, Rev. du Nord, XXVII, 1944, pp. 137-40; D. Roggen, Klaas Sluter voor zijn vertrek naar Dijon in 1385, Gentse Bijdragen, XI, 1945-48, pp. 7-40; H. Drouot, Sluter: Chichés à remplacer, Ann. de Bourgogne, XXI, 1949, pp. 147-50; F. van Thienen, Claus Sluter en de kunst te Dijon, Maandblad voor beeldende kunsten, XXVI, 1950, pp. 147-55; H. David, Claus Sluter, Paris, 1951; P. Quarré, La polychromie du Puits de Moïse, Arts plastiques, III, 1951, pp. 211-18; D. Roggen, Jehan Lomme en Klaas Sluter, Gentse Bijdragen, XIII, 1951, pp. 199-207; D. Roggen, Sluter et Tournai, Ann. XXXIIIᵉ Cong. de la Fédération archéol. et historique de Belgique, 1951, p. 592; F. Salet, Formation italienne de Claus Sluter?, B. mon., CX, 1952, pp. 84-86; S. Sulzberger, Claus Sluter et l'Italie, B. Acad. royale de Belgique, Classe des beaux-arts, XXXIV, 1952, pp. 90-106; S. Sulzberger, La formation de Claus Sluter, Brussels, 1952; P. Quarré, Les statues du portail de la Chartreuse de Champmol, BAFr, 1954-55, pp. 113-14; D. Roggen, Prae-sluteriaanse, sluteriaanse, post-sluteriaanse nederlandse sculptuur, Gentse Bijdragen, XVI, 1955-56, pp. 111-91; P. Gras, Deux "puits de Moïse" à Chalon-sur-Saône, Misc. D. Roggen, Antwerp, 1957, pp. 101-04; G. Zarnecki, Claus Sluter: Sculptor to Duke Philip the Bold, Apollo, LXXVI, 1962, pp. 271-76.

Henri PAUWELS

Illustrations: PLS. 77-80.

SŌAMI. Japanese painter and master of the tea ceremony. Son of Geiami and grandson of Nōami (1472?-1525/30), Sōami represented the third generation of the Ami family. Known also by the pseudonym Kangaku (his surname was Shinsō), he spent his entire life at the court of the Ashikaga as custodian of the archives, the art collections, and the calligraphic works of the shogun.

Sōami, a person of multiform talent, is the prototype of many later artists. As a painter he has left an extensive series of landscape paintings on fusuma in the Daisenin of the Daitokuji in Kyoto (PL. 82); one panel of such a painting is now in Cleveland (Mus. of Art). As a master of the tea ceremony (cha-no-yu) and the incense ceremony (kōdō) and as an artist of flower arranging (ikebana), he was outstanding for his originality, which was not without suggestions of Zen doctrine; as a landscape architect he has left unequivocal evidence of his talent in the gardens of the Ryūanji (VIII, PL. 448, FIG. 1082) and the Daitokuji in Kyoto and in that of Kinkakuji.

As a painter he was a follower of the Chinese Mu-ch'i (q.v.) and preferred, like his grandfather Nōami, landscapes with rounded hills and vast spatial depths, contrary to the tendency of his time, which preferred the rigid style of Hsia Kuei, Ma Yüan (qq.v.), and other Chinese artists of the "Northern School." In spite of the fact that he painted in the Chinese manner, with a strong and vigorous stroke, his paintings, especially those at the Daisenin mentioned above, are distinguished by that softness and lightness which can be found only in traditional Japanese painting (see YAMATO-E). For stylistic reasons, the Shōshō Hakkei (a series of eight lake views; PL. 81) and the Kōrō Nisei (Confucius and Lao-tzu), both at the Daisenin in Kyoto, are attributed to him.

His remarkable talent and familiarity with the art collections and archives of the shogun made him an exceptionally fine critic. The Onryūken nichiroku (a daily record) and other documents mention his activities as an art critic in the Bummei (1469-86) and Eishō (1504-20) eras. The Kundaikan Sayuchōki ("Account of the Treasures of the Lord"), the most ancient Japanese treatise on art criticism, is, in fact, attributed to him. This work, written in 1511, lists the paintings collected by the shogun and describes their stylistic characteristics with remarkable competence. Literary sources, however, consider this work the completion of a preceding book, begun by his grandfather, Nōami, in 1476. Tradition also ascribes to Sōami the authorship of another work, the Go shoku ki ("History of Decoration"); published in 1660 from notes written by Sōami between about 1521 and 1528, it deals with the interior decoration of dwellings, with particular reference to that of the shogun Yoshimasa (1436-90).

Antonio PRIORI

BIBLIOG. H. Minamoto, An Illustrated History of Japanese Art, Kyoto. 1935; N. Tsuda, Handbook of Japanese Art, Tokyo, 1935; K. Nakada, San Ami (Tōyō bijutsu bunko, 5), Tokyo, 1939 (in Jap.); Pageant of Japanese Art, II, 2, Tokyo, 1952; R. T. Paine and A. Soper, The Art and Architecture of Japan, Harmondsworth, 1955.

* *

Illustrations: PLS. 81, 82.

SOANE, SIR JOHN. English architect (b. near Goring, Berks., Sept. 10, 1753). At the age of fifteen Soan (as the name was then spelled) entered the London office of George Dance II, transferring some months later to that of Henry Holland, where he worked for several years. By winning the King's traveling studentship Soane was able to visit Italy (1778-80), there making the acquaintance of Thomas Pitt, later Lord Camelford, who was to be among his earliest patrons when the young architect returned to England and started his practice. Soane's first important works came in 1783, when he designed Blackfriars Bridge, Norwich, and a house at Letton, Norfolk, for B. G. Dillingham. A parsonage at Saxlingham and a house at Tendring were commissioned in 1784, followed by Shotesham and additions to Chillington in 1785, after which his practice grew rapidly. An introduction to Lord Camelford's cousin William Pitt, then Prime Minister, resulted in Soane's making additions to Holwood, Kent, in 1786; two years later the Prime Minister gave his support to Soane's successful application for the post of Architect to the Bank of England. In the course of the next forty years he was responsible for the enlargement of the Bank from a small nucleus to the great complex of buildings that constituted his finest work, although now only the outer wall remains of the original.

Up to 1790 Soane's designs were in the then-current idiom, influenced by Henry Holland and James Wyatt. With the financial security that came partly from the Bank appointment and partly from a legacy, his work from this date on took on a new character, embodying neoclassic ideas assimilated from such sources as M.-A. Laugier's Essai sur l'architecture. The result was a highly idiosyncratic style, classical in spirit but with the usual elements pared down to a minimum and often represented only by "token" orders or incised lines. The drawing room added to Wimpole, Cambs., is the earliest expression of this "Soane style," but its first important appearance came with the Bank Stock Office of 1791-92, where the practical requirements of security and fireproofing resulted in a remarkable composition of bays lit from above and vaulted with hollow tiles. From 1800 Soane became increasingly interested in attaining picturesque effects, attempting a combination of Gothic and classical elements that culminated in the Dulwich College Picture Gallery (1811) and the remarkable interiors of the old Law Courts (destroyed) in London. Although somewhat altered, Tyringham, Bucks. (1792), Pelwall, Staffs. (1822), and Soane's own country villa at Ealing, Pitzhanger Manor (1800), are the best surviving examples of his mature designs for private residences, while the Dulwich Art Gallery is a unique public work.

Soane was appointed Clerk of Works to the Royal Hospital, Chelsea, in 1807, rebuilding the Infirmary (destroyed), the secretary's office, and the stables. In 1815 he became one of the three architects attached to the Office of Works. Much of his work in this capacity is no longer extant, including the royal suite in the House of Lords (1822-23) and the State Paper Office (1829), but fragments remain in the present Treasury (originally Board of Trade), Whitehall, and at Nos. 10 and 11 Downing Street.

An outstanding collector of sculpture, paintings, books, and drawings, Soane took infinite care over their arrangement in the house in Lincoln's Inn Fields that he built in 1812. He lived there until his death in 1837, when, under an Act of Parliament, the house became a public museum named for him.

Dorothy STROUD

BIBLIOG. A. T. Bolton, The Works of Sir John Soane, London, 1924; J. N. Summerson, Soane: The Case-History of a Personal Style, J. of the Royal Inst. of British Architects, LVIII, 1951, pp. 83-89; J. N. Summerson, Sir John Soane, London, 1952; D. Stroud, The Architecture of Sir John Soane, London, 1961.

* *

SODOMA. Sobriquet of Giovanni Antonio Bazzi, Italian painter of the Renaissance (b. Vercelli, 1477; d. Siena, on the night of 14–15 Feb., 1549). Bazzi was technically a member of the Piedmontese school and was a pupil of Giovanni Spanzotti (ca. 1450–1526/28) for the seven years 1490–97. He was much influenced by Leonardo in the latter's Milanese phase. Probably in 1500 he went to Siena; he was certainly there in 1501. As he spent most of his life in Siena and came somewhat under the influence of Fra Bartolommeo and Raphael (qq.v.), Bazzi may also be reckoned a central Italian. He was twice in Rome, once about 1508 when he was painting in the Vatican and again in 1513 when he was working at the Farnesina for Agostino Chigi. His earliest important work is the series of frescoes in the Abbey of Monte Oliveto Maggiore (1505–08), which slightly antedates his first visit to Rome. These mostly concern the life and miracles of St. Benedict, and all have a spaciousness and freshness about them that Bazzi was not to preserve for long. They are light and facile in execution, with delicate bluish tones and a nice Umbrian sense of atmosphere and distance, occasionally combined with an arbitrary perspective. Bazzi's early work marks him as an artist of great talent, but there is an occasional ambiguity that is not altogether pleasing. His relatively early decline was due, in Giorgio Vasari's opinion, to lack of competition.

Bazzi's work is best seen in Siena and Rome, where perhaps half his works are concentrated. The reader is referred to Bernard Berenson's lists, s.v. Sodoma, but the following dated or datable paintings (all in Siena and all in fresco) may be selected for mention: scenes from the life of St. Catherine, 1518, in the Oratory of S. Bernardino (cf. XII, PL. 63); figures of saints, 1529–33, Palazzo Pubblico, Sala del Mappamondo; Madonna with SS. Sebastian and Bernardino, 1539, Capella di Piazza. Among the best-known of Bazzi's paintings are the *St. Sebastian* in the Uffizi and the *Judith* in the Pinacoteca, Siena. A *tondo* in the Louvre with figures of Love and Chastity (an identification generally accepted but appearing in Berenson's lists with a question mark) is also celebrated and reveals Bazzi's ability in composition within the particularly difficult roundel shape.

BIBLIOG. R. H. Cust, G. A. Bazzi, Hitherto Usually Styled "Sodoma," London, 1906; E. Jacobsen, Sodoma und das Cinquecento in Siena, Strasbourg, 1910.

Arthur McComb

SOGDIANA. The vast territory known as Sogdiana until the Arab conquest is situated between the Amu Darya (anc. Oxus) and Syr Darya (anc. Jaxartes) rivers. It consisted essentially of the arable or irrigable land in the middle valleys of these two rivers and their tributaries and in the valley of the Zeravshan. The lower valleys of the Amu Darya and Syr Darya were occupied by the settlements that formed Khwarizm (q.v.) and other centers in the Dzhety-Asar region that were of less importance.

Sogdiana had clearly defined borders and was inhabited by a people speaking an Indo-European language (Sogdian); however, it had a considerable cultural expansion after the founding of the Achaemenid empire. During the centuries following the Macedonian conquest until the first millennium A.D. (when the Turkic language replaced Sogdian), Sogdiana extended its influence toward the northeast beyond the Syr Darya, among the European type of peoples who spoke Indo-European languages of the Śaka type and who occupied the valleys of the upper Syr Darya, the Chu, and the Ili.

The history of these regions is known from the middle of the 6th century B.C., when Cyrus founded the Achaemenid empire. Discoveries by Russian archaeologists since the end of the 19th century have made it possible — in the absence of written documentation — to study the material civilizations and the cultures that emerged in these regions since about the first millennium B.C. The oases that were formed in the vicinity of the watercourses were gradually enlarged by a system of irrigation canals, and real towns were built. At the same time techniques were perfected, owing particularly to the utilization of iron.

These large irrigation systems appeared as early as the middle of the first millennium B.C. In the valley of the Zeravshan a vast network of canals was developed and the city of Afrasiyab (anc. Samarkand) was established. In the oasis of Merv a network that included the canal that irrigated the site of Gyaur Kale must have existed as early as the 7th–6th century B.C. During this period the irrigation system of the oasis of Kobadian was created on the left bank of the lower Kafirnigan, a tributary of the upper Amu Darya, a region that in antiquity was part of the northern territory of Bactria and where the important town of Kala-i-Mir arose. Either at this time or a little later the site of Eilatan in Fergana began to develop. At a later period other irrigation centers appeared north of the Syr Darya in the Chach region (Ak Tepe, Buzuk Tepe, Otrar, Sayram) and in the southern part of Tadzhikistan on the right bank of the Amu Darya (Key-Kobad-shakh, 3d–2d cent. B.C.).

For several centuries Sogdiana, together with its southern and northern peripheral territories, enjoyed considerable prosperity, first under the domination of the Achaemenid empire and later under Alexander the Great and his successors, the Seleucid and Bactrian kings. This prosperous era ended when the nomads of the northern steppe started to move toward Iran because they refused to recognize the authority of the newly founded Hsiung-nu empire in northern Asia.

For about four centuries (7th–3d cent. B.C.) the European type of nomads who seem to have been the descendants of the peoples of Andronovo occupied the whole of the Central Asian steppe from the confines of northern Asia to the Carpathian Mountains (see ASIA, CENTRAL). These were the Scythians, the Sauromatae, and the Sarmatians, and one part of them, the Śakas, or Sacae, lived on the borders of the settled regions of outer Iran, including Sogdiana. The Śakas, who were not yet acquainted with iron, seem to have had peaceful relations with the sedentary peoples whose economy complemented their own. Some of them had moved farther east at an undetermined period and had occupied a portion of northern Asia, either becoming sedentary in the western oases of the Tarim Basin or remaining nomad in the steppe of southern Mongolia, such as the Yüeh-chih and the Wu-sun, whose conditions during the 3d century B.C. have been described by Chinese sources.

The expansion of the Hsiung-nu empire, whose sovereigns defeated the Yüeh-chih and Wu-sun, led the latter people to move toward the west in order to escape its domination. At this time Sogdiana had regained its independence from the Greco-Bactrian kingdom with the help of the Śakas, even though they remained more or less dependent on them, since the Greek domination of Bactria had shifted toward India as early as the reign of Demetrios (ca. 190–175 B.C.), as attested to by some coins inscribed in Aramaean, while farther south the inscriptions are in Greek. Between 140 and 130 the Greco-Bactrian kingdom disappeared under the pressure of the Śakas, who were themselves driven out by the Yüeh-chih. The latter, having been forced to leave the Ili region where they had sought refuge, crossed Fergana, Chach, and Sogdiana and settled in Bactria. A short time later they founded some small states, which became unified and formed the Kushan empire (ca. 25 B.C.), whose center, which perhaps had been in Sogdiana, was transferred later to northwestern India. This new situation led to the weakening of the Kushan empire in Central Asia and, consequently (according to Chinese texts), to a partial conquest of their territory, including Sogdiana, by the Hsiung-nu Hu-yün, who apparently were real Huns.

A remarkable economic and cultural development occurred during the Kushan period. Thanks to the development of irrigation, vast desert areas were made habitable; agriculture and commerce expanded; iron, silver, gold, mercury, and cinnabar were mined; and stone was quarried in the Termez region. In this period the sedentary population lived in towns fortified by ramparts made of large sun-dried bricks and reinforced with square and, later, round towers, to which the sovereign's citadel was attached. Generally square, the towns varied in size, and some covered large areas (ca. 870 acres at Merv and ca. 250 acres at Afrasiyab). Smelters, jewelers, pot-

Principal centers of archaeological and artistic interest in Sogdiana and bordering areas. Key: (1) Modern national boundaries.

ters, stone cutters, and other craftsmen attained a high level of technical knowledge. It was in this environment that an art form developed remarkable for its originality in painting as well as sculpture.

The excavations of the past 40 years have brought to light entire cities whose importance could not have been imagined from the probings of the first 20 years of this century. The archaeological sites are grouped in sectors. The most important is located in the valley of the Zeravshan and includes Varakhsha, Paykand, Afrasiyab (the pre-Islamic site of Samarkand), Tali Barzu, Pyandzhikent, and Mug. In the Syr Darya valley are the fortified cities of Ak Tepe and Munchak Tepe and the settlements of Kaunchi Tepe and Burgulyuk. In the southern part of Sogdiana in the valley of the upper Amu Darya and some of its tributaries (Kobadian) are the sites of Termez, Airtam, Balalyk Tepe, Kala-i-Mir, and Key-Kobad-shakh; some of these were probably linked with ancient Bactria. Finally, the towns of the Talas and Chu valleys, such as Taraz, Saryg, and Ak-Beshim, must be considered as having been founded by Sogdians or eastern Iranians and inhabited by them up to the time of the Turkish conquest (ca. 10th cent.), following which their original language disappeared, which also happened in the oases of the Tarim and Turfan basins.

Most of these sites have been only partially excavated, especially the important towns; therefore only certain aspects of their architecture and art are known and it is not possible to describe their evolution, but only to examine some of their specific expressions at a given time. The art was influenced by the Greek conquest, which engendered the great Hellenistic trend, by ancient Iran, by India through the intermediary of Buddhism, and by the invasions of the Śakas, the Yüeh-chih,

and the Ephthalites. After the Moslem conquest during the 8th century a new, predominantly Arab style came into being, but certain types of buildings retained the previous architectural styles and some were probably linked with local art.

The characteristics of the cities of Sogdiana during the last centuries before our era are not well known. Key-Kobad-shakh was built about the 3d–2d century B.C.; it had a square plan — standard for all Central Asian cities of that period — and was surrounded by a wall of sun-dried brick, reinforced with square towers. During the Parthian period in Margiana the walls were also made of sun-dried brick and beaten earth; they had numerous loopholes and were reinforced with square towers, which by the 3d–4th century of our era were replaced by semicircular towers. At Key-Kobad-shakh the dwellings were situated within the surrounding defensive walls and were separated from them by a narrow passage. The vestibules of the houses were covered with a plaster of white alabaster. The lower layers of Kala-i-Mir go back to the 7th–6th century B.C.; those dating from the 3d–2d century B.C. have the same layout that is found at Key-Kobad-shakh.

Both these sites have yielded a considerable amount of pottery, much with a red slip, which is remarkable for the quality and fineness of the shapes. Characteristic is the large-footed cup, very widespread in Sogdiana and Fergana. Metal objects, cereal graters, and whetstones have also been found. Since similar pieces have been discovered at Begram in Afghanistan and north of Termez at Zar Tepe, it is evident that the civilization that existed throughout Sogdiana and the neighboring regions at that time was remarkably homogeneous.

The excavations at Afrasiyab also help to determine the level of civilization in Sogdiana during this period. Ceramics were highly developed and presented the same characteristics as those of Sogdiana and Fergana previously mentioned. Among the most interesting discoveries are some terra-cotta statuettes of rare artistic quality. Some of these represent local deities, such as Anāhitā and perhaps Siyāvash; others may have been inspired by Greek mythology.

During the Kushan period (see KUSHAN ART) the cities underwent a remarkable development. They were encircled by defensive walls. When they had a plan that was uniform, regular, and square, the districts were symmetrically arranged, as at Kala-i-Mir, Key-Kobad-shakh, and Toprak Kale in Khwarizm. Some cities were built on an irregular plan, such as Afrasiyab.

The discovery of remains of a potter's workshop at Afrasiyab, in a level corresponding to this period, with a stock of clay, statuette molds, and some vases ready for firing, and of some kilns of the same period at Airtam near Termez, at Munchak Tepe, and at other Central Asian sites shows that highly skilled craftsmen produced ceramic ware characterized by beautiful quality and by a red slip. These wares reveal some similarities of Roman ceramics of the same period.

The sites of Tali Barzu and Mug are of equal interest. Tali Barzu dates back to the Achaemenid period, and excavations have revealed several layers. The first two are of the 6th–5th and the 5th–4th century B.C. At that time the town was in the form of a fortified square, and the art and architecture had already reached a fairly high development. The subsequent two levels, which date from the 3d–2d century B.C. and the 1st century B.C.–2d century of our era, correspond to those of the towns already described. The fourth level appears to have continued until the end of the 6th or the beginning of the 7th century. It was during this period that the town was leveled and that a strong castle made of pisé with a donjon in the center was built. At this time Sogdiana became divided into small principalities, which, until the 8th century, were vassals of the empires that dominated northern Asia and that disappeared with the Arab conquest. The third and fourth levels have contributed much information on the Greco-Bactrian and Kushan periods. The Greek influence seems to have spread from the large centers, in particular Maracanda (Samarkand), and many terra-cotta statuettes have been found, as at Afrasiyab, representing Greek or Seleucid deities, as well as terra-cotta camels and other animals, horsemen, and numerous figures of Anāhitā. These statuettes, of which numerous examples have been discovered in Sogdiana and in its bordering regions as well as in the western part of the Tarim Basin (in particular at Khotan), seem to belong to the Kushan period. The type appears to have become widespread during the period when these regions enjoyed a certain unity. The large-footed cup is found in the same level at Tali Barzu and other sites in Sogdiana, the type having undergone some modifications in its proportions.

The site of Mug is a rocky spur at the junction of the Zeravshan and Kum rivers, on which a fortress in the form of an almost rectangular trapezoid was built. The lower part of the walls is made of schistose ashlar joined with loess and the upper part is made of sun-dried brick. The building is composed of four rooms vaulted with identical bricks, which probably supported one story as part of the construction. Numerous objects were discovered here: manuscripts; coarse pottery; wooden objects, particularly noteworthy for their finish; skins; fabrics, including some fragments of silk brocade, as well as cotton and woolen cloth of local manufacture; utensils of iron; and weapons. Of outstanding interest is a wooden shield covered with skin decorated with the representation of a horseman on a yellow background (see below). All the information collected indicates that Mug was approximately contemporaneous with Pyandzhikent and that it was destroyed at the time of the Arab conquest in the 8th century.

During the Kushan period Buddhism, aided and promoted by Kaniṣka and his successors, spread throughout Central Asia, and important buildings were erected in Sogdiana, Afghanistan, and the Tarim Basin. Two Buddhist monasteries have been discovered at Kara Tepe (FIG. 126) and Gengis Tepe near Termez (anc. Tarmita), founded by the Bactrian king Demetrios,

which include open-air buildings and rock-cut sanctuaries adorned with stone statues and wall paintings. Fragments of statues of Buddha and bodhisattvas have been found in other zones of the same region.

Buddhism must have reached Sogdiana at the same time, but no Buddhist site seems to have been discovered here. However, the very name of Bukhara, which comes from the Sanskrit *vihāra* (monastery), and the numerous Naubihar or Nobihar, from *navavihāra* (new monastery), which are found in Sogdiana and Iran, show the development of Buddhism in these regions. Two sites of later date have been discovered: one at Kuva and the other at Ak-Beshim. The Buddhist temple at Ak-Beshim probably dates from the late 7th or early 8th century. It appears that Buddhism began to die out in Sogdiana and Iran from the 5th or 6th century as a result of the development of Mazdaism during the Sassanian period. Apparently the only Buddhist communities that survived were outside the Sassanian empire, some north of Sogdiana, others south, particularly south of the Hindu Kush, despite the persecutions by the Ephthalites.

The temple at Ak-Beshim was built on a rectangular plan and, being constructed on a natural rise, had an entrance and a courtyard from which the central hall could be reached by a stairway. The central hall itself was on a lower level than the cella. The entrance portal was richly decorated with bas-reliefs in modeled clay painted in blue and representing mostly sprays of plants. The vast courtyard, surrounded by columned galleries, was reached by a vestibule. Access to the main hall

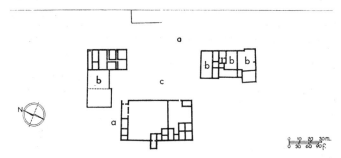

Kara Tepe, plan of the building complex around the main square: (*a*) Streets; (*b*) courtyards; (*c*) main square (*from Pugachenkova, 1958*).

was through a large door. This hall was lighted by openings in the ceiling, which rested on wooden beams supported by wooden columns. The walls were decorated with paintings executed on an alabaster coating and with bas-reliefs of modeled clay. Opposite the entrance were four statues of Buddha seated on high pedestals, which framed the doors leading to the cella and the circumambulation passage. The cella, reached by a stairway, was closed by a large door; the cella was built on a square plan and was covered by a cupola with a ceiling underneath it. The bronze idol was placed against the back wall. The gallery was vaulted and a long bench bearing statues and sculptured groups ran the length of it.

The cella of the Ak-Beshim temple is very similar to the cellae of several temples at Shikshim (Shorchuk) near Karashahr, as well as to certain temples of the same type at Dandan-uilik in Khotan (see KHOTANESE ART) and Bezeklik in Turfan (q.v.). However, most of them seem to be related to the cella of Temple I discovered at Pyandzhikent, which also originally had a circular gallery (later transformed) running around a hall and a cella, with, in addition, an open-air courtyard enclosed by walls, whose entrance was on the east, as it was at Ak-Beshim. This gives weight to the hypothesis that it was built by Sogdians who had settled in that region and were familiar with the building methods of Sogdiana as well as those of ancient Serindia (Kyzlasov, 1958).

The remains of the paintings and sculpture from Ak-Beshim are too fragmentary to make definite conclusions possible. The technique of molding the various parts of the statues in clay and fitting them to a coarse clay armature that rested on a wooden or reed support was also used in Serindia. The technique of molding ornaments and applying them to the walls also seems to be the same. The few remains of mural paintings recall motifs that are found particularly in the oasis of Turfan. These techniques are also encountered at Pyandzhikent and Tepe Marendzhap near Kabul. The folds of the garments and the medallions bordered with bead molding are elements encountered in the art of eastern Iran and Serindia.

Despite the spread of new ideas introduced by the Greeks and by Buddhism, the ancient beliefs survived. Some Greek deities were included in the traditional pantheon, among them Alexander deified. In Sogdiana as in Bactria, which became Tokharistan during the first centuries of our era, a large part of the population continued to worship Okhsho, the local deity of Vakhsh (Amu Darya), as well as the goddess Anāhitā and some secondary deities of the Indo-Iranian pantheon. Some clay statuettes representing a goddess have been found in the Termez region and at Key-Kobad-shakh. A small sanctuary, which may have been a fire temple, has been uncovered at Munchak Tepe. Important discoveries of mural paintings at Varakhshah and Pyandzhikent show that local cults had regained considerable importance around the 5th century.

The architecture of the Kushan period in Sogdiana and Tokharistan has been little studied because adequate documentation is lacking. The citadel of Tali Barzu dates from the first centuries of our era. On top of a hill was a fortified group of buildings, consisting of a high tower with narrow loopholes surrounded by a broad courtyard, itself protected by a square enclosure with towers at the corners. Several hundred small rooms with vaulted ceilings formed a single unit with the wall. The walls were made of beaten earth reinforced with sun-dried brick and covered with a coating of clay. A similar arrangement was used in the contemporaneous fortresses of Khwarizm. In Tokharistan beaten earth and large square sun-dried bricks seem to have been the material most utilized; stone was employed for capitals, column bases, cornices, and other decorative elements. Usually the buildings had flat wooden roofs supported by wooden columns with stone bases and Corinthian capitals of stone. The walls were often decorated with pilasters and coated with white stucco, and sometimes had paintings. The fragments of the stone frieze from Airtam (Leningrad, The Hermitage), which probably came from a Buddhist monastery, date from the 1st or 2d century of our era.

Ceramics underwent a remarkable development during this period. Two types have been found in Sogdiana and Tokharistan: one is of red clay covered with a red slip, sometimes brown in Tokharistan; the other is of gray clay with a gray or black slip, which is not generally characteristic of Sogdiana. The red pottery is in the form of cups with feet decorated in relief and vessels with handles in the form of animals, the latter deriving from the northern regions of Asia. Vessels with bands painted in red on a clear slip, jars of the oinochoe type, and vases with small modeled heads under the vertical handles are typical of the production of Sogdiana, and are also found in the Tarim Basin. The gray pottery found in Tokharistan consists mostly of flat cups with curved rims.

The monuments that have been studied in the Tashkent region in Chach, especially in the settlement of Kaunchi Tepe, afford an idea of the degree of civilization attained during the Kushan period. Vestiges of fortifications and buildings of beaten earth and sun-dried brick, covered by vaults of sun-dried brick, have been discovered. The artistic activity can be judged only from the ceramic ware: this is mostly handmade and includes jars, lids, vessels with vertical handles in the form of animals, and large, flat-bottomed bowls with grooved rims decorated with droplets of brown slip.

The collapse of the Kushan empire was followed by a confused period during which Sogdiana was divided into small feudal principalities that, under the authority of the Ephthalites, then the Turks and the Chinese, lasted until the Arab conquest in the 8th century. During this period some of the minor rulers in Sogdiana and Tokharistan built new capitals, some of which, discovered during the last 30 years, have revealed the remarkable art that flourished in these regions. Three particularly important sites have been discovered by Soviet archaeologists: Varakhsha and Pyandzhikent in Sogdiana and Balalyk Tepe in Tokharistan.

Before these important discoveries Sogdian painting was known solely from the shield discovered at Mug in 1933. On the skin that covers the shield an armed horseman is depicted against a yellow background; the horseman's head and the legs of the horse are missing. The horseman is armed with a straight sword, a dagger, a quiver and arrows, and two bows. He wears a caftan which comes below the knees, and holds in his left hand the handle of a weapon — probably a lance but perhaps a sort of scepter — which rests on his shoulder. According to Staviskii (1956), this horseman shows very close connections with the horses and riders portrayed in Room 13 of Sector VI at Pyandzhikent (see below). The Mug painting is remarkable for the firmness and flexibility of the drawing and the realism of the design.

Sogdian painting was, however, already known through a painting from the pre-Islamic period, discovered at Afrasiyab in 1913 by Viatkin (1927). This was a mural painting on which three human figures could be distinguished; it disintegrated after being exposed to the air and is known only from copies. In the light of present-day knowledge it can be surmised that the painting dates from the 6th–8th century; thus it would be roughly contemporaneous with the paintings of Pyandzhikent and Varakhsha.

The sites of Pyandzhikent and Varakhsha are of considerable interest because the archaeological remains are not those in which the influence of Buddhism, with all that this brought from India or eastern Iran, is manifest but those in which the Sogdian culture of the centuries preceding Arab conquest is evident. It is thus an art that is specifically Sogdian, both in sculpture and painting, a local art that was developed in Sogdiana in which the local artistic tendencies were mixed with various cultural elements coming from Iran and the Hellenistic East, undoubtedly through the intermediary of Greco-Bactrian art (see BACTRIAN ART).

The ruins of Pyandzhikent are those of an important center that existed from the 6th century and disappeared in the second half of the 8th century when it was destroyed by the Arabs. The ensemble has an irregular aspect; it includes the town proper (shahristān) surrounded by walls, the citadel farther west, both of which were built on hills, the buildings outside the walls forming a vast suburb east and southeast, and an immense necropolis south of the city. The excavations have been concentrated on the shahristān, which covers an area of about 47 acres, where the most interesting discoveries have been made: two temples designated as Temples I and II; a palace called Sector III, where the dwellings of the dignitaries were grouped into a single unit, located east of the temples; and another palace, Sector VI, southeast of Sector III. All these buildings are constructed of sun-dried brick. The remains of the wall paintings and sculpture discovered here are among the most interesting in Central Asia.

Temples I and II are built on the same plan (FIG. 130), with only a few differences in details. They comprise a group of main rooms erected on a high subfoundation, a vast courtyard, and a large number of rooms that form an enclosure around the courtyard. The first series of paintings was discovered in these temples.

In Temple I, Room 5, four male figures are depicted, three of whom, hands raised to the level of their faces, worship a haloed deity of larger size. In Room 10 on the west part of the north wall are two male figures seated cross-legged on a rug, holding small branches in bloom, with three fantastic animals above them; on the east part of the north wall the scene is divided in two parts: on the left a priest kneels before an altar and on the right are his five attendants divided into two groups; on the east wall three male figures are seated cross-legged, two represented full face holding goblets in one hand and small branches in bloom in the other (PL. 84). In Room 10-a a severely damaged painting represents about ten people engaged in what is probably a ritual dance.

In Temple II on the south wall of one room is a group of crowned horsemen with their arms raised in salute as if they were arriving at the shrine; its north wall has a badly damaged painting showing the heads of three horses facing west and several figures in the background. In the main hall on the central portion of the south wall is a scene of mourning (PL. 83) with women weeping over the body of a dead youth placed in an arcaded pavilion; another scene portrays three haloed deities, one of whom has four arms.

Sector III contains several important paintings. In Room 6 on the east and north walls a war scene has been preserved, with the goddess of victory watching over a battlefield where a group of figures is portrayed in black, white, and yellow against a red background. In Room 17 the west wall has a series of white horsemen outlined in black against a red background (PL. 85).

The paintings in Sector VI are equally as important as those in the two temples. In Room 1 the west portion of the north wall and part of the west wall have a group of figures feasting under a canopy (PL. 85); on the west portion of the south wall is a combat between two warriors on foot (PL. 86) and a woman playing a harp (PL. 84); the south portion of the west wall has a battle scene with many horsemen divided into two groups and a wounded warrior who has fallen between the feet of the horses. In Room 8 on the west portion of the north wall four female figures are depicted; one, adorned with small bells, is seated, and the other three are kneeling and holding jewelry and other objects in their outstretched hands (PL. 87). In Room 13 the north wall portrays horsemen and infantrymen who march in close ranks, followed by an elephant and, a little farther on, three musicians, one of whom is playing the Indian harp; on the north portion of the west wall the scenes are depicted in two registers: in one register are three figures, two of them playing tricktrack (PL. 86), and in the other register is a seated figure with two prisoners kneeling before him. A scene of another game of tricktrack from Room 13 is now in Leningrad (PL. 90). Many other fragments of paintings have survived, some with figures and others with geometric motifs of every kind.

These paintings were executed with the use of colored earths and mineral colors, applied by means of a fine layer of alabaster over a plaster of loess. The only exception is Temple II, where the layer of alabaster is missing.

According to D'iakonov (in Iakubovskii et al., 1954), it is possible to distinguish four styles in this ensemble. The first, represented by the paintings in Temple II, is the simplest and oldest. These paintings form a unit. The coloring of the ensemble is somewhat soft; yellow and red ocher and brown and cinnamon tones predominate; perhaps the blues have disappeared. The color range is thus somewhat poor, and the composition is rather conventional but simpler and more concise than in the other paintings; it is freer, asymmetrical, and tends to express emotion through the movement and gestures of the figures.

The second style is represented only by a bearded figure whose head is encircled by a halo, which appears in Room 10 of Temple I. This image differs radically from the other human faces represented at Pyandzhikent, as well as from those in the paintings of Bamian, in the Sassanian paintings, and in the paintings of the Tarim Basin. D'iakonov thinks that this painting has affinities with the Christian paintings of Byzantium and Transcaucasia; however, the affinity may be with Manichaean art (q.v.).

The third style is encountered in the major part of the paintings at Pyandzhikent that are found in Temple I and in Sectors III and VI. In spite of some basic differences, these paintings have so many common traits that they can be placed in the same group, in contrast to the paintings of the first two styles. All the human figures are represented in a more conventional way; the number of poses is limited, and even the position of the hands is restricted to a few rigorously defined variations; and the faces for the most part are shown in three-quarter view. A study of these paintings thus makes it possible to define a canon for the human figure established by the artists of that period: 1. frontal representation of figures seated cross-legged; 2. profile views of figures kneeling and resting on their heels; and 3. figures standing. In every category all the figures show the same relation in the proportions. The

drawing and contour lines are very supple and elegant; the poses are relaxed; the movements and gestures are affected, in contrast to the expressiveness and brutal force of the figures of the first style. Other characteristics of this style are the care for rendering details and the love for sumptuousness, which is expressed especially in the painting of the fabrics and rugs with gorgeous motifs. The background color is red, blue, or even black and constitutes a unified and monochrome field on which the figures and objects represented stand out. The paintings of Room 41 of Sector VI (PL. 89) seem to be related to this style.

Finally, there is a fourth style, represented by the paintings in Room 6 of Sector III, which is fairly close to the third style.

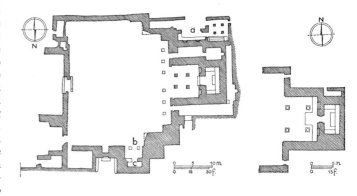

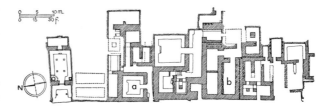

Pyandzhikent, plans. *Above, left*: Temple I; (*a*) Room 5; (*b*) Room 10; (*c*) Room 10-a; *right*: Temple II; *below*: Sector III; (*a*) Room 6; (*b*) Room 17 (*from Iakubovskii et al., 1954*).

One of these paintings represents a group of large seated figures; below this scene is a beribboned bird holding a jewel in its beak. This is a new version of the motif of a bird holding a pearl necklace in its beak, a motif of Sassanian origin that is also found at Bamian and at sites in the Tarim Basin.

According to D'iakonov, the first style is earlier than the third. The third style dates from the mid-7th and the early 8th century; in fact, these paintings were probably partially destroyed by the Arabs shortly after being completed. This date seems to be confirmed by the presence of a stirrup adorned with an eye in some of the pictures. The stirrup was already highly developed, since it is known that the nomads began to use the stirrup during the second half of the 6th century and that it was not yet used in Sassanian Iran at the time of the collapse of this empire in the mid-7th century. This is the reason why the stirrup must have been introduced in Sogdiana toward the end of the 6th century or the beginning of the 7th.

These paintings are approximately contemporaneous with some executed in the Tarim Basin, such as those of the oldest grottoes of Kumtura (VIII, PL. 405) and the later ones of Kizil (I, PLS. 478, 480, 481; VIII, PLS. 14, 401, 402, 404). Many examples show the relation between them. A figure with four arms at Pyandzhikent shows a definite relationship with a figure on a panel from Dandan-uilik (VIII, PL. 379). Other relations can be established between the paintings of the third style of Pyandzhikent and those of Afghanistan: Bamian (VIII, PL. 12), Kakrak (VIII, PL. 8), and Dukhtar-i-Noshirwan. Close similarities are apparent between the paintings of Pyandzhikent and those of Fondukistan, which apparently date from the 7th century. Other connections may also be established between these paintings and those of eastern Iran and the Tarim Basin. All of them formed a broad cultural unit having contacts with the cultures of bordering regions and assuming, according to time and place, special aspects owing to the influences of local traditions. This is also true of the paintings at Varakhsha and Balalyk Tepe (see below).

That sculpture at Pyandzhikent was highly developed is revealed by some fragments of stucco and the charred remains of carved wood that were parts of sculpture or architectural elements. On the west and south walls of a room in Temple II is a stucco panel, carved in relief, representing a marine landscape with a grotto, a stream, sea monsters, and people. Fragments of stucco — a human head, the head of a fantastic animal, a hand, and the fold of a garment — were found on the ground in the north part of Temple II. The wooden fragments (PL. 88) found in Sector III include a large semicircular slab that probably decorated an arched lintel on the interior of a building; a carved capital in the form of an octahedron whose faces are covered with leaves of different sizes forming a crown and completed on the corners by high, volute-shaped corbels; pieces decorated with a vine plant with leaves and clusters of grapes, an attribute of the Great Goddess; and bands ornamented with scales in the form of lozenges and rosettes. Other wooden fragments have been discovered in Temple I; the most important piece probably belonged to a zoomorphic or anthropomorphic image of the same type as those that adorn the walls of the palace at Varakhsha and on which a sort of wing can be distinguished with clearly visible feathers and the characteristic volute that decorate the wings of the reliefs at Varakhsha.

The discovery of these carved wooden fragments is important, but that of two female figures and the head of a woman is even more so, since, although they are in bad condition, they are outstanding works of art. The arms and feet of the two statues (PL. 88) are missing, and all the faces are severely damaged. The two figures, each 4 feet high, are true statues; only a narrow strip in the back is not carved. The hair is carefully coiffed, with large curls on the forehead and top of the head and waves on the back of the head. The bodies are nude to the hips. Each figure is adorned with a rich necklace and a long string of small bells to which another string of bells is attached and fastened at the shoulders and chest by round plaquettes, one of which has been preserved and represents a semihuman mask in relief. The skirt, of light material, falls in regular folds from a wide belt. The figures are thought to represent dancers.

These stucco and wooden sculptures reveal various influences, more or less modified by local art. Some of the influences were probably Hellenistic and reached Sogdiana through a tradition that originated in the Greco-Bactrian period or perhaps directly in the Parthian period. Others came from India through the intermediary of Greco-Buddhist art in Afghanistan or even directly, as is indicated by the sea monsters of the stucco relief in Temple II. The same influences are found in Serindia, where the wooden products of the Kucha region are decorated with bands decorated with scales in the form of lozenges and rosettes, which can also be found in the Khotan region.

The art of Pyandzhikent, although undisputably original, is related to the mural paintings and sculpture of Varakhsha as well as to the mural paintings of Balalyk Tepe. It is probably also related to the paintings and sculpture of Ak-Beshim and to the paintings of the shahristān near Ura Tepe in Tadzhikistan of which there are very few examples.

The excavations conducted in 1938 by Shishkin (1941) led to the discovery of mural paintings in the palace of Varakhsha. Further research between 1947 and 1952 resulted in the discovery of additional mural paintings (Shishkin, 1947, 1948, 1963).

The paintings are found in two rooms. On the walls of the first room is a frieze with a repeat motif representing a group of figures against a red background: a warrior, perhaps the king, is mounted on a white elephant, and the elephant keeper is depicted in his habitual place, on the animal's head; both are trying to drive back two wild beasts that are attacking the elephant from the front and the rear. In one group the

beasts are lions; in two others, leopards; and in two more, griffins. Above this frieze, running all around the hall, is another one, badly damaged, showing a procession of animals moving to the left, which are much smaller than those of the main frieze. Beneath the main frieze is an ornamental band. The second room has some very rich paintings on the south wall. The central scene probably represents a banquet in a palace; the main figure is seated in the center on a magnificent throne in the form of fantastic animals, placed in a courtly setting. On an adjoining wall some figures of mounted warriors moving toward the right were discovered. It is not possible to determine the relation between these two scenes.

Shishkin also discovered numerous fragments of a stucco decoration that had adorned the walls of two reception rooms at Varakhsha. This decoration was later removed and used as building stones, so that it is not possible to reconstruct it, but it was certainly composed of figural scenes alternating with decorative panels, like those found at Toprak Kale (see KHWARIZM). The entire complex represented hunting scenes on a background depicting a landscape with trees interlaced with vine plants; some birds with women's heads were perched in the trees. On this background the hunters stood out on two planes, in high and low relief, and the principal figures were distinguished by their larger size. The fleeing game seems to have consisted mostly of ibexes, gazelles, and antelopes. Above this ensemble ran a frieze representing partridges in movement; under it was another frieze representing a pond with fish, frogs, and snakes.

In his early articles Shishkin was inclined to date the paintings and sculpture to the 3d and 4th centuries; later he thought they might have been done between the 3d and 5th centuries; N. Solov'eva, in a note, speaks of the 5th and 6th centuries. According to Tolstov, these works belong to the 5th century. Iakubovskii maintains that they belong to the 5th and 6th centuries. Perhaps they should be assigned to a little later epoch. The study of the Varakhsha discoveries is not yet complete.

The third large site where important paintings of the 6th century have been discovered is Balalyk Tepe. The excavations, begun in 1953 under the direction of Albaum (1960), were concentrated on an aristocratic residence that included a temple. In contrast to the narrative character of the paintings of Varakhsha and Pyandzhikent, those of Balalyk Tepe treat only one theme: the banquet. A total of 47 men and women are depicted, magnificently clad and wearing numerous jewels; they hold cups, goblets, and mirrors. The body is generally in a frontal position, as at Pyandzhikent; the face is depicted frontally or in three-quarter view, and profile views are rare; the subjects look at their neighbors from the corners of their eyes. Except for a few scenes, the paintings are well preserved. The physical type of the personages is quite different from the figures at Pyandzhikent and Varakhsha; probably the people portrayed were not Sogdian.

BIBLIOG. V. L. Viatkin, Afrasiyab: Gorodishche bylogo Samarkanda (Afrasiyab: Site of the Former Samarkand), Tashkent, 1927; I. A. Vasil'ev, Sogdiiskii zamok na gore Mug (The Sogdian Castle on the Hill of Mug), Sogdiiskii sbornik (Sogdian Miscellany), Leningrad, 1934, pp. 18–32; G. V. Grigor'ev, Gorodishche Tali-Barzu (The Site of Tali Barzu), Trudy Otdela vostoka gosudarstvennogo Ermitazha, II, 1940, pp. 87–104; G. V. Grigor'ev, Kaunchi-tepe: Raskopki 1935 g. (Kaunchi Tepe: Excavations in 1935), Tashkent, 1940; G. V. Grigor'ev, Kratkii otchet o rabotakh iangiiul' skoi arkheologicheskoi ekspeditsii 1937 g. (Brief Report on the Work of the Archaeological Expedition to Yuangiiul in 1937), Tashkent, 1940; G. V. Grigor'ev, Poseleniia drevnego Sogda (Settlements of Ancient Sogdiana), KS, VI, 1940, pp. 24–34; A. Iu. Iakubovskii, Iz istorii arkheologicheskogo izucheniia Samarkanda (From the History of the Archaeological Investigation of Samarkand), Trudy Otdela vostoka gosudarstvennogo Ermitazha, II, 1940, pp. 285–337; A. Iu. Iakubovskii, Kratkii polevoi otchet o rabotakh zerafshanskoi arkheologicheskoi ekspeditsii (Brief Report on the Work of the Archaeological Expedition to Zeravshan), Trudy Otdela vostoka gosudarstvennogo Ermitazha, II, 1940, pp. 51–64; M. E. Masson, Termezskaia arkheologicheskaia kompleksnaia ekspeditsiia (The Inclusive Archaeological Expedition to Termez), KS, VIII, 1940, pp. 113–17; A. I. Terenozhkin, Pamiatniki material'noi kul'tury na Tashkentskom kanale (Monuments of Economic Culture on Tashkent's Canal), Izvestiia Uzbekskogo Filiala Akad. Nauk SSSR, IX, 1940, pp. 30–36; Trudy termezskoi arkheologicheskoi kompleksnoi ekspeditsii (Transactions of the Inclusive Archaeological Expedition to Termez), 2 vols., Tashkent, 1940–45; V. A. Shishkin, Issledovanie gorodishcha Varakhsha i ego okresnostei (Researches at the Site of Varakhsha and Its Environs), KS, X, 1941, pp. 3–15; G. V. Grigor'ev, Tali-Barzu kak pamiatnik do musul'manskogo Sogda (Tali Barzu as a Monument of Moslem Sogdiana), KS, XIII, 1946, pp. 150–53; E. G. Pchelina, Drevne-buddiiskii monastyr' v Kara-Tepe, Termez (An Ancient Buddhist Mon-astery at Kara Tepe, Termez), Doklady i soobshcheniia istoricheskogo fakul'teta Moskovskogo gosudarstvennogo univ., IV, 1946, pp. 52–56; A. N. Bernshtam, Sredneaziatskaia drevonst' i ee izucheniii za 30 let (Central Asiatic Antiquity and Its Study for 30 Years), Vestnik drevnei istorii, 1947, 3, pp. 83–94; V. F. Gaidukevich, Raboty farkhadskoi arkheologicheskoi ekspeditsii v Uzbekistane v 1943–44 gg. (Work of the Farkhad Archaeological Expedition in Uzbekistan, 1943–44), KS, XIV, 1947, pp. 92–109; V. V. Kesaev, Raskopki na Paikende (Excavations at Paykand), Soobshcheniia gosudarstvennogo Ermitazha, IV, 1947, pp. 26–29; V. A. Shishkin, Arkhi-tekturnaia dekoratsiia dvortsa v Varakhsha (Architectural Decoration of the Varakhsha Palace), Trudy Otdela vostoka gosudarstvennogo Ermitazha, IV, 1947, pp. 225–92; A. I. Terenozhkin, Arkheologicheskaia razvedka na gorodishche Afrasiab v 1945 g. (Archaeological Renaissance at the Site of Afrasiyab in 1945), KS, XVII, 1947, pp. 116–21; A. I. Terenozhkin, Vo-prosy istoriko-arkheologicheskoi periodizatsii drevnego Samarkanda (His-torical and Archaeological Questions on the Phases of Ancient Samarkand), Vestnik drevnei istorii, 1947, 4, pp. 127–35; V. A. Shishkin, Arkheologiche-skie raboty 1947 g. na gorodishche Varakhsha (Archaeological Work at the Site of Varakhsha in 1947), Izvestiia Akad. Nauk Uzbekskoi SSSR, V, 1948, pp. 62–70; A. I. Terenozhkin, Kholm Ak-Tepe bliz Tashkenta (The Ak Tepe Hill near Tashkent), Materialy po arkheologii Uzbekistana, Trudy Inst. istorii i arkheologii Akad. Nauk Uzbekskoi SSSR, I, 1948, pp. 71–134; S. P. Tolstov, Khorezmskaia arkheologo-etnograficheskaia ekspeditsiia Akademii Nauk SSSR 1947 g. (The Archaeological and Ethnographic Ex-pedition of the USSR Academy of Sciences to Khwarizm in 1947), Izvestiia Akad. Nauk, Ser. istorii i filosofi, V, 1948, pp. 182–92; V. L. Voronina, Ar-khitektura zamka Ak-Tepe (The Architecture of the Castle of Ak Tepe), Izvestiia, Nauk, Ser. istorii i filosofi, V, 1948, pp. 135–82; A. N. Bernshtam, Problemy drevnei istorii i etnogeneza iuzhnogo Kazakhstana (Problems of the Ancient History and Ethnogeny of Southern Kazakhstan), Izvestiia Akad. Nauk Kazakhskoi SSR, arkheol. ser., LXVII, 2, 1949, pp. 59–99; M. M. D'iakonov, Keramika Paikenda (Paykand Ceramics), KS, XXVIII, 1949, pp. 89–93; V. F. Gaidukevich, Keramicheskaia obzhigatel'naia Mun-chak-Tepe (The Ceramic Kiln of Munchak Tepe), KS, XXVIII, 1949, pp. 77–82; M. M. D'iakonov, Raboty Kafirniganskogo otryada (Work of the Kafirnigan Detachment), Trudy Sogdiiako-tadzhikskoi arkheologiche-skoi ekspeditsii, I (MIA, XV), 1950, pp. 147–86; A. Iu. Iakubovskii, Zhi-vopis' drevnego Piandzhikenta po materialam tadzhiksko-sogdiiskoi ek-speditsii 1948–59 gg. (Painting in Ancient Pyandzhikent according to the Materials of the Tadzhik-Sogdian Expedition of 1948–49), Izvestiia Akad. Nauk SSSR, Ser. istorii i filosofi, VII, 1950, pp. 472–91; M. E. Masson, K periodizatsii drevnei istorii Samarkanda (On the Phases of Samarkand's Ancient History), Vestnik drevnei istorii, 1950, 4, pp. 155–66; A. I. Terenozh-kin, Sogd i Chach (Sogdiana and Chach), KS, XXXIII, 1950, pp. 152–70; Trudy tadzhikskoi arkheologicheskoi ekspeditsii (Transactions of the Ar-chaeological Expedition to Tadzhikistan), 4 vols. (MIA, XV, XXXVII, LXVI, CXXIV), Moscow, Leningrad, 1950–64; S. S. Chernikov, Otchet o rabotakh vostochnokazakhstanskoi ekspeditsii 1948 g. (Report on the Work of the Expedition to Eastern Kazakhstan in 1948), Izdatel'stvo Akad. Nauk Kazakhskoi SSR, 108 (Arckheol. ser.), 3), 1951, pp. 64–80; M. E. Masson, Novye dannye po drevnei istorii Merva (New Elements in the Early History of Merv), Vestnik drevnei istorii, 1951, 4, pp. 89–101; A. I. Terenozhkin, Raskopki na gorodishche Afrasiab (Excavations on the Site of Afrasiyab), KS, XXXVI, 1951, pp. 136–40; S. P. Tolstov, Drevnii Khorezm (Ancient Khwarizm), Po sledam drevnikh kul'tur (On the Trail of Ancient Cultures), Moscow, 1951, pp. 169–208; A. N. Bernshtam, Istoriko-arkheologicheskie ocherki tsentral'nogo Tian-shana i Pamiro-Alaia (Historical and Archaeolog-ical Studies on the Central T'ien-shan and the Pamir-Alai, MIA, XXVI), Moscow, Leningrad, 1952; A. M. Belenitskii, Iz arkheologicheskikh rabot v Piandzhikente 1951 g. (Archaeological Work in Pyandzhikent in 1951), SA, XVIII, 1953, pp. 326–41; M. M. D'iakonov, Arkheologicheskie raboty v nizhnem techenii reki Kafirnikhan, Kobadian (Archaeological Work on the New Course of the Kafirnigan River, Kobadian), MIA, XXVII, 1953, pp. 253–93; M. M. D'iakonov, Slozhenie klassovogo obshchesva v severnoi Baktrii (The Structure of Social Classes in Northern Bactria), SA, XIX, 1954, pp. 121–40; A. Iu. Iakubovskii et al., Zhivopis' drevnego Piandzhi-kenta (Painting in Ancient Pyandzhikent), Moscow, 1954; B. Ia. Staviskii, O dvukh pamiatnikakh sogdiiskogo izobratel'nogo iskusstva (On Two Mon-uments of Sogdian Art), KS, LXI, 1956, pp. 63–64; G. Glaesser, Painting in ancient Pyandzhikent, East and West, VIII, 1957, pp. 199–215; A. M. Belenitskii, Nouvelles découvertes de sculptures et de peintures murales à Piandjikent, Arts asiatiques, V, 1958, pp. 163–83; L. R. Kyzlasov, Arkheo-logicheskie issledovaniia na gorodishche Ak-Beshim v 1953–54 gg. (Archaeo-logical Researches on the site of Ak-Beshim in 1953–54), Trudy kirgizskoi arkheologo-etnograficheskoi ekspeditsii, II, 1958, pp. 154–242; G. Puga-chenkova, Puti razvitiia arkhitektury iuzhnogo Turkmenistana pory rabov-ladeniia i feodalizma (The Development of Architecture in Southern Turk-menistan during the Time of the Slave-holding States and of Feudalism), Moscow, 1958; Skulptura i zhivopis' drevnego Piandzhikenta (Sculpture and Painting of Ancient Pyandzhikent), Moscow, 1959; L. I. Albaum, Balalyk-Tepe, Tashkent, 1960; A. L. Mongait, Archaeology in the U.S.S.R. (trans. M. W. Thompson), Harmondsworth, 1961; L. Hambis, Ak-Beshim et ses sanctuaries, CRAI, 1962, pp. 124–38; M. Bussagli, La peinture de l'Asie centrale, Geneva, 1963; V. A. Shishkin, Varakhsha, Moscow, 1963; T. V. Grek et al., Kara-Tepe. Buddiiskii peshchern'y monastyr' v starom Termeze (Kara Tepe. Buddhist Cave Monastery in Ancient Termez), Moscow, 1964. See also the bibliog. for KHWARIZM.

Louis HAMBIS

Illustrations: PLS. 83–90; 3 figs. in text.

SOMALILAND. Somalia (a republic formed by the union of Italian Somaliland with British Somaliland and independent since 1960) and French Somaliland (Côte française des Somalis) comprise a coastal area of eastern Africa bounded by Eritrea and Ethiopia to the north and west, the Indian Ocean to the east, and Kenya to the southwest. The coastal districts were the object of Asian migrations — especially by Arab, Persian, and Indian seamen and merchants — that have left important traces, particularly in architecture (see AZANIAN ART). The in-land regions, however, and today the coastal towns as well, are chiefly occupied by a population of Cushite origin (see CUSHITE CULTURES) that is responsible for recent artistic production in sculpture and the minor arts. European colonization has not caused any substantial changes in the artistic sphere, even though the residential districts in the major towns are planned and built on Western architectural lines.

SUMMARY. General characteristics (col. 134). Artistic production (col. 135): *Architecture; Sculpture and the minor arts.*

GENERAL CHARACTERISTICS. Along the coast, at various times in the early centuries of the Christian Era, towns were founded by settlers who came for the most part from Arabia and the Persian Gulf and who brought different cultures with them; at Berbera, for example, there are imposing remains of an aqueduct with tall arches that possibly dates from the Persian invasion in the 6th century. Along the coast of the Gulf of Aden these towns were subjected, probably shortly before the year 1000, to Cushite invasions, first by the Galla and then by the Somali, then to a brief Turkish occupation in the 16th century, with a subsequent period of slow decline resulting from historical events in the interior and perhaps also from the

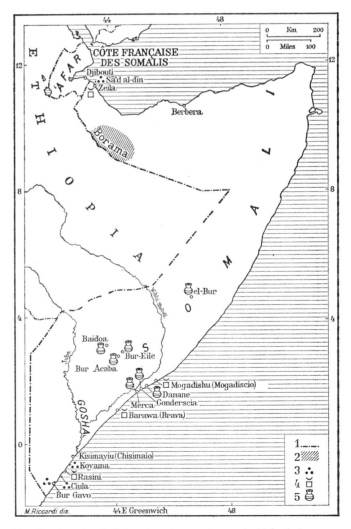

Somaliland, archaeological and modern centers and chief ethnic groups (in italic capitals). *Key:* (1) National boundaries; (2) Borama district with scattered archaeological remains; (3) archaeological centers; (4) centers with mosques; (5) pottery centers.

gradually increasing harshness of the climate. They preserve, however, many Arabo-Islamic cultural characteristics. Along the coast of the Indian Ocean, the Benadir towns, such as Mogadishu (Mogadiscio), Merca, and Brava (Barawa), enjoyed a rather protracted period of economic prosperity, preserving for a long time some of the characteristics of the original Arabo-Persian culture. They had begun to decline by the 17th century and were finally overrun by Somali nomads from the interior. The smaller centers, such as Gesira and Gondersha, to the south of Mogadishu, were soon reduced to little more than small fishing villages. Finally, other coastal towns farther south, which had their own cultural features and whose ruins are of great archaeological and artistic interest, sprang up on the Bagiuni (Juba) Islands and on the mainland around a sort of fiord at Bur Gavo (Bircao, Port Durnford).

At the end of the Somali migrations from the northeast to the southwest, with the resulting withdrawal of the Galla beyond the borders of Somaliland, small centers arose in recent times in the hinterland of Somalia. These are of some interest because of the craft industries that have developed there. The examples of rock art found scattered throughout the Somali territory, but most frequently in what was formerly British Somaliland and in Mijertins, do not seem to be of any great antiquity; they present symbolical geometric figures functioning as pictographs, and anthropomorphous and zoomorphic subjects.

ARTISTIC PRODUCTION. *Architecture.* In Somalia the surviving architectural monuments date from different periods and show superimposition of various elements that are usually inspired by motifs from Islamic-Oriental art; this is due to partial reconstructions and restorations carried out in recent times by artisans who were sometimes unskilled and of different origin from that of the original builders.

In French Somaliland there are no architectural monuments dating from past centuries, since Djibouti (Jibuti), the only town of any size, is of recent foundation, with a fine European residential quarter in addition to its modern mosques and administrative buildings. The small town of Zeila on the border of Somalia, which was once the port of entry into the Islamic state of Adal, is of little importance today: apart from a few masonry houses that reproduce the southern Arabian coastal style and perhaps date from the end of the 18th century, it offers nothing of note. Only a few ruins remain of a mosque that dates possibly from the 12th century. On the island of Sa'd ad-Din, opposite Zeila, are the ruins of a town, probably dating from the 15th century. About 15 centers with archaeological remains of varying extent and importance exist to the west of what was British Somaliland, in the Borama region and along the Ethiopian border; there are remains of houses, mosques, and tombs there, as well as traces of Oriental wares, especially Chinese porcelain, dating from various periods between the 12th century and the 18th. The ruins of northern Somaliland seem for the most part to be datable to a period of great commercial prosperity in the 15th or 16th century. Among the most remarkable remains are the mosque of Abasa, with its 12 pillars of different shapes, and the conical tomb of Au Boba. The towns on the Mijertins coast and those on the Indian Ocean as far as Somalia's 9th-century capital, Mogadishu, have no monuments worth mentioning.

Among the old mosques in Mogadishu, the best-known and most interesting artistically is the Masjid-i-Jāmi', in the Ḥamar-wēn district, built in A.D. 1238 and restored at various times, so that the original architecture has been partially transformed. It has lancet arches that recall the Fatimid style of the Egyptian mosques (see FATIMID ART). The minaret is cylindrical, with stringcourse moldings and small slit windows in the Arabo-Persian style of the 10th century. An inscription at the base bears the date A.H. 636 (A.D. 1238). The whole tower is plastered. The Arba'-rukun Mosque (1268), in Arabo-Persian style, has a slim, lofty minaret, probably of more recent construction. Around the mihrab, an Arabic inscription mentions one Khusrau, a Persian from Shiraz who founded or restored the mosque. Finally there is the Fakhr ad-Din Mosque (II, PL. 81; dated by Cerulli, 1926, to 1269), which, although now completely abandoned and in ruins, was formerly faced with marbles that were apparently removed toward the end of the 19th century by a representative of the Sultan of Zanzibar. Not far from the port, beside the little Persian-style Mosque of 'Abd-al-'Azīz (1300?), rises the large *manārah* tower, an ancient minaret in the same style as the minaret of the Masjid-i-Jāmi' in the Ḥamar-wēn. It has a square base and three tapering cylindrical sections; the last section has four high openings and is crowned by a conical roof. This minaret is not plastered, so the types of stone used for its construction can be seen. It has structural affinities with the Qomriyah Mosque in Baghdad (13th cent.) and with a number of Persian minarets of the 14th and 15th centuries, a fact suggesting that it was constructed after Mogadishu's great building period.

A few houses in Mogadishu have a certain artistic interest; they are "introverted" buildings usually, with large blind façades, a few small openings, and crenelations around the top. In the oldest houses in the Shangānī district, a characteristic feature is a kind of forepart open toward the outside, leading to the entrance, with a closed room above. This architectural feature is probably of Persian origin, and its function is to prevent dampness, since it helps to create drying air currents. Mogadishu's modern town hall in is in Moorish style.

At the important port of Merca there is the characteristic modern Mosque of Sheik 'Alī Maye, which is based on old architectural forms; the dome, consisting of a cylinder under a fluted cone, is reminiscent of Indian styles of architecture. At Brava, of Arab origin and a trading center since the Middle Ages, the Abūkar Sayyid mosque has a cylindrical dome topped by a conical section.

Also noteworthy is a distinctive kind of rectangular building in masonry with one or more floors, to be found in many coastal centers: this is the *garesa*, built for defense and to lodge the head of the village. Those in Mogadishu, Merca, and Brava date from the Oman (Uman) period (19th cent.). The one in Mogadishu was built (1870–80) by order of the Sultan of Zanzibar, Barghash ibn-Sa'īd, and was restored as faithfully as possible in 1933. Today it houses the museum.

In the Benadir coastal settlements there are many burial chapels, some older than others, usually in a state of neglect. They are whitewashed rectangular masonry buildings of various sizes. The most characteristic decorative elements are false domes in the center and lancet or multifoil arches or crenelations around the curvature. Among the more modern burial mosques, those of Sheik Ṣūfī and Sheik Muḥyī ad-Dīn in Mogadishu and that of Sharif Abū Bakr in Merca are of some artistic interest.

The Bagiuni Islands, lying off the Somalian coast to the south of Kismayu (Chisimaio), and Bur Gavo on the mainland, near the Kenya border, are areas of special historical and archaeological interest. In the Bagiuni Islands, near villages that are in a state of extreme decay, architectural monuments have survived that show an Arabo-Persian influence. The most interesting features here are funerary monuments with pillars in which are set porcelain vessels; phallic (?) pillar tombs (II, PL. 83; Bur Gavo); a stone mihrab among the ruins of a mosque on the island of Rasini (II, PL. 82, detail); and funerary inscriptions in Kufic characters (Koyama). It is believed that at Bur Gavo there was once an important port (Shungwaya), of which only a few tombs (possibly of Persian derivation) and the remains of the ramparts have survived.

Sculpture and the minor arts. At Chula (Ciula) in the Bagiuni Islands a few carved wooden doors have been found and also in the coastal towns where the ornamental motifs recall an Indo-Moslem style; some of these doors were perhaps made in the first years of the 19th century. The most characteristic, which is in the Mogadishu Museum, comes from the now-destroyed Garesa of Bargal (II, PL. 82), on the Mijertins coast, and bears the date A.H. 1230 (A.D. 1814). Contemporary wood carving is confined to neck rests (IV, PL. 86; made by the Hawiya and Digil Somali and in French Somaliland), the combs used by both sexes (IV, FIG. 169), spoons with finely engraved or carved handles (IV, FIG. 167), and various containers for liquids and food, often decorated with leather and cowrie shells and then painted (IV, PL. 85).

The pottery is made with reddish clays that, after firing, turn a light-brown color. Almost always a darker patina is obtained by spraying the vases, immediately after firing, with a liquid containing tannin. The most common forms are oval vases of different sizes, pots, bottles, and censers; they are decorated with crude geometric patterns, traced with sticks on the object as soon as it is formed. The most refined types come from Danane and Gondersha in the Merca region, the rougher examples from Bur Acaba and Bur Eybi (Bur Eile). Some coastal types are certainly of Arab origin, with some Indonesian influence.

Censers and braziers made by cold-working the soft, whitish limestone of El Bur are widespread throughout south-central Somalia. The engraved decoration repeats the patterns of the pottery.

The traditional hand-woven cotton fabrics (known commercially as Benadir cotton), with intersecting colored stripes, are made at Mogadishu and Baidoa and in the Lower Juba region. This craft, however, is rapidly declining. Carpets and mats woven in Somalia still show a certain artistic merit.

The most interesting Somalian handicraft products today are the leather goods made by the despised Yibir and Midgan castes: they produce chiefly shields, saddles, riding whips, bridles, amulets, and sandals. The art and handicrafts of the Afar, the Galla, and the Negroid minorities of the territory are much poorer in inspiration and more modest in their results.

The Eyle tribe, a Rahanwein subgroup occupying southern Somalia between the Webbi Shibeli and Juba rivers, makes modest goatskin masks that deserve mention: they seem rather foreign to the Cushite environment, but similar ones are to be found among the Negroid Gosha of the Lower Juba region and among the Boni tribe of Jubaland (Trans-Juba).

BIBLIOG. M. Guillain, Documents sur l'histoire, la géographie et le commerce de l'Afrique orientale, Paris, 1856; Robecchi Bricchetti, Somalia e Benadir, Milan, 1899; B. V. Vecchi, Vecchio Benadir, Milan, 1930; J. Parkinson, An Unsolved Riddle of Africa: Mysterious Ruins in Somaliland, ILN, CLXXXVI, 1935, pp. 126–27; N. Puccioni, Antropologia e etnografia delle genti della Somalia, III, Bologna, 1936; A. T. Curle, The Ruined Towns of Somaliland, Antiquity, XI, 1937, pp. 315–27; C. Massari, Maschere di danza degli Uaboni, AAE, LXXX–LXXXI, 1950–51, pp. 143–46; J. D. Clark, Dancing Masks from Somaliland, Man, LIII, 1953, pp. 49–51; G. Mathew, Recent Discoveries in East African Archaeology, Antiquity, XXVII, 1953, pp. 212–18; J. D. Clark, The Prehistoric Cultures of the Horn of Africa, Cambridge, 1954; V. L. Grottanelli, Pescatori dell'Oceano Indiano, Rome, 1955; I. M. Lewis, Peoples of the Horn of Africa, London, 1955; E. Cerulli, Somalia, 2 vols., Rome, 1957; M. Pirone, Le maschere di Bur Eybi, Somalia d'oggi, II, 2, 1957, pp. 37–39; I. M. Lewis, The Godhardunneh Cave Decorations of North-Eastern Somaliland, Man, LVIII, 1958, pp. 178–79; P. Graziosi, Graffiti rupestri in Migiurtinia (Somalia), AAE, XCI, 1961, pp. 153–63. Mogadishu: E. Cerulli, Iscrizioni e monumenti per la storia della Somalia, RSO, XI, 1926, pp. 7–8; U. Monneret de Villard, Note sulle influenze asiatiche nell'Africa Orientale, RSO, XXVII, 1938, pp. 303–49; E. Cerulli, Mogadiscio nel 1500 secondo i navigatori portoghesi, Terceiro Cong. do Mundo Portugues, Lisbon, 1941, pp. 54–55; U. Monneret de Villard, I minareti di Mogadiscio, Rass. di s. etiopici, III, 1943, pp. 127–30; G. Messana, Funzionalismo architettonico degli antichi costruttori mogadisciani, Somalia d'oggi, I, 1956; G. Messana, Note sull'architettura mogadisciana, Somalia d'oggi, I, 1956. Merca: G. Pantano, La città di Merca e la regione di Bimal nel Benadir, Livorno, 1910; G. Messana, Architettura monumentale mercana, Somalia d'oggi, II, 1957. Berbera: R. F. Burton, First Footsteps in East Africa, II, London, 1894, pp. 71–94.

Michele PIRONE

Illustration: 1 fig. in text.

SOUFFLOT, JACQUES GERMAIN. Foremost architect of the first phase of French neoclassicism and thus of the international neoclassic movement (b. Irancy, Yonne, July 22, 1713; d. Paris, Aug. 29, 1780). At the age of eighteen, having studied law unsuccessfully in Paris, Soufflot traveled to Italy, where, in 1733, he was admitted to the French Academy in Rome. By the beginning of 1739 he was in Lyons, where he published a book on St. Peter's and was soon after made a member of the local Academy. On April 12, 1741, he read an extraordinary paper, *De l'architecture Gothique*, in which, following the precepts of Michel de Fremin and Abbé Jean Louis de Cordemoy (1631–1713), he suggested employment of the proportions and structural finesse of Gothic cathedrals as basic principles in contemporary church design. These ideas were later taken up in Abbé Marc Antoine Laugier's *Essai sur l'architecture* (1752), but Soufflot himself found no immediate opportunity to apply them. He was overwhelmed with secular commissions in Lyons; his vast Hôtel Dieu (1742) must have accounted for his early reputation in Paris and for his selection as cicerone to Mme de Pompadour's brother, the Marquis de Marigny, future Directeur des Bâtiments, whom, together with the critic Jean Bernard Leblanc (1707–81) and the engraver Charles Nicolas Cochin (1715–90), he accompanied to Italy in 1750. They visited the new excavations at Herculaneum and the Doric temples at Paestum — which Soufflot was the first to measure — but he made no attempt to exploit these experiences as the basis for a revival of antique architecture (his *Suite de plans de trois temples antiques à Pestum* was not published until 1764). There can be no doubt, however, that under Marigny's patronage he intended to effect a reform in architecture in accordance with the rules and precedents handed down from antiquity, with Vitruvius as his guide.

Marigny was an equivocal patron: "Je ne veux point de chicorée moderne, je ne veux point de l'austère ancien, mezzo l'uno, mezzo l'altro," he decreed, and Soufflot felt bound to accede in the designs for both of Marigny's houses in Paris (ca. 1767 and 1769) and his garden pavilions at Ménars (after 1764; one of which survives). However, it was Marigny who secured Soufflot's greatest and most glorious commission, the Church of Ste-Geneviève, known as the Panthéon, in Paris (X, PL. 268). The approved plan, submitted in March, 1756, was in the shape of a Greek cross (X, FIG. 523). The cubic

bulk of the arms was broken by rows of roundheaded windows (subsequently filled in), and the structure was to have been topped with a small, ungainly dome over the crossing. To the west arm Soufflot added an imposing Corinthian portico derived from Baalbek, which brought into play a more authentic feeling for the splendors of the Roman world than had yet been known in France. But it was not only this sanction for archaeological accuracy that makes the church so important in the history of the neoclassic movement. The way in which the vaults and even the dome of the crossing were designed to rest on a grid of elegant freestanding Corinthian columns rather than the more usual piers (V, PL. 422) embodies another essential aspect of early neoclassic thought: a belief in structural refinement and its honest expression, based ultimately on a vital and engaging study of Gothic construction. Though Soufflot's church was classical in appearance, it was intended to be a paraphrase of Gothic structural arrangements.

As work went slowly ahead the audacious structure was vigorously attacked. Soufflot's chief adversary was the architect Pierre Patte (1723–1814), who held that empirical knowledge was essential for sound building construction. Instead, Soufflot and his friends, notably the engineer Jean Rodolphe Perronet (1708–94), stressed the development of an abstract theory of structures based on experiment and calculation. Patte's doctrine seemed to the members of the Academy cautious and provincial in relation to Soufflot's rationalism. Soufflot was invariably vindicated, even when the main supports of the crossing were found to be cracking due to unequal resistance in the stones. Defiantly, he issued a design in 1777 for the great dome, similar to that of St. Paul's in London, that was eventually built. The anxiety occasioned by its construction is said to have caused his death. But this did not end the controversy, nor was Patte championed when, toward the end of the century, the main supports were again found to be in danger of collapse. They were reinforced by Soufflot's disciple, Jean Baptiste Rondelet (1734–1829), the principal defender of structural rationalism.

BIBLIOG. J. Mondain-Monval, Correspondance de Soufflot avec les Directeurs des Bâtiments, 1758–1780, Paris, 1918; J. Mondain-Monval, Soufflot, sa vie, son œuvre, son esthétique, Paris, 1918; M. Mathieu, Pierre Patte, sa vie et son œuvre, Paris, 1940; M. Petzet, Soufflots Sainte-Geneviève und der Französische Kirchenbau des 18. Jahrhunderts, Berlin, 1961.

Robin MIDDLETON

SOUTH AFRICA. The British and Boer provinces of the Cape of Good Hope, Orange Free State, Natal, and Transvaal, which geographically compose the southernmost part of Africa, formed a separate nation in 1910 which was a member of the British Commonwealth and was named the Union of South Africa. In 1961 the Union of South Africa withdrew from the Commonwealth and became the Republic of South Africa. The discussion in this article of prehistoric and modern tribal art treats not only the territory of this nation but also that of South-West Africa, which is a mandated territory of the Republic of South Africa; for reasons of historical and cultural unity the British protectorate of Swaziland has also been included, as well as the independent nations of Botswana (formerly Bechuanaland) and Lesotho (formerly Basutoland). In all these regions there are many rock art monuments (see PALEO-AFRICAN CULTURES), although contemporary native production appears to be on a modest level.

European colonization, which began in 1652 with the occupation of the Cape by the Dutch East India Company, gave rise to an abundant and often original production, especially in architecture. In the southern and western districts some of the most important examples of Dutch colonial architecture were built. During the 19th century, with the beginning of the British domination (1814), ties with European artistic trends became increasingly close until, in the 20th century, South African artists began to take part in international movements.

SUMMARY. Prehistoric and modern indigenous production (col. 139): Rock art; Tribal art. Colonial and modern periods (col. 144). Modern centers (col. 146).

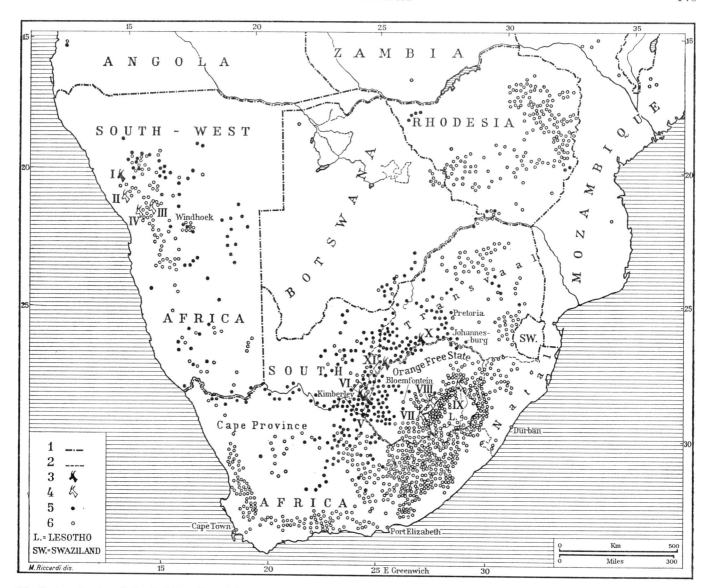

Distribution of rock art in South Africa. *Key*: (1) Modern political boundaries; (2) borders of the states; (3) major monumental sites of rock engravings; (4) major monumental sites of rock paintings; (5) isolated rock engravings; (6) isolated rock paintings. National monuments: I Twyfelfontein; II Brandberg; III Philipp cave (Erongo Mts.); IV Bushman Paradise; V Nooitgedacht; VI Driekops Eiland; VII Ventershoek No. 584; VIII Modderpoort; IX Schaapplaats No. 280; X Bosworth; XI Stowlands-on-Vaal.

PREHISTORIC AND MODERN INDIGENOUS PRODUCTION. The prehistoric invasions were from the north: first came Stone Age nomadic hunters, then Stone Age pastoralists, finally Iron Age pastoralists and agricultural pastoralists. The invasions in historic times have been by sea.

Stone Age peoples inhabited the country exclusively until sometime in the first millennium of our era, when they started to give way to Iron Age invaders. Later Stone Age peoples produced most of the rock engravings and rock paintings in which the country (in this context including Rhodesia and southern Mozambique, qq.v.) is still exceedingly rich. The earliest engravings may, however, date from the end of the Paleolithic period. Engraving and painting were probably contemporaneous developments, but it is unlikely that many of the surviving paintings are more than a few hundred years old. Both arts are traditionally attributed to the Bushmen, who practiced them within historic times, but it has been suggested that the Hottentots were painters too. During the 19th century both forms of art died out.

The Bushmen who survive today in the northern part of Cape Province, South-West Africa, and Botswana, live in sandy rather than rocky areas and have no knowledge of either art. Their decorative art is limited and is confined to patterns incised on ostrich-eggshell water bottles or stained on skin clothing. The Hottentots, however, no longer lead their traditional life.

The Iron Age peoples, whose descendants are loosely called "Bantu" (see BANTU CULTURES), came in successive migrations and settled in three main areas: the Ambo (Ovambo) and Herero (Damara)

in northern South-West Africa; the Sotho, Venda, Lemba, and some Thonga in eastern Botswana, the Transvaal, Orange Free State, and Lesotho; and the Nguni in the coastal area of Natal and of eastern Cape Province and Swaziland. The South African Bantu have not produced a spectacular art like the rock art of their Stone Age predecessors or the sculpture of the Bantu or Negro peoples farther north. It is accepted that some of the rock paintings and engravings were made by Bantu, but only as copyists.

The latest invasions of South Africa have been by Europeans (Portuguese in the east and Dutch and British in the southwest) from the 16th century onward and by Asians (Indians) in the southeast from the 19th century. The former follow Western European art traditions in their own work, and their effect on Bantu production has been threefold: to stimulate new materials and tools; to encourage the curio trade, for which a little good and much mediocre carving and modeling is produced; and to transplant Western art forms, so far resulting in some good but no remarkable work.

Rock art. The rock art is divided, with some overlapping, according to the topography of the country. Engravings are confined to the inner plateau, where they are found on rocky outcrops in the open. These petroglyphs are either incised (unbroken lines) or hammered (a series of small pits struck out of the rock). The incised designs are thought to be the older. Human figures and composite scenes are rare; the commonest subjects are single animals, hoofprints, and geometric forms (XI, PLS. 16, 19); the latter appear in great quantity at certain sites. As the map (FIG. 139) shows, there are sites in many

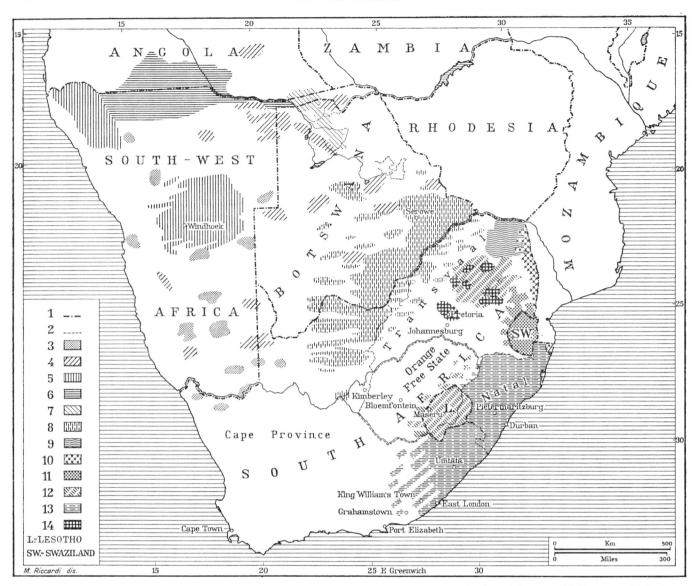

Distribution of the indigenous population of South Africa. *Key*: (1) Modern political boundaries; (2) borders of the states; (3) Hottentots; (4) Bushmen; (5) Herero; (6) Ambo; (7) Mbukushu; (8) Tswana; (9) Lemba; (10) Thonga; (11) Swazi; (12) Sotho; (13) Nguni; (14) Ndebele.

areas, but the greatest concentration and the finest examples are in western Orange Free State, particularly the Boshof and Fauresmith districts; in southwestern Transvaal, particularly the Klerksdorp, Rustenburg, Schweizer Reneke, and Krugersdorp districts; and in northwestern Cape Province, particularly the Vryburg, Herbert, and Kimberley districts. Probably the largest number at any single site is at Twyfelfontein, South-West Africa. Important incised work is found at Vosburg (near Victoria West) and along the border between Rustenburg and Klerksdorp. All engravings are protected by law, and the following sites have been proclaimed national monuments: Stowlands-on-Vaal Farm, Boshof District, Orange Free State; Bosworth Farm, near Klerksdorp, Transvaal; Driekops Eiland in the Riet River, Herbert District, Cape Province; Nooitgedacht, Kimberley District, Cape Province; Twyfelfontein, Outjo District, near Welwitschia, South-West Africa.

Paintings are found in rock shelters of the mountains that separate the plateau from the coast. The greatest concentrations are in southwestern and eastern Cape Province, eastern Orange Free State, Lesotho, and Natal — all four areas being contiguous. Especially rich districts are Clanwilliam, Albany, Queenstown, Wodehouse, Lady Grey, Elliot, and Maclear in the Cape; Ladybrand, Rouxville, Smithfield, and Zastron in the Orange Free State, Bergville and Estcourt in Natal; and Omaruru and Outjo in South-West Africa. There are many differences in style, the paintings in the southeast having more animation and a greater range of color than elsewhere. Subjects include single animals, animal groups at rest or in movement, and human beings engaged in various activities, especially hunting,

fighting, and dancing (XI, PLS. 20–24, 27, 28). Especially remarkable are those of obvious magical significance (IX, PL. 242; X, PL. 239). The site probably best known to the outside world is that of the "White Lady" of the Brandberg, South-West Africa. Like the engravings, all paintings are protected by law; the following sites have been proclaimed national monuments: Ventershoek Farm No. 584, Wepener District, Orange Free State (XI, PL. 22; a portion previously removed may be seen in the Musée de l'Homme, Paris); Mission of the Sacred Society, Modderpoort, Orange Free State; Schaapplaats Farm No. 280, near Clarens, Bethlehem District, Orange Free State; Brandberg, Omaruru District, near Omaruru, South-West Africa; Philipp Cave, Ameib Farm, Erongo Mts., near Omaruru, South-West Africa; Paula's Cave, Okapekaha Farm, Erongo Mts., near Omaruru, South-West Africa; Bushman Paradise, Grosse Spitzkoppe Farm, Swakopmund District, near Usakos, South-West Africa.

The museums of the country must also be considered important centers of rock art. Fine collections of engravings are housed in Pretoria (Old Mus.), Johannesburg (Archaeological Survey), Kimberley (Alexander McGregor Memorial Mus.), and Cape Town (South African Mus.). The last also has a fine collection of paintings.

Tribal art. Bantu art, nondecorative and decorative, is in decline. The carving of figures in wood has been practiced by the central group for ritual purposes, and children in the central and eastern groups model toy figures in clay. The main artistic development has been in decoration of useful objects, generally with flat, raised, or incised patterns, commonly based on triangles, circles, and chevrons, or with carving in the round, more often of animal than of human figures; symbolic patterns are found carved on divining tablets or bowls. There are general collections with good examples of former work in the museums in Cape Town (South African Mus.), Bloemfontein (Nat. Mus.), and Pretoria (Old Mus.).

The Nguni are noted for beadwork ornaments and wooden tobacco pipes and other wooden figures (II, PL. 131). Striking geometric designs of many colors are woven into a beadwork fabric. Pipe bowls and stems are decorated with carved figures and designs or with inlaid patterns of lead. The Cape Nguni live in the Transkeian Territories (chief town, Umtata), and the Natal Nguni live in Zululand and Natal. Examples of their crafts are in museums, primarily at East London (East London Mus.), King William's Town (Kaffrarian Mus.), and Pietermaritzburg (Voortrekker Mus.). A Nguni group in the Transvaal, the Ndebele, make extensive use of heavy but not highly patterned beadwork. More important is their mural decoration, a type of work originally adopted, as was their hut style, from the neighboring Sotho tribe but developed far beyond Sotho practice. The walls of huts and courtyards are covered with a variety of designs, the earliest ones geometric and worked in earth colors but now tending to portray as well such objects of interest as railway trains and often done with commercial paints. Some fine villages near Pretoria have now become show places.

The majority of the Tonga live in Mozambique, but those in the Transvaal are remarkable for their calabash work and the carved decoration of their wooden clubs, sticks, spoons, and headrests. There are fine collections of headrests at the Lemana Training Institution near Louis Trichardt and in the Africana Museum, Johannesburg.

The large Sotho group of Lesotho, Botswana, and the Transvaal also produces fine mural decoration, sometimes inlaid with small stones. They and the neighboring Venda (Bavenda) are well known for their excellent decorated pottery, with incised and painted designs, and for their coiled and woven basketwork. Clay vessels in the shape of birds are made by the Basuto, and the Bechuana produce fine engraved wooden containers (II, PL. 130). Among these tribes a few ritual figures and puppets are still found, the remains of what must once have been a considerable art, which gave rise to the curio trade in carved and branded figures that are sold along the Botswana railway.

The least given to the visual arts, as far as can be judged, are two of the South-West African groups, the Herero and the Bergdama. Of the original culture of the latter aboriginal group nothing now remains, and the Herero, a pastoral people, seem to have had no pottery or basketwork. Their wooden utensils were quite undecorated but of pleasing shape, as was the traditional headdress of the women.

This feeling for shape is also characteristic of the third South-West African group, the Ambo. Their fine basketwork is only slightly decorated, as is their pottery, but they were fine carvers of wood. Utensils, handles of implements, and ivory and copper ornaments were decorated with deeply ridged hatching. The women's hair styles are among the most ornamental in Africa. Specimens of South-West African production may be seen in the museum at Windhoek (Library Building) and elsewhere.

BIBLIOG. *General*: N. J. van Warmelo, A Preliminary Survey of the Bantu Tribes of South Africa, Dept. of Native Affairs, Ethn. Pub., V, Pretoria, 1935; A. J. H. Goodwin, The Bored Stones of South Africa, Ann. of the South African Mus., XXXVII, 1, 1947, pp. 1–210, map 12; C. D. Forde, Habitat, Economy and Society, London, 1952, pp. 24–31; W. M. Hailey, An African Survey (rev. ed.), London, 1957, pp. 1–11, 39–43, 72–74; J. D. Clark, The Prehistory of Southern Africa, Harmondsworth, 1959, pp. 253–313; L. J. P. Gaskin, A Bibliography of African Art, London, 1965. *Rock art*: M. H. Tongue, Bushman Paintings, Oxford, 1909; H. Obermaier and H. Kuhn, Bushman Art, Oxford, 1930; G. W. Stow, Rock Paintings in South Africa, London, 1930; L. Frobenius, Madsimu Dsangara, Berlin, 1931; M. Wilman, The Rock Engravings of Griqualand West and Bechuanaland, South Africa, Cambridge, Kimberley, 1933; J. and M. van der Riet, More Rock-paintings in South Africa, London, 1940; B. J. Craig, Rock Paintings and Petroglyphs of South and Central Africa, Bibliography of Prehistoric Art, Cape Town, 1947; W. W. Battiss, The Artists of the Rocks, Pretoria, 1948; W. W. Battiss, The Source of Art, Lantern, I, 1951, pp. 2–3, 145–46, 273–74, 352, II, 1952–53, pp. 107–08, 169, 315–16, 343; C. van Riet Lowe and B. D. Malan, The Monuments of South Africa, Pretoria, 1951, pp. 144, 154, 166; E. Rosenthal and A. J. H. Goodwin, Cave Artists of South Africa, Cape Town, 1953; H. Breuil, The White Lady of the Brandberg, London, 1955; C. van Riet Lowe, The Rock Engravings of Driekops Eiland, Proc. 2d Pan-African Cong. on Prehistory (Algiers, 1952), Paris, 1955; C. van Riet Lowe, The Distribution of Prehistoric Rock Engravings and Rock Paintings in South Africa, Union of South Africa Archaeol. Survey, Archaeol. Ser., VII, Pretoria, 1956; A. R. Willcox, Rock Paintings of the Drakensberg, London, 1956; H. Breuil, Philipp Cave, London, 1957; A. Viereck and J. Rudner, Twyfelfontein — a Centre of Prehistoric Art in South West Africa, B. of the South African Archaeol. Soc., XII, 1957, pp. 15–26; T. Johnson, H. Rabinowitz, and P. Sieff, Rock Paintings of the South West Cape, Cape Town, 1959; H. Breuil, Anibib and Omandumba and Other Erongo Sites, London, 1960; I. and J. Rudner, South African Prehistoric Paintings, Cape Town, 1960. *Tribal art*: H. P. N. Muller and J. N. Snelleman, Industrie des Cafres du Sud-Est de l'Afrique, Leiden, 1893; F. Christol, L'art dans l'Afrique Australe, Paris, 1911; F. von Luschan, Buschmann-Einritzungen auf Strausseneiern, ZfE, LV, 1923, pp. 31–40; E. M. Shaw, Native Pipes and Smoking in South Africa, Ann. of the South African Mus., XXIV, 1938, pp. 277–302; E. M. Shaw, South African Native Snuff-Boxes, Ann. of the South African Mus., XXIV, 1938, pp. 141–62; E. M. Shaw, Supplement to South African Native Snuff-Boxes, Ann. of the South African Mus., XXIV, 1938, pp. 221–52; A. J. D. Meiring, The Significance of the Engravings on Masarwa Egg-Shells (Kalahari), Fort Hare Pap., I, 1945, pp. 3–8; J. Walton, South African Peasant Architecture, African S., VII, 1948, pp. 139–45, fig. 12, 13, fig. 2; E. M. Shaw, South African Bantu Arts and Crafts, in E. Hellmann and L. Abrahams, Handbook of Race Relations in South Africa, Oxford, 1949, p. 628 ff.; L. Longmore, The A. A. Jaques Collection of Native Head-Rests, African Music Soc. Newsletter, I, 1951, pp. 26–28; A. J. D. Meiring, Some More Egg-Shell Engravings, Fort Hare Pap., I, 1951, pp. 255–56; W. W. Battiss, The Carvings of Isak of "Uitspan," Lantern, I, 1952, pp. 412–14; J. Walton, Carved Wooden Doors of the Bavenda, Man, LIV, 1954, p. 43; J. Walton, African Village, Pretoria, 1956, p. 143, pls. 98–104, fig. 53; J. Walton, Some Forms of Bushman Art, African Music Soc. J., I, 1957, pp. 27–32; P. Holz, A Visit to the Ndebele, Vigorous Art of a Primitive People, African World, 1957, pp. 13–14; W. W. Battiss, H. P. Junod, H. G. Franz, and J. W. Grossert, The Art of Africa, Pietermaritzburg, 1958; K. Schlosser, Bantu-Künstler in Süd-Afrika, Kiel, 1960.

E. Margaret SHAW

COLONIAL AND MODERN PERIODS. The history of modern architecture in the Republic of South Africa began in 1666 with the construction on the site of Van Riebeeck's fort of the castle of the Cape of Good Hope, which served as a supply base for the Dutch East India Company. Although it was successively reelaborated, its star-shaped plan still retains the characteristics of Renaissance military architecture. Near the castle many farms sprang up and the beginning of an urban center (first settlement, 1652), De Kaap (later Cape Town), concentrated around the market place. The main reason for the development of the colony was the supplying of ships with fruit and vegetables, and this also explains the layout of the oldest centers, which for that purpose were concentrated around the market places or greens and even today are rich in luxuriant gardens. The economy of the South African colony, which was primarily agricultural until the discovery of mineral deposits in the second half of the 19th century, determined not only the town planning but also the architecture of the first Dutch settlements (17th and 18th cent.). In the southern and western districts there are still many country homes and farmhouses that provide examples of the oldest, most typical Dutch colonial architecture of those years. Varied in plan, these houses generally have steeply sloping roofs and simple linear façades surmounted by gables decorated in relief. This type continued to be used without modification throughout the 18th century (e.g., Groot Constantia, 1692, in Constantia; Stellenberg House, 1790, in Kenilworth; Morgenster House, 1786, in Somerset West). The various regional styles of architecture are also characterized by their gables: the houses of the Cape peninsula have volutes; those of Stellenbosch and Somerset West have more complicated forms and more elaborate decoration; and those of Paarl are triangular, with slender little side columns.

The heavy Huguenot immigration contributed greatly to the colonization of the hinterland and to the development of rural construction (e.g., The Old Parsonage, 1786, today the Huguenot Museum, in Paarl). Toward the end of the 18th century, the gables in the region of the Cape were more richly decorated, primarily owing to the work of the German sculptor Anton Anreith (1754–1822), such as the gable of the wine cellar (1791) of Groot Constantia. Anreith, together with the French architect Michel Thibault, created many of the 18th-century houses still existing on Longmarket, Plein, and Strand Streets in Cape Town (the Kat Balcony is considered an outstanding masterpiece), the Drostdy Buildings in Tulbagh (1804), and others. These city residences are characterized by flat roofs, gables that are almost always triangular and decorated with stucco reliefs, and simple linear façades, sometimes divided by engaged pilaster strips, with large square windows. Outstanding among the few remaining 18th-century religious buildings is the well-preserved church of Tulbagh (1743; now a museum), which was inspired by contemporaneous Dutch religious architecture.

With the British occupation of 1806, the characteristics of colonial architecture changed. The urban centers, which were developing rapidly, were provided with large government and administrative buildings. Following European models, monumental architecture adopted the Neo-Gothic, Neo-Renaissance, Georgian, and neoclassic styles; the last was to persist until the first decade of the 20th century. Among the major architectural achievements of this kind are the administrative buildings in Pretoria, of which the finest example is the majestic neoclassic Union Buildings (1910–13) by Sir Herbert Baker, who was also responsible for the neoclassic reconstruction of the Anglican Cathedral (1901) in Cape Town.

The first examples of a South African style of architecture based on local tradition are found in the Boer rural communities (the Boer republic was founded in Natal in 1838) that were enveloped by the urban organization following on the discovery of deposits of diamonds (Hopetown, 1867) and of gold (Barberton, 1875), which attracted intensive European immigration. The cities that sprang up in the mining areas in the second half of the 19th century were soon to become the most important in the country: Johannesburg, Pretoria, Bloemfontein, Kimberley. Their establishment influenced the development of the coastal cities, and the reorganization of the ports: Cape Town, Durban, Port Elizabeth. Within a few years, between 1926 and 1930, architecture was modernized through the work of Rex Martienssen, W. G. McIntosh, and N. L. Hanson, who introduced the ideas of Gropius and Mies van der Rohe (qq.v.); during the 1930s these architects, who were in contact with European avant-garde architects such as Le Corbusier (q.v.), actively promoted the principles of functional architecture. After an interruption during the Second World War there was an extraordinary revival of industrial activity that was accompanied by the expansion of urban centers. Architecture underwent further changes and became oriented toward taller, vertical structures, the intensive exploitation of space, and the use of new materials such as metal and glass. At present the inspiration of the most recent tendencies of Brazilian architecture can be seen in Durban and in Pretoria, where there is an outstanding group of architects including A. L. Meiring, Director of the School of Architecture at Pretoria University, W. G. McIntosh, and Norman Eaton and the younger architects Hellmut Stauch and Philip Nel. The school of Johannesburg is represented by N. L. Hanson and John Fassler. Other important architects are Pryce Lewis, P. Connel, Thornton White, H. A. I. Watson, and R. Nixon. Among the buildings that best reflect the contemporary style of South African architecture, mention should be made of the Provincial Administration Building, the Mealie Industry Control Board, the Bank of South Africa, the Wachthuis Building, Greenwood House, and the impressive architectural group of the University in Pretoria; private homes such as the Harris house and the Bedo house and the Killarney and Berea housing developments in Johannesburg; the studios of the South African Broadcasting Corporation and the housing units in Cape Town; and the Dutch Reformed church in Parys (Orange Free State).

In contrast to architecture, painting and sculpture have shown themselves only slightly influenced by European trends. The first examples of painting are connected with the travel memoirs of European painters who were struck by the extraordinary South African landscapes. Samuel Daniell (1775–1811) published a noteworthy series of sketches and water colors illustrating the flora and fauna of South Africa. Thomas Baines (1820–75), the most prolific of 19th-century South African painters, excelled in landscapes and war scenes. The first painter of real artistic merit was Thomas W. Bowler (1813–69), who did engravings, water colors, drawings, and lithographs of foreshortened townscapes and views of the countryside surrounding Cape Town in a lively but traditional style, occasionally selling topical sketches to *The Illustrated London News*. At the beginning of the 20th century a radical change in painting technique occurred with the work of Hugo Naude (1869–1941) and Pieter Wenning (1873–1921), who were the first to introduce a richer and more brilliant palette in landscape painting, while Gwelo Goodman (1871–1939; also an architect and restorer of old Dutch houses in Cape Town), who used the neoimpressionist technique, and John Amshewitz (1882–1942) followed the romantic style. The painters began to look at Africa and its profuse natural vegetation with a different eye. Irma Stern and Maggie Laubser, who exerted a strong influence on the local school, may be set within the movement of German expressionism. Noteworthy among the other pioneers of South African modern painting are Wolf Kibel (1903–38), a Polish painter who arrived in Cape Town in 1929, and J. H. Pierneef (Pretoria, 1886–1957), who experimented with cubism.

Immediately after the Second World War, new trends emerged. Formal qualities that had also influenced European painting (geometric shapes, simplicity, schematization) were discovered in the primitive indigenous art. These new tendencies in painting are also found in industrial design, in fabrics, and in interior decoration. The inspiration is vast and varied, and artists draw it directly from objects of local craftsmanship and from the colors and shapes of the African landscape itself. Leading exponents of contemporary South African painting include Alexis Preller, Walter Battiss, Maurice van Essche, Erik Laubscher, Bettie Cilliers-Barnard, Douglas Portway, Rupert Shephard, Eleanor Esmonde-White, and Jean Welz. A small number of Bantu painters have established themselves, some as professionals, some as spare-time workers. Notable are G. Benghu, Buthelezi, J. K. Mohl, G. M. Pemba, and G. Sekoto.

South African sculpture is less profuse than painting, but it has an older tradition. The first well-known sculptor and architect was Anton Anreith (1754–1822), mentioned above, who decorated many

neoclassic pediments for private homes in Cape Town as well as the pulpits of the Dutch Reformed and Lutheran churches there. In the 19th century the chief exponent of commemorative sculpture was Anton van Wouw (b. Driebergen, Holland, 1862; d. Pretoria, 1945), who in the first years of the 20th century began to produce stylized figures of the pioneers and the natives. Most of his work is in Pretoria. The works of Moses Kottler (b. 1896) are also inspired by native life and local color. Since the beginning of the second decade of the 20th century, sculpture has also reflected European tendencies, although retaining the simplicity and schematization of the traditional local art.

Among the leading exponents of modern South African sculpture are Coert Steynberg (b. 1905), Lippy Lipschitz, Willem de Sanderez Hendriksz (1910–59), Eduardo Villa (b. 1920), and the Bantu artists Mvusi and L. Maurice; to these might be added the Bantu modelers H. Ntuli and S. Makoanyane.

MODERN CENTERS. Bloemfontein (Orange Free State). Founded in the middle of the 19th century, today it is an important commercial and industrial center. The town developed along a regular, orthogonal layout and is predominantly modern in appearance, although it also has examples of the local 19th-century architecture in such buildings as the First Raadsaal (1849; national monument), the Court of Appeal, and the National Museum (containing a large collection of fossils).

Cape Town. Seat of the Parliament of the Republic of South Africa, this is the oldest city in the country. It spreads out along a large bay that encloses one of the most active ports in all Africa. Between 1652 and 1666 the city arose near Fort van Riebeeck as a supply station for ships of the Dutch East India Company. At the end of the 17th century the town of De Kaap (later Cape Town) consisted of a group of houses clustered around Greenmarket Square and along Strand and Longmarket Streets. The subsequent growth of the Dutch colony brought about a rapid development of the town, which was extended on a regular layout and was provided with public buildings and large parks. The city was further developed during the period of English rule (19th cent.), which brought about a change in architectural style marked by European Neo-Gothic, Neo-Renaissance, and Georgian influences. Although there are still many Dutch colonial buildings, the appearance of the city today has been almost completely changed by the construction of entire new districts and the transformation of the old center according to the criteria of international modern architecture.

Among the buildings of the Dutch colonial period are the castle built to replace Van Riebeeck's fort in 1666 on a star-shaped plan (later reworked); the Old Town House, a monumental building of 1755 (restored in 1915), now a museum (Michaelis Collection of Flemish and Dutch paintings); the 18th-century Old Supreme Court Building; private homes such as the Koopmans De Wet House (1701; now a furniture museum), the Martin Melck House (1780), and many others with characteristic flat roofs and triangular gables decorated with figures, which stand along the old Longmarket, Plein, and Strand Streets. Almost all of them were the work of the French architect Thibault and the German sculptor Anreith. Of the oldest religious

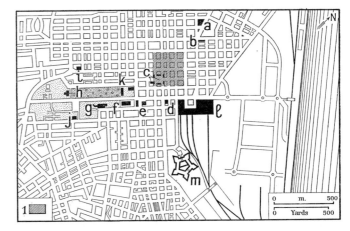

Cape Town, plan of the central zone. Key: (1) Original nucleus of the 17th century. Principal monuments: (a) Church of St. Andrew; (b) Customs Department; (c) Old Town House and Greenmarket Square; (d) Standard Bank; (e) Old Supreme Court Building and Dutch Reformed church; (f) Houses of Parliament; (g) Government House; (h) Botanical Gardens and South African Museum; (i) Lutheran church; (j) South African Gallery; (k) Public Library and new Anglican Cathedral of St. George; (l) railroad station; (m) castle.

architecture there remain the Presbyterian Church of St. Andrew, in the neoclassic style (1829), and the Dutch Reformed church, begun in 1699 but reconstructed in 1936; this last preserves the original steeple, as well as the pulpit by Anreith, who also decorated the pulpit in the old Lutheran church built at the beginning of the 19th century. The Botanical Gardens date from the period of the first Dutch settlement. They were created by Van Riebeeck to furnish vegetables for the ships of the Dutch East India Company and were the first of a series of splendid gardens that still adorn the old homes of the Dutch settlers and characterize the old urban center (e.g., Adderley Street).

Of a later date but outstanding for their massiveness and characteristic architecture are the Public Library, the South African Museum (containing a collection of native handicrafts and a zoological museum), the South African National Gallery (with an outstanding collection of old and modern paintings), and the new Anglican Cathedral of St. George, reconstructed in the neoclassic style (1901) by Sir Herbert Baker. Many buildings along the main thoroughfares of the city still exemplify traditional elements (the Customs Department, the railroad station, the Standard Bank, the Houses of Parliament, Government House, and the City Hall (completed 1905). Following the most modern international trends are various company headquarters, stores, and housing units recently constructed in the newly developed urban areas and in the nearby residential centers (e.g., housing development of Bellville). Near the city are Groote Schuur, the Prime Minister's residence (in Dutch colonial style with a large garden), and the complex of the University of Cape Town, founded in 1925.

Grahamstown (Cape Province). The town arose near a military post. It was founded by Colonel John Graham (1912) and developed rapidly. Today it is an important commercial and cultural center (including Rhodes University College) with interesting historical buildings such as the Albany Museum, the Anglican Cathedral of St. George (architect, Sir Giles Gilbert Scott), and the Roman Catholic St. Patrick's Cathedral.

Johannesburg (Transvaal). Johannesburg, the largest and most heavily populated city of the South African Republic, was established in 1886 near the newly discovered gold mines and developed along a regular, orthogonal plan, with wide, straight streets. Its outstanding modern building achievements place it, together with Pretoria, in the vanguard of contemporary architecture. There are a few buildings of historical interest: the City Hall and the Freemasons' Lodge (both neoclassic), the Anglican Cathedral, and some of the buildings of the old university. Chief among the modern constructions are the Public Library, the new railroad station, the South African Airways Terminal Building, the Netherlands Bank, the Twentieth Century-Fox Building, the Civic Theater (1962), and some parts of Witwatersrand University, founded in 1903 as the School of Mines and Technology. From the modernization carried out by the architects Rex Martienssen, N. L. Hanson, and W. G. McIntosh, an important urban center, with imposing buildings, skyscrapers, banks, and offices, has been developed (Eloff, Commissioner, Market, President, and Pritchard Streets). Recent large-scale industrial expansion has brought about the creation of new towns, the intensive utilization of the suburban areas of Jeppestown, Belgravia, Doornfontein, Berea, Parktown, and Yeoville, and the modernization of industrial and mining installations. Outstanding examples of the many new homes are the Harris house and the Bedo house. Particularly noteworthy among the large housing developments, built according to the most modern criteria, are those in the Berea and Killarney districts. The Johannesburg Art Gallery contains works by French, English, and South African artists.

Pietermaritzburg (Natal). Founded by the Dutch in 1839, this city has become an important cultural center. The old Dutch and English styles appear in the buildings of the Provincial Council, the Supreme Court, the Post Office, the Anglican Cathedral, and the Town Hall (with a picture gallery). An important historical building is the Church of the Vow, which was erected after the victory against the Zulus (1838); today it is a national monument and houses the Voortrekker Museum.

Port Elizabeth (Cape Province). The city is an important commercial and industrial center that developed in the 19th century around Fort Frederick, built in 1799 by the English colonel, Vandeleur. Today it is the third port of South Africa. The city is made up of five main agglomerations that form distinct districts. The port is the business district; The Hill is a residential quarter overlooking the bay; The Valley runs along the river; the North End is the industrial area; and the South End comprises the extensive suburbs. Among the most notable buildings is Fort Frederick, the first English construction in South Africa, now a national monument. Also note-

worthy are the Campanile, commemorating the first settlers in 1820, and the Boer War Horse Memorial.

Pretoria (Transvaal). The city was founded in 1855 by M. W. Pretorius in the richest mining area of the country; today it is the administrative capital. It contains imposing late-19th-century and early-20th-century public buildings. Outstanding are the Provincial Council Building and the Anglican Cathedral, both in the Neo-Renaissance style, facing the central square, the Union Buildings (1910–13) in the neoclassic style, with two wings and a large exedra, by Sir Herbert Baker; the City Hall, with an art gallery and extensive gardens containing a monument to Pretorius; the government offices; and the residences of the State President and the Prime Minister. Of historical interest are the Boer forts (national monuments), among which are the Skanskop (1897) and Klapperkop (1898); and the Voortrekker Memorial, a monument to the first settlers built in the form of a huge tapering block (1931–49), which houses a historical museum. Also of interest are the Transvaal Museum, containing geological, archaeological, and natural-history collections; the Old Museum, containing collections of native Bantu art; and Paul Kruger's House and Historical Museum. Included in the original plan of the city were many large parks, including Burgers Park (1875), with statues of historical figures, and Fountains Valley Nature Reserve, with botanical gardens and the National Zoological Gardens (1899).

In the 1930s, adopting the European functional style, urban renewal of the city was carried out by the architects Rex Martienssen, W. G. McIntosh, and N. L. Hanson. The industrial growth since the end of World War II has led to the creation of new suburbs and residential districts and of tall buildings in the administrative and commercial center. The latest building and city-planning projects are being carried out by local architects, including A. L. Meiring, Hellmut Stauch, Philip Nel, and Norman Eaton. The esthetic and technical tendencies of this group are inspired by contemporary developments in Brazilian architecture. Outstanding examples of recent architecture are the headquarters of the Bank of South Africa and of the Mealie Industry Control Board, the Transvaal Provincial Administration Building, the Wachthuis Building, Greenwood House, and the new section of the university, especially the amphitheater, the theater, the Public Hall, and the School of Music. Also of interest are the new industrial plants on the outskirts of the city and the modern town-planning approach in the new residential quarters.

Bibliog. In the Limelight, Spotlight, Sept. 19, 1947; Bantu Artists in Paris (Sokoto), Cape Times Mag. Section, Aug. 27, 1949; C. G. S. Damont, Samuel Makoanyane (Suto Clay-Modeller), Morija, 1951; R. H. W. Shepherd, An African Artist and His Message, The Work of G. M. Pemba, African World, 1952; Pemba the Artist, Drum, May, 1957, pp. 47–49; W. M. Howie, Contemporary Architecture in South Africa, Johannesburg, 1958; G. R. Naidoo, America Wants This Gangling Casual Artist (Mvusi), Drum, June, 1958, pp. 35–37; South African Tourist Corporation, South Africa, for the Visitor, Cape Town, 1959; D. Anderson, South African Art, Pretoria, n.d.; Our Art (cat. of South African painters and sculptors), Pretoria, n.d.

Francesco NEGRI ARNOLDI

Illustrations: 3 figs. in text.

SOUTH AMERICAN CULTURES. Among the indigenous cultures of the Americas (see AMERICAN CULTURES), those of the regions of South America east of the Andes, even though they underwent to a greater or lesser extent some influences of the higher Andean civilizations (see ANDEAN PROTOHISTORY), generally speaking had an autonomous artistic evolution, with numerous regional and tribal aspects. Compared with the archaeological finds, contemporary art appears poor in imagination and of a modest technical level; but it is precisely for these primitive characteristics that this art is of particular interest for the study of its origins.

The early artistic productions of northwestern Argentina and of Chile denote the presence of strong influences from the Central Andean civilizations, of whose complex this zone formed a political part in the period of Inca dominance. However, original styles of a high level were also developed there, especially in ceramics. These cultures therefore represent a separate phenomenon in the sphere of the other indigenous South American civilizations (see below).

SUMMARY. General characteristics (col. 149). Guiano-Amazonian culture (col. 154). Prehistoric cultures (col. 156): *Venezuela; The island of Marajó; Santarém; Maracá and Cunani; Early art of the middle and upper Amazon; Eastern Bolivia; The lower Paraná, Ar-*

gentina, and Chile; Early stone carving. Art of the contemporary South American Indians (col. 167): *Basketry; Wood carving and wood engraving; Wax and clay modeling; Masks; Featherwork; Body painting.* The Chaco (col. 173): *The Chiriguano; The Caduveo.* The Argentine plains nomads (col. 178). Tierra del Fuego (col. 178).

GENERAL CHARACTERISTICS. The contrast between the Andean cultures and those of the inhabitants of the forests and the Argentine pampas was probably not so marked as had been generally assumed. It is true that the tribes of the regions of the Amazon, the Chaco, and Patagonia never created states or founded towns, but neither were they submerged in complete barbarism. The influence of the great Andean empires reached far to the east, and the conquerors of the Brazilian coast and the Río de la Plata often received from the Indians accurate reports of the marvels of the Inca empire. In the American lowlands, however, there was no art comparable to that of Peru, Bolivia, or Colombia. The beauty of the feather-work, the originality and taste shown in certain forms of ceramics, and the striking large masks of beaten bark do not justify a comparison of the arts of the Indians of this part of South America with those of other peoples who, although their sur-roundings and way of life were similar, were of a different cultural level. Thus these arts, which have aroused only scant interest outside specialized circles, and, apart from a few archaeological pieces, have never been sought after by collectors, appear poor and limited compared, for instance, with those of New Guinea.

The poverty of this art can perhaps be attributed to decadence that rapidly overtook the tribes which had suffered, directly or indirectly, the effects of the European conquest; the slave trade and disease decimated once prosperous and powerful communities. Among "primitive" as well as among civilized peoples, the taste for perfection rarely survives the test of misery and insecurity. Mediocrity in artistic decoration, inattention to detail, and heaviness of form nearly always accompany social and economic decadence among Indian communities in contact with the white man.

There is little hope that archaeology will reveal artistic remains other than those of terra cotta and stone, since the climate of the tropical and subtropical plains destroys all other materials. Occasional references in old travel accounts and random pieces found by early explorers — for example the *duho,* or wooden seat of the Taino Indians, and a few Amazonian trumpets (Copenhagen, Nationalmus., and Leyden, Rijksmus. voor Volkenkunde) — indicate the existence of an art of wood carving which has no modern equivalent in the area. The ceramics of Marajó and Santarém, although inferior to those of ancient Peru, bear witness to the imagination and skill of the tribes which, soon after the white man settled in the region, became extinct.

Among the tribes of the forest and plains of the Chaco and Patagonia, art was only to a small extent inspired by religion. Apart from the masks which, in certain communities, represent the spirits, the Indians outside the Andean zone rarely gave material form to their gods, nor did they build temples or even rudimentary shrines. It is true that religious interpreta-tions have been suggested for the decorations of the pottery excavated at Santarém and Marajó, but these suggestions are quite arbitrary and fanciful.

The fundamentally democratic structure of these archaic communities did not favor the development of art; nowhere among the Indians were there chiefs or aristocratic groups powerful enough to promote its development by surrounding themselves with symbols of power and wealth. The slight distinctions of rank among individuals are evident only in the relative richness of feather decorations, bracelets, and lip ornaments.

The art of the primitive tribes of South America is essentially connected with personal adornment and everyday objects such as weapons, tools, and working utensils. Primarily decorative in character, this art is characterized by a relatively poor geometric style. From Guiana to the Chaco are found vases, baskets, objects made of tree bark, and clubs decorated with abstract designs consisting of whorls, key patterns, lozenges, triangles, and stippling. Rectilinear motifs predominate over curvilinear, a characteristic which distinguishes the modern works from those of the past. The prehistoric pottery from Marajó, Santarém, Guiana and environs, on the contrary, shows a certain predilection for curves, spirals, and serpentines. These motifs are also present in contemporary works, as can be seen in the incised decorations on Guianese clubs and in the beautiful patterns of the bark tunics of the Yurucari of eastern Bolivia, in which the designs recall flame and acanthus-leaf motifs.

The preference for abstract decoration did not exclude, however, attempts at figural art, examples of which exist among the arts of the Indians of the Uaupés and Içana river regions (northwest Brazil). The bark panels covering the fronts of their large *malocas* (communal huts) are generally decorated with geometric patterns including adjacent triangles, lozenges, and parallel lines. Sometimes these ornaments are replaced by more or less skilled portrayals of men and animals. Even in this art there is a tendency to transform abstract designs into pictures of animals or objects. Thus, a triangle, the base of which extends into hooks, often becomes a bird. Conversely, anthropomorphic figures may become purely geometrical designs. The figures traced on the hut posts are an example; on a rectangular body is a human head capped by a feather diadem. The figure is so stylized that, although it keeps its characteristic features, it has lost its anthropomorphic appearance.

In some respects the decorative art of the South American Indians is sufficiently uniform to make it possible to distinguish a few general characteristics. Thus, decorated surfaces are usually divided into rectangular sections having different motifs. In many tribes, the linear designs are less important than the areas which they delimit and which the artists try to bring out by uniform color or hatching. Krause (1912) is of the opinion that the Carajá Indians did not see decorative designs in the same way that we do. For them, the essential element was the surface bounded by the lines, and not the lines themselves. When the Indians reproduced the chief motifs of their art on paper, they were always at pains to hatch or stipple the areas enclosed between the lines. Krause also observes that it was often difficult for them to make a clear distinction between the design proper and the background against which it was set.

Ornaments — especially of feathers — can be classed as works of art when they reveal a concern for symmetry and rhythm in their forms or in the alternation of colors. Body painting constitutes one of the main forms of artistic expression among the South American Indians. Often this is a simple transposition onto the skin of the predominant decorative style of the tribe; thus the facial paintings of the Pano tribes of the Ucayali region are a faithful reproduction of the decorative elements of their pottery and textiles. It is also possible, however, for body painting to have a style of its own, often richer and more varied than that of other fields. The body painting of the Witoto Indians is a case in point.

The frequency with which certain decorative motifs recur in the arts of the Indians of the forest and of the Chaco is due both to the uniformity of their culture and to the widespread use of certain techniques over the continent. It is true that many of these designs are so simple that it is useless to try to determine their area of distribution. Many tribes (particularly those living on game and the fruits of the forest), such as the Guayakí, Sirionó, Nambicuara, and Waica, have virtually no art except a few ornaments not worthy of the name.

Even in the tribes in which an appreciation of beauty is evident, it is often difficult to distinguish between an art object and an object of a purely practical nature. The question arises for a number of handicraft products.

It is no doubt the simplicity and, it must be admitted, the poverty of the purely abstract **decorative** style which have led various scholars to draw from it hypotheses on the origins of Indian art in general. The Indians of the upper Xingú region (central Brazil), explored in 1886 by Karl von den Steinen, provided particularly rich material for ethnographical

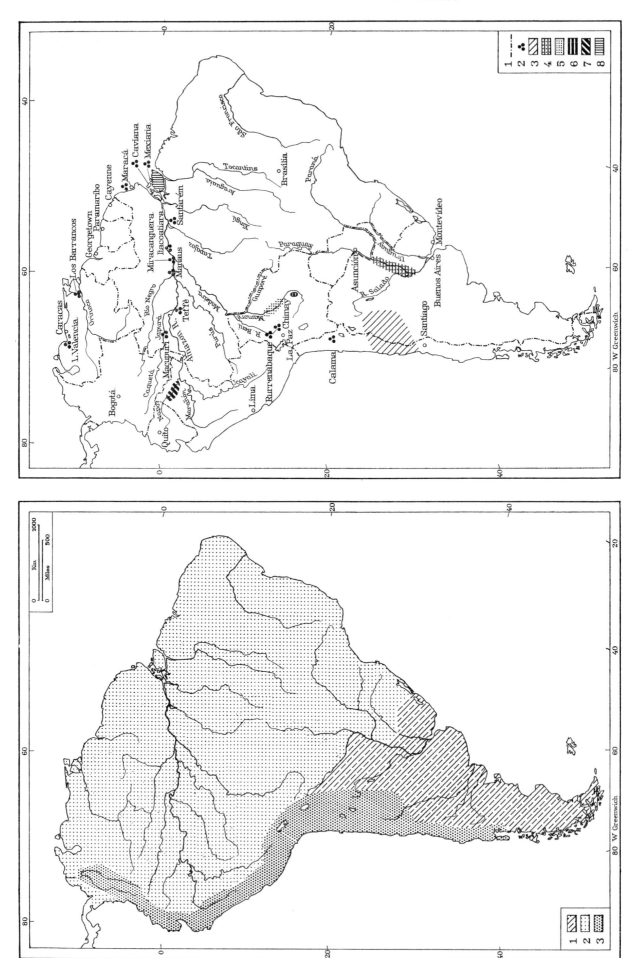

Left: Cultural areas of South America. *Key*: (1) Hunting and nomadic food-gathering cultures; (2) tropical forest cultures; (3) Andean civilization. *Right*: Distribution of the principal sites and areas of archaeological interest, exclusive of the great Andean civilizations. *Key*: (1) Political boundaries; (2) archaeological sites; (3) Andean civilizations. *Key*: (1) Hunting and nomadic food-gathering cultures; (2) tropical forest cultures; (3) Andean civilization. *Right*: Distribution of the principal sites and areas of archaeological interest, exclusive of the great Andean civilizations. *Key*: (1) Political boundaries; (2) archaeological sites; (3) Diaguita area; (4) the lower Paraná area; (5) the Mojo area; (6) the Río Palacios area; (7) the Napo River area; (8) the island of Marajó.

speculations. Most of the objects made by these Indians — oars, benches, flutes, masks, and spatulas for turning over cassava cakes — as well as the decoration of hut posts and walls are ornamented with designs in a characteristic style. These generally consist of series of lozenges or triangles with blackened angles. The Indians give names of animals or objects to these motifs. Thus the triangles are *uluri* — feminine *cache-sexe* made of palm leaves; the lozenges with blackened angles are *mereshu* — fish commonly found in the region; the series of triangles in rows are bats; the sinuous or zigzagging lines are serpents, and so forth. Karl von den Steinen (1894) sees in this nomenclature the proof that the decorative art of the Indians started from a realistic basis and developed toward geometrical and abstract forms. He thought it inconceivable that such simple ornaments should have sprung spontaneously from the artist's imagination, receiving only subsequently and purely by analogy the names of beings or things. The Carajá Indians of the Araguaia River, as Ehrenreich (1897) observed, give to the geometrical elements of their art names suggested to them by similarities between these designs and animal silhouettes, or by a detail peculiar to a single animal. Thus a number of motifs are called "serpent designs" because their pattern is similar to that of the dorsal scales of certain reptiles. This giving of names of animals or objects to geometrical designs because of a vague resemblance in no way proves that the artist's aim was to represent the latter in schematic form; the diversity of nomenclatures, which, for the same designs, vary from one community to the next, or even from one artist to the next, leaves no doubt as to the nonfigural nature of these decorative elements. The resemblance between a geometrical motif and a natural object, however, may be accentuated by the addition of details which turn an abstract design into a realistic design.

Another German ethnographer, Max Schmidt, who also explored the upper Xingú region, formulated a completely conflicting theory (1905) on the origins of art, a theory that caused such a stir that even Karl von den Steinen finally accepted it. A careful study of the methods used by the Indians in their basketmaking led him to the observation that, according to the type of palms and the direction in which the leaves crossed, different geometrical figures automatically resulted. In the so-called "twill" method of plaiting (see BASKETRY), which consists of passing the weft strands at right angles over or under two or more warp strands, with variations in the sequence, the result is inevitably a square crossed by diagonal lines. According to the rhythm adopted in the number of strands interwoven, the juxtaposition of four squares forms geometrical figures, particularly lozenges, crosses, and key patterns. These designs stand out clearly if warp and weft are of different colors. Comparing the motifs resulting from the technique of basketweaving with those which the Indians of the Xingú area use to decorate their masks, oars, and scoops for *beijú* (cassava), Max Schmidt (1905) pointed out their similarity and concluded that all the decorative art of these Indians was derived from basketry. He went so far as to write that "wherever palm trees grow and men use their leaves to make baskets, the same motifs and decorative themes result." Numerous objections can be raised to this hypothesis. Even if the *mereshu* lozenge recalls that which results from the twill technique, nothing proves that it derives from it, especially as its proportions are different and there is nothing in basketry which could account for the blackened angles. Also, why should a figure as elementary as the triangle (*uluri*) necessarily be considered as half a lozenge? Schmidt's hypothesis, even if it were proved correct, would moreover explain only the rectilinear decorations, without throwing any light on the origin of the circles and curves that also appear in the art of the Xingú region. Furthermore, the complex basketweaving motifs of the Guianese Indians do not seem to have had the influence one would expect on their other artistic productions. Although it is rash to consider the abstract style of the South American Indians as a transposition onto other materials of the designs directly resulting from the technique of basketmaking, it cannot be denied that in certain cases artists drew inspira-

tion from these designs. The most typical cases are those in which ceramic decorations reproduce not certain patterns decorating baskets, but the very texture of a basketwork object, such as a manioc press.

While some art historians were seeking the source of South American native art in a sort of artistic instinct, confined to the representation of realistic or abstract motifs, Raphael Karsten (1926), following Preuss (1921–23), disputed the validity of this assertion and linked almost all the art of the Indians to magic and religion. What were wrongly assumed to be the decorations of an object are actually, according to this author, charms against evil spirits. He explains the presence of animals or of motifs bearing animal names by the fact that demons often assume animal form. Rarely has a thesis been so confidently presented on such slight evidence. Working on analogies and suppositions, Karsten does not cite a single case in which the Indians affirm that the triangles or other patterns decorating everyday objects were traced for magic ends. The fact that ritual objects, such as rattles made from gourds, are painted or incised does not necessarily imply that the paintings and engravings have a religious significance. The symbolism of the Amazonian or Patagonian tribes is little developed, or has escaped the attention of ethnographers, for there is as yet no evidence, apart from the cases mentioned above, of the symbolical value of the designs traced on pottery or calabashes.

Little is known as yet about the social aspects of art among the South American Indians. One fact, however, must be borne in mind — the predominant part played by women in most artistic activities. Pottery-making, weaving, leatherwork, and the art of body painting are reserved for women. The only forms of artistic expression open to men are the modeling of animals in wax, basketmaking, and wood carving. Handicraft specialization, although not very marked, is to be found in several regions. The most notable example is that of the Warrau Indians of the Xingú, who have become the sole producers of pottery for all their neighbors.

Studying the art of the Carajá, Krause (1912) pointed out the contrast between the abstract character of the work produced by the women and the realism of that created by the men. In the course of the last half century the clay dolls (PLS. 101, 102) made by the Carajá women have changed in nature. They have lost their former conventionality and have become so realistic that certain contemporary Carajá artists depict scenes of everyday life. This development was prompted by the influence exerted by the men on the art of their women.

Although metallurgy was one of the chief forms of artistic expression in the Andean zone, to the east of the Andes it was known only among the Guianese Indians who, in the 18th century, still made ornaments and ceremonial objects of *guanín*, a gold and copper alloy. Among the modern Guianese tribes no trace remains of the goldsmiths' work mentioned by the travelers of the 17th and 18th centuries. Even the memory of it seems to have disappeared. The Indians of Colombia are known to have been highly skilled goldsmiths, and it is therefore not surprising if not only the goldsmiths' works but also the technical knowledge necessary for their execution penetrated among the Indians of Venezuela and thence among the Guianese Indians. The hypothesis attributing the discovery of the goldsmith's craft to Guianese Indians has little to support it.

Following contacts with Europeans, some tribes of the Chaco and Patagonia learned to make use of silver coins for ornaments of every sort, but this can in no wise be called an original art.

GUIANO-AMAZONIAN CULTURE. Guiano-Amazonian culture is both homogeneous in its most basic aspects and varied in its particular characteristics. The close interrelation between the Tupi-Guaraní, Arawakan, Carib, and Pano linguistic groups, to mention only a few, testifies to the great mixing of peoples and cultures that took place in the course of several centuries in the geographical area stretching from Guiana to the Chaco. The migrations of the Arawak, Tupi, and Carib tribes helped to disseminate techniques, rites, beliefs, and social institutions which accentuated still further the cultural uniformity of tribes whose economic systems were very similar or identical.

The way of life varies little from Guiana to the Mato Grosso. Cultivation is carried out on the burnt-plot system, manioc is the staple food, and hunting and fishing are important economic activities. The form of habitation is usually the large communal hut, which by itself constitutes the whole village. Clothing is sketchy, but feather ornaments of great variety are often magnificent. Basketwork is highly developed and the use of pottery is general.

Religious beliefs are based upon the fear of spirits and the rites are often propitiatory and defensive in nature. The social structure is based on the clan system.

Within this common background, isolation, local developments, and exchanges between neighboring communities, as well as influences from the Andean zone, have superimposed on these general characteristics an element of variety and differences which cannot be disregarded. As a rule, the greatest cultural homogeneity is to be found along the rivers or in their basins, so that regions characterized by a certain type of culture are called after rivers, such as the Río Negro, the Caiarí-Uaupés, the Xingú, and the Araguaia.

The Andean cultures of Colombia and the Argentine had a deep influence on the cultures of the forest peoples. Venezuela and Guiana were subject to cultural influences emanating from Colombia. Ecuadorian and Colombian influences converged in the tribes of the upper Amazon. The old Peruvian civilizations affected the tribes of eastern Bolivia and Chiquitos Province at a very early date. The military penetration of the Incas into the great Amazonian forest was not comparable in its effects to the conquests which they achieved in other directions. They did not establish themselves in the jungle and confined themselves to exploiting the hot valleys to which access was easy and where they could cultivate coca. The Amazonian forest, however, rose like an impenetrable wall.

Within this geographical area it is possible, following the distribution of the typical characteristics, to establish a certain number of cultural provinces. Considered from the artistic point of view, the only one relevant here, the classification established according to ethnographical criteria proves to be of little use. Artistic manifestations in many regions are in fact not rich or distinctive enough to make the esthetic criterion valid in a classification of the cultures. The decorative art of the Indians of the Montaña region has the originality and complexity necessary to define this cultural province, but what artistic elements can be chosen to distinguish the art of the Indians of the Guaporé region from that of the Paressí or the Nambicuara? Even the magnificent feather decorations of the Mundurucú and Apiacá of the Tapajoz River area do not justify the establishing of a cultural subdivision for these Indians, since the masterpieces of their *arte plumaria* have a counterpart among the Tupinamba of the Brazilian coast. Broadly speaking, the following artistic provinces can be distinguished: Guiana; the northwest of Brazil (basins of the Caiarí-Uaupés, Içana, and Apaporis rivers); the Montaña, that is, the Río Marañón; the upper tributaries of the Amazon, the Araguaia basin (Carajá) and that of the Xingú; and Paraguay (unfortunately little known). It has been necessary to eliminate a very large number of tribes whose art, at least such of it as is accessible, is too little developed for inclusion here. A clear distinction has been drawn between the arts which archaeology has revealed and those of contemporary Indians. Nothing is known about the ethnical affiliations of most of the tribes which have left vestiges of their art; and although a link between them and modern races is sometimes discernible, it is so tenuous that it would be confusing to put the past and the present on the same plane. The prehistoric cultures — in other words, those which disappeared before or shortly after the conquest — will therefore be considered first, and a special section will be devoted to the arts of the modern Indians. It would have been logical, in this description, to adopt the geographical order outlined here, but the differences between cultural provinces are often so slight that this plan would have involved much repetition. It therefore seemed preferable to treat tropical America as a whole, despite the cultural variations that exist within this area, extending from Guiana to the Chaco.

Two tribes whose art is particularly well known, the Chiriguano and Chané tribes, raised a difficult problem. The Chiriguano belong, by their ethnical origins and partially by their material civilization, to the cultural region of the tropics, but they were so strongly influenced by the Andean peoples that their art is linked with that of the south of Bolivia and the northwest of Argentina. The Caduveo, on the other hand, are a Chaco tribe which was influenced by an Arawak tribe, the Chané, whose civilization was more akin to that of the tropical tribes than to those of the Chaco. Since the documentation here is so full, the art of these two tribes has been treated in separate sections.

PREHISTORIC CULTURES. Archaeological study of the Amazon and Orinoco basins has been far from exhaustive. Methodical excavations undertaken in Venezuela and at the mouth of the Amazon have provided important chronological data and evidence that make it possible to establish links between the different sites, but they have revealed nothing about the prehistoric art of this part of South America which was already known through sporadic discoveries.

Santarém and the island of Marajó continue to figure as the two great centers of pre-Columbian art. The finds made on the mainland, notably in Venezuela, in Trinidad, and in Guiana, have simply confirmed the existence of a close link between the pottery of the West Indies and that of the South American mainland. The two ethnical groups occupying the West Indies at the time of their discovery belonged to the Arawakan and Carib linguistic families, which are now dispersed throughout the tropical regions of South America.

Several of the Indian cultures, known through pottery excavated by archaeologists, still flourished at the time of the arrival of the Europeans and survived at least until the 17th century (Santarém, Maracá, Aruã, etc.). There is no specific mention of their art in the chronicles of the first Amazonian explorers or in those of the Catholic missionaries, most probably because the products of the indigenous cultures were considered to be valueless by those early observers.

Venezuela. In a survey of art, it is difficult to take into account all the various cultural phases which scholars have established for Venezuela, for even if their criteria coincide with those of the art historian in the analysis of styles, a dry enumeration of the motifs decorating the potsherds would result in a catalogue which, despite its importance, would give the reader only a confused idea of the artistic works of vanished populations. This study will therefore be confined to a description of the objects through which the tribes who once lived from the Orinoco to the Andes gave expression to their esthetic sense. Here again knowledge of this art is limited almost exclusively to pottery, to a few stone or shell objects, and to rock inscriptions.

Judgment of their taste and technique is necessarily restricted in scope, since nothing is known of what these people produced in more perishable materials. Many South American tribes renowned among their contemporaries for the quality of their weaving and of the designs with which they decorated weapons and bark cloth have left nothing but coarse potsherds to testify to their art.

Following a custom which was widespread in tropical South America, the early inhabitants of Venezuela placed the bones of their dead in large vases, which they then grouped together in veritable cemeteries. As in Amazonia, the function of the funeral urns explains their anthropomorphic nature. Often the features of the human face are indicated in relief on the neck of the urn, as in the Valencia urns.

One of the characteristics of Venezuelan pottery, at least in some of its phases (Orinoco, La Cabrera, Valencia), is the predominance of modeled over painted decoration. Anthropomorphic or zoomorphic applied ornaments were disposed on the rim, the neck, or the sides of the vases. As this modeling is often worn away, the beings represented are not readily identifiable, leading prudent archaeologists to call them "biomorphic" or "vitamorphic." The archaeological sites abound with these ornaments, of which the finest specimens come from Los Barrancos on the lower Orinoco. In these, long deep grooves traced in the clay are combined with the modeling to form reliefs of an incisiveness and a vigor of execution lacking elsewhere. In the relatively old archaeological domain of La Cabrera, clay pipes with bowls shaped like a human being or an animal have been found.

Painted decoration becomes more important as the northwest of Venezuela and the Andes are approached, with applied ornament growing rare or being absent. Vases covered with slip are decorated with geometrical patterns arranged in bands or sectors. The proximity of the Andean cultures manifests itself in other ways — for example, tripod vases grow more common.

The significance of the terra-cotta statuettes of men and women, which are relatively numerous in regions as far removed from each other as Venezuela, Amazonia, and eastern Bolivia, as well as the West Indies and Central America, remains one of the riddles of American archaeology. In Venezuela they belong to two phases or archaeological cultures: those of Valencia and those of the Andes (PL. 91). These have in common a distinctive head shape, which is very broad for its height, but the examples from Valencia are much more rudimentary in their execution than are those of the Andes; the eyes and mouth are indicated by slits, the atrophied arms are shaped like handles, and the feet are nonexistent or mere stumps. Whereas the Valencia statuettes are all feminine, those of the Andes culture represent both sexes. The figure shown is standing, crouching, or sitting on a bench (the last type is always male). A common characteristic of these statuettes is the shape of the legs, which are disproportionately large and long in relation to the torso. Many of the figures are decorated with painted motifs, unlike the Valencia figurines, which are plain or decorated with engraved lines.

Among the archaeological finds of the Andes region are some very curious objects whose use is a mystery. They are slabs of stone (nephrite, serpentine, diorite) known as "broad-winged ornaments." Several types are known; on those of the Andean region the central triangular part is in relief and represents a human face. Some examples suggest the outline of a bat. Much has been written about the meaning of these objects, which have been found in similar form at Santa Marta in Colombia and in Central America as far north as Mexico. They have been successively identified as musical instruments, as pectorals (although the hole for hanging them is often missing), and as stylized representations of the bat god of the Maya. The difference in size of these objects, which range from about 1¼ in. to 28 in., intensifies the mystery. The shell specimens, which are naturally smaller, are sometimes topped by very stylized human heads and decorated with engravings in different designs. Excavations have also produced many nephrite and serpentine pendants carved in the shape of human figures or frogs. These pieces, which were perhaps amulets, are especially typical of the art of the Andean region.

The island of Marajó. Of all the civilizations of tropical South America, the most brilliant artistically was the work of the vanished people who, in the pre-Columbian period, occupied the center and the northeastern part of the island of Marajó. Thousands of pieces of pottery from this region are scattered in numerous museums. The discovery of these ceramics a century ago attracted the attention of the scientific world to this archaeological zone. Bold hypotheses were formulated to justify the presence of such a highly developed art in a part of America which was seemingly given over to savagery, for nothing in the configuration or the natural conditions of the island of Marajó could explain the advent of a civilization which was in many ways distinct from those of the Indian tribes of the historical era.

The island of Marajó, with an area of about 14,000 square miles, is the largest of the islands separating the mouth of the Amazon from the sea. Alluvial in formation, crossed by numerous rivers, dissected by swamps and lakes, it appears as a vast plain with its surface hardened and cracked by the sun during the dry season and flooded during the rainy period.

Documents and chronicles of the 17th and 18th centuries rarely mention the numerous tribes that peopled the island before it was laid waste by slave hunters and epidemics. The systematic excavations by Meggers and Evans (1960) at numerous points on the island have shown that the so-called "Marajó culture" — which came relatively late — was preceded by cultures of a different type. The first inhabitants — hunters and fishermen — knowing nothing of the art of pottery, left no trace of their existence. Some centuries after the beginning of the Christian Era (perhaps the 7th), some Indians whose cultural level was that of the contemporaneous Amazonian tribes settled on the island, introducing the culture known as Ananatuba (from the main site where its remains have been excavated). This first phase was followed by the Mangueiras and Formiga phases, which represent another intrusion of new tribes and cultures, ones that produced pottery of inferior quality.

The civilization that created the reputation of the island of Marajó was already fully developed when it was brought there. It is a mature art, with the benefit of a long tradition already apparent in the earliest archaeological periods. Where did the carriers of this civilization come from? Certainly from the north of South America, if not from still farther afield — perhaps from some region bordering on Colombia or the equator. The quality and complexity of its art suggest a society in which the idea of the division of labor was highly developed. It included influential members whose burial places were distinct from those of the common people, and it had a highly developed political system. To escape the floods, this mysterious tribe raised its dwelling places on artificial mounds often as much as 30 ft. high and 800 sq. ft. in area.

Such masses of earth can have been moved only by the coordinated efforts of groups under authoritative leaders. Many urns found in the burial mounds contained either bones or ashes. Certain geometrical patterns painted or engraved on the pottery are reminiscent of the decorative motifs of basketwork or marquetry. Knowledge of the art of weaving can be inferred from the existence of terra-cotta spindle whorls. The pottery of Marajó has the peculiarity, rarely found in South America (even in the Andean zone), of combining on a single piece different types of decoration. As well as painted, engraved, or champlevé motifs, there are molded or applied ornaments. It is just this simultaneous use of several decorative techniques that has made the classification of this pottery so difficult.

The receptacles vary greatly in shape and include cylindrical or globular vases, anthropomorphic jars, bowls (PL. 92), cups, and earthenware plates. The funeral urns (IV, PL. 452), by their size and wealth of decoration, rank among the finest examples of this pottery. The representation in relief of stylized human faces gives them a definitely anthropomorphic character. Richly decorated with engraved or fluted motifs, these urns usually also had ornate lids.

The art of ceramics, so highly developed in this archaeological phase, was applied to the making of objects which elsewhere were made with other materials. Among these, the strangest are the *tanga* (PL. 92), or convex triangular plaques made of very fine clay. These are thought to be feminine *cache-sexe* because of their shape, their size, and their proximity to women's skeletons. The plaques are covered with red and black patterns on a white background, which seem to imitate weaving or basketwork motifs. Round clay slabs on round bases are thought to be seats similar to those which the Indians of the forests still use. Engraved cylinders have been found which seem to have been ear or lip ornaments.

Religious significance has been attributed to small sculptures of seated figures with legs bent and arms on hips, whose phalloid appearance has been assumed by certain scholars to connect them to fertility rites.

The esthetic value of the pottery of Marajó lies more in the general shape of the vessels and in their painted and engraved decorations than in its molded ornamentation, which includes figures placed under the lips of certain vases, rather like caryatids; protuberances in the shape of human or animal heads projecting from the sides like rudimentary handles; and, on the rims of vases, moldings suggesting human or animal shapes (the only easily recognizable animal is the cayman, which often figures in relief on the necks or lips of ceremonial vases).

The most striking decoration is that obtained by hollowing out the surface of the receptacle, before or after firing, so that the remaining parts stand out in relief. This process has been likened to champlevé, although, strictly speaking, the term is not applicable here, since the hollow parts are not filled with a colored paste. The grooves, however, are often covered with a thick layer of white paint, which contrasts with the projecting parts (painted red or left uncolored). Sometimes the spaces separating the decorative motifs have been so finely hatched that the incisions, in their proximity to each other, produce an effect akin to that of champlevé.

The decoration may also be engraved in the slip which covers the surface of the vase. The grooves traced with a sharp tool are deep enough to reveal the natural color of the terracotta body. In receptacles painted in red over a white slip, the color of the slip appears in the groove. A black or brown band follows the outline of the engraved design.

On polychrome vases without engraving, the ornaments appear to be painted in white over a red, brown, or black ground, but actually these colors were applied with a brush on the white slip in a technique called "negative" decoration.

The ornamentation resulting from the technical processes described above is at first striking because of its complexity and diversity; yet when the motifs are analyzed, they are found to be based on a small number of fundamental motifs, such as simple or interwoven volutes, meanders, serpentine lines, S's, T's, tiered pyramids, "hands with spread fingers," and crosses inscribed in escutcheons.

A favorite motif among the ceramists was the human face, so stylized as to become almost a geometrical element. Confronted faces alternate to form kinds of ornamental bands, and two pairs of "eyes" (dots or circles separated by a long line) prove to be two heads facing in opposite directions. The contour of the head corresponds to two whorls between which dots and lines indicate the features of the face. The eyebrows and nose are sometimes suggested by a simple T. In many cases, modeling and painting are combined to represent a face or a figure in full. When the eyeball, shown in relief, is crossed by an oblique slit, the face, despite its stylization, assumes a sad or macabre expression.

Santarém. The second great artistic center of Amazonia is the town of Santarém. The torrential rains of the year 1922 washed through the streets of Santarém and revealed strange fragments of pottery shaped like human beings or animals. These remains, collected by Curt Nimuendajú (1952), as well as a very few intact pieces, revealed the existence of a previously unknown art. Its chief characteristic is the importance of molded decoration. It is true that the pottery of Marajó, as well as that of Guiana, included ornaments in relief and in the round, but these simply served to add a pleasing detail to objects whose esthetic value lay primarily in painted or engraved motifs. The taste for applied ornaments, protuberances, and twisted shapes is pushed to such exuberant excess in Santarém that the art has been called "rococo"; it has even been thought that the Jesuits had had some influence on it (an absurd hypothesis, since it is of pre-Columbian origin and is connected — as shall be seen — with certain artistic traditions of the West Indies and Guiana).

While almost nothing is known about the ethnography of Marajó, there is rather more information about the Indians of Santarém, the Tapajó, from whom the great tributary of the Amazon, the Tapajoz, derives its name.

The old chroniclers describe the Tapajó as a powerful and warlike tribe, greatly feared for their poisoned arrows. They worshiped painted idols and the mummified bodies of certain of their ancestors. No cemetery has been found which can be attributed to these Indians, perhaps because they shared the custom of many Amazonian tribes who pulverize the bones of their dead and drink them diluted in maize beer.

The variety of form and decoration complicates the analysis of the style of Santarém, which nonetheless follows very rigid conventions. A better idea can be formed of its originality by examining certain types of vases, for example those classified as "wide-base" vases (PL. 96; III, PL. 129) — vessels, either globular in shape or elongated, decorated with zoomorphic moldings in the round and having for handles two long protuberances shaped like birds' heads with inordinately long necks. These appendages in turn support animals (on one piece there is a bird and a mammal — probably a fox — playing a flute). The neck, which springs from the middle of the vase above a series of protruding rims, is considered a distinctive element of this art.

The potters of Santarém gave free play to their imagination in another category of pottery known as "caryatid dishes." These are round-bottomed bowls with straight sides supported by three small figures crouching on the edges of a base covered with engraved patterns. These "caryatids" are also to be found on the base of certain vases of the type described above.

Among the strangest innovations, and among the most successful artistically, are the dishes with a double edge joined by birds whose beaks form handles.

Anthropomorphic or portrait vases are rarer. Figures are modeled in a crouching position, following a convention that prevails in Amazonia in all representations of this type. What distinguishes the Santarém specimens from those of Marajó, for example, is the realism at which the artist aims. The features of the face are recognizably those of the Indians and the objects are readily identifiable. A terra-cotta statuette, from the same site, is even more remarkable in this respect: the figure has its head turned and resting on its right hand, and its left arm is hanging casually against its thigh. Another shows a woman with hands on hips (PL. 96).

Apart from the zoomorphic and anthropomorphic figures with which they are laden, some of these pieces have applied to their sides figures of snakes or frogs. In addition to the geometric patterns engraved in the clay (half circles, circles, oblique lines, spirals, etc.) human figures and animals are discernible, sometimes so stylized that it is difficult to distinguish them from the purely geometrical motifs. It is possible, as the Brazilian archaeologist F. Barata (1952) tried to prove, that many of the geometrical motifs are derived from realistic representations; the volutes, for example, seem to have originated in representations of coiled snakes. Certain spirals have, in fact, ophidian heads. But an inverse argument could be adduced: geometrical decoration may have been influenced by realistic themes, but it seems probable that in certain cases a characteristic peculiar to a zoological species — mottling of the skin, pattern of the scales or structure of the shell — was used to symbolize this species. This purely realistic representation may have been transformed into a simple geometric motif. This is apparently what happened with the squares of the tortoise's shell; after being used to symbolize the animal, they finally became an abstract decoration. The same is true of the "sun" motif used on vessels, which corresponds to the conventional representation of the eye on certain clay statues. The close connection between these motifs and the subjects they evoke gives special weight to Barata's interpretation.

It has been said that Tapajó pottery was a veritable catalogue of Amazonian fauna. In actual fact, a limited number of animals served as models for the artists, who represented them realistically enough to make identification relatively easy. The agouti, for instance, is represented in the sitting position it customarily adopts when nibbling fruit. The jaguar is not always very skillfully treated, but is easily recognizable by its open mouth and fangs. Birds were more often chosen as ornamental motifs than mammals. It is often difficult, however, to determine the species, except for those, such as vultures and toucans, having a very distinctive beak.

A large proportion of sculpture in the round is anthropomorphic, but a few details of ornamentation are indicated, such as feather diadems and cylinders set in the ears. Often the figures' hands are raised to the level of the mouth. The way in which the eye has been modeled assumes a certain importance for the archaeologist, since the convention adopted facilitates comparisons between different styles: sometimes it is a simple

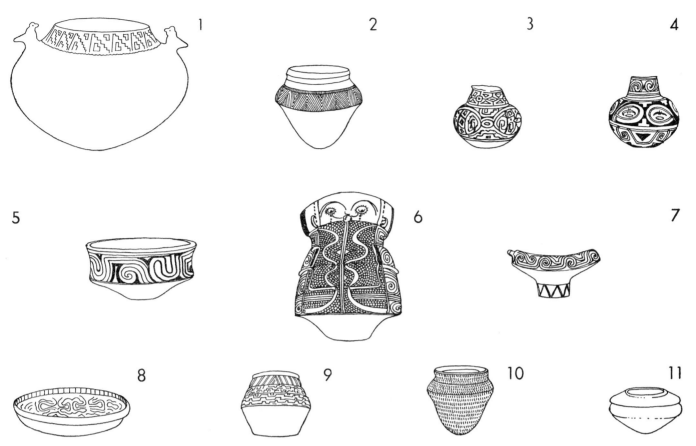

Formal and decorative typology of archaeological ceramics of the tropical forest area. (1, 2) Lower Paraná; (3, 4) Marajó; (5-7) Cunani; (8) Tupinamba; (9-11) Guaraní (*from Handbook of South American Indians, vol. III*).

protuberance, sometimes a protuberance surrounded by a concentric circle, sometimes a protuberance shaped like a coffee bean, and sometimes a ring in relief. Each of these types is to be found in the pottery of Amazonia and the West Indies, and it is with the help of the inferences which can be drawn from the proportion of each of these types that historical parallels have been established. Painting occupies only a secondary place in this pottery.

The art of Santarém, despite its undeniable originality, is not as isolated as might be supposed. Nordenskiöld (1930) had already drawn attention to the similarity between certain applied ornaments from Santarém and fragments of pottery from other regions of South America and from the West Indies. A bird's head from the island of Carriacou in the West Indies and another from Santarém are virtually interchangeable; the same is true of the vultures' heads found at Wakany (the Oyapock region in Guiana). The Palikur Indians stick feathers in the heads of the bird figures decorating their ceremonial benches; this would perhaps explain the orifice piercing the protuberance crowning the birds' heads from Santarém. The "caryatid" vases recall those which are so characteristic of the sculpture of the Talamanca Indians of Costa Rica and Chiriquí (Panama). The decorative moldings also suggest some remote influence from Central America.

H. C. Palmatary (1939), in her excellent comparative study of the art of Santarém, gives special significance to the motif of the double volute which figures in Cunani, Marajó, Santarém, and Manaus, and also in the West Indies and the southern United States. In this connection, one cannot overlook the numerous analogies between Amazonian art and that of the mounds of Mississippi, Florida, and Georgia in the United States.

A large number of clay pipes have been found in the region of Santarém. Their decoration is so clearly European in inspiration that they are thought with good reason to have been made in the missions under the direction of the Jesuits.

Maracá and Cunani. The decline and subsequent disappearance of the Marajó civilization shortly before the discovery of America did not mark the end of all artistic expression at the mouth of the Amazon. Two archaeological sites, Maracá and Cunani, to the north of Marajó, in Brazilian Guiana, have revealed pottery which, although inferior to that of Marajó, is nonetheless highly original. This is especially true of the secondary burial urns from Maracá, which represent a man or a woman sitting on a small bench, hands on knees (III, PL. 129). The cylindrical body, the tubular limbs, and the conical or rounded head forming the lid are reminiscent of stovepipe figures. Motifs painted in red or black on a white ground decorated these strange pieces, which have been dated from the immediately post-Columbian period, because they are decorated with bartered pearls. Other examples, probably of more recent date, are embellished with beards. The culture of Maracá appears as an enclave in a region dominated by the so-called "Mazagão" culture, which penetrated into Brazilian Guiana at a late date and persisted there in the centuries following the discovery of the Amazon until the extermination of the Indians there.

The art belonging to this phase is known by some twenty vases found on the banks of the Cunani River. They were found intact in two vaulted underground chambers; most of them contained ashes and bones. On the anthropomorphic urns, stylized relief and painting combine to represent human faces (always placed on the neck of the urn). The arms, breasts, and navel are applied to the body of the urn in decorative moldings (PL. 96). In shape, the most interesting pieces of these mortuary appointments are quadrangular basins with rims topped by molded animals. Red decoration on a cream background predominates, with squares and "commas" arranged in parallel bands.

In the islands of Caviana, Mexiana, and on the northern coast of Marajó, the archaeological remains may be those of a historically known race — the Aruã, an Arawak tribe which probably came from the north and was driven from the mainland to the islands by the races of the Aristé phase. There are many similarities between certain terra-cotta objects found in this zone and some West Indian specimens, but the art of the Aruã is far from presenting the quality and richness of that of Cunani or Marajó. Its most original contribution to Amazonian pottery was a technique of modeling which makes certain vases look as though they were made of overlapping pieces. Following a tradition which was almost general in Amazonia, the burial urns have an anthropomorphic character obtained by applied moldings.

Early art of the middle and upper Amazon. It is as yet unknown whether the art of Marajó and Santarém represents a kind of local development or whether this art is connected with a civilization that extended farther east, along the Amazon basin. Sporadic finds (Itacancura, Miracanguera, Manaus, and the Teffé, Japurá, and Napo rivers) make the second hypothesis plausible. Fragments of anthropomorphic and zoomorphic pottery found at Teffé are similar to the ornamental modeling of Santarém. On the other hand, a vase from Lake Macupy (Teffé), with diamonds inscribed one inside the other and with superimposed and opposed volutes standing out in relief, is more akin to the pottery of Marajó. The "champlevé" technique was also used at Manaus, especially on cups with circular bases. The archaeological sites of Manaus are rich in modeled ornaments in the style of Santarém. The funeral urns for secondary burial from Itacoatira, Miracanguera, and the Japurá River can be classed in the category of anthropomorphic vases; the features of the face, extremely simplified, stand out in relief below the neck of the vase. The pottery of the Napo and the Aguarico rivers, represented by funeral urns and bowls, combines three different orders of decoration: modeling, painting, and engraving. The affinities between the anthropomorphic vases of the Napo region and those of Marajó are so close that, at the time of their discovery, the possibility of direct importation from the lower Amazon was suggested.

A bulging of the legs similar to that on the anthropomorphic vases from Maracá can be explained by the custom of deforming the calf. A similar detail is visible on the burial urns from Miracanguera (site on the left bank of the Amazon, opposite the mouth of the Madeira). The terra-cotta pieces of this last region constitute a link between the style of the Napo region and that of the lower Amazon. There is a striking similarity between the red and black linear decoration on a white ground, which covers the outside of the vases from the Napo area, and the ornamentation in the same colors from the Ucayali region. The latter continues a tradition which goes far back in history.

Eastern Bolivia. There exists — as Nordenskiöld (1913) has pointed out — a certain analogy between the geographical setting in which the civilization of the Mojos developed and that which saw the birth and then the decline of the civilization of Marajó. There are the same expanses of territory alternately flooded and scorched by the sun, the same forests rising like islands of greenery on the horizon of the plains; but there is another and stranger similarity: the innumerable mounds raised by the early inhabitants — the Mojo Indians, who gave their name to the region. Many travelers have mentioned the wealth of archaeological remains covering these mounds. Only three of them, the mounds called Velarde, Hernmarck, and Masicito, were excavated by Nordenskiöld, who found a rich collection of terra-cotta objects.

The quality of the pottery from these sites confirms what the Jesuits who converted the Mojo Indians reported about their industry and their customs. These Indians, who belonged linguistically to the Arawakan family, were therefore related to the Taino of the West Indies, to the Manaus, the Aruã, and various other tribes of Venezuela and Guiana. The differences existing between the cultural state of the Mojos and that of the other Brazilian tribes can be explained by the influences exerted on them by the Andean tribes. It is to contacts with the latter that one must attribute the existence,

among the Mojos, of a priestly class and of temples where a jaguar god was worshiped in a complex ritual. The excavations of Mound Velarde have revealed two cultural strata. The older archaeological layer (lower Velarde) contained skeletons buried directly in the soil, bowls, tetrapod vases, applied ornaments, and painted shards decorated with a triangle with a volute, a motif which has also been found at Cochabamba and Mizque on vases of the Tiahuanaco period.

The pottery of the upper layer is perhaps the work of the Mojos, whose descendants still live near the mounds. The most typical pieces are secondary burial urns with three feet. Whereas these are ovoid at Mound Velarde, the burial urns found at Mound Hernmarck are globular and have bell-mouthed necks. The decoration varies somewhat from site to site. It is purely geometrical — S's, diamonds, hatched triangles — at Mound Velarde; at Mound Hernmarck, it includes, as well as linear motifs, S's, Y's, and bands, strange stylized faces separated by concentric circles. The better quality of the ornamentation, which can perhaps be explained by its later date, is all the stranger because the excavations undertaken by Nordenskiöld at Mound Velarde have made it possible to establish the existence of two successive cultures in the region.

The burial grounds of Mound Masicito (Mamoré River, southeast of Trinidad) reveal a rather aberrant culture: applied moldings, engraving (herringbone patterns, triangles, lines), and modeling having been preferred to painting for the decoration of the tripod vases. This ornamental technique is also found in the archaeological pottery of Covendo (Chimay) and on the tripod vases of the Palacios River area (province of Santa Cruz).

At Rurrenabaque a fine anthropomorphic urn has been found with a face modeled in quite realistic style. Some cups from the same site have a form of decoration similar to the style of the Tiahuanaco period.

Two traditions are therefore distinguishable in pottery: that with engraved decoration and that with painted decoration. Between the cultures characterized by these two techniques of decoration similarities are apparent which make it possible to class them in chronological order corresponding to the different periods of the Andean pottery of the Cochabamba valley, with which the pottery of the plains presents many analogies.

The lower Paraná, Argentina, and Chile. Although the remains of the art of the early peoples of the lower Paraná are geographically outside tropical America, their styles and techniques justify their inclusion in this survey.

On natural eminences, safe from the floodings of the numerous branches of the Paraná River in Argentine territory, pottery has been discovered which resembles that of the lower Amazon by its characteristic ornaments in the round. These served as handles or stood out from the sides of the vessel and generally represented animals, especially parrots, and (although rarely) human beings. Sometimes the modeling aims at realistic effects, but often it is stylized in such an extreme manner as to be audacious. Elementary geometrical patterns are engraved in these moldings.

Certain applied ornaments, cut out in animal shapes in slabs of clay, were also attached to the sides of the vessels and elaborated in order to give them a more realistic appearance or simply to enhance the artistic effect. The women of Paraná also modeled statuettes in clay; these have no decorative value and their function is unknown. Ordinary vases were also decorated with engraved motifs — wide, deep grooves characterized by slight hollows.

In northwestern Argentina and northern Chile many remains of roads, houses, villages, and fortresses, together with typical Inca ceramics, remain as a record of the military occupation of this land by the Inca armies toward the end of the 15th century. Prior to this period, the local cultures, although revealing the presence of some elements belonging to the central Andes (see ANDEAN PROTOHISTORY), had an independent, and in many respects original, development. The people lived primarily in isolated river valleys and mountain basins.

Archaeological studies of this area, although regular and

intensive, have necessarily been of a local nature; the cultural background therefore appears incomplete and does not permit a well-defined historical reconstruction. According to W. C. Bennett (1954), however, the three principal archaeological periods of the southern Andes (Los Barreales, Calchaquí or Diaguita, and Atacameño) probably correspond chronologically to the Mochica, Tiahuanaco, and Chimu cultures of Peru respectively (see PERU).

The earliest of these three periods had as its principal center of diffusion the area that has become the modern Argentine province of Catamarca (see ARGENTINA). The Diaguita Indians, carriers of the Los Barreales culture, built simple dwellings of adobe and undressed stone. They produced two different types of ceramics. The first had a black background and engraved decoration (anthropomorphic figures, birds, and pumas) and included cups, bowls, and goblets; the second was a polychrome ware with black, brown, and violet on a light-colored background, and its most common decorative theme was a curvilinear jaguar. Other finds from the Los Barreales culture include clay pipes carved as effigies, gold and copper objects, and bone ladles and flutes.

The second period represents the "classical" phase in the culture of the southern Andes, during which artistic production reached its peak. Scholars have identified it (also in its present denomination) with the Diaguita or Calchaquí people. The archaeological remains of this phase are primarily concentrated in the Argentine provinces of Tucumán and Salta, but many finds have been uncovered in every region of this cultural zone.

The Diaguita lived in large villages made up of round and rectangular houses of undressed stone and practiced farming on irrigated terraces. Occasionally stone columns decorated with geometric engravings have been found in Diaguita dwellings; it has been impossible to determine with any certainty whether the presence of these columns indicates that the buildings containing them were used for religious purposes. Outstanding among the Diaguita production are the infant burial urns (a fine polychrome ware), especially those of the Santa María type (PLS. 93, 97). The decoration found on these urns, consisting of zoomorphic figures and geometrical motifs, is also found in other, smaller clay objects such as cooking pots and bowls. The Santa María type of urn is diffused over the central part of this area; to the south (Belém), in the same period cruder urns, black on red, were produced with zoomorphic or anthropomorphic applied decorations above the handles. Affinities may be noted between some painted details of these urns and the early ceramics of Marajó and Cunani (see above). The same type of pottery is also found among the Diaguita of Chile, but there the urns are of finer workmanship and are smaller, ruling out their use as burial vessels (I, PL. 175). Chilean Diaguita ware continued to be made during the Inca occupation, but the period of its origin is unknown. It is also not known whether its two principal styles were in any way connected. The first of these comprises vessels with rather thick walls decorated in red, white, gray, and occasionally black; geometrical motifs predominate, especially zigzag lines, sometimes broken by a stylized face with some of the features in relief (PL. 98). The most common form is a bowl with a round base and straight or slightly swollen walls. The decoration of these bowls is confined to the outside surface. Another type consists of oval jars with the opening set asymmetrically in relation to the body so that it forms the outline of a duck (III, PL. 129). The similarities to southern Peruvian pottery and also to the Anasazi culture of the southwestern United States are clear (see NORTH AMERICAN CULTURES).

The second style of the Chilean Diaguita ceramics consists chiefly of round-based bowls having walls widening toward the top and made of a finer paste than that of the first type. Polychromy and external decoration are very similar to those of the first style but, unlike it, the inside of the bowl sometimes has representations of four small animals symmetrically arranged, painted in black on a white slip; the stylistic elements of these bowls are reminiscent of some types of Cuzco Incan vessels.

In addition to ceramics, mention should be made of the Diaguita works in cast copper or bronze; these include curved knives, thimbles, ceremonial axes (IX, PL. 499), and, especially, the sheet metal plaques with human figures in relief beside jaguars, or highly stylized human faces. The origins and derivation of Diaguita art remain an open question. Instead of the earlier and indiscriminate Peruvian attribution (to Tiahuanaco or to the Inca cultures, as the case may be) modern scholars tend to consider Diaguita art an original product, but one undeniably related to other South American styles that circulated in the archaeological period throughout the continent, stimulating local production and giving rise to new styles or to the reworking of earlier ones.

In the third phase of southern Andean archaeology, just before the Inca invasion, the military-political organization became stronger and crafts production declined to a primarily utilitarian level, while borrowings from Peruvian products and styles increased. The sole exception to this general decadence in the arts is represented by the culture of the Atacameño Indians located in the oasis of Calama in northern Chile. This culture was probably considerably earlier in origin than the Inca invasion, and it continued to develop almost undisturbed well into the colonial period. Indefatigable travelers who used the llama as a pack animal, the Atacameño also spread into northwestern Argentina and to other parts of Chile. The finds connected with their culture almost always come from tombs and are mostly wood products: parts of llama harnesses, bells with clappers, also made of wood, decorated boxes, small engraved and modeled panels, and tubes for snuff tobacco. Also in the Calama oasis, objects in pure Tiahuanacan style have been found, as well as ceramics similar to those of southern Peru, which certainly came to this area through trade exchanges in periods prior to the Inca domination.

Early stone carving. Stone carvings are rare in Amazonia, an area where rocky outcrops are confined to the plateaus and in which vast regions exist where there is not the smallest pebble. The attention of the early travelers was nonetheless caught by certain stone carvings. The Jesuits speak of "stone idols" in the sacred huts of the Tapajó Indians. It is in this connection that Heriarte (1874, p. 37) mentions the famous *muiraquita* — the amulets which enjoyed such prestige among the Indians and were the object of a brisk trade. He writes as follows: "It is commonly maintained that these stones are made on the Tapajoz River with a green clay which forms under the water. They fashion it in the water into long and round pearls, drinking cups, seats, birds, frogs and other figures. When the objects modeled in this way are withdrawn from the water, they change in the air into very hard green stones." Jade, nephrite, and Amazon-stone pendants, representing more or less stylized frogs, have in fact been discovered in various places of the lower Amazon. These precious objects were bartered as far afield as Guiana and the West Indies. The famous "green stones" were also used for the making of large lip ornaments which the coastal tribes, particularly the Tupinamba, wore in their lower lips.

The Goteborg Museum has three objects (of about 5, 6, and 11 in. in length) which are among the great masterpieces of stone carving in Amazonia. They come from the Trombetas River, and are made of slate. These so-called "idols" represent a crouching man whose head is imprisoned between the paws of a monster rising above him (PL. 95). The monster's back forms a large cavity, which suggests that the figure was used as a mortar or libation cup.

An explorer of the 17th century, Raoul d'Harcourt (1613), reports that the Indians of the Oyapock venerated an idol "shaped like a man squatting on his heels, his knees drawn up and his arms resting on his knees, his hands raised palm outward, gazing upward with his mouth agape." Except in a few details this description tallies with a stone statue (Paris, Musée de l'Homme) which is supposed to have come from the Río Uaupés, in northwestern Brazil. About $2\frac{1}{2}$ ft. tall, it represents a crouching figure with its hands clasping its chest. On the nape of its neck it had a protuberance (now broken off); on its chest a swelling is caused by an unidentifiable object. The legs are much too thin for the body. The only statue of this size found in Amazonia, it has never been possible to link this enigmatic work with a specific culture.

ART OF THE CONTEMPORARY SOUTH AMERICAN INDIANS. Neither in Guiana nor in Amazonia proper is there any modern pottery comparable to the early works of Santarém and the island of Marajó. It is true that the decoration of the pottery made by the tribes of the Ucayali and Huallaga recalls prehistoric vases sufficiently to justify the establishing of a historical link between them. The ornamental technique of modeling small figures on the body of the vase has persisted in a relatively rough form among the Indians of the upper Xingú. The Santarém region, which is characterized by an almost excessive use of decoration in the round, lies at the mouth of the Xingú, and the zoomorphic vases made by the Indians living on the upper reaches of the river perpetuate the influences of their ancestors.

From a technical and esthetic point of view, the pottery of the Cocama (PL. 102), Omágua, Conibo, Shipibo, and Chébero tribes, from the upper tributaries of the Amazon (the Marañón, Ucayali, and Huallaga rivers), occupies the first rank in tropical South America. The first explorers of Amazonia had already admired this pottery and had mentioned the variety of its motifs and the brilliance of its glaze. It is linked, if not by its form, at least by its ornamental themes, to the prehistoric pottery of the Napo River, of which numerous specimens have been excavated. Ceremonial pottery, from the point of view of shape, is confined to two chief types: bowls or cups with bulging sides and flat bases (PL. 102) and the large pitchers having a globular belly topped by a wide conical neck. The fineness of the paste and the quality of the glaze are two important characteristics of this pottery; but it is the geometrical decoration which chiefly gives it its originality. Disconcerting at first because of its variety, analysis shows it to be based on the imaginative grouping of a small number of abstract patterns: broken lines, zigzags, meanders, tiers, and sigmoid patterns grouped and, as it were, interwoven in different sectors. This decorative style — and herein lies one of its peculiarities — combines thick and thin streaks of color, in order either to accentuate the former or to decorate the spaces which they delimit. The decorative elements are often evenly spaced, but on some particularly elegant specimens a pleasing effect is obtained by the close succession of thick and thin parallel lines. The motifs are painted in black or in black and red on a cream background (Pano tribes). Among certain tribes (Yameo, Chayawita, and Omágua) the designs are painted in white against a red ground or in red against a white ground; in these, however, the ornamentation is traced with a less sure touch than on the specimens of the type which has black and red on cream. The style of this pottery tends to lose some of its vigor and complexity as it moves away from the basins of the Ucayali and the Huallaga, where it achieved its greatest purity (among the Pano and the Cocama). This pottery is becoming increasingly subject to the influence of European models, which detract from its esthetic worth and make its decline probable.

The basin of the Caiarí-Uaupés, the Içana, and the Apaporis also form, where pottery is concerned, a region where a style of undeniable artistic value prevails. The vases made by the various Arawak, Tucano, and Carib tribes do not have the elegance of shape and quality of paste of the pottery of the upper Amazon, but their geometrical decoration successfully uses meanders, herringbone patterns, triangles, and even curvilinear themes. In the rest of Guiana, pottery is no longer a means of artistic expression, with the possible exception of Galibí pottery, which has unfortunately become commercialized. The bird-shaped vases produced by the Indians and sold at Cayenne and Paramaribo are no longer linked with an old tradition, but this is not true of the motifs decorating them; these perpetuate, admittedly in degenerate form, genuinely Indian styles.

The pottery of the upper Xingú is the work of a single tribe, the Waura, who belong to the Arawakan family. This fact, first affirmed by Karl von den Steinen (op. cit.) and confirmed by other researchers, has greatly helped to consolidate the opinion of those who attribute a predilection for the art of ceramics to the members of this large linguistic family. It is in fact true that in many regions of tropical America, including the West Indies, it is certainly the Arawak who are the best ceramists.

The most striking characteristic of this pottery is its simplicity of shape combined with efforts at realism. The finest pieces are round bowls, rather like calabashes, to the sides of which have been applied various appendages in order to give the vessels the shape of an animal (in particular that of bats, toads, tortoises, armadillos, and, in short, any big-bellied animal whose appearance can be suggested by a rotund vase). The resemblance between the model and the piece of pottery is often accentuated by the meticulous representation of the scales or of some other anatomical peculiarity of the animal chosen. Sometimes the limbs and head of the animal, stylized to a degree, become mere decorative appendages. The bat was the favorite of Xingú pottery and served as a point of departure for a purely geometrical type of decoration.

Basketry. Previously in this article mention was made of the importance attributed to basketry as a source of inspiration of the decorative art of the forest Indians. Without denying that the motifs produced by the interweaving of different-colored elements were used as models for the decoration of other objects, it nonetheless seems dangerous to assume that all rectilinear motifs originate in basketry. This art achieved its highest point of perfection among the Indians of Guiana, whose mastery in this respect is unequaled in the rest of South America. They use nearly all known techniques except the spiral one. Yet it is really only the pieces made in the twill method that achieve truly artistic effects. The clever basketmaker can combine patterns produced by the regular interweaving of black and white elements to achieve skilled general effects and even realistic representations. Triangles, meanders, and diamonds are the most common motifs, but sometimes abstract designs give way to anthropomorphic or zoomorphic representations (II, PL 233). This evolution was favored by the nomenclature of decorative art that attributes to purely geometrical motifs the names of animals or plants. The animal, it is true, is often represented merely by the markings of its fur or the mottling of its skin, or else by some part of its anatomy — its paws, for example.

Twill basketmaking is common to most of the tribes of tropical America (II, PLS. 225, 230), but none of them produced such a variety of motifs in this art as the Indians of Guiana. Diamonds, rectangles, and cruciform patterns constitute the most common decorative motifs of the various baskets and sieves of which the Indians make such extensive use.

Wood carving and wood engraving. When considering the importance that wood plays in the techniques of the forest Indians, it seems surprising that it is so little used as an art material. Wood carving is in fact a little-developed art and has produced only mediocre pieces. The best examples are the seats hewn out of wooden blocks to which the carved addition of a head or a tail gives the shape of a bird (PL. 100), a tortoise, a jaguar, or some other animal. Pebbles or beads set in the carving like eyes give a realistic touch to the whole. This type of seat, which is particularly common in Guiana, is also to be found among the Indians of the upper Xingú. In this region, too, most of the seats represent birds, but sometimes also mammals, usually monkeys or jaguars.

The strange images of men or women which the Yagua and Witoto place on tombs as funerary monuments are so distinct in their naïve realism from the other forms of art of these tribes and from that of the neighboring peoples that one cannot help thinking that they imitate statues of saints familiar to the Indians. The term sculpture, on the other hand, can hardly be applied to the rough images carved from the trunks of trees by the Shipaya of the Xingú. Their neighbors, the Yuruna, had the reputation of being skillful carvers, but nothing remains of their art except a few wooden animals whose function is unknown.

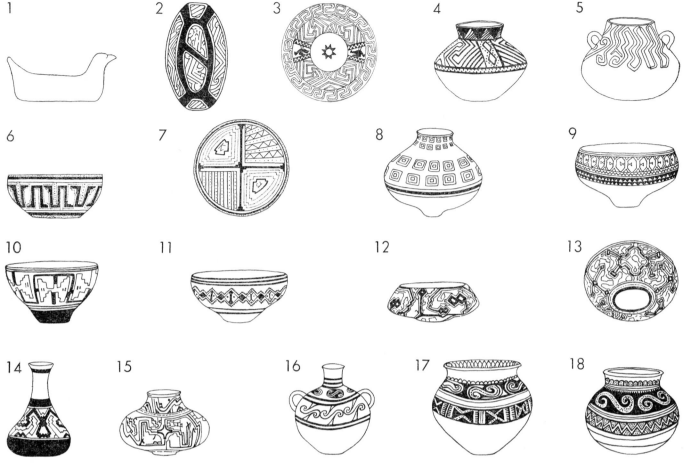

Decorative and formal typology of clay production of the contemporary tropical forest area. (1, 2) Caribs of Surinam; (3, 4) Arawaks of the Içana River; (5) Desana; (6, 7) Cocama of the upper Amazon; (8, 9) Coto; (10, 11) Cashibo; (12, 13) Chama; (14) Piro; (15) Panobo; (16–18) Chiriguano of eastern Bolivia (*from Handbook of South American Indians, vol. III*).

For certain feasts the Cubeo Indians of the Içana fix to their trumpets fish cut from wooden panels and decorated with engraved white lines. The dancers hold in their hands figures of birds or fish adorned with tufts of feathers. A similar custom exists among the tribes of the upper Xingú, where the dancers wear on their heads birds carved from soft wood. The tree-bark fish found in this region were no doubt dance accessories.

The manioc graters from Guiana can be described as artistic insofar as the stones or thorns set in their surface suggest geometrical designs (diamonds, meanders, etc.). Sometimes the panel itself is decorated with painted geometrical motifs.

Wood engraving reached a high degree of perfection in Guiana, where it is especially associated with clubs or tomahawks of hard wood. On the smooth surfaces the patterns stand out in white against a black ground; spirals, volutes, and circles alternate with rectilinear motifs (PL. 100). The ornamentation includes representations of human figures, more or less realistically conceived. Two or three of these figures are often shown side by side, so closely linked that they have a body or limbs in common. The representations of animals, which are rarer, are seldom as stylized as the anthropomorphic figures.

The art of wood engraving also includes calabashes engraved with geometrical patterns or animal profiles. The Indians attach little importance to calabashes, and so have never tried to make of them real works of art.

Wax and clay modeling. The Carajá Indians of the Araguaia have gained a certain reputation for their clay dolls (PLS. 101, 102). These represent both men and women; the female figures show large buttocks, almost in the style of the palaeolithic Venuses, with legs and arms missing or merely suggested by two sausagelike shapes. The hair, however, is represented with wax, and the breasts are always shown, even on the male figures. Whereas these clay dolls are all modeled by women, the boys and young men make wax figures and animals. These pieces, which are toys, vary in merit and sometimes reveal a sharp sense of observation, but as they are lacking in style and not fulfilling any real esthetic need, they do not embody a true artistic tradition. This is true not only of the Carajá, but of all the tribes where wax dolls have been found.

Masks. The South American Indians did not find in the masks the outstanding means of expression of which so many other cultures availed themselves, often turning the best of their inspiration to the execution of what today pass for masterpieces of "primitive" art (see IX, col. 561).

It is the use of large masks in beaten bark which constitutes one of the chief characteristics of the cultural province that includes the tribes of the Içana, the Caiarí-Uaupés, and the Solimões rivers in northwestern Brazil. These masks are a sort of cowl reaching below the knee and ending in a fiber skirt. They represent demons and nature spirits, usually conceived in the guise of animals. There are demons in the form of jaguars, vultures, butterflies, and even caterpillars and larvae. Whereas the mask of the jaguar demon is covered with spots suggesting the feline's coat, that of the other demons is decorated with geometrical themes apparently unrelated to zoological reality. The spectators, however, can easily identify the "demons" who come to visit them by the miming of the dancers. The ambiguity between the human and animal representation is increased by the fact that the animal masks have human heads. Some cowls are topped by a calabash in which eyes and a mouth have been cut. The masks of the Apaporis Indians are crowned with a wooden cylinder on which a face is painted and which has pieces of wood projecting at right angles from both sides to represent raised arms. Although the masks of this region are supposed to personify dread demons, there is nothing frightening about them and nothing suggesting a lowering vision of the supernatural world.

The same is not true of the Tucuna Indians, who live on the Solimões. Their vision of demons, at the same time terrifying and burlesque, inspires a style of masks unique in South America. Here again are found cowls of beaten bark, but the designs covering them evoke the features and attributes of monstrous creatures. Human or animal heads modeled in wax or carved in soft wood are attached to the cowls and heighten the strange and frightening appearance of the masked figures.

The masks of the Carajá Indians of the Araguaia are quite different in type, but also very curious. They take the shape of long basketwork cylinders, decorated with feathers, crowning the heads of the dancers, who are hidden under two or three superimposed fiber cloaks.

The masks of the upper Xingú are closely linked with dances having animal names, particularly those of fish. These dances are no doubt supposed to exert a good influence on hunting and fishing. There are several types of masks, some whose sole aim is to hide the person of the dancer, and others, more artistic in shape and decoration, which play the most important roles in the dances. These are carved from soft wood and include a kind of oval screen made of cloth stretched over a wooden frame. The carved heads are highly stylized; above the flat face is a bulging forehead from which springs the nose. The eyes are mere holes or perforated circles of mother of pearl. The mouth is missing or else is indicated by a few painted lines or piranha teeth attached with wax. On the cloth masks the eyes and nose are marked by circular protuberances and are arbitrarily placed. The empty surfaces are decorated with geometrical patterns, the lozenge with blackened angles (*mereshu*) being the most common motif. Some geometrical themes symbolize the animal personified by the dancer. Two juxtaposed triangles denote the piranha, and zigzags indicate a bird whose wings have a vaguely similar pattern. The connection between the geometrical figure and the distinguishing feature of the animal is often so tenuous that it cannot be discerned without interpretation by the Indians.

Featherwork. It is in their featherwork that the Indians of tropical America truly reveal their artistry. It is true that nature has given them incomparable materials, for this region is rich in birds whose brilliant plumage the Indians put to most ingenious uses. As Darcy and B. G. Ribeiro (1957) rightly observe, "the feather ornaments of the Brazilian Indians deserve the name works of art because they involve a highly developed technique, familiarity with the surrounding fauna and a sharpened sensibility which inspired their combinations of color and arrangements of shapes, following a long tradition." But one can only speak of the art of featherwork when the beauty of the feathers chosen is heightened by an effort of imagination, sensitivity, and technical skill which give to these objects an intrinsic artistic value.

Feather ornaments naturally offer a certain uniformity in general form and technical details, but a variety of styles is to be found, peculiar to a region or even to a single tribe. The origin of an ornament can be recognized from the special way it is made, from color combinations, or from the general structure of the ornament. Feather ornaments can be divided into two groups, according to whether they are mounted on a basketwork frame or tied together by threads or cloth and therefore flexible. The finest examples of the first group are the headdresses of the Aparai and Palikur, which are assembled the day before a celebration and dismounted the day after. The basketwork frame, consisting of a basketwork cylinder topped by a sort of handle, is completely hidden by bands of feathers, a fringe of which covers the dancer's face. The construction ends in an enormous crest made of long parrot's tail feathers, which are decorated with little chips of light wood covered with down and bristling with fine rods, which in turn carry beetles' wing cases. Strips of bark springing from the headdress hang down over the body.

The feather headdresses of the Chaco Indians are just as elaborate and consist of a diadem with a vertical shaft (V, PL. 267). The bases of the tail feathers are concealed by rows of shorter feathers and long feathered rods are stuck in the frame of the headdress.

In Guiana, feather diadems are held up by a basketwork cylinder, often with a projecting rim that tilts the feathers and makes them slant as though they were springing from the wearer's forehead. Bands of down feathers cover the lower part and hide the quills. The diadem may also be inserted in the band of a pliant straw wreath and so circle the head like a halo.

The technique of the ornaments of the second group is akin to that of mosaics. Small feathers of subtle colors are caught in the meshes of a closely woven net or stuck onto other feathers or onto objects. Whereas the ornaments of the first type might be called florid, the second owe their beauty to their meticulous workmanship, to the iridescence of their colors, and, in short, to a form of art so delicate that it has been compared to filigree work or to illuminated miniatures. Good examples are the famous feather caps of the Tupinamba and those of the Mundurucú Indians, which are like velvet in texture.

Mention should also be made of the capes of red ibis feathers worn by the Tupinamba Indians for their celebrations. The feathers, inserted into the knots of a net base, form a smooth surface often cut by a wide feather belt. These magnificent ornaments took the fancy of the sailors of the 16th century, who brought many of them back to Europe. Some are now in ethnographical museums (particularly in Florence, Mus. Naz. di Antropologia e Etnologia).

The art of featherwork has been most highly developed by the Urubu-kaa Indians of Brazil. Clad in their ornaments they look like fantastic birds. Their most magnificent decorations are diadems, fixed on cotton bands, whose rows of feathers in different shades produce iridescent color gradations. These Indians also make a kind of medallion by sticking very fine feathers of different colors onto a light foundation and so obtaining geometrical designs. These feather mosaics are used by the Indians as pendants, are attached to necklaces, or are decorations for the long feathers which they use as lip ornaments. They also use huge combs decorated with feather garlands.

Finally, among the works of feather art, one must mention the matting in which the Roucouyennes and Aparai Indians of Guiana insert ants or wasps and apply to the bodies of the initiates. These instruments of torture are animal-shaped and are covered with beautiful feather mosaics (see FEATHERWORK).

Body painting. Together with featherwork, body painting constitutes one of the most important forms of artistic expression among the Indians of the tropics. The annatto tree (*Bixa orellana*) provides them with a brilliant red paste, and the genipap (*Genipa americana*), with a black sap which, when it is daubed on the skin, does not fade for a week.

Body painting takes the form either of geometrical patterns or of irregularly alternating bands of different colors.

It is a pity that travelers and ethnographers have so rarely illustrated or described these ephemeral decorations, thus depriving us of valuable material for comparison. The style of the body painting is naturally related to the decorative themes ornamenting the pottery, basketwork, and wood carvings of a specific area, but the freedom of line inherent in the technique often promotes a play of fantasy and a freedom of expression not to be found in other productions. As it is impossible to make valid generalizations about this art, a description will merely be given of the forms it takes in some tribes, especially in the tribes of central Brazil, where it constitutes one of the chief artistic preoccupations of the tribe.

Among these peoples the paintings on the bodies of children, which are purely decorative, are the richest in motifs and the most successful. They are rather similar to the art of Marajó in the complexity of their designs, in the use of herringbone and checked patterns, in reticulate forms, and in skillful combinations of vertical and horizontal lines. The trunk and the limbs are treated separately and symmetrically following a longitudinal line which virtually divides the body into halves. Depending on the painter's talent, the network of straight or curved lines is more or less complicated or subtle in composition. The stylistic pattern does not seem to be rigid, and in fact in the course of her work the woman (the painters are always women) may change her theme, add lines, or accentuate motifs.

On the other hand, the paintings the women do on each others' bodies are based on a small number of models. The wide, oblique bands running from one shoulder to the opposite hip and a kind of striped "leotard" effect, extending halfway down the calf from a rounded neckline, seem to be their favorites. The faces, when they are not completely daubed with annatto, often have, running from the corners of the mouth to the ears, two checked trapezoids, coupled at the base, or two parallel bands, one red, going from one temple to the other and passing over the eyelids, and the other black, sometimes covering the lips and joining the maxillaries.

The men's body paintings are not very different from those of the women. Their trunks are also striped with black diagonal bands and they color not only their faces but also their feet and ankles. Some decorate the outsides of their calves with bold red stippling or a herringbone pattern. When their torsos are blackened, they leave a light triangle on the sternum, cut by a black vertical line.

The art of body painting reached a high degree of perfection among the Witoto and Bora Indians of the Putumayo River area. It takes the form of broad red surfaces edged with white which cover the thighs and both halves of the body. In outline, these meandering designs are reminiscent of camouflage patterns or of certain abstract paintings. The Indians of the Içana and the Apaporis regions are also noted for the beauty of their body paintings, which reproduce the favorite motifs of their decorative art — series of triangles linked by transverse lines.

As already mentioned, the Indians of the Montaña region transpose onto their bodies the main themes of their decorative art.

THE CHACO. In the heart of the South American continent, the Chaco forms a link between the Amazonian plain and the great Argentine pampas. It is a monotonous and unattractive flatland, alluvial in nature, and covered with dry vegetation consisting of thorny trees and bushes, brambles, and cacti. Forests alternate with savannas, marshes, and bare tracts covered with saline outcrops.

The Gran Chaco was — and to some extent still is — a vast natural reserve for the Indians. The native population is concentrated along or near the Paraguay and Paraná rivers, which cross the region from the north to the south, and along the Pilcomayo, the Bermejo, and the Río Salado, which cut it diagonally.

The Indians of the Chaco live chiefly on wild produce and on fish and game. There is little cultivation of the land. In comparison with the Chiriguano and the Caduveo, who, both by their way of life and by their artistic traditions, occupy a special place in the Chaco, the Toba, Mataco, Ashluslay, and Lengua Indians have only a relatively simple decorative art. Basketwork being almost nonexistent, these Indians transport their goods and the fruit they gather in nets made with fibers from the caraguata, which abounds in these desolate plains. They make bags of different sizes, either by interweaving the fibers or by using complex crochet techniques. By using strands of different colors (black, red), they achieve a geometrical pattern covering the whole surface of the net.

The cloth of the Indians of the Chaco is made on vertical looms, following the custom of the tribes of the Amazonian forest, but their motifs are unquestionably derived from old Peruvian models. The Indians have a predilection for rows of triangles, concentric diamonds, which, arranged in different sectors, destroy the symmetry of the design but increase its diversity. Different weaving techniques use very varying decorative themes. The bags and belts of wool woven on vertical looms are decorated with geometrical patterns which are much more regular but much more monotonous than the curious patterns which ornament these same objects when they are made with the wooden frame method of weaving. The process, which consists of distributing the decorative motifs in distinct sectors without aiming at symmetry or a general plan, probably has its origin in the habit of decorating separately each of the stag or otter skins which were once used to make the cloaks in which these Indians wrapped themselves. One of these cloaks, made up of fifteen different skins, is a veritable mosaic of geometrically decorated surfaces. Certain motifs (series of diamonds, triangles) reappear almost identically on several skins, but are separated by other areas where the decoration is different. Among the Lengua Indians cloaks have been found on which had been traced representations of animals and fantastic designs similar to those of the petroglyphs.

The pottery of the Chaco Indians is purely utilitarian; the circles and lines traced on it with resin reveal only a vague desire for artistic effect.

Tubular pipes are generally decorated with engraved, poker-work, or carved designs with quite skillful representations of animals and human figures. The men also decorate calabashes with engravings, either realistic or purely geometrical in character (VII, PL. 311).

The curious tubular pipes of the Payaguá Indians have formed the subject of several publications. These pipes are covered with relief ornamentation combining native geometrical themes with representations of human figures, animals, and trees. The designs are undeniably religious in nature and are connected with certain forms of occultism, of which the art of the Caduveo and the Chiriguano offers many examples.

The tattooing which covers the faces of the Toba and Pilagá women can be described as artistic. It consists chiefly of large cross-hatched triangles.

The Chiriguano. The pottery of the Chiriguano and Chané Indians of the Chaco belongs in style to the Andean zone. In fact, in our period it continues an artistic tradition peculiar to the pottery of the archaeological zone which stretches from the south of Bolivia to the north of Argentina and perhaps as far as the Chilean coast, in other words, the area once occupied by the Chica and Atacameño Indians, and those of the Quebrada de Humahuaca, in the province of Jujuy (Argentina; I, FIG. 711). The ancestors of the Chiriguano — the Guaraní from Paraguay — settled in the territories at the foot of the Andes, from the Argentine frontier to the province of Santa Cruz in Bolivia, at a relatively recent date (end of the 15th and beginning of the 16th century). When the Spanish conquered the basin of the Río de la Plata, the Guaraní were still migrating toward the borders of the Inca empire. The pottery of the Guaraní, identical to that of the Tupinamba (already described), was in every respect inferior to that of the Andean Indians. One of its distinctive characteristics was a form of ornamentation produced by series of impressions made with the fingernail on the surface of the vessels. This rather rough decoration was, and still is, very widespread among the Guaraní tribes. Often it has made it possible to identify archaeological strata. At the foot of the Andes, the Guaraní came into conflict with the Chané Indians, an Arawak tribe which had settled long ago in these parts. From direct contact with the civilized peoples of the mountains, the Chané had been so far influenced by them as to adopt their pottery, their weaving, the use of metal, and several other techniques. This encounter of an Andean and a tropical civilization gave rise to a hybrid culture, one which was intermediate between the two great cultural and geographical regions of South America.

The Chané were partially exterminated by the Chiriguano, who, like the Caribs in the West Indies, took the captive women into their tribes. These women imposed their artistic traditions on their captors and the traditions have remained unchanged. It is therefore a series of historical accidents that explains how the pottery of the Chica and Aracameño Indians, which today has disappeared, survived in a tribe whose culture was originally very different from theirs.

Despite the reputation which it enjoys, the art of pottery among the Chiriguano shows a certain lack of variety. Almost all its products are on the same model — that of the vessel with a more or less bulging body topped by a low neck splaying out at the rim. The anthropomorphic and zoomorphic vases are exceptional, as are the pedestal vases; they are interesting, however, because they are related to another artistic tradition, that of Amazonia. The decoration, painted in red and black on a cream ground, is, except in a few cases, geometrical. The traditional motifs are spirals, triangles with volutes, meanders set in series of triangles, scalloped bands, and opposed triangles. These decorative themes are to be found in the whole of the territory, but they enjoy different favor in different villages, so that it is possible to distinguish various styles in Chiriguano art as being peculiar to certain regions or even to certain villages. Spirals and triangles with volutes are the two patterns which

who were conquered by the more refined civilization of their subjects. The Caduveo belong to the Guaikurú linguistic family, whose modern representatives are the Toba and the Pilagá, whose way of life, social structure, and art can be considered typical of the Gran Chaco. The Caduveo, on the other hand, differ in so many respects from the tribes to which they are related that they form an independent cultural province. Already in the 16th century they exercised a sort of suzerainty over the Guaná Indians, who were closely related to the Chané subjugated by the Chiriguano. The Chané (or Chaná) were in the forefront of the groups of the Arawakan linguistic family who came from the basin of the Amazon and introduced into the semi-arid zone of the Gran Chaco the cultural traditions

Typology of decorative motifs of the Caduveo. (1–3) Body-painting motifs; (4, 5) applied decorative motifs (*from C. Lévi-Strauss, 1954*).

recur most frequently, although the way in which they are treated offers a wide range of variations. The calabashes in which the Chiriguano drink maize beer are decorated with engraved or poker-work patterns. Here again there is a close resemblance between certain motifs and those which decorate the calabashes found in the burial places of the Puna de Atacama and of the Calchaquí valleys. Today many calabashes are ornamented with designs representing men and animals, as well as with decorations of European inspiration. Calabash engraving, a masculine art, reflects much more than pottery — a feminine art — the influences to which the Chiriguano are subject as a result of their contacts with white men.

The Caduveo. The Caduveo Indians, who live on the northern borders of the Chaco, are, of all the South American tribes, the people whose artistic productions are best known. Their art, which has great originality, was treated in important studies by Lévi-Strauss (1954) and Darcy and B. G. Ribeiro (op. cit.).

The cultural and social history of the Caduveo is somewhat similar to that of the Chiriguano, for they were conquerors

characteristic of the tribes of the tropical forests. In the course of their migration, these tribes also came under Andean influences. The Caduveo, having asserted their supremacy over the Chané, assimilated the Chané culture, to which was added in the 18th century the influences transmitted by the Jesuit missionaries who settled among them. One can therefore distinguish a triple artistic tradition among these Indians: Amazonian, Andean, and European, although the last is only slight.

The decorative art, by far the most important art of the Caduveo, is strictly feminine and is geometrical; the art of wood carving, practiced by the men, is figural.

A description of the way in which the women execute their designs is relevant here. The artists divide the surface to be decorated into sections separated by lines (which contribute to the general effect). Then, without any preliminary sketching, they draw the motifs which occur to them, first fixing the main outlines and then completing them with ornamental details. They draw their inspiration from traditional styles, and give free play to their taste and inventiveness only in the arrangement of the elements prescribed by the culture. The variations which they introduce are minimal, but frequent enough to have promoted the development of this art.

At first sight the patterns preferred by the Caduveo women are disconcerting in their richness and diversity of themes; the effect produced depends less on the number of motifs than on the variety of their grouping. Curvilinear elements (volutes, loops, arabesques, tracery) are more common than rectilinear motifs (FIG. 175). The lines dividing the decorated surfaces into several zones are frequently highly embellished. Often, too, slender lines spring from the thick lines in order to frame the principal motif. This art, although highly abstract, has a vibrant, dynamic quality. Even more remarkable are the effects achieved through asymmetrical design in the facial paintings. In this connection Lévi-Strauss (op. cit.) writes: "Caduveo art pushes dislocation both further and less far. Less far because the face and body being worked on are a face and body of flesh and blood, which cannot be composed or recomposed without a hardly conceivable operation. The integrity of the real face is therefore respected, but it is nevertheless dislocated by systematic asymmetry, as a result of which its natural harmony is sacrificed to the artificial harmony of the painting. But just because this painting, instead of giving the image of a deformed face, in fact deforms a real face, the dislocation goes further than that already described. Apart from its decorative value, it has a subtle element of sadism which explains, at least partially, why the erotic appeal of the Caduveo women (expressed in and interpreted by the paintings) used to attract outlaws and adventurers to the shores of the Paraguay. It is also noticeable that the composition of the paintings around a double axis, horizontal and vertical, analyzes the face by a process of what might be called double subdivision: the painting recomposes the face, not in two profiles but in four quarters. The asymmetry therefore has a formal function, that of ensuring the distinction of the quarters; they would merge into two profiles if the fields were symmetrically repeated to right and left instead of being set point to point. Dislocation and subdivision are functionally linked."

With regard to facial paintings, it must be pointed out that certain motifs and themes were linked to rank and indicated the privileges of the nobility. The Caduveo used the stenciling method for their facial paintings and so were able to reproduce rapidly elementary motifs, which they combined according to their taste.

The motifs that figure in the composition of the facial paintings are also to be found on objects such as woven fans and the animal skins used for chairs or beds. The skins are also divided into quarters, following the type of asymmetry found in the facial paintings. Motifs such as meanders, broken lines, and right angles are more frequently found on the objects than on the human body.

From the point of view of both form and decoration, the pottery of the Caduveo deserves a special place in South American art. One of its original features is the use of small cords, made of many twisted strands, to imprint decorative patterns into the soft clay. Curvilinear decoration predominates (PL. 104), in particular a motif that suggests rosettes. Some rectilinear patterns evoke the triangles and tiers of the pottery of Tiahuanaco. The inside of the vases is decorated with red designs traced with the finger. The finest examples of this pottery usually combine five colors — terra-cotta red, the hematite red, the black of rosewood resin applied after firing, the glossy yellow of the angico, and white, which is smeared in the grooves formed by the impression of the cords.

Unlike the pottery of the Chiriguano, that of the Caduveo offers a great variety of shapes; some, for example square cups with rounded angles, have no equivalent elsewhere. Other vessels are shaped like a stylized bird (PL. 104). The most common types are long-necked pitchers (sometimes with two necks, as in Peruvian pottery). Rounded bowls are among the most ornate of the vessels (PL. 104).

The forms of art examined thus far are the work of women. That of the men, in particular weaving, is linked with the tradition of the Chaco. Belts and bags are woven on looms and decorated with geometrical patterns, diamonds, meanders, herringbone patterns, etc. The Caduveo used to embroider their cloths with glass beads and make bags of porcelain beads.

Wood carving is a limited artistic activity, since the men who have the monopoly of it confine themselves to carving pipe bowls and animals and dolls for the children (PL. 103). Although the latter have sometimes been taken for "idols," the Caduveo do not seem to have given them any religious significance. Many wooden objects, such as weavers' lathes, spindles, and spoons, can be classed as artistic objects because of their shape or because of the engraved or embossed motifs which ornament them.

Until quite recently the Caduveo also carved horn to make combs and diadems, to which they gave animal or geometrical forms.

THE ARGENTINE PLAINS NOMADS. The bands of Tehuelche and Puelche Indians who once wandered over the plains of the Argentine led too primitive an existence to be able to develop a plastic or decorative art of any importance. Having only simple shelters against the wind for dwelling places and using only the most rudimentary tools, the Patagonians had little opportunity to develop an artistic sense, but the desire for ornamentation reveals itself in the skin coats that were their principal clothing. These, made of the skins of various animals — wildcats, otters, and especially the guanaco — were sewn together and softened by repeated napping and the application of coats of grease. As the fur was worn against the body, the entire outside of the coat could be painted. The colors used were black, red, green, yellow, and blue, obtained from vegetables and pulverized ochers.

The decorated surface is usually divided into six sectors, each with a different type of decoration. On the edges and in the corners, the motifs were arranged so as to be seen to best effect when the coat was draped round the body. The central part was either painted uniformly or decorated with polychrome motifs arranged in three distinct zones.

The patterns were very simple — squares, diamonds, triangles, and crosses — but they were grouped in various ways. The impression of diversity resulted not only from the way in which the designs were juxtaposed, but also from the rhythm of the colors. The edges were decorated with a checkered pattern in three colors, with the checks forming diagonals or zigzags. The central designs were larger than the marginal ones and, unlike the latter, were not outlined in black. The chief motifs of this part of the coat were meanders, and rows of squares or crosses. Some of these motifs are similar to those which are still used to decorate Araucanian cloths, while others have striking affinities with the engraved patterns on the pottery of the prehistoric races who lived on the Atlantic seaboard from the lower Paraná to the Río Deseado. There are also close resemblances between the decorative motifs of the skin coats of the Patagonians and those of certain stone slabs, whose use is a mystery and which are covered with geometrical patterns — triangles, crosses, and diamonds.

The early Patagonians were strongly influenced by the Araucanian tribes who crossed the Cordillera de Agostini in the 17th century and invaded the Argentine pampas. They adopted in particular the jewelry, made with silver coins, which is the pride of the Araucanian women. There are the *topo* (pins used to fasten cloaks) with large flat or spherical heads, pectorals made with jointed parts, and crescent-shaped earrings. These large heavy pieces are often laden with pendants or charms, also of silver. The cloths, headbands, and belts are covered with small beads made of the same metal. The art of weaving, which was so highly developed among the Araucanians, was also adopted by the Patagonians, so that it was often difficult to distinguish Patagonian and Araucanian art merely by judging from outward appearances.

TIERRA DEL FUEGO. The tip of the South American continent and the islands around Cape Horn are the last inhabited lands of the Southern Hemisphere. Their climate is harsh; snow sometimes falls in full summer and the wind blows almost ceaselessly. There, in a desolate setting of fiords, islands, and glaciers, three Indian tribes still lived a few years ago: the Ona in Tierra del Fuego, the Yaghan (Yamana) near Cape Horn, and the Alacaluf in the canals of western Patagonia. These tribes differed not only in language but also in their way of life. The Ona were wandering huntsmen, essentially land-dwellers; the Yaghan and Alacaluf were fishermen whose life was spent on the water.

Like the Tehuelche, these Indians were poorly equipped, with only a few weapons and rudimentary tools. They led a nomadic life and had no more opportunity than the Patagonians to develop their esthetic sense; but it would be unjust and wrong to deny them all form of art, as some have done. During the initiation festivals, the young men learn to known the supreme god and the mysteries of the world. At this juncture masked men, representing various demons, come to spread terror among the women who have stayed in the camp. The masks, made of bark, are shaped like hoods and are decorated with black bands. The bodies of the masked figures are painted with horizontal stripes.

These designs, although roughly executed, nevertheless show a sense of symmetry and the desire to produce an esthetic effect. This is also evident in the fine grooves covering the bows of the Ona from end to end, which not only afford a better grip but are also pleasing to the eye.

Alfred MÉTRAUX

BIBLIOG. R. d'Harcourt, A Relation of a Voyage to Guiana, London, 1613; M. de Heriarte, Descripção do estado do Maranhão, Pará, Corujá e Rio das Amazonas, Vienna, 1874; L. Netto, Investigações sobre a archeologia brazileira, Arch. do Mus. Nac. (Rio de Janeiro), VI, 1885, pp. 257-555; K. von den Steinen, Unter den Naturvölkern Zentral-Brasilien, Berlin, 1894; G. Boggiani, I Caduvei, Rome, 1895; P. Ehrenreich, Anthropologische Studien über die Urbewohner Brasiliens vornehmlich der Staaten Matto Grosso, Goyaz und Amazonas (Purus-Gebiet), Brunswick, 1897; H. Meyer, Über die Kunst der Xingu-Indianer, XIVᵉ Cong. int. des Américanistes, Stuttgart, 1904, pp. 455-71; E. A. Goeldi, Excavações archeologicas em 1895, I: As cavernas dunerarias artificiaes dos Indios hoje extinctos no Rio Cunany (Goanany) e sua ceramica (Mem. do Mus. Goeldi, I, 1), Belém, 1905; T. Koch-Grünberg, Anfänge der Kunst im Urwald: Indianer-Handzeichnungen auf seinen Reisen in Brasilien gesammelt, Berlin, 1905; M. Schmidt, Indianerstudien in Zentralbrasilien, Berlin, 1905; T. Koch-Grünberg, Südamerikanische Felszeichnungen, Berlin, 1907; E. Boman, Antiquités de la région andine de la République Argentine et du désert d'Atacama, 2 vols., Paris, 1908; T. Koch-Grünberg, Zwei Jahre unter den Indianern: Reisen in Nordwest-Brasilien, 2 vols., Berlin, 1909-10; F. Krause, Die Kunst der Karaja-Indianer (Staat Goyaz, Brasilien), BA, II, 1912, pp. 1-31; E. Nordenskiöld, Urnengräber und Mounds im bolivianischen Flachlande, BA, III, 1913, pp. 205-55; F. F. Outes, Los asuntos decorativos biblicos en los objetos de ceremonial pagano payaguá, Anales Mus. nac. de h. natural de Buenos Aires, XXVI, 1915, pp. 383-401; K. T. Preuss, Religion und Mythologie der Uitoto-Textaufnahmen und Beobachtungen bei einen Indianerstamm in Kolumbien, Südamerika, 2 vols., Leipzig, Göttingen, 1921-23; F. Heger, Muyrakitas, Ann. XX Cong. int. de Americanistas, I, Rio de Janeiro, 1922, pp. 255-60; W. E. Roth, An Introductory Study of the Arts, Crafts and Customs of the Guiana Indians (BAE, Ann. Rep., XXXVIII, 1916-17), Washington, 1924, pp. 23-745; O. Bregante, Ensayo de clasificacion de la ceramica del noroeste argentino, Buenos Aires, 1926; R. Karsten, The Civilization of the South American Indians, London, New York, 1926; G. Montell, An Archaeological Collection from the Rio Loa Valley, Atacama, Skrifter Oslo Etn. Mus., V, 1926, pp. 1-46; M. Schmidt, Die technischen Voraussetzungen in der Ornamentik der Eingeborenen Südamerikas, Ipek, XXVI, 1926, pp. 142-74; H. Stolpe, Collected Essays in Ornamental Art: South America, Stockholm, 1927; H. Alberto Torres, Ceramica de Marajó, Rio de Janeiro, 1929; F. Krause, Das Kunstgewerbe der Naturvölker Südamerikas, in H. T. Bossert, Geschichte des Kunstgewerbes aller Zeiter und Völker, II, Berlin, 1929, pp. 245-68; S. K. Lothrop, Polychrome Guanaco Cloaks of Patagonia (Mus. of the Am. Indian, Heye Foundation, Contributions, VII, 6), New York, 1929; K. T. Preuss, Monumentale vorgeschichtliche Kunst, 2 vols., Göttingen, 1929; W. E. Roth, Additional Studies of the Arts, Crafts and Customs of the Guiana Indians, Washington, 1929; A. Métraux, Contribution à l'étude de l'archéologie du cours supérieur et moyen de l'Amazone, Rev. Mus. de la Plata, XXXII, 1930, pp. 145-85; A. Métraux, Etudes sur la civilisation des Indiens Chiriguano, Rev. Inst. de etn. de la Univ. nacional de Tucumán, I, 1930, pp. 295-494; E. Nordenskiöld, L'archéologie du bassin de l'Amazone (Ars americana, I), Paris, 1930; E. von Sydow, Die Kunst der Naturvölker, Berlin, 1932; A. Mordini, Les cultures précolombiennes du bas Amazone et leur développement artistique, XXIVᵉ Cong. int. des Américanistes, Hamburg, 1934, pp. 61-65; E. R. and D. L. Wagner, La civilización chaco-santiagueña y sus correlaciones con las del Viejo y Nuevo Mundo, Buenos Aires, 1934; H. Wassén, The Frog-motive Among the South American Indians: Ornamental Studies, Anthropos, XXIX, 1934, pp. 319-70; A. Mattos, Das origens da arte brasileira, Belo Horizonte, 1936; R. E. Latcham, Arqueologia de la región Atacameña, Santiago, 1938; H. C. Palmatary, Tapajó Pottery, Ethn. Studier, VIII, 1939, pp. 1-136. H. A. Torres, Arte indigena de Amazonia, Rio de Janeiro, 1940; R. Larco Hoyle, Los cupisniques, Lima, 1941; L. A. Acuña, El arte de los indios colombianos, 2d ed., Mexico City, 1942; A. Serrano, El arte decorativo de los Diaguitas, Córdoba, 1943; A. Kidder II, Archaeology of Northwestern Venezuela (Pap. Peabody Mus., XXVI, 1), Cambridge, Mass., 1944; C. Lévi-Strauss, Le dédoublement de la représentation dans les arts de l'Asie et de l'Amérique, Renaissance, II-III, 1944-45, pp. 168-86; F. Marquez Miranda,

Los Diaguitas, Rev. Mus. de la Plata, N.S., III, 1946, pp. 5-300; G. D. Howard, Prehistoric Ceramic Styles of Lowland South America: Their Distribution and History, New Haven, 1947; A. L. Kroeber, Art, HSAI, V, 1949, pp. 411-92; H. C. Palmatary, The Pottery of Marajó Island, Brazil (Tr. Am. Philosophical Soc., N.S., XXXIX, 3), Philadelphia, 1950; F. Barata, A arteoleira dos Tapajó, Rev. Mus. paulista, N.S., V, 1951, pp. 183-87; P. P. Hilbert, Contribução a arqueologia da ilha de Marajó (Pub. Inst. de antr. e etn. do Pará, V), Belém do Pará, 1952; J. Imbelloni, Dos nótulas sobre la alfareria del noroeste argentino, II: Las Urnas, Runa, V, 1952, pp. 84-109; C. Nimuendajú, The Tapajó, Kroeber Anthr. Soc. Pap., VI, 1952, pp. 1-25; F. Barata, A arte oleira dos Tapajó, III. Algunos elementos novos para a Tipologia de Santarém (Pub. Inst. de antr. e etn. do Pará, VI), Belém do Pará, 1953; F. Barata, Uma análise estilística da ceramica de Santarem, Cultura, V, 1953, pp. 185-205; N. H. Vera, Elementos de la decoración diaguita, La Rioja, 1953; W. C. Bennett, Ancient Arts of the Andes, New York, 1954; C. Lévi-Strauss, Tristes tropiques, Paris, 1954; V. Badano, Caracteres del arte plástico indígena del Parana inferior, Ann. XXXI Cong. int. de Americanistas, II, São Paulo, II, 1955, pp. 777-800; H. T. Bossert, Ornamente der Völker, Tübingen, 1955; G. H. S. Bushnell and A. Digby, Ancient American Pottery, London, 1955; A. A. Gerbrands, Masterpieces of Wood Carving from the Amazon Basin, Ann. XXXI Cong. int. de Americanistas, I, São Paulo, 1955, pp. 267-68; A. A. Gerbrands, Art as an Element of Culture, Especially in Negro Africa (Meded. Rijksmuseum voor volkenkunde, XII), Leyden, 1957; B. J. Meggers and C. Evans, Archaeological Investigations at the Mouth of the Amazon (BAE B. CLXVII), Washington, 1957; B. G. Ribeiro, Bases para uma classificação dos adornos plumarios dos indios do Brasil, Arch. Mus. Nacional, XLIII, 1957, pp. 59-120; D. and B. G. Ribeiro, Arte plumario dos indios Kaapor, Rio de Janeiro, 1957; C. Evans and B. J. Meggers, Archaeological Investigations in British Guiana (BAE B. CLXXVII), Washington, 1960; J. Imbelloni, Civiltà andine, Florence, 1960; A. Lommel, ed., Indianer vom Amazonas, Munich, 1960 (exhibition cat.); H. Nachtigall, Indianerkunst der Nord-Anden, Berlin, 1961; N. H. Vera, El arte ornamental diaguita, Santa Fe, 1961; D. Ribeiro, A arte dos indios Kadiuéu (Serviço de documentação, Ministerio da educação e saude), Rio de Janeiro, n.d.

Illustrations: PLS. 91-104; 4 figs. in text.

* *

SOUTINE, CHAIM. Russian painter attached to the school of Paris (b. Smilovitchi, near Minsk, Lithuania, 1894; d. Paris, Aug. 9, 1943). The tenth of eleven children of a poor Jewish tailor, Soutine was fascinated by art from early youth. After some preliminary instruction in Minsk, he entered the Academy in Vilna (Vilnius) in 1910 and in 1913 went to Paris, which thereafter became his permanent home. For a short time he studied with Fernand Cormon at the Ecole Nationale des Beaux-Arts but soon was working on his own. Like his friends Chagall and Modigliani, he remained independent of cubism and its allied styles, exploring instead Fauvism and the German expressionist tradition. He was in Céret (Pyrénées-Orientales) from 1920 to 1922 but otherwise, except for frequent summer travels in southern France, remained in Paris. Recognition of his work came slowly, forcing Soutine to live in Bohemian poverty until the late 1920s. Although he occasionally sold paintings, he did not participate in a major exhibition until 1927 and had his first one-man show only in 1935, at the Arts Club of Chicago. The 1920s were his most active period, but ulcers and other disorders plagued him continually and, after 1930, interfered seriously with his work. He lived in Champigny-sur-Veude (Indre-et-Loire) from 1941 to 1943 and died in Paris after an emergency operation.

Among Soutine's best-known paintings are *Self-Portrait at the Easel* (ca. 1917; New York, Coll. Mr. and Mrs. Henry Pearlman), *Landscape at Cagnes* (ca. 1922; New York, Coll. Mr. and Mrs. Ralph Colin), *Carcass of Beef* (ca. 1925; Buffalo, N.Y., Albright-Knox Art Gallery), *Dead Fowl* (ca. 1926; Art Institute of Chicago), *The Pastry Cook* (ca. 1927; New York, Coll. Lee Ault), and *House at Oisème* (1934; Lakeville, Conn., Coll. Richards H. Emerson). Soutine, painting and living in relative isolation, is celebrated chiefly for his paintings of the 1920s. As the heir of Tintoretto, El Greco, and Rembrandt, the last of whom he revered, he provided a vital link between Fauvism-expressionism and the abstract expressionism of the mid-century. The sinuous, ecstatic rhythms of his heavily pigmented canvases are complemented by the vigor and brilliance of his colors and reflect the rather convulsive, often agonized growth of Soutine's art (V, PLS. 140, 205).

BIBLIOG. E. Faure, Soutine, Paris, 1928; M. Wheeler, Chaim Soutine, New York, 1950; P. d'Ancona, Modigliani, Chagall, Soutine, Pascin, Milan, 1952; E. Szittya, Soutine et son temps, Paris, 1955.

Robert L. HERBERT

SPACE AND TIME. For many generations, space and time were considered opposing concepts, but in the 20th century there has been a tendency to connect them with one single act of perception. This change in attitude is due first and foremost to the work of mathematicians, Minkowsky and Einstein particularly, but it has also been promoted by the experiments and still more by the theories of artists, especially painters. The historiography of cubism, together with the analyses connected with the psychology of form and the lessons of the great Bauhaus masters, has certainly contributed to the diffusion of space and time problems and to awareness of their presence also in the art of the past. Further interest has been raised by cinematography, a visual form in which the time factor predominates and which makes possible the reading, as a temporal succession of events, of architectural, plastic, and even pictorial masterpieces whose internal rhythm is thus finally developed in a narrative way.

This article attempts to demonstrate that the space-time element is present in all artistic representation, although in very diverse and sometimes deceptive forms. To illustrate this demonstration, however, with examples drawn from all civilizations would be too ambitious an undertaking. Discussion is therefore confined to the art of western Europe from the 15th to the 20th century.

SUMMARY. Temporal expedients in the visual arts (col. 181). The nature of perception (col. 182). Representational systems (col. 185). The development of space and time concepts in Western art (col. 187): *The late Middle Ages; The transition to the Renaissance; The Renaissance; The modern period.* Conclusion (col. 202).

TEMPORAL EXPEDIENTS IN THE VISUAL ARTS. By traditional definition, the representational arts lie outside the time category since they produce static images that are two-dimensional (painting) or three-dimensional (sculpture). They are therefore structurally distinct from poetry and music, which develop within a physically prolonged time. Attempts at recovering, at least partially, the element foreign to each of them have, however, been made frequently both in the spatial and in the temporal arts; this has also been done by cinematography, which is both image (spatiality) and narration (time).

The limits that have been indicated are physical and do not exclude the possibility of suggesting space for poetry and time for the visual arts in a symbolic way. In literature and music there is no doubt, for example, that the melodic and rhythmic refrains and the presence of a unifying rhythm succeed in giving a sense of defined spatiality. In the visual arts, a "duration" of images, based on successive phases either of structure or of perception, has been obtained in different periods through a series of expedients. In prehistoric art (PL. 105) the images are superimposed without any attempt at spatial-temporal arrangement. With the geometric style there already appears a repetition of the same image or of an identical motif, which gives a sense of order and rhythmic continuity. It is the so-called "continuum" that characterizes not only abstract decoration (PL. 106) but also the figured decoration of entire civilizations, including that of Byzantium (PL. 107).

Another expedient for achieving the "duration" of the image is the system of representing a series of episodes simultaneously, in an identical setting or in a single work (PLS. 110, 111). Two other expedients should also be mentioned: the multiplicity of the perspective planes, which compel the eye to pass through a series of pictorial or plastic episodes that are often linked together in an unusual way (PL. 109); and the variety of viewing points, especially where monumental sculptures and large buildings are concerned.

In addition to this exploiting of internal formal structure, artists since antiquity have been able to compel the observer to a journey, physical or imagined, which objectively conditions the time needed for the enjoyment of the work. The most typical example is that of the labyrinth, especially when the itinerary remains largely a natural one. Here a modification or adaptation of the physical journey is used to create not only a time but a rhythm of enjoyment. Equally dramatic and de-

liberately planned is the ascent of the Mesopotamian ziggurats, of the pyramids and stairways of Central America, and of prehistoric mounds, which imitate the sacred mountain and make use of common and effective expedients to give to the journey a mysterious quality and a magical duration. For example, the slope of the path or stairway is calculated in such a way as to leave hidden until the last moment the summit where the ceremonies take place.

The idea of an enforced journey, corresponding to successive phases of initiation, is also found in the architecture and town planning of all civilizations (see ARCHITECTURE). The rhythm of the columns and arches in the Early Christian basilica leads up to the altar and apse; the Gothic ambulatory visually accompanies the procession around the relic; the large stairways of baroque palaces, with their hidden stages for the orchestras, provide an almost choreographic approach to the grand reception hall. The very placing of the building on a raised site, by turns visible to and hidden from anybody approaching, creates a sense of expectation and of progressive conquest.

Sculpture, too, when it is isolated and visible from all sides, demands a prolonged and rhythmically varying observation. In the baroque period, which took advantage of all the psychological factors to accentuate this type of variation, the simulation of movements was continued and completed in front of the onlooker: water, with the extreme mobility of its effects, was brought into the sculptural context, and the effect of changing sunlight on masses and backgrounds was calculated. The great decorative painting of the baroque period also participated in the "temporality" of architecture, to which it was connected through the variation and modulation of the spatial and temporal entities. The perception time, however, may be determined by exclusively pictorial means. One such device is the richness of the details, which compel a slow and minute observation; another, the obscurity of the theme, which requires interpretation; yet another, the presence of captions, which ultimately give every painting the character of a comic or tragic scene.

The cases cited are attempts to incorporate an element that is considered extrinsic; but a thorough knowledge of the nature of perception appears to prove that time is by no means a secondary formative factor of the image, even when it is generally thought to be absent.

* *

THE NATURE OF PERCEPTION. There is a widely held opinion that a visual image is instantaneously perceived. This opinion is clearly untenable. It is generally acknowledged that anybody with sensitivity enjoys stopping to look at a picture or a work of art. It is immaterial that some should speak of the pleasure the work gives them, others of analysis. The point beyond question is that in no case does the viewer grasp all the elements of an image — whether spatial or expressive — at first glance. What remains fixed in his memory as a reference point is not what he has seen but what he has apprehended. No experiment has ever made it possible to affirm that there is a reaction of the retina that does not involve the combination of a series of images. The retina is a part of the brain and not an instrument at the service of some superior element of our being which employs it for purposes independent of its own activity. Simple people calculate time on the basis of their experience; in a sense, they are unaware of its speed. They do not include it in the category of the infinitely small, and instead of regarding it as a physiological phenomenon to be calculated in terms of the speed of light, they estimate it in terms of the seconds of their watch. Nor has there been any explanation of how perceptive activity is divided between the rods and cones of the retina. Our eye never perceives a completely motionless spectacle. The movement of the universe is eternal and the activity of our brain constant.

Another reason that time is one of the fundamental conditions of all artistic perception is the fact that mobility is a correlative element of perception. To believe that it is possible to grasp a fixed image in its entirety with the fixed eye is sheer absurdity. Not only is vision binocular, but one eye alone can give the perception of an image in time, because, falling on any surface, the glance, following unknown laws, sweeps across the entire field of vision. The image is fixed but the perception of it is mobile. Seeing is an action; the mind is not passive, it registers an image that, moreover, is different for each observer.

Little of this is currently acknowledged. Today the success of art and of visual activities in general is so great that everybody claims to participate fully in a mental activity that, although general, is in fact unequally distributed among individuals. Some people may admit to having no ear for music, but nobody envisages the possibility of having no eye. Everyone discusses pictures and images as if the reading of them were a natural gift. It is commonly believed that a visual image is perceived by everyone in the same way. It is also believed that there are truths that can be communicated as isolated fragments of information. But in fact it is never the isolated elements that are the significant factor in a representational system, but rather their assembly and interrelation, and in order to understand this system of integration, it is essential to have first acquired — or naturally received — a capacity for deciphering the image and then to proceed in time to the exploration of the visual field or, in the case of sculpture and architecture, of the volumes, which are not thrown together by chance or nature but by the will of the artist.

If today the mechanism of seeing, observing, and interpreting representational works gives rise to so many false theories, this is mostly because the greater part of the public in viewing images follows criteria that are entirely different from those current during the past five centuries. For our contemporaries, photography and films are the chief reference points for the visual arts. Photography has spread the idea of the complete and instantaneous reading of any image. In this field, as elsewhere, the multiplication of images has resulted in the transformation of the very nature both of the image and of the act of perception. The number of images was once infinitely smaller than now. Even after printing had made it possible to produce a great number of prints from an engraving, people still continued to "read" and interpret pictures. Traditionally pictures always contained a whole series of allegorical or allusive meanings. It never occurred to anyone to question their value as an expressive language; they were considered as links in a chain of forms which could be explained one by another and which required an initiation in order to be correctly understood.

The function of images in the Middle Ages bears no relation to their function today. There were few images in medieval times. They were to be seen in public places, usually in the form of large-scale compositions and altarpieces. All the subjects were drawn from religion, in other words, from a fund of knowledge to which the very structure of medieval existence gave a lifelong familiarity. They demanded not the subtle deciphering practiced today but instantaneous reference to certain standards, which, however, involved the time element for any precise perception of the image. Pictures directed both the senses and the mind of the observer not to the passing spectacle of the exterior world but to knowledge that had evolved on a cultural level. They were the sum of experience and tradition. They impressed themselves upon the imagination in the course of prolonged contemplation or ceremonial presentation. Their significance matured and was assimilated slowly, and they were imbued with time not merely because they constituted a sort of long visual indoctrination but also because they were the repository of age-old wisdom. The observer drew upon both his visual and his intellectual memory, and in this way a space-time relationship was established that was very different from the one prevailing today.

The fact that the eye receives the light waves that carry the visual impression of objects was not unknown (see OPTICAL CONCEPTS). The question was whether it was the light particles emanating from objects that struck the retina, or the force of the eye's glance that lit up and revealed the objects. Already in the 14th and 15th centuries men like Fouquet and Leonardo da Vinci (qq.v.) were also aware of the fact that the eye has a curvature that plays its part in the reception of sensory stimuli upon the retina. But it was only with the discovery of photography that it was realized that an entire scene could be record-

ed in a flash and that a comparison could be established between the darkroom and vision. Although entirely questionable, this comparison bears witness to a total transformation of the relationship of images to space and time. The possibility of fixing the momentary coincidence of certain elements in a fleeting relationship which gives them special significance and which is in fact determined by the photographer's private train of thought, leads to the belief that this phenomenological dissection of the universe corresponds not to the realities of man's active and contemplative life but to the intention of nature itself. Man is experiencing a new kind of radical anthropomorphism. It is no longer to the gods or to God that he attributes his own interests and knowledge, but to matter. It is no less arbitrary, however, to imagine that the disposition of objects and human behavior reflect the interests and intentions of nature rather than those of the demiurge. The concept remains one of finality. The stability of the image is attributed to the universe, although the latter destroys the spectacle at the very moment of its perception.

These theories, which rest upon inadequate analysis, imply a rejection of time. The best proof of this is our absolute inability to recognize a subject that cannot be referred to criteria linked not to our artistic sensibility but to our culture. Any object from a civilization previously unknown gives rise to a host of conjectures. We see only what we know, or at least what we can integrate into a coherent system of expression, a system, therefore, that exists in time. It is not simply by using its senses that a child achieves control of its sensations; the same gesture may be repeated before it a thousand times but to no purpose unless it be placed in relation to other gestures. In other words, contact with space has no significance outside time. Moreover, there is no justification for attributing to men of the past knowledge and ways of thought identical to ours. It is impossible to believe that the eye, which registers only information and not scenes, has always operated in the same way throughout the centuries: since all vision occurs in time, no image can take shape without the participation of collective memory. Every image bears the dual imprint of a phenomenon and a consciousness. Even the phenomenon can exist only insofar as it is bound to what precedes, follows, and surrounds it. All consciousness is differential and therefore exists in time.

Whether it be a question of the necessary deciphering of a picture (in other words, of the conditions in which the eye explores the two-dimensional field of representation) or of the conditions in which the eye grasps those situations in the universe which are capable of supplying the fragmentary or episodic matter of the picture (in other words, of the relationship between vision and sensation), it has been shown that perceptive activity always implies, over and above the sensory impression, a mental activity that is inconceivable without the participation of the time factor. At this level it has been seen that the introduction of the time element in vision involves the intervention of memory. But this memory is different from that which is normally associated with acts of reminiscence. This is, so to speak, a present, immediate memory — a kind of "micromemory," or more precisely, a memory where time intervenes at phenomenological and not historical or merely conscious speed. This is not the place to examine how far this sort of physiological memory is identical with memory that can be analyzed on the level of social and historical consciousness. The main thing is to ascertain the participation of time in all spatial perception capable of producing a representational image.

The role played by transfers of memory in a given, well-defined historical situation and the divergence that necessarily exists between individual memories and collective memory will be examined later. But before approaching, on the basis of the concrete example of the Western civilizations of the last five centuries, the problem of the formation and mutations of a representational language necessarily based on the treatment of space and time, it should be remembered that, however great it may be, the importance of time in the phenomenological development of plastic vision exists only insofar as the creation of any representational language implies the projection in space of a sensation produced by the activity of nerve cells in the brain and then physically introduced into a space whose only connection with the space of artistic representation is a completely abstract one. Of course, the brain is in the same space as the landscape or the scene represented on the plastic surface or in the round by the artist. It belongs to the same universe and is governed by the same laws. But essentially, there remains the usual insoluble problem of unity and multiplicity, of identity and diversity. There is no life in the human sense of the term but that which is manifest in activities of a certain type, and the present aim is not to decipher the riddle of the universe but to get a better understanding of the objective conditions in which human endeavor operates. This study is not concerned with the problem of space-time in the universe as such, but simply with the way in which it informs, on the social and cultural level, works that are accessible to the sight and imagination.

Neither time nor space in homogeneous form is within human grasp — assuming that they even exist. Since the mind assimilates only human facts, the interpretation of universal facts can be undertaken only by means of analysis and the consideration of objects or events that fall into the main categories of our activities. Time can therefore be apprehended only insofar as certain phenomena possess qualities that are more or less stable and more or less associated with other series of facts; its interest lies not in its identity but in its variety. The same is true of space. An expanse that is homogeneous, infinite, and without mutation is the equivalent of death, a place of absolute fulfillment — in other words, a place where time and change have been abolished. The general assumption can therefore be made that the perception of space-time, upon which all artistic representation rests, always implies simultaneous attention to at least two types of consideration. Place is the present moment, time is memory; time differentiates while space unifies; time is the occasions, the events, the possibilities; space is the act and causality; time is distribution in the past or potentiality; space is distribution in reality and instantaneousness. The Chinese attribute to the "orients" (in other words, to the sectors of space), functions and qualities that Western civilizations classify in categories of time. There exists no standard classification of time and space elements. Every human community establishes between them a delicate equilibrium that is just as apparent in artistic works as it is in languages and institutions.

Visual perception of any image involves mental activity in two directions simultaneously. As the image is composed of elements, it acquires meaning when the material signs are correlated and when these elements are assumed to refer to composite wholes that are currently interpreted as objects by a given group of individuals; this is the domain of configurations, in other words, of space. The image, however, also acquires meaning when one considers that the spatial elements thus constituted assume reality only insofar as they refer to knowledge and values that the immediate sensory impression does not suffice to establish; this is the domain of memory or of the imaginary — in other words, of time. Thus space-time can be attributed neither to a single perception nor to opposing perceptions. No form of thought can be broken down into fragments. On the other hand, in no case do the elements cumulatively supply the principles of intellection. The categories of space and time are based not on different series of external facts but on the processes governing all mental activity.

REPRESENTATIONAL SYSTEMS. Since it is not only the representational elements and their current interpretations that vary from one generation to another but also the chains of thought and the body of knowledge upon which these interpretations are based, it is indispensable to replace the abstract analysis of the artistic phenomenon supposedly connected with the use of absolute space-time by a study of the specific situations in which, during the course of the 15th century in western Europe, one explanatory system was rejected and another elaborated. It is obviously arbitrary to seek to pin down the moment when one system supplants another. But it is perfectly clear that at certain moments the permanent process of modification involves a complete break and, more than a transposition of symbols, a mutation of the system. An attempt will therefore be made to describe both the origin and the stabilization of a system that for five hundred years has determined the understanding and the function of images.

It should first be stressed that the Gothic Middle Ages did not use only one artistic language. Between the style of the Paris workshop of Jean Pucelle (q.v.) and that of Simone Martini (q.v.) or between the stained glass of Chartres and Giotto (q.v.) there are differences that touch upon the very nature of the image. Neither was there a definite type of medieval man. The whole gamut of temperaments and beliefs existed between such men as Philip the Fair and St. Francis. This invalidates the naïve notion of a spirit of the age seeking its fulfillment in various forms of expression, of "infralanguages" aspiring to concrete form in symbols, and of great latent symbols rising to the surface through the more or less voluntary mediation of the artist. Yet the fact remains that all the forms of artistic expression chronologically grouped in the centuries of the Middle Ages made frequent use of certain signs common to all systems but never adopted certain structural forms that are characteristic of the following centuries. The problem, then, is to determine, on the one hand, the materials or component elements of the various medieval and Renaissance systems, and, on the other (and this is an entirely separate operation), to define the ways in which these elements were associated in both these periods. Visual representation can be explained not in terms of the more or less fixed elements of the repertory but only by the spatial-temporal associations that determine selection. As the fragment cannot define the whole, so the work cannot signify through its relation to purely sensorial data. Form is bound neither to the separate parts nor to reality, but to causality. It is not a reflection but a fabrication. Knowledge of all the elements never supplies the solution. The image, halfway between the real and the imaginary, is a system of comprehension; it is not the product of a free play of permutations. Syntheses are created following values that are sometimes extraneous. The image does not belong merely to the realm of information: it is creation, restrictive certainly, but intentional; it is method rather than description. It does not refer to what is already given but to what is intended.

If painting is considered as a regulated activity that is capable (like all manual and intellectual techniques) of evolving without ceasing to be itself and of engendering a series of objects or products that reveal as much about man as about nature, one should start by proposing the concept of the representational object, which is more accessible than that of the image. In fact, the more general term "cultural object" may also be used to define certain creations of a social group that do not necessarily take the form of artistic representation but fulfill the same functions. There are cultural objects that are not primarily regarded as the work of artists. Examples are objects like the cross and the Holy Grail or the throne and the ship, which impressed themselves on men's imaginations by virtue of their abstract meanings; having been adopted by a society from an ancient vocabulary, they were filled with meaning before they became established as forms. Generally speaking, that which specifically characterizes all representational activities is precisely their dialectic nature: concepts refer to expression and vice versa. Furthermore, in the case of very advanced societies, the creation of signs or objects with no reference whatsoever to a model is rare. The important thing is not to lose sight of the fact that representational signs arise not through the description of reality but as manifestations of mental processes. It is equally important to bear in mind that there exists, as a support for the systems of representation, a fund of signs and symbols which grew up in the mind through space-time and which are dialectically situated between reality, the perceived, and the imaginary. The fact that the dialectic relationship is therefore three-dimensional, not two-dimensional as is generally believed, is all-important. The failure to recognize this fact has been responsible for all the polemics over realism, from Plato and the iconoclasts down to the modern theorists of the reality of images.

It should be noted that societies do not possess representational objects in any definitely constituted form. The representational elements they use are sometimes universally applicable and at other times are split into parts that are reminiscent of other compositions. It may be said that representational language has its elementary and concrete particles that must be distinguished from the sign or symbol. A great difference exists between the fund of elements at the disposal of representational language and that utilized by verbal language. The elements of verbal language are homogeneous; they are real units set in a fixed relationship to one another and corresponding to an unchanging mechanism of the brain's phonetic activity. It is impossible to base the study of representational language on the simple application of the general laws of spoken language, because the elements of representational language are of an ambiguous nature, since they develop in space-time and thus combine elements from different levels of reality and intellection.

THE DEVELOPMENT OF SPACE AND TIME CONCEPTS IN WESTERN ART. In order to understand how a representational system evolved in Europe in the 15th century, it is necessary to discover not the absolute origin of the elements that were most commonly employed by the creators of the system, but rather the normal value that was attributed in about 1400 to the whole group of signs and symbols then in use in the Western world. These signs, of course, did not relate to nature. This does not mean that art had not shown highly developed realism and illusionistic tendencies. But the elements borrowed from reality were always organized within systems whose coherence depended on the acknowledgment of certain criteria of truth, implying reference to places and times distinct from those of daily life. It has been claimed that Greece and Rome depicted a world that was instable and incoherent, in which trees, rocks, and ships were freely distributed in nondimensional space against a background without scale. The ancients had their own criteria for "immediate" or "realistic" reference. This point of view implies, firstly, that all coherent representation of space necessitates belief in a spiritual finality, and secondly, that the two stages toward a rational representation of the universe have necessarily been that of the Middle Ages, when the symbolism of the visible and invisible was founded, and then that of the Renaissance, when the "correct" construction of a given space was discovered, implying a coincidence between Euclidean mathematics and the physical laws of the universe. This would mean that the Middle Ages discovered the reference required for an absolute value of time and the Renaissance the reference, which was just as necessary, for the physical reality of space.

The late Middle Ages. No more than in any other field does a sudden passage occur in the domain of space-time from the Middle Ages to modern times. The medieval world, far from approaching a decline at the end of the 14th century, was active and creative. Whether in politics, philosophy, or art, there was no lack of controversy and invention. The 14th century witnessed the development, for example, of the whole cycle of thought from Robert Grosseteste to Ockham that prepared the way, passing over the Humanism of the 15th century, for modern scientific thinking. In the arts, the esthetic current, far from being exhausted, was in full vigor.

Two principal centers oriented the movement of esthetic ideas: on the one hand, in the north, the princely courts that were offshoots of the reigning house of France, and on the other, the merchant towns and the cities of Italy that were seeking to free themselves from the excessive rigidity of the tradition of Rome and Byzantium. Art historians traditionally grant absolute priority to Italy because of the feeling that from there the whole modern world sprang fully armed, not so much through patient efforts at cultural development as through the sudden discovery, at the beginning of the 15th century, of a rational representational solution that annulled, so to speak, all the tentative efforts of preceding generations because it constituted the true norm of any objective vision of the world. This opinion leaves out of account the originality, and what is more, the personality of the Nordic world. The truth is that these two great

parallel cycles of esthetic speculation that developed in the course of the 14th century were both destined to shape the future.

If the innovating character of the 14th century and the duality of its poles of activity are accepted, the problem of the development of representational space-time can be seen in a new perspective: no longer as tending toward an invention that abruptly brought men back to the absolute truth of a normative form of vision forgotten since antiquity and suddenly rediscovered, but as the generator of a complex artistic code in which the Nordic and the Tuscan traditions finally merged.

It is difficult to compare the development of the visual arts north and south of the Alps, because neither the social conditions nor the technical traditions were identical. Yet it has been too hastily said that there is no relationship at all between the two regions. North of the Alps the great Franco-Flemish painting tradition developed not only through princely protectors but also through the rise of an urban society around Paris and several cities in Burgundy and Flanders. Mural decoration was supplanted in Gothic times by stained glass, which reached a high degree of perfection, certainly superior to the Italo-Byzantine decorative style, in spite of certain representational limitations. These resulted chiefly from the infinite fragmentation of the scenes imposed by the lead framework. Simultaneously there developed in the French cultural zone another representational art: that of illumination, which also imposed fragmented composition. With its stained glass and its miniatures, which should be considered as complementary, French Gothic painting constitutes a complete and outstanding type of visual art. It remains to be seen whether it played a part in that process of detachment from artistic traditions that led Italian artists to project their compositions in a modern space-time dimension, in which close ties were established between Christian legend and the spectacle of the world, and in which the realism of knowledge took precedence over the visionary world of faith.

First of all, it should be noted that the method of approaching or deciphering a work differs according to whether it is a large mural composition or an illustration. The reader of a manuscript demanded that the picture complete the idea he had formed from the text. As few people were even slightly capable of reading a text at that time, the public was one of clerics, not in the religious but in the intellectual sense of the term. Thus painting in the northern countries must be judged differently according to whether it is stained glass intended for the masses or manuscript illumination intended for a small elite. It is interesting to note, however, that there was no sharp division between the two genres throughout the 14th century. Illuminations were composed of episodes that were often set in lobed frameworks like segments of stained glass (see MINIATURES AND ILLUMINATION).

The representational art of the Franco-Flemish world of the 14th century had an extraordinary quality but also a certain dryness. It remained a minor art linked with writing and dependent on discursive thought. A peak in craftsmanship was reached in the output of the Paris workshops, but the Bible of Jean de Papeleu (Paris, Bib. de l'Arsenal, Ms. 5059), dating from 1317, the Psalter of Saint Louis and Blanche of Castile (Paris, Bib. de l'Arsenal, Ms. 1186), and the Belleville Breviary (VI, PL. 315), as well as *Le miroir historial* of King John (Paris, Bib. de l'Arsenal, Ms. 5080) and the Bible of Jean de Cis (de Sy; Paris, Bib. Nat., Ms. Fr. 15397), dating respectively from 1343 and 1356 at the latest, all give an impression of traditionalism in their inspiration. The traditionalism of Gothic art corresponds to that of contemporaneous Byzantine art and in no way detracts from the freshness and liveliness of the inspiration. The Gothic world of the north, like the Byzantine world, had its representational elements that determined place and time, these being much more frequently indicated anecdotally and by the portrayal of social customs than is the case in Italy. This art carried to their highest point both the taste for arabesque ornamentation and the refined representation of the human figure. On the other hand, by a curious mechanism of the creative imagination, it deliberately avoided any composition that in any way placed the episode in a context. The outside world is absent. The figures are always grouped in front of a neutral background, a sort of backdrop. This is an abstract and intellectual style, meant for the reader rather than the beholder. When, in about 1380, settings began to surround the figures in the works attributed to the apocryphal Maître aux Boquetaux, the Titus Livius of Charles V (Paris, Bib. Ste-Geneviève, Ms. 777), the *Grandes chroniques de France* (Paris, Bib. Nat., Ms. Fr. 2813), and John of Salisbury's *Policraticus* (Paris, Bib. Nat., Ms. 24287), affinities are apparent with the *Thebaid* by Francesco Traini (Pisa, Camposanto) or certain Sienese predella scenes. A composition like that in the *Grandes chroniques de France* showing the entry into Paris of Charles V and the Emperor Charles IV presents a boldly curved foreground such as appears later in the work of Fouquet. But even this composition has no spatial depth. Environment for the Parisian illuminators is entirely bound by the laws of verbal evocation. In the same way, because of this abstraction of space, time too is uniform. This is not at all the absolute time of divine vision. Time is unquestionably earthly, but historical sense is lacking.

This sort of abstract indifference to time and place led to a certain exaltation of man as the measure of all things. From this point of view, it is difficult to regard this art as backward. It belongs unmistakably to the feudal society of the day, with its great love of tales and its great indifference to any extraneous adventure. This world rejected the Crusades and, with Philip the Fair, rejected the faith. It was a secular society but not without a certain imagination, a society that was resolutely nonhistorical and therefore abstract, but not for that reason incapable of self-acceptance. This feudal world, which carried its way of life as far as the East, which was enthralled by tales whose spell was to hold captive another ten generations, had no artistic uneasiness. Everything was on a human scale, man being the author both of his destiny and of his environment. It is certainly not possible to accuse of banality and archaism a world without distance and without setting, a system of representation wherein the imaginary was confined to the rationalism of personal action, wherein a tale consisted in the linking of a succession of episodes, wherein the wonders of the present replaced legend and the stability of the human condition seemed absolute.

So far little attention has been paid to an evolution that was preparing, beyond the return to antiquity of the 15th century, certain forms of psychological humanism similar to that of Montaigne. The quality of this wave of artistic abstraction has been ignored. In its atemporal and abstract forms, Gothic art perfectly characterizes a whole historical age. But it is also a fact that this Gothic society, which reached its peak in the 14th century, was destined to undergo an immediate transformation. Recently attempts have been made to demonstrate that there is to be found in the art of the northern regions, with the exception of that of the French court, the origin of a new realism, which was steadily promoted by the use of the means discovered in Italy in the 14th century. More generally, however, art historians have tried to prove the Lombard origin of the imitation of the natural world, considered, together with the rational construction of a portion of space, as the basis of any "legitimate" vision and of all "true" representation of the universe. It would appear, however, that such hypotheses are as open to question historically as theoretically. Before discussing them further, however, it is necessary to examine the artistic developments that were taking place in Italy at this time.

The achievements of the Italian artists of the early 14th century can be assessed only in the context of the religious and artistic traditions that preceded them. For Byzantium the problem of place and time was a well-defined one. All representation was linked to the Christological dogma upon which the social hierarchy of the universe was based. The function of painting was therefore to materialize the dimensions of a space whose attributes were entirely determined by divine law. There was, so to speak, no figurative space: the space represented was actual, whether in the case of the walls and vaults of a church or on the surface of a picture. The universe was considered the material manifestation of God's thought. All space was real in the sense that represented space and actual space were

identical both with each other and with the universe. When a Byzantine painter decorated a church, he laid out his symbols in an order that reproduced the supernatural arrangement of the world. The Word alone existed. Painting was an initiation, an introduction to conceptual reality: invention was limited, since the image, the icon, was a reduction of an immutable prototype corresponding to a divine order, where place was also an immutable aspect of a hierarchic order of the good and where time was necessarily a reference to the prototype constituted by the episodes of a legend revealing an absolute order. Here time and place were therefore the means of expression of dialectic thought, which acted as mediator between spirit and matter (PL. 112; see BYZANTINE ART).

Western civilization, on the other hand, can be considered the daughter of heresy. Numerous heresies had of course existed in both Eastern and Western Christian worlds before the 14th century, but these heresies had engendered only timid representational forms. Above all, they had not penetrated the social structure to the point of obliging the Church to reach a compromise with the heretic body rather than condemn it outright. The whole history of the visual arts in the West springs from the fact that in the 13th century heresy took the form not of intellectual opposition but of a sentimental and spiritual claim. It was not without reason that the name "Spiritual" was given to all the monastic partisans of the doctrines that rejected the concepts of a human order strictly determined by a complete and final revelation that can only be respected and deeply meditated, substituting for it the concept of a partial, fragmentary revelation which is constantly in the process of fulfillment and which demands from each individual not mere devotional submission but an effort of the will, an active and constantly questioned adherence of his whole being. Once it has been admitted that the whole history of mankind consists not in the renewal of a collective act of thanksgiving and faith but in individual adhesion — which is necessary to the ever-indispensable realization of the creative act — belief, conduct, and the forms of representation all change. The aim of art is then no longer the repetition of a prototype; it becomes the instrument with which a group of individuals attribute devotional values to acts which no longer figure in the fixed tradition of Holy Writ but which seem, to some at least, to give actuality to the doctrinal teachings in the existing social context. At this point the artist is led to establish representational systems in which places and acts — in other words, events or times — come to express common values by the same token as the places and times fixed by tradition.

It is beyond question that the development of the visual arts in Europe is directly related to the social and religious movements that have stirred the social history of the West since the 13th century. It is because Giotto and his followers were so closely associated with the religious movement nearest to heresy, Franciscanism, that their work had such repercussions. Generally speaking, the 13th and 14th centuries were filled with the struggle of the monastic orders not only to make effective the mystical driving force that imposes upon men the will to live their faith but also to hold the excesses of free invention in check. Giotto himself was not the instrument of Spiritual Franciscanism but the agent of those official currents that aimed at disciplining the impulses threatening both social order and orthodoxy. The fact remains, nevertheless, that it was through his work that the dual problem of giving actuality to both places and times other than those of the Gospel tradition emerged as the generator of a truly modern artistic system (PL. 112; see GIOTTO).

The merit of an absolute discovery cannot be attributed to Giotto alone. There is no doubt that Giotto was the most perfect artist of his time, and it is owing to him that the system that would otherwise have remained a form of expression became a form of great art. It was not only in Florence, however, that the artists of the 14th century posed the problem of a representational expression of the current religious values linked to the forms of popular culture. In Siena, as well, efforts were made to create types of painting that differed from the pure Byzantine tradition. In the Pinacoteca of that city it is possible to see how the followers of painters in the Byzantine style such as Guido da Siena, the Master of the Blessed Gallerani, and the unknown artist of the altarpiece of St. John the Baptist endeavored to establish a new relation between the theme of the composition as a whole and the picturesque episodes of the lives of the saints. The effort to transfer the legendary episodes to the level of scenes in daily life constitutes the real intellectual innovation — that which renewed the whole concept of space-time. It is clear that in this field the Sienese played a leading part; it is also clear that the achievements of Duccio di Buoninsegna (q.v.) were based on premises akin to those of Giotto. This attempt to give actuality to sacred subjects introduces an element of invention and surprise that reappears sporadically and always disconcertingly throughout Western art until the time of Caravaggio (q.v.).

Finally, it is clear that with Duccio and the Sienese, form remained relatively close to tradition, and this is no doubt why their artistic innovations had fewer repercussions than those of Giotto. The same artistic material is to be found in Giotto and the Sienese: the town and the rocks, the cubiform building open on one side only, the tree, the altar, the door, and the column. It is easy to make an inventory of the common fund of representational forms and objects, which proves that it is the system and not the means that characterizes art. More exactly, it is the adaptation of the means to a system, which entails inevitable sacrifices and compromises. Moreover, it could be maintained that Giotto was a man of the early 14th century because he was the interpreter not of popular trends that were truly bold and innovative but rather of the tendencies of the established Church, which was determined to keep in check the heretical propensities of the time. It has been observed that Giotto, at Assisi itself, interpreted the legend of St. Francis in an anti-Spiritual sense, presenting him as the firm and faithful upholder of the Roman Church and the papacy. There was no question of turning art into an instrument of social and individual rebellion against the established order. A work of art is a confrontation point for the diverse tendencies of an age. The essential thing is this confrontation itself, which makes of the image something other than an icon expressing a truth formulated outside the boundaries of human endeavor. The new world of art, that of Giotto, was not in the least inspired by the faithful and direct observation of nature; it was a world of human action and earthly causality. Whether the subject was Francis (a Francis fully reconciled with the Church) or Scrovegni, who by the portrayal of his charitable principles hoped to redeem a life of usury, the aim of the image was to express the human desire to shape reality according to the existing social order. This is no longer the medieval universe inspired by clerics whose aim was to demonstrate to mankind the principles of a life directed by the application of an intangible doctrine. The evolution of Western art is linked with the development of a culture which no longer claims that all action is governed by the laws of revealed truth but which seeks to justify certain aspects of earthly life and to demonstrate, through the tangible presence of miracles, the immediate presence of a divinity more accessible through its teachings than through a mystical union that is not subject to the laws of space and time.

The transition to the Renaissance. With this change from a doctrine of symbolic immanence to a descriptive application of the structures and active values of earthly life, the Italian artists of the second half of the 14th century proposed a new kind of painting illustrating the presence of Christian morality in the world. It preached social action and the way of salvation for all; but its method of persuasion was an appeal to the imagination by showing Christ's action in this world. Place, which had been empyrean, was transferred to earthly reality, and absolute time was transferred to individual experience. The basis of art passed from idea to knowledge. The image no longer corresponded to a vision but to an experience. The search was no longer for the spatial figuration of eternity but for that of the world. Time and space were embodied not as absolute values but through the personal meditation of the artist and the collective memory of a social group. The elements of recollection were defined in terms of the laws governing the representational field and no longer according to the requirements of the cohesion of the myth.

It must now be established how far this enormous revolution had been accomplished by the beginning of the 15th century and what was the position of the artists of the Renaissance in relation to those of the 14th century. The cycle of mutations is infinitely slower than that of evolution. After a study of the deep changes that became manifest in 14th-century Italy, the question arises whether the contribution of the 15th century should in its turn be considered as development or transformation. The present aim is not to discuss the theories relating to the distant origins of realism and Western Humanism but radically to dispute the traditional view that in the years 1425-30 there occurred a sudden transformation in the forms and the spirit of Western cultures. In fact, the moment doubts are raised on the independently decisive influence of the process of bringing representational space into conformity with the secret codified some years later by Alberti, the work of Masaccio and his followers can no longer be considered either a necessary or a sufficient explanation of the Renaissance. Thus the question arises whether the obvious affinities that exist between the Tuscan and the Franco-Flemish experiments of the years 1390-1430 can be explained by the imitation of perspective methods, and where the precedence really lies. Even more pertinent is the question whether the international movement of these years coincided with a sudden cultural upsurge or whether, in the last analysis, it represented the culmination of a long-drawn-out development since Giotto. It should be remembered that Uccello painted himself in a famous predella (Paris, Louvre) together with Brunelleschi, Donatello, Manetti, and Giotto. Vasari and the academic age, however, promoted the idea of an artistic Renaissance that suddenly emerged fully armed from a wonderful formula in no way related to the esthetic or intellectual development of the preceding century.

It must be recognized, first, that the aim of art is the development of a true language, in other words, the establishment of an ordered system of signs and symbols that stabilize attitudes materializing the ephemeral aspects of the civilizing influence man wishes to exert upon the world, and second, that signs are significant because they coincide not with reality but with the totality of representations developed by a given society. If this is recognized, it would then seem that there is no break between Giotto and Masaccio and that in actual fact the 15th century in Europe constitutes the fulfillment of earlier attempts made predominantly in Italy since the time of Giotto.

In the course of the 14th century a whole series of space-time solutions appeared in Italy, none of which questioned the new principles of an art that was no longer attempting to materialize a vision but to define the efficacy and moral content of an action. One solution implied the opposition between the unity of the space painted and the plurality of the imaginary places. In Florence, for example, Pacino di Buonaguida depicted the Tree of Life (Florence, Acc.) growing up from the soil of the earth, the scene of the Fall, and rising into heaven, where Biblical personages sit enthroned in the hierarchic order established by the Church. Attached to the branches are episodes of a different temporal quality, absolute time being replaced by the relative time of human life. This work, therefore, summarizes human destiny by relating it to different spatial-temporal levels. In Siena there developed, from Simone Martini to Sassetta (qq.v.), the art of episodic narrative, through the use of representational material borrowed from all traditions but selected according to a limited number of values. These no longer referred to mystical qualities of the soul but determined the circumstantial settings of space and time — desert, town, countryside, and rock — that linked the two worlds of legend and reality. With the Lorenzettis (q.v.) there then appeared in Siena a direct description of the surrounding world. In Florence an iconography of salvation through works rather than through faith developed under the influence of the Dominicans. Certain rules for the linking of episodes may be distinguished; there exists a sort of rhetoric of narration in connected pictures. Certain types of composition recur with as much regularity as certain pictorial elements. The development of a new language can be observed, the creative effort being exerted on the level of both the invention of expressive elements and the linking of the episodes. In particular there evolved two types of representation that were destined to have the greatest success. One was the monumental composition like that by Andrea da Firenze in the Spanish Chapel in S. Maria Novella in Florence, where the various compositions suggest different places, some abstract, others pictorial, and where the Byzantine fiction of unitary and absolute space has entirely disappeared. The other was the elaborate decorative ensemble of medium size in which the saints are lined up in the panels of an altarpiece and the episodes are confined to the predella, thus maintaining the tradition exemplified by such works as Berlinghieri's *St. Francis* (VIII, PL. 181) in the Tuscan region. Here religious themes are visualized and projected for a specific public in imaginary acts (times) and episodes (places).

In the first half of the 14th century Italian artists used the repertory of pictorial objects that the school of Giotto had elaborated at the beginning of the century, using antique, Byzantine, and neorealist traditions. Toward the middle of the century a distinct evolution became apparent. A differentiation was established on other levels according to the nature of the subject. When Andrea da Firenze represented the life of St. Rainieri (Pisa, Campo Santo), he organized scenes in which everything was expressed through figures and accessories. Basically he was using a representational language identical with that of Franco-Flemish illumination: no background, distance, or evocation of a setting in any way different from that of contemporary life. The groups call to mind the realism of statuary, the great art of the time. In Spinello Aretino and Niccolò di Pietro Gerini picturesque settings make their appearance, but they still follow the Giottesque system of using nonrealistic but significant elements such as rocks, aediculas, etc. The insertion of several phases of the story into the same composition is, however, treated in a new way. The multiplicity of time, which at the beginning of the century had been expressed by the juxtaposition of separate scenes arranged around a central figure or theme, was thenceforth expressed by the articulation of the parts. This was still the method used by Masaccio and Masolino as well as by Gentile da Fabriano at the beginning of the 15th century.

At the same time, however, Andrea da Firenze used quite different methods in some of his compositions. In the Spanish Chapel of S. Maria Novella, the three great compositions covering the three walls utilize different methods of associating space and time: panoramic and unitary space with deep perspective, where everything converges on the central scene, in *The Crucifixion*; space without depth or illusionism in *The Triumph of St. Thomas Aquinas* (PL. 344), where the empyrean theme of Pacino di Buonaguida is taken up again, and the time and place are entirely abstract; the unfolding of a pictorial action across the surface of the fresco in *The Triumph of the Dominicans*. It is clear that the relation of time and space is here deliberately handled in such a way as to underline the complex possibilities of the picture. But it is also apparent that in Florence painters remained attached to strong artistic and intellectual traditions, from which even the greatest artists of the 15th century never freed themselves. This led to the linking of places to prototypes that were more symbolic than realistic and to the linking of time to moments of a legendary action defined by tradition and characterized by accessories evoking either the terms of a narrative or the ways of presenting the event paraliturgically. In all cases the event was related to a cycle of action foreign to the conditions of contemporaneous life and was placed in a uniform time. Only human life had any real temporal duration, the notion of a time determined by history being absent. This was still the stable world that, at every moment, concretized the thought of God.

This does not mean that the artists of this time were indifferent to their environment. The Biadaiolo Illuminator noted the busy spectacle of shops and market (VI, PL. 63), Andrea da Firenze painted the sermon and assassination of the 13th-century St. Peter Martyr (Florence, Spanish Chapel), and there were illustrations of chronicles. But clearly no direct relation was established between the thing seen and its representation. The aim of art was to establish values, traditions, beliefs, and lessons rather than to reproduce the spectacle of the world. More exactly, this second objective was limited to a small number of artists, many of whom were not Italian; their speculations, which suggested a complete reversal of the relations of space and time, were not accepted by the Western world as a whole because of the victorious resistance of 15th-century Italy.

As early as the middle of the 14th century in the Franco-Flemish world, which is considered to have been slower in its artistic development, original attempts were made to place organic series of pictures, revealing a new spirit, within nonabstract space and in nonlegendary time. It does not seem legitimate, however, to establish a connection between certain illustrations by the Paris circle of Jean Pucelle such as those of the Belleville Breviary (VI, PL. 315), probably dating from 1343, and the wonderful compositions of the Hours of the Maréchal de Boucicaut (Paris, Mus. Jacquemart-André, Ms. 2) and *Les Très Riches Heures du Duc de Berry* (Chantilly, Mus. Condé, IV, PL. 26; VI, PL. 65; IX, PLS. 137–140), both dating from the beginning of the 15th century. Certainly the idea of a realistic representation of, for example, the labors of the different months served as a basis for the great creations at the courts of the dukes. But once again, there is a misguided tendency to believe that it is the discovery of the theme that gives rise to pictorial innovation. In actual fact the representation of the labors of the months was a current theme in the decoration of cathedrals, and the Belleville Breviary did not in any way introduce a new concept of space-time relations in miniature painting. Its graphic style remained that of the Paris painters and did not establish a new relation between the image and the optical sensation, with the aim of representing not the external world but new social values. A new insight into the imaginary world of representational signs is to be found in the Boucicaut Hours and in *Les Très Riches Heures du Duc de Berry* in the relation that is established between the distant surroundings and the central scene and in the fact that a scene, based in this manner on a double level of actuality, refers solely to the pictorial quality of earthly life, without reference to any Gospel legend or any literary tradition. In *Les Très Riches Heures* the supernatural world of magic also finds a place with the figure of man at the center of the zodiac. The discovery of these new values did not lead to the complete rejection of pictorial and intellectual traditions; a new path was opened up, parallel to the old ones. Only very gradually does a real innovation transform a firmly constituted social group.

It would be arbitrary to try to interpret such works as the Boucicaut Hours with the intention of defining a single novel aspect. It is striking, on the contrary, to discover how many elements of this admirable work are to be found later in the most varied compositions. The Visitation scene, for example, reveals both a landscape with a single vanishing point and a group of figures suspended in a space that is foreign to the pictorial view of the world. The Coronation of the Virgin shows a similar group suspended in a space without scale, with an environment combining multiple elements, for example, the dais, which is related both to the alcove of the royal chamber in Pierre Salmon's *Réponses à Charles VI et Lamentation au roi sur son état* (X, PL. 77) and to the representations of the Trinity (Leningrad, Hermitage), of Jael and Sisera (known from a pen copy in the Landesmuseum in Brunswick, Germany), and of the Madonna and saints (pen copy in the Louvre), all three by the Master of Flémalle. However, the neutral background and the checkerboard floor in the Coronation of the Virgin are far from any attempt to reach a unity based on realistic vision. The Annunciation and St. Jerome are close to the Apocalypse of Louis I of Anjou (Angers, Mus. des Tapisseries) and to innumerable compositions based upon the architectural treatment, in oblique perspective for the most part, of a pictorial motif such as a throne, crib, bed, or the corner of a room. The dedication page foreshadows the divided composition of Masolino's *Founding of S. Maria Maggiore* (IX, PL. 374). The scene of the vigils of the dead is constructed on the exact principle of unitary perspective with a single vanishing point, while the Nativity and the Adoration of the Magi combine central vision with the suggestion of open space. Generally, the central episodes are detached and, so to speak, floating in a space that sometimes obeys the rules of perspective and sometimes is articulated according to the laws of the disposition of surfaces. It would be wrong to think that the deep connection between these different compositions is a particular way of seeing the world and of transposing it, following its own laws, onto a two-dimensional surface. What binds the episodes is, on the contrary, the intellectual elements that establish relations between places and times that are quite separate in nature. It does not follow that the works are unrealistic, artificial, or arbitrary in character. The ties of causality, according to which episodes and details combine in the memory to produce a satisfying total picture, have as much realistic value as the shifting reference to what is erroneously called the "seen object," which is simply the product of one of several possible visual combinations.

If the Boucicaut Hours may be regarded as one of the first masterpieces of modern painting, it is not because the painter has rendered certain details — the changing sky, light and shade, etc. — in an illusionistic manner but because he has set in properly differentiated relations fragments that are ordinarily isolated and alien to one another in visual experience. In other words, his results were achieved not through any following of normal operative vision but through his unaccustomed space-time combinations. It is a complete contradiction to present him as the pioneer of realism in the usual sense of the word. Certainly there is a realism of the imaginary, but its scale of values must be drawn not from a worldly scene that supposedly conforms to human reason but from the validity of arbitrary combinations, taking into account the knowledge and aspirations of a given society. This illusionism, the only one that plays any part in the domain of the arts, is not based on nature but on the experimental combining of elements.

The Renaissance. The study of 14th-century artistic developments shows that there is no foundation for the theories concerning realism in 15th-century painting, in the sense of the direct and faithful perception of a natural spectacle in which the artist and his public do not actively participate. The high quality of the art of the Van Eycks does not spring from the fact that it presented combinations of elements drawn bodily from reality following a method whose principles were furnished by the Italians. Indeed, this viewpoint involves a complete chronological paradox, since the Van Eycks were contemporaries of the Tuscan masters, while the unknown artist of the Boucicaut Hours, the Limbourgs, and the Master of Flémalle produced their masterpieces before Masolino, Masaccio, Donatello, and Brunelleschi. All this ideology derives from an academic interpretation of the art of 15th-century Italy and also from a surprising fidelity to the symbolist beliefs of the Middle Ages. The Italian and Franco-Flemish masters of the 15th century were great insofar as they introduced into painting not methods of mechanical or photographic reproduction or entirely arbitrary symbols, but a system based on the selection of elements from the totality of the experience and knowledge of their times.

In their belief that the illusionistic art of the 15th century arose out of a minute observation of nature, art historians have attempted to prove that the *taccuini* — the herbariums of the 14th century — had progressively led the artists of northern Italy to observe nature. It is not true that such attention to living natural details was first shown in Lombardy in the 14th century. As early as the 12th century, Gothic flora, particularly that of Notre-Dame in Paris, revealed interest in the smallest details of plant life. Of course, the plants in the *taccuini* are realistically represented, whereas on the Gothic capitals they are interpreted. But it would be sheer simplicity to believe that any painter, even a Pisanello, has ever painted the world as it really is. Visual "realism" is a modern doctrine, born of the difficulty that art historians find in examining the works of their time critically and appreciatively. Linear perspective does not give the painter the means of representing a fragment

of space realistically any more than the observation of detail provides him with the elements of a style. A painting of the 15th century is in no way made up of a series of realistic details grouped according to equally realistic optical laws. Illusionism does not arise from a greater or lesser degree of fidelity to reality. Painting is a thing of the mind, as Leonardo da Vinci said. The capacity for seeing and reproducing the elements observed in reality is common to all those who have an eye for observation just as others have an ear for music. It is as absurd to try to explain the style of Renaissance art through the presence, to be found in any age, of people with a gift for sketching as to attempt to explain Renaissance music by the precision of Josquin Deprès' musical ear.

The traditional explanation of the phenomenon of the Renaissance is based on the idea that the exterior world possesses a form that owes nothing to human intervention. The aim of art is then logically to discover the laws that permit the most faithful representation of the world, in other words, a realism based on knowledge. According to this thesis, Western societies in the 15th century rediscovered laws of which antiquity had already had a notion. Starting from a fragmentary approach, they progressively developed solutions that made possible the imitation of natural "microelements." They subsequently discovered the conceptual form of homogeneous and infinite space and rapidly constructed a representational system permitting the most faithful portrayal of the natural world. This traditional thesis is invalidated first by the impossibility of considering the whole merely as the sum total of the parts and second by another intellectual impossibility that must now be clarified.

Vision cannot be considered the product of a simple physiological activity: all representation is a cultural phenomenon. The fragments of a system can be incorporated in other systems and consequently cannot serve to characterize the system itself. Moreover, it is impossible to identify the image with the concept without careful analysis. The world is not a fixed datum to be interpreted from primary sources of information. A work of art denotes not something given but something conceived: the sign or symbol is not a substitute for reality but a means of approach and communication. The sign is determined not by the object but by perception. Schemes of thought coincide not with the total reality of the universe but with the approach to it. Their aim is to reveal not an absolute order but man's individual and social position. The image is distinct from both the object and the sign; it is situated in the imaginary and is an intermediary that partakes both of the nature of things and of the workings of the mind. Like mathematics, art develops a system of rules of deduction and combination that corresponds not to an innate faculty but to one particular type of activity. It strives to recognize the more or less stable and regular processes of optical perception, opening the way to an evaluation of probabilities. It founds styles on rough drafts or preliminary projects, aiming at establishing a causality rather than a faithful reflection of the original sensation. It is interested not in unique perceptions but in the repetitions of significant situations. Thus the aim of the artist is not to reproduce a spectacle in its phenomenological entirety but to constitute imaginary syntheses of elements drawn from various moments of experience — which are made present only by the memory — and inserted in a space that is inadequate for direct perception.

To illustrate this theory, an example can be taken from the period under discussion. The *Adoration of the Magi* by Gentile da Fabriano (Uffizi; VI, PLS. 84, 85) was the first great achievement of the new century south of the Alps. Usually it is considered as representing the legacy of the dying Middle Ages rather than the spirit of a new age, which is supposedly embodied in the art of Masaccio (q.v.) and the experiments of Brunelleschi (q.v.). However, the desire to attribute the great flowering of Italian art to a visual pseudorealism has led to the stressing of the relation between the meticulous details in the *Adoration of the Magi* and the sketchbooks both of Gentile himself and of his predecessors, such as Michelino da Besozzo and Giovannino de' Grassi, or those of his successor, Pisanello. Visual realism is considered by the critics such a universal solution that the minutely realistic observation in Gentile and the mathematical speculation on rationalized space of Brunelleschi are regarded as two aspects of a single tendency leading to the discovery of the intellectual laws of the universe. It is quite possible that an intellectual attitude may, in application, lead to methods that are seemingly distinct. The questionable point is whether either the integration of realistic details in the *Adoration of the Magi* or the speculation on mathematical space of Brunelleschi and Masaccio was the key to their inspiration and produced a visual realism that, in its universal validity, surpassed the limits of knowledge of their age.

In the complex composition of Gentile's *Adoration of the Magi* every detail is connected with a known model, or, more precisely, with a series of images in which each of the pictorial objects used has its function as an instrumental element of the language. The foreground on the left, the adoration proper, is a real synthesis of characteristic elements. The Virgin seated before the aedicula is to be found in Bartolo di Fredi and Taddeo Gaddi. Sketches of this motif exist, as well as more developed versions; it was known throughout the West and was apparently connected with the traditions of the *tableau vivant*. Adjoining the wall, where the little porch is a cross between the pictorial elements of house and cottage, is the grotto. Thus the artist has brought together the three variants of the traditional representation of the Nativity: grotto, manger, and dwelling. The synthesizing nature of the system is evident. Farther to the right, at the head of the procession, are the Magi, one of whom, the young prince, is the central figure in the picture. The composition develops from a central point through the careful linking of episodes that are connected by their meaning and differentiated by their style. It is impossible to grasp such a work at a single glance. Whereas the left side combines three formulas connected with the representation of an imaginary and ritual theme, the right side relates the picture to the contemporaneous world. The young prince is the exalted personification of youth in a society that was recovering from the terrible ravages of plague and internecine struggle. Military power is also exalted in the representation of the men of arms in the procession. The background of the picture, through which the procession winds its way, is full of episodes and pictorial elements: the town, castle, ship, and rock are all symbols communicating well-established messages.

Fifty years later, Cosimo the Elder had the walls of his private chapel decorated with another *Procession of the Magi* (VIII, PL. 193) by Benozzo Gozzoli (q.v.). This painting shows Cosimo's sons, clad in the lavish costumes of the times, riding toward the manger through a landscape closely related to that of Gentile. The scene unfolds in space over the walls of the chapel, but the imaginary route is identical with that enclosed within Gentile's frame. This demonstrates in the most absolute manner the role attributed to the temporal reading of a painting: men of the time reveled in the reading of pictures in which each detail was related to either a memory or an experience and in which an entire culture of chivalry was incorporated within the framework of contemporary life. The time and setting of a work expressed this plurality of the imaginary and the experience, of custom and aspiration. In no case did the picture refer to a homogeneous spectacle.

There can never be any fixed place or time in art, since there is no homogeneous place and time in thought. A representation arranged in such a way as to form an entirely coherent vision is unthinkable. The process of art does not consist in the ordering of elements grasped by the senses at a given moment and in a given form but in the realization of pictures, or organized systems, in which elements of the present, the past, and the future, of the real and the possible, of the visible and the virtual setting are associated. Permutations of elementary pictorial signs are intended not to give the spectator a more or less precise vision of a single spectacle but to multiply the organized combinations assimilated by the imagination to the innumerable spatial-temporal combinations that are made and unmade in the mind as soon as it selects and reorganizes raw perceptions — in other words, as soon as the senses, set in motion by contact with the universe, form spatial-temporal syntheses of reference and causality.

In reality it is not by multiplying the references to elements in the physical world that the analysis of a work of art of any kind can be deepened. It is necessary, on the contrary, to situate it in relation to the systems of values that predominate in a given human environment. The important factor is not the greater or lesser resemblance to the first impulse provoked by a phenomenon without any regular sequel but the mechanism that makes possible, within a single composition, the integration of elements originally alien to one another in space and time. In short, it is more interesting, as well as easier, to demonstrate the articulation of the narrative, the short cuts in thought that make the reading of a work possible in a way that is not rigidly fixed but is nonetheless oriented.

A study of the great compositions painted by Masaccio and Masolino (qq.v.) in Florence, Rome, and Castiglione Olona less than five years after Gentile's polyptych also shows that this problem of narrative technique, in other words, of space-time, is far more important than that of visual realism, in which the role of time is reduced by the existence of the alternative between the instantaneous and the infinite. For several centuries Masaccio has traditionally been considered the inventor of a new way of depicting the world, at the very moment when the Florentine theorists' speculation on space established the laws of a revival of the pictorial space of antiquity, which is also a form of realism based on knowledge. Alberti's treatise *Della pittura*, written about 1435, gave doctrinal form to a series of ideas that were widespread in the years 1420–40 in Humanist circles, particularly in Florence. With this treatise and the paintings of Masaccio and Masolino should be associated the famous life of Brunelleschi by Antonio Manetti, another cultured member of this group. It describes how Brunelleschi (q.v.), whose capacities as a theorist of architecture and spatial vision it is hardly necessary to emphasize, contrived two devices to study the representational possibilities of a spectacle hypothetically centered on a fixed station point that could, by a second hypothesis, be assimilated to the single eye of an observer placed in a chosen position (see XI, cols. 203–04, PL. 91). Later, especially after Vasari, it was deduced from this that certain Florentines in the years 1425–30 had defined the standard conditions of vision and that since that time art had found itself in possession of the necessary means for the exact representation of the external world.

In this way the tenet of visual realism originated, with a consequent weakening of the awareness of the role played by time in any perception of the visible world. However, no way has been found of demonstrating that the works of Masolino and Masaccio were conceived according to this unitary principle, in which space-time is replaced by a homogeneous space representing a world whose intrinsic form is quite independent of the completely relative values that an artist and his followers may strive to impose. *The Tribute Money* by Masaccio (IX, PL. 348), in the Brancacci Chapel, shows three episodes juxtaposed in a composition that has none of the qualities of space with a single vanishing point, axially constructed in relation to a fixed station point. The same applies to the Masolino fresco opposite, which represents St. Peter healing a cripple and raising Tabitha (IX, PL. 374). Here, on either side of a pictorial space suggesting a Florentine square, are inserted constructions serving as frames for the New Testament scenes, which are entirely foreign to the space and time in which the passing Florentines are moving. Legendary and present time coexist quite independently in a composition whose only unity is an imaginary one conditioned by knowledge and not by perception. The frescoes of the Brancacci Chapel are painted to be seen from a point about a third of the way down the chapel. There is therefore a unitary spatial arrangement, but only in the combination of the subjects, each one of them being differentiated. This shows that the work was conceived to be read in stages, the general impression being based on values distinct from those which make the parts intelligible.

There are, on the other hand, a number of other works by Masaccio and Masolino in which the hypotheses codified a little later in the treatises of Alberti play the principal role. An example is Masaccio's *Trinity* (IX, PL. 345). It should, however, be noted that the central figures of God the Father and Christ are here represented without foreshortening and that, if the architectural framework is traced out according to the rules of perspective and the single vanishing point, the placing of the figures against the receding background is differentiated. *The Founding of S. Maria Maggiore*, by Masolino (IX, PL. 374), offers a good example of landscape construction according to the rules of the single vanishing point, but it is clear that these rules concern only the lower part of the composition and that the upper part is based on a different esthetic system, which is essential to the contrast between heaven and earth, in other words, to the fundamental meaning of the picture. At S. Clemente in Rome some of Masolino's compositions show an attempt to apply rigorously the principles of linear perspective as codified by Alberti, for example, *The Death of St. Ambrose* or *St. Catherine and the Philosophers* (IX, PL. 378). Other paintings, however, are constructed on entirely different principles, the episodes being arranged against neutral backgrounds on the basis of their logical connection rather than their physical position in the visible space. *The Crucifixion* (X, PL. 484) is an example of panoramic composition that compels the eye to sweep across the entire painting: to the background vanishing point it opposes the mobile station point of the viewer.

It would be completely arbitrary to present the experiments of Brunelleschi and the theories of Alberti as reflecting the regular practice of contemporaneous painters. There is no doubt that these theories were known to painters like Masaccio, Masolino, Filippo Lippi (PL. 113), Angelico, Uccello, and Piero della Francesca (qq.v.), who sometimes used them to obtain special effects. But it cannot be maintained that these methods account for the essential forms of the art of 15th-century Italy. The existence of widespread speculation on the dimensions and unitary character of a homogeneous, infinitely divisible space that could be integrated into a Euclidean geometrical system is beyond discussion. However, it was a trend, both theoretical and empirical, which artists considered with a mixture of admiration and mistrust and which they did not follow exclusively. Between 1474 and 1478, Piero della Francesca wrote a treatise on perspective, *De prospectiva pingendi*, but it is obvious that he considered it a theoretical method that made it possible to calculate the parts of the composition but did not necessarily supersede all other methods. Throughout the 15th century in Italy the importance of the foreground, where the main figures have a plastic value of the first order, is at least equal to that of linear perspective. This tradition is certainly not negligible, since it is linked with the great works of Renaissance sculptors, particularly Michelangelo. On his return from Italy toward the middle of the century Fouquet sometimes used formulas deriving from Alberti's principles of unitary, immobile, and atemporal space; but he too considered them as representing merely one of several possible hypotheses. Moreover, he sometimes practiced a subtle organization of the composition that implied far greater visual realism, since, like Leonardo da Vinci, he acknowledged the influence of the curvature of the eyeball upon man's objective grasp of the world.

The theories traditional for generations in the academies have imposed a tendentious interpretation of the artistic developments of the Renaissance. This has given rise to a belief in the purely spatial character of representational art, and this belief has led historians to neglect everything in painting that belongs either to the field of time or to that of forms. It is impossible, however, to explain the development of visual art in 15th-century Italy through the supposed discovery of a procedure that facilitates the transfer of spatial arrangements, drawn bodily from those of the world of optical sensation, onto a two-dimensional wall or panel. The great transformation of art that occurred in the time of Van Eyck and Masaccio cannot be associated with the discovery of a system that does not involve the whole relation between man and the universe. It is not on the basis of the perception and development of purely spatial signs that one of the highest achievements of modern civilization was realized.

The modern period. In modern times, just when the diffusion of information is reaching a culmination, a radical change is taking place in forms of communication. Although nearly everyone now knows how to read, the number of people who are capable of studying a text and fully grasping its substance has decreased. The cycle that opened at the beginning of the 15th century with the multiplication of texts and later with Gutenberg's work is now closing. At the same time, the image as conceived and developed by those generations is ceasing to satisfy present needs. The image is never a substitute for the word but rather its complement. A civilization creates its spoken language and its visual language simultaneously. The crisis of contemporary art is evidence enough that a representational language can no more be adapted to the needs of all generations than can a verbal language or a system of mathematical thought.

This does not mean that from the end of the 14th century to the end of the 19th the same representational language reigned undisputed in the West, only then to disintegrate in a few decades. There is no doubt, however, that for five centuries invention remained within a certain structure, respecting a specific space-time relation. The Middle Ages respected the notion of a time in a way absolute and of a space determined by the structures of a world in conformity with the attributes of a divine will made accessible to man through revelation. The succeeding centuries respected a representational convention according to which the spatial setting of experience is apprehensible by the senses and reveals the qualities of a matter divisible, three-dimensionally, into surfaces and solids that can be transferred onto two-dimensional canvases, modeled by sculptors, and assembled by architects. Art became descriptive of a universe reduced to anthropomorphic norms. It was no longer God but nature that was humanized. An inventory was made of a world created for human societies, in terms of their knowledge, needs, and aspirations.

As long as beliefs and conventions prevailed over experience, nothing disturbed either the intellectual or the representational systems through which the exploration of the planet and the diffusion of ancient and medieval culture were accomplished. During this period the setting was "personalized," as it were. It was no longer conceived as the fixed scene of actions whose value was based on a uniform and universal law, but as the theater of human actions adapted to increasingly differentiated circumstances. Finally, the descriptive inventory of the planet, which had been explored in all its length and breadth, had nothing left to yield. At the same time man discovered his ability to modify the world. Renaissance man had attempted to assimilate the accumulated knowledge of the ancient world; 19th-century man became Faustian in his desire to impose his own will upon the universe.

The modern break with the traditional concept of space is no idle aspiration. Renaissance space-time could apparently have served as a framework for a culture enlarged to include traditions other than the Christian and the Greco-Roman had artists, on the basis of experience, not transformed the mechanism of the selective recording of optical sensations and the processes for articulating these sensations on a two-dimensional artistic screen. For a long time it was believed that impressionism (q.v.) consisted only in a modification of the use of color. The avant-garde painters, it was held, simply abandoned lines and contours in favor of a blurred vision whose sole object was to register the ephemeral and capricious effects of light. On this basis it was very difficult to explain the links between painters like Manet and Degas on the one hand and Monet and Sisley (qq.v.) on the other. In the end, impressionism was reduced to a short-lived formalistic fashion. The work of Cézanne and Gauguin (qq.v.) was excluded from the movement and even presented as a reaction. The result was an uncertain and even contradictory concept of the development of modern art.

There is still no clear perception of the link that has existed for a century between movements that are generally considered in the light of a disintegration of traditional artistic experience rather than as indications of a new artistic consciousness. Impressionism was not based simply on a subtler rendering of colored vision. Manet and Cézanne as well as Monet and Degas obviously rejected traditional academic practices; but what really bound them together was a positive doctrine that far exceeded mere techniques. For them the aim of art was to transfer onto canvas not a thing seen but a thing apprehended. They abandoned the idea that there exists in nature a series of objects corresponding to a nomenclature identical with our own and substituted an art based on intellectual perception for an art that presented a space supposedly ruled by the laws of Euclid. It thus becomes evident that Manet and Cézanne, Monet, Degas, and Gauguin were pursuing a common aim. What seems to be a succession of avant-garde movements that criticized and destroyed the experience of the past was in reality a great movement toward the intellectualization of all representational values. Space became an attribute of thought and no longer of matter, and in this evolution a new relation between space and time was established.

The representational art of the Renaissance drew on a double repertory of elements: nature insofar as it was subject to human control, and a collective memory composed of elements derived from a few limited sectors of history. The extension of the sectors of nature and history accessible to the painter's imagination has not played a decisive role in the great artistic revolution of the 19th and 20th centuries, any more than speculation on color and the fractioning of light. The vocabulary of pictorial language has grown, but its principles have remained unchanged. The awareness of pandemonium has added nothing to the system, and all those who, in the course of the 20th century, have tried to renew art by adding to its elements of information have succeeded only in spreading academicism.

That which, on the contrary, has assured the complete renewal of pictorial experience, in the field of time as in that of space, is the transference into the mind of the field of observation of the outside world. Anecdotes and events have lost their interest for the painter; gradually he has become interested solely in the possibility of conferring duration upon the configurations that he fixes on his canvas, no longer with the intention of providing the spectator with a double of the universe but as a testimony of his permanent efforts to find, in the shifting succession of his passive perceptions, elements of reference to be ordered in a way that suggests his rationality rather than external stimulus.

This mutation in the representational system of Western societies is undoubtedly similar to that of the 14th and 15th centuries. Both involved the adaptation of representational processes to the new values of a changing society. In both this was achieved through the modification of the relations between space and time, and the nature of the change was determined not by a greater fidelity to nature or by the discovery of more refined techniques but by the desire to satisfy new demands. In the Middle Ages a spectacle was judged in terms of actions and according to a scale of minutely gauged moral values. During the Renaissance the function of visual art was no longer to illustrate and justify a code of conduct but to explore the universe, nature having gradually taken the place of the gods. Finally, modern man has begun to think not in terms of maxims and legendary actions but in terms of the physical laws of the universe. No longer content to describe the different aspects of nature, he wishes to determine its laws. His predominant interest is the confrontation of phenomena — as they reach his consciousness through the filter of his senses — with the physical impulses that produce them. Whether mathematician, psychologist, ethnologist, or artist, he is no longer concerned with the concretizing of a morally ordered hierarchy of beings and objects where time and space are merely secondary contingencies, time being absolute and space a form of conceptualized extension. Nor is his present role to describe a universe whose bodies have the same appearance and the same meaning for both creature and creator, where time is historical and determined partly by material movements and partly by human actions, and where space is identified with Euclidean geometry, adapted to the activities and representations of Western man in the course of his exploration of the planet. Henceforth the aim of art is to give man one means, among others, of selecting from visual raw material those elements of reference which, once they have been isolated, can combine with one another to form ordered

syntheses. No more than in the past is art a reduced copy of nature: it remains a debate on the level of the imaginary, and it reveals more about the value judgments of an individual and his environment than about the configuration of the universe at a given moment.

CONCLUSION. The object of this study has been to establish the nature of the relations that, in a representational system, necessarily associate space and time. An attempt has been made to demonstrate that it was not by extending the art of meticulous reproduction from a blade of grass to the evocation of distant horizons, or by setting the product of raw sensations in a geometric frame prefabricated according to the dimensions of the universe and endowed like it with Euclidean coordinates, or by singling out positive elements drawn from the observation of mystical values that the Renaissance artists replaced one representational system by another. For the succeeding five centuries illusionism was based not on any of these factors but on the articulation of spatial values drawn from different moments of an individual's life and correlated with other values that were also spatial but referred to the experience of other men and other societies, who transmitted them through verbal as well as pictorial traditions. In other words, an illusionism of the imaginary replaced the illusionism of vision.

The transition from the Middle Ages to the Renaissance can also be explained not by the refinement of techniques and the senses but by a transformation in human relations. Knowledge ceased to be confined to events chosen by clerics in order to justify forms of conduct on the basis of a historical reconstruction of the concept of human destiny. When new series of actions, which had remained alive in the collective memory of society, began to attract interest, and when doubts arose as to the absolute unity of the human condition on the grounds of its variability according to time and place, the disruption of the medieval representational system resulted. Instead of the portrayal of a few standard situations universally determining human conduct, an inventory of memorable events was undertaken as well as a description of man's physical and social environment. The notion of diversity led to the multiplication of episodes as well as of objects. The simple relation of times and places ceased to be considered satisfactory the moment men enriched their knowledge of facts and events by assuming control of their own destiny. The result was necessarily a multiplication of the possible relations between immediate spatial perceptions and later temporal judgments, to which images give a causal value. The aim of art is not to record but to justify. Consequently, the historical study of the art of 15th-century Europe leads to a comparative study of the usages and values of the different social groups.

The study of space-time does not reveal qualities of matter but historical structures of experience. Of course all human experience, if it is to be valid, must preserve some links with reality; but this reality is on the level of perception and not of expression. In this sense the distinction of space and time corresponds to the twofold movement of differentiation and assimilation that characterizes all thought but not necessarily all nature. It seems just as legitimate to seek, in the analysis of esthetic phenomena, information regarding the human mind and society, as it is hazardous to presuppose a concordance between the mechanisms of thought and the laws of nature.

Consequently, by studying space and time in the history of the visual arts it is certainly possible to acquire a better knowledge of images, from both the artistic and the psychological point of view, but not to define the structure of the cosmos, since the object of art is not to produce miniature replicas of nature but to define human modes of behavior and interpretation. Every image is a fiction and therefore necessarily associates elements drawn from the present with others drawn from memory. Thus it becomes evident that one of the fundamental characteristics of the artistic image is its capacity for unifying elements of different origins and possessing different kinds of reality. This is one of the reasons visual art cannot be explained in terms of its adhesion to immediate reality. In the final analysis, every image implies not only a combination of temporal and spatial values but also an integration of elements fixed in relation to individual as well as collective experience. Whether spatial or temporal, the elements of the pictorial sign are largely drawn from the common fund of collective memory. A work is created only when an individual, the artist, adds some new principle of identification or some new operative suggestion to previous elements of reference. The introduction of an entropy, or complementary element, into any system will, of course, upset in their totality all the former relations of the parts.

The study of art demands an awareness that the individuality or form of objects is dependent on internal laws that are not fixed but discontinuous. Nor should there be any confusion between duration (which is the undefined permanence of a form) and time (which, like space, is a constituent attribute of this form). Space refers to the present structure of the thing extended, and time refers not to its permanence but to those of its constituent elements that are drawn from memory, that is, to successions of ideas that have already combined with others in the past. This is why, in the last analysis, the most apparent specificity of plastic form lies in space.

A representational object is not something stable possessing a definitive meaning. A work of art exists as such only for certain groups of individuals; in spite of its spatial character, it can exist only in time. It is necessarily composed of several elements belonging, as has just been said, to different moments of history; yet among these elements there are inevitably, in every spatialized system, a small number that condition the significance of all the others. It is to these elements, which act as a kind of catalyst, that reference should be made in order to understand and explain how systems possessing several spatial and temporal dimensions are finally integrated in an image or object whose extension is, by definition, limited to the present but which refers to many other experiences. Some of these may already have been fixed in a spatial dimension, while the reality of others may still be confined to the imagination.

In any image, time and space converge, and there is also a synthesis of the time that represents the artist's individual experience and of that which represents the collective experience of a social group. This is why deciphering is a necessary part of the appreciation of any work of art. First the spectator must try to analyze the pictorial field before him and compare its forms with his own selective experience. Then he must try to attach each of the constituent elements of the composite whole before his eyes to the fragmentary signs and symbols that have developed in his memory, not to the spectacle automatically supplied by the universe. It is not always easy for him to recognize the system of information and comprehension to which each of the elements adopted belongs. This means that no immediate and total perception of a work of art is really possible and that every work refers to a culture, not to nature. Any active reconstitution of a pictorial composition therefore involves replacing the representational signs in a space and time different from the space and time that allowed the artist to integrate his perceptions and his visual and mental information in a unified system. Hence an absolutely faithful perception of a work of art is as impossible as a direct perception of nature; hence, too, every pictorial sign takes its place in variable schemes of representation, which establish a dialogue between participants who are separated by time, space, and knowledge. Hence, finally, in a representational work, the whole, with its synthesis of diverse space and time, is more significant and more stable than the constituent elements.

Pierre FRANCASTEL

BIBLIOG. H. Minkowski, Raum und Zeit, Gesammelte Abhandlungen (ed. D. Hilbert), Leipzig, Berlin, 1911; O. Strnad, Einiges Theoretische zur Raumgestaltung, D. K. und Dekoration, XLI, 1918, pp. 39–68; H. R. Butler, Painter and Space, New York, 1923; L. von Weiher, Der Innenraum in der holländischen Malerei des 17. Jahrhunderts, Würzburg, 1937; H. Jantzen, Über den kunstgeschichtlichen Raumbegriff, SbMünchen, 1938, 5, pp. 1–44; M. S. Bunim, Space in Medieval Painting and the Forerunners of Perspective, New York, 1940; J. Pešina, Tektonický prostor a architektura u Giotta, Prague, 1945; W. M. Ivins, Art and Geometry, Cambridge, Mass., 1946; A. Berkman, Art and Space, New York, 1949; D. Frey, Raum und Zeit in der Kunst der afrikanisch-eurasiaschen Hochkulturen, Wiener Jhb. für Kg., XXVI–XXVII, 1949, pp. 173–288; P. Francastel, Peinture et société, Lyons, 1951 (bibliog.); Nouvelles conceptions de l'espace (XXᵉ siècle, N.S., 2), Paris, 1952; W. Lotz, Das Raumbild in der italienischen Architekturzeichnung der Renaissance, Mitt. der kunsthist. Inst. in Florenz, VII, 1953–56, pp. 193–226; H. Landolt, El espacio en la arquitectura barroca, Anales Buenos Aires Univ. Nac. Inst. de arte americano e investigaciones estéticas, 9, 1956, pp. 53–69; R. D. Martienssen, The Idea of Space in Greek Architecture, Johannesburg, 1956; H. Sedlmayr, Der Ruhm der Malkunst: Jan Vermeer "De schilderconst," Festschrift für H. Jantzen, Berlin, 1956, pp. 169–77; J. White, The Birth and Rebirth of Pictorial Space, London, 1957; B. Zevi, Architecture as Space (trans. M. Gendel), New York, 1957; C. Lapicque, Essais sur l'espace, l'art et la destinée, Paris, 1958; H. van Lier, Les arts de l'espace, 2d ed., Tournai, 1960; Construction de l'espace (XXᵉ siècle, N.S., 18), Paris, 1962; S. Giedion, Space, Time and Architecture, 4th ed., Cambridge, Mass., 1962; K. Badt, Raumphantasien und Raumillusionen, Cologne, 1963. See also the bibliogs. for ARCHITECTURE; CINEMATOGRAPHY; HUMAN FIGURE; PERSPECTIVE; PROPORTION; SYMBOLISM AND ALLEGORY; ZOOMORPHIC AND PLANT REPRESENTATIONS.

Illustrations: PLS. 105–116.

SPAIN. Spain (España), which occupies the greater part of the Iberian Peninsula and includes the Balearic and Canary islands, is bounded on the north by France and the Bay of Biscay, on the east and south by the Mediterranean Sea, and on the west by Portugal and the Atlantic Ocean. An important center of prehistoric artistic manifestations, Spain, because of its geographic proximity to Africa, served as a bridge for the influx of northern African cultures into Europe; of particular importance was the megalithic civilization, which flourished especially in Portugal (q.v.) and had extensive repercussions in the cultural evolution of central and western Europe as far as the Baltic countries. Spain has experienced several colonizations (Phoenician, Greek, Roman) and invasions (Visigothic, Moslem), which have left many remarkable traces. The nucleus of the modern state was established in 1492, when the Catholic Monarchs conquered the Arabs, who had ruled most of Spain, except for the northwesternmost part, since the 8th century.

SUMMARY. Cultural and artistic periods (col. 204): *Prehistory and protohistory; The ancient colonizations; Hispano-Roman and Early Christian periods; Visigothic influences; Asturias; Mozarabic and Hispano-Arabic styles; The Romanesque and the Gothic; The modern period; Folk art.* Monumental centers (col. 214): *Madrid; Castilla la Nueva; Extremadura; León; Galicia; Asturias; Castilla la Vieja; Provincias Vascongadas (Basque Provinces); Navarra; Aragón; Cataluña; Balearic Islands; Valencia; Murcia; Andalucía; Canary Islands; Gibraltar; Andorra.*

CULTURAL AND ARTISTIC PERIODS. *Prehistory and protohistory.* The Aurignacian period (about the 15th millennium B.C.) produced engravings and paintings in the Cantabrian area (the caves of La Clotilde de Santa Isabel and that of El Castillo, XI, PL. 274, both in Santander), in the center (Los Casares cave at Riba de Saelices, Guadalajara), and in the south of Spain (the cave of La Pileta at Benaoján, Málaga). Engravings on bone found in the caves of Altamira (Santander) and the small plaques of the cave of El Parpalló (Valencia) belong to the Solutrean period (about the 12th millennium B.C.). The art of the Magdalenian period (about the 10th millennium B.C) is more abundant and of finer quality. This art was predominantly zoomorphic, like that of the preceding periods, and reached its highest expression in the paintings of the caves of Altamira (XI, PLS. 268, 277, 278, 281, 282) and La Peña de Candamo near San Román de Candamo (Oviedo), with many representations of deer, bison, horses, and other fauna, painted forcefully, colorfully, and naturalistically. There is a profound contrast between the monumental style of this Cantabrian art and that of the paintings of the Spanish Levant region, which came later and were characterized by the abundance of small-scale human figures represented in a schematic manner, with a strong narrative sense and rhythmic feeling in the composition. Admirable examples of this art have been found in Cogul (Lérida); in Albarracín (XI, PL. 289), Calapatá, and Alcañiz (Teruel); in Morella la Vieja (XI, PL. 286), Ares del Maestre, and Albocácer (Castellón de la Plana); in Bicorp (Valencia; XI, PL. 288); in Boniches de la Sierra and Villar del Humo (Cuenca); and in Alpera and Minateda (Albacete). Although these paintings are later than the Magdalenian period, their exact date is still uncertain.

During the Neolithic Age that followed, a new transformation in style occurred: the earlier stylized figures became ideographs and signs that distorted the artistic motifs by arbitrary, perhaps symbolic additions. The paintings of La Graja, Peñarrubia, and Aldeaquemada (Jaén); of Almadén (Ciudad Real) and Casas Viejas (Cádiz); and of many other caves scattered throughout the south belong to this period, as do some small idols in stone or on bone plaques, with schematic drawings. Pottery also appeared, decorated with incisions or fingerprint designs that culminated in bell-shaped (campaniform) vessels with rich decoration; these vases were contemporary (ca. 2000 B.C.) with the megalithic architecture of the dolmens that spread from Andalucía and Algarve to the rest of the Peninsula. Outstanding examples of these structures are those at Menga (IX, PL. 431), Viera, and Romeral, in Antequera (Málaga); at Castilleja de Guzmán (Sevilla) and Soto (Huelva); at the settlement of Los Millares (Almería); and, during the decline of this culture, at the settlement of El Argar (Almería). Well into the Bronze Age (from ca. 1500 B.C.) an interesting culture developed in the Balearic Islands, with a wide variety and large number of monuments: settlements, talayoti, navetas, taulas, and other types (IX, PL. 406). The best examples have been found in Lluchmayor and Artá (Mallorca) and in Ciudadela, Alayor, Mahón, and Ferrerias (Menorca; IX, PL. 406); such fine objects of art as the bulls' heads from Costitx (Madrid, Mus. Arqueol. Nac.) also belong to this culture. (See also MEDITERRANEAN PROTOHISTORY; PREHISTORY.)

The ancient colonizations. From the 11th century B.C. the Mediterranean coasts and the south of Spain were visited by Phoenician sailors, who established colonies and commercial settlements there (Cádiz, Adra, Málaga) because they were particularly interested in obtaining metals (see PHOENICIAN-PUNIC ART). Some remains of these settlements have survived, such as the hypogea, the anthropoid sarcophagus, and some jewelry from Cádiz. The Carthaginians settled on Ibiza in the middle of the 7th century B.C.; abundant information on this culture is provided by the necropolis of Puig d'es Molins, where thousands of graves have preserved a vast quantity of sculptures, ceramics, and glassware (archaeological museums of Madrid, Barcelona, and Ibiza). Mention should also be made of the examples of goldwork from La Aliseda (Cáceres). The Greeks also reached Spain and in the 7th century founded settlements along the route to Tartessos; they founded Ampurias in the middle of the 6th century, followed by other colonies along the Mediterranean coast that survived until Roman times. Finds from these Greek settlements, although scarcer than those from the Punic ones, are of finer quality; they include some architectural remains of Ampurias, bronze and marble sculptures, ceramics, and metalwork.

The Iberian culture still remains one of the great unsolved problems of Hispanic art, despite the numerous remains that have been preserved from it. Its architecture, which seems to have been created without a knowledge of the classical elements of building, is known from excavations and text references to cities and towns: Galera, Toya, and Baza in Andalucía; La Bastida de Mogente, Liria, Elche, and Alcoy in Valencia; Ampurias, Tarragona, and Mataró in Cataluña (Catalonia); and Calaceite and Azaila in Aragón. The sculpture shows a high level of artistic development, with many small figurines in bronze; highly stylized ex-votos; the series of stone figures of priestesses and women making offerings found in Cerro de los Santos (Albacete; IX, PL. 408); figures of real and mythical animals that are often startling in their naturalism, such as the lion of Baena and the "Bicha de Balazote" (IX, PL. 408); the figured reliefs of Osuna; and many sculptures of varying origins. The local tradition mixed with the Phoenician, Carthaginian, and Greek artistic influences until it became an art with a personality of its own, which attained characteristics and refinements comparable to those of ancient Greece and which culminated in the "Lady of Elche" (IX, PL. 409). Another subject of great interest is the pottery painted in ochre found in the necropolises of this culture all along the Mediterranean coastlines, from the Pyrenees to Andalucía. A limited number of typical geometric motifs are distinguished from an extremely varied figural and floral repertory characterized by extraordinary spontaneity. The scenes portrayed on the Liria pottery, like the hunting scenes on the vase of Ampurias (IX, PL. 410) and on the urns of Callosa and Murcia, appear to be the direct successors of the prehistoric paintings in narrative style from the same region. Weapons, belt plaquettes, and metalwork complete the features of this culture, which acquired a greater importance because of its persistence through the long period of Roman colonization, because of the fact that characteristics of the various regions began to appear, and because of its relationship to the art of the Hispano-Celtic tribes. (See also MEDITERRANEAN, ANCIENT WESTERN.)

The art of the Celtic tribes developed between the 6th century B.C. and the Roman conquest. It was characterized by a more schematic linear style than that of the Iberian culture, while at the same time it revealed a lower and poorer cultural level. Three groups can be distinguished in this art: (1) the central plateau group, with settlements found in the provinces of Ávila, Salamanca, Zamora, and Burgos, such as Las Cogotas, with its large necropolis that has yielded numerous finds; (2) the Celtic-Iberian group, which was of a higher cultural level because of its proximity to the Aragonese-Iberian area

and which has offered the important pottery series found in Numancia (near mod. Soria) — this pottery had painted, sometimes polychromatic figures and decorative designs that surpass all Iberian art in their schematism; and (3) the Galician-Portuguese group, with numerous ruins of forts (Briteiros, Santa Tecla, Coaña) containing houses built on a round plan — this group displayed a preference for gold jewelry (this metal being abundant in the region at that time) such as the diadems, and torques (V, PL. 183) in the Museo Arqueológico Nacional, Museo Lázaro Galdiano, and Instituto de Valencia de Don Juan, of Madrid. (See also CELTIC ART.)

Hispano-Roman and Early Christian periods. The Roman domination, which lasted for more than six hundred years, beginning with the arrival of the Scipios in 219 B.C., completely changed the face of Spain, which from Augustus's time was divided into three large provinces: Tarraconensis, with its capital in Tarraco (mod. Tarragona); Baetica, with Corduba (mod. Córdoba) as its capital; and Lusitania, whose capital was Augusta Emerita (mod. Mérida). In an initial phase, until Augustus's death (A.D. 14), Romanization proceeded at an even pace, and the impressive monuments of Mérida, Tarragona, and Segovia (VII, PL. 244) were built, astounding the native population. During the period between Nero (54–68) and Trajan (98–117) the Hispanic peoples, with the exception of those in the northwest, were fully absorbed by Rome. In architectural decoration and in the popular portrait-sculptures in Beatica and Lusitania, Hispanic characteristics began to be recognizable. Between the reign of Hadrian (117–38) and that of Aurelian (270–75) building attained its greatest expansion, with luxurious villas in the countryside and costly constructions in the cities. With the Frankish invasion (257), however, a number of cities were laid waste; as the alarm spread throughout the land, new defensive walls rose, architecture lost its solidity, and sculpture grew poorer in quality. Finally, after Diocletian (305), due to the conflict between paganism and Christianity and between antiquity and the Middle Ages, art underwent changes that marked a prelude to the end of Roman art, which was finally swept away before the Germanic invasion in the early part of the 5th century.

The works of art preserved from this period in Spain are numerous and varied. Among the many public works there are road networks with bridges (Mérida, Alcántara, Alconétar, Salamanca), aqueducts (Tarragona, Segovia, Mérida, Sádaba), ports (Ampurias), lighthouse towers (Torre de Hércules in La Coruña), and irrigation systems (of Proserpina and of Cornalvos, in Mérida). There were military camps (Numancia); city walls of various types (Carmona, Barcelona, Zaragoza, Coria, Ampurias, Lugo, Tarragona) with their towers and gates; forums, tribunals, and market places (Tarragona, Ampurias, Clunia); fountains (Belo) and wells (Itálica, Mérida); monumental arches with one to three bays (Mérida, Bará, Cabanes, Medinaceli, Caparra, Martorell); temples (several in Tarragona and in Mérida, Belo, Barcelona, Vich, Sagunto, Itálica); necropolises (Carmona, Cádiz, Barcelona) and tombs (Fabara; Sádaba and Tarragona, VII, PL. 243; Barcelona; Mérida); baths (Itálica, Mérida, Barcelona, Badalona, Alange, Caldas de Montbuy); theaters (Mérida, Ronda la Vieja, Belo, Osuna, Sagunto, Clunia), amphitheaters (Itálica, Mérida, Tarragona, Ampurias), and circuses (Mérida, Toledo, Tarragona, Sagunto). There are many ruins of city buildings (Belo, Itálica, Córdoba, Ampurias, Mérida, Tarragona) and of country villas (Tossa, Navatejera, Cuevas de Vera, Fraga), as well as some pottery workshops and meat-curing houses.

Spanish sculpture of the Roman period presents many problems that have not yet been solved. In the beginning, Hellenistic works were copied, of which there are still some examples, especially in Baetica. Representations of classical deities were varied and numerous (Hercules, Venus, Diana, Bacchus, Jupiter, Ganymede, Mercury, and Pluto) — many of them found at Itálica and Mérida — in addition to Eastern gods (Isis, Mithras, Chronos). Portraiture is of particular interest in Hispano-Roman sculpture. There were portraits of emperors (Augustus, Trajan, Tiberius, Hadrian) and of other personages, usually clad in togas; those of popular type, although coarser, reveal strong racial characteristics. There are not many sarcophagi (Ager, Huesca, Barcelona, Tarragona, Madrid) or decorative reliefs; the capitals are like those commonly found elsewhere in the classical world, as are the altars. There are simple funerary reliefs, with interesting scenes from daily life; wall paintings; and an extensive series of mosaics showing various techniques and styles (Zaragoza, Barcelona, Itálica, Ampurias, Tarragona, Toledo). Glassware, ceramics, and gold and bronze works complete the varied panorama of the art of the Roman period in Spain. (See also HISPANO-ROMAN ART.)

There is almost no monument or archaeological trace of the first centuries of Christian culture in Spain. Not until the 4th century are such monuments found, and even then and in the following century architectural remains are rare (Centcelles, Mérida). Sculpture is better represented, with several statues, such as those of the Good

Shepherd (Sevilla and Almería), and many sarcophagi with historiated reliefs of varied iconography (Gerona, Tarragona, Barcelona, Zaragoza, Toledo). Most of them show a close relation to models common throughout the rest of the Western Roman Empire, and some of them even come from workshops outside Spain, but there are some late ones (5th cent.) that are undoubtedly of local origin (Tarragona). Mosaics were also important (Tarragona, Huesca, Mallorca). Some of them reflect North African artistic tendencies, especially in the 5th century, which marked the close of this brief artistic phase.

Visigothic influences. Under the Visigothic domination art in Spain was marked by two well-defined artistic tendencies. The North African one, which had already developed in the Early Christian period, was prevalent in Baetica and in church architecture of the 5th and 6th centuries; the other, Byzantine, tendency increased its influence in the 6th century and especially in the 7th, finally taking

(Palencia; XI, PL. 316) and in Quintanilla de las Vinas (Burgos) are built on the basilica plan, while those in San Pedro de la Mata (Toledo), in Bande (Orense), and in San Pedro de la Nave (Zamora; XI, PL. 316) are built on the Greek-cross plan. San Pedro de la Nave is perhaps the finest in its architectural forms, construction, and decoration (XI, PL. 321).

The sculpture of the period was of a merely secondary and decorative kind, subordinate to architecture; stone carvings with simple geometric decoration predominated, such as the socle in the Great Mosque of Córdoba and the friezes in several of the above-mentioned churches. There were few representations of human figures. Several sarcophagi of local workmanship have survived, decorated in Eastern style (Burgos, Écija, Alcaudete, Oviedo) with figures in relief. There was no well-defined and regular development of the capitals derived from classical prototypes, and other types, of Eastern origin, developed side by side with them. There are some interesting examples

Spain, principal medieval centers. *Key:* (1) Modern national boundaries; (2) Visigothic monuments; (3) Asturian centers; (4) Moslem centers; (5) Mozarabic centers; (6) Romanesque monuments; (7) early Gothic monuments; (8) later Gothic monuments.

shape in a national art that extended over almost the entire Peninsula, so that the 7th century, which was one of the darkest periods in Europe, marked a high point in Spain. In the architecture of the 5th and 6th centuries, the churches in Algezares (Murcia) and in San Pedro de Alcántara (Málaga) were particularly outstanding. From the 7th century several important churches have been preserved in their original structure without basic changes; they are built of large well-hewn dressed stones and have a projecting rectangular apse and horseshoe arches. In this group, the churches in Baños de Cerrato

to be found in Córdoba, Sevilla, and Toledo. In the 6th and 7th centuries Byzantine influence increased, as can be seen from the chancels, niches, pillars, and altar supports. Mérida was an important center whose influences extended to Córdoba, Toledo, Caceres, and Salamanca; other less important centers were in the Levant region and in Cataluña. Nothing is known about Visigothic painting.

The minor arts of the Visigothic period are outstanding in quality and abundance. The brooches and belt clasps show a deterioration of the Germanic type in the hands of the local craftsmen, while the products of the workshops where court commissions were executed show Byzantine influences. Two important finds have come from these workshops: those of Guarrazar (Toledo; V, PL. 61) and those of Torredonjimeno (Jaén), in which the votive crowns and crosses (now in various museums of Madrid, Paris, Barcelona, and Córdoba) are particularly fine. Most of the bronzes belong to the 7th century and consist of censers, small vases, and patens.

Asturias. Between the 8th and 10th centuries the highly important art of Asturias developed in northern Spain, confined to a small geographic area. Asturian architecture shows some interesting innovations. The oldest building is the church in Santianes, near Pravia, built 774–83; the little that remains shows its differences from Visigothic art as well as certain characteristics found in all the churches built in the first decades of the 9th century by Alfonso II el Casto (the Chaste) — in Oviedo, Cámara Santa and the churches of S. Tirso and of S. Julián de los Prados ("Santullano"; III, PL. 46; XI, PL. 318) — with small-course masonry, round-headed arches, pillars, and *chevets* on a three-apse plan. This art reached its peak in the short reign of Ramiro I (842–50) with three outstanding monuments — S. Cristina at Lena, near Pola de Lena (XI, PL. 317), and S. María de Naranco and S. Miguel de Lillo (XI, PL. 318), both on the outskirts of Oviedo — whose contemporaneous architecture and decoration show a reciprocal close connection. These structures are completely vaulted with transverse-rib arches, arcades on the interior and buttresses on the exterior, large windows or loggias, and a profusion of decorative sculpture of a decidedly Eastern character. In later Asturian art, while the most important churches (S. Salvador at Valdediós; III, PLS. 46, 47) are clearly derived from the style of Ramiro's time, another more modest group of churches of large size and with wooden roofs are basically related to the architecture of the period of Alfonso II, as is apparent in the churches of Santiago at Gobiendes, S. Adriano at Tuñón, S. Pedro at Nora, and S. Salvador at Priesca. In the 10th century there were some extensions of Asturian art toward Santiago de Compostela and León; in Cataluña the interesting and controversial group of churches of Tarrasa were built.

In almost all these Asturian churches there were decorative paintings, some of which have survived. Those of S. Julián de los Prados, with architectural motifs arranged in horizontal strips and with a limited color range, are particularly interesting.

The minor arts of the Asturian period are especially outstanding, particularly the religious goldwork, which includes examples such as the Cross of the Angels (808), the Cross of Victory (908), and the Caja de las Ágatas (910; XI, PL. 321), all in the Cámara Santa of Oviedo, and some gold-filigree objects, with enamel and cabochons, related in style to contemporaneous Germanic and northern Italian art. Also belonging to this period are the Caja de las Reliquias in the Cathedral of Astorga (León; XI, PL. 321), of gilded silver and repoussé work, and the communion table of the portable altar, covered with repoussé silver in a coarser style, from San Pedro de Roda.

Mozarabic and Hispano-Arabic styles. Mozarabic is the term applied to the art developed by the Spaniards who lived under Moslem rule; this art was in part derived from the old Hispanic tradition and in part affected by Islamic influences. Only in the regions reconquered by the Christians at a rather early period — and which were therefore areas of refuge for the Mozarabs, who were persecuted in the south — have any interesting works in this style been preserved. Chronologically it may be placed between the end of the 9th and the beginning of the 11th century. The churches were built in a great variety of styles, and the horseshoe arch was common; the main examples are S. Miguel at Escalada (León; X, PL. 197) and San Cebrián de Mazote (Valladolid), of the basilica type; Santiago de Peñalba (León), S. María at Bamba (Valladolid), and S. María at Lebeña (Santander), with some Byzantine features; and S. Millán de Suso at San Millán de la Cogolla (Logroño; X, PL. 197) and S. Baudilio (Baudel) at Casillas de Berlanga (Soria; X, PL. 196), with some influences from the Caliphate style. The Chapel of S. Miguel at Celanova (Orense; X, PL. 195) is a smaller version of Peñalba, and S. María at Melque (Toledo; X, PL. 195) is unique. In Cataluña this tendency was embodied in the basilica of S. Miguel de Cuxá (Rousillon), S. Pedro de Roda, the Abbey of S. María at Ripoll, and a number of small churches scattered throughout the region. In Aragón it can be found in part of the Monastery of S. Juan de la Peña.

This period was particularly outstanding in illuminated manuscripts. The Biblia Hispalense (10th cent.; Madrid, Bib. Nac., Ms. Vitrina 13.1) reflects the Caliphate style in its schematic drawings; the Bible of the Cathedral of León (920) is richer, and richest of all is the Commentary on the Apocalypse by Beatus of Liebana, illuminated by Magius (926; New York, Pierpont Morgan Lib., M. 644), who gave rise to a school of imitators up to the 11th century. These included Florencio, who illustrated the Bible now at S. Isidoro el Real in León (960); Obeco, the Beatus manuscript of Valcavado

(970; Valladolid, Bib., Col. de Sta Cruz); and Ende, the Beatus manuscript of Gerona (975; V, PL. 199). Some ivories (S. Millán de Suso; Louvre) and metalwork (the crosses of Peñalba and Mansilla de la Sierra) complete the various aspects of Mozarabic art (q.v.).

The Moslem styles in Spain, consisting of the Caliphate, Almohad, and Nasrid, developed their splendid phases from the 8th to the 15th century, with a continuation of their spirit in the so-called "Mudejar" art, derivatives of which may be traced to the present time. Nevertheless, the western European styles were those that prevailed and set the tone of Spanish art.

The Romanesque and the Gothic. The Romanesque was the first style that, transcending political boundaries, united the artistic life of the Christian kingdoms of the Peninsula. It arose as a kind of alien imposition begun in the most important buildings, but it immediately became nationalized, acquiring Spanish characteristics. Its distinguishing characteristics were ashlar masonry, more or less rusticated depending on the importance of the building; the round-headed arch; the cross-shaped plan covered by barrel or ribbed vaults on cross-shaped piers with capitals either richly decorated with plant motifs or historiated (without Hispanic precedents or any debt to models); the semicircular apse with exteriors having diagonal buttresses or engaged columns, projecting only slightly; blind arches; round-arch, single- or two-light windows; and bell towers, generally on a square plan but occasionally round. The outstanding monuments of this type are the Abbey of San Pedro de Roda (1022; XII, PL. 209) and S. Vicente at Cardona (1040; XII, PL. 210) in Cataluña; the Cathedral of Jaca (1063; XII, PL. 212) in Aragón; the monastery church at San Salvador de Leyre (1057) in Navarra; S. Martín at Frómista in Castilla (ca. 1066; XII, PL. 211); S. Isidoro in León (ca. 1080; XII, PL. 212); and Santiago de Compostela (begun in 1075; XII, PL. 213) in Galicia.

Examples of the wall paintings that decorated these churches and of the liturgical objects and furnishings that were used have survived, as have some of their religious images and some ivories, enamels, and woven cloth. This art surpassed all previous Christian art in Spain, contributing to the formation of a unified Hispanic national consciousness prior to the reconquest, and paved the way for future artistic innovations in the Peninsula. (See also ROMANESQUE ART.)

The iconographic freedom of Romanesque art aroused the austere protest of St. Bernard, who established the Cistercian order. In 1131 the monastery at Moreruela (Zamora) was founded in Spain by that order, which soon afterward built many other imposing constructions with special characteristics of their own: an extreme sobriety of decoration, the constant use of the pointed arch and of cross vaults, and a preference for high, square apses. Many of these principles were to be adopted later by the artistic style that, originating in France, was then enthusiastically accepted in Spain. The churches became stone skeletons, skillfully designed so that all their elements aimed at the achievement of elevation and transparency. The zeal for French renovation quickly reached Castilla; for the Cathedral of Ávila, one Fruchel had designed a three-aisle church with a double ambulatory encompassing the presbytery and with engaged supporting arches and cross vaults set symmetrically, which he combined with elements that were still Romanesque. The Cathedral of Cuenca was a Burgundian structure almost throughout, and shortly afterward, within a brief period, three large cathedrals of increasing Gothic purity were begun: those of Burgos (1221), Toledo (1227), and León (ca. 1250). Nevertheless, it was not these predominantly French-inspired examples that created a style, but rather those of a more Hispanic character. The 13th century marked the high point of the initial impetus that made it possible to undertake the building of the major Castilian cathedrals, subsequently perfected and completed throughout the 14th century, while the 15th century represented the attainment of the Spanish interpretation of the style that, through the brilliant age of the reign of the Catholic Monarchs, became more concerned with decoration than with structure and was to lead to the Renaissance.

In Cataluña the 13th century was rich in its own resources, which were expressed in the cathedrals of Lérida and Tarragona. In the Romanesque period Cataluña had already been more independent of France and its connection with Italy had been closer; in the Gothic period this tendency continued, oriented toward proportion and toward a simple and clear-cut type of structure in which each element was differentiated in terms of its function, with a preference for the single-nave plan with a polygonal *chevet*. This style was already fully developed in the 14th century, when the building of the large cathedrals of Barcelona, Gerona, and Palma de Mallorca (PL. 119; VI, PL. 308) were begun, in which French models were not copied but, rather, the customary predominantly vertical effect was perfected. This tendency led to the Church of S. María del Mar (1328–83), of extraordinary simplicity in its supporting elements and with great breadth and balance, whose supreme mastery and imposing quality found its culmination in the single aisle of the Cathedral of Gerona. In the 15th century the principal religious constructions had been completed and Cataluña's artists were able to devote themselves to the development of secular architecture, which was to have numerous outstanding examples. Aragón lagged slightly behind; in Valencia, where the style was smooth and plain, the splendid Lonja de la Seda (Silk Exchange) was built, which was modeled on the Lonja of Palma. In the Provincias Vascongadas (Basque Provinces) and in Navarra the Gothic style appeared late; it was richly decorated and was almost wholly French, owing to the close relationship between the ruling houses of Navarra and of France. (See also GOTHIC ART.)

The modern period. In the 16th century Castilla, abounding with ambition and opportunities (since it had ended the Moslem domination of Spain), discovered and began colonizing America and saw its king, Carlos I, become Holy Roman Emperor (as Charles V), the highest secular ruler of Christendom. Castilla shook off the traces of the Gothic style, which had been used to the limit of its creative

kingdom of Aragón remained somewhat peripheral to the new historical situation.

The art of the Renaissance period gradually evolved into the baroque style, expressing a state of mind arising out of the religious movement of the Counter Reformation. Forms became boldly complex; new solutions were sought, based on extreme elaboration and breaking down of classical elements; exuberant compositions were designed. This tendency appeared in all aspects of art, which finally lost the concept of the beauty of line. The baroque style soon became identified with the national character: independent and individual, allowing each artist and craftsman to create his own universe, limited only by his own imagination. The whole complex of political, philosophical, and scientific innovations introduced with the 18th century was necessary to bring this movement, with difficulty, to a brief halt in the interval represented by neoclassicism, which was quickly swept away by another individualistic movement, romanticism. Since then, throughout the 19th and 20th centuries, the multiplicity of coexisting art styles and forms has enabled each artist to express

Spain, principal modern centers and historical regions. *Key*: (1) Modern national boundaries; (2) regional boundaries.

possibilities, to follow the new trends that had arrived from Italy. The norms set by the Italian models, however, were too rigid for the Castilian creative temperament, which was intolerant of limitations; Spain preferred to create its own style, known as the plateresque (see RENAISSANCE, col. 123). The only Italian influences the plateresque retained were the round arch, the grotesque (in decoration), and the columns. It can therefore be said that, in fact, there were no purely Renaissance buildings in Spain until the brilliant works of Juan de Herrera (q.v.) in El Escorial and in Valladolid. Cathedrals, churches, and monasteries, palaces and public buildings, sprang up all over Spain, but especially in Castilla and its dependencies (including Andalucía), since the states formerly belonging to the

himself abundantly within the tendencies best suited to his temperament. (See also ART NOUVEAU; BAROQUE ART; ROMANTICISM.)

Folk art. Few countries in Europe present as rich and varied a folk art as Spain. It can be seen in the dwellings, adapted as they are to the different climatic zones of the Peninsula; in such characteristic types as the *casona* of Santander province; the Basque and Navarran *caserío* (village, cluster of houses); the Galician *hórreo* (storehouse); the *cortijo* (farmhouse) of Andalucía; the *barraca* (grass-roofed hut) of Valencia; the famous Mediterranean houses of Ibiza based on geometric volumes; and the *masía* of Cataluña, which may be a survival of the Roman country house — all perfectly suited to their environment and having details that are also used in the simpler forms of religious architecture. Furniture and household objects, of traditional and seldom-varying forms, must also be considered. These objects are solid, sturdy, made of jointed parts (woodwork), and often decorated with geometric motifs showing little diversity: seats (straight-backed chairs, armchairs, stools, and benches), tables, beds, *arguenos*, sideboards, chests, etc. (VIII, PL. 91).

Pottery, which is abundant and varied in the different regions, consists of plates, jars, casseroles, and deep vessels for cooking, eating, or drinking, in forms handed down through many generations and revealing a strong chromatic sense. Glassware also presents objects whose basic forms have not changed over the centuries, such as the *porrón* (glass wine pitcher with a long, narrow spout), which has slightly different forms and colors according to the various regions. Of traditional manufacture are the glasses of Mallorca, with elegant shapes and purity of color. Iron and repoussé work also form accessories to the home. Even today it is not unusual in small villages to find interesting examples of ironwork in grilles, crosses (V, PL. 350), weather vanes, pokers, bolts, hinges, and nails; these objects form one of the main attractions of the Museo de Cau Ferrat in Sitges (Barcelona), together with firedogs (IX, PL. 522) and objects of bronze, copper, or tin (braziers, pitchers, mortars) formerly used for domestic purposes.

Woven cloth, embroideries, and laces are also made, in keeping with the traditional forms required by regional dress. The study of the decorative elements in woven cloth and textiles is so complex, because of the quantity and variety of their motifs, that it would be difficult to note all the variations. In the production of petit point and lace, since the 17th century the outstanding centers have been Almagro, Granátula, and Manzanares; and since the 18th century, various towns of the coast of Cataluña. Regional dress is among the most varied and original in Europe — the natural consequence of the abundant meeting and merging of influences — and is heightened by jewelry characteristic of each region, commonly executed in filigee work.

Fans, toys, rustic carving, Christmas-crib figures, models of sailboats, painted ex-votos, whistles, ornamental compositions made of shells, popular prints, and *aleluyas* (small religious pictures with the word *aleluya* printed on them, thrown among the people on Easter Eve) are some of the other picturesque items of Spanish folk art. There are several museums whose main contents are objects of folk art, such as the Museo del Pueblo Español in Madrid, the Museo de Artes Populares in Barcelona, the regional museum of Ca'n Mulet in Palma, the Museo Etnográfico de Vizcaya in Bilbao, the Museo de Arte Popular in Ávila, the Museo Folklórico in Ripoll (Gerona), and the Museo del Mar in Luanco (Oviedo). (See also FOLK ART.)

BIBLIOG. *General*: Ars Hispaniae, Madrid, 1947 ff.; F. Jiménez Placer, Historia del arte español, 2 vols., Barcelona, 1955; J. Gudiol i Ricart, The Arts of Spain, Garden City, N.Y., 1964. See also the bibliog. for SPANISH AND PORTUGUESE ART. *Antiquity*: J. A. Ceán Bermúdez, Sumario de las antigüedas romanas que hay en España, Madrid, 1832; A. Schulten, ed., Fontes Hispaniae antiquae, Barcelona, 1922 ff.; R. Carpenter, The Greeks in Spain, London, New York, 1925; J. R. Mélida, Monumentos romanos en España, Madrid, 1925; A. del Castillo, La cultura del vaso campaniforme, Barcelona, 1928; E. Thouvenot, Essai sur la province romaine de Bétique, Paris, 1940; B. Taracena, La cerámica antigua española, Madrid, 1942; A. García y Bellido, La arquitectura entre los Iberos, Madrid, 1945; A. García y Bellido, Hispania Graeca, 2 vols., Barcelona, 1948; A. García y Bellido, Esculturas romanas de España y Portugal, 2 vols., Madrid, 1949; P. Bosch Gimpera, De la España primitiva a la España medieval, Estudios dedicados a Menéndez Pidal, II, Madrid, 1951, pp. 533-49; J. L. Cassani, Aportaciones al estudio del proceso de la romanización de España, Cuadernos de historia de España, XVIII, 1952, pp. 50-70; A. A. Castellán, Roma y España en la visión de Prudencio, Cuadernos de historia de España, XVII, 1952, pp. 20-45; A. García y Bellido, La peninsula ibérica en los comienzos de su historia, Madrid, 1952; M. Dolç, Hispania de Marcial: Contribución al conocimiento de la España antigua, Barcelona, 1953; J. Camon Aznar, Las artes y los pueblos de la España primitiva, Madrid, 1954; A. García y Bellido, Historia de España, I-II, Madrid, 1954-55 (bibliog.); F. J. Wiseman, Roman Spain, London, 1956; J. Caro Baroja, España primitiva y romana, Barcelona, 1957; A. Arribas, The Iberians, London, 1963. *Middle Ages*: M. Gómez Moreno, Iglesias mozárabes: Arte español de los siglos IX e XI, Madrid, 1919; H. Terrasse, L'art hispano-mauresque des origines au XIIIe siècle, Paris, 1922; E. Lambert, L'art gothique en Espagne aux XIIe et XIIIe siècles, Paris, 1931; E. Lambert, La civilization mozarabe, Hommage à Ernest Martinech: Etudes hispano-américaines, Paris, 1939, pp. 34-46; E. Bagué and J. Petit, La alta edad media, Barcelona, 1953; G. Marçais, L'architecture musulmane d'Occident, Paris, 1955; E. Bagué and J. Petit, La baja edad media, Barcelona, 1956; E. Lambert, Art musulman et art chrétien dans la Péninsule ibérique, Paris, 1958; G. Menéndez Pidal, Sobre miniatura española en la alta edad media: Corrientes culturales que revela, Madrid, 1958; H. Terrasse, Islam d'Espagne, Paris, 1958; L'art roman, Barcelona, 1961 (exhibition cat.); J. Puig i Cadafalch, L'art wisigothique et ses survivances, Paris, 1961. *Golden Age to the present*: B. Bevan, History of Spanish Architecture, London, 1938; E. Lafuente Ferrari, Breve historia de la pintura española, Madrid, 1946; E. Tormo y Monzó, Pintura, escultura y arquitectura en España: Estudios dispersos, Madrid, 1949; J. E. Cirlot, La pintura

abstracta, Barcelona, 1951; A. Igual Ubeda, El siglo de oro, Barcelona, 1951; J. A. Gaya Nuño, La pintura española en el medio siglo, Barcelona, 1952; J. M. de Azcarate, Monumentos españoles, 2d ed., 3 vols., Madrid, 1953-54; J. E. Cirlot, Del expresionismo a la abstracción, Barcelona, 1955; J. Mercader Riba, El siglo XIX, Barcelona, 1957; J. Pla y Cargol, Ciudades monumentales de España, Madrid, 1957; J. Reglá Campistol, El siglo XVIII, Barcelona, 1957; G. Kubler and M. Soria, Art and Architecture in Spain and Portugal and Their American Dominions, Harmondsworth, 1959 (bibliog.); J. Lees-Milne, Baroque in Spain and Portugal and Its Antecedents, London, 1960; C. Flores, Arquitectura española contemporanea, Madrid, 1961; J. A. Gaya Nuño, La arquitectura española en sus monumentos desaparecidos, Madrid, 1961. *Folk art*: I. de Palencia, El traje regional de España, Madrid, 1926; E. M. Aguilera, Los trajes populares de España, Barcelona, 1948; J. Subía Galter, El arte popular en España, Barcelona, 1948; R. Violant y Simorra, El Pirineo español, Madrid, 1949; R. Violant y Simorra, El arte popular española través del Museo de Industrias y Artes Populares, Barcelona, 1953.

MONUMENTAL CENTERS. Administratively, Spain is divided into 50 provinces that are historically grouped in 15 regions, corresponding, on the whole, to the states that arose during the Middle Ages. Some regions present considerable affinities, both historically and in their artistic expression: Galicia, Asturias, and León formed the early kingdom of León, which later joined the central block of the two Castillas. The present regions of Aragón, Cataluña, Valencia, and the Balearic Islands were part of the kingdom of Aragón. The Provincias Vascongadas (Basque Provinces) are linked artistically to Navarra, which was an independent nation. In the south, Andalucía constitutes a region with well-defined characteristics, and Extremadura displays the combined influences of León, Castilla, and Andalucía. Finally, the archipelago of the Canary Islands shows the direct influence of the Andalusian region.

In the following repertory the monumental centers are grouped by historical regions, beginning with Madrid, the nation's capital.

Madrid. Originally a Moslem town (some fragments of the outer wall remain), Madrid was reconquered at the end of the 11th century and was gradually resettled during the following centuries. The remains of the Torre de S. Nicolás, in the Mudejar style, and the Torre de S. Pedro el Real (14th cent.) have survived from this medieval stage. The Hospital de la Latina and S. Jerónimo el Real (1503-05), with a classical cloister (1612), are from the end of the 15th century. The Capilla del Obispo, a Renaissance structure with tombs and an altarpiece by the sculptor Francisco Giralte, is from the 16th century, as are the Torre de los Lujanes and the so-called "Casa de Cisneros" (1537). In 1561 Philip II established the capital in Madrid, and the period of the city's magnificence began, with many new religious constructions: the Convent of the Descalzas Reales, which has a classical façade and which comprises a church (reworked about 1750 by Diego de Villanueva) containing the tomb of Juana de Austria by Pompeo Leoni (1574), a stairway with paintings (1661-68), the Capilla del Milagro (1678), and a museum with paintings, sculptures, and goldwork; the Church of la Encarnación (1611-16), by Juan

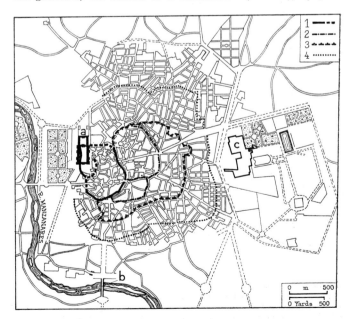

Madrid, plan of the city to end of 18th century. *Key:* (1) Outline of market walls and Moorish city; (2) boundary of medieval town; (3) outline of walls of 1566; (4) outline of walls of 1650. (*a*) Palacio Real; (*b*) Puente de Toledo; (*c*) Palacio del Buen Retiro (partially reconstructed).

Gómez de Mora (the interior renovated by Ventura Rodríguez in 1767); the Carmelite convent (1651); the Church of S. Andrés, with its adjoining Capilla de S. Isidro (1657–69; destroyed 1936, being rebuilt), which is an outstanding example of the baroque style in Madrid; the Abbey church of S. Plácido (1641–61), with a Dead Christ by Gregorio Fernández and the main altarpiece by Claudio Coello (1668); the Church of S. Ginés, with paintings by El Greco and Alonso Cano; the Church of S. Isidro el Real (FIG. 325); the Church of S. Antonio de los Alemanes (de los Portugueses; 1624–26), decorated with wall paintings by J. Carreño de Miranda and Luca Giordano (Lucas Jordán); and the Church of Las Comendadoras de San-

tiago, with a sacristy by Francisco Moradillo (1746). Outstanding among the secular constructions are the Plaza Mayor, by Juan Gómez de Mora (1617), with the statue of Philip III by Pietro Tacca; the Cárcel de Corte (1629; now the Ministry of Foreign Affairs); and the Ayuntamiento (City Hall), begun by J. Gómez de Mora (1640), with frescoes by A. Palomino de Castro y Velasco (1696) and a custodial by F. Álvarez (1560).

At the beginning of the 18th century there were several constructions by Pedro de Ribera, including the Hermitage of la Virgen del Puerto (1718; rebuilt 1950), the Puente de Toledo (ca. 1735), the Barracks of Conde-Duque de Olivares (1720), the Church of Montser-

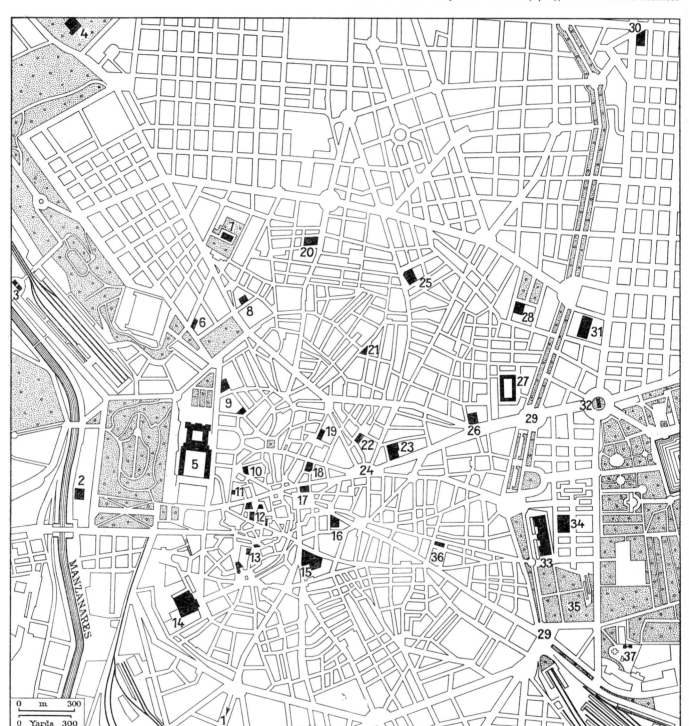

Madrid, plan of city center. Principal monuments: (1) to Puente de Toledo; (2) Hermitage of la Virgen del Puerto; (3) S. Antonio de la Florida; (4) Museo de América; (5) Palacio Real; (6) Museo Cerralbo; (7) Museo del Duque de Alba; (8) S. Marcos; (9) Museo del Pueblo Español and Church of la Encarnación; (10) Church of las Comendadoras de Santiago; (11) S. Nicolás; (12) Torre de los Lujanes, "Casa de Cisneros," Ayuntamiento, and Palacio Episcopal; (13) S. Andrés, Capilla del Obispo, and S. Pedro el Real; (14) S. Francisco el Grande; (15) S. Isidro; (16) Sta Cruz; (17) Plaza Mayor and Casa de la Panadería; (18) S. Ginés; (19) Convent of las Descalzas Reales; (20) Montserrat; (21) S. Antonio de los Alemanes; (22) Carmelite convent; (23) Customs House; (24) Puerta del Sol; (25) Hospicio de S. Fernando; (26) S. José; (27) Palacio de Buenavista; (28) Church of las Salesas Reales; (29–29) Paseo del Prado; (30) Museo Lázaro Galdiano; (31) Museo de Arte del Siglo XIX and Museo de Arte Contemporaneo; (32) Puerta de Alcalá; (33) Museo del Prado; (34) S. Jerónimo el Real; (35) Botanic Garden; (36) Museo de la Academia de la Historia; (37) Observatory.

at (1720), the Hospicio de S. Fernando (1729), and several palaces. Construction of the Palacio Real (FIG. 326) began in 1738 under the supervision of Giovanni Battista Sacchetti; it was decorated by Corrado Giaquinto (from 1753 to 1761), who was followed by Anton Raphael Mengs and Giovanni Battista Tiepolo. Noteworthy in the Palacio Real are the Salón del Trono (de Embajadores; de Reinos), the Salón de Gasparini (1765), the Sala de Porcelana (ca. 1770), the Salón de los Espejos, the Capilla Real (1749–57), the main staircase, the Royal Armory, the tapestries (almost 1,000 pieces; 15th–18th cent.), and the painting collection. Also from this period are the Palacio Liria (1773) and the Palacio de Buenavista (1772; now the War Office), the Oratory of the Caballero de Gracia (1789) by Juan de Villanueva, and the churches of S. José (1742); of SS Justo y Pastor (1745; now S. Miguel) by Giacomo Bonavia; of the Salesas Reales (1750) by Francisco Carlier; of S. Marcos by V. Rodríguez (1749); of S. Francisco el Grande by Francisco Cabezas (1768); of S. Antonio de la Florida, decorated by Goya (1798); and of las Escuelas Pías de S. Antón, with paintings by Goya. Other works of the period include the fountains of Cibeles, Neptuno, and Apolo (1777); the Puerta de Alcalá (1778) and the Puerta de Hierro; the Customs Houses (1769; now the Ministry of Finance) by Francisco Sabatini; and the Botanic Garden (1781) and the Observatory (1785), both by J. de Villanueva. The most important of Madrid's many museums is the Museo del Prado, in a building designed by J. de Villanueva (1785). It contains, among other works, the incomparable series of paintings by Velázquez, Goya's most brilliant paintings, and numerous examples by Murillo, Ribera, and El Greco. Foreign schools of painting are also well represented, particularly the French, Flemish, and Italian schools. Other important museums are the Museo de la Academia de S. Fernando (works by Goya, Zurbarán, Murillo, Ribera, and other artists of the 18th century and later); Museo Lázaro Galdiano (ivories, enamels, goldwork of various periods, medals, ceramics, glass, and weapons); Museo de la Real Academia de la Historia (has the missorium of Theodosius, 4th cent., and relics from the Monastery of Piedra, 1390); Instituto de Valencia de Don Juan (handicrafts of Spain, especially weaving, ceramics, embroideries, metals, furniture, jet, and glassware); Museo del Duque de Alba (paintings by Fra Angelico, Titian, Palma Vecchio, Ribera, El Greco, Rembrandt, Rubens, Goya); and Museo Cerralbo (paintings, drawings, weapons, furniture). Also of interest are the Museo Arqueológico Nacional, Museo de América, Museo Romántico, Museo Etnológico y Antropológico, Museo Nacional de Arte del Siglo XIX, Museo de Arte Contemporáneo, Museo Sorolla, Museo Nacional de Artes Decorativas, Museo del Pueblo Español, and Museo Municipal.

BIBLIOG. A. M. de Barcia y Pavón, Catálogo de la Colección de Dibujos originales de la Biblioteca Nacional, Madrid, 1906; A. F. Calvert, Madrid, London, New York, 1909; A. de Colmenares y Orgaz, Conde de Polentinos, Las casas del Ayuntamiento y la Plaza mayor de Madrid, Madrid, 1913, A. de Colmenares y Orgaz, Conde de Polentinos, La Plaza Mayor y la Casa Panadería, BSEE, XXI, 1913, pp. 37–62; E. Tormo y Monzó, En las Descalzas Reales, Madrid, 1917; E. Tormo y Monzó and F. J. Sánchez Cantón, Los tapices de la casa del Rey, 2 vols., Madrid, 1919; P. Gutiérrez Moreno, La ermita de Nuestra Señora del Puerto y su arquitecto P. Ribera, AE, VIII, 1927, pp. 219–22; E. Tormo y Monzó, Las iglesias del antiguo Madrid, 2 vols., Madrid, 1927; E. Tormo y Monzó, La visita a las colecciones artísticas de la Real Academia de San Fernando, Madrid, 1927; E. Harris, The Prado, London, New York, 1940; J. F. Guillén Tato, Catálogo-guía del Museo Naval, 9th ed., Burgos, 1945; F. Iñíguez, El arquitecto M. López de Aguado y la Alameda de Osuna, AEArte, XVIII, 1946, pp. 219–28; E. Tormo y Monzó, Las murallas y las torres, los portales y el Alcázar del Madrid de la Reconquista, Madrid, 1945; F. Pompey Salgueiro, Museo de Arte Moderno: Guía gráfica y espiritual, Madrid, 1946; A. Tamayo, Las iglesias barrocas madrileñas, Madrid, 1946; J. Bernia, Historia del Palacio de Santa Cruz, 1629–1950, Madrid, 1949; J. Cortés, Guía ilustrada de la Real Armería de Madrid, Madrid, 1950; J. A. Gaya Nuño, Guías artísticas de España: Madrid, 2d ed., Barcelona, 1950; J. Camón Aznar, Guía abreviada del Museo Lázaro, Madrid, 1951; F. Niño y Mas and P. Junquera de Vega, Guía ilustrada del Palacio Real de Madrid, Madrid, 1951; B. de Pantorba, Guía del Museo Sorolla, Madrid, 1951; E. Varela Hervias, La Casa de la Villa de Madrid, Madrid, 1951; F. J. Sánchez Cantón, Museo del Prado: Catálogo, Madrid, 1952; Museo Arqueológico Nacional: Guía, Madrid, 1954; H. B. Wehle, Art Treasures of the Prado Museum, New York, 1954; E. Lafuente Ferrari, Les fresques de San Antonio de la Florida, Geneva, 1955 (Eng. trans., S. Gilbert, New York, 1955); M. Rodríguez de Rivas, Museo Romántico, Madrid, 1956; C. Sanz-Pastor Fernández de Piérola, ed., Museo Cerralbo, Madrid, 1956; F. Chueca Goitia, Madrid y sitios reales, Barcelona, 1958; F. Baztán, Monumentos de Madrid, Madrid, 1959; J. M. Pita Andrade, El palacio de Liria, Madrid, 1959; M. Molina Campuzano, Planos de Madrid de los siglos XVII y XVIII, Madrid, 1960; A. Bonet Correa, Iglesias madrileñas del siglo XVII, Madrid, 1961; P. Junquera de Vega, Monasterio de las Descalzas Reales, Madrid, 1961 (Eng. trans., Madrid, 1962); F. Chueca Goitia, ed., Museo de Arte Contemporáneo, Madrid, 1962; J. J. Martín González, El Alcázar de Madrid en el siglo XVI, AEArte, XXXV, 1962, pp. 1–19.

Castilla la Nueva. This region consists of five provinces: Madrid, Guadalajara, Cuenca, Ciudad Real, and Toledo. The consolidation brought about by the reconquest made possible the development of several artistic centers. Between the 13th and 18th centuries Toledo was the most important, while Cuenca and Sigüenza were minor centers. During the 17th century and afterward Madrid flourished artistically, and its influence was extended in a series of royal residences of great interest.

BIBLIOG. J. M. Quadrado and V. de la Fuente, Castilla la Nueva, 3 vols., Barcelona, 1885–86; R. de Orueta y Duarte, La escultura funeraria en España, Madrid, 1919; M. Gómez-Moreno, Sobre el Renacimiento en Castilla, AEAA, I, 1925, pp. 1–40; F. Layna Serrano, Castillos de Guadalajara, Madrid, 1933; F. Layna Serrano, La provincia de Guadalajara, Madrid, 1948; F. Iñíguez Almech, Casas reales y jardines de Felipe II, Madrid, 1952; F. Chueca Goitia, Madrid y Sitios Reales, Barcelona, 1958; A. Sanz Serrano, Cuenca y su provincia, Barcelona, 1960.

Alarcón (Cuenca). Its medieval fortifications culminate in the castle. The Church of S. María has a plateresque portal (ca. 1555) and a large altarpiece (16th cent.). Other churches are S. Juan, La Trinidad, Santiago, and S. Domingo, all in poor condition.

BIBLIOG. M. Cardenal, Alarcón de las Altas Torres, BSEE, XXXI, 1923, pp. 281–83.

Alcalá de Henares (Madrid). This was the Roman city of Complutum, which under the Visigoths became an episcopal see. It affords a good example of Castilian city planning of the first half of the 17th century. The remains of the outer walls (14th cent.) are of brick and rubble masonry. Churches include the Magistral (1497–1509) by Pedro Gumiel; the church of the Bernardine nuns (1617–26; FIG. 327) by Sebastián de la Plaza, built on an oval plan and with paintings by Angelo Nardi; and the Jesuit church, with nave and transept of 1602–08 and with a main altarpiece by Francisco Bautista. The convent of the Carmelitas de la Imagen is located in a former aristocratic residence (16th cent.) with a particularly fine staircase. The façade of the University (Colegio Mayor de S. Ildefonso; 1541–53) is by Rodrigo Gil de Hontañón; the main hall was designed by Pedro Gumiel during the Mudejar renaissance. In the Colegio de S. Jerónimo is a trilobate Renaissance patio. The Archbishop's Palace (ca. 1540) is mostly by Alonso de Covarrubias.

BIBLIOG. P. de Madrazo y Kunst, La Universidad Complutense, Madrid, 1878; A. R. Tornero, Datos históricos de la ciudad de Alcalá de Henares, Alcalá de Henares, 1950; J. García Fernández, Sebastián de la Plaza, arquitecto, AEArte, XXIV, 1951, pp. 254–59; L. Torres Balbás, Complutum, Qual'at 'Abd al-Salām y Alcalá de Henares, BRAH, CXLIV, 1959, pp. 155–88; E. Tormo y Monzó, Alcalá de Henares, Madrid, n.d.

Almagro (Ciudad Real). The Dominican Monastery of la Asunción (16th cent.) has a cross-vaulted church without side aisles, as well as a Renaissance cloister. The 17th-century theater is the only one of that period in Spain preserved complete, together with its annexes and some of its original installations.

BIBLIOG. R. Ramírez de Arellano, Paseo artístico por el campo de Calatrava, Ciudad Real, 1894; J. Maldonado y Cocat, Las obras de restauración de la Plaza Mayor de Almagro, La Mancha, II, 6, 1962, pp. 65–73.

Aranjuez (Madrid). The Royal Palace was used by Fernando el Católico and Carlos V; Philip II commissioned Juan de Herrera to work on it (1564); construction was suspended in 1586, but it was resumed by P. Caro Idrogo (1715) and Santiago Bonavia (1744) and expanded by Francisco Sabatini (1772). The palace has a staircase by Santiago Bonavia, the Oratorio de la Reina with paintings by Francisco Bayeu (1790) and Mariano de Maella, the Salón del Trono, the Sala de Porcelana (1763–65), and a banquet hall decorated with paintings by Jacopo Amigoni (Amiconi) and Corrado Giaquinto, in addition to interesting furniture, clocks, tapestries, and many paintings. The park contains many fountains and the Jardín de la Isla and Jardín del Parterre, the latter with statues; in the Jardín del Príncipe there is a small neoclassical palace (1803) with fine decoration, known as the Casa del Labrador. The old town exemplifies an interesting city plan of the 18th century, with the main plaza and the Church of S. Antonio by Giacomo Bonavia (1768; FIG. 327).

BIBLIOG. E. Tormo y Monzó, Aranjuez, BSEE, XXXVII, 1929, pp. 1–20; E. Lafuente Ferrari, Sobre la Casa del Labrador y el arquitecto D. Isidro González Velázquez, AEAA, IX, 1933, pp. 68–71; L. M. Burillo Sole, Aranjuez artística, Aranjuez, 1958; A. Covaleda, Guía de Aranjuez, Madrid, 1958; J. J. Martín González, El palacio de Aranjuez en el siglo XVI, AEArte, 1962, pp. 237–54.

Atienza (Guadalajara). The castle was mentioned in documents as early as the 9th century, and its ruins date from the middle of the 12th century. The Church of S. María has a square Romanesque apse; La Trinidad reveals Mudejar influences in the apse and has a 13th-century crucifix. Other churches are S. Bartolomé, with Romanesque arcades; S. Gil, with Romanesque apse and three plateresque altarpieces; S. Francisco (14th cent.); and S. Juan, with a main altarpiece decorated with paintings by A. del Arco (17th cent.).

BIBLIOG. F. Layna Serrano, Atienza, BSEE, XLII, 1934, pp. 19–25; F. Layna Serrano, Historia de la villa de Atienza, Madrid, 1945.

Belmonte (Cuenca). An enormous outer wall encircles the original town and joins the castle, which was built in 1456 and is well preserved. The collegiate church of S. Bartolomé (15th cent.) has a nave and two aisles with cross vaults, a main altarpiece (17th cent.), some tombs of the 16th century, choir stalls from the Cathedral of Cuenca (1454), and an altarpiece of 1546.

BIBLIOG. R. Jurado Prieto, Notas informativas ilustradas referentes a la Villa de Belmonte de la provincia de Cuenca, Palma de Mallorca, 1952; B. Vázquez Gil, El Castillo del Belmonte, B. Asociación Española Amigos de los Castillos, II, 1954, pp. 177–81.

Boadilla del Monte (Madrid). The town contains the Palace of the Infante Don Luis, built by V. Rodríguez in the 18th century, with large halls and a chapel, and the Carmelite convent, with a brick church containing paintings by Francisco de Solís (17th cent.).

BIBLIOG. F. Martín Eztala, Excursión a Boadilla del Monte y a Villaviciosa de Odón, BSEE, XXXIV, 1926, pp. 183–98.

Buitrago (Madrid). The walled enclosure and castle made of brick (14th cent.) are Mudejar, with some older elements.

BIBLIOG. F. Suárez Bravo, De Buitrago a Turégano, BSEE, XXXVII, 1929, pp. 213–21; F. Layna Serrano, Castillos de Buitrago y Real de Manzanares, Madrid, 1935.

Cadalso de los Vidrios (Madrid). The Palacio de Villena (prior to 1534) has a Renaissance façade and a garden with balconies, arcades, and pavilions in the Italian style.

BIBLIOG. V. Lampérez y Romea, Arquitectura civil española, I, Madrid, 1922, pp. 481–83.

Calatrava la Nueva (Ciudad Real). The massive castle of the order of Calatrava (ca. 1217) contains a church with nave and two aisles that shows a mixture of the traditional Cistercian style with Castilian and Mudejar influences.

BIBLIOG. G. Cortezo y Collantes, El convento castillo de Calatrava la Nueva, BSEE, XXXIX, 1931, pp. 42–45; F. Cotta y Márquez de Prado, Descripción del Sacro Convento y Castillo de Calatrava la Nueva..., La Mancha, 1961, No. 1, pp. 35–76, No. 2, pp. 23–73.

Chinchón (Madrid). The church (16th cent.) contains a painting of the Assumption (1812) by Goya. The convent of the Poor Clares (17th cent.) and the Casa de la Cadena are also of interest.

Ciudad Real. There are remains of the ancient walls, with the Puerta de Toledo (1328), which has horseshoe arches set between two towers. The oldest part of the Cathedral (which is without side aisles) is the apse (15th cent.); the side chapels were completed in 1580. The altarpiece of the high altar is by Giraldo de Merlo, and there are also Gothic panel paintings. Other churches include Santiago (15th cent.) and S. Pedro.

BIBLIOG. R. Ramírez de Arellano, Ciudad Real artística, Ciudad Real, 1893.

Cogolludo (Guadalajara). The Palacio de Medinaceli (1492–95) is one of the oldest Renaissance palaces in Spain; it has some Gothic details and courtyard arcades of depressed arches. The parish church contains a painting by J. de Ribera (ca. 1630).

BIBLIOG. E. Lafuente Ferrari, Por las Alcarrías, BSEE, XXXVII, 1929, pp. 199–212.

Colmenar de Oreja (Madrid). The church, enlarged in 1553, has a nave and two aisles with Gothic piers; the chapel was designed by J. B. Monegro (1612). The church of the Augustinian nuns is the work of Fray Lorenzo de San Nicolás. The main plaza is arcaded.

BIBLIOG. L. Cervera Vera, Notas sobre la iglesia parroquial de Santa María la Mayor en Colmenar de Oreja, BSEE, LIII, 1949, pp. 113–68.

Colmenar Viejo (Madrid). The church (16th cent.), which shows a mixture of Gothic and Renaissance styles, has an altarpiece (1574–79) by A. Sánchez Coello, D. de Urbina, and F. Giralte.

BIBLIOG. D. García Rojo, Una excursión a Colmenar Viejo, BSEE XXVI, 1918, pp. 192–95.

Cuenca. The city is picturesquely located between the Júcar and Huécar rivers. It was mentioned in 834 during the Moorish occupation; it was reconquered by Alfonso VII (1177) and enjoyed a particularly brilliant period between the 13th and 16th centuries There are remains of the castle and parts of the walls. The Cathedral (1190–1250) has a Latin-cross plan with nave and two aisles, a wide chevet with an ambulatory, cross vaults, and a gallery. The Capilla Mayor, with a reja (screen) by H. de Arenas (16th cent.), contains a large altarpiece by V. Rodríguez (18th cent.); there is a screen in the coro, also by H. de Arenas, and simple choir stalls. The chapels contain a St. John the Evangelist (16th cent.); the altarpiece of the two St. Johns (16th cent.); the altarpiece of the Capilla de S. Martín (16th cent.); the tombs of the Montemayor family (15th cent.); the altar of St. Fabian and St. Sebastian (ca. 1551); the altarpiece of the Capilla de S. Elena (16th cent.); the Gothic altarpiece of the Capilla de Todos los Santos (15th cent.); the artesonado of the so-called "Capilla Honda" (16th cent.); the altarpiece of the Capilla de la Asunción, by Martín Gómez (16th cent.); the two Gothic tombs (14th cent.) in the Capilla de Santiago; the tombs (15th cent.) and the altarpieces by F. Yáñez de Almedina in the Capilla de los Caballeros (16th cent.); the plateresque group of the Capilla del los Muñoz; and the Calvary (13th cent.) and altarpiece (16th cent.) of the Capilla de S. Bartolomé. The Cathedral treasury contains a Byzantine reliquary (14th cent.), the episcopal crosiers of Juan Yáñez and of S. Julián, several pieces of goldwork, Gothic panels by Juan de Borgoña (16th cent.) and by Martín Gómez, two paintings by El Greco, liturgical embroideries and robes, and a number of tapestries (16th cent.) and sculpture.

Also noteworthy in the city are the Church of S. Pedro, built on a circular plan; the conventual church of S. Pablo, with a baroque façade; the church of the Hermitage of S. Antón, reworked by J. Martín de Aldehuela (1764); and the Chapel of Nuestra Señora de las Angustias. There are homes of aristocratic families in the Calle de San Pedro; the casas colgadas ("hanging houses") on the ravine of the Huécar River; the Ayuntamiento (1762); and the Casa de Beneficencia (1777).

BIBLIOG. J. Domínguez Bordona, Proceso inquisitorial contra el escultor Esteban Jamete, Madrid, 1933; F. Chueca, José Martín de Aldehuela, AE, XXVIII, 1944, pp. 9–28; A. González Palencia, Fuentes para la historia de Cuenca y su provincia, Cuenca, 1944 (bibliog.); J. M. Azcárate, Sobre el arco de Jamete, AEArte, XVIII, 1945, pp. 178–80; J. Hernández Perera, Exposición de arte antiguo en Cuenca, Cuenca, 1956; E. Fernández, Hernando de Arenas y sus rejas de la catedral de Cuenca, AEArte, XXX, 1957, pp. 287–93; F. Gómez de Travecedo, Nueva guía de Cuenca, Cuenca, 1958; V. Moragas Roger, Cuenca y Ciudad Encantada, Madrid, 1959; A. Sanz Serrano, La catedral de Cuenca, Cuenca, 1959; A. Sanz Serrano, Cuenca y su provincia, Barcelona, 1960.

Escalona (Toledo). The castle, originally Moslem, was rebuilt between 1435 and 1448. It has a square plan with irregular outer fortifications and watch towers. The interior contains Mudejar-Gothic stuccowork.

BIBLIOG. F. B. Navarro, Escalona, BSEE, III, 1895–96, pp. 21–32.

El Escorial (Madrid). The Monastery of S. Lorenzo el Real was founded by Philip II in 1561. The project for the architectural complex of the Escorial (XII, FIG. 126), which is set on a plan symbolically reproducing the gridiron on which the saint suffered his martyrdom, was made by Juan Bautista de Toledo (1562) and was completed by Juan de Herrera. It consists of a church flanked by the palace and the cloister, preceded by a patio on which a college and the monastery open. The church is a square basilica with a dome over the transept and a raised choir and presbytery. The Capilla Mayor has an altarpiece with sculpture by P. Leoni (1579) and paintings by F. Zuccari and P. Tibaldi; at the sides are the bronze tombs of Carlos I, Philip II, and their families, by P. Leoni. The vaults of the choir and presbytery are decorated with paintings by L. Cambiaso. The trascoro has a Christ by Cellini (1562). The Panteón de los Reyes is built on a design of Giovanni Batista Crescenzi (1617). The sacristy has an altarpiece by J. del Olmo (1685) with a crucifix by Pietro Tacca and a painting by Claudio Coello (1690); paintings by El Greco, José de Ribera, Veronese, Titian, Tintoretto, and others are also kept here. Surrounding the Patio de los Evangelistas is the cloister, with frescoes by P. Tibaldi and L. Giordano; the Salas Capitulares house a pinacoteca containing works by H. Bosch, Patinir, Rubens, Coxie, Velázquez, Ribera, Veronese, Titian, Tintoretto, Valdés Leal, El Greco, Rogier van der Weyden, J. Fernández Navarrete, and Alonso Cano. The library has frescoes by P. Tibaldi and N. Granello and many illuminated manuscripts (10th–16th cent.). The austere royal apartments of Philip II contain a selection of fine art works. In the gardens are the Casita de Arriba and the Casita del Príncipe (de Abajo; 1772); the latter contains charming decorations and paintings by Pannini, Teniers, and Goya.

Bibliog. F. de los Santos, Descripción breve del monasterio de San Lorenzo el Real de El Escorial, Madrid, 1657 (Eng. trans., London, 1760); J. de Sigüenza, Historia del monasterio de El Escorial, Madrid, 1881; J. Zarco Cuevas, Pintores españoles en S. Lorenzo el Real de El Escorial, Madrid, 1931; J. Zarco Cuevas, Pintores italianos en S. Lorenzo el Real de El Escorial, Madrid, 1931; J. A. Gaya Nuño, El Escorial, Madrid, 1947; H. Portabales Pichel, Maestros mayores, arquitectos y aparejadores de El Escorial, Madrid, 1952; F. Torres, El Escorial, Madrid, 1958; J. Zarco Cuevas and S. García, El Monasterio de San Lorenzo el Real de El Escorial y la Casita del Príncipe, new ed., Madrid, 1958; G. A. Davies, San Lorenzo el El Escorial: The Building of a Monastery, Proc. Leeds Philosophical and Lit. Soc., H. and Lit. Sec., X, 1962–63, pp. 127–36; El Escorial: IV Centenario de la fundación del Monasterio de San Lorenzo el Real, 2 vols., Madrid, 1963.

Getafe (Madrid). The Church of the Magdalena was built by J. Francés, following A. de Covarrubias' design (1541); it has a nave and two aisles separated by Doric columns. The altarpiece on the high altar is by Alonso Carbonell (1612), with paintings (1693) by A. Nardi, J. Leonardo, and F. Castello. The other altarpieces have paintings by A. Cano.

Bibliog. V. Gaspar, La iglesia de Santa María Magdalena de Getafe, BSEE, XXVI, 1918, pp. 189–91.

Guadalajara. The city was under Moorish domination and was reconquered in 1085 during the reign of Alfonso VI. It owes most of its monuments to the Mendoza del Infantado family, who were its feudal overlords. The bridge crossing the Henares River is Moorish (10th–11th cent.) with later reconstructions, and there are remains of Moorish walls. The Church of S. María de la Fuente is in Mudejar style with Moorish elements and later alterations. The apse of the Church of S. Gil (13th cent.) and that of the Church of S. Clara la Real (14th cent.) are also Mudejar, with traces of the Toledo style. In the Church of S. Francisco (15th cent.) the Panteón de los Duques del Infantado is modeled on the Panteón de los Reyes in the Escorial. The Capilla de los Urbina (1540), a brickwork fragment of the Church of S. Miguel, is in the Moorish style. The Church of S. Nicolás has 15th-century choir stalls and the tomb of Rodrigo de Campuzano (1488). Other noteworthy Renaissance churches are La Piedad, with portal by A. de Covarrubias (1526), S. Ginés, and Los Remedios. The Palacio del Infantado (ca. 1480) is mostly by Juan Guas, with richly decorated façade and central courtyard (1483) in the Mudejar-Gothic style. The Palacio de Mendoza (1507) is entirely in Renaissance style, with a courtyard having two architraved galleries.

Bibliog. E. Tormo y Monzó, Guadalajara, Madrid, 1917; L. Torres Balbás, El puente de Guadalajara, Al-Andalus, V, 1940, pp. 449–58; F. Layna Serrano, El palacio del Infantado en Guadalajara, Madrid, 1941; J. M. Azcárate, La fachada del Infantado y el estilo de Juan Guas, AEArte, XXIV, 1951, pp. 307–19; F. Layna Serrano, Castillos de Guadalajara, 2d ed., Madrid, 1960.

Illescas (Toledo). The Puerta de Ugena, the main entrance gate to the town, is Mudejar style. The Church of S. María de la Asunción, also Mudejar, was renovated in the 16th century; it has a nave and two aisles with cross vaults; the portal is plateresque and the Mudejar tower (possibly 14th cent.) is richly decorated. The Hospital de la Caridad has several paintings by El Greco and a church (1588–1600).

Bibliog. A. de Aguilar, Illescas: notas histórico-artísticas, BSEE, XXXV, 1927, pp. 120–37.

Loeches (Madrid). The wooden-roofed Renaissance church has portals in the austere Herreran style; the nave is separated from the side aisles by columns and round arches. The Dominican convent was built by A. Carbonell (1635–38).

Bibliog. M. A. López, Alonso Carbonell y la iglesia de Loeches, AEArte, XXV, 1952, pp. 167–69.

Lupiana (Guadalajara). The town has a Hieronymite monastery, S. Bartolomé. The church (1632) is in poor condition. There is a Renaissance cloister in the style of A. de Covarrubias, with two

stories on three sides and three on the south side, with round, semicircular, and architraved arches.

Manzanares el Real (Madrid). The castle of the Mendoza family (15th cent.), on which Juan Guas worked, includes a church in the Mudejar-Gothic style (13th cent.). There is a 16th-century parish church.

Bibliog. V. Lampérez y Romea, Los Mendoza del siglo XV y el castillo del Real de Manzanares, Madrid, 1916; F. Layna Serrano, Castillos de Buitrago y Real de Manzanares, Madrid, 1935.

Maqueda (Toledo). The town has a castle (15th cent.) built on a rectangular plan; the Torre de la Vela, in Mudejar style; the Church of S. María, with Mudejar apse (15th cent.); and the Castle of S. Silvestro (15th cent.), with a square plan.

Mondéjar (Guadalajara). The Gothic church of the Franciscan Monastery of S. Antonio (1509) is the earliest in Castilla to show Renaissance decorative motifs. The parish church (1516) displays a mixture of Gothic and Renaissance influences. Its main altarpiece (1554) is by J. B. Vázquez the Elder, N. de Vergara, A. de Covarrubias, and J. Correa de Vivar; it also contains the altarpiece of la Encarnación by the last-named.

Nuevo Baztán (Madrid). This town, built between 1709 and 1713 by José Churriguera, is a good example of 18th-century town planning, containing a church, a palace, two squares, and several blocks of houses.

El Pardo (Madrid). A royal residence since the Middle Ages, the palace was several times remodeled; it was reconstructed in 1604 after a fire and was subsequently enlarged by F. Sabatini (18th cent.). It has a square plan with towers at the corners and an inner court. There is a rich art collection, including works by G. Becerra, V. Carducho, J. de Mora, Bayeu, and F. González Velázquez, and an outstanding collection of Flemish and Spanish tapestries (16th–18th cent.). The church is by F. Carlier (1777). The garden is in the romantic style. The Casita del Príncipe (1784), by Juan de Villanueva, has a richly decorated façade (1791). Close by is the Palacio de la Zarzuela (1635) by F. Gómez de Mora and A. Carbonell; of interest also are the Torre de la Parada (1636) and the Real Quinta.

Bibliog. E. Tormo y Monzó, El Pardo, Madrid, 1920; J. Moreno Villa, La casita del Príncipe de El Pardo, AEAA, VIII, 1932, pp. 259–63; L. Calandre, El Palacio del Pardo, Madrid, 1953.

Pastrana (Guadalajara). There is an unfinished collegiate church (16th cent.) containing tapestries (15th cent.) whose cartoons are attributed to Nuno Gonçalves. The Palacio de Pastrana (1542) is severe and massive.

El Paular (Madrid). This Carthusian monastery was completed in 1440, but work on subsequent additions continued until the 18th century. The portal and the reja of the church, the vaults of the cloister, and the large altarpiece are in the flamboyant Gothic style (15th cent.). The Capilla del Tabernáculo and the stained-glass window behind the altar, designed by F. Hurtado Izquierdo (1718), are baroque.

Bibliog. A. L. Mayer, El retablo mayor de la iglesia de la cartuja del Paular, BSEE, XXXI, 1923, pp. 252–60; J. V. L. Brans, El Real monasterio de Santa María de El Paular, Madrid, 1956.

Riba de Saelices (Guadalajara). There are prehistoric rock engravings of animal figures in the Los Casares cave.

Bibliog. F. Layna Serrano, El poblado ibérico, el castro y la caverna prehistórica con relieves en Riba de Saelices, BSEE, XLI, 1933, pp. 177–84.

Sigüenza (Guadalajara). The origins of this town are Roman. Remains of the medieval walls survive; the castle (12th cent.; reconstructed 14th–15th cent.) contains a Romanesque chapel and was formerly the bishop's residence. The Cathedral (fig. 311) is Romanesque and Gothic (12th–14th cent.), with additions in the 16th and 17th centuries. On the outside it resembles a fortress; inside, it consists of a nave and two aisles, a transept with cimborio, and the Capilla Mayor with ambulatory. The sanctuary has a reja (1633), an altarpiece by the sculptor Giraldo de Merlo (1609–11), and the tombs of Alonso Carrillo de Albornoz and Gome Carrillo de Acuña (15th cent.); there is a Gothic pulpit (1485) and also a plateresque one by Martín de Vandoma (1572); the coro has stalls with Gothic tracery (1491) and a baroque screen (1649). The Capilla de la Anunciación has a plateresque *reja*, Mudejar decoration (1515), and a plateresque tomb; in the Capilla de S. Martín there is a Castilian altarpiece (15th cent.); the Capilla de S. Librada, with a sacristy, paintings by Juan de Pereda (1535), and the tomb of Fadrique of Portugal, forms a large plateresque ensemble, perhaps designed by A. de Covarrubias and completed before 1539. The Puerta del Pórfido leads into the cloister; the Capilla de las Reliquías is plateresque; the Capilla de SS Juan y Catalina (or de los Arce) has a number of 15th- and 16th-century Castilian sculptures (the tomb of Martín Vázquez de Arce, "El Doncel," is particularly outstanding) and panel paintings. The main sacristy is by A. de Covarrubias, Martín de Vandoma, and other artists (16th cent.). The Gothic and Renaissance cloister (1505) has several chapels and annexes, including the Museo Diocesano with Hispano-Arabic 12th-century textiles, Gothic religious images, a canvas by El Greco, 17th-century tapestries, and gold- and silverwork (16th–18th cent.). In the town are the Church of Nuestra Señora de los Huertos (16th cent.) and the Romanesque Church of Santiago (12th cent.). The district of San Roque is a town-planning development of the 18th century. The town also has the 16th-century Plaza Mayor and the Gothic residence of the Arce family.

BIBLIOG. M. Pérez Villaamil, La Catedral de Sigüenza, Madrid, 1899; T. Minguella y Arnedo de la Merced, Historia de la Diócesis de Sigüenza y de sus obispos, 3 vols., Madrid, 1910–13; E. Tormo y Monzó, Sigüenza, Madrid, 1929; A. de Federico, La Catedral de Sigüenza, Madrid, 1954; G. Sánchez Doncel, La Catedral de Sigüenza, Madrid, 1960.

Talavera de la Reina (Toledo). Some of the outer walls are preserved, including parts from the Roman period, the Torres Albarranas from the Moorish period, and the Puerta de Sevilla (16th cent.). The Church of S. María la Mayor, possibly begun by Maestro Alonso (14th cent.) and continued in the following century, is in the Mudejar-Gothic style; it has a large rose window with Flemish tracery and a Gothic cloister (15th cent.). The Church of Santiago (14th–15th cent.) has Mudejar façades. The Hermitage of la Virgen del Prado has socles and altarpieces (17th cent.) made with *azulejos* from the famous local workshops. There are several other churches and some aristocratic residences.

BIBLIOG. A Rumeu de Armas, Excursión histórico-artístico por Talavera, BSEE, XLV, 1941, pp. 55–58, 128–38, 214–20; I. Fernández Sánchez, Historia de Talavera de la Reina, Ms. 1560, Bib. Nac., Madrid.

Toledo (anc. Toletum). This was a city of the Carpetani, founded on a high outcrop of granite rocks; it was set there as a guard over the upper course of the Tagus River, which surrounds the city on three sides. It was first mentioned (as Toletum) in documents of 193 B.C.; under Augustus it was a *civitas stipendiaria* in the Conventus Carthaginiensis, and it was already famous for its blades in Roman times. It was the Visigothic capital from 579 until 711, when it fell under Moorish domination; it remained subject to the Caliphate of Córdoba for three centuries. In 1085 it was reconquered by Alfonso VI, King of Castile, and entered upon the period of its greatest splendor, becoming the capital of Spain under the reign of Carlos I. In 1561 Philip II transferred the capital to Madrid.

Enclosed between the Tagus River and the slopes of the Vega Hills, with no room for expansion, Toledo is a remarkable example of town planning, owing to the superposition and juxtaposition of monuments from different periods. The large circus (with a capacity of 20,000–30,000 spectators) dates from Roman times (2d cent.), as do an aqueduct and two bridges over the Tagus (extensively restored). The city wall, which rises up the hill, has been reworked several times; it retains elements from the Visigothic and Moorish periods; the Puerta Vieja de Bisagra (11th cent.), which is the only one preserved from the Moorish period; the Puerta del Sol, in the Mudejar style (14th cent.); the Puerta del Cambrón (restored 16th cent.); and the Puerta Nueva de Bisagra (15th cent.). Only two bridges give access to the city over the Tagus: the Puente de Alcántara, which is of Roman origin and is guarded by a turreted bridgehead in 15th-century Mudejar style and, across the river, by the Castle of S. Servando (14th cent.), now in ruins; and the Puente de S. Martín (13th cent.; rebuilt 14th cent.), guarded by three bridgeheads.

From the Moslem period (although probably transformed from a previous Visigothic church, whose capitals remain on the interior, are the Church of el Cristo de la Luz, a former mosque (980) with nine cupolas in the Cordoban style and a transept and apse added in the 12th century, and the Mosque of las Tornerías, a two-story building now in ruins, that was also built over an earlier Visigothic structure. The 10th-century Mozarabic churches of S. Justa, S. Eulalia, and S. Sebastián (the last having Visigothic elements of the 8th cent.) have all been restored in later periods. After the reconquest many churches were built in the Mudejar style: El Cristo de la Vega, which preserves its original apse; Santiago del Arrabal (13th cent.);

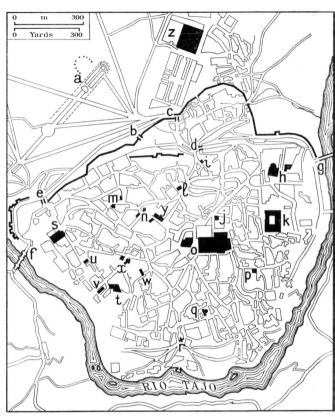

Toledo, plan. Principal monuments: (*a*) Roman circus; (*b*) Puerta Vieja de Bisagra; (*c*) Puerta Nueva de Bisagra; (*d*) Puerta del Sol; (*e*) Puerta del Cambrón; (*f*) Puerta de S. Martín; (*g*) Puerta de Alcántara; (*h*) Hospital de la Sta Cruz (Mus. Arqueol.) and La Concepción Franciscia; (*i*) El Cristo de la Luz; (*j*) Mosque of las Tornerías; (*k*) Alcázar; (*l*) S. Vicente (Mus. Parroquial); (*m*) S. Eulalia and S. Domingo el Antiguo; (*n*) Casa de Mesa, S. Clemente, and S. Pedro Mártir; (*o*) Cathedral and Archbishop's Palace; (*p*) SS. Justo y Pastor; (*q*) S. Andrés; (*r*) S. Sebastián; (*s*) S. Juan de los Reyes; (*t*) Museo y Casa del Greco; (*u*) S. María la Blanca; (*v*) El Tránsito; (*w*) Taller del Moro; (*x*) Palacio de Fuensalida and S. Tomé; (*y*) Church of S. Juan Bautista; (*z*) Hospital de S. Juan Bautista.

S. Vicente (1595, now the Museo Parroquial), with its original apse; S. Tomé, with a noteworthy Mudejar tower and, inside, the *Entombment of the Count of Orgaz* by El Greco; S. Miguel; and La Concepción Franciscia, with a dome decorated with colored *azulejos* (1422). The two former synagogues are also in the Mudejar style: S. María la Blanca (12th–13th cent.; a church since 1405), with nave and four aisles and octagonal pillars, and El Tránsito (1356; a church since 1492), consisting of a nave without side aisles and having *artesonados* inlaid with ivory. Fragments remain of the Taller del Moro (14th cent.), the Palacio de Fuensalida (15th cent.), the Palacio del Rey Don Pedro, and the Casa de Mesa.

Outstanding among the post-reconquest constructions is the Gothic Cathedral (VI, FIG. 491), with nave and four aisles, transept, and ambulatory, begun in 1227 and continued with important additions up to the 18th century. The main façade has three portals: the central one, the Puerta del Perdón (14th cent.), is richly decorated with Gothic sculpture, as are the Puerta del Reloj (13th cent.) and the Puerta de los Leones (15th cent.), opening onto the arms of the transept. The stained-glass windows (14th–18th cent.) are by P. Bonifacio, Juan de Cuesta, Gonzalo de Córdoba, N. de Vergara el Mozo, and others. The Capilla Mayor has an altarpiece (1502–04) decorated by many artists and showing scenes of Christ and the Virgin; on either side are royal tombs between Gothic sculptured decoration, and on the left, closing off the Capilla on the north side, is the tomb of Cardinal Mendoza, partly executed by Domenico di Alessandro Fancelli (16th cent.); the *reja*, flanked by two gilt pulpits, is the work of F. de Villalpando (1548). The crypt is by Diego Copin (1514). In the ambulatory the *transparente* by Narciso Tomé (1732). In the *coro*, or choir west of the crossing, the plateresque screen is by Domingo de Céspedes (1548); the lower stalls are by Rodrigo Alemán (1495) and the upper stalls by Alonso Berruguete and F. Bigarny (1539–45); the sculptured Transfiguration group is by Alonso Berruguete (1548); and the lecterns are by Nicolás de Vergara (1570). The "Virgen de la Blanca" figure (14th cent.) is over the altar. Among the side chapels, the Capilla de la Pila Bautismal (Baptistery) contains a bronze font (15th cent.) and Italian Gothic panel paintings; in the Capilla de la Descención de Nuestra Señora there are statues by F. Bigarny (1527); the Capilla de S. Juan (or de la Torre), which now contains the Cathedral treasury, has a platteresque door by A. de Covarrubias (1536) and a Mudejar ceiling; the Capilla Mozárabe contains frescoes by Juan de Borgoña (1514) and 15th-century panel paintings; the Capilla de S. Martín has a Gothic *reja* by Juan Francés and 15th-century panel paintings; the altarpieces in the Epifania and Concepción chapels are by Juan de Borgoña; the Capilla de S. Ildefonso contains the tomb of Cardinal Albornoz (14th cent.) and that of Bishop Alonso Carrillo de Albornoz (16th cent.) by Vasco de Zarza; in the Capilla de Santiago (or del Condestable) are the tombs of Álvaro de Luna and his wife and those of the archbishops Pedro de Luna and Juan de Cerezuela (15th cent.), as well as an altarpiece by Sancho de Zamora and Juan de Segovia (15th cent.); the platteresque Capilla de los Reyes Nuevos has several Gothic tomb sculptures and an altarpiece designed by V. Rodríguez with paintings by M. de Maella (18th cent.). The antechamber of the Sala Capitular has Mudejar *artesonados* by F. de Lara and wardrobes by G. Pardo (16th cent.); there is Mudejar stuccowork by Bernardino Bonifacio (1510) at the entrance to the Sala Capitular proper, a large square chamber with platteresque Mudejar *artesonados*, wall paintings by Juan de Borgoña (1508–11), and a series of portraits of archbishops of Toledo. The main sacristy, with vault frescoes by Giordano, has paintings by El Greco (the *Expolio*, or *Disrobing of Christ*, the Apostles series), Orrente, Pantoja, F. Ricci, Tristán, Goya, Bellini, Bassano, Giordano, Giaquinto, Van Dyck, and others. The sacristy also houses the so-called "San Luis Bible" (13th cent.) and other illuminated manuscripts, and many examples of weaving, embroidery, and lace (13th–18th cent.). In the Capilla de la Virgen del Sagrario, the Reliquary Room, and the treasury there are collections of gold- and silverwork; Romanesque reliquaries and crosiers with enamelwork; the reliquary of S. Eugenio; a wide variety of Gothic reliquaries, crosses, chalices, pyxes, trays, and urns; and a magnificent custodial by E. de Arfe (1515–24). The cloister (14th cent.) has wall paintings by Maella and Bayeu (1776–82); and in the Capilla de S. Blas there are 14th-century Italian Gothic paintings and the tomb of Archbishop Tenorio, signed by Fernán González (1399).

There are other interesting churches in the city: S. Andrés, which has Mudejar elements and altarpieces by Juan de Borgoña and Antonio de Comontes (16th cent.); SS Justo y Pastor, with the Mudejar Capilla del Cristo de la Columna (14th cent.); S. Domingo el Real, with an Early Christian sarcophagus; S. Juan de los Reyes, in the late Gothic style, designed by Juan Guas (ca. 1495; FIG. 319); S. Pedro Mártir, with wall paintings by G. B. del Mayno and several tombs; S. Domingo el Antiguo, with paintings by El Greco; and the various convents and monasteries.

Among the other monuments are the ruins of the Alcázar (16th cent.); the Ayuntamiento (17th cent.); the Archbishop's Palace, with Mudejar elements and a number of paintings; the Hospital de la Sta Cruz by E. Egas (1504–14; now the Museo Arqueológico Provincial), with a façade by A. de Covarrubias (1524) and a central patio; the Hospital de S. Juan Bautista (Hospital de Tavera or de Afuera, FIG. 317), designed by B. Bustamante and A. de Covarrubias (1541), with a platteresque double patio (1553), a church with the tomb of Cardinal Tavera by A. Berruguete (1559), the old pharmacy, and the Museo de la Fundación Duque de Lerma, arranged like a 16th-century Castilian palace with furniture, tapestries, and outstanding paintings by El Greco, Ribera, and others (16th–17th cent.); and the Museo y Casa del Greco, which is a suggestive re-creation of the artist's surroundings, with a fine group of paintings by him, as well as others by contemporaneous and 17th-century artists.

BIBLIOG. S. R. Parro, Toledo en la mano, Toledo, 1857; R. Amador de los Ríos, Toledo, Madrid, 1905; F. Pérez Sedano, Notas del archivo de la catedral de Toledo, Madrid, 1914; M. R. Zarco del Valle, Documentos de la catedral de Toledo, Madrid, 1914; R. Ramírez de Arellano, Catálogo de artífices qui trabajaron de Toledo, Toledo, 1920; E. Lambert, Tolède, Paris, 1925; E. Lambert, Les synagogues de Tolède, Rev. des études juives, LXXXIV, 1927, pp. 15–33; J. Ainaud de Lasarte, Toledo, Barcelona, 1947; M. de Cardona, Catálogo de la Fundación Duque de Lerma, Toledo, 1951; G. Téllez, La iglesia toledana, Toledo, 1953; G. Marañón, El Greco y Toledo, Madrid, 1956; M. Jorge Aragoneses, El primer credo epigráfico visigodo y otros restos coetáneos descubiertos en Toledo, AEArte, XXX, 1957, pp. 295–323; M. Jorge Aragoneses, Museo arqueológico de Toledo, Madrid, 1957; J. M. de Azcárate, La arquitectura gótica toledana del siglo XV, Madrid, 1958; C. Palencia Flores, Museo de la Santa Hermandad de Toledo, Toledo, 1958; P. Riera Vidal, Los judíos en Toledo y sus sinagogas, 1958 (Eng. trans., J. Macnab, Toledo, 1958); L. Torres Balbás, Por el Toledo mudéjar: el Toledo aparente y el oculto, Al-Andalus, XXIII, 1958, pp. 424–40; J. López de Alaya Álvarez de Toledo, Conde de Cedillo, Catálogo monumental de la Provincia de Toledo, Toledo, 1959; M. A. Martínez González y P. Puebla Gutiérrez, Toledo, Toledo, 1959; L. Moreno Nieto, La provincia de Toledo: Historia, monumentos, obras de arte, Toledo, 1960; A. Sierra Corella, Museo Parroquial de San Vicente, Toledo, n.d.

Torrelaguna (Madrid). The Gothic church of S. María Magdalena, with additions up to the 17th century, has a nave and two aisles, a platteresque raised choir, and three apses; it contains tombs, pulpits, and a main altarpiece (1752) with sculpture by L. S. Carmona. The town also contains the Renaissance residence of Juan de Salinas.

Uclés (Cuenca). This town is the headquarters of the military order of Santiago. There is a massive castle with a monastery beside it (16th–18th cent.), a church with a platteresque *chevet* and an austere façade, a chapter house with *artesonados* (1548), and a cloister (17th cent.) with a baroque portal (1735).

BIBLIOG. P. Quintero y Atauri, Uclés, 3 vols., Cadiz, 1913–15; J. M. de Azcárate, El convento de Uclés y Francisco de Luna, maestro de cantería, AEArte, XXIX, 1956, pp. 173–88; M. T. de Peña, Descripción de la villa de Uclés y de su convento-fortaleza, según el libro de las Visitaciones de la Orden de Santiago de 1508, La Mancha, II, 6, 1962, pp. 5–56.

Villaescusa de Haro (Cuenca). The town was an important center in the 15th and 16th centuries. It has a Gothic church with a Renaissance portal and the richly decorated Capilla de la Asunción (1507), which contains tombs, a *reja*, a Gothic vault, and a late Gothic altarpiece.

El Viso del Marqués (Ciudad Real). Has a church containing the tomb of Álvaro de Bazán (16th cent.); also his palace, which was designed by G. B. Castello (Bergamasco; 1564), with stuccowork and many painted decorations by César Arbasía and J. F. Peroli (16th cent.).

BIBLIOG. P. Alcalá Galiano, Palacio del marqués de Santa Cruz en el Viso, Madrid, 1888.

Extremadura. This region comprises two provinces: Cáceres and Badajoz. Originally inhabited by the Vettones and Turdulus, the region was extensively colonized by the Romans, who made Emerita Augusta (mod. Mérida) the capital of Lusitania. The Suevi and the Visigoths dominated the region before the coming of the Moors, who held it until Alfonso IX (1188–1230) reconquered it and incorporated it into his kingdom of León; with Fernando III it became a part of the kingdom of Castilla. Then began a brilliant period that lasted until the 17th century, with important centers such as Cáceres and Trujillo, known for their secular architecture, and Plasencia and Guadalupe, whose art developed around a religious nucleus.

BIBLIOG. N. Díaz y Pérez, Extremadura, Badajoz y Cáceres..., Barcelona, 1887; P. Hurtado y Pérez, Castillos, torres y casas fuertes de la provincia de Cáceres, Cáceres, 1912; J. R. Mélida y Alinari, Catálogo monumental de España: Provincia de Cáceres, 3 vols., Madrid, 1924; J. R. Mélida y Alinari, Catálogo monumental de España: Provincia de Badajoz, 3 vols., Madrid, 1925–26; M. A. Orti Belmonte, Cáceres y su provincia, Barcelona, 1954; A. Fernández Prada, Mudéjar en la Extremadura del Duero, BSEAAV, XXVIII, 1962, pp. 25–34.

Abadía (Cáceres). A former Cistercian abbey, this was later the palace of the dukes of Alba; it has a Mudejar patio of brick. The Italian-style gardens (16th cent.) are in poor condition.

BIBLIOG. T. Martín Gil, Una visita a los jardines de la Abadía, AE, XXIX, 1945, pp. 58–66.

Alcántara (Cáceres). There is a Roman bridge over the Tagus River; it has six arches and is 270 ft. long. In the center is a commemorative arch in honor of Trajan (ca. A.D. 105–06), extensively restored, and at one end is a small temple with a verse epigraph commemorating its architect, Caius Julius Lacer. In 1499 construction was begun on the new Monastery of S. Benito, birthplace of the knightly order of Alcántara, with a Gothic-Renaissance church by Pedro de Ibarra; the complex was finished in 1577. The parish church of S. María de Almocóbar, with a late Romanesque façade, contains the tomb of Antonio Bravo (16th cent.) and panels by Luis de Morales.

BIBLIOG. J. R. Mélida y Alinari, in R. Menéndez Pidal, Historia de España, II, Madrid, 1935, pp. 579–81 (bibliog.); L. Crema, Architettura romana, Turin, 1959, p. 216; G. Velo y Nieto, El castillo y plaza fuerte de Alcántara, B. Asociación Española Amigos de los Castillos, XI, 1963, pp. 175–98.

Badajoz. The Roman Pax Augusta, it preserves many of its Roman and Visigothic monuments. The Alcazaba (ca. 1170) has well-preserved walls and crenelated towers, such as the Torre de Espantaperros, octagonal and with blind arches, which houses the Museo Arqueológico Provincial. The Cathedral (1232–84) has the aspect of a fortress, with a severe tower (1240–1419); the *chevet* was reconstructed about 1600 and the portal in 1619. It has a nave and two aisles; the *coro* (1555) is by Jerónimo de Valencia; and the high altar

(1708) is Churrigueresque. Also of interest are the bronze tomb slab of Lorenzo Suárez de Figueroa (d. 1507), ambassador to Venice; canvases by Pedro Atanasio Bocanegra and José Antolínez; and a relief of the Virgin and Child, attributed to Desiderio da Settignano. The cloister is in the late Gothic style (1509–20).

BIBLIOG. Museo de Bellas Artes, Catálogo, Badajoz, 1943; L. Torres Balbás, La Alcazaba almohade de Badajoz, Al-Andalus, VI, 1941, pp. 168–203; A. Rodríguez Moñino, La escultura en Badajoz durante el siglo XVI, BSEAAV, XIII, 1946–47, pp. 101–31; J. Serra Rafols, La villa romana de la dehesa de "La Cocosa," Badajoz, 1952; A. Rodríguez Moñino, Los pintores badajoceños del siglo XVI, REE, XI, 1955, pp. 119–272; M. D. Gómez-Tejedor Cánovas, La catedral de Badajoz, Badajoz, 1958; J. M. Rubio Recio, Badajoz, REE, XVIII, 1962, pp. 225–71.

Cáceres. The Roman colony (Norba) was founded in the time of Augustus on the site of an earlier encampment. Only a few parts of the Roman walls survive, as well as a gate, now called the Arco del Cristo. The Almohads in the 12th century restored the walls and several towers (Torre de Bujaco, Torre Redonda, Torre Desmochada). S. María la Mayor, a Gothic church (15th–16th cent.) with nave and two aisles with cross vaulting, has a main altarpiece by the sculptors Guillén Ferrán and Balduc (de Balduque; 1547). The Church of Santiago, of Romanesque origin, was remodeled in the 15th and 16th centuries; it has a nave without side aisles and three apses, the central one with a plateresque *reja* by F. Núñez and an altarpiece by Alonso Berruguete (1557). The Church of S. Mateo (14th cent.) was erected over a mosque and was enlarged in the 16th century. The church of the Franciscan monastery is Gothic, and the Sanctuary of Nuestra Señora de la Montaña, with an altarpiece by José Churriguera, is baroque. There are many aristocratic residences: the Casa de los Golfines de Arriba (15th cent.); the Casa de los Golfines de Abajo (16th cent.), one of the finest; the Torre de Mayoralgo (16th cent.); and the Casa de las Veletas, which houses the Museo Provincial de Bellas Artes (Iberian and Roman remains, 17th-century paintings, folklore collection).

Nearby there are numerous ruins of a large encampment (Cáceres el Viejo) on a small ridge; the encampment is perfectly rectangular, with thick walls and gates, and has a moat running all around it. A. Schulten, who excavated the site, identified it as the Castra Caecilia, Quintus Caecilius Metellus's encampment of 79 B.C. in his campaign against Quintus Sertorius.

BIBLIOG. A. C. Floriano y Cumbreño, El retablo de Santiago, Cáceres, 1918; J. R. Mélida y Alinari, Catálogo monumental de España: Provincia de Cáceres, I, Madrid, 1924; A. Schulten and R. Paulsen, Castra Caecilia, AAnz, 1928, pp. 1–29, 1930, pp. 58–87, 1932, pp. 334–48; A. C. Floriano, El retablo de Santa María la Mayor de Cáceres, BSEAAV, VII, 1940–41, pp. 85–95; A. Schulten, Castra Caecilia, Atlantis, XV, 1940, pp. 181–91; L. Torres Balbás, Cáceres y su cerca almohade, Al-Andalus, XIII, 1948, pp. 446–72; J. Rosa Roque, Guía de Cáceres y su provincia, Cáceres, 1951; A. C. Floriano, Guía histórico artística de Cáceres, 2d ed., Cáceres, 1952; M. A. Orti Belmonte, Cáceres y su provincia, Barcelona, 1954; A. García y Bellido, EAA, s.v. Cáceres, II, 1959, p. 247 (bibliog.); C. Callejo, Cáceres monumental, Madrid, 1960; G. Velo y Nieto, El Arco de la Estrella, Cáceres, 1960.

Calera de León (Badajoz). The ancient monastery of the Knights of Santiago has a church (nave without side aisles) with cross vaulting and a polygonal apse; the cloister is of the 16th century. Nearby is another monastery of the Knights of Santiago, S. María de Tentudia (13th cent.), with a Mudejar cloister and church, containing altarpieces with *azulejos* signed by Francisco Niculoso (called Pisano; 1518).

BIBLIOG. J. R. Mélida y Alinari, Conventual santiaguista de Calera de León, BRAH, CI, 1932, pp. 359–61.

Caparra (Cáceres). There are many remains of the Roman Capera: the walls, a bridge over the Ambroz River, a basilica, an amphitheater, and a quadrifrons triumphal arch.

BIBLIOG. J. R. Mélida y Alinari, Monumentos romanos de España, Madrid, 1925, p. 129; A. C. Floriano, Excavaciones en la antigua Caparra, AEA, XVII, 1944, pp. 270–86; L. Crema, Architettura romana, Turin, 1959, p. 452.

Coria (Cáceres). Once the capital of the Vettones, it was named Caurium by the Romans. The walls, originally Roman, were reconstructed during the Middle Ages. The castle is of the 15th century. The Cathedral was reconstructed by Pedro de Ibarra in the 16th century; the side portal is Gothic-Renaissance and the main portal is plateresque. The nave (without side aisles) is cross-vaulted. There are Gothic choir stalls (1489), a baroque main altarpiece (18th cent.), tombs from the 15th and 16th centuries, and *rejas* and other works in wrought iron by C. Polo (18th cent.). It has a 14th-century cloister and a tower from the 18th century.

BIBLIOG. [E. Escobar Prieto, La catedral de Coria, BSEE, IX, 1901, pp. 245–52; J. R. Mélida y Alinari, Monumentos romanos de España, Madrid, 1925, pp. 45–46; T. Martín Gil, Hierros artísticos de la catedral de Coria, AE, XXVIII, 1944, pp. 134–48; A. Díaz Martos, Las murallas de Coria, REE, XII, 1956, pp. 263–95; M. Muñoz de San Pedro, Coria y el mantel de la Sagrada Cena, Madrid, 1961; E. Hübner, RE, s.v.

Garrovillas (Cáceres). Originally an Iberian settlement, the town still preserves many dolmens. The architecture is typically regional. The Church of S. María (15th cent.) and the Gothic Church of S. Pedro, with nave and two aisles, are interesting. Nearby, at the confluence of the Tajo and Almonte rivers, is Alconétar, with the ruins of a large Roman bridge, possibly a work from the time of Trajan.

BIBLIOG. T. Martín Gil, Excursiones a viejas ermitas, REE, I, 1945, pp. 147–60.

Guadalupe (Cáceres). The Hieronymite monastery (1389) has a fortresslike aspect; it is Mudejar in style with Gothic, Renaissance, and baroque elements. The Gothic church (14th cent.), with hammered bronze doors, has a nave and two aisles with cross vaulting. Outstanding are the *reja* of the Capilla Mayor, forged by Francisco de Salamanca and Juan de Ávila (1510–14); the main altarpiece by Giraldo de Merlo, Jorge Manuel Theotocopuli, and the painters Vincenzo Carducci (Carducho) and Eugenio Caxes; the tombs of the Velasco family by the Flemish Anequin de Egas Cueman; and the bronze baptismal font by Juan Francés (1402). In the anteroom of the sacristy are paintings by Juan Carreño de Miranda; in the sacristy are the famous St. Jerome series that Zurbarán painted in 1638–47 and a St. Jerome by the sculptor Pietro Torrigiani (16th cent.). The Camarín de la Virgen (1688–96) contains canvases by Lucas Jordán. In the treasury are goldwork, a noteworthy collection of embroidered robes for the Virgin, ornaments, frontals, and illuminated missals. The Mudejar cloister has a small Gothic-Mudejar pavilion of brick in the center (1405). In the town, with streets typical of the region, are a college and hostelry in Mudejar style (16th cent.).

BIBLIOG. J. Acemel and G. Rubio, Guía ilustrada del monasterio de Nuestra Señora de Guadalupe, Barcelona, 1912; G. Rubio, Historia de Nuestra Señora de Guadalupe, Barcelona, 1926; J. A. Gaya Nuño, Zurbarán en Guadalupe, Barcelona, 1951; A. Álvarez, Carlos V y el Real Monasterio de Guadalupe, Comillas, 1958; C. Callejo, El Monasterio de Guadalupe, Madrid, 1958; A. Álvarez, Breve guía histórico-artística del Real Monasterio de Guadalupe, Seville, 1961.

Jerez de los Caballeros (Badajoz). It is girded by walls and has a large castle of the Knights Templar. The Gothic Church of S. Miguel has a baroque portal and a tower in the Andalusian style; also of interest are the churches of S. María and S. Bartolomé (both 16th cent.).

Mérida (Badajoz). A colony of veterans (anc. Emerita Augusta) founded by Publius Carisius, a legate of Augustus, in 25 B.C. on the right bank of the Guadiana River, it became the capital of the province of Lusitania. Under the late Empire it was one of the largest and most prosperous cities of Spain. The modern city retains considerable traces of the Roman layout and many of the colony's monuments, including the theater (24 B.C.) and the amphitheater, from the Augustan period; the walls, with a double-vaulted gate, rebuilt in the Visigothic period; the circus, the best preserved in Spain, of uncertain date; two bridges, one over the Guadiana River, more than half a mile long, the other over the Albarregas, about 400 ft. long, both frequently restored; a triumphal arch ("Arch of Trajan"); and a large villa with paintings and mosaics of the 2d and 3d centuries of our era. Other Roman remains have been incorporated into later buildings: the Casona del Conde de los Corbos, built from the colonnade of the so-called "Temple of Diana"; the portico of the Capilla de S. Eulalia, with elements from the Temple of Mars; the monument to S. Eulalia, formed by a pedestal, three cylindrical Roman altars, and a Corinthian capital from the Augustan Temple of Concord; and a house that was a Romano-Christian basilica. By the Guadiana is the Alcazaba, built on a Roman foundation and reconstructed by the Moslems (835). The aqueducts of Los Milagros and of S. Lázaro are certainly works of the Augustan era, as are the cisterns of Proserpina and Cornalvo. The churches of S. Eulalia and of S. María la Mayor are medieval. The Museo Arqueológico has one of the richest collections of Roman statuary and Visigothic architectural and decorative elements in Spain.

BIBLIOG. J. R. Mélida y Alinari, Mérida, Barcelona, 1929; J. Serra Rafols, La Alcazaba de Mérida, AEA, XIX, 1946, pp. 334–45; M. Almagro Basch, Mérida, 2d ed., Mérida, 1961; A. Marcos Pous, La iglesia visigoda de San Pedro de Mérida, Akten VII. int. Kong. für Frühmittelalterforschung (1958), Graz, Cologne, 1962, pp. 104–30; A. García y Bellido, EAA, s.v. (bibliog.).

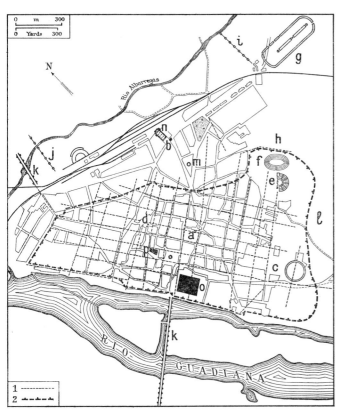

Mérida, archaeological plan. *Key:* (1) Roman drainage canals; (2) old walls. Principal Roman monuments: (*a*) "Temple of Diana"; (*b*) Temple of Mars; (*c*) site of Mithraeum; (*d*) "Arch of Trajan"; (*e*) theater; (*f*) amphitheater; (*g*) circus; (*h*) residential area (?); (*i*) aqueduct of S. Lázaro; (*j*) aqueduct of Los Milagros; (*k*) bridges; (*l*) necropolis. Principal medieval monuments: (*m*) monument to S. Eulalia; (*n*) Church of S. Eulalia; (*o*) Alcazaba; (*p*) Museo Arqueológico (*from M. Almagro Basch, 1961*).

Olivenza (Badajoz). The town preserves its walls and castle. The Church of S. María Magdalena has a plateresque portal; the interior is in the Manueline style, with nave and two aisles separated by twisted columns (16th cent.). The Church of S. María del Castillo was constructed about 1584 by Andrés de Arenas of Toledo in the Andalusian style. The façade of the Ayuntamiento is Manueline.

Plasencia (Cáceres). The walls (12th–13th cent.) are practically gone, although some of the gates remain. The bridges over the Jerte River are Gothic. The old cathedral, now the Church of S. María, has a nave and two aisles with cross vaulting and a Romanesque façade; the cloister is partly Romanesque; the chapter house has a pyramidal spire inspired by the Torre del Gallo of the Old Cathedral in Salamanca; there is a 14th-century tower. The architects Juan de Álava, A. de Covarrubias, Diego de Siloe, and R. Gil de Hontañón collaborated on the Catedral Nueva (New Cathedral), with nave and two aisles with tall pilasters and very complex vaulting. The altarpiece of the high altar is by the sculptor Gregorio Fernández and the painter F. Ricci (17th cent.); the choir stalls are Gothic, by Rodrigo Alemán (1492); the choir screen is by J. B. Celma (1604). The Cathedral museum contains paintings and codices. The Church of S. Nicolás contains the tomb of Bishop Carvajal. The Church of S. Martín has a main altarpiece painted by Luis de Morales (1565). The Church of S. Vicente (1464) contains a remarkable staircase (1577) and, in the sacristy, a frieze of *azulejos* from Talavera (16th cent.). There are Gothic and Renaissance patrician houses, such as the Casa del Deán, the Palacio de Mirabel, and the Casa de las Dos Torres.

BIBLIOG. V. Lampérez y Romea, La antigua sala capitular de la catedral de Plasencia, BSEE, IX, 1901, pp. 182–85; J. R. Mélida y Alinari, Dos retablos de azulejos de Talavera de la Reina existentes en Plasencia, BSEE, XXVII, 1919, pp. 56–61; F. Fernández Serrano, Artistas del libro litúrgico en Plasencia, BSEAAV, XVI, 1949–50, pp. 53–85; A. Fernández Prada, Historia y anales de la ciudad y obispado de Plasencia, Cáceres, 1952; M. del Carmen Pescados del Hoyo, El maestro Juan Alvares y la escalera del aire de Plasencia, REE, XV, 1959, pp. 397–404.

Talavera la Vieja (Cáceres). This was the Roman Augustobriga, from which are still preserved a tetrastyle temple, a forum with an impressive façade, and the ruins of an aqueduct. In the church there is an altarpiece with paintings by El Greco.

BIBLIOG. J. R. Mélida y Alinari, Monumentos romanos de la antigua Augustobriga, BRAH, LXXV, 1919, pp. 415–25; F. J. Sánchez Cantón, Viaje de un humanista español a las ruinas de Talavera la Vieja, AEAA, III, 1927, pp. 221–27; J. R. Mélida y Alinari, in R. Menéndez Pidal, Historia de España, II, Madrid, 1935, pp. 39–40, 591; A. Balil, FA, XII, 1957, no. 5853, XIV, 1959, no. 4739; E. Hübner, RE, s.v.

Trujillo (Cáceres). Trujillo was the Roman Turgalium. Sections of its medieval walls and of its Moorish castle, with four gates and strong walls, are still standing. The Church of S. María la Mayor (13th cent.) has a nave and two aisles with cross vaulting of the 15th century. The altarpiece of the high altar has 24 panels painted by Fernando Gallego (15th cent.). The Church of S. Francisco has a polychrome Virgin and Child (13th cent.). Notable among the many palaces are the plateresque Palacio del Marqués de la Conquista, with a corner balcony (16th cent.), and the Palacio del Duque de San Carlos (17th cent.).

BIBLIOG. F. Layna Serrano, Santa María la Mayor de Trujillo, BSEE, XLVII, 1943, pp. 243–58; F. Iñíguez Almech, Trujillo, Madrid, 1949.

Yuste (Cáceres). The Hieronymite monastery was founded at the beginning of the 15th century; the emperor Carlos V retired there in 1557 and died there the following year. Two patios are preserved, one Gothic and the other plateresque. The church has a nave without side aisles, with stellar vaulting and a raised choir. The simple palace has two stories with four rooms to each story.

BIBLIOG. D. M. de Alboraya, Historia del monasterio de Yuste, Madrid, 1906; J. J. Martín González, El palacio de Carlos V en Yuste, AEArte, XXIII, 1950, pp. 27–52, 235–52, XXIV, 1951, pp. 125–40; Cuacos de Yuste, Zaragoza, 1961.

Zafra (Badajoz). The Roman walls were reconstructed in the 15th century. The Alcázar was begun in 1437 by Lorenzo Suárez de Figueroa; it has a patio and Gothic-Mudejar ceilings in the chapel and in some of the rooms. The Church of la Candelaria (1546), with a Herreran façade, contains a 17th-century altarpiece with nine paintings by Zurbarán (1643–44). The Covent of S. Clara and the hospitals of Santiago and of S. Miguel are noteworthy.

BIBLIOG. M. L. Caturla, A retable by Zurbarán, BM, XCIV, 1952, pp. 47–48.

León. This region, corresponding to the ancient domain of the same name, comprises five provinces: León, Zamora, Salamanca, Valladolid, and Palencia. With a strongly established pre-Roman civilization, it entered on a rapid development during its Romanization, with important cities such as Legio VII (León), Palantia (Palencia), and Mirobriga (Ciudad Rodrigo). After the Visigothic and Moslem dominations, a brilliant and fecund medieval period began and the outstanding monuments in the Mozarabic, Romanesque, and Gothic styles were created. The productive phase lasted into the 16th and 17th centuries.

BIBLIOG. J. M. Quadrado, Asturias y León, Barcelona, 1885; J. M. Quadrado, Valladolid, Palencia, y Zamora, Barcelona, 1885; M. Gómez-Moreno, Iglesias mozárabes, 2 vols., Madrid, 1919; M. Gómez-Moreno, Catálogo monumental de España: León, 2 vols., Madrid, 1925–26; M. Gómez-Moreno, Catálogo monumental de España: Zamora, 2 vols., Madrid, 1927; F. Antón Casaseca, El arte románico zamorano, Zamora, 1929; R. Navarro García and R. Revilla Vielva, Catálogo monumental de la provincia de Palencia, 4 vols., Palencia, 1930–46; C. K. Hersey, The Salmantine Lanterns: Their Origins and Development, Cambridge, Mass., 1937; E. García Chico, Documentos para la historia del arte en Castilla, 3 vols., Valladolid, 1940–46; F. Antón Casaseca, Monasterios medievales de la provincia de Valladolid, Valladolid, 1942; A. Moro Gabriel, Los castillos de la provincia de Valladolid, Valladolid, 1952; J. E. Cirlot, Salamanca y su provincia, Barcelona, 1956; A. Gómez Martínez, Zamora y su provincia, Barcelona, 1958; E. García Chico, Partido judicial de Medina de Rioseco, Valladolid, 1959.

Aguilar de Campóo (Palencia). The town retains parts of its medieval walls, with various gates, such as the Puerta de Reinosa. The Benedictine Abbey of S. María la Real (12th–13th cent.) is in poor repair; its church was consecrated in 1222, and the cloister dates from 1209. The Church of S. Miguel contains some tombs (13th–16th cent.) and a 16th-century altarpiece. The town has a number of aristocratic houses.

BIBLIOG. V. Lampérez y Romea, El monasterio de Aguilar de Campóo, BSEE, XV, 1908, pp. 215–21; A. Fernández de Avilés, La collección Fontaneda en Aguilar de Campóo, RABM, LXVIII, 1960, pp. 757–79.

Alaejos (Valladolid). The 16th-century Church of S. María is a brick basilica with nave and two aisles. The vaults are ribbed, and the transept and Capilla Mayor have Mudejar *artesonados*. The main altarpiece was begun by Esteban Jordán in 1590.

BIBLIOG. J. J. Martín González, Esteban Jordán, Valladolid, 1952, pp. 89–92.

Alba de Tormes (Salamanca). The fortified tower of the ruined palace of the dukes of Alba contains paintings by Cristóbal Passini (1565). The town was once the center of Romanesque brick architecture with Mudejar elements. The Church of S. Juan has a Mudejar apse and two Romanesque aisles (12th cent.); there are Romanesque sculptures of the Virgin and Child and the Apostles. The Church of Santiago is brick and has Romanesque arches and cornices. The Church of S. Miguel is a mixture of Mudejar and Romanesque styles. The Carmelite convent, founded by St. Theresa in 1571, contains the tomb and relics of the foundress. In the vicinity of the town are the ruins of the Hieronymite Monastery of S. Leonardo (15th cent.).

BIBLIOG. E. Tormo y Monzó, Guía de Alba de Tormes, BRAH, XLVII, 1931, pp. 609–38.

La Alberca (Salamanca). The houses are built in a style typical of the region, in which granite is employed with latticework of wood. Medieval styles have survived in the local costumes. Nearby is the Monastery of las Bautecas, founded in 1597, surrounded by ruined hermitages.

Ampudia (Palencia). The 15th-century castle is square in plan and has several Gothic rooms with *artesonados*. In the Gothic collegiate church, where Gaspar de Solórzano worked (1541), there are a Renaissance pulpit and the Capilla de S. Ana; the reliefs on the altarpiece in the Capilla de S. Ildefonso, dating from before 1521, are attributed to F. Bigarny.

BIBLIOG. E. García Chico, Gaspar de Solórzano, maestro de cantería, BSEAAV, XV, 1948–49, pp. 169–79.

Arbás del Puerto (León). The village existed in the 12th century. The Church of S. María, founded by Alfonso VII, is Romanesque, with a cross-vaulted nave and two groin-vaulted aisles; it has three apses — the central one semicircular, with a noteworthy half dome with concave sections (*gallones*), the flanking ones square and barrel-vaulted — and richly decorated capitals and portals.

BIBLIOG. J. M. Luengo, Aportaciones para el estudio de la real colegiata de Santa María de Arbás del Puerto, AEArte, XIX, 1946, pp. 35–46.

Arcenillas (Zamora). There is an outstanding Gothic church that contains 15 panels from the main altarpiece of the Cathedral of Zamora, painted by Fernando Gallego in the 15th century.

Astorga (León). Of Roman origin (Asturica Augusta), Astorga preserves its Roman walls as well as sections of the medieval walls. The Romanesque Cathedral was reworked beginning in 1471, when a *chevet* in flamboyant Gothic style and the first two apses of the nave and aisles were constructed; in the second quarter of the 16th century the remaining part of the Romanesque building was razed and reconstructed in Gothic style under the direction of R. Gil de Hontañón. The baroque façade has a recessed portal (ca. 1660). The interior has a nave and two aisles and stellar vaulting; there is no transept. The Cathedral contains many works of art: a Romanesque Virgin and Child (12th cent.); an altarpiece in the Capilla Mayor carved by Gaspar Becerra (1558–62), to whom the pulpit is also attributed; tombs and altarpieces (16th–17th cent.); choir stalls (16th cent.); an Immaculate Conception by Gregorio Fernández; and stained-glass windows (16th cent.). The cloister and sacristy are of the 18th century. The treasury contains the crystal chalice of S. Toribio (10th–11th cent.) and ecclesiastical embroideries. Other churches are S. Julián, S. Bartolomé, S. María, and S. Francisco (13th cent.). The Ayuntamiento is of the 17th century. The Episcopal Palace is by A. Gaudí (1890). In the Museo Diocesano are a painted coffer (ca. 1300), panel paintings (15th–16th cent.), processional crosses (15th–16th cent.), a reliquary of the True Cross (12th cent.), a pyx by Sebastián de Encalada (16th cent.), the reliquary casket of Alfonso III the Great (10th cent.), and Romanesque remains from the early Cathedral.

BIBLIOG. S. Escanciana Nogueira, Una Inmaculada de Gregorio Fernández en la catedral de Astorga, AEArte, XXIII, 1950, pp. 73–77; J. M. Luengo, Los restos de la Sala Capitular del Real Convento de Santa Clara de Astorga, AEArte, XXIV, 1951, pp. 164–65; L. F. Matinot, Notas para una bibliografía astorgana, Astorga, 1955; J. M. Luengo, Astorga romana, Noticiario arqueol. hispánico, V, 1956–61, pp. 152–77.

Astudillo (Palencia). The walls with fortified towers and gates remain. The Church of S. María contains an altarpiece on which Hernando de Inestrosa worked (1570), and the tomb of Fernando Alonso. In the Church of S. Eugenia there are an altarpiece (15th cent.) and a monstrance of 1508. In the Church of S. Pedro the altarpiece is attributed to H. de Inestrosa; and there are various Gothic paintings. A simple Mudejar palace, constructed by order of Doña María de Padilla (1353), was later converted into the Convent of S. Clara.

BIBLIOG. A. Orejón Calvo, Historia documentada de la villa de Astudillo, Palencia, 1928.

Bamba (Valladolid). The Mozarabic church (S. María) was constructed about 920, employing abutments. The lower half has been reconstructed. The tympanum of the portal rests on brackets decorated with rosettes (1195). A Mozarabic capital serves as a holy-water font.

BIBLIOG. M. Gómez-Moreno, Iglesias mozárabes, I, Madrid, 1919, pp. 193–202.

Baños de Cerrato (Palencia). The Visigothic Church of S. Juan Bautista (FIG. 307) was dedicated by King Recceswinth in 661; its nave and two aisles are separated by horseshoe arches over columns with Corinthian capitals. The *chevet* has three square chapels.

BIBLIOG. J. Agapito y Revilla, La basílica visigoda de San Juan de Baños, Valladolid, 1902.

Becerril de Campos (Palencia). There are remains of the old walls, with a Gothic gate. In the town are the churches of S. Pelayo, S. María, S. Mario, and S. Martín, with several Gothic paintings and plateresque carvings; S. Pedro, with a Romanesque portal; and S. Eugenia, with a portal in the late Gothic style and paintings by Pedro Berruguete (15th cent.).

BIBLIOG. M. Pereda de la Reguera, Documentos y noticias inéditos, Altamira, 2–3, 1951, pp. 175–205; A. Redondo, Monografía histórica de Becerril de Campos, Palencia, 1953.

Béjar (Salamanca). Sections of its medieval walls remain. The Church of S. María is of the 13th century, that of S. Salvador of the 16th. The Alcázar del Duque de Osuna (16th cent.) has a classical patio.

Benavente (Zamora). Parts of the city walls remain. There are ruins of a castle with the Torre del Caracol (16th cent.). The Church of S. María del Azogue (12th–16th cent.) has a nave and two aisles, five Romanesque apses, and Romanesque portals in the transept; it contains a sculpture group of the Annunciation (13th cent.). The Church of S. Juan del Mercado, begun in 1182, has three Romanesque apses; the south portal is sculptured.

BIBLIOG. M. Gómez-Moreno, Dos iglesias románicas en Benavente, Arquitectura, XI, 1928, pp. 179–87.

Carracedo (León). The Benedictine monastery was founded in 1138; part of the church remains, and the entrance to the chapter house is of the Cistercian type. Near the monastery is a Gothic building (13th cent.), supposedly a royal palace, with three large halls.

BIBLIOG. E. Puyol, El monasterio de Carracedo, BRAH, XCII, 1928, pp. 19–22.

Carrión de los Condes (Palencia). The Church of S. María del Camino (12th cent.) has Romanesque sculptures on the façade. The Church of Santiago has a Romanesque frieze on the façade (1165), showing the Pantocrator with the Apostles. The Monastery of S. Zoilo contains tombs (13th cent.) in the Capilla de los Condes, one signed "Pedro," and a Renaissance cloister designed by Juan de Badajoz (1537).

BIBLIOG. R. Revilla Vielva, Sepulcros de los Beni Gómez, ITTM, I, 1949, pp. 39–41.

Cervera de Pisuerga (Palencia). In the Church of S. María del Camino (or del Castillo) is a Renaissance altarpiece over the high altar and another in the Capilla de S. Ana, both attributed to Felipe Bigarny. The town has several houses with heraldic shields.

BIBLIOG. M. Cagigal, Capilla de Santa Ana en Cervera des Río Pisuerga, BSEE, XXXII, 1924, pp. 40–41.

Cisneros (Palencia). In the Church of S. Pedro, containing some Gothic tombs, the ceilings and *artesonados* are Mudejar; the main altarpiece is by F. Giralte (before 1548). The Church of S. Facundo (16th cent.) and the Capilla de la Virgen del Castillo also have Mudejar ceilings.

Ciudad Rodrigo (Salamanca). The city preserves its Roman walls, three gates, and the Alcázar (14th cent.). The Cathedral was begun in 1165 and finished after 1230. The Romanesque Puerta de las Amajuelas in the transept has a sculptured tympanum; the west portal (Puerta de la Virgen) has sculptures of the 13th century. The interior has a nave and two aisles, a transept, foliated arches of Mudejar influence, groin vaults, and a Capilla Mayor with stellar vaulting (16th cent.). The choir stalls are by Rodrigo Alemán (1503); there are an alabaster altarpiece by Lucas Mitata (16th cent.) and several tombs. The cloister is by Benito Sánchez (14th cent.) and Pedro Güémez (16th cent.). The tower by Juan Sagarvinaga dates from 1765. In the city the Capilla de Cerralbo (1585–1685) has a painting by Ribera. The churches of S. Andrés and S. Pedro have Romanesque façades. The Ayuntamiento is in Renaissance style. There are several aristocratic residences, such as the Palacio del Marqués de los Altares (16th cent.), the Casa de los Miranda, and the Palacio de Montarco (15th–16th cent.).

BIBLIOG. M. Hernández Vegas, Ciudad Rodrigo, Salamanca, 1935; R. M. Quinn, Fernando Gallego and the Retablo of Ciudad Rodrigo, Tucson, 1961; M. Cabello y Lapiedra, Ciudad Rodrigo, Barcelona, n.d.

Cozuelos de Ojeda (Palencia). The Monastery of S. Eufemia was founded in 1185. The Romanesque church (12th cent.) is in the form of a Latin cross, with three semicircular apses.

BIBLIOG. M. A. García Guinea, La iglesia románica de Santa Eufemia de Cozuelos, AEArte, XXXII, 1959, pp. 295–311.

Dueñas (Palencia). The Church of S. María has a main altarpiece, carved choir stalls (both 16th cent.), a Gothic altarpiece, and several wall tombs (13th–16th cent.). Nearby is the Monastery of S. Isidro, founded in the 10th century, with a church (12th–13th cent.) that has been much modified.

BIBLIOG. F. Antón Casaseca, San Isidoro de Dueñas, AEArte, XXV, 1952, pp. 129–42; J. J. Martín González, La sillería de la iglesia de Santa María de Dueñas, AEArte, XXIX, 1956, pp. 117–23; R. Revilla Vielva, ed., Excavaciones en la villa romana del "Cercado de San Isidoro," Madrid, 1964.

La Espina (Valladolid). The Cistercian abbey was founded in 1147. The church (12th–13th cent.) has a nave and two aisles with cruciform pilasters; a transept; and the Capilla de los Vega (15th cent.), with stone urns used as sarcophagi and with stellar vaulting. The central apse dates from the 16th century. In the cloister, reconstructed in the 17th century, is a chapter house dating from the 12th–13th. The façade of the abbey dates from 1578 to 1584; the façade of the church is of the 18th century.

BIBLIOG. F. Antón Casaseca, Monasterios medievales de la provincia de Valladolid, Valladolid, 1942, p. 115.

Frómista (Palencia). The Romanesque Church of S. Martín (late 11th cent.) has a nave and two aisles, a transept, three round apses, an octagonal lantern over the crossing, and barrel vaults; the capitals are among the finest of Castilian Romanesque art. The Church of S. María del Castillo (14th–16th cent.) contains a painted altarpiece (ca. 1500) with panels by Juan de Flandes on the predella.

BIBLIOG. J. de Ciria, De Madrid a Frómista, BSEE, XII, 1904, pp. 219–24.

Gradefes (León). The Cistercian abbey was founded in 1168. The church was constructed as far as the transept in the first stage, with an ambulatory and three semicircular apsidal chapels; in the 13th or 14th century a short nave was added.

BIBLIOG. L. Torres Balbás, Sillerías de coro mudéjares, Al-Andalus, XIX, 1954, pp. 203–18.

Grajal de Campos (León). The castle (16th cent.), on a square plan, crenelated and flanked by round towers at each corner, was the first in Spain to be built with defenses to resist artillery. A palace (1540) was constructed by an architect who copied the patio and the stairway of the Archbishop's Palace in Alcalá de Henares.

BIBLIOG. J. M. Luengo, Las piezas de orfebrería de Grajal de Campos, AEArte, XIV, 1940–41, pp. 76–78.

Ledesma (Salamanca). The town is surrounded by well-preserved medieval walls. The Church of S. María (16th cent.) has a baroque altarpiece and some Gothic tombs. A medieval bridge spans the Tormes River. Nearby are remains of thermal baths, possibly Roman.

BIBLIOG. R. Aguirre Ibáñez, Arte y espíritu de la ciudad y su provincia, Salamanca, 1954.

León. The city is of Roman origin, from which era it retains its walls, although much restored in later times, and the thermae beneath the Cathedral. The most important medieval monument is the Church of S. Isidoro el Real (XII, FIG. 345); from its construction in the Romanesque period (it was founded in 1063) it preserves only the Panteón de los Reyes, with fine historiated capitals, and frescoes from the 12th century. The present church, with nave and two aisles, was constructed by Petrus Deustamben in the 12th century and has portals with excellent Romanesque statuary in the tympanums, capitals, and spandrels; within are an 11th-century baptismal font and a Gothic altarpiece. The treasury contains, among other things, an ivory reliquary casket (11th cent.), an enamel casket (12th cent.), and an agate chalice (11th cent.); the library possesses an illuminated Bible of 960.

The Cathedral (1258–ca. 1303) was built under the direction of Master Enrique and Juan Pérez. Statuary of the 13th century adorns the three portals of the façade and the south entrances. The interior consists of a nave and two aisles, a transept, triforium, and ambulatory; the magnificent stained-glass windows are from the 13th–16th centuries. Of the contents of the chapels the most outstanding are a Calvary by Juan de Balmaseda (1524) and the tombs of Ordoño II, Martín Rodríguez (both 13th cent.), and Rodrigo Álvarez. The altarpiece of the Capilla Mayor has paintings by Nicolás Francés (1427); also on the high altar is the silver custodial of S. Froilán, by Enrique de Arfe (1519). The *coro* has stalls by Juan de Malinas

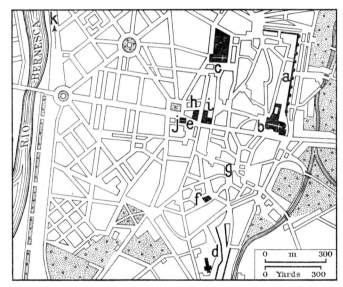

León, plan of city center. (*a*) Roman walls; (*b*) Cathedral; (*c*) S. Isidoro el Real; (*d*) S. Ana; (*e*) S. Marcelo; (*f*) S. María del Mercado; (*g*) Plaza of S. Martín; (*h*) Casa de los Botines; (*i*) Casa de los Guzmán; (*j*) Ayuntamiento; (*k*) S. Marcos.

(1467) and Diego Copín, of Holland (1475); the *trascoro* has reliefs by Esteban Jordán (1585). A vestibule with a Gothic doorway and containing a tomb with Romanesque sculpture leads into the cloister, dating from the 13th–14th century and completed in the 16th by Juan de Badajoz; noteworthy is another doorway, of walnut, dating from 1538. In the cloister there are frescoes by Nicolás Francés (1459) and Gothic tombs by Martín Fernández and Pedro Yáñez. Near the chapter house is the treasury, which contains Mudejar cabinets, Gothic sculpture, and codices and documents (8th–15th cent.).

Other churches are S. Marcelo (1588), with sculptures by Gregorio Fernández; Nuestra Señora del Mercado, Romanesque (12th cent.); S. Marina, with sculptures by Juan de Juni (ca. 1545); and S. Marcos (16th–18th cent.), with sacristy by Juan de Badajoz and choir stalls by G. Doncel (1542). The Museo Arqueológico Provincial, installed in the Convent of S. Marcos, contains, among other things, an ivory crucifix from the monastery of Carrizo (11th cent.) and the Mozarabic cross of Peñalba. Noteworthy secular buildings are the

Casa de los Guzmán (16th cent.; now the Diputación Provincial), the Ayuntamiento (16th cent.), and the Casa de los Botines, designed by A. Gaudí (ca. 1900).

BIBLIOG. A. Nieto, Guía del Museo Arqueológico de León, Madrid, 1925; F. J. Sánchez Cantón, Nicolás Francés, pintor, AEAA, I, 1925, pp. 41-65; J. Pérez Llamazares, Historia de la Colegiata de San Isidoro de León, León, 1927; J. C. Torbado, Catedral de León: Retablo de la capilla del Cristo, AEAA, VII, 1931, pp. 213-19; M. Gómez-Moreno, El arca de las reliquias de San Isidoro, AEAA, VIII, 1932, pp. 205-12; J. C. Torbado, El crucifijo del trascoro de la catedral de León, AEAA, VIII, 1932, pp. 49-52; G. Gaillard, León, Jaca, Compostelle, Paris, 1938; D. M. Robb, The Capitals of the Pantheon de los Reyes, AB, XXVII, 1945, pp. 165-74; J. J. Martín González, El Panteón Real de San Isidoro de León, BSEE, LIV, 1950, pp. 157-66; M. Domínguez Berrueta, La catedral de León, Madrid, 1951; M. Domínguez Berrueta, León, Barcelona, 1953; A. Cruz y Martín, Pinturas románicas del Panteón Real de San Isidoro de León, León, 1958; J. J. Martín González, La sillería de San Marcos, Goya, 29, 1958-59, pp. 279-83; A. García y Bellido, EAA, s.v.

Medina del Campo (Valladolid). The Church of S. Antolín (14th cent.) is built on the basilica plan, with nave and two aisles. It has a square Capilla Mayor from the 16th century; its altarpiece was finished in 1558 and is attributed to Juan Picardo. The Church of S. Miguel has a main altarpiece by Leonardo de Carrión (1567). The Church of la Magdalena was decorated by the Corral de Villalpando brothers (ca. 1558) and has a Calvary altarpiece by Esteban Jordán (1571). The Church of Santiago has an altarpiece attributed to Adrián Álvarez (16th cent.). The hospital was founded in 1591, with a church (1597) and patio (1619) by Juan de Tolosa. The Casa de las Dueñas (before 1556) has a façade of brick and a Renaissance patio attributed to Andrés de Nájera. The Casa Blanca is a square structure with a small patio decorated by the Corral de Villalpando brothers (1563). The Castillo de la Mota was reconstructed in brick by Fernando de Carreño about 1440, then enlarged and reconstructed by the Catholic Monarchs toward the end of the century.

BIBLIOG. J. Agapito y Revilla, La Casa Blanca en Medina del Campo, Arquitectura, I, 1918, pp. 149-57; E. García Chico, El templo de San Miguel de Medina, BSEAAV, X, 1943-44, pp. 103-22; E. García Chico, El palacio de las Dueñas de Medina del Campo, BSEAAV, XVI, 1949-50, pp. 87-110; E. García Chico, La Colegiata de Medina del Campo, Valladolid, 1957; J. M. Caamaño Martínez, El retablo de San Martín de Medina del Campo, BSEAAV, XXVII, 1961, pp. 31-44; E. García Chico, Catálogo monumental de la provincia de Valladolid: Medina del Campo, Valladolid, 1961.

Medina de Rioseco (Valladolid). The Church of S. María de Mediavilla (15th-16th cent.) is built on the basilica plan, with a nave and two aisles with stellar vaults; the octagonal Capilla Mayor has an altarpiece by Juan de Juni (1573) and Esteban Jordán (1585); the Capilla de los Benavente is square, with a dome on pendentives, with decorations by Jerónimo del Corral del Villalpando (1544-46) and an altarpiece by J. de Juni (1557). The Church of Santiago has a Renaissance façade designed by R. Gil de Hontañón and executed by Miguel de Espinosa. The Church of S. Francisco has a nave, without side aisles, with complex cross vaults; the lateral altars have plateresque altarpieces by Miguel de Espinosa with terra-cotta figures by J. de Juni; the pulpits are plateresque. The Church of Sta Cruz has a façade by Juan de Nates (ca. 1608) and an original dome over the sanctuary by Fray Diego del Castillo (1654).

BIBLIOG. E. García Chico, La capilla de los Benevente en Santa María de Rioseco, BSEAAV, II, 1933-34, pp. 319-58; E. García Chico, Medina de Rioseco, Valladolid, 1956; E. García Chico, Catálogo monumental de la provincia de Valladolid: Medina de Rioseco, 2d ed., Valladolid, 1960.

Moreruela (Zamora). The Cistercian abbey was founded in 1131. The church, begun in 1168, consists of nave and two aisles, transept, and ambulatory, a plan that influenced later Castilian and Leonese Gothic construction. The decoration is simple and austere. There is a barrel-vaulted sacristy; the chapter house in the cloister has square piers and ogival vaults.

BIBLIOG. M. Gómez-Moreno, El primer monasterio español de cistercienses: Moreruela, BSEE, XIV, 1906, pp. 97-105; M. P. Eydoux, L'abbatiale de Moreruela et l'architecture des églises cisterciennnes d'Espagne, Cîteaux in de Nederland, V, 1954, pp. 173-207; L. Torres Balbás, El monasterio bernardo de Moreruela, AEArte, XXVII, 1954, pp. 333-35; M. Cocheril, Apropos de la fondation de Moreruela, Cîteaux in de Nederland, XII, 1961, pp. 61-79.

Nava del Rey (Valladolid). The Church of los Santos Juanes (16th-17th cent.) is on the basilica plan, with nave and two aisles and three apses. The main altarpiece (1612-26), designed by Juan de Muniátegui, is the work of Francisco Velázquez and Gregorio Fernández.

BIBLIOG. E. García Chico, Una obra desconocida de Gregorio Fernández, BSEAAV, XVII, 1950-51, pp. 67-73; E. García Chico, La iglesia de San Juan de Nava del Rey, BSEAAV, XIX, 1952-53, pp. 143-51.

Olmedo (Valladolid). The 13th-century Church of S. Andrés consists of a nave without side aisles and a semicircular apse with round arches on the exterior. The Church of S. Miguel has nave and two aisles and a wide apse with barrel vaults. The chapel at the Monastery of la Mejorada (15th cent.) is square in plan and has a Mudejar dome with a circling band of decorative brickwork, supported by flying buttresses; it contains some tombs decorated with Gothic-Mudejar plasterwork. The Church of S. Juan, without side aisles, is Mudejar, as is the Arco de la Villa.

BIBLIOG. J. de Igual, Excursión a Olmedo, BSEE, VIII, 1900, pp. 97-99.

Palencia. This city, capital of the Celtic-Iberian Vaccaei, was conquered by the Romans and then by the Visigoths. It enjoyed a brilliant period during the Middle Ages. The present Cathedral, built over the 7th-century Visigothic crypt of St. Antolín, was begun in 1321 and finished in 1516. The side portals — Puerta de los Reyes (plateresque), Puerta de los Novios (early 16th cent.), and Puerta del Obispo (15th cent.) — are noteworthy. The interior consists of a nave and two aisles, transept, ambulatory, and triforium. The Capilla Mayor has a reja by Cristóbal Andino (1520); an altarpiece with sculptures by F. Bigarny (1505) and J. de Balmaseda (1519) and paintings by Juan de Flandes (1506); and, along its exterior wall, tombs of the Deán Enríquez (d. 1465), of the Abbot of Husillos (16th cent.), and of Diego de Guevara (d. 1509). The Capilla de S. Pedro was decorated by the Corral de Villalpando brothers (16th cent.). In the Capilla de Nuestra Señora la Blanca are interesting tombs. Noteworthy among the many altarpieces in the Cathedral are the one in the Sagrario (16th cent.); the one showing S. Ildefonso, possibly by Juan de Balmaseda (1525); and those in the Capilla de S. Gregorio (16th cent.). The pulpit ("de Cabeza de Vaca") is by Juan Ortiz (1541) and others. The decoration of the trascoro is in late Gothic style, perhaps by Juan de Ruesga (16th cent.); there is a triptych by Jan Joest von Kalkar (ca. 1505). The screen of the coro is by Gaspar Rodríguez (1571) and the Gothic choir stalls are by Luis Centellas. The door leading to the cloister is plateresque (1536). The Martyrdom of St. Sebastian by El Greco is in the sacristy (ca. 1580). The treasury contains a diptych by P. Berruguete, a monstrance in chased silver by Juan de Benavente (1581-85), numerous pieces of goldwork, and embroideries. The Gothic cloister is by Juan Gil de Hontañón (16th cent.); the chapter house has a canvas by Mateo Cerezo and Flemish tapestries (16th cent.).

The Church of S. Miguel (13th cent.) has a fortified Gothic tower. The Church of S. Pablo, founded in 1217, has a Gothic altarpiece in the Capilla del Deán Zapata (1516); in the Capilla Mayor are a 17th-century reja, plateresque altarpiece in polychromed wood, and the tombs of the Rojas family (16th-17th cent.). The 14th-century Church of S. Francisco has a large rose window and contains the tomb of Alonso Martínez (ca. 1500). The conventual church of S. Clara (15th cent.) is on the Greek-cross plan. The Museo Arqueológico Provincial contains prehistoric and Roman collections, some tombs (12th-13th cent.), and an altarpiece from Amusco (14th cent.).

BIBLIOG. E. García Chico, Bordadores palentinos, BSEAAV, X, 1943-44, pp. 207-12; E. García, Los tapices de Fonseca en la catedral, BSEAAV, XIII, 1946-47, pp. 173-96, XIV, 1947-48, pp. 189-203, XVI, 1949-50, pp. 143-49; E. García Chico, La custodia de la catedral de Palencia, BSEAAV, XIII, 1946-47, pp. 133-37; T. García Cuesta, La catedral de Palencia según los protocolos, BSEAAV, XIX, 1952-53, pp. 67-90, XX, 1953-54, pp. 91-142; J. San Martín Payo, Retablo mayor de la catedral de Palencia, ITTM, X, 1953, pp. 275-312; M. Vielva Ramos, La catedral de Palencia, Palencia, 1953; T. García Cuesta, Cinco rejas de la catedral de Palencia, BSEAAV, XXI-XXII, 1954-56, pp. 109-34; J. Milicua, Palencia monumental, Madrid, 1954; M. A. García Guinea, El arte románico en Palencia, Palencia, 1961.

Paredes de Nava (Palencia). Of pre-Roman origin, this town enjoyed great splendor during the Middle Ages. Among the various churches are S. María, with altarpieces of St. John the Evangelist (14th cent.) and of S. Antón by Manuel Álvarez (1558); S. Juan, with some Gothic paintings and others by P. Berruguete; and S. Eulalia, Gothic with modifications, containing a main altarpiece by E. Jordán (1556), a predella with paintings by P. Berruguete, Gothic and Renaissance woodcarvings and paintings, and a collection of goldwork and embroideries.

BIBLIOG. D. Angulo Iñíguez, Pedro Berruguete en Paredes de Nava, Barcelona, 1946; T. Teresa León, Templos paredeños, ITTM, IX, 1953, pp. 5-27.

Peñafiel (Valladolid). The magnificent castle was constructed mainly in the 14th century, on an elongated plan; it has double defensive walls and round towers along the wall, with the powerful Torre de Homenaje in the center. The church of the Monastery of S. Pablo, begun in 1324, has a Mudejar apse of Toledan influence, with foliated horseshoe arches; adjoining the church is the Capilla del Infante (1536), which recalls the art of Juan de Badajoz and the Corral de Villalpando brothers. Other churches are S. Miguel, attributed to Juan de Herrera; S. María, with a 16th-century altarpiece; and El Salvador, containing a processional cross (16th cent.).

BIBLIOG. J. R. Mélida y Alinari, El castillo de Peñafiel, BRAH, LXXI, 1917, pp. 58–67.

Peñalba de Santiago (León). The Mozarabic Church of Santiago (X, FIG. 365), built between 931 and 937, consists of a nave without side aisles and apses of horseshoe plan to the east and west; it is barrel-vaulted, with echinus molding, and has horseshoe arches. There are some remains of pre-Romanesque paintings.

BIBLIOG. M. Gómez-Moreno, Santiago de Peñalba, BSCE, IV, 1909–10, pp. 193–204; J. Menéndez Pidal, Las pinturas prerrománicas de la iglesia de Santiago de Peñalba, AEArte, XXIX, 1956, pp. 291–95; J. M. Luengo Martínez, De la Tebaida leonesa: Montes y Peñalba, Tierras de León, I, 2, 1961, pp. 25–41.

Ponferrada (León). The town is of Roman origin. The castle retains some sections from the 12th century. The Ayuntamiento (1692) is modeled on those of León and Astorga. The Church of Nuestra Señora de la Encina (1573) contains a Mary Magdalen by Gregorio Fernández.

BIBLIOG. J. M. Luengo Martínez, El castillo del Ponferrada, León, 1929; J. M. Luengo Martínez, El ayuntamiento de Ponferrada, BSEE, LII, 1944, pp. 280–92.

Sahagún (León). There are remains of a Benedictine monastery built 1121–1213 and of a church with a nave and two aisles. The Church of S. Lorenzo (13th cent.) is Mudejar, with nave and two aisles, three apses, and a square tower over the central apse; it contains an altarpiece by Guillén Doncel and Juan de Angés (1545). The Church of S. Tirso (12th cent.) is of brick and has a nave and two aisles covered by a wooden roof; the apses and the tower are Mudejar. The Santuario de la Peregrina, in a Franciscan convent founded in 1257, is Mudejar, as is the Hermitage of la Virgen del Río.

BIBLIOG. R. Escalona, Historia del Real monasterio de Sahagún, Madrid, 1782.

Salamanca. This city, the ancient Salmantica, is of pre-Roman origin; it was captured by Hannibal in 217 B.C. and became a Roman settlement. The bridge over the Tormes River is an important monument from this period. The city was destroyed by the Moors, but after the reconquest in the 11th century and subsequent repopulation in the early years of the 12th century it became an important center. Its many Romanesque churches date from this century: S. Martín, with some Gothic tombs; S. Marcos, on a round plan; S. Juan Bautista (or de Bárbalos); S. Cristóbal, now a school; S. Tomás Cantuariense, dedicated to St. Thomas à Becket; and S. Julián. The Catedral Vieja (Old Cathedral), also begun in the 12th century, was finished in the 13th under the supervision of various master builders; it has a nave and two aisles and a transept with a lantern tower (the Torre del Gallo) on sculptured pendentives at the crossing. Noteworthy are the capitals; the main altarpiece and the vault of the presbytery, with paintings by Nicolás Florentino (15th cent.); the enameled Virgen de la Vega (12th cent.); the series of tombs (13th–14th cent.) in the presbytery and the transept; the mural paintings (1262) in the Capilla de S. Martín; and the cloister, with the Capilla de S. Bartolomé, containing tombs of the Anaya family, and the Capilla de Talavera. The Catedral Nueva (New Cathedral), backed against the old, was begun in 1513 under the direction of R. Gil de Hontañón but was not finished until 1733. The three portals of the façade are richly decorated in plateresque style; there is a fine relief of Christ entering Jerusalem on the north portal (Puerta de Ramos). The tower and the central dome were not completed until the 18th century. In the interior, with a nave and two aisles, are Flemish stained-glass windows (1556); the Capilla Dorada (1525), with profuse decoration; and a Virgin and Child by Luis de Morales (16th cent.). The choir stalls are by José de Lara and Alejandro Carnicero (1725–33); the baroque *trascoro* has a St. John and a St. Anne in polychromed wood by Juan de Juni. In the Capilla de los Dolores is a Pietà by L. S. Carmona (18th cent.). One of the sacristies is by J. Sagarvinaga (1755) and contains a large 16th-century monstrance. The Museo Diocesano has paintings by Fernando and Francisco Gallego, Pedro Bello,

and Juan de Flandes, as well as sculptures and Hispano-Moorish textiles (12th cent.).

Other noteworthy religious buildings are the Dominican monastery, with a cloister (16th cent.) and a plateresque façade on the church, which has frescoes by Antonio Palomino (1705) and a main altarpiece by José Churriguera (1693); the Church of S. Benito, with late Gothic sculpture and tombs; the Church of el Espíritu Santo, with a plateresque façade and a Mudejar lower choir; the Convent of S. Isabel, with *artesonados*; the Convent of las Dueñas, with a Renaissance façade and patio; the church of the Bernardine Convent, by R. Gil de Hontañón; the Church of S. María de la Vega, with arcades from the Romanesque cloister (12th cent.); the Convent of las Augustinas Recoletas (1636), with paintings by Jusepe de Ribera (1635) and Giovanni Lanfranco on the altarpiece of the high altar; and the Clerecía (seminary), founded in 1614, with a baroque church and a cloister that is probably by Andrés García de Quiñones.

The University, which was already in existence in the 13th century, has a graceful plateresque façade. The Escuelas Menores (1533) has two plateresque portals on the south side and one on the east side. The Colegio del Arzobispo (Irish College), with façade, patio, and church by Diego de Siloe and J. de Álava, contains an altarpiece by Alonso Berruguete (1529). The Colegio de Calatrava is baroque, by J. de Churriguera (1717). The Colegio of Anaya, by J. Hermosilla (1760) and J. Sagarvinaga, has a neoclassic patio.

Among the medieval residences are the Torre del Clavero and the Casa de Doña María la Brava; from the late 15th and early 16th centuries are the Casa de las Conchas (so called because of the scallop shells decorating the façade) and the Casa de Abarca Maldonado (now the Museo Provincial de Bellas Artes); among Renaissance buildings are the Palacio de Monterrey (1539), the Palacio de Orellana (1576), the Casa de las Muertes, and the Casa de la Salina (now the Diputación Provincial). The Plaza Mayor, by A. de Churriguera (1729–55), is a good example of baroque city planning; the Ayuntamiento is by A. García de Quiñones.

BIBLIOG. M. Falcón y Ozcoidi, Salamanca artística y monumental, Salamanca, 1867; M. Gómez-Moreno, La capilla de la Universidad de Salamanca, BSCE, VI, 1913–14, pp. 321–29; M. Gómez-Moreno and F. J. Sánchez Cantón, El retablo de la catedral vieja de Salamanca, AEAA, IV, 1928, pp. 1–24; E. Tormo y Monzó, Las catedrales de Salamanca, Madrid, 1931; J. Camón Aznar, La iglesia del convento de Bernardas de Salamanca, AEArte, XIV, 1940–41, pp. 407–09; Marqués del Saltillo, La casa llamada de Fr. Luis de León en Salamanca, BSEE, XLV, 1941, pp. 11–19; J. González, El retablo del altar mayor de la Clerecía en Salamanca, AEArte, XV, 1942, pp. 346–50; J. González, La catedral vieja de Salamanca y el probable autor de la Torre del Gallo, AEArte, XVI, 1943, pp. 39–50; A. García Boiza, La iglesia y convento de Agustinas en Salamanca, Salamanca, 1945; A. García Boiza, Salamanca monumental, Madrid, 1950 (2d ed., 1959); F. Chueca Goitia, La catedral nueva de Salamanca, Salamanca, 1951; T. Prieto, Salamanca: la Ciudad de oro, Madrid, 1952; J. Camón Aznar, Salamanca, Madrid, 1953; J. M. Muñoz, Las murallas salmantinas y sus puertas, Zephyrus, IV, 1953, pp. 29–33; R. Aguirre Ibáñez, Arte y espíritu de la ciudad y su provincia, Salamanca, 1954; J. Gudiol Ricart, Las pinturas de Fernando Gallego en la Universidad de Salamanca, Goya, 13, 1956, pp. 8–13; J. M. Pita Andrade, La huella de Fonseca en Salamanca, CEG, XIV, 1959, pp. 209–32.

Saldaña (Palencia). In the Church of S. Miguel are some chapels with 16th-century altarpieces and tombs such as those of the Santander and Osorio families. The Church of Nuestra Señora del Valle is baroque. Among the patrician houses is that of the Marqués de la Valdavia.

San Andrés del Arroyo (Palencia). The convent is a daughter establishment of the one of Las Huelgas in Burgos, which was in existence in 1181. The church has a nave without side aisles and with a transept; the presbytery is octagonal, with a square chapel at each end. The cloister is Romanesque.

BIBLIOG. E. Almaraz, Monasterio de San Andrés del Arroyo, BRAH, XXXVI, 1900, pp. 210–18.

San Cebrián de Mazote (Valladolid). The wooden-roofed Mozarabic church (before 916) has a nave flanked by two aisles separated by horseshoe arches. It has a transept and three apses, the central apse of horseshoe plan and the ones on the sides square. The capitals are Corinthian.

BIBLIOG. V. Lampérez y Romea, La iglesia de San Cebrián de Mazote, BRAH, LXIX, 1916, pp. 231–34.

San Martín de Castañeda (Zamora). The town is of Visigothic origin. The church (12th cent.) is Romanesque, with nave and two aisles and three apses modeled after the Cathedral of Zamora.

San Miguel de Escalada (León). The Mozarabic church (X, FIG. 365) was founded by the Abbot Alfonso, who had emigrated from Córdoba; it was consecrated in 913. Its nave and two aisles are separated by horseshoe arches, and the roof is of wood; there are three apses of horseshoe plan and echinus molding around the vaulting. The tower (11th cent.) and side door are also Mozarabic.

BIBLIOG. M. Gómez-Moreno, Iglesias mozárabes, I, Madrid, 1919, pp. 141–62.

San Pedro de Dueñas (León). The monastery was founded by Abbot Pedro de Sahagún before 1107. The church has a nave and two aisles and three apses in Romanesque style, influenced by S. Isidoro el Real at León; other parts are in Mudejar and Gothic styles.

BIBLIOG. V. Lampérez y Romea, La iglesia de San Pedro de Dueñas, BSEE, XII, 1904, pp. 1–5.

San Pedro de la Nave (Zamora). The Visigothic church (7th cent.; XI, FIG. 667) has a nave and two aisles separated by trefoil arches on square pillars. There are barrel vaults, decorative molding, and historiated capitals.

BIBLIOG. E. Camps Cazorla, El visigotismo de San Pedro de la Nave, BSEAAV, VII, 1940–41, pp. 73–80.

San Pelayo de Perazancas (Palencia). The Romanesque church was erected in 1076 by Abbot Pelayo. It has a nave without side aisles; the apse has half-columns with a frieze along the curvature of the arches. There are Romanesque paintings of saints in the apse and of a bishop on one of the columns.

BIBLIOG. J. Gudiol Ricart, Las pinturas románicas de San Pelayo de Perazancas, ITTM, XVII, 1958, pp. 13–15.

Santa Marta de Tera (Zamora). The monastery existed as early as the 10th century; the church is Romanesque (12th cent.) on a Latin-cross plan, with an aisleless nave and a square apse. It has historiated capitals and Romanesque sculptures; along the walls are decorative friezes.

BIBLIOG. M. Gómez-Moreno, Santa Marta de Tera, BSEE, XVI, 1908, pp. 81–87.

Santiago de la Puebla (Salamanca). The large church (15th–16th cent.) has a nave and two aisles with groin vaulting. In the Gómez de Santiago chapel is a plateresque reja; there is an altarpiece by F. Bigarny and Diego de Siloe and sculpture and paintings of the 16th century.

Simancas (Valladolid). The Moorish castle was rebuilt in the 13th century and restored by Juan de Herrera (1564); it is now the Archivo General. In the Church of El Salvador the main altarpiece is by Inocencio Berruguete (1562); there are two other altarpieces, one a Pietà by Francisco de la Maza (16th cent.) and another by Gaspar de Tordesillas (1536).

Támara (Palencia). Some of its medieval fortifications remain. The Gothic Church of S. Hipólito (1334) has a nave and two aisles, three polygonal apses, a portal with splayed arches, and a tower designed by Rodrigo Gil de Hontañón. There are rejas, altarpieces (16th cent.), and choir stalls executed in 1577 by Hernando de Inestrosa.

BIBLIOG. R. Navarro García and R. Revilla Vielva, Catálogo monumental de la provincia de Palencia, I, Palencia, 1930, p. 25; M. Pereda de la Reguera, Rodrigo Gil de Hontañón, Santander, 1951, pp. ccx–ccxi.

Tordesillas (Valladolid). In the 15th-century Church of S. Antolín there is an altarpiece by Juan de Juni (ca. 1570) and the tomb of Alderete by Gaspar de Tordesillas (1550–62). The Convent of S. Clara, the former palace of Pedro el Cruel (ca. 1340), has a Mudejar façade, a small patio with horseshoe arches with floreated stuccowork along the spandrels, and baths of Moorish type. The aisleless church, with groin-vaulted nave, has a Mudejar ceiling (15th cent.) in the Capilla Mayor; the chapel of Fernán López Saldaña, constructed by Guillén de Rohán (1430), contains tombs and a triptych by Nicolás Francés.

BIBLIOG. V. Lampérez y Romea, El real monasterio de Santa Clara en Tordesillas, BSCE, VI, 1912–13, pp. 169–72; J. Agapito y Revilla, El sepulcro del comendador Alderete en San Antolín, AE, V, 1916, pp. 340–45; L. Torres Balbás, El Baño de Doña Leonor de Guzmán en el palacio de Tordesillas, Al-Andalus, XXIV, 1959, pp. 409–25.

Toro (Zamora). A good part of the medieval wall remains, and the bridge over the Duero River is from the 15th century, with later alterations. The Church of S. María la Mayor (1160–1240) has nave and two aisles, transept, three apses with ogival and barrel vaulting, and a lantern over the crossing. The west portal (13th cent.) is richly decorated with Gothic sculpture; the north portal is late Romanesque. The interior has 13th-century statuary, and in the sacristy are a relief of the Epiphany (16th cent.) and a Flemish painting of la Virgen de la Mosca. The Church of El Salvador is Mudejar (13th cent.), with nave and two aisles and three apses with decorated arcades. The Church of S. Lorenzo, also Mudejar (12th cent.), has a main altarpiece by Fernando Gallego (15th cent.) and Gothic tombs. S. Pedro del Olmo and S. María de la Vega (13th cent.) are also Mudejar. The Convent of Espíritu Santo has a large church (14th cent.) with a Mudejar roof over the aisleless nave; it contains the alabaster tomb of Doña Beatríz de Portugal (15th cent.). The Convent of the Mercedarias Descalzas in the Palacio de los Ulloa (15th cent.) has a Gothic patio.

BIBLIOG. L. Torres Balbás, Patio del convento de Mercedarias de Toro, Arquitectura, II, 1919, pp. 250–51; F. Casas y Ruiz del Arbol, Monumentos artísticos de Toro, 2 vols., San Sebastián, 1950.

Valbueno de Duero (Valladolid). The Cistercian abbey was founded in 1144. The church (12th–13th cent.) is well preserved and comprises a nave and two aisles, a transept, and five chapels in the chevet; it has ogival vaulting. Other buildings include the chapter house, the refectory, and a cloister (13th cent.) with pointed arches.

BIBLIOG. F. Antón Casaseca, Monasterios medioevales de la provincia de Valladolid: Santa María de Valbueno, BSEE, XXX, 1922, pp. 160–206.

Valencia de Don Juan (León). The castle was rebuilt in the 15th century, with tall towers that give it an unusual aspect. In the Church of S. Pedro is an altarpiece by Guillén Doncel (1543). The churches of S. Juan (14th cent.) and S. María are Mudejar.

BIBLIOG. A. Gutiérrez Cuñado, El retablo de Guillén Doncel, BSEAAV, IX, 1942–43, pp. 79–87.

Valladolid. The unfinished Cathedral is built on the site of the 11th-century Romanesque collegiate church; it was designed by Juan de Herrera about 1585 but was constructed slowly, with many important changes. In the Capilla Mayor are choir stalls by Juan de Juni and an altarpiece that the same sculptor made in 1551 for S. María la Antigua. The sacristy houses a monstrance by Juan de Arfe (1590) over 6 ft. high, whose main subject is Adam and Eve. The church of the Monastery of S. Pablo (nave without side aisles) has a flamboyant Gothic façade (15th cent.) by Simón de Colonia and two side portals richly decorated in Gothic style. The Colegio de S. Gregorio is also Gothic, with modifications by Juan Guas; it has a splendid façade, with heraldic ornament, and a patio with tall twisted columns on the first floor and a richly decorated arcaded gallery on the second floor. It now houses the Museo Nacional de Escultura, with an outstanding collection of Castilian religious sculpture of the 15th and 16th centuries. The Church of Santiago (15th–16th cent.) has an Epiphany altarpiece by Alonso Berruguete. S. Catalina has a crucifix by Juan de Juni (1571), and S. Isabel has a St. Francis by the same sculptor. The 16th-century Church of El Salvador has a sculptured Flemish altarpiece. The Church of la Magdalena (16th cent.) has an enormous escutcheon on the façade; within is an altarpiece by F. Giralte (16th cent.); the main altarpiece (1571–75) is by E. Jordán. Gregorio Fernández made the sculptures for the altarpiece (1613) of the Convent of las Huelgas, as well as various wood sculptures for the churches of la Vera Cruz, S. Miguel, and S. Martín. In the Church of Nuestra Señora de las Angustias, which has a façade by Juan de Nates (1597), is the "Virgen de los Cuchillos" by Juan de Juni. In the Church of Porta Coeli there are various paintings by Horacio Borgianni (17th cent.). The Augustinian monastery was designed by Ventura Rodríguez (1760). The Church of S. Ana, by Sabatini (1780), contains three canvases by Goya and three by Bayeu, as well as sculptures by Gregorio Fernández. Among the secular buildings, the Renaissance Colegio de Sta Cruz (1491) is outstanding; it contains the Beatus manuscript of Valcavado (970) in its library and houses the Museo Arqueológico Provincial. There are several Renaissance residences: the Palacio Valverde, the Palacio Real (now the Capitanía General), and the Casa del Sol. The University has a baroque façade (1715).

BIBLIOG. J. Martí y Monsó, Estudios histórico-artísticos, 2 vols., Valladolid, 1898–1901; J. Agapito y Revilla, La iglesia del convento de San Pablo y el Colegio de San Gregorio, Valladolid, 1911; J. Agapito y Revilla, La capilla de San Juan Bautista en la parroquia del Salvador, Valladolid, 1913; J. Agapito y Revilla, Una obra auténtica de Berruguete: El retablo de la Adoración de los Reyes en Santiago, BSCE, VI, 1913–14, pp. 121–33; E. García Chico, El barroco en Valladolid, BSEAAV, X, 1943–44, pp. 161–

68; C. Candeira Pérez, Guía del Museo Nacional de Escultura, Valladolid, 1945; M. A. García Guinea and F. Wattenberg, La iglesia de Santa María de la antigua de Valladolid, BSEAAV, XIII, 1946-47, pp. 147-72; F. Chueca Goitia, La catedral de Valladolid, Madrid, 1947; J. J. Martín González, La iglesia de la Magdalena en Valladolid, BSEAAV, XIV, 1947-48, pp. 205-14; J. J. Martín González, La arquitectura doméstica del Renacimiento en Valladolid, Valladolid, 1948; E. García Chico, Juan Guas y la capilla del colegio de San Gregorio, BSEAAV, XVI, 1949-50, pp. 200-01; J. J. Martín González, Guía histórico-artística de Valladolid, Valladolid, 1949; S. Rivera Manescau and F. Wattenberg, Las escavaciones de la Granja José Antonio de Valladolid, BSEAAV, XX, 1953-54, pp. 143-49; J. J. Martín González, Arquitectura dieciochesca vallisoletana, BSEAAV, XXI-XXII, 1954-56, pp. 29-37; G. Nieto Gallo, Valladolid, Barcelona, 1954; E. García Chico, Valladolid, Valladolid, 1958; J. J. Martín González, Anotaciones sobre la Plaza Mayor de Valladolid, BSEAAV, XXV, 1959, pp. 161-68; V. Rodríguez Valencia, La catedral de Valladolid, BSEAAV, XXVII, 1961, pp. 360-72; E. García Chico, La Cofradía penitencial de la Santa Vera Cruz, Valladolid, 1962.

Villafranca del Bierzo (León). The Romanesque churches of S. Juan (12th cent.) and Santiago (before 1190) have a nave without side aisles and richly decorated portals. The Church of S. Francisco has a Mudejar ceiling. The Church of S. María was reconstructed in 1535. The Jesuit college dates from 1647 and its church, with a baroque façade, from 1726.

BIBLIOG. M. Gómez-Moreno, Catálogo monumental de España: León, I, Madrid, 1925, p. 383; M. Pereda de la Reguera, Rodrigo Gil de Hontañón, Santander, 1951, pp. cxxviii-cxxxi.

Villagarcía de Campos (Valladolid). The collegiate church, founded in 1527, was constructed by Juan de la Vega after designs by Rodrigo Gil de Hontañón that were modified by Juan de Nates. The altarpiece of the high altar was designed by Juan de Herrera, with the reliefs in alabaster executed by Juan de Tordesillas (1579-82). The pulpit is by Andrés de Rada (16th cent.).

BIBLIOG. J. J. Martín González, El relicario de la Colegiata de Villagarcía de Campos, BSEAAV, XVIII, 1951-52, pp. 43-52; P. Pirri and others, Villagarcía de Campos: Historia de un pasado glorioso, Bilbao, 1952; E. García Chico, Los artistas de la colegiata de Villagarcía de Campos, BSEAAV, XX, 1953-54, pp. 43-80; J. J. Martín González, La colegiata de Villagarcía de Campos y la arquitectura herreriana, BSEAAV, XXIII, 1957, pp. 19-40.

Villalcázar de Sirga (Palencia). The Gothic Church of S. María la Blanca (13th cent.) has a side portal with two sculptured doors. The interior has a nave and two aisles, transept, and three rectangular apses. The tomb of the infante Don Felipe (d. 1274) and his wife, Doña Leonor Rodríguez de Castro, is especially fine; there are also some painted Gothic altarpieces.

BIBLIOG. A. Rubio Salán, Breve noticia de Villalcázar de Sirga y su templo, ITTM, VIII, 1952, pp. 27-45.

Villalón de Campos (Valladolid). The tower of the Church of S. Miguel was completed by Felipe Berrojo in 1692. In front of the church stands a Gothic-Renaissance column from the early 16th century.

Villalpando (Zamora). Sections of the 12th-century city wall remain; the Puerta de S. Andrés was begun in the 12th century and completed in the 16th. The Church of S. María la Antigua is Mudejar (13th cent.), with decorative arches in its three apses. In the same style are the churches of S. Nicolás and S. Pedro.

Villanueva de Cañedo (Salamanca). The Palacio de Fonseca (15th-16th cent.) mixes Gothic with Mudejar and Renaissance styles. It is built on a square plan with towers at the corners. The central patio, with two stories of arches, has Gothic parapets on three of its sides. The ceilings are Mudejar.

Zamora. The city walls are chiefly from the 12th century, with subsequent alterations; the Puerta de la Feria (known as the Arco de Doña Urraca), the Puerta de Olivares, and the Puerta de S. Ana form part of them. The bridge over the Duero is of the 13th century, with later reconstructions. The Cathedral is Romanesque (12th cent.), with a massive tower (ca. 1200) and a Gothic chevet (1496-1506); the Romanesque Puerta del Obispo is on the south façade. The interior has a cross-vaulted nave and two groin-vaulted aisles; there are square piers with three columns on each face; the barrel-vaulted transept has a lantern on pendentives at the crossing. The coro has a 16th-century screen, and stalls by Rodrigo Alemán (15th-16th cent.); in front of the presbytery are wrought-iron rejas and pulpits (16th cent.). Outstanding among the works of art are the altarpiece of Nuestra Señora la Calva (13th cent.); the altarpiece of the

high altar, sculptured by V. Rodríguez in 1772; the tomb of Juan de Grado (1507); the altarpiece of S. Ildefonso, painted by Fernando Gallego (1466); and the carved doors (16th cent.) to the sacristy and the cloister. In the Museo Catedralicio are sculptures by Bartolomé Ordóñez, a monstrance in plateresque style (1515) by Juan de Arfe and Master Claudio, and Flemish tapestries (16th-17th cent.). There is a group of Romanesque churches of the 12th century: S. Tomé, S. Cebrián, S. María la Nueva, Santiago el Viejo, S. Claudio de Olivares, Santiago del Burgo, S. Esteban, S. Isidoro, S. Pedro, S. María de la Orta, and La Magdalena, the last with a fine south portal and a Romanesque tomb (12th cent.). In S. Andrés is the tomb of Antonio Sotelo by Pompeo Leoni (1598). The Casa de los Momos (now the Audiencia) has a late Gothic façade. The Museo Provincial de Bellas Artes houses Roman steles, Visigothic objects from Villafáfila, medieval and Renaissance statuary, and paintings (16th-20th cent.).

BIBLIOG. F. Antón Casaseca, Estudio sobre el coro de la catedral de Zamora, Zamora, 1904; F. Antón Casaseca, El templo de Santa María Magdalena en Zamora, Zamora, 1910; M. Gómez-Moreno, La gran tapicería de la Guerra de Troya, AE, VIII, 1919, pp. 265-81; A. Gómez Martínez and B. Chillón Sampedro, Los tapices de la catedral de Zamora, Zamora, 1925; F. Antón Casaseca, Los relievos románicos de San Cipriano de Zamora, BSEE, XXXIV, 1926, pp. 167-75; A. Weyler, Una visita al catedral de Zamora, BSEE, XXXIV, 1926, pp. 61-71; M. Gómez-Moreno, Catálogo monumental de España: Zamora, 2 vols., Madrid, 1927; L. Torres Balbás, Las murallas de Zamora, BRAH, CXL, 1957, pp. 45-47; A. Gómez Martínez, Zamora y su provincia, Barcelona, 1958.

Galicia. After a period of Celtic culture, represented by various sites where abundant remains have been found, the region developed into an important Roman province. Following phases of domination by the Suevi, the Visigoths, and the Moslems, the development of Galicia was influenced by the international movement of pilgrims to Compostela. The flowering of the Romanesque style was not paralleled in the subsequent Gothic or Renaissance styles but had a worthy sequel in the brilliant Galician baroque, with its own unique character. The region is divided into four provinces: La Coruña, Lugo, Orense, and Pontevedra.

BIBLIOG. M. Murguía, Galicia, Barcelona, 1888; A. del Castillo, Guía artística de la provincia de Orense, Orense, 1928; P. Pérez Constanti, Diccionario de artistas en Galicia durante los siglos XVI y XVII, Santiago, 1930; J. Couselo Bouzas, Galicia artística en el siglo XVIII y primera mitad del XIX, Santiago, 1933; R. Otero Pedrayo, Guía de Galicia, 2d ed., Santiago, 1945; J. Carro García, Las catedrales gallegas, Buenos Aires, 1950; L. Torres Balbás, Monasterios cistercienses de Galicia, Santiago, 1954; M. Chamoso Lamas, La arquitectura barroca en Galicia, Madrid, 1955; E. Ferreira Arias, Monumentos en Galicia, Pontevedra, 1955; J. Filgueira Valverde and A. García Alén, Carta arqueológica de la provincia de Pontevedra, Pontevedra, 1957; J. M. Caamaño Martínez, El gótico en Galicia, Goya, 32, 1959, pp. 79-82; E. Álvarez, Vias romanas de Galicia, Zephyrus, XI, 1960, pp. 5-103; A. Bonet Correa, La arquitectura en Galicia durante el siglo XVII, Goya, 39, 1960, pp. 189-96; A. del Castillo López, La arquitectura de Galicia en la epoca de los Suevos, Bracara augusta, XI-XII, 1960-61, pp. 7-12; A. Rodríguez González, Documentos de arte gallego, BSEAAV, XXVII, 1961, pp. 297-315, XXVIII, 1962, pp. 245-50; J. M. Caamaño Martínez, Contribución al estudio del gótico en Galicia (Diocesis de Santiago), Valladolid, 1962; J. M. Pita Andrade, Visión actual del románico de Galicia, CEG, XVII, 1962, pp. 137-53; F. J. Sánchez Cantón, La vida en Galicia en los tiempos del arte románico, CEG, XVII, 1962, pp. 182-201; A. Gallego de Miguel, El arte del hierro en Galicia, Madrid, 1963; J. M. Pita Andrade, Observaciones sobre la decoración geométrica en el románico de Galicia, CEG, XVIII, 1963, pp. 35-56; J. Taboada Chivite, Los castillos, Vigo, 1963.

Bande (Orense). The Visigothic Church of S. Comba (7th cent.) has a Greek-cross plan, with a square Capilla Mayor, and barrel vaulting and, in the transept, splayed rib vaulting; the triumphal arch is horseshoe-shaped; the windows have stone tracery.

BIBLIOG. V. Lampérez y Romea, Iglesia de Santa Comba de San Torcuato de Bande, BRAH, LXXIX, 1921, pp. 107-09.

Betanzos (La Coruña). The Church of Santiago is late Romanesque, with a St. James on horseback on the tympanum. The Gothic Church of S. Francisco (ca. 1385) has a single aisle with lateral chapels, a transept, and three apses; it contains the tomb of F. Pérez de Andrade (d. 1397) and a statue of the Virgin (15th cent.). S. María de Azogue (14th cent.) has a nave and two aisles with wood roofing and three apses.

BIBLIOG. M. Martínez Santiso, Historia de la ciudad de Betanzos, Betanzos, 1892; V. Lampérez y Romea, La iglesia de San Francisco de Betanzos, BRAH, LXXIV, 1919, pp. 6-13.

Carboeiro (Pontevedra). The Monastery of S. Lorenzo (826) was reconstructed beginning 1171. It has a church with a nave and two aisles, a crypt, ambulatory, and three apsidal chapels. The central portal has a representation of the Elders of the Apocalypse, resembling the one in the Cathedral at Compostela.

Bibliog. E. Lambert, La influencia de Saint-Denis y la iglesia de Carboeiro, Arquitectura, VI, 1924, pp. 181–90; J. Filgueira y Valverde, San Lorenzo de Carboeiro, AEArte, XIV, 1940–41, pp. 59–68.

Celanova (Orense). The Benedictine Monastery of S. Salvador has a church by Melchor de Velasco Agüero (1661) with nave and two aisles and a baroque façade (1755). One cloister (1550) has round arches and groin vaulting; another cloister (1611–1722) is Ionic and baroque. In the garden the little Mozarabic Church of S. Miguel (10th cent.) has a single aisle, a transept, and an apse of horseshoe plan.

Bibliog. M. Chamoso Lamas, La iglesia conventual de Celanova y el barroco gallego, B. Mus. Arqueol. Orense, II, 1946, pp. 61–73.

La Coruña (anc. Ardobicum Curonium). The Church of S. María del Campo, begun at the end of the 12th century and finished in 1302, has a barrel-vaulted nave and two aisles without transept and a semicircular apse; the portal has a sculptured tympanum. Of the original Franciscan monastery little remains; its church has a single aisle, a transept, and three apses. The baroque Church of S. Jorge is by Domingo de Andrade (1693). The church of the Capuchin convent was commissioned in 1715 from Fernando de Casas y Novoa; it contains a St. Francis by Zurbarán. Stretches of the old city ramparts remain, with three sea gates: S. Miguel (1595), El Clavo (1676), and El Parrote (late 17th cent.). The circular Jardín de S. Carlos is noteworthy. The Museo Provincial de Bellas Artes has an archaeological collection, paintings of the 17th–20th centuries, ceramics of Sargadelos, and examples of Galician folk art. Nearby, the square Torre de Hércules, a Roman lighthouse reconstructed in 1791, is still in use.

Bibliog. M. Chamoso Lamas, La iglesia de Capuchinas de Coruña, AEArte, XV, 1942, pp. 222–30; I. Martínez Barbeito, Catálogo del Museo Provincial de Bellas Artes de La Coruña, La Coruña, 1957; C. Martínez Barbeito, La Coruña, Barcelona, 1959; L. Menéndez Pidal, Las últimas restauraciones en Santa María del Campo de La Coruña, CEG, XV, 1960, pp. 15–26.

El Ferrol del Caudillo (La Coruña). The church of the Franciscan monastery is of the 14th century. The Church of S. Julián was designed by J. Sánchez Bort (1763). The 18th-century city layout followed English models.

Bibliog. J. J. Martín González, Una obra ferrolana de Jualián Sánchez Bort, BSEAAV, XIV, 1947–48, pp. 216–21.

Lugo. The city was founded by the Celts; under Augustus it was called Lucus Augusti. Its Roman walls were reconstructed in the 3d century over older remains; they are laid out on a square plan with semicircular towers set at intervals and four gates, of which only one remains (Puerta del Carmen). Close to the Miño River are the remains of some Roman baths. The Cathedral was begun by Raimundo de Monforte in 1129; it has a nave and two aisles and a triforium up to the transept. The chancel and ambulatory are of the 14th century. Of note on the exterior are the Torre Vieja (16th cent.); the north portal, with a Romanesque Christ in Majesty on the tympanum; and the austere façade, built 1769–83 according to plans by J. Sánchez Bort and Miguel Ferro Caaveiro. The reliefs of the former altarpiece for the high altar are the work of Cornelis de Holanda (1531); the baroque Capilla de Nuestra Señora de los Ojos Grandes is by F. de Casas y Novoa (1726); the choir stalls are by Francisco Moure (1621). The sacristy (1678) and the chapter house (1683) are by Domingo de Andrade; the cloister was finished by Casas y Novoa in 1714. The single-aisled Church of S. Francisco (15th cent.) has a transept and three polygonal cross-vaulted apses. The Church of S. Domingo dates from the 14th century. The Ayuntamiento (16th cent.) was remodeled in 1736 by L. Ferro Caaveiro. The Museo Provincial contains Celtic and Roman collections, examples of folk art, and modern painting and sculpture. The Museo Diocesano del Seminario contains a 5th-century Visigothic plaque of Quiroga.

Bibliog. I. Portabales Nogueira, El coro de la catedral de Lugo, Lugo, 1915; M. Chamoso Lamas, El claustro de la catedral de Lugo, AEArte, XIV, 1940–41, pp. 133–37; M. Vázquez Seijas, Guía del Museo Provincial, Lugo, 1947; L. Vázquez de Parga, Nuevos restos romanos en Lugo, BCPML, III, 1948, pp. 133–40; M. Vázquez Seijas, Enterramientos romanos de Lugo, BCPML, III, 1948, pp. 194–200; A. López Acuña, Edificios lucenses del siglo XV, BCPML, V, 1950, pp. 90–96; F. Vázquez Saco, La catedral de

Lugo, Santiago, 1953; M. Vázquez Seijas, Fortalezas de Lugo y su provincia, Lugo, 1959; N. Peinado, Lugo monumental y artístico, Madrid, 1962; A. Schulten, RE, s.v. Lucus Augusti; see generally BCPML, 1946 ff.

Mondoñedo (Lugo). The Cathedral was begun in Romanesque style at the beginning of the 13th century and continued on Gothic lines; at the end of the 15th century the lateral apses were replaced by an ambulatory. It has a nave with flanking aisles and a transept; richly sculptured Romanesque columns support the groin vaulting. The façade is Romanesque and Gothic, with two baroque towers and a rose window. The trascoro has a 15th-century image of the Virgin ("la Inglesa") said to have been brought over from England at the Reformation. The Capilla de Nuestra Señora de los Remedios dates from 1738.

Bibliog. J. Villaamil y Castro, La catedral de Mondoñedo, Madrid, 1865; E. Lence-Santar y Guitian, Nuestra Señora la Grande o la Inglesa de la Catedral de Mondoñedo, CEG, VI, 1951, pp. 65–82.

Monforte de Lemos (Lugo). Sections of the girding medieval wall remain, as well as the 13th-century Puerta de la Alcazaba and the castle with a square tower. The late Gothic Church of S. Vicente del Pino (1539) has Renaissance details; the vaulting is decorated with complicated tracery. The main altarpiece is by Francisco Moure (1625), the altarpiece of S. Benito is by Juan de Muniátegui (1600), and the pulpit dates from the 17th century. The cloister was finished in 1780. The Colegio del Cardenal (now a residence of the Theological School) was designed by Andrés Ruiz (1592) with the participation of Juan de Tolosa. It has a church in the center with a patio on each side; Simón de Monasterio finished the church and the east patio between 1608 and 1619, and the other patio dates from the 18th century. The single-aisled church, with dome and vaulting that foreshadow the baroque, contains five panel paintings by Andrea del Sarto (16th cent.) and two canvases by El Greco, a marble crucifix by Valerio Cioli (1595), and a bronze kneeling statue of the founder, Cardinal Rodrigo de Castro, by Juan de Bolonia (Giambologna; 1598).

Bibliog. A. Cotarelo Valledor, El cardenal don Rodrigo de Castro y su fundación de Monforte de Lemos, 2 vols., Madrid, 1945–46; J. M. Pita Andrade, Monforte de Lemos, Santiago, 1952.

Montederramo (Orense). The Cistercian abbey dates from 1153 but was reconstructed in the 16th century by Juan and Pedro de la Sierra from designs by Juan de Tolosa. The church has a nave and two aisles with a dome over the crossing; it has an exceptionally deep Capilla Mayor. The façade was finished in 1607. There are two cloisters, one with Gothic and the other with Renaissance elements.

Bibliog. M. Chamoso Lamas, El monasterio de Montederramo, AEArte, XX, 1947, pp. 78–94.

Monterrey (Orense). The castle, overlooking the town of Verín, is perhaps the most important in Galicia. It was in existence by the 13th century. In addition to the fortifications and the Torre de Homenaje it contains a hospital of the 14th century, a Gothic church, and buildings of the 16th century.

Bibliog. J. Taboada Chivite, Monterrey: Resumen histórico y arqueológico, B. Mus. Arqueol. Orense, III, 1947, pp. 27–43; J. Taboada Chivite, Monterrey, Madrid, 1960; N. Peinado, El castillo de Monterrey, B. Asociación Españ. Amigos Castillos, XI, 1963, pp. 211–18.

Orense. The Cathedral was in construction from 1132 but is mainly a work of the 13th century. It has a nave and two aisles and a long transept, pointed arches, three apses, and groin vaulting. The Pórtico del Paraíso was copied from the Pórtico de la Gloria in Compostela; the portals of the transept are more original (13th cent.). The lantern over the crossing, attributed to Juan de Badajoz (1499–1505), combines Gothic and Hispano-Mauresque styles. In the cloisters are selected pieces from the Cathedral treasure: Limoge enamels (12th cent.), a monstrance by Isidro Montanos (ca. 1660), an enameled golden cross by Enrique de Arfe, and silver altar frontal by Pedro Garrido (18th cent.). The single-aisled Church of S. Francisco (14th cent.) has three polygonal apses and a long transept; the 14th-century cloister has some fine capitals. The Church of S. Eufemia is the work of Plácido Iglesias (18th cent.). The bridge spanning the Miño is built on a Roman foundation. The Museo Arqueológico Provincial, in the former episcopal palace (13th cent.), contains rich prehistoric, Roman, and Visigothic collections.

Bibliog. E. Leirós Fernández, La custodia de la catedral de Orense, BCPMO, XV, 1946, pp. 145–63; E. Leirós Fernández and J. M. Pita Andrade, El deambulatorio de la catedral de Orense, Santiago, 1948; J. M. Pita

Andrade, La construcción de la catedral de Orense, Madrid, 1954; M.
Chamoso Lamas, El Museo de la catedral de Orense, BCPMO, XVIII, 1956,
pp. 249–76; M. Chamoso Lamas, El puente romano de Orense, CEG, XI,
1956, pp. 5–30.

Osera (Orense). The Cistercian abbey has a church that was
consecrated in 1239; toward the end of the same century Fernán
Martínez constructed the lantern. The church has a nave and two
aisles, an ambulatory, and three apsidal chapels. The 16th-century
chapter house has groin vaulting supported by twisted columns.
There are three cloisters, the most important dating from the 15th
century.

BIBLIOG. L. Torres Balbás, Monasterios cistercienses de Galicia, Santiago, 1954; Guía de Osera, Orense, 1960.

Pontevedra. Sections of the old walls remain. The Gothic Church
of S. María la Mayor, designed by Juan de los Cuetos and Diego
Gil, has a nave and two aisles, a transept, a deep Capilla Mayor,
cluster piers, and complex groin vaulting. The façade by Cornelis
de Holanda (1541) is in the manner of a retable; the Capilla de S.
Miguel dates from 1522; and the tower was executed by Diego Fernández after 1549. The Church of S. Francisco (14th–15th cent.)
contains some 14th-century sepulchers in the Capilla Mayor; the portal
is dated 1229. Only the *chevet* remains of the Church of S. Domingo;
it is used today as the Museo Arqueológico y Lapidario. The chancel
was erected in 1331 and the lateral chapels in 1383. The Church of
S. Bartolomé (1696–1714) has large columns on the façade; inside is
a Magdalen by Gregorio Fernández. The Capilla de la Peregrina is
the work of Antonio Souto (1778–82). The town has a beautiful old
quarter with patrician houses (15th–18th cent.), particularly in the
Plaza de la Leña. The Museo de Pontevedra, installed in the houses
of Castro Monteagudo and García Flórez (18th cent.), contains ecclesiastical art, paintings, and Galician handicrafts. In the vicinity of
the town are a Benedictine monastery (S. Salvador de Lérez) with
a baroque doorway (1748) and the typical coastal village of Combarro.

BIBLIOG. J. Filgueira Valverde, A Fonte da Ferreria de Pontevedra,
Santiago, 1933; A. Pardo Villar, Historia del Convento de Santo Domingo,
Pontevedra, 1942; F. J. Sánchez Cantón, El Museo de Pontevedra, Santiago,
1950; F. J. Sánchez Cantón, Pontevedra, Santiago, 1963.

Ribadavia (Orense). This is the capital of the district of El Ri-
bero, rich in megalithic and Roman archaeology. The towers and
some sections of the old walls remain. The churches of Santiago
and of S. Juan are Romanesque, from the late 12th century. The
Church of S. Domingo dates from 1277. The town has arcaded streets
with houses typical of the region. In the vicinity of the town are the
remains of three monasteries: S. Clodio, with a Cistercian church
and two cloisters (16th–18th cent.); Francelos, with the pre-Romanesque Church of S. Ginés; and Melón.

BIBLIOG. M. Chamoso Lamas, Ribadavia, Santiago, 1951; M. Chamoso
Lamas, Descubrimiento de una necrópolis medieval en el castillo de Riba-
davia, CEG, VIII, 1953, pp. 436–40; J. Sánchez García, La iglesia de Santa
María de la Oliveira de Ribadavia, BCPMO, XX, 1959–60, pp. 245–54.

San Esteban de Ribas de Sil (Lugo). The monastery has a Mozarabic hermitage of the 10th century. The present church was
begun in 1184. There are three cloisters and a Romanesque stone
altarpiece.

BIBLIOG. M. Chamoso Lamas and F. Pons-Sorolla, El monasterio de
San Esteban de Ribas de Sil y su retablo de piedra, CEG, XIII, 1958, pp. 35–
42; M. Chamoso Lamas, El monasterio de Santa Cristina de Ribas de Sil,
CEG, XVII, 1962, pp. 202–08.

Santa Eulalia de Bóveda (Lugo). The church was perhaps a
Roman nymphaeum (4th–5th cent.). Almost subterranean, it is
rectangular in plan; there are interesting paintings on the walls and
vaults. The portico has two columns and horseshoe arches.

BIBLIOG. M. Chamoso Lamas, Sobre el origen del monumento soterrado
de Santa Eulalia de Boveda, CEG, VII, 1952, pp. 231–51; N. Arez Vázquez,
Santa Eulalia de Boveda: Dos lisiados y un monasterio, BCPML, VII,
1962, pp. 115–23.

Santa Marina de Aguas Santas (Orense). The church (1193)
has a nave and two aisles, three apses with pointed arches, and a
false triforium. In the vicinity stands a monument of Celtic type
and the prehistoric encampment of Armea.

BIBLIOG. J. Lorenzo Fernández, El monumento protohistórico de Aguas
Santas y los ritos funerarios en los Castros, CEG, III, 1948, pp. 157–212;
M. Chamoso Lamas, Santa Marina de Aguas Santas, CEG, X, 1955, pp. 41–88.

Santiago de Compostela (La Coruña). Of prehistoric and Roman
origins, the city of Compostela reached a considerable eminence
after the 9th century because of the pilgrimage to the tomb of the
Apostle James the Great (Santiago). The Cathedral (XII, FIG. 342)
is of the 11th and 12th centuries, with changes from various epochs.
The main façade (Fachada del Obradoiro) is by F. Casas y Novoa
(1750); the Fachada de la Azabachería was designed by Ventura
Rodríguez (1757); the Pórtico Real de la Quintana is by J. Peña de
Toro (1657–66). The Puerta Santa was built in 1611; the clock
tower was begun in the 14th century and finished by Domingo de
Andrade in 1676–80. The Puerta de las Platerías (11th–12th cent.)
is decorated with fine Romanesque sculptures on the tympanum,
jambs, and high frieze. Under the stairway of the Obradoiro is the
Romanesque crypt (ca. 1168–75), and immediately behind the Obradoiro is the Pórtico de la Gloria, a masterpiece of Romanesque art by
Master Matthew. The interior of the Cathedral is laid out in the form
of a Latin cross, with nave and two aisles, transept, ambulatory, and

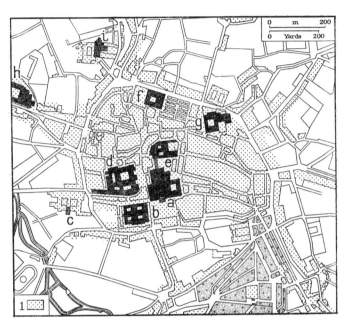

Santiago de Compostela, plan. *Key:* (1) Development to end of 18th century.
Principal monuments: (*a*) Cathedral; (*b*) Hospital Real; (*c*) S. Francisco;
(*d*) Monastery of S. Martín Pinario; (*e*) Monastery of S. Pelayo; (*f*) Monastery
of S. Agustín; (*g*) University; (*h*) Convent of S. Clara; (*i*) Monastery of S.
Domingo.

triforium. The nave is barrel-vaulted and flanked by groin-vaulted
aisles; there is a dome over the crossing. Many capitals and some
sculptures of the Romanesque period remain. In the Capilla Mayor
are a baroque altarpiece (17th cent.) and bronze pulpits by J. B.
Celma (16th cent.); the neoclassic Capilla de la Comunión (1771)
is by Miguel Ferro Caaveiro; the Capilla de la Corticela has a finely
sculptured Romanesque doorway; and the Capilla de las Reliquias,
by Juan de Álava (1527), contains a gold and silver monstrance by
Antonio de Arfe (1546) and baroque goldwork. The cloister was
begun by Juan de Álava (1521) and finished by Rodrigo Gil de Hontañón. The subsidiary buildings include the Archivo, which houses
the *Codex Calixtinus* (1149) and *Tumbo A* (12th–13th-cent. title deeds);
the library; and the chapter house (1751), which houses the Museo
Diocesano.

In the Palacio Arzobispal there are two Romanesque halls (ca.
1120) with sculptured corbels depicting banquet scenes. The Monastery of S. Martín Pinario, mentioned in the year 912, has a church
with a Renaissance façade (1598) and a main altarpiece by F. de Casas
y Novoa (1730). The Monastery of S. Pelayo contains Romanesque
statuary. The façade of the Convent of S. Clara (18th cent.) is by
Simón Rodríguez, who also designed the Church of S. Francisco.
The Capilla de las Angustias de Abajo (18th cent.) is by L. Ferro
Caaveiro. The Church of S. María de Sar (12th cent.) contains sections of the old Romanesque cloister. Notable among the secular
edifices are the Hospital Real (1501–11), after designs by Enrique
Egas; the Casa del Deán (1747); and the neoclassic Ayuntamiento,
by Carlos Lemaur (Charles Lemeaur). The University (1769–1805)
has a neoclassic façade; in the library is the illuminated Book of Hours
of Fernando I (1055).

BIBLIOG. K. J. Conant, The Early Architectural History of the Cathedral of Santiago de Compostela, Cambridge, Mass., 1926; S. Alcolea Gil, La Catedral de Santiago, Madrid, 1958; M. Chamoso Lamas, Santiago de Compostela, Barcelona, 1961; E. Kirschbaum, Die Grabungen unter der Kathedrale von Santiago de Compostela, RQ, LVI, 1961, pp. 234–54; J. Carro García, Del románico al barroco: Vega Verdugo y la capilla mayor de la catedral de Santiago, CEG, XVII, 1962, pp. 223–50; M. Chamoso Lamas, El Pórtico de las Platerías de Santiago de Compostela, Valencia, 1964.

Sobrado (La Coruña). Of the monastery (12th–13th cent.) there are scant remains; the church, with a baroque façade (1676) by Pedro Monteagudo, has a nave with flanking aisles and a dome over the crossing. There are three imposing cloisters (17th–18th cent.).

BIBLIOG. F. J. Sánchez Cantón, El monasterio de Sobrado, BRABASF, 2d Ser., XXII, 1928, pp. 130–37.

Túy (Pontevedra). A city of unknown antiquity, it was an episcopal see from the year 561. The Cathedral has the appearance of a fortress. The exterior walls, the transept, and the chancel were constructed by the beginning of the 13th century but remodeled toward the end of the 15th century; the main portal, with its Gothic sculptures and decoration, was completed before 1287. It has a Latin-cross plan, with a groin-vaulted nave and two aisles, a transept, three rectangular apses, and a triforium with blind arches. The cloister (1264) was reconstructed in 1408 and in 1464. The Church of S. Bartolomé is Romanesque in style, perhaps of the 12th century. The Church of S. Domingo is from 1330.

BIBLIOG. A. L. Mayer, The Decorated Portal of the Cathedral of Tuy, Apollo, II, 1925, pp. 8–12; J. Carro García, Alcazar y fortaleza de Tuy, CEG, VI, 1951, pp. 59–64; M. Fernández-Valdés Costas, La catedral de Tuy y su primitivo emplazamiento, CEG, VII, 1952, pp. 253–68.

Vigo (Pontevedra). The old quarter has typically Galician architecture (16th–18th cent.). The Church of Santiago is Gothic, with a Romanesque sculpture of the Saviour. The Church of S. María (1816) is neoclassic, designed by Melchor de Prado y Mariño. The Museo Municipal de Castrelos contains paintings by Francisco Collantes and others of various schools.

BIBLIOG. F. J. Sánchez Cantón, El salvador de Santiago de Vigo, Museo de Pontevedra, I, 1942, pp. 72–75; J. M. Álvarez Blázquez, Hallazgo de estelas funerarias romanas en Vigo, III Cong. Nac. Arqueol. (Galicia, 1953), Zaragoza, 1955, pp. 462–75.

Asturias. This region comprises a single province, Oviedo. The 9th and 10th centuries are particularly interesting artistically, and important monuments from this period remain.

BIBLIOG. J. M. Quadrado, Asturias y León, Barcelona, 1885; C. M. Vigil, Asturias monumental, epigráfica y diplomática, Oviedo, 1887; L. Menéndez Pidal, Los monumentos de Asturias, Madrid, 1954; H. Schlunk and M. Berenguer Alonso, La pintura mural asturiana en los siglos IX y X, Oviedo, 1957; J. M. de Luis, ed., Catálogo de las salas de Arte Asturiano Prerrománico del Museo Arqueológico Provincial, Oviedo, 1961; J. M. de Luis, Relaciones entre las arquitecturas asturianas y británica anteriores al siglo X, B. Inst. Estudios Asturianos, XVII, 1963, pp. 49–62; J. M. Pita Andrade, Arte asturiano, Madrid, 1963.

Amandi. The Romanesque Church of S. Juan (1134) has a nave without flanking aisles and a semicircular apse with a magnificent double arcade and fine capitals.

BIBLIOG. L. Menéndez Pidal, Los monumentos de Asturias, Madrid, 1954.

Covadonga. There is a sanctuary situated in a magnificent landscape. Nearby, a grotto contains the supposed tombs of the kings Pelayo and Alfonso I (8th cent.). Of the Church of S. Fernando the cloister (18th cent.) remains; it has round arches and contains some medieval tombs.

BIBLIOG. L. Menéndez Pidal, La cueva de Covadonga, Madrid, 1956; L. Menéndez Pidal, La cueva de Covadonga, Oviedo, 1958.

Lena. The Church of S. Cristina (9th cent.; XI, FIG. 667) is of the same structural plan and decorative order as S. María de Naranco. In the interior a single aisle with a narthex and a raised presbytery with an enclosure; above is a screen on three stilted arches with latticework, showing Mozarabic influence (10th cent.).

BIBLIOG. M. Jorge Aragoneses, En torno a la ermita de Santa Cristina de Lena: Nuevos hallazgos visigodos, AEArte, XXVII, 1954, pp. 147–54.

Llanes. There is a strong crenelated circular tower of the 13th century. S. María (13th cent. with later modifications) has a Romanesque portal; inside are a nave and two aisles with groin vaults and a main altarpiece (1517) with painting and sculpture.

BIBLIOG. J. F. Menéndez, Santa María de Llanes, Oviedo, 1925.

Nora. The Church of S. Pedro (10th cent.) shows influences of the Leonese-Mozarabic school; it has a vestibule, nave and two aisles, and three rectangular chapels.

BIBLIOG. M. Gómez-Moreno, Iglesias mozárabes, I, Madrid, 1919, pp. 86–88.

Oviedo. There are remains of the city walls of the 8th century. The Church of S. Tirso retains some elements from the 9th century. The Cathedral, begun in 1388 and finished in the early 16th century, consists of nave and two aisles, transept, ambulatory (17th cent.), and triforium; it has stellar vaulting. The Capilla del Rey Casto has a Gothic doorway with sculptures by Juan de Malinas (15th cent.) and Renaissance and baroque elements within. The choir stalls are from the 15th century, and the main altarpiece is by Benito Giralte and Juan de Balmaseda (1511–29). The Cámara Santa is a structure of two stories: the lower one (Capilla de S. Leocadia) has elements from the 9th century and the upper one (Capilla de S. Miguel), reconstructed in the 12th century, contains some of the finest Romanesque sculpture in Spain, six pilasters with magnificently sculptured Apostles, and various works of art of great importance, such as the Holy Casket (11th cent.), the Cross of the Angels (808) and the Cross of Victory (908), the Caja de las Agatas (10th cent.), several reliquaries, a Romanesque Christ of ivory (12th cent.), and three diptychs — one Byzantine (6th cent.), one Romanesque (12th cent.), and one Gothic (13th cent.). The cloister (14th–15th cent.) has a 13th-century chapter house and contains various Romanesque sculptures. In the Archivo is the *Liber Testamentorum* (ca. 1126). Other edifices are S. Domingo (16th cent.); the cloister of S. Vicente (14th cent.), now the Museo Arqueológico Provincial; the Monastery of S. Pelayo (18th cent.); the Hospicio Provincial, planned by V. Rodríguez and executed by Manuel Reguera (1768); and the baroque Palacio de Camposagrado (18th cent.).

In the vicinity of the city are the important Asturian churches of S. María de Naranco (848); S. Miguel de Lillo (ca. 848; XI, FIG. 667); and S. Julián de los Prados (first half of the 9th cent.; III, FIG. 95), which has remains of wall paintings.

BIBLIOG. A. Haupt, Die spanische-westgotische Halle zu Naranco und die nordlichen Königshallen, Mnh. für Kw., IX, 1916, pp. 242–63; F. Selgas, La basílica de San Julián de los Prados (Santullano) en Oviedo, Madrid, 1916; V. Lampérez y Romea, Nuevas investigaciones en la iglesia de San Miguel de Linio, BSEE, XXV, 1917, pp. 25–31; M. Duran, Capitales del claustro de la catedral de Oviedo, AE, XV, 1926, pp. 113–17, XVI, 1927, pp. 294–97; M. Gómez-Moreno, El retablo mayor de la catedral, AEAA, IX, 1933, pp. 1–20; M. Gómez-Moreno, El Arca Santa de Oviedo, AEArte, XVIII, 1945, pp. 125–36; J. Cuesta Fernández, Crónica del milenario de la Cámara Santa, Oviedo, 1947; J. Manzanares Rodríguez, Relieves románicos del antiguo claustro de la catedral, RUO, 2d Ser., I-II, 1950, pp. 113–28; H. Schlunk, The Crosses of Oviedo, AB, XXXII, 1950, pp. 91–114; R. Prieto Bances, Donacion de una iglesia a un altar, Cuadernos de h. de España, XVII, 1952, pp. 105–41; H. Schlunk, Las pinturas de Santullano, AEA, XXV, 1952, pp. 15–37; J. Cuesta Fernández, Guía de la catedral de Oviedo, Oviedo, 1957; J. Cuesta Fernández, La torre de la catedral de Oviedo, B. Inst. Estudios Asturianos, X, 1957, pp. 125–43; M. Fernández Avello, Reportaje a la catedral de Oviedo y su torre, B. Inst. Estudios Asturianos, XI, 1957, pp. 189–221; J. Cuesta Fernández, ed., XII Centenario de la fundación de Oviedo, Oviedo, 1961 (exhibition cat.); S. García Larragueta, Colección de documentos de la catedral de Oviedo, Oviedo, 1962; V. J. G. García, La iglesia de San Miguel de Liño, B. Inst. Estudios Asturianos, XVII, 1963, pp. 331–38.

Priesca. The Church of S. Salvador (921) has a nave and two aisles and three square-shaped chapels with barrel vaulting, the central one with wall arches.

BIBLIOG. J. R. Mélida y Alinari, La iglesia de San Salvador de Priesca, BRAH, LXI, 1912, pp. 125–28.

Salas. The collegiate church contains the tomb of the Grand Inquisitor Valdés, the work of Pompeo Leoni (1576–82), who also did the tombs of Valdés's parents, with praying figures. The Church of S. Martín encloses the remains of an earlier 10th-century building.

BIBLIOG. L. Menéndez Pidal, La antigua colegiata y palacio de Torre Salas, Academia, 3d Ser., VI, 1958, pp. 73–75.

Valdediós. S. Salvador (893; FIG. 307) has a nave and two aisles without transept, three chapels in its rectilinear *chevet*, and a vestibule;

it is barrel-vaulted and has some Mozarabic details. The Cistercian Church of S. María (1218) has nave and two aisles, transept, and three apses.

BIBLIOG. J. Fernández Meléndez, La basílica de San Salvador de Valdediós, BRAH, LXX, 1917, pp. 261–67; J. Menéndez, Santa María la Mayor de Valdediós, BSEE, XXVII, 1919, pp. 87–89; M. Berenguer Alonso, Breves notas sobre San Salvador de Valdediós, B. Inst. Estudios Asturianos, X, 1956, pp. 35–51.

Castilla la Vieja. In antiquity this region was populated by several Celtic-Iberian tribes that tenaciously opposed Roman domination. Under the Visigoths and the Moslems it suffered an interval of regression. After the reconquest and during the Middle Ages this region experienced a brilliant phase that lasted well into modern times. Romanesque, Gothic, and Renaissance monuments are abundant, particularly in the area of Burgos.

BIBLIOG. R. Amador de los Rios, Burgos, Barcelona, 1888; R. Amador de los Rios, Santander, Barcelona, 1891; E. Ortiz de la Torre, La montaña artística: Arquitectura religiosa, Santander, 1926; B. Taracena Aguirre and J. Tudela, Guía artística de Soria y su provincia, Soria, 1928; B. Taracena Aguirre, Carta arqueológica de España: Soria, Madrid, 1941; J. A. Gaya Nuño, El románico en la provincia de Logroño, BSEE, XLVI, 1942, pp. 81–97, 235–58; J. A. Gaya Nuño, El románico en la provincia de Soria, Madrid, 1946; M. Lasso de la Vega y López de Tejada, Marqués de Saltillo, Artistas y artifices sorianos de los siglos XVI y XVII, Madrid, 1948; C. Goicoechea Romano, Castillos de la Rioja, Logroño, 1949; O. Gil Farrés, Iglesias románicas de ladrillo en la provincia de Segovia, RABM, LVI, 1950, pp. 91–127; L. Huidobro Serna, El arte isabelino en Burgos y su provincia, BIFG, XXX, 1951, pp. 554–72; B. G. Proske, Castilian Sculpture: Gothic to Renaissance, New York, 1951; M. Pereda de la Reguera, Documentos y noticias inéditos de artífices de la Montaña, Altamira, 2–3, 1952, pp. 175–236; M. Villalpando and J. de Vera, Artistas segovianos del siglo XVI, Estudios segovianos, X, 1952, pp. 59–160; R. del Arco y Garay, Sepulcros de la Casa Real de Castilla, Madrid, 1954; S. Alcolea Gil, Segovia y su provincia, Barcelona, 1958; J. Pérez Carmona, Arquitectura y escultura románicas en la provincia de Burgos, Burgos, 1959; J. de Vera and M. Villalpando, Los castillos de Segovia, 2d ed., Segovia, 1961.

Ágreda (Soria). The Romanesque Church of Nuestra Señora de la Peña (1193), consisting of two naves of equal size side by side, contains Gothic panel paintings. The 16th-century Church of Nuestra Señora de los Milagros contains Aragonese altarpieces (15th cent.). The Gothic Church of S. Miguel has a Romanesque tower; within is a plateresque main altarpiece (ca. 1520). The Church of S. Juan (15th cent.) has a Romanesque portal and a Gothic nave; it has a baroque high altar and Gothic and plateresque altarpieces.

BIBLIOG. P. Fabo, Agreda, AE, V, 1916, pp. 305–22; M. Moreno y Moreno, Agreda: barbacana de Castilla, Soria, 1954.

Almazán (Soria). There are remains of the castle and the city walls with some of its gates (13th cent.). The Church of S. Miguel (12th cent.) has a nave and two aisles, an asymmetrical apse, a ribbed dome on crossed arches of Moslem style, and a stone Romanesque façade. The churches of S. Vicente and of Nuestra Señora del Campanario are Romanesque. The palace of the Hurtado de Mendoza family (15th–16th cent.) is one of many fine aristocratic houses.

BIBLIOG. V. Lampérez y Romea, San Miguel de Almazán, BSEE, IX, 1901, pp. 31–35; F. Zamora Lucas, El priorato de Santa María en Almazán, Celtiberia, XI, 1961, pp. 95–100.

Aranda de Duero (Burgos). The Church of S. María, with nave and two aisles, three apses, and a raised choir, has groin vaulting; the 16th-century façade and doorway are abundantly decorated. Within is an altarpiece by Gabriel de Pinedo (1611) and a pulpit by Miguel de Espinosa (ca. 1545). The Church of S. Juan (13th cent.) is noteworthy.

BIBLIOG. J. A. Quintana, El púlpito de Santa María de Aranda, BCMB, VII, 1928, pp. 269–71; F. Layna Serrano, Las iglesias de Aranda de Duero, BSEE, XLIX, 1941, pp. 181–205.

Arenas de San Pedro (Ávila). This town has interesting regional architecture. The castle (ca. 1400) is square, with round towers at the corners and square towers in the center of each side.

BIBLIOG. J. Serrano Cabo, Historia y geografía de Arenas de San Pedro y de las villas y pueblos de su partido, Ávila, 1925; E. Tormo y Monzó, Excursión a Arenas de San Pedro, BSEE, XXXVI, 1928, pp. 128–30.

Arévalo (Ávila). The remains of the city wall, the castle (a replica of the one at Coca), and the bridges over the Adaja and the Arevalillo are of Mudejar workmanship. The Church of S. Martín has two medieval brick towers and a Romanesque portal of the Segovian

type. Of the church of the Cistercian Abbey of Nuestra Señora de la Lugareja only the transept and three apses (13th cent.) remain; they are of brick with Mudejar decorations. S. Miguel contains a main altarpiece painted by Marcos de Pinilla (1508). In the Palacio de Villasanta is an Egyptian sarcophagus of green alabaster. In front of the Casa de las Cardenas is a stone bull from Carthaginian times.

BIBLIOG. Conde de Morales y los Rios, La Sociedad Española de Excursiones en Arévalo y Madrigal, BSEE, XXXVII, 1929, pp. 311–17; J. Supiot, La iglesia de la Lugareja en Arévalo, BSEAAV, IV, 1935–36, pp. 89–97; F. Sanz Vega, El retablo de San Miguel de Arévalo, AEArte, XXXI, 1958, pp. 243–46.

Ávila. A city of Roman origin, after a period of Moorish domination it was reconquered and repopulated (11th cent.). It is surrounded by the oldest and most complete medieval walls in Spain (about 1½ mi. in length) reinforced by 88 massive towers with several gates. The Cathedral was under construction in 1135; it was continued in Gothic style by Master Fruchel, and was finished in the 14th century. On the exterior, the *chevet*, built into the thickness of the city walls, and the Portada de los Apóstoles (13th cent.) are noteworthy. The interior has a nave and two aisles, a *chevet* with double ambulatory, a triforium, and ogival vaulting. The

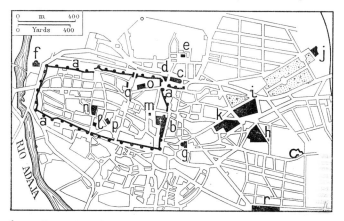

Ávila, plan. (*a*) Medieval walls; (*b*) Cathedral; (*c*) S. Vicente; (*d*) Museo Provincial; (*e*) S. Andrés; (*f*) S. Segundo; (*g*) S. Pedro; (*h*) Convent of las Gordillas; (*i*) Convent of S. Ana; (*j*) Convent of S. Antonio; (*k*) Convent of S. José; (*l*) S. Teresa; (*m*) Casa de Gonzalo Dávila; (*n*) Palacio de Polentinos; (*o*) Casa de los Águilas; (*p*) Casa de los Oñates; (*q*) Capilla de Mosén Rubín.

stained-glass windows are from the 15th and 16th centuries. In the Capilla Mayor is an altarpiece with sculptures by Vasco de la Zarza (1508) and paintings by Pedro Berruguete, Santa Cruz, and Juan de Borgoña; the sanctuary is by Vasco de la Zarza (1521). There are two hammered-iron pulpits in the transept, one Gothic by Juan Francés (15th cent.) and the other Renaissance by Llorente de Ávila (1523–38); to the sides are the plateresque altars of S. Catalina (1529) and S. Segundo (1548), designed by Vasco de la Zarza. In the *coro* the stalls (1534–44) were designed by Juan Rodríguez and Lucas Giraldo, the sculptors who also decorated the *trascoro* with abundant woodcarvings (1531–36). The *trassagrario* has Renaissance relief decorations and the tomb of Alfonso de Madrigal, a work by Vasco de la Zarza (1518). In the Museo de la Catedral is a monstrance by Juan de Arfe (1564), goldwork, sculptures, a Romanesque painted panel with episodes of the life of St. Paul, Castilian-Gothic panel paintings, a canvas by El Greco, illuminated missals, documents, and other objects.

The Church of S. Vicente (12th cent.; XII, FIG. 350) has a nave and two aisles, transept, three apses, and a crypt; fine specimens of Romanesque statuary decorate the portals and the tomb of SS. Vicente, Sabina, and Cristeta. The Monastery of S. Tomás (1482) has a Gothic church with a raised *coro* and high altar. Notable are the main altarpiece by Pedro Berruguete (1494–99); the tomb of Prince Juan, a work by Domenico di Alessandro Fancelli (1511); the tombs of H. Núñez de Arnalte and of Juan Dávila and his wife (16th cent.); and the Gothic choir stalls (ca. 1492). Of interest are the Romanesque churches of S. Andrés; S. Segundo, with the tomb of the saint by Juan de Juni (1572); S. Pedro; and S. Nicolás. The Capilla de Mosén Rubín is of the 16th century. There are many palaces, including the Gothic Casa de Gonzalo Dávila, the Palacio de Polentinos, the Casa de los Águilas, the Casa de los Oñates, and the Palacio de Benavides, which houses the Museo de Arte Popular.

BIBLIOG. I. de Benito Domínguez, Ermita y sepulcro de San Segundo, BSEE, I, 1893, pp. 29–32; E. M. Repullés y Vargas, Restauración de la casa de los Polentinos en Avila, BSEE, III, 1895–96, pp. 110–14; E. Tormo y Monzó, Avila, Madrid, 1917; E. Lambert, L'architecture bourguignonne et la cathédrale d'Avila, BM, LXXXIII, 1924, pp. 263–92; D. F. Darby, The Retable of Avila, Parnassus, I, 1929, p. 22; L. Moya, Fachada de la iglesia de Santa Teresa en Avila, Arquitectura, XI, 1929, pp. 347–54; W. Goldschmidt, El sepulcro de San Vicente en Avila, AEAA, XI, 1936, pp. 161–70; W. Goldschmidt, The West Portal of San Vicente at Avila, BM, LXXI, 1937, pp. 110–23; M. J. García Martín, Juan de Arfe y la custodia de Avila, BSEAAV, VIII, 1941–42, pp. 257–68; L. Cervera Vera, La iglesia de San José en Avila, BSEE, LIV, 1950, pp. 5–155 (bibliog.); S. Alcolea Gil, Avila monumental, Madrid, 1952; L. Cervera Vera, La capilla de San Segundo en la catedral de Avila, BSEE, LVI, 1952, pp. 181–229; L. Belmonte Díaz and A. de la Cruz Vaquero, Guía de Avila, Avila, 1951.

Berlanga de Duero (Soria). There is a castle (15th cent.) with double girding walls. The collegiate church was constructed (1526–30) by Juan de Rasines in Gothic-Renaissance style; on the basilica plan, it has nave and two aisles, transept, an unusual apse, and stellar vaulting above smooth cylindrical columns. In the Capilla de los Bravo de Laguna are the tombs of the founders and a sculptured and painted altarpiece (early 16th cent.). The Palacio de los Marqueses de Berlanga and the Hospital are of the 16th century.

BIBLIOG. La colegiata de Berlanga de Duero, Arquitectura, III, 1920, p. 103; M. Lasso de la Vega y López de Alaya, Marqués del Saltillo, La capilla del obispo de Coria en la colegiata de Berlanga, Celtiberia, II, 1951, pp. 385–86.

El Burgo de Osma (Soria). Sections of the city wall with the Puerta de S. Miguel remain. An early Romanesque church of the 12th century was replaced with the present Gothic Cathedral (begun 1232). The main portal (13th cent.) has Gothic statuary derived from the Burgos group. The interior consists of a nave and two aisles with chapels between the buttresses, a transept, and ogival vaulting; the ambulatory was constructed in the 18th century after plans by Juan de Villanueva. The main altarpiece (1550–54) was carved by Juan Picardo from designs by Juan de Juni; the grillwork of the Capilla Mayor and the coro was wrought by Juan Francés (1505). Of note are a Romanesque crucifix, the tomb of S. Pedro de Osma (1258), and several Gothic-Castilian panel paintings. The ancient chapter house has nine groin vaults over columns with historiated Romanesque capitals. The tower was constructed by Juan Sagarvinaga after plans by Domingo Ondátegui (1742); the late Gothic cloister (1505) has several chapels. The Museo Biblioteca Catedralicio contains a Beatus Apocalypse (1086), a collection of goldwork, and Hispano-Moorish textiles. The University of S. Catalina (ca. 1551) has a plateresque façade and an interesting patio. The façade of the Hospital is by Ignacio Moncalcán and Pedro Portela (1699). The Plaza Mayor dates from 1768 and has various noteworthy buildings.

In the vicinity are the ruins of the Roman city of Uxama Argelae on the road to ancient Numancia and Augustobriga; there is a theater built on the slope of a hill.

BIBLIOG. V. de la Fuente, Sepulcro de San Pedro de Osma, BRAH, II, 1882, pp. 31–34; F. Chueca Goitia, La arquitectura religiosa del siglo XVIII y las obras de Burgo de Osma, AEArte, XXII, 1949, pp. 287–315; V. Núñez, La catedral de Burgo de Osma, Burgo de Osma, 1949; V. Núñez, El retablo de la catedral de Burgo de Osma, BCMB, XXVIII, 1949, pp. 345–48; E. García Chico, El claustro de la catedral de Burgo de Osma, BSEAAV, XVIII, 1951–52, pp. 135–38; E. García Chico, Artistas que trabajaron en la catedral de Burgo de Osma, Celtiberia, VIII, 1956, pp. 7–18.

Burgos. In the city are the ruins of the castle, sections of the walls, and several gates: Arco de S. María, built in the 11th century but remodeled in the 16th; Arco de S. Martín, 14th century; and Arco de S. Esteban, of typically Toledan masonry. The Cathedral was erected after 1221 on the site of an earlier Romanesque church. The original plan (VI, FIG. 491) consisted of nave and two aisles, transept, ambulatory, and apsidal chapels (the chief architect of this first stage was Master Enrique, 1240–77); but subsequent additions (several chapels) partly modified the structure. The main façade has 13th-century sculpture, a rose window, and two towers with spires (15th cent.) by Juan de Colonia. The Puerta Alta de la Coronería (13th cent.) has Gothic statues similar to those on the south portal, the Puerta del Sarmental; the plateresque Puerta de la Pellejería is by Francisco de Colonia (1516). The altarpiece of the high altar is the work of various sculptors after designs by Rodrigo and Martín de la Haya (1562); the trassagrario has three reliefs by Felipe Bigarny (Vigarny; de Borgoña; 1499–1513), who also worked on the choir stalls (1507–12). In the coro is the gilt and enameled copper tomb statue of Bishop Mauricio (13th cent.); the trascoro has six pictures by Fray Juan Ricci (1654–59); and at the crossing is the richly ornamented Gothic-Renaissance cimborio with a stellar-vaulted dome. Of note in the various chapels are the altarpieces of S. Tecla (baroque),

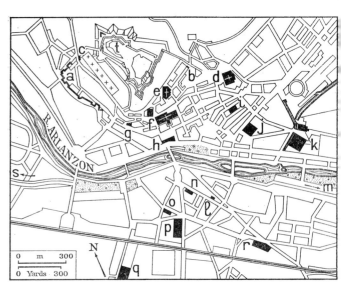

Burgos, plan. (a) Walls; (b) Arco de S. Esteban; (c) Arco de S. Martín; (d) S. Gil; (e) S. Esteban; (f) Cathedral and S. Nicolás; (g) S. Águeda; (h) Arco de S. María; (i) S. Lorenzo; (j) Casa del Cordón; (k) Hospital de S. Juan and S. Lesmes; (l) Casa de Miranda (Mus. Arqueol.); (m) to Abbey of Miraflores; (n) S. Luis; (o) SS. Cosme y Damián; (p) Hospital de la Concepción; (q) S. Dorotea; (r) S. Clara; (s) to Convent of las Huelgas; (t) castle.

of S. Ana (15th cent.), and of the Nativity (16th cent.); the Gothic tombs of Archdeacon Diez de Fuentepelayo, of Bishop Fontecha, of Pedro Fernández de Villegas, and of Bishop Alonso de Cartagena; and the Renaissance tombs of Bishop Acuña by the sculptor Diego de Siloe (1519) and of Gonzalo de Lerma by Felipe Bigarny (1524). The Capilla del Condestable, a work by Simón de Colonia (1494), is on an octagonal plan and has a decorated entrance arch, a reja by Cristóbal Andino (1523), an octagonal stellar vault, armorial escutcheons on the walls, and a main altarpiece (1523) by Felipe Bigarny and Diego de Siloe; in the center is the tomb of the Condestable and his wife. The sacristy of the chapel contains paintings and goldwork. In the north transept of the Cathedral the interior Escalera Dorada is by Diego de Siloe (1519), and at the end of the south transept is the entrance to the cloister, with 13th-century sculptures on the door stops, jambs, tympanum, and archivolt. The cloister, together with the Capilla de S. Catalina, houses the Museo Diocesano (Flemish tapestries, vestments, sculpture, panel paintings).

The Church of S. Esteban (1280–1350) contains Gothic and Renaissance sculpture; S. Lesmes has a Flemish altarpiece (16th cent.) and Renaissance panel paintings; S. Gil (14th cent.) has a Gothic altarpiece and Renaissance tombs; and S. Nicolás (15th cent.) has an ornate main altarpiece by Francisco de Colonia (1505) and Gothic panel paintings by the St. Nicholas Master. Other churches include S. Dorotea, S. Águeda, S. Clara, S. Lorenzo, and SS. Cosme y Damián. The Casa del Cordón (late 15th cent.) and the Renaissance Casa de Ángulo and Palacio de Castrofuerte are noteworthy, as are the Hospital de S. Juan (15th cent.) and the Hospital de la Concepción (1561). The Casa Consistorial (town hall) is by Ventura Rodríguez (1780). The Museo Arqueológico Provincial, housed in the Casa de Miranda (1545), contains Roman sculpture and epigraphs, mainly from ancient Clunia (mod. Santiago de Castro) and Lara; Visigothic and Mozarabic objects; tombs (14th–16th cent.); Moorish ivories (10th–11th cent.); the enameled altar screen of Silos (12th cent.); and Gothic and Renaissance sculpture and painting.

On the outskirts of the city stands the Carthusian Abbey of Miraflores; the church, finished in 1488 by Simón de Colonia, contains the magnificent tomb of Juan II and Isabel of Portugal (1489–93) and that of the Infante Alfonso (1493), both by Gil de Siloe, who also worked on the high altarpiece (1496–99), assisted by Diego de la Cruz; the choir stalls are by Martín Sánchez (1486), and there is an Annunciation by Pedro Berruguete. The Convent of las Huelgas (1187) has a church with numerous tombs of Castilian kings and infantes (13th–15th cent.) and a main cloister with Mudejar stuccowork; in the Zaguán is installed the excellent Museo de Ricas Telas, with a varied collection of 13th-century court costumes; the chapter house contains the so-called "Standard of las Navas." The Hospital del Rey, founded in the 12th century, was partly reconstructed in the 16th.

BIBLIOG. C. G. Villacampa, La capilla del Condestable de la catedral de Burgos, AEAA, VI, 1928, pp. 25–44; F. Tarin y Juaneda, La Cartuja de Miraflores, Burgos, 1930; F. B. Deknatel, The 13th Century Gothic

Sculpture of the Cathedrals of Burgos and León, AB, XVII, 1935, pp. 243–94; M. Martínez Burgos, La Casa del Cordón, Burgos, 1938; E. García de Quevedo, Bibliografía de la catedral de Burgos, BSEE, XLVII, 1943, pp. 70–78; L. Torres Balbás, El Hospital del Rey en Burgos, Al-Andalus, IX, 1944, pp. 190–98; M. Gómez-Moreno, El Panteón Real de las Huelgas de Burgos, Madrid, 1946; T. López Mata, El barrio y iglesia de San Esteban de Burgos, Burgos, 1946; J. L. Monteverde, El Museo de telas medievales del Real Monasterio de las Huelgas, BCPMB, XXVII, 1949, pp. 233–49; J. M. Navascués y de Juan, La nueva instalación del Museo Arqueológico de Burgos, BCPMB, XXVIII, 1949, pp. 1–5; T. López Mata, La catedral de Burgos, Burgos, 1950; J. A. Rodríguez Albo, El Monasterio de Santa María la Real de las Huelgas y el Hospital del Rey de Burgos, 3d ed., Burgos, 1950; M. Martínez Burgos, Iglesia de San Gil, Burgos, BIFG, XXX, 1951, pp. 675–703; M. Martínez Burgos, Puente, torre y arco de Santa María, Burgos, 1952; M. Martínez Burgos, En torno a la catedral de Burgos, BIFG, XXXII, 1953, pp. 414–24, 537–50, 600–16, 696–708, XXXIII, 1954, pp. 11–25, 118–33, 214–26, XXXIV, 1955, pp. 434–49, 851–63, XXXV, 1956, pp. 144–63, 314–37; I. García Rámila, Templos burgaleses: El del glorioso San Lesmes, patrón de la ciudad, RABM, LX, 1954, pp. 271–86; I. García Rámila, Casa y solar del Cid en Burgos, BIFG, XXXIV, 1955, pp. 657–65; M. Martínez Burgos, La iglesia de San Nicolás, BRAH, CXXXVIII, 1956, pp. 151–227; I. García Rámila, Algunas otras seleccionadoras y típicas estampas del vivir burgalés en los pasados siglos, BRAH, CXL, 1957, pp. 487–534; R. Osaba y Ruiz de Erenchun, La "Casa de Miranda," nuevo local del Museo Arqueológico de Burgos, RABM, LXIII, 1957, pp. 251–307; L. Huidobro Serna, La catedral de Burgos, Madrid, 1958; D. Mansilla, Capilla de la Presentación de Nuestra Señora en la catedral de Burgos, BIFG, XXXVII, 1958, pp. 322–37; T. López Mata, La Compañía de Jesús en Burgos, BIFG, XXXVIII, 1959, pp. 417–54; J. Pérez Carmona, Arquitectura y escultura románicas en la provincia de Burgos, Burgos, 1959; G. Avila y Díaz-Ubierna, Castillos de la provincia de Burgos, Burgos, 1961; G. Miguel Ojeda, Torres y castillos burgaleses, BIFG, XL, 1961, pp. 679–86, 717–27, XLI, 1962, pp. 41–49; J. Pérez Carmona, Historia y arte del partido de Salas de los Infantes, Burgense, III, 1962, pp. 349–76.

Calahorra (Logroño). This was the Calagurris Nassica of the Celts and the Iberians and the Calagurris Julia of the Romans. The Cathedral was renovated in the 15th century, and the apse and transept were reconstructed (1561–67) by Juan Pérez de Solarte. The Gothic north portal has Renaissance decorative details. The interior consists of a stellar-vaulted nave and two cross-vaulted aisles with lateral chapels between the buttresses, a transept, and an ambulatory with chapels. There are sculptured altarpieces (16th–18th cent.), 16th-century *rejas*, codices, and liturgical vestments. The Church of Santiago Apóstol is Herreran (1625), with a baroque tower (1777).

BIBLIOG. M. de Lecuona, La catedral de Calahorra, Berceo, II, 1946, pp. 63–109; M. de Lecuona, El escultor Juan Bazcardo y sus obras en la catedral de Calahorra, Principe de Viana, VII, 1946, pp. 27–41; M. de Lecuona, La Parroquia de Santiago de Calahorra, Berceo, XXIV, 1952, pp. 469–90, XXV, 1952, pp. 601–34.

Cañas (Logroño). The Cistercian abbey was established in 1171. Of the church, begun about 1236, only the apse and transept were constructed; it contains a 16th-century painted and carved altarpiece. The chapter house, with a central column supporting four ogival vaults, contains the tomb of the abbess Urraca López de Haro (late 14th cent.), of Castilian influence.

BIBLIOG. F. Sáenz y Andrés, Real monasterio de Santa María de San Salvador de Cañas, Cistercium, XIV, 1962, pp. 83–91, 147–54.

Casillas de Berlanga (Soria). In the vicinity of the village stands the Mozarabic church known as the Hermitage of S. Baudilio (Baudel) de Berlanga (11th cent.; X, PL. 196). Of rectangular plan, it has barrel vaulting over horseshoe arches that radiate from a central column, a vaulted apsidal chapel, and a tribune at the end. The walls and vaulting were once almost covered with paintings, but only fragments remain.

BIBLIOG. J. Garnelo, Descripción de las pinturas murales que decoran la ermita de San Baudelio en Casillas de Berlanga, BSEE, XXXII, 1924, pp. 96–109.

Castañeda (Santander). Although mentioned in the 11th century, the present church is Romanesque (12th cent., with later modifications); it has a single barrel-vaulted aisle, a transept with a dome on pendentives, and a central apse with blind arches; the tower is square. The church contains Gothic tombs (14th cent.).

BIBLIOG. A. Fernández Casanova, La iglesia de Santa Cruz de Castañeda, RABM, 3d Ser., XXXI, 1914, pp. 395–99.

Castro Urdiales (Santander). The Church of Nuestra Señora de la Anunciación is Gothic (13th–15th cent.), with nave and two aisles, transept, ambulatory, and triforium; it has cross vaulting and, on the outside, a system of double flying buttresses. The portal is in traditional Romanesque style; the tower is unfinished.

BIBLIOG. A. Pérez de Regules, La imagen de Santa María la Blanca de Castro Urdiales, Altamira, 1–3, 1955, pp. 342–50.

Cervatos (Santander). A monastery existed here in 999. The church, renovated in the 12th century and consecrated in 1199, has a single ogival-vaulted aisle, an apse with blind arches, and a polygonal tower at the lower end. In the church is a statue of the Virgin (13th cent.).

BIBLIOG. J. García de la Puente, La Colegiata de Cervatos, Bilbao, 1915.

Coca (Segovia). Possibly the Celtic-Iberian Cauca, the town reached its apogee in the 15th and 16th centuries. Sections of the city walls and one gate (Arco de la Villa) are preserved. The brick castle, on a square plan, has triple girding walls. The Church of S. María (16th cent.) is Gothic-Renaissance with a polygonal apse at each end of its Latin-cross arms; it contains the Renaissance tombs of the Fonseca family by Bartolomé Ordóñez and his pupils. The Torre de S. Nicolás is Mudejar.

BIBLIOG. M. López Otero and L. Torres Balbás, El castillo de Coca, BRAH, CXXXVIII, 1956, pp. 29–32; J. M. Pita Andrade, El castillo de Coca reconstruido, Goya, 28, 1959, pp. 210–16.

Covarrubias (Burgos). The town is of Roman origin. The Torre de Doña Urraca is of the 10th century and the city walls date from the reconquest. The collegiate church, with cross vaulting, has a nave and two aisles, a transept, and three rectilinear apses; its cloister (16th cent.) is decorated with openwork tracery. In the church are the tomb of Fernán González and that of his wife, Sancha, in a Roman sarcophagus from the 3d century. The Museo Parroquial contains embroidered vestments (15th–17th cent.), Castilian and Flemish panel paintings (15th cent.), goldwork (14th–18th cent.), and a Flemish triptych of the Epiphany.

BIBLIOG. R. Vargas, Covarrubias, AE, XIX, 1930, pp. 48–49; L. Huidobro Serna, El Museo parroquial de Covarrubias, BCPMB, XXVIII, 1949, pp. 59–60.

Cuéllar (Segovia). A center of Mudejar brick architecture, apparently derived from Sahagún, the town has seven churches of this type. S. Martín has a tower and three apses with blind arches and recessed windows. S. Esteban has a brick apse with blind arcades and contains tombs with Mudejar plasterwork (14th cent.). The portals of the Church of S. Andrés are Romanesque. The other churches are Santiago, S. Marina, El Salvador, and S. María del Castillo. The Hospital of S. María Magdalena is Gothic. In the Ayuntamiento is a diptych signed by Juan Fernández (15th cent.). The Sanctuary of Nuestra Señora del Henar is baroque.

BIBLIOG. G. de la Torre de Trassiera, Cuéllar, BSEE, II, 1894–95, pp. 199–215, 224–37, 241–46, IV, 1896–97, pp. 4–7, 21–26, 58–60, 70–75, 87–91, 102–09, 120–25, 140–44, 157–60, 177–84, 202–08, V, 1897–98, pp. 29–34, 67–74, 86–95, 102–12, 119–23, 131–34.

Gormaz (Soria). The castle was constructed in 965, with some additions in the 13th and 14th centuries. It is on an elongated plan, with a highly complex defense system. The walls, constructed in the Moorish manner, are reinforced with square towers; there are a *place d'armes*, a vaulted cistern, and a gate with Caliphate horseshoe arch; the Torre de Homenaje is Mudejar.

BIBLIOG. I. Gil, Gormaz, AE, II, 1913, pp. 408–20; J. A. Gaya Nuño, Gormaz, Al-Andalus, VIII, 1943, pp. 431–50; J. Gil Montero, El Castillo de Gormaz, B. Asociación Española de Amigos de los Castillos, II, 1954, pp. 296–98.

La Granja (Segovia). The royal palace was built around a farm and granary (*granja*) of the 16th century. The palace was begun by Teodoro Ardemans in 1721 and continued by Andrea Procaccini and Sempronio Subissati from 1727 to 1734 and by Giovanni Battista Sacchetti in 1736. The gardens, with their fountains, were finished in 1742; they contain various features of interest, such as the Esplanada de la Selva, the Carrera de Caballos, the Cascada Nueva, and the Plazoleta de las Ocho Calles. Fronting the gardens, the main façade of the palace has a portico with statues of the Seasons. Notable in the palace are the Patio de la Herradura and the opulently furnished rooms that constitute the Lower Gallery of Statues and the Official Gallery, both with richly decorated ceilings and walls and with numerous paintings. The tapestry collection of the Spanish kings is housed here. The collegiate church has a dome at the crossing and contains the tomb of Philip V and his wife (1756). In the town are the outlying buildings of the palace, all dating from the 17th century. In the Church of Nuestra Señora del Rosario are sculptures by Luis Salvador Carmona (1759).

BIBLIOG. R. Breñosa and J. M. Castellarnau, Guía y descripción del Real Sitio de San Ildefonso, Madrid, 1884; L. Pérez Bueno, Real Fábrica de Cristales de San Ildefonso, AE, XV, 1926, pp. 9–17; J. Digard, Les jardins de la Granja, Paris, 1934; Y. Bottineau, El panteón de Felipe V en la Granja, AEArte, XXVIII, 1955, pp. 263–66; J. Contreras y López de Alaya, Marqués de Lozoya, Palacios reales de la Granja de San Ildefonso y Riofrio, Madrid, 1961; Y. Bottineau, Las etapas de la construcción de la Granja, Goya, 46, 1962, pp. 260–68.

Gumiel de Izán (Burgos). The church has a Renaissance façade (1627); the nave and the two aisles are Gothic, as is the main altarpiece. There are two plateresque altarpieces and a baptismal font with carvings of the twelve Apostles (15th cent.). In the Museo Parroquial are some reliquary busts, several Romanesque capitals, and panel paintings (15th–16th cent.).

BIBLIOG. F. Palacios, Iglesia de Santa María en Gumiel de Izán, BCPMB, XXVI, 1947, pp. 479–90; F. Palacios, El Convento de San Pedro de Gumiel de Izán: panteón de los Guzmanes, BIFG, XXXI, 1952, pp. 179–90.

Haro (Logroño). The castle is in ruins and only vestiges of the walls remain. The Church of S. Tomás (nave and two aisles of equal height with stellar vaulting) was constructed under the supervision of Matías Francés (1515), Felipe Bigarny (1516–19), and Pedro de Rasines (1564–69). The plateresque portal (ca. 1525) is in the manner of a retable; there is a baroque altarpiece by Pedro Martínez (1730). The Ayuntamiento (ca. 1780) is neoclassic. Among the many aristocratic houses, the 16th-century Casa de Paternina is outstanding.

BIBLIOG. F. Layna Serrano, La ciudad de Haro, BSEE, XLIX, 1945, pp. 137–58.

Lebeña (Santander). The Mozarabic Church of S. María (ca. 930) is on a rectangular plan, with square pillars flanked by engaged columns with Corinthian capitals; it has barrel vaults at varying heights and horseshoe arches. The exterior is decorated with floral designs.

BIBLIOG. M. Gómez-Moreno, Iglesias mozárabes, I, Madrid, 1919, pp. 267–82.

Lerma (Burgos). The town provides an interesting example of urban planning, the work of the architect Francisco de Mora (1604–14) for the Duke of Lerma. The collegiate church, with nave and two aisles, was finished in 1617; it contains the tomb of Archbishop Cristóbal de Rojas, with a bronze kneeling statue, planned by Juan de Arfe and finished by Lesmes Fernández del Moral, following the style of Pompeo Leoni. The ducal palace dates from 1614.

BIBLIOG. G. Nieto Gallo, Los monumentos de Lerma, Madrid, 1959.

Logroño. A city of ancient origin, it was annexed by Castilla in 1076. A section of the city walls remains, and a gate with a blazon from the 16th century. The Church of S. Bartolomé (13th–15th cent.), with a Mudejar tower, has a portal with sculptures on the jambs and tympanum (14th cent.); the interior consists of short nave with flanking aisles, a transept, and three apses — the central one semicircular, the lateral ones square. The Church of S. María del Palacio (extensively altered), with nave and two aisles, three apses, and an octagonal dome on pendentives backed by a pyramidal tower, contains the statue of Nuestra Señora de la Antigua (12th cent.) and a Renaissance altarpiece. The Church of S. María la Redonda (15th–16th cent.), with nave and two aisles, has a basilican plan; it has stellar vaulting and simple cylindrical pillars without capitals, and contains an altarpiece of S. Ildefonso and sculptured choir stalls (both 16th cent.). The baroque, concave portal (1742–60), built like a retable, is flanked by twin towers constructed by Martín de Beratúa (ca. 1760). The Church of Santiago el Real has a Gothic nave and a baroque portal. The Museo de Arte contains many paintings, including a St. Francis by El Greco and two paintings by Vicente Carducho. The Museo del Seminario Diocesano is noteworthy.

BIBLIOG. J. M. Ruiz de Galarreta, Guía artística de Logroño, Logroño, 1948; M. V. Saenz Terreros, Colegiata de Santa Maria de la Redonda en Logroño, BSEE, LII, 1948, pp. 309–13; J. M. Ruiz de Galarreta, La portada de San Bartolomé de Logroño, Berceo, VII, 1952, pp. 125–32; J. Cantera Orive, El retablo mayor de Santiago el Real de Logroño, Berceo, XV, 1960, pp. 331–43; C. Goicoechea, Artistas y artífices riojanos, Berceo, XV, 1960, pp. 405–45; J. M. Ruiz de Galarreta and S. Alcolea, Logroño y su provincia, Barcelona, 1962.

Madrigal de las Altas Torres (Ávila). Parts of its Mudejar wall which formed a perfect circle, are preserved. The Puerta de Can talapiedra is flanked by fortified watchtowers; the Puerta de Medin is of simpler construction. The Romanesque-Mudejar Church S. Nicolás de Bari has apses decorated with blind arches, a towe resembling a minaret, a nave with Mudejar artesonado, and two aisle The Church of S. María del Castillo has Mudejar apses.

BIBLIOG. Conde de Morales de los Rios, La Sociedad Española d Excursiones en Arévalo y Madrigal, BSEE, XXXVII, 1929, pp. 311–1

Martín Muñoz de las Posadas (Segovia). The church has Gothic nave and a 16th-century apse. The main altarpiece is b Martín Imberto and others (ca. 1584); the tomb of Cardinal Dieg de Espinosa is by Pompeo Leoni (1577); there is a Crucifixion b El Greco. The Palacio del Cardenal (1572) is somber and classica with a fine Doric gate and round arches and corbeled architrave in the patio.

BIBLIOG. Conde de Cedillo, Martin Muñoz de las Posadas, BSEE XXXVIII, 1930, pp. 229–51.

Medinaceli (Soria). There is a three-span Roman arch of th 3d century with niches on the lateral openings; it is the only on of its kind in Spain. Parts of the Roman walls remain, as well a some from the Moslem era. The Gothic single-aisle Church o S. María (ca. 1530) contains tombs of the dukes of Medinacel The ducal palace (17th–18th cent.) and the many aristocratic house are notable.

BIBLIOG. M. Gómez-Moreno, El arco romano de Medinaceli, BRAH XC, 1927, pp. 260–62.

Moradillo de Sedano (Burgos). The fine single-aisled Romanesqu church (1188) has blind arches on the exterior. There are sculpture on the capitals and on the tympanum and archivolts of the portal

BIBLIOG. J. Martínez Santa-Olalla, La iglesia románica de Moradill de Sedano, AEAA, VI, 1930, pp. 267–75.

Nájera (Logroño). The Gothic Church of S. María la Rea (reconstructed 1422–53) has a nave and two aisles, a transept, an a plain chevet with gallery, and is cross-vaulted. The main altar piece is baroque (17th cent.). The stalls of the high choir are Gothic with only one figure, that of King García, done about 1495 by th sculptors Nicolás and Andrés. The low choir leads to the Panteó Real, with uniform tombs (16th cent.) and the Romanesque tom of Doña Blanca (ca. 1158), attributed to Master Leodegarius. Th Gothic cloister (1517–28) has Renaissance tracery and contain numerous tombs.

BIBLIOG. C. Garrán, El real monasterio de Santa María la Real d Nájera, Logroño, 1892; F. Fita, Santa María la Real de Nájera: Estudi crítico, BRAH, XXVI, 1895, pp. 155–98; I. Guadan y Gil, Monasteri de Santa María la Real de Nájera, Logroño, 1961.

Las Navas del Marqués (Ávila). The palace of the Marqués d las Navas (16th cent.) is rectangular, with towers at the corners the central doorway is flanked by two circular towers. The pati has Ionic columns and elliptical arches in the lower story and Dori columns and architraves in the upper.

BIBLIOG. F. Pérez Minguez, El castillo del Marqués de las Navas, AE VII, 1918, pp. 51–65.

Nieva (Segovia). The Dominican convent was founded b Enrique III and his wife, Catherine of Lancaster (14th cent.); th church, finished in 1432, has a side portal with Gothic statues an contains an altarpiece attributed to Alonso Berruguete. The iconog raphy of the cloister capitals is regional in character.

BIBLIOG. Conde de Cedillo, Santa Maria la Real de Nieva, BSEE XXXVIII, 1930, pp. 73–107.

Oña (Burgos). The Benedictine Abbey of S. Salvador was founde by Sancho the Great (1011). The church (13th–16th cent.), wit Romanesque elements in the façade, contains choir stalls attribute to Martín Sánchez; the tombs of Castilian kings and counts ar surmounted by Gothic canopies of wood, with geometric ornamenta tion (15th cent.). The Gothic cloister dates from the 16th century

BIBLIOG. E. Herrera Oria, Oña y su real monasterio, Madrid, 1917

Pedraza (Segovia). Situated atop a hill, this town, which ha preserved much of its 15th-century character, is girded by walls access being through an old gate (1561). The Plaza Mayor is arcaded. Of the once-numerous churches, only S. Juan, with its Romanesque tower, remains. The castle of the Velasco family (15th cent.) has Romanesque elements.

BIBLIOG. F. Suárez Bravo, Excursión por Pedraza, BSEE, XXXVII, 1929, pp. 213-21.

Peñaranda de Duero (Burgos). There is an unusual castle (15th cent.) on an elongated plan, with walls reinforced by semicircular towers; the Torre de Homenaje is square. The palace of the Condes de Miranda (ca. 1526) has a fine façade decorated with Roman busts and elegant windows. The rooms show a mixture of Gothic, Mudejar, and Renaissance styles. The patio has two stories with arches.

BIBLIOG. V. Lampérez y Romea, El palacio de los Condes de Miranda en Peñaranda de Duero, BSEE, XX, 1912, pp. 146-51; D. Jimeno, Peñaranda de Duero: Honor de villas castellanas, Burgos, 1961.

Piasca (Santander). The Abbey of S. María is mentioned in records of 933. The partly preserved Romanesque church (12th-14th cent.) has nave and two aisles, transept, and central apse with a decorated window. On the façade are Romanesque sculptures, and the doorway has pointed arches.

BIBLIOG. T. Maza y Solano, Santa Maria de Piasca, BBMP, I, 1919, pp. 128-41.

Puenteviesgo (Santander). Near the village are situated the caves of El Castillo and of La Pasiega, with prehistoric paintings of the Franco-Cantabrian type: figures of animals, outlines of hands, structural signs, and stylized human figures.

BIBLIOG. H. Alcalde del Rio and H. Breuil, Les cavernes de la région Cantabrique, Monaco, 1911; H. Breuil and others, La Pasiega à Puente Viesgo, Monaco, 1913; P. Graziosi, Palaeolithic Art, New York, 1960.

Quintanilla de las Viñas (Burgos). Of the 7th-century Visigothic church only the transept and the rectangular apse are preserved, with a main supporting horseshoe arch. The exterior and interior are decorated with friezes of reliefs.

BIBLIOG. E. Camps Cazorla, El visigotismo de Quintanilla de las Viñas, BSEAAV, VI, 1939-40, pp. 125-34; L. Grondijs, Une église manichéenne en Espagne, CRAI, 1952, pp. 490-97; E. Lambert, L'église visigothique de Quintanilla de las Viñas, CRAI, 1955, pp. 488-93.

Rebolledo de la Torre (Burgos). The south façade of the Romanesque church has a portico constructed by Juan de Piasca in 1186; it has round arches over double columns and sculptured corbels under the eaves. The Gothic single aisle of the church dates from the 16th century.

BIBLIOG. L. Torres Balbás, Un maestro del siglo XII, AEAA, I, 1925, pp. 321-22.

San Esteban de Gormaz (Soria). There are some remains of the walls; the medieval bridge over the Duero River was reconstructed in 1717. The Church of S. Miguel (12th cent.) has a single aisle, a semicircular apse, and a porticoed gallery toward the south, with rough capitals of curious iconography. The Church of Nuestra Señora del Rivero (12th cent.) is similar.

BIBLIOG. P. Artigas, Por tierras de gesta — San Esteban de Gormaz, BSEE, XXXIX, 1931, pp. 139-54, XL, 1932, pp. 39-49, 146-59, 221-35; T. Ortego y Frias, En torno al románico de San Esteban de Gormaz, Celtiberia, VII, 1957, pp. 79-103; T. Ortego y Frias, Las pinturas murales de la iglesia del Rivero en San Esteban de Gormaz, Celtiberia, IX, 1959, pp. 127-38.

San Juan de Ortega (Burgos). The monastery was constructed in 1138. The church has two aisles flanking the nave, a transept, a central polygonal apse with blind arches, and semicircular lateral apses. The tomb of the titular saint, with a Gothic canopy (1474), is enclosed by a plateresque railing.

BIBLIOG. M. Martínez Burgos, San Juan de Ortega, BCPMB, XXX, 1951, pp. 361-78.

San Millán de la Cogolla (Logroño). The monastic Church of S. Millán de Suso is Mozarabic (9th-10th cent., restored in 1030). Partly built into the mountain, it has two aisles with horseshoe arches and contains the Romanesque tomb of S. Millán (12th cent.). The Abbey of Yuso, founded in 537, was rebuilt in the 16th century.

The large church (1504-40) contains paintings by Fray Juan Ricci (ca. 1653), rejas, and carved lecterns. The trascoro is baroque (1765-69), and the sacristy (16th cent.) has baroque decoration. The ivorywork on the reliquary casket of S. Millán (1067-70), by Engelram and Rodolfo, and on that of S. Felices (ca. 1090) is notable.

BIBLIOG. C. Garrán, San Millán de la Cogolla y sus dos insignes monasterios, Logroño, 1929; J. M. Carriazo, El arca de los marfiles de San Millán de la Cogolla, AEAA, VII, 1931, pp. 167-69; E. Camps Cazorla, Los marfiles de San Millán de la Cogolla, Madrid, 1933; J. M. Ruiz de Galarreta, El retablo gótico de San Millán de la Cogolla, Berceo, XI, 1956, pp. 463.

San Quirce del Riopisuerga (Burgos). The Abbey was consecrated in 1147. The east and north portals of the church have Romanesque sculptures; inside are a nave, a semicircular apse with blind arches, and a dome at the crossing.

BIBLIOG. J. Pérez de Urbel and W. M. Whitehill, La iglesia románica de San Quirce, Madrid, 1931; F. Iñiguez Almech, La reparación de la abadía de San Quirce, Arquitectura, XVII, 1935, pp. 323-33.

San Vicente de la Sonsierra (Logroño). There are ruins of the city walls and the castle. The bridge over the Ebro River is of medieval origin. The single-aisle Church of S. María (1520-50) has an apsidal vault with concave sections (gallones) and a main altarpiece by Damián Forment.

Santa María del Campo (Burgos). The church (15th cent.) has nave and two aisles, transept, polygonal Capilla Mayor, and groin vaulting. The Renaissance tower at the front of the church is by Diego de Siloe (1527). The church contains fine choir stalls, tombs (16th cent.), and panel paintings by Pedro Berruguete (15th cent.).

BIBLIOG. V. Lampérez y Romea, Santa Maria del Campo, BSEE, XX, 1920, pp. 65-71.

Santa María de Huerta (Soria). The Cistercian abbey was established in 1162. The church (ca. 1202) has a nave and two aisles with ogival vaulting, a transept, and a chevet with five chapels, and contains the tomb of Rodrigo Jiménez de Rada (d. 1247), with a recumbent figure. The cloister (13th cent.) has a plateresque upper story (1535-47). The large refectory, begun in 1215, has sexpartite vaulting, large Gothic windows, and a pulpit for the lector.

BIBLIOG. E. Aguilar y Gamboa, Marqués de Cerralbo, El monasterio de Santa Maria de Huerta, Madrid, 1908; Conde de Morales y los Rios, El monasterio de Santa Maria de Huerta, BSEE, XXXV, 1927, pp. 257-62; M. T. Polvorosa López, Santa Maria la Real de Huerta, Santa Maria de Huerta, 1963.

Santander. On the site of an 8th-century abbey, the Gothic Cathedral (modified 16th and 18th cent.; largely rebuilt after 1941 fire) contains a 10th-century Moorish basin as a font. The Cathedral crypt (13th cent.), now used as a parish church, has cross-vaulted nave and two aisles, separated by cruciform clustered piers. The cloister (14th cent.), with ogival arches, has survived. In the Ayuntamiento is a portrait of Fernando VII by Goya (1814). The Museo Provincial de Prehistoria specializes in regional finds. The Museo Municipal de Pinturas contains canvases of the 17th-18th-century Spanish school and some of modern times.

BIBLIOG. Museo Provincial de Prehistoria, Catálogo, Santander, 1943; E. García Gómez, La inscripción de la pila árabe de Santander, Al-Andalus, XII, 1947, pp. 155-61; A. Hernández Morales, La cripta de la catedral de Santander, Santander, 1958.

Santillana del Mar (Santander). The whole town, because of its many interesting old buildings, has been declared a national monument. The Romanesque collegiate church (12th cent.), with a basilican plan, has a round tower. In the interior, the transept and the three apses have the original barrel vaulting; the ogival vaulting of the nave is of a later date. The cloister (late 12th cent., with restorations) has arches supported by double columns with richly decorated capitals, some historiated. Near the town are the caves of Altamira, with famous prehistoric rock paintings: bisons, horses, stags, boars, etc., painted in red, black, and ocher.

BIBLIOG. E. Cartailhac and H. Breuil, La caverne d'Altamira à Santillane près Santander (Espagne), Monaco, 1906; M. Escagedo Salmón, Santillana del Mar, Madrid, 1929; H. Breuil and H. Obermaier, The Cave of Altamira at Santillana del Mar (trans. M. E. Boyle), Madrid, 1935; E. Lafuente Ferrari, El libro de Santillana, Santander, 1956; A. Pérez de Regules, Santillana del Mar (trans. R. Studholme), Santander, 1958; M. Pereda de la Reguera, Santillana del Mar y Altamira, 6th ed., Santander, 1960.

Santo Domingo de la Calzada (Logroño). Sections of the 14th-century walls and towers are preserved. The Cathedral (begun ca. 1158) has its original Romanesque apse; the Capilla Mayor and the transept were reconstructed in 1529 by Juan de Rasines; the tower (1767), by Martín de Beratúa, and the south portal are baroque. The interior (nave and two aisles with gallery) has groin vaulting and historiated capitals. The main altarpiece is by Damián Forment (1537); the choir stalls are the work of Diego Guillén de Holanda and Andrés de Nájera (1521); the altarpiece of S. Andrés is attributed to Pedro Arbulo Marguvete (late 16th cent.). The sacristy (1602) has a Mexican monstrance (1659) and other goldwork.

BIBLIOG. N. Marcos Rupérez, El retablo mayor de Santo Domingo de la Calzada, BSEE, XXX, 1922, pp. 5–17; A. Prior Untoria, La Catedral Calceatense, Logroño, 1950.

Santo Domingo de Silos (Burgos). The Abbey was founded in 919 by Count Fernán González; it was later reconstructed, and its church was consecrated in 1088. Only the Romanesque cloister remains, with round arches supported by double columns with joined capitals, decorated with exceptionally fine Romanesque sculptures and complemented by the eight bas-reliefs on the piers at the corners. The south portal of the old church is of the 12th century. The Museo del Monasterio contains prehistoric and Roman exhibits, the Mozarabic chalice of S. Domingo (11th cent.), a copper Romanesque frontal with representations of the Apostles, and many examples of goldwork.

BIBLIOG. L. Serrano Péneda, Santo Domingo de Silos: Su historia y tesoro artístico, Burgos, 1926; G. Gaillard, L'église et le cloître de Silos, B. monumental, XCI, 1932, pp. 39–80; M. Gómez-Moreno, La urna de Santo Domingo de Silos, AEArte, XIV, 1940–41, pp. 493–502; S. González Salas, El castro de Yecla, Madrid, 1945; J. Pérez de Urbel, El claustro de Silos, 2d ed., Burgos, 1955; A. Ruiz, Abadía de Santo Domingo de Silos, Madrid, 1960.

Santo Toribio de Liébana (Santander). The monastery existed in the 8th century. The present church was built in 1256, with cross-vaulted nave and two aisles and three polygonal apses; one of the south portals is Romanesque. Over the Capilla del Camarín (18th cent.) is an extensively decorated dome.

BIBLIOG. E. Jusué Fernández, El monasterio de Santo Toribio de Liébana, Valladolid, 1921.

Sasamón (Burgos). The Church of S. María la Real has a nave and two aisles with cruciform pillars and ogival vaulting (13th cent.), a two-aisle transept, and five polygonal apses. It contains an altarpiece of Santiago (16th cent.) and some tapestries. The portal in the transept is a replica of the Puerta del Sarmental of the Cathedral of Burgos, and the cloister is a simplified version of the one at Burgos.

BIBLIOG. L. Huidobro Serna, Sasamón: villa de arte, BSCE, VI, 1911–12, pp. 59–63; T. López Mata, Santa María de Sasamón, BIFG, XXXII, 1953, pp. 551–53.

Segovia. The Roman aqueduct, from the time of Augustus, is about ½ mi. long and about 94 ft. at its maximum height. A large part of the walls (12th cent. and later) are in good condition, as are the Puertas de S. Andrés, S. Cebrián, and Santiago. The Alcázar (documented in 1122, but later changed) has a patio of 1592; the Torre de Homenaje (flanked with turrets; 15th cent.), the Salón de la Galera and Salón del Solio, and the Museo de Armas are noteworthy. The Romanesque churches include Sta Trinidad, with a porticoed gallery and the Capilla del Campo, containing 16th-century paintings; S. Esteban, with an airy 12th-century tower and an exterior cloister; S. Andrés (renovated but with its original apse); S. Martín, with a tower, fine exterior arcades, and a portal with 12th-century sculpture; and S. Millán (1111–23), with a Mozarabic tower, porticoes (13th cent.), and mural paintings in the interior. The 12-sided Church of la Vera Cruz (13th cent.), inspired by the Church of the Holy Sepulcher in Jerusalem, with central plan, has Romanesque portals; in the interior is a central two-story rotunda containing a replica of the Holy Sepulcher.

The Cathedral, designed by Juan Gil de Hontañón to replace the earlier building (destroyed), was begun in 1525 and finished in the 17th century; it is the latest example of the Gothic style in Spain, for only the portal (1620) and the cimborio at the crossing reflect the Escorial style. The interior is on a Latin-cross plan, with nave and two aisles, chapels between the buttresses, transept, chevet with ambulatory and chapels, and stellar vaulting. Noteworthy are the stained-glass windows (16th–17th cent.); the main altarpiece, designed by F. Sabatini (1772), with the ivory-and-silver Virgin of Peace (14th cent.); the Gothic stalls (15th cent.; some from the destroyed

cathedral) in the coro; and the trascoro, designed by Ventura Ro dríguez (1784). The chapels contain paintings by Francisco Camil (17th cent.), a 15th-century baptismal font, altarpieces by Pedr de Bolduque, a Deposition altarpiece designed by Juan de Jun (1571), a triptych by Ambrosius Benson (16th cent.), and Gothi rejas. The cloister (late 15th cent.), that of the old cathedral, contain small chapels and the Museo y Archivo de la Catedral, with painting by Luis de Ribera and Luis de Morales, sculptures (13th cent.) Brussels tapestries (17th cent.), a 17th-century monstrance, an manuscripts.

The Monastery of S. Antonio el Real was rebuilt in 1455; it church has a fine artesonado and a Flemish altarpiece (15th cent.) The Dominican Convent of Sta Cruz (now the Hospicio) has a richl ornamented portal (16th cent.). The Hieronymite Monastery of e Parral has a church with an altarpiece by Juan Rodríguez, who wit Lucas Giraldo, designed the tombs (ca. 1528) of Juan Pacheco an his wife, María Portocarrero; beside the elaborate late Gothic doorwa to the sacristy is the tomb of Beatriz Pacheco. The Dominican con vent, in a fortified mansion known as the Casa de Hércules, has 13th-century tower; the Church of S. Miguel (16th cent.) has portal with 12th-century sculpture; the Convent of S. Isabel has reja of 1507. The city has many interesting old mansions: Romanesqu (centered around the former Canonjías quarter); Gothic (Casa de Marqués de Lozoya, Casa de Arias Dávila); Renaissance (Casa de Marqués del Arco, Palacio Episcopal, Casa de los Marqueses d Moya); and the fortified Casa de los Picos, with a façade studde with faceted stones. The Museo Provincial de Bellas Artes contain an archaeological collection, Castilian panel paintings (15th–16th cent.) and canvases of the Madrid school (17th cent.). The deconsecrate Romanesque Church of S. Juan de los Caballeros houses the Muse Zuloaga (ceramics).

BIBLIOG. J. de Contreras, El monasterio de San Antonio el Real, BSEF XXVI, 1918, pp. 255–64; J. Contreras y López de Alaya, Marqués d Lozoya, La casa segoviana, BSEE, XXVII, 1919, pp. 107–13, 153–6 E. Tormo y Monzó, Cartilla excursionista, BSEE, XXVII, 1919, pp. 130–37 202–14; J. Tello y Dodero, Monasterio de Santa Maria de El Parral, Madri 1929; F. J. Cabello y Dodero, La arquitectura románica en Segovia, ES X, 1952, pp. 5–37; I. de Ceballos-Escalera, Segovia monumental, Madri 1953; S. Alcolea Gil, Segovia y su provincia, Barcelona, 1958; J. Contrera y López de Alaya, Marqués de Lozoya, La nueva instalación del Muse Provincial de Segovia, AEArte, XXXII, 1959, pp. 179–81; J. Contreras López de Alaya, Marqués de Lozoya, El alcázar de Segovia, Segovia, 196 M. J. Llorente Tabanera, El convento de Santa Cruz, Segovia, 1961; de Vera and M. Villalpando, Los castillos de Segovia, 2d ed., Segovia, 196 M. Quintanilla, Algunas notas sobre artifices segovianos (1560–1660), ES XIV, 1962, pp. 71–188; M. Villalpando, Orígenes y construcción de catedral de Segovia, ES, XIV, 1962, pp. 391–408.

Sepúlveda (Segovia). The Septempublica of the Romans, Se púlveda reached its most brilliant epoch during the medieval period There are remains of the castle and the city walls and gates. Th Church of el Salvador, whose apse dates from 1093, has a singl aisle with barrel vaulting and a porticoed gallery with simple capital The Romanesque Church of Nuestra Señora de la Peña has a port with variegated decorations and a tower constructed by Dominicu Iuliano in 1144. The Church of S. Justo (nave and two aisles) ha Romanesque sculpture in the crypt.

BIBLIOG. F. Suárez Bravo, De Buitrago a Turégano, pasado por Pe draza y Sepúlveda, BSEE, XXXVII, 1929, pp. 213–21; F. Hueso Rolland Las murallas de Sepúlveda, B. Asociación Española de Amigos de los Cas tillos, I, 1954, pp. 141–42.

Soria. Little remains of the castle and the city walls. The co legiate church (S. Pedro) was commissioned to Juan Martínez Muci (1551) and finished in 1573; it was modeled on the collegiate churc at Berlanga de Duero. In the interior are a nave and four aisle all of equal height, with cross vaulting. The main altarpiece is b Francisco del Río (1578), and the altarpiece of the Reliquias is b Gabriel de Pinedo (1600); there is a Flemish triptych from 155 Three wings of the old Romanesque cloister (12th cent.) show in fluences from the one at Santo Domingo de Silos. The Church o S. Domingo has a monumental Romanesque façade (12th cent.) The Romanesque Church of S. Juan de Rabanera (12th cent.) ha an aisleless nave, a dome on pendentives, and fluted columns wit fine capitals in the apse; the sculptured tympanum comes from th destroyed church of S. Nicolás. The cloister of the Monastery o S. Juan de Duero shows Oriental influences in its intersecting horse shoe arches. The church of the Hospital has an altarpiece by Gabrie de Pinedo (1597). The Renaissance palace of the counts of Gómar (1577) and the Casa de los Ríos, also of the Renaissance, are out standing. The Museo Numantino contains materials from the ex cavations at Numancia; of special interest is the pottery collection The Museo Celtibérico has collections of prehistoric and Roma remains.

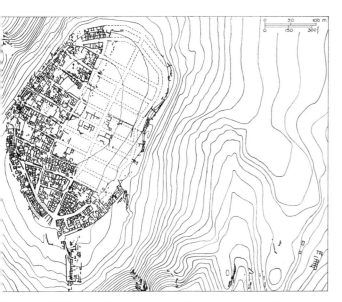

Numancia, Celtic and Roman ruins, with reconstruction of street plan.

Near the city are the ruins of the ancient city of Numancia, destroyed by the Romans in 133 B.C. Excavations have uncovered a large part of the Celtic and the Roman cities. The Celtic city, of Greek-inspired layout, was enclosed by walls almost 20 ft. thick; the city blocks are all the same size and the houses of a local type. The Roman city, which repeated the layout of the preceding city, had canals, wells, and small baths; the houses were still built on the native local plan, with a very few examples of the Hellenistic-Roman type.

BIBLIOG. T. Ramírez and L. Andrés, San Juan de Duero, Barcelona, 1904; J. R. Mélida y Alinari, La iglesia de San Juan de Rabanera en Soria, BSEE, XVIII, 1910, pp. 2–20; A. Schulten, RE, s.v.; A. Schulten, Numantia, 4 vols., Berlin, 1914–31; A. Schulten, Geschichte von Numantia, Munich, 1933; L. Torres Balbás, La influencia artística del Islam en los monumentos de Soria, Al-Andalus, V, 1940, pp. 465–67; M. A. and M. del P. Ridruejo Gil, Cuatro frontales románicos de Soria, AEArte, XVIII, 1945, pp. 97–106; J. A. Gaya Nuño, El románico en la provincia de Soria, Madrid, 1946; M. Moreno y Moreno, Soria turística y monumental, Soria, 1955.

Turégano (Segovia). The castle (10th cent., largely reconstructed in the 15th) is square in plan with cylindrical towers; it encloses a 13th-century church. In the village is a church with a Romanesque apse; the Plaza Mayor is arcaded.

BIBLIOG. G. M. Vergara, El castillo de Turégano, Segovia, 1893; F. Suárez Bravo, De Buitrago a Turégano, pasado por Pedraza y Sepúlveda, BSEE, XXXVII, 1929, pp. 213–21.

Provincias Vascongadas (Basque Provinces). This small region of northern Spain comprises the three provinces of Álava, Guipúzcoa, and Vizcaya, whose capitals are, respectively, Vitoria, San Sebastián, and Bilbao. Although less highly developed artistically than other regions, it nevertheless exhibits a definite and individual character in its adaptation of artistic influences from its important neighbors, Castilla and Navarra.

BIBLIOG. A. Pirala y Criada, Provincias vascongadas, Barcelona, 1885; C. de Castro, Catálogo monumental de España: Alava, Madrid, 1915; C. de Echegaray, Monumentos civiles de Guipúzcoa, Barcelona, 1921; J. de Yrizar, El "mudéjar" en Guipúzcoa, Arquitectura, IV, 1922, pp. 362–67; J. E. Delmas, Guía histórico-descriptiva del viajero en el Señorío de Vizcaya, Bilbao, 1944; J. A. Gaya Nuño, El románico en la provincia de Vizcaya, AEArte, XVII, 1944, pp. 24–40; P. de Zabalo, Arquitectura popular del país vasco, Buenos Aires, 1947; F. Sesmero Pérez, El arte del Renacimiento en Vizcaya, Bilbao, 1954; A. Aguirre Andrés, Materiales arqueológicos de Vizcaya, Bilbao, 1955; J. de Ybarra y Bergé, Lo romano en Vizcaya, Zumarraga, I, 1955, pp. 11–44; L. Michilena, Guipúzcoa en la época romana, B. Real Soc. vascongada de amigos del país, XII, 1956, pp. 69–94; J. de Ybarra y Bergé, Catálogo de monumentos de Vizcaya, 2 vols., Bilbao, 1958. See also B. Comisión de Monumentos de Vizcaya, Bilbao, 1909 ff.

Armentia (Álava). The town was an episcopal see in the 9th century. The Church of S. Andrés (12th cent., restored 18th cent.) has preserved Romanesque reliefs in the portico and on the capitals and statues of the Evangelists in the arches of the transept.

BIBLIOG. M. Díaz de Arcaya, Armentia, su obispado y su basilica de San Andrés, Vitoria, 1901; F. de Mendoza, Los relieves del pórtico de Armentia, Vitoria, 1913.

Bermeo (Vizcaya). The Church of S. Eufemia is Gothic, and the Franciscan convent (1357) has a Gothic cloister. In nearby Baquio, the Church of S. Pelayo has a square Romanesque apse.

BIBLIOG. I. Omaechevarria, Un claustro gótico en Vizcaya, B. Real Soc. vascongada de amigos del país, XIII, 1957, pp. 453–62.

Bilbao (Vizcaya). The Cathedral (formerly the Church of Santiago) was reconstructed in 1404; it has a nave and two aisles, transept, ambulatory, and triforium; the portal was designed by Martín Garita in 1581. The Church of S. Antón (1433) has a corner portico (1543) and a tower enlarged in 1775 by Gabriel de Capelastegui. The Church of la Encarnación has a 16th-century doorway and a 17th-century spire. The Church of S. Vicente de Albia (16th cent.) has cross vaulting above Tuscan columns. The Church of S. Nicolás de Bari (on an octagonal plan), reconstructed by Ignacio de Ibero (1743–56), contains numerous sculptures by Juan Pascual de Mena (ca. 1754). The Museo Arqueológico y Etnográfico is interesting. The Museo de Bellas Artes contains panel paintings and canvases by Spanish and other artists (13th–17th cent.); the Museo de Arte Moderno specializes in paintings and sculptures of the 19th and 20th centuries.

BIBLIOG. R. de Bastida, Los retablos y esculturas de la iglesia de San Nicolás de Bilbao, Arquitectura, VI, 1924, pp. 11–14; D. Roda, Museo de Bellas Artes de Bilbao, Bilbao, 1947; F. Sesmero Pérez, El pórtico de Santiago de Bilbao, BSEAAV, XIX, 1952–53, pp. 91–106.

Deva (Guipúzcoa). The Church of la Asunción has a 15th-century portal that shows the influence of the Franco-Navarrese school of sculpture. The interior of the church was remodeled in the 17th century by Juan Ortiz de Olaeta after plans by Juan de Aróstegui.

Durango (Vizcaya). The town has numerous patrician houses. The doorway of the Church of S. Ana was once a city gate. The Church of S. Pedro de Tavira, renovated in the 17th century, has a plateresque altarpiece. The Church of S. María de Ulibarri (15th–17th cent.) contains a main altarpiece by Martín Ruiz de Zubiate (1578). The stone Cross of Crutziaga (15th cent.) stands on the road to Vergara.

Eibar (Guipúzcoa). The Church of S. Andrés, whose orientation was reversed in the 16th century, has apses at each end of the nave and cross vaulting over four Corinthian columns; the portal is plateresque. The main altarpiece is by Andrés de Araoz and his son Juan (1567). There are two fine bronze lecterns (15th cent.).

Laguardia (Álava). The town, on a hilltop, with the ruins of a fortified castle, is surrounded by its old walls and gates. The Church of S. María de los Reyes (15th cent.) has a Renaissance apse and a Gothic portal with sculptured decoration; the main altarpiece is from the workshop of Juan Vascardo (16th cent.). The baroque Church of S. Juan Bautista (or El Pilar) contains a Gothic statue of the Virgin and a baptismal font of the 16th century. The Ayuntamiento (1574) and the many old mansions of the town are of interest.

BIBLIOG. F. López de Vallado, Santa María de los Reyes y San Juan Bautista de Laguardia, San Sebastián, 1921; J. M. de Mora, Noticia sobre las obras de arte de la iglesia de La Guardia, AEArte, XXXVI, 1963, pp. 65–71.

Lequeitio (Vizcaya). The Gothic Church of S. María is modeled on the Cathedral of Bilbao; the late Gothic gilded altarpiece (1510) over the high altar is by Juan García Crial.

BIBLIOG. E. Tormo y Monzó, Lequeitio, BSEE, XVIII, 1910, pp. 50–58.

Mondragón (Guipúzcoa). The Convent of S. Francisco, erected in 1582, has a main altar (1695) by Jacobo Ayesta and Rafael Larralde. The Ayuntamiento was built by Martín Carrera in 1746.

BIBLIOG. J. Ruiz de Larrinaga, Convento de San Francisco en Mondragón, Arch. Ibero-Americano, 47, 1952, pp. 297–346.

Oñate (Guipúzcoa). The 15th-century Church of S. Miguel has a nave and two aisles and a raised choir; it contains the Gothic tomb of the Count of Oñate and the plateresque sepulcher of Rodrigo Sáez de Mercado, sculptured in Granada by Diego de Siloe. The former university has a façade decorated by Pierre Picart in 1545; the patio has medallions in the style of Berruguete. The Ayuntamiento is by Manuel Carrera (1779–83).

BIBLIOG. J. A. de Lizarralde, Historia de la Universidad de Sancti Spiritus de Oñate, Tolosa, 1930.

Portugalete (Vizcaya). The Church of S. María has a nave and two aisles, with large pillars (14th–16th cent.); the main altarpiece was begun in 1533 by Guyot de Beaugrant and continued by his brother Jean after 1549; the altarpiece of the Epiphany is of the 16th century.

San Sebastián (Guipúzcoa). The Church of S. María, with a portal (1743–71) by Pedro Ignacio Lizardi, Miguel de Salazar, and Francisco de Ibero, contains several baroque altarpieces. The 16th-century Church of S. Vicente has a gilded altarpiece over the high altar by Ambrosio de Bengoechea and Juan de Iriarte (1583). The Convent of S. Telmo (1551), designed by Martín de Santiago, has a plateresque cloister; the former conventual chapel was decorated by José María Sert (1930–32) with a series of Basque-inspired paintings. The Museo Municipal de S. Telmo, located in the Convent, contains archaeological and folklore collections as well as paintings and sculpture (14th–20th cent.). The neoclassic Ayuntamiento (1829) was designed by Silvestre Pérez.

BIBLIOG. J. Peñuelas, La iglesia de Santa María en San Sebastián, BSEE, XXVI, 1918, pp. 265–71; G. Manso de Zúñiga, Historia del monasterio de San Telmo, San Sebastián, 1943; M. Oyarzun, San Sebastián: Sus calles y principales monumentos, San Sebastián, 1951; I. Arocena, Las murallas de San Sebastián, B. Real Soc. vascongada de amigos del país, XVIII, 1962, pp. 115–40.

Vitoria (Álava). The city preserves sections of its 13th-century walls. The Old Cathedral (14th–15th cent.) has a richly sculptured Gothic portal. The interior consists of nave and two aisles, a long transept, and a *chevet* with ambulatory; the triforium is decorated with tracery and has an openwork railing. In the chapels are Gothic and Renaissance tombs and many examples of gold- and silverwork. Modeled on the Old Cathedral, the Church of S. Pedro (14th cent.), with sculptures in the portal, contains bronze tombs of Italian workmanship and a Flemish panel painting from the 15th century. The Church of S. Miguel (14th cent.) contains a main altarpiece by Gregorio Fernández and Juan Velázquez (1624–32). The church of the Convent of S. Antonio has an altarpiece attributed to Gregorio Fernández (Hernández) and a Romanesque Virgen de los Remedios. Among the aristocratic mansions are the Gothic Casa del Portalón and Casa del Cordón and the Renaissance palaces of Bendaña, Villasuso, and Escoriaza-Esquivel. In the Plaza Nueva, by Justo Antonio de Olaguibel (1781–91), is the Casa Consistorial, with a Crucifixion by José Ribera. The Museo Provincial has prehistoric and Roman exhibits, panel paintings (15th–16th cent.), and canvases by José Ribera and Alonso Cano.

Near the city, the Sanctuary of Estíbaliz has a 12th-century Romanesque church with three fine apses; the richly decorated 13th-century portal has been widely copied. Within is an interesting Gothic baptismal font.

BIBLIOG. M. Diaz de Arcaya, La basílica de Nuestra Señora de Estíbaliz, Vitoria, 1900; E. de Pinedo, El santuario de Santa María de Estíbaliz, Madrid, 1940; A. de Apraiz, Las casas góticas llamadas "del Portalón" y "del Cordón" en Vitoria, BSEAAV, XVI, 1949–50, pp. 33–52; E. de Apraiz, El convento de San Francisco en Vitoria, RNA, IX, 1949, pp. 333–41; A. de Apraiz, El Museo de Vitoria, AEArte, XXIV, 1951, pp. 364–66; J. Cantera Orive, El pórtico y la portada de la catedral de Vitoria, Vitoria, 1951; A. de Apraiz, Los tímpanos de la catedral vieja de Vitoria, AEArte, XXVI, 1953, pp. 187–204; E. de Apraiz, La muralla del primitivo Vitoria, B. Real Soc. vascongada de amigos del país, IX, 1953, pp. 169–90.

Zumaya (Guipúzcoa). The Gothic Church of S. Pedro has a main altarpiece by J. de Anchieta (1577). Near the town is the Casa Museo Ignacio Zuloaga, which is housed in a 12th-century hermitage; in addition to works by Zuloaga, it contains paintings by El Greco and others.

Navarra. This region in the north of Spain, between the Pyrenees and the valley of the Ebro, consists of a single province, with its capital in Pamplona. Its distinctive character reflects its eventful history. It reached its artistic culmination during the Middle Ages, with many Romanesque and Gothic monuments testifying to its greatness.

BIBLIOG. P. de Madrazo y Kuntz, Navarra y Logroño, 3 vols., Barcelona, 1886; W. Bergmann, Studien zur volkstümlichen Kultur im Grenzgebiet von Hocharagón und Navarra, Hamburg, 1934; T. Biurrun Sotil, Las bellas artes en Navarra durante el Renacimiento, Pamplona, 1935; T. Biurrun Sotil, El arte románico en Navarra, Pamplona, 1936; D. Angulo Iñíguez, La pintura del Renacimiento en Navarra, Príncipe de Viana, IV, 1943, pp. 421–44, VIII, 1947, pp. 159–70; J. M. Lacarra and J. Gudiol Ricart, El primer románico en Navarra, Príncipe de Viana, V, 1944, pp. 221–

72; J. Yárnoz and M. López Otero, Ventura Rodríguez y su obra en Navarra, Madrid, 1944; J. Ramón Castro, Cuadernos de arte navarro, 2 vols., Pamplona, 1944–49; J. Yárnoz, Las iglesias octogonales en Navarra, Príncipe de Viana, VI, 1945, pp. 515–21; B. Taracena Aguirre and L. Vázquez de Parga, Excavaciones en Navarra: La Romanización, Príncipe de Viana, VII, 1946, pp. 413–69; B. Taracena Aguirre et al., Excavaciones en Navarra, 5 vols., Pamplona, 1947–57; J. E. Uranga Galdiano, Retablos navarros del Renacimiento, Pamplona, 1947; J. E. Cirlot, Guías Artísticas de España: Navarra, Barcelona, 1956; Museo de Navarra, Guía, Pamplona, 1956; R. Crozet, L'art roman en Navarre et en Aragon, Cah. civ. medievale, V, 1962, pp. 35–61. See also BMN, 1895 ff.

Artajona. Well-preserved defensive walls with crenelated towers gird the old part of the town. The fortified Church of S. Saturnino (12th–13th cent.), with a sculptured façade, contains a painted altarpiece over the high altar (1497). The Church of S. Pedro, with its Romanesque-Gothic portal, is from the same period. The 17th-century Hermitage of Nuestra Señora de Jerusalén contains a Byzantine statue of the Virgin, of gilded and enameled copper (13th cent.).

BIBLIOG. Conde de Morales de los Rios, La iglesia de San Saturnino en Artajona, BSEE, XXXVI, 1928, pp. 92–95.

Ayegui. Near the town, the Cistercian Abbey of Nuestra Señora de Irache (Hirache) has a somber Gothic-style church (12th–13th cent.) with a Romanesque apse and a 14th-century tower. The Gothic cloister has 16th-century elements.

BIBLIOG. C. Pellejero Soteras, Claustro de Irache, Príncipe de Viana, II, 5, 1941, pp. 15–33; J. E. Uranga Galdiano, Esculturas románicas del Real monasterio de Irache, Príncipe de Viana, III, 1942, pp. 9–20.

Estella. A town with Roman antecedents, it was important during the Middle Ages and is rich in artistic and historical monuments. The Church of S. Pedro de la Rúa has Romanesque portal and cloister. S. Miguel has a Romanesque portal with sculptured tympanum and contains Gothic panel paintings; S. Juan Bautista has a main altarpiece by Pierre Picart and Juan Imberto (1563–73). The sculptured Gothic portal that survives from the ruined Church of Sto Sepulcro is noteworthy. The Palacio de los Duques de Granada de Ega (now the Audiencia) is a remarkable Romanesque building (12th cent.). The Palacio de los Condes de San Cristóbal is in Renaissance style, as is the Casa Consistorial (town hall).

BIBLIOG. G. Lindemann, Die Skulpturen von Estella, Edwin Redslob zum 70. Geburtstag, Berlin, 1954, pp. 263–75; E. Lambert, L'ancien couvent des Dominicains à Estella, CAF, CXVII, 1959, pp. 125–28; J. Goñi Gaztambide, Historia del convento de Santo Domingo de Estella, Príncipe de Viana, XXII, 1961, pp. 11–64.

Fitero. The village rose around the Cistercian Abbey of S. María la Real (finished ca. 1250); its Gothic church has a Romanesque apse and contains a main altarpiece by Roland de Mois (1550). The cloister and the chapter house are exceptionally fine. In the treasury are a 10th-century Hispano-Moorish ivory coffer and a 13th-century enameled reliquary.

BIBLIOG. V. Lampérez y Romea, El real monasterio de Fitero en Navarra, BRAH, XLVI, 1905, pp. 286–300.

Huarte-Araquil. Near the village, the Sanctuary of S. Miguel de Excelsis has a Romanesque church that contains an enameled altarpiece of the 12th century.

BIBLIOG. M. Arigita y Lasa, Historia de la imagen y santuario de San Miguel de Excelcis, Pamplona, 1904; S. Huici Lazcano and V. Juaristi Sagarzazu, El santuario de San Miguel de Excelcis y su retablo esmaltado, Madrid, 1929.

Muruzábal. The church of the Templars' Monastery of Eunate exemplifies that order's typical plan; Romanesque in style, it has an octagonal plan with a loggia; the polygonal apse is decorated with blind arcading.

BIBLIOG. V. Lampérez y Romea, La iglesia de los templarios de Eunate, Madrid, 1907; E. Lambert, Le portique octagonal d'Eunate, B. monumental, LXXXIII, 1924, pp. 167–72.

Olite. Once the residence of the kings of Navarra, the town preserves parts of the walls and the ruins of the magnificent palacecastle. The town has many notable examples of civil architecture, which blend French Gothic and Mudejar styles. The Church of S. María la Real has a 14th-century sculptured façade and an atrium in Gothic style. The Church of S. Pedro has a Romanesque sculptured portal and an octagonal tower with a Gothic spire.

BIBLIOG. J. Albizu, Historia de la parroquia de San Pedro de Olite, Pamplona, 1915; J. Yárnoz, Iglesia parroquial de San Pedro de Olite, Príncipe de Viana, II, 5, 1941, pp. 8–15; J. Yárnoz, Palacio real de Olite, Príncipe de Viana, II, 2, 1941, pp. 13–35.

La Oliva. The Cistercian abbey was founded in 1134. The church, on a Latin-cross plan, was finished in 1198; its cross-vaulted nave and two aisles are Gothic, while the five apsidal chapels are Romanesque. There are also a Gothic cloister (14th cent.), a chapter house with ogival vaults over Romanesque columns, a library, and a refectory.

BIBLIOG. Conde de Morales de los Rios, El monasterio de Nuestra Señora de la Oliva, BSEE, XXXV, 1927, pp. 296–303; O. Larumbe, El monasterio de Nuestra Señora de la Oliva, Pamplona, 1930; J. Ramón Castro, Los retablos de los monasterios de la Oliva y Fitero, Príncipe de Viana, I, 3, 1941, pp. 13–26.

Pamplona. The city was founded by Pompeius Magnus in 75 B.C., perhaps on the site of a prehistoric settlement, although finds there cannot be dated before the 1st century of our era. Nothing is known of the city itself. Some mosaics and bronzes and a workshop for production of terra sigillata have been found. During the early Middle Ages the city was conquered by the Franks, the Visigoths, and the Moors. It was the capital of the kingdom of Navarra from the 10th to the 16th century, when it became part of the kingdom of Castilla. The Gothic Cathedral (1397–1525; VI, FIG. 493) has a neoclassic façade by Ventura Rodríguez (1783). In the interior (nave and two aisles, transept, chapels between the buttresses, and *chevet* with ambulatory and chapel) are the tomb of Charles the Noble of Navarra and his wife, by the Frenchman Janin Lomme of Tournai 1416); the 14th-century Caparroso altarpiece; a *reja* by Guillermo Ervenat (16th cent.); the Virgen de los Reyes (14th cent.) in the sanctuary; and various tombs (15th cent.). The doorway from the transept to the cloister (Puerta del Amparo) is richly sculptured on the jambs and tympanum. The cloister (14th–15th cent.), with the Capilla de la Barbazana, contains numerous sculptures in the French manner on the doorways (notably the Puerta de la Preciosa) and sepulchers. In the treasury is a panel painting of the Crucifixion 14th cent.), a Moorish ivory coffer (1005), and Gothic and Renaissance goldwork. Noteworthy are the churches of S. Cernín (S. Saturnino; 14th cent.), S. Nicolás (13th cent.), and S. Miguel, with an altarpiece by Juan de Anchieta (16th cent.). The Ayuntamiento has a baroque two-storied façade. The Casa de la Diputación contains canvases by Goya. The Museo de Navarra has a prehistoric collection, Roman mosaics, Moorish and Romanesque objects, Gothic murals, and 16th-century paintings from the Palacio del Cabo de Armería at Oriz.

BIBLIOG. E. Bertaux, Le tombeau de Charles le Noble à Pampelune, GBA, 3d Ser., XL, 1908, pp. 89–112; J. Albizu y Sáinz de Murieta, San Cernín, Pamplona, 1930; J. Ramón Castro, El Goya de la Diputación de Navarra, Príncipe de Viana, III, 1942, pp. 37–39; L. Torres Balbás, Filiación arquitectónica de la catedral de Pamplona, Príncipe de Viana, VII, 1946, pp. 471–508; L. Vázquez de Parga, Los capiteles historiados del claustro románico de la catedral de Pamplona, Príncipe de Viana, VIII, 1947, pp. 457–65; L. Vázquez de Parga, El Maestro del Refectorio de Pamplona, Príncipe de Viana, IX, 1948, pp. 145–51; A. Ubieto Arteta, La fecha de construcción del claustro románico de la catedral de Pamplona, Príncipe de Viana, XI, 1950, pp. 77–83; E. Lambert, La catedral de Pamplona, Príncipe de Viana, XII, 1951, pp. 9–35; L. Urabayen, Biografía de Pamplona, Pamplona, 1952; G. G. Callahan, Reevaluation of the Refectory Retable from the Cathedral at Pamplona, AB, XXXV, 1953, pp. 181–93; J. Idoate, Las fortificaciones de Pamplona a partir de la conquista de Navarra, Príncipe de Viana, XV, 1954, pp. 57–154; F. J. Sánchez Cantón, Les pinturas de Oriz y la Guerra de Sajonia, Pamplona, 1954; G. de Pamplona, La fecha de construcción de San Cernín de Pamplona, Príncipe de Viana, XVII, 1956, pp. 455–63; J. E. Uranga Galdiano, Las pinturas murales de Artaiz, AEArte, XXXI, 1958, pp. 253–54; M. A. Mezquíriz de Catalán, La excavación estratigráfica de Pompaelo, I: Campaña de 1956, Pamplona, 1958; G. Gaillard, Les sculptures romanes de la cathédrale de Pampelune au Musée de Navarre, B. Soc. nat. ant. de France, 1960, pp. 92–94.

Roncesvalles. The town, on the pilgrimage route to Compostela, rose around a Benedictine abbey founded in the 12th century. The early Gothic church, of French influence, contains Gothic sepulchers of the kings of Navarra; a Gothic statue of the Virgin of Sorrows, in wood covered with silver; and a 12th-century evangelistary. In the treasury are a Holy Family by Luis de Morales (16th cent.) and a Flemish triptych.

BIBLIOG. L. Vázquez de Parga, Esculturas góticas en Roncesvalles, Príncipe de Viana, V, 1944, p. 421; L. Torres Balbás, La iglesia de la Hospedería de Roncesvalles, Príncipe de Viana, VI, 1945, pp. 371–403; J. M. Lacarra, Roncesvalles, Pirineos, IV, 1948, pp. 355–84.

San Salvador de Leyre. The monastery has a Romanesque church of the 11th century whose sculptures reflect the style of Jaca; the sculptural decoration on the portal is noteworthy. The crypt, dating from the 11th century, has enormous capitals from an earlier structure of the 9th century. The other monastery buildings date from the 17th and 18th centuries.

BIBLIOG. G. Gaillard, La sculpture du XIᵉ siècle: Leyre et Ujué, B. Monumental, CXIII, 1955, pp. 237–49; E. Tyrell, Historia de la arquitectura románica de San Salvador de Leyre, Príncipe de Viana, XIX, 1958, pp. 305–35.

Sangüesa. There are remains of the medieval walls. The Church of S. María la Real (12th–13th cent.) has a sculptured portal by various Romanesque masters (Leodegarius, the Master of San Juan de la Peña, the Master of Jaca) that shows French influences. The church has three apses and an octagonal tower with a spire; it contains a 15th-century altarpiece and a Gothic monstrance. The Church of Santiago (12th cent.) has a Gothic portal and crenelated tower. The Church of el Salvador (14th cent.) contains an altarpiece by Juan de Berrueta (16th cent.). In the town are several Gothic and baroque palaces.

BIBLIOG. J. E. Uranga Galdiano, Las esculturas de Santa María la Real de Sangüesa, Pirineos, VI, 1950, pp. 53–66; C. M. Weber, La portada de Santa María la Real de Sangüesa, Príncipe de Viana, XX, 1959, pp. 139–86.

Tudela. The city, of very ancient origin, was under Moslem domination from 716 to 1114. The collegiate church (13th cent.), which was the cathedral until 1851, retains some elements of a mosque (9th cent.). Noteworthy is the Puerta del Juicio (ca. 1200), with sculptured groups depicting the Last Judgment. The church (cross-vaulted nave and two aisles, transept, and five apses) contains a Romanesque stone Virgin, the tomb of Chancellor Villaespesa and his wife (15th cent.), and several painted altarpieces: one over the main altar by Pedro Díaz de Oviedo (1487), one in the Capilla de la Esperanza by Bonanat Zaortiga (15th cent.), and that of S. Catalina. The stalls in the *coro* are by Esteban de Obray (ca. 1519). The cloister (12th cent.) has interesting carved capitals. The Church of la Magdalena (13th–16th cent.), with a sculptured portal and a square Romanesque tower, contains a 16th-century altarpiece. The Church of S. Nicolás has a Romanesque portal and Renaissance altarpieces.

BIBLIOG. J. Ramón Castro, Pedro Diaz de Oviedo y el retablo mayor de la catedral de Tudela, Príncipe de Viana, III, 1942, pp. 121–37; M. Gómez-Moreno, La mezquita mayor de Tudela, Príncipe de Viana, VI, 1945, pp. 9–27; F. Fuentes, Guía de la catedral de Tudela, Tudela, 1953; R. Crozet, Recherches sur la sculpture romane en Navarre et en Aragon, Cah. civ. medievale, II, 1959, pp. 333–70; A. de Egry, La escultura del claustro de la catedral de Tudela, Príncipe de Viana, XX, 1959, pp. 63–107.

Viana. The town preserves sections of the walls, gates, and several old mansions. The Church of S. María, with a magnificent Renaissance portal by Juan Goyaz and Juan de Oliva Arranótegui (1549–67), contains baroque altarpieces; the Capilla de S. Juan Bautista was decorated by Luis Paret y Alcázar in 1786. The Ayuntamiento dates from 1673.

Aragón. This region comprises the modern provinces of Huesca, Zaragoza, and Teruel; it extends from the Pyrenees to the central plain and is traversed by the Ebro River. All the artistic styles that flourished throughout Spain are well represented, with a special persistence of the Mudejar.

BIBLIOG. L. de Zaragoza and R. de Huesca, Teatro histórico de las iglesias del reino de Aragón, 9 vols., Pamplona, 1780–1807; J. M. Quadrado, Aragón, Barcelona, 1886; M. Abizando y Broto, Documentos para la historia literaria y artística de Aragón, 2 vols., Zaragoza, 1915–17; R. del Arco y Garay, Casas consistoriales de Aragón, Arquitectura, III, 1920, pp. 301–04, 333–39; A. Kingsley Porter, The Tomb of Doña Sancha and the Romanesque Art of Aragon, BM, XLV, 1924, pp. 165–79; R. del Arco y Garay, Aragón, Huesca, 1931 (biblig.); F. Iñiguez Almech, Sobre algunas bóvedas aragonesas de lazo, AEAA, VIII, 1932, pp. 37–47; F. Iñiguez Almech, Torres mudéjares aragonesas, AEAA, XIII, 1937, pp. 173–89; R. del Arco y Garay, Catálogo monumental de España: Huesca, 2 vols., Madrid, 1942; F. Abbad Rios, Estudios del Renacimiento aragonés, AEArte, XVIII, 1945, pp. 162–77, 317–46, XIX, 1946, pp. 217–27; R. del Arco y Garay, Sepulcros de la Casa Real de Aragón, Madrid, 1945; J. Galiay Sarañana, Prehistoria de Aragón, Zaragoza, 1945; J. Galiay Sarañana, La dominación romana en Aragón, Zaragoza, 1946; J. Galiay Sarañana, Arte mudéjar aragonés, Zaragoza, 1950; R. del Arco y Garay, La pintura en Aragón en el siglo XVII, SAA, VI, 1954, pp. 51–75; M. Almagro Basch, El arte rupestre del Bajo Aragón, Zaragoza, 1956; M. Almagro Basch et al., Prehistoria del Bajo Aragón, Zaragoza, 1956; F. Abbad Rios, Catálogo monumental de España: Zaragoza, Madrid, 1957; A. Durán Gudiol, Guía artística de Huesca y su provincia, Barcelona, 1957; F. Abbad Rios, Guía artística de la provincia de Zaragoza, Barcelona, 1958; S. Sebastián, Guía artística de Teruel y su provincia, Barcelona, 1959; F. B. Torralba Soriano, Guía artística de Aragón, Zaragoza, 1960; R. Crozet, L'art roman en Navarre et en Aragon, Cah. civ. medievale, V, 1962, pp. 35–61.

Agüero (Huesca). The Romanesque parish church contains a statue of the Virgin (13th cent.). The 12th-century Church of Santiago has three apses with sculptured capitals; the portal is by the Master of San Juan de la Peña.

BIBLIOG. R. del Arco y Garay, La inédita iglesia de Santiago en Agüero, Madrid, 1919; F. Abbad Rios, El Maestro románico de Agüero, Anales Inst. Arte Americano, III, 1950, pp. 15–25.

Ainsa (Huesca). There is a ruined castle with a pentagonal tower within an arcaded courtyard. The medieval walls still retain the entrance gates. The Romanesque church is from the 12th century, with a crypt and a cloister. The Plaza Mayor has preserved some Romanesque and Gothic elements.

BIBLIOG. A. Durán Gudiol, Guía artística de Huesca y su provincia, Barcelona, 1957.

Albarracín (Teruel). There are some remains of its Roman past. The well-preserved defensive walls have square towers. The Church of S. María is by Pierre Vedel (16th cent.). The Cathedral, remodeled in 1532, contains a 16th-century altarpiece of S. Pedro, seven remarkable Brussels tapestries of the 16th century, and fine goldwork. Near the town are caves with prehistoric rock paintings (Las Olivanas, Doña Clotilde, Navazo).

BIBLIOG. A. Sanz Serrano, La ciudad de los Aben-Racines, BSEE, LII, 1948, pp. 51–65; M. Almagro Basch, Un nuevo grupo de pinturas rupestres en Albarracín: "La Cueva de Doña Clotilde," Teruel, II, 1949, pp. 91–116; C. Tomás Laguía, Las capillas de la catedral de Albarracín, Teruel, XIV, 1955, pp. 151–86; M. García Miralles, Orígenes de la iglesia de Santa María de Albarracín, Teruel, XXIII, 1960, pp. 205–44.

Alcañiz (Teruel). The castle (12th cent.; restored 18th cent.) was erected by the Templars; the Torre de Homenaje and the Romanesque chapel preserve 14th-century mural paintings. The collegiate church has a Gothic tower and a magnificent baroque façade; it contains Gothic panel paintings. The arcaded Lonja (15th cent.) connects with the Renaissance Ayuntamiento. In the nearby Val del Charco del Agua Amarga are prehistoric paintings.

BIBLIOG. N. Sancho, Descripción de la ciudad de Alcañiz y sus afueras, Alcañiz, 1860; V. Bardaviu Ponz and R. Thouvenot, Fouilles dans la région d'Alcañiz, Bordeaux, 1930; J. Caruana Gómez de Barreda, El Castillo de Alcañiz, Teruel, XIII, 1955, pp. 5–116; C. Cid Priego, La colegiata de Alcañiz, Teruel, 1956; C. Cid Priego, Las pinturas murales del castillo de Alcañiz, Teruel, XX, 1958, pp. 5–100.

Alquézar (Huesca). The castle (11th–12th cent.) has double girding walls. The collegiate church, built by Juan Segura (1525–32), contains a 16th-century altarpiece over the main altar as well as several Gothic ones (15th cent.): one of S. Ana by the Master of Arguis, one of S. Quiteria by Juan de la Abadía, and one of the Passion; there is also a 13th-century crucifix. In the sacristy are paintings by Alonso Cano (15th cent.).

BIBLIOG. R. del Arco y Garay, El castillo de Alquézar, Linajes de Aragón, VII, 1916, pp. 54–57; A. Ubieto Arteta, La construcción de la colegiata de Alquézar, Pirineos, V, 1949, pp. 253–63.

Azaila (Teruel). Near the town are the ruins of an Iberian and Roman city on the Ebro. It had a large encircling wall with a moat and two entrances, and a system of paved streets. There were many houses of the Iberian type, a temple on the Iberian plan, and another on the Roman scheme; outside the walls there was a small bath complex. In addition, the characteristic painted pottery and other artifacts found here have provided interesting documentation on native life during the 1st and 2d centuries B.C.

BIBLIOG. J. Cabré Aguilo, Descripción del templo, AEAA, I, 1925, pp. 309–12; J. Cabré Aguilo, Azaila, Barcelona, 1929; L. Curtius, Zum Bronzekopf von Azaila und zu den Porträts des jugendlichen Augustus, RM, LV, 1940, pp. 36–64; J. Cabré Aguilo, Corpus Vasorum Hispanorum: Azaila, Madrid, 1944 (bibliog.).

Barbastro (Huesca). The town, prominent during the Roman era, was again an important center during the Moslem occupation until about 1100. The Cathedral, finished by Juan Segura in 1533 in Renaissance style, has Gothic elements; the stellar vaulting of the nave and flanking aisles is supported by slender pillars. Inside are a main altarpiece, begun by Damián Forment and finished by his pupils in 1604, and the altarpiece of S. Victorián (15th–16th cent.). There is a Museo Diocesano. The Ayuntamiento (15th cent.) and the arcaded Plaza Mayor, with houses of typical Aragonese architecture, are interesting.

BIBLIOG. M. Pano, Damián Forment en la catedral de Barbastro, Cultura española, I, 1906, pp. 812–19; R. del Arco y Garay, El arquitecto de la catedral de Barbastro, Arquitectura, V, 1923, pp. 349–54.

Barluenga (Huesca). The Church of S. Miguel contains some notable 13th-century frescoes; outstanding are those in the apse, by the artist who decorated the Church of S. Fructuoso in Bierge.

BIBLIOG. A. Durán Gudiol, Guía artística de Huesca y su provincia, Barcelona, 1957.

Calaceite (Teruel). The church has a baroque portal (ca. 1720). The town square is arcaded, and there are some fine patrician houses. Nearby is the Iberian settlement of San Antonio (4th–3d cent. B.C.).

BIBLIOG. W. Schüle, Reconstrucción del "Thymaterion" de Calaceite, AEA, XXXIII, 1960, pp. 157–60.

Calatayud (Zaragoza). This was once an Iberian city, which perhaps later became the Roman Bilbilis (ruins nearby). The Church of S. María, with an octagonal tower, has a Renaissance doorway by Juan de Talavera and Esteban de Obray (1526) and contains paintings by Pedro Aybar (1684), an Epiphany altarpiece by Tomás Giner (15th cent.), and Gothic paintings. The churches of S. Pedro de los Francos and S. Andrés are Mudejar; the Church of the Holy Sepulcher, founded in the 12th century, was reconstructed in 1613.

BIBLIOG. P. Savirón y Estévan, Iglesia de San Pedro Mártir: mudéjar de Calatayud, Mus. español de antigüedades, IX, 1878, pp. 387–97; V. Lafuente Alcántara, Historia de Calatayud, Calatayud, 1880; J. López Landa, Iglesias góticomudéjares del arcedianato de Calatayud, Arquitectura, V, 1923, pp. 125–34; Conde de Morales y los Rios, Excursión a Calatayud, BSEE, XXXVI, 1928, pp. 232–33; S. Amada Sanz, Portada y puertas de Santa María de Calatayud, BSEE, LI, 1947, pp. 177–209.

Casbas (Huesca). The Cistercian monastery was founded in 1172. Notable on the 12th-century church is the round-arched doorway with a chrismon on the tympanum; the choir stalls date from 1506 and the cloister is from the 15th century.

BIBLIOG. L. de la Figuera, El monasterio de Casbás, Arquitectura, III, 1920, pp. 102–03.

Caspe (Zaragoza). The Roman sepulcher on the bank of the Ebro River is a late-imperial square structure with fluted Corinthian columns. The 15th-century church has a portal with statues of the Apostles on the jambs (only three remain) and a statue of the Virgin on the trumeau. The interior has nave and two aisles and polygonal apses. It contains the sepulchers of the Master of the Order of St. John of Jerusalem, Juan Fernández de Heredia (15th cent.), and Bishop Martín García (16th cent.). The Plaza Mayor is almost circular, with ogival arcades.

BIBLIOG. M. Pellicer Catalán, Yacimientos arqueológicos en término de Caspe, II Cong. nac. de arqueol. (Madrid 1951), Zaragoza, 1952, pp. 389–96; A. Beltrán, Notas sobre un "kernos" hallado en Caspe, Caesaraugusta V, 1954, pp. 43–48.

Daroca (Zaragoza). The medieval wall, with many towers and two gates, is almost 2½ mi. long. The churches of S. Miguel and of S. Juan, both Romanesque, have 13th-century frescoes. The 16th-century collegiate church (S. María) contains the Gothic Capilla de los Corporales, with a 15th-century alabaster altarpiece. The Museo del Santíssimo Sacramento, housed in the church, contains the reliquary of the Corporales, by Pere (Pedro) Moragues (1384); the altarpiece of S. Martín, by Martín Bernat; panel paintings by Bartolomé Bermejo; and Gothic sculpture and goldwork.

BIBLIOG. F. Martorell, Pere Moragues i la custodia dels Corporals de Daroca, Rev. Est. Univ. Catalans, III, 1909, pp. 225–39; J. Cabré Aguilo, El tesoro artístico de los Corporales de Daroca, BSEE, XXX, 1922, pp. 275–93; L. Torres Balbás, La arquitectura mudéjar en Aragón: Las iglesias de Daroca, AEArte, XXV, 1952, pp. 209–21; F. Torralba Soriano, Iglesia colegial de Santa María de los Santos Corporales de Daroca, Zaragoza, 1954; J. Hernández Perera, Alabastros ingleses en España, Goya, 22, 1958, pp. 216–22.

Escatrón (Zaragoza). The Abbey of Rueda del Ebro, founded by Alfonso II of Aragón in 1182, is of the Cistercian type. The 13th-century church (nave and two aisles) has a rectilinear apse; the cloister has groin vaulting. There is a small octagonal pavilion in front of the refectory; other buildings include a chapter house and dormitories.

BIBLIOG. J. M. López Landa, El monasterio de Nuestra Señora de Rueda, Calatayud, 1922; G. M. Ojeda, Abadía de Rueda, BIFG, XXXVII, 1958, pp. 115–17; E. García Chico, La iglesia de Santa María de Rueda, BSEAAV, XXV, 1959, pp. 59–68.

Fabara (Zaragoza). An austere Roman sepulcher of the Augustan era is in the form of a temple *in antis*; it has a portico with two Doric columns and an Ionic frieze.

BIBLIOG. J. Puig i Cadafalch, L'arquitectura romana a Catalunya, Barcelona, 1934, p. 120.

Fraga (Huesca). The town was the Roman Gallica Flavia. In the remains of Villa Fortunatus are mosaics of the 2d century. The Romanesque Church of S. Pedro (12th cent.; later altered) has a Gothic vault and a tower. There are some patrician houses of the 16th century.

BIBLIOG. J. Salarrullana de Dios, Estudios históricos de la ciudad de Fraga, RABM, 3dS er., XLII, 1921, pp. 361–81, 491–512, XLIII, 1922, pp. 18–44, 197–234, 354–74; J. Serra Ráfols, La villa Fortunatus de Fraga, Ampurias, V, 1943, pp. 5–35.

Huesca. Of the ancient Roman Osca there are few remains, and equally little is preserved of the Moslem period, when the city was a major Moorish fortress. The main mosque was consecrated as a cathedral in 1097, but in the last quarter of the 13th century the present Gothic structure was begun (finished 1515). The principal portal has statuary of the 14th century. The interior consists of nave and two aisles, transept, five apses, and chapels between the buttresses; the windows, with ornate tracery, are by Francisco de Valdivieso (1516–18); the alabaster main altarpiece is by Damián Forment (1520–33); the Capilla de S. Joaquín is baroque and that S. Ana has an altarpiece in the Berruguete style. The choir stalls are by Nicolás de Berástegui (1587). The cloister is in ruins except for one wing erected in the 15th century. The parish house of the Cathedral contains the alabaster altarpiece of Montearagón, by Gil Morlanes the Elder (1506–12). The Museo Catedralicio contains murals from S. Fructuoso in Bierge (13th cent.); the altarpiece of the Coronation of the Virgin, by the painter Pedro Zuera (15th cent.); sculptures; chests with enamels (12th cent.); and the small silver altarpiece of the Virgin of Slas (1367). The Romanesque Monastery of S. Pedro el Viejo (1117) has a cloister with capitals by the Master of San Juan de la Peña; there is a Roman sarcophagus of the 2d century. The Sanctuary of S. María de Salas contains a 13th-century Virgin. The Museo Provincial exhibits prehistoric and Roman collections, Paleo-Christian mosaics, Romanesque capitals, and medieval and Renaissance paintings.

BIBLIOG. R. del Arco y Garay, El arte en Huesca durante el siglo XVI, BSEE, XXIII, 1915, pp. 188–97; R. del Arco y Garay, La catedral de Huesca, Huesca, 1924; R. del Arco y Garay, Catálogo monumental de España: Huesca, 2 vols., Madrid, 1942; R. del Arco y Garay, El Santuario de Nuestra Señora de Salas, AEArte, XIX, 1946, pp. 110–30; R. del Arco y Garay, La fábrica de la catedral de Huesca, AEArte, XXIV, 1951, pp. 321–27; R. del Arco y Garay, La sillería del coro de la catedral de Huesca, Zaragoza, 1953; R. del Arco y Garay, El retablo mayor de Montearagón, Zaragoza, 1954; S. Broto Aparicio, Huesca: corazón de los Pirineos, Huesca, 1955; A. Durán Gudiol, Huesca y su provincia, Barcelona, 1957.

Ibieca (Huesca). The Church of S. Miguel de Foces (1259) has a doorway in the late Romanesque style; mural paintings by the Master of Foces (ca. 1300) decorate the transept and four tombs, among them the sepulchers of Ximeno de Foces and his son Atón.

BIBLIOG. F. Lamolla, El templo de San Miguel de Foces, BRABASF, 2d Ser., XV, 1921, pp. 90–113.

Jaca (Huesca). Of pre-Roman origin, this city was the capital of the Jacetans and, in the 11th century, of the Kingdom of Aragón. The Cathedral (XII, FIG. 345) was begun, apparently, in 1076. Of the original structure it preserves the outside walls, the main portal, and the cloister vault of Moslem style. The chapels and the vaulting of the nave and flanking aisles were reconstructed in the 16th century. Notable are the plateresque Capilla de S. Miguel; the Capilla de S. Ana, with a 16th-century altarpiece; the Capilla de la Trinidad, with an altarpiece by Miguel de Ancheta (ca. 1570); the Gothic doorway to the cloister; the altarpieces of the Annunciation and of S. Jerónimo; and the tomb of Bishop Baquer. In the Benedictine convent is the sarcophagus of the Infanta Sancha (12th cent.). The Ayuntamiento (1544–46) is plateresque. Of interest are the Gothic bridges, the Palacio Episcopal, the citadel (1592), and the many patrician houses.

BIBLIOG. R. del Arco y Garay, La ciudad de Jaca, BSEE, XXIX, 1921, pp. 165–92; G. Gaillard, Les débuts de la sculpture romane espagnole: León, Jaca, Compostelle, Paris, 1938; R. del Arco y Garay, La ciudadela de Jaca, AEArte, XVIII, 1945, pp. 277–91.

Loarre (Huesca). The castle (Castillo Carreres; FIG. 309), the most important Romanesque fortification in Spain, has double girding walls with cylindrical towers and two gates; its Romanesque church has an interesting crypt and a nave with exceptionally fine sculpture on the capitals. The 15th-century church in the town has a square tower and contains Renaissance altarpieces and two 12th-century caskets with goldwork.

BIBLIOG. R. del Arco y Garay, El castillo real de Loarre, Madrid, 1917; L. de la Figuera, El castillo de Loarre, Arquitectura, VI, 1924, pp. 117–19; M. Chamoso Lamas, Revisión de formas constructivas en el castillo de Loarre, AEArte, XVI, 1943, pp. 384–98; V. Valenzuela Foved, El castillo de Loarre: Guía del turista, Huesca, 1957; E. Subiza Bernad, El castillo de Loarre en el compromiso de Caspe, Actas y Com. IV Cong. h. de la corona de Aragón (1955), Palma de Mallorca, 1959, p. 19–38.

Longares (Zaragoza). The 16th-century church, on a rectangular plan, has a nave and two aisles with Ionic columns, a rectilinear apse, and a tower that belonged to a mosque that once stood on the site; the church contains an altarpiece of Santiago (15th cent.), a plateresque main altarpiece, and fine Gothic and Renaissance goldwork.

BIBLIOG. M. de la Sala-Valdés y García-Sala, Historia de la villa de Longares, Zaragoza, 1936.

Muel (Zaragoza). The town is famous for its decorated ceramics (11th–18th cent.). On the pendentives of the Hermitage of Nuestra Señora de la Fuente are four frescoes of the Fathers of the Church by Francisco Goya (ca. 1770).

BIBLIOG. J. Galiay, Los alfares de Muel, Madrid, 1915; A. W. Frothingham, Aragonese Lustreware from Muel, Hispanic Notes, IV, 1944, pp. 78–91.

Nuévalos (Zaragoza). Near the town, beautifully situated in the wooded valley, is the Abbey of Piedra, founded by Alfonso II of Aragón in 1164; it is on the characteristic Cistercian plan (church, cloister, chapter house, etc.), with some later additions.

BIBLIOG. C. Sarthou Carreres, El monasterio de Piedra, Museum, V, 1916–17, pp. 345–76.

Roda de Isábena (Huesca). The streets and buildings have a typical medieval aspect. The parish church, formerly a cathedral (11th–13th cent.; nave and two aisles), has three apses; in the crypt, covered by rib vaulting, are the tomb of S. Ramón (12th cent.) and some 13th-century mural paintings; in one of the lateral apses are found paintings by the Master of Tahull (12th cent.). The church contains several medieval altarpieces, and the 12th-century cloister and small museum have objects of great interest.

BIBLIOG. P. Pach y Vistuer, Reseña histórica de la antigua y ilustre ciudad (hoy villa) ribagorzana de Roda, Barcelona, 1899; R. del Arco y Garay, La ex-catedral de Roda, BSEE, XXXI, 1923, pp. 28–43; F. Niño, Las mitras de Roda, AEArte, XIV, 1940–41, pp. 138–47.

Sádaba (Zaragoza). The Gothic church contains several altarpieces from the 15th and 16th centuries. The castle, on a square plan, has nine towers (13th cent.). Nearby are found the ruins of the Roman city Clarina, with the mausoleum of the Atilios (2d cent.), baths, and a 2d-century aqueduct.

BIBLIOG. J. R. Mélida y Alinari, Monumentos romanos de España, Madrid, 1925, passim; J. R. Mélida y Alinari, in R. Menéndez Pidal, Historia de España, II, Madrid, 1935, pp. 599, 609; I. Escagües Javierre, Las cinco villas de Aragón, Vitoria, 1944; J. Galiay Sarañana, Las excavaciones del Plan Nacional en los Bañales de Sádaba (Informes y Mem., Comisaría general de excavaciones arqueol., IV), Madrid, 1944; J. Galiay Sarañana, La dominación romana en Aragón, Zaragoza, 1946, passim; I. Escagües Javierre, Castillos olvidados de España, BSEE, LV, 1947, pp. 211–22; L. Crema, Architettura romana, Turin, 1959, pp. 330, 501; A. García y Bellido, La villa y el mausoleo romanos de Sádaba, Madrid, 1963.

San Juan de la Peña (Huesca). Sheltered under an enormous, projecting rock are the buildings of the Monasterio Viejo (FIG. 309), some parts dating from before the 10th century; the dormitory is of the 11th century, as is the lower church, with a funerary chapel (12th–14th cent.). The upper church (1094) has a sacristy and a royal pantheon; a Mozarabic door leads to the Romanesque cloister, which has richly sculptured 12th-century capitals by the Master of San Juan de la Peña. The Monasterio Nuevo (1675–1714) has a baroque façade.

BIBLIOG. J. Briz Martínez, Historia de San Juan de la Peña y de los Reyes de Aragón, Zaragoza, 1620; R. del Arco y Garay, El real monasterio de San Juan de la Peña, Jaca, 1919; R. del Arco y Garay, El claustro monacal de San Juan de la Peña, Zaragoza, 1952; V. Valenzuela Foved, San Juan de la Peña, 1956; V. Valenzuela Foved, Los monasterios de San Juan de la Peña y Santa Cruz de la Serós: Guía del visitante, Huesca, 1959.

Santa Cruz de la Serós (Huesca). The convent was founded in the year 992. The church (11th–12th cent.) has Romanesque portal and capitals and a tall square tower; the main altarpiece was painted in 1490. The parish church is also Romanesque.

BIBLIOG. R. del Arco y Garay, El monasterio de Santa Cruz de la Serós, Linajes de Aragón, IV, 1913, pp. 431–55; V. Valenzuela Foved, Los monasterios de San Juan de la Peña y Santa Cruz de la Serós: Guía del visitante, Huesca, 1959.

Sigena (Huesca). The convent, founded by Sancha of Aragón, was constructed after 1183. The Romanesque convent church (1188), with a magnificent portal, is built on the Latin-cross plan; in the central apse are mural paintings by the Master of Artajona (13th cent.).

BIBLIOG. M. de Pano y Ruata, El monasterio de Sigena: su historia y descripción, Lérida, 1883; R. del Arco y Garay, El real monasterio de Sigena, BSEE, XXIX, 1921, pp. 26–63; J. M. Estal, Culto de Felipe II a San Hermenegildo, Ciudad de Dios, CLXXIV, 1961, pp. 523–52.

Siresa (Huesca). The Monastery of S. Pedro is in the Visigothic tradition. The church, begun about 1088, has a single aisle, a transept, and a semicircular apse; it contains various painted altarpieces of the 15th century and other works of art.

BIBLIOG. R. del Arco y Garay, El real monasterio de Siresa, capilla real de Aragón, BSEE, XXVII, 1919, pp. 270–305.

Sos del Rey Católico (Zaragoza). There are some pre-Roman and Roman remains. Sections of the wall, with towers and gates, begun in 1137, are preserved. The Church of S. Esteban (12th cent.) has a crypt and a richly decorated Romanesque portal. The Palacio de Sada (before 1452) was altered in the 16th–17th century. The patrician houses and the arcaded streets give the town a medieval aspect.

BIBLIOG. T. Rios, Derrumbamiento de la casa donde nació Don Fernando el Católico, Arquitectura, VI, 1924, pp. 332–38; F. Abbad Rios, La iglesia de San Esteban en Sos, AEArte, XV, 1942, pp. 163–70; I. Escagües Javierre, Las Cinco Villas de Aragón, Vitoria, 1944.

Tarazona (Zaragoza). This was an ancient Iberian town called Turiasso by the Romans. The Cathedral (1235) has a nave and two aisles, chapels between the buttresses, and a triforium in the presbytery; at the crossing is a Mudejar lantern tower constructed by Juan Botero in 1519. The choir stalls are from 1464. Among the altarpieces are that of S. Juan Bautista, a 16th-century work by the sculptor Juan de Moreto (Moretti), and that of S. Catalina, by the painter Juan de Leví (15th cent.). The alabaster sepulchers of Pedro and Fernando Calvillo are Gothic. The cloister (1504) has Moorish latticework in the windows. The Church of la Magdalena has a fine Mudejar tower. Also of interest are the Palacio Episcopal (14th–15th cent.) and the Renaissance Ayuntamiento.

BIBLIOG. J. M. Sanz Artibucilla, Los artistas del coro de la catedral de Tarazona, SAA, I, 1945, pp. 31–38; F. Torralba Soriano, La catedral de Tarazona, Zaragoza, 1954; T. Pérez Urtubia, Tarazona, Zaragoza, 1956.

Teruel. The city, recaptured from the Moors in 1171, preserves sections of the 15th-century walls. The Cathedral has a Mudejar tower (1257); the apse was constructed in 1335 by Juzaff and other Moslems; the transept has a Mudejar lantern (ca. 1538) by Martín de Montalbán, and the nave is roofed by a painted *artesonado* (14th cent.). Notable in the Cathedral are the main altarpiece by Gabriel Joly (Joli; 1536), the choir screen by Master Cañamache (1486), the Coronation altarpiece (15th cent.), and the monstrance by Bernabé García de los Reyes (1742). The Church of S. Pedro, with Mudejar tower and apse, contains a 16th-century main altarpiece, the altarpiece of SS. Cosmas and Damian by Gabriel Joly, and several canvases by Antonio Bisquert (1620). The churches of S. Martín and el Salvador (13th cent.) have Mudejar towers. The aqueduct, built in the Roman style, is by Pierre Vedel (ca. 1550). From the 14th to the 17th century the city was an important center for the manufacture of decorated ceramics.

BIBLIOG. E. Gómez Ibáñez, Un rejero desconocido, BSEE, XXVI, 1918, pp. 169–71; R. García Guereta, Las torres de Teruel, Arquitectura, VII, 1925, pp. 97–124; J. Caruana Gómez de Barreda, Los puentes de Teruel, Teruel, III, 1950, pp. 35–65; J. Caruana Gómez de Barreda, Notas sobre la cerámica turolense, Teruel, V, 1951, pp. 83–109; M. Navarro Aranda, La arquitectura cristiana mudéjar de Teruel, Teruel, X, 1953, pp. 163–202; L. Torres Balbás, La iglesia de Santa María de Mediavilla, catedral de Teruel, AEArte, XXVI, 1953, pp. 81–97; M. Navarro Aranda, Las torres de Teruel, Zaragoza, 1954; J. Ibáñez Martín, Gabriel Yoly, Madrid, 1956;

E. Rabanaque Martín, El artesonado de la catedral de Teruel, Teruel, XVIII–XIX, 1957, pp. 143–202; A. Allanegui Félez, La evolución urbana de Teruel, Zaragoza, 1959; S. Sebastián, Teruel y su provincia, Barcelona, 1959; C. Tomás Laguía, Las capillas de la catedral de Teruel, Teruel, XXII, 1959, pp. 5–159. See generally Teruel, 1949 ff.

Uncastillo (Zaragoza). The castle is in bad repair. The Romanesque Church of S. María has a 14th-century fortified tower, a beautiful Romanesque doorway, and a cloister (1557) by Juan Larrandi. The Church of S. Martín (1179) has 16th-century altarpieces and Renaissance choir stalls and goldwork. The Romanesque S. Juan preserves important 13th-century wall paintings. The Ayuntamiento has a Renaissance façade.

BIBLIOG. E. Bayate Arbunies, El arte en la villa de Uncastillo, B. Mus. de Zaragoza, 2d Ser., II, 1942, pp. 53–72; F. Abbad Rios, El románico en Cinco Villas, Zaragoza, 1954; A. de Egry, Esculturas románicas inéditas en San Martín de Uncastillo, AEArte, XXXVI, 1963, pp. 181–87.

Veruela (Zaragoza). The Abbey of Veruela (1171), one of the oldest Cistercian houses in Spain, is built on the usual plan of this order; it is girded by high defensive walls with round towers and gates. The church has nave with flanking aisles, transept, and *chevet* with an ambulatory and contains various sepulchers. The cross-vaulted cloister has capitals of the Gothic type and an upper story in Renaissance style; adjoining is the early Gothic chapter house.

BIBLIOG. J. M. López Landa, Estudio arquitectónico del monasterio de Veruela, Lérida, 1918; J. M. Sanz Artibucilla, El Real monasterio de Veruela, SAA, II, 1945, pp. 29–36; P. Blanco Trias, El Real monasterio de Santa María de Veruela, Palma de Mallorca, 1949.

Zaragoza. Originally the Iberian Salduba, the city was called Caesaraugusta by the Romans; the Moors renamed it Sarakusta in the 8th century. Sections of the Roman walls are preserved, while the Castillo de la Aljafería (early 11th cent., later altered), with the original mosque, remains from the period of Moslem domination. The Seo (one of two co-cathedrals) is a Gothic edifice of the Catalan type (nave with flanking aisles and chapels between the buttresses); finished in the early part of the 15th century, it retains some elements of the earlier Romanesque edifice of the 12th century. The northeast exterior wall, decorated with a mosaic of brick and *azulejos*, the apse (14th cent.), and the *cimborio* (1501) are Mudejar. The tower (1682–90) beside the northwest façade is by the Italian Giovanni Battista Contini. The magnificent main altarpiece was begun by Pere (Pedro) Johan (1440) and finished by Hans de Suabia (1467); the plateresque *trascoro* is by Arnau de Bruselas (1557) and Tudelilla (Martín de Gaztelu, or de Tudela). The Capilla de S. Miguel (known as the Parroquieta) has a Mudejar dome and contains an altarpiece by Miguel de Ancheta (16th cent.) and the sepulcher of Archbishop de Luna by Pere (Pedro) Moragues (1382); other notable chapels in the Seo are that of S. Bernardo, with plateresque altarpiece and tombs, and that of S. Agustín, with an altarpiece by Gil Morlanes the Younger and Gabriel Joly (1520). The sacristy contains 14th-century reliquary busts and a monstrance by Pedro Lamaison (16th cent.). The Museo Diocesano, on the upper floor of the sacristy, has a large collection of Flemish and French tapestries (15th–16th cent.) and sketches by Goya and Francisco and Ramón Bayeu for the mural decoration of the Cathedral of Nuestra Señora del Pilar. That Cathedral was begun in 1681 on the site of an ancient chapel; it is a vast baroque edifice with a nave and two aisles and contains the lavish Capilla de la Virgen del Pilar by Ventura Rodríguez. The main altarpiece is by Damián Forment (1509), and the *coro* is by Esteban de Obray and Nicolás Lobato (1544). The vaulting has frescoes by Antonio González Velázquez I, Francisco Bayeu, and Goya (18th cent.). The Gothic Church of S. Pablo contains a wooden main altarpiece by Damián Forment (1511) and tapestries after cartoons by Raphael. The Church of S. Engracia has a plateresque doorway by the two Gil Morlanes and contains some Paleo-Christian sarcophaguses. Among the many Renaissance buildings the Palacio de los Morlanes, the Lonja, the Real Maestranza, and the Audiencia (1551) are noteworthy. The Museo Provincial de Bellas Artes has Iberian, Roman, and Moslem exhibits; medieval, Renaissance, and 17th-century paintings and sculpture; and some portraits by Goya. On the outskirts of the city is the Carthusian Monastery of Aula Dei; the church contains some magnificent frescoes by Goya (1774).

BIBLIOG. A. and P. Gascón de Gotor, Zaragoza artística, monumental y histórica, 2 vols., Zaragoza, 1890–91; J. Galiay, El Castillo de la Aljafería, Zaragoza, 1960; R. del Arco y Garay, El coro de la catedral del Pilar en Zaragoza, BSEE, XXXIII, 1925, pp. 161–65; Museo de Bellas Artes de Zaragoza, Catálogo, Zaragoza, 1929; R. Revilla Vielva, Catálogo de las antigüedades que se conservan en Patio Arabe del Museo Arqueológico Nacional, Madrid, 1932, pp. 13–83; J. Camón Aznar, La Lonja de Zaragoza, Universidad, X, 1933, pp. 397–412; M. La Sala, Estudios histórico-artísticos de Zaragoza, Zaragoza, 1933; A. Gascón de Gotor, La Torre Nueva de Zaragoza (proceso y ajusticiamiento), Zaragoza, 1943; F. Abbad Rios, La Seo y el Pilar de Zaragoza, Madrid, 1948; F. Torralba Soriano, La insigne Iglesia de San Pablo de Zaragoza, Zaragoza, 1950; F. Abbad Rios, Guías artísticas de España: Zaragoza, Barcelona, 1952; J. Albareda Piazuelo, El retablo de San Bernardo de la Seo de Zaragoza, Zaragoza, 1952; F. Torralba Soriano, Real seminario de San Carlos Borromeo de Zaragoza, Zaragoza, 1952; F. Torralba Soriano, Los tapices de Zaragoza, Zaragoza, 1953; F. Abbad Rios, Catálogo monumental de España: Zaragoza, 2 vols., Madrid, 1958; F. Abbad Rios, Provincia de Zaragoza, Barcelona, 1958; J. M. Madurell Marimón, La capilla de la Inmaculada Concepción de la Seo de Zaragoza, Tarragona, 1958; J. M. Madurell Marimón, La Aljafería Real de Zaragoza, Madrid, 1961; A. San Vicente, La capilla de San Miguel del Patronato Zaporta en la Seo de Zaragoza, AEArte, XXXVI, 1963, pp. 99–118.

Cataluña. Geographically constituting almost a bridge between Europe and the Iberian Peninsula, this region has always occupied a leading place in the history of Spanish art. An important center before the period of colonizations, Cataluña was readily Romanized. Art in the region flourished during the Romanesque period and, especially, during the Gothic, which marks its greatest artistic epoch. After a decline during the Renaissance, the baroque period signaled the beginning of a revival and the advance of Cataluña toward the preeminent position which it reached at the end of the 19th century and still maintains. The region comprises four modern provinces: Barcelona, Tarragona, Lérida, and Gerona.

BIBLIOG. J. Puig i Cadafalch, L'arquitectura románica a Catalunya, 3 vols., Barcelona, 1909–18; J. Gudiol Cunill, Nocions d'arqueología sagrada catalana, 2d ed., 2 vols., Barcelona, 1931–32; A. Duran i Sanpere, Los retablos de piedra, 2 vols., Barcelona, 1933; J. Fontanels Ráfols, Pere Blay i l'arquitectura del Renaixement a Catalunya, Barcelona, 1934; J. Puig i Cadafalch et al., L'arquitectura romana a Catalunya, Barcelona, 1934; R. Filangieri di Candida et al., L'architecture gothique civile en Catalogne, Mataró, 1935; P. Lavedan, L'architecture gothique religieuse en Catalogne, Valence et Baléares, Paris, 1935; P. Bosch Gimpera, L'art grec a Catalunya, Barcelona, 1937; J. C. Serra Ráfols et al., Carta arqueológica de Barcelona, Madrid, 1945; J. Gudiol Ricart, Historia de la pintura gótica a Cataluña, Barcelona, 1947; P. de Palol Salellas, Gerona, Barcelona, 1953; J. Gudiol Ricart, Provincia de Barcelona, Barcelona, 1954; Junta de Museos, Guía de los Museos de arte, historia y arqueología de la provincia de Barcelona, Barcelona, 1954; J. Gudiol Ricart, Cataluña, Barcelona, 1955; Junta de Museos, Obras de los Museos de las provincias de Tarragona, Lérida y Gerona, Barcelona, 1956; S. Alcolea Gil, Lérida y su provincia, Barcelona, 1957; P. Deffontaines and M. Durliat, Espagne du Levant, Paris, 1957; J. Folch y Torres et al., L'art català, 2 vols., Barcelona, 1957–61; J. Gudiol Ricart et al., Historia de la pintura en Cataluña, Madrid, 1957; J. Gudiol Ricart, Tarragona y su provincia, Barcelona, 1958; C. Martinell, Arquitectura i escultura barroques a Catalunya, Barcelona, 1959; E. Junyent, Catalogne romane, 2 vols., Paris, 1960–61; Notas de arqueología de Cataluña y Baléares, Ampurias, XXII–XXIII, 1960–61, pp. 323–63; M. Durliat, Art catalan, Paris, 1963; E. Junyent, L'arquitectura religiosa en la Catalunya carolingia, Barcelona, 1963.

Ager (Lérida). There are remains of the Roman walls and ruins of the collegiate church of S. Pedro, dating from 1056. In the parish church is a Roman sarcophagus with mythological scenes (3d cent.) and a monstrance in Barcelonian style (17th cent.).

BIBLIOG. P. Sanaluja, Historia de la villa de Ager, Barcelona, 1961.

Agramunt (Lérida). The 13th-century church has a late Romanesque portal. The interior has a nave and two aisles, sharply pointed vaulting, and capitals signed by French sculptors.

BIBLIOG. J. Font i Rius, La Mare de Déu del Castell, Barcelona, 1958.

Bañolas (Gerona). The town is of Roman origin. The church of the Monastery of S. Esteban contains an altarpiece dedicated to the Virgin (15th cent.) by the Master of Bañolas and a reliquary urn of S. Martirián (15th cent.), possibly by Francisco Artau. The parish church is Gothic. The Museo Arqueológico Comarcal houses prehistoric and Roman collections. Near the town stands the Romanesque Church of S. María de Porqueras (12th cent.).

BIBLIOG. L.-G. Constans, Dos obras maestras del arte gótico en Bañolas, Barcelona, 1947; L.-G. Constans, Bañolas, Bañolas, 1951.

Barcelona. The Carthaginian city of Barcino (3d cent. B.C.), perhaps built on the site of an earlier native center, was conquered by the Romans, who called it Colonia Julia Augusta Pia Faventia Barcino. It was sacked by the barbarians in A.D. 263 and was later dominated by the Visigoths (5th cent.) and by the Moors (8th cent.). From the Roman period there remain sections of the encircling walls (4th cent.), with rectangular towers at intervals and round towers at the corners; the remains of the praetorium gate; the temple of Augustus (1st cent.), a peripteric hexastyle; two colonnaded porticoes,

one of them from the 1st century of our era that perhaps belonged to a bath complex; and a pagan necropolis (1st–4th cent.) and a Christian one (3d cent.). There is also an Early Christian church. Nothing remains of the Moorish era.

The Gothic Cathedral (VI, FIG. 494), built on the site of a Romanesque structure that was consecrated in 1058, was begun in 1248 and finished in the 15th century, except for the modern principal façade. The Puerta de S. Ivo, of a sober and restrained aspect, dates from the 13th century, while the Puerta de la Piedad and the Puerta de S. Eulalia are of the 15th century. The interior (nave and two aisles) has chapels between the buttresses, a *chevet* with radiating chapels, and a crypt dedicated to S. Eulalia, with the relics of the saint and an Italian sepulcher (ca. 1327). The stained glass of the clerestory windows and the lectern and stalls in the *coro* are of the 15th century; the *trascoro* is dedicated with marble reliefs by Bartolomé Ordóñez (1518). The high altarpiece is of the 14th century; other notable altarpieces are that of SS. Cosme y Damián, by Miguel Nadal (ca. 1454), that of the Transfiguration, by Bernardo Martorell (ca. 1450), and that of S. Gabriel, by Luis Borrassá (14th cent.). The many sepulchers include that of S. Olegario, with a statue by Pedro Sanglada (Pere Ça-Anglada; 1406); that of Doña Sancha Jiménez de Cabrera, by Pedro Oller (1436); and that of Bishop Escales, by Antonio Canet (1409). The cloister (14th–15th cent.) has historiated capitals, a fountain in a pavilion, and Gothic sepulchers and *rejas*. In the Museo Capitular are a Pietà by Bartolomé Bermejo (1490) and other Gothic paintings. In the Cathedral treasury are the Missal of S. Eulalia by Rafael Destorrents (1403), a jeweled monstrance of the 15th century, the silver throne (1395–1410) of King Martin of Aragón, and an enameled processional cross by Francisco Vilardell (1383). S. Ana, a Gothic church, erected in 1146, is modeled after the Church of the Holy Sepulcher in Jerusalem; S. María del Pino (14th cent.) has a fine Romanesque door from an older building; S. María del Mar, designed by Ramón Despuig and Berenguer Montagud (1329), has a wide nave and two narrow aisles of equal height separated by slender, gracious pillars; and SS. Justo y Pastor, begun in 1342, has two octagonal towers. The Monastery of Pedralbes was founded by Doña Elisenda de Moncada in 1326; in the church is the tomb of the foundress, and the cloister contains paintings by Ferrer Bassa (1346). The Capilla de S. Águeda, adjacent to the Palacio Real Mayor, was constructed by Bertrán Riquer in 1302; it has an altarpiece painted by Jaime Huguet (ca. 1466).

Outstanding among secular Gothic architecture are the Tinell (Great Hall of the aforementioned Palacio Real Mayor) by Guillermo Carbonell (1370); the Pía Almoina (15th cent.); and the Palacio de la Generalidad (15th cent. and later), which has a medallion of St. George and the Dragon by Pere (Pedro) Johan over the main doorway, a patio by Marcos Safont (Marc Çafont; 1425), and the Capilla de S. Jorge. The Casa Consistorial (mostly of the 19th cent.) preserves a Gothic façade by Arnau Bargués (1402) and the Salón de Ciento (1373), a fine Gothic hall. The Antiguo Hospital de la Sta Cruz (VI, FIG. 495), begun in 1401, now houses the Biblioteca Central de Cataluña. The Reales Atarazanas (14th-cent. arsenal and covered shipyards) is today the Museo Marítimo. The Lonja, a neoclassic edifice begun in 1763, preserves a Gothic great hall by Pedro Arvey (1386). There is a group of modern edifices by Antonio Gaudí: the Güell palace and park, the Batlló and Milá houses, and the Church of the Sagrada Familia, of which only the east façade has been completed. The Museo Arqueológico features Iberian, Greek, Punic, and Roman exhibits. The Museo de Arte de Cataluña has important Romanesque sculptures and paintings (murals and panels); Gothic altarpieces and sculptures from Cataluña, Aragón, Valencia, and Castilla; and canvases by Velázquez, Zurbarán, Ribera, Goya, and El Greco. Other museums include the Museo de Arte Moderno, the Museo Picasso, the Museo de Artes Decorativas, the Museo Federico Maré, and the Museo Diocesano.

BIBLIOG. A. A. Pi y Arimón, Barcelona antigua y moderna, Barcelona, 1854; J. Puig i Cadafalch and J. Miret y Sans, El Palau de la Diputacio General de Catalunya, AIEC, III, 1909–10, pp. 385–480; J. Mas, Guía itinerario de la catedral de Barcelona, Barcelona, 1916; M. Trens, Catalogo del Museo Diocesano de Barcelona, Barcelona, 1916; B. Bassegoda y Amigó, Santa María de la Mar, 2 vols., Barcelona, 1925–27; N. M. Rubío i Tudurá, Jardines de Barcelona, Barcelona, 1936; Junta de Museus, Catáleg del Museu d'Art de Catalunya, Barcelona, 1936; M. Trens, Ferrer Bassá i les pintures de Pedralbes, Barcelona, 1936; A. Duran y Sampere, La Casa de la Ciudad: Vestigios de la Barcelona romana, Ampurias, V, 1943, pp. 53–77; Divulgación Histórica, Varios trabajos en Barcelona, Barcelona, 1945–59; J. Ainaud de Lasarte, J. Gudiol and F. P. Verrié, La ciudad de Barcelona, 2 vols., Madrid, 1947; A. Duran y Sampere, La Casa de la Ciudad, Barcelona, 1951; A. Duran y Sampere, El barrio gótico de Barcelona, Barcelona, 1952; J. Gudiol Ricart, Barcelone, Barcelona, 1952; Museo Federico Marés, Catálogo, Barcelona, 1952; J. Puig Boada, Templo de la Sagrada Familia, Barcelona, 1952; F. P. Verrié, Barcelona antigua, Madrid, 1952; Museo de Arte Moderno, Guía, Barcelona, 1953; F. Caret, De Sant Pere e Sant Pau, Barcelona, 1958; A. Florensa Ferrer, Las murallas romanos de la ciudad, Barcelona, 1958;

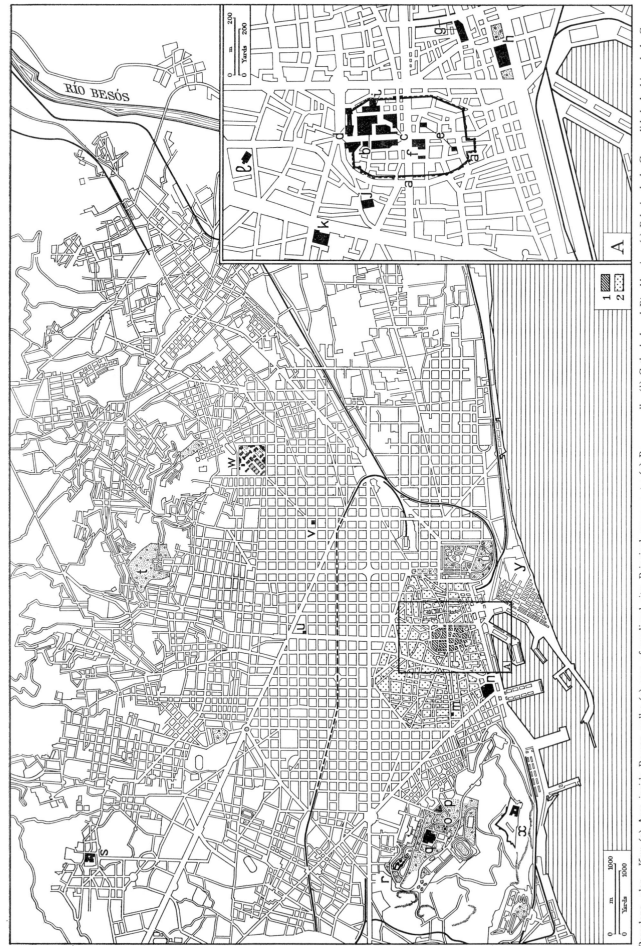

RÍO BESÓS

A

1
2

Barcelona, plan. *Key:* (1) Area inside Roman walls; (2) area of medieval city. Principal monuments: (*a*) Roman walls; (*b*) Cathedral and Pia Almoina; (*c*) Palacio de la Generalidad, Archivo de la Corona de Aragón, and Casas Canonicales; (*d*) Palacio Episcopal and Casa del Arcediano; (*e*) SS. Justo y Pastor and Capilla de los Templarios; (*f*) Casa Consistorial and Palacio Centelles; (*g*) S. María del Mar; (*h*) Lonja; (*i*) Palacio Real Mayor and Capilla de S. Agueda; (*j*) S. María del Pino; (*k*) Palacio de la Virreina (Mus. de Artes Decorativas); (*l*) S. Ana; (*m*) S. Pablo del Campo; (*n*) Reales Ataranazas; (*o*) Museo Etnológico y Colonial; (*p*) Museo Arqueológico; (*q*) Museo de Arte de Cataluña; (*r*) Museo de Arte Popular; (*s*) Monastery of Pedralbes; (*t*) Güell park; (*v*) Sagrada Familia; (*w*) Hospital de la Sta Cruz; (*x*) Castillo Montjuich; (*y*) Barceloneta quarter.

CAF, CXVII (Catalogne), 1959, passim; A. Balil, El mosaico romano en la Iglesia de San Miguel, Barcelona, 1960; A. Balil, Las murallas romanas de Barcelona, Madrid, 1961; A. García y Bellido, EAA, s.v.; F. Carreras y Candi, La ciudad de Barcelona, Barcelona, n.d.

Bellpuig (Lérida). The town is dominated by the ruins of an old castle. In the church is the marble sepulcher of Ramón de Cardona, signed by Giovanni Merliano (Marigliano, known as Giovanni da Nola; 1531).

Bellpuig de les Avellanes (Lérida). A Premonstratensian monastery founded in 1166; the 14th-century church, with an imposing apse, was used as the pantheon of some of the counts of Urgel. The cloister is late Romanesque.

BIBLIOG. C. Rocafort y Sansó, Bellpuig de los Avellanas, Barcelona, 1906; E. Corredera, El monasterio de Santa María de Bellpuig de los Avellanas, Ilerda, XVII, 1959, pp. 137–64.

Besalú (Gerona). Once the seat of the domain of the counts of Besalú, the town has arcaded streets and a medieval bridge. The Romanesque Church of S. María (1055) is in ruins. The Monastery of S. Pedro (12th cent.) has a church with noteworthy sculptural decoration. S. Vicente, another Romanesque church, has been recently restored.

BIBLIOG. J. Francés, Sobre la declaración de monumento histórico-artístico del puente de Besalú, Academia, 3d Ser., I, 1952, pp. 357–58; G. Gaillard, Besalú, CAF, CXII, 1956, pp. 236–46.

Caldas de Montbuy (Barcelona). The Roman baths survive. In the parish church is a Romanesque Christ in Majesty (12th cent.); the portal is baroque (1701).

BIBLIOG. J. Gudiol Ricart, Provincia de Barcelona, Barcelona, 1954; C. Pallas, Las termas romanas de Caldas de Montbuy, San Jorge, XXVI, 1957, pp. 44–46.

Cardona (Barcelona). Part of the girding walls remains. The castle on the height encloses the Romanesque Church of S. Vicente, which is in Lombard style (1040). There is also a Gothic church with medieval paintings, sculptures, and goldwork.

BIBLIOG. J. Ballaró Casas and J. Serra Vilaró, Historia de Cardona, Barcelona, 1906; J. Serra Vilaró, El castillo de Cardona, Cardona, 1954.

Castellón de Ampurias (Gerona). There is a Gothic church with a Romanesque battlemented tower; the main portal was constructed by Antonio Antigoni (15th cent.). The church contains an alabaster main altarpiece by the sculptor Vicente Borrás (1483) and various Gothic sepulchers.

BIBLIOG. J. Subías Galter, Les taules gòtiques de Castello d'Empurias, Gerona, 1930.

Cervera (Lérida). The collegiate church (S. María; 13th–15th cent.) has an octagonal bell tower of 1431; the arms of the transept terminate in a pentagonal wall. There are various sepulchers from the 14th century, a statue of the Virgin and Child (13th cent.), and a processional cross by Bernat Llopart (1435). The Church of S. Pedro el Gros is on a circular plan (11th cent.). The Ayuntamiento by Francisco Puig (1677, enlarged in the 18th cent.) and the University (18th cent.), with an altarpiece by Jaime Padró in its chapel, are baroque. The Museo Comarcal exhibits Gothic panel paintings.

Estany (Barcelona). The Abbey of S. María del Estany has a Romanesque-Gothic church (consecrated 1133) of great artistic interest; it contains an alabaster Virgin and Child (14th cent.), and the magnificent Romanesque cloister has historiated capitals (12th–13th cent.).

BIBLIOG. J. Codina Puigsaulens, Monestir de Santa Maria de l'Estany, Barcelona, 1926; E. Junyent, El monasterio del Estany, Ausa, III, 1960, pp. 441–63.

Gerona. Sections of the old Roman city of Gerunda, which was possibly built on the site of an Iberian settlement, are preserved. The Gothic Cathedral, begun in 1312 on the site of the former 11th-century building, has Romanesque elements: the so-called "Torre de Carlomagno" and the cloister, with historiated capitals (12th cent.). The south portal, with statues of the Apostles (only two remain), is of the 15th century. The baroque façade (1607), with a grand stairway, was remodeled in the 18th century. The aisleless nave (1417–1598), the

widest in European Gothic architecture, terminates in three arches that lead into the *chevet*, which has an ambulatory and nine radiating chapels. The Capilla Mayor has a Romanesque altar table (11th cent.), a silver altarpiece by Master Bartomeu (1320) and Pere Berneç (1358), and a silver canopy (14th cent.). The stained-glass windows are of the 14th century; the *coro* has an episcopal chair (1351). There are sepulchers of the 14th century (those of Arnau and Bertrán de Montrodón, of Pedro de Rocaberti, of Guillermo de Vilamarí, and of Count Ramón Berenguer II and his wife, Ermisindis) and of the 15th century (those of Berenguer de Anglesola, of Dalmau and Bernardo de Raset, and of Bernardo de Pau). In the Cathedral museum are the famous tapestry of the Creation (11th cent.); embroidered frontals (14th–15th cent.); Gothic paintings; Romanesque and Gothic sculptures; a Beatus manuscript (975); and a Moorish silver casket of Cordovan workmanship (10th cent.). The Church of S. Félix (13th cent.) surmounted by a truncated spire; the church contains eight sarcophagi, two Roman and the others of the 4th century; the sepulcher of S. Narciso by Juan de Tournai (1328); and an alabaster Dead Christ (15th cent.). S. Pedro de Galligans (12th cent.), which houses the Museo Arqueológico Provincial, has a Romanesque church and cloister (both 12th cent.). The Church of S. Nicolás (12th cent.) is Romanesque. The Monastery of S. Daniel, founded in the 11th century, has a Romanesque cloister and a 14th-century shrine. The Monastery of S. Domingo, now a barracks, has a Gothic church and cloister. Of interest are the so-called "Baños Árabes," dating in their present form from the 13th century. The Museo Diocesano contains Romanesque sculptures and paintings (murals and panels), Gothic and 16th-century altarpieces, textiles, and goldwork.

BIBLIOG. J. Puig i Cadafalch, Els banys de Girona i la influencia moresca a Catalunya, AIEC, V, 1913–14, pp. 687–728; E. Serra Ráfols, La nau de la Sea de Girona, Miscel-lania Puig i Cadafalch, I, Barcelona, 1947, pp. 185–204; J. Marqués Casanovas, Origen y vicisitudes de la Plaza de los Apostoles de Gerona, AIEG, III, 1948, pp. 226–45; J. Pla Cargol, La provincia de Gerona, 3d ed., Gerona, 1949; M. Oliva Prat, Catálogo de los vidrios del Museo Arqueológico de Gerona, AIEG, V, 1950, pp. 113–67; C. Cid Priego, La iconografia del claustro de la catedral de Gerona, AIEG, VI, 1951, pp. 5–118; L. Font, Gerona: La Catedral y el Museo Diocesano, Gerona, 1952; J. Pla Cargol, Gerona arqueológica y monumental, Gerona, 1952 (5th ed., 1961); J. Marqués Casanovas, La fachada de la catedral de Gerona, AIEG, X, 1955, pp. 285–316; J. Marqués Casanovas, Guía del Museo Diocesano de Gerona, Gerona, 1955; P. de Palol Salellas, Gerona monumental, Barcelona, 1955; E. Lambert, Saint-Félix de Gérone, CAF, CXII, 1956, pp. 220–25; P. Lavedan, La Cathédrale de Gérone, CAF, CXII, 1956, pp. 226–35; P. de Palol Salellas, Une broderie catalane d'époque romane: La Genèse de Gérone, CahA, VIII, 1956, pp. 175–214, IX, 1957, pp. 219–51; J. M. Coll, Historia sucinta del Convento de Santo Domingo, AIEG, XII, 1958, pp. 1–28; C. Battle Gallart, Solución al problema de las dos sinagogas de Gerona, Sefarad, XIX, 1959, pp. 301–20; J. Marqués Casanovas, Apuntes históricos sobre el Palacio episcopal de Gerona, AIEG, XIV, 1960, pp. 263–306; J. M. Madurell Marimón, Obras de plateros barceloneses en iglesias gerundenses (1392–1698), AIEG, XV, 1961–62, pp. 103–201; M. Oliva Prat, Noticias sobre iglesias prerromanicas gerundenses, Rev. de Gerona, VIII, 1962, pp. 65–89.

Lérida. Originally an Iberian settlement, it later became the Roman Ilerda. It was captured by the Moors in the late 8th century and reconquered in 1149. The castle, known as La Zuda, preserves Moorish elements, although it was remodeled in the 13th and 14th centuries. Beside it stands the Old Cathedral (Seo Antigua), begun in 1203 under the direction of Pedro Coma and P. de Pennafreita and consecrated in 1278; the cloister is Gothic (14th cent.); the octagonal steeple was finished by Carlos Galtés in 1416. The Puerta de la Anunciata and the Puerta de los Infantes (Porta dels Fillols) are Romanesque; the Puerta de los Apóstoles is Gothic. The interior has a nave and two aisles, a wide transept, three apses, and an octagonal lantern tower. The Church of S. Lorenzo has three polygonal apses (13th cent.) and an octagonal tower (15th cent.); it contains four sculptured altarpieces of the school of Lérida (14th cent.), dedicated to S. Lorenzo, S. Úrsula, S. Pedro, and S. Lucía. The New Cathedral (1764–90) was designed by Pedro Cermeño. The Ayuntamiento, or Pahería (13th cent.), has a fine façade and contains an illuminated codex (14th cent.) and an altarpiece by Jaime Ferrer II (ca. 1440). The Gothic Hospital of S. María (15th cent.) houses the Museo del Instituto de Estudios Ilerdenses, with an archaeological collection. The Museo del Seminario contains Romanesque and Gothic paintings and sculpture.

BIBLIOG. C. Martinell, La Seu Nova de Lleida, Valls, 1926; J. Bergós Massó, La catedral vella de Lleida, Barcelona, 1928; J. Fusté Vila, Museo Arqueológico del Seminario sobre el Lleida, Lérida, 1933; J. Bergós Massó, L'escultura a la Seu Vella de Lleida, Barcelona, 1935; M. Gomá Pujadas, La capilla de la Epifani de la Seo antigua de Lérida, Ilerda, II, 1944, pp. 325–36; J. Maluquer de Motes, La provincia de Lérida durante el eneolítico, bronce y primera edad de hierro, Lérida, 1945; Guía gráfica de Lérida y provincia, Lérida, 1950; R. Borras Vilaplana, Una escuela de arte neoclásico en Lérida y la Catedral Nueva de la misma, Ilerda, XIII, 1955, pp. 95–118; J. Lladonoso, La ciutat de Lleida, Barcelona, 1956; E. Lambert, La cathédrale de Lérida, CAF, CXVII, 1959, pp. 136–43; C. Pérez de Puertas and J. M. Nadal Gaya, El Ayuntamiento de Lérida, Lérida, 1961.

Manresa (Barcelona). The town, the Roman Munorisa, is in the shape of an amphitheater; it has a Roman bridge and sections of the medieval walls. The present building of the Church of S. María de la Seo was begun in 1328, but fragments of the original Romanesque edifice (1020) survive (one section of the cloister and of the north portal, 12th cent.); the building was finished in 1596, except for the modern west façade. In the interior (nave and two aisles) the vaulting of the aisles also covers the chapels between the internal buttresses; the altarpiece of the Holy Ghost is by Pedro Serra (1394). The small museum (Mus. de la Colegiata), housed on the upper floor of the portico, contains several notable altarpieces — of S. Marco, attributed to Ramón Destorrents (14th cent.); of S. Nicolás, painted by Jaime Cabrera (1406); and of the Trinity, by Gabriel Guardia (ca. 1500) — a Holy Entombment by Luis Borrassá (1410), a Romanesque crucifix of the 12th century, and an altar frontal embroidered by the Florentine Geri di Lapo (1340). The Museo Municipal houses archaeological remains and Catalan ceramics (12th–14th cent.).

BIBLIOG. J. Sarret y Arbós, Art i artistes manresans, Manresa, 1916; J. Sarret y Arbós, Historia religiosa de Manresa: Iglesies i Convents, Manresa, 1924; J. Gudiol Ricart, El retablo del "Sant Esperit" de Manresa, Manresa, 1954; M. Durliat, Notre-Dame-de L'Aurore à Manresa, CAF, CXVII, 1959, pp. 199–207.

Martorell (Barcelona). This was the Telobis of the Romans. A Roman triumphal arch is at the entrance of the so-called "Puente del Diablo" over the Llobregat River. The Museo Santacana has collections of architectural fragments and Catalan ceramics. In the Museo Municipal are Roman remains and local ceramics.

BIBLIOG. F. Santacana Romeu, Catáleg il-lustrat del Museu Santacana de Martorell, Barcelona, 1909; F. B. Verrié, Martorell y su Museo Municipal, San Jorge, 23, 1956, pp. 1–3; I. Coplas, El puente del diablo en Martorell, San Jorge, 44, 1961, pp. 34–39.

Montblanch (Tarragona). Parts of the girding wall remain, with square towers and the gates of Bover and of S. Jorge. There are some medieval residences, as well as a medieval bridge. The Church of S. María, begun in 1352 by the Englishman Raynardus dez Fonoyll, has a single nave with chapels between the buttresses; the façade is baroque (1653). The church contains a Gothic statue of the Virgin, and the altarpiece of SS Bernabé y Bernardo (14th cent.). The Church of S. Miguel has a Romanesque façade and a Gothic interior. The Sanctuary of the Serra has an alabaster Virgin from the 14th century. The Gothic hospital has a 16th-century cloister.

Montserrat, Monastery of (Barcelona). Located among rugged cliffs at an altitude of almost 3,000 ft., the Monastery was founded in the 11th century by Abbot Oliva of Ripoll, on a site where hermitages had existed since the 9th century. A Romanesque portal and remains of the Gothic cloister are preserved. The 16th-century church contains a Romanesque statue of the Black Virgin (12th cent.) in the sumptuous Camarín. There are several museums, including a picture gallery (works by Fray Juan Ricci, Caravaggio, El Greco, Pedro Berruguete, and Luis Morales), an interesting library, and the Museo Bíblico. There are many chapels and hermitages situated in the Montserrat range, including the church of the Monastery of S. Cecilia (11th cent.).

BIBLIOG. A. M. Albareda, Historia de Montserrat, Montserrat, 1931 (2d ed., 1946); J. Leonard et al., Montserrat, Barcelona, 1959; J. M. de Sagarra, Montserrat, 5th ed., Barcelona, 1959 (Eng. trans., J. Forrester); F. B. Verrié, Montserrat, Madrid, n.d.

Olot (Gerona). The Church of S. Esteban contains a canvas by El Greco and several baroque altarpieces. In the public park is the Museo de Arte Moderno, with paintings and sculpture by Catalan artists. The Museo Municipal contains ceramics and archaeological remains.

Poblet (Tarragona). The Cistercian Abbey of S. María de Poblet (FIG. 311), founded by Ramón Berenguer IV in 1150, was sacked and burned in 1835, but it has been carefully restored. The nucleus of the Abbey is surrounded by triple walls; near the fortified Puerta Dorada (1493) are the chapel of S. Jorge (1442) and the Romanesque chapel of S. Catalina; in the third wall is the Puerta Real (14th cent.). The Church has a baroque façade (1669); the interior (12th–14th cent.) has a barrel-vaulted nave, two cross-vaulted aisles, a transept, and a chevet with ambulatory. The Capilla Mayor contains an altarpiece by Damián Forment (1527); the sepulchers of the kings of Cataluña and Aragón have been restored. The cloister (late Romanesque

and Gothic), with cross vaults and a hexagonal fountain pavilion, leads into the refectory, the kitchen, and the fine Gothic chapter house (13th cent.). The Palacio del Rey Martín was begun by Arnau Bargués (ca. 1392).

BIBLIOG. L. Doménech y Montaner, Historia y arquitectura del Monestir de Poblet, Barcelona, 1925 (2d ed., 1928); C. Martinell, El monestir de Poblet, Barcelona, 1927; J. Gudiol Ricart, Las esculturas del palacio del rey Don Martin en Poblet, BAT, XLV, 1945, pp. 51–53; F. Marés, Las tumbas reales de Poblet, Barcelona, 1952; J. E. Cirlot, Tarragona, Poblet y Santas Creus, Madrid, 1956; C. Martinell, Monastères cisterciens de Poblet et de Santes Creus, CAF, CXVII, 1959, pp. 98–128; The Abbey of Poblet (trans. P. Nadal), Poblet, 1960; F. A. Vilarrubias, El altar del Santo Sepulcro del Real Monasterio de Santa Maria de Poblet, Poblet, 1960; F. A. Vilarrubias, La antigua Capilla de las Reliquias del Real Monasterio de Poblet, Poblet, 1961; F. A. Vilarrubias, La restauración de Poblet, Poblet, 1961; F. Marés, Las tumbas reales de los Monarcas de Cataluña y Aragón del Real Monasterio de Santa María de Poblet, Barcelona, 1963.

Reus (Tarragona). The 16th-century Church of S. Pedro, by Benito Otger (Oger), has an octagonal tower. The Casa de Bofarull has a room with paintings by Pedro Pablo (Pere Pau) Montaña; there are several noteworthy mansions from the 18th century. The Museo Municipal Prim-Rull contains prehistoric, Iberian, and Roman collections, as well as local ceramics (15th–16th cent.). The Archivo Municipal contains an illuminated missal (1363) from the workshop of Ramón Destorrents.

Ripoll (Gerona). The Monastery of S. María was founded in 888; it was destroyed in 1835 and carefully restored in 1887. The Church (S. María; XII, FIG. 342) preserves the imposing Romanesque façade (12th cent.), covered with sculptures depicting Biblical scenes. The transept has seven apses; in the interior (nave and four aisles) is the sepulcher of Ramón Berenguer III (12th cent.). The two-storied cloister, begun in the 12th century and completed in the 16th, has beautiful columns with historiated capitals. The Museo Folklórico is installed in the 14th-century Church of S. Pedro.

BIBLIOG. J. Gudiol, Iconografia de la portada de Ripoll, Barcelona, 1909; E. Junyent, La basílica del Monasterio de Santa María de Ripoll, 2d ed., Ripoll, 1955; G. Gaillard, Ripoll, CAF, CXVII, 1959, pp. 144–64; C. Cid Priego, El proceso de disgregación de los monumentos y la restauración de la Portada de Ripoll, Rev. de Gerona, VII, 1961, 16, pp. 33–41, 17, pp. 45–58, VIII, 1962, 18, pp. 43–55.

San Cugat del Vallés (Barcelona). The Benedictine abbey is of Paleo-Christian origin. The Church (13th–14th cent.; nave and two aisles, cimborio over the crossing, with a notable rose window, contains the tomb of Abbot Otón (14th cent.) and 16th-century altarpieces. The Romanesque cloister (12th cent.) has capitals by Arnaldus Gatell. In the chapter house is an altarpiece of All Saints by Pedro Serra (1375).

BIBLIOG. J. de Peray y March, Monografía histórica de Sant Cugat del Vallés, Barcelona, 1907; J. Baltrusaitis, Les chapiteaux de Sant Cugat del Vallés, Paris, 1931; S. Alcolea, Le monastère de Sant Cugat del Vallés, CAF, CXVII, 1959, pp. 178–88; J. Gudiol i Cunill, Sant Cugat del Vallés, Barcelona, n.d.

San Fructuoso de Bages (Barcelona). The Benedictine Abbey of S. Benito de Bages (de Bogea) has a 13th-century church. The cloister (12th cent.) has carved capitals of Caliphate type from an earlier cloister.

BIBLIOG. G. Gaillard, San Benet de Bages, CAF, CXVII, 1959, pp. 208–14.

San Juan de las Abadesas (Gerona). The convent was founded in 887. The collegiate church (FIG. 307), consecrated in 1150, shows French influence; built on the Greek-cross plan, with three apses, it contains Romanesque capitals, a 13th-century sculptured wooden Calvary, an altarpiece of the White Virgin, and the tomb of the Blessed Miró (14th cent.). A 15th-century cloister adjoins the church.

BIBLIOG. P. Parassols, Historia de San Juan de la Abadesas, Barcelona, 1890; J. Danés, La Vall y el Monastir de Sant Joan de las Abadesas, Barcelona, 1912; G. Gaillard, Sant Joan de las Abadesas, CAF, CXVII, 1959, pp. 160–64.

San Martín de Ampurias (Gerona). Near this village on the Gulf of Rosas are the ruins of Ampurias, which was founded by Greek settlers about 580 B.C. and which enjoyed a flourishing economic life. As the Greek city expanded, the part to the north became known as "Palaia polis" and the southern part as "Nea polis." In the time of Caesar a Roman colony was established outside the Greek city. The remains of the Greek city include the encircling cyclopean walls from the beginning of the 5th century B.C.; the sacred area comprising the temples of Aesklepios and of Jupiter-Serapis (?), from the Hellenistic period; a stoa from the 2d century B.C.; and a necropolis with

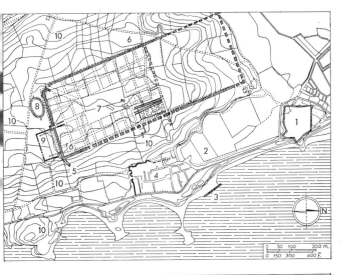

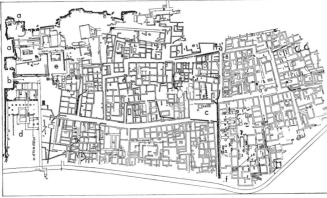

Ampurias. *Above*: general archaeological plan. (1) "Palaia polis"; (2) port district; (3) Greco-Roman pier; (4) "Nea polis"; (5) walls of native city; (6) walls of Roman colony; (7) forum (?); (8) amphitheater; (9) gymnasium; (10) necropolises. *Below*: area excavated in "Nea polis" plan. (*a*) Walls; (*b*) gate; (*c*) agora; (*d*) Temple of Jupiter-Serapis (?); (*e*) Temple of Aesklepios; (*f*) Christian basilica (*from M. Almagro, 1957*).

objects imported from Corinth, Rhodes, and Chalcis. The Roman city, which has been only slightly excavated, is girded by well-preserved walls (mid-1st cent. B.C.); it also contains an amphitheater, a large town villa (?), a cistern 65 ft. long, and a temple surrounded by porticoes, all dating from the 1st and 2d centuries of our era. The Museo Monográfico, on the site, contains many objects from the Greek and Roman cities, although the most important pieces have been moved to the Museo Arqueológico in Barcelona.

BIBLIOG. A. Schulten, Ampurias: Eine Griechenstadt am iberische Strande, Leipzig, 1907; J. Puig i Cadafalch, Les excavacions d'Empuries, AIEC, II, 1908, pp. 150–94; P. Bosch y Gimpera, La colonia greca d'Empuries, AIEC, VI, 1915–20, pp. 694–712; M. Almagro Basch, Estratigrafia de la ciudad helenistico-romana de Ampurias, AEA, XX, 1947, pp. 179–99; A. García y Bellido, Hispania Graeca, 3 vols., Barcelona, 1948, passim; M. Almagro Basch, El recinto sepulcral romano tardio de "El Castelet," AEA, XXIV, 1951, pp. 99–116; M. Almagro Basch, La necropolis de Ampurias, I, Barcelona, 1953; M. Almagro Basch, Ampurias, Barcelona, 1957; M. Almagro Basch, EAA, I, 1958, s.v. (bibliog.); P. de Palol Salellas, Hallazgos de la Ampurias romano-cristiana y visigoda, VIII corsi di cultura sull'arte ravennate e bizantina, Ravenna, 1961, pp. 195–206; M. Almagro Basch and P. de Palol Salellas, Los restos arqueológicos paleocristianos y altomedievales de Ampurias, Rev. de Gerona, VIII, 1962, pp. 27–91.

San Pedro de Roda (Gerona). Of the Benedictine monastery founded in the 9th century only the walls, two towers, and the church remain. The church, the principal monument of Catalan Romanesque before the Lombard influence, was consecrated in 1022; it has a nave and two aisles, three apses (the central one with an ambulatory without chapels), barrel vaults, and a crypt.

BIBLIOG. A de Falguera, Sant Pere de Roda, Barcelona, 1906; J. Subias Galter, El monestir de Sant Pere de Roda, Barcelona, 1948; J. Subias Galter, El monestir de Sant Pere de Roda, Anales Inst. de estudios ampurdanensis, I, 1959, pp. 79–89.

Santa Coloma de Queralt (Tarragona). The medieval parish church contains an altarpiece of S. Lorenzo by Jordi de Deu (1386). S. María de Belloc (13th cent.), with a Romanesque façade, contains two sepulchers of the counts of Queralt by Pedro Ciroll and Pedro Aguilar (14th cent.).

Santas Creus (Tarragona). The Cistercian Abbey, founded in 1169, follows the general architectural plan of that order. The church (12th–13th cent.) has a round-arched portal with a pointed window above; built on the Latin-cross plan, it has a nave with flanking aisles, five chapels in the *chevet*, Gothic vaulting, and a lantern at the crossing. Among the many magnificent tombs are that of Pedro the Great and that of Jaime II and his wife, Blanche d'Anjou, by Pedro Bonull (Bonhuyl; 1314). The cloister (1313–41), decorated with flamboyant Gothic tracery, is perhaps by the Englishman Raynardus dez Fonoyll; there is a small hexagonal fountain pavilion. The chapter house and the dependencies (dormitories, storeroom, refectory, and kitchen) are interesting. There are remains of the royal palace (14th cent.) and of a Romanesque cloister (1163).

BIBLIOG. J. Puig i Cadafalch, Un maestre anglés contracta l'istora del Claustro de Santes Creus, AIEC, VII, 1921–26, pp. 123–38; C. Martinell, El monestir de Santes Creus, Barcelona, 1929; G. Lo Bue di Lemos, Le tombe di Pietro III d'Aragona e di Ruggero di Lauria, Arch. storico siciliano, 3d Ser., VII, 1955, pp. 279–86; J. E. Cirlot, Tarragona, Poblet y Santas Creus, Madrid, 1956; Guía histórico-descriptiva del Real Monasterio de Santas Creus, Barcelona, 1959; C. Martinell, Monastères cisterciens de Poblet et de Santes Creus, CAF, CXVII, 1959, pp. 98–128; J. Vives y Miret, Las sepulturas en Santes Creus de los nobles fallecidos en la conquista de Mallorca, Tarragona, 1959.

Seo de Urgel (Lérida). The Romanesque Cathedral (12th cent.), constructed by Raimundus Lambardus, has barrel-vaulted nave and transept, rib-vaulted side aisles, and five apses, the central one with an exterior gallery. It contains an image of the Virgen de Andorra (12th cent.), a Beatus manuscript (11th cent.), a chalice by Galcerán de Vilanova (15th cent.), a magnificent ciborium (15th–16th cent.), a Romanesque enameled cross, the reliquary of Arabell (1516), and a reliquary urn of S. Ermengol made by P. Llopart (1755). The cloister has fine historiated capitals. The Museo Diocesano is in the Romanesque Church of S. Miguel.

BIBLIOG. V. Serra y Boldú, Seo de Urgel, Barcelona, 1930; J. Corts Peyret, Historia de la Seo de Urgel, Barcelona, 1953.

Solsona (Lérida). There are remains of the city walls. The original single-aisled Romanesque Cathedral was greatly altered in the 14th and 15th centuries; in the cloister the Capilla de la Virgen del Claustro has a 12th-century statue of the Virgin. The Palacio Episcopal (1779) houses the Museum Archaeologicum Diocesanum, containing prehistoric objects, Romanesque mural paintings from the churches of S. Quirce in Pedret and of S. Pablo in Caserras, Romanesque panel paintings from Sagás (Sagars) and San Jaime de Frontanyá, and Gothic paintings, sculpture, and goldwork.

Tahull (Lérida). The town is famous for its two Romanesque churches, S. María and S. Clemente, which were consecrated in 1123. Each church has a nave with flanking aisles, three apses, and a freestanding bell tower (that of S. María has been restored several times). The frescoes from these two churches, now in Barcelona (Mus. de Arte de Cataluña), are the most important of the Catalonian Romanesque and show some similarities to contemporaneous Piedmontese mural painting.

Tarragona. The city, whose origins are uncertain (perhaps the Iberian Cissa), appears to have been in existence as early as 530 B.C. In 218 B.C. it was conquered by Scipio, and under Augustus it became the capital (Tarraco) of Hispania Citerior, or Tarraconensis. The city rises on three large terraces. The first, the acropolis, is surrounded by megalithic walls, probably built during the first Roman occupation, having remains of six gates, three of which are still in use; it contained the famous Temple of Augustus, built in A.D. 15, of which only a few architectural elements remain, and the Temple of Jupiter Ammon, which has also disappeared. The second terrace included the forum, known only from documentary sources, with the *praetorium* (the so-called "Palacio de Augusto," or "Torreón de Pilatos"), an imposing civic structure of the 1st century of our era; also on this terrace was a triumphal arch of Augustus, of which only the base survives. The third terrace held the amphitheater and the circus, both of which have been preserved in part. In the lower part of the city were a theater, a slaughterhouse, and the temples of Eastern deities, all built in the 1st and 2d centuries of our era. There is a Christian necropolis with a basilica and about one thousand graves (3d–6th cent.) *in situ*; the Museo Paleocristiano houses the most important finds from the necropolis. The Cathedral, built between 1171 and 1331 on the site of a former mosque, retains an imposing Romanesque apse resembling a fortress; the bell tower, with a Romanesque base, is unfinished. The rest of the building reflects the various stylistic phases of Gothic art, which are particularly evident in the west façade (the main portal has sculptures by Master Bartomeu), begun in 1278 and also unfinished. The austere interior has a nave and two aisles divided by massive cluster piers. The frontal of the main altar is by Pere (Pedro) Johan. The Romanesque cloister (12th–13th cent.) has historiated capitals and preserves a fragment of the frieze from the Temple of Jupiter. The ruins of the Church of S. María del Milacre date from the Romanesque period (12th cent.). The churches of S. Pablo, of the Enseñanza, and of S. Tecla la Vieja (which now houses the sculpture and epigraphic collection of the Museo Diocesano) are from the 13th century. Of note are the Museo Arqueológico Provincial, the Museo Molas, and the Paseo Arqueológico (a promenade adorned with antique fragments).

In the vicinity are the remains of the Roman aqueduct ("Puente de las Ferreras"; 1st cent.) with 11 lower arches and 25 upper ones. On the road to Barcelona are a Roman mausoleum of the 1st century of our era known as the "Torre de los Escipiones" and the Arco de Bará (2d cent.).

Bibliog. L. Pons de Icart, Libro de las grandezas y cosas memorables de Tarragona, Lérida, 1572; B. Hernández Sanahuja, El Pretoria de Augusto, Tarragona, 1880; B. Lewis, The Antiquities of Tarragona, AJA, XXXVII, 1880, pp. 1–29; J. Serra Ráfols, Baetulo-Blanda (Forma conventus Tarraconensis, 1), Barcelona, 1928; L. Doménech i Montaner, Centcelles, Barcelona, 1931; J. Puig i Cadafalch, L'arquitectura romana a Catalunya, Barcelona, 1934; S. Capdevila, La Seu de Tarragona, Barcelona, 1935; J. R. Mélida y Alinari, in R. Menéndez Pidal, Historia de España, II, Madrid, 1935, pp. 402–07, 599; J. Puig i Cadafalch, La Basilica de Tarragona, Barcelona, 1936; L. Bonet Garí, Excavaciones en Tarragona en el solar del Banco Vitalicio, Ampurias, III, 1941, pp. 141–44; B. Hernández Sanahuja, Templo de Octaviano Augusto en Tarragona, BAT, XLIV, 1944, pp. 25–36; A. Nogues Farré, Restos del circo romano de Tarragona, BAT, XLIV, 1944, pp. 2–5; P. Battle Huguet, Los tapices de la Catedral primada de Tarragona, Tarragona, 1946; C. Cid Priego, El monumento conocido por Torre de los Escipiones en Tarragona, Ampurias, IX–X, 1947–48, pp. 137–69; A. Schulten, Tarraco, Barcelona, 1948; J. Serra Vilaró, La necrópolis de San Fructuoso, 1948; J. Serra Vilaró, La muralla de Tarragona, AEA, XXII, 1949, pp. 221–36; D. Ripoll, La cronologia de las murallas de Tarragona, Ampurias, XIII, 1951, pp. 175–80; P. Battle Huguet, Las pinturas góticas de la Catedral de Tarragona y de su Museo Diocesano, BAT, LII, 1952, pp. 197–218; F. Camprubi, El monumento paleocristiano de Centcelles, Barcelona, 1952; J. Martínez de Santaolalla, Las murallas ciclopeas de Tarragona, BAT, LII, 1952, pp. 20–24; D. Ripoll, Plano parcial de las bovedas del circo romano de Tarragona, BAT, LII, 1952, pp. 41–48; S. Ventura Solsona, Noticia de las excavaciones en curso en el Anfiteatro de Tarragona, AEA, XXVII, 1954, pp. 259–80; P. Battle Huguet, Tarragona, CAF, CXVII, 1959, pp. 215–24, J. Serra Vilaró, Sant Miguel del Pla, Tarragona, 1959; J. Serra Vilaró, Santa Tecla la Vieja, Tarragona, 1960; P. Battle Huguet, El retablo mayor de la catedral de Tarragona, Tarragona, 1961.

Tarrasa (Barcelona). The Roman Egara, the town is known for its three pre-Romanesque churches. S. María, with a 9th-century apse and a 12th-century nave, contains a painted stone altarpiece (10th cent.) and Romanesque murals (12th cent.). S. Miguel, of Visigothic origin, was enlarged in the 10th century; the crypt contains 12th-century mural paintings. S. Pedro has a trilobed apse (9th cent.) and a vaulted nave (12th cent.); traces of 10th-century murals remain. The Museo Textil Biosca contains Coptic and Hispano-Moorish textiles. Near the town, the former Carthusian Monastery of Vallparadís (also called the castle of Vallparadís, or of Egara) dates from the 12th century; it is now a museum containing medieval paintings and sculpture and ancient Catalan ceramics.

Bibliog. J. Soler Palet, Egara-Termasa, 2d ed., Tarrasa, 1928; J. Puig i Cadafalch, La Seu visigotica d'Egara, Barcelona, 1936; J. Serra Ráfols and E. de Fortuny, Excavaciones en Santa Maria de Egara (Tarrasa), Madrid, 1949; F. Torrelas, Las colecciones del Museo Textil Biosca, Tarrasa, 1949; S. Cardús, Belleses i records del temple del Sant Esperit de Terrassa, Tarrasa, 1955; E. Junyent, Las iglesias de la antigua sede de Egara, Ampurias, XVII–XVIII, 1955–56, pp. 79–96; J. Ainaud de Lasarte, Les églises d'Egara, CAF, CXVII, 1959, pp. 189–98; L. Monreal y Tejada, El castillo-cartuja de Vallparadis en Tarrasa, San Jorge, 33, 1959, pp. 72–77.

Tortosa (Tarragona). This was the Roman Dertosa. There are ruins of the Castillo de la Zuda. The Cathedral is built on the site formerly occupied by a Roman temple; the present edifice, begun in 1347 under the direction of Benito Dalguayre, was finished in the 18th century. The beautiful double ambulatory has chapels separated by screens of Gothic tracery. The Capilla Mayor has a sculptured altarpiece (1351) with paintings by Francesco d'Oberto; the Capilla de la Sta Cinta is baroque. The 14th-century cloister has a baroque portal (1705). The Palacio Episcopal has a Gothic patio and a chapel with an altarpiece by Jaime Huguet (15th cent.). The Convent of S. Luis (1544) has a plateresque portal and a two-storied patio. The Museo

Archivo Municipal, housed in the former Dominican monastery, contains Roman statuary, Visigothic pilasters, and ceramics.

Bibliog. C. Gracia, Un retablo inédito de la catedral de Tortosa, Barcelona, 1923; J. Matamoros, La catedral de Tortosa, Tortosa, 1932; F. González Cirer, El arte gótico en Tortosa, La Zuda, V, 1959, pp. 675–84.

Tossa de Mar (Gerona). Of the Roman Turissa there are remains of a villa (1st–4th cent.). There are remains of the medieval walls and castle. The Museo Municipal exhibits objects from the Roman excavations and modern paintings.

Bibliog. J. and J. M. Ainaud de Lasarte, Tossa, Barcelona, 1957.

Valls (Tarragona). The Gothic Church of S. Juan Bautista, built by Bartolomé Roig (1570), has a wide single aisle with 14 chapels between the buttresses. There are various works by the sculptor Luis Bonifás y Massó (1730–86); the Capilla del Rosario has walls decorated with 14th-century *azulejos* depicting the Battle of Lepanto.

Bibliog. F. de Moragas, L'art, els artistes i els artesans de Valls, BAT, XXI, 1921, pp. 15–17, 43–44, 65–67, 76–77, XXII, 1922, pp. 105–07, 143–47, 194–96, 216–22, 232–36; C. Martinell, Cappella de N.a S.ra del Roses i ses pinturas en rajoles vidriades, Valls, 1924.

Vich (Barcelona). This was the Iberian and Roman Ausa. A Roman temple is still standing. There are medieval bridges, walls, and houses. The Cathedral, founded in 1038 and rebuilt in the neoclassic style in 1803, preserves a Romanesque crypt and bell tower (11th cent.) and a Gothic cloister (14th cent.). The interior is decorated with murals by José María Sert (1945). It contains an alabaster main altarpiece by Pedro Oller (1427), a processional cross (1394) by Juan Carbonell, and the silver sarcophagus of Bishop Bernardo Calvó by Juan Matons (1728). The Museo Arqueológico Artístico Episcopal contains early Catalan mural and panel paintings, Romanesque and Gothic sculptures, and textiles and embroideries.

Bibliog. Museo Arqueológico Artístico Episcopal de Vich, Catálogo, Vich, 1893; J. Gudiol y Cunill, Vich y el Museo Episcopal, Vich, 1921; E. Junyent, La catedral de Vich y la decoración de Santa Maria de Ripoll, Barcelona, 1949; E. Junyent, El castillo de Montcada, Ausonia, 29, 1959, pp. 261–70; E. Junyent, La Cathédrale de Vich et le Musée Episcopal, CAF, CXVII, 1959, pp. 165–77; E. Junyent, El retablo mayor de la catedral de Vich, Vich, 1959.

Villanueva y Geltrú (Barcelona). The Church of S. María contains a noteworthy baroque altarpiece (17th cent.). The Casa Papiol has painted rooms and furniture of the 18th and 19th centuries. The Museo Balaguer, housed in the medieval Castillo de La Geltrú, has Mozarabic furniture, ceramics, Egyptian and Roman antiquities, and a large collection of paintings, including *The Annunciation* by El Greco and works by Giovan Battista (Juan Bautista) del Mayno, Juan Carreño de Miranda, and Juan Antonio de Frías y Escalante.

Baleares (Balearic Islands). The archipelago consists of three main islands, Mallorca, Menorca, and Ibiza, and several smaller ones. From the middle of the 2d millennium B.C. until the Roman conquest, Mallorca had a flourishing Bronze Age culture. There were many fortified villages and megalithic structures such as the *talayoti*, the *navetas*, and the *taulas* (see VI, col. 686). Ibiza was settled by the Carthaginians. The islands became part of the Roman Empire (123 B.C.) and then of the Byzantine Empire (A.D. 534); there followed five centuries of Moslem domination, until the reconquest by Jaime I in 1229. The Baleares experienced a brilliant artistic period during the Middle Ages.

Bibliog. A. Furió, Diccionario de los profesores de las Bellas Artes en Mallorca, Palma de Mallorca, 1839; P. Piferrer, Mallorca, Barcelona, 1842; J. Colominas Roca, L'edad del bronze a Mallorca, Barcelona, 1920; M. Alcover, El Islam en Mallorca (707–1232) y la Cruzada Pisano-Catalina (1113–1115), Palma de Mallorca, 1930; F. P. Verrié, Guías artísticas de España: Mallorca, Barcelona, 1948; J. Vidal Isern, Arte árabe en Mallorca, BAC, XX, 1949, pp. 177–84; C. Bauzá, M. Roger, and B. Guasp, Los castillos roqueros de Mallorca, Palma de Mallorca, 1952; G. Llompart, Bibliografía arqueológica de las Baleares (Mallorca y Menorca), Palma de Mallorca, 1958; J. Mascaró i Pasarius, Els monuments megalítics a l'illa de Menorca, Barcelona, 1958; B. Ferra Perello, Techos artísticos en la Isla de Mallorca: Cruces de piedra, Palma de Mallorca, 1959; M. Durliat, La arquitectura mallorquina en la primera mitad del siglo XIV, Goya, 41, 1961, pp. 314–21; M. Durliat, L'art dans le royaume de Majorque, Paris, 1962. See also BSAL, Palma de Mallorca, 1885 ff.

Alcudia (Mallorca). A substantial part of its walls remain, with a gate flanked by square towers with battlements (14th cent.). The Oratory of S. Ana is from the 13th century. The parish church contains Gothic panel paintings. In the vicinity are ruins of the Roman city of Pollentia, destroyed by the Vandals; there are remains of a theater, dwellings, and a necropolis.

BIBLIOG. A. Schulten, RE, s.v. Pollentia; L. R. Amoros, Excavaciones en Pollentia, Palma de Mallorca, 1950; L. Bernabò Brea, Il teatro antico di Pollentia, RSLig, XVII, 1951, pp. 18–29; M. Almagro Basch and L. R. Amoros, Excavaciones en la necrópolis romana de Can Fanals de Pollentia, Ampurias, XV–XVI, 1953–54, pp. 237–77; A. Balil, FA, XIII, 1958, no. 4740.

Artá (Mallorca). There is a Franciscan cloister dating from the 17th century. The Museo Regional has a collection of small bronze statues (2d cent. B.C.) originally from Son Favar. In the vicinity are prehistoric remains (Sa Canova, Ses Païsses, El Claper dels Gegants).

BIBLIOG. G. Lilliu and F. Biancoforte, Primi scavi del villaggio talaio-tico de Ses-Paises (Arta, Maiorca), Ann. Facoltà di Lettere . . . dell'Univ. di Cagliari, XXVII, 1959, pp. 31–74.

Ciudadela (Menorca). There are remains of the early walls. The streets are arcaded, and the Vigo, Martorell, and Torresaura palaces are especially interesting. The Cathedral, begun in 1300, has a neo-classic south façade (1814), a Gothic lateral portal, and a polygonal presbytery. The baroque Church of Nuestra Señora del Rosario (1701) has a Churrigueresque portal. In the vicinity of the town are megalithic monuments (Naveta dels Tudons; settlements of Torre Llafuda and Son Carlá).

BIBLIOG. M. Santaolalla, L'état actuel de l'archéologie dans l'île de Minorque, Barcelona, 1937 (bibliog.); F. Durán Cañameras, Notas arqueo-lógicas de Menorca, Ampurias, V, 1943, pp. 37–52; J. Malunquer de Motes, in R. Menéndez Pidal, Historia de España, I, Madrid, 1947, pp. 717–51; Revista de Menorca, sp. no., 1948, pp. 239–330; J. Maluquer de Motes Sobre la cueva de "Na Figuera" en Parelli, Arch. Preh. Lev., III, 1952, pp. 195–98; A. Balil, FA, XIII, 1958, no. 4658; P. de Palol Salellas, Basílicas paleocristianas en la isla de Menorca, Baleares, Festschrift F. Gerke, Baden-Baden, 1962, pp. 39–53; M. L. Serra Belabre, Fortificaciones medievales del campo de Menorca, Rev. de Menorca, LIII, 1962, pp. 89–105.

Felanitx (Mallorca). The church is Gothic, with later additions. The Santuario de S. Salvador (14th cent.) contains a sculptured altarpiece in Mallorcan Gothic style (15th cent.). The Castillo de Santueri retains many sections constructed in the 14th century.

BIBLIOG. B. Guasp Gelabert, Antiguas ermitañas en Mallorca, Ana-lecta sacra tarraconensia, XXIV, 1951, pp. 131–37.

Ibiza. The town was the Ebusus founded by the Carthaginians. Its walls and fortifications date from 1554 to 1585; near the Puerta de las Tablas are Roman statues. The single-aisled Cathedral, with a square tower, is Gothic with baroque remodeling. It contains a monstrance in the form of a small temple (15th cent.) and Gothic panel paintings. The façade of the Curia is Gothic. The Church of S. Domingo is baroque. Nearby, in the village of Jesús, is a church containing an altarpiece of the Virgen de los Ángeles by the Osonas (15th cent.). The Museo Arqueológico has a rich collection of objects of Punic origin. There are remains of a Carthaginian necropolis at Puig d'es Molins and of Carthaginian sanctuaries at Isla Plana, at Cueva d'es Cuyram, and at Puig d'en Valls. The rural sections of the island are characterized by whitewashed cubical houses.

BIBLIOG. A. Vives y Escudero, Estudio de arqueología cartaginesa: La necrópolis de Ibiza, Madrid, 1917; C. Roman y Ferrer, Excavaciones en diversos lugares de la isla de Ibiza (Mem. Junta Sup. Exc. y Ant., 28–7, 43–8, 58–5, 80–10), Madrid, 1918–25; J. Serra Ráfols, Les îles Baléares, Barcelona, 1929; J. Colominas Roca, Les terracuites cartaginese d'Eivissa, Barcelona, 1938; I. Macabich, Notas sobre Ibiza púnico-romana, AEA, XX, 1947, pp. 129–37; L. Figini, Diario i illustrato di Ibiza, Domus, 263, 1951, pp. 43–52; J. M. Blázquez and E. Escandell, Nuevos objetos arqueológicos ebusitanos, Zephyrus, XI, 1960, pp. 165–77; G. Gualandi, EAA, s.v. (bibliog.).

Inca (Mallorca). The church (13th cent., remodeled in the 18th cent.) has a Gothic bell tower. Within are painted altarpieces (14th cent.) and a Gothic panel painting of the Virgin and Child (1373) by Juan Daurer. In the vicinity are the Santuario de S. Magdalena del Puig; and the Monastery of Nuestra Señora de Lluch, mainly from the 17th and 18th centuries, with some medieval elements; it contains a 14th-century Virgin and Child.

BIBLIOG. B. Guasp Gelabert, Antiguas ermitañas en Mallorca, Analecta sacra tarraconensia, XXIV, 1951, pp. 131–37; J. Obrador Socias, Santa Maria de Lluch: Historia de su colegiata, Palma de Mallorca, 1952.

Mahón (Menorca). The town was founded by the Carthaginians and was the Portus Magonis of the Romans. Near the port entrance are the ruins of the Castillo de S. Felipe. The single-aisled Church of S. María dates from 1287 and was reconstructed in 1772; it contains a processional cross by P. Marcer (ca. 1625). The Church of S. Francisco and that of the Virgen del Carmen are of the 18th century.

The Ayuntamiento was built in 1613 and restored in 1789. The Museo de Bellas Artes has noteworthy archaeological collections. The Villa Carlos quarter (George Town), erected by the English (1711), has an urban plan that was later copied in Barcelona and El Ferrol del Caudillo. Nearby are the megalithic complexes of Trepucó and Talatí.

BIBLIOG. J. Gutiérrez, Autor y fecha de la cruz procesional de Santa Maria de Mahon, Rev. de Menorca, 1949, p. 176.

Manacor (Mallorca). The parish church retains Gothic elements. Of interest is the Dominican monastery, with a church and a cloister. The crenelated Torre del Palau and Torre de Ses Puntes are medieval. Among the fine patrician houses is the Puigdorfila. The Museo Arqueológico contains prehistoric objects and Paleo-Christian art from the Basilica of Son Peretó, including a mosaic by one Baleria (5th cent.).

BIBLIOG. J. Ferrer Manaset, La gran basílica de Son Peretó, Manacor, Palma de Mallorca, 1953; B. Pinya, El Museo arqueológico y la basílica pri-mitiva de Manacor, Palma de Mallorca, 1953.

Muro (Mallorca). The town has a Gothic church containing an altarpiece of S. Miguel (1374) by the painter Juan Daurer, an altar-piece of S. Margarita (15th cent.), and a Gothic monstrance and other goldwork.

BIBLIOG. F. P. Verrié, Guías artísticas de España: Mallorca, Barcelona, 1948.

Palma de Mallorca. The most important monument is the Ca-thedral, begun in the early 14th century with the Capilla de la Santí-sima Trinidad in the chevet; the Capilla Real was completed about 1327; the nave and two aisles, with high vaults on slim octagonal pil-lars and with chapels between the buttresses, were completed in 1529. Among the principal masters were Berenguer Ostales, J. Mates, Guillermo Morey, and Guillén (Guillermo) Sagrera. The Puerta del Mirador (14th cent.) is richly ornamented; the principal portal (1594) is by Miguel Verger; the Puerta de la Almoina dates from 1498. The bell tower is from the 15th century. There are rose windows and other large stained-glass windows. In the interior are Gothic sculptures and altarpieces, plateresque pulpits (1531), sculptured choir stalls, and Gothic sepulchers. In the Museo de la Catedral are ecclesiastical ornaments, Gothic panel paintings, illuminated codices, goldwork, and tapestries. Other Gothic churches are S. Miguel, S. Nicolás, S. Eulalia, and Sta Cruz. The Church of S. Francisco (13th cent.), with a fine cloister, contains the tomb of Ramón Lull. From the baroque period are the churches of Montesión, La Merced, Nuestra Señora del Socorro, and S. Antonio Abad.

There are Moorish baths from the 11th century; in the castle, or Almudaina, is the Gothic Capilla de S. Ana. The Lonja (1426–52), by G. Sagrera, is built on a rectangular plan, with rich portals and angular turrets. The large hall has slim spiral pillars; the Museo Pro-vincial is located here. Patrician residences include the Casa Villa-longa and Casa del Marqués de Palmer (16th cent.). The Museo Dio-cesano, in the Palacio Episcopal, contains a Balearic archaeological collection, Gothic sculptures, and painted altarpieces. There is a notable altarpiece of S. Bernardo (14th cent.) in the Museo de la Sociedad Arqueológica Luliana. In the suburb of Génova is the Museo Regional de C'an Mulet. Nearby is the Castillo de Bellver, now the Museo Municipal.

BIBLIOG. G. Forteza, El Claustre de Sant Francesc, BSAL, XXVI, 1935, pp. 113–23; P. Lavedan, Palma de Majorque et les îles Baleares, Paris, 1936; H. E. Wethey, Guillermo Sagrera, AB, XXI, 1939, pp. 44–60; G. M. de Jovellanos, La catedral de Palma..., Palma de Mallorca, 1945; E. Sagristá, La catedral de la Plana, Castellón de la Plana, 1948; E. Sagristá, Los retablos góticos de la catedral de Palma de Mallorca, BSCC, XXVI, 1950, pp. 36–57; J. V. Verdaguer, El castillo de Bellver, Palma de Mallorca, 1951; A. Mulet, C'an Mulet de Génova, Palma de Mallorca, 1952; Museo de la lonja, Catálogo, Palma de Mallorca, 1952; E. Sagristá, La catedral de Mallorca: El enigma de la Capilla de la Trinidad, BSCC, XXVIII, 1952, pp. 3–28, 226–61; B. Minya Forteza, Antiguo monasterio de Santa Margarita de Palma de Mallorca, Palma de Mallorca, 1953; A. Jiménez Vidal, La portada de San Francisco de Asis, BSAL, XXXI, 1955–56, pp. 226–35; M. Durliat, Les artistes de Perpignan et de Montpellier à Majorque au début du XIV⁰ siècle, B. Soc. Nat. Ant. de France, 1956, pp. 75–77; M. Durliat, Le château de Bellver à Majorque, Etudes roussillonnaises, V, 1956, pp. 197–212; G. Rossello-Bardoy, Sobre los "Baños árabes" de Palma de Mallorca, Palma de Mallorca, 1956; P. A. Matheu Mulet, Palma de Mallorca monumental, Ma-drid, 1958; J. Vidal Isern, Castillos de Mallorca: El oratorio de San Miguel de Campanet, Palma de Mallorca, 1959; M. Durliat, La construction de la cathédrale de Palma de Majorque au XIVᵉ siècle, Mouseion: Studien aus Kunst und Geschichte für Otto H. Förster, Cologne, 1960, pp. 115–23; J. Miralles Sbert, Las reliquias y relicarios de la catedral de Mallorca (ed. L. Pérez), Palma de Mallorca, 1961; G. Sabater, El castillo de Bellver, Palma de Mallorca, 1962.

Pollensa (Mallorca). The Dominican cloister is noteworthy. The Oratory of the Roser Vell (Old Rosary) contains Gothic panel paintings, including one of the Luis Borrassá school. Nearby is the Castillo del Rey.

BIBLIOG. B. Guasp Gelabert, Antiguas ermitañas en Mallorca, Analecta sacra tarraconensia, XXIV, 1951, pp. 131-37.

Valldemosa (Mallorca). The Carthusian monaster ywas established in 1399, but the present buildings date mainly from the 18th century. Its church contains frescoes by Fray Manuel Bayeu; the conventual complex also includes a cloister and the ancient pharmacy.

BIBLIOG. J. Cirera, Algunos documentos relativos a la construcción de la iglesia de Valldemosa, BSAL, XXXI, 1955-56, pp. 301-05; E. Sans, Los monumentos megaliticos de Valldemosa, BSAL, XXXI, 1955-56, pp. 269-71.

Valencia. The old Mediterranean kingdom of Valencia comprises three modern provinces: Castellón de la Plana, Valencia, and Alicante. The region has noteworthy remains of pre- and protohistoric civilizations, as well as of the Roman era. Following the period of domination by the Moors, whose artistic influence is scarcely visible today, a strong Gothic style marked by local characteristics flourished in the region. Although less important than the rest of the Peninsula during the 16th century, Valencia experienced a dramatic resurgence in artistic expression at the beginning of the baroque period.

BIBLIOG. Baron de Alcahalí, Diccionario biográfico de artistas valencianos, Valencia, 1897; J. Sanchís Sivera, Pintores medievales en Valencia, Valencia, 1914; L. Tramoyeres Blasco, La arquitectura gótica en el Maestrazgo, AAV, V, 1919, pp. 5-47; E. Tormo y Monzó and J. Dantin Cereceda, Levante, Madrid, 1923; J. Sanchís Sivera, La escultura valenciana en la Edad Media, Valencia, 1924; J. Sanchís Sivera, Orfebrería valenciana en la Edad Media, Valencia, 1924; J. Sanchís Sivera, Maestros de obras y lapicidas valencianos en la Edad Media, Valencia, 1925; M. A. Orellana, Biografía pictórica Valentina, Madrid, 1930; F. Llorca, La escuela valenciana de arquitectos, Valencia, 1933; F. Garín Ortiz de Taranco, Aspectos de la arquitectura gótica valenciana, Valencia, 1935; J. Obermaier, Nouvelles études sur l'art rupestre du Levant espagnol, Anthropologie, XLVII, 1937, pp. 477-98; T. García, Mosaicos romanos de la provincia de Valencia, Cartagena, 1949; M. González Martí, Cerámica del Levante español, Barcelona, 1952; A. Beltrán, Guías artísticas de España: Valencia, Barcelona, 1953; J. Mateo, Castillos de la provincia de Alicante, Alicante, 1953; C. Sarthou Carreres, Valencia monumental, Valencia, 1954; S. Roda, El camino de dolor del estilo mudéjar en el reino de Valencia, ACCV, XVIII, 1957, pp. 1-24; F. Figueras Pacheco and D. Fletcher Valls, Bibliografía arqueológica de la provincia de Alicante, Alicante, 1958.

Albocácer (Castellón de la Plana). The Church of S. Juan (13th cent.) contains an altarpiece of the Santos Juanes, perhaps by Domingo Valls (14th cent.). In the small Gothic church known as the Hermitage of the Virgen de la Esperanza (1408) is a Valencian altarpiece from the 15th century. Prehistoric rock paintings are found in various sections of the gorge of Valltorta (Cueva del Civil, Cueva de los Caballos).

BIBLIOG. H. Obermaier and P. Wernert, Les pintures rupestres del barranco de Valltorta, Madrid, 1919.

Alcoy (Alicante). Near the modern town, on a hill called "La Serreta," are the remains of an Iberian settlement with a sanctuary dating mainly from the early Empire although of pre-Roman origin (5th cent. B.C.). The Museo Arqueológico Municipal, in the Ayuntamiento Viejo (16th cent.), contains exhibits of Iberian and Roman artifacts, *azulejos* of the folk-art type, and Valencian panel paintings (16th cent.).

BIBLIOG. C. Visedo Moltó, Excavaciones en La Serreta de Alcoy (Mem. Junta Sup. Exc. y Ant., 41), Madrid, 1921-22; A. Miró, Bibliografía de Alcoy, Alicante, 1958; C. Visedo Moltó, Alcoy: Geologia, prehistoria, Alcoy, 1959.

Alicante. The city, perhaps on the site of the Roman colony of Lucentum, rises in amphitheater fashion below the isolated rock on which stands the Castillo de S. Bárbara. The Church of S. Nicolás de Bari (1616-62), built by Agustín Bernardino and Martín de Uceta, contains the Capilla del Sacramento, with lavish baroque decorations by Juan Bautista Borja (1738). The Gothic Church of S. María has a baroque portal by Manuel Violat (1721-24); it contains a painting by Rodrigo de Osona (15th cent.). The Ayuntamiento, with a baroque façade (18th cent.), and the Consulado del Mar (1785-95) are noteworthy. The Museo Arqueológico Provincial, in the Diputación, contains the dolium of Lucentum; prehistoric, Punic, and Ibero-Roman artifacts; and a collection of terra sigillata.

BIBLIOG. V. Martinez Morella, La colegiata de San Nicolás de Alicante, Alicante, 1951; J. Lafuente Vidal, El Castillo de Santa Bárbara de Alicante, Alicante, 1952; J. Lafuente Vidal, Las ruinas de la antigua Lucentum, Alicante, 1954; G. Vidal Tur, Quadros existentes en la Diputación Provincial de Alicante, Alicante, 1956; J. Lafuente Vidal, Alicante en la edad antigua, 2d ed., Alicante, 1957; C. López Jiménez, Una obra de Salzillo en Alicante, Murcia, 1958; J. Llorca Pillet, Estudio histórico-artístico sobre la Colegiata de San Nicolás de Bari de Alicante, Alicante, 1958; F. Figueras Pacheco, Dos mil años atras: Las ciudades, el puerto y la necrópolis de la Albufereta, Alicante, 1959; F. Figueras Pacheco, El castillo de Santa Bárbara de Alicante, Alicante, 1962.

Castellón de la Plana. The Gothic Church of S. María was constructed by Miguel García in 1409; consecrated in 1549, it was remodeled in baroque style in 1645. The portal has a canopied arch, the interior has a single aisle with a polygonal Capilla Mayor; the octagonal tower dates from 1604. The Ayuntamiento is baroque (1689-1716). The Museo Provincial de Bellas Artes exhibits medieval Valencian panel paintings, heraldic shields (14th cent.), archaeological pieces, and ceramics.

BIBLIOG. A. Peyrat y Roca, La iglesia mayor de Castellón, Castellón de la Plana, 1894; E. Codina Armengot, Artistas y artesanos del siglo XVIII en la villa de Castellón, Castellón de la Plana, 1946; E. Codina Armengot, El Museo Provincial de Bellas Artes y las colecciones de la Diputación, Castellón de la Plana, 1946; D. Fletcher Valls and J. Alcacer Grau, Avance a una arqueología romana de la provincia de Castellón, Castellón de la Plana, 1956; V. Traver Tomas, El Palacio-castillo de Bechi, Castellón de la Plana, 1961.

Elche (Alicante). The ancient Iberian settlement of Ilici, known to the Phoenicians as Helike, it was enlarged by the Romans, who called it Ilici Augusta. The Church of S. María (1673-1767), modeled on S. Nicolás de Bari in Alicante, has a fine baroque portal; the Capilla de la Comunión is attributed to Jaime Bort Miliá. The Museo Municipal has prehistoric, Hellenistic, Iberian, and Roman collections.

BIBLIOG. B. Bono y Barber, La basílica de Santa María de Elche, Valencia-Attracción, 24, 1952, pp. 14-15; A. Ramos Folqués, Memoria de las excavaciones practicadas en la Alcudia, Elche (Alicante), Not. arqueol. hispánico, III-IV, 1954-55, pp. 102-13; S. and J. Gomez Brufal, Bibliografía de Elche: Bibliografía alicantina, Alicante, 1957.

Gandía (Valencia). The Gothic collegiate church (14th cent., enlarged in the 16th cent.) has two fine Gothic portals. The Palacio de los Duques (16th-18th cent.) contains the magnificently decorated Borgia apartments. The Convent of S. Clara (15th cent.) contains an altarpiece by Pablo de San Leocadio (de Aregio). Nearby is the cave of El Parpalló, which has yielded much prehistoric material.

BIBLIOG. P. Solá y Cervos, El palacio ducal de Gandia, Barcelona, 1904; L. Pericot y García, La cueva del Parpalló, Madrid, 1942; J. Giner Ferrer, La Colegiata de Gandia: Apuntes históricos, Valencia, 1944.

Játiva (Valencia). This was the Roman Saetabis, which afterward became a Visigothic episcopal see. The large fortified castle, which dates from the 15th century, retains some Moorish elements. The Hermitage of S. Félix, a small Mozarabic church, has a Romanesque portal and a Gothic interior (13th cent.) containing various Valencian painted altarpieces of the 15th century. The collegiate church, begun in 1596, apparently after plans by J. Pavia, contains Gothic altarpieces, as does the Church of S. Pedro. The Museo Municipal, housed in the former Almudín, or Lonja del Trigo (wheat exchange; 1548), contains a Moorish basin (11th cent.), Moorish architectural elements from the Palacio de Pinohermoso (13th cent.), and paintings (16th-20th cent.).

BIBLIOG. C. Sarthou Carreres, El Museo Municipal de Játiva, Valencia, 1947; C. Sarthou Carreres, San Félix de Játiva, BSEE, LV, 1947, pp. 161-75; C. Sarthou Carreres, Los monumentos nacionales de Játiva, BSEE, LIX, 1951, pp. 105-20.

Liria (Valencia). This was the Edeta of the Iberians and the Lauro of the Romans. It has yielded many finds of Iberian pottery and Roman mosaics. The Church of la Sangre (14th cent.) has a Romanesque-Gothic portal. The Church of el Buen Pastor has Gothic frescoes. The parish church (La Asunción; 1627-72), designed by Martín Orinda, has a grandiose baroque façade. The palace of the dukes of Berwick y Alba, now the Ayuntamiento, is in Renaissance style.

BIBLIOG. V. Ferrán, En torno al escultor Raimundo Capuz, AEArte, XXVI, 1949, pp. 358-59; J. M. Pita Andrade, El Palacio de Liria, Madrid, 1959.

Morella (Castellón de la Plana). The town, the Castra Aelia of the Romans, is dominated by a massive castle and is girded by walls, on which Domingo Zoroball worked (1358), with 14 towers and 4 gates. The Gothic Church of S. María la Mayor, begun in 1273 and consecrated in 1394, has two exceptional portals decorated with figures of the Apostles and the Virgin (14th cent.); in the interior nave and two aisles, without transept or ambulatory) the rasied *coro* is reached by a stairway (decorated by Antonio Sancho about 1470) that winds around one of its four supporting pillars. The Convent of S. Francisco (1272) and the Gothic Church of S. Juan (15th cent.) are noteworthy. Nearby are prehistoric rock paintings in the caves of Morella la Vieja.

BIBLIOG. E. Hernández Pacheco, Las pinturas rupestres de Morella la Vella, Madrid, 1918; E. Tormo y Monzó, Iglesia arciprestal de Santa María de Morella, BRAH, XC, 1927, pp. 28–36; M. Milián Boix, Morella, BSEE, XXXVIII, 1930, pp. 280–87; A. Sanchez Gozalbo, Pintores de Morella, Castellón de la Plana, 1943; M. Milián Boix, Real convento de San Francisco de Morella, Penyagolosa, 4, 1958, pp. 24–33.

Orihuela (Alicante). This was the Aurariola of Roman times, called Origüela by the Moors. The Cathedral, begun in the 14th century, has a presbytery with stellar vaulting with spirally twisted ribs (15th cent.) and an ambulatory dating from the 16th century. The Puerta de la Anunciación is attributed to Jerónimo Quijano (ca. 1550); the Puerta de las Cadenas and the south portal are Gothic. The Church of Santiago (15th cent.) has a fine late Gothic façade; the baroque Church of S. Domingo, by Pedro Quintana (1654–59), contains a St. Michael by the painter Pablo de San Leocadio (de Arezio; 16th cent.). The former university, begun by Juan Anglés (1552) and continued in the 17th century, has two cloisters and a refectory decorated with *azulejos*. The Museo Diocesano contains sculpture and paintings from the 16th and 17th centuries, including a St. Thomas Aquinas painted by Diego Velázquez (ca. 1631).

BIBLIOG. J. Garcia Soriano, El Colegio de Predicadores y la Universidad de Orihuela, Murcia, 1918; P. Gutiérrez Moreno, La capilla mayor y el crocero de la catedral de Orihuela, AEA, X, 1934, pp. 21–25; J. Garcia Soriano, El Museo de Orihuela, Valencia, 1937; J. C. López Jiménez, Consideraciones en torno al arte en Orihuela, ACCV, XXI, 1960, pp. 160–78.

Peñíscola (Castellón de la Plana). The town is built high on a rocky peninsula. The fortress (13th–15th cent.) was the residence of the antipope Benedict XIII (Pedro de Luna); the 13th-century church has a semicircular apse and barrel vaulting; the Torre de Homenaje bears the coat-of-arms of the Luna family. The walls surrounding the town were constructed by Bautista Antonelli (16th cent.).

BIBLIOG. J. Rico de Estasen, Peñíscola y el Papa Luna, Madrid, 1957.

Requena (Valencia). There are remains of the walls and of the 15th-century castle. The old city has retained its medieval appearance, and in the narrow streets are many Gothic houses. The churches of S. María (15th cent., restored ca. 1730) and S. Salvador (1480–1533, restored in 1710–12) have late Gothic portals. The 13th-century Church of S. Nicolás was altered in 1787.

Sagunto (Valencia). Originally an Iberian city of Greek origin, Saguntum was allied with the Romans against Carthage. There are many remains of its Roman period: theater (2d cent. B.C., with later additions), circus (of the Christian era), and necropolis. The Church of S. María, begun in 1334, has two Gothic portals. The Church of S. Salvador retains elements from the 13th century. The Museo del Teatro Romano and the Museo Saguntino are noteworthy. Above the town lie the ruins of the castle, the so-called "Acrópolis," exhibiting architecture from various epochs: Iberian and Roman foundations with Moorish and medieval additions. Nearby there is a Roman temple of the republican period.

BIBLIOG. A. Chabret, Sagunto: Su historia y sus monumentos, 2 vols., Barcelona, 1888; A. Schulten, RE, s.v. Saguntum; M. Gonzalez Simancas, Excavaciones en Sagunto (Mem. Junta Sup. Exc. y Ant., 48), Madrid, 1923 (bibliog.); A. García y Bellido, Un templo romano arcáico en Valencia, AEA, X, 1947, pp. 149–51; P. Beltrán Villagrasa, Excavaciones en Sagunto, Not. arqueol. hispánico, III–IV, 1954–55, pp. 131–68; D. Fletcher Valls, Obras e restauración en el teatro romano de Sagunto, AEA, XXVIII, 1955, pp. 345–9; L. Piles Ros, La judería de Sagunto, Sefarad, XVII, 1957, pp. 352–73; A. Blanco Jiménez, Sagunto, Sagunto, 1958; S. Bru y Vidal, Notas de arqueología saguntina, Arch. preh. lev., VII, 1958, pp. 147–71; S. Bru y Vidal, Datos para el estudio del circo romano de Sagunto, Arch. preh. lev., X, 1963, pp. 207–26.

Segorbe (Castellón de la Plana). There are some well-preserved sections of the old walls of the Roman Segobriga. The Cathedral (15th–16th cent., remodeled in the 18th cent.) contains altarpieces by P. Serra, Jaime Baço Jacomart, Juan Rexach, and the so-called "Master of Segorbe" (15th cent.); panel paintings by Vicente Masip (1530); an Italian relief of the Virgin and Child, attributed to Desi-

derio da Settignano; sepulchers; and goldwork. The 13th-century Church of S. Pedro is Gothic. Nearby are the imposing ruins of the 14th-century Carthusian Monastery of Valldecristo.

BIBLIOG. C. Sarthou Carreres, La ex-cartuja de Vall de Cristo, BSEE, XXVIII, 1920, pp. 86–93; C. Torres, Las murallas de Segorbe, BSEE, XXIX, 1921, pp. 223–26.

Valencia. The city was founded in 139 or 138 B.C. on the site of a former Greek settlement. Sacked by the Romans in 75 B.C., it was rebuilt and named Valentia Edetanorum; later it came under the domination of the Goths and then of the Arabs. There are Iberian and Roman remains and some from the Early Christian and the Moorish period, such as the baths, the so-called "Baños del Almirante" (11th–13th cent.). The city was reconquered in 1238 by Jaime I of Aragón. Outstanding among monuments built after the reconquest is the Cathedral, begun in 1262 and finished before 1376. The south portal (Portada del Palau; 13th cent.) is Romanesque, derived from that of the Cathedral of Lérida; the Gothic north portal (Puerta de los Apóstoles; 14th cent.) is richly ornamented with statues and is surmounted by a magnificent rose window; the concave main portal, in the baroque style, is by Konrad Rudolph (1703). Beside the main façade rises the octagonal bell tower (Torre del Miguelete; 1381–1424), built by Andrés Juliá, Juan Franch, and Martí Lobet. The Gothic interior was reworked during the baroque period; over the crossing is an octagonal lantern tower (14th cent.) with windows. The wings of the main altarpiece have 12 scenes from the life of the Virgin painted by Fernando Yáñez de Almedina and Fernando Llanos; the Capilla del Sto Cáliz has alabaster reliefs by Giuliano Fiorentino (15th cent.). Other chapels have Gothic panel paintings by Jacomart and the Master of San Narciso; canvases by Pablo de San Leocadio, Vicente Masip, Juan de Juanes, and Goya (1799); a St. Sebastian painted by Pedro Orrente (17th cent.); and a Virgin and Child by the sculptor Juan de Castellnou (1458). In the Church of S. Martín there is a bronze statue of the titular saint (1494) attributed to Piers (Pedro) de Becker. The Church of S. Nicolás contains a Calvary by Rodrigo de Osona (1476) and paintings by Juan de Juanes and Yáñez. S. Augustín is Gothic, as is the apse of S. Juan del Hospital. The Convent of S. Domingo has a Gothic cloister (14th–15th cent.); the chapter house, with a vault on four freestanding columns, contains the double tomb of the Boyl family (15th cent.); the Capilla de los Reyes (1437–52), with the sepulcher of the marquises of Cenete, has an altar frontal with paintings by Isaac Hermes (16th cent.). The Monastery of S. Miguel de los Reyes (ca. 1590–1644) has a baroque portal. The Colegio del Patriarca (or de Corpus Christi), founded by Blessed Juan de Ribera and begun by Guillermo (Guillén) del Rey (1586), has a Renaissance cloister and a fine picture gallery containing works by Dirk Bouts, Yáñez, El Greco, Pablo de San Leocadio, and Luis Morales. The tower of the Church of S. Catalina was built by Juan Bautista Viñas (1688); the Church of Nuestra Señora de los Desamparados has a dome decorated with paintings by Antonio Palomino (1701).

In secular architecture the outstanding works include the Lonja de la Seda (silk exchange), a Gothic structure built by Pedro Compte (1482–98); the Palacio de la Generalidad, with the magnificent Salón de las Cortes, which has a Renaissance *artesonado* by Ginés Linares (1540); the Gothic Casa del Almirante and the Palacio del Marqués de Dos Aguas (which houses the Museo Nacional de Cerámica), with a rococo portal; and the Torres de Serranos (a gate by P. Balaguer; 14th cent.) and the Torres de Cuarte, built by Pedro Bonfill (1441–60). The Museo Provincial de Bellas Artes contains a large collection of Valencian Gothic panel paintings and canvases by Velázquez and Goya.

BIBLIOG. J. Martínez Aloy, La casa de la Diputación de Valencia, 2 vols., Valencia, 1909–10; J. Sanchís Sivera, La catedral de Valencia, Valencia, 1909; M. Ferrandis Torres, El monasterio de San Miguel de los Reyes, BSEE, XXVI, 1918, pp. 180–88; A. Monforte, El convento de Santo Domingo, BSEE, XXVI, 1918, pp. 161–68; J. Barberá Sentamans, Catálogo del Museo Diocesano, Valencia, 1923; E. Tormo y Monzó, Valencia: Los Museos, Madrid, 1932; F. Almela Vives, La Lonja de Valencia, Valencia, 1935; J. Feo García, Nota sobre la supuesta destrucción de la antigua Tyris, Emerita, XII, 1944, pp. 129–36; D. Fletcher Valls et al., Repertorio de bibliografía arqueológica valenciana, 3 vols., Valencia, 1951–60; P. A. Pérez Ruiz, La Fe, la historia y el arte en el antiguo convento de predicadores de Valencia, Valencia, 1951; G. Ros Fillol, Murallas de Valencia, Valencia, 1951; C. Sarthou Carreres, Valencia monumental, Valencia, 1954; F. Garín Ortiz de Taranco, Guía del Museo de Bellas Artes, Valencia, 1955; L. Bellido, La iglesia de San Esteban de Valencia, Academia, 3d Ser., V, 1955–57, pp. 165–66; M. Sanchís Guarner, Les barraques valencianes, Barcelona, 1957; F. Almela Vives, Destrucción y dispersión del tesoro artístico valenciano, Valencia, 1958; S. Carreres Zacarés, El patio de los naranjos de la Lonja de Valencia, ACCV, XIX, 1958, pp. 1–24; E. Domínguez González, Guía del Museo Nacional de Cerámica, Valencia, 1958; F. Almela Vives, Pere Balaguer y las torres de Serranos, AAV, XXX, 1959, pp. 27–39; F. Garin Ortiz de Taranco, Valencia monumental, Madrid, 1959; J. Toledo Girau,

Inventarios del Palacio Real de Valencia e la muerte de doña María, esposa de Alfonso el Magnánimo, Valencia, 1961; M. Tarradell, La fundació de la ciutat de Valencia, Barcelona, 1962.

Villena (Alicante). Rising on a height in the center of the town is a 15th-century castle with double girding wall; the square Torre de Homenaje, originally Moorish, has been altered. The Church of Santiago is late Gothic (16th cent.); the interior has ogival vaulting over spiral and sharply fluted columns; it contains a noteworthy altarpiece of polychromed wood (1540) by Jerónimo Quijano.

BIBLIOG. M. de Assas, Monumentos arquitectónicos de España: Iglesia de Santiago de Villena, Madrid, 1878; M. Belén Portillo, Santiago de Villena y el gótico "Reyes Católicos" en el sudeste español, AEArte, XXXVI, 1963, pp. 74–78.

Murcia. This region, whose artistic expression has been a blending of Andalusian, Castilian, and Mediterranean influences, comprises the provinces of Murcia (on the Mediterranean) and Albacete (on the plateau to the north). The province of Murcia experienced an outstanding baroque period; Albacete is noted chiefly for its Renaissance monuments.

BIBLIOG. R. Amador de los Rios, Murcia y Albacete, Barcelona, 1889; A. Baquero Almania, Los profesores de las Bellas Artes murcianos, Murcia, 1913; E. Tormo y Monzó, Levante, Madrid, 1923; J. Espin Rael, Artistas y artifices levantinos, Lorca, 1931; L. M. Lluvia and M. López Guzmán, La cerámica murciana decorada, Murcia, 1951; D. Sánchez Jara and L. Ayuso Vicente, Salzillo, Madrid, 1951; A. E. Pérez Sánchez, Iglesias mudéjares del Reino de Murcia, AE, XXIII, 1960, pp. 85–112; A. E. Pérez Sánchez, Murcia-Albacete y sus provincias, Barcelona, 1961.

Albacete. The Renaissance Cathedral (formerly Church of S. Juan Bautista; 16th cent., restored after 1936) has nave and two aisles and three Gothic apses; it contains 16th-century paintings and a plateresque sepulcher. The Museo Arqueológico Provincial, in the Diputación Provincial, contains prehistoric, Iberian, and Roman exhibits.

BIBLIOG. A. García y Bellido, El Museo de Albacete, AEA, XVII, 1944, pp. 98–100; A. E. Pérez Sánchez, Murcia-Albacete y sus provincias, Barcelona, 1961. See also Anales del Seminario de Historia de Albacete, passim.

Alcaraz (Albacete). The castle and city walls are Moorish; the castle contains remains of the Gothic Church of S. María. Around the Plaza Mayor are many fine buildings: the Lonja del Corregidor (1518); the Torre del Tardón (1568), by Bartolomé Flores; the Ayuntamiento (1588), with a plateresque portal (ca. 1530); and the Pósito (1592). The Church of la Trinidad, by P. Cobo (1486), with a 16th-century tower, has nave and two aisles with stellar vaulting; it contains some late-15th-century sculpture. The Church of S. Miguel dates from the 16th century.

BIBLIOG. J. Marco Hidalgo, Estudios para la historia de la ciudad de Alcaraz, RABM, 3d Ser., XXI, 1909, pp. 208–33; J. Carrascosa González, Las torres de la ciudad de Alcaraz, n.p., 1929; M. Manzano Monís, La plaza de Alcaraz y Andrés de Vandelvira, BSSE, LIV, 1946, pp. 157–85.

Almansa (Albacete). The town lies at the foot of a Moorish castle (rebuilt in the 15th cent.). The parish church has Gothic, Renaissance, and neoclassic elements. The Palacio de los Condes de Cirat has a façade of 1575 and an Ionic patio. Nearby, at Alpera, are prehistoric rock paintings (Cueva de la Vieja, Cueva del Queso). On the Cerro de los Santos are remains of an Iberian sanctuary (4th cent. B.C.).

BIBLIOG. J. de Rada y Delgado, Antigüedades del Cerro de los Santos, n. p., 1875; A. Fernández de Avilés, Las primeras investigaciones en el Cerro de los Santos, BSEAAV, XV, 1948–49, pp. 57–70 (bibliog.); A. García y Bellido, in R. Menéndez Pidal, Historia de España, I, 3, Madrid, 1954, pp. 483–541.

Caravaca (Murcia). The town has a large castle (15th cent.). The Church of S. Salvador (1534–1600), with nave and two aisles of equal height and with stellar vaulting on Ionic columns, contains canvases, sculpture, and a processional cross (15th cent.). The Church of Sta Cruz, Herreran with a baroque façade, contains panel paintings by Fernando Llanos (16th cent.), canvases by Antonio Arias (17th cent.), and Hispano-Moorish textiles.

BIBLIOG. A. E. Pérez Sánchez, Murcia-Albacete y sus provincias, Barcelona, 1961.

Cartagena (Murcia). This was the Roman Carthago Nova; remaining from the Roman period is the sepulcher of a member of the gens Cornelia, the so-called "Torre Ciega." The baroque Church of S. María de Gracia has sculpture by Francisco Salzillo (Zarcillo). The Museo Arqueológico Municipal contains Roman sculpture and

mining tools and some Iberian objects. The city was a center fc the production of decorated porcelain in the 19th century.

BIBLIOG. M. González Simancas, Excavaciones de Cartagena (Men Junta Sup. Exc. y Ant., 102), Madrid, 1929; A. Fernández de Avilés, Museo Arqueológico Municipal de Cartagena, AEA, XVII, 1944, pp. 8c 91; E. Calandre, La loza de Cartagena, AEArte, XXII, 1949, pp. 239–5 A. Beltrán, El plano arqueológico de Cartagena, AEA, XXV, 1952, pp. 47 82; A. García y Bellido, EAA, s.v.

Chinchilla de Monte Aragón (Albacete). The town was a stron[g] hold during the centuries of the reconquest. There is a castle from the 15th century. The Church of S. María del Salvador, with 15th century nave and Renaissance apse (probably by E. Hamete, or J mete), contains a fine *reja* (1503) by Antón de Viveros, panel paintin[g] (16th cent.), embroideries, goldwork, and outstanding *artesonad[o]* in the sacristy. The Ayuntamiento has a baroque façade and a pla eresque lateral portal of 1590.

BIBLIOG. A. E. Pérez Sánchez, Murcia-Albacete y sus provincia[s] Barcelona, 1961.

El Cigarralejo (Murcia). The large Iberian sanctuary of] Cigarralejo, near Mula, dates from the 4th century B.C. and w[a] dedicated to a goddess who was a protective deity of horses; it consi[s] of a sacred building and many annexes for worship. It was destroy[e] during the 3d century B.C., rebuilt, and destroyed again in the 2 century B.C. The excavations have yielded many ex-votos. Near[l] is a large Iberian necropolis.

BIBLIOG. E. Cuadrado Diaz, Excavaciones en el Santuario Iberi del Cigarralejo (Mem. Com. Prov. Gen. de Exc., 21), Madrid, 1950; Cuadrado Diaz, Excavaciones en El Cigarralejo, Not. arqueol. hispánic II, 1953, pp. 80–101; A. García y Bellido, in R. Menéndez Pidal, Histor de España, I, 3, Madrid, 1954, pp. 327–32; E. Cuadrado Diaz, Die iberisc[h] Siedlung von El Cigarralejo bei Murcia, Jhb. Röm-german. Zentralmu Mainz, VIII, 1961, pp. 26–37.

Hellín (Albacete). This was the Illunum of the Romans. T[h] church of the Franciscan monastery dates from the 15th and 16 centuries, and there is a 16th-century church with a plateresque port[a] There are interesting patrician houses. In the vicinity are the pr historic rock paintings of Minateda, among the most important the Spanish Levant.

BIBLIOG. E. Martínez García, Hierros artisticos de Hellin, Macana I, 1952, pp. 135–37.

Jumilla (Murcia). The Church of Santiago has a late Goth nave with transept and a Renaissance *chevet* (1562). The main alta piece (1583) is by Francisco and Diego de Ayala. The castle (15 cent.) retains some Moorish elements. The Monastery of S. A has a Scourging at the Pillar (1756) by Francisco Salzillo.

BIBLIOG. D. Sánchez Jara and L. Ayuso Vicente, Salzillo, Madr 1951.

Murcia. The city retains few remnants of its Moslem and mediev past. The Cathedral, on the site of a former mosque, was razed abo 1320; the present building was begun in 1394 and was consecrat[e] in 1465. The Puerta de los Apóstoles dates from about 1440; t[h] Puerta de las Cadenas (1512–15) is ascribed to Francesco Torni; t[h] tower, begun by him in 1521, was continued in the 16th century Jacopo Torni (both Tornis were known as l'Indaco, also Florenti and Jerónimo Quijano and was completed in the 18th century. T[h] magnificent baroque façade (1736–54) was designed by Jaime Bc Milia. The Gothic interior has nave and two aisles, transept, and ar bulatory; the choir has a *reja* by Antón de Viveros and stalls (156 by Rafael de León. The Capilla de los Vélez is late Gothic (1507 with stellar vaulting; the 16th-century Capilla de los Junterone on an elliptical plan, contains many sculptures; the altarpiece of Miguel (15th cent.) is Valencian; the baptismal chapel is Renaissanc the sacristy, with a fine doorway that may be by Jerónimo Quijan contains Renaissance cabinetwork. Also of interest within the C thedral complex are the Museo Diocesano, containing a Roman s[a] cophagus with Muses, Gothic statuary, a double altarpiece by Barna da Modena (14th cent.), panel paintings by Fernando Llanos (16 cent.), and sculpture by Salzillo; and the treasury, containing monstrance (1677) and other goldwork. Other churches of intere are S. Esteban (1560), built for the Jesuits by Bartolomé Bustamant with a Renaissance façade; the Virgen del Carmen and S. Juan Ba tista (both, 18th cent.); La Merced (1560), with a Churrigu100resq portal; and S. Nicolás, with sculpture by Alonso Cano. The Palac Episcopal, by Baltasar Canestro, dates from 1748. The Museo A queológico Provincial contains Iberian, Roman, and Visigothic c[o] ections; the Museo Provincial de Bellas Artes exhibits panel paintings nd canvases (16th–17th cent.) by the Murcian school; the Museo Salzillo contains famous works by this sculptor (1707–83). Near the ity are the Santuario de la Fuensanta (17th cent.) and the Monastery f la Nora, the latter with a baroque church containing a St. Jerome 1755) by Salzillo.

BIBLIOG. M. González Simancas, La catedral de Murcia, RABM, 3d er., XXIV, 1911, pp. 510–38; Museo Provincial de Bellas Artes de Murcia, Catálogo, Murcia, 1927; E. Tormo y Monzó, La capilla de los Vélez en a catedral de Murcia, BRAH, XC, 1927, pp. 263–78; A. Fernández de vilés, El sarcófago de las Musas y Maestros de la catedral de Murcia, AEArte, XVII, 1944, pp. 325–62; S. García de Pruneda, El retablo de anta Lucía en la catedral de Murcia, BSEE, LV, 1947, pp. 79–88; D. ánchez Jara, Orfebrería murciana, Madrid, 1950; J. Sánchez Moreno, Miscelánea sobre escultura en Murcia, Anales Univ. de Murcia, I, 1951– 2, pp. 77–98; C. Lozano Guirao, Baltazar Canestro y el palacio episcopal e Murcia, AEArte, XXV, 1952, pp. 53–58; C. Lozano Guirao, Arquitectura arroca en Murcia, AEArte, XXVI, 1953, pp. 285–93; M. Jorge Aragonenses, d., Museo Arqueológico de Murcia, Madrid, 1956; M. Jorge Arangonenses, l Museo Diocesano de Murcia, AEArte, XXXII, 1959, pp. 267–69; M. orge Aragonenses, El Museo Salzillo de Murcia, AEArte, XXXII, 1959, p. 360–62.

Andalucía. This region, which occupies the whole meridional one of the Peninsula, comprises eight provinces: Almería, Jaén, Granada, Málaga, Córdoba, Sevilla, Cádiz, and Huelva. It has lways been a region of intense artistic expression, reaching a high rtistic level during the Moslem period (8th–15th cent.) and showing qual vigor and quality in the Gothic, Renaissance, and baroque eriods.

BIBLIOG. La escultura en Andalucía, 3 vols., Seville, 1927; Documentos ara la historia del arte en Andalucía, 10 vols., Seville, 1934–46; E. Romero e Torres, Catálogo monumental de España: Cádiz, 2 vols., Madrid, 1934; Hernández Díaz, A. Sancho Corbacho, and F. Collantes de Teran, Catá- go arqueológico y artístico de la provincia de Sevilla, 4 vols., Seville, 1939– 5; R. Thouvenot, Essai sur la province romaine de Bétique, Paris, 1940; . Lambert, Les mosquées de type andalou en Espagne et en Afrique du Jord, Al-Andalus, XIV, 1949, pp. 273–89; A. Sancho Corbacho, Arquitectura arroca sevillana del siglo XVIII, Madrid, 1952; F. Collantes de Teran, os castillos del reino de Sevilla, Arch. hispalense, XVIII, 1953, pp. 117– 5; J. Hernández Díaz, Aportaciones al estudio de la imaginería barroca ndaluza, Arch. hispalense, XVIII, 1953, pp. 9–15; J. M. Pemán, Andalucía, arcelona, 1958.

Alcalá de Guadaira (Sevilla). Here was the most important Mu- ejar castle (14th cent.) in Andalucía, with remains of an earlier Al- ohad structure. The ruined subterranean storerooms, cisterns, eep, and donjon (15th cent.) still survive. The church of the Convent f S. Clara contains an altarpiece with reliefs by Juan Martínez Iontañés.

BIBLIOG. L. Torres Balbás, Dos obras de arquitectura almohade: La ezquita de Cuatrohabitan y el castillo del Alcalá de Guadaira, Al-Andalus, I, 1941, pp. 204–16.

Alcalá la Real (Jaén). The Castillo de la Mota dates from the Ioorish period, with later additions (13th–15th cent.); the church of the 13th–14th century, enlarged in the 16th century. The abbot's alace is of the 16th century. The Charles V fountain is plateresque.

BIBLIOG. S. Sanguinetti, El palacio abacial de Alcalá la Real, Reconstruc- ón, XV, 1954, pp. 121–26.

Almería. Originally founded by the Phoenicians, this was the ortus Magnus of the Romans. Named al-Mariyat by the Moors, was a Moslem seaport and industrial center until the 12th century. here are ruins of the strong Moorish Alcazaba, which contains the 5th-century Torreón del Homenaje and the Church of S. Juan, ith vestiges of an old mosque. The fortresslike Cathedral, with ur massive towers, is late Gothic (1524–43); the two portals and fa- de are by Juan de Orea (1550–73), who also designed the choir alls and the sacristy. The Church of Santiago, with a tall bell tower, as Mudejar ceilings. The Museo Arqueológico Provincial exhibits rehistoric finds and Paleo-Christian sculptures.

BIBLIOG. V. Lampérez y Romea, La catedral de Almería, BSEE, XV, 07, pp. 69–74; S. Espinosa Orozco, Almería, Almería, 1950; A. García Bellido, Las dos figuras del Buen Pastor de Gádor, AEA, XXIII, 1950, . 3–12; L. Torres Balbás, La mezquita mayor de Almería, Al-Andalus, VIII, 1953, pp. 412–30; B. Martín del Rey, Guía ilustrada en Almería su provincia, Almería, 1957; J. Goytisolo, Campos de Níjar, 2d ed., Bar- ona, 1961; G. Menéndez Pidal, La capa de Fermo, BRAH, CXLVII, 61, pp. 169–76.

Almonaster la Real (Huelva). Within the ruined castle can be en the remains of a small mosque (11th–12th cent.). The Mudejar

parish church has a 16th-century doorway in the Portuguese Manueline manner.

BIBLIOG. J. Rodríguez Cano, La ermita del castillo de Almonaster la Real, Al-Andalus, II, 1934, pp. 364–66; F. Pérez Embid, La portada manuelina de Almonaster la Real, AEArte, XVII, 1944, pp. 270–78.

Antequera (Málaga). This was the Roman fortified city of Anti- caria. There are remains of the Moorish Alcazaba, with the Torre Mocha and battlemented towers (13th cent.). The churches of S. María la Mayor, S. Sebastián, and S. Juan Bautista are of the 16th century; the churches of the Remedios, S. Isidro, and S. Agustín are baroque. Close to the town are three dolmens: Cueva de Menga, Cueva del Romeral, and Cueva de Viera (ca. 2000 B.C.).

BIBLIOG. A. García y Yegros, Historia de la antigüedad y nobleza de la ciudad de Antequera, Antequera, 1915; A. de Burgos Oms, Monumentos artísticos de Ronda y Antequera, Málaga, 1940; J. M. Fernández, Las iglesias de Antequera, Málaga, 1943; S. Giménez Reyna and A. García y Bellido, Antigüedades romanas de Antequera, AEA, XXI, 1948, pp. 48–68; F. Arri- bas, Iglesia colonial de Antequera, BSEAAV, XVI, 1949–50, pp. 189–94; M. Gómez-Moreno, Arquitectura tartesia: La necropoli de Antequera, Misc. h. arte y arqueol., I, 1949, pp. 105–30; L. Torres Balbás, Antequera islámica, Al-Andalus, XVI, 1951, pp. 427–54; M. Catena Sevilla, Iglesia del convento de Madre de Dios de Antequera, AEArte, XXX, 1957, pp. 71–74.

Aracena (Huelva). The Church of Nuestra Señora del Dolor Mayor was constructed by the Templars (13th–14th cent.) over the former mosque of the 12th-century Moorish castle; the minaret (12th cent.) survives. Of note is the Church of la Asunción (16th cent.). The church of the Carmelite convent contains an altarpiece by Juan Giralte (1562).

BIBLIOG. J. A. Vázquez, Guía de la Gruta de las maravillas, Aracena y la Sierra, Seville, 1936; J. Fernández Díaz, Estudios de imaginería andaluza, Arch. hispalense, XX, 1954, pp. 202–06; J. A. Vázquez, El signo de Solomon en la iglesia del castillo de Aracena, Arch. hispalense, XXVI, 1957, pp. 101–05.

Arcos de la Frontera (Cádiz). The Church of S. María de la Asun- ción has a fine façade (15th–16th cent.); it contains a main altarpiece by Jerónimo Fernández (Hernández; 1586) and baroque choir stalls (1734–44); in the apse are noteworthy murals from the 14th century. The Church of S. Pedro, built on the site of a Moorish fortress, contains an altarpiece of 1539 by Ferdinand Sturm (Hernando Stur- mio), paintings by Zurbarán and Francisco Pacheco, and Moorish banners won in battle. The baroque Hospital de la Caridad (1740– 64) has a fine patio. The castle-palace of the dukes of Osuna retains its ancient fortifications; the Palacio de Águila has a splendid Mudejar façade.

BIBLIOG. M. Mancheño Olivares, La iglesia parroquial de Arcos de la Frontera, Arcos de la Frontera, 1896; C. Pemán y Pemartín, Las pinturas murales de Santa María de Arcos, AEAA, IV, 1928, pp. 139–54; A. Do- mínguez Ortiz, Documentos para la historia de Sevilla y su antiguo Reino, Arch. hispalense, XXXII, 1960, pp. 263–74.

El Argar (Almería). This prehistoric village represents the deca- dence of the first Bronze Age in Spain (1500–1000 B.C.). There are remains of dwellings on a rectangular plan and, around the citadel, numerous tombs, as well as examples of pottery of a very dark hue and bronze weapons and bracelets of archaic shape.

BIBLIOG. H. L. Siret, Les premières âges du métal dans le sud-est de l'Espagne, Antwerp, 1887; J. de Mata Carriazo, in R. Menéndez Pidal, Historia de España, I, 1, Madrid, 1947, pp. 758–94; S. Puglisi, EAA, s.v. (bibliog.).

Baena (Córdoba). The town is dominated by the Moorish castle; the upper part of the town, the Almedina, is surrounded by the old walls. The Church of S. María la Mayor contains plateresque altar- piece and *reja.* The Church of Nuestra Señora de Guadalupe (16th cent.) contains some interesting Mudejar octagonal *artesonados.* The church of the Convent of la Madre de Dios has a Gothic-Renaissance doorway and porch with a noteworthy carving of the Annunciation; within are fine Mudejar ceilings.

Baeza (Jaén). This was the Roman Vivatia. The Cathedral, re- built (1567–93) by Andrés de Vandelvira and Alonso Barba, preserves two portals from the earlier Gothic structure; the façade dates from 1587. Inside (nave and two aisles with vaulting supported by Corin- thian columns) are several fine altarpieces, a wrought-iron pulpit (1580), and a baroque monstrance (1714). The Church of S. Andrés (1500–20) has a Renaissance tower and a plateresque portal; the Ca- pilla Mayor is by Vandelvira (1562), who also designed the Church of S. Francisco (1546; now in ruins). Secular buildings include the

Ayuntamiento, with a plateresque façade (1559); the Casa del Pópulo (ca. 1530); the Gothic-Renaissance Palacio de Benavente; and the Fountain of S. María (1574), in the form of a triumphal arch.

BIBLIOG. V. Lampérez y Romea, La casa de Corregidores y carcel de Baeza, BRAH, LXX, 1917, pp. 207-10; V. Lampérez y Romea, La Casa del Pópulo en Baeza, BRABASF, XIII, 1919, pp. 129-32; F. Escolano Gómez, La custodia de la catedral de Baeza, AEAA, XII, 1936, pp. 179-90; F. Escolano Gómez and D. Angulo Iñíguez, Tablas sevillanas en San Andrés de Baeza, AEArte, XVII, 1944, pp. 316-19; R. Ortega y Sagristá, Algunas capillas de la catedral de Baeza, Paisaje, 105, 1958, pp. 1855-57; J. Chamorro Lozano, La catedral de Baeza, B. Inst. Estudios Gienenses, VI, 22, 1959, pp. 10-37; R. Vaño Silvestre, La iglesia de Santa Cruz de Baeza, B. Inst. Estudios Gienenses, VI, 21, 1959, pp. 9-20.

Cádiz. Founded by the Phoenicians and later known as Gades, it became the Julia Augusta Gaditana of the Romans. Although one of the oldest cities in Europe, it retains only a necropolis (8th-3d cent. B.C.) from its distant past. The city is almost entirely surrounded by 17th-century walls. The New Cathedral, begun in 1720 after plans by Vicente Acero and finished in 1838, has nave with flanking aisles and domes over the transept and the main chapel; the choir stalls (1702) are by Agustín and Miguel de Perea. The Old Cathedral (officially the Parroquia de Sta Cruz), originally of the 13th century but rebuilt in 1602, contains a notable baroque altarpiece (1650). The conventual Church of S. Domingo has a portal from 1675; the Oratory of S. Felipe Neri (1679), with an Immaculate Conception by Murillo, is on an elliptical plan, as is the Sta Cueva (18th cent.), with paintings by Goya. The Church of Nuestra Señora del Carmen (18th cent.) has baroque bell cots of South American influence. The Capuchin Church of S. Catalina (1641) has paintings by Murillo. The Hospital de Mujeres (1740) has a St. Francis by El Greco in the chapel. The Casa de las Cadenas has a doorway by Giacomo Antonio Ponzanelli (Ponsonelli; 1692). The Museo Arqueológico Provincial contains prehistoric collections, a Punic sarcophagus in the shape of a human figure (5th cent. B.C.), and Roman statuary. The Museo de Bellas Artes has a series of paintings by Zurbarán from the Cartuja of Jerez.

BIBLIOG. J. Urrutia, Descripción histórico-artística de la catedral de Cádiz, Cádiz, 1843; P. Quintero, La necrópolis anteromana de Cádiz, BSEE, XXII, 1914 pp. 81-107; J. Ezquerra del Bayo, Las pinturas de Goya en el oratorio de Santa Cueva, AE, XVII, 1928, pp. 388-91; P. Gutiérrez Moreno, La cúpula de Vicente Acero para la Catedral de Cádiz, AEAA, IV, 1928, pp. 183-86; C. Pemán y Pemartín, Sobre el San Francisco de El Greco en Cádiz, AEAA, VI, 1930, pp. 77-78; E. Romero de Torres, Catálogo monumental de España: Provincia de Cádiz, 2 vols., Madrid, 1934; H. Sancho de Sopranis, Los Vandelvira en Cádiz, AEArte, XXI, 1948, pp. 43-54; E. Kukahn, Sarcófago sidonio de Cádiz, AEA, XXIV, 1951, pp. 23-34; C. Pemán y Pemartín, Catálogo del Museo de Bellas Artes de Cádiz, Cádiz, 1952; R. Moreno Criado, Iglesias de Cádiz, Cádiz, 1953; H. Sancho de Sopranis, Para la historia artística de Cádiz en el siglo XVII, Arch. hispalense, XXI, 1955, pp. 53-65; C. Pemán y Pemartín, Arquitectura barroca gaditana, AEArte, XXVIII, 1955, pp. 199-206; J. A. Baird, The Retables of Cádiz and Jerez in the 17th and 18th Centuries, Anales Inst. Investigaciones Esteticas, 26, 1957, pp. 39-49; M. Guillen Roson, Monumentos de Cádiz, Cádiz, 1960; E. García y Bellido, EAA, s.v.

La Calahorra (Granada). The palace (1509-12) was constructed by Lorenzo Vázques for the Marquis of Cenete. The interior was decorated by Lombard artists in the Italian Renaissance style. The square marble patio has doorways strongly influenced by the plateresque style.

BIBLIOG. C. Justi, Der Baumeister des Schlosses La Calahorra, Jhb-PreussKSamml, XII, 1891, pp. 224-26; V. Lampérez y Romea, El castillo de la Calahorra, BSEE, XXII, 1914, pp. 1-28; V. Escribano Ucalay, La Calahorra: Casa de los Caballeros de Santiago: Plaza de la Corredora, Córdoba, 1961.

Carmona (Sevilla). The town, once the Roman Carmo, retains a definite Moorish stamp. The two city gates (Puerta de Sevilla and Puerta de Córdoba), originally Roman, were restyled by the Moors. The Alcázar de Abajo (now in ruins) is a Moorish fortress built on Roman foundations; the Alcázar de Arriba (also in ruins) is Gothic. The late Gothic Church of S. María has a fine Moorish patio; within the church is an altarpiece by N. Ortega and Juan Bautista Vázquez the Elder (1559-65). The Churrigueresque Church of el Salvador (early 18th cent.) contains a main altarpiece by J. Maestre (1722). Outside the town is a vast Roman necropolis (2d cent. B.C.-4th cent.) with about 900 tombs; the Museo de la Necrópolis contains objects from the site.

BIBLIOG. E. Hübner, RE, s.v.; G. Bonsor, Colonies agricoles préromaines de la Vallée du Bétis, RA, 3d Ser., XXXV, 1899, pp. 126-59, 232-325, 376-91; G. Bonsor, The Archaeological Sketch-book of the Roman Necropolis at Carmona, New York, 1931; J. R. Mélida y Alinari, in R.

Menéndez Pidal, Historia de España, II, Madrid, 1935, passim; B. Taracena Aguirre, Las murallas de Carmona, AEA, XV, 1942, pp. 348-51; A. Balil, FA, XIV, 1959, no. 4778.

Córdoba. The ancient Iberian settlement became the Roman city of Corduba, birthplace of the Senecas; remains from the Roman epoch include a bridge over the Guadalquivir (which has been reconstructed many times) and sections of the walls. During the time of the Caliphate (8th-10th cent.) it was the foremost city in western Europe, with 3,000 mosques, 300 public baths, and numerous magnificent palaces. There are remains of the Moorish walls, with the Puerta de Sevilla (prior to the 10th cent.) and the Puerta de Almodóvar. The former Great Mosque was begun by ʿAbd-ar-Rahmān I (ca. 780) and was enlarged by ʿAbd-ar-Rahmān II (822-52), Ḥakam II, and al-Manṣūr (10th cent.); its conversion into a cathedral in the 13th century and alterations after 1523 left it mutilated. Rectangular in plan (570 by 450 ft.), it is enclosed by a massive, battlemented wall with various doorways of Moorish (that of S. Esteban is the finest) Mudejar, and other styles; within the wall is the notable Patio de los Naranjos; the tower (1593-1664) encloses the original minaret of the mosque. The interior consists of 19 aisles separated by horseshoe and semicircular arches over columns with Roman, Visigothic, and Moorish capitals; the "Lucernario" (Capilla de Nuestra Señora de Villaviciosa) and the mihrab are intricately decorated with stuccowork and mosaics. Notable in the Cathedral are an Annunciation by Pedro de Córdoba (1475), the stalls in the coro by Pedro Duque Cornejo (1758), 18th-century pulpits, a monstrance by Enrique de Arfe (1518), Renaissance altarpieces, 17th-century sculptures and canvases, and fine goldwork. Other churches include S. Juan (now Sagrado Corazón) with a 9th-century minaret; S. Marina, with Gothic portal and Renaissance tower; and S. Nicolás, with 15th-century mural paintings. In the Hospital de Agudos is the Gothic-Mudejar Capilla de S. Bartolomé (13th-15th cent.). The Casa de las Campanas (14th cent.) and the Casa de los Caballeros de Santiago (14th-15th cent.) are Mudejar; the Palacio del Marqués de Fuensanta and the Palacio de los Villalones are in Renaissance style. In the old Jewish quarter is the synagogue of the 14th century, decorated with stuccowork similar to that found in Granada. The Museo Arqueológico Provincial, housed in the Renaissance Palacio de Don Jerónimo Páez, contains Iberian, Roman, Visigothic, and Moslem collections. The Museo Provincial de Bellas Artes has 16th-century paintings, canvases of the Andalusian school of the 17th century, and a collection of drawings. The Museo Julio Romero de Torres contains work by this painter.

BIBLIOG. P. de Madrazo, Córdoba, Barcelona, 1884; R. Ramírez de Arellano, Diccionario de artistas de Córdoba, Madrid, 1893; M. A. Ortiz Belmonte, La sillería del coro de la catedral de Córdoba, AE, VIII, 1919, pp. 237-58; R. Ramírez de Arellano, Historia de Córdoba, 4 vols., Ciudad Real, 1919; J. de la Torre, El puente romano de Córdoba, B. Real Acad. Córdoba, I, 1922, p. 87; O. Nogales, El antiguo Hospital de la Caridad actual Museo de Bellas Artes, B. Real Acad. Córdoba, III, 1924, pp. 365-75; R. Castejón y Martínez de Arrizala, La casa del Gran Capitán, B. Real Acad. Córdoba, VII, 1928, pp. 199-222; R. Castejón y Martínez de Arrizala, Córdoba califal, B. Real Acad. Córdoba, VIII, 1929, pp. 253-339; R. Castejón y Martínez de Arrizala, Guía de Córdoba, Madrid, 1930; A. de la Torre y del Cerro, Obras en la torre de la catedral de Córdoba en los siglos XVI y XVII, B. Real Acad. Córdoba, IX, 1930, pp. 297-323; E. Lambert, Las tres primeras etapas constructivas de la mezquita de Córdoba, Al-Andalus, III, 1935, pp. 139-43; M. Ocaña Jiménez, Las puertas de la Medina de Córdoba, Al-Andalus, III, 1935, pp. 143-51; D. Angulo Iñíguez, Pintores cordobeses del Renacimiento, AEArte, XVII, 1944, pp. 226-44; R. Aguilar Priego, Datos sobre la restauración del Mihrab de la mezquita de Córdoba, B. Real Acad. Córdoba, XVI, 1945, pp. 31-58, 139-67; R. Aguilar Priego, Bosquejo histórico de la ejecución del coro de la catedral de Córdoba, B. Real Acad. Córdoba, XVII, 1946, pp. 173-214; R. Aguilar Priego, Bosquejo histórico de la ejecución de los púlpitos de la catedral de Córdoba, B. Real Acad. de Córdoba, XVIII, 1947, pp. 189-200; S. Alcolea Gil, Guía artística de España: Córdoba, Barcelona, 1951 (bibliog.); E. Lambert, La grande Mosquée de Cordoue et l'art byzantine, VI⁰ Cong. int. d'études byz. (1948), II, Paris, 1951, pp. 225-32; L. Torres Balbás, La mezquita de Córdoba y las ruinas de Madinat-al-Zahra, Madrid, 1952; E. Camps Cazorla, Módulo, proporciones y composición en la arquitectura califal cordobesa, Madrid, 1953; E. Lévi-Provençal, Histoire de l'Espagne musulmane, III, Paris, 1953; R. Aguilar Priego, La capilla mayor del convento de Santa Isabel, B. Real Acad. Córdoba, XXV, 1954, pp. 189-238; Al-Sayyid Salem, Cronología de la mezquita mayor de Córdoba, Al-Andalus, XIX, 1954, pp. 393-401; R. Aguilar Priego, Obras en la torre de la catedral de Córdoba desde el siglo XVII hasta nuestros días, B. Real Acad. Córdoba, XXVII, 1956, pp. 27-42; S. de los Santos Gener, Las artes en Córdoba durante la dominación de los pueblos germánicos, B. Real Acad. Córdoba, XXIX, 1958, pp. 147-92; V. Escribano Ucelay, Urbanización de Córdoba medieval y actuales ideas sobre urbanismo, Córdoba, 1960; A. García y Bellido, EAA, s.v.

Estepa (Sevilla). The town was the Iberian Astapa. The Church of S. María is Gothic-Mudejar; S. Sebastián is plateresque. The tower of the Church of la Victoria dates from 1760. The churches of the Virgen del Carmen (1718), of la Asunción (1749), and of the Virgen de los Remedios (1754) are baroque, as is the Palacio de los Cerverales

Granada. The city, located on the northwestern slopes of the Sierra Nevada, was the Iberian Elibyrge, known as Illiberis to the Romans and the Visigoths. It was only during the period of the Moorish domination that Granada became an important center. During the 11th century it was ruled by the Zirids, after the fall of the Ommiads. From the end of the 11th to the middle of the 12th century it was under Almoravid rule, then under that of the Almohads. The Nasrid dynasty lasted for some 250 years (beginning in 1241), until the city was reconquered by the Christians in 1492. The long period of Moslem domination has left extensive and marked traces in Granada. Of the 11th century are the Moorish walls (built over earlier Visigothic foundations) with square and semicircular towers; the Torres Bermejas, on Monte Mauror; and the Bañuelo, a Moorish bath that preserves Visigothic capitals. The Puerta de Elvira is the principal gate of the 12th-century belt of the walls. The Cuarto Real de S. Domingo, with fine *azulejos* and *artesonados*, and the Casa de los Girones are 13th-century Moorish mansions decorated with elegant stuccowork. The Alcázar de Genil preserves elements of a magnificent Moorish palace (14th cent.) that stood on the site. The Casa del Carbón (early 14th cent.) is a notable example of a Moorish hostelry. The Alcazaba, on the cliffs of the Alhambra hill, was a Moorish fortress from the 11th century, but the remaining walls and towers date from the 13th century. The Generalife, which was the country residence of the Moorish rulers, is a group of pavilions whose decoration dates from 1319; recent excavations here have uncovered remains of Moorish baths, wells, and dwellings.

The monument for which Granada is famous, the Alhambra, is a superposition of the successive royal residences of the Nasrid rulers. The complex is arranged around the two large courts called the Patio de los Arrayanes (Court of the Myrtles) and the Patio de los Leones (Court of the Lions). The former, with porticoes on its short sides and two fountains in the center, is connected, through the Sala de la Barca, which is ornamented by two white-marble sculptured niches, with the Salón de Embajadores, which occupies the entire Torre de Comares and which has profuse, highly refined decoration. The Patio de los Leones, begun in 1377, is surrounded by an arcade supported by white-marble columns with traces of polychromy on their stalactite capitals; in the center there is a fountain with 12 lions. This court gives access to the Sala de las Dos Hermanas, with a roof formed of stuccoed vaulting; to the Sala de los Reyes, decorated with stalactites; and to the Sala de los Abencerrajes. The Museo Arqueológico de la Alhambra contains the Alhambra Vase, the finest example of Hispano-Moorish ceramics. Other Moslem buildings in the city include the Casa del Cabildo Antiguo (the former Moslem madrasah, or college), with an octagonal Moorish dome and a minaret, and the Dār al-Horra, the palace of the princesses.

The Cathedral was begun in Gothic style (apse) by Enrique Egas, continued in Renaissance style by Diego de Siloe (beginning in 1528), and finished in 1703; the façade is by Alonso Cano (1667). The interior has a nave and four aisles with chapels between the buttresses; the circular Capilla Mayor has sculpture by Alonso Cano and marble pulpits by Francisco Hurtado Izquierdo (1713). Adjoining the Cathedral is the Capilla Real (Royal Chapel), which is an earlier structure (1505–21) designed by Enrique Egas and built as the pantheon of Ferdinand and Isabella; of note are the monument to the Catholic Monarchs by the Florentine Domenico di Alessandro Fancelli (1517), the monument to Felipe I and Juana by Bartolomé Ordóñez (1526), the *reja* made by Master Bartolomé de Jaén, and the main altarpiece by Felipe Bigarny (Vigarny; de Borgoña; 1520–22). The Museo de la Capilla Real, in the sacristy of the chapel, has canvases (from Isabella's collection) by Rogier van der Weyden, Hans Memling, Dirk (Thierry) Bouts, Botticelli, and Pedro Berruguete. Also adjoining the Cathedral is the Sagrario, a parish church (18th cent.) designed by Francisco Hurtado Izquierdo. Other churches include S. Jerónimo, by Jacopo Torni (l'Indaco; also Florentín) and Diego de Siloe; S. José, with a Moorish minaret (10th cent.) and sculpture by Siloe and José de Mora; S. Antonio Abad, with sculpture by Pedro de Mena; Nuestra Señora de las Angustias, with a baroque *camarín*, or niche (1712) on the wall behind the main altar; and S. Domingo, with the *camarín* of the Virgen del Rosario (1726) in Granadine late baroque style. The church of the Cartuja has a ciborium (1704) by Hurtado Izquierdo and a rococo sacristy; the church (1737–59) of the Hospital de S. Juan de Dios has a rich baroque façade.

Outstanding among the secular edifices built after the reconquest is the Palacio de Carlos V (16th cent.), which adjoins the Alhambra; designed by Pedro Machuca in the Italian Renaissance style, it has a circular courtyard; the upper floor houses the Museo Provincial de Bellas Artes, with sculpture and paintings of the Andalusian school. Other notable post-reconquest buildings are the Hospital Real de Dementes (1504); the Casa de los Tiros (16th cent.); the Curia, with a Doric-columned courtyard (1534) and painted decoration; the Cancillería (1587), the former law courts, now the Audiencia; and the Casa de Castril, with a Renaissance façade (1539), which houses the Museo Arqueológico Provincial (prehistoric, Iberian, Roman, Visigothic, and Moorish collections).

BIBLIOG. F. Pí y Margall, Granada, Jaén, Málaga y Almería, Barcelona, 1885; M. Gómez-Moreno, Guía de Granada, Granada, 1892; A. Gallego Burín, Los Menas, los Moras y los Roldanes, AEAA, I, 1925, pp. 323–31; M. Gómez-Moreno, En la capilla real de Granada, AEAA, I, 1925, pp. 245–88; F. Henriquez de Jorquera, Anales de Granada (ed. A. Marin Ocete), 2 vols., Granada, 1934; D. Angulo Iñiguez, Miniaturistas y pintores granadinos del Renacimiento, BRAH, CXVI, 1945, pp. 141–82; A. Gallego y Burín, Guía de Granada, 2d ed., 2 vols., Granada, 1946; M. Gómez-Moreno, Monumentos arquitectonicos de la provincia de Granada, Misc. H. Arte y Arqueol., I, 1949, pp. 347–90; R. C. Taylor, Francisco Hurtado and His School, AB, XXXII, 1950, pp. 25–61; L. Torres Balbás, La Alhambra y el Generalife, Madrid, 1950; F. Prieto-Moreno, Los jardines de Granada, Madrid, 1952; A. Gallego y Burín, La Capilla Real de Granada, Madrid, 1952; A. Gallego y Burín, Nuevos datos sobre la Capilla Real, BSEE, LVII, 1953, pp. 9–116; H. E. Wethey, Discípulos granadinos de Alonso Cano, AEArte, XXVII, 1954, pp. 25–34; F. P. Bargebuhr, The Alhambra Palace of the 11th Century, Warburg, XIX, 1956, pp. 192–258; A. Gallego y Burín, El barroco granadino, Madrid, 1956; E. E. Rosenthal, A Renaissance "Copy" of the Holy Sepulchre, JSAH, XVII, 1958, pp. 2–11; J. Lavalleye, Considerations sur les primitifs flamands conservés à la Capilla Real de Grenade, B. Classe Beaux-Arts Acad. royale de Belgique, XLI, 1959, pp. 21–29; S. Alcolea Gil, Granada, Barcelona, 1960; M. Antequera, The Alhambra and the Generalife (trans. C. Taylor), Granada, 1961; A. Gallego y Burín, Granada, Madrid, 1961; E. E. Rosenthal, The Cathedral of Granada: A Study in the Spanish Reniassance, Princeton, 1961; A. Gallego Morell, ed., Casa de los Tiros, Granada, 1962; A. C. Taylor, La sacristía de la Catuja de Granada y sus autores, AEArte, XXXV, 1962, pp. 135–72; A. Gallego y Burín, La Alhambra, Granada, 1963. See also the numerous articles of L. Torres Balbás in Al-Andalus, 1933 ff., and elsewhere.

Guadix (Granada). A town of ancient origin, Guadix was the Roman Acci. There are remains of the 9th-century walls, with square towers, and of the 10th-century Alcazaba. The Cathedral was influenced by the one in Granada; begun by Diego de Siloe in 1549, the building was completed (1710–96) by Vicente Acero and Gaspar Cayón; the façade, with a strong tower, is baroque. Of note in the interior are the Capilla de S. Torcuato, on a round plan, and the pulpits by Torcuato Ruiz del Peral (1737). The Church of S. Ana has a Mudejar ceiling; the Church of Santiago has a plateresque portal (1540).

BIBLIOG. A. Gallego y Burín, El barroco granadino, Madrid, 1956.

Huelva. Probably founded by the Phoenicians, Huelva occupies the site of the Roman Onuba. The Church of S. Pedro, with traces of a former mosque, is in Mudejar style, with later alterations (1772). The baroque Cathedral, the church of the former Convent of la Merced, has an unusual façade (1605). There are a relief of the Circumcision by Juan Martínez Montañés and paintings by Francisco Pacheco in the Church of S. Francisco (16th cent.). The Sanctuary of Nuestra Señora de la Cinta has fine *artesonados*; in the Church of la Immaculada Concepción (16th cent.) are paintings by Zurbarán and fine choir stalls. The Museo Arqueológico Provincial contains exhibits of prehistoric and Roman artifacts. Nearby are ruins of an aqueduct, probably from the Moslem period.

Jaén. Important during the Roman epoch as Aurinx, or Auringis, Jaén was later the capital of the Moorish principality of Jayyan. Moorish baths of the 11th century remain. The Castillo de S. Catalina, originally Moorish, was rebuilt in the 13th century. The Arco de S. Lorenzo has a chapel (15th cent.) with Moorish decoration. The Cathedral, constructed on the site of an ancient mosque, was begun at the end of the 15th century, continued by Andrés de Vandelvira from 1548, and finished in 1691 with a façade by Eufrasio López de Rojas. The nave and side aisles are of equal height; the elliptical ciborium is by Ventura Rodríguez (1764). The choir stalls date from about 1520; the altarpiece of S. Pedro de Osma is by Pedro Machuca (1546). In the Mudejar Church of S. Andrés is the Santa Capilla (1517), with a beautiful *reja* by Master Bartolomé (16th cent.). S. Ildefonso (14th cent.) has a portal by Vandelvira. The Gothic Church of la Magdalena contains a Crucifixion (16th cent.) attributed to Jacopo Torni (l'Indaco, also Florentín). In the convent of the Bernardines are canvases by Angelo Nardi.

BIBLIOG. N. Sentenach, Tenebrario en la catedral de Jaén, BSEE, I, 1893–94, pp. 88–90; M. Gómez-Moreno, Sillería de coro de la catedral de Jaén, AE, XXVI, 3, 1941, pp. 3–6; R. Ortega y Sagristá, Alonso Barba: Maestro mayor de la catedral de Jaén, Paisaje, VIII, 1951, pp. 121–24; L. González López, El Museo Provincial de Bellas Artes, Paisaje, IX, 1952, pp. 417–21; J. Chamarro Lozano, Guía artística y monumental de la ciudad de Jaén, Jaén, 1954; R. Ortega y Sagristá, La capilla de los Maya de Santa María Magdalena de Jaén, B. Inst. Estudios Gienenses, I, 1954, pp. 109–16; F. Pinero Jiménez and J. Martínez Romero, La catedral de Jaén, Jaén, 1954; R. Palomino Gutiérrez, Guía y planos de Jaén y provincia, Jaén, 1955; S. de Morales, Castillos y murallas del Santo Reino de Jaén, Jaén, 1959; J. Hernández Perera, La Sagrada Familia de P. Machuca en la catedral de Jaén, AEArte, XXXIII, 1960, pp. 79–81.

Jerez de la Frontera (Cádiz). The ancient Ceret of the Visigoths, Jerez was a Moorish stronghold until the 13th century. There are remains of the Roman walls near the Alcázar, a quadrangular fortress with two towers (the octagonal one is from the 15th cent.) that includes a chapel (13th cent.), Moorish baths, and a Renaissance palace. The collegiate church (S. Salvador) preserves Gothic elements from the earlier (13th cent.) building; the present edifice was begun by Diego Moreno Meléndez (1695) and finished by Torcuato Cayón de la Vega (1755). The Gothic Church of S. Miguel (ca. 1430) has a neoclassic façade (1672-1701) and a tower by Moreno Meléndez; the main altarpiece is by Juan Martínez Montañés (1625) and José de Arce. The portals of the 13th-century Church of Santiago are late Gothic. The Church of S. Dionisio has a tower with Mudejar decoration. The Casa del Cabildo Viejo, in Renaissance style, was built by Andrés de Ribera and others in 1575; here is housed the Colección Arqueológica Municipal, with Roman remains and a Greek helmet of the 7th century B.C. Notable among the many old mansions is the Renaissance Casa de Ponce de León. Near the town stands the Cartuja, founded toward the end of the 15th century; in ruins from 1835 to 1949, it has now been restored. Of note are the main portal, by Andrés de Ribera (1571); the Gothic church, with a baroque façade (1667); the Gothic cloister; and the Renaissance portal of the refectory.

Bibliog. L. M. Cabello Lapiedra, La Cartuja de Jerez, BSEE, XXVI, 1918, pp. 241-54; F. Giménez Placer, La labor de Montañes en el retablo de San Miguel de Jerez, AEArte, XIV, 1940-41, pp. 517-41; F. Giménez Placer, Montañes y Arce en el retablo de San Miguel de Jerez, AEArte, XIV, 1940-41, pp. 345-64; M. Esteve Guerrero, Jerez de la Frontera: Guía oficial de arte, 2d ed., Jerez de la Frontera, 1952; H. Sancho de Sopranis, El retablo mayor de San Marcos de Jerez, Arch. hispalense, XVII, 1952, pp. 141-53; M. Gómez-Moreno, La restauración de la Cartuja de Jerez, Academia, II, 1953, pp. 79-80; H. Sancho de Sopranis, La capilla capitular de la Concepción de la iglesia del convento de San Francisco el Real de Jerez de la Frontera, 1739-1777, Jerez de la Frontera, 1962.

Málaga. Founded by the Phoenicians as Malaca, it was colonized by the Carthaginians and later conquered by the Romans. In the 8th century it came under Moorish rule, which lasted until 1487. The city lies at the foot of a hill surmounted by the ruins of the Castillo de Gibralfaro (of Phoenician origin but rebuilt by Yūsuf I in the 14th cent.), which is joined by remains of a wall to the Alcazaba, an 11th-century Moorish fortress built on earlier ruins (restored). In the restored rooms of the Alcazaba palace is housed the Museo Arqueológico Provincial. The marketplace, built on the site of the old Moorish arsenal, preserves a horseshoe-shaped white-marble portal (1333-54). The Cathedral was begun in 1528 and finished in the 18th century, with the intervention of Diego de Siloe and Andrés de Vandelvira (16th cent.), José de Bada (1722), and Antonio Ramos (1755). Of note in the interior are the choir stalls, by Pedro de Mena (1658); the 16th-century altarpiece of S. Bárbara; and an altarpiece by Juan de Villanueva; there are also paintings and sculptures from the 16th and 17th centuries. The adjoining Church of the Sagrario has a late Gothic portal; within are some Castilian plateresque altarpieces. The Church of the Virgen de la Victoria has a baroque camarín (1693). The Church of S. Felipe Neri is by Ventura Rodríguez (1778). The Palacio Episcopal is by Antonio Ramos (1776) and the Aduana (Customs House) by M. Martín Rodríguez (1787). The Museo Provincial de Bellas Artes exhibits sculpture and paintings from the 16th and 17th centuries; it also has a good modern-painting collection.

Bibliog. M. Bolea y Sintes, Descripción de la catedral de Málaga, Málaga, 1894; A. Murillo, Museo Provincial de Bellas Artes de Málaga, Málaga, 1933; F. J. Sánchez Cantón, Pinturas y esculturas de colecciones madrileñas, Madrid, 1943; J. Remboury, La Alcazaba de Málaga, Málaga, 1945; J. Temboury and F. Chueca Goitia, José Martín de la Aldehuela y sus obras en Málaga, AE, XXIX, 1945, pp. 37-57, XXXI, 1947, pp. 7-19; S. Giménez Reyna, Memoria arqueológica de la Provincia de Málaga hasta 1946, Madrid, 1947; A. Llordén, Los maestros plateros malagueños de los siglos XVI-XVII, Málaga, 1947; A. Bueno Muñoz, El libro de Málaga, Málaga, 1950; A. Llordén, El insigne maestro escultor Fernando Ortiz, Ciudad de Dios, CLXIV, 1952, pp. 579-602, CLXV, 1953, pp. 312-44; H. E. Wethey, Juan Niño de Guevara, Academia, II, 1953, pp. 135-42; J. Temboury, La orfebrería religiosa en Málaga, Málaga, 1954; A. Llordén, El ingeniero y escultor granadino Pedro de Mena y Medrano, Ciudad de Dios, CLXVIII, 1955, pp. 313-76; F. Percheles, Las calles de Málaga, Málaga, 1955; A. Llordén, El tabernáculo de la Santa Iglesia catedral malagueña, Gibralfaro, VII, 1957, pp. 3-16; D. Vázquez Otero, Castillos y paisajes malagueños, Madrid, 1960; L. Torres Balbás, La Alcazaba y la catedral de Málaga, Madrid, 1960; A. Llordén, Arquitectos y canteros malagueños, Avila, 1962.

Medina az-Zahra (Córdoba). The remains of the palace (begun by 'Abd-ar-Rahmān III in 936, continued by Ḥakam II, and abandoned in 1011) consist of a complex of buildings arranged in terraces.

Excavations have permitted the restoration of two pavilions and several halls. The small museum exhibits fragments of columns and mosaics and artifacts found on the site.

Bibliog. R. Jiménez Amigo et al., Excavaciones en Medina az-Zahra (Córdoba), 2 vols., Madrid, 1924-26; R. Velázquez Bosco, Medina Azahara, Madrid, 1924; M. Ocaña Jiménez, Obras de al-Ḥakam II en Madīnat al-Zahrā', Al-Andalus, VI, 1941, pp. 157-68; R. Castejón Martínez de Arrizala, Excavaciones del plan nacional en Medina Azahara, Madrid, 1945; L. Torres Balbás, Excavaciones en Madīnat al-Zahrā', Al-Andalus, XI, 1946, pp. 439-42; L. Torres Balbás, La mezquita de Córdoba y las ruinas de Madinat al-Zahra, Madrid, 1960.

Los Millares (Almería). Located on a hill surrounded on three sides by the Andarax River, the remains of the prehistoric settlement after which the Los Millares culture has been named, include sections of the surrounding wall and numerous dwellings and cisterns. Farther up the hill are remains of large dolmenlike collective tombs with central and secondary chambers and long dromos, often sectioned off. The culture of the village, of neolithic type, can be traced chronologically from the last centuries of the 3d millennium to the first centuries of the 2d millennium B.C.

Bibliog. P. Bosch y Gimpera, Etnología de la península ibérica, Barcelona, 1932, passim; G. V. Leisner, Die Megalithgräber der iberischen Halbinsel, I, Berlin, 1943; A. del Castillo, in R. Menéndez Pidal, Historia de España, I, 1, Madrid, 1947, pp. 531-97 (bibliog.); A. Almagro Basch and A. Arribas, Avance de la primera campaña de excavaciones en los Millares, Actas IV Cong. Int. de Ciencias Prehistóricas y Protohistóricas (1954), Saragossa, 1956, pp. 419-26; E. Castaldi, EAA, s.v.

Niebla (Huelva). The surrounding wall, Moorish for the most part, is almost completely preserved, although some sections are in ruins; it has square towers and fine gates. The Gothic-Mudejar Church of S. María de la Granada (13th cent., reconstructed 15th cent.) has a Mozarabic horseshoe-arched doorway from the earlier 10th-century building. The Church of S. Martín shows Almohad influences in the horseshoe arches that separate the nave from the flanking aisles. The façade of the Ayuntamiento is Gothic-Mudejar.

Bibliog. J. P. Droop, Excavations at Niebla . . ., Ann. Archaeol. and Anthr., XII, 1925, pp. 175-206; J. Hernández Díaz, La ruta de Colón las torres del Condado de Niebla, Madrid, 1946.

Osuna (Sevilla). The remains of the Roman Urso are scarce and poorly explored, but many examples of native sculpture from the 1st and 2d centuries B.C. have been found. The Renaissance collegiate church, with the adjacent Capilla del Sto Sepulcro and the Patio de Capellán, dates from 1534; in the church is a Crucifixion by Jusepe de Ribera. The Church of S. Domingo (1531) contains a Renaissance altarpiece by Antonio Alfián (1564). The bell tower of the Church of la Merced is by Alonso Ruiz Florindo (1767-75). In the vicinity is a Roman necropolis (Cuevas de Osuna).

Bibliog. A. Engel and P. Paris, Une forteresse ibérique à Osuna (fouilles de 1903), Nouv. arch. des missions scientifiques et littéraires, XIII, 1906, pp. 357-491; R. Grosse, RE, s.v.; A. D'Ors, Epigrafía iurídica de la España Romana, Madrid, 1953, passim; A. García y Bellido, in R. Menéndez Pidal, Historia de España, I, 3, Madrid, 1954, pp. 541-57, 586-88.

Peal de Becerro (Jaén). Here is located the necropolis of the Iberian city of Tugia (6th-3d cent. B.C.), which later was conquered by the Romans. Among the tombs is a large one with five chambers.

Bibliog. J. Cabré Aguiló, Arquitectura hispánica: El sepulcro de Toya, AEAA, I, 1925, pp. 73-101.

Priego de Córdoba (Córdoba). The square castle, with towers in the corners and on the sides, is of the Moorish epoch, with late additions. The town is noted for its baroque churches: the Sagrario of the Church of la Asunción by F. X. A. Pedraxas (1784), to whom are also attributed the Sagrario of the Church of S. Pedro and the Chapel of S. Nicasio (generally called "La Aurora"; 1771); the Church of Nuestra Señora de las Mercedes (1775); S. Francisco (1771), with an interesting façade; and the Church of Nuestra Señora de las Angustias (1783).

Bibliog. R. C. Taylor, Francisco Hurtado and His School, AB, XXXII, 1950, pp. 25-61; D. Angulo Iñíguez, El castillo de Priego de Córdoba, Real Acad. Córdoba, XXIV, 1952, pp. 322-27.

Puerto de Santa María (Cádiz). The Castillo de S. Marcos has a fortified church that preserves Moorish elements. The Church of Nuestra Señora de los Milagros, rebuilt at the end of the 15th century and again in the 17th century, has a portal (the so-called "Puerta del Sol") of the school of Diego de Siloe. The Church of S. Francisco

ontains a baroque altarpiece, as does the domed church of the Capuchin convent. There are a number of palaces and patrician mansions,
mainly baroque, such as the Palacio del Marqués de Villa Real de
Purullena.

BIBLIOG. L. Torres Balbás, La mezquita de Al-Qanatir y el santuario
de Alfonso el Sabio en el Puerto de Santa Maria, Al-Andalus, VII, 1942,
p. 417–37; H. Sancho de Sopranis, Charles de Valera, Hispania, XI, 1952,
p. 413–540; H. Sancho de Sopranis, Notas y documentos para la historia
de la iglesia del Señor San Miguel, convento de San Francisco Observante
del Puerto de Santa Maria, Arch. ibero-américano, XIII, 1953, pp. 441–504.

Ronda (Málaga). The Roman Arunda, Ronda is located in an
almost impregnable position in the mountains. Divided in two parts
by a deep gorge (known as El Tajo), the town retains its old Moorish
quarter, with narrow and winding streets, in the southern part. There
are remains of the Alcazaba, the Moorish fortress that was destroyed
in the 19th century, and the Arco del Cristo and the Puerta de Almo-
abar with horseshoe arches. Other noteworthy remains of Moorish
structures include the 14th-century baths, with three vaulted chambers; the minaret that was incorporated in the destroyed Church of
S. Sebastián; and the Casa del Rey Moro (11th cent., restored), with
terraced gardens. The Church of S. María la Mayor (16th–17th cent.)
was built over an old mosque, from which there remain the mihrab
and the minaret; the richly decorated apse is modeled on the one in
the Cathedral in Málaga. The Church of la Encarnación dates from
the 16th century. Of note are the Plaza de Toros (1784) and the Puente
Nuevo (1740–88), a bridge by José Martín de Aldehuela. The Casa
de Mondragón has a Renaissance façade and two galleried patios.
Near the town, at Ronda la Vieja, are the ruins of the Roman city
of Acinipo, with an amphitheater and a circus.

BIBLIOG. J. Cascales y Muñoz, Una excursión desde Sevilla, BSEE,
IV, 1896–97, pp. 113–16; A. Palomeque Torres, Notas antiguas y modernas
sobre las ruinas del teatro romano di Acinipo (Ronda la Vieja), AEA, XVI,
1943, pp. 220–27; L. Torres Balbás, La acrópolis musulmana de Ronda, Al-
Andalus, IX, 1944, pp. 449–81.

Santiponce (Sevilla). The Monastery of S. Isidoro del Campo,
founded in 1291 and built in the 14th century, has two Gothic churches
of unequal height joined by an arch contiguous with the two apses
and having a single transept. One of these churches has a main altarpiece of wood (1613–19) by Juan Martínez Montañés, who also made
the effigies (1609) to replace the original statues on the tombs of the
founders; the other church has a Mudejar portal. The Patio de los
Muertos is in Mudejar style and contains mural paintings (15th–16th
cent.). The Patio de los Evangelistas has frescoes in grisaille. Near
the village are the ruins of the Roman Italica, founded by Scipio
Africanus in 206 B.C. There are remains of the walls, with a gate;

a large amphitheater (1st–2d cent. A.D.); a theater; two baths from
Hadrian's era (the so-called "Baños de la Reina Mora" and "Los
Palacios"); and several houses with mosaics.

BIBLIOG. M. Wegner, Italica, Gymnasium, LXI, 1954, pp. 427–38
(bibliog.); A. García y Bellido, Colonia Aelia Augusta (Italica), Madrid,
1960; A. García y Bellido, EAA, s.v. Italica.

Sevilla. The ancient Hispalis, the city is of Iberian origin; it was
conquered by the Phoenicians, the Greeks, the Carthaginians, and
the Romans. A prosperous center during the five centuries of Moorish
domination (712–1248), Sevilla flourished artistically under the rule
of the Almohads, beginning in 1146. Extant from the Moorish period
are sections of the walls; the Torre de la Plata and the Torre del Oro
(1220); the Patio de los Naranjos, adjoining the Cathedral (once the
courtyard of the ancient mosque); the Giralda (1184–98), the minaret
from the same mosque; and sections of the Alcázar (see below). The
Cathedral, begun in 1401 and consecrated in 1506, owes its plan (nave
and four aisles — with side aisles — that extend beyond the transept;
square east end with a small apse) and its great size (ca. 400 by 250
ft.) to its having been erected on the site of the mosque. It has nine
portals, some with terra-cotta sculptures by Lorenzo Mercadante
(1453) and Pedro Millán (ca. 1500). In the apse, behind the Capilla
Mayor, is the Capilla Real, finished in 1575, which contains a silver
reliquary (1717) of S. Fernando. The stained-glass windows date
from the 16th to the 19th century, the earliest being by Cristóbal
Alemán (1504), Arnao de Vergara, and Vicente Menardo. The
coro has a screen by Francisco de Salamanca (1519) and Gothic-
Mudejar choir stalls by Nufro Sánchez and Pieter Dancart (1475–
78). The Capilla Mayor has a reja (1518–33) by Francisco de Salamanca and Sancho Muñoz, pulpits by Francisco de Salamanca
(1531), and a carved altarpiece begun by Pieter Dancart in 1482.
Among works of interest in the chapels are numerous wood carvings
and paintings (15th–17th cent.): a statue of the Virgen del Pilar
by Pedro Millán (ca. 1500), an altarpiece by Ferdinand Sturm
(Hernando Sturmio; 1555), a painting of St. James by Juan de las
Roelas (1609), Murillo's St. Anthony (1656), the Espousals of the Vir-
gin by Juan Valdés Leal (1667), the panel paintings of the Altar del
Nacimiento (1555) and the Altar de la Concepción (or de la Gamba,
1561) by Luis de Vargas, panel paintings by Pedro de Campaña
(Peter de Kempener, 1555) in the Capilla del Mariscal, an Immaculate
Conception by Juan Martínez Montañés, and a terra-cotta relief by
Andrea della Robbia. Notable sepulchers are those of Gonzalo de
Mena (15th cent.), Cardinal Juan de Cervantes (by Lorenzo Mer-
cadante; 1458), and Cardinal Hurtado de Mendoza (by Domenico di
Alessandro Fancelli; 1509). In the Sacristía de los Cálices, designed by
Diego de Riaño (1529), are a Crucifixion, the masterpiece of Juan
Martínez Montañés (1603); panel paintings by Juan Núñez (15th

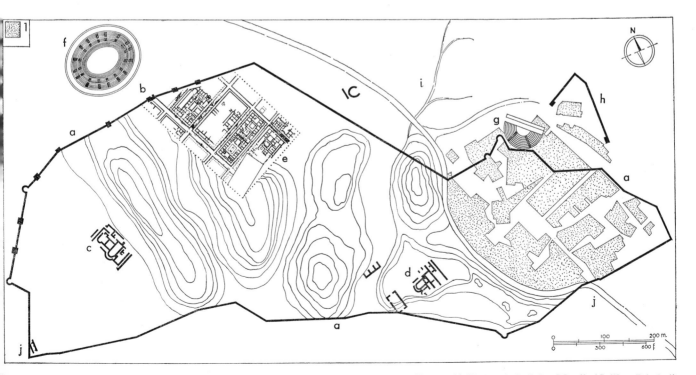

Santiponce and ancient Italica, plan. Key: (1) Modern town. Roman remains: (a) Walls; (b) gate; (c) "Baños de la Reina Mora"; (d) "Los Palacios";
(e) excavated area; (f) amphitheater; (g) theater; (h) pier of river port(?); (i, j) pagan and Christian necropolises (from A. García y Bellido, 1960).

cent.) and Alejo Fernández (16th cent.); and canvases by Murillo, Valdés Leal, Zurbarán, Luis Tristán, Francisco Reina, and Goya. Of note in the Sacristía Mayor are the sculptured doors by Master Guillén (1548); the Tenebrario (1559–62), a bronze candelabrum designed by Hernán Ruiz and executed by Bartolomé Morel and Pedro Delgado; and a silver monstrance by Juan de Arfe (1580–87). The Sala de Ornamentos contains an extensive collection of embroideries (16th–19th cent.), and in the anteroom of the chapter house are choir books (15th–17th cent.) and illuminated manuscripts. The chapter house (1530–92), on an elliptical plan, is decorated with white-marble reliefs and has works by Murillo. On one side of the Patio de los Naranjos is the Biblioteca Colombina, containing the manuscripts of Christopher Columbus, and on the other side is the Sagrario (17th cent.; now a parish church), which contains an altarpiece with sculpture by Pedro Roldán. Other churches include S. Ana (1280), with a Romanesque portal and panel paintings by Pedro de Campaña, Alejo Fernández, and Sturm (1553); S. Vicente (14th cent.), with a Deposition by the sculptor Andrés de Ocampo (1603); S. Isidoro (14th cent.), with a main altarpiece by Juan de las Roelas (1613); Omnes Sancti and S. Marcos, both with Mudejar towers; S. Andrés

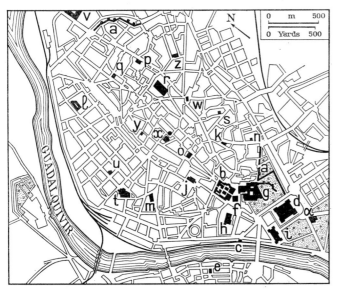

Sevilla, plan of city center. Monuments: (a) Roman walls; (b) Cathedral; (c) Torre del Oro; (d) Fábrica de Tabacos; (e) S. Ana; (f) Lonja; (g) Alcázar; (h) Hospital de la Caridad; (i) Palacio de S. Telmo; (j) Ayuntamiento; (k) Convent of la Madre de Dios; (l) S. Clara; (m) S. María Magdalena; (n) S. María la Blanca; (o) S. Salvador; (p) S. Luis; (q) Omnes Sancti; (r) Casa de las Dueñas; (s) Casa de Pilatos; (t) Museo de Bellas Artes; (u) S. Vicente; (v) Hospital de la Sangre; (w) S. Catalina; (x) University; (y) S. Andrés; (z) Convent of S. Paula; (a) to Museo Arqueológico.

(14th–15th cent.), with works by Alonso Cano, Gaspar Núñez Delgado, and Alonso Vázquez; S. Pedro, with a fine bell tower; and S. Catalina, with beautiful *artesonados* and a baroque Capilla del Sacramento. The Church of S. María la Blanca, a synagogue until 1391 and rebuilt as a baroque church in the 17th century, contains paintings by Luis de Vargas (1564) and Murillo; the Church of S. Salvador (1671–1712), built on the site of a mosque, incorporates elements of the ancient minaret in its tower. The Convent of S. Paula, founded in 1475, has a Gothic portal with terra-cotta decorations (16th cent.) by Francisco Niculoso (called Pisano) surrounding medallions of saints by Pedro Millán; the church has beautiful Mudejar *artesonados* (17th cent.), fine *azulejos*, and sculpture by Alonso Cano and Juan Martínez Montañés (1637). In the church of the Convent of la Madre de Dios are Mudejar *artesonados* (1562), sculptures by Jerónimo Fernández (Hernández), and a fine *reja* (1571). Socles of *azulejos* (1575), *artesonados*, and sculptures by Martínez Montañés decorate the church of the Convent of S. Clara; in the gardens stands the battlemented Torre de Don Fadrique (13th cent.). The polychrome statue called the "Cristo de la Expiración," by Francisco Antonio Gijón (1682), is in the small Church of el Patrocinio. The Church of S. María Magdalena, built 1692–1724 by Leonardo de Figueroa, contains sculptures of the 17th century, two paintings by Zurbarán, and Mudejar decoration in the Capilla de la Quinta Angustia.

The Alcázar preserves some elements from the Almohad epoch (defensive outer walls and towers, Puerta del León; 12th cent.), but it is mainly a Mudejar palace (1364–66) from the time of Pedro el Cruel. Outstanding are the façade (1364); the Patio de las Doncellas, with magnificent *azulejos*; the Salón de Embajadores (16th cent.);

and the Salón de Carlos V, with fine 16th-century ceilings. In the gardens is the Pabellón de Carlos V, built by Juan Hernández in 1543. The Casa de las Dueñas, or del Duque de Alba (15th cent.), contains a magnificent patio and a Gothic chapel with *azulejos*. The Casa de Pilatos (16th cent.) has an interesting patio with four Roman statues from Italica; the Casa de Arguijo has a painted ceiling (1601). The Hospital de la Caridad (1647) has paintings by Valdés Leal and Murillo. The Ayuntamiento, with notable plateresque ornamentation on the east façade, dates from the 16th century. The Archivo de Indias is located in the former Lonja, designed by Juan de Herrera. The Palacio de S. Telmo was designed by Leonardo de Figueroa (18th cent.). The Museo Arqueológico Provincial has prehistoric collections and a large group of Roman mosaics and statuary from Italica. The Museo Provincial de Bellas Artes, housed in the former Convent of la Merced, contains paintings of the Sevillian school.

Near the town is an aqueduct with 401 arches in two orders that was restored several times during the Middle Ages and in modern times; in the surrounding area there are noteworthy remains of dolmens from the Los Millares culture, the most important being that of Matarubilla.

Bibliog. *Antiquity*: A. Engel, Fouilles executées aux environs de Séville, RA, XVII, 1892, pp. 87–92; E. Saavedra and J. R. Mélida y Alinari Las murallas romanas de Sevilla, BRAH, L, 1907, pp. 438–41; J. R. Mélida y Alinari, El antiguo acueducto hispalense conocido con el nombre de "Caños de Carmona," BRAH, LVIII, 1911, pp. 518–22; J. Hernández Díaz, A. Sancho Corbacho, and F. Collantes de Teran, Catálogo arqueológico y artístico de la provincia de Sevilla, 4 vols., Seville, 1939–55; J. de Mata Carriazo, Las murallas de Sevilla, Arch. hispalense, XV, 1951, pp. 9–39; A. Schulten, RE, s.v. *Medieval and modern periods*: F. González de León Noticia artística y curiosa de todos los edificios públicos de Sevilla, Seville 1844; J. Gestoso y Pérez, Sevilla monumental y artística, 3 vols., Seville 1889–92; J. Gestoso y Pérez, Diccionario de artifices de Sevilla, 2 vols. Seville, 1899–1900; J. Gestoso y Pérez, Catálogo de las pinturas y esculturas del Museo de Sevilla, Madrid, 1912; B. Vega, El patio de la mezquita en El Salvador de Sevilla, BSEE, XXVI, 1918, pp. 18–21; C. López Martínez Arquitectos, pintores y escultores vecinos de Sevilla, Seville, 1928; P. Gutiérrez Moreno, La Capilla sevillana de la Quinta Angustia, AEAA, V 1929, pp. 233–45; C. López Martínez, El templo de la Madre de Dios de Sevilla, Seville, 1930; D. Angulo Iñiguez, Arquitectura mudéjar sevillana de los siglos XIII, XIV y XV, BSEE, XL, 1932, pp. 165–212, 245–93, XLI 1933, pp. 1–35; E. Lambert, L'art gothique à Séville, après la Reconquête RA, 5th Ser., XXXVI, 1932, pp. 155–65; L. Torres Balbás, Las torres de Oro y de la Plata en Sevilla, AEAA, XI, 1934, pp. 89–104; A. Camacho Baños, El templo de San Luis de Sevilla, Seville, 1935; J. Hernández Díaz, La Universidad hispalense y sus obras de arte, Madrid, 1942; L. Torres Balbás, Notas sobre Sevilla en la época musulmana, Al-Andalus, X, 1945 pp. 177–96; L. Torres Balbás, La primitiva mezquita mayor de Sevilla, Al-Andalus, XI, 1946, pp. 425–39; S. Montoto, La catedral y el Alcázar de Sevilla, Madrid, 1948; J. Guerrero Lovillo, Sevilla: Guía artística, Barcelona 1952; A. Martín de la Torre, Via crucis a la Cruz del Campo, Arch. hispalense, XVI, 1952, pp. 49–104; A. Sancho Corbacho, Arquitectura barroca sevillana del siglo XVIII, Madrid, 1952; F. Collantes de Teran, Los castillos del Reino de Sevilla, Arch. hispalense, XVIII, 1953, pp. 117–85; J. Guerrero Lovillo, La puerta de Córdoba en la cerca de Sevilla, Al-Andalus, XVIII, 1953, pp. 178–87; J. González Moreno, El convento de San Antonio de Padua de Sevilla, Arch. hispalense, XX, 1954, pp. 9–25; L. Torres Balbás, La torre de la iglesia de San Marcos de Sevilla, Al-Andalus, XIX, 1954, pp. 421–39; I. Turmo, Bordados y bordadores sevillanos, Seville, 1955; C. Fernández Chicarro El Museo Arqueológico Provincial de Sevilla, Madrid, 1957; J. González Moreno, Guía histórico-artística de la Casa de Pilatos, Seville, 1960; J. Romero y Murube, El Alcázar de Sevilla, Madrid, 1960.

Tarifa (Cádiz). The castle, finished in 960, preserves the original Moorish walls and towers, such as the Torre de Guzmán. The Church of S. María is built over an earlier mosque, utilizing Roman columns in its construction. Near the town are the remains of the Roman Bolonia, or Belo, which include sections of the wall (1st cent. B.C.) with two gates (one flanked by two columns), as well as a capitolium, with three identical small temples, a nymphaeum, a colonnaded street, numerous houses of Roman type, and fish-preservation works (all 1st–2d cent. A.D.).

Bibliog. R. Amador de los Rios, Lápida arábiga del castillo de Tarifa, BSEE, 1895–96, pp. 17–19; E. Hübner, RE, s.v.; P. Paris et al., Fouilles de Bolonia, Bordeaux, 1923; J. R. Mélida y Alinari, in R. Menéndez Pidal, Historia de España, II, Madrid, 1935, passim; M. Cagiano de Azevedo, I Capitolia nel mondo romano, MPontAcc, V, 1940, pp. 1–76 at 36; L. Crema, Architettura romana, Turin, 1959, p. 382; F. Bordejé, El milenario del castillo de Tarifa, B. Asociación española de amigos de los castillos, VIII, 1960, pp. 173–92.

Úbeda (Jaén). The town was a Moslem stronghold until 1234. The collegiate church (S. María de los Reales Alcázares; 13th cent.), with nave and two aisles, has fine *rejas* by Master Bartolomé (16th cent.); noteworthy are the façade (1615–46) and the Gothic cloister. Other churches include S. Clara, with a Mudejar portal; S. Pedro, of Romanesque origin; the Gothic S. Pablo (14th–15th cent.), with a 16th-century plateresque tower; El Salvador, designed by Diego le Siloe and executed in 1540 by Andrés de Vandelvira, with an altar-piece by Alonso Berruguete; and S. Nicolás de Bari, with a late Gothic south portal (1505) and a Renaissance west portal by Vandelvira (1566). There are good examples of Renaissance secular architecture: the Ayuntamiento (the former Casa de las Cadenas), the Palacio de Vela de los Cobos, with galleries and balconies, and the Hospital de Santiago (1562–75), all by Vandelvira; the Palacio de Mancera; the Casa de las Torres; and the Casa de los Salvajes.

BIBLIOG. J. R. Mélida y Alinari, El Hospital e iglesia de Santiago en Úbeda, BRAH, LXIX, 1916, pp. 33–38; M. Campos, Guía artística y histórica de Úbeda, Úbeda, 1928; M. Muro García, Úbeda monumental, Madrid, 1928; R. Martos López, Monumentos de Úbeda: La casa de las Torres, Úbeda, 1948; R. Martos López, La iglesia del Salvador, Úbeda, 1951; F. Chueca Goitia, Andrés de Vandelvira, Madrid, 1954; J. Molina Hipólito, Guía de Úbeda, Úbeda, 1959; J. Pasquau Guerrero, Admirable, ero . . . , Oretania, 7, 1961, pp. 19–21.

Canarias (Canary Islands). The archipelago, situated in the Atlantic Ocean, comprises seven islands: Gran Canaria, Tenerife, La Palma, Gomera, Lanzarote, Hierro, and Fuerteventura, divided into two provinces after 1927. The art of Canarias, which flourished in the 17th and 18th centuries, is mainly a reflection and adaptation of Andalusian and Portuguese stylistic trends.

BIBLIOG. J. de Viera y Clavijo, Historia general de las Islas Canarias, vols., Santa Cruz de Tenerife, 1950–52; C. Dervenn, Les Canaries, Paris, 1954; P. de Panthou, Iles canaries, Paris, 1954; J. Hernández Perera, Orfebrería de Canarias, Madrid, 1955; D. Martínez de la Peña y González, Las cubiertas de estilo portugués en Tenerife, AEArte, XXVIII, 1955, pp. 313–21; P. Tarquis Todavia, Juan de Miranda, Rev. de Historia, XXI, 1955, pp. 89–99; J. Lodwick, The Forbidden Coast, London, 1956; J. J. Martín González, La influencia de Montañés en Tenerife, AEArte, XXXII, 1959, pp. 322–24; M. Tarquis and A. Vizcaya, Documentos para la historia del arte en las Islas Canarias, I, La Laguna, 1959; E. Wustmann, Las Canarias, Radebeul, 1963.

La Laguna (Tenerife). The Cathedral (nave and four aisles) has a façade (1819) modeled on that in Pamplona; noteworthy are the numerous examples of goldwork in the treasury. The Church of la Concepción (nave and two aisles with Mudejar elements, 16th cent.) contains baroque choir and lecterns and, in the Capilla de S. Bartolomé (1714), fine Portuguese-style *artesonados*. The Universidad Vieja dates from the 17th century. The Palacio Episcopal (18th cent.) has a façade with reliefs and a patio. In the Palacio de los Nava Grimón is a ceiling in the Portuguese manner over the stairway.

BIBLIOG. J. Hernández Perera, Ventura Rodriguez y la fachada de la catedral de La Laguna, Las Ciencias, XXIII, 1958, pp. 697–705.

La Orotava (Tenerife). The Church of la Concepción, by A. de Llanera (1768), has a baroque façade; the interior (nave and two aisles) has composite capitals on the columns, barrel vaulting, and a lantern over the crossing. It contains a neoclassic sanctuary designed by Ventura Rodríguez and executed by the Genoese J. Gaggini (1823), a St. John the Evangelist by José Luján Pérez (18th cent.), and goldwork. The Church of S. Juan has a Dolorosa by Luján Pérez and a Scourging at the Pillar attributed to Luisa Roldán. Of note is the Casa de los Machado.

BIBLIOG. J. Hernández Perera, Planos de Ventura Rodríguez para la Concepción, Rev. de Historia, XVI, 1950, pp. 142–61.

Las Palmas (Gran Canaria). The Cathedral (S. Ana; 1497–1570), designed by Diego Alonso Montaude, was restored in 1781 and 1820, with the neoclassic façade of that epoch; the Gothic interior is stellar-vaulted. There are a Dolorosa and a Crucifix by Luján Pérez and some 18th-century goldwork by Damián de Castro and others. The churches of S. Domingo, S. Agustín, and S. Francisco have baroque sculpture by Luján Pérez. In the aristocratic Vegueta quarter are noteworthy patrician mansions (16th–18th cent.). The Museo Canario contains archaeological collections. The Museo Provincial de Bellas Artes, installed in the 15th-century Casa de Colón, has canvases from the 17th century and later.

BIBLIOG. J. Pérez de Barradas, El Museo Canario, Las Palmas, 1944; E. Marco Dorta, Planos y dibujos del Archivo de la catedral de Las Palmas, Las Palmas, 1946; E. Marco Dorta, Pedro de Llerena: arquitecto de la catedral, Rev. de Historia Canaria, XXIV, 1958, pp. 123–27; J. Hernández Perera, Sobre los arquitectos de la catedral de Las Palmas, 1500–70, Mus. Canario, 73–74, 1960, pp. 255–305.

Santa Cruz de Tenerife. The Church of la Concepción, reconstructed in 1652, has a nave with 18th-century *artesonados* and four aisles with side chapels. The Church of S. Francisco (1680, altered 18th cent.) has *artesonados*, as do the churches of the Orden Tercera

(1760) and el Pilar (1755). Of typically Canarian architecture is the Palacio de los Carta (1752), with Mudejar and Flemish elements. The Museo Municipal contains archaeological objects, as well as paintings by Bernardo Germán Llorente, Juan de Miranda, and Luis de la Cruz y Ríos.

BIBLIOG. J. Francés, Palacio de los Carta, Academia, 3d Ser., II, 1952, pp. 512–13; L. Diego Cuscoy, El libro de Tenerife, Santa Cruz de Tenerife, 1957.

Gibraltar. The town and fortress on the Rock of Gibraltar (anc. Calpe), which has been a British colony since 1713, have a military aspect. The Moorish castle was begun by Tariq in the 8th century. Of note are the Moorish baths (13th cent.) and the Torre de la Calahorra (1342–44), constructed by Sultan Abu Inan.

BIBLIOG. H. M. Field, Gibraltar, New York, 1888; L. Torres Balbás, The Moorish Baths at Gibraltar, Ann. J. Gibraltar Soc., 1930, pp. 54–57; L. Torres Balbás, Gibraltar, llave y guarda del reino de España, Al-Andalus, VII, 1942, pp. 168–216; J. C. de Luna, Historia de Gibraltar, Madrid, 1944; M. R. Edmonds, Guide to Tangier, Torremolinos, Gibraltar, 2d ed., Tangier, 1960.

Andorra. An independent state, Andorra is under the joint jurisdiction of France and the Bishop of Seo de Urgel (Spain). It occupies an area of 175 sq. mi. in the Pyrenees and its capital is Andorra la Viella. Throughout the state are small Romanesque churches with porticoes and bell towers. Noteworthy are S. Coloma, with a round tower (12th cent.); S. Miguel d'Engolasters; the belfry at Encamp; S. Romá de les Bons (1163); and S. Joan de Caselles (12th cent.), which is the best preserved.

BIBLIOG. D. de Bellmunt, L'Andorre et ses beautés, Toulouse, 1952; L. Capdevila, Libre d'Andorra, Barcelona, 1958; S. Deane, The Road to Andorra, London, 1960.

José GUDIOL

Illustrations: 15 figs. in text.

SPANISH AND PORTUGUESE ART. The development of Spanish and Portuguese art is inextricably linked to the history of the small Christian states in the north of the Peninsula. After the Christian reconquest, which began at the end of the 11th century, these states maintained their independence until the Catholic Monarchs united Spain in the last half of the 15th century. The towns in the southern part of the Peninsula also developed during the Middle Ages, but their growth stemmed from the Hispano-Moresque spirit and was determined by it. Although the Hispano-Moresque tradition was by then already in its decline, it left a profound mark on the art of the time and was to persist in the Mudejar style, which remained long after all Moslem influence had disappeared as a political power in the Peninsula (see MOORISH STYLE). When Spain and Portugal were securely established, expansion began in the vast territories of the Americas; these colonial manifestations are dealt with briefly in the final section of this article (see also AMERICAS: ART SINCE COLUMBUS and articles on individual countries).

In the 16th century, the art of the Iberian Peninsula entered a particularly brilliant phase, with many outstanding works. Nevertheless, the Peninsula had little influence in the formation and development of the various schools of art that prevailed in Europe. It would seem that its spirit, which is expressed with an unmistakable character in the arts, had a greater capacity for the absorption of outside influences than for the creation and diffusion of its own original concepts. (See also BAROQUE ART; EUROPEAN MODERN MOVEMENTS; GOTHIC ART; MOORISH STYLE; MOZARABIC ART; RENAISSANCE; ROMANESQUE ART.)

SUMMARY. I. Spain: The Romanesque (col. 307): *Architecture and sculpture; Painting.* The Gothic (col. 310): *Architecture; Sculpture; Painting.* The Hispano-Moresque (col. 314): *Caliphate period; Almohad period; Nasrid period; Mudejar style.* The Renaissance (col. 317): *Architecture; Sculpture; Painting; Minor arts.* The baroque (col. 324): *Architecture; Sculpture; Painting.* The neoclassic (col. 332): *Architecture; Sculpture; Painting; Minor arts.* The modern period (col. 335): *Architecture; Sculpture; Painting.* Diffusion of Spanish art (col. 338). II. Portugal: Architecture, sculpture, and painting (col. 339): *The Middle Ages; The 16th–20th century.* Minor arts (col. 342). III. Colonial manifestations (col. 343).

I. SPAIN. THE ROMANESQUE. *Architecture and sculpture.*
In Spain, Romanesque art evolved in the inaccessible mountain
regions in the north that were not affected by the Moslem
occupation; from these regions it extended to the areas that
were reclaimed for Christianity before the end of the 12th
century and in general remained confined to the area north

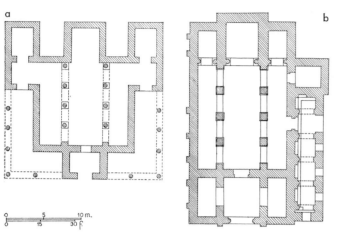

Spanish pre-Romanesque churches, plans. (*a*) Baños de Cerrato, S. Juan
Bautista, 7th cent., reconstructed plan (*from B. Bevan, 1938, p. 11*); (*b*)
Val de Dios, S. Salvador, 893 (*from Ars Hispaniae, II, 1947, p. 379*).

of the Tagus River. The Spanish Romanesque was the result
of impulses that had come from beyond the Pyrenees and had
fused with Visigothic, Mozarabic (q.v.), and Asturian artistic
expressions. Three centers in particular show a certain autonomy
in their artistic development; Catalonia, Aragon-Navarra, and
Castile-León-Galicia. The styles of the last two are especially
close, since both centers were traversed by the pilgrim route
to Santiago de Compostela.

Early Catalonian Romanesque showed strong Carolingian
influence (see CAROLINGIAN PERIOD). Its most notable monuments
are the monastery church of San Pedro de Roda (XII, PL. 209),
the 11th-century sculptures at San Genés les Fonts (Saint-
Genis-des-Fontaines; XI, PL. 311), Sureda (Sorède, Roussillon,
Church of S. Andrés), Besalú, and San Miguel de Fluviá,
and finally, the great 12th-century portal of Ripoll (XII, PL. 250).
The Lombard influence, which was to give unity to Catalonian
Romanesque until the end of the 12th century, had already
made itself felt in the 11th century; examples are S. Vicente
at Cardona (XII, PL. 210) and S. Clemente (1123) at Tahull
(Lérida). In the Church of S. Miguel de Cuxá (Saint-Michel,
Roussillon) and in those of San Juan de las Abadesas (Gerona;
FIG. 307), Serrabone, Elne, and Cabestany (Roussillon), and
Covet (Lérida), and in the cloisters of the monastery of San Cugat
de Vallés (Barcelona) are representative pieces of the sculpture
of the period. The cathedrals of Lérida and Tarragona (13th
cent.) are examples of late Catalonian Romanesque; they also
show adaptations of structural elements taken from Cistercian
monasteries.

Early Romanesque style in the Navarra-Aragon area is to
be found in the Pyrenees in several small churches showing
Mozarabic influences; it culminated in the monastery church
of San Salvador de Leyre (XII, PL. 209). The style was continued
in the Cathedral of Jaca (XII, PLS. 212, 248, FIG. 345), important
because of its quality and influence, and was further developed
in Loarre (FIG. 309; XII, PL. 234), Sos, Uncastillo, San Juan
de la Peña (FIG. 309), Pamplona, Huesca, Estella, Tudela
(FIG. 307), and elsewhere in many buildings of outstanding
architecture, ornamented by sculptures that were executed by
clearly identifiable masters. This group provides a link between
the great Toulouse school (XII, PL. 236) and that which evolved
in Castile, León, and Galicia during the 11th and 12th centuries
along the pilgrim route. The latter group's important monuments
are the churches at León (PL. 122; XII, PLS. 212, 248, FIG. 345),
Frómista (XII, PL. 211), and Santiago de Compostela itself
(XII, FIG. 342), with its Puerta de las Platerías (XII, PL. 249)
and Pórtico de la Gloria, the latter executed by Master Matthew

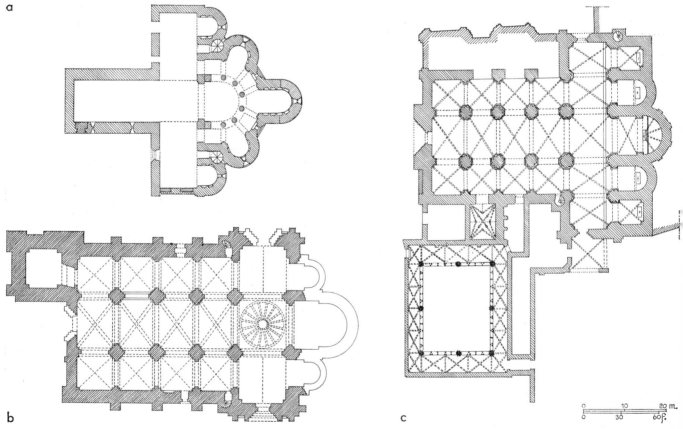

Spanish Romanesque churches, 12th cent., plans. (*a*) San Juan de las Abadesas, collegiate church, reconstruction of plan; (*b*) Zamora, Cathedral;
(*c*) Tudela, collegiate church (*from Ars Hispaniae, V, 1948, pp. 48, 262, 173*).

a   b   c

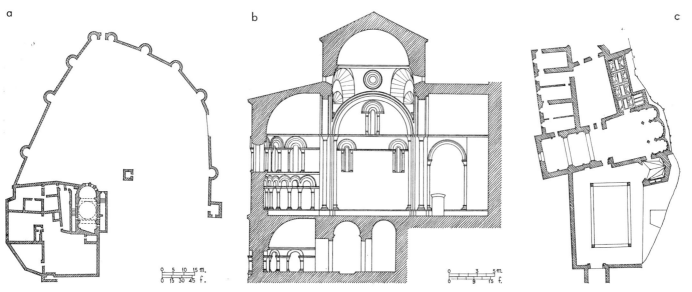

Spanish Romanesque building complexes, late 11th cent. Castle of Loarre; (*a*) general plan, (*b*) section of church (*from V. Lampérez y Romea, 1930, pp. 354, 355*); (*c*) San Juan de la Peña, monastery, plan (*from Ars Hispaniae, V, 1948, p. 138*).

(1189–1192). Other noteworthy monuments of the period are the monastery of S. Pedro de Arlanza, near Burgos, the imposing cloister of S. Domingo de Silos (11th–12th cent.; XII, PL. 257; XIV, PL. 465), the Santander group (at Cervatos, Castañeda, and Santillana), the church of Carrión de los Condes, the cathedrals of Zamora (PL. 117; FIG. 307) and Salamanca, and the collegiate church of Toro (XII, PL. 214) and the many churches in Burgos province; the Church of S. Domingo and the cloisters of the churches of S. Pedro and S. Juan de Duero at Soria, as well as the numerous churches in Soria province, many of them with the characteristic porticoed galleries that are also frequent in Segovia (XII, PL. 215); the center of Ávila, with its walls (PL. 118; XII, PL. 235) and its Basilica of S. Vicente (XII, PL. 215, FIG. 350); and finally, the Cámara Santa of Oviedo.

The sculpture of the Romanesque period was especially rich in crucifixes and images of the Virgin, including such fine examples as the Deposition from Erill la Vall (divided between Vich, Mus. Episcopal, and Barcelona, Mus. de Arte de Cataluña), the Majestad Batlló (Barcelona, Mus. de Arte de Cataluña), the Virgen de la Vega in the Old Cathedral of Salamanca, and the Virgins in the Cathedral of Toledo. Equally remarkable are the ivory sculptures such as the cross of Fernando I and Sancha (1063; XII, PL. 281) and the plaques (1070–90) of San Millán de la Cogolla. (See also ROMANESQUE ART, col. 455.)

Painting. Some magnificent examples of Romanesque painting have been preserved in Spain. In Catalonia, besides the early examples at Tarrasa (10th cent.) and S. Quirce in Pedret (11th cent.), there is a 12th-century group, including both wall paintings and panels, that combines traditional elements with Byzantine influences, probably introduced by artists traveling from Italy. There are splendid wall paintings from the churches of Tahull (S. Clemente and S. María) and Seo de Urgel (XII, PLS. 270–72), Bohí, Ginestarre de Cardós, Esterri de Aneu (S. María), and Sorpe (S. Pedro) and from the monastery of S. Pedro de Burgal near Escaló (all, Barcelona, Mus. de Arte de Cataluña), as well as from Osormort (Vich, Mus. Episcopal). The panels — altar frontals and baldachinos — include outstanding examples from Durro (XII, PL. 271), Tabérnoles and Aviá (S. María; both, Barcelona, Mus. de Arte de Cataluña), Torelló and Sagás near Vich (PL. 127), Espinelvas, and Ribas (XII, PL. 244). The Catalan Romanesque tradition continued into the 13th century. The altar frontal of Suriguerola (Barcelona, Mus. de Arte de Cataluña) dates from this period and contains some Gothic elements. The Romanesque in the Castile-León area includes the paintings in S. Baudilio (X,

PL. 196), and in the Church of Sta Cruz at Maderuelo (VII, PL. 375) and the Panteón de los Reyes series in S. Isidoro in León, the most important in Spain (XII, PL. 243).

THE GOTHIC. *Architecture.* Following the establishment of Cistercian architecture (e.g., the monasteries of Moreruela in León; Poblet; FIG. 312, and Santas Creus in Catalonia; see GOTHIC ART, col. 488), the development of the Gothic style in Spain during the 13th century pursued two courses: the first, evolved in the cathedrals of Ávila, Sigüenza (PL. 119; FIG. 311), and Cuenca in Castile, Túy in Galicia, and Ciudad Rodrigo in León, continued the Cistercian tradition, incorporating elements acquired through contacts beyond the Pyrenees; the other course developed as a result of the introduction of an advanced French Gothic style. The latter course is well exemplified in the Cathedral of Toledo (PL. 122; VI, PL. 305) and especially in the cathedrals of Burgos (VI, PL. 306, FIG. 491) and León (VI, PL. 304, FIG. 492), which were the work of Master Enrique (Henri), a Frenchman by birth. During the 14th century in Castile and León work was continued on constructions begun in the previous century, while in Catalonia buildings were constructed in the autonomous style of the Catalonian Gothic tradition. This style was simple almost to the point of functionalism, as can be seen in such notable buildings as the early church of the monastery of S. Domingo at Gerona (begun 1253); the monastery church of Pedralbes (1325); S. María del Pino (ca. 1322), S. María del Mar (1328), and the Chapel of S. Águeda (the former chapel of the royal palace; ca. 1310), in Barcelona; and the cathedrals of Barcelona (VI, FIG. 494) and Gerona (FIG. 311), the latter with a single very wide aisle (ca. 1385). Fine examples outside of Catalonia are the cathedrals of Palma de Mallorca (PL. 119; VI, PL. 308), Valencia, Huesca, Pamplona (PL. 119; VI, FIG. 493), and Vitoria (VI, PL. 305).

In the 15th century flamboyant Gothic became prevalent in Spain. The great Cathedral of Seville (PL. 123) was built, and German-Flemish influences were widespread. These influences, combined with the Mudejar tradition, gave rise to Gothic buildings with exuberant ornamentation, such as S. Pablo and S. Gregorio (VI, PL. 356) in Valladolid, S. María at Aranda de Duero, S. Juan de los Reyes in Toledo (IV, PL. 400), El Parral and Sta Cruz in Segovia, and the Carthusian monasteries of El Paular, near Madrid, and Miraflores in Burgos. It also produced sumptuous chapels in various cathedrals, such as the Chapel of Santiago in Toledo, the Condestable Chapel in Burgos (VI, PL. 306), and the Velez Chapel in Murcia, southern Spain. Secular buildings in the Gothic style include the *lonjas*

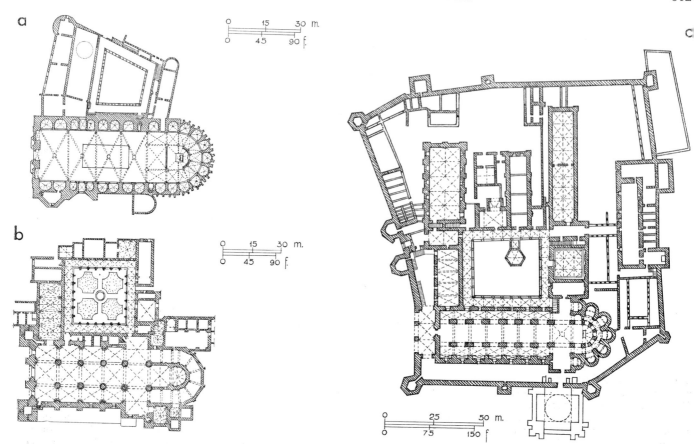

Spanish religious complexes, 12th–15th cent., plans. (a) Gerona, Cathedral; (b) Sigüenza, Cathedral, early 13th cent. (from Ars Hispaniae, VII, 1952, pp. 198, 55); (c) Poblet, monastery (from B. Bevan, 1938, p. 73).

(market halls, or exchanges) of Barcelona, Palma de Mallorca, and Valencia; the arsenal in Barcelona (PL. 121); public buildings such as the Ayuntamiento (town hall) and Palacio de la Generalidad (seat of the ancient Catalan parliament) in Barcelona; castles and fortifications such as those in Olite (Navarra), Bellver on Mallorca, and Manzanares el Real, near Madrid, and the Torres de Serranos, the old city gate of Valencia; and palatial residences such as the Palace of the Duques del Infantado in Guadalajara and the Casa del las Conchas in Salamanca. A prolongation of the Gothic style into the 16th century can be seen in the cathedrals of Segovia (VI, PL. 307) and Salamanca.

ARTISTS. Arnau Bargués, builder of the Ayuntamiento of Barcelona (1400) and the Palacio del Rey Martín at Poblet (F. P. Verrié, Arnau Bargués y sus obras, Divulgación histórica de Barcelona, IV, 1947, pp. 146–52). – Juan de Colonia (Hans von Cöln), d. 1481; active in Burgos ca. 1442, built the Cathedral's towers, various chapels also attributed to him. – Simón de Colonia (son of Juan), d. ca. 1511; active from 1480 to his death; chief work the Condestable Chapel in Burgos Cathedral (F. Arribas Arranz, Simón de Colonia en Valladolid, BSEAAV, V, 1934, pp. 153–66; M. Martínez Burgos, Colonias y Siloes, BIFG, XIV, 1956, pp. 144–63). – Pedro Compte, active at Valencia, where he completed Cathedral (1480) and built the Lonja de la Seda (1482–98). – Enrique Egas, renowned figure of end of 15th–beginning of 16th century, active at Toledo, Santiago de Compostela, Granada, and elsewhere (J. M. Azcárate, La labor de Egas en el Hospital Real de Santiago, Misc. Dr. D. Roggen, Antwerp, 1957, pp. 15–23). – Master Enrique (Henri), d. 1277, architect of cathedrals of Burgos and León. – Jaime Fabré (of Mallorca), master of works at Cathedral of Barcelona (1317–39). – Master Fruchel, d. 1192; began Cathedral at Ávila. – Juan Guas, d. 1496; son of the Lyonese Pedro Guas, active at Toledo (ca. 1453), Segovia, Guadalajara, Toledo, and elsewhere; completed fusion of Flemish flamboyant Gothic and Toledan Mudejar Gothic styles (A. Hernández, Juan Guas, maestro de obras de la Catedral de Segovia, BSEAAV, XIII, 1946–47, pp. 57–100; E. Garcia Chico, Juan Guas y la capilla del colegio de San Gregorio, BSEAAV, XVI, 1949–50, pp. 200–01; J. M. Azcárate, Sobre el origen de Juan Guas, AEArte, XXIII, 1950, pp. 255–56; J. M. Azcárate, La fachada del palacio del Infantado y

el estilo de Juan Guas, AEArte, XXIV, 1951, pp. 307–19; J. M. Azcárate, La obra toledana de Juan Guas, AEArte, XXIX, 1956, pp. 9–42; J. V. L. Brans, Juan Guas escultor, Goya, 36, 1960, pp. 362–67). – Master Martin, d. 1234; architect of Cathedral of Toledo. – Marc Safont, active at Barcelona (Palacio de la Generalidad, 1418–34). – Guillén (Guillermo) Sagrera, d. 1456; architect and sculptor, active 1397–1434; works include Puerta del Mirador of Cathedral of Palma, Lonja of Palma, and Hall of the Barons of Castel Nuovo in Naples (1452) (H. E. Wethey, Guillermo Sagrera, AB, XXI, 1939, pp. 44–60).

Sculpture. Sculpture was largely concentrated on the decoration of church doors and other portals and on tomb ornamentation. Splendid 13th-century groups of sculptures are to be found in the Cathedral of Burgos — on the Puerta del Sarmental (VI, PL. 354), with its tympanum by the Master of the Beau Dieu of Amiens — and that of León: the relief panels and the portal in the vestibule of the cloister, the statues on towers and, particularly, on the main portal with its "Virgen Blanca" (VI, PL. 355; attributed to Master Enrique), as well as the tympanums, archivolts, and doorjambs on this and other portals of the Cathedral.

French influence was combined with local Spanish developments in Castile and León and produced, at the end of the 13th century, such works as the funerary monuments in Villalcázar de Sirga (Palencia). This style persisted into the 15th century, when its composition became more involved. Catalonia produced a continuous line of masters, beginning in the late 13th century with Master Bartolomé, creator of the Virgin on the main portal of the Tarragona Cathedral, and continuing into the 14th century with Pedro Bonull (Bonhuyl, Bonncil; tomb of Jaime II and his wife, Blanche of Anjou, 1314, in Santas Creus), the master known as Aloy (retable of the Sastras Chapel in the Cathedral of Tarragona, 1368), Jaime Cascalls (retable of Corneilla-de-Conflent, 1345), and Pedro Moragues (tomb of Archbishop Lope Fernández de Luna, ca. 1381, in Zaragoza). In addition, a trend toward an Italianate style developed in the 14th century with the sarcophagus of S. Eulalia (Cathedral of Barcelona), the tomb of Archbishop Juan de Aragón (Cathedral of Tarragona), and the numerous altarpieces of the prolific Lérida group. The 14th century was a brilliant period also in Navarra and the Basque Provinces. Dating from this period are the sculptures on the Puerta Preciosa of the cloister of the Cathedral of Pamplona, the Epiphany group by J. Perut in the same cathedral, and the Olite, Vitoria, and La Guardia groups.

In Catalonia the work of Pedro Sanglada (Pere Ça-Anglada) marks the transition to the 15th century (e.g., figure on the tomb of S. Olegarius in the Cathedral of Barcelona). Prominent artists in the first half of the 15th century were Pedro Oller (retable of the Cathedral of Vich) and Pere Joan (decoration of the Palacio de la Generalidad in Barcelona and the altarpieces in the cathedrals of Zaragoza and Tarragona; VI, PL. 357). The Flemish influence began to penetrate Castile toward the middle of the 15th century. Outstanding works of this period are in the Cathedral of Toledo (the tombs of the De Luna family and the Puerta de los Leones; PL. 122), in Guadalupe (the tomb of Alonso de Velasco), and in Sigüenza (among several, the fine tomb of "El Doncel"; VI, PL. 357). For a brief time Lorenzo Mercadante of Brittany worked in Seville. All these works, however, were a mere prelude to the splendid heights reached at the end of the century with the sculptures in Toledo (VI, PLS. 355, 357), the altarpieces in the Carthusian monasteries of Burgos (PL. 124) and El Paular and in the Cathedral of Seville, and the choir stalls by Rodrigo Alemán in Toledo, Plasencia, Ciudad Rodrigo, and Zamora.

ARTISTS. Aloy, fl. 1340–68. – Master Bartolomé, 13th–14th cent.; active at Gerona and Tarragona – Jaime Cascalls, fl. 1345–77. – Pere Joan, active 1398–1458. – Janin Lomme of Tournai, active in Navarra 1411–44 (D. Roggen, Doornikse grafplastiek in het sticht: Jehann Lomme en Klaas Sluter, Gentse bijdragen tot de kg., XIII, 1951, pp. 193–207). – Lorenzo Mercadante, of Brittany, worked in Seville 1454–67. – Pedro Moragues, fl. 1369–87 (A. M. Albareda, Pere Moragues: Escultor i orfebre (segle XIV), EUC, XXII, 1936, pp. 499–524). – Gil Morlanes the Elder, active in Aragon 1482–1515 (M. Serrano y Sanz, Gil Morlanes, escultor, Zaragoza, 1919). – Pedro Sanglada (Pere Ça-Anglada), fl. 1394–1406. – Gil de Siloe, fl. 1486–1505 (H. E. Wethey, Gil de Siloe and His School, Cambridge, Mass., 1936).

Painting. Gothic painting in Spain was characterized by four distinct phases, although they were not contemporaneous in the different regions. The linear Gothic style, developed from the Romanesque style, is well represented in Catalonia, in wall paintings at Puigcerdá (VI, PL. 370), Lérida (VI, PL. 326), and Barcelona and on various altar frontals; in Aragon, in the city of Teruel; in Navarra, in the impressive series of works by Juan Oliver (VI, PL. 373), Roque de Artajona, and the Master of Olite, among others; and in Castile, in the Old Cathedral of Salamanca (PL. 127) and in the altarpieces of S. Millán in San Millán de la Cogolla. The Italo-Gothic style, which was derived from the Florentine and Sienese schools and flourished during the second half of the 14th century, was introduced in Barcelona by Ferrer Bassa (VI, PL. 374); it was further developed by Ramón Destorrents and continued by Jaime Serra (PL. 127) and his brother Pedro. Almost at the same time, similar progress was being made in Lérida, Tarragona, and Valencia. The transition to the International Gothic style was effected gradually during the first years of the 15th century. In Catalonia this style was represented by L. Borrassá (PL. 128; VI, PL. 335), Ramón de Mur, and Bernardo Martorell; in Valencia by Lorenzo Zaragoza (altarpiece of Jérica), Andrés Marzál de Sax (Altarpiece of St. George, London, Vict. and Alb.), and Pedro Nicolau; in Aragon by Juan de Leví (altarpiece of Tarazona), Bonanat Zaortiga (altarpiece of Tudela), the Retascón Master, and the Lanaja Master. Foreign artists introduced the style in Castile: Gherardo Starnina (IX, PL. 7) in Toledo, Dello Delli in Salamanca (altarpiece of high altar and vault in the Old Cathedral), and Nicolás Francés in León (altarpiece and cloister of the Cathedral). Finally, in the second half of the 15th century, the Hispano-

Flemish style developed as an adaptation of the Van Eycks' innovations. Initiated by Luis Dalmau (PL. 128), this style was firmly established by Bartolomé Bermejo (PL. 135), who was active in Valencia, in Aragon, where he founded a school, and in Catalonia (Pietà, 1490, in the Cathedral of Barcelona). It attained its finest expression in Castile, where it was introduced by Jorge Inglés (altarpiece with the portrait of the Marquis of Santillana) and was taken up by Fernando Gallego (altarpieces of Salamanca, PL. 129, and of Zamora, Ciudad Rodrigo, Trujillo, and Tóro) and by the Master of S. Ildefonso, the Luna Master, and the Ávila Master. The last group to adopt this style was that of Pedro Berruguete (PL. 129) and his followers, the Master of the Catholic Monarchs, the St. Nicholas Master, the Burgos Master, the Master of S. María del Campo (also known as Master of the Large Figures), and Alonso de Sedano. In Catalonia, the foremost exponent of this style was Jaime Huguet (PL. 129), a man who was sensitive and profound in his simplicity and whose influence extended as far as Aragon. Noteworthy artists of the period in Andalusia were Pedro de Córdoba, Juan Sánchez de Castro, and Juan Núñez.

ARTISTS. Ferrer Bassa, active from 1324, d. 1348; produced illuminations, altarpieces, and frescoes (M. Rodríguez Codolá, Las pinturas murales de Ferrer Bassa: Su importancia y descripción, Museum, VII, 1927, pp. 67–84; M. Trens, Ferrer Bassa i les pintures de Pedralbes, Barcelona, 1936). – Bartolomé Bermejo, of Córdoba, active in Valencia, Aragon (1474–77), and Barcelona (1486–95); numerous works of Flemish derivation without Renaissance traits (E. Tormo y Monzo, Bartolomé Bermejo: El más recio de los primitivos españoles, AEAA, II, 1926, pp. 11–97; J. M. Brown, Dos obras tempranas de Bartolomé Bermejo y su relación con Flandes, AEArte, XXXVI, 1963, pp. 269–79). – Pedro Berruguete, b. Paredes de Nava (Palencia) ca. 1450, d. ca. 1504; trained in the Hispano-Flemish school; at Urbino, Italy, in 1477, working for Federigo da Montefeltro; active in Spain from 1483 to his death; many works at Paredes de Nava, Ávila, Palencia, and Burgos (Monastery of Miraflores), in the Prado, and elsewhere; had numerous followers (G. Gamba, Pedro Berruguete, Dedalo, VII, 1927, pp. 638–62; R. Lainez Alcalá, Pedro Berruguete, Madrid, 1935; G. Hulin de Loo, Pedro Berruguete et les portraits d'Urbin, Brussels, 1942; D. Angulo Iñiguez, Pedro Berruguete en Paredes de Nava, Barcelona, 1946; Musée des Beaux-Arts, Ghent, Juste de Gand, Berruguete et la cour d'Urbino, Brussels, 1957 [cat.]; C. Bernis, Pedro Berruguete y la moda, AEArte, XXXII, 1959, pp. 9–28). – Luis Borrassá, b. Gerona ca. 1360, d. Barcelona 1426; noted for more than thirty altarpieces (J. Gudiol i Ricart, Borrassà, Barcelona, 1953). – Luis Dalmau, sent by Alfonso V to Flanders in 1431 and in Valencia by 1436. – Ramón Destorrents, active at Barcelona 1351–91 as painter of illuminations and altarpieces (F. P. Verrié, Más sobre Destorrents: "Dos contratos trescencistas de aprendizaje de pintor," ABMAB, II, 3, 1944, pp. 63–65; F. P. Verrié, Una obra documentada de Ramón Destorrents, ABMAB, VI, 1948, pp. 321–40). – Juan de Flandes, Flemish painter in the service of Queen Isabella of Castile, active in Spain 1496–1515; works at Salamanca, Palencia, Madrid, and elsewhere (F. J. Sánchez Cantón, El retablo de la Reina Católica, AEAA, VI, 1930, pp. 97–133, VII, 1931, pp. 149–52; C. Eisler, Juan de Flandes's St. Michael and St. Francis, BMMA, N.S., XVIII, 1959–60, pp. 129–37; E. Bermejo, Juan de Flandes, Madrid, 1962). – Nicolás Francés, active at León from before 1434 until his death in 1468 (F. J. Sánchez Cantón, Maestro Nicolás Francés, pintor, AEAA, I, 1925, pp. 41–65). – Fernando Gallego, notable activity 1466–1506 (J. A. Gaya Nuño, Fernando Gallego, Madrid, 1958; R. M. Quinn, Fernando Gallego and the Retablo of Ciudad Rodrigo, Tucson, 1961). – Jaime Huguet, b. Valls (Tarragona) ca. 1415, d. Barcelona 1492, worked at Zaragoza, Tarragona, and Barcelona; works in many museums in Spain and elsewhere (B. Rowland, Jr., Jaime Huguet, Cambridge, Mass., 1932; J. Gudiol i Ricart and J. Ainaud de Lasarte, Huguet, Barcelona, 1948 [bibliog.]; J. Ainaud de Lasarte, Jaime Huguet, Madrid, 1955). – Jorge Inglés, mentioned in 1455 (F. J. Sánchez Cantón, Maestro Jorge Inglés, BSEE, XXV, 1917, pp. 99–105, XXVI, 1918, pp. 27–31). – Bernardo Martorell, active from 1427 to his death in 1452; altarpiece of St. George (Louvre; Art Inst. of Chicago), Altarpiece of the Saviour (Barcelona, Cath.), and the altarpiece in Pubol (Gerona), other works in Barcelona (Mus. de Arte Cataluña) and elsewhere (J. Gudiol i Ricart, Bernardo Martorell, Madrid, 1959. – Andrés Marzál de Sax, of German origin, active at Valencia 1393–1410.

THE HISPANO-MORESQUE. Following the defeat of the Visigoths in the battle of 711 near the Guadalete River, the Moslems rapidly extended their sway and became solidly entrenched in most parts of the Peninsula. Their political influence prevailed until the 11th century, but beginning with the fall of the Caliphate of Córdoba and through the subsequent division of the region into separate kingdoms or *taifas*, it declined steadily. The Christian reconquest brought about a gradual unification of the Christian kingdoms until they formed a single state, and the final Moslem defeat at Granada in 1492 destroyed the Moslem power in Spain (see ISLAM; MOORISH STYLE).

Caliphate period. The most important work of the period of the Western Caliphate of Córdoba is the Great Mosque in Córdoba (VIII, PL. 148; X, PLS. 161, 163), which was begun by 'Abd-ar-Raḥmān I about 780 and subsequently enlarged by 'Abd-ar-Raḥmān II (in 833–48), Hakam II (in 961–68), and al-Manṣur (ca. 987). Despite later alterations, this building is for the most part well preserved. It is built on a rectangular plan (VIII, FIG. 338) including a large courtyard and has low façades. The multiple aisles of the great hall are separated by columns, many of them taken from Roman or Visigothic sites. The columns support horseshoe arches above which are placed semicircular arches (X, PL. 162). The Mosque's elaborate decoration culminates in the so-called "Lucernario" (Capilla de Nuestra Señora de Villaviciosa; X, PL. 163) and the mihrab (PL. 277; III, PL. 7; VIII, PL. 148), which has intersecting polylobed arches, mosaics, and reliefs with geometric, floral, and calligraphic designs. Near Córdoba are the ruins of what was once the brilliant court city of Medina az-Zahra, whose construction was begun by 'Abd-ar-Raḥmān III in 936; its monumental aspect and refinement were unparalleled in Europe at the time. Soon after its completion in 1011 it was destroyed and abandoned. Dating from the Caliphate period are several other buildings in Córdoba, as well as the mosque in Tudela (Navarra), now in ruins, and the formidable castle of Gormaz (Soria). Examples of sculpture are the *pilas* (massive sculptured stone blocks) in Seville (Mus. Arqueol.) and in the Alhambra in Granada, as well as the decorative marble tablets from Málaga, Baena, and Córdoba (all, Córdoba, Mus. Arqueol.) Similar technical perfection and fine decoration are to be found in the various crafts and minor-arts products of the period, such as the series of ivories from the caliphal workshops of the 10th and 11th centuries; outstanding pieces are the cylindrical jars in Madrid (Mus. Arqueol. Nac.), Paris (Louvre), and London (Vict. and Alb.) and the small caskets of Pamplona Cathedral, Silos (Burgos, Mus. Histórico y Artístico), and Palencia (Madrid, Mus. Arqueol. Nac.), decorated with geometric and floral reliefs, human and animal figures, and calligraphic motifs. Other products from the caliphal workshops include the ceramics found at Elvira, near Granada, and Medina az-Zahra, objects in bronze and gold, and textiles.

Relics of the Caliphate period have survived in some of the kingdoms founded after the fall of the Caliphate: in Toledo the old Puerta Visagra, Las Tornerías mosque, and the Mosque Church of Cristo de la Luz; in Zaragoza the Aljafería, built between 1047 and 1081 and presently being restored; in Málaga most of the Alcazaba (1057–63) and its palace; and the well-preserved Alcazaba in Almería and the one in Granada, as well as the 11th-century baths in Granada.

Almohad period. The brief period in which the Almohads ruled Spain (11th–12th cent.) offers few, but nevertheless remarkable, examples of art works. One is the fine tower called the Giralda, completed about 1195 as the minaret of Seville's main mosque. On an equally high artistic level are the remains of the courtyard of the same mosque, as well as the Torre del Oro, also in Seville, and the town walls of Cáceres and Badajoz in Estremadura. During the Almohad era the minor arts and architectural ornamentation continued to develop and, while retaining the caliphal tradition, tended to stress abstraction of forms (see MOORISH STYLE, col. 310).

Nasrid period. In the middle of the 13th century Moslem power in Spain was restricted to the kingdom of Granada under the rule of the Nasrid (Nazari) dynasty. In this kingdom the brilliant Nasrid art developed for two centuries, excelling

in the use of ornamental elements to cover and adorn the basic simplicity of its structures. New and original forms arose — for instance in the capitals of columns — and the minor arts prospered. The masterpiece of the period, the Alhambra in Granada (FIG. 316; VIII, PL. 149; X, PLS. 166–68, 171), is

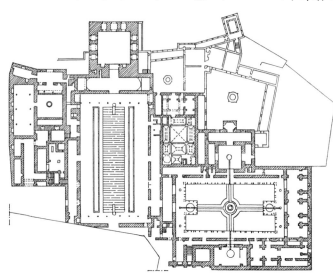

Granada, the Alhambra, plan (*from A. Lurcat, Formes, composition et lois d'harmonie, Paris, 1954–55*).

made up of a vast grouping of palaces, with many balconies, courtyards, and gardens, the whole surrounded by a massive wall. Begun by Muhammad I ibn-al-Aḥmar in 1238 and completed by his successors, the Alhambra has been preserved with few alterations. The refined sensitivity of the artists who built it is reflected in doors such as the Puerta de la Justicia and towers such as the Torre de las Infantas (PL. 223) and the Torre de la Cautiva and in the apartments surrounding the Cuarto de Comares (X, PL. 168) and the Patio de los Leones (Court of the Lions; X, PL. 167). There are numerous cupolas of Mozarabic derivation and much stucco and glazed tile (*azulejos*) embellished with a rich variety of brilliant colors. Less important are the Generalife, with its graceful gardens, and the remains of several other structures in the city of Granada: the Casa del Carbón (the former *funduq*), the Dār al-Horra (palace of the royal princesses), and various minarets and residences.

The Nasrid minor arts are equally refined and superior in quality. Notable among the ceramics are the Alhambra Vase (X, PL. 169) and the large Fortuny Tile (X, PL. 160). The skilled workmanship is also apparent in tooled and embossed leatherwork, silk weaving (Almería and Málaga), ivory, metal- and goldwork, wood carving, and other crafts.

Mudejar style. Long before the end of the Moslem reign in Granada (1492), the influence of the architectural, decorative, and applied arts of Spanish Islam had penetrated the Christian kingdoms of the reconquest and had given rise to the Mudejar style (see MOORISH STYLE, col. 320), a survival of the Hispano-Moresque style, which was to persist until the 18th century. It was kept alive in certain areas partly because the Islamic building techniques, based on the use of brick, were suited to the available materials in these regions. Mudejar art often maintained a certain purity of style, both in its preference for brick as a building material and in its use of decorative elements such as blind arches, interlace, and geometric ornament; but in other instances it engendered hybrid formulas in which Gothic and Renaissance elements were mixed in varying degrees with Hispano-Moresque features.

There are several important centers of Mudejar art. In Andalusia it is represented at Córdoba, in the synagogue and the Royal Chapel of the Cathedral, and at Seville in the parts of the Alcázar that were built by Pedro I in 1364–66 (façade, Patio de las Doncellas, Patio de las Muñecas, and Salón de

Embajadores, which are similar to contemporaneous works in Granada) and in the many Mudejar churches and palaces of the city. In New Castile, Toledo contains Mudejar churches, synagogues, residences, and monasteries, and Guadalupe has a famous monastery; in Old Castile and León there are many churches (Madrigal de las Altas Torres, Arévalo, Cuéllar, Toro, Sahagún) public buildings, palaces (Tordesillas), and castles (Coca, PL. 121; Medina del Campo, FIG. 318; and Arévalo). Aragon presents a personality and force of its own that are expressed in the abundance of its towers as well as their variety (Teruel, Zaragoza, Calatayud, Utebo, Tauste), in the *cimborios* of its churches (Zaragoza, Teruel, Tarazona), in its cupolas embellished with geometric interlace, in its façades decorated with brick and ceramic facing, and in its stuccowork.

Other Mudejar elements, as abundant as they were varied, are the vaulted ceilings, roofs and cupolas of carved polychrome wood, *azulejos* floors and socles, decorative stuccoes, and wood carvings. The influence of the Mudejar style on the minor arts was extensive, and there are many fine examples of furniture, textiles, rugs, tooled leather, ceramics, and metal objects.

THE RENAISSANCE. *Architecture*. Spanish architecture of the Renaissance followed two stylistic trends. One was the style known as plateresque, with a prevalence of decorative elements, sometimes retaining a simplified Gothic structure; the other was derived from the great models of the Italian Renaissance but with a profoundly Spanish character and a geometric treatment of volumes. Because of historical conditions

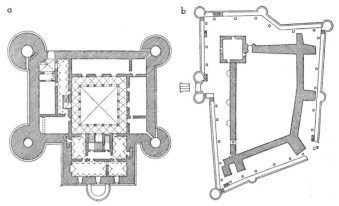

Spanish fortifications, 16th cent., plans. (*a*) Calahorra, Granada, castle; (*from Ars Hispaniae, XI, 1953, p. 36*); (*b*) Medina del Campo, castle (*from Lampérez y Romea, 1922, p. 267*).

at the beginning of the 16th century, marked by the leading role of Castile in the unification of Spain, and because trade with the new lands of America improved the economy of Andalusia, it was natural that the nation's wealth should become concentrated in these two regions and that the most important examples of the architecture of this period should have been built there.

Among early works, mention should be made of those by

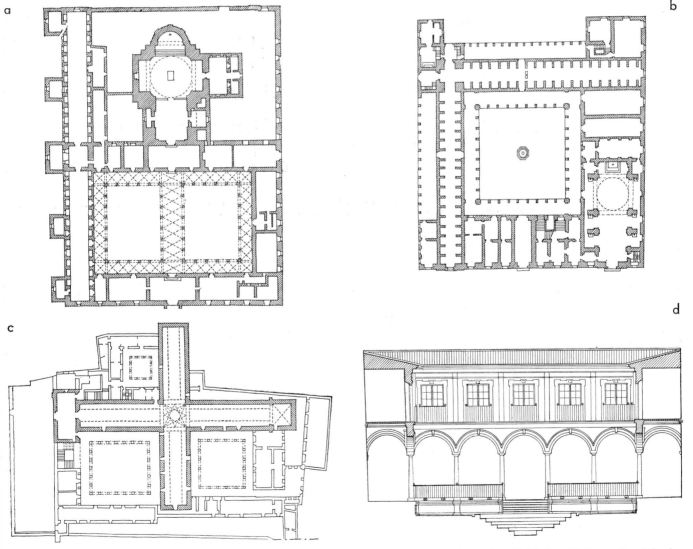

Spanish secular buildings, 16th–17th cent. (*a*) Toledo, Hospital de S. Juan Bautista (Afuera Hospital), plan; (*b*) Medina del Campo, hospital, plan; (*c*) Toledo, Hospital de Sta. Cruz, plan; (*d*) Seville, Hospital de Venerables, section of court (*from Ars Hispaniae, XI, 1953; XIV, 1957*).

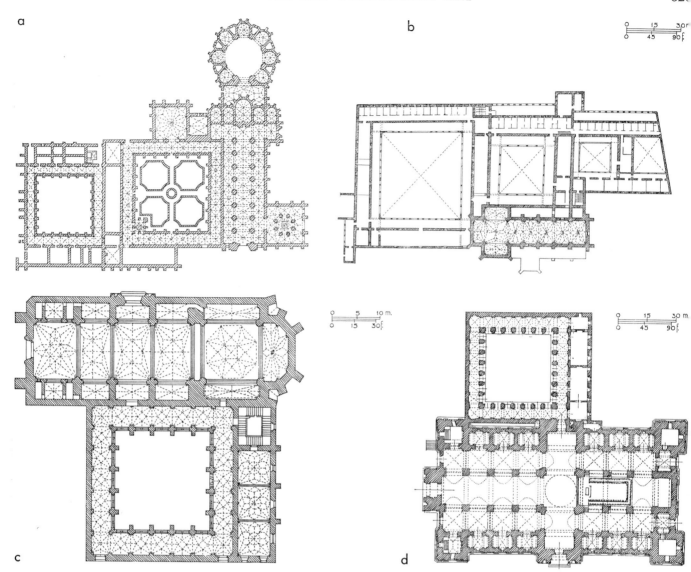

Religious building complexes, 14th-16th cent., plans. (*a*) Batalha, Portugal, Monastery of S. Maria da Vitória (*from W. C. Watson, Portuguese Architecture, London, 1908, p. 81*); (*b*) Ávila, Spain, Monastery of S. Tomás, 15th cent.; (*c*) Toledo, Spain, S. Juan de los Reyes, 15th cent. (*from Ars Hispaniae, VII, 1952, pp. 339, 340*); (*d*) Valladolid, Spain, Cathedral, 16th cent. (*from Ars Hispaniae, XI, 1953, p. 378*).

Lorenzo Vázquez in Valladolid (Colegio de Sta Cruz, 1492), Cogolludo (PL. 123), and in Mondéjar in Guadalajara Province. Alonso de Covarrubias was active in Toledo — where he built the hospitals of Sta Cruz and S. Juan Bautista (Hospital de Tavera, or de Afuera) and the Reyes Nuevos Chapel in the Cathedral — and Rodrigo Gil de Hontañón in Alcalá de Henares (PL. 123) and in Salamanca (Palacio de Monterrey), the city where the plateresque style reached its culmination in such works as the New Cathedral, the University, the churches of S. Esteban and Espiritu Santo, and the Irish College. In many Castilian cities such as Burgos, Segovia, León, and Valladolid there are numerous churches and palaces decorated in the characteristic plateresque style, with grotesque symbolic figures and innumerable windows, doors, and courtyards. Derivatives of this style can be seen in Galicia (Santiago de Compostela) and Estremadura (Plasencia, Trujillo, Cáceres). In Andalusia the early Renaissance art flourished with such eminent artists as Diego de Siloe — cathedrals of Granada (PL. 131) and Málaga — and Andrés de Vandelvira (churches and secular buildings of Jaén, Úbeda, and Baenza), who were the leaders of important schools, and the lesser figure of Pedro Machuca (Palace of Charles V; XII, PL. 102). In the regions of Aragon, Valencia, Catalonia, the Balearic Islands, Murcia, the Basque Provinces, and Navarra the Renaissance produced buildings that bore some original characteristics but were, in general, artistically inferior to those of Castile and Andalusia, owing to a lack of architects of strong creative personality.

In the last third of the 16th century the Spanish Renaissance entered a new phase, dominated by Juan Bautista de Toledo and Juan de Herrera (q.v.) centering around the Escorial, an austere and refined construction built between 1563 and 1584 (PL. 131; VII, PLS. 221-223). The later works of Juan de Herrera (Cathedral of Valladolid, FIG. 320; III, PL. 316; VII, PL. 224; the Lonja of Seville) continued this trend. His disciples and followers gradually developed the forms that were to lead to the baroque style.

ARTISTS. Alonso de Covarrubias, 1488-1570 (V. Garcia Rey, El famoso arquitecto Alonso de Covarrubias, Arquitectura, IX, 1927, pp. 167-75, 207-12, 311-19, 375-80, 415-20, X, 1928, pp. 3-7, 95-99, 202-03, 236-37, 268-69, 297-99). – Rodrigo Gil de Hontañón, son of the architect Juan Gil de Hontañón, active 1523-77 (M. Pereda de la Reguera, Rodrigo Gil de Hontañón, Santander, 1951; J. Contreras y López de Alaya, Marqués de Lozoya, Rodrigo Gil de Hontañón en Segovia, Santander, 1962). – Juan de Herrera (q.v.), ca. 1530-1597, active at Escorial from 1563 (A. Ruiz de Arcaute, Juan de Herrera, Madrid, 1936; M. López Serrano, Trazas de Juan de Herrera y sus seguidores para el Monasterio del Escorial, Madrid, 1944; F. Chueca Goitia, Herrera y el herrerianismo, Goya, 56-57, 1963, pp. 98-115). – Pedro Machuca, active 1520-50 (M. Gómez-Moreno, Las águilas del Renacimiento español, Madrid, 1941). – Diego de Siloe, ca. 1495-1563, son of sculptor-architect Gil de Siloe

M. Gómez-Moreno, Diego Siloe, Granada, 1963). – Juan Bautista de Toledo, d. 1567; summoned from Naples in 1559 by Philip II. – Andrés de Vandelvira, 1509–75 (F. Chueca Goitia, Andrés de Vandelvira, Madrid, 1954). – Lorenzo Vázquez, active 1487–ca. 1510 (M. Gómez-Moreno, Hacia Lorenzo Vázquez, AEAA, I, 1925, pp. 7–40).

Sculpture. Despite the fact that during the 15th century the first influences of the Italian Renaissance had already reached Spain, for instance with Giuliano Fiorentino (Juliá lo Florenti) in Valencia, this trend did not win acceptance until after 1500, with the activity of Domenico di Alessandro Fancelli

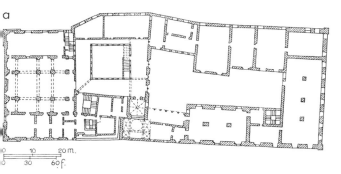

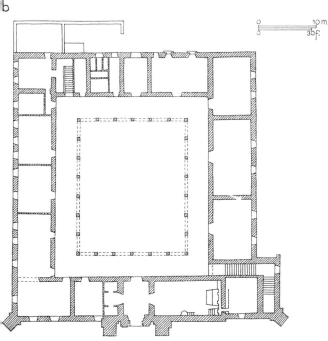

Spanish secular buildings, 16th cent., plans. (*a*) Barcelona, Casa de la Diputación (*from Lampérez y Romea, 1922, p. 61*); (*b*) Oñate, University (*from Ars Hispaniae, XI, 1953, p. 347*).

and other masters. Among the first Spanish artists to adopt the new esthetic forms were Damián Forment from Valencia, the leader of a prolific school in Aragon. In Castile, during the first quarter of the 16th century, the outstanding figures were Vasco de la Zarza in Ávila and Felipe Bigarny (Vigarny; de Borgoña) in Burgos and Toledo. In Andalusia the most important artists were Jacopo Torni (called L'Indaco, also Florentín) and Pietro Torrigiano. Of greater importance were three Italian-trained Castilian sculptors: Bartolomé Ordoñez (PL. 139), who worked on the choir of Barcelona Cathedral and the tombs of Philip I and his wife Juana in the Capilla Real of the Cathedral of Granada; Diego de Siloe (PL. 140), mentioned above as an architect, who worked on various tombs and altarpieces in Burgos Cathedral and who was later active in Granada, where he executed his principal works; and Alonso Berruguete (q.v.; PL. 141), son of the painter Pedro, who had the most personal style of the three and whose sculpture reveals

an elegant mannerism already imbued with the baroque spirit. Notable among Alonso Berruguete's works are the altarpieces of the monastery of La Mejorada at Olmedo and of S. Benito at Valladolid (parts of both in Valladolid, Mus. Nac. de Escultura), the stalls in the high choir of the Toledo Cathedral (XII, PL. 102), which he carved together with Felipe Bigarny, and the tomb of Cardinal Juan de Tavera in the church of the Hospital de Tavera in Toledo.

Contemporary with Berruguete and rivaling him in fame was the Frenchman Juan de Juni (PL. 141). Fully adhering to Castilian esthetic principles, he created works (at Segovia, Medina de Rioseco, and Valladolid; IV, PL. 210) that exerted a strong influence in the last third of the century, when this trend was merged with the mannerism of Gaspar Becerra (altarpiece in Astorga Cathedral).

Prolific schools arose in Valladolid, Palencia, and Burgos, as well as in La Rioja and the Basque-Navarra regions. By the last third of the 16th century the Valladolid school began to decline, with the sculptor Esteban Jordán, a lesser artist than Juan de Anchieta, who emerged as the most brilliant representative of Michelangelesque mannerism, being active in the Basque and Navarra regions and in Aragon. Meanwhile, in Seville, sculpture workshops were being established that were to become the basis of the great Andalusian school of baroque sculpture. Another school matured around the court, but it was to have only a few followers. It was primarily made up of Italian artists such as Leone Leoni and Pompeo Leoni (El Escorial, XII, PL. 102; Descalzas Reales; the Prado) or artists trained in Italian art. At the same time the Toledo school of sculpture (Juan Bautista Monegro), based on Spanish national traditions, was losing its influence.

ARTISTS. Juan de Anchieta, b. Azpeitia (Guipúzcoa) ca. 1540, probably trained in Italy; active ca. 1588 (J. Camón Aznar, El escultor Juan de Ancheta, Pamplona, 1943). – Gaspar Becerra, b. Baeza (Jaén) ca. 1520, d. 1568; educated in Italy, returned to Castile 1557 (E. Tormo y Monzó, Gaspar Becerra, BSEE, XX, 1912, pp. 65–97, XXI, 1913, pp. 117-57, 241–65). – Alonso Berruguete (q.v.), b. ca. 1488, d. Toledo 1561 (R. de Orueta y Duarte, Berruguete y su obra, Madrid, 1917; M. Gómez-Moreno, Las águilas del renacimiento español, Madrid, 1941; J. A. Gaya Nuño, Alonso Berruguete en Toledo, Barcelona, 1944; F. de Cossio, Alonso Berruguete, Valladolid, 1948; Alonso Berruguete, Madrid, 1961 [cat.]). – Damián Forment, d. Santo Domingo de la Calzada (Logroño) 1540, active Valencia beginning of 16th cent., later founded workshop at Zaragoza (M. Abizanda y Broto, Damian Forment, Barcelona, 1942; C. R. Post, The Paintings of Damián Forment, Miscellànea Puig i Cadafalch, I, Barcelona, 1951, pp. 213–23). – Esteban Jordán, b. ca. 1530, d. Valladolid 1598 (A. de Apraiz, Esteban Jordán, Valladolid, 1952). – Juan de Juní, b. León ca. 1533, d. Valladolid 1577 (E. Garcia Chico, Juan de Juni, Valladolid, 1949; J. J. Martín González, Juan de Juní, Madrid, 1954; J. J. Martín González, Juan de Juní y Juan de Angés el Mozo en Orense, Cuadernos de estudios gallegos, XVII, 1962, pp. 68–82). – Pompeo Leoni, b. 1533, d. Madrid 1608; son of the Milanese Leone Leoni (see ITALIAN ART); in Spain after 1556 (B. G. Proske, Pompeo Leoni: Work in Marble and Alabaster in Relation to Spanish Sculpture, New York, 1956). – Bartolomé Ordóñez, b. Burgos, d. Carrara, Italy, 1520 (M. E. Gómez-Moreno, Bartolomé Ordóñez, Madrid, 1956). – Juan Bautista Monegro, ca. 1545–1621, worked at El Escorial and Toledo (V. Garcia Rey, Juan Bautista Monegro: Escultor y arquitecto, BSEE, XXXIX, 1931, pp. 109–25, 183–89, XL, 1932, pp. 22–38, 129–45, XLI, 1933, pp. 148–52, 205–24, XLII, 1934, pp. 202–23, XLIII, 1935, pp. 53–72, 211–37). – Felipe Bigarny (Vigarny), d. Toledo 1542; arrived at Burgos in 1498 (T. López Mata, La capilla de la Presentación y Felipe de Vigarny, BIFG, XXXV, 1956, pp. 245–64; M. Martínez Burgos, En torno a la catedral de Burgos II, BIFG, XXXV, 1956, pp. 144–63; M. Martínez Burgos, Más sobre la capilla de la Presentación y su autor Felipe Vigarni, BIFG, XXXV, 1956, pp. 314–37). — Vasco de la Zarza, d. 1524; known after 1499, worked at Ávila and Toledo (M. Gómez-Moreno, Vasco de la Zarza, escultor, BSCE, IV, 1909–10, pp. 149–58).

Painting. In the first quarter of the 16th century the formulas of the 15th century, characterized for the most part by Flemish influence, were gradually abandoned, and an Italianate style derived from the great masters of the late 15th century was adopted. In Catalonia the German Anye Bru (PL. 129) in his altarpiece in the Abbey church of San Cugat del Vallés maintained a certain compromise between the Gothic and Venetian styles, while in Castile the Flemish tradition persisted until the second decade of the 16th century, largely as a result of the extensive work of Juan de Flandes (PL. 136) in Palencia. Juan de Borgoña, who succeeeded Pedro Berruguete in the execution of the Ávila altarpiece, was active in Toledo. His followers included Antonio de Comontes, Pedro de Cisneros, and the Astorga Master. In Valencia, painters of this early period include the Osonas and Pablo de San Leocadio; Fernando Yáñez de Almedina and Fernando de Llanos reflect the style of Leonardo da Vinci (altarpiece of high altar, Valencia Cathedral, 1506). Later, Vicente Masip and his son, Vicente Juan (known as Juan de Juanes; PL. 143) were outstanding in this area.

In Andalusia, after Alejo Fernández (PL. 143), three Flemish painters achieved prominence: Ferdinando Sturm (Hernando Sturmio), Frans (Francisco) Frutet, and Pieter de Kempener (Pedro de Campaña; PL. 143). The latter had lived in Italy, where he was influenced by Raphael. Luis de Vargas and Pablo de Céspedes mark the steady advance toward realism. In Estremadura, Luis de Morales (PL. 145; XII, PL. 102) came to the fore; he was commonly known as "El Divino" because of the mystical inspiration of his many works.

A new movement of Italian mannerist influences reached Spain when Italian artists were brought there to decorate the recently completed monastery of El Escorial, foremost among them Luca Cambiaso, Federico Zuccari, and Pellegrino Tibaldi. The Spanish painter from La Rioja, Juan Fernández de Navarrete, known as "El Mudo" ("the deaf-mute"), was important in this group.

A notable change occurred with the arrival of two painters of greater artistic importance whose styles were completely different. They were the Netherlander, Anthonis Mor, and the Greek, Domingo Teotocópuli, known as El Greco (q.v.). Mor, a meticulous and effective portrait painter (V, PL. 293; IX, PL. 297) was the teacher of Alonso Sánchez Coello (IX, PL. 297) and Juan Pantoja de la Cruz; he originated many of the concepts that led to the brilliant realism of the 17th century. El Greco, in contrast, brought from his native land of Crete the influence of the ancient icons in the Byzantine tradition and combined these elements with powerful expressions of the baroque and mannerist tendencies that he had absorbed during his stay in Venice and Rome. In Toledo he found a second home where he painted many works, among which *The Entombment of the Count of Orgaz* (VI, PLS. 454, 455) and *The Martyrdom of St. Maurice* (VI, PL. 459) deserve special mention. Because of the pronounced individuality of his style, El Greco left no school of disciples; Luis Tristán (PL. 148) is almost the only artist who can be called a follower of El Greco.

ARTISTS. Juan de Borgoña, active at Toledo 1495–1536 (?), principal works preserved there in the Cathedral (D. Angulo Iñíguez, Juan de Borgoña, Madrid, 1954; A. Condorelli, Il problema di Juan de Borgoña, Comm, XI, 1960, pp. 56–59). – Pedro de Campaña, b. Brussels; in Seville 1537–63, where he was the most important Raphaelite painter (D. Angulo Iñíguez, Pedro de Campaña, Seville, 1951). – Pablo de Céspedes, b. Córdoba ca. 1540, d. 1608; went to Rome, returned ca. 1577 (F. M. Tubino, Pablo de Céspedes, Madrid, 1868; M. Gómez-Moreno, El gran Pablo de Céspedes, BRA, XIX, 1948, p. 63). – Alejo Fernández, German, d. 1545/46; went to Córdoba 1496, to Seville 1508, where his style was dominant until his death (D. Angulo Iñíguez, Alejo Fernández, Seville, 1946; D. G. Carter, A Crucifix by Alejo Fernández, B. R. I. School of Design, Mus. Notes, March, 1963, pp. 1–17). – Juan Fernández de Navarrete, d. 1579; follower of the Venetian school, active at El Escorial after 1568 (J. Zarco Cuevas, Juan Fernández de Navarrete, AE, X, 1930, pp. 106–17). – Juan de Juanes, b. Valencia ca. 1500, son of the painter Vicente Masip; numerous works manifest Raphael's influence (A. Igual Ubeda, Juan de Juanes, Barcelona, 1943; A. Dotor y Municio, Juan de Juanes, Gerona, 1945). – Luis de Morales, b. ca. 1510, d. Badajoz ca. 1586; trained as mannerist, influenced by Leonardo (E. du Gué Trapier, Luis de Morales and Leonardesque Influences in Spain, New York, 1953; J. A. Gaya Nuño, Luis de Morales, Madrid, 1961; I. Bäcksbacka, Luis de Morales, Helsinki, 1962). – Rodrigo de Osuna, father and son of same name; father active in Valencia 1464, introduced Renaissance Quattrocento into Spain; active 1505–13, combined father's style with other Italian influences (E. Tormo y Monzo, Rodrigo de Osona, padre e hijo,

y su escuela, AEAA, VIII, 1932, pp. 101–47, IX, 1933, pp. 153–214). – Juan Pantoja de la Cruz, ca. 1553–1608; principal disciple of Sánchez Coello in portraiture (F. J. Sánchez Cantón, Sobre la vida y obras de Juan Pantoja de la Cruz, AEArte, XX, 1947, pp. 95–120; H. Friedmann, A Painting by Pantoja and the Legend of the Partridge of St. Nicholas of Tolentino, AQ, XXII, 1959, pp. 45–55). – Alonso Sánchez Coello, of Valencia, 1531–88, pupil in Flanders of Anthonis Mor, disciple of Titian, principal Spanish portraitist of his period (F. de San Roman, Alonso Sánchez Coello, BRA Toledo, XI, 1930, pp. 158–209; J. Sánchez Coello Reynalte, Alonso Sánchez Coello, Ilustraciones a su biografia, Lisbon, 1938). – Luis de Vargas, ca. 1506–68, lived many years in Italy, returned to Seville 1553. – Fernando Yáñez de la Almedina, Castilian, trained in Italy, arrived Valencia 1506 with Fernando de Llanos; influenced by Leonardo; work at Valencia, Cuenca, and elsewhere (F. M. Garín Ortiz de Taranco, Yáñez de la Almedina: Pintor español, Valencia, 1953).

Minor arts. The 16th-century craftsmen of Spain produced magnificent works in ceramics, textiles, furniture, and other minor arts. Especially notable are the creations of the goldsmiths and ironworkers. The Arfe family of goldsmiths — Enrique, Antonio, and Juan — executed many of the great tabernacles and custodials of the Spanish cathedrals (VI, PL. 389). The most important works of wrought iron are the remarkable *rejas* (grilles, screens), ranging from the vast screens in the cathedrals (VI, PL. 306) to small fire screens (IX, PL. 518). Noteworthy makers of *rejas* were Cristóbal Andino, Francisco de Villalpando, and Hernando de Arenas.

ARTISTS. Arfe family of goldsmiths: Enrique, German, worked in León 1501, last recorded activity 1545, made custodials for Cathedrals of Sahagún, Córdoba (1518), and Toledo (1515–23), also processional crosses and other objects. Antonio, his son, b. ca. 1510 made custodials of Santiago de Compostela (1539–45) and Medina de Rioseco (1552–54); in Madrid 1574. Juan, Antonio's son, b. León 1535, d. Madrid 1603; made custodials at Ávila (1564–71), Seville (1580–87), and Valladolid (1587–90) (J. Sánchez Cantón, Los Arfe, Madrid, 1920).

THE BAROQUE. In Spain, the baroque style — using the term in its broadest sense — covered a period corresponding roughly to the Hapsburg and Bourbon reigns in Spain. It flourished from about the end of the 16th century until the second third of the 18th; in the last third of the 18th century it entered its final phases, showing increasing signs of transition to the neoclassic. In 1562 Philip II (r. 1556–98) made Madrid the capital of Spain; and the interest that succeeding monarchs took in embellishing the city rapidly transformed it into an artistic center. The kingdom of Castile — which by then included León and Galicia — and that of Andalusia continued their dominating influence, while Valencia and Murcia experienced a phase of particular splendor, and Catalonia, in the course of the 18th century, slowly began to shake off the crippling effects of the War of the Spanish Succession (1701–13/14).

Architecture. The influence of the Escorial school was particularly strong in early Castilian baroque. The Plaza Mayor in Madrid, designed in 1617 by Juan Gómez de Mora, dates from this period. Juan Gómez was probably also the creator of that city's old Cárcel de Corte (now the Foreign Office). The Italian Giovanni Battista Crescenzi, who devoted a large part of his efforts to decorative and scenographic work, introduced the taste for marble and bronze facings in the Panteón de los Reyes of the Escorial. In the city of Madrid, the outstanding religious monuments of the period are the Cathedral of S. Isidro (1661; FIG. 325), built by Francesco Bautista (PL. 132); the Church of Las Comendadoras de Santiago by Francisco de Herrera the Younger and José del Olmo; and the S. Isidro Chapel in the Church of S. Andrés by Pedro de la Torre and Sebastiano de Herrera Barnuevo (1669).

The Churriguera family (see CHURRIGUERESQUE STYLE), of Catalan origin, was numerous and productive: José Benito made the large altarpiece of S. Esteban in Salamanca (1693; III, PL. 319) and, between 1709 and 1713, designed the urban complex of Nuevo Baztán (Madrid); his brother Joaquín built

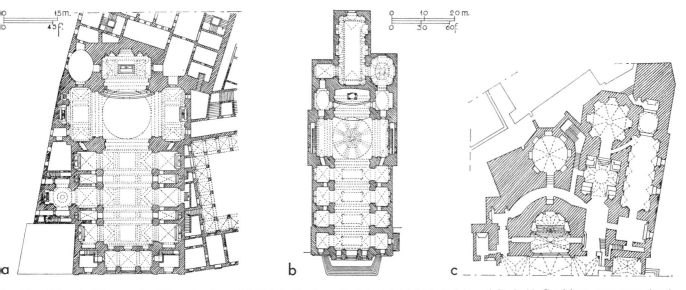

Spanish religious buildings, 17th–18th cent., plans. (*a*) Toledo, S. Juan Bautista; (*b*) Madrid, S. Isidro el Real; (*c*) Guadalupe, monastery church, apse area and adjacent chapels (*from Ars Hispaniae, XIV, 1957, pp. 58, 17*).

the Colegio de Calatrava (PL. 133); while Alberto, the third brother, built the church in Orgaz (province of Toledo; 1738) and participated in the construction of the Plaza Mayor (1729; III, PL. 316) and the Church of S. Sebastián (1731) in Salamanca. The architect Andrés García de Quiñones (fl. ca. 1750) was also active in Salamanca: he completed the Clerecía, begun by Juan Gómez de Mora (III, PL. 317), and the Plaza Mayor.

In Madrid, Pedro de Ribera was the most important architect of the first third of the 18th century; he built the hermitage of the Virgen del Puerto (PL. 134), the churches of S. Cayetano and Montserrat (1720), the Toledo Bridge (1719), the Barracks of Conde-Duque Olivares, the Hospicio de S. Fernando (1722) — whose portal testified to the artist's passion for tempestuous baroque ornamentation — and various private residences. Another artist of the period was Narciso Tomé, creator of the façade of the University of Valladolid (1715; II, PL. 160) and of the *transparente* of the Cathedral of Toledo (1721–32; II, PL. 161), in which the interplay of irregular curves enhances the baroque effect.

The baroque spirit gave a strong impulse to building throughout the north of Spain. In Galicia, at the end of the 17th century and during the first half of the 18th, the constructions that both completed and marred Santiago de Compostela were erected. The bell tower on the main façade was built about 1670 by José Peña de Toro, from Salamanca; and the clock tower in 1680 by Domingo de Andrade. The main façade itself (PL. 134) was completed in 1738 by Fernando de Casas y Novoa, together with the other tower and the nave. Interesting works in Catalonia include those of Fray José de la Concepción; those of the various members of the Morató family; and those of Pedro Martín Cermeño and Francisco Sabatini (the churches of Nuestra Señora de Belén, la Merced, and S. Miguel del Puerto and the Palacio de la Virreina in Barcelona; and the New Cathedral in Lérida, 1761–81). In Santander and in the Basque region the influence of the varied and interesting palaces and church towers of the period extended as far as El Burgo de Osma (Valladolid) and Logroño.

In the Valencia region, noteworthy work was done by Juan Bautista Pérez in the chancel of Valencia Cathedral (1674), by Corrado Rodulfo (Konrad Rudolph) on the portal of the same building, and by Hipólito Rovira y Brocandel and Ignacio Vergara in the palace of the Marqués de Dos Aguas (PL. 137; II, PL. 160). In Murcia the façade of the Cathedral (PL. 134) was built about 1737 by Jaime Bort y Miliá; it is one of the foremost examples of Spanish rococo. There was a remarkable growth in building activity in Andalusia: in Granada, Alonso Cano (q.v.) built the main façade of the Cathedral (1667;

PL. 132) and Francisco Hurtado Izquierdo worked on the Cartuja (1702), which was only completed many years later. Seville was a center of architectural activity; Leonardo de Figueroa (ca. 1650–1730), among others, built many churches (La Magdalena, El Salvador, S. Luis; PL. 138), palaces (S. Telmo; II, PL. 162), and hospitals. These buildings had their counterparts in smaller Andalusian towns such as Fuentes de Andalucía — where Juan Ruiz Florindo and his son, Alonso Ruiz Florindo, were active — Écija (FIG. 326), Priego de Córdoba, and Estepa. Also noteworthy are the completion of the Cathedral of Jaén (façade by Eufrasio López de Rojas y Almansa, ca. 1670); various buildings in Córdoba, Málaga (Virgen de la Victoria), and Jerez de la Frontera (the Colegiata and other churches, as well as palaces); and the New Cathedral of Cádiz, which was originally designed by Vicente Acero (ca. 1720), then modified first by Torcuato Cayón de la Vega and again later by Juan Daura.

In Castile, beginning with the second third of the 18th century, the court buildings in Madrid and the neighboring royal residences were constructed. The first was the Palace of La Granja at San Ildefonso near Segovia; the participating artists were Teodoro Ardemans (1719), Andrea Procaccini, Sempronio Subissati (1727–34), and Giovanni Battista Sacchetti (1736). Work on the gardens was supervised by René Carlier and executed by Etienne Boutelou (Boutelet) with various collaborators. Construction of the Royal Palace in Madrid (PL. 241; FIG. 326; II, PL. 160) was begun in 1738 from plans

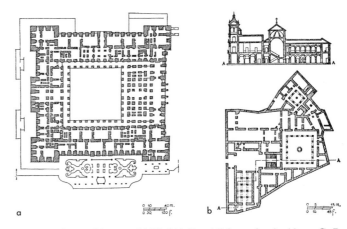

Spanish palaces, 18th cent. (*a*) Madrid, Royal Palace, plan (architect, G. B. Sacchetti); (*b*) Écija, Valverde Palace, section and plan (*from Kubler and Soria, 1959, pp. 44, 56*).

drawn up by G. B. Sacchetti; it was in use by 1764. In Aranjuez the old 16th-century palace was completed by Pedro Caro Idogro (1728) and Santiago Bonavia (1748), and the city itself was replanned. The palace at El Pardo, near Madrid, rebuilt by Francisco de Mora after 1604, was enlarged by Francisco Sabatini in 1772; the result was a palace that, although entirely Spanish, still reflected various Mediterranean and northern European influences. A most important effect of this active building program under the Bourbon kings was to provide a school for a new generation of Spanish architects, whose principal figures were Ventura Rodríguez (1707–85) and Juan de Villanueva (1739–1811).

center. The dominant style in Castile was that of Valladoli as represented by Gregorio Fernández (PL. 142) — successo to Juan de Juni (PL. 141) — whose art is characterized by strong religious tone. Fernández was the creator of numerou versions of the Crucifixion, the Dead Christ, Our Lady o Sorrows, the Pietà (II, PL. 178), and the Immaculate Conception in which the heads are especially impressive in their emotiona power. Madrid as the court city attracted artists of man origins, without, however, originating a school of sculpture as it did in painting. Among Madrid sculptors the Portugues Manuel Pereyra, whose work is distinguished by sober realism is noteworthy. In Andalusia the main centers of activity wer

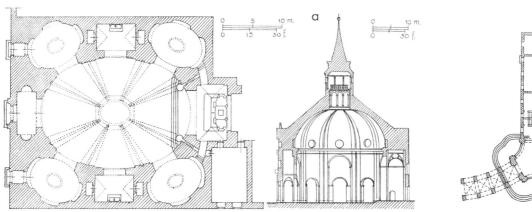
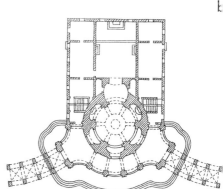

Spanish religious buildings, 17th–18th cent. (a) Alcalá de Henares, church of the Bernardine nuns, plan and longitudinal section (from Ars Hispaniae XIV, 1957, p. 15); (b) Aranjuez, S. Antonio, plan (from Kubler and Soria, 1959, p. 47).

ARTISTS. Vicente Acero, worked on Cathedral of Guadix 1714–20, on New Cathedral of Cádiz 1720–29, then in Seville (P. Gutiérrez Moreno, La cúpula del maestro Vicente Acero para la nueva catedral de Cádiz, AEAA, IV, 1928, pp. 183–86). – José Martín de Aldehuela, worked at Teruel (before 1750), Cuenca (1750–67), and Málaga (F. Chueca, J. M. de Aldehuela, AE, XXIX, 1944, pp. 29–37; J. Temboury and F. Chueca, J. M. de Aldehuela y sus obras en Málaga, AE, XXX, 1945, pp. 37–57, XXXII, 1947, pp. 7–19). – Domingo de Andrade, active at Santiago de Compostela in second half of 17th century (S. González García Paz, Sobre Domingo de Andrade, AEAA, XI, 1935, pp. 279–82). – Francisco Bautista, 1594–1679; earliest among architects of Jesuit churches in Spain; works in Alcalá de Henares, Toledo, and Madrid (E. Tormo y Monzo, Pintura, scultura y arquitectura en España; Estudios dispersos, Madrid, 1949, pp. 415–74). – Fernando de Casas y Novoa, d. 1749; active in Galicia from 1711, continued de Andrade's work; works in Lugo, La Coruña, and Santiago de Compostela. – Churriguera family (see CHURRIGUERESQUE STYLE). – Leonardo de Figueroa, b. Utiel (Valencia) ca. 1650, d. 1730; chief activity in Seville. – Juan Gómez de Mora, 1586–1646; continued work of Francisco de Mora; displayed Italian influences; works in Madrid, Salamanca, Alcalá de Henares, and elsewhere. – Francisco Hurtado Izquierdo, 1669–1725; works in Málaga and Granada (Cartuja; Sagrario of the Cathedral), also Cartuja of El Paular near Madrid (R. C. Taylor, Francisco Hurtado and His School, AB, XXXII, 1950, pp. 25–61). – Francisco de Mora, pupil and successor of Juan de Herrera, builder of town of Lerma (Burgos; 1604–14), other works in Madrid and Ávila (L. Cervera Vera, Arquitectos y escultores del retablo y enterramientos de la capilla mayor de la iglesia del desaparecido Convento de Merced de Madrid, Madrid, 1948). – Pedro de Ribera, ca. 1683–1742, great master of the Ayuntamiento of Madrid, with many works there and in Salamanca (J. Delgado Martín, La fuente de la fama del arquitecto Pedro de Ribera, BSEE, LI, 1943, pp. 224–40). – Narciso Tomé, d. 1742; active from 1715; displayed audacity and originality in his transparente for Toledo Cathedral; high altar for León Cathedral, only partly preserved (F. Chueca Goitia, Narciso Tomé: Una incógnita del barroco español, Goya, 49, 1962, pp. 12–21).

Sculpture. In the early, realistic phase of baroque sculpture, polychrome images became dominant, and there was a marked decrease of the monumental and funerary sculpture that had been so abundant in the previous century. At the same time Castile lost its leading position and was gradually replaced by Andalusia, which reached its peak at this time as an artistic

Seville and Granada. These cities were closely related an appear as scarcely distinguishable branches of a single school characterized by a classic balance that avoids violence an exaggeration. The outstanding exponent of this school wa Juan Martínez Montañés (1568–1649), creator of variou Crucifixions and figures of the Christ Child, as well as th altarpiece and other works (1609) in the monastery of S. Isidor del Campo near Seville, in addition to many versions of th Immaculate Conception. Montañés had a workshop witl numerous disciples; notable among them was Juan de Mes (1586–1621), who carved several Crucifixions, some very moving such as his figure of Christ in agony (1622) at Vergara (Guipúzcoa). A step toward clarity of form and pure beauty cal be observed in the work of Alonso Cano (q.v.; PL. 142), who like the great artists of the Renaissance, was a painter an architect as well as a sculptor. He exerted enormous influenc not only in Andalusia but also in Madrid. Cano's most distin guished disciple was Pedro de Mena (1628–1688; PL. 142 XII, PL. 377). He went to Málaga in 1658 to work on the choi stalls of the Cathedral and later took up residence in tha city, where he was active until his death. At the same tim the Mora family became active in Granada. One of them José de Mora, was the most impassioned of the Andalusia sculptors; his religious sculpture (representations of the Crucifixion, the Ecce Homo, and Our Lady of Sorrows) is unrivaled Diego de Mora, who died in 1729, provided the link betwee the Cano tradition and the art of the 18th century.

At the end of the 17th century a new and powerful influenc arrived from Italy, represented by Bernini's tumultuous and picturesque style, and reached its highest development in Andalusia Its leading exponent was Pedro Roldán (1624–1700), most o whose work is in Seville, his masterpiece being the large altarpiec of the Hospital de la Caridad (1670). His daughter Luisa known as La Roldana, was one of his two chief disciples, althougl she worked independently; the other was his grandson, Pedro Duque Cornejo (1677–1757), active in Seville, Granada, E Paular, and Córdoba. Torcuato Ruiz del Peral (1708–73) despite his strong attraction to the baroque, was a faithfu follower of Cano. He was active in Guadix (Granada), bu most of his surviving sculpture is in the city of Granada; hi work represents the final stage of the Granada school. The work of the Castilian group of sculptors of this period lacked individuality, hence Castile readily yielded to the academic tendencies that dominated the second half of the 18th century. During this period the eastern regions of Spain produced some sculptors of stature. Luis Bonifás y Massó (1730–86) was active in Catalonia; his work is of uneven quality and shows a greater interest in form than in expression. Ignacio Vergara worked in Valencia, and Francisco Salzillo (Zarcillo, 1707–81) in Murcia; the latter is the purest representative of the Italian trend in Spanish baroque sculpture, as well as the artist most deeply inspired by the national popular spirit. The work of José Luján Pérez of the Canary Islands is somewhat comparable.

ARTISTS. Luis Bonifás y Massó, ca. 1730–86; settled at Valls, produced numerous works in Catalonia, of which only a small part is preserved (C. Martinell, El escultor Luis Bonifás y Massó, Barcelona, 1948). – Alonso Cano, 1601–67, architect, sculptor, painter; created high altar of S. María at Lebrija (1629), near Seville; worked in Madrid (1638–52 and 1657–59) and Granada (M. Martínez Chumillas, Alonso Cano, Madrid, 1948; E. Díaz-Jiménez y Molleda, El escultor Alonso Cano, Madrid, 1954; M. E. Gómez-Moreno, Alonso Cano, Madrid, 1954 [cat.]; H. E. Wethey, Alonso Cano, Princeton, 1955). – Gregorio Fernández, of Galicia, active in Valladolid after 1605; works in El Pardo (Madrid), Segovia, Valladolid, and elsewhere (M. Gómez-Moreno, Gregorio Fernández, Madrid, 1935; E. Garcia Chigo, Gregorio Fernández, Valladolid, 1952). – José Luján Pérez, b. Guia (island of Grand Canary) 1756, d. 1815; continued Andalusian tradition of sculpture; works in Las Palmas, La Laguna, Santa Cruz de Tenerife, and elsewhere (S. Tejera, Don José Luján Pérez, Madrid, 1914). – Juan Martínez Montañés, b. Alcalá la Real (Jaén) 1568, d. 1649; pupil of Pablo de Rojas in Granada; active in Seville after 1588, greater part of work preserved there and in neighboring cities (Homenaje a Martínez Montañés, B. bellas artes (Sevilla), IV, 1939, pp. 1–179; M. E. Gómez-Moreno, Juan Martínez Montañés, Barcelona, 1942; C. López Martínez, San Jerónimo penitente: magnífica escultura de Juan Martínez Montañés, Seville, 1948; J. Hernández Díaz, Juan Martínez Montañés, Seville, 1949). – Pedro de Mena y Medrano, b. Granada 1628, d. 1688; worked in Granada with Alonso Cano; went to Málaga (1658), made short trip to Madrid and Toledo (ca. 1663); works in Granada, Córdoba, and Madrid (R. de Orueta y Duarte, Pedro de Mena, Madrid, 1914; Pedro de Mena, escultor; Homenaje en su tercer centenario, Málaga, 1928; E. Orozco Díaz, Devoción y barroquismo en las dolorosas de Pedro de Mena, Goya, 52, 1963, pp. 235–41). – José de Mora, b. Baza (Granada) 1642, d. 1724; worked in Madrid as sculptor to Charles II, returned to Granada 1680 (A. Gallego Burin, Tres familias de escultores; Los Menas, los Moras y los Roldanes, AEAA, I, 1925, pp. 323–31; A. Gallego Burin, José de Mora, escultor: Su vida y su obra, Granada, 1926; R. de Orueta y Duarte, Sobre José de Mora, AEAA, III, 1927, pp. 71–75). – Pedro Roldán, b. Antequera 1624, d. 1700; educated in Granada, worked in Seville, where greater part of work is preserved; other works in Jerez de la Frontera, Jaén, and elsewhere (M. D. Salazar y Bermúdez, Pedro Roldán: Su vida, Madrid, 1955). – Torcuato Ruiz del Peral, b. Esfiliana (Granada) 1708, d. 1773; pupil of Diego de Mora in Granada, where he continued to live (A. Gallego Burin, Un escultor del siglo XVIII: Torcuato Ruíz del Peral, B. Granada Univ., VIII, 1936, pp. 341–416). – Francisco Salzillo (Zarcillo), 1707–81, son of the Italian Nicolò Zarcillo; lived in Murcia, where greater part of work is preserved (J. Sánchez Moreno, Vida y obra de Francisco Salzillo, Murcia, 1945; D. Sánchez Jara and L. Ayuso Vicente, Salzillo, Madrid, 1951; J. Torres Fontes, ed., Museo Salzillo: Guía, Murcia, Madrid, 1959).

Painting. The 17th century was the most distinguished period in Spanish painting, during which great masters emerged in several centers. The royal painting collection, which contained a wealth of Italian baroque and Flemish paintings, was a perennial source of inspiration and study — almost substituting for journeys abroad — for the fortunate artists who were connected with the court. The transformation of the 16th-century style was marked by the fusion of baroque art with realism and with the preference for the somber "tenebrist" palette and the chiaroscuro of Caravaggio (q.v.) and other painters known as the *tenebrosi*. This tendency was introduced by Francisco Ribalta (1556–1628; PL. 147; II, PL. 188), who worked in Valencia, and Jusepe (José) de Ribera (q.v.; PL. 155; II, PL. 192), also of Valencia, who was to become an important figure in the Neapolitan school. The Toledo school was continued by Luis Tristán (PL. 148), El Greco's disciple, and

Pedro Orrente (ca. 1570–1627), a follower of the Bassanos (q.v.). In Madrid Juan Bautista (Giovan Battista) Mayno (II, PL. 189), Philip IV's drawing master, gave a Caravaggesque stamp to the style of the group of painters descended from the mannerists of the Escorial.

Diego Velázquez (q.v.; 1599–1660), who studied in Seville under Francisco Pacheco (XII, PL. 376) and settled in Madrid in 1623, marked the peak of Spanish painting. His chief contribution was a highly personal style in which economy of means and mastery of space and light triumph over pure form. After his early tenebrist period he painted, as official painter to Philip IV, his wonderful portraits of the royal family (PL. 150; II, PL. 190; XIV, PLS. 326, 328) and of dwarfs and buffoons (XIV, PL. 327). Following his first visit to Italy he returned to Spain in 1631, painted the magnificent *Surrender of Breda* (1635; VII, PL. 276), and continued his steady progress to *Las Meninas*, of 1656 (XIV, PLS. 330, 331). Despite his lengthy stay in Madrid, Velázquez had little influence on the painting of that city — less, indeed, than Rubens or Van Dyck — precisely because his style was so strongly personal.

Contemporary with Velázquez were the painters who formed the first generation of the school of Madrid. Its outstanding members were Fray Juan Rizi (Ricci; 1600–81) and Antonio de Pereda (ca. 1608–78; PL. 151). Their disciples included Juan de Pareja (PL. 144), Juan Bautista Martínez del Mazo (PL. 149), and, in a later generation, Juan Carreño de Miranda (PL. 149; II, PL. 191), Francisco Rizi, Francisco de Herrera the Younger, Mateo Cerezo (PL. 147), José Antolínez, Juan Antonio de Frías y Escalante, Juan Martín Cabezalero, and Claudio Coello (q.v.). With Coello (1642–93) the great baroque period in Madrid came to a close; his principal work is the picture of Charles II and his court venerating the miraculous Host (*La Sagrada Forma*; II, PL. 191) at the Escorial. The Neapolitan Luca Giordano (Lucas Jordán; 1632–1705; PL. 352; V, PL. 226) was summoned to Madrid in 1692 by Charles II (r. 1665–1700) and remained there until 1702. The strong influence that his fluent and brilliant style exerted there is evidenced in the large wall decorations by Antonio Palomino, who was also the first Spanish art historian.

At the same time in Andalusia, several fine painters worked in Córdoba and Granada and especially in Seville, which was the region's most important center. In Granada Fray Juan Sánchez Cotán painted his famous still lifes (II, PL. 184). Other members of this school were the previously mentioned Alonso Cano (PL. 147), whose representations of the Immaculate Conception are particularly beautiful, Pedro Atanasio Bocanegra, Juan de Sevilla, Pedro de Moya, and José Risueño. In Córdoba the work of Antonio del Castillo was outstanding, while Francisco de Zurbarán (q.v.; XIII, PL. 201) dominated the scene in Seville. Despite certain primitive features in his painting, Zurbarán wrought a radical change by simplifying technique and chromatic range and by his use of light as a mystical element. Particularly effective are his still lifes and paintings of religious, in which he imparts a singular quality to the texture of the habits. Bartolomé Esteban Murillo (q.v.) was particularly esteemed; he blended the refined technique of the period with a feeling for the popular image that, in his religious paintings, satisfied the fervor of the broad public but sometimes, in its superficial aspects, obscures the profound and strictly pictorial beauty of his work. Murillo's best-known subjects are genre scenes such as the *The Pie Eater* (PL. 156). The great artist Juan de Valdés Leal (1622–90) met with a similar fate, although for different reasons. In his *Allegory of Death* (II, PL. 188) and his *Finis Gloriae Mundi* (PL. 148) in Seville, the Spanish sense of the dramatic is combined with a 17th-century leaning toward allegory to produce terrifying images. Valdés Leal was a true painter of intense baroque leanings who finally achieved an original style in his use of light and of realistic detail. The Seville school was continued by a series of painters who cultivated Murillo's style until well into the 18th century. Besides these main Andalusian centers may be mentioned the activity of Jerónimo Jacinto de Espinosa in Valencia, Senén Vila and Mateo Gilarte in Murcia, and Jusepe Martínez and Vicente Verdusán in Aragon.

In the first half of the 18th century, forms and tendencies that had been highly developed in the preceding century were still prevalent, and a large number of foreign artists were summoned to the court, among them the Frenchmen Michel-Ange Houasse, Jean Ranc, and Louis Michel Van Loo and the Italian Jacopo Amigoni (Amiconi). Representative of these influences were Teodoro Ardemans and Juan Garcia de Miranda the Elder in Madrid; Domingo Martínez, Bernardo Germán Llorente, and Alonso Miguel de Tobar (Tovar) in Seville; José Risueño in Granada; Pablo Rabiella (Raviella) in Zaragoza; and Antonio Viladomat in Barcelona. New academic ideas were consolidated by the establishment of the Academia de S. Fernando in Madrid (1752), an event which was to have a decisive influence on the course of Spanish art in the second half of the 18th century.

ARTISTS. José Antolínez, of Madrid, 1635–75, pupil of Francisco Rizi; painted Virgins according to personal concept (M. S. Soria, José Antolínes: Retratos y otras obras, AEArte, XXIX, 1956, pp. 1–8; D. Angulo Iñiguez, José Antolínez, Madrid, 1957). – Juan de Arellano, 1614–76; master of flower painting; PL. 201 (J. Cavestany, ed., Floreros y bodegones en la pintura española, Madrid, 1935–40). – Alonso Cano, painter and sculptor (see above). – Juan Carreño de Miranda, b. Avilés (Asturias) 1614, d. 1685; court painter from 1671, portraitist of Charles II, painter of religious paintings showing Flemish influence (P. Penzol, Un pintor asturiano en la corte de Carlos II, B. Inst. estudios asturianos, XIII, 1959, pp. 15–26; D. Berjano Escobar, El pintor Juan Carreño de Miranda, Madrid, n.d.). – Antonio del Castillo, active at Córdoba, where most of his work is found (F. J. Sánchez Cantón, Dos cuadros fechados de Antonio del Castillo, AEAA, XIII, 1937, pp. 159–61). – Mateo Cerezo, b. Burgos ca. 1626, d. Madrid 1666; excellent colorist, elegant and beautiful forms (E. Tormo y Monzo, Mateo Cerezo, AEAA, III, 1927, pp. 245–74). – Claudio Coello (q.v.), 1642–93, painter of numerous portraits, altar paintings, and frescoes (J. A. Gaya Nuño, Claudio Coello, Madrid, 1957). – Francisco Collantes, 1599–1656, pupil of Vicente Carducho (Carducci); famous as painter of Biblical themes with landscape backgrounds (PL. 144) and of landscapes with small figures (J. A. Gaya Nuño, En el centenario de Collantes, Goya, 10, 1956, pp. 222–29; A. E. Pérez Sánchez, Algunas obras inéditas y nuevas consideraciones en torno a Collantes, AEArte, XXXV, 1962, pp. 253–63). – Juan Antonio de Frías y Escalante, b. Córdoba ca. 1633, d. Madrid 1670; pupil of Francisco Rizi; painted lively and colorful canvases (E. Lafuente Ferrari, Escalante en Navarra y otras notas sobre el pintor, Principe de Viana, II, 1941, pp. 8–23; E. Lafuente Ferrari, Nuevas notas sobre Escalante, Arte Español, XXIX, 1944, pp. 29–37). – Jerónimo Jacinto de Espinosa, pupil of Ribalta; worked in Valencia (L. Tramoyeres Blasco, El pintor Jerónimo Jacinto de Espinosa, Arch. de arte valenciano, I, 1915, pp. 127–41, II, 1916, pp. 3–15; G. Gómez Carbonell, Jerónimo Jacinto de Espinosa, Anales Univ. Valencia, 1930–31). – Francisco de Herrera the Elder (PL. 147), ca. 1576–1656; active in Seville; impetuous and violent work (J. S. Thacher, The Paintings of Francisco de Herrera the Elder, AB, XIX, 1936, pp. 324–80; J. A. Gaya Nuño, Semblanza de Herrera el Viejo, Goya, 35, 1960, pp. 277–84). – Francisco de Herrera the Younger, of Seville, 1622–85, son of foregoing; studied in Italy and worked in Seville and Madrid. – Juan Bautista Martínez del Mazo, d. 1667; collaborator of Velázquez; painted portraits and landscapes (J. A. Gaya Nuño, Juan Bautista del Mazo: el gran discípulo de Velázquez, Varia Velásqueña, I, Madrid, 1960, pp. 471–81; J. López Navio, Matrimonio de Juan Bautista del Mazo con la hija de Velázquez, AEArte, XXXIII, 1960, pp. 387–419). – Juan Bautista (Giovan Battista) Mayno, b. Pastrana (Guadalajara) ca. 1568, d. 1649; style resembles El Greco's, displaying fondness for clear, mild colors (E. Harris, Aportaciones para el estudio de J. B. Mayno, REA, XXXVII, 1935, pp. 333–39; A. Garcia Figar, Fr. J. B. Mayno: pintor español, Goya, 25, 1958, pp. 6–12). – Pedro Orrente, b. Montealegre (Albacete) ca. 1570, d. 1627; worked in Montealegre, Valencia, and Toledo; style resembles El Greco's; painted religious and pastoral scenes reminiscent of Bassano (E. Lafuente Ferrari, Pedro Orrente y el perdido retablo de Villarejo de Salvanés, AEA, XIV, 1940–41, pp. 503–16; J. C. López Jiménez, Sobre pinturas varias, una escultura y el testamento de Orrente, Arch. de arte valenciano, XXX, 1959, pp. 62–76). – Antonio Palomino, b. Bujalance (Córdoba) ca. 1655, d. 1726; most prolific fresco painter in Spain; works in Valencia (1701), Salamanca (1705), Granada (1712), El Paular (1723) and elsewhere (J. A. Gaya Nuño, En el centenario de Palomino, Goya, 5, 1955, pp. 265–74; R. Aguilar, Nuevos datos para la historia de Palomino, Córdoba, 1958). – Antonio de Pereda, ca. 1608–78, b. Valladolid ca. 1608, d. 1678; worked in Madrid, produced excellent bodegones, still lifes (Academia de S. Fernando, Madrid), and altarpieces (E.

Tormo y Monzo, Antonio de Pereda, Valladolid, 1916). – Francisco Ribalta, b. Solsona ca. 1565, d. Valencia 1628; lived in Madrid ca 1582–97; originated school that survived into 18th cent. (D. F. Darby, Francisco Ribalta and His School, Cambridge, Mass., 1938; J. Ainaud y Lasarte, Ribalta y Caravaggio, ABMAB, V, 1947, pp. 345–413; C. G. Espresati, Ribalta, Barcelona, 1948; J. Mateo Blanco, Estancia en Italia e influencias italianas de Ribalta, SAA, X–XII, 1961, pp. 165–79). – Jusepe (José) de Ribera (q.v.), b. Játiva ca. 1591, d. Naples 1652; in Naples from 1616 (A. L. Mayer, Jusepe de Ribera, Leipzig, 1923; J. Pla y Cargol, Ribera y Zurbarán, 4th ed., Gerona, Madrid, 1944; E. du Gué Trapier, Ribera, New York, 1952; D. F. Darby, Ribera and the Wise Men, AB, XLIV, 1962, pp. 279–307). Francisco Rizi (Ricci), 1608–85, b. Madrid 1608, d. 1685; collaborator of Carreño; prolific and able decorator; painter of frescoes (Toledo) and altarpieces (D. Angulo Iñiguez, Francisco Rizi: Su vida: Quadros religiosos fechados anteriores a 1670, AEArte, XXI, 1958, pp. 89–115; D. Angulo Iñiguez, Francisco Rizi, AEArte, XXV, 1962, pp. 95–122). – Fray Juan Rizi (Ricci), b. Madrid 1600, d. 1681; brother of foregoing and a Benedictine monk; worked in various monasteries (San Millán de la Cogolla, Burgos, Montserrat); resided in Italy from 1662 until death (E. Tormo y Monzo, C. Gusí and E. Lafuente Ferrari, La voda y la obra de Fr. Juan Rizi, Madrid, 1930). – Juan de las Roelas, ca. 1560–1625; worked at Valladolid and Seville, where he settled and originated school (D. Angulo Iñiguez, Juan de Roelas: Aportaciones para su estudio, AEAA, I, 1925, pp. 103–09). – Fray Juan Sánchez Cotán, 1560–1627, b. Orgaz (Toledo) ca. 1560, d. 1627; worked in Toledo and Granada (E. Orozco Díaz, El pintor certujo Sánchez Cotán y el realismo español, Clavileño, III, 16, 1952, pp. 18–28; M. L. Caturla, Zurbarán... con unas notas sobre Fr. Juan Sánchez Cotán por Emilio Orozco Díaz..., Madrid, 1953 [cat.]; E. Orozco Díaz, Realismo y religiosidad en la pintura de Sánchez Cotán, Goya, 1, 1954, pp. 19–28). – Luis Tristán, worked at Toledo in El Greco's studio; style akin to Ribera's and Ribalta's (F. de B. de San Román, Noticias para la biografía del pintor Luis Tristán, Toledo, 1924; F. de B. de San Román, Noticias nuevas para la biografía del pintor Luis Tristán, B. Real Acad. de bellas artes y ciencias históricas de Toledo, V, 1924, pp. 113–39; A. Aragonés de la Encarnación, El pintor Luis Tristán, B. Real Acad. de bellas artes y ciencias históricas de Toledo, VI, 1925, pp. 1–58; D. Angulo Iñiguez, Algunas obras de Luis Tristán, AEArte, XIX, 1956, pp. 265–73). – Juan de Valdés Leal, of Seville, 1622–90; trained in Córdoba, settled in Seville after 1656; represents final splendor of Seville school (J. Gestoso, Biografía del pintor Juan de Valdés Leal, Seville, 1918; T. S. R. Boase, Christ Bearing the Cross, attributed to Valdés Leal, at Magdalen College, Oxford: A Study in Taste, London, New York, 1955; E. du Gué Trapier, Valdés Leal: Baroque Concept of Death and Suffering in His Paintings, New York, 1956; E. du Gué Trapier, Valdés Leal, New York, 1960).

THE NEOCLASSIC. About the middle of the 18th century the feeling arose throughout Europe that a change was needed in art if it was to keep pace with the new philosophical, political, and scientific concepts of the time. The tendency was to condemn everything superfluous and stress all that was rational, which was, without doubt, one of the causes of the great surge in architecture in this period. The organization of art studies by the state became inevitable and was based on international academic trends that reached Spain through French and Italian models.

Architecture. During the reign of Charles III (1716–88) Spain experienced a period of economic prosperity that enabled the government to patronize the artistic activity of three great architects: Ventura Rodriguez (1717–85), Francisco Sabatini (1721–97), and Juan de Villanueva (1739–1811). Ventura Rodríguez, a disciple of Filippo Juvara (q.v.) and a direct heir to the influence of the baroque art of Rome, was able to adapt to the times so successfully that, without abandoning the baroque tradition, he was reputed in his day, and almost until modern times, to be one of the most intransigent neoclassicists. The large number of works to his credit and their widespread influence throughout the country made Rodríguez the true originator of the impulse to renewal. The work of the Italian Sabatini (Puerta de Alcalá and Ministry of Finance in Madrid) although highly interesting and of considerable originality, was not of major importance. Juan de Villanueva, an artist with a stronger personality, followed the new European trends, at the same time revealing his enthusiasm for the architecture of the Escorial. No other Spanish architect knew or used classi-

art so well; the best example of his work is the Prado in Madrid. Silvestre Pérez and other talented followers continued Villanueva's style until the middle of the 19th century. In the second half of the 18th century Madrid, renewed and embellished, was the great artistic center of Spain, while the regional schools of architecture, rooted as they were in the baroque tradition, declined in the face of increased academic intervention in the designs of both civic and religious buildings. Nevertheless, certain interesting buildings were constructed by the regional schools, such as the Lonja in Barcelona, created by Juan Soler Faneca in 1772.

ARTISTS. Ventura Rodríguez, b. Ciempozuelos (Madrid) 1717, d. 1785; worked 40 years on royal buildings; Ceán Bermúdeg (1800) lists 140 of his projects, many of them carried into effect throughout Spain by his pupils and assistants (F. Chueca, Ventura Rodríguez y la escuela barocca romana, AEArte, XV, 1942, pp. 185–210; J. Simon and F. Chueca, Ventura Rodríguez en los Estudios Reales de Madrid, AEArte, XVII, 1944, pp. 245–63; F. Iñiguez, La formación de Ventura Rodríguez, AEArte, XXII, 1949, pp. 137–48). – Francisco Sabatini, 1721–97; arrived in Spain in 1760 from Palermo and Rome; pupil of Luigi Vanvitelli; worked particularly on royal buildings (Rev. nacional de arquitectura, V, 1946, pp. 232–39). – Juan de Villanueva, of Madrid, 1739–1811, son of a sculptor; studied seven years in Rome and, after return, worked on the Escorial (1768–73), Burgo de Osma (1770), Casita de Arriba and Casita de Abajo at El Escorial (1773); Casita del Príncipe at El Pardo (1784); in Madrid, the Botanic Garden (1781), Prado (1785), Oratory of Caballero de Gracia (1789), and Observatory (1790) (C. de Miguel and F. Chueca, La vida y las obras del arquitecto Juan de Villanueva [ed. F. Chueca Goitia], Madrid, 1949; A. Bonet Correa, Los retablos de la iglesia de las Calatravas de Madrid, AEArte, XXXV, 1962, pp. 21–49).

Sculpture. Neoclassicism as expounded by Antonio Canova (q.v.) and Bertel Thorvaldsen did not become firmly established in Spain until 1800, for sculpture, the neoclassic art par excellence, had to struggle constantly against the deep-rooted baroque tradition. It remained a superficial art in Spain, and in many cases neoclassicism was limited to the repainting of older polychrome statues in white. With the advent of the academies, however, the study of technique was reinstituted after a long period of neglect due to baroque conventions, which tended to solve the problems of drapery by using a base of stiffened cloth. Madrid became the most important art center of the period, while Barcelona gradually emerged as the foremost among the provincial centers.

The most important figures of the early academic phase were Luis Salvador Carmona (1709–67), who was a classicist in his interest in nude studies and his concern with proportion; Juan Pascual de Mena (1707–84), who combined complete mastery of the classical forms with a preference for religious subjects; Robert Michel (ca. 1720–86), whose figures are graceful and animated; and Manuel Alvarez (1727–97), who worked with precision and refined taste. The last sculptors to devote themselves to religious images were active during the period of transition to the 19th century; noteworthy among them were José Ginés (1768–1823) and Ramón Amadeu (1745–1821). Sculptors working in the more truly neoclassic style prevailed in the first half of the 19th century, including such figures as Juan Adán (1741–1816) — who, however, still represents the transitional period; José Alvarez y Cubero (1768–1827), called the Spanish Canova, who was the most eminent of the Spanish neoclassic sculptors; Damián Campeny y Estrany (1771–1855), devoted to neoclassic canons and prolific in the production of mythological pieces; and, an important follower of this trend, Antonio Solá (1787–1861).

ARTISTS. Juan Adán, b. Tarazona 1741, d. 1816; studied at Zaragoza and Rome, returned to Spain 1776; worked in Lérida and, after 1782, Madrid (E. Pardo Canalís, El escultor Juan Adán, SAA, 7–9, 1957, pp. 5–63). – José Alvarez Cubero, b. Priego de Córdoba 1768, d. 1827; studied in Madrid, Paris, and Rome, where he lived for 20 years; returned to Spain 1826. – Ramón Amadeu, 1745–1821, pupil of Luis Bonifás; devoted himself particularly to Nativity scenes and religious images (C. Martinell, El escultor Ramón Amadeu: Su formacion y su obra, ABMAB, III, 1945, pp. 157–88). – Damián Cam-

peny y Estrany, b. Mataró 1771, d. 1855; studied in Barcelona and later in Rome (1796–1816), then returned to Barcelona. – Luis Salvador Carmona, 1709–67; worked in La Granja and Madrid; numerous scattered religious sculptures (J. Moreno Villa, Memoria del escultor Luis Salvador Carmona, AEAA, VIII, 1932, pp. 98–99). – Juan Pascual de Mena, 1707–84, director of Academia de S. Fernando, Madrid; numerous works in Madrid. – Antonio Solá, b. Barcelona 1787, d. 1861; removed to Rome when very young and spent most of his life there (A. Palau, Venus y Cupido..., AEArte, XIV, 1940–41, pp. 456–60; J. Rius Serra, El grupo de Daoiz y Velarde de Antonio Solá, AEA, XX, 1947, pp. 335–38).

Painting. Through the activity of the Italian Corrado Giaquinto (in Spain 1753), who had a profound influence on Spanish art, the academic tendencies produced an artificial and conventional painting style, lacking in force and artistic conviction. One of the chief exponents of this trend was the German Anton Raphael Mengs (1728–79), who arrived in Madrid in 1761; more consistent in his writing than in his painting, he left a deep impression on such artists as Mariano S. de Maella, Gregorio Ferro, Francisco Bayeu, the members of the González Velázquez family, José del Castillo, and even Goya and, later, Vicente Lopéz y Portaña. Giovanni Battista Tiepolo (q.v.) was summoned to Madrid to decorate the Royal Palace in 1762, but his work and that of his sons exerted little influence. Luis Meléndez (1716–80; PL. 201) and Luis Paret y Alcázar (1749–99) revealed original artistic personalities, but the dominating genius of the time was Francisco Goya (q.v.).

Working with a minimum of classical references, Goya was the best representative of the transformation of the rococo style into the pathos of romanticism. His work marks the opening of art to the imagery of fantasy and the continuation of Velázquez' tradition in the striving for economy of means. In these aspects Goya can be considered a precursor of modern artistic trends. After studying in Zaragoza and Madrid and in Italy, he painted in the Cathedral of Nuestra Señora del Pilar in Zaragoza and in 1775 established his residence in Madrid, where he painted cartoons for the Royal Tapestry Factory. His personality gradually matured during the last decade of the century; from this period are the series of etchings *Los Caprichos* (IV, PL. 440; VI, PL. 402) and his penetrating portraits. After 1808, the beginning of the Napoleonic War in Spain, he expressed his vision of the horrors of war in the scenes known as *Los desastres de la guerra*. In the years following the return of peace (1814) Goya painted superb portraits; but his dislike for commissions and models, together with his predilection for the imaginative and the fantastic, made him turn more and more toward the sombre treatment of subjects, as can be seen in his *pinturas negras* ("black paintings") and his *Disparates* ("follies"). He was ill at ease in the absolutist Madrid of Ferdinand VII's reign (1814–33), and when he was close to eighty he moved to Bordeaux in France, where he died. Shortly thereafter appreciation of his work and personality began to grow, and it has increased ever since.

Vicente López y Portaña (1772–1850), a highly productive artist who typified the traditional tendency, was especially distinguished in the field of portrait painting. The weak neoclassic pictorial style was chiefly represented by José Madrazo y Agudo (1781–1859), José Aparicio (1773–1838), and Juan Antonio Ribera y Fernández (1779–1860). Local schools developed during this period especially in Valencia, Barcelona, Zaragoza, and Seville.

ARTISTS. Francisco Bayeu, b. Zaragoza 1734, d. 1795; studied in Zaragoza and Madrid, where he settled; frescoes in Toledo, Zaragoza and Madrid (Royal Palace); also portraits and religious paintings (V. de Sambricio, Francisco Bayeu, Madrid, 1955). – José del Castillo, 1737–93, particularly noted for cartoons for tapestries (V. de Sambricio, José del Castillo, Madrid, 1957). – Vicente López y Portaña, of Valencia, 1772–1850; pupil of Maella; court painter after 1814: impeccabile portraitist, also produced religious paintings and decorative frescoes (A. Méndez Casal and M. González Martí, Vicente Lopez, Valencia, n.d.; J. Contreras y López de Alaya, Marqués de Lozoya, Vicente López, Barcelona, 1943 [cat.]). – Mariano S. de Maella, of Valencia, 1739–1819; studied in Italy, follower of A. R. Mengs; work included portraits, frescoes for royal palaces,

SPANISH AND PORTUGUESE ART

religious paintings. – Luis Meléndez, 1716–80, b. Naples (?) 1716, d. 1780; studied in Rome, settled in Madrid ca. 1750; painter of miniatures and *bodegones* (F. J. Sánchez Cantón, El autorretrato de Luis Meléndez en el Museo del Louvre, AEAA, V, 1929, pp. 197–98; M. S. Soria, Firmas de Luis Meléndez, AEArte, XXI, 1948, pp. 215–17). – Anton Raphael Mengs, b. Aussig (Bohemia) 1728, d. Rome 1779; summoned to Madrid 1761 by Charles III, lived there until 1769 and from 1774 to 1776; painted portraits and religious subjects, also frescoes (F. Sánchez Cantón, Antonio F. Mengs, Madrid, 1929 [cat.]). – Luis Paret y Alcázar, b. Madrid 1749, d. 1799; pupil of the Frenchman Charles François de la Traverse (1726–80); traveled in Europe; painted flowers, landscapes, genre scenes, portraits, and religious subjects (O. Delgado, Luis Paret y Alcázar, Madrid, 1957; X. de Salas, Aportaciones a la obra de Luis Paret y Alcázar, AEArte, XXXV, 1962, pp. 123–33).

Minor arts. During the 18th century the production of textiles, furniture, silverwork, and ceramics attained a high level. Traditional products were improved and new ones were created. In the Madrid area, which was the most receptive to innovation and had the greatest means at its disposal, the quantity and quality of production advanced steadily. This process was favored by the founding of a large number of factories, most of them owned by foreigners under royal protection, that were intended to furnish and decorate the royal residences. Silk weaving flourished in Valencia, as did cotton weaving in Catalonia. Fine work was produced in Madrid at the Royal Embroidery Factory (directed by Matteo Gasparini from 1764 to 1774), the Royal Tapestry Factory of Santa Barbara, the Royal Cabinetwork Factory (active from 1763), the Royal Silversmiths' School (founded in 1778 and directed by Antonio Martínez), and the Royal Bronze Factory; in the ceramics workshops of Madrid (Buen Retiro Palace) and Alcora; in the Royal Crystal Factory of Segovia (La Granja); in the Royal Stone Workshops, founded in 1763; and in the ivory workshops of the various royal palaces.

THE MODERN PERIOD. The spirit of romanticism gave rise, in a sense, to many of the changing stylistic facets of modern art. During the course of the 19th century, short-lived movements began to succeed one another rapidly, so that artists at any given time represented the most varied trends. The artistic supremacy of Paris was established by the middle of the century; as a result, many phases of Spanish art in the modern period reflect trends that were born and developed in Paris, often by Spanish artists who found that the French capital offered a more favorable artistic climate for their activity.

Architecture. Dominated by an academic orientation and hampered by the crisis in style caused by the Industrial Revolution, the architecture of the 19th century produced few works of merit. The interest in archaeology, beginning in the second third of the century and becoming more pronounced during the last third, called forth the modernist reaction, charged with baroque feeling but also with premonitions of a new style. In Catalonia, Antonio Gaudí (q.v.) was outstanding; he designed the Church of the Sagrada Familia (unfinished; I, PL. 467) and the Güell Park in Barcelona (I, PL. 466) and the Episcopal Palace of Astorga, among many other works. Castile continued the neoclassic tradition, revived the Mudejar style, and constructed buildings along modified or transformed Renaissance lines, until the advent of new building methods. In the 20th century, architecture slowly began to break away from the ornamentalism that had been cultivated in Catalonia by Luis Doménech y Montaner and from the Neo-Gothic tendency of José Puig y Cadafalch. In the first decades of the 20th century the trend to the monumental and Neo-Renaissance styles still prevailed; only about 1930 did the influence of functionalism reach Spain through the work of José Luis Sert and other able architects. In Madrid, the work on the University City (most of it destroyed during the Civil War and since rebuilt on a new plan) and the building of several skyscrapers (e.g., the Telephone Exchange) made possible a certain degree of innovation in construction, although this was not always correlated with esthetic quality. A synthesis of the tradition of brick architecture with functionalism seemed possible,

although most buildings followed more or less classicist formulas in the prevailing stylized version.

Sculpture. Following neoclassicism, a tendency toward realism developed in the second half of the 19th century with such figures as Venancio Vallmitjana, Jerónimo Suñol, and Ricardo Bellver. Agustín Querol was the most typical representative of *fin-de-siècle* modernism, which was continued in the realism of Mariano Benlliure. During the transition to the 20th century, Catalonia took the lead in Spanish sculpture with the work of Miguel Blay and José Llimona. The sculpture of the first decades of the 20th century tended toward a moderate expressionism with Victorio Macho, Emiliano Barral, and Rodriguez Santiago Bonome, and toward the approach of Auguste Rodin and Aristide Maillol (qq.v.) with the work of Nemesio Mogrobejo, Julio Antonio, José Clará, Enrique Casanovas, Manolo (Manuel Martínez Hugué), and Pablo Gargallo in his traditional aspects; Gargallo's chief contribution, however, was his revival of the technique of sculpture in wrought iron, which he learned in Paris and in which he was followed by Julio González. Among the Spanish abstract sculptors of the later years of the century are Angel Ferrant (1891–1959), Oteiza (Jorge de Oteiza Embil; b. 1908), Eudaldo Serra (b. 1911), and Eduardo Chillida (b. 1924; V, PL. 146).

ARTISTS. Ricardo Bellver, b. Madrid 1845, d. 1912; lived in Rome 1874, thereafter almost exclusively in Madrid. – Mariano Benlliure, b. Valencia 1862, d. Madrid 1947; worked in Rome and Paris, active in Madrid (F. Alcantara, Mariano Benlliure, Nuestro tiempo, II, 1902, pp. 113–44; C. de Quevedo Pessanha, Vida artística de Mariano Benlliure, Madrid, 1947; P. Tuero-O'Donnell, Mariano Benlliure o recuerdos de una familia, Barcelona, 1962). – Miguel Blay, 1866–1936, studied in Paris under Meunier; one of the most finished sculptors of turn of century. – José Clará, b. Olot (Gerona) 1878, d. Barcelona 1958; studied in Toulouse and Paris; worked in Paris and Barcelona (J. Teixidor, La evolución plástica del arte de José Clará, ABMAB, I, 1941, pp. 13–29; J. Teixidor, José Clará, Barcelona, 1945). – José Llimona, b. Barcelona 1864, d. 1934; profoundly affected by Quattrocento sculpture, which he studied in Italy. – Agustín Querol, b. Tortosa (Tarragona) 1860, d. Madrid 1909; pupil of Vallmitjana brothers; studied in Rome, then settled in Madrid (C. Rudy, Modern Spanish Sculpture: The Work of Don Agustín Querol, Studio, XXXVII, 1906, pp. 300–06). – Jerónimo Suñol, 1840–1902, best Catalan sculptor of romantic era; pupil of Vallmitjana brothers; studied in Rome; worked in Madrid. – Agapito (d. 1905) and Venancio (1828–1919) Vallmitjana (brothers), of Barcelona, where most of their artistic production is found (M. Rodriguez Codolá, Venancio y Agapito Vallmitjiana, Barcelona, 1946).

Painting. Romanticism, breaking with the artificiality of neoclassicism, often turned to themes drawn from popular life. This trend had many followers in Andalusia, particularly Valeriano D. Becquer and M. Rodríguez de Guzmán. Another tendency followed the course set by Goya and included Leonardo Alenza (1807–45), Francisco Lameyer (1825–77), and Eugenio Lucas y Padilla (1824–70). Pictorial concepts found expression in drawing, lithography, and other techniques of illustration that flourished in the 19th century. Romantic landscape painting, following the models of the Scottish painter David Roberts (1796–1864), who was in Spain from 1832 to 1833, was cultivated by Genaro Pérez Villaamil (1807–54) and Francisco Javier Parcerisa (1803–75). There was a parallel interest in line and drawing — an extension of the neoclassic style — represented by the portraitist Federico de Madrazo (1815–94) and the group of Catalan Nazarenes such as Joaquín Espalter (1809–80) and Claudio Lorenzale (1815–89).

The painting of historical scenes underwent considerable development in the second half of the century by such artists as Antonio Gisbert, José Casado del Alisal, and José Moreno Carbonero. This trend later evolved into genre painting and representations of provincial life. Two important figures of the period were Eduardo Rosales (1836–73) and Mariano Fortuny (1838–74). The latter, founder of a long-lived school and celebrated in his day, cultivated an affected style, although his watercolors and sketches show greater flexibility. During the same period landscape painting evolved as an independent genre, launched by the prolific artist Carlos de Haes (1829–98).

Belgian by birth. Prominent among the artists who followed him were Casimiro Sainz (1853-98) and Martín Rico (1833-1908) in Madrid and, in Catalonia, Ramón Marti Alsina (1826-94), — who also painted figures — and Joaquín Vayreda (1843-94), founder of the fertile school of Olot (Gerona).

Impressionism reached Spain toward the end of the 19th century, preceded by the luminism of Joaquín Sorolla (1863-1923); noteworthy artists working in this style were the Castilian Aureliano de Beruete (1845-1912), the Asturian Darío de Regoyos (1857-1913), and the Catalonians Eliseo Meifren (1859-1940), Francisco Gimeno (1858-1938), and Joaquín Mir (1873-1940). Other notable artists were Ramón Casas (1866-1932) in Catalonia and the interesting painter Isidro Nonell (1873-1911). The grandiose decorative style of Hermengildo Anglada Camarasa (1872-1959) brought 19th-century art to its close.

Spanish painters of the 20th century can be divided into three basic groups: the revolutionary artists who joined the school of Paris and helped to change the face of world painting — from cubism to surrealism — with such artists as Pablo Picasso, Joan Miró, Salvador Dali (qq.v.), and Antonio Clavé (b. 1913); the traditionalists, represented by Fernando Alvárez de Sotomayor (b. 1875) and Manuel Benedito (b. 1875); and a third group who sought a synthesis of values, their point of departure being the lonely, dramatic, and profound art of José Gutiérrez Solana (1886-1945). Among the artists of the last group, the most notable are Benjamín Palencia (b. 1902), Godofredo Ortega Muñoz (b. 1905), and Rafael Zabaleta (b. 1907) of the school of Madrid; and José Mompou (b. 1888), Miguel Villá (b. 1905), Jaime Mercadé (b. 1889), and C. Olivé Busquets of the school of Barcelona. Also noteworthy is the work of Javier Nogués (1874-1941), Francisco Galí (b. 1880), Pedro Gastó (b. 1909), and Pedro Pruna (b. 1904), all of Barcelona. Most of the artists of the later years of the century either paint in a schematic style derived from Picasso's work after 1930 or devote themselves to abstractionism; there are also, however, influential efforts to return to a sensitive and effective representational art.

ARTISTS. Leonardo Alenza, of Madrid, 1807-45; prolific draftsman of popular themes, portraits, and other pictorial types (C. Palencia y Alvarez Tubau, Leonardo Alenza, Madrid, n.d.). - Aureliano de Beruete, of Madrid, 1845-1912; painted landscapes, preferably of Madrid and its environs (R. D. Faraldo, Aureliano de Beruete, Barcelona, 1949). - Ramón Casas, b. Barcelona 1866, d. 1932; worked in Paris, Madrid, Granada; produced admirable easel portraits and drawings (J. M. Jordà, Ramón Casas: pintor, Barcelona, 1931; J. F. Ráfols, Ramón Casas: dibujante, Barcelona, 1949; J. F. Ráfols, Ramón Casas: pintor, Barcelona, 1949). - Mariano Fortuny, b. Reus (Tarragona) 1838, d. Rome 1874; trained in Barcelona; resided in Rome (1857), traveled in Africa and Europe (A. Mestres, La Vicaria de Fortuny, Barcelona, 1927; J. C. Daviller, Fortuny, Milan, 1930; A. Maseras, El pintor Fortuny, Barcelona, 1938; Exposición Fortuny, Barcelona, 1940 [cat.]; F. Pompey Salgueira, Fortuny, Madrid, 1953). - Francisco Gimeno, b. Tortosa, (Tarragona) 1858 d. Barcelona 1938; painted interiors, admirable figures, still lifes, vibrant landscapes (J. Serra, Francisco Gimeno, Barcelona, 1951; J. Cortés, El pintor Gimeno, Barcelona, 1958). - José Gutiérrez Solana, b. Madrid 1886, d. 1945; hardly left Spain and was little influenced by Paris; moving, sober, and forceful work (R. Gómez de la Cerna, José Gutierrez Solana, Buenos Aires, 1944; M. Sánchez Camargó, Solana, Madrid, 1945 [2d ed. 1962]; J. Francés, José Gutiérrez Solana y su obra, Gerona, 1947; J. López Jiménez [B. de Pantorba, pseud.], José Gutiérrez Solana, Barcelona, 1952). - Eugenio Lucas Padilla, b. Alcalá de Henares (Madrid) 1824, d. Madrid 1870; disciple of Goya; painted taurine themes; traveled in Africa and Europe; work uneven (E. du Gué Trapier, Eugenio Lucas y Padillá, New York, 1940; J. A. Gaya Nuño, Eugenio Lucas, Barcelona, 1948). - Federico de Madrazo, b. Rome 1815, d. Madrid 1894; son of neoclassic painter José; studied in Rome and Paris; portraitist of court and of Madrid aristocracy (M. de Madrazo, Federico de Madrazo, 2 vols., Madrid, 1921). - Isidro Nonell, of Barcelona, 1873-1913; studied in Barcelona; sensitive temperament with preference for humble themes; admirable still lifes (J. Merli, Isidro Nonell, Barcelona, 1938; C. Nonell, Isidro Nonnell: Su vida y su obra, Madrid, 1963). - Genaro Pérez Villaamil, b. El Ferrol de Caudillo (La Coruña) 1807, d. 1854, traveled in Europe (A. Méndez Casal, Jenaro Pérez Villaamil, Madrid, 1923; J. A. Gaya Nuño, En el centenario de Villa-

amil, Goya, 1, 1954, pp. 29-34; L. Menéndez Pidal, Varios dibujos del pintor Jenaro Pérez Villaamil en el Museo Provincial de Oviedo, B. Inst. de estudios asturianos, XIV, 1960, pp. 353-79). - Darío de Regoyos, b. Ribadesella (Asturias) 1857, d. Barcelona 1913; studied in Madrid; worked in Belgium and later in Spain (R. Benet, Regoyos, Barcelona, 1946; A. García Miñor, El pintor Dario de Regoyos y su época, Oviedo, 1958). - Eduardo Rosales, b. Madrid 1836, d. Madrid 1873; studied in Madrid; lived many years in Rome (J. López Jiménez [B. de Pantorba, pseud.], Eduardo Rosales: Ensayo biográfico y crítico, Madrid, 1937; X. de Salas, "El testamento de Isabel la Católica", pintura de Eduardo Rosales, AE, XXXVII, 1953, pp. 108-33). - Joaquín Sorolla, b. Valencia 1863, d. Cercedilla (Madrid) 1923; worked in Rome and Paris; masterful depiction of Mediterranean light with decisive, quick stroke; also painted portraits (L. Williams, The Art of Joaquín Sorolla, New York, 1926; J. López Jiménez [B. de Pantorba, pseud.], Sorolla: Esbozo biográfico y critico, Gerona, 1944; J. López Jiménez [B. de Pantorba, pseud.], La vida y la obra de Joaquín Sorolla, Madrid, 1953; R. M. Anderson, Costumes Painted by Sorolla in His "Provinces of Spain", New York, 1957; J. Manaut Vigliette, Crónica del pintor Joaquín Sorolla, Madrid 1964).

DIFFUSION OF SPANISH ART. Spanish influence on the development of European schools of art has been slight: none of the major medieval European currents appears to have originated in Spain; nor can it be said that any of Spain's great artists — Huguet, Berruguete, Velázquez, Zurbarán, Valdés Leal — were influential outside their country, in the way that Giotto, Van Eyck, Titian, Rubens, and many others were (Ribera, who became one of the central figures of the Neapolitan school, is unique).

Little is known of the origins of the Romanesque and its relation to the arts of the nations that were created after the fall of the Roman Empire, hence it is impossible to say in which country the Romanesque achieved definition as a style. The most credible and widely held opinion is that the earliest evolution of Romanesque art took place in France, although many historians, such as Kingsley Porter (1923) and Dieulafoy (1910) assign a leading role to Spain. If Romanesque art was born of the fusion of Roman traditions with Oriental influences, Spain could, indeed, have been the birthplace. The Gothic style arrived in Spain fully matured, and the role of Spain was limited to carrying it to other countries in slightly modified versions. Because of Catalonian expansion throughout the Mediterranean, the Gothic style in Sicily is little more than a derivative of Catalonian Gothic, especially in the field of secular architecture, and the same is true of Sardinia, which was also receptive to Catalonian influence; in Cyprus also, the Gothic developed in a form reminiscent of that of the Spanish Levant; and a 14th-century Catalonian panel found its way to the Monastery of St. Catherine on Mount Sinai. Neither the art of Andorra nor that of Roussillon and Cerdagne (both today part of France), however, can be included within the framework of Catalonian expansion; rather, they must be viewed as belonging to the art of Catalonia itself, to which both Roussillon and Cerdagne belonged until the second half of the 17th century.

Hispano-Moresque art, powerful and prestigious, also radiated clearly recognizable influences, the most powerful stream directed toward Morocco — where, indeed, its force has not yet waned; another reaching into the Sicily of the Norman kings; and a third insinuating itself into Western Christian art. That art, especially, reveals an assimilation of various Moorish elements into the Romanesque, even certain structural forms such as the vaults of Córdoba with transverse arches (VIII, PL. 148; X, PLS. 163, 439), which were used, for example, in the monks' kitchen of Durham Cathedral (14th cent.) in England. This type of vault was familiar to Leonardo da Vinci and to the Italian architect Guarino Guarini (q.v.) who, it appears, traveled through Spain 1666-68. Guarini made use of it in the Sta Sindone Chapel (1657-94) and in the Church of S. Lorenzo (1666-79; II, PL. 143), both in Turin, and in the Church of the Somaschi in Messina.

It is not possible in this survey to study in detail the multiple aspects of Spanish influences in the arts of those countries of the New World which were discovered and colonized by Spain and whose cultural life for three centuries reflected that of the mother country. From the regions that are today part of the United States (California, New Mexico) to the southermost points of Argentina and Chile, the trends that succeeded one another in Spanish art are manifested. This influence was exerted in various ways; hence Hispano-American art has many facets, which are extremely interesting but have as yet been only superficially explored. At times the influence was direct, brought by Spanish artists who crossed the ocean or by paintings or works of sculpture that were sent to the New World. At other times it stemmed from individuals, usually friars, who, although they had little knowledge of architecture, were obliged by circumstances to supervise contruction work; they drew on their memories of what they had seen in Spain, sometimes with astonishing results. Finally, another path of influence consisted in copies made by native artists of art works that had been brought to the New World. The most interesting works are precisely those in which the native artists interpreted the work of the Spanish masters in their own way. To a lesser extent this occurred also in the Philippines (q.v.).

Among the great Spanish masters only Goya, after his death, exerted a lasting influence in France, more through the intellectuals there than through the artists. There was a certain amount of interest in Velázquez, although it frequently degenerated into triviality. In any case, the particularly Spanish aspects of Goya's art, those which constitute his authentic personality and relate him to other Spanish artists, made no mark on international art. Pablo Picasso, the greatest 20th-century painter, who has contributed so much to the development of contemporary art, has succeeded in communicating one of the basic aspects of Spanish artistic expression: a breaking down of form combined with a rapid technique. Picasso's significance is undeniable, and with him Spanish art has assumed an important role in the world, even though this has occurred through the school of Paris.

II. PORTUGAL: ARCHITECTURE, SCULPTURE, AND PAINTING. *The Middle Ages.* The history of Portuguese art as such begins with the founding of the nation in the 12th century. The few pre-Romanesque churches are all in the northern part of the country. Examples are S. Pedro of Balsemão, near Lamego; S. Frutuoso, near Braga (7th cent.); and the Mozarabic church at Lourosa (920). Romanesque art (q.v.) was introduced in Portugal by French prelates and artists and spread to the south in the wake of the reconquest. It is essentially an architectonic style with little decoration of portals, apses, and triforiums. Façades seldom have figural sculpture; symbolic iconography is found mainly at the Cathedral of Braga and the churches of S. Salvador in Bravães and S. Pedro in Rates. The outstanding monuments of the period are the cathedrals of Braga, Coimbra (XII, PL. 215), and Lisbon (PL. 120), after which many buildings were patterned; the polygonal church of the Templars in Tomar; and the Domus Municipalis (PL. 120) in Bragança. The Cathedral of Évora (13th cent.) combines Romanesque with early Gothic tendencies. Tomb sculpture is rare, but there are simple examples in Guimarães (soc. Martins Sarmento) and Alcobaça (Mus. Soáres dos Reis). There was no Romanesque painting of importance.

Because the Romanesque style was deeply rooted in Portugal, the Gothic did not become prevalent in architecture until the 14th century. The Abbey of S. Maria at Alcobaça (12th–13th cent.; VI, PLS. 308, 309), built by French monks, follows the Cistercian plan; it displays the Gothic spirit that attained magnificent expression in the Monastery of S. Maria da Vitória at Batalha (PL. 120; FIG. 319, *a*), begun in 1388 by Afonso Domingues, who supervised its construction until about 1402. The architect Huguet continued the work until 1438, adding ornamentation inspired by the English Gothic style.

Sculpture in the 14th century was chiefly made for tombs and developed in three main centers: Lisbon, 1325–50 (tombs of King Diniz at Odivelas and of Afonso IV in the Cathedral of Lisbon); Évora, 1320–40; and Coimbra, the most important, where sculpture reached its high point about 1360 with the tombs of Pedro I and Inés de Castro (PL. 124). These are the work

of an anonymous artist; their iconography, technique, and composition place them among the outstanding works of European sculpture of this period. In the 15th century the Monastery of S. Maria da Vitória was the focal point of a style that bore traces of English influence. Toward the end of this century another artist from Coimbra, Diogo Pires the Elder, continued the national tradition instituted by João Afonso and brought the 15th-century style of sculpture to an end.

Only a few vestiges of 14th- and early-15th-century painting have survived, although the names of several artists have come down through history. The third quarter of the 15th century is dominated by the personality of Nuno Gonçalves (active 1450–71), who was court painter to Afonso V and who executed the polyptych of St. Vincent (PL. 126). There was little painting in the last quarter of the 15th century but noteworthy examples of this period are the triptych of St. Clare in Coimbra and the *Ecce Homo* in Lisbon (Mus. Nac. de Arte Antiga).

The 16th–20th century. Portugal's new wealth following the discovery of the route around the Cape of Good Hope to India, together with the preference of King Manuel (r. 1495–1521) for sumptuousness, resulted in the so-called "Manueline" style of the 16th century. Two early monuments of this time are the Church of Jesus in Setúbal, designed in 1492 by the Frenchman Diogo Boytac, and Nossa Senhora do Pópulo in Caldas de Rainha (1500). An important school developed around Batalha, where one of the creators of the style, Mateus Fernandes the Elder (d. 1515), received his training and where Boytac applied Manueline ornamentation to the Capelas Imperfeitas (Unfinished Chapels). Boytac is credited with the design and construction (1500–16) of the monastery of the Hieronymites (Jerónimos) in Belém. Diogo and Francisco de Arruda created such characteristic monuments as the church nave and the famous windows of the Church of the Templars in Tomar and the Tower of Belém. This style did not take long to develop and its influence, especially in the regional schools, spread during the reign of João III (1521–57).

Manueline sculpture followed several trends: one, whose chief exponent was Diogo Pires the Younger, continued the medieval tradition; another was evolved by the Basques working in the north and by the collaborators of João de Castilho in Belém; another was developed by wood carvers, who for the most part were Flemish or German; and still another, developed by the French, introduced some Italian Renaissance forms.

The new interest in painting was primarily due to the Flemish artists who worked in Portugal, such as Francisco Henriques (PL. 130), active 1500–18, whose work had a wide influence. Workshops were active in Viseu and, above all, in Lisbon, which had a clearly defined school and was the hub of pictorial activity in Portugal. Noteworthy among the painters of the period were Frei Carlos, who worked in the second quarter of the 16th century and continued the Flemish tradition; Vasco Fernandes (ca. 1475–ca. 1542), from Viseu, who painted the panels for the high altar of the Cathedral of Lamego (1506–11); Cristóvão de Figueiredo (PL. 130), one of the artists of the altarpiece for the main altar of the Monastery of Sta Cruz (1522–30) in Coimbra and of the altarpiece at Ferreirim (1533–34). The impressive unity of style among painters during the Manueline period persisted in the following period as well. (See also GOTHIC ART.)

In 1517, before the end of the reign of King Manuel, João and Diogo de Castilho and the French sculptors introduced Lombard themes at Belém, Tomar, and Coimbra. Their influence was first felt in the decorative arts and later in architecture. The principal centers of this trend were Coimbra (Diogo de Castilho and João de Ruão, or Jean de Rouen), Tomar (João de Castilho), and Évora, tending more toward the Italian manner (Diogo de Torralva). Miguel de Arruda and Afonso Alvares were outstanding artists who emerged during the middle of the 16th century. Alvares initiated a new trend with the cathedrals of Leiria (begun 1551) and Portalegre (begun before 1560). When Philip II of Spain became King of Portugal as well, he appointed Filippo Terzi as Master of Royal Works, and under Terzi's leadership a school of architects flourished that rivaled that of El Escorial. Terzi's best work was the Church of S. Vicente de Fora in Lisbon (PL. 131; FIG. 341, a). Renaissance sculpture was introduced by Nicolas Chanterene, who was undoubtedly French and who was active

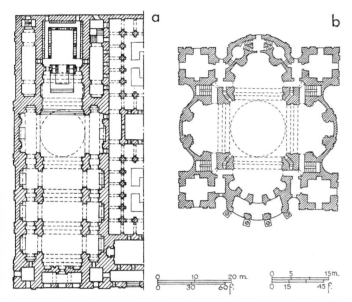

Portuguese religious buildings, 16th–17th cent., plans. (a) Lisbon, S. Vicente de Fora (architect, Filippo Terzi); (b) Lisbon, S. Engrácia (architects, João Nunes Tinoco and João Antunes) (*from Kubler and Soria, 1959, pp. 105, 109*).

in Portugal ca. 1415–51; his most important pieces are to be found in Coimbra, Sintra, and Évora. The work of another Frenchman, Filipe Udarte (Hodart), is less refined but more forceful and vigorous; a precursor of the baroque, he was active in Portugal 1530–36. João de Ruão (1530–80) was a prolific artist whose work, graceful and simple, had much influence in the Mondego Valley. Renaissance painting in Portugal was varied and heterogeneous, reflecting the struggle between the traditional trends and the strong Italian influences introduced in Portugal by João III.

In the 17th century there was a repetitiousness in the plans of buildings that, together with the sober ornamentation that characterized the period, made architecture during the first three quarters of the century somewhat monotonous. Noted architects of the period were Pedro Nunes Tinoco, his son João, Leonardo Turriano, and his sons João and Diogo. Later the Portuguese baroque attained greater originality, especially in ornamentation and in the use of gilded and carved polychrome altarpieces. The architect João Antunes (active 1683–1734) was outstanding at the end of the century; he particularly favored the central plan (Lisbon, S. Engrácia, FIG. 341, b). The differences in architecture between the north and the south of Portugal became pronounced during the reign of João V (1706–50). João Frederico Ludovice (PL. 137), a German trained in Italy, was the dominant personality in Lisbon and Évora; between 1717 and 1730 he built the Palace-Monastery of Mafra (FIG. 342), which was to be the training ground of a number of architects, including Mateus Vicente de Oliveira and Reinaldo Manuel dos Sants, whose royal palace at Queluz (PL. 137) and Basilica da Estrêla in Lisbon expressed a more truly national Portuguese style. In the north, Nicolò Nasoni, active in Oporto 1732–73, made an original contribution to the baroque style, different from both the Italian tendency and Ludovice's style. The palaces were enriched with splendid granite ornamentation, whitewashed walls, and tile panels, which give a fresh, cheerful, and colorful effect. There was a new development in the decorative carving of altarpieces: toward the middle of the 17th century classicism lost its purity and broke down into various baroque trends. In the 18th century architectural plans became more varied and complex; the use of gilded and poly-

chrome carvings was extended from the altarpieces to the entire apse and even to chapel walls.

The foremost and most original example of sculpture of the second half of the 17th century is that is the Cistercian Abbey of S. Maria at Alcobaça. The most important sculptors of the 18th century were José de Almeida (1700–69) and Joaquim Machado de Castro (1732–1822); the latter was the creator of the equestrian statue of King José Manuel in Lisbon and of charming Nativity scenes, a genre also cultivated by António Ferreira. Seventeenth-century painting, in the first decades under Spanish influence, developed two tendencies: the religious, in keeping with the dominant spirit of the century, and the portrait. In the middle of the century the leading figure was Domingos Vieira, of Lisbon, who painted portraits with exquisite sensitivity. Several foreign painters worked in Portugal during the 18th century; noteworthy among them were P. A. Quillard and J. Pillement. Outstanding Portuguese artists of the period include Francisco Vieira de Matos (known as Vieira Lusitano), Francisco Vieira (known as Vieira Portuense), and Domingos António de Sequiera (1768–1837; PL. 149), whose life bears a curious similarity to Goya's.

The greater part of the 19th century was not a favorable period for Portuguese architecture, either religious or secular. The second half of the century, however, produced an outstanding architect, José Luis Monteiro. Raul Lino is responsible for the most important activity in the first quarter of the 20th century. In sculpture António Soares dos Reis, who had a strong artistic personality, was active in the last quarter of the 19th century; the best of his followers was António Teixeira Lopes. The renewal of painting under the stimulus of romanticism was late, dating only from the second half of the 19th century. About 1880, realism was launched, producing a generation of brilliant artists such as António Carvalho da Silva Porto (1850–

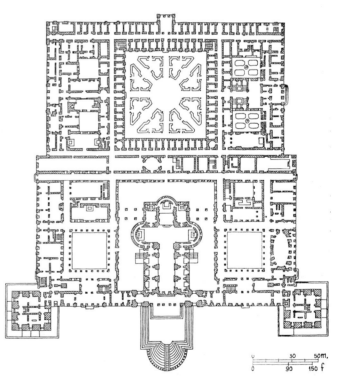

Mafra (Portugal). Palace-monastery, 1717–70, plan (architect, J. F. Ludovice) (*from Kubler and Soria, 1959, p. 111*).

92) and Columbano Bordalo Pinheiro (1857–1934), the latter a painter of excellent portraits and elegant still lifes.

MINOR ARTS. There are few examples of pre-Romanesque gold- and silverwork in Portugal. Romanesque pieces in this medium have the same characteristics as the architecture of the period: there is a marked French influence and a preference for sober and stylized form. The work executed during the reign of King Diniz (1279–1325) achieved brilliance, and there are many elegant and well-executed examples from the 15th century. The Manueline period was characterized by great originality in' decorative forms, which were naturalistic, and by reduced proportions in chalices, custodials, and patens (Lisbon, Coimbra, Oporto, Guimarães, Braga, Setúbal, Évora, Vila Franca, etc.) designed by Gil Vicente, Master João, and other gold- and silversmiths. Renaissance gold- and silverwork was no longer Portuguese-inspired but was rather an assimilation of a foreign and erudite art. After the 15th century secular gold- and silverwork gained new importance, as can be seen from the jars, water jugs, trays, and salvers, which constitute the richest, most numerous, and most authentically Portuguese examples of the period. The outstanding 17th-century example is the reredos and altar frontal of the Cathedral of Oporto (1632–78), which was executed by Manuel Guedes, Manuel de Sousa, and others. (See also GOLD- AND SILVERWORK.)

Examples of Gothic furniture are scarce, and the furniture of the 16th century reflects Spanish and Indian influences. The 17th century provides more examples and more originality than any other period in the history of Portuguese furniture. Pieces from this were often executed in precious woods in the style known as Indo-Portuguese. The 18th century was characterized by two fundamental influences: the English style and, in the last quarter of the century, the French Louis XVI style. (See also FURNITURE.)

The oldest production of ceramics appears to date from the 16th century. The influence of Chinese and Italian ceramics was strong, the latter especially for its Renaissance themes transmitted through Spain and Flanders. These two influences were felt throughout the 17th century, but the Oriental influence dominated until the middle of the 18th century; the glazed ceramics of the period are of finer design, color, and quality of enamel but lack the originality and decorative forcefulness of the 17th-century ceramics. In the second half of the 18th century, ceramics production received new impetus in the factories of Lisbon, Oporto, and Coimbra, owing to the Marquês of Pombal's personal interest in it. (See also CERAMICS.) The porcelain industry in Portugal was launched in 1824 when José Ferreira Pinto Basto founded the Vista Alegre factory, which is still active. Its production was particularly fine in the 19th century under the directorships of V. Chartier-Rousseau and G. Fortier, both Frenchmen.

The originality of Portuguese tiles lies not in their technique or decorative themes but in the wide range of their application, which was greater than in any other country. For three centuries, beginning with the 16th, tilework replaced tapestry and frescoes. In the 18th century the main tile workshops were in Lisbon; the most noteworthy artists were António and Policarpo Oliveira Bernardes, Nicolau de Freitas, and Bartolomeu Antunes. Glass manufacture was unimportant until the 18th century, when João V founded a glass factory. The Marinha Grande factory, founded by Guillermo Stephens in 1769 and still in operation, was much influenced by the English, and the Vista Alegre factory has followed the same tendency.

Ivory carving was for the most part an Indo-Portuguese art, with examples from the 16th to the 18th century.

Trade with the Orient stimulated a taste for Persian and Indo-Persian tapestry. As early as the 17th century Portugal was producing a type of tapestry known as *tapices de Arraiolos*; these pieces were of Indo-Persian inspiration and were more properly embroideries rather than true tapestries. The tapestry factory founded in Tavira during the reign of José Manuel (1750–77) did not prosper. Quilts and laces of Oriental inspiration were also produced by skilled craftsmen.

III. COLONIAL MANIFESTATIONS. Discovered and colonized by Spain and Portugal, the fertile territories of the Americas rapidly developed a flourishing art. In general they may be said to have followed the trends that reached them from the mother countries; there were, however, variations owing to indigenous interpretation of the models and the need to adapt them to the locally available means. Indigenous influence is limited, for all practical purposes, to decoration, characterized

by a strong feeling for color and ornamentation and by the use of the wealth of motifs, with excellent results. (See also AMERICAS: ART SINCE COLUMBUS.)

In Mexico (q.v.) examples of late Gothic architecture include the Cathedral of Mexico City, which has a plan derived from the Segovia-Salamanca group; the Monastery of S. Francisco in Cholula (1552); and the Actopan cloister and the open chapels (the one at Tepozcolula is noteworthy), for which there was no precedent in Spain. The Renaissance style is evident in the cathedrals of Mexico City (FIG. 344, *a*), Puebla (II, PL.

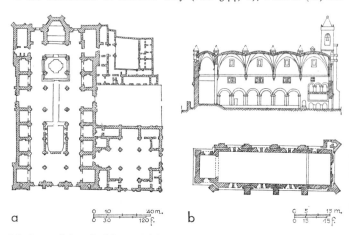

a   b

Mexican religious buildings. (*a*) Mexico City, Cathedral, plan; (*b*) Tepeaca (Puebla), Franciscan church, section and plan of lower story (*from Kubler and Soria, 1959, pp. 72, 74*).

163), and Mérida (FIG. 344), while many works show a successful interpretation of the plateresque style, of which the Capilla Real (Royal Chapel) in Cholula is a remarkable example. The Herreran style did not readily penetrate (towers of S. Francisco at Tlaxcala and of the Cathedral of Durango), but colonial architecture found its most satisfactory expression in the baroque style. Powerfully original and exceptionally fine buildings were constructed during the baroque period; at times they were superior to their European counterparts and occasionally even influenced the latter. There are two main groups, each with many variants: the academic style, created by professional architects (cathedrals, city churches, large monasteries), and the popular style, which was almost entirely the work of indigenous artists. The use of the dome was frequent, as was an overcharged ornamentation on façades and altarpieces. Among innumer-

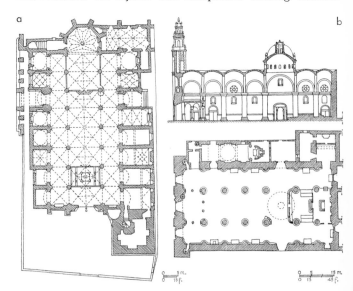

a   b

Religious buildings, Central America and Antilles, 16th cent. (*a*) Santo Domingo, Dominican Republic, Cathedral of S. Domingo, plan; (*b*) Mérida (Yucatán), Mexico, Cathedral, section and plan (*from Kubler and Soria, 1959, pp. 64, 67*).

ble examples perhaps the most successful and refined is the Sagrario Metropolitano (PL. 152) — adjoining, but not part of, the Cathedral of Mexico City — completed in 1768 and designed by Lorenzo Rodríguez. Magnificent palaces derived from Andalusian models are to be found in Mexico City and Puebla. Manuel Tolsá was the foremost exponent of the academic style.

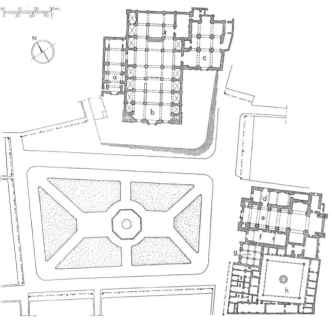

Cuzco, Peru, Plaza de Armas churches, plans. (a) Church of Jesús y María La Sagrada Familia); (b) Cathedral; (c) Church of El Triunfo (or El Sagrario); (d) Chapel of Nuestra Señora de Loreto; (e) Church of the Jesuits; (f) Chapel of St. Ignatius; (g) University (former Jesuit house); (h) patio (from l'Arhitettura, No. 31, 1958, p. 46).

Many works of painting and sculpture were imported from Spain. Beginning with the 16th century there are interesting mural decorations, as in Acolmán and Actopan, and painters such as Simón Pereyns worked in Mexico City. In the 17th century the workshops of Baltasar de Echave the Elder and his son (the Younger) were outstanding; in the 18th century Miguel Cabrera was a particularly prolific artist. Until the end of the 18th century sculpture was the work of anonymous craftsmen. José Villegas produced interesting work in Puebla, and the Valencian Manuel Tolsá, author of the famous equestrian statue of Charles IV, worked in Mexico City. After the Conquest the gold- and silversmiths adapted their traditional styles to European forms. In Mexico City, Puebla, and Oaxaca there are admirable examples of grilles also based on Spanish models.

The viceroyalty of Peru (q.v.) constituted the chief artistic center in South America, with influence extending northward as far as Quito and the old viceroyalty of New Granada (Colombia) and southward to Chile, Bolivia, and Argentina. Examples of the Spanish Gothic style are practically nonexistent in this region, and there are only a few buildings in the Renaissance style; the works of Francisco Becerra are notable (cathedrals of Lima and Cuzco; I, PL. 140). The addition of several elements (Mudejar, Incan, Eastern) to the Hispanic gave rise between 1650 and 1800 to the elaborate and interesting Peruvian baroque style that had its expression in three principal groups: that of Lima (Palacio de Torre Tagle), that of Cuzco (magnificent palaces and churches; FIG. 345), and that of northern Peru, with its center in Arequipa showing the strongest native influence. In Argentina the best group of Hispanic works is to be found in Córdoba (Cathedral; La Compañía church); the largest number of aristocratic residences are in Salta. In what is now Ecuador, Quito was an important artistic center, related to Cuzco.

Painting had a wide development in Peru, although it was less influenced by indigenous trends than it was in Mexico.

There were no great figures but many admirable artists. In the 16th century many paintings were imported, and there was an immigration of artists such as Angelino Medoro and Mateo Pérez de Alesio. The so-called "Cuzco school" is of great interest. It had its origins in the 17th century, attaining its most brilliant phase in the 18th century. Chiefly the work of native artists, ingenuous and technically primitive, its themes were almost entirely religious. This school's production was considerable and the extent of its influence enormous. Miguel de Santiago (d. 1673) and his nephew Nicolás Javier Goríbar painted in Quito and Gregorio Vázquez (1638–1711) in Bogotá.

Sculpture, which was popular in tone and highly varied, was also abundant in Peru. Many excellent Spanish pieces were brought to Lima, where such artists as Pedro Noguera (17th cent.) and Baltazar Gavilán (18th cent.) worked. The workshops of Cuzco were of greater importance and produced such notable works as the pulpit of S. Blas, attributed to Juan Tomás Tuyru Tupac. Sculpture in Quito was almost always of wood. The outstanding artist there was Father Carlos in the second half of the 17th century, but the local tradition was continued throughout the 18th century.

There was no artistic activity in the vast territory of Brazil until the end of the 17th century. Art flourished in the 18th century, when the colony became economically important. In the second half of the 18th century artistic forms appeared that broke way from Portuguese influence and assumed their own local personlity. Baía (formerly Bahia) is perhaps the Brazilian city of the strongest colonial character, with its church of Nossa Senhora do Pilar and other monuments. In the last third of the 18th century a highly esteemed architect and sculptor, António Francisco Lisboa (1730–1814), known as "O Aleijadinho," was active in the state of Minas Gerais. His works include the churches of S. Francisco in Ouro Preto (1766) and in São João d'El Rey (1774–1804; FIG. 346) and the important groups of sculptures in the Bom Jesus de Matozinhos church in Congonhas do Campo (PL. 154; I, PL. 143).

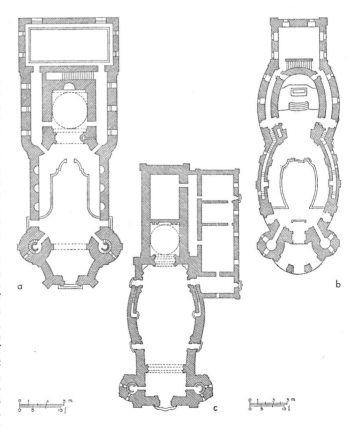

Brazilian religious buildings, 18th cent., plans. (a) Ouro Preto. S. Francisco (architect, A. F. Lisboa, known as "O Aleijadinho ") (from Architectural Review, 662, 1952, p. 95); (b) Ouro Preto, Capela do Rosário (from Kubler and Soria, 1959, pp. 118, 119); (c) Sao João d'El Rey, S. Francisco (architect, A. F. Lisboa, "O Aleijadinho") (from Architectural Review, 662, 1952, p. 94).

Bibliog. *Spain*: *a. General works*: A. A. Palomino de Castro y Velasco, El museo pictórico y escala óptica, 2 vols., Madrid, 1715–24 (repr. 1947); A. Ponz, Viaje de España, Madrid, 1785 (new ed. by C. M. del Rivero, Madrid, 1947); J. A. Ceán Bermúdez, Diccionario histórico de los más illustres profesores de las Bellas Artes en España, 6 vols., Madrid, 1800; E. Llaguno y Amirolas, Noticia de los arquitectos de la arquitectura en España, 4 vols., Madrid, 1829; M. Menéndez y Pelayo, Historia de las ideas estéticas en España, 5 vols. in 8, Madrid, 1883–91; C. Muñoz y Manzano, Conde de la Viñaza, Adiciones al diccionario de J. A. Ceán Bermúdez, 4 vols., Madrid, 1889–94; V. Lampérez y Romea, La arquitectura civil española, 2 vols., Madrid, 1922; F. J. Sánchez Cantón, Fuentes literarias para la historia del arte español, 5 vols., Madrid, 1923–41; G. Weise, Spanische Plastik aus sieben Jahrhunderten, 4 vols. in 6, Reutlungen, 1923–39; C. R. Post, A History of Spanish Painting, 12 vols., in 18, Cambridge, Mass., 1930–60; J. Contreras y López de Alaya, Marqués de Lozoya, Historia del arte hispánico, 5 vols., Barcelona, 1931–49; B. Bevan, History of Spanish Architecture, London, 1938; M. E. Gómez-Moreno, Breve historia de la escultura española, 2d ed., Madrid, 1951; J. M. de Azcarate, Monumentos españoles, 2d ed., 3 vols., Madrid, 1953–54; E. Lafuente Ferrari, Historia de la pintura española, 4th ed., Madrid, 1953; L. Torres Bálbas et al., Resumen histórico del urbanismo en España, Madrid, 1954; F. Jiménez Placer, Historia del arte español, 2 vols., Barcelona, 1955; G. Kubler and M. Soria, Art and Architecture in Spain and Portugal and Their American Dominions (1500–1800), Harmondsworth, 1959; J. Gudiol i Ricart and S. Alcolea, Hispania, 2 vols., Barcelona, 1962.

b. Romanesque: A. Kingsley Porter, Romanesque Sculpture of the Pilgrimage Roads, I, V, VI, Boston, 1923; C. L. Kuhn, Romanesque Mural Paintings of Catalonia, Cambridge, Mass., 1930; M. Gómez-Moreno, El arte románico español, Madrid, 1934; W. M. Whitehill, Spanish Romanesque Architecture of the 11th Century, London, 1941; J. Gudiol and J. A. Gaya Nuño, Arquitectura y escultura románicas (Ars Hispaniae, V), Madrid, 1948; J. Pijoan and J. Gudiol, Les pintures murales romàniques da Catalunya, Barcelona, 1948; W. W. S. Cook and J. Gudiol i Ricart, Pintura y imaginería románicas (Ars Hispaniae, VI), Madrid, 1950; E. W. Anthony, Romanesque Frescoes, Princeton, 1951; K. J. Conant, Carolingian and Romanesque Architecture, Harmondsworth, 1959; M. Durliat, Hispania romanica, Vienna, 1962.

c. Gothic: G. E. Street, Some Account of Gothic Architecture in Spain (ed. G. G. King), 2 vols., London, 1914; A. Duran i Sanpere, Los retablos de pietra, 2 vols., Barcelona, 1923–34; L. Torres Bálbas, Inventaire et classification des monastères cisterciens espagnoles, Actes Cong. d'h. de l'art (Paris, 1921), II, Paris, 1924, pp. 119–25; A. L. Mayer, Gotik in Spanien, Leipzig, 1928; V. Lampérez y Romea, Historia de la arquitectura cristiana española en la Edad Media, 2d ed., 3 vols., Madrid, 1930; F. B. Deknatel, The 13th Century Gothic Sculpture of the Cathedral of Burgos and Leon, AB, XVII, 1935, pp. 243–394; B. G. Proske, Castilian Sculpture: Gothic to Renaissance, New York, 1951; L. Torres Bálbas, Arquitectura gótica (Ars Hispaniae, VII), Madrid, 1952; E. Bague, La alta Edad Media, Barcelona, 1953; J. Gudiol, Pintura gótica (Ars Hispaniae, IX), Madrid, 1955; A. Duran and J. Ainaud, Escultura gótica (Ars Hispaniae, XIII), Madrid, 1956; J. Camón Aznar, Pintura española medieval, Goya, 54, 1963, pp. 344–54.

d. Hispano-Moresque art: G. G. King, Mudejar, Bryn Mawr, 1927; H. Terrasse, L'art hispano-mauresque des origines au XIIIe siècle, Paris, 1932; L. Torres Bálbas, Arte almohade, arte nazarí, arte mudéjar (Ars Hispaniae, IV), Madrid, 1949; M. Gómez-Moreno, Arte arabe español hasta los almoshades: Arte mozarabe (Ars Hispaniae, III), Madrid, 1951; L. Torres Bálbas, La mezquita de Córdoba y Madinat al-Zahra, Madrid, 1952; E. Camps y Cazorla, Módulo, proporciones y composición en la arquitectura califal cordobesa, Madrid, 1953; L. Torres Bálbas, La Alhambra y el Generalife, Madrid, 1954; L. Torres Bálbas, Artes almorávides y almohade, Madrid, 1955; E. Lambert, Art musulman et art chrètien dans la Péninsule ibérique, Paris, 1958; H. Terrasse, Islam d'Espagne, Paris, 1958, F. García Romo, Lo pre-musulmán (visigodo), lo hispano-musulmán y lo mozárabe en el arte, Principe de Viana, XXIII, 1962, pp. 213–37.

e. Renaissance art: A. N. Prentice, Renaissance Architecture and Ornament in Spain, London, 1893; P. M. de Artinano, ed., Exposición de tejidos españoles, Madrid, 1917 (cat.); A. Byne and M. Stapley, Spanish Architecture of the 16th Century, New York, London, 1917; Marqués de Valverde, Exposición de lencería y encajes españoles del siglo XVI al XIX, Madrid, 1925 (cat.); J. Ferrandis, Marfiles y azabaches españoles, Barcelona, 1928; J. F. Ráfols, Arquitectura del renacimiento español, Barcelona, 1929; M. Gómez-Moreno, La escultura del Renacimiento en España, Barcelona, 1931; A. Saló Marco, El estilo renacimiento español, Barcelona, 1931; J. Ferrandis, ed., Exposición de alfombras antiguas españolas, Madrid, 1933 (cat.); G. Glück, Arte del renacimiento fuera de Italia, Barcelona, 1936; M. Gómez-Moreno, Las águilas del Renacimiento español, Madrid, 1941; J. Camón Aznar, La arquitectura plateresca, Madrid, 1945; A. Igual Ubeda, El Siglo de Oro, Barcelona, 1951; M. Trens, Las custodias españols, Barcelona, 1952; F. Chueca Goitia, Arquitectura del siglo XVI (Ars Hispaniae, XI), Madrid, 1953; D. Angulo Iñíguez, Pintura del Renacimiento (Ars Hispaniae, XII), Madrid, 1955; J. Hernández Perera, Escultores florentinos en España, Madrid, 1957; J. Contreras y López de Alaya, Marqués de Lozoya, Escultura de Carrara en España, Madrid, 1957; G. Weise, Die Plastik der Renaissance und des Frühbarock im nördlichen Spanien, 2 vols., Tübingen, 1957–59; J. M. de Azcárate, Escultura del siglo XVI (Ars Hispaniae, XIII), Madrid, 1958; J. Camón Aznar, La arquitectura y la orfebreria españolas del siglo XVI, Madrid, 1959; J. Camón Aznar, La escultura y la rejeria españolas del siglo XVI, Madrid, 1961.

f. The 17th and 18th centuries: M. Pérez Vilaamil, Artes y industrias del Buen Retiro, Madrid, 1904; O. Schubert, Geschichte des Barock in Spanien, Esslingen, 1908; A. de Beruete y Moret, The School of Madrid, London, 1909; A. Mayer, Die Sevillaner Malerschule, Leipzig, 1911; J. Cavestany et al., Exposición del Antiguo Madrid, Madrid, 1926 (cat.); D. Angulo Iñíguez, La escultura en Andalucia, 3 vols., Seville, 1927–36;
A. Igual Ubeda and F. Morote Chapa, Diccionario biográfico de escultor
valencianos del siglo XVIII, Castellón de la Plana, 1933; J. Cavestan
ed., Floreros y bodegones en la pintura española, Madrid, 1935–40 (1 vo
cat.); W. Weisbach, Spanish Baroque Art, Cambridge, 1941; L. Pérez Buen
La Real Fábrica de Cristales de San Ildefonso (la Granja), Madrid, 194
F. Chueca Goitia, Los arquitectos neoclásicos y sus ideas estéticas, RI
I, 2, 1943, pp. 19–49; J. Selva, El arte en España durante los Borbones, Ba
celona, 1943; M. Escrivá de Romani, Conde de Casal, Historia de la cer
mica de Alcora, Madrid, 1945; E. Lafuente Ferrari, La pintura españo
del siglo XVII, Barcelona, 1945; G. Pillement, La sculpture baroque esp
gnole, Paris, 1945; E. M. Aguilera, Pintores españoles del siglo XVII
Barcelona, 1946; M. Lorente Junquera, La evolución arquitectónica en Esp
ña en los siglos XVIII y XIX, AE, XXXI, 1946, pp. 76–79, XXXII, 194
pp. 102–10; F. Jiménez Placer, El arte neoclásico y romántico españo
Barcelona, 1948; J. M. Echalecu, Los talleres reales de ebanistería, bronc
y bordados, AEArte, XXVIII, 1955, pp. 237–59; A. W. Frothingham, Cap
dimonte and Buen Retiro Porcelains, New York, 1955; G. Kubler, Arquite
tura de los siglos XVII y XVIII (Ars Hispaniae, XIV), Madrid, 1957;
Pardo Canalís, Escultura neoclásica española, Madrid, 1958; J. J. Mart
González, Escultura barroca castellana, Madrid, 1959; S. Rodrígue
García, El arte de la sedas valencianas en el siglo XVIII, Valencia, 195
Y. Bottineau, L'art de cour dans l'Espagne de Philippe V, 1700–46, Bordeau
1960; M. del Socorro González de Arribas and F. Arribas Arranz, Notici
y documentos para la historia del arte en España durante el siglo XVII
BSEAAU, XXVII, 1961, pp. 131–296.

g. The 19th and 20th centuries: M. Ossorio y Bernard, Galería bio
gráfica de artistas españoles del siglo XIX, Madrid, 1883–84; A. de Berue
y Moret, Historia de la pintura española del siglo XIX, Madrid, 1926;
Elias, L'escultura catalana moderna, Barcelona, 1926; J. López Jimén
(B. de Pantorba, pseud.), El paisaje y los paisajistas españoles, Madrid, 194
A. Cirici Pellicer, Los Nazarenos catalanes, ABMAB, III, 2, 1945, pp. 59
93; J. López Jiménez (B. de Pantorba, pseud.), Historia y critica de las Ex
posiciones Nacionales de Bellas Artes, Madrid, 1948; J. F. Ráfols, Mode
nismo y modernistas, Barcelona, 1949; E. Lafuente Ferrari, Medio sig
de pintura española, Madrid, 1950; P. Cirici Pellicer, El arte modernis
catalán, Barcelona, 1951; J. A. Gaya Nuño, La pintura española del med
siglo, Barcelona, 1952; M. Sánchez Camargo, Pintura española conten
poranea, Madrid, 1954; J. F. Ráfols, El arte romántico en España, Barcelon
1954; V. Marrero, El tradicionalismo español del siglo XIX, Madrid, 195
J. A. Gaya Nuño, Escultura española contemporanea, Madrid, 1957;
Mercader Riba, El siglo XIX, Barcelona, 1957; H.-R. Hitchcock, Architectur
19th and 20th Centuries, Harmondsworth, 1958; F. Novotny, Painting an
Sculpture in Europe, 1780–1880, Harmondsworth, 1960.

h. Expansion and influence of Spanish art: G. Guarini, Architettur
civile, Turin, 1737; A. Rubio y Lluch, Els Castells catalans de la Grec
continental, AIEC, II, 1908, pp. 364–425; M. Dieulafoy, Les premièr
peintures de l'école catalane, CRAI, 1910, pp. 324–30; C. Aru, Storia del
pittura in Sardegna nel secolo XV, AIEC, IV, 1911–12, pp. 508–2
E. Mâle, La mosquée de Cordoue et les églises de l'Auvergne et du Vela
Rev. de l'art ancien et moderne, 1911, pp. 81–89; R. Filangieri di Candid
Architettura e scultura catalana in Campania nel secolo XV, BSCC, X
1930, pp. 121–36; E. Lambert, L'Hôpital Saint-Blaise et son église hispano
mauresque, Al-Andalus, V, 1940, pp. 179–87; E. Tormo y Monzó, Monu
mentos de españoles en Roma y de portugueses y hispano-americanos, 2 vols
Madrid, 1942; D. Angulo Iñíguez, ed., Historia del arte hispano-american
3 vols., Barcelona, 1945–56; J. Adhemar, Essai sur les débuts de l'influen
de Goya en France au XIXe siècle, Paris, 1947; E. Lafuente Ferrari, Ant
cedentes, coincidencias y influencias del arte de Goya, Madrid, 1947; M. Gó
mez-Moreno, El arte árabe español hasta los almohades, Ars Hispania
II, Madrid, 1951, pp. 192–96, 282–96.

Portugal: *a. General*: A. Raczinski, Les arts en Portugal, Paris, 184
A. Raczinski, Dictionnaire historico-artistique du Portugal, Paris, 184
Biblioteca Nacional, Guia de Portugal, 3 vols., Lisbon, 1924–44; J. Contre
ras y Lopez de Alaya, Marqués de Lozoya, Historia del arte hispánic
5 vols., Barcelona, 1931–49; E. Lavagnino, Gli artisti in Portogallo, Rom
1940; A. de Lacerda et al., Historia de arte em Portugal, 3 vols., Porto, 1942
53; Acadamia Nacional de Belas Artes, Inventario artístico de Portuga
5 vols., Lisbon, 1943–55; E. Lambert, L'art en Espagne et au Portuga
Paris, 1945; J. Barreira, Arte portuguesa, Lisbon, 1946; J. van der Els
Le Portugal, Paris, 1951; R. dos Santos, Historia del arte portugués, Barc
lona, 1960.

b. Monographs: J. de Figueiredo, Da architectura manuelina, Coimbr
1885; A. Haupt, Die Baukunst der Renaissance in Portugal, 2 vols., Fran
furt am Main, 1890–95; F. M. de Sousa Viterbo, Dicionario historico e do
cumental dos arquitectos portugueses, 3 vols., Lisbon, 1899–1922; F. M
de Sousa Viterbo, Noticia de algunos pintores portugueses, 3 vols., Lisbo
1903–06, Coimbra, 1911; W. C. Watson, Portuguese Architecture, Londo
1908; V. Correia, Pintores portugueses des seculos XV e XVI, Coimbr
1928; V. Correia, Batalha, 2 vols., Porto, 1929–31; E. Korradi, Alcobaç
Porto, 1929; R. dos Santos, Sequeira y Goya, Madrid, 1929; C. Davi
Evora, Porto, 1930; C. de Passos, Nicolás Nasoni y Luis Chiari, Port
1931; L. X. da Costa, As Belas Artes plásticas em Portugal durante o sécul
XVIII, Lisbon, 1935; R. C. Smith, João Frederico Ludovice: An 18t
Century Architect in Portugal, AB, XVIII, 1936, pp. 273–370; D. de Maced
Emredor dos presepios portugueses, Lisbon, 1940; E. Soares, Historia d
gravura artística em Portugal, 2 vols., Lisbon, 1940–41; L. V. Aldemira,
pintor Columbano, B. Acad. Nacional Belas Artes, IX, 1941, pp. 51–5
A. A. Bernardy, Portogallo e Roma, Rome, 1941; D. de Macedo, Antoni
Teixeira Lopes, B. Acad. Nacional Belas Artes, X, 1942, pp. 7–12; A. Ca
doso Pinto, Domingo Vieira e ñao Domingos Barbosa, Lisbon, 1943;
Costa Torres, A arquitectura dos descobrimentos e o renascimento ibéric
Braga, 1943; A. de Lucena, Pintura portuguesa do romanticismo, Lisbo
1943; F. de Pamplona, Un século de pintura e escultura em Portugal (183
1930), Porto, 1943; L. Reis Santos, Estudos de pintura antiga, Lisbon, 194

. Pérez Embid, El mudejarismo en la architectura portuguese de la epoca manuelina, Seville, 1944 (2d ed. 1955); D. de Macedo, Soares dos Reis, Lison, 1945; L. Reis Santos, Vasco Fernandes e os pintores de Viseu do século XVI, Lisbon, 1946; T. Espanca, Notas sobre os pintores em Avora (sec. XVI-XVII), Evora, 1947; R. dos Santos, A escultura em Portugal, 2 vols., Lisbon, 1948-50; A. de Magalhaes, Nasoni e la igreja dos Clerigos, Porto, 1950, R. dos Santos, O estilo manuelino, Lisbon, 1952; G. Bazin, Morphologie du retable portugais, Belas Artes, V, 1953; pp. 3–28; J. B. Bury, Late Baroque and Rococo in North Portugal, J. Soc. Arch. H., XV, 3, 1956, p. 7–15; A. de Carvalho, A escultura em Mafra, 2d ed., Mafra, 1956; R. dos Santos, O românico em Portugal, Lisbon, 1956; R. dos Santos, Os primitivos portugueses, 3d ed., Lisbon, 1958; C. de Azevedo, Arte cristã na India portuguesa, Lisbon, 1959; A. de Carvalho, Dom João V e a arte do seu tempo, Mafra, 1962.

c. Minor arts: J. de Vasconcellos, Cerámica portuguesa, Porto, 1884; Queiroz, Cerámica portugueza, Lisbon, 1907; L. Costa, A ourivesaria e s nossos artistas, Porto, 1917; J. Pessanha, O cális de ouro do mosteiro de Alcobaça: A porcelana em Portugal (primeiras tentativas), Coimbra, 1923; . de Passos, O altar de prata da Sé portuense, Porto, 1939; V. Valente, Porcelana artística portuguesa, Porto, 1949; R. dos Santos and I. Quilho, Ourivesaria portuguesa nas colecões particulares, Lisbon, 1959; R. dos Santos, Faiança portuguesa, I, Porto, 1960.

Latin America: a. *General*: D. Angulo Iñíguez, Planos de monumentos arquitectónicos de América y Filipinas existentes en el Archivo de Indias, vols., Seville, 1933–39; D. Angulo Iñíguez, ed., Historia del arte hispanoamericano, 3 vols., Barcelona, 1945–56; R. C. Smith and E. Wilder, A Guide to the Art of Latin America, Washington, 1948; G. Kubler and M. Soria, Art and Architecture in Spain and Portugal and Their American Dominions (1500–1800), Harmondsworth, 1959; F. Cali, L'art des conquistadors, Paris, 1960 (Eng. trans., B. Rhys, The Spanish Arts of Latin America, New York, 1961); E. Marco Dorte, Fuentes para la historia del arte hispano-americano, 2d ed., Seville, 1960.

b. *Monographs*: F. Diez Barroso, El arte en Nueva España, Mexico City, 1921; M. Toussaint and J. R. Benitez, Iglesias de México, 6 vols., Mexico City, 1924–27; F. Cossio de Pomar, Pintura colonial: Escuela cuzueña, Cuzco, 1928; J. G. Navarro. La escultura en el Ecuador (sec. XVI-XVIII), Madrid, 1929; M. Toussaint, La pintura en México durante el siglo XVI, Mexico City, 1936; A. Mattos, Historia de arte brasileira, 2 vols., Belo Horizonte, 1937; R. Newcomb, Spanish Colonial Architecture in the United States, New York, 1937; Serviço do Patrimonio Historico e Artistico Nacional, Revista, Rio de Janeiro, 1937 ff.; G. Hernández de Alba, Teatro del arte colonial, Bogotá, 1938; A. Velázquez, Tres siglos de pintura colonial mexicana, Mexico City, 1939; J. Fernández, Catálogo de construcciones religiosas del estado de Hidalgo, 2 vols., Mexico City, 1940–42; H. Pedrosa, O Aleijadinho, São Paulo, 1940; A. Benavides, La arquitectura en el virreinato del Perù y en la capitania general de Chile, Santiago de Chile, 1941; J. Moreno Villa, La escultura colonial mexicana, Mexico City, 1942; J. M. dos Reis, Historia da pintura no Brasil, São Paulo, 1944; J. Fernández, Catálogo de construcciones religiosas del estado de Yucatán, 2 vols., Mexico City, 1945; J. G. Navarro, Religious Architecture in Quito, New York, 1945; M. Toussaint, Arte mudéjar en América, Mexico City, 1946; J. B. Couto, Diálogo sobre la historia de la pintura en México, Mexico City, 1947; G. Giraldo Jaramillo, La pintura en Colombia, Mexico City, 1948; G. Kubler, Mexican Architecture in the 16th Century, 2 vols., New Haven, 1948; J. Moreno Villa, Lo mexicano en las artes plásticas, Mexico City, 1948; A. M. Ribera and H. Schenone, El arte de la imaginería en el Río de la Plata, Buenos Aires, 1948; M. Romero de Terreros, Grabados y grabadores en la Nueva España, Mexico City, 1948; M. Toussaint, Arte colonial en México, Mexico City, 1948; H. E. Wethey, Colonial Architecture and Sculpture in Perù, Cambridge, Mass., 1949; F. de la Maza, Los retablos dorados de Nueva España, Mexico City, 1950; E. W. Weismann, Mexico in Sculpture, Cambridge, Mass., 1950; P. Kelemen, Baroque and Rococo in Latin America, New York, 1951; M. Romero de Terreros, El arte en México durante el virreinato, Mexico City, 1951; P. F. Santos, O barocco e o jesuitico na arquitectura do Brasil, Rio de Janeiro, 1951; H. Berlin, Historia de la imaginería colonial en Guatemala, Guatemala City, 1952; E. W. Palm, Los monumentos arquitectónicos de la Española, 2 vols., Ciudad Trujillo, 1955; G. Bazin, L'architecture religieuse baroque au Brésil, 2 vols., Paris, 1956–58; M. S. Soria, La pintura del siglo XVI en Sudamérica, Buenos Aires, 1956; P. F. Damaz, Art in Latin American Architecture, New York, 1963. See also the bibliogs. for articles on particular Latin American nations.

José GUDIOL and Santiago ALCOLEA

Illustrations: PLS. 117–156; 18 figs. in text.

STAGE DESIGN. See SCENOGRAPHY.

STAINED GLASS.

The unique decorative effect of stained glass derives essentially from its translucence. It is, in effect, a painting on light, composed of glass panes of different colors joined by a network of narrow lead strips and inserted into a metal framework. These compositions were used to seal windows and other wall apertures. In medieval religious structures, especially, stained glass assumed the decorative function once assigned to mosaics (q.v.). Although there were earlier examples, the use of stained glass became widespread in the 12th century, when architectural forms were tending away from flat expanses of wall toward a more dynamic articulation and a consequent lightening of stress on wall surfaces (see also GOTHIC ART and ROMANESQUE ART). Important works in stained glass that remain *in situ* are also discussed in the geographical articles on the countries in which they are located.

SUMMARY. Technique (col. 350). The history of stained glass from the Middle Ages to modern times (col. 354).

TECHNIQUE. The origin of stained glass lies in the ancient practice of using glass as a translucent screen for sealing windows and other types of apertures. The excavations of Beni Hasan in Egypt have brought to light fragments of flat poured glass, which date from the beginning of the 2d millennium B.C. and probably formed part of translucent window closures. Common use of colored glass for this purpose dates to Roman times. (It was probably at that time that blown glass was developed to replace molded glass, permitting the production of extremely thin transparent sheets.) Examples of blown glass have been found in Rome and in various cities of the Roman Empire (see GLASS).

In Early Christian architecture, translucent screens of natural materials such as alabaster and selenite were preferred, but glass was also employed. It was mounted in wooden frameworks (remains of which have been found in S. Apollinare in Classe, Ravenna) and in pierced screens (transennae) of stone (e.g., marble), stucco, or bronze (see LATE-ANTIQUE AND EARLY CHRISTIAN ART). There is clear evidence of glass windows in early medieval religious buildings. A passage in St. Gregory of Tours's *De gloria martyrum*, one of his books of miracles, narrates that the glass panes of the church of Yzeures-sur-Creuse (Indre-et-Loire), between Turenne and Berry, were removed from their frame by a thief who thought they were infused with precious metals. This indicates that in the 6th century there existed stained glass mounted in wooden frames: "Fenestras ex more habens quae vitro lignis incluso clauduntur." Other references are found in Venantius Fortunatus, who praises the stained glass of the Cathedral of Notre-Dame in Paris and of the Basilica of St-Martin in Tours; in Paulus Silentiarius, who extols the colored windows of St. Sophia in Constantinople; in Apollinaris Sidonius, who praises those in the chapel of the Maccabees, erected in Lyons about 450; and in Prudentius, who compares the stained glass of S. Paolo fuori le Mura in Rome to spring flowers. Other mentions of colored glass panes appear in the *Liber pontificalis romanus* (those in St. Peter's) and in the works of St. John Chrysostom, St. Jerome, and Lactantius, among others. But all these windows must have been composed of pieces of glass that were colored throughout rather than painted, and it is likely that they bore no depictions.

A singular technique developed in the Islamic East: the vitreous fragments were "let into" a stucco trellis, thereby giving rise to the creation of original compositions with fine architectonic and plant motifs by alternating stucco and glass. Among the first examples of this technique are those that came to light in the excavations of the winter palace of the Ommiad caliph Hishām (d. 743) at Khirbat al-Mafjar, near Jericho. This technique enjoyed particular success in Egypt during the 12th and 13th centuries (e.g., the window of the mausoleum of the Abbasside caliphs in Cairo) and was continued in Islamic art (e.g., panes in the Dome of the Rock, Jerusalem, ca. 1528; examples in the Vict. and Alb.). It is very probable that the same technique was introduced in the Byzantine Empire and thence spread to those areas of Europe where stucco (q.v.) enjoyed particular favor.

All these techniques employing transparent glass have little in common, however, with stained glass as it developed in the West from about the period of the 9th–10th century. The first precise references to the existence of figural stained glass appear in texts of this period. It is true that the passage on stained glass in the little poem in which Ratpertus, a Benedictine monk of Saint Gallen, describes to his colleague Notker Balbulus the consecration of the convent of the Fraumünster in Zurich in 853 leaves some doubt as to whether the panes were actually painted or figured. But explicit evidence is contained in a life of St. Ludger, Bishop of Münster, written about 864, which tells of a blind maiden who, thanks to a miracle performed by St. Ludger, regained her sight in the Abbey church of Werden an der Ruhr as the growing light of dawn began to reveal the figures in the glowing windows ("aurora iam rubescente et luce paulatim per fenestras irradiante imagines in eis factas monstrare digito coepit"). A chronicle written in 995 by Richerus, a monk at the Abbey of St-Remi in Reims, in speaking of works carried out in the Cathedral by order of Adalbéron, Bishop of Reims (969–88), explicitly mentions windows containing representations of stories ("fenestris deversis continentibus historias"). Figured stained glass probably had its beginnings in the Carolingian period in concomitance with the splendid florescence of the minor arts. Certainly connected with this development is a small glass composition with a cruciform motif found at Séry-les-Mézières (Aisne), which must have been the translucent cover of a reliquary chest, datable to the 9th century. The dating of glass fragments of a head found at Lorsch, in the Rhineland, has caused extensive discussion: some scholars assign the work to the Carolingian period, while others vigorously challenge this dating. Similar discussion has been aroused by a head of Christ discovered about 1880 at Wissembourg in Alsace (now in Strasbourg, Mus. de l'Œuvre Notre-Dame); this work shows affinities with the Lorsch fragment, which, despite the controversy surrounding it, is probably datable to the Carolingian period. Another incunabulum of stained glass, destroyed in World War II, was a head from the crypt of the Cathedral of Magdeburg that could be dated to about the year 1000. Stylistically this work was clearly related to the Ottonian miniature.

With the Lorsch, Wissembourg, and Magdeburg fragments begins the consecutive story of Western stained glass, which was to develop into one of the richest aspects of medieval pictorial art. As early as the Romanesque and, above all, in the Gothic period stained glass became in much of the West one of the most important techniques — when it was not actually the foremost technique — of painting. As has been indicated above, for the Roman period and the early Middle Ages an idea of the appearance of stained glass and the procedures used can be acquired only by integrating the scant archaeological evidence with a minute and careful examination of written sources. Beginning with the late 11th and the early 12th century the innumerable surviving examples of stained glass make possible firsthand knowledge of its characteristics and direct observation of every technical detail of the execution, mounting, and so on. Furthermore, the technical data are codified in the *Schedula diversarum artium*, whose author, although he signed himself Theophilus, has been identified by some scholars as a monk-artist named Rogkerus (or Rugerus) who was active at the beginning of the 12th century in the Benedictine abbey at Helmarshausen in Saxony.

The model was the same size as the pane that was to be executed and was drawn, according to Theophilus, with a lead or tin point on a wooden panel smeared with chalk. The wooden panel was successively replaced by more easily handled materials — cloth, parchment, paper — until, beginning well in the 15th century, the use of cardboard, an Italian innovation, became prevalent.

On top of the prepared model the pieces of glass of different colors were arranged. To obtain various gradations of color in the vitreous paste, mineral salts, oxides of iron, copper, cobalt, manganese, and so on were added during fusion to the sand and other component elements of the glass (potash, and later soda). In many cases the pieces of colored glass were composed of two layers: one of clear glass and a thinner layer of colored glass, which was fused to the first by a process known as "flashing." This was normal practice in the case of red glass because the copper salts gave the glass such a strong color and such a dark tonality that it would become completely opaque at a certain thickness. Double panes were also used in combinations of yellow and red, white and blue, and green and red. In other cases the layer of red glass was placed between two layers of clear glass. The use of flashed panes made possible the practice of sgraffito — that is, of scraping away the thin red film until the surface of the clear glass was exposed. This technique, dating from the end of the 13th century, was extensively applied in the 14th century and, most particularly, in the 15th. In less common use was "Venetian glass," which German glass masters employed at the end of the 15th century and in the 16th century. This glass, which was probably made at Murano, consisted of thin rods of glass of different colors incorporated in the body of clear glass during fusion.

After the glass had been cut with an incandescent iron point or, beginning in the 15th century, with a diamond point, so as to correspond exactly to the shapes indicated in the model, it was mounted in a provisional frame in such a way as to permit the glass master to check the over-all effect of the composition and to proceed to the painting of the single pieces. This operation was carried out with a dark-colored tint, called "grisaille," made of a powder of crushed glass, metallic salts (iron and copper oxides), and other pulverized minerals (Theophilus recommended "Greek sapphire," and Antonio da Pisa, cobalt) dissolved in wine or some other liquid (resins and gums were later added to render the mixture more adherent to glass). This process is of primary significance in the creation of stained glass, which, far from being simply a mosaic of glass and lead, is in the truest sense of the word both painting with glass and painting on glass at the same time. More than one type of grisaille was used. In many stained-glass windows one can clearly discern two different tints, one black and the other brown, of different chemical composition; in certain Austrian stained glass of the 14th century the use of a green grisaille has been noted. The panes were painted mainly on the inner side, but they were in many cases also painted sketchily on the outer side; sometimes even the most important elements of the painting were traced on the outer face of the glass. Ignorance of this fact, only recently discovered, has been the cause of serious damage in the restoration of old stained glass; for, while the inner surface of the glass was treated with maximum care, the outer surface was subjected to radical cleaning that removed much of the original painting along with incrustations, dust, and mold.

The role of grisaille in the over-all production of stained glass is highly important. In the first place, it is used to modify at least partially the tonality of the glass; for colors absorb light in varying degrees (as has been noted in the case of red glass), and it is the painter's task to regulate the translucence in order to obtain a homogeneous general effect — a problem that was studied in detail by Viollet-le-Duc (q.v.; 1868). In this manner, for example, blue glass that was particularly vivid in one panel could in certain cases be given a patina of grisaille to diminish the intensity of the blue for the sake of the total effect. Grisaille was also employed near the lead separating two panes of different tonality in order to attenuate the contrast between two overlively colors. Finally, grisaille — and this was its principal use — was employed to outline the details of the drawing, the lineaments of faces, the folds of drapery, and so on, as well as to create the modeling that would give the impression of volume.

The application of the grisaille was not a single operation. First the lines were drawn with a thin brush. When the painted lines had dried, the coating of tint used for modeling was applied with a larger brush of badger hair and with a broad, flat brush to make the layer of paint uniform. Then a part of the grisaille coat was removed so that the light could shine through. This was done with a very stiff brush of fitch and with other brushes and rods (and often with the brush handles), metal points, and so on. Thus the artist could control the distribution of the grisaille, reduce its thickness, and even reexpose the glass itself to obtain clear lines and zones of light. With another brush the artist would proceed to the final retouching.

As one can see, in the art of painting glass the operation of applying the tint and that of removing it were equally important; for the glass master painted not only with grisaille and the juxtaposition of colored glass but also with the light that filtered through the pane. Thus, for example, the edge of a stained-glass window was generally painted with a thick layer of grisaille, which was then abraded with wooden and iron points to produce beads, frets, and other decorative elements such as tendrils, leaves, and animals, that would stand out clearly against the dark ground.

The manner of tracing the lines of the design and of applying the modeling varied from period to period, from city to city, and from one master to another. In one window dark, opaque tones will prevail; in another much of the tint will have been removed to obtain greater brightness; in a third the modeling will have been applied in most delicate superimposed layers; and in still another the effect of modeling will have been achieved by purely graphic means, with close-set fine lines. These modifications and varieties of techniques, as well as differences in the choice of colors, are attributable exclusively to stylistic developments and consequently pertain to the history of style in stained glass.

Grisaille, though extensively used, generally did not allow for radical modifications in the color. Consequently, where a variation in color was needed it was necessary to insert a piece of glass of the required color as well as a strip of lead to join the two zones. The separation of colors is generally very distinct, passing directly from one color zone to the next with no other modulations than those obtained with grisaille. Alterations in the color of a glass pane, so that there would be two distinct colors in a single piece, became possible (aside from the use of sgraffito on double panes) only with the introduction of "silver stain," a compound of metallic salts that was applied to the exterior face of the glass and assumed a golden look in firing. This important technical achievement, known in the East since the early Middle Ages, was adopted and came into common use in France only in the 14th century. While grisaille remained the principal means of obtaining chiaroscuro effects, the innovation of silver stain made possible a modification of color even within a single part of the surface of a pane. In a single fragment that contains a white and a golden zone, for example, a motif of architectural decoration may vary from white to yellow, and the blond hair of a figure may be obtained on the same piece of white glass that was used for the face. Silver stain can be used on colored glass as well as on clear glass — for example, with blue to produce green. Later, another coloring agent, known in France as "Jean Cousin" for the artist who seems to have been the first to use it, was introduced. Red in color, from a base of trioxide of iron, this coloring agent represents a middle way between grisaille and enameling. Finally, beginning in the second quarter of the 16th century, the use of enamels — that is, of vitreous pastes colored with metallic oxides (generally composed of powdered glass containing lead and various combinations of borosilicates) — completely revolutionized the methods of working stained glass and offered the possibility of imparting different colors to a single piece of glass. This innovation made the use of different panes of various colors superfluous and hence destroyed the very concept of stained glass as a colored mosaic.

Once painted, the glass was submitted to another firing, which permanently fixed the grisaille by vitrifying one of its components, the powdered glass. When the firing was successful the parts covered with grisaille were much more resistant to atmospheric agents than those which were not. Occasionally, because of defective firing, the grisaille was not satisfactorily fixed, in which case it would end by falling away and being almost completely erased. In certain cases, particularly for retouching, "cold techniques" were also used — that is, oil colors were applied, and these were naturally far less resistant than the vitrified grisaille.

Then the pieces of glass were set into the leading. The deep-grooved double strips of lead held together the various pieces of glass and emphasized the contours of the images. (Large windows were made in units that were subsequently fitted into an iron "armature.") This technique of joining stained glass is somewhat similar to that of enamels (q.v.), in which the elements of vitreous paste are held together by thin copper or bronze wires. In a great many cases modern restoration has replaced the old lead strips with others, causing very serious damage; for the purity, precision, and sensitivity of the old mountings are inimitable, and the substitution of the leads has often changed the effect of the design of stained glass, rendering the outlines of the figures mechanical and flat.

After the leading the stained glass was finally fitted into the window by means of an iron frame, which had replaced the earlier wooden ones that were still in use in the 12th century for windows of small dimensions. In the 12th century the design of the mounting was extremely simple, consisting of vertical supports and transverse bars spaced about 2 ft. to 2 ft., 8 in., apart so as to form more or less equal squares. From the end of the 12th century this design was replaced to a large extent by the so-called "medallion forms" — circles, quatrefoils, lozenges — that intersected in quadrilobes or were set concentrically, following the decorative scheme of the stained glass and dividing the surface into panels and zones of diverse shape and composition.

However, not all the problems relating to stained glass can be discussed within the context of a simple exposition of techniques. The rapid development, widespread diffusion, and extraordinary popularity of stained glass from the 12th to the 16th century cannot, of course, be accounted for in a study limited to the mechanics of its technological evolution. Materials and techniques alone cannot explain the exceptional success or the flourishing stylistic development of stained glass. On the contrary, it is clearly demonstrable that in many instances specific technical solutions were adopted not as a result of fortuitous discoveries but under the impulse of profound esthetic exigencies. For example, silver stain was thought to have been used first in the monochrome (grisaille) stained-glass window donated to the Cathedral of Chartres by Canon Thierry in 1328; but J. Lafond ["Un Vitrail au Mesnil-Villeman (1313) et les origines du jaune d'argent," BAFr, 1954–55, pp. 93–95] has shown that this coloring agent was employed as early as 1313 in a stained-glass window for the church of Mesnil-Villeman. The most interesting aspect of Lafond's research, however, is his proof of the prior existence of a formula for silver stain in a Spanish manuscript, the Lapidario of Alfonso X of Castile and León (r. 1252–84); this formula was translated from a Hebrew text for the King in about 1279. Furthermore, Lafond has proved that this technique had been used extensively in Egypt for the decoration of glass, perhaps as early as the 6th century, but certainly between the 8th and 12th centuries. This is a clear case of how a technical expedient that had been long available in the objective sense came to be employed at a specific time and in answer to specific cultural needs. Similar observations can be made regarding the mutations in the manufacture of glass, an element of primary importance in the evolution of the art of stained-glass windows that was likewise conditioned by stylistic evolution, which, as L. Grodecki has pointed out, spurred the master glaziers to seek out one specific kind of glass and not another. In this case, too, the history of style and the history of technique are indissolubly linked.

THE HISTORY OF STAINED GLASS FROM THE MIDDLE AGES TO MODERN TIMES. French and German historians have long been attempting to clarify the complex problems of medieval stained glass, the reasons for its ever-increasing employment, its exceptional prestige, and its vigorous, unarrested development. Since such causes are undoubtedly to be sought in the general cultural situation in which the phenomenon of stained glass emerged, study has concentrated especially on bringing to light the correspondences that can be found in stained glass and the suggestions for it provided by contemporary philosophical, liturgical, and religious thought. There is no lack of examples in medieval literature of the place held by stained glass in liturgical symbolism. From Rabanus Maurus to Honorius of Autun, to Siccardus of Cremona, to Durandus of Mende, from the Carolingian period (q.v.) to the end of the 13th century, the glass windows of churches, which allowed the light to pass through and offered protection from storms, were likened to, or actually identified with, the prophets, the Apostles, the doctors of the church, or the Holy Scriptures, in short, with all that enlightens the faithful and shields them from evil. In his Rationale Divinorum Officiorum Gulielmus Durandus of Mende wrote: "The glass windows in a church are Holy Scriptures which expel the wind and the rain, that is all things hurtful, but transmit the light of the true Sun, that is God, into the hearts of the faithful" (J. Neale and B. Webb, trans., *Symbolism of Churches and Church Ornaments*, Leeds, 1843, p. 297). For that matter, the medieval symbolism of light and the theories of its origin and divine qualities could only enhance the prestige of glass, an exceptional material that admitted light without obstructing it or being damaged by it. Finally, the splendid, glowing colors of stained glass gave it a value equal to that of precious stones, whose magical qualities were celebrated in the lapidaries, and made the church the terrestrial equivalent of the New Jerusalem with its luminous walls of gems.

Although this cultural situation seems (and certainly was) particularly favorable to the success of painting on glass, the fact remains that it is all but impossible to distinguish how much the success of a technique is inspired and brought about by specific cultural needs and how much its highest achievements themselves have contributed to modifying and influencing the cultural milieu. An important problem in the history of stained glass is that of its relationship with architecture. The close bond between the two is immediately apparent. The ever-increasing importance of windows in Gothic churches, culminating in the creation of airy cages with diaphanous walls (e.g., the Ste-Chapelle in Paris and the Church of St-Urbain in Troyes), was a fundamental factor in the development of stained glass. But the relationship between stained glass and architecture is far from being explained by the subordination of the one to the other. It has been pointed out that the deepening of the color range of stained glass at the end of the 12th century led directly to the heightening and widening of windows and, therefore, to larger and larger apertures in the wall surfaces (cf. VI, PL. 314).

Parallel to the evolution of cultural perspective and stylistic tendencies, the function of stained glass underwent changes: a filter and modulator of light in Gothic churches, it became a gleaming plaque of color emulating mosaic or glazed terracotta in Renaissance churches (e.g., in S. Maria del Fiore, the Cathedral of Florence). Equally variable was the relationship between stained glass and the various techniques of painting. In the stained glass of the second half of the 12th century, particularly in northeastern France and the Rhineland, affinities with enamelwork are evident, while in that of the mid-13th century there are clear connections with contemporary illumination (as seen, for example, in the stained glass of the Ste-Chapelle). In 15th- and 16th-century stained glass, instead, relationships with fresco painting, other painting media, and engraving are more apparent. In turn, these genres were often influenced by stained glass. The celebrated manuscripts of the *Bible moralisée* executed in a Parisian "atelier" about the middle of the 13th century show a marked influence from contemporary stained glass in the disposition of the scenes and in the decoration. The way in which the medallions with illustrations are arranged on the page recalls stained-glass composition in a lancet window. This influence is also evidenced by the ornamental border that frames the page and by the elegant trilobate motifs set in the lateral spaces unoccupied by the medallions. Other French miniatures of the end of the 13th century appear to have been variously influenced by the technique of stained glass. The contours of the figures are highly accentuated, an emphasis that clearly reveals an effort to imitate the lead strips that hold together the pieces of glass. This is an obvious case of the transference of expressive means from one technique to another. In fact, every period has had its guiding techniques, that is to say, techniques that because of the high quality and novelty of their results have acquired such prestige that they become exemplars for other techniques, which in attempting the same results come to share the same manner of expression.

A final fundamental problem in the history of stained glass is that of the relationship between the artist who conceives the work and the executor, between the painter who creates the model and the master glazier who carries it out. This problem, which in certain aspects resembles that of the relationship between painter and engraver, is especially important to the history of European stained glass of the Renaissance. Although there is frequently precise documentation regarding the creator and executor of many stained-glass works, there are clear indications

that the same problem also exists for earlier periods, when the distinction between "artist" and "artisan," "creator" and "executor" had not yet been made. The close relationships, for example, between certain panes of stained glass in the Cathedral of Chartres and certain sculptures in the same Cathedral and between certain stained-glass panes in the Ste-Chapelle and certain contemporary Parisian miniatures (cf. VI, PL. 28g) extend so far beyond mere influence as to suggest the hypothesis of common authorship.

Nevertheless, when speaking of the design of a stained-glass window provided by a particular artist, one would do well to distinguish between different cases. It is one matter if the artist designs a cartoon of the same format as the stained-glass window or if he himself paints the single pieces of glass after they have been cut by the master glazier, as Cennino Cennini advised in his *Libro dell'Arte*; and it is another matter if the artist merely provides a design, which the master glazier reproduces on a larger scale and then transfers to glass. In the latter case, the artist's contribution is purely compositional, and the relationship of his drawing to the finished stained glass has the same value as that of the engravings of — let us say — Albrecht Dürer, Il Rosso (qq.v.), Marcantonio Raimondi, or Heinrich Aldegrever, whose graphic works were frequently copied in 16th-century stained glass. It is difficult, at the least, to preserve certain personal characteristics of style and manner in the passage from drawing to cartoon and from cartoon to glass. In the first case, if the designer has closely followed the work of the master glazier in order to ensure against betrayal of his manner and intentions in the passage from cartoon to glass, one can speak of a genuine transference not only of a compositional idea but also of authentic expressive elements.

In France, the Low Countries, and Germany the personalities of the master glaziers, often both creators and executors, were of great importance. Among such 15th- and 16th-century masters were Peter Hemmel of Andlau, André Robin, Arnaud de Moles, Jean and Nicolas Le Prince, Romain Buron (PL. 177), Dirck Pietersz. and Wouter Pietersz. I Crabeth, and Aert van Oort, known as Arnoult de Nimègue. Contributions to the creation of stained glass were also made by outstanding painters, including the Master of the Aix Annunciation, the Master of Moulins, Lukas Moser, Hans Holbein the Younger, and Dürer. In Italy, especially in central Italy, the personality of the designer was always more prominent than that of the glazier. Among the former were Lorenzo Ghiberti, Paolo Uccello, Donatello, Andrea del Castagno, Alesso Baldovinetti (qq.v.), and Mariotto di Nardo. Among the latter were Niccolò di Pietro Tedesco, Bernardo di Francesco, Fra Bartolomeo di Pietro da Perugia, Guido di Niccolò da Pelago, Domenico di Piero da Pisa, Francesco di Giovanni, and Angiolo Lippi (PL. 170). This situation was already partially established in the 14th century. As Cennini notes, "It is true that this occupation is not much practiced by our profession and is practiced more by those who make a business of it. And ordinarily those masters who do the work possess more skill than draftsmanship, and they are almost forced to turn for help on the drawing to some one who possesses finished craftsmanship, that is, to one of all-round, good ability" (trans. D. V. Thompson, 1932–33, chap. CLXXI). It is clear from the tenor of this passage that in Italy at that time the master glaziers were regarded as practical men, clearly subordinate to the painters, that is, to those who possessed "finished craftsmanship." The only Renaissance master glazier working in central Italy to acquire and retain great fame, precisely because of his own personality — however one judges his achievements — which was not that of a simple executor, and because of his exceptional technical skill, was the Frenchman Guglielmo de Marcillat (d. Arezzo, 1529; PL. 179). The situation in northern Italy was quite different from that in Florence. In northern Italy the great master glaziers were far more intimately involved in the creation of stained glass than the Florentine craftsmen were. These disparities in the relative position of designer and executor are clearly rooted in deep divergences in cultural outlook and in differing values placed on the relationship between various techniques and between the ideation and the intervening execution.

The master glazier is more than a passive executor of the idea of others. His own sensibilities and formal intuition have a decisive influence on the results obtained. Such operations as the choosing and cutting of the individual pieces of glass, the leading of the panes, and, most of all, the grisaille painting of the various fragments involve far more than mere habit or experience. Perfect knowledge of instruments and material and complete mastery of techniques, permitting the coordination of the various means toward a specific end, are capacities that often go beyond the area of pure technique into that of expression.

The history of stained glass is long and uneven. The great medieval flowering of stained glass — attended in the literature of art by the pages dedicated to it in the *Schedula diversarum artium* of Theophilus and in the *De coloribus et artibus romanorum* of Heraclius (i.e., the part of this curious treatise that concerns stained glass and consists of texts from different periods back to the 13th century), and later, at the end of the 14th century, in the *Trattato* of Master Antonio da Pisa and in the chapter on painting on glass in Cennini's *Libro dell'Arte* — was followed, with no less dedication and with equally fine results, by the ambitious 15th-century works. During this period the general characteristics of stained glass underwent fundamental changes, both in the range of colors and in the compositional schemes.

The earliest great stained-glass cycles that survive largely intact date from the 12th century. For those of Augsburg Cathedral, the Abbey church of St-Denis, and the cathedrals of Chartres, Poitiers, and Le Mans there is general agreement about dating, thus affirming that in connection with the stained glass of the preceding period nothing remains but written documents and a few debatable fragments. In general, 12th-century stained glass exhibits a close, though variable, relationship with the minor arts, and the varicolored panes seem to try to emulate the splendor and limpidity of precious stones. Abbot Suger, in his account of works accomplished during his tenure at St-Denis (*De rebus in sua administratione gestis*), praises the "saphirorum materia" of the stained-glass panes he had commissioned for his church. Enamel, the technique that produced masterpieces in the Carolingian and Ottonian periods, was the model to which the master glaziers often looked for inspiration. The color range employed in this period was already, on the whole, that which would be used until the end of the Middle Ages. The general tonality tended to be light, inclined toward a transparency that was only slightly modified by the application of grisaille, as if the artists wanted to be faithful to the lucid radiance of earlier unpainted glass panes. The centers of greatest importance for the history of stained glass in this period are France and Germany.

In France there were various tendencies, some of which were opposed and some of which overlapped. One very important tendency is represented by a group of stained-glass windows in the western region — at Le Mans, Poitiers, Angers — outstanding among which are a fragmentary Assumption in Le Mans Cathedral (ca. 1145; PL. 159) and the Crucifixion window of Poitiers Cathedral (ca. 1165; PL. 157), which was donated by Henry II of England and his wife, Eleanor of Aquitaine. These windows show close connections with contemporary miniatures and wall painting of the region, and they are completely Romanesque in their vehement expressiveness and in the imaginative distortion of forms. Another tendency of great moment had its center in the Abbey of St-Denis, where Abbot Suger commissioned the painting, by numerous masters "from different regions," of six windows with figures and others that were to be purely decorative for the choir of the Abbey church, which was built between 1140 and 1144. These panes have survived in extremely fragmentary condition. In any case, the surviving panels do not reveal affinities with either the agitated Romanesque expressiveness of the western region or the achievements of the earliest Gothic sculpture, both of which were finding expression at that time on the portals of the Abbey church. Instead, the stained glass has a rather sophisticated and refined appearance that relates it to goldsmiths' work and to some miniatures of northern France. The stained glass of St-Denis is also exceptionally important from the standpoint of iconography; such themes as the tree of Jesse, with Christ's genealogy, and the concordance of the Old and New Testaments, which are treated here, were to have great popularity. Strongly influenced by these works are the three stained-glass windows in the façade of the Cathedral of Chartres (ca. 1155; PLS. 158, 162). Although iconography and compositional suggestions from St-Denis are equally noticeable in all three windows, the situation is different as far as style is concerned. At Chartres the influences from St-Denis in the Jesse-tree window are opposed by other inspirations from western France in the windows depicting the infancy of Christ and the Passion.

In central and southeastern France predominance of Byzantinesque stylistic elements, probably transmitted from Lombardy, is evident in stained glass as well as in wall painting and miniatures. Examples include the windows of the small church of Le Champs (Isère; ca. 1160), those of the Chapel of St. Peter in the Cathedral of Lyons (ca. 1180–90), and the earliest ones in the Cathedral of Notre-Dame in Clermont-Ferrand (ca. 1190). In the stained glass of the northeast — for instance, in the windows of the Cathedral of St-Etienne in Châlons-sur-Marne (PL. 158) — there are substantial affinities with the stylistic schemes of Mosan goldwork. Also in eastern France the stained-glass windows of St-Remi in Reims (ca. 1175–1200; PL. 158), which were destroyed in large part during World War I, elaborate in a Gothic and monumental fashion certain elements in the windows of the Cathedral of St-Etienne in Châlons-sur-Marne; this is the most advanced and modern point reached by glass painting in the 12th century, as well as that in which the connections with early Gothic sculpture are strongest. Less modern and more closely tied to a certain Romanesque courtliness are the Alsatian stained-glass windows, which to a great extent show contact with the fundamentally conservative Germanic sphere. Examples include the St. Timothy from Neuwiller (ca. 1150–60; now in Paris, Mus. de Cluny); the Virgin in the Church of Ste-Ségolène in Metz (ca. 1160–70); the Virgin in the center of the north rose window in the church of Wissembourg; and, above all, the many stained-glass windows dating from the end of the 12th and the beginning of the 13th century in the Cathedral of Strasbourg.

The case of Germanic stained glass in the 12th century is quite different from that of French stained glass. First of all, far less survives, and often in such a fragmentary state that it is impossible to outline a plausible general picture of it. The most important cycle is represented by the five figures of prophets in Augsburg Cathedral (PL. 161), which can perhaps be dated about 1130. Of later works all that remains are fragments and single panels, among which are St. Nicholas from Oberndorf, now in the Eisenach museum; a Crucifixion, with lacunae, from Reichenau, now in the Darmstadt Landesmuseum; various fragments of a cycle that adorned the apse of the Church of St. Patroklus in Soest; and two exceptionally fine tondos from Ingelheim in the Palatinate, formerly in the Staatliche Museen in Berlin, which were destroyed during World War II. A more consistent group of works can be grouped around another stained-glass window signed by Master Gherlacus, with scenes from the life of Moses (PL. 160), in which the link with the art of the Mosan enamelers is very marked.

Despite the incomplete picture presented by the few surviving windows, it is possible to make some observations on the general characteristics of 12th-century Germanic stained glass. In the first place, it is very closely bound to the techniques of the minor arts, even more so than contemporary French stained glass. Germanic stained glass of the 12th century is also marked by an insistent elaboration of forms that achieves accents of minute elegance in the backgrounds of rinceaux and in the rich borders of plant motifs. It has rightly been confirmed that the difference in scope of French and Germanic stained glass in this period is clearly discernible. French stained glass was created in the service of Gothic architecture and designed for the large windows of the new religious edifices, which prescribed the form and dimensions of the stained glass and gave it an authentic monumental quality. The Germanic stained glass of this period was designed for the narrow apertures of Romanesque churches, and its function and relation to the wall surface were radically different from those between wall and window in Gothic architecture. Thus Romanesque architecture not only limited the dimensions of Germanic stained glass but at the same time imposed on it a precious character.

In the Germanic cultural area — the influence of which is also clearly discernible in the use of particular types of foliated ornamentation — there are other stained-glass windows produced in centers that were peripheral to the main centers of the Rhineland. Among such works are the Virgin and Child from the little church of Flums (Saint Gallen canton), now in the Schweizerisches Landesmuseum in Zurich; the St. Martin from Bjerreby Taasinge, now in the Nationalmuseet in Copenhagen; and the Magdalen from Weitensfeld (ca. 1170; PL. 161).

A distinct trend in 12th-century stained glass is represented by the so-called "Cistercian grisailles," which adorned abbey windows. Following the precepts of St. Bernard of Clairvaux, these stained-glass windows bear no figural representations and consist of simple decorative interlaces that continue older ornamental forms. Among the windows of this type are those of Eberbach (now in Wiesbaden, Landesmus.) and the former Convent of Marienstatt, both in Germany; of Heiligenkreuz, near Vienna (13th cent.); and of Obazine, Beaulieu-sur-Dordogne, Bonlieu, and Pontigny, all in France.

The 13th century opened with the colossal undertaking at Chartres. In little more than thirty years — between 1200 and 1236, approximately — the stained-glass windows for the Cathedral were all but completed. The Chartres cycle remains the greatest monument, the apogee, of medieval painting on glass. It represents an outstandingly successful realization of narrative stained glass, in which the legendary scenes are arranged in medallions and grouped to form quatrefoils and superposed circles or lozenges — a formula that was to be applied throughout France (VI, PL. 299). Meanwhile, at the end of the 12th century, the color range of stained-glass windows had been notably darkened. Chartres itself is an example of this development, as attested by a comparison of the limpid stained-glass windows dating from the 12th century on the façade with those of the nave, which are stronger and deeper in tone.

Masters of the most diverse origin and experience came together in the Chartres workshop. Some were archaizers, influenced by the Romanesque art of the western region (e.g., the Master of the St. Lubin Window); others were more modern, that is, exponents of that serene Gothic classicism which was emerging during those years in the statuary of Chartres and Amiens (e.g., the Master of the Life of the Virgin; the Charlemagne Master, PL. 162; the St. James Master); and still others were in contact with the north (Soissons, Saint-Quentin) or with the Parisian milieu. Openly innovative personalities were responsible for some of the tall windows in the choir and transept, including the two large rose windows on the south and north (PL. 165), as well as for the exceptional window with St. Denis giving the oriflamme to Clement of Metz, in which the splendid face of the young warrior recalls the statuary of the south portal of the Cathedral. The influence of Chartres was dominant in all France. Glass masters and entire units of artisans from the immense workshop of Jean de Beauce were later employed to produce stained glass for other cathedrals. For example, in Rouen there worked a certain Clément of Chartres, the only 13th-century glass master known to us by name. Furthermore, as we have seen, Chartres was not dominated by the presence of a single great master, but it was marked, rather, by the almost contemporaneous activity of artists from various regions with highly diverse interests and training.

A similar situation presents itself in the Cathedral of Bourges, which houses another exceptional complex of 13th-century stained glass (VI, PL. 290). The iconographic program of Bourges is more organic than that of Chartres, where the iconography is confused and full of repetitions. As Grodecki has suggested (*Le vitrail français*, 1958, p. 139a), the iconographic program may have been formulated by Guillaume de Donjon, who was archbishop of Bourges from 1199 to 1209, when the Cathedral was being built. The principal artists who worked there were the Master of the Good Samaritan, whose late Romanesque conception recalls that of the Master of the St. Lubin Window at Chartres; the Master of the *Nouvelle Alliance*, who is close to the classical Gothic style of Chartres; and the Master of the

Relics of St. Stephen, the most modern and Gothic of the three. The last-mentioned artist ranks along with the authors of the south and north rose windows and some of the lancets at Chartres and the exceptional, but later (ca. 1255), SS. Gervasius and Protasius window in the Cathedral of Le Mans as one of the greatest 13th-century painters in France.

Although the cathedrals of Chartres and Bourges house the most extensive and significant cycles of the early 13th century, the history of French stained glass during this period comprises far more than just these two centers. The cultural diversification that had been emerging throughout the 12th century continued to develop, and the traditional centers maintained their importance in the west (Le Mans, Angers, Poitiers), in central France (Lyons), and in the east (Reims, Orbais, Troyes). Other centers in the north assumed great importance in the early years of the century (Laon, Soissons, Saint-Quentin). It is hard to say anything about Paris in this period because of the scarcity and extremely fragmentary quality of what has survived. Both Chartres and Bourges exercised great influence on other large undertakings in Gothic France, particularly on the stained-glass windows of Sens and Auxerre cathedrals. Unfortunately, a high percentage of the many 13th-century windows (more than 1,000, consisting of a total of some 20,000 scenes) remain altogether unpublished, so their arrangement can only be outlined at present.

There was a decided change toward the middle of the century; until then the prevailing scheme provided that the lower windows of the aisles be dedicated to hagiographic and legendary themes and to episodes from the Holy Scriptures, which were disposed in scenes and framed by medallions (which, in turn, were grouped in diverse combinations), and the higher windows were generally devoted to a single personage (often an Apostle or a prophet) framed by an architectural setting. The evolution of Gothic architecture in the 13th century altered the relationship between the lower and higher windows, which was resolved in certain cases by a single tall window, such as those of the Ste-Chapelle. The format of the window also changed as a result of the introduction of vertical masonry elements that divided it into two or more tall and narrow compartments. Compositions were altered accordingly and there prevailed a scheme of simple superposition of panels — ovals, tondos, multifoils, and so on; even the lancets came to include several personages placed one above the other.

Of fundamental importance is the stained-glass cycle in the Ste-Chapelle in Paris (PL. 163), which was erected between 1243 and 1248 to house relics of the True Cross. The 1 windows with superposed medallions represent, along with the Chartres and Bourges cycles, one of the high points of 13th-century stained glass. The vital and spasmodic style of the 1,13 scenes derives from that of the stained-glass windows of the Chapel of the Virgin in the Church of St-Germain-des-Prés (1232–45; now in the former Abbey church at Saint-Denis and the Victoria and Albert Museum). The stained glass of the Ste-Chapelle exerted great influence on French stained glass in the second half of the 13th century (e.g., Tours, Le Mans).

In Germany the 13th-century stained glass reveals the existence of two major stylistic currents that were used alternately and that were in certain cases superimposed. One was more receptive to Gothic influences from France and had its centers in the west — in Cologne (St. Kunibert, ca. 1220–30), in Bücken (the Abbey church, ca. 1240–50), in Freiburg im Breisgau and in Marburg (the Church of St. Elizabeth, ca. 1235–50). French Gothic influences, which are evident in compositional elements, in the polylobate compartments, and so on, alternate with the sumptuous taste of the late Romanesque, deriving from the tradition of Gherlacus and from "scholarly" stained glass. The other tendency is unabashedly Romanesque and conservative, closely related to contemporary Thuringian-Saxon miniatures, and assimilates Byzantine influences. The most important stained-glass windows of the last-mentioned widely popular style — to which are related the stained-glass windows of the Upper Church of S. Francesco in Assisi, as well as some examples on the Swedish island of Gotland — are those of the Franciscan church in Erfurt (PL. 164). In the secnd half of the 13th century Gothic elements became more pronounced and prevalent. From this period date some of the windows in the transept, nave, and side aisles of the Cathedral of Strasbourg (ca. 1250–70), those of Naumburg Cathedral (ca. 1250), and others in Frankfurt am Main (Historisches Mus.; Städelsches Kunstinst.), in the church of the former Benedictine abbey in Mönchen-Gladbach, in the Stadtkirche of Bad Wimpfen im Berg (ca. 1270–80), and in Darmstadt (Landesmus.; from the collegiate church of Bad Wimpfen im Tal). The most important examples of 13th-century stained glass in Austria are the windows of the collegiate church in Ardagger (ca. 1230–40), the extremely beautiful tondo with the Deposition in the Cathedral of Gurk (ca. 1270), and windows in the Church of St. Barthlmä in Friesach (ca. 1260–70), the Walpurgiskapelle at Sankt Michael, near Leoben (ca. 1290–95), and the Church of St. Nikolaus at Pichl. The outstanding 13th-century complex in Switzerland is the rose window in the south transept of the Cathedral of Lausanne (ca. 1230), which is related to French stained glass and may have been executed by the master glazier Pierre of Arras.

Thirteenth-century English stained glass includes some splendid works, which show close affinities with French models. Among the most significant works are the windows in the Trinity Chapel of Canterbury Cathedral, the largest English glass cycle of the 13th century, in which connections with the stained glass of Sens are clear; the rose window in the north great transept of Lincoln Cathedral; the medallions now in the Jerusalem Chamber of Westminster Abbey; and windows in the Church of the Birth of Our Lady in Madley (Herefordshire).

In Italy the oldest stained-glass windows are those of the choir of the Upper Church of S. Francesco in Assisi (ca. 1240–50), which are by German masters who may have worked earlier in the Franciscan church of the discalced friars (the Barfüsserkirche) in Erfurt (PL. 164). The windows of the north transept (PL. 164), probably the work of an Alsatian master, date from about the end of the 13th century and influenced the windows of the south transept, which were painted by more archaizing Italian masters. The design of a window in the oculus of the apse of the Cathedral of Siena (PL. 166) has been attributed to Duccio di Buoninsegna (q.v.) and identified with a stained-glass window that documents prove the Sienese master executed about 1288 — a date that seems too early, however, for the window in question. Among the other rare windows of this period in Italy are the two tondos depicting the Death of the Virgin in the Cathedral Treasury of Aosta, perhaps a work of the end of the 12th century; these reveal contacts with the Germanic sphere, as well as with the unusual window of the Ascension in the small church at Le Champ (Isère) and with the panel of the Madonna and Child in the Sanctuary of the Madonna della Grotta, near Siena, which stylistically recalls the forms of the 13th-century painter Guido da Siena.

The 14th century was a period of particular importance for the history of stained glass. The relationships with painting, including the miniature, became even closer (partly because of the new, genuinely pictorial possibilities offered by the introduction of silver stain), and the notable stylistic changes in these other painting techniques during the course of the century immediately and significantly influenced glass painting. The color range also changed, and ever more frequently the figures stand out against the lightest of backgrounds, against whites and yellows only subtly suffused with a shading of grisaille. Aside from the change in color range, the most important factors in the history of 14th-century stained glass are the successive introduction, first, of the expressive style and the tendency to achieve a semblance of volume through the use of shading that were characteristic of the works of the Parisian miniaturist Honoré and, second, of the new spatial effects of Giotto (q.v.). The latter development was of great consequence in glass painting, introducing the element of depth, which contravened the entire previous history of this technique and put in crisis the hitherto prevailing concept of stained glass as a "translucent carpet." The great innovations made by Italian painters in the depiction of space introduced a third dimension in composition, and spatial illusionism made its entry into stained glass.

The 14th century saw an extraordinary flourishing of imaginary, fantastic architecture in stained-glass windows throughout Europe, with successive archivolts, projecting corbels, opened-out domes and baldachins, and a budding of balconies and belvederes. Throughout Europe — from Königsfelden to Strasbourg, from Rouen to Evreux (PL. 167), from Auxerre to Vienna — an effect of existing and habitable space was sought in stained-glass compositions. The first endeavors were limited to minor architectural elements that could suggest space, evoking the setting of the representation. The frames, which in the 14th century assumed increasing importance in providing a setting for the large figures in the windows, came to protrude from the surface and stand out against the diaphanous wall. Beyond the authentic architecture there opened the imaginary and deceptive architectural effects within the window. Counterfeit frames repeated and enriched the lines of the windows, creating striking effects.

In the course of the 14th century France's preeminence, absolute in preceding centuries, gradually diminished and finally disappeared. Other centers acquired great importance, from Austria to Switzerland, Italy, Alsace, and Germany. In France the stained glass of Ste-Radegonde in Poitiers (PL. 167), completed at the beginning of the century, advanced a new formula that placed the figures on a light background and allowed the scenes to range freely over the entire field of the glass panel rather than confining them in compartments. The windows of St-Pierre in Chartres (ca. 1315) — of generally deeper colors, which are frequently adjoined by light grisailles — were strongly influenced by Honoré's expressionism. The window donated by Canon Thierry to Chartres Cathedral in 1328 is particularly important for the precocious and extensive use of silver stain and for the elaboration of the scenes against a grisaille background with a marvelous harmony of light on light colors. The region of France that has preserved the largest quantity of 14th-century stained glass and the most important cycles is Normandy. Since Parisian stained glass of the period is almost completely lost, that of Normandy provides the best evidence from which to trace the history of 14th-century stained glass in France. The most important cycles are those of the Cathedral and the Church of St-Ouen in Rouen, the Abbey church of Jumièges, and the Cathedral of Evreux (PL. 167). The stained glass of Evreux Cathedral was donated by bishops, feudal lords, and kings of France and constitutes an exceptional series, created throughout the course of the century, in which the different steps in stylistic evolution can be traced. Another well-defined cultural area rich in stained glass is Alsace, where tendencies converged and mixed. Two tendencies — one of Parisian origin, which was dramatic and attentive to a delicate and shaded rendering of personages, and another of Italian origin, which keenly explored spatial effects — had particularly interesting encounters and developments in Alsace. Examples are the cycles of the childhood of the Virgin and the life of Christ and the Passion in the south aisle of Strasbourg Cathedral; the scenes of the childhood of Christ and the Passion from the Dominican church of Strasbourg and now in the Church of St-Guillaume and the Chapel of St-Laurent in the Cathedral; and a window from the Church of St-Etienne in Mulhouse, now in the Protestant church of the same city.

One of the most interesting cycles of the century is preserved in the Franciscan church of the former Hapsburg abbey at Königsfelden near Brugg, in the Swiss canton of Aargau, which dates from about 1330 and represents an exceptionally early instance of Giottesque influence in the north. Among the other more significant 14th-century stained-glass windows in Switzerland are those of the Church of St. Laurentius in Oberkirch-Frauenfeld (Thurgau; ca. 1310–20), the Cistercian church of Kappel (Zurich; ca. 1325–30), the Abbey of Hauterive (Fribourg; ca. 1330), and the Church of Blumenstein (Bern).

In the Swabian town of Esslingen in Germany the splendid cycles in the Church of St. Dionysius (end of the 13th cent.), the Franciscan church (ca. 1300), and the Frauenkirche (ca. 1320–30; PL. 168) show marked contacts with Alsatian works and with the new Parisian pictorial style of Honoré. Other notably beautiful examples are found in the Cistercian church of Heiligkreuztal (ca. 1312), in the Cathedral of Freiburg im Breisgau, in the parish church of Amelungsborn (ca. 1330–40; this cycle, which showed particularly close affinities with Italian works, was largely destroyed in 1945), and in Regensburg Cathedral. In the second half of the century there spread that tendency to develop the scenes within imaginary and spacious architectural settings which had led to the previously mentioned notable achievements in France. Among the examples are the stained-glass windows of the Cathedral choir in Erfurt (ca. 1360–70) and the Jakobskirche in Rothenburg (ca. 1380–1420). But the most spectacular manifestations of this tendency are found in Austria — in the Sanctuary of St. Maria at Strassengel (ca. 1350), near Graz, from which some of the panes are now in the Victoria and Albert Museum; in the monastery church at Viktring in the province of Carinthia; and, above all, in Vienna, in the Church of St. Maria am Gestade and the Cathedral of St. Stephan, where the stained-glass windows of the Ducal Chapel (ca. 1390) represent the absolute masterpiece of Austrian 14th-century stained glass.

Italy occupies a leading place in the 14th-century history of European stained glass owing to the impetuous development of this technique that accompanied the general flourishing of Gothic architecture and especially to the collaboration of great artistic personalities in the field. In the works of this period one of the basic problems in the history of stained glass presents itself with utmost clarity — that of the relationship between creator and executor. In 14th-century Italy the design of stained-glass windows was generally the work of painters and not of master glaziers. Consequently, it sometimes happens that a group of works which is extremely similar in technical realization will reveal marked stylistic inconsistency; such is the case, for example, of the windows of the Lower Church of S. Francesco in Assisi, where it is presumed that a single atelier executed the designs of different painters. Among the painters who provided designs for stained-glass windows in Florence were Taddeo and Agnolo Gaddi (Sta Croce and S. Maria del Fiore), Maso di Banco (Sta Croce), the great anonymous artist known as the Master of Figline (Sta Croce), Pacino di Buonaguida (Sta Croce), Andrea Bonaiuti, known as Andrea da Firenze (S. Maria Novella), Niccolò di Pietro Gerini (S. Maria Novella), and perhaps even Lorenzo Monaco and other painters of his circle (Orsanmichele). The results were not always up to the artistic level of the original designs, and it is clear that a beautiful design was often poorly executed because of inadequacies on the part of the master glaziers. Among the master glaziers who worked in Florence were Bernardo di Francesco, Antonio and Domenico di Piero da Pisa, Leonardo di Simone, Angiolo Lippi and his son Biagio, and the Germans Niccolò di Pietro and his son Guido di Niccolò. Among the artists who provided designs for stained-glass windows outside Florence were Ambrogio Lorenzetti, to whom is attributed a panel with the archangel Michael in the Palazzo Pubblico in Siena; Lorenzo Maitani, who probably designed the large window in the apse of Orvieto Cathedral, which was magnificently executed (completed 1434) by Giovanni di Bonino of Assisi, the greatest master glazier in 14th-century Italy; and Mariotto di Nardo, who furnished the design for the beautiful window of the Church of S. Domenico in Perugia, which was ably executed (1411) by the Dominican friar Bartolommeo di Pietro of the same city. The authorship of the stained-glass windows in the Lower Church of S. Francesco in Assisi is problematical. Among the oldest of these windows are those of the chapels of John the Baptist and St. Peter of Alcantara, which are strongly marked by Byzantine elements and are not devoid of Germanic echoes, particularly in the framing and decorative motifs. Furthermore, the types of mixtilineal compartments that enclose the images in the various windows of the Lower Church are inspired by Germanic schemes which are characteristic of the atelier that executed the windows. But the authors of the designs were certainly Italians with tendencies variously marked by Florence and Siena. It is difficult to discern, as has often been attempted, a firm suggestion of Simone Martini in the stained-glass windows of the Chapel of St. Martin. But it is very probable, as Toesca (*Tr*) proposes, that the design for the windows in the Chapel of St. Louis

(or of St. Stephen) is by the same master who frescoed the pen dentives of the vaulting in the Church of S. Chiara in Assi (R. Longhi has attempted to identify this artist as Buffalmacco The most important windows in the Lower Church are those the Chapel of St. Anthony of Padua, which were masterfull executed by an eminent glazier, probably the same Giovann di Bonino who had worked in Orvieto. These windows mu have been designed by a great artist who has remained anony mous, but the exceptional quality of these windows causes the to stand out among all the panes of the neighboring chapels.

In England the history of 14th-century stained glass can b traced particularly well in the large churches of the north an the Midlands: in York Cathedral, which preserved the mo important and finest 14th-century cycles, with various window (some of which are closely linked with Norman examples) tha are datable to between 1310 and 1340; in Gloucester Cathedr. (ca. 1350); and in Tewkesbury Abbey. Other notable 14th century stained glass is that of Wells Cathedral (Somerset of Merton College at Oxford (ca. 1300–10), and of various rur. parish churches, such as those of Eaton Bishop (Herefordshire Fladbury (Worcestershire), and Deerhurst (Gloucestershire In many ways the stylistic development of English stained glas corresponded to that of France. It was similar in the growin use of architectural elements to enclose the scenes and singl figures and in the extensive use of grisaille. English stained glas of this period naturally reflects elements from contemporar indigenous paintings, including the use of concise, convention forms of expression (e.g., the Virgin in the parish church c Fladbury). Toward the end of the 14th century English staine glass made an intelligent, highly refined contribution of ex ceptional quality to the new International Gothic style, as seer for example, in the windows of the chapel of Winchester Colleg (ca. 1393) and in the tondo showing the angel appearing to th shepherds (PL. 168).

In the 14th century the Low Countries produced interestin examples of painting on glass: the two kneeling donors (ca 1350) in the Musée Royaux d'Art et d'Histoire in Brussels and most particularly, the exceptionally beautiful window of the Cru cifixion (ca. 1387–98) in the Church of St-Eustache at Sicher in Brabant (PL. 171).

At the end of the 14th century the period of the Internationa Gothic style opened in the history of European stained glass All crafts and techniques swiftly embraced the new style. Som extremely interesting and fine works of this stylistic phase ca be found in painting on glass. Two tendencies met and becam interwoven within this style: a naturalistic inclination that assim ilated the new modes of depicting space and certain realisti trends in contemporary sculpture (such as those found in work by the Parler family of Prague), which first became predominan in the Germanic regions (e.g., the stained-glass windows of th choir of Erfurt Cathedral and of the Jakobskirche in Rothenburg) and a more subtle, elegant, cultivated, and gracious tendenc that showed affinities with certain developments in miniatur painting, which finally prevailed. Certain stylistic elements cam to be used in new ways and to far different effect than they ha been originally. Thus, for example, the introduction of archi tectural elements in the composition of scenes, which ha represented a step toward realism in the first half of the 14th century, at this time often served to secure and reinforce effect of unreality — that is, fragile, fantastic structures were provided as settings for attenuated images. These developments are at tested in France by the stained-glass windows of Bourges and Evreux; in Germany, by the cycle in the Besserer Chapel o Ulm Cathedral (PL. 171); in Alsace, by some of the windows i the church of Sélestat (PL. 172); in Belgium, by those of the Basilica of St. Martin in Halle; in England, by windows in the chapel of Winchester College and York Cathedral; and in Italy by Lorenzo Ghiberti's (q.v.) windows for S. Maria del Fiore the Cathedral of Florence.

The significant changes brought about in painting by Italy and Flanders had a deep and widespread influence on stained glass of the 15th century, which includes exceptional works by masters of the highest level. At the same time, however, many characteristics peculiar to the technique of stained glass were disappearing, and the history of stained glass finally came to coincide completely with that of painting in general, though there remained the problem of the relationship between creation and execution that had emerged earlier.

In France the most refined qualities of 15th-century painting, the difficult balance between Italian synthesis of form and Flemish particularization, were reflected in painting on glass. Among the outstanding personalities were the master of the window of Jacques Cœur (PL. 169), who worked in Bourges between 1440 and 1450, and André Robin, who at about the same time worked for King René of Anjou (a rose window in the Cathedral of St-Maurice in Angers). Great painters such as the Master of Moulins and the Master of the Aix Annunciation provided designs for stained glass, but the execution was often somewhat inferior to the original design. Among the most significant works of the century are the rose window of the Ste-Chapelle in Paris and stained-glass windows in the Cathedral of Tours (ca. 1460), the Ste-Chapelle of Riom, the Cathedral of Le Mans, the Cathedral of St-Etienne and the Church of St-Bonnet in Bourges, and the cathedrals of Troyes and Chalon-sur-Saône. Normandy also retains some very rich examples of stained glass from this period (e.g., in the Cathedral of Rouen, the church of Caudebec-en-Caux, the Cathedral of Evreux, and the Church of Notre-Dame in Louviers).

In Germany the outstanding master was the Alsatian Peter Hemmel of Andlau (ca. 1420/25–ca. 1505), who worked in Strasbourg and was chief of an atelier that worked in an area extending from Austria to Lorraine and produced windows for the Besserer Chapel of the Cathedral of Ulm (PL. 171), the Benedictine Abbey church of Walburg (1461), the churches of St-Guillaume and La Madeleine in Strasbourg, the Church of St. Georg in Tübingen, the Church of St. Peter and the church of the Kloster Nonnberg in Salzburg, the Church of St. Lorenz in Nürnberg, and the Frauenkirche in Munich. Reflections of Peter Hemmel's art are also evident in the stained-glass window with St. Catherine in the Church of S. Nazzaro Maggiore in Milan. Of particular interest are the links between Hemmel and contemporary engravers and painters active in the region of the Upper Rhine, among them the Karlsruhe Master, Martin Schongauer (q.v.), and Master E. S. The birth and rapid development of engraving had notable consequences for the history of stained glass. The rapid and widespread diffusion of the new technique rendered possible a familiarity with the compositional ideas and even the style of great artists throughout a vast area, in which geographical distances thus constituted an ever less important limitation. Especially relevant in this respect are the small windows attributed to the Master of the Housebook, an extraordinarily fine painter, draftsman, and engraver, who worked about 1480 in the Middle Rhine (PL. 174; VI, PL. 6).

In Austria the amazing windows produced in Vienna at the end of the 14th century were succeeded by only a few works in stained glass that are worthy of mention — those in the chapel of the Castle of Wiener Neustadt, the pilgrimage church of St. Leonhard in Tamsweg, the Chapel of St. Leonhard in Murau, and the chapter house of Klosterneuburg.

In Switzerland the choir of the Cathedral of Bern contains a 15th-century cycle of first importance, which was begun in 1441 and finished about 20 years later. Among those engaged in this work was the master Hans Acker of Ulm. This cycle is rather heterogeneous and uneven both iconographically and stylistically, owing in part to the multiplicity of commissioners. Swabian artists and others with Alsatian training worked on the choir windows, in which there are reminiscences of the courtly Gothic style as well as Flemish traits and elements of the style of Konrad Witz (q.v.). A phenomenon of great importance, especially in Switzerland, was the success of secular stained glass — windows painted with the arms of a city, a canton, a family (PL. 175), a community, or a corporation, which were made to adorn the windows not of chapels but of municipal chambers.

In Italy stained glass was widely used in the 15th century both in Renaissance structures and in the last great Gothic centers of the north. In Florence the major artists executed designs for stained glass: for the Cathedral, Paolo Uccello (a Nativity, PL. 170; and a Resurrection), Donatello (a Coronation of the

Virgin), Andrea del Castagno (a Deposition); for the Pazzi Chapel, Alesso Baldovinetti; for S. Maria Novella, Domenico Ghirlandajo and Filippino Lippi; and for Sto Spirito, Perugino. Filippo Lippi also designed stained-glass windows for the Cathedral of Prato; some of the window designs of the Cathedral of Lucca have been attributed to Sandro Botticelli; and Baldovinetti designed those of the Cathedral of Pisa. A German master glazier, Fra Jakob Griesinger (Jacopo da Ulm; 1407–93), said by tradition to have accidentally discovered silver stain, worked in Bologna; and in the same city designs for stained glass were provided by Michele di Matteo (window of the fourth chapel on the right aisle of S. Petronio, 1466), Francesco del Cossa (S. Giovanni in Monte), Lorenzo Costa the Elder, and Francesco Francia. The Bolognese workshop of the Cabrini family was also important in the last half of the 15th century. In Umbria the few surviving 15th-century stained-glass windows are the work of Fiorenzo di Lorenzo and Bartolomeo Caporali. The large stained-glass window in the Church of SS. Giovanni e Paolo (or S. Zanipolo) in Venice is attributed to Girolamo Mocetto. The most active region for stained glass was Lombardy. Destruction, alteration, and restoration have unfortunately modified and in large part annihilated the splendid glass created in the 15th century for the Cathedral of Milan, leaving only a few traces of the windows executed in the early part of the century. Nevertheless, the windows attributed to Vincenzo Foppa (PL. 173) and those by Niccolò da Varallo and Cristofor de' Mottis testify to the exceptional quality of 15th-century Lombard stained glass and the extremely close rapport between creators and executors. Consequently these works do not exhibit that gap in quality between design and execution which is characteristic of some Florentine stained glass. There are other notably beautiful stained-glass works in Pavia, particularly in the Certosa, where some of the windows were executed after designs by Il Bergognone (Ambrogio da Fossano). Active in Piedmont were Spanzotti (1455–1526/28), mentioned in a document as a painter of stained glass (e.g., the window from the Sanctuary of Crea Monferrato now in the Museo Civico in Turin), and other noteworthy masters, among them an outstanding anonymous artist who did the windows of Aosta Cathedral and those from the Castle of Issogne (PL. 173). This anonymous master is not identifiable with Spanzotti.

The 15th century in England was marked by very beautiful stained-glass windows, chiefly in the parish churches of small towns rather than in the large cathedrals. Nevertheless the growing use of spatial effects in painting on glass resulted in the gradual elimination of commissions to English painters, who were reluctant and incapable of consistently following this new stylistic development. Commissions were given instead to Flemish workshops, whose hegemony was unchallenged in the 16th century. The most important English master glazier whose works have survived was John Prudde (Pruddle) of Westminster, author of the splendid windows in the Beauchamp Chapel of the Church of St. Mary in Warwick, the most beautiful English stained glass of the century. Another artist known by name was John Glazier, who was responsible for the windows of the antechapel of All Souls College in Oxford. In the east the school of Norwich was active (windows of St. Peter Mancroft in Norwich, churches of East Harling in Norfolk and Long Melford in Suffolk); in the north, the school of York (All Saints on North Street and St. Martin's in York, the priory church at Great Malvern in Worcestershire). Although English cathedrals do not contain many 15th-century windows (among the most beautiful is one in Canterbury Cathedral depicting the wife of Edward IV, Elizabeth Woodville, at prayer), there are strikingly handsome works in stained glass in many minor churches, such as those of Diddington (Huntingdonshire), Ludlow (Shropshire), and Fairford (Gloucestershire).

In Belgium important 15th-century stained-glass windows adorn the Church of St-Gommaire in Lier. In these works is seen the influence of great Flemish paintings — of Rogier van der Weyden and Dirk Bouts (qq.v.). Among the artists who worked on these windows was Rombout II Keldermans of Louvain, brother-in-law of Bouts. Other important windows, showing the definite influence of Hugo van der Goes (q.v.), are conserved in the Church of SS. Pierre-Paul et Guidon in Anderlecht, a suburb of Brussels. Another significant example — though much reworked in the 19th century — is the large cycle in the Cathedral of Tournai by Aert van Ort (Arnould de Nemègue, who later worked in Normandy and then in Antwerp), which is datable to about 1490–1500.

The technique of stained glass enjoyed a great florescence in 15th-century Spain, where notable works had also been produced in earlier centuries for León Cathedral (13th- and 14th-century windows, of which these show close contact with France), for Gerona Cathedral (14th century), and for the church of the Monastery of Pedralbes in Barcelona, where Ferrer Bassa worked (14th-century windows reflecting Italian models). In Spain there is documentation of the activity of many foreign masters in the 15th century (in the first half, in particular), including Nicolás Colin of the diocese of Troyes in Catalonia, Thierry (Tarrinus) des Mes (Metz?) in Saragossa, and Pere Nicol in Tarragona; at the same time stained-glass windows based on designs by Spanish masters (e.g., Luis Borrassá) were being commissioned in Flanders. Among the most beautiful extant windows are those of the Chapel of St. Andrew in the Cathedral of Barcelona (designed by Luis Borrassá); the chapter room of the Monastery of Pedralbes; the apse of the Cathedral of Seo de Urgel; the Basilica of S. María del Mar in Barcelona (1460; by Antonio Llonye, who had previously worked at Avigliana in Piedmont and at Toulouse); the Cathedral of León [window by Juan de Argr (Angers?), ca. 1419–24; windows designed by Nicolás Francés (d. 1468)]; and the Cathedral of Toledo [windows donated by Archbishop Sancho de Rojas (ca. 1415–22); windows of Archbishop Alonso Carrillo (1447–82)]. With the unification of Spain under the Catholic monarchs there began a new period in the history of Spanish stained glass. In the last quarter of the century a Flemish mode spread in Spain just as it did elsewhere. The most significant cycles of this period are those of the Cathedral of Toledo, where there worked a Master Enrique, who was of German origin, and of the Cathedral of Seville.

While stained glass suffered a drastic decline in 16th-century Italy, it continued to thrive in the northern countries — even in Lombardy — in conjunction with late Gothic architecture. In France, Romain Buron (PL. 177), the Le Princes (windows in Rouen, Beauvais, etc.), and Arnaud de Moles (Auch, ca. 1507–13) surpassed the achievements in other fields of contemporary painting. The crisis of the Renaissance, which overturned the great tradition of 15th-century French painting, spared stained glass, probably due in part to its organic and indispensable relationship to late Gothic architecture. The influence of engraving on stained glass became increasingly specific and widespread, and the graphic works of Dürer, Aldegrever, and Lucas van Leyden were the source of numerous stained-glass windows in Europe. In this exceptional flourishing (as Emile Mâle has noted, the 16th century was, together with the 13th century, the richest in the production of stained glass) the specific problems of this technique underwent major changes. The scenes are unified and are no longer contained within the lancets of the windows; elaborate architectural backgrounds frame the scenes and suggest illusionistic spatial openings that modify the Gothic structural elements in order to advance a particular repertory of Renaissance forms, which are bizarrely juxtaposed and interwoven with syntactical uncertainty. In an accounting of the original contributions made by stained glass to the history of artistic forms, 16th-century stained glass, despite its abundance, would not occupy a leading position. Among the noteworthy examples of 16th-century French stained glass mention should be made of the windows of the church of Brou (ca. 1530), which are Flemish in design but French in execution, and those of St-Nizier in Troyes. Equally noteworthy for their stained glass are the Church of St-Acceul in Ecouen; the Church of St-Martin in Montmorency (PL. 174); Notre-Dame-la-Riche in Tours; and Notre-Dame-en-Vaux and the Cathedral in Châlons-sur-Marne, as well as many churches in Paris (St-Merry, St-Gervais, St-Etienne-du-Mont, St-Germain-l'Auxerrois), the Cathedral of Autun, and the Cathedral and Church of St-Bonnet in Bourges.

While stained glass had had a not unimportant role in tl churches of the early Renaissance, the situation changed rapid in the architecture of the High Renaissance; and in manneris baroque, rococo, and neoclassic architecture it had no place all. Profound changes had occurred in the conception of spa and in the reciprocal relationship of architectural element The evocative and varying effects produced by light from colore windows were no longer compatible with the new mode of treatir interior space. Consequently, in Italy stained glass all but di appeared in the course of the 16th century. In the first years the century Guglielmo de Marcillat had worked in Arezz (PL. 179) and in Rome. He was an admirable executor bu not at all exceptional as a creator. Then, aside from the wor that continued in the important late Gothic workshop of tl Cathedral of Milan, the only memorable Italian works are tl grisailles of the Certosa of Galluzzo (or Val d'Ema) and thos of the Biblioteca Laurenziana in Florence (PL. 175), along wit a few other examples in Bologna, Perugia, and Siena (whe Pastorino di Giovan Michele de' Pastorini, a pupil of Marcilla worked in the Cathedral). The great Cathedral workshop Milan continued in operation throughout the 16th centur producing important works that still require study. In the late works northern European elements were increasingly predom nant. For many years the most active artist in the Milan work shop was a German, Konrad Much (Corrado de Mochis) Cologne. His successor, from 1572 to 1599, was a Flemin Valerius van Diependaele (Profundavalle), who descended fro a family of glaziers of Louvain. Among the Italians who pr vided windows for the Cathedral of Milan were Biagio and Gi seppe Arcimboldi, Pellegrino Tibaldi (windows of the SS. Qua tro Coronati, executed in 1568–70 by Konrad Much), and Carl Urbini.

In the art of stained glass the 16th century was marke by the growing domination of masters from the Low Countrie who enjoyed exceptional prestige throughout Europe, and whe by way of their cartoons and because of the executors of thei designs, came close to monopolizing the technique. The painter of the 16th century, like those of the 15th, often furnishe designs for stained-glass windows — from Bernart van Orle (PL. 176) to Hieronymous Bosch (lost designs for the Cathedr of 's Hertogenbosch), to Michiel van Coxie, to Lucas de Heer to Lambert Lombard, to Hendrik and Dirk van Balen. Amon the most famous Flemish executors of stained glass were th already-mentioned Aert van Ort (Arnould de Nimègue), wh worked at Rouen, Tournai, Malines, Hoogstraeten, and Ant werp; Nicolaus (Claes) Rombouts, author of important window in Brussels (SS. Michel and Gudule), Mons (Ste-Waudru Lier (St-Gommaire), and Liège (St-Jacques); Dirk Veller who created cartoons for windows in King's College Chape at Oxford; Dick and Wouter Pietersz. I Crabeth, who did th spectacular windows of the Church of St. John in Gouda (Ne therlands); and Jan II Hack (Haeck), Jacob I Floris de Vriend and Hendrik van der Broek (known in connection with a windov in Perugia as Arrigo Fiammingo). In 16th-century Spain tru dynasties of Flemish masters were active: Alberto and Nicolá de Holanda, father and son who worked in Ávila, Toledo, Burgos Segovia, and Salamanca; and Arnao de Flandes and his sons Ar nao de Vergara and Nicolás de Vergara the Elder (d. 1574) as well as the latter's sons, Nicolás de Vergara the Younger an Juan de Vergara. The Vergara family was responsible for muc of the 16th-century stained glass in the cathedrals of Burgos Toledo, Segovia, Seville, and Granada.

The development of stained glass in Germany was fo the most part arrested by the Reformation, which radicall modified liturgical objects and church furnishings (see REFORMA TION AND COUNTER REFORMATION). In the first decades of th century there were some large workshops that were engaged i stained-glass production, such as those in Cologne, Freiburg and Nürnberg, which executed windows based on designs b the foremost contemporary German masters, including Albrech Dürer (windows of St. Sebald in Nürnberg), Hans Baldung Grien, Hans Burgkmair the Elder (q.v.), Jorg Breu, Barthe Bruyn the Elder, Hans von Kulmbach, and such anonymou Cologne masters as the Master of the St. Bartholomew Altar he Master of the Holy Kinship (Sippenmeister), and the St. Severin Master. Also related to the German ambient is the splendid cycle by the Alsatian Valentin Busch in the choir of Metz Cathedral (1520–40). Subsequently, German stained glass, like Swiss stained glass (PL. 180), turned to the middle-class and secular decoration of heraldic windows.

In the 17th century there remained several active workshops in France — in Paris (windows in St-Merry, St-Médard, St-Eustache, St-Gervais, St-Etienne-du-Mont) and in Rouen Troyes, Bourges, and Toulouse. The most celebrated master glaziers in France were Louis and Nicolas Pinaigrier and, above all, Linard Gontier of Troyes. Likewise active were the Flemish ateliers in Brussels (SS. Michel and Gudule), Louvain, Mons. and Antwerp [Jean de Caumont, Jean Baptist and Pierre van der Veken (Veecken), Abraham van Diepenbeeck, Jan de La Baer (Barre), Theodor van Thulden, Jean de Loose]. In Germany and even more so in Switzerland the tradition of small secular windows continued. In England there are noteworthy 17th-century windows at Oxford by two Flemish masters, Bernard van Linge and his son Abraham. England also conserves 18th-century stained glass of considerable interest. Elsewhere in the 18th century — as was sadly pointed out toward the end of the 18th century in the important treatise by the French author Le Vieil (1774) — the technique was dying out. By his time it had become more similar to painting on porcelain than to traditional painting on glass and was based on the application of vitrified enamels over a clear ground. Among the most important figures, who provided stained glass chiefly for the chapels of the colleges at Oxford, were the brothers Joshua and William Price, as well as the latter's son William the Younger windows for New College, Queen's College, and Christ Church in Oxford, and also for Westminster Abbey and the church of Great Witley); William Peckitt (York Cathedral, New College and Oriel College in Oxford, Trinity College in Cambridge, and at Rothwell in Yorkshire and Audley End in Essex), who also worked for Horace Walpole (1717–97), the father of the Gothic revival; Francis Eginton (1737–1805); James Pearson (d. 1805); and Thomas Jervais (d. 1801), who, after designs by Sir Joshua Reynolds (q.v.), executed a Nativity and a series of Virtues for the chapel of New College at Oxford.

The 19th century witnessed an impressive revival of stained glass throughout Europe, which was nurtured by the doctrines of romanticism (q.v.) and by a renewed interest in medieval art. Many studies concerning the history of stained glass were undertaken, technical experiments were carried out to rediscover the "lost secrets" of coloring glass panes and painting with glazes, and the plain windows of old churches were replaced by painted glass. Great energy was poured into colossal and often catastrophic restoration projects, involving cleaning, releading, and even, unfortunately, the completion and supplementation of the great medieval cycles. The years between 1815 and 1830 were crucial to the history of 19th-century stained glass. In France the Sèvres factory made small windows that were reproductions of old pictures, while G. Bontemps, director of the Choisy-le-Roy factory, rediscovered the forgotten formula for red pot metal. In Italy there were the first attempts of G. B. Bertini (1799–1849), founder of the Milanese Bertini dynasty, which was to have Milan Cathedral as its chief base of operation. In England this was the golden age of the firm of Betton & Evans of Shrewsbury, and in Germany Siegmund Frank (1770–1847), the Nürnberg porcelain painter, was frequently working in stained glass.

The years after 1830 marked the triumph of Sèvres in France. Famous paintings, including Proud'hon's *Assumption*, were copied in glass, while Ingres, Eugène Devéria, and other celebrated painters provided cartoons for the stained-glass windows of the Sèvres church, and Delacroix painted sketches for windows in the Chapelle Royale in Dreux, for which Ingres also furnished window designs. But the idea of mechanically copying paintings in glass and the romantic and "troubadour" taste were challenged by a group of architects and medievalists including Jean Baptiste Antoine Lassus, Eugène Emmanuel Viollet-le-Duc (q.v.), and Adolphe Napoléon Didron. The ideas of the "scientific romanticists" prevailed and soon became official with the

support of Prosper Mérimée, who was then central inspector of the Service des Monuments Historiques. The years between 1840 and 1860, approximately, were marked by extensive restoration projects and flourishing Neo-Gothic construction. Also, the problem of furnishings came to the fore, and Viollet-le-Duc, Lassus, and many others designed gold and silver objects, various ornaments, and, above all, stained glass. *The Annales Archéologiques*, founded in 1844 under the direction of Didron, was the spokesman for the Neo-Gothicists, and the Parisian Church of St-Germain-l'Auxerrois was their "classroom." The 1839 window for this church, planned by the glazier Steinheil with the advice of Lassus and Didron, was the 19th century's first "legendary" window (i.e., inspired by the 13th-century type with scenes from the lives of saints), a type that came to enjoy particular popularity. Meanwhile, the development of stained-glass ateliers in France was extremely rapid: in 1835 there were three, and by 1849 there were about forty-five. Notable master glaziers were Antoine Lusson, who worked in Le Mans on projects of Viollet-le-Duc, Lassus, and others; Henri Gérente, who in 1847 won the competition for the restoration of the stained-glass windows of the Ste-Chapelle; Maréchal de Metz (1801–87), who provided windows for many churches in Paris; and Prosper Lafaye and the above-mentioned Steinheil (PL. 163), who continued to be advised by the group associated with the *Annales Archéologiques*. In these years there appeared studies of stained glass produced by those scholars who were most directly involved in the movement: Viollet-le-Duc wrote the fundamental article, "Vitrail," for his *Dictionnaire raisonné de l'architecture du XIe au XVIe siècle* (Vol. IX, 1868); F. de Lasteyrie published his *Histoire de la peinture sur verre* (1853–56); and monographs appeared on the windows of the cathedrals of Bourges (Cahier and Martin, 1841–44), Tours (Bourassé and Manceau, 1849), Tournai, Chartres (Lassus, Amaury-Duval, 1855), Auch (Caneto, 1857), and Le Mans (Hucher, 1864). These works are the finest results of the romantic-archaeological experiment, which was positive in the field of studies, mediocre in artistic achievement, and completely unsuccessful in the area of restoration. Although these architect-archaeologists hoped to become authentic "maîtres d'œuvre," expert in the most varied techniques, mass production had already eliminated many possibilities of contact and collaboration. In the meantime fine examples of antique painting on glass that had been put aside because of too impetuous and hasty restoration now entered into the private art market, only to be dispersed in museums and collections in Europe and America — though some were installed in churches, particularly in England. Germany, Italy, and England, in spite of an exuberant production, did not experience the committed and rigorous attempt to save antique stained glass that was undertaken in France between 1840 and 1860. A particularly interesting development in England was the collaboration of Edward Burne-Jones and William Morris, which achieved some successful results. But the most remarkable occurrence in the field of stained glass after the "archaeological" movement was the revival of secular stained glass between 1890 and 1900. It was the period of reaction to impressionism, the period of the cloisonnists, or synthetists, of the school of Pont-Aven, and, above all, of the appearance of Art Nouveau (q.v.), which was chiefly concerned with domestic furnishings (see also V, cols. 185–186). In 1895 the merchant Siegfrid Bing exhibited in Paris stained-glass windows executed by Louis Comfort Tiffany (1848–1933) and based on cartoons by Toulouse-Lautrec, Pierre Bonnard, J. Edouard Vuillard (qq.v.), Félix Vallotton, Paul Sérusier, and Ker-Xavier Roussel. Art Nouveau stained glass was fashionable for some years throughout Europe. Later, symbolism prevailed, with Jan Thorn-Prikker (1868–1932) as its most celebrated exponent. In French Switzerland the competition for the windows of Fribourg Cathedral marked a new revival of religious stained glass, a field in which Maurice Denis (1870–1943) was to achieve distinction. Thus stained glass returned, though with different forms and purposes, to the ground of archaeological stained glass — that is, to the decoration of religious buildings.

Contemporary efforts in stained glass differ in nature from those of the 19th century. It is no longer a question of presenting the faithful with intellectual, didactic, and edificatory suggestions, but, rather, a question of exploring the emotional force of light and color, which is, after all, one of the principal problems that recurs throughout the history of stained glass. The search for new techniques, intended as new means of expression and pursued because they can be introduced organically into some aspects of modern life, has fostered a revival in stained glass similar to that in tapestry. In modern architecture the use of certain materials, such as reinforced concrete and steel, has once more made it possible for stained glass to function as a translucent wall, as it does in the Ste-Chapelle and in the Church of St-Urbain in Troyes. The leading French painters — Matisse (PL. 178; Chapel of the Rosary in Vence), Braque, Léger (Church of Sacre Cœur in Audincourt, 1951), Rouault (the church at Assy), Chagall (qq.v.), and Jacques Villon (Metz Cathedral; see DUCHAMP BROTHERS), Marcel Gromaire (b. 1892), Alfred Manessier (b. 1911), and others — have worked in this medium, either providing cartoons or actually painting and assembling windows. In France there are many fine examples of the new stained-glass technique in cathedral chapels and country churches. Contemporary stained glass is deeply engaged in the struggle for the renewal of religious art in a time when the church is neither the only nor the chief source of appeal to man's emotions. Precisely because it is closely linked to technical possibilities and requirements the stained-glass revival remains somewhat irresolute.

BIBLIOG. *a. Early sources*: A. Neri. L'arte vetraria distinta in libri sette, Florence, 1612; Heraclius, De coloribus et artibus romanorum (Quellenschr. f. Kg. u. Kunsttechnik, IV), Vienna, 1873; Theophilus (called also Rugerus), Schedula diversarum artium (Quellenschr. f. Kg. u. Kunsttechnik, VII, Vienna, 1874 (for the chap. on stained glass, see G. Bontemps, trans., Deuxième livre de l'Essai sur divers arts par Théophile, Paris, 1876); Antonio da Pisa, Trattato, see R. Brück, Der Tractat des Meisters Antonio von Pisa über die Glasmalerei, RepfKw, XXV, 1902, pp. 240–69; Anonimo senese, De la pratica di comporre finestre a vetri colorati, ed. A. Lusini, La Diana, V, 1930, pp. 261–90; C. Cennini, Il libro dell'arte, ed. and trans. D. V. Thompson, 2 vols., New Haven, London, 1932–33.

b. History, technique, and restoration: P. Le Vieil, L'art de la peinture sur verre et de la vitrerie, Paris, 1774; A. Brongniart, Mémoire sur la peinture sur verre, Paris, 1829; E. H. Langlois, Essai historique et descriptif sur la peinture sur verre, ancienne et moderne . . . suivi de la biographie des plus célèbres peintres-verriers, Rouen, 1832; M. A. Gessert, Geschichte der Glasmalerei, Stuttgart, Tübingen, 1839; E. Thibaud, Considérations historiques et critiques sur les vitraux anciens et modernes et sur la peinture sur verre, Clermont, Paris, 1842; J. Ballantine, A Treatise on Painted Glass, London, 1845; G. Bontemps, Peinture sur verre au XIXe siècle, Paris, 1845; F. de Lasteyrie, Histoire de la peinture sur verre, 2 vols., Paris, 1853–56; A. Lenoir, Musée des monuments français: Histoire de la peinture sur verre, 7th ed., Paris, 1856; F. de Lasteyrie, La peinture sur verre au dixneuvième siècle, GBA, IX, 1861, pp. 129–42; J. Labarte, Histoire des arts industriels au moyen âge et à l'époque de la renaissance, IV, Paris, 1866; G. Bontemps, Guide du verrier: Traité historique et pratique de la fabrication des verres, cristaux, vitraux, Paris, 1868; E. E. Viollet-le-Duc, Vitrail, in Dictionnaire raisonné de l'architecture française du XIe au XVIe siècle, IX, Paris, 1868 (F. P. Smith trans., Atlanta, 1946); N. H. J. Westlake, A History of Design in Painted Glass, 4 vols., London, 1881–84; E. Garnier, Histoire de la verrerie et de l'émaillerie, Tours, 1886; K. Schaefer, Ornamentale Glasmalereien des Mittelalters und der Renaissance, Berlin, 1888; F. Jaennicke, Handbuch der Glasmalerei, Stuttgart, 1890; K. Elis, Handbuch der Mosaik- und Glasmalerei, Leipzig, 1891; O. Merson, Les vitraux, Paris, 1895; L. A. Ottin, Le vitrail, son histoire, ses manifestations diverses, Paris, 1896 (with bibliog.); L. F. Day, Windows: A Book about Stained and Painted Glass, London, 1897 (3d ed., 1909); Stained Glass Association of America, Stained Glass: A Quarterly Devoted to the Craft of Painted and Stained Glass, 1907ff.; L. A. Ottin, L'art de faire un vitrail, 3d ed., Paris, 1908; N. Heaton, The Foundations of Stained Glass Work, J. of the Royal Soc. of Arts, LVIII, 1910, pp. 454–70; L. Magne, Décor du verre: Gobeleterie, mosaïque, vitrail, Paris, 1913 (2d ed., 1927); A. J. de H. Bushnell, Storied Windows: A Traveller's Introduction to the Study of Old Church Glass, from the Twelfth Century to the Renaissance, Especially in France, Edinburgh, 1914; J. L. Fischer, Handbuch der Glasmalerei, Leipzig, 1914 (with bibliog.); J. A. Knowles, The Technique of Glass Painting in Medieval and Renaissance Times, J. of the Royal Soc. of Arts, LXII, 1914, pp. 568–85; A. H. Schmarsow, Kompositionsgesetze romanischer Glasgemälde in frühgotischen Kirchenfenstern, Leipzig, 1916; A. Werck, Stained Glass: A Handbook on the Art of Stained and Painted Glass, Its Origin and Development from the Time of Charlemagne to Its Decadence (850–1650 A.D.), New York, 1922; E. W. Twining, The Art and Craft of Stained Glass, London, New York, 1928; C. W. Whall, Stained Glass Work: A Text-book for Students and Workers in Glass, London, 1931; A Brief, Annotated Bibliography on Stained Glass, Liturgical Arts, VI, 1937, pp. 84–90; C. J. Connick, Adventures in Light and Color: An Introduction to the Stained Glass Craft, New York, 1937; M. T. Engels, Zur Problematik der mittelalterlichen Glasmalerei, Berlin, 1937; O. Freytag, Hinterglasmalerei, ihre künstlerische Eigenart und Arbeitsweise in Vergangenheit und Gegenwart, Ravensburg, 1937; J. A. F. Divine, Stained Glass Craft, London, 1940; J. Lafond, Pratique de peinture sur verre, Rouen, 1943; L. Grodecki, Le vitrail et l'architecture a XIIe et au XIIIe siècles, GBA, XXXVI, 1949, pp. 5–24; H. Wentzel, Glasmaler und Maler im Mittelalter, ZfKw, III, 1949, pp. 53–62; E. von Witzleben, Gotische Farbfenster, Baden-Baden, 1949; W. J. Drake, A Dictionar of Glasspainters and "Glaysers" of the Tenth to the Eighteenth Centurie New York, 1955; H. G. Franz, Neue Funde zur Geschichte des Glasfensters Forsch. u. Fortschritte, XXIX, 1955, pp. 306–12; E. Frodl-Kraft, Architektur im Abbild ihre Spiegelung in der Glasmalerei, Wien. Jhb. f. Kg XVII, 1955, pp. 7–13; W. E. S. Turner, Our Forefathers in Glass, J. of th Soc. of Glass Tech., XXXIX, 1955, pp. 404–12; J. Verrier, De la conservation et de la mise en valeur des vitraux anciens, Les Mon. Historiques de France, I, 1955, pp. 20–26; H. G. Franz, Les fenêtres circulaires de la cathédrale de Cefalú et le problème de l'origine de la "rose" du Moyen Âge CahA, IX, 1957, pp. 253–70; H. Wentzel, Arbeitstagung zum "Corpu Vitrearum Medii Aevi," Kunstchronik, X, 1957, pp. 217–19; E. L. Armitage Stained Glass: History, Technology and Practice, London, 1959; A. van de Boom, De Kunst der glazeniers in Europa, 1100–1600, Amsterdam, 196 G. Frenzel, Schwarzloterhaltung und Schwarzlotrestaurierung bei mittelalterlichen Glasgemälden, ZfKg, XXIII, 1960, pp. 1–18; E. Frodl-Kraf Beobachtungen zur Technik und Konservierung mittelalterlicher Glasmalereien, Ö. Z. f. K. u. Denkmalpflege, XIV, 1960, pp. 79–86; W. Lowe, Th Conservation of Stained Glass, S. in Conservation, V, 1960, pp. 139–4 J. Lafond, La technique du vitrail: Aperçus nouveaux, Art de France, I 1962, pp. 246–48; J. Taralon, Le colloque international d'Erfurt et la sauvegarde des vitraux anciens, Les Mon. Historiques de la France, VIII, 1962 pp. 231–46; H. Wentzel, Vierte Arbeitstagung zum "Corpus Vitrearu Medii Aevi" in Erfurt, Kunstchronik, XV, 1962, pp. 311–15; L. Grodecki La quatrième réunion internationale du Corpus Vitrearum Medii Aevi ses enseignements, B. Monumental, CXXI, 1963, pp. 73–82.

c. Corpus Vitrearum Medi Aevi: A series devoted to the publicatio of stained glass throughout the world. The following volumes have s far been published: E. J. Beer, Die Glasmalereien der Schweiz vom 12. bi zum Beginn des 14. Jahrhunderts, Basel, 1956; H. Wentzel, Die Glasmalereien in Schwaben von 1200–1350, Berlin, 1958; M. Aubert, L. Grodecki J. Lafond, and J. Verrier, Les vitraux de Notre-Dame et de la Sainte-Chapell de Paris, Paris, 1959; J. Helbig, Les vitraux médiévaux conservés en Belgique 1200–1500, Brussels, 1961; E. Frodl-Kraft, Die mittelalterlichen Glasgemälde in Wien, Graz, 1962; A. Anderson, S. Christré, C. A. Nordman and A. Roussell, Die Glasmalereien des Mittelalters in Skandinavien, Stockholm, 1964; E. J. Beer, Die Glasmalereien der Schweiz aus dem 14. and 15 Jahrhundert, Basel, 1965.

d. Catalogues of important collections: J. Schinnerer, Katalog der Glasgemälde des Bayerischen National Museums, Munich, 1908; H. Schmitz Die Glasgemälde des Königlichen Kunstgewerbemuseums in Berlin, Berlin 1913; A Guide to the Collections of Stained Glass, Victoria and Alber Museum, London, 1936; A. von Schneider, Die Glasgemälde des Badische Landesmuseums Karlsruhe, Freiburg im Breisgau, 1950.

e. Exhibition catalogues: Stained Glass of France, 13th–16th Centuries Springfield, Mass., Museum of Fine Arts, Springfield, 1939; Alte Glasmalerei der Schweiz, Zurich, 1945; Meisterwerke alter deutscher Glasmalerei Munich, Bayerisches Landesmuseum, Munich, 1947; Vitraux de Franc du XIe au XVIe siècle, Paris, Musée des Arts Décoratifs, 2d ed., Paris, 1953 Cathédrales: Sculptures, vitraux, objets d'art, manuscrits des XIIe et XIII siècles, Louvre, Paris, 1962.

f. Individual countries: *France*: For the bibliog. up to 1934, see J. Verrier Vitraux, in Les études sur les arts appliqués à l'industrie du Ve au XVIII siècle en France de 1834 à 1934, CAF, 1934, pp. 292–97; for more recent bibliog., see M. Aubert, Le vitrail en France, Paris, 1946 (2d ed., 1953); L vitrail français, Paris, 1958 (the fundamental work, with texts by M. Aubert A. Chastel, L. Grodecki, J. J. Gruber, J. Lafond, F. Mathey, J. Taralon J. Verrier). The following are the most important subsequent studies A. Chichereau, Saint-Etienne de Bourges: Architecture et vitraux, Paris 1958; L. Grodecki, Une scène de la vie de Saint Benoît provenant de Saint Denis au Musée de Cluny, RArts, VIII, 1958, pp. 161–71; P. Ahnne and V Beyer, Les vitraux de la Cathédrale de Strasbourg, Strasbourg, 1959; E Castelnuovo, Vetrate francesi, Paragone, X, 113, 1959, pp. 44–66; L. Grodecki, Vitrail, B. Monumental, CXVII, 1959, pp. 76–82; L. Grodecki, Le vitraux de Châlons-sur-Marne et l'art mosan, Acts of the 19th Int. Cong on the H. of Art, Paris, 1959, pp. 183–90; J. Lafond, Vitraux français en Angleterre: Wilton (XIIe et XIIIe siècles), BAFr, 1959, pp. 241–43; J. Simon Les vitraux de Saint-Remi à Reims, Les Mon. Historiques de la France, V 1959, pp. 1–25; G. Wildenstein, Jacques Pinaigrier, son inventaire, GBA LIII, 1959, pp. 283–94; P. Frankl, Die Glasmalereien der Wilhelmerkirch in Strassburg, Baden-Baden, 1960; L. Grodecki, Vitrail, B. Monumental CXVIII, 1960, pp. 222–26; L. Grodecki, Les vitraux soissonnais du Louvre du Musée Marmottan et des collections américaines, RArts, X, 1960, pp. 163–78; J. R. Johnson, Studies in the Early Stained Glass of Chartres Cathedral New York, 1960 (thesis, Columbia Univ.); L. Grodecki, Un group de vitraux français du XIIe siecle, in Festschrift Hans R. Hahnloser, zum 60. Geburtstag 1959, ed. E. J. Beer, Basel, Stuttgart, 1961, pp. 289–98; L. Grodecki Les vitraux de Saint-Denis: L'enfance du Christ, in De Artibus Opuscul XL, Essays in Honor of Erwin Panofsky, I, New York, 1961, pp. 170–86 J. R. Johnson, The Tree of Jesse Window of Chartres: Laudes Regiae Speculum, XXXVI, 1, 1961; L. Grodecki, Vitrail, B. Monumental, CXX 1962, pp. 92–103; Y. Delaporte, L'art du vitrail aux XIIe et XIIIe siècles Chartres, 1963; P. Frankl, The Chronology of the Stained Glass in Chartre Cathedral, AB, XLV, 1963, pp. 301–22. *Germany*: H. Wentzel, Meisterwerke der Glasmalerei, Berlin, 1951 (2d ed., 1954; with essential bibliog to date); D. Rentsch, Glasmalerei des frühen vierzehnten Jahrhunderts i Ost-Mitteldeutschland, Cologne, 1958; D. Rentsch, Zur Rekonstruktion de

Jungfrauenfensters" im Ostchor des Naumburgers Doms, Kunstchronik, XII, 1959, pp. 130–31; H. Wentzel, Zur Diskussion um die Farbverglasung es Domes zu Speyer, Kunstchronik, XII, 1959, pp. 331–35; G. Frenzel, 'eit Hirschvogel: Eine Nürnberger Glasmalerwerkstatt der Dürerzeit, .fKg, XXIII, 1960, pp. 193–210; G. Frenzel, Entwurf und Ausführung in er Nürnberger Glasmalerei der Dürerzeit, ZfKw, XV, 1961, pp. 31–59; ;. Frenzel, Zur Diskussion um die Farbverglasung des Domes zu Speyer, Kunstchronik, XIV, 1961, pp. 8–10; K. A. Knappe, Albrecht Dürer und das 3amberger Fenster in St. Sebald in Nürnberg, Nürnberg, 1961; K. A. Knappe, Baldung als Entwerfer der Glasgemälde in Grossgründlach, ZfKw, XV, 1961, pp. 60–80; E. Schürer von Witzleben, Die Regensburger Domenster, Kunstchronik, XV, 1961, pp. 293–94; H. Seifert, Alte und neue 'enster im Ulmer Münster, Königstein im Taunus, 1962. Switzerland: H. Oidtmann, Geschichte der Schweizerischen Glasmalerei, Leipzig, 1905 with bibliog.); H. Lehmann, Zur Geschichte der Glasmalerei in der Schweiz Mit. der antiquarischen Gesellschaft in Zürich, XXVI, 4), Zurich, 1906–2; A. Glaser, Die Basler Glasmalerei im 16. Jahrhundert seit Hans Holbein . j., Winterthur, 1937; H. Lehmann, Geschichte der Luzerner Glasmalerei on den Anfängen bis zu Beginn des 18. Jahrhunderts, Lucerne, 1941; '. Hofer, Die Glasmalereien des Berner Münsterchors, Das Werk, XXXIII, 946, pp. 21–28; A. Scheidegger, Die Berner Glasmalerei von 1540 bis 580 (Berner Schr. zur K., IV), Bern, 1947; F. Zschokke, Mediaeval Stained Glass of Switzerland, trans. D. Cooper, London, 1947; M. Stettler, Stained Glass of the Early Fourteenth Century from the Church of Koenigsfelden, New York, 1949; H. R. Hahnloser, Chorfenster und Altäre des Berner Münsers, Bern, 1950; E. J. Beer, Die Rose der Kathedrale von Lausanne und der osmologische Bilderkreis des Mittelalters, Bern, 1952; P. Boesch, Zur Geschichte der Freiburger Glasmalerei, ZSAKg, XIII, 1952, pp. 65–82; '. Boesch, Notizen zu den Glasgemälden in Wettingen, ZSAKg, XIII, 953, pp. 248–54; J. Schneider, Die Standesscheiben von Lukas Zeiner im 'agsatzungssaal zu Baden, Basel, 1954; M. Stettler, Alte Glasmalerei im ochweiz, Zurich, 1953; P. Boesch, Schiessen auf den toten Vater: Ein beiebtes Motiv der Schweizerischen Glasmaler, ZSAKg, XV, 1954, pp. 87–2; P. Boesch, Die Schweizerische Glasmalerei, Basel, 1955 (with bibliog.); L. Fischel, Die Berner Chorfenster: Ihre künstlerische Herkunft, ZfKw, XV, 1961, pp. 1–30; B. Anderes, Die spätgotische Glasmalerei in Freiburg i. Ü.: Ein Beitrag zur Geschichte der schweizerischen Glasmalerei, Freiburg, 963. Italy: G. Marchini, Vetrate italiane, Milan, 1955 (with bibliog. to late; Eng. trans., Italian Stained Glass Windows, New York, 1957); F. 3ologna, Vetrate del Maestro di Figline, BArte, XLI, 1956, pp. 193–99; M. Salmi, Lorenzo Ghiberti e la pittura, in Scritti di storia dell'arte in onore i Lionello Venturi, I, Rome, 1956, pp. 223–37; C. Verga, Una finestra del Duomo di Crema, Arte Lombarda, II, 1956, pp. 156–65; E. Castelnuovo, Vetrate italiane, Paragone, IX, 103, 1958, pp. 3–24; C. Volpe, Tre vetrate erraresi e il Rinascimento a Bologna, Arte antica e moderna, I, 1958, pp. 23–7; W. Cohn, Zur Ikonographie der Glasfenster von Orsanmichele, Mit. es Kunsthist. Inst. in Florenz, IX, 1959, pp. 1–12; C. L. Ragghianti, 'ilippino Lippi a Lucca: L'Altare Magrini, nuovi problemi e nuove soluzioni, CrArte, VII, 1960, pp. 47–53; M. Salmi, Tre vetrate fiorentine del primo Cinascimento, in Festscrift Hans R. Hahnloser, zum 60. Geburstag 1959, d. E. J. Beer, Basel, Stuttgart, 1961, pp. 317–22. Spain: J. Ainaud de Laarte, Vidrieras, Ars Hispaniae, X, Madrid, 1952, pp. 374–97 (with bibliog., 2. 408). England: J. Carter, Specimens of the Ancient Sculpture and Painting Now Remaining in England, from the Earliest Period to the Reign of Henry VIII, London, 1838 (new ed., 1887); O. B. Carter, A Series of the Ancient Painted Glass of Winchester Cathedral, London, 1845; C. Winston, An Inquiry into the Difference of Style Observable in Ancient Glass Paintings, Especially in England: With Hints on Glass Painting, Oxford, 1847 (new ed., 2 vols., 1867); M. Drake, A History of English Glass Painting, London, 1912 New York, 1913); H. Arnold, Stained Glass of the Middle Ages in England nd France, London, 1913 (2d ed., 1955); P. Nelson, Ancient Painted Glass n England 1170–1500, London, 1913; W. P. Littlechild, A Short Account f King's College Chapel, 2d ed., Cambridge, Eng., 1921; F. S. Eden, Anient Stained and Painted Glass, Cambridge, Eng., 1933; F. Harrison, Stained Glass of York Minster, London, New York, 1937; C. Woodforde, English Stained Glass and Glass Painters in the Fourteenth Century, Proc. of the 3r. Acad., XXV, 1940, pp. 29–49; C. Woodforde, English Stained and Paintd Glass, Oxford, 1954 (with bibliog.); J. Baker, English Stained Glass, London, 1960 (with bibliog.). Austria: F. Kieslinger, Gotische Glasmalerei n Österreich bis 1450, Vienna, 1928; O. Pächt, Zur jüngsten Literatur über lie gotische Tafel und Glasmalerei Österreichs, Kritische Berichte zur Kg., II, 1928–29, pp. 161–75; F. Kieslinger, Die Glasmalerei in Österreich, in Abriss ihrer Geschichte, Vienna, 1947. Holland and Belgium: A. van ler Boom, Monumentale glasschilderkunst in Nederland, The Hague, 1940 I.; J. Helbig, De glasschilderkunst in Belgie: Repertorium en documenten, 2 vols., Antwerp, 1943–51 (with extensive bibliog.); J. Helbig, L'évolution lu décor architectural dans le vitrail belge pendant le premier quart du XVIe iècle, P. van der Koninklijke Commissie voor Monumenten en Landschapen, III, 1951–52, pp. 9–20; L. Devliegher, Enkele Brugse glasramen uit iet einde der XVe eeuw, Rev. belge, XXIII, 1954, pp. 197–202; B. Bijtelaar, De geschilderde glazen van de Oude Kerk te Amsterdam, Oud Holland, LXXI, 1956, pp. 204–11; F. Winkler, Eine flämische Folge von Rundscheien der Sakramente, Pantheon, XIX, 1961, pp. 284–88. Other countries: W. Bramzelius, Die hinduistische Pantheon Glasmalerei: Eine ethnograohische, religions- und kunstgeschichtliche Studie über die hinduistische Glasgemälde im Staatlichen Ethnographischen Museum zu Stockholm (Int. Archiv f. Ethn., XXXIV, Sup.), Leiden, 1937; C. Brailoiu, Les icones payannes roumaines peintes sous verre, Formes et couleurs, VII, 1, 1945; J. Roosval, Gotländsk vitriarius, Stockholm, 1950; E. Lambert, Vitraux de couleur dans l'art musulman du Moyen-âge, in Hommage à Georges Marçais, II, Paris, 1957, pp. 107–09; J. G. Lloyd, Stained Glass in America, Jenkintown, Pa., 1963.

g. 20th century: G. Janneau, Modern Glass, London, New York, 1931; J. Jajczay, Die ungarische Kirchenkunst der Gegenwart, Budapest, 1938;

The British Society of Master Glass Painters, A Directory of Stained Glass Windows Executed within the Past Twenty Years, London, 1939; R. Hess, Neue Glasmalerei in der Schweiz: Eine Wegleitung zu den Standorten und ein Verzeichnis der Künstler, Basel, 1939; E. Frei, The Future of Stained Glass, Arch. Record, CIII, 1948, pp. 120–27; H. Junecke, Mosaiken und Glasmalereien der Gegenwart, Z. f. K., IV, 1950, pp. 251–83; J. Baker, Stained Glass Today, Arch. Yb., VI, 1955, pp. 157–64; Farbige Steine und leuchtendes Glas im Bau, Baumeister, LII, 1955, pp. 294–308; B. Spence, The Coventry Windows, Arch. and Building News, CCX, 1956, pp. 190–95; M. Duchamp, From the Green Box, trans. G. H. Hamilton, New Haven, 1957; J. Schreiter, Die Glasmalerei unseres Jahrhunderts, Das Werk, XII, 5–6, 1958, pp. 3–13; R. Sowers, Reflections on Some New Stained Glass in Europe, Craft Horizons, XVIII, 1958, pp. 32–37; Glasmalerei und Mosaik in Deutschland 1957–62, Das Münster, XV, 1962, pp. 409–69, XVI, 1963, pp. 1–48; O. Knapp, Architektur- und Bauglas in Vergangenheit und Gegenwart, 2d ed., Halle, 1962; J. Leymarie, ed., Chagall's Jerusalem Windows, New York, 1962.

Enrico CASTELNUOVO

Illustrations: PLS. 157–180.

STEEN, JAN. Dutch painter (b. Leiden, ca. 1626; d. Leiden, 1679). Steen was the son of a Leiden brewer. His teachers are not known, though Adriaen van Ostade, Jan van Goyen (qq.v.), and Nicolaus Knüpfer have been mentioned. Records indicate that in 1646 he was a student at the local university and that two years later he was one of the founding members of the painters' guild. He married a daughter of Jan van Goyen in 1649, and she bore him four children, two of whom became artists. Steen probably was a Catholic; his children were baptized in Catholic churches. His wife died in 1669 and four years later he remarried. One son was born from his second marriage.

Steen is known to have lived at The Hague (1649–54), Delft (1654–56), Warmond (1656–60), Haarlem (1661–70), and Leiden (1670–79). His father leased a brewery for him in Delft, and he managed that enterprise between 1654 and 1657. In 1672 he obtained permission to keep an inn at Leiden. In 1672–73 he was an officer of the painters' guild at Leiden, and in 1674 he served as its dean. The various self-portraits of the artist (Amsterdam, Rijksmus.; Lugano, Thyssen-Bornemisza Coll.) seem to bear out the notion, derived from this framework of facts, that Steen was an enterprising, possibly restless man, endowed with considerable mental and physical vitality.

Steen occupies a unique place in Dutch art. He is the only Dutch painter of rank who can be called a true humorist. Like Molière, to whom he has been compared and whose life span paralleled his almost exactly, Steen treated the contemporary scene as one vast comedy of manners — often including himself among the chief actors. It is likely that some of Steen's Biblical and classical themes (The Wrath of Ahasuerus, Birmingham, England, Barber Inst. of Fine Arts; Antony and Cleopatra, Göttingen, Universitätsgal.) were inspired by the contemporaneous stage. Steen also painted groups of amateur actors (The Rhetoricians, Brussels, Mus. Royaux B.A.; Worcester, Mass., Art Mus.), in their noisy gatherings.

The majority of Steen's pictures are genre scenes. Like Jordaens, whose influence on the artist is obvious, Steen moralizes with a twinkle in his eye. He was inexhaustible in depicting characteristic situations in Dutch life, whether it was a young woman putting on her stockings (1663; London, Buckingham Palace, Royal Colls.) or groups of frolickers (V, PLS. 314, 317; X, PL. 508). Skillful in his renderings of still life, animals, costumes, and motion, he was unequaled as a student of human character. In the mobile faces of his actors one finds expressions of sly cunning, gross sensuousness, drunken stupor, and raging fury, but there are few pictures in which he did not include a smiling face, and he is especially engaging in his observation of the behavior of children. If Steen's emphasis on anecdote and his indefatigable desire to entertain occasionally fail to move the modern viewer, his technical mastery is beyond reproach. One of the subtlest and most accomplished colorists of his age, Steen ranks in his best works with such masters as Terborch, Metsu, and De Hooch (qq.v.) and can even be compared with Vermeer (q.v.). Unfortunately his large output includes works that were done hastily, and it is further clouded by the many copies of inferior quality made by his imitators.

MAJOR WORKS. *The Feast of St. Nicholas* (Amsterdam, Rijksmus.). – *The Wedding Contract* (Brunswick, Germany, Herzog-Anton-Ulrich Mus.). – *Twelfth Night* (1668; Kassel, Staat. Gemäldegal.). – *The Poultry Yard* (1660), *The Quack Doctor*, and *The Doctor's Visit* (all, The Hague, Mauritshuis). – *The World Upside Down* (III, PL. 424). – *The Twelfth-night Feast* (Boston, Mus. of Fine Arts).

BIBLIOG. A. Bredius, Jan Steen, Amsterdam, 1927; F. Schmidt Degener, Jan Steen, London, 1927; C. H. de Jonge, Jan Steen, Amsterdam, 1939; W. Martin, Jan Steen, Amsterdam, 1954; Jan Steen, The Hague, 1958 (cat.).

Julius S. HELD

STEPPE CULTURES. The art of the steppe, also termed the "animal style" and formerly known by the vague appelation "migration art," is one of the most interesting and important phenomena in art history because of its duration and geographic spread and because of the numerous historical and stylistic problems that it poses. The chief subject of steppe art was the animal figure, and its treatment was essentially naturalistic. Chronologically steppe art took root in the first half of the 2d millennium B.C. and continued through the end of the 1st millennium of our era. Geographically it stretched from the plain of the Hwang-ho River (Yellow River) in China to the Hungarian steppe (FIG. 375). In its formation were combined the most disparate elements derived from the ancient Near East, China, pre-Islamic Iran, and even the Hellenistic world. Although these elements were always reworked on the basis of local experience and taste, which varied according to area and period, they were linked to almost homogeneous social and technical conditions and to a style that passed from realism (perhaps of eastern Siberian origin) to conventionalized expression that probably originated in ancient Iran and Asia Minor.

Steppe art flourished with the spread of metalworking, without, however, excluding other media, especially wood. Its enormous vitality, based on vigor of stylization and expressive power, can be judged by its protracted survivals and artistic repercussions in Europe and Asia. In Europe, through the contacts of the Huns with the Germanic populations, the most characteristic motifs spread northward and exerted a profound influence on the art of the vikings and the early Christian art of northern Europe (see EUROPE, BARBARIAN). The last Asiatic survival appears in the bronze objects that the Tibetans call

ton-t'i, or *gnam-lcags*, which were introduced by the Karlu Turks (the Gar-log of Tibetan tradition) and used as amulets Throughout the Scandinavian peninsula, from Finland t Lapland and elsewhere, animal motifs deriving from the steppe repertory recur in popular art (textiles and embroidery), thoug they lost their original stylistic vigor with the passage of time an the adoption of new techniques. This survival confirms the vitality of an impressive artistic phenomenon that was felt ove a vast area (see also ASIA, CENTRAL; ASIATIC PROTOHISTORY CHINESE ART; GOLD- AND SILVERWORK; GRECO-BOSPORAN AN SCYTHIAN ART; HUNGARY; IRANIAN PRE-SASSANIAN ART CULTURES KUSHAN ART; METALWORK; MONGOLIAN ART; ORDOS; PARTHIA ART; SIBERIAN CULTURES).

SUMMARY. General considerations (col. 376). The stylistic for mation (col. 379): *The Andronovo and Karasuk cultures; Caucasia The Pontic migration; The Scythian influence; The Tagar period The Hunno-Sarmatian period.* Conclusion (col. 404).

GENERAL CONSIDERATIONS. Steppe art, despite its over-al consistency, can be divided into three main stylistic trend that correspond to the three distinct historical and geographi areas of Scythia (the southern zone of European Russia), Alta (southwest Asiatic Russia), and Ordos (central Inner Mongolia) There are, in addition, various stylistic phases that are distinc in time and indicate a considerable chronological evolution Other minor trends limited to specific geographic areas ar not always precisely definable because of exchanges and contact maintained with neighboring movements and with the whol of the vast territory where nomad influence prevailed.

For social, religious, and economic reasons steppe art wa always bound to the animal motif. Undoubtedly some stylistic and iconographic elements were of exceptional duration or re mained practically constant throughout the development o the art. This relative homogeneity, which gradually increased is the fundamental problem raised by steppe art and is connected in turn, with the problem of origins. The many theories formu lated on these points can be divided into two main groups (1) theories citing the uniform social and economic condition of the steppe as determinants of the similarities and continuitie in style and iconography; and (2) theories explaining the same phenomena as the natural outcome of a single, specific cente or area of origin.

Concerning the first group of theories, the steppe worl

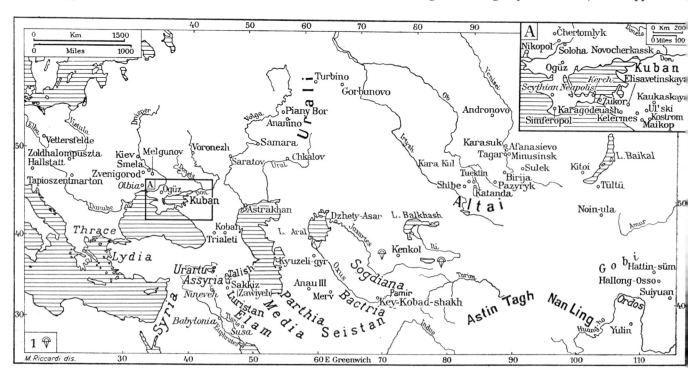

Principal centers of the diffusion area of steppe art. Key: (1) Necropolis of the Wu-sun people.

as based on a specialized, generally nomadic economy that
not only molded the social structure but also affected every
facet of life. Certainly a relative homogeneity and slowness
in social evolution favored the formation of a fairly uniform
style. And undoubtedly these factors affected the choice of
subject matter, giving rise to the predominance of the animal
style in steppe art. However, survivals and irradiations of steppe
art occurred in extremely different geographic zones and among
extremely dissimilar cultures (e.g., the Parthians, the Germanic
peoples, the Scandinavian navigators, the Christian communities
of Ireland and Italy) and cannot be explained strictly in terms
of similar socioeconomic structure. Therefore, steppe art must
also be viewed as the expression of a collective and autonomous
sensibility capable of vigorously assimilating and reworking
various components acquired through contact. The characteristics of the steppe peoples were undoubtedly suited to the
formation of an autonomous stylistic tendency, even though the
population belonged to different ethnic stocks variously affected
by the sedentary civilizations surrounding them.

For exactly these reasons it is possible to set aside Chlenova's (1962) several reservations to theories falling within the
first category that have been formulated by Soviet scholars.
It is true that animal figures occur frequently in the art of the
ancient Near East and that they were, in fact, of primary importance in the art of ancient Iran. In rebuttal it can be argued
that the cultural and social environment of the civilizations of
Mesopotamia, Syria, and Asia Minor was so far removed from
that of the nomad world that, diffusions and exchanges aside,
it would be impossible to look to the Near East for the principal origin of such a profoundly different stylistic evolution,
which was endowed, moreover, with a vigor unknown to the
sedentary civilizations. A second reservation to theories within
the first category points out the nonexistence of an animal style
among peoples that can be considered in many ways analogous
in development and cultural level to the Eurasian nomads. The
analogies in question are extremely vague, however, and a true
environmental and social similarity to the steppe cannot be found
outside that area, even among those other nomadic populations
who replaced the horse with the dromedary. Theories falling
within the first group are therefore acceptable within the limits
indicated above, even though they do not deal directly with
the stylistic problem or that of subsequent evolution.

The theories of the second group can be subdivided according
to the general area and the specific center to which the genesis
of steppe art is being attributed. Excluding the unacceptable
hypothesis of its derivation from Ionian art, first suggested by
Furtwängler (1883) and later taken up again by Farmakovsky
1914) and by S. Prusevskaya, the theory of an irradiation from
Pontus, in Asia Minor, toward Siberia, which still has some supporters, is perfectly well-grounded if it is regarded as the
simple record of a current of influences moving eastward from
the Scythian area, carrying Greek elements along with it and
influencing Altaic art. The validity of the inverse hypothesis
of a westerly movement, formulated by Minns (1913), is equally
evident but has similar limitations, serving only to identify
a stream of influences that reached the Scythian world from the
Altai region and, more generally, from western Siberia. It is
instead much more difficult to establish a precise genetic relation
between Scythian art and that of Karasuk (the first Altaic period
of steppe art) because of stylistic factors and of the fluctuations
in the chronologies suggested for the latter art. But there is no
doubt about the existence of a bilateral exchange, which is made
more complex by the ties connecting Karasuk art with Chinese
cultures. The possibility that Scythian art and that of the first
Altaic period may share a common origin, to be sought outside
their respective areas of expansion, appears rather unlikely if
an attempt is made to find the original center in the region north
of the taiga (Borovka, 1928; Strzygowsky, 1930; Minns, 1942),
also because the Scythian animal style cannot be dissociated from
the weapons and harness through which it is expressed (Chlenova, 1962). If, instead, such a zone of origin is sought in the
mountains surrounding the northern part of the Mesopotamian
area, there is at least the certainty of identifying a current of
influences that had wide repercussions in the steppe area;

and, while these influences may not have been the determining
factor in the Scythian and Altaic stylistic development, they are
undoubtedly of far from negligible significance.

In the light of present knowledge, it may be concluded
that the art of the steppe displays all the features of an autonomous stylistic phenomenon favored and partly determined
by socioeconomic conditions. Steppe art evolved slowly owing
to the restraints inherent in specialization and in the natural
environment, but on this account it was no less vital nor was it
perfectly uniform. The various elements that impinged on it
were assimilated and transformed by a brilliant and highly
developed taste, so that the very intensity of foreign influences
gave rise to alterations and variations in the fundamental unity
of this art. The essentially naturalistic character of steppe art
does not preclude numerous instances of stylization that reflected the particular taste of the artist and his public. The transformation of the image in ornamental terms, which hardly
ever implied the loss of representational clarity, was in fact
a common feature of the entire production of the steppe; yet,
viewing steppe art as a whole, it is possible to perceive a succession of transformations and phases in which the efforts to create
volume were reduced in favor of a flat, linear stylization, as
well as a later tendency toward heaviness of forms, together with
a predominance of polychromy that was achieved by means of
openwork and incrustations with precious and semiprecious
stones. Another typical characteristic of steppe art in its late
phase was the presence of the human figure in scenes of various
meaning and the use of compositions that were no longer symbolic but fully descriptive.

The origin and especially the evolution of steppe art were
undoubtedly linked to exchanges and reciprocal influences
among the various groups and clans that arose from, or were
at least encouraged by, trade movements, which were certainly
more intense than previously suspected; because of its geographic expanse and its comparatively high population density,
the internal trade movements of the steppe made it one of the
major market areas of ancient times. It is, moreover, possible
to identify the presence of circumstances linked with the balance
of power established at various times by the peoples of the steppe
with the sedentary civilizations. Yet another underlying factor
was that tendency toward specialization in the field of metalworking resulting from a highly particularized outlook and from
religious factors associated with shamanism (q.v.). Migration,
in some instances of considerable historical significance, now
appears to have been a less important determinant of internal
cultural evolution than was formerly thought. Instead, the
regions where nomads and sedentaries intermingled have acquired major importance. Such regions were almost always
quite vast and characterized by an unmistakable cultural physiognomy owing to the fact that the boundaries separating the
nomad and sedentary worlds — opposed and yet complementary
— were neither fixed nor clearly marked but consisted, rather,
of strips of land that were in some cases hundreds of miles
wide. In certain respects the entire Ordos area — though it
experienced internal historical and evolutionary forces — can
be considered a true zone of interpenetration between China and
the steppe, even though it was subject to various vicissitudes
that increased or reduced the actual geographic extent of the
regions dominated by the nomad and sedentary worlds and its
culture was, in any case, exposed to the varying intensity of
expansive forces from either side. Another buffer area, at the
borders of the Iranian world, was ancient Khwarizm (q.v.),
where the villages with wall dwellings (6th–4th cent. B.C.;
see below) seem to indicate a high degree of interpenetration,
since they were occupied by a stock-raising people on the way
to becoming sedentary and therefore represent an intermediate
stage of social organization between that of the breeder-shepherds
and that of the sedentary farmers.

Evidence of the importance of the boundary areas does not
alter the fact that some migrations did play a truly remarkable
role in the evolution of the art of the steppe as determining factors in the diffusion of particular tendencies or stylistic traits.
Relevant cases are the so-called "Pontic migration" (Heine-
Geldern, 1951); the displacements of the Sarmatian groups,

undoubtedly connected with the movements of the Parthians (see VIII, cols. 279–284; PARTHIAN ART) and of the Yüeh-chih (see GANDHARA; KUSHAN ART); and the movements of the Huns (which as a historical event now appears to have been far from unitary because of the recurrent use of the term "Hun" for different populations).

It should be noted that with the advance of studies in this field the problem of origins and derivation has been related to that of contacts and connections between different cultures and tendencies within and outside the nomad world; thus, among other considerations, the general character of steppe art appears to be the possible result of exchanges and contacts between the nomad world of Central Asia (see ASIA, CENTRAL) and a series of internal and, above all, external cultures. It must not be forgotten that the main subject of steppe art, the animal figure, is typical of the protohistoric art of Mesopotamia, and particularly of Iran, where there have been found simplified images that anticipate very vigorous stylizations without totally excluding highly effective realistic representations. The tendency toward stylization that was typical of the more ancient phases of Iranian vase painting may well constitute an antecedent of considerable importance in the evolution of nomad art through a slow penetration from south to north. However, even in the neolithic phase, the protohistoric cultures of Lake Baikal also produced, albeit sporadically, animal figures carved out of bone or incised on stone, varying from a naturalistic realism of considerable effectiveness to the figural conventions of the metal age. The Kitoi period (2500–1800 B.C.; see II, cols. 12–13), which is perhaps chronologically related to the Afanasievo culture (2500–1500 B.C.) and marks the peak of the Lake Baikal fishing cultures, saw the use of ocher in tombs, a result of ritual aspersions of the corpse; an attempt can therefore be made to connect the Kitoi period with a series of roughly contemporaneous cultures extending from Europe to China, touching Iran (q.v.) in the cultures of Tepe Sialk and related centers. Incontrovertible proof of commercial relations between Kitoi and China is documented by the graphite particles contained in the earliest Chinese jades, which can for this very reason be identified as coming from the north. Furthermore, the Kitoi jade production displays forms unknown to China, as well as others that the Chinese imitated, only occasionally retaining their original symbolic meaning. Thus it is clear that the exchanges and contacts on the steppe cover immense areas and go back almost to the limits of prehistory. The problem of the genesis and stylistic evolution of steppe art thus becomes complicated but at the same time partly clarified because the area subjected to nomad domination may have drawn inspirations and ideas even from very distant lands through a complex process of movements and exchanges. This in no way diminishes its creative genius but, rather, suggests a long preparation that corresponds in part to the slow formation of the characteristic specialized economy of the nomads. Therefore, instead of following a line of investigation based on direct derivation, it may be more profitable to examine the various stylistic components revealed by the art of the steppe in order to outline as clearly as possible the characteristics and phases of an artistic phenomenon that is especially deserving of attention since it constitutes the main focus of stylistic integration between Europe and Asia, which was achieved — it should be noted — even by way of brutal clashes that profoundly affected the history of the two continents.

THE STYLISTIC FORMATION. *The Andronovo and Karasuk cultures.* The Aëneolithic culture known as Andronovo began between 2000 and 1700 B.C. and came to an end, owing to exhaustion or transformation, approximately half a millennium later. The name Andronovo has come to indicate a complex of regional cultures that extended over very vast territories, from the Ural basin on the west to the Yenisei basin on the east, and from the region of Omsk on the north to the south coast of the Aral Sea, where the Khwarizm culture of Tazabagyab covered a further large expanse of land. Andronovo tomb furnishings are quite rich in metal objects (bronze, gold, tin), especially in the late period, which shows a marked progress

in metalworking. It has also been established that the exploitation of the Kazakhstan tin mines began with the full development of Andronovo culture in about the 14th century B.C. while, almost contemporaneously, copper mining was intensified both in the Altai region and farther west. The bearers of the Andronovo culture were farmers for whom stock raising (sheep, cattle, horses), which was markedly on the increase provided a sufficiently integrated economy that enabled them to reduce hunting to the level of an occasional and primarily protective activity. The structure of the tombs, which were underground chambers, links Andronovo with the Srubnaya culture of east-central Russia, although the occasional cremation rites attest to a variety of funeral customs that may reflect a ethnic variant.

Adronovo culture reveals an absolute prevalence of geometric decoration, often characterized by highly original motifs that were applied to both clay and metal. This culture, in its various expressions, undoubtedly falls within a typical geometrically oriented phase that includes the synchronous cultures of central Russia (beginning with Seima, which embraced the Oka River region and part of the Volga basin) and some encampments on the eastern slope of the Ural Mountains. Ornamental motifs identical — or very nearly so — to those of Andronovo clay production are found on celts with long tubular sockets from both Seima and Andronovo; the same motifs are generally found throughout the metal production of the Sino-Siberian interpenetration area (Suiyuan, Ordos; PLS. 184, 185). Since it is quite likely, according to the hypothesis formulated by Loeh (1956), that some bronzes from Suiyuan and the Ordos usually dated to later periods are, on the contrary, earlier than 1300 B.C. yet another synchronism is established that connects these bronzes chronologically as well as stylistically (since they, too, belong to a geometrically oriented phase) with the period of Andronovo and related cultures. Considering that in the western extreme of Asia the carriers of this same culture, who settled in the Ural basin, undoubtedly used metalliferous minerals from the Volga basin, that the Andronovo spearheads correspond perfectly with those of the Seima culture (including the decoration), and that similar spearheads in silver appeared in the treasure of Borodino (Bessarabia; ca. 1800 B.C.), it becomes clear that a large part of the Eurasian world was most likely covered at the beginning of the 2d millennium by a belt of contiguous and probably related cultures, which occupied most of the steppe (excluding the southern agricultural civilizations, which differed profoundly from the others in every respect) and coincided in part with the diffusion area (including Antalya and Iran) of the above-mentioned socketed celts.

In this unique cultural context, in which contacts were facilitated by the easy communications on the steppe, the animal motif suddenly emerged, coinciding closely with the formation of a new economic and social structure corresponding to the way of life of the so-called "early nomads," which derived partly from the Andronovo peoples and partly from other groups that had penetrated the area of this culture and later reached the steppe belt. The animal motif was not, however, limited to the area of these cultures. In Chinese civilization the animal imagery of the fantastic t'ao-t'ieh (II, PL. 10, FIG. 26) developed in that period and began to appear on the veined geometric background of the bronzes, gradually becoming more evident and simultaneously losing its peculiar expressive quality. Perhaps the t'ao-t'ieh owed its origin to a meeting between the characteristic geometricizing trend mentioned above and an animal iconography deriving from, or at least nourished by, the north through the peoples of Lake Baikal, whose cultural attitudes resembled those that were typical of certain of the so-called "proto-Chinese" peoples. The stylization of a few jade tigers from Hsi-pei kang and of some human figures from An-yang seems to confirm the possibility of northern inspiration. At any rate, the characteristic stylization of art of the steppe depended only in part on the Chinese temper, the creative power of which was expressed mainly in the image of the t'ao-t'ieh. Furthermore, the possibility that the animal motif may have come from other regions cannot be ruled out; in fact, together with the Lake Baikal antecedents, due account should be taken of those final mas-

movements of peoples from ethnic groups in a formative stage of development which entered already-defined culture areas and crystallized, so to speak, into the historical Indo-European peoples. Above all, it should not be forgotten that the various cultures which had flowered in Iranian territory from time immemorial showed a marked preference for the animal figure, both stylized and realistic, and attributed to it an esthetic significance that has no precise counterpart in the art of the Near East — except perhaps in the culture of Hassuna, although this may be due to exchanges and interpenetration between the two areas. The period treated here corresponds, however, to the Kassite invasion, to which it is no longer possible to relate the Luristan production, which undoubtedly belongs to a much later period (see VIII, cols. 254–260). Between the 19th and 13th centuries B.C. Iran went through a phase of mere stylistic continuation preceding the rise of fragmented stylistic tendencies such as those of the pre-Luristan cultures (all belonging, it seems, to a period after the 12th century B.C.); these tendencies were quite similar in tone to steppe art, although they were often considerably differentiated in the formal aspects. An Iranian source of inspiration for the art of the steppe may be sought in apparently minor cultures (e.g., Hasanlu; Amlash, XIV, PL. 459), which probably occurred later than the 12th century but were nevertheless in a position to affect, if not the origin, at least the stylistic development of nomad art, and particularly in the remarkably advanced metalwork of Elam (Susiana), which attained political autonomy in about 1200 B.C. It is probable that some elements destined to become typical of Scythian art were drawn from Elam, such as the "zoomorphic joint" (a beast's head with wide-open jaws that hold the blade) of an Elamite ax discovered at Chuga Zanbil that has the name of King Untash-Huban incised on its blade and is therefore datable about 1250 B.C. The ax in question is very similar in shape to the earliest Luristan axes and probably reelaborates a motif used in the 2d millennium B.C. by the civilization of the Near East, but its diffusion in Scythian art may have resulted from an Elamite irradiation rather than from direct contact with the Near East. In fact, the stylistic interpretation peculiar to the typical animal figure of steppe art corresponds more closely to Iranian than to Near Eastern interpretations. Striking though sporadic similarities can also be observed among creations of the steppe, Hittite works, and, more rarely, examples from Mitannian art (the Kirkuk tablets, 2d millennium B.C., Iraq; XII, PL. 524).

It is by now established that the fall of the second Hittite empire (ca. 1200 B.C.) caused a wide diffusion of motifs and themes that had developed in the area it had dominated. This irradiation seems to have extended as far as the borders of China (O. Sirén, *A History of Early Chinese Art*, London, 1930), perhaps the result of an exodus of specialized craftsmen, and certainly affected the Iranian territory, where traces remained even in somewhat later periods. Consequently, the genesis of the animal motif turns out to be more complex than might be expected owing to the variety of possible sources of inspiration.

The area of the steppe appears, in fact, to have been occupied by two different peoples, who were complementary to a certain extent and able to influence the genesis and evolution of steppe art. In the northeast there were the Lake Baikal cultures and, subsequently, the Chinese interpretation of the animal figure apart from the *t'ao-t'ieh*; in the southwest, on the other hand, the Iranian area and the Caucasus (the latter an area of reelaboration and contact that witnessed the flowering of the art of Talish, tentatively dated 1550–1200 B.C.) were associated with the Hittite world of Asia Minor. It is as yet impossible to establish a precise priority of inspiration regarding steppe art. At any rate, the antiquity of the Lake Baikal cultures finds a parallel in the millenarian animal-art tradition of Iran, which, on the other hand, displays characteristics that closely correspond to the production of the steppe both in the tendency to stylization and in the essentially ornamental rendering of the animal figure (very different from the expressionist aim of the Chinese *t'ao-t'ieh*), though symbolic meanings are not lacking. The Karasuk culture, which was the basis of the whole subsequent evolution of steppe art, was undeniably affected to a great extent by Chinese influence, and it can be said, furthermore, that the emergence of the animal style in the area of the steppe (and therefore in the nomad cultures) is proved to have been closely and variously linked with the evolution of the whole surrounding cultural world. Also, it can easily be inferred that the inspiration supplied by the neighboring regions reached maturity in the Karasuk culture only because of its specialized society based on stock raising, which was thus inclined to attribute magicoreligious and symbolic significance to the various forms of animal life because of the effects they produced on its economic and spiritual structure. On the other hand, the Scythoid masses to the west and east must have been more deeply affected by the Iranian irradiation, due less to an instinctive correspondence in taste than to the presence of peripheral currents of exchange, albeit rudimentary, that were stimulated and sustained by the characteristic economic disparity between the cultures of the south and that of the steppe; at the same time, the Scythoid masses tended to gravitate toward the south along the steppe areas that penetrated Iranian territory. On the contrary, the nomad masses coming from the north were affected by the Chinese irradiation and were also exposed to the influence of the Lake Baikal cultures.

According to the dates suggested by S. Kiselev and accepted by both Jettmar (1954) and Loehr (1956), the Karasuk culture flourished between 1220 and 700 B.C., although Teplukhov (1929) dated it at least two centuries later. This culture developed around the center of Minusinsk in the Altai region but also extended to numerous isolated localities in the middle basin of the Irtysh River and, apparently, spread out through Mongolia toward the Hwang-ho River. If Kiselev's dates are accurate, as they appear to be, the Karasuk culture would be contemporaneous with the Shang phase of An-yang and with the first and part of the second Chou period. At any rate, from the very beginning Karasuk received typological inspirations, decorative motifs, and stylistic elements from China, though this influence was limited to metalwork since the considerable Karasuk pottery production seems to have been autonomous. Karasuk nevertheless displays original features, which it apparently transmitted to the eastern cultures of the Middle Urals (e.g., the so-called "Turbino phase" of the Gorbunovo culture, 12th cent. B.C.). At a much later period Karasuk was undoubtedly responsible for the transmission of certain Chinese motifs to the Luristan bronzeworkers; among these the goat head with the horns falling back and welded to the neck is outstanding (see II, col. 24). It is not known, however, whether this enrichment of the Luristan repertory resulted from the diffusion of a particular type of object — in this instance the typical curved knives with handles in the shape of goat heads — or from an actual stylistic irradiation. In either case, the influence of Karasuk is undeniable because the bearers of this culture are definitely to be credited with both the intensification of exchanges with China and the diffusion of the curved knives either directly or, instead, indirectly by imitation (which even suggests their possible use as tender in the trade dealings between Karasuk and China). Concerning the complex problem of the stylistic relationships between the Karasuk culture and Scythian art there is absolutely no doubt as to the specific role played by the Karasuk culture, which assimilated inspirations from the east and transmitted them to the west, diffusing them over a vast area, so that Karasuk influences are perceptible even in regions surrounding the Aral Sea.

The large number of Karasuk tombs indicates a remarkable population increase over preceding settlements in the area, and the human remains found in them show an overwhelming prevalence of brachycephali in contrast to the marked dolichocephalic characteristics of their predecessors. Evidently there occurred a large-scale population movement from the north, since a culture with characteristics similar to those of Karasuk evolved in the Lake Baikal region and, furthermore, elements found north of Lake Balkhash can, according to Jettmar, hypothetically be linked with Karasuk. It is therefore quite probable that the bearers of this culture belonged to the Paleo-Asiatic groups that moved southward from the forest region and spread out over the steppe. The full significance of this movement, which resulted in superimpositions and interpenetrations, cannot be fully defined at present, despite the data from various areas collected by Soviet scholars. Without ruling out an intermingling with Mongoloid groups, it was precisely this movement — as a result of which the Altai became the foremost region of Siberian metalwork — that was the main origin of those populations with which the China of the Chou period (1027–256 B.C.) came into early contact and which are identified by Chinese sources, beginning in the 8th century, as the Hsün-yü, Hsien-yün, and Hün-yü, all of which resemble (but are perhaps independent of) the designation Hsiung-nu, the name by which we know the peoples who created the first great empire of the steppe (see below).

The Karasuk culture coincided with an intensification of stock raising (especially sheep) and the introduction of the camel as a pack animal; hence there was an emphasis on stock raising and grazing that was detrimental to agriculture, which had been characteristic of the Andronovo culture. At the same time, the southerly migrations of the Paleo-Asiatic masses may have been accompanied by the displacement of small groups from east to west. Rather than acquiring the character of a migratory phenomenon, as Kiselev assumes, this displacement was probably only an exodus of specialized craftsmen (blacksmiths and smelters) and fugitives provoked by the overthrow of the Shang dynasty (1026 B.C.?) and the beginning of the Chou period, though the exact motives (possibly religious as well as political) underlying this hypothetical exodus are far from clear. The small number of people involved in this migration in no way excludes rather wide cultural repercussions, and it is highly probable that such a phenomenon determined the development of the Chinese component in Karasuk art. It is evident that the Sino-Siberian creations of the phase under discussion had, at least in part, a prolonged persistence — as attested, for example, by the echoes they produced in Luristan art — which proves that they were thoroughly consonant with the taste of the nomad populations and related groups.

The undeniable Chinese origin of some works and types of works does not, however, justify the formulation of hypotheses claiming a single source of inspiration for the animal-style art of the steppe. In fact, a whole series of different data confirms the multiplicity of sources of inspiration, even though the Karasuk culture appears to be entirely free of sufficiently identifiable western influences. In the western part of the steppe belt, where the Scythian style prevailed, highly stylized animal figures (especially water fowl) appear in the vase painting of various Ural stations belonging to the Bor II phase, which is datable, according to M. Gimbutas (1956), to the 12th or 11th century B.C. Such figures were undoubtedly a coarse reelaboration of Iranian trends that became established with the first diffusion of metalworking in the area of the Bor culture. Most probably the metalworking technique reached the Ural areas from the Caucasus, which strongly indicates that the road connecting Iran with the Ural Mountains, frequently used in the Achaemenid and Sassanian periods, was open by the end of the 2d millennium B.C. Southern influences seem therefore to have had considerable importance in the evolution of the Ural settlements, which appear to be interpenetration cultures and partly related to the Karasuk culture, from which they received and to which they perhaps offered inspirations of various kinds.

Caucasia. The Caucasus also appears to have been a connecting area between different cultures and is characterized by a considerable autonomy of development and esthetic creativity. Directly or indirectly, the area was probably influenced by the rising Scythian art, the Pontic migration (see below), and steppe art as a whole. It is certain that in the 2d millennium B.C. some regions south of the Caucasus area, as far as the Zagros Mountains of Iran and beyond, were already occupied by Indo-European peoples such as the Kassites; very likely all of Azerbaijan in Caucasia was a point of departure for the movements of these masses. Even the fall of the Hittite empire in Asia Minor was probably caused by the thrust of peoples coming from Caucasia, apparently connected with the Cimmerian groups. The characteristic features of the metal production

(particularly weapons) diffused in the Hittite territories in th north of Asia Minor and of the Caucasus and in northern Ira suggest a series of migrations that may have had a direct impac on India. Evidence provided by the Caucasus region and regior affected by migrations from that area indicates the formatio of the Cimmerian masses out of the peoples belonging to th western Pontic culture. At the same time there was a slo crystallization of the future Scythians into a well-defined ethn structure, a phenomenon that must have resulted also from th attraction exerted by an area that was still scarcely populatec

Reaching its culmination in the Caucasus region and in th Pontic cultures was the spiral as the dominant element of geometricizing ornamentation. Preference for the spiral as decorative motif probably affected the rendering of the anim figure in its most stylized aspects. The coiled, almost discoid representations of the later phases of the dominance of the spira beginning with the Tagar period (700–300 B.C.), and the styliz tion based on the contiguous rings formed by the clawed paw of beasts of prey are probably due to the persistence of a sens bility that regarded the curved line and the circle as basic el ments of ornamentation (PL. 182). At a relatively early perio an interest in the animal style began to develop in the Caucasia region, in the cultures both of the Kuban and of the Sovi Talish, south of Baku, and extended into Iranian territory. Th Talish culture had considerable echoes in the Ossetian region t the north, where a geometrically oriented phase (Digora A was succeeded by the emergence of animal motifs (Digora I 11th–7th cent. B.C.), as well as in the settlements of the Gan Karabakh group (now Soviet Armenia), which are probabl more ancient if the data derived from the accompanying Assyr ian material [objects bearing the name of King Adadnira (I?); r. 1305–1277 B.C.] are exact. The Talish culture exerte a clear influence on that of Levlar, west of Lake Sevan, wit which, according to C. Schaeffer (1948), it was contemporaneou The intensity of this contact suggests a conquest and subse quent cultural superimposition. Contacts between Talish an Levlar were interrupted by the rise of the Van empire — th is, Urartu (q.v.) — which thrust a wedge into the intermediat territory.

This brief examination of the function and importance c the Caucasian area and the surrounding regions should b concluded by pointing out some other data. Although th Talish culture was in a sense a separate phenomenon and ab sorbed to varying degrees east-to-west irradiations from th neighboring zones of Transcaucasia and Ciscaucasia, there a also definite connections between the Caucasian and Irania cultures. These relationships concern not only the last phas of Tepe Sialk (gray-black ware; see CERAMICS) but also the cu tures of Hasanlu, Khurvin, and Amlash, all of which develope animal motifs in their metalwork and pottery production (vas decoration and animal-shaped vessels). Between the end c the 2d millennium and the beginning of the 1st, the norther Iranian territory underwent a process of comparative unificatio in the arts; ties between this region and the Caucasian regior appear in the cultures of Talish and Levlar, later becoming eve more obvious in the production of Urartu. The Kuban culture which declined in the weak phase known as "recent Kuban (PL. 183), exerted influence as far as the Volga and Kama riv basins; while the Kuban culture (PL. 181), deriving its nam from an Ossetian center north of the Daryal Pass, sprea as far as Stavropol in the Caucasus and faced on the Blac Sea near Novorossisk. Thus we see the extent and artistic v tality of these southern regions, which probably contribute directly to the evolution of steppe art. Stylistically, a part of th characteristic motifs of the art of the southern regions even ha prolonged correspondences in Caucasian, Kuban, Koban, an Hittite art, especially in minor details and, more rarely, in th Caucasian production, in the attempts to stylize legs, horn and tails into circles or spirals. Possibly derived from Kuba is the same treatment of the animal figure (goat or deer) with th four legs close together in the standing position, typical of th early phases of the art of this area, although static representatio is certainly alien to the southern area of inspiration and w developed above all in the Ordos region.

Karasuk art was the first clear Siberian manifestation of the animal style, which was continued by the Tagar culture, forming part of the so-called "triad of the steppe" (i.e., Scythia, Tagar, and Ordos). However, an endless series of cultures spread over a vast area concerned themselves, in different spirit, with the same esthetic problem, thereby reducing the importance of the Karasuk period, which nevertheless remains the first indisputable manifestation of an artistic outlook peculiar to the nomad world.

The Pontic migration. For almost three centuries after the beginning of the 1st millennium B.C. there occurred large-scale movements and transformations that affected a huge area from the Black Sea to China and beyond, reaching their peak in the 9th and 8th centuries B.C. The well-known and reliable hypothesis formulated by Heine-Geldern (1951) identifies the dominant movement in this complex series of events as an eastward migratory thrust, placing its culmination in the withdrawal of the Western Chou, who in 770 B.C. moved their capital to Loyang because of the pressure of the barbarians and feudal revolts. This same migration was responsible for the diffusion in the Chinese area of objects deriving from the West and connected with the Caucasian and Hallstatt productions. Chinese production reveals ties with Hallstatt C [the "iron phase" in the nomenclature of P. Reineke (*Altertümer unserer heidnischen Vorzeit*, V, 1911)], as well as with Hallstatt B, which is in turn related to, if not identical with, the Urn-field culture (see V, cols. 269–271).

Certain forms of axes, daggers, and buckles as well as ornamental motifs (spirals, S motifs, meanders, Greek frets) thus reached the Chinese territory and, according to the hypothesis advanced by Heine-Geldern, descended southward as far as Indochina as the result of a split in the main migratory stream. This hypothesis explains the obvious analogies (noted by Janse, 1934) between the Caucasian and Hallstatt productions and the Ordos bronzes, which Heine-Geldern dates between the end of the 2d millennium and the beginning of the Han period (206 B.C.). However, Heine-Geldern's attempts to explain the presence of populations belonging to the western Indo-European group in Central Asia may be based excessively on migratory movements. Although Soviet archaeological research in the basin of the lower Oxus River (mod. Amu Darya) and on the Jaxartes River (mod. Syr Darya) stresses the mobility of the local Scythoid population, it also acknowledges the presence of settled groups of breeders and farmers who created irrigation systems, varied and complex handicrafts, and numerous urban centers. Tolstov (1960) has observed that the concept of the classic nomad was alien to these groups and reflected a very different cultural configuration. Nonetheless, mobility was carefully preserved by their social structure and became dominant when circumstances demanded it. This new evaluation of the Scythoid groups of Central Asia somewhat reduces the probable exactness of the hypothesis concerning the Pontic migration.

Other hypotheses, adopting somewhat different chronologies, explain the similarities between Hallstatt and Ordos by various types of contacts and attribute great importance to other movements that led Caucasian ethnic types to push westward and settle in Bosnia and Central Europe. However, there is no proof that the easterly Pontic migration reached the territories south of the Aral Sea. The fact that there are Indo-European groups in Central Asia speaking western-type languages is explainable either by a west-to-east movement that occurred in the period under discussion or by a much earlier eastward movement by Indo-Europeans originally located between the peoples of the Pontic steppe and those of Central Europe. Perhaps the Pontic migration should be interpreted as a continuous displacement of organized human masses. In any case, it is established that there was a stylistic and typological diffusion, whatever the historical background, which was responsible for the characteristic aspects of steppe art; that it followed a west-to-east direction; and that it illuminates the role played by western cultures as sources of inspiration for those of the Chinese era. This easterly expansion, along the shortest and easiest paths of communication, joined the two poles of the animal-style art: the Cimmerian (later

Scythian) area and the Ordos. Although the Altai was situated outside the main line of expansion, it was able to receive, directly or indirectly, influences from west or east (PL. 187). Whether Heine-Geldern's hypothesis is accepted, or whether only the stylistic irradiation rather than the population movement is considered, the point of departure of the influences and inspirations that reached the Ordos and spread to the neighboring areas that were best prepared to accept them must be sought in southeastern Europe and in the Caucasus. In those regions originated the complex spiral and S-shaped ornamentation and the use of *pointillé* work and of plaited and discoid motifs (often beaded). Even the stylized contortion found in some animal figures — the curled-animal motif (*animal enroulé*) and the contorted-animal motif (see ORDOS for examples of both) — has a Caucasian origin, whether it reached the east directly or through Iranian mediation. The bronze figurines of the lions of Hasanlu (Louvre; Teheran, Archaeol. Mus.) show in fact a flattening of the muzzle and a treatment of the rictus not unknown in Caucasian works (which, however, accentuate the geometric character of the decorative elements); these same characteristics may be traceable to Hittite inspirations. At any rate, the Caucasian contribution was significant, considering that at the beginning of the 1st millennium B.C. the local production was connected with that of Iran (even with the Luristan bronzes of a considerably later period) and with that of the contemporaneous and later Khwarizmian cultures of Turkestan, which should perhaps be attributed to the Massagetae.

Classical sources beginning with Herodotus (IV, 12) testify to a very deep ethnic transformation that implies the displacement of Cimmerian groups in Caucasia as a result of Scythian pressure. Recent Soviet discoveries of pre-Scythian entrenched fields in this area rule out the total disappearance of the Cimmerians. Their culture remains obscure, although undoubtedly they were in close contact with the cultures of Caucasia, Thrace, and Illyria. Very little is known about their artistic activity, which was developed in a territory filled with influences from Anatolia and the Aegean. Probably Cimmerian art does not lend itself to exact identification but reflects a stylistic tendency that spread over a vast area, influencing the various phases of the Pontic pre-Scythian production. Hančar's hypothesis (1934) identifying the Cimmerians with the bearers of Hallstatt culture is rejected by those who regard the latter people as Celts or proto-Celts. (The Celts unquestionably assimilated Hallstatt culture and contributed to its diffusion; see CELTIC ART.) The series of displacements effected by the Cimmerians in historical times (documented by various sources, especially Assyrian and classical) appears unquestionable; their pressure toward the south is at the root of R. Ghirshman's hypothesis attributing the Luristan production proper to a trend of Medo-Cimmerian art and dating it no earlier than the 8th century B.C. (*Iran from the Earliest Times to the Islamic Conquest*, London, 1954; see also VIII, cols. 254–260). The Cimmerian element in this case contributed to the particular vigor of the Luristan animal motifs and to the similarities between Luristan art and some Caucasus bronzes datable to the beginning of the 1st millennium B.C. The more recent hypothesis of Barnett (1962), however, perceives in the local Mannai culture an aspect of Median art pervaded by Urartian influences; this hypothesis is substantiated by the Zawiyeh finds (II, PL. 4; VI, PLS. 248, 249; VIII, PLS. 124, 125) and by other stylistically similar works from the Pontic area. The wide diffusion of works of this kind suggests the possibility of influences from the little-known art of the Medes (through trade and stylistic irradiations), which would indicate the artistic prestige it enjoyed, as clearly confirmed by Achaemenid inscriptions. It can be seen, therefore, that in the course of a few centuries the art of an enormous area closely connected with that of the steppe became more complex and lively than was previously suspected. Migratory currents and cultural as well as iconographic and stylistic irradiation crossed and were superimposed in an uninterrupted exchange of basic elements that affected different civilizations and cultures, while under closer analysis they are seen to have been fragmented into minor trends and reveal the coexistence of opposed and genetically different orientations. The art of the area in question, which included a large part of Iran, was undoubtedly bound to animal motifs and was thus, from the standpoint of subject matter, complementary to the area in which steppe art flourished; it was practically an autonomous province in which there appeared stylistic trends that were capable, in turn, of influencing the art of the steppe in a variety of ways. Apart from these influences, there are also the ties that link the art of Luristan to Altaic and Chinese art, as the result of an east-to-west irradiation, and the undeniable consonances between Median production and the art of Urartu and the coast of the Black Sea, as seen in the treatment of eagle heads from Zawiyeh to Kelermes and beyond and in the Caucasus (Kaukaskaya). It is very possible that it is precisely in the Pontic area — in view of the persistence of the stylistic tendency that led to the use of the spiral and S motif in ornamentation — that the origin of the animal figures coiled into a circle or twisted into an S which prevailed in the steppe art from the Tagar period onward is to be sought (see below). Historical documentation testifies to the presence of the curled-animal figure in the Ordos, in the Minusinsk region (Tagar), in various places in western Siberia, and in Scythian art (e.g., Simferopol in the Crimea). Tagar may possibly have conveyed this motif to Scythian art, but the great success enjoyed by this stylized form (of which the earliest prototypes perhaps came from the Near East) is undoubtedly connected with the widespread favor enjoyed by the spiral. The adaptation of this motif to the animal style was achieved simply by substituting the elongated body of the animal for the winding geometric line. As for the S-shaped forms — that is, the contorted figures of various animals (for the most part herbivorous) — the necessary transformation, though complicated in appearance, was not in fact much different, considering the wide diffusion of the double opposed-spiral motif in Pontic and Caucasian decoration. It is likely that this particular interpretation of the animal figure acquired its definite form in China and later spread westward by way of the Ordos; it is also possible that it originally derived from a western inspiration that spread eastward and then returned to the areas of its origin with the substitution of a representational element (the animal) for an abstract geometric motif.

Despite the many problems posed by the hypothesis of the Pontic migration, the movement is fundamental in the study of the animal art of the steppe. The Pontic migration assimilated developments differing in origin and style but similar in substance, conveying them eastward toward rich reelaboration and unexpected survivals.

The Scythian influence. The Scythian masses, which replaced the Cimmerian groups in southern Russia, pushed the latter forward in different directions over a wide geographic area. The resulting society was ethnically heterogeneous, according to Soviet scholars, and contained at least three coexisting cultures: Scythian culture proper (the Royal Scyths), based on racial homogeneity and organized into agricultural and nomadic tribes; various tribes of shepherds and farmers of differing origins; and the Sindo-Maeotic culture on the east coast of the Sea of Azov and along the Kuban River. Scythian domination extended for some time as far west as the Danube basin in the heart of Europe. Classical sources stretched the Scythian boundaries eastward to reach to the Altai Mountains. Beyond that, to the borders of the Chinese area, a "second Scythia" included other peoples and other lands, which have been unfortunately associated with Scythia proper in a general nomenclature that has led to the groundless hypothesis of a so-called "Scythian phase," indicating a specific level of material culture. The existence of these peoples of the "second Scythia" is abundantly confirmed by Indian, Iranian, and Chinese sources in addition to the classical texts; these Scythoid masses did, in fact, constitute the so-called "Outer Iran," an immense cultural world traditionally hostile to the Iranian empires, which nonetheless transmitted and elaborated the achievements of Iranian and other civilizations and contributed independently to the cultural evolution of Asia (René Grousset, *L'Iran extérieur: Son art*, Paris, 1932).

Scythian production proper represents one grouping of the so-called "triad of the steppe." The first Scythian thrust may have been directly or indirectly responsible for the Pontic migration and rapidly reached the slopes of the Caucasus. It was followed by a second wave that flowed over beyond the Caucasus range, spreading into Armenia and Azerbaijan. The Scythians also played a role in the history of the Near East through their complex relations with Urartu in Turkey, with Assyria (whose allies they became after reducing Assyrian power), with the Medes (who eventually destroyed Scythia), and with other peoples to the east and west. The presence of Scythian groups in an area, incidentally, cannot be fully established by the appearance of distinctly Scythian objects; a combination of various types of evidence is necessary.

Between the earliest data concerning the Royal Scyths and the first secure archaeological documentation there is a gap of approximately two centuries, during which the formative period of Scythian esthetic development occurred. An invaluable clue to a later, but still early, phase of Scythian art is the previously mentioned treasure of Zawiyeh from northern Iran, consisting of numerous works from about the last quarter of the 7th century B.C. collected in a bronze coffin (see VIII, cols. 260–267). These works display different artistic trends (Assyrian, Scythian, Assyro-Scythian, Mannaian) and testify to the

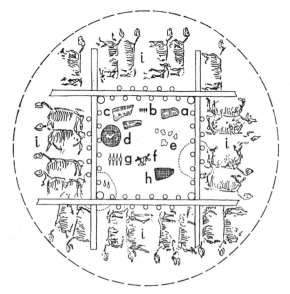

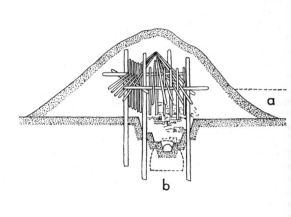

Kostromskaya, mound graves. *Left*: Plan: (*a*) Grindstone; (*b*) arrows; (*c*) leather quivers; (*d*) iron shield with deer; (*e*) potsherds; (*f*) bits; (*g*) iron spearhead (*h*) scale armor; (*i*) skeletons of horses buried with the deceased. *Right*: Section: (*a*) Stratum with horse skeletons; (*b*) lowest chamber (*from Talbot Rice, 1957*)

success of the Scythian interpretation of the animal motif. The Zawiyeh works are approximately contemporaneous with the earliest Scythian tombs of the Crimea (Termir Goa near Kerch, Lake Zukor in the Taman Peninsula) but antedate the large tomb complexes of Kelermes, Melgunov, and Kostromskaya Stanitsa (FIG. 387; I, PL. 437; VI, PLS. 463, 464). The composite nature of the art of Zawiyeh is revealed by a magnificent gold breastplate (Teheran, Archaeol. Mus.), the upper section of which contains a lynx motif at each of the narrow ends. The breastplate is Urartian in type. The lynx, however, is an animal typical of the Central Asian steppelands. Apparently the Scythian interpretation of some motifs was already well established at this time, since the lynx is rendered in Scythian style. The eclecticism of Zawiyeh art reveals a phase in which heterogeneous components were prevalent. The late dating of the Zawiyeh finds (7th cent. B.C.) unfortunately prohibits them from being used to demonstrate a derivation of Scythian art from the northern Iranian trends.

Another motif from Zawiyeh is that of the stags in a flying gallop, their antlers transformed into an almost purely ornamental band stretching above the body (PL. 186; VI, PL. 463); this same stylization of the stag is also found in the Tagar production, though as an isolated figure, and on a horse from the Ordos region (ca. 1st cent. B.C.). Stylized heads of birds of prey in the Urartian manner were used not only at Zawiyeh but also in the Scythian art of Kuban (PL. 183; VIII, PL. 125) and generally in the coastal regions of the Black Sea. The origin of this type of stylized figure has been sought in the Lagash seals. Undoubtedly some heads of predatory birds were inspired by the stylization documented in Urartu and at Zawiyeh, as were certain Altaic heads. It is not yet clear, however, whether the Urartu and Zawiyeh versions were of Scythian origin or of a Median-Urartian admixture, or even the result of a Cimmerian inspiration assimilated by the Mannai culture and adapted to the local style. There is no doubt that other motifs, including some re-elaborated in the Scythian manner, indicate a Siberian provenance and perhaps even a Siberian formal origin (e.g., the lynxes of the gold breastplate). The combined whole of the components absorbed by such works seems to have been steadily enriched by new elements more or less akin to the Scythian creations but actually alien to Scythian art proper. This indicates that the animal art of the steppe was already mature in many of its formal aspects at the time the Zawiyeh works were placed in the coffin and that the Scythian trend undoubtedly assimilated Siberian inspirations, at least in subject matter, thus reflecting a development in taste similar to that established in other regions.

Since the Scythian area proper was exposed to many influences developed through direct contact or trade routes, its art proceeded within various and occasionally coexisting trends and was able to utilize heterogeneous components, blending them into an essentially new vision. The typical character of Scythian art depends largely on a style evolved from this meeting of different influences and from experiments during the early formative stage. The salient features of the art are stylization, distortion, and whimsy, along with a certain naturalistic approach that can be partly attributed to Greek influence. The tendency to stylization and to distortion persisted for a long time; the last Scythian works found in Central Europe retained their original characteristics, preserving vague reminiscences of motifs from Mesopotamia, the Hittite world, Caucasia, and areas farther east (PL. 186). Scythian art also reflects a connection of the animal figure with hunting magic and a correspondence to the social and economic organization of the world from which it derived. Thus there are similarities in Scythian art to other artistic trends from different regions that also underwent a corresponding social evolution. These analogies in social development were partly responsible for the irradiation of Scythian art and enabled the Scythian world to absorb related foreign elements. The naturalistic trend became accentuated in the later phases, producing profound transformations brought about by contacts with Greek civilization. Eventually the vast imaginative and expressive wealth of Greek art stifled some of the creative capacities of Scythian culture, which in turn left considerable traces of its animal motifs in the tomb decorations of the Scythian captains of Mycenae.

Woodworking undoubtedly represented a significant preparatory stage for metalworking in the Scythian area, as it did elsewhere in the art of the steppe. Perhaps in an earlier hunting stage the proto-Scythians sculptured bone, easing the way for a ready adaptation of metalworking to deliberate figure distortion and to a full exploitation of the decorative possibilities of the superposition of several figures on the body of a main figure.

At the time of its greatest splendor, Scythian art revealed a limited range of prevailing subjects: the curled animal, the goat figure (II, PL. 13), and animals in combat (usually a herbivorous and a carnivorous animal; PL. 187; FIG. 390). The battle plaque, imbued with magical significance, was less widespread here than elsewhere (e.g., western Siberia), although possibly

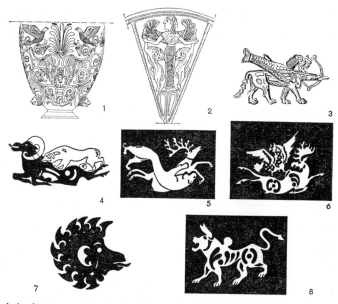

Animal representations in Scythian and steppe art. Engraving on metal: (1) Chertomlyk, detail of electrum kumis jug, 4th cent. B.C.; (2) Kelermes, detail of the Great Goddess from the gilded and engraved silver mirror, 7th–6th cent. B.C.; (3) Melgunov, detail of the gold sword sheath. Pazyryk saddlecloth designs, Barrow I, 5th cent. B.C.: (4–6) animal combat; (7) ram's head; (8) lion (*from Talbot Rice, 1957*).

some of the Siberian specimens have a Scythian origin. The theme of animal combat is interpreted in Scythian culture in an almost heraldic spirit, appearing more idealized and less charged with the expressive power characteristic of similar interpretations from Ordos and from the later Sarmatian phase, when the artist delighted in a crude realism and in an extraordinary and highly refined effect of slow motion. Perhaps the symbolic significance of these works depicting animal combat varied considerably according to area, since it seems unlikely that the same ideas could correspond to both the idealizing attitude of the Scythian world and the crude realism of the eastern and Sarmatian cultures. There is nothing, however, to document these symbolic variations except a difference in style.

Gradually the old style of animal art proved insufficient to satisfy the esthetic needs of the Scythian area (PL. 191); from various directions there came new inspirations that led not only to the representation of the human figure but even to an art partially pervaded by a ceremonial spirit abounding in naturalistic accents and individualized characterizations of personages. This was the period of the maximum Greek influence preceding the uncontrollable Sarmatian pressure from the east that ended the Scythian domination and caused the dispersion of the Scythian mercenaries, who were no longer called upon to fight in distant lands.

The Tagar period. The cultural and stylistic period known as Tagar is named for a small island on the Yenisei River near Minusinsk. The Tagar period (700–300 B.C.) is defined by some authors as the culture of the kurgans of Minusinsk because the numerous Tagar tombs there are the largest and most important finds belonging to this culture. Family tombs of the pit type with ceilings of stone slabs, they are covered with mounds of earth and surrounded by rectangular enclosures, marked either by enormous stones placed at the four corners or by an uninterrupted perimeter of somewhat smaller, though sizable, stones. In many respects the Tagar culture is a continuation and further development of the Karasuk, but it also acquired distinct stylistic characteristics as a result of advances in metalworking, which reached new heights in the Tagar period. There was, however, a marked delay in the use of iron, probably due to the abundance of copper and tin, which encouraged the use of bronze.

The bearers of the Tagar culture were mainly farmers. Vast canal-irrigation systems, sometimes hewn out of rock over short distances, can still be identified despite strong wind erosion. Some fortified settlements have also been found. Although stock raising remained a supplementary activity, seasonal livestock movements influenced the mobility of the Tagar groups. The importance of the horse as a draft and saddle animal became predominant in the Altai area during the Tagar period, as documented by the numerous bits and bridles of bronze and later of iron.

Although Kiselev (1951) divides Tagar culture into three phases, not all specialists agree on the first phase, whose origins Kiselev dates back to the 10th century B.C.; or the last phase, which he continues to the 1st century B.C. The Tagar culture proper experienced two distinct periods of florescence: from about 700 B.C. to 500 B.C., and from about 500 B.C. to 300 B.C. The first period continued the preceding Karasuk culture. During the second period new social factors arose, as indicated by impressive kurgans such as the one at Salbyk with a perimeter of over 1,600 ft. and an enclosure of colossal stones, some weighing between 20 and 30 tons. Such kurgans were obviously reserved for the ruling families. Other changes in funeral customs and tomb furnishings evidence a transformation of the society in the direction of warlike strength and domination by an increasingly oppressive central power. This transformation seems to have also affected the style of metal objects, which began to show dynamic forms that were highly stylized and almost monumental despite their limited size. The second Tagar period exhausted itself after laying the groundwork for new societies that gave life to the Hunno-Sarmatian phase.

Tagar, together with Ordos and the Scythian area, is part of the "triad of the steppe" and represents a fundamental aspect of the trend of figural animal art. The two geographically extreme areas of Ordos and Scythia reacted on each other through the mediations of Tagar. There is a possibility that Tagar culture was the result of Scythian and Iranian influence through irradiations or contacts between different populations; or, on the other hand, that Tagar may have strongly affected animal-art trends of western Europe and Iran. Probably both are true to some degree. Tagar was definitely responsible for the Chinese-oriented and Sino-Siberian accents observed in the Luristan bronzes; here its role as a link between east and west can be fully established.

Tagar art, with its particular similarities to the art of Ordos and Scythia and to the composite works of Zawiyeh, developed at a time when steppe art was becoming unified in its principal characteristics, although certain regional differences were preserved. Tagar was the first steppe culture to develop on a broad scale the standing figure of the goatlike animal almost unknown to Scythian art, which favored the stag in a flying gallop (PL. 186), a motif that also appeared frequently in Tagar production, but possibly not before its second phase. The stag may have originated in Scythia or, more likely, in its peripheral regions, since the theme of the flying gallop was fully developed in the Zawiyeh goat and deer figures and has antecedents in the Kirkuk seals. The precise role of Tagar in diffusing the curled-animal figures in their westward return, following a prior easterly diffusion, remains unclear, since the chronology of the findings is unverifiable. The intensity of Tagar's bilateral exchanges with Ordos and Scythia in no way alters its stylistic autonomy and its role as liaison between east and west. In fact, the Scythian tendency to stylization appears reduced (although

still evident) in Tagar works; the stylistic character of Tagar was sufficiently marked to influence the heavy sculptural quality of Chinese bronzes from the Warring States period (IX, PL. 175, 498), which further confirms reciprocal influences between these regions.

The evolution of Tagar art shows a certain relationship between the social structure and the animal-style art of the steppe, reflecting a slow change from a society in the formative stage to a highly organized society that simultaneously pursued agriculture (to a limited extent) and stock raising (increasingly developed) and was oriented toward growing mobility and centralization of political and religious power. In a certain sense the Tagar phase reveals the most complete expression of steppe art, owing to its felicitous combination of realistic tendencies and power of stylization.

The origin of the Tagar culture, though far from clear, resulted in part from the cultural transformation of an area that witnessed an increase in population density and widespread use of the horse as a saddle animal. It is highly doubtful that such a transformation was determined by outside forces. More probably it depended on local factors, since cranial measurements indicate no significant physical differences between the bearers of this culture and those of the Karasuk period. Regarding artistic activity, the Tagar creations are unquestionably original. The many trends by which Tagar art could have been affected — at least hypothetically — were either of western origin (through direct irradiation or indirectly through reflections from the Pontic migration that reached Tagar by way of the Ordos) or definitely eastern (Chinese and, once again, from the Ordos), nor should the vast southern regions be overlooked, since it was the domain of Scythoid groups that readily received and reelaborated both the Iranian irradiation and Scytho-Caucasian inspirations, along with limited, though clear, artistic and technological influences from Karasuk. Thus, some works from northern and eastern Kazakhstan, ascribed to the 8th–7th century B.C., reveal by their stylization a Scythian influence or, at least, a similarity to Scythian works that cannot be entirely accidental; this similarity assumes greater significance in relation to other contemporaneous creations — unquestionably attributable to Tagar — that stand out by comparison. These problems are now attracting the attention of scholars specialized in the study of the southern regions, which appear to be not only an area of contact but also the source of new creations, and they again pose and emphasize the complex problem of the art of the Medes, which originated in an area of interpenetration, an art that was very vigorous, according to available sources, as well as autonomous. Nor should it be forgotten that from the cultural formations that developed on the peripheries of Outer Iran, which are also interpenetration cultures (e.g., the one known as Yaz Tepe), bronze plaques have been found that are similar to Karasuk creations. The culture of Yaz Tepe, which flourished in the lower Murghab basin in ancient Margiana, displays in its first phase (datable 950–700 B.C.) materials that can be associated with the Iranian culture of Necropolis B at Tepe Sialk and with the Caucasian cultures documented at Novocherkassk as well as with the above-mentioned Karasuk influences. If no further changes occur in the chronological scale that now appears to be the most probable, this would constitute proof of a Karasuk irradiation prior to that of Tagar. The latter was the continuation of the Karasuk culture and demonstrates beyond question the vitality and expansive power of Altaic art and of the rich Altaic repertory, which was partially absorbed by sedentary cultures as well. The dwelling centers of Yaz Tepe, the larger of which had a central fortress, and the complex network of irrigation canals reveal a distinctly sedentary way of life. The Yaz Tepe gray-paste earthenware corresponds perfectly to that of Necropolis B of Tepe Sialk and, in subsequent Yaz Tepe phases, to that of the Persian-Achaemenid levels of the villages of Susa and Nad-i-'ali. As Masson (1958) has pointed out, the painted ceramics of the first Yaz Tepe phase constitute a subtantial antecedent for ceramics found by R. Ghirshman at Susa ("Village perse-achéménide," Mém. de la Mission Archéol. en Iran, Mission de Susiane, XXXVI, Paris, 1954). This may also indicate within the heart of ancient Persia an influence from e eastern Iranian area, perhaps achieved through the Medes; or this conjecture, however, there are numerous gaps in a ng chain of correlations, and no definite proofs. The trilobate rowheads, usually attributed to the Scythian groups, make eir appearance only in the third phase of Yaz Tepe. Undoubt-lly prevalent in the first and second phases were two-lobed rowheads similar to those from Dagestan and from the first hase of the Koban culture. All this reveals a striking cultural ntinuity unaffected by outside influences and proves that the nes east of Iran proper were not merely transit areas for the omadic migratory waves but also a cradle of civilization and of e composite cultures referred to in classical sources. In addi-on to Margiana, Khwarizm in the basin of the lower Oxus iver also displays a basically similar cultural character. This nfirms the characteristic structures and function of all (or arly all) the cultures of Outer Iran.

The phase of Khwarizm that appears to be contemporaneous ith Yaz Tepe I is known as the Amirabad culture (ca. 1000–o B.C.). According to Soviet archaeologists, this culture was e product of the Massagetae or of the Alans (Alani). As a rotohistorical phase it preceded a stage of sedentary breeders, ocumented by the so-called "culture of the villages with wall wellings." The black or gray-black Amirabad ceramics deco-ted with a herringbone pattern appear connected with western eramics and motifs in use in the Iranian cultural sphere. The nportance of Amirabad is that it preserves incised and graffito eometric decoration.

Amirabad preceded the formation of a state (6th cent.–4th ent. B.C.) which encompassed the culture of the villages with all dwellings and caused Khwarizm to enter a historical phase. ext came the culture of Kangyu (Chin., K'ang-ch'ü; 4th cent. .c.–1st cent. of our era), designating a group of stock raisers ttled east of Sogdiana proper and northeast of the area dom-ated by the Wu-sun, who probably were racially similar to e Sarmatians and subsequently played an important role in e history of Central Asia.

The culture of the villages with wall dwellings was the result f a long history of a sedentary social organization centered ound stock raising. The rectangular defensive walls were over ft. thick and contained dwellings, warehouses, and sheds. he empty enclosed area was used for the gathering of herds d flocks, the stock raisers' only wealth (VIII, FIG. 1002). his culture apparently spread over a vast area, including the axartes River basin. It was clearly in contrast with the social ructure of the classic nomad culture, in which dwellings were lt tents and defense was based on particular techniques of arfare associated with the very nature of the nomad. The vil-ges with wall dwellings, with their moats, crenelations, towers, rowhead-shaped loopholes, and fortifications in front of the ccess gates, reveal an entirely different way of life and social onception, certainly closer to that of the southern farmers than that of the evolving nomad masses. The vitality and attraction f the sedentary life, however, was to become in subsequent enturies a threat to the nomad peoples from a psychological s well as organizational point of view; without exception, they esorted at first to any possible means to avoid it and occasionally nployed cruel and drastic solutions.

The western irradiation of both the Karasuk and Tagar ultures appears indisputable, but it must have been accompanied y bilateral exchanges, the extent of which is not yet fully estab-shed. The relations between Tagar and Ordos to the east were earer, more intense, and more continuous; the small eastern ingdom of the Chou (1027–256 B.C.), in the great bend of the wang-ho River, grew from a small border state federated with e Shang into a military power of the first magnitude that re-laced its former rulers. This transformation is related to the ontacts maintained by the Chinese world with Central Asia d to pressures from the Siberian area and from the more south-rn zones.

In the figural arts of the Chou period (see III, cols. 480–490) e first stylistic phase, up to about the year 900 B.C., is designated in-Chou, or ancient Chou, and exhibits no fundamental nnovations (III, PL. 224). With the second phase, known as liddle Chou, which lasted until the 7th century B.C., the style of

the bronzes underwent a marked transformation and new tenden-cies developed in the animal-art production (III, PLS. 223, 226, 229). The entire Chou period, including the Warring States period (by which time the political power of the dynasty had practically vanished, so that the last rulers retained only a certain religious prestige), was a feudal phase — that is, a period of fragmentation — in contrast to the Shang period, which was more unified and more broadly based on the slave system. The Chou period witnessed, however, the rise and establishment of Confucianism (q.v.), the basis of the subsequent imperial and bureaucratic organization of China. The relative break-down of the Chinese area into feudal divisions implies a greater possibility of exchanges and contacts with the steppe world with which we are concerned, the development of parallel or diverging trade movements, and a closer link with border cul-tures and the more remote ones of Central Asia. The great Ordos production, notwithstanding its antecedents (pointed out by Loehr, 1956), was concentrated in the last centuries preceding the Christian era and retained the character of an art that was intermediate between two different cultural worlds. Thus there evolved in the Ordos a particular style, which, despite the comparative clarity, delighted in complex stylizations, entan-gled figures, and forced and unreal combinations of various life forms. An ornamental tendency prevailed, which originated with the heaviness and striking forcefulness of the openwork animal figures on the battle plaques; these were always depicted as if in slow and purposeful movement. Perhaps the innate sty-listic sensibility of the Paleo-Asiatic groups that came to the south drew new vigor from the means of expression provided by the Chinese and Altaic experiences. Even though the contacts between the Ordos and Siberia date from a very early period and are well established, the abundant and widespread Ordos pro-duction certainly coincides with the so-called "Hunno-Sarma-tian" period, which followed the Tagar period and constituted another evolutionary stage in the art of the steppe.

The Hunno-Sarmatian period. This period, termed "Hunno-Sarmatian" by Soviet scholars, extended from about 300 to 100 B.C. It was particularly rich in historical, political, and cul-tural phenomena that influenced the subsequent evolution of Eurasia as a whole and developed some of the premises estab-lished in the preceding centuries. This period witnessed the rise of the first of the great nomad empires, that of the Hsiung-nu, which was to become the unyielding enemy of Han China. Soon afterward, by the forceful action of Shih Huang-ti (r. 221–206 B.C.) of the Ch'in dynasty, the Chinese region was organized into a centralized state, enormously increasing its political and military power.

At the other end of the continent an even more far-reaching though shorter-lived phenomenon had been in existence for some time. There the Achaemenid empire had unified the ancient Near East and absorbed all its composite cultures, imbuing them with a more humane conception of life that enabled it to effect an immense concordance of peoples from Egypt to Bactria in southwest Asia. Achaemenid art incorporated various strains (e.g., Egyptian, Greek, Median, Assyrian, Urartian, various local trends) but despite its eclecticism was a thoroughly Ira-nian art, as evidenced by monuments and inscriptions. It was also an extremely vital art and underwent wide diffusion, espe-cially in its later period and even after the fall of the empire. Evidence of this diffusion can be found even in the Ural zone in the metal plates of the Irano-Scythian type (Bashkiria near the Yuryuzan River; end of 6th cent. – beginning of 5th cent. B.C.), in the bronze plate of a strictly Achaemenid type from the Kama River basin, and in a plate discovered in the Ufa region (Kuganak Valley). In the same area the vases, bearing Aramaic inscriptions, and the fine iron sword with an enameled gold hilt from the necropolis of Prokhorovka also provide decisive and very clear evidence of an Achaemenid irradiation — all the more so as the Egyptian objects found in the tombs of the Caucasus also seem to have reached there from Iran rather than from the Greek colonies of the Black Sea, as some authors have suggested. There was undoubtedly an influx of trade stimulated by occasional exchanges connected with political-diplomatic contacts; the route on which this trade was expedited was partly the same as the itinerary indicated by Herodotus (IX, 16, 27), connecting Scythia and Kazakhstan via the Ural Mountains. The traffic along this route, which had been active since very early times, appears to have intensified during the Achaemenid period. According to some scholars, the westward extension of the area in which mirrors with animal-shaped handles are found was connected with the trade movements along this route. Taking into account the almost complete lack of Greek pre-Hellenistic objects in the region of the Ural Mountains and of the Volga and the comparative abundance of Iranian and Caucasian objects, it becomes clear that these areas were exposed to an Iranian cultural irradiation from the 7th to 4th century B.C. Curiously enough, this irradiation apparently became even more intense when the Achaemenid empire fell before the attacks of Alexander and exerted a considerable effect on the cultural evolution of the Sarmatian tribes. This extraordinary survival (also manifested in other regions, starting with India) may have been due to an exodus of craftsmen and Iranian fugitives that affected both the Ural area and the Altaic zone, where the Achaemenid irradiation was combined with a far from negligible persistence of Scythian elements. Trade exchanges between the empire and the semidesert Tarim basin region of Central Asia are attested only by a few textile fragments woven in the Iranian manner, but the contact was certainly more intense than the sparse documentation would indicate. Instead, the rich furnishings from the complex of underground chamber tombs at Pazyryk (southeastern end of the Altai massif) clearly prove a strong Iranian irradiation (FIG. 397; PLS. 23, 24, 188–190). Recent finds in Kazakhstan show that the trade route reaching this region from Scythia through the Ural Mountains was traversed by prevailingly Scythian movements and by other Iranian movements of the pre-Achaemenid and Achaemenid periods. In the eastern part of Kazakhstan numerous small reliefs in gold with animal figures reveal a Scytho-Siberian contact (the Siberian component inspired by Tagar), which is confirmed by more northern finds in which the Scythian or Scythian-oriented trend prevails. Elsewhere some rare but important finds evidence vague Iranian influences and other influences of true Achaemenid type, sometimes blended with a Scythian or Scytho-Sarmatian component (e.g., the Scytho-Iranian plates of the Ural Mountains).

Probably this diffusion did not occur through the Caucasus alone. The Caucasian Kangyu (Kankju) culture, which flourished on the lower Oxus River and along the west coast of the Aral Sea, must have acted as an intermediary for a considerable portion of the Iranian irradiation toward the Altai Mountains, both through occasional exchanges and through continuous or organized trade movements. The Oxus Treasure, with its many works of purest Achaemenid inspiration, proves the dependence of that area on the great tradition of Iranian imperial art. It is not difficult to identify in the Kangyu culture some ethnic, iconographic, and structural elements (e.g., fortified funerary constructions in a circular plan; VIII, FIG. 1003) of the Outer Iranian or, more generally, western type; these were, however, always reelaborated by the Iranian genius. The Achaemenid irradiation in its various forms was therefore quite vast and was to be essential to the stylistic formation of the period under discussion.

Concerning the Altaic production and Pazyryk kurgans of this period, consideration must be given to some of the problems relating to the ethnic composition of this area and of Central Asia as a whole. Beginning with the 10th century B.C., the Mongoloid elements of the Eurasian steppe, which were already partly mixed with the dolichocephalic masses of the Europoids, began a westward movement that lasted until after the 6th century of our era, though in various forms and with contradictory aims. This movement of Mongoloid groups appears to be the outcome of a westward dispersion that much later involved organized displacements of masses with a well-defined social and economic structure who were capable of creating vast empires, as in the case of the T'u-chüeh (Turks). Prior to the 3d century B.C. a considerable infiltration of Mongoloid elements occurred in eastern Turkmenistan, and probably spearhead

groups of Mongoloid elements even reached the Volga. At th beginning of the 3d century the Minusinsk basin, which had bee inhabited until then by an almost pure Europoid populatio received a Mongoloid thrust that profoundly changed its ethn composition. The dispersion of Mongoloid elements as far the northern slopes of the T'ien-shan Mountains and the Ball hash steppe, as well as westward, may be related to pressu by Paleo-Asiatic peoples from the north (from the large Siberia forest belt); it could also be connected with the groups calle Hsiung-nu by Chinese sources, probably composed of Paleo Asiatics mixed with some Mongoloid elements, or with that va group of peoples known as Huns. Undoubtedly the Minusins area and the entire Altai zone saw a high increase in populatio density at this time, and wider use was made of iron, which wa worked with a more advanced technique. This middle Iro Age culture became established very rapidly in the Altai, re vealing considerable Scythian contributions, perhaps via th cultures of the Sauromatians (proto-Sarmatians) settled in eas ern Russia and on the Ural River.

The monumental Pazyryk complex, composed of five larg stone-topped kurgans lined with timber, is undoubtedly th most important and well known in the Altai area. Next in im portance are the two kurgans of Bashadar and two others Tuektin. Because these kurgans were frozen many objec made of wood, leather, cloth, and metal pieces survived an escaped looting. The Pazyryk culture began at the end of th 5th century B.C. or, according to Rudenko (1948), at the beginnin of the 6th, though many other scholars date it between th 3d and the 1st century. The most important and strikin creation of the Altaic peoples, it also appears to have bee connected with many other trends already established on th Asian continent. According to Kiselev (1951), Pazyryk ab sorbed two different artistic tendencies, one of which derive from the last phase of the Tagar culture, on which there wer Scythian influences, and the other from the Central Asian noma culture of the Huns, the Śaka (Sacae), or the Massagetae. I the art of Pazyryk scholars are actually confronted by two clea components: the local elements, already pervaded by Scythia influences; and the style designated as "Hunnish," which wa responsible for similarities to the art documented in the tomb of Noin-ula (PL. 190), ascribed to the Hsiung-nu princes, whic transmitted Ordos elements and anticipated certain moti and types found in the barbarian art of the West, especially tha connected with Attila's Huns. Since, however, it is impossible t delineate accurately the ties that linked the various groups know as Huns, it is advisable to consider the name as purely conver tional and as being useful to indicate that some Pazyryk moti are also found among the populations that fall within the contre versial problem of the Huns. The Sarmatian or Śaka componen in the art of Pazyryk is revealed in the use of fretwork, pol chromy, and some typical animal shapes, but it appears hardl separable from iconographic and stylistic reminiscences ev denced by the Luristan production and by other Iranian trenc of the protohistoric period. The ribbon-shaped stylization Luristan, which influenced the threadlike and dismembere style of the Ch'ang-sha lacquers (VIII, PL. 413), exists in a intermediate phase at Pazyryk in the decoration of some leath and textile objects, which therefore document the west-to-ea path followed by this figural tendency (PL. 190). Achaemeni elements reached the Altai area both directly and indirectl through the Outer Iranian component, whether Śaka or Sarm tian. The correspondences to the Iranian trends that evolve prior to the formation of the empire have made more difficu accurate identification of the Achaemenid component. Th does not alter the fact that the new ethnic makeup of the Alta peoples resulted in a style remarkably similar to the Irania pre-Achaemenid and Achaemenid creations, thus justifyin the attribution of all the artistic activity of the period to a near homogeneous artistic trend (hence the appellation Hunne Sarmatian) in which the Iranian (or Outer Iranian) compone played a major role, as is the case with true Sarmatian work This conclusion does not imply a Pan-Iranian vision, which a concept is certainly subject to criticism, especially since th various components of pre-Achaemenid Iranian art, beginnir with the Luristan bronzes, reveal Central Asian and Sino-Siberian contributions as well as Chinese elements reinterpreted through Altaic or, more generally, Siberian intervention; this does not conceal, however, a process of stylistic unification in the art of Eurasia, in which heterogeneous components were combined with undeniable artistic genius. Thus, at Pazyryk there are to be found, together with a marked prevalence of profile representations (FIG. 397), frontal figures of outstanding quality in which Achaemenid elements are assimilated, despite the absolute rejection of the frontal view by Iranian imperial art. Perhaps the use of the frontal view can be traced back to the Chinese scheme of the *t'ao-t'ieh*; but certainly the Luristan frontal figures are much closer to the Pazyryk creations in time and style. Some representations of the griffin (FIG. 397) or fantastic eagles (PL. 192) can be connected with particular Iranian interpretations of the griffin (VIII, PLS. 125, 140, 142), but in other cases the griffin image becomes a decidedly local and isolated creation because of the prominence given to a carnivorous quadruped, possibly a panther.

especially of the planes and projecting of the muzzles. A metal plaque, among the very few that escaped the looters, appears to be Achaemenid or at least of clearly Iranian inspiration in the heraldic arrangement of the two animals framing it and in the treatment of their bodies. On openwork textiles and leather the Iranian motif of the cock or facing cocks was transformed into an exquisite decorative element reflecting the local style (FIG. 397; II, FIG. 31). The spirit that animated these figures is probably connected with hunting magic and the symbolic concepts of the nomad world. It is different from the spirit informing the Iranian creations, all of which are subject to symbolic and religious values of a more intellectual type and which, in any case, display accents alien to the nomad world.

There is no doubt that direct relations connected the Altai area and the Achaemenid empire. This is proved by a splendid Persian carpet (PL. 190), the earliest known, which was preserved by ice in Barrow V; by the small textile fragment decorated with a row of lions passant reproduced in keeping with a scheme that was very common in some of the jewelry of Achaemenid Iran;

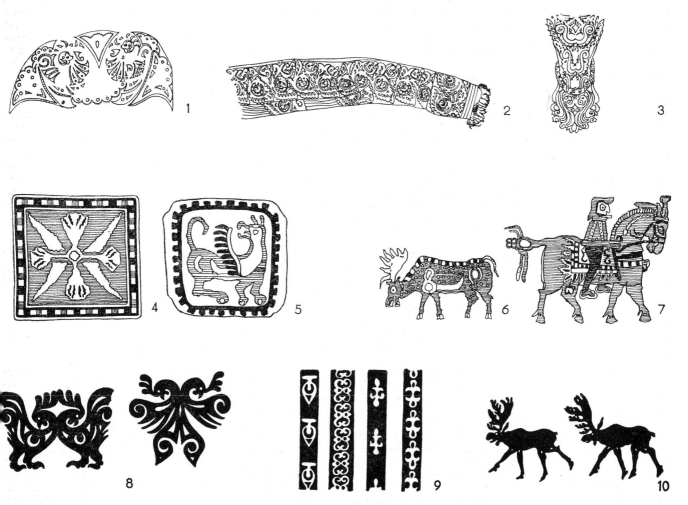

Pazyryk, decorative motifs in tomb furnishings of the kurgans. Embroidery on women's garments, Barrow II, 4th cent. B.C.: (1) Trimming on dress bodice; (2) sleeve from dress; (3) trimming on stocking. Details of carpets, Barrow V, 5th cent. B.C.: (4) Star-shaped motif; (5) griffin; (6) elk; (7) horseman. Openwork leather: (8) Stylized cocks, Barrow I, 5th cent. B.C.; (9) saddle straps: Barrow I, 5th cent. B.C.; (10) elks, Barrow II, 4th cent. B.C. (*from Talbot Rice, 1957*).

The unsolved problem of the eagle is greatly complicated by its diffusion as a symbol in all the territories of Central Asia, by its presence in the Luristan bronzes, too frequently overlooked, and by its unquestionable connection with the griffin (PL. 24). Achaemenid accents also appear, ranging from the treatment of the eye to the typical motifs known as "apple and pear" and "dot within parentheses" (PL. 190, top; FIG. 397), to a whole series of stylized plant motifs of Near Eastern origin, to the schematization of the reliefs of the muscular volumes and

and by other artifacts. Equally clear evidence of Achaemenid irradiation in the Altai area is provided by more or less obvious Greek touches (long denied by most scholars). Sometimes these works appear to be autonomous products of local art (e.g., small anthropomorphic masks used as harness decoration), but closer examination of them reveals very clear iconographic antecedents derived from the Greco-Hellenistic world. The local spirit was constantly superimposed on external components; it took satisfaction in ornamental stylization, in the sharp intersection of planes, in the elongation of bodies, and in the transformation of tails and horns into continuous motifs that were almost thick, fluid, uninterrupted lines. The art of Pazyryk reveals a highly developed sense of symmetry that by adapting particular forms of stylization made full use of them; through brilliant and autonomous inspiration there was an emphasis of the ornamental quality inherent in the animal heads and bodies, which often provides striking effects derived from the arrangement of shapes, qualities of the material used (particularly wood), and adaptation of the composition to the dimensions of the material. Wood production was almost always of high quality (PLS. 23, 24). Sculptors often deliberately left the work unfinished so that the sketchy quality of the whole set off the more expressive parts of the figure, which were always rendered with great precision. When the wood was incised, the figures were enriched by volutes and ornamental details and acquired an effect of weight and slowness of movement, closely relating them to the Ordos battle plaques.

A predominant role was played everywhere by the contorted S-shaped animal, which also appears as a frequent motif in tattoos, thus displaying its full ornamental value and its consonance with the taste of the Pazyryk peoples, who may have been the only Siberian group to practice tattooing. In this practice they were similar to some Scythian, Scythoid, or Sarmatian groups. Striking documentation of this custom appears on the body of a chieftain, preserved by ice, who died in battle and was buried in Barrow N2. The upper part of his body was decorated in patterns of nomad animal style. Wounded in the head, the chief was subsequently scalped, indicating that the Pazyryk people fought against other groups whose barbaric customs were not unlike those of the Scythians. The survivors replaced the chief's scalp with a tightly sewn fur skullcap.

While the presence of horse skeletons in the tombs recalls the Scythian custom of equine sacrifice, it also suggests a similar Chinese custom widespread in the Shang period and subsequently discarded. The use of reindeer masks on the horses seems to indicate that the Pazyryk people had recently discontinued raising reindeer in favor of horses. Nevertheless the reindeer continued to be the most sacred animal for the Pazyryk people, as was the stag for the Scythians; this is borne out by the use of the reindeer masks, which were intended to disguise the horse in afterlife, and by the frequent representations of reindeer (II, FIG. 31). It is therefore likely, though not established, that the Pazyryk people had a northern origin. That they were distinct from the Hsiung-nu is indicated by the fact that Chinese sources, which are usually well informed on the customs of the Hsiung-nu, their traditional enemies, make no mention of tattoos.

The available data concerning the ethnic compositions of the Pazyryk peoples are admittedly very contradictory. Even the cephalic indexes noted by Soviet scholars lend themselves only to hypothetical interpretations that do not clarify the evolution of this group or of the inhabitants of the Altai range. There is the possibility, clearly attested by certain aspects of the artistic production, that what occurred here was a slow unification of usage and customs, as well as interpenetration and superimposition factors. Even if this process did not simultaneously affect the whole mass of the nomads, it was apparently widespread, as is revealed by the numerous stylistic and iconographic contacts and by the extensive similarities and correspondences observed in implements and ornamental objects. Thus the term Hunno-Sarmatian, however inaccurate and perhaps erroneous it may be, finds some justification in that it clearly reflects the unifying process referred to above and brings out the similarities among the cultures of peoples belonging to different racial stocks. In addition to the Pazyryk group and the kurgans connected with it, there were in this area other variants of a deeply rooted cultural background; new nomad masses related directly or indirectly to Attila's Huns were later to draw on them. These variants are documented in various places in the kurgans of Shibe (PL. 24; some kurgans are dated fairly accurately owing to the presence of Chinese lacquers from the 1st cent. B.C.), in the Katanda finds (characterized by a huge quantity of buttons and by some survivals of the Scythian style), and in the highly stylized finds of Kara Kul (containing undeniably Sarmatian elements and objects).

A probable relationship is that of the Hsiung-nu with Tashtyk culture on the upper Yenisei River in the Minusinsk district which flourished between the 1st century B.C. and the 5th century of our era; some Soviet scholars, however, believe Tashtyk to have been produced by the ancestors of the Kirghiz (see I cols. 820–822). In any case, the period of Tashtyk ascendancy which was later than that of Pazyryk, greatly alters the problem. By this time the term Hsiung-nu in the Chinese sources had already broadened, since large portions of these groups had entered the sphere of Chinese culture and had been thoroughly assimilated by it. Tashtyk also displays considerable Chinese influences, and these form the basis of the attributed dates. It is characterized by an even wider use of iron and by a twofold burial system: large hypogean tombs belonging to the rulers and pit graves, probably those of the subject peoples. Tashtyk was obviously a composite culture, heir to the last phase of Tagar and therefore connected with all the other Altai cultures; from these, however, it differed considerably (PL. 25). Tashtyk is further characterized by the presence of death masks, sometimes made directly from the face of the corpse, thus proving the presence of Europoid groups (similar to the Afanasievo peoples) as well as other Mongoloid strains. This complicates the problem of ethnic composition, made all the more difficult since bodies were either cremated or interred, or in rare cases mummified. The tombs also contain anthropomorphous figurines sewn into Chinese silks, intended to "replace" the deceased in the period immediately following death; this was customary, even in recent times, among various Siberian tribes. The presence in the tombs of Chinese parasols coincided with similar finds in the Noin-ula tombs of Outer Mongolia, which are believed to be those of the princes of the Hsiung-nu. The parasols, which were Chinese symbols of power and nobility conferred upon chiefs of confederate or dependent tribes, are evidence of political relations between Tashtyk and China. Cultural relations between these two groups are amply documented by tomb furnishings composed of directly imported objects and other items (e.g., bows symbolically broken, arrows with gilt heads, bridle bits of small dimensions similar in shape to those used by Attila's Huns) which prove that Tashtyk material culture followed autonomous tendencies partly derived from the preceding Altaic tradition, although frequently employing Chinese craftsmen.

The tombs of Noin-ula are very similar to Altaic tombs and were probably constructed about the beginning of our era. (A Chinese lacquer cup from Noin-ula bears an inscription attributed to 2 B.C.) Local evidence of the animal style in Noin-ula is relatively scarce: all that remains is a magnificent woolen tapestry with leather appliqués (PL. 190) on which rested a large sarcophagus and a few metal ornaments, some in gold and silver; most of the objects, including all those of obvious commercial value, have disappeared because of looting. The surviving animal figures, especially those of the large tapestry, show extraordinary similarities to the production of Pazyryk. The autonomous objects recovered at Noin-ula reveal a marked stylistic similarity between the Altaic production and that of the Chinese-oriented areas, proving the strong persistence of a very individual stylistic sensibility and suggesting the considerable extent to which the movements of the Hsiung-nu contributed in the diffusion and unification of animal-style art.

This stylistic unification was also influenced by displacement of the Sarmatian and related masses, although it is difficult to reconstruct the complex process with accuracy. The burial grounds in the Talas River basin, west of Lake Issyk Kul, show beyond doubt that a material culture in many ways similar to those examined above extended toward the Oxus basin and Fergana, becoming part of an ancient and uninterrupted evolutionary context that already displayed elements favorable to the assimilation of the new tendencies. Statistics based on anthropometric measurements do not indicate ethnic modification that would suggest large-scale population movements, migratory or otherwise. In fact, the burial grounds of Kenkol and Kyz-art as well as the human remains brought to light in centers related to them (e.g., Arpa, Atbac, Zon-Alai, Maada, and Kyzyl Kum) display striking anthropometric similarities to the remains found in the tombs ascribed to the Wu-sun, who were peoples of Sarmatian type. Thus the hypothesis of a Hsiung-nu displacement from east to west, first conjectured on the basis of inaccurate diffusion percentages and cranial measurements, becomes untenable, even though the presence of these peoples in the neighboring region is documented by the unquestionable testimony of the Chinese sources.

On the other hand, cranial and anthropometric measurements taken by Ginzburg and Zhirov (1946) on remains from the large necropolis of Besh Shatir on the right bank of the Ili River in Sinkiang (flowing into Lake Balkhash) prove that the clearly Europoid basis of the local populations was mixed with the Mongolian type or a type with brachycephalic characteristics hypothetically attributed to contacts with the Hsiung-nu. However, nothing here reveals large-scale Hsiung-nu displacements or migratory movements, since the racial mixture appears to have resulted from proximity, which also implies cultural interpenetration and exchange.

Perhaps such exchanges gave rise to the so-called "Sarmatian style," which was not devoid of elements already established in the Pazyryk works. Trade exchanges and, above all, a correspondence in stylistic sensibility were certainly responsible for the presence of Sarmatian or Scytho-Sarmatian works in Siberia. Common to some Pazyryk works and many Sarmatian products is the use of simple geometric elements to obtain decorative or relief effects on the body of animal figures. The polychromy of the northern openwork cloths had some parallels with the incrustations of precious stones on Sarmatian jewelry. In both these trends the human figure appears frequently — in Pazyryk as an ornamental motif on masks and in religious and genre scenes, and in Sarmatian art combined with animal figures in hunting and perhaps epic scenes. Stylistic differences between the Altai and Sarmatian production are very slight in some cases. Occasionally they are caused by external factors such as the material used or the functional purpose of the work (e.g., openwork appliqués for clothes and belts that were designed to be set off by color contrasts).

Most of the metal production of Pazyryk has been lost, and there is no way of knowing the precise origin of some works, often of great worth, found in the Altai range and elsewhere in Siberia; they may be either local or imported. For this reason the Sarmatian style does not always lend itself readily to a precise definition with respect to the corresponding Altaic production. However, certain specific, recurrent elements in the Sarmatian style do constitute a criterion for differentiation: treatment of horns in the Hittite manner; a weaker feeling for line; the reduction or absence of ornamental plant motifs; the stylized realism of tree images; a revival of geometric motifs, particularly of interlace motifs in the minor works; and differences in proportion within a single composition.

The Scythian influence reached Pazyryk and other contemporaneous Altai centers through the mediation of the proto-Sarmatians, the so-called "Sauromatians" of classical nomenclature, which has been revived by Soviet scholars. However, the immense Central Asian territory inhabited by Śaka groups and Sarmatian peoples, such as the Wu-sun, was also long open to western influences, Scythian and Iranian in particular, and to other influences from the Altai, especially Tagar, which were connected in turn with Ordos trends.

It was this Central Asian region that witnessed the rise of characteristic attitudes and aspects of community life, of which the clearest expression was the armored horseman, the antithesis of the archer-horseman to whom the nomadic hordes owed their impact and their fame for being warlike. Besides, as has already been noted, Soviet research tends to emphasize the stock-raising nature of the peoples between the Oxus and Jaxartes basins, as well as some neighboring territories, who were highly mobile but already sedentarized to some extent. On the other hand, it is as yet impossible to affirm with any accuracy the real foundation of the attractive hypothesis formulated by some Soviet specialists of the Massagetae diffusion of true nomadism in the Asiatic steppe. It therefore remains doubtful whether this way of life, implying the establishment of the complex and highly specialized economy of the shepherd-stock raiser, was really due to Indo-European groups (more or less mixed with Europoid peoples) who would have transmitted it to other, Paleo-Asiatic and Mongoloid, groups who were irresistibly attracted by the obvious advantages of the new system as compared with hunting and harvesting, or whose type of agriculture had been arrested at a rudimentary stage because of climatic factors and in spite of remarkable technical means (e.g., the above-mentioned irrigation canals of the Altai area). It is certain, however, that the true nomadic economy was preceded by a long period of preparation and that it was the result of a combination of various factors and the contributions of different populations.

Although Chinese sources record that the way of life of a portion of the peoples (probably Indo-European) inhabiting the southern belt of Central Asia was similar to that of the Hsiung-nu (and therefore unquestionably nomadic), Soviet investigations reveal that the Sarmatian and Śaka populations of the western zone of the same area had an entirely different social structure and wholly distinct outlook on life. The difference in conception is clearly demonstrated not only by the prevalence of armored horseman but also by the fortified dwelling centers and the connection of the latter to commemorative and funerary traditions and concepts. This difference in concepts was probably due to the development of certain local situations and to Sarmatian and Śaka interpenetration within sedentary civilizations, that of Iran in particular.

In the extensive continuum of Indo-European peoples, who were Outer Iranian and therefore linguistically homogeneous, from the western borders of the Chinese area to the Scythian area (including the Tarim basin, the steppe regions south of the Aral Sea, and the Caspian and Ural steppelands), a great migration of peoples occurred between the 3d century B.C. and the 1st century of our era. Divided into three vast waves that spread over different but approximately adjoining territories, it was further broken up into successive thrusts. This was an upheaval that was to be decisive for the future history of Eurasia and included nomad and seminomad groups who participated for opposing reasons. The first group to make a start, for reasons that are not yet clear, was the Sarmatians. They began from the ancient settlements of the Sauromatians and the so-called "proto-Aorsi" (Soviet terminology) from the Volga and Ural steppelands in a series of approximately simultaneous thrusts heading southward beyond the Caucasus and westward. The thrust overran the Scythian territory and affected even the Bosporan Greco-Scythian kingdom of the Spartocids. During the Early Christian era it still showed considerable vitality in the movements of the Jazyges and the Roxolani. Dispersing the Scythian groups of southern Russia and confining the remainder within narrow territories, the Sarmatian wave put an end to Scythian culture, which had long become the product of interpenetration between nomads and highly civilized sedentary peoples such as the Greeks, and replaced it with Sarmatian culture. The Sarmatian thrust, like the others, crystallized into a political state, but it was of limited importance and duration. Instead, the Parthian thrust, coming down from the north, restored the entire Iranian territory to the domination of Iranian peoples and gave rise to the Arsacid kingdom that later played an important role in the history of Europe and Asia.

The third thrust, by a people whom the Chinese sources call Yüeh-chih, poses a series of almost insoluble problems. The movement was the product of profound changes in the Central Asian balance, which had resulted from clashes between the Hsiung-nu and China. Other groups were affected, including the Sai-wang (apparently a Śaka group) and the Wu-sun. The thrust of the Yüeh-chih was divided into consecutive phases and directly or indirectly determined the formation of the great Kushan empire (see KUSHAN ART) as well as a vast series of displacements.

The migrations revived an interest in the animal figure over a tremendous area, with emphasis on Central Asian stylization. The persistence of the animal-style trend also appears in contacts with Hellenistic currents. These contacts were established in almost all of the area affected by the migratory waves. Interest in the animal figure and the occasional survival of iconographic and stylistic tendencies associated with steppe art in jewelry, the minor arts, and certain decorative motifs appeared even when the prevailing artistic trends were those of the Irano-Hellenistic type or of a classical Western nature. The original importance of the Yüeh-chih is still not known, nor is the extent to which the representational trends of the Sarmatians coincided with ancient Yüeh-chih art, of which nothing remains. Some works discovered in the regions dominated by the Kushans are considered Sarmatian and seem to show a similarity to Kushan style. The Sarmatians, the Parthians, and the Kushans showed a strong preference for the frontal figure but did not discard the profile representation (VIII, PLS. 411, 412; XI, PLS. 56, 57). The Sarmatians and related groups used the frontal convention to full advantage, with a number of ingenious devices in specific details, in scenes depicting animal combat, reflecting a stylistic feeling that was practically nonexistent in Altai production. On an entirely different level, the highest expressions of Parthian and Kushan production reveal a persistent predilection for the frontal view, which in the light of the data available appears to have originated in Central Asia. The increased importance of the human figure in Sarmatian art indicates a remarkable change in the spirit underlying steppe production. This is connected with epic and legendary traditions, which had come to prevail over purely animal motifs to the point of replacing them.

The great migration that occurred from the 3d century B.C. to the 1st century of our era thus appears to be a movement of masses highly differentiated from a social and organizational point of view, combining sedentary and nomadic populations. Its repercussions were far-reaching. For instance, the fully armored horseman, whose diffusion was aided by the migration, influenced the art of war in many countries and affected the medieval conception of chivalry, although by way of Iran. Despite the variety of cultural and social levels of peoples participating in this series of invasions and migrations, the cultural effects were uniform; particular trends prevailed which modified other contributions (whatever the cultural level of their source) that did not coincide with the dominant tendencies. If there was any one area that assumed the role of cultural irradiation center, whether the irradiation followed the direction of migration or whether the center filtered influences that internally transformed the nomadic masses of the group, it could only have been the region south of the Aral Sea (with some extension west and perhaps east). This was a region of interpenetration, open to active Scythian and Iranian influences and all they imply in terms of foreign components, which explains why Sarmatian art — an art that was perhaps close to that of the Yüeh-chih and very similar to that of the Parthians — introduced a new artistic outlook, a different spatial sense, and compositional values and subject matter little known, if at all, to the Altaic trends. According to this interpretation, the Sarmatian trend must have been the artistic expression of a different concept of life — specifically that of Outer Iran — which was capable of creating many differences in the essentially homogeneous cultural world of the Asiatic steppe. The diverse historical destinies of the Altaic groups (inaccurately called "Huns") and the Indo-European groups of the south are obvious proof of this differentiation. Thus, taking into account certain cultural differences, the supposed "unity" of the Hunno-Sarmatian period can be refuted or viewed as purely conventional despite the many correspondences between the Altaic and southern Indo-European groups in style, material culture, funerary mores, and various customs that testify to exchanges and contacts. And, in fact, the denomination used by Soviet scholars tends to stress the unitary values and correspondences between the two groups, whereas the new researches being conducted by Soviet specialists, as well as stylistic analyses directed toward pointing out the full validity of the various trends, may well bring about a critical reevaluation of the current interpretation and chronological subdivision, which may even have to be abandoned. In fact, no consideration has been given to the predominance of the female members in the social organization of the southern

groups and the Kushans (matriarchy, gynecocracy), which i abundantly confirmed by some sources, such as the Syrian poe and Christian theologian Bardesanes (154–223?).

Further differences between the two groups include the use of coarse gray ceramic ware in an area spreading from Bactria to the Black Sea coast, while polished red-clay ceramic were commonly used by the Kushans and the Alans of the lowe Volga. There is still some doubt as to the origins of the long straight, double-edged swords, which Werner (1956) believe to be Hunnish but which may actually be Sarmatian according to recent data that conflict with material provided by the Odintsovka culture of the upper Ob River. A complete list of the differences and similarities is too lengthy to be dealt with in the scope of the present discussion, the primary objective o' which is to point out the major distinctions between the southern peoples, who for the most part remained alien to the nomac way of life, and the Paleo-Asiatic and Altaic masses, which were to determine several successive stages of the historical evolutior of Asia.

In conclusion, it seems possible to state that the Iraniar area proper and the region known as Outer Iran had considerable importance in the formation of the last phase of steppe art and its subsequent evolution. The former exerted its influence through irradiation, the latter by direct contribution partly derived from the Iranian diffusion. Exchanges and contacts similarities and correspondences among the various trends are part of a historical picture which scholars may never be able to analyze in detail; from the standpoint of artistic creation it is advisable to remember that the similarities and correspondences among the various trends are just as important as their differences and stylistic contrasts, however slight, and that either of these aspects taken singly affords only a partial and inaccurate vision of a major phenomenon that seems to join within a single evolutionary process peoples still obscured by the mists of protohistory and others on the verge of creating fully developed high civilizations.

CONCLUSION. The Hunnic masses of Attila's empire were partly responsible for the success enjoyed by the animal style in Europe, where it was promptly absorbed by the Scandinaviar and Germanic peoples and became widespread under various aspects throughout the early Middle Ages (see EUROPE, BARBARIAN). Many different factors contributed to the conferring on Attila's Huns a particular and far from negligible role in the diffusion of animal-style motifs; besides, the presence of the typical caldrons with mushroom-shaped handles in the Danube basin and the western diffusion of the asymmetrical bow clearly establish the connection of the Huns themselves with the Asiatic cultural world and their function as bearers of some aspects of its artistic production as well as particular features of its material culture. The origin of these caldrons is probably to be sought in the Altai area, from which they seem to have spread both eastward and westward over a huge area stretching from northern Mongolia to the region of Perm, to the Volga valley and to the Hungarian Corridor. Moreover, the terra-cotta imitations of these same caldrons brought to light at Dzhety-Asa show that the influence of Hunnic culture reached the lowe Jaxartes River. Although the Hunnic caldrons were created for practical purposes, they were obviously inspired by a particular stylistic feeling. The style had already reached the Wes through the Sarmatian groups, whose influence on the Goth and the western Alamanni was considerable.

The great pathways along which the animal style spread were the Danube route and the "northern way," already traveled by the Goths at the time of their displacement toward southern Russia. The style later proceeded westward, affecting the Franks and the Alamanni, and became even more widespread and important in connection with the movements of the Avar and the Lombards. In Scandinavia the whole of Viking art even more than the preceding Vendel style (V, PL. 94), felt the effect of the steppe creations. The animal figure became in practice an Asiatic component in the decoration and religiou symbolism of European pre-Romanesque art (q.v.). Possibly certain archaic Greek accents received from the ancient Orient

STEPPE CULTURES

nd the Iranian world (both Achaemenid and Parthian) retained ome vitality, and in different ways and for different reasons ormed actual stylistic sedimentations that reemerged with the lecline of classicism (W. Deonna, "Quelques conventions primitives de l'art grec," REG, XXIII, 105, 1910, pp. 329–401).

It is certain that an Irano-Sassanian irradiation affected a arge part of Europe, including its barbarian areas. However, or the most original component of decoration in the periods rior to the Romanesque revival, the whole of Europe was ndebted to steppe art, which brought with it elements capable f revitalizing the ancient stylistic sedimentations and contemoraneous influences. For example, in European art the symbolsm attributed to the larva of the cicada alluded to the Resurrecion, but it undoubtedly originated in China during the Shang eriod, where it stood for the undifferentiated and unorganized ootentiality of life. Similar meanings of genesis and derivation re also revealed by the composite animal masks, the stylized hapes of fish and horses, and the eagle heads adopted as ornanental and symbolic motifs in Merovingian and Scandinavian rt (q.v.), clearly showing their Scythian or Sarmatian descent. Even the contorted animal typical of Altaic art is found in Meroingian metalwork and in the sculptural decoration of the Abruzzi churches built before A.D. 1000. The snakelike monster terminatng in a head at each end and represented as a curled S was not xclusive to the Ordos but also appeared in Scythia, Koban, China, Gaul, Scandinavia, and Italy, and almost contemporaeously became a frequent motif in the pictorial compositions f Kizil (Qyzyl; see KUCHA) that had visions of hell as their ubject matter.

There is no doubt as to the importance acquired by the animal motif in Europe, where its success elevated it from a marginal and secondary element to an almost constant position of primary importance (see GOLD- AND SILVERWORK). Of course, the original symbolic meanings connected with hunting magic disappeared and were replaced by other meanings, which in only a few cases vaguely corresponded to the original. In fact, the animal figure in Europe often tended to acquire a monstrous aspect totally distinct from the characteristic realism of steppe art and its elegant stylizations. Such a tendency reflected a need of the medieval European world to express an imaginary realm created by new metaphysical values; this coincided with Iranian trends of the monstrous beast (e.g., Luristan, XIV, PL. 462; see MONSTROUS AND IMAGINARY SUBJECTS), which were pervaded with an eschatological symbolism entirely adaptable to Christian values. For similar reasons early medieval art absorbed other animal-art creations (e.g., the winged horse) unknown to the steppe repertory and probably traceable to contributions from Sassanian Iran (see SASSANIAN ART). In other cases the animal motif blended with the geometric interpretation of decorative themes and was gradually outweighed by the latter, which eventually assumed an absolute prevalence; this occurred very clearly in the Scandinavian world (cf. XIV, PL. 463). The ancient geometric premises of steppe art again assumed dominance, although in different forms conditioned by the new environment and the experience of the centuries.

In Asia, animal-style art slowly became exhausted, ultimately surviving only in the previously mentioned bronze objects the Tibetans call ton-t'i, or gnam-lcags. These were presumably introduced into Tibet by the Karluk Turks and remained in use as amulets until quite recently. Even these works, which are often more interesting for their religious and historical significance than for their artistic quality, reveal persistences of ancient symbolic compositions and stylistic accents dating back to very remote periods. It is possible to identify adaptations to local symbolism in the gnam-lcags, combined with slavish imitations of the Ordos creations and Sino-Siberian works, although in other works Chinese elements predominate. Perhaps the symbolism contained in these imitations also found in the Tibetan religious environment a corresponding local meaning. However, this is mainly a case of accidental adaptations and coincidence. All that can be said with certainty is that the repetition of form did not go far beyond the survival of a typical figure determined by external factors.

The survival of steppe art was even more prolonged in other motifs, reaching the present age through themes clearly derived from animal art in the handicrafts and popular decoration of Scandinavia (including embroidery). Such persistences testify to the validity of steppe art. The interest it arouses is justified by the specific problems connected with it, by the historical occurrences that accompanied its evolution, and by the numerous general problems connected with it, such as the relation between realism and social conditions, the origin of realism, and the relation between realism and stylization. Along with the art of barbarian Europe and Asia, steppe art represents the most profound and complete synthesis between East and West in the fields of esthetics and iconography, and sometimes even in symbolism.

BIBLIOG. A. Furtwängler, Goldfund von Vettersfelde, Berlin, 1883; W. Radloff, Aus Sibirien, Leipzig, 1884; N. Kondakov, J. Tolstoi, and S. Reinach, Antiquités de la Russie meridionale, Paris, 1891; E. H. Minns, Scythians and Greeks, Cambridge, 1913; B. V. Farmakovsky, Arkhaicheskii period v Rossii (The Archaic Period in Russia), Materialy po arkheologii Rossii, XXXIV, 1914, pp. 15–78; M. I. Rostovtsev, Une trouvaille de l'époque gréco-sarmate de Kertch au Louvre et au Musée de Saint-Germain, MPiot, XXVI, 1923, pp. 99–163; G. Borovka, Scythian Art, London, New York, 1928; J. G. Andersson, Der Weg über die Steppen, BMFEA, I, 1929, pp. 143–63; M. I. Rostovtsev, The Animal Style in South Russia and China, Princeton, 1929; M. I. Rostovtsev, Srednaia Aziia, Rossiia, Kitai i zverinyi stil' (Central Asia, Russia, China and the Animal Style), Prague, 1929; S. A. Teplukhov, Opyt klassifikatsii drevnikh metallicheskikh kul'tur minusinskogo kraia (A Tentative Classification of Ancient Metal Cultures in the Minusinsk Region), Materialy po etn., IV, 1929, pp. 41–58; J. Strzygowsky, Asiens bildende Kunst in Stichproben: ihr Wesen und ihre Entwicklung, Augsburg, 1930; M. I. Rostovtsev, Skythien und der Bosporus, I: Kritische Übersicht der schriftlichen und archäologischen Quellen, Berlin, 1931; W. P. Yetts, Chinese Contact with Luristan Bronzes, BM, LIX, 1931, pp. 76–81; J. G. Andersson, Hunting Magic in the Animal Style, BMFEA, IV, 1932, pp. 221–317; M. I. Rostovtsev, L'art gréco-sarmate et l'art chinois de l'époque des Han, Paris, 1932; C. Trever, Excavations in Northern Mongolia, Leningrad, 1932; J. G. Andersson, Selected Ordos Bronzes, BMFEA, V, 1933, pp. 143–54; A. Salmony, Sino-Siberian Art in the Collection of C. T. Loo, Paris, 1933; F. Hančar, Zum Problem des "kaukasischen" Tierstils, Wiener Beiträge zur Kunst- und Kulturgeschichte Asiens, IX, 1934, pp. 3–34; O. Janse, Le style du Houai et ses affinités, RAA, VIII, 1934, pp. 159–81; O. J. Maenchen-Helfen, Die Träger des Tierstils im Osten, Wiener Beiträge zur Kunst- und Kulturgeschichte Asiens, IX, 1934, pp. 61–68; B. Karlgren, Ordos and Huai, BMFEA, IX, 1937, pp. 97–112; A. N. Bernshtam, Iz istorii Gunnov I v. do n.e. (History of the Huns of the 1st Century A.D.), Sovestskoe Vostokvedenie, I, 1940, pp. 49–77; A. N. Bernshtam, Kenkol'skii mogil'nik (Sepulchers of Kenkol') (Arkheologicheskie ekspeditsii gosudarstvennogo Ermitazha, II), Leningrad, 1940; E. H. Minns, The Art of the Northern Nomads, Proc. Br. Acad., XXVIII, 1942, pp. 47–99; J. H. Gaul, Observations on the Bronze Age in the Yenisei Valley, Siberia, Peabody Mus. Pap., XX, 1943, pp. 149–86; V. V. Ginzburg, Materialy po antropologii Gunnov i Sakov (Materials for the Anthropology of the Huns and Saka), Sovetskaia etn., 4, 1946, pp. 207–10; G. F. Debets, Paleoantropologiia SSSR (Paleoanthropology of the USSR) (Trudy Inst. etn. SSSR, N.S., IV), Moscow, 1948; S. I. Rudenko, Vforoj Pazyrykskij kurgan, Leningrad, 1948 (Ger. trans., Der zweite Kurgan von Pazyryk, Berlin, 1951); C. Schaeffer, Stratigraphie comparée et chronologie de l'Asie occidentale (III°-II° millénaires), London, 1948; M. Bussagli, Bronze Objects Collected by Professor Tucci in Tibet, AAs, XII, 1949, pp. 331–47; T. G. Frisch, Scythian Art and Some Chinese Parallels, O. Art, II, 1949–50, pp. 6–24, 57–67; V. V. Ginzburg and E. V. Zhirov, Antropologicheskie materialy iz Kenkol' skogo katakombnogo mogil'nika v doline reki Talas Kirgizskoi SSSR (Anthropological Material from the Kenkol' Catacomb Sepulcher in the Talas Valley), Sbornik Muz. antr. i etn. Akad. Nauk SSSR, X, 1949, pp. 213–65; M. Loehr, Ordos Daggers and Knives: New Material, Classification and Chronology, AAs, XII, 1949, pp. 23–83, XIV, 1951, pp. 77–162; M. Loehr, Tools and Weapons from Anyang and Siberian Analogies, AJA, LIII, 1949, pp. 126–44; K. Jettmar, The Karasuk Culture and Its Southeastern Affinities, BMFEA, XXII, 1950, pp. 83–126; A. P. Okladnikov, Arkeologicheskie issledovaniia v nizoviakh reki Selengi (Archaeological Researches in the Lower Basin of the Selenga), KS, XXXV, 1950, pp. 85–90; G. Vernadsky, The Eurasian Nomads and Their Art in the History of Civilization, Saeculum, I, 1950, pp. 74–86; R. Heine-Geldern, Das Tocharer-Problem und die Pontische Wanderung, Saeculum II, 1951, pp. 225–55; S. V. Kiselev, Drevniaia istoriia iuzhnoi Sibiri (Ancient History of Southern Siberia), Moscow, Leningrad, 1951; G. Vernadsky, Die sarmatische Hintergrund der germanische Völkerwanderung, Saeculum, II, 1951, pp. 340–92; R. D. Barnett and W. Watson, Russian Excavations in Armenia, Iraq, XIV, 1952, pp. 132–47; N. Fettich, Die Chronologie der siberischen Goldfunde der Ermitage, Acta O. Acad. Sc. Hungaricae, II, 1952, pp. 251–68; M. P. Griaznov, Pamiatniki Karasukskogo etapa v tsentral'noi Kazakhstane (Monuments of the Karasuk Stage in Central Kazakhstan), Sovetskaia arkheol., XVI, 1952, pp. 129–62; F. Hančar, The Eurasia Animal Style and the Altai Complex, AAs, XV, 1952, pp. 171–94; N. T. Terenozhkin, Pamiatniki predskifskogo perioda na Ukraine (Monuments of the Pre-Scythian Period in the Ukraine), KS, XLVII, 1952, pp. 3–14; K. Jettmar, Hunnen und Hsiung-nu: Ein archäologisches Problem, Arch. für Völkerkunde, I–VII, 1953, pp. 166–80; K. Jettmar, Les plus anciennes civilizations d'eleveurs d'Asie Centrale, Cah. d'h. mondiale, I, 1954, pp. 760–83; K. V. Sal'nikov, Abachevskaia kul'tura na iuzhnom Urale (The Abachev Culture in the Southern Urals), Sovetskaia arkheol., XXI, 1954, pp. 52–94; T. Sulimirski, Scythian

Antiquities in Western Asia, AAs, XVII, 1954, pp. 282–318; R. Barthélemy-Vogels, Notes on Siberian Art of the Karasuk and Tagar Periods, O. Art, N.S., I, 1955, pp. 100–03; N. N. Bondar', Torgovye snosheniia Ol'bii s Skifiei v VI–V vv. do n.e. (Commercial Relations of Olbia with the Scythians in the 6th–5th Centuries B.C.), Sovetskaia arkheol., XXII, 1955, pp. 58–80; N. L. Chlenova, O kul'turakh bronzovoi epokhi lesostepnoi zony zapadnoi Sibiri (On the Bronze Age Civilization of the Forest Zone of Western Siberia), Sovetskaia arkheol., XXIII, 1955, pp. 38–57; A. J. Terenozhkin, K voprosu ob etnicheskoi prinadlezhnosti lesostepnykh plemen severnogo prichërnomor'ia v skifskoe vremia (The Problem of Ethnic Affinity of the Forest Zone's Tribes on the North Coast of the Black Sea in Scythian Times), Sovetskaia arkheol., XXIV, 1955, pp. 6–28; R. D. Barnett, The Treasure of Ziwiye, Iraq, XVII, 1956, pp. 111–16; N. L. Chlenova, Trudy kirgizskoi arkheologo-etnograficheskoi ekspeditsii (Acts of the Kirghiz Archaeologico-ethnographic Expedition), I, Moscow, 1956; M. Gimbutas, Borodino, Seima, and Their Contemporaries, ProcPrSoc, XXII, 1956, pp. 143–73; M. Loehr, Chinese Bronze Age Weapons, Ann Arbor, Mich., 1956; B. Svoboda and D. Končer, Neue Denkmäler antiker Toreutik (Mon. Archaeol., IV), Prague, 1956; J. Werner, Beiträge zur Archäologie des Attila Reiches (AbhAkMünchen, N.S., XXXVIII), Munich, 1956 (rev. by O. J. Maenchen-Helfen, Speculum, XXXIII, 1958, pp. 159–66); D. Carter, The Symbol of the Beast: The Animal Style Art of Eurasia, New York, 1957; B. Goldman, Luristan Pitchers, AAs, XX, 1957, pp. 251–64; L. Hambis, Représentations aquiliformes dans l'art de la steppe, CRAI, 1957, pp. 57–64; S. H. Hansford, The Seligmann Collection of Oriental Art, I: Chinese, Central Asian and Luristan Bronzes and Chinese Jades and Sculptures, London, 1957; C. Hopkins, Oriental Elements in the Hallstatt Culture, AJA, LXI, 1957, pp. 333–39; E. D. Phillips, New Light on the Ancient History of the Eurasian Steppe, AJA, LXI, 1957, pp. 269–80; T. Talbot Rice, The Scythians, London, 1957; S. van Rensselaer Cammann, The Animal Style Art of Eurasia, J. of Asian S., XVII, 1958, pp. 323–39; A. Godard, Les bronzes du Louristan, Orientalia Romana, I, 1958, pp. 51–72; M. P. Griaznov and A. Bulgakov, L'art ancien de l'Altai, Leningrad, 1958; K. Grønbech, The Steppe Region in World History, ActaO, XXIII, 1958–59, pp. 43–56, XXIV, 1959, pp. 15–28; B. M. Masson, Problema drevnei Bactrii i novii arkheologicheskii materialy (The Problem of Ancient Bactria and New Archaeological Material), SA, 1958, pp. 49–65; J. Moreau, Die Welt der Kelten, Stuttgart, 1958; J. J. Rudenko, The Mythological Eagle, the Gryphon, the Winged Lion and the Wolf in the Art of Northern Nomads, AAs, XXI, 1958–59, pp. 49–65; P. Amandry, Toreutique achémenide, Antike Kunst, II, 1959, pp. 38–56; G. Azarpay, Some Classical and Near Eastern Motifs in the Art of Pazyryk, AAs, XXII, 1959, pp. 313–39; L. Hambis, Le mythe de l'aigle et ses représentations artistiques en Eurasie septentrionale, Arts Asiatiques, VI, 1959, pp. 3–12; J. F. Haskins, Sarmatian Gold Collected by Peter the Great, VII: The Demidov Gift and Conclusions, AAs, XXII, 1959, pp. 64–78; O. J. Maenchen-Helfen, The Ethnic Name Hun, Studia Serica Bernhard Karlgren Dedicata, Copenhagen, 1959, pp. 223–38; A. Mongait, Archaeology in the USSR, Moscow, 1959; A. P. Okladnikov, Ancient Population of Siberia and Its Cultures, Cambridge, Mass., 1959; J. A. H. Potratz, Die Skythen und Vorderasien, Orientalia, N.S., XXVIII, 1959, pp. 57–73; H. Samadi, Les découvertes fortuites; I, Mazanderan et Gilan, II, Kalardash, III, Garmabac, IV, Amlash, Arts Asiatiques, VI, 1959, pp. 175–94; J. M. Zamotorin, Otnositel'naia khronologiia Pazyrykskikh kurganov (Relative Chronology of the Pazyryk Kurgans), SA, 1959, pp. 21–30; A. C. Margulan, Discovery of New Bronze Age Monuments in Central Kazakhstan, 25th Int. Cong. of Orientalists, III, Moscow, 1960, pp. 22–30; J. A. H. Potratz, Skythische Kunst, Orientalia, N.S., XXIX, 1960, pp. 46–62; S. P. Tolstov, Scythians of the Aral Sea Area and Khorezm, 25th Int. Cong. of Orientalists, III, Moscow, 1960, pp. 22–30; J. F. Haskins, Targhyn the Hero, Aq-Zhunus the Beautiful and Peter's Siberian Gold, Ars Orientalis, IV, 1961, pp. 153–69; S. P. Tolstov, Les Scythes de l'Aral et le Khorezm, Iranica Antiqua, I, 1961, pp. 42–92; R. D. Barnett, Median Art, Iranica Antiqua, II, 1962, pp. 77–95; VI Cong. int. des sc. préhistoriques et proto-historiques: Les rapports et les informations des archéologues de l'URSS, Moscow, 1962 (reports by N. L. Chlenova et al.); G. Frumlin, Archaeology in Soviet Central Asia, II: Kazakhstan, Central Asian Rev., XI, 1963, pp. 13–29. See also the bibliogs. for: ASIA, CENTRAL; ASIATIC PROTOHISTORY; GRECO-BOSPORAN AND SCYTHIAN ART; ORDOS.

Mario BUSSAGLI

Illustrations: PLS. 181–192; 4 figs. in text.

STIJL, DE. See EUROPEAN MODERN MOVEMENTS; NON-OBJECTIVE ART.

STILL LIFE. The type of painting that depicts inanimate objects as its sole theme, in harmony with a particular bent of expressive taste, belongs to a well-defined phase of modern European art, that is, essentially to the baroque. Yet it forms part of a much wider trend — common to other epochs and cultures, even though attaining some of its most refined and sensitive expressions in the modern Western world — toward motifs of artistic inspiration unconnected to religious or historico-political necessity but drawn from the visible reality of the moment (see GENRE AND SECULAR SUBJECTS; LANDSCAPE IN ART). In this way, still life takes on, within the limits of its special iconographic range, a somehow exemplary character — both through the polemic charge that it carries in its relation t courtly painting and through the scope that it offers to th artistic imagination of certain artists.

SUMMARY. Terminology (col. 408). Elements of still life i ancient painting (col. 408). Origins of still life as an independen genre in the West: late Gothic to early 17th century (col. 410). Sti life as an independent genre from the 17th to the 19th century (co 415): Rubens and Snyders. Fruit and flower painting. The 17th centur in the Netherlands. The 17th century in Flanders and France. Th 17th century in Spain. Caravaggesque still life. The Lombard The Neapolitans. Late baroque to the 19th century. Aspects of Fa Eastern art comparable with Western still life (col. 430).

TERMINOLOGY. The Italian locution "natura morta," un known in the very early literature, was, as the excellent stud by Sulzberger (1945) made clear, coined in the middle of th 18th century with a disparaging implication, almost as if were being opposed to the "natura vivente" of the courtl genres of paintings, which were the only ones recognized b the academic tradition. In the early historiography of art beginning with Vasari, there is mention of "natural objects animals, cloth, instruments, vases, landscapes, apartment houses and greenery" and, as Vorenkamp (1934) has documented similar references (to pictures of fruit, flowers, luncheons banquets, etc.) appear to have been employed in Dutch inventories before 1650, when the expression "vie coye" wa used for the first time. In the ateliers of the Low Countrie this term was soon translated into "stilleven," which correspond to the term "stillstehende Sachen" that Joachim von Sandrar applied to the works of his student Sebastian Stosskopf (1597–1657), and in Germany and in England into "Stilleben" an "still life," respectively. In Italy, as Longhi points out, thes expressions had a counterpart in the locution "soggetti e og getti di ferma" used in 17th-century criticism.

Thus, the expression "natura morta" appears to be distortion of the older designation, which stressed rather th immobility and quietness of the subject or, perhaps better its motionless and silent life. But the variations that hav been contrived to correct the distortion have not been successful and the term, like so many others coined with similar intent has now become firmly established in the literature and ha shed the derogatory connotation that it had in the beginning The English term "still life" requires no apologia.

Stefano BOTTARI

ELEMENTS OF STILL LIFE IN ANCIENT PAINTING. The concep of "still life" can obviously not be legitimately dated back t the classical world except in terms of similarity of impulse even though the influence that ancient painting had on th painting of the Renaissance (q.v.) may somehow account fo the occasional references to antique motifs in the actua beginnings of this type of art (see below, Fruit and flowe painting).

The words "ropography" and "rhyparography," sometime equated with "still life," have (in accordance with their deriva tion from the Greek words rhopographos and rhyparographos different connotations, signifying, respectively, the painting o petty things and the painting of garbage or litter; thus th former pertains more to genre painting and the latter to tromp l'oeil, in which plants, fruit, and animals killed in hunting o fishing have no place (PLS. 193–195). However, the mor precise designation for this kind of representation, asarotun (Gr., asarotos oikos, "unswept house"), and the specific attribu tion of it to the mosaic artist Sosos, active in Pergamon in th 3d–2d century B.C. (PL. 195; see MOSAICS), makes it clear tha first for the Greeks and then for the Romans these subject represented merely the whim of the commissioners of th works, realized through the technical virtuosity of the artists and are not classifiable in a definite genre of art. Proof of al this is the inclusion in some critical quarters in this categor of the mosaic artist Hephaistion because his signature appeare on a scroll representing a crumpled piece of paper, which i clearly a trompe l'oeil. It should be noted that this artis o was active in Pergamon itself in the first part of the 2d century B.C. (see HELLENISTIC ART); in other words, there can e defined within the area of the artistic culture of Pergamon certain taste for what is nowadays called by some illusionism nd by others "painted reality."

To some the term *xenion* has seemed to relate more closely) still-life painting because Vitruvius (VI, vii, 30) states that e Greeks gave this name to those gifts of food which it was ustomary for gentlefolk to present to their guests. Probably e subjects of certain pictures were designated in this manner; ut even in this case a term of iconographic interpretation iould not be confused with a genre of painting.

This is not to deny the existence of still-life painting in a sense milar to that which art criticism applies to a whole genre of iodern painting, even though we cannot include certain ianifestations that only by an overbold transposition of ideas in be, or ever have been, called "still life." Thus the rep- sentations of fruit, foliage, and animals placed near the ead in Eastern reliefs and paintings cannot be defined as ill lifes, nor can the offerings to the dead represented on reek vases. These form an integral part of figural contexts, nd it would be arbitrary to consider them apart as constituting genre by themselves. A certain value of thematic independence iight be attributed to those plant and animal elements or roups of elements (and small sketches of implements, vases, iasks, etc.) which so often appear in the painted decorations f Hellenistic and Roman houses and tombs and sometimes so in the reliefs. But these tend to serve a purely decorative inction, like that of architectural elements, when they are ot grouped with more precise intention as the subject of a picture."

Though the still life of antiquity may appear to extend ver a fairly wide geographical area and a number of centuries, :tually it belongs to a limited phase of culture — that is, to lellenistic art, and in particular to the centers of Pergamon, lexandria, and Rome. In respect to Rome, it should be iade clear, however, that still life appeared there in the age - from the second half of the 2d century B.C. to the days of ie Antonines — when that city came on the scene in the orld of art as the last center promulgating Hellenistic culture, hich it did with varying intensity but without any substantial reak in cultural continuity. The limited number of pictures iat can be included in the category of still life comes, in fact, most exclusively from Rome, Ostia, Pompeii, and Hercula- eum. Because they belong to the artistic phase that, especially : the beginning, proclaims an indisputable derivation from the lellenistic world, the first still lifes are customarily attributed » that world, being centered in Pergamon and Alexandria, ›r the former seems to have given rise to illusionist painting id the latter is generally credited with a special taste for the etailed and the picturesque; but this is all a matter of conjecture.

The documented products are still, practically speaking, iose of the Roman world, from the mosaic of the House of ie Faun representing a cat and birds (VII, PL. 191) dating om the 2d century B.C. — if this can be called a still life — » the mosaic with a basket of flowers from the Villa of the uintilii on the Appian Way (Vat. Mus.), which is of the ntonine age (if its exuberant restoration does not require to be considered a 19th-century work). In this manner iere is formed a chronological curve covering a definite aspect f the Roman artistic culture which is commonly known as Ieo-Attic (see NEO-ATTIC STYLES): in effect, a cold, almost :holastic reconstruction of phases of Greek art, especially ttic, but also of the Hellenistic art of Asia Minor and Alex- ldria, drawing from them schemes and motifs that are repeated most mechanically both in the whole and in details.

But that which in the Greek world makes its appeal through ie particular — the poetry of detail, an almost Theocritean :valuation of the confrontation of nature and man — becomes i the Roman world (perhaps through the deterioration of the ›ncept of mimesis as imitation of nature) merely an impulse ›ward the display of technical knowledge, which takes shape ot as artistry but as an exaggerated virtuosity of artistic expertise.

The small pictures of glass cups and fruit of the triclinium

of the House of Livia on the Palatine, the *xenion* with votive offerings from Herculaneum (Naples, Mus. Naz.), mosaics with fish from Pompeii (VII, PL. 179), and the cock beside the fruit basket in Naples (VII, PL. 190) — to cite but a scant sampling of a rather monotonous though numerically abundant repertory — form part of this pictorial phase, which clearly demonstrates its narrow artistic boundaries.

In the age of the Severans this taste disappeared, only to reappear later — in the 4th century — and to continue in the 5th and also the 6th century in the squares of mosaic floors, where in the individual emblemata appear trays of fruit (the plump ripe figs at Piazza Armerina) and baskets with plants and fruit (certain floors in Aquileia). Even in these cases, however, the designation "still life" gives proof of the great elasticity of the term.

It should be obvious that the position of secondary impor- tance that the above-mentioned pictures held almost constantly in the repertory of wall decorations of the Hellenistic-Roman world and the repetition of the motifs in squares of the floors make implausible the religiosymbolic interpretation of these still lifes that is sometimes suggested.

Michelangelo CAGIANO DE AZEVEDO

ORIGINS OF STILL LIFE AS AN INDEPENDENT GENRE IN THE WEST: LATE GOTHIC TO EARLY 17TH CENTURY. During the 14th century, elements from real life and from nature began to appear regularly in painting. In fact it was in the late medieval period that the tendency toward visualization became pre- dominant, and it was in the late Gothic that the interest in descriptive detail arose. This interest, which in Italy, with rare exceptions, was to remain confined within schemes of formal abstractions, as will be seen later, was in contrast given free play in Franco-Flemish art and in the art of neighboring areas (Burgundy, Provence, Spain) and dependencies (Naples and Sicily). Thus, after the exceptional precedents of the miniatures of the late 14th and the early 15th century — witness the sharpness of detail in *Les Très Riches Heures du Duc de Berry* (IV, PL. 26; VI, PL. 65; IX, PLS. 137–140) — it is principally the great Flemish painting of the 15th century that offers penetrating glimpses of still life in pictures of religious subjects (see FLEMISH AND DUTCH ART). The inclusion here of Provençal painting is supported, for example, by the splendid shelf full of objects in the Jeremiah panel by the Master of the Annunciation of Aix (PL. 196), and what was said above about the dependencies is confirmed by the equally splendid achieve- ment of Colantonio in Naples (PL. 196).

Italy never attained to such descriptive verve, at least not in the course of the 15th century. It is true, of course, that as early as the first decade of the 14th century, in Padua, Giotto (q.v.) painted some elements that could be called still life, but it is likewise true that they keep pace with the extremely measured cadence of his style and always appear in a subordinate position. When they achieve autonomy, as they do for instance in the "Secret Chapels" on the triumphal arch of the Scrovegni Chapel, they seem to be linked, in the record of the classical tradition, to the exigencies of illusionistic perspective, the same requirements as are presented by a Taddeo Gaddi, a Matteo Giovannetti da Viterbo, and by others, down to Masolino himself. The beginnings of still-life painting in Italy maintained this twofold attachment to realism and to the perspective- illusionist requirement even in the painting of the Quattrocento, when it was chiefly in intarsia that these found application. It is indeed rather significant that the quest for a formula of an ideal character — that is, rigorously geometric and per- spective — caused the masters of inlay (q.v.) to represent objects rather than flowers and fruit (PL. 196). In short, the early Renaissance proper was profoundly averse to the episodic, the *tranche de vie*, and placed the occasional example of still-life painting on the level of other exercises in perspective, such as imaginary city views (I, PL. 308) and actual studies in pure geometric form. Indeed it took the pressure of the Flemish taste to repopulate with naturalistic elements the increasingly deserted scene of Tuscan Renaissance painting after the tendency to abstraction had progressed to its absolute limit in the hands of painters from Paolo Uccello to Piero della Francesca (qq.v.).

In this way the vases of flowers in the Portinari triptych (V, PL. 281; XIV, PL. 468) by Hugo van der Goes (q.v.), brought to Florence soon after 1475, stand as the signpost of a new inclination toward episodic realism, and the effects of this are already visible in the altarpiece by Luca Signorelli (q.v.) in Perugia, as well as in all the works of Domenico Ghirlandajo (q.v.), the master who most frankly undertook the task of reintroducing the daily chronicle into the historical picture.

It was not by mere chance that all the centers and artists in 15th-century Italy who showed themselves receptive to elements of still life were in touch with Flanders, artistically, commercially, or politically: from the Naples of Colantonio, to the Sicily of Antonello da Messina (q.v.), the Venice of Vittore Carpaccio (q.v.). And it was really Venice that at the beginning of the 16th century produced the first true Italian still life in the work of Jacopo de' Barbari (PL. 199), whose ties with the northern, especially the Germanic, world can hardly be overestimated. In the course of the 16th century the gradual ascendancy of the Humanistic position in Italian painting opened the way to a richer proliferation of naturalistic elements in paintings of subjects both sacred and profane. It must, however, be emphasized that the various still-life elements, though still subordinate in function, often catered to the taste for a vision of nature that was in a certain sense abstract or, to use another term, nonrealistic. This drift is evident, for instance, in the famous *St. Cecilia* of Raphael in the Pinacoteca, Bologna (XII, PL. 367), in which the group of musical instruments (their execution, as Vasari records, was delegated by the master to Giovanni da Udine) stands almost by itself, like a painting within a larger painting. The same effect was to be created later, perhaps after Raphael's example, by Prospero Fontana (1512–97) in his large *Deposition* in the same gallery.

Somewhat different is the case of the great Lombard painters, in whom the interest in everyday reality is expressed with more immediacy, in accents in a way more congenial to the creations of the masters of northern Europe, though without their sharp and slightly pedantic minutiae. Thus in the works of Moretto da Brescia (q.v.) and Il Romanino (XII, PL. 71), to cite only the most famous, the still-life elements are perfectly balanced with the other elements of the compositions, for the mood of placid naturalism governed artistic invention, laying the foundations for a tradition that was not to be interrupted for almost two centuries. After the first two decades of the Cinquecento, with the new tendencies of mannerism (q.v.), naturalistic elements became predominant more or less everywhere in Italian painting. Introducing realistic details into the, by and large, nonrealistic conceptions, almost as if to compensate for the capriciousness of the invention and the intensity of the stylization, was one of the characteristic aspects of mannerism and one that almost engendered a situation similar to that of the late Gothic, from which the still-life impulse had emerged.

However, the real history of still-life painting as an independent genre does not correspond exactly with this trail of naturalistic elements, of occasional digressions and annotations. There is reason to suppose that paintings identical in subject with what is called "still life" originated in the 15th century with definite and independent aims. On the back of a portrait by Memling in Lugano there is a representation of a vase of flowers that is undoubtedly one of the earliest still lifes known (PL. 197). The custom of decorating the reverse of portraits was widespread in the 15th century, and very often it was a heraldic or symbolic element that was represented. Thus it is probable that the flowers painted by Memling had some particular significance relating to the personage represented (see SYMBOLISM AND ALLEGORY). In any case, this is in keeping with the earliest and most widespread interpolations of still life, namely, the vases with lilies in depictions of the Annunciation, which were clearly symbolic of the purity of the Virgin.

In the course of the 16th century, and even more in the following century, "still life" assumed a dominant symbolic

and allegorical significance — the theme "Vanitas vanitatum. Sometimes this meaning is manifest, as when a luxurian composition of flowers or of fruit is set alongside a skull, t represent the contrast between life and death and the triump of the latter; sometimes, more subtly, a blemish on the golde skin of a fruit, a petal falling from a rose, a mouse gnawin a hazelnut, a candle being consumed by its flame, stands a a symbol of the transience of physical beauty and the corrodir action of time upon it.

In the course of the 17th century, the "vanitas," adoptin the fixed iconography of a skull resting on a book betwee an hourglass and a candle, sometimes with a withering flowe in the foreground (PL. 206), became a type in its own righ intended for the cells of monks or the chambers of the faithfu Through the motif of the "vanitas," the still life found substantive justification in the rigorous atmosphere of the a of the Counter Reformation, and this is undoubtedly one of the factors that contributed to its emergence and to its existenc as an independent genre.

Another factor must have been a desire on the part of a patrons with scientific interests to have exact reproductions of flora, fauna, and minerals: this would accord with the reviv of the studies of nature that characterized the end of the 16t century. Predominating in this group were pictures of flower and we have precise testimony — for example, in the wor of Jan Brueghel the Elder ("Velvet" Brueghel; 1568–1625) that artists took considerable trouble to obtain the variou plants requested by the commissioners of the paintings an then reproduced them with absolute fidelity. This explain the often pedantically detailed treatment and the extremel meticulous execution of these scientific still lifes.

However, it seems indisputable that there must also hav been another root, entirely secular, of still life. This is a matte of the gradual multiplication of those naturalistic and descriptiv elements that appeared in religious painting from the late Gothi on, and it is logical that such a development should hav occurred in the northern countries, where this tendency ha always been more marked.

In Flanders, as early as the period 1550–75, Pieter Aertse (q.v.) began to produce pictures in which the religious subjec appears in the background, while the entire foreground i conspicuously occupied by such objects as were to becom the most usual motifs of still life (V, PL. 294). In Aertsen' *Christ in the House of Mary and Martha* (PL. 198), which i signed and dated 1553, and in his *Christ and the Adultere* in Frankfurt am Main (Städelches Kunstinst.), signed an dated 1559, the religious scenes can almost be said to disappea behind the great displays of objects that stand out in the fore ground. Aertsen's nephew Joachim Beuckelaer (ca. 1530–c 1574) followed in his footsteps, as is demonstrated by Beucke laer's various versions of *Christ in the House of Mary and Marth* dated 1565 and 1566 (e.g., Brussels, Mus. Royaux B.A., an Amsterdam, Rijksmus.). This lack of interest in the religiou scenes and the keen interest shown, on the other hand, i "still lifes" is emphasized by the great number of fowl, fish fruit, and vegetable markets that form the fundamental theme of the works of the two masters. It must also have been i the circle of Pieter Aertsen that the type of painting showin a spread table, which was later to have wide circulation through out Europe, took shape.

Alongside of, or parallel to, this type of still life ther developed in this period another, which either sprang fro the allegorical representation of the seasons or, more simpl set down typical still-life elements within a landscape. A example of the latter case is supplied by Abraham Bloemae (1564–1651), author of a landscape (Amsterdam, Rijksmus. in which the foreground is made up, however, of a super and luxuriant display of vegetables. For the allegorical rep resentation of the seasons may be cited the Sienese painte Astolfo Petrazzi (1579–1665), whose painting *Winter*, a norther landscape (private coll.), has been published by Del Brav (1961), together with two of the same artist's striking sti lifes in Siena (Coll. Chigi-Saracini).

But more can be gained from a consideration of the sprea

in Italy of the more typical formula of the Aertsenian still life. Everything points to the possibility of finding the missing link in the period of Vincenzo Campi (1536–91), who was active mainly in his native town of Cremona. The connection between the works of the Dutch master and the paintings of Campi — especially the five canvases in the Castle of Kirchheim representing poultry, fruit, and fish venders (one painting is dated 1578) and the versions of some of them in the Brera, in Milan (PL. 198; VI, PL. 69) — is apparent and is generally recognized by scholars. Probably Campi saw the works of Aertsen or of Beuckelaer in his native town, from which at that time the merchant and banker Giancarlo Affaitati had established a close and complex network of contacts with the Netherlands. In any case, the works of Vincenzo Campi met with great favor; his brother Antonio points out that his still lifes were highly esteemed not only in Milan but also in "numberless other places in Italy and even in Spain, where many have been sent" — and where, it may be added, Vincenzo himself went in 1584. Evidence of his success is that in Bolognese circles he was promptly imitated by Bartolomeo Passarotti (1529–92; IX, PL. 297), as is documented by Passarotti's two paintings, one with a display of meat and one with a display of fish, both with figures, in Rome (Gall. Naz.), and by his much more significant *Poulterers* in Florence (Coll. R. Longhi). The Campi influence continued to be evident in the work of Carlo Antonio Procaccini (ca. 1555–1605), who, according to Malvasia, was highly regarded in Milan as a painter of "frutta e fiori" (a general designation applied to still lifes) — a fact that, provided the attribution is reliable, is confirmed by the *Cellier d'une grande maison* in Besançon (Mus. B.A.) and even (by way of Passarotti) by the work of Annibale Carracci, whose canvas *The Butcher's Shop* (III, PL. 83) is an important example. Furthermore, one must take into account the repercussions that were felt in the Florentine ambience by Empoli (Jacopo Chimenti; 1551–1640) and in the Spanish ambience by Alejandro de Loarte, by whom there is a signed still life (*bodegón*) dated 1626, and even before that (by way of Passarotti) in the works of Juan Esteban, who left a thoroughly Passarottian still life signed and dated 1606. The two last-mentioned artists provided the incentive, even if merely on the thematic level, for the much more directly observed and compelling works of Velázquez (q.v.), as is evidenced by that master's early work *The Servant*, in Chicago (VI, PL. 71), and also by his *Christ in the House of Martha* in London (Nat. Gall.), which is cited here because in its foreground there are two women busy in the kitchen, while the religious scene proper, not without precedent in earlier examples, is confined, like a smaller picture within a larger one, to a corner of the background.

In the Bolognese ambience, the epilogue to this type — and at the same time the most spirited statement of it — was the work of Paolo Antonio Barbieri (1603–49). In this genre Barbieri's most typical works are the *Spice Shop* (1637) in Spoleto (Mus. Civ.) and the *Poultry Vender* in Pesaro (Mus. Civ.), in which the remote northern inspiration is annulled by an immediate and compelling brushwork that shows greater concern with the subtle play of values — painting which in these aspects recalls the works of Velázquez himself. The Bolognese epilogue is not to be regarded as the end of the ramifications of this kind of painting, for at the height of the baroque it reappears, conjured up once more by Luca Giordano (1632–1705) in his painting *The Cook* (Rome, Gall. Doria Pamphili).

All the works cited thus far as links in the chain of modern Western still-life painting are characterized by the scheme of composition termed "archaic" (with objects aligned separately, in diffused lighting, and painted in precise detail), which has connections, as suggested above, with schemes of mannerist origin. Mannerist beginnings figure also in the compositions, so widespread at the beginning of the 17th century, with large tables, lengthened in perspective, the better to display the rows of dishes upon them bearing various culinary specialties, fruit, and flowers; significant examples are presented by the works of Osias Beert (d. 1625), Clara Peeters (active 1611–48), and, especially, Jan van Kessel the Elder (1626–79), who,

after the time of Rubens, remained a faithful follower of "Velvet" Brueghel (typical Van Kessel works are the two *Fruit and Flowers* in the Gall. Doria Pamphili, Rome). In Italy this kind of painting had a belated and curious application in the works of the "fiorante" Bartolommeo Bimbi (1648–ca. 1725), as is documented by a signed canvas of 1699, with a "sampling of pears" in a baroque setting, in storage in the Uffizi. But even earlier, in a by now re-formed state — that is, reduced to a few, essential elements — it had found expression in the works of Fede Galizia (1578?–ca. 1630), who in this vein had achieved similar, though more controlled effects than those of Jacob van Hulsdonck (1582–1647). The still life of the Counter Reformation, in fact, effected a reshaping of the more archaic still life.

The archaic type of still life with allegorical or scientific import and the type derived from Aertsen, with religious subject relegated to the background or frankly depicting fruit or fish venders or butchers' shops, are the earliest instances of the genre. But these were soon followed by other types, which, blending and merging, gave rise to the prolific production of the 17th and 18th centuries.

To begin with, the record must mention the birth of the so-called "Caravaggesque" still life, the prototypes of which, if not by Caravaggio (q.v.) himself — he may never have painted an independent still life (his early pictures with one figure and baskets of fruit recall the compositions of Aertsen but in their simplicity achieved a much higher artistic value) — certainly come from Caravaggio's immediate circle in Rome, particularly Tommaso Salini (PL. 200), and date from not later than the second decade of the 17th century. Thus Rome became as important a center as Flanders and Spain. In Rome the Lombard-Bolognese type of still life, derived from Pieter Aertsen and imported by such followers of the Carraccis (q.v.) as Pietro Paolo Bonzi, known as Il Gobbo dei Carracci (d. between 1633 and 1644), encountered and blended with the Caravaggesque type in the orbit of the studio, or "academy," of Giovanni Battista Crescenzi (ca. 1577–1660), later being diffused and subsequently transformed and developed by contact with local taste in Spain and Naples.

Indeed it was probably in Rome that still life was finally liberated from allegorical and scientific content — which had also been its justification. In the atmosphere of skepticism toward the Church and toward traditional culture, in which, like the works of the Bamboccianti (q.v.) and the "Lutheran" masters of Utrecht, the religious or allegorical picture with naturalistic figures of Caravaggesque invention was transformed into the genre scene, the still life also became autonomous — that is, valid in and for itself. This liberation from subject matter — which produced the "battles without history" of Pieter van Laer (Il Bamboccio; 1592–1642) and Michelangelo Cerquozzi (1602–60; VII, PL. 276), the concerts without allegory of Bartolomeo Manfredi (II, PL. 179) and Valentin de Boulogne (1594–1632; II, PL. 179; V, PL. 399), and the pure still lifes of Salini and Cerquozzi — is of the greatest interest in the history and evolution of the genre.

Thus, after the first two decades of the century, the production of still lifes freely multiplied, from Rome to Naples, to Spain, and to Northern Europe. In Flanders, during the third and fourth decades of the century, both the still life of fruit and flowers and the still life after the manner of Aertsen became radically renovated in the dynamic and baroque direction of the art of Rubens, and the great exuberant compositions of Frans Snyders (1579–1657) and of Jan Fyt (1611–61) came into being.

From this point on, the succession of different types of still life and their intricate interrelation within the genre make a unitary treatment inadvisable. For purposes of exposition the discussion must be divided into several distinct sections, of necessity artificially structured. It suffices to keep in mind that a certain amount of crossing over of elements from one type of still life to another took place throughout and that the sequence of the treatment is not necessarily chronological. For instance, Caravaggesque still life, which will be discussed after the Rubensian, in point of fact preceded it in time.

STILL LIFE AS AN INDEPENDENT GENRE FROM THE 17TH TO THE 19TH CENTURY. *Rubens and Snyders.* The mannerist compositional scheme appears to have been suddenly interrupted in Flanders; the painters of Antwerp having been dispersed as a result of the religious struggles, the works of Peter Paul Rubens (q.v.), who was one of the creators, if not the sole creator, of the baroque in Europe, immediately came to the fore. The rather calculated and somewhat shadowy style that had prevailed was succeeded by the warmth, the impetuousness, the burst of light and color of baroque painting and its total commitment to bold and resounding loftiness and grandeur: in short, the silence of the old compositions yielded to the thundering clamor of the new.

The start is to be found in works of Rubens himself, although it is not certain whether the great master ever painted still lifes proper. The attribution to him of the Louvre painting *Philopoemen Recognized by an Old Woman*, a larger version of which is in Nantes (Mus. B.A.), is not definitive, and the painting is alternatively attributed to Anton van Dyck (q.v.); whatever may be the judgment rendered on the figures of the mythological scene confined to the left margin of the canvas, it is quite certain that the bold conception of the large display of game and vegetables was realized in the inspired and brilliant terms of Rubensian painting, if not directly by the master, then by one of his followers, possibly Frans Snyders.

Snyders must be considered the most genuine interpreter, in this particular field, of the Rubensian style, starting with the second decade of the century, when he abandoned the more archaic modes, of Brueghelian derivation (fixed in a more precise and detailed definition, more direct and more carefully executed, as in the *Fruit Shop*, The Hermitage, Leningrad; and *Fruit on a Table*, Statens Mus. for Kunst, Copenhagen), and executed works conceived with greater swiftness and immediacy, for example, the *Game Merchant* in Oslo (II, PL. 207), perhaps the most striking masterpiece of this second trend, and the large canvas with game, fruit, and vegetables in Brussels (Mus. Royaux B.A.). Snyders's works were widely diffused not only in Flanders but throughout Europe (PL. 203; VI, PL. 73). His style was carried to France by Nicasius Bernaerts (1620–78), who worked there for a long time; Juriaen Jacobsz. (1625/26–1685) took it to the Netherlands, and Jan Fyt disseminated it in France and Italy, in both of which countries he had lived (PL. 205; V, PL. 311). Even before Fyt came to Genoa, Jan Roos, also known as Giovanni Rosa (1591–1638), was in residence there. Roos's favorite theme was animals, and this was immediately taken up and imitated by such artists as Anton Maria Vassallo (in whose work the Caravaggesque is so strong that his painting *The Kitchen*, formerly in the Cook Collection in Richmond, Surrey, was long attributed to Velázquez), Sinibaldo Scorza (1589–1631), Antonio Travi (1608–65), and Giovanni Benedetto Castiglione, known as Il Grechetto (1616–70).

This account of Genoese painting of Flemish derivation would be incomplete without mention of the fact that as early as the first decades of the century such artists as Rubens, Cornelis de Wael (1592–1667), and Van Dyck had left works in Genoa or had actually sojourned there, as had Pieter Boel (ca. 1622–74), another talented follower of Snyders, about the middle of the century — all of whom had contributed to solidifying the taste for the painting of animals. Thus it becomes clear how Bernardo Strozzi (1581–1644; II, PL. 202), not without links to Rubensian techniques, could realize in the Genoese milieu so fresh and light a work as the famous *Cook* in the Palazzo Rosso, Genoa. It should be added that this circulation of ideas was also fruitful in its impact on Lombard painters, influencing the activity of Angelo Maria Crivelli (d. ca. 1730), Francesco Londonio (1723–83), Giorgio Durante (1685–1755), and others, as well as the Piacentine artist Felice Boselli (1650–1732); all these bridge the boundaries of the Seicento and reach into the heart of 18th-century painting, when the traits of the archaic still life were incorporated into Arcadian scenes or transposed to a frankly decorative level. In Roman and Neapolitan circles the works of Snyders found — even though indirectly, through his followers — a popularizer in Pietro Navarra, the reconstruction of whose artistic personality was begun by Zeri (1959) through the attribution to him of sever canvases in the Galleria Pallavicini in Rome. Also affecte at least in certain aspects, was the work of Arcangelo Resa (1670–1740; represented in Faenza, Pin., and elsewhere) an more especially, of Baldassare de Caro (1689–1750), a proli artist (trained, so far as is known, in the atelier of Andr Belvedere; PL. 207), who is represented in museums in Naple Pesaro, and Piacenza and in many private collections.

Fruit and flower painting. The fascination of antiquity n only played a decisive part in relation to the illusionist traditic but also influenced other types of still lifes — above all, flow painting. In this trend, grotesques (PL. 195, *above*), known throug out the 15th century but very much in vogue at the end of th century as a consequence of the discovery of the grottoes Nero's Domus Aurea (VII, PL. 215), were crucial. Ma painters devoted themselves to the study of the antique decor tions thus brought to light, but their application in decorati terms, which was vital to the development of flower paintin took place under the aegis of Raphael, chiefly in the worl of Giovanni da Udine, who can be termed an *ante littera* master of still life, since it was to him, according to Vasa that Raphael entrusted the execution of "all the musical instru ments" at the "feet" of St. Cecilia. Sterling (1959) and Cau (1961) have published two Neapolitan copies of grotesque from models by Giovanni da Udine, in which the old mot seems to have been renewed by a Raphaelism revised from natur

The very early dates of these copies (1538 and 1555) lea us to suppose that the representation of vases of flowers — eve though we find the type developing in Flanders and in th Netherlands — originated from stimuli ripening in the spher of the Italian Renaissance. Even in the case of mannerist sti life, discussed above, the primary stimulus, antedating i development in the works of Aertsen, seems to have deriv from Italian sources, particularly the paintings of Jacop Bassano (q.v.).

In the north, the first vases of flowers modeled on th antique style appeared in the works of Jan Sadeler (155c 1600) and Roelant Savery (1576 or 1578–1639). These we individual vases of flowers against a light background or enclose within a niche, but before long, as was often the case in th genre, there emerged various specialities: flowers in a glas flowers in a pot, flowers in a bunch, and so on. From thes precedents, which reecho also the tradition of the Flemis miniature, began the great development that this kind of paintir underwent, particularly in the first three decades of the 17 century, in the works of Jacques (Jacob II) de Gheyn (1569 1629), Osias Beert (d. 1625), Ambrosius I Bosschaert (157 1645), Jacob van Hulsdonck (1582–1647), Clara Peeter Alexander Adriaenssen (1587–1661), and then "Velvet" Bruegh and Daniel Seghers (1590–1661), the last two of whom live for a time in Italy. Brueghel was already in Italy in the la decade of the century, at the time, therefore, when the fir still lifes of Caravaggio, if he ever did paint independent sti lifes, would have appeared (according to the sources, at leas these would have been "fiori"). Seghers was in Rome for tw years toward the end of the firs, quarter of the new centur and Rubens availed himself of the collaboration of the youn Jesuit.

In the works of these artists the subtle and delicate quali of Flemish painting, reflecting the influence of the miniatur unites with the more robust and intense qualities of Dutc painting. The flower paintings of Ambrosius Bosschaert a characterized by pale hues against light, cool skies (V, PL. 329 while a gamut of more vivid, lively colors, combined with tl utmost perfectionism, characterizes the works of the elder Ja Brueghel, in which the artist, with the precision of a botanis combined a great variety of flowers. This type of paintir had wide circulation throughout Europe, while in the countri of its origin it underwent a further development in tl second half of the century in the work of Willem van d Aelst (1625/26–ca. 1683); Rachel Ruysch (1664–1756), who paintings, with their cool and refined tonalities, are marke by the zeal of supreme craftsmanship; and, toward the en f the century, in the work of Jan van Huijsum (ca. 1682–749), in which virtuosity had hardened into an academic mold V, PL. 312).

In Italy, despite the Renaissance precedents and the inferences drawn from the inlaid marble decorations that began to embellish the churches at the height of the 16th century, flower painting rose under the standard of the Flemish tradition, even though in the course of its development it availed itself of the grand example of the Caravaggesque models. The fact is that between the Flemish tradition and the Caravaggesque there was an irreconcilable divergence: the former tended toward a close-range, delicate, and precise vision, as of a herbarium, even though the light, with its unbroken fixity, mysteriously transforms the magnificent display of flowers, while the latter tended toward a more natural vision with flowers and colors alive, or brought back to life by the animating effect of the light.

The legacy of the mannerist tradition is encountered in the many anonymous flower paintings, which, especially in the Roman ambience, manifest their derivation from the relief carving on large decorative candlesticks and from the inlaid marble decorations already cited. From this anonymity there emerge two remarkable figures, Mario Nuzzi, called Mario de' Fiori (ca. 1603–73), and Giacomo Recco (active ca. 1627), who have taken on importance through the researches of Zeri (1959) and Causa (1961). The paintings of both are rooted in the mannerist style, tinged with reflections from Brueghel; but, while the work of Recco remains anchored to archaic compositional schemes, that of Nuzzi assumes a brighter and gayer tonality, which in the Roman ambience was to have even more exuberant sequelae in the works of the followers of Nuzzi who have been brought back from oblivion by Zeri: Zenone Varelli, Giovanni Stanchi (b. ca. 1645), and Brugnoli.

The works of the Flemish "fioranti," particularly those of Brueghel and Seghers, were not altogether unknown to the Roman and Neapolitan group of painters, but it appears they exercised a more decisive influence on the artists of Milan. There the style of Brueghel was echoed by Fede Galizia (1578–1630), who was active in the decades bridging the turn of the century (fruit and flower paintings in Pin. Ambrosiana, Milan; Wadsworth Atheneum, Hartford, Conn.; and in private collections in Milan and elsewhere, including the Coll. Vitale Bloch, Paris). The Brueghel mode was wearily continued by many other less important artists, in a certain sense, anchored to retardataire style: Giuseppe Vincenzino, Gilardo da Lodi, and the Cremonese painter Margherita Caffi.

But the work of Fede Galizia in the Milanese ambience may also be cited as a reflection of the reshaping that was given to the more archaic still-life compositions all over Europe at the beginning of the 17th century. Thus her small canvases of fruit and flowers, though not untouched in her latest phase by the luministic revelation of a Caravaggio (typical is the Fruit and Flowers in the Wadsworth Atheneum, Hartford, Conn.), make their place on the international scene at a singularly interesting period in the history of still life and, because of their common origins, afford a remarkable parallel to the works of Jacob van Hulsdonck, as is evident if one of her small bunches of flowers is compared to his picture with similar subject in the Hoogendijk Gallery, Amsterdam. In the quiet and modest life of her reserved yet elegant images, ever suspended on the thin thread that joins naturalism and design, Longhi has seen an extraordinary crossing of "technical devotion with the neo-Thomistic tendencies of the Counter Reformation." No doubt in their finely woven texture, in that rare mixture of abstraction and realism — in the abstraction which crystallizes the realism and in the realism which, if it does not dissolve, smooths and softens the crystalline forms of the abstraction — there is a strong vein that stems from what is now usually characterized as the "mannerist poetic" and that, in any case, can be dated back to the most archaic phase of the history of the esthetic of still life.

Contemporaneously with Fede Galizia, specifically between 1581 and 1631, there was active in Milan another artist of mannerist and Lombard lineage — Panfilo Nuvolone (active 1581–1631). In his still lifes (one signed and dated 1620 in a private collection in Milan; others in the St. Lucas Gallery, Vienna) the style of Brueghel had only a marginal influence; on the other hand, more marked are the typical aspects of Lombard naturalism, that "sfoggio di pittura" of which Lanzi speaks — the wide painted background for the design, the clear, limpid exuberance of color, and the swift brushstroke, almost anticipating the baroque works of Spadino (see below).

The 17th century in the Netherlands. Concurrently with flower painting there appeared and developed in the Low Countries the theme, with its variations, of the spread table, now laid frugally, now in a more elaborate and showy manner — often with symbolic implication, particularly as handled by the school of Leiden, in the works of David Bailly (1584–1657) and his followers, the brothers Pieter (active 1632–54) and Harmen (Herman) van Steenwyck (1612–after 1656; PL. 206). This type of picture appeared at the same time in Flanders and the Netherlands but had a more continuous development in the Netherlands because most of the Flemish painters had had to abandon their centers of activity owing to the religious struggles. In this area too the Flemish artists diverge from the Dutch on account of the differing origins of their artistic tradition. The works of the Flemings — after the earliest, still mannerist-derived examples, in which, upon tables enlarged in perspective and slightly tilted (to display to greater advantage the various specialities, painted with the utmost fidelity, almost like a collection of samples of the different species) — are characterized by fineness of execution. The Dutch paintings on the other hand — works by Jan Jansz. den Uyl (1596–1640), Pieter Claesz. (V, PL. 311), and Willem Claesz. Heda (PL. 202; II, PL. 216), as well as by the German-born Gotthardt de Wedig (1583–1641) — are characterized by compositions of greater concentration and simplicity, based on diagonal axes, conforming to which there prevails a coloristic (and in the case of Gotthardt de Wedig often even tenebrist) tonality that is intense and muted, held to a few shades, cool and low-pitched, and tending in some cases toward monochrome. These are in a certain sense re-formed still lifes, in which the episodic multiplicity of the objects is reorganized into the essence of a single episode to form a more telling and coherent representational scheme. It was the archaic type of still life, which, supplanting the type that was mannerist in origin, was also to have international circulation, as may have already been gathered.

An important center in the Netherlands, besides Haarlem and Leiden, where the above-mentioned artists were active, and Amsterdam, which had a cosmopolitan character, was The Hague. Here the most renowned artist was Abraham van Beyeren (ca. 1620–90), in whose works the vivid displays of fish and the spread tables rise to what might be called monumental expressiveness (PL. 202; II, PL. 216). His themes have elements in common with those of Jan Davidsz. de Heem (1606–83/84), who introduced into the quiet and subdued course of Dutch still life the compositional grandeur and lush exuberance of Flemish painting, especially of the school of Antwerp. Jan Davidsz. de Heem had a follower in Andrea Benedetti of Modena (active ca. 1636–49), who was working in Antwerp about the middle of the century, and, through Benedetti, in Cristoforo Monari of Reggio Emilia (d. 1720), who continued the De Heem style well into the first two decades of the 18th century.

Aside from the Flemish incursion of De Heem, Dutch still-life painting underwent a notable change through the influence, albeit indirect, of the mysterious and captivating art of Rembrandt (q.v.). In a sense, this change can be understood as a modernization of the traditional characteristics of Dutch painting — that is, a heightening of luministic and coloristic aspects and an emphasis on the play of reflections and transparencies in compositions become more sumptuous and imposing. The most gifted artist in this sense, and perhaps the greatest of all Dutch still-life painters, was Willem Kalf (1622–93), in whose lavishly elegant and grandly ordered compositions transparencies and reflections are brought into play with the utmost subtlety against the dense texture of colors glowing with a dusky luminosity (PL. 202; V, PL. 313). Besides the pictures of this type, which belong to the later period of Kalf's activity, well-known works include the interiors of kitchens (Rome, Gall. Naz.; Berlin, Staat. Mus.; Rotterdam, Mus. Boymans-van Beuningen), which belong to his youthful period, about the middle of the century, when he was living in Paris and was most likely in touch with other painters of the same genre, such as Egbert van der Poel (ca. 1621–64), Pieter van den Bosch (1613–after 1663), and Frans Ryckhals (after 1600–1647).

The 17th century in Flanders and France. From the beginning of the century, groups of Flemish painters were working in almost all the European centers, scattered, as we have seen, as a consequence of the intolerance of the Spanish occupation toward the new religious sects. One school established itself in Germany, settling in the Rhineland, in Frankfurt am Main, and elsewhere; another in France, particularly in Paris, where their center was in the Saint-Hippolyte and Saint-Germain-des-Prés sections and where they organized themselves into a corporation. Some Flemish artists went to Italy, among them Lodewik Susi (Turin, Rome; documented 1616–20; PL. 201). Others went to Spain, more specifically to Madrid; among these was Juan van der Hamen, who must have been in that city as early as 1595, since a son, who presumably continued his work (no paintings by the father are known) and who added León to the family name, was born there in 1596 (Cavestany, 1940).

The activities of all these painters spread everywhere the more archaic type of still life but at the same time fitted it into the various local traditions. In other words, in this type of still life the Flemish origin does not obscure the essential features or aspects of the native tradition — German or French, Italian or Spanish. In Germany the activity of the Flemish painters was very important to the formation of the Hamburg painter Georg Flegel (1563–1638), whose still lifes (principally in the museums of Darmstadt, Augsburg, and Frankfurt am Main, in which city his life ended) join a graphic sense of reality, worked out through the subtle accentuation of light values, to the Flemish-derived archaic compositional pattern.

Flegel's was not an isolated case; it was repeated in the formation and development of the Alsatian artist Sebastian Stosskopf (1597–1657), almost all of whose works have now been brought together in Strasbourg (Mus. B.A.). The case of Stosskopf, however, is far more complex, in that his initial style, in which Flemish and German motifs converged, underwent in the Parisian ambience a distillation through which the artist achieved his clearer and simpler statements, more delicately articulated in a rediscovered spatial dimension. In Paris the archaic style of the Flemish still life began to spread in the time of Henry IV, but it had wider diffusion during the reign of Louis XIII, when such artists as Stosskopf, Jacques Linard (ca. 1600–45), François Garnier (d. 1672), Louise Moillon (1610–96), René Nourisson (documented 1644–50), and above all the great Baugin were active. These painters had a trait in common in their simplification of the somewhat dispersed themes of Flemish painting: in that subtlety, of a geometrical or at least an intellectualistic order, that they introduced into the presentation of objects — in that clarity, the fruit at once of rationalism and of imagination, that illumines all their works. The typical case, as has been suggested, is provided by Baugin (baptismal name unknown; probably active 1620–40), three of whose paintings are known: *Books and Papers by Candlelight* (PL. 201) and the Louvre's *The Five Senses* and *Dessert with Wafers.* These, especially the last, are works of a compelling clarity and surpassing optic lucidity that thus attain to the level, within the tradition of Caravaggesque patterns, of Zurbarán's rigorousness. Analogies in the French milieu, as Sterling (1959) has noted, are to be found in the works of Georges de la Tour (q.v.) and the brothers Le Nain (q.v.).

From 1640 to 1650, approximately, new ferments from diverse quarters began to affect the direction of the still life. First there was the Caravaggesque current, by which even Louise Moillon seems to have been affected, since she lighted

up with luministic reflections the fine Flemish design of he *Grapes, Apples, and Melons,* signed and dated 1637 (America private coll.; Sterling, 1959, pl. 46), in which the vine branche laden with bunches of grapes, the fruit, and the melons ar arranged in unusual breadth over the whole canvas. Th Caravaggesque influence is even more clear-cut in the worl of René Nourisson and Pierre Dupuis (1610–82). Then the were the Dutch currents, attributable principally to the presenc in Paris of Willem Kalf from about 1642 to 1646, the yea when Dutch-inspired rustic interiors also began to appear i the circle of the brothers Le Nain and even in the work c Stosskopf.

But, in the second half of the century, this crisis of transi tion between the "old world" and the baroque had — at leas insofar as it touched the fundamental line of developmer in this type of painting — an outcome that was in a certai sense academic because of the imperious imposition of th new taste, which was dictated by the orientation of the Cour In France, through the rising power of the Academy, whic monopolized the activity of the painters, the ties with Roma courtly painting were consolidated, and public favor turne to such artists as Jean Baptiste Monnoyer (1634–99), whos showy pictures present a significant affinity with those c Francesco Fieravino, also known as Il Maltese (active 1650–80 whom he may have met in Rome, and of Jean Belin de Fontena (1653–1715), in whose pictures the court taste is exuberantl and ornately expressed on a base of classicizing academisrm During this same time, following in the steps of the Flemin Nicasius Bernaerts, who, as has been mentioned, had settle in France and become a member of the Academy, Françoi Desportes (1661–1743) was reelaborating the traditional theme in a formula already 18th-century in its elegance (PL. 207)

The 17th century in Spain. As in no other country, stil life in Spain was to attract the greatest artists and so to attai above and beyond any question of specialization, to the leve of the great artistic expressions: it engaged the efforts of Cotán Velázquez, and Zurbarán, for example, and the tradition ca be said to have continued down to Goya. Here, too, connection with Italy and the Low Countries were decisive. Mentio has already been made, apropos of the spread of the manneris schemes, of the trip of Vincenzo Campi to Spain in 1584 and of the importance of his works and the kindred works o Passarotti, not only for such lesser artists as Juan Estebar and Alejandro de Loarte but also — if only as a margina stimulus — for the great Velázquez himself.

The same connections can be cited in the case of fruit an flower painting, which had an enormous diffusion and which in its origins, was bound up with the school of Giovanni d Udine, though independent personalities soon began to brea away from the orbit of this school. Among them was Bla de Ledesma (active under Philip II, 1556–98), whose activit may have come to a close within the 16th century and who mus have exercised a considerable influence beyond the restricte Spanish sphere, since paintings very similar to those that bea his signature — among them the magnificent *Still Life* with fruits a basket of cherries, a cut red watermelon, flowers in a vase and mushrooms (from a Swiss private collection, shown ir the exhibition "La nature morte et son inspiration," Paris 1960) — appeared also in the Neapolitan milieu, from which apart from works by Luca Forte (see below), there unfortunatel remain only the names of a few artists, such as Ambrosiell Faro and Antonio Mariano, mentioned in the sources as th forerunners of the local genre painters. As for the Flemisl influence, prompt mention should be made of the works o Juan van der Hamen, who probably, as has been said, move to Madrid about 1595, and then of the circle of the "fioranti, what with Juan de Arellano (1614–76), the most noted of th Spanish painters of flowers (PL. 201), producing works recalling those of Seghers.

As was stated above, there are known to us no paintings by the elder Van der Hamen, but it is probably possible to form an idea of his works from those of his son Juan van de Hamen y León (1596–1631; PL. 201); in any case, it is certain that they must have played an important part, one that was not merely stimulating but even decisive, in the emergence and development of the great still-life painting of Spain.

In the first place, the possibility cannot be overlooked that Van der Hamen had considerable influence on Blas de Ledesma, the more so since the two were court painters at the same time in Madrid. More than this, however, it is worth noting that in the works of Blas de Ledesma there are already apparent — whether or not sensitized by a precocious Caravaggism — some of the essential characteristics of Spanish still-life painting. The compositions of this patriarch of painting contain humble objects of daily use, and these are arranged on the tables which frame them, between the shadow of the background and the light that streams in from the side, with that calculated pursuit of symmetry which is one of the deepest strains in the rigorousness of the Spanish spirit. As Sterling (1959) has noted, the objects, thus situated between light and shadow, assume the aspect of a frieze and are redeemed from their lowliness by the authoritative stamp of the style. At this level, a part no less important than that of Blas de Ledesma must have been played by Juan de Labrador, whose artistic personality can be reconstructed on the basis of the reputation he enjoyed, as recorded in early writings, in France (Félibien praised his work) and in England, and on the basis of several paintings of fruit, particularly one at Hampton Court, attributed to him in the catalogue of the collection of Charles I of England. In these pictures, which bear the mark of the influence of Caravaggio's earlier works, humble things acquire that monumental dimension which was later to characterize the far more rigorous and concisely stated works of Zurbarán and Cotán. In the course of Spanish painting the still life of Flemish origin was most prolifically represented by Juan van der Hamen y León, whose works (e.g., the *Vases, Cakes, and Box* in the Thyssen-Bornemisza Coll., Lugano) have, not without reason, carried the weight of attribution to Zurbarán himself.

Juan Sánchez Cotán (1561–1627) was a student of Blas de Ledesma in Toledo and probably saw the works of Juan de Labrador in the early 1600s. In any case, if, as seems likely, Cotán's *Quince, Cabbage, Melon, and Cucumber* (II, PL. 184) is identifiable with one of the eleven still lifes described in the inventory of his properties that he drew up in 1603, when he entered the Carthusian Order, it must be agreed that at the beginning of the century (1602 at the latest) his style was already so fully formed that he could produce one of the supreme masterpieces of painting. As in his other works, the few everyday objects (some set down on a surface, others suspended on strings) are here too enclosed within a perspective framing and stand out in a somehow metaphysical dimension against the dark background or on the window sill. Thus there is set up among the realistic yet so simply relieved forms a transcendent equilibrium, a kind of magic dimension, and all things, from forms to colors, become immutable, like attributes of the eternal. Lowly objects, rigorous style, intense values, supreme truthfulness: these are aspects of the essence of the Spanish spirit, its mystic exaltation and unequivocal rigorousness. This was to be the painting of the Counter Reformation, toned down and strung on the taut thread of an inflexible rationalism; but this is painting with no trace of pietism or devotionalism, wholly concentrated as it is on the equilibrium of balanced values and immersed in the need, so deeply felt by the Spanish culture of that time, for harmony and geometrical grandeur.

Francisco de Zurbarán (q.v.) appears to have started from Cotán, even though in his work (PL. 201) the geometric ardor and the formal polish seem to be worked into the more archaic schemes of a Blas de Ledesma. The fact remains that in his paintings interest is concentrated on the illumining of the colors in a fixed, unreal light, so that the formal refinement and monumental relief of his canvases assume a metaphysical and hermetic splendor. Thus the Caravaggesque interpretation appears to have filtered through in a subtler form, more genuinely adapted to the deep inwardness of Spanish spirituality, in which there figure dreams of an atavistic tradition that, by way of the Arabs, seems to go back to the geometric speculation of ancient hermetic Egypt. Velázquez apart, the continuation

of Spanish still life was to be in the hands of followers of these great masters, particularly of Zurbarán, only a few of whom are known by name, for instance, Pedro de Camprobín (active ca. 1660); a great many other still lifes — and there are some that attained to a perfection of a kind that recalls the works of the school of Bergamo — remain anonymous.

In the course of the second half of the 17th century the mysterious "vita silenzia" of the great Spanish still life was overtaken by the spread of the baroque movement, as a consequence, among other things, of the arrival of artists from Italy, especially from Naples, noteworthy examples being Luca Giordano and, in his train, Giuseppe Recco.

Caravaggesque still life. Many aspects of still life, though elaborated and developed in Flanders and the Netherlands as we have seen, had their origins in Italian mannerism and often returned to Italy with the specialization of the Flemish and Dutch painters. But the great still-life painting in Italy was quite another matter. It had its beginnings in the revolutionary works of Caravaggio (q.v.), who (as quoted in a letter of Vincenzo Giustiniani to Teodoro Amideni) said that "it required of him as much craftsmanship to paint a good picture of flowers as of figures," and thus intentionally rejected and upset the hierarchy of the genres of the academic tradition. Still life was thus elevated all at once to the level of great painting. With this statement Caravaggio in effect confirms his predilection for painting compounded of immediacy and truth and concerned only with rendering "values" in the reality of natural light. This capturing on canvas of "arranged" simple objects meant, in fact, calling attention to values in a more arresting manner, rendering more vibrant and dramatic the relief of light and shadow, of forms and colors. That this was understood by the writers of the time is evidenced by the chapter on painting in the work by Father Francesco Lana entitled *Prodromo, ovvero saggio di alcune invenzioni nuove premesso all'Arte Maestra* (Brescia, 1670); as has been pointed out by a profound student of the baroque, E. Raimondo (*Letteratura Barocca*, 1961, p. 277), Lana speaks of the "great usefulness" of "painting from life various kinds of fruit ... because fruit, flowers, and the like have very vivid colors, and the light striking them shows more distinctly the contrast between highlights and shadows." Besides, he goes on, "in painting these objects there comes about a certain sincerity in working, which delights and heartens" because "in painting these things we have great freedom and liberty to vary them, making leaves, flowers, fruit here more and there less rich in color, these with one, others with another, different, shape."

The *Basket of Fruit* in the Pinacoteca Ambrosiana, Milan, which Caravaggio painted in Rome prior to 1596, is not only — assuming it was a separate work and not, as has been suggested, a portion of a larger painting — the first example of independent still life but also a model of truth and style, and as such aligns itself with all the other elements of still life that, early and late, Caravaggio included in his pictures. That he could conceive of a simple basket of fruit as the subject of a painting means that he was impelled toward the pure values in painting, in this particular case, light and shadow, which endow a representation with qualities of style and high rigorousness, and that he was at the same time waging war on the large, pompous canvases of official painting. It was, in short, a protest — just as it was in protest that humble people were used in the religious pictures of Caravaggio, a reference to the unadorned simplicity and humility of the evangelical tradition and the primitive church as opposed to the regalia and the pomp of the official Church Triumphant.

The works of Caravaggio had great repercussions at once in the Roman ambience, where they suited an ever-widening taste and met the demands of collectors, art lovers, and dealers. Indeed, it should be noted that in the first decades of the *seicento* the taste for still life became popular among art collectors to the point where brisk and intense trade and exchange were established, as is recorded in the correspondence carried on by "Velvet" Brueghel and Ercole Bianchi, secretary to Cardinal Federico Borromeo. In Rome, the stronghold of

Caravaggesque still life was the previously mentioned "academy" of Giovanni Battista Crescenzi. The most active exponents were Crescenzi himself, Tommaso Salini, and Pier Paolo Bonzi. Unfortunately, no still lifes by Crescenzi have been definitely traced either in Italy (one in Rome, Gall. Naz., has been claimed for him by Longhi) or in Spain, whither, as is known from the sources, some made their way. However, if we dwell on the words in which Baglione describes works of Crescenzi ("He made . . . an extremely beautiful display of glassware, diversely represented; some glasses dimmed by frost, others with fruit in water; wineglasses and glasses of different shapes"), we cannot but be struck by the resemblance to those in which he and Bellori describe similar works of Caravaggio. Baglione speaks of a painting of a "youth playing a lute" with "a carafe of flowers filled with water in which one can easily distinguish the reflections of a window and other objects in the room. On the flowers is fresh dew which is rendered with exquisite accuracy." Says Bellori: "He painted a carafe of flowers in which he showed the transparency of the glass and of the water and in which one can see the reflection of a window in the room; the flowers are sprinkled with the freshest dew drops."

A different situation obtains in the case of Salini (PL. 200) and Bonzi (both born in 1575 and active for about the first three decades of the 17th century): rather large groups of their works are known as a result of researches in recent years. The thematic material of these two artists is still mannerist, as appears, for instance, from Salini's *Woman Buying Eggs* (Minneapolis, Inst. of Arts; Sterling, 1959, PL. 53) and *Fruiterer* (Milan, Coll. Orsi; Testori, 1958) and from some *bodegones* with fruit vendors by Bonzi (Battisti, 1954; Bottari, 1960). But if the themes were still mannerist (concerning Bonzi, derivation from the Carraccis has been suggested), composition and style were altogether Caravaggesque, and of the two artists the one who followed Caravaggio with more profound fidelity was Salini, the pupil or, as he was called, "guardian angel" of Baglione — it was almost as if Salini were seeking forgiveness for the famous "spying" that led to Baglione's libel suit of 1603 against Caravaggio. Certainly Caravaggesque, though connected with a similar orientation in Spanish painting, is the way the objects are aligned, almost as if in a frieze, between the shadow of the background and the light that streams down from side or front, as in the *Still Life* in Washington, D.C. (Nat. Gall., Kress Coll.), that Longhi has attributed to Caravaggio himself. Caravaggesque, too, is the arresting precision with which light and shadow give clearness and relief, reality and tangibility, to the various images. It is precisely this sense of reality and concreteness, of accessibility and familiarity of the various objects enclosed in the picture, that differentiates the Caravaggesque Italian still lifes from comparable Spanish depictions, which are always steeped in a surreal and visionary aura. It is also what distinguishes Italian Caravaggism vis-à-vis French examples, as becomes clear in comparing one of the later still lifes of Bonzi (e.g., the painting in the Pin. della Congregazione di Carità, Modena) and the above-mentioned Flemish-influenced *Grapes, Apples, and Melons* by Louise Moillon.

The naturalism of the vision, in short, acted upon the thematic material of mannerist origin, and separated from that context, with a final, passionate definition of values, the independent still life of the 17th century. It should be added, however, that the activities of the Crescenzi-Salini-Bonzi triad do not cover the entire Caravaggesque sector of the Roman ambience: mention must also be made of the artist for whom Longhi has proposed the tentative designation "Pensioner of Saraceni" (author of the *Cook in the Kitchen* in the Galleria Corsini, Florence) and of the much more important and significant artist Cecco del Caravaggio. The well-known *Interior with a Man Holding a Recorder* in the Ashmolean Museum, Oxford, which Longhi (1943) attributes to Cecco, has superb elements of still life both in the background and in the foreground: the mute objects so delicately poised in the cryptic light that strikes the cupboard in the background — an effect foreshadowing the works of Carlo Magini — and the objects arranged in the foreground with subtle and calculated interplay in the rays of a full, flooding brightness. The same qualities reappear in two independent

still lifes belonging to a private collection in Rome, in which the fineness of the draftsmanship and the clear contrasts of light and dark confirm the French origin of this painter, as suspected by Longhi.

Note should be taken here of the elements of still life that appear in the paintings of two other artists of the Roman milieu: Bartolommeo Manfredi (1580/82–1620/21) and Michelangelo di Campidoglio (1610–70). Within the compass of Manfredi's work may perhaps be explained, if not included, two charming still lifes with flowers, one in Boston (*Poppies in a Wine Flask*, Mus. of Fine Arts) and the other in Forlì (Pin. Com.), which are attributed, respectively, in apparent disregard of chronology, to Caravaggio and to Cagnacci (Guido Canlassi, 1601–81), a painter active several decades later. Michelangelo di Campidoglio, known chiefly through the mention that Pascoli makes of him in the life of Mario Nuzzi, appears, from various indications, to be connected with the style of Bonzi.

The Lombards. The Caravaggesque still life emerged, as we have seen, in the Roman environment, where it inspired an immediate following, with parallel developments in Lombardy, as well as noteworthy ramifications in various directions, including, in a special way, Naples. Naples is singled out because we can regard as an episode of Caravaggism, even though peripheral, the activity of the Lucchese artist Simone del Tintore (active ca. 1630–70), who is often linked with Tommaso Salini — a connection deriving from the naturalism of Tintore's teacher, the Lucchese painter Pietro Paolini (1603–81). In his known works (in private and public collections in Lucca and Florence) Tintore attains in some aspects, particularly in the representation of rare natural species, to effects resembling those of the Neapolitan artist Paolo Porpora (PL. 205), perhaps through common sources of inspiration.

In Lombardy, Bergamo — Caravaggio's native town — was a center unto itself, dominated by an eminent artistic figure, Evaristo Baschenis (1617–77), author of a group of still lifes that rank among the greatest of all time. At the same time he was painting still lifes with characteristic musical instruments (lutes, mandores, flutes, guitars, violins, spinets, etc.; PL. 209), and even before, Baschenis must have been applying himself to creating compositions with game, birds, fish, pottery, meat, and so on. The arrangements of the latter work, while still showing traces of the Caravaggesque idiom, seem not unrelated to the contemporary paintings of the circle of Zurbarán in Spain, probably arriving in Lombardy with the Spanish conquerors. Extremely significant in this connection are a *bodegón* in Milan (Coll. Treccani degli Alfieri; Angelini, 1946, pl. 28) and the *Still Life* by David Barrera with a piece of bread, a silvery pitcher, and some green apples around a fruit basket, signed and dated 1642, in Florence (Palazzo Davanzati). Unfortunately, we know very little of Baschenis — only that he received commissions when he was still very young and applied himself to painting "soggetti di ferma." The few available dates do not permit the arrangement of the surviving works in a tenable chronological order.

At any rate, the name of Baschenis remains linked, rather than to still lifes with provisions, to musical instruments (PL. 209; II, PL. 184), and in considering these one must not dismiss the possibility that the Bergamask solitary was directly inspired by works of Caravaggio himself — keeping in mind, for example, the musical instruments in the *Amor Victorious* (III, PL. 33). And it should be noted that, while the Spanish-derived still lifes were imitated, if not in the paintings of Giuseppe Recco in whose work other decisive factors could have intervened, certainly in some works by Paolo Antonio Barbieri — compare the *Still Life with Fine Chocolate* in Modena (Gall. Campori) with Baschenis' display of fish in Rome (Coll. L. Albertini) — the still lifes with musical instruments, aside from a few scattered local imitations, had, one might say, no followers and remained a form of expression peculiar to the Bergamask artist. In these works (in collections and museums in Bergamo and Milan, Mus. Royaux B.A., Brussels; etc.) there is an utter rigorousness that invests the magic repose of the instruments with a mysterious monumentality and lends to the glaze of their color

ivid glow. This repose bears within itself the sense of the du-
ation of time: the past is in the dust that has settled on the in-
truments and the dimension of the present is in the mark left
y the brush of fingers. Motionless life, nourished on imme-
norial silence — it is these aspects of Baschenis that recall
he works of Vermeer (q.v.), and that inspired Longhi to describe
im as a "local Vermeer sacrificed in the provinces."

In the Bergamask ambience Baschenis had imitators and
ollowers, as has been indicated, but these — from the prolific
Bartolomeo Bettera (1624–87) to the 18th-century painter
Antonio Gianlisi (represented in Cremona, Mus. Ala Ponzone;
1 Piacenza, Coll. Alberoni; and in private collections) — were
ngaged by the more external and showy aspects of the Berga-
nask master rather than his deeper and more subtle qualities.
They adorned their paintings with musical instruments, tapes-
ries, and vases of flowers or set them in the open against a
ackground of Arcadian gardens. Similar works are those of
Pier Francesco Cittadini (1616–81; represented in Modena,
Gall. Estense; Bologna, Opera Pia dei Vergognosi, Church of
he Madonna di Galliera, Palazzo Com.; etc.), a Milanese who
ettled in Bologna and whose trip to Rome and contacts with
eghers and Nuzzi never erased his Lombard origins or his
elations with the Bergamask world.

A Lombard — and Bergamask — background also contrib-
ted to the development of Giuseppe Recco (see below).
Here it is of interest to stress that the activity in Rome of Francesco Fieravino, during the second half of the century, apparently
annot be fully accounted for except on the basis of a connection
vith the Bergamask milieu. This is not to deny that the work
f Fieravino, known as Il Maltese (paintings in the museums
f Modena and Grenoble; Royal Colls., Hampton Court Palace,
London; private collections), had a more courtly and lively
one, more baroque accents — had, in other words, aspects
hat in the Roman milieu made a particular impression on Jean
Baptiste Monnoyer and were transposed by him to the pageantry
f Louis XIV at Versailles.

The Neapolitans. The connections between the Neapolitan
enre painters and the Caravaggesque tradition were strength-
ned in the Roman ambience between 1630 and 1640, but
hey must have been of much longer standing in Naples, perhaps
nediated there by the contributions of Spanish painters. The
arliest still lifes that can be claimed for the Neapolitan school
resent singular likenesses to the Spanish examples, and even
Luca Forte seems, in his early work, to be not unaware of the
vork of a Blas de Ledesma. Such canvases as the two still lifes
y Luca Forte brought to light by Sterling (1959; the one
vith the inscription "Don Joseph Carrafa" in the Ringling
Mus., Sarasota, Fla., the other in a European private coll.)
re still in the line of the Spanish tradition. From this the artist
vas to separate himself only when he was in the Roman milieu,
1 contact first with the works of Crescenzi (possibly including
he above-mentioned still life in the Gall. Naz. attributed to
Crescenzi by Longhi), then of Salini, and last but not least of
Pier Paolo Bonzi, as is suggested by the Luca Forte still lifes
1 New York (Acquavella Coll.) and the one in Bologna (Coll.
Molinari Pradelli). It appears, then, that the works of Luca
Forte, even when they give way to decorative tendencies, are all
aced with a whimsical and pervasive naturalness, in which
eappears a vein of the clearest, purest Caravaggism.

Present knowledge warrants the assumption that the work
f Luca Forte acted as a stimulating influence on the most tal-
nted Neapolitan artists, especially Paolo Porpora (1617–ca.
673). Whatever his origins, this painter, now become much
etter known through the research of Causa (1951), early aligned
imself in the direction indicated by Luca Forte. This applies
specially to Porpora's stylistic tone, certainly not to his themes,
vhich, particularly in his later period — when his vision also
xpanded toward the baroque, if, as Causa maintains, the large
anvas with flowers formerly in the Chigi-Saracini Collection
which Zeri attributes to Karel van Vogelaer) is really his —
ecame much richer and more elaborate and included motifs
rom other sources. These sources include, for example, the
vork of Otto Marseus van Schrieck (1619–78), who was in

Rome for a few years with Matthias Withoos (1621 or 1627–
1703), about the middle of the century; Franz Werner von Tamm
(1658–1724), who was in Rome, where he was known as Monsù
Daprait, in the 1680s; perhaps even Abraham Begeyn (1637/38–
97), whose authorship of a still life set in a landscape background
(Rome, Gall. Naz.) was established by Hoogewerff (1923–24);
and finally Nicola Lachtropius (active ca. 1656–1700). Through
the influence of these artists, Porpora produced, along with
paintings with floral motifs, others in which the foreground
shows the mysterious ferment of life in the undergrowth, with
strange and exotic vegetable and animal species (mushrooms,
reptiles, frogs, tortoises, etc.; PL. 205). But in Porpora's work,
in contrast to what occurs in the work of the artists cited and
of the above-mentioned Simone del Tintore, these motifs lose
their small-scaled strangeness and acquire the strength of exceptional luministic clearness and vibrant formal relief, as is
seen in a canvas in the Museo di Capodimonte, Naples (lent
by the Banco di Napoli), and in a painting in the Musée des
Beaux-Arts in Strasbourg, still attributed to Franz Werner
von Tamm.

A different case is that of Giuseppe Recco (1634–95), son
of Giacomo, both of whom have been mentioned above. On
the basis of his early Lombard training — as De Deminici
(1742–44) informs us and as is documented by a still life in London (Nicholson Coll.) and one in Bologna (Coll. Molinari Pradelli) and by the painting with a display of glasses in Warsaw
(Nat. Mus.) — Recco improved upon parental models, that
is to say, flower paintings, before he changed the themes of
his still lifes, addressing himself to the painting of fish and am-
plifying the scheme of the pictures by an atmospheric dimension, arresting and compact, and charged with dense reflections, a dimension in which are found echoes of baroque
painting. On the basis of the most reliable chronology of his
works it can be held that his change of themes and also of style
came about (rather than from Lombard and Bergamask stimuli)
within the Neapolitan ambience, probably through his contacts
with such Spanish painters as Francisco de Herrera the Younger
(1622–85), who is cited by early writers and was known in Naples
as "the Spaniard of the fish." On the other hand, the few pictures of other subjects, for instance, Recco's *Kitchen* in Vienna
(Kunsthist. Mus.), signed and dated 1675, also offer clear evidence of his contacts with Spanish culture, reinforced by a
trip to Spain made prior to the one of his last years. But Recco
unquestionably reached his peak of expressive intensity in his
displays of fish, which kindle with phosphorescent reflections,
against atmospheric backgrounds, fish that seem in their incandescence to have just been pulled from the sea (examples in
Naples, PL. 204; Besançon, Mus. B.A.; Madrid, Prado; Florence,
Uffizi; Udine, Mus. Civ.; and in Italian and other private collections).

Often confused with the works of Giuseppe Recco are those
of Giuseppe Ruopolo, the archaic severity of whose compositions
— for example the initialed *Still Life* in Bologna (Coll. Molinari Pradelli) as well as canvases in Naples (Mus. di Capodimonte) and still lifes with fruit, lemons, and citrons in various
private collections — probably means, as Causa (1961) has
suggested, that he was older than the better-known Giovan
Battista Ruopolo (PL. 205), who, together with Abraham Brueghel (PL. 205), poured baroque modes into Neapolitan still-life
painting. But the similarity from the point of view of composition
and choice of subject finds little corroboration in the more intimate and special aspects of the painters' idioms: the works
of Recco are characterized by a relation of light and dark that
serves to reinforce and define the forms, while in those of Giuseppe Ruopolo the forms, instead of being drawn close within
the confines of a luminous definition, expand in the continuing
ebullition of color.

In these artists the bond with the Caravaggesque tradition
remained more or less strong but at last dissolved into the expanded spaciousness of modes more specifically baroque. This
is particularly true of Giuseppe Recco. In the case of others,
the bond with the Caravaggesque tradition remained more alive
and engrossing, probably through the mediation of other sources, for example the works of Cecco del Caravaggio and the re-

stored works of the Flemish painter Lodewik Susi, who became known in Italy (where he was, as has been indicated above, in the second decade of the century) as Lodovico de Susio (PL. 201). Such was the case with Giovan Battista Recco, whose works are distinguished from those of his brother by a more precise compositional balance (quest for symmetry, or equivalences), a more static tone, and a firmer incidence of light. On the basis of certain signed or initialed works, among them a painting in Naples (Coll. Astarita), Carpegna (1961) has essayed a reconstruction of this singular personality. But to the works that he has cited others can be added, including a signed canvas in a private collection in Catania which may mark the transition to the *Interior of a Pantry* in Palermo (Gall. Naz. della Sicilia) and to several others (at least two of them signed). The peculiar circumstances of the origin of the work of Giovan Battista Recco explain the similarities, despite the difference in period and in stylistic influences, between his work and that of Felice Boselli, of Arcangelo Resani, of Tommaso Realfonzo, and, finally, of the Fano painter Carlo Magini, who, in a more general sense, is associated with the neoarchaic movement of 18th-century still-life painting.

Late baroque to the 19th century. At midcentury, first in the Roman and then in the Neapolitan milieu, the course of still life was the outcome of the ever more marked opening up of the baroque taste toward grandiloquence, lavishness, and artifice. In an orbit still in certain aspects Caravaggesque, the transitional was accomplished by the works of Michelangelo Cerquozzi (1602–60), whose artistic formation, at least insofar as this genre of painting is concerned, appears to have taken place in the ambience of Pier Paolo Bonzi, as was also the case with the elusive Michelangelo di Campidoglio. Canvases by Cerquozzi such as *Snail Gathering* (Rome, Coll. Briganti) and *Vine Branches* (Modena, Gall. Campori) in certain aspects refer back to the esthetic of Bonzi, but the way in which the compositional elements expand into the landscape is an indication of a new orientation, or, as has been said, of the transition to the "still life-landscape" that accompanied the development of this genre in a baroque direction.

Some northern European painters moved along the same lines as Cerquozzi. Among these were Abraham Brueghel (PL. 205), who, aided by assistants and followers, carried on an intense activity first in Rome and then, from 1671 on, in Naples (represented in public and private collections in Naples, Bari, Turin, Amsterdam, Brussels, Leningrad, Stockholm, and elsewhere); Christian Berentz (1658–1722), a painter of showy, bright, cool still lifes with crystal, animals, and fruit (Rome, Gall. Pallavicini and Gall. Corsini; Pesaro, Mus. Civ.; Naples, Mus. di Capodimonte); and Karel van Vogelaer (1653–95), known in Roman circles as Carlo dei Fiori because of his large, sumptuous, pyramidal arrangements of flowers (Rome, Gall. Pallavicini; Prato, Mus. Com.; etc.).

Along the same lines, but more directly linked with the works of Cerquozzi, moved many Italian painters, among whom should be singled out the still-obscure Giovanni Paolo Spadino (active ca. 1687; represented in the Palazzo dei Conservatori, Pin. Capitolina, Rome; Pin. Com., Montefortino; Mus. Com., Prato; Coll. Roccamodoro-Ramelli, Porto San Giorgio; Mus. Fesch, Ajaccio; Wadsworth Atheneum, Hartford, Conn.; and many private collections). He felt not only the influence of Abraham Brueghel but also, and more especially, that of Giovan Battista Ruopolo, the outstanding and most widely followed exponent of baroque still life in Naples, where Spadino sometimes worked, and not without reciprocal influence, with Brueghel himself. From the various phases of Giovan Battista Ruopolo — that is, from his youthful period, when, in rivalry with Giuseppe, he painted fabulous displays of fish in rosy, clear colors, like the one in Stockholm (Nationalmus.), dated 1653, to his Roman period, when he strengthened his connections with the ambience of Cerquozzi, and to his later, Neapolitan period, when he competed with Brueghel — the numerous group of Neapolitan genre painters of the day took their models. Among these were Onofrio Loth (ca. 1650–1717), Francesco della Quosta (d. 1723), and Aniello Ascione (active ca. 1680–1708), who with

refined virtuosity popularized the traits of Ruopolo's earli manner, still derived from Cerquozzi. Some of these artist Francesco della Quosta, for one, collaborated also with Lu Giordano and others, including Gaetano Cusati (d. ca. 172 and Nicola Malinconico (ca. 1654–1721), and they assimilate the Giordanesque style to the point where their works were ofte confused with the master's.

But the golden age of still-life painting was now over, an the rich and lively works of the time were, at best, purely de orative. The only exceptions are the refined works of Andr Belvedere (PL. 207), who probably developed artistically wit Porpora but not without contacts with the works of Giova Battista Ruopolo and of Abraham Brueghel. The frothy ligh ness of Belvedere's flower paintings is a reflection of the gra of the 18th-century mentality, a grace compounded of a kee sense of values and, most of all, of a consummate sense of pr portion that conditions the elegance and expressive intensit of his work. His pictures with water birds drifting o flowery ponds and his paintings with tulips, hydrangeas, and forth evoke with dreamlike suggestion an enchanted world subtle elegance. These were the qualities that made Belvedere work so successful in his time; during the years from 1694 1700, when he lived in Spain, they won him the favor of th court of Charles II. Works by Belvedere are preserved Naples (Mus. di Capodimonte), in Madrid (Prado), in Sorren (Mus. Correale di Terranova), and in Florence (Pitti).

As we have seen, beginning with the second half of th 17th century, that is, with the adoption of the baroque styl still life tended to diverge from its original significance (objec in repose, and hence investigated in their essence or transfigure by the rhythm both of the forms and of the colors and ligh and to take on accents and traits more purely decorative. Thes aspects became increasingly predominant in the course of th 18th century, when finally an entirely decorative purpose w assigned to still life — that is, still-life paintings were used overdoors, as screens to conceal fireplaces and doorways, as decorative elements in furniture. Nor were the still lif of even the greatest painters of the century spared these function the two famous *Shelves with Books* by Giuseppe Maria Cresp (1665–1747) in the Conservatorio di Musica G. B. Martin Bologna, were painted to conceal doorways; *The White Tabl cloth* by Jean Baptiste Simeon Chardin (q.v.), now in the A Institute of Chicago, originally served as a fireplace scree some of the still lifes of the above-mentioned François De portes and of Jean Baptiste Oudry (1686–1755) were conceive as overdoors; and some of the vibrant flower pictures of Francesc Guardi (1712–93), traced through the diligent research of Fiocc (1950), were painted as overdoors or fireplace screens. In con formity with the intended uses and also in keeping with th current taste, which delighted in perspective-illusionistic s lutions in decoration, many of the still lifes of this period see to have recovered that illusionistic character which they ha in antiquity and again in the 15th and 16th centuries. Here th two previously mentioned *Shelves with Books* by Crespi rep resent a rather significant paradigm.

Clearly, the characteristics indicated, which remain manife in the abundant and yet carefully executed artisan productio are forgotten in the painting of the great masters in the fac of the tremendous artistic commitment of the works, eve though in some cases — Chardin's *White Tablecloth* is a instance — recalling the purpose of the works may be of us in understanding and interpreting them.

What characterizes the works of an Oudry, for exampl is not their ornamental intent but the melodic unfolding of th design and the juxtaposition of the clear, open, luminous tone The works of Crespi (the canvases in storage in the Uffizi, Florence, and those in the Coll. Cassa di Risparmio, Bologn come to mind) are characteristic for the bold essentiality line and for the mercurial and luminous effervescence of th intense colors; absorbing the stimulus derived from Fyt (th canvases with displays of game as a theme), the depiction game once more became the pretext for the kindling of ligh and color. The works of Chardin — whether they represe flowers (e.g., the beautiful *Vase of Flowers* in Edinburgh, Na

Gall. of Scotland), furred or feathered animals (PL. 207), or interiors of kitchens with their appurtenances, or groups of knickknacks (e.g., the well-known *Still Life with Pipe* in the Louvre) — are distinguished for the vital rhythm that links the objects in the compositions, for the subtle harmony with which full and empty areas, forms and spaces, are disposed, and for the no less effective and evocative harmony with which colors echo and attract one another. For these qualities of composition, in which there is no trace of the "inventory" that persisted even in the late Flemish and Dutch paintings, the Bolognese Crespi may rightly be called a forerunner of Chardin.

The freedom of these artists vis-à-vis the traditional models is typified by the manner in which Francesco Guardi composed and painted his vases and baskets of flowers, which, after all, consists in the same animation, the same nervous, scintillating rapidity of stroke, and the same exuberant, spreading, luxuriant colors that characterize his *vedute* and his *capricci* (see GUARDI).

With these artists the still life surmounted, in certain respects, the traditional schemes and reached the level of great painting more than ever before. But it must be said that these were really exceptional cases in the area of still-life painting, that appanage of the true genre painters, who continued their activity also at this time but by now had declined to the status of survivors. Thus it is not without cause that these artists, except for Chardin, had no actual following; on the other hand, the followers of Chardin, though preserving a certain freedom, brought still life back to traditional lines. Among them Roland de La Porte was a disenchanted imitator of the forms of the master — as were, though less rigorously, Anne Vallayer-Coster (1744–1818) and Michel Bruno Bellangé (ca. 1726–93). Only Jean Jacques Bachelier and the Swiss painter Jean Etienne Liotard (1702–89), who had their training in France, managed, though feeling the influence of the master, to remain independent of him. This independence in the works of Liotard is accentuated in subtle and refined echoings of the forms of the great 17th-century age of still life. In Italy the œvre of the Rovigo nun Elisabetta Marchioni (active ca. 1700; works in Rovigo, Italy, Pin. dell'Acc. dei Concordi) offer a parallel: her flowery "altar frontals" superimpose the imaginative manner of Guardi upon that of Margherita Caffi, who at the end of the previous century had enjoyed great success at the courts of Tirol and Spain (many of her signed paintings are preserved in private collections in Spain and in the Academia de S. Fernando, Madrid), to the point of arousing the interest of Guardi himself, who in some instances may have imitated her.

But more pertinent than these episodes is the revival that took place in the second half of the century of the more archaic types of still life — a revival that was participated in by such artists as, to mention only the more important, Luis Eugenio Meléndez (1716–80), who won the reputation of being the Spanish Chardin and adorned the royal palaces with still lifes intended as decoration [represented by many works in the Prado PL. 201) and one in the Mus. of Fine Arts, Boston], and Carlo Magini (1720–1806) from Fano, who, following the example of the Lombard tradition, restored an everyday, familiar character to the surrealism of the works of such artists as Cecco del Caravaggio, and who was followed or imitated in this respect by the Rimini painter Nicola Levoli (1730–1801) and by the Faenza artist Pietro Piani (1770–1810).

As we have seen, in the course of the 18th century the high points of still-life painting were the works of the great artists whose paintings place them outside the traditional schemes, even though the thematic material was retained, and the works of the more gifted of the genre painters, who reintroduced, in a perceptible revival, the more archaic schemes of still life.

This same phenomenon occurred during the first half of the 19th century, after the "genres" had disappeared with the decline of the prestige of the Academy, and after the classicizing euphoria wholly centered on the anthropomorphic vision of "Greek" sculpture (see NEOCLASSIC STYLES) had subsided; then painters in various quarters who were no longer oriented to the traditional schools began to reintroduce the themes of "natura morta." In this connection, the works of Eugène Delacroix PL. 208), Gustave Courbet, and Jean Baptiste Camille Corot

(qq.v.) are extremely significant, as are the paintings of the lesser but still significant artist Adolphe Monticelli (1824–86), who took up and simplified the baroque of Jean Baptiste Monnoyer with a dedication that was almost pre-Cézannesque. Delacroix and Corot, even though in a different spirit and with different purposes, took up again the traditional motifs of the Flemish and Dutch still life, while Courbet, in some works of powerful import, seems to have reelaborated in terms of his own realism the motifs of Giovan Battista Ruopolo and of Spadino, that is to say, the motifs of 17th-century Neapolitan still life.

In this period, only in connection with the still lifes of Goya (1746–1828; PL. 208) and, later, Edouard Manet (q.v.; PL. 208) can a break with the past be spoken of: Goya almost humanized the elements that formed part of his compositions by charging them with an immediate, brutal inner power of expression, and the elements of the compositions assumed a relief and a dimension so monumental as to become emblematic for the orientation of modern and contemporary expressionism; Manet drew in the boundaries of the vision, eliminating the static implication from the traditional formula of the still life (objects in repose) by imbuing the vision with a sense of dynamic immediacy.

For the impressionists more generally speaking, however, it cannot be said that there existed a specific problem of still life. Henri Fantin-Latour (q.v.; PL. 210) and Pierre Auguste Renoir (q.v.; PL. 211), for instance, reposited in the more or less accentuated pagan gaiety of their painting the themes and moods of a Chardin, with a franker attention to the problems of light, or rather of the *plein-air* that constitutes the secret charm of their art. Claude Monet (q.v.) restated in still lifes the terms of his vision, which was also centered on the problems of light but in a more direct and brusque manner.

What has been said about the impressionists, or the painters now classified under this label, can be said more emphatically of Paul Cézanne (q.v.), who, on the one hand, took up the aspects of the problems with which the impressionists were concerned — as is now historically known despite arbitrary opinions to the contrary that were aired for a time — and, on the other hand, introduced into the orbit of those problems new accents that endowed images with greater concreteness (PL. 211; III, PLS. 184, 185; XI, PL. 96). In Cézanne there is not, in fact, the surrender of the impressionists to the phenomenological aspects of nature; rather there is a dynamic reconstitution of them through the sometimes ruthless light of the image and of the imagination: a subtly intellectualistic commitment, which by restoring reality of shapes and space to the semblances of nature gave rise to a new dimension, along which contemporary painting was to travel a great distance. In this sense, it can be said that if his earlier still lifes appear to be reelaborations of themes and motifs seen in museums, the later ones provide vital evidence of his continual experimentation and are symbolic of his mind and vision.

After Cézanne and the fantastic still lifes of Vincent van Gogh (q.v.), and with the advent of cubism and expressionism, the history of still life, which was by then completely unrelated to its traditional schemes or even to the faintest recollection of tradition, became the history of contemporary painting itself, that is, of "pure" painting. Since the days of the cubist "decompositions" of Pablo Picasso and Georges Braque (qq.v.; II, PLS. 349, 350), it can be said that contemporary painters, by concentrating on still life, have found a way to shake off every encumbering illustrative apparatus and every claim of objectivity and to concentrate interest exclusively on pure values. In Italy this was the case with Giorgio Morandi, who devoted himself almost solely to painting infinite variations of a few constant themes: bottles, apples, and insignificant everyday objects (PL. 211; IV, PL. 444; V, PL. 149). In conclusion, however, it can be stated that all the painting of the present century, even that of the most bold, revolutionary, and innovating movements, tends to take on the configuration of still life. (See also CUBISM AND FUTURISM; EUROPEAN MODERN MOVEMENTS; NONOBJECTIVE ART.)

Stefano BOTTARI

ASPECTS OF FAR EASTERN ART COMPARABLE WITH WESTERN STILL LIFE. Various categories of painting, based on the subject represented, are distinguished in the Chinese treatises emanating from the academies, and these types correspond in their methodological approach to the Western classification that gave rise to such a definition as that implicit in the term "still life."

The anonymous catalogue (*Hsüan-ho hua p'u*) of the collection of the emperor Hui-tsung, which has a preface bearing the date 1120, but which in the entirety of its present form is assignable to the beginning of the 14th century, lists ten categories of subjects in order of importance. Of these, the eighth, ninth, and tenth (in other words, the least important) are flowers and birds (*huaniao*), ink-painted bamboos (*mo-chu*), and vegetables and fruit (*su-kuo*). It should be stated at once, however, that this grading of values was not universally accepted — in particular, not by artists who specialized in a given subject, for instance, the landscapist Mi Fei (q.v.; 1052–1107), who put landscape (*shan-shui*), the sixth category, in first place — and also that there is no evidence of the existence of either the sixth category or the eighth, ninth, and tenth before the period of the Five Dynasties (907–60). In any case, the last of the ten categories does offer works comparable with Western still life; and the scant importance almost universally attached to it does not differ much from that granted to still life in many Western critical sources, among them Malvasia, Lanzi, and Salvator Rosa (q.v.). In a certain sense, the tenth category corresponds closely to the fruit and flower painting of the Western world (PL. 202). The works in the two preceding categories, by virtue of the symbolic values concentrated in them and because of the fact that they were fragments of a lesser life, lyrically interpreted as expressions of a state of mind, can be considered not "natura morta" but, if anything, "natura vivente." But all the categories represent the search for the essential and constant principle (*li*) inborn in things.

As for style, naturally one does not look to China for that virtuosic realism and that predilection for constructing illusionistic volumes in space typical of pre-19th-century still lifes, even if in these latter we find a continuous effort to render the visible essence of the things depicted. Rather, we find those distinctive elements of Chinese painting, speed of execution and certitude of brushstroke. Likewise, in the Chinese compositions that concern us here there is no seeking after ornamental values for their own sake; these are shunned as dangerously beclouding that deeper truth which was defined by Su Tung-p'o (Su Shih; 1036–1101) as "the constant principle of things." Thus the similarity between Chinese compositions (and Japanese works derived from them) and Western still lifes is distinctly limited, so that few works can be considered in the present context.

Without question the most important is the painting entitled *Persimmons* (X, PL. 201), which, together with *Chestnuts* and *Rose Mallows in Rain* (X, PL. 201), is attributed to Mu-Ch'i (q.v.). The ink spots that describe the fruits in the first-mentioned work even manage to convey their compact mass, concentrating into a magnificent serenity the flash of an impassioned inspiration. The *Chestnuts*, too, may be regarded as cognate to still life by reason of its particular structure, which presents the subject of the painting isolated in the center of the area of the available background. But here, as in the *Persimmons* and in many other Chinese and Japanese pictorial compositions, there is at work the symbolic component of the Ch'an (Jap., Zen) current in Buddhism (q.v.), which often unfolds through obscure meanderings that are not always clarified by the inscriptions. But surely, whatever the symbolic import of the *Persimmons* and the *Chestnuts*, the prodigiousness of the intuiton that produced them and the extraordinary skill of the author, an absolute master of his medium, is not altered. However, in certain works symbolism, patent or hidden, is all-pervasive: thus in the painting of the Japanese master Ekaku Hakuin (1685–1768; see also VIII, PL. 315) representing a beetle, or beater for husking rice, the symbolic reference to the Sixth Ch'an Patriarch, Hui-Nêng (637–713), who husked rice for eight months in the barns of the monastery, is manifest, and the allusive inscription that accompanies the work confirms it. Quite different is the symbolism found in another work by the same artist, which represents a candlestick with a candle burning in it. The inscription reads: "The light shines with a cut wick,

the heart glows with the practice of Dharma." Similarly, th? composition of Eiboku Suiō (1716–89) in which a broom an? a bamboo box (to contain a scroll) are juxtaposed represents by depicting their symbols, the legendary Chinese sages Han shan and Shih-tê.

The examples cited, which could easily be multiplied (c? PL. 212), illustrate the ascendancy of the symbolic implicatio? over the representational aspect of the object depicted: thus even in those works that seem to come closest in conception to th? still life of the West the divergence — not of style alone — i? very clear. Such compositions as the *Field Flowers* by Wang Shih-min (1592–1680; see WANG SHIH-MIN, CHIEN, HUI, AN? YUAN-CH'I), now in Stockholm (Östasiatiska Mus.), and th? motif of flowers in a basket that appears in several prints turn on the lyric expression of a state of mind through the represen? tation of elements of the natural world and hence do not trul? correspond to Western still life.

Mario BUSSAGLI

SOURCES. Vasari; G. Baglione, Le vite de' pittori, scultori et architetti dal pontificato di Gregorio XIII del 1572, in fino a' tempi di papa di Urban? Ottauo nel 1642, Rome, 1642; A. Félibien des Avaux, Entretiens sur les vie? et sur les ouvrages des plus excellens peintres anciens et modernes, 5 vols. Paris, 1666–88; J. von Sandrart, L'academia todesca...: Oder, teutsch? Akademie..., 2 vols., Nürnberg, Frankfurt am Main, 1675–79; C. C? Malvasia, Felsina pittrice, 2 vols., Bologna, 1678; L. Pascoli, Vite de' pittor? scultori ed architetti moderni..., 2 vols., Rome, 1730–36; B. de Dominic? Vite de' pittori ed architetti napoletani..., 3 vols., Naples, 1742–44; F? Bartoli, Notizie delle pitture... d'Italia, 2 vols., Venice, 1776; L. Lanz? Storia pittorica dell'Italia, Florence, 1792.

BIBLIOG. *General*: H. Wichmann, ed., Meister des Stillebens, Leipzig 1926; H. Furst, The Art of Still-life Painting, London, New York, 192? E. Badelt, Das Stilleben als bürgerliches Bildthema und seine Entwicklun? von Anfängen bis zur Gegenwart, Würzburg, 1938; U. Christoffel, Natur? morte, Kunstwerk, II, 7, 1948, pp. 5–12; M. J. Friedländer, Landscape Portrait, Still-life: Their Origin and Development (trans. R. F. C. Hull? Oxford, 1949; I. Mackintosh, Paintings of Flowers, Scottish Rev., IV, 4 1952–53, pp. 7–101; A. Gwynne-Jones, Introduction to Still-life, Ne? York, 1954; A. Kübler, Zu unserem Aprilheft: Stilleben, D? 1954, 4, p. 6 (see entire issue); A. Sergeev, Uchebnii natyurmort (Techniqu? of Still Life), Moscow, 1955; J. Bernström and B. Rapp, Iconographica Stockholm, 1957; J. A. Gaya Nuño, Eternidad de un genero, Rev. de idea? estéticas, XVI, 1958, pp. 187–202; G. Raimondi, Perché natura morta? Comunità, XII, 59, 1958, pp. 74–83; A. Ioannou, L'objet dans la natur? morte, peinture de chevalet, Paris, 1959; C. Sterling, La nature morte d? l'antiquité à nos jours, 2d ed., Paris, 1959 (bibliog.; Eng. trans.), J. Emmons London, New York, 1959); W. S. Walter, Still Life Painting, London, 196? E. H. Gombrich, Tradition and Expression in Western Still Life, BM? CIII, 1961, pp. 175–80; S. H. Pavière, A Dictionary of Flower, Fruit an? Still Life Painters, 3 vols. in 4, Leigh-on-Sea, 1962–64.

Catalogues of exhibitions and collections: Galerie Bernheim-Jeune, Cen? ans de nature morte, Paris, 1907; La nature morte hollandaise, Brussels, 192? Fogg Art Museum, Still-life, Cambridge, Mass., 1931 (introd. by G. B? Washburn); Museum Boymans, Cent quinze natures mortes de 1480 à 193? Rotterdam, 1933; J. Cavestany, Floreros y bodegones en la pintura español? Madrid, 1940; L. M. Costa, Algumas "naturezas mortas" no Museu naciona? de belas artes, Anuario Mus. nac. de belas artes, VII, 1945, pp. 129–58 Galerie Charpentier, La vie silencieuse, Paris, 1946; G. Briganti, ed., Na? ture morte del '600–'700, Rome, 1947; Galerie de l'Elysée, Natures morte? des écoles espagnole, française, flamande et hollandaise, Paris, 1950; C? Sterling, ed., La nature morte de l'antiquité à nos jours (Mus. de l'Orangerie) Paris, 1952 (reviewed by V. Bloch, BM, XCIV, 1952, pp. 208–09); A. Duhau? Le Peintre, 46, 1952, pp. 14–15; R. Longhi, Paragone, III, 38, 1952, pp. 46? 52; R. Michau, Le Peintre, 47, 1952, pp. 12–13; Arcade Gallery, The Ar? of Still-life, 1600–1700, London, 1953 (pref. by V. Bloch); A. Chudzikowski ed., Holenderska i flamandzka martwa natura XVIII wieku (17th Centur? Dutch and Flemish Still-life Painting), Warsaw, 1954; H. Haug, Nature? mortes du Musée des Beaux-Arts de Strasbourg, Strasbourg, 1954; Museum Boymans, Vier eeuwen stilleven in Frankrijk, Rotterdam, 1954 (introd. b? C. Sterling); M. Allemand, ed., Natures mortes, Saint-Etienne, 1955; J? Białostocki, ed., Wystawa malarstwa włoskiego w zbiorach polskich (Exhi? bition of Italian Painting in Polish Collections), Warsaw, 1956; Musée de? Beaux-Arts, Natures mortes d'hier et d'aujourd'hui, Besançon, 1956; L? Salerno and others, Il Seicento europeo, Rome, 1957; Il Settecento a Roma? Rome, 1959; Silent World: Exhibition of Still Life Paintings by Old Masters London, 1960; A. Wertheimer, ed., La nature morte et son inspiration (Gal? André Weill), Paris, 1960; Baltimore Museum of Art, Fruit and Flowers Baltimore, 1961; L. J. Bol, Nederlandse stilleven uit de 17de eeuw, Dordrecht 1962; Z. van Boér, Stilleben på gavnø, Copenhagen, 1964; La natura morta italiana, Milan, 1964 (exhibition at Naples, Zurich, Rotterdam; bibliog.? Newark Museum Associates, The Golden Age of Spanish Still-life Painting Newark, N.J., 1964.

The term "still life": A. P. A. Vorenkamp, Bijdrage tot de geschiedeni? van het hollandsch stilleven in de 17de eeuw, Leiden, 1934; S. Sulzberger La nature morte: Son évolution depuis l'antiquité jusqu'à la Renaissance Brussels, 1945 (unpub. diss.); H. Haug, Natures mortes du Musée des Beaux Arts de Strasbourg, Strasbourg, 1954; C. Sterling, La nature morte de l'an? tiquité à nos jours, 2d ed., Paris, 1959, pp. 41–42.

Antiquity: Overbeck, SQ, nos. 2158–60; G. Lippold, RE, s.v. 'Ρωπο-άφος, 'Ρυπαρογράφος; H. G. Beyen, Über Stilleben aus Pompeji und Hercu-neum, The Hague, 1928; P. Marconi, La pittura dei Romani, Rome, 1929; . E. Rizzo, Pittura ellenistico-romana, Milan, 1929; O. Elia, Pitture murali mosaici del Museo Nazionale di Napoli, Naples, 1932; G. E. Rizzo, Speci-en sulle pitture di natura morta, Rome, 1935; S. Ferri, Plinio il Vecchio, ome, 1946, p. 113; D. Casella, La frutta nella pittura pompeiana, Pompe-na: Studi per il II centenario degli scavi di Pompei, Naples, 1950, pp. 355–; A. Palombi, La fauna marina nei mosaici e nei dipinti, Pompeiana, aples, 1950, pp. 425–55; A. Maiuri, La "nature morte" dans la peinture de ompéi, in C. Sterling, ed., La nature morte de l'antiquité à nos jours (Mus. l'Orangerie), Paris, 1952, pp. vii–xii; K. Schefold, Pompeianische Wand-alerei: Sinne und Ideengeschichte, Basel, 1952; F. Eckstein, Unter-chungen über die Stilleben aus Pompeji und Herculaneum, Berlin, 1957; . Sgatti, Caratteri della "natura morta" pompeiana, AC, IX, 1957, pp. 174–; J.-M. Croisille, Les natures mortes campaniennes, Brussels, 1965 (bib-g.).

Middle Ages, Renaissance, mannerism: F. Arcangeli, Tarsie, Rome, 43; G. Briganti, Il Manierismo e Pellegrino Tibaldi, Rome, 1945; S. osia, Valore e significato della "natura morta" nella tradizione critica, Acme, , 1952, pp. 329–47; M. Faré, Les origines de la nature morte dans la peinture objects du Moyen Age et de la Renaissance, Paris, 1952; C. de Tolnay, es origines de la nature morte moderne, RArts, II, 1952, pp. 151–52; C. Tolnay, Notes sur les origines de la nature morte, RArts, III, 1953, . 66–67; I. Bergström, Revival of Antique Illusionistic Wall-painting in enaissance Art, Göteborg, 1957; A. Parronchi, Postilla sul neo-gaddismo gli anni 1423–25, Paragone, XII, 137, 1961, pp. 19–26; C. de Tolnay, ostilla sulla origine della natura morta moderna, RArte, XXXVI, 1961–, pp. 3–10.

Flemish painters: J. Silvers, Joachim Beuckelaer, JhbPreussKSamml, XXIV, 1911, pp. 185–212; A. Bredius, De Bloemschilders Bosschaert, ud-Holland, XXXI, 1913, pp. 137–40; C. Benedict, Un peintre oublié e natures mortes: Osias Beert, L'amour de l'art, XIX, 1938, pp. 307–14; . Boström, A Still-life Painting, by J. Beuckelaer, Oud-Holland, LXIII, 48, pp. 122–28; E. Greindl, Jan Fyt: Peintre de fleurs, Misc. Leo van uyvelde, Brussels, 1949, pp. 163–65; M. L. Hairs, Osias Beert l'Ancien: eintre de fleurs, Rev. belge d'archéol. et d'h. de l'art, XX, 1951, pp. 237–; R. Gennaille, L'œuvre de Pieter Aertsen, GBA, XLIV, 1954, pp. 267–; M. L. Hairs, Les peintres flamands de fleurs au XVIIe siècle, Brussels 55; E. Greindl, Les peintres flamands de nature morte au XVIIe siècle, russels, 1956 (bibliog.); I. Bergström, Osias Beert the Elder as a Collabo-tor of Rubens, BM, XCIX, 1957, pp. 120–21; L. J. Bol, The Bosschaert ynasty: Painters of Flowers and Fruit, Leigh-on-Sea, 1960.

Dutch painters: A. Bredius, Jan Jansz. Uyl, Oud-Holland, XXXV, 917, pp. 193–95, XXXVIII, 1920, p. 126; I. Blok, Abraham van Beyeren, nze kunst, XXXIII, 1918, pp. 159–65; I. Blok, Willem Kalf, Onze kunst, XXV, 1919, pp. 85–94, 137–45; R. Warner, Dutch and Flemish Flower nd Fruit Painters of the 17th and 18th Centuries, London, 1928; E. Zar-owska, La nature morte hollandaise: Ses principaux représentants, ses rigines, ses influences, Brussels, Maastricht, 1929; R. Renraw, The Art f Rachel Ruysch, The Connoisseur, XCII, 1933, pp. 397–99; P. de Boer, an Jansz. den Uyl, Oud-Holland, LVII, 1940, pp. 49–64; H. E. van Gelder, eda, Beyeren, Kalf, Amsterdam, 1941; N. R. A. Vroom, De schilders van et monochrome banketje, Amsterdam, 1945; R. van Luttervelt, Schilders van et stilleven, Naarden, 1947; M. Salinger, Early Flower Paintings, BMMA, .S., VIII, 1949–50, pp. 253–61; M. H. Grant, ed., The Twelve Months f Flowers by Jacob van Huysum, Leigh-on-Sea, 1950; J. Bruyn, David ailly, Oud-Holland, LXVI, 1951, pp. 148–64, 212–27; I. Bergström, Dutch till-life Painting in the 17th Century (trans. C. Hedström and G. Taylor), ondon, 1956; P. Gamelbo, Dutch Still-life Painting from the 16th to the 8th Centuries in Danish Collections, Copenhagen, 1960.

Still life in Italy: *a. General*: M. Marangoni, Valori malnoti o trascu-ti della pittura italiana del Seicento, RArte, X, 1917, pp. 1–31 (repr. in rte barocca, 2d ed., Florence, 1953, pp. 1–35); G. J. Hoogewerff, Nature orte italiane del Seicento e del Settecento, Dedalo, IV, 1923–24, pp. 599–24, 710–30; G. Delogu, Pittori minori liguri, lombardi, piemontesi del Sei-ento e del Settecento, Venice, 1931; F. Zeri, La Galleria Spada in Roma, lorence, 1952; U. Prota-Giurleo, Pittori napoletani del Seicento, Naples, 953; N. di Carpegna, Pittori fiamminghi e olandesi nella Galleria Nazionale 'Arte Antica, Rome, 1954; R. Causa, Pittura napoletana dal XV al XIX ecolo, Bergamo, 1957; N. di Carpegna, Pittori napoletani del '600 e del 700, Rome, 1958; F. Zeri, La Galleria Pallavicini in Roma, Florence, 1959; . Delogu, Natura morta italiana, Bergamo, 1962. *b. Single artists or chools*: M. Perotti, I pittori Campi da Cremona, Milan, 1932; R. Longhi, ltimi studi sul Caravaggio e la sua cerchia, Proporzioni, I, 1943, pp. 5–3; L. Angelini, Evaristo Baschenis, Bergamo, 1946; G. Fiocco, Francesco uardi, Arte veneta, IV, 1950, pp. 76–85; R. Longhi, Un momento impor-nte per la storia della natura morta, Paragone, I, 1, 1950, pp. 34–39; R. ausa, Paolo Porpora e il primo tempo della "natura morta" napoletana, aragone, II, 15, 1951, pp. 30–36; A. Puerari, La Pinacoteca di Cremona, lorence, 1951, pp. 176–78 (the "fioranti"); F. Zeri, Giuseppe Recco: Una atura morta giovanile, Paragone, III, 33, 1952, pp. 37–38; E. Battisti, Pro-lo del Gobbo dei Carracci, Comm, V, 1954, pp. 290–302; G. Briganti, ristoforo Monari, Paragone, V, 55, 1954, pp. 40–42; G. Briganti, Michelan-elo Cerquozzi pittore di nature morte, Paragone, V, 53, 1954, pp. 47–52; . Delogu, Novità su Charles Magini peintre à Fano, Emporium, CXX, 954, pp. 247–58; G. Incisa della Rocchetta, Un dipinto dello Spadino in ampidoglio, B. Mus. Com. di Roma, I, 1954, pp. 6–8; H. Swarzenski, aravaggio and Still-life Painting, BMFA, LII, 1954, pp. 22–38; G. Testori, ature morte di Tommaso Salini, Paragone, V, 51, 1954, pp. 20–25; L. auli Naldi, Carlo Magini pittore di nature morte del secolo XVIII, Paragone, V, 48, 1954, pp. 57–60; J. Thuillier, Les tableaux du Cardinal-onlce, Oeil, 34, 1957, pp. 33–41; G. Testori, Nature morte di Tommaso Realfonzo, Paragone, IX, 97, 1958, pp. 63–67; F. Arcangeli, Maestri della pittura del Seicento emiliano, Bologna, 1959, pp. 279–80 (the Forlì "fiori"; exhibition cat.); A. Berne-Joffroy, Le Dossier Caravage, Paris, 1959; G. Delogu, Ancora sul Magini pittore di "nature morte," Emporium, CXXIX, 1959, pp. 67–70; L. Servolini, Carlo Magini, Milan, 1959; F. Arisi, Il Museo Civico di Piacenza, Piacenza, 1960, pp. 230–37 (bibliog.); S. Bottari, La "bella" raccoglitrice di frutta, Arte antica e moderna, III, 1960, pp. 413–16 (A. Brueghel); S. Bottari, Due "nature morte" dell'Empoli, Arte antica e moderna, III, 1960, pp. 75–76; S. Bottari, Un'opera di Pietro Paolo Bonzi, Arte antica e moderna, III, 1960, pp. 290–95; S. Bottari, Una segnalazione per C. Berentz, Arte antica e moderna, III, 1960, pp. 416–17; R. Causa, La peinture italienne au XVIIIe siècle, Paris, 1960 (A. Belvedere; bibliog.); G. Delogu, Nature morte dell'Empoli, Emporium, CXXXI, 1960, pp. 195–98; K. M. Malitskaia, A Still-life Painting of Jacopo da Empoli in the State Museum of Fine Arts (in Rus.), Trudy Gosudarstvennogo muzeia izobrazitel'nykh iskusstv, Moscow, 1960, pp. 200–10; F. Arcangeli, Il fratello del Guercino, Arte antica e moderna, IV, 1961, pp. 325–43; G. Bargellesi, Arcangelo Resani, Emporium, CXXXIII, 1961, pp. 153–57; S. Bottari, Appunti sui Recco, Arte antica e moderna, IV, 1961, pp. 354–61; N. di Carpegna, I Recco: Note e contributi, BArte, XLVI, 1961, pp. 123–32; R. Causa, Un avvio per Giacomo Recco, Arte antica e moderna, IV, 1961, pp. 344–53; C. Del Bravo, Due nature morte di Astolfo Petrazzi, Paragone, XII, 139, 1961, pp. 58–59; C. Del Bravo, Una figura con natura morta del Seicento toscano, Arte antica e moderna, IV, 1961, pp. 322–24; L. Zauli Naldi, Nicola Levoli e le sue nature morte, Paragone, XII, 141, 1961, pp. 40–42; R. Causa, Luca Forte e il primo tempo della natura morta napoletana, Paragone, XIII, 145, 1962, pp. 41–48; G. Maggi, Attualità della natura morta, Antichità viva, I, 1962, pp. 9–13 (Simone del Tintore); S. Bottari, Fede Galizia, Arte antica e moderna, VI, 1963, pp. 309–18; A. Quintavalle Ghidiglia, Cristoforo Munari e la natura morta emiliana, Parma, 1964.

Still life in France: H. Haug, Un nouveau tableau de Jacques Linard, B. Mus. de France, VII, 1935, pp. 63–64; C. Benedict, A propos de quelques natures mortes de l'époque Louis XIII, Maandblad voor beeldende kunsten, XXIV, 1948, pp. 29–34; H. Haug, Sébastian Stoskopff: Peintre de natures mortes (1597–1657), Arch. alsaciennes d'h. de l'art, XVI, 1948, pp. 23–72; H. Haug, Trois peintres strasbourgeois, RArts, II, 1952, pp. 137–50; M. Faré, Baugin: Peintre de natures mortes, B. Soc. d'h. de l'art fr., 1955, pp. 15–26; W. J. Müller, Der Maler Georg Flegel und die Anfänge des Stillebens, Frankfurt am Main, 1956; J. Wilhelm, Louise Moillon, Oeil, 21, 1956, pp. 6–11; C. Benedict, Notes sur Jacques Linard, Et. d'art, 13, 1957–58, pp. 5–45; A. P. de Mirimonde, Deux natures mortes du XVIIe siècle français aux musées de la Fère et de Chaumont, RArts, VII, 1957, pp. 218–24; I. Elles, Das Stilleben in der französischen Malerei des 19. Jahrhunderts, Zurich, 1958; M. Faré, Nature et nature morte au XVIIe siècle, GBA, LI, 1958, pp. 253–66; J.-F. Revel, Linard, Conaissance des arts, 79, 1958, pp. 5–45; M. Faré, Attrait de la nature morte au XVIIe siècle, GBA, LIII, 1959, pp. 129–44; H. Haug, Sébastian Stoskopff, Oeil, 76, 1961, pp. 22–35; C. Benedict, Petits maîtres de la nature morte en France, Oeil, 91–92, 1962, pp. 38–45; M. Faré, La nature morte en France: Son histoire et son évolution du XVIIe au XXe siècle, 2 vols., Geneva, 1962 (bibliog.); J. W. McCoubry, The Revival of Chardin in French Still-life Painting, AB, XLVI, 1964, pp. 39–53; A. P. de Mirimonde, Les œuvres françaises à sujet de musique au musée du Louvre: Natures mortes des XVIIe, XVIIIe et XIXe siècles, Rev. du Louvre, XV, 1965, pp. 51–58, 111–24.

Still life in Spain: J. Cavestany, Pintores españoles de flores, Arte español, VI, 1922–23, pp. 124–35; E. Lafuente Ferrari, La peinture de bodegones en Espagne, GBA, XIV, 1935, pp. 169–83; G. Oña Iribarren, 165 firmas de pintores tomadas de cuadros de flores y bodegones, Madrid, 1944 (Flemish and Italian as well as Spanish painters); H. P. G. Seckel, F. de Zurbarán as a Painter of Still-life, GBA, XXX, 1946, pp. 279–300; M. S. Soria, Notas sobre algunos bodegones españoles del siglo XVII, AEArte, XXXII, 1959, pp. 273–80; W. Jordan, Juan van der Hamen y León: A Madrilenian Still-life Painter, Marsyas, XII, 1964–65, pp. 52–69.

Still life in the United States: W. Born, Still-life Painting in America, New York, 1947; A. Frankenstein, After the Hunt: William Michael Harnett and Other American Still Life Painter 1870–1900, Berkeley, Los Angeles, 1953.

The Far East: See the bibliog. for CHINESE ART.

* *

Illustrations: PLS. 193–212.

STOSS (STOSZ), VEIT. Sculptor, painter, and engraver (d. Nürnberg, 1533), active in Nürnberg and in Kraków, where his name was spelled Wit Stwosz. The date of his birth is given as 1438 by J. Neudörfer, who in 1547 compiled short biographies of Nürnberg artists, but later writers suggest 1447. His name first appears in a document of 1477, when he gave up his citizenship before the City Council of Nürnberg; since he had not previously acquired it he must have inherited it from one or both of his parents. The commission that called Stoss to Kraków was the high altar for the Church of the Virgin Mary (Panny Marii), which he began in 1477 and completed in 1489. The altar, which is of enormous dimensions (ca. 43 ft. high and ca. 36 ft. wide, with some of the statues in the shrine rising to a height of 9 ft.) depicts, with statues in the round, the Death and Assumption of the Virgin. An outer pair of stationary wings and an inner pair of movable wings show — when the latter are closed — twelve scenes in relief from the life of Christ and the Virgin; when the inner wings are open, six reliefs with similar themes are revealed and flank the statues in the shrine. In the architectural superstructure the Coronation of the Virgin is represented, and on the predella there is a Tree of Jesse. Large dimensions are not uncommon in altars of the time: the altarpiece by Michael Pacher (q.v.) for the church at Sankt Wolfgang am Ambersee, near Salzburg, was executed in the same period.

The main source of Stoss's style was Nicolaus Gerhaert van Leyden, who first appeared along the Middle Rhine in 1462 and then spent some years in Strasbourg before he was called in 1469 to Vienna, where he died early in the 1470s. The cometlike emergence of this great sculptor (evidently a Dutchman) had a notable effect in southern Germany from about 1470 on. In many places — in Alsace and Swabia, in Nürnberg and Passau, as well as in Vienna — students adopted the luminosity of his surface treatment, the bold *contrapposto* of his figures, and the bold undercutting of his draperies. There are indications that a Gerhaert pupil was working in Nürnberg before Stoss left for Kraków. This master, who has been identified, perhaps erroneously, by Lossnitzer (1912) with a Simon Lainberger mentioned in documents, may have created the figures of the high altar in the Church of St. Georg at Nördlingen. But Stoss may also have seen works by Gerhaert himself: the similarities between Stoss's large sandstone crucifix, also in the Church of the Virgin Mary in Kraków, and Gerhaert's sculpture of the same subject (1467) in the old cemetery of Baden-Baden are probably indicative of first-hand observation of the latter's work.

In the austere expression of the faces (e.g., the St. John in the central group of the Kraków altar) there are features that seem to be typically Franconian and — apart from the more monumental character of Stoss's work — show affinities with facial expressions in the paintings of Michael Wolgemut, though in Stoss's works this austerity has a monumental quality that is lacking in Wolgemut's. The same monumentality of expression and sculptural form is seen in the head of King Casimir IV Jagello on his tomb in the Chapel of the Holy Cross in the Cathedral on the Wawel in Kraków, a work which Stoss finished and signed in 1492; the bold treatment of draperies and the choice of material (red marble) recall Gerhaert's monument for Emperor Frederick III in the Cathedral of St. Stephan in Vienna. During the last years of Stoss's residence in Poland he executed the red-marble tomb slab of the primate Zbigniew Oleśnicki (1493) in the Cathedral of Gniezno; the monument of Bishop Peter Moszyński (d. 1493) in the Cathedral of Włoclawek; and a sandstone relief depicting Christ and Apostles on the Mount of Olives (PL. 214).

When the Kraków altar was thoroughly cleaned in 1932–33 the elaborate coloring of the statues and the relief figures and the entirely painted relief backgrounds were found to be practically intact under the heavy overpainting. The composition of the reliefs — the high horizon; the broken outlines and drapery folds; and, whenever possible, numerous figures — is echoed in the ten engravings that have been preserved. Although none of them repeats a subject represented on the altar, they constitute a useful exercise for a sculptor who had to grapple with three-dimensional representation on a two-dimensional surface. To the modern observer the nervous sensitivity of their broken lines and the problematic character of their spatialization have a strong appeal. Chronologically, they accompany Stoss's work on the altar and go beyond it to the end of his stay in Kraków.

In 1496 Stoss returned to Nürnberg, where his citizenship was immediately reinstated. By 1499 he had completed three large sandstone reliefs for the choir of St. Sebald, depicting the Last Supper, Christ on the Mount of Olives (with reminiscences of the same scene in Kraków), and Christ taken prisoner, in which a ferocious soldier in Polish costume with a huge

scimitar is a free version of a similar figure in Stoss's engraving of the Raising of Lazarus. The donor of these reliefs, Pa Volckamer, also commissioned two linden statues to be place above them — a Man of Sorrows and a *mater dolorosa*. Th large crucifix in St. Lorenz, Nürnberg (originally in St. Sebald with the loincloth fluttering in a wildly twisting curve, mu coincide in date with the linden statue of the Virgin and Chil (VI, PL. 133) that he carved for the façade of the house he ha bought in the year of his return from Kraków. The latter wo reflects the composition of the engraving B.3 (P.6) in the Gra phische Sammlung in Munich, but the style is softer and th outlines are more rounded. The figure of St. Roch in th Guadagni Chapel of SS. Annunziata in Florence is placed b C. T. Müller (ThB, s.v.) in the same period — that is, betwee 1500 and 1503, which may be a few years too early.

This magnificent and extremely powerful work, for whic there is no documentation prior to 1523, when it was fir described in SS. Annunziata, was much admired by Vasar (I, p. 167) who called it a "miracolo di legno" and found th natural expression and the perfect arrangement of the draperie particularly praiseworthy. Like other statues that followe it, Stoss's sculpture of St. Roch was left unpainted, and the mor ochrome splendor of the wood recommended itself to a Renais sance taste that was beginning to appear in the north.

His activities as an artist were interrupted in 1503 by tu bulent events, during which the passionate character of th master clashed with the laws of bourgeois society. A merchan in whose enterprises Stoss had invested 1,000 florins, defrauded him of that sum; in the lawsuit that followed Stoss produce an acknowledgment of debt on which he himself had forge the signature of the merchant. The forgery was discovered, an according to the law of the times Stoss might have received death sentence had not the Bishop of Würzburg and other pleaded for him. Owing to their efforts the sentence was re duced to branding through both cheeks. Furthermore, he wa enjoined not to leave the city for the rest of his life. Instead he fled to Münnerstadt, the home of his son-in-law, who imme diately — and entirely on his own — began a dispute wit the city of Nürnberg that he continued for the next 14 year In 1505, however, Stoss returned to Nürnberg, and in the follow ing year, to the annoyance of the City Council, the Holy Roma emperor Maximilian I repealed the sentence of 1503.

During his stay at Münnerstadt Stoss painted the figure and reliefs on Tilman Riemenschneider's (q.v.) altar of S Mary Magdalene (1491/92) in the parish church and adde to the altar four wings with paintings illustrating the legen of St. Cilian in hard, light, and strangely clashing colors. O his return to Nürnberg he found his workshop closed and as sistants dispersed, and the churches refused to order altarpiece from him. A larger-than-life-size unpainted linden figure St. Andrew on a pillar in the choir of St. Sebald, executed (ca 1506) for a member of the Tucher family, shows a new, les turbulent monumentality and resembles that of St. Roch i Florence. The somewhat later crucifix (ca. 1510) in the Churc of Ognissanti in Florence (formerly in S. Salvatore al Monte is a product of the workshop that Stoss was beginning to rebuild The closely related crucifix of the same years from the Hospita of the Holy Ghost in Nürnberg (now, Germanisches Nat. Mus.), on which the original colors are well preserved, has mor claim to being a work by Stoss himself. The final developmen in his art is seen in the unpainted sculpture of Christ on th Cross that was donated to St. Sebald by Niclas Wickel in 152c by now, calmness in expression and outline — showing in par the influence of Dürer (q.v.) — had become characteristic o the work of the last 10 years of Stoss's activity. The same re straint, more evolved than in the figure of St. Andrew in S Sebald, is found in the unpainted linden statue of St. Paul i the Church of St. Lorenz, which was made in 1513 for Anto Kress.

In 1516 the typically Florentine subject of the young Tobia with the archangel Raphael was entrusted to Stoss by Raffael Torrigiani, a Florentine silk merchant, who commissioned th work for the Carmelite church in Nürnberg. The two unpainted figures (1516–18; PL. 213), half life-size, were later removed

St. Jakob and are now in the Germanisches National-Museum. There followed, in 1517–18, the group of the Annunciation in St. Lorenz, Stoss's best-known work, in which the two main figures, painted and larger than life-size, are accompanied by eight smaller angels — all placed within a frame in the form of a rosary suspended from the vault of the choir. More and more the concentration of sculptural force in the body seems to absorb the exuberance of the draperies. The final development is seen in the boxwood statuette of the Virgin and Child in the Victoria and Albert Museum, London. In this work, as well as in the Bamberg altar, the stabilizing influence of Dürer is unmistakable. When the Bamberg altar, commissioned in 1520 for the Carmelite monastery by the prior Andreas Stoss, son of the artist, was almost ready for delivery in 1523, the adherents of the Reformation forced Andreas out of the city; the Carmelites refused to accept the altar, which was placed in the Bamberg parish church not until a decade after the master's death and in 1937 was transferred to the Cathedral. An original drawing for the center of the altar, showing the inner wings open, is in the Muzeum Archeologiczne in Kraków. [Other drawings by Stoss depict the Presentation in the Temple (1505; Berlin, Kupferstichkabinett) and St. Anne with the Virgin, a preparatory drawing for one of his several groups of that subject (ca. 1510; Budapest, Nat. Mus.).] The Bamberg altar consists of an Adoration of the Shepherds in the center and four reliefs — all that were completed of 8 or perhaps 12 planned — in the wings. The absence of color, except for a light glaze on the faces, is not a result of the unfinished state, but, rather, of the consideration that color could only harm the powerful concentration of forms, in which all unnecessary detail is suppressed.

Stoss, blind and very advanced in age, died in 1533. While younger contemporaries, such as Hans Leinberger (1470?–after 1530), indulged in an emotional semibaroque, Stoss with his passionate temperament never allowed gesture or expression to overshadow the sculptural power of form.

SOURCES: J. Neudörfer, Nachrichten von Künstlern und Werkleuten deselbst [in Nürnberg] aus dem Jahre 1547, ed. G. W. K. Lochner (Quellenschr. f. Kg. u. Kunsttechnik, X), Vienna, 1875, pp. 84–115; J. von Sandrart, l'Academia tedesca . . . oder, Teutsche Academie, 3 vols., Nürnberg, Frankfurt, 1675–79, ed. A. R. Peltzer, Munich, 1925; J. G. Doppelmayr, Historische Nachricht von den Nürnbergischen Mathematicis und Künstlern, Nürnberg, 1730, p. 191 ff.; C. G. von Murr, Beschreibung der vornehmsten Merkwürdigkeiten in Nürnberg, 2 vols., Nürnberg, 1778–1801; A. Grabowski, Starożytności historyczne Polskie, Cracow, 1840, p. 437 ff.; J. Baader, Beiträge zur Kunstgeschichte Nürnbergs, Nördlingen, 1860; T. Hampe, Nürnberger Ratsverlässe (Quellenschr. f. Kg. u. Kunsttechnik, N.S., XI), Vienna, 1904, no. 644 ff.; A. Gümbel, Eine neue archivalische Dürernotiz: Zur Veitstossforschung, RepfKw, XXXI, 1908, pp. 138–43; A. Gümbel, Archivalische Beiträge zur Stossbiographie, RepfKw, XXXVI, 1913, pp. 66–85, 343–56.

BIBLIOG.: H. Weizäcker, Veit Stoss als Maler, JhbPreussKSamml, XVIII, 1897, pp. 61–72; B. Daun, Beiträge zur Stoss-Forschung, Leipzig, 1903; B. Daun, Veit Stoss, Bielefeld, Leipzig, 1906; F. Kopera, Wit Stwosz w Krakowie, Rocznik Krakowski, X, 1907; H. Voss, Eine Madonnenstatuette des Veit Stoss im South Kensington Museum, RepfKw, XXXI, 1908, p. 528–30; H. Voss, Zwei unerkannte Werke des Veit Stosz in florentiner Kirchen, JhbPreussKSamml, XXIX, 1908, pp. 20–29; M. Lossnitzer, Veit Stoss, die Herkunft seiner Kunst, seine Werke und sein Leben, Leipzig, 1912; E. Baumeister, Veit Stoss: Nachbildungen seiner Kupferstiche (Graphische Gesellschaft, XVII), Berlin, 1913; B. Daun, Veit Stoss und seine Schule in Deutschland, Polen, Ungarn, und Siebenbürgen, Leipzig, 1916; W. von Grolman, Zur Würdigung des Veit Stoss, Mnh. f. Kw., XI, 1918, pp. 297–309, XII, 1919, pp. 14–25; W. A. Baillie-Grohman, A Work by Veit Stoss, BM, XXXV, 1919, pp. 129–36; L. Dami, Un San Rocco di Veit Stoss, Dedalo, I, 1920–21, pp. 418–20; A. Feulner, Die deutsche Plastik des sechzehnten Jahrhunderts, Florence, 1926, pp. 24 ff., 60; E. F. Bange, Die Kleinplastik der deutschen Renaissance, Florence, 1928, p. 34 ff.; M. Lehrs, Geschichte und kritischer Katalog des deutschen, niederländischen und französischen Kupferstichs im XV. Jahrhundert, VIII, Leipzig, 1932, p. 243 ff.; Katalog der Veit Stoss-Ausstellung im Germanischen Museum, Nürnberg, 1933; C. T. Müller, Veit Stoss in Krakau, MJhb, N.S., X, 1933, pp. 27–58; R. Schaffer, Veit Stoss: Ein Lebensbild, Nürnberg, 1933; H. Wilm, Veit Stoss als Kupferstecher, Pantheon, XII, 1933, pp. 250–51; P. Frankastel, Guy Stoss et le rétable de Notre-Dame de Cracovie, GBA, XI, 1934, pp. 272–87; S. Detloff, Die Quellen der Kunst des Veit Stoss, Warsaw, 1935 (Ger. summary); A. Stange, Bemerkungen zur Kunst des Veit Stoss, in Festschrift Heinrich Wölfflin zum siebzigsten Geburtstage, Dresden, 1935, pp. 152–59; E. Lutze, Die "Italienischen" Werke des Veit Stoss, Pantheon, XIX, 1937, pp. 183–89; E. Lutze, Veit Stoss, Berlin, 1938; C. T. Müller, ThB, XXXII, 1938, s.v. (with bibliog.); E. Kloss, Veit Stoss, der Krakauer Marienaltar, Berlin, 1944; A. Bochnak, Wit Stwosz w Polsce,

Warsaw, 1950; E. Buchner, Veit Stoss als Maler, Wallraf-Richartz-Jhb., XIV, 1952, pp. 111–28; E. Egg, Veit Stoss in Tirol, ZfKg, XVI, 1953, pp. 202–07; A. Feulner and C. T. Müller, Geschichte der deutschen Plastik, Munich, 1953, p. 360 ff.

Martin WEINBERGER

Illustrations: PLS. 213–214.

STRUCTURAL TYPES AND METHODS.

This article develops and complements the themes discussed in the article on architecture (q.v.), considering them in another perspective; it is an analytical study of the components of architecture in their technical, morphological, and typological aspects.

The evolution of architecture is here considered in a historicocritical context, that is, in relation to the cultural traditions and expressions of various ages and peoples and according to available materials and functional requirements. The article includes discussions of the historical development of architectural elements such as the column, cornice, and capital and of such structural types as the basilica and theater. It is organized in three closely interrelated and interdependent sections: structures, structural members, and structural types.

The distinction according to which the article is organized in a sense reiterates the distinction made by Vitruvius among the fundamental requisites of architecture; thus structural members would be linked with the Vitruvian concept of *firmitas*, architectural and decorative elements would be connected with *venustas*, and structural types would correspond to the concept of *utilitas*. These subjects are here considered singly — not, however, as isolated factors but as interrelated elements that are fused to form an esthetic unity, i.e., the architectural work. The technical aspects of architecture — formal and functional — are to be considered not as independent and isolated but as objective elements on which is imposed the architect's subjective vision. The objective elements determine the basic principles according to which a spatial-temporal form (the architectural work) is executed by the architect and ideally endowed by him with artistic expression.

The article considers various building techniques as implemental in architectural expressions; it demonstrates the relation between formal and decorative elements and the artistic expression; and it discusses structural types as related historically and functionally.

SUMMARY. I. Structures. Pseudoarchitectural spaces (col. 438). Primitive structures (col. 440). Basic materials and techniques (col. 444): *Wooden structures; Stone and brick structures: a. Walls; b. Roofs: arches, vaults, and domes; Metal and reinforced concrete structures.* II. Structural elements (col. 470). Base elements (col. 471): *Bases of buildings; Floorings; Stairs.* Wall elements (col. 483): *Moldings.* Wall apertures (col. 491): *Doorways and portals; Windows; Other types.* Pillars (col. 509). Terminal or superstructure elements (col. 527): *The orders.* III. Structural types (col. 547). Dwellings (col. 549): *Houses; Palaces; Villas.* Religious buildings (col. 564): *Protohistoric and ancient Eastern structures; Greek and Roman temples; Churches; Mosques; Synagogues; Religious edifices in India, China, and Japan; Pre-Columbian American temples; Monastic buildings.* Public buildings (col. 586): *Assembly buildings; Theaters and sports installations; Castles and defensive structures; Public service buildings; Commercial buildings.* Funerary structures (col. 618).

I. STRUCTURES. PSEUDOARCHITECTURAL SPACES. A structure (from the Latin *struere*), in the general sense, is any object produced with the intention of delimiting space, making it fulfill specific requirements of individual and community life.

Even the most elementary form of structure, such as the simple alignment of permanently superimposed materials, creates, as does a line drawn on a sheet of paper, an objective definition of space. A more complex articulation of structures, when they delimit a portion of space on more than one side, creates — at least potentially — an enclosed space.

According to the specific functions that structures — as objects delimiting space — are intended to fulfill, they can be distinguished as follows: (1) Sheltering structures, which may form simple windbreaks or contribute in delimiting portions of space that are either undefined or already partly defined by natural factors. Sheltering structures include those placed at the entrances of caves and those which function as enclosing or connecting elements between supporting structural members; those elements which subdivide a defined space into several internal parts may also be considered sheltering structures because of their similar function. (2) Supporting structures, which, while functioning as shelters, are independently stable and can simultaneously function as supports. Often, depending on the materials of which the sheltering structures are made or on the way in which such materials are utilized, the supporting function is assigned to special structural members that are constituted differently from the sheltering structures. (3) Sheltering, supporting, and covering structures, which fulfill those functions simultaneously, as for instance, simple huts with inclined converging walls and domical structures that rest on the ground. A practical distinction is made between supporting structures in elevation (usually vertical) and covering structures superposed on them. Covering structures may, in turn, function simultaneously as shelters and supports, if the material used is suited to both these purposes.

Structures can also be distinguished according to the materials of which they are formed. These materials fundamentally condition the structure's shape as well as its functionality, while not absolutely determining them. The materials themselves have a primarily instrumental value; more important is the way in which they are used in relation to the functions of the structure, that is, the way in which the various building techniques are applied to them (these techniques are quite similar even when applied to markedly different materials).

Although the function and the materials of structures can be distinguished empirically, they are closely interrelated and are considered here as a whole, within the framework of the historical development of the basic structural forms. (The subdivision according to the principal building materials is to be understood as a convenience adopted for purposes of organization of this article.)

As mentioned above, each portion of space delimited by more than one structural element constitutes, at least potentially, an enclosed space. It should be specified here that this concept of enclosed space has a broader meaning, since it comprises not only the spaces enclosed by structures but also those pseudoarchitectural spaces caused by the removal of earth, rock, and large tree trunks. Such pseudoarchitectural spaces include some primitive types of shelter and tunnels dug for purposes of communication, mining, and so forth. Pseudoarchitectural spaces may be composed of several natural chambers, contiguous and communicating, divided by natural partitions; more often these spaces are integrated by man-made structural elements which subdivide the space more conveniently and which may also function as facings for the natural walls or serve as partial or total closing of the entrance.

Spaces obtained by excavation and completed by structural elements have been made to serve as dwellings by different peoples in various epochs — from the primitive caves, whose access could be protected or hidden by plant tangles, to the more complex *sassi*, still inhabited at Matera, where an architectural structure erected against the rock face extends and completes a dwelling hewn out of the rock. In ancient times such spaces were more commonly used as religious and burial sites, as in the small burial grottoes of Mediterranean protohistory, the Egyptian rock-cut hypogeums and temples, the Hal Saflieni hypogeum in Malta, the rock-cut tombs in Phrygia and Etruria, the Jewish and Christian catacombs scattered throughout various regions of the Mediterranean basin, the hermits' caves in southern Italy and Sicily, and the rock-cut temples in India.

When a specific artistic expression is intended in a pseudo-architectural space, the complementary structural elements are often entirely similar in form to those in real enclosed architectural spaces, since their function is similar. It is evident that real structural elements influenced the treatment of the natural interior walls and screens, which are often worked so as to imitate typical structural forms, as in many Central Asian rock-cut temples. (See ASIA, CENTRAL; KHOTANESE ART; KUCHA;

TUN-HUANG; TURFAN.) In Egypt, the interior halls of hypogeums such as those at Beni Hasan (IV, PL. 346) are decorated with columns, capitals, beams, niches, and simulated door with jambs and lintels, all carved directly in the rock, an similar reproductions of enclosed architectural spaces are be seen in the rock-cut temples of Nubia — from those Abu Simbel, where the rock façade is carved to imitate th pylons typical of the temples of the New Kingdom, to tha at Garf Husein, where the hall with pillars, beams, and statu of Ramses II excavated in the rock appears as a practicall uninterrupted development and continuity of the form an style of the temple's porticoed courtyard.

The diffusion of pseudoarchitectural spaces that reprodu the forms of an architectural space was widespread. Suc spaces range from those in which the interior walls are almo entirely bare of decoration and the rock façade is carved to imitat the front of a palace (IV, PL. 457; VIII, PL. 136) to those in whic the plans and distribution of the rooms and the structur elements of surface buildings are imitated in undergroun spaces used as dwellings (Phoenician dwellings at 'Amrit an near Sidon). These spaces exist most commonly in tomb where the ideal transition between the realms of life and death a basic concern of many ancient cults, was evoked in the façade the layout of the rooms, and the imitation of the structur elements, which repeat features typical of dwellings. Reproduc tions of the exteriors of dwellings are to be seen in the roc tombs of Iran, Phrygia, Lycia, and Etruria, while interiors ar reproduced in Etruscan tombs, notably the tomb of the Chair and Shields at Cerveteri (IV, PL. 458) and the tomb of the Vo lumnii near Perugia.

Notable examples of underground places of worship tha reproduce the interior structures of similar surface building are the many temples of Buddhist and Brahman India (se GUPTA, SCHOOL OF; INDIAN ART) at Ajanta (I, PL. 40), Elephanta Ellora (VII, PL. 468), Karli (VII, PL. 451), and the caves of th Bamian valleys (see INDO-IRANIAN ART). In the Western worl the grottoes excavated by the monks of the Eastern rite in Apuli (9th–13th cent.) are often of a complex plan that recalls tha of domed Byzantine churches; similarly complex effects hav been achieved in the large ossuary-church carved out of th granite of the Valle de los Caídos, near Madrid.

PRIMITIVE STRUCTURES. The most elementary structures ar those that function as shelters, that is, huts and tents. The appear in even the simplest cultures, in almost all the inhabite zones of the earth, and presumably were common amon prehistoric societies, although no traces remain from the mor remote ages. These shelters were usually productions of nonspecialized type and were executed directly by the individua (or family) who was to make use of the dwelling and who, i most cases, faithfully reproduced the type that had becom peculiar to his tribe. Some structural forms may persist withi a culture because of a special ritual significance connected wit their execution (see SEX AND EROTICA; TOWN PLANNING). To trac the historical development and geographic incidence of thes structures is a complex and difficult task, so they are considere here in typological groups.

Sheltering structures include those which constitute th integrating elements of pseudoarchitectural spaces (e.g., wattle or walls of superposed stones placed before the openings o caves) as well as those which are used as windbreaks by som seminomadic peoples; these windbreaks are made up of brush wood, strips of bark, and the like and are set at a slant or sup ported by small posts driven obliquely into the ground. A mor advanced form of windbreak, found in Australia, is forme by two small vertical poles atop which rests a third horizonta pole from which layers of bark hang down to the ground a an angle on either side; this structure represents a transitiona stage between the windbreak proper and the hut of triangula transverse section.

Huts are relatively permanent constructions, usually com posed of plant materials. Some of these materials (saplings branches, bamboo canes) are used for the basic framewor and act as supports for lighter materials (straw, bark, etc.

hat are occasionally mixed with mud. Huts may be simple, with a single surface forming walls and roof, or composite, with walls and roof distinct from each other (FIG. 549).

The most common simple huts, all of which are circular in plan, have a conical structure (made up of a series of straight poles driven at angles into the ground so as to converge at the top), a beehive structure (composed of flexible saplings driven vertically into the ground and bent to meet at the top, held fast by small saplings or ropes arranged in horizontal circles;

PL. 215), or a domed structure (composed of a series of flexible poles that are curved at the top and intersect to form parallel arches that are graduated in size from the central, highest arch; a second similar series of arches intersects these, forming a domical framework that is connected by ropes in horizontal circles).

An intermediate stage between the simple and composite hut is represented by the hut with a triangular transverse section and a rectangular plan, which, as mentioned above,

Constructions in various materials. (1–8) Stone constructions: (1) Granada (Spain), dolmen (2d millennium B.C.), plan and section; (2) Egypt, Pyramid of Cheops (4th dynasty), relieving chambers above the funerary cell of the Pharaoh, section; (3) pre-Columbian Peru, funerary monument (*kulpi*), section; (4) Kerch (U.S.S.R.), kurgan (tumulus tomb; 4th–3d cent. B.C.), plan and section; (5) Alberobello (Apulia), trullo, section; (6) Aegina (Greece), temple of Aphaia (early 5th cent. B.C.), section; (7) Rome, Castrum Praetorium, external walls, partial elevation and section (1st century); (8) Cashel (Ireland), Cormac's Chapel (12th cent.), section. (9–14) Wooden constructions: (9) reconstruction of a neolithic hut of the Michelsberg culture (Germany; beginning of 2d millennium B.C.), section; (10) Vaupés River (Colombia), collective hut, perspective view; (11) Brazil, supporting posts of Caraja Indian dwellings, perspective view; (12) Canada, semi-interred hut of the Salish Indians, section; (13) Varzug (U.S.S.R.), Church of the Dormition (17th cent.), section; (14) Chichester, St. Mary's Hospital (14th cent.), section. (15–17) Metal constructions: (15) London, Victoria Station (19th cent.), section; (16) Philadelphia, Broad Street Station (19th cent.), section; (17) San Francisco, Oakland Bay Bridge (20th cent.), section. (18–20) Reinforced-concrete constructions: (18) Orbetello (Italy), hangar (by P. L. Nervi; 20th cent.), section; (19) Bricy (Orléans, France), hangar (20th cent.), section; (20) Mexico, project for a chapel (by Felix Candela; 20th cent.).

elaborates the scheme of the Australian windbreak; in this type of hut, two walls are composed of a series of slanting poles joined at the top, where they are sometimes connected and often supported by a ridgepole that rests on two or more vertical posts; the two end walls consist, instead, of light vertical poles sometimes linked by horizontal rods. Another type of hut is similarly rectangular or square in plan but is semicircular in cross section; it is composed of a number of flexible arched poles, with two vertical end walls that are sometimes closed by boards.

Huts of the composite type usually have vertical wall structures formed by posts driven into the ground, more or less spaced and connected by horizontal, diagonal, or intersecting ropes. These huts usually are circular, rectangular, or square in plan; polygonal-plan huts appear rarely. Hut roofs are almost never flat; the prevailing roof types follow the schemes of simple huts. Among the most common types of roof are the conical roof used on circular huts, widespread throughout Africa and formed by radiating poles tied together at the top (this roof often rests on a central supporting post), and the pitched roof, which is a simple structure that rests on the rectangle formed by the walls and is triangular in transverse section, with a ridgepole. More advanced forms of pitched roofs used in the islands of the Pacific have a rudimentary system of trusses, with tie beams that link the slanting elements horizontally; these trusses bear the weight of the ridgepole and the roofing (IX, PL. 543).

Another development of this structural scheme has four sections of covering members, the lower sides of which rest on the walls. When the four covering members converge and meet they form a pyramid or pavilion roof; when two trapezoidal sections slope down from the ridgepole and two triangular sections slope down from the ends of this pole, they form a hipped roof. There are some rare examples of composite huts in which the roofing structures form a barrel vault; in these the outward thrust that the curved poles transmit to the walls with which they are joined is countered by a system of ties placed like bowstrings (as in the communal houses of the extinct Tupinamba tribe of Brazil).

In huts where the longer sides are straight and the shorter ones are semicircular, the roof structures consist of a pitched roof with two semiconical sections at either end. A highly unusual structural system is employed in the earth lodges of North America; it consists of two concentric circles of vertical poles, of which those in the interior circle are higher; the tops of the poles are linked in two circles of horizontal beams; on these beams rests a series of smaller beams laid radially from the inner circle across to the outer circle and then down to the ground. The whole is covered with a thick layer of branches, bark, and pressed mud, forming a sort of tumulus with a circular opening at the center that serves as an outlet for smoke.

The structural methods used in building huts are substantially identical whether the construction rests directly on the ground or is raised on piles or tree branches; when the hut is raised, however, special devices are used to implant the supporting structures, and a floor is built.

The fundamental characteristic of tents is that they can easily be dismantled and transported; since remote times, they have been used mainly by nomadic peoples and by armies. The supporting structures in tents, which generally consist of light wooden poles, are clearly distinct from the covering of hides, mats, and the like, which rests on them and which is often held taut by means of stakes that pin its lower edges to the ground; other stakes often serve as attachments for ties that secure the supporting structures themselves.

Although there are special connecting devices between the various elements which compose tents and which permit their easy dismantling and reassemblage, tent shapes are remarkably similar to those of huts, and tents can similarly be distinguished as of simple structure or composite structure. Among the first, the most common types are those with a conical structure (the tepee, found in various parts of America and Asia) and those with a domed structure (the wigwam of eastern North America and similar tents in South America and East Africa

that have more or less complex systems of intersecting arche and coverings of hides or mats).

Among the simple tents with a square or rectangular plan the most elementary is the A tent, which repeats the schem of the huts that have a triangular transverse section; in thes tents the covering is attached by means of cords and stake driven into the ground. Other elementary tent shapes have supporting structure that consists of two or three rows c vertical posts on which the covering is loosely laid, as in th Patagonian toldo, or held taut by ties; the second system used in Arab and in Iranian tents, in which a further devic is introduced — short T-shaped horizontal elements superpose on the supporting poles to prevent rents in the covering.

Among the composite-structure tents, that of the Asiati nomad is notable; it is circular in plan with a latticework hurd forming its perimeter. The covering may be domed (as i those of the Turkic tribes) or, more frequently, conical (a in those of the Mongols, the Kalmucks, and other peoples c Central Asia), with the radiating poles that rest on the cylindrica walls held in place at the top by a small rigid cap that eliminate the need for a central supporting post.

In the ancient West, tents were widely used by armies Caesar and Pliny often mention the tents with which the Roma army was equipped, which were of various types: simple, wit a triangular transverse section (*tentorium*), or composite (*ta bernaculum*), with a rectangular or circular plan. The tent of medieval and modern times in the Western and Islami worlds are structurally complex in shape; they are general circular in plan or in the shape of a pavilion and are sometime subdivided into several rooms. In modern tents the supportin structures often consist of tubular elements, made of ligh alloys, which fit into one another or are connected by joint these are real metal structures (see below) and can be of grea size and complexity, as are those used by circuses.

BASIC MATERIALS AND TECHNIQUES. The erection of structure that can be defined as architectural only in a broad sense, suc as huts and tents, requires the solution of relatively comple problems, especially the stability and the reciprocal articulatio of supporting and covering structural elements. Although th evolution of hut and tent structures and their transition to tru architectural structures is not clear, there is a general relatio between the two kinds of structures, and in this sense hut and tents can be termed "pre-architectural." Often the technica solutions arrived at in the construction of huts and tents ar based on fundamental building principles that also are applie in true architectural structures. However, true architectura structures pose a greater number of specific problems, especiall in their component materials and in the technical processe that are to be applied to them.

These processes, which give the structure its basic form can consist of simple systems of superimposition or, in th covering structural elements, systems of juxtaposition of mor or less finished materials and arrangements of supportin elements — as distinct from sheltering elements — so that the will interact with the physical stress created in the structure such arrangements of supporting structures are known a armatures or frameworks.

The use of either of these processes is determined by th proposed function of the structure, climatic conditions, th degree of technical knowledge, and the availability of labo and raw materials and of facilities for processing them.

The construction materials most commonly used throughou the ages are wood and stone; earth and clay are used in mixture with fragments of wood, leaves, and small stones and are als employed in the manufacture of bricks. Because the technique applied to these diverse materials are basically similar, the are occasionally used interchangeably (e.g., wooden structura elements are sometimes employed in techniques more frequentl and more properly applied to stone constructions, and vice versa) Examples of this interchange — which often is indicative of persistence of taste rather than a lack of technical development — can be found in the discussion of individual structural type (see below).

Wooden structures. The use of wooden structures has been idespread from ancient times in various cultural spheres and almost all the regions of the earth that are rich in forests, hatever their particular climatic conditions. Edifices of many nds have been built entirely of wooden structural elements: vellings, storehouses, places of meeting and worship, theaters, idges, and small fortifications; presently the use of all-wood ructures is generally restricted to single dwellings and other uildings of limited size and to buildings in rural districts.

Wooden structures are often combined with other types of ructures, especially when the utilization of various materials economically advantageous. The use of wooden structures the construction of the load-bearing elements of roofs has rsisted in many regions. The woods most frequently used structural elements are oak, chestnut, and all the resinous oods (fir, pine, pitch pine, etc.).

In buildings consisting entirely of wooden structures, the oright supporting elements (perimeter walls) are of either solid frame construction.

Solid walls are formed by the horizontal superposition of aterials (or, occasionally, by their vertical arrangement), as en logs roughly planed on two sides are stacked one upon e other; the logs in two walls of this type are joined at the rners by means of plain joints, or end-lap joints (halving). he interiors of constructions made by this method are often led with boarding for insulation. A more advanced form of lid wooden structure is composed of squared logs, closely ted by means of tongue-and-groove joints. Structures of is type generally rest on a foundation of dry walling (without ortar) that isolates and protects the lumber from the humidity the ground. This structural method was applied in the West small religious buildings (as in the Church of St. Maria inor, Lund, Sweden, and in St. Andrew's Church in Green- ead, Essex, England, both 11th cent.) and to dwellings, cluding some large ones (palace at Lojsta, Sweden), until the ginning of the Middle Ages. It is still used in eastern Europe or example, in Russian *izba*s and in Poland); in Alpine regions, here it is limited to the construction of huts and haylofts L. 215); and in Canada.

In frame construction, vertical timbers or posts are connected horizontal members (binders or girders) by means of joints rengthened by nails or wooden pins. When the interstices the framework are very wide, diagonal braces are inserted them from corner to corner in order to strengthen the structure id to prevent the deformation of the various elements.

The frame method was widely used in the ancient world, Egypt, and in Asia Minor; it was known to the Etruscans id to the Romans, who called it *opus craticium* and adopted it r use in both exterior and interior walls (as in the so-called :relliswork" house in Herculaneum) and for building machines war and other constructions. It often appears in Far Eastern onstructions, in which the horizontal members are bamboo nes inserted into holes drilled in larger, vertical canes; wooden ns hold the horizontal members in place. In Oriental con- ruction the interstices of the framework are generally of rather nall dimensions, and there are no diagonal reinforcing elements. he frame method of building later became widespread in the orthern regions of Europe from the Middle Ages until the rth century; it was used in dwellings and sometimes also in ligious buildings, such as the church of Borgund in Sogn ovince, Norway (12th cent.). The balloon-frame type of ooden structure was developed in America by George Wash- gton Snow at the beginning of the 19th century. The balloon ame is composed of small pieces of lumber (scantlings or uds, i.e., vertical timber members) which run to the height the roof and to which the floor joists are nailed; it is frequently sed on the North American continent in the construction of wellings and was the first type of structural method to include andardized and prefabricated elements.

There are many different ways in which a frame structure n be completed: it can be covered entirely with boarding with panels of other materials (e.g., terra cotta); or often e structural members are left visible and the spaces between em are filled in with wooden panels, mud mixed with

straw, or stone or brick masonry that is then plastered over. The second method was used in Roman constructions and in the half-timbered buildings of north-central Europe, where, especially in the Gothic period, the wooden elements remained exposed, creating a highly decorative contrast with the filling material (I, PL. 398; V, PL. 354; VI, PL. 431).

Wooden roof structures often have been and are presently used in buildings in which the supporting structures are made of different materials. These roof structures display a remarkable variety; the most frequently used are flat structures and struc- tures of triangular section that support pitched roofs (FIG. 447, 8–12). Rarely, wooden structures are shaped into vaults or — in central-plan buildings — cones or domes.

Flat structures best serve as roofs only in regions with a dry climate (e.g., ancient Egypt). However, they are widely used as horizontal partitions in multistoried buildings; constructed so that their upper surfaces are practicable as floors, they generally consist of parallel supporting members of considerable strength. These parallel beams are called joists and are placed at brief intervals (14–28 in.); normally they rest on the wall structures of the long sides of the space which they cover. A special building device, used as early as Roman times, distributes the weight of the joists by resting their ends on stone templets or on beams running alongside the wall structures and supported in turn by stone brackets, known as corbels. In roofing over areas of great size, frequent use is made of a compound system in which binding joists (beams that span the opening from wall to wall) placed far apart support common joists (beams that directly support the floor) set close together. Boards are laid on this supporting framework. The covering structure thus formed may function as a floor; when it functions solely as a roof its upper surface may be protected by various materials. The beams on the lower surface may be hidden by the ceiling or left exposed, in which case they are often decorated. Building techniques used in the construc- tion of flat roofs have remained practically unchanged, even though the supporting beams may now be made of metal or of reinforced concrete.

The most elementary but rarest type of pitched timber roof is the simple span roof that repeats the principle of the ridgepole supported by central posts. The triangular truss was known to the Romans and was the prototype of king-post and queen-post trusses. In the simple triangular truss, or king-post truss, two beams lying close to and parallel with the slope of the roof (principal rafters) are linked at their bases by a horizontal timber (tie beam). Set into their apex is a vertical member (known as the king post, crown post, or, in the United States, joggle post) that extends down to the tie beam (IV, PL. 195). The head of the king post supports the ridgepole; horizontal beams (purlins) are set at right angles to the rafters. The ridgepole and purlins connect the trusses and support the common rafters and roofing. Since the 18th century the king post, which is suspended from the rafters, has usually been connected to the tie beam by means of a metal U-strap that prevents excessive flexure. Two struts (braces) are fixed between the base of the king post and the principal rafters (FIG. 447, 11). In the queen-post truss, generally used for wider spans, the central post is replaced by two posts at either side of the center, held firm by a straining beam at the top.

These two types of trusses, either separately or in combina- tion, were common in Early Christian architecture (S. Apollinare in Classe, Ravenna, II, PL. 431). During the Romanesque period in central Italy they were used to span the naves, while vaulted roofs generally covered the aisles. A type of roof truss used in China consisted of superposed queen-post and king-post trusses (III, FIG. 357).

Another elementary roof form is the trussed-rafter roof, which is composed of pairs of rafters and does not have a ridgepole. The outward thrust exerted by the rafters is contained by a horizontal tie beam at the level of the wall plate, by braces, or by a collar beam approximately halfway up their length that allows more light and headroom. In the arched trussed-rafter roof curved timbers connect the rafters and collar beams.

Roofs. (1–7) Flat roofs: (1–2) wooden: (1) Saqqara (Egypt), roof of the tomb of Aha (3d millennium), projection; (2) Knossos (Crete), funera temple (2d millennium), reconstructed elevation; (3–5) stone: (3) Karnak, hypostyle hall of the Temple of Amen (13th cent. B.C.), projection of roofi structures; (4) Orissa (India), Hindu temple roof (8th cent.), projection; (5) Peru, roof of pre-Columbian tomb (*kulpi*), elevation; (6) met al: st frame roof supported by Vierendeel girders (20th cent.), projection. (7) Stone coffering, plan and section, and wooden coffering, plan. (8–12) Woode roofs: (8) roof structure of huts of the Jarua Indios (Peru); (9) roof structure typical of Buddhist architecture (China, Canton; Japan, Kamakura), sectio (10) detail of roof structure with brackets (Japan, Engakuji, 13th cent.), projection; (11) king-post truss, section; (12) truss of the Polonceau typ with two struts, section. (13–16) Rood elements used in various types of buildings: (13) reconstruction of a wooden roof on a wood and stone e tablature (Thermon, Greece, Temple of Apollo, 7th cent. B.C.), projection; (14) reconstruction of the terminal elements of an Etruscan-Italic roo projection; (15) reinforced-concrete terrace roof (20th cent.), section; (16) flat wooden roof (20th cent.), section.

The collar-braced roof has a ridgepole; the principal rafters are linked together by a collar beam. In such a roof, braces added below the collar beam to link it with the principal rafters form what is known as an arch-braced truss. In the hammer-beam truss, which was used mainly in England in the Gothic period, the thrust is transmitted to a point as low as possible on the supporting wall. Each truss consists of the two principal rafters, hammer beams with struts, curved braces, and collar beams. The hammer beam appears to be, but does not function

as, a tie beam from which the central part has been remove If it is sculptured, the hammer beam is called an angel bear Notable examples of the hammer-beam truss can be found Westminster Hall, London (VI, PL. 426), and the Hall Hampton Court Palace, Middlesex (VI, PL. 430).

In the arched trussed-rafter roof, the collar beam or arc braced roof, and the hammer-beam roof, the structural elemen generally remain visible. Occasionally they are filled in to crea a round- or pointed-arch ceiling, either trefoil or cinquefoil

ection (as in the church of Södra Råda, Varmland, Sweden); such ceilings are sometimes called carinate (Cathedral of Aquileia, PL. 227; S. Zeno, Verona, XII, PL. 220).

Trusses have been most highly developed in countries that abound in timber construction. In such countries the beams tend to be more slender and are usually used in great numbers. In St-Germain-des-Prés in Paris as many as seven radially arranged struts prevent the flexure of the rafters, discharging their weight onto the tie beam; there is, in addition, a straining beam that intersects some of the struts. In the Romanesque church of Maulbronn in southern Germany, the rafters are strengthened by a tie beam, a straining beam, and two struts that distribute the weight of these beams onto two different points of the tie beam.

Some wooden constructions include structures that, although of special shapes, are based on building methods similar to those used in roofing structures. This is especially true of wooden bridges, which have existed since ancient times and are widely used in primitive cultures; wooden bridges still appear frequently in the Far East, while in the West they are found mainly as temporary bridges or small bridges. Bridges are often built of vertical structures in stone or brick and the rest in wood; an example is the bridge — about two-thirds of a mile long — that Trajan had built on the Danube by Apollodoros of Damascus (ca. A.D. 104; I, PL. 324). Such structures are noteworthy because of the extent to which the more technically evolved among them influenced building techniques in iron structures.

The simplest type of bridge consists of logs thrown across a stream or crevice. The ends of the bridge generally rest on a substructure consisting of abutments; intermediate supports or piers are constructed when the bridge has more than one span. These supports are usually of masonry but may also take the form of piles driven into the ground. The long beams or girders, known as stringers or joists, that constitute the span of the bridge are covered with transverse beams that form the deck. These reinforce the stringers and give them lateral rigidity; in order to transmit the stress, lateral braces are placed between the main supporting elements. This bracing can consist of simple struts or even of a complex arch, which, if flattened, can itself form the deck of the bridge, as, for example, in many Oriental bridges. A type of timber truss bridge that was developed in the 16th century by the Italian Andrea Palladio limited the flection of the girders by means of trusses rising on either side of the deck. Timber bridges were often covered to protect the deck. Examples are found in almost all forested zones, from those of the United States, where the covered wooden bridge became a characteristic feature of the landscape of the northeastern region, to those of Tibet and Switzerland, where one of the oldest examples exists: the Kapellbrücke in Lucerne (1333).

Stone and brick structures. The use of stone building materials dates to remote times. At first the use of stone was generally related to specific environmental factors (thus it was common in regions rich in loose stones or where stone was easily quarried and processed) and functional requirements when particular conditions of stability and resistance were required). Structural forms such as those described above have persisted until modern times in cultures in which the technique of building stone structures is highly developed. In such cultures the techniques used may be somewhat similar to those used in wooden structures or they may tend to the formal imitation of the latter; nevertheless, they display unique characteristics, especially in the solution of the problems inherent in the material.

The technical and functional aspects of this type of structure have developed in direct relation to concepts that tend to exploit the degree of resistance of the materials employed in accordance with their natural or artificial conformation, with their arrangement, and finally, with the use of joining elements (pins, cramps, and cements).

Generally similar to stone structures — in their conception and in the building methods used — are structures composed of artificially formed blocks or bricks, especially those composed of a clay mixture that is either sun-dried, burnt, or baked in a kiln.

The most elementary method of construction of stone structures is the superposition of blocks of material whose stability is ensured by the force of gravity. This system was applied specifically in the building of megalithic structures. The development of megalithic structures was related to the various ways of shaping the blocks so that they would cohere better and so that their weight would be distributed more evenly. Some types of covering structures composed simply of a slab or of a stone beam of large dimensions resting on two or more vertical supports are based on the same principle of gravity. Such structures are examples of the post-and-lintel method used in primitive constructions such as the lichavens, or trilithons, of the British Isles, in which the supporting elements are two huge stones driven into the ground. Similar to these are the dolmens, funerary structures consisting of vertical stones covered by a single slab that forms a huge stone table (PLS. 216, 219); in the area of diffusion of the dolmens, which includes western Europe, the British Isles, Scandinavia, Syria, Palestine, Persia, India, and even Korea and North Africa, there appear other constructions that are structural developments of the dolmens themselves; among these are the *allées couvertes* that are found in France, in the department of Morbihan, and in Corsica. They are galleries composed of large vertical and horizontal stone slabs (FIG. 441, 1; V, PLS. 160, 161). The post-and-lintel method of construction has been frequently used and has undergone various developments in architecture throughout the ages. One of its earliest manifestations is the talayot of the Balearic Islands. These circular or elliptical tombs have a covering formed of large stone slabs arranged radially; the slabs rest on walls of superposed blocks and are further supported by a central pillar formed of blocks that are progressively larger toward the top.

The most highly developed and outstanding architectural examples of covering structures achieved by means of the post-and-lintel method are the Egyptian hypostyle halls, where the pillars and stone beams support flat roofs in a manner found also in wooden structures (FIG. 447, 3). Similar techniques are used in the roofs of Indian sanctuaries of the Gupta and post-Gupta period (VII, PL. 142; FIG. 447, 4). The post-and-lintel method is the fundamental structural scheme of Hellenic and pre-Hellenic religious and monumental architecture; however, in these as in Etruscan and occasionally also in Roman architecture, the roofing was composed of gabled wooden structures.

The post-and-lintel method is more usual (and still employed) in framing apertures in walls (doors and windows).

a. Walls. The simple superposition of irregularly shaped stone blocks, held up solely by the force of gravity, was the origin of all masonry techniques. Primitive examples of this type, still being produced in primitive cultures, display a rudimentary knowledge of structural composition in the intuitive selection of large stones and in the insertion of pebbles or earth and straw between the large stones to ensure their cohesion. When this type of masonry was composed of unusually large stones it was known as Cyclopean and generally was not used for wall elements proper, but rather in scarps, steeply inclined supports for embankments. Masonry composed of stones of moderate dimensions has generally been used in protective structures and boundary walls.

The transition was brief from the selection of the large stones to the working of them; they were rough-hewn and were laid with irregular joints and a limited use of filling chips. There are numerous examples of this type of stone construction, known as pseudopolygonal work, particularly in the area of the Mediterranean cultures, from the Near East to Greece and Italy (PL. 220). Later the stone blocks were hewn to polygonal shapes, at first rather irregular, with rudimentary rustication; the sides of the blocks did not fit precisely and the interstices were filled with stone chips or other materials. These polygonal stones were later worked to regular shapes with polished faces, and the blocks were closely fitted. More advanced masonry consisted of blocks hewn to trapezoidal shapes and laid side by side in superposed, though often discontinuous, horizontal courses. The more compact masonries achieved with polygonal work resisted the displacement caused by sinking of the ground or war damage. Polygonal masonry (also sometimes termed Cyclopean when the blocks are of extraordinary size; cf. I, PLS 154, 155) was used well into the Roman period, as in the Pont du Gard (PL. 216), and was widely used for the constructions of city walls and later as supports for embankments, foundations, and bases of buildings, especially temples. It was used in the ancient Western world (in particular in the Apennine region of central Italy) and also in pre-Columbian America, where the walls in Cuzco, Peru (I, PL. 153) are noteworthy for their technical perfection. This type of masonry was also used in the Far East, particularly Japan, where the walls often are concave and diminish in width at the top.

It would seem that the logical development of polygonal construction led to the use of squared stone blocks, of more or less uniform size, known as ashlars. However, the opinion is now widely held that the transition from polygonal work to squared ashlars was not the result of a logical development but was, instead, caused by differences in the stone itself. The shape given to the stone was often determined by variations in the hardness of the material and consequent ease or difficulty in working it; also, occasionally sedimentary rock was quarried so that the blocks extracted were already roughly square in shape. In some places two ways of using stone coexist, and sometimes polygonal work is superposed on ashlar walls.

Where stone was scarce and there was instead an abundance of loose clayey soil, clay was a prime material. It was generally mixed with straw and water; the mixture was placed inside box molds where it was left to dry or shaped into small squared bricks that were sun-dried or baked in kilns. Pisé de terre, or rammed-earth construction, is walling of damp earth, sometimes mixed with concrete, that is rammed or cast in wooden forms. Brickwork was widely used by the ancient cultures that arose along the banks of large rivers: the Egyptian, Chaldean, Assyrian, and Persian (in the last two, bricks were occasionally glazed). It was common also in the coastal areas of Peru.

The Egyptians had widely adopted ashlar masonry for the walls of palaces and temples, for the mastabas and the pyramids (PL. 216); so had the Phoenicians and, in a coarser manner, so had the Sardinians in some nuraghi (S. Sarbana near Nuoro; Santu Antine at Torralba, IX, PL. 401). It was used by peoples of the pre-Hellenic cultures (the dromos of the so-called "Treasury of Atreus," IV, PL. 68).

Stone ashlar masonry was used by the Etruscans, Greeks, and Romans in various ways. Although the Etruscan ashlar generally lacked a constant unit of measure, the blocks of the necropolis of Crocefisso del Tufo, at Orvieto, are carefully dressed cubical ashlar. The Greeks created a system in which groups of two, three, or four ashlars placed lengthwise, parallel to the face of the wall (stretchers), alternated with one ashlar block placed at right angles across the wall itself (diatonos, or more commonly, headers). They also used alternating courses of markedly different heights (pseudoisodomic masonry). In isodomic masonry all the blocks are used as headers in diatonous courses, that is, with the longer side across the wall. In order to limit possible displacements of the structures, the vertical joints of the ashlar in two superimposed courses did not coincide; instead, they occurred halfway along the length of the ashlars below them.

In Roman opus quadratum (saxum quadratum, Vitruvius, De architectura, II, 8; PL. 216), the ashlars are typically placed in alternate courses of stretchers and headers. Generally the ashlars are twice as long as they are high, but opus quadratum may also be simply squared stone masonry. This type of masonry has survived to modern times without substantial variation. Occasionally, especially during the Middle Ages, masonries consisting exclusively of headers were again used, as were those made of small cubical blocks.

In order that the stone blocks might cohere better, the Greeks, and later the Romans, adopted the system of close

fitting known as anathyrosis: the point of contact between th blocks in a course of ashlars was along a smooth narrow borde made around the ends of the blocks, which were concave an roughly finished. Often, especially in columns and entablature the ashlars were connected by means of wooden or metal cramp and dowels, inserted into holes and anchored in molten lea Cramps were known to the Egyptians, who used wooden ree shaped and dovetail cramps. Other methods of linking th blocks were used in some constructions in India and in pr Columbian America, where the internal faces of the block were so shaped as to achieve simple joints between the block themselves.

As noted above, in primitive stone structures variou materials were interposed between the blocks to make then cohere; often these mixtures were applied in a soft state an later hardened to constitute proper cement. Mixtures of mu and straw were used in the Sardinian nuraghi, while cla mixtures were used in the pre-Hellenic world, in Egypt, an in India to cement both stone blocks and mud bricks; gypsum based mixtures were occasionally used in constructions other cultures of the Mediterranean and of Sassanian Persi finally, special mixtures based on coral lime were compose in Oceania and others based on lime with small granite fragmen were created in Rhodesia, while in Mesopotamia the cementin substance was sometimes made of bitumen.

The Romans produced cementing substances based on lim mixed with river sand, lapilli, powdered stone, and, above a pozzuolana, which when combined with lime forms an extremel hard mortar. This was used in the construction of masonrie in which the stone elements (also known as aggregate, rubbl or caementa) were of small size and were mixed with the morta to form a conglomerate, a sort of artificial rock; this type masonry, called opus caementicium, or rubblework, was generall executed by throwing or laying the stone rubble into timbe frames and then pouring the mortar over it. The timbe shuttering was removed after the mixture had set. Opus cae menticium provided a quick and easy method of building wall and remained in use for a long time, especially in foundations numerous examples survive from the Middle Ages, for instanc in S. Pietro in Agliate, in the baptisteries in Galliano (ca. 100 XI, PL. 323) and Biella, and in the towers of Bologna an Tuscania, and it still continues in use. The mixture differ according to place and period; sometimes it is used in alternat layers of large stones and smaller aggregate embedded in morta The concrete was generally left without facing only in founda tion works. In upright structures the concrete was alway faced with masonry of a different type that would be decorativ and protect the less resistant concrete nucleus from the element

Stone facings are a development of the building processe described above. A common type of facing is composed small blocks embedded in the mortar of the opus caementiciun in Roman architecture, this was used in arrangements tha were characteristic of different periods and so provide a valuabl basis for dating surviving works. In the earliest works, th level surfaces of the broken stone or rubble made up the fac of the structure (FIG. 453, 16); then, as the result of a gradua tendency to differentiate the external and internal portion o the wall, the materials were processed separately. At th beginning of the 2d century B.C., the external elements wer composed of small conical blocks with a rough-hewn polygona base that formed the facing; these blocks were arranged i irregular patterns, and this work is known as opus incertu (PL. 217; FIG. 453, 15). Toward the end of the republica period, the blocks used to face rubblework walls were almos uniform in size. They were pyramidal in shape, and the smoot square base formed the surface while the truncate or pointe end was set into the body of the wall. These blocks were arrange in rows set at a 45-degree angle, and the whole is known a opus reticulatum (PL. 217; FIG. 453, 10). A process that marke the transition between opus incertum and opus reticulatum i the first half of the 1st century B.C. employed small blocks i irregular courses.

Outside Rome, toward the end of the republican perio opus vittatum was widely used for facings; it consisted o

Masonry. (1–4) **Types** of polygonal work (after Lugli); (5) Pompeian stone-masonry pattern; (6) Greek masonry (Priene); (7) *opus vittatum*; (8) masonry in timber-framed bricks resting on stone (Zincirli); (9) mixed work in stone and brick (Roman); (10); *opus reticulatum* (Roman). (11–17) Various masonry patterns: (11) arrangements of blocks in Greek and Roman rectangular masonry; (12–13) Mixed work with rectangular masonry and concrete masonry; (14) Wall facing in rectangular masonry (with internal concrete work). (15–17) Concrete work: (15–16) *opus incertum*; (17) rubble work with a facing of dressed (or trimmed) blocks. (18–21) Rusticated masonry: (18) plain; (19–21) diamondpoint. (22–33) Wall apertures: (22) trilithic; (23–24) with lintels; (25) with superimposed lintels; (26–29) flat arches; (27–28) flat arches with relieving arches; (30–33) false arches: (30) monolithic; (31) ogee (Buddhist); (32) corbelled; (33) polylobate (Moghul); (34) wedge-arch with keystone; (35) round arch with irregular voussoirs (Sassanian); (36) round arch (Greek); (37) round arch with molded voussoirs (Romanesque); (38) brick relieving arches (Roman); (39) pointed segmental arch (Moghul); (40) lancet arch (Gothic); (41–46) types of trabeated windows and doors: (41) tapered (Andean); (42) tapered (Etruscan); (43) with crossed mullions (French Renaissance); (44) tapered (Greek); (45) with rusticated decoration (Renaissance); (46) with pediment (Renaissance); (47–52) types of arched windows and doors: (47) two-light mullioned window in brick (Byzantine); (48) three-light mullioned window in ashlar blocks (Romanesque); (49) lancet window (English late Gothic); (50) four-centered arched window (English late Gothic); (51) two-light mullioned window (Italian Renaissance); (52) arched doorway with rustication (late Italian Renaissance); (53) wheel, or rose, window (medieval); (54) bow-window (English), section and elevation.

horizontal courses of small rectangular blocks. Similar to this was a facing consisting of small cube-shaped or almost cubical elements, used mainly in Gaul (hence the name *opus gallicum*) and in Britain through the Middle Ages up to the Gothic era (Church of S. Elia, Castel Sant'Elia, near Nepi; cathedrals of Civita Castellana, III, PL. 478, Caserta Vecchia, VIII, PL. 175, and Troia, XII, PL. 223; and, generally, the Romanesque buildings of western and northern Europe). A facing of rectangular stone slabs arranged in alternately inclined courses to form a herringbone pattern (*opus spicatum*) was used almost exclusively in certain areas of Cisalpine Gaul and the Rhone Valley.

The Romans also used facings of large stone and marble blocks arranged either as stretchers or as *opus quadratum*, often rusticated. This highly decorative facing was applied mainly to monumental buildings; it persisted in the Romanesque and Gothic periods and was widely used in Renaissance architecture. Probably under the influence of Islamic architecture, in which rustication often appears, and perhaps following some Etruscan examples, rusticated facings were used in Italy in the bases of towers (the tower at Tarquinia, Torre delle Ore in Lucca, Torre Grossa in San Gimignano), in the castle at Gioia del Colle (13th cent.), in Palazzo Vecchio in Florence, and in the Palazzo Comunale of Città di Castello (14th cent.); they also appear in the Pitti and Strozzi palaces and in the lower part of the Palazzo Medici-Riccardi in Florence (XII, PL. 4), in the Palazzo dei Diamanti in Ferrara, where the rustication is diamond-pointed (FIG. 453, 19–21; XII, PL. 12), and elsewhere.

The Romans were responsible for the development of brick structures in the West, although these had already been used, as mentioned above, in the cultures of the Mediterranean basin and the Near East, India, China, and pre-Columbian America. From the end of the reign of Augustus, Roman builders substituted bricks baked in kilns for sun-dried bricks. The baked bricks were usually square, with a constant thickness of about 1½ in.; the smallest were *bessales*, approximately 8 in. square, the *sesquipedales* measured 18 in. square, and the largest were the *bipedales*, 2 ft. square. Occasionally bricks of different shapes were produced for special constructions (e.g., those used in the round pillars of the tomb known as "La Conocchia," near Santa Maria Capua Vetere). Triangular bricks obtained by breaking the *bessales* along the diagonal were employed only for the facing of a nucleus of rubblework. Rectangular bricks are mentioned by Vitruvius, and some examples were found in Lydia and in northern Italy; apparently they were used only rarely.

The bricks were joined by special mortars, always of a lime and pozzuolana base. Because the bricks were usually square in shape, they were aligned in rows, arranged so that the vertical joints did not coincide (PL. 217).

There was greater variety in the arrangement of bricks in the Byzantine period; this variety is also evident from the Middle Ages to modern times, that is, since it became customary to produce rectangular bricks. The most common bonds used in brickwork generally repeat those previously used by the Greeks and Romans for the laying of ashlars. English bond consists of alternate courses of headers and stretchers and is the equivalent of *opus quadratum*. Flemish bond adopted the Greek system of stretchers and headers alternating in a single course. The stretching or running bond is composed exclusively of stretchers. The heading bond uses the perfectly isodomic scheme: all the bricks are laid as headers, with the end placed toward the face of the wall. Among the many variations are the monk or Yorkshire bond, in which two stretchers are followed by a header in each course, and the Flemish diagonal bond, in which a course of stretchers alternates with a course of alternating headers and stretchers, creating a diagonal pattern. In the building of partitions, bricks were placed on end with their broadest sides forming the surface of the wall. Perforated bricks are a recent development; they are much lighter than traditional bricks and have scored surfaces to attain more perfect adhesion of the mortar.

Brickwork structures are often left unplastered to highlight the decorative and chromatic value of the material. Often, too, the structure itself is brought into relief by tracing the green mortar beds with the edge of the trowel (e.g., S. Maria in Cosmedin, Rome); this is known as jointing. The shaping of green mortar joints with any tool other than a trowel (e.g., a round or V-shaped instrument) is known as tooling; concave joints are hollowed out by tooling them with a round bar. Another technique used in brickwork is pointing, which is the raking-out of mortar joints and then filling them with a surface mortar; this technique allows the use of mortar in different colors.

In order to ensure greater stability, especially in more fragile structures, it has been a common practice in various cultures throughout the ages to use different structural methods and sometimes different materials in a single building (FIG. 453, 8). As in wood-frame structures, load-bearing and supporting structures are distinguished from filling elements. Aside from the jambs and lintels of doors and windows, which were generally made of more resistant materials than the rest of the masonry, rectangular frameworks or piers occasionally were built with large stone blocks; the interstices were filled with *opus incertum* or cast concrete. Examples of such masonries exist in the areas of diffusion of the Phoenician culture (Cagliari and Nora), of the Hellenic influence (Delos), and of the Roman (Pompeii) and also probably the Byzantine (Selinunte) cultures. *Opus mixtum* is typical of Roman constructions; it was used from about 50 B.C to about the end of the 2d century of the Christian Era and consisted of horizontal — and occasionally also vertical — brickwork bands interspersed with *opus reticulatum* (as in some structures in Ostia Antica). Another typical Roman masonry is *opus listatum*, or *opus vittatum mixtum*, which consists in the alternation of one or more horizontal courses of small stone blocks with courses of bricks (FIG. 453, 12). *Opus listatum*, which was used in Pompeii and Herculaneum but became particularly widespread after the end of the 3d century of the Christian Era, was subsequently adopted by Byzantine builders, who, as in the fortifications in Salonika, interposed a set of five brick courses in stone masonry at intervals of about 4½ ft. More often the Byzantines alternated two brick courses with three courses of small stone blocks that were bound by a large quantity of mortar; thus the brick courses constituted progressive bonding levels for the entire structure, including the internal concrete nucleus. After the 8th century the Franks introduced horizontal brick courses into the stone facing of *opus gallicum*.

During the Middle Ages composite structures became common in the Western world; decorative elements were introduced in the chromatic alternation of the various materials, which gives greater variety of design to the curtain walls; some instances of this occurred also in Byzantine architecture (PL. 217). In the Church of S. Nazario at Montechiaro d'Asti (12th cent.), courses of stone and brick were alternated; many Veronese buildings of the Romanesque age show the same technique. In Lombardy, from the 10th to the 11th century, brick courses alternating with stone were sometimes composed of bricks laid in a herringbone pattern for purely decorative purposes. These decorative techniques were the prototypes of those used in curtain walls composed of varicolored marbles in alternate bands, which give their characteristic appearance to many buildings in Pisa, Pistoia, Siena, and many other cities of Tuscany and also of Lombardy (e.g., the *broletti*, or courts of justice, in Piacenza and Como).

b. Roofs: arches, vaults, and domes. In some civilizations, particularly the Egyptian, stone was used to build flat roofing structures based on the post-and-lintel method. The principles applied in these structures apply also to those types of roofing which are similar in form to arches, vaults, and domes and which constitute a transitional stage between the post-and-lintel method proper and other methods that rely for their stability on the force of gravity. In this type of structure the roof is formed of blocks that are superposed in a slightly progressive projection (corbeling) until they converge at the vertex (I, PL. 413); sometimes the opening is closed by a slab.

In the ancient world, from the time of the earliest precedents in Egypt and Mesopotamia, in the 3d millennium B.C., the area of diffusion of corbeled roofing was a vast one. In Egypt, where this type of roofing was at first executed with sun-dried bricks and later with stone blocks, its most advanced form was the semicylindrical pseudovault (barrel vault), in which the surface of the stone blocks was shaped to a curve. Also in Egypt and Mesopotamia, by an ingenious arrangement of sun-dried bricks in inclined concentric rows, pseudodomical coverings were achieved. From the second half of the 2d millennium B.C. the same structural scheme was widely used in the conoid nstructions (tholoi) typical of Mycenaean architecture (e.g., e so-called "Treasury of Atreus"; IV, PL. 68, FIG. 105) and, er, in other western Mediterranean civilizations, as in some ruscan tombs (e.g., that from Casale Marittimo, near Volterra, which the large closing slab is supported by a central pillar; PL. 26), the Sardinian nuraghi (PL. 222; IX, PL. 402), the si of Pantelleria, the *navetas* of the Balearic Islands (IX, PL. 6), and other types of tumuli in the Scythian region (e.g., at of Kerch, which has a pseudovault in the dromos and pseudodome of corbeled courses over the tomb; PL. 224; , PL. 470, FIG. 854). There are more recent examples in some ligious buildings in Ireland (Oratory of Gallerus, Dingle, unty Kerry, 7th–8th cent.), in the trulli of Apulia (PL. 244, 3. 441, 5; V, PLS. 337, 354), in the dwellings of the Mesopo-mian Kurds, and in the igloos of the arctic regions.

The peoples of Mesopotamia and of Turkistan, and espe-lly those of Persia (Khorasan and Bactria), conceived a similar ethod of roofing square areas, one that spread to Armenia, edieval India, and various regions of Europe. This method known as anomalous vaulting and consists in arranging one slabs to form concentric polygons which are set one upon e other at a 45-degree angle and which diminish in size until e opening at the top can be closed with a single block (FIG. 7, 7). Another type of covering, widely used in Mesopotamia d Assyria, in Egypt, and later in the Byzantine world, rep-sents an intermediate method between that of corbeled blocks d that of true vaulting; series of contiguous arches are placed parallel supporting walls to form a barrel vault. The arches e slightly inclined so that one rests upon the other, and the ed for temporary centering is thus eliminated because the ight of each brick interacts with the adjacent bricks in the me arch and with those in the preceding arch.

A true arch is a structure composed of bricks or wedge-aped stone blocks known as voussoirs that are disposed over curved surface and held together by reciprocal thrust, the ight of each element affecting the adjoining ones not vertically t obliquely. The supports of the arch are subject to thrusts at tend to displace them toward the outside; these thrusts n be balanced by contiguous arches, by a strengthening of supports, or by chains or ties placed under the arch itself. ne component parts of the arch are as follows: The vertical ele-nts on which the arch rests (columns, pillars, or walls) are utments; above the abutments are the imposts, that is, the embers (usually formed of moldings) on which the ends of the h rest; the level at which an arch springs from its supports called the springing line; the distance between the abutments the springing line is known as the span; the rise is the distance m the springing line to the central voussoir, called the key-ne, at the crown of the arch. The inner curve, or visible under-rface of an arch, is called the intrados, and the outer surface known as the extrados. The faces of the arch are its lateral rfaces; the depth of the arch is the distance between its two es. As in any other masonry structure, the surfaces on which voussoirs or bricks are joined are called joints. Among the ussoirs or bricks, those set obliquely at 30 degrees with re-ect to the horizontal are particularly important; they are called unches, and up to their level the voussoirs generally remain place even when the central part of the arch is missing, since friction between the surfaces of the voussoirs is sufficient hold them together. This friction replaces the thrust gen-ited by the higher voussoirs. During the building of an h it is usually necessary to support the component elements th a temporary wooden frame, known as centering, which is aped to conform to the curve of the intrados; this is removed ce the arch has been completed.

The most common shape of an arch is that with a single ter. (By the center of an arch is meant the center of the circle ose radius determines the curve of the intrados.) If the center on the level of the springing line the arch is called round, Ro-n, or semicircular (e.g., Rome, S. Sabina, PL. 220). If the ter falls below that level the arch is called segmental or de-essed (e.g., Cyrene, Temple of Apollo, PL. 220). If the center extremely low the intrados of the arch is almost horizontal; h an arch is called straight or flat and has both the appearance

and the function of a lintel (FIG. 453, 26–29). Often a round arch is built above it to carry the weight of the superposed ma-sonry; the round arch discharges this weight on the ends of the lintel and related supports (posts or jambs; FIG. 453, 27, 28).

Single-center arches were the most widely used in ancient Eastern architecture and in Roman constructions. They were built with various arrangements of voussoirs and bricks; often the convergence of the joints did not coincide with the center of the arch itself but was placed higher (this was necessary especially in flat arches). The Assyrians and Babylonians, who built huge arches as city gates (gate of the Palace of Sargon II at Dur Sharrukin, mod. Khorsabad; Ishtar Gate, IX, PL. 494), generally used courses of sun-dried bricks in a very oblique ar-rangement that created the need for filling with pieces of brick in the key. This arrangement facilitated the laying of the various elements without centering or with centering only in the highest part of the arch. The Romans, instead, usually preferred to arrange the voussoirs with all the joints convergent toward the center of the arch, thus achieving a perfectly regular struc-ture. Often during the imperial age, in order to increase the re-sistance of the arch to the superposed weight, the Romans used two or more concentric arches (FIG. 453, 38). They sometimes also used wedge-shaped bricks in order to be able to reduce the thickness of the mortar to a minimum, thus giving the arches greater resistance. In Early Christian and Byzantine architec-ture the center of convergence of the joints was made to fall lower than that of the intrados.

Examples of arches built with stone voussoirs, rather than bricks, are rare in the ancient East. Stone voussoirs were more widely used by the Etruscans and the Romans almost exclusively for round or flat arches in town gates (Rome, arch in the Servian Wall, PL. 220) and in bridges. At first the arches were built with trapezoidal voussoirs that formed a curved extrados sur-face. During the imperial age more frequent use was made of arches composed of pentagonal voussoirs that formed a stepped extrados line; this type of arch, in which the voussoirs are often rusticated, had many applications in Renaissance ar-chitecture (as in the portals of Palazzo Farnese and Villa Giulia, Rome, XII, PLS. 56, 89). Eastern arches also were built with a polygonal extrados. To prevent the possible reciprocal move-ment of the voissoirs, they were frequently joined by metal ties. The Romans sometimes worked the voussoirs so that they fitted one into the other; the method of interlocking blocks was later applied in the building of round arches throughout the Byzantine and Arab world in the medieval period.

The curve of the arch can have two, three, or more centers. When it has two centers, and they fall on the same horizontal springing line, the arch is a pointed arch (FIG. 453, 40). This type of arch — light and load being equal — creates less hori-zontal pressure on the supports than the round or, especially, the depressed arch. When the two centers are internal to the span, the arch is a drop arch; if the centers are at the ends, the arch is called equilateral; if they are external, the arch is known as a lancet arch (FIG. 453, 49).

The pointed arch was known in ancient times and is found again as a well-defined element in Islamic architecture (where it generally was raised on piers); it has been used in Persia since the 8th century, in Syria and Egypt since the 9th century, and later appeared in Armenia, India, and Turkey. The inter-lacing of several round or pointed arches creates a series of small pointed arches; this decorative structure originated in the Islamic world and later spread to southern Italy (Amalfi, Chiostro di Paradiso; Monreale, façade and apse of the Cathedral). The pointed arch is typical of Gothic architecture, which used it in almost all its forms; at first the segmental pointed arch prevailed, and later the equilateral arch predominated. The many va-riants on these types became characteristic of certain artistic centers; among them are a type of arch that is composed of a pointed arch subtended by a depressed or segmental arch, and the Tudor arch, typical of 16th-century England, which is a depressed four-centered arch.

In the common three-centered or basket-handle arch the intermediate center has a radius greater than the radii of the lateral ones. The lateral centers are usually on the springing line while the other is below the springing line, precisely at the meeting point of two straight lines passing through the extreme internal points of the small arches and their respective centers; the curve of this arch is continuous and similar to a semi-ellipse. The three-centered arch is rarely found in ancient constructions but is more frequently seen in buildings of the modern era. The ogee arch (PL. 221), in which each side is both concave and convex, is typical of Spanish Islamic buildings; in the 14th century it was commonly used also in Venice. In the horse-shoe arch the center or centers fall above the springing line. This type of arch, at first round (PL. 221) and later pointed, was widely used by the Visigoths and by the Moslems, especially in Andalusia (portal of St. Sebastian in the Great Mosque in Córdoba) and the Maghrib, from the second half of the 8th century. It persisted in some Romanesque and Gothic constructions in southern Italy (Caserta Vecchia, Cathedral) and also in Gothic buildings in Venice.

Various other decorative arches were developed: among them are the trefoil and multifoil (or cusped) arches of the Arabo-Hispanic world and of late-Gothic Venice, where various types of interlaced arches resting on common supports are also to be found (cf. arches in the Palazzo Papale, Viterbo, PL. 221). They can also be seen in Florence in the portals of Orsanmichele (VI, PL. 338). The unusual arches in the patio of Salamanca University (16th cent.) are formed of concave and convex curves with angular connections.

For special purposes arches were built with the two imposts or abutments at different levels. These are called rampant arches; they have different centers for each side and may be pointed or round. They are generally used to support flights of stairs. Quadrant arches were often used in the Gothic period as the bridges of flying buttresses (PL. 228; VI, PL. 299). They have one center and are segments, generally half, of a true arch.

The structure of the vault is directly derived from that of the arch: a vault is an arched covering, either a ceiling or a roof. It can be defined geometrically as the curve resulting from the movement of a directrix. Thus semicircular or barrel vaults (also known as wagon or tunnel vaults) are produced by a round-headed directrix (FIG. 461, 1); other vaults have curves that correspond to semi-elliptical, segmental, and pointed arches. The vault is perpendicular if the directrix moves perpendicularly to its plane; it is out of the perpendicular if the movement is inclined with respect to the horizontal, with a corresponding inclination of the springing line (as in vaults roofing flights of stairs). When the movement takes place outside the plane of the directrix around a vertical axis inside it, the vault is annular. When, instead, the axis of rotation is also the axis of symmetry of the directrix, the vault is round; such vaults are properly called cupolas or domes when their base circumference coincides with or is less than that of the wall structures of the space they are meant to cover. If, instead, the base circumference of the vault circumscribes that of the supporting structures, the covering is known as a sail vault or a simple dome (called by some a domical vault, but not to be confused with a cloister vault; see below). The sail vault, which can rest on a square, hexagonal, octagonal, or other polygonal base, must be visualized in the form of a hemispherical calotte from which sections of the hemispherical surface in a number corresponding to the number of sides of the base have been cut by the vertical planes of the supports. In another type of vault, built to support spiral staircases, the directrix can have a helicoidal movement; this type is called the *vis de Saint-Gilles*, taking its name from the staircase in the abbey of Saint-Gilles-du-Gard in Provence.

When the vault is formed by the intersection of two or more simple vaults, it is known as a compound vault. The most common vaults of this type are the cross vault and the cloister vault, which is also known, especially in Britain, as a domical vault. To understand the form of these structures one must visualize a barrel vault cut by two vertical planes through the diagonals of the plan. Of the four sections of cylindrical surface thus obtained, the two that rest on the imposts are called sections and the other two are known as webs or cells. The curved edges formed by the intersection of vaulting surfaces are called groins.

The cross vault, also known as a groin vault, is general composed of four webs resting on the corners of a quadrangu area (FIG. 461, 8), its sides are formed of four arches, next each of which another cross vault can be built. Some spec types of cross vaults, built in Europe in the Middle Ages coverings for square or, more often, rectangular rooms, a sexpartite. They are formed of six webs resting on six piers; t sides of the vault have a single web each, while the other t sides have two webs each (FIG. 461, 10).

The cloister vault, which is built on a square or, occasional octagonal plan, is formed of four or eight sections and rests the perimetral walls of the space to be covered; as the numb of sections is increased, this type of vault tends to take the sha of a true dome (FIG. 461, 4, 41).

When the plan of the room to be covered is rectangu and the difference between the short and the long sides not great, the cloister vault is composed of two sections wi a semielliptical directrix on the short sides, at a lower level wi respect to the sections laid on the long sides. If the difference length is considerable, a barrel vault can be built to rest on the lo sides, with two sections of a cloister vault resting on the othe

Simple vaults (i.e., barrel vaults) — generally round-head — were built with sun-dried rectangular bricks by the Sumeria in the tombs of Ur as early as the 3d millennium B.C. Th were more widely used in Babylon, where they were seen Strabo (*Geography*, XVI, i, 5), who took them to be a structu form brought about by the scarcity of timber in that regio and they were also frequently employed in Egypt, perhaps b ginning with the 12th dynasty: it has been suggested (H schler) that the hypostyle hall in the first palace of Ramses I (20th dynasty) at Medinet Habu was covered by a barrel vau This type of vault is also found in Achaemenid Persia and in t Hellenistic world (especially in burial chambers in Macedoni

Vaulting was widely used by the Romans, who elaborat structural techniques and developed to a high degree almc all its potentials. At first they used large stone slabs arrang radially in curves to form the vault, inserting smaller slabs a mortar between the stones; later they used *opus caementiciu* casting the mortar mixed with pebbles directly on the centerin In this way they achieved vaults which were at least apparent monolithic and which should, therefore, not have exerted a thrust on the supports; however, because *opus caementicium* not very resistant to tensile stress, the stress was the same as the vaulting were made of ashlars. From the 1st century of t Christian Era the Romans fractioned the concrete mass of t vaults by means of transverse arches or ribs which were lai interconnected at intervals by means of *bipedales* bricks; t mortar was cast in the interstices formed by this structure. Th the load was concentrated in the ribs, which were better suit to resist, especially until the mortar was completely s and large regular blocks of concrete were formed. The ri were sometimes emphasized in the intrados of the vault means of coffers (lacunars).

Although vaults built in concrete work were typical of t Roman world, examples of stone ashlar vaults that were rei forced by an upper stratum of concrete appeared especially in t provinces of Syria, Africa, and Cisalpine and Transalpine Gai

The problem of reinforcing the supports to balance t outward thrust exerted by the barrel vault was resolved by t Romans in a variety of ways. The obvious solution was to thic en the supports themselves. Another device was to set mass of masonry or brickwork at right angles to the supports. Su masses, set at intervals, are called buttresses; when the outsi edge slopes downward they are known as spur buttresses scarp walls. In the Portico of Aemilia (2d cent. B.C.), a seri of parallel barrel vaults abutted reciprocally; this technique buttressing with vaults is similar to that used by the Egyptia in the hypostyle hall of the first palace of Ramses III. In t main nymphaeum of the so-called "Villa of Cicero" at Form the thrust of the large central vault, which rests on a trabeat colonnade, is balanced by two smaller parallel vaults that conv part of the thrust onto the perimetral walls. In the nymphaeu near S. Antonio in Tivoli, the vault rests on a colonnade th frames some arches firmly anchored to the perimetral wall.

Vaults. (1) Barrel vault; (2) pointed barrel vault; (3–5) types of cloister vaults; (6–8) types of cross, or groin, vaults: (6) intersecting barrel vaults; (7) barrel vault with semicircular intersecting vault; (8) intersecting semicircular vaults; (9) Gothic rib vault; (10) sexpartite vault; (11–12) ribbed groin vaults; (13) various arrangements of bricks used in vault construction; (14) three-range barrel vault, projection; (15) transverse and longitudinal sections of a vault (Rome, Tabularium; 1st cent. B.C.); (16) small vaults with alternate axes (Nîmes, amphitheater, 1st cent.); (17) springing line of Roman rib vault (Rome, Severan constructions on the Palatine); (18) Islamic rib vault; (19) dome on squinches; (20) dome on pendentives (Byzantine); (21) corbelled roof or pseudodome, plan and section (Karalar, Asia Minor; 1st cent. B.C.); (22) ribbed dome with oculus (Rome, Baths of Diocletian), section; (23) coffered dome with oculus (Rome, Pantheon), section; (24–25) decagonal ribbed dome on pendentives (Rome, nymphaeum of the Horti Liciniani ?, the so-called "Temple of Minerva Medica," 4th cent.), section and plan; (26) buttress (Gothic), section and plan; (27) flying buttress (Gothic), section; (28, 29) dome on octagonal base (Rome, Baths of Caracalla), plan and projection; (30) pattern of brickwork in a squinch; (31) pendentive with stalactite decoration (Islamic); (32–33) Islamic honeycomb vaults; (34) impost of a vault (Gothic; Castel del Monte). (35–41) Domes, sections: (35) ovoid stilted domes (Iran, Palace of Fīrūzbādād, Sassanian period); (36) spherical stilted dome on a square plan (Palermo, S. Giovanni degli Eremiti, 12th cent.); (37) cloister, or domical, vault (Parma Cathedral, 13th cent.); (38) ribbed dome on a drum (Todi, S. Maria della Consolazione, 16th cent.); (39) triple dome (London, St. Paul's, 17th cent.); (40) double dome (Versailles, chapel, 17th cent.); (41) octagonal cloister, or domical, vault in reinforced concrete (Leipzig, Market Hall; by Deschinger and Ritter; 20th cent.). (42–47) Various external shapes of domes (Islamic; 12th–16th cent.).

These methods of containing the thrust of the central vault were widely applied also in the Middle Ages, particularly in the Romanesque period. The buttress and scarp-wall method found in some 9th-century churches in the Spanish province of Asturias (as in S. Maria de Naranco and S. Miguel de Lillo, both near Oviedo; XI, PL. 318); the presbytery of S. Ambrogio in Milan is flanked by bays covered with cross vaults. In other churches barrel-vaulted central naves are flanked by aisles with cross vaults that convey the thrust to determined points on the outer walls; these points are reinforced by buttresses (as in Notre-Dame-du-Port in Clermont-Ferrand). Sometimes the main vault is also reinforced by ribs, which concentrate part of the thrust on their imposts, balancing it by means of cross vaults and external buttresses (Notre-Dame in Paray-le-Monial). The problem of containing the thrust was resolved in many other ways: for example, by balancing the main vault with two small lateral quadrant vaults (St-Trophime in Arles), with rampant-arch vaults, or with a series of halved groin vaults, often stilted. All these vaults discharged the thrust at a point low on the supports so that windows could be placed above the level of the lateral vaults to light the nave directly. Frequently a vaulted gallery was superposed over the vaulted side aisles for use as a women's gallery. Such a gallery, however, precluded the possibility of directly lighting the nave, except from the ends.

The Byzantines often balanced the thrust of their vaults by means of tie rods, usually wooden and occasionally iron; these were placed under the vault generally at haunch level — sometimes at impost level — and were attached to beams that were embedded laterally in the masonry supports of the vault. The Arabs and the Venetians often followed this example in their need to create light constructions because of the unstable terrain on which they built.

Sail (or simple) vaults and cloister vaults were rarely used in the Roman period. The most notable examples of the first type are those in a rectangular hall in a villa of the Augustan age at Minori near Amalfi and in the lower cell of the so-called "Sedia del Diavolo" in Rome. Cloister vaults appeared in the Sanctuary of Hercules at Tivoli and in the Tabularium in Rome, where a series of cloister vaults rested on arches. Sail vaults also were rare elsewhere and in later periods; they were used frequently only in Byzantine architecture, where they sometimes rose on a polygonal plan, in an intermediate form combining the features of sail vaults and cross vaults.

More frequently used in ancient Roman architecture were true cross vaults, which gave a feeling of uninterrupted space to large rooms covered by two or more such vaults or to adjoining rooms; they were used in monumental dimensions in the Baths of Titus, of Caracalla, and of Diocletian and in the hall of Trajan's Market (PL. 222), where they have a rectangular base. The thrust of the three cross vaults of the nave of the Basilica of Maxentius or of Constantine in Rome was borne by huge buttresses, which were steadied by three barrel vaults in each aisle (IX, PL. 36); the barrel vaults were lower than the vault of the nave, so that it was possible to make windows in the upper part of the walls of the nave. This method of construction reappeared in the churches of the Counter Reformation, where the vaulted nave is flanked by chapels whose partitions form the buttresses of the central vault.

The cross (or groin) vault fell into disuse in the Byzantine period and the early Middle Ages (exceptions were the vaults of triangular, square, and rhomboidal plan of the Church of S. Sofia at Benevento, 8th cent., and perhaps those in the crypt of the Old Cathedral, in Brescia, 9th cent.). However, it became the prevailing structural form of Romanesque and later of Gothic architecture.

The first Romanesque cross vaults were generally made of stone, sometimes with large, roughly arranged slabs but more often with small, imperfectly squared blocks bonded with great quantities of mortar. The extrados was covered in cast concrete; especially in northern Italy and in Germany such vaults were often stilted. When several cross (or groin) vaults are aligned to cover a single space, such as the nave of a church, each vault is set within two transverse arches (Fr. arcs doubleaux) springing from the wall or piers that connect them with the adjoining vaults, and within two longitudinal arches (Fr. arcs formerets), parallel to the axis of the nave, that connect the piers. These vaults are known as rib vaults, and the method is called rib-and-panel vaulting. Vaults of a greater span, such as that of the nave of S. Ambrogio in Milan (XII, PL. 216), are further supported at the groins by two diagonal ribs (ogives), which intersect at the common crown point, either passing one through the other or, in a more evolved structural phase, being closed by a central stone block (boss) that acts as a keystone for both. The six-arch complex, known as sexpartite vaulting, acts as

a permanent centering for the vault and discharges its weight on specific points of the vertical structures (FIG. 461, 10).

Gothic builders further developed and elaborated the structural method. In Gothic architecture the arcs doubleaux and arcs formerets and sometimes the ogives were pointed arches; sexpartite vaulting was common (as in the cathedrals of Amiens, Bourges, and Laon; I, PL. 386; VI, PL. 295, FIGS. 471-472). Especially in the late Gothic period, other ribs were added to the vaulting: liernes (short intermediate ribs that do not spring from the impost and are not ridge ribs) connect the bosses of the main ribs with those of the tiercerons, which are other intermediate ribs that rise from the impost to meet the liernes. Thus the visible armature of the vault is increased, creating a decorative effect augmented by the molding of the vault's various elements and often giving rise to imaginative treatments of form that are partly independent of structural requirements. (See GOTHIC ART.)

The triangular compartments (webs) of the vault between the diagonal ribs are generally filled in with carefully dressed stone ashlars that are joined by mortar. The arrangement of the ashlars varies, but it usually follows one of four patterns: courses perpendicular to the arches framing each section, courses perpendicular to the diagonal ribs, curved courses rising toward the diagonal ribs, or circular courses, each on a horizontal plane, as in a dome. These patterns prevailed respectively in the Île de France, in the Anglo-Norman sphere of influence, in southwestern France, and in Spain.

In interiors covered with cross vaults the thrust of the vault was customarily balanced by means of similar vaults covering parallel and adjoining areas (e.g., side aisles) and by means of buttresses. In addition, structures that tend increasingly to discharge their own weight on specific points rather than on the mass of the walls were conceived; the vertical supports of the imposts were molded to give the appearance of a sheaf of ribs (clustered, compound, or grouped piers); and finally the thrust of the vaults of the nave was transmitted to the buttresses (which were often strengthened by pinnacles above them) by means of quadrant arches (flying buttresses). Thus the walls tended increasingly to become simple webs of stone between the supporting elements; this made possible the construction of extremely large windows.

In the modern era many varied types of vaults have been used; cloister vaults, barrel vaults ending in cloister vaults, and skiff vaults have been commonly employed when it was planned to decorate the intrados with frescoes or stuccoes. The structure of the dome is based on the principles of the statics of vaulted structures and is closely related to the structure of cloister vaults. The earliest examples of domes (dating from the beginning of the 2d millennium B.C.) have been found in Mesopotamia and in Egypt. Such domes were generally ovoid rather than spherical (repeating the form of pseudodomes); they were used to cover not only circular-plan rooms but also rooms with a square plan, in which case the impost of the dome was joined to the perimetral walls by means of arched elements (squinches) or small triangular sections of spherical vaults (pendentives; FIG. 461, 19, 20).

Domes were less widely used in ancient times than other vaults; after the Eastern examples mentioned above, they did not appear again until the time of the Romans. Often they were a development of cloister vaults built on a polygonal plan, as in the octagonal hall of the Domus Aurea and in the lower nymphaeum of the Domus Augustana, both in Rome, and in the umbrella vault of the vestibule of the Piazza d'Oro in Hadrian's Villa at Tivoli, all of which were open at the top, with an oculus. There were examples of hemispherical vaults (i.e., true domes) perhaps as early as the time of the construction of the Sanctuary of Fortuna Primigenia at Palestrina and surely at the begining of the Augustan period, in the thermal hall known as the Temple of Mercury at Baia. Only rarely were pointed domes built, as in the so-called "Temple of Diana" at Baia and in the tomb of the Plautii near Tivoli.

In Roman architecture domes were joined to the perimetral walls of square and polygonal rooms by means of squinches or more simply, by triangular slabs that rested on the walls at the corners; pendentives were used less frequently, as in the upper cell of the "Sedia del Diavolo" in Rome and in the tomb known as "Torraccio della Cecchina" near Rome. Sometimes the dome was simply laid on a drum, as in the "Temple of Venus" at Baia, where the dome is composed of concave webs on stilted arches, which alternate with a sort of convex rib. The insertion of ribs in a dome to reduce its weight was a technique widely applied by the Romans, who used coffers running in horizontal and vertical rows, as in the Pantheon (FIG. 461, 23), or ribs rising to the crown, as in the Villa dei Sette Bassi in Rome.

When the vertical masonry structure required reinforcement, this was achieved not so much by external buttresses as by very thick walls into which large interior niches were built; in the Temple of Portunus(?) such niches are placed precisely between the imposts of the ribs. This expedient, intended to lighten the piers, is to be found in various other later buildings (e.g., in the mausoleum in Diocletian's Palace at Split). In the nymphaeum of the Horti Liciniani (?) in Rome, the so-called "Temple of Minerva Medica," recesses are formed by projecting wall structures that create a more complex structural articulation (FIG. 461, 24, 25; IX, PL. 37). Another way of balancing the thrust of the dome was that of surrounding the springing line with an annular barrel vault, as in the Mausoleum of Constantina (S. Costanza; IX, PL. 38) in Rome and S. Maria Maggiore at Nocera Superiore; this device was used in various other Early Christian buildings.

The use of domical coverings in cast concrete disappeared in the West in the 4th century of the Christian Era, and survivals in Early Christian architecture were rare. Domes continued to be used in the East to cover baptisteries, martyriums, and churches, but these domes were made of brick, except in Syria where they were generally built of perfectly dressed ashlars.

According to the theories of some scholars it is precisely from the Christian East, rather than from any continuity of Roman structural traditions, that the system of domical coverings spread again to the Byzantine Empire and from there to Islam and hence to the medieval West.

In late Roman imperial architecture a constant effort was made to reduce the weight of the domes, and various devices were applied to this end. A typical device was that of forming the structures of hollow clay pots or tubes; these had been used — at least occasionally — in Rome and in Africa since the 2d century for the construction of barrel vaults over furnaces and in insulating structures. Later there began the production of pots specifically created to be inserted into one another in vertical or in horizontal rows; domes built of this material could be constructed without centering and were widely used in Italy in the Byzantine era (e.g., those of the Baptistery of the Orthodox and of S. Vitale in Ravenna). Another device, which in practice resulted in thrustless domes, was that of using curved tiles. Their concave faces were placed alternately upward and downward, with the narrower part always toward the intrados of the dome; in this way the rows of tiles were interconnected and could not spread. However, for the most part domes were built of bricks; they were often reinforced by vertical ribs projecting on the intrados, as in Hagia Sophia in Istanbul. The joining of the imposts of the dome to the walls of the square or polygonal room that it covered was generally carried out through the traditional system of squinches or pendentives placed at the corners.

Particularly noteworthy are the ways in which the Byzantines counteracted the thrust of the dome: while in more modest examples they limited themselves to containing it by means of ties (one on each side, or occasionally two diagonal ones), more often they provided solutions reflecting their preference for complex spatial articulations that, in the multiplicity of the enclosed spaces, create lively lighting effects (I, PLS. 378, 379). They balanced the thrust of the domes by means of other vaulted coverings that received these thrusts along their entire line of action; both barrel vaults and semidome niches were suited to this purpose and were sometimes used together on the four sides of the supporting structures. This device is used in Hagia Sophia at Istanbul, where the dome rests on four arches connected by pendentives: on two sides the thrust is balanced by two

large semidomes, supported in turn by two other, smaller semidomes placed at 45-degree angles, while on the other two sides the arches are supported by powerful buttresses, which were added later to keep the dome from collapsing (II, PL. 428, FIG. 774). In the Church of the Holy Apostles (Apostoleion) in Athens the central dome rests on four barrel vaults that in turn convey its thrust to four semidomes; in addition, the thrusts of the barrel vaults are balanced by four more small domes and by small semidomes placed at 45-degree angles to the others.

A different method was applied in S. Vitale in Ravenna, where solutions that had been known to the Romans for covering polygonal buildings were revived in part. Here, the drum of the dome is supported by large semicircular vaulted niches; the niches open out through two superposed orders of arches into a two-storied octagonal ambulatory, whose vaulting supports the arches (I, PL. 384; II, FIG. 775). This plan was perhaps inspired by that of S. Lorenzo Maggiore in Milan and is similar to that of the Church of SS. Sergius and Bacchus in Istanbul (II, FIG. 771), which has a melon dome (also known as an umbrella or pumpkin dome) composed of curvilinear flutings or segments. In the latter church, however, there is no drum and the impost surface is placed directly on the niches (II, PL. 426, FIG. 770). In the West, the Palatine Chapel at Aachen recalls the plans of these churches.

Another typically Byzantine structure is that which sets dome against dome (as in buildings having a central dome and four smaller ones at the sides), connecting them by means of barrel vaults or round arches. This structural scheme spread to the West, and examples can be found in S. Marco in Venice (XII, PL. 220) and in churches of southern Italy (La Cattolica at Stilo, XI, PL. 323; S. Marco at Rossano) and France (Cathedral of St-Front in Périgueux; Cathedral of Angoulême).

The influence of Byzantine architecture is evident in Arab constructions; however in the latter the domes were generally stilted and — after the 10th century — were often ribbed to create special decorative effects, as in the Great Mosque in Córdoba (VIII, PL. 148; X, PL. 439). The joining of the dome to the square-plan wall structures was carried out mainly by means of squinches; however, during the Ottoman Empire the use of pendentives prevailed. The closing of the dome was generally pointed (i.e., the inclination of the bricks was constant from the point at which the angle formed by them with the horizontal springing line would become too great for them to be laid without centering), and the practice of containing the thrust by means of tie rods persisted.

The Byzantine influence in the construction of domes is evident also in Russia, Serbia, Moldavia, and Walachia, where the domes were set on high drums with openings for light. The connection with the perimetral walls was generally achieved in Serbia by means of pendentives and in Russia by both pendentives and squinches.

Domed constructions of the medieval West, especially those built on a central plan, were based on Byzantine or Eastern models. There was a widespread revival of the method of balancing the thrust of the main dome by means of a perimetral vaulted gallery (Baptistery in Santa Severina, Calabria; Church of S. Tomaso in Lémine at Almenno San Bartolomeo, near Bergamo), or by using three or even four lateral semidomes ("Trigona" church at Cittadella dei Maccari, near Noto; baptisteries of Biella and Galliano; Church of S. Fedele, Como). A grouping of several domes was favored in southern Italy, in Sicily (where the domes repeated the form of Islamic domes, with a high cylindrical drum), and at Padua, in S. Antonio (VIII, PL. 174). The stilted dome of Pisa Cathedral (XII, PL. 222) may well have been inspired by Islamic models.

Ribbed domes were frequently used as coverings for polygonal areas, as in the cathedrals of Mainz and Limburg an der Lahn (PL. 225) and in the baptistery of Cremona and Parma (I, PL. 297). The techniques of dome construction were applied throughout the Middle Ages to the building of semidomes to cover apses.

In the early Renaissance, Brunelleschi built the dome of the Cathedral in Florence without centering; he resorted, among other things, to herringbone masonry courses — which had been used in ancient times — portions of which were progressively laid in a spiral. In his central-plan constructions (the Old Sacristy of S. Lorenzo and the Pazzi Chapel, both in Florence; II, PL. 368) Brunelleschi also took up the system of balancing the thrust of the ribbed dome — composed of webs between stilted ribs on pendentives — by four arches or barrel vaults, one on each side of the enclosure. In subsequent developments on this structural scheme the barrel vaults lead into semicircular apses and, diagonally, there are four smaller domes whose thrusts, as in Bramante's project for St. Peter's, are carried by the piers of other smaller spherical vaults. (This scheme was used in S. Maria della Consolazione in Todi, VIII, PL. 206; XII, PL. 51.) Some examples of this scheme were created in the baroque age, but more widely used in this period was a similar scheme that called for a central space whose vaulted covering rests on at least the greater part of the perimetral walls; the thrusts of the vault are balanced by vaulted niches arranged around the perimeter (as in S. Andrea al Quirinale in Rome, II, PL. 268; S. Giacomo in Augusta in Rome; S. Caterina in Asti).

During the Renaissance and later in the baroque period, some large domes were built with ribs and a double shell (e.g., Brunelleschi's dome for Florence Cathedral, II, FIG. 655; Madonna del Calcinaio, XII, FIG. 23b); the origin of such structures, however, is to be sought in much earlier constructions, both in Italy and the Middle East. Double-shell domes were much lighter than solid ones and facilitated inspection of the structure.

Marcello SALVATORI

Metal and reinforced concrete structures. The possibility of building metal structures, treated theoretically by the Venetian Fausto Veranzio, who, in his treatise *Machinae Novae* (1617), illustrated a project for an iron bridge, began to find practical applications in Great Britain, precisely in the construction of bridges, in the last decades of the 18th century.

The first bridge of this type, the bridge over the Severn River near Broseley (PL. 265), consists of a cast-iron arch spanning the distance between masonry abutments. On this arch rest rectilinear girders. The use of cast-iron elements is found again in the bridge on the Wear River at Monkwearmouth (ca. 1798–99) and in the single-span bridge that Thomas Telford designed in 1801 to replace the old London Bridge.

In all these constructions the erection of the metal girders, which were joined by bolts, was carried out in accordance with structural schemes that are closely related to those of other types of structures, especially of similar wooden structures. In many of the earliest metal constructions the use of new materials did not give rise to new structural forms: there was a tendency, later strengthened by the ideals of the Gothic revival, to endow the new structural elements with the appearance of the traditional ones. This tendency is evident in the cast-iron columns that had been used since 1780 for utility buildings and became the characteristic formal elements of the Royal Pavilion in Brighton, built by John Nash about 1820; the court of the Science Museum of Oxford University (Deane and Woodward, 1855–60), covered with pointed-arch vaulting; and the Church of St-Eugène in Paris (1854) by L. A. Boileau.

It was not long before architects attempted to give full scope to the structural possibilities of metal. Examples of this trend are the first suspension bridges, from that by James Finley over Jacob's Creek (1801) in Fayette County, Pa., to the Menai Straits Bridge (1819–25) by Telford in Wales and the Clifton Bridge (ca. 1837) by I. K. Brunel near Bristol, England. In these bridges long chains forming catenaries were anchored to the top of large piers, supporting, by means of tie bars, the rectilinear girders on which the roadway lies. This structural system cannot be considered wholly original, since it more or less consciously repeats the models of ancient Chinese and Andean wooden bridges; nevertheless, in its use of metal elements it presents solutions that are unique in form. These bridges inspired subsequent constructions in Europe (Fribourg Bridge, in Switzerland, Elizabeth Bridge in Budapest) and in America (Brooklyn Bridge, New York, 1872–75, I, PL. 82; Golden Gate Bridge, San Francisco, 1933–37).

Almost contemporaneously, and especially in Paris, architects began to construct vaults and domes by means of an iron or copper framework of vertical arches connected by parallel rings (as in Paris in the roofing of the Halle au Blé, 1811, the Marché de la Madeleine, 1824; the Galerie d'Orléans in the Palais Royal, 1829–31; and the large greenhouse of the Botanical Gardens, 1833).

Technical developments fostered by the Industrial Revolution led to the replacement of cast-iron elements with wrought-iron beams and, after the invention of the Bessemer process (1844), with steel beams. These innovations gave great impulse to the use of metal structures.

Developing a theme that had been experimented with previously, H. Labrouste built the Bibliothèque Ste-Geneviève in Paris (PL. 228), in which all the supporting structures — columns, arches, and floor beams — are made of iron. He applied the same technique in the Reading Room of the Bibliothèque Nationale (1858–68). It was used also by J. Bogardus in New York (a factory building in Centre Street, 1848; Harper's Building, 1854) and by J. Paxton, whose Crystal Palace for the Great Exhibition of 1851 in London was the first example of a building with a wholly metal structure composed of prefabricated structural members (V, PL. 188). The Crystal Palace, which spread over an area of approximately 214,500 sq. ft., was dismantled and reassembled in 1854 at Sydenham; it was destroyed by fire in 1936.

In these buildings, as in the Menier chocolate factory at Noisiel, near Paris (J. Saulnier, 1871–72), the Home Life Insurance Building in Chicago (W. Le Baron Jenney, 1884–85), and the Tacoma Building in Chicago (W. Holabird, 1886), which are among the earliest true skeleton-framed buildings, the load is carried by the metal girders, while masonry is used alternately with increasingly broad glass surfaces as cladding.

An important innovation of this time was the adoption of steel lattice girders, standardized prefabricated structural elements that made possible the construction of slightly flexible buildings of comparatively limited weight and cost. Another major innovation was the insertion of hinges (points at which the members are free to rotate slightly) at the main points of support of the structural elements: the principal thrusts discharged themselves on these hinges. A system of hinged arches was used in the central railway station of Frankfurt am Main. The most outstanding application of the system of hinged structural elements is in the huge Hall of Machines (PL. 228), which F. Dutert and Contamin built for the Paris Exhibition of 1889 and in which the apex of the immense roof is made up of hinged elements.

For the same exhibition Gustave Eiffel built his tower (V, PLS. 99, 189), in which he applied a variation of the system of arched pylons that he had experimented with in the bridge over the Duero (Douro) River (1875) and in the Garabit Viaduct (ca. 1880), on the Truyère. This system inspired B. Baker and J. Fowler in their Firth of Forth bridge in Scotland (1883–88), in which they created original solutions in their use of tie bars and tubular struts.

By the end of the penultimate decade of the 19th century, the basic principles of modern steel construction had been formulated. Steel structures no longer recalled wooden prototypes, nor were they realized simply as rigid cages composed of vertical and horizontal elements; instead, they were conceived in dynamic structural forms.

While there was a persistent tendency (especially in such public buildings as railroad stations, large stores, galleries, and religious edifices) to disguise structural elements under traditional shapes or to use them in systems based on the post-and-lintel method, this tendency was accompanied by a trend toward structural methods better suited to the intrinsic possibilities of the materials used. Such methods were employed by the Art Nouveau movement (q.v.), especially in architectural works by V. Horta in Brussels (L'Innovation department store; I, PLS. 415, 424, 468; V, PL. 99), H. P. Berlage in Amsterdam (Bourse, 1896–1903), F. Jourdain (V, PL. 99) and H. Guimard in Paris (auditorium of the destroyed Humbert de Romans building in Rue St-Didier; and Métro station entrances), and contemporaneously by the American rationalist movement (L. H. Sullivan and D. Adler in the Wainwright Building in St. Louis, Mo., PL. 218; I, PL. 86, and in the Carson Pirie Scott & Company store in Chicago, I, PL. 86). The structural solutions proposed by these movements were subsequently developed and repeated.

Metal structures have been largely replaced in constructions in Europe by structures in reinforced concrete, which is undoubtedly more economical — except for the construction of floors, roofing elements, or temporary scaffoldings. The use of metal structures persists in the United States and in Japan, where notable technical progress has been made in building methods whereby the planes of the cantilevered floors are inserted into a central supporting structure and the exterior walls function solely as cladding (also known as curtain walls, or skin). Important steel constructions have been executed recently, often using elements molded in sections, sometimes also using metal sheeting and glass as cladding. Among such constructions are the apartment houses at 845-860 Lake Shore Drive and Crown Hall (Illinois Institute of Technology) in Chicago, both by Mies van der Rohe, the General Motors Technical Center in Warren, Mich. (I, PL. 94), by Eero Saarinen, the Eagle Rock Playground House in Los Angeles, Calif., by Richard Neutra, and, in Europe, the heating plant in Cachan by F. Vitale and J. Fichot, the low-cost housing blocks in Metz by J. M. Lafon, the roofing of a savings bank in Florence by G. Michelucci, and an office building in Via Torino in Rome by Adalberto Libera.

The most advanced contemporary building methods tend toward the use of prefabricated structural elements, which are designed either to be used in predetermined forms in series (as in the Dymaxion constructions of Buckminster Fuller) or to be adaptable to extremely varied constructions. Much attention has been given to the problem of the connection of these elements by means of fixed joints for profiled or corner elements but mainly by means of a nodal system. Using this system Fuller developed the "geodesic" dome (VIII, PL. 62), whose structure is based on elementary geometrical figures; Konrad Wachsmann conceived systems that are based on the use of prefabricated tubular structural elements combined by means of three-dimensional swivel connectors — a development of the rudimentary systems used by Contamin. Wachsmann's system permitted the realization of structures in which there is an integration of dynamic forces, open to unlimited possibilities of composition. Wachsmann claims that the building can be developed indirectly by means of the multiplication of the cell, that is, it is always adaptable to subsequent enlargements.

Technical developments in the use of metal structures were parallel to — and sometimes interacted with — developments in reinforced-concrete structures. In the final decades of the 19th century, almost simultaneously in France and in the United States, concrete structural elements in building foundations were reinforced by metal bars inserted into them. These were the first applications of reinforced concrete (ferro-concrete). As early as 1850 J. L. Lambot had built, merely as an experiment, a canoe made up of a light metal frame completely covered with concrete. In 1867 Joseph Monnier built cylindrical tanks in reinforced concrete and obtained a patent for a method of constructing foundations for buildings; in the same year François Coignet used concrete with metal reinforcement for the foundation piers of the buildings of the Paris Exhibition. Similar use of reinforced concrete can be seen in some buildings erected in the United States by Thaddeus Hyatt and in the Montauk (Block) Building by John Root in Chicago (1883), which rests on a concrete bed that is strengthened by a network of steel rails.

At this time two German engineers, G. Wayss and M. Koenen, were experimenting with the possibility of building-beams in which the metal reinforcement, composed of a lattice of thin bars or rods of iron or steel, might be arranged so as to integrate the resistance to compressive stress typical of concrete with the resistance to tensile stress characteristic of iron. The solution of this problem made possible the use of concrete beams cast in wooden molds in situ, the metal reinforcement having already been placed inside the molds.

Developing this technique in 1890 Françoise Hennebique produced compound beams — mainly load-bearing girders and arched girders for vaulted structures — which were patented in 1892. Two years later the first building in reinforced concrete was built: the Church of St-Jean-de-Montmartre in Paris, by Anatole de Baudot; a second — a house in Lincoln's Inn Fields — was built in London in 1895 by W. Simmons. Progress in the use of reinforced-concrete structures was made by Auguste Perret in Paris in the house at Rue Franklin 25 bis (V, PL. 102), and by T. Garnier, who, in his project for the Cité Industrielle (1901-04), foresaw the use of such structures on a vast scale, as in his plans for hospitals and the stadium of Lyons, which were carried out later. Important examples of reinforced-concrete structures are the complicated ribbing of the dome in the Jahrhunderthalle in Wrocław by Max Berg (PL. 229) and the parabolic arcades of the hangars at Orly (1916; destroyed) by E. Freyssinet.

In these constructions, reinforced-concrete structures make up compact and unitary compositions of vertical and horizontal elements that are connected by plane surfaces (floors, walls, etc.), often also made of reinforced concrete or — in vaults or domes — of monolithic ribs, in accordance with structural schemes that reflect contemporary developments in the use of metal structures.

This construction method is both practical and versatile; it is the one most frequently used in modern building, in the supporting framework, in covering structures (floors, vaults, domes, and trusses), and in base elements (e.g., *pilotis*; IX, PL. 107).

Studies of the dynamic principles of concrete structures led to the development of prestressed concrete, which permitted the manufacture of highly resistant prefabricated structural elements. In prestressed concrete, cracking and tensile forces are eliminated or reduced by introducing internal stress into the metal reinforcement either before or immediately after the concrete is poured. In addition reinforced concrete can be modeled to an extent previously unknown in building materials. Some structures in this material are conceived in accordance with a coordination and a dynamic concentration of the lines of force — as, for instance, mushroom-slab structures (used for the first time by R. Maillart in the Lagerhaus in Zurich, 1908, and later in the Federal Grain Depots at Altdorf, 1912, where the vertical supporting elements are organically connected with the covering structures). This type of construction made possibile the widespread use of large cantilevered covering structures such as the roof of the grandstand at the Zarzuela race track near Madrid by E. Torroja. Maillart used reinforced-concrete stiffened arch slabs in several bridges in Switzerland — the Valtschiel bridge in Graubünden Canton (1925), the railroad bridge at Klosters (1930), the Schwandbach bridge near Schwarzenburg (1933), and the Aire bridge near Geneva (designed 1938, built 1952-54). He had also used reinforced concrete in the bridge at Tavanasa (PL. 265).

Because of its intrinsic plasticity, reinforced concrete can be modeled into another type of structure, creating spatial solutions that are original and devoid of any geometrical harshness, as in the work of German architects of expressionist inspiration.

The Italian Pier Luigi Nervi has used prestressed concrete (in prefabricated structural units) in the geodetic vaults of a hangar at Orbetello airport (I, PL. 415), the Palazzo delle Esposizioni in Turin (1948-50), and the Palazzetto dello Sport (V, PL. 117) and the Palazzo dello Sport (1959) in Rome.

Oreste FERRARI

II. STRUCTURAL ELEMENTS. The fundamental parts of a building are brought into being by means of the various structural elements (previously examined), from the supports to the roofing parts, that distinguish dimension and mark out portions of space, thus making the building usable for the particular purposes for which it is intended. These elements, therefore, do not combine to form a simple and undifferentiated shell, but even in their purely instrumental and technical aspects — that is, in the peculiarities of the building processes, as they appear in relation to the various possibilities of shaping and of utilization of specific materials — they imply intrinsic formal qualifications.

Such formal qualifications are expressed in the context of the architectural work first of all in relation to specific functional requirements; in other words, where the elements form special, functionally characterized parts of the building (base areas, terminal and connecting elements of the walls, framing of doors, windows, etc., isolated supporting elements, cresting of the entire building, and the superstructures).

Secondly, the same formal qualifications evade the merely deterministic limit of those instrumental and technical aspects to become characterized, to a greater or lesser extent, by their relation to the specific esthetic intentions of the builder, in giving certain elements greater or lesser relief, more or less accentuated values, in accordance not only with trends in fashion or stylistic innovations, but also with different conceptions of architectural space. Consequently, within the sphere of the total unity of the formative process of the space which is expressed in the architectural work there appear various possibilities of coordinating the parts of a building; quite often, and especially in the cultures that are normally defined as classical, these possibilities find a system and concrete terminology in the architectural orders, which are not, however, always and absolutely binding.

It can also happen, however, that the formal arrangement of structural elements has little or no relation to the function of the building, either because traditionally stabilized forms persist, or because purely decorative values tend to prevail.

From the various relationships that spring up between the functional and technical requirements of architecture, on the one hand, and the expressive intentions, on the other, derives the phenomenological complexity of all those structural elements that have been mentioned, and which can be considered as constituting the constructive and decorative morphology of architecture. It is this aspect of structural elements (which, however, it must be remembered, cannot be separated except by a conceptual abstraction from the architectural work as a whole) that is examined below in its historical phenomenology and in its essential formal characteristics.

BASE ELEMENTS. *Bases of buildings.* The base area is that part of the construction which acts as intermediary between the building proper and the surfaces, whether natural or artificial, which constitute the ground.

Rudimentary bases are found in some primitive constructions in which, between the ground and the vertical members, were interposed layers of resistant material (usually stone), the purpose of which was both to endow the structures themselves with a uniform supporting surface on unleveled land and to avoid deterioration such as that caused by standing water and creeping vegetation.

In everyday language, improper use is normally made of the terms that specifically define the various types of base elements — terms originally employed to designate particular and precise forms of base area and used for specific types of building or for specific parts of them have in fact acquired in current usage wider and vaguer meanings. It is therefore deemed advisable to proceed here with a preliminary clarification of the terminology of base elements, distinguishing as far as possible those which form the supporting structures of a building as a whole (or of more than one building) from those which represent only the supporting structures of some parts of the building itself.

Elements of the first type, which are all included in the general definition of base, constitute a platform (which can also be formed by an embankment or even by a whole floor of the building) upon which rests the portion of the building actually in elevation. In Greek architecture an element of this type is the stylobate: strictly speaking this term should indicate only the stone slabs placed immediately under the columns; nevertheless it is generally used to define the whole surface on which the columns rest. By extension, therefore, "stilobate" came to mean the whole stepped base, which it would be more correct to call "crepidoma." In Italic and Roman architecture, the base of the whole temple is called the podium.

The various base elements of single parts of buildings ar⁹ often undifferentiatedly included in the term "bases" but more exact terminology distinguishes them as follows: (1) th⁹ base, the part with which the pier (and particularly the column ends on the floor in its lower part (by extension of the term the word "base" is used for the foot of any vertical structur⁹ and particularly for what should properly be called "socle" (2) the socle, a projecting member at the foot of a wall or pier normally running along the whole length of the wall; (3) the ped⁹ estal, properly, the isolated (or projecting from the wall) ele ment which supports a column or an ornament such as a statu⁹ or vase; (4) the plinth, the square stone block under the roun⁹ base of a column (the plinth may be considered as the lowes⁹ square member of a base); (5) the dado, both the lower par⁹ of a wall (generally interior) when it is treated apart and als⁹ the square prism, also known as the "die," which is that par⁹ of a pedestal between its base and surbase or cornice.

The custom of building base areas upon which whole constructions stood gave rise in many cultures of the ancient worl⁹ to characteristic architectural forms, especially when th⁹ constructions were intended for religious purposes (e.g., th⁹ Indian stupa). Parallelepiped bases are sometimes found i⁹ Egypt, at least after the 12th dynasty, in some small periptera⁹ sanctuaries, in the terraced temples built on mountain slopes and in the temples for which an outstanding monumental appearance was desired, such as Luxor. In some small temple⁹ of the Middle and New Kingdoms (as well as those of the Late Period) the base area is surrounded by a parapet (see IV, PL 379, *above*).

Terraced bases are common in Mesopotamian constructions because of the nature of the soil, which tends to be very moist In Achaemenid Persia buildings were constructed on high platforms to which access was gained by means of stairs; examples are the Masjid-i-Sulaymān (Mosque of Solomon), where the artificial terracing, achieved in part by leveling a portion of the mountainside, is enclosed by sloping megalithic structures interrupted by ten staircases (see VIII, col. 267), and also Bard-i-Nisande, Pasargardae, and Persepolis. Stepped bases are rather rare and appear only in funerary buildings such as the so-called "Tomb of Cyrus" at Pasargardae (VIII, PL. 126).

A constant motif of Greek religious architecture, at least until the 5th century, was, as has been mentioned, the crepidoma, usually built with squared blocks and stepped. The upper step, sometimes different from the others in height and shaping, is called the stylobate: in many cases, for instance, in the Parthenon and in the Propylaea in Athens (I, PL. 396; III, PL. 337), the *krepidoma* rests on yet another base, which is, rather, its ground foundation.

In Etruscan architecture and later in Roman architecture, the platforms, or podiums, on which the constructions (mostly religious) rise are not stepped but are uniform in volume throughout their height and are generally open in front with a flight of stairs (PL. 240). In Etruscan architecture — especially in funerary constructions after the 7th century B.C. — the whole stone wall sometimes takes the shape of a podium, composed of a lower socle, more or less projecting and roughly molded, a smooth vertical or slightly inclined zone, and an upper zone with bands and moldings slightly projecting and receding. The tombs at Cerveteri (IV, PL. 456) and the façades of Castel d'Asso and of Norchia and its necropolis of S. Giuliano present pertinent examples. True podiums are mostly to be found in temples and tend to become characteristic forms resulting from the superposition of a smooth or patterned socle, a flat vertical zone, and one or more moldings constituting a rudimentary surbase.

It is more or less in these forms that the podium occurs in Roman architecture from the time between the 4th–3d century B.C. and the end of the Republican Age (Temple C in Largo Argentina, Rome; the temples at Gabii; the "Temple of Vesta," Tivoli; and the "Temple of Hercules," Cori, VII, PL. 201). In Roman architecture the podium generally represents a planimetrically continuous base surface (as for instance in the so-called "Temple of Fortuna Virilis" in Rome, PL. 252), sometimes of considerable height (as in the "Temple of the Dioscuri" in Rome, where it consists of two superposed areas). It some-mes appears profiled and projecting in correspondence with the columns (Temple of Vesta in the Roman Forum), or else is interrupted to form isolated pedestals supporting the columns themselves (façade of the Temple of Minerva Asisium, Assisi).

Base members of the same type in the shape of a pedestal or of a continuous or variously profiled stylobate were frequently adopted in the Greek and in the Roman world also for other types of buildings, such as funerary monuments, theatrical sets, and triumphal arches (V, PL. 470; IX, PL. 35).

In the West, ever since the Early Christian and medieval periods, despite the considerable variety of the solutions, the use of base platforms or of podiums has not been particularly widespread. There were a few, but these resulted from the particular character of the terrain and were related to the particular purpose of the building. Notable exceptions are represented by certain Renaissance, mannerist, baroque, and 19th-century buildings in which the influence of antiquity led to the adoption of podiums, platforms, or socles to form bases.

In Egyptian buildings it is sometimes the first course of masonry which forms a sort of socle by projecting slightly; elsewhere (temple at Luxor) this is formed by bands, also slightly projecting. Blocks of stone placed so as to form high socles are frequently to be observed in Asia Minor, in Mesopotamia, in Hittite constructions, and in northern Syria. The brick walls often rested on wide courses of masonry; a typical device is that of the socles composed of orthostats or of base bands with figural and decorative motifs in relief, painted or covered with glazed tiles (VII, PL. 287).

In Crete, particularly in the palaces of Knossos and Phaistos, there are socles formed by strongly projecting stone blocks arranged in two courses of different heights receding progressively or else placed so as to form seats; in the interior parts, the dadoes of the walls were sometimes faced with large slabs of gypsum alabaster.

At Mycenae sometimes the socle is covered with marble orthostats. This is a device that was to become constant in the walls of the cellas of Greek temples (it was already in use in the Heraion at Olympia, ca. 600 B.C.). Sometimes the revetment slabs rest on one or two courses of slightly projecting stones, which take the shape of flat bands (temple of Aphaia at Aegina) or of a flat band surmounted by another projecting one ("Theseion" of Athens; Temple of Olympian Zeus, Agrigento). In a more evolved form, and particularly in the Ionic temples such as the temples on the Ilissos and of Athena Nike (I, PL. 92) and in the Erechtheion, the lower part of the socle is molded like the bases of the columns. Subsequently, in the Hellenistic period and in Rome, a type of socle became established which was composed of a molded base, one or more courses of revetment slabs, and a molded cornice.

A particular type of dado, used especially for interiors, is that consisting of a revetment of various colored marble slabs (crustae), which sometimes make up ornamental or geometric motifs; this type spread to Rome in the late imperial period and survived into Early Christian and Byzantine architecture, sometimes in the form of a slab worked in *opus sectile* (for instance in the basilica of Junius Bassus, in S. Sabina, and in S. Costanza, all in Rome, and in the religious buildings in Ravenna).

In the Middle Ages, building bases were usually very low except where there were particular irregularities of the ground, and they projected only slightly from the masonry facing, corresponding to the external buttresses set within the base, which was occasionally ornamented by one or more moldings. In Gothic architecture the base became much higher, and instead of enclosing the buttresses, it followed their external outline and was marked out by one or more molded profiles, or by a sloping cornice molding (as in the Cathedral of Amiens, VI, PL. 296; and in Wells Cathedral, VI, PL. 310). In the façades of the great cathedrals (Reims, Rouen, etc.) the base often consisted of a high uninterrupted plinth on which rested the statue columns.

In the Renaissance there was a return to the associations and to the moldings exemplified by the classic models. Two solutions prevailed. One consisted of extending the molding of the base of the vertical element (pilaster, half column, column) to the socle of the whole wall, as in the Pazzi Chapel in Florence (II, PL. 367) and in the wall of the cella of the Tempietto of S. Pietro in Montorio, Rome. Quite often such a molding is placed above a smooth socle, as in the Church of S. Biagio, in Montepulciano, and in the Serra Chapel of S. Giacomo degli Spagnuoli (now Sacro Cuore di Maria) in Rome. The other solution adopted a base socle that imitated a continuous podium (as in the façade of S. Maria di Loreto, Rome) or a podium planimetrically profiled in the shape of a pedestal in correspondence with the vertical elements, as in the Farnesina (XI, PL. 120). Sometimes, especially since the beginning of the 16th century, the two systems are combined to form a more complex whole. In addition to these typical solutions, certain abbreviations, simplifications, and variants were often introduced; such are the types of uninterrupted socles, more or less high and projecting and concluded at the top by a simple band or by a torus on which the bases rest directly, used earlier by Alberti in the façade of the Tempio Malatestiano (I, PLS. 51, 52); this system was to be used often in the 16th century and in the baroque period, following the example of Bramante in the Belvedere courtyard (Vatican; II, FIG. 605). Sometimes the area in the shape of a pedestal, above which begins the façade, in turn rests on a socle, and may be defined by moldings or not.

A different solution for socles was introduced in the palaces with rusticated bases or entire façades. In such cases the ashlar reaches down to the ground or ends at the bottom with a simple smooth band, which may be projecting but sometimes may be receding with respect to the plumb of the rustication. In some other cases, the lower part of the rustication forms a sloping surface delimited on the upper part by a torus, in accordance with solutions typical of military architecture (Palazzo dei Diamanti, Ferrara, XII, PL. 12; Palazzo Tabarelli, in Trent; Palazzo Farnese, Gradoli; Palazzo Bocchi, Bologna). In other examples the base socle projects to form a seat, as in the palaces of the Medici (XII, PL. 4), Strozzi (XII, PL. 5), Rucellai (I, PL. 55), and Gondi, in Florence; the Palazzo Del Monte, Monte San Savino, and in the Palazzo dei Tribunali, by Bramante, the Palazzo Farnese, and the Villa Giulia, in Rome (XII, PL. 89).

Many Renaissance buildings lacked a socle (Palazzo Venezia, Rome) and in many others the socle was limited to the corners of the construction, being eliminated or reduced to a minimum — to a simple and low vertical slab — at the foot of the walls. Mannerism (q.v.) and baroque art did not in substance add any new schemes to those in use during the Renaissance; rather, the same schemes were used, but with a greater freedom in the combining of the various elements, in simplifying the various solutions, or, conversely, in complicating them.

In neoclassicism and in the 19th-century revivals, past solutions were adapted or reelaborated and varied slightly, often eclectically, without achieving any particularly notable results, except occasionally, in the last years of the 19th century, in the refined modeling of details.

Subsequently, the desire for renewal expressed through a greater adherence to facts and to practical and objective content (functionalism as well as structural, technological, and economic, distributive rationality) led contemporary architecture to approach the problem of the base structures of the building in a new and different way, for the most part reducing them to smooth, vertical socles, made of slabs of natural or artificial materials (the Stoclet house by J. Hoffmann in Brussels and, in general, the works of T. Garnier, of A. Perret, of P. H. Berlage, etc.): but often, and especially when the wall is made of resistant materials, the socle is eliminated altogether.

Arnaldo BRUSCHI

Floorings. The upper face of the base platforms and that of the floors in many-storied constructions are generally covered with materials that are more or less compact and resistant to wear to form a layer that constitutes the flooring (see INTERIOR DECORATION AND DESIGN). In primitive constructions flooring consists simply of a layer of beaten earth or clay, in which may also be incorporated small fragments of stone or straw. Within the sphere of more evolved cultures, especially in buildings intended for dwellings, the custom persisted of forming the floor by means of clay and mortar mixes. Such floors were found frequently in ancient Mesopotamia, in India, and in the Far East. In Rome, during the imperial age, a type of flooring similar to these was widely used; it consisted of a layer of concrete covered with another layer of a mixture (know as *opus signinum*) of minute pottery shards and mortar in which were inserted small pieces of stone arranged to form geometric designs or, in a subsequent period, thickly laid loose pebbles (*pavimentum barbaricum*); another type of flooring mixture was that called *graecanicum*, formed of coal, ashes, and lime. Even in modern times, especially in rural constructions and in factories and warehouses, flooring made up of cast concrete mortar is frequently used.

In the ancient world, the layer of beaten earth was usually covered with another material, such as brick or gypsum, on which was then applied a layer of plaster, which in ancient Egypt and in Crete was sometimes painted with ornamental motifs. At Pompeii the *opus signinum* was occasionally covered with colored plaster. The most widespread type of flooring in ancient times was, however, that composed of stone elements of various dimensions.

In Egyptian temples and tombs, and later also in the palaces, the flooring was, even in the early periods, composed of large stone slabs (granite, limestone, sandstone, basalt, and sometimes alabaster), irregular in shape but regularly joined by cement. Floors of this type are found also in Achaemenid Persia (at Susa they are even composed of polychrome marble slabs), in the Phoenician constructions, and in Crete, where the interstices between the stones were generally filled in with white or red plaster; and also in pre-Columbian America, in India, and in China, where floors were often built with polygonal stone slabs like those used for road pavements. The use of perfectly square slabs, occasionally adopted at Mycenae, became common in the Hellenic world: in most cases such floors were superimposed on the stylobate, resting on a concrete layer or on rows of bricks, as in the Temple of Apollo at Delphi.

Also of widespread use in Greece was a floor composed of pebbles — white and black — closely set in the concrete layer and arranged to form geometric or figural motifs. These floors were thus created in the mosaic process from which developed the techniques that were to find particular favor in Rome: the *lithostrota*, in which irregular pieces of colored stone and marble were inserted variously on a background of irregular tesserae of white limestone (see for instance the *lithostroton* in the sanctuary of Fortuna Primigenia, in Palestrina); and the *tessellata*, the technique of mosaic proper, composed only of uniform tesserae, of which very numerous examples are to be found, either in purely ornamental compositions or — more often — with figures (see MOSAICS; I, PLS. 22–28; VII, PL. 197; X, PL. 176).

Mosaic floors continued to be used in the Early Christian period, with regional variations in ornamental motifs and in the colors of the tesserae. Many mosaic church pavements have been preserved in Yugoslavia, in the Syro-Palestinian area, and in Africa. Among the floors illustrating secular subjects, mention should be made of that in the Great Palace of the Emperors, Istanbul, variously dated in the 5th and 6th centuries (II, PL. 437; VII, PL. 372). With the establishment of the Byzantine style, the trend in floor decoration was toward abstract repeated motifs, geometric figures, imitations of Eastern fabrics and carpets, and highly stylized plant motifs.

Mosaic floors are not lacking in the later Byzantine period, but they are rare and in the East are limited to geometric designs (St. Luke, in Phocis; Mount Athos; Trebizond); in Italy motifs derived from Eastern fabrics are common (S. Marco, Venice; S. Maria del Patir, Rossano; Otranto Cathedral; X, PL. 190). But the type of flooring which became most widespread in the area of Byzantium beginning with the 9th century was that called *opus alexandrinum*, formed by marbles and vitreous pastes of various colors, cut and arranged so as to form a geometric pattern dotted with large disks of precious materials (floor in the Church of S. Sofia, Nicaea). This is the type of flooring which in the West enjoyed greatest favor in south-central Italy, and which evolved into the so-called *opera campana* (Salerno Cathedral) in southern Italy (perhaps derived directly from the work of the *quadratari* summoned by Abbot Desiderius

from Byzantium) and the "Cosmatesque" type in Lazio (se COSMATI; III, PL. 483). In northern Italy, as well as in southern France, mosaic floors continued to be used, although with • rough technique (see ROMANESQUE ART).

In the West, a resurgence of figural themes occurred i• the 9th century (floor of Ivrea Cathedral, with allegorical fig ures inspired by the miniatures of the Warmondo codices) an• particularly, in the Romanesque period, in northern Italy (floo• of S. Michele, Pavia, with the story of Theseus and the Mino taur; that of Cremona Cathedral, illustrating the Psychomachy that of Aosta Cathedral, with the Labors of the Months; thos• of the Leone Museum, Vercelli, and of S. Marco, Venice, wit• imaginary scenes; and that of S. Colombano, Bobbio, wit• Biblical scenes).

Mosaic floors are not infrequently found in subsequent pe riods, but figural or naturalistic compositions became rare• (except, of course, in the reworkings of classical themes durin• the period of neoclassicism); geometric patterns prevailed, or in the Veneto region, arrangements of tesserae in various shade• of the same color (Palazzo del Te, Mantua, floors designed b• Giulio Romano). Also characteristic is the so-called "Palladia• floor," composed of minute irregular fragments of colored marbl• bound with plaster (usually red); this technique lies somewher• between that of mosaic proper and that of the "mixture" floors• and has been continuously used, even into modern times.

Another type of floor, using stone elements, which appeare• in Rome in the republican period and was to persist for a lon• time in the West, is *opus sectile*, composed of stones and slab• of colored marbles of various shapes composed into ornamenta• patterns or simple figural designs (see INLAY; VIII, PL. 79, 81•

A particular form of inlay called niello was subsequentl• developed in Tuscany, which, according to Vasari, "imitate• subjects painted in chiaroscuro." It is created by filling hollow• in marble slabs with a black mixture based on pitch. The tech nique is derived from that of the *opus interassile* of the Roman• (which, however, was never used for flooring) in which strip• of colored marble were inserted in the hollows. Examples of thi• process in the 13th century are the floor of the Baptistery o• Florence (VIII, PL. 82); that of Siena Cathedral (VIII, PL. 86• begun at the end of the 14th century, with Biblical scenes from designs by Matteo di Giovanni, and continued in the 16th centur• by Domenico Beccafumi; and the floor of Lucca Cathedra• with designs by Antonio Federighi.

Floors in colored marble inlay are rather rare in the Gothi• period (during which, nevertheless, some examples are to b• found of floors with emblematic motifs, as in the "labyrinths" of the cathedrals of Chartres, Reims, and Amiens); they were• however, widely adopted in the Renaissance and baroque pe riods, with magnificent realizations of ornamental motifs (floo• of the Biblioteca Laurenziana, Florence, which reproduces th• design of the ceiling).

Brick floors were used in the ancient Orient, particularl• in Mesopotamia, where large terra-cotta squares were place• on a layer of beaten earth covered with bitumen. In Rom• there appeared floors composed of small rectangular brick• arranged in a herringbone pattern (*opus spicatum*), or of squar• or hexagonal bricks. Terra-cotta slabs were also used, althoug• infrequently, in China and in other regions of the Far East• The use of brick for flooring became common in Europe durin• the Romanesque period and has persisted in modern times• In general, in floorings of this type, the shape and arrangemen• of the brick paving tiles create hexagonal, diamond, and sta• patterns; quite often, through the use of suitably shaped pavin• tiles in two different colors, the floors composed recall those o• marble inlay (floor by G. Vasari in the Hall of Leo X, Palazz• Vecchio, Florence, VIII, PL. 102). Also frequent were combi nations of brick sections with sections of marble or majolica• In the Gothic period and throughout the 16th century, in Franc• and in northern Europe generally, widespread use was mad• of floors composed of paving tiles on which were stamped dec orative motifs; into the hollowed-out design white or colore• clay was poured and the tiles were then fired with a lead glaze• These are known as *carreaux plombés* (examples in the Châtea• de Blois).

Floors of glazed tiles became widespread from the end of the 13th century, probably following the example of Islam (see CERAMICS). The paving tiles, square or hexagonal and decorated with heraldic motifs, plant ornament, stylized animal figures, and so on, usually formed patterns in bands, octagons, or chess-board designs. The first European production centers were the Hispano-Moorish ones of Manises and Valencia, which supplied the glazed tesserae (aliceres) and the polygonal paving tiles (azulejos) with which, especially in the kingdom of Aragon, were composed floors of various patterns and the dadoes known as alicatados. Soon, however, the production of majolica paving tiles spread elsewhere; in Italy, at the end of the 13th century, local production supplied paving tiles to decorate the steps of the Upper Church of S. Francesco, Assisi, and, at the beginning of the 14th century, those of the Church of S. Maria Donnaregina, Naples. Other 14th-century examples of this kind are to be found in the Cathedral and in the Abbey of St. Paul, Utrecht; in France; and in Burgundy. In the 15th century the use of tile floors spread in Italy (Borgia Apartments in the Vatican; S. Silvestro al Quirinale, Rome; Palazzo Vecchio, Florence, ascribed to Luca della Robbia the Younger; S. Giovanni a Carbonara, Naples) and gave rise to an uninterrupted tradition, of which numerous 16th-century examples are to be found in Bologna, in Tuscany, in Viterbo, and also outside Italy (but with materials of Italian production, such as those from the Montelupo workshops, presented by Cosimo II to Marie de' Médicis in 1611). This tradition was to have particularly felicitous moments in the baroque period, especially in southern Italy, where floor decoration was often conceived as an organic complement of architectural design and reflects the styles of contemporary painting (floor of the Concezione at Montecalvario in Naples, designed by Domenico Antonio Vaccaro, and that of S. Michele at Anacapri) or perpetuates figures from the popular figural repertory.

Among the other important flooring materials is wood, which has certainly been utilized since remote times — although, of course, no examples are extant — and is still commonly used. The most common type is a floor composed of boards, occasionally caulked in the interstices with oakum and bitumen, in imitation of ship decks. In the modern period wooden floors have also been composed with inlay or with small geometric elements, which often make up ornamental patterns.

Metal floor coverings have been used only exceptionally, and for sumptuary purposes: in Biblical tradition the floor of the holy of holies in the Temple of Jerusalem was covered with a sheet of gold, and the same seems to have been true of the floor of part of the hypostyle hall in Karnak in Egypt; in the East, the floor of the pagoda in Phnom-Penh (Cambodia) is of engraved silver.

In contemporary architecture frequent use is made of such materials as linoleum, rubber, gres, and vinyl mixtures. From a decorative point of view, the floor is more strictly qualified as a chromatic surface in accordance with the environmental ensemble of the ceiling and of the walls. Moreover, the floor, in its internal structure, is conceived as a functional element, that is to say it may be equipped to contain heating systems (as the Romans did with the hypocaust) and electric wiring.

Stairs. Among the most important architectural elements connected with the base areas of buildings are those whose function is to provide access from one floor to the next. These may consist simply of an inclined plane with a smooth surface, or may be divided into small successively placed plane surfaces, that is to say, steps. In the first case — of which applications have always been rare — the inclination must obviously be limited; in the second case, it is possible instead to have more marked inclinations, but these should at any rate always be contained within specific ratios associated with the rise and with the width of the surface of the steps. Each section of steps included between two landings is called a "flight"; the whole is the "staircase." Rectangular treads are called "fliers"; triangular or wedge-shaped ones are known as "winders."

Stairs display great structural and formal variations in relation to their dimensions, their placement, and the materials of which they are built.

In wooden or iron stairs each flight is generally made up of two or more parallel and sloping boards or beams, called the string or stringer, on which the steps rest. The string can either have its upper edge cut into steps with the treads overhanging, or can be connected to the treads by triangular elements; alternatively the treads and risers can be housed in the face. In stone stairs the structures supporting the steps can consist of a compact shaped base, a rampant vault, a quadrant vault, or several adjoining round-headed arches of progressively increasing height; similar constructions, especially the vaulted ones, are to be found in brick stairs.

A greater structural complexity is, of course, to be observed when the stairs are not made up of one or more straight flights along a single axis, but of several flights grouped into a square, rectangular, polygonal, or T-shaped plan, or else of curved runs on a circular, elliptical, or "horseshoe" plan. In these cases the flights may be continuous, as is typical of flights on a circular plan or of spiral staircases, which have in fact a continuous helical movement; otherwise, the connection between the various flights is formed by horizontal planes known as landings. The use of iron and of reinforced concrete has furthermore allowed the development of the self-supporting staircase, that is to say, one with each step supported at its front by the step below and with only one end built into a wall (also achieved, although rarely, in the Middle Ages, with other materials), and the development of stairs in which the supporting members are slabs resting at either end on cantilevered landings.

The internal stairs of buildings are normally contained within a supporting framework or cage (walls or piers) which carries the flights and landings. Wellhole stairs leave an open space about which the stairs, whether consising only of fliers, or of fliers and winders, turn. The steps of a circular staircase may wind around an upright which is known as a "newel" or "newel post." Stairs with straight flights having the main post at the foot, as well as a secondary post at a landing which supports the outer string of each of the two flights it separates, are called "newel staircases."

These elementary structural schemes have had widely varied applications, in which flights of compound shapes were differently combined. Of the stairs with straight flights built along a single axis and often alternated with landings, numerous examples are to be found since ancient times and within various cultures. These were generally external stairs, to which a particular formal or symbolic significance was often attached. Such were the stairs which gave access to the tops of the bases on which rose the Assyrian, Babylonian (PL. 242), and sometimes the Egyptian temples, many constructions of pre-Sassanian Persia (VIII, PL. 126), and the stairs on the fronts of the podiums of Etruscan and Roman temples (PL. 252), and those of the pyramids and religious buildings of the Mayas (PL. 240), of Islamic India, of Burma (PLS. 240, 243), of Indonesia, and of medieval Japan (VIII, PLS. 282, 284, 285).

External stairs with straight flights are often found in the architecture of the medieval West, especially in the Gothic period, running along the façades of the buildings (Palazzo dei Consoli, Gubbio; Palazzo del Popolo, Orvieto) or against one of the internal walls of the courtyards, as in the Ca' d'Oro in Venice (VI, FIG. 539), in the Palazzo del Podestà (Bargello) in Florence, in the Castel Nuovo in Naples, and in many other examples of civil constructions in which the stairs themselves are often covered by roofs supported by small pillars, arches, or other means. External straight stairs are also found in subsequent periods, notable examples being the Scala dei Giganti in the Palazzo Ducale in Venice, those of Palladio's "La Rotonda" in Vicenza (XI, PL. 31), and those in the Villa Piovene at Lonedo; these inspired many of the Palladian derivations in Great Britain and elsewhere. Straight stairs became an almost constant motif of the façades of Renaissance and baroque churches, although in these cases they often formed a base member on a rectangular or curvilinear plan, with successively receding planes. In addition to facing the entrance portals, such an element — which can also be considered as a form derived from the Greek *krepidoma* — is sometimes found on the sides or at the back of churches (apse of S. Maria Maggiore in Rome, by C. Rainaldi; II, PL. 132).

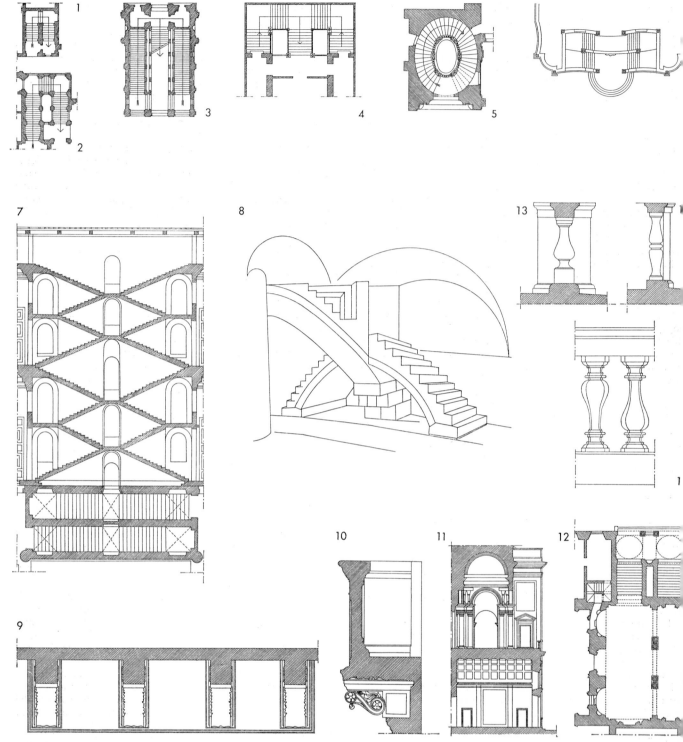

Stairs, balconies, and loggias. (1–8) Stairs. (1–6) Plans: (1) with partition; (2) wellhole stairs; (3) opposed flights, "scissors" scheme; (4) monumen
staircase; (5) spiral stairs with central open well; (6) external staircase of the 18th century; (7) double straight stairs, from a project by Pallad
section and plan; (8) Rome, Colosseum, stairs on rampant arches, perspective drawing. (9–10) Italian Renaissance balcony, plan and section. (11–12) Itali
Renaissance loggia, section and plan. (13–14) Balusters: (13) Renaissance, section; (14) baroque.

Among the various forms of combinations of straight flights
for external stairs, the simplest one, flights set at a right angle,
had already been adopted by the Persians at Persepolis and at
Susa and appears again frequently in the medieval West (as
in the *profferli* — a local term for external stairs — of the houses
in Viterbo, PL. 240); in Spain and in southern Italy such stairs
are for the most part placed in the courtyards and roofed.

It is mostly in the architecture of the Renaissance and baroque periods that both external and internal stairs acquired
striking monumentality and the most complex forms of combi-

nations of straight flights are to be found. These, reproducir
a scheme which the Romans had already adopted, though n
for staircases (in, for instance, the sanctuary of Fortuna Prim
genia at Palestrina; VII, FIG. 399), can have opposed ar
convergent flights, as in the Palazzo Senatorio (IX, FIG. 90
in the Piazza del Campidoglio in Rome, by Michelangel
in the Villa Repeta at Campiglia dei Berici, by Palladio; an
in a more complex form, also by Palladio, in the Villa F
scari ("La Malcontenta") and in the Villa Badoer at Fratta P
lesine. The same scheme is also to be found, adapted in comp

itions of several elements, in the castle of Racconigi by Guarino Guarini (VII, PL. 106); in the Church of the Annunziata at Grignasco by B. A. Vittone; and later in Chiswick House (Middlesex) by R. Boyle (ca. 1725; VI, PL. 441).

Another typical scheme is the T-shaped one, composed of a rectilinear flight leading to a landing, from which diverge two opposed flights. This was apparently conceived by Francesco di Giorgio (q.v.) among the most striking examples are those by Primaticcio at Fontainebleau and others in which the motif of the divergent flights is often completed by that of the subsequent convergent flights (Nymphenburg Palace by Agostino Barelli, 1664; Albergo dei Poveri, Naples, by F. Fuga, begun 1751).

These same schemes were applied also for combinations of elliptical flights, as in the villa of Poggio a Caiano by Sangallo (q.v.; XII, PL. 387) and, in more complex forms, in the horseshoe-shaped flights of steps at Fontainebleau by J. Ducerceau (PL. 241). Rectilinear and curvilinear flights were also combined, on occasion, with results of great scenographic effect like that achieved by Vignola at Caprarola (XIV, PL. 371).

Interior stairs display a greater variety of structural schemes and of shapes. Rare in the ancient Orient, interior stairs were more frequent in Egypt, in the tombs, in the pyramids, and often in the pylons flanking the entrance to the temples (as at Karnak); they were also common in the Cretan and Mycenaean palaces and fortifications (sometimes inside the thickness of the walls) as well as in some Sardinian nuraghi.

In Greece, stairs were sometimes built to give access to the upper galleries of temples (Temple of Zeus, Olympia); in Magna Graecia and in Sicily temples often had two winding staircases at either side of the cella (Paestum, Temple of Athena; VII, FIG. 126). In the Hellenistic period the use of interior stairs spread also to private dwellings (in which the gynaeceum was normally on an upper floor) and to other civil constructions, such as the arcades (Stoa of Attalos and eastern arcade of the Asklepieion in Athens).

Roman architecture applied new and varied structural forms, especially in supporting structures with rampant barrel or cross vaults, as in the Baths of Caracalla and in the Aurelian walls, by means of which it became possible to build both stairs turned around a central core and wellhole stairs, of which the first examples are to be found in Rome in the Pantheon and in the Temple of Venus and Roma.

The Romans also built stairs covered by vaults (Tabularium, Baths of Diocletian, Basilica of Maxentius) and complicated systems of flight connection, like those in use in the amphitheaters, where often two short convergent flights led to a third flight, following a sort of reverse T-shaped scheme. Spiral staircases were quite common (like that, for instance, inside Trajan's Column), while those with self-supporting steps, as in the Villa dei Sette Bassi, were very rare. Finally, special architectural structures were conceived, distinct from the whole of the building, in which the stairs were contained (stair towers). Within this great variety of forms in the Greek and Roman world the prevailing intent was to give the stairs purely practical functions; but there are examples of monumental stairs, as in the Great Altar of Zeus at Pergamon (VII, PL. 172; FIG. 296) and in the Propylaea of the Temple of Baalbek.

A clearly utilitarian character is obvious in the stairs of medieval architecture, which reproduced the types already conceived by the Romans; however, spiral staircases were more frequent, especially those inside bell-towers (Pisa) or stair towers, such as that of S. Vitale in Ravenna (II, FIG. 775), those of St. Michael in Hildesheim (X, FIG. 881), and those at Castel del Monte (VI, FIG. 536). In the Gothic period, in fact, the theme of the spiral staircases evolved into particular shapes, since the supporting structure was composed not of cylindrical masonry but of small pillars and open arches. Derivations of this structural and decorative type persisted for a long time; examples include the stairs of Palazzo Contarini (the so-called "bovolo") in Venice, ascribed to Giovanni Candi (end of the 15th century); the stairs of the Château de Blois in France (IX, PL. 317) — which are, however, polygonal in plan; and those of the choir of St-Etienne-du-Mont, Paris, ascribed to Philibert Delorme (q.v.).

In the early Renaissance, stairs rarely possessed monumental character. It was not until the beginning of the 16th century that — as already mentioned — stairs acquired a considerable importance in the architectural conception. Throughout the baroque period they were often treated as a sort of introduction to the decorative unity of the whole (as with the stairs of the presbytery of S. Stefano in Florence, PL. 241) and often as the fulcrum of the spatial articulation of the building itself.

The schemes already described in connection with external stairs were again used: rather rarely that with rectilinear flights along a single axis (as in the stairs of the Biblioteca Laurenziana, IX, PL. 540, and in the Scala Regia in the Vatican, II, PL. 270); more often the T-shaped one, which was, however, generally completed by other connecting elements to prolong or repeat the movement of the first flights. Examples of this T-scheme are the Escalera Dorada by Diego de Silos in Burgos, second decade of the 16th century; the large staircases of Genoa University by Baccio Bartolommeo del Bianco (II, FIG. 285); those of the Monastery of S. Giorgio Maggiore in Venice by B. Longhena, and of the Palazzo Reale in Naples by A. Picchiatti (1651); and those by L. Le Vau the Younger at Versailles (1671), by P. Canali in the Palazzo Cloetta-Fantuzzi in Bologna (1680), and by C. Fontana (q.v.) in the Palazzo Reale in Genoa (ca. 1705).

The motif of the two divergent flights which then make a 180 degree turn and converge again was carried out in the large staircase of the Palazzo Madama in Turin, by Juvara. Another shape quite typical of late mannerist and baroque architecture is that of the staircases known as "imperial," in which a central flight is succeeded, after a landing, by two flights with a divergent course or, viceversa, where two side flights are succeeded by a third central one: examples are those by J. Bautista de Toledo and Juan de Herrera at the Escorial (1563–84); by J. B. Neumann at Würzburg (VI, PL. 148); by Juvara in the Royal Palace in Turin (the so-called "stair of the scissors," begun 1720); by L. Vanvitelli in the royal palace in Caserta (VIII, PL. 226); and by G. B. Sacchetti in the royal palace in Madrid (PL. 241).

Stairs with a central supporting structure were also frequent, especially in the 16th century (suffice it to recall those of Palazzo Farnese in Rome and those by Sansovino in the Palazzo Ducale and in the Biblioteca Marciana in Venice), often also with an open supporting structure, as in the Palazzo Spinola in Genoa. Wellhole stairs had multiform schemes of an imposing scenographic layout, particularly in the baroque period; the flights adhere to all four sides of the cage with small landings at intervals, or else at every three flights there is a wide landing lighted by large windows or open like a loggia (stairs of S. Juan de los Reyes, 1504, and of the hospital of Sta Cruz, 1504–14, both in Toledo, by Enrique Egas, which constitute the precedents for those by F. Mansart in the Château de Blois, 1635–38, those of the Château de Maisons-Lafitte, IX, FIG. 479, and all the similar constructions which were repeated throughout Europe into the 19th century).

The same structural schemes recur frequently in the stairs with curvilinear flights, on an elliptical plan (like those by Borromini in Palazzo Barberini and by Mascherino in the Quirinale, Rome) in which is repeated the motif of the central supports of paired columns, or with convergent flights (Borromini's plan for the Palazzo Carpegna, Rome, II, FIG. 551; stairs of the Palazzo Carignano, Turin, by Guarino Guarini).

A particular type of spiral staircase, for which some medieval precedents exist (Collège des Bernardins, Paris) as well as some examples in Leonardo's drawings, is that with two (or more) parallel spirals. Already realized in the first half of the 16th century in the Château de Chambord (I, PL. 387), this type reappeared often in Italy, Spain, and Germany.

In many other cases, finally, baroque stairs are so varied in shape that they evade a detailed analysis of formal schemes and tend rather to appear as organisms which realize a dynamically open and multiplied spatiality with lively effects of light and shade. In this connection should be mentioned the elliptical stairs supported by open structures in the Episcopal Palace in Bruchsal by J. B. Neumann (1723), decorated with stuccoes by J. M. Feichtmayr; and the complicated combinations of different structural themes used by F. Sanfelice in Naples, as in the double stairs converging in a single landing in Palazzo Serra di Cassano, in those with two wells in Palazzo Sanfelice (1728), and the imperial stairs in Palazzo di Maio on Via Foria.

Stairs in modern architecture — after the interval of Art Nouveau, during which they still represented opportunities to create movement in interior decoration themes — generally resume primarily practical functions and therefore cease to represent a decorative element. Moreover, the variety of structural forms made possible by the use of new materials gave rise to specific forms, an example of which may be seen in the spiral staircases by Gropius (q.v.) in the administration building at the Werkbund Exhibition, Cologne, 1914, and by P. L. Nervi in the city stadium in Florence. Worthy of mention also are the stairs composed of prefabricated elements by Alvar Aalto; in these the shape of the steps is such that it can be adapted to various inclinations by varying the ratio between the rise and the tread.

Finally, stairs represent a considerable element in landscape architecture and in town planning. In the first case, obviously, they contribute in creating picturesque effects, whether they have a distributive function among the various terraces (as in the Villa Garzoni at Collodi, near Pescia, in the Villa Aldobrandini in Frascati, in the Orangerie of Versailles, and at Schönbrunn Castle, Vienna), or whether they form more complex perspective articulations (as in the Villa d'Este in Tivoli; VIII, PL. 432). In town planning, on the other hand, the original practical functions of stairs — as conceived in ancient Greece (in Athens, in Assos) and in the Roman world (at Praeneste, mod. Palestrina), and in the Middle Ages in Rome, Siena, Perugia, Naples, Genoa, Amalfi, Spoleto — were combined, during the Renaissance and baroque periods, with intentions of scenographic monumentality. In this connection also many examples could be mentioned, from the famous flight of steps leading to the Campidoglio and that of Trinità dei Monti (by F. de Sanctis, 1723–25) in Rome, to others, less well-known but worthy of mention, such as the steps of the sanctuary of S. Maria della Scala at Massafra.

Oreste FERRARI

WALL ELEMENTS. Quite often, and even in buildings for which no particular esthetic value was intended, the walls are characterized by formal features which stand in more or less direct relation to the functional structural aspects of the walls themselves, to their dimensions, and to their placement. Sometimes these features are decorative elements applied to the walls, such as painted plasters, mosaic facings, revetments in polychrome marbles, in natural or glazed brickwork, in slabs of various materials, and in reliefs. Even though, in many cases, these decorations assume a wholly independent character, sometimes to the point of seemingly obliterating the wall itself (in the sense of the spatial limit it represents), a relation between such decorations and this "limit" persists with regard to the unity of the architectural work.

In many other cases, however, the wall structure itself has an intrinsic and independent formal value, which contributes in supporting, specifying, and deepening the technical, structural, and functional motives in the light of clear expressive and decorative requirements.

Within many cultures masonry curtain walls were deliberately left in view, and sometimes were imitated by incising the plaster facing, such elaborations often serving to emphasize and give greater relief to the structure. In masonry, for example, this was a achieved by paying special attention to the shape, dimension, and position of the elements, or by attempting combinations of different materials, as in the Roman use of courses of stone blocks and bricks; this device was widely adopted by Byzantine builders, who subsequently relied on color effects obtained by the arrangement of bricks in decorative geometric compositions, often enriched with majolica inserts. A classical derivation is to be attributed to the marble facings of the Romanesque Byzantine buildings, and the two-colored ("zebrawork") facings of the Pisan Romanesque style were perhaps a subsequent development based on local traditions.

In Islamic architecture frequent use was made of ornamentation made up of bands or of series of arches composed of stone arranged to form star-shapes and other geometric patterns (technique similar to, though not identical with, the inlay process in that it was here inserted into the actual structure of the walls. Various examples of this type of decoration are found in Moslem influenced art, especially in Spain and southern Italy (Salerno Gaeta, Caserta Vecchia, Ravello, Pontone near Scala, Monreale Cefalù, Forza d'Agrò, S. Giovanni Vecchio at Stilo, etc.), a well as in the Byzantine world (St. Luke of Stiris, Phocis; Pa nagia Parigoritissa, at Arta, 13th century, PL. 217; and at Mistr in the Peloponnesus, PL. 255).

From the period of the Renaissance to the 19th centur the leaving in view of wall structures became less frequen and certain forms of facing were composed in ways similar t the structures themselves (rustication, etc.). In some trend of contemporary architecture a marked tendency to give promi nence to the structural materials is apparent, and a widesprea custom is that of leaving in view pillars and walls of reinforce concrete, just as they appear after the removal of the form

* *

Moldings. The surface of the wall is also defined in relatio to the other elements to which it is connected by molding The latter is the result of the profiling of an architectura member running on the surface and involving a series of pro jections and recesses which, originally at least, inspired b factors of various kinds (structural, technological, etc.), shap the surface, with insertions of a type generically similar to sculp tural ones, through the relief acquired by the shapes under th light (see ORNAMENTATION). Molding is an architectural eleme which can be executed with any type of material and is connecte in origin to the processes of woodworking. The projectio of a single course of stone blocks from a flat wall can be consid ered as a molding; but in a more general sense, molding i in the words of Choisy, "the abstract art of accentuating th masses," of separating, underlining, or giving greater reli to the various parts of the wall surface and its elements. Ind vidual moldings are combined to form bases, pedestals, cornice door and window frames, crestings, and other elements. Suc combinations of moldings vary according to culture and perio they are either more or less free and variable, or they are regulate by precise (sometimes very strict) rules and customs, as in class cal architecture (see below, *The orders*). Historically speakin molding, in the strict sense of the word, made its appearanc only when man achieved tools capable of shaping the materi used. In Egypt, for instance, its use spread and became regulate beginning with the Middle Kingdom and consisted most gen erally of flat elements (listels or bands), concave element (cove, "Egyptian gorge," or cavetto, FIG. 487, no. 2), and conve elements (astragal or bead or torus), in regular association an applied to the cornices of walls or to wall members (socles, plinth bases, door and window spaces, framing of surfaces, corners buildings, etc.). Sometimes the cresting of the constructio was concluded by a row of snakelike figures (ureaus) with characteristic S-shaped profile (the so-called "cobra," or khe kes, cresting; IV, PL. 330).

Such types of molding and their elementary combination spread to the Mediterranean area and eastward as far as Persi where, at a later time, in the Achaemenid period and as la as the Sassanian, evidence is to be found of the use of molde elements having Egyptian influence. In Persia, however, th Greek influence is also present, as in the so-called "Tomb c Cyrus" at Pasargadae (VIII, PL. 126); in the Achaemenid perio moreover, is found the projecting band enriched with dentils — as in classical Greek architecture (VIII, PL. 137); and, in th capitals and bases of the columns, a more complex and refine sometimes exuberant, combination of curvilinear molding, used, for the most part carved with simple motifs of a vague phytomorphic type (PL. 231; VIII, FIG. 274). In Mesopotami where the use of the solid brick wall prevailed, moldings wer generally limited to flat listels or decorated bands.

Cretan architecture, and even more, Mycenaean, show th use of flat profiles (listels or smooth bands, often arranged i parallel zones and sometimes decorated with reliefs for the most part of the plant motifs; reworkings of motifs derived from the Egyptian and Eastern ornamental repertory) or concave and convex profiles, quite similar to the types diffused from Egypt. It is, however, at Mycenae that there are found the earliest Western examples of moldings proper in organic compositions of several different elements — flat, concave, or convex — of various sizes, such as the molding with a flat listel, the semicircular one, the quarter-round or convex (cavetto and scotia) and the concave types (ovolo and thumb), and the concave-convex S-shaped one (cyma recta). Not much more is offered by the pre-Hellenic architecture of western Asia and of the Aegean area, where the moldings were little more than variously projecting bands or curved elements, characterized in the Phoenician sphere, to a greater or lesser degree, by an unadorned and rough appearance.

In Etruria, contemporaneously with the Greek examples, the use of moldings, particularly in the profiles of bases and tombs, developed with considerable scope and originality and with a preference for effects of vigorous sobriety, also accentuated by the use of coarse-grained materials such as tufa, peperino, and limestone. The effects are obtained by sharp contrasts between smooth areas and profiled parts. In addition to flat bands, astragals, or tori of different sizes, sometimes connected by small coves, much use was made (in bases, podiums, and capitals) of the typical quarter-round molding; beginning in the 7th and 6th centuries B.C., moldings with a concave "bird's beak" overhang made their appearance and were often used to conclude the double-curve cyma reversa. The tombs — especially those in the necropolises of Castel d'Asso, Norchia, S. Giuliano, Blera, Cerveteri, and Sovana — the ruins of Marzabotto, the paintings of Tarquinia (columns of the Tomb of the Lionesses), and the gates of Volterra and of Perugia (V, PL. 48), among others, provide characteristic examples, some of them strongly influenced by the Hellenic world.

The Greeks display a much more systematic and, in a certain sense, rational use of molding, not only in relation to functional, technological, and structural factors, but with a view to the effects of light, shadow, and reflections, of particular optical conditions, and so forth. The basic elements of Greek molding are in substance the same as those used in the Mediterranean area and in western Asia: that is, flat (band, listel, dentils, etc.) or curvilinear (scotia, cavetto, torus, astragal, cyma recta, cyma reversa, bird's beak) elements, but the Greek way of associating them was strictly regulated by custom. Thus, if a curved molding of any type was placed in a diffused light, the tendency was to deprive it of softness by the adoption of a vigorous profile; if instead the sun struck it directly, the same type of molding acquired a more rounded shape. The shape of the Greek molding was, moreover, related to the characteristics of the material employed. A single type of molding may display a different profile according to whether it is made of terra cotta, as in the archaic temples, or traced in soft or porous stone, as in the so-called "Temple of Concordia" in Agrigento, or carved in a compact material such as Pentelic marble, as in the Parthenon. The shape of the moldings varies, furthermore, in the various architectural orders. In the Doric, though the use of flat moldings definitely prevails, especially in the entablature (for instance, that of the "Temple of Neptune" at Paestum, PL. 252, or that of the peribolos of the Parthenon), the infrequent curved moldings display vigorous and harsh profiles. In the Ionic order there is more scope for moldings; they are often decorated and carved with elegant and varied shapes, rich in sinuous profiles, and are sometimes vigorously accentuated.

Other differences are naturally to be placed in relation to the different periods of Greek architecture, even though in substance the same general trends are preserved. Thus the archaic orders display simple moldings with wide, vigorous profiles, as for example in the entablature of Temple C at Selinunte, and in the capitals of the "basilica," of the "Temple of Ceres," and of the "Temple of Neptune" at Paestum. In the 5th century, the moldings acquired a refined elegance and tension, as in the Parthenon (VII, PL. 399), in the Temple of Apollo Epikourios at Bassae

(VII, PL. 399), and especially in the Erechtheion (III, PL. 341). In the Hellenistic period some typical Doric profiles, such as the echinus, became more rigid, while some curved moldings of Ionic style became softer in profile.

In Roman architecture, in the Sullan period and in the last years of the Republic various stylistic components were blended and the profiles of the members sometimes drew near to Hellenistic elegance, as for example in the so-called "Temple of Hercules" at Cori (VII, PL. 201), in some Pompeian examples (PL. 247), and at Palestrina (anc. Praeneste); while elsewhere in the podiums of some temples an almost harsh simplicity of shapes, unknown to the Hellenic world, recalled the Etruscan-Italic models. This is especially notable in the profiles of the podium of Temple C in Largo Argentina in Rome (second half of the 4th century B.C.), of the Lanuvium "capitolium" (end of 4th cent. B.C.), of the Temple of Gabii (ca. end of 3d cent. B.C.). However, in the examples from this period and subsequently, it is possible to note a process of stabilization in the profiles of the individual curved moldings, which tend to elementary geometric forms and to an arrangement of combinations within precise rules that was to end in a limited vocabulary of elements. According to the Renaissance theorizations, based on the study of Roman monuments, such elements were limited to the following: the listel (or taenia), the dentil, the astragal of semicircular section, (which differs only in size and position from torus molding), the quarter-round ovolo, the cyma recta or reversa of convex-concave section, and the scotia with a curve larger than a semicircle, utilized in bases of the Attic type. All these moldings can remain smooth or, excepting the listel and the scotia, they can be ornamented with such motifs as the dentil, the bead and reel, and the egg and dart. They can, of course, be carried out in various materials (marble, stucco, terra cotta, bronze).

Roman architecture, substantially indifferent to detail and basically concerned with over-all spatial composition, preferred shapes which were regularly geometrical and of constant proportions and which were therefore easy to execute and reproduce. Nevertheless, traces of the Hellenic refinement and of the old sculptural style survived at least until the Augustan period. Between the last part of the 1st century B.C. and the early years of the 1st century of our era, Roman moldings often display sharp and clear profiles, and the vertical planes (listels, dripstones) are sometimes (as in the Theater of Marcellus) slightly inclined in order to accentuate the effects of light. However, in many cases, as for example in the moldings of the Temple of Apollo Sosianus and of the "Temple of Concordia," decorative motifs (even if somewhat overabundant) were used to achieve effects of refinement and richness. Under the Antonines the trend toward ornamental exuberance was accentuated and resulted in combinations of moldings overloaded with ornamentation in which the sculptural values tended to fade into a more markedly pictorial and chiaroscuro conception. Regional variations also appeared and became progressively more accentuated. In the West moldings and their ornamentation often tended to a certain heaviness and solemnity resulting from rounded and vigorous forms, while a greater angularity in profiles is to be noted in the moldings of the Eastern Empire. In the latter, beginning in the 3d century, sculptural decoration tended to be reduced to superficial incisions carried out with a drill, in a process which later came into use throughout the Empire. In this technique each member, especially in the entablature, was underlined by the black drilled holes, which by contrast gave a certain transparency to the shadows and restored vigor to the outlines when viewed from a distance. Between the 4th and the 6th century regional differentiations were further accentuated. The Latin molding often appears round and soft (entablature and cornices of S. Costanza and of the so-called "Temple of Romulus," IX, PL. 41) and the projections are sometimes flattened.

In the Byzantine area, the classical molding with its characteristic decorations disappeared and was replaced by a series of alternating surfaces (almost always flat) enriched with repeated fretwork motifs, usually floral (Hagia Sophia, II, PL. 429, and SS. Sergius and Bacchus, II, PL. 426, in Constantinople). In a later period (11th–14th cent.) moldings — especially exter-

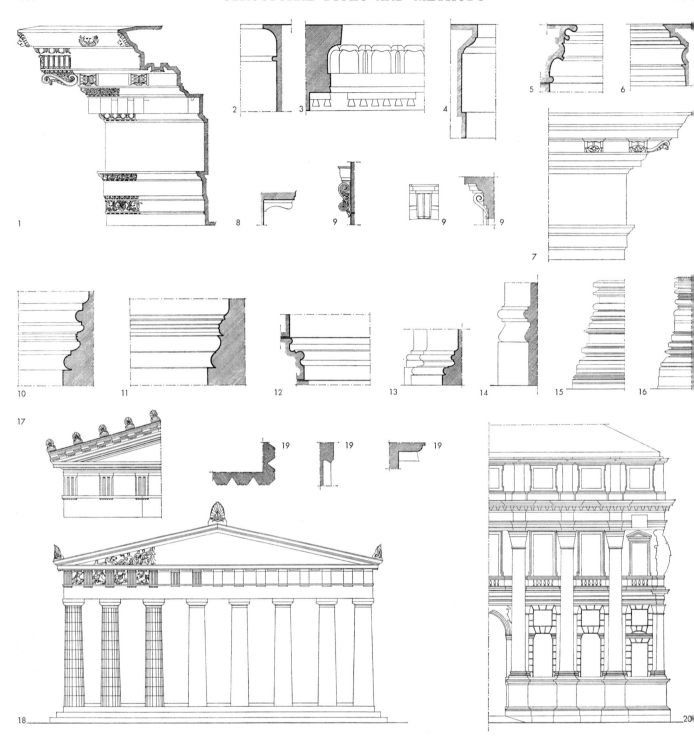

Molding. (1–7) Crown moldings: (1) Complete entablature, face and section (Rome, Temple of Castor and Pollux; early 1st cent.); cornice profiles: (2) Egyptian cyma or crown; (3) Greek cyma (Locri, Magna Graecia); (4) Etruscan-Italic cyma (Gabi); (5) Gothic crown molding; (6) Renaissance crown molding; (7) Renaissance entablature with corbel tables; front view (Venice, Palazzo Grimani). (8–9) Types of mutules and corbels, Greek and Renaissance, in a crown molding. (10–16) Base moldings: (10) Greek (Athens, Stoa of Attalos); (11) Roman (Pantheon); (12) Gothic; (13) Renaissance; (14) baroque; (15–16) medieval Indian (Khajuraho, Temple of Laksmana, 10th cent.). (17) Front with antefixes, Doric entablature, and frieze with triglyphs (Krimissa, Magna Graecia, Temple of Apollo Alaeus). (18) Composition of the Doric order: pediment, cornice, frieze, architrave, columns, and stylobate (Athens, Parthenon). (19) Plan and section of a triglyph. (20) Composition of the order and of various types of moldings from a project by Andrea Palladio.

nal ones — were achieved by a characteristic arrangement of the bricks (radiating patterns, dentils, etc.), often alternated with marble or stone in basically chromatic effects (see BYZANTINE ART).

In the West during the Middle Ages the character of molding, which always remained secondary to sculptural decoration, changed to a considerable extent, although it was still based on more or less complex combinations, often fanciful and changeable, of curvilinear, convex, and concave profiles separated in most cases by listels, flat bands, and decorated bands. Regional

variations, however, led to the introduction of completely new types and combinations of molding elements. There is, therefore, a great variety of styles which would be very difficult to classify. In Italy, in the regions of Tuscany, Lazio, Umbria, and Campania, the Roman influence remained quite strong. In some areas of southern France, such as Auvergne, even in constructions which were quite advanced architecturally, the molding was rather simple; but in Poitiers, where the cornices of the Baptistery of St-Jean clearly recall the late-Roman equivalents,

eavy and complicated forms prevailed; in Burgundy and Pro-
ence, where the vigorous profiles suggest Roman models (at
utun, Cluny, etc.) and where a surprising delicacy of outline
also found (at Montmajour and in Arles), the art of molding
as highly developed. Some scholars have pointed out a certain
milarity to Syrian profiles (e.g., at Vézelay and in St-Ruf
ar Avignon), which is also to be found in the Norman Ro-
anesque period (e.g., at St-Nicolas in Caen). Arch frames and
le posts of portals are often richly carved.

In the Gothic period the reworking of some of the principles
the Greek molding led to completely new formal results,
nsistent with an evolution begun in the Romanesque period.
general characteristic, which clearly distinguishes the moldings
this period, is the association of curves and countercurves
lowing a continuous or broken profile and separated by slight
liefs without the interposition of flat bands. This typical use
curves confers upon the structures a notable dynamism.
nother general characteristic (especially in the Gothic style of
e Île-de-France and in its derivations) is, moreover, the exclu-
on of decoration from the surface of moldings. In the late
othic period the profiles of architectural members were often
mplicated by the adoption of smaller dimensions and of con-
uous rhythmical alternations.

In Italy Gothic profiles, lacking for the most part the French
gicality and adopted for purely decorative purposes, often
splay lines tending more to roundness (with the frequent use
torus moldings, smooth or sometimes "cable-carved") as,
r example, in the base of the façade of Orvieto Cathedral
I, PL. 333), or else they display considerable simplicity, as
the Florentine production of the 14th century (Cathedral
d bell tower, Orsanmichele, and Loggia della Signoria). In
ombardy, in Bologna, and in Siena, moldings and decorations
ere often of decorative terra cotta.

In the Renaissance, Brunelleschi (q.v.) clearly used the Roman
odels, although with considerable freedom, in his combinations
various types of molding (as in the portico of the Ospedale
gli Innocenti, II, PL. 366, in the chapels of S. Lorenzo, in
e chapels of Sto Spirito, II, PLS. 370, 371, and in the Pazzi
aapel, I, PL. 417). The moldings of L. B. Alberti (q.v.) were
oser to the classical models; he gave them a voluminous and
ulptural interpretation and also altered them freely, as for
ample in the cornices of the Palazzo Rucellai (I, PL. 55) and
S. Maria Novella (I, PL. 53) in Florence.

The styles set by the examples of Brunelleschi and Alberti
ere followed for the most part during the 15th century in
uscany, while in Lombardy, for instance in the works of G. A.
nadeo (such as the Certosa in Pavia, VIII, PL. 195), the same
assical motifs either were combined in an exuberant and con-
sed way or were translated into shapes which recall the late
othic tradition. This also occurred in Venice and later in
ance, in Catalonia, in the regions of southern Italy under
talan influence (especially Naples), in Burgundy, and in
anders.

Bramante (q.v.), influenced by the charm of Lombard dec-
ation while in Milan, displayed in Rome a strong adherence
the classical prototypes (as in some parts of the Tempietto
S. Pietro in Montorio; I, PL. 305) and drew from the Roman
onuments a formal idiom composed of elements, profiles, and
gulated combinations newly adapted to the style of the period.
the 16th century the morphological elements and their as-
ciations were essentially Roman and Bramantesque; and yet
e variety in the character of the profiles is quite remarkable
there is the linear, almost Hellenistic, purity of Peruzzi in
e Farnesina (XI, PL. 120) and in the Palazzo Massimo (XI,
. 121; XII, PL. 52); the free sobriety of Raphael; the archaic
ength of Antonio da Sangallo the Elder; the vigorous solem-
ry of Antonio da Sangallo the Younger; the exuberant richness
Sansovino and Sanmicheli; and the controlled austerity of
lladio. Furthermore, it was a typical problem of the 16th
ntury to fix within set rules the individual shapes and the
mbinations of the moldings; this problem was dealt with
length in the treatises by Sebastiano Serlio, Giacomo da Vi-
ola, and Palladio and was the subject of debates by academies
ch as the Vitruviana.

Michelangelo, in an attempt to endow the surfaces of the
architectural members with greater dynamism by a vigorous
sculptural modeling of the parts, interpreted the classical profiles
in a very personal way, distorting, as it were, the static, solemn,
and sometimes slightly inert geometry of the traditional profiles;
thus concavities became more concave and taut, the hollows
and convexities of the cymae were accentuated, the ovoli and the
tori became more swollen, and single moldings were sometimes
isolated by deep incisions with a curved profile. The composition of the moldings was regulated by a marked and dramatic
concentration at certain points, accentuated by contrasting areas
of bareness. Characteristic of Michelangelo's interpretations are,
in Florence, the profiles of the architectural and decorative
elements of the New Sacristy (IX, PLS. 530, 531) and the other
realizations of the S. Lorenzo group and those of the Biblioteca Laurenziana (I, PL. 418; IX, PL. 540); and, in Rome,
those of the façade of the Palazzo dei Conservatori, of the
staircase of the Palazzo Senatorio, of the windows on the
last floor of the courtyard and of the large cornice of Palazzo
Farnese, of the members of the tribune of St. Peter's, of the Sforza
chapel in S. Maria Maggiore, and of Porta Pia. Some mannerist
architects (especially the Florentines) often adopted solutions
suggested by Michelangelo; others, like Vignola, were sensitive to his teachings, with a view more to the expansion of the
architectural vocabulary, to the simplification and strengthening
of the profiles, than to the distortion of the molding profiles.
This was not the case for some artists of the last mannerist
generation, like Giacomo della Porta and Maderno, who tended
to accentuate the effects in an almost expressionist manner along
the guide lines set by Michelangelo, whose treatments of moldings
thus became part of the repertory of almost all the Roman architects who worked during the late 16th and the early 17th
century and, later (and more exaggeratedly), of the baroque
architects.

The use of stucco (q.v.) instead of stone or marble often
permitted bolder solutions. Quite typical of these styles, which
often, at least until the middle of the 18th century, showed remarkable variety in execution, are the works of Borromini,
Bernini, Pietro da Cortona, Carlo Rainaldi, Guarini, and G.
Valvassori.

A marked freedom in molding styles is noticeable in the baroque production of the late 16th, 17th, and 18th centuries in
Germany, and especially in Spain; where more decorative styles
often prevail; a greater adherence to classicist traditions (although
with a certain independence in the geometric patterns) is to be
noted in France and in Great Britain, where a preference for
the Bramantesque and Palladian prototypes, often known only
through the drawings of the treatise writers, remained. The
tradition of Roman molding survived here and there throughout
Europe, especially with architects of more avowedly classicist
tendencies.

The passion for the study of the works of the past in the neoclassic period and in the eclectic 19th century allowed an often
quite accentuated adherence to the models of antiquity. Architects and builders made frequent use of Vignola's popular
manual, which suggested profiles and combinations with a method
of easy and practical application.

In contemporary architecture, after finally discarding the
traditional forms no longer in harmony with new building methods, molding became an element closely allied to the technique,
structure, and function of the building.

Outside of the Western tradition, the use of moldings displays no outstanding peculiarities. Rare examples are to be
found in the medieval Islamic world of shapes derived from the
classical Iranian transition, such as the moldings of the cornice
of the Pīr-i-'Ālamdār in Damghan (Iran, 11th cent.) and those
framing the portals and windows of mihrabs (such as that of the
Masjid-i-Jāmi' of Isfahan, ca. 1310; VII, PL. 403).

A certain interest in moldings is to be found in some examples
of ancient India in which projecting bands were inserted in the
crowning of façades; these display a reverse-cyma profile in the
upper part and it has been conjectured by some scholars that this
motif reproduced in solid form the curve which is naturally
acquired by the edge of a clay terrace under the action of rain.

Later, a more significant use of moldings is to be found in the bases of buildings (usually in bands, often decorated and delimited by slightly projecting listels), in the frames of portals (in the dentil molding in the 5th–6th century Temple of Viṣṇu Daśāvatāra at Deogarh; VII, PL. 137), and in the profiles of capitals, such as those of the chaitya of Karli (VII, PL. 451), of the caves of Ajanta (5th–6th cent.) and of Ellora (7th cent.; VII, PL. 468). The Aśoka period drew from some Persian motifs, and subsequent contacts with the Seljuks gave greater diffusion to typically Hellenistic ornaments such as ovoli and meanders. In the 11th century moldings were used to shape the profiles of the columns of a Jain building at Halebid (VII, PL. 485) and, up to the 18th century, formed the profiles of bases of buildings and of colonnades, as in the 17th–18th century temple of Rameshwarasm, Madras (VII, PL. 487).

Similar shapes spread also to Indonesia and are found, for instance, in the Borobudur, and in the base of the Candi Pawon (8th–9th cent.), both in Java (VIII, PLS. 30, 34). Apart from these, the use of moldings in the Western sense is almost unknown to the architecture of the Far East.

Arnaldo BRUSCHI

WALL APERTURES. The functional need to interrupt the continuity of the walls, that is, to create openings to provide access to the various rooms of the buildings (doors) or to admit light and air (windows, etc.), obviously gives rise to a number of structural problems. These are solved with the technical means available to the various cultures (trilithic, or post-and-lintel system, arched structures, pseudo-arched structures, etc.) and are, by their nature, rich in expressive possibilities.

Since remotest antiquity there has existed the aim of giving a particular formal definition to the structural and technological elements of openings — the jambs, lintels, arches, and window sills; this definition was often extended to the wall areas immediately surrounding the openings.

The types of formal definition can vary from the simple proportioning of the size of the openings to deliberate emphasis of the structural elements which form the openings achieved by means of moldings (and other more complex elements) of a more properly sculptural or, more rarely, pictorial character.

The use, the shape, and the function of the openings therefore display varied aspects, which should be considered in general in their close relationship to different forms of artistic production, in the framework of stylistic developments, and, in particular, as the individual expressive aims of the creators.

In the present treatment the various types of openings are considered separately in the historical framework of their essential developments.

Doorways and portals. In Egyptian and Mediterranean antiquity the prevailing type of doorway was that based on the trilithic system, either with a rectangular or slightly trapezoidal opening, or with progressively projecting blocks. In Egyptian tombs, temple enclosures, pylons, and other such structures, the typical form was the trabeated construction with supports formed by the ashlar courses of the wall, which either continued into the projecting doorjambs or, more often, formed independent jambs. Jambs and lintels were in many cases profusely decorated and painted in many colors. In the false door of the south tomb of the funerary precinct of King Zozer at Saqqara (ca. 2950 B.C.), the lintel is decorated with hieroglyphs and projects slightly. In the New Kingdom the doorway with jambs and a high lintel without a crown molding existed, particularly in tomb interiors; among typical examples are the granite doorway of the Temple of Hatshepsut at Deir el-Baḥrī and that of the Temple of Seti I at Abydos. Other, more complex, doorways reflect wooden models translated more or less faithfully into stone, as in the examples in the mortuary temple of King Mycerinos, in a mastaba at Giza (4th dynasty), in the 5th-dynasty tomb of the priest Ptahhotep, and in various other tombs at Saqqara.

The doorway crowned with a concave cyma, almost always fluted, was used from the time of the early dynasties and was undoubtedly the most widespread type, especially in temp enclosures; often inserted into the propylon or in the pylo it frequently reached large dimensions. In such doorways t frames are almost always tapered upward and are profuse decorated. The whole of the portal is normally projecting w respect to the wall surface. A rather common type of doorw in Ptolemaic temple enclosures displays, probably for functio reasons, lintel and crown molding interrupted in the central pa Examples of this type of doorframe are to be found in the porti of the large courtyard of the Temple of Horus at Edfu (I PL. 380) and in the courtyard of the small temple at Medi Habu, at Thebes. Portals with the usual Egyptian entablatu supported by columns of the edicule type are found o rarely; a portal of this type, with a strong soffit and stur fluted columns with papyrus-motif capitals, appears in t chapels of Gebel Silsileh and reveals a marked appreciation the effects of light and shadow.

In the Mediterranean area, typical and remarkable examp of trapezoidal trilithic doors are found in the so-called "meg lithic temples" in Malta, where, from the second half of t 2d millennium B.C., pillars, lintels, and jambs are often enrich with decorative effects achieved by the thick dotting of the su faces with a marteline (temple of Mnaidra; IX, PL. 426). In S dinia the doorways of the nuraghi consist of a simple interrupt of the megalithic structure; they are topped by a lintel, whi sometimes (as in the entrance to the small temple of Serra C rios), is slightly arched. In Sicily, the rock tombs of the Cast luccio culture (1600–1400 B.C.) display doorways closed by sla carved with spiral motifs; and the entrance to a tomb at Cas bile (ca. 1000 B.C.), south of Syracuse, is defined by fram marked with parallel and progressively recessed bands and w a typically curved profile, clearly demonstrating the desire enrich the opening (IX, PL. 435). Similar frames, also decorat are to be found in the rock tombs (*domus de janas*) in Sardin In the upper part of other types of doorways, as at Samos a at Phigalia, one or more of the blocks forming the jamb proj to reduce the length of the architrave but do not display a particular decorative elements in addition to the specific str tural characteristics.

In Minoan Crete, the frames or cornices of doorways (a also of windows) were often made of wood, sometimes defi by bands painted with ornamental motifs. The frames of t larger and more important doorways were, however, of carv stone. The well-known faïence plaques in the Heraklion A chaeological Museum (IV, FIG. 87) reproduce Cretan hous having doors and windows that are rectangular or square w one, two, or three lights; they always have lintels and are fram by polychromed beams.

In Mycenaean Greece, the façades of the tholos tombs a provide examples of doorways based on the post-and-lintel sy tem. The opening, sometimes tapezoidal, is in most ca framed with simple stone moldings, the frame being creat by the oversailing courses of the wall blocks and occasiona flanked by half columns in inverted truncated-cone shap The sturdy monolithic lintel is in some examples richly deco ted with superimposed horizontal bands or moldings, formi almost an entablature or crown molding. The doors of the cades of the tholoi of Mycenae and of Orchomenos (Boeoti with half columns decorating the openings, are related to so entrances to Minoan palaces; the decorations also utilise eleme and motifs of Cretan origin. Above the lintel an opening in t shape of an equilateral triangle (needed to relieve the lin of the weight of the superimposed wall) came to character this construction (see the reconstruction of the façade of t "Treasury of Atreus" and the Lion Gate at Mycenae (IV, P 68, 69, FIG. 105).

In Achaemenid Persia doors and windows based on the tr beated system display for the most part, as in the palaces Persepolis, a rectangular frame, often molded with flat bar (smooth or decorated with rosettes) of varying size and recess from the outside toward the opening. Above the frame, t crown cornice takes the shape of the Egyptian cornice consisti of an astragal (or torus), a cove, and a terminal listel; sometim the astragal is decorated by a series of beads and reels, and t

ncave cove is carved with three orders of flutes. The inner
de of the jamb is sometimes decorated in low relief, as seen
the ruins of Persepolis. Certain decorative accents appear
have been inspired by wooden architecture (as in the "Tomb
Cyrus") at Pasargadae and in the rock tomb of Darius at
aqsh-i-Rustam (VIII, PLS. 126, 136, FIG. 275). At Hatra the
agment of a portal displays more elaborate moldings and
anthus-leaf reliefs in the obviously Greek-influenced lintel.
the Sassanian period, the Achaemenid type of door with a
ollow crown molding was reproduced in stucco in the palace
Firuzabad and elaborated by the insertion of a round-headed
ch. The base of the great jambs of the Gate of Xerxes at Per-
polis was decorated with demons and bulls with human heads
calling similar Assyrian constructions. In other cases, as in
e so-called "tower of the sacred fire" at Naqsh-i-Rustam (VIII,
.. 137), the upper-door frame ends with two lateral corbel-
e projections (*parotides*) and is crowned by a molding quite
e that of the "Tomb of Cyrus" at Pasargadae.

In Etruria a particularly characteristic and widespread type
doorway was that with a trapezoidal opening framed by a
mple molded band projecting from the lintel and connected
the jambs by two brackets (*projecturae*), sometimes with a
pical bird's-beak profile ("Tomb of the Cornice," Cerveteri,
.. 235; François tomb, Vulci).

In classical Greece doorways were characterized almost
ithout exception by rectangular or slightly trapezoidal openings
mited by jambs and straight lintels, more or less projecting at
e sides. They were sometimes decorated geometrically with
e basic moldings typical of the Hellenic repertory. Often,
p to the 5th century and beyond, as for example, in the Athe-
ian Propylaea, the shape is a simple trilithon without any
articular decorative elaborations.

The doorways of the Doric temples were often trapezoidal
d of great size and generally reflected the simplicity typical
the Doric order. The jambs followed the slant of the opening
d the enframement in most cases was devoid of ornamentation,
eing marked toward the outside by a small, soberly molded
order. The doorways of Ionic buildings, however, sometimes
isplay a horizontal crown cornice resting on two modillions;
mong the most significant examples is the framing of the door
f the Erechtheion (FIG. 453, no. 44), which has a wide flat
and marked by listels and astragals and decorated with rosettes
relief. The area surrounding the opening is broken up by
arious simple moldings; the crown cornice, only slightly
rojecting, is formed by an undercornice with an egg-and-tongue
olding which forms a connection with the frame by a supporting
orona superimposed on a farther-projecting band. Similar
hemes recur frequently in Roman architecture, as in the door-
ay of the Doric "Temple of Hercules" at Cori (VII, PL. 201)
d in those of the arcaded terrace of the sanctuary of Fortuna
rimigenia at Palestrina, and persisted until a late period, although
ith some variations and changes at various times and places.

A simpler type of doorway, also of widespread use, was
at of the simple frame, plain, with flat bands, or with moldings,
laced to enclose a rectangular, square, or, more rarely, an
rched opening (examples seen in the Ara Pacis, in Trajan's
orum, etc., and in certain Byzantine examples). In yet another
ype the modillions were eliminated and a frieze and a cornice
ere placed above the lintel to form a complete entablature,
s in the door of the "Temple of Vesta" at Tivoli.

The doorway of the Pantheon is of this type; it is formed by
frame profiled with the typical moldings of the Ionic architrave
urrounding the opening on three sides and is surmounted by
slightly convex frieze on which rests an entablature composed
f the usual elements (bed molding, gutter, and cyma).

Other types of doorway take up and reelaborate the Hel-
nistic pattern in the edicule or tabernacle plan, consisting of
architectural order (columns, half columns, or pilaster strips
pporting an entablature which is sometimes profiled together
ith the supports) placed to enclose the opening and defined
most cases by the usual types of frame. When the columns
e detached from the wall, the edicule doorway becomes a
rothyrum (a small vestibule), as in the so-called "Tower of
e Winds" in Athens.

These and similar systems were also used in doorways with
arched openings, which, in the ancient world, had considerable
development within certain cultures. The use of arched door
openings was particularly widespread in Mesopotamia. Sargon's
palace at Khorsabad (722–705 B.C.; anc. Dur Sharrukin) has an
arched doorway flanked by tall rectangular towers; the door
jambs are decorated with figures of winged bulls with human
heads in the same scheme adopted for other Assyrian monuments (e.g., at Nimrud) and the round-headed archivolt is
brought into relief by a band, decorated with rosettes and
human figures, which follows the curve of the arch and continues horizontally at the sides, forming the omega-shaped
mixtilineal profile that was to occur frequently in western Asia,
at least until the Byzantine period. In the neo-Babylonian
period (612–538 B.C.) polychrome reliefs on glazed bricks were
used to compose ornamental friezes, as in the Ishtar Gate
(IX, PL. 494). In Sassanian Persia there were doorways with
an arch-shaped opening, as in the palace of Ctesiphon (XII,
PL. 397), and, occasionally, doorways with actual arches, joined
to the jambs by applied stucco, which was also used to line
the intrados (e.g., the Firuzabad Gate).

Traces of Eastern influence can perhaps be perceived in
the shape, if not in the structure, of certain arched doorways
in Western rock tombs of the protohistoric era, for example,
those at Fordongianus in Sardinia, which have cornices with
bands or tori in relief, and that of the Tomb of the Painted
Lions in Cerveteri. Also to be noted are the composite shapes
(architraved and arched doorways) in the doorways with lunettes
in the Tomb of the Casetta at Cerveteri.

Arched doorways were not unknown in the Hellenistic world
proper, as is shown by that of the so-called "sacred way" of
Kekropoulis (later, anc. Palairos), which is, however, a pseudo-
arched doorway, and the remains of many other doorways at
Delos, Pergamum, Priene, and in other places both in the
Greek peninsula and in Asia Minor.

The Etruscan-Italic influence was mainly responsible for the
widespread use of arched doorways in the Roman world. However, frequently the opening was based on purely structural
factors, especially in the building of private houses and minor
constructions, in which doorways were constructed with rectangular openings and horizontal or very slightly curved flat
arches, as can be seen in the houses of Ostia (House of Diana,
PL. 246). In town gates, even those with decorated enframements, a preference is evident for simple shapes and plain
moldings on the imposts, jambs, and lintels (e.g., the gates of
Saepinum and the so-called "Arch of Augustus" at Fano).

At the end of the 1st century B.C. the edicule type of
construction began to be used more frequently, especially in
town gates and in triumphal arches; the arch was enclosed by
an architectural order, usually surmounted by a horizontal cornice and a triangular pediment, as in the gates of Spello, Rimini,
and Ravenna, in the Porta Maggiore (Rome), in the Arch of
the Gavi, the Gate of the Lions, and the Porta dei Borsari
(all, Verona; PL. 235). Another, less common, type of opening
is that in which an arch, usually molded, is superimposed
directly on a pilaster strip or a column by means of the interposed entablature.

After the 4th century there was a departure from the classical shapes in the framing of openings, with either the traditional system of coordinating the elements being abandoned or
the traditional profiles of the moldings being distorted. The
strong influence of the classic trabeated opening remained,
however, and is perceptible in the doors of S. Salvatore in
Spoleto (4th–5th cent.), where the horizontal crown cornice on
a high frieze and the tall lateral modillions are covered with
exuberant decoration (I, PL. 416; IX, PL. 46). This influence
remained strong in Rome from the Early Christian period to
the high Middle Ages and beyond, often strengthened by the
custom of utilizing decorative fragments taken from ancient
monuments (e.g., in S. Sabina and in S. Giorgio in Velabro).
The classical elements with a simple frame molded with smooth
or carved bands and with or without a cornice are also often
found, as in S. Costanza.

The doorway of the Mausoleum of Galla Placidia (Ravenna),

with a simple band and a decorated lintel, is enclosed by a small, slightly projecting frame; those of the Mausoleum of Theodoric, with a crown cornice, display highly sculptural moldings. The doorway with a simple molded frame and a rectangular opening is sometimes found also in the Romanesque period, as in S. Miniato in Florence. The edicule type with columns and trabeated crown cornice (e.g., the doorway of the Oratory of St. John the Baptist in the Lateran Baptistery; 461–468) survived and gave rise to more or less free interpretations that marked the beginning of new medieval types of doorways. Quite faithful derivations were to appear later, as in the doorway of the Oratory of S. Zenone in S. Prassede (9th cent.), Rome, where Roman and contemporaneous elements are combined into a strongly classically oriented whole. In the basilica of Cimitile, the Cappella dei Martiri (ca. 900) shows a revived interest in the scheme of the architectural motif of the *prothyrum*; and in the Christian architecture of some Eastern regions such as Syria and Cilicia, preference for molded cornices persisted through the 7th century. In some Syrian churches (e.g., in the chapel of Khirbet Tēzîn; II, PL. 422) the frame at the beginning of the jamb curls into a large volute.

In the 12th and 13th centuries, in south-central Italy, the portals (and windows) of the Cosmati (q.v.) were characterized by a strong adherence to classical influences. The doors, often surmounted with a lunette, are for the most part surrounded by a simple frame, the surface of which, divided into panels, is decorated with ornamental motifs in polychrome mosaics (as in S. Lorenzo fuori le Mura and SS. Giovanni e Paolo in Rome; in the atrium of Civita Castellana; and in the façade of S. Maria di Castello at Tarquinia, III, PL. 478). Freely distorted interpretations of Roman schemes are to be noted throughout the Middle Ages, from the Carolingian and Ottonian period up to the Romanesque portals of S. Pietro in Ciel d'Oro (Pavia) and of the side of St-Sernin (Toulouse).

A type of entrance found in some Early Christian churches in Rome (S. Pudenziana, S. Clemente, S. Pietro in Vincoli, S. Vitale, SS. Giovanni e Paolo, etc.) is that consisting of three-arched openings; this type is also common in the Early Christian churches of Greece, and it appears at a later date in S. Maria de Naranco, Spain (848), and at Pomposa, Italy (10th cent.).

In the Western Middle Ages, trabeated doors are rather rare and appear in some minor examples or in environments more closely tied to classical traditions, as in Tuscany. A more widespread type of doorway was that which combined the rectangular lintel with a superimposed relieving arch of clearly Roman origin. This type of door was given monumental interpretation in the "Golden Gate" (Porta Aurea) of Split (Yugoslavia), where the flat-arch lintel is surmounted by a large arch with a projecting and richly molded frame (IX, PL. 34). This scheme appeared, between the 8th and the 11th centuries, in a great number of examples, with or without a lunette recessed in the relieving arch, as in S. Maria in Valle, in Cividale; in S. Pietro (ca. 8th cent.), near Ferentino; in Pieve di Arliano (11th cent.); in S. Frediano, in Lucca; and in the basilica of Castel Sant'Elia.

The lintel is generally a monolithic block and, for a better structural functioning, sometimes has a greater height in the center than at the ends; in this shape it is sometimes found in France (e.g., in the church of Notre-Dame-du-Port, in Clermont-Ferrand), but examples are not lacking in other places. In many cases the load borne by the lintel is relieved by the lateral insertion of large modillions. Toward the 11th century, this type of door was complicated by the introduction — soon to become general — of concentric arches placed to enclose the opening (as in the main door of S. Ambrogio, Milan, and that of St-Etienne in Caen (1066–1086). This type of portal, used mostly in walls of considerable thickness, displays a remarkable variety of special solutions, while retaining for the most part the aspect of an embrasure with successive setbacks formed by concentric recessed arches (or archivolts) resting on pillars or columns. A lunette was placed above the lintel. Among the most important examples of such are S. Michele (XII, PL. 219) and S. Pietro in Ciel d'Oro, in Pavia; S. Abbondio, in Como (XII, PL. 219); the cathedrals of Modena and Parma; the bap-

tistery of Parma; St-Trophime, in Arles (XII, PL. 245); Notre-Dame-la-Grande, in Poitiers (XII, PL. 202); La Trinité a St-Etienne, in Caen; St-Sernin in Toulouse; the cathedrals Autun, Lucca, and Ferrara; S. Ciriaco and S. Maria de Piazza in Ancona; S. Pietro and S. Maria Maggiore in Tuscani S. Marco in Venice; the Palazzo Comunale of Perugia; St. Peter in Hirsau; St. Martin, in Worms; and the cathedrals of Spey and Mainz. A variation of this scheme is to be noted in t rear doorway of S. Fedele, in Como, where instead of t concentric recessed arches there is a crown formed by a ser of recessed triangular elements (mitre-crown).

In France, the type of portal with concentric arches acquir greater dimensions and a pillar or trumeau was inserted at t center to support the lintel or tympanum. Typical exampl are those of the churches of Ste-Madeleine, in Vézelay (109 1132), and St-Pierre, in Moissac. This type was adopted Spain (S. Vicente, in Ávila), in Germany, and in Scandinav In rare cases, as in Strasbourg Cathedral, two portals of th type are coupled. For the most part, the archivolts are cover with ornamentation, sometimes figural; in France, where t interest in sculpture was greatest, a series of statues was insert between the columns along the splay of the opening, as in t portal of St-Trophime in Arles (XII, PL. 245), of the church Parthenay, of Autun Cathedral, and of the Church of Ste-Cro in Bordeaux. Sometimes the portal with concentric arches h the outermost arch enclosed by an oblique triangular pedimen or, especially in Germany in the 12th century, it is set with a rectangle (cathedrals of Mainz, XII, PL. 225, Maulbron Alpirsbach). Especially in Italian Romanesque architectu (Lombardy, Veneto, Emilia, Le Marche, Apulia), this type portal is often preceded by a more or less projecting vestibu (or *prothyrum*), generally formed by a small vault supporte by columns, with which it is architecturally connected, ar covered by a gabled roof. The two (or more) lateral colum sometimes rest on an element typical of the portals of t 12th and 13th centuries — the column-bearing figure (usually crouching wild beast, for instance a lion), which can also placed as a support of the door jamb.

The use of column-bearing beasts can probably be trace to Mesopotamia and Anatolia. Figures of animals used direct supports for doors are not lacking also in Rome, pa ticularly in the Cosmatesque production of the 12th and 13th ce turies, as in S. Lorenzo fuori le Mura and SS. Giovanni e Paol Outstanding examples of column-bearing beasts as supports the columns of the vestibule appear in the cathedrals of Moden (XII, PL. 219), Piacenza (PL. 238), Ferrara, and Parma, in t Baptistery of Cremona, in S. Zeno in Verona, and in S. Ciria in Ancona (XII, PL. 221). In Ferrara (VIII, PL. 171) the out columns of the vestibule are supported by human figures restin in turn on the backs of wild beasts. Sometimes, as in t cathedrals of Ruvo di Puglia (VIII, PL. 172) and Altamur column-bearing animals are placed at the bases of the later columns, at the sides of the portals with concentric arches, an at the impost of the outermost arch. In S. Nicola in Bari t column-bearing beasts are pensile, that is, they rest on corbe (XII, PL. 223).

Two-storied vestibules, by means of which the portal connected with the superimposed window (or niche), appea for instance, on the façade of the cathedrals of Piacenza (PL. 23 and Ferrara and on the façade and the side of Modena Cathedr (XII, PL. 219). The archivolt of the upper story has an arche intrados (in Modena it has a depressed arch in the vestibu of the façade and is divided into three arches in the lateral on over which is, in most cases, a gabled roof.

The Gothic period did not witness a radical transformatic of the Romanesque portal with concentric arches supported b pillars and small columns; but the depth of the embrasu increased and its component elements were set closer togeth and became more slender and numerous. Arches were almo always pointed; the decorations of the jambs, of the column and of the recessed archivolts acquired new relief; exubera ornamentation often composed of a multitude of human figur placed side by side and superimposed spread to all the element and a gable placed on the outer archivolt and often flanked b

wo pinnacles normally crowned the whole, which often pro-
ected quite sharply from the surface of the building (Notre-
Dame in Paris, cathedrals of Chartres, Reims, Bourges, Rouen),
and sometimes formed a vestibule or even a portico, as in the
orthwest façade of Chartres. In Italy Gothic portals often
reelaborated the basically Romanesque scheme but were less
xuberantly decorated and retained the emphasis on the struc-
ural framework of the portal, thus avoiding an excessive ver-
cality (cf. VIII, PL. 184). In Tuscany, particularly in civil
rchitecture, a characteristic type of portal was that having a
imple stone frame with a superimposed pointed-arch lunette
s, for instance, in the Palazzo del Podestà in Florence (13th-
4th cent.). In Siena, this type was occasionally done in brick,
and sometimes a rectangular aperture was pierced in the lunette,
s in the Palazzo Tolomei. In Venice elaborate shapes were
dopted for decorative purposes, as in the Porta della Carta
oining the Doges' Palace with S. Marco.

In early English Gothic works the scheme with concentric
ointed arches on small columns retained considerable sim-
licity and adherence to the French models, but it was enriched
and weighted down in the Decorated style, as in the portal of
t. John's in Norfolk, and later reverted to a new simplicity
i the Perpendicular style, when the pointed arch surrounding
he opening was sometimes inserted into a rectangle defined by
ertical and horizontal moldings (Merton College, Oxford;
t. Peter's Church, Kettering). French influence was strong
i Germany, in the portals of the cathedrals of Cologne (VI,
LS. 321, 322), Erfurt, and Marburg, and also in some Spanish
hurches, such as Burgos Cathedral; but in Spain, particularly
fter the 14th century, the tendency was to vary and complicate
he French scheme by the insertion of fanciful combinations
and interlacings of pointed arches and exuberant decoration
monastery of Batalha, Church of S. Gregorio, VI, PL. 356,
and monastery of S. Pablo, Valladolid; Capilla de los Reyes in
Granada Cathedral; Church of Sta Cruz, Segovia). In France,
i the late Gothic period, the earlier schemes were often dis-
orted and given refined decorative interpretations, as in the
orth and door of Strasbourg Cathedral and in the side portal of
lbi Cathedral; in other cases the early Gothic scheme was
etained, though with more slender architectural members and
icher decoration, as, for instance, in the cathedrals of Tours
nd Orléans and in the south wing of Beauvais. In civil archi-
ecture simpler portals were general; they commonly had many-
entered or depressed arches, as in the Hôtel de Cluny (1485),
aris, in the Château de Josselin (Brittany, 16th cent.), and in
he Palais de Justice, Rouen (1493–1508). These shapes, oc-
asionally interpreted with classical moldings and motifs, were
o survive into the early French Renaissance (as in some of
he castles of the Loire and of Brittany). The late Gothic portal
nown as "Durazzo Gothic" and common in the civil architecture
f Catalonia and southern Italy displays a depressed arch enclosed
vithin a frame marked out by tori or other moldings, some of
vhich cut outward at the level of the imposts of the arch.

Almost all the types of doorway of the Roman period reappeared during the Renaissance; they were more or less faithful
eproductions of classical models, with minor variations in-
roduced in the proportions and in the use and combination
f the traditional classical elements. In the 15th century a
vide variety of sculptural decorations was used to elaborate
he traditional architectural structure; these included triangular
nd semicircular pediments, festoons, plaits, strigils in the
riezes and frames, and figural sculptures. Thus there was a
evived use of the type of door with a simple molded frame,
vith either a rectangular or a round-headed arched opening,
nd with moldings generally taken from the classical repertory.
Brunelleschi's characteristic molded frame, with or without
he interposition of a decorated entablature, was, from his
arliest period, surmounted with a cornice supporting a triangular tympanum which could vary in shape from a flattened
o an isosceles triangle (as in the works of Francesco di Giorgio;
.v.). Among the Renaissance doorways with a tympanum
rame are those of the Pazzi Chapel in Florence (II, PL. 367),
f the Tempio Malatestiano in Rimini (I, PLS. 51, 52), of
. Maria delle Carceri in Prato, and of S. Maria del Popolo

in Rome. This type, more or less closely reproducing the doorway of the Pantheon, was also used by Vignola (e.g., in the
doorway of S. Andrea in Via Flaminia, in Rome; I, PL. 305),
by Palladio, and by many other architects of 16th-century Italy.
The same formal scheme was often adopted for windows, as
in Brunelleschi's portico of the Ospedale degli Innocenti (II,
PL. 366) and in the apse of the Pavia Cathedral and that of
S. Maria delle Consolazione in Todi. A variant of this type
was the opening with a simple horizontal cornice supported by
side modillions, used both for doorways (e.g., in Palazzo Rucellai,
in Florence, I, PL. 55; in S. Sebastiano, in Mantua; and in
S. Pietro in Montorio, I, PL. 305; in Palazzo Massimo alle
Colonne, XI, PL. 121; and in the Church of S. Damaso in
Rome) and for windows (in the Villa di Poggio a Caiano, near
Pistoia, and in many of the Sangallo palaces). This same type
of opening was also set under a triangular tympanum (as in the
Palazzo dei Diamanti, in Ferrara) or a semicircular tympanum
or, as in some windows by Vignola (e.g., in the Villa Giulia,
in Rome, XII, PL. 89), finished by a volute decoration. This
last type was to be used in the 16th and 17th centuries and in
the neoclassic period throughout Europe and particularly in
French (e.g., in the Louvre) and English (in the Banqueting
House in London, by Inigo Jones; II, PL. 147) Renaissance
structures. Another frequently used type was that framed by
an edicule, with a rectangular or arched opening (usually with
a molded frame) flanked by columns or pilaster strips supporting a simple horizontal entablature or a triangular or curved
tympanum.

In the 15th century these schemes were often quite free
and richly decorated. In one 15th-century variant, particularly
widespread in the area of Florentine influence and often adopted
for the framing of tombs, altars, and chapels, the horizontal
cornice of the entablature is surmounted by a lunette (usually
depressed and defined by a frame) whose span is smaller than
the cornice and has leaves at either end bearing a double volute
or sculptural decoration. Significant examples of this type are
the portal of Sta Croce and the interior door of Sto Spirito
in Florence. Interpretations of the same motif appear in the
Veneto in, for example, the portals of S. Zaccaria and of
S. Maria dei Miracoli, Venice. The lunette usually encloses a
geometric design, figures, or a shell motif, as in the doorway
of the Church of Corpus Domini in Bologna (1478–91). The
edicule doorway or window scheme had already been adopted
in the early 15th century in the Florentine area, probably
deriving its inspiration from Romanesque monuments. Thus
it is found in examples by Donatello with a tympanum entablature in the outside niche (edicule), such as that housing
the statue of St. George in Orsanmichele and that of the Old
Sacristy of S. Lorenzo; a more subtly ornamented example is
Michelozzo's door of the Chapel of the Novitiate in Sta Croce.
The edicule type of opening, with varied details, was fairly
common in the second half of the 15th century in central and
northern Italy; examples are found in the Church of the Madonna del Calcinaio, near Cortona, in the Cathedral of Città
di Castello, in the Palazzo Ducale in Urbino (PL. 237), in the
Doges' Palace and in the Scuola Grande di S. Marco (VIII,
PL. 198) in Venice, and in Michelozzo's portal of the Medici
Bank (XII, PL. 3) in Milan.

In the 16th century, the more classically oriented architects
(the two Antonio da Sangallos, Raphael, Sanmicheli, Palladio,
Michelangelo) made wide use of the edicule scheme, which
thus made its way into the repertory of European classicizing
motifs, surviving throughout the mannerist and baroque periods,
permeating the French, English, and Spanish classicism of the
16th, 17th, and 18th centuries and influencing the neoclassic
and eclectic styles. In mannerist and baroque architecture the
scheme was often complicated by the insertion of rusticated
ashlar surfaces between the elements of the architectural order
or in the frame, by the profiling and breaking of the pediments,
by the duplication of the supporting elements, and by the variation of the moldings. Another whole series of doors and windows
that may still be called "edicule" in type involves the utilization of an arch (or archivolt) placed above the architectural
order to conclude the motif (column, half column, pilaster strip,

and entablature, profiled in most cases in correspondence with the jambs, and including a curved pediment). One of the earliest and most representative examples of this type is Alberti's portal for S. Maria Novella in Florence, the scheme of which influenced many portals, tabernacles, and funerary monuments of the second half of the 15th century. Further classicizing elaborations of this type of opening occurred in the 16th century, in the works of Sanmicheli, Sansovino, and Palladio. The combination of the arched motif with the entablature order gave rise to the so-called "Serlian" (after the style of Serlio) motif, already applied in the sphere of Bramante's Roman followers (Antonio da Sangallo the Younger, Raphael, Sanmicheli), and then by Palladio, who was to transmit it to the English classicizing styles.

Another type of doorway and window opening, based on the stressing of the purely structural factors of the arched opening, was the type sometimes called "rustic," of which the best-known example is the portal of the Palazzo Pitti, in Florence, in which large rusticated ashlars form the jambs and the frame of the arch without projections or moldings. Also in Florence, the portals of the Quaratesi (II, PL. 373), Guadagni, Medici (XII, PL. 4), Strozzi, and Gondi (PL. 246) palaces are similar, but in these the jambs and the rusticated arch often enclose a molded frame which defines the opening. The extrados of the rusticated arch often does not correspond to the curve of the opening but follows instead a line, not perfectly concentric with it, which obtains an increase in the thickness of the arched lintel proceeding from the impost to the key. In the 16th century a variant of the type (perhaps introduced for the first time by Bramante in the doorway to the courtyard of the Belvedere, in the Vatican, and often used by his followers) influenced the Florentine scheme with Roman structural motifs, in most cases isolating the ashlars of the portal from the facing of the adjacent wall and often alternating rusticated ashlars of two different heights and strongly accentuating the width of the voussoirs of the arch proceeding toward the keystone, so that the extrados acquires an outline tending to the pointed arch. Typical examples are the portals of the Palazzo Vidoni (1515) in Rome, of the Palazzo Pandolfini (1516–1520) in Florence, of the Palazzo Farnese in Rome (XII, PL. 56), of the Palazzo Gagnoni (now Grugni) at Montepulciano, and of the castle at Nepi. The type, however, was to spread particularly through the works of Antonio da Sangallo, especially in central Italy; it later became part of the common repertory of 16th-century architecture, undergoing many reelaborations and variants. This is the type which the mannerist architects, sometimes deriving their inspiration from the suggestions made by Serlio in his treatise of 1537, were to utilize most frequently — adapting, varying, and sometimes corrupting the scheme (as through the insertion of parts of a classical architectural order).

Both the edicule type of portal and the rusticated one were often set, from the 16th to the 18th century, under a balcony with small balusters; examples may be seen in the Palazzo Gagnoni-Grugni, Montepulciano; the Palazzo Sacrati, Ferrara; the Palazzo Bocchi, Bologna; and in Rome in the Palazzo Sciarra, the Palazzo della Cancelleria, Villa Giulia, the Palazzo Barberini, and the Palazzo Odescalchi. Such a balcony was not infrequently architecturally associated with the window above it, as was earlier done in Palazzo Venezia in Rome (15th cent.) and in some 16th-century structures (Palazzo Farnese, Rome), and constituted, on occasion, the predominant element of the façade (Villa Giulia, Rome; Ospedale Maggiore, Milan; Jordaens' house in Antwerp). In some rare cases, especially in the mannerist period, the human figure acquired great importance or was even adopted as the principal motif of the scheme (as in the portals and windows forming a grotesque mask in Palazzetto Zuccari in Rome; IX, PL. 314).

In the 17th and 18th centuries, through the development of the method and approach of Michelangelo and his followers, in the use and reelaboration of the 16th-century styles, and in application of the classical repertory of motifs, a new enthusiasm arose for exploring and expanding the formal potential of the traditionally established limits. Totally new elements, therefore, were rare, and the general schemes are almost never altered; but

the use and combination of the elements resulted in numerou examples that varied widely from one to another.

The great innovators in architecture of the Roman 17th cer tury and their Italian, German, and Spanish baroque followe found new solutions for the problem of wall openings; thes are difficult to define from a typological point of view, but ar always endowed with a marked individuality. They go beyon mere free interpretation of the architectural orders: the clea elementary logic of the architectural order was altered to con form to new combinations and rhythms, was contradicted b the omission of traditionally established members or by th insertion of new ornamental elements; the profiles of the mold ings were made to follow richer, more elaborate, and mor complex lines than the classical ones in order to achieve sculp tural emphasis and linear and decorative rhythms. Among th significant examples of doorways, windows, and niche frame the most representative of these innovations are those of mannerist type used by Maderno in the façade of S. Susann (1603; II, PL. 137) and in St. Peter's (1607–1612; IX, PL. 541 among others are the windows by Borromini on the top floo of the connecting structure between the façade and the wing of Palazzo Barberini (II, PL. 134) and, also by Borromini, th various openings in the façade and in the interior of the Orator of the Filippini and the doorways and windows of S. Agnes in Agone, of the Palazzo di Propaganda Fide, and of S. Mari dei Sette Dolori (all, Rome). No less original are the solution of Bernini, sometimes aimed at achieving perspective effects suffice it to recall the arcades of the third level of Palazzo Bar berini (II, PL. 134) and the semidomed portal with a vestibul on columns of S. Andrea al Quirinale (II, PL. 270). Pietr da Cortona should be mentioned for his original solutions i the churches of S. Maria in Via Lata and SS. Luca e Martin (XI, PL. 172), and in the portico of S. Maria della Pace.

The markedly baroque forms adopted by Guarini in Palazz Carignano, in the Collegio dei Nobili, and in S. Lorenzo (Turin were to be widely diffused, especially in Catholic countries although they were often corrupted by classicizing recollection and local styles. In France, from the 16th century, the clas sicizing influence was frequently blended with traditional form to interpret the functional architectural elements in a decorativ way, as in some rusticated portals in which the motif of th ashlar is marked by a purely linear and pictorial definition

Sometimes mannerist, baroque, and classical schemes wer blended to form openings of simple but elegant shape, as i the portals of the stables and of the riding field at Versaille or in the portal of the Château de Marly. More abundant dec oration was used in interior openings, which became the vehicle for the ornamental subtleties of the rococo style.

Throughout the 17th century and well into the 18th, Englan was to remain faithful to the classical tradition, particularly i the works of Inigo Jones and the various Palladian architects although it did not lack, in the works of C. Wren and John Vanbrugh, examples of the sculptural power of the baroqu style, as in Blenheim Palace (VI, PL. 436). A greater complexit and freedom in shapes, still influenced by mannerist and eve late Gothic styles, is to be noted in Flanders and in the Nether lands, as in the doors and windows of the Jesuit churches i Antwerp and Louvain (II, PLS. 148, 149). In the Germani countries there was a more marked emphasis on decoration with frequent insertion of ornamental motifs and figural sculp ture in schemes stemming from the Italian baroque style blende with French variations. Typical examples of Germanic portal and windows of this period are those created by J. B. Neumann for the Residenz at Würzburg (II, PL. 152), by M. D. Pöppel mann for the gate pavilion of the Zwinger of Dresden (II PL. 155), and by J. L. von Hildebrandt for works such as th Belvedere Palace and the palace of Prince Eugene in Vienn (II, PLS. 158, 159). An original example of a portal in which the human figure has great importance is that of the Thur Palace in Prague (II, PL. 159). In Spain, in Portugal, and i Latin America, late Gothic, mannerist, and baroque scheme are blended in conceptions that are often highly original, es pecially those of the Churrigueresque style (q.v.). Some altar frames and retables, such as that of S. Esteban in Salamanc nd the famous *transparente* (II, PL. 161) of Toledo Cathedral, re of this type. Points of contact with the Spanish styles, vhich do not necessarily imply a derivation, can be found in ontemporaneous works in southern Italy, in Sicily, and es-ecially in Lecce, all conceived with a view to architectural lecoration.

The tendency to return to the styles of classical antiquity, lways present in 17th- and early-18th-century Italy, France, nd England, became stronger toward the middle of the 18th cen-ury, with architects retaining at first certain elements — espe-ially the decorative — of the rococo style. But the styles derived rom late-Hellenistic formal themes of the newly excavated 'ompeii and Herculaneum were quickly accepted (examples nay be seen in Piranesi's façade of S. Maria del Priorato, X, 'L. 267; and in such works of the Adam brothers as the entrance o Syon House, Middlesex, 1773, the interior doorways of Kedleston Hall, Derbyshire, X, PL. 271, and the doorways of Osterley Park House, VIII, PLS. 110, 111).

The Pompeian influence was to persist in Europe at least o the end of the period of Napoleon's empire, especially in nteriors and in the slender and elegant forms of doorways and of enframements of more or less direct archaeological inspira-ion. Shortly before and during the French Revolution, how-ver, some architects — especially of the French school (Cléris-eau, Ledoux, Boullée) — eliminated all decoration of openings n the search for functional purity. Forms from classical an-iquity and especially Greek Doric architecture supplied the major inspiration in this stage of neoclassicism, even though a ew architects turned to other traditions (Gothic, Moslem, Chinese, Egyptian) for new ideas. Quite soon imitations of all the forms of the past were admitted into the schemes of door-ways and windows and their elements; a hybrid and uncontrolled eclecticism resulted, which only rarely produced tasteful and original works.

Toward the end of the 19th century the progressive archi-tects of Europe and America began to seek new solutions for doors and windows; even though traditional and conserv-ative schemes were the bases of their designs, they were radi-cally renewed, as for instance by Victor Horta in the Tassel House in Brussels (1893); by C. R. Mackintosh in the art school in Glasgow (1898–1909); by L. Sullivan in the Audito-rium Building in Chicago (1886–89) and in the Wainwright Building in Saint Louis (1890); by Otto Wagner in his Viennese works; by J. M. Olbrich in the Sezession Haus in Vienna and in the Exhibitions Palace and the dwellings of the artists' colony in Darmstadt; by J. Hoffmann in the Stoclet house in Brussels (V, PL. 102); by Berlage in the Stock Exchange in Amsterdam; by R. D'Aronco in his works in Italy and in Turkey (I, PLS. 467, 468); by E. Basile in his Roman and Sicilian works; and by E. Saarinen in the Finnish pavilion at the Paris Exhibition (1900). But, apart from the first works by Frank Lloyd Wright in North America, some works by P. Behrens (q.v.) and by H. Poelzig, and the earliest works of Le Courbusier (q.v.) and Gropius in the model factory of the Werkbund Exhibition in Cologne (1914), little more than a marked simplification of traditional motifs was achieved until mid-20th century. At this time there emerged a trend toward overcoming the concept of the opening as a "hole in the wall" and treating it instead as an interruption of a plane surface. This treatment became usual in modern architecture and in most cases eliminated all enframe-ment and independent decorative accents of the opening.

In the ancient civilizations outside Europe, the most charac-teristic forms of doorways are those based on the trilithic system to form openings which are usually tapered into a trapezoid shape, as displayed by the portals of pre-Columbian America. As in European megalithic constructions, the jambs can be formed by the same ashlars as the wall (as in the Cyclopean walls of Sacsahuaman, in Machu Picchu) or by monolithic elements (as also in Machu Picchu, in Cuzco, and in Colquam-pata; I, PLS. 148, 150, 151, 152). Another characteristic solution is the double, or rebated, doorframe, that is, one with a second jamb set back with respect to the wall surface to form a sort of simple, flat stepped molding which often continues into the threshold. Sometimes, as in Machu Picchu, the lintel is carved

with figures in relief. In some cases, as at Chiprak (near Lima), the trabeated trapezoidal door is inserted in a tall niche which duplicates its shape; in others the openings are based on the corbeled-arch system (the doorway in the façade at Uxmal and of the gateway at Labná, Mexico; X, PLS. 9, 11).

In the Islamic world, although shapes of doorways in use since ancient times frequently persisted (for instance, the arched openings made of stone voussoirs in northern Syria), others were inspired by Early Christian models (as in the entrance of the Great Mosque of Damascus, A.D. 706–715, X, PL. 378; and in the 9th-century minaret of the Great Mosque at Kairouan); in these a trabeated opening is set under a simple relieving arch with a recessed lunette or is inscribed within an arch supported by columns. More typical are the horseshoe-arched openings, of which there are numerous and varied examples, from the simple doorway in the above-mentioned Kairouan mosque to the fa-mous so-called "St. Sebastian's Doorway" in the Great Mosque in Córdoba (855–856 A.D.). Also characteristic is the portal with a slightly depressed pointed arch and a double- or triple-arched lintel (in stone and brick, sometimes progressively set back), as in the town gates of Baghdad, Raqqa (A.D. 722), and Ukhaidir (8th–9th cent.).

In China, the doorways of buildings — trabeated or, more rarely, arched — are little defined except for smooth or carved enframements. More elaborate shapes appear in town gates, such as that of Chü-yung, which is arched but has a polygonal intrados and rich decoration carved on its front. The monu-mental portals called *p'ai-lou* (III, PLS. 293, 294) are also usually trabeated and have several arched openings; like the Indian torana, they display shapes and decoration partly derived from those of wooden portals. In Japan the very concept of "door" in the Western sense is lacking; entrance openings generally consist of a simple interruption in the continuity of the wall, defined by the supporting structural elements and provided with shutters or sliding panels (this treatment was to find great acceptance in the works of modern Western architects).

In ancient India, such openings as the torana of the en-closure of Stupa No. 1 and Stupa No. 3 at Sanchi (1st cent. B.C.), richly decorated with figures and other motifs in relief, were inspired by the shapes of earlier wooden portals (II, PL. 405). One type, formed by a rectangular opening flanked by carved pilaster strips with a figured capital supporting an arch, also decorated with figures, is to be found in the Ananta Gumphā (Khandagiri, Orissa, ca. 25 B.C.–A.D. 25; VII, PL. 443) and, later, at the entrance to the Temple of Sūrya at Modhera (11th cent.). The entrance to Cave No. 19 at Ajanta (6th cent.; VII, PL. 454), displays, however, a rectangular opening with an edicule frame formed by columns and a sort of entablature with mainly straight moldings; the whole is surmounted by a large open parabolic arch. The edicule type appears again in the Temple of Pārśvanātha at Khajuraho (11th cent.; VII, PL. 472). In later examples such as the fort at Gwalior (18th cent.), the intrados of the arch is reduced by voussoirs projecting like a corbel, in an archaic scheme earlier utilized in Borobudur in Java (8th cent.; VIII, PL. 30). In many other constructions, such as the Taj Mahal at Agra (17th cent.; VII, PL. 498), the solutions are Occidento-Islamic combinations.

Windows. In the ancient world windows were not a prom-inent architectural feature; however, some Egyptian examples deserve special mention. The great window of the royal pavilion at Medinet Habu is square and has a thick sill on which two jambs rest; their decoration continues along the end of the lintel, which has no superimposed cornice and is in turn orna-mented by a winged disk. Another example in the same build-ing has a frame in strong relief with decorated jambs and a complete crown molding surmounted by decorations carved in the wall above it. It seems that as early as the period of the Old Kingdom a type of window was used which was often of horizontal proportions, was closed by a stone grating and oc-casionally had many lights; an example of this type is reproduced on the Sarcophagus of Mykerinos. Similar in type were the windows of the hypostyle hall in the Temple of Amen at Karnak. Of the same type is the window divided by seven faceted mullions with Hathor capitals from the temple of Dendera (now in London, Br. Mus.).

In the pre-Hellenic world windows were square or rectangular and generally had only one light, as illustrated by the Cretan glazed-pottery tablets of the Heraklion Museum. Among the rare examples in Greek architecture of windows associated with the Doric order is that in the so-called "Temple of Concordia" in Agrigento (PL. 219), where the intrados of the architrave slopes back, forming an opening with a mixtilinear profile. In the western façade of the Erechtheion there are trapezoidal windows of the Ionic order enclosed within a smooth frame concluded by a perimetral molding that follows the external outline of the slanting jambs and of the lintel, which projects slightly at the sides of the jambs (i.e., forming a lintel with *parotides*). But, in general, in Greek and Hellenistic architecture the use of windows was sporadic and became more common only at a relatively late period, as in the temple of Labraunda in Asia Minor or in that of Palmyra.

In Roman architecture the schemes used for doorways were often adopted for windows. Thus there are the trabeated type, with the frame and cornice supported by modillions (at Palestrina in the Temple of Fortuna Primigenia, PL. 212; and in the "Temple of the Sibyl" at Tivoli); the type with a frame and complete entablature; and, especially in the imperial period, the edicule type, characterized by the architectural order enclosing the rectangular or arched opening. As was later to happen in the Renaissance, the terminal cornice was a simple horizontal; or was set under a triangular, curved (as in the Porta dei Borsari in Verona, PL. 235, and in the hemicycle of Trajan's Forum in Rome), or broken pediment (as in Trajan's Forum, at Baalbek, and in the nymphaeum of Gerasa); or was placed under an ornamental *fastigium* with volutes or palmettes (e. g., in the mausoleum under St. Peter's in Rome and in the Tycheum of Sahamen). Another type, also reproduced in the Renaissance, was formed by the supports of the architectural order set directly under an arch, which was occasionally — as in some examples in Verona — inscribed within a rectangle defined by a molding.

In Etruscan-Italic architecture, and later mainly in Roman, wide use was made of round-arched windows (these were to become typical of the side walls of the Christian basilicas); flat-arched windows were less common. During the late Roman imperial age the round-arched type was to develop into shapes that were decorative to a certain extent, as in the large windows of the thermae of the "basilica" of Trier, where the arched opening is enclosed by successively recessed concentric arches. But in buildings of this type, another kind of window is also very frequent and is, in fact, known as "thermal"; this is a semicircular window divided into three lights by mullions (e.g., in the baths of Caracalla and of Diocletian and in the basilica of Maxentius) and was to be reproduced in Hagia Sophia (II, PL. 428) in Istanbul and later in works by Sangallo, Palladio, and Longhena and in a few 19th-century examples.

The shapes and solutions typical of Roman and Hellenistic architecture spread throughout the Empire, where they were adopted with many variations until quite a late period. Later still, a remarkable solution appears in the windows of some Syrian buildings of the 5th, 6th, and 7th centuries, where the frames of the jambs and of the arch continue horizontally at the level of the lower part of the opening and join the frame of the jamb of the adjoining window, thus forming a sort of uninterrupted molding linking the various openings together (II, PL. 422). This motif, transformed, was later to make its way into Armenian Moslem architecture and into some medieval European architecture (the Cuba in Palermo, St. Peter's in Hirsau). In the Syrian churches the frames of windows and of doors sometimes form a large outward-curling volute at the foot of the jambs, as in the chapel of Khirbet Tezim. Contemporaneously, in Armenia and in Cilicia the frame was often limited to the arched lintel, which, however, ended with horizontal sections as in the basilicas of Kadırlı (Cilicia; II, PL. 422), of Ereruk (5th–7th cent.; I, PL. 426) and of Echmiadzin and in the Cathedral of Ani (10th cent.) in Armenia. In the latter, the molded or richly carved archivolts are occasionally associated

with jambs covered with purely decorative sculptures and enclos rectangular or arched openings (I, PLS. 433, 435).

Except in cases of strict adherence to the types used fo doors, the church windows of the early Middle Ages and o the Romanesque period are generally very small, mostly round arched, and of more or less elongated proportions. They are almost always characterized by an embrasure splayed both outward and inward to admit more light. For the simple round headed window a not infrequent variant involves the use o two or more concentric arches (as in the windows of S. Tom maso in Lémine in Almenno San Bartolomeo; of S. Bassano in Lodi; in the apse of S. Maria Maggiore in Bergamo; o Cremona Cathedral; of S. Pietro in Grado; of Murano Ca thedral; and of some Sicilian bell towers and secular buildings) the impost of which can be with or without a corbel table Other variants, with a different character according to the region and the monument, mark the jamb by the insertion o small columns or pilaster strips (as in S. Abbondio, in Como in the Baptistery in Florence; and in St-Sernin, in Toulouse) On occasion the window with a single light flanked by smal columns is inscribed within a projecting arch supported in turr by small columns which, as at Maria Laach (XII, PL. 225) are pensile and rest on corbels. In Norman Romanesque architecture, and particularly in its derivatives in Great Britain, the archivolt, or surround, was often decorated with typical zigzag motifs in relief, as was also done in the arcades of porticoes and portals. Sometimes round-arched, and later pointed-arched, windows have multifoil stone traceried moldings; this is a type which was to enjoy great favor in various European regions and also in Italy, for instance in Lombardy, where the surrounds were often made of brick (e.g., the window of the Casa dei Panigarola; PL. 236).

Beginning in the Byzantine period and then (and especially) in the Romanesque period, use was made (concurrently with the rectangular type with a simple frame) of windows divided into two or more lights; these are certainly direct descendants of the type used in 3d-century Roman residential architecture and later in some Early Christian churches in Rome.

In medieval two-, three-, and multilight windows, the opening is often divided by small columns supporting arches. Such types of window appear frequently in bell towers and in civil architecture up to the 13th and 14th centuries and beyond (bell towers in Lombardy, Emilia, Apulia, the Rhineland, and France; XII, PLS. 205, 219, 225, 228) and can be classified into many subspecies, which vary or elaborate the simple two-light (or three- or multilight) scheme with each outer arch resting directly on the wall and on intermediate columns. In one of these variants the arches are double-profiled and the small columns are coupled (e.g., in the façade of S. Zeno in Verona). Quite frequently, in the Romanesque architecture of the Lombard, French, and Flemish schools, a two- or three-light window of the simple type is inserted in a single blind arch which encloses the whole, as in the two-light windows of the Cathedral in Trier, of Maria Laach, and of St. Peter's at Hirsau (12th cent.) or the three-light windows of Modena Cathedral (begun 1099). In some exceptional cases, the two- or three-light window is enclosed by a trilobed arch (e.g., at Andernach, ca. 1200). In later derivatives of the two- and many-light types, from the 13th to the 15th century the round-headed arch was abandoned in favor of the pointed or mixtilineal arch, and the over-all appearance varied according to the materials used, the different shapes of the elements, and the greater or lesser amount of decoration.

In Gothic constructions of the 13th century in the Île-de-France, the window, almost always in stained glass and often historiated, acquired new breadth, and the trend was to go beyond the concept of the "hole in the wall" and to arrive at the idea of a wall with a glazed surface from pillar to pillar. The opening itself, large and usually rectangular, was set under a pointed arch and subdivided by secondary stone elements (tracery) with intersecting ribs forming two- or three-light windows. The tracery of the lunette was formed by molded ribs in designs generally based on the combination of circles and segments of circles inscribed within a circle to form a

e which connects with the mullions. The designs formed
the sum of the elements varies widely in the different pe-
ls and places. Until the beginning of the 13th century, the
thic window inserted in a pointed arch was still a two-light
dow with interior pointed arches and a simple circle pierced
the spandrel above the lights (plate tracery). Later (late
h–early 14th cent.) the circle was often divided to form a
oil, and the spandrel above the two-light window was some-
es subdivided into curved triangles with internally lobed
files (as in St-Urbain in Troyes; 1260), to form a design
t was to become characteristic of the 14th century (St-Nazaire
Carcassonne, transept at Meaux, St-Ouen in Rouen, etc.).
the 15th century, the custom was to extend the moldings
the mullions to form complex designs based on curves and
ntercurves which break up the various fields into a web of
nterrupted tracery of varying pattern (flowing tracery). Out-
e France, though the same general schemes were usually
epted, simpler geometric designs were often adopted. In
gland, during and after the 15th century, windows were
lved which were simply divided by several vertical mullions
ssed by transoms (bar tracery) and crowned by a pointed
h, sometimes depressed; the whole was enclosed within a
are hood molding. This same scheme was also used in the
h century in Venice, in south-central Italy, and in Spain.
In the Renaissance, mannerist, and baroque periods windows
quently reproduced the schemes of doors and portals, often
n developing such schemes in a sort of counterpoint between
ilar motifs (PL. 237). Nevertheless, elaborations of particular
es were not lacking. For instance, the motif of the arch on
architectural order gave rise to a type of window, perhaps
wn from a Roman type or from classicist interpretations of
Gothic schemes, which was to become particularly wide-
ead in Rome and in Lazio and which displays an arch on a
aster strip inserted within a rectangle crowned by a cornice.
e spandrels between the arch and the rectangle generally
r a decorative motif (a roundel or a rosette). Among the
ny examples are those of the Cancelleria, the Palazzo del
ago, the Palazzo Ricci, the Palazzo Vacca, and the Palazzo
der, all in Rome. Antonio da Sangallo the Younger used this
e of window in the first project for Palazzo Baldassini, but in
16th century the type was abandoned except in some build-
s in the provinces. Other variants, also in a many-light version,
re to appear in Venice as an evolution of late Gothic types.
In the meanwhile, from the beginning of the 15th century,
er types of windows developed along with the classically
ented types, which were to remain in use throughout the
tury. In all of Europe, in the late Gothic period, use had
n made of the rectangular opening divided vertically and
rizontally by stone mullions and transoms. In the 15th cen-
y this design, elaborated by moldings and elements drawn
m the Roman repertory, led to the "cross window" (i.e.,
h one mullion and one transom intersecting in a Latin
ss) adopted in such Roman palaces as the Palazzo Venezia
II, PL. 14), the Palazzo dei Penitenziari, and the Palazzo
pranica, and in some works by Giuliano da Sangallo (as in
Villa di Poggio a Caiano, IV, PL. 191; XII, PL. 387).
milar types, but often with stronger decorative accents in
e elements or with late Gothic motifs, were used until the
ddle of the 16th century in the castles of the Loire Valley
ois, IX, PL. 317; Chambord; Fougères; Chaumont; Am-
ise; Villandry; Azay-le-Rideau, XII, PL. 101), sometimes with
re than one transom and often with the whole enclosed
thin two pilaster strips topped by an entablature, as in some
rman (Erfurt), Flemish, and English buildings.
The two-light window with a small column and small arches
closed by a larger arch persisted in the large Florentine
laces of the 15th century, with a more or less free adaptation
the elements to classical shapes, as for instance in the Palazzo
aratesi (II, PL. 373), the Palazzo Medici-Riccardi (XII,
, 4), the Palazzo Strozzi, and the Palazzo Gondi (XIII, PL. 246).
berti gave this type a personal interpretation by inserting a
tel at the impost level of the arch in the Palazzo Rucellai
Florence, and his example was followed by Rossellino in
e Palazzo Piccolomini in Pienza. In Venice, in the first years

of the 16th century, elaborations of the type found in the
Palazzo Medici were used in the Palazzo Vendramin and the
Palazzo Corner-Spinelli (XII, PL. 11).

Two-light windows with a superimposed lintel were not
common in the 15th century. Some examples are to be found
in works by the northern schools and in southern Italy (in the
style known as "Durazzo" Gothic) in which the upper part of
the opening is decorated by a richly pierced marble panel (e.g.,
in houses at Carinola, Fondi, Roccamonfina). In central Italy,
a two-light window with a lintel is to be seen on the façade
of S. Bernardino, in Urbino. More frequently, in the architecture of central and northern Europe (especially in residential
architecture) between the 15th and 17th centuries, but sometimes also in Italy, the two- or many-light window acquired
the shape of a cross window or was combined with other types.
Thus, for instance, in the Ospedale di Sto Spirito in Rome, a
two-light window (now restored) was set within a larger window
with a classic frame and cornice; in the Castle of Heidelberg
(VI, PL. 138) an edicule window encloses an opening divided
in two by a herma.

From the middle of the 16th century the Renaissance schemes
were often elaborated by the repetition of the elements — especially of columns or pilaster strips — supporting the entablature
in edicule windows; sometimes there were obvious attempts at
perspective effects, and often elements of a more properly
sculptural nature, such as coats of arms, plant motifs, and
medallions with figures or protomas, were inserted between the
moldings to represent links between the various structural members. A characteristic type, the first examples of which are the
windows on the ground floor of Palazzo Medici in Florence, is
the so-called *finestra inginocchiata*, with the usual cornice but
with a sill supported by two sturdy modillions set on the same
axis as the window posts, which they extend.

Windows in present-day architecture emphasize, even more
than doors, the abandonment of the "hole in the wall" concept;
since the wall itself can, because of the elimination of its load-
bearing function, be executed in transparent material, windows
as such are unnecessary. Thus a new integration of solids and
voids and of the internal and the external space of the building
becomes possible (PL. 218).

In Islamic architecture windows, especially in religious buildings, often mirror the shapes and morphological elements of
the Western type. The arched window, occurring more frequently than the type with a lintel, can have one light inscribed
within a rectangular frame, or many lights inscribed within a
slightly recessed arch. The jambs are often flanked by small
columns, and the archivolt is connected by horizontal bands to
the archivolt of the adjacent windows (as in the Mosque of
Ibn-Tūlūn). In many other cases horseshoe or polylobed arches
are used (as in the mosque of Samarra, middle of the 9th cent.);
these shapes were later to spread to the West (as in the transept
of the Cathedral of Caserta Vecchia). A characteristic device
is the filling of the opening with an openwork marble screen
with complicated geometric interlace, as in the famous windows
of the Great Mosque in Damascus (8th cent.), those of the
already mentioned Mosque of Ibn-Tūlūn, and, in India, those
of the mausoleum at Fathpur Sikri and of the Mosque of Sīdī-
Sayyid at Ahmadabad (16th cent.; VII, PL. 496). In India it is
the windows of the various Moslem types which most often
display complex and original decorative patterns.

In the Far East there are, in general, no particular accen-
tuations of the purely structural elements of windows.

Other types. In centric Roman architecture, frequent use
was made of circular openings (oculi) placed at the crown
of the dome or, more rarely and in a late period, on the
drum or in correspondence with the curve of the vault, as for
instance in the octagonal hall of the Villa of the Gordians, in
Tor de' Schiavi. This type persisted in Roman Early Christian
architecture (in the first Basilica S. Agnese and perhaps in
S. Maria Maggiore) and was combined or alternated with other
types of openings, as in SS. Giovanni e Paolo, where the oculi
are placed above round-arched windows, or in S. Stefano Rotondo, where an oculus is placed between two cruciform openings.

In medieval architecture the round window often appeared; it became in the late Romanesque and in the Gothic period the rose window, in which the opening is normally filled with tracery, pierced or otherwise, composing a decorative pattern. As early as the Abbey of Pomposa round windows appeared, defined by a masonry ring and filled with decorative bands and pierced motifs. In Lombard architecture simple smooth stone lintels define the opening, which is often highly splayed, as in the apse of S. Fedele and that of S. Carpoforo, in Como. In Pavia round windows in concentric circles were adopted instead, as in the façades of S. Michele (XII, PL. 219) and of S. Pietro in Ciel d'Oro, following a type, widespread in European Romanesque architecture, which was to remain in use until the 13th century, with variants of proportions and of profiles, from Tuscany to Apulia, in France, and in Germany. In some structures such windows acquired a shape other than circular; some were hexagonal (as in the Abbey of Maria Laach) and some lozenge-shaped. Something of the sort had already existed in the decorative repertory of some Armenian churches and in some churches of the Byzantine Middle Ages. In the Gothic period trilobed and quadrilobed windows were sometimes used (as in the upper part of the façade of S. Chiara, in Naples). In the 13th century the internal elements of the oculus tended for the most part to be replaced by a radiating pattern of stone elements in a design in which the principal radii are linked to one another by means of small arches of which the extrados serves as the starting point for the secondary radii.

In the 13th and 14th centuries the circular oculus acquired new importance and larger dimensions throughout the Western world. They appeared in façades in the shape of large rose windows; especially in the Île-de-France and in regions influenced by French culture, rose windows were sometimes of such great size as to cover much of the façade. In the 14th century, to balance as far as possible the surfaces of the various sections, the ribs of the tracery were no longer made to converge toward the center and the radial tracery was transformed into a kind of network of straight and curved lines. In the 15th and 16th centuries such a network was formed by wavy interlacing lines, as in the rose windows of the transepts at Beauvais, of the portals of St-Germain-l'Auxerrois and of the Ste-Chapelle (Paris). In some Gothic schools, as for instance in Champagne and in the area of Soissons, the opening in which the rose window is inserted has an ogival shape (Cathedral and cloister of St. Nicasius in Rheims; St-Jean-des-Vignes in Soissons).

Oculi and rose windows were often used in the Renaissance, and in the 15th century in particular. Thus Brunelleschi gave a classical shape to the large oculi of the drum under the dome of S. Maria del Fiore (Florence); he used circular windows in the lunettes of the chapels of S. Lorenzo, in the Old Sacristy in the same church, and in the Pazzi Chapel (II, PLS. 365, 367, 368), and he went so far as to superimpose them on round-arched windows in the façade of the Palazzo di Parte Guelfa. The same motif is found in Palazzo Quaratesi, also in Florence (II, PL. 373). Brunelleschi made frequent use of molded rings that might be considered blind oculi. Similar elements, occasionally more sculptural and decorative, appear in Alberti's architecture; they are sometimes in the shape of triumphal crowns, as in the Tempio Malatestiano in Rimini, and sometimes in the shape of a large rose window with a simple molded frame, as on the façade of S. Maria Novella (I, PL. 53).

The rose window with a molded frame appears quite frequently on the façades of 15th century Roman churches (such as S. Maria del Popolo, S. Agostino, S. Maria dell'Anima, S. Pietro in Montorio), in many churches of Tuscany (notably S. Maria del Calcinaio at Cortona), in Lombardy (especially at the end of the 15th century in Milan: S. Maria presso S. Satiro, S. Maria delle Grazie, monastery of S. Ambrogio), in Umbria and the Marches, and elsewhere.

In baroque architecture circular, oval, and lobed openings were frequently used. Among the most significant examples are the rose windows of the façades of St-Paul-St-Louis in Paris (by F. Derand, 1634), S. Gaetano in Florence (by G. Silvani, 1645), Sta Croce in Lecce, and the oval windows in the

lower part of the façade of S. Carlo alle Quattro Fonta (Rome) by Borromini. Openings of this kind were even mc frequently used in bell towers, in the drums of domes, and the domes themselves (S. Carlo al Corso, Rome, by Pietro Cortona; Chapel of the Holy Shroud, Turin, by G. Guari church of Valinotto, near Carignano, by B. Vittone, 1738-17: Val-de-Grâce, by F. Mansart, Paris, begun 1645). In Ven the custom was widespread of inserting a simple circular ope ing into the tympanums of the façades (S. Nicolò da Tolentir by A. Tirali).

It is also possible to discuss here a related architectu device: simulated apertures. Since very early times blind (that to say, not pierced) doors and windows have been used for stru tural emphasis or for pure decoration. In many cases it wou be more accurate to call these recessed areas "niches"; th were, in fact, often intended to house a statue or other dec rative element, thus creating, by the mediation of the frames, formal relationship between plastic and architectural elemen In certain cultures, and especially in sepulchral or religio buildings, the blind door (such as those in Egyptian toml was used mainly for symbolic or ritual reasons.

The formal schemes of blind doors and blind windows not differ substantially from those adopted for true archite tural elements; it would therefore be superfluous to descri the various types except for a few instances in which the mo of the simulated opening has become characteristic of t particular spatial conceptions of the architectural work.

In Roman architecture simulated openings and niches occ frequently, either with molded or with (sometimes elaborate aedicule openings. Characteristic shapes are to be noted in t *frontes scaenae* of theaters, in town gates (e.g., Porta Nigra Trier, the gate of Gerasa, Porta Aurea at Split, the city ga at Nîmes, V, PL. 471), and sometimes in bridges (e.g., "Brid of Tiberius" on the Marecchia River at Rimini), in triumpl arches (e.g., the Arch of Augustus at Aosta, the Arch of Titt XII, PL. 131, and the Arch of Janus, IX, PL. 35; Rome), sepulchral monuments (as in the so-called "Canocchia" ne Capua), in thermal buildings, and in religious structures.

The attempt to articulate the surfaces by means of recess and indications of depth is manifested in medieval architectu in ways that were to acquire the typical aspect of the bli arcade. Originally a structural motif intended to articulate t mass of the wall, the blind arcade soon became a comm architectural device, sometimes merely decorative, and appear in a large variety of shapes.

The blind arcade appeared quite often also in the archite ture of the Renaissance, inspired for the most part by classi examples, as in the façade of the Tempio Malatestiano in Rim and in S. Maria dei Miracoli in Venice. A more systemat use of false openings, within a general tendency to emphasi the profiles of architectural elements, was to be typical Brunelleschi, who also inserted blind oculi at the tops of lunett in the pendentives of the domes, and in the spandrels, som times so as to enclose decorative figures within them (as in tl Old Sacristy of S. Lorenzo, in the Pazzi Chapel, and in tl Portico degli Innocenti, all Florence). Brunelleschi's examp was followed in other Renaissance creations such as Mich angelo's works in S. Lorenzo and in the Biblioteca Laurenzia (Florence) and in Porta Pia (Rome), from which so ma mannerist works were derived.

In baroque architecture false niches and openings were us which sometimes acquired fanciful shapes and were often great depth (as, in Rome, the façade of S. Susanna, by Maderr in Paris, the Val-de-Grâce, by F. Mansart).

The niche and the edicule, often enclosing a sculptur element (generally a statue), were also much-used device especially from the Gothic period onward. Like the blin openings, these forms correspond generally to the general a coeval structural shapes of the openings; therefore, it is su ficient to refer to the descriptions of the relevant architectur elements and to the examples illustrated under other heading

The use of false openings or niches was frequent also Eastern cultures. In the architecture of the Islamic world, typical element is the mihrab, a niche in the wall of the sanctua a mosque indicating the direction of Mecca; but decorative se openings also appeared in various other types of construc- n, as in the upper part of the "Baghdad Door" at Raqq.

India and the Far East, wide use is made of niches for ulptures, which have no particular formal accentuation to stinguish them from the other openings in the wall surface cept for the profile, which is often polylobed.

The custom of articulating the wall by means of niches was o known in pre-Columbian America (I, PLS. 150, 157; III, . 485; X, PLS. 11, 22). In the area of the central coast (Cajamar- illa) and elsewhere a frequent motif is that of niches (or, ther, of false windows with trapezoidal openings) defined romatically, for instance in red on a yellow wall.

PILLARS. A pillar is the freestanding vertical architectural ment, almost always either rhythmically repeated or asso- ited with continuous wall structures, that constitutes a sup- rt for other structures. Its purpose is to permit, functionally, e reduction of the planimetric dimensions and, structurally, e concentration of the stresses on areas of relatively limited rface.

The pillar can vary in shape in a number of ways while taining the appearance of a prismatic solid of polygonal sec- n or of a cylindrical solid of circular or elliptical section, or can be composed of complex combinations and intersections solids (as in compound or clustered piers).

Pillars generally consist of: a main element, with a more or ss marked vertical development, known as the shaft, trunk, fust, which can be monolithic or composed of superimposed ums or ashlars; a base, consisting of one or more elements linth, socle, pedestal) in the lower part serving as an inter- ediary between the shaft and its horizontal support or foun- tion; the crowning element or elements (capital, dosseret, lvin, impost block) between the shaft and the superincum- nt structures. The elements comprising the lower zone and, uch more rarely, those constituting the upper zone of the pport can present points in common or a relationship with e corresponding areas of the contiguous wall.

From a morphological and structural-functional point of ew, the pillar can be isolated and possess an actual supporting nction (as in the pillar of an Egyptian construction or the lumn of the peribolos of a Greek temple); it can be isolated d without a supporting function (as, for instance, in com- emorative columns); it can have only the appearance of a pporting, partially supporting, or totally non-supporting func- n (e.g., in the columns set in correspondence with the vault posts in the central halls of Roman thermae, in the Basilica Maxentius and in many other examples of a similar applica- n in the Renaissance); or it may be engaged, or part of the all itself, in the shape of a pillar, buttress, pilaster strip, laster, half column, or else of an encased column with the nction (depending upon the individual need) of structural ticulation and of reinforcement of the supporting wall, or mply as a device for formally defining the wall. Thus the llar often plays an essential role in the organization of the ructure and in the determination of the architectural masses, a linking or connecting element of visual interruption; it ntributes to the definition of the spatial limits of the architec- ral organism, so that it plays a considerable role in charac- rizing a work of architecture by its appearance, by the type material utilized, by the structural method adopted (trabeated arcuated), by the technical means and methods used to carry out, and by the combination of its component elements.

The various types of pillar, though distinct in their specific pects, are characterized by their relationship to structural and nctional requirements and to the architectural space which is hieved through them. Thus, within the scope of this article, is deemed advisable to deal with pillars and the elements hich make up the various types of pillars (bases, shafts, pitals, pulvins) not on the basis of criteria of descriptive menclature, but rather within the various cultural and historic ameworks.

In Egypt, in the architecture of the Old and Middle King- ms, the most elementary shape of pillar — simple, square,

and generally monolithic — frequently recurs. Examples of this type, without a base and with the surfaces completely smooth, are to be found in the Hall of the Pillars in the Valley Temple of King Chephren (IV, PL. 332) and, with a simple square base, in the necropolis of Saqqara, the Tomb of Prince Sirenpowet II, near Aswan (IV, PL. 346), and in the so-called "Festival Hall" of King Thutmosis III at Karnak. Sometimes the square pil- lars of a later period, all without capitals, taper slightly towards the top, as at Abu Simbel.

The elementary structural shape of the square pillar was enriched, from very early times, with carved and colored dec- orations on two or on all four faces. In the so-called "Hall of the Annals" in the Temple of Amen at Karnak papyrus and lotus stalks carved on the faces with an exceptional purity of line defined the surfaces by means of vertical accents sug- gesting fluting, and the stylized flower becomes a capital-like termination, thus emphasizing the vertical dimensions of the pillars themselves — which are slightly tapering — without im- pairing their tectonic sturdiness.

Often the decoration of the faces of the pillar consists of hieroglyphs, painted or carved, as in the small pavilion of Sesostris I at Karnak (IV, PL. 345); in numerous other con- structions, especially in the Ramesside period, this minute dec- oration is tidily arranged on the faces, but leaves the corners and the end posts uncovered, thus emphasizing the structural shape and the volumetric solidity of the pillar.

In all these pillar types the architrave generally rests directly on the shaft; only in the Ramesside period, at Karnak, did square pillars surmounted by square capitals with an Egyptian gorge molding appear. Square abacus capitals were generally placed over polygonal pillars, that is, those which, by means of successive bevelings of the corners, acquired the appearance of six- or eight-sided prisms. An early tomb at Saqqara has quadrangular pillars with beveled corners; a regular octagon is found at Beni Hasan in the portico of the Tomb of Prince Amenemhet and in the interior of the tomb are sixteen-sided pillars, slightly concave, resting on circular bases (IV, PL. 346). This type of pillar, sometimes called an Egyptian "proto-Doric" column, was particularly common in the sepulchral caves of the 12th and 13th dynasties. There are also examples to be found at Karnak and in the atrium of the chapel of Anubis in the Temple of Queen Hatshepsut at Deir el-Bahri, near Thebes (IV, PL. 356), where the shaft of the pillar, formed by superim- posed drums, is quite slender and the capital consists of a squared abacus flush with the front facets of the support and with the surface of the sturdy architrave on which is superim- posed the typical Egyptian gorge molding. This represents, therefore, a more or less constant compositional arrangement of the various parts of the trabeated system, which may perhaps be considered a prototype of the Greek orders of architecture. The shaft of such pillars usually taper (very slightly in archaic examples) most markedly in New Kingdom examples; there is, however, no trace of entasis, that is, the swelling of the middle part of the shaft. Polygonal pillars are also sometimes decorated with hieroglyphs on some of the eight or sixteen faces (as at Kalabsha). In some cases, they also display a figured capital — the so-called "Hathor capital" (PL. 230), formed by a head of the goddess Hathor, sometimes with the headdress in the shape of a sistrum (the instrument sacred to Hathor), sur- mounted by an edicule.

A particular type of pillar is that which bears a statue of a god engaged in one of its faces; according to the god rep- resented (Osiris or Hathor), these pillars are usually called "Osiride" or "Hathoric" pillars (some remarkable examples are to be seen in the Ramesseum at Thebes; IV, PL. 358).

The type of support prevailing in Egyptian monumental architecture was, however, the column, which appears in a remarkable variety of shapes. These shapes can, nevertheless, be reduced to three ideal models: the papyrus column (PL. 230), the campaniform column, and the palmiform column (PL. 230; IV, FIG. 682). Normally, the Egyptian column consisted of a shaft, generally monolithic, a capital, and, almost always, a base.

In discussing the utilization of columns in the architectural complex it should be noted that in all the periods of Egyptian architecture the relationship of the columns to the entablatures and the intercolumniations is extremely varied, so that it is virtually impossible to speak of a "system," as is done for the classical orders of architecture. There appears to have been not only a lack of any kind of constant interrelationship between the parts, but, on the contrary, columns of the same type and diameter in varying heights, or different types of columns of equal height and diameter can be found in a single building.

In the last period of Egyptian architecture, particularly in smaller buildings, the intercolumniation is closed by walls up to half or one-third the height of the column (e.g., the Temple of Amen at Hibis in the Kharga Oasis, IV, PL. 379; Temple of Horus at Edfu, IV, PL. 380; the Kiosk at Philae). In some cases, half columns are set against the face of the wall, as in the tomb enclosure of King Zoser at Saqqara (IV, PL. 330), where they are without bases, have smooth, tapered shafts, and are terminated in capitals in the shape of half-opened papyrus buds.

In this same monumental complex there are examples of tapered columns with shafts having the appearance of a sheaf of reeds; these are set on wide, low circular bases and are, therefore, early types of the "bundle" or bundled papyrus column, which was later to be widely used. Columns of this type sometimes had a capital formed by buds and flowers continuing from the reeds and connected to the architrave by means of a flat tablet or abacus; the whole was decorated in brilliant colors. Another type of column in the funerary monument of King Zoser has a more strongly tapering shaft with concave flutes and a peculiar capital with two pendent leaflike projections; it is very probable that this type of column was derived from the wooden one that in turn derived from the tree trunk hewn with special curved adzes and having brackets inserted to support cult images. As early as the Old Kingdom, however, the papyrus column was in use (IV, FIG. 682).

At Abusir, in the sanctuary of the Temple of King Sahura (5th dynasty) the shaft of the columns is in the shape of a sheaf of lotus buds; at Beni Hasan, in the interior of the Tomb of Prince Khety (12th dynasty, ca. 1900 B.C.), there is a quadri-lobed column with a stiffly tapering shaft (IV, PL. 346). Four sturdy semi-cylindrical protuberances (stalks or fascicles) form the shaft, and near their tops four listels are inserted vertically, representing the hanging ends of smaller buds. Five parallel rings bind together the upper part of the four grouped stalks; above the binding the capital develops into the shape of truncated lotus buds. The columns rest on wide, flattened circular bases with beveled edges. In columns of this type the grouped stalks can be four or six in number and they are circular in section. Most of the bud capitals, however, use the papyrus motif; the lotus bud capital is much rarer, and was used chiefly in the Old Kingdom. The papyrus capital is similar to the lotus, although the buds between the single flowers are lacking and the flowers can, in turn, be decorated at the base with small pointed leaves. The stalk displays distinctive characteristics, namely the triangular section of the ribs (imitating the papyrus stalk) and, especially, the tapering followed by a swelling (entasis) immediately above the base, which was often decorated with papyrus leaves.

Examples of bundled lotus or papyrus columns of heavier proportions and with each lobe grooved survive at Tell el 'Amarna in the Tomb of Ai (ca. 1360 B.C.). Thus, between the first and second Theban empires the bundled papyrus column was partially transformed. In the colonnade of Amenhotep III at Luxor (IV, PL. 357, FIG. 682) the comprehensive surface approached the cylindrical shape through an evident process of simplification. The fascicles, or ribs, of the shaft were softened and terminated in a circular drum under the capital; the tapering became less marked and the swelling at the base very slight. The capital acquired a more geometric shape and was rounded in its lower part; the buds were transformed into slender ribs converging toward the tall, quadrangular abacus. Another example of the same type at Luxor has very close set reeds and the circular parallel lashings at the top are repeated at the bottom and at the middle of the shaft; while at the base of the capital with its very tall abacus, a crown of heavy stylized

leaves is arranged between the ribs. The horizontal rings a the leaf decoration are polychromed. At Medinet Habu t simplification of the type is even more marked. The geomet scheme of the whole is still the same in its general lines, b the reeding of the shaft has disappeared and has been replac by polychrome decoration and hieroglyphs, and traces of persist only in short vertical incisions on a small portion of t cylindrical surface, which is slightly tapering. Light strip also mark the shaft horizontally under the squat capital, whi has a decorated abacus. The base, which is circular, has this case a rolled edge somewhat in the shape of a mass torus (that is, almost semicircular in section) and is ligh carved with hieroglyphs. A final and extreme transformati of the type is noticeable in the courtyard of Ramses II in t Temple of Amen-Mut-Khonsu at Luxor, and at Karnak in t Temple of Khonsu and in the hypostyle hall of the Temple Amen, where the cylindrical shaft (smooth and tapering), t very tall capital and the abacus are all profusely decorated w adjoining bands of stylized drawings and hieroglyphs. T elements, which originally were naturalistic, had by then l all meaning and imitative value. This last type of column called "monostyle" because it lacks ribs.

In the campaniform (bell-shaped) column (also called "op lotus," after the shape of the capital) the shaft is smooth a cylindrical, without reeds, but is often decorated in low rel or carved hieroglyphs. Under the capital, this type also d plays the superimposed rings (generally five in number). T capital, in the shape of an inverted bell, is almost always de orated in its lower part with pointed leaves, from which spri flowers with slender vertical stems set parallel to each other underline the compact geometric surface on which they a drawn and painted. Between the capital and the architrave sort of cubical abacus is normally inserted. In most cases t latter does not project beyond the upper diameter of the colur and therefore appears to be set back with respect to the proje tion of the capital, which thus acquires more of a decorati (rather than supporting) function. This column, which beg to be widely used in the time of the second Theban empi acquired certain characteristics in particular examples, in th the shaft could vary widely in appearance, proportions, amou of taper, and decoration, and the capital could be more or l expanded and projecting and display a more or less rigid profi Thus, in the columns of the first courtyard at Medinet Ha the proportions are massive, the shaft is only slightly taper and is clumsy and without ornaments; the capital (the or decorated part) is slender and only slightly projecting. In t colonnade of Amenhotep III at Luxor (IV, PL. 357) the sha of the columns are slimmer, while the capital, of very wi proportions, has a more rigid and more vertical profile. even more slender proportions are the columns in the centr nave of the hypostyle hall at Karnak; there the shaft is ve slender, tapered with an almost imperceptible decrease in t section, the capital is very projecting and the whole is profuse and richly decorated (IV, FIG. 682). A much more taperi profile and a lower part rounded to resemble a bulb (as in t columns with a papyrus capital) are displayed by the shafts the columns of the central nave in the hypostyle hall of t Ramesseum in Thebes. The decoration, carved or painted, concentrated in the lower part of the column, at its upper te mination under the rings, and in the capital; the central pa of the shaft is smooth and undecorated. The capital has bell-shaped profile and remarkable strength and elegance. all these examples the column rests on a base of the usual ty (a smooth disk), more or less large and thick, with vertical beveled edges.

The palmiform column generally has a smooth, cylindri shaft and is characterized by a capital imitating bundled pal leaves springing from the shaft and falling back toward t ground (IV, FIG. 682); this type appears at Abusir, in th sanctuary of the Temple of King Sahura (5th dynasty). In t temple of Soleb (Nubia; built by Thutmosis III and re-bu by Amenhotep III, 18th dynasty) some columns have a capit which seems inspired by a bunch of palm leaves; they spri from a circular shaft to which they are connected by the usu five-ring necking. In curving outward, each highly stylized leaf forms a sort of lobe. A similar example is provided by the columns of the Temple of Seti I at Sesebi in Nubia, where the capitals display leaves with a more marked relief, terminating with lobes of an accented and modeled profile, where the recollection of natural shapes appears strongly transformed. A much more obvious naturalistic reference is to be found in later examples, especially in those of the Ptolemaic age, for instance, in the Temple of Horus, at Edfu, where the smooth columns have palm-shaped capitals (similar to those of Soleb and Sesebi) but with more lengthened proportions and more naturalistic accents (IV, PL. 380). Other examples of palmiform columns, with more or less complicated capitals, are in the atrium of Nectanebo II (358–341 B.C.), added to the Temple of Amen at Hibis, in the Kharga Oasis. The small temple of Nectanebo on the island of Philae shows some variants of the same theme, with a complication of shapes typical of the late period, when different motifs were mixed in a markedly realistic style. The column, bulbous in its lower part, seems to emerge from a bush of triangular leaves and displays flutes (triangular in section) in the upper part of the shaft above the usual series of five smooth rings. In some cases the capital bears only delicately carved palm leaves, while in other examples of the type with a bell-shaped profile (e.g., the typical one of the pavilion of Nectanebo at Philae), half-open lotus flowers are inserted between the palm leaves. Here the capital is surmounted with a very tall cube decorated on each of its four faces with a head of Hathor, above which stands the usual small edicule which often accompanies the Hathor capital. This obviously indicates an eclectic adoption of various motifs, so that this capital could properly be called "composite."

A type of column with a peculiar capital is found at Karnak in the reception hall of Thutmosis III. It consists of a squat column tapering downwards (with an increase in the diameter proceeding from the base to the top), on which rests a capital in the shape of a suspended bell (that is, the reverse of the usual bell-shaped capital). The smooth shaft is encircled by rings, underneath which a vertical band lengthens and widens and then spreads out at its upper end to meet the lower edges of the capital, which is decorated with leaves shaped like a curved acute-angled triangle with the tip pointing downwards, and supports an abacus in the shape of a cube with the sides tangent to the upper circular section of the bell and the four corners projecting with respect to its profile. Columns of this type, with a suspended-bell capital, seem to have existed in wood in a much earlier period, as is shown by the reproductions of columns or piers in representations of edicules of the Old Kingdom.

A preference for complicated shapes of capitals was characteristic of the late period. These were normally placed on cylindrical columns with smooth shafts, common since the Ramesside period. Columns with different capitals are often grouped to form a portico or the front of a building (as in the already-mentioned portico of the Temple of Amen at Hibis in the Kharga Oasis; in the front of the large courtyard of the Temple of Horus at Edfu; in the Temple of Isis at Philae). Among the earlier examples those that mainly persisted were the palm-shaped one, sometimes with the insertion of dates or other ornaments or flowers among the leaves, and the bell-shaped one, often modeled on the lotus, which was, however, complicated by being covered with varied and rich floral ornaments of which stems and flowers project in relief from the horizontal rings at the upper end of the shaft of the column. While retaining the bell shape in their overall form, many capitals of this period (8th cent. B.C. – 2nd cent. of our era) display dense and complicated interlacings of flowers, stems or leaves in relief and projecting more or less from the general outline. These did not become widespread in the temples until the beginning of the 30th dynasty, but their shapes had been developed in the Ramesside period.

In Mesopotamia masonry pillars were utilized very early, but for the most part they had no clear definition and were treated essentially as part of the walls. The palace of Lagash (mod. Telloh) displays "polystyle" pillars, composed of four brick columns grouped in a cluster and then plastered to form a single pillar resting on a square socle. At Uruk there were columns covered with mosaic decoration (X, PL. 172). However, columns were not widely used in a country where wood and stone were rather scarce and in a type of architecture in which the brick and the vault prevailed. At Khorsabad and at Nimrud there were columns with a bulb-shaped capital with rounded moldings and a base not unlike the capital. The sculptural reproductions of kiosks show squat monolithic columns with a torus-shaped circular base and a capital with volutes connected to the architrave by a sort of pulvin, or impost block, in the shape of an inverted truncated pyramid with stepped edges. The capital vaguely resembles the later Phoenician capitals and the Greek Ionic type. In some cases there seems to have been a mixture, in the same building, of very different types of columns and of capitals.

In the Hittite culture, especially in the imperial period (1450–1200 B.C.), quadrangular pillars were particularly common and only later was the column with a decorated base and capital adopted. During the first half of the 1st millennium B.C. Syro-Hittite architecture adopted the column with a wooden shaft in the shape of an inverted truncated cone tapering downward, resting on round basalt bases: examples of this type stood in the Palace of Yarim-Lim at Alalakh (northern Syria). Some component elements of the column are of considerable interest, since they were to reappear as motifs typical of Minoan architecture. Toward the middle of the 1st millennium, the base of the columns, at first composed of a single circular element, was enriched by elaborate sculptural decoration which reveals an Assyrian influence interpreted with great originality. Some bases were flanked by massive figures of lions and sphinxes, as at Zinçirli (I, PL. 523) and at Tell Taynat. In the bīt-hilani of the Palace of Kaparu (8th century B.C.) at Tell Halaf the shafts of the columns were replaced by telamons consisting of human figures resting on lions or bulls. In other cases, as at Tell Taynat, the base of the column was enriched with complex motifs of cordons, rosettes, and palmettes. Within the same cultural sphere there was utilized at Megiddo (9th–8th cent. B.C.) a typical capital composed of two volutes springing from the sides of a triangle (I, PL. 526). These are capitals of the so-called "proto-Ionic" type, to be found in a more or less elaborate version in Cyprus in the 6th century and also in the Ionic-Asiatic environment and in Etruria, but whose origin is probably to be found in Syro-Palestinian architecture.

In paleo-Mediterranean and European megalithic architecture wide use was made of monoliths as supports. Examples are to be found in the dolmens, in the Maltese temples, in the talayotic architecture of the Balearic islands (with hypostyle halls similar to the Egyptian), and in the nuraghic architecture of Sardinia.

In the Cretan-Mycenaean culture quadrangular pillars, monolithic or otherwise, with smooth shafts, were used from the earliest period, in both interiors and exteriors of palaces and tombs. They were generally colored and supported decorated cornices; in addition to a technical and architectural function, it seems that they also had a magic or religious and ritual significance. Some piers, such as those in the sanctuary of the Palace of Knossos, are decorated with the often-repeated emblem of the double ax (labrys). Sometimes in Crete, as at Hagia Triada, square pillars were alternated with isolated wooden columns. A small clay model of a sanctuary from the Palace of Knossos shows a temple with three columns surmounted by sacred doves. The columns, squat and cylindrical, are set close together and rest on simple drum bases; each one seems to support, by means of a sturdy abacus resting directly on the shaft, a pair of cylindrical beams forming the main framework of the roofing.

The rhyton with pugilists and bull-racing scenes from Hagia Triada (IV, PL. 59) shows columns without a base, of massive proportions, tapering into a cone and with a strange termination consisting of a quadrangular capital framed by circles (perhaps hinting at cylindrical roofing beams).

Another type of column, more typically Minoan and Mycenaean, seems to have derived from a simple tree trunk with the diameter larger at the top (i.e., an inverted truncated cone), to provide a larger bearing surface for the beam supporting the roof.

The Hall of the Columns in the Palace of Knossos must have displayed massive columns of this type on low circular bases and capitals composed of a sort of echinus in the shape of a large torus supporting a projecting abacus.

Some frescoes of the sanctuary in the Palace of Knossos represent columns, similar but of more slender proportions and with more elaborate capitals showing a profile based on the combination of large tori or astragals.

The inverted-cone column persisted without undergoing substantial changes and without acquiring fixed proportions or precise types of bases or capitals until the high period of Mycenaean architecture.

The half columns in the façade of the "Treasury of Atreus" (IV, FIG. 107) at Mycenae, tapering slightly downward, display more elongated and elegant proportions, with quadrangular and stepped bases. The shafts are richly decorated with smooth chevrons or meandering spirals, evidently related to the painted and sculptured designs typical of Minoan and Mycenaean handicrafts.

In the last Mycenaean period a similar type of column appears in the Lion Gate at Mycenae (IV, PL. 69). Resting on a square plinth, the sturdy shaft tapers downward quite sharply; the simple capital displays similarities to the painted examples at Knossos. An astragal connected by a sort of scotia to a large torus, raised and projecting, acts as a necking. In this example, the column is set below an element which might be called an entablature; it is, in fact, composed of a beam (which could also be interpreted as an abacus) supporting a series of small adjoining beams, circular in section, placed to support the covering. Sometimes, as in the Minoan agora of Hagia Triada, there are examples of columns superimposed in two orders.

In Phoenicia and Cyprus, both in pillars (normally rectangular in section) and columns, shaft and capital are generally carved from a single block. Columns do not seem to have been very widely used; they were of small dimensions and were utilized primarily for ornamental purposes. The shafts were generally smooth. On the whole, there were no pillars or columns peculiar to the Phoenicians; motifs applied elsewhere were eclectically repeated.

Some pillars, as for instance the square one at Gebal, seem to echo in the capital the Egyptian motif of the cyma reversa on a projecting astragal, used here as a necking; the whole is surmounted with a sort of squared abacus. A capital from Golgoi (Cyprus) displays a simple curved echinus supporting a robust abacus; another capital from Edde, near Byblos, is characterized by a very slightly projecting echinus with a strange concave profile and an abacus.

Some Cypriot capitals of the 6th century, which surmounted pillars or rectangular steles placed as tombstones, reveal a mixture of Mesopotamian and Egyptian decorative elements which results in a general shape vaguely resembling the Ionic style. One of the simplest of these, from Famagusta, displays, carved on the two faces, two rather accentuated volutes starting from superimposed horizontal bands at the top of the shaft. In other capitals from Athienu (second half of the 6th cent. B.C.) the volutes — at the base of which is inserted a triangle which separates them — are set below a series of two or three reversed smaller volutes (IV, PL. 96). An example of the same type (Met. Mus.), also from Athienu, displays at the center two upright sphinxes facing each other across a palmette. Capitals of this type were often surmounted by a sort of abacus consisting of three increasingly projecting tablets of which the rims were sometimes decorated with carved chevrons.

Other terminations of Cypriot funerary steles in limestone display two crouching lions (or two winged female sphinxes) set back to back to form a decorative motif that recalls the capitals of Persepolis (IV, PL. 96).

Cypriot eclecticism is also documented by a Hathor capital from Larnaca, Cyprus (ca. 500 B.C.; PL. 230). Other Cypriot capitals, however, display more original shapes: one from Athienu in the shape of an inverted bell (kalathos) is almost hemispheri-

cal; it is truncated at the base and incised with coil designs and is surmounted by a light, projecting abacus; another, from the same place, has a kalathos decorated with branches and small leaves and has a strong trapezoidal abacus with slightly concave rims decorated, on three superimposed rows separated by listels, with the chevron motif. Following Egyptian and Mesopotamian examples, the Phoenicians utilized (probably only in small constructions) slender small columns of wood or metal with fanciful capitals, perhaps of the volute type.

In the architecture of the Anatolian peninsula, as in Phrygia, columns show frequent influences of classical architecture, with original interpretations in the proportions and in the shape of the capitals. A tomb at Ayazim has a column with a kalathos capital, with vertical grooves at the top of the shaft, and a termination consisting of three thin parallel incisions. This is connected with the entablature by a slightly projecting abacus.

The column had great importance in the architecture of Achaemenid Persia; it consisted originally of a wooden shaft on a stone base and it imitated models created previously in the Sumerian culture (the use of wooden columns persisted in that region up to the 9th–10th cent. of our era). The Achaemenid column, with its base, capital, and entablature, made up a formally unitary whole with a tendency to constant proportional ratios in the various parts and in the intercolumniation (very wide in archaic examples and later narrower), thus giving rise to something which approached the concept of an architectural order.

A constant characteristic of the Achaemenid column is its slenderness; for instance, in the so-called "Palace of the 36 columns" at Persepolis and in the façade of the Tomb of Darius I at Naqsh-I Rustam, the height of the column, including base and capital, is 12 times the diameter of the shaft.

The shafts, slightly tapering, almost always display rather shallow but numerous flutes (32 at Isthar). The base, always present in Achaemenid columns, shows a great variety of shapes from one building to another; there are simple black marble disks supporting white limestone shafts (Palace of Cyrus at Pasargadae); there are low quadrangular plinths on which are superimposed large tori with horizontal fluting (portico at Pasargadae); in the Tomb of Darius I and in the central colonnade of the Palace of Xerxes, there are square plinths with smooth tori superimposed. But the most typically Persian base, which appears at Persepolis and at Susa, is bell-shaped and has a vertical ornamental plant motif. A smooth torus is superimposed on the bell and is connected to the shaft by astragals and listels forming a complex molding (PL. 231; VII, FIG. 274).

A peculiarity of the Achaemenid column is that the capital is in fact an impost block, usually composed of a sculptured representation of the foreparts of two animals, supporting the architrave and the cornice. The animals of the capital, usually bulls (but sometimes griffins, human-faced bulls, or unicorns) are set with the legs and the body parallel to the architrave forming in elevation a right angle with respect to the shaft of the column on which they are directly superimposed without any intermediate elements. Such is the case, for instance, in the previously mentioned tomb at Naqsh-I Rustam and in the east portico of the Palace of Xerxes at Persepolis (VIII, FIG. 274). But in other cases, between the shaft proper and the capital some characteristic architectural members are introduced: for instance, in the apadana at Persepolis and in the Palace of Artaxerxes at Susa there are successively superimposed on the shaft a ring of drooping sepals, a sort of palm-leaf capital with a papyrus flower at the center of each element (corolla capital), at each side two pairs of vertical volute scrolls set one within the other, and, finally, the capital proper with bull figures. This type is known as the "Persian composite" capital. The Persians generally avoided the problem of the placing of the capital at the corner of a building, and preferred to conclude the porticoes with solid walls (antae) or other corner elements in order to have at the corner a wall or a pilaster on which to rest the entablature. Only in the hypostyle hall of the Palace of Xerxes does the corner seem to have been occupied by a column (according to the reconstruction by G. Perrot and C. Chipiez, *Histoire de l'art dans l'antiquité*, Paris, 1882-1914).

Although various types of pillars used in the classical world are dealt with separately in this article in the section on the orders of architecture (see below), mention should be made here of a type of capital which was used in the Greek world in a limited cultural area and at an archaic period without ever being set within the rules of a true architectural order. It is the Aeolic capital, named after the region where it was developed — Asiatic Aeolia (it is also, rather improperly, called "proto-Ionic"). The most characteristic examples are those from Neandria consisting of two large volutes rising above a smooth torus and two rings of leaves; between the volutes is an open palmette (PL. 230). Similar examples were used both in Anatolia and in the Aegean islands (VII, PL. 36). The Aeolic capital seems to have been used predominantly in interiors or to crown steles or votive columns such as those from the Acropolis of Athens or those of the Clazomenian sarcophagi (ca. 500 B.C.). It is possible that the leaf element connecting the shaft with the volute of the Aeolic capital represents by itself another type of capital (known as the leaf capital), which appears to be associated with shapes common in Achaemenid Persia. It was, however, primarily in the Etruscan sphere that the Aeolic capital was given a particular and very free interpretation, with double superimposed volutes, as can be seen in the Tomb of the Capitals at Cerveteri (PL. 230). Between the 4th and the

Vertical elements: pedestals, columns, and capitals. (1-5) Typical elements, schematized in elevation and plan: (1) pier; (2) column; (3) pilaster; (4) Greek Atlamon; (5) figural pilaster (late Renaissance). (6) Plans of piers, pilasters, and of cruciform piers in reinforced concrete. (7-10) Plans of columns: (7) Doric; (8) Ionic with view of capital; (9) Ionic corner; (10) half-column. (11-17) Capitals: (11) Aeolic (Neandria, 6th cent. B.C.); (12) Doric (Selinunte, Temple G; 6th cent. B.C.); (13) Mairya (Pāṭaliputra, India); (14) Ionic, with base (Priene, Temple of Athena; 4th cent. B.C.); (15) Corinthian (Rome, Temple of Castor and Pollux; 1st cent.); (16) composite (Pompeii, 1st cent. B.C.); (17) Renaissance (Venice, Palazzo Grimani, 15th-16th cent.). (18-20) Classical orders, elevations: (18) Doric; (19) Ionic; (20) Corinthian. (21-23) Types of polygonal piers used in Indian architecture, elevations and plans: (21) Buddhist; (22) Hindu; (23) Moslem.

2d century B.C. the volute type was often combined with naturalistic interpretations, giving rise to several variants in the number, position, and character of the volutes. A highly esthetic interpretation of the type with only two facing volutes was given, in the 3d century B.C., to the polychrome capitals of the Tomb of the Reliefs at Cerveteri (VIII, PL. 95), where the volutes springing vertically from the necking are repeated on the four faces of the element.

In late Roman architecture, in Early Christian architecture, and in the first stage of Byzantine architecture, the use of supports in the shape of pillars and, much more frequently, of columns persisted. The supports generally consisted of the same basic elements of the similar classical supports, but the connection between such elements was carried out in ways which had by then already fundamentally departed from that of the traditional order and tended rather to achieve effects of a pictorial-chromatic nature typical of all the art of that period. This also occurred in the frequent cases in which elements taken from ancient monuments were utilized again; only rarely were such elements uniform, as in S. Sabina in Rome; much more often, the elements used were of various origins, of different sizes, aligned on bases of different heights.

In Byzantine architecture and in the regions which were most sensitive to its influence, conspicuous modifications occurred in capitals, which were most generally supported by smooth columns. The change of fundamental importance consisted in the gradual replacement of the abacus with concave sides by an abacus with straight sides, better suited to bear the weight of the arch (by then used almost everywhere instead of the architrave), and in the splitting of the capital into two superimposed areas. This type of capital, known as the "impost capital," resulted from the combination of a capital, usually Corinthian but sometimes Ionic, with a very wide upper part decorated in the course of the 5th century with protomas or whole animal figures (prototypes of this kind of capital are found, though rarely, in late antiquity, as at Ephesus). In some cases the first area has the shape and the structure of a basket (basket capital) or it can be decorated with vine or acanthus scrolls (capitals from Salona, Belgrade Mus.). In the 6th century the upper part of the capital acquired the characteristic shape of an inverted truncated pyramid (pulvin or dosseret), usually smooth or decorated with a simple cross or monograms (e.g., in Hagia Sofia at Istanbul). Also in the 6th century, the capital sometimes appeared as an inverted truncated pyramid surmounted by a smooth or decorated abacus. From the point of view of style, the shape tended gradually to become geometric and the decoration to spread profusely on the surface. This evolution can be followed very clearly from the capitals of the 5th century with acanthus leaves, in which, from a chiaroscuro achieved by drilling holes and by emphasizing the leaf shapes (as in the so-called "wind-blown" capitals with folded acanthus leaves in Ravenna, in S. Apollinare in Classe), the trend was toward an increasingly evident stylization with a preference for "acanthus spinosus" (that is, with pointed leaves) covering the faces of the capital with a flat openwork pattern (e.g., 6th-cent. capital, Ravenna, Mus. Nazionale; capitals in Hagia Sofia and SS. Sergius and Bacchus in Istanbul; II, PLS. 426, 429).

Much more limited use was made in the Byzantine period of pillars, pilaster strips, and half columns; the first were sometimes monolithic on a square plan, but in most cases took the shape of a simple masonry and structure element. In Syria and in Armenia, especially after the 6th–7th centuries, rudimentary clustered pillars were elaborated. The shapes of the Byzantine capitals found a particular interpretation in these same regions, where simpler types also appeared, cylinder- or bulb-shaped (and sometimes also with superimposed bulbous elements), often decorated with carvings which were to spread in the medieval Slavic world and in early Islamic architecture.

Through the Carolingian, Ottonian, and Romanesque periods, columns were still in frequent use; they often had a perfectly cylindrical shaft, that is, without tapering or entasis, although such devices persisted in some cases, especially in Italy, Provence, and Auvergne. The shaft, monolithic or composed of several drums, was generally smooth, but some examples

are available of shafts with plain or cabled fluting (mostly in Provence, as in St-Quinin at Vaison; V, PL. 375), shafts with cabling (S. Cristina de Lena, in Spain, 9th cent.) or with decorations, whether geometric designs or figures, carved on the surface of the cylinder. In the Romanesque period, large shafts composed of superimposed drums sometimes displayed fluting or a typical chevron decoration, as for instance in Durham Cathedral (VI, PL. 425) and in St. Peter's at Northampton.

In various regions more elaborate forms, often displaying great imagination, were created for the small columns of cloisters, pulpits, baldaquins, and external loggias. These forms included coupled columns (in France, at Moissac and St-Trophime in Arles; in Spain, in the monastery of S. Domingo de Silos), columns decorated with geometric motifs (Monreale, Palermo), columns with a twisted shaft (loggia of Lucca Cathedral) or with a knotted shaft (cloister of S. Sofia at Benevento), and columns decorated with mosaics (as in the Cosmatesque cloisters).

In addition to columns, isolated pillars or piers were frequently used after the early Middle Ages; these were for the most part quadrangular in plan, sometimes considered as a portion of wall or as mere unelaborated structural elements, therefore devoid of base and capital or provided only with the rudiments of such members. In the long period of architectural experimentation in Europe from the 7th to the 10th century, a type of composite pillar was gradually worked out on the basis of Roman and Eastern models: this consisted of a central nucleus and of various elements combined and incorporated into a whole with a complex perimeter (clustered pier). The shape and the general arrangement of the various structural members of the clustered pier are related to the superincumbent arched structures which it supports. The clustered pier is normally composed of a central nucleus, against which rest half columns and pilaster strips. It almost always retains the elements typical of the column — a base and a capital.

In its general outline and in the majority of cases, the base acquires the typical shape of the "Attic" base, composed of two tori separated by a trochylus or a scotia: the whole rests on a plinth, often placed in turn on a pedestal. Sometimes this typical form, never totally discarded, was temporarily replaced (especially in the 8th, 9th, and 10th centuries) by a simple element of transition — a truncated pyramid with beveled corners — intended to connect the cylinder of the shaft with the quadrangular socle. Thus the shapes of the connection used for the bases are not unlike those utilized in the capital to solve the same structural problem. Especially from the 11th century on, perhaps on the basis of late Roman examples, the angles of the square plinth not occupied by the circular base are filled by tongues (or claws or griffes) set diagonally and often decorated with carved plant motifs. The plinth, almost always a parallelepiped on a square plan, is often superimposed on a pedestal in the shape of a truncated pyramid.

The capital is no longer in proportion to the height of the column as it was in classical times; it can be monolithic or, when it is part of a polystyle pillar, obtained from several stone blocks. Medieval capitals were extremely varied in shape, but the abacus was much more important than in the preceding periods and was often shaped in relation to the vault above it. The capitals can be grouped into a number of types, subtypes, and variants, some derived from the free imitation, utilization, and reelaboration of classical models, particularly the Corinthian and the Roman composite (revivals of the latter are to be found, for instance, in a capital from Fulda and in the capital of the lower order of the gateway of the Abbey of Lorsch). Similar types survived, at least until the 12th century, in Provence, in Tuscany (S. Miniato and SS Apostoli in Florence, Pisa Cathedral, and others), and in Lazio.

The structural problem of the connection between the circular shaft of the column and the square abacus inspired many different schemes from the 9th century on. For example, capitals formed by the section of a sphere with four vertical and one horizontal plane (cubical, or cushion, capital) were created. Characteristic examples of this type, which was to spread especially during and after the Ottonian period, to the Rhenish area, to Lombardy and Emilia, to France (e.g., in Champagne d to England (in Norman-English Romanesque architecture) e those in St. Michael in Hildesheim, in the crypt of Speyer athedral, and in S. Abbondio in Como. Another type of pital was based on a truncated pyramid with beveled corners s was earlier used in the 9th century in S. María de Naranco). ariants of the type, in which the geometric shape was modified approach a basket shape or that of an inverted truncated ne, often with blunt or rounded-off corners, are to be found Germany (in Augsburg, in the cathedrals of Quedlinburg d Mainz, in St. Godehard in Hildesheim); in France (at armoutier and widely in Auvergne, Burgundy, and Cham-gne); and in England (Peterborough, Durham). This last type as sometimes covered with carved stylized decoration or plant otifs (leaves, palmettes), drawn from the classical or Byzantine pertory, or they introduced decorative motifs of braids, ribbon terlacing, and imaginary animals of Eastern inspiration.

Many other capitals, difficult to classify precisely, are dec-ated with human or animal figures, and are mainly sculptural xpressions (frequently the case in Italy, for instance in Pavia, S. Michele; in Tuscany, especially in the region of Arezzo, the parish churches of Romena, Gropina, Stia, and Arezzo; Apulia, in S. Nicola in Bari; and in Sicily, in Monreale). here are in France striking examples at Vézelay and in the oister of St-Trophime in Arles. Another type of capital, used rticularly in the small columns of the two-light windows of ell towers or in the arcades of cloisters, is that of decidedly ctangular plan and with side-corbels, called a bracket capital loister of S. Sofia at Benevento). Quite frequent also were e corruptions of the various types which utilized formal hemes and decorative motifs of several origins, as in the capi-ls of the crypt of Jouarre (III, PL. 388), those of the church Saint-Aignan-sur-Cher, of the cloister of St-Trophime in rles (I, PL. 385), of Durham Cathedral (VI, PL. 425), of the rium of S. Ambrogio in Milan, of S. Pantaleon in Cologne, d of Würzburg Cathedral. In general, in 10th–11th-century ork it is possible to perceive an attempt to bring into relief e formal structure of the capital by favoring massive, rough, d bare shapes; in the 12th–13th-century work the general end seemed to be a return to sculptural motifs.

The abacus acquired a very sturdy and massive shape, con-sting generally of an inverted truncated pyramid, and normally ojected quite strongly below the springer of the arch. Par-cularly in the Carolingian and Ottonian periods it is possible perceive a certain reference to classical models: for instance, ere is, as early as the Palatine Chapel at Aachen, a very tall pe of abacus, consisting of a simple square parallelepiped rming a cube crowned by a cornice (III, PL. 52); such is so the case in the Abbey of Corvey, where the abacus is rmed by a sort of fragment of classical type of architrave rmounted by a cornice with dentils and small modillions, d in St. Michael in Hildesheim. Similar solutions are to found in Tuscany, particularly in Florence. In the Ottonian d Romanesque periods, however, the abacus was normally of ore limited height and resulted from the free combination of rved and flat moldings, more or less correctly reproduced om Roman and Eastern examples, and was contained within scheme in the shape of an inverted truncated pyramid, as in . Michael in Hildesheim and in the churches of Tournus, ssen, Quedlinburg, and Maulbronn. A trend already begun the 10th and 11th centuries, for instance at Auxerre, and ther marked in the 12th century, tends to do away with the stinction between the bell of the capital and the abacus and hieves a unitary whole, as in St. Godehard in Hildesheim, the Abbey of Maria Laach, in Speyer, in Worms, in Naum-rg, and in Würzburg.

The supporting element acquired more individualized charac-ristics in the Gothic period; in fact, by developing the Roman-que tendency to articulate the structure in depth, it was ansformed in the Île-de-France into a true cluster of elements, ch placed to support the ribs of the superincumbent structures ransverse arches of the nave, or doubleaux, diagonal arches, ofing arches, relieving arches above windows). The decision carry down to the ground the ribs (often of circular section) the superincumbent structures was made initially only for

the supports set against the face of a wall (engaged compound piers, as in the side aisles of Notre-Dame in Paris); while the independent ones used to subdivide the aisles have, at least until the beginning of the 13th century (choir of St-Denis, Notre-Dame, cathedrals of Noyon and Laon; VI, PL. 295), the shape of a cylindrical pillar (without tapering or entasis) with a base and a pedestal, and are topped by a capital concluded by an abacus, on which are interrupted the ribs, shaped like slender columns, proceeding from the vault. But already in the pillars of the portico of Notre-Dame (of a slightly later date than the nave) the four principal ribs, corresponding to the transverse arches, reach down to the ground addorsed to the cylindrical shaft; and during the first quarter of the 13th cen-tury this solution was adopted for the pillars of the cathedrals of Amiens, Reims, and Soissons (VI, PLS. 292, 300). In Bourges, perhaps for the first time, the ribs corresponding to all the structures were extended on the shaft of the pillar (VI, PL. 297), which was articulated (as in the nave of St-Denis) into a cluster of slim columns (fuseaux) until in some cases they completely hide the original cylindrical nucleus, which, however, through-out the 13th century, generally remains visible in the back-ground. But quite soon, every single column was articulated, in turn, in relation to the articulation of the profile of the corresponding structure. Thus, for example, at St-Urbain in Troyes three torus-shaped elements, grouped into a trefoil, constitute the extension of similar ribs. This solution became established and spread throughout the 14th century until it resulted in pillars of extremely complicated plan, in which the elements became much more slender and tended to assimilate their profiles completely with that of the superincumbent mem-bers. In the 15th and 16th centuries capitals — and any other interruption — were sometimes eliminated, and the support could display a shaft composed of ribs which extend those of the vault, or a smooth shaft, mostly circular, which interrupts the ribs above it.

Gothic bases and capitals also acquired various shapes ac-cording to the different periods. The base of the pier, which was square in plan in the earliest examples, was often modified by the rounding off of the corners for the purpose of making the element less cumbersome (choir in Chartres), or by the removal of the whole corner along a vertical plane (choir of Notre-Dame in Paris). In other cases, as in Chartres and Reims, when the pillars of the central nave are flanked by slim columns, each of them has its own base, while the whole is placed above an octagonal platform. When the columns are very numerous the bases are retained, but the general platform is usually lacking. The passage between pedestal and plinth of the base is carried out in most cases by the insertion of a curved molding. The circular base of the column rests on a quadran-gular plinth, and the triangular areas left free by the base are still connected to the latter by means of carved tongues. Toward the end of the first half of the 13th century the triangular spaces left on the plinth were sometimes eliminated by causing the base to project beyond the sides of the plinth, which eventually suggested the insertion of small corbels as supports for the overhanging portions of the base. Another solution consisted simply of replacing the square plinth by a polygonal plinth. After the 13th century, base and plinth followed the outline of the ribs or columns set against the shaft and were connected to the socle by means of complex intersections of elements (e.g., in the choir of St-Nazaire at Carcassonne). In the late Gothic period, in an attempt to abolish any horizontal line which might interrupt the prevailing vertical movement of the whole, the bases of the attached shafts of the clustered pier were set at different levels and staggered: for instance, the base of the central column could be placed directly above the pedestal, the bases of the principal rib shafts a little higher, and the bases of the secondary shafts could be inserted at a third level; each base rested on an independent pedestal which in turn intersected and interpenetrated the other elements belonging to the other members.

In the 15th and 16th centuries, the support took the shape of a large cylindrical pillar and the pedestal, the plinth, and the base, despite the tendency to blend the various elements nto a single whole, almost always acquired greater simplicity of shape. Contemporaneously, from the 12th to the 14th century, the profile of the column base was gradually modified. In fact, in the 12th century and at the beginning of the 13th, the base retained in substance (although distorted) the classical profile of the "Attic" base; but starting with the 13th century there can be perceived a progressive trend to emphasize the sculptural effects, by interposing between the two tori a scotia of lesser height but of greater depth. The two tori were gradually placed closer to each other from the end of the 13th century and through the 14th; the scotia was replaced by a thin incision, until it was completely eliminated in the 15th century, and the two tori were set directly one on top of the other. The outlines of the single moldings, according to place and circumstance, acquired a rounded profile (formed by complex curves) or, more often, a highly angular one.

The Gothic capital (PL. 234) generally consisted of three basic parts: the terminal necking of the shaft (usually formed by a torus-shaped molding), the leaf bell, and the abacus. As in the Romanesque equivalent, the height of the Gothic capital is not in direct proportion to the height of the support, so much so that in some buildings similar pillars are topped by capitals of different size. Moreover, with the exception of cases like that of Soissons Cathedral, all the capitals have different shapes. The profile of the bell, or chalice (*corbeille*), of the Gothic capital is curved, often quite slender, widens toward the top, and is enveloped by a sculptural decoration consisting almost exclusively of foliage arranged in rows and often treated with a lively naturalistic feeling. In the 12th century, leaves with ragged outlines were discarded in favor of shapes with more even outlines. In the 13th century the lines acquired greater slenderness, the shapes became more slim and crescent-shaped and sometimes were enriched with a simple and austere decoration of fine nervation and ragged edges terminating in a sort of bud or curl (crocket; Abbey of Fossanova, PL. 234). These leaves spread over the whole surface of the basket, curved and folded under the four corners of the abacus. Toward the middle and at the end of the 13th century the outline became more ragged and the decorations tended to overcome their traditional limits and invade the abacus to an increasing extent; at the same time a more marked realism was displayed in the sculptural interpretation of the plant elements. The general character became more decorative and less monumental, as, from 1240, in the additional bays of the central nave of Reims Cathedral. The 14th- and 15th-century trend was toward a greater sobriety in the use of carved ornamentation, which soon took the shape of thistles or of curled leaves with ragged edges, and was inserted with great freedom on the nucleus of the bare bell, which appears as the extension — beyond the necking — of the cylindrical shaft of the columns of the clustered pillar. From about 1250, when the column or shafts attached to the pier began to be considered as actual extensions of the ribs above, the abacus was judged a useless element and the capital was eventually reduced to the necking which marked its lower margin, and to a tuft or cluster of plants in place of the bell, the latter having been replaced by the ribs themselves. Sometimes, in the 14th century, even the cluster of leaves was discarded and only the necking was left. From the end of the 15th century the necking also disappeared and the ribs of the superincumbent vaults, after reaching a node where they met and interpenetrated geometrically, proceeded vertically to form a pillar, as in St-Ouen in Rouen (15th cent.), or they came to an end by being inserted into a small cylindrical column, without any element of interruption to mark the point where the rib ends and the pillar begins. These last solutions were frequent until the 16th century in France (Colmar), in Germany (Esslingen), and in Spain (Segovia). In Great Britain, sometimes, as in the cathedrals of York and Gloucester, the capital remained at the starting point of the curves of the ribs and often, especially in the Perpendicular style, its height was reduced (as at Wolborough, Devon).

At the end of the Gothic period the leafed bell element disappeared completely and the whole of the capital, which was quite squat, was made up of a series of curved moldings;

in other cases, still later, when the decorative repertory ha already come to include Renaissance elements and the sha had become round or octagonal, the capital was enriched wit heraldic devices or classically inspired motifs (garlands, volute grotesques, etc.), as is often the case in the Loire area (Chap of St-Hubert, Amboise, 15th cent.), in Normandy, in Burgund in Germany, and in the Flemish countries.

Throughout the 12th century the abacus of the Gothi capital was square in plan, as it was in the Romanesque perioc but quite often, as in Notre-Dame in Laon, and frequently i the 13th century, the corners were more markedly blunted But when, in the 13th century, the moldings forming the rib above the abacus were inscribed within a rectangular, trapezoida or triangular perimeter, the abacus lost its square shape i favor of the polygon or triangle, which adhered more close to the outlines of the ribs it supported. In Normandy, whe the square shape became outdated, an abacus on a circular pla was frequently adopted. Such a shape was often utilized i England in the Early English period, as in the nave of Lincol Cathedral and in the portico of Ely Cathedral, and it was als introduced in the Scandinavian countries.

Other variants are the lobed and mixtilinear shapes. Th height of the Gothic abacus is remarkably variable, even thoug a trend can be perceived, with the passing of time, toward gradual loss of importance of this element, until its total disap pearance during the 14th century. The edge of the abacu was profiled by curved moldings separated at times by listels o limited height. Sometimes a decorative motif — usually leave (north portico of Chartres Cathedral) or dentils (S. Maria d Fiore in Florence) — was inserted between the moldings. I Italy, the square abacus, almost always sturdier in appearanc and with simpler moldings (as in S. Maria Novella in Florence survived until the 15th century, when it was replaced by th classical types.

For the basic types of the supports in the architecture the Renaissance, see below, *The orders*.

In the neoclassic period, a more accurate and broade knowledge of ancient models led to a more faithful imitation them, but also to the tendency toward an eclectic combinatio of various stylistic elements, which was to persist through th 19th century, without ever achieving a real integration betwee the forms imitated and the architectural works produced. was rather the utilization of new building materials, such cast iron, that since the beginning of the 19th century favore the working out of new types of supports which, though sti formally characterized by the eclectic reference to tradition types, display a peculiar slenderness. The taste for supports the shape of slim columns is also evident, from the end of th 18th century, in the adoption in interior decoration of archite tural solutions drawn from the so-called "styles" of Roma painting (decoration of some interiors in the palace of Tsarsk Selo, 1781, carried out for Catherine II by the architect Chameron, perhaps after designs by Clérisseau, and the mar arrangements created by C. Percier and L. Fontaine in th first years of the 19th century).

Cast iron and ingot iron were well suited to the making light and slender supports, and in England, between 1818 an 1821, John Nash adopted very slim small columns in cast iro with naturalistic capitals of vaguely Eastern inspiration in th Royal Pavilion in Brighton. The use of some styles of th past in supports generally characterizes the 19th century. a few works, such as J. Paxton's Crystal Palace in London (185 H. Labrouste's Bibliothèque Ste-Geneviève (1843–61), and th reading room of the Bibliothèque Nationale in Paris (1862–68 an honest artistic intent is perceptible in the utilization of su porting elements whose shape is based on the exploitation the esthetic possibilities implicit in the new material.

Attempts at renewal took place between the end of th 19th century and the early 20th; personal and refined transl tions of eclectically selected motifs into present-day terms we adopted by V. Horta (e.g., in the stair columns of the hou in Rue de Turin, Brussels) and later by the masters of A Nouveau, by Berlage (Stock Exchange in Amsterdam, 1898 1903), by L. Sullivan in his American works, by Otto Wagne nd more resolutely by Adolf Loos, J. Hoffmann, P. Behrens, nd by the French pioneers of reinforced concrete, A. Perret nd T. Garnier. The pillar and, above all, the column of the raditional type were still used, at least until about 1920, in nany attempts at renovating the shapes of the past and dapting them to the new taste by means of a synthesis of the lements and the simplification of decoration (which, however, d to architectural hybrids of often very doubtful effect). Only few Scandinavian works, often of modest dimensions and omantic tone, occasionally achieved a certain validity, as for xample the supports of H. and K. Sirén's "Chapel in the Vood" (1918–20) in Otaniemi, Finland, and the columns of he Forest Crematorium in Stockholm (1935–40) by E. G. Asplund. A much more certain taste is displayed by the attempts of Perret to renew the traditional styles through the se of columns, often with inverted tapering, whose shapes and etails (bases, capitals) were consequent upon the new structural rinciples laid down by reinforced concrete. Such principles, ke those peculiar to metal constructions, were subsequently to revail to a considerable extent in determining the shape of the upports which in present-day architecture are characterized in ost cases by their functional and structural value.

                    Arnaldo BRUSCHI

In the earliest Islamic architecture supports often reproduced lassical shapes and their Byzantine derivations; in some cases s in the original Aqsa Mosque in Jerusalem and in the Great Iosque in Damascus) original Roman columns were used which ad Ionic and Corinthian capitals. The influence of the clas-cal shapes is evident also in the columns with a smooth and lightly tapered shaft on bases of the "Attic" type and with aguely Corinthian capitals in the interior of the Dome of the ock in Jerusalem (7th cent.), of the Mosque of 'Amr in Cairo, f the Great Mosque of Kairouan (VIII, PL. 146), and of the ireat Mosque of Córdoba (VIII, PL. 148; X, PL. 162), where ere are many pulvins similar to those which had by then ecome common in the Byzantine cultural area. Corinthian nodels also inspired the capitals of the Mosque of Sammara nd of that of Ibn-Ṭūlūn at Fostat, where acanthus leaves are eplaced by vine scrolls and volutes by trilobate plant motifs. Composite capitals were the inspiration in the Palace of the aliphs at Medina az-Zahra (10th cent.; X, PL. 163), where aturalistic motifs, treated to achieve an accentuated styliza-on by means of deep drillings, are reduced to arabesques ith minimal luministic — and no longer plastic — sculptural fects.

Islamic architecture, though it inherited and reinterpreted lassical shapes also in the entablature, did not accept the rinciples of the systematic rules peculiar to the orders of rchitecture. In fact, it utilized those forms with considerable reedom, adopting original compositional solutions, often alter-ating pillars and columns, and conceiving new and simplified apital shapes, as in the entrance portico of Mshattā. Structural eculiarities were frequent, for example, the T-shaped pillars : Samarra and the cruciform piers in the cistern arcades at .amla, the piers with engaged columns which are in turn sus-ained by columns, as in Córdoba, or with encased columns, s in Samarra. Many of these peculiarities were transmitted to nedieval European architecture. It should be borne in mind nat often the columns were not made of marble, but rather f plastered bricks painted to imitate marble.

In the architecture of ancient India such a great variety of upport shapes appear that it would be difficult to define them rpologically. Even in examining only a few examples, it be-omes clear that the types range from the very simple square r octagonal pillars without bases or capitals of some rock nctuaries of the 1st century B.C. to the types having a tall quare base and a bracket capital which appears to be a schematic duction of the Corinthian capital (such as those reproduced a 2d-cent. relief from Amarāvati; VII, PL. 445), or those owing more evident relation to Hellenistic shapes in the base f the "Attic" type on a square plinth and the capital with anthus leaves and volutes, between which is inserted the

figure of a god (such as that reproduced in a 2d-cent. relief from the monastery of Loriyan Tangai; VII, PL. 449).

The memorial columns which appeared in Buddhist India in the Maurya period, and particularly during the reign of Aśoka (3d cent. B.C.), consisted of a tall, smooth, and slightly tapered shaft, sometimes without a base or resting on a simple square plinth, with a reeded or cabled bell-shaped capital derived from the Achaemenid capitals. This capital is connected by means of a simple concave or convex molding to an abacus (often decorated in relief with animal figures, cart wheels, or other motifs) on which rests a sculptured group (II, PLS. 399, 401). This formal scheme is echoed in the pillars of the chaitya of Beḍsā (1st cent. B.C.; II, PL. 401), where the tapered octagonal shaft rises on a bulb-shaped base, under which is a small quadrangular stepped plinth; the whole is topped by a bell-shaped capital with an abacus surmounted by a sculptured group. Except for the greater height of the plinth under the base, and the absence of tapering in the shaft and reeding in the capital, the pillars of the chaitya of Karli (VII, PL. 451) and of Kanheri (2d cent.) are similar. The capital of Iranian derivation utilized in the pillars of Aśoka appears again, in different interpretations, as in the iron column which Kumā-ragupta I had erected (ca. A.D. 415) near Mathura (now in Delhi) and later in Temple 17 at Sanchi (VII, PL. 140), where the short octagonal shaft rests on a tall square base, and the abacus acquires the shape of a basket full of trailing leaves.

More fanciful shapes are to be noted between the 5th and the 6th century in other types of pillars, such as those at Ajanta. There the shaft tends to be cylindrical and not tapered, but it is subdivided into several superimposed sections, with flutes or spiral grooves, alternated with bands of varying height bear-ing carved plant motifs (PL. 231; VII, PLS. 140, 141, 454, 455). The base can consist of some polygonal convex moldings (as in the façade of Cave 19) or of a tall square plinth, which becomes octagonal at a certain point and bears sculptural orna-mentation (interiors of caves 1 and 19). At the top, the shaft narrows and acquires, more or less, the appearance of a slightly flattened semispherical cap on which is a carved necking and a capital in the shape of a large fluted torus; this is surmounted by an abacus, also ornamented, and by a capital, more or less bracketed, with figures in relief.

The pillars of Ajanta are an example of the great inventive-ness of the Indian builders, which led them to renew, constantly and for each building, the shape of the supports.

Another, almost extreme, case of the variety of these archi-tectural elements in Indian art can be noted in the pillars of a 12th-century Jainist religious building (basti) at Halebid (VII, PL. 485); there the base consists of a tall rectangular dado resting on a square, molded plinth ornamented on all four faces with small edicules carved with figures of gods, and the shaft is made up of a dense succession of moldings in strong relief, of short sections with a marked entasis, and of bands decorated with plant motifs in relief. This is obviously an isolated case, of which the equivalent is not to be found in any other shape of support (see JAINISM).

Many other pillars, generally rectangular or octagonal, have the shaft completely covered with carved decorations in more or less wide bands, which divide into various sections; although the structural concept of base, shaft, and capital is retained, it is completely hidden by the ornamentation itself (interior of the Temple of Sūrya at Modhera, 11th cent.; VII, PL. 483). Later the elements composing the support were more distinctly marked, although they were still richly decorated. At Madura (Madras), the Temple of Mīnākṣī (17th cent.; VII, PL. 493) has interior pillars composed of figures sculptured almost in the round; and at Rameshwaram, also in Madras (18th cent.; VII, PL. 487), the pillars in the temple corridor rest on a high molded socle and have a very tall base, a rather short and con-spicuous rectangular shaft, and modillions carved with volutes and plant and animal motifs (PL. 231) which reduce to a con-siderable extent the width of the ceiling beams.

In the architecture of the Far East, especially in China, supports in the shape of pillars or columns generally have no particular formal emphasis and retain in practice the simple structural appearance of the primitive wooden constructions of the Shang-Yin period, when a simple smooth shaft was set on a circular stone or bronze base, as in the temples of An-yang and Cheng-chou.

Almost exactly similar methods of support were used in Korea and in Japan. In Shintoist architecture, the support was provided by a structural complex of ornamental brackets; in the Edo period the method of connecting the supports with the roofing elements was modified structurally, and preference was given to jointed solutions, that is, without brackets (VIII, PLS. 322–325), as is still done. See JAPANESE ART.

* *

TERMINAL AND SUPERSTRUCTURE ELEMENTS. Architectural solutions for the terminal parts of buildings were generally suggested in the various periods by the structural, technological, and functional problems of the structures (type of roof, protection of the underlying area, disposition of rain water, etc.). These elements, however, acquired a formal definition depending on the degree to which it was desired to integrate them in the architectural work.

In the architecture of the ancient Eastern and the Mediterranean world terminal elements of walls generally appear in the shape of a lesser or greater projection, flat or molded, often drawn from elements typical of structures carried out in other materials. Thus, for instance, a clear reference to wooden structures can be perceived in the typical Egyptian cornices, usually consisting of an architrave, a thin astragal, and a projecting hollow, or gorge, molding (Egyptian gorge) terminating in a vertical band which may vary in height — in other words, a cornice that is in every way similar to those described earlier as being utilized above doors and windows and often decorated with symbolic or merely decorative motifs (see above, *Moldings*).

Another stone interpretation of wooden structural shapes is to be found in the rather unusual crowning of the portico of the Tomb of Amenemhet II at Beni Hasan; it is in the shape of an architrave surmounted with a flat cornice profiled with dentils in its lower part. Another unusual type of crowning is that with semicircular merlons, such as that in the Royal Pavilion of Ramses III at Medinet Habu (IV, PL. 359).

Stepped triangular or trapezoidal merlons, made of bricks, often glazed or painted, normally terminated monumental Mesopotamian constructions.

The crowning cornices of Cretan-Mycenaean buildings, as they are documented by the illustrations in the Museum of Heraklion (IV, FIG. 87), reveal, particularly in the motif of the adjoining disks which can be interpreted as the heads of small beams, the derivation or translation into decorative terms of clearly structural wooden elements. A shape interpretative of wooden structures can also be perceived in the alternate metope and triglyph frieze which appears at Knossos and later at Mycenae and Tiryas, which is considered by some as the predecessor of the Doric frieze.

Other examples of the transposition of wooden structural elements into stone are the cornices with dentils, frequent in Phoenicia and in Cyprus, and especially those of the rock tombs of Lycia, in the Anatolian region, inspired by roofing systems with jointed beams (I, PLS. 533, 534), as for instance in the tombs of Pinara, Kenibachi, Phellos, and, particularly, Antiphellos. Some of these are crowned by a triangular pediment or by a tympanum in the shape of a pointed arch. The frontal with pediment was in use also in Phrygia (as in the so-called "Tomb of Midas") and showed characteristics that suggest points of contact with the Hellenic solutions.

In Persia, the entablature, probably of wood, ran above the capitals with back-to-back animals and consisted normally of an architrave on which rested small beams placed very close together and supporting a boarding, on which was superimposed a wooden or brick parapet, sometimes ornamented and terminated by the crenelations which were customary in the Mesopotamian culture.

Although the types of crowning in use in the classical world will be dealt with below in the section on the orders, mention must be made here of a few solutions of late imperial Roman

architecture which do not, strictly speaking, fall within the structure of the orders. Sometimes, in fact, the crowning an architectural work consisted simply of the upper part, cornice, of the entablature, or of an architrave and cornice Particularly in Diocletian's time, wide use was made of a particular shape of cornice with stone modillions that has no structural links with the other parts of the wall, as for instance the Curia (IX, PL. 33) and in the Baths of Diocletian in Rom This type of crowning cornice was to be used, in more or less distorted versions, in some Early Christian, Byzantine, and medieval architectural works such as the Baptistery of St-Jea in Poitiers, the Palatine Chapel in Aachen, the Torhalle Lorsch, and frequently in the architecture of Rome and Laz until the Romanesque period. At that point, as had alread happened in some Byzantine constructions (Mausoleum of Gal Placidia, Ravenna), such a shape tended to be replaced by fre combinations of stone or, more often, brick elements, givin rise to various types of medieval cornices, among them th "saw-toothed" cornice, so called because of the diagonal a rangement of the elements placed to form progressively mo marked projections.

In the Roman period, and previously in city gates and the fortified town walls, crenelation had been widespread; th merlons were mostly rectangular, but sometimes were of tria gular shape. The rectangular shape was usually applied to th battlemented walls of medieval fortifications and sometimes a few palaces or fortified churches, particularly in Italy and France; this type of crenelation was later to be differentiate according to the shape of the merlons ("Guelph" type ar "Ghibelline" type).

In Roman architecture — in a few sporadic cases and most in the eastern sphere — a terrace with parapet was superin posed on the usual terminal entablature; in the imperial peric it was more common to superimpose a low story or wall (atti above the principal entablature, as for instance in the forun of Augustus, Nerva, and Trajan and in many memorial arche These provided examples for the introduction of similar el ments in the architecture of the Renaissance, mannerist, ar baroque periods (Porta Pia and Porta Flaminia in Rome; I PL. 542).

In the late imperial and in the Early Christian period, th type of terminal element (crowning) consisting of a simp projection of the roof was also often used in monumental arch tecture; such was the case in many churches of the 4th ar 5th centuries, even though the termination of the wall w sometimes underlined by a simple masonry projection or by rudimentary cornice.

During the early Middle Ages, new types of terminal wa elements appeared; these, used particularly in Italy and in th Rhineland, consisted of simple corbel tables supported by a cading, as had already been done at an earlier date in the e terior of the Baptistery of the Orthodox in Ravenna (5th cent Such a solution should very probably be considered as th simplification and development of the use of arcades resting columns supported by corbels. The use of cornices support by arcadings and resting on simple stone corbels persisted to the late Middle Ages, particularly in northern Italy; it w adopted, in addition to horizontal cornices (e.g., along the si of the building), also in façades with gables, the small arch being arranged along the axis perpendicular to the slant distorted into small asymmetrical arches so as to keep th springers and the supporting corbels along vertical axes (as S. Michele in Pavia). Characteristic interpretations of th scheme, which was common to almost all the European Roma esque schools, are noted in the dimension and rhythm of t small arcades, in the shape of the corbels (sometimes in t form of a figure), and in the treatment of the voussoirs.

Another type of medieval terminal element, in use from t Carolingian period until the 12th century, consisted of a co nice, set directly on the wall, on which rested the first cour of tiles, without the interposition of a gutter to throw off ra water. The lip of the cornice was generally — and particula in French Romanesque architecture — ornamented with simp moldings that varied in appearance according to the differe egions; dentils and small modillions of widely varying shapes — often set within a concave molding — were frequently inserted between these moldings (St-Trophime in Arles). Other types of crowning, quite widespread throughout the Romanesque period, consist of cornices in the shape of a small corbel table, the corbels being of various shapes. Their profiles were occasionally classically oriented, but more frequently, new shapes were introduced, sometimes enriched by figural elements (human or animal heads, as in St-Trophime in Arles and in Notre-Dame-des-Doms in Avignon; strong stylizations of plantlike shapes, as at Vézelay). In Tuscany and in northern Latium the use of this type of cornice persisted until at least the 14th century, with the occasional superimposition of several orders of corbels, giving rise to more complex types, which were still current in the 15th century. Particularly in France, all of these cornices were often crowned by pierced-stone crestings that sometimes followed the slant of the roofs or marked the ridge. During the Romanesque period the projection of the crowning cornice was seldom used to support a valley (or gutter) to collect rain water, but when it was so used (especially in the region of Poitou) the outward lip of the stone gutter rose to form a low wall (sometimes molded) or parapet (occasionally pierced) and was characterized by the presence of gargoyles, as in the Church of Notre-Dame-la-Grande in Poitiers and in the choir of the abbey at Saint-Savin-sur-Gartempe, giving rise to a stylistic mode that was to spread throughout Gothic Europe. The gutterless cornice was retained in more modest constructions, however, as late as the 13th century. In large buildings frequent use was made of a simple band, often molded into a cyma without a dripstone and with modillions that sometimes took the shape of a leaf or other plant element. In the Gothic period, however, the profile of the cornice tended to be schematized; it generally consisted of a lower area with a concave profile ornamented with leaf or curl (crocket) motifs, in relief and more or less projecting, and of an upper molded area comprising a dripstone. Among the many examples of Gothic crowning cornices are that of St-Denis (12th cent.) and those of the cathedrals of Noyon, Paris, Sens, and Amiens. After the 13th century the gargoyles (or spouts), almost always sharply projecting, varied in shape; they were often carved in the shape of imaginary or monstrous beasts, perhaps symbolizing diabolic personifications flying about around the sanctuary. Among the most remarkable are those of St-Denis, Notre-Dame, Chartres, Reims, Amiens, and Dijon, and of the Château de Blois (IX, PL. 317). Gargoyles survived in central and northern Europe and in Spain until the 16th century, sometimes in shapes drawn from the classical decorative repertory, and sometimes retaining the traditional Gothic shapes.

The cornice with gutter and gargoyle was often completed, especially in the late Gothic period, by a stone parapet (or balustrade) pierced with mixtilineal geometrical patterns similar to window tracery, as in the cathedrals of Strasbourg, Troyes, Senlis, and Cologne, and in the Ste-Chapelle in Paris.

A type of crowning used particularly for town walls, towers, city gates, and fortified buildings comprises a strongly projecting parapet — usually crenelated — resting on sturdy corbels of a distinctly vertical profile connected by small arches, resulting in a sort of crowning gallery. Originating in functional requirements in the time of the Crusades and often adopted during the 12th and 13th centuries (Carcassonne, Coucy), crownings of this type found in the 14th and 15th centuries widespread applications that were differentiated by the type of corbel and by the profile of the connecting arches and merlons. Not infrequently (particularly in Italy, in Florence, Siena, and Rome) these crownings were also used in civil and religious architecture (Palazzo Venezia, Rome, XII, PL. 14; S. Maria del Fiore, Florence, X, PL. 295); at a later date they appeared in French castles and in the municipal buildings of Flemish and Germanic countries and survived well into the 16th century, sometimes as fanciful variants of the original defensive function.

In Venice in the 14th and 15th centuries wide use was made of crenelated terminal elements consisting of a row of small triangular or mixtilineal cusps, solid or pierced, as for instance in the Doge's Palace (VI, PL. 340) and in the Ca' d'Oro

(I, PL. 380) and, after the 15th century, in many minor buildings. Similar elements in classical shapes were apparently planned to crown the large upper arch (which, however, was not built) of the Tempio Malatestiano, and Alberti utilized them above the entablature of the small temple of the Holy Sepulcher in the Rucellai chapel in Florence.

In Italy from the 15th century, and later throughout Europe into the 20th century, the most common types of terminal elements of buildings were entablatures or cornices derived from the Roman orders of architecture; but these were by no means the only solutions. In the 15th century, in the Florentine environment, much use was made of the terminal device that had been common in the Middle Ages — that consisting of a marked projection of the roof, of which the small beams rested on corbels (usually wooden) often progressively overhanging in superimposed orders; the modified version of this terminal element was formed by a cornice with classical moldings, on which large wooden corbels composed of small beams rested directly. The corbels were molded, superimposed, and increasingly jutting, until they achieved remarkable projections, as in the Palazzo Pazzi-Quaratesi (restored) and the Palazzo Guadagni in Florence (II, PL. 373; XII, PL. 54) and in the Palazzo Grifoni in San Miniato, as well as in many Tuscan villas, where they persisted until a much later date. A variant of this type is that in which, above a cornice or a classical entablature, the eaves take the shape of a flat, coffered undersurface, as in the loggia of S. Maria delle Grazie in Arezzo (ca. 1490). Another type of 15th-century crowning is that of the Palazzo Spannocchi in Siena, where a corbel table with a molded edge and a flat undersurface rests upon large, tall stone corbels between which decorative medallions are inserted on the wall; this clearly reveals a return to medieval solutions, perhaps modified by that of the trabeated design with corbels in the frieze adopted by Alberti in the Palazzo Rucellai in Florence (I, PL. 55), inspired by the Colosseum.

Michelozzo seems to have been the first to introduce, in the Palazzo Medici, the crowning consisting of a stone "top cornice," strongly projecting and almost always on modillions, that repeats the prescribed shapes of the cornice of a classical entablature from which the frieze and architrave have been discarded, the architrave being sometimes only vaguely outlined on the wall, as in the Palazzo Strozzi, by a large torus. This solution was to become common in the 16th century, generally with less marked projections than in the 15th century, and sometimes with a frieze inserted or with the whole deviating somewhat from the classical models and given personal interpretations, as in Michelangelo's top cornice on the Palazzo Farnese (Rome; XII, PL. 56).

In façades with superimposed architectural orders the problem of adapting the height of the trabeated cornice of the classical type to the height of the entire front, rather than to the height of the last order of the façade, and thus bringing into relief the importance of the terminal entablature with respect to that of the orders below, led to several variants; also it resulted in the adoption of the type of entablature proposed by Alberti and characterized by a frieze on modillions, which was in fact used in the 16th century in the cloister of S. Maria della Pace in Rome (II, PL. 345) and later, with different characteristics, by Sanmicheli in the courtyard of the Palazzo Canossa and in the door of S. Zeno in Verona and in the Palazzo Cornaro in Venice. One of these two variants, conceived by Vignola, has inserted in the frieze large molded brackets, markedly vertical in profile, on which rest the modillions of a classical cornice (as in the top cornice of the Palazzo Farnese, Caprarola). This type was to have many applications and variants in the work of the mannerist and baroque architects (Bernini, Borromini, B. Longhena, F. Fuga). Another solution of the same problem, introduced by Peruzzi in the Farnesina (XI, PL. 120), greatly increased the height of the frieze between the architrave and the cornice to the point at which windows could be pierced into it; reproduced by Sansovino in the Libreria Vecchia di S. Marco in Venice and by Sanmicheli in the Palazzo Roncale in Rovigo, this solution was to be frequently applied in the mannerist and baroque periods. Another solution adopted occasionally in these periods and also by Inigo Jones in the Banqueting House in Whitehall, London (II, PL. 147), emphasizes, by the insertion of friezes or other elements, the area corresponding to the capitals of the uppermost order.

In the 18th century, as a development of the crowning element with a simple cornice (without frieze or architrave), wide use was made, especially in the civil architecture of some Italian regions, of terminal elements consisting of a large, curved, projecting cove in which the gutter was generally inserted.

All these types of terminal elements (only after the middle of the 16th century were most of them equipped in their upper part with channels, or gutters, for the drainage of rain water) can be crowned by a parapet, consisting almost always of small balusters, that is, vertical stone elements with variously molded shafts supporting a cornice and sometimes alternated with sections of wall in the form of a pilaster. The baluster used by Brunelleschi in the Palazzo Pitti (Florence, II, PL. 372) acquired in the 15th and 16th centuries shapes that were often derived from decorative elements of the classical repertory (especially candelabra). Thus, balusters appeared with a shaft swelling above and below a narrow center, or as small columns narrowing at the bottom, like those adopted in the mannerist and baroque periods, when the shafts often were square, octagonal, triangular, or mixtilineal, and the profiles were fancifully altered (for instance, as Borromini used, in the cloister of S. Carlino alle Quattro Fontane, II, PL. 303, balusters narrow at the top and bottom and swollen in the middle). Parapets with balusters were superimposed on terminal entablatures as early as Bramante's Tempietto of S. Pietro in Montorio (ca. 1503; I, PL. 305), but their utilization in this way, to crown façades, was to spread particularly after the middle of the century. The solid wall elements separating the rows of balusters often served as a base for statues or other ornaments. Carlo Maderno and the architects of the 17th and 18th centuries utilized these balustrades in religious architecture, occasionally arranging them along a slanting line above the frontals of the façades, as in the Church of S. Susanna, Rome (II, PL. 137).

Following some Roman examples, the top cornice of buildings can also be surmounted with a solid area, consisting of a more or less high wall (parapet) or of a low story (attic).

The crowning of the façade with a pediment was reserved for religious architecture, even though horizontal top cornices also appear in this type of construction. Such a pediment is mostly in the shape of a triangular tympanum, as was the case in the 15th century in the façades (among others) of S. Maria Novella in Florence (I, PL. 53), of S. Maria del Popolo and of S. Agostino in Rome, and of S. Sebastiano and of S. Andrea in Mantua (I, PLS. 56, 57). In Venice some religious buildings of the late 15th century bore crownings with curved tympanums (S. Maria dei Miracoli, S. Zaccaria, and S. Michele, and the Scuola Grande di S. Marco); the inspirations may have come from Alberti's project for the Tempio Malatestiano to insert a curved tympanum in a façade. Michelangelo used with great freedom triangular, curved, broken, and profiled pediments, often inserting one into the other to form a single pediment. Moreover, following Alberti's example (façade of S. Maria Novella in Florence), connecting parts in the shape of scrolls were inserted to link two parts of the façade of different heights; during the mannerist period and in the 17th century such scrolls acquired varied and fanciful forms — festoons, palm fronds (S. Marcello al Corso in Rome; VIII, PL. 223), and angel wings.

In the French Renaissance the use of tall, steeply pitched roofs led to the insertion above the classically inspired crowning of structures (dormer windows, skylights, mansards) intended to admit light into the rooms under the roof. Such structures were often framed with complex shapes and were often characterized by decorative devices intended to link the structure with the façade below. Sometimes the terminal element was broken and rhythmically articulated by the insertion of triangular and curved pediments (as in the façade of the Louvre by Pierre Lescot) or, above the top cornice, of decorative cresting fancifully carved.

From the middle of the 17th to the end of the 18th century, the crowning structures developed in Italy and France were

the models for all of Europe and for the colonial countries. From the end of the 18th century to the beginning of the 20th the various revivals produced no original solutions. The dependence upon past styles persisted through the first quarter of the 20th century, even though the shapes were sometimes freely interpreted with a view to rationalization or to translation into more modern terms. The solutions adopted by various architects between 1890 and 1920 differ from each other to a considerable extent and are hard to classify into types, even though the intent to simplify and to adhere to functional, structural, technological, and economic factors is evident. After World War I the masters of contemporary architecture — Gropius, Le Corbusier, Mendelsohn, Oud, and Aalto, among others — often adopted horizontal terminal elements in structures in which, after the elimination of any overhang or elaborate projection or crowning, the wall itself forms a terminal element and is protected only by a simple coping of stone or metal (as in the Steiner house in Vienna by Adolf Loos, 1910). Another solution much used between the two world wars originated in such movements as Dutch neoplasticism and drew inspiration from the work of Frank Lloyd Wright; in this solution the terminal element of the building became a simple horizontal slab, more or less projecting in the shape of a cantilever roof, as in the Schroeder house in Utrecht by G. T. Rietveld (1924), in some of W. M. Dudok's works in Hilversum, in the pavilion at the Barcelona Exposition by Mies van der Rohe (1929), and in the Columbus Haus by Mendelsohn in Berlin (1931).

Arnaldo Bruschi

In the Eastern world the terminal parts of buildings are not always characterized by a marked formal definition.

In Islamic architecture, the exterior walls of even monumental buildings often lack a crowning element, as do the lateral walls of the Great Mosque of Kairouan (9th cent.), or simple parapets with gargoyles are used, as in the courtyard of the same mosque (X, PL. 164). In many other cases there is only a concave cornice, of limited size and decorated or not, which is occasionally supported by small brackets or modillions (sides and on the façade of the Great Mosque of Damascus, X, PL. 378; and the so-called "Mosque of the Three Doors" at Kairouan). Quite typical of the Islamic architecture of north Africa is the crenelation, inspired by ancient Eastern examples, with arched merlons (Gate of Baghdad, minarets of Kairouan and of Tlemcen; X, PL. 165) or with triangular stepped merlons (corner tower of the ṣaḥn of the Great Mosque of Damascus). This type of crowning acquired a decidedly decorative character in the ziyāda of the Ibn-Ṭūlūn Mosque (Cairo), where, above a cornice decorated with rosettes, there runs a pierced and crenelated balustrade, of a type which unquestionably greatly influenced the Romanesque and Gothic architecture of Venice. Among these types, the crowning that was to persist longest was that with triangular merlons, which later acquired fanciful crested shapes.

The terminal elements of Indian religious buildings are highly complex, forming at the same time both crowning and roofing (which are completely covered with crowded adjoining moldings and carved bands), and are so different from one building to the next that they cannot be strictly defined. These crownings are a purely ornamental (often figural) conception of the conclusion of the architectural whole, as can be seen in many buildings of the Gupta period (VII, PL. 142) and later over a long period in many monuments, such as the temple of Khajurāho (VII, PL. 472) and of Bhuvaneśśvara in Orissa (11th cent.; VII, PL. 482) and the Temple of Viṣṇu in Madras (17th cent.; VII, PL. 493). Only where the Islamic influence was strongest did terminal elements consisting of molded cornices appear; these were overhanging with parapets (Mausoleum of Sikandar Lōdī in Delhi, 15th cent.; VIII, PL. 16) or, more often, obviously Islamic merlons.

In China and Japan, the connecting element between the supporting structures and the roofing consisted simply of a purely functional complex of superimposed beams and brackets which, nevertheless, achieved a peculiar formal characterization even

:fore the custom was adopted (in China from the time of the
.ng and Liao dynasties; in Japan from the Momoyama period)
decorating such elements with reliefs and paintings. It is in
ese cultural areas that the roof itself becomes a sort of ter-
inal element, clearly decorative in character and often broken
» into various superimposed roofs; sometimes the decorative
nction was emphasized by sculptural and painted ornament.

* *

The orders. Within the sphere of the civilizations of clas-
cal antiquity the fundamental architectural elements can be
.tegorized on the basis of criteria that rule their mutual relations
id make them into an autonomous whole. This whole consti-
tes the order of architecture in which the structural elements of
building, from base to roof, are determined in such a way
at each one of them is inseparable from that whole to which
is bound by specific correspondences. Thus, while in other
iltures it has been possible to examine separately the individual
ements, in the cultures in which the orders of architecture
ere established canons, the same elements (base, column,
ipital, entablature) must necessarily be viewed as a whole.
he order of architecture has been considered ever since classical
itiquity as an organic unity of the various elements that com-
ise it. At the base of the formalization of the various elements
' the order there is the artistic concept or, perhaps more
irrectly, the technique (τέχνη) of the imitation of nature, not
much in the sense of naturalistic mimesis (as existed in other
vilizations of the ancient Eastern and Mediterranean worlds)
i in an organic-structural correspondence to the natural order
' things, so that the architectural order is seen as a symbol-
aage of the universe. In other words, the principle of the order
: architecture is in substance an interpretation of those pro-
irtions, of those ratios of analogy, between the various members
iat are typical of the Greek ideal vision of the cosmos and that
iabled such philosophers as Diodorus to distinguish the har-
.onious proportioning (συμμετρία) of the Greek structural
iethods from the structural composition of the Egyptians.

The theoretical formulation of this principle is found in
itruvius, who, taking up the Greek concept of man as the image
f the macrocosm, states " . . . for without symmetry and pro-
irtion no temple can have a regular plan; that is, it must have
1 exact proportion worked out after the fashion of a finely
iaped human body. . . . Therefore, if Nature has planned
ie human body so that the members correspond in their pro-
irtions to its complete configuration, the ancients seem to have
ad reason in determining that in the execution of their works
ley should observe an exact adjustment of the several members
» the general pattern of the plan" (*De architectura,* ed. Loeb
lass. Library, III, i, 1, 4). In the Renaissance this con-
:pt was revived and elaborated; Michelangelo was to write
i one of his letters (G. Milanesi, *Le lettere di Michelangelo
'uonarroti,* Florence, 1875) that "there is no doubt that the mem-
:rs of architecture derive from the members of man." Thus,
ie order of architecture is the result of a vision of things in pro-
iund relation to the human sphere.

Other civilizations, to be sure, have manifested the concept
f a relationship between the various architectural elements based
n the ideal analogy with the fundamental principles of nat-
ralistic forms (cf. E. Panofsky, *Meaning in the Visual Arts,*
Iew York, 1955); but it is only in the orders of architecture that
iis concept is a rigid requirement for organic unity. A sympto-
iatic confirmation of this is found in the fact that the various
rders, in the interest of the principle of "fitness," were often
iund typologically defined in the architectural whole. Thus,
ir instance, from the 5th century B.C. in Attica, the Doric order
:ems to have been utilized particularly in larger temples and
ie Ionic order in buildings of smaller size. Moreover, the Ion-
: order, at least in western Greece, seems better suited to in-
:riors; indeed, it is found in the interior of buildings with
)oric exteriors (the so-called "Temple of Ceres" at Paestum;
he Temple of Apollo Epikourios at Bassae, anc. Phigalia, III,
IG. 669). Vitruvius himself suggests its use in portico interiors.
'he Corinthian order was preferred for small buildings of
prevalently ornamental nature and for interiors. In the Ren-

aissance, even though in practice there was greater freedom
in the use of the various orders, the treatises prescribed special
modes of utilization: the Tuscan order for structures requiring
an appearance of strength and simplicity, such as town gates
and country houses; the Doric order (which V. Scamozzi called
the "Herculean") for sturdy works and for first levels of buildings;
the Ionic order (which Scamozzi called "matronly") for works
requiring loftiness; the Corinthian (which Scamozzi called "vir-
ginal") reserved for monumental buildings; and finally, the
Composite order could be used interchangeably with the Ionic
and the Corinthian where monumentality was to be stressed.

It is precisely because of their fundamental adherence to
organic structure that the orders of architecture are not ruled
by fixed and invariable laws but only by norms or ideal canons
that can find concrete form in expressively and quantitatively
different ways in each structure, depending upon historical framework and the creator; but their exactitude of shape and proportion has made it possible to use them as compositional constants and as essential instruments for defining architectural
space.

Each order of architecture is composed of two fundamental
parts based on the trabeated system: the vertical element of
support (column and, by analogy, pillar and pilaster) with all
of its constituent elements; and the horizontal element borne
by the supports (the entablature, consisting of an architrave,
a frieze, and a cornice). The static function of these elements
can be real (structural or supporting order) or simulated (ornamental order).

From the 7th–6th century B.C. two basic orders were created
in Greece: the Doric order and the Ionic order, both considered
by the Greek historians themselves as building methods peculiar to specific cultures. The other orders constitute what might
be called subspecies, or variants, of the two basic orders; such are
the Aeolic (sometimes called proto-Ionic) and Corinthian orders,
Greek in origin, and the Tuscan and Composite orders, created
within the Etruscan-Roman sphere. All these orders and their
subsequent derivations and variants came to be used throughout
the ancient Western world, were revived during the Renaissance,
and survived in general use until the beginning of the 20th
century.

The Doric order (PL. 233; FIG. 487) is that in which the
concept of the architectural order is expressed in its fullness
and exactitude. It is in this order that the translation of a timber
construction method into a stone technique is particularly apparent. Vitruvius himself confirmed this hypothesis, which was,
however, refuted by some scholars (cf. H. Hübsch, *Über griechische Architektur,* Heidelberg, 1822), who maintained that the
order was created in stone.

In the Doric order the column (FIG. 517), consisting of a
fluted shaft with a more or less marked entasis, generally lacks
a base and begins directly at the stylobate. It is connected to the
entablature by means of a capital, always consisting of a lower
part in the form of a spreading convex molding (echinus) and
of an upper part in the shape of a square, flat slab (abacus).
The entire capital is generally made of a single block. The connection between the upper part of the shaft and the echinus
is effected by the insertion of other secondary elements.

The entablature is made up of three basic parts: architrave, frieze, and cornice (FIG. 487). The architrave is formed
by large rectangular blocks joined exactly in the middle of the
abacus, and it is divided from the frieze by a fillet called the
taenia. The frieze, made of vertical rectangular blocks, is divided into square panels (metopes), which can be smooth, painted,
or carved, by grooved triglyphs. The position of the triglyph
is marked below the taenia by a listel (the regula) with a series
of small truncated cones (guttae). The cornice consists of a bed
molding flush with the triglyphs and projecting part, the corona
(I, FIG. 602). The bed molding can be an ovolo, a cyma reversa,
a bird's beak, or a square corbel molding. On the soffit of the
undercut and inclined corona, thin flat rectangular slabs (mutules)
with 18 guttae are carved in correspondence with the triglyphs
and regulae. Crowning the whole is a gutter molding, or sima,
which may be in the shape of a simple convex molding, a cyma
recta, or a cyma reversa (the gutter molding is often also called

the cymatium, but this is a usage that is better avoided). Along the sides of the structure, at regular intervals, the gutter is pierced by rain spouts (almost always in the shape of an open-mouthed lion's head; VII, PL. 57). When there are no spouts, the cornice is ornamented with antefixes (VII, PLS. 38, 56, 57) and the top cornice becomes a sima. The apex of the pediment and the four corners of the temple are adorned with acroteria (VII, PL. 41), often shaped like human figures (VII, PLS. 41, 61).

These basic elements of the Doric order, although they remain typologically constant, display many variations in shape in relation to chronological and geographic factors. For instance, the column sometimes had (as at Eleusis and in the Temple of Olympian Zeus at Agrigento) a rudimentary circular base; the shaft could display more or less marked tapering and entasis (or no entasis at all); and the number of flutes varied (in the archaic age, between 16 and 24; later, about 20). But there are also Doric shafts without flutes from the Hellenistic age (as in the Temple of Nemesis at Rhamnous; III, FIG. 663) or only partly fluted (Temple of Apollo at Delos; Temple of Athena Polias Nikephorus at Pergamon). All the elements of the entablature display characteristic variations, especially in the archaic period. The architrave was sometimes decorated with reliefs, as in the Temple of Athena at Assos (end of 6th cent. B.C.), and the taenia can be molded, as for instance in the "Temple of Ceres" at Paestum. In the frieze of the Sanctuary of Hera on the river Sele the triglyphs taper upward, but this is uncommon; and in some ancient examples mentioned by Europides the place of the metopes was empty. In general the metopes are decorated with carved human figures or with paintings.

Until the 4th century the plane surface of the triglyph was generally on a level with that of the architrave; from the Hellenistic period on it was instead the outer surface of the metope that was level with the architrave, with the triglyph projecting, even though it was on a level with the taenia. The alternation of triglyphs and metopes followed, at least through the 5th century, rules that prescribed the position of the triglyphs on an axis with the column and the metopes on an axis with the intercolumniation. As a result of this arrangement a problem arose in the arrangement of the triglyphs at the corner of the building. In fact, by retaining the position of the triglyph on an axis with the corner column, the abacus of the capital would have projected too far with respect to the entablature, and the thrust of the roofing would have been borne eccentrically by the column. Therefore the Greeks, wishing the frieze to be concluded at the corner by a triglyph, discarded the custom of having the axis of this triglyph correspond to the axis of the column, so that in the archaic period either the last metope was considerably wider than the others or the corner triglyph was wider than the others (e.g., in Temple C at Selinunte). Another solution, used from the 5th century on, required the reduction of the dimensions of one or more intercolumniations near the corner of the building and, therefore, sacrificed the traditional perfect coincidence between the axis of the intermediate triglyph and the axis of the intercolumniations. In the Roman period the position of the end triglyph is generally on an axis with the column and a solid element was inserted at the end of the frieze (corner half-metope). Commonly in the Hellenistic and Roman periods, as a consequence of the tendency to widen the intercolumniations and to reduce the height of the entablature, the result was not only one triglyph, but two or even three in correspondence to each intercolumniation, as in the stoa of Athena at Pergamon (VII, FIG. 297) and in the Temple of Hercules at Cori (VII, PL. 201).

In the archaic period pilasters (antae) terminating the walls of the pronaos show various solutions; they may be in the form of a pillar, tapered (Basilica of Paestum) or not (Temple G at Selinunte), in the form of a column (Temple D at Selinunte), or of a smooth pilaster. The capitals of the antae, different from those of the columns, are of various types; sometimes they are the cavetto (in the archaic period, as in the Basilica of Paestum), and sometimes, from the 5th century on, the bird's beak, with a variety of profiles.

In the Etruscan-Italic world, especially from the 5th and 4th centuries, Doric forms were used, but generally only for deco-

rative purposes, and were frequently associated in eclectic combinations with elements typical of other orders. Thus, for instance, the rock façades of the "Doric tombs" of Norchia display in a general arrangement of the Doric type with a triglyph frieze, insertions of Ionic elements (the dentils in the corona) and local survivals of Tuscan elements in a whole devoid of true syntactic coordination.

Roman variants of the Doric order (of which the Theater of Marcellus became a sort of model prototype) were to serve as a basis for the analysis of the order in the Renaissance by such theorists as Serlio, Vasari, Vignola, and Palladio and applications of it in such works as Bramante's "Tempietto" of S Pietro in Montorio (1503; I, PL. 305) and the many others by the Sangallo family, Sanmicheli, and Palladio. In France, under Henri II, following the example of the Italians and under the direct influence of Serlio, French architects such as Jean Goujon and Jean Bullant (Château d'Ecouen, ca. 1560) also adopted Doric forms, which they enriched with exuberant sculptural decoration. In the 17th and 18th centuries the Doric order was infrequently used in Italy, but conspicuous applications of it appeared in France, especially in the works of F. Mansart, and in Great Britain, where Robert Adam utilized the Doric order in the interior of Syon House (Middlesex; 1762–70) and J. Stuart built a reproduction of a Greek Doric temple at Hayley, near Birmingham (1758). In the late 18th and early 19th centuries revivals of the Doric style, which was identified as the ideal concept of classicism, were common; subsequent revivals occurred in 19th-century eclecticism and even in modern architecture (as in the above-mentioned "Chapel in the Wood").

The Ionic order, the "canonical" order of classical architecture (PL. 233; FIG. 517), is, generally speaking, the result of a process of systematic coordination of elements originating in the western Asiatic world (and especially in the coastal area of Anatolia known as Ionia), which were quite probably derived from wooden structural types. The definition of its basic elements was achieved in the 7th century, but the Ionic order did not reach its full maturity, so to speak, until the 5th century in Athens.

Richness of ornamentation in moldings is typical of the Ionic order. According to the shape of the basic moldings themselves, different motifs were chosen (e.g., egg-and-dart or egg-and-tongue on ovolo moldings; bead-and-reel on the astragal, bead-and-tongue for the cyma reversa; see ORNAMENTATION X, FIG. 839). Schematically, the Ionic order is composed of a column (resting on a circular base superimposed on a plinth) that has a slender and only slightly tapered shaft topped by a capital with spiral volutes, and an entablature in which the architrave (or epistyle) is formed by progressively projecting fascias. The frieze, when it is present, is smooth or ornamented with uninterrupted figures in relief (zoophorus); the horizontal cornice is without mutules. In late examples small square blocks, or dentils, were placed immediately under the cornice.

As in the Doric order, the concrete applications of the Ionic order show different variations in relation to chronological and geographical factors. The plinth, frequent in archaic examples, was no longer used in such Attic constructions of the 5th century as the Erechtheion, but was to reappear during the Hellenistic period, in some rare cases in an octagonal shape, as in the Temple of Apollo Didymos, near Miletus. From the middle of the 6th century, the base proper appeared in shapes made possible by the then new methods of turning. The Ionic base has several variants: the type known as Samian, utilized by the architect Theodoros in the Heraion of Samos (ca. 560 B.C.), is composed of two superimposed elements, a circular base (or spira) and a superimposed torus, both with shallow horizontal flutes; the Ephesian type, as found in the Temple of Artemis at Ephesus (ca. 550 B.C.), has both torus and spira elaborated so as to break up the profile. The torus is molded with a triple curve carved with a heart-and-dart pattern or with the flutes divided by simple fillets. The spira has pairs of convex pipings, at its top, center, and bottom. Such a base evolved into the so-called "Ionic base," widely used, at least until the 3d century B.C., in the eastern areas of Greek influence, as in the Temple of Athena Polias at Priene, where the upper torus rests on two superimposed scotias. At the beginning of the classical period Attic architects worked out type that, with some variants, was to enjoy great popularity the Roman period, during which it retained the name of "At-" base (see above, *Terminal elements*). It is the type found the temple on the Ilissos and, on the Acropolis, in the emple of Nike Apteros, and in the Erechtheion (II, PLS. 51,). Even when the other members remain smooth, the upper rus is often ornamented with horizontal flutes. About the iddle of the 5th century a new type appeared, displaying even greater simplification of shapes. In this case the torus, direct contact with the stylobate, disappears or is reduced to ninimum, while the scotia is strongly developed and its upward nt emphasized. It is the type evidenced in the internal order the Temple of Apollo Epikourios at Bassae (Phigalia; VII, .. 399) and, with the scotia more or less prevailing, for instance, Palatitsa in southern Macedonia and in the Leonidaion of lympia.

The shaft of the Ionic column is normally fluted; the archaic lumns of Ephesus have as many as 40 flutes, but later the num-r seems to have decreased to 24. The flutes of the Ionic shaft, stead of meeting in a sharp edge, as in the Doric order, are parated by a flat interval or by a fillet achieved by chamfer-g the acute angle of the edge.

The Ionic capital consists of an echinus, almost always or-imented with the egg-and-dart motif, placed at the top of the aaft and bearing the typical element with horizontal volutes, nnected to the architrave by a thin abacus which is often dec--ated. Perhaps the earliest Ionic capital known is that of the tive column of the Naxians at Delphi (ca. 570 B.C.; VII, PL.]), where the echinus is obtained from the flutes of the column, hich terminate in drooping leaves. The triangular connecting arface between echinus and volutes is ornamented by a small ve-leafed palmette. Generically to be included in this type are ue capitals of the Temple of Artemis at Ephesus, which in-ired many archaic examples. In some examples at Delos single palmette separates the two volutes and the shaft ends a sort of necking ring. In the later examples of the 5th century, ue echinus settles into the shape of a torus molding enriched ith egg-and-dart motifs, this ornamentation being repeated the abacus and in the cornices. The line connecting the two olutes arches downward (as in the capitals of the now destroyed :mple on the Ilissos and in other examples at Gela and at elinunte). The sides of the volutes, called cushion (or volute) olls, resemble concave reels.

A characteristic example of the archaic Ionic capital is found the north colonnade of the Erechtheion, where the form of ue echinus and the downward-falling connecting line between ue two volutes became constant elements. The spiral of the olutes narrows progressively, terminating in an eye marked y a metal rosette. Between echinus and shaft is a large collar and decorated with palmettes and delimited in its lower part y a fillet and above by an astragal with a bead-and-reel pattern. he outside rolls and volutes are also ornamented by three eries of beads and reels, while the echinus is surmounted by a raided motif.

Special solutions were adopted for corner capitals. Begin-ing in the 5th century it was customary, in order to have the olutes appear on all four faces, to distort the capital somewhat, naking it asymmetrical by canting the angle volute along the iagonal. Toward the end of the 5th century, in about 430 and perhaps for the first time in the Temple at Bassae), the iagonal volutes were set at 45°; thus the rolls were eliminated n the internal faces and the capital was made symmetrical. rom that time, and throughout the Hellenistic and Roman eriods, two types of capitals coexisted: the cushion, or bolster, apital that seems to have prevailed in Ionia and the four-sided apital with diagonal volutes prevailing in Greece, in Macedonia, nd in the Italic sphere (as at Pompeii).

The architrave generally consists, as already mentioned, of three fascias, gradually higher and more projecting, of which he terminal one is crowned by a projecting molding or by a ombination of different moldings, almost always enriched with he traditional decorative motifs: palmettes, egg and tongue, ead and reel. Completely smooth architraves, as in the Doric rder, are quite exceptional (e.g., the temple on the Ilissos, ca.

450 B.C.). In the orders of Lycia, which were archaic in influence, the architrave is often subdivided into two rather than three fascias. The frieze (also known as the zoophorus and character-ized by uninterrupted ornamentation in animal forms), which is lacking in archaic examples, and not found in the small "Loggia of the Caryatids" in the Erechtheion, seems nevertheless to have appeared at about the end of the 6th century (e.g., in the Treas-ury of the Siphnians at Delphi, ca. 530) and to have spread through European Greece and also in the Doric area (in Asia it was not in use until the beginning of the 4th century or later).

Concerning the cornice, it is sufficient to note that while in the examples of archaic Asiatic Greece dentils are often present above the bed molding, they are for the most part lacking in Athenian structures except in a few rare examples such as the above-mentioned "Loggia of the Caryatids" (II, PL. 52).

The Ionic pediment often tends to be less steeply pitched than the Doric. The connection between the horizontal cornice and the slanting cornice is carried out by eliminating the sima, which is retained only in the raking part and is continued along the sides of the temple. Under the oblique sima the other mem-bers of the cornice (corona and bed molding) continue, though often with slight changes. In Greece, the pediment was often filled with sculpture, while in Rome and later, during the Ren-aissance, it usually was left plain.

When it is utilized in the internal parts of buildings, the Ionic order, like the Doric, is simplified through the elimination of the corona and often also of the frieze. The antae, or terminal pilasters of the pronaos walls, become pilaster strips, and special capitals are used with them. A common type of capital used in this connection consists of an echinus, delimited by astragals and decorated in the traditional way, on which is superimposed a cyma reversa topped by a small abacus with a molded upper edge. In other cases, antae and Ionic pillars, particularly in the eastern Greek area (Propylaea of Priene and Temple of Apollo of Didyma, VII, PL. 150), display flattened capitals, laterally enclosed by small vertical volutes that delimit an area taken up by an ornamental relief with various motifs, including fig-ures. The base of the anta, on the other hand, is often much more closely related to the base of the corresponding column, as in the Erechtheion.

From the standpoint of the relationship between the various structures, it can be noted that there being no correspondences between the elements of the frieze and the column (as in the Doric order), the position of the column is not determined by the elements of the entablature, nor is there any need to bring the corner columns closer together. Normally, therefore, in Ionic colonnades the intercolumniations are all alike. Nevertheless, in some examples (e.g., the Temple of Nike Apteros), perhaps for reasons of optical correction, the end intercolumniations are narrower than the central one. On the other hand, as in the Doric order, a varying proportional ratio persists between the base diameter and the height of the column, which gradually became more slender. In the Temple of Nike Apteros the height of the column, including base and capital, is equal to approxi-mately $7\frac{1}{2}$ diameters, but in the temple on the Ilissos it equals approximately 8 diameters; in the Erechtheion it is slightly over $8\frac{1}{2}$, and in the temples of Bassae (Phigalia) and Miletus almost 9 diameters are reached; in the Propylaea of Athens and in the Temple of Athena Polias at Priene, the height equals about 10 diameters. As the whole became more slender and the height of the entablature decreased, the intercolumniation also tended to narrow. The Temple of Nike Apteros has an inter-columniation equaling two diameters (sistyle type), the Erech-theion's is about $2\frac{1}{2}$ diameters (approaching the eustyle type); but in the Temple of Athena Polias at Priene it is equal to $1\frac{2}{3}$ diameters, and in the Temple of Apollo at Didyma it equals $1\frac{1}{2}$ diameters (pycnostyle). On the basis of the theories pro-pounded by the Alexandrian theoreticians, Vitruvius prescribed that in civil buildings the intercolumniations should be wider than in temples.

Outside the spatial and cultural limits of classical-Hellenistic Greece the use of the Ionic order spread rather slowly and was freely subjected to various interpretations that resulted, finally, in a form that was later to be known as the Composite order.

At the end of the Republican period, there spread from Sicily into Italy (particularly at Pompeii and in Rome) the scheme of the Ionic capital with four equal faces and diagonal volutes, which was to be found later also at Aquileia and in Provence. Sometimes the ring of egg-and-dart molding is modified, in this type, into an echinus with strong, deep carvings; from the volutes vertical palmettes rise to break the continuity of the connection between the volutes themselves, which are massive and sturdy, often having a convex rather than concave profile (VII, PL. 57).

In Rome, from the 1st century B.C. and during the Empire, faithful adherence to the Hellenistic prototypes prevailed; often the volutes are flattened and connected by less winding and more geometric lines, as in the Temple of Fortuna Virilis (PL. 252), very close to the Ionic style of Hermogenes described by Vitruvius. This type was subsequently retained, for instance in the Theater of Marcellus and again, at a late date, in the Baths of Diocletian. Numerous and varied capitals of this type were reused in Christian basilicas (e.g., S. Maria Maggiore, S. Lorenzo fuori le Mura). In some cases, as in the Colosseum (PL. 232), the tendency is to simplify the type and make it sturdier; elsewhere, as in the Temple of Saturn, by the adoption of the capital with four symmetrical faces, the volutes were separated and made to spring out from the egg-and-dart echinus, under which are set other carved moldings, obtaining an overall result that recalls the upper part of the Composite order and that seems to blend Ionic and Tuscan elements.

The classical type of capital with volutes on only two sides and having rolls continued to be utilized in the Early Christian and Byzantine periods, as for instance in S. Demetrius in Salonika, even though in these cases it cannot be said to be part of an order, since it has lost every syntactic link with the other elements. The capitals of some Christian constructions in Rome (e.g., S. Stefano on the Via Latina and S. Stefano Rotondo, IX, PL. 39) are of this type in that they display a more synthesized over-all appearance, cylindrical volutes, and an echinus without carvings. This type is sometimes found in simplified and rudimentary forms in the Middle Ages, particularly in Italy. Worthy of mention are those in the front of the Chapel of St. Zenone in S. Prassede (9th cent.) and of the portico of S. Lorenzo in Lucina, where one of the capitals has cylindrical volutes formed by tightly wound spirals.

Greater fidelity to ancient models is found in the Roman works of the 12th and 13th centuries, as in the portico of the Cathedral of Civita Castellana (I, PL. 302), in S. Lorenzo fuori le Mura, and in the cloister of St. John Lateran.

The revival of the classical elements in the 15th century seems to have favored the Corinthian and Composite orders rather than the Ionic, but there were occasional uses of columns with smooth shafts and Ionic capitals with rolls connected to the shaft by means of a necking (as in Masaccio's Holy Trinity, IX, PL. 345, in S. Maria Novella, Florence, perhaps inspired by Brunelleschi). That this type with a necking — which in fact appears occasionally also much later — was very much to the early-15th-century Florentine taste is evidenced by the fact that it was utilized by Donatello in the tabernacle of Orsanmichele, by A. Cavalcanti in the balusters of the pulpit of S. Maria Novella, by Michelozzo in the library and in the cloister of S. Marco, and in paintings by Masolino and by Fra Angelico. Moreover, Donatello utilized the Ionic order in the doorways of the Old Sacristy of S. Lorenzo and to support the pulpits of the same church. Giuliano da Sangallo used Ionic columns in the atrium of the Church of S. Maria Maddalena dei Pazzi (XII, PL. 387) and adopted them as the symbol of classicism in the entrance gallery of Poggio a Caiano (XII, PL. 387), although he inserted a tall necking under the capital, following a type introduced by Michelozzo in the shrine of the Crucifix in S. Miniato al Monte. This hybrid type enjoyed a certain amount of popularity around the end of the 15th century, and was revived a number of times as late as the 17th and 18th centuries also outside Florence, for instance in Naples in Castel Nuovo, in Urbino in the Cappella del Perdono (II, PL. 337), in Rome in Vignola's Villa Giulia, and elsewhere.

In Rome, Bramante sought inspiration in the Temple of Fortuna Virilis and the Theater of Marcellus for the cloister of S. Maria della Pace (II, PL. 345), the Belvedere courtyard, and in a more concise and massive interpretation, the spiral staircase of the Vatican (II, PL. 345). After Bramante and Giuliano da Sangallo, Antonio da Sangallo the Younger (Palazzo Farnese), Peruzzi (Palazzo Massimo), Sanmicheli, Sansovino, Vignola, Ammannati, and Palladio (XI, PL. 352) utilized the Ionic order in its "pure" form, drawn from the study of Roman monuments and of Vitruvius; Serlio, Vignola, Palladio, and others formulated theories about its shapes and proportions. The prevailing model was the Ionic capital with two volutes and rolls, which Michelangelo interpreted most originally in a marked sculptural sense, and introducing a variant in which the part linking the deeply hollowed-out volutes is narrowed to the utmost, the astragal under the egg-and-dart echinus is eliminated, the capital is separated from the shaft by a necking, and (a typical element) the eyes of the volutes are linked by a hanging festoon, as may be seen in the capitals of the Ionic columns of the portico of the Palazzo dei Conservatori (IX, PL. 542) and of the window of St. Peter's. This type, sometimes called the "Michelangelesque capital," enjoyed particular favor throughout Europe in the late mannerist and baroque periods.

In the neoclassic period, in view of the broader knowledge of Greek and Hellenistic models, the trend was to favor Attic and Asiatic capitals, sometimes interpreted with great refinement.

The Corinthian order (PL. 233, FIG. 517) was considered in ancient times, essentially as a variant of the Ionic, of which it retained the basic elements while displaying greater ornamental richness. Vitruvius characterized the Corinthian order by stating that it "does not differ from the Ionic as to proportions, other than by the greater height of the capital." In fact, the capital is the most clearly characteristic element of the Corinthian order. Vitruvius relates the legend of the invention of the Corinthian capital by the sculptor and goldsmith Kallimachos, who was said to have drawn his inspiration from a basket placed on the tomb of a Corinthian girl; but some scholars (C. Chipiez, 1876; A. Choisy, Histoire de l'architecture, Paris, 1899) have deemed it probable that the Corinthian capital derived from the translation into stone of metal ornamental elements applied onto a cylindrical shaft. A more reliable hypothesis traces the origin of the Corinthian capital to an elaboration of ornamental elements of plant origin from the southeastern Mediterranean area (Egypt, Mesopotamia, Syro-Hittite sphere, and Phoenicia) and Hellenized Asia. A. Riegl (1883) referred to this hypothesis when he declared the origin of the acanthus motif to be a translation in relief and a naturalistic interpretation of the traditional palmette motif.

One of the earliest examples of the Corinthian capital seems to be that (now lost) of the Temple of Apollo at Bassae (Phigalia; ca. 420 B.C.), which some authorities consider to be earlier than the temple itself and to have been utilized for the temple by Iktinos. The various representations made of this capital all agree in showing the essential typological elements of the Corinthian capital as already well defined: the molded abacus with concave sides and projecting corners rests on a cylindrical or slightly conical bell widening at the top and ornamented above the necking at the end of the shaft by one or two rows of small leaves above which, in correspondence with the diagonal axes, unfold four larger acanthus leaves from which spring four slender, projecting, vertical volutes supporting a molded abacus with concave sides and projecting corners terminating with a small cornice in its upper part; between the volutes, on each of the four faces, are set two smaller volutes (helices) crowned by a palmette. This whole constitutes perhaps the first example of the forms that were to develop (with different shapes and positions of the various parts) into the type of capital used in the funerary monument of Lysikrates (335 B.C.), where the lower part consists of a crown of lanceolate leaves from which rise eight large, curved, spiny acanthus leaves, above which unroll freely the corner volutes rising naturalistically from acanthus tufts, out of which spring vine tendrils curled into helices crowned by a palmette that spreads to the abacus.

The various interpretations of the Corinthian theme developed in the Etruscan-Italic area between the 3d and 2d cen-ries B.C. generally distort plastically the various elements, can be seen for instance in the Porta Marzia in Perugia, where e whole is quite flattened, with low volutes and a wide base ing from a single crown of leaves.

A type peculiar to the Greek-Italic sphere is that in which e central helices are widely separated from each other and m the abacus and are often accompanied by other plant corations; under the abacus is a large projecting flower in ong relief with six petals separate from each other; moreover, e leaves of the second crown often spread only slightly beyond e end of those of the lower crown. This type of capital, which rhaps originated in Sicily, was widespread between the 2d d the 1st century B.C. throughout continental Italy (see the pitals of the "Temple of the Sibyl" at Rivoli, those in the Sanctary of Fortuna Primigenia at Palestrina, others at Aquileia, North Africa, and in Crete) and influenced works of later riods (Temple of Minerva, Assisi; the Colosseum, Rome). me capitals of this type, probably from the Tabularium in me, display, perhaps for the first time, smooth rather than rved leaves with the details of the foliage eliminated as in the rta Maggiore and in the Colosseum (PL. 232), Rome.

From the Augustan period onward the Corinthian capital s used in its Roman "pure" shape. The over-all proportions came more slender, the profile more jagged, and the acanthus ves (sometimes replaced by olive leaves), carved or, occasionly, smooth, were normally very projecting and arranged in two perimposed orders of equal height. The volutes spring from acanthus tuft, of which the leaves just touch their lower ternal part and support them; the two central volutes (helices), metimes interlaced, acquire strong relief as they proceed ward the axis of the front of the capital and remain only ghtly lower than the corner volute. At the center of the abacus, ten shaped into a concave molding and crowned by an ovolo, inserted an ornamental element, generally a rosette in strong lief (FIG. 517).

In shapes more or less similar to these, the Corinthian pital had wide diffusion in Roman architecture: suffice it recall the elements of such temples as that of Venus Genetrix, Mars Ultor, of the Dioscuri, of Antoninus and Faustina, of piter Stator, and those of the Pantheon. In fanciful variants the type, based on examples already carried out in Magna raecia (in Taranto, Lecce, Pompeii, Paestum) and in the Etrusn-Italic area (Vulci, Sovana, Chiusi, Volterra), figured parts e inserted between the elements, sometimes replacing them together. In the interior of the Temple of Mars Ultor the corner lutes are replaced by winged horses; in the Temple of Concord Roman Forum) the volutes are formed by rams; and, in the later pitals, from the time of Antoninus and Severus, there are serted such motifs as trophies of arms or figures of gods, as the capital of the last column of the Appian Way in Brindisi.

As concerns the other constituent elements of the Corinthian der, there are no important variations of the Ionic order apart om the insertion of supporting elements of the cornice and the tablature, that is to say, of modillions. This insertion, which ermitted a greater projection of the cornice, became usual in ome during the last period of the Republic and in the Augustan ge (even though Vitruvius deemed it to be contrary to good adition) and was to be transmitted to the architecture of the enaissance. The most common shape of modillion is the reersed one (i.e., with the spiral curling downward; Temple f Venus Genetrix and the Pantheon, Rome), its lower part ostly ornamented with carved foliage; quite frequently the tervals between modillions, in the soffit of the corona, are ecorated by coffers with a carved rosette in their center. Inequent use was made in Roman architecture of the modillion ith a straight, vertical face, that, resting on the architrave, takes p the whole height of the frieze and directly supports the orona, projecting slightly from the latter (e.g., the cornice of ne topmost order of the Colosseum). This type was to be ken up in the Renaissance by L. B. Alberti, Bramante, Sanicheli, and, in the mannerist period, by Vignola and his folowers; in the baroque period it was elaborated with various hapes of modillions, of which the lower parts were sometimes uted in an imitation of Doric triglyphs.

In the amalgamation of elements taken from the Ionic and Corinthian orders and known as the Composite order, the typical capital is formed from the lower part of the Corinthian capital, of which it retains the two crowns of leaves, with the four volutes of the symmetrical Ionic capital, separated from each other, coming out of an echinus enriched with the egg-and-dart motif and supporting an abacus of the Corinthian type. Remote prototypes of these shapes can be found in Ionic capitals with the necking band decorated by a frieze, like the previously mentioned ones of the Erechtheion. Some types of Composite capital had wide diffusion, especially from the Flavian period; notable among them, in that they are particularly characterized, are those of the Porta dei Borsari in Verona (PL. 235) and those of the Arch of Titus, of the Baths of Diocletian, and of the Lateran Baptistery in Rome. In a late period, highly simplified forms appeared, with a single circle of leaves schematically outlined (House of Eros and Psyche at Ostia, atrium of the Church of S. Vitale in Rome) or with a single crown of leaves without carvings (5th-cent. capitals in S. Prassede at Rome). The Composite type not infrequently displays the insertion — between the decorative elements — of figured motifs, as in the Baths of Caracalla, Rome (PL. 233).

The traditional division of the orders, as established by historians and by treatises (from Vitruvius to Vasari, Serlio, Vignola, and Scamozzi), includes the order known as Tuscan. This order, however, should be considered, rather than an archaic variant or a simplification of the Doric order, as the result of the partially autonomous Italic elaboration of an architraved wooden structure. At least initially (that is to say, within the sphere of Etruscan culture) the Tuscan forms did not achieve the typical syntactical system of the true order.

Even in the Roman period a true Tuscan order, autonomous and clearly distinguished from the Doric by characteristics of its own, had not been developed, but rather a sort of syncretism was achieved by the occasional insertion of shapes of Italic derivation into a Doric-Hellenistic complex. According to Vitruvius, the Tuscan order is distinguished by the column with a smooth shaft and circular base on a plinth, a capital with abacus (at first round, later square), an echinus with a roundish profile and a necking, and an entablature without a frieze (or, subsequently, with a frieze but without triglyphs) and usually faced with polychrome terra-cotta antefixes and crowned, in lieu of a cornice, by the eaves of the roof (V, FIGS. 127, 131). Because of the wooden entablature, which persisted until a relatively late period, the intercolumniations could be much wider than in the Doric order, so that the whole seemed to be very light and could be richly ornamented with friezes, antefixes, acroteria, and statues.

Examples surviving from the Italic sphere as early as the 7th–5th century B.C., notwithstanding their relatively limited number and, sometimes, the difficulty of their identification, nevertheless show the development and increasingly widespread use of a type of column of which the characteristics progressively became constant. Some of them, like the capital with abacus and echinus and the occasionally extreme tapering and entasis of the shaft, derive in all likelihood from the Hellenic sphere; thus it is possible to distinguish reflections of Mycenaean models in the columns tapered downward (in a reversed truncated cone), echoes of eastern Mediterranean traditions in the capitals with cylindrical abacus and base in the form of a large torus; however, in the eclectic wavering among various influences and interpretations, it is possible to single out a line of continuity in the original and constant elaboration of a type of column that can appropriately be termed "Tuscan." On an archaic urn of the 6th–5th century B.C. from Chiusi (Berlin, Staat. Mus.) there is shown a column with a smooth, very tapered shaft marked at the bottom by a listel under an astragal and with a base in the form of a spreading convex molding. The capital probably had a circular abacus, as in some examples of Paestum, Pompeii, and Minturno in which the abacus projects only very slightly from the echinus; between the echinus and the top of the column there is, finally, a band forming a sort of necking. From approximately the same period, the spreading base is found in other examples at Chiusi (where, occasionally, a small torus is inserted between the base and the bottom of the shaft) and in the stele "of the Satyr" from Fiesole (Florence, Mus. Archeol.) in a smooth, slightly tapered small column, with a capital formed by the superimposition of an astragal, of a rather swollen echinus, and of a thin abacus. Between the 6th and 5th centuries this type seems to have been widespread throughout Etruria; examples are found at Vignanello (Viterbo), where the column, placed as a support in a chamber tomb, has a smooth shaft with a strong conical tapering and rests on a spreading base on a listel. The capital, with a thin square abacus and an echinus in a quarter-circle, is separated from the shaft by an astragal. In the painted cave of Blera (anc. Bleva) the shaft is massive, smooth, and strongly tapered; the base is the simple spreading type; and the very tall abacus is circular and of the same diameter as the echinus. The columns in the paintings in the Tomb of the Lionesses at Tarquinia show a smooth, slightly tapered shaft and a capital with a thin abacus and a very swollen and projecting echinus, under which is inserted a sort of necking with a bird's-beak profile (recalling the anthemion of the archaic capitals at Paestum), delimited at the top of the shaft by an astragal. In the Tomb of Pulcella at Tarquinia, a column tapered downward in a reversed truncated cone displays a capital with a thin abacus and a swollen echinus separated from the shaft by means of the usual astragal. In the famous columns of the "great gymnasium" of Pompeii, combined with elements characteristic of the Doric order (such as the capital with a projecting echinus and a very marked entasis), there appear the smooth shaft of Italic tradition, an outline of necking under the echinus, and a simple circular base on a plinth. In the column at Vulci, perhaps incorrectly reconstructed in the 19th century on the basis of fragments found in the tumulus of the Cuccumella, typically Tuscan elements such as the smooth shaft with a moderate tapering and without entasis, a double astragal at the top of the shaft, and a base consisting of a large torus between two plinths or listels are combined with a capital with a massive abacus and a flattened and projecting echinus of the archaic Doric type.

There can, therefore, be observed, between the 7th and the 4th century B.C., the affirmation and stabilization of some constituent elements characteristic of the Tuscan column, which can be summarized as follows: a capital with abacus and echinus connected to the shaft by a more or less developed necking; a smooth shaft with moderate tapering and often without entasis; a circular base on a plinth, generally molded either in the form of a spreading convex molding or in a more or less toruslike shape. As for the other component elements of the Tuscan order, it can be noted that the entablature, as it appears in the surviving clay fragments placed as facing for wooden beams, is superimposed on a more or less projecting cornice, often vertically fluted, or on an architrave richly decorated with fascias. The frontal seems to have originally displayed an open pediment. This solution later appeared together with, and then was replaced by, that with a closed pediment filled with figures, as in the Greek examples.

As already mentioned, between the 3d and the 1st century B.C. all these characteristic forms were established and coordinated, so that it is possible to speak, from that period onward, of a Tuscan order proper. Among the first examples of the true Tuscan order is the south temple of the Foro Olitorio (Rome; 2d cent. B.C.), which may be considered as a precedent for the subsequent applications of the system in the Roman world. At that period the column, with a generally smooth shaft and with slight tapering and entasis, rested on a base on a square plinth, the base often formed by a simple torus with a superimposed astragal; this scheme was occasionally complicated by the insertion of a cyma reversa, as in the first order of the Colosseum (PL. 232), or by the adoption of the Attic base. The capital is generally composed of a low abacus with a terminal cornice, an echinus with a quarter-circle profile (or ovolo), and a smooth necking delimited by a small torus in its lower part; in some cases, as in the memorial columns of Trajan and Marcus Aurelius in Rome, the echinus is carved with an egg-and-tongue pattern, following the example of Hellenistic models, or sometimes, rather than an ovolo, it is in the form of a cyma recta (e.g., in the amphitheater of Verona and in the forum of Ostia).

Finally, the entablature is normally composed of an architra with fascias of the Ionic type, of a smooth frieze, and of a simp bed molding with dentils similar to the Doric type.

The Roman examples gave rise to the subsequent reelab rations that were to appear in the works of the Cosmati and of t Vassalletti families (cloister of S. Paolo fuori le Mura in Ron III, PL. 480) and then frequently in the architecture of the Re aissance and up to quite recent times. From the 16th centu onward the reelaborations were often strengthened in an attem to differentiate clearly between the Tuscan and the Doric. these Renaissance works the architrave was often smooth a was delimited above by a fillet (or taenia), the frieze was witho triglyphs, and the bed molding was reduced to one or two simp moldings in the form of a cyma reversa (Vignola) or cyma rec (Palladio); the capital consisted of abacus, echinus in the form an ovolo enriched with an egg-and-dart band, and neckir the base was usually formed by a simple torus. Sometimes t frieze was eliminated and an architraved entablature was adopte A particularly concise interpretation of the Tuscan order w given by Inigo Jones in St. Paul's (1631–38) in Covent Garde London, where he placed on columns of the usual type an enta lature consisting only of a tall, smooth architrave direct supporting a cornice formed by small, projecting beams.

In the 17th century interpretations of the Tuscan order we used by Bernini (colonnade of St. Peter's at Rome), by Ju Hardouin-Mansart (orangery of Versailles, 1681–86), and Great Britain by Christopher Wren and his followers (163 1723). In France, as late as the 19th century, some architec attempted purely structural interpretations of the Tuscan ord Thus E. Gilbert (1793–1874) created in his hospice at Ch renton (1838) some porticoes consisting of columns with circular abacus supporting an entablature with a wooden a chitrave and a cornice formed by the small beams of the ro alternated with brick panels ornamented with rosettes.

More recently, in the eclectic styles of the late 19th centu and then in the classicizing styles of the early 20th centur inspiration was sought in examples of the Roman or Renaissan Tuscan order, but these were often misinterpreted.

At least from the time of the Hellenistic age, elements ty ical of different orders were mixed, as had happened in the fo mative stages of the Tuscan order. To consider only the histo ically more conspicuous examples and those less bound to inc dental factors, suffice it to recall the applications of the Dor entablature to the Ionic column found in Magna Graecia: small so-called "Temple of Empedocles" at Selinunte (4th–3 cent. B.C.); the "Oratory" of Phalaris and the "Tomb of Theror in Agrigento (beginning of the 1st cent. B.C.); the Temple Apollo and other Pompeian buildings. This combination ha also spread to the Asiatic sphere, at least from the 2d centur at Ptolemais and later in the "Tomb of Absalom" in Jerusale (VIII, PL. 331), where the Ionic column is surmounted by Doric entablature, with triglyphs, crowned by a cornice with a Egyptian gorge molding.

A not infrequent combination, that of Doric and Corinthia elements, was accepted even by Vitruvius; an example ma be seen in the "Italic Temple" (3d–2d cent. B.C.) at Paestun where columns with a Corinthian capital with figured elemen support an entablature with a frieze and triglyphs and a be molding with dentils. Similar combinations are found in th Hellenistic sphere (tombs of Petra) in a small tholos near th right hemicycle of the first terrace of the Sanctuary of Fortun Primigenia at Palestrina, and in the small propylaea of Eleus (middle of the 1st cent. B.C.), where the capital is fanciful composed of a hexagonal abacus, to the sides of which corre spond alternately three plant motifs and three griffins, all risin from a crown of acanthus leaves. Other examples of the fusio of Doric and Corinthian orders are found in the Arch of Augustu in Aosta, in a portico of Apamea (2d cent.) in which the colum have spiral grooves, in a mausoleum at Ghirza, and in example at Leptis Magna.

In addition to these eclectic mixtures of elements of differe orders, there are combinations more in harmony with the system atic spirit of the orders, whether by the alternation or the su perimposition of different orders, or by the combination of th

chitraved and arched systems. In classical Greece until the
5h century B.C. it was customary to superimpose — generally
a the pronaos of a temple — only two Doric orders, as in the
»-called "Temple of Neptune" at Paestum, in the Temple
f Athena Aphaia at Aegina (I, PL. 332), and in the Temple of
eus at Olympia. The two superimposed columns are often
a a precise dimensional ratio deriving from the fact that the pro-
le of the upper shaft is usually the exact extension of that of
ae lower shaft (as in the "Temple of Neptune," Paestum).

In the Hellenistic period (3d–2d cent.), with the diffusion
f two-storied porticoes, the custom began of superimposing
vo different orders (porticoes of the Pergamene type); the Doric
rder was generally at the lower floor and the Ionic (sometimes
ith a triglyph frieze) on the upper story, as in the stoa of Athena
a Pergamon, and later at Delphi and in Athens. In these exam-
les the upper order is considerably smaller than the lower
VII, FIG. 297).

In a building at Tegea, according to Pausanias, the Doric
rder was utilized in the lower floor, and the Corinthian on the
pper one. In the basilica at Pompeii, continuing this custom,
Corinthian order of limited height is superimposed on an Ionic
rder.

Freer and more complex superimpositions matured during the
ellenistic period, for instance in the "Palace of the Columns"
f Ptolemais (2d–1st cent. B.C.), and are echoed in the rock
çades of Petra. In Roman architecture the superimposition
f two similar orders persisted, as in the two Tuscan orders, in
ae amphitheaters of Nîmes and Verona, in the Porta Palatina
a Turin, and as in the two Corinthian orders in buildings of
more decorative nature (e.g., in the "Tour d'Horloge" at Aix-
a-Provence). But quite often freer solutions can be observed,
ven though, in the light of a certain real or simulated structural
gic, the trend was to place the sturdier orders below. The
aost natural superimposition seems therefore to be that which
roceeded upward from the Doric (or Tuscan) order, to the
onic, the Corinthian, and the Composite. Thus, in Rome, in
ae Tabularium a Corinthian order is superimposed on a Doric;
a the Theater of Marcellus a Corinthian is superimposed on an
onic; in the Colosseum Corinthian orders are superimposed
n an Ionic and on a Tuscan respectively; at Arles there is a
orinthian on a Tuscan. But in the same type of construcon in the 2d century the arrangement is freer, as in the amphi-
teater of Thysdrus (mod. El Djem) in Tunisia (where, starting
om the bottom, the arrangement is Composite, Corinthian,
omposite).

The Roman system of coordination of the superimposed
rders was followed in the Renaissance as early as in Alberti's
rst works (façade of the Tempio Malatestiano in Rimini, the
alazzo Rucellai in Florence; I, PLS. 52, 54, 55) and by other
rchitects of the second half of the 15th century until the more
nature achievements of Bramante and up to the mannerist and
aroque periods. The upper orders are generally only slightly
naller than the lower; only rarely is the upper order markedly
naller than that on which it is superimposed (as for instance
a the interior of the Medici Chapel by Michelangelo). In the
6th century, in the mannerist period, and in the neoclassicism
f the 17th–18th century, until the 19th century, in cases where
ae superimposed orders were not similar the Roman system
vas adopted of placing the sturdier, heavier order below.

The simplest combination of architraved order and arch is
nat which, by reducing in substance the order to a decorative
aotif, caused it to be placed to frame an arched opening, and
» become part of the wall. Already rudimentarily outlined in
ome Etruscan monuments (such as the Porta Marzia in Perugia),
nis solution became usual in Rome from the Republican period
n. There the arch was framed by the Corinthian order (as in
ae Sanctuary of Fortuna Primigenia at Palestrina), by the Doric
rder (in the Tabularium in Rome), or by the Doric or Tuscan
rder (in the Sanctuary of Hercules at Tivoli). In these examples
ae orders consist of half columns projecting from the wall
tructure. Such an arrangement was also to be adopted in trium-
hal arches (such as those of Augustus in Aosta and Rimini).
a these monuments the tendency was to insert the supports
f the order in increasingly greater relief, as in the Arch of the

Gavi in Verona, until they were completely detached from the
wall, as in the Arch of Septimius Severus and that of Constantine in Rome and of Caracalla in Tebessa. In many other cases
the half columns were replaced by pilaster strips, as in the city
gate of Nîmes (V, PL. 471). The pilaster strips are sometimes
rusticated, as in the theaters of Aosta and Verona.

The theme of the arch framed by the order enjoyed particular favor in the Renaissance, at first with some free interpretations by Brunelleschi, Alberti, and their followers. A revival
of the motif, in a spirit more or less close to the Roman prototypes, occurred in the last years of the 15th century in Rome,
for instance in the courtyard of the Palazzo Venezia, and in the
first years of the 16th century in Bramante's cloister of S. Maria
della Pace. From then on, and especially within the circle of
Bramante's followers (Peruzzi, Sangallo, Sansovino), it became
one of the most typical motifs of 16th-century classicism in Rome;
and, after about 1530, it was adopted and utilized on a wide
scale in central and northern Italy in works of considerable importance (courtyard of the Palazzo Farnese, Farnesina, Villa
Madama, portico of S. Maria in Domnica, in Rome; Library
of S. Marco and Loggetta of S. Marco, 1537, in Venice; portico
of the piazza of Loreto; fortresses of Civita Castellana and Montefiascone).

In the mannerist period, this motif, theorized in the treatises in its shapes and proportional ratios, became one of the main
elements of European architecture, even though it was often
complicated in practical applications by the adoption of pilaster
strips and rusticated arches or by the combination with other
elements. Moreover, this motif took hold as a basic element in
the internal structure of the walls in churches with a single
aisle and in the so-called "Jesuit" chapels, spreading throughout
Europe and to the Spanish colonies in America. Though often
subjected to very personal interpretations, this motif was accepted and utilized by the major architects of the European baroque
period and it persisted until the eclectic experiments of the 19th
century and of the first years of the 20th. A variant of the motif,
adopted by Borromini and by Bernini in the final project for the
Louvre, encloses two stories of arcades within a single gigantic
order. Other variants insert in the order stilted, flat, and many-
centered arches with perspective splays. The spandrels between
the arch and the order of architecture were also subjected to
various decorative treatments, especially during the mannerist
and baroque periods. A synthesis of the motif, established in
Rome with the works of Vignola, Giacomo della Porta, and
Maderno and later utilized in the 17th and 18th centuries, frames
the arch with a sort of simplified order with pilaster strips without a capital and with a schematic entablature.

Finally, mention must be made of a typical arrangement of
the architectural order: that which couples and disposes rhythmically the supports (pilaster strips, half columns, or columns)
on one or more levels to give movement to the continuous surface of the wall or to frame the arch or other opening. The use
of coupled columns or pilaster strips was not unusual in Roman
architecture, especially in triumphal arches and on the fronts
of nymphaea or theater stages, but the spreading and regulation
of the system into a rhythmical repetition on a surface is typical
of the Renaissance.

L. B. Alberti utilized coupled pilaster strips to frame an
arch in the walls of the nave of S. Andrea, Mantua, giving rise
to an arrangement that was to appear again in many mannerist
and baroque interiors (Church of the Gesù, IX, PL. 312; St.
John Lateran, Rome). In the last years of the 15th century
the façade of the Palazzo della Cancelleria in Rome displayed
this arrangement for the first time on a large scale and with the
superimposition of levels; it was repeated soon afterwards in
the Palazzo Torlonia. Bramante was to use it with greater
precision in the courtyard of the Belvedere (II, PL. 346). Subsequently, the motif of the coupled supports spread rapidly
and became part of the repertory of classical architecture. Raphael used it in the Palazzo Vidoni (Caffarelli), and Peruzzi utilized
it in the Palazzo Massimo (ca. 1536), both in Rome.

Sanmicheli (Porta Palio, Verona), Sansovino (Loggetta of
S. Marco, Venice), Palladio (Palazzo Thiene, Vicenza), and
Vignola (Church of the Gesù, Rome) all adopted this motif

in façades, as did Michelangelo, who superimposed it on two stories in the project for the façade of S. Lorenzo (Florence) and later, with marked sculptural power, in the vestibule of the Biblioteca Laurenziana (Florence) and then in the internal and external drums of St. Peter's dome (Rome). In his treatise, Serlio mentions several examples of façades defined by the coupling of the supports, and the motif is utilized in numberless cases in mannerist and baroque architecture and in the eclectic revivals of the 19th century.

The coupling of columns or, more rarely, of pillars to support arches is also frequent; suffice it to recall the courtyard of the Palazzo Marino in Milan by G. Alessi, and the courtyard of Genoa University by B. Bianco.

Arnaldo BRUSCHI

III. STRUCTURAL TYPES. A study of structural types must include those constructions without internal space and also those in which the internal space is only a simple shelter or an area without well-defined characteristics. First among these are constructions of a funerary, ritual, or commemorative nature (see MONUMENTS), whose elements are volumetrically and plastically defined but which are not intended as sculptures: these include menhir steles, tumuli, steles, so-called "high places" set on platforms, Mesopotamian ziggurats, and Indian stupas (PLS. 242, 243). Obelisks, honorary columns and arches, fountains, and other monuments in public squares and roads assume the function of real and proper urban accessories. In a broader sense, bridges and often ramps and exterior staircases (PLS. 240, 241) are also constructions without real interior space.

Constructions that enclose an internal space may be said to be of three types:

1. Constructions in which space is delimited only or principally along a certain perimeter, as in rudimentary enclosures, town walls, ancient theaters, amphitheaters and circuses, and modern stadiums.

2. Constructions that delimit a single unit of space by means of a perimeter and a roof. This unit is often subdivided into several distinct areas or rooms by partitions or other elements with more or less accentuated structural functions (columns, pillars) that articulate the space without impairing its basic unitary nature. The interior space may be circular or polygonal in form, but it is always on a central plan — as in huts and tents, in some dwellings, and frequently in buildings used for worship or entertainment; examples range from the principal types of primitive dwellings, from the talayoti of the Balearic Islands to the *trulli* of Apulia, from the Pantheon to the Temple of Vesta and the Mausoleum of Augustus in Rome, from

S. Costanza in Rome to numerous baptisteries, martyriums, and churches of the Early Christian period to the present, from medieval theaters to the sports arenas of Rome, New Haven (Yale University), São Paulo (Brazil), Atlanta (Georgia), and Montevideo — planned, respectively, by Pier Luigi Nervi, E. Saarinen, I. de Castro Mello, R. Aeck, and A. Miller and L. Rios — and to the geodesic domes of Buckminster Fuller. The interior space may be square or rectangular in form, as often in huts and tents, dwellings and places of worship, sheds, workshops, barracks, hangars, and buildings for assembly and entertainment; among innumerable examples are the Egyptian hypostyle halls, the Iranian *apadana*, the Creto-Mycenaean megarons, Greek temples, Etrusco-Italic and Roman temples, Roman and, later, Christian basilicas, and many types of dwellings in the Far East. Constructions consisting of a single square or rectangular room (rarely those of circular or polygonal form) are the nucleus of those constructions in which a more complex articulation and more specific functional qualifications of rooms are effected, not by subdivisions but by means of an organic multiplication of the rooms. Although this can be carried out within a single square or rectangular perimeter, it can also give rise to spatial multiplicity.

3. Constructions with multiple rooms arranged in extension or elevation. Those arranged in extension may follow several layouts: a succession of rooms along a single axis (as in some hilani of Syro-Hittite origin); a disposition of rooms along the sides of a central axis (as in early Etruscan dwellings and the palace at Ctesiphon); a more or less symmetrical arrangement of rooms around three or four sides of a central area (courtyard, atrium, peristyle; as in many types of ancient dwellings, in Hellenistic *stoai* and the exedras, cloisters, and arcades, modeled on them, up to modern times). The layout of the rooms may be the result of the grouping of distinct and interdependent buildings, as in such advanced types as Roman thermae and villas, medieval monastic complexes, modern buildings (schools, workshops, technical buildings), in which an open concept of the architectural work has been adopted. Constructions that develop in a vertical sense consist simply of rooms placed one atop the other (sometimes, and even more simply, a single room is subdivided horizontally by means of floors), not necessarily intercommunicating; examples are to be found in Sardinian *nuraghi*, in some Roman tombs, in buildings of the Hellenistic east (in Lycia and Phrygia), and later in the Mausoleum of Theodoric in Ravenna. The type is rarely used in places of worship built on a central plan, in which a lower room is often built half underground, forming a crypt, as in Bramante's Tempietto of S. Pietro in Montorio in Rome; it is more

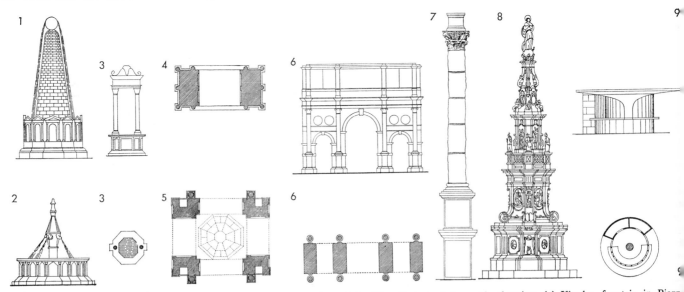

Decorative urban structures. (1–2) Fountains: (1) Rome, reconstruction of the Meta Sudante (4th cent.), elevation; (2) Viterbo, fountain in Piazza S. Caterina (14th cent.), elevation. (3) Viterbo, design for a Renaissance well, elevation and plan. (4–6) Commemorative arches: (4) Aosta, Arch of Augustus (1st cent.), plan; (5) Tripoli, Arch of Marcus Aurelius (2d cent.), plan; (6) Rome, Arch of Constantine (early 4th cent.), with three barrel vaults, elevation and plan. (7) Mainz, "Column of Jupiter" (1st cent.), elevation; (8) Naples, Guglia dell'Immacolata (18th cent.), elevation; (9) Zurich, refreshment kiosk (20th cent.), elevation and plan.

equently applied in constructions designed to fulfill a special
nction, such as bell towers, minarets, and lighthouses.

The scheme of multiple rooms in extension can be used in
uildings of more than one floor. In such cases it is not neces-
ry that the layout of rooms on one floor reproduce exactly
at of the rooms of the floor below. This scheme was adopted
om the very earliest times for simple dwellings (as shown in
e terra cottas in Heraklion, IV, FIG. 87, and as later used
the Roman insula). It was often used in villas, palaces, and
stles, later became the dominant system of building, and has
mained so up to the present.

The general scheme of constructions with several rooms
d floors can have functional variations: areas on several floors
n be joined unitarily; other areas can be limited to a single
oor; rooms can be created in special forms to suit special
rposes (halls, auditoriums, theaters, chapterhouses, gym-
siums, laboratories, etc.). This is true also of many buildings
at are designed for sports and of those in which one or more
ctors are intended for collective use (monasteries, barracks,
hools).

The following is a review of the various types of buildings
hich, in the course of history, are important as having devel-
ed characteristic treatments of internal space.

DWELLINGS. *Houses.* Although the use of pseudoarchitectural
aces such as grottoes and caverns for shelter was still wide-
read at the end of the mesolithic and especially during the
eolithic period, the progressive tendency of the community
ward agriculture favored the development of such relatively
ermanent constructions as huts. Traces of primitive huts that
ate from the third millennium show that these were generally
ected in the variety of forms discussed above under *Structures.*
hese huts generally consisted of a single room. The floor
as slightly sunken and was covered with a stratum of beaten
rth, often protected against water seepage by a base of stone
ixed with mortar; a hole in the center of the room functioned
the hearth. Although any reconstruction of these buildings
hypothetical, it is possible to deduce from the forms of
nerary urns from Latium and the Villanova culture (III,

been reiterated in the *tholoi,* in classical temples, and in Christian
central-plan buildings.

Primitive huts were often grouped in villages surrounded
by rudimentary defense systems such as palisades or ditches
(as at Murgia Timone and Murgecchia in Lucania, in the
Vibrata valley, and at Castelluccio near Syracuse) or stone walls
(as at Branco Grande di Camarina). Collective dwellings existed
in the Mediterranean area and in Central Europe from the
Neolithic period. Remains of such dwellings have been found
in Westphalia and in Poland (Brześć Kujawski). They were
similar to the constructions of the present-day Tupi people of
the western Amazon area, in which several families live together
in a large single dwelling. During the Neolithic period and
more often later in the metal ages, palafitte dwellings were
grouped in lake villages; they were built on platforms supported
by poles near the lake shore, and connected to it by means of
removable gangplanks (as at Ansbach and on the Federsee in
Germany, and on lakes Como, Varese, Iseo, and Garda). Similar
to the lake villages were those of the Bronze Age that were
composed of dwellings built on piles over ground that was dry
but subject to flooding, such as those of the Po valley between
Mella and Oglio.

These single-family huts, generally built on a rectangular
plan and placed very close together, were grouped around a
square or circular open space (dwellings in the village of
Kolomijščina, near Kiev, are arranged in two concentric circles,
with all entrances facing the center of the enclosure). Such
groupings, in effect, resulted in an embryonic town layout (see
TOWN PLANNING) and also probably provided the point of
departure for the rational arrangement of rooms in multiroomed
unitary constructions.

From the remote past the type of the single-roomed hut
has been related to types of masonry constructions that were
generally built on a circular plan or with apses. In these more
advanced constructions there were important variations in the
arrangement of the rooms; in the nuraghi these were placed
one above the other; in a primitive form of megaron with apses
there was a continuation of the side walls and a subdivision
into several rooms along the continuation.

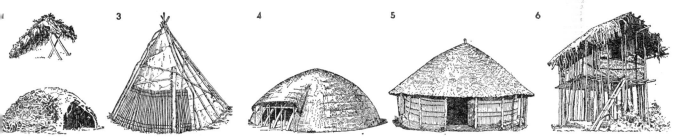

rimitive single-unit dwellings. (1) Senoi shelter (Malay Peninsula). Simple huts: (2) beehive hut of the Bushmen (South Africa); (3) wigwam of the
innebago tribe (North America); (4) hut of the Ganda tribe (Uganda). Composite huts: (5) circular-plan hut of the Monvu tribe (Haute Uelle,
ongo); (6) rectangular-plan hut on piles of the Tapiro tribe (New Guinea).

L. 124) and from observations at the excavation of the Ger-
alus on the Palatine Hill in Rome that these dwellings had
estitudinate roofs and sometimes also small porches in front
f the main entrance and along the sides, which contained
indows. The single-roomed hut is still widely used among
rimitive peoples and in more developed regions serves as
mporary living or storage space. The huts were the basic
orm from which domestic architecture developed. From the
arliest protohistory onward there existed an increasing tend-
ncy to build in more stable materials (e.g., stone, unbaked
rick). The circular or rectangular plans of the hut dwellings
re an important aspect of their grouping as types: these plans
an be distinguished historically and geographically (e.g., the
revalence of circular-plan types in the most ancient Mediter-
anean protohistorical period, the dominance of the rectangular-
lan type in European protohistory and the early historical
eriod; see EUROPEAN PROTOHISTORY; MEDITERRANEAN PROTO-
ISTORY). The scheme of the circular hut persisted and has

Rock-cut dwellings were often composed of several rooms,
as were the wall-grottoes of the Matmata in Tunis, where
additional rooms were excavated radially around a central one,
and the *sassi* in Matera, where rooms created by means of
masonry structures are added to those cut into the rock.

Similar divisions by multiple partitions are also to be found
in large pavilion tents such as those used by the Roman army
and by the nomadic peoples of the Near East and North Africa.

The elementary forms of multiroomed houses were, therefore, those in which a single room was subdivided into several
sectors: a typical example is the Mycenaean megaron, in which
the rectangular hall — with a semicircular apse at one end that
later disappeared — enclosed within a single perimeter a room
open at the front with columns (*in antis*) and a second room
behind it. Another typical form is that of the ancient Egyptian
houses of the Upper Kingdom (ideally reconstructed from small
clay models, the so-called "soulhouses," from the necropolis of
Rifeh; remains of the houses, which were built of extremely

perishable materials (wood or unbaked bricks), are rare. In these houses one side of an enclosed courtyard was the site of a square or rectangular building containing a room placed on the axis of the entrance and other smaller rooms located at right angles to the larger one. Later these buildings came to have a second story, reached by an exterior stairway. The buildings were usually roofed by a terrace. An intermediate form between the megaron and the Egyptian house of the type described was that used by the Hittites, an example of which is to be found in Boğazköy. Houses of this type were sometimes completed by a courtyard placed on one side of the building (as at Kültepe). In several large Egyptian dwellings dating from the Middle Kingdom (the villages of Lahun and Hawara) a more complex principle of organization tended to distinguish the various rooms by specific functions, thus eliminating multipurpose rooms. The side of the house facing the end of the courtyard given over to living rooms and reception rooms centered around a hypostyle hall, while other rooms housing the domestic facilities and crafts activities and rooms limited to men, women, or children were placed along the adjoining two sides of the courtyard. Thus the area was divided into three nuclei, and this division soon evolved into a system whereby four blocks of buildings formed the four sides of a central courtyard. A variation of this scheme appeared in the plan of the house of the Vizier Nakht in Tell el 'Amarna, with its tripartite arrangement (FIG. 553, 6). Off a projecting vestibule was the first nucleus, consisting of reception hall flanked by smaller rooms. At the center of the house was a large hall with a second reception room on one side and small rooms on the others, from which a corridor led to the third nucleus — the living quarters, with sitting room in the middle and bedroom suites on either side; the master suite is accessible also from the outside by means of a small stairway. The three-sided and four-sided schemes are more or less exactly reproduced in numerous examples of ancient houses both in and outside of Europe. The scheme with buildings on three sides of the courtyard, for example, can be seen in the remains of Assyrian and Babylonian (Assur) houses and is also evident in the Moslem world and particularly in Turkey, with precise functional differentiation of the three domestic nuclei: one reserved for the men, one for the women, and one set apart for living and reception rooms. This layout also was used in pre-Columbian houses, especially in the Olmec and Toltec cultures. The scheme with rooms on all four sides of the courtyard, often completed by two courtyards placed at the front and back of the building, also occurred frequently in Assyria (where the building itself often rose above earthwork foundations and had sections with two stories), in Phoenicia, sometimes in parts of northern India, and in China. Chinese dwellings are based on a protohistoric architectural complex known as the Ming-t'ang, which had a square space in the center (t'ien-ching) surrounded by four groups of rooms (see INTERIOR DECORATION AND DESIGN, cols. 204–205).

Similar forms were developed in the ancient West. Etruscan dwellings, as reflected in the tombs that reproduce their forms (VIII, PL. 95), give evidence of such a variety of plans that it is impossible to speak of a typical Etruscan or Etrusco-Italic dwelling. The tombs provide evidence of types of dwellings with two cells on the same axis (the Campana tomb at Veii) or with cells placed symmetrically on two or three sides of a larger central room (François tomb at Vulci, tomb of the Volumnii in Perugia). Probably the most common type of Etruscan house was that built on a more or less rectangular plan, with an open central area. The tomb of the Marcareccia in Tarquinia and the cinerary urn from Poggio Gaiella, near Chiusi (formerly Berlin, Staat. Mus.), reproduce in an elementary form the single-roomed building with compluvium (opening in the center of the roof). This type of building presumably rose in the center of an enclosed courtyard, to the interior sides of which were attached small outbuildings housing the domestic facilities. The whole constituted the nucleus of a distributive system oriented toward the interior. Later several roofed areas were added along the sides of the enclosure; of the exterior a few small apertures served for ventilation rather than as windows, and these unbroken expanses of wall gave the house a fortresslike

aspect. In this the type is similar to that of Egyptian a Middle Eastern dwellings.

A rational and organic disposition of rooms similar to tl found in the examples of tomb architecture mentioned abo (at Cerveteri, Castel d'Asso, Blera, and Norchia) is characteris of some examples of the type, which has been reconstruct mainly from literary evidence that refers more properly to Italic and Roman type. In this type an entrance corrid without a roof (fauces) led to a rectangular central area (atriu partially covered by a sloping roof. The roof, which was su ported at the four corners by corbeling, sloped downwa toward the compluvium, which directed the rain water into t impluvium (shallow basin) below. One end of the atrium, whi was flanked by two or more rooms, gave onto a larger roo (tablinum) covered by a pitched roof, connected in turn wi two or more rooms, also roofed; often there was a garden the rear of the house. The tablinum was the center of t house and served as the central hall and reception room: was often flanked by two smaller rooms or recesses (ala which isolated the tablinum from the rooms at the sides the atrium.

The plan of the atrium house persisted in other types Etruscan dwellings, including those multistoried ones discover at Marzabotto. These, however, contained several nuclei at are the prototype of the insula (multifamily, multistory dwe ings such as those at Ostia Antica, near Rome). The same pl was taken up in the Roman and Pompeian domus type, whi also strongly reflected Hellenistic dwelling types.

A study of later dwellings at Priene and Delos reveals th the traditional megaron type, in which the nucleus consisted a hall with a vestibule in antis opening onto a central courtya flanked by other rooms and with a corridor (VII, FIG. 30. underwent a transition to other forms in which there were tv courtyards or in which the nucleus around which the roon are grouped, sometimes on two levels, takes the form of peristyle, as at Delos (VII, FIG. 305). At the same time a cle distinction is made between the functions of the rooms (as the House of the Masks), with a part reserved for men (andr nitis), another for women (gynaikonitis), and others for rece tion, guests, the library, and the art gallery (see HELLENISTIC AR1

The Roman domus, especially in examples at Pompeii ar Herculaneum, combines elements of the traditional Etrusc Italic atrium house with Hellenistic elements (peristyles, exedra gardens). Examples of this fusion are the House of Pan (FIG. 553, 10), the House of the Faun (VII, FIG. 402, lowe the House of the Silver Wedding (PL. 247), and the House the Citharist — all at Pompeii.

The entrance to the typical domus was through a vestibu (known as vestibulum or fauces) which — often flanked by tabe nae, or shops — opened directly onto the street and precede the entrance doorway, from which the fauces led to the atriu with its impluvium. The atrium was called Tuscan if the ro was of the type that sloped inward (VIII, PL. 96), was know as tetrastyle if the roof was supported by columns at the fou corners, and was called Corinthian if the number of supportir columns was greater. If the roof channeled the rain away fro the compluvium, the atrium was called displuviate, and it w known as testudinate if it was completely roofed over. In tl last type there was no impluvium.

The tablinum was generally located on the longitudinal ax of the atrium. It soon lost its air of intimacy and opened o toward the peristyle that lay beyond, thus linking in a sing architectural expression the two nuclei that Italic and Hellenist tradition had conceived of as self-sufficient and independen The alae, or wings at the sides, of the tablinum led into th colonnades of the peristyle, off which were various room tricliniums (dining rooms), oeci (reception rooms), and exedra The first typical dining rooms, with couches placed around th mensa, were located in various areas of the domus; there wa an outdoor dining room for use in pleasant weather. The oe and the exedras, instead, were reception areas and were als used for celebrations; they were often tetrastyle or Corinthiar and were always richly decorated. They communicated, gel erally by means of loggias or other apertures, with the viridariu

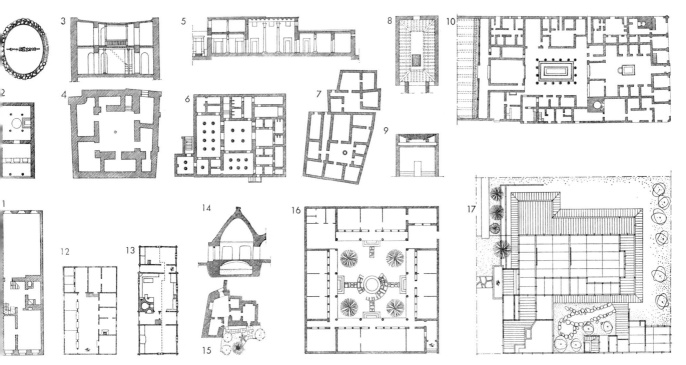

Historical development of the single-unit dwelling. (1) Germany, neolithic circular-plan dwelling, plan; (2) Tiryns, Mycenaean megaron (13th cent. B.C.), plan; (3–4) Ur, Mesopotamian private house (ca. 2000 B.C.), section and plan; (5) reconstruction of an Egyptian private house, section; (6) Tell 'Amarna (Egypt), house of the Vizier Nakht (14th cent. B.C.), plan; (7) Athens, private house (5th cent. B.C.), plan; (8–9) reconstruction of the Italic atrium, plan and section; (10) Pompeii, House of Pansa (2d cent. B.C.), plan; (11) Spremberg (Germany), typical terrace house (15th–16th cent.), plan; (12) Steinheim (Westphalia), typical working-class house (18th cent.), plan; (13) northern Scandinavia, typical wooden house, plan; (14–15) Alberobello, trullo, section and plan; (16) Peking, typical house on an East–West street, plan; (17) Japanese house, after 15th- and 16th- century prototypes, plan.

garden) beyond. This was enclosed by high walls and accentuated the unitary perspective vision that began in the atrium.

A radical transformation of the typical *domus* plan, which was in fact a total rejection of it, occurred when intensive urban construction made necessary the widespread use of buildings composed of apartments built on several stories to be rented to a number of families. During the last years of the Republic this type of construction had appeared occasionally as in the so-called "trelliswork" house at Herculaneum and several houses near the amphitheater at Pompeii; it was, however, in imperial times that the insula became common. In this structure the horizontal scheme of the traditional *domus* plan was abandoned in favor of more ancient schemes such as those of the Etruscan houses of Marzabotto; thus it assumed a vertical expression that was adaptable to contemporary life and to the diverse needs of the heterogeneous Roman population. Insofar as possible, the rooms were no longer oriented around an internal space but opened toward the outside; the courtyard facilitated the distribution of the rooms and provided a source of illumination. A corridor connecting the apartments ran along the outer perimeter of the insula or around the sides of the courtyard, according to whether the exterior was open on one or two sides (as in the House of Diana at Ostia, PL. 246).

The courtyards were often connected with the principal streets running along the sides of the blocks by means of walks, which were sometimes colonnaded. Access to the upper stories was by steep stairways in masonry or wood, generally of one flight per story; the stairways were reached from the courtyard or the *angiportus* (narrow covered alley), or directly from the street. They were so located within the insula that they might serve several apartments at the same time. These apartments (*cenacula*) consisted generally of an indistinct series of identical rooms, sometimes divided by wooden partitions; the rooms were utilized according to the needs, customs, and way of life of the tenant.

Rudimentary collective sanitary facilities were grouped around the stair well, and there was a single water fountain in the courtyard. There seems to have been no kitchen area in the apartments, and no evidence of chimneys or heating

installations has been found in the walls. Ventilation was afforded by the wide rectangular openings, often in the form of two- and three-light windows, which were placed symmetrically in the exterior walls.

The insula, built entirely in masonry with the brick structure left exposed, opened onto the street at ground level in long rows of tabernae with colonnades. Some insulas opened onto the alleys. (Sometimes the owner reserved the entire ground floor of the insula for his own residence.)

Balconies (*maeiana*) projected from the upper stories of the insula; they were supported by barrel vaults springing from heavy travertine corbels or, more rarely, from constructions in wooden raftering. These balconies often formed a continuous terrace along the façade of the house, alternating with colonnades or taking their place if the street was narrow.

Under Augustus the insulas rose as high as 70 ft., this being the maximum permitted by law for the height of façades overlooking the street. Over the courtyards, however, the addition of attics and various wooden superstructures must have added to this already elevated limit and greatly altered the aspect of the buildings.

The grouping of several similar buildings in unitary complexes resulted in a form typical of Ostia — the insulas of Serapis and of the Aurighi (FIG. 555, 1). These groupings of several insulas appeared in vast complexes, such as those, also at Ostia, called the *case a giardino* (garden houses) and the *casette tipo* (typical small houses). Both are made up of small two-story blocks divided by streets, with similar apartments arranged in series. The rationally repeated scheme of these complexes was one of the origins of unitary town planning.

Luciano PONTUALE

The plan of the Roman *domus* persisted, however, in the construction of minor buildings in the early Middle Ages in Italy and western Europe. The proportions of the *domus* were gradually diminished as the atrium was eliminated and the peristyle was reduced to a modest courtyard. A stairway to the upper story or stories stood on one side of the courtyard

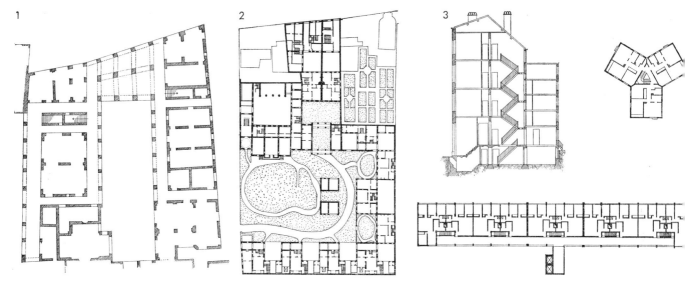

Multiple-unit dwellings. (1) Ostia, insula of the Aurighi (2d cent. B.C.), plan; (2) Paris, houses by C. Ledoux (18th cent.), plan; (3) Paris, hou on Boulevard Haussmann (19th cent.), section; (4) Saint-Cloud, apartment block (20th cent.), plan; (5) Caracas, corridor house (20th cent.), plan.

or against one of the side walls on the building's exterior. Along the front were shops, taverns, and stables, and, above them, windows. Reception areas were no longer distinguished from domestic areas, except that in most cases bedrooms and rooms for servants were on the upper floors.

To this type, which followed the traditional model, was added a more simple one in which the yard stood at the back of the house and all the rooms were located in a single block, arranged around a large room that was entered directly from the main entrance or through a short corridor. This layout was reproduced on the upper floor, where the entrance to the rooms was usually on one side. Sometimes there was a small balcony on the upper floor or a covered veranda or terrace on the roof. Constructions of this type were widespread in western Europe. In Spain the Arabs introduced their interpretation of the *domus* type, with the rooms placed around a central courtyard (patio). The Byzantine-Arab type of house was widely used in southern Italy. This type had rectangular rooms roofed with barrel vaults or low domes located on several, but not all, sides of an open space; the house was often T-, L-, or U-shaped.

In northern Europe, the principal feature of the house often was a great hall, which was repeated on the upper floors; off this hall were the living quarters.

In Great Britain before the 12th century, the hall was sometimes divided by aisles, as at Oakham. The great hall remained important in later British manor houses, some of which were fortified (Stokesay Castle, ca. 1280–90; see GREAT BRITAIN, col. 737).

Medieval town houses in France were multistoried constructions with narrow façades that gave onto the street and with courtyards at the back. The ground floor often served as a shop, and sometimes there was a second building at the end of the courtyard (see GOTHIC ART, col. 482).

In the 15th and 16th centuries, there was still a notable variety in the layout of the rooms of houses, which in Europe, at least, retained the characteristics of the single-family dwelling (FIG. 553, 11, 12, 13). However, in the 16th century, and more often in succeeding centuries, town houses once more became multifamily dwellings, taking up and simplifying the forms of the more aristocratic palace, adapting the palace plan to diverse functions, and recalling more or less intentionally the model of the ancient Roman insula. Rooms were arranged in several apartments on each floor according to purely utilitarian criteria and no longer followed any typical scheme.

There is a wide variety of examples of similar constructions in modern architecture. The problem of a more rational order that serves the demands of family life, within limits dictated by social, economic, and urbanistic concerns, has been a fun damental one in modern architecture. Independently of solu tions designed to fulfill the client's demands, architects of th rank of Hans Scharoun, Adolf Loos, J. P. J. Oud, Walte Gropius, and G. Terragni have carried out important exper ments directed toward solutions that combine the advantage of standardization with a variety of architectural potential an an esthetic sense. The modular concepts applied in the housin units (*unités d'habitation*) by Le Corbusier in Marseilles (I, PL. 38 are an example of this attempt to integrate the dwelling int the urban complex and to insert both in turn into their su roundings. The new architectural types presently being deve oped are conceived not as rigid compositional schemes, b rather in terms of "open" spatial elements that are adaptab to varying functions, as in houses with walls that can be free composed and shifted and in prefabricated and expandab houses such as those produced by Gropius, R. Rapson, D. Rur nels, and Buckminster Fuller.

Palaces. Very early in the history of Mediterranean an Near Eastern cultures there is evidence of the development a type of building that was intended both as the residence the chief official of the community and as a civil and religio center. Often, therefore, this type included reception room audience halls, administrative offices, archives, places of worshi and soldiers' quarters. The rooms were arranged in a fashio that is, in general, inspired by basic dwelling plans; howeve the palace of ancient times cannot be considered merely larger and more elaborate development of the house. Th coordination of several nuclei of rooms, functionally differer tiated and yet closely interconnected, gives rise to the type an its characteristics. These characteristics may vary among pala buildings within the same culture, but have been transmitte to and repeated in palaces constructed in different perio and places.

Palaces are distinguished by their official character, eithe as residences of a sovereign, an archbishop, or bishop, or public buildings (e.g., seats of legislature). This official chara ter is to be distinguished from the private nature of elabora town houses and of villas, which are more or less pretentiou rural or suburban dwellings generally surrounded by a par A castle is a fortified palace and as such is treated below und *Fortifications.*

With the possible exception of the "Palace of the Inca" Lake Titicaca, Bolivia (I, FIG. 355), the palaces of pre-Colum bian America do not seem to have been royal residences. Cuzco and Chan-Chan in Peru (FIG. 557, 2) communal livin quarters or small houses were grouped within walled zone

The so-called Mayan "palaces" often were simply buildings with many rooms and were used not so much for residences as, perhaps, for workshops and storerooms. The most striking palaces are in Yucatan, where they are raised on platforms. The so-called "Nunnery Quadrangle" (cf. MIDDLE AMERICAN PROTOHISTORY, col. 40; X, PLS. 8, 9) is a complex of four buildings built around a courtyard. The Mixtec archaeological site of Mitla has several palaces consisting of rooms laid out around quadrangular porticoes (X, FIG. 68).

Among the most ancient of princely dwellings are the royal palaces of Egypt, which, like less important houses, were built of sun-baked brick and wood. From the New Kingdom there are remains of the Palace of Amenhotep III at Malkata; this building was lacking in an organized plan. The appearance of the interiors may be deduced from representations in wall paintings and from the layout of the hypogeum tombs at Tell el 'Amarna (XIV, PL. 128), where several royal palaces were laid out along monumental lines with both state and private royal apartments set in a symmetrical scheme. The North Palace, with a garden court opening from the halls north of the throne room, apparently was for purely official purposes. It was connected with the royal living quarters by a bridge over a roadway.

Colonnaded porches and monumental gateways were important architectural elements in Egyptian palace buildings. Sometimes palaces were annexed to mortuary temples, as in the Rameseum of Thebes (see EGYPTIAN ART, col. 677). Here the palace was not conceived of as a permanent residence and consisted only of the essential official and private chambers (colonnaded court and throne room, sleeping quarters) with a balconied "window of appearances" opening into the temple hall.

In Dur Sharrukin in Mesopotamia the citadel within the city enclosed the palace of Sargon II and the ziggurat (I, FIG. 870; X, FIG. 777). Access to the palace, which was set on a terrace, was by a ramp which led into a court through a monumental arched gateway flanked by towers. On the left was a group of temples, on the right were service quarters and administrative offices, and facing the entrance stood the private and residential apartments. On the other side of these was another court around which were grouped the state rooms. The turreted walls of the citadel and the varying heights of the architectural groups contributed to the lively aspect of the whole.

This scheme was amplified in the palace near the Ishar Gates in Babylon, which was built by Nabopolassar and later enlarged by Nebuchadnezzar II. A series of five courtyards lay side by side, and off the largest of these was an immense throne room. Distinct from the palace, but part of the complex, was a massive fortress. The entire complex was enclosed by high bastions that delimited it (IX, FIG. 783).

The freedom of composition evident in Assyrian palaces inspired the construction of the royal dwellings of Achaemenid Persia, for example, those at Masjid-i-Sulaymān and at Badr Nishanda, where the rooms were grouped around a triple liwan. This division into three enclosed asymmetrically placed nuclei was repeated in the palace of Cyrus at Pasargadae, where they

are not adjacent, however. The first contained a monumental entrance hall with two rows of four columns. The second rose on a terrace about 220 yd. from the entrance and functioned as an audience hall. The third was the reception hall and had a triple liwan along the façade. A similar scheme was used in the palaces of Darius at Persepolis (VIII, FIG. 229) and Susa, the second of which was reconstructed by Artaxerxes II (see IRANIAN PRE-SASSANIAN ART CULTURES, cols. 267–273).

The Iranian palace complex was conceived as a free architectural expression, unlimited by town-planning concepts and enlivened by its variety of forms, which included high, decorated bases with ramps and stairways. The open forms of the audience hall were later replaced, especially in Sassanian architecture, by areas that were contained by the structures of the palace. The most typical element of this architecture was the barrel-vaulted liwan, which was open along the façade, as at Firuzabad (XII, FIG. 705), Sarvistan (XII, FIG. 707), Ashur, and Ctesiphon (see PARTHIAN ART; SASSANIAN ART).

A complex articulation of rooms was achieved in another manner in Cretan palaces, where the functions of royal residence and place of worship were more explicitly defined. The ideal center of the palace was the megaron, around which the various rooms and nuclei were freely grouped and were connected by colonnades, small courtyards, and terraces. The location of the buildings on various levels created pleasing effects of perspective. This lively articulation of the rooms, effected within the sphere of a unitary whole, was a conscious expression of the Cretan builders, as is evident in the few remains of the early stages of construction of the palaces of Knossos, Phaistos, and Mallia (FIG. 557, 1). In these, the variety of the nuclei, which at Knossos and Phaistos included an embryonic peristyle and a theater, contributed to the architectural articulation of the buildings, as did the alternation of the open façades of the megaron with other closed ones and the concept of the central courtyard as an open space, as used at both Knossos (IV, FIG. 85) and Phaistos, where it was preceded by a grand staircase that accentuated its scenographic aspect.

The megaron also formed the center of the Mycenaean palace complex, at least from the time of the Middle Mycenaean period (1500–1400 B.C.). However, unlike those in the area of Cretan culture, Mycenaean palaces assumed a more clearly defensive character, as at Mycenae itself (IV, FIG. 108) and in the acropolis at Tiryns (IV, FIG. 111). The rooms were generally grouped asymmetrically along the axis formed by the propylaea, the partly colonnaded courtyard, and the megaron. At Tiryns the basic form was repeated in megaronlike rooms adjacent to the nucleus. The palace at Tiryns, with its aspect of a small fortified citadel, returned to an organization that, though somewhat fragmentary, was oriented around a central nucleus.

It was almost exclusively during the archaic period that the Greeks built palaces; these were based on eastern examples, as in the palace of Vuni in Cyprus (IV, FIG. 181). The entrance was flanked by a prothyron (vestibule) that led to two vast rooms and thence to a colonnaded courtyard surrounded by other rooms, including, at the end, an audience chamber. Later

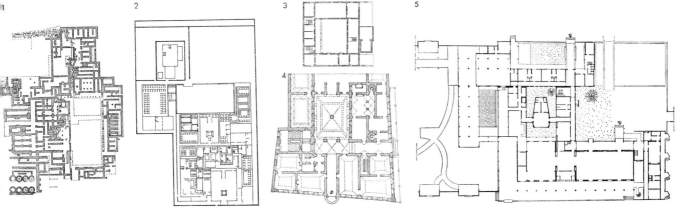

Palaces, plans. (1) Mallia (Crete), palace (2d millennium B.C.); (2) Chan-Chan (Peru), enclosure of the "first palace" (13th–14th cent.); (3) Palermo, Palazzo Abatelli (15th cent.); (4) Rome, Palazzo Mattei (16th cent.); (5) locality on the Persian Gulf, sheik's palace (20th cent.).

elaborations of the palace recall the plans of Mycenaean palaces: the entrance was transformed into a kind of megaron, the audience chamber was divided in two, and the location of the entrance was reversed.

In Rome (see ROMAN IMPERIAL ART), the Imperial Palace built by Augustus on the Palatine Hill (whence the etymology of *palatium*) was presumably originally a typical patrician *domus*, even though it was later enriched with new elements. This was probably also true of the palace built by Tiberius (A.D. 30) and enlarged by Caligula (A.D. 40), about which little is known other than its general form and location. Nero's Domus Aurea on the Oppian Hill introduced new architectural forms and inaugurated a new type of Roman palace (XII, FIG. 522). Its plan was a departure from those usual in the architecture of the period and was linked, in its rooms laid out along a straight line, to the open plan of the colonnaded villa. A more precise and individual aspect was given to the palace complex built by Domitian on the Palatine Hill. It was formed of two adjacent nuclei (XII, FIG. 519, 19, 21). One, the Domus Flavia, consisted of a *domus* with peristyle surrounded by three halls ("royal hall," *lararium*, and basilica), tablinum, nymphaeums, and baths. To one side of the Domus Flavia was the Domus Augustana, which was built on the plan of the *domus* with two peristyles. The entire complex rose at different levels on the hill and was bounded on the east by a large stadium and the Baths of Septimius Severus.

In a later period the nature of the palace as an imperial residence (sometimes a patrician one), assumed a military character, incorporating features of the *castrum* and *castellum*. A basic example is the Palace of Diocletian at Split, Yugoslavia (IX, FIG. 91). This was enclosed by a turreted wall which, on the southern side facing the sea, had open galleries; on the other sides of the wall were gates (Porta Aurea, Porta Argentea, Porta Ferrea) flanked by towers. Inside, two rectilinear roads crossed at right angles, repeating the positioning of the *cardo* and the *decumanus* and subdividing the complex into quarters that were distinguished by function. This rigidly geometric layout was partially relieved by the widening of the main street, on which stood the mausoleum of the emperor, a small temple, and the entrance to the imperial residence (IX, FIG. 91, 6, 5, 7 respectively). It may be said that this wide area in the palace complex corresponded to the peristyle. The Palace of Diocletian and the Imperial Palace on the Palatine Hill served as models for similar constructions of the late Roman imperial period, as at Antioch, Salonika (palace complex of Galerius, IX, FIG. 90), and Trier. These, in turn, inspired many medieval castles.

In the early Middle Ages, the few palaces that are well documented do not differ significantly in type from Roman palaces. The Palace of Theodoric in Ravenna probably was derived from previous types in some of its principal parts. The Lateran Palace in Rome reproduced more or less exactly the plan of the Roman *domus* (according to the description in the *Liber pontificalis*, at the time of Leo III this building had a peristyle and a triclinium with apses). The Palace of Charlemagne at Aachen, built by Odo of Metz in 792, followed earlier examples. The other Carolingian palace at Ingelheim differed in that the front side of the courtyard may have been free of buildings (it was presumably colonnaded) and the palace had a second, semicircular courtyard. This scheme, with the courtyard open at the front, had also been used in Constantinople, in the so-called "Palace of Justinian," in which large portals and balconies on the façade of the end building created a rich ornamental effect. It was used again, also in Constantinople, in the later Tekfur Sarayi, where there is a marked sense of the form of the building, and where the façade was decorated with ornamental brickwork.

The schemes of Roman buildings were taken up in the older Moslem palaces, which also show the influence of more recent Western expressions. Thus the axial scheme of the type used in Diocletian's palace at Split reappeared in the Dār al-Imāra of Merv, in the palace of the Caliph al-Mutasim in Samarra, and later, in the 10th century, in that of al-Bahr, Algeria. In these constructions were introduced compositional accents in elevation that are unique, especially in the shape of the entrance wing, which generally included the audience chamber, preceded by one or four liwans placed radially and with vaulted roofing.

Moslem palaces (see ISLAM, cols. 342–346) generally followed the tripartite division: one section contained guardhouses, storerooms, and a prayer hall; another housed the court of honor and basilican hall with a triconch throne room; and the third contained the private apartments of the caliph. This division appeared in Ommiad and Abbasside architecture (see OMMIAD SCHOOLS, cols. 749–751, and ABBASSIDE ART, cols. 6, 7) and was still evident in the Alhambra (cf. VIII, FIG. 335; see also Medina az-Zahra, X, FIG. 305). In later palaces, as in those in Isfahan and Istanbul, the plan was freer and centered around courtyards, pavilions, and liwans (FIG. 557, 5). Indian palace architecture, of which there are many examples in Rajasthan, was influenced mainly by the Moghul palaces at Agra, Delhi, and Lahore.

In the West, from the beginning of the Romanesque period up to the beginning of the 14th century a simpler form of palace became common. In most cases these were inserted into the layout of the town; they were differentiated on the exterior from common houses in only a few aspects such as larger and more decorative doors and windows and the presence of towers. On the interior this type of building was divided into two parts, one for reception purposes and the other more properly residential. The first included a vast hall, a chapel, and a number of smaller rooms in which the official activities of the owner were carried out. The second, much more simple and less formal, was composed of a series of private chambers located in the inmost part of the house and often distributed so as to create two separate apartments — one for summer and one for winter — both of which opened into a garden at the rear with large balconies, loggias, and roof terraces. The colonnaded courtyard admitted light and air to the interior rooms on the upper floors. An outdoor staircase led from the courtyard to the piano nobile (the principal story, generally the second story) and was the principal means of access to floors. The remaining free space served such various purposes as housing for the guard, armory, and storerooms.

Among the few variants of this compositional scheme, that common in Venice until the 16th century is notable. In Venetian palaces the lower story of the façade on the canal, often colonnaded or with superposed open galleries, opened into a large hall that ran the entire length of the building and was generally repeated on the floor above; the rooms were aligned along one side of this axis. If there was a courtyard, its main function was to divide the space, separating the rooms.

In the northern countries the rooms converged on three sides of the great entrance hall. However, especially during the late Gothic period, aristocratic dwellings took on a form that cannot wholly accurately be described as that of a palace, both because it was based on the plan of the castle, and because it was more magnificent than that of the ordinary house; in most cases this form was conceived with maximum freedom in its grouping of different nuclei, and, therefore, also in its volumetric aspect. The Hôtel Jacques-Cœur in Bourges (V, PL. 381 FIG. 658) is an example of the rejection of any schematic form and any axial design.

In Tuscany in the late Gothic period the palace had been isolated from contact with other buildings and placed as a freestanding unit surrounded by streets and squares (Palazzo Davanzati in Florence, Palazzo Tolomei in Siena), foreshadowing the later development of the Renaissance palace.

The typical palace of the Renaissance was a unitary construction, geometrically conceived (see RENAISSANCE ART). The façade or façades (usually similar) were articulated by a rhythmical series of apertures. Generally on three stories, each decorated with one of the three orders, the Renaissance palace repeated internally the measured rhythm of the façades with a system of intersecting axes around a large arcaded courtyard. The rooms were oriented outward and were connected by corridors along the courtyard façade. The various functions were generally divided among three floors: on the lower story were the doorkeeper's rooms, storerooms, rooms for supplementary facilities and for business; on the second story (piano nobile) as a series of similar rooms, set one after the other, surrounding a large central hall which, placed on the axis of the main façade, was often two stories high and served as the center of all official and social activities (the dimensions of the hall sometimes were concealed on the exterior, but in other examples were reflected in the modeling of the façade — in balconies, in large or more closely placed windows, or in other special architectural devices.) On the third story were the family rooms, bedrooms, dining rooms, and those used for domestic activities. The topmost story, often a mezzanine, contained the servants' quarters.

This basic plan, used as early as the 15th century in the Medici-Riccardi, Strozzi, and Rucellai palaces in Florence (XII, FIGS. 14, 21b), was the model for almost every Italian Renaissance palace up to the 16th century (Palazzo Vidoni and Palazzo Farnese in Rome, XII, FIG. 80). The scheme remained substantially the same, with variations dictated by geographic, functional, and creative considerations. A different interpretation of the Renaissance palace emerged in the stately châteaux built by French nobility, especially in the Loire region.

With the baroque period (see BAROQUE ART) the traditional palace plan inherited from the Renaissance did not change, but was rendered more complex, with emphasis on the plan's formal and spatial values, on the juxtaposition of volume and a more expressive style (II, FIGS. 285, 289, 293). In the division of the building into three stories the Renaissance plan persisted, while there was a more frequent use of mezzanines, which sometimes extended through the entire building. The characteristics of the mezzanines were subordinated to the nature of the rooms below them, which they often overlooked.

On the piano nobile the use of large reception rooms was accentuated. In this period they linked the smaller rooms grouped around them and because of their particular size conditioned the design of the entire building. The reception area generally consisted of the main hall and a series of small lounges of elliptical, circular, or mixtilinear shape. The representative character of these rooms was often clearly expressed on the exterior by a closer positioning of the windows or by masonry projections in the center of the façade, as in Piedmontese palaces, where the structure of the central hall was reflected on the façade (cf. Palazzo Carignano, Turin, VII, PL. 104). The extension of the building in successive architectural masses united to the main building along a continuous transverse axis created new problems of form and layout that were resolved by the architect Juvara (q.v.), whose work foreshadowed the palaces of 18th-century France and England. Juvara transmitted his style to Spain, where he executed the Royal Palace in Madrid (I, PL. 160).

Occasionally the desire for a geometric definition of volume precluded such solutions, as in the Palazzo Barberini in Rome, in which the main hall, two stories high, is not demarcated in the façade, which is filled in with a double row of windows (I, PL. 134).

The use of scenographic solutions in the architectural treatment of rooms of a highly ceremonial or official character, earlier a concern of the Renaissance architects, recurred in the baroque conception of the perspective of atrium, courtyard, and main staircase. The measured effects of space used in the Renaissance were replaced in this period by more scenographic effects aimed at a spatial synthesis of the three elements in perspective. The best examples of these effects are in palaces in Genoa, Rome, and the Piedmont region (Palazzo Balbi, Genoa, VIII, PL. 226; Palazzo Carignano, Turin; the Barberini and Braschi palaces, Rome).

Later the staircase, which was the focus of the plan, added to its specific functions of communication and distribution the new function of an indirect source of light for the interior rooms it served, thus heightening that illusionistic effect of spatial freedom typical of the 17th and 18th centuries (cf. the stair hall of the Residenz of Würzburg, VI, FIG. 187).

Palace plans reflected these developments elsewhere in Europe: the baroque style in England is evident in Blenheim Palace, Oxfordshire (II, FIG. 285); the Czernin Palace in Prague (I, PL. 159) is a fine example of the style as transmitted to

Czechoslovakia by Italian architects; the castles of Rosenborg and Christiansborg show the plan as adapted in Denmark in the 17th and 18th centuries, respectively; in Vienna the Belvedere is notable for the sculptural treatment of its façade (II, PL. 158, cf. FIG. 289).

A return to the classical lines of ancient models gave new impetus to the construction of palaces in the late 18th and 19th century. Among these neoclassic buildings were the Skórzewski Palace in Lubostroń, Poland (X, PL. 273) and, in Russia, the English Palace in Peterhof (X, FIG. 535b), the Elagin Palace (X, FIG. 535d), and the New Mikhail Palace (X, FIG. 539), all of which were planned, at least in part, by architects from Italy.

The traditional concept of the palace has gradually disappeared in the 20th century, especially since the decline of the monarchical system has eliminated the need for new residences to serve elaborate court functions. The modern palace — that is, public building — serves very different purposes and has evolved as a distinct type (see below).

Villas. A villa is a building or complex of buildings that serves as a residence, in which the relation of architectural and natural elements is intentional. The simple association of building and garden does not necessarily denote a villa. Many dwellings and palaces in ancient Egypt and the East rose among gardens and parks and were, furthermore, completed by structures — colonnades, exedras, terraces, kiosks — that established a continuity between the main building and the garden (see LANDSCAPE ARCHITECTURE), but are not considered villas.

According to the above definition the first true villa of the ancient world was the Roman villa of the late Republican and imperial eras, mentioned above with reference to the *domus* type. In the Roman villa spacious development of the peristyle and the articulation of functionally differentiated building nuclei were more than a simple organic expansion of the *domus*; they represented the creation of a new type of building complex.

The form of the *domus* is repeated in part in the Roman country villa, where, for utilitarian reasons, the atrium was replaced by a courtyard in the form of a peristyle, which also served as a farmyard. Although the villa type presents no consistent plan, evidence in Cato (*De agricoltura*, I, iii, 10), Columella (*De re rustica*, I, 6), and Vitruvius (*De architectura*, VI, vii, 9) and the remains of the villa in Boscoreale known as "La Pisanella" indicate that this type of construction (at least during the imperial period) must have consisted of not less than five main groups of rooms: the owner's quarters, quarters for the servants and the farmer-manager, rooms for equipment and facilities, shelters for the animals, and storerooms. In many cases (as was noted by Seneca in describing the villa of Scipio Africanus; *Ad Lucilium*, Ep. 86), the country villa was surrounded by strong walls that had the air of true fortifications.

The solely utilitarian nature of the country villa tended to diminish about the 2d century B.C., as the part dedicated to agricultural activity became distinct from the residential quarters. In this transition the peristyle assumed greater importance. The fortresslike character of the outer walls was transformed by the insertion of a colonnade, at first located before the main entrance (as in the Villa of Diomede, Pompeii) and later extended along three sides of the villa (early stages of the "Villa of the Mysteries," Pompeii), thus presenting a view of the surrounding landscape to those rooms which previously had been oriented exclusively inward around the atrium. The entrance was moved to the opposite side of the house and opened onto the peristyle, which thus became the new center of the building. The construction as a whole was open and dominated the surrounding countryside with wide, airy galleries. The atrium became a simple connecting element between the various rooms of lesser importance. The general distributive order of the rooms, however, remained unitary and was contained within a single rigidly rectangular space.

During the imperial age the concept of the villa as a center of amusement and entertainment was emphasized, while its function as a farm unit remained unchanged.

Because of the freedom of arrangement of the building nuclei and their variety in number and character, there emerged no consistent villa plan. The villa ranged from the country type, contained within a more or less compact block (as the villa at Sirmione or the villa near Anguillara, whose façade was an immense semicircular exedra), to a type with a more irregular scheme (villas at Pompeii and Herculaneum and Domitian's villa near Alba Longa). In these types the *domus* nucleus still dominated and conditioned the plan of the entire complex; in later examples (the villa of Vedio Pollione at Posillipo and Hellenistic villas in the Phlegraean Fields) the *domus* plan became secondary.

In the 1st century of the Christian era villa complexes were built on multiple axes with polyhedric pavilions. They were adapted to the terrain, sometimes dominating it, and were composed of structures on different levels, with terracing and imposing multistoried masonry constructions. The principal zones were often divided into groups of several rooms placed to the north and south so as to enjoy greater amounts of sunshine throughout the changing seasons. In his *De re rustica*, written in the Augustan era, Varro recommended that villas be provided with gymnasiums, colonnades, peristyles, entrance halls, cryptoportici, exedras, loggias, and nymphaeums, all facing south.

In such complexes the residential area proper gradually developed into a single autonomous element, while the entire villa complex was divided into groupings set freely in varying compositions, seemingly asymmetrical, which attained their most monumental expressions at the time of the height of the Empire with the addition of theaters, baths, and hippodromes.

Hadrian's Villa at Tivoli (XII, FIG. 531) and the Roman villa at Casale, near Piazza Armerina (IX, FIG. 95), are typical of such monumental complexes. In both the *domus* plan had disappeared and the various groups of structures were arranged according to a plan that followed the natural contours of the area. This careful adaptation of architecture to terrain gave a sense of the free and organic conception of the entire complex. This freedom was expressed in the interrelated groupings of the various monumental areas of the villa, each of which had an internal plan. The single members of the various groups were arranged symmetrically, in traditional types. Hadrian's Villa at Tivoli, for example, is organized along three principal axial systems that are interconnected. The first group, made up of the two libraries, the palace, and the buildings in the Piazza d'Oro, is connected by the theater to the Stadium and the Poikile. This second group is connected to the great and small baths, the Canopus, and the Temple of Serapis on a third axis (XII, FIG. 531).

Among other types of villas were those called "colonnaded villas," known from numerous paintings and from remains found in Campania (Stabiae). They were generally formed of a single rectangular building, usually L- or U-shaped; along the front of the building was a colonnade through which the rooms were lighted directly from outside, there being no peristyle.

In the Middle Ages the house with garden had no characteristics that substantially distinguished it from other dwellings.

However, Moslem architects had more precise intentions regarding the characterization of a residential building in relation to the garden in which it stood. What remains of the constructions in Spain (Seville, Córdoba) and Sicily (Palermo) and derivatives in southern Italy (Rufolo at Ravello) indicates that, while retaining a closed plan with either inner or rear courtyard, the whole enclosed by high walls, they sought an ideal continuity between the courtyard and the garden around it. Galleries that open onto the courtyard are a distinguishing feature of the type.

In Italy during the 15th and 16th centuries the villa finally assumed more definite characteristics: those of the Tuscan villas, whose simple form was inspired by the rustic house (as in the villas at Careggi, XII, FIG. 21; Cafaggiolo, VIII, PL. 191; and Poggio a Caiano, VIII, PL. 428; XII, FIG. 683), and those in Rome, which were small palaces with less compact plans elaborated by galleries on the ground floor (e.g., the Farnesina in Rome, XI, FIG. 273; Villa Lante at Bagnaia, near Viterbo,

VIII, PL. 433). Later villas consisted of palaces integrated wi gardens by means of exedras, lateral colonnades, staircases, a other architectural elements, as in Villa Giulia in Rome (VI FIG. 1087), Palazzo Farnese at Caprarola (IX, FIG. 465), Vi d'Este at Tivoli (VIII, PL. 432), and Villa Aldobrandini at Fi scati (VIII, PL. 433).

In the Veneto region Palladio effectively integrated the buil ing nucleus with the landscape in Villa Trissino in Meledo extending the construction into the landscape area. In Vi Barbaro at Maser, the building is the terminal element in a pe spective view of the park (VIII, PL. 434), as also in Villa Piove at Lonedo. The same integral relationship can be seen in t Villa Cornaro at Piombino Dese and Villa Capra ("La Rotunda near Vicenza, where the front and sides are opened by galleri (XI, FIG. 69). Palladio's schemes continued in use in Ita until the 18th century (as in Villa Albani in Rome and Vi Cordellina at Montecchio Maggiore) and spread to Englai and central and eastern Europe, where Palladian models we considered the ideal in villa planning.

The architects of the baroque style turned to the mode of 16th-century Rome: the villa was built as a palace that mig be either large or rather small (lodge), with wide galleries ground level and on the upper stories, often linked to its pa by means of scenographic elements — stairways or covered a cades that sometimes served to connect the main building wi other subordinate nuclei (nymphaeums, exedras, terraces, fou tains, kiosks, imitation ruins, artificial grottoes).

These types of villas spread throughout Europe, existi contemporaneously with constructions that were larger, mo elaborate interpretations of rustic models, as especially in Engli country houses, the rural dwellings of a landed aristocracy (s GREAT BRITAIN, col. 737). Another contemporary develo ment led to the transformation of castles, which had by th become obsolete, into the French châteaux.

In more recent times there has been an eclectic and co fused return to Renaissance and baroque models, together wi a tendency toward the exotic in 19th-century villa architectur In the modern villa there is an attempt at a more organic it tegration of architecture and nature, whether in garden or op countryside. Examples of this concept are the Mensendie country home designed by Richard Neutra (VIII, PL. 45 and Frank Lloyd Wright's Kaufmann house (Falling Wate Pa.; I, PL. 91).

It is to be noted that even in areas where landscape ga dening has attained a high degree of perfection, as in Chir and Japan, there are, in the architectural sense, no particul characteristics of buildings with gardens that admit them classification as villas; in general these buildings repeat form typical of common dwellings.

RELIGIOUS BUILDINGS. It is generally believed that, among types of buildings, those intended as places of worship prese the most easily distinguished types. The mention of the Egypti or Greek temple, the Christian basilica, the mosque, or t pagoda seems to conjure up the image of a building stereotyp However, a study of the historical development of vario religions and their rites reveals that buildings inspired by th same religion may differ markedly in different regions ar periods. In regard to these buildings, therefore, it will necessary to mention both their general characteristics and the principal differences.

Protohistoric and ancient Eastern structures. In many prehi toric and primitive cultures there was often no liturgical defin tion of the ritual, and the room or rooms used for the rit were not distinguished architecturally in any special way. Suc rites usually were held in one of the interior rooms of the hou of the priest or witch doctor, where the ritual accessories ha been gathered. More precise characteristics can be found the sacred places (sanctuaries, votive shrines, shelters for th object of worship) and the huts where the initiation rites of t young took place. These were usually larger than huts use as dwellings and were often enclosed within one or more fenc that had symbolic connotations.

Presumably, places of worship were constructed mainly in wood during the prehistoric era in the West, but the only remains of such places are such megalithic constructions as dolmens, the lichavens of the British Isles, the *allées couvertes* of Morbihan in France, the stone enclosures (*alignements*) in France, and the sanctuaries of Stonehenge and Avebury in England (PL. 252; V, PLS. 164, 165). Other megalithic constructions designed as places of worship are of a later period. In plan these are generally circular (the well-temple at Santa Vittoria di Serri, Sardinia, IX, FIG. 607) or elliptical (the neolithic temples of Hagar Qim and Hal Tarxien in Malta, built as a series of rooms along an axis, with raised apse areas, IX, FIG. 418).

found near Persepolis. In the palaces of Ashur (Assur), Kuh-i Khwaja, and Hatra (XI, FIG. 111) from the Parthian era, the liwan (a vaulted room closed on three sides and open on the fourth) is introduced; it reappears in the Sassanian period in the palace at Firuzabad (XII, FIG. 705), in the 'Imārat-i-Khusrau at Qaṣr-i Shīrīn, and, later, in other buildings in more complex forms (see IRANIAN PRE-SASSANIAN ART CULTURES; PARTHIAN ART; SASSANIAN ART, col. 711).

A more complex type of sacred building is to be found in Egypt. A basic distinction must be made between temples dedicated to the celebration of funeral rites and those reserved for worship. The first, both religious and commemorative in

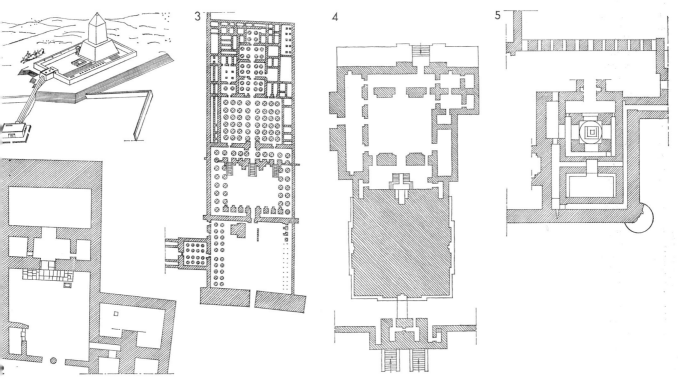

Temples of the ancient East. (1) Abu Gurob (Egypt), sun temple of Neuserra (5th dynasty, 15th cent. B.C.), reconstruction; (2) Alalakh (Syria), temple from Level 1 B (13th cent. B.C.), plan; (3) Thebes (Egypt), Ramaseum (13th cent. B.C.), plan; (4) Kar-Tukulti-Ninurta (Mesopotamia), Temple of Ashur (late 13th cent. B.C.), plan; (5) Kuh-i-Khwaja (Iran), Parthian temple (1st–2d cent.), plan.

It is probable that ritual functions were carried out in dwellings, as must have been the case, for example, in the Sardinian nuraghi and the talayoti of the Balearic Islands (IX, FIG. 611). In ancient Mesopotamia, enclosed shrines constituted the embryo of the temple, but the principal place of worship was the stepped pyramid (ziggurat), with its complex symbolism (PL. 242; I, FIG. 867; III, PL. 485). The symbolic pyramid- or cone-shaped building without internal space can be found in various cultural areas; among these were probably the Egyptian pyramids, such as that of Zoser, at Saqqara (IV, PL. 329), and more certainly the stepped pyramids of pre-Columbian America, from those of Teotihuacán (PL. 242), Chichén Itzá (X, PL. 35), and Tajín (III, PL. 485; X, PL. 22) — all in Mexico — to those of Tikal in Guatemala (PL. 253), along with some constructions in Asia.

In Achaemenid Persia there were no true temples. At Pasargadae (XIV, PL. 476) and Naqsh-i-Rustam (VIII, PL. 137) there were towers, probably temples for the preservation of the sacred fire. At Susa the fire temple, or *ayādanā*, was of a type elaborated on in later architecture. It consisted of a square courtyard surrounded on three sides by a corridor; on the fourth side was a colonnade of paired columns with a door leading to a square room, whose roof was supported by four columns, where the sacred fire was housed. (More common sites of worship during this period were fire altars erected in the open, cf. XIV, PL. 477.) The fire temple at Susa was the model for the relatively rare examples of similar structures

nature, is typified by the mortuary precinct of King Zoser, where the pyramid rises in the center (IV, FIG. 633). Other examples are the temple of Mentuhotep II (Nebhepetra), in which a ramp leads to an enclosure with a square terrace, at one end of which is the pyramid surrounded by a colonnade (IV, FIG. 653), and the temple of Queen Hatshepsut, with ramps leading to two large terraces rising on pillared galleries (PL. 252; IV, PL. 356, FIG. 671), behind which a hypostyle hall was cut into the rock. These temples combined the forms of the terrace temple and those of the hypogeum temple, which was also common (as in Abu Simbel). The temple reserved for worship, in its schematic and elementary form, consisted of an enclosure preceded by an avenue flanked with statues and ending in a pylon gateway. This opened onto a vast courtyard, usually square, surrounded on three or all four sides by a colonnade. At one end was the hypostyle hall, often slightly raised and preceded by a flight of steps; beyond were the cells of the sanctuary and other rooms (a typical example is the Temple of Khonsu at Karnak, IV, FIG. 675). In other temple layouts successions of pylons stood at the entrances to the various parts, as in the Temple of Amen at Karnak (IV, FIG. 668), and the number of elements was increased, not necessarily following a single axis, as in the temple at Luxor (IV, FIG. 673). Other variants of the plan affected the location of the colonnade in the first courtyard, the shape of the entrances, the construction of the hypostyle hall, and the composition of the cella and adjoining rooms; such variants were used in temples of the Ptolemaic era: that of Horus at Edfu (IV, FIG. 699) and that of Sobek and Haroeris at Kom Ombo (IV, FIG. 700).

Greek and Roman temples. In its essential form, and in regard to the principal chamber (naos: sanctuary; also called cella), the Greek temple derives from the Creto-Mycenaean megaron. The temple *in antis* is a direct imitation of the megaron. Temples of this type have a columned pronaos (porch) limited by the pilasters that terminate the side walls of the naos. The pronaos supports the entablature and pediment (in several archaic examples, such as Temple A at Prinias in Crete, there is only one square pillar at the center of the pronaos between the antae; FIG. 569, 3); a similar but smaller porch (*opisthodomos*) was sometimes built at the back. When there is a line of columns across the porch in front of the antae the temple is called prostyle and when there is a line of columns also along the back it is called amphiprostyle (FIG. 569, 3). Inside there could be a line of columns on one or two levels, supporting the crown of the roof and dividing the room into two naves. At the end of the naos was an inner sanctuary (*adyton*) in which the image of the god was kept. The center of worship was, therefore, the naos, which might be all that the temple consisted of, as in many small temples of the *in antis* type, or, rarely, the prostyle type. More commonly the naos was contained within a group of columns that supported an entablature, the whole resting on a three-stepped platform (*krepidoma*). Temples with a single file of columns surrounding the naos are called peripteral. If there are two rows of columns around the naos the temple is called dipteral. Pseudodipteral temples are similar to dipteral ones, but the inner line of columns is omitted on the sides of the naos. In pseudoperipteral temples the single line of columns around the naos is engaged at the sides of the building. Usually, the number of the side columns was double that of the front columns plus one. These were ideal schemes and were not necessarily followed; there are countless variants (FIG. 569).

Among the Doric temples, Temple C at Selinunte (FIG. 569, 5) is noteworthy. The cella had an anteroom and *adyton* and lacked pronaos and *opisthodomos*. A double row of columns at the front creates the effect of an inner porch. Temple G at Selinunte was pseudoperipteral with eight columns on the front (octastyle), a naos and *opisthodomos* (VII, FIG. 123). Two rows of columns divided the naos into three aisles. The double row of columns on the front, and the three-aisled naos appear again in the Temple of Apollo at Syracuse (VII, FIG. 121). At Paestum the naos of the "Basilica" was divided by a single row of columns. There were three columns in the pronaos instead of two, and along the front were nine columns (enneastyle). Temple G at Selinunte and the Temple of Athena (Ceres?) at Paestum also have three-sided prostyle porches in front of the pronaos (VII, FIG. 126), and the so-called "Temple of Neptune" at Paestum was of the type with the inner colonnade in two superimposed orders. A more unusual solution was adopted in the Temple of Olympian Zeus in Agrigento, where the columns were engaged by a perimeter wall which rose only to half height at the front, where Atlantes were probably placed in the spaces between the columns to act as intermediate supports for the entablature. The temple was pseudoperipteral on all sides; its huge naos was divided into three aisles by two rows of pillars.

In Greece the temples of Zeus at Nemea, of Nemesis at Rhamnous, and of Asklepios at Epidauros were peripteral; each had a naos without an *adyton*, and the second was without an *opisthodomos* (III, FIG. 661). In the Temple of Zeus at Olympia the naos was divided into three aisles, and in the Parthenon, which was octastyle, the naos was divided into two separate parts, each with its own pronaos and prostyle (III, FIG. 661). This last feature was perhaps the result of a special veneration of the image of Athena and a desire not to conceal it in a private *adyton* but to permit access to it. In the Hellenistic era, a more emotional concept of worship and the search for more striking effects of light led to substantial variations in the general plan of temples. While the Temple of Artemis Leukophryene at Magnesia (FIG. 569) was based on traditional

models, the dipteral Temple of Hera at Samos had a doubl row of columns in the deep pronaos (VII, FIG. 85). The sam was true of the Artemision at Ephesos, where the double r₀ of columns extended from the porch into the unroofed na (VII, FIG. 82). The plan was similar to that of the Egypti₂ hypostyle halls, with their forests of columns. A similar effe was achieved in the dipteral Didymaion at Miletos, which h twelve columns in the pronaos (FIG. 569, 8).

The effort to achieve effects of light within a geometrica defined space fostered the development of the round temp plan; these temples were few in number and generally h₂ one circle of columns outside the sanctuary and another insi₄ it (as in the Tholos of Epidauros).

The Etruscan temple was only partially similar to the arch₂ Greek temple, judging from reconstructions made according descriptions by Vitruvius (*De architectura*, IV, 7). The temp rose on a high podium preceded by a flight of steps and w divided in two parts: the porch, with rows of four widely spac₄ columns of the Tuscan or proto-Ionic type, and the sanctuar which was subdivided into three rooms, the largest at the cent₄ each of which was dedicated to a different god (FIG. 569, 1 V, FIGS. 127 lower, 129b, c). Sometimes the sanctuary wa single room, flanked by two *alae* or covered *ambulacra*. Rarel the sanctuary was narrower and was flanked with a row columns; this form is known as the *periptera sine postico*.

Roman temple architecture fused elements from Etrusc₄ Italic tradition with others of Greek origin. From the Etrusca it adopted the podium, the clear distinction between porch ar cella, and the division of the cella into three parts. From tl Greeks were derived the compositional elements of the Ion and Corinthian orders and the peripteral and pseudoperipter treatment. There also existed such unusual plans as that ₄ the Temple of Venus and Roma, a pseudodipteral temple wi two cellae with apses placed back to back in the center. Tl circular temple was favored; some (Temple B in Larç Argentina, VII, FIG. 397; "Temple of Vesta" at Tivoli, VI PL. 201) were inspired by the *tholoi* of the Hellenistic perio₄ while others were more complex structures roofed with dom₄ and vaulting (the Pantheon, FIG. 569, 14; I, PL. 401). Templ₄ appeared in Latium sometimes as parts of sanctuaries, whic were monumentally conceived organic complexes of single buil₄ ings built around a temple. Their development may be con pared with that whereby the Roman house, with the *domus* ₄ its nucleus, expanded to form a villa or palace. There was transition from the relatively simple sanctuary at Gabii (a temp of Juno set on a podium, preceded by a kind of cavea, wit the whole complex surrounded on three sides by colonnade and the somewhat similar Sanctuary of Hercules at Tivoli (VI FIG. 401) to the extremely complicated forms of the sanctuar of Fortuna Primigenia at Palestrina, with converging ramp exedras, and colonnades at different levels (VII, FIG. 399).

Churches. The construction of the first monumental edific₄ of Christian worship began after the official recognition ₄ Christianity (A.D. 313). They may be divided generically int two groups: those built on a longitudinal plan and those bui on a central plan. Originally the two types had different func tions (except in some special cases): longitudinal-plan church₄ were built for the Eucharistic synaxis, and central-plan edific₄ for commemorative and baptismal purposes. This distinctio did not endure except in the cases of the baptisteries and maus₀ leums, since the martyriums gradually took on the functions ₄ the buildings of longitudinal plan, and, with the establishmer of the Byzantine style and the disappearance of the martyrium₄ the typical plan of the Eastern church was a central one, whil₄ with few exceptions, the Western church retained the longitudi nal plan.

The derivation of Christian edifices of worship from sever₂ prototypes of Late Antiquity has been discussed elsewhere (s₄ LATE-ANTIQUE AND EARLY CHRISTIAN ART, col. 80). But th₄ Christian monuments display forms that are very different fror known and traditional ones, forms that were greatly influence by differences in liturgy and in functional requirements. Struc tures of varying nature and characteristics were often built ₀

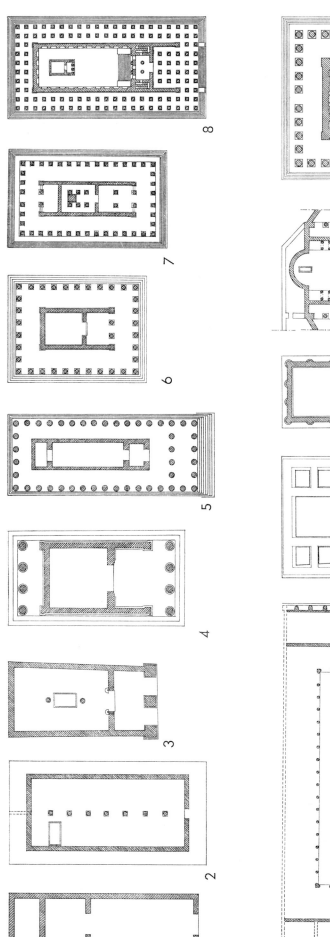

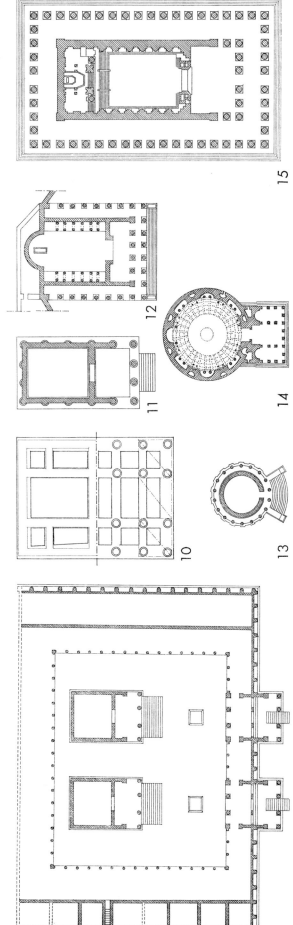

Classical temples, plans. (1–9) Greek temples: (1) Selinunte, megaron (6th cent. B.C.); (2) Neandria (Turkey), temple (7th–6th cent. B.C.); (3) Prinias (Crete), Temple A (7th cent. B.C.); (4) Athens, amphiprostyle temple on the Ilissos (5th cent. B.C.); (5) Selinunte, peripteral Temple C (6th cent. B.C.); (6) Lagina (Turkey), pseudodipteral Temple of Hecate (2d–1st cent. B.C.); (7) Magnesia-on-the-Maeander (Turkey), pseudodipteral Temple of Artemis (2d cent. B.C.); (8) Didyma, near Miletos (Turkey), dipteral Temple of Apollo (begun 4th cent. B.C.); (9) Coos (Greece), sanctuary in the port area (2d cent. B.C.). (10) Pyrgi (Italy), Etruscan temple (5th cent. B.C.), reconstruction. (11–15) Roman temples: (11) Tivoli, pseudo-peripteral temple (mid-2d cent. B.C.); (12) Rome, Temple of Mars Ultor (Augustan age); (13) Rome, Temple of Vesta (3d cent.); (14) Rome, Pantheon (2d cent.); (15) Baalbek, pseudodipteral Temple of Jupiter Heliopolitanus (1st–2d cent.).

similar bases, with differences that were sometimes attributable mainly to differences in local supplies of building materials (bricks in the West, stone in Syria, etc.).

Early Christian edifices were often ancient buildings that were adapted to the new cult, as in many African basilicas, the basilica of Antalya in Asia Minor, and the basilica of the Parthenon in Greece; other Christian churches were constructed with material taken from older buildings. The principal difference between Early Christian buildings and the religious edifices of the ancient world is the more complex concept of internal space in Christian buildings, as opposed to what may be defined as the unbroken quality of space in the classical temple. Unlike the temple, the internal space of the Christian building must be adequate to contain the entire congregation if necessary. The basic concept of Christian architecture is not so much that of a rhythmic counterbalancing of the parts as that of the relation of internal space to the rite.

Longitudinal-plan edifices that are classified as basilicas (this type also includes chapels and minor rooms built on a basilica plan) generally consist of two principal elements: the nave and the sanctuary, opening directly into each other along the same axis. The rectangular nave may be divided into aisles, generally by arcades; the nave is usually of larger dimensions than the side aisles. The aisles may number three, five, or as many as seven or nine, as in the North African basilicas of St. Cyprian and Damus el-Karita, both in Carthage. Rarely, the elements that divided the aisles were trabeated, as in S. Maria Maggiore in Rome. Sometimes trabeation is alternated with a system of arches, as in the old St. Peter's in Rome, where the architrave was used in the nave and the arch in the aisles. In Syria, pillars were used in place of columns; coupled supports were known in Africa, and there are examples of columns alternating with pillars, notably in St. Demetrios in Salonika (II, FIG. 763). The columns that delimit the nave support a section of wall that contains windows and is called the clerestory.

In some basilicas, as at Stobi in Macedonia, low marble walls (*plutei*) formed partitions between the aisles; in others the columns rested on high stylobates that separated the side aisles from the central nave. In Greece stone benches were sometimes placed along the aisle walls for use by worshipers (as in the basilica of Lechaion). Sometimes the two side aisles were divided into two levels and the upper floor was reserved for women (called the gynaeceum, or women's gallery); earlier in the East, this gallery was sometimes reserved for the catechumens and was therefore called the *catechumenion*. The women's gallery and the lower level of the aisle opened onto the nave through a series of columns surmounted by arches (and, rarely, through a series of small trabeated piers). This two-level division was sometimes extended along the inside of the façade (as in St. Demetrios in Salonika and St. John in Studion in Istanbul). The parapet of the women's gallery was formed by marble *plutei*. When the nave was vaulted, as in basilicas in Asia Minor, the basilica was of the Anatolian type; a truss roof over the nave was characteristic of the Hellenistic type. In Syria transverse arches under a flat roof were common.

The large arch that spanned almost the entire width of the nave at one end was called the triumphal arch; this led to the sanctuary, a raised area that formed the apse, which was almost always semicircular (it was sometimes horseshoe-shaped, as in the triapsidal basilica in Vaison-la-Romaine, France). In rare cases, the sanctuary was quadrangular (as in some churches in southern Syria). The apse might contain one or more arched windows. The space that included the apse and was enclosed by low quadrangular screen walls (*cancelli*) extending into the nave (in African churches this area occupied almost the entire length of the nave, as in the Basilica of Douimes at Carthage, IX, FIG. 86) took the name of sanctuary, chancel, presbytery, or, in the Eastern churches, bema. The screen was made of panels of wood, stone, or marble, and precious metals (cf. that in Hagia Sophia in Istanbul); carved panels in the screen are called *plutei*, those pierced in openwork are known as *transennae*. Small posts were interposed between the panels and were sometimes used as a high plinth for columns that supported an architrave from which lights, curtains, and even icons were hung. In Byzantine churches the screen came to be known the *iconostasis*; in its center stood an arched door that led the sanctuary. The sanctuary was thus clearly delimited a was barred to the worshipers, who could, however, see the r being performed at the altar, which was generally placed front of the raised apse, with ciborium above it (cf. XI, PL. 32 In African basilicas the altar was situated almost at the cen of the nave (as in the basilica built over the judiciary basil at Sabratha). Access to the apse proper was gained by mea of steps, either centrally placed or located on each side (as most African churches). Around the curved wall of the ap was a bench (*subsellium*) used by the clergy, and at the cen of the curve, in certain basilicas, stood the episcopal thro (cf. III, PL. 477).

At the center and to the right of the nave, outside the e closure, stood an ambo, or pulpit. In the West from the 5th ce tury on, there were generally two ambos, which formed p of the choir enclosure, which extended beyond the apse ir the nave (as in S. Clemente in Rome, III, PL. 477).

In Syrian churches can be found structures in the nave the form of an exedra with a throne; these are believed to ha been ambos (cf. J. Lassus, *Sanctuaires Chrétiens de Syr* Paris, 1947).

The sanctuary was sometimes quite complex. In Syria a in areas under Syrian influence the tripartite sanctuary w common: the apse was flanked by two rooms with square apsidal ends entered from the aisles and communicating wi the sanctuary through side doors. They were probably t *pastophoria*, or sacristies, although one may perhaps have fun tioned as a martyrium (cf. J. Lassus, ibid). These rooms we later used as the *prothesis*, where the priests robed, and t *diakonikon*, where offerings were collected. In Egypt (in t basilicas at Dendera and Deir el-Abied and Deir el-Ahm III, FIG. 803) trefoil apses were used, flanked by *pastophor* There are also some examples of apses with an internal, ope arched ambulatory (e.g., S. Giovanni, Cimitile, Campania, Ital In Africa the apse was delimited either by three arches or an architrave with an arch at the center. The presence of crypt under the apse was rare (there are crypts in St. Demetri in Salonika and in the 5th-century basilica at Stobi, Yugoslavi (The use of a crypt under the cross vault was limited to ma tyriums such as that of St. John in Ephesos; see BYZANTI ART, cols. 764, 772, FIGS. 765, 772.) Early Christian basilic often incorporated a narthex, that is, a porch extending t length of the façade and communicating with the nave throu doors. (The narthex is not to be confused with that arm the atrium that abuts the church.) The narthex was sometim a simple structure, with arcades that opened onto the exteri as in the basilica of Sabratha, which ended in two side aps and was divided, as was general in Syria, into three parts (i. with two side rooms). The lateral rooms sometimes acted supports and bases for the towers of the façade. The narth might also extend in one or two rooms projecting beyond t sides of the building that were probably used as *diakonika* (as in the basilicas of Brauron and Nicopolis in Greece, I FIG. 767). When there is a second, inner, narthex, it was usual built on two levels, the lower opening onto the nave throug arches, and the upper opening into the galleries through communicating loggia. In African basilicas, where there we often two opposite apses, with the entrance to the nave on o side, the place of the narthex is often occupied by a raised ap which probably housed the bodies of the martyrs.

Sometimes, especially in the West, a transverse structu that was not necessarily visible from the outside was insert between the apse and the nave, giving the building the for of a cross, as in the Roman basilicas of the era of Constanti This transept, in turn, might be divided by columns and th form a more complex bema (as in St. Demetrios, Salonika, I FIG. 763). Sometimes, also, the transept was inserted at a po about two-thirds along the length of the nave, giving rise the cruciform plan, and sometimes it terminated in two aps The exterior of the basilica was extremely simple; doors a windows were framed by sculptural decorations, almost alwa plant motifs (see ZOOMORPHIC AND PLANT REPRESENTATION

Christian, Jewish, and Moslem places of worship. (1–18) Christian: (1) Rome, S. Sabina (5th cent.), plan; (2) Rheims, St-Remi (11th–12th cent.), plan; (3) Lyons, St-Jean (13th–15th cent.), plan; (4) Salzburg, Franziskanerkirche (14th cent.), plan; (5) Gaibach (Germany), parish church (18th cent.), plan; (6) Qal'at Sim'ān (Syria), baptistery, plan (5th cent.); (7) Rome, St. John Lateran, Baptistery (4th cent.), plan; (8–9) Nocera, baptistery (5th cent.), plan and section; (10) Milan, S. Lorenzo (4th cent.), plan; (11) Ephesus, St. John (4th cent.), section; (12) Daphne, Byzantine church (11th cent.), plan; (13) Barcelona, Sagrada Familia (19th cent.), plan; (14) Heckington (England), bell tower (13th cent.), section; (15) Rome, S. Agnese fuori le Mura (7th cent.), section; (16) Durham (England), cathedral, section (13th cent.); (17) Anagni, cathedral, section showing the crypt, (11th–13th cent.); (18) Speyer, cathedral, plan of the crypt (11th cent.). (19–20) Synagogues: (19) Ostia, synagogue (3d–4th cent.), plan; (20) St. Paul, (Minnesota), Mount Zion Temple and community center (by E. Mendelsohn; 20th cent.), plan; (21–22) Mosque of al-Guyūshī (Egypt; 11th cent.), plan and section.

the façade was usually in three sections that followed the outline of the aisles and nave, with the center section higher and ending in a triangular apex. The doors, numbering from one to five, were on the same axes as the aisles, and the central door was always larger. One or two rows of windows were set into the upper part of the façade, which, especially in Greece, was sometimes crowned by a kind of pediment. In Greek basilicas there was generally only one door, but this was divided into sections formed by two or three arches supported by columns. Sometimes the side doors were preceded by vestibules (as in the basilica of Sinhar, Syria). The apse was either included in the perimeter of the exterior walls, which presented a rectilinear form (as in basilica of Perge, Anatolia; basilica of Kleious, Lesbos, etc.), or projected in semicircular or horseshoe shape. From the 5th century, especially in the East, the exterior of the apse was often given polygonal form (as in St. John in

Studion, Istanbul, II, FIG. 762). The apse sometimes had exterior stepped buttresses (as in St. Mennas, Egypt, IX, FIG. 86a, and the basilica in Nicopolis, II, FIG. 767) or engaged columns (basilica in Qalb Lauzeh, Syria). The roofing of the basilica was generally formed by pitched roofs over the nave and transept, a shed roof over the side aisles, and a semi-cone-shaped roof over the apse.

A structure which was not always present in the basilica, but which appeared frequently, especially in the West and along the coast of Anatolia and what was then Palestine, was the atrium, on the axis of the basilica, but standing as an independent spatial unit. Quadrangular in shape, it had colonnades on four interior sides and was enclosed on the exterior by high walls. In the center stood a fountain — the *cantharus* or *phiale* — for ritual ablutions. (In some examples, the water flowed from a nymphaeum complex, as in Basilica A at Philippi.) In Syrian churches, instead of an atrium there was a simple courtyard on the southern side of the basilica.

Frequently the basilica plan was elaborated by the addition of rooms, often not clearly identified, but mentioned by sources, that communicated with the basilica through doors. Most important of these was the baptistery (which more often, and especially in the West, was a separate edifice). This was built on a central plan; it had a basin for immersion in the center and was roofed with a dome (for various baptistery plans, see below).

In Africa and what was then Palestine, the baptistery was almost always on the same axis as the church; it was located behind the apse and was incorporated within the perimeter wall of the basilica (as in the basilica at Emmaus). In a few examples (the Basilica at Poreč, Yugoslavia) the baptistery stood on the west side of the porch, on the same axis as the church. Baptisteries in African churches always included a small apse, and the basin was placed under a canopy. Sometimes there were also small thermal edifices communicating with the baptistery (as at Philippi, at Nea Anchialos in Greece, and at Thamugadi in Africa).

Among other rectangular rooms connected to the basilica and variously placed without any fixed order were the *catechumenion*, a room used for the instruction of the catechumens, and the *consignatorium*, near the baptistery, for the celebration of confirmation; sometimes there were rooms for carrying out exorcisms, small martyriums that were often triconch (as in basilicas in Salonika and Tebessa, and in Roman basilicas *extra moenia*) or cruciform (as in S. Maria Formosa, Pulj), and mausoleums, such as the tomb of Constantine in the Church of the Holy Apostles in Istanbul and that of Constantina in S. Costanza in Rome (IX, FIG. 98) and the so-called "Mausoleum of Galla Placidia" in Ravenna (III, PL. 425, a cruciform building that was attached to the basilica-plan Church of Sta Croce, destroyed).

The basilica complex often had an exterior aspect common to such Late-Antique complexes as thermae, that of a group of buildings not placed according to a preordained and symmetrical plan. In the *domus ecclesiae*, in 4th-century Syria, as well as the above-mentioned additional rooms, the basilica complex included houses for priests and buildings as yet not identified.

Central-plan edifices included buildings with different functions: martyriums or edifices dedicated to saints or marking sacred sites; mausoleums or funerary monuments; and baptisteries. In later times the type also included churches. The central plan was especially suitable for these types of buildings because it could fittingly house a central important element. The outer perimeter of these edifices was perfectly circular (hence the name "rotunda") or polygonal; if polygonal, it was generally octagonal, especially in the martyrium (as in the Church of the Ascension on the Mount of Olives and the Martyrium of St. Philip at Hierapolis, Turkey). There were also ten-sided constructions (e.g., the Mausoleum of Theodoric in Ravenna, IV, PL. 457). In Armenia the quatrefoil plan was widely used. When edifices were built on a square plan the interior space was frequently modified to become circular (as in the Church of SS. Sergius and Bacchus at Bosra), hexagonal, or octagonal in form (as in the Church of St. George in Zorava, mod. Ezraa). The interior walls of central-plan buildings were

often articulated by niches. In other examples there was [an] ambulatory that created a more complex articulation of the int[e]rior space (as in S. Costanza in Rome, IX, FIG. 98b); sometim[es] the ambulatory was divided into two levels (S. Vitale, in Ravenna). In central-plan buildings used for the Eucharistic synaxis a[nd] in many martyriums the orientation of the building is mark[ed] by a small projecting apse that contains the altar.

Central-plan edifices include cruciform-plan buildings; t[he] typical eastern version of this plan was in the form of a Gre[ek] cross, that is, with four arms of equal length. This plan appea[rs] in two versions: the free-cross plan, and the cross-in-squa[re]. In the first, the form of the arms is visible on the exterior ([as] in the Martyrium of St. Babilas, II, FIG. 764; and the so-call[ed] "Mausoleum of Galla Placidia," Ravenna) and there may [be] a single nave (e.g., the Martyrium of St. Babilas) or three nav[es] (the Church of St. Simeon Stylites the Elder at Qal'at Sim'[an,] Syria). The crossing at the intersection of the arms may be squa[re] or polygonal. The crossing was almost always covered by [a] dome, except in Syria, where it was roofed by a pyramidal stru[c]ture. In the most complex cruciform edifices, a smaller cup[ola] was sometimes placed over the end of each arm. Cruciform[-] plan buildings continued to be built in the middle Byzanti[ne] period in Armenia and in northern Anatolia (e.g., St. Soph[ia,] Trebizond), but they were most widely used in medieval E[u]rope (see below).

In buildings on a cross-in-square plan the arms of the cro[ss] are contained within square solid masonry perimeter wa[lls] (as in the Church of the Apostles and Martyrs, Jerash, [II,] FIG. 766); the arms are formed of rows of columns that exte[nd] from a square central area usually delimited by four piers a[nd] called the crossing. The cross-in-square edifice became, exce[pt] for rare cases, the canonical type of post-iconoclastic Byzanti[ne] church. In the Romanesque period churches were sometim[es] built in imitation of the Holy Sepulcher (e.g., the churches [of] the Knights Templars); these often had two stories and we[re] sometimes connected with a basilica-plan edifice (e.g., the Chur[ch] of S. Maria do Olival in Tomar, Portugal), following the exampl[e] of the Anastasis in Jerusalem. Separate baptisteries, situat[ed] beside episcopal churches or cathedrals, also continued to [be] built as central-plan edifices; one of the most recent exampl[es] is the Baptistery at Pisa (14th century). Later the baptism[al] font was included in a chapel of the church itself.

During the Carolingian period the longitudinal plan conti[n]ued to be used in hall churches (III, cols. 82–89, FIG. 8[7,] which reproduced the earliest form of Christian religious buil[d]ings. The hall church consists of a nave with aisles that a[re] equal to the nave in height or, occasionally, of a single ais[le;] it may have either semicircular apses or a rectangular chanc[el] with or without contiguous rectangular chapels. Sometim[es] there are lateral chapels that form a kind of transept. In Lati[n-] cross churches (in which the nave arm is the longest; III, co[ls.] 94–97, FIG. 95) the transept was not clearly identifiable on t[he] interior because of narrow arcading. One type of Carolingi[an] church had facing chancels, or apses (III, cols. 93–94, F[IG.] 93); this feature was retained until the end of the Romanesqu[e] period.

An innovation at the west end of the church was the wes[t]work (*Westwerk*: cf. III, cols. 89–93, PL. 44; X, PL. 456), a stru[c]ture placed transversally at the end of the nave. It ended in tw[o] towers, sometimes with opposing apsidioles (small, seconda[ry] apses), and often a central lantern tower was built over the pri[n]cipal chamber (as in St.-Riquier, Centula, III, FIG. 91). On t[he] interior the westwork was usually on two levels, subdivide[d] into rooms. The gallery on the second level was open an[d] overlooked the nave (III, PL. 45); it was reserved for the emper[or] and often contained a throne. The corner rooms in the towe[rs] on the same level were usually used as chapels, and the low[er] level served as a burial ground.

During the Ottonian period the *Westbau* appeared at th[e] western end of the church; this was a more complex mult[i-] storied structure, sometimes with an apse and sometimes in t[he] form of groupings of towers (e.g., Essen and Trier cathedra[ls,] X, col. 877, FIG. 879 lower, PL. 459). The lantern tower, whic[h] contained windows and had a pyramid-shaped roof, stood ov[er] e crossing — that is, where the transept crossed the nave (as St. Michael in Hildesheim, X, FIG. 881, PL. 455). Towers ften flanked the apse and the transept, giving the entire edifice a upward thrust. (For more specific information on the development of church architecture, see also CAROLINGIAN ART, ols. 82–104; FLEMISH AND DUTCH ART, cols. 402–403, 404–406; TTONIAN ART, cols. 874–881; PRE-ROMANESQUE ART, cols. 641–43, 645–647, 652, 663–666.)

The westwork continued to be of great importance in Romanque architecture (cf. XII, col. 373), although its external charcteristics were gradually assimilated into those of the façades northern churches. In the Romanesque period was introduced system of vaulting (the *gebundene* system; XII, col. 372), in hich the single bay of the nave is balanced by the two vaulted ays of the side aisles, and every second pier is specially reinforced form a compound column. The choir and altar (this space also known as the chancel) were located in the apse, directly ove the crypt, and were often raised above the level of the nave. Ottonian churches crypts under the choir or transept were ly rarely accessible from the nave (as in St. Georg in Oberzell, , PL. 463). In Italian churches central or lateral staircases led rectly from the nave to the crypt, which was often visible rough the columns or supports upon which the chancel was ised (as in Modena Cathedral, III, PL. 17, XII, FIG. 359; S. eno, Verona, XII, PL. 220; S. Vincenzo, Galliano, XI, PL. 324). ften there was a screen at the entrance of the chancel; this reen was analogous to the iconostasis of the Greek churches and as surmounted by a gallery (rood loft, in England) that served a passage. In English churches it was called the chancel reen (or rood screen, if surmounted by the rood, or cross; I, PL. 425); it is known in French as the *jube*, in German as e *Lettner*, and in Italian as the *pontile*.

In French Romanesque churches the rectangular plan preominated and the two facing apses or transepts disappeared. maller lateral apses at the ends of the side aisles flanked the ntral projecting apse. The *chevet* also appeared; this was apse surrounded by an ambulatory off which there might or ight not be radiating chapels. At first separated, in the Gothic riod the radiating chapels became contiguous. The *chevet* found not only in French but also in German, English, and panish Romanesque and Gothic churches (cf. XII, col. 320, G. 342b, PLS. 199–201). Transepts sometimes ended in sidioles, thus giving the church a triapsidal plan (e.g., Angers athedral, V, FIG. 655; St. Elizabeth, Marburg, VI, FIG. 512). or further details on the rich variety of ecclesiastical architecture roughout Europe in this period see also ROMANESQUE ART: pain: cols. 338–348, 349–353 (cf. also MOZARABIC ART); France: ls. 318–334; Italy: cols. 354–366; Germany and Central Europe: ls. 366–378; England: cols. 378–381; Scandinavia: cols. 381–385.

With the introduction of flying buttresses, the women's llery over the aisles was replaced by the triforium, or blindory, a sort of gallery set into the thickness of the wall; it was ghted by a series of three-arch openings onto the nave (see OTHIC ART, cols. 472–474). Sometimes the triforium encompassed e entire interior (VI, PLS. 292, 297, 312). (It should be noted at the term triforium is often erroneously used for gallery general.) Above the triforium was a range of windows, called earstory (or clerestory), that lighted the nave.

During the Gothic period ground plans evolved with and ithout aisles, with particular emphasis on the *chevet* and bsidiary chapels set along the aisles between the flying butesses. There were many local and regional variations (see OTHIC ART: France: cols. 468–480; Low Countries and Switzernd: cols. 486–488; England: cols. 499–510; Germany and Central Europe: cols. 511–525).

In the Renaissance period both the longitudinal and centraled plans characteristic of Western and Eastern churches, reectively, were used. New developments in the treatment of erspective led to a more lucid concept of interior space. In runelleschi's Latin-cross Church of Sto Spirito in Florence I, PL. 370, FIG. 658) the perspective continuity was emphasized y means of the colonnades that surround the transept and e square presbytery. In S. Andrea in Mantua (I, PL. 58, G. 204), which is also on a Latin-cross plan, Alberti created

the type of single-nave church with side chapels that recalled the plan of the Basilica of Maxentius in Rome; this same type was the model for the mannerist churches of Vignola (e.g., Church of the Gesù, Rome, XI, FIG. 899) and was later reproduced by the Jesuits in the American mission churches.

Once the liturgy had been established, the various forms of Christian edifices for worship were created almost solely as artistic expressions. The elliptical, oval, and mixtilinear plans of many baroque churches are only variations of the basic type of Christian church. No new types emerged during the 18th and 19th centuries; at the most, original and highly individualistic architectural expressions were clearly reflected in such edifices as the Church of the Sagrada Familia in Barcelona, by Antonio Gaudí.

Only recently has the drive to give new impetus to the formal architectural repertory produced works that aim at creating a closer relation between the worshipers and the liturgical rite. Important examples of these works are the church by O. Niemeyer in Pampulha (Brazil), that by A. Aalto in Imatra (Finland; V, PL. 118), the chapel by Le Corbusier at Ronchamp, and that by G. Michelucci on the Autostrada del Sole near Florence.

The central plan has permitted great freedom of expression to architects of different periods up to the present; some notable examples are the Palatine Chapel in Aachen (III, FIG. 102, 5), S. Marco in Venice (I, FIG. 643, third row), the Pazzi Chapel (II, FIG. 662) and S. Maria degli Angeli (II, FIG. 659) in Florence, the Tempietto of S. Pietro in Montorio (II, FIG. 602), the plans by Michelangelo and Bramante for St. Peter's in Rome (II, FIG. 607), Michelangelo's New Sacristy in S. Lorenzo in Florence (IX, FIG. 892), and Borromini's S. Giovanni in Oleo in Rome.

The bell tower is an important architectural element, widely used as an adjunct to the church. The first use of bells is attributed to S. Paolino, bishop of Nola in Campania (409–32). However, the oldest examples of bell towers are found not in Campania but in the city of Ravenna, where they are cylindrical structures, as at S. Apollinare in Classe (II, PL. 430; VIII, FIG. 411a) and the Cathedral. In another early example, St-Martin in Tours, the tower is placed over the apse. Throughout the Middle Ages and up to the Gothic period, the bell tower usually took the form of a high tower with the belfry on top. Built in a variety of shapes, they were generally inspired by eastern towers and lighthouses and were, therefore, square or polygonal; often they were multiform and tapered. The tower was usually placed beside the church façade or was connected to it. There are some examples of towers standing beside the apse, as in S. Abbondio in Como and the Cathedral of Ivrea. In churches with westworks, as in the Cathedral of Speyer (VI, FIG. 159a), the two towers of the westwork probably served as bell towers; this model was widely adopted in Central and Northern Europe during the Gothic period. At this time there persisted in Italy the custom of building the bell tower as a separate structure situated at one side of the façade. Rarely is the bell tower otherwise situated: in S. Fedele in Albenga it is located at the front of the church on an axis with the main door; in Saint-Benoît-sur-Loire in France and in Cistercian churches it is placed at the top of the tower above the crossing.

The bell tower gradually disappeared as an autonomous architectural element. In the small Abbey church of Saint-Generoux in France (10th century) and later in S. Claudio at Spello, it was a simple openwork supporting structure (from which the bells were suspended) rising above the façade. It was more frequently used in baroque architecture and even later in the form of a small lateral tower or towers that were part of the church façade.

Mosques. The mosque was primarily a prayer hall where the faithful could gather (see ISLAM, col. 336 ff.). Its pre-Islamic prototype was a simple enclosed open space (*muṣallā*) where prayers were recited. The principal requirement of a mosque was that its orientation (*qibla*) be directed toward the Kaaba in Mecca. This permitted the adaptation of existing Christian edifices for use as mosques, as in the majority of 7th-century Syrian Christian churches and in 14th-century churches in

Constantinople (e.g., Hagia Sophia, SS. Sergius and Bacchus). When necessary, Moslem architects constructed a *qibla* wall on the interior of the building to show the direction of the orientation and inverted the position of the entrance (as in Syria, where Christian churches were oriented toward the East). In Persia the apadana was transformed into an edifice of Moslem worship (cf. K. A. C. Creswell, *A Short Account of Early Muslim Architecture*, Harmondsworth, 1958, pp. 7–8).

The first mosques were constructed during the 7th century. Their characteristic features varied somewhat according to local architectural traditions. The traditional Arab courtyard mosque consisted of a large courtyard (*ṣaḥn*) in the center of which ablution fountains were generally placed (X, PL. 445). This courtyard was usually enclosed by a series of arcades (*riwāq*). The *qibla* side of the courtyard had a deeper *riwāq* with more aisles. Sometime early in the development of Islamic architecture a semicircular niche (mihrab; this was sometimes, but rarely, square in plan, as in the Great Mosque of Samarra) was built into the *qibla* wall; this indicated the direction of the Kaaba. The aisles lay parallel to the *qibla* wall (as in the Mosque of Ibn-Ṭūlūn, Cairo; see TULUNID ART) or were perpendicular to it (as in the Great Mosque of Córdoba and that of Kairouan, VIII, FIGS. 337, 338, where they attained an impressive number).

In those mosques with aisles parallel to the *qibla* there was usually a higher central transept that cut across them, indicating the location of the mihrab (as in the Great Mosque of Damascus, VIII, FIG. 338; X, PL. 378). In those mosques with aisles perpendicular to the *qibla*, the broader central aisle indicated the location of the mihrab (as in the Great Mosque of Kairouan, X, PL. 164, VIII, FIG. 337). The aisles were separated by columns that directly supported the roof, as in areas of Persian influence (the Great Mosque of Samarra), or were divided by columns with round or pointed horseshoe arches (X, PL. 162). Sometimes the arches were supported by columns alternating with piers (as at Córdoba) or by piers alone (the Great Mosque of Samarra; the Mosque of Ibn-Ṭūlūn, Cairo). Vaulted roofs were used (the Great Mosque at Susa). In the 9th century the use of a dome in front of the mihrab became widespread. To the right of the mihrab was the mimbar, a wooden, or occasionally stone, lectern or pulpit. To the left stood a richly decorated wooden enclosure called the *maqṣūra*, which was reserved for the nobility. In some mosques, as in that of 'Alā-ud-Dīn in Konya, a curtained enclosure was reserved for women.

Another type of mosque was introduced by the Turks in Anatolia (see OTTOMAN SCHOOLS); it had a domed roof of Byzantine derivation, and was most widely used from the 13th century onward. It always was built on a square plan, and its form ranged from that of a simple sanctuary consisting of a single cella and a large central dome, as in the Mosque of Alaeddin in Bursa (X, FIG. 857c), to that with a small dome over every bay, as in Zincirli Kuyu Mosque (X, FIG. 857d). More complex forms incorporated a series of liwans (rooms open toward the outside; cf. ABBASSIDE ART, col. 6), thus merging in a single building the functions of mosque and madrasah (as in the Mosque of Murat I, X, FIG. 857a); the plan of these buildings generally called for a transverse colonnade with domes that led into the sanctuary, which was square, with two liwans in the wings and one projecting on the main axis. All these areas were roofed by domes which were visible on the exterior. After the 15th century even more complex forms emerged, showing strong Byzantine influence; for example, the Mosque of Sultan Sulaymān in Istanbul (X, PL. 444) repeats the design of Hagia Sophia (cf. also X, PL. 448).

In Persia the typical mosque plan included elements derived from both Zoroastrian fire temples and Iranian madrasahs. The so-called "kiosk" type, in which a domed area was preceded by a liwan or open anteroom, was a direct derivation from the fire temples. In the liwan mosque the kiosk plan was combined with that of the madrasah, a cruciform plan in which the arms projecting from the central court consisted of four large liwans. The first liwan mosque, known through sources, was that of Dar-El-Mara, built in the mid-8th century. This type took on a more elaborate form in the Masjid-i-Jāmi' in Isfahan (VIII, FIG. 339), which had four liwans on the axes of the central

courtyard, and a sanctuary in which the mihrab was precede by a square, domed area.

Beginning with Ommiad times a characteristic feature the mosque was the minaret, a tower used for the call to praye (see ISLAM, col. 340; VIII, FIG. 343). This was placed at th front of the courtyard in a line with the mihrab, in a corne of the courtyard, or outside it. In the Seljuk period the minare were attached to the front of the liwan and their number wa increased to two (see also OTTOMAN SCHOOLS, col. 856).

Synagogues. Historical data concerning the most ancie Jewish places of worship are extremely summary. From Biblic sources it can be deduced that the Temple of Solomon (VII FIG. 901) was approximately similar in shape to the pre-Helleni megaron or to Syrian temples such as that of Tell Ta'ina The Temple of Herod in Jerusalem was a basilica-plan buildin located on the south side of a great square. It had a women court and a sanctuary court (see JEWISH ART, cols. 904–905 Synagogues in Galilee under the Roman occupation from the 2 century B.C. onward were generally on a basilica plan; the nav was surrounded on three sides by aisles and there was a galler over the main aisle. The façade always faced Jerusalem. A example of this type is the Synagogue of Capernaum (VII FIG. 910). In later constructions the apse indicated the building orientation.

During the Middle Ages there were two distinct synagogu types; these reflected the schism between the Jewish commu nities existing in the Moslem world and in the Christian on In Moslem-dominated areas, as in Toledo, the synagogue wa on a basilica plan with several aisles, and the Ark of the La was set in the wall that faced Jerusalem. In Christian area however, Jewish communities constructed less monument synagogues, with only one aisle or with two aisles divided b a row of columns (VIII, PL. 335). The Ark did not have a fixe place, as in Spanish synagogues. In the center, in both type stood a platform (the almenar, or bema) on which the Ark the Law was placed during prayer. Since the construction women's galleries was not possible, the area reserved fo women was either on a level with the rest of the building or wa slightly sunken (as in the Synagogue of Carpentras, near Av gnon). Apart from these particular interior arrangements, syn agogues had no other characteristic structures or forms. Thei architecture has mirrored the expressions of Western art throug the baroque period up to the present, as in the Beth Sholo Synagogue in Philadelphia, designed by Frank Lloyd Wrigh

Religious edifices in India, China, and Japan. The divers forms of Indian religious architecture are linked to the variou cults and can be grouped according to two types: stupas (thes are edifices whose internal space is not articulated; their functio is not only religious, but also commemorative, funerary, an cosmological; see BUDDHISM, cols. 678–679) and buildings tha can be considered true temples (these have an internal spac that holds groups of worshipers; their characteristics diffe according to the area in which they were built). There are n remains of the wooden structures of the earliest examples of bot these types, but their principal characteristics may be deduce from later sculptures and, especially, from those rock-cut sanc tuaries, also called "chaitya halls," which clearly are imitatio of freestanding buildings of the period.

The stupa originally consisted of a tumulus erected as th tomb of a ruler or holy man. Its basic form was that of a moun topped by a central post and surrounded by a fence of woode uprights and crossbars, with a gateway made of two upright and from one to three crossbars. At the time of Asoka (273 36 B.C.), with the spread of the Buddhist religion, there wa an increase in the construction of stupas, which diminished i importance as funerary monuments and took on the characte of true shrines, erected over relics of either the Buddha or hi servant followers. Their rigorously geometric structure ha a religio-cosmological significance (see BUDDHIST PRIMITIV SCHOOLS, cols. 709–711). In the Gupta period the stupas had th aspect of towers, often rising on platforms with smaller stupa at the four corners, with sculptural decoration on their base his type of stupa, variously interpreted, is found in Java, Thailand, and Tibet (see INDIAN ART, col. 957).

In Gandhara (cf. VI, cols. 34–35) the stupa took on a very much more elaborate aspect; it was a multilevel structure consisting of a high platform, a drum, and the stupa itself, so arranged as to form a true tower. Sculptural decoration was extended to the body of the stupa itself. In the late Andhra period the proportions of the traditional stupa with the semidome were so enlarged as to require a complicated internal brick supporting structure (see ANDHRA, cols. 404–405).

The oldest extant temple structures are the rock-cut chaitya halls (see II, cols. 719–722), with an apse and columns forming aisles. Its similarity to the plan of Christian basilicas is accidental. Within the curve of the apse there was a rock-cut stupa, positioned so that the worshipers might walk around it (VII, PL. 141). The entrance to the chaitya hall was imposing and rich in sculpture; the doors might number from one to three, and were often preceded by a type of porch with columns. Above the door, a horseshoe-arched window, called a "chaitya window," provided light for the interior. Wooden structures were often used on the façade (VII, PL. 454) and in the transverse ribs on the interior.

Some freestanding buildings were based on the rock-cut sanctuary type, which continued to be built. The Temple of Durgā at Aihole is one of the first freestanding Hindu temples (, PL. 220; VII, FIG. 960). This type of building (the *vesara* temple) had a barrel roof and its use was generally restricted to western India and the Deccan.

The early freestanding Hindu temple consisted simply of a roofed cella. The addition of a small portico created an *in antis* type (see GUPTA ART; VII, PL. 140, above). By the end of the 6th century, the temple consisted of a sanctuary set on a square platform on which the public stood to assist at the services. Secondary chapels were set up along the steps leading to the platform or at its four corners. An open mandapa (porch) might be added in front for the temple dances; sometimes a covered gallery for circumambulation surrounded the sanctuary proper.

In the Indo-Aryan (*nāgara*) type of temple the spire or sikhara (see GUPTA ART, col. 255) gradually came to form the entire roof of the sanctuary. Typical of northern and central India, this type had its most impressive examples in the Liṅgarāja temple of Bhuvaneshwar (III, PL. 485; VII PL. 482, FIG. 970). In the Dravidian type of temple the roof is in the form of a stepped pyramid and only the topmost spire is called the sikhara.

The plans and proportions of the Hindu temples were closely governed by metaphysical factors; because of this, the sikhara, for instance, must measure twice the height or width of the temple.

In the Dravidian architecture of southern India the basic elements that served as models for later temple structures can be clearly seen in the temple complex of Kailāsanātha at Kanchipuram (IV, PL. 255): the mandapa (porch), the ardhamandapa (pillared porch; IV, PL. 257), the small surrounding cells, the gopura (entrance tower to the temple enclosure; IV, PL. 260), and the vimana (towered sanctuary; IV, PL. 257 above). (See also VII, FIG. 961.)

A fine example of the blending of northern and southern traditions is the Keśava temple in Somnathpur, Mysore (PL. 253; VII, PL. 484). The star-shaped plan of the temple is made up of three shrines grouped around a central pillared hall and the high podium. The sikharas do not display the curved form typical of northern temples but are constructed in steps.

In later Indian architecture an analogous type of temple for every religion became the rule. The central plan was replaced by an axial layout, as in the Liṅgarāja temple of Bhuvaneshwar, in which the various elements (vimana, mandapa, ardhamandapa, etc.) were aligned in a continuous structure. In these edifices the roof and the decoration are both particularly important. From the base to the roof the buildings were covered with dense sculptural decorations of a religious nature. In one sense the sculpture nullified the architectural values; this was also true of the decorative elements in the inner rooms. (For a further discussion of temples see the following articles: ANDHRA, cols. 403–404, 406, 408; BUDDHIST PRIMITIVE SCHOOLS, cols. 719–721; DECCAN ART, especially cols. 263, 265–267;

DRAVIDIAN ART, cols. 447–451; GANDHARA, col. 34; HINDUISM, cols. 431–435; INDIAN ART, cols. 958–960, 969–975, cf. text figures; INDONESIAN CULTURES, cols. 63–64, 65–72, 75–80; JAINISM, cols. 788–792; KASHMIR ART, cols. 965–970; KHMER ART; KHOTANESE ART; KUSHAN ART, col. 1047. For the development of the stupa and temple outside India see also: BURMESE ART; CEYLONESE ART; CHAM, SCHOOL OF; SIAMESE ART; TIBETAN ART; VIETNAMESE ART.)

In Indo-Moslem areas temples reflected forms inherited from Iran (see INDO-MOSLEM SCHOOLS), while in some area of Kashmir there were fire temples.

In pre-Buddhist Chinese architecture, whose main forms were retained in Buddhist buildings, the temple often consisted of a simple wooden pavilion, on a rectangular plan, with the typical *t'ing* roof supported by pillars and brackets. The building was always built in bays with extra rows of columns added when a deeper building was required. Few wooden buildings have survived in China; contemporary buildings in Japan offer the best examples of type and general layout (see CHINESE ART, cols. 516–518). Large buildings of the T'ang period generally had four colonnades plus an extra one for a portico. They were on raised platforms, reached by one or more flights of stairs. The entrance was never under the gables but always in the middle of the southern façade. Generally the temple buildings, with the exception of pagodas, were one or two stories high. All these features can be seen in the main hall of the Fo-kuang-ssŭ on Wu-t'ai-shan in Shansi (ca. 875; III, FIG. 515), which consists of a single story of seven by four bays covered by a hipped roof. There are doors in five bays of the southern façade. A similar structure is found in the *kondō* of the Tōshōdaiji at Nara (VIII, FIG. 854). The Huan-yin hall of the Tulo-ssŭ at Chi-hsien, built around a huge statue of Kuan-yin, has two stories (FIG. 583, 6; III, FIG. 536). Japanese temple complexes (see JAPAN, cols. 811–812, cf. the Hall of the Great Buddha at Tōdaiji, PL. 253, below right) generally consisted of temple, relic shrine, bell tower, one or two pagodas (PL. 253, below left), library, and dwellings for the monks, all arranged axially and enclosed within walls with great gateways (see JAPANESE ART, cols. 849–850).

Most surviving examples of Sung and Liao architecture are in northern China (see CHINESE ART, cols. 535–538). In the important temple complex of Lung-hsing-ssŭ in Chêng-ting the oldest edifice is the Mani hall, a square building of seven bays, with an unusual entrance with a hip-and-gable roof on all four sides.

A unique temple complex (or complexes) is that in Peking (III, cols. 426–427, PL. 286, FIG. 427), which consists of the Temple of Heaven (III, PL. 286), Hall of the Annual Prayers (PL. 253, below center), and Temple of Agriculture complex.

The pagoda, which had existed in pre-Buddhist China simply as a tall wooden tower with pent roofs defining the actual stories, took on the significance of a stupa. It was then generally made of brick or stone and its horizontal divisions were marked by simple intermediate cornices of corbeled masonry (see CHINESE ART, cols. 516–517). The larger the pagoda, the more solid its structure; there was an interior staircase that gave access to openings in each level and an aisle on the ground floor where there were images in niches. In northern pagodas the staircase and upper levels were often missing. Early pagodas were generally on a square plan; in the Sung era the pagoda was often hexagonal or octagonal (III, PL. 273; see CHINESE ART, cols. 537–538). The Great Gander Pagoda (III, PL. 273) and the Small Gander Pagoda at Sian (see CHINESE ART, col. 516) and the Fan pagoda of the Kuohsiang-ssŭ at Kaifeng (III, PL. 273) were all square in plan. At first pagodas were aligned with the main temple in the temple complex; later two pagodas appeared, one on either side of the temple; and finally the pagoda was situated outside the complex itself.

The first Shinto shrines imitated the indigenous thatched hut. The complex usually consisted of two structures, the sanctuary and the hall for worshipers, often connected by a raised, covered platform. (For terminology of the various parts of the buildings and a complete discussion of styles see SHINTOISM; see also JAPANESE ART, col. 847.)

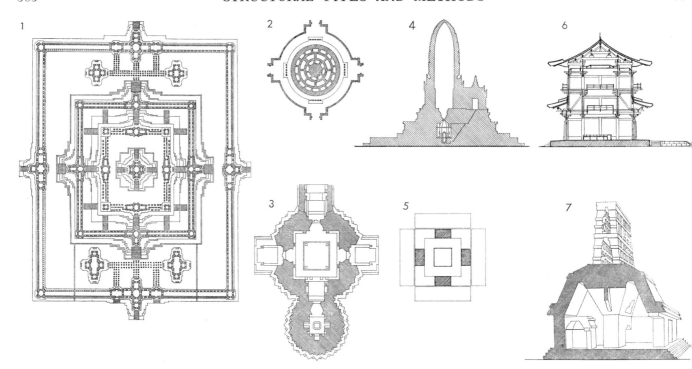

Oriental and pre-Columbian American temples. (1) Angkor (Cambodia), Baphuon (late 11th cent.), plan; (2) Nagarjunakonda (India), stupa (2d-3 cent.), plan; (3) Dumbal (India), temple of Dodabasavanna (12th cent.), plan; (4–5) Ayudhya (Ayuthia; Thailand), Wat Rājapūraṇa (15th cent. section and plan; (6) Chih-hsien (Hopei prov., China), Tu-lo-ssŭ, Hall of Kuan-yin (10th cent.), section; (7) Palenque (Chiapas, Mexico), Temple the Inscriptions (4th–10th cent.), section.

Pre-Columbian American temples. Typical of South and Middle American pre-Columbian religious edifices is the pyramid or high platform topped by a temple. In the Andean area (see ANDEAN PROTOHISTORY, cols. 360–362) pyramids or terraced structures often had multiple functions, and it is not clear whether they were mainly defensive, devotional, or ceremonial structures, observatories, or combinations of these.

Early temples in Middle America (MIDDLE AMERICAN PROTOHISTORY, col. 7) were pyramids topped by simple wooden huts. These developed into elaborately carved structures, such as the Temple of Quetzalcoatl in Teotihuacán (X, col. 18, PL. 6). Mayan temples were erected on high and narrow pyramids (PL. 253; X, cols. 27–28, 39–40). Only priests were permitted to enter the temple itself; public ceremonies were performed in front of the temple. At Palenque the temples were composed of an anteroom running across the width of the building and three rooms opening off it at the far end; of these the center room is the largest and is the sanctuary. The Temple of the Inscriptions (FIG. 583, 7) has a crypt beneath it.

At Monte Albán the Zapotecs set three temples on a platform or pyramid (X, col. 44). The Totonac Pyramid of the Niches in El Tajín (III, PL. 485; X, cols. 46–47, PL. 22) is especially notable. (For descriptions of Toltec and Aztec structures see X, cols. 56–57, 63–64.)

* *

Monastic buildings. Edifices or complexes of buildings that are designed as residences for communities of priests have been used in many societies. However, little is known about the characteristic structures of this type as it appeared in the proximity of Egyptian temples and Greek and Roman sanctuaries, where it also functioned as a shelter for pilgrims.

With the rise of the Christian monastic orders in the Middle Ages the clearly drawn organization of the monastic community was reflected in the layout of the building complex, which served as residence and center of religious and social activity for the community and which acquired equally clearly defined structural characteristics.

The first monasteries were built in Egypt and in the area of Syria and Palestine during the course of the 4th century,

as complexes of independent buildings enclosed by high wall and sometimes fortified. The main building was the basilic (cf. III, col. 803). Most important among the buildings in whic the community lived were the refectory, the dormitory, whic was composed of groups of single cells or single cells with a sma chapel (as in Bawi, Egypt), and a guesthouse; these building have been identified with certainty in most monastic complexe as in that of Qal'at Sim'ān, which includes the Church of S Simeon Stylites (IX, FIG. 89). In some monasteries, especiall in Egypt, such as those of Deir Mar Antonius and Deir Ma Boulos (still in existence, but largely rebuilt), a defense towe that is similar to a keep was erected within the walls. A coordi nated plan, probably of Syrian derivation, is evident in the for tified monastery of Tebessa (Algeria), which was built in the 5t or 6th century. This consisted of a central basilica with a tre foil martyrium; the monks' cells, which were placed agains the basilica's perimeter wall; a garden in front of the basilic enclosed by *plutei*; a hospice; and a burial ground.

The Byzantine monastery is characterized by a freedor of placement of the various edifices within the walled enclosur and for this reason no consistent structural types can be distin guished (cf. the Nea Moni in Keos, 11th cent., and the monas teries on Mount Athos). The rock-cut monasteries of Cappa docia are similarly conceived.

In the West, Irish monasteries were rather modest complexe made up of scattered groups of very poor buildings. The firs clearly defined layouts of monastic buildings date to the Ca olingian and Ottonian eras and are characterized by the regula placement and coordination of the buildings inside the walle enclosure. These characteristics are especially evident in th plan of the Benedictine Monastery of St. Gall (see CAROLINGIA PERIOD), where the dormitory and refectory were placed alon the sides of the cloister, thus forming a nucleus of building that was the model for later monastery complexes, especiall those of the Benedictines. In the reconstruction of the 11th century monastery of Cluny, the chapter house opened onto th cloister on the south side of the church; the other residentia buildings were grouped around a secondary cloister. Stable guesthouses, and refectories for pilgrims were placed near th entrance to the enclosure (V, FIG. 653).

Thus the monastery took on a form that foreshadowed the gular layout of building units typical of town planning. With nly minor exceptions, this general plan has remained unchanged p to modern times.

Fernanda de' MAFFEI

The typical Benedictine abbey complex was arranged around cloister with a garden (*paradeisos*) and central fountain. One de of the cloister generally abutted the side of the church, nd another, obviously, partially abutted the transept. Ideally, ne chapter house (prescribed by Benedictine rule, and later y almost all other orders, as the meeting place for the monks) as an extension of the transept (cf. VIII, FIG. 409). The side the cloister opposite the side of the church was often re-rved for the refectory, although sometimes this was inserted right angles on the same side, as at Fontenay (V, FIG. 654) nd Fossanova (VI, FIG. 533), and for dormitories. Opposite ne chapter house stood the reception rooms and entrance. ther dormitories were located on the upper floors of the rious buildings. To this nucleus were added other smaller oisters or courtyards, around which were arranged rooms for e novitiate, the schools, the kitchens, the sanitary facilities hese often constituted separate groups of buildings), and other rposes (commissary, *scriptoria*, laboratories, shelters for do-estic animals, and storerooms). On the periphery of the mon-tic complex (as in the Abbey of Cluny) were the hospice, spital, and quarters for the laity. The courtyard behind the se was generally used as a burial ground.

The plan of the monastic complex, originated by the Ben-lictines, became formally established in the monasteries of e Cistercian order, at least with regard to the typical nucleus ound the main cloister (cf. VI, FIG. 162). Along the side on hich stood the chapter house (which gradually took on eater importance and often had several aisles), the sacristy, e library, the chapel, and the abbot's lodgings were grouped. Variations of this scheme appeared in Carthusian monas-ries, in which church, chapter house, and refectory were nerally grouped around a small cloister, while the monastic icleus proper consisted of a larger cloister, around which re the cells of the individual monks, each with its small getable garden. In these monasteries the rooms to which the ity were admitted were reduced to an indispensable minimum.

In the monasteries that were built along the pilgrim routes d in the Holy Land, many of them by the knightly orders the Templars and Hospitalers, greater importance was given those buildings destined to shelter pilgrims and to house e sick. It should also be mentioned that in later stages of velopment in several Benedictine monasteries (such as those Montecassino and Cava dei Tirreni) and some Carthusian onasteries (such as that of Galluzzo, near Florence; PL. 261) ere was an enlargement, if not an outright predominance ithin the monastic complex, of those rooms given over to aritable activities and to the teaching of the novices and the laity.

The general characteristics of the plans described above mained constant throughout the Gothic period (VI, FIGS. 2-494, 496, 499, 505) and later. From the Renaissance on-ard, a more compact layout replaced the free and basically ganic grouping of several building nuclei that had character-ed medieval monastic complexes. The Renaissance scheme cluded within a unitary and structurally homogeneous building rious rooms that were nevertheless functionally separate. me examples are El Escorial, by J. B. de Toledo and Juan Herrera (1563–64; XII, FIG. 126); the Certosa di S. Lorenzo Padua (founded in 1306, completely rebuilt in the 17th and th centuries), which like El Escorial had a symbolic plan that presented the gridiron of St. Lawrence; the Oratorio dei Fi-ppini in Rome, begun in 1637 by Borromini (II, FIG. 285); and the Jesuit mission complexes in South America.

No other culture produced such complex and monumental onastic edifices as did the West, which developed and extend-l them throughout Christendom into the Near East and the untries of Orthodox rite.

The Moslem madrasahs were schools of theology and law ther than true monasteries. They were generally cruciform

in plan, with four liwans connected by dormitories around a central court (VIII, FIGS. 339, 340; cols. 339–340) and subdivided — at least in the bigger complexes — according to the four Orthodox rites (Malikite, Hanafite, Hanbalite, and Shafite).

The monastic complexes of Buddhism had a spiritual im-portance equal to those of Christianity. There were, however, much simpler architectural types. They were composed of huts, or more often, grottoes (viharas), in which the monks lived (the cells were called *parivena*), as at Karli, Ajanta, and Bamian (FIG. 611, 2). In addition to the rock-cut monastic complex there were those made up of freestanding buildings (*samghārāma*), constructed on square or rectangular plans, in which the cells were grouped around the main hall (*caityagṛha*), which some-times had apses or was perfectly rectangular and preceded by an atrium; at first the stupa and later the statue of the Buddha stood in this atrium. Although there were many variations, this basic plan, often so elaborated by the addition of various other buildings that the entire complex took on the aspect of a citadel, spread throughout the Buddhist Orient from Tibet to China and later served as the model for Hindu monasteries (math).

Shintoist temples also included monastic complexes within their walls. These were simple in plan and consisted of small buildings placed symmetrically around the sanctuary; they repeated the forms of Japanese rural dwellings.

PUBLIC BUILDINGS. *Assembly buildings*. In autocratic socie-ties rooms set aside for assembly and the exercise of civil or religious power are commonly included in the palace of the sovereign, or within the complexes of sacred buildings.

In ancient times it was, to all effects, only in the Greco-Roman world that such buildings began to take on the form of structural types that were well defined and endowed with particular functionality.

In ancient Greece, apart from those types of building that were related to the town plan (see TOWN PLANNING) and had a rather generic function for the community (such as the colon-nades and stoas that surrounded the agora), there were two main types of assembly building: the *bouleuterion* and the *ekklesiaste-rion*, used respectively for assemblies of the senate and of the people. These sometimes were built in the form of a theater or odeon (see below), which often also served to house assemblies (e.g., those at Priene, FIG. 587, and Miletos; see HELLENISTIC ART, col. 302, FIG. 302).

Other types of assembly buildings were built on the plan of the hypostyle hall; the hall at Delos (VII, FIG. 298) was built on a rectangular plan, with two concentric peristyles and another row of columns along the main axis that support the roof, which was raised at the center to allow lighting from above. This structural form may be derived from the Telesterion of Eleusis (VII, FIG. 787) by Iktinos and from Egyptian struc-tures; it was further developed in the Thersilion at Megalopolis, in which columns were arranged in the form of five concentric rectangles converging on a central podium from which the orator spoke.

The distributive plan of internal space in the Hellenistic hypostyle hall was probably the model for that of the Roman basilica. The basilica at Pompeii is an example of a Roman adaptation of the Hellenistic form (see HELLENISTIC ART, cols. 298–299).

The Basilica Julia, begun by Caesar and rebuilt by Augustus, represented another phase in the development of this type. As reconstructed by several scholars, it probably consisted of a rectangular hall with a colonnade on three sides; it was unroofed at the center, and was somewhat similar to a peristyle. The Basilica Ulpia (I, FIG. 513) in Trajan's Forum was the model for the type that spread throughout the Roman Empire, from Leptis Magna to Smyrna. It was a rectangular hall, with en-trances on the long sides and projecting apses on the shorter sides. There were double aisles of columns on all four sides of the interior; square piers separated them from the central space and from one another.

In the Basilica of Maxentius (FIG. 587, 6, 7) there was a radical transformation of the plan and structures of the ancient basilica. Following the example of the great central halls in

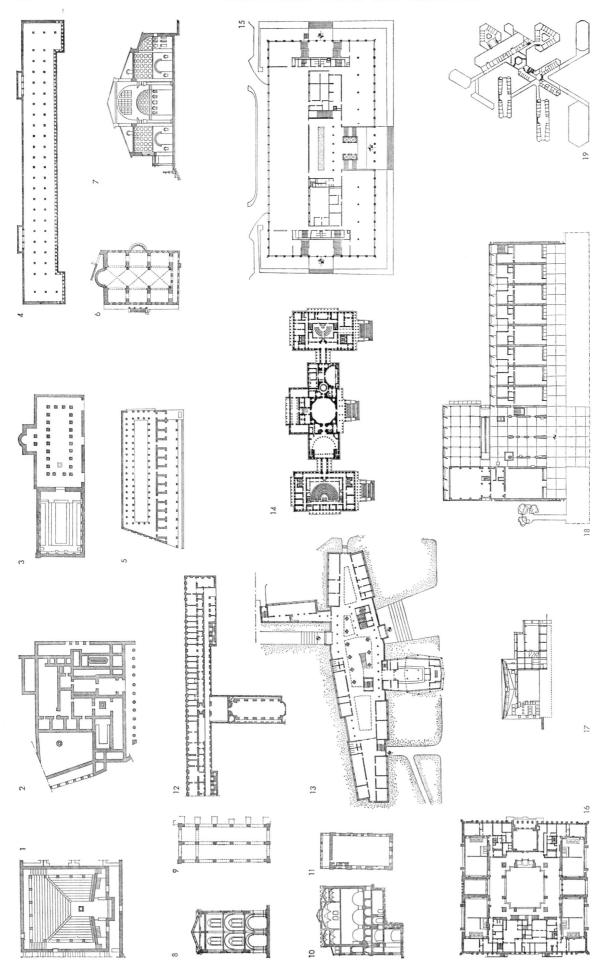

Assembly halls, administrative buildings, and courts of law. (1) Priene (Turkey), Ekklesiasterion (late 2d-early 1st cent. B.C.), plan; (2) Olympia (Greece), Prytanaeion (5th cent. B.C.), plan; (3) Sabratha (Libya), basilica and curia (3d cent.), plan; (4) Megalopolis (Greece), Stoa of Philip (2d cent. B.C.), reconstruction of plan; (5) Rome, Basilica Aemilia (1st cent. B.C.), plan; (6–7) Rome, Basilica of Maxentius (4th cent.), plan and section; (8) Florence, Orsanmichele (14th cent.), plan; (10–11) Gubbio, Palazzo dei Consoli (13th–14th cent.), section and plan; (12) Budapest, town hall (18th cent.), plan; (13) Lünen (Germany), city hall (by W. Rausch and S. Stein; 20th cent.), plan; (14) Washington, D.C., Capitol (18th–19th cent.), plan; (15) London, United States Embassy (by E. Saarinen; 20th cent.), ground floor plan; (16) Sioux City (Iowa), Woodburg Court House (20th cent.), plan; (17–18) Chandigarh (India), High Courts of Justice (by Le Corbusier; 20th cent.).

the thermae, the lateral aisles were divided into three zones by walls at right angles to the nave, and these zones were roofed with barrel vaulting; this plan was taken up again by Alberti (e.g., in S. Andrea in Mantua) and still later by mannerist architects.

Among other Roman public edifices mention should be made of the Curia (Senate chamber; PL. 250; IX, PL. 33), a square or oblong hall, with a series of risers along the longer sides and sometimes with a *comitium* at the end; this type of structure may have been inspired by the form of the Greek gymnasium. The Tabularium in Rome (PL. 250) had an arched colonnade and, probably, a trabeated loggia above it; level with the openings in the colonnade were the rooms housing the state archives.

In the Middle Ages the type of edifice opened on the ground floor by a colonnade — the same plan used by the Romans in the Tabularium — was taken up again in the development of the municipal palace. This type of building was among the most characteristic expressions of medieval civic architecture; it generally consisted of a two-story building with a room on the ground floor behind the portico. In Central and Northern Europe it was almost always divided into two aisles, together with a larger hall on the first floor. Typical elements were the second-story loggia on the façade, from which officials addressed the public; the bell tower, where the archives were usually kept; the treasury; and the prison. Other rooms housed the lodgings of the mayor, the guard, and administrative offices.

There are countless examples of this type of structure, from the Romanesque version at La Réole in France to the *broletti* of Milan, Bergamo, Brescia, and Monza (FIG. 587, 9) and from the *hôtels de ville* of Saint-Omer, Noyon, and Arras in France to the town halls of San Gimignano, Todi, and Gubbio in Italy.

The growing complexity of administrative functions brought about by the economic and urban development of the medieval communes gave rise to more complicated forms, such as those of the Palazzo del Comune (della Ragione) in Verona and the Doges' Palace in Venice, which has a central courtyard (VI, PL. 340). Other public buildings copied the forms of palaces of the aristocracy, and developed on diverse plans and on several stories, while preserving an aspect that remained typical and representative, as in the Altstadt-Rathaus in Brunswick, Germany, the Palazzo Pubblico of Siena (VI, PL. 339), and the Palazzo dei Priori in Volterra (PL. 251). It was not unusual to find a functional distinction made among several buildings, according to which the courthouse might be distinguished from the town hall, as in Padua, where there is a Palazzo della Ragione, or courthouse, and in Pistoia, where there were three principal public buildings: the mayor's palace (Palazzo del Podestà), the so-called "palace of the people's captain" (Palazzo del Capitano del Popolo; cf. VIII, PL. 186), and that of the commune (Palazzo Comunale). In Florence a distinction was made between the palace of the mayor (Palazzo del Podestà, VIII, PL. 184) and the palace of the commune (Palazzo Vecchio).

During the Renaissance in Central and Northern Europe, where the fall of feudalism concentrated political and economic power in the hands of the trading middle class, the town hall was often the seat of the business offices (for the guilds and corporations) of the community.

Other types were developed at this time, conceived in connection with the emergence of more complex political forms that transcended the commune. Examples of such types are the Palazzo Senatorio by Michelangelo, in Rome, and the Uffizi by Vasari in Florence (IX, FIG. 470).

After the Napoleonic administrative reforms, which centralized and unified the bureaucratic structure of the French government, there was an increase in the number of public buildings throughout 19th-century Europe (e.g., ministries, parliaments, courthouses). In most cases these were older buildings that had been erected for other purposes (e.g., monasteries, palaces, castles) and adapted to their new functions. The new buildings that were constructed reflected a variety of stylistic forms and often were typical examples of neoclassic styles (q.v.) and the Gothic Revival. Sometimes, especially in parliamentary halls, there was greater awareness of functional requirements and a search for more interesting structural solutions.

Some modern public buildings have established new structural types that reflect current architectural trends. Examples of these are the *hôtel de ville* of the Paris surburb of Boulogne-Billancourt, designed by Garnier and Debat-Ponsan; the town hall of Hilversum, Norway, by W. M. Dudok (V, PL. 106); the Ministry of Health and Education in Rio de Janeiro by Costa, Niemeyer, and others (I, PL. 142); the Chandigarh complex by Le Corbusier (FIG. 587, 17–18; IX, PL. 108); and the governmental buildings in Brasilia (XIV, PL. 173).

Theaters and sports installations. The theater as an architectural entity originated in Greece, on the site of performances of ritual choruses and dances connected with the cult of Dionysos. The rites were performed in a circular space around an altar; this space was known as the orchestra. The participants observed the rites from a concave slope, usually in the side of a hill, where they sat on rudimentary steps that were either natural formations or man-made constructions.

The form of the Greek theater may have been derived in part from that of the theaters of the Minoan court, which were traditionally square (C. Anti, *Teatri Greci Arcaici*, Padua, 1947, pp. 289–91). The archaic theaters of the palaces of Phaistos and Knossos (IV, FIG. 85), like those of Hellas before the 5th century B.C., had a square orchestra and a more or less trapezoidal auditorium (see CRETAN-MYCENAEAN ART, cols. 80, 87). The first important example of a semicircular theater dates to the era of Hieron I in Syracuse; this was the theater built in 460 B.C. by Demokopos (FIG. 591, 1; VII, PL. 55). In the 4th century B.C. appeared examples of an auditorium constructed completely in stone, as in those at Epidauros (370–60 B.C.; III, PL. 340; XI, PL. 194) and Megalopolis (350–330 B.C.).

The earliest dramas were performed in the orchestra in front of a simple portable backdrop of canvas (*skene*). Before long this primitive canvas backdrop was replaced with a permanent one consisting of a rectangular wooden structure that functioned as a backdrop and provided space for a storeroom and dressing room for the actors. In a short time this structure took on such importance that it was no longer merely a backdrop but became an integral part of the action, as the performers entered and exited from it. (See SCENOGRAPHY, cols. 748–752.)

In the time of Aeschylus the *skene* was enlarged and elaborated according to the specific requirements of the performance. As early as the second half of the 5th century B.C. movable wooden backdrops were replaced by a fixed *skene* in masonry, of a more precise architectural nature, generally reproducing the façade of a building, such as a palace or a royal residence (XII, FIG. 749). The actors entered the orchestra from ramps (*paradoi*) on either side.

As the drama developed in Hellenistic times the addition of a raised stage in front of the *skene* became necessary to bring the actors more clearly into view. This stage was known as the *logeion* and its façade was called the *proskenion* (proscenium; cf. XII, FIG. 749, B–C). The *skene* was built on two levels; the lower level (*hyposkenion*) was used to house dressing rooms and storerooms for the stage apparatus.

The *paraskenia* were wings that flanked the *skene*, which was generally slightly recessed between them (as in the theaters of Segesta, VII, FIG. 301, and Tyndaris).

The tiered auditorium was usually divided into three distinct sectors (*kerkides*), reserved, in ascending order, for the magistrates and priests, the soldiers, and the people. The seats were further divided at intervals by a network of radial flights of steps and horizontal passages (*diazomata*) that provided outlets for the individual sectors.

Another type of building for public entertainment, in widespread use during the Hellenistic period, was the odeon, designed for musical performances and similar not only to the theater but also to the *bouleuterion*, in which an auditorium was placed within the rectangular masonry structure that supported the roof.

In Roman times the theater became a regular addition to the public edifices of the forums of the more important cities only during the 1st century B.C. The small stone theater of Pompeii dates to 75 B.C.; actually, an odeon, this was the first of its type and differed in its structural forms from the traditional Greek odea, although in its general plan it derived directly from them (FIG. 591, 2).

The Roman theater, unlike the Greek theater, was generally built on level ground; the cavea, or auditorium, rested on a mighty and complex system of sloping radial substructures that formed, on its outside perimeter, an imposing architectural structure with several superimposed orders. Under the cavea, among the large structures supporting the tiers, were the entrances to the various sectors, placed according to a studied network of passageways that led from the ground-floor colonnades by means of a system

of steps and semicircular corridors to the many openings into the cavea (*vomitoria*).

The semicircular cavea was divided into three principal sectors, or *maeniana:* the *ima cavea, media cavea,* and *summa cavea,* reserved, respectively, for the magistrates, the citizens and soldiers, and the plebs. Above the uppermost sectors of seats there often was a covered gallery (*porticus in summa gradatione*), where a mixed public stood to watch those performances which attracted a greater number of spectators than usual. These differing sectors of seats were separated by narrow semicircular corridors (*praecinctiones*); each sector was surrounded

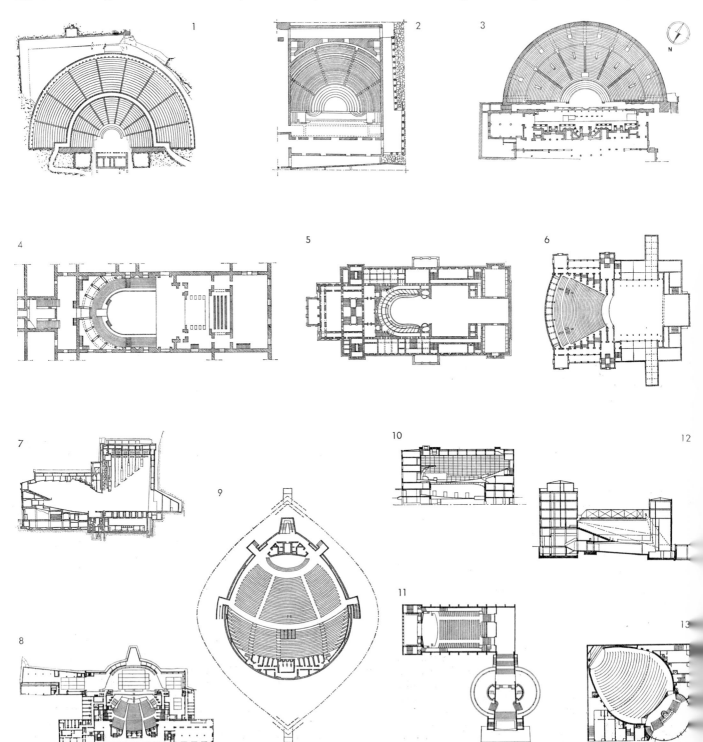

Theaters and auditoriums. (1) Syracuse, Greek theater (3d cent. B.C.), plan; (2) Pompeii, *odeon* (1st cent. B.C.), plan; (3) Mérida (Spain), Roman theater, plan (Augustan age); (4) Parma, Teatro Farnese (16th cent.), plan; (5) Budapest, State Opera House (19th cent.), plan; (6) Bayreuth (Germany), Festspielhaus (19th cent.), plan; (7–8) Salzburg, Festspielhaus (by C. Holzmeister; 20th cent.), section and plan; (9) Berlin, Congress Hall (by H. A. Stubbins; 20th cent.), plan; (10–11) Hälsingborg (Sweden), auditorium (20th cent.), section and plan; (12) Stuttgart, Universum cinema (20th cent.), section; (13) Stockholm, Vicktoria cinema (20th cent.), ground floor plan.

a parapet (*balteus*). Since the semicircular orchestra (Latin *nistra*) was no longer a functional part of the drama, as it had en in Greek times, its width was diminished and inside its rve were placed three concentric rows of steps reserved for e seats of senators, priests, and important personages. Thus e orchestra became an integral part of the auditorium.

The façade (*frons scaenae*) of the stage building (*scaena*) as as high as the *summa cavea* and, especially in the late im-rial age, was structurally elaborated with several superimposed ders of columns alternated with semicircular or square niches. he *frons scaenae* had three openings (*hospitalia*), which served entrances for the actors and which led to the dressing rooms side the stage building (*postscaenium*). The main door (*porta gia*) opened in the center of the *scaena*, and was flanked by e other two. Sometimes, in addition to the monumental stone aena special wooden scenery flats were used; they either were ovable (*scaena ductilis*) or were mounted on prisms that could turned (*scaena vertilis*). The *scaena* was generally longer an that of Greek theaters; most often its length was twice e diameter of the orchestra.

The stage (*pulpitum*) was generally deeper and lower than ose of Greek theaters; it was built only slightly higher than e level of the orchestra so as to permit those seated in the very st rows to follow the action.

Between the cavea and the *scaena*, two symmetrical covered trances had the same function as the Greek *paradoi*; they ermitted direct entrance to the orchestra level and to the first ws of seats in the cavea. The boxes (*tribunalia*) were always aced above these two entrances and were reserved for the mag-trates in charge of the performances and for the Vestal Vir-ns. With the addition of the *tribunalia*, which linked the cavea d the stage, the theater had become a single architectural it. (See also ROMAN ART OF THE EASTERN EMPIRE, cols. 292–4; ROMAN IMPERIAL ART, cols. 514–516.)

After the Roman era the drama suffered a sharp decline the West; no performances were given and no theaters were ilt. During the Middle Ages mystery plays, enactments of cred events, were presented on the porches of churches or the church square; morality plays were mounted on carts in ultiple scenes with a minimum of scenery. (See SCENOGRAPHY, ls. 753–759, FIG. 757.)

It was only with the Renaissance that the renewed interest ancient culture brought about a revival of the Greek and Ro-an classic drama. The first Renaissance theaters were built wood and had a decidedly temporary air; this type, in use ntil the middle of the 16th century, can be reconstructed om drawings by Serlio. The general plan was entirely based classical schemes, from which it derived the semicircular uditorium, with places of honor in the first rows, and the sub-ivision into sectors by corridors and radial ramps. The raised ont part of the stage also reflected classic schemes, while the ar part, with the floor inclined, reflected a new concept of erspective space. A series of wings added to the illusion of epth. Examples of this construction were the court theaters of e Gonzagas in Mantua and the Este family in Ferrara, hich are known only from sources.

The first public theater conceived as an autonomous archi-ctural unit was the Teatro Olimpico in Vicenza, built by Pal-dio about 1575 (IX, PL. 312, FIG. 465). In this theater, which as an elliptical auditorium, a first attempt was made to extend e scenic effects and the dramatic action beyond the limits of the onumental architectural *frons scaenae*, which, in homage to the lassical theater, was the basic scenographic element. To this nd, seven city streets, conceived in perspective, extended ra-ially from the traditional doors in the classical *frons scaenae*, hich in itself was no longer adequate; it could not produce those lusory scenic effects required by 16th-century drama and by a ew concept of perspective (XII, PL. 425).

Other important attempts at representing illusionary space d at isolating it from any dimensional or real contact with the uditorium were made in 1588 in the theater of Sabbioneta by camozzi (XII, FIG. 100) and in 1618 in the Teatro Farnese in arma (PL. 258; FIG. 591, 4) by G. B. Aleotti. These signaled e birth of the Italian type of theater; the auditorium was

lengthened into a U shape and the *frons scaenae* disappeared. A simple partition (the proscenium) divided the theater, creating the spatial duality characteristic of the modern theater: the real, architectural space of the auditorium and the illusionary per-spective space of the stage.

The U-shaped auditorium was further developed in the baroque age, especially in theaters designed by Andrea Seghizzi in Venice (1630) and Bologna (1640), and in those by the Galli Bibiena family (cf. VIII, PL. 106), in which reception areas were added to the theater and the entire complex was enclosed within a perimeter that on the exterior only partially suggested the shape of the auditorium.

Meanwhile, other important modifications were inspired by other types of theaters that had been conceived in Europe, especially in England and Spain. In Spain the typical form was that of the *corrales*, temporary theaters on a rectangular or square plan; in these the action was performed at the center of a courtyard, around which was placed a series of super-posed open galleries (see also SCENOGRAPHY, cols. 760–61).

Luciano PONTUALE

The typical Elizabethan theater in England was inspired by and somewhat resembled the arenas used for bear-baiting (see SCENOGRAPHY, col. 760). As reconstructed from a drawing of the Swan Theater by John de Witt (ca. 1596), the theater was a circular, roofless building. The square stage extended into the stalls, which were placed in a circle. On the stage there was a sort of loggia supported by two columns, which func-tioned as scenery; sometimes the action took place on the upper level, and sometimes this was reserved for privileged spectators. The stage was composed of three distinct areas: front stage, rear stage (the part between the columns), and upper stage (the small loggia above). All around the stalls, which were reserved for the people (groundlings), ran galleries in superim-posed orders.

This type of theater plan was later combined with that of the English private theater, which echoed the rectangular form of the hall, was roofed over, and had the seats aligned in three rows along three sides. The most common form of theater from the 17th to the 19th century was known as the "French theater." This was composed of stalls and galleries or boxes placed in superimposed series around an elliptical auditorium, facing a stage that was generally rectilinear.

This form, some examples of which have endured up to the present, was eventually opposed by that of the "German theater," which was first achieved in the Festspielhaus in Bayreuth, built in 1871 by Brückwald, who based his work on studies by Semper; the architect was inspired and directed by Richard Wagner. The plan recalled those of the theaters of the ancient world, and in particular, that of the odeon; there were no stalls or galleries, the auditorium was curved (or, later, semicircular or rectangular) and was separated from the stage by a slightly sunken level, in which the orchestra played (FIG. 591, 6). The auditorium and stage areas were clearly distinguished from each other, and this distinction was obvious also on the theater's exterior, because of the greater height of the stage loft, which was often covered by a dome.

The model of the Bayreuth theater was taken up and elab-orated in the Covent Garden Theater in London, the Chicago Civic Opera House, and the Shakespeare Memorial Theater in Stratford-on-Avon and was to be the basis for many modern forms. In modern theaters, however, there has been a tend-ency to minimize the distinction between auditorium and stage in order to achieve more immediate dramatic effects, by pro-jecting the stage into the auditorium area, by placing the stage so that it is almost surrounded by the auditorium (theater designed by Oskar Strnad), or by creating an almost circular stage into which a wedge-shaped sector of the auditorium was introduced [partly effected in the theater designed by Henry van de Velde (1914) for the Werkbund Exhibition at Cologne and later in the plan of the so-called "simultaneous theater" created by A. Pronaszko and S. Syrkus].

Noteworthy in this attempt to achieve an emotional integration of action and audience are the plans by Walter Gropius for the *Totaltheater* (1926) conceived by Erwin Piscator and for a theater in Kharkov (1930). The theater thus conceived has greater functional flexibility, since it can be used for stage performances or as an auditorium, conference hall, or cinema. Notable examples of more recent theater design are the Philharmonic concert hall in West Berlin, built from plans by Hans Scharoun (1956), and the Sydney Opera House, an all-concrete building with shell-shaped roof structures designed by Jørn Utzon (1957).

While many types of buildings that house sports installations function as places where one or several sports can be presented to the public, others serve primarily for the practice of sports and do not necessarily include facilities for spectators.

Such edifices have taken on characteristic structural forms only in the Greek and Roman eras and in modern times. With the exception of the patios for ritual ball games built in pre-Columbian America (PL. 256; X, PL. 36; see X, cols. 29, 57), other cultures and eras did not produce well-defined types of edifices, even though highly developed and spectacular forms of sporting activity were practiced and special buildings were sometimes designed for such activities.

In ancient Greece the panhellenic games (Olympic, Pythian, Nemean, and Isthmian) were held in stadiums that were essentially composed of a track, six hundred feet long, around which were stepped seats or a glacis of earth, as at Olympia, with the two longer sides generally rectilinear (the sides were not always parallel, and at Delphi they were slightly convex; of the shorter sides, one was also rectilinear, and the other was semicircular, FIG. 597, 1). The location of the stadium, like that of the theater, was determined by the terrain. The stadiums of Athens and Messene were situated in a long valley; at Delphi only one of the longer sides was placed against a natural incline, while the other was supported by an earthen bank. The stepped seats were not necessarily uniform in height along the perimeter and sometimes rose higher along one of the longer sides. On the track, marked by a plinth or stone curb or a small canal containing running water, two straight lines designated the starting and finishing points. Entrances to the stadium were located halfway along the longer sides and at the corners between these and the shorter sides.

This plan has been reconstructed from the remains of the stadiums at Olympia and Epidauros (PL. 257; the only exception seems to have been the stadium at Miletos, where the stepped seats ran only along the longer sides and where the shorter sides were also rectilinear); it was similar in form to the hippodrome, such as that at Olympia where the games of the xxv Olympiad were held in 680 B.C. (Pausanias, V, *viii*, 8). The track of the hippodrome was much broader, however.

The forms of hippodrome and stadium were further developed by the Romans in their circuses, which also employed some of the structural aspects of the theater.

* * *

The Roman circus, as it appeared during the Imperial age (e.g., Circus Flaminius; Circus Maximus, FIG. 597, 3; Circus of Maxentius, PL. 257), generally consisted of two long parallel sectors of stepped seats connected by semicircular sectors and of an arena in which there was a long central dividing wall, or spina, marking the track. As in the theaters, the tiers of seats were divided into various *maeniana*, which were separated by corridors and entered through *vomitoria* and *transennae*. On the lowest level was the podium, the sector reserved for important guests; the upper rows of steps were generally protected by a loggia. The emperor's box (*pulvinar*) was located on the first level at the center of one of the longer sides; and that of the judges (*tribunal judicum*) was situated opposite the finish line. The box for the *editor spectaculorum*, the magistrate who organized and presided over the spectacles, was at the center of one of the semicircular end sections, above the *porta triumphalis*, through which processions and contestants entered. Opposite this entrance rose the *carceres*, stalls from which the competing chariots entered the arena. The *carceres* also had

the so-called "pump gate" in the center, and their sides ended in two high towers (*oppida*).

The *porta libitinensis*, which opened into one of the longer sides of the circus, served for the removal of dead or wounded contestants and animals. Two secondary doors were also placed between the corner towers of the *carceres* and the seats. The central spina divided the arena along an oblique line that allowed a wider space for the entrance of chariots into the first course. At the end of the spina rose two metae, around which the chariots had to make seven laps for a total distance of about $2^1/_4$ mi.

The distance between the metae was always constant; the spina was often decorated with groups of trophies, columns, and statues and sometimes was enlivened by water displays that were fed from a canal (*euripus*). The spina also contained various service rooms.

Although the word amphitheater is Greek in origin, it designates the place where gladiatorial games were held. These were completely unknown to the Hellenic world, but were popular among Etruscan and Italic peoples who, according to Vitruvius, attributed to such combats a ritual meaning. These contests also became popular with the Romans, who at first held them in their forums. According to Pliny (*Naturalis Historia*, XXXVI), the first amphitheater was built by Caius Curio. The amphitheater reflected the structural type of the theater. It was elliptic in shape and had a sloping auditorium sometimes supported by vaulted radial structures, similar to those used in the cavea of theaters. The arena itself was also elliptic and served for gladiatorial games as well as for hunts (*venationes*), naval battles (*naumachiae*), and performances of drama or the dance. (See ROMAN IMPERIAL ART, cols. 516–517.)

The arena was surrounded by a wall about 7 to 12 ft. high (sometimes a protective net was stretched above the wall), behind which was the podium, reserved for senators, Vestals, magistrates, and high-ranking military authorities. The tiers of seats in this official sector were interrupted at the ends of the main axis of the ellipse by two principal gates opening into the arena, one for the entrance of parades of combatants, the other for the removal of the bodies of victims of the games. At the two ends of the lesser axis of the ellipse stood the *pulvinaria*, one for the emperor and the other for high officials. The different sectors of seats (usually three) were reserved for different social classes; these sectors were subdivided and had entrances and systems of corridors very similar to those of the theater. Access to the topmost sector (*maenianum summum*) was provided in diverse ways. In the amphitheaters at Pompei (PL. 256) and Pulj it was effected by means of external systems of stairs that were joined to the walls themselves. In the Roman Colosseum a more organic system of corridors and internal staircases was used (FIG. 597, 4); this was adopted in all later amphitheaters.

The arena of the Colosseum, as well as those of many other amphitheaters (e.g., Santa Maria Capua Vetere, Verona), had an elaborate system of substructures that were used to house technical apparatus and animals' cages.

Other types of sports buildings were developed during the Hellenistic period. These were the gymnasium, an outdoor exercise ground, and the palaestra, indoor rooms for such sports as wrestling and boxing (see HELLENISTIC ART, col. 303). These edifices were not designed to accommodate spectators, but were intended as places where various sports might be practiced; the terms gymnasium and palaestra came to be identified with each other (FIG. 597, 2). Throughout the Roman world, especially at Pompeii, Herculaneum, and Rome, similar structures were incorporated into the thermae complex (cf. XI, FIGS. 295, 296).

Luciano PONTUALE

In modern times no new types of sports edifices appeared before the last decades of the 19th century. (Such earlier developments as riding schools and stables, FIG. 597, 5; fencing halls, gymnasiums; and polygonal shooting ranges generally had no distinguishing structural types.) The broader social base of spectator participation in sporting events and the rise of new forms of sporting contests in recent times has brought about

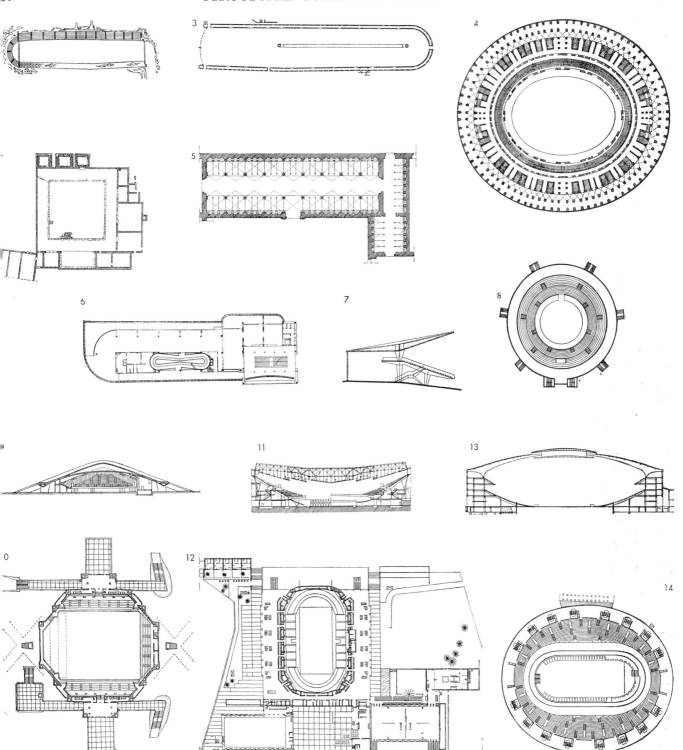

Sports installations. (1) Delphi (Greece), stadium (5th cent. B.C., with later additions), plan; (2) Delos (Greece), gymnasium (3d cent. B.C.), plan; (3) Rome, Circus Maximus (2d cent.), plan; (4) Rome, Colosseum (1st cent.), plan; (5) Rome, Palazzo Doria Pamphili, stables (18th cent.), plan; (6) Warsaw, hippodrome (20th cent.), plan of the main stand; (7) Rome, Tor di Valle hippodrome (by J. Lafuente, G. Rebecchini, P. Vietti Violi; 20th cent.), section of grandstand; (8) Madrid, Plaza de Toros (20th cent.), plan; (9–10) Niigata, sports palace (by E. Miyagawa; 20th cent.), section and plan; (11–12) Vienna, municipal sports complex (R. Ranier; 20th cent.), section of main building and plan of complex; (13–14) Dortmund, Westphalenhalle (by W. Höltje; 20th cent.), section and plan.

a number of widely varied types of sports edifices, based on Greco-Roman models.

The type of construction most widely used and most adaptable to various kinds of sports competitions is the stadium, which is also the form most similar to that of the ancient amphitheater. The modern stadium is usually built in the shape of an elongated ellipse (PL. 257, FIG. 597, 13–14).

The use of reinforced concrete structures (pioneered by Tony Garnier in the Lyons stadium), with their potential for articulation, permits freer solutions in the construction of stairs, entrance corridors, and rooms housing technical facilities. These structures can also be used to build cantilevered roofs over vast sectors of seats (FIG. 597, 7). The first large stadium to be completely roofed over was planned by Kiewitt and Sohrmann for St. Louis, Mo. (1929). New architectural solutions have led to the erection of stadiums on a circular plan.

For other types of sports that do not require extensive playing fields, the stadium plan has been adapted to suit specific needs: as in stands overlooking race tracks, tennis courts, and swimming pools, whether or not these are roofed over (FIG. 597, 6–7). The sports palace, usually a circular structure with a domed roof in reinforced concrete or stressed metal elements, has been widely used for the presentation of many kinds of sports and spectacles (V, FIG. 244).

In some sports installations the surface on which the sport is practiced demands special architectural solutions, as in bicycle-racing tracks, and, above all, in motor-racing arenas, where the centrifugal force caused by the speed of the cars is balanced by the banking of the track at the curves. Swimming pools and winter sports installations also require special architectural and technical solutions (V, FIG. 243).

Installations designed primarily to house exercise facilities, such as gymnasiums, are generally based on a common type, which is adapted to suit specific requirements (FIG. 597, 9–10).

Castles and defensive structures. Many areas inhabited by early man give evidence of rudimentary enclosures of a defensive nature, consisting of palisades strengthened by ramparts of earth, such as those found at present among primitive peoples in central, western, and southern Africa (Congo, Togoland, Mali, Rhodesia, Tanzania, Zambia; FIG. 601, 1), and in Indonesia and New Zealand (the Maori *pa*).

In more advanced cultures these enclosures were formed by megalithic walls that surrounded the settlement or pivoted on natural protective barriers. Examples of this are the walls of Troy and those surrounding the settlements of Alatri, Ferentinum, and Arpino, the Celtic *oppida*, and villages in Zambia and pre-Columbian America (e.g., Cuzco). Other defensive walls enclose smaller groups of buildings that are usually situated on an elevation, as in the towns of Tiryns and in Osuna, Gerona, Sagunto, and Numancia in Spain, the prehistoric fortified villages (*castellieri*) of the Venezia Giulia Region, and the *casteliars* of Gaul. The last two were the prototypes of the castle and the fortress.

Because of their clearly functional nature, walled enclosures tend to be fundamentally similar in various cultures. In the ancient Mediterranean world, in Nubia and Mesopotamia, in China and in pre-Columbian America defensive walls were monumental brick structures, often sloping, backed by earthen ramparts. Along the top there was a walkway, which was often protected by battlements or balustrades; circular or, more often, square towers were placed at intervals, rising to a height above that of the walls. The defensive apparatus was concentrated around the gates in the walls, and these gates were often flanked by towers (e.g., the Ishtar gate in Babylon; IX, PL. 494). The towers emphasized the monumental character of the gates themselves. It was probably from the defensive function of the turreted gateway that the Egyptian pylon was derived, as at Medinet Habu (FIG. 601, 8; IV, PL. 359).

The characteristics of Hellenic and Etruscan defensive enclosures were retained in Roman town walls and in the long walls marking the frontiers (limes) of the Empire; Roman walls were interrupted at regular intervals by square battlemented towers, reinforced by earth ramparts (*vallum*). Ditches were dug along the perimeter of the wall.

Noteworthy changes were introduced in the walls built in Rome by Aurelian (270–75) and completed in 279 by successors Tacitus, Florian, and Probus. In these a covered gallery ran along the interior of the wall; the type of gateway with two semicircular towers and a second gallery on top became the rule, as in the Porta S. Sebastiano and the Porta S. Paolo (anc. Porta Ostiensis, PL. 248; cf. also FIG. 601, 10). The defensive wall retained this form throughout the Middle Ages and into the early Renaissance — that is, as long as it remained in use.

The passive defense afforded by a system of walls was usually supplemented by special fortifications which housed concentrations of soldiers and which were equipped with defensive weapons; these installations were generally placed near the gates and in other strategic positions. Examples of this type of construction date back to ancient times and even to primitive peoples and were used also in the ancient East (e.g., the Thinite

fortresses of Kom el Ahmar and Abydos, both in Egypt, an the fortress of Babylon).

The basic characteristics of the fortress type may be see in the Euryelos castle, which was the pivot of the defensiv walls of the Epipolae section of Syracuse (FIG. 601, 6). Thi was an imposing complex surrounded by three ditches tha were linked by means of tunnels; it had a projecting emplace ment for war engines. There was a bastion at the front wit a drawbridge, behind which rose five towers that formed th front of the internal defensive system. Roman builders wer only partly inspired by this construction in their fortification along the limes and at bridgeheads such as those at Castra Div tensia (mod. Deutz), near Cologne, and Rigomagus (mod Remagen), near Coblenz. The Roman *castellum* was a fortifie *castrum* (Caesar, *De Bello Gallico*, III, 1) and was generally a larg square or rectangular enclosure with towers, usually cylindrical at the corners and along the sides.

No important variations on this plan appeared during Lat Antiquity, the Early Middle Ages, and the Byzantine period The form also persisted in the East (FIG. 601, 13–16), wher the Ommiad rulers modeled their palaces on Roman *castella* as in the palace of Mshattā (VIII, FIG. 345). In the Wes ancient buildings, such as the Mausoleum of Hadrian and th tomb of Caecilia Metella in Rome, were often adapted fo defensive purposes and transformed into fortresses.

In the pre-Romanesque and especially during the Roman esque period the castle took on a new and clearly defined form developing around the tower (keep), which was both residenc and fortress, and which constituted the principal defensiv element of the entire castle complex. The keep was originall built on a square plan (as that of Langeais, built in 994 b Fulk III Nerra, Count of Anjou), with buttressed walls. I was two stories high, with the entrance by means of stairs o a drawbridge leading only to the upper floor. In the 11th an 12th centuries the keep took on the circular form (as at Fréteva Mondoubleau, and Châteaudun) that was to be typical in th future, with only rare exceptions. (See FRANCE, cols. 527, 529 ROMANESQUE ART, col. 336.)

Fortifications in Great Britain originally took the form o the Saxon *burh*, which consisted mainly of a mound and woode palisade. In the Romanesque period a more permanent struc ture, the Norman *castel*, was introduced. By the 12th centur the round keep had been replaced by the rectangular one, a in the White Tower of London (VI, FIG. 751). One of the bes examples of 12th-century English castles is Kenilworth (FIG. 601 7; see also XII, col. 732, PL. 235).

At a later stage of development of castles in the West, tw keeps were connected by tangential walls. Later the castle wa surrounded by a wall with corner towers protected by a dee ditch. Château-Gaillard at Les Andelys, built in 1196 (V col. 337; VI, cols. 484–485, FIG. 485), was a unitary constructio in which the buttressed keep was surrounded by turreted walls The keep's function as an isolated defensive element was hence forth fulfilled by the ravelin and the rondel, both detache outer works communicating with the castle by means of covered passageway (caponier). New kinds of defensive ele ments appeared, such as the small towers that projected from the upper corners of the keep, the openings (machicolations between the corbels of the parapet, from which projectiles coul be hurled at attackers below, and the postern gate. The Roman esque castle type was reproduced throughout the Holy Lan by the Crusaders, who remodeled ancient Byzantine and Om miad constructions (e.g., Le Crac des Chevaliers).

In Italy the keep was almost always incorporated withi the castle complex (cf. XII, FIG. 688); in Scandinavia and i England castles were built on French Crusader models. Th original concept of the keep persisted only in the tower-hous within Italian towns (as in Florence, Siena, San Gimignano and Bologna, PL. 249).

In the Gothic period fortified castles became widesprea throughout France, sometimes enclosing entire towns, as a Carcassonne (I, PL. 392; V, FIG. 658), Angers, Avignon (V PL. 381), and Aiguesmortes (V, FIG. 659), and even abbeys an churches were fortified. (See GOTHIC ART, cols. 484–486.) Th

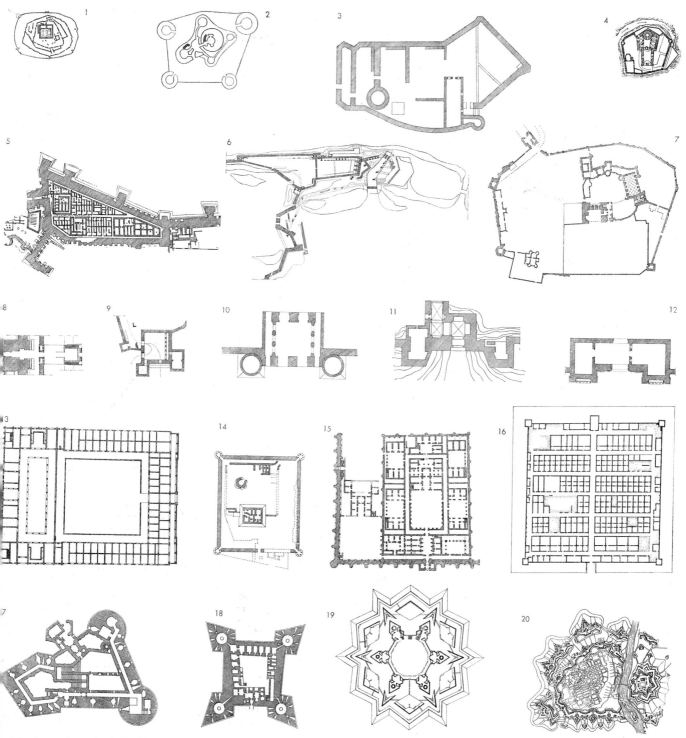

ortifications, plans. (1–4) Fortified dwellings and isolated castles: (1) Tabora (Tanzania), fortified residence of Nyamwezi chief; (2) Barumini (Sar-
inia), nuraghe Su Nuraxi (8th–7th cent. B.C.); (3) Puebla de Alcócer (Spain), castle (14th cent.); (4) Burgschwalbach (Germany), castle (14th cent.).
–7) Fortresses and citadels: (5) Uronarti (Egypt), fortress (2d millennium B.C.); (6) Syracuse, Euryelos castle (4th cent. B.C.); (7) Kenilworth (England),
tadel (14th–16th cent.). (8–12) City gates: (8) Medinet Habu (Egypt), gate in the mortuary complex of Ramses III (12th cent. B.C.); (9) Pergamon
urkey), gate (2d cent. B.C.); (10) Turin, Porta Palatina (Augustan age); (11) Jerusalem, Damascus Gate (16th cent.); (12) Perugia, Porta S. Pietro
5th cent.). (13–16) Fortified complexes with castrum layouts: (13) Xanten (anc. Vetera), castrum (3d cent.?); (14) Khwarizm (mod. Khoresm district
.S.S.R.), fortified complex (7th–8th cent.); (15) Karbala (Iraq), Castle of Uhaidir (8th cent.); (16) Hong Kong, fortification (18th cent.). (17–20) Bas-
ned fortifications: (17) Ostia, castle (16th cent.); (18) Barletta, castle (16th cent.); (19) project for a bastioned fortress on a star plan, from F. de
archi (*Della architettura militare*, Brescia, 1599); (20) Alexandria, fortifications (19th cent.).

revailing tendency to incorporate the keep in the castle com-
lex, defending the most vulnerable position, was evident in
Varkworth Castle in Northumberland (VI, cols. 736–737,
G. 735).

Château Villandraut (VI, FIG. 486), built around a central
ourtyard, was based on Moslem constructions and was itself
e prototype of many other castles in Provence and throughout

Europe, from Bodiam Castle, Sussex (VI, FIG. 511), to Castel
Nuovo in Naples (XII, PL. 7). This compact form was used
throughout the area ruled by Frederick II of Swabia, as in
Castel del Monte, near Andria (VI, col. 535, PL. 340, FIG. 536).

This development of military architecture was paralleled in
Germany (see GERMAN ART, col. 166; GERMANY, cols. 218–219;
and GOTHIC ART, cols. 515, 525).

The advent of artillery brought about many changes in the castle (cf. V, col. 529; VI, cols. 525, 736). The keep, which was especially vulnerable, became less important, and the towers were adapted as artillery positions; they were built lower in height and in shapes that would both lessen the effect of a hit and permit a wide range of fire. They were most often built as bastions on a triangular plan with the vertex projecting outward and were protected in turn by ravelins, similar triangular works (FIG. 601, 19). This so-called "bastioned order" characterized military architecture of the period, especially in Italy, where fortresses were designed by Leonardo da Vinci (cf. IX, PL. 118), Michelangelo, and Baccio Pontelli (PL. 249, FIG. 601, 17); it had been first used in the bastion of Porta al Parlascio in Pisa (see BRUNELLESCHI, cols. 660–61).

These new structural features brought about a gradual differentiation between the fortress, which was used exclusively for military purposes, and the castle, which had become an aristocratic residence that sometimes retained the defensive elements of towers and the ditch, and which later drew inspiration from Italian *palazzo* models.

Public service buildings. Among the edifices designed to serve the needs of the general public, several distinct types are evident. Such buildings as hospitals, schools, and libraries have specific functions, and their development as types has remained quite closely connected to their fulfillment of those functions. In other public service buildings, there has been a wider latitude for expression.

In the ancient world the sick were treated in quarters (*iatreia*) added to the doctor's own residence and were sheltered in special rooms in temples dedicated to Aesculapius (cf. XII, FIG. 285 i). Sometimes shelters for the sick rose next to large sanctuaries or near thermal springs. These shelters were generally large rooms that could house many persons at the same time. Small buildings used as infirmaries (valetudinaria) may have been built near some permanent military bases and were also included in the homes of some of the more important Roman families. Remains of the valetudinarium of the *castrum* of Xanten (anc. Vetera) in Germany indicate that such buildings were square, had a central courtyard, and consisted of four large rooms subdivided into small cells.

In the Early Christian period, the sick were cared for in a complex of rooms (xenodochium) flanking a place of worship, as in the xenodochium of Pammachius (4th cent.) at Porto near Rome, in which a basilica was surrounded on three sides by corridors and large rooms, or wards. This connection with places of worship continued into the period when hospital buildings had taken on the characteristics of a structural type. Among the earliest examples of such edifices were the hospitals (*māristāns*) of the Arabs, such as the one founded in Baghdad in 979 by 'Adud al-Daula, which had several clinics. Later examples were that attached to the mosque of Sultan Qalā'ūn in Cairo (1285) and that added to the Seljuk mosque of Divriği (13th cent.; XII, FIG. 873).

In the West the construction of hospitals was begun by St. Jerome and continued by the orders of the Templars and, later, the Hospitalers, who cared for pilgrims and Crusaders in the Holy Land from the 12th century onward. The buildings erected by these orders, and, in particular, the hospital of S. Maria Latina in Jerusalem, were inspired by the model of the Roman valetudinarium, as it had been interpreted in Moslem architecture. They consisted of four large wards surrounding a square courtyard. The infirmary at the abbey of Saint Gallen in Switzerland (9th cent.) had a similar plan.

This same plan was common in the Gothic period, when the hospital building was no longer a secondary element in a monastery complex, but an autonomous structure. Among the various service facilities, the pharmacy often took on particular importance. The vaulted wards were arranged around a courtyard and often were divided into two aisles by a row of columns or pillars. There are several surviving examples of such Gothic hospitals: those of Monte Frumentario at Assisi and S. Maria della Scala in Siena (both 13th cent.) and the Hospital de la Santa Cruz in Barcelona (14th cent.; VI, FIG. 495). French hospitals of this period did not follow the courtyard plan. They consisted of a large rectangular sickroom with one or several aisles, as in the hospitals of Angers (V, PL. 380), Beaune, Tonnerre, and Chartres (VI, FIG. 482 a, b; see GOTHIC ART, col. 481).

The Gothic type, which was retained in the now-destroyed Pammatone hospital in Genoa, built in the early 15th century, was not substantially modified by Renaissance architects. It inspired Filarete's plan for the Ospedale Maggiore in Milan (XII, FIG. 14), which had eight internal courtyards and a large central courtyard. Brunelleschi turned to the single-ward plan in his Ospedale degli Innocenti in Florence. These two plans were widely used during the Renaissance. The courtyard type may be found in the Scuola Grande di S. Marco in Venice, and the single-ward type appears in the Roman Hospital of Sto Spirito in Sassia (PL. 260), which has a wide, square entrance hall.

These two types appeared in later periods in countless variations, as in the Hospital of St-Louis in Paris designed by Claude Vellefaux (1607), and that of S. Gallicano in Rome (1725–26) designed by Filippo Raguzzini.

In 18th-century England there first appeared the hospital complex made up of several specialized clinics (polyclinic; e.g. St. Bartholomew's Hospital in London, 1730, and the hospital at Plymouth naval base, 1764); this has become an almost universal type and is presently still in use. Techniques of medicine have had a profound influence on the development of the structural types of various edifices for the care of the sick and have led to the creation of such specialized edifices as sanatoria, convalescent homes, clinics, dispensaries, and research centers. While modern hospitals have been built to conform to the rationalist view of architecture (e.g., the sanatorium by B. Bijvoet and J. Duiker at Hilversum, 1928; the hospital by Eric Mendelsohn in Haifa, 1937; and the sanatorium at Paimio, by A. Aalto, I, PL. 2), there has been an attempt to render the building more welcoming and cheerful (cf. PL. 260, center left).

It is known that buildings designed specifically to contain large collections of documents or written texts existed in the ancient East, particularly in Mesopotamia, and it has been possible to reconstruct the plans of the Library of Alexandria, which was an annex of the Mouseion, and those of Antioch and Pella.

The first surely documented library conceived as an autonomous architectural unit was that of Pergamon, founded by

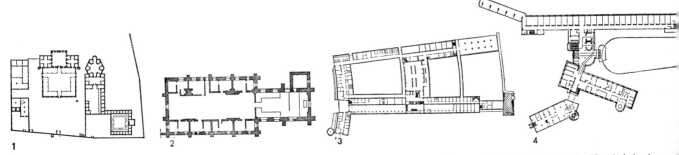

Hospitals, plans: (1) Edirne (Turkey), hospital and medical school (15th–16th cent.); (2) Chichester (England), St. Mary's Hospital (13th cent.); (3) Tel Aviv, Beilinson Hospital, ground floor (by A. Sharon and B. Idelson; 20th cent.); (4) Paimio (Finland), sanatorium (by A. Aalto; 20th cent.).

imenes II (195–159 B.C.). It was rather small and was com-
sed of only four rooms laid out in a line beside a portico;
e room, larger than the others, had a podium around three sides
at probably served as a base for statues. On a high pedestal at
e entrance stood a copy of the *Athena Parthenos* of Phidias.

Roman libraries had no more distinct characteristics. What
s probably the first public library, conceived by Caesar and
ilt by C. Asinius Pollio, probably consisted of a series of
oms placed around a peristyle; this was also true of the library
used in the portico of the Temple of Apollo on the Palatine.
he same general layout was used in libraries in private villas
g., that of the Villa of the Papyri at Herculaneum). In im-
rial times libraries were generally made up of two rooms
ne for Greek and the other for Latin works) each with an
se and rectangular niches that held the written works.

The library of Celsus at Ephesus (2d cent.; FIG. 605, 1)
s a rectangular building with a series of aediculas on two
vels of the façade and three doors that gave onto a single
rge hall. There were three niches in each of the side walls
d on the wall opposite the entrance there was an apse flanked
niches. Around three sides was a colonnade that framed
e niches and supported an interior loggia. The same scheme
s used in Hadrian's library in Athens, in which the entrance
as on one of the shorter sides. The library of the Basilica
lpia in Trajan's Forum was, instead, composed of two rec-
ngular buildings, one on either side of the rectangular court-
rd at whose center stood Trajan's column.

The library of the Domus Aurea had a different plan. This
was a rectangular building in which there was a vast central
semicircular area, around which opened rooms for the book
collections. In a later stage of development this layout was
used in Numidia in the library at Thamugadi (2d cent.), a
U-shaped building that enclosed three sides of a peristyle; the
main, semicircular hall faced the open side of the peristyle. In
all these libraries the main hall was the most important element;
there was no reading room as such.

In the Middle Ages, libraries were incorporated into monastic complexes and no longer appeared as autonomous architectural units. They retained the central plan, with a single large
room that was often divided into two aisles by a row of pillars
and with cupboards and shelves along the walls. They were
fitted out with a series of seats and took on the character of
true reading rooms; they also served as scriptoria for scribes
working on the transcription of codices. In the Moslem world
medieval libraries added to madrasahs retained functional distinctions between rooms used for different purposes, as in those
in which the volumes were kept, offices, and the reading room,
which was usually central (FIG. 605, 5).

During the Renaissance and up to the baroque period, the
library's characteristic element was the large reading room, with
or without shelves, around which service rooms were placed
without any particular functional coordination (FIG. 605, 2).
Typical among these were the library of the Convento di
S. Marco in Florence by Michelozzo (PL. 259; XII, FIG. 28),

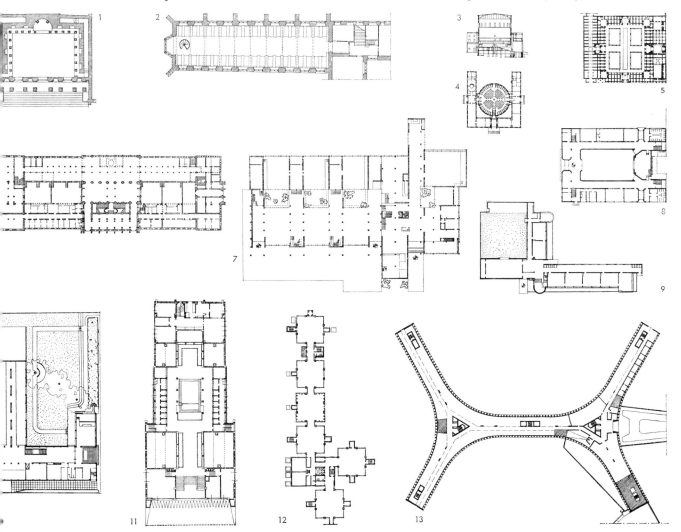

braries, schools, and research facilities. (1) Ephesus (Turkey), library of Celsus (2d cent.), plan; (2) Cambridge, St. John's College, library (16th cent.),
an; (3–4) Stockholm, City Library (by E. Gunnar Asplund; 20th cent.), section and plan; (5) Isfahan (Iran), madrasah of the Chahār Bāgh (early
th cent.), plan; (6) Budapest, university building (19th cent.), plan; (7) Barcelona, University Law School (by Giráldez Dávila, Lopez Iñigo, and Subías
ges; 20th cent.), plan; (8) Celle (Germany), school with a central atrium (by Otto Häsler; 20th cent.), plan; (9) Hilversum (Holland), Valerius School
y W. Dudok; 20th cent.), plan; (10) Bern, Museum of Natural History (20th cent.), ground floor plan; (11) Turin, Acquarium-reptile house (by
Venturelli; 20th cent.), plan; (12) Pennsylvania (U.S.A.) University Richards Medical Laboratories (by Louis Kahn; 20th cent.), plan; (13) La Grande
ice), I.B.M. laboratories, plan of office floor (by M. Breuer; 20th cent.).

and the Biblioteca Malatestiana in Cesena (XII, FIG. 28), whose three aisles echo the basilica plan. There was another type with a single hall that was not subdivided; examples are the Piccolomini library in Siena Cathedral, the Biblioteca Laurenziana in Florence, the library of El Escorial, the *Salone* of the Biblioteca Casanatense in Rome (PL. 259), and the Biblioteca dei Gerolomini in Naples. The plan of the Libreria Vecchia in Venice, designed by Sansovino (XII, FIG. 77), was more complex.

It was only at the end of the 18th century and particularly during the 19th century that the library once more became an autonomous edifice, functionally conceived according to its special contents and services. In the Bibliothèque Ste-Geneviève (PL. 228) and the reading room of the Bibliothèque Nationale in Paris, both by Henri Labrouste (see above), new structural methods were used to resolve specific functional needs, as also in the reading room of the British Museum in London, where the stacks converge on the circular reading room with its radially-placed seats, and in O. Wagner's plan for the university library in Vienna (1910). These were typical of plans in which the service rooms were coordinated around one or more reading rooms (FIG. 605, 3-4). More modern buildings have tended toward more complex arrangements that are determined by technical requirements such as lighting, ventilation, and soundproofing, as in Alvar Aalto's library at Vyborg (PL. 259; V, FIG. 240; cf. also I, PL. 141).

In spite of the elevated levels of their teaching and a clear awareness of public interest in the instruction of the young, the ancient Eastern and Mediterranean cultures did not develop architectural units specifically intended as schools. No such buildings are known in ancient Egypt, Mesopotamia, or Persia. The Greek gymnasium was a place for physical exercise (see above), and only occasionally were meetings of a cultural or didactic nature held there. The Romans did not construct buildings for use as schools. The nature of teaching in the ancient world, based as it was on the initiative of private teachers or tutors, precluded the organization of schools and did not create a demand for constructions answering particular functional needs. Teaching was carried out in public places (e.g., under the colonnades, as documented by students' *graffiti* on the walls and pillars of the Basilica Argentaria in Caesar's Forum in Rome) or in the houses of teachers or students, in ordinary rooms which were adapted as classrooms; there is some sculptural and pictorial evidence of this (the relief from Neumagen, VI, PL. 61; a fresco from Pompeii, now in Naples, Mus. Naz.).

In the Middle Ages teaching became the prerogative of the clergy, and classes were held in the homes of parish priests (a custom initiated in Italy, this became common throughout the Christian world after the Council of Vaison, in 529). The very few schools that sprang up under lay initiative, such as the palace school founded by Charlemagne at Aachen, were housed in edifices that primarily served other purposes, as were the cathedral and monastic schools of the time.

In the 12th century, with the rise of universities in the form of student-teacher corporations, private at first and later under the patronage of church and secular authorities, edifices were built with the specific function of housing schools (as at Bologna, Padua, Salerno, Salamanca, and Naples). These buildings provided lodgings for students, who were grouped according to their nationalities; they were similar to palace structures and had no distinguishing architectural characteristics. The halls, such as that in the medical school in Salerno, were simple rooms, sometimes very large, and were divided into several aisles.

The beginnings of a clearly defined type of school building first appeared in the Oxford colleges (New College, 1386, VI, FIG. 510), in which the adaptation of plans that were typical of private palaces or abbey complexes reflected the communal spirit of Gothic universities. Medieval university complexes, which included within the same building or unitary groups of buildings such elements as study rooms, libraries, and lodgings for students and teachers, provided a model that has endured up to the present. A certain uniformity of scholastic structures

was established, but these were not so highly specialized as preclude the utilization of buildings erected for other purpose especially monasteries, and their adaptation as schools.

School construction of the 19th and early 20th century w still based on the concept of the school as a series of unifor halls, together with the minimum essential service areas. T School at Celle (FIG. 605, 8) is an example of the transiti from these older types to a more rational school architectu The demands created by a reorganization of didactic activi and by new systems of teaching that require the active c laboration of the student have brought about structural innov tions that clearly distinguish the modern school building different levels and fields of instruction (V, PLS. 107, 11 FIGS. 242, upper, lower; 248). The Bauhaus in Dessau Walter Gropius is perhaps the most important example school construction of the expression of purpose in form (192 26; VII, PL. 81, FIG. 176). The principal achievements in scho design in Europe and America have followed rational mod (FIG. 605, 9, 10, 12; I, PLS. 93, 141, lower).

Other types of structures that serve the public are relat to traffic and tourism, from bridges and rail and air termin (PLS. 265, 266, FIG. 609) to hotels and inns (PL. 261, FIG. 61 8-11).

Railway stations and terminals have very precise function requirements, but these have often become secondary consider tions in the face of attempts to give monumental or symbol significance to such buildings. The result has often been exaggerated eclecticism (sometimes, however, of some wort as in the stations of the Métro in Paris, designed by H. Guimar that has precluded the development of well-defined types. specific type began to emerge with the construction of the lar train sheds with arched roofs in cast-iron, in Paddington (185 and St. Pancras (1868) stations in London. These great cover halls that housed passenger and freight terminals, along wi various public services, gave impetus to the development of more clearly defined station type. Recent examples of th development are the Central Station in Florence by G. M chelucci, the Central Station in Rome, and the airport termin of Zurich, Orly (Paris), Fiumicino (Rome; by R. Morandi a associates, PL. 266), and New York (Trans World Airlin Flight Center, by Eero Saarinen, XI, PL. 398).

Buildings for lodging of travelers were common in the a cient world. In Greece they were erected near temples ar sanctuaries and were called καταγώγια; these are known almo exclusively from literary sources. Thucydides (III, lxiii, 3) me tions one near the Heraion of Plataia, and Pausanias (v, xv, describes the Leonidaion at Olympia as a building compos of a peristyle surrounded by rooms. Near the Temple Asklepios at Epidauros a square building with four inner cour yards housed pilgrims in about 160 small rooms on two floor Greek private inns (πανδοκεῖα) and Roman inns (*hospitia, deve soria,* and *cauponae*), mentioned by many sources, were n very different from common dwellings.

St. Basil of Cesaraea founded the first καταγώγιον for Chri tian pilgrims and during the Middle Ages hotel activity w carried out mainly by the monastic orders in the buildir complexes that they erected along the route leading to sanctuari and to the Holy Land; these complexes almost always includ guesthouses. These usually were large dormitories, sometim with two or more aisles; some smaller rooms were reserved f more important guests, and these could, if necessary, also ser as hospitals or infirmaries. Many of these buildings have r mained in a fair state of preservation and give evidence considerable capacity. *La Guide des Pèlerins* by Amery Pica (12th cent.) documents the complex organization of hospic administered by the Cluniac monks along the pilgrim rou to Santiago de Compostela.

The few private hotels (*hospitia* or *hostariae*) that existed to the 10th–11th century were merely ordinary dwellings us as inns.

The hotels of the Gothic and Renaissance periods had distinguishing characteristics. The few examples that have su vived in Italy (the Albergo dell'Orso, the Della Corona, ar the Del Sole in Rome, as well as the Leon Bianco and t

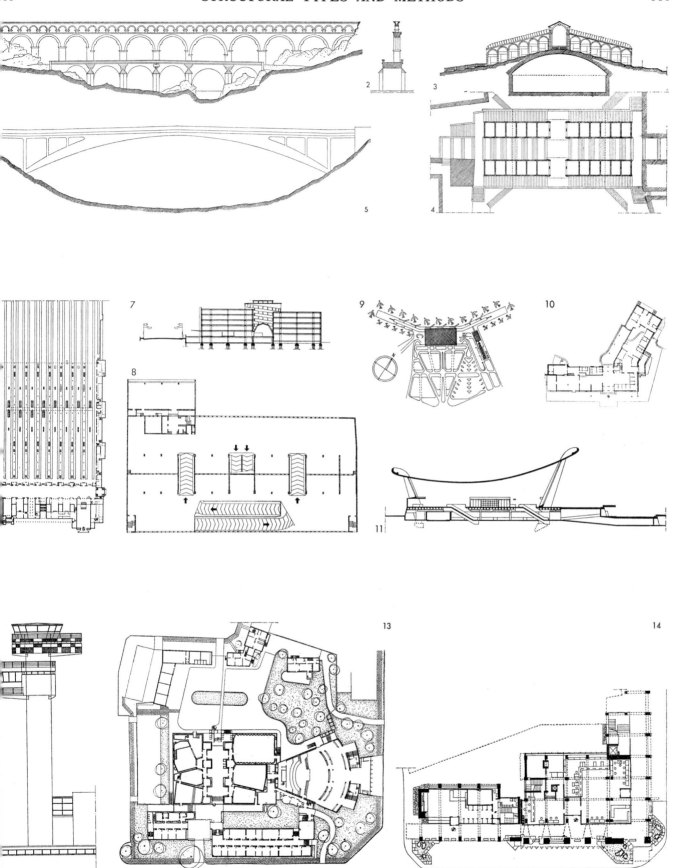

Structures for transit and communications. (1–5) Bridges: (1–2) near Nîmes, Pont du Gard, elevation and section (Augustan era); (3–4) Venice, Rialto Bridge, section and plan (16th cent.); (5) near Bern, reinforced-concrete bridge (20th cent.), elevation. (6–11) Rail and traffic Terminals: (6) Stuttgart, railway station (by P. Bonaty and F. E. Scholer; 20th cent.), plan; (7) Venice, multistory garage, section (20th cent.); (8) London, Aldersgate, garage, plan (20th cent.). (9–11) Airports: (9) Fiumicino, Leonardo da Vinci Airport (by R. Morandi and associates; 20th cent.), plan; (10) Sondica (Spain), airport terminal (20th cent.), plan; (11) Washington, Dulles International Airport Terminal building (by E. Saarinen; 20th cent.), section. (12–14) Communications centers: (12) Fiumicino, Leonardo da Vinci Airport, control tower; (13) Copenhagen, radio center (by V. Lauritzen; 20th cent.), plan; (14) Cortina d'Ampezzo (Italy), postal, telephone, and telegraph center (20th cent.), plan.

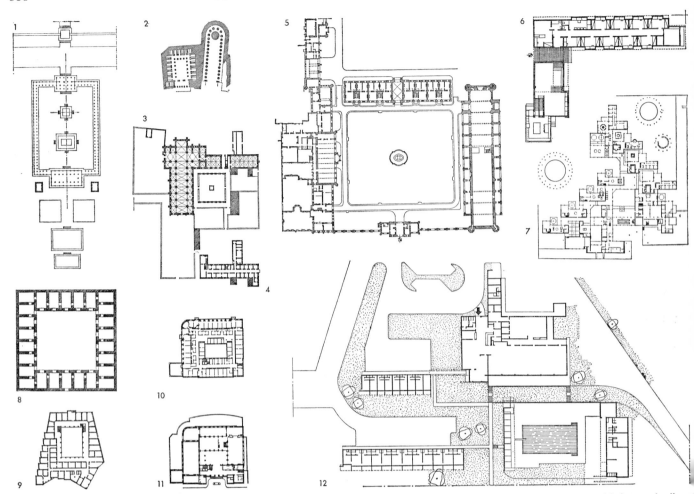

Collective dwellings, plans. (1) Osaka (Japan), monastery of Shitennō (6th cent.); (2) Kondane (India), rock-cut monastery (chaitya and vihara; 1st cent. B.C.); (3–4) S. Galgano (Siena), church and monastery, ground floor and dormitory floor (13th cent.); (5) Cambridge, Magdalene College (16th–20th cent.); (6) Oslo, girls' boarding school (20th cent.); (7) Amsterdam, boys' boarding school (20th cent.); (8) Kunar Siah (Iran), caravanserai (probably Sassanian period); (9) Istanbul, Khan of Hasan Paşa (18th cent.); (10–11) Bern, Hotel Bellevue, upper floor and ground floor (19th–20th cent.); (12) San Pedro (California), residential center (20th cent.).

Cavalletto in Venice) are similar to private houses. More marked distinctions are to be found in the hotels of central and northern Europe and the British Isles, where there was an inner court-yard with a loggia or where the rooms were grouped into very small apartments. More notable characteristics can be found in the buildings constructed by European merchants in the East, where entrance to Arab dwellings was forbidden and there was a consequent lack of accommodation for non-Arab travelers. These buildings also served as trade stations, and they were probably inspired by those structures (guesthouses or caravan-saries, known as khan or han, or *funduq*) which in the Islamic world provided shelter for travelers and caravans. They were often fortified (I, PL. 13; VIII, PL. 161) and in Iran and Iraq they were based on the model of the madrasah. They were always imposing buildings with considerable capacity (FIG. 611, 8, 9; cf. ISLAM, col. 346, OTTOMAN SCHOOLS, cols. 863–864).

Only when hotel activity was undertaken on an industrial level, that is, during the 19th century, did there appear a true hotel type. A noteworthy early example was the Tremont House in Boston (I, PL. 80, FIG. 254). The arrangement of reception and service areas became increasingly rational in rela-tion to the special characteristics of each building: its location (on a main highway, as a motel; near an airport or terminal) and purpose (city hotel, vacation resort, health resort, residen-tial hotel; cf. PL. 261).

* *

In aqueducts and reservoirs the functional nature of the structure predominates, as in the imposing Roman aqueducts than ran above ground (*aquae pensiles*). These were accurately

described by Frontinus in his *De aquis urbis Romae* (1st cent of the Christian era); they consisted of a continuous series o arches supporting the conduit (PL. 265). Collection of th water was effected in large masonry tanks (*castella aquae o dividicula*; e.g., that of Nîmes), often decorated on the exterio with architectural elements, or in reservoirs in the form o enormous halls subdivided into several chambers by piers tha supported the vaulted roof (as at Chieti, one of many extant)

Systems of aqueducts similar to those of the Roman wer used in later periods, especially when it was necessary to conve water across deep valleys; examples are the aqueducts of Sul mona (1256) and Spoleto (Ponte delle Torri; 14th century and the bridge with three rows of superposed arches that carrie the aqueduct (1753–56) by Luigi Vanvitelli across the valle near Maddaloni. Reservoirs deriving from the Roman mode were known during the Middle Ages in the West, the Byzan tine world, and Islam (the reservoir of Ramla, about 789)

In modern times the builders of reservoirs often sought t conceal their functional characteristics by resorting to a mor or less eclectic monumentality, as in the Cisternone at Leghor by Poccianti (PL. 264) and the water tank at Poznán (1911) b Hans Poelzig. However, more recent constructions have achiev ed a synthesis of function and form (the water tower at Örebr PL. 264).

Fountains serve a monumental purpose and appear in man forms; they usually combine architectural and sculptural ele ments and should be considered in their relation to town plan ning and landscaping (PL. 264, left center, right above).

The thermae type of structure is constant and has bee much more clearly defined even from its beginnings. Durin

e Roman era the strictly utilitarian and essentially hygienic
nction of public baths (known in the Greek world, as at
ssos, Athens, and Sybaris; see HELLENISTIC ART, col. 303) was
odified and became more complex. Roman thermae had
quired a broad social significance as early as the Republican
riod (see ROMAN IMPERIAL ART, cols. 519, 529). In addition
the various bathing facilities, they included *xysti* (parklike
aces where games were held) and *ambulationes*. Poetry read-
gs, concerts, and lectures were given in the thermae complexes,
nich became centers of social activity. This combination of
nctions in a structure that incorporated features of the Hel-
nistic gymnasium and the traditional Italic bath, made the
ermae one of the most important and representative examples
 Roman architecture and favored their spread to the cities of the
ovinces (see ROMAN ART OF THE EASTERN EMPIRE, cols. 295–296).

In the less complex thermae there was a simple sequence of
rious bathing rooms that followed a linear or annular scheme.
his scheme was enriched by the insertion of various halls
tween the main ones, usually in order to allow for gradual
justments to changes in temperature. The order of the main
oms was rigidly determined by the function of the building:
om the *apodyterium*, or dressing room, the bather passed
rough the *frigidarium* and *tepidarium* to the *calidarium*, which
is the center of the thermae. Sometimes, in addition to the
vered or colonnaded rooms that served as rest rooms and
eeting halls, in the more complex types of thermae a hall
r steam baths (the *laconicum*) was placed near the *calidarium*.
 order to return from the *calidarium* to the dressing room

in thermae that were arranged on a linear scheme, the bather
was obliged to retrace his steps, and each room was, therefore,
subject to constant traffic. The adoption of an annular scheme
avoided this inconvenience; the bather moved along one-way
passages from the dressing room through a series of rooms heated
to gradually higher temperatures to the *calidarium*, whence
he could return to the dressing room by passing through the
tepidarium and *frigidarium*. This annular scheme was used
in the large thermae south of Thamugadi, the small thermae
at Madauros (Numidia) and the Baths of Faustina at Miletus
(XII, FIG. 296).

Some thermae had two nuclei that provided separate bath
complexes for the two sexes and had somewhat different characteristics. Examples of these constructions exist at Pompeii
and Herculaneum, as well as at Badenweiler, Lambaesis (mod.
Lambessa) and Vieil-Evreux. In these complexes, which were
distinguished by their linear distributive system, one of the main
halls was sometimes common to both sectors (e.g., the *calidarium*,
and, rarely, the *tepidarium* or *frigidarium*).

The monumental imperial thermae complexes were derived
from these various schemes (PL. 264; XII, FIG. 530). The *frigidarium*, *tepidarium*, and *calidarium* were generally placed along
the principal minor axis of the complex and were surrounded by
rooms heated to different temperatures, through which the bather
could go from the *apodyterium* to the *calidarium*.

In such complexes there was also a large cold-water outdoor
swimming pool (*natatio*) connected to the *frigidarium*; there were
semicircular rooms (*heliocamini*), for sunbathing and conver-

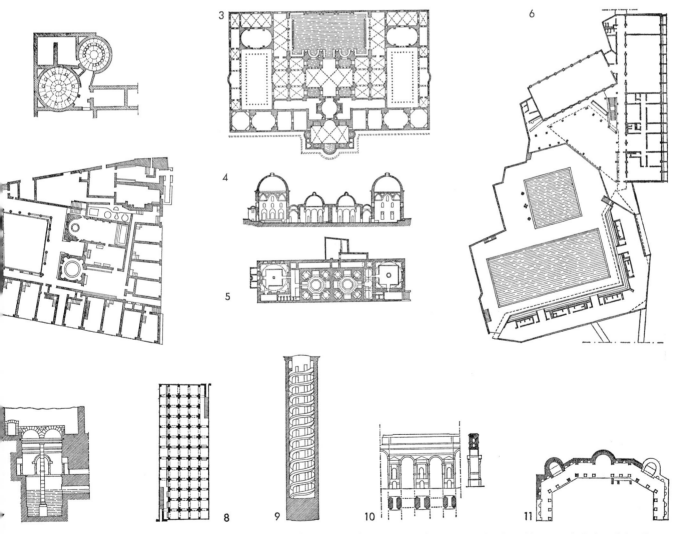

ructures for the use and conservation of water. (1–6) Thermae: (1) Ouniadai (Greece), baths (5th cent. B.C.), plan; (2) Pompeii, Baths of the Forum
st cent. B.C.), plan; (3) Rome, Baths of Diocletian (4th cent.), plan; (4–5) Istanbul, bath of Haseki Hurrem (16th cent.), section and plan;
) Caracas, University swimming pool complex (by C. Villanueva; 20th cent.), plan; (7) Island of Roda (Cairo), Nilometer (restored 9th cent.), section;
) Bacoli (Italy), Piscina Mirabilis (Augustan era), plan; (9) Orvieto, Pozzo di S. Patrizio (16th cent.), section; (10) Rome, acqueduct over Porta
aggiore (1st cent.), elevation, plan, section; (11) Amman (Jordan), triapsidal nymphaeum (3d cent.), plan.

sation, as well as gymnasiums, colonnades, and areas designed for recreation, games, and walks. The various elements were disposed along the two main axes, which met in the *frigidarium*, which was the unitary center of the entire complex.

The thermae was surrounded by a vast space and a rectangular enclosure, along the sides of which were located the various service areas (guardians' quarters, water tanks, woodsheds) and meeting halls, nymphaeums, and exedra-like structures for theatricals, as in the baths of Trajan, Caracalla, and Diocletian in Rome.

Public thermae as they had been known during the Roman age all but disappeared from the beginning of the Christian era onward; sometimes they appeared as very small buildings, as at Philippi (3d cent.), generally annexed to baptisteries.

Luciano PONTUALE

Public baths (hammam) were widespread throughout the Moslem world. Al-Walid I followed the model of the late Roman imperial complexes in the hammam that he built next to the audience chamber of Qusayr 'Amra (early 8th cent.). This small building was decorated with paintings and was composed of three rooms, a rectangular chamber with barrel-vaulting (*apodyterium*), a square room with cross-vaulting (*tepidarium*), and another square room with a dome (*calidarium*). (See also OTTOMAN SCHOOLS, cols. 862–863.)

Very little evidence exists regarding medieval baths, which were constructed exclusively for therapeutic purposes at hot springs. The illuminations of the codex *De balneis puteolanis* by Pietro da Eboli (13th cent., Rome, Bibl. Angelica, MS 1474) show structural elements of Roman origin and others in Byzantine style. Modern spas present no well-defined types.

Commercial and industrial buildings. Although there exi important indirect evidence of an evolved and complex organi tion of commerce in the ancient world, documentation relat to places and buildings set apart for trade in Egypt and the N East is scant.

More certain information is available regarding anci commerce in the Greek world. Trade was carried out mai in the agora, which contained the shops and stalls of retail trad (FIG. 615, 1), and in the ports, where exchanges of goods w affected in and near large warehouses (*emporia*). In the Rom era retail trade was usually carried on in shops (tabernae), whi were usually located in the exterior walls of dwellings or on ground floors of the *insulae*. Their form was relatively unifor but each had different features related to the type of trade which it was intended. Numerous reliefs and paintings dep the interior aspects of these shops, and many fairly well-preserv examples exist, especially at Herculaneum (e.g., the wine sh next to the House of Neptune and Amphitrite), Pompeii (t Thermopolium of Asellinae; the laundry in Via di Mercur the shop of the metalworker Verus), and Ostia Antica (varic tabernae and the Thermopolium in Via di Diana, PL. 262).

Next to the forum, which partly retained the function commercial center of the city, rose buildings designed exclusiv for trade; these markets, which were often covered (*macell* housed groups of shops. An example was Trajan's Mar in Rome, where the various shops were located on five stori The fourth story led into a large cross-vaulted hall, onto whi other shops opened (PL. 222). Other examples can be found Thamugadi, Leptis Magna, Pompeii, and Pozzuoli (the so-call "Serapeum"). More specialized forms appeared in those buil ings designed for the regulation of commerce (*mensae ponder riae*, for checking weights, and *annonae*), and above all in lar

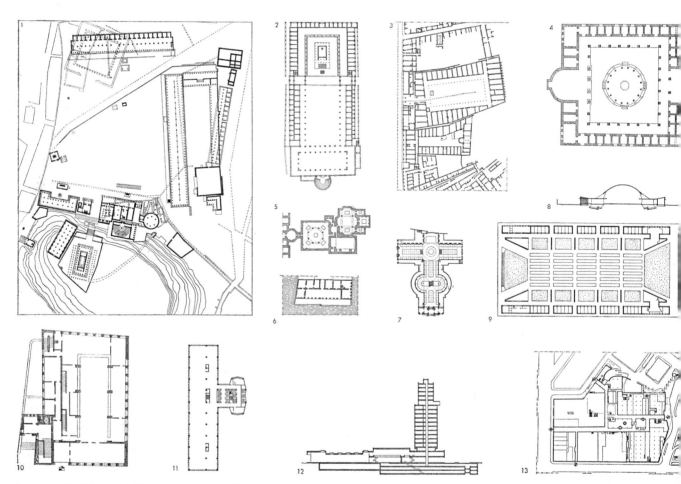

Commercial buildings. (1) Athens, agora, plan in Hellenistic era; (2) Augusta Raurica (mod. Augst), forum (1st cent. B.C.), plan; (3) Ostia, group of hor (2d cent.), plan; (4) Pozzuoli, *macellum* (1st–2d cent.), plan; (5) Kasan (Iran), bazaar of Haggi Sayyid Husayn (19th cent.), plan; (6) Venice, Fondaco Turchi (13th cent.) plan; (7) Ixelles (Belgium), Halles (19th cent.), plan; (8–9) Pescia (Italy), flower market (by Brizzi, Gori, Ricci, and Savioli; 20th cen section and plan; (10) Jerusalem, Anglo-Palestine bank (20th cent.), plan; (11) Pittsburgh (U.S.A.), office building in Golden Triangle (20th cent.), pl (12–13) Rochester (U.S.A.), Midtown Plaza (20th cent.), section and plan.

arehouses (*horrea*), subdivided into numerous rooms arranged round courtyards; the *horrea* also housed the administrative fices of those merchants who had been awarded contracts for e management of the warehouses. Among the important pes, Agrippa's Market in Rome, easily recognizable in the *orma Urbis*, and the many warehouses at Ostia Antica, among em the Horrea Epagathiana et Epaphroditiana, are noteworthy.

In the medieval West small-scale commercial activity connued to be carried out in shops that had no distinguishing ructural features other than a low window beside the door at served as a counter. The porticoes and ground-floor oms of the town halls were often fitted out as markets. Market uildings must have existed during the Romanesque period, nce that of Clermont-en-Beauvais was transformed into the wn hall in 1147.

European trading stations in the East were modeled on e *funduq*. The bazaar quarter (*sūq*) typical of Arab towns IG. 615, 5) may have been the model for those sections which ill exist in many Western cities, in which a number of similar ops are grouped together in a single street or square (see TTOMAN SCHOOLS, col. 864).

During the Gothic period the wholesale market for a single pe of goods appeared in Europe. The old covered market Paris and the loggia that was later transformed into the Church Orsanmichele in Florence were erected as markets. Many pects of trade and financial activity were conducted in the ouses of the entrepreneurs.

This relatively modest repertory of types of commercial uildings had no significant further development until the th century, when new practical needs determined the construcon of buildings that were more functional. It was at this me that the great banking institutions and stock exchanges took a typical structural forms (FIG. 615, 10). An increase in longistance trade resulted in the designing of huge warehouses with ecific functions (silos, refrigeration chambers). The structure retail trade underwent profound changes, and the first large epartment stores were built (the Marshall Field wholesale store Chicago by Henry Richardson, I, PL. 84; and the Carson irie Scott & Co. store in Chicago by Louis Sullivan, I, PL. 86; 'Innovation store built in 1901 in Brussels by Horta; La Saaritaine store in Paris by Jourdain, V, PL. 99). These have ad important developments in modern times, and similar pes of structures have influenced town planning. In Europe d the United States, especially, they have often been combined form a nucleus of commercial buildings (e.g., shopping centers ich as Northland Center, 1954, near Detroit, and Southdale enter, 1956, near Minneapolis, both by Victor Gruen), which clearly distinct from residential areas (PL. 262, below left d right; FIG. 615, 11-13). Wholesale market and warehouse buildings have undergone a development parallel to that of industrial buildings, in which function and versatility of the structural forms are emphasized (FIG. 615, 8-9).

From ancient times until the end of the 18th century — that is, as long as productive activity remained exclusively on a craft level — production was carried out in the homes of the craftsmen themselves. Among the few types of edifices that had clearly defined structural characteristics were arsenals and shipyards, ironworks and kilns, mills, and specialized manufacturing installations, whose structural development, in fact, did not always occur simultaneously with technical developments. Some specialized production was realized in installations that were often simply more or less unitary groupings of crafts workshops.

The advent of industrial systems of production, with their more complex organization, gave rise to structural solutions that were completely new and are still developing rapidly and in myriad forms.

Industrial buildings in the 19th century and the beginning of the 20th century consisted of sheds — usually of the large dimensions made possible by the use of new structural techniques in iron, steel, and reinforced concrete — inside which various technical equipment was placed. The forms and structures of these buildings presented the typical structural characteristics of the shed (FIG. 617, 2-4). Industrial structures continued to reflect a generic and uniform concept of the technical building; enlargement of the plant was achieved by multiplying the various building nuclei, as is evident in photographs of the Krupp works in Essen in 1860 and 1880 reproduced by B. Zevi (*Storia dell'architettura moderna*, Turin, 1950, pl. 13), and in Tony Garnier's project for a *cité industrielle*.

This rigid concept of industrial architecture has produced buildings which are formally and functionally valid but which are irrevocably bound to those productive processes for which they were designed. Rationalist European and American architecture has opposed this concept, insisting on an awareness of various factors: constant developments in technology, the trend toward "integral-cycle" productivity in larger industries, and the demand for a high degree of flexibility in relation to production needs. The Fagus factories (PL. 218; V, PL. 103, FIG. 229) and those erected for the Werkbund Exhibition in Cologne (1914) marked the transition from a static and programmatic concept of industrial architecture to a more dynamic and rational one. The reaction and interaction of these two concepts has resulted in the great variety of types of modern industrial buildings (PL. 263, FIG. 617; cf. V, PL. 110, below).

FUNERARY STRUCTURES. Funerary structures have been important in almost all civilizations from the most ancient times. They have been regarded as equally or only slightly less sacred

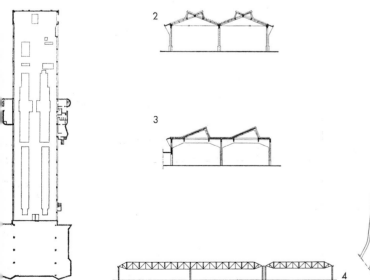

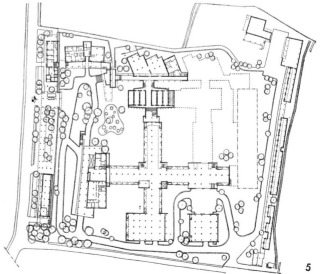

dustrial buildings. (1) Fors (Sweden), paper factory (by R. Erskine; 20th cent.), plan; (2-3) typical industrial sheds, sections; (4) Zurich-Kloten rport maintenance hangars (20th cent.), section; (5) Pozzuoli, Olivetti industrial complex (by Luigi Cosenza; 20th cent.), plan.

than religious edifices and have often been given more emphasis than the dwellings of the living. This reflects the awareness of the spiritual nature of such structures and relates them to the broad concept of monuments (q.v.). (See also ESCHATOLOGY.) The construction of funerary buildings has constituted one of the most remarkable manifestations of the art of various civilizations, and has provided some noteworthy examples of the fusion of architecture and sculpture.

Types of funerary structures have varied within civilizations and eras, as in Egypt during the Thinite period, when tumulus tombs (as at Abydos) and house tombs (as at Memphis) appeared simultaneously, and, later, pyramids attached to surface funerary temples were built at the same time as hypogeum tombs. In the Hellenistic and Roman worlds funerary structures that appeared contemporaneously included the hypogeum with a tumulus, that with a courtyard and peristyle, that with a monu-

Funerary edifices. (1) Egypt, mastaba (4th dynasty), section; (2) Abusir (Egypt), pyramid of King Sahura (5th dynasty), section. (3-8) Hypogeum tombs; (3) Fakhraka (Iran), rock-cut tomb (Median period), elevation and plan; (4) Tarquinia, Tomb of the Mercareccia (3d-2d cent. B.C.), section and plan; (5) Alexandria (Egypt), El-Wardān hypogeum (Roman era), plan; (6) China, royal tomb of the Yin period, section and plan; (7) Rome, so-called "Sedia del Diavolo" (2d cent.), section; (8) Ostia Antica (Rome), Isola Sacra, Tomb 29 (2d cent.), plan. (9-13) Circular-plan buildings: (9) Galera (Spain), Tomb 75, section and plan (4th-3d cent. B.C.); (10) Mycenae (Greece), so-called "Treasury of Atreus," section and plan (15th cent. B.C.); (11) Cortona (Italy), so-called "Tomb of Pythagoras" (Hellenistic era), section and plan; (12) Rome, Mausoleum of Augustus (1st cent.), section and plan; (13) Ravenna, Mausoleum of Theodoric (6th cent.), section and plan; (14) Cnidus (Greece), Tomb of the Lions (4th cent. B.C.), section and plan; (15) Ghirza (Libya), spire mausoleum (4th cent.), elevation; (16) Sultaniya (Iran), mausoleum of Öljeitü (14th cent.), plan; (17) Verona, tomb of Mastino II della Scala (14th cent.), elevation; (18) Monte Grappa (Italy), ossuary and mausoleum (20th cent.), plan.

ental façade, the tomb in the form of a small temple, the he-
oon, and the mausoleum.

There follows a list of the principal types of funerary
ructures used throughout the ages:

Tumulus tombs (FIG. 619, 1,2,9). These were generally
eometric in form and sometimes had no internal space. They
ometimes enclosed rooms that reproduced the dwellings of
ne living, but these had no structural reference to the exterior
f the tumulus. This was the form of the mastabas of Egypt,
f which the pyramids may be considered an evolved form
V, PL. 332, FIGS. 634, 641); the pseudo-domed tholoi of Crete
nd Mycenae (PL. 224), and their developments in southern
aly (Cumae); the Lidia tumuli (Sardis) and the Etruscan
muli (Cerveteri, Vetulonia, Casale Marittimo, Populonia),
hich generally consisted of an earthen mound above a stone
ase (PL. 242, IV, PL. 456).

Hypogeum tombs (FIG. 619, 3-8). This type was totally
r partially cut out of rock, and the interior often reproduced
pical freestanding architectural forms, sometimes including
açades that imitated architectural elements. These tombs were
so widely used in the ancient world: important examples exist
n Egypt (tombs at Aswan and Beni Hassan, IV, PL. 346, FIG.
59; and at Thebes, IV, FIG. 677), in Achaemenid Persia (tomb
f Darius I at Naqsh-i Rustam, VIII, PL. 136), among the Etrus-
ans (hypogeum of the Volumnii, the rock-cut necropolises near
rosseto and Viterbo), in the Hellenistic world (Alexandria;
yprus; Petra, VII, FIGS. 308, 309; XII, PL. 193), and in the Ro-
an world (the tomb of the Scipioni on the Via Appia).

Funerary temples. These edifices were typical of ancient
gypt; in early times they were part of the pyramid complex
he funerary precinct of King Zoser, near Saqqara, IV, PL. 329,
IG. 633) and later were built as autonomous structures (cf. IV,
IGS. 653, 658, 671, 676).

Mausoleums (FIG. 619, 11-14, 16, 18). This type was a monu-
ental derivation of the tumulus (it includes architectural
ements on the exterior of the tumulus). It was especially
ommon in the Hellenistic world (e.g., at Belevi, Mylasa, and
lalicarnassus; the so-called "Tomb of Theron" at Agrigento,
L. 232), and in the Roman world (the Tomb of Caecilia Metella,
nd the Mausoleum of Augustus, FIG. 619, 12, in Rome; that
f L. Munatius Plancus at Gaeta, and the so-called "Tour de
Horloge" in Aix-en-Provence).

The mausoleum type was taken up in the Christian world
. Costanza in Rome; the mausoleums of Galla Placidia and
heodoric in Ravenna, FIG. 619, 13; IV, PLS. 457, 458). It
ecame associated with that type of sacred edifice built on
central plan (martyrium) and later with the funerary chapel
f Renaissance and baroque architecture. The same form
ppeared in the Moslem world (the tombs of the Mamelukes
n Cairo, VIII, PL. 162) and in Moslem India (Mausoleum of
ultan Sikandar Lōdī in Delhi, VIII, PL. 16; tomb of Akbar
n Sikandra, VIII, PL. 166). (See also FIG. 619, 16; VII, PL. 400.)

Tombs in the form of small temples. These generally
onsisted of an architectural element atop a tumulus (as at
elphi, or in the Oratory of Phalaris at Agrigento) or a pedestal
s was common in Rome along the Via Appia and throughout
ne imperial world in general). In most cases these elements
ad no true internal space and reproduced the forms of small
emples. This type of tomb is related to the heroon, which is
building erected over a hypogeum room (that of Kalydon sug-
ests a palaestra). It also influenced such structures as the tomb
nown as La Conocchia at Santa Maria Capua Vetere; that of
arsina near Forlì (IV, PL. 456); and the so-called "Tomb of
bsalom" near Jerusalem (VIII, PL. 331).

Edicules (FIG. 619, 17). This typical form of late medieval
nerary architecture was partly derived from the tomb in the
hape of a small temple and was later distinguished by more
dividual structural features (as in the tombs of the Glossatori
n Bologna and those of the Scaligeri family in Verona, I, PL.
80). During the Gothic period, this type of tomb lost its autono-
ous architectural character and became an essentially sculptural
ement located in chapels or churches (the tomb of St. Dominic
y Nicola Pisano and collaborators, X, PL. 326; the tomb of
t. Peter Martyr by Giovanni di Balduccio, VI, PL. 367; tomb

of Doge Niccolò Tron by Antonio Rizzo, VIII, PL. 198). Later
such tombs were placed against the walls of the church, taking
on an almost exclusively sculptural character; the architectural
element was reduced to a framework for the sculptural elements,
usually taking the form of a baldaquin or aedicule. Early
examples of this development were the tomb of Leonardo Bruni
by Bernardo Rossellino and that of Carlo Marsuppini by Desiderio da Settignano (XII, PL. 16). These models were elaborated in many versions during the Renaissance, culminating
in the complex monumental works by Michelangelo in the New
Sacristy of S. Lorenzo (IX, PL. 530) and those by Bernini
(II, PLS. 167, 275) and Algardi (II, PL. 168).

These basic types of funerary buildings have persisted
up to the present. Recent changes in the concept of the funerary
monument have led to developments of considerable artistic
value, such as the Liebknecht-Luxemburg monument in Berlin
by Mies van der Rohe (1926) and the memorial park of the
Fosse Ardeatine in Rome (1949, IV, PL. 459).

* *

BIBLIOG. *General*: E. E. Viollet-le-Duc, Dictionnaire raisonné de l'architecture française du XI au XIX siècle, Paris, 1854–69; A. Choisy, L'art
de bâtir chez les Romains, Paris, 1873; G. Gozzadini, Note per studi sul-
l'architettura civile in Bologna dal sec. XIII al XIV, Modena, 1877; C.
Daremberg, E. Saglio, Dictionnaire des Antiquités grecques et romaines,
Paris, 1877–1912; Perrot-Chipiez, 1882–1903; A. Choisy, L'art de bâtir
chez les Byzantines, Paris, 1883; M. Dieulafoy, L'art antique de la Perse,
Paris, 1884–89; J. Durm, Die Baukunst der Griechen, Darmstadt, 1892;
A. Riegl, Stilfragen, Berlin, 1893; V. Graniello, Stili di architettura, Naples,
1894; B. Fletcher, The Influence of Material in Architecture, London,
1897; A. Choisy, Histoire de l'architecture, Paris, 1899; A. Riegl, Spätrom-
ische Kunstindustrie, Vienna, 1901; J. Strzygowski, Orient oder Rom,
Leipzig, 1901; A. Venturi, Storia dell'Arte Italiana, Milan, 1901–39; J.
Strzygowski, Kleinasien, ein Neuland der Kunstgeschichte, Leipzig, 1903;
A. Kingsley Porter, Medieval Architecture, New York, 1909; W. Deonna,
Les lois et les rythmes dans l'art, Paris, 1914; G. T. Rivoira, Architettura
musulmana, sue origini e suo sviluppo, Milan, 1914; J. Strzygowski, Die
Baukunst der Armenier und Europa, Leipzig, 1918; J. Baum, Baukunst
und dekorative Plastik der Fruhrenaissance in Italien, Stuttgart, 1920; D.
Donghi, Manuale dell'architetto, Turin, 1920; G. Giovannoni, Elementi
delle fabbriche, Rome, 1920; L. Cloquet, Les lois des proportions dans
l'architecture, Revue de l'Art chrétien, 1920, pp. 340 ff.; E. Panofsky, Entwicklung der Proportionslehre als Abbid der Stil, Monatshefte für Kunstwissenschaft, XIV, 1921; U. Tarchi, L'architettura e l'arte musulmana in
Egitto e nella Palestina, Turin, 1922; G. Jéquier, Manuel d'archéologie
égyptienne, Paris, 1924; R. Atkinson, H. Bagenal, Theory and Elements
of Architecture, London, New York, 1926; M. Salmi, L'architettura romanica in Toscana, Milan, 1927; P. Toesca, Storia dell'arte italiana dalle
origini alla fine del secolo XIII, Turin, 1927; M. Hürlimann, Indien, Berlin,
1928; A. Grenier, Manuel d'archéologie gallo-romaine, Paris, 1931–60;
K.A.C. Creswell, Early Muslim Architecture, Oxford, 1932–40; P. Abraham,
Viollet-le-Duc et le rationalisme médiéval, Paris, 1934; T. Fischer, Zwei
Vorträge über Proportionen, Munich, Berlin, 1934; J. A. Hamilton, Byzan-
tine Architecture and Decoration, New York, London, 1934; G. B. Milani,
Le forme architettoniche, Milan, 1934; N. Pevsner, Pioneers of the Modern
Movement, from William Morris to Walter Gropius, London, 1936; R.
Paribeni, Architettura dell'Oriente antico, Bergamo, 1937; B. Fletcher, A
History of Architecture on the Comparative Method, London, 1938 (17th
rev. ed., London, 1961; with bibliog.); H.-R. Hitchcock, In the Nature of
Materials, New York, 1942; M. E. Blake, Ancient Roman Construction in
Italy from the Prehistoric Period to Augustus, Washington, 1947; G. Nicco
Fasola, Rapporti tra tecnica ed arte, Metron, 1947, pp. 26–33; J. B. Ward
Perkins, The Italian Element in Late Roman and Early Medieval Architec-
ture, London, 1947; G. Bandmann, Die Bauformen des Mittelalters, Bonn,
1949; A. Nava, La teoria di Viollet-le-Duc e "l'architettura funzionale,"
CrArte, II, 29, 1949, pp. 230–41; W. B. Dinsmoor, The Architecture of
Ancient Greece, London, 1950; P. L. Nervi, La proporzione nella tecnica,
Domus, 264–65, 1951, pp. 45–47; H. de Caboga, Etude concernant le pro-
blême d'une typologie, Rapperswil, 1952; R. Wittkower, Systems of Proportion, Architect's Year Book, v, 1953, pp. 9–18; B. Zevi, Storia dell'architettura moderna, Turin, 1950; T. Hamlin, Forms and Functions of Twentieth-
century Architecture, New York, 1952; R. T. Paine, A. Soper, The Art
and Architecture of Japan, Harmondsworth, 1955; L. Barbiano di Belgioioso,
Per una fenomenologia dei caratteri distributivi degli edifici, Aut Aut, 38,
1956; L. Galmozzi, Proposte per una classificazione e definizione razionale
dei tre principi costruttivi dell'architettura, Florence, 1956; D. Mustilli,
L. von Matt, Architettura romana, Genoa, 1958; H. Busch, B. Lohse,
Baukunst der Gotik in Europa, Frankfurt, 1958; K. J. Conant, Carolingian
and Romanesque Architecture, 800 to 1200, Harmondsworth, Baltimore,
1959; P. Selz, M. Constantine, Art Nouveau, New York, 1960; P. Frankl,
Gothic Architecture, Harmondsworth, Baltimore, 1962; J. Joedicke,
Shell Architecture, London, New York, 1963; E. Hempel, Baroque Art and
Architecture in Central Europe, Baltimore, 1965; R. Krautheimer, Early
Christian and Byzantine Architecture, Baltimore, 1965; W. L. MacDonald,
The Architecture of the Roman Empire, New Haven, 1965; R. Wittkower,
Art and Architecture in Italy, 1600 to 1750, Harmondsworth, Baltimore,
1965; J. White, Art and Architecture in Italy, 1250 to 1400, Baltimore,
1966. *Structural methods and materials*: J. White, T. F. Pritchard, On
Cementitious Architecture as Applicable to the Construction of Bridges,

with the First Introduction of Iron for Arches of a Large Span, London, 1832; L. Runge, Beiträge zur Kenntniss der Backstein-Architektur Italiens, Berlin, 1846; W. Fairbairn, On the Application of Cast and Wrought Iron for Building Purposes, London, 1854; P. Lacroix, E. A. Bégin, F. Sere, Le livre d'or des métiers: histoire de la charpenterie, Paris, 1858; J. H. Parker, De variis structurarum generibus penes romanos veteres, Rome, 1868; G. E. Street, Brick and Marble in the Middle Ages, London, 1874; J. Lacroux, C. Détain, Constructions en briques, Paris, 1878–86; G. Eiffel, W. A. Eddy, The Eiffel Tower, Report of the Smithsonian Institution, Washington, 1889, pp. 729–35, 736–43; G. A. Breymann, H. Lang, Allgemeine Bauconstructionslehre: I, Die Constructionen in Stein, Leipzig, 1879–80, II. Die Konstruktionen in Holz, Leipzig, 1883–84; L. Dietrichson, H. Munthe, Die Holzbaukunst Norwegens, Berlin, 1893; O. Stiehl, Der Backsteinbau Romanischer Zeit, Leipzig, 1898; G. B. Milani, L'ossatura murale: studio statico costruttivo ed estetico-proporzionale degli organismi architettonici, Turin, 1900; F. Hussen, Maçons et tailleurs de pierre, Paris, 1903; E. Charles, Development of Architectural Art from Structural Requirements and Nature of Materials, J. of the Royal Inst. of British Architects, XII, 1905, pp. 457–88; A. G. Meyers, Eisenbauten, Esslingen, 1907; A. Kingsley Porter, The Construction of Lombardic and Gothic Vaults, New Haven, London, 1911; E. B. van Deman, Methods of Determining the Date of Roman Concrete Monuments, J. of the Am. Inst. of Architects, XVI, 1912, pp. 2–3; E. L. Ransome, A. Saurbrey, Reinforced Concrete Buildings, New York, 1912; G. Weickle, Süd-westliche europäische Megalitkultur, Würzburg, 1912; P. Séjourné, Grands voutes, Bourges, 1913–16; C. Ward, Medieval Church Vaulting, Princeton, 1915; P. Augros, Béton armé: possibilités techniques et architecturales, Paris, 1923; F. B. Andrews, The Medieval Builder and His Methods, Oxford, 1925; G. Giovannoni, La tecnica della costruzione presso i romani, Rome, 1925; G. T. Rivoira, Roman Architecture and its Principles of Construction under the Empire (trans., G. McN. Rushforth, Oxford, 1925); C. Roccatelli, E. Verdozzi, Brickwork in Italy, Chicago, 1925; T. P. Bennett, Architectural Design in Concrete, London, 1927; G. Cozzo, Ingegneria romana, Rome, 1928; S. Giedion, Bauen in Frankreich: Eisen, Eisenbeton, Leipzig, 1928; J. Vischer, L. Hilbersheimer, Beton als Gestalter, Stuttgart, 1928; G. Giovannoni, La tecnica delle costruzioni romane a volta, Atti della Soc. It. per il Progresso delle Scienze, XVII, Rome, 1930; A. Giannelli, Capriata, EI, VIII; E. Freyssinet, Les ponts en béton armé de trés grande portée, L'Architecture Vivante, IX, 35, 1931, pp. 5–16; P. Morton Shand, Steel and Concrete, A Historical Survey, The Architectural Review, LXXII, 1932, pp. 169–79; D. Knoop, G. P. Jones, The Medieval Mason, Manchester, 1933; H. Stolper, Bauten in Holz, Stuttgart, 1933; E. Lambert, Les coupoles des grandes mosquées, Atti del Cong. Internaz. di Storia d'Arte, XIV, 1936; C. B. Andrews, The Early Iron Bridges of the British Isles, The Architectural Review, LXXX, 1936, pp. 63–68; W. B. Douglas, Carpentry and Joinery, London, 1937; A. Rava, Architettura della coupole nell'arte neoclassica, AttiStArch, I, 1936, Florence, 1938, pp. 117–55; G. de Angelis d'Ossat, Sugli edifici ottagonali a cupola nell'antichità e nel Medio Evo, AttiStArch, I, 1936, Florence, 1938, pp. 13–24; R. Neutra, Rivoluzione della struttura, Domus, 128, 1938, pp. 8–15; H. D. Roberts, A History of the Royal Pavilion at Brighton, London, 1939; G. de Angelis d'Ossat, La forma e la costruzione della cupola nell'architettura romana, Atti del III Convegno Naz. di Storia dell'Architettura, Rome, 1938, pp. 246 ff.; S. B. Hamilton, The Use of Cast Iron in Building, Tr. of the Newcomen Soc., XXI, 1940–41, pp. 139–55; G. de Angelis d'Ossat, Nuovi date sulle volte costruite con vasi fittile, Palladio, V, 1941, pp. 241 ff.; F. Wachsmuth, Der Backsteinbau, seine Entwicklungesgänge und Einzelbildungen in Morgen und Abendland, Marburg, 1942; R. Billig, Chronologische Probleme der römischen Konkret: Verkleindung, Opuscula Archeol. Inst. Rom. Sueciae, III, 1944, pp. 124 ff.; S. Chermayeff, Structure and the Aesthetic Experience, Mag. of Art, XXXIX, 1946, pp. 190–94; L. Torres Balbos, Bovedas romanas sobre arcos de resalto, AEA, LXIV, 1946, pp. 173–208; M. Rumpler-Schlacter, Le triomphe de la coupole dans l'architecture byzantine, Strasbourg, 1947; E. Goethals, Bogen, Gewelxen, Koepels, Brussels, n.d. (Fr. trans. Brussels, 1947); J. G. Peirson, The Work of the Bridge Builders, London, 1948; J. Gloag, D. Bridgwater, a History of Cast Iron in Architecture, London, 1948; S. B. Hamilton, Old Cast-Iron Structures, Structural Engineer, N.S., XXVII, 1949, p. 183; H. Straub, Die Geschichte der Bauingenierkunst, Basel, 1949; Perret et l'histoire du beton armé, Techniques et Architecture, IX, 1–2, 1949–50; T. Bannister, The First Iron-Framed Buildings, The Architectural Review, CVII, 1950, pp. 231–46; L. Michaels, Contemporary Structure in Architecture, New York, 1950; M. Pallottino, La Sardegna Nuragica, Rome, 1950; H.-R. Hitchcock, Early Cast Iron Façades, The Architectural Review, CIX, 1951, pp. 113–16; P. Gutierrez Moreno, Estructuras de plementerías pétreas de bóvedas de cricería estrellada, AEA, XXIV, 1951, pp. 251–53; N. Pevsner, High Victorian Design; a Study of the Exhibits of 1851, London, 1951; L. Moretti, Struttura come forma, Spazio, III, 6, 1951–52, pp. 21–30; T. F. Hamlin, Forms and Functions of Twentieth-Century Architecture, New York, 1952; L. Moretti, Struttura e sequenze di spazi, Spazio, VII, 1952–53, pp. 9–20; P. L. Nervi, Scienze e arte del costruire, Rome, 1954; P. A. Michelis, E aesthetik tes architektonikes ton beton-arme, Athens, 1955; P. L. Nervi, Costruire correttamente, Milan, 1955; W. Rave, Das Domekalgewölbe, Deutsche Kunst und Denkmalpflege, I, 1955, pp. 33–43; H. Reuther, Das Platzlgewölbe der Barockzeit, Deutsche Kunst und Denkmalpflege, II, 1955, pp. 212–39; A. M. Romanini, Les premières voutes sexpartites en Italie, Bulletin Monumental, CXIII, 3, 1955, pp. 179–91; P. L. Nervi, Structures, New York, 1956; M. Rumpler-Schlacter, La Coupole dans l'architecture byzantine et musulmane, Strasbourg, 1956; G. Lugli, La tecnica edilizia romana con particolare riguardo a Roma e Lazio, Rome, 1957; L. Laurenzi, Precedenti dell'architettura bizantine a volta, Corso di Cultura sull'arte Ravennate e Bizantina, II, 1958, pp. 71–85; G. Daniel, The Megalith Builders of Western Europe, New York, 1959; A. Terzaghi, Origini e sviluppo della cupola ad arconi intrecciati nell'architettura barocca del Piemonte, Atti del X Cong. di Storia dell'Architettura, Rome, 1959, pp. 369–79; B. Virdis, Le volte nell'architettura, Rome, 1960; K. Wachsmann, Una svolta nella costruzione, Milan, 1960; C. Siegel, Strukturformen in der modernen Architektur, Munich, 1960; G. Bovini, L'impiego di tubi fittili nelle volte degli antichi edifici di culto ravennate, Felix Ravenna, XXX, 1960, p. 79–99; P. Héliot, Remarques sur les voûtes d'arête et sur les coupoles dans l'architecture romane, RA, I, 1961, pp. 167–90; S. Bettini, Tra Oriente e Occidente; origini della crociera d'ogive, Quaderni dell'Istituto di Storia dell'Architettura, 31–48, 1961, pp. 83–92; G. Lilliu, I nuraghi, Cagliari, 1962; L. H. Heydenreich, Strukturprincipien der Florentiner Frührenaissance Architektur: "Prospectiva aedificandi," Acts of the 20th Int. Cong. on the History of Art, II, 2, Princeton, 1963, pp. 108–23; G. Rohlfs, Primitive costruzioni a cupola in Europa, Florence, 1963. *Structural elements: a. Pavements, columns, and decorative elements*: E. Müntz, Les pavements historiés du IV au XII siècle, Etudes Iconographiques et Archéologiques sur le Moyen Age, 1 ser., Paris, 1887; J. Bühlmann, Die Bauformenlehre, Handbuch der Architektur, I, 2, Darmstadt, 1896; G. Foucart, Histoire de l'ordre lotiforme; étude d'archéologie égyptienne, Paris, 1897; L. Borchardt, Die Aegyptische Pflanzensäule, Berlin, 1897; W. P. P. Longfellow, The Column and the Arch; Essays on Architectural History, New York, 1899; G. Tesorone, A proposito dei pavimenti majolicati delle chiese napoletane, Napoli Nobilissima, XI, 1901, pp. 115–24; R. H. H. Cust, The Pavement Masters of Siena (1369–1562), London, 1901; H. Wallis, The Majolica Pavement Tiles of the Fifteenth Century, London, 1902; J. Font y Gumà, Rajolas Valencianas y Catalanas, Barcelona, 1905; H. Pfiefer, Die Formenlehre des Ornaments, Stuttgart, 1906; H. Sohrmann, Die altindische Säule; ein beitrag zur Säulenkunde, Dresden, 1906; M. Dieulafoy, Le rythme modulaire du temple de Salomon, Acad. des Inscriptions et Belles-Lettres, Paris, 1913; E. Madoni, Pavimento del battistero fiorentino, Brescia, 1913; R. Filangieri di Candida Gonzaga, Per il pavimento della cappella di S. Gianni Caracciolo nella chiesa di S. Giovanni a Carbonara in Napoli, Faenza, 1915; U. Monneret de Villard, I dati storici relativi ai mosaici pavimentali cristiani in Lombardia, Milan, 1916; G. Ferrari, La terracotta e pavimenti in laterizio nell'arte Italiana, Milan, 1928; G. Ballardini, An Unknown Della Robbia Tile-work Floor, BM, LV, 1929, pp. 212 ff.; M. E. Blake, The Pavements of the Roman Buildings of the Republic and Early Empire, MAARome, VIII, 1930, pp. 1–159; L. Crema, Pavimento, EI, XXVI; R. Kautsch, Spätanike Kapelle, Berlin, Leipzig, 1936; R. Kautsch, Kapellstudien, Berlin, Leipzig, 1936; E. Pernice, Hellenistische Kunst in Pompeij, Pavimento v. figürlichen Mosaiken, Berlin, 1938; A. Lane, The Spanish Tiles in the Castel Sant'Angelo, Faenza, 1939; A. Lane, Guide to the Collection of Tiles, Victoria and Albert Museum, London, 1939; D. Levi, Antioch Mosaic Pavements, Princeton, 1941; R. Krautheimer, Introduction to an "Iconography of Medieval Architecture," Warburg, V, 1942; R. Naumann, Das Hausmodell vom Tell Halaf und die nach unten verjnten Säulen Nordsyriens, Jhb. für Kleinasiatische Forsch., 1953, pp. 246–66; G. Gullini, I mosaici di Palestrina, Rome, 1956; G. V. Gentili, La Villa Erculea di Piazza Armerina: i mosaici figurati, Rome, 1959; E. Lavagnino, Elementi decorativi di origine gotica nell'architettura del XIII secolo nell'Italia centro-Meridionale, Acts of the XX Int. Cong. of the History of Art, I, 3, Princeton, 1963, pp. 168–82. *b. The orders*: S. Serlio, Regole generali di architettura, Venice, 1537–51; H. Blum, Quinque columnarum exacta descriptio, Tiguri, 1550, Zurich, 1554; J. Bullant, Règle generale d'architecture de cinq manieres de colonnes... suivant les règles et doctrines de Vitruve, Paris, 1564; G. Barozzi da Vignola, Regole delli cinque ordini di architettura, Venice, 1570; A. Capra, La nuova architettura famigliare, Bologna, 1678; B. J. Lauterbach, Proporzione de' cinque ordini di architettura, Leipzig, 1706; A. Pompei (Michel Sanmicheli), Li cinque ordini dell'architettura civile, Verona, 1735; G. B. Piranesi, Della magnificenza ed architettura dei Romani, Rome, 1761; J. Antoine, Traité d'architecture ou proportions des trois ordres grecs, Treves, 1768; D. C. Cerato, Nuovo metodo per insegnare li cinque ordini d'architettura civile conforme le regole di Palladio e di Scamozzi, Padua, 1784; G. Richardson, Treatise on the Five Orders, London, 1787; C. Normand, Nouveau parallèle des ordres d'architecture des Grecs et des Romains, Paris, 1819; H. Hübsch, Uber griechische Architektur, Heidelberg, 1822; M. Aures, Nouvelle theorie du module deduite du texte même de Vitruve, Nîmes, 1862; J. Mauch, Die Architektonische Ordnungen der Griechen und der Römer, Berlin, 1875; C. Chipiez, Histoire critique des origines et de la formation des ordres grecs, Paris, 1876; O. Puchstein, Das Ionische Capitell, Wpr, 1887; C. Chipiez, Le systeme modulaire et les proportions dans l'architecture greque, Paris, 1891; P. Tincolini, Comparazione degli ordini di architettura antich e moderni, Florence, 1895; V. Mortet, La mesure et les proportions de colonnes antiques d'aprés quelques compilations et commentaires anterieurs au XII siècle, Paris, 1898; M. Groote, Ionischen Kapitelle, Strasbourg, 1905; R. Lichtenberg, Die ionische Säule, Leipzig, 1907; G. Homolle, L'origine du chapiteau corintien, RA, 1910; F. von Luscan, Entstehung und Kerkunst, Leipzig, 1912; E. Wurz, Der Ursprung der Kretisch-mykenischen Säulen, Munich, 1913; G. Patroni, Il capitello composito, Miscellane Stampini, Turin, 1921, pp. 151 ff.; G. P. Stevens, The Entasis of Roman Columns, Rome, 1924; P. Montuoro, L'origine della decorazione frontale, MemLinc, s. VI, 1, 1925, pp. 273–344; E. R. Wurz, Die Entstehung de Säulenbasen des Altertums unter Berucksichtigung verwandster Kapitelle, Heidelberg, 1925; G. Giovannoni, L'ordine protodorico greco, Architettur e Arti Decorativi, II, 1929–30, 12, pp. 529–39; W. Andrae, Die inoisch Säule, Bauform oder Symbol?, Berlin, 1933; P. Fontana, Osservazione intorno ai rapporti di Vitruvio con la teorica dell'architettura del Rinascimento, Miscellanea di Storia d'Arte in Onore di J. B. Supino, Florence, 1933; F. Krischen, Werden und Wesen der ionischen Formensprache, Antike und Abendland, 1946, pp. 77–94; W. Andrae, Die Griechisch Säulenordnungen, Kleinasien und Byzanz, Istanb. Forschungen, XVII, 1950, 1, pp. 1–9; C. J. Moe, I numeri di Vitruvio, Milan, 1951; M. Cavallar Le proporzioni canoniche... nei trattatisti di Architettura, Atti della Società di Ingegneri e Architetti, Turin, 1952; L. Polacco, Tuscanicae Dispositiones, Padua, 1952; P. Amandry, Le colonne des Naxiens et le portiqu des Athéniens, FD, II, Paris, 1953; J. Boardman, Chian and Early Ioni Architecture, AntJ, LXVI, 3, 1962, pp. 249–54. *Structural types: a. Domest* hitecture: A. Darcel, De l'architecture civile au Moyen Age, GBA, XII, 62, 4, pp. 350–65, 5, pp. 447–64; R. Burri, Sulle forme e caratteri dell'rchitettura civile e sulle cause delle loro variazioni, Mem... Roma, 1873; E. Viollet-le-Duc, The Habitations of Man in All Ages, Boston, London, 76; A. von Essenwein, Romanisch und Gothik Architektur: II, Der Wohnu, Darmstadt, 1889–1902; L. de Beylié, L'abitation byzantine, Grenoble, 04; W. Rostovtzeff, Pompeiianische Landschaften und römische Villen, I, XXIX, 1904, pp. 124 ff.; W. Dörpfeld, Kretische, mykenische und homerhe Paläste, Actes du Ier Cong. Int. d'Archéologie, Athens, 1905; A. n Essenwein, Der Wohnbau des Mittelalters, Leipzig, 1908; B. Patzak, e Renaissance und Barockvilla, Leipzig, 1910; A. Colasanti, Case e pazi di Roma, Milan, 1912; B. Patzak, Palast und Villa in Toscana, Leipzig, 13; E. R. Flecter, Das italische Atriumhaus, Zurich, 1914; F. Pfuhl, rgriechische und Griechische Haustypen, Zurich, 1914; G. Calza, La eeminenza dell'insula nell'edilizia romana, MaLinc, XXVIII, 1916; H. Glück, egaron, Hilani und Apadana, Vienna, 1922; A. Haupt, Palast-Architektur n Ober-Italien und Toskana, Berlin, 1922; A. Gargana, La casa etrusca, ilan, 1924; K. M. Swoboda, Römische und Romanische Paläste, Vienna, 24; P. Wolf, Wohnung und Siedlung, Berlin, 1926; F. Delmann, Haus d Hof in Altertum, Berlin, 1927; H. Field, M. Bunney, English Domestic chitecture of the XVII and XVIII Centuries, Cleveland, London, 1928; . Spano, L'origine e l'evoluzione della casa italica, B. dell'Università per ranieri, Perugia, 1935; A. Gargana, Tombe etrusche rupestri e case rone, Atti del III Conv. Naz. di Storia dell'Architettura, Rome, 1938, . 33–38; B. M. Felletti May, La casa e l'arredamento, Civ. Romana, XV, 40; G. Fiocco, La casa antica veneziana, RendLinc, CCCXLVI, 1940, pp. 38 ff.; Paribeni, Le dimore dei "potentiores" nel Basso Impero, RoemMitt, , 1940, pp. 135 ff.; A. Maiuri, Lezioni sulla casa romana e pompeiiana, aples, 1948; G. Becatti, Case ostiense del tardo Impero, Rome, 1948; Chiolini, I caratteri distributivi degli antichi edifici, Milan, 1950; A. aiuri, La casa a Pompeii, Naples, 1951; P. Grimal, Les villes romaines, ris, 1954; G. Chierici, Il trullo, Atti del IX Cong. Naz. di Storia dell'Architettura, Bari, 1955, pp. 203–07; G. Chierici, Il palazzo italiano dal c. XI al sec. XIX, Milan, 1957; J. W. Graham, The Central Court as inoan Bull Ring, AJA, LXI, 1957, pp. 255–62; V. Mosca, Architettura mestica en Sardegna, Cagliari, 1957; K. M. Swoboda, Palazzi antichi e edievali, B. del Centro di Studi per la Storia dell'architettura, XI, 1957, . 3–32; G. A. Mansuelli, Le ville del mondo romanico, Milan, 1958; . Cagiano de Azevedo, Admiranda Palatia, I palazzi imperiali e le resinze tetrarchiche, B. del Centro di Studi di Storia dell'Architettura, XIV, 59, pp. 3–24; J. W. Graham, The Residential Quarter of the Minoan lace, AJA, LXIII, 1959, pp. 47–52; G. Tosi, Il palazzo principesco delrcaismo greco alla Domus Flavia, Arte Antica e Moderna, VII, 1959, . 241–60; D. de Chapeaurouge, Der Ursprung des modernen Glashausen, te e moderne Kunst, V, 1960, pp. 14–19; J. W. Graham, The Minoan nit of Length and Minoan Palace Planning, AJA, LXIV, 1960, pp. 335–41; Maretto, L'edilizia gotica veneziana, Rome, 1960; A. Schott, Minoische d Mykenische Palasthöfe, Jhrh. der Osterreichischen Inst. in Wien, XLV, 60, pp. 68–80; K. M. Swoboda, The Problem of Iconography of Late ntique and Early Medieval Palaces, J. of the Soc. of Architectural Historians, XX, 1961, pp. 78–89; I. Lavin, The House of the Lord; Aspects the Role of Palace Triclinia in the Architecture of Late Antiquity and e Early Middle Ages, AB, XLIV, 1962, pp. 1–27; J. Ackermann, Sources the Renaissance Villa, Acts of the 20th Int. Cong. of the H. of Art, Princen, 1963, vol. II, part 1, pp. 6–18. *b. Religious architecture*: H. Hübsch, Ionuments de l'architecture chrétienne depuis Constantin jusqu'à Charleagne, Paris, 1866; G. Dehio, G. von Bezold, Die Kirchliche Baukunst r Abendlandes, Stuttgart, 1892–1901; F. Witting, Die Anfänge Christlicher rchitektur, Gedanken über Wesen und Entstehung der christlichen Basilika, rasbourg, 1902; A. Riegl, Zur Entstehung der altchristlichen Basilika, Jh. r Zentralkommission für Erforschung der Kunst, N.S., I, 1903, pp. 195–6; H. Thiersch, Pharos, Leipzig, Berlin, 1909; J. J. Stryzygowski, Urrung der christlichen Kirchenkunst, Leipzig, 1920; B. Melchers, China: , Der Tempelbau, Hagen, 1921; J. Braun, Der Christliche Altar in seiner schichtlichen Entwicklung, Munich, 1924; H. W. Beyer, Der svrischen irchenbau, Berlin, 1925; R. Schultze, Basilika, Berlin, Leipzig, 1928; A. aybon, Les temples du Japon, architecture et sculpture, Paris, 1931; . Sedlmayr, Geschichte des Iustinianischen Architektursystem, Bizantinche Z., 1935, p. 38; O. Gruber, Das Westwerk, Z. des deutschen Vereins r Kunstwissenschaft, 3, 1936; R. Krautheimer, Corpus basilicarum christianarum Romae, I, Città del Vaticano, 1937–54; C. Ceschi, Architettura ei templi megalitici di Malta, Rome, 1939; F. Despoulieres, Les cryptes 1 France et l'influence du culte des réliques sur l'architecture religieuse, aris, 1941; G. Rodenwalt, W. Hege, Griechische Tempel, Berlin, 1941; H. Grinnell, Greek Temples, New York, 1943; A. Grabar, Martyrium, Paris, 1946; S. Kramrisch, The Hindu Temple, Calcutta, 1946; E. Gabrici, empio greco e tempio italico nelle loro più antiche fasi, Atti del VII Cong. az. di Storia dell'Architettura, Palermo, 1950, pp. 223–38; R. Rey, L'art es cloîtres romans, Toulouse, 1955; F. Oelmann, Homerische Tempel und ordeurasiatische Opfermahlhäuser, BJ, CLVII, 1957, pp. 11–52; G. Matthiae, asiliche paleocristiane con ingresso e polifora, BArte, XLII, 1957, pp. 107–21; . Krautheimer, Il transetto nella basilica paleocristiana, Actes du Vème ong. Intern. d'Archéologie Chrétienne, Aix-en-Provence, 1954, pp. 238–90; I. van Doren, Les Sacrario; une catégorie méconnue d'edifices sacrés chez s romains, L'Antiquité Classique, XXVII, 1958, pp. 38 ff.; A. Andréon, rigine e formazione dell'architettura templare etrusco-italica, RendPontAcc, XXII, 1959–60, pp. 21 ff.; G. Urban, Die Kirchenbaukunst des Quattrocento Roma, Römische J. H., 1961–62, pp. 73 ff.; A. Khatchatrian, Les baptistères paléochrétiens, Paris, 1962; G. de Angelis d'Ossat, Tipologia architettonica dei battisteri paleocristiani, Corso di Cultura sull'arte Ravennate Bizantina, Ravenna, 1963, pp. 122–29. *c. Other types*: C. Tetti, Discorso elle fortificazioni, Venice, 1575; G. Fonda, Elementi di architettura civile militare, Rome, 1764; E. King, Munimenta antiqua, or Observations on ncient Castles, London, 1782; L. Gozlan, Les châteaux de France, Paris, 857; A. Gosset Traité de la construction du théâtre, Paris, 1876; G. Gozzadini, Note per studi sull'architettura civile in Bologna del sec. XIII al XIV, Modena, 1877; J. von Schlosser, Das abendländische klosteranlage der frühern Mittelalters, Vienna, 1889; E. Pollack, Hippodromica, Leipzig, 1890; K. Wernicke, Olympische Beitrage, V: Der Hippodrom, Jdl, IX, 1894, pp. 190 ff.; A. Griesebach, Das Deutsche Rathaus der Renaissance, Berlin, 1907; B. Ebhardt, Die Burgen Italiens, Berlin, 1909; P. N. Schultze, Das Schloss, Munich, 1910; E. N. Gardiner, Greek Athletic Sports and Festivals, London, 1910; M. Bieber, Die Denkmäler zu Theaterwesen im Altertum, Berlin, 1920; L. Piccinato, L'architettura del moderno albergo, Architettura e Arti Decorativi, IV, 1924–25, pp. 201–77; J. Hammond, B. Hammond, The Rise of Modern Industry, London, 1925; O. Navarre, Le théâtre grec, Paris, 1925; A. Mazzoni, Architettura ferroviaria, Architettura e Arti Decorativi, VI, 1926–27, pp. 193–279; G. Patroni, L'origine degli archi trionfali romani, Historia, I, 1927; A. Nicoll, The Development of the Theatre, London, Bombay, Sydney, 1927; E. Lowy, Die Anfänge des Triumphbogens, Jbh. SammlWien, n.f., 11, 1928, pp. 1–40; A. Fellheimer, Modern Railway Passenger Terminals, The Architectural Forum, LIII, 6, 1930, pp. 655–62; E. J. Neutra, Terminals? – Transfer!, The Architectural Record, LXVIII, 8, 1930, pp. 99–104; R. W. Sexton, American Theatre of To-Day, New York, I, 1927, II, 1930; G. Libertini, Il teatro antico e la sua evoluzione, Catania, 1932; M. P. Nilsson, The origin of the Triumphal Arch, Corolla Gustavo Adolpho, Lund, 1932; E. B. Van Deman, The Building of Roman Aqueducts, Washington, 1934; T. Ashby, I. A. Richmond, The Aqueducts of Ancient Rome, Oxford, 1935; F. Frigerio, Antiche porte di città italiche e romane, Como, 1935; F. Milkau, Geschichte der Bibliotheken im Alten Orient, Leipzig, 1935; H. Lorenz, Untersuchungen zum Praetorium, Halle, 1936; B. Moretti, Teatri, Milan, 1936; C. L. Ragghianti, Architetture scolastiche e loro significato, CrArte, 1936, 6, pp. 299–300; B. Ebhardt, Der Wehrbau Europas in Mittelalters, Berlin, 1939; G. Pagano, Architettura industriale in Italia, LeArti, I, 1939, pp. 258 ff.; F. di Capua, Appunti sull'origine e lo sviluppo delle terme romane, Rend Napoli, XX, 1940; F. Krischen, Antike Rathäuser, Berlin, 1941; T. Cochran, W. Miller, The Age of Enterprise, A Social History of Industrial America, New York, 1942; G. de Angelis d'Ossat, Technica costruttiva e impianto delle terme, Rome, 1943; H. Stern, Notes sur l'architecture des châteaux omeyyades, Ars Islamica, XI-XII, 1946, pp. 72–97; C. Anti, Teatri greci arcaici, Padua, 1947; M. Aubert, L'architecture cistercienne en France, Paris, 1947; R. J. Neutra, Scali marittimi, Metron, 13, 1947, pp. 36–55; S. Pastorini, Architettura scolastica negli edifici rinascimentali, L'Ultima, III, 28, 1948, pp. 23 ff.; G. Lugli, Porte di città antiche ad ordini di archi sovrapposti, Archaeol. Cristiana, I, 1949; C. Barman, an Introduction to Railway Architecture, London, 1950; E. Gentili, Architettura dell'industria, Comunità, IV, 8, 1950, pp. 46 ff.; C. L. V. Meeks, The Life of a Form: A History of the Train Shed, The Architectural Review, CX, 1951, pp. 163–73; F. R. Wylie, Industrial Buildings, J. of the Royal Inst. of British Architects, LVIII, 1951, pp. 309–14; C. W. Condit, The Rise of the Skyscraper, Chicago, 1952; W. W. Caudill, Toward Better School Design, New York, 1954; G. A. Mansuelli, El arco honorifico en el desarrollo de la arquitectura romana, Archivo Español de Arqueologia, XXVII, 89–90, 1954, pp. 93–178; T. Sidney, A History of Fortification from 3000 B.C. to 1700 A.D., Melbourne, 1955; M. Wentmeyer, Babilonske og Assiriske arkiven og biblioteker, Copenhagen, 1955; V. Gruen, The Planned Shopping Centers in America, Zodiac, I, 1957, pp. 159–68; H. B. Harvey, Early Industrial Architecture, J. of the Royal Inst. of British Architects, LXVI, 1959, pp. 316–24; P. du Colombier, La naissance des châteaux en France, La Rev. des Deux-Mondes, 1960, pp. 448–60; J. Fichten, The Construction of Gothic Cathedrals, a Study of Medieval Vault Erection, Oxford, 1961; A. Neppi Modona, Gli edifici teatrali greci e romani, Florence, 1961; S. Sitwell, Die Grossen Schlösser Europas, Berlin, 1961; F. Gobelin, Les châteaux de France, Paris, 1962; M. Pallottino, Arco onorario e trionfale, EAA, I, pp. 588–99.

Oreste FERRARI

Individual elements of the figures illustrating this article have been adapted from various sources, including: (General) Viollet-le-Duc, 1854–69; Choisy, 1899; A. Springer and C. Ricci, *Manuale di Storia dell'arte*, Bergamo, 1927; Fletcher, 1938; G. Tucci, *Le civiltà dell'Oriente*, 4 vols., Rome, 1962; G. V. Egle, *Forme e stili dell'architettura*, Turin, 1966; (Egyptian and ancient Eastern architecture) E. B. Smith, *Egyptian Architecture as Cultural Expression*, New York, 1938; J. Vaudier, *Manuel d'archéologie egyptienne*, II, 1, 2, Paris, 1952–55; M. Frankfort, *Art and Architecture of the Ancient Orient*, Harmondsworth, 1954; (Greek, Roman, and Byzantine architecture) Chipiez, 1876; Dinsmoor, 1950; A. W. Lawrence, *Greek Architecture*, Harmondsworth, 1957; Lugli, 1957; L. Crema, *L'architettura romana*, Enciclopedia classica, IV, Rome, 1958; H. Berve, G. Gruben, and M. Hirmer, *I templi greci*, Florence, 1962; D. Talbot Rice, *Byzantine Art*, Harmondsworth, 1962; D. S. Robertson, *Handbook of Greek and Roman Architecture*, Cambridge, 1963; (Islamic architecture) Rivoira, 1914; E. T. Richmond, *Moslem Architecture*, London, 1926; Creswell, 1932–40; (Romanesque and Gothic architecture) A. W. Clapham, *Romanesque Architecture in Western Europe*, Oxford, 1936; Conant, 1959; H. Weigert, *Baukunst der Romanik in Europa*, Frankfurt, 1959; Frankl, 1962; (Renaissance, baroque, and rococo architecture) A. Venturi, *L'architettura del quattrocento*, Milan, 1923–24; D. Frey, *The Architecture of the Renaissance from Brunelleschi to Michelangelo*, The Hague, 1925; A. Venturi, *L'architettura del cinquecento*, Milan, 1938–40; W. Hager, *Die Bauten des deutschen Barok*, 1942; L. Hautecoeur, *Histoire de l'architecture classique en France*, Paris 1943–57; Chierici, 1957; J. Summerson, *Architecture in Britain 1530–1830*, London, 1953; (Modern architecture) A. Sartoris, *Encyclopédie de l'architecture nouvelle*, 3 vols., Milan, 1957; H.-R. Hitchcock, *Architecture of the Nineteenth and Twentieth Centuries*, 2 vols., Baltimore, 1958; L. Benevolo. *Storia dell'architettura moderna*, Bari, 1960; and such periodicals as *Architectural Forum*; *Architectural Record*; *Architectural Review*; and *L'Architecture d'aujourd'hui.*

Illustrations: PLS. 215–266; 28 figs. in text.

STUART, GILBERT. Early American portrait painter (b. North Kingstown, R. I., Dec. 3, 1755; d. Boston, Mass., July 9, 1828). Before he was twenty Stuart produced a few stiff likenesses with the aid of the Scotsman Cosmo Alexander, with whom he made a brief journey to Edinburgh in 1772. From 1775 to 1793 he lived in England and Ireland, first as an impoverished student who was befriended by Benjamin West, and later, from 1780, as an accomplished technician whose likenesses of his London patrons equaled the best portraits in the Royal Academy exhibitions. After a stay of about five years in Dublin he returned to paint in New York, Philadelphia, and Washington; in 1805 he moved to Boston, where he lived for 23 years until his death.

Such works of his English period as *The Skater* (ca. 1782; Washington, D. C., Nat. Gall.) and *Henrietta Vane* (1782–83; Northampton, Mass., Smith College Mus. of Art) reveal his indebtedness to Gainsborough and Reynolds (qq.v.). By the time of his *Mrs. Richard Yates* (ca. 1793; Washington, D. C., Nat. Gall., Mellon Coll.), he had achieved his own direct, masterly style; the portrait *Mrs. Timothy Pickering* (1818; Pittsburgh, Carnegie Inst.) indicates how little that style varied in his prolific American years. In his *Thomas Jefferson* (1799; Brunswick, Me., Bowdoin College, Mus. of Fine Arts) he presented a figure of handsome dignity. His numerous portraits of George Washington were replicas of three works done from life: the Vaughan bust portrait (Washington, D.C., Nat. Gall.) of 1795; the Lansdowne full-length (Philadelphia, Pennsylvania Acad. of the Fine Arts) of 1796, and the unfinished painting owned by the Boston Athenaeum since 1831 (on loan, Boston, Mus. of Fine Arts) of the same year. Stuart dominated the art of portrait painting of his day, and many prominent people sat for him, including John Adams (I, PL. 102) and four other presidents. His work and his advice shaped the styles of many younger artists, among them Thomas Sully, John Wesley Jarvis, Samuel Morse (q.v.), Ezra Ames, Chester Harding, John Neagle, and Matthew Jouett. Exclusively a portraitist, he preferred to show his subject at bust length against a plain brown or gray background that enhanced his glowing flesh tones and brilliantly summarized costumes. His procedure, based on English methods, was orderly and sure: a swift blocking in of the principal forms in monochrome followed by the application of a few colors in simple mixtures as transparent glazes or as deft accents with a loaded brush. His completed canvases reflect a luminous and untroubled harmony and a sketchlike freshness. Some critics credit him with powers of penetrating the human personality, while others consider his realism to be only superficial; but all concede that he possessed amazingly keen powers of observation and great breadth of style.

BIBLIOG. L. Park, Gilbert Stuart, An Illustrated Descriptive List of His Works, 4 vols., New York, 1926; W. T. Whitley, Gilbert Stuart, Cambridge, Mass., 1932; J. H. Morgan, Gilbert Stuart and His Pupils, New York, 1939; J. T. Flexner, Gilbert Stuart: A Great Life in Brief, New York, 1955.

Oliver W. LARKIN

STUCCO. The use of stucco ranges from the simple protective covering of structures (see STRUCTURAL TYPES AND METHODS) and the providing of the support for wall paintings (see PAINTING) to the modeling of sculptures in relief and in the round (see SCULPTURE). However, because of its fineness and its capacity for being worked the material lends itself especially to a decorative function, the modeling of relief on large surfaces and the accentuating of architectural elements — a function that through the development of a technical artistic tradition already existing in limited areas in the ancient world and in medieval Europe and Asia achieved more effective expressions and attained to independent esthetic stature particularly during the Renaissance (q.v.) and the periods of baroque art and rococo (qq.v.).

SUMMARY. The technique of stuccowork (col. 628). Antiquity and the Middle Ages (col. 629): *The ancient civilizations; Late antiquity, Byzantium, and medieval Europe.* Iran, India, and Central Asia (col. 638). The Islamic world (col. 642). Pre-Columbian America (col. 643). European stuccowork from the Renaissance onward (col. 644).

THE TECHNIQUE OF STUCCOWORK. From very early tin the slow-setting plaster known as "stucco" — a mixture genera of lime, washed sand, and gypsum in varying proportions has been used to provide a homogeneous covering for archittural surfaces and for the modeling and refining of works of scul ture. In the most ancient examples of the application of stuc it is noteworthy that the process was almost always employ with a view to the subsequent application of color.

In classical antiquity the preparation of ground surfac of white stucco was the necessary preliminary to many wor of painting. In Roman times still-soft stucco, handled as easily malleable mass, was applied to the plastered wall w the aid of special spatulas or even with the fingers alone; the case of friezes and rosettes involving recurrent motifs, sp cial molds and forms were used. Vitruvius (VII, iii–vi) a Pliny (XXXVI, lv, 176) describe early methods of obtaining go stucco mixtures; Pliny (XXV, xliv, 153) records that Lysistrat of Sicyon was the first to model "a likeness in plaster . . . fro the living face" and to use the "method of pouring wax into th plaster mold and then making final corrections on the w cast."

The material used for medieval stuccoes was generally gy sum plaster mixed with sand and small quantities of lime. T proportions of the mixture were almost constant, but the were exceptions: at Malles Venosta (III, PL. 60) and at Gern gny-des-Prés (III, PL. 51) lime was used in greater proportio but always together with gypsum plaster; at Disentis (cant of Graubünden, Switzerland) only lime and sand were used produce a mixture known as "stucco forte," or hard stucc

The traces of iron, aluminum sesquioxide, and magnesiu oxide found in one fragment of the Church of S. Salvato in Brescia can undoubtedly be explained as impurities, b the greater proportions of these elements found in other fra ments of this church, and at Malles Venosta, seem to represe an expedient employed to retard the setting of the material a thus to facilitate the refinement of the modeling. The stuc was worked directly on the wall (as in the crypt in the Chur of S. Salvatore), or on reeds that were interwoven and fasten with nails (as in other parts of this church), or on wood (as in th Church of St-Julien in Brioude and the Cathedral of Notr Dame in Alet); the mixture was then shaped with modelir tools, rasps, and files.

The stuccowork associated with the Byzantine traditic exhibits a dense and sharply incised treatment intended simulate the carving of precious substances: this constitut presumptive evidence that the material was no longer worke before it had set but was allowed to dry and then carved. Th technique, transmitted to the Arab world by Byzantine-train craftsmen, is seen in the stuccoes of the Alhambra, in Granac (X, PLS. 166, 167), and of Medina az-Zahra, near Córdob where, through intricate carving and artful finish, the effe of ivorywork was reproduced with the utmost finesse.

During the Gothic and Renaissance periods there flourishe a type of plasterwork — called "pastiglia" — that was use in the decoration of interiors and furniture. This modelin was carried out in the familiar impasto of gesso, marble powde and size, in some cases spread on linen cloth that had previousl been applied to the wood surface; the modeled elements wer then painted or gilded. The 15th-century *Libro dell'Arte* Cennino Cennini contains interesting technical information o methods of preparing gesso and applying it to panels. In th wood sculptures of the 14th and 15th centuries, stucco serve as a connecting element between the underlying structure an the chromatic coating (this is the "albatura gypsi" of whic Theophilus Presbyter speaks in his *Diversarum artium schedula* Besides being applied to wood, it was combined in some case with papier-mâché to achieve graceful results in the composite media category.

A passage in Vasari's life of Giovanni da Udine is illuminatin on the technical aspect of stucco decoration in Raphaelesqu circles: "Digging in the ruins and remains of the Palace of Titu in the hope of finding figures, certain rooms were discovere completely buried under the ground, which were full of littl grotesques, small figures, and scenes, with other ornaments c ucco in low-relief. Whereupon, Giovanni going with Raffaello, ho was taken to see them, were struck with amazement, both e one and the other, at the freshness, beauty and excellence f those works.... These grotesques..., with their delicate rnaments of stucco divided by various fields of color, and with eir little scenes so pleasing and beautiful, entered so deeply to the heart and mind of Giovanni, that, having devoted him-lf to the study of them,... he succeeded in executing them ith facility and grace, lacking nothing save a knowledge of the ethod of making the stucco.... Now many before him... ad exercised their wits on this, but... had not found the true ethod of making stucco similar to that which had been discov-ed in those ancient chambers and grottoes. But at that time orks were being executed in lime and pozzolana,... and Gio-anni, after considering that method of working with lime and ozzolana, began to try if he could succeed in making figures low-relief; and so, pursuing his experiments, he contrived make them as he desired in every part, save that the outer urface did not come out with the delicacy and finish that the ncient works possessed, nor yet so white. On which account e began to think that it might be necessary to mix with the hite lime of travertine, in place of pozzolana, some substance hite in colour; whereupon, after making trial of various mate-als, he caused chips of travertine to be pounded, and found at it answered passing well, but that still the work was of a vid rather than a pure white, and also rough and granular. ut finally, having caused chips of the whitest marble that could e found to be pounded and reduced to a fine powder, and then fted, he mixed it with white lime of travertine, and discovered hat thus he had succeeded without any doubt in making the rue stucco of the ancients, with all the properties that he had esired therein" (Vasari, *Lives*, London, 1912, trans. G. du C. le Vere).

In the High Renaissance, stucco also appears, combined vith other elements, in sgraffito, or scratched architectural rnament. The lines of the cartoon were "pounced" onto the ayers of cement and stucco in two or more colors applied to he exterior of buildings. The broader areas of the composition vere exposed by removing the top layer with a special blade, nd the outlines of the design were then incised with the point f a knife.

Concurrently, stuccowork found interesting applications in nterior decorations of imitation marble, a fashion that was to volve to a point of prodigious technical excellence in the 17th nd 18th centuries, especially in the ambit of the Germanic ococo. It was in fact during the baroque period that stucco-vork underwent its most interesting technical variations, in the reations of the great dynasties of modelers. In these families f stuccoworkers, which flourished particularly in the north f Italy and in the south of the Germanic countries, many ad-anced technical procedures were handed down as secrets; of hese only the faintest echo remains in the specification books f certain craftsmen of the end of the 19th century.

* *

ANTIQUITY AND THE MIDDLE AGES. *The ancient civilizations.* Its inherent perishability as a material, which has rendered evi-lence particularly scarce, makes it impossible to say whether the se of stucco, which appears to be very ancient, has followed a constant line or represents the stylistic option of those artists who saw in it a material easily adaptable to the expression of their deas or a substitute for more valuable and costly substances.

In ancient Egypt, the use of stucco is evidenced in the 18th dynasty by products of the sculptural workshops of Tell el Amarna: portraits in plaster of Amenhotep III and Amenho-tep IV and of members of the royal court (Berlin, Staat. Mus.; IV, PL. 375). In the case of the celebrated bust of Nefertiti (XII, PL. 489), however, this material was used only to supple-ment the limestone in which the bust was carved. The plaster portrait technique can be connected to a procedure that was practiced in the Old Kingdom, probably motivated by the same quest for permanence as gave rise to the so-called "reserve heads." The linen-wrapped head of the deceased was coated with plaster, which was then modeled to approximate a portrait; two

such plaster masks from mummies, dating from the First Inter-mediate Period, are in Boston (Mus. of Fine Arts). Sometimes the plaster coating was applied to the entire linen-wrapped body. It is thought that the cartonnage masks of the First Intermediate Period and the cartonnage coffins of the Middle Kingdom may have been suggested by these plaster coatings, to which the fu-neral masks of stuccoed and painted cloth, of the Ptolemaic period (IX, PL. 353) are also related.

In the Cretan world, at about the middle of the 2d millen-nium, stucco was used for large compositions in low relief, as is known from the painted reliefs, among them the one with the charging bull (PL. 267), the procession with the cupbearer, and the shield fresco found in the palace of Knossos. But the art seems not to have been limited to that palace (Graham, 1962; see also J. D. S. Pendlebury, *The Archaeology of Crete*, London, 1942, p. 158). In the Mycenaean world the isolated discovery at Mycenae of a female head made of stucco (IV, PL. 72) provides no basis for establishing the comparative extent to which this material was used in the Mycenaean royal palace (see CRETAN-MYCENAEAN ART).

As is proved by the pediments of the archaic temples of the Acropolis (II, PL. 39), the use of stucco for finishing sculpture made of porous materials and situated on the outside of buildings was widespread in Greece in the 6th century B.C. But there must also have been actual sculptural forms entirely composed of stucco since Pausianias (VIII, 22, 7) questions whether certain figures of birds on the roof of the Temple of Artemis at Stym-phalos in Arcadia were carved in stucco or in wood.

However, given the passion for marble and the refined tech-nique of working it in the classical period, stucco works must have been very rare, being confined to the decoration of walls as a substitute for marble. But this use must have been wide-spread, to judge from the fact that Solon prohibited the adorn-ment of tombs with stuccowork (Cicero, *De legibus*, II, 26, 64-65) in summoning the Athenians to a regime of "austerity."

In the Alexandrian ambience — at least so far as can be de-duced from the finds — stucco had a very special application. It was used not for large reliefs or for figures sculptured in the round but for small reliefs that were models for or casts from silverwork. An extensive series of these models was found in Egypt, with the largest group coming from Mit Rahina (now in Hildesheim, Germany, Pelizaeus Mus.). On fields of various types are depicted Neoptolemos, the Pleiades, Eros with a goose, Scylla, a sea dragon, and the Labors of Hercules. If the attribution of the prototypes to the 3d century B.C. is accepted, the actual execution of the casts can be placed either in that century (A. Adriani) or in the 1st century of our era (A. Ippel). In the opinion of O. Rubensohn they came from the workshop of a silversmith, who used them to reproduce various figures on the embossed or cast silver plate that was so fashionable at that time and in that culture. The same provenance is assigned to a plaster disk (Alexandria, Greco-Roman Mus.) with two pro-files, one of a man and one of a woman, which have been iden-tified as portraying Ptolemy I Soter (r. 323-285) and Berenike I; if, as maintained by Adriani, the metal original dates from the subsequent reign of Ptolemy II Philadelphus (285-246), the plaster copy could be only slightly later in date and hence con-temporaneous with the models or casts from Mit Rahina, as dated in Adriani's hypothesis.

Similar objects form part of the extraordinary hoard discov-ered at Begram (anc. Kapisi), stopping place on the great east-ern caravan route and capital of Kapisa, a region of Hellenistic-Roman culture situated in what is now Afghanistan. There are about forty circular emblemata (VII, PL. 195) and nine isolated pieces suitable for the sides of cylindrical beakers. The subjects of these range from individual profiles of diminutive satyrs to entire figures of divinities and complex scenes of the Diony-sian thiasos, or worship, to typically Alexandrian rural landscapes. On one of the beakers the Pharos of Alexandria appears; Adriani's dating of this piece also is early (3d cent. B.C.), but there are later examples, so that the span covers the entire Hellenistic-Roman period. The plaster models from Egypt (fomerly Berlin, Bissing Coll.) that were used for the mass production of a statue of Hermes Diskobolos have been ascribed to the early imperial age; stucco molds intended for similar uses are well known, and there is a large collection of them in Cairo (Egyptian Mus.).

Nothing is known of stucco decoration in Hellenistic architecture, a type of decoration that on the basis of certain indications must be presumed. It existed in such regions as Mesopotamia and Iran, which were often under Greek influence, and in such regions as Etruria and, later, Rome, which actually shared the Greek cultural experience.

To begin with Etruria, a widely known example is the Tomb of the Reliefs in the necropolis of Cerveteri (PL. 268; VIII, PL. 95). On the walls and pilasters of this complex hypogeum there appear in stucco not only architectural elements but also representations of arms, household utensils, and mythological creatures. These stuccoes date from the height of the Hellenistic period. The famous François Tomb in Vulci (VII, PL. 260), which is also variously dated within a wide span extending from the end of the 4th to the beginning of the 1st century B.C., had parts related to its architectural elements decorated in stucco.

It is thus difficult to reject the hypothesis of a similar use of stucco in Hellenistic buildings, which, moreover, seems to be documented by various monuments in the East. In Jerusalem the Herodian entry known as the Double Gate has decorative stuccowork in the vaults. The use of stucco is known in Parthian art (q.v.), even though — as has been suggested — it may have had a Nabataean origin by way of Iran. This theory must be taken to relate only to the use of the material, not to the manner of using it, considering the dates of the monuments containing stuccowork and the area of their diffusion: from the 1st to the 3d century they were spread over the entire Parthian area — in other words, in the region where contacts between the East and West were particularly close and fruitful. What this means is that in the daily osmosis of experiences, certain ones were accepted from the West and translated "at sight" — that is, they were understood not in terms of structural logic but only in their external aspect. In this way the stucco decoration of coffered ceilings or interior moldings was transferred to the external friezes of the architraves of the individual architectonic partitions, as in the façade of the palace at Ashur (Assur), datable about A.D. 200. Stucco was used as a substitute for marble; some ornamental motifs were derived from the East, but the design of the façade is a Parthian interpretation of Hellenistic modes and styles. The contamination of style is even more evident at Kuh-i-Khwaja, where meanders and Greek frets are found together with the well-known Eastern rosettes formed by intersecting circles.

The Sassanids continued this style, but in accents more clearly revealing the impact of Hellenistic culture. Nor is this impact surprising when it is recalled that Western craftsmen (i.e., from Asia Minor) held as prisoners of war were employed by Shāpur I in the construction of Bishapur after the defeat of Valerian.

The use of stucco in the Roman world and in the West in general had a very different development, but here too Hellenistic precedents, though undocumented, must be assumed. New and decisive information may perhaps be forthcoming from the study of Neo-Attic casts of classical sculptures discovered at Baia. Moreover, the beginning of the use of applied stucco for architectural decoration coincides with Sulla's conquest of Campania — a very significant indication, which presupposes the existence of stuccowork in the Hellenistic world and reveals the path of its entrance into Rome. It was in Rome that the earliest important examples of stucco appeared, in the House of the Griffins on the Palatine (PL. 276), in the vault of the House of the Farnesina (PL. 270), and in the Basilica of Porta Maggiore (PL. 269). In point of fact, the lunette in the House of the Griffins showing two griffins heraldically confronted among rinceaux dates from the first half of the 2d century B.C.; in design and execution it evinces the Alexandrian taste as widely expressed in toreutic works.

The stuccoes in the House of the Farnesina (PL. 270; IX, PL. 4) are later. Their use shows an untrammeled freedom of expression. The artist did not feel himself bound to a partitioning of the vaults that would correspond to the coffers of a ceiling or to some other acceptable architectural form; instead, in fiel delineated with delicate spatial balance, he scattered imaginati airy, bucolic, and mythological landscapes, alternating the with squares of mythological scenes totally dominated by hum figures. The style of this artist cannot be considered apart fro that of the golden-yellow landscapes on the black walls of t same house or of the cubicula of Boscotrecase. However, tl master remains isolated, for even though extremely finishe the stuccoes in the underground Basilica of Porta Maggic (PL. 269), which is only a little later in date, are undoubtec of lesser artistic quality. The decorative partitioning of the va bears certain similarities to the Farnesina, but there are landscapes, and the mythological scenes unfold with a certa rigidity of modeling and a mannered definition of volumes th cannot compare to the light and ethereal style of the plaste work in the Farnesina. Of particular importance is the stuc depicting the story of Sappho (PL. 271) in the concha of tl apse of the Basilica of Porta Maggiore.

The fanciful richness of image and scene characterizi the group of stuccoes just examined became restrained, and ev suppressed, from the Julio-Claudian period on, so that geometr partitioning, and thereby the ornamental rather than the illu trative element, gained the upper hand. Moreover, particular in the areas of provincial culture, stucco often complement the pictorial decoration, with dubious stylistic results. Stucc was also frequently covered by painting. In ceilings there w widespread use of coffered partitioning, often simply whit as in the arcades of the Colosseum, but not infrequently painte as in certain rooms that were incorporated into the later Dom Flavia on the Palatine and therefore remained a part of its su structure, and in the famous room of the Villa of Livia at Prin Porta (Mus. Naz. Romano; VII, PL. 208), which is of the Cla dian period. However, in other buildings the complicate partitioning becomes whimsical — as, for example, in Nero Domus Aurea (cf. VII, PL. 215), about which our only sourc of knowledge are old drawings and engravings and some sca remains which tell us that the palace owes its name to the go leaf applied to stucco moldings. But a wealth of similar, eve though minor, geometric motifs is found in the stuccoes the Portico of Caligula in the Domus Tiberiana on the Palatir and in the House of the Golden Cupids in Pompeii. On the oth hand, a cryptoporticus of the Villa of Domitian at Castel Gandol contains a solemn, figural wall decoration. Figures with a scul tured appearance, molded with a monumental feeling, are see on the balconies of a building with Style IV wall decoratio (see HELLENISTIC ART), whose panels contain smaller mythologic scenes. A counterpart in the provincial style is a similar Pompeia wall in Naples (A. Ruesch, *Guida illustrata del Museo Naziona di Napoli*, 1911, nos. 828–30); in Pompeii the walls of the Temp of Isis as well as those of the Stabian Baths (PL. 270) have simila decoration but of a higher order. Also noteworthy is the friez with scenes from the *Iliad* in the House of the Cryptoporticu (PL. 271).

The large stucco vaults in Hadrian's Villa at Tivoli are in th unmistakable style of the Emperor — who revitalized the Gree artistic legacy, but via a cool and academic Neo-Attic vision c it. As in all other fields, here too there is a clear division betwee the products belonging to the imperial circle and those whicl in contrast, arose out of the taste of the popular culture (se ROMAN IMPERIAL ART; ITALO-ROMAN FOLK ART).

In the 2d century stucco was widely used, and this is conspic uously documented by several sumptuous tombs. The stucc left white, was particularly fine and smooth and was worked wit a refined craftsmanship that proves the existence of a class o highly expert artisans. The principal tombs are the catacom under the Church of S. Sebastiano in Rome, which has ceiling with hexagons and grapevine leaves, and the Tomb of the Valer on Via Latina (VII, PL. 215), in which the vault is divided int squares and circles, as in similar painted tombs, but by a patter of moldings of extreme lightness and precision of carving. O its walls there are small mythological figures in small square supported by twining acanthus also enclosing small figures Again in the coeval Tomb of the Pancratii appears the use o squares containing figures of a certain type together with colore

ackgrounds that relieve the brightness of the stuccowork.
lore magnificent, indeed monumental, is the Tomb of the Va-
rii in the necropolis under St. Peter's. It has large, almost
fe-size figures placed in the niches in the walls. The figures
nd the architectural elements are all in stucco. A columba-
um, unfortunately destroyed, which was formerly on the Via
ortuense had a vault studded with circles, and every niche in
ne loculi terminated in a shell.

A unique funerary monument is the one from Thuburbo
Iajus in Tunis (Mus. du Bardo), datable in the second half
f the 2d century. On a large square base surmounted by a
linth with floral borders are stucco reliefs with a *sella curulis*
nd scenes of the subjugation of the barbarians. A similar
ucco relief in New York (Met. Mus., acc. no. 09.221.37)
nows a barbarian kneeling before the emperor Antoninus Pius
. 138–161).

In the latter part of the 2d century stucco was also used in
lithraeums for sculptural compositions of considerable size
nd interest. The most important is the one with Mithras and
ne bull under the Church of S. Prisca in Rome. Besides this
rge relief there were other, secondary figures here, also exe-
uted in stucco. The scantiness of the remains makes it impossi-
le to form a precise idea of the style of these works. In Rome
nere was another stucco relief, now lost, in a Mithraeum near
ne Ponte Mammolo. An inscription in Stixneusiedl, Austria, doc-
ments a similar relief of the same period, when this site was
art of the ancient Roman province of Noricum.

The 3d century is rather scant of stuccowork. However,
ne vault of the large mausoleum called the Tor de' Schiavi
lust have been decorated with stucco coffers. The mausoleum
nat was later transformed into the Church of S. Marina at
rdea, near Rome, had similar decoration. Tomb N in the ne-
ropolis of the Isola Sacra at Ostia is more remarkable, not
nly for all its figural scenes, inspired by episodes from the heroic
oems and from mythology, but also because the stucco figurines
ere executed in the workshop, perhaps by means of molds,
nd then attached to the wall with metal supports, instead of
eing modeled directly on the wall in the usual way.

Also notable for its singularity is a cylindrical stucco beak-
r depicting Adam in the terrestrial paradise (Rome, Coll. A.
onsoli; photos 656–60, Mus. Pepoli, Trapani). In all prob-
bility this served as a model for ivory or bone engraving
r for metal embossing. Its date cannot be earlier than the end
f the 4th century.

Stucco was used as a coating for architecture and sculpture
n Spain during the 3d and 4th centuries, as is documented at
'arragona and Barcelona by statues, by tombstones decorated
ith a cross, and by other monuments. Stuccowork also existed
n the churches of Africa, where its use continued until the 5th
entury.

Michelangelo CAGIANO DE AZEVEDO

Late antiquity, Byzantium, and medieval Europe. Stuccowork continued to be used as a complement to architecture,
nd in northern Italy it was used in the ornamentation of arches
nd vaults in the Roman fashion and as an intermediate band
etween the marble socle and the mosaics. An ancient example
s found in the Church of S. Lorenzo Maggiore in Milan (ca.
25): the band of leaves and fruit in the splay of a window em-
rasure.

Of prime importance are the polychromed stuccoes in the
ctagonal Baptistery of the Orthodox in Ravenna (PL. 273; IX,
LS. 45, 66, 72; X, PL. 441). The stuccowork ornaments the
pper of two superposed arcades; this upper arcade forms an
ntermediate zone between the ground story and the cupola.
On each of the eight sides of the structure the decoration of this
one is articulated in a motif of three arches supported by col-
mns. In each triplet of arches the central, larger, one frames
he window, while the smaller, side, ones contain aediculas,
ne with a semicircular and one with a triangular pediment.
n each aedicula a prophet is represented in high relief against
n illusionistic perspective background. The prophets (the
ork of many artists) are dressed in tunic and fluttering pallium,
vith a book or scroll in hand, and depicted in the act of taking

a step. In each of the pediments of the aediculas there is a shell,
and in the spaces above the pediments and beneath the arches
there are pairs of small confronted animals flanking a vase or
basket and episodes from the Old and New Testaments: Daniel and the lions, Christ trampling the lion and the adder,
Jonah and the whale (for symmetry, two whales), and Christ
flanked by the apostles Peter and Paul (*Traditio legis*). Among
the minor features of the stucco decoration is the ornamentation
of the soffits of the arches: bands of rosettes and of vine motifs
and some compartments with representations of birds. Each
of the triplets of arches is embraced by a large arch, and the
lunettes of these eight main arches were originally embellished
with stuccowork executed in a technique still partly classical;
unfortunately this was destroyed in the 19th century in the mistaken belief that it represented 17th-century restoration, and
the rich designs of animal and plant motifs have been reproduced
in modern fresco painting.

The style and details of the compositions and the subjects
represented in these stuccoes lead us to believe that they are
all of the same period as the mosaics (ca. 450). The theory
that they are works from the time of Maximian, Archbishop
of Ravenna 546–56, even if plausible from certain aspects, is
not substantiated by the evidence (Kostof, 1965).

In the Church of Sta Croce in Ravenna, now for the most
part destroyed, there were, according to the 9th-century chronicler Agnellus, gilded and silvered stuccoes ("gipsea metala
sculta"; *Codex pontificalis ecclesiae ravennatis*, ed. A. Testi-
Rasponi, Bologna, 1924, p. 119), and the Basilica Ursiana, likewise destroyed, had similar stuccowork, in panels with human
figures and animals ("et hinc atque illinc gipseis metalis diversa
hominum animaliumque et quadrupedum enigmata inciserunt
et valde optime composuerunt"; *ib.*, p. 67).

Stuccowork in the Byzantine ambit was ornamental in character and of moderate importance. In the Church of S. Vitale
in Ravenna (PL. 273), the heavy rinceaux with flat, thick acanthus
leaves, deeply grooved in the middle, that adorn one wall are
directly comparable with those of the frames of the side entrance
to the esonarthex of Hagia Sophia, in Constantinople, which
is of the 6th century. A barrel vault divided into coffers has large
leaves of isolated vines reminiscent of the cornices in the women's
galleries in Hagia Sophia. The rinceaux in the arches in S. Vitale are similar to those on the wall: in one arch, cornucopias
were added; in another, there are thin rinceaux that wind into
classicizing volutes, round as a cord in section, from which
leaves and small clusters branch off. The motifs in the arcades
of the lower floor of the presbytery are geometrical: juxtaposed
circles with small rosettes and overlapping leaves and tangential
octagons with varied rosettes.

There are also 6th-century stucco decorations in the soffits
of the arches of the left aisle in the Euphrasian Cathedral in
Poreč, Yugoslavia. However, the composition here is closer
to the classical tradition. It can be surmised that in Ravenna's
S. Vitale labored Constantinopolitan craftsmen and in Poreč
local stuccoworkers, firmly anchored to the Roman taste for
breadth and variety of motif. The geometric motifs at Poreč
are various: circles alternating with hexagons, octagons alternating with small squares, circles alternating with rhombi, and tangential and overlapping circles. In the coffers there are small
animals and flowers. One of the soffits is decorated with cornucopias and tenuous acanthus leaves and with large volutes
filled with baskets of fruit and palmettes.

In the West during the 7th, 8th, and 9th centuries, stucco
was used for large sculptural compositions. Appropriately
gilded and enriched with spherules of vitreous pastes, it was
used to imitate large works of goldsmithery. This was the result
of the enthusiasm for precious metals and gems, the prohibitive
cost of mosaics with glass tesserae, the declining taste for massiveness in sculpture, and the gradual abandonment of the stone
quarries.

There are numerous references to stucco in the early sources:
Isidore of Seville, at the beginning of the 7th century, and Rabanus Maurus and the Caroline Books, in the 9th century, cite
stucco, together with painting, marble, wood, and terra cotta,
as a medium for the creation of images. The life of St. Angilbert

by Anscher speaks of large stucco compositions — gilded like mosaics and colored ("mirifico opere ex gipso figuratae et auro musivo aliisque pretiosis coloribus pulcherrime compositae sunt") — representing the Passion, the Ascension, the Resurrection, and the Nativity.

Nothing has come down to us from the 7th century, but the use of stucco, together with mosaic, in the no-longer-extant Church of St-Saturnin of Angers, which was founded in that century, is noted in a life (ca. 1100) of the Bishop of Angers at the time of the church's founding. But there are evidences, notable for quality if not for quantity, ascribed to the 8th, 9th, and 10th centuries; the stuccoes in question were used alone in figural and decorative ensembles and also as frames and ornamentation for frescoes. Unfortunately, their chronology is as yet controversial.

The stucco decorations attributed to the 8th century consist of graceful openwork motifs with grape leaves and clusters branching in a double row from a light, undulating stem; palmettes; small intertwining arches; and rosettes with slender radiating leaves. This type of ornament is seen in two Italian structures generally assigned to the 8th century: the Church of S. Maria in Valle in Cividale del Friuli and the Church of S. Salvatore in Brescia (PLS. 274, 275). In all probability these motifs and the use of the openwork technique reflect Byzantine influence; motifs of exactly the same type, consonant with the taste then current in eastern Mediterranean regions, are found in Ommiad monuments, which were in many cases executed by Byzantine artists.

At Cividale, the figures of saints aligned against a wall (PL. 274; XI, PL. 324), some wearing magnificent jewel-studded robes and holding ornate crowns or orbiculi, are precious monuments of Byzantinizing fashion and taste. The airy rinceaux with openwork grape leaves and clusters on the arch of the entrance door and the terminal fretwork seem to be of the period of the Ommiad palaces of Qaṣr al-Ḥayr al-Gharbī (727) and Khirbat al-Mafjar (ca. 740) and of the pulpit panels at Kairouan (862–63; see OMMIAD SCHOOLS). However, there is also a suggestion of barbarian art in the knotted, Nordic interlace in the armilla of the window as well as in the openwork palmettes. The frescoes, with frontal figures of saints against an architectural perspective background, also appear to be inspired by early Byzantine taste; they may originally have appeared as large enamels in a brilliant composition of imitation goldwork. In fact, the glass cabochons set in the centers of the daisies of the horizontal band and of the archivolt of the doorway in imitation of precious stones correspond to the gems represented in the robes of the saints.

Similar ornaments, with the typical glass spherules (PL. 275), are found in the stuccoes of the intrados and of the cornices of the arches in the Church of S. Salvatore in Brescia, which has been excavated and reconstructed with care and skill. Under the floors of this church were also discovered foundations of an older building, but the closeness of the Brescian pieces to those of Cividale in style and technique has led many scholars to ascribe this three-aisled church to the time of King Desiderius and Queen Ansa, founders of the monastery — that is, to the period 756–76. In S. Salvatore the walls of the nave had fresco panels, and the archivolts below were decorated with stuccoes showing wickerlike interlace, leaf rinceaux and grape clusters, and large rosettes with diagonal palmettes (a typical motif of the 8th cent.; cf. the tympanum and pluteus, Mus. Arch., Cividale del Friuli). In the arched lintels there were small intertwined arches, acanthus leaves, and interlace; in the smooth band there were daisies with glass insets. The third quarter of the 8th century is the dating allowed by the majority of scholars, but others propose the Ottonian period, pointing out the relation between the stuccoes of Cividale and the frescoes in the Church of S. Sebastiano al Palatino in Rome, which may date from 977–99, and the 10th-century Byzantine frescoes in southern Italy. The 10th-century dating of the stuccoes in S. Salvatore in Brescia is subscribed to by their discoverer.

The stuccoes of the Church of St. Martin in Disentis (Grisons), which come from a large figural composition, also appear to go back to the 8th century. Unfortunately, it was not possible

to reassemble the many fragments of figures (more than seven heads, in addition to hands, feet, and pieces of garments), o naments, and frames; these are stored in cases in a room of t monastery.

Great interest attaches to the stuccoes of Malles Venosi which are unanimously ascribed to the beginning of the 9 century. They framed the frescoes in the three apses of the ba wall of S. Benedetto, a small church that was a chapel of t monastery of nearby Münster (founded ca. 800). There were s small columns with Nordic openwork interlace, capitals su mounted by wild animals, and archivolts with palmettes ar rinceaux having stems strung with cornucopias and a bord of double openwork arches.

In the 9th century the artistic picture changed because t direct influence of Byzantium ceased; after this, even thou Constantinople abandoned many of its outposts, there was continuation of the frequent influx into Italy of Byzanti works of art, which were imported and sought after becau of their magnificence and the value placed upon them.

The relative certainty of their dating (ca. 806) lends impo tance to the stucco fragments from the oratory in Germigny des-Prés. These pieces (Orléans, Mus. B.-A.) include rosette broad and flat interlace, and rinceaux with shallow-groove leaves.

This technique and this sculptural style, which present flat and sfumato modeling, appear again in the ornamentatic of the ciborium in the Church of S. Ambrogio in Milan (X PL. 325), another of the important monuments whose dating controversial. This work consists of four arches surmounted h pediments. On the tympanums are represented the Redeem between SS. Peter and Paul; St. Ambrose between SS. Gerv sius and Protasius, who are embracing two monks, one of who is offering a model of the ciborium; a holy bishop venerated t two men bowed in prayer; and a female saint venerated by tv women (PL. 278). Many of the iconographic elements — tt attitudes, the jeweled crowns, the angels, the hands, and tt dove that appears behind the heads of the saints — go bac to a very ancient tradition; and, as has been indicated, the rii ceaux and interweaving arches may well be attributed on tt basis of design and technique to the 9th century. In contras the internal vault, a ribbed cross, is Romanesque, and certai details, such as the little leaves on the bands under the feet the personages and on the upper borders of the pediments well as the treatment of the folds and certain postures of tt figures, find parallels in the Ottonian period. An assured chro ological attribution is not possible, though on the basis of tt form of the horseshoe arches and the placing of the bases of tt columns on the Early Christian floor an attribution to the tin of Angilbert, Bishop of Milan (824–59), might be considere On the other hand, the supporters of the later, Ottonian, datir have many valid arguments.

Other Italian examples from the 9th century are the remai of a ceiling with Carolingian daisies in stucco and fragmen of a cornice found in the crypts of S. Prassede (817) and S. Marc in Rome (827–44). In France, a capital in the crypt of the Churc of St-Germain in Auxerre should be noted (III, PL. 49).

The stuccoes in the vault of the Chapel of St. Ulrich in Mür ster, Switzerland, which decorate the lintels of the arches wit rich foliage and the diagonal arches of the cross vault with sma curving vine branches, can probably be dated to the end of th 10th century. On the imposts appear the symbols of the Evar gelists, and in the pendentives of the vault there are four ange (PL. 275).

The stuccoes of the arches in the crypt of the Church c S. Salvatore in Brescia consist of thin leaves in profile, some c which are curled. A fragment with frontal acanthus leaves be tween two rows of small beads has been excavated. The techniqu in these stuccoes is quite different from that used in the uppe church. Considering the simplicity of the layout of the cryp it is not unlikely that these stuccoes belong to the end of the 10t or the beginning of the 11th century.

The stuccoes in the crypt of the Abbey church (consecrate 1021) in Quedlinburg, Germany, should also be attributed t the Ottonian period. It has pillars and intermediate archivol ith leaves on small twisted columns. Of a slightly later period the composition representing the Baptism of Christ in the Church of St. Johann in Münster, Switzerland. The iconography is new. The Baptist stands beside Christ, who is emerging from the waves of the river, but he is not making the ritual gesture of baptism. On the other side an angel is holding out a mantle to Jesus, above whose head flies a dove.

Stucco remained in favor during the 11th century until the increasing establishment of stone sculpture caused it to take a secondary role. In France it appears only as ornamentation in the capitals of St-Remi in Reims. In Italy, on the other hand, stucco was employed from 1070 to 1100 in figural compositions and in ornaments in the presbytery of the Church of S. Ambrogio, Milan (I, PL. 384), which was erected in the 11th century. The large arches of the vault were covered by a band of rinceaux in stucco. On the imposts there were the symbols of the Evangelists.

At Lomello, in the Church of S. Maria Maggiore — a building that can be dated about 1070, rather than 1025, on the basis of discoveries made in the course of restoration — there is a stucco torso in relief between the windows, which indicates that here too, as at Cividale del Friuli, there was a procession of saints.

Other stucco elements, perhaps a bit earlier in date, were found in the Church of S. Pietro in Acqui. To a period not far removed can be assigned both the stuccoes and the frescoes that decorate the Church of S. Pietro al Monte in Civate: it is probable that in accordance with the general rule these decorations were contemporaneous with the structure (which is similar to the Church of S. Maria Maggiore in Lomello). An elaborate ciborium incorporates arches with pediments on whose tympanums are represented the Crucifixion, the empty Holy Sepulcher with the Angel and the Marys; Christ between SS. Peter and Paul, and Christ in a mandorla between two angels. The borders of the tympanums are decorated with leaves and scrolls. Two walls of the crypt have enormous compositions in stucco: the Crucifixion, the Dormition of the Virgin, the Presentation of Jesus in the Temple. Rich parastades with rinceaux alternate with figural scenes, and the capitals are also covered with foliage in stucco. The plutei of the church and the crypt are also of stucco; two have rampant animals and two have interlace in a style characteristic of the earliest Romanesque, so the date of about 1080 seems well founded. In the stuccowork at Civate there is also a clearly discernible Byzantine influence, which is a characteristic of much of the sculptural work in this medium in Italy and Germany, as a result of the close cultural as well as political ties between the West and Byzantium during the Ottonian period.

In the church at Aulla in Tuscany there were other stucco fragments from the end of the 11th century (or the beginning of the 12th) — decorative panels and a figure of an abbot.

Stucco was rarely used in Italy in the 12th century. In France there are two known examples of 12th-century stuccowork: the tympanum of Brioude (Haute Loire), which was still intact about 1830 (Christ in a glory flanked by two angels and ten Apostles) but has since for the most part been destroyed, and an ornamental fragment from the archivolt in Alet (Aude).

In contrast, in Germany stucco reliefs and decorations of the 12th century are numerous and important. While in the other countries of Europe the sculptors of the time customarily worked in stone with a chisel, in many German cities the artists, often of great talent, remaining faithful to the ancient tradition, worked and modeled lime and gypsum plaster with a stick. Sometimes, as in the Holy Sepulcher (ca. 1100–20) in the Church of St. Cyriakus in Gernrode, statues of stucco were framed by ornamental bands of stone. Among others, there remain the depictions of Christ (PL. 278) and the Virgin from a "Noli me tangere," the Marys at the Tomb, and a figure of a saint (the Magdalen).

At Gandersheim (1110–25) there are fine statues of Apostles. Two very beautiful torsos of Apostles, richly draped in clinging robes with elaborate borders (ca. 1130–35), come from nearby Clus. In the Cathedral of Erfurt (ca. 1160) an altar decoration shows the Virgin and Child under an arch dominated by the Maiestas Domini. On the sides there are two bishops and underneath, in a row, eight martyrs.

A fine, though little-known, stucco sculpture is the large parapet from a Benedictine church in Gröningen, Westphalia. In the center of this work (East Berlin, Staat. Mus.) Christ is shown enthroned in the heavens; from his open hands two scrolls unroll toward the Apostles, ten in number, seated on high-backed chairs on either side.

The latest of the monumental works in this group are associated with Hildesheim and Halberstadt. From the Church of St. Michael in Hildesheim come the pleasing images of saints (ca. 1186) in the Staatliche Museen in East Berlin. Dressed in clinging, pleated garments that appear to reflect the Byzantine tradition, they are depicted unrolling scrolls. Conserved in the church itself are two large compositions (ca. 1197) on the choir screens, which are articulated into blind arches. The northern one (PL. 278) is enlivened with representations of the Virgin and Apostles standing under canopies with lobed cupolas and buildings seen in perspective. The last important German figural composition in stucco is the relief in the Liebfrauenkirche in Halberstadt (end of 12th cent.) with Christ and Apostles framed in arches. The attitudes and drapery are already close to the Gothic taste.

Minor remains of stucco ornamentation are preserved in other churches in Germany. Notable among these are capitals in the monastery churches of Drübeck, Ilsenburg, and Bad Segeberg and in the Cathedral of Lübeck, as well as doorways in Ratekau and Süsel. Of particular interest are the three tomb slabs of the abbesses in the collegiate church of Quedlinburg (ca. 1130), which are very similar to the figures in Clus. It was the tradition of the convent to have such funerary reliefs executed in stucco; others, dating up to the end of the 12th century, have also been found there.

                                                         Daria De Bernardi

IRAN, INDIA, AND CENTRAL ASIA. Stucco with a base of plaster, generally mixed with other materials (as a rule, powdered marble), was frequently used in Iranian art. The artists of the Parthian and Sassanian periods achieved magnificent effects in figural as well as ornamental architectural decoration both by molding fresh plaster and by carving into a thick facing of hardened plaster. The type of monuments — for example, the palaces with vast ceremonial halls (liwans) — offered large surfaces to be decorated, and the construction materials employed (brick and ashlar) entailed the use of facings and veneers. Hence the importance assumed by stucco, a medium in which the richness of polychrome could be added to the nuances of the relief and the variety of motifs.

Architectural stuccoes assumed great importance in this area as early as the Parthian period (3d cent. B.C.–3d cent. of our era). The façade is known to have been the object of particular attention on the basis of the reconstruction of the elaborate stucco decoration of the façade of the Parthian palace of Ashur (Assur). Beautiful stucco decorations were also discovered by E. Herzfeld in the Parthian palace on the island of Kuh-i-Khwaja on Lake Hamun (1st cent.). Hollowed-out triangles and other motifs derived from the Greek meander are seen side by side with Asiatic merlons, and an entire panel is decorated with a pattern of overlapping circles.

The remains from the Sassanian period (3d–7th cent.) are more numerous and better known. Though the great rupestral reliefs are the masterpieces of Sassanian sculpture, the figural stucco works are by no means unimportant. Some of these were produced by fine artists working in the tradition of stone sculpture. Stucco busts and heads drawing inspiration from the stone sculptures of Hatra were a part of architectural ensembles; such were the busts of Shāpur II (or of Bahrām Gūr) and of the queen that must have adorned the façade of the palace of Kish; such were the women's heads incised in square panels that, again at Kish, alternate with fleurons on the barrel vaults of a liwan. Although the busts and heads in high relief are not, properly speaking, portraits, nevertheless they give an impression of strength and dignity that suggests the high rank of the personages represented.

STUCCO

Quite exceptionally, a work composed of plaques separately molded and then assembled draws its inspiration from a theme glorifying the *roi chasseur* represented in the scenes of the royal hunt in rupestral bas-reliefs. Such a panel in the Philadelphia Museum of Art, probably representing Fīrūz II, or Peroz (457–84), is made up of six units: in one plaque the king is shown attacked by two boars, which in another plaque he overcomes. The two panels that form the middle section show the whole herd of boars in rout.

Many stucco works, while still of a figural character, nevertheless primarily fulfilled a decorative function. Numerous motifs — for example, women's heads framed by foliage and animals (mythical or real) enclosed in a beaded circle — were incised on easily assembled quadrangular panels. Two tendencies exist side by side in the representation of animals; either naturalism predominates or a decorative stylization schematizes the forms. The famous boar's head from Damghan, the winged dragon with peacock's tail (simurgh), the wings and fluttering ribbons accompanying a mouflon, are heraldic in style, while the representations of the bear, the watering deer, or the running dog are pleasing for their vitality and naturalness. Sometimes the two tendencies coexist in one motif, as in the rearing ibexes flanking a tree, a motif that comes down from the ancient and symbolic tree of life.

Ctesiphon, Kish, Bishapur, and Damghan are the principal sites that have yielded figural decorative remains together with others of a more exclusively ornamental nature (XII, PL. 399). In the latter category diverse elements meet: architectural, geometric, and plant-form. Purely architectural ornament is rather limited: moldings (including the Egyptian "gorge", or cavetto, above niches; Firuzabad, |3d cent.), friezes of niches with concave tympanums adorned with a shell, and frames of horizontal and vertical bands.

The panels covering the walls afforded the possibility of juxtaposing geometric motifs in every direction. The simplest elements are broken lines and series of hollowed-out circles and concentric lozenges. The meander patterns are sometimes elaborated by being intertwined through the elongation of one of the arms or being arranged diagonally. Tangential circles are also subject to variation: interlacing divides each circle into four sections, thus creating quatrefoil motifs, to which are joined elongated petals or a linear pattern.

Plant motifs are no less important in the decorative repertory. Sometimes, as in the case of the motif formed by supple stems, grape leaves, and very often grape clusters (Ṭāq-i-Bustān, Ctesiphon), the ornamentation is in a free style. In other cases it is more conventional and is dominated by geometric and linear designs; the acanthus leaf, stylized, devitalized, and treated as a polylobed palmette, frequently appears in this type of ornamentation. Sometimes four palmettes are arranged crosswise, forming a quadrangular pattern that can combine with medallions. Half palmettes, or folded acanthus leaves in profile, are seen in numerous combinations: forming a frame around other elements, such as the pomegranate; or, in series of opposing pairs, forming a more or less complex rinceau; or with the profiled leaves addorsed and forming a fleuron within a heart-shaped motif created by the in-curving stems. The art of Islam, like the art of Central Asia (Turkistan, Russia, China), also took up these variations and drew extensively upon the vast decorative repertory created in the art of stuccowork. Certain patterns even reached China by way of Tun-huang (q.v.). As in Sassanian Iran, and notably during the same period, sculptured and painted stucco had also been used extensively in Chorasmia and Sogdiana (q.v.), where geometric and floral patterns adorned the stuccoed walls of the great halls of Toprakkala (3d cent.) and Varakhsha (ca. 6th cent.).

During the first six centuries of our era, stucco was used extensively at only a few sites in the various provinces extending from the Punjab to Bactria. This immense area, unified at the beginning of this period by the powerful Kushan dynasty, saw the emergence and evolution of a Buddhist art that was very distinctive though born of various influences. But in Gandhara as in Swat (the great centers of the development of this art) schist was the principal material used in sculpture and in architectural ornamentation, and it was only from about t end of the 3d century, and near the borders of this region (Ta ila, in the Punjab, and Hadda, near Jalalabad), that the use stucco became general and led to a renewal of artistic tren (PL. 272; VI, PL. 20).

However, finds made at Taxila in the Scytho-Parthi city of Sirkap show that the use of stucco was already knov from the beginning of our era. The court of an apsidal temp was decorated with bas-reliefs made of a mixture of lime a small pieces of broken stone. The heads worked in this rath coarse stucco combine Hellenistic contributions such as the typ of the satyr and the bearded thinker (VI, PL. 14) with loc details such as turbans. At the other end of the Kushan territor at Kunduz, in Bactria, in a small monastery of uncertain da (ca. 3d cent.?), some heads fashioned of plaster of medioc quality were discovered by J. Hackin (II, PLS. 85, 88). T features, classical in type, in some cases softened and Orient izing, are framed by thick curls, and one of the heads wea the tall Iranian headgear known as a Phrygian cap (II, PL. 8 A few plaster face masks have been found at Shotorak, b elsewhere, in the numerous monasteries along the old rou from Hadda to Bactra, clay mixed with horsehair or shredd straw and covered with a thin coat of plaster was used in li of stone or true stucco. At Bamian (3d–7th cent.), Tepe Maren zhap, and Fondukistan (7th cent.) this inferior material, pain ed, was used in the same way as stucco for the ornamental faci of walls and ceilings, and for reliefs. As with stucco, a layer clay mixed with other materials, and rather thin in proportio coated the coarse surface of the colossal Buddhas of Bami and the mass of modeled clay in the *personnages* of Fonduk stan (VIII, PLS. 4, 6, 7). At both sites sculptural motifs bo rowed from the decorative repertory of Iran or of Kushan ar Gupta India complemented the architecture.

The rise of the Indo-Afghan school appears to have coincid with the decline of the sculpture workshops of Gandhara, which the schist that was readily available in the locality ha been almost solely used. The favor found by stucco seems tally not only with reasons of economy and of ease of productic of this material in regions remote from quarries but also wi an evolution of taste and of artistic tendencies, since in t Gandharan sites of Takht-i-Bahi and Sahr-i-Bahlol stucco scul tures are found side by side with stone. They belong to a rath late period (4th–5th cent.?), often to that of the rebuilding monuments, as attested by the sanctuary of Butkara I at Mingo (Swat), which has been brought to light by Italian excavation

The great centers of development of this school were t numerous monasteries of Hadda and those located near t Kushan city of Taxila, which were built, rebuilt, or enlarge during the 4th and 5th centuries (e.g., Jaulian, Mohrā Morādu At these sites, and during this period, stucco was used to fa the masonry of every type of building: stupa, chapel, and ha Accessory to architecture, it served for the creation of sculptur as well as ornamental decoration. Being a very hard materi it was used for the pilasters, capitals, cornices, arcades, and co soles that decorated the various stories of the stupa. The ca itals were most frequently of a pseudo-Corinthian type in whic modified acanthi were variously interpreted, sometimes wi small Buddhas or animals interspersed among them. Crouchir warriors, bearded figures, and winged genii served as atlante Series of niches separated by pilasters were aligned on the bas or drums of the stupas. These niches, which were surmounte by molded arcades — trapezoidal, arched, or trilobed — frame statues of the Buddha, who was sometimes accompanied b disciples. The decoration was modeled in the fresh stucco, the heightened with colors (yellow, red, black) and sometimes wit gilt; black often served to accentuate the relief by substitutin for or intensifying shadows. The statues were executed separate and later attached by means of sticks, which formed tenon According to Barthoux (1930), the stucco employed was har and of good quality; it was made of pulverized limestone an siccative oil or glue. Apricot gum and even egg yolk may hav been used as binding agents.

The statues, the backs of which were always placed again the wall of the stupas or chapels, represented the Buddh

ated, standing at ease, or walking. In larger works — some which were colossal — the bodies were made of artificial ndstone or clay coated with a layer of stucco, and folds were odeled in this medium. The head was made separately, the ce, of the classical type, being molded, while the hair and the rs, which were added on, were modeled, as were all works smaller size.

Stupas of smaller dimensions were decorated with numerous s-reliefs, arranged in friezes or framed by arcades. But rtually all that has remained of this decoration in its profusion d animation is a number of small heads. At Hadda, in partic- ar, these show great diversity and an extreme intensity of pression: the smiling and adorned heads of divinities or laymen e seen side by side with the harsh features of barbarians and arriors, while the faces of kindly young monks or grave and nsive ascetics contrast with the terrifying and monstrous deousness of demons. At Taxila a few groups are better pre- rved, and in the retinue of the Buddha there are sometimes nors wearing the local Kushan costume.

Although the stucco art of Hadda and Taxila at first borrowed s forms, themes, and patterns from the schist art of Gandhara, modified them and infused them with new life. Suppleness, imation, and imagination are in general the predominant qual- ies of works modeled in stucco — a technique that also calls r skill and spontaneity of execution. The postures and the apery are also remarkable for their naturalness and freedom, e folds and fabrics of the costumes allowing the modeling and xibility of the body to be discerned. Only the hair of the Bud- na, at first wavy and *mouvante*, tended to become schematized d conventional in more evolved pieces. This marked the be- nning of one of the tendencies in Central Asian art (Tarim asin) that borrowed so many details from the works of Hadda. hus the Gandhara school of stucco diffused its traditions in rious directions, often to remote regions. The Buddhist nters of Kashmir are its most direct successors; at Akhnur well as Uskur (7th–8th cent.), works in terra cotta or un- aked clay took up and modified its forms.

True gypsum-based stucco was used only sporadically in hinese Turkistan. In the Buddhist centers that extended helonwise to the north and south of the Tarim Basin the scar- ty of stone and even of lime for the making of stucco led to e use primarily of clayey earth mixed with vegetable or animal bers. However, stucco was not unknown in this region; it as used for certain rather exceptional large images — for stance, a colossal Buddha of which fragments in hard stucco ere found by Pelliot at Maurī-Tim, near Kashgar. Stucco was so employed for smaller pieces and, when mixed with hard aterials, for the molds designed to obtain the various sculptural d architectural decorative elements made of clay. A. von Le oq also reported that at Kumtura — and in rupestral sanctuaries a few other sites — the cult images of the seated Buddha were metimes coarsely carved in stone and then coated with a layer f modeled stucco. The head was made separately, and only e stone core has survived. Plaster was also used for the paint- pavements of both excavated and constructed sanctuaries Tumshuk, Kizil, etc.), and some fragile figurines of pure plaster ere found at Tumshuk (PL. 272; I, PL. 476), Duldur-akhur, horchuk, and other sites; some of these figurines were rein- rced by means of a small interior rod of iron. Stucco may have een more easily obtainable at sites located on the South Road f the Silk Route), where Sir Aurel Stein reported its use for the cing of walls and the bas-reliefs placed against them (e.g., Rawak) and for sanctuary sculptures. At Dandan-uilik in articular a hard material described as plaster of Paris was found. he works in clay were also primed for painting with a thin yer of whitewash or plaster; thus the classification of the mate- al as "stuccoed clay" is warranted.

Aside from texture, there is nothing to distinguish the few orks of true stucco from those of relatively fine clay. Both ere modeled only rarely; generally molded, they were painted colors and sometimes gilded with gold leaf. In the case of edium-size and large images, a wooden armature covered with raw or bundles of reeds served as support for the head and arious parts of the body. For these, a mass of rather coarse clay was sketchily shaped on the armature; next, a layer of finer and more homogeneous material — stucco or clay — was applied over this rough figure. It was then modeled (for the body) or else received the imprint of a mold for its final form, which was often complemented by the application of separately molded details (jewelry of all sorts; various elements of costume and hairdress). Sculpture in the round was virtually unknown, and subjects treated in high relief were placed against the wall, to which they were secured by means of wooden pegs.

In the monasteries of Central Asia, sculpture played much the same role as it did in those of Hadda and Taxila. Cult images of the Buddha (in some cases colossal), of the bodhisattvas, of secondary deities or guardians of the temples and of space (*dvā- rapāla, lokapala*) were placed in the sanctuaries; statues of the Buddha or bas-reliefs of various sizes were aligned on the stupas or in the chapels; and sculptural ornamentation was abundant. Various elements hark back to classical origins (the Gorgonian mask, the laureled torus) or to Indian sources (undulating stems, the lotus rosette), but many go back principally to the repertory of Sassanian Iran (checkerboard patterns, rinceaux with poly- lobed leaves, birds). Although the iconography, the themes, and the forms appear to have been borrowed at first, from the tradi- tions of the Gandhara school of stucco, their artistic realization soon — during the 5th and 6th centuries — took on a distinctive aspect. Various contributions from Gupta India, Sassanian Iran, and Sogdiana came to be mingled together and transformed by local taste, which tended to render all elements more decorative and often more conventional. Thus it produced an original style that was later (after the 7th cent.) modified by Chinese influences, chiefly in the Turfan region.

Madeleine HALLADE

THE ISLAMIC WORLD. Stucco, inherited from Hellenistic art via the Byzantines, the Sassanids, and the Buddhists of Cen- tral Asia, has played a most important role in Islamic art (see ISLAM and related articles referred to therein). For one thing, the desert climate of North Africa, Spain, and southwest and Cen- tral Asia is very favorable to its preservation. In addition, the shortage of good stone and of timber in many parts of these areas recommends stucco as the best material available locally for the exterior and, more especially, the interior embellishment of buildings. And then the character of Islamic decoration, the coating of vast surfaces with intricate patterns of infinitely var- ied designs rich in contrasts of light and color, demanded an easily moldable, low-cost medium. It follows that no design is peculiar to stucco: the motifs used might be executed as well in other materials. Though stucco dominated the vast interior wall surfaces, conspicuous details such as mihrabs, tombstones, and entrance arches would be executed in marble or tiles, and ceiling beams, mimbars, tomb screens, and doors in wood; exteriors would be executed in sun- or kiln-baked bricks, the cruder workmanship sufficing for the view from a distance. Generally stucco was applied direct to the rough (rubble or brick) wall; in North Africa and Spain it was also molded into large slabs mounted on a wooden framework. The complicated *mu- qarnas* ceilings of later times were also in many cases modeled over a wooden skeleton.

Several techniques of stucco carving evolved. The seminat- uralistic imitation of floral and even figural motifs was still known during the Ommiad caliphate of Syria (661–750) but not later. Two stucco-carving techniques came to predominate: one entailed cutting vertically into the flat surface, leaving the design raised as on a printing block; in the other the cutting was done so as to achieve a beveled edge. The former technique was applied sometimes in several layers, the deeper ones forming a background for the more prominent principal design; sometimes the outlines were rounded off, or rounding off was combined with the beveling of motifs; sometimes the larger surfaces were roughened by a technique of picking holes in them, which created a rich chiaroscuro effect. In most cases the stucco reliefs were painted — gilt, red, and cobalt blue (sometimes also green and black) serving for the background, and gold, white, yellow, and red for the foreground. From the 10th to the 14th century, human and animal figures in heraldic style were occasionally introduced.

The chief regions in which stucco decoration was prominent were Iraq, Iran, and Turkistan, North Africa west of Egypt, and northwestern India. During the period of their dominance the fashion for stucco spread to Syria, Egypt, Turkey, and central India and the Deccan; with their decline it was supplanted by stone decoration. After the 12th century, and at an increasing rate in the period of the 14th–17th century, stucco was all but superseded in the sphere of Irano-Turkic culture by polychrome tiles, but it retained its importance for the intricate muqarnas ceilings.

In Ommiad Syria stucco decoration was used as early as the time of the Great Mosque of Damascus (705-11; X, PL. 378), the Qaṣr-al Ḥayr al-Gharbī (40 mi. from Palmyra), and, most notably, the palace of Khirbat al-Mafjar (near Jericho), erected by Hishām, with its amazing figural sculptures in the Sassanian and ancient Eastern tradition, even including a portrait statue (X, PL. 382). In the period of the Abbasside caliphs of Baghdad (750–1258) stucco became the most common medium of decoration (I, PL. 4). The walls of the palaces of Samarra (VIII, PL. 151) reveal four different tendencies, reflecting Hellenistic, Iranian, and Central Asian sources (in the last-mentioned the beveled technique predominated). The Samarra style spread to Iran, where it was a factor in the 10th century and survived even into the 12th, and to Egypt, where its principal monument is the Mosque of Ibn-Ṭūlūn (XIV, PL. 191). In Egypt it continued to be in fashion also under the Fatimid caliphs [909–1171; the mosques of al-Ḥākim, al-Azhar (both, V, PL. 246), and al-Guyūshī, the Mashhad of Sayyida Ruqayya, etc., in Cairo], but afterwards played only a subsidiary role (Mosque of Sultan Ḥasan, tomb of the daughter of Barsbāī, etc.). However, it became the most common form of decoration in the Maghrib, from Tunisia to Morocco [Tunis, Tlemcen (X, PL. 165), Timmal, Fez, Marrakech, Rabat, etc.] and in Spain [Great Mosque of Córdoba (PL. 277), Patio del Yeso in the Alcázar of Seville, the Alhambra and Generalife in Granada, the Aljafería in Saragossa, etc.]. The most famous monuments are in North Africa and Spain: the Saʿadid tombs in Marrakech (16th cent.) and the Alhambra (14th cent.), both of an astonishing wealth of intricate ornamental designs. The tradition continued also in Christian Spain.

The best-known monuments of the Mudejar style are the Alcázar of Seville, the chapel of the Alcázar of Córdoba, the Archbishop's Palace in Alcalá de Henares, and the Church of S. María la Blanca, El Tránsito, the Casa de Mesa, and the Palace of Conde de Esteban in Toledo.

In Iran and Turkistan stuccowork experienced its golden age under Seljuk and early Mongol rule from the 11th through the 14th century [in Qazvin, the Ḥaydariya; in Hamadan, the Gunbad-i-ʿAlaviyān; in Linjan, the Pīr-i-Bakrān; in Bistam, the mausoleum of Bāyazīd al Bisṭāmī; in Isfahan, the Masjid-i-Jāmiʿ (VII, PL. 403); in Varamin, the Masjid-i-Jāmiʿ]. Thereafter, the application of stucco became more and more restricted, until it was used only for the muqarnas ceiling and occasional wall panels (e.g., the Imāmzāda Karrār in Buzan, 1534).

In the late 15th and the early 16th century, stucco decoration had a renaissance in India, especially under the Lōdī and Sūr dynasties of Delhi (Lōdī Mosque at Khairpur, built by Abū-Amjad, 1494) and the Barīdshāhs of Bidar. It even found an echo in the semi-Islamic palaces of the Hindu emperors of Vijayanagar. In late-17th- and 18th-century India stucco was revived as a substitute for marble, but with seminaturalistic floral designs. The same development is seen in the architecture of 18th- and 19th-century Turkey, which paralleled the European rococo.

Hermann GOETZ

PRE-COLUMBIAN AMERICA. Sculpture in stucco, either in the round or in relief, is absent in the civilizations of ethnological interest and appears only within the archaeological civilization of the Mayas, mainly in the classic period. In addition, there are a few exceptional stuccoes from the post-classic period, such as those at Tulum, in Quintana Roo, where some stucco panels that decorated the architrave of the buildings were discovered.

The site where stucco decoration and sculpture reached the highest level was Palenque — in the Palace group and in t̶ crypt of the Temple of the Inscriptions. In the former archite tural complex the façades below and above the central moldi⸜ were decorated with stucco bas-reliefs of exquisite workma⸜ ship (X, PL. 16). In the crypt, besides a fine mural frieze, pro⸜ ably of a religious nature, there have been recovered two stuc⸜ heads, sculptured in the round, which represent one of the lo⸜ iest heights reached by Mayan art of the classic period (VI PL. 398; X, PL. 17).

Works in stucco have also been found in other Mayan ce⸜ ters that were influenced by Palenque. At Comalcalco in Taba⸜ co, about 90 miles northwest of Palenque, three walls of a tom⸜ are decorated with stucco bas-reliefs; on each of these sid⸜ three human figures are depicted. At Acancéh in northe⸜ Yucatán the upper part of the façade of a structure brought light in 1952 was decorated with a stucco panel showing a com⸜ position of animals, birds, and reptiles. Still perceptible a⸜ traces of the original painting, in which a light turquoise col⸜ predominates.

Another fine example of decoration in stucco comes fro⸜ Uaxactún in Petén. Here the sides of the great Pyramid E V sub were ornamented with large stucco masks of anthropomo⸜ phous and ophiomorphous subjects. A recent discovery ma⸜ at Xunantunich, a site in the district of Cayo, British Hondura⸜ is a panel of remarkable size, entirely of stucco, decorated wi⸜ grotesque masks, glyphs, and ornamental figures (PL. 268 It appears that the stucco decoration of façades was comm⸜ in Mayan architecture of the classic period, but owing to t̶ perishability of the material only a small fraction of this stucc⸜ work has survived (see MIDDLE AMERICAN PROTOHISTORY).

* *

EUROPEAN STUCCOWORK FROM THE RENAISSANCE ONWAR⸜ Although the use of stuccowork as architectural decoratic⸜ practically ceased in the period of the International Goth⸜ style, it found special application is some of the minor ar⸜ In late Gothic and early Renaissance furniture, "pastigli⸜ ornamentation was very popular. Modeled in bas-relief ar⸜ gilded or painted, it constituted a rich decoration, especia⸜ on chests (cassoni). An important example of this productio⸜ which fits into the transition style between Gothic and Renai⸜ sance, is a chest with a wedding scene by a Tuscan artist of t̶ early 15th century (PL. 279). Stucco is similarly handled in mar⸜ polyptychs of the period, where halos and rays typically rendere⸜ in low, finely incised relief form elegant connecting elemen⸜ between the painted figures and the gilded areas in the bac⸜ ground. To the mature Renaissance style•(ca. 1475) belongs⸜ magnificent chest, likewise gilded and of Tuscan workmanshi⸜ which is preserved in the Palazzo Venezia in Rome (PL. 279 The figures, which show traces of Antonio Pollaiuolo's mann⸜ (see XI, PL. 184), are strongly modeled on the sides of the ches⸜ enlivening the sobriety of its lines. In another type of che⸜ popular in northern Italy until the mid-16th century, the dens⸜ minute decoration displays the by-now usual arabesques ar⸜ spirals of classicizing type, but with a horror vacui and a⸜ attention to naturalistic detail still partaking of the Internation⸜ Gothic style.

Pastiglia ornament is also found on small caskets used ⸜ hold money and precious objects. Dominant in the decoratic⸜ of these caskets are the brilliant colors of the reliefs, which stan⸜ out against backgrounds likewise painted in vivid colors. Th⸜ typical production "in miniature" has its best-known appl⸜ cation in tabernacles and frames, in some of which the reli⸜ attains effects of particular delicacy.

Stuccowork as a complement of large-scale wooden sculptu⸜ — of which a great many significant examples are known, bot⸜ in the Tuscan region and in the Veneto, in elegant Sansovin⸜ esque renditions of the Virgin and Child — should be mention⸜ here in passing.

A triumphant revival of stuccowork as architectural decor⸜ tion was to take place under the sway of Raphael's genius. Abou⸜ 1515, concurrently with the renewed interest in architectu⸜ and antiquities, there appeared in his work a new type of dec⸜ oration of interiors in which stucco was treated now with a gen⸜

ngraver's sharpness, now with a softness yielding chromatic ffects. It was used alternately with painting in detailed mytho-ogical scenes, putti, and festoons, which conferred on the basic ructure of walls and vaults the illusion of a far more varied terplay of architectural elements.

With the appreciation in the early 16th century for ancient oldwork, toreutics, the refinements of niello decoration, and the reciousness of engraved gems found in excavations, the popular-y of elaborate relief ornament was only to be expected. Stucco elief offered the rapid invention of the modelers a chance to tain effects imitating intaglio, cameo, and inlay of precious aterials.

Together with the admirable decorative program of the atican Logge (XI, PL. 431) should be grouped the exquisite rnaments in the conched niches in the Stufetta of Cardinal ibbiena in Castel Sant'Angelo. The sophisticated prelate anted a room for displaying a small antique Venus that had een given him and entrusted Raphael and his pupils with the sk of creating a Renaissance interpretation of a small Roman ath. The decoration suggested by thermal buildings was ap-lied with a far more mature complexity of themes and solutions the loggia of the Villa Madama (VIII, PL. 206; XII, PL. 51), here stucco was employed in the creation of a subtle and concise lay of pictorial elements that accentuates every architectural ovement (PL. 285).

Giulio Romano, who had played such an important role in he Villa Madama, was to make himself the interpreter and prop-gator of the new decorative style — again in the interior of build-gs — in Mantua, when he moved to that city. In the Sala el Sole in the Palazzo del Te the vault is divided into lozenges hat frame slender figures inspired by the coins and engraved gems f the classical world. The Hellenistic grace of the extremely elicate motifs, poised as it were in the subtle web of panels, ood out against the subdued tints of the backgrounds, now bliterated through an unconscionable remodeling in the early 9th century. A probable contribution to this room by the young rancesco Primaticcio (q.v.), corroborated by a comparison ith two drawings in the Uffizi, would illuminate in a striking anner the antecedents of the celebrated decorations at Fontaine-leau (V, PL. 395); in these a recollection of the classicizing ights of Giulio Romano, mingled with exquisite Parmese uches, was to produce — with the collaboration of outstanding ssistants such as Jean Goujon (q.v.) — the elegant stuccoing f the Gallery of Francis I (PL. 281) and the rooms surrounding , a work of prime importance for the formation of the French enaissance.

The most gifted among Primaticcio's colleagues in the Pa-zzo del Te must have been a certain Giovanni Battista Scultori il Mantovano; 1503–75) mentioned by Vasari, whose work an be seen in the Sala degli Stucchi. Here the subtle harmonies f decoration in the Alexandrian taste have given way to a far ore deliberate and ceremonious classicism. In the mytholog-al figures framed by the coffers that subdivide the barrel ault, and in the double frieze with figures of armed and mount-d men, the iconography and the sculptural execution of the odies convey the solemnity of a programmatic return to the ntique.

The stylistic characteristics of the decoration evolved in iulio Romano's circle are found in the Galleria dei Mesi in he Palazzo Ducale, also in Mantua, where many features of the illa Madama are repeated with greater exuberance in the relief nd color, and also in the house that the artist built for himself, here the interior echoes many of the motifs of the external rchitecture. In this house there is an original mantelpiece with stucco-decorated hood, of which an interesting preparatory tudy is preserved in the Louvre; it is one of the first examples f a type that was to be widely disseminated, with a vast repertory f motifs, in northern Italy and especially in the Veneto. How uch imagination Giulio Romano and so many others after im (e.g., Vincenzo Scamozzi, q.v.) put into the invention f new forms and sculptural ornaments for mantelpieces is shown y the quantity and quality of the drawings, which deserve hat would prove a most useful chronological and typological lassification.

Many further examples of decoration executed by crafts-men in Giulio Romano's circle could be cited. Suffice it to men-tion Fornarotto's work in the Palazzo del Giardino at Sabbioneta, where the lavishness of the reliefs — enriched by gilding and color — are vivid testimony to the influence that must have been exerted by the rooms of the Palazzo del Te.

This taste was not limited to northern Italy. In Germany stucco reliefs alternating with paintings of grotesques — almost exclusively the work of Italian craftsmen — complemented the characteristic massiveness of the local Renaissance architecture. Interesting interpretations of Raphaelesque decoration were executed in the Residenz in Munich and in the Fugger House in Augsburg. North Italian elements of technique and style were propagated throughout eastern Europe, almost invariably by Italian artists, but they were revived in special forms re-flecting the late arrival of the Renaissance in these areas. Some arresting decorative schemes were executed in Bohemia, for example, by mid-16th-century craftsmen: in the castle at Bu-čovice, a room with exquisite ornamentation that is mannerist in flavor and, in some ways, already prebaroque; in the palace at Kratochvíle, ornaments echoing Italian Renaissance motifs despite a persistence of popular and local stylistic elements; and in the castle at Nelahozeves, a mantelpiece of a type that originated in the Veneto.

Returning to the Roman sphere, it should be noted that the subtle linearism of decoration by Raphael's circle, inspired by examples of the Augustan Era, finally gave way to the ponder-ous and robust severity of Sangallesque ornament (such as that in the Chapel of Cardinal Alborense in the Church of S. Giacomo degli Spagnoli), which was doubtless influenced by a study of reliefs in late Roman thermal buildings.

Attributable to stuccoworkers still practicing in the first manner are the very delicate ceiling ornaments in the Palazzo Farnese at Caprarola (especially the ones in perspective in the Sala delle Colonne), in which the elegance of line stands out against pale green and soft pink backgrounds. Notable too are the dec-orations in the villa of Pope Julius III (Villa Giulia), which accord so well with the taste of Giacomo de Vignola and Bar-tolommeo Ammanati (qq.v.).

Of the architects active in Rome who favored stucco ornament to finish off their work, the most versatile was Pirro Ligorio. In the Casino of Pius IV in the Vatican Gardens (VIII, PL. 429; XII, PL. 89) the decoration both in the interior (where it echoes the patterns of the classical nymphaea) and on the exter-ior takes on substance and proliferates with such vitality that it seems an end in itself, as if detached from the architecture (PL. 280); in the Piccolo Casino, or "Kaffeehaus," the architect even tried to avoid providing window space, in order to make room for an abundance of reliefs that almost disrupt the serene Renaissance equilibrium of the original architectural conception.

With the work of Giulio Mazzoni in the Palazzo Spada (PL. 288; IX, PL. 311) and in the Sala Regia in the Vatican (ca. 1560; IX, PL. 294) there triumphed a tendency toward overstated plasticity. Eventually figures were projected in the round, so that, together with the jutting shields, tablets, and friezes, they emulated the freedom of structural members, while the dense web of color in the ornamentation — subtly and coherently elegant as it was — smothered the underlying structures.

In Rome this style finally anticipated many aspects of the baroque, but in Tuscany the sober serenity of the Renaissance was preserved. It is seen in the decorations of Baldassare Peruzzi (q.v.) for the Castle of Belcaro, in which the plastic ele-ment serves as a felicitous link between the plain interior of the loggia and the exterior. In the Villa Medici at Poggio a Caiano, stuccoes crown the famous frescoes in the great hall and enrich the Loggia of Leo X, where the white and gold motifs, still in the Roman tradition, do not in the least disturb the balance of architectural lines.

In the context of Tuscan mannerism were devised those small rooms which, in the dwellings of the gentry, were used as repos-itories for money, jewels, and collections of precious objects. A typical example is the Tesoretto in the Palazzo Vecchio in Florence designed by Vasari (ca. 1560), where in the skillfully utilized space the sculptural decoration of the ceiling contrasts with the dark wood of the cabinet doors on the walls.

Roman artists and Roman influences were responsible for some interesting and original decorations in Genoese buildings. The highly skillful Lucio Romano collaborated with Perino del Vaga in the work on the Loggia degli Eroi in the Palazzo Doria (ca. 1530). Recollections of the Vatican Logge and the Villa Madama in this work inspired a serene and measured classicism that was to characterize the decoration of many Genoese interiors of the period — the very rich decoration in the hall of the Villa Cambiaso by Andrea and Ottavio Semino (ca. 1550), very close to the taste of Perino del Vaga; the decoration in the reception room of the Villa delle Peschiere, marked by such a sense of measure as to appear almost frozen; and the decoration of Marcello Sparzo in the Villa Scassi at Sampierdarena (ca. 1560). Still in Genoa, in the Palazzo Cataldi, the presence is noted of another school of decorators given to more exuberant plastic effects; in the reception room, where stucco alternates with painting in a harmonious variety of iconographic motifs, the decorations of G. B. Castello (Bergamasco) and his assistants (ca. 1565) show a tendency toward stylistic solutions that anticipate the baroque.

The importance of the diffusion of ornament of Raphaelesque inspiration throughout Italy is attested by the work of the circle of Pellegrino Tibaldi in Bologna in the mid-16th century. While the architecture and reliefs in an elegant mantelpiece in the Palazzo dell'Università exhibit a subtle linearism still in the spirit of the early Renaissance, the decoration of S. Giacomo Maggiore attains an equilibrium between a pictorialism of Roman origin and a fanciful richness that is already fully mannerist. The same harmonious balance of motifs is found in the decorations, by craftsmen of Tibaldi's circle, in the Palazzo Ferretti in Ancona.

The presence in Venice of the very active Giovanni da Udine for the decoration of the Palazzo Grimani in the S. Maria Formosa quarter (ca. 1540) was of signal importance for the formation of a group that was to interpret Roman classicism with a remarkable variety of solutions. Indeed, notable iconographic and stylistic exchanges took place while his work in the rooms and interior stairway of the Palazzo Grimani was being completed and the decorations of Jacopo Sansovino, who had come to Venice in the 1530s, were taking shape. Sansovino undertook, among other projects, the decoration of the stairway of the Biblioteca Vecchia di S. Marco, which also engaged the ready versatility of Alessandro Vittoria, then at the beginning of his career (ca. 1560). To Sansovino and his assistants must also be credited, in the Doges' Palace, the splendid Scala d'Oro (PL. 282) and the conception of the superb ornamental scheme in the Sala delle Quattro Porte (PL. 287); in this room, perhaps by Palladio, a harmonious union was achieved between the stuccoes of G. B. Cambi (called Bombarda) and the paintings of Titian and Tintoretto.

Echoes of the taste responsible for the splendor of these rooms are found not only in numerous Venetian interiors, such as the Camera dell'Archivio in the Scuola di S. Rocco, but also outside Venice. At Urbino, in the little chapel in the Palazzo Ducale, where pure decoration accompanies representational panels that offer some ingenious perspective solutions, the reliefs of Federico Brandani partake of the Raphaelesque style of ornamentation but are also very close to the production of Venetian modelers in the lively swirl of volutes in the cartouches and especially in painterly effects that contrast with the sharpness of line. The very beautiful crèche in the Oratorio di S. Giuseppe, also in Urbino, is likewise the work of Brandani.

In the Veneto, among the assistants of Sansovino who worked in stucco should be mentioned Tiziano Minio. Though trained in Padua with Donatello and Riccio (Andrea Briosco) as his models, he was no more than an uninspired follower incapable of raising himself above an ordinary level of production. His works, spontaneous in their modeling and almost vulgar in their vitality, though lacking any flash of imagination, give an idea of the taste that prevailed in the artistic craftsmanship of the time.

It was Alessandro Vittoria who achieved in the plastic rendering of forms a softness of chromatic transitions that was a legacy of the great contemporary school of Venetian painting. Of particular interest are the mantelpieces in the Palazzo Vendramin Calergi, where the stuccoes of the hoods, attributed to Vittoria and his circle on the basis of recently discovered drawings, blossom forth in the form of cartouches, volutes, and figures from classical marble architecture. The pictorial vivacity of Vittoria's sculptural style is also found in the chromatic subtleties of the stuccoes at Maser (PL. 281; VIII, PL. 434), as well as in the decoration of the Chapel of the Sacrament in S. Giuliano in Venice. Likewise to be traced to Vittoria and his workshop are the statues of the Seasons in the Villa Pisani in Montagnana, whose modeling in numerous ways reflects the influence of the painting style then triumphant in Venice. In this statuary may be found the ties between the Venetian mannerist movement and the baroque elements in the sculpture of Camillo Mariani (PL. 284; XII, PL. 86).

In 17th-century Rome there were still many decorations (the roster of designers and craftsmen is too long to list) in the late mannerist tradition covering religious and secular buildings — sometimes with excessive redundance. Such was the style of Giovanni Vasanzio (creator of carved and inlaid furniture and cabinets); though his exterior ornamentation for the Casino of Villa Borghese has survived, that of the interior disappeared as the result of a renovation in the neoclassic period, with the exception of echoes of it in the aviary.

The same decorative spirit, which animated the architecture only superficially, achieved particularly fine pictorial effects in interiors, especially in the dense web of reliefs covering pilasters, ceilings, and intrados of aisles and chapels. One of the most important and effective examples of this tendency is found in Rome in the sculptural decorations of the Chapel of the Crucifix in the Church of S. Giovanni dei Fiorentini, in which elongated figures are set against the flattened (a schiacciato) perspectives of the background with a graceful surface play of light that is skillfully emphasized by the gilded highlights.

In contrast, in the more fully developed baroque tendency the sculptural decoration became much more intimately integrated with the architecture. Sculptural decoration conceived together with the architectural plan found its most brilliant application in the work of Bernini, notably in the churches of Castel Gandolfo and Ariccia (PL. 286). In Rome, mention should be made of well-known decorations in the Church of S. Andrea al Quirinale (II, PL. 268) and, in the Vatican, those of the Scala Regia (II, PL. 270) and the Sala Ducale. In the last appears one of the first examples of exuberant drapery, a motif that, applied to the working of stucco, was to have great success up to the 18th century. Among the many names of collaborators and followers of Bernini encountered in traversing baroque Rome, that of Antonio Raggi stands out because of the lively individual accent of his work. His imagination and ability as a sculptor are exemplified — aside from work in the already mentioned Bernini creations — by the medallion on the façade of the Church of S. Marcello, the statues in the Church of S. Maria dell'Umiltà, and the magnificent decorative complex in the Church of the Gesù (PL. 289; II, PL. 166), which fit well into the stylistic orbit of Giovanni Battista Gaulli (I, PL. 171).

To this imaginative exuberance and technical virtuosity Borromini's decorations in a sense offer a contrast. In the white and gilded ceilings of the Palazzo Falconieri (II, PL. 310) the variety of cultural components is balanced in the equilibrium of an intentional, emblematic simplicity in which the naturalistic elements almost harden into an elegant and rarefied abstraction. And this stylistic rigor, which was a constant in Borromini's creations, culminated in the sculptural decoration of the Church of St. John Lateran (PL. 286; II, PL. 309), where every hint of hedonism is purged in the tension of the palms and laurels that accentuate the linear purity of the architecture and of the cornices that set off the remains of the early basilica.

The evolution of the varied components of the idiom of Pietro da Cortona (q.v.) is indicative of the importance of the circulation of decorative elements in the Roman environment. While in the Palazzo Barberini, in Rome, the sculptural elements had been limited — with tempered classicism — to enriching only the cornices, in Florence, in the Pitti Palace (many of the skilled craftsmen came from Rome), there was a more luxuriant flowering of ornamentation, which found its most effective expression in the individual pictorial likeness (e.g., the busts of Medici in the Sala di Venere). This maturation of style, articulated along lines parallel to the plans for the interior of the Church of SS. Luca e Martina in the Roman Forum (XI, PL. 173), is attested by the interesting preparatory designs, which start from a Renaissance mood of purity and proportion and develop into forms that are totally baroque.

Even to list all the most significant ensembles of stucco decoration in the Roman area would be impossible here. Among the most noteworthy are those in the Church of S. Maria della Vittoria (ca. 1620), designed by Carlo Maderno, who was also responsible, with the collaboration of Giovanni Battista Ricci and Martino Ferabosco, for the magnificent ceilings of the portico of St. Peter's and the Cappella Paolina in the Palazzo del Quirinale (PL. 283), and for the stucco decorations of the staircase of the Palazzo Mattei (modeled by Donato Maggi), which partially derive from the mannerist style (PL. 283).

Of prime importance, too, are the decorations of the Cappella del Sacramento in St. Peter's, which are probably from designs based on Pietro da Cortona's and those conceived by Alessandro Algardi for the casino of the Villa Doria-Pamphili and for the Church of St. John Lateran. Not to be omitted from this listing are the decorations by Giacomo Antonio Fancelli in the Church of S. Carlo al Corso and in the Chiesa Nuova (S. Maria in Vallicella), those by Giovanni Grossi in the Church of S. Nicola dei Lorenesi, and those by the Bernini circle in the Church of S. Carlo ai Catinari and the Church of S. Maria del Popolo.

In the evolution from the baroque to the "barocchetto" there were minor personalities who contributed to architecture some attractive ensembles of sculptural ornament. Typical examples are seen in the production of Filippo Carcani, who worked in many Roman churches during the second half of the century, and in the work of Antonio Gherardi. In the Cappella Avila in the Church of S. Maria in Trastevere (ca. 1680) the sculptural element is integral to the fanciful eccentricity of the architectural invention: in the small dome supported by angels poised in the atmosphere appear those solutions of aerial perspective that Gherardi had previously worked out in fresco painting.

In the second half of the century numerous schools of stuccoworkers branched out from the Roman ambience to work all over Italy, creating actual dynasties of *plasticatori* (modelers), who in the following century — in the sphere of the rococo — were to flourish in the major European artistic centers. Interesting examples of this handing down of stylistic and iconographic elements are found in northern Italy, especially in Lombardy. In this connection mention should be made of the decorations of Giovanni Battista Barberini of Laino, whose reliefs for the interior of the Church of S. Cecilia in Como (PL. 290) foreshadow the graceful 18th-century products of Italian stuccoworkers that were to be diffused throughout Europe.

During this typical phase of transition from the baroque to the *rocaille* emerged the outstanding, and in a certain sense isolated, personality of the Palermitan Giacomo Serpotta (1656–1732), whose family training (he came from an old family of modelers and carvers) was interspersed with influences from the Roman ambience. His work in stucco — a medium that from a technical point of view requires quickness and extemporaneity in improvisation — is expressed in forms of prodigious vitality and exuberance. In the rooms decorated by Serpotta (PL. 289; I, PL. 169; XII, PL. 172), which give evidence of a gradual approach to the style that was to become the rococo, symbolic feminine figures succeed one another, their solemnity giving way to a well-mannered 18th-century decorum — delicate chiaroscural transitions in the dynamism of the now very famous figures of infants (the successors of those of Antonio Raggi and François Duquesnoy), micrographic vibrations in the overlapping of movements and drapery that crowd the small sacred scenes.

While in Italy, during the 17th and 18th centuries, the handling of stuccowork was evolving from forms of baroque exuberance toward those of the full-fledged rococo, in France and England it was growing into a style marked by a more austere and tranquil classicism.

In France, during the first half of the 17th century, architects and decorators, from an innate sense of restraint, drew away from the bold ventures and flights of fancy that had characterized the age. In a rigorous process of simplification ornamentation was consistently subordinated to emphasis on the architectural structure. In the decoration of French interiors in the second half of the century a more harmonious balance was achieved between the tendency to emphasize the sculptural decoration through the use of tapestries and polychrome marble and the need to give prominence to the significance of the architecture. Walls and ceilings were barer, marked off by simple borders and central rosettes. But in addition to new ideas that were at once decorative and practical, such as the mantelpieces conceived by Jules Hardouin Mansart, other solutions of a purely ornamental nature appeared, such as the famous shell which was to become the emblem of the *rocaille*. Mansart, Charles Lebrun, and Robert de Cotte struck a balance between the tendencies toward baroque fancy and classicizing equilibrium. The contribution of plasterwork decoration in such celebrated French state rooms as the Hall of Mirrors in Versailles (V, PL. 409) is well known, but stuccowork also flourished in many towns in the French provinces. An extremely interesting set of examples is found in the decorations of interiors in Montpellier, datable in the last quarter of the 17th century, for which many very elegant preliminary drawings are known. In the elaborate fireplace of the Hôtel de Castries and in the ceilings of the Hôtel de Manse and of other similar structures, stucco treated as a very hard material, without the tractability conducive to summary effects or to colorism, takes on the high finish of marble.

In 17th-century England the production of stucco decorations, starting with graceful stylizations of late Renaissance forms, reached at the end of the century the level of genuine and very elegant artistic expression. One of the first 17th-century examples is the ceiling (ca. 1624) of the Great Chamber in Castle Ashby, Northamptonshire, in which the stylization of the coats of arms, tablets, and other late mannerist elements evidence the taste for clearly drawn line and for a sense of proportion that was later to have a most successful development.

A tendency toward forms defined with greater plasticity and further advanced in the baroque direction is found in the "Double Cube Room" in Wilton House (ca. 1650), where sculptural ornament serves as a valuable and coherent connective element, framing the famous canvases of Van Dyck in the architecture of Inigo Jones (VIII, PL. 341).

The taste for sculptural extravaganza reached its height in the baroque virtuosity of the ceilings in Astley Hall, Chorley, Lancashire (ca. 1670), but the prevailing trend until the neoclassic period was toward sober, controlled decoration, which tended to accentuate a delicate chromatic component. Typical examples are the ceilings of Dunsland House, Holsworthy, Devon (ca. 1680), and of Denham Place, Denham, Buckinghamshire (1688–1701), which anticipated motifs that were to appear in French decorations a century later. Consonant with the elegant purity and proportion of this classicism are large decorative schemes like that of Clandon Park, near Guildford, Surrey (ca. 1720), which is attributable to Giuseppe Artaria (1697–1769), whose overall restraint is enlivened by the inspired invention with which the details of the decorations are worked out (PL. 292). Of singular interest are the sculptures sometimes attributed to the Anglo-Dane Charles Stanley (1703–61) in Stoneleigh Abbey, Kenilworth (PL. 294); here the severity of the English handling of stucco in imitation of marble is softened by subtle, chiaroscuro transitions. Such effects were also achieved in the very delicate panels and cornices (ca. 1740) in Wallington Hall, Cambo, Northumberland, where the presence of numerous Italian stucco artists appears certain.

Throughout the 17th century plasterwork decorations virtually always complemented other ornamentation of rarer materials in the great architectural complexes, ecclesiastic and secular; with the rococo their use was extended to the residences (less grandiose but still always marked by a tone of elegance) of the well-to-do middle class.

Study of stylistic developments in the art of stuccowork in 18th-century Venice affords one of the most typical examples of this spreading of a more sophisticated style of life, which coincided with an evolution in customs and in taste. In the sitting-room of the Palazzo Widmann-Foscari, in the S. Canciano quarter, the floral motifs of the ceilings and the heavy cornices bordering the walls display a vital sculptural concept of 17th-century cast, which also firmly underlies the many decorations by the same craftsmen in the Palazzo Bolani in the S. Trovaso quarter and in the Palazzo Barbaro in the S. Stefano quarter.

The custom of surrounding all phases of everyday living with elegance caused small rooms, boudoirs, and rooms with alcoves to be preferred to large reception halls. Adapted as it was to the new proportions and functions of rooms, stucco decoration became an indispensable element. Thus the heavy overhangs, the imposing volutes, and the chubby putti were eliminated in favor of airy surfaces of garlands, flourishes, love knots, and *chinoiserie* landscapes, in a relief that was shallower but enriched by subtle coloring and delicate gilding. One of the most typical of the small private apartments is the Casino della Procuratessa Venier at the Ponte dei Barattieri, which retains intact its plaster decoration, marked by a delicacy and *brio* that are unmatched. Ornamentation by the same circle of stuccoworkers is found in the Palazzo Vitturi-Veronese and in a sitting-room of the Palazzo Vendramin ai Carmini, where motifs of garlands on a palest yellow ground frame finely wrought Chinese scenes.

Mention should also be made of the motif of the stucco alcove, which was gradually substituted for the heavy, sculpturesque bed hangings of the baroque period and was to be very popular in European interior architecture throughout the 18th century. One of the most noteworthy in Venice is preserved in the Palazzo Barbarigo at S. Maria del Giglio (PL. 292).

Memorable among 18th-century Italian stucco decorations are those by Filippo Juvara (q.v.) and his circle. In his Piedmont workshops plaster ornamentation was preferred to marble facing. Among the many stuccoworkers associated with Juvara, Pietro Filippo Somazzo and Carlo Papa were outstanding. To the same circle of stuccoworkers that executed the ideas of Juvara can be attributed the magnificent decorations in the royal hunting lodge at Stupinigi and those on the branching staircase in the Palazzo Reale of Turin.

In Spain there arose during the 18th century a particular type of stucco decoration that was born of the exuberance of the local baroque. The most sumptuous example of these sumptuous decorations that cover walls and vaulted ceilings almost to suffocation is found in the Cartuja in Granada (PL. 291; XII, PL. 169). They comprise a prototype that was to have wide application as a complement to church architecture in Latin America, where, interpreted with oppressive profuseness, it assumed a popular tone, intermingled with local iconographical elements (PL. 152).

But the triumph of 18th-century stuccowork was to come about within the ambit of German rococo. It has been said that in Germany the decoration of interiors took on an aspect of uniformity because some plasterworkers moved from place to place, producing to order works that in a sense prefigure modern mass production. It was even possible to buy modeled ornaments for application to walls and ceilings, but this occurred only in the case of products of lesser quality. A mere comparison of the great decorative cycles of the various German towns is sufficient to indicate quickly the fundamental differences. For example, substantial divergences are noted if the decorations of the Residenz of Würzburg (II, PL. 153; VI, PL. 148) are compared with those by François de Cuvilliés for the Nymphenburg Palace (VI, PL. 148) and the Amalienburg (VIII, PL. 117; XII, PL. 166) or with the less noted ones of the Palais Thurn und Taxis in Frankfurt am Main. In Prussia, just as the exterior of buildings presents the continuation of classicizing elements still bearing the stamp of Palladio, so the interiors show very moderate use of *rocaille* extravaganzas. With the work of the Hoppenhaupt brothers, Johann Michael II and Johann Christian,

there developed a style that was to win the favor of Frederick the Great, whose predilection was for the stated simplicity of French theoretics. It was in the course of the taking hold of this style that such works as the decorations of the Blumenzimmer in the Palace of Sanssouci, Potsdam (ca. 1750; X, PL. 272) and the Goldene Galerie in the Charlottenburg Palace, Berlin were created. Special note may well be taken of the decoration by Georg Wenzeslaus von Knobelsdorff and Johann August Nahl the Elder (ca. 1740), who left free large portions of the walls, merely adorning them with the subtlest of floral garlands (XII, PL. 163).

In southern Germany the decorative imagination of the stuccoworkers expressed itself with much more freedom and vitality. Itinerant artists from the south must have had a role of prime importance in the internationalization of the rococo. Perhaps the stuccoworkers of Wessobrunn offer the most significant example of this. Setting out from that Bavarian town — where, in addition to the works of the families of *plasticatori* from northern Italy, there were very active influences deriving from Italian decorations — they diffused the stylistic and iconographic motifs of the rococo throughout Europe, to Berlin, to Amsterdam, to Warsaw, and to Paris.

But the art of the German stuccoworkers was manifested in the fullness of its imagination and boldness of technical solutions in the interiors of the churches in southern Germany. From the Augustinian church of Weltenburg (ca. 1720; VI, PL. 142) — in which the reliefs cover all the structural parts but are also combined with marble and stone elements — plasterwork decoration underwent an evolution in which one of the most notable steps was the Augustinian church in Rohr, where Egid Quirin Asam (see ASAM, THE BROTHERS) worked on the architectural decoration and on the famous group of the Assumption (VI, PL. 145). In the latter work the stucco, supported by an armature of wood and straw, is enriched by patinated surfaces on which the color has acquired effects of particular delicacy. In the Abbey church of Osterhofen (ca. 1735), the stucco ornamentation is even more exuberant (PL. 297). In addition to the niches there are decorated pilasters and columns paneled in imitation marble. There are many groups completely in the round, some by E. Q. Asam. A comparison has been drawn between the statues of Faith and Hope here and those of the altar in the Church of S. Ignazio in Rome, and in connection with the group of donors reference has been made to the Bernini figures leaning out of the sides of the chapel in the Church of S. Maria della Vittoria in Rome. However, the similarities can be limited almost exclusively to the iconography, so greatly were the stylistic starting points altered by the exuberant imagination of the German modelers. Not to be overlooked are the decorations in Diessen (XII, PL. 168) and Zwiefalten (ca. 1750; X, PL. 440; XII, PL. 164). The pilgrimage church of Zwiefalten has magnificent altars by Johann Michael II Feichtmayr and lively figures of prophets that can be attributed to Joseph Christian, whose *Baptism of Christ* in Ottobeuren (PL. 293) is marked by the same stylistic exuberance. In Ottobeuren and in Rott am Inn there flourished a type of statuary in stucco that on the highest stylistic level achieved special effects of technical dexterity. In the pilgrimage church of Steinhausen (XII, PL. 167) the reliefs blend with the frescoes of the vaults, and the standard naturalistic repertory was enriched with new motifs based on local fauna.

In Italy the stuccoes of the period of transition from the rococo to the neoclassic (see NEOCLASSIC STYLES) reached a high point in the art of Piranesi (q.v.); in the decorative ensemble of the Church of S. Maria del Priorato in Rome (PL. 295) the imagination not only of the architect, but, even more, that of the decorator rouses admiration. Though there are still elements of rococo taste in the altar, analysis of the ornamentation of the walls, ceiling, and façade yields a sense of the neoclassical characterized by strong originality. The reliefs — in which so much nostalgia for a glorious past are expressed in style so full of future — were executed by the sculptor and stucco artist Tommaso Righi (1727–1802). Superb preliminary drawings are preserved in the Pierpont Morgan Library in New York.

The neoclassic movement in England comprehended a new type of stucco ornamentation that had its consummate expression n the production of Robert Adam (PL. 296) and his circle (see DAM, ROBERT AND JAMES). The decorative designs executed fter Robert Adam's return from Italy give evidence (under the nfluence of Piranesi) of his study of Roman stuccoes, both classical and Renaissance, especially those of the Villa Madama. among the many projects of outstanding importance with which e was occupied between 1760 and 1770 were Kedleston Hall, Derbyshire (X, PL. 271), Osterly Park House, Osterly, Middlesex (VIII, PLS. 110, 111; X, PL. 270), and Syon House, Middlesex (VI, PL. 442); in all these houses the stuccoes often stand ut on a ground of the most delicate color, alternating with pictoial ornamentation in a coherence of style that also embraces urniture, rugs, and other accessories. This type of ornamentation radually replaced the tectonic massiveness of the Georgian nteriors with a decorative scheme that attenuates and almost disguises the essentiality of the structural features, endowing olumns, architraves, and vaults with an air of lightness and legance.

France reached the detached sophistication of neoclassicism through a distillation of the motifs of *rocaille*, which reached ts zenith in the ornamentation of the Hôtel de Soubise (now he Archives Nationales) in Paris (XII, PL. 162) and in the decoration of many of the interiors of Versailles (V, PL. 421).

Among the most beautiful neoclassical decorative complexes n which stucco ornamentation plays an important role are those onceived by François Joseph Bélanger for the Bagatelle in Paris. If Louis Martin Berthault's project for the decoration of Madame Récamier's boudoir (X, FIG. 543) had been executed, most exquisite example of this style (which became heavier during the Empire) would have been ours to admire.

In Italy mention should be made of the decorative cycles of the royal palaces in Naples (X, PL. 435) and Caserta (VIII, L. 111), where a certain tendency of forms and motifs to become heavier is noticeable in the ostentation and in the quality of the whole. A more refined artistry is found in the ornament f the Tuscan ambience: a typical example is the bath of Maria Luisa in the Pitti Palace in Florence (VIII, PL. 118). In Milan, Giocondo Albertolli left his particularly elegant stamp on the reliefs in the bath of the Palazzo Reale. In the palace's Salone delle Cariatidi a tendency toward an accentuated plasticity makes tself felt.

In Europe during the entire 19th century motifs of preceding epochs were repeated and combined with eclectic taste. In the 20th century, except for a passing vogue for relief decorations n the ambit of Art Nouveau (q.v.), the fashion for stucco decoration declined into the sphere of a mass production without rtistic significance.

Gemma CORTESE DI DOMENICO

BIBLIOG. *Antiquity*: Fensterbuch, RE, s.v. Stuck; T. Venturini Papini, La pittura ad encausto e l'arte degli stucchi al tempo di Augusto, Rome, 901; O. Rubensohn, Hellenistisches Silbergerät in antiken Gypsabgüssen, Berlin, 1911; W. von Bissing, Mitteilungen aus meiner Sammlung, IV, AM, XXXVII, 1912, pp. 69–72; A. Ippel and G. Röder, Die Denkmäler es Pelizaeus Museum zu Hildesheim, Berlin, 1921; G. Lugli, La decorazione dei colombari romani, Architettura e arti decorative, I, 1921–22, p. 219–41; G. Bendinelli, Le volte a stucco di antichi edifici romani, Architettura e arti decorative, II, 1922–23, pp. 97–107; E. L. Wadsworth, Stucco Reliefs of the 1st and 2d Centuries Still Extant in Rome, MAARome, V, 1924, pp. 9–102; G. Calza, Ostia: Rinvenimenti nell'Isola Sacra, NSc, 928, pp. 133–75 at 151; M. Morgensen, La Glyptothèque Ny Carlsberg: a collection égyptienne, Copenhagen, 1930; A. Ippel, Guss und Treibarbeit in Silber (Wpr, 97), Berlin, 1937; A. Adriani, Contributo all'iconografia lei Tolemei, V. B. Soc. archéol. d'Alexandrie, XXXII, 1938, pp. 77–111; N. C. Debevoise, The Origin of Decorative Stucco, AJA, XLV, 1941, pp. 45–1; G. Röder, Lebensgrosse Tonmodelle aus einer altägyptischen Bildhauerverkstatt, JhbPreussKSamml, LXII, 1941, pp. 145–70; B. Goldman, The allover Pattern in Mesopotamian Stuccowork, Berytus, X, 1950–51, pp. 13–c; A. Merlin and L. Poinssot, Guide du Musée Alaoui (ed. P. Quoniam), th ed., Tunis, 1950, p. 71; F. Sanguinetti, La chiesa di S. Marina in Ardea, Palladio, N.S., IV, 1954, pp. 81–84; A. Adriani, Segnalazioni alessandrine, , AC, VII, 1955, pp. 124–38; M. J. Vermaseren, Corpus inscriptionum et nonumentorum religionis mithriacae, 2 vols., The Hague, 1956–60; C. Picard, Sur un "naiskos" inédit de Cybèle au Musée du Caire, MPiot, XLIX, 1957, pp. 41–65; W. Wolf, Die Kunst Ägyptens, Stuttgart, 1957; S. Marinatos, Kreta und das Mykenische Hellas, Munich, 1959; D. E. Strong, A Group of Roman Stucco Reliefs, BMQ, XXI, 1959, pp. 98–102; C. Roth, ewish Art, New York, 1961; N. Dacos, Les stucs du Colisée: Vestiges archéologiques et dessins de la Renaissance, Latomus, XXI, 1962, pp. 334–5; J. W. Graham, The Palace of Crete, Princeton, N.J., 1962; A. Lucas, ncient Egyptian Materials and Industries, 4th ed., London, 1963.

The medieval West: a. General: E. A. Stückelberg, Langobardische Plastik, Kempten, 1909; H. Beenken, Romanische Skulptur in Deutschland, Leipzig, 1924 (rev. by A. Kingsley Porter, Speculum, I, 1926, pp. 233–42); E. Panofsky, Die deutsche Plastik des 11. bis 13. Jahrhunderts, 2 vols., Munich, Florence, 1924; P. Deschamps, Etude sur la renaissance de la sculpture en France à l'époque romane, BM, LXXXIV, 1925, pp. 5–98; P. Verzone, Note sui rilievi in stucco dell'alto medioevo nell'Italia settentrionale, Le Arti, IV, 1941–42, pp. 121–28; G. de Francovich, Arte carolingia ed ottoniana in Lombardia, Römische Jhb. für Kg., VI, 1942–44, pp. 115–255 at 116; G. de Francovich, Problemi della pittura e della scultura preromanica, I problemi dell'Europa post-carolingia (Settimane di Studio di Spoleto, II), Spoleto, 1955, pp. 355–519 at 370; Atti VIII Cong. int. di s. sull'alto medioevo, I, Milan, 1962, passim. *b. Single localities and monuments*: D. Bartolini, La sotterranea confessione della romana basilica di S. Marco, Rome, 1844; J. Lahondès, Alet, CAF, LXVIII, 1906, pp. 103–07; J. Garber, Die Karolingische St. Benediktkirche in Mals, Z. Ferdinandeums, LIX, 1915, pp. 1–61; A. Gaudy, Die kirchliche Baudenkmäler der Schweiz, Berlin, 1922, pp. 67–72; J. Shapley, The Stuccos of S. Vitale, Studien zur Kunst der Ostens (Festschrift J. Strzygowski), Vienna, 1923, pp. 19–32; C. Albizzati, Il ciborio carolingio nella basilica Ambrosiana di Milano, RendPontAcc, II, 1924, pp. 197–265; W. W. S. Cook, The Stucco Altar-frontals of Catalonia, Art S., II, 1924, pp. 41–81; P. Deschamps, Saint-Julien de Brioude, B. Soc. Nat. des Ant. de France, 1924, pp. 206–13; J. Hubert, Germigny-des-Prés, CAF, XCII, 1930, pp. 534–68; F. Berndt, Stuckplastik in frühmittelalterlichen Sachsen: Ihre Bedeutung und Technik, Hanover, 1932; L. Bréhier, Le portail nord de St.-Julien de Brioude et son ancien décor de stuc, Brioude, 1932; V. Mesturino, La basilica latina di S. Pietro, Turin, 1934; P. Toesca, Monumenti dell'antica abbazia di S. Pietro al monte di Civate, Florence, 1942; H. P. L'Orange, L'originaria decorazione del tempietto cividalese, Atti II Cong. int. di s. sull'alto medioevo, Spoleto, 1953, pp. 95–113; H. Torp, Note sugli affreschi più antichi dell'Oratorio di S. Maria in Valle a Cividale, Atti II Cong. int. di s. sull'alto medioevo, Spoleto, 1953, pp. 81–94; W. Arslan, Storia di Milano, III, Milan, 1954, pp. 569–86; H. Beseler and H. Roggenkamp, Die Michaeliskirche in Hildesheim, Berlin, 1954, passim; P. Deschamps, A propos des pierres à décor d'Entrelacs et des stucs de Saint-Jean de Mustair, Akten III, Int. Kong. für Frühmittelalterforschung (1951), Olten, Lausanne, 1954, pp. 253–70; I. Müller and O. Steimann, Zur Disentiser Frühgeschichte, Akten III. Int. Long. für Frühmittelalterforschung (1951), Olten, Lausanne, 1954, pp. 133–49; C. Casalone, Ricerche sul battistero della cattedrale di Ravenna, RIASA, N.S., VIII, 1959, pp. 202–68; E. Schaffran, Stuckfragmente aus der Pfarrkirche in Suhr bei Aarau, Erlangen, 1959; A. Peroni, La decorazione a stucco in S. Salvatore a Brescia, Arte lombarda, V, 1960, pp. 187–220; G. Panazza and A. Peroni, La chiesa di S. Salvatore di Brescia (Atti VIII Cong. int. di s. sull'alto medioevo, II), Milan, 1962; S. K. Kostof, The Orthodox Baptistery of Ravenna, New Haven, London, 1965.

Iran: N. C. Debevoise, A Portrait of Kobad I, B. Art Inst. of Chicago, XXIV, 1930, p. 10; M. S. Dimand, Sasanian Wall Decoration in Stucco, BMMA, XXVI, 1931, pp. 193–95; A. U. Pope, The Historic Significance of Stucco Decoration in Persian Architecture, AB, XVI, 1934, pp. 321–32; J. H. Schmidt, Figürliche sasanidische Stuckdekorationen aus Ktesiphon, Ars Islamica, IV, 1937, pp. 175–84; SPA, I, pp. 411–44, 493–578, 601–45; K. Erdman, Die Kunst Irans zur Zeit der Sasaniden, Berlin, 1943; A. Christensen, L'Iran sous les Sassanides, 2d ed., Copenhagen, Paris, 1944; G. Contenau, Arts et styles de l'Asie antérieure, Paris, 1948; H. Lenzen, Zur relativen Chronologie der sasanidischen Stuckarbeiten, AAnz, LXVII, 1952, cols. 188–221; U. Monneret de Villard, L'arte iranica, Verona, 1954; see also the bibliog. for SASSANIAN ART.

India, Bactria, Central Asia: A. Foucher, L'art gréco-bouddhique du Gandhāra, I, Paris, 1905; A. Grünwedel, Bericht über archäologischen Arbeiten in Idikutschari und Umgebung im Winter 1902–03, Munich, 1906; A. Stein, Ancient Khotan, 2 vols., Oxford, 1907; S. Oldenburg, Russkaia turkestanskaia ekspeditsiia, 1909–10 (The Russian Turkestan Expedition, 1909–10), St. Petersburg, 1914; A. Stein, Serindia, 4 vols., Oxford, 1921; A. von Le Coq and E. Waldschmidt, Die buddhistische Spätantike in Mittelasien, 7 vols., Berlin, 1922–33; A. von Le Coq, Bilderatlas zur Kunst- und Kulturgeschichte Mittel-Asiens, Berlin, 1925; E. Waldschmidt, Gandhara — Kutscha — Turfan: Eine Einführung in die frühmittelalterliche Kunst Zentralasiens, Leipzig, 1925; A. Godard, Y. Godard and J. Hackin, Les antiquités bouddhiques de Bāmiyān, Paris, 1908; A. Stein, Innermost Asia, 4 vols., Oxford, 1928; J. Barthoux, Les fouilles de Haḍḍa, Paris, 1930; J. Strzygowski, The Afghan Stuccos of the N.R.F. Collection, Paris, New York, 1932; J. Hackin, Guide-catalogue du Musée Guimet, Paris, 1933; J. Hackin and J. Carl, Nouvelles recherches archéologiques à Bāmiyān, Paris, 1933; R. C. Kak, Ancient Monuments of Kashmir, London, 1933; K. Otani, Shin Saiiki ki: New Records on Central Asia, being Several Reports by the Otani Mission, 2 vols., Tokyo, 1937; C. L. Fabri, Buddhist Baroque in Kashmir, Asia, XXXIX, 1939, pp. 593–98; J. Meunié, Shotorak, Paris, 1942; J. Marshall, Taxila, 3 vols., London, 1951; M. Bussagli, L'influsso classico ed iranico sull'arte dell'Asia centrale, RIASA, N.S., II, 1953, pp. 171–262; M. Bussagli, Osservazioni sulla persistenza delle forme ellenistiche nell'arte del Gandhāra, RIASA, N.S., V–VI, 1956–57, pp. 149–247; J. Hackin, J. Carl and J. Meunié, Diverses recherches archéologiques en Afghanistan (1930–40), Paris, 1959; D. Faccenna, Mingora: Site of Butkara, I, Reports on the Campaigns 1956–58 in Swat, IsMEO, Rep. & Mem., I, 1962, pp. 3–169.

Islam: D. Hill and O. Grabar, Islamic Architecture and Its Decoration, Chicago, 1966; see also the bibliogs. for FATIMID ART; ILKHAN ART; ISLAM; MOGHUL SCHOOL; MOORISH STYLE; MOZARABIC ART; OMMIAD SCHOOLS; etc.

Pre-Columbian America: see the bibliog. for MIDDLE AMERICAN PROTO-HISTORY.

Modern period: G. P. Bankart, The Art of the Plasterer, London, New York, 1908; G. Ferrari, Lo stucco nell'arte italiana, Milan, 1910; R. Lentini, ed., Le scolture e gli stucchi di Giacomo Serpotta, Turin, 1911; R. Brayda, Stucchi ed affreschi del real castello del Valentino, Turin, 1913; R. Plaul, Die Stuckdecken in Sachsen, Berlin, 1920; R. Paribeni, Un'arte intermittente, Rass. d'arte, N.S., IX, 1922, pp. 175–84; I. Dalchow, Italienische Stukkatoren und ihre Ornamentik in der bayerischen Architektur um 1700, Bad Wörishofen, 1928; D. Frazzoni, L'imbianchino, decoratore — stuccatore, 2d ed., Milan, 1928; M. Ciartroso Lorenzetti, Stucchi veneziani del '700, Le tre Venezie, July, 1929, pp. 45–50; R. Pascual Diaz, Arte de Locar el estuco, escrito en el siglo XVIII, AEA, XXIV, 1932, pp. 237–42; W. Buchner, Der Stukkator Johann Baptist Modler von Kösslarn, Passau, 1936; L. Simona, L'arte dello stucco nel cantone Ticino, 2 vols., Bellinzona, 1938–49; G. Romano, Scultori, stuccatori e ceramisti italiani in Germania, L'Illustrazione romana, I, July 1939, pp. 9–13; A. Ayscough, Country House Baroque, London, 1940; M. von Klebelsberg, Stuckarbeiten des 16. und 17. Jahrhunderts in Nordtirol, Veröffentlichungen Ferdinandeums, XX–XV, 1940–45, pp. 175–214; J. Zykan, Barocker Stuck und seine Pflege, D. K. und Denkmalpflege, 1942–43, VIII–VIII; H. Hoffmann, Barockstukkatur im Zürich, ZfSAKg, X, 1948–49, pp. 155–68; A. Staring, 17-eeuws stucwerk in het Oosten des lands, NedKhJb, II, 1948–49, pp. 316–40; G. Morazzoni, Stucchi italiani, Milan, 1950; L. Döry, Die Stukkaturen der Bandlwerkzeit in Nassau und Hessen, Frankfurt am Main, 1954; F. Windisch-Graetz, Gold, Stuck und edle Hölzer, Alte und moderne K., III, 1958, pp. 4–8; J. Claparède, Gypseries montpellieraines de la seconde moitié du XVIIIᵉ siècle, Arte antica e moderna, V, 1962, pp. 267–79; G. Mariacher, Ambienti italiani del '500, Milan, 1962; A. Ress, Der Würzburger Dom-Stuck, D. K. und Denkmalpflege, 1962, pp. 103–26; T. Breuer, Die italienischen Stukkatoren in den Stiftsgebäuden von Ottobeuren, Z. der d. Vereins für Kw., XVII, 1963, pp. 231–59; E. Arslan, Gli stuccatori del barocco al rococo (Arte e artisti dei laghi lombardi, II), Como, 1964.

• •

Illustrations: PLS. 267–298.

SUBLIME, THE. See TRAGEDY AND THE SUBLIME.

SUDAN. The eastern Sudan, "the land of the black men" (Ar., Bilad-es-Sudan) south of Egypt, was known as the Anglo-Egyptian Sudan before it became the Republic of Sudan in 1956. It covers the Nile Valley south of the Second Cataract and is bordered by Libya, Chad, and the Central African Republic on the west, by the Nile-Congo watershed on the southwest by Uganda and Kenya on the south, and by Ethiopia and the Red Sea on the east. The population is mainly made up of Sudanese and Nilotic ethnic groups with a high proportion of Arabs (see NILOTIC CULTURES; SUDANESE CULTURES). Although there is little historical data for the southern region up to very recent times, the northern part of Sudan has been in contact with Egypt since the beginning of historical times (see NUBIAN ART) as its location along the caravan routes crossing Africa from east to west made it an important center of cultural exchange. Sudan's contacts with European culture have not produced any significant artistic trends.

SUMMARY. Cultural and artistic phases (col. 655): *Prehistory; Period of Egyptian domination; The Napatan dynasties and the Meroitic period; The Christian period; The Fung kingdom; Contemporary indigenous art.* Monumental centers (col. 661).

CULTURAL AND ARTISTIC PHASES. *Prehistory.* Pebble tools as old as any human artifact have been found in the oldest gravels of the Nile. North of Khartoum the Acheulean hand-ax culture developed normally, but in the southern half of the country paleolithic tools are absent. Fine bifacial lanceheads of the Aterian-Sangoan-Stillbay complex occur near Khartoum, but no Aterian arrowheads have been found, and the bow was probably brought to the Sudan by mesolithic hunters of the Capsian-Wilton complex. The oldest rock engravings of wild animals were made by paleolithic hunters, but thousands of years of quarrying rock along the Nile have destroyed most of them, although pictures of elephants and giraffes survive in the Second Cataract area and no doubt also in the northwest desert.

About 7000 B.C. mesolithic Negroes hunting and fishing along the Nile near Khartoum used harpoons of bone and made large bowls of well-fired unburnished pottery, decorated externally with catfish spines. This is the earliest pottery so far known; indeed, pottery may have been invented along the Nile not far from Khartoum. The earlier form ("Wavy Line" ware) is confined to this area; the later form ("Dotted Wavy Line" ware) has been traced across Africa through the Ennedi Plateau to the northwestern Hoggar Mountains. Pottery was thus diffused by a widespread and long-lived neolithic culture in the Sahara; this area was at first reasonably well watered,

but as it gradually dried up, people carrying forms of the Saharan neolithic culture were driven out into surrounding countries. Two such groups entered the Nile Valley, one in the Fayum and the other in the Khartoum area; the latter gave rise to the Khartoum neolithic culture (site at Shaheinab). Features of the culture carried by these two groups include burnished pottery, ground cutting edges on some stone implements, bone harpoons with holes for attachment of the line (Sudan but not Fayum), shell fishhooks (also Sudan only), and beads of blue-green amazonite (probably from northeast Tibesti).

The Khartoum neolithic culture was ancestral to the Badarian civilization of Upper Egypt. The date of the first domestication of cattle in Africa is unknown, but it goes back to the Badarian era (ca. 4000 B.C.). The earliest rock pictures of cattle are found in the eastern desert, in Lower Nubia, and in the western desert (once steppe) at Jebel Oweinat, at Eghei in northeast Tibesti, and in the Hoggar Mountains. Most of the cattle depicted are long-horned, though a few are short-horned. Occasionally, one or both horns are shown double. These are attributed by Winkler (1938–39) to people that he calls "Autochthonous Mountain dwellers" (perhaps predynastic, ca. 3500 B.C.).

Period of Egyptian domination. The earliest datable picture in Sudan is a rock engraving near the Second Cataract recording the conquest of this area by Zer, the third king of the 1st dynasty of Egypt (ca. 3000 B.C.). The conquered country is represented by a man holding a ceremonial bow with spiral ends, a type that is still used by Dinka witch doctors as part of their insignia. Beautiful rippled pottery (related to Badarian pottery) made by the local inhabitants has been excavated at Faras and has been found near Khartoum and as far afield as Grassy Valley in the desert to the west. These people, known to archaeologists as the A Group, were probably wiped out by later Egyptian slave raids.

After the collapse of the Old Kingdom of Egypt a cattle-owning people, known as the C Group, lived in the northern Sudan (ca. 2250–2100 B.C.). Their art was largely confined to pottery — bowls of black ware decorated with infinite variations of incised decoration sometimes tastefully filled with different colors (X, PL. 364). Their graves were circular, flat-topped structures in stone, alongside of which large slabs of white stone with rough pictures of cattle scratched on them were sometimes erected. No doubt the C Group made some of the rock pictures of cattle to be found in this area. In their graves they placed clay figurines of women and cattle to provide the dead with what they valued most in life.

About 2000 B.C. northern Sudan was occupied by the Egyptian Middle Kingdom and strongly held by a series of elaborate forts stretching from Lower Nubia to Semna, 50 miles south of the Second Cataract. A trading post was set up at Kerma, the home of a native chieftain, 150 miles south of Semna at the downstream end of the fertile and navigable reach then known as Kush and now as Dongola. At the trading station the Egyptians introduced the manufacture of faïence vessels (X, PL. 369), beads, and copper objects, which at first they no doubt bartered for gold and other goods. They taught these crafts to the men of Kush, and after the collapse of the Middle Kingdom, when the forts were burned by a people glad to see their Egyptian conquerors depart, Kush remained strong enough to intrigue with the Hyksos in Lower Egypt against the Egyptian resistance that was growing up at Thebes. It was probably during the enthusiastic earlier years of independence from Egypt that Kerma produced the first black-topped red pottery beakers ever made in the Nile Valley, numerous copper daggers and short swords with ivory handles of a type not made in Egypt, and a blue-glazed quartz couch for their ruler. It must have been the arrival at this time (as presents to the chieftain of Kush) of Hyksos bone inlay work, such as has been found at Gaza and Sedment, that inspired the craftsmen of Kush to decorate bed footboards with fine bone and ivory inlays of African subjects (X, PL. 364). In this work Kerma showed a far higher degree of taste and humor than the Hyksos. They also decorated leather caps with mica cutouts in patterns similar to those they had developed for their inlays; among these there are birds with two heads that reminded Reisner (1923) of Babylonian and Syro-Hittite designs, although he was not prepared, as is the present author, to admit Asiatic influence.

In the war of liberation in Egypt, Thebes employed considerable numbers of Beja troops from the Red Sea hills. Their graves are found from Cusae, the Hyksos frontier, southward and are known to archaeologists as the Pan Graves. Their art is negligible, consisting of black-topped bowls far inferior in quality to Kerma ware and bowls decorated with deep incisions. They painted the skulls of animals sacrificed at the funeral feast with crude colored patterns, and on one skull there has survived an important sketch of a Pan Grave soldier with his ax and sling.

In the expansion that followed the expulsion of the Hyksos the Egyptians occupied the northern Sudan, including the whole of Kush, thus extinguishing the joy of independence and putting an end to

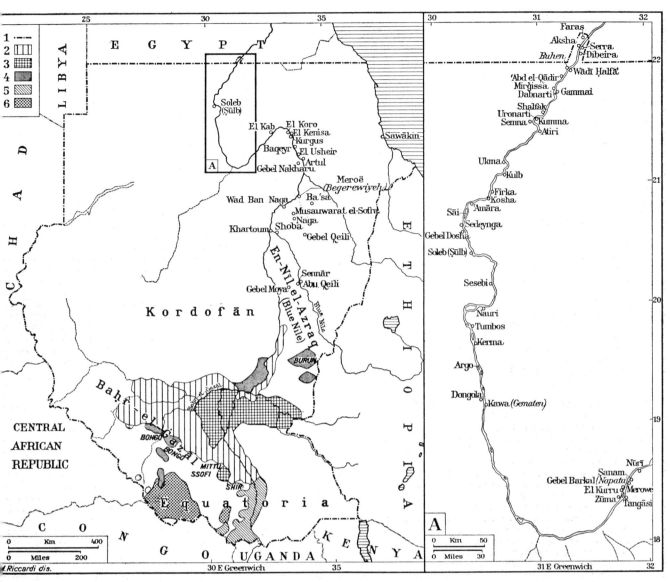

lan, principal centers of historic and artistic interest and distribution of the principal ethnic groups with artistic production (ethnic names in sans-
f capital letters). *Key:* (1) Modern national boundaries. Zones of distribution: (2) the Dinka; (3) the Nuer; (4) the Shilluk; (5) the Bari; (6) the Azande.

native art. The northern Sudan now became part of Egypt and its thoroughly Egyptian, as represented by fine temples, most notably Temple of Amenhotep III at Soleb (Sulb), and their contents, :h as the two fine red granite lions from Sulb (one in the Br. Mus.).)ser contact with the Negroes south of Kush caused the Sudan influence Egyptian art. Negresses and monkeys imported to Egypt slaves and pets are frequent art motifs, and southern peoples, mals, and natural products appear in representations of the southern)ute; in contradistinction to the northern tribute not a single Su- 1ese work of art is shown.

A rock inscription at Kurgus beyond the Fourth Cataract marks frontier under Thutmosis I (1530–1520 B.C.). In it he is represent- as a huge lion, and the god Amen (Amon, Amun) as a bull. Rough)ies of these animal petroglyphs occur on rocks in the vicinity, : they are only rough imitative scribbles and not art. They do, .vever, suggest that Egyptian wall paintings and reliefs inspired na- e petroglyphs and rock pictures.

The Napatan dynasties and the Meroitic period. When the Kushites Napata conquered Egypt as reformers (750–660 B.C.), they acted Egyptians, for they had been educated to the task by the Egyptian ests of Gebel Barkal. Thus the temples and pyramids they built 1 the statues, *shawabtis* (funerary figures), amulets, and other ects produced under the Kushites were all the work of Egyptian ftsmen (X, PLS. 365, 366). The Kushites were eventually driven m Egypt by the Assyrians, whose forces were armed with the novel tal iron; in 591 B.C. the Saites, who had come to power with Assyr- help, sent an expedition against Napata in which Greeks and

Carians also armed with iron weapons were the spearhead. Their sack of Napata led to the transfer of the capital to Meroë and to the introduction of ironworking on a considerable scale (whence it spread west and south into Africa).

Meroë, a kingdom of Egyptian origin, was thus more or less cut off from Egypt, and it survived, though slowly degenerating, for nearly a thousand years (590 B.C.–ca. A.D. 325). It eventually developed a script in which Meroitic was written, but apart from its painted pottery it developed hardly any art of its own in that long period. Even the pottery was basically inspired by foreign ideas. Imports of Greek and later Roman pottery were considerable between the Ptolemaic period and the 2d century of our era, but foreign styles and motifs were adapted rather than copied slavishly by the native artists — that is, they recast what they so readily borrowed in a typically Meroitic fashion. The result has been described as a hybrid offspring of Greece and Egypt. Garlands of ivy and vine are examples of this borrowing, long retained and slowly degenerating. Processions of birds or animals, which originated in Asia, were borrowed from Greece. Greek satyrs and other Bacchic figures can still be recognized despite their adapta- tion. Animals are sometimes severely stylized as in Egypt. But, at times, the native affection for animals, birds, and plant forms breaks through: giraffes graze on treetops, running guinea fowl pick up seeds, a hunter sets out with a large hound, or (on a bronze bowl) the head cowman brings the milk from the herd to the lady sitting with her women outside the grass hut (X, PLS. 368, 370, 371). Later, Roman wares (terra sigillata, stamped and barbotine) were copied as well as imported, and Roman pottery shapes were adopted.

In contrast to the unnaturally slim female figures of Ptolemaic art, Meroë had a different standard of female beauty, and increasingly obese females were represented in relief scenes in temples and pyramid chapels that remained basically Egyptian in inspiration. A few new deities were introduced into the Egyptian pantheon, and the dress of deities and royalty gradually became less Egyptian. In the 1st century of our era rare innovations appear as the result of Indian influence — the lion-headed god Apezemek (Apedemak), the Meroitic form of the Egyptian Bes, is in one instance represented with three heads and two pairs of arms, and a king is shown riding an elephant.

In the 2d-3d century stone statues of a human-headed bird, the so-called "Ba statues," were placed outside Meroitic tombs. The Meroitic Ba statue soon ceased to resemble a bird and took on human form, fully representing the deceased as he was known in life, with all his insignia, though still retaining the bird tail and sometimes the wings. These statues were later made in pottery.

After the fall of Meroë (ca. A.D. 325) Meroitic cultural influence survived among the X Group, or Nobatae, of the northern Sudan, and probably along the Blue and White Nile south of Khartoum, though no excavation has yet been done there; shards of highly burnished ware with incised patterns, in which botanical motifs predominate, probably belong to this period. Silver bowls, dishes, and flagons, bronze lamps and bowls, and inlaid chests are found in the richer X Group graves of Nubia, but they are mostly products of Byzantine Egypt of the 5th and 6th centuries. Even the royal insignia, including crowns incrusted with semiprecious stones in Byzantine style with many Meroitic motifs — rams' heads, uraei (sometimes winged), and busts of Isis wearing the atef crown — were probably made in Egypt. International trade at this time was particularly flourishing, for among the objects found in a royal grave at Ballana there is a bronze censer in the form of a grotesque lion that had been made in China, while degenerate copies of Byzantine bronze lamps, such as are common in X Group graves, have been found in a grave on the Gold Coast (now Ghana; q.v.).

The Christian period. In the latter half of the 6th century the northern Sudan became nominally Christian; but in the art of Christian Nubia only the pottery is truly indigenous. This is still mainly in the Meroitic tradition, consisting of a white ware with patterns, including Christian motifs, painted in dark brown and of a hard, polished red ware with stamped patterns. Church architecture and mural paintings are purely Coptic in inspiration (see COPTIC ART). The latter, which frequently include mounted saints, inspired crude rock paintings of horsemen in northern Kordofan and in Darfur, where a monastery with two tiny churches of red brick has recently been identified at Ain Farah. There the terracing of the hillsides is well done and extensive, and it is probable that all the terracing of the Darfur hills owes its origin to Christian Nubia. In the 13th century Islam advancing from the west put an end to Christianity in Darfur, and in the following century Moslem attacks from Egypt overwhelmed the Christian kingdom of Dongola. The forts that were built in the last phase of Dongola's resistance to Islam were all of European inspiration.

The Fung kingdom. At the beginning of the 16th century, the Moslem kingdom of the Fung arose, with its capital at Sennar on the Blue Nile. Only at Abu Geili has any Fung pottery been recognized to date; brown flat-bottomed bowls with incised decoration are characteristic. The royal insignia of the Fung included a horned headdress derived from Meroë (through Christian Nubia) and a royal stool (*kukur*) imported from West Africa. It is probable that the Fung dynasty was a branch of the Moslem royal family of Bornu in northern Nigeria. A degenerate Fung kingdom was destroyed by Turkish forces in 1821.

Anthony J. ARKELL

Contemporary indigenous art. The Kordofan and Blue Nile region is undoubtedly one of the poorest in artistic production, and only the Nuba (in southern Kordofan) and the Burun (in the Blue Nile area) deserve mention here. The Nuba are known primarily for their production of quite fine pottery and for their execution of frescoes and reliefs on buildings. L. Frobenius has also noted the presence of wood sculptures standing in their "men's houses." At the time of the harvest the heads of families, through their religious authorities, evidently make offerings of food to these anthropomorphic statuettes. The Burun (a small group living near the border of Ethiopia) sometimes decorate the façades of their houses with rather realistic animal figurines. Rock drawings of similar workmanship are also attributed ot them.

In the region of Bahr el Ghazal and the Upper Nile, among the few tribes whose sculptural works are known, the Dinka (more accurately called the Jieng or Jang) should be mentioned first. The various Nilotic tribes such as the Padang, the Bor, the Agar, and the Rek, which are collectively designated as the Dinka, occasionally model clay images depicting large cattle, goats, and wild animals such as

the elephant. It is quite possible that they have no religious or tri significance but are merely toys. G. Schweinfurth, who was the fi to note the existence of these sculptures, believes they are made the Dinka children, while other authorities think they are made the adults, which is certainly true of the wooden, generally amorphe statuettes found among the Bor, who probably use them for purpo of black magic.

The Nuer, who live in the Upper Nile region, more specifica in the triangle formed by Bahr el Zeraf and Bahr el Jebel, also ma identical statuettes in potter's clay. Some large head-shaped pip have been collected that can probably be attributed to them (unl they are of Dinka origin); in these both the plastic conception and t finish show a higher artistic level.

Among the Luo of the North, living in the same province, t Shilluk are particularly noteworthy. This Nilotic group also produ zoomorphic clay figurines that portray horned animals and are prc ably used as "fertility charms" (*deang*). Masks are also attribut to the Shilluk, some examples of which can be seen in German m seums. They are made primarily of highly perishable materials l the fruit of the gourd tree (only the teeth of the beings depicted made of more solid material such as fish bones or wood) and are enti ly covered with dung. These masks are generally curved in for and they are conceived and executed in an extremely primitive mann with nothing but holes for the eyes, nose, and mouth. Although th masks have a somewhat anthropomorphic appearance, they are actua representations of animals like the leopard and other wild quadrupe Their purpose is still unclear; some authorities — E. von Sydo for example — believe they are used in dances imitating certain a mals. Statuettes are also found among the Shilluk. According Westermann (1912) and Hofmayer (1925) the culture hero Nyika is probably represented in the dwellings dedicated to the ancest of one of the ancient Shilluk kings.

The Bongo, who live in various parts of Bahr el Ghazal as w as outside this province, have long been known as skillful woodworke Once more Schweinfurth was the first to point this out and, at t same time, to draw attention to the presence among them of lar sculptures in the form of stakes, which are set in rows at the entra of the palisades enclosing the villages or quite near the huts of the c people to commemorate dead persons of fame. Other more realis commemorative sculptures were discovered earlier among the sa population group. They were kept in their owner's house and p trayed dead persons whom he loved, as well as murdered relativ Again according to Schweinfurth such sculptures were used in tracki down people involved in a murder. The same author claims to ha seen pipes with anthropomorphic bowls among the Bongo. A ha of anthropomorphic type found among them is similar to those ma by the Azande who live farther south (see SUDANESE CULTURE Schweinfurth also points out that funerary sculptures decorated w glass beads, similar to those of the Bongo, existed at one time amo the neighboring Mittu and Sofi. Cummins (1911) has noted t existence of wood sculptures among the Golo, who live between t Wau and Boro rivers.

In the province of Equatoria the foremost producers of sculptu works are the Bari, a cluster of tribes living along both banks of t Nile, among which the Bari tribe itself and the neighboring Mond and Shir are particularly noteworthy. The Bari carve crude m and female figurines in wood, as was already noted by Schweinfu and W. Junker late in the 19th century; because of their tree-tru shape these works are classified as *Pfahlplastik* ("paliform sculpture Many of these statuettes, which are about 19 in. high, are in Europe museums. Most of them have rather small spherical or cone-shap heads; arms that hang stiffly at either side of a thin torso or that a an integral part of it; and slim legs that are slightly parted. It is fr quently assumed that these figurines represent or honor ancesto However, there is no substantial ground for this opinion. C. Seligman expresses serious doubts concerning the Bari origin these figures, pointing out that they have never had a place in th people's religious system. The anthropomorphic sculptures attribut to the neighboring Mondari bear such a marked resemblance to t above-mentioned Bari figurines that they may readily be confuse Among the Bari, Cook (1940) has observed crudely made stone funera figurines, one of which depicts a well-known rain maker in the regic

The sculptural works of the Azande living around Tambu Maridi, and Yambio (most of the Azande live in the Congo and neig boring Ubangi-Shari) unquestionably bear the mark of a more b anced and highly developed civilization. This people is especia known for its water jars adorned with representations of human hea string instruments with similar decorations, and large zoomorph drums with slits. Three-dimensional sculptures portraying wh humans or animals seem to be rare among the Azande of Suda while they are more numerous among the Azande of the northeaste Congo.

Herman BURSSENS

BIBLIOG. *The origins to the Fung kingdom*: F. Cailliaud, Voyage à Meroe
ıu fleuve blanc, 4 vols., Paris, 1826–27; C. R. Lepsius, Denkmäler aus
:ypten und Aethiopien, 12 vols., Berlin, 1849–59; E. A. W. Budge, The
·rptian Sudan: Its History and Monuments, 2 vols., London, Philadelphia,
7; G. S. Mileham, Churches in Lower Nubia, Philadelphia, 1910; C.
Woolley and D. Randall-MacIver, Karanog, 2 vols., Philadelphia, 1910;
V. Crowfoot, The Island of Meroe, London, 1911; J. Garstang and others,
roe: The City of the Ethiopians, Oxford, 1911; S. Clarke, Christian Antiq-
es in the Nile Valley, Oxford, 1912; F. L. Griffith, Oxford Excavations
Nubia, Liverpool Univ. Ann. of Archaeol. and Anthr., VIII, 1921, pp. 1–18,
·104, IX, 1922, pp. 67–134, X, 1923, pp. 73–179, XI, 1924, pp. 115–
141–80, XII, 1925, pp. 57–172, XIII, 1926, pp. 17–37, 49–93, XIV,
5, pp. 57–116, XV, 1928, pp. 63–88; G. A. Reisner, Excavations at Kerma,
ols., Cambridge, Mass., 1923; G. Brunton, Sedment, I, London, 1924;
M. Flinders Petrie, Ancient Gaza, IV, London, 1934; U. Monneret de
lard, La Nubia medioevale, 4 vols., Cairo, 1935–57; G. Steindorff, Aniba,
ols., Glückstadt-Hamburg, 1935–37; G. Brunton, Mostagedda, London,
7; H. A. Winkler, Rock-drawings of Southern Upper Egypt, 2 vols.,
ndon, 1938–39; I. E. S. Edwards, The Prudhoe Lions, Liverpool Univ.
n. of Archaeol. and Anthr., XXVI, 1939, pp. 3–9; J. H. Dunbar, The
:k Pictures of Lower Nubia, Cairo, 1941; W. B. Emery, Nubian Treasure,
ndon, 1948; A. J. Arkell, Early Khartoum, Oxford, 1949; D. Dunham,
·al Cemeteries of Kush, I: El Kurru, Boston, 1950; A. J. Arkell, Meroe
I India, Aspects of Archaeology in Britain and Beyond, London, 1951,
32–38; O. G. S. Crawford and F. Addison, The Wellcome Excavations
·he Sudan, III: Abu Geili, Oxford, 1951; PM, VII; S. E. Chapman and
Dunham, Royal Cemeteries of Kush, III: Decorated Chapels of the
roitic Pyramids at Meroe and Barkal, Boston, 1952; A. J. Arkell, Shahei-
·, Oxford, 1953; O. G. S. Crawford, Castles and Churches in the Middle
·e Region (Sudan Ant. Service, Occasional Pap., 2), Khartoum, 1953;
sh, Khartoum, 1953 ff.; D. Dunham, Royal Cemeteries of Kush, II:
:ri, Boston, 1955; D. Dunham, Royal Cemeteries of Kush, IV: Royal
mbs at Meroe and Barkal, Boston, 1957; W. S. Smith, The Art and Ar-
tecture of Ancient Egypt, London, 1958; G. A. Reisner, D. Dunham and
lanssen, Second Cataract Forts, I, Boston, 1960; A. J. Arkell, A History
the Sudan to A.D. 1821, London, 1961; K. Michalowski, Faras (Feuilles
onaises 1961–62), Warsaw, 1962, 1965; Comite Español de la UNESCO
·a Nubia, Madrid, 1963–65; M. P. Fouchet, Rescued Treasures of Egypt,
w York, Toronto, 1965.

Contemporary indigenous art: G. Schweinfurth, Im Herzen von Afrika,
ols., Leipzig, 1874; G. Schweinfurth, Artes Africanae, London, Leipzig,
·5; W. Junker, Reisen in Africa 1875–76, Vienna, 1889; S. L. Cummins,
ıtribes of the Bahr-el-Ghazal Dinkas, JRAI, XXXIV, 1905, pp. 149–
S. L. Cummins, Golo Models and Songs, Man, XI, 1911, pp. 132–33;
G. Seligman, An Avungura Drum, Man, XI, 1911, p. 17; L. Frobenius,
d Afrika sprach, 3 vols., Berlin, 1912–13; D. Westermann, The Shilluk
·ple: Their Language and Folklore, Berlin, 1912; C. G. Seligman, A
ıgo Funerary Figure, Man, XVII, 1917, pp. 97–98; L. Frobenius, Das
·ekannte Afrika, Munich, 1923; C. G. and B. Z. Seligman, Some Little-
·wn Tribes of the Southern Sudan, JRAI, LV, 1924, pp. 15–36; W.
fmayr, Die Shilluk: Geschichte, Religion und Leben eines Niloten-
mmes, Mödling, 1925; E. Vatter, Religiöse Plastik der Naturvölker,
nkfurt am Main, 1926; H. Baumann, Afrikanisches Kunstgewerbe, in
T. Bossert, Geschichte des Kunstgewerbes aller Zeiten und Völker, II,
·lin, 1929, pp. 51–148; C. G. and B. Z. Seligman, Pagan Tribes of the
·otic Sudan, London, 1932; G. O. Whitehead and T. Thomas, Carved
·oden Figures from the White Nile, Compte Rendu, II· Cong. int. des
anthr. et ethn., Copenhagen, 1938, pp. 265–66; R. C. Cook, A Bari Stone,
R, XXIII, 1940, p. 191; F. H. Lem, Sudanese Sculpture, London, 1949;
Boccassino, Il contributo delle antiche fonti sulla religione dei Latuca,
·bo, Bari, Denca, Nuer e altre popolazioni, Ann. lateranensi, XV, 1951,
79–143; R. Boccassino, Primo supplemento alla documentazione sulla
·gione e sulla magia delle popolazioni nilotiche fornita dai musei di etno-
fia, Ann. lateranensi, XVII, 1953, pp. 9–54; D. Paulme, Carved Figures
·m the White Nile in the Musée de l'Homme, Man, LIII, 1953, pp. 113–
W. Schmalenbach, L'art nègre, Basel, 1953; F. H. Lem, The Art of the
·dan, in Brooklyn Mus., Masterpieces of African Art, Brooklyn, N.Y.,
·4, pp. 17–21; E. von Sydow, Afrikanische Plastik, Berlin, 1954; P. Ger-
nn, Zur Ornamentik im Kunsthandwerk des Mittelsudans, in W. Lang
al., Von fremden Völkern und Kulturen, Düsseldorf, 1955, pp. 153–60;
Boccassino, Secondo supplemento di documenti per lo studio della reli-
ne e della magia delle popolazioni nilotiche, forniti dai musei di etnografia,
n. lateranensi, XXI, 1957, pp. 98–114; E. Leuzinger, Afrika: Kunst
· Negervölker, Baden-Baden, 1959.

Bibliographies: R. L. Hill, A Bibliography of the Anglo-Egyptian Sudan,
ıdon, 1939; Abdel Rahman el Nasri, A Bibliography of the Sudan, 1938–
·8, London, New York, 1962.

MONUMENTAL CENTERS. Sites, beginning in the north, are de-
ibed according to the course of the Nile, near which most of them
·· situated. In each subhead (l) or (r) following the name of the
·e indicates that it is on the left or right bank looking downstream.
he capital, Khartoum, is discussed first.) All ancient remains be-
·een the First Cataract and Kosha, except for those which have been
·noved, are situated within the backup area of the Aswan dam.
To avoid repetition, the following notes describe the chief fea-
·es of typical Sudanese temples and churches. Temples, whether
New Kingdom or Napatan date, usually follow the normal plan
·an Egyptian temple: (i) a rectangular plan; (ii) a processional way
·d pylon; (iii) a forecourt; (iv) a hypostyle hall; (v) a pronaos; and

(vi) a sanctuary containing the god's shrine, often surrounded by
subsidiary shrines and storerooms. The exterior was decorated with
reliefs of the king and gods, and the interiors of the pylon and forecourt with reliefs depicting the king's public acts (e.g., foreign victories); the rest of the interior reliefs largely depicted offering and ritual
scenes. The usual materials were stone (sandstone) and brick (of
unbaked mud). Meroitic temples tended to deviate from this type.

Churches were usually built of unbaked brick or of brick (of
baked mud), sometimes combined with stone. The basic plan included the following features: (i) a square or rectangular ground plan;
(ii) north and south entrances; (iii) three west rooms; (iv) a nave and
two aisles; (v) a sanctuary with an apsidal end and with an imposing
arch; and (vi) two small sacristies flanking the sanctuary. The roof
was flat (with vaulted aisles and nave) or domed, while a larger type
of church had upper galleries reached by an interior southwest staircase. The walls were often decorated with painted scenes.

Khartoum (Khartum, el-Ḥarṭūm). The capital of Sudan is
situated on the left bank of the Blue Nile just before it joins the White
Nile. A mesolithic site and necropolis were situated in this area.
After the destruction (1885) of the original urban center (1820–23),
the city was rebuilt by the British in 1898 on a master plan by Lord
Kitchener that provided for a series of squares cut by large thoroughfares running in a north-south direction and intersected by smaller
diagonal streets. The city has a picturesque appearance, with its many
stone and brick buildings, generally two stories high, surrounded
by gardens of typical 19th-century English design. The government
and other principal buildings, often characterized by numerous con-
cessions — above all, ornamental (Arab arches, etc.) — to traditional
architecture, are ranged along the river and on Gordon Avenue which
runs parallel but not next to the Nile. Among the main structures
are the Palace (1899), formerly seat of the governor general, with
three stories, arcaded verandas on the two top stories, and a fine loggia; in front of the Palace there is a bronze statue of General Gordon
mounted on a camel. Gordon College (since 1951 incorporated in the
University College of Khartoum) is a two-storied building with
arched windows. Surrounding the Palace are various government
buildings, the Sudan Club, the Mudiria (the governor's residence),
the mosque, and Coptic, Anglican, Maronite, Greek, and Roman
Catholic churches. Along the right bank there is an extensive suburb
characterized by low mud-brick and stone houses. A road and railroad bridge (1910) connects this section with the main urban center.
Another bridge (1928) joins the Blue and the White Nile. The Sudan
National Museum contains mostly archaeological remains and houses
some of the dismantled temples and other remains that have been
saved from the backup area of the Aswan dam.

BIBLIOG. P. F. Martin, The Sudan in Evolution, London, 1921; C.
E. J. Walkley, The Story of Khartoum, SNR, XVIII, 1936, pp. 221–41,
XIX, 1937, pp. 71–92; A. J. Arkell, Early Khartoum, Oxford, 1949; EB, s.v.

Faras (l). The capital of Christian Nobadia, the kingdom of the
Nobatae (ca. 6th–12th cent.), Faras is important for the study of Christian Nubian art and architecture, although earlier remains exist
elsewhere. In the northeast there stood a stone temple of Tutankhamen, the inscribed blocks of which were reused in a nearby Meroitic cemetery. To the northwest there are two domed brick churches
called the northern and the southern church. A Meroitic ditch and
well-built stone and brick walls, with bastions and corner towers,
enclose a riverside mound that was probably the site of a Middle
Kingdom fort. Temples of Thutmosis III and Ramses II once stood
here. The principal monuments (brick) are the Great Church, with
wall paintings in Coptic style, and an adjoining monastery; a bishop's
palace; the Citadel Church (dated partly by adjoining bishops' tombs),
with 100 wall paintings, some in a fine Greco-Byzantine style but
including many Nubian elements (portraits of contemporary rulers
and bishops). Most of the existing paintings date from the 10th
and 11th centuries, but the underlying paintings are from about the
9th century. (Most of the frescoes have been removed; many were
offered to Poland.) The paintings of the River Gate Church are similar in style. The site also includes Meroitic, Christian, and Islamic
houses and fortifications, and slightly north of the mound there are
pottery kilns that provided important stratified material for the study
of the development of Christian pottery. South of the town site are
Hathor Rock, which contained a rock temple of Ramses II and Hatshepsut (relics in Khartoum, Sudan Nat. Mus.) and the Church of
Nabindiffi. To the northwest are A and C Group cemeteries.

BIBLIOG. G. S. Mileham, Churches in Lower Nubia, Philadelphia,
1910, pp. 37–45; S. Clarke, Christian Antiquities in the Nile Valley, Oxford,
1912, pp. 66–70; U. Monneret de Villard, La Nubia medioevale, I–II, Cairo,
1935, pp. 188–200; PM, VII, pp. 124–27; W. J. Adams, An Introductory
Classification of Christian Nubian Pottery, Kush, X, 1962, pp. 245–88;
K. Michalowski, New Discoveries at Faras in Nubia, Archaeology, XV,

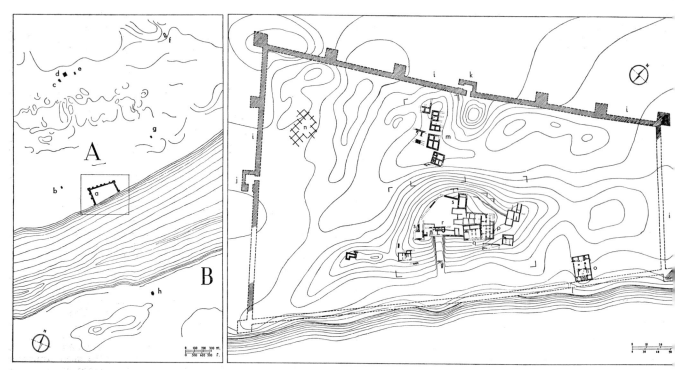

Faras and the surrounding area; in the enlargement at the right, the plan of the fortress. (A) Faras zone; (B) Adindan zone. (a) Fort; (b) Hat Rock and the Church of Nabindiffi; (c) southern church; (d) western palace; (e) northern church; (f) Anchorite grotto; (g) remains of a Meroitic cemet and a temple of Tutankhamen; (h) northern church; (i) wall of the Meroitic fortress; (j) south gate; (k) west gate; (l) remains of a postern toward the riv (m) remains of Meroitic houses; (n) remains of the Great Church; (o) River Gate Church; (p) Citadel Church; (q) monastery; (r) chapels; (s) remains a citadel from the Arab period (from U. Monneret de Villard, 1935, and from K. Michalowski, in Archaeology, XV, 1962, and Kush, X, 1962).

1962, pp. 112–20; K. Michalowski, Polish Excavations at Faras, Kush, X, 1962, pp. 220–44, XI, 1963, pp. 227–34, XII, 1964, pp. 195–207; P. Huard, A propos des Buchrânes a corne déformée de Faras, Kush, XII, 1964, pp. 63–81; T. Save-Söderbergh, Preliminary Report of the Scandinavian Joint Expedition: Archaeological Investigations between Faras and Gemai, Kush, XII, 1964, pp. 19–39.

Serra (Sarra) East (r). The riverbank fort (probably Middle Kingdom) with brick walls and a rock-cut ditch was later occupied by a Christian town with a small two-storied church. To the north and south there are two domed brick churches, and one mile farther south stands a large brick church.

BIBLIOG. S. Clarke, Christian Antiquities in the Nile Valley, Oxford, 1912, pp. 59–66; U. Monneret de Villard, La Nubia medioevale, I-II, Cairo, 1935, pp. 200–05; PM, VII, p. 128.

Aksha (l). The stone temple was dedicated by Ramses II to his own statue. The fine stylized reliefs were for the most part destroyed, and the forecourt was reused as a church.

BIBLIOG. PM, VII, pp. 127–28; J. Vercoutter, Preliminary Report on the Excavations at Aksha, Kush, X, 1962, pp. 109–17; J. Vercoutter, Excavations at Aksha, Kush, XI, 1963, pp. 131–40; J. de Heinzelin, Le soussol du Temple d'Aksha, Kush, XII, 1964, pp. 102–10.

Dibeira (Debeira) (r). The rock-cut tomb of Djehuty-hetep, a Nubian prince serving under Hatshepsut, is the only known decorated New Kingdom chamber tomb in the Sudan. The first of its several chambers has wall paintings of Djehuty-hetep hunting, inspecting a plantation, and feasting. Both the style and motifs are purely Egyptian. An inner shrine contains statues of the owner and his family, but only later burials were found in the reused tomb.

BIBLIOG. PM, VII, p. 128; T. H. Thabit, The Tomb of Djehuty-Hetep Prince of Serra, Kush, V, 1957, pp. 81–86; H. Wilde, Une danse nubienne d'epoque pharaonique, Kush, VII, 1959, pp. 76–90; T. Save-Söderbergh, The Paintings in the Tomb of Djehuty-hetep at Debeira, Kush, VIII, 1960, pp. 25–44; P. E. Shinnie, The University of Ghana Expedition at Debeira West, Kush, XI, 1963, pp. 257–63, XII, 1964, pp. 208–15.

Buhen (l). An important ancient military and administrative center, the site is basic for the study of Egyptian military architecture. In the northwest there is a fortified town (4th–5th dynasties), the only one of its kind known so far in the Sudan. To the south stands a brick Middle Kingdom fort (ca. 500 sq. ft.), the plan of which is repeated with some modifications in all Middle Kingdom Nubian forts. The

towered walls (ca. 40 ft. high and 13 ft. thick) were fronted b wide ditch and had bastioned ramparts with archer's loopholes. the west side a massive towered gateway with drawbridge led i a town with a regular plan, while two river gates on the east were link with quays. During the New Kingdom the fort was enclosed a new ditch and a towered wall, within which a town develop East of the fort there was a brick temple (with the name of Ahm inscribed on a doorway), which was restored by Amenhotep II. the northeast corner of the fort, probably on a Middle Kingdom tem site, Hatshepsut built a peripteral stone temple with fine reliefs, which Thutmosis III made slight additions. Parts of both these te ples are now in the Sudan National Museum in Khartoum. La Middle and New Kingdom cemeteries have been discovered, a Christian remains include a brick church south of the New Kingd wall.

BIBLIOG. U. Monneret de Villard, La nubia medioevale, I-II, Ca 1935, pp. 212–13; PM, VII, pp. 129–39; W. B. Emery, Preliminary Repo Kush, VII, 1959, pp. 7–14, VIII, 1960, pp. 7–10, IX, 1961, pp. 81– X, 1962, pp. 106–08, XI, 1963, pp. 116–20, XII, 1964, pp. 43–46.

Kor (l). The fortified trading post has triple walls and bastio (Middle Kingdom, New Kingdom). New Kingdom and later ce eteries are situated nearby.

BIBLIOG. PM, VII, p. 140; J. Vercoutter, Kor est-il Iken?, Ku III, 1955, pp. 4–19.

Abd el-Qadir (l). The small brick church has wall paintings provincial style of favorite Nubian subjects: Christ Enthroned, t Trinity, the Fiery Furnace, and the Nativity. The principal scer are behind the altar and on the aisle walls and include a portrait a contemporary Nubian ruler.

BIBLIOG. F. L. Griffith, Oxford Excavations in Nubia, Liverp Univ. Ann. of Archaeol. and Anthr., XV, 1928, pp. 63–88.

Mirgissa (l). A Middle Kingdom brick fort of the Buhen ty has unusual double walls on the north, west, and south. A stone temp (18th and 19th dynasties) stood in the northwest corner.

BIBLIOG. PM, VII, p. 142; G. A. Reisner, The Egyptian Forts fr Halfa to Semna, Kush, VIII, 1960, pp. 11–24 at 17; N. F. Wheeler, Dia of the Excavation of Mirgissa Fort, Kush, IX, 1961, pp. 87–179; J. Vercoutt Excavations at Mirgissa, Kush, XII, 1964, pp. 57–62.

Dabnarti. On this island in the Nile, just opposite from the Mirgissa fort, there is a brick fort with projecting spurs (probably Middle Kingdom).

BIBLIOG. PM, VII, p. 142; J. W. Ruby, Preliminary Report of the University of California Expedition to Dabnarti, Kush, XII, 1964, pp. 54–56.

Gammai (Gemai) (r). The southernmost known A Group cemetery and two Meroitic or X Group cemeteries are located here.

BIBLIOG. PM, VII, pp. 142–43.

Shalfak (l). On a hilltop there is a Middle Kingdom brick fort (ca. 280 × 155 ft.) based on the Buhen type, which illustrates the modifications imposed on the Second Cataract forts by their irregular sites: stone foundations, the absence of a lower rampart, the very thick wall towers, and the enormously developed spur wall (ca. 386 ft. long) defending the approaches. Inside the fort there is a town.

BIBLIOG. PM, VII, p. 143; G. A. Reisner, The Egyptian Forts from Halfa to Semna, Kush, VIII, 1960, pp. 11–24 at 16.

Uronarti (Geziret el-Melik). On this island in the Nile there is a brick fort of Sesostris III resembling Shalfak in plan and containing a single-chamber stone temple of Thutmosis III (fragments in Khartoum, Sudan Nat. Mus.; Boston, Mus. of Fine Arts).

BIBLIOG. PM, VII, pp. 143–44; G. A. Reisner, The Egyptian Forts from Halfa to Semna, Kush, VIII, 1960, pp. 11–24 at 13.

Semna (l). The brick fort at Semna with the one at Kumna (see below) marked the Middle Kingdom frontier. L-shaped in plan (ca. 528 × 500 ft.), it was defended by a glacis, ditch, and strong towered walls (X, FIG. 732). In the eastern area stood the single-chamber stone Temple of Thutmosis III, with relief decorations and with east and west porticoes, as well as the brick Temple of Taharqa. The Temple of Thutmosis has been completely dismantled for the Sudan National Museum.

BIBLIOG. PM, VII, pp. 144–51; G. A. Reisner, D. Dunham and J. Janssen, Second Cataract Forts, I, Boston, 1960; R. A. Caminos, Surveying Semna Gharbi, Kush, XII, 1964, pp. 82–86.

Kumma (r). A square brick fort of the Middle Kingdom contained a stone and mud-brick temple from the period of Thutmosis III and Amenhotep II with fine reliefs (temple remains now in Khartoum, Sudan Nat. Mus.).

BIBLIOG. PM, VII, pp. 151–56; G. A. Reisner, D. Dunham and J. Janssen, Second Cataract Forts, I, Boston, 1960.

Susinarti Island. A large stone-walled Christian fort of unusual triangular shape has towers at each corner and remains of crude huts within.

BIBLIOG. H. N. Chittick, Antiquities of the Batn el Hajar, Kush, V, 1957, pp. 42–48.

Ukma East (r). A rectangular stone-walled Christian fort has a semicircular northeast corner tower and contains a brick church.

BIBLIOG. H. N. Chittick, Antiquities of the Batn el Hajar, Kush, V, 1957, pp. 42–48.

Kulubnarti. On this island in the Nile opposite Kulb there is a Christian town with a two-storied brick church containing remains of wall paintings.

BIBLIOG. S. Clarke, Christian Antiquities in the Nile Valley, Oxford, 1912, pp. 49–50; U. Monneret de Villard, La Nubia medioevale, I–II, Cairo, 1935, p. 234; P. L. Shinnie, A Christian Nubian Painting, Kush, II, 1955, pp. 96–97.

Kulb (l). The ruined brick church on a stone platform, without nave or aisles, is covered by a dome.

BIBLIOG. S. Clarke, Christian Antiquities in the Nile Valley, Oxford, 1912, p. 45 ff.; U. Monneret de Villard, La Nubia medioevale, I–II, Cairo, 1935, p. 234.

Firka (r). The transition from X Group to Christian culture has been revealed by three large necropolises: A (X Group mounds, 5th-6th cent.), B (transitional, late 6th cent.), and C (Christian). Some fine metal objects came from these cemeteries (Khartoum, Sudan Nat. Mus.; Oxford, Ashmolean Mus.).

BIBLIOG. L. P. Kirwan, The Oxford University Excavations at Firka, Oxford, 1939.

Amara (l). This typical fortified Sudanese town of the 18th and 19th dynasties had buttressed brick walls. The Temple of Ramses II in the northeast corner contained fine stylized reliefs, including a Syrian war scene and copies of the "Marriage" and "Dream" steles of Abu Simbel. In the town four building levels have been distinguished, dating respectively to Seti I, Ramses II, and Ramses III (that is, to the years 1313–1167 B.C.), or possibly to the 25th dynasty (712–663 B.C.). East of the town there was a small brick building connected with a Nubian snake cult.

BIBLIOG. PM, VII, pp. 157–64.

Sai. On the northern tip of this island in the Nile there are the remains (four stone columns) of a church, while on the east bank lies a town site with stratified levels dating to the New Kingdom, Meroitic, X Group, Christian and late Christian, and 16th-century Arab or Turkish periods. The surrounding stone walls are probably Christian with Turkish additions, while a massive brick wall in the interior may be part of a New Kingdom fort. Temple blocks of the 18th and 19th dynasties and a small Meroitic temple exist. Southwest of the fort are 25th dynasty and X Group cemeteries, while the south is occupied by several Kerma and hundreds of Kerma-Nubian mound graves.

BIBLIOG. U. Monneret de Villard, La Nubia medioevale, I–II, Cairo, 1935, pp. 238–39; PM, VII, pp. 164–66; J. Vercoutter, Excavations at Sai 1955–57, Kush, VI, 1958, pp. 144–69.

Gebel Doshah (l). There is a rock-cut shrine of Thutmosis III with reliefs.

BIBLIOG. PM, VII, p. 165.

Soleb (Sulb) (l). The New Kingdom temple, one of the finest in the Sudan, was founded by Thutmosis III and almost entirely built by Amenhotep III. The final stone complex was a grandiose version of the normal temple plan and was decorated with reliefs of the highest quality. In its earlier phases a processional way led to a pool that was linked to the river by a long canal, which was later filled in to form a causeway. The double brick walls of the enclosure, with towered outer faces, formed an area of about 450 × 540 ft., which was later enlarged with similar walls.

Southeast of the temple lies the town (unexcavated), and a little farther in the same direction there is a cemetery with a few Kerma-Nubian graves and 45 New Kingdom family tombs, some with a pyramidal superstructure and chapel — the earliest known examples of this form in the Sudan.

BIBLIOG. PM, VII, pp. 169–72; M. Schiff Giorgini, Preliminary Reports, Kush, VI, 1958, pp. 82–98, VII, 1959, pp. 154–70, IX, 1961, pp. 182–97, X, 1962, pp. 152–69, XIV, 1964, pp. 87–95; J. M. A. Janssen, A Brief Description of the Decoration of Room II of the Temple of Soleb, Kush, VII, 1959, pp. 198–209; J. Leclant, Le sarcophage de Ouabset de la nécropole de Soleb, Kush, XI, 1963, pp. 141–58.

Sesebi (l). This typical but eroded New Kingdom Sudanese town was built largely by Akhenaten and occupied into the 19th dynasty. Each of the buttressed brick walls is pierced by gateways leading into a well-laid-out town with several 'Amarna-type houses. The two temples are unusual. The larger (ca. 190 × 160 ft.), situated in the northwest corner, was built of stone in the time of Akhenaten and was altered by Seti I. It consisted of three adjoining sanctuaries, the central one having a relief-decorated crypt; in front of the sanctuaries there was a court enclosed by a stone wall. Another temple — possibly a sun temple of Akhenaten — in the northeast corner had two courts, one 6 ft. higher than the other.

BIBLIOG. PM, VII, pp. 172–74.

Kerma (r). This is the site of a native town and a fortified Egyptian trading post during the Middle Kingdom and Second Intermediate Period and of a cemetery including burials of the native kings of the area. The town has mostly disappeared through wind erosion, but the original post consisted of a solid brick rectangle with rooms on top; buildings were later added toward the east and west. To the north lies a cemetery in which the grave types (mounds), burial customs (including numerous human sacrifices), and grave goods are clearly Sudanese but show considerable Egyptian influence, as illustrated by two rectangular brick funerary chapels with wall paintings in Egyptian style and numerous imported objects, notably the beautiful Middle Kingdom statue of Lady Sennuwy (Boston, Mus. of Fine Arts). It is also possible to trace the development of distinctively Sudanese products, such as ivory inlays, mica ornaments, bronze daggers, and pottery (see X, cols. 731–732, PLS. 364, 369).

BIBLIOG. PM, VII, pp. 175–80.

Dongola (r.) The capital of the Christian kingdom of Mukurra (6th–14th cent.), it has a rectangular brick church with five vaulted corridors on the ground floor and a chamber surrounded by a corridor on the upper. The edifice was converted into a mosque in 1317.

BIBLIOG. S. Clarke, Christian Antiquities in the Nile Valley, Oxford, 1912, pp. 43–44; U. Monneret de Villard, La Nubia medioevale, I–II, Cairo, 1935, pp. 246–48; O. G. S. Crawford, The Fung Kingdom of Sennar, London, 1951; PM, VII, p. 193; P. L. Shinnie, Old Dongola Church, Kush, III, 1955, pp. 97–98.

Kawa (Gematen) (r.) A great religious center, this site has important architectural remains mainly of the 25th dynasty (751–656 B.C.). From east to west the principal monuments are as follows: Temple A was originally a stone shrine with reliefs and a brick court built by Tutankhamen; a brick court was added by Taharqa (688–663 B.C.), the whole being about 125 × 56 ft. Adjacent Temple B (89 × 50 ft.) was founded by Amenhotep III but was rebuilt in brick by Harsiotef (404–369 B.C.) and in stone by Aryamani. Northeast of Temple B is the west kiosk, a halting place for the god's bark during processions, erected between 70 and 2 B.C. East of the kiosk, an avenue that was once flanked by statues of rams bearing representations of Taharqa (Merowe Mus.; Br. Mus.) leads to the grandiose stone Temple T (ca. 226 × 117 ft.), which was built under the same ruler. The plan is normal, but the reliefs, carved by Memphite and Sudanese craftsmen, contain unusual elements. In the first court reliefs depicting the king as a sphinx trampling his enemies are close copies of 5th- and 6th-dynasty royal reliefs from Abusir and Saqqara, while on the walls of the hypostyle hall the scenes of the god's procession include a well-preserved native orchestra; the other reliefs are more conventional.

Notable finds from Temples T and A include steles (Copenhagen, Ny Carlsberg Glyptotek; Merowe Mus.; Br. Mus.), fragments of statues, a fine bronze head (Arnekhamani; Br. Mus.), and a New Kingdom gold statuette (Oxford, Ashmolean Mus.).

East of Temple T there is a poorly preserved brick temple, and northwest of this a stone kiosk with columned sides and curtain walls (probably 18–2 B.C.).

BIBLIOG. M. F. L. Macadam, The Temples of Kawa, 2 vols., Oxford, 1949–55; PM, VII, pp. 180–92.

Zuma (r.) There are large mound graves, possibly a royal cemetery of the Upper Nobatae, as well as many pyramids.

BIBLIOG. PM, VII, p. 193.

Tangasi (l.) Large mound graves, possibly royal burials of the Upper Nobatae, and pyramids are located here.

BIBLIOG. PM, VII, p. 193; P. L. Shinnie, Excavations at Tanqasi, Kush, II, 1954, pp. 66–85.

El Kurru (r.) The royal cemetery of the 25th dynasty (apart from that of Taharqa at Nuri) until the reign of Tanwetamani (663–656 B.C.) shows the development from the early mound graves of the dynasty's predecessors through the stone mastaba form to the stone pyramid with external chapel and underground stairway tomb that remained the basic type of royal burial until the end of the Meroitic period (ca. A.D. 350). The earliest example of the latter type is the tomb of Piankhy (751–716 B.C.). The usual size of each complex is about 33 × 50 ft. Mastabas were used for wealthy, nonroyal burials, and the mound grave remained characteristic of the lower-class burials. The chapels do not preserve their decoration, but several funerary chambers are painted in good Egyptian style (especially tombs 5 and 16). Numerous fine objects, especially ivory carvings and bronzes, recovered from the tombs show strong Egyptian influence (see also X, cols. 737–738).

BIBLIOG. PM, VII, pp. 195–98.

Sanam (l.) The denuded site contained a stone temple of Taharqa reproducing the plan of Temple T in Kawa. The entire temple was originally covered in reliefs; a copy of the procession scenes at Ka[...] and interesting details of wheeled carts and riders on horseback [...] main. Foundation and endowment inscriptions of Taharqa we[...] found. East of the temple, there was a brick treasury containing[...] regular series of rooms, and west of the temple, a cemetery dating fr[...] Piankhy to Amtalqua showing mixed Egyptian and Sudanese bur[...] customs. (Remains from the temple are in Oxford, Ashmolean Mu[...] and Berlin, Staat. Mus.)

BIBLIOG. PM, VII, pp. 198–203.

Wadi Ghazali (l.) A massive dry-masonry wall encloses a chur[...] and numerous monastery buildings. The church, of dressed sto[...] and red brick, was built in two phases — an earlier one with colum[...] and a flat roof and a later one with stone pillars supporting vau[...] Outside the north door there is a square baptistry with a stone ta[...] and brick dome — the only known baptistry in the Sudan. Christi[...] cemeteries are found toward the east, southeast, and south, the l[...] with numerous inscribed tiles. The Ghazali pottery forms a ba[...] for the Christian Nubian corpus (Khartoum, Sudan Nat. Mus.).

BIBLIOG. P. L. Shinnie and H. N. Chittick, Ghazali: A Monaste[...] in the Northern Sudan (Sudan Ant. Service, Occasional Pap., V), Khartou[...] 1961.

Gebel Barkal (Napata) (r.) Here was founded Napata, the N[...] Kingdom frontier town and capital of the Kushite kings until abo[...] 590 B.C. At the foot of the great rock Gebel Barkal — a Sudanese A[...] Simbel — there is a Temple of Amen (B 500), with a shrine of Ra[...] ses II on the east side (X, FIG. 733, PL. 365). Piankhy and Tahar[...] added a new stone casing and a west chapel, while a third pylon w[...] built during the Meroitic period. Over eighteen entire or fragmenta[...] statues were recovered from B 500 and B 800, including life-size [...] over-life-size royal statues, dating from Taharqa to Aspelta (X, p[...] 366), as well as one of Akhraten, all of which are excellent exampl[...] of the art of the period (Boston, Mus. of Fine Arts; Merowe Mus[...]

West of B 500 lies an undecorated stone temple, B 600 (ca. [...] cent. B.C.), and west of B 600 there is a stone temple of Atlaner[...] and Senkamanisken, B 700 (643–623 B.C.), probably on a 19th-dynas[...] site. The relief-decorated sanctuary of B 700 contained a fine sculptur[...] altar of Atlanersa (653–643 B.C.; Boston, Mus. of Fine Arts). Templ[...] B 600 and B 700 are simple in plan, each having a columned for[...] court, sanctuary, and the typical Meroitic addition of a column[...] portico. Farther south lies temple B 800, to which Piankhy and lat[...] kings added the complex B 900; both of these originally had reli[...] decoration. To the west lie temples 200 and 300, rock-cut Am[...] temples of Taharqa, one on a Ramses II site. To the west there a[...] cemeteries, used only sporadically for royal burials (3d–1st ce[...] B.C.) but employing the typical pyramidal tomb. The preserved chap[...] decoration, along with that of Meroë, is the chief source for the d[...] velopment of Meroitic funerary-chapel reliefs.

BIBLIOG. PM, VII, pp. 203–23; S. E. Chapman and D. Dunha[...] Royal Cemeteries of Kush, III: Decorated Chapels of the Meroitic Pyrami[...] at Meroe and Barkal, Boston, 1952; D. Dunham, Royal Cemeteries of Kus[...] IV: Royal Tombs at Meroe and Barkal, Boston, 1957.

Nuri (l.) This site of a royal cemetery was in use from Tahar[...] until Nastasen (336–315 B.C.). The tomb type is the pyramid compl[...] (usual size, 98 ft. on each side of the base) developed at El Kurr[...] some chapel decoration in relief is preserved, while several funera[...] chambers had painted or incised decoration (X, PL. 367). Numero[...] objects — sarcophagi of Anlamani and Aspelta and fine metal objec[...] — continue to show strong Egyptian influence. Other buildings, fro[...] west to east, are a stone funerary chapel (500); a brick church (10c[...] in which important Napatan royal steles were reused as floor slab[...] a stone mortuary chapel (600); and a partly rock-cut late Napat[...] funerary chapel (400).

BIBLIOG. PM, VII, pp. 223–33; D. Dunham, Royal Cemeteries of Kus[...] II: Nuri, Boston, 1955.

El Kab (r.) This and several of the following sites are importa[...] for the study of Sudanese Christian fortifications, on which the[...] was possibly European influence by way of the Crusades. The nort[...] ern fortress is typical: roughly rectangular (165 × 363 ft.) with dr[...] masonry walls, oval bastions at each corner and on the sides, and[...] single gate defended by a reentrant. To the south there is a small[...] irregular complex with rectangular buildings, probably of later dat[...]

BIBLIOG. O. G. S. Crawford, Castles and Churches in the Midd[...] Nile Region (Sudan Ant. Service, Occasional Pap., II), Khartoum, 195[...] pp. 10–14.

El Koro (l). A Christian stone fort of El Kab type with corner towers is located here. To the south there are two mosques, one of which was originally a church. A tile in the Christian cemetery seems to bear the date 917.

BIBLIOG. O. G. S. Crawford, Castles and Churches in the Middle Nile Region (Sudan Ant. Service, Occasional Pap., II), Khartoum, 1953, pp. 31-35.

Kurgus (r). The southernmost of the known rock inscriptions of Thutmosis I and Thutmosis III may have marked the frontier. There are also the remains of a brick fort.

BIBLIOG. PM, VII, p. 233.

Suakin (Sawakin). This is the best example of the Red Sea architectural style in Sudan. Situated on an oval island in the Red Sea, the town was built in three phases: the earliest, including two mosques, from the 15th-16th century; the middle phase, to which most of the buildings belong; and, finally, the coarser, larger buildings of the Egyptian occupation (19th cent.). The two- and three-storied houses of stone and coral are of standard Islamic type; *mashrabiyas* (grilles) and projecting wooden balconies, often elaborately decorated, are characteristic.

BIBLIOG. D. H. Matthews, The Red Sea Style, Kush, I, 1953, pp. 60-86; D. H. Matthews, Suakin Postscript, Kush, III, 1955, pp. 99-111.

Artul Island. The rectangular stone church is now a mosque.

BIBLIOG. O. G. S. Crawford, Castles and Churches in the Middle Nile Region (Sudan Ant. Service, Occasional Pap., II), Khartoum, 1953, pp. 14-15.

Tarfava (r). A Christian stone fort of the El Kab type with an inner and outer enclosure stands here.

BIBLIOG. O. G. S. Crawford, Castles and Churches in the Middle Nile Region (Sudan Ant. Service, Occasional Pap., II), Khartoum, 1953, pp. 15-17.

Gandeisi Island. There is a Christian stone fort of the El Kab type, with a red brick church to the north of it.

BIBLIOG. O. G. S. Crawford, Castles and Churches in the Middle Nile Region (Sudan Ant. Service, Occasional Pap., II), Khartoum, 1953, pp. 26-30.

Baqeir (l). The Christian stone fort is of the El Kab type.

BIBLIOG. O. G. S. Crawford, Castles and Churches in the Middle Nile Region (Sudan Ant. Service, Occasional Pap., II), Khartoum, 1953, pp. 30-31.

El Usheir Island. A Christian stone fort of the El Kab type with chevaux-de-frise of pointed stones is situated here. To the south there is a trapezoidal red-brick church with nine columns.

BIBLIOG. O. G. S. Crawford, Castles and Churches in the Middle Nile Region (Sudan Ant. Service, Occasional Pap., II), Khartoum, 1953, pp. 19-24.

Gebel Nakharu (l). A square, well-built stone fort has bastions of possible Meroitic origin.

BIBLIOG. O. G. S. Crawford, Castles and Churches in the Middle Nile Region (Sudan Ant. Service, Occasional Pap., II), Khartoum, 1953, pp. 17-19.

Fura Wells (l). At this site, in the desert west of the Nile, there is a rectangular Meroitic stone fort with rectangular bastions.

BIBLIOG. O. G. S. Crawford, Castles and Churches in the Middle Nile Region (Sudan Ant. Service, Occasional Pap., II), Khartoum, 1953, pp. 36-39.

Meroë (Begerewiyeh) (r). An important town in the 25th dynasty, became the royal capital, probably about 591 B.C., and remained so until the kingdom fell about A.D. 350. From north to south the main monuments are the Temple of Isis, notable for the use of glazed tiles as floor and wall decoration and for two, great columnar statues (X, PL. 368), and the City of the Kings, a brick-walled town in which the most important elements were the northern area with palaces;

the frescoed chamber (292) with wall paintings of a king, queen, and officials, outside of which a large bronze head of Augustus was found (looted from Egypt ca. 24 B.C.; now Br. Mus.); the royal baths possibly built under Roman influence about the time of Natakamani (2 B.C.-A.D. 23). The baths had an elaborate water-supply and drainage system, and the colonnaded pool was decorated with glazed tiles, wall paintings, and notable statuary of classical and Sudanese inspiration (X, PL. 368). Similar statues came from the Late Palace (750) southeast of the town.

Adjoining the eastern town wall is the Temple of Amen (ca. 400 × 165 ft.), built prior to 463 B.C., largely in brick but with some relief-decorated stone areas. Farther east there are three temples, distinctive Meroitic types, each built on an artificial mound: the Lion Temple (probably before 463 B.C.) and the nearby shrine (no. 70), both simple two-chambered buildings; and the Sun Temple, which may have been in the time of Aspelta, possibly under Greek influence. A stone-walled platform decorated with reliefs based on local scenes supported a sanctuary with glazed-tile and relief decoration and a surrounding colonnade. South of the town there is a shrine of Apis.

The necropolises stretching along the east of the site consist of the north cemetery (royal burials, ca. 275 B.C.-A.D. 350), the south cemetery (burials dating from the 25th dynasty and royal burials of ca. 300-275 B.C.), the west cemetery (queens and nobility), and the commoners' cemeteries. The royal cemeteries form a basis for study of the chronological sequence of the kings and illustrate varying periods of prosperity and strong Egyptian influence or of decline and isolation. The royal grave type is the normal stone pyramid, but the latest and poorest are of red brick (X, PL. 367). The surviving funerary chapel decoration (with that of Gebel Barkal) illustrates the stylistic and iconographic changes in Meroitic art (PL. 330; X, PL. 371); numerous objects of classical, Egyptian, and Sudanese inspiration were recovered from the plundered tombs (VI, PL. 241; X, PL. 370). The commoners' mound graves also show an archaeological progression of grave types and burial goods continuing into the post-Meroitic period.

BIBLIOG. PM, VII, pp. 235-61; S. E. Chapman and D. Dunham, Royal Cemeteries of Kush, III: Decorated Chapels of the Meroitic Pyramids at Meroe and Barkal, Boston, 1952; D. Dunham, Royal Cemeteries of Kush, IV: Royal Tombs at Meroe and Barkal, Boston, 1957; F. F. Gadallah, Meroitic Problems and a Comprehensive Meroitic Bibliography, Kush, XI, 1963, pp. 196-216.

Ba'sa (r). A large circular Meroitic enclosure contains five stone lions; east of this there is a red-brick sanctuary surrounded by a colonnade, probably connected with a lion-god cult as it contained seven stone lions, four of which are now in Khartoum (Sudan Nat. Mus.).

BIBLIOG. PM, VII, p. 262.

Wad Ban Naga (r). There are two temples and a settlement, now almost completely destroyed.

BIBLIOG. PM, VII, p. 263.

Musauwarat el-Sofra. This site, 19 miles east of the Nile, is (with Naga) an important source for Meroitic art at a period when there were Greek, Roman, and Indian as well as Egyptian influences; although based on Egyptian prototypes the relief work is distinctively Sudanese in the depiction of physical types, dress, ornament, and motifs drawn from local beliefs and scenes. A walled enclosure (ca. 690 × 900 ft.) contains, among other ruins, three temples, the north and east ones being Meroitic temples of simple plan. The Great Temple consists of a stone platform (ca. 72 × 52 ft.) supporting a single-chamber sanctuary surrounded by a colonnade; the plan and some of the column decoration on the east portico (dancing boys, wrestlers) suggest Greek influence. An elaborate stone complex surrounds the temple.

To the east there is a group of temples. The northern one (Hintze II A) is a single-chamber Meroitic temple with the remains of relief decoration; and the southern one (Hintze II D) is a Meroitic temple with entrance court, forecourt, and sanctuary. The central Lion Temple (Hintze II C) is of great importance: a single-chamber stone temple, it was dedicated by Arnekhamani (Hintze: 235-218 B.C.) to Apezemek (Apedemak), a lion-god unknown in the Egyptian pantheon, who may have been the Meroitic national god since lion temples occur on other sites. The exterior reliefs (largely preserved) depict Apezemek, Sebejmeker (Sbwjmkr; another strictly Sudanese god), Egyptian gods, and the king. The interior scenes, with the king and Apezemek, contain unusual elements (e.g., the two elephants on which Apezemek stands). The lower parts of the columns were decorated with gold leaf and the upper parts bear unusual reliefs (e.g., winged lionesses as well as more conventional ones). Near the temple, but not belonging to it, were two sculptured groups each rep-

Meroë, plan of the ancient city and the zones of the necropolises. *Key:* (1) Modern village of Begerewiyeh; (2) excavated areas with superimposed remai of different periods. Principal monuments: (*a*) City walls; (*b*) royal baths; (*c*) early Meroitic palace; (*d*) middle Meroitic palace; (*e*) observatory; (columned hall; (*g*) frescoed chamber 292; (*h*) remains of a temple; (*i*) building of a later period; (*j*) rectangular enclosure; (*k*) Temple of Amen; (kiosk; (*m*) late palace 750; (*n*) Temple of Isis; (*o*) to the shrine of Apis; (*p*) Lion Temple; (*q*) shrine 70; (*r*) Sun Temple; (*s*) to the north necropoli (*t*) to the middle necropolis; (*u*) to the north pyramids; (*v*) to the south necropolises (*after Garstang et al., 1911*).

resenting three elaborately decorated animal heads. A low oval wall surrounded the temple. East of the Lion Temple is a stone-walled enclosure, possibly defensive, of a type found on other Meroitic sites. To the south there is a small, late Meroitic temple.

BIBLIOG. PM, VII, pp. 264–67; F. Hintze, Preliminary Report on the Butana Expedition 1958, Kush, VII, 1959, pp. 171–96; F. Hintze, Preliminary Report on the Excavations at Musawwarat, Kush, X, 1962, pp. 170–202, XI, 1963, pp. 217–26.

Naga. This large town site southwest of Musauwarat el-Sofra has several well-known monuments. Besides a temple with the re-

mains of two large exterior statues, there is, to the southwest of the single-chamber stone Lion Temple (Queen Amanitere, 2 B.C A.D. 23), on which there are exterior reliefs, including a unique figu of the lion-god Apezemec with three heads and four arms — sugge tive of Indian iconography — and a lion-headed serpent. The i terior reliefs of the same temple include three full-face depictio of gods, two bearded and the third with a rayed halo, possibly owi to Roman influence (X, PL. 371; XI, PL. 355). East of the Lion Temp there is a small stone kiosk almost completely Greco-Roman in sty (X, PL. 367). Farther to the east stands a stone temple of Amen (N takamani and Queen Amanitere). Approached by a flight of ste d an "avenue of rams" with a kiosk, it consists of a pylon, a forecourt, onaos, and sanctuary with surrounding complex (ca. 66×105 ft.). liefs of the gods and the king and queen decorate the walls. Slightly the south is the South Temple with a triple sanctuary (largely deded), and south of this, two reservoirs and a peripteral temple. ne stone East Temple is decorated with reliefs and is the earliestown monument at Naga. There are cemeteries to the north and uth of the town site.

BIBLIOG. PM, VII, pp. 267–72; F. Hintze, Preliminary Report on the tana Expedition 1958, Kush, VII, 1959, pp. 171–96 at 183.

Shaheinab (l). The settlement is the "type" site of the Khartoum olithic.

BIBLIOG. A. J. Arkell, Shaheinab, Oxford, 1953.

Gebel Qeili (r). Here a rock bears a striking victory relief of King erakarer (1st cent. of our era), shown as a solar god with a rayed n-disk "halo," and realistically depicted falling enemies.

BIBLIOG. F. Hintze, Preliminary Report on the Butana Expedition 58, Kush, VII, 1959, pp. 171–96 at 189.

Soba (r). Possibly occupied in Meroitic times, Soba was the caal of Christian Alwa. Trial excavation has revealed three building els and recovered a corpus of Christian pottery and datable glass. ba flourished from the 9th to the 12th century.

BIBLIOG. P. L. Shinnie, Excavations at Soba (Sudan Ant. Service, casional Pap., III), Khartoum, 1955.

Sennar. This site on the Blue Nile contains extensive cemeteries, m which came a scarab of Shabako (ca. 707–696 B.C.) and other ects (Khartoum, Sudan Nat. Mus.).

BIBLIOG. PM, VII, p. 273.

Zankor. Approximately 300 miles west of the White Nile, the vn ruins (red brick and stone) on this site may be Meroitic.

BIBLIOG. A. E. D. Penn, The Ruins of Zankor, SNR, XIV, 1931, pp. 179–84.

Uri. The legendary capital of the Tungur kingdom (ca. 8th- e 12th cent.), this site has an irregular stone-walled town containing o palace complexes of dry masonry. Both the earlier lower palace d the larger and later upper palace have oval enclosure walls, aunce platforms reached by steps, and numerous circular huts. The tforms and some of the masonry recall Meroitic building practices.

BIBLIOG. A. J. Arkell, Darfur Antiquities III, SNR, XXVII, 1946, 185–202; H. G. Balfour-Paul, History and Antiquities of Darfur (Sudan t. Mus. Pamphlet, 3), Khartoum, 1955.

Ain Farah. The most westerly Christian site identified in the dan, it has two red brick churches and a monastery (9th–13th cent., possibly as early as A.D. 700).

BIBLIOG. A. J. Arkell, Darfur Antiquities I, SNR, XIX, 1936, pp. 301– A. J. Arkell, A Christian Church and Monastery at Ain Farah, Darfur, sh, VII, 1959, pp. 115–19.

Turra. In this area there are a number of medieval remains of ying dates. Gebel Kusi was a walled construction of Tungur date, wing a tendency to rectangular building when compared with later remains at Fur (16th–17th cent.). The Fur palaces, apparently ated to the palaces of Bornu, consist of a circular stone-walled area taining circular buildings.

BIBLIOG. A. J. Arkell, Darfur Antiquities II, SNR, XX, 1937, pp. 91–

Shoba. Capital of the Fur sultan Muḥammad Teirab (1752–85), oba is a good example of Islamic architecture. The oval stone ensures of the larger palace and the oval earthwork ramparts of the aller palace seem to be related to the earlier Fur palaces, but, inad, the interior buildings are rectangular with complex room plans. ne buildings of both palaces are of brick and two-storied and conn columned rooms. South of the smaller palace there is a redck mosque with 47 brick columns.

BIBLIOG. H. G. Balfour-Paul, Sultans' Palaces in Darfur and Waddai, sh, II, 1954, pp. 5–18.

Wara. Earlier a Tungur capital and later the old capital of the Wadai sultanate, this site has 18th–19th-century remains. Within a circular brick-faced stone wall there is a complex of square buildings, including a two-storied house, a square keep, and a brick platform supporting a tower. A mosque with a hexagonal minaret is situated west of the main enclosure.

BIBLIOG. H. G. Balfour-Paul, Sultans' Palaces in Darfur and Waddai, Kush, II, 1954, pp. 5–18 at 11.

Abu Geili (l). The site consists of a Meroitic settlement and a possible Fung cemetery with the only known corpus of Fung pottery.

BIBLIOG. O. G. S. Crawford and F. Addison, Wellcome Excavations in the Sudan, III: Abu Geili, Oxford, 1951,

Gebel Moya (l). This large Meroitic settlement site has yielded a considerable quantity of pottery and other objects.

BIBLIOG. F. Addison, Wellcome Excavations in the Sudan, I: Gebel Moya, Oxford, 1949; F. Addison, Second Thoughts on Gebel Moya, Kush, IV, 1956, pp. 4–18.

David O'Connor

Illustrations: 3 figs. in text.

SUDANESE CULTURES. The cultures termed Sudanese extend over vast interior territories of northern Africa: the breadth of this geographical horizon, the key location of the Sudan as a transit area of the great caravan routes, and the consequent openness to external influences from various sources brought about the emergence, particularly in the field of artistic production, of a number of regional or tribal aspects resting on a remarkably homogeneous base (see AFRICAN CULTURES). Prehistoric and archaeological studies, though very promising, at least as regards the area of Chad, are still in the initial stages, but easily identifiable within the contemporary indigenous production are differing styles, some typically Sudanese, others influenced by the neighboring Bantu and Guinean cultures. Toward the north and east the artistic manifestations gradually become more modest and closer to the artisan level, whether because of Islamic influence or because of the proximity of the Nilotic cultures.

SUMMARY. General observations on Sudanese sculpture and minor arts (col. 674). History of the Sudanese kingdoms and peoples (col. 678). Western Sudanese cultures (col. 680): *The Bambara; The Malinke; The Dogon; The Mossi; The Bobo; The Lobi group; The Senufo.* Cultures of the central and eastern Sudan (col. 702): *The Chad civilization; The Bongo; The Azande; The Peul; The Hausa; The Nupe, the Jukun, and other peoples of the Nigerian upland plain.* Sudanese cultures in the Congo (col. 708). Architecture (col. 711).

GENERAL OBSERVATIONS ON SUDANESE SCULPTURE AND MINOR ARTS. The Sudanese cultures cover regions bordered on the north by Saharan, on the east by Hamitic and Semitic, on the south by Bantu, and on the southwest by Guinean culture areas (see BANTU CULTURES; GUINEAN CULTURES; NILOTIC CULTURES; SAHARAN-BERBER CULTURES). This wide horizontal band is characterized, as to vegetation, by two zones: the arid savanna in the north and the grassy savanna in the south, with some small areas of wooded savanna.

From the point of view of the artistic production of these cultures, the observation must be made, to start with, that toward the east and toward the north — that is to say, toward the Saharan boundaries — artistic manifestations become at the same time rarer and less varied; moreover, esthetic quality declines, at least so far as the sculptural arts are concerned. The regions where the plastic arts are almost or entirely nonexistent are those where Islamic influence was felt in a direct and relatively constant manner, but this observation by no means exhausts the matter. The interpretation of the strictures of the Koran as condemning the representation of living beings may well have stemmed from a particular orthodox sect; it may also have been made necessary by the conditions of the milieu upon which it was imposed. To the extent that for the

Sudanese Negro, and for the African Negro in general, the image always reflects that for which it doubles (and as such is capable of containing or receiving a portion of its life force), the image is virtually alive. It can therefore be assumed that what in the suras of the Koran aimed only at prohibiting any representation likely to support an idolatrous cult was in the Negro African context necessarily extended to every representation; in fact, virtually any representation or depiction is in Negro Africa reinterpreted as a religious function on the plane of animism.

In other words, the mechanics of Islamic influence on the African cultures that it affected must be described in terms of dynamism, by the reciprocal action of the confronted forces. If the coercion exercised by the Arab invaders was a factor in the gradual disappearance of the production of sculptural art, this was only because the sociological situation it created was such as to profoundly modify the very bases of the African societies. Thus the decline must be attributed not solely to the force of Islamic religious dictates but to a collapse or modification of the Negro African societies as well, a collapse and modification that favored the setting up of the rules of Islam. On the other hand, the decline took place not only in the regions that were in contact with Islam but spread over the whole of Africa, and in the last 50 years it has steadily accelerated. The origin of this process must be sought not in individual causes but in the complex they formed, which brought about the conditions of their efficacy. From the very first, Christianity, like Islam, when it began to gain a foothold in Negro Africa was strictly iconoclastic. For the missionaries the statuettes and the masks were the expressions of a paganism that it was their aim to uproot by destroying its visible signs. Moreover, according to the system of esthetic references prevailing among the missionaries, those works that are admired today had no artistic value. Thus an entire literature bears the record of impressive autos-da-fé. The appearance of Negro African churches accentuated the iconoclastic frenzy. This methodical destruction of objects of sculpture was not, however, a really decisive factor in the gradual abandonment of artistic practices: it provoked secondary effects that were effective because they operated in a favorable milieu.

In short, the present decline of Negro African sculptural arts is the result of an overthrow of the social structures that ensured the cohesion and legitimacy of the ideals embodied in and by the works. This overthrow has given rise to conditions in which certain elements have succeeded in playing an outstanding but nonetheless secondary part. Colonialism is in itself a complex fact that has provoked reactions whose degree of complexity is no less great. The slave trade disintegrated most African societies, at the level of their institutions as well as of their demography and economy; moreover, it created a psychological climate of uncertainty and insecurity in which every effort felt itself threatened even before it achieved its purpose. Lastly, it brought about the weakening of the societies and the rupture of the bonds which had kept them together, so that the invaders were met by relatively slight resistance to the new situation they created and the new ideals they endeavored to impose. All these elements would seem to have created conditions that deprived the Negro African cultures of any possibility of internal evolution and fixed them in a conservatism which — forcing the creative impulse to regress to "mannerism," then to impoverish itself in the purely academic — has considerably weakened the creative current, to the point of drying it up in many regions and perverting it in others.

Thus in speaking of the sculptural productions of the Sudanese cultures it must not be lost sight of that they constitute a body of works that henceforth can be disposed in formally closed series — that is, practically in styles that have been brought to completion. If a revival of Sudanese arts, and more generally of African arts, is to take place, it will no doubt be accomplished in the direction of a continuity that will give it a specifically Sudanese, or African, character but at the same time, as M. Leiris (1955) has suggested, it will mark a break with the sculptural formulas hitherto employed.

Since, as it appears, treating of Sudanese arts involves dealing with formally closed series and perfected styles, an effo to place these series chronologically seems indicated — to cat the moment in which these styles were formed, if possib and to determine to what extent they represent a break wi previously existing styles. The problem is a particularly delica one: given the available data, even to state it fully is not possib Because Sudanese sculptures are mainly carved in wood ar because environmental conditions are extremely unfavorable their preservation, the masks and statuettes that form the subje of the present analysis can hardly be more than 150 to 2(years old. There are rare exceptions. A small number of ob jects reached Europe between the rediscovery of Africa in th 15th century and its systematic exploration in the second ha of the 19th century. (An inventory of these would be of i estimable value in enabling the ethnologist and the historian African civilizations to establish the series of references essenti to the setting up of a chronology of Negro African sculptural arts

Moreover, even in Africa, some relatively ancient pieces ca still be found. Thus the discovery in 1931, by the Daka Djibouti Mission, of the shelter of Barna (Cliff of Bandiagar in Mali (formerly French Sudan) brought to light four masl (PL. 304) identified as having been used in the celebration the Sigui. Since the festival was celebrated every 60 year and since the last Sigui took place at the beginning of tt 20th century, it was determined (a new mask being require for every celebration) that the fourth of these masks — tt most ancient — could probably be placed between 1725 ar 1730 (Griaule, 1938, p. 245, fig. 2).

Aside from the rarity of such discoveries, objects of th antiquity discovered under such conditions are so fragile th they cannot withstand the rigors of even the slightest transpo tation and must be examined in situ. F. M. Olbrechts (194 succeeded in drawing up a methodological series capable helping to establish a chronology of Negro African arts, but seems improbable that such a body of methods can make possible to discover works of styles earlier than those alreac known, except perhaps in the old European collections. Tt interest that would attach to research that would group togethe concrete data capable of laying the foundations of a differenti analysis of the arts produced in the midst of one and the san society at different stages of its evolution is obvious. Tt effects of time, and incidentally of vandalism, which have take their toll of wood sculptures — metal, stone, ivory, and eve earthenware objects being affected by these factors to a less degree — constitute a considerable hindrance to research. The limit its scope, depriving it to a certain extent of a tempor perspective in regard to its development. Hence elements whicl once gathered, would help to define historical or at least chror ological landmarks are doubly precious, and the importane that invests African archaeology in this particular situatic cannot be too highly stressed (see PALEO-AFRICAN CULTURES

But here again difficulty arises. The discovery of a site - or of several sites — in a particular place is not in itself suff ciently conclusive to lay the foundations of a chronology the arts in that region, owing to the movements that have take place in the interior of Negro Africa. A relation between th art whose remains have been brought to light by archaeolog and the one that was still vigorous half a century ago canne be established without proof that those remains and the mo recent products were shaped by the same population. Howeve the still-new archaeology of western Africa is destined to pe form outstanding services in the elucidation of the problem posed by the present-day arts. The excavations undertaken b B. Fagg in Nigeria and by A. Masson-Detourbet and J. I Lebeuf in the region of Lake Chad and in northern Cameroo are henceforth capable of indicating directions and fixir landmarks.

This does not exhaust the problems surrounding the stud of Sudanese cultures. It has been seen that material knowledg of these cultures is incomplete. Similarly, the conceptual know edge available is almost always conjectural. A culture canne be reduced to an inventory of its material aspects alone. Objec not only have a form, which is a matter of their visual aspe alone, they also convey a meaning assigned to them by tho

ho fashioned them and for whom they were fashioned. These
jects were designed for particular purposes, and the ways in
hich they are handled often react upon their form. Lastly,
eir function not only justifies their existence but actually
duces their creation. It is clear that this complex — form,
eaning, use, and function — can be defined only in relation
the cultures in which these objects are produced.

In most cases the records necessary to place the material
e lacking. An even more serious feature is the fact that the
companying documents are often not only incomplete but
so forged. Lack of documentation, where it is most acutely
lt, cannot be compensated for by the comparative or analogical
ethod. The mere fact that the same form and the same theme
e found at the heart of two different populations in no way
arrants the conclusion that this particular form or theme
presents an identity of use and function or that it is clothed
th the same meaning. For the use as well as the meaning
d the function of an object having a definite form can be
asped only through detailed analyses and by investigation *in
u*. It is in fact currently observed that the form, and some-
nes even the conditions of use, of a certain object emigrate
om its culture of origin. In the course of such migration the
rms and conditions of use undergo adaptation. Such adapta-
n obeys quite precise laws: the importance of a borrowing
s much less in the fact itself than in the similarity of situa-
ns it implies and in the reinterpretation to which the borrowed
ject becomes subject. Similarly, within the same population
form can outlive itself and endure even when its original
eaning has been lost or forgotten — that is, its meaning has
d to be reinvented.

It seems useful to reaffirm these principles of methodology
view of the fact that the efforts that have been made to define
e cultures in their most positive aspects have led, through
cessive particularization, to a crystallization of the cultures
der discussion into stable and immutable systems. Though
ch crystallization may be useful at a certain stage of research,
loses its value when raised to the status of a dogma that is
nstantly referred to without question as to its validity. It
uld seem much more logical to view a culture as a state of
uilibrium that is preserved by the various movements that
ke place within it than as a rigid mechanism whose function-
g is impeccable and whose diverse parts are susceptible to
t even the slightest alteration.

A general criterion determining the cultures dealt with in
e present article has been the practice, to whatever degree,
the plastic arts — carving, modeling, and painting. Products
lated to the arts of adornment — jewelry, weaving, leather-
orking — may well be dealt with separately; by their very
ture these items of artistic production are more closely linked
commerce than are those of the plastic arts, and they form
e basis of a trade that does not necessarily take into account
ltural frontiers. Secondly, the Sudanese cultures that will be

considered are the continental cultures, those which owing to
their geographical position have been relatively protected from
strongly marked influences or which have succeeded in assimilating the influences to which they may have been exposed.

It is far from the intention of this study to make an exhaustive inventory of the Sudanese cultures. As has been indicated,
the plastic arts have been taken as a criterion, since the study
of sculpture seems most capable of shedding light on the societies
where it is practiced: the works are varied, rich, and plastically
of a high standard; the societies that have produced them enjoy
a privileged position.

It has been possible to deal with the subject of architecture
only briefly (see below), notwithstanding its considerable importance. Although a movement in this direction is taking
shape, there is still a lack of actual data on buildings, and thus
the problems cannot be stated with precision in their entirety.
The ethnographic literature of course includes photographs,
sometimes drawings, more frequently descriptions of dwellings
and of the complexes in which they are arranged. There is
even available, but to a lesser extent, information on the "symbolism" that enters into the plan of a house and on the sociological implications of the distribution of the buildings within a
single architectural complex. But coordination of the available
information and methodical intensive and extensive research in
this field have only begun. It is an indication of the proportions
of the task to be accomplished in this field that in most cases
the ground plan, that irreplaceable document, is missing.

Jean LAUDE

HISTORY OF THE SUDANESE KINGDOMS AND PEOPLES. As a
result of historical, environmental, and economic conditions
similar to those that obtained in the kingdoms on the Guinean
coast (see GUINEAN CULTURES) between the 9th and the 17th century, vast empires were also established in western and central
Sudan. Their wealth and power were noted in the contemporary
chronicles of Arab travelers, which made medieval Europe aware
of their existence. As in the case of the Guinean kingdoms,
the introduction of ironworking was one of the basic factors in
the establishment of large states. International commerce along
the many caravan routes leading to the north and east and
crossing the Sudan in all directions afforded a constant source
of wealth, made possible frequent exchanges, and led to the
formation of large caravan crossroads that later became true
cities. These cities were not mere commercial centers; they
were also centers of learning and seats of courts that were
organized with luxury and pomp.

Of these large centers, which, as the Arabian chronicles
relate, ranked with the greatest European cities of the time,
either nothing at all remains but a few insignificant ruins or
all traces have completely vanished: wars, sackings, abandonment, and the inexorable work of time have virtually erased

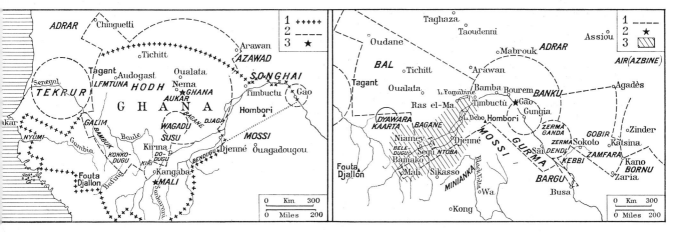

danese kingdoms and peoples. *Left*: Expansion of the Mali and Ghana kingdoms: (1) Approximate reconstruction of the limits of extension of the
ali kingdom (11th–15th cent.); (2) approximate reconstruction of the limits of extension of the Ghana kingdom (9th–11th cent.); (3) original nuclei
the kingdoms. *Right*: Expansion of the Songhai kingdom: (1) Approximate reconstruction of the limits of extension of the Songhai kingdom (15th–
th cent.); (2) original nucleus of the kingdom; (3) Bambara empire (17th cent.).

them from the map. Timbuktu, Djenné, Gao, and Kumbi Saleh were great capitals with large populations and beautiful buildings. They were established according to a planning code that provided for various types of residential quarters surrounded by agricultural areas with huts of perishable material for the working classes.

While, nominally at least, Islam triumphed in the cities, not only as a religion but also as a conditioner of the cultural and social life, the rural folk remained attached to the ancient traditions. It was owing to this fundamental conservatism of the people that, despite external influences, international commerce, and the new Islamic religious faith, the Sudanese empires retained a decidedly "African" character, which, with the inevitable variations, found parallels in the Bantu (see BANTU CULTURES) and Guinean kingdoms. The expansionist drive of the larger empires that succeeded one another in the Sudanese territory was arrested in the north and south by two formidable natural barriers: the desert and the forest. Nevertheless, the Sudanese states acted as commercial intermediaries between the north and the south, making it possible for Guinean gold to cross the desert and reach Europe and setting in motion the advance of European commodities, especially salt — and in all probability, also the ironworking techniques — toward the people living in the forest. The oldest empire was Ghana, or Gana (not to be confused with the modern state of that name on the Gulf of Guinea). The Arab chronicles mention it as a powerful centralized state at the beginning of the 9th century, so the remote origins of this kingdom must be placed even further back, to the very first centuries of the Christian era. It is most likely that the foundations of what was to become a great power were laid in the period when the knowledge of metallurgy was introduced into the area, enabling its possessors to triumph over their neighbors who had remained in the Stone Age.

Like all the other states of the western Sudan, Ghana had a typical savanna culture based on a mixed agricultural-pastoral economy, from this point of view no different from the tribal cultures of the mass of the population. However, it was different in that it developed a complex bureaucracy, built up a large, well-equipped army, promoted commerce on an international scale, and had an urban court in a setting of Oriental splendor. All these cultural elements are found again, in more or less identical form, in the other Sudanese "imperial" civilizations.

In 1067, when the work of the Arab geographer al-Bakrī familiarized Europe with the splendors of Ghana — which are even more amazing if compared with European feudalism — the Almoravids of Morocco had already been besieging that empire for 13 years, attracted more by the mirage of its riches than by a desire for territorial expansion. It took them more than 22 years to subjugate Ghana and conquer its capital (which may perhaps be identified with the Kumbi Saleh of recent excavations). When Ghana was subjugated by the Almoravids, it extended from the Atlantic to the middle of the Niger and northward as far as Mauritania. The victorious Almoravids soon abandoned the vast conquered territory; but by then it was so radically undermined that it easily fell prey to the neighboring Susu, who occupied it and reduced the inhabitants to slavery.

At the same time that Ghana disappeared as a geographic and historical entity a new Sudanese empire came to the fore. In 1213, Mali (or Melle), which had existed as a state as early as the 11th century, was transformed into an empire by Allakoi Keita. Twenty-five years later it had become so powerful that the new sovereign, Sundiata, attacked the Susu who had occupied Ghana. In 1240, they conquered and destroyed Ghana's capital, and farther south — perhaps at Niani or at Jeriba on the upper Niger — built the first Mali capital. Later, the large cities of this empire were Timbuktu and Djenné, especially beginning with the reign of Mansa Musa, who considerably enlarged his territory (its vastness was calculated in terms of "four months of walking") at the expense of the Songhai empire on the middle Niger. Gao, the capital of the Songhai empire, was occupied in 1325.

In power, wealth, and "civilization" Mali far surpassed Ghana. The cities were embellished with outstanding mon-

uments, and, in addition to being commercial and religiou centers, they also became internationally known centers learning, as is attested by, among other sources, the work Leo Africanus (ca. 1525), written two centuries after the ap gee of Timbuktu. Peace extending over so vast an area cause commerce to prosper, despite occasional raids and attacks l other peoples, such as the sacking of Timbuktu in 1333 by t Mossi.

At the height of its splendor Mali extended over all of weste Africa. On the south its borders reached the rain forest, beyor which were the gold countries. On the northwest it reach to Senegal and on the northeast to Air. Mali's representativ maintained diplomatic relations, as equals, with the sulta of Morocco and the king of Portugal.

The decline of Mali coincided with the establishment, alo the middle Niger, of the Songhai empire, the most importa and developed of the Sudanese states, which resisted extern attacks longer than its predecessors. Its fall, in the 17th centur marked the end of the great period of Sudanese history.

States of lesser importance, historically and territorial were established by the Hausa (capital at Kano), by the Bamba (Ségou and Kaarta), and by the Fulbe (Masina, Fouta Djallo in Bagirmi, Wadai, and Kanem-Bornu and on the savan between the Niger and the Nile. Among the minor stat Kanem-Bornu was the most important both because it fulfill a civilizing function in a vast area of central Africa and becau the Sao archaeological civilization was developed within i territorial sphere.

Unfortunately, when the Europeans began to penetrate t interior of western Africa almost nothing survived of the wo derful cultural achievements of the past. The populatio had resumed their tribal lives, the cities had disappeared, ar the small local courts preserved only a dim recollection of the former splendor. However, something had remained: a milita organization that still evoked admiration in the second half the 19th century, a marked inclination toward commerce, and flourishing crafts production that often reached the level of ar

Currently, peoples such as the Malinke and the Songh who in the past played distinguished roles as creators of empir and bearers of advanced cultures, are not culturally distinguis able from neighboring peoples whose achievements had r mained on the tribal level.

Ernesta CERULLI

WESTERN SUDANESE CULTURES. In terms of the scheme work out for the western Sudanese cultures by Baumann and Weste mann (1948), the cultures here treated belong to the Upp Niger cercle (formed by a successive belt of races and cultur that extends from the Sahara to the forests of Guinea) and t Volta cercle (formed by a group of populations enclosed with the loop of the Niger). The population of what Baumann ter the Western Atlantic cercle (extending over the center of t virgin rain forest, from Senegal to Bandama, on the Ivory Coas are not dealt with because, although they constitute a who with certain clearly defined Sudanese features, they have acquir characteristics that are peculiar to them and that are the resu at least so far as artistic manifestations are concerned, of combination of continental and Atlantic plastic solutions. comparison of drawings made in 1886 of two statuettes and Nimba mask at Petit Talabonche (A. Coffinières de Nordec Voyage au Pays des Bagos et du Rio Nunez, Paris, 1886) wi currently known statuettes and masks of the same type revea a marked softening of forms and a gradual abandonment of t characteristic Sudanese linearity. Moreover, a population su as that of the Guros, which Baumann places in the Weste Atlantic cercle, belongs so far as its art is concerned to a regic influenced by Guinean cultures (q.v.), more specifically by t Baule culture, to which the products are unquestionably relate

Taking into consideration in both regions only the tw most representative and best-known populations, the Dog and the Bambara, it is noted first of all that both belong to t Mande group. On the other hand, the societies made up these populations are linked by a very complex relation not on among themselves but also with other populations.

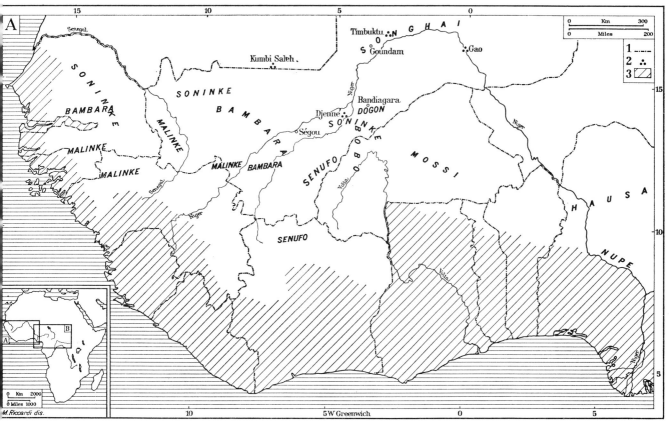

stribution of the principal archaeological centers and ethnic groups in the area of the Sudanese cultures: (*A*) Area of the western Sudanese cultures. y: (1) Political boundaries; (2) archaeological sites; (3) area of Guinean cultures. Inset at lower left indicates western (*A*) and eastern (*B*) Sudanese areas.

It should not be lost sight of that in Negro Africa — inas-
uch as the forces exerted by the cultures under consideration
e actually in equilibrium from a qualitative and a quantitative
ndpoint — the phenomena of acculturation are always defined
a movement of reciprocity. The mutual loans that the exist-
g African cultures make to one another and the reinterpreta-
ns to which these loans are subject do not tend, however,
represent a rather unstable syncretism; rather, they modify
ch of these cultures and change them into an original culture.

Care must therefore be exercised, on one hand, not to
cumscribe the cultures of the western Sudan too narrowly
d, on the other, to differentiate them from one another, de-
ibing their gradual differentiation, starting with the common
bstratum from which they emerge. These differences will
course here be noted only in the field of the arts and, more
ecisely, through the analysis of form.

The Bambara. The main body of the Sudanese population
made up of Bambara. The name Bambara (lit., "infidel") —
e term applied to them by their Moslem neighbors — shows
arly the resistance this population offered to Islam.

The Bambara claim to have come from Mande, that is,
m the region where there stood the capitals that succeeded
e another in the ancient kingdom of Mali (or Malle). From
e 14th to the 17th century they were organized into small
iefdoms more or less subject to the neighboring empires.
the 17th century a Peul penetration into the region brought
out the foundation of two empires, one of which was the em-
e of Ségou. At the same time a mixed Peul and Bambara
stocracy was created. The Bambara economy is mainly
sed on agriculture (millet, fonio, rice, and maize) and, to a
ser degree, on cattle-raising and gardening. However, living
symbiosis with the Bozo (generally recognized as the first
cupants of the riverain territories of the Niger), the Bambara
rned from them the techniques of fishing. The social struc-
res reveal a political system founded upon the preeminence of

priests, heads of the families, and old men. From a religious
point of view, an apparently very complex system unites the
various activities of the society as a whole, and even seems to
govern them. The core of this system would appear to be the
concepts relating to the idea of the "person."

Bambara art is mainly an art of wood sculpture. Its products,
while not so varied as those of Dogon art (see below), can nevertheless be classified in different series according to the circumstances of their use. Taken as a whole they form a corpus that
includes masks (and mask tops, or headpieces), ancestor figures,
objects of *art mobilier*, and musical instruments. The masks
and headpieces are used during the ritual performances connected
with the social and religious life of the group and vary from one
to another of the secret societies to whose functioning they
contribute. There follows a brief account of three of these societies: the Komo, the Koré, and the N'tomo (or Ceble).

The N'tomo (lit., "grouping"), or Ceble (lit., "red man"),
is an association of the uncircumcised; it is headed by a chief,
who is assisted by a functionary who performs the sacrifices
and by a master of ceremonies. At the time of the harvest
all the members of the N'tomo participate in the collective
tasks of the village. In payment they receive millet or other
gifts in kind, which are automatically turned over to the common
fund of the association. The N'tomo fulfill an educational function that can be observed in operation at the level of the individual and within the society at large; it develops a sense of
solidarity among all its members and between them and the
community in whose activities it participates.

The N'tomo has five ritual objects (which are rudimentary
musical instruments), whips, and, lastly, a mask — which would
appear to be the earliest authenticated object from within the
Bambara society. The masks typically represent a human face
surmounted by straight horns which vary in number (five,
six, sometimes eight). The forehead and the horns are decorated
with cowrie shells and red berries (*Linociera sudarica*) affixed
with latex (Lem, 1947, pls. 30, 31). Other N'tomo masks, of

a notably different style, have only two horns; these are antelopian, slightly curved and finely wrought, and between them stands a female figurine (ibid., pl. 32).

The known masks used in the ritual ceremonies of the N'tomo constitute a relatively homogeneous series with clearly defined characteristics. However, they are not uniform, and noteworthy differences in the elements of representation as well as in the fashioning are readily apparent. As a rule, the mask has a very high forehead, which according to Dieterlen (1951) endows the face with a "beneficial power." But this forehead is treated either as a curved volume detached from the flat, triangular surface of the face (Lem, 1947, pl. 30) or as a half sphere that at the arch of the eyebrows breaks abruptly away from the retreating face (ibid., pl. 31). In the first case the concern of the sculptor appears to be to compose a whole with sinuous surfaces and not to show too distinct an interruption of continuity between them. In the second case the face has been conceived as a plane whose verticality is stressed by the straight bridge of the nose; it has been carved out within a mass delimited by the line of the forehead continued past the break of the eyebrows. The two examples just cited were found in the village of Néguéna and seem to have come from Macina. It is tempting to relate these masks, at least so far as the general representational aspect is concerned, to a Senufo mask (Trowell, 1954, pl. 29) surmounted by six straight horns. The Senufo mask incontestably reveals an infusion of Guinean influences and an explicit relation, in its plastic treatment, to certain gold masks of the Baule. A mask with a figurine collected in the Kenedougou district (ibid., pl. 32) is a greatly elaborated work in which an acute feeling for straight lines and sharp ridges (bridge of the nose, eye sockets, half-opened lips) is knowingly combined with an almost voluptuous feeling for modulated, curved volumes (forehead, eyelids). The horns, whose spirals are simulated by carved circumflex markings, and the figurine between them reveal a construction in accordance with the lines of vertical stress that form a characteristic aspect of Sudanese art in general.

The iconography of these masks has not as yet formed the subject of methodical elucidation. However, their function, like that of all other Sudanese masks, appears to be to ensnare and fasten a wandering power of a malignant nature (particularly antagonistic to fecundity) that normally dwells in the foreskin or clitoris of the uncircumcised. This power, the wanzo, departs from a member of the N'tomo at the moment of circumcision and establishes itself in the mask. From then on the mask is the repository of the life of the uncircumcised person who wears it, handles it, or offers it sacrifices. It is closely related to the altar, which houses the wanzo of those who die uncircumcised. The mask-altar duality thus "confers upon the N'tomo responsibility for the life of the adolescents and gives it such power that this society of youths is, to a certain extent, held in awe by the adults who have left it" (Dieterlen, op. cit.).

The Komo is an association whose membership is restricted to the circumcised (excluding the griots, or musicians, bards, and genealogists). This society has a well-defined age-based hierarchy. It is subject to the authority of a chief, preferably chosen from the caste of the smiths, whose position is hereditary. In practice the association intervenes in all manifestations that concern the whole community, whether technical (agriculture, craftsmanship), juridical, or political and economic, as well as those that, though from a certain point of view public, more particularly concern the individual (birth, circumcision and initiation, marriage, funerals). Custodian of traditional beliefs, the Komo's duty is to ensure that they are respected, to provide comment, and to teach and study them thoroughly. Thus the Komo appears to form the political backbone of the Bambara society at the village level; at the same time it incarnates the highest religious power in the sense that it is responsible for all — men, animals, and plants. Lastly, the recruiting of the members of the Komo leads to the creation of actual social classes: the entrance ceremony and the participation in the rites entail a considerable outlay, which not all villagers can afford. Certain conversions to Islam have been attributed to this fact (Dieterlen, op. cit.).

The material used in the ritual performances of the Komo

consists of a mask, boli (ritual objects, including small altars and musical instruments, including bells, flutes, and iron an wooden trumpets. Some of the wooden trumpets end in representation of a human head (Minotaure, II, 1933, p. 22 The Komo mask can be anthropomorph or zoomorph in typ its character depends upon the village where the ceremon is celebrated (Konodimini, panther; Sungoba, stork; Banan koroni, eagle; Banumgubula, elephant; Segubugu, vulture; etc But most often it combines elements drawn from different an mals. Affixed to the top of the head of these masks are copp arrows and amulets, ammunition against undesirables (tl noninitiated, women, and children). These masks would see to be the work of the smiths. Their appearance is interprete in a symbolic sense: the eyes are large so that the Komo ca "see and unveil everything," the nostrils are wide so that tl Komo can "smell everything, smell out the good and the ev of things," and the ears are enormous so that the Komo ca "hear everything, even the things each man secretly utte in his heart." As to the chin, it is "square, a sign of purit decision, and second sight" (Dieterlen, op. cit.). It is, howeve difficult to state with certainty whether the mask's forms are function of this symbolism or whether this symbolism is a reinte pretation of the forms. In fact, a form survives longer than tl meanings attached to it, and as soon as these meanings ha been forgotten (even if the forms survive in their initial gener aspect) they are gradually replaced by others. The moveme can, moreover, go in the opposite direction: the forms can l gradually oriented toward their strict reduction to the meanin ascribed to them.

The Koré is an association that performs most particular the rites related to the various spatial concepts (the sky, tl cardinal points, space) and to the atmospheric manifestatio (especially rain) of Faro, a mythical being designated as tl "master of the reorganizing world of the universe." This socie is closely linked to the Komo, and an individual in a positic to meet the outlay involved can belong to both.

The ritual performances of the Koré consist of a rehears of the contests that the celestial genii engaged in with the un bridled elements to obtain the rains necessary to mankin The chief properties are the disguises by means of which tl individual dancer identifies himself with the individual gen The participators in the ritual performance mime the gestu and depict the sufferings of the genii. "Among the membe some are designated to play the part of the Koré duga [li 'vulture'] during the ceremonies: masked and brandishir green branches in each hand, they straddle a wooden hors the Koré dugaso. Thus equipped, they represent the Ko genii mounted on their winged horses, ready to assault the sk One of them wears a mask, the Koré ku, representing the a cestor of the group" (Dieterlen, op. cit.). The Koré dug whose special status in the social order parallels that of tl griot, has the right to mock the most sacred things.

A sculptural treatment quite different from that of the oth known Bambara masks is seen in a mask collected in the regic of Koutiala that was used in the course of these performanc (Lem, 1947, pl. 33). Apparently very ancient, it represents human head with two small straight horns springing from tl base of the forehead. This work is remarkable in that the trea ment is convex — that is, the sculptor "in penetrating tl block of wood, had had to foresee and arrange the subsidia exterior masses from which he will extract the details of tl face" (Lavachéry, 1954). A mask of a different style used the ritual performances of the Koré, part of the costume wo by the Koré duga, was found by the Dakar-Djibouti Missi (1931–33) at Sangaso (region of Koutiala). The mask (Min taure, II, 1933, pp. 20–21, A and center) represents an anim head: the ears are long, and bent slightly forward; the forehea consisting of a bulbous mass, overhangs an oblique plane which rectangular holes (the eyes) have been bored and fro which a trapezoidal volume (the nose) stands out; where tl mouth would normally be, the mask protrudes (the muzzl Another type of mask, used in the same ritual performances, co sists of a hood whose top — made of esparto grass — is su mounted by a bifrontal figurine representing the male-fema principle. (This occurrence of the male-female principle in a cosmographic context invites comparison with the ancient Chinese division of space on the basis of yang and yin.) Of this type of mask only this example, found in the Kenedougou, survives (Lem, 1947, pl. 38). From the point of view of form the figurine may be described as the product of the separation, or the orthogonal disposition, of planes. Works such as this, resorting to curved volumes only in the representation of the breasts, are particularly characteristic of the Sudanese tendency to use straight lines almost exclusively to define dynamics and to create rhythm by the opposition rather than by the confluence of lines.

The variety demonstrated by the few examples cited suggests that the masks used in the ritual performances of the Koré are more diverse in their representational elements and in their morphology than the literature indicates. The Koré ceremonies bring — or have brought — into play complicated scenarios in which the mythological characters are fairly numerous and have well-defined roles. Each mask possesses its own individuality: it represents a definite character, with a definite role and having a specific name and destiny. An iconography of Bambara art (similar to the one made for the Dogon masks), worked out on the level of representation and meaning rather than on the level of general and spiritual conceptions, would make it possible to grasp the mythology. The fact has sometimes been lost sight of — in the course of many attempts to interpret Sudanese art strictly through the general principles of religion or the details of symbolism — that a specific work gives concrete form to only one aspect of such principles or symbolism, and that it is the outcome of an activity that contributes to the definition (or alteration) and the direction (or transformation) of the principles. Within an African society the work of art appears not as an optional and superfluous manifestation illustrating an aspect of a metaphysics or of a cosmogony; it is essential in that it makes manifest concepts that would rapidly disintegrate if not given tangible form.

A type of association found throughout the region of the Bambara is the Fla-n-kuru. The members are youths who have been initiated at the same time; they carry out together the agricultural tasks (clearing, sowing, harvesting), under the authority of the head of the family or village community. In the celebrations held at the beginning and the end of the growing season their dancers, in ritual dress and masks, execute ceremonial performances related to ancient agrarian rites.

A body of sculptured works of remarkable homogeneity comprises the antelope headpieces, called Segoni-kun, that constitute the main element of the costume of the dancers, who represent in these performances the tji wara (lit., "the great cultivators"; PLS. 309, 329). The dancers mimic the attitudes and movements of antelopes in the bush.

Although they form a homogeneous series the individual antelope headpieces vary greatly. The ones portraying male antelopes (the sex of the animal is often explicit) are larger; the ones representing female antelopes, in addition to being smaller, are simpler; sometimes a fawn is borne on the back of the doe.

All these headpieces have this main characteristic: they are designed as though meant to be viewed in profile. They are extremely schematic, interest being centered on the neck (and mane) and the head (and horns). The head is long and narrow, conceived entirely in terms of parallel longitudinal lines that delimit the subordinate masses, which successively recede (nose, cheeks). On the forehead a double horizontal band is often carved. (This detail appears also in the faces of certain statuettes constructed on the same principles.) The horns are generally straight, but a spiral effect is achieved by parallel circumflex lines carefully incised. In some cases the horns have small metal bands (or carved ones) around them. The male antelopes have elaborate openwork manes. These antelope headpieces (Lem, 1947, pls. 19–29) are actually like "drawings" carved out of wood, precisely defining a two-dimensional entity, the rhythmic structure of which is achieved by contrasting straight lines and arabesques without hindrance to their development in space (Trowell, 1954, pl. 28). On the

forehead or the top of the mane of certain Segoni-kun stand small male or female figurines (ibid., pl. 29c).

A number of associations in addition to the Fla-n-kuru are connected with the celebration of agrarian rites. Of a type quite distinct from societies such as the N'tomo, the Komo, and the Koré, these would appear to be mutual-help organizations, with a strongly established hierarchy, whose members carry out in common all the work entailed in the life of the village. To one of these associations, the N'tieko society, whose rites take place at the begining and the end of the cultivation season, belongs the headpiece of a mask (Lem, 1947, pl. 16) that establishes a close connection between agrarian rites and the ancestor cult.

This recent headpiece, collected in the village of Séla in the region of San, is a fairly large bifrontal composition (ca. 57 in. high) representing the "chain of ancestors." The base supports a bifrontal bust and head of a woman; from each temple of the woman's head protrudes (on a sticklike neck) a bifrontal head of the same proportions, from the temples of which, in turn, project two smaller heads. In short, this piece depicts eight ancestors on each of its sides. In regard to the carving, all the heads are treated uniformly by means of identical plastic conventions: the forehead is formed by a spherical volume overhanging the face proper, which is treated as a flat triangular surface and is divided in half by the straight, thin ridge of the nose. A comparison of the plastic treatment of this face with that of a N'tomo mask (Lem, 1947, pl. 31), of certain ancestor statuettes (ibid., pls. 15, 17), and of certain Marka masks (Schmalenback, 1952, pl. 58; Plass, 1957, pl. 2) reveals a remarkable unity of style, which is also demonstrated by a thorough analysis of the modeling of the faces of the antelopes represented on the top of the Segoni-kun masks and of the figures on certain wooden door locks. From the point of view of form these stylistic conventions are in clear opposition to those that govern the carving of other Bambara works, not only masks but also fertility and ancestor figures (Lem, 1947, pls. 34, 35), which bear witness to entirely different concepts in that they are sculptured altogether in continuous curved masses with no thought given to separation of planes.

According to Lem, these two statuettes are ancient. Since the ancestor chain from Séla is recent, the possibility presents itself that the works carved according to linear principles, with clearly marked ridges, may be the result of a gradual schematization of ancient forms. The hypothesis suggested by Lavachéry, in which the "concave" and the "convex" are distinguished in the styles (with various transition styles between them), attributes anteriority to the concave style, the flowering of which Lavachéry saw principally in the Sudanese cultures. But the perspective of the research alters markedly in view of the fact that the examples just cited seem to demonstrate only that the Sudanese populations produced works in the convex style but also that these works were probably produced earlier than those belonging to the concave style. It is not in fact a question of showing which system is prior to the other: it is not possible to attribute to the characteristics of a concave style the function of a criterion of "primitivity"; first it has to be demonstrated that what took place was a shift from one system to another, and then that this shift corresponded to a transformation in the culture as the result of an internal evolution, or of accepted, tolerated, and assimilated external influences, or lastly — and this appears to be more consistent with concrete reality — of a process that, having allowed the external influences to be accepted, accelerated the progress of an internal evolution that had already begun in another connection.

According to Lem, the three great centers of production of Bambara art are the regions of Bamako, Furu (in the region of Buguni), and Kinian (which straddles the three areas of Sikasso, Koutiala, and Ségou). If the regions where one encounters objects belonging more particularly to the convex style are marked out on a map, it is seen that these regions are at the same time rather far from areas converted to Islam and areas in which the pressure of Islam could make itself felt and that they are close to the regions of the Guinean cultures.

It therefore seems legitimate to question whether the schematic sculptured works — that is, those in the concave style — do not betray an Islamic influence (noticeable in the tendency to render forms geometrically), and whether the works belonging to the more complex style — in other words, the convex style — do not reveal a Guinean influence (noticeable in a tendency to treat surfaces in continuous planes, if not to conceive volumes in the round). Moreover, even if these two influences have prevailed to different degrees, qualitatively and quantitatively speaking, they by no means exclude one another and may well have been simultaneous. Thus, even if the reality of these influences has been clearly demonstrated, conclusions about them should not be drawn in order to solve the problem mentioned earlier. Distributing the products of Bambara art on a single horizontal (geographical) scale does not exhaust the complexity of its development. The postulation of a development of Bambara art according to a vertical (historical) scale clearly requires not only objects that can be used as landmarks but also archives attesting to the chronology. At the same time, to follow this formal evolution requires understanding of the evolution of the concepts, attitudes, and representations rendered concrete by the forms. To collectors the Bambara statues — the *noumoumani*, or "little men of the smiths" (Kjersmeier, 1935, 1) — seem to have been overshadowed by the masks, especially by the Segoni-kun. It must be admitted that, even though a certain number of examples are known, these statues have not been the object of methodical study; in actual fact, only sporadic information as to their meaning and their function is available. They are usually fairly large (in some cases over 4 ft. in height), at least compared with others carved in Negro Africa. The various types include statues with "reliquaries"; ancestor figures, male and female (PLS. 305, 310); small fertility figures; and "double statues" similar to those which, among the Dogon, represent the duality "heaven-earth" and, according to Baumann, represent the principle of generation (Baumann and Westermann, 1948).

A female figure of considerable antiquity, apparently from Macina in the region of Touna-Neguena (Lem, 1947, pls. 14, 15), is unusual in having a small shutter opening into the belly, in which a hollow has been carved out to receive a ritual preparation. From this shutter protrudes a head carved in high relief, and another head protrudes from the back of the statue. The legs are treated rather schematically. The fashioning of the figure's head is similar to that seen in the bifrontal "chain of ancestors" described above. These two sculptures can be related to each other not only because of the stylistic analogies they present but also because of common representational elements. The statue seems to manifest concepts linked both to the ancestor cult and to fertility, as is evidenced by the small figures carved on the back and the belly and by the unquestionably ritual intent of the "reliquary" feature.

From a stylistic point of view this statue — the peculiarity of the reliquary aspect aside — appears to belong to the same group as a series of other Bambara works (cf. Lem, 1947, pl. 17) and of sculptures carved within other Sudanese societies. As far as general style is concerned, the links are readily apparent between the heads of these two statues and that of a figure that seems to be Soninke (Lavachéry, 1951, p. 50, fig. 1-A; attributed by him to the Malinke). These works are treated in an angular way; the planes are clearly separated and discontinuous and are placed either in parallel or orthogonally. It is possible to establish a fairly continuous line connecting these various works: they would seem to represent, if not landmarks, at least stylistic references that suggest adaptation of the same style through the genius of different populations observing general conventions. In accordance with these conventions the sculptor is at pains to build vertical planes, to reduce his structural schemes to straight intersecting lines, and to delimit each of his volumes by enclosing them with incised lines. But the principle of linearity is not absolute, and the Bambara artist not only has a sense of rounding off but also can conceive and use curved volumes, which he does not link by a continuous joining but juxtaposes in rhythmic compositions. An exception that presents a problem is a statue representing a woman seated on a stool (Underwood, 1951, pl. 1; Trowell, 1954, pl. 1-A). Attributed by Underwood

to the Baga and by Trowell to the Bambara, the work is in fact identical in its general structure to the above-mentioned sculpture attributed by Lavachéry to the Malinke. However, there is an important difference between the two works — specifically in the sculptural treatment of the heads. The head of the Malinke sculpture differs from that of the Bambara sculpture in the same way as do the Baga masks and statues of the Nimba type, such as the above-mentioned examples drawn in 1886 by Coffinières de Nordeck and those currently known. In the work attributed to the Malinke the treatment of the head is articulated through the intersection of planes bound by sharp lines. In the Bambara work the treatment of the head evidences a tendency toward the exclusive utilization of curved lines, a softening of the lines that enclose and separate the volumes, and a release of the volumes on the rounded surface of the face.

Mention must also be made of other Bambara sculpture: the dolls formerly given to young girls to ensure numerous offspring; the *merekun*, a large, puppetlike figure held above the head by the masked dancer (Lem, 1947, pl. 13); and statues of twins that served in case of the death of one twin to replace the deceased at the survivor's side. [Their function is compared by Lavachéry (1954) to that of the "Ibeji" of the Yoruba (VII, PL. 130).] Finally, the Bambara sculptors make wooden locks. Widely dispersed, such locks become real works of art in the Sudan, among the Bambara and the Dogon, and even among the Malinke, where they are treated more schematically (Paulme, 1956, fig. 5). Among the Bambara, the designs in the central part include anthropomorphs, zoomorphs (caymans, lizards, tortoises, birds), and other motifs (crescent moon, wooden clogs). These works are fairly close to those of the Dogon, but they manifest a more marked tendency toward the schematization of forms as well as toward ornamentation of a geometric type (Lem, 1947, pl. 18).

In reviewing the salient features of Bambara art it can be said that from a general morphological point of view, two systems of image-making can be distinguished. The first tends to reduce forms to their rhythmical structure by developing them either on one plane, as in the case of the antelope headpieces, or by combining different parallel or orthogonally overlapping planes. The works in this style evidence a method of connecting the inner space created within the sculpture and the outer space into which the works are integrated. The second system of image refrains from defining an unbroken continuity among the different surfaces that limit the volumes and, instead, softens and links the successive surfaces by a relative modulation. The two systems seem to be separated by a period of time, but one cannot ascertain which of the two styles is earlier.

From the ethnological point of view it must be said of Bambara art that even though, mainly as a result of the work of G. Dieterlen, the background against which this art stands out is known, for the most part detailed knowledge of the meaning, the conditions of its use, and sometimes even the function of the individual object is lacking. The function of the masks, as well as that of the statuettes, consists mainly in the ensnaring of immaterial forces that could work evil if they were free. Moreover the statues seem to manifest, at least in some cases, the permanence of tradition within the village and to root the society in the movement that shaped or is still shaping it. The function of the ancestor cult is at the same time to serve as a reminder of the origin of the society and to determine for the future the development of that movement whose first stirrings took place *illo tempore*.

As for the attitudes that this art makes concrete and evokes within the Bambara society, masks and statues are — or have been — fashioned by individuals belonging to a particular caste, that of the smiths. These artisans, whose vocation and status are at once technical and religious, and who manifest by the very nature of their work the fundamental ambiguousness inherent in the sacred, are throughout Negro Africa, as Clément (1948) has pointed out, the object of an ambivalent feeling which can be characterized, in the apt phrase of Lavachéry (1954), as "reverential disdain." To this factor must be added one growing out of the existence of the various "secret societies" briefly mentioned above, which, chiefly because of the economic membership, hold the political and religious power of the ¹lage and constitute real "social classes." To these social ¹sses correspond various degrees of initiation. The store of ¹owledge — and, consequently, the authority — of a Bambara ¹o has the means to belong to several societies is more important ¹n that of another who is a member of only one society. The ¹mbara is fully aware of this state of affairs.

Now, inasmuch as the various aspects of knowledge not only ¹m the object of gradual oral instruction but also are rendered ¹o tangible forms, the question arises as to what attitudes ¹se forms evoke in the noninitiated (when they are allowed ¹see them) or in the partially initiated. They disclose their ¹itents only to those who are already acquainted with them, ¹se who by the very fact of their initiation have direct access ¹them and, consequently, do not depend upon their material ¹mulation. But these forms seem not only to be the account ¹the expression of the concepts they make manifest but also ¹have within the Bambara society a function *qua* forms — that ¹to say, they are valued on the esthetic level. So deeply do ¹se forms embody collective ideals that they reveal, beyond ¹se ideals, a fundamental attitude with regard to the universe ¹the part of those who created these forms and for whom they ¹ve been created; more precisely, they define quite exactly ¹ relation in which the Bambara find themselves in respect ¹the external world. This relation can be described as repre-¹iting man's minimum psychological distance from what ¹rrounds him. The Bambara does attempt to perceive and place ¹nself as what he would be objectively, but he sees himself, ¹ a person, in an intimate relation with the universe, with ¹ich he feels a sense of close solidarity. This relation signifies ¹ither an absorption of man by the natural environment that ¹rounds him nor a projection of man onto his natural environ-¹nt; it is thought of as reciprocal. Thus is it not expressed ¹actly in the terms of the classic dilemma of "cosmomorphism" ¹d "anthropomorphism." From a genetic point of view it ¹ould seem to mark the impulse by which man perceives him-¹f as a person whose destiny is linked to that of the universe, ¹that he acts on himself in acting on the universe. Art therefore ¹ssesses here an operating function that transcends the one at-¹buted to it within the society; objectively, it favors a grasp ¹awareness and appears as a factor of action and an element of ¹dual individuation tending to wrench man out of his web ¹cosmogonic relations in order to establish him as an individual.

The Malinke. The most characteristic and widespread pop-¹ation of the Mande-tan group (Baumann and Westermann, ¹48), the Malinke live in isolated colonies in the regions of ¹per Senegal and Gambia and the sources of the Niger and Bani ¹ers. They appear to have been converted to Islam perhaps as ¹rly as the 12th century. This fact is of fundamental importance, ¹least so far as the development of the Malinke arts is concerned, ¹it led to an almost complete disappearance of sculpture. ¹ily among the Malinke of Guinea, who are somewhat removed ¹m the mainstream of the group, are carved works found. ¹amples, however, are rare and seldom reproduced. The stat-¹ttes are fertility figures; like the Bambara statuettes, they ¹ called *noumoumani* (Kjersmeier, 1935, I, fig. 3). The masks ¹ mostly zoomorph in character. The undeniable relation be-¹een certain works of Bambara and Malinke sculpture has been ¹ited above. What distinguishes Malinke sculpture is its clearer ¹idency to render forms schematically. Lavachéry (1954) ¹und in the shaping of the trunk and breasts "a certain grace ¹at the Bambara have never attained"; he also noted that ¹e features of the face are inscribed in a plane that, instead ¹being vertical, "protrudes obliquely starting from the eye-¹ow ridges," and commented on the delicacy of the ornaments ¹d other details. On the other hand, in certain headpieces ¹ stricter reduction of forms to their geometric elements is ¹rticularly evident. In one example (*Le musée vivant*, XXXVI-¹XVII, p. 83, fig. 47) the head of the antelope is, in fact, ¹duced to a tridimensional symbol constructed as an orthogonal ¹tersection of planes. The idea of the antelope is indicated only ¹ the two ears and the two straight horns standing out on ¹e same plane. This headpiece may well be compared with

a pair of Bozo wooden clappers (Paulme, 1956, fig. 4), the carving of which seems to mark the crossing over from a style in which the figural elements are still immediately legible to a style in which these elements are "abstracted" to the point of being legible only to members of the society that conceived them. The top of these clappers represents a human head in profile, on which the hair is indicated by a series of five parallel triangular planes. The blades are decorated on each face with a geometric motif, pyrograved and polychromed, that probably renders in concrete form symbolic concepts that have not as yet been de-ciphered.

The Dogon. A population that has been the object of intense study from the point of view of social structure (Paulme, 1940) as well as of ritual performances (especially through the work of Griaule and his colleagues), the Dogon, owing to their priv-ileged geographical position, were successful in resisting external influences for a fairly long time. If in the course of the centuries infiltrations did take place, the cultural features thus conveyed were reinterpreted in such a way as to be readily assimilated. The migratory movements of the Dogon would appear to have started from Mande, where the Dogon claim to originate and whence they scattered to the Bandiagara cliffs. Their arrival in certain villages has been dated in some cases by deduction based on the masks found in shelters; masks were carved every 60 years, as was mentioned earlier in connection with the Sigui.

Although politically they constitute a very fragmentary population, the Dogon are very much aware of their common origin and combine love for the land they occupy with an acute sense of unity. In every village authority is vested in a council of the elders. The economy is mainly agrarian, but — and their myths preserve the recollection of this — the Dogon originally formed a population of hunters, who fairly early sought lands for cultivation, probably because of the gradual disappearance of big game. The artisan group is made up mainly of smiths belonging to castes, weavers who turn to account a craft common to the whole of Sudan, and, lastly, potters and shoemakers.

Against the background of this patriarchal, agricultural organization stands out a complex religious system that ensures the cohesion of the whole group and of its activities. This relig-ious system, with its manifold symbolic implications, is es-sentially based upon the ancestor cult and the concept of the person. It is immediately apparent that the material products of the Dogon culture are related to this religious system; sculp-ture, *art mobilier*, architecture, techniques of weaving, and make-up and choreography (taken as a whole) manifest a relation-ship at various levels to one or more aspects of this system. Thus Dogon art cannot be considered apart from the ideals it incarnates and the ends it is expected to attain.

Masks are used during certain ceremonies related to rituals of purification. Their origin, their fabrication, and the circum-stances of their use are attested by a complicated myth (Griaule, 1947). Of this myth it need only be detailed here that the mask and the fibers of the costume constitute funerary trappings whose appearance incited the presence of death but later served to minimize the effects it had provoked. Pure and impure at the same time, the mask appears as an image cut out in the likeness of a dead being (man or animal) and intended to capture the "life force" that escaped from the being at the moment of death. This life force, the *nyama*, if permitted to wander freely could cause the most serious trouble within the society. Once ensnared, it becomes not only innocuous but actually beneficent; it is recovered to the advantage of the whole society. Thus an inter-esting motif can be discerned: the actor who in the part that devolves upon him in the ritual performance must incarnate a person or an animal endeavors to attract the *nyama* of the being he mimes. But this *nyama* is dangerous, and he must therefore protect himself against its effects. In this perspective the mask appears at once as the image in which the life force will be ensnared and as the protective screen designed to protect the dancer from its malignant effects.

Conceived under this dual aspect, the function of the mask is, in a certain sense, specific; at the same time it is linked to the general function of the ritual performance. This performance consists mainly in the repetition of the primordial events that led to the creation of the world (M. Eliade, *Mythe de l'éternel retour*, Paris, 1948). Thus assuring the validity, reality, and duration of these gestures and acts, on the one hand, and of their results, on the other, the ritual performance at the same time accumulates the life forces in order to pour them back into the common reservoir of the society.

This triple function of the ritual performance in general and of the mask in particular is embodied in forms and gestures whose meaning must be grasped within the society in which they are perceived. The complexity of the symbolism of the masks is suggested by two examples: the *kanaga* mask and the *maison à étages* mask. The first of these is meant to be the "particular representation of a cosmogony which it exhibits on the public square"; the second presents "the complete universal system in colors and movement" (Griaule, *Présence Africaine*, X–XI, 1951). They confirm the fact that the ritual performance is supposed to be not only a commemoration but also a reestablishment of the primordial events that led to the creation of the world. But since knowledge of this symbolism depends upon degree of initiation, that is, upon social status, the meaning of the masks differs from one individual to another. The meaning attached to a mask is not so clear that it reveals itself instantly and appears far less to be a quality inherent in the object than an activity produced in the milieu in which the object is modeled and used.

The Dogon mask can be made of bark or of plaited fibers trimmed with cowries or it can be carved in wood. Masks of the last type are more numerous and more varied; they represent animals — antelopes, hyenas, monkeys (PL. 303), hares, lions, crocodiles, birds — or human beings of various types — the old man, the old woman, the hunter, the magician, the shoemaker, the young girl, the brigand (PL. 304). There are also masks of a mixed type, representing at the same time a human being and an animal, but the result is never hybrid as the two images are clearly differentiated.

The Dogon masks on the whole possess fairly well-defined characteristics, and the margin of invention left to the sculptor is relatively scant. Nevertheless, the objects belonging to a series are not marked by monotonous repetition. The differences are not in style but in execution, and the technical differences of course affect the form of the carved object. With rare exceptions the mask is made from a single piece of wood. It is sometimes carved within the circumference of the cylinder formed by the trunk of a tree. The mask is nearly always hollowed out, the secondary volumes (nose, lips, eyes) emerging within the main volume that envelops them. On the other hand, the mask is made up of a series of distinct planes, clearly separated but clearly interrelated. The connections between the various elements are so conceived that each element is perceived "analytically" and at the same time enters into a general rhythm that, accentuating the masses and the hollows in their reciprocal relation, demonstrates their inevitability. The mask thus appears to require the perception of each one of its parts, which have respectively the value of independent symbols. The general meaning that will be seen in the mask depends at once on the presence of these different elements and on their arrangement vis-à-vis one another.

But the mask must not be seen merely as an organic and independent volume. By its very nature it is not intended to stand out against the background of a flat surface, and consequently it could not be reduced to a relief. It is in fact conceived as varying with movement in a three-dimensional space, to which it is thus related. Owing to the extreme rapidity and complexity of the choreography the mask can be grasped only in a process of perception broken into a series of successive and incomplete views, which are never identical and can merge only in the innermost consciousness. Hence the elements of meaning it is responsible for must be represented on a scale and in a rhythmic relation that enable them to be perceived immediately: the details are not very numerous and they are enlarged, simplified to the essential, rigorously delimited forms. Thus the masks used in the liveliest dances present a more angular aspect and are made up of more clearly separated planes than the masks

worn in less complicated, slower figures. The masks used this second type of dance present a volume with careful modulated curves (Griaule, 1947, fig. 23). The general construction remains vertical (underlined by the straight ridge the nose), but the masses are joined continuously — that they do not form separate compartments — nor is one ma directly opposed to the adjacent ones. Thus the Dogon sculpt is quite capable of representing, when necessary, the delimiti surfaces of the volumes in a continuous development: he know how to soften these surfaces until they form curved or spheric volumes.

The spatial conceptions that these two systems embo reveal the Dogon as expressing, on the one hand, the feelin of man's belonging to the world and, on the other, of mar fear of letting himself be engulfed by the world. This twofo feeling is related to the dual notion of "person," by which t mask must capture and ensnare the life force of the being represents and, at the same time, protect its wearer against t effects of this force. The ritual as a whole, conceived as esthetic manifestation, aims at establishing a relationship wi the world such as may guarantee man's participation and, multaneously, at creating a series of intermediaries through t manipulation of which man is able to defend himself against h absorption into the world and to individualize himself as a perso In its very oppositions this double function defines a dynam system that can only favor, in the development of its practic the evolution of the institution to which it is linked and of t culture that expresses it and that it expresses. This evoluti proceeds, more precisely, in the direction of a gradual individua ization and also of a laicization of the ritual performance. / Griaule (1938) points out, the introduction of new masks is striking illustration of this.

The available information concerning the Dogon statu and statuettes is relatively scant. To this author's knowled these works have not been the subject of systematic stud Among the problems they raise is that of the reason for strikir stylistic differences among them. A case in point is a wood statue discovered by D. Paulme-Schaeffner and D. Lifchi in 1935 in the village of Yayé in the region of Mopti; it represen a hermaphrodite figure (Griaule, 1947, fig. 33) that is ver different in style from the Dogon sculpture known today. T discoverers established that this was a work belonging to a cu abandoned by the people who had preceded the Dogon this area.

A discovery of this kind invites the application of historic perspective to the problems raised by Dogon sculpture — th is, the consideration of a single theme, in this case the primordi couple. It is incontestable that there is a difference between t double statue of the Barnes Foundation, Merion, Pa. (Len 1947, pl. 1), and that of the Musée de la France d'Outre-Me Paris (ibid., pl. 6). Moreover, comparison of the plastic trea ment of these human figures with that of smaller statues, suc as the hermaphrodite horseman in the Musée de l'Homm Paris (Griaule, 1947, fig. 34), shows conclusively that these wor belong to well-differentiated stylistic series. If the same then depicting identical subjects can be treated differently, t question arises *ipso facto* whether the stylistic differences ob served are due to the fact that the works examined have bee fashioned in different periods or to the fact that they come fro far-removed centers of production. So far as the two doub statues are concerned, if the information as to their origin correct, both originate from the Hombori region. Hence would be logical to suppose that these two objects represer two styles deriving from two different traditions. But this giv no indication as to the period of time that may have elapse between the making of the two objects. A style does not d at the moment in which another tends to replace it; in perio of transition an old style may continue to be manifested eve though there is a tendency toward a new style. Still, the ob servation, made apropos of Western art, that "a new style im plies the appearance of a new attitude of man toward the world (P. Francastel, *Peinture et Société*, Lyon, 1951) seems all th more applicable here precisely because Dogon art is rooted i an intransigent tradition.

The data supplied by ethnography inform us, first of all, that a common origin is attributed in mythology to the ancestor statues and to the great mask (sometimes called "mother of the masks"), the term *waguem* (lit., "ancestors") being "applied to the altars of ancestors and to their accessory statuettes, as well as to the altar of the great mask and the wood itself" (Griaule, 1947). Furthermore, the ancestor statues, like the masks, have the function of capturing and ensnaring the life force. Lastly, while the masks are meant to be exhibited during ritual performances that take place in the public square, the ancestor statuettes must be hidden in the recesses of the family, clan, or village sanctuary.

But at the same time, these statuettes give tangible form to a number of concepts subsumed in the myth. A statue from the sanctuary of Orosongo, for instance, representing a horseman holding a lance in his right fist, appears to represent the vicar of the Creator mounted on the first horse that ever came out of the ark of the world (Griaule, *Zodiaque*, v, 1951, pl. 1). As such, it would seem to recount an event that took place in primordial times and became part of the creation myth. Its symbolic implications aside, such an object raises several questions. First, it must be asked in what period the horse appeared in this region of Africa. This information would make it possible, not to date the object, to determine the approximate period at which this theme was defined. According to Baumann (1948) the horse was introduced in the Sudan by the Mossi. Connecting this and other facts with the above-mentioned tradition that the Dogon were originally a population of hunters leads to the conjecture that the Dogon formed their system of thought in connection with that of the Mossi and that the theme of the horse, in particular, appears precisely in the context of an encounter between the Mossi and Dogon cultures. Account must also be taken of another indication. A Bambara headpiece in the form of a helmet surmounted by a horseman leaning on a lance (Lem, 1947, pls. 36, 37) is identical in every detail to the statuette from the Orosongo sanctuary. It would appear to be extremely ancient, and the Bambara among whom it was purchased were unable to explain its purpose. Whether it is of Dogon origin or belongs to a similar system of thought whose implications have been forgotten by the Bambara is a question that can clearly not be answered with certainty. On the other hand, it seems that a common substratum underlies the Bambara, Dogon, and Mossi cultures and that this substratum could originally have taken shape and been diffused among the Mossi.

An examination of the statuette from the Orosongo sanctuary shows, among other things, that from the point of view of its interpretation by the Dogon themselves this work is a reference to an important cosmogonic event. But, at the same time, it constitutes a barrier designed to prevent the noninitiated from gaining a deeper knowledge of the content of the cosmogony or, as Griaule (*Zodiaque*, v, 1951) put it, to "lead the common man away from a profound reading of genesis." This remark gives us a glimpse of the sociological situation of Dogon art and, beyond this, of the conditions of its development. In sum, the understanding of the most secret mysteries of the mythology is restricted to a particular class of individuals (the hierarchy of the initiated) and is achieved through the perception of abstract signs. The explicit work of art, while making manifest part of the mythology, would appear to be a trompe l'oeil designed to hide the essential from the uninitiated. Appearing within the Dogon society as a substitute for knowledge (or as incomplete knowledge), diverting knowledge or impeding it at a certain point, art meant for those who will never be educated would therefore appear to possess less religious content than the abstract signs whose fathoming is reserved for the initiated. Consequently, the purely artistic aspect of the works tends to develop at the expense of the complex religious meanings to which they refer.

Here begins a process that can only end in the secularization of art. Intended for those who have and must have only limited knowledge of the symbolism, art creates in the popular consciousness the conditions by which the restricted symbolism it reveals can only become poorer. The noninitiate can react either by reinterpreting these works (and this in accordance with his own needs) or by taking an attitude toward these works that justifies and authorizes esthetic judgment and perception. He thus projects onto these works, in relation to himself and to his status of noninitiate, a set of representations that have to do with him in his situation, which, in turn, determines the content he recognizes in them. Freer than the initiate — who is enmeshed in a network of rites, observances, and meanings whose efficacy is guaranteed by strict respect for tradition — the noninitiate is the repository of the living forces of evolution in the society.

In Dogon sculpture three series, each defined by well-differentiated characteristics, can be distinguished. The first is exemplified by the double statue in the Musée de la France d'Outre-Mer in Paris. The two figures are in a standing position. The woman's arms hang the length of the body, from which they are not detached, and the hands cover the knees. The man's left arm encircles the shoulders of the woman. The legs are slightly bent and are quadrangular in section; their slight dimensions give them little importance compared to the trunk. The woman's breasts are small and close together, set at the base of the neck. The man's chest is formed by a rectangular volume, upon which are engraved vertically opposite angles. In both cases the neck, a simple cylinder, is excessively elongated, and the head is in the shape of a sharply outlined crest of a helmet. The hair is indicated by lightly incised oblique grooves. The face is slightly concave, hollowed out within the mass of the head, and the nose, a trihedron, stands out from it. The eyes are simply holes pierced at the top of shallow cavities. Despite its small size (under 15 in.) the whole structure has a very clear monumental and architectural character. The general rhythm arises from the simple orthogonal balance of vertical and horizontal lines, a principle also well exemplified by a Dogon lock (Griaule, 1947, fig. 55).

The double statue of the Barnes Foundation in Merion, Pa., shows quite another style, although the positions of the figures and the basic architectonic scheme of this group and the one discussed above are virtually identical. Here the man and woman are seated on a stool (whose carved legs represent small squatting figures), and they are slenderer, particularly as to the limbs. Further, the trunks are almost entirely covered with shallow and delicate geometric engraved patterns (chevrons, crossbars). The shoulders and the chest form a single mass, from which stems the upper limbs; this volume is clearly demarcated from the trunk. Also contraposed to the cylindrical volume of the trunk is the continuous mass of the ensemble of the lower limbs and pelvis. The trunk, like the shaft of a column, joins two quadrangular masses that could be compared respectively to a plinth and a capital; the whole is thus made up of volumes that do not follow one another in linked continuity but are juxtaposed in a rhythmic counterbalance that describes each one separately. This system has been deliberately conceived: the sculptor has emphasized it by exactly delimiting each volume — even the secondary ones — by engraved strokes.

If these two double statues belong to two periods of Dogon sculpture, to two paradigmatic and limited types around which other groups could be ranged, they were undoubtedly conceived in relation to a single master scheme. That the statue in the Musée de la France d'Outre-Mer appears to be unique in style may be taken to argue that it is more ancient than the one of the Barnes Foundation, since some works unquestionably resembling the latter are known. If this hypothesis were to be confirmed, the line of development of Dogon art would be seen as one of increasing mannerism rather than of progressive schematization. But in actuality, in the series of works referred to as *art mobilier*, comprising locks, granary shutters, and the like, it is evident that when these are surmounted by human figurines or when human figurines stand out in relief against the background, they combine solutions borrowed from each of the two styles.

Still to be considered is a series of small statuettes, either freestanding or incorporated into other objects, in which case they undergo a plastic treatment that depends in part on the nature of the object. On a lock (PL. 302) or a granary shutter (PL. 301) they are conceived as true reliefs and stand out against the background of a flat surface. On the lid of a ceremonial cup, or urn (PL. 310), or even on the top of an unguent container (Paulme, 1956, fig. 6), they come closer to being sculpture in the proper sense. Moreover, even though these objects are the materialization of mythical events, in most cases they are meant for daily use and their function is primarily of a material order; the religious factor enters only to the extent that it supplies a certain number of appropriate themes. If a row of ancestors is portrayed on a granary shutter, it is because the "ancestors-fecundity-fertility" chain is a natural association for the sculptor to make. As for the freestanding statuettes, these form a special series that maintains a stylistic relation with the ones mentioned above, without, however, being of identical workmanship. The volumes are more supple and less angular. Moreover, they manifest a certain sense of movement (PL. 306). They often represent a figure (female or hermaphrodite) with arms raised toward heaven in an attitude that may represent supplication (Griaule, 1947, fig. 36). Their function is essentially religious: these are the ancestor figures and mythical personages called, according to Kjersmeier (1935, I), *degue* (lit., "little relatives"). There is as yet no study of these objects that makes it possible to consider Dogon art in its entirety by establishing the connections between the various series of products that to date have been studied strictly from the point of view of their mythological implications, their specific functions, and their iconography at the expense of analysis of their stylistic differences.

The relation that links the Dogon to the esthetic universe he has created appears to be the result of a past evolution and is itself still in evolution (Griaule, 1938). In describing this relation it should be said that the esthetic function of a work — mask, statuette, or piece of *art mobilier* — is deeply felt by the Dogon himself, both as such and as a guarantee of the efficacy of the rite in which the work figures. This may well lead, insofar as the symbolic complex in which the Dogon moves (and of which he has a varying knowledge according to his degree of initiation) reveals the existence of an analytical intellectual activity, to a consideration of various aspects involved in the modalities of the process of esthetic perception. This perception at once reveals to the Dogon that the work of art operates as a means by which he, through immediately legible signs, apprehends himself in the context of the world that surrounds him and of the society to which he belongs. Instead of being referred to a transcendent reality, which these signs disclose and fulfill, he is referred to himself, to his own material situation and his status in the society — which are thus, if not justified, at least made clear. He realizes his membership in a collectivity where his role is defined and in a universe whose destiny appears to him to be intertwined with his own. Now this double realization does not consist merely in the revelation of its object: it is truly a process that creates its object. The Dogon apprehends himself in the world, from which he is distinct, in the process of analysis by which he delineates it. But he also apprehends the world through the symbols to which he reduces it. The symbols he has created are, in a sense, mobile elements, which he uses and manipulates and through whose agency he possesses power over the world.

If a parallel development is discernible in the statuettes and masks as well as in the architecture (PLS. 299, 300; Griaule, *Présence Africaine*, X–XI, 1951), in the rock paintings (Griaule, 1938) as well as in the *art mobilier* and the textiles (Griaule, *Zodiaque*, V, 1951), and if stylistic and institutional connections are apparent among the various series of products examined, it is not because Dogon art, an original creation, gives expression to a body of lore, a knowledge that preceded it: Dogon art is the means by which this learning and the expression of it have been slowly elaborated.

The Mossi. A population grouped in two feudal states, the respective capitals of which are Ouahigouya and Ouagadougou, the Mossi appear to have come from the east, from a region situated beyond the Niger, in the 11th century. They later conquered Dagomba and Gambaga, and their power then gradually extended toward the north. During the same period they penetrated southward as far as Wa, on the Black Volta,

and eastward into Gurma. In the 16th century the great Mos⟨ kingdom collapsed as a consequence of conflicts with the kin⟨ doms of Songhai and Mali. A people of warlike beginning⟨ the Mossi possess a historic tradition. Their social organizatio⟨ subject to the authority of their ruler, the Mogho-Naba, a rigid hierarchy. The aristocracy provides a cadre of fun⟨ tionaries, subordinate to whom are the peasants, the craftsm⟨ in their castes, and lastly the slaves.

The Mossi would seem to have absorbed an indigeno⟨ population, the Fulse (or Kurumba), whose customs were simil⟨ to those of the Dogon and the Bambara. Although it was on⟨ in the cities that Islam came close to taking root, the Mossi cultu⟨ reveals certain Islamic characteristics, perhaps as a result ⟨ influences radiating from the court of the Mogho-Naba. T⟨ Mossi religion appears to manifest a twofold system corr⟨ sponding to a distribution of the society into well-defined classe⟨ On the one hand, the religion of the peasant classes (and of t⟨ conquered populations) seems similar to that of other Sudane⟨ populations, being founded mainly on a dualism evidence⟨ by belief in the existence of a "heaven-earth" duality and ⟨ an agrarian cult. On the other hand, the religion of the aristo⟨ racy appears to be based on a "monothéisme approximatif⟨ (Hardy, 1927).

Mossi art borrows most of its stylistic conventions fro⟨ Dogon and Bambara art; its works are chiefly the masks use⟨ during ritual performances. There are, however, some statuette⟨ which are rather rare and probably ancient works. An exampl⟨ collected in Yatenga — a standing figure of a woman, the fac⟨ bearing traces of white highlights (Lem, 1947, pl. 9) — is ⟨ great interest. The style of this statuette is at variance with th⟨ rigid linearity that is, for the most part, the rule in Sudane⟨ sculpture; its general aspect is sinuous, as if the body had n⟨ skeleton, and the joints of the lower and upper limbs are hard⟨ indicated, as if the limbs were pliant. The piece brings to min⟨ certain Dogon figural concepts and representations, connecte⟨ with the genii of water, the *nummo*, whose limbs were flexib⟨ and without joints (Griaule, 1948).

A female figurine of a type similar to the statuette just de⟨ scribed is found surmounting certain antelope masks; affixe⟨ to a thin wooden board rising above the horns, these figures ar⟨ not reliefs as they are attached to the board 'n only three plac⟨ (Lem, 1947, pl. 10).

The Mossi mask as a rule represents the head of a large kob⟨ antelope and is elongated at the back by a cut-out and pyro⟨ graved wooden board. This board looks like an actual coat ⟨ arms bearing polychrome charges (whose character is unques⟨ tionably emblematic, but whose meaning has not as yet bee⟨ elucidated. The ensemble is of the most elegant workmanshi⟨ both the mask proper and the thin board surmounting it. (⟨ comparable type is the Dogon *maison à étages* mask previous⟨ described.) When the mask represents a male antelope, th⟨ horns are straight; in the case of a doe, they are curved and th⟨ thin board is completed by a feminine figure. All the Moss⟨ masks of this type are designated by the name *waôngo* (pl⟨ *wando*). They are encountered in the Fulse villages (whic⟨ are also the smiths' villages), being used in the course of ritua⟨ performances given by the associations of young people. Th⟨ masks and their accessories are in the custody of the "chie⟨ of the earth," a priest whose authority coexists, in the Fuls⟨ villages, with that of the Mogho-Naba's delegate. This doubl⟨ authority points up the coexistence within the Mossi societie⟨ of the dual religious system mentioned above. According t⟨ Paulme (1956), the Mossi society has features that sugges⟨ "the survival of an agrarian cult, where masks play a par⟨ comparable perhaps to that which still holds good today amon⟨ the Bambara and the Bobo."

To this series of objects must be added the headpieces rep⟨ resenting the head of a male equine antelope used in the ritua⟨ ceremonies of the Fulse. The known examples of this Fuls⟨ headpiece are thought to number well under a dozen (Fagg, 1963⟨ there are three identical specimens: in Paris (Mus. de l'Homme⟨ Griaule, 1947, fig. 25), in Baltimore (Mus. of Art., Wurtzburge⟨ Coll.; Plass, 1956; pl. 4-A), and in Geneva (private coll.; Lem⟨ 1947, pl. 12). Because it is based on the antelope motif, th⟨

pe inevitably calls to mind the Segoni-kun of the Bambara. Although a similarity in use and function to the Bambara works an indeed be noted, the Mossi examples represent an original creation, at least from the aspect of form and perhaps also of significance. The plastic treatment differs considerably: whereas the Segoni-kun the forms unfold dynamically in two-dimensional terms through the bold exploitation of the rhythmic resources afforded by the contrast between broken lines and arabesques, the Fulse headpiece develops in three-dimensional forms, not as a silhouette but as a volume, its four sides blazoned with emblematic polychrome designs (black, ocher, red, and white) of a geometric aspect.

Mossi sculptures in metal are also known. Contemporary bronze figurines (cast by the lost-wax method) representing scenes from daily life, made at a center in Ouagadougou, are on the level of export art and are of scant interest (Paulme, 1956). Of greater interest are statuettes (modeled by the strip method) that portray the deceased Mogho-Naba accompanied by relatives. These statuettes, executed by a specially appointed smith at the death of each Mogho-Naba, were placed in a special hut in the village of the royal burial ground. Figurines similar in style and type are found among the Bobo (Lem, 1947).

The Bobo. Inhabiting the region between the cities of San, Bobo-Diulasso, Diébougou, and Dédougou, the Bobo were already established when the Mossi appeared. They are essentially farmers, organized in large patriarchal families, and very much attached to their fields and villages. The practiced arts are sculpture in wood, painting, and bronze casting by the lost-wax process. So far as the sculpture in wood is concerned, it depends stylistically on a general effect common to certain aspects of Mossi and Dogon art.

The sculptured products of the Bobo are chiefly masks; freestanding sculpture (PL. 309) is rare. Mention should be made of their small square or rectangular stools, which frequently have a handle carved in the form of a human head. A remarkable example — a striking adaptation of utility to representation — has such a handle, which is in the likeness of a man on his hands and knees; the horizontal element, formed by his trunk, is engraved with geometric motifs (Griaule, 1947, pl. 61). Bobo youths carry these objects slung over the shoulder by a cord (Lem, 1947).

The Bobo masks appear in connection with rites for the dead, including a feast held at the beginning of the agricultural season. They would seem to represent the guardian spirits of the village and are rather varied in form. Generally polychrome, they simulate either animals (cock, buffalo, antelope) or individual types (e.g., a young Peul girl). One such mask, very schematic in style and adorned with motifs of a geometric type, succeeds in combining, in restrained fashion, human and animal features (Lem, 1947, pl. 58); it is rightly compared by Lem with a Baga mask (ibid., pl. 59). On the other hand, the large Bobo masks, with their circular faces surmounted by a blazoned small plank, call to mind not only the great masks of the Dogon and Mossi but also a mask that the Baga have never allowed to be photographed, the *bansundyi*: "a painted fretworked board which may be up to twenty feet in height. It has a sinuous outline and is completed at the summit by two feathers or by a strip of fabric that floats in the wind" (Paulme, 1956). There are hints here of an identical original schema, which was differentiated into the various manifestations presently known in this group of societies, which, having evolved a culture based on a link between agrarian and funeral rites, possess similar economies and social organizations.

Painting, like sculpture, yields common manifestations to populations often very distant from one another. Bobo painting, which is closely linked to architecture, the external and internal walls being covered with polychrome motifs of a geometric cast, can be compared to the paintings seen, for example, among the Senufo, the Minianka, and the Grunshi (Baumann and Westermann, 1948).

Mural art among the Bobo is not restricted to painting. In fact, the Bobo — like the Senufo, the Grunshi, the Dogon, and the Fon of Dahomey — possess an art of low relief in mud

(directly incorporated into the wall) and in wood (shutters, doors). Common motifs in these low reliefs are twins, a paired man and woman, horned animals, birds, snakes, and lizards. These figures are probably linked to concepts of fecundity. To judge from a panel forming the entrance to the antechamber of the house of a village chief — found at Sikasso but coming from the region of Folona — the Bobo artist, even when he borrows motifs from neighboring populations, remains faithful to a highly schematized style and to the distribution of his motifs on a flat, blazoned surface (Lem, 1947, pl. 64).

In describing Bobo art heraldic terminology is used deliberately, since of all the Sudanese arts it is the one most aptly characterized by means of this special vocabulary. The Bobo thinks much more in terms of surface than of volume. Still, the Bobo undoubtedly practices true sculpture and is not unaware of the treatment of volumes; in particular, he carves statues (Kjersmeier, 1935, I, pl. 32) and masks of helmet type, sometimes with the crest surmounted by a small statue (Fagg, 1953, pl. v). Nevertheless, in most of its products Bobo art shows a predilection for the treatment of polychrome surfaces, upon which — particularly on the circle or the oval of the face — slight relief is sometimes indicated, designed to give greater emphasis to the circles that define the contours. This tendency of Bobo art to express itself for the most part in surface treatment coincides with extreme schematization of forms as well as skillful use of polychromy. A photograph of a group of participants in a ritual performance (Paulme, 1956, pl. III) demonstrates the degree of variety that Bobo masks achieve with a limited number of motifs (checkered patterns, chevrons, crossbars, crescents) and suggests the sense of harmony and of the distribution of colors (ochers, blacks, some reds) of the Bobo artisans.

Jean LAUDE

The Lobi group. The various tribes that make up the Lobi population (Lobi, Kulango, Dorossié, Gan, Dian, Birifor, etc.) are located along the boundary zone between Upper Volta, the Ivory Coast, and Ghana. The artistic level of their sculptural production is extremely low. The only feature peculiar to the Lobi culture worthy of mention is the three-legged wooden stool, on one of whose legs a small head wearing the tribal helmet headdress is often carved.

The metal objects, inspired by plant motifs, are the same as those of the Bobo and Mossi. The copper pendants, worn for protective purposes, are shaped like a sheathed knife, the dreaded horned viper, or, more often, the chameleon. Certain whistles are made in the form of a stylized human figure.

Ernesta CERULLI

The Senufo. Also known as the Siena, the Senufo inhabit the regions situated between the southeastern part of former French Sudan and the north of the Ivory Coast. The center from which they would appear to have spread out is in the southern region, in the vicinity of Korhogo, where, in fact, the greatest number of sculptured objects can be found. Except as concerns the settlements on the Ivory Coast, Senufo customs are relatively little known. Descendants of a first group of invaders from the southwest (Baumann and Westermann, 1948), the Senufo are a somewhat dispersed agricultural people. They have not favored martial pursuits and have built fortified villages, with *pisé de terre* walls on the model of the Sudanese *tata*, only to defend themselves against possible invaders. Thus more than once they have come under the domination of foreigners of Mande stock.

Like the other Sudanese, the Senufo have secret societies linked to agrarian and funerary rites. The predominant organization is the Lo society, found in every village (Goldwater, 1964). The artistic output of the Senufo comprises statuettes of various sizes, masks, and objects of *art mobilier* including heddle pulleys, carved doors, and rhythm pounders. The masks can be divided into two main series, differing in form — face masks and helmet masks.

The most common of the several types of helmet masks are

those termed *gbon* by M. Prouteaux ("Notes sur certains rites magico-religieux de la Haute Côte d'Ivoire," *L'Anthropologie*, XXIX, 1918-19, pp. 37-52), which have acquired the designation "firespitter" (PL. 304). The *gbon* dances with a whip in his hand to the rhythm of drums, horns, and voices. He is subject to a fine if he is seen by a noninitiate, especially a woman. The music that accompanies his performance is supposed to attract the sorcerers irresistibly. The powers attributed to this mask mainly concern fire; the wearer can sit without danger on a brazier or burn a witch inside his house without its catching fire.

The firespitter masks are zoomorph in form and very large. Many examples are surmounted by a more or less stylized representation of a chameleon (Lem, 1947, pl. 54). Others are of the Janiform type (ibid., pl. 55). In certain of the firespitter masks, contamination of the animal representation by human features, particularly as to nose and eyes, has been observed (Paulme, 1956, pl. v). Such masks have therefore sometimes been interpreted as representing a cynocephalus, but they are now thought to represent the head of a hyena (Fagg, 1953, pl. xv); they are worn by members of the Korubla secret society.

Fashioned according to an essentially horizontal construction scheme, the firespitter masks are not without certain similarities to the Banda masks of the Baga of former French Guinea (Paulme, 1956, pl. IV), but the Banda mask is less sculptural and more schematic and, owing to the polychrome motifs on its outer surfaces, more decorative. The firespitter mask looks almost like an independent sculpture closed in upon itself. It is formed by curved volumes, carefully modulated, which barely contrast with the slightly sunken plane of the face. The powerfulness of these volumes is sometimes relieved by secondary motifs directly grafted onto them. These motifs act as vectors, which from a structural point of view mark the outline of a movement and direct the eye (PL. 304). In certain examples the characteristic chameleon that surmounts the top of the skull is schematized to the point of being reduced to its dorsal curve, with one interruption to indicate the head (Paulme, 1956, pl. v).

In these objects the structural schemes seem infinitely more complex than those of the works belonging to cultures more distant from the coast. However, Senufo art is an art of transition, which borrows certain characteristics from pure Sudanese art (notably in the pains it takes almost never to conceive surfaces as outer skins totally imprisoning the volumes) and from the art of the Guinean cultures (particularly in the tendency to soften the surfaces and modulate them in unbroken continuity); proof of this is to be found in certain styles of representation that prevail, for instance, among the Baule, an example of which is a heddle pulley that is similar to the firespitter mask but less ornate in conception (Fagg, 1953, pl. XIIₑ).

A particularly clear example of the analogies that may exist between certain works of Senufo art and certain works of Guinean art — more precisely that of the Baule — is found in the Senufo face mask known as *kpélié* (PL. 304), which is carved in shallow relief that is surrounded by motifs flattened laterally to the same plane. Generally anthropomorph in type, these masks are in most cases surmounted by the representation of a bird, sometimes extremely stylized. Although such works, carved in soft wood with European tools and crudely tinted with aniline, have been mass produced for export, these should not be used as the basis for judgment of the whole series of masks of this type. Two beautiful antique specimens (Lem, 1947, pls. 52, 53) differ slightly from each other. The first offers the eye a convex surface, though the mask is appreciably sunken in the region of the face. In contrast, the second mask (which was found in the region of Korhogo) appears as a more clearly concave volume and, in profile, is almost totally curvilinear; the hornbull surmounting the forehead is reduced to its elemental geometric terms — the straight line that indicates the body and the curved one that indicates the long beak. More particularly, the first of these two masks reveals a conception fairly close to that followed in the making of certain Baule masks, of the Gu type (Paulme, 1956, pl. xi i). In any case there are incontestable signs of a relationship here.

The Senufo face masks appear to represent a mythical character, the "bird-woman." The bird theme is a persistent motif in Senufo art, so much so that some of its avatars should be detailed here. In one "bird-woman" mask (Lem, 1947, pl. 50) the figure is the result of a combination of anthropomorph and ornithomorph motifs, while in other examples the bird is clearly distinguished from the female figure it surmounts. A mask of an unusual type for Senufo territory (Plass, 1957, pl. 11) appears to represent a buffalo (?), the head of which is surmounted by four extremely stylized hornbills (?).

The bird motif is also treated independently of the mask as an isolated sculpture or in groups. As a freestanding sculpture a figure of a bird sometimes adorns the hut consecrated to the protecting genii of the village (PL. 308; Lem, 1947, pl. 48). An example (ibid., pl. 49) shows a bird supporting a smaller bird on each of its outspread wings; on its back is a female figurine, and two other birds, also with outspread wings, are attached to its tail with a metal rod. Fastened to the end of a staff, with colored scarves tied to its edges, such a sculpture might lead the movements of a group of dancers belonging to a secret society. During the dances known as *kurbi* these birds, "male and female in couples," appear to play the same part as the Segoni-kun of the Bambara — that is, they are "totemic representations of the ancestors of the tribe taking part in rituals commemorating very ancient family and agrarian rites" (Lem, 1947). Finally, mention must be made of the bird motif on the top of heddle pulleys, on the lid of unguent boxes, and in the low reliefs decorating the doors of the antechamber of the village chiefs, where this bird motif is associated with representations of iguanas and tortoises, masks, and riders bearing lances (Allemand, 1956, fig. 74). This motif doubtless refers to themes or events of a mythological order whose exact significance the present state of knowledge does not make clear.

The Senufo bird seems to be either an avatar of a demiurge which is supposed, in the beginning, to have revealed the practice of certain techniques (which would explain its appearance on such objects as tools and heddle pulleys and its use during dances performed in the course of agrarian rites), or an avatar of an ancestor, as observed in other regions of Negro Africa where the bird is associated with the snake, which would be linked to certain concepts relating to fecundity and birth and, more precisely, to the death-and-rebirth cycle (which would explain its appearance on female ancestor masks).

Senufo sculpture has often been the object of relatively disparaging judgments, which perhaps may be attributed to the influence of Delafosse (1908-09). To the present author such judgments seem unjustified. Senufo sculptures not only show great variety in their functions and their general aspect but often reveal remarkable vigor and great freedom of structure as well as a certain sense of rhythm. Foremost are the small statuettes said to be fecundity fetishes; these were given to "nubile young girls who were, in the past, meant to keep them all their lives as a token of maternity" (Lem, 1947, pls. 39, 47). These statuettes, which today are regarded as merely dolls, were buried with their owners. Also noteworthy are groups representing a female figure and a male figure on a single base, intended for twin infants (ibid., pls. 42, 43); small separated twin figures (male and female), used for purposes of divination (ibid., pl. 46); and ritual female figures carved on a heavy base to form rhythm pounders, used for the dances of the Lo initiation society (ibid., pls, 44, 45). Lastly, besides this group, there are ancestor statuettes — some fairly similar to those used for divination (Trowell, 1954, pl. XXXIV B), others in a rather different style, particularly in the elongated treatment of the body (Allemand, 1956, figs. 18, 20). Most of these statuettes represent standing figures (PLS. 306, 310), but there are some seated female figures. A remarkable example, and one that is rather typical of Senufo sculpture, shows a woman seated on a semicircular stool. The arms are bent at the elbow; the breasts are not pendent but project forward; the face is thin, and the facial angle acute. On the head is borne a large jar (Allemand, 1956, fig. 16). The Sudanese linearity softens here, without, however, causing the sculpture to lose its monumental character. The volumes are delicately defined, without interruption of

e over-all rhythm; this rhythm derives from the contrast be-
een vertical and horizontal (or oblique) elements sufficiently
assive to have weight but not so massive as to unbalance
e whole.

Another group of statuettes is a series representing a mounted
rseman holding a lance (Allemand, 1956, fig. 22; Trowell,
54, pl. XXXIV A). The appearance of this motif carved in low
ief on doors in conjunction with masks, hornbills, and a har-
st scene has been mentioned. It would be difficult not to re-
ll in this connection the Dogon statuette from the Orosongo
nctuary and the representation that crowns certain Bambara
adpieces. In the case of the Senufo statuettes, however, the
rse is rather clumsily executed, and in certain specimens its
ce is human (Clouzot and Level, 1924, pl. 14).

To sum up, Senufo art appears as an essentially sculptural
c in the strict sense of the word, despite the fact that the works
e generally small. While remaining particularly faithful to
gorously defined structural schemes, it combines certain features
the Sudanese plastic sense with the more voluptuous sense of
rm that characterizes Guinean sculpture, and it is profoundly
iginal in its most successful expressions. When it does not
ult in a hybrid juxtaposition, it achieves a real synthesis,
ich it establishes as its special quality. Though the ideals
incarnates are but dimly understood, everything points to a
rtain community of concepts and representations with the
rs of the Dogon; this could be based on common origin of the
pulations concerned, or it could have been forged in the course
a history that linked these populations in relative political
ity. Moreover, if certain Guinean motifs do appear, it is
eresting to note that they concern a particular attitude toward
jects whose function is conceived in closer connection to
istic values. One cannot speak of a free art — a fiction that
es not apply even to Western arts. However, the Senufo
ists very often supply a foreign market, so the demand that
verns the production of carved works is not fulfilled solely
the local level and determined by local needs. "The Senufo
ulptors, well-known craftsmen in ancient Sudan, supplied with
ual portable objects many populations who lacked craftsmen.

As clientele they had all the minor potentates and village or
settlement chiefs to whom they furnished badges of dignity
in the form of staffs with carved handles and of small chairs. ..."
(Lem, 1947). It is undoubtedly with this production that one
must connect certain works cast by the lost-wax process, among
them a beautiful command staff crowned by a masked figure
holding a knife and various attributes and standing on a base
composed of two addorsed antelope protomas (Allemand,
1956, fig. 8). Senufo art certainly did not radiate very far
beyond the center of its production, but its diffusion is indicative
of its recognized significance on the artistic level and of its
ability to arouse interest beyond the circles of its creators and
those for whom they produced their works.

CULTURES OF THE CENTRAL AND EASTERN SUDAN. It is difficult to make a distinct separation between the central and
eastern Sudan, since "the historical fate and the civilization
of these two regions are very similar" (Baumann and Westermann, 1948). The most noteworthy cultures of these two regions
will therefore be dealt with together.

The Chad civilization. The most important culture in this
area insofar as the figural arts are concerned — the Chad
civilization — can be traced to an ancient population, the Sao,
whose present descendants are the Kotoko. The Sao would
seem to have been, to the west and the north, the builders
of Kano and the drillers of a well between Tanout and Agadès.
Certain ruins in the Djourab and the Bahr-el-Ghazal are thought
to be the remains of structures they erected. To the east they
appear to have dwelt in the neighborhood of Lake Fitri and the
region of Moyto, and toward the south their presence has been
traced at Wase, Bïa, and along the Chari (Shari) up to Mandjafa
and Bousso (Lebeuf and Masson-Detourbet, 1950). In general,
traditional sources agree that the Sao came from the east, but
so far as physical type is concerned the testimony is contradictory:
dark-skinned according to some, and fair-skinned according
to others. Actually, the populations designated under the name
Sao would seem to have belonged to successive waves of

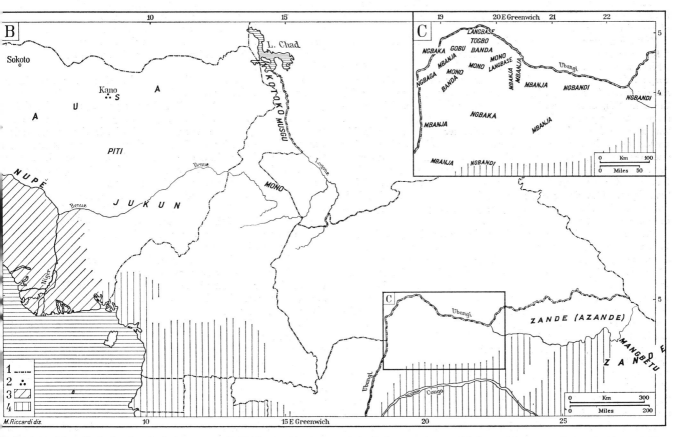

stribution of the principal archaeological centers and ethnic groups in the area of the Sudanese cultures; (B) Area of the eastern Sudanese cultures. *Key:* Political boundaries; (2) archaeological sites; (3) area of the Guinean cultures; (4) area of the Bantu cultures. Inset C shows a detail of the bend of the Ubanghi.

immigrants. There is little historical information about the peoples. It is known that in the 7th century there was a massacre of a group of dark-skinned Sao in the Bilma oasis, over 300 mi. from Lake Chad.

The Chad civilization flourished mainly in the Chari Delta, where, in about 950, the Sao settled. There they lived in peace until the 13th century, the period in which the sovereigns of Kanem-Bornu tried to extend their empire at the expense of the Sao. This period of incessant and bloody struggles ended at the close of the 16th century, when the Sao disappear from the chronicles (Lebeuf, 1951).

The material from the Chad civilization, excavated in the course of numerous expedition, is considerable, yet it probably represents only a first contribution to the knowledge of a civilization for which much evidence has yet to be exhumed. In this region, where stone is lacking, clay was the preferred material, made use of by the builders of cities as well as the artists and craftsmen, who created an extremely diversified body of works, ranging from jars to statuettes and including spindle whorls, weights for fish nets, and toys. No information has come down to us concerning the composition and treatment of the *pâte* used by the ancient Sao, but it must be borne in mind that "the technique of pottery being among those which evolve the least, or the most slowly, present usage reproduces ancient practices" (Lebeuf and Masson-Detourbet, 1950). The substances used were not of uniform quality; in some instances objects modeled of a fine clay are found next to others modeled in a coarse earth mingled with particles refractory to firing. The method of fashioning vases was the process of coiling. But sometimes the ancient Sao also used molds (exterior or interior) in the form of baskets. Probably the assembling of the large funerary urns had to be carried out in several operations; the bottom, pressed against a "mold" of basketwork or fragments of terra cotta, was then wedged into loose soil so that the worker could finish it. Sometimes it was "soldered" to the belly of the urn with a plaster made of earth during the process of execution. The firing methods are not yet known with certainty, though some characteristics of the objects that have been dug up suggest that the heating was carried out in an open fire. To such crude firing can be attributed the fragility and poor state of preservation of certain bulky pieces.

The funerary urns, some of which reach a height of about 5 ft., are generally ovoid and slightly narrowed under the neck, which widens at the opening to allow for the passage of the corpse. They are decorated on the exterior with motifs of geometric type, but everything points to a symbolic meaning for these motifs, among which chevrons predominate. Vases belonging to the period of the most recent occupation of the knolls, which were found buried on the perimeter of towns or inside enclosures, held verses of the Koran deemed effective in keeping enemies away and checking epidemics. In general, the funerary urns and the pottery — ritual as well as domestic — of the ancient Sao reveal a remarkable mastery in both execution and firing technique. The decorations are varied, and different "styles" can be distinguished, but the mystery of the symbols expressed in them has not yet been fathomed.

More spectacular are the various pink-colored clay sculptures that have been dug up in most of the strata. These statuettes are of different styles and types. The two main categories into which Lebeuf (1951) has divided them are "deified ancestors" and "masked dancers." The function of the statuettes is essentially religious. More precisely, these statuettes, like all the Sudanese works of this type mentioned so far, are meant to contain a vital force that must be trapped in order to be controlled and used. They are related to the cult of the dead.

These works, which cannot as yet be grouped in chronological order, all manifest marked stylistic differences from one another. And yet, above and beyond these differences, it is possible to distinguish Sao sculpture in terms of a stylistic generalization: "eyes with a lack-luster stare, an excessively large, protuberant mouth, a nose jutting out on the forehead to the point of becoming a horn at the top of the skull, flat chin, no ears or, on the contrary, amply projecting ears" (Lebeuf, 1951).

The statuettes of deified ancestors are among the most beautiful. With the exception of one, which is placed on t• short, slightly bent legs (Lebeuf and Masson-Detourbet, 19: fig. 12), they rise from a massive plinth without any indicati• of lower limbs. One example, the central figure from the Ta sanctuary, is marked by particularly delicate workmanship a• nobility of execution (ibid., fig. 13). Its mass is powerful wit out being heavy. The rigid arms, closely attached to the bod are of a piece with it, and the shoulders are broad and squa• A crossed ornament on the breast appears to be a prolongati• of the necklace. Incised on the shoulders and on either si• of the breast are chevron motifs. The handling of the he• contrasts, in its "baroque" quality, with the severity that go• erns the treatment of the body. The lips, stretched wid protrude like ledges. The nose is short and turned up. T• eyes are made of "shells" slit laterally, in this case with no i• dication of the eyebrow ridges. A fan-shaped beard is suggest• by the striae incised on the chin. Despite their relatively sm• size (the largest are barely 14 in. tall), these statuettes are u• deniably monumental in aspect (III, PL. 126; IV, PL. 20•

The contrast between the hieratic character and sobri• of the lower volumes and the expressive dynamism of the he• does not negate the unity of the work; rather, it is resolved a unity of presence (in the theatrical sense of the word), and th raises the question of the link that connected the style of the• works to their function. It has been noted that at Tago "t• disposition of the premises allows one to suppose that the thr• central statues constituted the main interest; as representatio• of the founder of the city and of his descendants, they c• symbolize the succession of the first chiefs" (Lebeuf and Masso• Detourbet, 1950). Moreover, the complex ritual of the enthro• ing of the prince indicates the importance of the bonds linki• the new king to his ancestors. From this point of view it see• that tradition is felt not at all as mere fidelity to a complet• past; it is felt, rather, as a continual, dynamic reaffirmatio• of the past by the present. Thus the essential function of the• ever-present figures is not to recall the past but, on the contra• to deny it as past and to show its permanence and consta• reality. The king acts as an interpreter and consequently more than the representative of the people; he is an incarnatio• of them. Each new king — and thus also the people — tak• upon himself the original acts that directed the foundation the towns and repeats them, not as a simulacrum but as a realit by virtue of gestures and rites that precisely embody the mean• of these acts.

The "masked dancers" seem to be of coarser material a• workmanship. Their aspect is massive, with a striking dispr• portion between the "mask" and its support (Lebeuf and Ma• son-Detourbet, 1951, figs. 8, 9). To judge from these zo• morph masks, in the ancient Chad civilization there exist• ceremonies — similar to those performed, for that matter, • the whole of the Sudan — connected with both funeral a• agrarian rites. But, whereas no examples of Dogon, Bamba• or Senufo statuettes representing masked figures are present• known, this evidence indicates that the ancient Sao deem• it necessary somehow to "double" the ritual performances • the presentation of the members of the corps of dancers appea• ing in them. In other words, the ritual performance, itself a• institution within the society in which it takes place, is inst• tutionalized to a further degree, insofar as it offers to anoth• field of artistic activity a repertory of figural themes — a si• uation similar to that of the European artists of the late Midd• Ages, who reproduced on their canvases sacred performance• given under church auspices.

What need does this "secondary expression" of the ritu• performance fill? As has already been mentioned, the ritu• performance rehearses primordial events that must periodical• be "renewed," or brought up to date, in order to guarantee an• assure the reality and meaning of daily life. This "recharging• must be done periodically. Since the effects it should produ• extend over a certain span of time (after which the ceremo• must be celebrated anew), the ritual performance in itself is n• conceived as being ephemeral. But as soon as it is given objecti• form in representations of masked dancers, which are them• selves meant to produce certain results, the purport of th•

eremony has become in its turn one that another mechanism aspires to produce. In other words, the function of the ritual performance is no longer felt to be exercising itself efficaciously though without being strengthened and guaranteed. To make images of characters who exhibit themselves in a ritual performance means that the intrinsic efficacy of the performance is no longer completely relied on. In the ritual performance there undoubtedly still exists a religious content, but this content has been transformed to the degree that it has been rendered objective. Thus it seems as if at a given moment the ritual performance was perceived visually and no longer as a complete whole whose function was guaranteed by forms of participation that mobilized the entire being, with consciousness intervening only in the immediate recognition of the signs and symbols involved. The fact that the ways of participating in the ritual performance could have been — and must have been — defined through an agent (i.e., through the representation of masked dancers) indicates that the theatrical aspect of this performance tended gradually to put the ritual aspect into the background.

A certain number of clay statues representing animals are among the artifacts of the Chad civilization. Less numerous and less varied than the deified ancestors and the masked dancers, these were probably connected with religious performances, but their exact role in the cult has not yet been determined. It is thought that some of these statuettes "replaced the animals the people intended to kill or those which had really been killed during a day's hunting" (Lebeuf and Masson-Detourbet, 1951, figs. 44–47). Porcupines, hippopotamuses (exclusively in the sanctuaries of Drik and Tago), and sea mammals are represented.

The ancient Sao also modeled clay likenesses of human heads, which are markedly different in style. In some cases they were intended as stoppers to close bottles that contained beverages for the deceased they were supposed to represent (ibid., figs. 18–20). Other examples, not treated in the round but made in the shape of a quoit, have extremely stylized faces (ibid., figs. 22, 28). According to local traditions, these objects were modeled to celebrate the birth of a child, and sacrifices as well as offerings were made to them to ward off the mortal illnesses that might otherwise be transmitted to the newborn by wandering spirits (Lebeuf and Masson-Detourbet, 1951). Some of these quoit-shaped heads were buried at the foot of trees reputed to be the dwelling places of genii. Others were worn as pendants on the wrist and around the neck. Still others — the bulkier ones — were kept in houses or in public sanctuaries. These heads call to mind the famous little pendant masks of the Baule, made of gold (VI, PL. 288), and those of the Benin, made of ivory (VII, PL. 112), and they may be linked by virtue of an identical function with the small ma of northeast Liberia (G. W. Harley, "Masks as Agents of Social Control," in Northeast Liberia, Cambridge, Mass., 1950).

Sao art was by no means solely an art of pottery. Bronze casting was practiced contemporaneously, and the finds reveal a mastery implying "a long industrial past" (R. Lantier, in Lebeuf and Masson-Detourbet, 1950). The discoveries consist mainly of items of personal adornment: armlets and wrist bracelets; anklets; beads for stringing; earrings; necklace pendants and trinkets in the form of heads of gazelles (Midigué), crocodiles (Mahaya), and ducks (Woulki, Mahaya, Makari); a ring decorated with the representation of this same bird (Woulki); and breastplates (Midigué). Some libation cups, probably for ritual purposes, also came to light at Midigué (Lebeuf and Masson-Detourbet, 1951, figs. 41, 42–48, 49, 50).

Many of these bronze pieces show the kind of extremely delicate decoration that would be difficult for even a skillful chaser to execute. "Cordons, torsades, plaitings, and braids can be found on almost all the decorated pieces, and the spiral motif is often repeated" (Hamelin, 1952–53). In fact, the complexity and delicacy of these motifs were made possible by the existence of a close link joining the lost-wax technique with techniques of decoration.

Of the modeling and casting techniques of the ancient Sao, their descendants, the Kotoko, have retained almost nothing. This is an example of the almost total disappearance of a once

flourishing art — a disappearance for which Islam and colonization can be held accountable. However, skill in modeling has not diminished. Adolescent Kotoko girls make waxen dolls that reveal perfect taste. These dolls, modeled over a straw core, are by no means merely toys; they are images of the children that their makers hope to have when they become women. The typical doll has a very clean-cut body that serves as a support for finely modeled ornaments. "The hair is plaited and curled, the wrists are covered with minute rings and the lower limbs disappear under a complicated juxtaposition of spirals and volutes. The chest is often covered with a breast-plate that recalls the heavy silver jewellery of the elegant Kotoko female potters" (J. P. Lebeuf, "Dolls of Black Africa," Marco Polo, Aug., 1956, p. 59, n. 22).

The Bongo. The regions occupied by the ancient Sao do not, of course, mark a definite boundary to the east of which figural art is no longer to be found. Though no study of Sudanese sculptures can disregard, for example, the production of the Azande (see below), it must be recognized that this is work of poor quality and little variety. The possibility must not be excluded that some eastern Sudanese populations do model — or have modeled in a certain epoch of their history — wooden or earthenware statuettes and masks. No precise evidence that such works exist or have existed is available; so far as is known, they have not been the object of any commentary, nor have they ever been published. The Bongo, whom Baumann relates to the Sara, carved a certain number of wooden objects, four-legged stools in particular, and were also acquainted with a ceramic art (practiced by the women), particularly pipe bowls (X, PL. 331) decorated with human heads (Baxter and Butt, 1953). Sculptured poles erected over tombs have been attributed to the Sara as well as to the Bongo. These anthropomorphous images are of rather rough and summary workmanship. The head is barely set off from the trunk; at the sides, two puny arms are scarcely distinguishable from the body (Baumann and Westermann, 1948, fig. 271).

The Azande. A certain reputation in the arts of ceramics and woodcarving as well as basketwork has been acquired by the Azande (Zande). Their sculptural products are strictly utilitarian, such as seats and pottery (III, PL. 125). Well known in this field is an artist by the name of Kisanga, "one of the finest carvers in the whole kingdom of Goudwe" (Evans-Pritchard, 1937). Sometimes attributed to the Azande are works in a pure Mangbetu style (Lavachéry, 1954). To the same Azande there have been attributed certain figures (20 ft. and over in height) scattered over the savanna in the Bahr el Ghazal — that is, in a region peopled by the Sara. Lastly, among both the Azande and the Makere "some decorative sculptures which, in general terms, correspond to the Mangbetu objects," but differ from them "in stylistic and morphological details, such as the shape of the eyes, the ears, etc.," have been pointed out (Maesen, 1950). However, the British Museum has a male figure labeled Azande whose general form and details in no way recall the Mangbetu works (Schmalenbach, 1952, fig. 136).

If indeed a figural art exists among the populations of the center and the east of the Sudan, it is little known. But there is always the possibility that ancient works no longer in use exist in these regions or that chance finds will be brought to light by archaeologists. However, the relative absence in the eastern Sudanese cultures of illustrated documents, when not attributable to direct or indirect Islamic influence, means that the most elementary data are lacking. Whether the artistic vein of these populations dried up in a remote period of their history or whether these populations never felt the need of incarnating in works of art their religious and social principles, it is undoubtedly at the level of social structure and its evolution that a hypothesis should be sought. But, as has been pointed out, a society explains the art that is produced in its midst far less than the society itself is explained in certain of its essential aspects by this same art.

At this point, a brief account should be given of two particular cultures which, though they have produced no sculptural works, have become famous for the production of various objects characterized by a genuinely esthetic character: the Peul and the Hausa.

The Peul. Since they form, in the main, pastoral societies, the Peul (Fulbe, Fulani) are seminomads. Thus the conditions of their existence limit them to material that will not hinder them in their movements. Among the shepherds, art is limited to the production of utilitarian objects. In wood, the Peul carve chiefly containers for milk. These receptacles are soberly decorated with geometric motifs; some handsome specimens are to be found in the Musée de l'Homme in Paris. Besides these wooden vessels, mention must be made of the decorated gourds. The sides of these are engraved by the women — in particular the Bororo women — with schematized anthropomorphous motifs (H. Brandt, *Les Nomades du soleil*, Lausanne, 1956, p. 66). The Bororo women also execute very fine embroidery with yarn of vividly colored wool.

A certain number of Peul societies have become sedentary. Among those that occupy the *cercle* of the Upper Niger, the craftsmen are grouped in castes: the *drawambe* (weavers), the *laobe* (wood carvers), the *abarbe* (goldsmiths and leatherworkers), the *wayube* (smiths, potters), the *mabbe* (singers), and so on. However, in Senegal the Fulbe "despise those who exercise ancient trades, such as potters, smiths, or wood carvers, and honor those who practice more modern trades, such as weavers and saddlers, leatherworkers. . . ." (Baumann and Westermann, 1948). The artistic or artisan production of the Peul does not appear to be peculiar to their own culture. The indigenous culture of the Peul seems to manifest itself mainly at the level of literary and poetical expression.

The Hausa. A population of merchants whose economic power was maintained in Negro Africa until the 19th century, when the Peul reduced them politically to servitude, the Hausa gained fame mainly through their achievements in applied arts (weaving and jewelry) and decoration (leatherwork). The richly embroidered *boubou* is well known, as are their techniques for preparing woven materials. By beating them with a special beater, they succeed in giving the materials a metallic luster. Moreover, they are acquainted with the batik technique. In the pearl- and cord-decorated earrings of the Hausa women can be seen an influence of Oriental origin.

A molding technique is practiced by the Hausa in modeling boxes and containers, which are used in the whole of western Sudan and as far as the Sahara, where the Tuareg have adopted them. Another technique of the Hausa involves stretching a wet animal skin on a clay mold; once it has dried, the skin shrinks and retains the shape it has been given when the mold is broken (H. Balfour, "The Tandu Industry in Northern Nigeria and its Affinities Elsewhere," in *Essays Presented to G. Seligman*, London, 1934, pp. 5–17). Two origins can be suggested for this technique: the lost-wax process and the gesture of the potter, who applies a cake of damp clay to the upturned bottom of a pottery model (Paulme, 1956).

Hausa leatherwork is justly renowned. Saddles, bags, and the like are made of beautiful skins, which are sewn together and decorated with applied geometrical motifs in resplendent colors (reds, greens). These objects are fairly similar to those of the Tuareg.

Jean LAUDE

The Nupe, the Jukun, and other peoples of the Nigerian upland plain. There remains much to be discovered pertaining to the artistic production of the tribes in this zone. Archaeological investigation along the Niger River has already led to remarkable results. The figurines of Jebba and Tada, which are stylistically connected to the great Guinean artifacts, are products of the Nupe, dating back to the time of their large-scale migrations under the guidance of the cultural hero Tsoede. Other products of the Nupe, also of the archaeological age, are known (PL. 312). Conspicuous among these is the bronze figure of a seated man, which is almost life-size and realistic in its corpulent nudity. W. Fagg (1963) attributes this statue to the 15th century.

The production of the Nupe, who have embraced Isla but still preserve many traces of their original paganism, limited to admirable works of artisanship (PL. 316; III, PL. 12 VII, PL. 340), which show not only a similarity to the Hau style but also derivations and influences from the ancient Me iterranean and Oriental civilizations. Particularly remarkabl are embossed brass objects with floral and spiral motifs, indig dyed fabrics, and wall paintings. In comparison with the tec nical level of the crafts production the sculptural produc seem crude and uneven. Since old examples are very rare, it not possible to establish whether the qualitative poverty the plastic arts existed from the beginning or was a result the introduction of Islam. The various masks are extreme simple and almost all have horns; it appears that one — b certainly not their only — function was to intimidate the wome The few sculptures of any value, including one lovely do clearly show Yoruba influences.

Only fragmentary information is available for the numero other tribes of this area, especially as pertains to their artis production. Among the Dakakari, horned masks are used du ing funerals, and hollow wooden statues depicting the decease with open mouths showing teeth and with real hair, are plac on the tombs together with miniature anthropomorph and zo morph figurines. Ceramic funerary objects, made by the wome are of six different types; the older of these are by far the mo refined works. Hausa influences are noticeable in the cra of this tribe (e.g., small bowls and decorated spoons) and al in the ornamental motifs. Among the Tiv (IX, PL. 156), pa of wooden figures called *kombuhumba*, probably connected wi fertility rites, are placed before the doors of dwellings. The people appear also to model life-sized clay figures of anim and men.

The plastic art of the Jukun is more complex and refine On a naturalistic background there are developed forms, som times simple and sometimes complex, showing a certain tenden toward geometricization and stylization. For example, som times the masks are of an imaginative abstract type; at oth times they are plainly geometric. The masks are used in co nection with funeral rites; they are related to the worship dead leaders, whose "double" is imprisoned (here again found a belief held by other Sudanese populations, such as t Bambara, Dogon, etc.), and to the fear of particular spiri There are also zoomorph masks that depict the buffalo, t crocodile, the monkey, and so on.

The sculpture, which is very rare, generally shows "cubisti tendencies: elongated bodies, heads flattened at the sides, lar protruding mouths, and contrasts of projecting and recedi planes (PL. 311). Some of the figurines represent Achidong, t god of the dead and of thunder.

Information about the upland-plain tribes of Bauchi and t so-called Nigerian "pagan belt" is even more scarce. The form peoples (Yergum, Ankwe, Gurka, Angas) produce a cru paliform sculpture whose function is unknown and two typ of masks: a horned mask, which is connected with initiati rites, and a plate-shaped mask, which is associated with hunti ceremonies. The latter groups (Tiv, Bachama, Bata, Piti, et are known for their decorated earthenware (PL. 316) and f brass personal ornaments of some artistic merit.

Ernesta CERULLI

SUDANESE CULTURES IN THE CONGO. It is a striking fact th the some two millions of Sudanese peoples living in the northe part of the former Belgian Congo have a much less conspicuo artistic production than the Bantu-speaking tribes in t southern part of this area (see CONGO). Sculptures in the rou and masks are fairly rare, and the articles of everyday use wi anthropomorph, zoomorph, or simply geometric ornament a not very numerous. Apart from this, the artistic quality of the Sudanese products is uneven; alongside some fine works the are other pieces notable only for the simplicity of conceptio schematic representation, and rough elaboration. Answers the question why both the quantity and the quality of t products are so far behind those of the Bantu-speaking trib

ust perforce be in the realm of the hypothetical. The humid
avannas inhabited by the Congo Sudanese are hardly substan-
ally different from those extending to the south of the equator.
hus it does not seem likely that the lack of a flourishing
culptural art could be a consequence of the natural surround-
ngs. Nor can the way of life, the family organization, or the
eligious system be held responsible. It is more probable that
ne prolonged migrations (up to recent times), together with
ne absence of consolidated, centrally ruled realms (or other
olidly constructed societies) in early times, constitute the
asic cause of the general artistic underdevelopment. It is in
act striking that where a tendency to consolidation is found
r where some sort of central authority exists, as in the case of
ne Azande and Mangbetu tribes, there is also found more artistic
roduction than in other northern Sudanese Congo tribes.

Among the tribes that produce — or have produced —
culpture, five merit particular attention: to the west, the Banda,
Igbaka (Bwaka), and Ngbandi, inhabiting the Ubangi and
Tongala areas; to the east, the afore-mentioned Azande and
Mangbetu tribes, inhabiting the upper and lower Uele areas.

The Banda, an ethnic group numbering about 321,000,
as mainly established itself in neighboring Ubanghi-Shari (see
FRICA, FRENCH EQUATORIAL). In the Congo it is represented
y the Mbanja, Togbo, Mono, Gobu, and Langbase tribes,
mong others. A number of human and animal figures and some
asks and ornamented utensils are attributed to the Mbanja
PL. 314). Stylistically the anthropomorph sculptures call to mind
nose of the Ngbaka and Ngbandi. These are wooden figures
ith roundish heads (the foreheads show vertically aligned
ttoo points), lean trunklike bodies, stiff arms, and legs positioned
ightly apart; rough and polished surfaces alternate. The mean-
.g of these figures is shrouded in mystery. It is possible that
ey are commemorative images. It is certain that most of them
e more elaborate than the human and animal figures that are
tended to serve as fetishes. The zoomorph representations
clude both quadrupeds and birds. The former enter into
unting magic; the birds are placed on the top of certain huts,
ut it is not known for what purpose. Some animal figures are
ade of clay, like the nearly life-sized sepulchral statues that
casionally came to light in earlier days.

The few specimens of masks ascribed to the Mbanja are used
uring the rite that accompanies the circumcision of the young
en. Most of them are flatly executed wooden specimens with
schematic representation of a human face. Their artistic value
not great. More successful are some pipes decorated with a
presentation of a small human head and the similarly treated
ringed instruments.

The Togbo are known to have produced a few characteristic
atues: plump, heavy human figures, about 20 in. high, with
e face altogether flat and the back of the head globular in
ape. They may perhaps represent the important spirit Nga-
la. It should not be overlooked that the Togbo also use sculp-
res in other connections — for instance, to cure barrenness
women and in obtaining forgiveness after committing an
justice.

So far as is known, the Togbo make no masks. Nor do their
ighbors the Mono, the Gobu, and the Langbase; these three
bes are represented only by a number of roughly carved wooden
pulchral statues.

The Ngbaka produce much more sculpture (PL. 314). In
ost cases the figures represent Seto and his wife Nabo, two
irits who play a very important part in the Ngbaka's lives;
eir statues are placed by the huts that contain the spirits of
e ancestors. Other figures are fetishes, thought to afford
otection against illness and infirmity. Roughly carved zoo-
orph figures serve as hunting fetishes.

Like the Mbanja, from whom they have in fact taken over
is custom, the Ngbaka use masks during the circumcision
es. There is a marked resemblance between the examples
oduced by the two tribes; indeed, they are practically indis-
nguishable, especially since they are generally made with
eat simplicity and finished carelessly. During these rites all
rts of objects (e.g., mouth disks and sticks) with graphic orna-
ent and polychrome painting are used.

A fairly large number of stringed instruments and pipes are
found among the Ngbaka. In general, the images on these show
a rather wide variety of styles, but in the case of the stringed instruments the figures are always corpulent (the resonance box
forms the trunk), with a globular head and short legs. The pipes,
on the other hand, are almost indistinguishable from those of
the Mbanja. It should be added that in earlier times the Ngbaka
customarily adorned the tombs of their notables with almost
life-sized recumbent or standing clay figures.

The plastic art ascribed to the Ngbandi is stylistically
more homogeneous than that of the Ngbaka. The salient feature
of the figures is the upward-pointing triangle carved into the
headdress of each statue. The purpose of such figures — whether
ancestral, commemorative, or sepulchral — is not always clear.
The *kokoro* (witch doctors) and the *bendo* (fortunetellers) use
other types of figures, sometimes along with masks, while
performing their functions. On the other hand, to proclaim
their courage the *lombé* (warriors) formerly wore on their upper
arm a small stick carved to represent a human head.

The work of numerous Azande sculptors provides evidence
of a more highly diversified culture. The Azande are in fact
a conglomerate of tribes under the leadership of two ruling groups
— in the west, the Abandia (Bandya), and in the east, the Avungara. The influence of the latter in particular has made itself
strongly felt. At the courts of the Azande potentates there developed a type of art that might, with the necessary qualifications,
be labeled "court art." However, the arrival of the Europeans
toward the end of the past century, when the Azande realm had
just begun to be consolidated, so greatly curtailed the power
of the princes as to make conditions unfavorable for further
development of this art. Nevertheless, especially in the field
of applied art, works of high artistic quality are found (PLS.
313, 316; III, PL. 125). Finely shaped ceramic representations of
human heads are seen on harps and other stringed instruments,
pipes, and utensils such as spoons. The harps are frequently
crowned by a small head; in several cases an anthropomorph
shape was devised for the entire instrument; these examples
have a tiny head, a long neck (the sounding board), and long,
heavy legs. The few known statues in the same style have much
more realistic proportions, but they show a similar stylization,
which makes it easy to ascertain their origin. Highly decorative,
too, are the monumental grooved drums found especially in the
Avungara area.

A kind of sculpture that is totally different in style and purpose from the above-cited examples of plastic and applied art
is found among the Azande. This is the so-called *yanda* image,
the existence of which was ascertained as early as 1925 by
Lagae (1926), though practically no examples were known until
recently. These are anthropomorph (or in exceptional cases
zoomorph) statuettes of wood or terra cotta. They are used by
the *abandakpa*, or local leaders, of the secret Mani sect, an
association whose members gather in order to perform magic.
The statuettes assure among other things the welfare of their
owners, the *abandakpa*, and of such Mani adherents as claim
this protection. Most of the *yanda* images are fashioned in a
highly schematic style; some are finished with care, others
sketchily. Still, in more than one case striking plastic results
have been achieved with extremely simple stylistic means.

Within this Mani sect, the leaders sometimes used to wear
masks during great celebrations; these masks now serve only
a decorative purpose. All the known examples are very simply
executed; stylistically they bear resemblances to the bulk of the
masks of the northern Congo.

Akin to the court art of the Azande is the similar art produced by the Mangbetu, who live farther south. In fact, from
the beginning of the 19th century, when Nebingbale laid the
foundations of the Mangbetu realm through his clever policy
of conquest and subjugation, flourishing courts sprang up;
that of Munza, with its impressive architecture, was particularly
brilliant.

The accounts of Lang (1918) describe the passion of Okondo,
the last prince of this dynasty, for art; this ruler employed a
number of sculptors in ivory and wood, who rivaled one another
in the quest for perfection. Taken as a whole, however, the plastic

art of the Mangbetu appears limited in scope, especially in regard to variety of forms. Apart from the standing figures (of which only some 20 or 30 remain), artistic production includes little beyond bark and wood boxes (VII, PL. 326), harps, daggers, hairpins, and pipes (PL. 313). The forms are mainly anthropomorph (the pipes sometimes show monkey figures). The handles of the sickle-shaped parade knives (the so-called *trombach*) and the ivory horns, some of which are even adorned with engravings showing scenes from everyday life, also come under the heading of works of applied art. Special mention must be made of the graceful globular terra-cotta jars with the top in the form of a woman's head; these are often devised to convey the impression of a complete figure. A striking feature here is the typical elongated skull, with headdress giving a halo effect (PL. 316; III, PL. 126). This hypertrophy, which is characteristic of the Mangbetu and related groups, is evident in most of their plastic work, whether in wood (VII, PL. 398), ivory, or ceramic. The style, characterized by a rather naturalistic vision coupled with a degree of refinement, also shows a certain unity despite the variety of materials used.

With regard to the social and religious function of the Mangbetu plastic works very little is known. Whether the male and female figures are ancestors or represent the deified ancestor and cultural hero Adzapane and his wife remains an open question. It is certain, however, that the Mangbetu seldom place such images on their graves. The bark boxes, which were at one time erroneously thought to be honey boxes, are simply used to hold all sorts of more or less valuable trifles as well as *ngula* powder. As for the jars, in addition to serving as containers for liquids, they confer on their owners a higher social standing. Although certain signs indicate that ceramics of this type are not very old, the possibility that these jars originally served cultic purposes cannot be excluded a priori.

Herman BURSSENS

ARCHITECTURE. Heirs to the great medieval empires and to foreign architectural traditions brought to them over the great commercial routes of which the area of Sudanese civilization was a focal point for many centuries, the Sudanese peoples developed special architectural forms that broke away both from the modest, typically African constructions and from forms introduced by Islam and other more advanced civilizations and constituted original interpretations and modifications of the varied cultural influences.

Above all, it should be pointed out that the thatched hut is not absent. On the contrary, it is still the preferred habitation of the more backward marginal tribes. On the other hand, from the western Sudan to northern Nigeria, in Upper Volta as well as in the northern territories of Ghana and Togoland, and among the Kotoko and Musgu of Chad, the technique of clay construction is widespread. This technique, though perhaps not originated by ancient Mediterranean, Oriental, and, later, also Islamic trends, was at least fostered by them.

Not only palaces, fortresses, and mosques but also entire villages are constructed in clay, either with superimposed blocks or with sun-dried bricks (Bambara, Dogon, Bobo). The Dogon villages almost always lean against a rocky wall and are difficult to reach. In addition to family dwellings, each village includes a certain number of buildings for community use, among which are temples, houses for the men, houses for girls in menses, and granaries (PLS. 299, 300).

The dwellings, whose plan corresponds to a complex cosmic symbolism, are quadrangular with slightly sloping walls and a terraced roof. The house invariably has more than one story, and life revolves around an interior courtyard. The façade is in almost every instance decorated with 80 niches, whose function is more symbolic than decorative; in fact, certain ritual implements are kept in them.

The circular or square granaries have conical, straw roofs and are decorated with bas-reliefs. The wooden parts — doors, columns, locks, and shutters — always have relief carvings with figures and designs of symbolic significance (PLS. 301, 302).

Fortified villages and towns with walls that encircle or reinforce strategic positions are found virtually everywhere – from northern Nigeria to Upper Volta, from the northern territories of Ghana and Togoland to Chad. These systems of construction used in the past have largely fallen into disuse or have deteriorated technically. Outstanding examples of fortified dwellings are the so-called "castles" of the Tamberma in Togo. They are either circular or oval and contain many rooms for varied uses (dormitory, kitchen) and large tower-shaped granaries that open onto a central space which functions as courtyard and stockyard.

Other notable examples of Sudanese architecture are the mosque in Mopti, the dwellings of the Musgu of Logone (south of Lake Chad), and the old center of Bida, capital of the Nupe kingdom. The first, which shows marked influences of the architecture of the Mauritanians (see SAHARAN-BERBER CULTURES) reveals certain characteristic traits: the supporting beams that extend above the walls, the tall pinnacles, and the crenelated walls.

One of the boldest and most unusual examples of African clay-construction techniques is represented by the villages of the Musgu. These are very high beehive structures, whose exterior walls, decorated with large ribs in relief, are made impermeable by a covering of clay and dung (PL. 300).

The old center of the city of Bida, which had about 60,000 inhabitants at the time of the British occupation, had perimetric walls more than 12 miles long. The city was divided into sections separated from one another by open spaces. Each family nucleus lived in its own enclosure, inside which rose various cylindro-conical huts with clay walls, often decorated with reliefs, and grass roofs. The enclosures opened toward the outside by a doorway (*katamba*) decorated with designs indicating the occupation and social status of the inhabitants. The royal palaces were of imposing size, with walls decorated in relief and painted.

Unfortunately, there exists no comprehensive study of Sudanese architecture. Systematic research on the symbolism of the dwellings and on the sociological implications of the distribution of the constructions within a city, village, or architectural complex is only in its beginnings. The archaeological investigations begun on old inhabited areas like those at Kumbi Saleh which was probably the capital of the medieval empire of Ghana may augment our present knowledge of the origins of Sudanese architecture.

Ernesta CERULLI

BIBLIOG. *Prehistory and archaeology*: J. P. Laffitte, Les grottes peintes du Soudan, La Nature, XXXVIII, July 9, 1910, pp. 85–86; F. de Zeltner, Les grottes à peintures du Soudan Français, L'Anthropologie, XXI, 1910, pp. 1–2; G. Luquet, À propos des peintures des grottes soudanaises, L'Anthropologie, XXIII, 1913, pp. 337–38; A. Schaeffner, Peintures rupestres de Songo, Le Minotaure, I–II, 1933, pp. 9, 52–55; M. Griaule, Peintures rupestres de Soudan Français, Rev. de synthèse, IV, 1934, pp. 187–89; J.-P. Lebeuf, Les fouilles dans la région du Chari et du Tchad, L'Anthropologie, XLII, 1938, pp. 147–48; L. Perois, Les dessins rupestres du poste de G à Bamako (Grotte de Medinakouri), NIFAN, XXVII, 1945, pp. 1, 1; J.-P. Lebeuf and A. Masson-Detourbet, La civilisation du Tchad, suivi d'une étude sur les bronzes Sao par R. Lantier, Paris, 1950; J.-P. Lebeuf and A. Masson-Detourbet, L'art ancien du Tchad, CahArt, XXVI, 1951, pp. 7–28; J.-P. Lebeuf, L'art du delta du Chari, Présence africaine, X–XI, 1951, pp. 96–102; P. Hamelin, Les bronzes du Tchad, Tribus, N.S., II–III, 1952–53, pp. 379–99; P. Huard, Recherches rupestres au Tchad, Tropique, VIII–IX, 1952, pp. 40–45, X, 1952, pp. 38–46, I, 1953, pp. 35–48; P. Huard, Gravures rupestres des confins nigéro-tchadiens, BIFAN, XV, 1953, pp. 156–81; P. Jaeger, Précisions au sujet des sites rupestres de la région de Kita, NIFAN, LX, 1953, pp. 97–99; A. Leroi-Gourhan and J. Poirier, Ethnologie de l'Union Française, I: Afrique, Paris, 1953; G. Szumowski, Notes sur la grotte préhistorique de Bamako, NIFAN, LI, 1953, pp. 35–40; J. Henninger, Abris sous rocher de la région de Bobo-Dioulasso, NIFAN, LVI, 1954, pp. 97–99; R. Mauny, Gravures, peintures et inscriptions rupestres de l'Ouest Africain (Initiations africaines, XI), Dakar, 1954; A. and J.-P. Lebeuf, Monuments symboliques du palais royal de Logone-Birni, JSA, XXV, 1955, pp. 27–34; J.-P. Lebeuf, L'archéologie de la région du Tchad, Actes Pan-Afr. Cong. on Prehistory (4th, Leopoldville, 1959), II, Tervuren, 1962, pp. 427–36.

Sudanese empires: C. Monteil, Les empires du Mali, Paris, 1930; Meek, A Sudanese Kingdom, London, 1931; C. Monteil, Une cité soudanaise: Djénné, Paris, 1932; J. Beraud-Villars, L'empire de Gao, Paris, 1942; L. Tauxier, Histoire des Bambara, Paris, 1942; H. Baumann and D. Westermann, Les peuples et les civilisations de l'Afrique, Paris, 1948; R. Mauny, L'Afrique occidentale d'après les auteurs arabes anciens, NIFAN, XL, 1947, pp. 6–7; R. Mauny and R. Thomassey, Campagne de fouilles de 1950

Koumbi Saleh, BIFAN, XIII, 1951, pp. 438–75, XVIII, 1956, pp. 117–40; R. Mauny, Notes d'archéologie au sujet de Gao, BIFAN, XIII, 1951, pp. 837–52; S. F. Nadel, A Black Byzantium: The Kingdom of Nupe in Nigeria, 3d ed., London, New York, 1951; D. Westermann, Geschichte Afrikas: Staatenbildung südlich der Sahara, Cologne, 1952; G. P. Murdock, Africa: Its Peoples and Their Culture History, New York, London, 1959; B. Davidson, Old Africa Rediscovered, London, 1960.

Contemporary artistic production: H. Clouzot and A. Level, Sculptures africaines et océaniennes, Paris, 1924; G. Hardy, L'art nègre, Paris, 1927; Casques et masques de danses du Soudan Français, Minotaure, II, 1933, pp. 20–21; C. Kjersmeier, Centres de style de la sculpture nègre africaine, 4 vols., Paris, Copenhagen, 1935–38; H. Baumann and D. Westermann, Völkerkunde von Afrika, Essen, 1940; F. M. Olbrechts, Bijdrage tot de kennis van de chronologie der Afrikaanse Plastiek (Mém. Inst. Royal Colonial Belge, X, 2), Brussels, 1941; M. Griaule, Arts de l'Afrique noire, Paris, 1947; F. H. Lem, Sculptures soudanaises, Paris, 1947 (Eng. trans., Paris, 1949; bibliog.); P. Clement, Le forgeron en Afrique Noire, Rev. geog. humaine et d'ethn., I, 2, 1948, pp. 35–58; Le musée vivant, XXXVI–XXXVII, Paris, 1948; G. Ballandier, Les conditions sociologiques de l'art noir, Présence africaine, X–XI, 1951, pp. 58–71; M. Griaule, Art et symbole en Afrique Noire, Zodiaque, V, 1951, pp. 1–35; M. Griaule, Les symboles des arts africains, Présence africaine, X–XI, 1951, pp. 12–24; H. Lavachéry, L'art nègre et son destin, Présence africaine, X–XI, 1951, pp. 38–57; J. C. Pauvert, Approche de l'art africain noir, Présence africaine, X–XI, 1951, pp. 72–84; L. Underwood, Figures in Wood of West Africa, London, 1951; W. Schmalenbach, L'art nègre, Paris, Basel, 1952; W. Fagg, The Webster Plass Collection of African Art, London, 1953; H. Lavachéry, Statuaire de l'Afrique Noire, Neuchâtel, 1954; M. Trowell, Classical African Sculpture, London, 1954; M. Leiris, The African Negroes and the Arts of Carving and Sculpture, in UNESCO, Interrelations of Cultures, Paris, 1955, pp. 318–51; M. Allemand, L'art de l'Afrique Noire et l'époque nègre de quelques artistes contemporains, Saint-Etienne, 1956; D. Paulme, Sculptures de l'Afrique Noire, Paris, 1956; M. Plass, African Tribal Sculpture, Philadelphia, 1957.

Regional styles of the Western Sudan: M. Delafosse, Le peuple sénoufo ou siéna, Rev. des ét. ethn. et sociologiques, I–II, 1908–09, pp. 1–107; J. Cremer, Matériaux d'ethnographie et de linguistique soudanaises, III–IV: Les Bobo, Paris, 1924–27; A. A. Dim Delobsom, Les danses mossies et leur signification, Rev. anthr., XLII, 1932, pp. 169–73; M. Griaule, Mission Dakar-Djibouti: Rapport général, JSA, II, 1932, pp. 113–22, 229–38; M. Griaule, Masques Dogons, Paris, 1938; D. Paulme, Organisation sociale des Dogon, Paris, 1940; F. H. Lem, Au sujet d'une statuette sénoufo, BIFAN, I–IV, 1941, pp. 175–81; M. Griaule, Dieux d'eau, Paris, 1948; M. Griaule, L'image du monde au Soudan, JSA, XIX, 1949, pp. 81–88; D. Zahan, Aperçu sur la pensée théogonique des Dogon, Cah. int. de sociologie, V, 1949, pp. 120–33; A. Dieterlen, Essai sur la religion bambara, Paris, 1951; P. G. Clamens, Curieuse statue de cuivre sénoufo, NIFAN, LVII, 1953, pp. 14–15; V. Pâques, Les Bambara, Paris, 1954; J. Rouch, Les Songhay, Paris, 1954; D. Forde, Peoples of the Niger-Benue Confluence, London, 1955; H. D. Gunn, Pagan Peoples of the Central Area of Northern Nigeria, London, 1956; R. Holas, Les Sénoufo y compris les Minianka, Paris, 1957; M. Palau Marti, Les Dogon, Paris, 1957; A. M. D. Lebeuf, Les populations du Tchad nord du Xe parallèle, Paris, 1959; R. Goldwater, ed., Bambara Sculpture from the Western Sudan, New York, 1960; H. D. Gunn and F. P. Conant, Peoples of the Middle Niger Region: Northern Nigeria, London, 1960; E. Leuzinger, Africa Nera, 2d ed., Milan, 1961; W. Fagg, Nigerian Images, London, 1963; R. Goldwater, Senufo Sculpture from West Africa, New York, 1964.

Styles of the Congo Sudanese: C. van Overbergh, Les Mangbetu (Coll. de monographies ethn., IV), Brussels, 1909; H. Lang, Famous Ivory Treasures of a Negro King, Am. Mus. J., XVIII, 1918, pp. 527–52; R. C. Lagae, Les Azande ou Niam-Niam (Congo Bib., XVIII), Brussels, 1926; H. Baumann, Die materielle Kultur der Azande und Mangbetu, BA, XI, 1927, pp. 1–129; B. O. Tanghe, De Ngbandi naar het Leven geschetst (Congo Bib., XXIX), Bruges, 1929; H. Kerels, L'art chez les Mangbetu, Beaux-Arts, VII, 198, 1936, pp. 22–23; E. E. Evans-Pritchard, Witchcraft, Oracles and Magic among the Azande, Oxford, 1937; J. Maes, Sculpture décorative ou symbolique des instruments de musique du Congo Belge (Artes Africanae CII), Brussels, 1937; G. D. Perier, Un édifice d'art mangbetu, Beaux-Arts, VII, 250, 1937, pp. 25–27; J. Maes, Kabila- en Grafbeelden uit Kongo, Ann. Mus. van Belgisch Congo, II, 2–3), Brussels, 1938–39; R. Gaffé, La Sculpture au Congo belge, Paris, Brussels, 1945; P. T. W. Baxter and A. Butt, The Azande and Related Peoples of the Anglo-Egyptian Sudan and Belgian Congo, London, 1953; E. von Sydow, Afrikanische Plastik, Berlin, 1954; H. Burssens, La fonction de la sculpture traditionnelle chez les Ngbaka, Brousse, XI, 1958, pp. 10–28; H. Burssens, Les peuplades de l'entre Congo-Ubangi (Ngbandi, Ngbaka, Mbandja, Ngombe et Gens d'Eau) (Monographies ethn., IV), Tervuren, 1958; H. Burssens, Sculptuur in Ngbandi-stijl: Een bijdrage tot de Studie van de Plastiek van Noord-Kongo, Kongo-Overzee, XXIV, 1–2, 1958, pp. 1–52; H. Burssens, Yanda-beelden bij de Azande (Centraal Afrika), Handelingen van het XXIIIe Vlaams Filologenkongress, Brussels, 1959, pp. 255–59; H. Burssens, Enkele Landemaskers uit Uele, Congo-Tervuren, VI, 4, 1960, pp. 101–08.

Illustrations: PLS. 299–316; 3 figs. in text.

SULLIVAN. LOUIS HENRI. American architect (b. Boston, Sept. 3, 1856; d. Chicago, 1924). Sullivan attended Massachusetts Institute of Technology, Cambridge, Mass., in 1872, worked in the office of Furness & Hewitt, Philadelphia, in 1873,

and studied at the Ecole des Beaux-Arts, Paris, in 1874. He worked in several Chicago offices, including that of William Le Baron Jenney, from 1875 to 1879, before joining the firm of Dankmar Adler in 1879, where he became a full partner in 1881. The partnership dissolved in 1895, after which Sullivan continued alone, with a declining private practice, until his death. He is known primarily for his influential designs of tall commercial buildings, as the teacher of Frank Lloyd Wright (q.v.), as a master ornamentalist, and for his social-architectural criticism.

Not an engineering innovator, Sullivan's main task in skyscraper design was to establish an external shell that would harmonize visually with the space disposition and construction of the tall building. And despite the popularity of his dictum, "form follows function," he was not a functionalist, since Sullivan saw materials and construction only as points of departure, not as determinants, of form.

Sullivan's first major work was the Auditorium Building in Chicago (1886–89), a large hotel-office-theater (now occupied by Roosevelt College); its traditional masonry form derived directly from the Marshall Field Wholesale Store in Chicago (I, PL. 84; now demolished) by Henry Hobson Richardson (q.v.). His first major physical statement of skyscraper design was the Wainwright Building in St. Louis (1890–91; PL. 218; I, PL. 86), a ten-story, U-shaped commercial structure. The lower two stories are of smooth-surfaced masonry, while the upper levels are organized within an orderly grid of cellular units that rise to the tenth story. An explosion of decorative terra cotta terminates the composition. The division into three horizontal elements and the visual reinforcement of corners are familiar Renaissance compositional devices, applied here to the new problem of packaging a tall building. Verticality is emphasized by the recessed spandrels and by extra verticals between the structural-steel members. Thus the orderly veneer does not express the structural-steel frame within. The Guaranty Building in Buffalo, N.Y. (1894–95; I, PL. 87), Sullivan's most successful tall building, carries out the Wainwright scheme in a more refined manner. As an innovation, Sullivan exposed vertical supporting members at ground level, thus anticipating the elevated slab of later masters, such as Le Corbusier and Mies van der Rohe (qq.v.). Sullivan's last major work, executed without Adler, was the Schlesinger & Mayer Department Store (now Carson Pirie Scott & Co.; I, PL. 86), built in Chicago 1899–1904. A stack of horizontal layers of open display space, the building has little interior distinction; its outside, however, is significant. The two-storied base is sheathed in vigorous Art Nouveau (q.v.) cast-iron ornament (I, PL. 469), while above, interior space is expressed by a horizontally emphasized grid. The composition terminates at the twelfth story with a roof that hovers above a deeply recessed horizontal band of glass.

With the ambition to mold modern commercial buildings into a form that would rank them with the great ancient, medieval, and Renaissance works of the past, Sullivan saw himself as an architectural Walt Whitman, imposing physical form upon modern American technological, democratic society. (See also AMERICAS: ART SINCE COLUMBUS, cols. 257–259; EUROPEAN MODERN MOVEMENTS, col. 223.)

SELECTED WRITINGS. The Tall Office Building Artistically Considered, Lippincott's, March, 1896, pp. 403–09; A System of Architectural Ornament According with a Philosophy of Man's Powers, Washington, 1924; Kindergarten Chats and Other Writings, New York, 1947; The Autobiography of an Idea, New York, 1956; Democracy: A Man-Search, Detroit. 1961.

BIBLIOG. F. L. Wright, Genius and the Mobocracy, New York, 1949; H. Morrison, Louis Sullivan, Prophet of Modern Architecture, New York, 1952; J. Szarkowski, The Idea of Louis Sullivan, Minneapolis, 1956; A. Bush-Brown, Louis Sullivan, New York, 1960; W. Connely, Louis Sullivan as He Lived, New York, 1960; S. Paul, Louis Sullivan, An Architect in American Thought, Englewood Cliffs, 1962; J. M. Jacobus, "Sullivan," Encyclopaedia of Modern Architecture, London, 1963.

Theodore M. BROWN

SUPREMATISM. See EUROPEAN MODERN MOVEMENTS; NON-OBJECTIVE ART.

SURREALISM. This was a movement of ideas that developed between World Wars I and II and was particularly prolific in the field of figural art. It derived from the French symbolist culture, from Apollinaire, and, most immediately, from Dada. Surrealism was given a precise theoretical formulation in the first surrealist manifesto published by André Breton in 1924. Surrealism fulfilled two functions: it opposed and loosened the formalist rigidity of cubism, and it introduced a new subject matter into modern art — the irrational and the unconscious. The surrealists were among the first to see the importance of Freudian theory in relation to the arts. Surrealism escaped from the historico-chronological limits of its original polemic phase, and its impact has been broad and lasting (see EUROPEAN MODERN MOVEMENTS).

SUMMARY. Dada and the origins of surrealism (col. 715). Surrealist theory and the development of the movement (col. 721). Characteristics of surrealist art (col. 725).

DADA AND THE ORIGINS OF SURREALISM. Among the different trends in the development of modern art the anarchonihilistic movement of Dada occupies a special position. World-wide in its action, it attacked with irony, humor, and cynicism the established but shaken moral, political, esthetic, and metaphysical concepts of Europe and America during and after World War I.

The first "organized" Dada group was formed in Zurich in 1916; it consisted of the Romanians Tristan Tzara and Marcel Janco, the Germans Richard Hülsenbeck and Hugo Ball, and the Franco-Alsatian Jean (Hans) Arp. Looking for a stage name for a singer in the German-French dictionary, they came upon the word "Dada," which means hobbyhorse, and adopted it for their group.

Dada was both a literary and an artistic movement. It cannot be considered only as a stylistic trend, as cubism, futurism, and expressionism, which preceded it, were, but also as a rebellious attitude of the mind, a drug, an intoxicant. Born of chaos and with the intention of creating confusion, Dada was in fact a demonstration against any and every form of art conceived in the traditional and even modern spirit as a constructive representational or symbol-creating activity, and it denied that art in general was a spiritual manifestation to be taken seriously. "We like neither art nor artists," declared Jacques Vaché in his Lettres de guerre (Paris, 1919). All art appeared quite senseless to a group that took a name for their activities through which they intended to show that they had given up every hope for human intelligence and were expecting still more insanity in the future. Nevertheless, the major artists connected with the Dada movement, such as Arp and Max Ernst, produced a highly spontaneous technique and inventive "imagery" and their artistic spirit led them to further explorations of form and content. Dada is so closely bound up with the rise and development of surrealism and with certain tendencies in fantastic and abstract art that historically it should be regarded as a generator of ideas rather than as a merely destructive and purely temporary caprice.

Inasmuch as it was a reaction against World War I, which had revealed the hollowness of many bourgeois illusions, Dada in its own self-ridicule aimed at the destruction and negation of all values. Measured by the standard of the tragedy through which Europe was living at that time and by the complex nature of the problems awaiting solution, Dada revealed itself as frivolous. And that was what its high priests wanted it to be. It was Dada that André Breton was referring to when he spoke of "black humor" (Guggenheim, 1942). Vaché (op. cit.), who greatly influenced Breton, saw in humor "a sense of the theatrical inutility and joylessness of everything, when one has become aware." In such a state of mind nothing can be built or created. "Jacques Vaché's good fortune," wrote Breton (1924), "is to have produced nothing. He always kicked aside the work of art, that ball and chain that holds back the soul after death."

The Dadaists wanted to bring about a radical change. The first thing to do, therefore, was to create a *tabula rasa* without

a thought of what should come after. This was the reas behind the urge toward frantic destruction, systematic disor and negation, and the total confusion of which Tzara a Hülsenbeck were masters. "We are a furious wind," wr Tzara (1918), "tearing in pieces the linen of the clouds and the prayers, clearing the way for the great spectacle of disast the conflagration, the decomposition." Its technique of attra ing attention to itself by means of journalistic advertising tri (VI, FIG. 685) reveals Dada as an odd mixture of sensatio exhibitionism and revolt. Its method was to create scandal diversions, a method practiced by the futurists before it a by the surrealists after it. In 1921 the movement was sp and soon afterward Dada came to an end. Georges Ribemo Dessaignes in his *Histoire de Dada* (1931) defines the fact that led to its demise: "Born of an urge toward freedom a life, and conscious of the weakness and the strength of human mind, Dada saw clearly that it could work tow nothing but its own dissolution. It was well aware of its o bankruptcy, and when its time came it made no defens Dada had performed its task. After cubism, futurism, Da and what grew out of them, ideas on art had undergone su a change that the *status quo* in the old sense was no lon possible. Dada had demonstrated against the materialist a pragmatic mind that had led mankind into a world war. Ho ever, the Dadaist spirit is still active in present-day art: *brut*, tachism, and "Neo-Dada" (see EUROPEAN MODERN MO MENTS; MODERNISM).

In 1936 Georges Hugnet, one of the first historians of Da wrote: "Dada is ageless, it has no parents, it stands alo making no distinction between what is and what is not. No c has a right to ignore Dada" (in Barr, *Fantastic Art*, 193

Marcel Duchamp said in an interview in 1947: "Dada v an extreme protest against the physical side of painting. It v a metaphysical attitude. It was intimately and consciously volved with literature. It was a sort of nihilism to which I still very sympathetic. It was a way to get out of a state mind — to avoid being influenced by one's environment, or immediate past: to get away from clichés — to get free . . Dada was very serviceable as a purgative" (in Sweeney, 194

In 1957 Hugnet wrote: "Dada was the embodiment of liber of laughter, of disdain, of humor. It was insolent, disinterest and without weight, it was spontaneity and inventiveness, the things that are today dead . . . . All anti-literature becom automatically literature. And all anti-art changes to banali May Dada save us from this lot." In the same year Mar Janco proclaimed: "Dada will last. Not so much because the experiments and literary excesses that gave birth to s realism but rather because of the creation of the prophe spirit found in the works of Arp, in the poetry and the art Klee, in the picturesque illustration-series of Richter, in abstract films of Eggeling and Richter, in our attempts in mu painting and abstract plastic works, and in the beautiful tap tries of Sophie Taeuber. Dada was anything but a hoax; was a turning on the road opening up wide horizons to modern mind. It lasts, and will last as long as the spirit negation contains the ferment of the future" (in Verkauf, 195 And Hülsenbeck: "I am quite conscious of the fact that I treating Dada as a living idea, as if it still existed. I have of given expression to this, for example, in an essay I wrote the periodical *Transition*, shortly after emigrating to the Uni States. 'Dada lives' was the title of that essay and I believ then, as I do now, that there exists a kind of a Dadaist m a Dadaist fundamental way of life that is not only characteris of our time but is congruent with many assertions of mode thought" (ibid.).

The French architectural historian, Auguste Choisy, sa "All tendencies are best characterized by their abuses" (*Histo de l'Architecture*, Paris, 1899). The mainspring of the Da movement was the urge to undermine all cultural conceptio that no longer seemed to correspond to the new reality. C of love for the cultural values whose genuineness was call into question by a murderous war and its consequences, t Dadaists threw up their hands in despair and sought to attr attention to themselves to show that there was something wro

h the *condition humaine* and that reality was quite different
m the illusions of it in which people still lived. Here problems
re touched upon that belong to the spiritual tradition of man:
and religion, ethics and metaphysics. The work of destruc-
n begun by the war was being carried to its bitter end by a
cidal attempt on the part of intellectuals gone mad. A second
rld war has shaken the world, but a second Dada movement
not followed as its aftermath. This time it was not necessary,
modern man had no illusions to lose.

Postwar humanity is trying through the medium of existen-
ism to arrive at a definition of existence and being. Existen-
ism is not hostile to art, as literary Dada was; on the con-
ry, it sees in art a means "to remake the world by showing
as it is, yet as if its source were in human freedom" (J.-P.
tre, *Situations*, II, Paris, 1948). As a form of humanism,
stentialism seeks to move men to action that will change
world. There is a relationship between Dada and existen-
ism. The spiritual crisis of our times, caused by the impact
science and technology, of which the two world wars were
ptoms, continues unabated. Out of a consciousness that
old spiritual positions were untenable, authors such as Paul
léry and André Gide supported Dada. Gide demanded in
 nouvelles nourritures (Paris, 1935) that youth not accept life
it is offered to them by man. But Valéry, speaking in 1939
the mind and its power of transformation in times in which
cumstances material and political are different, pleaded for
highest and finest culture to be preserved, "the culture of
lly great art that is marked by purity of form and rigor of
ught" (*Regards sur le monde actuel*, Paris, 1945).

Pessimism is found in Dada as well as in existentialism.
vertheless — and this is important — the artist sublimates his
simism in an artistic form, a process that of itself constitutes
anifestation of vitality and of the ordering power of the
d. Why Dada turned its arms against art and why it wanted
deprive man of the consciousness of his possible greatness
 dignity are closely bound up with the war mentality. The
daists had to use words and plastic elements in order to
ress their protest, but these words and elements were pro-
med anti-art. "Art in any form is an infantile sickness, the
st childish form of magic," proclaimed Hülsenbeck (in Soer-
, 1926). Quite logically he, like many others, later found
 way into the camp of the social revolution. Even at the
y beginning of his Dadaist activity he wanted to "create
rature with a revolver in his pocket" (ibid.).

If two or more poems were recited simultaneously at a
da gathering so that none of them could be understood, the
ention back of this demonstration was clear: to show that
istic expression was a *quantité négligeable*, that meaning was
aningless, and that art was nonsense. At the same time a
w of this nature reveals itself as naturalism of a profoundly
uman sort. The human mind is selective in its intake of
terial and its assimilation of impressions, and here this
chological law was deliberately affronted. If a newspaper
icle or a poem by Tzara was read aloud to the simultaneous
ompaniment of bells, rattles, or drums (bruitist poem, a
urist idea), this was a way of expressing the fact that the
ublesome outer world is invading and oppressing the ego to
h an extent that the ego is overcome and surrenders uncon-
ionally. A bruitist poem describes a streetcar as it is, the
chanical essence of a streetcar, where the regular rhythm of
 machine is blended with the yawning of the passengers.
lsenbeck wrote in *En avant Dada* (1920): "While I become
cessively conscious that yesterday I boxed the ears of an
 lady and that an hour ago I washed my hands, the screech
 the brakes of an electric streetcar and the noise of a tile
ing off a neighboring roof strike my ears, and my eye — my
er and my inner eye — is immediately on the lookout to
ture a quick sense of life from these happenings. Out of
se common simultaneous events of the everyday life around
 — the Dada circus, noise, shouts, steam whistles, fronts of
ses, and the smell of veal cutlets — an impulse arises within
, driving me to direct action, to becoming, to the great X,
 unknown quantity." What is expressed here is the simul-
eity of the senseless hodgepodge of all things. "While Herr

Schulze reads, the Balkan Express crosses the bridge at Nisch,
a pig squeals in butcher Nuttke's cellar" (ibid.). Seen critically,
this is nothing but the world in all its fragmentation, invading
an individual in the great city, so that the person no longer
has the power to create a hierarchy of values among all these
impressions. It is just this passivity, this being lost, that constitutes the essential Dada, not that Dada has given up the
individual or become anti-individualistic. However, the confused collectivist ideas in Dada soon transformed themselves in
Germany and France into political concepts and activities.

"Dada means nothing," wrote Tzara in the Dada manifesto
of 1918. But as a symbol it does signify something. It signifies
a process of fermentation in which a number of different elements are included: social and political, pacifist and revolutionary, antireligious and antiesthetic, premechanistic and idealistic. Satire and bluff complete the gigantic chaos.

In discussing the visual productions of Dada it must be
borne in mind that Dada cannot be considered as an isolated
phenomenon, any more than cubism or futurism can. Apart
from the fact that Dada was bound up to a great extent with
these movements (see CUBISM AND FUTURISM) in its formal
speculations, it was for artists like Jean Arp and Max Ernst
(qq.v.) a transition stage or a starting point for their first efforts.
Ernst, at first very much a Dadaist, concentrated more and
more on the "subconscious" in artistic experience and even
technique; this made him the first "surrealist" artist. His surrealist art was dominated by Dadaist principles, from which
for a long time it did not entirely free itself. Arp in his drawings, collages, wood engravings, and wood reliefs was basically
a purely abstract artist always conscious of the beauty of form,
who joined the Dada movement and used it as a vehicle for
his artistic aspirations.

It is not Dada but cubism that must be regarded as the
decisive break with tradition, establishing the revolutionary
spirit that was also present in Dada. The cubist spirit made
everything possible; it proclaimed absolute freedom, but that
this freedom could be handled only by artists of the highest
integrity without falling into the license of anarchy is demonstrated by the theories of Dada. Inspired by the cubists, who
used newspaper, sand, wood, and so forth, the futurists carried
still further the revolution in materials and gave the Dadaists
the courage to carry this revolution to its extreme. Sand, hair,
post-office receipts, string, inflated bank notes, bus tickets,
broken glass — all these materials were used by the Dadaists to
express a new chaotic, devalued reality (see MEDIA, COMPOSITE).
Dada also developed new devices, procedures, and techniques
such as dynamism and bruitism, simultaneism or the superimposition of images (derived from futurism and often used by
Picabia), photomontage and collage (derived from the cubist
papier collé), the "improvement" of prints to give the represented
object a Dada twist (used by Ernst), automatic drawing, and
the uncontrolled arrangement of shapes (practiced by Arp).
Christian Schad produced "schadographs" (photographs based
on the collage principle), Man Ray "rayographs" (photos made
without a lens), and Hans Richter and Viking Eggeling "abstract" films (see CINEMATOGRAPHY; PHOTOGRAPHY).

There is a social aspect to all this that deserves consideration.
These innovations and methods robbed art of its precious,
quasi-sacred character, tore it from its splendid isolation, and
forced it to share in the dirt and noise of the street. As early
as 1910 the futurist manifesto on painting of April 11 demanded
of the artist: "Exalt every kind of originality, of boldness, of
extreme violence. . . . Rebel against the tyranny of the words
'harmony' and 'good taste' " (in Barr, *Cubism and Abstract
Art*, 1936).

The new material is for the Dadaist "a reference to the
absolutely self-evident" in the domain of humanity of that
which actually pervades its existence. This is literally a great
step forward. It then forms, as Hülsenbeck said, "part and
parcel of life itself" (in Motherwell, 1951). This statement is
simply the identification of art and reality, or rather art and
the lowest type of reality, that is, the disappearance of art in
"rubbish" reality. Art, however, is the conquest of reality by
the spirit of man. Between art and reality stands man.

In 1913 the Spanish painter Francis Picabia declared himself in favor of amorphism. From an ideological viewpoint this is important, for the amorphous is the unformed, the formless, and here in a sense it is exalted to the rank of form. Picabia's "amorphous" pictures, a satire on abstract art, contained nothing but the signature "Popaul Picador."

Kurt Schwitters in his collages, collage reliefs (IX, PL. 397), and constructions tried to demonstrate that the human mind is capable of creating "beauty" even out of rubbish, of ordering and organizing rubbish in the sense that the first man in the Bible was formed out of the dust of the earth. He called his creations "Merz," from the fragment of the word "Kommerz" used in one of his collages. This mentality has, however, still another humanist implication. "When bits of paper and newspaper advertisements are stuck in pictures, and when one sees in a picture objects collected out of the ash-pit, then it is finally clear," remarked Nikolai Berdyaev, "that dissolution has gone beyond all measure and that a process of dehumanization has set in" (*The Meaning of History*, London, 1936).

Marcel Duchamp (see DUCHAMP BROTHERS) was the first painter to display a decidedly Dadaist turn of mind. As early as 1911, in pictures such as the *Coffee Mill*, he showed his opposition to the cubist dictation of form, which in his *Bachelors* of 1914 was completely left behind. In the same year Duchamp produced his first "ready-made," an ordinary bottle rack, signed as a work of art, and *Pharmacy*, which was an "improvement" of a cheap landscape lithograph. The early work of Duchamp and of Picabia — for example, Picabia's abstractions of 1912-13, which were provided with Dadaist titles such as *Catch as Catch Can* (V, PL. 132), or his drawings with a "mechanistic" theme done in 1915 for the review *291* — has been called proto-Dada or pre-Dada. These works, however, can be counted among the most authentic Dada productions. The nomenclature "proto-Dada" or "pre-Dada" attaches too much attention to the fact that the name "Dada" was invented only in 1916. The Dada spirit and works animated by it existed before this date, and the beginning of Dada should rightly be put at 1911.

Duchamp as an artist is one of the most fascinating Dadaist personalities. He has genuine talent as a painter and possesses great sensibility. Although he displayed an adventurous spirit, he strove for a formal synthesis of biological and mechanical forms of existence. Constructivism, as an engineer might understand the word, was part of his make-up. His tendency to use mechanomorphic forms instead of living and organic ones (a tendency developed by Boccioni and Léger) found expression in his *Nude Descending a Staircase* paintings (No. 1, 1911; No. 2, 1912; No. 3, 1916, IV, PL. 79 — all Philadelphia, Mus. of Art, Arensberg Coll.). Duchamp also painted other works of a similar kind, for example, *Le roi et la reine entourés des nus vites* (*The King and Queen Surrounded by Swift Nudes*, 1912, Philadelphia, Mus. of Art, Arensberg Coll.) and *Le passage de la Vierge à la Mariée* (PL. 319), which were inspired by futurist dynamism. His ready-mades, such as the urinal entitled *Fountain* and signed R. Mutt (1917), and "improved" ready-mades, such as the bird cage filled with marble lumps of sugar called *Why Not Sneeze?* (1921, Philadelphia, Mus. of Art, Arensberg Coll.), were not only intended, as Hugnet (in Barr, *Fantastic Art*, 1936) wrote, "to signify Duchamp's disgust for art and his complete admiration for ready-made objects." They were also manifestations of Duchamp's metaphysical eloquence: art is to be negated and its place taken by everyday objects; "material" culture is to be recognized as the only really existing one; and this material culture is to be ridiculed and to be represented only by the ordinary, the mean, and the banal. Thus the machinelike, the mechanical, has vanquished the spiritual.

Duchamp demonstrates the anti-idealistic debasement of humanity through his personal predilections. He painted on glass and made the cracks in it himself to show how "fragile and fugitive" he considered cultural values to be. In 1920 he exhibited a picture of the Mona Lisa with a moustache, which was entitled *L.H.O.O.Q.*, at a Dada manifestation in Paris. What the petit bourgeois in his ignorance admires, not because of its immanent value but because it is famous as a "great

work of art," must be made ridiculous; however, art itself debased by such an act. Duchamp's gesture also has a su realist significance. His most important work, a painting glass entitled *La mariée mise à nu par ses célibataires, mê* (*The Bride Stripped Bare by Her Bachelors, Even*; 1915-2 Philadelphia, Mus. of Art, Arensberg Coll.), also reveals train of thought anticipating that of the later surrealists, w hardly surpassed it from the artistic point of view.

Duchamp published 94 facsimile reproductions of documen relating to this strange work in 1934, consisting mostly of lit scraps of paper on which he had jotted down fragments thoughts about the work in various cafés. These form an a companiment to the birth and growth of his opus, though th hardly explain it. He gave up art in 1923 to devote hims to chess, and has published a book on chess in which t course of whole games can be followed on transparent pag There is something symbolic in his decision to quit the fie of art. It symbolizes his time as well as his temperament a his peculiar mind. He is to our mechanistic age what Arth Rimbaud was to the age of the symbolists. Rimbaud turn his back on poetry after having achieved fame as a poet in very early years. In order not to quit the stage of art in silen Duchamp prepared his *Boîte-en-valise* in 1942, which was d tributed in an edition of 20 numbers. In this his entire œu is shown in miniature models and reproductions; here his pri cipal opus (on cellophane instead of glass) as well as his stylis development can be studied.

Arp's and Ernst's *Fatagaga* series of collages also anticipa the surrealist idiom. *Fatagaga*, an acronym for *fabrication tableaux garantis gazométriques*, means nothing — it is pure no sense — and is an ironic imitation of the language of adve tising brochures and scientific catalogues. In these *Fataga* collages old prints and illustrations are combined with painti with the conscious aim of producing erotic or other associatio

Ernst's inexhaustible fantasy is shown in all his Dada works whether they are drawings or constructions, such *Dada-Plastik* (1920), or "improvements" of technical, biologic or commercial engravings, which bear long titles such as *I pressions mécaniques rehaussées de couleurs* (1920), *Plantati farcineuse hydropique parasite* (1921), and *The gramineous cycle garnished with bells the dappled fire damps and the echin derms bending the spine to look for caresses* (1920-21).

In Arp's work the law of chance plays a part distinct fro the conscious labor of composition. He cut out pieces of pap colored on one side, shuffled them around, and then turn them over and pasted them on a cardboard, preserving t pattern of shapes and the arrangements of colors which he h obtained by chance. Chance, amorphism, and chaos go ha in hand as do necessity, form, and creation. In his automa drawings, collages (IX, PL. 394), and wood reliefs (PL. 31 Arp wanted to eliminate the conscious side of art productio Only after chance had its way could taste and the critical mi of the artist act, but only to a limited degree. The chan element as a device of the subconscious, of the urge toward primary state of experience, has played a decisive role in mode art since Dada and surrealism, and its importance has be stressed particularly in nongeometric abstract art (tachism, acti painting). It also occurs in modern philosophic and scienti thought. In existentialist philosophy the acceptance of absolu chance is rejected just as is that of absolute necessity. In scien the concept of chance became important when the classic concept of causality was shattered by the new research atomic physics.

In New York Duchamp's attitude inspired that of the Ame can Man Ray, who made his name as a photographer and the inventor of the rayograph. Like Duchamp, Ernst, a Picabia, he later belonged to the surrealist group. In his Dada period Man Ray also constructed objects containing elemen extraneous to painting (*Collage transatlantique*, 1920; *Cadea* 1921, a flatiron with nails on its ironing surface, New Yor Mus. of Mod. Art) and objects of everyday use. Picabia, w was living in New York at this time, was occupied wi problems similar to those of Duchamp, but artistically he w less talented.

Picabia began as a cubist. In his Dadaist period he tried o represent the whole complexity of modern life by means of mechanical contrivances, perhaps with a view to showing their absurdity. *La Novia* (1917, New York, Robert Motherwell Coll.), *Parade amoureuse* (1918, Paris, Coll. Mme. André Breton), and *Cannibalisme* (1919) depict machines that do not make sense, for they can never work and have no purpose.

In Germany there were Dada groups in Berlin, Cologne, and Hannover. Hülsenbeck brought Dada from Zurich to Berlin; George Grosz, Johannes Baader, John Heartfield, Hannah Höch, Walter Mehring, Raoul Hausmann, and Franz Jung were the best-known members of the Berlin group. Ernst, Arp, and Baargeld (Alfred Grünewald) founded a Dada group in Cologne, and Schwitters established one in Hannover.

Many reviews and manifestoes were published by the various Dada groups. The review *291*, published in New York in 1915, was the first to appear, with contributions by Apollinaire, Picasso, Modigliani, Arp, Jakob van Hoddis, Tzara, Hülsenbeck, Janco, and Blaise Cendrars. In 1916 in Zurich Tzara published the first Dada manifesto, *La première aventure céleste de M. Antipyrine*, illustrated by Janco, and Hülsenbeck brought out his *Phantastische Gebete*, with woodcuts by Arp, and his *Schalaben Schalomai Schalomezomai*, with drawings by Arp. In 1917 Duchamp published the periodicals *The Blind Man* and *Rongwrong* in New York, Picabia founded the review *391* in Barcelona, *Dada 1* and *Dada 2* appeared in Zurich, and the literary review *Nord-Sud*, which was favorably inclined to Dada, was published in Paris, with contributions by Apollinaire, Pierre Reverdy, Max Jacob, Breton, Philippe Soupault, and Louis Aragon.

In 1918 *Dada 3* appeared in Zurich, and Hülsenbeck published *Club Dada* and *Der Dada* in Berlin. In 1919 the review *Littérature* in Paris took up the Dada line. It was directed by Breton, Soupault, and Aragon with the collaboration of Paul Eluard. In Zurich *Dada 4* and *5* appeared under the title *Anthologie Dada*, and *Der Zeltweg* was also published there. In Cologne Baargeld founded the Dada newspaper *Der Ventilator* in 1919. In 1920 the *Bulletin Dada*, Paul Eluard's *Proverbe*, *Dadaphone*, and Picabia's *Cannibale* were published in Paris, and *Littérature* brought out twenty-three Dada manifestoes. The same year *Die Schammade* appeared in Cologne and *Dada Almanach* in Berlin.

SURREALIST THEORY AND THE DEVELOPMENT OF THE MOVEMENT. What happened in the endless discussions before and while the break between Dada and surrealism took place, that is, from 1922 until 1924, the year when the new faction adopted the name of surrealism and the first surrealist manifesto by André Breton was published, was the crystallization of the early surrealist ideology. The new faction, made up of former Dadaists under the leadership of Breton, found a mouthpiece in the new series of the review *Littérature*. The essential fact is that the purely negative, destructive, cynical spirit of Dada represented by Tzara was replaced by a new mental orientation toward the irrational. Strongly influenced by Sigmund Freud, the new movement found its spiritual center in the exaltation (theoretically) of the antirational. What remained of the Dada spirit was the basic attitude of revolt — revolt against all established values of an idealistic and also political nature. This led in 1930 to a temporary and partial adherence to the Communist program (first number of *Le surréalisme au service de la révolution*).

In the field of art the anti-art attitude of Dada theoreticians appeared in a milder form as condemnation of any kind of estheticism and of any purely formalistic attempt in art. Georges Hugnet, one of the historians of the movement, says: "Surrealist painting should not be judged from an artistic or plastic point of view; it may be conceded that a painter should be able to paint, but nevertheless surrealist painting must not be judged by artistic quality" (in Barr, *Fantastic Art*, 1936). The surrealist is not an esthete but an investigator and experimenter who extends his research into every field in an attempt to get to the bottom of things. Nevertheless, when Pierre Naville in the third number of *La révolution surréaliste* declared the impossi-

bility of creating a genuine surrealist visual art, Breton replied with his volume *Le surréalisme et la peinture* (1928) in the positive. The element of change and the passive, automatic quality of producing art (discovered before the surrealist term "automatism" was established) acquired a new significance in connection with the notion of the subconscious. New techniques were developed that were a direct continuation of those favored in the Dada era (collage, *frottage*, etc.). Through the emphasis on the irrational, dreams, and fantastic, even abnormal, states of mind, new elements entered both in the stylistic sense and in regard to subject matter. Surrealism became an independent trend in art.

When Breton tried to set up a constructive program against the nihilism of the Dada movement, he approached the task with the intention of enlisting the cooperation of all the intellectuals at a Congrès de l'esprit moderne in 1922. The failure of this Congress, which, however, precipitated the breakup of the Dada movement, brought a new spiritual force into the center of interest, prompted by a strange personal experience that Breton described in his first manifesto of surrealism. He discovered the significance for man of the free flow of imagination, especially that offered him in his dream life. Breton was a poet and, during World War I, a practicing psychiatrist, schooled in the methods of Freudian psychoanalysis. His discovery that Freudian theory and also its clinical methods offered a new tool to the arts was revolutionary. The clinical methods of psychoanalysis led Breton to automatism, and the teaching of Freud to a new synthesis of the real and the irrational. "I believe," he wrote in the manifesto, "in the future resolution of these two states — outwardly so contradictory — which are dream and reality, into a sort of absolute reality, a *surreality*, so to speak" (Breton, 1955).

Breton chose the name "surrealism" in honor of the poet Guillaume Apollinaire, who applied the description "surrealist" to his play *Les mamelles de Tirésias-drame surréaliste* (1917). But as early as 1910 Apollinaire had alluded to pictures by Chagall as surnatural. What lies at the back of both the surreal and the surnatural is the urge toward exploring truth through ethnology and imagination, so as to be able to form a completely new picture of humanity, a proposition very dear to Apollinaire. And that the element of surprise would play an important part in this exploration was to him very agreeable. Both Apollinaire and Breton rejected the word "supernaturalism," which derives from Gérard de Nerval and was also used by Thomas Carlyle in *Sartor Resartus*. In a letter to Paul Dermée in March, 1917, Apollinaire wrote: "Everything considered, I believe, in fact, that it is better to adopt the term 'surrealism' rather than 'surnaturalism,' which I have already used. Surrealism does not yet exist in the dictionaries and it will be simpler to handle than surnaturalism, which has already been applied by the philosophers" (in Nadeau, 1945).

The word "surrealism" leads back to the forerunners of the movement; or, rather, surrealism itself is only one form of appearance in a spiritual process that in its antirationalistic attitude goes back to the romantic movement. Ideologically, the first precursor was Gérard de Nerval, who in his novel *Aurélia, ou le rêve et la vie* (Paris, 1855) speaks of "the overflowing of the dream into the life of reality." He suffered a temporary loss of reason, and in describing this experience in the preface to his book *Les filles de feu* (Paris, 1854) he used the word "supernatural" to express its magic and its quality of belonging to a realm beyond that of sensible nature.

Charles Baudelaire must be mentioned on account of his Satanism and the nervous tension that governed his mind, which he called *mélancolie irritée*. Baudelaire was also aware of a new unity proceeding from the fusion of two worlds: "To take possession immediately of a revealed Paradise on this earth itself," he wrote in *L'Art romantique* (Paris, 1931).

The capacity for Baudelaire's *sorcellerie évocatoire* took in Arthur Rimbaud an almost desperate step forward. "Change life," demands Rimbaud in his *Une saison en enfer*. Of the poet he says that he is "truly a thief of fire, like Prometheus." He declares that "one must be a seer, become a seer." The poet arrives at this through a long, immense, and intentional intemperateness of all the senses. "He becomes among all men the great sufferer, the great criminal, the accursed, and also the great sage, for he stands before the Unknown" (*Œuvres*, Paris, 1898).

Lautréamont (Isidore Ducasse) made the deepest impression of all on the surrealists. The crescendo of individual dissatisfaction, of social revolt, and of the thirst for freedom and the urge toward deep and secret knowledge are expressed in his work. In Lautréamont's *Poésies* and in *Les chants de Maldoror*, an epic of Luciferian spirit, not only are human society, morals, and reason accused but God himself is made responsible for the appalling atrocity that constitutes life. "I have received life like a wound.... I desire that the Creator shall contemplate the gaping crevasse of this gash for all the hours of His eternity. That is the punishment I inflict upon him" (*Œuvres complètes*, Paris, 1938).

Alfred Jarry tore from the face of life its idyllic and hypocritical mask. The figure he created, Ubu (in *Ubu roi, Ubu enchaîné*), is a "hideous presentation of combined cupidity, cowardice, gluttony, lechery, bourgeois respectability, philosophical wisdom, and sharp, dangerous cunning" (Lemaitre, 1941).

Stéphane Mallarmé's symbolism was also important for the surrealists, because it introduced the breakup of traditional grammatical associations between words and their objective meanings and discovered the symbolic character of words, their value in themselves, all of which was a poetic process, antilogical and antirational. This tendency led in art to the discovery of symbolic signs as evidenced in the work of Klee, Miró, Masson, and others, as it led also to the deep sigh of André Gide: "Ah, who will deliver our spirit from the heavy chains of logic?" (*Les nouvelles nourritures*, Paris, 1935).

In addition to these literary precursors, surrealism was influenced by Hegel's philosophy. In the introduction to his *Phänomenologie des Geistes* (1807) Hegel says: "Beauty without power hates the spirit because the spirit demands of her what she is unable to give. But it is not the life that quails before death and would preserve itself from destruction, but the life that accepts and renews itself in death that is the life of the spirit." In this antiesthetic thought and in the idea of the ambiguity of life the basic tenets of surrealism can be recognized. Hegel's importance for surrealism must be particularly stressed. Breton said of him: "Hegel attacked all the problems at present held to be the most difficult in the field of poetry and art and he did so with an unparalleled lucidity, and for the greater part he solved them. Even today it is of Hegel that we must inquire as to whether the activity of surrealism is well- or ill-founded" (Breton and Eluard, 1938).

In his first manifesto Breton gave the following philosophical definition of surrealism: "Surrealism is based on the belief in the superior reality of certain forms of association heretofore neglected, in the omnipotence of the dream, and in the disinterested play of thought. It leads to the permanent destruction of all other psychic mechanisms and to its substitution for them in the solution of the principal problems of life." The method or technique of arriving at tangible results in this sense is defined by Breton as "pure psychic automatism by which it is intended to express, either verbally or in writing, the true function of thought. Thought dictated in the absence of all control exerted by reason, and outside all esthetic or moral preoccupations" (Breton, 1955). Breton and Philippe Soupault wrote down the first automatic texts, some of which were published under the title *Les champs magnétiques* (Paris, 1921). This was after being tormented, since 1919, by a series of hallucinatory visions in which the direct cause and origin of surrealism can be seen.

On the heels of automatic writing came the automatic fashioning of objects. Arp's use of the law of chance and Ernst's collages have already been mentioned in connection with Dada. Upon these collages and, later, *frottages*, other automatic methods followed. One was decalcomania: "With a large brush spread black gouache, more or less diluted in places, on a sheet of smooth white paper that you will immediately cover with a smilar sheet on which you exert a medium pressure with the back of your hand. Lift this second sheet slowly.... Process discovered by Oscar Dominguez in 1936" (Breton, 1955). Another was

"exquisite corpse" (*cadavre exquis*): "A game of folded pape played by several people, who compose a sentence or drawin without anyone seeing the preceding collaboration" (ibid.) Other techniques and methods were surrealist objects, that is objects with a symbolic function made by artists (Dali), as dis tinguished from found objects (*objets trouvés*) or objects o surrealist character, ready-mades, or merely assisted objects smoke pictures (Paalen); rayographs; composite images (in fluence of Arcimboldi; cf. V, PL. 240); fantastic perspectiv and trompe l'oeil to achieve a dreamlike atmosphere; an combination of real and painted objects. Of all these methods known as "passive methods," Max Ernst wrote in 1933: "Th investigations into the mechanism of inspiration that have beer ardently pursued by the surrealists lead them to the discover of certain techniques, poetic in essence and devised to remove th work of art from the sway of the so-called conscious faculties These techniques, which cast a spell over reason, taste, and th conscious will, have made possible a vigorous application o surrealist principles to drawing, to painting, and even, to a¤ extent, to photography. These processes, some of which, espe cially collage, were employed before the advent of surrealism are now modified and systematized by surrealism, making i possible for certain people to represent on paper or on canva the dumbfounding photograph of their thoughts and of thei desires" (Ernst, 1948). It was Dali who contributed an activ method in 1930, which he called "paranoiac-critical activity."

Although surrealism first manifested itself as a literary movement, it wanted to be regarded as a philosophy of life, ¤ metaphysical attitude toward the whole of human existence, and a method of investigation rather than as a theory of art and literature. All the strivings of surrealism to break the fetters of convention and of logical thought in order to gain access to the unfettered and unconscious imagination have one aim to provoke a "crisis of consciousness," according to the second manifesto of surrealism (1930; in Breton, 1955). Dream accounts automatic texts, automatic drawings or paintings, all these prod ucts of psychic activity "offer a key capable of opening indef initely that box of multiple depths called man" (ibid.). In the same way as Freud speaks of dream censorship and of the sup pression of the unconscious by the conscious mind, the surreal ists speak of the necessity of a censorship of all accepted forms o traditional thinking. Reason, intellect, and consciousness are so many walls that stand between the real human self and the universe, and no means of breaking through these walls — sar casm, irony, ridicule, challenge through absurdity — is to be despised if it serves the purpose. All moral and esthetic laws are to be regarded as mere prejudices, and humor, objective humor as Breton calls it, is the chosen weapon for the enlight enment of humanity. This humor differs in spirit and intentior from that of Dada in that it is directed systematically to ¤ constructive end: that of gaining access to the surreal, or rather of dragging the surreal out of its dark retreat so that the miracle of life may be experienced.

In his struggle against that rationalism which holds dowr the inner forces of life, Breton attacked "the hatred of the mar velous wherever it rages." Where is the marvelous to be found "It comes to light within reality. It comes to light in dreams obsessions, preoccupations, in sleep, fear, love, chance; in hallu cinations, pretended disorders, follies, idle wanderings, poetry the supernatural and the unusual, in empiricism, in superreal ity" (in Barr, *Fantastic Art*, 1936). In the first surrealist mani festo Breton declared that "the marvelous is always beautiful everything marvelous is beautiful. Nothing but the marvelous is beautiful." And in his book *Nadja* (Paris, 1928) he stated "Beauty will be convulsive or it will not be." The "esthetic credo of surrealism" is to be found in these two statements The problem of the beautiful and the ugly rooted by tradition in classic Greek art and valid throughout the centuries up to its reversion in Gustave Courbet's statement *Le beau c'est l¤ laid* is not touched by this surrealist position. The aim of sur realism was to disturb, and it pursued this aim by breaking through the conventional, the seemingly ordered, using the instrument of surprise that forces us to take notice. This element of surprise was expressed by Lautréamont, whom Breton (1934 uoted: "Beautiful as the chance meeting on a dissecting table f a sewing machine and an umbrella." In this use of the term, ne beautiful is eliminated and replaced by something else. Convulsive beauty will be erotic-veiled, explosive-stable, magic-circumstantial or it will not be" (Breton and Eluard, 1938).

The surrealists' claim of being able to lure the unconscious ut of its hiding place has never been substantiated. An analysis f works by Dali, Magritte, Delvaux, or Tanguy, for instance, hows that they were planned and must have required considrable conscious effort. This would, however, apply only o the technical and compositional side of the painting. In surealism the content is more important. Is the content in a *frotage* by Ernst or a painting by Masson subconscious? What ppears to be depicted on surrealist canvases is *manifest content*, visual appearances similar to the images or items experienced n a dream. Such images are not unconscious and no unconcious inspiration is necessary to paint them.... If we say nat surrealist art depicts incongruous objects and dream imges in planned arrangements, we have pretty well described it, nd the theories of creativity based on tapping the unconscious eem unnecessary" (Gordon, 1951).

A further question presents itself: To what degree can the ubjective unconscious present in their work, as the surrealists nsist it is, claim universal validity? Dali says: "The subconscious as a symbolic language that is truly a universal language, for :... speaks with the vocabulary of the great vital constants – sexual instinct, feeling of death, physical notion of the enigma f space — these vital constants are universally echoed in every uman being. To understand an esthetic picture, training in ppreciation is necessary, cultural and intellectual preparation. 'or surrealism the only requisite is a receptive and intuitive uman being" (in Levy, 1936). Scientific critics have decisively ejected this claim of universal validity. "Dali's assertion vould demand a fixed response to surrealist symbolism, that is, hat surrealist symbolism be objective. If dreams could similarly e interpreted, psychoanalysis would be unnecessary — the atient's latent content would be immediately apparent to nyone, including the patient himself" (Gordon, 1951; Aiken, 945). The surrealist synthesis of the content of the unconscious is one in name only," says Gauss (1949); "it is a new label for eality." Gauss sees in surrealism "no necessary movement rom a given thesis to its opposite" (ibid.).

The first group exhibition of surrealist painting was held n Paris in 1925, and a second exhibition took place there the ollowing year. Other collective exhibitions were held in 1928 Paris), 1933 (Paris), 1935 (Copenhagen and Tenerife), 1936 London), 1938 (Paris and Amsterdam), 1940 (Mexico), and 942 (New York). In 1930 and 1936 exhibits of surrealist bjects with a symbolic function were held in Paris. The first xclusively surrealist exhibition in the United States took place n Hartford, Conn., in 1931, and was followed by one in New 'ork in 1932. After the war there were international exhibitions n 1947 (Paris), 1948 (Prague and Santiago, Chile), 1960 (Paris nd New York), and 1964 (Paris).

Dali and the Spanish film maker Luis Buñuel collaborated n two surrealist films: *Un chien andalou* (1928) and *L'Age 'or* (1930). Jean Cocteau produced the surrealist film *Blood f a Poet* in 1930 (III, PL. 332). See also CINEMATOGRAPHY.

Important surrealist publications, in addition to those lready cited, included Breton and Eluard's book of automatic exts entitled *L'Immaculée conception* (Paris, 1930), Breton's ook *Les vases communicants* (Paris, 1930), the review *Minotaure* Paris, 1933–38), and the magazine *VVV* (New York, 1942–44). After the war surrealist periodicals continued to be published, uch as *Medium* (Paris, 1954–55), *Le surréalisme, même* (Paris, 956–59), and *Bief* (Paris, 1958–60).

CHARACTERISTICS OF SURREALIST ART. Max Ernst (q.v.) was ne of the founders of surrealism in Paris in 1924. He defines urrealist collage as "the exploitation of the chance meeting f two distant realities on an unfamiliar plane, or ... the culture f systematic displacement and its effects" (*Beyond Painting*, 948). Inspired by the cubist *papiers collés*, Ernst developed his technique by cutting out parts of old engravings from ad-

venture and love stories or illustrations from technical treatises and publicity catalogues and combining them to achieve what the surrealists like to call "the irrational." Ernst says: "He who speaks of collage speaks of the irrational." The main works produced with this technique are *Les malheurs des immortels* (1922), a series of collages with poems by Eluard, and the collage novels *La femme 100 têtes* (1929), *Rêve d'une petite fille* (1930), and *Une semaine de bonté* (1934).

Besides this conscious technique, which was intended to produce rational or irrational associations, Ernst invented the half-automatic method of *frottage*, which he described in *Beyond Painting* as follows: "The *frottage* process — based simply on the intensification of the irritability of the mind's faculties by appropriate technical means, excluding all conscious mental guidance (of reason, taste, or morals) and reducing to a minimum the active part of what has hitherto been called the 'author' of the work — was consequently revealed as the true equivalent of ... automatic writing." The technique consists in placing paper over an object and rubbing a stick of graphite on the paper; this makes the veins of the wood, the web of the tissues, or the ribs of the leaves appear. Ernst discovered the process as a result of a visual obsession, which he has described in *Beyond Painting*. The principal work produced with this technique is the *Histoire naturelle* (1926).

Ernst was haunted by fever visions, hallucinations, and the dread of nothingness. His contact with occult, magic, and witchcraft powers dates from 1906. A shock in his youth gave birth to the bird imagery in his work. The obsession tormented him until he created his *Monument to the Birds* (oil) in 1927 (Paris, Coll. Vicomtesse de Noailles). Ernst has identified himself with Loplop, the Bird Superior (*A 100,000 Doves*, 1927, Paris, Coll. Mme Simone Collinet; *Loplop Introduces*, 1929–30, Chicago, Mr. and Mrs. Edwin Bergman Coll.), and the bird motif is represented in his later works, although in a more abstract manner (*After Me, Sleep*, 1958, Paris, Mus. Nat. d'Art Mod.).

Other themes of Ernst group themselves into dream imagery (*Revolution by Night*, 1923, London, Roland Penrose Coll.; *The Horde*, 1927, V, PL. 134; *Swamp Angel*, *The Stolen Mirror*, both 1940; here the artist often seems to emulate the grainy structure of his *frottages* in oil painting) and visions of sun or moon with forests or other landscapes (*Lune en Bouteilles*, XI, PL. 372; *The Great Forest*, 1927, PL. 320; *Moon over Wellfleet*, 1942; *Summer Night in Arizona*, 1943, Bridgewater, Conn., Mr. and Mrs. Julien Levy Coll.). The shapes of primitive idols enter his work in both painting and sculpture, relating the magic visions of the past to the wish fulfillment of the unconsciousness in the present (*Lunar Asparagus*, 1935, PL. 325; *Gay*, 1935, New York, Mr. and Mrs. Joseph Slifka Coll.; mural sculptures in the artist's home at St-Martin d'Ardèche in France, 1938; *Moon Mad*, 1944, Bridgewater, Conn., Mr. and Mrs. Julien Levy Coll.; *The King Playing with the Queen*, 1944, New York, Mus. of Mod. Art). The concept of convulsive beauty is exemplified in *The Elephant of the Celebes*, 1921, and *The Joy of Living*, 1936 (both London, Roland Penrose Coll.). A geometric element enters in the 1940s (*Euclid*, 1945, Houston, Mr. and Mrs. John de Menil Coll.; *Head of a Young Girl*, 1948), a cosmic trend in the 1950s (*The Earth Seen from Mars*, *The Earth Seen from Pluto*, both 1955), and finally an animistic-geometric-abstract element (*Imponderables*, 1957; *Doubt*, 1957; *Four Crystalline Temperaments*, 1957). Ernst has also illustrated works by Breton, Eluard, René Crevel, Jacques Baron, Benjamin Péret, and others. It is only with Ernst that one can speak of a surrealist painting which has developed special means of expression.

The step from Ernst to Salvador Dali (q.v.) is the step from psychology to psychiatry. Dali's violent and unbalanced temperament could not be satisfied with the established methods of surrealism. Dreams and automatism were too passive for him. He sought for an active element to "materialize the images of concrete irrationality" (Dali, 1930). As method he believed he could achieve this through the paranoiac-critical activity, and as technique through the use of a three-dimensional realism rendered with photographic clarity and an overemphasized perspective (infinity, the feeling of being lost and deserted in dream or life) that derives from Chirico (q.v.).

Dali looks upon this paranoiac-critical activity as "a systematic violent irruption of a man's desire into the world," a "spontaneous method of irrational understanding based upon the interpretative critical association of delirious phenomena" (Dali, 1935). The activist element is to be sought in the fact that "the images which paranoiac thought may suddenly release will not merely spring from the subconscious; the force of their paranoiac power will itself be at the service of the unconscious" (Dali, 1930). Tangible realism dominates in Dali's work because the visual logic of the picture makes itself felt in the sense that the dreamlike, the paranoiac accent, can only be conveyed to the beholder when the objects are neither stylized nor rendered in an abstract manner but are factually represented (*The Dream*, 1931, Paris, Coll. Félix Labisse; *The Average Fine and Invisible Harp*, 1932, Paris, Coll. Vicomtesse de Noailles; *Puzzle of Autumn*, 1936; *Impressions of Africa*, 1938, V, PL. 133). Only in this way can that moment of surprise be realized through which the subjective "irrationalism" of Dali expresses itself. For this reason Dali speaks of his own pictures as "hand-painted dream photographs."

Paranoia plays both a direct and an indirect part in Dali's make-up: direct, inasmuch as he declares that madness is the common base of the human spirit; indirect, inasmuch as he sees in madness a means of revolt. "I believe the moment is at hand when by paranoiac and active advance of the mind it will be possible (simultaneously with automatism and other passive states) to systematize confusion and thus to help discredit completely the world of reality . . . . Only the violence and duration of your hardened dream can resist the hideous mechanical civilization that is your enemy" (Dali, 1930).

Paranoia is a chronic mental disease that is characterized by systematized delusions, with or without hallucinations, of grandeur and persecution. There is a decidedly megalomaniac trait in Dali's character. He has said that when he was seven he wanted to be Napoleon and that his ambition has been increasing ever since then. Two themes with typically Freudian connotations dominate his work from 1930 to 1934: the legend of William Tell and the tragic myth of Millet's *Angelus* (*The Old Age of William Tell*, 1931, Paris, Coll. Vicomtesse de Noailles; *The Atavisms of Twilight*, 1933–34, Switzerland, priv. coll.). They fascinate him, as did the copy of Vermeer's *Lacemaker* that his father had in his office. Countless symbols of persecution mania, in particlar sharp instruments, symbols of mutilation, and sexual fetishes, are found in Dali's later pictures. Some of them are taken from Krafft-Ebing's case histories of paranoia. These symbols indicate sexual perversion, the transitoriness of time (ants, the melting watch), necrophilia, and even leanings toward coprophagy, and they are the true expression of a person to whom excrement, blood, and putrefaction are the cardinal images of life (*Accommodations of Desire*, 1929, Santa Barbara, Calif., Wright Ludington Coll.; *Illumined Pleasures*, 1929, New York, Mr. and Mrs. Sidney Janis Coll.; *The Persistence of Memory*, 1931, New York, Mus. of Mod. Art; *The Specter of Sex Appeal*, 1934, Coll. Mme Gala Dali; *The Cavalier of Death*, 1935, Belgium, priv. coll., 1936, X, PL. 139; *Boiled Beans*, 1936, X, PL. 139; *Metamorphoses of Narcissus*, 1936–37, XI, PL. 374; *Imperial Violets*, 1938, New York, Mus. of Mod. Art; *Apparition of Face and Fruit Dish on a Beach*, 1938, Hartford, Conn., Wadsworth Atheneum).

For the analysis of his personality the fact that Dali is a Catalonian imaginatively gifted and brought up in the tradition of the spirit of the Inquisition is of decisive importance. Dali calls the Spanish the most irrational people in the world.

The difference between the paranoiac and Dali is that one is really ill while the other merely simulates illness. In his hatred of all that is rational and mechanical, Dali fell into another extreme, that of an obsession with insane subjectivism. Dali's work does not, however, reproduce paranoiac conditions. Scientific authority denies their authenticity.

The demoniac condition forms part of the human psyche. It may, under the stress of assaults to which the inner life is exposed, come into the foreground in the development of the individual and even of whole epochs. Surrealist art has sougl its forerunners in the magic art of the primitives, in the dar age of the late Romanesque, in mannerism, or in individual fig ures such as Bosch, Pieter Bruegel the Elder, Goya, Fusel Francesco de Nomé ("Monsu Desiderio"), and others. A who series of such figures from the 15th century down to artists lik Redon, Chagall, and Chirico has been analyzed. Dali's doub images and multiple images are derived technically from Arcin boldi (*The Invisible Man*, 1929–33, Coll. Mme Gala Dal *Paranoiac Face*, 1934–35). Bracelli and Larmessin also hav directly influenced Dali.

About 1937–38 Dali felt the impact of the Renaissance an stated that psychopathology no longer interested him. He no wished to perfect his techniques and express the new conceptio of physics with it. Since then Dali has produced paintings ‹ both scientific and religious subject matter in a style emulatir Vermeer, Chardin, and Hubert and Jan van Eyck, often combinir the religious past and the scientific present into one aspect an using split or exploded forms (*Basket of Bread*, 1945, Lea *Atomica*, 1948, *The Maximum Speed of Raphael's Madonn* 1954, all three, Coll. Mme Gala Dali). Other religious painting include *The Madonna of Port Lligat*, 1950 (Canada, Lady Jame Dunn Coll.), *The Christ of St. John of the Cross*, 1951 (Glasgov Art Gall. and Mus.), and *The Sacrament of the Last Suppe* 1955 (PL. 328).

Dali, in addition to being a good technician in oil and wate color, is a fine draftsman. His drawings and pastels and the 1c illustrations to Dante's *La Divina Commedia* (1954) show I is a great master in the traditional mannerist sense. He ha illustrated other books, produced lithographs for *Don Quixo* (1946), made films (*Un chien andalou, L'Age d'or*), designe sets and costumes for ballets (*Sentimental Colloquy* and *The Ma Tristan*, XII, PL. 447), designed surrealist jewelry, painte society portraits, created advertisements (XI, PL. 396), an written several more or less autobiographical novels.

Yves Tanguy joined the surrealists in 1925 and his fir work shows influences of Ernst, Masson, and Miró. But ‹ early as 1927 he found his personal style (*A Large Pictu which is a Landscape*, Saigon, Coll. Mme Henri Hoppeno *Extinction of Useless Lights*, New York, Mus. of Mod. Ar *Mama, Papa is Wounded!*, PL. 321). During 1928 and 192 his style became completely mature (*The Mood of Now*, Pari Coll. Mme Simone Collinet; *Old Horizon*, New York, Pien Matisse Gall.; *The Lovers*, priv. coll.). After a journey to Afric in 1930 and 1931 a new element entered, inspired by some cu rious African rock formations (*The Armoire of Proteus*, Pari Coll. André Breton). Mineral forms started to replace the veg etal forms formerly used. The color scheme was more comple: and especially after his arrival in America in 1939 became mo audacious (*Indefinite Divisibility*, 1942, Buffalo, Albright-Kno Art Gall.; *Slowly Toward the North*, 1942, New York, Mu of Mod. Art). The end of World War II was reflected in work such as *The Closing Days*, 1944 (Port Chester, N.Y., Hug Chisholm Coll.), *Closed Sea, Wide World*, 1944 (New Yor Pierre Matisse Gall.), and *The Rapidity of Sleep*, 1945 (PL. 321 The climax of his work was reached in 1954 with the monument composition *Multiplication of the Arcs* (XI, PL. 372).

Two significant elements are found in Tanguy's indefinab world. Space is expressed by perspective means, but not, i the manner of Chirico, with the help of architecture but throug an empty infinity like that of a desert whose distances have r air and are often bounded by no horizon. It is characterize further by dark threatening shadows that a sharp artificial ligl throws into the picture and by the indication of a misty atmo phere and vague shapes of clouds. This is a dream world, ste ile, or as it might have been before the beginning of the act ‹ creation. Tanguy enlivens this dead atmosphere with artifici beings that he sets there instead of the organic and inorgan life that exists on earth. It is not easy to place exactly these form of Tanguy's — where they belong and where they come from Up to a certain point it can be said that Arp's abstract form influenced Tanguy. These forms have a strong power of sug gestion. The idea that arises in the mind of the beholder is poetic one in the sense that the imagination is stimulated, but ‹

same time it is never satisfied. With the half-dreamy, half-
structed character inherent in them, Tanguy likes to remain
the twilight condition that he prefers in his inner experiences.
seems to reawaken within himself primitive modes of thought
imagination, and in this a reflection of the evolution theory
be recognized, but as an urge and not as an object of rational
earch.

An art like Tanguy's is only possible in a highly developed
entific age. Without this science, whose poetic equivalent
wishes to create (the scientific beyond, as it were), such an
as his is unthinkable. In the evolution of his art positive
logical formations and astronomical phases can be observed.
st the age of gaseous formations (1927–29) and the solidi-
ng phenomena in lavalike formations that followed (1930–31),
n bone formations combined with crystal formations; then
in purely rational elements, geometric lines of relationship,
aight and angular, or forms reminiscent of the models of
anic molecules — a mixture of abstract and biomorphic forms.
e constructive element in this phantom world lies in the su-
imposition of the artist's personal will upon the mystical
erience called up in man by such elemental phenomena as
ce, water, air, light, wind, and the shapes of bones. Breton
28) said of Tanguy's art that in it "the figures of the past
future coexist like various characters in a drama which is
yet unraveled but which is already finished in the author's
nd." Some of Tanguy's drawings radiate a great precision and
stical beauty. As form appearances they may be regarded
abstract, for which reason it is possible to speak, in connection
h this artist, of abstract surrealism.

Paul Delvaux has been a surrealist since 1936. His biographer,
ude Spaak, lays stress in two passages of his book (1948)
the relationship of Delvaux to surrealism. "Delvaux is a
realist," he says. "In the surrealist camp to which, I repeat,
vould be absurd to deny that he belonged, Delvaux has never
n an isolated figure."

Delvaux's work in the beginning owed much to the ideas
Magritte — and stylistically even more to Chirico — but Del-
ux is a painter with an exquisite poetic vision and by no means
academic surrealist like Magritte. Delvaux's world is a dream
rld in the sense in which Pindar saw life, as the dream of
hade, or in the sense of Calderón de la Barca's Life is a Dream,
Shakespeare's The Tempest, which denies reality to the dreamer
nself: "We are such stuff as dreams are made on . . . ." The
posite forces in this dream world of Delvaux are the young
men and Death (The Courtesans, 1943, Bridgewater, Conn.,
r. and Mrs. Julien Levy Coll.; Venus Asleep, 1944, PL. 321)
the realm of the moon in its still enchantment (The Lunar
ty, 1944, New York, Alex Salkon Coll.). There is a spell of
auty — in the traditional, not convulsive, sense — upon it,
both the human figures and the architecture (Nocturnal Garden,
42, property of the artist; The First Rose, 1946, Brussels, Coll.
n L. Merckx; The Staircase, 1948, Cleveland, Mus. of Art).
eternal question seems to float around these quiet figures.
ly occasionally is there an intrusion of waking reality in the
ape of strange appearances in clothes (Le Cortège en Dentelles,
36, Coll. Jean Giron) or interiors of Victorian taste (Woman
d Rose, 1936, Hollywood, Albert Lewin Coll.; Night Train,
47, Brussels, Coll. Jean L. Merckx) or the 20th-century man
o, buttoned up and reading his newspaper, passes life by
thout seeing it (Man in the Street, 1940, Brussels, Coll.
bert Giron). With Delvaux, as with Chirico, the perspective
infinity of distance, melancholy, an Ingres-like classicism, a
ging for the ideal. Although everything in Delvaux's world
ms equivocal and mysterious, nothing in it is painful. One
cepts the riddle of life as it is stated in the immobility of the
es and the poses of the figures (Village of the Sirens, 1942,
ll. Théo Léger). These pictures do not speak to the intellect
t directly to the emotions, and from there they seep slowly
o the consciousness.

The realm of doctrinaire or academic surrealism is exempli-
d by the work of René Magritte, Pierre Roy, and Léonor
ni. Magritte's paintings include The Difficult Passage, 1926
russels, Coll. G. Niels), The False Mirror, 1928 (V, PL. 144),
volution, 1934 (Choisel, France, Coll. Claude Spaak), The Red

Model, 1935 (Stockholm, Moderna Museet), Nostalgia, 1941
(London, E. L. T. Mesens Coll.), The Carnival of the Wise,
1947 (Brussels, Coll. Robert de Keyn), Presence of Mind, 1958
(priv. coll.), and The Great War, 1964 (Paris, Gal. Alexandre
Iolas). Typical examples of Roy's work are Daylight Saving
Time, 1929 (New York, Mus. of Mod. Art), Rural Electrifi-
cation, 1930 (Hartford, Conn., Wadsworth Atheneum), St.
Michael's Summer, 1932 (Paris, Mus. Nat. d'Art Mod.), Fortune
at Rest, The Guitars, and Coral and Pastels. Léonor Fini's
pictures include The Initials, 1936, Sphingue noire guettant le
sommeil d'un jeune homme, 1947 (Coll. Georges Sébastien),
The End of the World, 1950, and La guardienne à l'œuf noir,
1955. These works have in common the use of trompe l'oeil,
a sharply delineated three-dimensional space without atmosphere,
the juxtaposition of incongruent objects, and the exploitation of
current surrealist symbolism (the bird, the snake, the tree without leaves, the plaster torso, candlelight, the double image,
flooded space, erotic symbols, etc.). The emphasis that the
surrealists have given to the libido, their sexual "revolution,"
is to be seen as a protest against the Christian doctrine of original
sin. It did not lead to any concept harmonizing body and soul,
or to the abolition of the dualism involved, but rather to an
excessive, even pornographic, cult of sex.

The work of Arp, Man Ray, Picabia, and Duchamp has already been mentioned in connection with Dada. The ways
of Picabia and Breton parted as early as 1921. In 1930 Picabia
turned his back on surrealism altogether, and in 1945 he became
exclusively abstract (a style that he had practiced as early as
1909). In 1949 he exhibited his paintings as "sur-irrealist"
works, abstract compositions with titles such as Tu ne le ven-
dras jamais and Sens dessus-dessous, Je ne veux plus peindre,
Quel est le titre. From his "ironic machines" up to his latest
works, his style always showed a predominance of the linear
element with the use of two or more superimposed images (PL.
319). Duchamp was one of the organizers of the international
exhibition of surrealism in 1947 in Paris. He exhibited Rain
Room and Labyrinth and produced a cover in relief for the catalogue.

André Masson started his career as a cubist. He attracted
the attention of Breton and exhibited with the surrealists from
1924 to 1928 (The Four Elements, 1923–24, Paris, Coll. Dr.
Tchernia-Jéramec; Nude in an Interior, 1924; Battle of Fishes,
1927, PL. 320; Dead Horses, 1927, Coll. Alphonse Kann; Animals
Devouring Themselves, 1928, New York, Mus. of Mod. Art).
Masson himself said: "Fundamentally I am more a sympathizer
with surrealism than a surrealist or a nonsurrealist . . . . With
me surrealism has been a cyclic affair. I was one of the first
group of surrealists. Then in a manner of speaking I became
separated from them. But I am actually more a surrealist in
my illustrations than in my painting. Perhaps it is really that
my romanticism appears surrealist" (in Sweeney, 1946).

In fact, Masson has not a surrealist mind but an elemental
mind. His mind is turned toward the elemental experience and
his work belongs essentially to the trend of fantastic art. He
brings the states of passion (solitude, fascination, generation, sadism, androgyny, masochism, attraction, repulsion)
into relationship with the seven conditions (élan, reunion, friction, gyration, sowing, separation, fall), and these in their turn
are associated with elements of the Middle Ages (air, water,
fire, and earth). Heraclitus is for him the essential philosopher
(Heraclitus, 1943). Heraclitus is to be seen as the forerunner
of Bergson, James, and above all of the existentialist philosophers
Heidegger, Jaspers, and Sartre. Masson is the existentialist
artist kat exochen. The notion of necessity in life gives way in
the modern interpretation of Heraclitus to tychism: everything happens by change. In Masson's art the idea propulsion
is at least as important as its pictorial rendering (Don Quixote's
Vigil, 1933; Daphne, 1933; Narcissus, 1934; Ibdes in Aragon,
1935, PL. 318; Ophelia, 1937; Gradiva, 1939; Goethe and the
Metamorphosis of the Plant, 1940; Sybil, 1944, property of the
artist; Bread, 1944, Geneva, Gal. Krugier). "Painting can be
a subtle means to give movement to philosophic thought — but
above all to elaborate it . . . . The idea that the realm of concrete
forms is near to that of ideas will one time come to all painters,"

wrote Dubuffet in *Peintres initiatiques d'Alfonso Ossorio* (Paris, 1951).

Masson's mind may be likened to the two parts of a scale. In one part lie mystical, metaphysical, mythicoirrational knowledge and values of beauty; in the other part lies scientific, critical, adventurous rationalism. This establishes him as a true representative of our times. He has too calculating a brain, too conscious an inner life, but he longs to be at the opposite pole. Poles attract him, and his thought and his art are to be understood in the light of this polarity. Masson "knows" what mysticism is but he can no longer feel it. His art illustrates his ideas (this is particularly true of his drawings) and is also dependent on them. An interesting phenomenon is encountered in his book *Anatomy of My Universe* (1943): the text is mystical or metaphysical, irrationally conceived, and the drawings are constructivist and rational. The literary influences lead us back to astrology, alchemy, magic, and also depth psychology, whereas the stylistic influences are those of the Renaissance and its successors (e.g., Leonardo da Vinci, Bracelli, Larmessin, and Piranesi). Other books by Masson such as *Nocturnal Note-book* (1944) and *Mythologies* (1938) complement this picture. Existentialist man stands isolated; but not only that. The brain-man Masson looks upon him as an automaton, although a very complicated one, more complicated than Albertus Magnus saw him or than Condillac's sensualist automaton. Basically it is the existentialist automaton of Heidegger that recalls the problems of the Double and of Narcissus: one evolves from the cradle to the tomb, the other carries its own death with it like a cast shadow.

Masson observes life with impassioned meditation. "I know that I am surrounded by the irrational. I let my reason go as far as I can. It traverses the court of objects and reaches finally a waste land of infinite desolation; it is a truly human place, which creates its own time." Here Masson is both existentialist and surrealist, especially in the imagery of the desert. His *Dream of a Future Desert* is a modern apocalyptic vision of that future which science may bear in its lap. He buries himself "in the darkness of the earth, a seed eager to burst out toward the light of day" (*La terre ensemencée*, 1945). Salvation lies only in beauty and mystery; Masson experiences "the fraternity of the natural kingdoms. The unity of the cosmos. There is nothing inanimate in the world; a correspondence exists between the virtues of minerals, plants, stars, and animal bodies." And there is "no hierarchy in the cycle of natural forms. The royal structure of the human body is no more beautiful than the Radiolaria, an oceanic star with solid rays." He knows the sacred figure 5 of the Pythagoreans, just as he knows the geometry of beauty, the laws of the golden section, and the laws of the various orders of architecture; but all intellectually, theoretically. Then again he feels himself to be near to the magic myth of the primitives (*Primitive*, 1947, V, PL. 138), and the totality of all this dominates in his astrological conception of the emblematic man who symbolizes the universe in his own proper person, ever changeable under the power of knowledge. The frontiers in Masson's thought are so flowing that this in itself would leave the door open for the existentialist to find his way to the essential.

A strong abstract element in various forms enters Masson's later work (*End of Summer*, 1955; *Lightning, Sadness of a Spring Day*, both 1956; *Tumulus I*, 1957). In 1963 he was commissioned to paint a new ceiling for the Odéon in Paris, which he completed in 1965.

Joan Miró (q.v.) was connected with the surrealists from 1924 to 1930. Nothing can better characterize his work, his position in modern art in general, and his relationship to surrealism in particular than his own words: "I am attaching more and more importance to the subject matter of my work. To me it seems vital that a rich and robust theme should be present to give the spectator an immediate blow between the eyes before a second thought can interpose. In this way poetry, pictorially expressed, speaks its own language." He also said, "I like Odilon Redon, Paul Klee, and Kandinsky for their spirit. I like Picasso and Matisse as pure painting — from the point of view of plasticity. Both points of view are important."

Whereas Prévert and Ribemont-Dessaignes (1956) and E[l] (1954) like to stress that Miró is a surrealist, there is m[uch] truth in Queneau's (1948) assertion : "Notwithstanding [the] reputation Miró's painting is not surrealist, although at cert[ain] periods in his life he has made use of surrealist and even D[adaist] 'methods.' Miró's painting is not surrealist because, apart fr[om] certain periods ... it is a matter of painting and not of me[re] or ultra- or nonpainting." Although Breton (1928) said t[hat] Mirò was "perhaps the most surrealist of us all," this statem[ent] depends on how surrealism is defined. Surrealism was a sou[rce] of inspiration to Miró from 1924 on, but nothing more. Th[ere] is no automatism, no nonsense-verse mentality, as in Ern[st's] subtitles, no obscene sexualism, no black humor, but the [joie] *de vivre* of a truly naïve personality. Miró, like Klee, belo[ngs] to modern fantastic art.

Miró may be seen as a giant child playing with the appe[ar]ances of the world as a child plays with a ball. All these appe[ar]ances take on an astonishing form, just as surprising as it is n[ew.] No speculation as to progress or usefulness intervenes to trou[ble] this blithe spirit or disturb the primacy and freshness of manner of observation. The world for Miró is a happy and m[ys]terious home, not a torture chamber. Curiosity and a play[ful] joy in life dominate. Joy breaks through the clouds of the mys[tery] through the utilitarian ideas of the grown-up, through th[e] absurd seriousness that makes a hell of the world. It is rema[rk]able how in our time this joy of life blossomed into stra[nge] flower. With Miró it took a clownish-primitive form.

He began to paint in an expressionist-cubist, even Fau[ve] style until in 1922 or 1923 he embarked on a surprising n[ew] vision. Pictures such as *The Carbide Lamp*, 1922–23 (N[ew] York, Mus. of Mod. Art) and *The Tilled Field*, 1923–24 (Radn[or,] Pa., Mr. and Mrs. Henry Clifford Coll.) were painted bef[ore] the first surrealist manifest saw the light of day. Under [the] impact of surrealism Miró painted *Carnival of Harlequi[n]* 1924–25 (PL. 322) with its frantic movement of semiabstr[act] forms. Miró wandered through the forest of rich suggesti[on] offered by modern art, taking what he needed, as well as from [the] abstractionists (Kandinsky) and above all from Klee. Klee v[as] not so full-blooded as the Spaniard, and yet in him there v[as] that same varying direction of the spirit that led Miró also [to] the art of the child, to the art of the primitives (see PRIMITIVIS[M]) and finally to the primitivity of mankind as far back as to [the] engraved pebbles from La Colombière (IV, PL. 261; XI, [PL.] 246).

The pictorial elements in Miró's art are composed to a gr[eat] extent of pictographs or ideograms. Not only can a Miró p[ic]ture be enjoyed but it can also be read like hieroglyphics or C[hi]nese characters. His pictures are written just as much as th[ey] are painted. Sign equals idea equals form. Miró's style can [be] called a hieroglyphic style.

Miró's vocabulary consists of pictorial symbols, plas[tic] metaphors, not dream symbols. In *Catalan Landscapes*, 19[?] (New York, Mus. of Mod. Art) the central figure is a hunt[er.] He holds a knife in one hand and a dead hare in the oth[er.] The long vertical object is his gun and the spherical shape [is] the pellet that killed the animal. In the foreground is an anim[al,] probably a dog. There is humor in Miró's pictures, an impi[sh] seriousness that escapes all attempts at definition. The lette[rs] S A R D are used partly as a compositional element (cubist), b[ut] they may also suggest the word *sardana*, a Catalonian dan[ce] which indicates the mood of the picture. A tree is represent[ed] by a circular cross section to which a leaf is attached. On t[he] sea a ship flies the Catalonian flag. The sun is a heart with te[n]tacles. The eye of the painter is on the horizon line.

Miró also introduces himself by way of a sense organ in *The Tilled Field*, where the silence of the landscape is bei[ng] overheard by a big ear, growing, as it were, out of a tree trun[k] just as the watchful eyes are seeing the landscape. Also depict[ed] are a triangle (it might be a palette) and color running out [of] a tube. Thus the person of the painter comes into the pictu[re.] In the painting is an airplane with a "Klee" ladder. The ladd[er] occurs also in Miró's *Dog Barking at the Moon*, 1926 (Phil[a]delphia, Mus. of Art), where the dog's yearning is symboliz[ed] by the ladder up which (if it really existed) he would climb

the animal in the moon. In connection with Miró, Leiris (1926, 1947) speaks of "little equations" and of a "Miró-glyphic dictionary, mi-hieroglyphic." Queneau found that Miró's female figures in two pictures, *Two Personages in Love with a Woman* and *Women with Disarranged Hair Saluting the Waxing of the Moon*, are identical with the Chinese character signifying "woman." The futurist device of the line-force is used in *Person Throwing a Stone at a Bird*, 1926 (New York, Mus. of Mod. Art). Birds make their appearance in Miró's pictures through different pictographs; so do stars and women (V, PL. 135). In a painting depicting a family the mother is represented by means of surrealist sexual signs. The Duchamp moustache of the father appears as a symbol of virility.

In his later work Miró achieves great power through increased simplicity, intensified color, and abstraction (PL. 327). The literary element recedes into the background and is sublimated into poetic content. Geometric figures, vibrating electrically charged lines, sharply defined color forms, or, again, tracts of intense color with indefinite limits above and beyond which his line leads a life of its own: these are the means used by Miró for his poetic painting. There have been attempts to reckon him among the abstract painters, but he would have none of it. "As if the signs that I transcribe on a canvas, at the moment when they correspond to a concrete representation of my mind, were not profoundly real and did not belong to the world of reality." Nor was he greatly in sympathy with the rigid cubist program. He spoke of the necessity of transcribing the cubist plasticity to arrive at poetry: "I can see no difference between painting and poetry. Sometimes I illustrate my canvases with poetic phrases and vice versa. The Chinese, these lords of the spirit, did they not do this also?" Here it is in his own words: "*Phrases poétiques*, sentences that consist of words and connections of words symbolized by written signs." That is his style.

Miró has also produced objects, engravings, etchings (XI, PL. 333), and lithographs, illustrated literary works, and created ceramics (since 1942) and sculptures (since 1950). He collaborated with Ernst on the sets and and costumes for Diaghilev's ballet *Roméo et Juliette* in 1925 and designed the scenery and costumes for Massine's ballet *Jeux d'enfants* in 1932. He painted murals for the Spanish Pavilion at the Exposition Internationale in Paris in 1937, visited America in 1947 and 1951 to complete the murals for the Terrace-Plaza Hotel in Cincinnati and for Harvard University, and finished the murals for the UNESCO building in Paris in 1959.

The strong attraction exerted by the personalities clustering round the nucleus of the surrealist effort and the liberating effect of its theses can be seen in the work of artists closely connected with the movement such as Hans Bellmer and his eroticism, Stanley William Hayter, and Roberto Matta Echauren. Hayter produced typically surrealist works from 1933 to 1939 (e.g., *Chiromancy*, 1935). The works of Hayter, Masson, Picabia, and others are at the root of American action painting (e.g., Jackson Pollock).

Matta exchanged the study of modern architecture with Le Corbusier (1934/35) for the company and inspiration of the surrealists in 1937. His art, in which a jewellike crystal motif has a central role (I, PL. 146; V, PL. 134), has affiliations with Tanguy's earlier work and with that of Duchamp in the mid-1940s, but it is more abstract than Tanguy and less mechanistic than Duchamp. Animism and anthropomorphic symbolism (in his work from 1952 on) play an essential part. Like Masson, Matta is a painter of ideas: metamorphosis (*The Morphology of Desire*, 1938, Mill Valley, Calif., Gordon Onslow-Ford Coll.), anguish and trembling (*The Disasters of Mysticism*, 1942, New Canaan, Conn., James Thrall Soby Coll.), mind (*The Prisoner of Light*, 1943, New York, Edgar J. Kaufmann, Jr., Coll.), the astral world (*Illminonde*, 1943, Cincinnati, Mr. and Mrs. Thomas C. Adler Coll.; *The Vertigo of Eros*, 1944, New York, Mus. of Mod Art; *The Revolt of the Contraries*, 1944, New York, Mus. of Mod. Art; *The Revolt of the Contraries*, 1944, New York, priv. coll.), the great invisibles (*The Heart Players*, 1945, Santa Barbara, Calif., Wright Ludington Coll.), man's fate (*Being With*, 1946, property of the artist), and biological growth and germination (*Dawn*, 1952–57; *To Give Painless Light*, 1960, priv. coll.).

Jean Dubuffet's *art brut* (V, PL. 147; IX, PL. 398), Alfonso Ossorio's painting, and the work of Henri Michaux, Wols (A. O. W. Schulze; V, PL. 147; X, PL. 339), and Camille Bryen (the forerunners of tachism) are unthinkable without the surrealist and, in the case of Dubuffet, even Dadaist spirit.

Breton (1928) also claimed Wifredo Lam as a surrealist. Lam joined the movement in 1939. His painting has its roots deep in tropical voodoo magic and poetry. He revives in his painting old mystical experiences (*Malembo*, 1942, NewYork, Pierre Matisse Gall.; *The Jungle*, 1943, New York, Mus. of Mod. Art; *Idol.*, 1944; *Fear*, 1949; *The Light That Goes Up*, 1950; *Rumblings of Earth*, 1950, New York, Solomon R. Guggenheim Mus.).

The transautomatism and grammar of vision of Hundertwasser (Friedrich Stowasser) obviously have their roots in surrealism. His style is visionary, abstract (XI, PL. 372), his phraseology is surrealist (PL. 324; *Target in the Green Cloud*, 1956, Vienna, Coll. Walter Wellek; *Sun Drops*, 1956, Stockholm, Coll. Kurt and Agnes Kristiansson; *Resistance to the Stream*, 1956, Milan, Coll. Dr. Graziano Laurini; *Gas Flames Together with the Flames of the Holy Spirit*, 1957, Paris, Coll. Hèlene Kamer; *The Yellow River*, formerly called *The Beautiful Tip of the Tongue*, 1963, Paris, Coll. Mme Marteau).

Victor Brauner, who exhibited with the surrealists as early as 1933, also uses primitive myths to rediscover the soul and its innermost needs. His art is magic, not surrealist; it is an attempt to create images with the intention of conjuring up the good offices of the eternal powers to help modern man (*The Interior Life*, 1939; *The Lovers*, 1943, property of the artist; *Pantacular Progression*, 1948, New York, Mus. of Mod. Art; *The World*, 1950; *To Be Tearing out Being*, 1951; *Spread of Thought*, 1956, New York, Solomon R. Guggenheim Mus.).

Francis Bacon is a man who cannot find his way back to myth. He is without illusions and the feeling for human dignity, screaming with anxiety in his existentialist nothingness. He depicts, with a psychotically meticulous eagerness, different stages of this nihilistic hell in sequence; it is a Kafka world of refined self-torture and emptiness, of a debased mankind left without refuge even in the belief that there is hope if not for man then at least for God. Bacon's visions display in a cold process the inner trembling, the slow and perpetual dying, the terror of loneliness, of helplessness, of vacuum (PL. 324; V, PL. 145). It is a cold process because it does not arise out of the despair of the heart but out of the cruelty of the brain. It is not cold, however, in the way that Dali and Magritte are cold in their manner of execution; it is cold in conception.

Bacon depicts man in a most pitiful condition, man who, in all his grandeur (the pope!), is more miserable than the animal, because cursed with knowledge and the blackness of his own soul — deprived of the grace and the power to bring into subjection his self-destructive, self-humiliating urge (*Figure with Monkey*, 1951, London, Hanover, Gall., and Cambridge, Eng., F. J. Anscombe Coll.; *Study after Velázquez's Portrait of Pope Innocent X*, 1953, New York, Mr. and Mrs. William A. M. Burden Coll.; *Sphinx*, 1954, London, Marlborough Fine Art).

In his more recent work Bacon has been inspired by the work and fate of Van Gogh. The macabre quality that is Bacon's credo and strength penetrated even here. This is not color; it is blood and excrement; it is loneliness and death under the killing sun of the south, which is personified in the shape of the great and solitary genius of vision. The fate of the artist, the fate of man, whose presence is surrounded by might, dread, and annihilation, this is existentialist nihilism par excellence (*Study for Portrait of Van Gogh I*, 1956, London, Mr. and Mrs. R. J. Sainsbury Coll.; *II*, 1957, Netley, Hants., Mr. and Mrs. Anthony Hubbard Coll.; *III*, 1957, New York, Joseph H. Hirchhorn Coll.; *IV*, 1957, London, Tate Gall.).

Surrealism was not limited to painting and objects. Ernst (PL. 325), Miró, and Masson have produced sculptures. Arp is basically a sculptor, though not a surrealist one (PL. 325). Only in the wood reliefs (V, PL. 132; X, PL. 336), where the law of chance entered into the arrangement of the single elements and a certain exclusion of conscious creation in the formative process that produced the shapes itself, and in the basic forms of his sculptures that go back to *objets trouvés* and sometimes to erotic themes, can he be called a surrealist. His art is essentially abstract.

The sculptor Alberto Giacometti (q.v.) worked under the influence of cubism from 1925 to 1928, when he evolved a style that can be described as drawing in space. Beginning in 1930, inspired by surrealism, he produced constructions in a cage (XII, PL. 522) and also a series of constructions with movable parts. He contributed poems, articles, and drawings to surrealist periodicals. His style became extremely diversified, ranging from pure abstraction to schematic naturalism until his mature style emerged about 1945. Giacometti is also a painter, and from 1947 on he began to paint and draw intensively.

Germaine Richier's macabre work has assimilated some of Giacometti's metaphysical surrealism and form speech. Richier covers her elongated, worm-eaten or corroded, and spiderlike shapes with a texture reminiscent of bark, an allusion to the biological metamorphosis of man and tree, a theme well known in classical Greek mythology but here treated with all the decadence and morbidity typical of 20th-century man. Man ceases to be man, and, degraded into a lower order of life, becomes a vegetable.

Francis Bacon's work has influenced that of Graham Sutherland (q. v.; PL. 322; V, PL. 145) and Reg Butler. Butler moves between the animism with which he endows his machinelike constructions and the tendency to identify man with lower animal organisms such as insects. The latter idea had already attracted artists such as Odilon Redon, James Ensor (qq.v.), and Masson and writers such as Franz Kafka, but in Butler's case, as well as that of César (Baldiccini), primitive magic conceptions are translated into the realm of mechanized civilization, thus giving expression to the paralyzing effect of the machine age. Jacques Delahaye (PL. 326), Lynn Chadwick (PL. 325), John Hoskin, and others are working along the same lines as Richier and Butler.

Although artists are still creating works in the surrealist idiom, there is no possibility of a renaissance of the doctrinaire Freudian attitude. The recent developments in art have shown that it is in step with Jung's statement ("Der Gegensatz Freud und Jung," in *Seelenprobleme der Gegenwart*, Zurich, 1931): "We moderns are bound to revive the spirit, that is, to make elemental experiences. This is the only possibility of breaking through the magic circle of biological happenings."

BIBLIOG. F. Picabia, Poèmes et dessins de la fille née sans mère, Lausanne, 1918; F. Picabia, Rateliers platoniques, Lausanne, 1918; T. Tzara, Manifesto Dada, 1918 (repr. in Motherwell, 1951, q.v.); F. Picabia, Pensées sans language, Paris, 1919; F. Picabia, Poésies Ron-Ron, Lausanne, 1919; F. Picabia, Jésus Christ Rastaquouère, Paris, 1920; F. Picabia, Unique Eunuque (pref. by T. Tzara), Paris, 1920; R. Hülsenbeck, En avant Dada: Eine Geschichte des Dadaismus, Hannover, 1920 (repr. in Motherwell, 1951, q.v.); A. Breton, Francis Picabia (pref. to Cat. Dalman), Paris, 1922; M. Ernst, Les malheurs des immortels, Paris, 1922 (trans. G. Chisholm, Misfortunes of the Immortals, New York, 1943); H. Prinzhorn, Bildnerei des Geisteskranken, Ein Beitrag zur Psychologie der Gestaltung, Berlin, 1922; A. Breton, Les pas perdus, Paris, 1924; M. Ernst, Histoire naturelle (introd. by H. Arp), Paris, 1926; F. Lehel, Notre art dément, Paris, 1926; M. Leiris, Joan Miró, Little Review, Spring-Summer, 1926; A. Soergel, Dichtung und Dichter der Zeit, Eine Schilderung der deutschen Literatur der letzten Jahrzehnte, Neue Folge, im Banne des Expressionismus, Leipzig, 1926; J. Frois Witman, Preliminary Psychoanalytical Considerations of Modern Art, Arch. of Psychoanalysis, I, pt. 4, 1927, pp. 891–941; A. Breton, Le surréalisme et la peinture, Paris, 1928 (2d ed., New York, 1945); M. Ernst, La femme 100 têtes, Paris, 1929; L. Aragon, La peinture au défi, Paris, 1930 (pref, to cat. of exhibition at Gal. Goemans); S. Dali, La femme visible, Paris, 1930; M. Ernst Rêve d'une petite fille qui voulu entrer au Carmel, Paris, 1930; S. Dali, L'Amour et la mémoire, Paris, 1931; K. Jaspers, Die geistige Situation der Zeit, Berlin, Leipzig, 1931; G. Ribemont-Dessaignes, Histoire de Dada, Paris, 1931; S. Dali, Babaouo, précédé d'un abrégé d'une histoire critique du cinema et suivi de Guillaume Tell, Paris, 1932; G. Hugnet, L'Esprit Dada dans la peinture, CahArt, VII, 1932, 1–2, pp. 57–65, 6–7, pp. 281–85, 8–10, pp. 358–64, IX, 1934, 1–4, pp. 109–14 (English trans. in Barr. Fantastic Art, 1936, q.v.); A. Masson, Massacre, Paris, 1932; A. Breton, Qu'est-ce que le Surréalisme?, Brussels, 1934; M. Duchamp, La mariée mise à nu par ses célibataires, même, Paris, 1934; M. Ernst, Une semaine de bonté ou les sept éléments capitaux, Paris, 1934; Man Ray, Photographies, 1920–1934, Hartford, Conn., 1934; A. Masson, Sacrifices, Paris, 1934; S. Dali, Conquest of the Irrational, New York, 1935; A. H. Barr, Jr., Cubism and Abstract Art, New York, 1936; A. H. Barr, Jr., Fantastic Art, Dada, Surrealism, New York, 1936; G. Duthuit, Ou allez-vous Miró?, CahArt, no. 8–10, 1936, pp. 261–64; J. Levy, Surrealism, New York, 1936; S. Dali, Metamorphosis of Narcissus, New York, 1937; M. Ernst, Œuvre de 1919 à 1936, Ed. CahArt, Paris, 1937; Man Ray, La photographie n'est pas l'art (introd. by A. Breton), Paris, 1937; A. Masson, Métamorphose, Paris, 1937; A. Breton and P. Eluard, Dictionnaire abrégé du surréalisme, Paris, 1938; J. Cazaux, Surréalisme et psychologie, Paris, 1938; A. Masson, Mythologies, Paris, 1938; B. Champigneulle, L'Inquiétude dans l'art d'aujourd'hui, Paris, 1939; R. Huyghe, La peinture française. Les contemporains, Paris, 1939; G. Lemaitre, From Cubism to Surrealism in French Literature, Cambridge, Mass., 1941 (rev. ed., 1947); J. T. Soby, Salvador Dali, New York, 1941; J. J. Sweeney, Joan Miró, New York, 1941; M. Duchamp, Boîte-en-valise, contenant la reproduction des 69 principales œuvres de Marcel Duchamp, New York, 1942; P. Guggenheim, Art of This Century, New York, 1942; A. Masson, Anatomy of My Universe, New York, 1943; S. Dali, Hidden Faces, New York, 1944; A. Masson, Nocturnal Notebook, New York, 1944; H. Michaux, L'Espace de dedans, Paris, 1944 (Selected Writings, The Space within, London, 1952); J. Aiken, Psychological Aspects of Surrealism, J. for Clinical Psychopathology and Psychotherapy, 7, 1945, pp. 32–42; A. Breton, Anthologie de l'humour noir, Paris, 1945; C. Bryen, Les cloîtres du vent, Paris, 1945; A. Césaire, Wifredo Lam, CahArt, 1945–46, pp. 357–61; R. Gaffé, Paul Delvaux ou les rêves eveillés, Brussels, 1945; M. Nadeau, Histoire du surréalisme, Paris, 1945 (trans. R. Howard, New York, 1965); Wols, First Exhibition, Paris, 1945 (Cat. Drouin); A. Masson, Bestiaire, New York, Paris, 1946; J. J. Sweeney, Eleven Europeans in America, New York, 1946; M. Tapié, Mirobolus, Macadam et Cie., Hautes pâtes de J. Dubuffet, Paris, 1946; R. Guilly, Wols, Paris, 1947; A. Breton and M. Duchamp, eds., Le surréalisme en 1947, Paris, 1947; Interview with Miró, in Possibilities, Problems of Contemporary Art, New York, 1947; L. Krestovskaia, La laideur dans l'art à travers les âges, Paris, 1947; M. Leiris, The Prints of Joan Miró (Cat. Valentin), New York, 1947; M. Leiris and G. Limbour, André Masson and His Universe, Geneva, 1947; G. Limbour, Joan Miró, Souvenirs sur un peintre, Arts de France, no. 17–18, 1947, p. 47; A. Masson, Designs for Hamlet (Cat. Arts Council), London, 1947; S. Alexandrian, Victor Brauner ou la Clé des Mythes, Progression Mythologique de Victor Brauner, Paris, 1948; H. Arp, On My Way, Poetry and Essays, 1912–1947, New York, 1948; A. H. Barr, Jr., Painting and Sculpture in the Museum of Modern Art, New York, 1948; S. Dali, 50 Secrets of Magic Craftsmanship, New York, 1948; S. Dali, The Secret Life of Salvador Dali, London, 1948 (new enlarged ed., New York, 1961); Paul Delvaux (Cat. Drouin), Paris, 1948; M. Ernst, Beyond Painting and Other Writings by the Artist and His Friends, New York, 1948; C. Greenberg, Joan Miró New York, 1948; H. Michaux (Cat. Drouin), Paris, 1948; J. Ortega y Gasset The Dehumanization of Art, and Notes on the Novel, Princeton, 1948; R Queneau, Joan Miró ou le poète prehistorique, Geneva, 1948; L. Scutenaire René Magritte, Antwerp, 1948; C. Spaak, Paul Delvaux, Antwerp, 1948 C. Bryen (Cat. Gal. des deux îles), Paris, 1949; J. Dubuffet, L'Art bru préféré aux arts culturels (Cat. Drouin), Paris, 1949; C. E. Gauss, The Aesthetic Theories, of French Artists, Baltimore, 1949; J. J. Sweeney, Modern Art and Tradition, Three Lectures on Modern Art, New York, 1949; Hans Bellmer, 25 reproductions, 1934–1950, Paris, 1950; J. Bousquet and M Tapié, Max Ernst, Cat. of exhibition at Gal. Drouin, Paris, 1950; L. Kirstein Symbolic Realism in American Painting (cat.), London, 1950; Psychopathological Art, International Congress of Psychiatry, Paris, 1950; M. Raymond From Baudelaire to Surrealism (Documents in Modern Art, A Series), New York, 1950; F. Reitman, Psychotic Art, A Study of the Art Products of the Mentally Ill, London, 1950; S. Dali (Cat. Lefèvre), London, 1951; M. Ernst Gemälde und Graphik, 1920–1950, Brühl, 1951; D. A. Gordon, Experimental Psychology and Modern Painting, J. of Aesthetics and Art Criticism IX, no. 3, Mar. 1951, pp. 227–43; H. and S. Janis, Marcel Duchamp, Anti Artist, in Motherwell, 1951, q.v.; Wifredo Lam (Cat. Inst. of Contemporar Arts), London, 1951; M. Leiris, Pierres pour un Alberto Giacometti, i Derrière le miroir (Cat. Maeght), Paris, 1951; R. Motherwell, The Dad Painters and Poets, an Anthology, New York, 1951; J. Audiberti, C. Bryer L'ouvre-boîte, Colloque abhumaniste, 2d ed., Paris, 1952; K. Bauch Abendländische Kunst, Düsseldorf, 1952; Dessins par Wifredo Lam, Cah Art, 2, 1952, pp. 202–04; E. Fromm, The Forgotten Language, An Introduc tion to the Understanding of Dreams, Fairy Tales and Myths, London, 195 R. Gaffé, Peinture à travers Dada et le surréalisme, Brussels, 1952; A. (Ritchie, Sculpture of the Twentieth Century, New York, 1952; P. A. Soroki Social Philosophies of An Age of Crisis, London, 1952; Max Ernst, Ca Knokke-Le-Zoute, Brussels, 1953; D. H. Kahnweiler, André Masson (Ca Valentin), New York, 1953; G. Limbour, Tableau bon lavain à vous de cui la pâte, l'art brut de Jean Dubuffet, Paris, 1953; S. Alexandrian, Victor Brau ner l'illuminateur, Paris, 1954; Cat. of the XXVII International Bienna of Art, Venice, 1954; S. Dali (cat.), Rome, 1954; S. Dali, Io, Salvador Da Rome, 1954; F. Elgar, Miró, in Dictionnaire de la peinture moderne, Pari 1954 (Bib. Aldine des Arts, 30); Le Fantastique dans l'Art Belge, De Bosc à Magritte, Les Arts Plastiques, Brussels (special no.), 1954; J. A. Hadfiel Dreams and Nightmares, London, 1954; A. Huxley, The Doors of Perceptio London, 1954; J. P. Hodin, Les phases freudiennes et jungiennes du su réalisme, in La Biennale et l'avenir du surréalisme, Les Arts Plastique Brussels (special no.), 1954; J.-P. Sartre, Les Peintures de Giacometti, Derrière le miroir (Cat. Maeght), Paris, 1954; F. Alquie, Philosophie du Su réalisme, Paris, 1955; A. Breton, Premier manifeste du surréalisme, Poiss Soluble (1924), in A. Breton, Les manifestes du surréalisme, Paris, 195 M. Brion, Léonor Fini, Paris, 1955; R. Butler (Cat. Valentin with pr by R. Penrose), New York, 1955; M. Clarac-Sérou, Francis Bacon (Ca Inst. of Contemporary Arts), London, 1955; A. Giacometti (Cat. A Council), London, 1955; C. Giedion-Welcker, Contemporary Sculptur An Evolution in Volume and Space, London, 1955 (rev. and enlarg ed., 1961); G. Richier (Cat. Hanover), London, 1955; A. C. Ritch The New Decade, Twenty-two European Painters and Sculptors, N York, 1955; Pierre Roy (Cat. Jeffress), London, 1955; J. T. Soby, Y Tanguy, New York, 1955; C. Bryen, Jepeinsje, Révolution de l'infigu no. 51, Autumn 1956, pp. 20–22; S. Dali, Les cocus du vieil art moder Paris, 1956; E. Glissant, Matta, Terres nouvelles (Cat. Dragon), Paris, 195 J. P. Hodin, The Cultural Psychology of Sigmund Freud, in The Dilem of Being Modern, London, 1956; J. P. Hodin, A Madonna Motif in the Wo

Munch and Dali, in The Dilemma of Being Modern, London, 1956; A. Masson, Métamorphose de l'Artiste, Geneva, 1956; H. Michaux, Parcours, 1939 à 1956 (Cat. Drouin), Paris, 1956; Paintings by Max Ernst (Cat. Matthiesen), London, 1956; L. Pauwels, Salvador Dali, Aujourd'hui-même (pref. to Cat. Knokke-Le-Zoute), Brussels, 1956; J. Prévert and G. Ribemont-Dessaignes, Joan Miró, Paris, 1956; G. Richier (Cat. Mus. Nat. d'Art Mod.), Paris, 1956; Francis Bacon (Cat. Hanover, London, 1957; R. Bertelé, Henri Michaux (Poètes d'aujourd'hui, 5), Paris, 1957; G. Buffet-Picabia, Francis Picabia (1879–1953), in Aires abstraites (pref. by J. Arp), Geneva, 1957; J. Dubuffet, Tableaux d'assemblages (Cat. Rive Droite, prepared by L. Limbour), Paris, 1957; J. Genêt, L'Atelier d'Alberto Giacometti, in Derrière le miroir (Cat. Maeght), Paris, 1957; S. W. Hayter, Exhibition of Paintings, Drawings, and Engravings, from 1927 to 1957 (Cat. Whitechapel, with pref. by B. Robertson), London, 1957; J. P. Hodin, Francis Bacon, Artistes Anglais et étrangers, Quadrum, 4, 1957, p. 178; J. P. Hodin, Ben Nicholson, The Meaning of His Art, London, 1957; G. Hugnet, L'aventure Dada, 1916–1922 (introd. by T. Tzara), Paris, 1957; Hundertwasser, Meine Augen bind müde (Cat. Gal. St. Stephan), Vienna 1957; A. Masson, Peintures récentes et ancienne (Cat. Leiris), Paris, 1957; H. Michaux, L'infini turbulent, Paris, 1957; Miró, The Graphic Work, Das graphische Werk, L'œuvre graphique, Museum Hans Lange, Krefeld, Haus am Walsee, Berlin, Städtische Galerie, Munich, Kölnischer Künstlerverein, Cologne, Kestner-gesellschaft, Hannover, Kunsthalle, Hamburg (cat.), 1957; P. Restany, Hundertwasser, Paris, 1957; W. Rubin, Matta, B. of Mus. of Mod. Art, XV, 1, 1957; W. Verkauf, Dada, Monograph of a Movement, New York, 1957; Jacques Villon, Raymond Duchamp-Villon, Marcel Duchamp (Cat. Guggenheim, with pref. by J. J. Sweeney), New York, 1957; Max Ernst (Cat. Creuzevault), Paris, 1958; C. Giedion-Welcker, Jean Arp, London, 1958; M. Tapié, Dali, New York, 1958; P. Waldberg, Max Ernst, Paris, 1958; J. Breton and J. L. Bédouin, Storia del surrealismo, 2 vols., Milan, 1960; F. Cowles, The Case of Salvador Dali, London, 1959; Exposition internationale du surréalisme, Paris, 1959–1960, Gal. Cordier, Paris, 1959; G. R. Hocke, Die Welt als Labyrinth, Manier und Manie in der Europäischen Kunst, Hamburg, 1959; M. Jean, History of Surrealist Painting, New York, 1960; P. Waldberg, Le surréalisme et ses affinités à Paris, Quadrum, 8, Brussels, 1960; J. L. Bédouin, Vingt ans de surréalisme, 1939–1959, Paris, 1961; A. Breton, Les manifestes du surréalisme (new ed.), Paris, 1962; R. Descharnes, The World of Salvador Dali, New York, 1962; Y. Duplessis, Surrealism, New York, 1962; M. Josephson, Life among the Surrealists, a Memoir, New York, 1962; R. Alley, Francis Bacon (introd. by J. Rothenstein), New York, 1964; S. Dali, Journal d'un génie, Paris, 1964; R. Hülsenbeck, Dada, eine literarische Dokumentation, Hamburg, 1964; S. Dali, 1910–1965 (cat.), Gall. of Mod. Art, New York, 1965; H. Richter, Dada, Art and Anti-art, New York, 1965; P. Waldberg, Surrealism, New York, 1965.

Josef P. Hodin

Illustrations: PLS. 317–328.

SUTHERLAND, Graham.

SUTHERLAND, Graham. Modern English painter (b. London, Aug. 24, 1903). At the age of sixteen he became an apprentice in engineering at Derby but left after one year to study painting in London. Enrolled at the Goldsmiths' College School of Art (1921–26), he became skilled in engraving and later taught this subject at the Chelsea School of Art. By the early 1930s he had established a reputation in London for his prints depicting rustic scenes in the manner of Samuel Palmer. With the depression, sales fell off and Sutherland turned successfully to designing for posters and fabrics, while continuing to teach. His primary interest in painting the English landscape sent him on sketching tours to Kent, Sussex, Dorset, and later Wales. The bold and romantic character of the Welsh countryside impressed him profoundly and played a part in the change from his early style. By the middle of the decade he had rejected scenic charm to concentrate on features of form and color that better expressed his emerging personal vision. His color in these years was rich, dark, and glowing. His drawing and composition, although based on nature, emphasized strong patterns and semiabstract design. In 1936 he participated in the International Surrealist Exhibition in London and saw for the first time the strange forms of Jean Miró, Salvador Dali, and Max Ernst (qq.v.). A few years later Pablo Picasso's (q.v.) Guernica sketches left their mark on his imagery. But with or without these surrealist influences, Sutherland's own vision was turning instinctively toward the strange and mysterious aspects of nature, particularly toward configurations of plants, trees, or rocks that suggested human anatomy, often as ghostlike apparitions. At the same time his landscapes had recognizable aspects of the visual world, so that the elements of fantasy and strangeness are tempered by the familiarity of everyday English environment.

Sutherland's appointment as a war artist (1939–44) produced some of the most vivid and artistically significant works to come out of wartime England: sketches of bombed dwellings, burned-out office buildings, wrecked locomotives, and the like. In 1944, invited to paint an Agony in the Garden in the Church of St. Matthew, Northampton, he hesitated, then obtained permission to substitute a Crucifixion, but did not finish it until nearly three years later. This large painting may be said to summarize Sutherland's wartime experiences and to express his own religious feelings as a convert to Catholicism. Inspired by Grünewald's tragic Christ of the Isenheim Altar (VII, PLS. 86, 88), Sutherland discovered a personal idiom for this theme in thorn trees (PL. 322), which were transformed in his vision to the crown of thorns, symbol of suffering and salvation. A few other religious paintings followed, as well as the huge tapestry, Christ in Glory in the Tetramorph (begun 1952), for the new Cathedral of Coventry.

In the late 1940s Sutherland's painting began to develop the maturity and consistent high quality of his later years. The landscape space became shallower, allowing greater concentration on objects. The tonality of his color became lighter and less moody, although, as always, richly decorative. At times one detects similarities to the painting of his friend Francis Bacon. After Sutherland's move to France (frequent sojourns in Menton since 1947), his increasing contact with the works of the great French contemporaries Picasso, Matisse, Braque, Miró, and Bonnard no doubt contributed to the enrichment and strengthening of his later painting, as did the landscape of the Riviera, particularly for its bright light and the harsh forms and colors it gives to the rocky hills, red soil, and blue sea. Sutherland's brooding vision was aroused, too, by the exotic flora of the south: palms, artichokes, banana leaves, which, like the boulders and gnarled oaks of England, he transformed into fantasies. To this enlarged repertory of flora were later added a number of images from the world of animals—toads, snakes, bats, monkeys—which, as interpreted by Sutherland, have the same mysterious, foreboding quality as his plant forms (V, PL. 145).

A somewhat different but equally important phase of his work is the series of portraits begun with that of Somerset Maugham in 1949 and including such distinguished sitters as Lord Beaverbrook and Winston Churchill. Decidedly not in the official academic tradition, they are nonetheless realistic representations, but informal in pose and often uniquely revealing of the individual character. In effect Sutherland observes his sitter with the same penetrating attention to detail that marks his approach to nature, although fantasy is ruled out.

Sutherland's intense personal vision, his ambivalent metaphors, his capacity to evoke an inner feeling of "presence," together with an original and significant use of form and color have given him a prominent place in modern art. In the judgment of many, he is the foremost English painter of the 20th century.

BIBLIOG. D. Cooper, The Work of Graham Sutherland, 2d ed. London, 1962 (with critical biography, list of works, annotated bibliography; abundantly illustrated, incl. several plates in color); A. Revai, The Coventry Tapestry, London, 1962.

Henry R. Hope

SWEDEN.

SWEDEN. Sweden consists of the southern and eastern parts of the Scandinavian peninsula, the islands of Gotland and Öland, and some smaller islands of the Baltic Sea. The name Sweden first appears in the 8th-century Anglo-Saxon poem Beowulf under the form Swiorice, or realm of the Svear. From prehistoric to early Christian times the artistic phenomena that developed in this territory were retarded and isolated in comparison with those of the rest of the European continent, although they did not lack originality (e.g., naturalistic and schematic rock engravings, figures and scenes on stones and goldwork of the Viking era, wooden churches). With the spread of Christianity, and especially in modern times, Sweden became increasingly involved in the development of European artistic culture and styles, and has achieved autonomous avant-garde artistic expression in the modern world.

SUMMARY. Protohistory (col. 739). Barbarian and early Christian art (col. 739). Romanesque and Gothic art (col. 740). The 16th and 17th centuries (col. 742). The 18th and 19th centuries (col. 746). The modern period (col. 751). Monumental centers (col. 753): *Stockholm; Dalarna; Uppland; Västmanland; Närke; Södermanland; Vastergotland; Östergötland; Gotland; Småland; Öland; Skåne (Scania).*

PROTOHISTORY. The earliest examples of Swedish art date from the late Stone Age and the Bronze Age. They include pottery, weapons, and decorative and ritual objects of fine craftsmanship. The many rock engravings dating from this period, too, show a lively artistic imagination in their use of forms, which include human beings, animals, ships, and magical signs (V, PLS. 180, 181). The early engravings are naturalistic pictures of animals, often life-size, while the later ones are more or less stylized. There is strong evidence that the northern rock engravings (in Norrland) are connected with hunting magic, whereas the southern ones (chiefly in Bohuslän) are intended to evoke fecundity.

Sweden, principal historical and artistic centers. Key: (1) National boundaries; (2) medieval monuments; (3) modern monuments; (4) 12th-century abbeys; (5) castles.

BARBARIAN AND EARLY CHRISTIAN ART. At the beginning of the age of the great migrations (5th cent.) and throughout the Vendel era (550–800) and the Viking era, a great variety of artistic production bears witness to a highly developed and integrated civilization, where the ruling class loved display and where traditions of craftsmanship were well established (V, PLS. 63–68, 70–73, 85, 89, 93–95; X, PL. 438; XII, PL. 411). As might be expected, the finest and most elaborate items are the weapons. Such discoveries as those in Uppland (notably the rich grave finds in the parish of Vendel), in Östergötland, and on the island of Gotland have revealed a decorative art that, within the framework of primitive Germanic zoomorphic ornament, is among the finest in Europe from that period (see EUROPE, BARBARIAN; SCANDINAVIAN ART; ZOOMORPHIC AND PLANT REPRESENTATIONS). Through Sweden's widely ramified trade channels this art was stimulated by many foreign civilizations, but the influences were assimilated and converted into an indigenous national style.

On the island of Gotland a special kind of sculpture began to develop in the 6th century. It consisted in low reliefs executed on prepared limestone surfaces and subsequently painted (V, PLS. 81, 90). These so-called "picture stones" (*bildstenar*) were erected to commemorate and honor a friend or kinsman. They were embellished with ornamental motifs or figures, or both; the figural scenes usually depicted warriors, horsemen, and ships with dramatic simplicity, their subjects often being taken from the ancient Norse sagas. This art form had three periods of flowering: in the 6th century, about 700, and about 1000. During the last period the figural scenes were increasingly replaced by zoomorphic ornament and runic characters that formed decorative interlacings. This distinctive style, the so-called "runestone" style, from then on dominated the decoration of domestic utensils, metalwork, and weapons, as well as memorial stones and sarcophagi, and finally even the wood carvings of the stave churches (XI, PL. 328; XII, PL. 414; XIV, PL. 463). It is characterized by widespread formalism and by stylized animal forms interlacing to produce an impression of supple vitality. Its centers were mainly in Gotland and the eastern provinces to the north and south of Lake Mälaren, but itinerant artists also introduced it in other parts of the country.

Christianity was late in gaining a footing in Sweden (11th cent.); Gamla (Old) Uppsala, the last stronghold of paganism, was not conquered until about 1130. Along with the new religion, new forms entered the arts, although tenaciously opposed by the traditional ornamentation. Little remains of the first churches, built of wood, the so-called "stave churches" such as St. Mary Minor in Lund and the churches in Hemse and Eke (Gotland), dating from the 12th century. The only example that has survived intact is the 13th-century church at Hedared. These stave churches were built of forked, interlocking logs, usually of oak (see X, col. 721). They were constructed on a rectangular plan, with corner posts and intermediate supports — a plan probably modeled to some extent on pagan temples. Gamla Uppsala's pagan temple, for example, appears to have consisted of a square hall with aisles on all four sides and with corner pillars and intermediate supports. According to Adam of Bremen (11th cent.) the interior was adorned with gold and contained three statues of the Old Norse gods Odin, Thor, and Frey.

ROMANESQUE AND GOTHIC ART. The pagan forms survived for a long time, but during the 12th century they were strongly modified under the influence of Romanesque art (q.v.). A mixture of forms resulted, especially in sculptural decoration.

In about 1000 the town of Sigtuna became a center of Christianity, and several large churches were built there. The ruins of three of these churches — St. Per, St. Olaf, and St. Lars — still exist St. Per, with its apse, transepts, central tower, and reduced west end, is typical of European Romanesque church architecture at its height. The central tower also dominates St. Olaf, but the forms here have a distinctly local character. The ancient Cathedral of Gamla Uppsala, which probably was erected on the site of the old pagan temple, incorporates elements borrowed from both St. Per and St. Olaf. These churches derived from Romanesque models, but with markedly individual characteristics, are the precursors of Romanesque architecture in central Sweden. Church architecture in western Sweden reveals Anglo-Saxon or Norman influence in the 11th century but finally tended more toward German ecclesiastical architecture.

During the 12th century, with the building of its large Cathedral, Lund became a center of the arts, and influences from there spread all over southern Sweden and Gotland. The Cathedral is a large basilica with two west towers; there is a large crypt extending under the transept, choir, and apse. During the earlier period of construction until about 1130 (while Donatus was directing the work), the ornamentation was dominated by Como-Lombard influences, but subsequently (under Regnerus's direction) archaic and sometimes Byzantine stylistic features were increasingly used.

On the island of Gotland, which the Goths had long ago made an important center of trade, there was a rich and original flowering of religious art in the 12th and 13th centuries. Sculpture from here was to a large extent exported to countries around the Baltic Sea. Several wood sculptures revealing German influence have been preserved. The finest examples of Gotland sculpture are the Viklau Virgin (Stockholm, Statens Historiska Mus.) and the crucifixes of the churches in Väte and Hemse (1170–90). The old zoomorphic ornament lived on in Gotland and sometimes combined with Romanesque forms, as for instance in Master Hegvald's richly expressive art (fonts from Vänge, Etelhem, Stanga, Hälla). Besides Hegvald there were many highly original artists, several of whom had no doubt worked on the Cathedral of Lund, for example, Master Byzantios, whose style bespeaks Lombard influence, and the so-called "Magister Majestatis," whose work is vigorous and severely ordered (XII, PL. 267). The Gotland churches of the 12th century are characterized by their richly sculptured façades and are in general highly ornamented.

When the Cistercians came to Sweden in the 12th century they introduced new artistic ideas. With their first abbey, Alvastra (in Östergötland), founded in 1140 and completed in 1185, they launched their Burgundian architectural style, which involved a new vault construction with groins and pointed arches. The nearest model for Alvastra Abbey was the Abbey church of Fontenay (PL. 223). Similar Cistercian abbeys are Nydala (Småland) and Roma (Gotland). In about 1150 monks from Alvastra founded Varnhem Abbey, for whose church the closest model was the reconstructed Abbey church at Clairvaux, although the Gothic style was not consistently carried through.

Swedish church architecture of the Gothic period (see GOTHIC ART) shows a rather strong national stamp, especially in the small village churches. A marked preference for heavy, compact walls with few ornamental details persisted. Throughout Scandinavia the elements of Gothic architecture were adopted in the same manner as in northern Germany. The smooth wall was retained and buttresses were used, but there were no flying buttresses. In Sweden, particularly in Gotland, the usual 13th-century church plan comprised a straight-ended choir of the hall-church type, a long nave, and a west tower. Brick was the standard building material, especially in central and southern Sweden. Among the large churches built at this time are the Church of St. Mary in Sigtuna and the cathedrals of Strängnäs and Uppsala, the last of which reveals a return to the basilica type. Many foreign influences are apparent in the churches of this period. In northern Götaland (Östergötland and Gotland) an architecture developed that was inspired by the late Romanesque architecture of Westphalia and Saxony. French influence was not confined to the Cistercians' Burgundian style: the Gothic cathedrals of northern France also served as architectural examples. The typically Gothic style of the Cathedral of Uppsala was modeled on Notre-Dame in Paris (VI, PL. 293). In some respects the Cathedral of Skara is also reminiscent of French Gothic, while the Church of St. Petri in Malmö is similar to St. Mary's Church in Lübeck, which shows French influence. In a few cases English Gothic influences are also apparent. Between approximately 1280 and 1310 the Franciscans built their church, the Riddarholmskyrka, in Stockholm, which has a lofty and spacious interior, representative of the simpler and more severe architecture favored by the Franciscans and Dominicans. Vadstena Abbey church (beginning of the 15th cent.) is the prototype of the Brigittine Order's church building; its hall-like interior has a dignified simplicity. In the 15th century countless Swedish churches were rebuilt, many of them being given large west towers, wide choirs, and simple, unified interiors.

Nothing remains of the earliest secular architecture, which was wood. The medieval castles were of two main types. The first was a round or square tower of stone, its approaches probably protected by wooden fortifications or by moats. Trade centers sprang up in the shelter of such castles (Stockholm, Visby). The original Stockholm castle was a round tower called Tre Kronor (Three Crowns), built in the late 12th century. (Even after several additions had been made, the tower continued to form the core of the castle until the end of the 17th century.) Similar round towers constituted the original nucleus of other castles, such as those at Borgholm, Kalmar, and Hälsingborg. They were meant only for defense and seldom served as residences. The second type of castle, from which originated the residential castles of the later Middle Ages, consisted of several wings, built of stone or wood, or both, sometimes surmounted by a defensive tower and surrounded by a ringwall (Näs on Visingsö, Kalmar). In about 1250 the Tre Kronor tower in Stockholm was surrounded by a residential castle with royal apartments, a great hall, a chapel, and other court premises, and on the north side a defensive castle was built with a surrounding wall and fortified towers at the four corners. Subsequently similar fortifications were built at several strategic places. At the end of the 13th century similar castles were built at Kalmar (a well-preserved example), Örebro, Nyköping, Bjärka-Säby, Åhus, and Malmöhus. Of the extensive ramparts that surrounded several towns in the Middle Ages only one is preserved, that of Visby (Gotland), which was completed in about 1300 and is one of the longest still to be seen in Europe. Gotland is also noteworthy for its palacelike stone houses built by rich merchants (Hästnäs, Lauks, Bringes).

Swedish sculpture of the Gothic period was influenced by the Cistercians' French tendencies and, during the best period, by the Chartres and Reims schools (e.g., the Öja Master). The French style reached Sweden in much of the late Gothic sculpture arriving from England and Germany. The most important center of late Gothic sculpture was the workshop of Uppsala Cathedral. During the 13th and 14th centuries a number of original artists were also at work on Gotland. These included the Tingstäde Master, the Hejnum Master, the Bunge Master, and the mid-14th-century master known as "Egypticus," whose sculpture is distinguished by its severity and dignity. In about 1400 this style was replaced by the cosmopolitan Court style with its lyrical complacency and lack of vigor. It reached Sweden through Lübeck, whose sculptors at this time provided sculptures and altarpieces for churches all over Scandinavia. During the 15th century there was a reversal of taste, resulting in a realistic art of individual character, full of vigor and expressiveness. This art was still influenced by the Lübeck school: the finest piece, by Bernt Notke (a Lübeck artist active in Stockholm 1484-96), is a large wood sculpture of St. George and the dragon (VI, PL. 133), offered in 1489 as an ex-voto in Stockholm's Storkyrkau ("great church"), St. Nikolai. An artist prominent as both sculptor and architect was Adam van Düren, from Westphalia, who came to Sweden in about 1480 to work on the choir of the Cathedral of Linköping. He did some of the finest figure carving in late medieval Scandinavian art, for instance on Archbishop Birger Gunnarsson's tomb in Lund Cathedral and on the remarkable wellhead in the crypt of that Cathedral. During his 45 years of activity in Scandinavia he designed, among other buildings, the Glimmingehus (1499-1507), a castle that in its monumental compactness retains the character of the medieval stone house. Toward the end of the 15th century new concepts began to dominate Swedish art, as Flemish art became increasingly important.

Medieval Swedish mural painting developed in permanent contact with the stylistic currents dominating the Continent, yet this did not prevent national characteristics and individual styles from flourishing. Mural painting is in fact the only artistic field in which a sustained, independent national evolution can be observed. Romanesque mural painting is particularly well represented in Skåne, Östergötland, and Gotland. Many of the Gothic mural paintings of the early and middle periods have been lost (they adorned wooden roofs, which, during the 15th century, were generally replaced by brick vaulting), but late Gothic murals have survived all over the country, and especially in the province of Uppland. Walls and vaults were covered with lively groups of figures and intertwining leaves. During the 15th century the ornamental pampres and interlacing leaves grew increasingly important, giving churches the appearance of brilliant bowers. A lively epic talent, a keen eye for reality, and strong characterization distinguish the highly expressive paintings of Albertus, executed in the last third of the 15th century in the area around Lake Mälaren (for example, in the churches of Härkeberga and Härnevi). Albertus was the first great painter of scenes of Swedish life, and his work was much imitated.

THE 16TH AND 17TH CENTURIES. In 1527, during the reign of Gustaf Vasa (1496-1560), the Reformation reached Sweden. This period was characterized by domestic consolidation, centralization, and concentration of royal power. It was no longer the Church but the court that commissioned works of art, and in some cultural fields there was a striking break with earlier traditions. Gothic art was regarded as Catholic and Renaissance art as Protestant. The Gothic style lived on for a considerable time in religious art. The foremost Swedish reformers were not iconoclasts, and initially the Renaissance style was confined to such church fittings as pulpits and pews, and to funerary monuments.

The most important monuments of the 16th century were the large royal castles which were built in different parts of the country to accommodate the court on its frequent travels and which were heavily fortified because of the political unrest of the period. These defense considerations dominated Swedish palace building until the beginning of the 17th century, when royal building activity diminished for some time and the nobility became the principal builders of residences. Gustaf Vasa's first large edifice was Gripsholm Castle, the plan of which was a compact, irregular hexagon with four massive round towers at the corners. Gustaf Vasa's elder son, Erik XIV, who had a keen esthetic sense, decorated the castles magnificently, and the second son, John III, who was passionately interested in building, completed their construction.

The most important royal castles still extant (in their original form or rebuilt) are those of Vadstena, Uppsala, Stockholm, Västerås, Kalmar, Svartsjö, Örbyhus, and Kronoberg. These castles are generally characterized by an irregular layout and compact, massive construction. Their decoration is sober but shows fine stonecutting in the details. Their style is based on practical considerations and has a marked Swedish quality. The Renaissance style was introduced into Sweden (from about 1540) mainly from Germany and the Netherlands, initially by foreign craftsmen brought in for the purpose. The finest of these was Guillaume Boyens (Willem Boy; ca. 1520-92), who worked both as an architect and as a sculptor. He represented the Flemish Renaissance style, and among other activities he participated in the rebuilding of the castles of Stockholm and Svartsjö. Under John III he designed a number of churches in Stockholm, including the finest religious monument of that period, the Church of St. Jakob (1588-93), a square hall church with columns, nine stellar vaults, and a narrower choir.

By the end of the 15th century Stockholm had become a vital center of the arts, and its artistic production, which was mainly of a popular nature, was to a large extent exported to the provinces. Toward the middle of the 16th century an official court art developed in Sweden. Its chief exponents were foreign artists, who were principally portraitists (Jakob Binck, Dominicus Verwilt, Johan Baptista van Uther) and mural painters (for example, Arent Lambrechts). During the Vasa period figural painting was used especially to decorate buildings. The chief works are lost, but among those preserved is a series of fresco paintings by Arent Lambrechts in the "Gray Hall" of Kalmar Castle that constitutes a typical example of the mannerism of the Netherlands. Decorative painting still retained a certain medieval character, for example in the common interlacing motifs of flowers and fruit. Gustaf Vasa insisted that the foreigners should also teach young Swedish artists. One of the principal teachers was Johan Baptista van Uther, who helped found a national tradition of portraiture.

During the first half of the 16th century sculpture was in abeyance. A new evolution was initiated only after 1550, when Gustaf Vasa and his sons commissioned a number of foreign sculptors to embellish their new palaces with ornate windows, stately portals, and, at a later stage, roof sculptures and magnificent gables. Another important development was that of funerary art, for which Vadstena became a main center. The most prominent representative of the Dutch and Flemish Renaissance in Sweden was the versatile Guillaume Boyens, who created the splendid tomb of Gustaf Vasa and his queens in Uppsala Cathedral. Second in prominence to Boyens was the fine sculptor Hans Fleming (d. 1623), whose works included the gable figures at Vadstena Castle.

At the beginning of the 17th century, Sweden established itself as a leading European power, a position that it retained during the larger part of the century. This political prominence called for grandiose settings, which were created through widespread building activity, chiefly in the towns. In Stockholm, where this activity was at its peak about 1640, tall houses with magnificent gables were erected. The palaces were characterized by the picturesque grouping of their buildings and by gaily decorated façades, elaborate windows, sculptured friezes, *chaines*, towers and spires with weather vanes, and roofs richly ornamented with sculptures, pinnacles, etc. All this decoration was designed to embody the splendor that the period demanded from the arts. Sculpture, too, which was closely linked with architecture, went through a period of prosperity.

During the first half of the 17th century, architecture was dominated by a German-Dutch style, whose main representatives were Christian Julius Dötebar (the Tyska Kyrka, or German Church of St. Gertrud, the Torstensson Palace, and the Petersen House, all in Stockholm); Hans Jakob Kristler (the Makalös Palace, now destroyed, which was the great attraction of the period; Jacobsdal Palace, now called Ulriksdal); and Kasper Panten (rebuilding of Tre Kronor Castle; Vibyholm Castle). One of the best-preserved monuments of this period is Tyresö church, an original building designed by Hans Ferster.

In about 1640, a classical austerity was introduced into architecture, by Simon de la Vallée (d. 1642), who was one of the designers of the Riddarhus ("house of the nobility," until 1866 the assembly house of the Council of Nobles in Stockholm), which was inspired by the Luxembourg Palace in Paris. His other buildings include Tidö Castle (Västmanland) and Rosberg Castle, which are in a style derived mainly from the French and Dutch Renaissance. Shortly afterward a Dutch variant of Palladianism left important traces in Swedish architecture, for example in the De Geer House (now known as the Ebba Brahe House) in Stockholm and in Finspång Castle. The main exponent of this style was a Dutch architect, Justus Vinckeboons (Vingboons), the designer of the central building of the Riddarhus, which has perhaps the most beautiful façade in Stockholm. The order of pilasters contrasts rhythmically with the wall surface, which is decorated with trophies and sandstone festoons. The form of the roof is that of the typically Swedish *säteritak* (manor-house roof), which consists of two tiered sections — either sloping or curved — usually separated by a short vertical section. (This form of roof construction became frequent during the 17th and 18th centuries.)

Between 1660 and 1680, when peace had returned, there was a period of unprecedented building activity in Sweden. Swedish magnates vied with one another in building magnificent castles and manor houses. The leading architects of this period were Jean de la Vallée (1620–96) and Nicodemus Tessin the Elder (1615–81), who often worked in collaboration. As Royal Architect, Jean de la Vallée supervised state constructions, but on several occasions Tessin completed the building work. De la Vallée finished the Riddarhus and built the Bonde Palace (later the Rådhus) in Stockholm. The Bonde Palace, with its wide central building flanked on both sides by courtyards, shows French influence. De la Vallée built a number of minor castles for the nobility, such as Runsa in Uppland (externally

the best-preserved baroque castle in Sweden) and supervised rebuilding of Karlberg Castle in the French style. He was also creator of the Oxenstierna Palace in Stockholm (ca. 1650), wh anticipates the classic Roman baroque a quarter of a century bef this style became predominant in Sweden. By building the Chu of St. Katarina, which has a square plan with a projecting rectan on each side, and the octagonal Hedvig Eleonora Church, Jean de Vallée definitively introduced into Sweden the brick church b on a central plan. The somewhat grandiose baroque style of chu was in fact hardly in keeping with the orthodox Lutheran faith p vailing in Sweden at the time; this simple piety was more faithf expressed by the wooden village church, often built on a cen plan, with a small central tower and a shingled façade, tarred or pain red, and frequently with a *säteritak* and a bell cote.

In 1653 Nicodemus Tessin the Elder returned from a tour abr with impressions from many different countries, which he then tra lated into an eclectic classicistic style. His most important chu is Kalmar Cathedral, which was influenced by the Roman baroc While his earlier town palaces generally followed French traditi (for instance, the Rosenhane and Bååth palaces in Stockholm), works of his old age tended mainly to the Italian style, for exam the Riksbank (Bank of Sweden) with its blocklike mass scarc broken by the close window cornices and the floor divisions. Tessi principal creation, however, was Drottningholm Palace outs Stockholm, begun in 1662. This was the most stately and represen tive palace of the period. The main building consists of a thr storied rectangle with pavilions at the corners. On either side ext two-storied wings, each enclosing its courtyard; the corners of th wings are also marked by pavilions. Most of Tessin the Eld country palaces were built in this style, which may be described French baroque with traditional Swedish additions, for instance typical roof line of the *säteritak*. One of the best palaces that he b for the nobility is Mälsåker in Södermanland.

With Nicodemus Tessin the Younger (1654–1728; appoin Royal Architect in 1681), the Roman baroque, adapted to Swec conditions, was definitively introduced. The architectural s that Tessin the Younger launched was based on pragmatic princip Although an eclectic with regard to details, he had a genuine ta for creating original, well-proportioned buildings. His outstand work is the Royal Palace in Stockholm. The old palace having b destroyed by fire in 1697 — when even its original core, the Kronor tower, collapsed — he had complete freedom in the of reconstruction. He adopted the Roman type of façade, with roque sculptural details, but the total effect was original lar because of the balancing of the masses. He considered the pa as merely part of a larger whole and planned a bridge lined statues that was to lead from the north façade of the palace ac the Norrström to the present Gustaf Adolf Square, where a l church serving as a royal burial place was to close the prosp The church was to be flanked by two identical palaces to the east west. The project for these palaces was taken up again during 18th century and partly carried out in the twin edifices of the Cr Prince's Palace and the Royal Opera House (the latter now demolish The Roman style is also obvious in Tessin's own house in Stockh and in the plans and interior decoration of his churches. The pri palaces he built often reflect French currents, for example Sten Castle (Uppland) and Sturefors (Östergötland); also as a landsc architect he tended toward the French style of Le Nôtre (q.v.).

From the beginning of the 17th century, sculpture and paint as well as architecture, reflected Sweden's newly won positio dominance. Painting had stagnated under the guild system, anc order to achieve its renewal foreign artists were again encoura to work in Sweden. The numerous sculptors (chiefly Germans Dutchmen) who immigrated in the third decade of the century schooled in the mannerism of Giambologna (q.v.), which predc nated until the 1660s and the "auricular" (convoluted) style also tained its influence on sculptural decoration until that period. about 1630 a fundamental influence was exerted by Aris Clae (Gustav Banér's funerary monument in Uppsala Cathedral, tha Carl Banér at Danderyd, etc.), Heinrich Wilhelm (funerary monum in the Riddarholmskyrka, Tyresö church, Uppsala Cathedral, e and Joest Henne. Henne worked on the richly decorated Pete House in Gamla Stan, Stockholm's oldest section, where he also e ed several of the splendid portals of this period (e.g., the port the Tyska Kyrka, or German Church). His chief work is Ma Brahe's tomb in Västerås Cathedral. This style, dominated strong sense of movement, was further represented by Markus bel, Christian Pfund, Christian Julius Dötebar, and Heinrich B (the portal and pediments of Tidö Castle, the portals of the Ch of St. Jakob).

With the appearance of the Palladian style in architecture, sc ture was subjected to more austere classical ideals, especially thr the influence of Jean Baptist Dusart (Dieussart). He executed statues on the roof of the Riddarhus and the many sculptures (since lost) in the park of Jacobsdal (now Ulriksdal). Nicolas Millich (Millincks) from Antwerp, who contributed greatly to the development of Swedish sculpture, executed a number of statues destined for the staircase at Drottningholm; during the 1670s and 1680s he did several portrait busts of members of the royal family. The Roman baroque style, introduced by Tessin the Younger into architecture, is also found in the ecclesiastical art of Burchardt Precht (1651–1738; pulpits in the Storkyrka in Stockholm and in Uppsala Cathedral, altarpieces for Uppsala Cathedral, now in Stockholm's Gustaf Vasa Church). At the end of the century Paris and Versailles rather than Rome were the centers of artistic influence. Tessin the Younger recruited several artists from Paris for the decoration of Stockholm's Royal Palace; among them were the sculptors René Chauveau and Bernard Fouquet. Chauveau's works include the reliefs with themes from Ovid's *Metamorphoses* on the south façade of the palace. Fouquet was entrusted with the more important works in the sculptural decoration of the palace.

During the second and third decades of the 17th century, under Gustaf Adolf, national traditions lived on in pictorial art, chiefly in the works of Holher Hansson and Cornelius Arendtson, whose portraits are dominated by an increasing naturalism and a feeling of space. The evolution of painting was also influenced, however, by foreign artists, such as Jakob Hoefnagel and Jakob Henrik Elbfas, who was active in Sweden from 1622 until his death in 1664. At the time of Christina's coronation (1644), Sweden's cultural life was at its peak. The country was in close touch with European cultural centers, and the queen, who realized that the Thirty Years' War had left Sweden culturally backward, invited foreign men of letters, scientists, and artists to help remedy this situation. Her strong cultural interests were shared by a number of Swedish magnates, who sometimes surrounded themselves with a complete staff of artists and craftsmen in order to satisfy their new demands for princely splendor. Thus a large number of artists, headed by Johan Werner the Elder and the Younger, worked in Per Brahe's castle of Visingsborg. The most important private patron of the arts was Count Magnus Gabriel de la Gardie, who commissioned the building or rebuilding of many churches. The artists who worked for him included Nicolas Vallari (monumental painting), David Beck, Elbfas, David Klöcker Ehrenstrahl, and Pierre Signac, the miniaturist. During this period the country acquired considerable art collections, largely as spoils of war.

Toward the middle of the century Van Dyck's pupil David Beck and the Frenchman Sébastien Bourdon were the leading portrait painters. The miniaturist of the court was Alexander Cooper, and its most outstanding engraver was Jeremias Falck. In 1654 Jürgen Ovens arrived in Sweden from Holstein. He did large paintings of contemporary events such as coronations and royal weddings.

During the second half of the 17th century Swedish painting consolidated itself, owing especially to the extremely productive Ehrenstrahl (1629–98) and also in part to Martin Mytens the Elder (1648–1736) and to the numerous pupils of both these artists. Ehrenstrahl was the most versatile and outstanding painter of this period. He painted numerous ceilings (Drottningholm, the Riddarhus), where he depicted the enormous visions and ponderous classical allegories of the baroque era. Impressive at least in size are the two huge religious paintings, dating from the 1790s, *The Crucifixion* and *The Day of Judgment* (now in the Storkyrka), which show the influence of both Michelangelo and Rubens. Although his fame among his contemporaries was based on his large, erudite compositions, he is more admired today for his many landscapes and animal and genre pictures. These show a remarkable, fresh approach to reality. Several of the animal and hunting pieces that he did for the sports-loving King Charles XI are faithful and spontaneous descriptions of Swedish nature. His chief influence, however, was as a painter of baroque-style portraits in allegorical settings. In 1686 Johan Sylvius (d. 1695), a painter in the monumental style, returned from England, where his commissions had included work at Windsor Castle. Sylvius participated in the decoration of various buildings, his most notable work being at Drottningholm, where he painted, among other things, the bold trompe l'œil perspectives on the staircase.

During the second half of the 17th century a less pretentious fashion gained favor: still lifes and animal and genre paintings. This realistic art was popular particularly with bourgeois collectors, the artists usually being Dutch or Flemish visitors. In about 1640 Allart van Everdingen spent some time in Sweden, drawing subjects for his paintings from the Göteborg area. These highly romantic forest and mountain landscapes with their impetuous waterfalls were adopted as pictorial themes by such painters as Jacob van Ruisdael (q.v.). The Dutch still-life and animal painter Govert Camphuysen was active in Sweden 1652–63, and his objective representation of reality helped to found the Swedish realistic tradition. Others working in the same spirit were the Swedish still-life painter Christian von Thum (d. 1696), a master of Stockholm's guild of painters, and

Cornelius Vermeulen (van der Meulen; 1642–92), whose works include an extremely faithful view of Stockholm painted in oils (Broxvic, Coll. O. Taube von Block). Johan Johnsen (ca. 1650–1705) specialized in a purely decorative kind of still life (often flower pieces) and also did a number of gouache landscapes with ruins. In 1683 Johann Philip Lemke of Nürnberg was commissioned to perpetuate Sweden's victorious struggle for power in a sequence of monumental battle scenes, to be placed in two galleries at Drottningholm Castle. These paintings were based mainly on the sketches of Erik Dahlberg (1625–1703), which were done on the spot. Most important was the large volume of prints, *Suecia antiqua et hodierna* (Stockholm, 1716), on which Erik Dahlberg had worked for several decades; its 469 copperplates of Swedish towns, castles, manor houses, and monuments of the past were assembled, according to the author, "in order that foreigners may see what greatness and beauty our fatherland holds." This publication laid the foundations of topographic art in Sweden.

Toward the end of the 17th century the great flourishing of the arts slowly declined, largely as a result of war and *Realpolitik*. Many outstanding young artists began seeking their fortunes in other countries. In 1695 Johan Richter (1665–1745) settled in Venice, where he became one of the first Venetian panorama painters. One of Ehrenstrahl's pupils, Michael Dahl (1656–1743), who settled in London in 1682, gained a reputation there as a portraitist and influenced many Swedish artists through his somewhat sentimental art. With his most gifted pupil, Hans Hysing (1678–1752), a prominent portraitist, he helped to found the Academy of Painting in London. Another outstanding apprentice of Ehrenstrahl was David Richter the Elder (1662–1735), who in the 1690s went abroad and painted portraits and landscapes at several German courts. David von Krafft (1655–1724) was the only really remarkable pupil of Ehrenstrahl who remained in Sweden during the hard years of war during and immediately after the reign of Charles XII. His art was an important point of departure for the Swedish portrait tradition of the new century.

THE 18TH AND 19TH CENTURIES. Charles XII was a great military hero, but after his death in 1718 Sweden was left impoverished in every respect. Its principal industries were paralyzed by an economic crisis, and its population was devastated by epidemics. In these conditions the arts did not thrive, and one by one the finest artists left Sweden. All efforts, however, were concentrated on the country's economic rehabilitation, and soon after 1720 the foundations were laid for a new and brilliant era in Swedish civilization. After a pause of twenty years building was resumed on the Stockholm Royal Palace, which for several decades remained the focal point for Swedish art and handicrafts. Around it various institutions were founded, for example in 1735 the Kungliga Ritareakademi (Royal Academy of Draftsmen), which later became the Kungliga Akademi för de Fria Konsterna (Royal Academy of Fine Arts), and in 1752 the Superintendency, which supervised all the constructions of the state and thus strongly influenced Swedish architecture.

The transition from the painting of the Caroline period to the new, brilliant, rococo art was marked especially by three portraitists, the popular Johan Henrik Scheffel (1690–1781), Olof Arenius (1701–66), and Lorenz Pasch the Elder (1702–66). This transitional style of the first part of the 18th century was considerably influenced by David von Krafft, the French Régence, and the Swedish painters in London, Dahl and Hysing.

About 1730 the rococo style was introduced into Sweden, mainly by Carl Hårleman, Guillaume Taraval, and Gustaf Lundberg. The architect Hårleman (1700–53) was in charge of the Stockholm Palace construction, which had reached the stage of interior decoration. He called in a number of French and Italian artists of the new school, but their stay in Sweden was short; for reasons of economy official circles were more inclined to favor domestic talent. The most important foreign painter was Taraval (1701–50), who arrived in 1732. In his ceilings and the panels above the doors in the Royal Palace he displayed a vivacious charm that recalls the paintings of François Lemoyne. He was an unselfish and influential teacher and protector of young Swedish artists and became the natural leader of the Konstakademi (Academy of Arts) during its initial period. Among his pupils was Johan Pasch (1706–69), who eventually became the leading painter of monumental and decorative pieces of that period. The most important sculptors were Charles Guillaume Cousin (active in Sweden ca. 1737–47), Jacques Philippe Bouchardon, and Pierre Hubert Larchevêque (in Sweden 1755–76). The latter also worked for the Marieberg porcelain manufactory.

Hårleman, whose tasks included not only royal palaces but also more humble dwellings, was important as the creator of the Swedish type of manor house. The first example is Svartsjö Castle, dating from the 1730s; this was followed by Åkerö, Svindersvik, Övedskloster, and others. Hårleman transformed the proud mansions of the Caroline period, which were designed more for show than for convenience, into pleasant and practical country houses. This style was adopted by his numerous pupils. Carl Johan Cronstedt (1709–79) built several manor houses (Svenby, Myrö, and others) entirely in the spirit of his predecessor. He was, however, more important as an engineer, notably for his invention of the Swedish glazed-tile stove with a serpentine flue, which provided extremely efficient domestic heating. Carl Fredrik Adelcrantz (1716–93) created the most genuine rococo building in Sweden, the small pleasure palace called Kina Slott (the Chinese Pavilion) in the Drottningholm grounds. It was built in the 1760s and was so named because it replaced a Chinese-style wooden palace dating from the beginning of the 1750s. It is a graceful building with dark-red panels and green Greek frets against sand-colored wall surfaces, corners in the form of palm trunks, and a blue-green, tent-shaped roof, suggesting folds of fabric and decorated with hanging bells. Later Adelcrantz became the main exponent of the more rigid Gustavian style (a Swedish adaptation of the Louis XVI style), as for instance in the Royal Opera House built for Gustaf III in Stockholm. This was a harmonious building with a rusticated ground floor, two upper floors with pilasters, and a central portion forming a pillared ressaut. Eventually he adopted the classical style, building (in 1780) the east façade of the old mint in Stockholm in the form of a Doric temple. His other buildings include the Ruuth Palace (now Vattenfallsstyrelsens House) and the Adolf Fredrik Church in Stockholm.

The architect Jean Eric Rehn (1717–93) was influenced by Hårleman in his designs of the 1750s (e.g., Stora Väsby in Uppland), but during the following decade he developed a new style (Erstavik Castle in Södermanland and Gimo Castle in Uppland). He was a skillful engraver and draftsman, and for a time he taught Crown Prince Gustaf (III) these arts. His chief contribution, however, was in the sphere of interior decoration and handicrafts. In the decoration of numerous interiors he contributed to the creation of the Gustavian style. After 1745, following lengthy studies in Paris, he became the chief designer for the silk manufactories in Sweden, a position that enabled him to exert a predominant influence on the evolution of handicrafts during the second half of the century. This period was a golden age for Swedish handicrafts (especially textiles and porcelain), their prosperity being largely due to state subsidies.

In the course of the 18th century several Swedish painters earned themselves positions of eminence abroad, especially Gustaf Lundberg, Carl Gustaf Pilo, Peter Adolf Hall, and Niclas Lafrensen. Lundberg (1695–1786) dominated pastel painting in Paris from the beginning of the 1720s. His brilliant technique and superlative skill brought him great success in aristocratic circles. After his return to Sweden in 1745 he caused a complete revolution in Swedish portrait painting. Alexander Roslin (1718–93) acquired a reputation in Paris at the beginning of the 1750s. His somewhat superficial but extremely elegant manner, which exploits sensuous qualities with refinement, epitomizes the pictorial ideals of the rococo (V, PL. 415). In 1774 he made a short visit to Sweden, where, among other portraits, he painted the members of the royal family (Stockholm, Nationalmus.); after this visit he was called by Catherine the Great to St. Petersburg. For several decades, starting in the 1740s, Pilo and his following of Swedish artists played a dominant part in Danish painting. Pilo (ca. 1711–92), perhaps Sweden's most famous colorist, was painter to the Danish court and director of the Danish Royal Academy of Fine Arts. He used a highly personal style and softly blending colors. His portraits are remarkable for their refined spirituality; in the 1770s certain romantic features appeared in his figural compositions. After returning to Sweden in 1772, he created his finest masterpieces. Johan Edvard Mandelberg (1730–86), who, after studying with François Boucher, came under the influence of Johann Joachim Winckelmann and Anton Raphael Mengs, made a noteworthy contribution as a painter of historical, monumental, and decorative pieces in Denmark (e.g., in the palaces of Fredensborg and Christiansborg). He set a fashion in Danish historical painting in the classical style.

After studying with Joseph Vernet in Paris, Johan Sevenbom (Säfvenboom, 1721–84) returned to Stockholm and laid the foundations of Swedish landscape painting. He executed a number of harbor pictures in the style of Vernet and a sequence of six monumental views of Swedish royal countryseats, destined for one of the galleries in Stockholm's Royal Palace (now in Nyköping, Södermanlands Läns Mus.). His chief work consists of 15 large views of Stockholm (1764–84; Stockholm, Rådhuset), which are distinguished by their objective realism.

The Gustavian period (1772–1810) was strongly influenced by the personality of Gustaf III (d. 1792). Stylistically it directly continued and developed the art of the preceding period, with a growing tendency toward neoclassic forms. The tender, slightly allusive painting of the rococo period became increasingly plastic and realistic, while retaining its charm and spirituality. After successful activities abroad, Per Krafft the Elder (1724–93; court painter in Poland) and Lorenz Pasch the Younger (1733–1805) returned to Sweden,

where they laid the foundations of the new Gustavian portrait style. Krafft adopted a rather bourgeois style, and many of his portraits, especially those of children, have the appearance of calm genre pictures. Both artists were skillful colorists. Peter Adolf Hall (1739–93), who gave new life to the gouache miniature, settled in Paris in 1766 as court painter. His swift impressionistic touch and his refined manner earned him international fame. Adolf Ulric Wertmüller (1715–1811), a pupil of Joseph Marie Vien, was an accomplished portraitist. His works include a painting of Marie Antoinette and her children (Stockholm, Nationalmus.) and a portrait of George Washington (one of several replicas, New York, Met. Mus.), done after Wertmüller had emigrated to North America. Carl Fredrik von Breda (1759–1818), who studied with Sir Joshua Reynolds (q.v.), made himself a reputation in England. His portraits are done in an expressive style, occasionally with a lyrical scene as background. After he returned to Sweden in 1796, his romantic art exerted a salutary influence on Swedish painting, which at that time was pursuing classical ideals.

A typical representative of the rococo period was Niclas Lafrensen (Lavreince) the Younger (1737–1807), who between 1771 and 1791, while living in Paris, successfully depicted Parisian manners in provocative gouache paintings. His technically exquisite boudoir scenes and depictions of amorous intrigues, often frivolously portrayed, spread all over Europe in the form of engravings and color prints. After returning to Sweden he devoted himself chiefly to miniature painting. The pictorial work of Per Hilleström (1732–1816) is perhaps more interesting from a historical than from an esthetic point of view. After many years of activity as Sweden's outstanding haute lisse weaver, he turned to painting in the 1770s. His objective depiction of everyday life became popular in a society where cultural leadership was passing from the aristocracy to the middle class. He rendered bourgeois interiors, depicted the work in mines and forges, and painted still lifes and landscapes, park scenes and episodes of rustic life with sympathy, simplicity, and a personal touch, albeit sometimes a trifle heavily.

Landscape painting was used mainly to decorate walls or door panels. Johan Filip Korn (1728–96) was a prolific painter in this ornamental, idyllic genre. Elias Martin (1739–1818) achieved unprecedented excellence as a landscape painter, working with great success in London from 1768 to 1780. In his highly personal work he expressed his love of nature in harmonious, spontaneous, and uninhibited form. He painted large romantic-idyllic landscapes in oils, often with a religious undertone. He attained unquestioned mastery in water colors, concentrating on light and atmosphere and achieving realistic interpretation of nature in this medium. Pehr Hörberg (1746–1816), who was much admired by the subsequent romantic generation, was an artist of independent bent. In his baroque style he created countless altarpieces and religious paintings of compelling sincerity.

From 1780 neoclassic ideals were influential. Gustaf III's Italian journey in 1783–84 officially promoted the interest in antiquity. The central figure of the neoclassic movement was the sculptor Johan Tobias Sergel (1740–1814), who returned to Sweden in 1779 after 12 years in Rome. Except for his extraordinary portrait busts and portrait medallions, he used traditional themes from the neoclassic repertory of ancient mythology. His sculptural work, however, unlike that of most of his contemporaries, never settled into a lifeless formalism, but retained a Dionysiac touch, owing to his natural disposition and to the fact that he was first trained in the late baroque era. Together with Carl August Ehrensvärd, the art philosopher and admiral (1745–1800), and Louis Masreliez, the decorative painter (1748–1810), Sergel formed a triumvirate that drew its inspiration from antiquity. Ehrensvärd, like Sergel, was one of the finest draftsmen in Swedish art history, not only from a technical point of view but also through his capacity for translating thought and feeling spontaneously into images. He expressed his intense admiration for antiquity in two fascinating books, De fria konsters filosofi (1786) and Resa til Italien (1816), which describes his Italian travels. Masreliez abandoned historical painting after a promising start (he studied with Vien) and devoted himself to decorative interior painting in the style of the time, for example in the courtyseat of Haga and the Crown Prince's Palace. This style was inspired by Pompeian wall paintings and Raphael's grotesques (V, PL. 239). Louis Jean Desprez (1743–1804), who was engaged in Rome by Gustaf III in 1784, cultivated a solemn and theatrical form of classicism. The theater was the king's passion, and Desprez was employed as a scene painter, as well as working as an artist and architect. His abundant imagination always enabled him to offer impressive solutions for the king's fantastic construction projects, but his designs were rarely executed. The outstanding landscape architect of the period was Fredrik Magnus Piper (1746–1824), who was chiefly responsible for the introduction of the English-style park (Haga, Drottningholm, Forsmark, etc.; see VIII, FIG. 1098).

It was Erik Palmstedt (1741–1803) who, after building the Stockholm Börhus (stock exchange), finally broke with rococo tradition in architecture. In the neoclassic style he built, among other things,

ustaf III's theater at Gripsholm Castle and the Stockholm Tullhus
ustomhouse). Olof Tempelman (1745–1816; Gustaf III's pavilion
Haga, the present town hall of Härnösand) and Carl Fredrik
ndvall (1754–1831; library and auditorium at Uppsala University,
järnsund Castle in Närke) used classical elements almost exclusively.
s a reaction against this deliberately antique type of architecture,
simplified and more bourgeois variety of the neoclassic style was
troduced about 1818, mainly by Fredrik Blom (1781–1851).
is bourgeois version of the French Empire style influenced landscape
chitecture in the Stockholm area during the greater part of the 19th
ntury. Swedish architecture in the French Empire style (ca. 1810–
) differed considerably from the Greco-Roman taste that prevailed
the rest of Europe. The purely classical components (columns
d temple gables) soon disappeared, and sumptuousness gave place
a practical and objective simplicity. By about 1840 the neoclassic
vle had lost its impact, and during the subsequent period up to
70 the over-all European pattern of stylistic eclecticism was followed
Swedish architects in their search for various inspirations from the
st. In the early 1830s, Romanesque and Gothic formal elements
appeared. In his later works Fredrik Blom often followed this
nd (Admiralty House, Skeppsholmen, Stockholm), but the most
tstanding representative of the Neo-Gothic school was Axel Ny-
röm (1793–1868; the Bishop's Palace in Lund). About the middle
the century a medieval romanticism manifested itself, but only
oradically. In Sweden as elsewhere stylistic eclecticism influenced
e 19th century as a whole. The architecture of the period was
spired not only by the Romanesque and Gothic styles but also by
e early and High Renaissance and the baroque. Among the archi-
cts best known for revivals of past styles were Fredrik Wilhelm
holander (1816–81), who showed great skill in combining the various
chitectural components of the Renaissance, and Johan Fredrik
bom (1817–1900). Between 1840 and 1870 the façades of buildings
ere increasingly broken up by windows and richly varied ornament,
ith the result that the architectural components often lost their tecton-
implications.

Despite manifold influences resulting from frequent contacts
ith the successive centers of European art, Swedish 19th-century
inting had a marked character of its own and only rarely showed
y direct affiliation with the fashions current elsewhere. On the whole,
was characterized by idealism, moralism, sentimentalism, and anecdo-
l and epic tendencies — all having the common denominator of
creasing realism.

Political circumstances in Sweden promoted appreciation of na-
nal cultural traditions, and from about 1810 Swedish cultural life
as dominated by a marked nationalistic current, which expressed
elf programmatically in the so-called "Gothic League" (Gö-
ska Förbund), founded in 1811. This group endeavored to revive
everyday life and in the arts what were commonly believed to have
en the ancient Swedish virtues, and the world of Norse legend was
this time considered to provide a repertory of artistic themes
tter adapted to the Swedish temperament than Greco-Roman
ythology and history, which had long been predominant. This
tionalistic attitude led to a deliberate but not very concentrated
successful effort to break loose from the classicist tradition in the
ts. This tendency must be regarded as part of the striving for artis-
renewal that was evident throughout Europe about 1800. Even
its purest form, this Gothicism did not appear as a unified trend
ithin the visual arts, although several artists sporadically had re-
urse to Norse themes. The most persistent was the sculptor Bengt
land Fogelberg (1786–1854), who for more than 25 years searched
r an adequate rendering of Norse legends. The attempt culminated
his three huge statues of the gods Odin, Thor, and Balder (1830–44;
ockholm, Nationalmus.), which, despite their Norse character, show
assicistic formal qualities.

The classicistic art of portraiture was continued in the 19th century
David's pupil Per Krafft the Younger (1777–1863), who combined
rmal rigor, clear colors, and dignity in the delineation of the human
rm with an amplified realism. Since, however, classicism emphasized
andeur and dignity of content, historical painting supplanted por-
aiture as the most esteemed pictorial genre. The efforts made to
sist young historical artists nonetheless produced meager results,
obably because this genre was unlucrative and was generally cul-
vated in an artificial atmosphere. In the preceding century Jonas
offman (1731–80) had made a promising start with subjects from
assical mythology and history, but his career was short. Apart from
s work as a portraitist, Adolf Ulric Wertmüller painted mythological
bjects with an attractive softness and sensuality. The leading painter
historical pieces during the first half of the century was Johan
ustaf Sandberg (1782–1854), who drew his subjects exclusively
om Swedish history. Classicistic historical painting was also pro-
ced in a weakened form by the prolific Fredrik Westin (1782–
62); it is interesting to observe how in his work the heroic ideals
classicism give way to effeminate sentimentalism.

The opposition between cold idealism and sensual realism also
affected sculpture during the first half of the 19th century. This is
clearly reflected in Sergel's favorite pupil Johan Niklas Byström
(1783–1848). While his huge marble statues of royal personages generally give an impression of complete lifelessness, his mythological
figures and groups, especially those with erotic themes, display fine
qualities, particularly in their combination of formal elegance and
sensuous charm. Erik Gustav Göthe (1779–1838) and Carl Gustaf
Qvarnström (1810–67) treated classical subjects more realistically.
The work of Johan Peter Molin (1814–73) is also characterized
by increasing formal realism and sentimentalism.

Norse subjects, supplemented with themes from early Swedish
history, came into favor again after 1850, above all in the paintings
— full of figures and dramatic events — by Mårten Eskil Winge (1825–
96) and Johan August Malmström (1829–1901). This national current
led to more important artistic results in two other genres: the depiction
of nature myths and scenes of Swedish life. Swedish village life
was realistically depicted with a wealth of picturesque detail by
objective painters such as Sandberg, Wilhelm Wallander (1821–88),
and Christian Didrik Forssell (1777–1852). The nature-myth genre
belongs within romanticism, not only because of its literary substance,
but also formally, through the merging of all the details and the diffused
coloring. Following these trends, painters such as Nils Johan Blommér
(1816–53), Johan Zacharias Blackstadius (1816–98), and Malmström
generally tried to interpret the inner life of nature in evocative, cre-
puscular pictures. These are connected with romantic landscape
painting, of which the finest representative is Carl Johan Fahlcrantz (1774–1861). There are none of the usual decorative figures
in his landscapes and no literary symbolic subjects; he used scenery
merely to convey an atmosphere. He often made careful topographical
studies as a preliminary, but then transformed the composition into
a romantic landscape by strong contrasts of light and effects suggestive
of distance. He was active as a teacher for a long time, Michael Gustaf
Anckarsvärd and Johan Kristian Berger being among his pupils.

Between 1840 and 1870 pictorial art reached a new flowering.
Following the example of a group of Norwegian painters, several
young Swedish artists were chiefly active in Düsseldorf throughout
the 1850s, notably Carl Henrik d'Unker, August Jernberg, Bengt
Nordenberg, Wilhelm Wallander, Axel and Jakob Kulle, and Kilian
Christoffer Zoll. Scenes from everyday life were the main concern
of these painters, who played a leading part in Swedish art of two
decades. They often used idealized anecdotal topics drawn from town
or village life. Among the Düsseldorf artists there were also several
landscape painters, for example Johan Edvard Bergh and Axel Wilhelm
Nordgren. Carl Wahlbom (1810–58) appears as the most capable
historical painter; in his violent scenes of war he revived the memory
of Sweden's age of glory. He also had recourse to Norse subjects.
An ambitious use of color, often related to this epic art, is apparent
in figure painters such as Johan Fredrik Höckert (1826–66) and Egron
Lundgren (1815–75). Lundgren spent most of his life abroad, mainly
in London, where he was much admired by Queen Victoria and the
English aristocracy. His water-color sketches are imbued with light
and brilliantly transform the outer world into poetic impressions.

A large number of landscape painters belonging to this generation
finally consolidated the landscape tradition founded during the preceding century. The abundant landscape production includes formally
astringent compositions of a topographic nature (Gustaf Wilhelm
Palm, Joseph Magnus Stäck); realistic pieces in the old Dutch tradition (Nils Andersson), some of them imbued with a lyrical atmosphere (Petter Gabriel Wickenberg); and a more dramatic, emotional
art, which combines the early romantic landscape (Fahlcrantz) with
the new detailed naturalism. A leading representative of this expressive
landscape painting was Markus Larsson (1825–64), whose dramatic
renderings of the fury of the elements often conveyed a tragic foreboding of disaster. Lars Teodor Billing (1817–92) was the only artist
connected with French plein-air painting, but this type of painting
was without influence in Sweden until the 1870s.

In the 1870s there was a period of great cultural activity in Sweden,
during which realistic tendencies became increasingly evident. Architecture also reflected this trend. A functional rather than imaginative treatment of the wall established itself, while decorative motifs
assumed the appearance of actual structural components. The illusory
use of plaster was abandoned in favor of more solid materials. Helgo
Zetterwall (1831–1907), the most typical representative of the period,
was the first architect to restore the solidity and weight of the wall.
These trends, along with an increasing demand for convenience and
comfort, continued until the end of the century. Houses were, so to
speak, created from the inside, and the interior design influenced the
appearance of the façade (for instance through a more sparing use of
windows). There was a desire for genuineness of both materials and
function, but nevertheless a certain predilection for historical details
persisted. This is apparent in the work of Isak Gustaf Clason
(1856–1930; Hallwyl Palace, now Hallwylska Mus. and Nordiska

Mus., both in Stockholm; Norrköping Town Hall). The compactness of the walls and the sculptural weight of the details were intensified. In the 1890s there was a predilection for the picturesque, an asymmetrical subdivision of buildings, and the frequent addition of towers.

In the 1870s Swedish landscape painting was strongly influenced by early French plein-air painting (Barbizon school), while still retaining its particular tone of lyrical intimacy (Alfred Wahlberg, Gustav Rydberg, Oskar Törnå, Per Ekström). Carl Frederik Hill (1849–1911) executed during his short painting career (he was overcome by insanity at the age of thirty) some of the finest works in Swedish landscape painting. His way of creating great forms with colors has affinities with the technique of Cézanne (q.v.). He produced — like Ernst Josephson ten years later — bold drawings in India ink or crayon that have a timeless, visionary poignancy. The young painters of this decade drew their chief inspiration from Munich (Georg von Rosen, Carl Gustaf Hellquist, Julius Kronberg) and Paris (Nils Forsberg the Elder, Gustaf Cederström, Hugo Salmson). In the 1880s the problems of color and light predominated, brighter colors were used, and human figures in outdoor surroundings constituted the most frequent subject. Many young Swedish artists went to study in France. The young painters of the 1880s and the following decades were a heterogeneous group. Their only common characteristic was a rapid transition through the various artistic phases of the time — from the objective recording of outdoor reality (the 1880s) through a somewhat dispirited emotional romanticism imbued with literature (the 1890s) to the various individual forms of synthesism (from the beginning of the 20th century). Remarkable among the young *fin de siècle* artists were Ernst Josephson, the most luminous colorist of them all, Carl Larsson, Karl Nordström, the brilliant Anders Zorn, Helmer Osslund, Eugène Jansson, Carl Wilhelmsson, and Ivan Agueli. The famous writer August Strindberg (1849–1912) occupies a place apart as an amateur artist; in the 1890s he created a number of extraordinary paintings, in oils applied with a palette knife, which anticipate "informal art."

The 19th century was not a favorable period for sculpture. The innovators at the end of the century were Karl Peter Hasselberg (naturalistic sensualism) and Christian Eriksson (incipient conventionalization). Carl Eldh and Carl Milles inaugurated the sculpture of the 20th century.

THE MODERN PERIOD. During the first decades of the 20th century the leading architects followed the trends of the 1890s, respecting local traditions and advocating natural constructional materials and free grouping of buildings. Among these architects were Ragnar Östberg (Stockholm City Hall, 1911–23), Erik Lallerstedt (Polytechnical School, Stockholm, 1914–22), Lars Wahlman (Engelbrekt Church, Stockholm, 1906–11), and Carl Westman (Stockholm Law Courts, 1911–15). The trend in favor of loosely grouped, acentric complexes was followed by a reaction that, in the 1920s, took the form of a return to a rigid classicist style of architecture. This reaction was represented by Ivar Tengbom (Concert Hall, Stockholm), Gunnar Asplund (Municipal Library, Stockholm), and Sigurd Lewerentz. After the Stockholm Exhibition in 1930, functionalism came strongly to the fore, and Swedish architecture has since been chiefly concerned with ambitious residential and town-planning projects (V, PLS. 113, 114; XIV, PLS. 158, 159, 176).

Internationalism is the salient characteristic of contemporary painting and sculpture in Sweden. Swedish artists have given more or less personal interpretations of the major trends in modern art. Good taste and high average quality have compensated for the lack of really great achievement. In the years after 1910 the influence of Matisse (q.v.), especially, resulted in a vital, flamboyant, and highly decorative style of painting with a deliberately modern touch (Isaac Grünewald, Leander Engström, Tor Bjurström, Sigrid Hjertén). Nils von Dardel (1888–1943) was late offshoot of the decadent Continental *fin de siècle*, revealed a personal, somewhat diabolical style, characterized by refinement and artificial naïveté. About 1920 several artists tried, sporadically, to adapt the creative principles of cubism. The work of Viking Eggeling (1880–1925) is historically interesting. He was an intentionally active experimenter and theorist who created a sort of scroll painting (1919–20) consisting of sequences of interrelated geometric figures. One of these scroll paintings, *The Diagonal Symphony*, was made into a motion picture in 1921; it is one of the first abstract films (see CINEMATOGRAPHY). Gösta Adrian-Nilsson, who was active in the spirit of the futurists and the Blaue Reiter (see EUROPEAN MODERN MOVEMENTS), strongly championed abstractionism. In the 1920s there was a tendency toward absolutely lucid and ordered formal expression; this manifested itself partly in a retrospective, eclectic neoclassicism (architecture and sculpture), partly in the support of the purist ideals of the Neue Sachlichkeit (Arvid Fougstedt), and, to a lesser extent, in neoplasticism (Otto Carlsund). This striving toward simplicity also had a certain moral bias, consisting in a new

appreciation of the naïve and spontaneous (Eric Hallström, Herbe Lindqvist). The expressionism of the 1930s covered a wide ran of attitudes; some artists tended toward pathos (Vera Nilsson, S Derkert), others were visionary romantics (Carl Kylberg); some we lyrical (Ivan Ivarson) and others witty and playful (Ragnar Sandberg Related to this expressionist art are the coarse primitivism of Br Hjorth's paintings and sculpture, Sven Erixson's spontaneous deligh in the material world and his poetical interpretations of commonpla subjects, and Evert Lundquist's terse portrayals of basic psychologic states. Sculpture has progressed from a monumental compactne (Bror Marklund) toward a disintegration of volume, movement, an dynamic space (Arne Jones). The 1950s were the years of concretis which was most eloquently represented by Olle Baertling. It wa followed by many forms of "informal art," all of them abundant represented (Endre Nemes, T. Renquist, C. F. Reuterswärd, Gunna Larsson, Albert Johansson).

BIBLIOG. *General*: L. Looström, Den svenska Konstakademien 173: 1835, Stockholm, 1887; Svenska slott och herresäten, Stockholm, 19c ff.; S. Curman and J. Roosval, ed., Sveriges kyrkor, Stockholm, 1912 f A. L. Romdahl and J. Roosval, ed., Svensk konsthistoria, Stockholm, 191 Sveriges städer nu och fordom, 5 vols., Stockholm, 1915–26; H. Ahlebe et al., ed., Svenska trädgårdskonsten, 2 vols., Stockholm, 1931–35; S. Ka ling, Trädgårdskonsten i Sverige intill Le Nôtrestilens genombrott, Stoc holm, 1931; J. Roosval, Swedish Art, Princeton, 1932; E. Hultmark, Kun Akademiens för de fria konsterna utställningar 1794–1887, Stockholr 1935; A. Hahr, Architecture in Sweden: A Survey, Stockholm, 1938; I Lundberg, Byggnadskonsten i Sverige 1000–1650, 2 vols., Stockholr 1940–48; G. Nässström, Forna dagars Sverige, 3 vols., Stockholm, 1941–6 E. Lundberg, Svensk bostad, Stockholm, 1942; H. Cornell, Den svens konstens historia, Stockholm, 1944 (2d ed., 2 vols., 1959); A. Lindblor Sveriges konsthistoria, 3 vols., Stockholm, 1944–46; U. Thersner, Ford och närvarande Sverige (ed. G. Boëthius and C. T. Thäberg), Stockholr 1946; G. Lilja, ed., Svenskt konstnärslexikon, 4 vols., Malmö, 1952–6 Svensk skulptur från Sergel till 1900-talets början, Stockholm, 1952; ↲ Lindblom, Svensk konst, Stockholm, 1960; P. Grate et al., ed., Trésors d'a suédois: Des temps préhistoriques au XIX⁰ siècle, Malmö, 1963 (cat

Prehistory and protohistory: O. Almgren, Sveriges fasta fornlämning från hednatiden, Uppsala, 1934; S. Curman et al., ed., Tiotusen år i Sverig Stockholm, 1945; E. Oxenstierna, Järnålder, guldålder, Stockholm, 195 J. Brøndsted, The Vikings, Harmondsworth, 1960; Rannsakningar eft antikviteter, I, Stockholm, 1960; M. Stenberger, Det forntida Sverige, Stoc holm, 1964.

Middle Ages: A. Lindblom, La peinture gothique en Suède et en Norvèg Stockholm, 1916; A. Branting and A. Lindblom, Medeltida vävnader o broderier i Sverige, 2 vols., Uppsala, Stockholm, 1928–29 (Eng. trans., M dieval Embroideries and Textiles in Sweden, 2 vols., Stockholm, 193: A. Hahr, Nordiska borgar från medeltid och renässans, Uppsala, 1930; Boëthius, Hallar, tempel och stavkyrkor, Stockholm, 1931; H. Cornell ar S. Wallin, Uppsvenska målarskolor på 1400-talet, Stockholm, 1933; A. B relius, Konstens historia i Sverige, I, 2 vols., Lund, 1943–59; N. P. Tidmar Så byggde Nordens gotiker, Visby, 1946; A. Andersson, English Influen in Norwegian and Swedish Figure Sculpture in Wood 1220–1270, Stoc holm, 1949; W. Holmqvist, Sveriges forntid och medeltid: Kulturhistori bildatlas, Malmö, 1949; B. G. Söderberg, Svenska kyrkomålningar fr medeltiden, Stockholm, 1951; H. Cornell and S. Wallin, Uppsvenska ky komålningar från 1500-talet, Stockholm, 1953; A. Andersson, Silber Abendmahlsgeräte in Schweden aus dem 14. Jahrhundert, Stockholm, 195 E. Lundberg, Albertus Pictor, Stockholm, 1961.

Modern era: A. Hahr, Konst och konstnärer vid Magnus Gabriel De Gardies hof, Uppsala, 1905; E. Dahlberg, Suecia antiqua et hodierna, Stoc holm, 1924; H. Ahlberg, Swedish Architecture of the 20th Century, Londo 1925; G. Nordensvan, Svensk konst och svenska konstnärer i 19⁰ århundrad 2 vols., Stockholm, 1925–28; E. Wettergren, L'art décoratif moderne Suède, Malmö, 1925; W. Nisser, Michael Dahl and the Contemporary Swe ish School of Painting, Uppsala, 1927; R. Josephson, Nicodemus Tess d. y., 2 vols., Stockholm, 1930–31; W. Nisser, Konst och hantverk i Vising borgs grevskap på Per Brahe d. y.:s tid, 2 vols., Stockholm, 1931; H. Rabé Träskulptur och snickarkonst i Uppsverige under renässans och baroc Stockholm, 1934; K. E. Steneberg, Vasarenässansens porträttkonst, Stoc holm, 1935; G. Selling, Svenska herrgårdshem under 1700-talet, Stockholr 1937; A. Johnson, Recent Swedish Architecture, J. Br. Arch., XLVI, 193 pp. 217–27; N. G. Wollin, Desprez en Suède 1784–1804, Stockholm, 193 B. Wennberg, Svenska målare i Danmark under 1700-talet, Lund, 194 A. Militello, Scansen e i musei all'aperto della Svezia, Le vie del mond XII, 1942, pp. 849–58; B. Waldén, Nicolaes Millich och hans krets, Stoc holm, 1942; S. Strömbom, ed., Fem stora gustavianer, Stockholm, 194 Svensk konstkrönika under 100 år, Stockholm, 1944; S. Strömbom, Kons närsförbundets historia, I, Stockholm, 1945; A. Sjöblom, David Klöck Ehrenstrahl, Malmö, 1947; B. Hellner, Järnsmidet i vasatidens dekorati konst, Stockholm, 1948; W. Nisser, Die italienischen Skizzenbücher v Erik Jönson Dahlberg und David Klöcker Ehrenstrahl, Uppsala, 1948; M. Lugli, Aspetti dell'urbanistica svedese, Rass. critica di arch., II, 194 pp. 3–40; G. Axel-Nilsson, Dekorativ stenhuggarkonst i yngre vasati Lund, 1950; E. Blomberg, Ernst Josephson, Stockholm, 1951; B. Rap Djur och stilleben i karolinskt måleri, Stockholm, 1951; A. Anderberg, C Hill, Malmö, 1952; C. Hernmarck, Svenskt 1700-tal, Stockholm, 1954; Söderberg, Den svenska konsten under 1900-talet, Stockholm, 1955; E. Steneberg, Kristinatidens måleri, Malmö, 1955; R. Josephson, Serge fantasi, 2 vols., Stockholm, 1956; S. Fogelmarck, Carl Fredrik Adelcran arkitekt, Stockholm, 1957; G. E. Kidder Smith, Sweden Builds, 2d e New York, 1957; H.-R. Hitchcock, Architecture: 19th and 20th Centuri

Harmondsworth, 1958; A. Tuulse, Castles of the Western World, London, 1958; S. B. Lundwall, Generationsväxlingen inom romantikens klassicism, Stockholm, 1960; G. Eimer, Carl Gustaf Wrangel: som byggherre i Pommern i Sverige, Stockholm, 1961; G. W. Lundberg, Roslin: Liv och verk, 2 vols., Malmö, 1961; Svenska arkitekters riksförbund, ed., New Architecture in Sweden: A Decade of Swedish Building, Stockholm, 1961; M. Hofrén, Nordsvenska studier och essayer, Kalmar, 1962.

MONUMENTAL CENTERS. The description of monumental centers begins with Stockholm and is then arranged according to provinces, from north to south.

Stockholm. According to tradition, the capital of Sweden was founded in the middle of the 13th century, when a large castle was built around one of the two defense towers that had been constructed a century earlier. The nucleus of the town — the section known as "The City between the Bridges" or Gamla Stan ("the old town") — still reveals a medieval layout. There are remains of the walls of the 13th-century castle in the north wing of the present Royal Palace. The main structure of several burghers' houses dating from the 14th and 15th centuries has survived, and a number of tall, stepped gables of the late Middle Ages are still visible. Of the ramparts that encircled medieval Stockholm only two towers remain, dating from the second half of the 15th century. Both are on Riddarholmen island, one forming part of the Wrangel Palace, the other the so-called "Birger Jarl's Tower." The original 13th-century city church is partly preserved in the present Storkyrka ("great church"), St. Nikolai, which has a Gothic interior, while the exterior is in the classicistic style of the 18th century. The church contains Bernt Notke's sculpture of St. George and the dragon (installed 1489). On the neighboring Riddarholm is the Riddarholmskyrka, a Franciscan church dating from the 13th century (used since the 17th century as a royal burial place).

The 17th century was a period of great urban development for Stockholm. There are a number of interesting examples of the richly decorated architectural style that prevailed in northern Europe in the first half of the 17th century, one such example being the Petersen House (near Munkbron), dating from 1645-49. This picturesque, late Renaissance style is also evident in the Church of St. Jakob (begun in the 16th century) — particularly in the elaborate portals and the interior with its stellar vaulting (ca. 1640) — as well as in the Tyska Kyrka, or German Church, which was given its present form by Hans Jakob Kristler in about 1640. At the same time several architects (Simon de la Vallée, Justus Vinckeboons, Jean de la Vallée) started work on the Riddarhus, which was the first large palace in Stockholm to display the new classicistic ideals, introduced from Holland. A number of public and private palaces dating from the second half of the 17th century, most of them built by Jean de la Vallée and Nicodemus Tessin the Elder, are characterized by this simpler and more monumental style, for example the Wrangel Palace and the Rosenhane Palace, both on Riddarholmen; the Bonde Palace, the Oxenstierna Palace, and the Bååth Palace on Blasieholmen; the Old City Hall (now Stadsmuseet) in the Södermalm section; and the old Riksbank (Bank of Sweden).

Jean de la Vallée, later assisted by Tessin the Elder, also built the Church of St. Katarina and the Hedvig Eleonora Church, which were the first churches in Stockholm to be built on a completely central plan. In 1680 Tessin the Younger's plan for the Royal Palace (which was to replace the old castle, destroyed by fire) introduced the Roman baroque into Sweden. In the same spirit Tessin the Younger

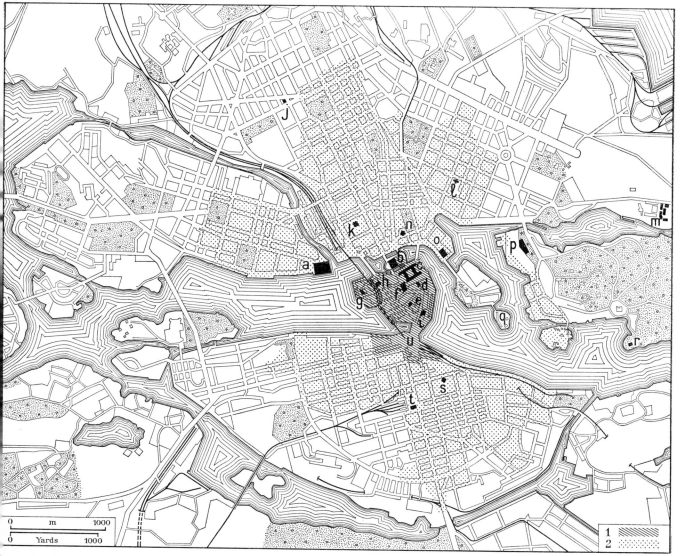

Stockholm, city center. *Key*: (1) Medieval city nucleus; (2) 17th-19th-cent. expansion. Principal monuments: (*a*) Kungsholmen Town Hall; (*b*) Helgeandsholmen; (*c*) Royal Palace; (*d*) Overståthållarpalatset (Governor's Palace); (*e*) Tyska Kyrkan (German Church); (*f*) Börhuset (stock exchange) and Storkyrkan (Great Church); (*g*) tower of Wrangel Palace and Birger Jarl's Tower; (*h*) Riddarhuset; (*i*) Tullhuset (customhouse); (*j*) Gustaf Vasa Church; (*k*) Church of St. Klara; (*l*) Hedvig Eleonora Church; (*m*) Statens Etnografiska Museum; (*n*) Church of St. Jakob; (*o*) Nationalmuseum; (*p*) Nordiska Museet; (*q*) Kastellholmen; (*r*) Waldemarsudde; (*s*) Church of St. Katarina; (*t*) Old City Hall (now Stadsmuseet); (*u*) Slussen.

built his own house (ca. 1690). The Royal Palace was not completed until 1750; the exterior reflects Tessin the Younger's plan, while the interior, executed under the direction of Carl Hårleman, is mainly rococo. One of the most outstanding rococo monuments is the Börhus (stock exchange), designed by Erik Palmstedt and completed in 1776. Subsequently, a more austere style following the classical pattern manifested itself in such buildings as the Adolf Fredrik Church by Carl Fredrik Adelcrantz, the Crown Prince's Palace (now the Ministry of Foreign Affairs, built as a counterpart to Adelcrantz's now demolished Royal Opera House), and the Tullhus (customhouse) by Palmstedt, which has an entirely undecorated rusticated façade.

On the outskirts of the capital the most outstanding monument is Drottningholm Palace (on the island of Lovön), Sweden's foremost royal countryseat and the most impressive example of Swedish baroque architecture. It was built by Tessin the Elder (from 1662), who also created the garden, which is typical of the landscape architecture of the time. The rococo interior decoration was chiefly the work of Hårleman and Jean Eric Rehn. At Drottningholm there is also the most genuinely rococo building in Sweden, the small pleasure palace called Kina Slott (the Chinese Pavilion). The remains of the English park with its Gothic tower reveal the taste of another period. Jacobsdal Palace (now called Ulriksdal) was built about 1640 under the direction of Hans Jakob Kristler; little remains of the garden, which was richly furnished with examples of baroque architecture. Karlberg Castle was built about 1630; after 1670 it was rebuilt in the grandiose baroque style of the Caroline era. Gustaf III's countryseat at Haga (built by Olaf Tempelman in 1787) is a typical product of Gustavian culture. This applies particularly to the interior decoration (now completely restored), but also to the English park, which was planned by Fredrik Magnus Piper.

Modern architecture is well represented in Stockholm by such public buildings as the City Hall designed by Ragnar Ostberg (1911–23), the Law Courts by Carl Westman (1911–15), the Municipal Library by Gunnar Asplund (1921–28), and the Concert Hall, designed in the style of a Greek temple by Ivar Tengbom (1926). The Engelbrekt Church by Lars Wahlman (1906–11) and Erik Lallerstedt's Polytechnical School (1914–22) are other notable examples of 20th-century architecture. The burial chapels at Skogskyrkogården — Asplund's last work — are interesting for their combination of architectural design and landscape planning. Several large town-planning schemes have been carried out in Stockholm's outlying districts, notably at Kvarnholmen, Årsta, Vällingby, and Farsta.

Museums and galleries: Nationalmuseum (ancient and modern painting and sculpture, prints and drawings); Östasiatiska Museet (Oriental art); Egyptiska Museet; Statens Historiska Museum; Nordiska Museet (Swedish culture, notably folk art); Stadsmuseet (archaeological and historical collections); Statens Etnografiska Museum; Skansen (prototype of Scandinavian open-air ethnographical museums); Millesgården (former home of Carl Milles, containing the sculptor's art collections and many of his works).

BIBLIOG. R. Josephson, Stadsbyggnadskonst i Stockholm intill år 1800, Stockholm, 1918; G. Upmark et al., ed., Stockholmsbilder från fem århundraden 1523–1923, 2 vols., Stockholm, 1922–23; A. Lindblom, Stockholms slott genom seklerna, Uppsala, 1925; H. Wahlin and J. Svedelius, ed., Stockholm nu och fordom, Stockholm, 1925; N. G. A. Wollin, Drottningholms lustträdgård och park, Stockholm, 1927; R. Josephson, Stockholm, Stockholm, 1928; M. Olsson, ed., Stockholms slotts historia, 3 vols., Stockholm, 1940–41; T. O. Nordberg, Stockholm i tolv vandringar: Byggnader och monument, Stockholm, 1946; H. Alm, The Old Town of Stockholm, Stockholm, 1947; M. A. Ohlsson, Stormaktstidens privatpalats i Stockholm, Stockholm, 1951; M. von Platen, ed., Stockholm 1252–1952, Stockholm, 1951; S. Fogelmarck et al., Bilder från Drottningholm, Stockholm, 1952; G. Hesselman, Historik över byggnadsyrket i Stockholm, 1250–1950, Stockholm, 1952; N. Ahnlund, Stockholms historia före Gustav Vasa, Stockholm, 1953; R. Hentzel, G. Munthe, and G. Sahlberg, The Wonderful Adventures of Stockholm, Stockholm, 1953; M. Rydbeck and A. Andersson, Stockholm som medeltida konstcentrum, Stockholm, 1953; S. Fogelmarck, Carl Fredrik Adelcrantz: arkitekt, Stockholm, 1957.

Dalarna. The churches of Dalarna are characterized by large, bright interiors, richly colored and often decorated in the baroque style. The province has a great variety of folk art of high artistic quality. In the village of Sundborn is the painter Carl Larsson's farm, Lilla Hyttnäs; this early-20th-century home has had a strong influence on Swedish domestic interiors.

BIBLIOG. A. L. Romdahl, Carl Larsson som etsare, Stockholm, 1913; G. Boëthius, Dalarna (Dalecarlia): A Description of Its Scenery, Its People and Its Culture, Stockholm, 1930; S. Svärdström, Dalmålningarna och deras förlagor, Stockholm, 1949; H. Cornell, Den svenska konstens historia, 2d ed., II, Stockholm, 1959; E. Forssman, Medeltida träskulptur i Dalarna, Falun, 1961.

Falun. Interesting monuments of this old mountain town include the Kopparberg Church (15th cent.) and the Kristina Church, which was built in 1642–55 by Hans Ferster following the same basic plan as the church of St. Jakob in Stockholm. There is also a 17th-century town hall. The Dalarnas Museum has archaeological collections, church art, and folk art.

BIBLIOG. E. Lyberg, Falu stad och borgare före 1641, Falun, 1940; G. Eckström, Kristine kyrka, Falun, 1950.

Leksand. The church of Leksand was built at the end of the 13th century and enlarged in the 15th and 17th centuries. In the 18th century it was given a typical low central tower with an onion-shaped cupola.

BIBLIOG. G. Boëthius, Dalarnas högsta kyrktorn, Dalarnas hembygdsbok, 1942, pp. 51–64; A. Lindblom, Sveriges konsthistoria, II, Stockholm, 1944, pp. 471–72; K. Hedlund, I Leksand, Leksand, 1960.

Stora Tuna. The 15th-century church of Stora Tuna is an impressive three-aisled hall church built of stone with brick ornamentation. The stellar vaulting has medieval frescoes.

BIBLIOG. A. Lindblom, Sveriges konsthistoria, I, Stockholm, 1944, pp. 240–41; O. Bolling, ed., Stora Tuna, Stora Tuna, 1959.

Torsång. The church here is of stone with brick ornamentation and dates from the middle of the 14th century. The picturesque church square has a shingled bell cote and a number of red stalls, formerly used to stable horses during church services.

Uppland. This province has many castles of different periods. They include Rydboholm Castle, where three wings were added in the 16th century to a massive medieval central tower; Vik Castle, which, in spite of 17th-century modifications, has retained the character of a 15th-century fortified residence; Rosersberg Castle, a 17th-century building designed by Simon de la Vallée; and Gimo Castle, built about 1760 by Jean Eric Rehn in typical Gustavian style.

BIBLIOG. O. Almgren, Upplands fornminnen, Uppsala, 1912; G. Upmark, Rydboholm: Några ord om Gustav Vasas fädernegård, Hävd och hembygd, 1923, pp. 21–28; A. Hahr, Gimo slotts anläggning, Upplands fornminnesförenings tidskrift, X, 1925–26, pp. 21–28; N. G. Wollin, Rosersberg, Stockholm, 1930; H. Cornell, Den svenska konstens historia, Stockholm, 1944.

Birka. Björkö, an island in Lake Mälaren, is one of the areas in Sweden richest in ancient remains. On it lies the town of Birka, which in the 9th and 10th centuries was one of the country's most prosperous trade centers. A number of burial mounds and fortifications encircling the ancient town are still visible here.

BIBLIOG. A. Schück, Studier rörande det svenska stadsväsendets uppkomst och äldsta utveckling, Stockholm, 1926; H. Arbman, Birka, I, 2 vols., Stockholm, 1940–43.

Färentuna. Färentuna church is one of the four churches in Uppland with an east tower; it has late Gothic frescoes and a baroque pulpit and choir screen.

Härkeberga. The church in Härkeberga is famous for its frescoes by Albertus (late 15th cent.), who executed paintings in some twenty churches in Uppland (e.g., Härnevi); it also has a triumphal crucifix dating from the best Gothic period and a Gustavian pulpit.

BIBLIOG. Å. Nisbeth, Härkeberga kyrka, Uppsala, 1956; E. Lundberg, Kyrkan som bilderbok, Svenska Turistföreningens årsskrift, 1962, pp. 175–94.

Grönsö. The castle here was built at the beginning of the 17th century in late northern European Renaissance style. It has, among other features, six richly decorated 17th-century ceilings in a good state of preservation, as well as mural paintings.

BIBLIOG. S. Wallin, Grönsö: hemmet i ett stort uppländskt herrgårdshus, Stockholm, 1952.

Östra Ryd. The church here contains frescoes by Johannes Ivan (15th cent.) and fittings dating from the late Middle Ages, as well as a large collection of paintings, acquired during the Swedish campaigns on the Continent during the years of political expansion.

BIBLIOG. F. Westberg, Östra Ryds kyrka i Roslagen, Julhälsning till församl. i ärkestiftet, 1926, pp. 167–70; T. O. Nordberg, Östra Ryds tavelsamling, Stockholm, 1929.

Sigtuna. This ancient town has a main square with several typical 18th-century wooden buildings, one of which is the picturesque Town Hall. Nearby is the Church of St. Mary (formerly the Domin-

n church), the major part of which was completed in 1255. There
remains of the stone churches of St. Per and St. Olaf and of the
ver of St. Lars, dating from about 1100; for a long time these build-
s exerted a strong influence on church architecture in this part of
eden.

BIBLIOG. O. Almgren, Upplands fornminnen, Uppsala, 1912; H.
rnell, Sigtuna och Gamla Uppsala, Stockholm, 1920; G. Hallström et
ed., Från det gamla Sigtuna, Uppsala, 1923; J. Roosval, Une voûte à
vures du XIe siècle à Sigtuna, Medieval S. in Memory of A. Kingsley
ter, II, Cambridge, Mass., 1939, pp. 689–97; E. Floderus, Sigtuna, Stock-
m, 1941; C. Munthe, Sigtuna, Svenska Turistföreningens årsskrift,
2, pp. 245–56.

Skokloster. This castle, built in the middle of the 17th century,
a square plan with octagonal towers at the corners. The interior
a good example of Swedish 17th-century decoration. The castle
tains, among other things, a rich collection of arms and armor.
e nearby church, consecrated in 1300, is one of the oldest brick
rches in the area round Lake Mälaren.

BIBLIOG. E. Andrén, Skokloster, Stockholm, 1948; G. Eimer, Carl
staf Wrangel: Som byggherre i Pommern och Sverige, Stockholm, 1961.

Solna. The church here is one of Uppland's three round churches
ing from the 12th century (the others being the churches of Brom-
and Munsö); its interior was decorated by the masters known
Peter (second half of 15th cent.) and Albertus.

BIBLIOG. A. R. G. Tydén, Solna slott och fornminnen, Stockholm,
6; R. Stenberg, Solna kyrka, Uppsala, 1946.

Spånga. Spånga church is a 13th-century building, with additions
ing from the 15th and 17th centuries. It has late Gothic frescoes
formerly contained a remarkable 12th-century reliquary (now
Stockholm, Statens Historiska Mus.).

BIBLIOG. I. Henschen, Spånga kyrka, Uppsala, 1949; A. Tuulse and
Lindqvist, Spånga och Hässelby kyrkor, Stockholms kyrkor, VIII, 1959,
85–230.

Steninge. Built in the 17th century following designs by Tessin
Younger, this country mansion is in the Italian baroque style
thus differs from other countryseats in Sweden.

BIBLIOG. A Lindblom, Sveriges konsthistoria, II, Stockholm, 1944,
433, 441–42.

Täby. The church of Täby is one of the most interesting medieval
rches in the area; it has mural paintings by Albertus and fine
ramental fittings, such as the late medieval altarpiece.

Tensta. The church here is one of the most remarkable rural
rches in Uppland. The blind arches of the brick walls are unique
a Swedish village church. The walls and vaults are decorated with
ntings by Johannes Rosenrod (ca. 1430), and the altarpiece is
rhaps by Bernt Notke.

BIBLIOG. F. Nordström, Tensta kyrka, Uppsala, 1951; E. Lundberg,
rkan som bilderbok, Svenska Turistföreningens årsskrift, 1962, pp.
–94.

Uppsala. This town is an episcopal seat and has the oldest uni-
rsity in Sweden. Its Cathedral, the largest in Scandinavia, is in the
thic style of northern France; one of its first architects was a French-
n, Etienne de Bonneuil (late 13th cent.). It consists of a nave with
o side aisles and numerous chapels to the north and south, a transept,
d a choir with an ambulatory and chapels. When consecrated in
35, the church had two small west towers (subsequently heightened)
d ridge pinnacles. The Bondkyrka (Church of the Trinity), which
adjacent, dates from the 12th century but was modified during the
er Middle Ages; the main structure of the church is of stone, but
e cross-vaulting of the nave is of brick. The exterior has tall brick
bles. Uppsala Castle was begun about 1540 by Gustaf Vasa. John
engaged the architect Francesco Parr (Pahr) to continue the work,
d after 1620 (under Gustaf II Adolf) Kasper Panten was put in
arge. The present imposing structure, flanked by two massive
und towers that give the edifice its characteristic outline, was built
ut 1600. Seventeenth-century buildings include the Skytteanum
d Gustavianum (until the end of the 19th century the true nucleus
the university).
Museums: Universitetets Samlingar i Gustavianum (Swedish and
yptian antiquities, ecclesiastical and other art); Upplandsmuseet
wedish history and ethnography); Disagården (open-air museum).

Some miles to the north of Uppsala is Gamla (Old) Uppsala,
the last stronghold of paganism in Sweden. In an area where prehistoric remains abound there are the enormous sepulchral mounds known
as "Kungshögarna." Parts of Sweden's oldest cathedral (ca. 1100)
are visible in the present stone church, which has a nave without
aisles (ca. 1300).

BIBLIOG. O. Almgren, Upplands fornminnen, Uppsala, 1912; H. Cornell, Sigtuna och Gamla Uppsala, Stockholm, 1920; A. Hahr, Uppsala
slott och dess rikssal, Stockholm, 1932; G. Boëthius and A. Romdahl, Uppsala domkyrka 1258–1435, Uppsala, 1935; M. Åmark, Uppsala domkyrka
genom åtta århundraden, Uppsala, 1938; A. Hahr, Uppsala domkyrka under
1300-talets första hälft, Kyrkohistorisk årsskrift, XL, 1940, pp. 47–127;
S. Lindqvist, Gamla Uppsala kyrka, Fornvännen, XLVI, 1951, pp. 219–50;
F. Nordström, Studier i Uppsala domkyrkas äldsta byggnadshistoria, Stockholm, 1953; O. Herrlin et al., ed., Uppsala ärkestift i ord och bild, Stockholm,
1954.

Vendel. Situated in an area rich in prehistoric burial places,
Vendel has a church that has changed little since the 15th century.
Its oldest part is the sacristy, which is one of Sweden's best-preserved
ecclesiastical interiors in the early Gothic style. The nave is covered
with paintings by Johannes Ivan (1451).

BIBLIOG. O. Lundberg, ed., Vendel i fynd och forskning, Stockholm,
1938; H. Alm and A. Tollstén, Vendels kyrka, Uppsala, 1947.

Västmanland. This province is related architecturally to Uppland. Medieval architecture is mainly represented by the Gothic style
in stone and brick. Gables are often adorned with patterns in brick
facing, and occasionally towers also have this form of decoration.
Church towers are frequent, but there are many churches with a
detached bell cote instead of a tower. Among the castles of interest
in Västmanland are Ängsö Castle, a medieval fortress enlarged first
in the 17th century and again about 1740; Fullerö Castle, which
has architectural similarities with the Riddarhus in Stockholm and
contains a valuable collection of paintings and sculpture, including
works by Jacques Philippe Bouchardon, Charles Guillaume Cousin,
and Johan Tobias Sergel; and Strömsholm Castle, which was rebuilt
about 1670 by Tessin the Elder in typical Caroline style. The parish
of Badelunda in this province is one of the richest areas in Sweden
in relics of the Iron Age.

BIBLIOG. A. G. Bäckström, Strömsholm förr och nu, Strömsholm, 1924;
A. Lindblom, Sveriges konsthistoria, II, Stockholm, 1944; L. Rask, ed.,
Västmanland, Stockholm, 1956; STF, Resehandböcker: Vad skall jag se i
Västmanland och Närke?, Stockholm, 1960.

Dingtuna. The church here dates from the Middle Ages. Its
tower may originally have been a separate fortified tower; the stellar
vaulting was added in the 15th century and decorated with interesting
paintings by Albertus.

BIBLIOG. H. Cornell, Den svenska konstens historia, Stockholm, 1944,
pp. 142–44.

Kila. Kila church (14th cent.) has a fine late medieval interior,
with an altarpiece, a triumphal crucifix, and wood sculptures dating
from the 15th century.

BIBLIOG. S. Erixon, Kila, Stockholm, 1946; I. Schnell, Kila kyrka,
Nyköping, 1948.

Tidö. Tidö castle was built in the second quarter of the 17th
century in a French classicistic style; the entrance and façade were
designed in the northern European mannerist style by Heinrich Blume.

BIBLIOG. N. Berg, Tidö slottskapell, Julbok för Västerås' stift, 1926,
pp. 87–93; A. Lindblom, Sveriges konsthistoria, II, Stockholm, 1944, pp. 357–
58, 393, 398, 403, 407.

Västerås. The present Cathedral in Västerås is in the German
late Gothic style, but the original building was considerably older.
In the 15th century it was reconstructed with a nave and four aisles
extending to the tall, bright choir. Inside there are some magnificent
late medieval altarpieces. Västerås Castle is one of the old fortresses
restored in the 16th century by Gustaf Vasa. It is a compact square
construction, and, like most of the Vasa castles, served not only as
a fortress but also as a royal residence.
Museums: Vallby Friluftsmuseum (open-air museum of Swedish
culture); Västerås Konstgalleri; Västmanlands Läns Museum (archaeology, ecclesiastical art, Swedish history and ethnography).

BIBLIOG. S. Drakenberg, Västerås genom tiderna, Västerås, 1942;
Västerås, Uppsala, 1946; G. Ekström et al., ed., Västerås stift i ord och bild,
Stockholm, 1951.

Närke. The Hjortsberga area in this province is interesting for its prehistoric remains. Närke also has a number of noteworthy religious monuments. At Riseberga there are the ruins of a 12th-century Cistercian abbey. Glanshammar church, originally built in the 12th century and later enlarged, has a number of medieval wood sculptures and interesting 16th-century frescoes.

Bibliog. A. Lindblom, Sveriges konsthistoria, II, Stockholm, 1944; STF, Resehandböcker: Vad skall jag se i Västmanland och Närke?, Stockholm, 1960.

Örebro. This is the largest town in the province of Närke and one of the oldest in Sweden; since the late Middle Ages it has been an important trade center. The castle is a compact square construction with four massive round towers at the corners. The oldest parts of the fortress date from the 13th century; its present plan and dimensions are chiefly the result of additions carried out between 1573 and 1627. The Church of St. Nikolai (second half of 13th cent.) was built of limestone and shows English architectural influences. The Örebrö Läns Museum has archaeological, ethnographic, and church-art collections, as well as a number of modern art works.

Bibliog. Örebro, Uppsala, 1945; B. Waldén, Sankt Nikolai kyrka i Örebro, 3d ed., Örebro, 1948; B. Waldén, Örebro slott, Örebro, 1960.

Södermanland. This province is rich in relics of the remote past. These include what is perhaps Sweden's most remarkable runic inscription, the so-called "Sigurd inscription," incised on a rock on Ramsundsberget; the text, encircled by winding runes, is combined with lively scenes from Norse legends (Sigurd fighting the dragon Fafnir). Södermanland also has many castles and mansions. Some are medieval in origin, for example Julita Manor, a 12th-century Cistercian abbey reconstructed in the 18th century and now used as a museum of Södermanland folk art. Several of the 17th-century castles were designed by Tessin the Elder; they include Mälsåker Castle and Fiholm Castle (a building in the Franco-Dutch Renaissance style on which Simon de la Vallée also worked). Tessin the Elder probably also designed Eriksberg Castle, which has some large ceiling paintings by David Klöcker Ehrenstrahl. Sandemar Castle, a wooden edifice dating from the 1690s, is one of the best-preserved Caroline buildings in Sweden, while Sturehov Castle, designed by Adelcrantz (ca. 1780), is one of the finest examples of a Gustavian mansion.

Bibliog. STF, Årsskrift, Stockholm, 1927; G. Upmark, Eriksberg, Svenska turistföreningens årsskrift, 1927, pp. 100–16; Sörmländska kyrkor, Nyköping, 1940 ff.; S. Svärdström, En julitasommar, Fataburen, 1942, pp. 7–30; K. Bonde, Ericsbergs slottskyrka, Till hembygden, XLI, 1944, pp. 14–19; A. Lindblom, Sveriges konsthistoria, II, Stockholm, 1944; S. Wallin, Julita kyrka, Nyköping, 1945; N. Sundquist, Julita kloster, Fataburen, 1951, pp. 153–62; I. Schnell, Sörmland genom tiderna, Nyköping, 1952; S. Fogelmarck, Carl Fredrik Adelcrantz: Arkitekt, Stockholm, 1957, pp. 87–97, 467; M. Lagerquist, Julita gård i Södermanland, Fataburen, 1957, pp. 29–56; S. B. F. Janson, The Runes of Sweden, Stockholm, 1962.

Botkyrka. The stone church of Botkyrka was consecrated by Sweden's first archbishop, Stefan, in 1176; its altarpiece is a particularly fine example of early-16th-century Flemish workmanship.

Jäder. The church here, which dates back to the 12th century, was modified in the 17th century by Jean de la Vallée and Tessin the Elder; it contains many interesting fittings.

Ludgo. The area around Ludgo is particularly rich in runestones. Ludgo church, which dates from the early Middle Ages, has sandstone sculptures (ca. 1400) and an altarpiece attributed to Burchardt Precht.

Bibliog. STF, Resehandböcker: Mälarlandskapen, Stockholm, 1939; E. Bohrn, Ludgo kyrka, Nyköping, 1944.

Mariefred. This town was named after the Carthusian monastery of Pax Mariae. Gripsholm Castle nearby is one of the most remarkable castles of the Vasa period. It was originally built about 1380, and remains of this construction are still to be seen in the northwest corner of the present building. The present exterior dates from the 16th century, with a few 17th- and 18th-century additions. The interior decoration faithfully reflects Renaissance, Gustavian, and neoclassic styles. Gripsholm contains one of the largest portrait collections in Europe.

Bibliog. A. Flentzberg, Ett kyrkojubileum, Till hembygden, XXII, 1925, pp. 93–116; P. O. Westlund, Mariefreds och Kärnbo kyrkor, Nyköping, 1945; P. O. Westlund, Gripsholm under Vasatiden, Stockholm, 1949; N. G. Wallin, Gripsholmsföreningen och restaureringen på 1980-talet,

Kungl. Vitt. H. och Antik. Akad. Handl., LXXI, 1950, pp. 149–213; P. Westlund, Gripsholm under den karolinska tiden, Stockholm, 1953; B. Malmberg, Gripsholm: Ett slott och dess konstskatter, Stockholm, 1958; A. Tuulse, Gustav Vasas reformationstavlor, Malmö, 1958.

Nyköping. This royal seat is rich in historical associations. regular layout of the town was planned in the 17th century by J de la Vallée. The Church of St. Nikolai is a 12th-century buildi with a later bell cote (1692). The Nyköpingshus consists of an in fortress with wings enclosing two courtyards, the whole surroun by ramparts. During the second half of the 16th century the medi castle was transformed into a Renaissance palace, which fell i disrepair after a fire in 1665. The Governor's Palace, which n houses the Södermanlands Läns Museum, was built in the precir of the castle in the 18th century.

Bibliog. E. Bohrn, Nyköping, Stockholm, 1937; E. Bohrn, Nyköpi renässansslott och Herkules Mida, Stockholm, 1941; E. Lundberg, Sa Nikolai kyrka, Nyköping, 1947.

Strängnäs. This is the episcopal seat of Södermanland and of the oldest towns in Sweden. The Cathedral was built in the mid of the 13th century by the Dominicans in the form of a three-ais brick hall church. The latest noteworthy changes were made in 15th century, when the massive west tower and the spacious chan with an ambulatory were added; the chapels along the nave w converted into richly adorned funerary chapels after the Reformati The Cathedral is a typical example of the mendicant friar's large, s ple churches; it contains many interesting fittings. It is surroun by buildings of historical interest, such as Kort Rogge's episco mansion (the Roggeborg, late 15th cent.), the present Bishop's Pal (1650), and the Paulin House (17th cent.). In the Roggeborg i museum containing historical and ecclesiastical art collections.

Bibliog. I. N. Fehr, Strängnäs domkyrka, Strängnäs, 1925; S. Wa Den klassika Strängnäsvyn, Fataburen, 1947, pp. 7–16; E. Bohrn, Sträng domkyrka, 2d ed., Nyköping, 1959; H. Jägerstad, Strängnäs stads histo Strängnäs, 1959.

Tumbo. Tumbo church was built of stone in the first half the 12th century, and the vaulting was added in the 15th centu its interior is rich in medieval fittings.

Bibliog. STF, Resehandböcker: Mälarlandskapen, Stockholm, 19 S. Boëthius, Tumbo kyrka, Nyköping, 1948.

Tyresö. The church here, designed by Hans Ferster and con crated in 1641, is a typical example of the religious architecture Sweden's golden age; it has remarkable fittings, notably the pul (one of the finest pieces of 17th-century woodwork in Sweden) a a 17th-century sepulchral monument by the court sculptor Heinr Wilhelm. Tyresö Castle is medieval in origin, but its present fo dates from the first half of the 17th century.

Västergötland. At Ekornavallen, near Skara, there are ma ancient remains such as megalithic tombs, stone cists, tumuli, a monoliths. Another noteworthy monument in this province is ruined abbey at Gudhem, which was the first women's abbey to founded in Sweden (probably in 1161). Other religious monume include Husaby church (12th cent.), which is built of sandstone, w a large west tower, and which contains a remarkable 13th-cent episcopal chair; Suntak church, an unusually pure Romanesc structure; and Hedared church, which is a 13th-century stave chur Västergötland also has several castles that are characteristic examp of the architectural styles of different periods. Mariedal Cast probably designed by Jean de la Vallée at the beginning of the i century, is a good example of a baroque Swedish countryseat, wh Stora Ek, designed by Jean Eric Rehn, is a typical rococo manor hou

Bibliog. E. Fischer, Västergötlands romanska stenkost, Götebo 1918; E. Fischer, Västergötlands kyrkliga konst under medeltiden, Gö borg, 1920; A. Svahn, Husaby kyrka, källa och ruin, Lidköping, 1927; Cornell, Den svenska konstens historia, Stockholm, 1944; A. Lindbl Sveriges konsthistoria, Stockholm, 1944; G. Ewald, Hedareds stavkyr Alingsås, 1958.

Göteborg (Gothenburg). This town, founded at the beginn of the 17th century, is the second largest in Sweden. Its architect is predominantly modern. The East India Company building v designed by Hårleman in the middle of the 18th century. The Cat dral was rebuilt in a heavy classicistic style following the designs Karl Wilhelm Carlberg (1802–15). In 1937 Gunnar Asplund enlar the neoclassic Town Hall without destroying its stylistic homogenei Another notable example of 20th-century architecture is the Conc Hall, designed by Nils Ejnar Eriksson (1931–35).

Museums: Arkeologiska Museet; Etnografiska Museet; Göteorgs Konstmuseum (ancient art, Italian art of the 16th and 17th enturies, and modern art); Sjöfartsmuseet (maritime museum).

Bibliog. A. F. E. Baeckström, Studier i Göteborgs byggnadshistoria öre 1814, Stockholm, 1923; H. Almquist, Göteborgs historia, 2 vols., Göeborg, 1929–35; G. Munthe and K. W. Gullers, Gothenburg: Sweden's Gateway the the West, Stockholm, 1948; O. Thulin, ed., Göteborg, Göteorg, 1948; E. Liljer et al., Göteborg, Malmö, 1952; K. Hjern, Göteborg konsten, Göteborg, 1961; R. Söderberg, Modern Swedish Art, Stockholm, 1963.

Götene. The 12th-century church here has remained comparatively unchanged; the cross-vaulting was added later and is decorated with paintings — notably a *Passion* — by Master Amund (ca. 1490). The church has interesting medieval fittings.

Bibliog. E. Fischer, Västergötlands kyrkliga konst under medeltiden, Göteborg, 1920.

Läckö. Large portions of Läckö Castle date from the Middle Ages, when it was the castle of the bishops of Skara; it was converted to its present form in the 17th century, when it was lavishly decorated with paintings, sculpture, and stuccowork. There are 16th-century paintings in the medieval Bishop's Room.

Bibliog. A. Hahr, Läckö slott och andra de la Gardieska monumentalbyggnader i Västergötland, Göteborg, 1923; Ä. Noreen, Läckö slott, 4th ed., Stockholm, 1962.

Skara. Västergötland's oldest town, Skara flourished chiefly in the pre-Christian period. Its present plan still partially reveals the medieval street system. The Cathedral dates from the 12th century and is the oldest in Sweden after Lund. It has a nave with two aisles, a transept, and two west towers; it was rebuilt in the first half of the 14th century in typical French Gothic style. The Chapter House was built about 1740. The Västergötlands Museum had good archaeological and church-art collections.

Bibliog. A. L. Romdahl and S. Dahlgren, Skara domkyrkas byggnadshistoria, Uppsala, 1928; E. Lundberg, Den äldsta stenkatedralen i Skara, Festskrift till Martin Olsson, Stockholm, 1936, pp. 25–36; S. Welin, Skara domkyrka, Skara, 1943; H. Widéen, Skara domkyrka, Skara, 1949; H. Widéen, Konstrond i en gammal kyrka, Paletten, 1950, pp. 70–80.

Torpa. There is a medieval fortress here, which was enlarged in the 16th and early 17th centuries; the Riddarsal (Great Hall) has well-preserved Renaissance paintings, and the chapel is a fine example of a richly decorated baroque interior.

Bibliog. R. Stenbock, Torpa, Torpa, 1925; P. O. Westlund, Torpa slott, Stockholm, 1942.

Varnhem. The abbey at Varnhem (founded 12th cent.) is modeled on the abbey at Clairvaux; it is ruined except for the church, which was restored in the second half of the 17th century.

Bibliog. L. E. Williams, Varnhem Abbey, Sweden, J. Royal Inst. Br. Arch., 3d ser., XXXVII, 1929, pp. 49–54; A. Lindblom, Sveriges konsthistoria, I, Stockholm, 1944, pp. 84–86, 88–91; A. Forssén, Varnhem, 7th ed., Stockholm, 1962.

Östergötland. One of the most remarkable monuments in Östergötland is the runestone (Rökstenen) at Rök. This stone is just over 8 ft. tall, and its runic inscriptions — among the oldest surviving examples of Swedish poetry — rank with the most remarkable early written documents in Europe. The province also has interesting ecclesiastical monuments, for example the Cistercian foundations at Alvastra and Vreta. Alvastra, founded toward the middle of the 12th century, is the oldest abbey in Sweden; the church, now a ruin, was modeled on the church of Fontenay Abbey. Vreta Abbey, consecrated in 1162, was the first Swedish women's abbey founded by the Cistercians; its church is an enlargement of an older Romanesque church. Vårdsberga church (12th cent.) is the only round church left in Östergötland, while Tidersrum church (1300) is one of the oldest surviving wooden buildings in Sweden. The earliest Romanesque art of the province was influenced by the art of Skåne. The church at Rogslösa is famous for its 12th-century wrought-iron door, and Ask church — an unusually pure Romanesque structure — contains interesting examples of medieval metalwork, vault frescoes, and wood sculpture. In the 18th century about half the medieval churches in Östergötland were rebuilt in the style of large classical temples. Some of the castles are built in the Dutch classicistic style, for example Finspång Castle (ca. 1660), which has a pedimented façade and large pilasters,

and Sturefors Castle (ca. 1700), which was designed by Tessin the Younger and served as a model for several 18th-century Swedish manor houses.

Bibliog. O. von Friesen, Rökstenen, Stockholm, 1920; A. Nordén, Östergötlands bronsålder, 2 vols., Linköping, 1925–26; B. Cnattingius and E. Lundberg, Östgötska landskyrkor, Linköping, 1930; O. Frödin, Den äldsta klosterkyrkan i Alvastra, Fornvännen, XXVIII, 1933, pp. 168–81; H. Cornell, Den svenska konstens historia, Stockholm, 1944; A. Lindblom, Sveriges konsthistoria, Stockholm, 1944; B. Berthelson, Studier i Birgittinerordens byggnadsskick, Lund, 1946; A. Borelius, Romanesque Mural Paintings in Östergötland, Stockholm, 1956; H. Arbman, Östgötar från urtid till Birgitta, Lund, 1957; E. Lundberg, Vreta kloster, 4th ed., Stockholm, 1958; S. B. F. Janson, The Runes of Sweden, Stockholm, 1962; I. Swartling, Alvastra kloster, 3d ed., Stockholm, 1962.

Linköping. This royal residence and episcopal seat has a Cathedral that, despite several changes made during the Middle Ages, has remained comparatively intact. It is a three-aisled hall church, with an apse of the same height as the body of the church, an ambulatory, and three chapels. Linköping Castle was built at the end of the 15th century as a fortified episcopal residence. In the 16th century three low wings enclosing a courtyard were added; it was restored in the 18th century. In the Östergötlands och Linköpings Stads Museum there are collections of archaeological pieces, medieval art, and Swedish paintings of the 18th and 19th centuries.

Bibliog. A. L. Romdahl, Linköpings domkyrka 1232–1498, Göteborg, 1932; B. Cnattingius, Linköpings slott, Meddelanden från Östergötlands fornminnes- och museifören., 1935–36, pp. 27–52; J. Roosval, Studier i Linköpings domkyrka, Stockholm, 1955; H. Tigerström, St. Larskyrkan i Linköping under 900 år, Linköping, 1958; H. Schück, Ecclesia Lincopensis, Stockholm, 1959.

Vadstena. This town in the fertile Östgöta plain near Lake Vättern has retained its medieval character. Vadstena Abbey was founded about 1340. The plan of its church — a three-aisled hall, with five stellar vaults over each aisle and a square choir to the west — is based on indications left by St. Bridget in her *Revelations*. The church, which was consecrated in 1430 and is the mother church of the Brigittine order, is impressive in its spacious and harmonious simplicity. It contains some fine sculptures by Johannes Junge of Lübeck (a group with St. Anne and St. Bridget, first half of 15th cent.). The rest of the abbey has undergone considerable changes. Vadstena Castle was begun in 1545 by Gustaf Vasa as a fortress on a square plan with four corner towers. About 1570 important additions were made by Arendt de Roy, who was succeeded by Hans Fleming; as a result the main building, provided with a monumental central tower and adorned with magnificent gables, was extended to the front bastions. In Storgatan there is a Gothic tower with a stepped gable, the Red Tower, which was once part of the now demolished Church of St. Per. Of interest among the older buildings are the Engelbrekt House (which in its present form dates back to the 16th century), the Town Hall with its fortified tower (15th cent.), the medieval Helgeandshus ("house of the Holy Ghost"), the Bishop's Palace (1574), and the Mårten Skinnare House (late medieval).

Bibliog. F. Klemming, Vadstena slott, Stockholm, 1921; A. Lindblom, Vadstena, Stockholm, 1925; B. Berthelson, Studier i birgittinerordens byggnadsskick, I, Lund, 1947; I. Anderson, Gården Vastenis och klostret i Watzstena: preliminär redogörelse, Fornvännen, LIII, 1958, pp. 258–71; A. Lindblom, Johan III och Vadstena nunnekloster, Stockholm, 1961; P. O. Westlund, Vadstena slott, 2d ed., Stockholm, 1961.

Gotland. The province of Gotland, with its capital, Visby, occupies a special place in the history of Swedish medieval art (church architecture, sculpture, and stained glass). Apart from the many interesting relics of the remote past, most of the monuments date from a period extending from the middle of the 12th century to the end of the 14th century. During this period Gotland enjoyed a material and spiritual well-being of an unusually high order, which enabled each little parish to build a richly appointed stone church. Few of the earliest churches remain; they were of the Romanesque order, with a long nave, a choir, an apse, and sometimes a west tower. Here and there Lombard influence is discernible (e.g., the north portal of Hablingbo church), and in some churches the paintings show Russo-Byzantine features (e.g., Garde and Källunge). The first result of the contact with France was the building of the Cistercian Abbey of Roma (1164); the group of three windows in the east wall of the choir is typical of several Gotland churches. Influences from Germany (especially Westphalia) manifested themselves at the end of the 12th century and became more pronounced during the 13th century. They are apparent in wide three-aisled hall churches, the vaulting of which is usually supported by four round or square pillars (St. Mary in Visby); in the smaller village churches there is often only a single pillar (Vall church). Massive church towers are typical (Stenkyrka, Tingstäde). The Gothic influence is visible mainly in the architectural details, as the general church structures retained their massive compactness. Several churches have frescoes and splendid medieval stained glass (the choir of Lye church has stained glass dating from about 1325). Gotland is richer in stained glass than any other area in Scandinavia, and stone sculpture also flourished there during the Middle Ages. Notable examples of medieval domestic architecture are the palatial stone houses such as Lauks and Stora Hästnäs (ca. 1270) that were built by wealthy Gotland merchants.

BIBLIOG. C. R. af Ugglas, Gotlands medeltida träskulptur, Stockholm, 1915; J. Roosval, Die Steinmeister Gotlands, Stockholm, 1918; S. Lindqvist, Gotlands Bildsteine, 2 vols., Stockholm, 1941–42; M. Stenberger, Die Schatzfunde Gotlands der Wikingerzeit, 2 vols., Stockholm, 1947–58; J. Roosval, Gotländsk vitrarius, Stockholm, 1950; J. Roosval, Den gotländske ciceronen, 2d ed., Stockholm, 1950.

Bunge. The church here, built about 1300, is one of the most richly decorated in Gotland. The interior has extensive frescoes dating from the second half of the 14th century; to the northeast of the church are the impressive ruins of the medieval presbytery. Bunge also has an interesting open-air museum, where exhibits include old Gotland buildings and one of the largest and best-preserved picture stones from this province.

Garde. This parish has a church (12th cent.) with choir carvings and a richly sculptured portal by the so-called "Master Egypticus" (ca. 1325); some of the original fittings are still extant, such as the baptismal font by Master Byzantios and a triumphal crucifix (12th cent.). The churchyard wall with its ogival embrasures is typically medieval in character.

Gothem. The church in Gothem, with its unusually tall towers, makes an interesting architectural group with the compact ruins of the medieval defense works and the gate with a stepped gable facing the presbytery. The church has vault frescoes dating from the end of the 13th century.

BIBLIOG. J. Roosval, Die Kirchen Gotlands, Stockholm, 1911; G. Svahnström, Gothems prästgård, Gotländskt arkiv, 1941, pp. 59–78; A. Lindblom, Sveriges konsthistoria, I, Stockholm, 1944, pp. 280–81.

Lojsta. The church here (1199–1250) has fine 13th-century stained glass as well as wall and vault frescoes dating from the 13th o the 16th century.

BIBLIOG. J. Roosval, Die Kirchen Gotlands, Stockholm, 1911; G. Boëthius and I. Nihlén, Lojsta hall, Fornvännen, XXVII, 1932, pp. 342–55.

Visby. This town was an important trading center during the Viking era and the Middle Ages. Its ramparts, which are about 2 miles long and include a gallery, a moat, drawbridges, and 44 towers, are among the most remarkable and best-preserved in Europe. They were first erected in the 12th century and vary in height from about 19 to 33 ft. The Kruttorn ("gunpowder tower"), which is still older, was heightened and reinforced during the 13th and 14th centuries, when most of the other towers were added. The nucleus of the town has preserved its medieval character. Among the many medieval churches, only St. Mary, the present Cathedral, has remained intact. It is a three-aisled hall church built of limestone, with two east towers and a fortified west tower; it contains a number of interesting funerary monuments, notably some epitaphs dating from the second half of the 16th century. St. Nikolai (originally the Dominican church) is the most impressive of the ruined churches; it was enlarged during the 13th century and again about 1400. The 13th-century Helgeandskyrka (Church of the Holy Ghost) is a two-storied octagonal building. Under the ruins of St. Clemens the foundations of three older churches have been excavated, the oldest of which probably dates from the end of the 11th century. St. Katarina (the Franciscan church) was originally built in the first half of the 13th century and was reconstructed about 1410. The Drottenkyrka (Church of Our Lord) and St. Lars are closely related; the latter is in the shape of a Greek cross. Among the numerous medieval secular buildings the best-preserved are the Gamla Apotek ("old pharmacy") and the Liljehorn House, a seven-storied mansion with a stepped gable dating from the 13th century. Among later buildings the Burmeister House (16th cent., rebuilt ca. 1650) and the Town Hall, designed in the 18th century by Carl Hårleman, deserve special mention. The Gotlands Fornsal is a museum containing a remarkable collection of prehistoric and medieval art, as well as collections illustrating country and urban life in Gotland.

BIBLIOG. H. Wåhlin, Wisby and the Ancient Civilization of Gotland, Stockholm, 1926; P. Sörensen, Visby, Copenhagen, 1935; E. Hejneman et al., ed., Visby stift i ord och bild, Stockholm, 1950; O. Janse, Visby stadsmur, 3d ed., Stockholm, 1962; E. Lundberg, Visby, 3d ed., Stockholm, 1962.

Småland. The most noteworthy prehistoric site in Småland is Smålands Stenar, where there are five large stone circles that serve as places of council and religious ritual. Småland is a densely foreste province, and consequently during the Middle Ages the churche here were built of wood rather than of stone. Occasionally the were fortified, for example the 12th-century church at Kläckeberg Many churces in Småland are shingled and red in color (Bottnaryc Näshult, Tutaryd), and their construction shows a native skill in th use of wood. Often they were modified in the 17th and 18th centuries Several churches contain interesting works of art. Among these ar the paintings on the wooden ceiling of the abandoned church a Dädesjö (ca. 1275) and an altarpiece attributed to Bernt Notke in th 17th-century church at Djursdala.

BIBLIOG. E. H. G. Wrangel, Småländska kulturbilder, Lund, 1925 B. Blomqvist, Studier i Smålands romanska stenkonst, Lund, 1929; S Erixon, Allmogemålningar från Småland och Halland, Stockholm, 1930 O. Lidén, Västra Smålands äldsta bebyggelsehistoria i belysning av des stenålderskulturer, Hyltén Cavallius förening. årsbok, 1936, pp. 155–213 I. Rudmark, Djursdala kyrka genom tiderna, Linköping, 1941; M. Hofrén Pataholm, Stockholm, 1946; H. Schiller, Småland, Stockholm, 1953; STF Resehandböcker: Vad skall jag se i Småland och Bleckinge?, Stockholm, 1959

Kalmar. There are numerous ancient remains in the vicinity o Kalmar, indicating that from early times it was an urban center. I the middle of the 13th century it was probably Sweden's largest town After a fire at the end of the 17th century the town was rebuilt o a typically baroque plan, with regular blocks and straight streets Stortorget (the main square) is one of the most interesting in Sweden it is dominated by the 17th-century Cathedral and surrounded by typical 18th-century wooden houses. Kalmar Castle is of ancien origin; its nucleus is the medieval tower, which remained the centra building when in the 16th century the edifice was transformed into the finest castle of the period by Gustaf Vasa and his sons, Erik XIV and John III. It was given impressive fortifications and towers and exquisite Renaissance decoration. The so-called "King's Room" has Renaissance decoration, executed for Erik XIV, that is unequaled in Scandinavia, and the soberly ornamented portals and the fountain in the inner courtyard are also fine examples of Renaissance style. The Cathedral, which is on a central plan, was designed by Tessin the Elder in Roman baroque style (begun ca. 1660). The Town Hall dates from the end of the 17th century, as do the Dahm and Casten houses. The town has many important examples of 18th-century architecture.

Museums: Kalmar Läns Museum (archaeological and ethnographic collections); Konstmuseet.

BIBLIOG. H. Alving, Kalmar och Borgholm, Stockholm, 1925; P. G. Berggren, Kalmar stad och dess historia (ed. M. Hofrén), 2d ed., Kalmar, 1936; M. Olsson, Kalmar slotts historia, 2 vols., Stockholm, 1944–61; M. Hofrén, Kalmar domkyrka, Kalmar, 1952.

Nydala. Nydala Abbey, founded about 1140, was inspired by the Cistercian abbey at Fontenay; the apse and transept of the original Abbey church were incorporated in the present church, which was built in 1688.

BIBLIOG. E. Lundberg, Nydala klosterkyrka, Meddelanden från Norra Smålands fornminnes- och Jönköpings läns hembygdsförb., XVI, 1943, pp. 31–39; A. Lindblom, Sveriges konsthistoria, I, Stockholm, 1944, passim.

Öland. This province has runestones dating from early Christian times, elaborately engraved with zoomorphic decorative motifs. There are also a number of interesting churches in the region, for example the well-preserved 12th-century church of Resmo, Vickleby church (with an interesting early Gothic portal), and Gärdslösa church (rebuilt 13th and 14th cent.), which is perhaps the most beautiful church in the province. Certain wooden portions surviving in the oldest churches show a high level of craftsmanship. Many churches had battlemented west towers for defense purposes, and some also had east towers. The medieval stone sculpture of this province is closely connected with that of Gotland.

BIBLIOG. S. Söderberg and E. Brate, Ölands runinskrifter, Stockholm, 1906; B. Palm, L. Landin, and O. Nordmark, ed., Öland, 3 vols., Kalmar, 1948–49; B. Palm, ed., Vickleby: En sockenbeskrivning, Vickleby, 1956; STF, Resehandböcker: Vad skall jag se på Öland?, Stockholm, 1958.

Borgholm. Originally a medieval fishing hamlet, Borgholm was mentioned in 1281 as a fortified place. The fortress — one of the largest ruined castles in Europe — is a square edifice with massive round corner towers. Its present dimensions were the result of enlargements carried out during the reign of John III (end of 16th cent.) following designs by Dominikus Parr (Pahr). On the landward side the castle was equipped with bastions in accordance with the Italian fortification system.

BIBLIOG. E. E. Areen, Borgholm, Stockholm, 1924; Z. Lakociński, ›rgholms slotts medeltida byggnadshistoria, Kalmar läns fornminnesrenings Meddel., XXIX, 1941, pp. 85–107; B. Palm et al., ed., Öland, I, Kalmar, 1949, pp. 307–526.

Gråborg. This is the largest of the ancient strongholds in Öland ıd dates from about A.D. 500. The walls, which are nearly 2000 ft. ıng, were still used in the 17th century as a refuge by the local populaın. In the early days of Christianity Gråborg was probably also a ıce of pilgrimage.

BIBLIOG. M. Stenberger, Anteckningar om Gråborg, Meddelanden ılmar läns fornminnesförening, XIV, 1926, pp. 60–75; M. Stenberger, ınanstorps borg och Gråborg samt Ölands övriga fornminnen, Stockholm, 34.

Ismanstorp. This is a remarkable ancient fortress, dating from •out A.D. 500. Its walls, which are 1350 ft. long, enclose a network narrow streets and a round market place.

BIBLIOG. M. Stenberger, Ismanstorps borg och Gråborg samt Ölands ·riga fornminnen, Stockholm, 1934.

Skåne (Scania). This is Sweden's southernmost province, conıered from Denmark in 1658. It is rich in medieval and Renaissance ›onuments, among which are some notable examples of church ·chitecture. The Heligkorskyrka (Church of the Holy Cross) in ılby, founded in 1060, is the oldest stone church left in Scandinavia; ·contains Gothic frescoes and fine medieval fittings. Gumlösa church ›nsecrated 1191) and Maglar church (ca. 1200) are early examples brick churches; the second is a typical Scanian village church, ·chitecturally influenced by Lund Cathedral. The church of Valle·rga (ca. 1200) is the only round church left in Skåne. Finja has an ıusually pure Romanesque church, which has some of the finest ›omanesque frescoes in the province, while some of the oldest can be found in Övraby church. Hällestad church has vault frescoes ıat are probably by the Vittskövle Master (15th cent.), and in the ılls of the church are some remarkable runestones.

The fact that Skåne is a flourishing agricultural province in a ·rategically exposed position accounts for its many fortified castles ıd residences. Of the medieval castle of Hälsingborg only the tall ·ärnan tower has survived. The Glimmingehus at Glemminge, ·gun in 1499 by Adam van Düren, is the only medieval castle in ·candinavia left entirely unchanged. Tosterup Castle, in spite of ılargements and restorations carried out in the 17th and 18th centu·s, exemplifies the early fortified castle with towers and moats. Torə Castle (mid-16th cent.) was also built for defense purposes and ıs remained comparatively unchanged. The castle of Trolle-Ljunby ·629) is a moated building, but otherwise residential requirements ıve here superseded defense considerations. Skarhult Castle, which ıas first built in the late Middle Ages, has an exterior that is essenılly of the 17th century; it contains a fine collection of paintings. ıe of the best-preserved Scanian Renaissance castles is Rosendal ·arly 17th cent.), a brick edifice with two wings. Övedskloster at ·ved is one of the finest rococo monuments in Sweden; it was built in ·765–76 by Carl Hårleman, and the interior was partly decorated ·y Jean Eric Rehn. Other castles in Skåne include Svaneholm, which built on a square plan (begun 1530, enlarged 18th cent.); Svenstorp, ·hich was probably designed by Hans Steenvinkel the Elder (ca. ·590); and Maltesholm (ca. 1630), where the architectural style is a ·anish adaptation of Dutch Renaissance style.

BIBLIOG. A. Hahr, Skånska borgar, 4 vols., Stockholm, 1914–22; O. ·ydbeck and E. Wrangel, ed., Äldre kyrklig konst i Skåne, Lund, 1921; . M. Bååth, ed., Hälsingborgs historia, 2 vols. in 4, Hälsingborg, 1925– ·; E. Lundberg, Torups slott, Skånes hembygdsförbunds årsbok, 1933, ›. 103–22; T. Mårtensson, Hälsingborgs slott under medeltiden, Hälsing·rg, 1934; M. Rydbeck, Skånes stenmästare före 1200, Lund, 1936; J. E. ·orssander, Skånska kalkmålningar, Skånes hembygdsförbunds årsbok, ·939, pp. 56–74; O. Rydbeck, Dalby heligkorskyrkas förhall och dess restaur·ing, Årsberättelse kungliga humanistiska vetenskaps-samfundet i Lund, ·40–41, pp. 212–33; E. Andrén, Övedskloster, Svenska turistföreningens ·sskrift, 1943, pp. 238–44; M. Rydbeck, Valvslagning och kalkmålningar ·skånska kyrkor, Lund, 1943; H. Cornell, Den svenska konstens historia, ·ockholm, 1944; A. Lindblom, Sveriges konsthistoria, Stockholm, 1944; .. Cinthio, Remains of the Cloister of the Monastery of Dalby, Årsberät·lse kungliga humanistiska vetenskaps-samfundet i Lund, 1946–47, pp. 204–); A. Hedwall, Maltesholm: En herrgårdskrönika, Gärds härads hembygds·renings årsbok, XIV, 1949, pp. 53–64; N. G. Sandblad, Skånsk stads·anekonst och stadsarkitektur intill 1658, Lund, 1949; A. Tuulse, Kärnan ·Hälsingborg, Fornvännen, XLIV, 1949, pp. 103–18; Slott, herresäten och ·ıngsgårdar i Skåne, Malmö, 1950; T. Mårtensson, K. Gierow, and A. ·estin, Sancta Maria kyrka i Hälsingborg, Hälsingborg, 1951; B. G. Sö·erberg, Svenska kyrkomålningar från medeltiden, Stockholm, 1951, pp. 188–); STF, Resehandböcker: Skåne, 6th ed., Stockholm, 1951; A. Borelius, ·kånes medeltida monumentalmåleri, Stockholm, 1954; H. Schiller, Skar·ılt — Böckernas Slott, Svenska Hem, 1954, pp. 217–20; R. Norberg,

Dalby kyrka, Uppsala, 1956; A. Åberg, Skånska slott och deras herrar, Stockholm, 1960; S. Anjou, Heligkorskyrkan i Dalby, 3d ed., Stockholm, 1961; STF, Årsskrift 1961: Skåne, Stockholm, 1961.

Bäckaskog. Bäckaskog Manor was a monastery in the Middle Ages and later became a royal residence. The present castle, dating from the 17th and 18th centuries, rests on medieval foundations and consists of several buildings picturesquely grouped around a large courtyard. The church dates from the 13th century.

BIBLIOG. S. Nordenskjöld, Några bilder från Bäckaskog i flydda tider, Handlingar ang. Villands härad, XII, 1955, pp. 55–59.

Krageholm. The castle here dates back to the 14th century. In the 16th century it was converted into a typical Scanian Renaissance castle on a square plan with a fortified tower; it was rebuilt again in the 18th century.

BIBLIOG. STF, Resehandböcker: Skåne, 6th ed., Stockholm, 1951.

Kristianstad. The plan of Kristianstad is typical of a 17th-century fortified town. There are a number of houses dating from the second half of the 17th century. The Trefaldighetskyrka (Trinity Church), consecrated in 1628, is a good example of Protestant church architecture in a mixture of late Gothic and Renaissance styles; it is a hall church with impressive sandstone ornamentation on a brick exterior. The Kristianstads Museum has collections illustrating local history and culture.

BIBLIOG. M. Lundborg, Heliga Trefaldighetskyrkan i Kristianstad, Kristianstad, 1928; W. Karlson, Några skulptörer, snickare och målare i Kristianstads läns kyrkor vid 1700-talets mitt, Skånes hembygdsförbunds årsbok, 1944, pp. 45–65; A. Lindblom, Sveriges konsthistoria, II, Stockholm, 1944, pp. 345, 362–67; K. Enghoff, Kristianstads historia 1614–1948, Kristianstad, 1949.

Lund. This town is historically richer than any other town in southern Sweden. The town plan has, on the whole, retained its medieval character, with many single-storied half-timbered houses, often with high roofs. The Cathedral, which is one of Scandinavia's most remarkable churches, is a vaulted basilica with a vast crypt under the transept, choir, and apse. The apse and south portal are masterpieces of 12th-century Lombard style. The church of St. Peter's Monastery is the only surviving example of Lund's ancient abbey churches. The Kingshus (now the university library) was originally built as a royal residence in 1578. Southeast of the Cathedral is the library of the former St. Lawrence Monastery; it is a medieval brick construction.

Museums: Universitetets Historiska Museum (important prehistoric, medieval, and Renaissance collections); Universitetets Konstmuseum; Universitetets Klassiska Institutionen och Antikmuseet; Kulturhistoriska Museet.

BIBLIOG. O. Rydbeck and E. Wrangel, ed., Äldre kyrklig konst i Skåne, Lund, 1921; E. Wrangel, Lunds domkyrkas konsthistoria, Lund, 1923; W. Anderson, Lund, Bari och Compostella, Studier i konstvetenskap tillädnade Ewert Wrangel, Lund, 1928, pp. 1–28; M. Rydbeck, Skånes stenmästare före 1200, Lund, 1936; K. Gierow, Lunds domkyrka i litteraturen, Lund, 1946; A. Borelius, Skånes medeltida monumentalmåleri, Stockholm, 1954; E. Cinthio, Lunds domkyrka under romansk tid, Lund, 1957; E. Cinthio, The Oldest Bishop Churches in Lund and Antiquarian Observations in Connection with the Restoration of Lund Cathedral, Med. från Lunds Univ. H. Mus., 1960, pp. 73–106.

Malmö. This is the third largest town in Sweden. It was founded in the 13th century and still has characteristic half-timbered houses and a number of Renaissance houses with magnificent gables (e.g., the Jörgen Kock House). The Church of St. Petri was built in the 14th century in a Gallicized version of the Lübeck Gothic style; it is a three-aisled cruciform church with a massive square west tower. The gables of the transept and chapels are richly ornamented with stone facing. The church has many elaborately carved furnishings of the Renaissance and baroque periods. The Malmöhus is a moated castle, built in the 15th century and reconstructed in the first half of the 16th century; only the gatehouse, the north wing, and the north tower have survived. The Town Hall was originally built in 1546. Among the 20th-century buildings is the city theater, by David Helldén, Erik Lallerstedt, and Sigurd Lewerentz, which is located in a park. The Friluftsstad ("open-air city") at Malmö, built in 1944, is an interesting example of residential town planning. The Malmö Museum, which contains historical and art collections, is located in the Malmöhus.

BIBLIOG. H. Wåhlin, Malmö, Stockholm, 1926; N. G. Sandblad, Malmö residens byggnadshistoria, Lund, 1931; E. Lundberg, Malmöhus, Ord och bild, 1932, pp. 523–32; E. Wrangel et al., Malmö genom 600 år, Malmö, 1940; Slott, herresäten och kungsgårdar i Skåne, Malmö, 1950.

Skabersjö. The castle here, which dates from about 1620, is a towered fortress, surrounded by ramparts and moats; in the 18th century it was converted into a residence. Its chapel dates from the 12th century.

BIBLIOG. STF, Resehandböcker: Skåne, 6th ed., Stockholm, 1951.

Vittskövle. The castle here is a typical 16th-century fortress built on a quadrangular plan with massive corner towers. The chapel has interesting 15th-century mural paintings by the Vittskövle Master.

BIBLIOG. E. Liedman, Vittskövle kyrka, Vittskövle, 1944; A. Lindblom, Sveriges konsthistoria, II, Stockholm, 1944, pp. 348–50; A. Hedwall, Vittskövle, Gärds härads hembygdsförenings årsbok, XV, 1950, pp. 47–64.

Ystad. The center of this town contains many medieval buildings and half-timbered houses of the 16th and 17th centuries (the Pilgränd House, 1400; the Angel House, 1600). The Church of St. Mary is a three-aisled church with a straight-ended choir and an ambulatory; it has a square west tower. The exterior of the choir has three gables. The aspect of the church was mainly determined in the 13th and 17th centuries. St. Petri, begun about 1260, has a square, stepped-gable tower; it formed part of the Franciscan monastery, of which the main building and one wing remain.

Museums: Ystads Konstmuseum (Swedish and Danish art of recent centuries); Klostermuseet (archaeological and local-history collections).

BIBLIOG. R. Wåhlin, Ystad, Stockholm, 1928; N. G. Sandblad and A. Tuulse, Hans Räffns gård i Ystad, Skrifter utg. av Ystads fornminnesförening, VI, 1952, pp. 5–74; C. Wallin, Santa Birgittas kapell i Ystad, Stockholm, 1961.

Gunnar BEREFELT

Illustrations: 2 figs. in text.

SWITZERLAND. The Swiss Confederation, situated in the heart of Europe, grew progressively from 1291 to 1814 through alliances, commercial transactions, and conquests. Heterogeneously composed from both a racial and linguistic point of view, it shares the cultures of the bordering territories — southern Germany, the Upper Rhine region, Austria, France, and Italy. This cultural multiplicity was encouraged by strong topographical differences, the dualism of Catholic and Protestant regions, and the federalist structure of the country. Thus there was never a single predominant cultural center.

SUMMARY. Historical and artistic periods (col. 767): *Prehistory and protohistory; Roman period; The Early Christian to the Carolingian period (4th–10th cent.); Romanesque art; Gothic art; The Renaissance; Baroque art; Neoclassicism and the 19th century; Modern period.* Historical topography (col. 775). Artistic and monumental centers (col. 775): *Bern; Basel; Solothurn; Aargau; Zurich; Schaffhausen; Saint Gallen; Schwyz; Lucerne; Graubünden; Ticino; Valais; Fribourg; Vaud; Geneva; Neuchâtel.*

HISTORICAL AND ARTISTIC PERIODS. *Prehistory and protohistory.* There are paleolithic finds from caves high in the Alps and in the Jura; the Wildkirchli shrine on the Säntis at an altitude of 5,000 ft. is the oldest stone (dry wall) sanctuary known. From caves in the canton of Schaffhausen have come representations of animals incised on bone; there are no cave paintings. In the middle and late Stone Age there were settlements of dwellings on the shores of lakes and in marshes as well as hill settlements and cave dwellings. The discovery in 1853 of the lake dwellings on the Lake of Zurich by Ferdinand Keller (1800–81) was the point of departure for research on lake dwellings in general. In the late Bronze Age (Hallstatt A and B) lake dwellings flourished once more along the Swiss lakes. Besides abundant local finds, there are a few rare imported pieces (the Hallstatt gold bowl in Zurich, the Greek bronze hydra from Grächwill in the canton of Bern, and gold jewelry from Erstfeld, canton of Uri). Celtic finds from the Iron Age come from La Tène on the Lake of Neuchâtel and Basel, where painted ceramics were also found. (See CELTIC ART; EUROPEAN PROTOHISTORY; PREHISTORY.)

Roman period. In the 1st century B.C. most of the country was inhabited by Celtic Helvetii, while eastern Switzerland was populated by Rhaetians. In 58 B.C. the Helvetii and neighboring peoples wandered to France after the destruction of 12 of their cities and 400 villages but they were defeated by Caesar and forced to return home in order to help protect the Rhine border as "foederati." There

arose large colonial cities such as Augusta Raurica (Augst), Aventic (Avenches), Colonia Julia Equestris (Nyon), and Genava (Gene as well as many market towns, smaller villages (*vici*), and cour properties (*villa rustica*) that spread over the land to the foothills the Alps. In the 4th century, when cities such Augst and Avenc lay in ruins as a result of German raids, the more important s tlements such as Basel, Chur, Lausanne, Olten, Solothurn Zurza and Zurich were transformed into fortresses. As early as A.D. Vindonissa (Windisch, near Brugg) was established not far fr the Rhine front as one of the principal military camps. In the . century, a dense row of towers was built along the Rhine. Rema of monumental buildings are the theater at Augst (ca. 330 ft. in ameter), the amphitheater at Windisch (ca. 360 ft. in diameter), city walls at Avenches. Mosaic finds are fairly extensive, but rema of wall paintings are scarce. An impressive number of small bro sculptures have been found. Among the larger sculptures the m significant are the fragments from Martigny in the Musée Historic du Valère in Sion, the golden bust of the emperor Marcus Aure from Avenches (V, PL. 479), and the head of a young Helvetian in Historisches Museum of Bern. The minor arts are represented two treasures: gold jewelry from Obfelden-Lunnern (canton of Z rich) and a silver table service from Augst (4th cent.; discovered 1962).

The Early Christian to the Carolingian period (4th–10th cen The oldest surviving ecclesiastical monument is the Baptistery Riva San Vitale (canton of Ticino; 5th–6th cent.). There are foun tions of Early Christian churches in Saint-Maurice (canton of Val where a sanctuary was built over the martyr's grave in 380 and n constructions were added in the 5th, 6th, and 8th centuries) as w as in the episcopal sees of Geneva, Augst, and Chur and in castles s as that of Zurzach. At Avenches and Windisch excavations have to be made. In 455 German Switzerland was settled by the pa Alamanni and western Switzerland by the Christian Burgundia Monasteries arose at a very early date: Romainmôtier in the mid of the 5th century and Saint-Maurice about 515. Itinerant Ir monks began to Christianize the Alamanni in about 600; and in 6 St. Gallus founded a monastery in eastern Switzerland at prese day Saint Gallen. Architecture of monumental character did reappear until the time of Charlemagne, who in 780–86 founded Monastery of St. Johann at Münster (canton of Graubünden), which there was constructed the type of triple-apsed hall church Eastern origin that was used by the Swiss well into the 12th cent (III, FIG. 87). A unique architectural-historical document is the id plan of a monastery (preserved in the monastery library at Sa Gallen) that was probably drawn up in the period 820–30 at Reich nau; the columned basilica had a double choir, a crypt, and two fre standing circular towers. In Saint-Maurice a basilica with a dou choir was built about 787. The foundations of the Fraumünster Zurich (founded 853; plan used with variations in 1030 at Be münster) indicate a transept with three apses.

Early Christian sculpture is represented by the altar relief fr the Church of St-Germain in Geneva (5th cent.) and the relief of t Good Shepherd (Christ carrying the lamb on his shoulders) in Sai Maurice (4th–6th cent.). For the succeeding centuries the m significant artistic relics are the metal objects found in tombs: b buckles, fibulae, and ornamental plaques. Some extremely rare 7 century pieces from church treasures are the reliquaries in Sai Maurice and Beromünster, and the crosier of Germanus in Délémo The increased building activity during the 8th century also produc altar enclosures, chancel barriers (III, PL. 60), and ambos with Lo bard braid decoration such as those in Chur, Münster, Schänis, R mainmôtier, and Saint-Maurice. The only surviving large-sca sculptures are the stucco fragments from Disentis. In Beromünst and Saint Gallen there are small ivory sculptures in relief. The pri itive stone Crucifixion reliefs (10th cent.) from Herznach and Mü chenwiler provide rare evidence of the workmanship of the perio

Medieval painting began with the Irish manuscripts of the 8 century at Saint Gallen, but these works were of course importe The monastery developed its own painting school in the 9th centur The most monumental example of Carolingian painting is the de oration for the Church of St. Johann in Münster (ca. 800; III, 57), executed by northern Italian painters, in which the Roman tr dition incorporates Eastern and Germanic elements (see CAROLINGI PERIOD; EUROPE, BARBARIAN).

Romanesque Art. About the year 1000 there was built a group basilican churches showing Lombard influences, with piers and o or three apses, but without transepts (e.g., the churches of Amsoldin en, Spiez, Schönenwerd, Zurzach, and Biasca, and the Church S. Biagio in Bellinzona). In the churches of Saint-Sulpice (Vauc Saint-Imier (Bern canton), and Saint-Pierre-de-Clages (Valais) t east end has a transept and a central tower; at Einsiedeln and Mu there are twin towers on the façade. A number of churches influenced by Cluny were then built with transept and stepped choir chapels — for example, those of Romainmôtier, Payerne, Rüeggisberg (near Bern), and Schaffhausen. The late Romanesque episcopal churches of Basel and Chur, the Grossmünster of Zurich, and the church at Saint-Ursanne (near Basel) differ from the more systematic structures built for religious orders.

The entrance richest with figural sculpture is the St. Gallus portal of the Cathedral of Basel (ca. 1180–90). There are architectural sculptures — above all, capitals — mainly in the churches of Grandson, Payerne, and Neuchâtel, in the Grossmünster of Zurich, in the cathedrals of Basel, Chur, and Geneva, and in the Church of Notre-Dame-de-Valère in Sion. There are stone reliefs in the Cathedral of Basel and stucco works at Münster. The most important wood sculptures are preserved in the Schweizerisches Landesmuseum in Zurich. Apart from any remains of wall paintings, mostly in smaller churches, there is a remarkable wooden ceiling in the church of Zillis (Graubünden), with 153 painted panels dating from the years 1130–40. The earliest evidence of stained glass (ca. 1150) is the Madonna from Flums in the Landesmuseum in Zurich. Book illumination has been preserved mainly at Saint Gallen, at Einsiedeln, and — the best and most original — at Engelberg. The main examples of the goldsmith's art are the Henry II Altarpiece from the Cathedral of Basel (Paris, Mus. de Cluny, VI, PL. 263) and the cross in the Engelberg monastery (ca. 1200).

Gothic art. The most important early Gothic building is the Cathedral of Lausanne, begun in 1173 in Burgundian style and influenced by the Cathedral of Laon. Lausanne Cathedral had an influence on the completion of the Cathedral of Geneva, which like Notre-Dame-de-Valère in Sion shows Cistercian elements. Of the seven Cistercian churches in Swiss territory those in Bonmont, Hauterive, Kappel, and Wettingen (with baroque additions) have survived. Late Gothic French cathedral art is visible only in the Cathedral of Basel (the main portal, 1260; the glass enclosure of the choir, ca. 1360). In addition to 13th- and 14th-century construction on cathedral scale (e.g., Church of St-François in Lausanne), a series of more severe Franciscan and Dominican basilicas without transept or towers was built, for example, in Basel, Zurich, Bern, Lucerne, and Königsfelden. Many parish and collegiate churches (in Basel and in the small towns of Aargau) follow this pattern. In Fribourg the first monumental city parish church was begun in 1283, and work on the Cathedral of Bern started in 1421. The main buildings of the late Gothic period are the Church of St. Oswald in Zug (begun 1478) and the Wasserkirche in Zurich (1479–84) by the Bavarian architect Hans Felder the Elder. The German model of the hall church with freestanding piers was followed in the Church of St. Leonhard in Basel (1490) and in the transformation of the church of Münster (1492). Ulrich Ruffiner from Prismell (Val Sesia) built public halls in Raron (1512) and Savièse (1923) in the canton of Valais. Architects from Prismell (now Riva, in Val Sesia) played a prominent role in Swiss building during the 16th century.

In the 12th and 13th centuries the plans of the Swiss cities were for the most part established; some of the cities had developed on Roman and early medieval substrata (Basel, Zurich, and Geneva), and others had arisen on new ground (Bern, Fribourg, etc.). The most extensive medieval fortification sites in existence are in Fribourg, Murten, Lucerne, and Schaffhausen; there are also wooden bridges of the period in Lucerne. The most important secular buildings are the town halls of Basel, Bern, Fribourg, Sursee, and Zug. There are well-preserved strongholds in German Switzerland at Lenzburg, Wyburg, and Thun; in western Switzerland at Chillon, Champvent, Aigle, Vufflens, Neuchâtel, and Estavayer; and in Ticino at Bellinzona. Valeria-Sion and Muttenz, near Basel, are church citadels.

There are stone sculptures on the side portal of Lausanne Cathedral (ca. 1230–50), on the main façade of Basel Cathedral (13th–15th cent.), and on the portals of Fribourg Cathedral (14th–15th cent.) and Bern Cathedral (1485–1501). To these should be added the 15 statues that compose the tomb of the counts of Neuchâtel (14th cent.; Notre-Dame, Neuchâtel) and the large stone figures of the Entombment group (1433) in Fribourg Cathedral. In the leading 14th-century school of wood sculpture (region of Lake Constance) mysticism was predominant (the group of figures with Christ and St. John in the monastery church at Sankt Katharinenthal, as well as the many Pietàs). In the 15th and 16th centuries Basel was the main center, the dominant style being that of the Upper Rhineland. At the same time there was a great influx of Swabian carved altars, even as far as Graubünden and Ticino.

Painting of the 14th and 15th centuries is represented mainly by cycles of wall paintings. The first important personality in easel painting is Konrad Witz of Basel, a master of powerful realism (XIV, PLS. 427–430). Also influenced by realism from about 1500 were the studios in various cities of the Masters of the Carnation, who were

so known because that flower was used as a signature. The last Gothic artist, showing tendencies toward the Renaissance, was Hans Fries (ca. 1465–1520) from Fribourg. Three exceptional stained-glass works remain: the rose window on the façade of Lausanne Cathedral (1250) and the cycles in Königsfelden (ca. 1325–30) and Bern Cathedral (1439–55). The most original book illuminations were of a secular character: the Manessa Codex (first half of 14th cent.; IV, PL. 26) and a series of illuminated picture chronicles (ca. 1470–1515) that testify to a growing national consciousness. The chief examples of Gothic goldsmith's art are the church treasures in Basel (Historisches Mus.), Beromünster, Chur, and Saint-Maurice. Basel was also a center of tapestry production in the 15th century (see GOTHIC ART).

The Renaissance. Italian Renaissance architecture is to be found in the canton of Ticino: the façade of S. Lorenzo in Lugano (begun 1514); the Collegiate Church of SS. Peter and Steven in Bellinzona (begun 1514); the Church of S. Francesco in Locarno (1528–38); the Church of the Madonna del Ponte near Brissago (1528); and Sta Croce in Riva San Vitale (end of 16th cent.). There are some Renaissance buildings in central Switzerland: in Lucerne, the Knights' Palace (Ritterscher Palast; begun 1557) the Town Hall (begun 1601), the colonnaded Tuscan halls of the otherwise German Hofkirche (begun 1633); the Franciscan monastery near Werthenstein; and the interiors of the churches in Stans (begun 1641) and Sachseln (begun 1672). The Stockalper Palace in Brig (canton of Valais), with its colonnaded courtyard belongs to the same period. Western Switzerland has French Renaissance architecture with a Gothic tendency such as in the former *préfecture* in Fribourg (1581–83), the Maison des Halles in Neuchâtel (1569–75), and the Town Hall (begun 1556) and Maison Turrettini (1617–20), both in Geneva. A northern Renaissance style of forbidding character is seen in the Geltenzunft (Wine Guild) and the Spiesshof in Basel (1580) and the former Zeughaus (Arsenal) in Schaffhausen (1617).

Architectural sculpture is to be found in the Church of S. Lorenzo in Lugano and in the Knights' Palace in Lucerne. Outstanding achievements were the Swiss fountains, particularly the 16th-century works with mannerist columns and figures in Bern and Fribourg. Church sculpture flourished again in the first third of the 17th century in Fribourg (altar in the former Augustine monastery) and in Lucerne (Hofkirche).

In painting, Lombard art predominated in Ticino. The greatest work is the *Passion* by Bernardino Luini (1529) in S. Maria degli Angioli in Lugano (see also XII, PL. 62), from which derives a cycle of paintings in S. Maria delle Grazie in Bellinzona. In both places, as well as in Locarno and Morcote, there are other murals of the period. Renaissance painting in German Switzerland comes from Augsburg, which the Holbein family left about 1515–16 in order to settle in Basel. Apart from the outstanding figure of Hans Holbein the Younger, the best of Swiss art during the period of the mercenaries and the Reformation was represented by Niklaus Manuel Deutsch the Elder from Bern (ca. 1484–1530; XII, PL. 106); Urs Graf from Solothurn (ca. 1485–1527; VI, PL. 136), who depicted the life of the mercenaries in drawings; and Hans Leu the Younger from Zurich (ca. 1490–1531). After an intermediate generation of craftsmen, a new artistic peak was reached in the work of the mannerist Tobias Stimmer (1539–84; VI, PL. 135; IX, PL. 259). Stained glass, both religious and secular, remained a special achievement of the Swiss and was encouraged by the custom of donating windows to new buildings; the making of stained glass died out only at the beginning of the 18th century. Book illumination also flourished.

Baroque art. Almost all of the baroque churches in German Switzerland were built by south Germans who came predominantly from the Voralberg. The first baroque churches to be built were the Jesuit churches of Lucerne (begun 1666,) and Solothurn (begun 1680). Then followed churches on the Voralberg model — hall churches with pilasters and galleries — by Franz Beer (Rheinau, Bellelay, Sankt Urban) and by Caspar Moosbrugger (in Seedorf, with cupola; in Disentis, III, FIG. 87; and in Engelberg). The Romanesque basilica of Muri was rebuilt (1647) with an octagonal central area. At Einsiedeln, in 1719, a church with several open areas centered within a hall was built in the middle of an impressive symmetrical monastery. In Saint Gallen Cathedral (begun 1755) one can see the fusion of space in an already neoclassical manner by means of the insertion of a rotunda between aisles of equal length. The last great edifice of the period is the Church of St. Ursus in Solothurn (begun 1763), which is strongly imbued with classical elements. From about 1740 to the beginning of the 19th century, the Singer and Purtschert families of architects built late baroque hall-type parish churches in central Switzerland (Sarnen, Schwyz, Willisau, Pfaffnau). Protestant churches reached their greatest development only in the 18th century. After the church on the Fusterie (Temple Neuf) in Geneva (1708–10) the most monumental church is the Church of the Holy

Ghost (Heiliggeistkirche, 1726) in Bern. The churches of Yverdon and Morges are also representative. Smaller churches were built especially in the canton of Zurich, where a type was developed with a square, rectangular, octagonal, or oval hall with galleries.

In secular architecture Switzerland does not possess great urban edifices and castles. The most imposing civic buildings were erected in Bern. Throughout Switzerland town palaces and country estates provide evidence of French influence on the life of the patricians who ruled until 1798. Bern, Basel, and Zurich produced some remarkable architects, but in the west Frenchmen were employed and in the German regions architects from southern Germany. Fine wooden bridges were built by Johann Ulrich Grubenmann. Stuccoworkers, who were important as decorators of interiors and façades, came from Ticino, from Wessobrunn in Bavaria, and from the Vorarlberg; Zurich and Schaffhausen had some local masters. The art of wrought iron for church railings was centered in Constance.

Sculpture of the period is almost entirely limited to the Catholic regions, where it has traits of folk art (as in southern Germany and Austria). Hans Ulrich Räber (Reber), Michael Hartmann, and Kaspar Tüfel worked in Lucerne; Peter Frölicher in Solothurn; the Reiff (Reyff) family in Fribourg; the Ritz family and Anton Sigristen (Sigrist) in the canton of Valais; and Johann Baptist Babel in Einsiedeln. Associates and followers of the above-mentioned sculptors included the south German Asam brothers (q.v.), Joseph Anton Feichtmayr (XII, PL. 173), and Christian Wenzinger. Johann August Nahl the Elder from Berlin and north Italians, such as Diego Francesco Carlone, were active in Bern.

In painting, church ceilings and altarpieces were executed mainly by south German painters such as Jakob Christoph Stauder, Cosmas Damian Asam, Franz Ludwig Hermann, Franz Joseph Spiegler, and Christian Wenzinger; by Ticino artists such as Francesco Innocenzo Toriani, Francesco Antonio Giorgioli, Giovanni Antonio Torricelli, and Giuseppe Antonio Petrini; or by Italians, among them Giuseppe Appiani. The most important painter from Ticino was Giovanni Serodine (1600–30). The most important portrait painters of the 17th century were Samuel Hoffmann (Zurich) and Kaspar Meglinger (Lucerne), and of the 18th century, Johann Rudolf Huber the Elder and the Younger and Emanuel Handmann (Basel), Jean Etienne Liotard (Geneva; V, PL. 201), Johann Melchior Wyrsch (Unterwald), and Anton Graff (Winterthur; VI, PL. 155). The goldsmith's art flourished in many places.

Neoclassicism and the 19th century. Classicism, which had been introduced in the Church of St. Ursus in Solothurn. manifested itself mainly in secular buildings — first in the Neuchâtel Town Hall (1782) and in the "Kirschgarten" town house (1777) in Basel. In the first third of the 19th century neoclassical buildings were constructed mainly in Geneva and Aarau. The principal architect of the late phase was Melchior Berri (1801–54) from Basel, who was trained in Karlsruhe. Out of this neoclassicism grew a Renaissance revival; its most outstanding representative was Gottfried Semper (1803–79), who taught from 1855 to 1871 at the Federal Institute of Technology (Eidgenössische Technische Hochschule) in Zurich and left works in Zurich and Winterthur. The organic continuation of this style was the revival of baroque art by Johann Jakob Stehlin II (1826–94) from Basel. A revival of Gothic art also prospered in the 19th century with Ferdinand Stadler (1813–70) from Zurich as its leading exponent. Romanticism of the Munich school was represented by Amadäus Lukas Merian (1808–89) in Basel.

Alexander Trippel (1744–93), his pupil Joseph Anton Christen (1767–1838), and Jean Jacques Pradier (1792–1852) were neoclassic sculptors. Bertel Thorwaldsen (q.v.) was active in Lucerne (III, PL. 391; VII, PL. 389; X, PLS. 252, 279).

In this period many diverse personalities existed among painters. The most important romantic painter, Johann Heinrich Füssli (Henry Fuseli; q.v.), emigrated to England. Among the numerous landscape painters Kaspar Wolf, a painter of Alpine landscapes (1735–98) and Jakob Christoph Miville (1786–1836) created effective works. Louis Léopold Robert (1794–1835) was the idealizer of Italian life. Jacques Laurent Agasse (1767–1849) became an animal painter in England. The mountain landscapes of Alexander Calame (1810–64), still in the pathetic-heroic vein, led to realism and to the "intimate landscapes" of Barthélemy Menn (1815–93) and Robert Zünd (1827–1909). A realistic animal painter was Rudolf Koller (1828–1905). Frank Buchser (1828–90) and Albert Anker (1831–1910) were painters of human figures and situations. The great master of symbolic-mythological idealism was Arnold Böcklin (q.v.; 1827–1901), and to the same school belonged Ernst Stückelberg (1831–1903) and Albert Welti (1862–1912). Swiss painters of the period preferred to be trained in Munich. Special mention must be made of the north Italian Giovanni Segantini (1858–99; XI, PL. 442), who worked in Graubünden. The realism and idealism of 19th-century history, landscape, genre, portrait, and mythological-symbolic painting were united in the work of Ferdinand Hodler (q.v.; 1853–1918), whose independent spirit transformed these currents into a new art.

Modern period. In architecture, Karl Moser (1860–1936) at first designed buildings (in Basel, Zurich, Lucerne) in which the various historical styles were freely mixed but later, starting with the Church of St. Antonius in Basel (1925), he turned to construction in concrete under the influence of the Perret brothers of Paris (see PERRET). The appearance in Switzerland of a varied and at times daringly experimental religious architecture was accompanied by a renewed interest in wall painting and stained glass, vestments, goldwork, and sculptural treatments of altars and architectural features. In secular buildings, since the 1930s, the stimulus from the German Bauhaus has taken effect in a discreet form. The outstanding Swiss architect of this period, Le Corbusier (q.v.), worked in other countries, but through his teaching and his pupils his influence returned to his native country.

Carl Burckhardt (1878–1923) from Basel was one of the initiators of modern sculpture. The following generation — H. Haller and K. Geiser, and others — preferred the simple figure without symbolic significance or exaggerated expression. A tendency toward abstraction has come to predominate.

After the Munich school of painting and Hodler, Paris became the focal center for painters such as Cuno Amiet (b. 1868), Giovanni and Augusto Giacometti (1868–1943; 1877–1947) and Félix Vallotton (1865–1925). At the time of expressionism certain painters — Paul Klee (q.v.; V, PL. 137; VIII, PLS. 391–394; X, PL. 335; XI, PL. 333), Otto Meyer-Amden (b. 1881) and others — again turned to Germany. A solitary figure was the "peintre naif" Adolf Didtrich (b. 1877). In contemporary Swiss art no particular trend (figurative, surrealist or abstract) predominates, and no national coloring is evident. Switzerland produces graphic works of the highest quality. (See also EUROPEAN MODERN MOVEMENTS.)

BIBLIOG. *General works*: J. R. Rahn, Geschichte der bildenden Künste in der Schweiz von den ältesten Zeiten bis rum Schlusse des Mittelalters, Zurich, 1876; Schweizergeschichtliches Repertorium, I, J. L. Brandstetter and H. Barth, Repertorium über die Zeit- und Sammelschriften der Jahr 1812–1890, Basel, 1892, II, H. Barth, Repertorium über die Zeit- und Sammelschriften der Jahre 1891–1900, Basel, 1906, III, Allgemein Geschichtsforschende Gesellschaft der Schweiz, Bibliographie der in Zeit- und Sammelschriften der Jahre 1901–1912 (Quel. zur Schweizer Geschichte, N.S IV, Abteilung Handbücher, VI) Basel, 1943; J. Gantner and A. Reinle, Kunstgeschichte der Schweiz von den Anfängen bis zum Beginn des 20 Jahrhunderts, 4 vols., Frauenfeld, Leipzig, 1936–62; P. Meyer, Schweizerische Stilkunde von der Vorzeit bis zur Gegenwart, Zurich, 1942; P. Ganz, Geschichte der Kunst in der Schweiz von den Anfängen bis zur Mitte de 17. Jahrhunderts, Basel, 1960.
Statistical and geographical works: C. Brun, Schweizerisches Künstler Lexikon, 4 vols., Frauenfeld, 1905–17; Schweizerischer Ingenieur- un Architektenverein, Das Bürgerhaus in der Schweiz, 30 vols., Zurich, 1907 37; Die Kunstdenkmäler der Schweiz, 51 vols., Basel, 1927–65; M. Guid Dizionario degli artisti Ticinesi, Rome, 1932; H. Jenny, Kunstführer de Schweiz, Küssnacht, 1934 (2d ed., Bern, 1946); U. Donati, Breve stor: di artisti Ticinesi, Bellinzona, 1936; U. Donati, Artisti Ticinesi a Rom: Bellinzona, 1942; Congrès archéologique de France, CX° session tenue e Suisse romande en 1952, Paris, 1953.
Periodicals: Anzeiger für Schweizerische Altertumskunde, Zurich 1868–1938 (cont. in ZfSAKg, 1933 ff.; Jahrbuch der Schweizerischen G sellschaft für Urgeschichte, Frauenfeld, 1909 to date; Jahrbuch für Kun und Kunstpflege in der Schweiz, 5 vols., Zurich, 1913–29; Das Wer Schweizerische Zeitschrift für Baukunst, Gewerbe, Malerei und Plasti Bern, 1914 ff.; Ur-Schweiz, Mitteilungen zur Ur- und Frühgeschichte d Schweiz, Basel, 1937 ff.
Regional bibliography: H. Rott, Quellen und Forschungen zur Süddeu schen und Schweizerischen Kunstgeschichte im XV. und XVI. Jahrundert 3 vols., in 6, Stuttgart, 1933–38; G. Amweg, Les arts dans le Jura bernois à Bienne, 2 vols., Porrentruy, 1937–41; W. Déonna, Les arts à Genève, d origines à la fin du XVII° siècle, Geneva, 1942; A. Knoepfli, Kunstgeschich des Bodenseeraumes, I, Constance, 1961.

TOPICAL PUBLICATIONS: *a. Architecture*: J. Braun, Die Kirchenbaut der deutschen Jesuiten, published in 4 parts, Freiburg im Breisgau, 190: 10; A. Gaudy, Die kirchlichen Baudenkmäler der Schweiz, Berlin, 1922–2 H. Hoffmann, Bürgerbauten der alten Schweiz, Frauenfeld, 1931; H. Hof mann, Schweizer Rat und Zunftstuben, Frauenfeld, 1933; P. Meyer, D schweizerische Bürgerhaus und Bauernhaus (Schweizer Kunst, II), Bas 1946; H. Reinhardt, Die kirchliche Baukunst in der Schweiz (Schweiz Kunst, III) Basel, 1947; R. Weiss, Häuser und Landschaften der Schwe Erlenbach, Zurich, Stuttgart, 1959; G. Germann, Der protestantische K chenbau in der Schweiz von der Reformation bis zur Romantik, Zurich 1963. *b. Sculpture*: P. Meintel, Schweizer Brunnen, Frauenfeld, 19: W. Déonna, La sculpture suisse des origines à la fin du XVI° siècle, Bas 1946; P. L. Ganz and T. Seeger, Das Chorgestühl in der Schweiz, Fraue feld, 1946. *c. Painting*: P. Ganz, Handzeichnungen Schweizerischer Meis: des XV.–XVIII. Jahrhunderts, 3 vols., Basel, 1904–08; H. Lehmann, Z Geschichte der Glasmalerei in der Schweiz, Mit. der antiquarischen Gese schaft, Zürich, XXVI, 4, 1906–10; V. H. Bourgeois, La peinture décorat dans le canton de Vaud des l'époque romaine jusqu'au XVIII° siècle, La ne, 1910; H. Göbel, Wandteppiche, 3 vols. in 6, Leipzig, Berlin, 1923– D. Baud-Bovy, Les maîtres de la gravure suisse, Geneva, 1935; L. Gielly, cole genevois de peinture, Geneva, 1935; A. Bruckner, ed., Scriptoria dii aevi helvetica, Denkmäler schweizerisches Schreibkunst des Mittelrs, 9 vols., 1935–64; P. Bianconi, La pittura medioevale nel canton Tio, 2 vols., Bellinzona, 1936–39; H. Lehmann, Geschichte der Luzerner smalerei von den Anfängen bis zu Beginn des 18. Jahrhunderts, Lucerne, 1; W. Hugelshofer, Schweizer Kleinmeister, Zurich, 1943; A. Neuler, La peinture à Genève de 1700 à 1900, Geneva, 1945; G. de Traz, stoire de la peinture suisse, Geneva, 1945; H. Keller, Winterthurer Kleinister 1700–1830, Winterthur, 1947; A. Bovy, La peinture suisse de 1600 900, Basel, 1948; P. L. Ganz, Die Malerei des Mittelalters und des 16. rhunderts in der Schweiz, (Schweizer Kunst, Bd. 5) Basel, 1950.

Prehistory: J. Heierli, Die archäologische Karte des Kantons Aargau, rgau, 1899; J. Heierli, Urgeschichte der Schweiz, Zurich, 1901; E. Major, llische Ansiedlung mit Gräberfeld bei Basel, Basel, 1940; O. Tschumi, geschichte der Schweiz, Frauenfeld, 1949; Schweizerische Gesellschaft Urgeschichte, Repertorium der Ur- und Frühgeschischte der Schweiz, rich, 1955–61.

Roman period: T. Mommsen, Die Schweiz in römischer Zeit, Mit. antiquarischen Gesellschaft, IX, Zürich, 1853–56, Gesammelte Schriften, Berlin, 1908, pp. 352–89; F. Stähelin, Die Schweiz in römischer Zeit, sel, 1931 (2d ed.), 1948 (3d ed.); C. Simonett, Die römischen Bronzetuetten der Schweiz, Berlin, 1939; E. Howald and E. Meyer, Die röche Schweiz, Texte und Inschriften mit Übersetzung, Zurich, 1940; Déonna, L'art romain en Suisse, Geneva, 1942; E. Meyer, Die Schweiz Altertum, Bern, 1946; W. Drack, Die römische Wandmalerei der Schweiz, sel, 1950; R. Fellmann, Basel in römischer Zeit, Basel, 1955; Basler Halle Mustermesse, Die Schweiz zur Römerzeit (cat. by R. Fellmann), Basel, 57; W. Drack, Die Römer in der Schweiz, Repetorium der Ur- und ihgeschichte, IV, Zurich, 1958.

The Early Christian to the Carolingian period: S. Guyer, Die christlichen nkmäler des 1. Jahrtausends in der Schweiz, Leipzig, 1907; M. Besson, L'art bare dans l'ancienne diocèse de Lausanne, Lausanne, 1909; S. Steinmanndtbeck, Herkunft und Verbreitung des Dreiapsidenchores, ZfSAKg, I, 39, pp. 65–95; S. Steinmann-Brodtbeck, Das Baptisterium von Riva San ale, ZfSAKg, III, 1941, pp. 193–240; L. Mazenod, L'art primitif en Suisse, neva, 1942; J. Baum, Frühmittelalterliche Denkmäler der Schweiz und ihrer chbarländer, Bern, 1943; H. Reinhardt and R. Laur-Belart, Die Kirche von hen, ZfSAKg, V, 1943, pp. 129–48; P. Bouffard, Nécropoles Burgondes la Suisse, Geneva, Nyon, 1945; Congrès International pour l'Étude Haut Moyen Age, 3d, Lausanne, 1951; Fröhmittelalterliche Kunst in Alpenländern, Actes du IIIe Congrès International pour l'Étude du ut Moyen Age, 4–9 Septembre 1951, Lausanne, 1954; 700. Jahre Stadt rsee, 1256–1956, Sursee, 1956; R. Moosbrugger-Leu, Der Abtsstab des Germanus, Ur-Schweiz, XX, 1956, pp. 54–56; H. R. Sennhauser, Die hmittelalterliche Kirche auf Burg, Zurzach, Badener Neujahrsblätter, 57; L. Hertig, Entwicklungsgeschichte der Krypta in der Schweiz, Biel, 58 (Studien zur Baugeschichte des frühen und hohen Mittelalters), Zuh, 1958; Die Schweiz in Frühmittelalter, Repertorium für Ur- und Frühchichte der Schweiz, V, Basel, 1959; J. Duft, Studien zum St. Galler osterplan, Mit. zur Vaterländischen Geschichte, XLII, 1962; H. R. Sennuser, Die Kirchenbauten der ersten Jahrtausends in der Schweiz, Basel, 1936.

Romanesque art: *a. Architecture*: A. Fraefel and A. Gaudy, Baugechichte der Stifts- und Pfarrkirche in Schennis und ihrer Kapellen, ssau, 1913; E. A. Stückelberg, Denkmäler des Königreichs Hochburgund d Vornehmlich in d. Westschweiz, Mit. der antiquarischen Gesellschaft, X, Zurich, 1925, pp. 1–45; J. Hecht, Der romanische Kirchenbau des denseegebietes, Basel, 1928; K. Escher, Die Münster von Schaffhausen, ur und St. Gallen, Frauenfeld, 1932; M. Grütter, Die romanischen Kirn am Thunersee, Indicateur d'antiquités Suisses, Zurich, 1932, pp. 118– 204–18, 272–85; H. Reinhardt, Das erste Münster zu Schaffhausen und Frage der Doppelturmfassade am Oberrhein, Indicateur d'antiquités isses, Zurich, 1935, pp. 241–57; A. Reinle, Die hl. Verena von Zurzach, sel, 1948; W. Sulser and A. Heubach, Die Restaurierung der romanischen rche von Spiez, ZfSAKg, XI, 1950, pp. 150–66; G. Loertscher, Die nanische Stiftskirche von Schönenwerd, Basel, 1952. *b. Sculpture and inting*: E. Poeschel, Die romanischen Deckengemälde von Zillis, Erlench, Zurich, 1941; G. de Traz, L'art roman en Suisse, Geneva, 1943; Brenk, Die romanische Wandmalerei in der Schweiz (Basler Studien r Kg., n.f. 5) Basel, 1963.

Gothic art. *a. Architecture*: J. R. Rahn, Die mittelalterlichen Kirchen s Cistercienserordens in der Schweiz, Mit. der antiquarischen Gesellaft, XVIII, Zurich, 1872–75, pp. 63–88; E. Rehfuss, Hans Felder, ein ätgotischen Baumeister, Innsbruck, 1922; J. Oberst, Die mittelalterliche chitektur der Dominikaner und Franziskaner in der Schweiz, Zurich, 27; R. Riggenbach, Ulrich Ruffiner von Prismell und die Bauten der hinerzeit im Wallis, Brig, 1934; A. M. Bucher, Baugeschichte der Pfarrche Weggis, Vitznau, 1956; F. Bucher, Notre Dame de Bonmont und die sterzienserabteien der Schweiz, Bern, 1957. *b. Sculpture*: E. M. Blaser, tische Bildwerke der Kathedrale von Lausanne, Basel, 1918; I. Futterer, tische Bildwerke der deutschen Schweiz, 1220–1440, Augsburg, 1930; Kaufmann-Hagenbach, Die Basler Plastik des fünfzehnten und frühen hzehnten Jahrhunderts (Basler St. zur Kg. Bd. 10) Basel, 1952. *c. Paint*: J. Zemp, Die schweizerischen Bilderchroniken und ihre Architekturrstellung, Zurich, 1897; W. Hugelshofer, Die Zürcher Malerei bis zum sgang der Spätgotik, Mit. der antiquarischen Gesellschaft, XXX, Zurich, 5, 1928–29; W. Muschoz and E. A. Gessler, ed., Die Schweizer Bilderroniken des 15./16. Jahrhunderts, Zurich, 1941; J. Gantner, Konrad Witz, enna, 1943; P. M. Moullet, Les maîtres à l'Œillet, Basel, 1943; P. L. nz, Meister Konrad Witz von Rottweil, Bern, Olten, 1947; A. Stange, utsche Malerei der Gotik, VII, Berlin, 1955.

The Renaissance: *a. Architecture*: R. Rahn, Zur Geschichte der Renaisce-Architektur in der Schweiz, RepfKw, V, 1881, pp. 1–20; C. Chiesa, L'architecttura del Rinascimento nel Cantone Ticino, Bellinzona, 1934 P. Felder, Die Hofkirche St. Leodegar und Mauritius in Luzern, (Basler Studien zur Kg. Bd. 17) Basel, 1958; H. Aepli, Der westschweizerische Profanbau der Renaissance, 1550–1680, Freiburg, 1960. *b. Painting*: R. Rahn, Die Malereien aus dem Renaissancezeitalter in der italienischen Schweiz, RepfKw, 1889, pp. 1–18; P. Ganz, Malerei, der Frührenaissance in der Schweiz, Zurich, 1924; W. Hugelshofer, Das Werk des Zürcher Malers Hans Leu, Indicateur d'antiquités Suisse, XXVI, Zurich, 1924, pp. 28–42; W. Hugelshofer, Schweizer Handzeichnungen des 15. und 16. Jahrhunderts, Freiburg im Breisgau, 1928; W. Hugelshofer, Einige Luzerner Maler im ersten Viertel des 16. Jahrhunderts, Geschichtsfreund, LXXXIII, Stans, 1928, pp. 76–103; H. A. Schmid, Die Wandgemälde im Festsaal des Klosters St. Georgen in Stein a. Rhein aus dem Jahrs 1515/16, Frauenfeld, 1936; M. Bendel, Tobias Stimmer, Leben und Werke, Zurich, 1940; G. Schmidt and A. M. Cetto, Schweizer Malerei und Zeichnung in 15. und 16. Jahrhundert, Basel, 1940; C. de Mandach and H. Koegler, Niklaus Manuel Deutsch, Basel, 1941; A. A. Schmid, Untersuchungen zur Buchmalarei des 16. Jahrhunderts in der Schweiz, Olten, 1954.

Baroque art: *a. Architecture*: J. Zemp, Wallfahrtskirchen im Kanton Luzern, Lucerne, 1893; F. Gysi, Die Entwicklung der kirchlichen Architektur in der deutschen Schweiz im 17. und 18. Jahrhundert, Aarau, 1914; E. Aftergut, Reformierte Kirchen im Kt. Zürich von der Reformation bis zur Romantik, Berlin, 1922; L. Birchler, Einsiedeln und sein Architekt Bruder Gaspar Moosbrugger, Augsburg, 1924; M. Lüthi, Bürgerliche Innendekoration des Spätbarocks und Rokokos in der deutschen Schweiz, Zurich, 1927; A. M. Zendrelli, Graubündner Baumeister und Stukkatoren in deutschen Landen zur Barock- und Rokokozeit, Zurich, 1930; H. Hoffmann, Die führenden Architekten der Vorarlberger Schule in der Schweiz, Franz Beer, Caspar Moosbrugger, Peter Thumb, Zeitschrift für Schweizerische Geschichte, XI, 1931, pp. 354–70; E. Gradmann and A. M. Ceto, Schweizer Malerei und Zeichnung im 17. und 18. Jahrhundert, Basel, 1944; H. Landolt and T. Seeger, Schweizer Barockkirchen, Frauenfeld, 1948; A. Reinle, Ein Fund barocker Kirchen- und Klosterpläne, ZfSAKg, XI, 1950, pp. 216–47, XII, 1951, pp. 1921; A. Reinle, Luigi Ferdinando Marsigli, Nachtrag zu "Ein Fund barocker Kirchen- und Klosterpläne" in ZAK 1950/ 51, ZfSAKg, XIII, 1952, pp. 170–81; A. M. Zendrelli, I Magistri Grigioni, architetti e costruttori, scultori, stuccatori e pittori, dal 16 al 18 secolo, Poschiavo, 1958; N. Lieb, and F. Dieth, Die Vorarlberger Barockbaumeister, Munich, 1960. *b. Sculpture*: L. Simona, L'arte dello stucco nel Canton Ticino, Bellinzona, 1938; G. Pfulg, Jean-François Reyff, sculpteur fribourgeois et son atelier, Archives de la Soc. d'h. du canton de Fribourg, VII, 1950; O. Steinmann, Der Bildhauer Johann Ritz von Selkingen und seine Werkstatt, Disentis, 1952; A. Reinle, Hans Ulrich Räber und Michael Hartmann, die Hauptmeister der Luzerner Barockplastik, Innerschweiz Jhb., XIX–XX, 1960. *c. Painting*: D. Baud-Bovy, L'ancienne école genevoise de peinture, Geneva, 1924; O. Waser, Anton Graff, Frauenfeld, 1926; G. de Traz, Liotard, Paris, 1928; H. Helmerking, Samuel Hofmann, ein Zürcher Maler des 17. Jahrhunderts, Uster, 1928; P. Fischer, Der Maler Johann Melchior Wyrsch von Byochs, sein Leben und Werk, Lucerne, 1938; E. Gradmann and A. M. Cetto, Schweizer Malerei und Zeichnung im 17. und 18. Jahrundert, Basel, 1944; L. Fromer-Imobersteg, Die Entwicklung der schweizerischen Landschaftsmalerei im 18. und frühen 19, Jahrundert, (Basler St. zur Kg., III), Basel, 1945; R. Longhi, Giovanni Serodine, Florence, 1954; A. Eeinle, Der Luzerner Maler Kaspar Meglinger, Innerschweiz. Jhb., XVII–XVIII, 1954; W. Schönenberger, Giovanni Serodine, pittore di Ascona (Basler St. zur Kg., XIV), Basel, 1957.

Neoclassicism and the 19th century: *a. Architecture*: H. Bemper, Gottfried Semper, ein Bild seines Lebens und Wirkens, Berlin, 1880; J. J. Stehlin, Architektonische Mitteilungen aus Basel, Stuttgart, 1893; Festschrift zur fünfzigjährigen Bestehens des eidgenössischen Polytechnikums, II, Frauenfeld, 1905; A. Pfister, Melchior Berri, Basler Jahrbuch, 1931, 1936; H, Hoffmann, Die Klassizistische Baukunst in Zürich, Mit. der antiquarischen Gesellschaft, Zurich, XXXI, 2, 1933; A. Krayer, Die Baumeister- und Künstlerfamilie Stadler in Zürich und ihre Beziehungen zur Kunst im 19. Jahrhundert, Darmstadt, 1948; C. Zoerge von Manteuffel, Die Baukunst Gottfried Sempers, Freiburg im Breisgau, 1952; B. I. Polasek, Johann Georg Müller, ein Schweizer Architekt, Dichter und Maler (Neujahrsblatt hrg. vom Hist. Verein des Kanton St. Gallen), XCVII, Saint Gallen, 1957; B. Carl, Klassizismus, 1770–1860 (Die Architektur der Schweiz) I, Zurich, 1963. *b. Sculpture*: A. Etex, Jean Pradier, Paris, 1859: C. H. Vogler, Der Bildhauer Alexander Trippel aus Schaffhausen (Neujahrsblatt des Kunstvereins zu Schaffhausen, 1892, 1893), I–II, 1892–93; H. von Matt, Josef Anton Maria Christens, sein Leben, sein Werk und seine Zeit, Lucerne, 1957. *c. Painting*: F. Feuillet de Conches, Léopold Robert, Paris, 1848; C. Clément, Léopold Robert d'après sa correspondance inédite, Paris, 1875; C. Clément, Gleyre, Geneva, Neuenberg, 1878; E. Rambert, Alexandre Calame, Paris, 1884; F. Servaes, Giovanni Segantini, Vienna, 1902; J. H. Heer, Die Schweizerische Malerei des 19. Jahrhunders, Leipzig, 1906; M. Lehrs, Karl Stauffer, Bern, Dresden, 1907; W. L. Lehmann, Albert Welti (Neujahrsblatt der Zürcher Kunstgesellschaft, 1913), Zurich, 1913; C. A. Loosli, Ferdinand Hodler, Zurich, 1919; E. Bender, Das Leben Ferdinand Hodlers, Zurich, 1921; C. A. Loosli, Ferdinand Hodler, Leben, Werk und Nachlass, 4 vols., Bern, 1921–24; H. A. Schmid, Arnold Böcklin, 4 vols., Basel, 1922; E. Bender, Die Kunst Ferdinand Hodlers, Zurich, 1923; W. Barth, Arnold Böcklin, Frauenfeld, Leipzig, 1928; S. Rocheblave, Ernst Stöckelberg, sa vie, son œuvre, Paris, Lausanne, 1931; H. Uhde-Bernays, Robert Zünd, Landschaftsmaler, Basel, 1934; G. Wälchli, Frank Buchser, Zurich, Leipzig, 1941; M. Huggler and A. M. Cetto, Schweizer Malerei im 19. Jahrhundert, Basel, 1942; R. Toepffer, Œuvres complètes, 25 vols., Geneva, 1942–47; H. Rumpel, Beiträge zu einer Charakteristik der schweizerischen Malerei des 19. Jahrhunderts, Zurich, 1943; G. Wälchli, Martin Disteli, Zurich, 1943; Die Lithographie in der Schweiz und die verwandten Techniken, Zurich, 1944; P. Wescher, Die Romantik in der Schweizer Malerei, Frauenfeld, 1946; V. Huber, Schweizer Landschaftsmaler, das intime Landschaftsbild im 19. Jahrhudnert, Zurich, 1949; H. Lanz, Der Basler Maler Jakob Christoph Miville, Basel, 1954; J. Brüschweiler, Barthélemy Menn, Zurich, 1960.

Modern period: W. Schäfer, Die moderne Malerei der deutschen Schweiz, Frauenfeld, Leipzig, 1924; Ars Sacra, Schweizerisches Jb. für Christliche Kunst, Basel, 1927 ff.; W. Barth, Carl Burckhardt, der Bildhauer und Maler, Zurich, Leipzig, 1935; H. Kienzle, Karl Moser, (Neujahrsblatt der Zürcher Kunstgesellschaft, 1937) Zurich, 1937; M. Bill, ed., Moderne Schweizer Architektur, 10 parts issued in loose plates, 1938–44, 1949 (1 vol. ed.); Dr. h. c. Hans Bernouilli zum 75. Geburstag am 17. Februar 1951, Bern, 1951; M. Joray, La sculpture moderne en Suisse, Neuchâtel, 1955–59 (Ger. ed., Schweizer Plastik der Gegenwart, Neuchâtel, 1955–59). See also the periodical Werk.

HISTORICAL TOPOGRAPHY. The Swiss Confederation is made up of 22 cantons in which coexist four languages — French, German, Italian, Romansh (Ladin) — and two main religious groups — Protestants and Catholics. The following list gives the names of the cantons in alphabetical order and indicates for each one the official language or languages and the year in which it joined the Confederation: Aargau, German, 1414; Appenzell, German, 1513; Basel, German, 1501; Bern, French and German, 1353; Fribourg, French and German, 1481; Geneva, French, 1814; Glarus, German, 1353; Graubünden, German, Italian, and Romansh, 1803; Lucerne, German, 1847; Neuchâtel, French, 1814; Saint Gallen, German, 1454; Schaffhausen, German, 1501; Schwyz, German, 1291; Solothurn, German, 1481; Thurgau, German, 1803; Ticino, Italian, 1503; Unterwalden, German, 1291; Uri, German, 1291; Valais, French and German, 1815; Vaud, French, 1803; Zug, German, 1353; Zurich, German, 1353.

The places of archaeological and artistic interest are grouped according to cantons in a geographical order. Bern, the capital, is first.

ARTISTIC AND MONUMENTAL CENTERS. *Bern*. Bern. Capital of the Confederation Bern was founded in about 1160 by Berchtold IV

of Zähringen, became an imperial city in 1218, entered the Confederation in 1353, and from the 16th to the 18th century was the m powerful political member of the Confederation. The city, whi lies on a tongue-shaped plateau along the Aare river, developed gra ually toward the west, where the new parts of the city have arise Characteristic of the old town are the long parallel streets lined wi pillared arcades (*Lauben*) and the many 16th-century fountains wi brightly painted central figures. Little remains of the fortificatio except for the clock tower known as the Zeitglockenturm.

The most important church is the late Gothic Cathedral (Münst of St. Vincent, begun in 1421 by Matthias Ensinger of Ulm a for the most part completed around 1588 by Daniel Heintz of Prisme the tower was capped with a helm roof in 1893; the main portal (1485–1501) by Erhard Küng, with a Last Judgment and the W and Foolish Virgins in bas-relief, is the last Gothic church portal such a vast scale. The largest 16th-century sculptural ensemble composed of the 87 figured keystones on the choir vaulting (complete 1517). The five windows (ca. 1439–55) in the choir form the larg group of stained glass after that of Königsfelden; they are by vario artists, some of whom are well known. The choir stalls are by Jak Rüsch (1522–25) after a design by the painter Nikolaus Manuel Renaissance style with Lombard influences. The Heiliggeistkirc (Church of the Holy Ghost; 1726–29) by Nikolaus Schiltknec the largest and artistically most important baroque Protestant chur in Switzerland, shows French and English influences; its interior lined on all sides with colossal Corinthian columns and galleries abo Gothic arches.

Among the civic buildings the Gothic Town Hall (1406–17) important, with a hall with circular pillars on the ground floor and raftered ceiling dating from the time of construction. The power a prestige of the Bernese state in the baroque period are manifested the public buildings, such as the Stift (cantonal government) by Albrec Stürler (1735–48), the Kornhaus by Hans Jakob Dünz III (1711–1

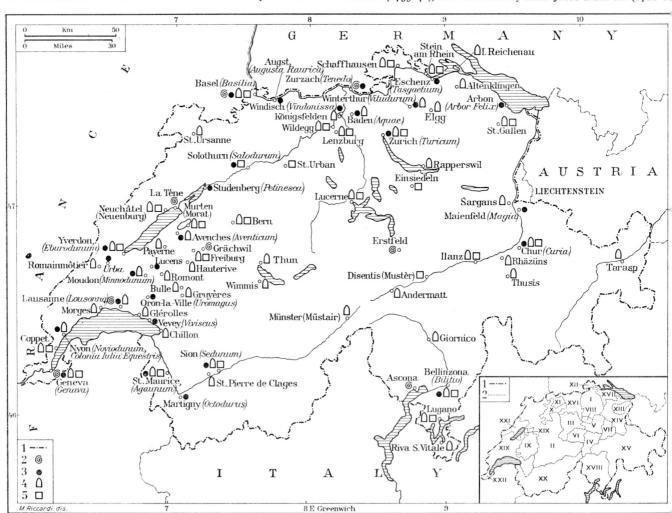

Switzerland, principal artistic centers. *Key*: (1) Modern national boundaries; (2) settlements and sites with remains from the Bronze and Iron A (3) centers and sites with remains from the Roman period; (4) centers with medieval monuments; (5) centers with monuments from modern times. Ins Administrative subdivisions. *Key*: (1) Modern national boundaries; (2) cantonal boundaries. Cantons: I Zurich; II Bern; III Lucerne; IV U V Schwyz; VI Unterwalden; VII Glarus; VIII Zug; IX Fribourg; X Solothurn; XI Basel; XII Schaffhausen; XIII Appenzell; XIV Saint Galle XV Graubünden; XVI Aargau; XVII Thurgau; XVIII Ticino; XIX Vaud; XX Valais; XXI Neuchâtel; XXII Geneva.

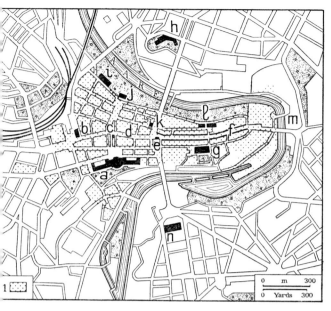

ern, plan of the center. *Key*: (1) Area built before the beginning of the 19th century. Principal monuments: (*a*) Bundesplatz and Bundeshaus; (*b*) Heiliggeistkirche; (*c*) Käfigturm; (*d*) Marktgasse; (*e*) Zeitglockenturm; (*f*) Gerechtigkeitsgasse; (*g*) Cathedral (Münster); (*h*) Casino on the Schänzli; (*i*) Kunstmuseum; (*j*) Waisenhaus (Orphanage); (*k*) Gewerbemuseum; (*l*) Rathaus (Town Hall) and Peter- und Paulkirche; (*m*) Nydegg Bridge; (*n*) Historisches Museum.

and the Ankenwaag (1755–60; rebuilt as a library in 1787–94), as well as buildings by Niklaus Sprüngling — the Hauptwache (1766–68), the Hôtel de Musique (1767–70), and the Bibliotheksgalerie, of which only the original façade remains (1772–75). Among the 18th-century houses of the nobility the Erlacherhof, the two Wattenwyl houses, and the Fischer house on Amstshausgasse are outstanding.

The Historisches Bernisches Museum contains an archaeological collection and precious textiles from the Burgundian spoils of 1476 and from the church treasures of Königsfelden, Lausanne, and Bern. The Kunstmuseum houses Renaissance paintings, works by Bernese and Swiss painters, a collection of contemporary art, and since 1947 the Paul Klee Foundation.

BIBLIOG. Schweizerischer Ingenieur- und Architektenverein, Das Bürgerhaus in der Schweiz, XI, 2, 1922; H. Bloesch and M. Steinmann, Das Berner Münster, Bern, 1938; Die Kunstdenkmäler der Schweiz, XIX, XVIII, XL, XLIV, 1947–59; H. R. Hahnloser, Chorfenster und Altäre des Berner Münsters, Bern, 1950.

Basel. Basel (Bâle). Capital of the canton, situated on the banks of the Rhine, the city owes its development to its geographical position between the French and German borders. In 374 the emperor Valentinian ordered the construction of the Robur fortress. In about 400 Basel became an episcopal see, in 912–19 it was part of Upper Burgundy, and in 1006 became part of the German Empire. In 1431–49 the Council of Basel took place there; the university was founded in 1460; in 1501 Basel joined the Confederation; and in 1529 it experienced the Reformation.

The city's town plan is based on a Roman settlement on the Münsterhügel (Cathedral Hill) that was later replaced by a late Roman castrum. In 1225 the first bridge was built across the Rhine and the foundations of Klein Basel (Little Basel) were laid on the right bank. The earthquake of 1356 caused much destruction. The last medieval wall with 40 towers that surrounded the city was built in 1389. Until the 19th century Basel maintained the character of a fortified military-religious town. Of the fortress there remains the impressive Spalen Gate, built about 1398, with sculptural ornamentation of the Parler school. The Fischmarkt Brunnen (end of 14th cent.), a fountain with a central column and figures, is the oldest in Switzerland.

The most important church is the Cathedral (Münster, formerly St. Mary's). Behind the choir are the foundations of a Carolingian chapel with three apses. A section of the Ottonian cathedral, consecrated in 1019, can be seen on the west façade, under St. George's tower. The present building dates mainly from 1185–1200; it is a late Romanesque basilica of red sandstone with galleries over pointed arches, a transept, a crypt, and, originally, an open ambulatory. In the transept there is the Gallus Portal, the richest Romanesque portal with sculptured figures in Switzerland; there is also sculptural orna-

mentation on the capitals of the choir ambulatory of the crypt, and of the galleries. The Gothic west façade with figures was begun in about 1260; it was transformed after the earthquake of 1356 and enriched with new sculptures in the 14th and 15th centuries and with towers on bases of dissimilar construction — St. George's tower on the north (1421–29) and St. Martin's tower on the south (finished 1488–1500). In the years 1357–63 the upper part of the choir was rebuilt with a Gothic glass enclosure by Johann Parler from Gmünd. Remains of the furnishings are the Romanesque relief panels with the Apostles (III, PL. 18) and the legend of St. Vincent (ca. 1000) and the Gothic tombs (13th–15th cent.) of bishops and nobility, among them the tomb of Empress Anna von Hohenberg, wife of Rudolf of Hapsburg. The two cloisters have architectural fragments of the 14th and 15th centuries. The Gothic bishop's residence dates from 1451–58. The Cathedral square is well preserved and has Gothic, baroque, and classical buildings around it.

Other churches include St. Martin, a basilica with circular piers built about 1356. The Franciscan Barfüsserkirche (Church of the Discalced Friars) dates from 1298–1350; a basilica with three naves and circular piers, it is the most impressive church of a mendicant order in the country. St. Leonhard, once a collegiate church of the Augustinians, was built on elevated land like a fortress; it has a Romanesque crypt like those in the Hallenkirchen of the 11th century, a choir built around 1356, and a nave (1489–1521) built by Hans Niesenberger from Graz in the form of a hall with freestanding piers — a form that is rare in Switzerland. St. Peter, a 14th-century basilica with circular piers, has some 15th-century wall paintings. St. Alban, formerly a Cluniac monastery church, is a Gothic edifice of the end of the 13th century with a single nave and remains of a Romanesque cloister (ca. 1100). The Dominican Predigerkirche (Preacher's Church) is a basilica with a single aisle and circular piers (ca. 1356); the choir dates from 1261–69. Remains of the famous *Dance of Death* of the middle of the 15th century, once on the cemetery wall, are now in the Historisches Museum. St. Theodore, a basilica with circular piers, was started in 1422. The former Carthusian monastery (begun 1408) was rebuilt beginning in 1487. The sumptuous Gothic visitors' room dates from 1509. Of the church only the choir remains. St. Clara, a former convent of the Clarist nuns, is still mostly a 14th-century basilica with circular piers. The former Convent

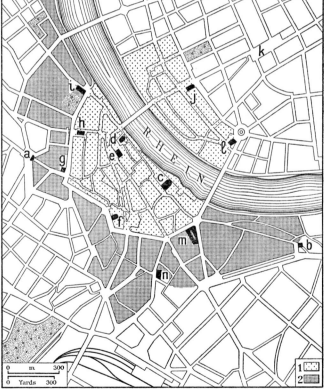

Basel, plan of the center. *Key*: (1) Area built within the 13th-century walls; (2) area built within the fortified walls of the second half of the 14th century. Principal monuments: (*a*) Spalen Gate; (*b*) St. Alban's Gate; (*c*) Cathedral; (*d*) Church of St. Martin; (*e*) Rathaus (Town Hall) and marketplace; (*f*) Church of St. Leonhard; (*g*) Gewerbemuseum; (*h*) Church of St. Peter; (*i*) Predigerkirche (Preacher's Church); (*j*) Church of St. Clara; (*k*) Fairgrounds (Merse); (*l*) Church of St. Theodore; (*m*) Kunstmuseum; (*n*) Kirschgarten Museum.

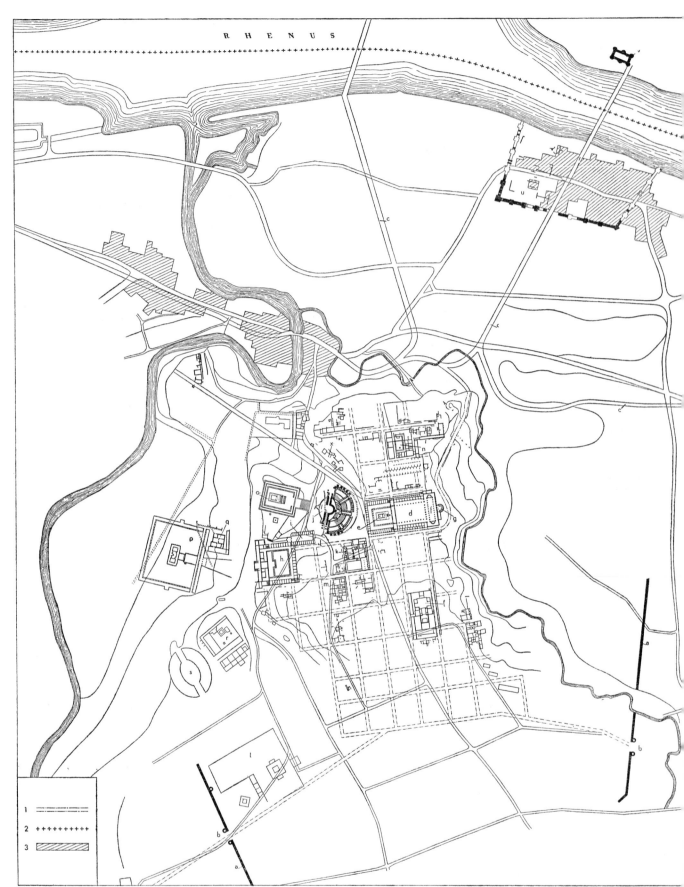

Augusta Raurica (Augst), plan. *Key*: (1) Roman street plan; (2) modern boundary between Switzerland and Germany; (3) modern zone. Princi
monuments and constructions; (*a*) Walls; (*b*) gates; (*c*) Roman streets outside the city limits; (*d*) main forum; (*e*) Temple of Jupiter; (*f*) basilica; (*g*) cur
(*h*) southern forum; (*i*) smaller forum; (*j*) theater, with remains of an older theater and a later amphitheater; (*k*) women's baths; (*l*) central bat
(*m*) workshops and residential section; (*n*) peristyle buildings; (*o*) temple; (*p*) shrine; (*q*) sacred baths; (*r*) Gallo-Roman temple; (*s*) amphitheat
(*t*) sacred enclosure; (*u*) Castrum Rauracense; (*v*) bridgehead (*after R. LaurBelart, 1959*).

f Klingental (Augustinian nuns) has an exceptionally elongated church vith a single nave (1278–93). St. Elizabeth (1859–65), built by Ferdinand Stadler, is the most important work in the Swiss Neo-Gothic tyle. St. Paul (1898–1901), by Karl Moser, is in Neo-Romanesque tyle. By the same architect is St. Antonius (begun 1925), the first oncrete church in Switzerland.

The Rathaus (Town Hall) has a main building (1504–14) with n elegant façade decorated with sculpture above an open court nd the Council Chamber (1512–14). The Baden (Badischer) Railway Station (1912–13) is by Karl Moser. Among residential buildings he Renaissance is represented by the Geltenzunfthaus and by the Spiesshof (both 1578). Outstanding among the many baroque houses f the nobility are the Markgräflerhof by De Risse (1698–1705), he house of the Wild family by J. J. Fechter (1762–63), and the White House and Blue House by Samuel Werenfels (1763–70). From the arly classicist period there is the Kirschgarten House (1777–80) y Johann Ulrich Büchel. The principal country house is the Sandrube (1745–51), also by Fechter.

The major museum is the Kunstmuseum, which contains important late Gothic and Renaissance German and Swiss paintings nd a large collection of modern European paintings. The Historisches Museum in the Barfüsserkirche houses fine medieval sculpture, tapestries, and goldsmiths' work. The Kirchsgarten Museum preserves nainly 17th- and 18th-century Basel interiors. The Stadt- und Münster-museum contains sculpture and casts, principally from the Cathedral. The Museum für Völkerkunde und Schweizerisches Museum ür Volkskunde houses important collections of primitive and folk art.

BIBLIOG. R. Wackernagel, Das Kirchen- und Schulgut des Kantons Basel-Stadt (Basel-Historische und Antiquarische Gesellschaft, Beiträge ur Geschichte Basels, XIII), Basel, 1889; E. A. Stückelberg, Die ältesten Basler Porträts, Basel, 1923; Schweizerischer Ingenieur- und Architekten-verein, Das Bürgerhaus in der Schweiz, XVII, XXXII, XXXIII, 1926–31; I. Reinhardt, Das Basler Münster, Die Spätromnaische Bauperiode des Basler Münsters vom Ende des 12. Jahrhunderts, Basel, 1926; Die Kunst-enkmäler der Schweiz, III–IV, XII, 1932–33, 1941; M. Moullet, Die Galluspforte des Basler Münsters, Basel, Leipzig, 1938; H. Reinhardt, Das Basler Münster, Basel, 1939.

Augst (Augusta Raurica). A Roman colonial city founded in 44 .C., Augst flourished in the 2d century and was destroyed by the Alamanni in about A.D. 260. The city was built along the left bank f the Rhine, mostly on a hilly plateau, and had a regular network f roads and insulae of about 180 × 216 ft. The only surviving building is the theater (diam., 328 ft.), the axis, of which was based on a emple. To the east of the theater was the town's central complex vith the Temple of Jupiter, the main forum, the transversally situated basilica (after the manner of the Basilica Ulpia in Rome), and the circular curia, all built along the same axis, as were similiar buildings in Paris and Saint-Bertrand-de-Comminges. Other temple zones, baths, nd shoppings quarters have been excavated. There are no city walls, ut only remains of an attempt at fortification. There is a museum nd a reconstruction of a Roman house.

In the wake of the new fortifications along the Rhine front (ca. 97) the Castrum Rauracense was built close to the Rhine (today he village of Kaiseraugst). It has an irregular rectangular form and ections of the surrounding walls remain. There are traces of two ridges over the Rhine. In 1960, under the Gothic parish church, here were excavated the foundations of a primitive Christian church a hall with an apse and two pastophoria, ca. 400). In 1962 a silver reasure was uncovered that had been buried about 350 and consisted rincipally of pieces from a sumptuous table service.

BIBLIOG. Jahresberichte der Stiftung Pro Augusta Raurica, Basler Zeitschrift für Geschichte und Altertumskunde, 1901 ff.; F. Frey, Führer urch die Ruinen von Augusta Raurica, Liestal, 1907; F. Stähelin, Die Schweiz in römischer Zeit, Basel, 1948, pp. 597–604; R. Laur-Belart, Uber ie Colonia Raurica und den Ursprung von Basel, Basel, 1957; R. Laur-Belart, Führer durch Augusta Raurica (Auftrag der Historischen und Anti-quarischen Gesellschaft zu Basel, Stiftung Pro Augusta Raurica), Basel, 959; L. Rochetti, EA, s.v.

Solothurn. Solothurn (Soleure, Soletta). The capital of the canton, t is situated in the Aare River valley. The town was begun as an pen Roman *vicus*, Salodurum; in late Roman times it was replaced y a bell-shaped castle, most likely with bridges over the Aare. In bout 300, the local saints Ursus and Victor, members of the Theban egion, were martyred there. A free city of the Empire, from 1218, t joined the Confederation in 1481 and in 1828 became the seat of he bishop of Basel.

The medieval town grew out of the Roman castrum. Of the fortiications only the Basel Gate (1504–08) remains and part of the ba-oque bastions designed in 1667 by Francesco Polata. There are several 6th-century fountains with figures in the Bernese and western Swiss nanner. Before the wide steps of the Cathedral there are two baroque

fountains by J. B. Babel (ca. 1775). The Cathedral of SS. Ursus and Victor, built in 1763–73 by Gaetano Matteo Pisoni and his nephew Paolo Antonio from Ascona, is the most important late baroque and early classical church in Switzerland. It has monumental open steps reminiscent of the early Italian baroque and French classicism. The severe façade has sculpture by Babel. The church is basilican with a row of chapels, a choir, and rounded transept aisles; the central dome has a low drum. Only one of the two towers at the head of the choir was erected to its full height; the east end is decidedly baroque. The Professorenkirche, the former Jesuit church (1680–88), was probably built according to the plan of Heinrich Mayer and P. F. Demers. It is a towerless, squat, short building with an ornate Italianate fa-çade and stands in the middle of a row of houses; the nave has pilasters and galleries, with stuccowork from Ticino, in part executed by the Neuroni brothers. The 17th- and 18th-century patrician and country houses show French influence. The Städtisches Museum contains the main collection of the 19th-century painter Frank Buchser.

BIBLIOG. J. R. Rahn, Die mittelalterlichen Kunstdenkmäler des Cantons Solothurn, Zurich, 1893; J. Braun, Die Kirchenbauten der deutschen Je-suiten, II, Freiburg im Bresgau, 1910, pp. 236–43; F. Schwendimann, St. Ursen, Kathedrals des Bistrums Basel und Pfarrkirche von Solothurn, Solothurn, 1928; Schweizerischer Ingenieur- und Architektenverein, Das Bürgerhaus in der Schweiz, XXI, 1929.

Aargau. Königsfelden. The church once belonged to a convent of Clarist nuns. Built in the years 1310–30 on the spot where King Albert I of Hapsburg was murdered, it is a basilica with three aisles — a plan that was typical of the churches of the mendicant orders. The choir contains the most important cycle of stained glass in Switzerland, executed in the years 1325–30 and showing influences of the Upper Rhineland.

BIBLIOG. Schweizerischer Ingenieur- und Architektenverein, Das Bürgerhaus in der Schweiz, XIII, 1924; Die Kunstdenkmäler der Schweiz, III, 1932; M. Stettler, Königsfelden, Farbenfenster des 14. Jahrhunderts, Laupen bei Bern, 1949.

Windisch (Vindonissa). Founded about A.D. 17 as a military camp for the reinforcement of the neighboring Rhine front, this Roman site lies on a plateau above the confluence of the Aare and Reuss rivers; a Celtic *oppidum* had previously occupied the same site, which has been thoroughly excavated since 1897. The plan is of an irregular polygonal shape with four towers. There was also a *vicus*, a forum, and an amphitheater (360 × 321 ft.), the latter being the only remaining visible building. The church — since 517 an episcopal see — has not been explored. The finds from Windisch are in the Vindonissa Museum in Brugg.

BIBLIOG. F. Stähelin, Die Schweiz in Römischer Zeit, Basel, 1948, pp. 623–33; R. Fellmann, Die Principia des Legionslagers Vindonissa und das Zentralgebäude der römischen Lager und Kastelle, Brugg, 1958; Jahresberichte der Gesellschaft Pro Vindonissa, Basel, 1956 ff.

Zurich. Zurich. The capital of the canton is situated on the Limmat and Sihl rivers and on the banks of the Lake of Zurich. The Roman *vicus* Turicum with a bridge was a Gallo-Rhaetian customs station. About A.D. 370 a Roman castle with seven towers and three gates was erected on the Lindenhof hill above the Limmat river. A Carolingian palace built within the castle walls was renovated under the Emperor Otto I. Zurich was designated a *civitas* in 929 and became a free city of the Empire in 1218. The medieval fortifications with 17 towers were destroyed beginning in 1833.

Among the most important churches is the Grossmünster, founded in Carolingian times. The choir and the double crypt (ca. 1100) were modeled after the Cathedral of Speyer, while the nave with galleries (ca. 1230) followed the model of S. Ambrogio in Milan. The main basilica was completed in 1250. The sculptural decorations (capitals) are mainly Lombard in style with stylistic borrowings from Como, Pavia, and Catalonia; the towers were completed in Gothic style by Stefan Rützenstorfer (1490), and their remarkable Neo-Gothic crowns were designed by J. C. Vögeli (1783); the cloister dates from 1200, and the older parts were rebuilt in 1851. The Frau-münster was founded in 853 by Louis (II) the German, and the church was consecrated in 874. Excavations have revealed remains of the Carolingian basilica. The present rectangular choir is late Romanesque of the 13th century and the main body is 14th-century Gothic. The Dominican Predigerkirche has a nave dating from about 1270 that was transformed into early baroque in the years 1611–14; the mid-14th-century choir has been rebuilt. The Wasserkirche, built on an early medieval religious site, is a Gothic building (1479–84) by Hans Felder with an austere hall and lierne vaulting. The Neu-münster is a neoclassic building by Leonard Zeugheer (1836–39).

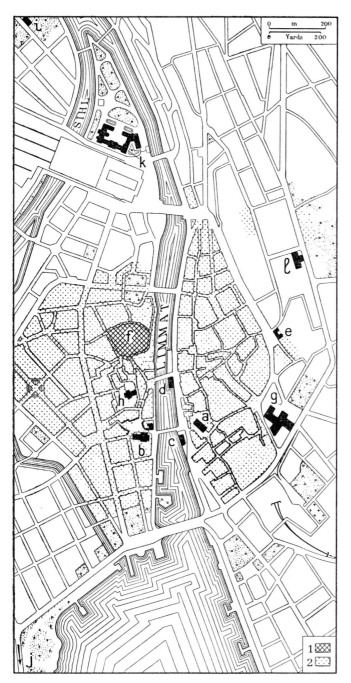

Zurich, plan of the center. *Key:* (1) Original nucleus; (2) area developed up to the 19th century. Principal monuments: (*a*) Grossmünster; (*b*) Fraumünster, Zunfthaus (Guildhall) zur Meise, and Zunfthaus zur Waag; (*c*) Wasserkirche; (*d*) Rathaus (Town Hall); (*e*) Haus zum Rechberg; (*f*) Lindenhof and the Schipfe; (*g*) Kunsthaus; (*h*) Church of St. Peter; (*i*) Kunstgewerbemuseum; (*j*) to the Rietberg Museum; (*k*) Schweizerisches Landesmuseum; (*l*) Sammlung für Völkerkund der Universität.

The Rathaus (1694–98) is by an unknown architect; its outer appearance is decidedly Renaissance. The former orphanage (Waisenhaus) is by G. M. Pisoni (1765–71). The Cantonal School (1839–42) is a neoclassic building by Gustav Albert Wegmann on the model of Karl Friedrich Schinkel's (q.v.) Bauakademie in Berlin. The Federal Institute of Technology (1861–64) was built by Gottfried Semper in Neo-Renaissance style and is the best example of its kind in Switzerland. In the same style are the main railroad station built by Jakob Friedrich Wanner (1865–71) and the buildings on Bahnhofstrasse. The transition to the modern style is seen in Karl Moser's Kunsthaus (1909–10) and the University (1911–14).

Among the guildhalls are the Gothic Rüden (15th cent.) and the Saffran (1719–23) and Zimmerleute (1708), the last two in a restrained baroque style; the rococo guildhall known as the Zunfthaus zur Meise (1752–57) by David Morf is the most sumptuous building

of that period in Zurich. By the same architect is the Haus zum Rechberg (1759–70), a most elegant private home. Country houses outside the city include the Muraltengut (1777–82), Schönbühl (1838) by Hans Conrad Stadler, and Rietberg (originally Wesendonck, 1853–57 by Leonard Zeugheer. The patrician houses of the 16th–18th century usually have bay windows as was the custom in eastern Switzerland

The main museums are the Schweizerisches Landesmuseum (painting, sculpture, and artifacts from ancient times to 1800); the Kunsthaus (painting, sculpture, and drawings from the late Middle Ages to the present time); the Rietberg Museum (Von der Heyd collection of art from eastern Asia, Indonesia, and Peru); and the Kunstgewerbemuseum. There are collections of drawings in the Eidgenössische Technische Hochschule and the Zentralbibliothek.

BIBLIOG. J. R. Rahn, H. Zeller-Werdmüller and J. Zomp, Das Fraumünster in Zürich, Mit. der Antiquarischen Gesellschaft Zürich, XXV 1–4, Zurich, 1900–03; Schweizerischer Ingenieur- und Architektenverein Das Bürgerhaus in der Schweiz, IX, 1921, XVIII, 1927; C. Escher, Di beiden Zürcher Münster, Frauenfeld, 1928; H. Hoffmann, Die Klassizis tische Baukunst in Zürich, Mit. der Antiquarischen Gesellschaft Zürich XXXI, 2, Zurich, 1933; Die Kunstdenkmäler der Schweiz, VII, 1938, X 1939, XV, 1943, XXII, 1949, XXVII, 1952; H. Wiesmann and H. Hoff mann, Das Grossmünster in Zurich, Mit. der Antiquarischen Gesellschaf Zürich, XXXII, 1–4; 1937–42; E. Vogt and H. Herter, Wasserkirche un Helmhaus in Zürich, Zurich, 1943; R. Zürcher, Die künstlerische Kultu im Kanton Zürich, Zurich, 1943; E. Vogt, Der Lindenhof in Zürich, Zürich 1948; E. Vogt, Zur Baugeschichte des Fraumünsters in Zürich. ZfSAKg XIX, 1959, pp. 133–63.

Schaffhausen. Schaffhausen (Schaffhouse). Capital of the canton situated on the right bank of the Rhine, the town was founded in 104 and the Benedictine All Saints (Allerheiligen) Monastery in 1049 Schaffhausen became a free city in 1218 and a Hapsburg dominion in 1330; in 1510 it joined the Confederation. An impressive land mark, situated on a hill above the city, is the Munot (1564–85), a cir cular fortress 170 ft. in diameter with a ramp and a tower — the onl edifice built according to Albrecht Dürer's theories on fortifications

The Cathedral (Münster), once the church of the former Al Saints Monastery, was built in the years 1090–1103, although evi dence of an earlier building (1049–65) has been unearthed; it i an important example of the Hirsau school of building (see VI, co 210). A severe basilica with transept, it has a choir and side chapel that show the influence of Cluny; the tower (ca. 1200) is Romanesque In the museum there is a 13th-century donor's tomb. The cloiste was rebuilt in the late Middle Ages with Romanesque elements. Th monastery buildings date from the 12th–16th century. St. John, 15th-century Gothic basilica with piers and three aisles, was enlarge in 1515 by the addition of two vaulted side aisles. On the console of the arches there is early Renaissance sculpture (1517).

The Gothic Rathaus (Town Hall), completed in 1412, contain sumptuous carved woodwork (1624–25). The Zeughaus (Arsenal in German Renaissance style is by Johann Jakob Meyer (1617) The Gothic Haus zum Ritter (1492, 1566) has a façade repainte in 1939 with a copy of the original decoration (1568–70) in late Ren aissance style by Tobias Stimmer. The detached original mural are in the Museum zu Allerheiligen. There are many baroque house of the 17th and 18th centuries with the customary bay windows o eastern Switzerland. The local stucco school of Samuel Höscheler Johann Jakob Schärrer, and Johann Ulrich Schnetzler executed man ceilings as well as the façade of the Haus zum Steinbock (ca. 1750)

The Museum zu Allerheiligen has a famous late Roman onyx cameo in a 13th-century setting. There is also a picture galler (Gemäldesammlung des Kunstvereins in Imthurneum).

BIBLIOG. Schweizerischer Ingenieur- und Architektenverein, Da Bürgerhaus in der Schweiz, VI, 1918; J. Stamm, Schaffhausen Deckenplastik Neujahrsblatt des Kunstvereins und des Historisch-Antiquarischen Verein Schaffhausen, XVII, 1911, XVIII, 1913, XIX, 1914; D. F. Rittmeyer Beiträge zur Geschichte der Goldschmiedehandwerks in Schaffhausen Schaffhauser Beiträge zur Vaterländischen Geschichte, XXIV, 1947; Di Kunstdenkmäler der Schweiz, XXVI, 1951; L. Birchler, Grabungen unte dem Münster in Schaffhausen, Actes du XVII° Cong. Int. d'H. de l'art The Hague, 1955, pp. 119–24; W. Drack, Zur Baugeschichte des Münster zu Schaffhausen, ZfSAKg, XVII, 1957, pp. 14–45.

Stein am Rhein. The city was founded in the 11th century In 1002–07 the Benedictine Monastery of St. George was establishe (closed in 1525). The monastery church (early 12th cent.) is a ba silica with columns, three aisles, and no transept; it originally ha a façade with twin towers. The cloister and the monastery building are late Gothic. The ceremonial hall in the monastery was decorate in 1515–16 by Thomas Schmid and Ambrosius Holbein with Ren aissance wall paintings and is one of the most important early Ren aissance monuments in the country. Schmid also executed the paint ings on the façade of the Haus zum weissen Adler.

BIBLIOG. Die Kunstdenkmäler der Schweiz, XXVIII–XXIV, 1950; A. Schmid, Die Wandgemälde im Festsaal des Klosters St. Georgen in ein am Rhein, Frauenfeld, 1950.

Saint Gallen. Saint Gallen (Saint-Gall). The city is capital of e canton. In 612 the Irish itinerant monk Gallus settled here in e mountains and founded a monastic community that later came der Benedictine rule (747–48; the monastery was closed in 1805). the Carolingian and Ottonian periods the monastery was an im-rtant cultural center. Gradually a town grew up around it, and in e 10th century the first ring of city walls was built. Saint Gallen tained the status of city in about 1170 and joined the Confederation 1454. The fortifications have for the most part been demolished.

The Cathedral (Stiftskirche), once the monastery church, is built on the foundations of earlier Carolingian church; it is a rococo ilding erected in the years 1755–66, with the nave and rotunda after signs by Peter Thumb, which were further developed by Giovanni aspare Bagnato, Gabriel Loser, and Johann Michael Been. The oir and the interesting convex-concave façade with twin towers e by Beer and Loser. The nave and the choir are of the hall type th pilasters, but without galleries, and there is an inserted rotunda. ue façade sculptures of the rotunda, the stucco reliefs, and the inte-r rotunda frescoes are by Christian Wenzinger. Joseph Anton ichtmayr executed the sculptures of the east façade, the splendid oir stalls, and the confessionals. The Stiftsbibliothek (1758–67), estive rococo room with stuccoes by Hans Georg and Mathias II gl of Wessobrunn and paintings by Joseph Wannenmacher, uses an important collection of manuscripts with Irish, Carolingian d Romanesque miniatures (I, PL. 282; X, PL. 72) as well as ivory ok covers, the Tuotilo diptych (cf. III, col. 118), and other early edieval works. St. Lawrence (1413), a three-aisled basilica with lars, was rebuilt in Neo-Gothic style in 1851–53. St. Magnus a cruciform church of the 11th century.

The older secular buildings have for the most part been destroyed. ry typical are the sometimes two-storied bay windows decorated th sculpture on the 17th- and 18th-century houses. The Kunst-iseum has a small collection of Swiss paintings; the Historisches iuseum contains examples of the minor arts; and the Gewerbe-iseum houses a collection of lace and textiles.

BIBLIOG. G. Scherrer, Verzeichnis der Handschriften der Stiftsbiblio-ek St. Gallen, Halle, 1875; J. L. Meyer, Die Erker der Stadt St. Gal-, Saint Gallen, 1883; Schweizerischer Ingenieur- und Architektenverein, is Bürgerhaus in der Schweiz, III, 1913, XXIX, 1937; A. Hardegger, Schlatter, and T. Schiess, Die Baudenkmäler, der Stadt St. Gallen, int Gallen, 1922; D. F. Rittmeyer, Zur Geschichte des Goldschmiede-adwerk in der Stadt St. Gallen, Saint Gallen, 1930; Die Kunstdenkmäler r Schweiz, XXV, 1951, XXXVII, 1956; J. Duft and P. Meyer, Die Irischen iniaturen der Stiftsbibliothek St. Gallen, Olten, Bern, 1953–54 (Eng. ., The Irish Miniatures in the Abbey Library of St. Gall, Olten, New rk, 1954); E. G. Rüsch, Tuotilo, Mönch und Künstler (Mitt. zur Vater-dischen Geschichte, XLI) Saint Gallen, 1953; J. Duft, Studien zum St. llen Klosterplan, Saint Gallen, 1962; P. H. Boerlin, Die Stiftskirche St. illen, Basel, 1963; J. Duft, Hochfeste im Gallus-Kloster, die Miniaturen Sacramentarium Codex 341 (11. Jahrhundert), Beuron, 1963.

Schwyz. Einsiedeln. This village and pilgrimage center was ilt up around the Benedictine monastery founded in 934 on the ot where St. Meinrad had built his hermitage. One of the largest mmetrical monastery complexes in the baroque style, it was begun 1704 by Caspar Moosbrugger and completed in 1770. The rectan-lar monastery complex is divided into four courtyards by the church d transverse sections. The church (Stiftskirche; begun 1719) is Moosbrugger, under the influence of the engineer and naturalist iigi Ferdinando Marsigli from Bologna; it is in the form of succes-e open spaces with an octagon over one of the chapels (the Gna-nkapelle). There is stuccowork, architectural sculpture, and ceiling inting by the Asam brothers and other sculptures by Diego Fran-sco Carlone and Johann Baptist Babel. Before the monastery, ose central part is made up of the twin-towered convex church ;ade, there is a vast square with arcades based on designs of the ilanese Paolo Bianchi; in the center there is an older fountain iebfrauenbrunnen).

BIBLIOG. P. A. Kuhn, Der jetzige Stiftsbau Maria Einsiedeln, Einsie-ln, 1913; L. Birchler, Einsiedeln und sein Architekt Bruder Caspar Moos-ugger, Augsburg, 1924; Die Kunstdenkmäler der Schweiz, I–II, 1927-; M. Huggler, Die romanische Kirche in Einsiedeln, Anz. f. Schweizer-he Altertumskunde, III, 1934, pp. 180–97; Schwezerischer Ingenieur-d Architektenverein, Das Bürgerhaus in der Schweiz, IV, 1940; W. Op-nheimer, Die Baufinanzierung des Klosters Einsiedeln im Rahmen seiner irtschaftgeschichte, Einsiedeln, 1949; A. Reinle, Ein Fund barocker rchen- und Klosterpläne, ZfSAKg, XI, 1950, pp. 216–47, XII, 1951, . 1–21; A. Reinle, Luigi Ferdinando Marsigli, Nachtrag zu "Ein Fund rocker Kirchen- und Klosterpläne" in ZAK 1950/51, ZfSAKg, XIII, 1952, . 170–81; P. R. Henggeler, Der Einsiedler Klosterplatz, ZfSAKg, XV, 1954.

Lucerne. Lucerne (Luzern). Capital of the canton, Lucerne is situated on the Lake of the Four Forest Cantons at a point where the river Reuss enters the lake, so the city is divided into two parts by the river. A Benedictine monastery was founded there in the middle of the 8th century, a town developed around it in about 1180. On the Musegghill there are still some 3,000 ft. of outer fortifications (ca. 1400) with nine towers; the two covered wooden bridges (Kappell-brücke and Spreuerbrücke) extended the fortifications to the other side of the river; they were decorated with picture cycles in the 17th century.

The Hofkirche (St. Leodegar) is a basilica with piers, which was begun in 1633 by Jakob Kurrer in the style of the German Renaissance; Nikolaus Geissler provided its sculptural ornamentation. The twin towers are in the late Gothic style (1506–16). The Franziskanerkirche (ca. 1270–80) is baroque. The Jesuit church, begun in 1666 by Vorarlberg and Jesuit artists, was completed by Heinrich Mayer. It is a monumental single-aisle basilica with galleries above the chapels. The decorations are according to the designs of Heinrich Mayer. The Knights' Palace (Ritter'sche Palast), later the Jesuit College and now the seat of the cantonal government, was begun in 1557 in the Florentine Renaissance style with a rustic façade and a colonnaded courtyard. The Rathaus, begun in 1602 by Anton Isenmann from Prismell, is an Italian Renaissance building with richly paneled rooms; the Hall of Archives (1696) is baroque. Most of the patrician and middle-class houses are in the baroque style of the 17th and 18th centuries. In the vicinity there are the early baroque pilgrimage churches of Hergiswald (with a *casa santa*) and Blatten (richly dec-orated with sculpture by Hans Ulrich Räber and Michael Hart-mann).

BIBLIOG. Schweizerischer Ingenieur- und Architektenverein, Das Bür-gerhaus in der Schweiz, VIII, 1920; D. F. Rittmeyer, Geschichte der Lu-zerner Silber- und Goldschmiedekunst von den Anfängen bis zur Gegen-wart, Lucerne, 1941; H. Lehmann, Geschichte der Luzerner Glasmalerei von den Anfängen bis zu Beginn des 18. Jahrhunderts, Lucerne, 1942; H. P. Landolt, Die Jesuitenkirche in Luzern (Basler St. zur Kg., IV), Basel, 1947; Die Kunstdenkmäler der Schweiz, XXX, 1953; P. Felder, Die Hof-kirche St. Leodegar und St. Mauritius in Luzern (Basler St. zur Kg., XVII) Basel, 1958.

Sankt Urban. The former Cistercian monastery was founded in 1194 (closed in 1848). The baroque complex of the Vorarlberg type was begun in 1711 by Franz Beer. The most important baroque choir stalls (1701–07) are by Peter Frölicher, Ursus Füeg, and Victor Wüest. About 1255–80, the brickworks of the monastery produced richly decorated brick pieces, the most important of which are pre-served in St. Urban, in the Historisches Museums of Bern and Lu-cerne, and in the Schweizerisches Landesmuseum of Zurich.

BIBLIOG. H. Meyer-Rahn, Das Chorgestühl in der Kirche der ehemali-gen Cisterzienser-Abtei St. Urban, Lucerne, 1913; Die Kunstdenkmäler der Schweiz, V–VI, 1934–35; R. Schnyder, Die Baukeramik und der mittel-alterliche Backsteinbau des Zisterzienserklosters St. Urban, Bern, 1958.

Graubünden. Chur. Capital of the canton the city lies at the foot of the Cathedral hill, known as the Hof. The Roman settlement, which later became a fortified castle, was called Curia (Itinerarium Antonini, ca. 280; Peutinger Tables, 4th cent); it became an episcopal see in 451. The Cathedral (ca. 1155–1272) is a heavy, primitive late Romanesque basilica with three aisles, no transept, pointed arcades, and a rectangular choir and crypt. There is a Romanesque portal with steps, capitals with carved figures, and four columns with fig-ures of the Apostles that stand before the crypt. The Carolingian relief panels on the altars come from the choir stalls. The Gothic high altar is by Jakob Russ (1492), and the tabernacle by Klaus von Feld-kirch (1484). The Cathedral treasure includes Romanesque and Gothic works and early Christian textiles. The Episcopal Palace was rebuilt in baroque style in 1733; the *Dance of Death* frescoes (after Holbein; 1543) are now in the Rätisches Museum. St. Martin (1474-91), built by Steffan Klain, has a lierne vault in the nave and in the choir; parts of the walls of the Carolingian three-aisled church (8th cent.) were used in the present building. St. Regula, completed in 1500, has lierne vaulting in the nave and choir. St. Luzi (begun 1150), the Romanesque church of a Premonstratensian monastery, has a single aisle; it is partially transformed into a Gothic building. There is a circular Carolingian crypt from the first half of the 8th century preceded by a Romanesque hall crypt (ca. 1150).

The Gothic Rathaus (town hall) is from the 15th and 16th cen-turies, and the dignified patrician houses from the 17th and 18th cen-turies. The Rätisches Museum contains a historical collection.

BIBLIOG. Schweizerischer Ingenieur- und Architektenverein, Das Bürgerhaus in der Schweiz, XII, XIV, XVI, 1923–25; Die Kunstdenkmäler der Schweiz, VII, X, XIV, XXII, XXVII, 1932–41; W. Sulser, Die St. Luziuskirche in Chur, Frühmittelalterliche Kunst in den Alpenländern,

Akten zum III. Internationalen Kongress für Frühmittelalterforschungen, Olten, Lausanne, 1954, pp. 151–66; E. Doberer, Die ursprüngliche Bestimmung der Apostelsäulen im Dom zu Chur, ZfSAKg, XIX, 1959, pp. 17–43; W. Sulser, Die St. Stephanskirche zu Chur, Akten zum VII. Internationalen Kongress für Frühmittelalterforschungen, Graz, Cologne, 1961.

Münster (Müstair). The Benedictine Convent of St. Johann was founded in Carolingian times (ca. 780–90). The church of the convent (ca. 800; III, FIG. 87), a hall with three apses, was transformed in 1492 into a three-aisled church through the introduction of columns and arches; the frescoes (ca. 800), mostly well-preserved, constitute the largest cycle of paintings of the Carolingian period (II, PL. 287, III, PL. 57). In about 1280 Romanesque paintings were superimposed on the older frescoes in the apses. There are Carolingian ornamental reliefs and Romanesque stucco sculptures (ca. 1087; relief of the Baptism of Christ, a life-size statue of Charlemagne, etc.).

BIBLIOG. J. Zerm and R. Durrer, Das Kloster St. Johann zu Münster in Graubünden, Mitt. der Schweiz. Gesellschaft für Erhaltung historischer Kunstdenkmäler, V–VII, Geneva, 1906–10; Die Kunstdenkmäler der Schweiz, V, 1934; L. Birchler, Zur Karolingischen Architektur und Malerei in Münster-Müstair, Frühmittelalterliche Kunst in den Alpenländern, Akten zum II. Internationalen Kongress für Frühmittelalterforschungen, Olten, Lausanne, 1954, pp. 167–252; G. de Francovich, Problemi della pittura e della scultura preromanica, I problemi comuni dell'Europa post-Carolingia, Settimana di studio del Centro Italiano di Studi sull'Alto Medioevo, II, Spoleto, 1955; C. Simonett, Die Bauernhäuser des Kantons Graubünden, Basel, 1965.

Ticino. Bellinzona. Capital of the canton, it was in the Middle Ages a fortified outpost for the defense of Milan against invasion from the North; in 1503 it joined the Confederation and became a barrier against Italy. Above the city tower three fortresses combined with town walls that were mostly built by Milanese architects in the second half of the 15th century: the Great Castle (Castello Grande), Montebello, and Sasso Corbaro.

The collegiate church (begun 1518; built over a long period) has chapels between pilasters. S. Biagio (in Ravecchia, near Bellinzona) is an early Romanesque basilica with piers (11th cent.) and contains frescoes from the end of the 14th and the 15th century. The Franciscan Church of S. Maria delle Grazie (ca. 1481–95) has only one aisle and a row of chapels on one side. A great cycle of frescoes depicts the life of Christ (1495–1505); other frescoes, in part from the school of Gaudenzio Ferrari, date form the same period. The Historisches Museum is in Montebello Castle.

BIBLIOG. A. Zeller, Die Schlösser von Bellinzona, Z. f. Bauwesen, LV, 1905, pp. 439–67; Commissione Cantonale dei Monumenti Storici ed Artistici, Monumenti storici ed artistici del Cantone Ticino, 3 vols., Milan, 1912–14; Schweizerischer Ingenieur- und Architektenverein, Das Bürgerhaus in der Schweiz, XXVI, 1934, XXVIII, 1938; Commissione Cantonale dei Monumenti Storici ed Artistici, Inventario delle cose d'arte e di antichità (ed. P. Bianconi), I, Bellinzona, 1948; Ticino, Dipartimento della Pubblica Educazione, Inventario delle cose d'arte e di antichità, (ed. V. Gilardoni), II, Bellinzona, 1955.

Lugano. The city is picturesquely situated along the northern end of the Lake of Lugano. It is Italian in character since it was formerly part of Italy. The Cathedral of S. Lorenzo, a Romanesque basilica with piers, rebuilt in the 13th century, is notable for its richly decorated monumental façade (1517), the purest Renaissance work in Switzerland. The church of the former Franciscan monastery, S. Maria degli Angioli (begun 1499), has a row of chapels, on one side of the nave. It is known for a great fresco of the Crucifixion, with a multitude of figures, by Bernardino Luini (1529) and for its other 16th-century wall paintings (especially in the Cappella Camuzio). Other churches include S. Rocco and Madonna di Loreto (16th cent.) S. Antonio in baroque style, and S. Carlo (1640).

Among the baroque patrician houses, the most important is the Palazzo Riva (now the Banca della Svizzera Italiana). There is a classical Town Hall with a pillared courtyard (1844–45). Statues and monuments by Vincenzo Vela adorn the city. The Museo di Belle Arti is in the Villa Ciani. The Thyssen-Bornemisza Collection in the Villa Favorita is notable.

BIBLIOG. C. Chiesa, L'architettura del rinascimento nel Cantone Ticino, Bellinzona, 1934; Schweizerischer Ingenieur- und Architektenverein, Das Bürgerhaus in der Schweiz, XXVI, 1934, XXVIII, 1938.

Valais. Sion (Sitten). The city dates back to Roman times, when it was known as Sedenum, and became an episcopal see in 580. It is dominated by two rocky cliffs surmounted by the castles of Valeria and Tourbillon. Of the city walls only a corner tower (1200) remains. The fortress of Valeria was the seat of the Cathedral chapter from the middle of the 11th century until 1798. It is about 490 ft. long, includes parts dating from the 12th to 15th century,

and is dominated by a collegiate church. The latter, massively R manesque from the outside, has a spacious early Gothic interior wi transept and polygonal choir; begun in the first third of the 12 century and completed in the second third of the 13th century, it related to the cathedrals of Lausanne and Geneva. The choir scre is early Gothic. There are Romanesque capitals with figures of primitive type and wall paintings of the 15th century. On the we wall, there is an organ with painted shutters (ca. 1435). The origina Romanesque Cathedral of Notre-Dame was rebuilt in Gothic sty at the end of the 15th century; it retains a Romanesque tower capp with a conical stone roof. The Cathedral treasure includes reliquari and textiles of the 8th–10th and 14th centuries.

Secular buildings include the ruins of the bishop's castle, Tourb lon, which was begun in 1294; the Supersaxo House (1505) has notable wooden Gothic ceiling. In the Musée Historique du Valè there are Roman finds, medieval sculpture, and other objects.

BIBLIOG. V. van Berchem and T. van Muyden, Le château de Valè à Sion, Geneva, 1904; M. Holderegger, Die Kirche von Valeria bei Sitte Zurich, 1930; Schweizerischer Ingenieur- und Architektenverein, D Bürgerhaus in der Schweiz, XXVII, 1935.

Saint-Maurice (Saint-Maurice d'Agaune). At first it was t important Celtic town of Agaunum and then became a Roman m itary and customs station. At the end of the 4th century Bish Theodore built a rectangular tomb sanctuary for St. Maurice and I Theban legion who were martyred here, and it rapidly became place of pilgrimage. In the 5th century the construction, situat at the foot of a cliff, was enlarged with a polygonal apse. In 515 a abbey was founded by the Burgundian king Sigismund, who resid here, and near the older building a three-aisled basilica and a re tangular baptistery were constructed. At the end of the 8th centu the older parts were reused in the construction of a basilica with double choir and polygonal apses over circular crypts. At the begi ning of the 11th century transformations and additions were mad but these were replaced in the 17th century by a late Gothic constru tion, although the Romanesque tower was kept. The church treasu of Carolingian and Romanesque objects is one of the best in Swi zerland.

BIBLIOG. E. Aubert, Trésor de l'abbaye de Saint-Maurice d'Agaur Paris, 1872; M. Besson, Monasterium Acaunense, Fribourg, 1913; P. Scha mann, Vase en sardonyx monté sur cloisonnés en or à l'abbaye de Sair Maurice d'Agaune, ZfSAKg, VII, 1945, pp. 1–22; A. Alföldi, Die Gol kanne von St. Maurice d'Agaune, ZfSAKg, X, 1948, pp. 1–27; L. Blond Les basiliques d'Agaune, Vallesia, B. Ann. de la Bib. et des Arch. Cantona du Valais, des Mus. de Valère et de la Majorie, III, 1948, pp. 9–57, IV, pp. 1 28, V, pp. 167–84, VI, pp. 1–17, VIII, pp. 5–18; L. Blondel, L. Hall and L. Birchler, Saint-Maurice d'Agaune, les anciennes basiliques, Sair Maurice, 1951; O. Homburger, Früh- und Hochmittelalterliche Stücke i Schatz des Augustinerchorherrenstiftes von Saint-Maurice und in der K thedrale zu Sitten, Frühmittelalterliche Kunst in den Alpenländern, Actes III⁰ Congres International pour l'Etude du Haut Moyen-Age, Olten, La sanne, 1954, pp. 339–53.

Fribourg. Fribourg (Freiburg). Like Bern, the city was found by Duke Berchtold IV of Zähringen in 1178; it joined the Confeder tion in 1481, and in the baroque period became, with Lucerne, t most important Catholic center of the country; since 1613 it h been an episcopal see. It is the best preserved medieval city in Sw zerland with very extensive fortifications. There are many Renaissan fountains with a central column and figures by Hans Gieng and Ha Geiler (mid-16th cent.).

St. Nicholas Cathedral has a nave and side aisles (begun 128 a central tower (ca. 1370–1400), and a late Gothic choir (1627–3 by Daniel Heintz II and Peter Winter, both from Prismell. On t main and side portals there are 14th and 15th-century sculpture Inside there are an important group of figures depicting the Entom ment (1433), carved choir stalls (1462–64), and a rare choir scre (1464–66). Notre-Dame is a 12th-century church renovated in t Louis XVI style (1785–87). The Augustinian Church of St. Mauri 1255–1311) is a basilica with round piers and an important Renaissan high altar by Peter Spring (ca. 1610–18). The church of the Cisterci Convent of Maigrauge is early Gothic (1255–84). The church the Franciscan monastery (Couvent des Cordeliers) has a choir (125 81), a nave (1745), a high altar by one of the Carnation Masters (148c a lateral late Gothic altar (ca. 1513), and early Gothic choir stalls (c 1280). In the cloister there is a cycle of wall paintings depicting scen from the life of Mary (ca. 1440). The Gothic Jesuit Church of S Michael (1604–13) is in the form of a basilica with chapels and g leries; in 1756–57 the hall was rebuilt in rococo style. The church the Ursuline convent is from 1653–55; the Church of the Visitati is a quatrefoil building with a dome and lierne vaulting (1653–5 the Loreto Chapel is from 1647–48; all three buildings are baroqu Gothic works by Hans Franz Reiff (Reyff). The Gothic chapel castle Pérolles (ca. 1520) has stained-glass windows of the same period. The Town Hospital has a central chapel with a cupola (1581–99).

The Gothic Town Hall (1500–22) has upper stories by Hans Felder the Younger. There are many Gothic houses with freestone façles and ornamental tracery. The former *préfecture* (1583–86) is the French Renaissance style. The baroque patrician houses are dignified in character. The Musée Cantonal d'Art et d'Histoire located in the former *préfecture*; the Musée des Arts et Metiers is the Castle Pérolles.

BIBLIOG. Schweizerischer Ingenieur- und Architektenverein, Das Bürgerhaus in der Schweiz, XX, 1928; Die Kunstdenkmäler der Schweiz, 1930, III, 1932; H. Reiners, Fribourg pittoresque et artistique, Fribourg, Augsburg, 1930.

Vaud. Lausanne. Capital of the canton, the city is situated on a steep hill above the Lake of Geneva. The fortifications have almost completely disappeared. It was founded as a Helvetic *oppidum* on the Cathedral Hill and as a Roman *vicus*, Lousanna, on the beach at Vidy; the latter was abandoned in 400 and consequently the old *oppidum* was transformed into a castrum. About 600, the episcopal see of Aventicum (Avenches) was transferred to Lausanne. In 1536, the city was subjugated by Bern and the Reformation was introduced. Vaud became an independent canton in 1803.

The Cathedral of Notre-Dame is built on the foundations of the Roman *castrum* and of a Carolingian and early Romanesque basilica. Begun in 1175 and consecrated in 1275, it is the largest Gothic building in Switzerland (ca. 318 ft. in length), — a basilica with three aisles, narthex, transept, choir ambulatory, two towers over the transepts, a central tower, and one completed façade tower; is entirely in the French style. The south portal is decorated with a wealth of early Gothic figures (second quarter of 13th cent.). The rose window in the north transept with its stained-glass cycle of pictures from the middle of the 13th century is the first great monument in stained glass in Switzerland. The choir stalls are from the 13th and 14th centuries, and the bishops' and nobles' tombs from the 13th and 14th centuries. The precious late Gothic tapestries, in particular those depicting the life of Julius Caesar, are now in the Bern Historisches Museum. St-François, a Franciscan church of the second half of the 13th century, was rebuilt in the 14th century.

The bishop's castle dates from the beginning of the 15th century. The Town Hall is an early baroque building (1674–78) by Abraham de Crousaz. The Old Hospital (1766–71; present Collège Scientifique) by Rodolphe de Crousaz is the largest baroque building. The Musée Cantonal des Beaux-Arts has a collection of Swiss paintings.

BIBLIOG. J. Stammler, Le trésor de la cathédrale de Lausanne, Lausanne, 1902; E. M. Blaser, Gotische Bildwerke der Kathedrale von Lausanne, Basel, 1918; Schweizerischer Ingenieur- und Architektenverein, Das Bürgerhaus der Schweiz, XV, 1925, XXV, 1933.

Avenches (Aventicum). An important town of the Helvetii on a steep hill, under the Romans the city spread out into the plain. Vespasian (who spent his youth in Aventicum) raised it to the rank of a colony in about 73/74, but it was destroyed by the Alamanni in about 260. There is a regularly planned network of roads with *insulae* about 310 × 230 ft. in area. Of the polygonal city wall with about 80 towers and 5 gates only parts — mainly by the east gate — are preserved. The amphitheater (ca. 350 ft. in diameter) lies on the slope of a hill. Because of a column, called Le Cigognier, which has remained *in situ*, the temple can easily be reconstructed. The baths have in part been laid bare. A valuable relic is the gold embossed bust of the emperor Marcus Aurelius discovered in 1939 (V, PL. 479).

The Musée Romain is housed in a medieval tower by the amphitheater. On the hill there is a late Gothic castle that was rebuilt in the French Renaissance style (1565–68).

BIBLIOG. B. de l'Association Pro Aventico, 1887 ff.; E. Stähelin, Die Schweiz in römischer Zeit, 3d ed., Basel, 1948, pp. 604–11 (with bibliog.); Rocchetti, EAA, s.v.

Payerne. Here, on his country property, Bishop Marius of Lausanne consecrated a church in 587. The present church, built over late Roman secular buildings, is the most impressive early Romanesque edifice in Switzerland. The main body, with a west wing, is a three-aisled vaulted basilica with circular piers (first half of 11th cent.); the transept and the Burgundian stepped choir with four chapels date from the 12th century. In the nave there are primitive sculptured capitals; the sculptures in the choir are of a later date. The narthex has Romanesque frescoes. There are remains of the Romanesque monastery.

BIBLIOG. J. R. Rahn, L'église abbatiale de Payerne, Lausanne, 1893; A. Schmid, Akten zum VII. Internationalen Kongress für Frühmittelalterforschungen, Graz, Cologne, 1962.

Romainmôtier. The monastery, which was founded in the middle of the 5th century, came under the authority of Cluny in 966–81 and was closed in 1537. Excavations have revealed foundations that are identical with those of 7th- and 8th century churches: a hall church with an apse and symmetrical quadrangular annexes. The present building, for the most part of the 11th century, consists of a vaulted basilica with a transept. The choir and two side chapels, as well as the three apses, were extended and enclosed in a rectangular form in the 14th century. Toward the west there is a narthex of the 12th century with two superimposed three-aisled halls. The relief panel from an ambo is of the 7th century.

BIBLIOG. A. Naef, Les phases constructives de l'Eglise de Romainmôtier, Anz. f. Schw. Altertumskunde, N.S., VII, 1905–06, pp. 210–30; J. Zemp, Die Kirche von Romainmôtier, Z. f. Geschichte der Arch., Heidelberg, 1908, pp. 89–110; M. Reymond, A. Bonard, and H. Chastellain, Histoire de Romainmôtier, Lausanne, new ed., 1928; S. Brodtbeck, Les voûtes romanes de l'Eglise de Romainmôtier, B. monumental, XCV, 1936, pp. 473–505; E. Bach, L'ambon de Baulmes et les ambons de Saint-Maurice et de Romainmôtier, Mélanges d'histoire et de la littérature offerts à Monsieur Charles Gilliard, Lausanne, 1944, pp. 114–32.

Geneva. Geneva (Genève). The city, capital of the canton, is situated on the Lake of Geneva and is divided by the Rhone into an old town on the hill that still conserves its ancient aspect and a modern city along the shores of the lake. First a Celtic *oppidum*, then a Roman *vicus* (Genua, Genava) with a bridge and port, in late Roman times it was fortified. It became an espiscopal see in about 400 and was one of the most important centers of the Swiss Reformation. Linked with some cantons of the Confederation in 1526 and 1584, it entered the latter completely in 1814.

The Cathedral of St-Pierre was begun in the late 4th or early 5th century as a basilica on the emplacement of a Roman temple; it was replaced by the Burgundian king Sigismond in 513–15 by a much larger one, with a rotonda behind the choir, that was demolished at the end of the 10th century. The present structure was started in the 12th century in the Romanesque style (lower parts of the nave and choir to the level of the capitals) and was completed in the Gothic style in the 13th and 14th centuries. It is a basilica with nave and side aisles, a transept, and triforium. There is a late Gothic lateral chapel (Maccabean Chapel; begun 1406) and an early classical west façade in the form of a temple portico by Benedetto Alfieri (1752–56). The Cathedral has Romanesque and Gothic carved capitals and choir stalls of the end of the 15th century.

Ste-Marie Madeleine, mainly from 1334 and 1444–53, was built over apse churches of the 7th and 8th–9th centuries. St-Germain (begun 1334) was built over a church of the end of the 4th century that was transformed in the 6th century. There are fragments of an altar relief dating as far back as the 5th century. St-Gervais (15th cent.), a vaulted hall church with a row of chapels, has a crypt with an ambulatory of the 8th–9th century that is a relic of a Carolingian palace chapel. The foundations of the Burgundian royal palace and its chapel have been found through excavation. The Burgundian chapel dedicated to St. Victor, built at the end of the 5th century and destroyed in 1535, was a circular building; its existence has been ascertained from documents. The church on the Fusterie (Temple Neuf; 1707–10), built after plans by Vennes, has an interior entirely encircled by columns and galleries and served as a prototype for the Church of the Holy Ghost in Bern.

The Gothic Town Hall (15th cent.) had later additions (a tower with ramp) in the French Renaissance style. In 1617 the building was enlarged to include a colonnaded hall and arcades in heavy Renaissance style after plans by Faule Petitot. The Maison Turrettini by Jean Pattac is of the same period. There are many stately 18th-century patrician houses in the French style, which are the most imposing town houses in Switzerland. Especially noteworthy are the palatial Maison Lullin (now Maison de Saussure) by Joseph Abeille (1707–12), the Maison Mallet by Jean François Blondel (1721), and the uniform row of four houses on the Rue des Granges (begun 1720). Of equal grandeur are the country estates at Eaux-Vives, Genthod, and Varembé. Classicism is represented by the Palais Eynard (1817–21) of the philhellenic Eynard family and by the Musée Rath (1824–26) by Samuel Vaucher.

There are no fountains with figures because of the Calvinist opposition to images. The Rousseau memorial monument (1834–35) is by James Pradier. The Reformation monument dates from 1909–17.

The Musée d'Art et d'Histoire has a fine altar by Konrad Witz and a collection of 18th and 19th century paintings.

BIBLIOG. D. Baud-Bovy, Peintres genevois du XVIIIème et du XIXème siècle Geneva, 1903; C. Martin, Saint-Pierre, ancienne cathédrale de Genève, Geneva, 1909–10; C. Martin, Le Temple-Neuf de Genève, Geneva, 1910; Schweizrischer Ingenieur- und Architektenverein, Das Bürgerhaus in der Schweiz, II, 1912; Genava, B. Mus. d'Art et d'H. de Genève, 1923 ff.; D. Baud-Bovy, L'ancienne école genevoise de peinture, Geneva, 1924; L. Blondel, Les premiers édifices chrétiens de Genève, Genava, XI, 1933, pp. 77-101 (with bibliog.); W. Déonna, Les arts à Genève des origines à la fin du XVIIIᵉ siècle, Geneva, 1942; L. Blondel, Le développement urbain de Genève à travers les siècles, Geneva, Nyon, 1946.

Neuchâtel. Neuchâtel (Neuenburg). The capital of the canton is situated on the borders of the lake of the same name. The fort of Novum Castellum is mentioned for the first time in 1011; it soon developed into a city, spreading to the east toward the lake. Under Prussian rule from 1707 to 1856, it then joined the Confederation.

On the fortress hill, which has a castle and a church, impressive remains of a dungeon and moat have been unearthed. The Tour des Prisons (Prison Tower) dates from the 10th to the 15th century. There is a Renaissance fountain with figures (16th cent.). The collegiate church (Stiftskirche) has a choir with three apses and a Romanesque portal (end of 12th cent.); the main building has three aisles, a transept, and a Gothic central tower (13th cent.). The tomb of the counts of Neuchâtel with many figures is the most important Gothic tomb in Switzerland (1372; some of the statues were added later). The castle of the counts (12th-15th cent.) has architectural ornamentation from the late 12th century. The Town Hall is a monumental early classical building by Pierre Adrien Paris (1784-90). The Maison des Halles (1569-75) by Laurent Perrot is in the strongly Gothicizing style of the western Swiss Renaissance. There are many patrician houses of the 18th century in the French style; the Hôtel du Peyrou (1764-71) was built according to plans by Erasmus Ritter from Bern. Also noteworthy are the Maison de Marval (1609) and the Maison Montmollin (1686). The Musée des Beaux-Arts contains Swiss 18th- and 19th-century paintings.

BIBLIOG. Schweizerischer Ingenieur- und Architektenverein, Das Bürgerhaus in der Schweiz, XXIV, 1932; A. Lombard, L'église collégiale de Neuchâtel, Neuchâtel, 1931; Die Kunstdenkmäler der Schweiz, XXXIII, 1955.

Adolf REINLE

Illustrations: 5 figs. in text.

SYMBOLISM AND ALLEGORY.

The practice of signifying a thing by means of something else that stands for it — in other words, its symbol (Gr. σύμβολον, "a sign") — is a widespread phenomenon in the visual arts, of special relevance in the transmission and modification of images (see ICONOGRAPHY AND ICONOLOGY). Whatever its definition and application in philosophical, religious, literary, and other spheres, symbolism always involves the substitution of signs and thus has its roots in visual experience, the dimension of imagination and of artistic expression; objectively, the symbol does not arise from esthetic experience but forms part of the cultural patrimony, from which it is selected for purposes of artistic expression.

In symbolic representation there is an immediate and direct relation between the chosen symbol or sign and the thing signified, implying a spontaneous, reciprocal correspondence — indeed, almost an identification — between them; the thing signified is conceived as being implicit in the symbol, which thus has a well-nigh magical and uniquely summary quality. This explains, among other things, the deep connection between symbolism and the religious imagination.

On a more intellectualized plane, there are allusive or substitutive representations that have their origin not so much in the substitution of signs as in a correspondence of concepts: these are designated by the term "allegory" (Gr. ἀλληγορία, "description of something in the guise of something else"). In allegory the sign is always something other than the thing signified; they always remain distinct and separate entities, and there is no direct or unambiguous relation between them; rather, this relation is established through a deliberate transposition of meaning. The reference is first and foremost an intellectual one (hence the distinction between allegory and myth, for the latter introduces an element of imagination). In allegory, then, not only is the thing signified of more value as a concept than the image that signifies it, but it remains independent of the sign, might well be expressed in some other way, and, in any case, tends to overshadow the image itself, which is merely a means to an end. The relation between allegory and art presupposes a criterion of interpretation: on account of the

radical difference between the sign and the thing signified, t image (if it is an artistic one) has allegorical significance wh it is interpreted allegorically, but its esthetic significance autonomous and subject to esthetic interpretation. It is th duality that has given rise to the phenomenon of allegorizatio the attempt to provide a retrospective allegorical interpretation works whose authors had in mind a very different purpose fro that attributed to the work at a later time. This phenomen illustrates clearly the predominantly intellectualistic nature allegory; indeed, it was this tendency that, in certain cultur and periods, particularly in the Middle Ages, developed in a general set of interpretative rules applied not only to th works of classical antiquity but to all human activities as we as to literature and art.

Among the processes peculiar to symbolism and allego. is that of personification, conspicuous examples of which a found in the figural arts. Personification consists in concretizi a concept in a human or animal form that is considered correspond to it; hence personification can be held to be mainl allegorical. However, allegory cannot be identified entirely wi personification (although this opinion is frequently held), becau just as there are many allegories that are not personification so also there are personifications (as, for example, of the season rivers, or parts of the world) that are more metaphors tha anything else and can be said to be allegories only in an extende meaning of the word. Nevertheless, for the purposes of th article, no distinction will be made between such personification and true allegories.

Despite their fundamental difference, it is sometimes difficu to distinguish between symbolism and allegory in the histo of art and of iconography, and they are frequently either confuse or identified with each other. In this article they have therefo been considered together in the discussion of theoretical problem and concepts. In the study of individual artistic manifestation however, an attempt has been made, wherever possible, distinguish between the two phenomena, recognizing the primar profound, and universal nature of the symbol, as opposed allegorical representations that are characteristic of specific an well-defined artistic traditions.

SUMMARY. I. Symbolical and allegorical conceptions of art in th Western world: The Middle Ages (col. 793). From the Renaissan to the 19th century (col. 795). The modern period (col. 798). I Artistic manifestations: The ancient Middle East (col. 802). Gree and Rome (col. 805). The Judaeo-Christian tradition (col. 808 Early Christian and Byzantine art (col. 810). The Western worl (col. 811): *The Middle Ages; From the Renaissance to the 19th centur Recent and contemporary movements.* The East (col. 827): *Islam India; China and Japan.* The pre-Columbian Mexican and Andea civilizations (col. 834). Primitive cultures (col. 835).

I. SYMBOLICAL AND ALLEGORICAL CONCEPTIONS OF ART I THE WESTERN WORLD. While it remains true that symbolis and allegory are not in themselves factors in the esthetic qualit of works of art, these means of expression frequently refle certain general tendencies in the formative processes of that ar On the phenomenological plane, there is a consistent relationshi between symbolism and allegory on the one side and art o the other. It is on this plane that artistic manifestations ma be seen to be more or less explicitly connected with symbolic or allegorical conceptions of art, so that a basic symbolical c allegorical orientation is found at the root of the creative ac Even when the symbolical and allegorical conceptions of ar are not explicit, the respective theoretical postulates are s clearly distinct from each other in actual artistic practice tha these conceptions constitute pointers to the basic polarities c the phenomenology of the creative processes, tending respectivel to the general symbolization or allegorization of artistic form

Symbolical conceptions of art are those in which the intrinsi identity of the sign and the thing signified is fundamental; a artistic images, therefore, being by their very nature signs c something else, constitute symbolic forms that of themselve identify the thing signified, which only in them can find it fullest expression. In allegorical conceptions of art, on th other hand, the meaning is never held to be implicit in the sig ut is merely associated with it, so that the more specifically rtistic element in the work of art, the image, is regarded as ie temporary clothing of a meaning which is not identical ith it but which rather finds its most complete and appropriate xpression in the conceptual formulation, to which the artistic mage serves merely as an introduction.

Considered on the phenomenological plane, symbolism and llegory constitute particularly interesting aspects of the history nd criticism of art and of esthetics. Whereas allegory, however, , of interest mainly as a historical phenomenon connected with onceptions of art as an intrumental form of higher idealisms n the Middle Ages, during the Counter Reformation, etc.), ymbolism has become, particularly in recent times, a general sthetic conception that sees the whole of art, from its pro- esses to its true essence, as symbolic form.

Oreste FERRARI

THE MIDDLE AGES. Symbolism and allegory in Early Christian art drew directly on the example and poetic images f Holy Scripture, especially the Gospels. The need for a rider conceptual and cultural basis was soon felt, however, oth as a consequence of the gradual rejection of the naturalistic alues of figural representation and as a result of the fight against eresy that favored the creation of a theologically orthodox onography. This conceptual basis was derived from a number f philosophical and literary works from which the visual rts largely borrowed both their thematic repertory and their ymbolizing and allegorizing processes. There can be no doubt s to the importance of the medieval texts on rhetoric and rammar that drew a close parallel between etymology and llegory: of prime importance in this connection was the vast ncyclopedic work of Isidore of Seville, the *Etymologiae*. Another ctor was the interpretation in literature of the writings of reek and Latin poets and philosophers as Christian allegories. t goes without saying that interest was mainly concentrated on ie allegorical exegesis of Scripture, which in itself is pregnant rith allegorical and symbolical passages, and of the works of ie Fathers of the Church and of the Christian philosophers: was these writings which gave rise to a taste for the parallel resentation of episodes from the Old and New Testaments.

The most prolific trend expressed in allegorical form the arly Christian symbols and created completely new allegorical mages capable of expressing the ideals of the new culture. t is interesting, because of the undeniable repercussions of this rend in the visual arts, to note that the process of allegorization realized mainly through personification) tended to move in two uite separate directions: on the one hand there was the tendency o portray the allegorical images in a static fashion, as in the ersonifications of the virtues in the writings of John Climacus 7th cent.), in Alcuin of York's *Dialogus de rhetorica et de irtutibus* (796), and in the works of Rabanus Maurus (784–856); n the other there was the tendency to present these images in narrative context based on the conflict between good and vil, as in Prudentius's *Psychomachia* (384–410), which describes he conflict between Faith (Christ) and Sodom and Gomorrah, he vices that tempt Lot (the human soul).

There were also allegorical images that were not strictly eligious — e.g., the Arts of the trivium and quadrivium and he Liberal and Mechanical Arts that appear in such early vorks as those of Philo Judaeus and St. Augustine and more articularly in Martianus Capella and in Theodulf of Orléans's Carolingian poems, where the signs of the zodiac also are ersonified allegorically. The allegorizing of scientific and istorical thought was also very common, so that science and istory were reduced to a general picture with moralistic over- ones, as in the *Topographia christiana* of Cosmas Indicopleustes mid-6th cent.; known through later copies); the *Differentiarium*, he *De natura rerum*, the *Chronicon*, and the *De viris illustribus* f Isidore of Seville; the historical and cosmographical works f the Venerable Bede; and Rabanus Maurus's *De universo*, vhich opened the way to a type of encyclopedic treatise that vas to culminate in the famous Specula (*Speculum naturale*, *peculum doctrinale*, and *Speculum historiale*) of Vincent of

Beauvais. The moral bestiaries of the Romanesque period also fall within this category of scientific-allegorical treatises.

Literary and philosophical works in which full-scale allegor- izing and symbolizing phenomena are apparent are of interest here both because of their more or less direct repercussions on the visual arts and, more especially, because these works afford a clue to the thought processes underlying such phe- nomena. Although there was no systematic formulation of a theoretical awareness of the symbolical and allegorical nature of the visual arts, this awareness was nevertheless the basis of medieval esthetics. It should be noted that this aspect of the visual arts began to be emphasized decisively when it became necessary to furnish a theologically sound justification for figural art in order to confute the iconoclastic heresy; Pope Gregory the Great at the end of the 6th century (*Epistulae*, III, IV) and Pope Gregory II in the first half of the 8th (in a letter addressed to the initiator of the iconoclastic controversy, Leo the Isaurian) offered a theoretical basis for symbolism and allegory in medieval art, enunciating the concept that was to be further elaborated toward the end of the 8th century by Pope Adrian I (in a letter concerning images written to Emperor Constantine VI and the regent, later Empress Irene), that art must "show the invisible by means of the visible" (*demonstrare invisibilia per visibilia*) so that "our mind may be stirred by the spiritual through con- templation of the image" (*mens nostra rapiatur spirituali affectu per contemplationem figuratae imaginis*).

Medieval theorizing concerning symbolism and allegory was, however, not based exclusively on these premises. At the end of the 8th century, the *Libri Carolini* (ca. 794) discussed the problem from a slightly different angle, which might, to a certain extent, be termed the secular point of view. According to this text, works of art were to be admired for their crafts- manship and the quality of the materials rather than for their devotional fervor. The Carolingian culture did not deny the symbolical-allegorical quality of such works of art but distin- guished it from their strictly esthetic value, which was independent of the theological or didactic aims of allegory and symbolism. Although this viewpoint permitted a purely esthetic apprecia- tion of the visual arts, it implicitly confirmed what Rabanus Maurus had already suggested in his *Carmina* (Carmen XXX, addressed to Bonosus), namely, that art, as compared with the written word, was inadequate for the expression of concepts: even the *Libri Carolini* called for the use of clarifying titles and superscriptions on images.

An awareness of the esthetic value of a work of art survived throughout the Middle Ages and was, in fact, inseparable from the theory of symbolism and allegory that developed as a result especially of the great influence of the writings of Pseudo- Dionysius from the 9th century onward. In these writings, particularly in his *De coelesti hierarchia* (860) as translated, with commentary, by John Scotus Erigena, the symbolical and allegorical value and the esthetic quality of a work of art are seen as quite distinct though complementary aspects of universal beauty, of which the work of art is at once a symbol and an allegory: hence allegory acquired a new function, that of con- firming the world of the senses, which led to a renewed interest in art as such. It is significant that an exceptionally enthusiastic promoter of major artistic enterprises, Abbot Suger, should have drawn inspiration from Pseudo-Dionysius and Erigena. It was while Abbot Suger was supervising the construction of the Abbey of St. Denis (consecrated in 1144) that their writings aroused renewed interest and that Hugh of St. Victor wrote his *Commentaria in hierarchiam coelestem Sancti Dionisii* (1137), which propounded a theory of allegory differing from that of Erigena in that, although it postulates a more radical distinction between visible and invisible beauty, it nevertheless regards the former as an image of the latter: an image which is essential for the knowledge of things invisible and which ends by assuming a more marked instrumental function "in showing the invisible wisdom of God" (*ad manifestandum invisibilem Dei sapientiam*). The work of Hugh of St. Victor, like that of Richard of St. Victor, who was to carry it further, constitutes the fullest theoretical definition of medieval allegory and of a critical method that sought to recognize in the features of visible beauty (*color*, *formatio*) those of the invisible (*sensus, significatio*); it should be noted, however, that this in no way implied underestimating one as compared with the other (see especially Richard of St. Victor's *Benjamin major*). The general lines of these concepts were elaborated by St. Thomas Aquinas, for whom earthly things were "*spiritualia sub metaphoris corporalium*," and later by Dionysius the Carthusian (d. 1471), who applied a totally allegorical interpretation to naturalistic data, in close parallel with the fundamentally unrealistic and distorted interpretations of symbolism that Huizinga (1965) discerned in the "naturalism" of 15th-century Franco-Flemish art.

A hint of a different attitude, largely rejecting the relation between the two types of beauty (visible and invisible), is implicit in the thought of St. Bernard of Clairvaux: in his famous invective (*Apologia ad Guillelmum sancti Theodorici abbatem*, ca. 1123–25) against the "deformed beauty and beautifully formed deformity" (*deformis formositas ac formosa deformitas*) of carvings in cloisters, the recognition of the esthetic autonomy of the work of art is carried so far that the work of art is not only considered inadequate for the expression of theological concepts but is even held to be a distraction from meditating on them. Clearly, however, this view does not amount to a theological rejection of art; rather it is an indication of the requirements of a new spirituality (see CRITICISM, col. 124–25).

Goffredo ROSATI and Oreste FERRARI

FROM THE RENAISSANCE TO THE 19TH CENTURY. During the Renaissance, with the works of Lorenzo Ghiberti, Leon Battista Alberti (qq.v.), and Antonio Manetti, art history and criticism began to achieve an independent and conscious idea of their own tasks; among the problems of art theory and criticism, allegory, which continued to arouse unreserved enthusiasm, was frequently and specifically treated. Alberti, stimulated by the idea of the social and educational function of art, affirmed for the first time the dignity of painting and particularly of narrative painting (*pittura di historie*) in his *Trattato della Pittura* (ca. 1435). Alberti's attitude is an indication of the tendency to substitute intellectual for spiritual interests; more common, however, was the attempt to establish a balance between the two, as is apparent from the plans for the ideal city of Sforzinda in the *Trattato di architettura* (ca. 1461–64) of Antonio Filarete (q.v.) and from the mystical and symbolical significance imputed to numbers by Fra Luca Pacioli (*De divina proportione*, 1497).

One symptom of this trend was the great popularity enjoyed from 1419 onward by Horapollon's *Hieroglyphica*, a sort of catalogue, with commentary, of the signs and symbols used in ancient Egyptian writing, probably compiled by an Egyptian or Byzantine grammarian about the time of Theodosius II (408–50). Alberti was familiar with the *Hieroglyphica* (*De re aedificatoria*, 1485, VIII, 4), as were Filarete and Leonardo da Vinci; in 1505 this work was printed by Aldus Manutius and in 1514 was translated into German by Dürer's friend, Willibald Pirckheimer. The influence of the *Hieroglyphica* can also be detected in Francesco Colonna's *Hypnerotomachia Poliphili*, published by Aldus in 1499; the descriptions of the symbolical aspects of imaginary ancient monuments and of ruins that occur so frequently in this famous tale form part of a general approach (acknowledged in the book's subtitle, *Ubi humana omnia non nisi somnium esse docet*) that interprets allegorically the evidences of decay and of mystery in these works.

These texts served as works of reference for the countless specialized treatises that appeared in the course of the 16th century in the form of collections of symbols and allegorical images from which artists could draw. The first such treatise, and unquestionably one of the best, was the *Emblemata* (1531) of Andrea Alciati: "emblemata" because it consisted mainly of personifications and allusive representations, although genuine allegories were also included. There followed the *Hieroglyphica* of Piero Valeriano (1556), whose work incorporated the lost work of his uncle, Fra Urbano Valeriano (a scholar who lived at the courts of Leo X and Clement VII), intended as an amplification of Horapollon's *Hieroglyphica*. Other such treatises included *Le Imprese Illustri*, by Giordano Ruscelli (1556), based

on the works of Alciati and Valeriano; and the *Hieroglyphic* of Jean Becan van Gorp (Goropius Becanus; 1580), who, in the wake of Horapollon, indulged in strange disquisition concerning the shape of the letters of the alphabet, seekin in them an independent and occult meaning. The greatest c the allegorists was Cesare Ripa, author of the famous *Iconologi* published in 1593, which went through 10 further edition before 1764 (III, PL. 202). Ripa constituted in a sense th epitome of a tradition and was to exercise considerable influenc on later literature on the subject; even the term "iconology was thereafter to be generally taken to mean the theory o allegorical personification. His work enjoyed great success an was much used by poets and artists; it was with good reaso considered the key to allegory in the 17th and 18th centuries The treatises on classical mythology are also closely linke with allegory in art; among the most important of these treatise should be mentioned the *Immagini degli dei degli antichi* (155(and 1571) of Vincenzo Cartari.

These authors of treatises were joined by a galaxy of writer interested in allegory, while others represented the manneris taste for abstruse metaphysics and the distorted concepts o astrological speculation; one example is the *De sculptura* o Pomponius Gauricus (1504), in which the author presentee his arcane interpretation of physiognomy, which, he claimed could reveal the specific symbolic nature of every part of th human body. Other theoretical works dealing with the magica and occult symbolism of the Renaissance include the *De verb mirifico* (1494) of Johann Reuchlin, the *De occulta philosophi* (1531) of Cornelius Agrippa of Nettesheim, the writings o A. Theophrastus Bombastus von Hohenheim, known as Pa racelsus (*Opus paragranum*, 1565; *Opus paramirum*, 1575), an(the prophetical writings (*Centuries*, 1555) of Nostradamu (Michel de Notredame).

There is a real and more consistent relationship betwee the concept of allegory and artistic practice in the writings o art historians of the mannerist period, some of which reflec the personal experience of the authors themselves. This is tru above all of Giorgio Vasari (q.v.), who, in his *Ragionament* (published posthumously in 1588), a commentary on the painting done by him in the Palazzo Vecchio in Florence, gives a ful explanation of the allegories in the Medici *studiolo*; Vasari who knew Piero Valeriano personally, also discussed the subjec at length in his *Lives* (*Le Vite*) and *Correspondence* (*Il Carteggi di Giorgio Vasari*), particularly in his correspondence wit Vincenzo Borghini. In sum, he considered it permissible fo the artist to "treat philosophy in fables."

Next in importance is Giovanni Paolo Lomazzo, who wa acquainted with the writings of all the leading allegorists, from Horapollon to Alciati, Valeriano, and Cartari; in his *Trattat dell'arte della pittura* (1584) he expounded a Neoplatonic concep of beauty as a Platonic "idea" that painting expressed in visibl form for the satisfaction of the intellect rather than the senses he went so far as to link the various kinds of painting with th astrological signs and with numbers, according to a complicatec symbolical system, and in Books VI and VII of his treatise h gives a repertory of classical and Christian allegorical figures

Mention should also be made here of Anton Francesc(Doni, who introduced into his *Disegno partito in più ragionament* (1549) a personification of sculpture that has obvious links wit Albrecht Dürer's *Melencolia I* (III, PL. 203) and who, in hi *Le Pitture* (1564), gave a new interpretation of the allegorie of Petrarch's *Trionfi*. Not to be overlooked also is Lodovic(Dolce's *L'Aretino, o dialogo della pittura* (1557), in which th author discussed allegory and symbolism in connection wit the theory of "decorum," that is, the appropriateness of forn to content and purpose in the work of art, a theme that hac already inspired Giovan Battista Armenini. Paolo Giovio, frien(and collaborator of Vasari, wrote a *Dialogo* (*Discourse on Em blems and Commentary on the Mottoes and Themes of Art an(Love which are commonly called Emblems*; 1560); and Raffaell(Borghini, in his *Il Riposo* (1584), showed particular appreciatio of allegory and departed from academic tradition by constan references to actual works of art.

Interest in allegory increased among churchmen confronte(

ith the problems that arose in critical phases of the Reforma-
on and Counter Reformation (q.v.). St. Ignatius Loyola in
s *Spiritual Exercises* (1522) had already recognized the place
the imagination, visualizing dynamically and dramatically
e problems of the soul, in meditation, which he considered
 indispensable step in the spiritual life. Giovanni Andrea
ilio (Gilio da Fabriano) confirmed the educational and devo-
onal functions of art in his *Due dialoghi ... degli errori de'
ttori* (1564) and, in classifying sacred themes, sanctioned the
se of allegory if it was clear and comprehensible and was
tended to inspire devotion. In his *De picturis et imaginibus
cris* (1570), Johannes Molanus (Jan Vermuelen) clearly ex-
essed the approach to allegory that was favored at the time,
rticularly in ecclesiastical circles; Cardinal Federigo Borromeo
voted a chapter of his *De pictura sacra* (1620–24) to sacred
nblems, with special reference to the Early Christian symbols
d those taken from the Scriptures; and Cardinal Gabriele
aleotti, in his *Discorso intorno alle immagini sacre e profane
582), laid further emphasis on the devotional function of the
legorical image, as did Antonio Possevino in his *Tractatio
 poësi et pictura ethica, humana et fabulosa ...* (1593).

The allegorical conception of art continued to prevail over
e symbolical in the 17th century. Lorenzo Pignoria brought
it a new edition of Andrea Alciati's *Emblemata* in 1618, and
out the same time a number of other interesting treatises
ppeared: the *Amorum emblemata* (1608; IV, PL. 404) and
moris divini emblemata (1610) of the painter Otto Vaenius
·an Veen); the *Nucleus emblematum* of G. Rollenhagen (1611–13);
d three weighty volumes by Nicolas Caussin, *Electorum
mbolorum et parabolarum historicarum syntagmata* (Paris, 1618),
olystor *Symbolicus, electrorum symbolorum et parabolarum
storicarum stromata* (Paris, 1618), and *De symbolica Aegip-
orum sapientia* (Cologne, 1623). These were followed by the
ieroglifici morali of Fra Vincenzo Ricci (Naples, 1626); the
ithor quoted Valeriano repeatedly but never Ripa, though
is obvious that his work follows closely that of Ripa, whose
mplexities he carried to an extreme. In 1644 Jean Baudoin
anslated Ripa's *Iconologia* into French, it was translated into
·erman in 1699 and then into English (*Iconologia or Moral
mblems*, London, 1709).

Goffredo ROSATI

The works of both Ripa and Alciati must have served as
urces for Emanuele Tesauro in his treatise, *Il Cannocchiale
·ristotelico* (1655), which contains an exhaustive treatment of
isual and verbal-visual symbols and allegories. Tesauro's
eatise contains the most exhaustive and organic treatment of
te baroque conception of art as an ingenious visual statement
f a mental process that confers a specific value on images as
gns carrying preestablished and universally recognizable
neanings, and a reading of it is indispensable to the iconographic
iterpretation of the baroque art that developed from this
onception. He deals with symbols and allegories on the basis
f concepts of metaphor, which may be attributive (the signifying
f a concept by means of, for example, insignia or instruments
elated to it), or may be based on ambiguity of facts (representa-
on of a person by means of something else of the same name)
r on hypotyposis of facts (representation of action by liveliness,
orcefulness, and movement), or may be an abbreviated state-
nent or glancing allusion to facts. He distinguishes emblems
om devices (both of them symbolic metaphors with a sensory
nd an intellectual significance): the device has a recondite
neaning, accessible only to those who have the key to it, whereas
ne emblem is an immediately comprehensible symbol, composed
f figures and words, signifying something relating to human
xistence.

For Giambattista Vico, in his *Principi di una scienza nuova
721, rev. ed. 1730), pictorial symbolism constituted the poetic
nguage of the heroic ages, preceding verbal poetic imagery:
By a necessity of human nature, poetic style arose before
rose style; just as, by the same necessity, the fables, or im-
ginative universals, arose before the rational or philosophic
niversals which were formed through the medium of prose
peech" (*The New Science of Giambattista Vico*, trans. T. G.

Bergin and M. H. Fisch, Ithaca, 1948, p. 138). Vico linked
to this proposition the development of medieval heraldry as
well as the devices of medals and coins and the emblems that
were so widespread in baroque art. His work paralleled Tesauro's
closely in many respects.

Rosario ASSUNTO

In addition to the treatise writers, art historians and theorists
also concerned themselves with allegory. Giovanni Baglione
(*Le vite di pittori ...*, Rome, 1642) showed little interest in
learned and complex inventions; such tales and allegories,
however, aroused the enthusiasm of Carlo Ridolfi (*Le mara-
viglie dell'arte ...*, Venice, 1648); of André Félibien, who
discussed the allegories of Nicolas Poussin (XI, col. 559) in
particular (*Entretiens ...*, Paris, 1666); and above all of Giovanni Pietro Bellori, who devoted almost the whole of his *De-
scrizione delle immagini dipinte da Raffaello da Urbino nelle
camere del Palazzo Apostolico Vaticano* (Rome, 1695) to interpretation of the allegories. He asserted, with evident pride,
in his *Le Vite* (1672), that he himself had suggested the original
concept for the complex allegories painted by Carlo Maratti
in honor of Clement IX in the Palazzo Altieri in Rome. Bellori's
appreciation of allegory, which fully accorded with classicist
theory, was paralleled by that of Carlo Cesare Malvasia (*Felsina
Pittrice*, Bologna, 1678), of the imaginative Giovanni Battista
Passeri (*Vite de' pittori ...*, Rome, 1772) and of Filippo Baldinucci (*Notizie de' professori del disegno ...*, Florence, 1681–1728).

Among those with a taste for the bizarre and the abstruse
in figural allegory should be mentioned Giovanni Bonifacio,
who, in his *L'arte de' cenni* (Vicenza, 1616), devoted the tenth
chapter of Book II to poets and painters; and Athanasius Kircher,
whose *Oedypus aegyptiacus* (Rome, 1652–54) showed that he
was well acquainted with the work of Horapollon and discussed
Egyptian hieroglyphics, for which he offered a magical, theosoph-
ical, and "mysteriosophic" interpretation.

In the first half of the 18th century came the beginnings
of a radical clarification of the problems connected with allegory,
largely as a result of the gradual elimination of the halo of
pseudo doctrine that had formerly attached itself to allegory.
Art historians, however, continued their appreciation of allegory
(e.g., Lione Pascoli, *Vite de' pittori ...*, Rome, 1730–36); and
further treatises were written on the subject: in 1740, Cesare
Orlandi published a new edition of Ripa's *Iconologia*, to which
he added a lengthy introduction, which is of particular interest
because of its reference to the complex decoration of the Church
of S. Maria della Pietà dei Sangro in Naples.

By the time Jean-Baptiste Boudard's *Iconologie* (1759) had
been published (Boudard was acquainted with the works of
Ripa, Alciati, and Valeriano), the general tone had already
changed. The crisis in allegorical culture, of which there were
traces in Boudard's work, became fully apparent in the second
half of the century with the statement of neoclassical theories
by Johann Joachim Winckelmann. He discussed allegory
specifically in his *Versuch einer Allegorie, besonders für die Kunst*
(1766), reaffirming the importance of Horapollon, Valeriano,
and Ripa (whose *Iconologia* he regarded as an artists' manual),
but he was also the first to point out the need for serious criticism
of traditional allegory; in fact, he devoted a portion of his essay
to criticism, frequently severe, of allegorical works. He went
on to identify lucidly the directions in which allegory had found
its greatest richness of expression and added a detailed catalogue
of allegories, mainly from antiquity, together with a series of
suggestions for classicist themes in symbolical or allegorical
representations. It may well be that his intention was to develop
this theory to the point of presenting a new iconology to suit
neoclassical taste; however, all that remains is this rough outline.
The new neoclassical iconology was, in fact, produced (again
in Germany) by Karl Wilhelm Ramler (1788) but did not enjoy
much success. The golden age of allegory was over, never
to return.

THE MODERN PERIOD. Neither criticism nor esthetic thought
was particularly concerned with symbolism and allegory during
the 19th century. Indeed, romanticism and the individualistic

exaltation of liberty of expression could not admit the conventional ties that form certain aspects of symbolism and allegory. Although allegorizing processes can be detected in the work of painters and sculptors, they rested on no specific substructure of art criticism or theory and bore little relation — as will be seen in a later section of this article — to the esthetic that gave rise to the symbolist movement of the final decades of the century (see EUROPEAN MODERN MOVEMENTS).

In the 20th century symbolism and allegory became a specialized art-historical interest of students of iconography, esthetics, and the history of criticism. Foremost among these is Emile Mâle, whose *L'art religieux après le Concile de Trente* (Paris, 1932) examines the allegory of the Counter Reformation and post-Reformation periods and evaluates Cesare Ripa's *Iconologia* from a critical point of view. Erna Mandowsky, too, was to return to this theme in her *Untersuchungen zur Ikonologie der Cesare Ripa* (1934), in which she gave a list of works inspired by themes taken from Ripa's work. P. D'Ancona (1923) published a survey of the iconography of specific medieval allegorical figures. Raimond van Marle was another who concerned himself with the Middle Ages and the Renaissance; in his *Iconographie* (1931-32) he presented a great mass of material, although not all of it had been sifted with a vigorously critical eye. The work of Erwin Panofsky (1939) is of prime importance for its new methodological approach and the results achieved in specific fields (see ICONOGRAPHY AND ICONOLOGY, cols. 774-77). Louis Réau (1955-59) is another who has done excellent work in the field of allegorical iconography. The various stages in the history of allegory have been well illustrated by J. Schlosser in *Die Kunstliteratur* (1924). Max J. Friedländer (1942) proclaimed the fundamentally symbolic nature of art and distinguished between symbolism and allegory. In discussing symbolist poetry of the 19th century, Arnold Hauser (1951) considered also the relations among allegory, symbolism, and metaphor and came to a negative conclusion concerning the value of allegory, which he termed "the simple, plain and to some extent superfluous transcription of an idea which gains nothing by being translated from one sphere to another."

Finally, from the strictly theoretical and critical point of view, Benedetto Croce (1926) devoted some important notes to the subject of allegory. His opinion was completely negative: according to him, allegory was simply the "conventional and arbitrary linking" of a concept or thought and an image, according to which "this image is held to represent that concept." He described allegory as "a form of code writing" using graphic images; for this reason allegory must be regarded as "necessarily alien to poetry."

Goffredo ROSATI

While modern writings on the subject can claim to have finally placed the problems of symbolism and allegory on the level of historical analysis, in practice they have relegated them to a position closer to the boundaries of esthetics. Another approach in dealing particularly with symbolism (and to a certain extent also with allegory) sees in it not only historically localized phenomena or the external factors conditioning artistic practice but also certain other aspects that are basically inseparable from such practice. Indeed, a widespread revival of symbolical and allegorical conceptions of art, accompanied by critical interpretations that view works of art from a symbolical or allegorical point of view, is now apparent in various sectors of contemporary culture. Among these concepts is semantics, which, in the general sense, is the study of the relations between verbal, visual, or acoustical signs and their meaning. The specific fields in which semantics is applied are linguistics, logic, and psychology, but — inasmuch as the images of painting and sculpture, as well as the spatial forms of architecture, can be (and often are) regarded as the visual expressions of a mental process similar to the verbal statements studied in linguistics — painting, sculpture, and architecture can also be studied with a view to determining, in a strictly scientific way, the relations between these signs and the meanings they carry, thereby deepening knowledge of the arts in their structure as well as the reconstruction of their origin. From this point of view, the semantics of art coincides with the general theory and philosphy of art itself, appearing as semantic esthetics, which regards all art as a system of signs and symbols whose value the same as the relation they bear to a meaning. This is no unquestionably accepted by all scholars, and one must distinguish between semantic esthetics and asymbolic esthetics, by which is meant both the esthetics that absolutely denies the symbolical nature of art (or at least of some art forms, such a painting, sculpture, and architecture) and that which, while not denying the symbolical nature of artistic forms, places the esthetic value and interest of art as such in the form of the sign or symbol itself, independent of the meaning it embodies.

In treating of modern concepts of symbolism it is essential too, to refer to theories based on psychology and on philosophy the former see in art one aspect of the general symbolizing activity of the psyche; the latter regard it as one of the activities of the human mind and therefore study it from the point of view of its affinities and points of difference in relation to other forms of knowledge. The first category covers psychoanalysis Jungian analytical psychology, and Gestalt psychology; the second category includes Ernst Cassirer's philosophy of symbolic forms and also that of Susanne Langer, who has formulated an organic system of esthetics based on the conception of art as a symbolizing activity.

Sigmund Freud's analyses of dreams led him to conclude that symbols indirectly represent objects, relationships, and situations present in the unconscious. On the basis of this premise (which Freud himself, in 1922, applied to the interpretation of Leonardo da Vinci's art) it became possible to study art images as the product of the unconscious symbolizing of the psyche. Since psychoanalysis constitutes a method of investigation and therapy that sets out (to use Freud's own definition) to enable man "to draw the best out of himself and to "render him as far as possible capable of joy," it may be regarded as a kind of lay, worldly soteriology, a science that leads to salvation in this world; it therefore reproduces in purely profane and earthly dimension the attitude to art of the medieval conscience. This analogy between the psychoanalytical conception of art and that peculiar to medieval religious soteriology extends also to the passage, common to both from symbolism to allegory.

Based as it is on the analogy between artistic activity and the so-called "dream process," which represents in dream images those thoughts which are latent in the waking state, the psychoanalytical conception of art distinguishes in works of art both a manifest content and a latent content that must be brought to light by interpretation. The images which constitute the manifest content and which are in fact symbols fashioned by unconscious mental processes are seen to be allegories with respect to their latent content; the passage from the manifest to the latent content therefore appears to be analogous to that from the literal to the allegorical sense in the traditional conception of allegory. Being symbolical in origin, art images are according to the psychoanalytical conception, allegorical in structure, in that once the latent content has been brought to the surface it overshadows the manifest content from which it has been freed, just as an awareness of allegorical significance tends to overshadow literal significance. The contribution of psychoanalysis to the current revival of symbolical-allegorical conceptions of art can thus be seen as a vindication of the symbolizing activity of the unconscious and of the allegorical process as a form of mediation between the unconscious and the conscious. The psychoanalytical conception of art therefore provides a primarily psychological theory that, as applied to art combines the concepts of symbolism and of allegory.

The analytical psychology of Carl Gustav Jung (1931, 1948 1963) and his school differs from Freudian psychoanalysis in its conception of art and its symbolism. To Jung, art was a psychological activity and as such was to be subjected to psychological analysis — only in its formal aspects, however, and not in its essence, which could be the object of esthetic study only. Jung gave Freudian psychoanalysis full credit for having delved into the "prehistory" of the work of art; nevertheless, in Jung's opinion the limitations of the psychoanalytical conception in the fact that it shifts the discussion to a broad human plane that is by no means specific to the artist and is, in any case, of no importance from the point of view of his art.

In the Jungian view, art may be either symbolic or semiotic. Those works of art are symbolic which embody primordial images, the archetypes of the collective unconscious; semiotic works of art are those dominated by energies springing from the individual unconscious. A parallel can be drawn between this classification of symbolic and semiotic works of art and that of symbolical and allegorical works. Insofar as the collective unconscious does not constitute a whole made up of innate images but rather a mere potential whose images appear only in the finished work of art, works of art which give shape to the archetypes of the collective unconscious are symbolical: entities both in themselves and as archetypal images which dominate history, in the course of which they recur every time the creative imagination is freely exercised. In symbolical works of art, therefore, the unity between the art and its meaning is such that the meaning itself can be conceived only in imaginative form; the work of art is symbolical in that it is the individualization of images that in their essence transcend the individual. In the semiotic work of art, on the other hand, the unity of the art and its meaning is such that once the consciousness has been made aware (or reminded) of the meaning, this becomes completely separated from the image and stands alone, just as the allegorical sense in traditional allegory becomes separated from the literal sense and stands on its own. Thus the Jungian conception, in its study and interpretation of art, plays its part in rehabilitating the symbol (because only in and through the symbolizing activity can man become aware of the archetypes present in the collective unconscious) and also, though only indirectly, allegory. The relation between the symbol and its latent meaning is not therapeutic-soteriological in the Freudian sense but one of revelation: by translating primordial images into the language of its own time, symbolic art opens up to all "the way to the deepest sources of life" and works unceasingly for the education of the contemporary spirit by revealing the forms of which it has greatest need.

In his rigorous application of the theoretical principles of the "psychology of form," Rudolf Arnheim (1954) reached the conclusion that all art is symbolical. Gestalt psychology is based on the principle that vision does not consist merely in the recording of sensations but is a process of evaluation conferring an order and a meaning on reality. True of vision in general, this is particularly true of the artist's vision. In the act of seeing, judgment is not simply something added by the intellect but inherent in the very act, so that far more is apprehended than registered on the retina: in the light of this theory of vision, Arnheim asserts that the perceptive scheme of a work of art acts as interpreter for the idea the work of art is meant to express, and that the subject matter is closely bound up with this perceptive scheme, the unity of scheme and subject constituting a concrete application of an abstract theme.

All art is therefore symbolical because it helps man to understand the world and himself, inasmuch as the artist presents to mankind what he himself has understood and regards as true. Comprehension and presentation are inseparable from vision and from the visualizing activity, in which artistic activity is made concrete; the artistic image is not, therefore, a substitute for something that could be formulated in another way but is itself that which it signifies. The symbolical conceptions derived from Gestalt psychology thus contribute to the current rehabilitation of the symbolic nature of art in that, presupposing the indivisibility of evaluation and vision, they justify the conception of a symbol as an inseparable unity of sign and thing signified, a unity intrinsic to art as such. Gestalt psychology thus, on strictly scientific premises, recognizes the symbolic nature of art in precisely that quality which makes it art: in form, which, for the visual arts, is visible form.

Ernst Cassirer, however, in his *Philosophie der symbolischen Formen*, arrived at a recognition of the symbolic nature of art from purely speculative premises. According to Cassirer, the symbol is a freely chosen sign in which the spirit perceives simultaneously the object, itself, and the laws of its own formativeness. In every symbol, a new and previously nonexistent synthesis of "ego" and "world" is created, a union of the subjective and the objective. Partaking in this symbolizing function are all true, autonomous, and original trends of consciousness, which are distinguished from one another by the diversity of their symbolic forms. Symbolic forms are, therefore, the channels through which the spirit objectifies itself — in other words reveals itself: art, science, myth, religion, all exist in a world of images (*Bildwelten*) that is something more than a simple reflection of data, because in them and through them the mere existence of experience receives a specific meaning, an appropriate ideal content. The feature peculiar to art as a symbolic form is that in it the image is appreciated for itself, simply as an image: it does not have to be stripped of itself and its content in order to fulfil its function. Hence in art, images acquire a wholly immanent significance, becoming the pure expression of the creative force of the spirit. In Cassirer's view, then, the symbolical quality of art lies in the fact that it is a spiritual form in which the spirit reveals itself and grasps the depth of being: in art the unity of symbol and thing signified is absolute.

There is a connection between Cassirer's philosophy and Susanne K. Langer's esthetics; conceiving art as symbolization that occurs in the affective faculties, she defines the forms of art as affective symbols, in which the meaning factor is not descried logically but rather perceived as quality. In opposition to logical positivism, Langer defends the cognitive value of the language of presentative symbols, which differ from discursive symbols in that the latter are translatable whereas the former are not and are therefore unverifiable. The symbolical quality of art lies in the correspondence of the symbolic form to the form of a vital experience without any conventional reference to a preordained meaning; every work of art is a symbol that can neither be broken down into factors nor be built up by a synthesis of the elements that enter into it. In this indivisible unity of the artistic form — a symbol of a sentiment whose structure varies according to the variations of what Langer calls the "primary illusion" of the individual arts — is found the unity of self and *Alter* that makes art not a mere diversion but a means of giving form to life.

Rosario ASSUNTO

II. ARTISTIC MANIFESTATIONS. THE ANCIENT MIDDLE EAST. In Egypt, as far back as the predynastic and protodynastic eras, symbolic representations, or emblems, were commonly used to denote both administrative areas (IV, PL. 323, cols. 715-16) and the exploits of the pharaoh, depicted as a bull destroying city walls or attacking his enemies (IV, PLS. 323, 324, cols. 623-24). This concept of the "heavenly bull," the bull-like power of the pharaoh, is recalled, in the Trinite period, by the bull-hoof supports used for beds. The regality and power of the pharaoh were connected with the representation of the sphinx, the symbolic meaning of which is made apparent by the reliefs in which it tramples on its overthrown adversaries; the habitual attitude of the sphinx, however (also constituting an expression of pharaonic power), is one of calm majesty (IV, PLS. 333, 354). Still another symbol associated with the pharaoh was the uraeus, or sacred asp (X, FIG. 843, no. 13), personifying the protecting goddess of his sovereignty. (See also IV, col. 716.)

A series of ideograms dating from the archaic period of Egyptian history has a symbolic value that goes well beyond their semantic symbolism as seen merely from the point of view of graphic convention (see CALLIGRAPHY AND EPIGRAPHY; III, PL. 2). Thus the ideogram *ankh* (X, FIG. 843, no. 23) occurs frequently in the iconography of monumental reliefs and statues as a symbol of life in scenes in which the various divinities present it to the pharaoh (IV, PL. 365). The ideogram *sm*, meaning "to unite," entwined with the papyrus and lotus plants, forms an emblem symbolizing the union of Upper and Lower Egypt and appears frequently on the sides of the cubiform thrones on which the pharaohs are seated in the classic iconography of statuary (PL. 331; IV, PL. 340). The ideogram *djed* was less popular than the other two; it was an Osirian symbol and denoted stability (PL. 330; IV, PL. 215).

Personifications of abstract ideas present a special problem;

predominant among them is Maat, "truth-justice," represented as a woman with an ostrich feather on her head. The divinization of abstractions probably led the Egyptians to believe that the truth-justice goddess did, in fact, resemble their image of her; the same may be said of Shay (Fate), Ronpet (Year), Ahket (the Flood Season), Peit (Spring), Sokhet (the Fertile Soil), Amenti (the West), Shemu (Summer), and Ḥa (the Desert), all of which, however, were far less popular in the figural arts. The frequent cosmological portrayals of the goddess Nut (the Sky), her body an arch supported by Shu (Air), who in turn rests on Geb (the Earth; III, PL. 487), and the depictions of the pharaoh suckled by the sacred cow, were regarded by the Egyptians as concrete realities and not as allegorical fictions. (See also IV, col. 309.)

Among the most important Egyptian symbols — and one that seems to have migrated widely — is the solar disk, often winged, representing the sun god (PL. 330; IV, PL. 391). During the attempted monotheistic reform of Akhenaten (14th cent. B.C.) this was the only representation of the divinity permitted; the sun disk of that period was often shown with rays in the form of human arms (IV, PL. 215).

In Mesopotamia, symbolic representations were used almost exclusively to denote the divinity. Some of the symbols revealing the presence and identity of a divine personage (see DIVINITIES) occur among the earliest ideograms of cuneiform writing in the first centuries of the 3d millennium B.C. They normally appear, particularly in carvings on gems and seals (q.v.), as complements to portrayals of the divinity. Occasionally, however, even in such ancient monuments as the Naram-Sin stele (I, PL. 507), the symbols themselves constitute the representation of the divinities; in Old Babylonian glyptics, the inscriptions carved on the seals mention divinities for whom only the symbols appear in the figural part of the seal. In the Kassite, or Middle Babylonian, era, symbolic representations of the divinity underwent a marked development, particularly when used on boundary stones (*kudurru*; PL. 331; II, PL. 20; IX, PL. 486), where various symbols often appear in superimposed registers (see IX, cols. 770–71), and in glyptics, where a similar tendency to dispense with the anthropomorphic representation of the divinity prevailed. Secondary themes that served to fill in the gaps in both Old Babylonian and Kassite glyptics probably have a symbolic value, but their significance is not clear. In reliefs and glyptics of the 1st millennium B.C., the function of divine symbols once again became complementary as the anthropomorphic representation of the divinity predominated (IX, PL. 495), except in the representation of the national god Ashur (Assur), whose composite symbol, consisting of a winged disk from which emerges the bearded bust of a man sometimes hurling arrows, was later adopted for the Persian god Ahura Mazda (IV, PL. 216; XII, PL. 525).

The preeminent symbol of divinity and hence of royal power was the horned tiara, placed on a throne. Among cosmological symbols was the solar disk of Shamash, the sun god (IX, PL. 495), who was also symbolized by the lion. A river uniting two human heads was a common symbol of Apsu, the god of rivers; Ea, the god of the oceans, appears as a goat-headed fish. (See also IV, col. 390.)

In the Syrian and Anatolian worlds there are few symbols whose meaning can be identified with any degree of accuracy, with the exception of the so-called "Cappadocian symbol" (a four-pointed star with volutes and spirals between the points), which is connected with the concept of royalty, and the countless ideograms used in Hittite hieroglyphics (III, PL. 3). Unlike the Egyptian ideograms, these were, however, never adopted in the figural arts. The symbology of the Syrian themes remains uncertain and is in any case nearly always obscure, so much so that it is commonly believed that, especially in the Phoenician world, the motifs may have been mainly ornamental.

Paolo MATTHIAE

Iranian art is deeply symbolical. In fact, it may be said that, particularly in certain periods, there is a deliberate effort to transfigure symbolically not only religious beliefs but also historical and geographic reality as well (see IRANIAN PRE-SASSANIAN

ART CULTURES; SASSANIAN ART). The symbolism of prehisto[r] and protohistoric Iran is no different from that of the neig[h] boring territories of the same era, especially, in its more primiti[ve] forms, that connected with fertility and fecundity. In spite [of] systematic efforts to interpret it, its meaning, remain, in t[he] last analysis, obstinately obscure.

The encounter between the figural trends of Mesopotam[ia] (q.v.) and those of the steppe (see ASIATIC PROTOHISTOR[Y, col. 23 ff.; STEPPE CULTURES) was of vital importance in the d[e]velopment of the symbolism of Iranian art. Even as early [as] the Luristan bronzes (8th cent. B.C.; see VIII, col. 254 ff.) — in which is found that symbolism of animals and the hunt (VI[I], PL. 139; XIV, PLS. 462, 463) which was to prove so popular [in] Achaemenian and post-Achaemenian art (VIII, PLS. 130, 13[?,] 138–140) — it is possible to detect the effects of this encount[er] which constituted a facet of the wider phenomenon of the e[x]pansion of the Mesopotamian civilization (see IRANIAN PR[E-] SASSANIAN ART CULTURES, cols. 254–59). How profound the si[g]nificance of Mesopotamian symbolism was in the Achaemen[ian] period is to be seen in the cylinder seals, which frequently be[ar] the representation of the palm, symbolizing the Tree of Li[fe,] accompanied by two genii or fantastic beasts, usually wing[ed] (XII, PL. 525, no. 6). Although the iconographic inspiration w[as] Mesopotamian in origin, the concept of the Tree of Life was n[ot] foreign to the religious patrimony of pre-Islamic Iran (X[,] PL. 514), and it is a theme that recurs in the Avesta and in Pa[h]lavi texts. Sometimes the seals depict a hero battling with [a] monster with the body of a horned and winged lion (XII, P[L.] 525, no. 9), a symbolical scheme common in Mesopotamian a[rt.]

There is also a specifically Iranian symbolism on the cy[l]inder seals, however, even though the forms are traceable [in] large part to the earlier iconographic traditions of the East a[nd] to Egypt. An outstanding example is the winged solar dis[k,] symbol of the supreme god of Mazdaism, Ahura Mazd[a.] Sometimes the sun disk appears above the Tree of Life, as [in] the glyptics of Mesopotamia and Syria; or (both in seals and [in] the larger Achaemenian rock carvings) the disk may be depict[ed] with a human bust in the center, according to an iconograph[y] that was common also in Babylonian and Assyrian art. Aga[in] the iconography may be modified in a way that seems pecul[iar] to Iran: in some of the seals, the human bust no longer emerg[es] from the center of the sun disk but is inscribed in a circle plac[ed] below it and supported on either side by two hybrid genii wi[th] either human or bird faces (XII, PL. 525, no. 5).

The symbolism of animals and hunting scenes on the Acha[e]menian seals commonly had an astral significance, which w[as] carried over in part into Sassanian art (q.v.). The sun-sky g[od] was conceived as a hunter, pursuing and driving before him t[he] constellations, personified in animal form for each season (t[he] bear for winter, the stag for spring, the lion for summer). [In] this symbology the bull is often the personification of the sun go[d;] on Sassanian seals the lion, the griffin, the horse, and the hipp[o]griff also appear as solar symbols, and a triple animal proton[?] sometimes represented the path of the sun across the sky. (S[ee] also IRANIAN PRE-SASSANIAN ART CULTURES; SASSANIAN ART.)

The central symbol of Zoroastrianism (q.v.), and pre-Islam[ic] Iranian religious feeling generally, was fire, the son of Ahu[ra] Mazda, signifying the life of the macrocosm and the microcos[m.] The symbolism of fire, which recurs constantly in Iranian a[rt,] became a constant theme of Sassanian numismatics, in whi[ch] the basic iconography (with a number of variations) is a fi[re] altar set between two standing, armed figures (III, PL. 39[?,] no. 12; XIV, PL. 477). An interesting and original symbol[ic] detail is added on some coins: a crowned human head appea[rs] in the flames on the altar, probably an expression of the *xvarna[h]* a symbol of the splendor and prosperity of the Iranian king[.]

In the Sassanian era there was a major development in roy[al] symbolism, known from coins and seals of the period showi[ng] the royal diadem, on which the sun and moon are almost a[l]ways represented to symbolize the cosmic conception of Sass[a]nian kingship (XII, PL. 525, nos. 10 and 12). Similar cosmologic[al] expressions of the royal power appear on the "Cup of Khusrau["] and elsewhere in Sassanian art (III, PL. 490; XII, PLS. 395, 40[?,] 407). See also III, col. 840; IV, cols. 717–18.

The soul-bird, or senmurv, was a symbol that found characteristic iconographic expression in Iran (XII, PL. 406; XIV,
. 458); it recalls, to a certain extent, the symbolic meanings
attached to the phoenix, and there are other traces of this same
symbology.

Whatever their diffusion outside the Iranian world, the Mith-
aic mysteries are unquestionably of Iranian origin. There
are clear traces of the central act of these mysteries, the killing
of the bull by Mithras, even in the religious tradition of Maz-
ism. But in the mysteries of Mithras, alongside the Iranian
contribution, other heterogeneous symbolisms arose, creating a
composite and eclectic symbolism and iconography. Moreover,
the mystery nature of the Mithraic religion induced the ini-
tates to conceal the meaning of their sacred representations:
thus allegory took the place of symbolism.

Finally, a constantly recurring symbolic representation shows,
on Achaemenian cylinder seals, two winged beings beside the
Tree of Life or at the edge of the sun disk: these figures, Cauti
and Cautopati, reappear as torchbearers, one with uplifted and
the other with inverted torch, in Mithraic representations,
probably as personifications of the sun at the equinoxes. They
appear, too, on either side of the fire altar on Sassanian coins,
where one is surmounted by the sun symbol and the other by
the moon symbol — representing not ontological opposition
between the two symbols but rather their complementary nature,
at the basis of the concepts of interdependence between opposing
elements that are characteristic of the ancient Iranian religion
and other cults of the East.

Gherardo GNOLI

GREECE AND ROME. Forms and figures to which may be
attributed a symbolic value in that they refer to a hidden meaning
are rare in archaic Greek art; it shows no basic predisposition
toward symbolism. The explanation lies in the peculiar and
close link between archaic Greek art and the ancient religion:
a religion that, as Kerényi (1940) says, was essentially, if not exclusively, mythological in character and had no sacred writings in
the strictly theological and doctrinal sense of the word but
rather narratives of mythical events (the Homeric poems and the
Works and Days of Hesiod). Archaic Greek art, which was
inspired specifically by the mythological tales of the Homeric
epics and the writings of Hesiod and drew from them its basic
iconographic themes, is thus the visible manifestation of that
mythological content, to which it referred directly and explicitly
by way of illustration, and not of symbolical exposition (see
MYTH AND FABLE). So long as this close relationship between
the mythological religion and the forms of artistic expression
continued, there could be no symbolism in the true sense. Beginning with the 5th century B.C., however, when there was a
crisis in religious belief, this relationship became less close and
intellectualistic references to mythological allegories appeared,
in an attempt to salvage a mythological and religious past which
was no longer understood in the rationalistic world of the Soph-
ists but which nevertheless, for ethicopolitical reasons, could
not be abandoned.

* *

In the visual arts there was a far wider range of allegorical
phenomena than in literature and philosophy but also a much
vaguer distinction between personification and allegory proper.
Although the progressive increase in the number of allegories
began about this time, some monuments of the allegorical type
date as far back as the 7th century B.C.: from that era may be
dated the Thanatos, Hypnos, Nyx, Dike and Adikia, and Eris
and Phobos on the famous chest of Kypselos at Olympia described by Pausanias (Description of Greece, v, 17). All these personifications are found on the vases of a later age (IV, PL. 168),
together with Mania, Apate, Oistros, Lyssa, Ananke, and the
Poinai — all personifications of abstract concepts based on religious or simply current moral conventions that here assumed
human lineaments and behaved as men.

Lists of personifications are readily available in the studies
of Pottier (1889–90) and others; it cannot have been long before
an iconographic repertory was established that served as a more

or less direct source for the images found on various Greek
and Roman monuments and in paintings, sculpture, and reliefs:
surely a genius loci can be seen in the marble group of the "Farnese Bull" (XII, PL. 121), and another on the Ficoroni cist (V,
PL. 50). Yet another example is the painting from Herculaneum
depicting Telephos and Herakles before Arcadia (VII, PL. 193).
In this discussion, however, it is of more concern — rather
than summarizing once again the main types of allegorical
representation — to outline the general problems presented by
allegory with special reference to the specific phenomenology
of the major forms of artistic expression in the Greek and Roman
civilizations: ceramics, wall paintings, and sculpture.

Much of the ceramics production of antiquity was intended
exclusively for sacred or funerary use and was therefore found
among tomb furnishings; this function throws light on the
meaning of the various images that occur. Much information
is to be derived from the vast repertory of figures represented:
all the gods, Olympian and pre-Olympian alike, have their place,
as has the whole of mythology, with scenes of joy and sorrow
(II, PLS. 46, 47; X, PL. 243), as well as the entire epic cycle —
a favorite theme, almost as if to denote the great sacred value
attached to a mythology recalled to life and reproduced in action
by disguised human beings; in addition there is the colossal
cycle of Dionysos with the bacchantes, the satyrs, and Seilenos
(II, PLS. 38, 54; III, PLS. 349, 376), not to speak of funeral scenes
proper (IV, PL. 461; VII, PL. 77). In short, all the traditions
dearest and most sacred to the Greeks found expression in the
decoration of Greek and even of Italic ceramics. The sacred and
the profane, the ancient and the contemporary, the real and the
imaginary, alternate with and are superimposed on one another
without any special hierarchy or preference, rather as they must
have coexisted in the common thoughts and beliefs of the time.

In the translatio from this life to the next, the Greek dead
became young and handsome — kaloi — and thus made their
entry into mythology. They became "heroes" or demigods;
they were transformed into Dionysii, satyrs, nymphs, or bacchantes; they became Demetrii in Athens; they took on the features
of Hercules on Roman sarcophagi; they were Joviales in some
provinces of the Empire; they became Hermetes, Artemides,
and the like. Representation on funerary urns is therefore
cathartic and so directly allegorical. There is a double translatio
— from Olympus to the world beyond the grave and from there
to the world of the living: three worlds coexisting side by side,
each of which might be assimilated to the others. Even the pan-
Athenian amphoras exemplify this attitude: the allegorical significance of the usual figured representation is, in fact, the
"transhumanization" of the dead man into a young athlete
and victor. The same may also be said of the famous pinaces
of Locri (IV, PL. 218; V, PL. 429; VII, PL. 75), in a technique
that combines relief and painting. Here is expressed the allegory
of the Greeks, for whom Hades and Persephone, gods and men,
scenes of life and death are intermingled in a special world that
is neither that of the living nor that of the dead but rather the
allegorical place where the unreal becomes real and vice versa
and where the two live side by side, blended by a natural mysticism.

From literary references — almost the only source of knowledge of the paintings of antiquity — it is known that Parrhasios painted the Athenian Demos and Arete; Pausias, a Methe
or Drunkenness; Euphranor, a Demokratis and a Demos; and
Apelles, a War and a Triumph. All these are, however, obviously
personifications rather than allegories in the true sense of the
word. The only documented allegory is the famous Calumny
painted by Apelles and described by Lucian: half a score of
personifications acting in a scene that referred to an experience
of the painter himself in his relations with Ptolemy.

The tomb paintings and the ornamental and decorative
ones from Pompeii give some idea of the great paintings of
antiquity; the Pompeian ones (VII, PLS. 190, 368) are frequently
not without a vague erotic or at least sensual meaning designed
to titillate the householder. In a different category is (whatever
its interpretation) the magnificent cycle of paintings (the hieros
gamos, the suckling of the kid symbolizing the initiate, the ritual
scourging) in the Villa of the Mysteries at Pompeii (IV, PL.

168; VII, PL. 203). Of clearer allegorical significance and in full analogy with the vase paintings are the paintings in tombs depicting scenes of everyday life, rebirth and continuation of life, and the like; the representations of bloody scenes and of monsters must also have had a cathartic purpose transcending the form in allegorizing it.

The same forms of allegorization recur in the statuary of the 5th century B.C. (see CLASSIC ART): athletic bodies, divinities, and portraits (III, PL. 372) were transposed into a noble form — not that of any particular man or god but that conceived as characterizing a physically and ethically ideal beauty. Beginning in the 4th century B.C., however (see HELLENISTIC ART), there was an increasingly strong tendency to a more complex type of personification, subtle, hedonistic, and mystical, and allegory became a substantial coefficient in art. The most striking aspect of the phenomenon is the broadening of the iconographic repertory of allegories and personifications: e.g., the Eirene and Ploutos by Kephisodotos (III, PL. 373), the Aphrodite, Pothos, and Himeros by Skopas (PL. 42), the Eros by Praxiteles, the Hypnos by Skopas, the Samothracian Nike (VII, PL. 177), and, in particular, the "Tyche of Antioch" (VII, PL. 157) by Eutichides.

Together with the Tyche may be mentioned the famous statue of the Nile with 16 putti symbolizing its floods (PL. 338): the symbolical waters course down the pedestal of the statue, and even the marble strands of the god's beard seem to turn to liquid and flow down in streams. The Tiber was also personified, and later the Danube, in a half-bust on Trajan's Column (PL. 109) and on the Column of Marcus Aurelius: the back view of the Danube figure constitutes a further allegory, one that is military and political in character, signifying that the Roman armies had defeated and trodden on the "back" of the river. Among similar Roman personifications are that of Saturnia Tellus in the Ara Pacis (III, PL. 488), personifying Earth with her breezes, her fertile soil, and her waters; the personification of Africa as an elephant; and the innumerable personifications of Rome and the cities and provinces of the Empire (PL. 339). Of the many examples of allegorical scenes may be mentioned the one on Trajan's Column showing Jupiter taking part in the battle against the Dacians and the bust of Night intervening from the rocks to break off a dangerous engagement; the one on the Arch of Benevento where Jupiter seems to be handing over the scepter (the thunderbolt) to the emperor who will represent him on earth; and the scene on the Column of Marcus Aurelius where the ample fleece of Jupiter Pluvius is transformed into streams of water running down onto the parched rocks (PL. 337). One might add the Hadrianic slabs in the Palazzo dei Conservatori, one of which depicts the apotheosis of the empress (XII, PL. 298); the base of the Antonine Column, also showing an apotheosis; the Monument of the Haterii, which undoubtedly depicts the preparation of the great catafalque for an apotheosis (IV, PL. 454); and the allegories of the Triumphal Arch of Galerius in Salonika (XII, PL. 198).

Even more widespread and typical was the allegorical adjunct on funerary monuments, where there is a repetition of the phenomenon already studied in relation to funerary urns: the Harpy Tomb in the Xanthos necropolis (I, PL. 537) with its strange mixture of personages living and dead, winged monsters that snatch at souls (IV, PL. 167), and various animals; the Heroon of Trysa (VII, PL. 354) with its series of bas-reliefs — Amazonomachies, centauromachies, scenes from the *Odyssey*, etc. — even though time has obscured some of the allegorical meanings; and the more obvious allegory of the twelve *aure oceanidi* that was placed between the columns of the "Nereid Monument" in Xanthos (ca. 370 B.C.).

It is in tomb statuary especially that allegory reigns supreme. The herm, an extremely ancient sepulchral symbol, was revived in the form of the late steles and reliefs with the same connotation (III, PL. 357; IV, PL. 450; VII, PL. 46). The nude virile funerary statue — the kouros — that replaced the herm was a transposition of the effigy of the dead man to that world of youth and beauty which those who survived him liked to picture to themselves. The winged monsters that once had snatched and lacerated became sirens, sphinxes, and harpies (VII, PL. 23); the half-busts so common in Magna Graecia and in Cyre-

naica recall Demeter-Ge, the Earth Mother, whose body the earth that produces men, plants, and animals and th gathers them all once again to her breast to prepare a new l The same type of allegory is apparent in the Erotes with cross legs or downcast gaze; the Thanatos and Hypnos; the h reclining dead, with the lower half of the body seeming disappear into the sarcophagus; and the sleeping forms w their faithful dog and little guarding servant (VII, PL. 51).

The allegorical overtones are even clearer in the funer banquet scenes where the divinized dead man reclines at meal with the living, from whom he does not differ forma (VII, PL. 14). The dead-man-become-a-god continues to l among the living, who in turn are transported, ideally, to world beyond the grave; above, the protoma of a horse — ancient demon of death — warns that the festal gathering ex only in the yearnings of the living. But it is in the figu steles, particularly the Attic ones (II, PL. 53), that the measur and almost dreamy expression is fixed in statuesque forms t would be meaningless were they not illuminated by a spec form of allegorical *translatio* peculiar to the mentality and spi of the Greeks, consisting in the inversion of the two wor and the indiscriminate juxtaposition of the dead and the livi (III, PL. 369). The dead man or woman is the youngest a most beautiful person in the group and is surrounded by t loving care of relatives, who well know that their dear one no more and that their own names will soon be recorded on t architrave of the stele. But they appear to be unaware of the s reality: the dead one lives on in their midst and, silent and drea like, they relive with him one of their joyous family gatherin

The sarcophaghi of the Roman era, whether they dep scenes from real life — weddings, sacrifices, the palest games — or take their themes from Greek mythology, comprehensible only as allegories. In the first type it is t *translatio* from everyday reality to the world beyond the gra that is signified; the second represents — though in forced a inadequate fashion — an application of the ancient Gre cathartic principle according to which the dead man laid in sarcophagus decorated in this way seemed better able to beco purified and worthy of immortality. Thus the entire Dion sian cycle lives once more, as also the labors of Hercules, t massacre of the children of Niobe, the Oresteia, Meleag Alcestis, Phaedra, Actaeon, and the rest. The numerous chitectural sarcophagi with small columns, which came to Ror from the East, are also closely bound up with the concept the apotheosis of the dead man, who appears at the center the composition, already exalted to the rank of hero and flank by divinities (XII, PL. 195).

Another fairly common type of Roman sarcophagus bea representations of battles between Romans and barbaria (2d and 3d cent.; XII, PLS. 302, 507). There are two possib allegorical interpretations for these: they may represent continuation of the Greek tradition of Amazonomachies, ce tauromachies, and the like, in which the victory of the superi over the inferior civilization vindicates the vitality and surviv of the sovereign people and of the dead man; or, alternative they may be connected with that aspect of Hellenistic thoug and late Greco-Roman philosophy in which the vanquishe fallen or taken prisoner, naturally evoke greater pity and sy pathy than the proud victors. One may recall, for instance, t moving scenes depicted on the lid of the Amendola sarcophag in the Capitoline Museum; but in fact, this same approach w already apparent on the Column of Trajan. A similar allegoric interpretation is possible for the great Pergamon frieze (V PLS. 172–174), in which the Giants inspire respect and sympat and are perhaps less bloodthirsty than the Olympians: the latt in this instance, being the Romans and the Giants being t Anatolians, who would succumb, admittedly, but would displ their nobility and ancient civilization in so doing, like the Gian and Titans in comparison with the Olympians.

Silvio FERRI

THE JUDAEO-CHRISTIAN TRADITION. There was an abunda treasure of symbols in the Jewish world to which the fir Christians, in the Middle East, were largely oriented; the clo entification between symbol and thing signified, however, giving the former a merely semantic value, reduced the symbols nost to the level of hieroglyphics or pictograms, without pri- ary artistic intent or value: it is no coincidence that signs ade up of letters played a large part, with a rich variety of eanings for individual letters or groups of letters. From these ne also the image possessing an almost autonomous value, ch as the fish (ΙΧΘΥΣ), for the name of Jesus; the alpha and ega, usually with the cross (Felix sarcophagus, Ravenna, . 342); and the Chi-Rho monogram, which developed from a ere sign denoting the name of Christ into the emblem that nstantine placed on his helmet (as seen in the splendid Ti- um coin) and on the famous labarum and which came to be pled, denoting the Trinity, in the mosaic decoration of the ult of the Albenga Baptistery dating from the second half the 5th century — contemporary with the Menorah of the a'aran synagogue: the comparison could hardly be more sig- icant.

The interchangeability of meanings also extended to actions d signs — the so-called "seals" (a term applied to both cumcision and baptism), as well as the sign imprinted on a ne (the famous Gnostic abraxas) or the sign made on the rson: the sign of the cross, for example (which eventually veloped in art into the splendor of the *crux gemmata*), or the cross denoting a Christian, which was scratched on the tues of pagan divinities almost as a form of exorcism, as on e Praxitelian head of Aphrodite in the National Museum Athens (G. E. Rizzo, Praxiteles, Milan, 1932, p. 28, XLIII).

Symbolism was deeply rooted in the Judaic mentality: as Justin points out (Dialogus XC, in Migne, PG, vi, 690), ll things spoken by the Prophets were shrouded in parables d figures," and the teaching of Christ, too, was couched in rables. A typical example of such Biblical similitude is Jacob's ing prophecy (Gen. 49: 1–27), in which Jacob's children are ened to animals in their virtues and faults: "Judah is a lion's elp . . . Issachar is a strong ass . . . Dan shall be a serpent the way . . . Naphtali is a hind let loose . . . Benjamin shall en as a wolf . . . ." The transition from verbal to visual tement in these and other prophecies, especially those of Eze- l and from the Apocalypse, proved a rich source for Christian nography (see CHRISTIANITY). From the Gospels may be ntioned especially the parable of the Good Shepherd, which s especially favored in the early Church (see below).

The sign ceased to be identical with its signification almost ultaneously among Jews and among Christians. The change me about partly from the disappearance of the need to speak idden language in order to conceal the cult and partly from e influence of Hellenistic-Roman culture — which tended to e an art form to every figured manifestation — and from the wing need to decorate religious buildings and other cult ales (III, PL. 101; VII, PL. 405).

The Menorah (III, PL. 103; VIII, PL. 333), or seven-branched ndlestick, soon became the central symbol of Judaism (see WISH ART), often shown flanking the Torah, or tablets of the w: the decorations of the catacombs of Beth Shearim include me twenty variations of the Menorah. Other symbols were e lion (standing for the Lion of Judah) and the sacrificial p, a symbol of the Temple. Decorations on door jambs and tels also include magical symbols such as the "Shield of David" xagram and the five-pointed (or later, six-pointed) star, or ntacle, known as the "Seal of Solomon" (Synagogue of Ca- rnaum).

Other examples of interest are "Davithea Eleleth," a symbolic age showing David in priestly garb bearing in one hand the re and in the other the golden bell; the drawing of the Lord- avros in the Bruce Papyrus; the graffiti on the Khirbet Kil- steles and in the Dominus Flevit necropolis in Jerusalem here a number of seven-branched candlesticks are represented); d the mystical-cosmological symbolism of the staircase in e Christian monastery at Beth ha-Shitta (near Neth Shan) a relatively late work, although built before the year 427.

Michelangelo CAGIANO DE AZEVEDO

EARLY CHRISTIAN AND BYZANTINE ART. Early Christian symbolism expressed something natural and joyous, almost as if the eschatological message, and even persecution and martyr- dom, were nothing but an invitation to future happiness. It is this idyllic quality and simplicity of Early Christian symbolism which accounts for the greater popularity of the parable as com- pared with allegory in its true sense: the parable is linked with a specific and homely example (the Good Shepherd or the la- borers in the vineyard), whereas allegory is based on a rational or at least intellectual generalization. The tendency to symbolism rather than to allegory was especially deeply rooted in Byzantine art (q.v.), which was inclined to depreciate the naturalistic aspects of representational art: a typical example is the representation of the Transfiguration in the apsidal mosaic in S. Apollinare in Classe, Ravenna (X, PL. 181).

Among the symbolic representations may be mentioned the vintage scenes in the circular mosaic in the Mausoleum of Constantia (Church of S. Costanza) in Rome and the count- less illustrations of the seasons, which were favored because of their cyclic allusion to death and resurrection. Examples of the latter are to be found in the catacombs of Priscilla, of Callix- tus, and of Praetextatus (the Crypt of St. Januarius, second half of the 4th cent.); in the Catacomb of Domitilla (the so-called "crypt of the millers"); and in a cubiculum in the Catacomb of SS. Peter and Marcellinus "ad duas lauros" (4th cent.; see CATACOMBS; CHRISTIANITY). Certain symbols of this early pe- riod were to remain characteristic and unchanged in all Christian art. Chief among these, appearing first in the 4th–5th century, were the Apocalyptic symbols of the Evangelists (mosaics in S. Pudenziana and in S. Paolo fuori le Mura, Rome; Sigwald altar frontal, Cividale, PL. 342).

Interest in allegory nevertheless manifested itself fairly early. On the border line between symbolism and allegory are the countless depictions of the Good Shepherd (catacombs of Callixtus, of Praetextatus, and of Domitilla; Catacomb of SS. Peter and Marcellinus, II, PL. 281, X, PL. 482; statues and sarcophagi in the Vatican, III, PL. 304, IX, PL. 63; "Mauso- leum of Galla Placidia," Ravenna, X, PL. 179) and those of doves, of peacocks, and of stags drinking from the Fountain of Life; and representations of a ship or anchor (PL. 341), or of a ship guided by a beacon, symbolizing salvation or the journey toward it.

Definitely allegorical are the representations in which the lamb ceases to be a simple symbol of Christ and assumes a differ- ent meaning: alluding to sacrifice, as on the cover of the 5th- century Gospel book in Milan (PL. 341); or, in the form of a lamb among wolves, alluding to the episode of Susanna and the elders (Rome, Catacomb of Praetextatus, mid-4th cent.); or indicating the Apostles or the faithful (PL. 342). Even more explicit allegorical intentions are apparent in scenes drawn from the Gospels (the Loaves and Fishes, PL. 341) and in rep- resentations such as that of St. Peter in a boat supporting a net full of fishes as the mystical fisher of men (fragment of 4th- cent. sarcophagus, Rome, S. Sebastiano); that of Christ as the helmsman guiding the ship of the Church with the Evangelists at the oars (fragments of 4th-cent. Spoleto sarcophagus, Vatican, Lat. Mus.); the 4th-century lamp in the form of a boat with Christ and an orant (or the Apostles Peter and Paul?; IX, PL. 89); the Traditio Legis (III, PL. 304; IX, PLS. 63, 65); and the Traditio Clavium (mosaics in the side niches of S. Costanza, Rome; and the personifications of the Ecclesia ex circumcisione and ex gentibus in the S. Sabina mosaics in Rome (III, PL. 314).

Especially interesting are the allegorizations of classical myths, which, because of their tenor of mystery, salvation, and resurrection, were held to be acceptable to the new Christian ideals. The myth of Orpheus found various expressions (PL. 342; III, PL. 98), sometimes in the form of the Good Shepherd (Catacomb of Callixtus), as did that of Eros and Psyche, an allegory of salvation and immortality (Catacomb of Domitilla).

The intention of imbuing the work of art with symbolical or allegorical significance extended to all creative activity. With reference to architecture, the whole of Christian religious literature, from St. Paulinus of Nola (353–431) and St. Eucherius (d. ca. 449) down to the 13th-century Guillaume Durand of Mende and Honorius of Autun, is full of precepts and recommendations designed to give such significance to every part of the sacred edifice. Great importance was attached to the orientation of the church to the east, and special attention was directed to the symbolism of light as expressed in the illumination as well as in the use of precious metals and glowing colors; the concept of the basilican church as a symbol of the Church maternally gathering the faithful in her arms was set forth as early as the *Constitutiones apostolicae* (largely 4th cent.), and the later central plan was seen as a cosmological symbol; still later, the cross, the central symbol of Christianity, was embodied in the Latin-cross and Greek-cross plans.

Goffredo ROSATI

THE WESTERN WORLD. *The Middle Ages.* In medieval art (whether connected with religious experience or related to civic life, love, political institutions, or military forces), systems of visual signs and symbols occupy a highly important position because of the predominantly symbolical and allegorical character medieval culture attributed to art in general and to the visual and architectural arts in particular. The recourse to conventional and ideographic signs having a preestablished and universally accepted meaning and to symbolic images that refer, in the common mind, to specific meanings (independent of the form in which they are developed by individual artists) is, obviously, fundamental to such a conception of art. Among the signs or symbols of the first sort that denote an indirect but clearly recognizable meaning are the lion, for strength; the eagle, for majesty; the serpent, for shrewdness; and the dove, for innocence.

Visual symbols are numerous in the Christian tradition, particularly for the symbolic depiction of Christ (the lamb, the fish, the pelican, the gryphon, the phoenix, III, PL. 303; the sacred monogram — the Chi-Rho or chrismon, I, PL. 281, FIG. 452; the cross with vine scrolls or acanthus rinceaux growing out of it); of God the Father (the hand; see IV, cols. 408–09, PL. 228); of the Holy Spirit (the dove, the tongues of fire; II, PL. 284; III, PL. 110; IV, PL. 229; V, PLS. 215, 216; see DIVINITIES, cols. 411–13); and of the Trinity, for which sometimes figural and sometimes geometrical forms were used, or a combination of the two, with or without verbal signs (IV, PLS. 230–232; cols. 413–17; see also CHRISTIANITY; IMAGES AND ICONOCLASM). The symbols of the Evangelists, too, form part of this medieval patrimony whose meaning was universally known and accepted; they are frequently found as attributes with the "Evangelist portraits" in medieval Gospel books (I, PLS. 276, 282; X, PLS. 72, 74, 462, 471).

Calligraphy, especially in the early medieval period, in manuscripts for liturgical use, had a dual symbolic value, both verbal and figural; ornamented and accompanied by the figural forms that were an integral part of it, it was thus made intelligible even to those who were unable to read and grasp its verbal exposition.

On the secular level, heraldry afforded a vast field for the application of signs and symbols during the medieval period. In heraldry the figures, borders, and tinctures, the divisions on shields, and the shapes of crowns and helmets were all signs carrying well-defined and universally recognizable meanings (see EMBLEMS AND INSIGNIA). Although the signs used in coats-of-arms and military insignia were of extremely ancient origin, heraldry as it is now known arose in the 11th and 12th centuries and probably began to take definitive shape at the time of the first Crusades. In medieval heraldry the tinctures, devices, and figures were not purely decorative motifs but, rather, specific signs; their use was governed by rules that no individual imagination might violate in designing a coat-of-arms. The cross on the shield of the Crusaders is one of the first heraldic signs whose origins can be dated with certainty, and from this cross certain formal modifications were derived, such as the Maltese cross, the cross of Lorraine, and the flowered cross (with the bars ending in fleur-de-lys), found in family, city, and regional coats-of-arms and on those of religious military orders such as the Knights of St. John of Jerusalem (Knights of Rhodes; Knights of Malta) and the Teutonic Knights.

Religious heraldic symbolism also enters into other mediev art forms, both as specific content, an understanding of whi can help to place individual works in their historical or cultu environment, and as iconographic themes or motifs in whi the meaning of these signs is broadened (see ICONOGRAPHY A ICONOLOGY). This heraldic or religious-heraldic symbolism w to enter into, for example, the tapestries of the 15th and 16 centuries produced in the workshops of French Burgun Among the most famous of these are the "Lady and the U corn" tapestries (PL. 393); their iconography is clearly bas on a heraldic code that in turn was often derived from t medieval bestiaries, in which the form of each animal convey symbolic meanings, and from herbals in which plants had si ilar symbolic meanings.

Another repertory of pictorial or calligraphic-pictorial sy bolism in the medieval period consisted of magical signs; t gether with those of religion and heraldry, these signs we frequently included in the works of art of the time (they a believed to be present even in the ornamentation of Romanesq and Gothic churches) and often determined the iconograph content of such works (see MAGIC). These magical signs a of extremely ancient origin; scholars in this field date some them to the early Neolithic. During the medieval period ma cal signs developed along several lines: the apotropaic, whi adopted certain images as signs to ward off evil, attributing them a power to exorcise malignant forces (see MONSTROUS A IMAGINARY SUBJECTS), and which often, like heraldry, drew the bestiaries and herbals for the images it used (the more less fantastic beasts ornamenting the gallery and windows o side the east choir of Worms Cathedral are believed to ha had an apotropaic function); the astrological (see ASTRONO AND ASTROLOGY); and the cabalistic, whose signs, of Arab origin, were of a hieroglyphic type and designated supernatu entities. A characteristic of the concept held with regard hieroglyphic signs and the function assigned them was the bel that whoever drew certain signs under a given set of conditio while pronouncing certain formulas would find himself face face with the being represented by such signs. These, the were signs that, under given conditions, were literally identi with the thing signified — that is, they were representativ and not merely indicative or metaphorical, signs.

Rosario ASSUNTO

After the hiatus caused by the barbarian invasions, whi produced almost exclusively symbolical representations (e. the carved panels in the Baptistery of the collegiate chur of Cividale and those of the Cathedral of Modena), allegori tendencies revived, in the atmosphere of the Carolingian artis revival, following a well-defined course based on a spiritu reality that was to support it until the dawn of the Renaissan An early allegorical representation of a strictly religious natu is the Carolingian representation of Christ in glory, while belo an angel holds a soul on his knee, defending it from lions a other enemies by which it is assailed (ivory cover of Psalter Charles the Bald; III, PL. 62).

From the 11th century onward a specific and more clea identifiable iconography developed, especially for doctri allegories — that is, representations connected, at least in inte tion, with problems of theology, ecclesiastical organization, met odology, and Church history. First among such doctrin allegorical subjects are the Church and Synagogue personi cations such as the Mater Ecclesia from an 11th-century Mo tecassino Exultet (PL. 343); the Ecclesia with angels battling w demons in the 12th-century *Hortus deliciarum* of Herrad v Landsberg (fol. 225v; modern copy from a lost original) and t Teaching Synagogue and the Synagogue cursed by Chri bearing on their yellow standards the scorpion, medieval syml of evil and falsehood and, often, specifically of the *perfidi iuda* (Sienese miniature in an early-14th-century Bible; Paris, B Nat., Cod. fr. 9561, fol. 98r). Sometimes these portrayals doctrinal conflict betray the influence of the dramatic repr sentations of Prudentius's *Psychomachia*; thus there are scen of *altercationes* (there are clear links with the contempora ligious theater) or of the Archangel Raphael intervening to ush the head of the Synagogue, whose standard is broken Antelami's *Deposition*, Parma Cathedral; I, PL. 292).

Among ascetical allegories may be mentioned the Ladder Paradise of John Climacus in an 11th–12th-century miniature Rome, Bib. Vat.; reverse side of cover of Cod. vat. gr. 394). et another frequently occurring doctrinal-mystical subject allegory is the tree. As the Tree of the Cross it occurs in the psidal mosaic in the Church of S. Clemente, Rome (12th cent.; , PL. 194); it becomes the Tree of Life, linking up scenes in the fe of Christ in accordance with the teaching of St. Bonaventure fresco, S. Maria Maggiore, Bergamo, 1347; altarpiece by acino di Buonaguida, Florence, PL. 343); it appears as a genea- gical tree (Tree of Jesse by Benedetto Antelami, door jambs Parma Baptistery; Psalter of Queen Ingeborg, early 13th nt., Chantilly, Mus. Condé, Ms. 1695, fol. 14v; Cavallini (?) escoes, Naples, Cathedral; reliefs by Lorenzo Maitani, fa- de of Cathedral, Orvieto) and as an allegory of life (B. Ante- mi, XII, PL. 252); and it is further developed in the Franciscan nealogical tree in Taddeo Gaddi's fresco in the refectory f Sta Croce, Florence.

Among the less directly doctrinal allegories in medieval art, ne most common are the personifications of the virtues and vices; addition to the theological virtues (faith, hope, and charity) d cardinal virtues (prudence, justice, fortitude, and tem- erance), there is a whole constellation of minor spiritual qual- ies. Among the most interesting groups of the virtues are e holy-water stoup in S. Giovanni Fuorcivitas, Pistoia, by iovanni Pisano (PL. 345); Andrea Pisano's bronze door for e Baptistery in Florence, where Humility completes the Vir- es (I, PL. 229); the marble panels by the same artist for the ampanile in Florence (the seven traditional Virtues); and an alian miniature showing the Virtues beneath the cloak of Theol- gy (Paris, Bib. Nat., Cod. it. 112). The Virtues also frequently ake their appearance on the tombs of saints (tomb of St. Peter artyr in Milan; tomb of St. Augustine in S. Pietro in Ciel 'Oro, Pavia, 1362) and of popes and rulers (tomb of Clement II Bamberg Cathedral, 1237; sarcophagus of Mastino II and that f Cansignorio della Scala in Verona; Paschal candlestick in . Domenico Maggiore, Naples, with nine figures of Virtues ade by Tino di Camaino for the tomb of Philip of Taranto).

Depictions of the subsidiary virtues alone are rare. It was r more common for these qualities to appear as accessories to e principal virtues in more or less complex orders and group- gs, as in the Antelami carvings in the Parma Baptistery and the carved decoration of Andrea Orcagna's tabernacle in Or- nmichele, Florence. It is even rarer to find the vices repre- nted alone, and where this does occur, it is usually only as minor decorative detail: a holy-water stoup in the Cathedral f Cremona that may previously have been a capital, dating om the 12th century, has rough reliefs with demons or vices; d a fine capital in Vézelay (Church of La Madeleine) depicts ust and Anger. The common practice was to show Virtues d Vices together, doing battle or counterbalancing one an- ther or paired off symbolically, as was done, though as yet not accordance with any rigorous scheme, in the pavement mo- ics in Cremona Cathedral (Cruelty, Impiety, Faith, and Dis- ord) and in the mosaic from the Church of S. Maria del Po- olo in Pavia (Pavia, Mus. Civ.) with Faith and Discord. A hematic organization of the theme is found in the reliefs on e façade of the Cathedral of Piacenza and in the sculptures f Chartres, Notre-Dame in Paris (VI, PL. 349), and Strasbourg athedral (VII, PL. 376); Giotto's frescoes in the Scrovegni hapel in Padua (III, PLS. 211, 392) are another outstanding xample. The counterpoise of themes lends interest to a min- ture by Nicolò da Bologna (1354) showing the Virtues, the ices, and the Liberal Arts; the miniature appears at the be- inning of the Giovanni Andrea manuscript *Novella super uinque libros decretalium* (Milan, Bib. Ambrosiana). There is lso a curious set of Virtues and Vices portrayed as animals in e 14th-century miniatures adorning the *Fiore di virtù* (Florence, ib. Naz., Cod. II, vi, 15). An example of the opposition of ositive and negative qualities is seen on the capitals of the ortal of the Cathedral of Piacenza (1122), which bear rep-

resentations of Avarice, Humility, Anger, and Patience; Tad- deo Gaddi's Truth and Falsehood in the Tribunale di Mer- canzia frescoes of Orsanmichele, Florence, may also be cited.

The narrative type of allegory of the Virtues is more com- plex: thus, for example, in the pavements of S. Michele in Pavia and of the Cathedral of Cremona and on the portico of the Cathedral of Lucca (S. Martino) there are depictions of The- seus slaying the Minotaur; on the tomb of Clement II at Bem- berg, Fortitude is symbolized by Samson slaying the lion; and in the Pisa Baptistery, Nicola Pisano depicted Hercules with the same meaning. A similar example is provided by the two well- known marble reliefs in S. Marco in Venice: one of these (3d cent.) shows Hercules carrying the Erymanthian boar; the other (13th cent.) bears, as an allegory of salvation, a parallel scene of a man with a stag in his arms trampling on a dragon.

The allegorical representation of the psychomachia, or conflict between the Virtues and Vices, was common. Some of the loveliest psychomachias are the French ones of the age of chivalry: on the portal of St-Pierre-de-la-Tour, Aulnay- de-Saintonge (PL. 345); on a capital in the choir of Notre-Dame- du-Port in Clermont-Ferrand (by Maestro Roberto, 12th cent.), where there is also a personification of Anger; and on the main portals of Strasbourg Cathedral and of Notre-Dame in Paris. In Italy the theme is found in the Romanesque pavements of S. Benedetto Po at Polirone and of the cathedrals of Ivrea and Pavia; in Cremona is the iconographic variant of the Vices bat- tling one another; and in the sculptures of the Cathedral of Mo- dena, Wiligelmo depicted Truth tearing out the tongue of False- hood (XII, PL. 255). In the mosaics of the Baptistery of S. Marco in Venice (mid-14th cent.) the Virtues are seen trampling on Death, and the Powers conquer the Demons; sometimes it is Christ Himself who intervenes in the battle, as in a miniature in a 12th-century Exultet (Rome, Bib. Casanatense), where He is shown transfixing the demon.

The vows and special virtues of the religious life also have their place in this category; the Franciscan order especially played an important part in directing allegory and personifi- cation toward devotional forms capable of arousing an immediate emotional response. The most outstanding examples of this are provided by the Master of the Assisi Vault in his allegories of the vows of the order, Poverty, Chastity, and Obedience. Particularly beautiful are the Mystical Marriage of St. Francis to Poverty (PL. 344) and the Chastity in her many-towered castle defended by Purity (Munditia) and Fortitude while a blindfolded Cupid and Passion are driven out by Death and Repentance. This same spiritual climate is shared by the Giotto frescoes in the Bardi Chapel of Sta Croce, Florence (VI, PLS. 206, 207) and by the Mystical Marriage of St. Francis to Pov- erty from the Sansepolcro altarpiece (first half of 14th cent.; Chantilly, Mus. Condé).

The Virtues were often combined with the Liberal Arts, as on the central pulpit support in Pisa Cathedral, by Giovanni Pisano (three Theological Virtues and eight Arts); on the tomb of Robert of Anjou, by Giovanni and Pace Bertini (da Firenze) in S. Chiara, Naples (1343–45); and on the reliefs of the Campanile of the Cathedral of Florence, where the Mechanical Arts are also represented, all being embodied in historical or legendary figures who excelled in a particular discipline (I, PLS. 231, 232; XIV, PL. 276). There are specific personifications of the Liberal Arts by the Pisanos on the central column of the pulpit in Siena Cathedral and on some panels of the Fontana Maggiore in Pe- rugia. Music was of special interest because of the demands of the liturgy; a capital in the campanile of the Cathedral of Modena represents David, personifying Music, and the Dance (1170); a 14th-century miniature in the *De arytmetica* of Boethius (X, PL. 232) and another of the same period in the *Liber saecularum litterarum* of Cassiodorus (Paris, Bib. Nat., Cod. lat. 8500) have personifications of Music; and a series of marble reliefs in Cluny from the late 11th century show personifications of the eight Gregorian modes (XII, PL. 240).

Representations of the mechanical arts, or crafts, are less common, and such examples as there are do not always adhere rigidly to the classification given by Vincent of Beauvais in his *Speculum doctrinale* (*lanificium, armatura, navigatio, agricultura, venatio, medicina,* and *theatrica*) but tend rather to refer to local guilds and activities. In addition to the panels of the Campanile in Florence mentioned above may be cited the seven mural reliefs of the donor guilds on the columns in the Cathedral of Piacenza (ca. 1150) and the crafts depicted beneath the great arch of the portal of S. Marco, Venice (14th cent.), which refer in particular to shipbuilding and other maritime activities in addition to the customary trades.

Death and Eternal Life also were remarkably represented, although at first they had no fixed and stabilized iconography. Death was a winged crone in a 4th-century ivory (Br. Mus.); together with Sleep, personified as a young man, also winged, she greets the soul of a dead man. In a Byzantine miniature in the *Topographia christiana* of Cosmas Indicopleustes (9th cent., from 6th-cent. original; Rome, Bib. Vat., Cod. vat. gr. 699, fol. 56r) there is a representation of Enoch with Time (an old man) and Death (a dark-skinned young man). The Fountain of Life occurs in the Godescalc Gospels (781; III, PL. 55) and in the Gospels of St. Médard of Soissons (Paris, Bib. Nat., Cod. lat. 8850, fol. 6v). In 9th-century Byzantine art, St. Basil appears between the figures of Celestial Life and Earthly Life in the *Sacra Parallela* of St. John Damascene (Paris, Bib. Nat., Cod. gr. 923, fol. 272).

In the later Middle Ages allegories of death, as of life, became ever more imaginative (see ESCHATOLOGY). The personified Death alone has a varied iconography, ranging from the early single figures, with nothing of the macabre, in an 11th-century miniature in the Uta Codex (Munich, Staatsbib., Clm. 13601, fol. 94) and on the ivory Cross of Gunhild of the same period (Copenhagen, Nationalmus.), the blind Death in Notre-Dame, Paris (ca. 1220), and the sculpture on the west front of Strasbourg Cathedral, down to the more complex figures depicted in the *Documenti d'Amore* by Francesco da Barberino (Bib. Vat., Cod. barb. 4076 and 4077) and in a painting by Bartolo di Fredi, who portrayed Death as a knight (Lucignano, S. Francesco). One of the most original and fanciful themes of the later Middle Ages was the Triumph of Death; many representations (Subiaco, PL. 346; Pisa, IV, PL. 468) link it with the legend of the three living and the three dead.

The contingencies of human existence are another frequent subject of allegory, represented in two iconographic forms. One of these, Byzantine in origin, portrays a winged youth, with wheels or globes beneath his feet, holding scales, while another figure crowns him; this can be interpreted as an allegory not only of Life but of Time or Opportunity (Fortune). It recurs in a miniature in the *Ladder of Paradise* by John Climacus (late 11th cent.; Bib. Vat., Cod. vat. gr. 394), where the counterbalancing personification of Death also appears; and in a marble relief in the Cathedral of Torcello that may have been part of an ambo (early 12th cent.). The second form is taken from the Christianized Buddhist legend of Barlaam and Josaphat: one example is the relief by Benedetto Antelami in the Parma Baptistery showing Josaphat in a tree eating honey while the dragon lies in wait below. The same scene, with minor variations, appears in a bas-relief on the door of the Chapel of S. Isidoro in S. Marco, Venice (early 14th cent.); in other examples the beast has put the young protagonist to flight and caused him to take refuge in a tree (miniature, Bib. Vat., Cod. barb. gr. 372, fol. 237v; late-13th-cent. marble panel, Ferrara, Mus. dell'Opera del Duomo).

The various ages of man, too, were allegorized, mainly in connection with the astronomical cycles. Once again it is Antelami who provides a fine example (Parma Baptistery), connected with the Gospel parable of the laborers in the vineyard and with the planets; some decades later, in the crypt frescoes in Anagni Cathedral, the four ages of man were depicted in relation to the seasons, the four elements, and the four temperaments, the whole being based on the scheme for the *mundi continuatio* taken from Plato's *Timaeus*.

The states of life are allegorized in representations of the active and the contemplative life on one of the portals of Chartres Cathedral (mid-13th cent.). Other representations adhere more closely to practical reality and social relations: a miniature in the Glossary of Bishop Solomon of Constance (school of

Ratisbon, mid-12th cent.; Munich, Staatsbib., Clm. 1300 depicts Cupidity, Opulence, Riches, Poverty, and Fortun This last introduces a theme, firmly rooted in literary traditio that had great popular appeal and lent itself to both caricatu and satire: namely, the Wheel of Fortune, or the insecuri of the human lot. Sculptors of the Romanesque era feature this theme countless times, particularly in the rose windov on church façades.

Representations of the Months occur fairly frequently church portals; they are found as isolated portrayals on tl portals of the Pisa Baptistery and on the façade of S. Pietr Spoleto. More often, however, they appear as complete cycle as on the architrave of S. Zeno in Verona, in the Parma Ba tistery together with Spring and Winter by Antelami or h assistants, on the main portal of Parma Cathedral and (thoug now broken up) that of Ferrara (VIII, PL. 171), on the port of the Pieve di S. Maria in Arezzo (PL. 345; XII, PL. 256), the second arch of the main portal of S. Marco in Venic in the porch of Cremona Cathedral, on the Porta della Pescher of the Cathedral of Modena, in the cloister of Sta Sofia in Ben vento, and on the Fontana Maggiore in Perugia (X, PL. 325 Outside Italy, the Months are found in the sculpture of V zelay, Amiens (II, PL. 24), Notre-Dame in Paris, and the we portal of Salzburg Cathedral.

The Year and the Seasons were also frequently personifie A highly complex example of this treatment of the Year is th in the mosaic pavement of S. Savino, Piacenza (12th cent. enclosed in a circle recalling the Wheel of Fortune and supporte by Atlas is the figure of Time, seated on a throne and holdir the Sun and the Moon in his hand; around him are dispose the Cardinal Virtues. The Year was also depicted surrounde by the Months, as in the pavement in Aosta Cathedral (11t cent.). A lovely cycle devoted to the Seasons is the series nine reliefs on the bronze doors of Augsburg Cathedral (mi 11th cent.; IX, PL. 508); and they appear in the reliefs in Notr Dame, Paris (1210–20), and in Rheims Cathedral (1260–70 on some of the Romanesque capitals in the Musée du Farinie Cluny (13th cent.), and in the Lorenzetti frescoes in the Palazz Pubblico in Siena.

Also fairly numerous are the cosmological allegories (s ASTRONOMY AND ASTROLOGY). Among the elements, Earth an Water (often with the Sun and Moon) occur most frequentl mainly in relation to scenes of the Crucifixion; Water may af pear in representations of the Baptism of Christ (ivory cov of the Codex Aureus Esternacencis, Nürnberg, Germanisch Nationalmus.; binding of the "Pax of Duke Orso," 8th–9t cent., Cividale, Mus. Arch.). There are allegorical represent tions of the four elements (water, air, earth, fire) in the 11t century Bamberg Gospels (Munich, Staatsbib., Clm. 4453 where they are portrayed surrounding the figure of Chris in the Parma Baptistery frescoes (second half of 13th cent. where they are related to the Seasons; and in the *Libro di Gius* (Rome, Gabinetto Naz. delle Stampe, Fondo Naz. 2826), whe the four elements are depicted as animals: the chameleon (air the salamander (fire), the fish (water), and the mole (earth Individual elements, too, have at times been given allegoric treatment: the Air on a capital of the Church of La Madelein Vézelay; Water on a relief in Bamberg Cathedral (1237); an Earth frequently in the Exultets of southern Italy, such as a 11th-century one at Bari (Cath. Arch.).

Images of Night occur frequently (Rome, Bib. Vat., Co palat. gr. 431, 7th–8th cent., from 5th-cent. original); in a mi iature in a 10th-century Greek Psalter (Paris, Bib. Nat., Co gr. 139), the prophet Isaiah stands between Night and Daw and in a miniature dating from about 975 Night is personifie in the figure of a blindfolded woman (Berlin, Staatsbib., Co theol. lat., fol. 192). Allegories of Day and Night appear al in nonreligious or less directly religious contexts (the Sun an the Moon in the Barlaam fable by Antelami, XII, PL. 252; t blind Night led by Day, portal of north transept of Chartr Cathedral, ca. 1120).

These various allegories reached the peak of their develoj ment in the great cycles comprising all the elements of theolo ical, moral, and literary knowledge. One such cycle appea n the tomb of St. Peter Martyr in S. Eustorgio, Milan (VI, L. 367); the caryatids represent the theological and cardinal irtues, the series being rounded off with Obedience. Another xample is Pietro di Puccio's fresco in the Camposanto, Pisa 390), where the Universe is supported by the Word; in the nter is the Earth, surrounded by concentric circles of the four ements, then by the seven planets, and finally by the nine oirs of angels. A third and most complete doctrinal cycle from e Middle Ages comprises the frescoes by Andrea da Firenze the Spanish Chapel of S. Maria Novella, Florence (ca. 1370), hich form a veritable scholastic encyclopedia of the learned ominican order (PL. 344; III, PL. 314). These cycles establish clear link between the various allegories, all of which have eir place in the vision of a systematically ordered world: in e center is the most specifically doctrinal element; around is and connected with it — with their respective functions d even on their respective hierarchical levels — are the non-octrinal elements that represent the various ways in which ligious doctrine is manifested and implemented in morals, ulture, and everyday life.

Allegorical personifications of geographical units were rel-tively unimportant in the Middle Ages, but a few may be cited: e parts of the world depicted as half figures in the Echter-ach Gospels (Paris, Bib. Nat., Cod. lat. 9389); the personi-cations of the various peoples to whom the Apostles first reached the Gospel (12th cent., Pentecost mosaic, Venice, . Marco); and the Peutinger map (III, PL. 493), a German opy (ca. 1200) of a 4th-century map of the world depicting the ities of Rome, Constantinople, and Antioch as queens on thrones. certain allegorical-political value was sometimes attached to ersonifications of cities: Rome symbolized the Holy Roman mpire in the Vivian Bible (First Bible of Charles the Bald; aris, Bib. Nat., Ms. lat. 1), and in Taddeo di Bartolo's frescoes the Palazzo Pubblico in Siena the figure of Religio stands r republican Rome. Other cities, too, are symbolized, for xample Capua in the woman's head from the (destroyed) iumphal arch of Frederick II (1233; Capua, Mus. Provinciale ampano). Political pride and a consciousness of power led a theme that frequently came to the fore in Venetian art, amely, the glorification of Venice herself, personified in a great ariety of ways; one is exemplified in the relief on the Doges' alace (mid-14th cent.), which depicts Venezia Regina as Jus-ice, wearing a crown and seated on two lions. Other allegories f cities may represent scenes of invocation and submission: isa, personified, places herself under the protection of St. Ur-ula in a late-14th-century painting attributed to Turino Vanni Pisa, Mus. Naz.). Alliance and solidarity are expressed in the epresentation of Chiusi bearing grain to Perugia, by the isanos, on the lower basin of the Fontana Maggiore in Perugia.

Politically allegory also played a part in coronation scenes PL. 347), particularly when kings, popes, and emperors are hown being consecrated by Christ, the Virgin, or saints, thus onfirming their authority as coming from God. Among the oveliest and most complex political-social allegories of the entire Middle Ages are Ambrogio Lorenzetti's frescoes (ca. 1340) n the Palazzo Pubblico in Siena, depicting Good Government nd Bad Government, with the Liberal Arts, the Seasons, the igns of the zodiac, and the Planets framing the main scenes IX, PLS. 194–196). Good Government was frequently depicted lsewhere, too, especially on the Biccherna tablets (Siena, Arch. di Stato). Bad Government, more rarely shown, tended o appear in the form of a "fleeced" or plundered Commune: ccording to Vasari, Giotto treated this subject in a lost fresco n the Palazzo del Podestà in Florence, and there is an extant xample among the various allegories on the tomb of Bishop Guido Tarlati in the Cathedral of Arezzo, by Agostino di Gio-anni and Agnolo di Ventura da Siena (1330).

Classical themes continued to be interpreted allegorically n accordance with the tenets of medieval Christian spirituality: o those already mentioned may be added the sibyls, who are iven a religious significance in the Sant'Angelo in Formis hurches frescoes (11th cent.) and on the pulpits by Giovanni isano in Pisa Cathedral (VI, PL. 214) and in S. Andrea in Pi-toia (III, PL. 312). In other examples the classical subjects

convey their original meaning, or one very close to it: for in-stance, the Wiligelmo funerary Genius (XIV, PL. 425) and the Siren figures in Modena Cathedral. The figures of the Muses are normally depicted in conjunction with the Liberal Arts, as in the miniatures of the panegyric executed in Italy about 1340 in honor of Robert of Anjou (Br. Mus.).

The not infrequent allegorical representations centered about the theme of Love are more decidedly profane in treat-ment and illustrate a subtle vein of spiritualized and courtly hedonism that was characteristic of the entire Middle Ages. Love is generally symbolized by Cupid, as in the miniatures of the Roman de la Rose (Vienna, Nat. Bib., Cod. 2592, fol. 13v) and those of a manuscript by Guillaume de Machaut (Paris, Bib. Nat., Cod. fr. 1584, fol. D.). Of particular interest from this point of view are the miniatures devised by Francesco da Bar-berino for his Documenti d'Amore (PL. 348): they include per-sonifications of Sacred and Profane Love and the allegory of the Castle of Love, which also figures in some French Gothic ivories (Florence, Mus. Naz.; Venice, Mus. Correr). Yet other hedonistic themes are the Fountain of Life or Fountain of Youth that restores strength to those who bathe in it (14th-cent. ivo-ries; Louvre, Paris) and the Garden of Virtues (miniature in La Somme le Roi, 1279; Paris, Bib. Mazarine, Ms. 870, fol. 61v).

From the repertory of fables with their associated morals are derived yet other representations that are only incidentally allegorical; a 12th-century relief showing the fox, feigning death, with the hens on the façade of S. Pietro, Spoleto, and the sim-ilar reliefs in Modena Cathedral (X, PL. 253); a capital bear-ing the stork and the fox in the cloister of S. Orso, Aosta (12th cent.). Other representations turn such themes into a sort of caricature of monastic life: Brother Wolf in a cowl with a fleeing ram, also on the façade of S. Pietro, Spoleto; a hooded wolf on the bishop's throne training a kid (Rome, cloister of S. Paolo fuori le Mura; 13th cent.).

The same popular fancy is found in the sly moralizations of celebrated figures and episodes or legends of antiquity. Alexander the Great and Adam are often linked because of their culpable curiosity, and Alexander is depicted in his grotesque attempt to rise to heaven on a throne drawn by griffins (pave-ment in Otranto Cathedral, X, PL. 190; relief on north façade of S. Marco, Venice). Alexander and Campaspe, Aristotle and Phyllis, Vergil and the lady who, in the legend, kept him sus-pended in a basket, are the butt of countless representations designed to ridicule love: Aristotle is depicted ridden by his anything-but-respectful pupil (PL. 348), especially on ivory caskets produced in France in the 13th and 14th centuries (Florence, Mus. Naz.; Cologne, Church of St. Ursula), in a relief on the façade of Lyons Cathedral, and on a capital in the Church of St-Pierre in Caen (14th cent.); Vergil was also slung in a pannier from the window in a miniature in the Gran Can-zoniere of Heidelberg (first half of 14th cent.). These are, how-ever, little more than apologues and illustrated fables to which the medieval bent for allegory gave a moralistic interpretation.

Goffredo ROSATI

From the Renaissance to the 19th century. Renaissance in-terest in symbolism was confined largely to emblematic signs, cryptograms, and insignia (see EMBLEMS AND INSIGNIA); heral-dic and magical symbolism thus survived and entered into both the content and the iconographic motifs of Renaissance art. Heraldic devices, either directly derived from medieval heraldry or newly invented, appeared on buildings and in other works of art as signs of their sponsor's desire to commemorate himself, or someone dear to him, or outstanding events in his political or military career. Such signs, in addition to their cultural significance, were used by artists as decorative formal elements: an outstanding example is the entwined initials S (Sigismondo) and I (Isotta) and the iconographic sign of the elephant in the interior of the Tempio Malatestiano at Rimini (I, PL. 51; IV, PLS. 400, 402). The bees of the Barberini coat-of-arms were to determine the iconographic content in the fresco by Pietro da Cortona on the ceiling of the main salon of Palazzo Barberini in Rome (II, PL. 176); and in the little Bernini fountain in Rome known as the Fontanella delle Api the same heraldic element, serving both an emblematic and an ornamental function, was to determine the entire composition of the work.

The signs of the zodiac also found widespread use. Their function was not only ornamental but also magicoastrological, as in the *De sphaera* of the Este family (II, PL. 25), probably dating from the last decades of the 15th century in Lombardy. In this codex, too, as in most manuscripts illuminated for noble and princely families, one entire page is made up of heraldic signs and related emblems: the Visconti and Sforza shields surmounted by their respective crests; a right hand emerging from a cloud, the symbol of the Almighty, here signifying the divine protection invoked on the two families; pitched tents encamped in a landscape divided in half by a pine tree with golden cones — probably an augury of wealth; and an unleashed white dog seated at the foot, perhaps intended to signify fidelity. Other pages show mixed signs combining calligraphic, representational, and geometric elements as visual references to concepts of physics, astronomy, and astrology. Astrological signs carved in wood (see ASTRONOMY AND ASTROLOGY) were also frequent in the 15th century.

In north-central Europe magicocabalistic symbolism was to exert great influence on the iconography of the 15th and 16th centuries. The work of Hieronymus Bosch (q.v.) is full of magical and occult symbols; some of his paintings (*Seven Deadly Sins*, Madrid, Prado; *Marriage at Cana*, Rotterdam, Boymans-Van Beuningen Mus.) are iconographically determined by the occult repertory of symbols (see MAGIC). Occult symbolism continued to find expression in later centuries, particularly in the illustrations of cabalistic literature; and it achieved new importance for the secret societies of the 18th and 19th centuries, together with the ancient devices of the medieval craft guilds, to which these societies attached ethical, religious, and political meanings (PL. 353).

Another field in which such symbolism found application in the Renaissance period was that of games (see GAMES AND TOYS). In playing cards (III, PL. 201; VI, PL. 10), whose use in Europe appears to date from the end of the 14th century, heraldic and magical signs acquired a new function, while often retaining their own original functions and features. The relation of the sign to the meaning defined by the rules of the different games became, in playing cards, the iconographic content governing their artistic appearance.

Beginning with the 15th century, the development of cartography connected with geographical discoveries provided a repertory of iconic signs and images denoting places, animals and plants typical of the newly discovered or explored lands, and customs of their peoples, which entered iconography as designations of exotic countries or of the vastness of the earth (Vasari, PL. 355; III, PLS. 488, 495; see COSMOLOGY AND CARTOGRAPHY). Examples of this iconographic assimilation of cartographic symbols are the figure of the parrot, used in allegorical paintings to indicate the American countries, and that of the savage.

Rosario ASSUNTO

The Renaissance inherited from the Middle Ages a taste for allegory, which continued to be regarded as one of the best means of conveying concepts. There was, however, a profound change in the primary motive underlying allegory. Faith no longer constituted the only ideal point of reference and therefore of convergence of the spiritual and practical life of man, with the result that specifically religious idealisms become distinct from — without ever being opposed to — other idealisms affecting the structure and perspective of the conception of the world. Hence there was no longer that bond with a single higher truth which had provided a systematic framework for allegory in the art of the Middle Ages: the fundamental disposition toward allegory ceased to reflect the spiritual need to understand and explain all things in a vision organically related to that single higher truth.

Medieval allegorical themes continued to be used for definitely religious subjects, as in such representations as the Mystical Wheel and the so-called "Lex Amoris" on the Armadio

degli Argenti made by Fra Angelico's assistants for SS. Annu ziata (Florence, Mus. di S. Marco); Lorenzo Monaco's *Pie* (Florence, Accademia), with the instruments of the Passio and (in a more imaginative and mystical vein) the fresco of Chr in the winepress by Bergognone (Ambrogio da Fossano; Mila Church of S. Maria Incoronata). Other themes, which h first been elaborated in the Middle Ages within the framewo of doctrinal belief, lent themselves to adaptation to the ne ethical convictions, not all of which were any longer unequiv cally subordinated to the religious credo. The Virtues we depicted over and over again (often the full canonical series the cardinal and theological virtues), as on a Lombard paint chest from the late 15th century (Milan, Coll. Bagatti Valsecch in the reliefs by Agostino di Duccio on the doorposts of S. Be nardino in Perugia and those (in collaboration with Matteo d Pasti) in the Tempio Malatestiano in Rimini, in the reliefs l Pollaiuolo (q.v.) in the monuments to Sixtus IV and Innoce VIII (XI, PL. 186), and in the same artist's paintings for t Tribunale di Mercanzia in Orsanmichele, Florence (XI, PL. 18 Individual Virtues were also fairly common, with specific re erence to the use for which they were intended: thus th might appear on tombs as a reminder of the virtues practic by the deceased.

A factor in the popularity of this theme was that it le itself to dynamic compositions, depicting the conflict betwe the Virtues and Vices not merely with reference to the spiritu theme of the psychomachia, as in the Middle Ages, but rath with the intention of exalting another quality admired by Re aissance man, namely heroism. Isolated representations Virtues and Vices or of Vices alone are relatively rare, but the are countless representations of Virtue — visualized as a sing quality, analogous to the Latin *virtus* — defeating Vice (II PL. 468). Another token of the new spirit that gave this ancie allegorical theme new life is the fact that Virtue is sometim identified with Wisdom (Mantegna, *Triumph of Virtue*, I PL. 327; Bartholomeus Spranger, *Triumph of Wisdom*, Vienn Kunsthist. Mus.; medal for Gianello della Torre attribute to Leone Leoni in which Wisdom is explicitly called Virtu in accordance with the Humanistic cult of knowledge, whic produced allegorical representations ranging from Hans Ba dung-Grien's (IX, PL. 255) to Raphael's *School of Athe* (XI, PL. 426; see RAPHAEL) and Titian's *Wisdom* in the Librer Vecchia di S. Marco, Venice (see TITIAN).

The Liberal Arts, too, no longer looked upon as an emanatio of Divine Wisdom but rather as an essential element of t dignity of the human personality that cultivates and protec them, recurred frequently in Renaissance allegorical work frequently assimilated to the Muses, in representations of Pa nassus (Mantegna's, IX, PL. 327; Raphael's in the Stanza del Segnatura in the Vatican, I, PL. 307). This aspect was furthe emphasized in some later and more complex works in norther Europe, typical examples of which are the depiction of the Ar slumbering in wartime, by Lucas de Heere (Turin, Gall. S bauda), and the work by Bartholomeus Spranger showing th Arts with Time, obviously connected with the concept of Fam (Braunschweig, Herzog-Anton-Ulrich-Mus.). Isolated all gories of the individual arts were also common, such as th Architecture (Florence, Mus. Naz.) and Astronomy (Vienn Kunsthist. Mus.) sculptures by Giambologna (q.v.).

This tendency in Renaissance allegory to exalt the activ virtues in man gave rise to the long series of works that, inspire by Petrarch, took Triumphs as their theme. The Triumph as such, frequently depicted together, appear in miniatures, i the engravings for the 1493 Venetian edition of Petrarch' *Trionfi*, on the chests painted by Pesellino (Boston, Isabell Stewart Gardner Mus.) and by Jacopo del Sellaio (Fiesol Mus. Bandini), and elsewhere. The theme of the Triumph was thereafter slowly transformed into that of the apotheos of a particular person (IX, PL. 11), and this iconographic typ was to flourish in the age of mannerism and above all in the ba roque period. Connected with this are the representations c groups of famous persons, as in the miniatures of the *Imagine pictae virorum illustrium* by Leonardo Molinari da Besozzo (M lan, Crespi Coll.) and in the cycles of paintings in the Castell ella Manta in Piemonte (VI, PL. 64) and those by Andrea del Castagno (q.v.) from the Villa Pandolfini, Legnaia (I, PL. 245).

Love was another theme much favored by Renaissance hedonism, and its iconography was varied, though it was often a development of Gothic originals: in addition to the Triumph of Love (PL. 348; VIII, PL. 246), there were the Fountain of Love and the Garden of Love (PL. 348; VIII, PL. 427). There are countless examples of these in Italian, French (Master of the Banderoles), and German (Master of the Gardens of Love) engravings, on majolica ware (there is a whole series of *piatti amatori*, or "lover plates," from Faenza, Tuscany, and Deruta, 15th–16th cent.), on *deschi da parto* or birth trays (PL. 348), in frescoes (at Castello della Manta; VIII, PL. 427), and in tapestries (*Triumph of Venus*, by Francesco del Cossa; IV, PL. 2). Love is sometimes linked with Chastity, seen as a spiritual quality ennobling love. The most celebrated allegory of chastity was the "Lady with the Unicorn," which was common particularly in France (PL. 398; X, PL. 84).

Another theme dear to medieval allegory that recurred in the course of the Renaissance was the personification of Life, as on the pavement of the Cathedral of Siena (original, Mus. dell'Opera del Duomo) — although this was more common in northern European art, in the form of the Fountain of Life, for instance, in Jan van Eyck's Mystical Lamb polyptych (V, PL. 216). Death, too, had its place, whether as a theme for the Triumphs (Triumph of Death, IV, PL. 468) or in the traditional form (which survived particularly in French art) of the meeting of the three living and the three dead (Jean Colombe's miniature for the Laval Hours; Paris, Bib. Nat., Cod. lat. 920, fol. 190) or of the Dance of Death (VI, PL. 369).

In a narrative form, Death and the Lovers, Death and the Knight (PL. 346), and Death and the Maiden were frequent themes. These and similar representations were particularly popular in German art, from Dürer's engravings (IV, PLS. 297, 301) to Hans Baldung-Grien's paintings (IV, PL. 468). An interesting variation on the theme of Death is that which personifies it in the mortal remains of René d'Anjou, in a French miniature in the Hours of King René (1437; Br. Mus., Egerton Ms. 1070, fol. 55).

The Months continued to appear in allegories and lent themselves to highly narrative treatment: in the miniatures of the Limbourgs for the *Très Riches Heures du Duc de Berry* (VI, PL. 65; IX, PLS. 137, 138); in the miniatures by Simon Bening and his assistants for the Grimani Breviary (X, PL. 80); in the Torre dell'Aquila frescoes at the Castello del Buonconsiglio (VI, PL. 64) and in the Palazzo Schifanoia frescoes in Ferrara by Francesco del Cossa (II, PL. 25; IV, PLS. 1–3, 5); and in the tondi by Luca della Robbia (q.v.) in London (II, PL. 27). Representations of the Seasons were even more common: in Ferrarese painting (XII, PL. 33), in Paolo Veronese's frescoes at Maser (XIV, PL. 345), and in the statues by Giovanni Battista Caccini, Taddeo Landini, and Pierre Franqueville of the Ponte Sta Trinita in Florence.

Cities, regions, and nations, too, continued to be personified: Giambologna blended his allegory of victorious Virtue with that of Florence (Florence, Mus. Naz.); there are also Niccolò Tribolo's figure of Fiesole (Florence, Boboli Gardens), Giambologna's figure of the Appennine (VIII, PL. 430), the celebrated Bavaria by Hubert Gerhard (Munich, Schloss Nymphenburg), and finally the various portrayals of Venice and her glory in the Doges' Palace (PL. 355). In comparison with this profusion of political themes, those of even purely generic social significance are relatively rare: a miniature by Jean Bourdichon (formerly Amiens, Coll. Masson) depicting the Four Estates, and an engraving by Hans Weiditz portraying the Tree of the Social States, in a German version of Petrarch's *De remediis utriusque fortunae* by Sebastian Brant (*Glücksbuch*, Augsburg, 1532).

It will be seen, therefore, that allegorical art was extremely widespread throughout the Renaissance; but closer scrutiny indicates its basic limitations. The examples cited reveal that the taste for allegory as such was particularly marked in those areas which were exposed to the spirit of the Renaissance more or less on the rebound or indirectly, whereas in the work of those artists who were in the forefront of the Renaissance, allegory occupies a secondary position, serving a mainly decorative purpose. It would be quite wrong to regard as primarily allegorical, and therefore as affording a specifically allegorical interpretation (even though they retain a certain allegorical character), such works as Botticelli's Spring (III, PL. 302), the "Restello" panels of Giovanni Bellini (II, PL. 260), Piero di Cosimo's *Allegory* (Washington, D.C., Nat. Gall., Kress Coll.), *The Tempest* (VI, PL. 186) or the *Three Philosophers* (VI, PLS. 190, 191) by Giorgione, Titian's *Sacred and Profane Love* (XIV, PL. 94), Correggio's frescoes in the Camera di S. Paolo (III, PLS. 465), Pontormo's frescoes of the Seasons at Poggio a Caiano (IV, PL. 201) — which are, if anything, idyllic rather than allegorical representations — Dürer's *Melencolia I* (III, PL. 203), Michelangelo's *Day and Night, Dawn and Evening* on the Medici Tombs (IX, PLS. 530, 531; XII, PL. 60) and the figures of the Prisoners for the tomb of Julius II, and the *Parable of the Blind* by Pieter Brueghel the Elder (q.v.; II, PL. 358). These are all works in which a higher sense and a more complex conception of existence, of the world, and of the spirit transcend the merely allegorical concept that served as a vehicle for the creative process, as a means and not an end in the mind of the artist. It should be mentioned in passing that modern iconological studies acknowledge this differing attitude to allegory on the part of the Renaissance masters and therefore regard the allegorical content as entirely secondary in the critical interpretation of their works, rather than as absolute and conventional indications of their content: this point has been emphasized by Panofsky (1961) in his work on Correggio's Camera di S. Paolo.

The same thing may be said of mannerism (q.v.), though here the attitude to allegory differs from that of Renaissance art. At the moment when it became apparent that the formal equilibrium of the Renaissance had well-nigh reached a point beyond which there would be a danger of its becoming crystallized, art began to be intellectualized, turning inward on itself and expressing itself in near-abstract formal values, turning once more to allegory in search of a conceptual point of reference. But this was sought almost as a means of escape, with an intellectual subtlety which was by no means unaware of the instability of the concepts themselves. Thus there are frequent examples of the contamination of themes, which, because they lack conceptual clarity, end by overlapping, with the result that the whole is relatively indecipherable from the specifically allegorical point of view: it will be sufficient to cite as examples the frescoes of Giulio Romano and his pupils in the Palazzo del Te at Mantua (IX, PL. 298) and, above all, the celebrated painting by Bronzino (q.v.) with Venus, Cupid, Folly, and Time (IX, PL. 292), which may be interpreted as an allegory of Truth and Calumny or as an allegory of Lust. Basically, the complex allegorical web of the great mannerist historical and celebrative works betrays a spiritual unrest arising from a consciousness of the transitory nature of the very deeds and undertakings which they are intended to exalt. Giorgio Vasari (q.v.), aware of how very vague was the reference to a conceptual significance in these allegories, even felt it necessary to write a commentary on his own frescoes in the Sala degli Elementi of the Palazzo Vecchio in Florence. Thus a fundamental skepticism is evident with regard to both form and content and, as a logical consequence, with regard to the very relationship between the two.

In order to obviate this dissociation, the Counter Reformation endeavored to create a fully decipherable and unequivocal iconography. The 25th session of the Council of Trent was devoted to the figural arts, but the result was a series of purely exterior precepts, which gave rise to some novel themes (as, for example, the symbols of the spiritual attributes of the Virgin, taken from the litanies) but which ultimately only pushed allegory still further toward the periphery of art.

Toward the end of the 16th century a marked reaction to late-mannerist formalism became apparent, due partly to a changed attitude to allegory. On the one hand, Caravaggio (q.v.) rejected absolutely any intellectualistic connection between form and content and therefore, by implication, ruled out allegory altogether. A few of his paintings, such as the

Bacchino Malato (III, PL. 35) and *Amor Victorious* (III, PL. 33), convey a note that does not spring entirely from the predominant naturalistic intent, but this note is not so much an allegorical as an elegiac theme running parallel to the naturalistic aim; when, later, he tried his hand at a subject most often handled allegorically, the Works of Mercy (III, PL. 40), the result was a scene of such striking realism and so closely in accordance with the concrete evidence of the facts represented as to be clearly quite the contrary of allegory. The Carraccis (q.v.), on the other hand, displayed a certain fresh interest in allegorical representations: thus, for instance, in the decoration of the Galleria Farnese in Rome, there are depictions of the Virtues and of Eros and Anteros, as well as Domenichino's *Woman with a Unicorn* (III, PL. 392) symbolizing Chastity; and in the mythological scenes taken from Ovid's *Metamorphoses* there is a general allegorizing theme that Bellori pointed out.

This propensity for allegory in 17th-century classicism had basically the same roots as baroque allegory; indeed, it was baroque spirituality that restored allegory to favor as a result of the conception of art that had been formulated on both a critical and a theoretical basis by 17th-century writers from Bellori onward (see BAROQUE ART; CRITICISM). In this view, art required as its instrument a relation between form and content that would enable it to communicate the conceptual essence — in other words, allegory (and, to a certain extent, also the symbol and the emblem). It is this conception that methodically coordinated the vast range of baroque allegorical themes with all their iconographic complexities.

Outstanding among these is the theme of glorification and apotheosis, above all the apotheosis of religion, or rather of a triumphant Catholicism emerging from the crisis of the Reformation: *Faith Victorious*, by Jean-Baptiste Théodon, and *Religion Driving Out Heresy*, by P. Legros (II, PL. 177), on the altar of St. Ignatius in the Gesù in Rome; the Victory of Faith over Heresy in two paintings by Luca Giordano in Germany (Pommersfelden, Castle); the *Triumph of the Name of Jesus*, by Giovanni Battista Gaulli (II, PL. 171); the glory of the Church expressed symbolically rather than allegorically by Bernini (q.v.) in the Cathedra Petri (II, PL. 135). The theme was extended to include also the glorification of the religious orders that had played an active part in bringing about the victory of the Church.

The theme of apotheosis was frequently applied also to the great men or families of the time, as in the glorification of Urban VIII Barberini by Pietro da Cortona (II, PL. 176), of the Medici by Luca Giordano (Florence, Palazzo Medici-Riccardi), and, by Tiepolo (q.v.), of the Rezzonico family (Venice, Ca' Rezzonico), of the Pisani (XIV, PL. 61), and of Spain and the Spanish monarchy (Madrid, Palacio Real). Other representations glorifying the deeds of historical figures give an allegorical version of historical events, such as the canvases by Rubens (q.v.) in the Louvre depicting the life of Marie de Médicis (X, PL. 251), Tiepolo's frescoes of the marriage of Barbarossa and Beatrice di Borgogna (Würzburg, Residenz), and the fresco by Giovanni Coli and Filippo Gherardi with the allegory of the Battle of Lepanto (Rome, Palazzo Colonna). The use of mythological figures for allegorical glorification was common: besides those already mentioned one might cite the frescoes by Ciro Ferri and Pietro da Cortona in Florence (XI, PLS. 167, 170).

It is characteristic of baroque allegory that it tends to reach beyond the immediate and traditional subject matter to allude to still other meanings by a complex web of references and associations, using allegory to convey a discursive complex rather than a single and well-nigh immutable meaning (PLS. 350, 351). An example of this is the Four Seasons series (XI, PL. 147) by Poussin (q.v.), in which the traditional meaning attached to the seasons is associated with other and more complex religious themes: Spring symbolizes the world *ante legem*, Autumn the world *sub lege*, Summer the world *sub gratia*, and Winter, depicted as a flood, the Last Judgment and Redemption.

Even in the baroque era there were, of course, many allegories based solely on traditional themes and handled in the older way. Baroque allegory is better characterized, however, by

brief reference to some of the new themes peculiar to it. Among these are the philosophical allegories, or "moralities," as the were termed by Salvator Rosa (q.v.), who himself produced few in satirical vein (*Fortuna*, London, Marlborough Gall *Justice among the Shepherds*, Vienna, Kunsthist. Mus.). Thi theme is linked with that of the vanity of all earthly things tha do not survive death, with the *Memento mori*, symptom of totally different spirituality from that of the Renaissance, whic had produced so many representations of fame and its triumph The countless macabre figures that were so common on tomb and monuments are offshoots of this theme. Another allegoric theme that found favor in the 17th and 18th centuries was th Five Senses (PL. 352; V, PL. 298), depicted in the paintings c Theodor Rombouts, Michael Sweerts, Sebastien Stosskop Jacques Linard, and many others.

These tendencies of baroque art had an effect in architecture too, in the form of symbolization. The same spirit that ha given new vigor and material to allegorical representation mo tivated, for example, the architectural organization of the in terior of SS. Trinità in Turin, by Ascanio Vittozzi, who symbol ized the Trinity by incorporating in his trilobed design variou tripled elements (three doors, three altars, etc.). Moreover Vittozzi's design provided a precedent for the analogous schem by Borromini for the Church of S. Ivo alla Sapienza in Rome reflecting the shape of the bee in the arms of the Barberin pope, Urban VIII (II, FIG. 556). The allusion to the ecumenica apostolate conveyed by the shape of the Bernini colonnade o St. Peter's (I, PL. 403; II, PL. 269) is another example; and th allusive intent was even more explicit in the Church of St. Charle Borromeo in Vienna, built for Charles VI, emperor of Austria by Fischer von Erlach (q.v.); in the two freestanding spira columns in front of the church (II, PL. 155), depicting storie from the life of St. Charles Borromeo, Hans Sedlmayr (*Johann Bernhard Fischer von Ehrlach*, Vienna, 1956, p. 128) has seer an allusion to Constancy and Fortitude, the device of the Em peror, constituting a complex symbolism interweaving the im perial with the sacred.

Oreste FERRARI (with
contributions by Goffredo ROSATI)

One of the aspects of the gradual abandonment of the ba roque tradition in the course of the 18th century was the chang in the attitude of artists themselves to both symbolism and al legory. Where the baroque artist had looked upon art as a sor of explanatory discourse and hence regarded symbol and allegory as technical means to that end, now, under the influence of il luminist thought, a new relation of art to ideology was estab lished: the artist, aiming to represent a rational, and therefore his torically verifiable, signification, sought new expressive means to manifest this in his work. The most significant example o this search is provided by William Hogarth (q.v.). He based his art on what is defined as "wit," an imaginative faculty establishing with penetration and without rhetorical artific the relation of form to content. Hogarth's art tends to demon strate its meaning, and that meaning is a moral principle: thus his most famous works are satirical and not allegorical (VI PLS. 293–295). Basically, it is the conceptual and doctrinal structure on which allegory and symbolism had traditionally rested that was here called into question, and in practice, i was never again to be recovered; the proof that allegory had definitively ceased to be valid would be found in Goya (q.v.) A certain interest in some forms of allegorical representation still persisted in the 18th century, as in the work of Danie Chodowiecki, who was influenced to a certain extent by Ho garth, and that of Francesco Bartolozzi, whose allegorical themes for engravings were suggested by Angelica Kauffman (X, PL. 282), G. Hamilton (X, PL. 283), and Francis Wheatley However, these were but isolated manifestations on the fringe of the different and already all-pervading attitude that romanti cism was to make its own and develop.

In the earliest stages of romanticism, the visionary and pas sionate images of William Blake (II, PL. 296; VI, PL. 445) and Henry Fuseli (qq.v.) were anything but allegorical, nor could there be any question of allegory in such works as *Liberty*

Guiding the People (XII, PL. 313), by the young Eugène Delacroix (q.v.), in which the emotional fervor turns the very concept of liberty into a concrete thing of the moment. It is rather in neoclassical art that there was more frequent recourse to allegorical figures, drawn, of course, from the antique repertory (X, PL. 252): one of many examples that might be mentioned is the *Parnassus* by Anton Mengs at Villa Albani, Rome. The later developments of romantic art confirmed its lack of interest in allegory. It was only when romanticism was already in decline, with the growth of the trends that were to come together in the symbolist poetics of the end of the century, that some tendencies that might be described as symbolical or allegorical made their appearance: for example, in the works of the English Pre-Raphaelites and the German Nazarenes (see PRE-RAPHAELISM AND RELATED MOVEMENTS), Hans von Marées, Franz von Stuck, and especially Arnold Böcklin (VI, PL. 158).

In the age of romanticism, allegory and symbolism were reserved almost exclusively for works of a celebrative and "official" nature; generally speaking, throughout the 19th century and well into the 20th, this form of art tended to make up in quantity what it lacked in quality, and it is therefore of more interest to social history than to art history. It should be added that, under the impetus of livelier and more immediate themes, 19th-century allegory succeeded, at least partially, in throwing off the shackles of its own rhetorical conventionality, as in those allegories based on politicosocial themes or on the ideals of movements aiming at the formation of a national consciousness (VI, PLS. 397, 399). Here too, however, satire proved the most effective mode of expression (IV, PLS. 118–120) and, in fact, the only one that made it possible to express with compelling immediacy the popular sentiments, opinions, and aspirations.

* *

Recent and contemporary movements. During the last three decades of the 19th century, symbolism once again became a specific and conscious means of expression in French literature, and the phenomenon soon found an echo in the visual arts: there was renewed interest in early romanticism of the visionary kind to be found in Blake (I, PL. 309; XII, PL. 316) and Fuseli (XII, PL. 308; XIV, PL. 187), and what had been held to be peculiar to the word was now attributed to the image and then to line and to color. The literary origins of the phenomenon are apparent, from the point of view of content, in the work of Gustave Moreau, Rodolphe Bresdin (who turned back to northern European sources, from Altdorfer to Dürer), Félicien Rops, and, finally, Pierre Puvis de Chavannes (q.v.) — who, however, grafted symbolist intent onto the formalistic tradition of Parnassian purism and, unlike the others, sometimes adopted more specifically allegorical figures (*Peace and War*, 1861, and *Ave Picardia Nutrix*, both Amiens, Mus. de Picardie; the murals of the Sorbonne amphitheater, with allegories of Literature, Science, and the Arts; the *Sacred Grove*, XI, PL. 305). The chief exponent of the French symbolist school in art was Odilon Redon (q.v.), in whose painting symbolism found its most complete formal expression, evoking subjective and not empiric reality (XI, PL. 371).

Gaugin (q.v.), too, had literary contacts, in particular with Mallarmé, after his return to Paris in 1890; he had first shown interest in the problems of symbolist expression during his earlier sojourn in Brittany. His position in this field is unique, however, and literary suggestions in his paintings are only marginal (VI, PLS. 26–32). The so-called "Pont-Aven school" was centered around Gaugin; Louis Anquetin (1861–1932) and Emile Bernard (1868–1941) were its most prominent personalities. In its clear perception of the basic character of Gauguin's art, it tended toward an emblematic rather than a specifically symbolical formal synthesism. An undoubted continuity with symbolist poetics is more apparent in the work of those artists who recognized Redon as their master and centered around the *Revue Blanche*: the Nabis and in particular J. Edouard Vuillard (V, PL. 122), the early Pierre Bonnard (qq.v.), Paul Sérusier, and the early Maurice Denis (see EUROPEAN MODERN MOVEMENTS).

At almost the same time, and in more or less close connection with French symbolism, similar trends became apparent in other European countries: in England, where the impetus had to a certain extent been given by the Pre-Raphaelites (Dante Gabriel Rossetti, XI, PL. 301; E. Burne-Jones, XI, PLS. 305, 306; William Holman Hunt, XI, PL. 304) and the Victorian estheticism of Aubrey Beardsley (q.v.); in Switzerland with Ferdinand Hodler (q.v.; V, PL. 210); in Holland with Jan Toorop (XI, PL. 381); in Germany with A. Kubin (V, PL. 212). On a different level, with motivations borrowed from existentialist thought, are the paintings of the Norwegian Edvard Munch (q.v.): the symbolical element does not here refer to an undifferentiated subjective state but is conditioned by a more precise expressive intention and by clearly definable emotion as an existential circumstance (V, PL. 116). Vienna was yet another symbolist center, where Gustav Klimt was the focal point of a large group of artists (among then Munch and Hodler) that formed the nucleus of the Sezession movement in 1897. In Klimt's painting, however, which was undoubtedly motivated by a reaction against the leveling down of personality threatened by the modern world, there is a frequent passage from symbolism to allegory (XI, PL. 371).

In its rapid diffusion, symbolist poetics lost some of its original components, and, in addition, manifested its estheticizing and formalist character, becoming a form of taste that was to exert wide influence on various forms of artistic expression. The symbolism that had come into being as an aspiration toward *poésie pure* thus became a formal principle, a style, which was widely applied in the so-called "useful arts" and in decoration — and all this, basically, without any internal contradiction, because its own radical estheticism, applied to all fields of production, offered a precarious but immediate solution to the conflict between the life of the spirit and practical life, of which society at the end of the 19th century was already acutely aware. Hence the symbolist influence on the English arts and crafts movement (particularly on the work of Charles Rennie Mackintosh, q.v.; I, PLS. 468, 469) and above all on the genesis of Art Nouveau (q.v.), largely due to the Vienna Sezession. It will here suffice to mention the symbolist influence, on architecture and on objects of everyday use, of the Belgians Victor Horta (I, PLS. 415, 424, 468; V, PL. 99) and Henry van de Velde (q.v.; I, PL. 469; VII, PLS. 325, 342), the Austrian Josef Hoffmann (V, PL. 102), the German August Endell, the Frenchmen Hector Guimard (VI, PL. 278) and Emile Gallé, the Swiss Hermann Obrist, the American Louis C. Tiffany (VI, PL. 239), and the Italian Raimondo D'Aronco (I, PLS. 424, 467, 468). In the more specifically figural field, symbolism, in its special Viennese Sezession form, exerted influence on the early work of Ernst Kirchner, Ernst Barlach, and Wassily Kandinsky (qq.v.; V PLS. 126, 264; VIII, PLS. 347–349).

Symbolism is also the theoretical base of surrealism (q.v.): of special note is its development in the work of Max Ernst, where it is once again possible to speak of the symbol in its original connotation (PLS. 320, 325; V, PL. 134; XI, PL. 372). In the case of Paul Klee (q.v.), however, no symbolic intent as such can be posited, but rather an operative process that, having identified the poetic images in the layers of the unconscious, renders them pictorially as denoting themselves and nothing else (V, PL. 137; VIII, PLS. 391–394; IX, PL. 397). Metaphysical painting falls halfway between symbol and allegory: while an echo of Böcklin's symbolism survives in the work of Giorgio de Chirico (q.v.; V, PL. 133) and Alberto Savinio, in practice metaphysical images have an emblematic rather than a specifically symbolic value.

It is thus apparent that symbolism, in this sense, has gradually come to constitute one of the basic polarities of modern artistic expression, to which, at least theoretically, programmatic realism could be contraposed. In fact, however, this dualism has already been overcome, in — to cite the most significant example — the art of Pablo Picasso (q.v.; IV, PLS. 75, 443; IX, PL. 393; XI, PLS. 141–146). His conception of artistic activity as an engaged involvement in reality leads to the rejection of any preconceived image existing in itself and outside that act (itself realistic) which creates it; hence also to the rejection of any categorical distinction between form and content and any possible intellectualistic mediation between the two. For this reason Picasso's art is all the more "realistic" — in other words, all the more an active involvement in reality — the more it does not refer back to any meaning other than that which it is in itself, thus manifesting itself as a unity of the sign and the signified: in other words, a symbol. Picasso's art, from *Guernica* (VII, PL. 278) to *War and Peace* (XI, PL. 145), provides the clearest illustration of the modern theory of art as symbolic form and, on the critical plane, clearly shows that one may not regard as allegories works whose meaning, in actual fact, is not a conceptual one but a direct product of emotion and reality.

The esthetic justification of other forms of artistic expression is implicit in this conception of art as symbolic form: on the one hand, those forms, of rationalistic inspiration, which consider art to be a highly qualified and therefore symbolically exemplary praxis — the conception on which the teachings of Walter Gropius (q.v.) and the Bauhaus are based; and on the other, the more recent forms of expression that conceive art as an existential event or an epistemological metaphor of human behavior, such as *art informal*. It is this basis which serves to justify the more explicit and recent recourse to more specifically symbolical means of expression in those forms of art which, when they are not merely epigonic manifestations, constitute a profitable salvaging of surrealist suggestions (see EUROPEAN MODERN MOVEMENTS).

Oreste FERRARI

THE EAST. *Islam*. The spiritual world of the Koran immediately following its revelation and up to the time of the great Hellenizing influence of the translations of the Greek philosophers (9th-10th cent.) was one of monolithic and radical monotheism, ruling out absolutely (by analyzing minutely all possibilities of "idolatry") any autonomy of the non-God in relation to God. All values were concentrated in the personal and transcendent God, including the fullness of life itself. This caused an outlook of radical distrust with regard to all the arts, in which lurk hidden dangers of idolatry. The figural arts would not only make man a creator like God but would produce symbolic entities living too autonomous a significative life in opposition to the one significant being, God. Music was identified with frivolity, and the dance even more so. Even poetry was looked at askance in the earliest days of Islam. It is no exaggeration to say that in primitive Islam the only true art was that whose direct creator was God Himself, in other words, the only true art was His word, the Koran.

The impossibility of using "objects" external to God as symbols, coupled with the invisibility of God, meant that the only thing in which the symbolic tendency of the early Moslem could find outlet was the word of God, the Koran, even in its external forms. Groups of letters or phrases taken from the Koran and woven together artistically therefore constituted an important source of symbolic expression, and psychologically they took the place (and continue to do so) of the Christian sacred image; their outward form is purely decorative, since they are merely letters ingeniously woven together, while their interior form (since they are "words") may be clearer and more direct and vivid than an image (XII, PLS. 346, 347). But the Koran also contains narratives — of a special sort and vaguely allusive — of symbolized facts (the mysterious journey of Moses, accompanied by the even more mysterious Khidr, to the Water of Life; Alexander the Great turned into a legendary figure, IV, PL. 408; Gog and Magog; the Seven Sleepers of Ephesus); and moreover, with the acceptance of the ancient pre-Islamic rite of Mecca in a form purified of polytheism, Islam introduced into the bare asymbolic monotheism that constitutes its very essence the symbolic ritual of the pilgrimage to Mecca and the holiness of the Ka'ba and of the Black Stone. The purification of these sacred objects from polytheism lay above all in the fact that they were "historicized" — that is, connected with specific historic events: X became a holy place because the Prophet Y in the year Z passed nearby or did something memorable there. All the same, in the psychological life of the believer, this monotheistic "historicized" sacredness differs very little from "archaic" sacredness.

In primitive Islam, then, there were three orders of symbols

or, better, three possible starting points for symbols: (1) t[h]e divine allusive words enshrined in the decorative form of t[he] letters; (2) the mysterious accounts of the Koran and, in gener[al] all those parts of the Koran known as *mutashabih* ("ambiguous[,]" though this term is controversial and might even mean "symb[ol]ical"); (3) the archaic objects and sacred rites which had be[en] monotheistically revaluated by providing them with a histori[c] background but which nevertheless still retained powerful sy[m]bolic associations.

After the 9th-10th century, and with an astonishing facul[ty] for assimilation, Islam added to its original Koranic elemen[ts] a wide range of materials drawn largely from the Hellenist[ic] and Iranian world, so rich in potential symbolism. Thus the[re] came into being a whole Neoplatonic demythologized symbolis[m] (the myth being, of course, completely foreign to Islam) [in] which the Neoplatonic "ideas" seem to blend with the "angel[s]" of ancient Iran, living an anemic and semiautonomous life (VII PL. 143). This symbolism never found expression in plast[ic] form, however; its greatest outlet was in neo-Persian poetr[y] which is especially rich in complex symbolic imagery. At th[e] same time, allegory continued to be used and indeed becam[e] more profound in contact with cabalistic doctrines from vario[us] sources (late Jewish, etc.); in Islam (in view of the slight im portance attached to the figural arts) allegory easily took t[he] form of allegorizing the letters of the Arab alphabet.

This outlook on symbol and allegory resulted in a dange[r]ous artistic crisis in modern Moslem cultures (those followi[ng] contact with European influence). In European culture, whe[re] symbol and allegory frequently assumed plastic and corpore[al] forms in the absence of any prohibition in this regard, once t[he] symbol has declined or lost its value, there remains its embo[d]iment, realism. But when, as a result of European influe[nce] modern Islamic culture too begins to devaluate the symbo[l] all that remains is empty decorative lines to replace which so[me] sort of imitative realism is desperately sought.

Alessandro BAUSANI

India. There are few religions in which the symbol h[as] played as important a part as it has in the religions of ancie[nt] India. The peoples of ancient India were generally able [to] imagine the inexplicable forces of nature only in anthropomo[r]phic form. To differentiate these beings exterior identificati[on] marks were required, that is, symbols that would make the[m] immediately recognizable. Yet their creation and function w[as] not exclusively the work of speculation, although speculati[ve] thinking may have played some part in their development an[d,] in fact, did create in later times specific, although rather mea[n]ingless, symbols (e.g., the figure of Prajñāpāramitā in Mah[a]yana Buddhism). In many cases they were the fruits of a na[t]ural development, even if today it is not always possible [to] ascertain their original form and thereby their innermost mea[n]ing. Many of the symbols may have been lifted from a sphe[re] of simple concepts or natural environment that somewhe[re] sometime must have been valid; and from the symbols them selves something of the environment in which a mythologic[al] figure came into being or from which it received part of i[ts] nature can be inferred.

The linga, that is, the image of the god Śiva's male gene[r]ative organ (I, PL. 224; VII, PL. 476), which existed as ear[ly] as the Harappa culture, testifies to a definite fertility aspe[ct] of the god. The bull as Śiva's mount (I, PLS. 222, 225; I[?] PL. 258) and the "lunar crescent" (actually the horns of a bu[ll] on the god's head are derived from the prehistoric cult of t[he] bull that had once extended throughout the Mediterrane[an] area and had reached India. The necklace of skulls worn [by] Śiva and the bloody severed head carried by the feared go[d]dess Kālī indicate the part taken by the wild head-hunting trib[es] in determining this grisly aspect of Śiva's domain. The thi[rd] or forehead eye of Śiva, his shakti (female counterpart), Gaṇe[śa,] Kārttikeya, and various other figures of the Hindu pantheo[n] and particularly of Mahayana Buddhism, show the comm[on] basic origin of all these figures. Finally, weapons such as t[he] club and the bow as attributes of a divinity also signify th[e]

bes who used these weapons probably contributed some ele-
ent to the conceptual complex. The ancient Greek identifi-
tion of Viṣṇu, who generally had the club, disk, conch, and
tus as his attributes (X, PL. 296), with Hercules may have
sulted from the fact that the club was common to both. How-
er, Śiva's customary attributes — trident or trisula, bow,
um (ḍamaru), rope, and club, as well as the black snake as
sacrificial cord (VII, PLS. 136, 233, 477) — reveal influences
om a completely different background; the drum in particular
dicates a close connection with the world of magic.

Not all divine symbols can at present be explained so plau-
bly; still problematical, for instance, is why the war god Kārt-
keya should have been awarded the peacock as his mount and,
nsequently, as his symbol. But regardless of whether their
iginal meaning is known, the mounts of the gods are to be
en as symbols, and they not only denote the gods themselves
t are also manifestations of the gods' divine essence. Also
lid as symbols of the divinities are their manifold attributes
well as the number of limbs or heads (PL. 460; X, PL. 297;
I, PL. 3), hand gestures or mudras (II, FIG. 690; VII,
s. 452, 462), and attitudes. All these symbols are combined
ith one another in a multitude of ways, so that the religious
stem of Hinduism (q.v.) and especially that of Mahayana
uddhism (see BUDDHISM) seems interwoven with a net of
zzling elements — elements that simultaneously indicate their
ovenance from various times, culture phases, and tribes. Only
selection of symbols from the various realms of life can give
idea of this unique chapter of Indian culture, which left
mark also on India's religion and art.

The animal symbols of the most important divinities, whose
aktis also have the same animals, include the white bull
andi of Śiva and the black buffalo of the Lord of Death,
ama. A special form of Śiva's shakti, Durgā Mahiṣamardinī
estroyer of the buffalo demon Mahiṣa; IV, PL. 171), is, like
e Babylonian Ishtar and the Cybele of Asia Minor, accompanied
y the lion (I, PL. 225). The lion is also the mount of Heramba
he Nepalese form of Gaṇeśa) and of the Buddha represented
the planet Mercury. The elephant Airāvata is identified as
e mount of the king of the gods, Indra; sometimes an elephant
also attributed to the planet Saturn. Only in isolated or local
ses does the camel seem to have been associated with the planet
enus. The ram or goat is associated with the fire god Agni,
antelope with the wind god Vāyu. The boar represents the
ird incarnation, or avatar, of Viṣṇu (VII, PL. 232). A mouse
rat is considered the vehicle of Gaṇeśa (VII, PL. 227), and a
t is sometimes associated with the planet Venus. The horse
ccaiḥśravas is also Indra's mount, and his chariot is drawn by
un horses. Horses pull the car of the sun god Sūrya (IV, PL.
21; IX, PL. 178; XI, PL. 6). The chariots of the various Tibetan
lanet gods are drawn by boars, horses, and Indian cuckoos.
he gander is the symbol of the god Brahmā (IV, PL. 222;
II, PL. 232); the peacock that of Kārttikeya; and the owl
at of Cāmuṇḍā, a terrifying manifestation of Śiva's shakti.
avens and vultures were attributed to the unlucky planet
turn. Garuḍa or Garutmat, Viṣṇu's mount, is a fantastic bird
eature with human features, which seems to have developed
om the winged solar disk of the ancient Orient.

Hinduism adopted a few symbols from the element of water.
he makara (I, FIG. 410; X, FIG. 843, no. 15), a sea monster,
the mount of the water god Varuṇa and also the emblem of
e love god Kāmadeva. The crocodile is associated with the
ver goddess Gaṅgā. The tortoise is the token of the river god-
ess Yamunā, represents the second incarnation of Viṣṇu, and
the image of the visible heaven. Viṣṇu's first incarnation is
a fish. An over-all view of the representatives of the animal
ngdom that appear in Hinduism as symbolic figures discloses
at in this respect India presents a remarkable parallel to the
ncient Near East (Tell Halaf in Syria; Egypt), and some of these
mbolical associations must have existed in India even before
e Aryan influence made itself felt.

The 24 tirthankaras of the art of Jainism (q.v.) can be identi-
ed by the characterizing signs attached to them. Their em-
lems are generally animals, for example, the bull of Ṛṣabha-
atha and the elephant of Ajitanātha.

In all three of India's religions the footprint has a symbolic significance. The Ṛgveda mentions the three steps of
Viṣṇu with which he is said to have taken possession of the whole
universe; owing to this he is also called Trivikrama ("three
steps"; X, PL. 296). The footprint is venerated in many places
as a cult object, such as the Viṣṇupad ("Viṣṇu's Footprint")
Temple in Gaya. In Buddhism and Jainism the Buddha's and
Mahāvīra's footprints are objects of worship (VII, PL. 412).
The print of the hand (IV, PL. 205) is also endowed with a symbolic, above all an apotropaic, effect.

In Buddhism and Jainism there are certain symbolic omens
that are said to herald the appearance of a world savior or universal monarch (chakravartin). One of them was the dream the
savior's mother, Māyā, had at the time of his conception (II,
PL. 407; XI, PL. 84). Buddhist legend recounts that the future
Buddha entered the womb of his mother in the image of a white
elephant; thus it was natural that the Buddhists should choose
the elephant as a symbol of the Buddha. Other signs heralding
the superhuman nature of a world savior and therefore to be
considered as symbols were the 32 major physical and physiognomic characteristics and the 80 minor ones by which nature
desired to announce externally, as it were, the future dignity
of their bearer.

The Buddhists also venerate the following symbols: the
Bo tree under which the Buddha received Enlightenment (II,
PLS. 376, 407; VII, PL. 442; X, PL. 247); the triratna ("three
gems"), representing the Buddha, the Law or Dharma, and the
Community (VII, PL. 412); and the stupa, containing the mas-
ter's relics or commemorating an event in the story of salvation
(II, PLS. 404, 411; IV, PL. 457; VII, PLS. 445, 448; see also II,
cols. 678–79 and 709–10).

The "Eight Auspicious Symbols" of Jain iconography are
illustrated in manuscripts. The swastika, a very ancient symbol,
is, in Jain belief, an attribute of an arhat, or saint; it is depicted
on the arhat's palm with the signs for sun and moon and indicates that he has already reached omniscience. The śrīvatsa
in its simplest form is similar to a blossom with four oval petals;
in a further development it becomes an eight-pointed star or
an eight-petaled blossom. The śrīvatsa corresponds to the hair
whorl on Viṣṇu's and Kṛṣṇa's breast and also decorates that of
an arhat. The nandyāvartana is a type of swastika with complicated, arabesquelike double lines. The varddhamanāka, a wide-
bellied, richly decorated vase on a slender foot with a lid decorated with three peaks, is reminiscent of a motif on Indo-
Scythian coins; it seems to have been an artistically worked
powder jar. The other symbols are the bhadrāsana, a throne
with curving feet and upholstered back; the kalaśa, a vase; the
matsya-yugma, a pair of fishes; and the darpaṇa, a mirror.

One of the most characteristic symbols of Indian art from
earliest times, which decorates the national flag, is the spoked
wheel. In the oldest hymns of the Ṛgveda the sun was repeatedly compared with a wheel (cakra). The Buddha is said to
have set the Wheel of the Law (dharmacakra) in motion with
his First Preaching in the Deer Park at Sarnath (PL. 333; II,
PLS. 376, 400, 401). The Wheel of Life not only symbolizes the
Buddha and the nirvanic plane with which he is coessential but
also represents the eternal revolution of samsara (the endless
cycle of incarnations). This symbol spread over the Buddhist
lands of Asia and also seems to have influenced the West from
the 12th century on in a form acceptable to Western thought,
that is, as the Wheel of Fortune (PL. 340). The oldest extant
representation of the Wheel of Life is found in a fragmentary
fresco in Cave XVII at Ajanta (ca. A.D. 500). It is first described
in the Divyāvadāna (XIII, XIX, and XXI), a Buddhist text that
may belong to the 2d century of our era. The wheel is kept
turning by a three-eyed demon and a number of other symbols
explain its inner being and its effect. On the hub are shown three
animals, a bird, a snake, and a pig, which represent respectively
the three basic evils, lust, hate, and delusion. The area between
the hub and the rim is divided by spokes into five or six sections
that are meant to convey to the observer the conditions of
existence of the various realms of life (gods, men, animals,
spirits, infernal beings, and sometimes semidivine beings) according to Buddhist concepts. On the rim itself, and at times

outside it, are depicted the 12 nidanas (causes of finite existence); these are represented in the form of symbols, which are not always identical on the various monuments. The demon symbolizes karma, that is, the transcendent successions of thought, word, and deed which keep the wheel in eternal movement and effect the constant ascent and descent of beings.

Color is an important element in the symbolism of Indian art. The world mountain, Meru, is conceived of as four different colors corresponding to the four principal directions (see COSMOLOGY AND CARTOGRAPHY). In Hinduism the five incarnations of Śiva are associated with a color and a direction: Sadojāta (west, white), Vāmadeva (north, red), Tatpuruṣa (east, yellow), Aghora (south, black), and Īśāna (center, crystal clear). In Jainism the tirthankaras are associated with the colors gold, red, white, green, blue, and black. The Tantric deities are also differentiated by colors and directions: Vairocana (center, white), Akṣobhya (east, blue), Ratnasambhava (south, yellow), Amitābha (west, red), and Amoghasiddi (north, green).

Willibald KIRFEL

Allegory, too, has an important place in Indian art, especially in the form of personification. Kubera, the Lord of Wealth and king of the yakshas (tutelary deities who guard the treasures of the earth), has nine *nidhi*, or divine treasures, which are personified as his attendants. Two are especially noteworthy: Śaṅkha (conch) and Padma (lotus). Sometimes the yakshas are depicted spouting conches or lotus rhizomes full of gold coins, and as auspicious figures signifying prosperity they are often painted or carved on the doorposts of homes and temple entrances. Prosperity is also suggested by a woman standing on a lotus peering around an overflowing vase or *pūrṇaghaṭa* and pressing her breast. As the same Sanskrit word (*pāyas*) denotes both water and milk, this image personifies prosperity both in an idealized maternal aspect and as the earth overflowing with milk and honey from an abundance of water.

A river in general is depicted in feminine form with a pitcher in her hand. In an early Buddhist relief from Amaravati (Br. Mus.) a flowing stream is personified as a damsel carrying food on a tray and water in a jug; this theme also appears in contemporaneous Kushan sculpture. This figural tradition survived through the centuries, and in a Sena sculpture of the 12th century Gaṅgā, the personification of the Ganges River, is depicted with a pitcher in her hand; however, the mandāra (coral) tree behind her, which symbolizes her connection with heaven, identifies her with the celestial river *suranimnagā*. The personifications of the rivers are distinguished by their mounts: the *makara* for Gaṅgā, the tortoise for Yamunā, and the swan for Sarasvatī. Gaṅgā and Yamunā personified and sometimes symbolized as *pūrṇaghaṭa* often flank doorways of Gupta and early medieval temples in northern India and the Deccan (I, PL. 226). Mountains are also personified in Indian art. In the relief at Elephanta depicting the marriage of Śiva and Pārvatī (VII, PL. 467), Himavat, the personification of the Himalaya, and his consort are shown beside their daughter Pārvatī. Pārvatī's wedding is also portrayed at Ellora (VII, PL. 468), where the whole story of the mountain maid is narrated. Himavat and his queen are shown conversing with the sages headed by Brahmā, whom Śiva had sent to ask for Pārvatī's hand.

One of the most charming poetic creations is the personification of dawn as a beautiful damsel unveiling slowly and revealing her beauty. On the sculptured column of the 1st century B.C. at Lālā Bhagat near Lucknow, two swans at the top carry a banner to herald the approach of the dawn. Below is the sun in his glorious chariot, preceded by the dwarfish *vālakhilya* sages and the beautiful nymph of dawn, her robes fluttering in the wind. Below that is a peacock whose outspread tail suggests the joyous atmosphere; the arch formed by his tail indicates the horizon. The joy of the maid of the lotus pond when greeted by the rays of the sun as she opens her eyes is suggested by a representation of Paṅkajaśrī, the beauty of the lotus lake.

The seasons and musical modes are also personified. The month of Madhu in spring is depicted as the friend of Mādana (Cupid). The musical modes (XI, PL. 415) are either masculine (*rāga*) or feminine (*rāgiṇī*). One of the most importa melodies, Toḍi, is represented as a charming damsel who a tracts the deer by playing her lute.

Victory is represented as a goddess, Jayaśrī, waiting, garla in hand, to woo the victor when two equally matched herc fight. The concept of the city personified as a goddess was qu popular. An Indo-Parthian coin shows the goddess of the ci approaching the victorious king with a garland in her hand welcome him as her lord.

Lakṣmī is associated with royal prosperity and is depict holding a large lotus like an umbrella over the king. The u brella and the chowry are emblems of sovereignty (VI, PL. 1 and the goddess of prosperity is shown on Gupta coins with chowry resting on her shoulder, standing in attendance on t king. In other Gupta coins Lakṣmī is shown seated on a thro with her feet resting on a lotus (III, PL. 400) or seated on t back of a lion, the animal itself being the symbol of the roy throne.

Mādana or love personified as Cupid has two consorts, R (passion) and Tṛṣṇā (lust), who are depicted in a carving of t Pala school from Bihar (Calcutta, Indian Mus.). A very popu theme in Buddhist art is the temptation of the Buddha befc his Enlightenment (II, PL. 377; VI, PL. 18; VIII, PL. 404), whe all the passions are personified as the daughters of the tempt Māra. Passion is symbolized by amorous couples (*mithuna* in several medieval temples, particularly those at Konarak a Khajuraho (VII, PLS. 393, 473; XII, PL. 565; see also VII, co 439–40 and 690).

Beauty personified is conceived as the enchanting dams Mohinī, the form into which Viṣṇu transformed himself distract the *dānava*s (demons) who, along with the devas (god were participating in the Churning of the Milky Ocean f ambrosia. The *dānava*s took the liquor by force from the dev who turned to Viṣṇu for help. In the twinkling of an eye Viṣ assumed the guise of a damsel of ravishing beauty. The *dān* vas were so entranced by her beauty that they willingly gave t ambrosia to the devas. The Churning of the Milky Ocean depicted in the east gallery at Angkor Wat in Cambodia. Anoth personification of Beauty was Tilottamā, a damsel born from t thigh of Nārāyaṇa; her name signifies that she is composed particles of beauty that constitute the essence of perfectio A representation of Tilottamā is found in the panel of Na and Nārāyaṇa at Deogarh (VII, PL. 459).

Calambur ŚIVARAMAMURTI

China and Japan. The symbol appears in the earliest artis manifestations in China, in the Neolithic or the early Bron Age (15th–12th cent. B.C.): the primitive ideograms found on t Shang-Yin oracle bones and elsewhere are themselves a form symbolic representation of concepts or ideas, and Karlgre (1930), moreover, has related these inscriptions to the phall symbolism of the stakes symbolizing the soil god, She (see D VINITIES, col. 401). Many of the earliest objects in jade, bronz and other materials must have had symbolical significance, b it should be kept in mind that the meanings attributed to the in later texts may have been speculatively created long aft their original significance had been forgotten; it is by no mea unusual for a variety of meanings to be attached to the san object or graphic symbol, according to the interpreter or scho of thought.

Cosmological symbolism assumed distinctive forms at early stage. One of the most ancient symbols is the *pi* (I PL. 31; VI, PL. 49), a perforated jade disk believed to have bee used to locate the center of the heavens, the pole, and therel determine the five cardinal directions (the fifth, for the Chines being the zenith) and establish the calendar on the basis of t seasonal rotations of the constellations (see ASTRONOMY AN ASTROLOGY, cols. 79–81). From this use the *pi* is thought eve tually to have become a symbol of the heavens and of divin power, later extended to represent the imperial power (s CHINESE ART, cols. 79–80). Its counterpart is the *ts'ung*, a ja tube symbolizing the earth (see SEX AND EROTICA, col. 894 The five directions came to be associated, in a complicat ries of symbolic relationships, with the five colors and five elements that entered into Chinese cosmology as interpreted by the school of the Five Elements, as well as with stars, tastes and odors, musical notes, and other mystical correspondences. Another very ancient symbol is the circle within which the two opposing halves, the yin and yang — symbolizing the union of the two opposing forms of cosmic energy, the "male" and "female" principles — pursue and complement each other.

The Sun and Moon were frequently personified with their symbols or attributes, often in animal form: the Sun was commonly identified by the crow, his ritual animal, and the Moon by his accompanying hare and toad, even in areas of western Asia where the influence of Chinese mythology was secondary to that of India, as in the Tun-huang caves; in addition, the Sun and Moon (also identified as the legendary kings Fu-Hsi and Nü-kua) commonly bore a compass and a square (II, PL. 30). This symbolism entered into the mythology of Taoism (q.v.) and appears in representations of the Paradise of the West, accompanying Hsi-wang-mu, the Western Mother Queen; it extended to Japan and to Korea, where it is found as late as the 4th century. (See also ESCHATOLOGY, cols. 817–19.) The animals of the so-called "Chinese zodiac" (mouse, ox, tiger, hare, dragon, serpent, horse, goat, monkey, cock, dog, and pig), known in Chinese art since the beginning of our era, became particularly important in the T'ang period and appear among tomb figures both in China and in Japan, spreading also to Tibet, Mongolia, Korea, and Indochina. This cycle of animals, still important today in Chinese astrology, is believed to have originated in central Asia; outside of China, often only the figure of the dragon continued to show the Chinese influence (I, PL. 19; see ASTRONOMY AND ASTROLOGY, cols. 77–78).

Chinese cosmological symbolism found particularly interesting expression in architecture, as Stein (1957) has pointed out in relation to the traditional Chinese house plan, dating from the Han and Chou periods and persisting to the present day. The replacement of the Buddhist stupa form by the pagoda, too, reflects the Chinese notion of multiple superimposed worlds, with the square or octagonal base as a reference to the four cardinal points surrounding a central one. The plan of the Temple of Heaven in Peking illustrates the full development of cosmological concepts in architecture. (See COSMOLOGY AND CARTOGRAPHY, cols. 846–47.)

The dragon, prominent in Chinese art from its earliest beginnings (II, FIG. 26), survived through the ages, as a symbol of earth's fertility (the east, the rainmaker), a royal emblem, and an apotropaic sign (II, PL. 15; III, PLS. 229, 278, 280; VI, PL. 50; XIV, PL. 32). Birds seem to have been considered particularly propitious symbols: the phoenix is almost always seen in funeral representations and recurs, together with peacocks, mandarin ducks, and magpies, on Sui and T'ang mirrors used in the wedding ceremony. In Japan, too, the mandarin duck was the symbol of conjugal love. The folk art of China is rich in symbols: animals and birds, plants and flowers in particular are used for their symbolical meaning as well as their decorative value. Thus the peony signifies social distinction; the peach (XIV, PL. 457) and the tortoise, longevity; and the pomegranate, children.

Confucianism (q.v.), in its stress on ethics and its endeavor to eliminate the irrational, made no use of symbolism, but with Taoism (q.v.) the ancient symbols flourished once more and new ones were added. The school of the Soothsayers was based on the interpretation of specific graphic signs (the eight trigrams, or pa-kua; the sixty-four hexagrams; see MAGIC) symbolizing the various forces and aspects of the cosmos; and the school of the Five Elements, already alluded to, was also important in the development and interpretation of symbols. A whole pantheon of secondary divinities, some of them legendary and some historical figures, came to be associated with the forces of nature and with every aspect of daily life, finding symbolical and allegorical representation in both arts and crafts (PLS. 384, 385; see DIVINITIES, cols. 402–03). It was with the advent of Buddhism, however, that a whole new repertory of symbols entered Chinese art, with the Buddhist and Jain emblems — the fiery wheel, the conch, the state umbrella, the canopy, the lotus,

the vase, the pair of fishes, and the knot — assuming special importance as ornamental motifs (X, FIG. 843).

Japan (see JAPANESE ART) saw a somewhat similar development. As in many prehistoric or primitive cultures, the earliest art showed a strongly phallic symbolism (batons and pillars, stakes and clubs). The haniwa (funeral figures), paralleling the mortuary cult of China and other Oriental cultures, reflected in part a magical-cosmological symbolism. Shintoism (q.v.) made use of an aniconic symbolism, symbolizing the deities by their attributes, and gave rise to no iconography expressing the religious ideology. As in China, it was the diffusion of Buddhism that brought a new range of symbolism to Japan (PL. 334), eventually contributing to the anthropomorphic personification of the later syncretist forms of Shintoism (IV, PLS. 224, 225). Finally, a development of special importance in Japan was the heraldic emblem; as early as the 8th century, coats-of-arms analogous to those of medieval and Renaissance Europe were in use, appearing by the 13th–14th century on kimonos (IV, PL. 9) and on the insignia of warriors. Cities, too, often adopted arms, and to this day many commercial houses display the family arms as a trademark. (See EMBLEMS AND INSIGNIA, col. 723.)

This section incorporates material contributed by Lionello Lanciotti.

                                                     * *

THE PRE-COLUMBIAN MEXICAN AND ANDEAN CIVILIZATIONS. All the artistic production of the ancient American civilizations, ranging from architecture to codices, reflects — at times realistically but more often symbolically — the elaborate cosmological-religious conceptions of these peoples; in part the symbolism is obvious and easy to interpret, but some of it (as with a great part of the Maya graphic signs) has remained incomprehensible. Among examples taken from architecture may be cited the Tajín Pyramid of the Niches (III, PL. 485; X, PL. 22), in which the 365 niches symbolize the days of the solar year and therefore the passage of time. With time, too, are connected symbolically some of the most significant Aztec and Mayan sculptures, such as the tonalamatl (II, PL. 19), or calendar stone, on which are represented symbols of the year and of time, the centerpiece being the image of the sun, which is one of the predominating figures in the Aztec pantheon. The entire monolithic temple of Malinalco, with its entrances in the shape of a serpent's jaws and its sculptures representing an Eagle Knight and a Tiger Knight, is a symbol of the solar cycle, as are the 360 steps leading to the ancient sun temple in Mexico City. (See also ANDEAN PROTOHISTORY; ASTRONOMY AND ASTROLOGY, col. 83; COSMOLOGY, col. 849; MIDDLE AMERICAN PROTOHISTORY.)

A figure closely resembling the St. Andrew's cross, which occurs frequently in Aztec art and was for long erroneously held to denote Christian influence in Mexico prior to the advent of Cortés, may be a symbol of the four cardinal points or may represent human crossbones, symbol of death, of sacrifice, or even of night. A complex symbolism was bound up, in ancient Mexico, with colors, which in turn were linked with the cardinal points, with the gods, and with the very composition of things (for example, red indicated the skin, fire, blood, sunlight); other symbolic meanings were embodied in stones and metals (thus jade was a symbol of the year, of water, and of rain, and turquoise a symbol of light); animals, too, had their part to play (the serpent, the owl, and the alligator or crocodile were symbols of the year; a spiny crocodile skin symbolized the earth).

A classic example of the ancient Mexican use of symbolism is the image of the god of rain, Tlaloc (PL. 332; IV, PL. 465; VI, PL. 52; X, PLS. 6, 19): the three symbols that — either singly or together — denote the god (circled eyes, protruding fangs, and a forked tongue or scroll) may either appear on a naturalistic face or may indicate it symbolically (X, PLS. 6, 19). The Aztec deity Uitzilpochtli, god of war, is distinguished by a beaked mask resembling a hummingbird (symbol of the souls of warriors). Most of the Mexican deities were simply personifications of natural phenomena (cf. Xolotl, IV, PL. 227).

Less well known but equally varied and complex is the symbolism of ancient Peru as it is reflected in art. This symbolism seems to have been absent from architecture, although the countless terraced pyramids (I, PL. 163) could well symbolize the vault of heaven as in ancient Mexico, while those pyramids which are unterraced but which are provided with access ramps could symbolize the cosmic mountain. Symbolism is indeed apparent, however, in the few extant sculptures in stone, of which the outstanding example is the renowned half-feline half-gorgon monster of the Raimondi Stele (I, PL. 167). The symbolism of ancient Peru finds its chief expression in pottery, particularly in the Tiahuanaco, Mochica, Chimu, and Nazca styles.

In the Mochica and Chimu pottery, the figures with their heads adorned with a sort of helmet bearing two rays or horns are symbols of the moon (I, PL. 180); there are various representations of varieties of beans bearing markings that are probably pictorial symbols whose meaning is unknown; and the "trophy heads" that occur so frequently in Nazca pottery, as well as the stepped motif (I, PL. 203), which spread from Tiahuanaco to all the other styles of the coastal areas of Peru, would seem to be symbols of fertility, like the phallic symbolism of the serpent. Beasts of prey (I, PLS. 195, 200), particularly the puma (I, PLS. 202, 206) and the fox, as well as the serpent and the owl (I, PL. 178), were symbols of the ruling class, and it is quite probable that they also possessed a totemic significance; animals which are fleet of foot, as well as birds, frequently represented messengers; sunlight and the sun god were symbolized by rayed circles and by the use of gold; and the snail or a spiral stood for the terraces of the pyramid-temple or of the sacred mountain (I, PL. 194). Similar symbolical features are to be found in the textiles (I, PLS. 170, 171, 183) and jewelry (I, PLS. 214, 216, 217) of these peoples.

Ernesta CERULLI

PRIMITIVE CULTURES. It is characteristic of the symbolism of the so-called primitive peoples that little or no distinction is made between image and reality: what happens in dreams is considered as real, and the acts in which a wish is prefigured and expressed are expected to bring it to realization. Ignorant of scientific methods and knowledge, primitive man assumes the existence of relationships, on the basis of similarities of form or other correspondences, where none exist. Here, then, the symbol assumes a dynamic quality: it is not only a sign standing for something else but also brings that something else into being.

Among the lowest-level groups, with a poor material culture and undeveloped ritual, such as the Pygmies, symbolism is scarce and insignificant. On the level above, the more developed hunting cultures, symbolism arises particularly out of the endeavor to ensure successful hunting. Like the more recent hunters, early Palaeolithic man appears to have pierced his image of an animal with an arrow so as to magically ensure success in the hunt (IX, PL. 241; XI, PLS. 269, 271); and the representation of mating animals was believed to sustain by magic the supply and the multiplication of the animals pictured. Rock art thus often mirrored the hunter's conception of the world, and even in the earliest period the prevailing shamanism (q.v.) can be recognized in many incantation scenes, such as the black-and-red paintings at Lascaux, showing a bison together with a bird-headed man and a bird on a pole (XI, PL. 264).

Among nomad herding peoples, the art of making utensils is often the only one to have attained a high degree of development; the symbolical element here is chiefly in the decoration and ornamentation. Among the early nomads of Eurasia, next to the individual animal motif, which was a mark of identification and a sign of descent and clan membership, the theme of animals attacking other animals was a favorite (XIV, PL. 463; see ASIATIC PROTOHISTORY). According to one interpretation (J. G. Andersson, 1932), its origins lie in the chase with trained animals and birds, and it was meant to magically guarantee the success of the chase. Another theory (Alföldi, 1934) explains it as a reflection of tribal or clan traditions, for the deer represented the clan mother for the equestrian nomads, and a beast of prey the clan father; the interbreeding of these two animals, which never mate in nature, was then presented in the form of pursuit and victorious domination.

Cult and celebrations contributed to the development much of the primitive symbolism in art. In cult it is, above a the imagined primordial events that are dramatized. Mc primitive peoples attributed special importance to initiation ce emonies. In addition to masks (IX, PLS. 251, 354–359) a ritual dance paraphernalia, mention should be made of ancest and totem figures with their various specific local forms, such the *uli* (IX, PL. 448; white wood sculpture painted red a black with emphasized breasts and phallus) and the *malam gan* (IX, PLS. 447, 448) of New Ireland; the totem poles of t Northwest Coast American Indians (X, PL. 350), which a based on the representation of a (generally animal) protecti spirit and clan ancestor; the ancestor skulls with face model over in white clay and real human hair, from New Guin (IV, PL. 449); the *korwar* figures (wooden standing, seated, crouching human figures with large heads, thought to be t dwelling place of the spirit of the dead and at times also fitt out as a skull container; New Guinea, q.v.; see also POLYNESI CULTURES); figures of gods in wood, stone, metal, bone, or oth material, such as the Polynesian tikis (XI, PL. 198), which a exist as small, artistic, particularly charming pendants in nep rite (VI, PL. 52; XI, PL. 200); artificially constructed monste used in coming-of-age celebrations, mostly in the form of a mals, each ritually devouring the initiant and then disgorgi him, thus enacting rebirth in the sense of "death and becoming and the bull-roarers, flat, often decorated, wooden boar that in Australian, Melanesian, and some African and Americ cultures (qq.v.) are swung around with a string, the resulti humming sound being meant to produce spirit voices or to c forth some other magico-religious effect (II, PL. 66; IX, PL. 1 XIV, PL. 114; see also MUSICAL INSTRUMENTS, cols. 438–4

Mention must also be made of the sites of worship and t sacred structures, even among undeveloped peoples. Usua they are full of symbols and in their grandeur can often be f vorably compared to the religious architecture of the high cultures — e.g., the great house in New Guinea and in parts Africa (see III, cols. 850–51; X, col. 499). Particularly interes ing are the kivas, the cult rooms of the Pueblo and other India of the Southwestern United States, with their altars and sa paintings (PL. 329; X, PL. 239) as well as the cult objects in u there. The paintings are made of variously colored sand a depict rain clouds and lightning; each color and each geometi figure has a specific meaning (see NORTH AMERICAN CULTURE col. 707). Sunflowers, maize, rainbows, and stepped desig are among the symbols that recur on the cult objects.

The significance of a symbol is extremely variable: its mea ing can change from one people to another and even from o group to another of the same people, so that it is impossible accept unquestioningly as a general definition the interpretati of the meaning given to a symbol by a given people or grou Thus in Africa among the Dogon the cross of Lorraine appea as a superstructure on a mask and is variously explained as bird in flight (a hunting symbol), as the symbol of the crocodi and even, according to some, as a symbol of the balance b tween heaven and earth. In individual cases the particul meaning is revealed through the mythical, religious, or oth traditions of the group: thus the frequent appearance of t chameleon in the art of western Africa is explained by t widespread legend that it was to have brought immortali to man but moved so slowly that other animals overtook and the great significance of the antelope as a mask headpie in the cult dances of the Bambara of the Sudan (PLS. 307, 3 329) is explained by the part played by this animal as the cl emblem of this people. (See MASKS, cols. 548–49; MYTH A FABLE, cols. 497–99.)

Animal symbolism holds a high place in the art of primiti peoples. The particular popularity of the snake almost ever where is to be attributed partly to the fact that, in one form another, it is found in almost all mythologies (see also SEX A EROTICA, cols. 895–96). Also widespread, at least in Africa, t South Seas, and Malaya, is the lizard (II, PL. 61; X, PL. 13 XI, PL. 207). The "ram's horn" motif has attracted particul attention; it is especially widespread among the nomad her ers of southern Siberia (II, PLS. 6, 11; see ASIATIC PROT

STORY, col. 24), but it also appears in Indonesia, Polynesia, and Melanesia, as well as in eastern Europe and North Africa. Its origins have been sought in China, where Tanew (1941–) related it to the pattern on a clay impression from Long (in northern Korea), which, according to his interpretation, refers to the three Chinese divisions of the cosmos; it is also apparently related to the archaic motif of the four pairs of feathers with the sun symbol in the center (Hentze, 1951). Thus it would appear that this animal symbol, considered a ram's horn by the Turkoman, Kirghiz, and other nomads, and whose occurrence and meaning in Berber and Yoruba Africa was favored and influenced by the widespread ram myths and ram cults, basically a cosmological sign.

Plant symbolism is rare in the ornamentation of primitive peoples, and when it occurs it can usually be traced to the influence of the high cultures, as with the lotus in primitive ornamentation in India. Geometric ornament with symbolic significance is common, with the sun and the moon among the most widespread motifs: concentric circles, a circle with rays, circle of rays with an inscribed cross, a wheeling cross or cross with whirling rays, the swastika, etc. appear as sun symbols, and the moon also is often represented by similar circles. But caution is recommended in interpreting this geometric ornamentation, for a sign may have one meaning here, another there, just as the same object may be expressed by one sign here and another there. The zigzag, often standing for lightning (as among the Navaho; PL. 329) or for the snake, is seen as representing a river by the Chukchi Eskimos and as mountains by the Chinese. A row of zigzags, one of the favorite Jakut ornaments, is called "tent ornament" on Kumiss containers but it is also called "mare's-nipple design." The triangle, often comprising the zigzag design, is frequently related to the vagina and therefore interpreted as the symbol for the female in general and specifically for female fecundity. In North America, according to Boas (1955), who put special emphasis on the variations in meaning of this sign, it has the following significances: in the United States Southwest the equilateral triangle with lines extending downward from the base is the cloud from which pours the desired rain; for the Plains Indians the triangle is the sign of the tent, fastened with tent pegs to the ground; for others it is a mountain with rivers springing from its base; while on the Alaskan coast it is the paw of a bear.

An especially fine example of the migration of symbols and their reinterpretation in different cultures is offered by the Ashanti (Ghana) interpretation of the swastika (VII, PL. 128) as a monkey's foot. Different meanings can exist even within the same group. The Dakota men interpret a diamond-shaped figure with triangular appendages as a fallen enemy, while the women speak of it as a turtle, a fertility symbol among them (Wissler, 1904).

Ferdinand HERRMANN

SOURCES. F. Colonna, Hypnerotomachia Poliphili, Venice, 1499 and 1545, Paris, 1546, 1553, and 1561; Horapollon, Hieroglyphica, Venice, 1505 (Eng. trans., G. Boas, The Hieroglyphics of Horapollo, New York, 1950); Alciati, Emblemata, Augsburg, 1531, Paris, 1534, Lyons, 1550, Basel, 1582, Padua, 1626; Vasari; G. P. Valeriano, Hieroglyphica, Basel, 1556, Lyon, 1576, Leipzig, 1592, Venice, 1602; J. van Gorp, Hieroglyphica, Antwerp, 1580; G. P. Lomazzo, Trattato dell'arte della pittura, Milan, 1584 (Eng. trans., R. Haydock, Oxford, 1598); C. Ripa, Iconologia, Rome (?), 1593 and 1603, Padua, 1611, 1618, and 1630, Paris, 1644, Amsterdam, 1644, Venice, 1645 and 1669 (Eng. trans., Iconologia, London, 1709); E. Tesauro, Il canocchiale aristotelico, Turin, 1654; A. Félibien des Avaux, Entretiens sur les vies et sur les ouvrages des plus excellens peintres anciens et modernes, Paris, 1666–88, London, 1705, Amsterdam, 1706; G. P. Bellori, Vite de' pittori, scultori et architetti moderni, Rome, 1762; G. B. Vico, La scienza nuova (1730–44); ed. N. Abbagnano, Turin, 1952.

BIBLIOG. a. General: J. B. Boudard, Iconologie, Parma, 1759; J. J. Winckelmann, Versuch einer Allegorie, besonders für die Kunst, Dresden, 1766; K. W. Ramler, Allegorische Personen zum Gebrauch der bildenden Künstler, Berlin, 1788; K. H. Heydenreich, Aesthetisches Wörterbuch über die bildenden Künste, Leipzig, 1793; E. E. Goldsmith, Sacred Symbols in Art, New York, 1912; J. Burckhardt, Die Allegorie in den Künsten, in Vorträge 1844–87, Basel, 1919 (4th ed.); M. Ghyka, Le nombre d'or, 2 vols., Paris, 1931–52; R. van Marle, Iconographie, The Hague, 1931–32; E. Mandowsky, Untersuchungen zur Ikonologie des Cesare Ripa, Hamburg, 1934; S. Lewis, The Allegory of Love, Oxford, 1936; K. von Baudissin, Auf der Suche nach dem Sinngehalt, JhbPreussKSamml, LVII, 1936, pp. 88–97; Panofsky, Studies in Iconology, New York, 1939; W. M. Urban, Language and Reality, London, 1939; J. Seznec, La survivance des dieux antiques,

London, 1940 (Eng. trans., B. F. Sessions, The Survival of the Pagan Gods, New York, 1953, rev. ed.); C. Morris, Signs, Language and Behavior, New York, 1946; O. Brendel and U. Middeldorf, Correspondence, AB, XXIX, 1947, pp. 65–69; E. Droulers, Dictionnaire des attributs, allégories, emblèmes et symbols, Turnhout, 1948; E. H. Gombrich, Icones Symbolicae: The Visual Image in Neo-Platonic Thought, Warburg, XI, 1948, pp. 163–92; E. Wind, The Eloquence of the Symbol, BM, XCII, 1950, pp. 349–50; C. Funck-Hellet, De la proportion: L'équerre des maîtres d'oeuvre, Paris, 1951; A. Hauser, The Social History of Art, 2 vols., London, New York, 1951; I, Bergström, Disguised Symbolism in Madonna Pictures and Still-life, BM, XCVII, 1955, pp. 303–08, 342–49; Schlosser; ISMEO, Le symbolisme cosmique des monuments religieux, Actes de la conference internationale ... à Rome, avril-mai 1955, Rome, 1957; R. Tuve, Allegorical Imagery, Princeton, 1966; Warburg (passim).

b. Modern theories: S. Freud, Eine Kindheitserinnerung des Leonardo da Vinci, Leipzig, 1910 (Eng. trans., A. A. Brill, Leonardo da Vinci: A Psychosexual Study of an Infantile Reminiscence, New York, 1916); E. Cassirer, Die Philosophie der symbolischen Formen, 3 vols., Berlin, 1923–29; E. Cassirer, Sprache und Mythos, Leipzig, Berlin, 1925 (Eng. trans., S. K. Langer, Language and Myth, New York, London, 1946); B. Croce, Sulla natura della allegoria, Nuovi saggi di estetica, 2d ed., Bari, 1926; C. G. Jung, Seelenprobleme der Gegenwart, Zurich, 1931; S. Freud, Neue Folge der Vorlesungen zur Einführung in die Psychoanalyse, Vienna, 1933 (Eng. trans., W. J. H. Sprott, New Introductory Lectures on Psycho-Analysis, New York, 1933); S. Freud, A General Introduction to Psychoanalysis, Garden City, 1943; E. Cassirer, Essay on Man, New Haven, London, 1944; C. G. Jung, Symbolik des Geistes; Studien über psychische Phänomenologie, Zurich, 1948; S. Weil, La connaissance surnaturelle, Paris, 1950; S. K. Langer, Philosophy in a New Key, Cambridge, Mass., 1951 (3d ed., 1957); M. Eliade, Images et Symboles, Paris, 1952 (Eng. trans., P. Mairet, Images and Symbols, New York, 1961); R. A. Schwaller de Lubicz, Etude du symbole et de la symbolique, Cairo, 1952; S. K. Langer, Feeling and Form: A Theory of Art Developed from Philosophy in a New Key, New York, 1953; R. Arnheim, Art and Visual Perception: a Psychology of the Creative Eye, Berkeley, 1954; S. K. Langer, Problems of Art, New York, 1957; C. G. Jung, Die Beziehungen Zwischen dem Ich und dem Unbewussten, Zurich, 1963 (rev. ed.).

c. Ancient Middle East: F. Cumont, Textes et monuments figurés relatifs aux mystères de Mithra, Brussels, 1896–99; K. Frank, Bilder und Symbole babylonisch-assyrischer Götter, Leipzig, 1906; A. Grohmann, Göttersymbole und Symboltiere auf südarabischen Denkmälern, Vienna, 1914; J. De Morgan, Manuel de numismatique orientale, Paris, 1923; SPA, I; E. D. Van Buren, Symbols of the Gods in Mesopotamian Art, Rome, 1945; G. Jéquier, Considérations sur les religions égyptiennes, Neuchâtel, 1946; E. Porada, Mesopotamian Art in Cylinder Seals of the Pierpont Morgan Library, New York, 1947; H. Bonnet, Reallexikon der Ägyptischen Religionsgeschichte, Berlin, 1952; S. Schott, Symbol und Zauber als Grundform altägyptischen Denkens, Studium generale, VI, 5, 1953, pp. 278–88; H. Jacobsohn, Die symbolische Bedeutung des göttlichen Pharaonentums für den ägyptischen Menschen, Cong. Int. di Storia delle Religioni, Atti VIII, Rome, Apr. 17–23, 1955, Florence, 1956, pp. 230–33; M. J. Vermaseren, Corpus Inscriptionum et Monumentorum Religionis Mithraicae, The Hague, 1956–60; G. A. Wainwright, The Cappadocian Symbol, Anatolian S., VI, 1956, pp. 137–43; A. Bausani, Persia religiosa, Milan, 1959; R. T. R. Clark, Myth and Symbol in Ancient Egypt, London, 1959; L. Van den Berghe, Archéologie de l'Iran ancien, Leiden, 1959; H. Corbin, Terre céleste et corps de résurrection, Paris, 1960; J. Duchesne-Guillemin, Symbolik des Parsismus, Stuttgart, 1961; J. Duchesne-Guillemin, La religion de l'Iran ancien, Paris, 1962; A. Godard, L'art de l'Iran, Paris, 1962 (Eng. trans., A. M. Heron, The Art of Iran, New York, 1965); E. Porada, Alt-Iran, Baden-Baden, 1962 (Eng. trans., The Art of Ancient Iran; Pre-Islamic Cultures, New York, 1965); B. L. Goff, Symbols of Prehistoric Mesopotamia, New Haven, 1963.

d. Greece and Rome: E. Pottier, Les représentations allégoriques dans la peinture des vases grecs, Monuments grecs, XVII–XVIII, 1889–90, pp. 1–33; J. Hastings, ed., Encyclopaedia of Religion and Ethics, 12 vols., 1908–21, s.v. Allegory, Symbolism; E. Strong, Apotheosis and After Life: Three Lectures on Certain Phases of Art and Religion in the Roman Empire, London, 1915; R. P. Hinks, Myth and Allegory in Ancient Art, London, 1939; K. Kerényi, La religione antica nelle sue linee fondamentali, Bologna, 1940 (Eng. trans., The Religion of the Greeks and Romans, London, 1962); F. Cumont, Recherches sur le symbolisme funéraire des Romains, Paris, 1942; E. Will, Le relief cultuel gréco-romain; contribution à l'histoire de l'art de l'Empire romain, Paris, 1955.

e. Judaeo-Christian tradition: A. N. Didron, Iconographie chrétienne, Paris, 1843 (Eng. trans., E. J. Millington, Christian Iconography, London, 1886); E. R. Goodenough, Jewish Symbols in the Greco-Roman Period, 6 vols., New York, 1953–65; G. Ferguson, Signs and Symbols in Christian Art, New York, 1954; L. Réau, Iconographie de l'art chrétien, Paris, 1955–58; M. Guarducci, I graffiti sotto la Confessione di S. Pietro in Vaticano, Vatican City, 1958; C. R. Morey, ed., The Gold-Glass Collection of the Vatican Library, Vatican City, 1959; J. Daniélou, Les symboles chrétiens primitifs, Paris, 1961; P. E. Testa, Studio esegetico archeologico sul simbolismo dei giudeo-cristiani della Chiesa Madre di Gerusalemme, Jerusalem, 1961; P. E. Testa, Il simbolismo dei giudeocristiani, Jerusalem, 1962; M. Cagiano de Azevedo, Il patrimonio figurativo della Bibbia all'inizio dell'alto Medioevo, Settimane di Studio del Centro italiano di S. Sull'alto Medioevo, X: La Bibbia nell'Alto Medioevo, Apr. 26–May 2, 1962, Spoleto, 1963, pp. 341–86.

f. Early Christian and medieval art: P. D'Ancona, Le rappresentazioni allegoriche delle Arti Liberali nel Medio Evo e nel Rinascimento, L'Arte, V, 1902, pp. 137–55, 211–28, 269–89, 370–85; A. Muñoz, Le rappresentazioni allegoriche della vita nell'arte bizantina, L'arte, VII, 1904, pp. 130–45, IX, 1906, pp. 212–16; M. Förster, Adams Erschaffung und Namengebung, Archiv f. Religionswissenschaft, XI, 1908, pp. 477–529; B. Fedi, Il simbolismo cristiano nell'arte romanica, Florence, 1915; P. D'Ancona, L'uomo e le sue opere nelle figurazioni italiane del Medioevo, Florence, 1923; J. Sauer,

Symbolik des Kirchengebäudes und seiner Ausstattung in der Auffassung des Mittelalters, Freiburg im Breisgau, 1924; J. von Schlosser, Präludien, Berlin, 1927; J. Baltrušaitis, Études sur l'art médiéval en Géorgie et en Arménie, Paris, 1929; H. Flanders Dunbar, Symbolism in Mediaeval Thought, and Its Consummation in the Divine Comedy, New Haven, 1929; J. Baltrušaitis, La stilistique ornementale dans la sculpture romane, Paris, 1931; R. Bauerreis, Arbor vitae: Der "Lebensbaum" und seine Verwendung in Liturgie, Kunst und Breauchtum des Abendlandes, Munich, 1938; R. Hinks, Myth and Allegory in Ancient Art, London, 1939; F. Saxl, A Spiritual Encyclopedia of the Later Middle Ages, Warburg, V, 1942, pp. 82–142; N. Scheffer, Symbolism of the Russian Icon, GBA, XXV, 1944, pp. 77–94; E. De Bruyne, Études d'esthétique médiévale, Bruges, 1946; M. A. Alexander, The Symbolism of Christianity, Archaeol., III, 4, 1950, pp. 242–47; M.-D. Chenu, L'homme et la nature: Perspectives sur la renaissance du XIIe siècle, Arch. d'h. doctrinale et lit. du Moyen Age, XIX, 1952, pp. 39–66; M. C. d'Alverny, Le cosmos symbolique du XIIe siècle, Arch. d'h. doctrinale et lit. du Moyen Age, XX, 1953, pp. 69 ff.; L. Hautecoeur, Mystique et architecture, symbolisme du cercle et de la coupole, Paris, 1954; M. M. Davy, Essai sur la symbolique romane, Paris, 1955 (new ed., Initiation à la symbolique romane, XIIe siècle, Paris, 1964); J. Huizinga, The Waning of the Middle Ages, Harmondsworth, 1965.

g. Renaissance and baroque: H. Tetius, Aedes Barberinae, Rome, 1642; H. Janitschek, Die Gesellschaft der Renaissance in Italien und die Kunst, Stuttgart, 1879; H. Tietze, Programme und Entwürfe zu den grossen oesterreichischen Barock-fresken, JhbKhSammlWien, XXX, 1911, pp. 1–28; K. Giehlow, Die Hieroglyphenkunde des Humanismus in der Allegorie der Renaissance, JhbKhSammlWien, XXXII, 1915, pp. 1–229; L. Volkmann, Bilderschriften der Renaissance, Leipzig, 1923, Nieuwkoop, 1962; Mâle, IV; K. L. Schwarz, Zum aesthetischen Problem des "Programma" und der Symbolik und Allegorik in der Barocken Malerei, Wiener Jhb. f. Kg., XI, 1937, pp. 79–88; M. Praz, Studies in Seventeenth-Century Imagery, 2 vols., London, 1939–47 (2d expanded ed., Rome, 1964); E. Castelli, ed., Umanesimo e Simbolismo, Atti del IV Convegno Int. di S. Umanistici, Venezia, Sept. 19–21, Padua, 1958 (see especially E. Castelli, Umanesimo e simbolismo involontario, pp. 17–21; H. Sedlmayr, Idee einer Kritischen Symbolik, pp. 75–89; E. Battisti, Simbolo e classicismo, pp. 214–33; R. Volmat, Mecanisme inconscient et symbolisme dans certaines peintures de la Renaissance, pp. 305–17); E. Panofsky, The Iconography of Correggio's Camera di San Paolo, London, 1961.

h. Neoclassicism and romanticism: L. Volkmann, Die Hieroglyphen der deutschen Romantiker, Münch. Jhb. der bildenden K., III, N.S., 1926, pp. 157–86; E. Mâle, La clef des allégories peintes et sculptées au XVIIe et au XVIIIe siècle en Italie, Rev. des deux mondes, XCVII, 1927, pp. 106–29; M. Praz, La carne, la morte e il diavolo nella letteratura romantica, Milan, Rome, 1930 (Eng. trans., A. Davidson, The Romantic Agony, New York, 1956, 2d ed.); A. Pigler, Barockthemen, eine Auswahl von Verzeichnissen des 17. und 18. Jahrhunderts, 2 vols., Berlin, Budapest, 1956; E. Honig, Re-Creating Authority in Allegory, J. of Aesthetics, XVI, 1957, pp. 180–93; E. Honig, In Defense of Allegory, The Kenyon Review, XX, 1958, pp. 1–19.

i. Recent and contemporary movements: J. Moréas, Le symbolisme, Figaro Littéraire, Sept. 18, 1886; A. Aurier, Le symbolisme en peinture: Paul Gauguin, Mercure de France, March, 1891; A. Mellerio, Le Mouvement idéaliste en peinture, Paris, 1896; W. Kandinsky, Über das Geistige in der Kunst, Munich, 1912 (Eng. trans., H. Rebay, On the Spiritual in Art, New York, 1946); M. Denis, Théories, 1890–1910, du symbolisme et de Gauguin vers un nouvel ordre classique, Paris, 1920 (4th ed.); P. Martino, Parnasse et Symbolisme, Paris, 1925; B. A. Morisette, Aspects fondamentaux de l'esthétique symboliste, Clermont-Ferrand, 1932; M. Raymond, De Baudelaire au surréalisme, Paris, 1933; M. J. Friedländer, On Art and Connoisseurship, London, 1942; B. Dorival, Les étapes de la peinture française contemporaine, I, Paris, 1943; W. Gaunt, The Aesthetic Adventure, New York, 1945; W. R. Valentiner, Origins of Modern Sculpture, New York, 1946; A. H. Barr, Jr., ed., Fantastic Art, Dada, Surrealism, New York, 1947 (3d rev. ed.); C. Chassé, Le mouvement symboliste dans l'art du XIXe siècle, Paris, 1947; C. Seeley, Notes on the Use of Symbols in contemporary Painting, AQ, II, 1948, pp. 324–34; G. C. Argan, Picasso: Il simbolo e il mito, S. e note, Rome, 1955; J. Rewald, Post-Impressionism from Van Gogh to Gauguin, New York, 1956; M. Calvesi, Il futurismo di Boccioni: formazione e tempi, Arte antica e moderna, II, 1958, pp. 149–69; J. Lethève, Impressionistes et symbolistes devant la presse, Paris, 1959; P. Selz and M. Constantine, Art Nouveau, New York, 1960; The Museum of Modern Art, New York, Odilon Redon, Gustave Moreau, Rodolphe Bresdin, Garden City, 1961; G. Ballo, La grafica simbolista italiana, Cat. della XXXI Biennale, Venice, 1962; G. Dorfles, Simbolo, comunicazione, consumo, Turin, 1962; L. P. Finizio, La grafica simbolistica italiana, Arte oggi, IV, 14, 1962, pp. 24–27.

j. Islam: See bibliog. for ISLAM.

k. India: J. Fergusson, Tree and Serpent Worship, London, 1880; A. C. A. Foucher, Etude sur l'iconographie bouddhique de l'Inde, 2 vols., Paris, 1900–05; G. Weicker, Der Seelenvogel in der antiken Literatur und Kunst, Leipzig, 1902; T. A. G. Rao, Elements of Hindu Iconography, 4 vols., Madras, 1914–16; M. Anesaki, Buddhist Art in Its Relation to Buddhist Ideals, Boston, New York, 1915; A. K. Coomaraswamy, The Mirror of Gesture, Cambridge, Mass., 1917; A. C. A. Foucher, The Beginnings of Buddhist Art and Other Essays in Indian and Central-Asian Archaeology, London, Paris, 1917; W. Kirfel, Die Kosmographie der Inder, Bonn, Leipzig, 1920; J. Przyluski, La roue de la vie à Ajantā, JA, 1920, p. 314 ff.; N. B. Bhattacharya, The Indian Buddhist Iconography, London, 1924; J. P. Vogel, Indian Serpent-lore, London, 1926; A. K. Coomaraswamy, Yakṣa, 2 vols., Washington, 1928–31; A. Getty, The Gods of Northern Buddhism, 2d ed., Oxford, 1928; B. Barua, Gayā and Buddha-Gayā, 2 vols., Calcutta, 1931–34; J. Hackin et al., Asiatic Mythology, London, 1932; J. Przyluski, Le symbolisme du pilier de Sarnath, in Mél. Linossier, II, Paris, 1932, p. 484 ff.; A. C. A. Foucher, On the Iconography of the Buddha's Nativity, Delhi, 1934; A. K. Coomaraswamy, Elements of Buddhist Iconography, Cambridge, 1935; G. Jouveau-Dubreuil, Iconography of Southern In Paris, 1937; B. Rowland, Buddha and the Sun-god, Zalmoxis, I, 1938, pp. 6 84; E. Benda, Der vedische Ursprung des symbolischen Buddhabild Leipzig, 1940; H. Zimmer, Myths and Symbols in Indian Art and civili tion, New York, London, 1946; W. Kirfel, Die dreiköpfige Gottheit, Bo 1948; J. Auboyer, Le trône et son symbolisme dans l'Inde ancienne, Pa 1949; H. Demoulin-Bernard, Le lion dans l'art de l'Inde ancienne, M de France, XIV, 1949, pp. 205–07; G. Tucci, Teoria e pratica della manda Rome, 1949; J. Gonda, Aspects of Early Viṣṇuism, Utrecht, 1954; S. Kram risch, The Art of India, London, 1955; O. Śivaramamurti, Sanskrit Lite ture and Art, Delhi, 1955; H. Zimmer, The Art of Indian Asia, 2 vo New York, 1955; J. N. Banerjea, The Development of Hindu Iconograp 2d ed., Calcutta, 1956; B. Rowland, The Art and Architecture of India, B timore, 1956; E. Zannas and J. Auboyer, Khajurāho, The Hague, 19

l. China and Japan: B. Laufer, Jade: A Study in Chinese Archaeolo and Religion, Chicago, 1912 (2d ed., South Pasadena, 1946); B. Karlgr Some Fecundity Symbols in Ancient China, BMFEA, II, 1930, pp. 1– W. A. Thorpe, Creatures of the Chinese Zodiac, Apollo, XI, 1930, pp. 1 13; C. Hentze, Die Sakralbronzen und ihre Bedeutung in den frühchine schen Kulturen, Antwerp, 1941; A. Bulling, The Meaning of China's M Ancient Art, Leiden, 1952; A. Salmony, Antler and Tongue: An Essay Ancient Chinese Symbolism and Its Implications, Ascona, 1954; R. Ste L'habitat, le monde et le corps humain en Extrême-Orient et en Haute As JA, 1957, pp. 37–74; E. D. Saunders, Mudrā; A Study of Symbolic Gestu in Japanese Buddhist Sculpture, New York, 1960.

m. Pre-Columbian Mexican and Andean civilizations: G. C. Vailla The Atzecs of Mexico; Origin, Rise and Fall of the Aztec Nation, Gard City, 1941, Harmondsworth, 1950, 1956, Baltimore, 1960; J. E. S. Thomps Aquatic Symbolism Common to Various Centers of the Classic Period Meso-America, Selected Pap. of the XXIX Int. Cong. of Americanis Chigaco, 1951, pp. 31–36; H. Hoppenot, Mexique, magie maya, Lausan 1954; A. R. Sawyer, Collection Nathan Cummings d'art ancien du Pér (Musée des arts décoratifs, Palais du Louvre, mars-mai 1956), Paris, 19 (cat.); W. Krickeberg, Altmexikanische Kulturen, Berlin, 1956; H. Fe Explanation of the Nasca Iconography, Proc. of the 32d Int. Cong. of Am icanists, Copengagen, 1958, pp. 388–94; J. Imbelloni, Civiltà andine, Fl ence, 1959; H. Trimborn, Das alte Amerika, Stuttgart, 1959.

n. Primitive cultures: K. Weule, Die Eidechse als Ornament in Afri Festschr. f. Adolf Bastian, Berlin, 1896; C. Wissler, Decorative Art of Sioux Indians, Am. Mus. of Natural H. B., XVIII, 3, Dec. 17, 1904, pp. 2 77; M. Heydrich, Afrikanische Ornamentik, Leiden, 1914; H. T. Boss Geschichte des Kunstgewerbes aller Zeiten und Völker, 6 vols., Berlin, 19 35; J. G. Andersson, Hunting Magic in the Animal Style, BMFEA, I 1932, pp. 221–317; L. Frobenius, Kulturgeschichte Afrikas: Prolegom zu einer Historischen Gestaltlehre, Zurich, 1933; A. Alföldi, Zur histo schen Bestimmung der Avarenfunde, ESA, IX, 1934, pp. 285–307; Bittremieux, Symbolisme in de Negerkunst, Brussels, 1937; T. Tanew, I Ornament "Die Elbėtiza," IPEK, XV–XVI, 1941–42, pp. 170–97; G. Tichelman, Tooverteekens en Symbolen van Indonesië, The Hague, 19 K. Birket-Smith, Geschichte der Kultur, Zurich, 1946 (2d ed.); L. Ada Primitive Art, Harmondsworth, 1949 (2d rev. ed.); C. Hentze, Bronzeger Kultbauten, Religion im ältesten China der Shang-Zeit, Antwerp, 1951; Dittmer, Die Kunst der Naturvölker, Zurich, 1952; U. Johansen, Die namentik der Jakuten, Hamburg, 1954; F. Boas, Das Geschöpf des sechst Tages, Berlin, 1955 (Eng. trans., The Mind of Primitive Man, New Yo 1965, rev. ed.); F. Boas, Primitive Art, New York, 1955; P. Germann, Z Ornamentik im Kunsthandwerk des Mittelsudans, Festschr. f. H. Plisch Düsseldorf, 1955; F. Hančar, Die Kunst der frühen Nomaden Eurasie Kleine Kunstgeschichte der Vorzeit und der Naturvölker, Stuttgart, 19 F. Herrmann, ed., Symbolik der Religionen, I–XIII, 1958–66 (also sub quent issues); E. Leuzinger, Kunst der Negervölker, Baden-Baden, 19

* *

SYRIA. Constituted in 1920 after the dismemberment the Ottoman Empire and under French mandate from 1922 1941, the Syrian Arab Republic of today covers a territo that coincides only in part with the geographic and histo area of ancient Syria. While its territory today stretches in part of northern Mesopotamia, it no longer includes eith Lebanon (q.v.) or the Hatay province of Turkey (q.v.), wi which it nevertheless forms an organic historicocultural who

In antiquity Syria was the focal point of historical and arti tic development of the entire region comprised between t Nile and the Euphrates (see ASIA, WEST: ANCIENT ART; PHOEN CIAN-PUNIC ART; SYRO-PALESTINIAN ART), and it continued hold this role throughout the Hellenistic, Roman, and Ear Christian periods, which left a great abundance of splend monuments in the country (see LATE-ANTIQUE AND EARLY CHRI TIAN ART; ROMAN ART OF THE EASTERN EMPIRE). After bei invaded by the Persians on the eve of the Arab conquest, Sy became, as the center of the Islamic empire, part of a vast cultu complex (see ISLAM). The breaking up of this empire broug into power a succession of local dynasties, all of which, exce during the interval of the Crusades (see GOTHIC ART, col. 48 ROMANESQUE ART), were exponents of Arab culture, and su sequently brought Syria under the sway of larger states (Mam ukes, Ottoman Turks) whose numerous but not very significant cultural vestiges also belong to the Islamic tradition (see MAME-LUKE ART; OTTOMAN SCHOOLS).

SUMMARY. Historical and artistic outline (col. 841): *Ancient Oriental influences; Greco-Roman and Early Christian influences; The Islamic conquest and the Crusades; Modern period.* Monumental centers (col. 848).

HISTORICAL AND ARTISTIC OUTLINE. *Ancient Oriental influences.* The most ancient artistic manifestations in Syria — the neolithic structures at Ugarit (5000 B.C.) and the rock engravings of Demir Qapu — are important but few in number; generally speaking, it may be said that the region remained unaffected by the artistic development in neighboring areas. Only the northern part of the country seems to manifest any evidence of activity in the Mesopotamian artistic tradition; and the cultural influence of Egypt was to reach Syria only later, from the south and across its Mediterranean coastline. The pottery of Tell Halaf (named after a town in Syria but found in abundance from northern Mesopotamia to the Mediterranean) and that of al-'Ubaid show, however, that in the 4th millennium B.C. Syrian art was developing as part of a vast civilization that embraced almost all of the Near East, producing its most noteworthy monuments in Mesopotamia (see IRAQ, col. 287). Mesopotamian currents came to the fore even more strongly in the 3d millennium, with the development of Sumerian civilization: while the steles of Jebelet el-Beida are merely coarse imitations of Sumerian models, there was a rich artistic production in pre-Sargonic Mari (I, PLS. 502, 503; IV, PL. 16; XII, PL. 484) with iconographic and stylistic characteristics that indicate western influence. In addition, there were in the 3d millennium works with a decidedly local character — stylistically perhaps not entirely successful, but certainly highly original: witness the carved male heads and an interesting series of small idols with large eyes found at Tell Brak (see MESOPOTAMIA, col. 746) and other isolated pieces of sculpture found at Hama and Tell Nebi Mend.

Ancient Syrian art reached a peak in the 2d millennium B.C., and it was certainly no mere chance that this coincided with a period of lively political activity, manifested first in the independent city-states (Mari epoch) and later in the founding of the Mitannian kingdom and of the autonomous cities of Ugarit, Carchemish (Karkemiš, in Turkey), and Aleppo. In northern Syria, Mesopotamian influence was still strong: the palaces of Mari (IX, PL. 483; XIV, PL. 128) and Ugarit resemble Sumero-Akkadian models, but new elements of a local character are also present, especially in Mari. An acquaintance with Egyptian work is evident in the pictorial decoration of Mari (IX, PL. 482), particularly in the liveliness of certain scenes and in the iconography itself — for instance, in the scene showing Negroes climbing on palm trees (I, PL. 513). Mari sculpture (IX, PLS. 484, 485, 491) represents the most independent manifestation of art on the periphery of the Babylonian kingdom. In contrast with the situation in the 3d millennium, outside influences were profoundly modified in Syrian work, and the static Old Baby-

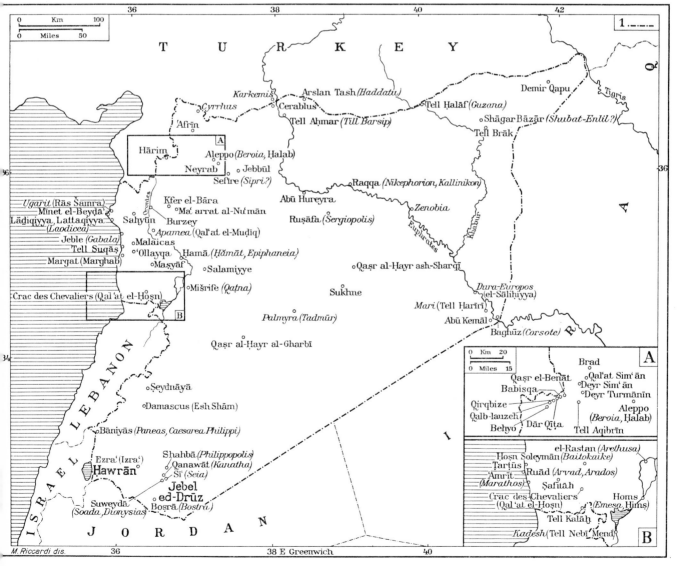

Syria, principal sites of archaeological or artistic interest. Key: (1) Modern national boundaries.

Ionian glyptic style was replaced by a production that shows great originality in composition and in its sense of volume. The most significant phenomenon in the 2d millennium, however, was the appearance of new cultural trends, some Mycenaean but chiefly from Egypt. The flourishing art of Ugarit, ranging from steles (XI, PL. 130) to metal statuary (PLS. 360, 361; XI, PL. 129), from ivorywork (VIII, PL. 237) to gem engraving and toreutics (X, PL. 401; XI, PL. 131), shows the variety of the artists' response to Egyptian models, which they followed with greater or lesser faithfulness but which can always be recognized. Alongside the manifestations with a more or less obvious foreign imprint, there are also from the 2d millennium works of a typically local character, even though these are limited in number and type. The sculptured heads from Gabbula (mod. Jebbul) and Qatna (mod. Mishrife) are among the best works of Syrian art; and even in architecture, strong local influence is evident in the plans of the temples of Ugarit and of the large public edifices of Alalakh (in the Hatay province of Turkey).

The political situation, which had become stabilized through the balance of power achieved by neighboring states, underwent deep changes toward the end of the 2d millennium. The invasions of the Peoples of the Sea, which destroyed the Hittite kingdom and limited Egypt's power to the African continent, created a political vacuum that was filled by a new ethnic group, the Aramaeans; soon afterward, these and the peripheral populations formerly under Hittite domination set up new urban political units engaged in a struggle for supremacy. These urban centers gave rise to an artistic style that, in the domain of handicrafts such as ivories (PL. 363) and wrought metals, was no longer derivative, even though Egyptian and, later, Assyrian motifs continued to play a noteworthy role. The most typical examples of the architecture of the 1st millennium are found at Guzana (mod. Tell Halaf). The palace of Kaparu there (I, FIG. 879), with its rich decoration of architectural sculpture and its orthostats carved in relief, is a structure whose splendor is equaled only by its originality; it is a typical *bît-hilani*, having the vestibule and inner hall wider than they are deep; the origins of this form, not yet entirely clear, seem to be rooted in the Syria of the 2d millennium. The sculpture of the 1st millennium seems rather primitive and constitutes an interesting example of a search for particularized expression on the basis of outside influences. The reliefs found at Damascus, Aleppo, Til Barsip (mod. Tell Ahmar), Neyrab (I, PL. 525; IV, PL. 450), Hama, and Homs present a diversity of characteristics and different degrees of eclecticism. The Assyrian conquest in the 8th century B.C. marked the end of the search for renewal in Syrian art: while on the one hand there was an ever-stronger current of Oriental influence (Assyrian and then Iranian), on the other the first signs of Hellenic penetration appeared — at first indirect, through contact with Cyprus, and later, during the Greco-Roman period, direct.

Giovanni GARBINI

Greco-Roman and Early Christian influences. The Greco-Roman period is represented in Syria at numerous sites marked by noteworthy ruins (see ROMAN ART OF THE EASTERN EMPIRE). The city layout based on the checkerboard pattern, of which the first examples were produced in Greece as early as the 5th century B.C. by the architect Hippodamos of Miletos, was adopted by the Seleucids during the Hellenistic period in the new cities they founded as well as in the older ones, whenever possible. Dura-Europos, which was abandoned early, has retained intact the grid design of its streets, which form identical rectangular blocks with uniform proportions of 5 to 2. Though less obvious, this layout is recognizable also elsewhere: in its pure state, at Cyrrhus (Kyrrhos); or covered by later constructions of various inspiration, at Antioch (mod. Antakya, now in Turkish territory), Laodicea (mod. Latakia), Beroea (mod. Aleppo), and Damascus; or modified by the Romans, at Apamea; or belatedly and imperfectly adapted, at Palmyra. A remarkably well-preserved Roman city layout patterned on a military camp, with two main intersecting streets forming the axes and terminating at the gates of a rectangular perimeter wall,

can be found at Philippopolis (mod. Shahba), and its basic line can also be seen at Bostra (mod. Bosra). The trend toward axial architecture and monumental perspective which characterize the imperial period and which, in Rome itself, is linked with the name of the Syrian architect Apollodoros of Damascus is illustrated in an original manner in Syria by the tall colonnade which line the transverse artery at Apamea and Palmyra (XI, PL. 190) and which are combined with the traditionally Hellenistic checkerboard design of the secondary streets. At Palmyra the plan of the square agora surrounded by porticoes is also in the Hellenistic tradition, whereas the arches which mark the street intersections and serve as links for the colonnades are definitely of Roman inspiration, like the city gates and tetrapylons still standing at Bostra, Philippopolis, Damascus, and Laodicea.

Greek and Roman influence also resulted in the construction of numerous buildings in the Western style. Syria contains many theaters, of which several have been recently excavated or restored. The principal ones are at Palmyra, Gabala (mod. Jeble), Apamea, and Cyrrhus in the north, and at Philippopolis Kanatha (mod. Qanawat), and Bostra in the south. In the field of religious architecture, the imperial period was one of intense building activity: numerous old, indigenous sanctuaries were embellished with colonnades and provided with temples. Important vestiges can still be found at Damascus, Baetocaece (mod. Hosn Soleyman), Kanatha, and, in particular, at Palmyra (XII, PL. 191). However, just as Greek and Latin names were often given to Semitic deities who nevertheless retained their own character and vitality, so the Corinthian colonnade erected to adorn these sanctuaries remained a form of decoration that nowhere replaced the traditional architectural structure required by the old cults.

Other manifestations of Greek and Roman influence in Syria must also be mentioned. The extensive coinage of money by many cities as an expression of their municipal autonomy is of esthetic as well as documentary interest. The mosaics from Antioch (IX, PL. 76; X, PL. 177), Palmyra, and the Jebel ed-Druz show not only the favor in which the technique was held but also, through the subject matter, the wide dissemination of imported mythological themes. The decorative sculpture and statuary (XII, PL. 193) as well as the mural paintings of certain tombs have the marks of a style that the newcomers had already brought to perfection in their own lands. However, it must be remembered that this influence affected, rather belatedly, a country whose old civilization and millennial traditions had been subjected to many earlier influences. Even in the new cities, Greco-Roman art in Syria remained a composite art, a trend contrasting with other trends without actually affecting them and losing some of its vigor as it got farther away from the coast, from its Mediterranean wellsprings.

The Roman penetration toward the Euphrates was mostly of a military nature; it left significant vestiges in the flagstone pavements of their strategic roads, the milestones, and the defense works of the limes. Art and religion, on the other hand, were affected only slowly and superficially. At Palmyra, as already mentioned, as well as at Damascus and Baetocaece, the typical structure of the old Semitic sanctuaries was preserved in spite of the wide use of colonnades to embellish their courts. The architecture of the temples of Bel and of Baal-shamin also show the persistence of Oriental characteristics: the cella is lighted by windows and equipped with a thalamos (and, in the former with staircases); in both the cornice is surmounted by graduated merlons. The series of dated capitals that have survived show that the bronze foliage applied onto a roughly hewn corbel or the scrolled capitals without foliage, typical of the first half of the 1st century, were replaced by the Corinthian capital only in the 2d century of our era. Similarly, it was only in the 2d century that the funeral towers, which had their origin in an ancient type of indigenous monument, began to disappear at Palmyra and that the first obvious signs of Western influence appeared in the sculptured or painted decorations of the hypogeums (XII, PLS. 193, 196). In fact, Palmyrene sculpture, so abundant until the 3d century, consistently retained its Oriental character, which found expression in its conventions its style, and in the costume of its subjects (XI, PLS. 54, 56); his sculpture was linked, as has been shown, to the vast field of Parthian art (q.v.; see also ROMAN ART OF THE EASTERN EMPIRE, col. 307), which at the time spread as far as the Indus.

Among the more remarkable artistic manifestations of the beginning of our era in Syria, mention should also be made of the basalt sculptures of Hauran, important in the history of religions and showing a curious alliance of Roman influence with local traditions; the handsome silver-plated and bronze helmets with face masks from Emesa (mod. Homs; XII, PL. 97) and Tell Um Hauran (Damascus, Nat. Mus.); and particularly the decorations painted by the Palmyrenes (XII, PL. 96), the Jews (VIII, PLS. 333, 335–337), and the Christians on the walls of their respective sanctuaries at Dura-Europos — miraculously preserved vestiges of a probably widely used but fragile technique — whose esthetic value equals their iconographic interest.

Thus began at Dura-Europos, during the first half of the 3d century, the rise of a Christian art of which a further stage of development is illustrated a little later by the sculptured symbols on the north gate of the retaining wall at Rusafa (Seriopolis) and which, from the 5th century onward, reached an incomparable flowering with the churches in northern Syria, in Hauran, and at Rusafa.

The profusion of ruins, evidence of numerous settlements in the calcareous plateau region of northern Syria, where water is scarce and the terrain rocky, poses a problem to which a plausible solution has recently been found. While the plateau does not lend itself to grain cultivation, it could, on the other hand, support the growth of trees, which could take root in the rocky basins where some soil accumulates. Still, even if the rainwater collected during the winter and kept in large cisterns could just satisfy the needs of a large population, the cultivation of vines and olive trees alone could not provide it with the means to obtain the food and manufactured products it required unless the crops were assured of a regular market. A political situation stable enough to guarantee both the security of the long-term investment such crops require and the free trade essential for the shipment of wine and oil to distant points — necessary prerequisites for such a way of life — was, in fact, the condition Syria enjoyed at the beginning of our era under the Pax Romana and until the Arab conquest. This explains the astonishing wealth of constructions that rose between the 1st and 7th centuries in what is at first sight so poorly endowed a region.

The attention of early travelers in this region was naturally first attracted by the churches. But churches are seldom isolated, and it would be arbitrary to dissociate them from the architectural compounds of which they were an integral part. Some large settlements such as Breij and Turmanin rose around monasteries devoted to agriculture; others, with their bazaars and their inns, around one that was a center of pilgrimage, as at Telanissus (mod. Deir Sim'an); elsewhere, the presses and farms were grouped around rural villas, as at Bamuqqa, Qirqize, and Behyo. Brad, an administrative and trade center, and Kfer el-Bara, an agricultural as well as industrial center equipped for large-scale production of wine and oil, are two communities that are remarkable for their size and the diversity of their buildings.

Christianity, whose origins were linked so closely with Syria, found its monumental expression very early: Dura-Europos already had a church when it was destroyed in 256; in 379 the emperor Theodosius founded a basilica, subsequently dedicated to St. John the Baptist, in the sanctuary of Jupiter-Hadad in Damascus. Several important sanctuaries were built at Rusafa near the tomb of St. Sergius soon after his death in 305; the emperor Justinian I had several churches built at Palmyra; and the Hauran and Jebel ed-Druz regions, where bishoprics were numerous, also contained many churches and monasteries. However, it was in northern Syria above all that Christianity expressed itself through an extraordinary architectural development. Numerous authors have drawn attention to the important part played by Syria in the evolution of primitive Christian architecture, the exceptional interest of certain basilicas, and their

historical, artistic, and religious significance (see LATE-ANTIQUE AND EARLY CHRISTIAN ART, col. 85). A striking feature is the remarkable uniformity of the architecture in the limestone plateau region bounded on the west by the cleft of the Orontes and Afrine valleys; there in the midst of the rubble of collapsed buildings appear, even to this day, the ruins of some isolated church, such as that at Qalb Lauzeh, or of monastery buildings, as at Kfer el-Bara or Telanissus. This unity of style can be attributed to the use of the same material and of the same technique in cutting and setting stone. However, the homogeneity of the sculptured decorations that were progressively adapted to the new structural forms is just as striking. This has led to the hypothesis that itinerant teams of workers took their style and methods from site to site. Thus a great school of builders and sculptors developed and worked in northern Syria until the 7th century. Whatever the part that may be attributed to them in the development of Byzantine art (see II, col. 763) and, later, of Western Christian art, the structures they left are evidence enough of the important role they played until the Moslem conquest put an end to their extraordinary and flourishing activity.

Paul COLLART

The Islamic conquest and the Crusades. Moslem art, after its rudimentary beginnings at the time of the Prophet himself and of his first successors, produced its first great manifestation in Syria during the Ommiad period (see OMMIAD SCHOOLS). As was only natural, it was essentially receptive at this time and still showed signs of the preexisting Hellenistic-Roman and Byzantine traditions, sometimes combined with Iranian and Mesopotamian influences. Thus the principal monument that has come down to us from that period, the Ommiad mosque at Damascus (in which the original ancient structure is still recognizable beneath the later transformations), reproduces the Hellenistic-Roman scheme of the agora with a basilica (VIII, FIG. 338; X, PL. 378); and the sanctuary itself, which consists of three parallel arcades cut by a transept with a cupola in the middle, is reminiscent of the typical layout of the Christian churches of Syria and Armenia. The rich mosaic ornamentation, which has in part been preserved (II, PL. 441; VII, PL. 407; VIII, PL. 145; X, PLS. 379, 380, 386), is — from obvious stylistic characteristics and from explicit mention in Arab sources — clearly the work of Byzantine craftsmen using Byzantine models. The other great architectural monument of the Ommiad period, the Dome of the Rock at Jerusalem, which is outside the territory of present-day Syria, confirms the derivation of the new Moslem art from the Christian architecture that preceded it. Predominantly Oriental, and more specifically Irano-Mesopotamian, influences are visible, on the other hand, in the remains of Ommiad desert castles and palaces, both in present-day Syria (Qaṣr al-Hayr al-Gharbī and Qaṣr al-Hayr ash-Sharqī; X, FIG. 751) and in Jordan (Khirbat al-Mafjar; Mshattā, VIII, FIG. 345; Quṣayr 'Amra, X, FIG. 749); generally on a square plan, they are surrounded by strong walls with a single monumental door reinforced by towers. Their stucco, fresco, and mosaic ornamentation (X, PLS. 381–384) testifies to the meeting and combination, in varying degrees, of the two great currents — the Hellenistic-Byzantine and the Irano-Mesopotamian — upon which the most ancient Islamic art in Syria was based. The natural predominance of the Hellenistic element later receded when the cultural and political center of Islam moved eastward, but it never completely disappeared from the successive phases of Moslem art.

There is almost nothing left in Syria from the early Abbasside period or the Hamdanid, Fatimid, and Seljuk periods before the time of the Crusades. Certain monuments in Damascus (the hospital, or *māristān*, of Nūr ad-Dīn) and Aleppo (the madrasahs of Khān al-Tūtūn and Shād Bakht) date back to the 12th century, while from the end of the 12th and from the 13th century (the Ayyubid period) there are still many religious and secular monuments, among which first place belongs to the citadel complex at Aleppo. But the greater part of the inheritance of Islamic art in Syria dates from the various Mameluke periods (see MAMELUKE ART): in the mosques, madrasahs, funeral chapels, baths, and fountains — just as in Egypt, where the political and cultural climate was similar — a composite art prevailed, drawing its inspiration from all parts of the Moslem world and, through the monuments of the crusaders, even from Christendom.

Alongside architecture (the victory of the most rigid orthodoxy having eliminated painting and sculpture) there were the decorative arts, which were particularly rich in Mameluke times: ceramics (III, PL. 142), toreutics, and above all glass (VI, PL. 227; VIII, PL. 157), in which Syria carried on its great classical and Hellenistic traditions. The magnificent pieces of gilt and enameled glass (cups, glasses, bottles, mosque lanterns) produced by the workshops of Antioch, Damascus, and Aleppo between the 12th and 16th centuries are among the most precious treasures of European and Oriental museums and private collections.

Little was added to this period of intense activity by the Ottoman domination; at that time, Syrian artists copied rather feebly, and with rather limited means, the architectural and ornamental models of Ottoman art, whose most original and powerful accomplishments are to be found in Constantinople and in Anatolia. Syria, like Egypt, was relegated to the position of a neglected province, although isolated single monuments of great nobility, such as the al-'Aẓm (Azem) Palace at Damascus (PL. 247), still testified to the creative capacity existing on Syrian territory even in such a period of decadence. The political rebirth of modern times, in Syria as elsewhere, manifests a double tendency: an effort to link up with the local artistic traditions and the importation of the most modern currents in Western art.

Francesco GABRIELI

The military orders of crusaders that arose in the 12th and 13th centuries built, frequently over preexisting Arab fortresses or archaeological remains, many fortresses and castles, of which several examples have survived. Almost all the castles, which were erected on heights or at strategic points, show a quadrangular plan and one or more enclosure walls with towers and strong bastions. Inside stood the keep, the church, and several rooms, the largest of which was the hall in which the order met. Among the Arab and crusader castles and fortresses of which interesting vestiges still remain are Qal'at el-Muḍīq (built on the acropolis of Apamea), Saône (mod. Sahyūn), and Burzey, all near Laodicea; the White Castle, the Red Castle, and the Castle of the King's Daughter, all near Tortosa (mod. Tartus); Margat (mod. Marqab), 'Ollyaqa, El Kahf, and Maṣyāf; Qal'at es-Subaybi, near Baniyas in southern Syria; Bassuet (mod. Basut), near 'Afrin; and Le Crac des Chevaliers (mod. Qal'at el-Ḥoṣn). Of many other castles, famous in their day, only insignificant ruins remain. In many cases Arab or crusader fortresses form, even today, the central nucleus (that is, the citadel) of cities and large towns that developed in the Middle Ages and grew in modern times; for example, the citadels, still intact, of Damascus, Aleppo, and Tortosa and of numerous small centers such as Baniyas and Bostra (whose fortress was erected around and over the Roman theater). Many monasteries arose or were rebuilt at the time of the Crusades and were often provided with powerful defense works, as at Qaṣr el-Benāt. Other examples are the monastery of Sardenaye (mod. Seydnaya), with its many open sepulchral grottoes in the surrounding rocks, and that of St. George (near Le Crac des Chevaliers); the latter, founded by Justinian I and refashioned in the 12th and 13th centuries, has a treasure rich in church vestments and vessels and icons.

Modern period. Almost all the large centers of Syria can today be divided into an ancient section, which has kept its typical medieval road network, and a new one that has sprung up outside the city walls (which still exist almost everywhere) along the lines of modern town planning. There is little architecture derived from or inspired by Western models of the 16th–19th centuries, and wherever this occurs it is almost always in connection with Catholic, Orthodox, or Protestant religious edifices. Far more remarkable and decisive, during this period, was the Ottoman influence. It is only recently, and in the

large centers, that international planning and architectur criteria have been adopted. The cities that, in this field, hav developed and changed most are Damascus and Latakia.

BIBLIOG. *General*: E. G. Rey, Voyage dans le Haouran et aux bore de la Mer Morte exécuté pendant les annés 1857–58, Paris, 1860; J. I Porter, Five Years in Damascus, with travels and researches in Palmyr Lebanon and the Hauran, 2 vols., London, 1855; E. Isambert and A. Chav vet, Itinéraire descriptif, historique et archéologique de l'Orient. III, Syr et Palestine, Paris, 1881–82; E. Honigmann, RE, s.v. Syria; Bibliothèqu archéologique et historique, Institut français d'archéologie de Beyrout Paris, 1921 ff.; H. Lammens, La Syrie: Précis historique, 2 vols., Beiru 1921; Syria, 1921 ff.; H. Baraude (pseudonym of J. Tupinier), Au pays d mirage, Syrie et Palestine, Paris, 1924; R. Dussaud, Topographie historiqu de la Syrie antique et médiévale, Paris, 1927; R. Dussaud, P. Deschamp and H. Seyrig, La Syrie antique et médiévale illustrée, Paris, 1931; W Wegener, Syrien, Irak, Iran, Leipzig, 1943; R. Fedden, Syria, Londoi 1946; C. Cahen, Note additionelle à deux ouvrage d'archéologie orienta médiévale, Cahiers techniques de l'art, II, Strasbourg, 1949, pp. 83–9 E. Will, La tour funéraire de la Syrie et les monuments apparentés, Syri XXVI, 1949. pp. 258–312; Les annales archéologiques de Syrie, 1951 fl P. Collart, S. Abdul-Hak, and A. Dillon, Syria: Problems of preservatic and presentation of sites and monuments, Paris, 1954; P. K. Hitti, Histoi of Syria, London, New York, 1957.

Antiquity and Early Christian period: M. de Vogüe, Syrie centrale: A chitecture civile et religieuse du I⁰ʳ au VII⁰ siècle, 2 vols., Paris, 1865–7 R. Röhricht, Syria sacra, Z. des Deutschen Palästina-Vereins, X, Leipzi 1887, pp. 1–48; R. Dussaud and F. Macler, Voyage archéologique au Sa et dans le Djebel ed Drûz, Paris, 1901; H. C. Butler, American Archaeologic Expedition to Syria in 1899–1900, II, Architecture and Other arts, Ne York, 1903; H. C. Butler, Princeton University Archaeological Expeditio to Syria in 1904–05 and 1909, II, Architecture, Section A, Southern Syri Section B, Northern Syria, Leyden, 1907–22; Syrie du Nord (Institut frar cais d'archéologie orientale, Mémoires, XXV, LXXVI, LXXVIII), 3 vols Cairo, 1909–55; H. W. Beyer, Der syrische Kirchenbau (Studien zur sp tantiken Kg.), Berlin, 1925; H. C. Butler, Early Churches in Syria, Princeton 1929; S. Guyer, Le rôle de l'art de la Syrie et de la Mésopotamie à l'époqu byzantine, Syria, XIV, 1933, pp. 56–70; D. Schlumberger, Les formes ar ciennes du chapiteau corinthien en Syrie, en Palestine et en Arabie, Syri XIV, 1933, pp. 283–317; A. Poidebard, La trace de Rome dans le dése de Syrie, 2 vols., Paris, 1934; J. Strzygowski, L'ancien art chrétien de Syri Paris, 1936; D. Krencker and W. Zschietzschmann, Römische Tempel i Syrien (Archäologisches Institut des deutschen Reiches, Denkmäler antik Architektur, Bd. V), 2 vols., Berlin, Leipzig, 1938; J. Mattern, A travers le villes mortes de Haute Syrie: Promenades archéologiques en 1928, 192 1931, Beirut, 1944; J. Lassus, Sanctuaires chrétiens de Syria, Paris, 194 D. Schlumberger, La Palmyrène du Nord-Ouest, Paris, 1951; E. Frézoul Les théâtres romains de Syrie, Ann. Archaeol. de Syrie, II, 1952, pp. 46–10 D. Sourdel, Les cultes du Hauran à l'époque romaine, Paris, 1952; G. Tch lenko, Villages antiques de la Syrie du Nord, le Massif du Bélus à l'époqu romaine, 3 vols., Paris, 1953–58; R. W. Enrich, ed., Relative Chronol gies in Old World Archaeology, Chicago, 1954; M. I. Rostovtzeff, Syria an the East, Cambridge Ancient History, VII, 1954, pp. 155–96; R. Dussau La pénétration des Arabes en Syrie avant l'Islam, Paris, 1955; H. Frankfor The Art and architecture of the Ancient Orient, Harmondsworth, Baltimor 1958; E. Frézouls, Recherches sur les théâtres de l'Orient syrien, Syri XXXVI, 1959, pp. 202–28; J. Nasrallah, Bas-reliefs chrétiens inconnu de Syrie, Syria, XXXVIII, 1961, pp. 35–53; K. A. Kitchen, Suppilulium and the Amarna Pharaohs: A Study in Relative Chronology (Liverpoc Monographs in Archaeology and Oriental Studies, V), Liverpool, 196: P. Matthiae, Ars Syra: Contributi alla storia dell'arte figurativa siriana dell età del medio e tardo bronzo (Università di Roma, Centro di Studi Semitic Serie Archeologica, IV), Rome, 1962; R. W. Enrich, ed., Chronologies i Old World Archaeology, Chicago, London, 1965.

Islamic period: M. Gaudefroy-Demombynes, La Syrie à l'époque d Mamelouks d'après les auteurs arabes, Paris, 1923; K. A. C. Creswell, Earl Muslim Architecture: Umayyads, Early 'Abbāsids and Tūlūnids, 2 vols Oxford, 1932–40; J. Sauvaget, L'architecture musulmane en Syrie, RA VIII, 1934, pp. 19–51; J. Sauvaget, Les monuments ayyoubides de Dama Paris, 1938–48; J. Sauvaget, Remarques sur les monuments omeyyades, Châteaux de Syrie, JA, CCXXXI, 1939, pp. 1–59; H. Stern, Notes sur l'ai chitecture des châteaux omeyyades, Ars Islamica, XI–XII, 1946, pp. 72–9

MONUMENTAL CENTERS. Damascus (Heb., Dammeseq; Aram Darmeseq; Gr., Δαμασκός; Ar., Dimeshq, Esh Sham). The preser capital of Syria is one of the most ancient centers in the country The city, whose name is probably not Semitic and is to be found early as the beginning of the 2d millennium B.C., became in the 10t century B.C. the capital of a powerful Aramaic state, which was fre quently at war with the Israelites and later with the Assyrians; i 732 it was subdued by the latter, who put an end to its independence The most famous monument of the Aramaic period was the gre Temple of Hadad, which was transformed successively into the sanc tuary of Jupiter Damascenus, the Church of St. John the Baptis and the Great Mosque. The only vestige of the Aramaic period a bas-relief representing a sphinx (9th cent.; Nat. Mus.). From th Seleucid period the city has kept the orthogonal plan of the streets from Roman times there remain the line of the city walls and, on th colonnaded Darb al-Mustakim ("Street called Straight"), the ruin a monumental arch and of the eastern gate to the city (Bāb Sharqī). ound the Great Mosque there are the remains of the sanctuary Jupiter Damascenus, the most remarkable being, to the west, the Corinthian colonnade of one of the propylaea of the peribolos h beautiful fragments of the arches.

The Great Mosque (Ommiad Mosque), the most important oslem monument in the city, was built under the caliph al-Walīd I 5–15) within the enclosure of the temple of Jupiter Damascenus, on the site of the demolished church of St. John the Baptist. though it has several times been wrecked and buried, and has been atly restored in modern times, the Mosque still possesses at least e original structure and plan (VIII, FIG. 338) and a part of the orna-

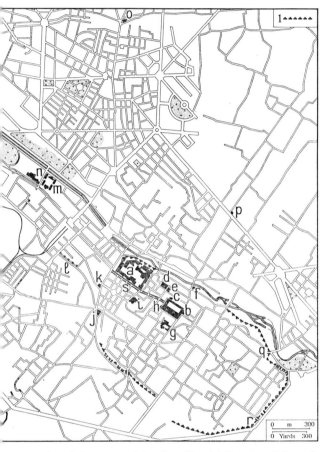

amascus, plan of the center of the city. *Key*: (1) Remains of the 12th- ntury city walls. Principal monuments: (*a*) Citadel; (*b*) Great Mosque mmiad Mosque); (*c*) Mausoleum of Saladin; (*d*) 'Ādiliya Madrasah; (*e*) hiriya Madrasah; (*f*) Bāb al-Farādīs; (*g*) Azem Palace; (*h*) ancient gateway the Temple of Jupiter; (*i*) Māristān of Nūr ad-Dīn; (*j*) Mosque of Sinān sha; (*k*) Darwīshiya Mosque; (*l*) Roman aqueduct; (*m*) Tekkiya; (*n*) Na- nal Museum; (*o*) Mardāniya Mosque; (*p*) Bāb Tūmā; (*q*) Bāb Sharpī (east e); Sūq al-Ḥamīdiya.

entation that, in the Middle Ages, caused it to be one of the wonders Islam. The rectangular courtyard has, on three sides, porticoes th arches on columns; the fourth side opens onto the prayer hall, ich is also rectangular and is divided into three arcades with arches columns, as in the Syrian basilicas. A transept cuts it perpen- cularly along the axis of the mihrab; above the point of intersection the two axes is the dome. In the portico and the vestibule of the ayer hall itself, the original precious mosaics of Byzantine style, ade by Syrian craftsmen in iconoclastic times, were brought to light the 1920s. One of the three minarets, the "minaret of Jesus," linked with Moslem eschatological beliefs (the return of Christ at e end of the world to fight the Antichrist).

Near the Great Mosque stands the Mausoleum of Saladin (12th nt., restored in the 19th), which with the 'Ādiliya and Ẓāhiriya adrasahs and the citadel, constitutes the principal group of Ayyubid d Mameluke monuments in Damascus. The 'Ādiliya, which is w the seat of the Arab Academy, contained the tomb of Malik 'Ādil, brother of Saladin, while the Ẓāhiriya, with its mosaic orna- entation and rich library, shelters the tomb of the sultan Baybars I -Malik al-Ẓāhir). The memory of Nūr ad-Dīn, the Zangid pred- essor of Saladin in the fight against the crusaders, is kept alive

by the hospital (*māristān*) which he founded and by his own tomb (1172) with its stalactite-decorated cupola. From the Ottoman pe- riod are the Azem (al-'Aẓm) Palace (18th cent.), a magnificent example of a private residence with its typical division into two separate parts for men and women (selamlik and haremlik), splendid marbles, ce- ramics, and painted woodwork; the Darwīshiya Mosque with the mausoleum of its founder; and several of the innumerable khans or caravansaries that stud the old city. Other Moslem monuments are to be found in the ancient suburb (now a suburban quarter) of Sa- lihiye (the Mardāniya Mosque, the Mausoleum of Jaharkas, the Mau- soleum of Muḥyī ad-Dīn ibn-'Arabī). Vast and numerous *sūqs* (markets), both covered and open (Sūq al-Arwām, Sūq al-Ḥamīdiya), and many baths complete the characteristic Oriental aspect of the Syrian metropolis.

In the 20th century the city has developed to the north and south of the old urban nucleus and has acquired specimens of modern ar- chitecture (which are still, to a great degree, linked to the traditional style), such as the buildings that house the law courts and the Figeh Water Company, the Central Post Office, and the Hejaz Railroad Station, as well as the churches of the Jesuits and of the Franciscans, the Greek Catholic and Orthodox churches, and the National Mu- seum, in which are collected precious architectural, sculptural, and other remains from the Roman, Early Christian, and medieval periods. The modern installations of the Damascus International Fair and the new Syrian Universal complex are more recent and come closer to the style and construction standards of contemporary international architecture.

BIBLIOG. J. L. Porter, Five years in Damascus, with travels and research- es in Palmyra, Lebanon and the Hauran, 2 vols., London, 1855; Benzing- er, RE, s.v., Damaskos; C. Watzinger and K. Wulzinger, Damaskus, die Islamische Stadt (Wissenschaftliche Veröffentlichungen des deutsch-tür- kischen Denkmalschutz-Kommandos, V) Berlin, 1924; R. Dussaud, Le temple de Jupiter Damascénien et ses transformations aux époques chrétienne et musulmane, Syria, III, 1922, pp. 219–250; J. Sauvaget, Les monuments histo- riques de Damas, Beirut, 1932; J. Sauvaget et al., Les monuments ayyoubides de Damas, 4 vols., Paris, 1938–50; W. Herzfeld, Damascus, Studies in architec- ture, Ars Islamica, IX, 1942, pp. 1–53; X, 1943, pp. 13–70, XI–XII, 1946, pp. 1–71; J. Sauvaget, Le plan de antique Damas, Syria, XXVI, 1949, pp. 314–58; S. Abdul-Hak and A. Abdul-Hak, Catalogue illustrée du Dé- partement des antiquités greco-romaines au Musée de Damas, Damascus, 1951; Catalogue des expositions des découvertes archéologiques au Musée de Damas, Damascus, 1952; Les Guides Bleus, Moyen-Orient, Paris, 1956; S. Abdul-Hak, K. Moaz, Aspects de l'ancienne Damas, Damascus, n.d.; E. Will, EAA, s.v.; J. Witmar, Étude sur l'aménagement de la ville ancienne de Damas par l'assainissement de l'existant, Ann. Archéol. de Syrie, XI– XII, 1961–62, pp. 19–44; On the mosaics of the Great Mosque: R. Etting- hausen, Arab Painting, Geneva, 1962, pp. 22–28.

Aleppo (Accadian, Khallaba; Hittite, Khalap; Gr., Βέροια; Rom., Beroea; Ar., Haleb). One of the oldest cities in Syria, in the 2d millennium B.C. it was the capital of the state of Yamhab, which played a political part of the greatest importance. It was destroyed toward the end of the millennium and was of little importance in the following one, for the political center of the region had moved to the neighboring city of Arpad. The lack of any archaeological excavations explains the extreme scarcity of remains dating from the most ancient period of the city: a bas-relief representing two facing genii, which belong to the Syro-Anatolian figural repertory, and a pair of basalt lions are the most important remains from the beginning of the 1st millennium B.C. In Hellenistic times, Seleucus Nicator introduced a Macedonian colony into the city, which took the Macedonian name of Beroia (Lat., Beroea). Of the Hellenistic-Roman city, there remain the foundations of the perimeter wall (upon which were constructed the medieval bastions), the Hippodamian plan, the citadel (now oc- cupied by buildings of the Islamic period), and the Temple of Zeus- Hadad, which was later replaced first by a Byzantine cathedral and then by the Madrasah Ḥalawiya.

After Damascus, Aleppo is the Syrian city richest in Moslem monuments, mostly of the Ayyubid and Mameluke periods. The Jāmi' al-Kabīr (Great Mosque), founded about 715, belongs in its present state to the 11th and 12th centuries; it has a Seljuk minaret, decorated with Kufic inscriptions, and a beautiful mimbar of carved wood (15th cent.). The Madrasah Ḥalawiya opposite is the adaptation (12th cent.) of the former Byzantine cathedral. Other mosques are the Jāmi' al-Fustuq (14th cent.), the Bahrāmiya, the Jāmi' al-Tūtah (whose façade shows Fatimid elements), and those of Alṭūnbughā, al-Utrush, and al-Tawāshī (all of the Mameluke period). Especially noteworthy is the Madrasah al-Firdaus (Madrasah of Paradise) of 1235; its stalactite-decorated portal and courtyard with liwan and porticoes make it probably the loveliest Islamic architectural complex in Syria. Among the mausoleums, mention should be made of those of the Ayyubid prince al-Ẓāhir Ghāzī, son of Saladin, and of the Mam- eluke governor Khā'ir Bey. But the most imposing monumental complex is that of the citadel, built by the above-mentioned al-Ẓāhir

Ghāzī at the end of the 12th century and beginning of the 13th and restored by the Mameluke sultan Khalīl in 1292; the superb portal, preceded by a bridge and flanked by two towers, gave access to the fortress through a passageway with several right angles, in accordance with an old fortification technique. The inside, which is now in ruins, still shows traces of baths and of two mosques, besides a well and other architectural fragments. Also noteworthy are the three main gates of the city (Bāb an-Naṣr, Bāb Anṭākiya, and Bāb Qinnasrīn), all of the Ayyubid period, as well as the various markets (Sūq al-'Aṭṭārīn, Sūq al-Saqaṭiya, Sūq al-Qaṣṣābiya, etc.), which, along with the numerous khans (caravansaries), give Aleppo a decidedly medieval character and color.

The city grew considerably in the 17th century, at which time there arose impressive buildings in the Ottoman style, such as the Khān al-Wazīr (caravansary with a monumental entrance), and Khān al-Ṣābūn, with rich sculptured ornamentation on the façade. Also dating from the 17th century are many artistically decorated private houses, such as those that bear the names of Dallal, Sayagh, and Sadar, all of them grouped together in the picturesque Jedeideh quarter. Other remarkable buildings are the Greek Orthodox and Latin churches. The urban development of Aleppo and the increase in building are recent; new quarters have grown up (e.g. that of Aziziye), with modern dwelling houses, schools, colleges (e.g. that of the Holy Land), hotels, and public buildings. The city also boasts a rich Archaeological Museum, and a Library, housed in the Madrasah Sharafiya, where precious illuminated manuscripts are kept.

BIBLIOG. J. Sauvaget, Inventaire des monuments musulmans de la ville d'Alep, Rev. des Et. Islamiques, V, 1931, pp. 59–114; G. Ploix de Routrou, Le Musée national d'Alep, Aleppo, 1932; J. Sauvaget, Le "tell" d'Alep, Mélanges syriens offerts à Monsieur René Dussaud, Paris, 1939, pp. 59–65; J. Sauvaget, Alep: Essai sur le développement d'une grande ville Syrienne des origines au milieu du XIXᵉ siècle, 2 vols., Paris, 1941; S. Saouaf, Aleppo, Visitors' Guide, Aleppo, 1953; E. Herzfeld, Inscriptions et monuments d'Alep (Syrie du Nord, II–III, Institut français d'archéologie orientale, Mémoires, LXXVI, LXXVIII) Cairo, 1954–55; E. Will, EAA, s.v. Beroia.

'Amrit (Gr., Μάραθος; Rom., Marathus). This place was perhaps mentioned by Thutmosis III; tombs from the 2d millennium B.C. have been brought to light. A stele with a relief representing a Phoenician deity may be dated to the middle of the 1st millennium. Of a slightly later date is a series of monuments still visible above ground: two small temples in the Egyptian style and some tombs. Quite well known are the so-called "Maghāzil" ("spindles"), two cylindrical funerary edifices; one has four lions' heads disposed around the base, while the cylindrical structure itself terminates in a hemisphere. Excavations have been carried out at the sanctuary known as "al-Ma'abad," a small sacred edifice standing in the middle of a great court near a spring. From the city itself have come many votive statues, more or less mutilated, which can be dated to the 4th or 3d century B.C.

BIBLIOG. E. Honigmann, RE, s.v. Marathos; M. Dunand, Les sculptures de la favissa du temple de Amrit, BMBeyrouth, VII, 1944–45, pp. 99–107, VIII, 1946–48, pp. 81–107; M. Dunand, Recherches archéologiques dans la région de Marathus, note préliminaire, Ann. Archéol. de Syrie, III, 1953, pp. 165–170; M. Dunand, Nessib Saliby, and Agop Khirichian, Les fouilles d'Amrith en 1954, rapport préliminaire, Ann. Archéol. de Syrie, IV–V, 1954–55, pp. 189–204; M. Dunand and Nassib Saliby, Rapport préliminaire sur les fouilles d'Amrith en 1955, Ann. Archéol. de Syrie, VI, 1956, pp. 3–10; S. Abdul-Hak, Découvertes archéologiques récentes dans les sites Greco-Romains de Syrie, Part 3, Amrith, Annales Archéologiques de Syrie, VIII–IX, 1958, pp. 86–90; G. Garbini, EAA, s.v. Marathos; M. Dunand and Nessib Saliby, Le sanctuaire d'Amrith, rapport préliminaire, Ann. Archéol. de Syrie, XI–XII, 1961–62, pp. 3–12.

Apamea (Gr., Απάμεια; Rom., Apamea ad Orontem; Ar., Qal'at el-Mudiq). The site of this city occupies a position dominating the marshy plain of the Orontes. In the vast field of ruins of Apamea it is still possible to see scattered fragments of its monuments above ground. Occupied by the Macedonians, it became one of the centers of the Seleucid kingdom and the capital of a satrapy of northern Syria. In 64 B.C. it was conquered by Pompey, who destroyed its citadel. The city was built on a regular plan and had two main arteries crossing at right angles and terminating at the principal gates; at the central crossroad stood the baths and a palaestra. From the Corinthian columns of the porticoes, built in the 2d century of our era along the main north–south artery, have been found architraves with elements of the three orders; here and there, consoles supported statues of emperors or of private citizens. There are also remains of the theater, of a quadrilobate basilica, of a triclinium (with mosaics, now in Brussels, Mus. Royaux d'Art et d'H., and in Damascus, Mus. Nat.), of a synagogue with a mosaic, and of a basilica with three aisles. Outside the city walls are the necropolises.

BIBLIOG. Benzinger, RE, s.v. Apameia; H. C. Butler, American Archæ logical Expedition to Syria in 1899–1900, II, Architecture and Other A New York, 1903, pp. 52–57; F. Mayence, La deuxième campagne de fou Belges, à Apamée, B. des Mus. Royaux d'Art et d'H. de Bruxelles, 1931, pp. 42–45, reprinted AntC, I, 1932; H. Seyrig, Sur les ères quelques villes de Syrie: Apamée, Syria, XXVII, 1950, pp. 15–20; E. s.v. Apamea di Siria.

Arslan Tash (Accadian, Haddatu). Founded in Assyrian tim Haddatu was a royal provincial residence on the road from Assy to Syria. Remains of the city walls (with three gates), of a temple, a of two Assyrian palaces were dug up by a French mission in 19 The great palace, founded by Tiglathpileser III (745–727 B.C.)

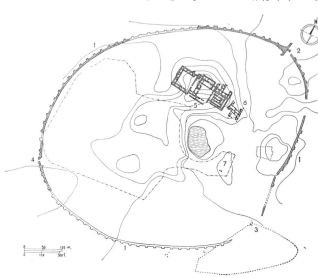

Arslan Tash, of the site (1) Wall; (2) north gate; (3) east gate; (4) west g (5) palace of Tiglathpileser III; (6) palace "of the ivories"; (7) site of two salt bulls, remains of the entrance to an Assyrian temple (*from F. Thure Dangin et al., 1931*).

of special interest for its *bît-hilani* structure; adjacent was a smal and older building in which were found a number of carved iv plaques (Louvre; Aleppo, Nat. Mus.). Some of the ivories proba ornamented a bed which an inscription states to be that of Haza King of Damascus; the bed appears to have been offered in trib by his son Benhadad III to the Assyrian king, Adadnirari III, w transported it from Damascus to Haddatu. At this site, too, h been found various reliefs representing warriors (Istanbul, Archae Mus.), in which Assyrian influence is evident to a degree. There a also vestiges of the Hellenistic period.

BIBLIOG. F. Thureau-Dangin et al., Arslan-Tash, 2 vols., Paris, 19

Arvad (Gr., Άραδος; Rom., Aradus; Ar., Ruad). A rocky isla opposite Tartus. As a Phoenician city, it expanded along the co and founded both Marathus (mod. 'Amrit) and Antaradus (m Tartus). The entire island was surrounded by a powerful polygo wall, except for the part where the port lay: in this section, rema of columns are still to be seen. Preliminary excavations have reveal inscriptions, coins, scarabs, and tombs for cremated remains. Th are fragments of architectural decoration and sculpture from vario periods. In the 13th century an Arab castle was built overlooking port; the island's walls had been razed by Muawiyah, the first govern of Syria after the Arab conquest.

BIBLIOG. E. Renan, Mission de Phénicie, Paris, 1864, pp. 19–42; Benzinger, RE, s.v. Arados; R. Savignac, Une visite à l'île de Rouad, Rev Biblique, 1916, pp. 565–592; J. G. Milne, The coinage of Aradus in the H lenistic period, Iraq, V, 1938, pp. 12–21; H. Seyrig, Aradus et Baetocae Syria, XXVIII, 1951, pp. 191–206; H. Seyrig, Aradus et sa pérée sous rois séleucides, Syria, XXVIII, 1951, pp. 206–220; G. Garbini, EAA, s Arados.

Baetocaece (Gr., Βαιτοκαίκη; Ar., Hisn Sulayman, Hosn Sol man). A dependency of Arvad situated 30 miles inland from Tart it is one of the most remarkable examples of those mountain sanctuar of indigenous Semitic construction scattered in the Lebanon hills which the architects of the Roman imperial period liked to add te ples and colonnades. Inside a trapezoidal surrounding wall of magn cent proportions, whose monumental gates are decorated with b

iefs and inscriptions, may be seen the remains of an Ionic temple
I an altar. Another temple, not far away, is part of a group of partic-
rly well-built structures.

BIBLIOG. D. Krender and W. Zschietzschmann, Römische Tempel in
ien, Berlin, Leipzig, 1938, pp. 65–101; H. Seyrig, Aradus et Baetocécé,
ia, XXVIII, 1951, pp. 191–206; H. Seyrig, Aradus et sa pérée sous les
s séleucides, Syria, XXVIII, 1951, pp. 206–220.

Bosra (Bib., Bossora; Gr., Βόσσορα, Βόστρα; Rom., Nova Trajana
stra; Ar., Busra Eski Sham). Situated in the fertile Hauran region,
ir the southern border of Syria, Bosra was one of the principal towns
the Nabataean kingdom and later became the capital of the Roman
ovince of Arabia, which was added to the Empire by Trajan's
ieral Cornelius Palma (A.D. 106). The topography of the ancient
tlement is still clearly indicated by the city's rectilinear main street,
 former decumanus. Several columns of its porticoes and a gate
its western end are still standing. Along the street can be seen a
onumental three-bayed arch, ruins of the baths, and four tall Co-
thian columns which may have been part of a nymphaeum.
Bosra has one of the largest, most beautiful, and most complete
man theaters in existence; it presents, moreover, some quite re-
irkable particularities in the structure of the slanted vaults that sup-
rt the tiers, in the arrangement of the small stairways that lead to
e tiers, and in the wonderful decoration of the *frons scaenae*.
The city is also important for its Christian monuments. While
inscription is the only thing left to recall the oldest church of the
y, dedicated to the Virgin in the 5th century by Archbishop Anti-
er, parts of the imposing basilica built in 512/13 by Archbishop
ian — one of the first examples of a large church with a central
in and cupola — still survive.

BIBLIOG. M. de Vogüé, Syrie centrale: Architecture civile et religieuse
Ier au VIIe siècle, 2 vols., Paris, 1865–77, pp. 40, 63–67; Benzinger, RE,
, Bostra; R. E. Brünnow and A. v. Domaszewski, Die Provincia
abia, III, Strasbourg, 1909, pp. 1–84; H. C. Butler, Princeton University
chaeological Expeditions to Syria in 1904–05 and 1909, Section 2A (South-
ı Syria), Leyden, 1919, pp. 215–295; H. C. Butler, Early Churches in
ria, Princeton, 1929, pp. 124–27; J. W. Crowfoot, Churches at Bosra and
maria-Sebaste (British School of Archaeology in Jerusalem, Supplementary
per IV) London, 1937; E. Frezouls, Les théâtres romains de Syrie, Ann.
chaéol. de Syrie, II, 1952, pp. 69–79; E. Ouéchek and S. Mougdad, Bosra,
mascus, 1954; E. Will, EAA, s.v. Bostra.

Brad (Barad). This is the site of one of the largest basilicas of
rthern Syria. Built between 395 and 402, it had three aisles and an
se flanked by prothesis and diaconicon that opened onto the lateral
les. In the center of the nave was an exedra for the empty throne,
iich was used as an ambo. A chapel, dedicated to various saints,
s added to the north aisle in the 5th century.

BIBLIOG. H. C. Butler, Early Churches in Syria, Princeton, 1929, p. 34;
Lassus, Sanctuaires chrétiens de Syrie, Paris, 1947, p. 168; G. Tchalenko,
llages antiques de la Syrie du Nord, le massif du Bélus à l'époque romaine,
vols., Paris, 1953–58.

Corsote (Gr., Κορσωτή; Ar., Baghuz). The site has been identified
du Mesnil du Buisson (1948) as the classical Corsote, mentioned
Xenophon. The place dates from very remote times, as is proved
the finds of pottery of the Samarra type (5th millennium B.C.).
oove the surface of the ground are still to be seen certain funerary
vers of the 2d and 3d centuries of our era, resembling those at
Imyra.

BIBLIOG. R. Du Mesnil du Bousson, Baghouz, l'ancienne Corsôtê;
 tell archaïque et la nécropole de l'âge du bronze, Leiden, 1948.

Le Crac des Chevaliers (Ar., Hosn el-Arhad, Qal'at el-Hosn).
ais fortress was enlarged and strengthened by the Order of Hospi-
ers in the 12th and 13th centuries; they added defensive works,
aqueduct (which is in ruins), a powerful keep, a 12th-century
urch, and a great hall. The castle is the most important and the
st preserved of all those built in the area by the various religious
ders.

Cyrrhus (Gr., Κύρρος, Ἁγιούπολις, Κύρος; Ar., Qurus). A
leucid colony on the northern border of Syria, this was in Roman
nes an important frontier post and military camp. At the end of the
century, SS. Cosmas and Damian suffered martyrdom here, and
er their tomb was built an important basilica. Relatively decadent
the middle of the 5th century, the town was rebuilt by Justinian,
d in 637 it was occupied by the Arabs. The acropolis was surrounded
 a massive wall; at the summit stood the keep, with four towers,
ree of them square and one circular. In the lower part of the town,

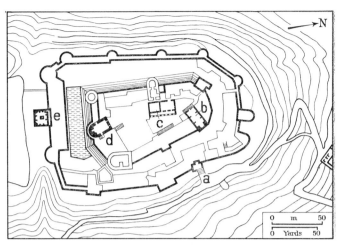

Le Crac des Chevaliers, plan. (*a*) Entrance; (*b*) chapel; (*c*) great hall; (*d*)
central tower; (*e*) rectangular tower (*after a plan by F. Anus*).

which was quite extensive, can still be recognized the orthogonal
plan of the streets and the arcades that bordered the main thorough-
fare. Abutting on the city wall is a rectangular construction with
towers and a monumental entrance; inside, the plan of a church with
three aisles and a narthex can be distinguished. A large theater of
the 2d century of our era stood in the center of the city, built against
the slope of the acropolis. Outside the walls were the cemeteries, in
one of which there is a hexagonal mausoleum in excellent condition.
Also outside, two bridges of definitely Roman type are to be noted.

BIBLIOG. Honigmann, RE, s.v. Κύρρος; E. Frézouls, Les théâtres romains de Syrie, Ann. Archéol. de Syrie, II, 1952, pp. 58–66; E. Frézouls,
Recherches sur la ville de Cyrrhus, Ann. Archéol. de Syrie, IV–V, 1954,
pp. 89–128; E. Lissi, EAA, s.v. Kyrros.

Demir Qapu. Not far from this village are to be found pecked
rock engravings attributed to the Neolithic age but perhaps more
recent. They represent animals (cervids and bovids for the most part)
and human figures, the latter each carrying a bow or long sticks (or
spears); in some cases the human figures are combined with the animals
in groups portrayed in varying attitudes.

BIBLIOG. F. von Luschan, Über Petroglyphen bei Assuan und Demir-
Kapu, ZfE, LIV, 1922; H. T. Bossert, Altsyrien; Kunst und Handwerk
in Cypern, Syrien, Palästina, Transjordanien und Arabien von den Anfängen bis zum völligen Aufgehen in der griechisch-romischen Kultur, Tübingen, 1951.

Dura-Europos (Gr., Δοῦρα Εὔρωπος; Rom., Dura Europos).
The city, near modern Salahiye, was probably founded by a Seleucid
satrap at the end of the 4th century B.C.; afterward it was occupied
by the Parthians and later became a Roman colony. It was conquered
and destroyed by the Sassanids in A.D. 256. The city extends above the
Euphrates, on a plateau bordered by two narrow gorges leading down
to the river. As a caravan center and a river port it occupied a strategic and economic position of great importance. The original plan
probably dates back — as does the perimeter wall, which was later
rebuilt — to the Seleucid period. It was built on the checkerboard
pattern originated by the architect Hippodamos of Miletos. On one
of the two hills stood the governor's palace, while the military headquarters and a temple were erected on the acropolis. Another temple
and the market were in the center of the city. Under the Parthians
the city was rebuilt and flourished. The already existing monuments
were enlarged and new ones were constructed, among them a splendid
palace in the citadel and numerous sanctuaries that contained magnificent paintings. Among the important temples were those dedicated to
Artemis Nanaia, to Atargatis, to Zeus Megistos, to Artemis Azzanathcona, to Aphlad, to Adonis, to Zeus Kyrios, and to Zeus Theos.
Another sanctuary, dedicated by the inhabitants of Palmyra to their
gods or genii, stood at the northwestern corner of the city. Also remarkable are the houses of Babylonian type, the market, the porticoes,
and the shops.

In the following period, that of the Roman occupation, Dura
lost its importance as a caravan city, and underwent profound economic
changes, becoming a strategic stronghold. The Romans built there the
extensive Palace of the Dux and reinforced the city walls and the towers
in defense against the danger of the Sassanid Persians. Apart from the
military edifices there are also religious ones of great artistic interest,
among others a Christian church (IX, FIG. 79), a synagogue, and a
Mithraeum, all three decorated with paintings.

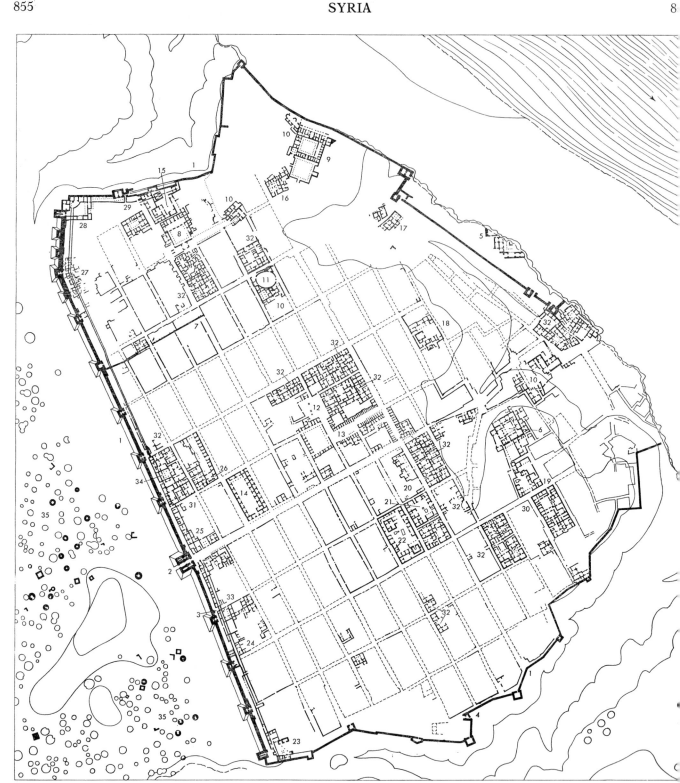

Dura-Europos, plan of the site. (1) City wall; (2) main (Palmyra) gate; (3) subsidiary gate; (4) south gate; (5) citadel and its palace; (6) military hea
quarters on the acropolis; (7) wall of the Roman encampment; (8) praetorium; (9) Palace of the Dux; (10) Roman baths; (11) amphitheater of the milit
forces; (12) area of the Hellenistic agora; (13) markets; (14) warehouses; (15) Temple of Artemis Azzanathcona; (16) *dolichenum*; (17) Roman milit
chapel; (18) Temple of Zeus Rheos; (19) Temple of Zeus Olympius, later of Zeus Magistos; (20) Temple of the Gaddē; (21) Temple of Atargatis; (
Temple of Apollo and Artemis, later of Artemis Nanaia; (23) Temple of Aphlad; (24) Temple of Zeus Kyrios; (25) Temple of Tyche; (26) Temple
Adonis; (27) Mithraeum; (28) Temple of Bel (?), known as the Temple of the Palmyrene Gods; (29) an officer's house; (30) House of Lysias; (31) Ho
of the Scribes; (32) dwelling houses; (33) Christian church; (34) synagogue; (35) necropolis area (*from The Excavations at Dura-Europos, Prelimin
report of the 9th season, New Haven, 1944*).

Bibliog. F. Cumont, Fouilles de Doura-Europos (1922–1923), Paris, 1926; Yale University, The excavations at Dura-Europos, conducted by Yale University and the French Academy of Inscriptions and Letters, Preliminary report, 10 vol., New Haven, 1929–52; M. I. Rostovtzeff, Dura-Europos and its Art, Oxford, 1938; M. I. Rostovtzeff, The foundation of Dura-Europos on the Euphrates, Seminarium Kondakovianum, X, 1938, pp. 99–106; R. du Mesnil du Buisson, Les peintres de la synagogue de Doura-Europos, 245–256 après J.-C., Rome, 1939; A. Pagliaro, Le isc zioni pahlaviche della sinagoga di Dura-Europo, RendLinc, VII, vol. 1940–41, pp. 578–616; H. F. Pearson, A Guide to the Synagogue of Dou Europes, Beirut, 1939; Yale University, The excavations at Dura-Euro conducted by Yale University and the French Academy of Inscriptions a Letters, Final reports, New Haven, 1943–   ; A. Pagliaro, Date e pittori ne sinagoga di Dura-Europos, RSO, XXVIII, 1953, pp. 170–73; R. N. Frye,

Gillian, H. Ingholt, and C. B. Welles, Inscriptions from Dura-Europos, ale Classical Studies, XIV, 1955, pp. 123–213; E. R. Goodenough, The aintings of the Dura-Europos Synagogue, Israel Exploration J., VIII, 58, pp. 69–79; M. I. Rostovtzeff, A. Perkins, EAA, s.v.

Ezraa (Ezra'; Rom., Zorava). This town in the Hauran, has two im-ortant churches, dedicated to St. George (515) and to Mār Elias 42). The former, which is the better preserved, is built on an octag-al plan and surmounted by a dome.

BIBLIOG. M. de Vogüé, Syrie centrale: Architecture civile et religieuse, Paris, 1865, pp. 61–62; H. C. Butler, American Archaeological Expedition Syria in 1899–1900, II, Architecture and Other arts, New York, 1903, . 411–413; H. C. Butler, Early Churches in Syria, Princeton, 1929, pp. 122–, 125.

Hama (Aram., h m t; Heb., Hamath; Gr., 'Επιφάνεια; Rom., piphania). This city, whose oldest settlement dates back to Neo-hic times (5th millennium B.C.) acquired a certain importance only ward the end of the 2d millennium, when Aramaic and neo-Hittite eoples established a small state that took an active part in the polit-al vicissitudes of the times. Destroyed by the Assyrian king Sargon in 720 B.C., it was rebuilt in Hellenistic times. From the 3d mil-nnium B.C. traces have been found of houses with apses, which show relationship with the Aegean world. From the Aramaic period there main, besides a few ivories and pieces of sculpture, vestiges of the tadel and of the royal palace, as well as the monumental entrance te to the citadel. From the Greco-Roman period there are vestiges the checkerboard street plan and a few sculptures, among which small replica of the so-called "Sosandra of Kalamis" (sometimes nown as "Aspasia") is of great interest (Damascus, Nat. Mus.).

The present city, thanks to its position on the Orontes, to its rdens, and to its norias (Ar., na'ūra, wheel for lifting water), is one the smaller Syrian centers that have kept intact their Oriental aracter and fascination. Noteworthy among the monumental build-gs are the Jāmi' al-Kabīr (Great Mosque, adapted from an old hristian church), with an octagonal minaret and the adjacent mau-leum of Malik al-Muẓaffar III (1284–98), and the Jāmi' al-Ḥayyāt Mosque of the Serpents) of the Mameluke period, with the tomb of e historian Abū'l-Fidā (1332), who was sultan of the little city. he Jāmi' Nūrī, with its magnificent carved wooden mimbar and its lack-and-white minaret, is of the 12th century. The Bait al-'Aẓm Azem Palace), once the residence of the pasha who founded the palace Damascus bearing the same name, is more modest than the latter ut is interesting as an example of a wealthy private house of Otto-an style, with courtyards at different levels, inlaidwork, majolica, d 18th-century paintings.

BIBLIOG. M. Sobernheim, Encyclopédie de l'Islam, II, Paris, Leiden, 27, p. 256; H. Ingholt, Rapport préliminaire sur la première campagne des uilles de Hama, Copenhagen, 1934; P. J. Riis, Remains of a Roman Build-g in Hāma, Syria, Berytus, II, 1935, pp. 34–39; H. Ingholt, Rapport pré-minaire sur sept campagnes de fouilles à Hama en Syrie (1932–38), Copen-agen, 1940; P. J. Riis, Les cimetières à crémation (Copenhagen, National-useet, Skrifter, Større beretninger, I) Copenhagen, 1948; E. Fugmann, 'architecture des périodes préhellénistiques, Copenhagen, 1958; G. Gar-ni, EAA, s.v.

Homs (Gr., Έμεσα, Έμισα, Έμισσα; Rom., Emesa, Emissa, emisa; Ar., Hims). The city stands in the middle of a broad plain ar the river Orontes. Its beginnings appear to date back to very cient times, but the first mention of it is to be found only in the oman era. It was the home of Julia Domna, Mammaea, Helio-abalus, and Alexander Severus. Under Heliogabalus it obtained the atus of a metropolis and enjoyed a period of great prosperity. There as a temple dedicated to Baal, in whose honor were celebrated games hich are commemorated on coins. The remains of the temple robably lie underneath the Jāmi' al-Kabīr (Great Mosque), which turn occupies the site of an old Christian church. Outside the me-ieval walls are two funerary towers on a square plan with a central aircase, which date back to the first centuries of our era. In the nderground chapel of Bāb Sbā' are interesting paintings of the 5th ntury, and nearby are the underground remains of the ancient mon-stery. The royal necropolis to the west of the city has yielded a umber of valuable objects dating from the 1st century of our era Damascus, Nat. Mus.); they include a helmet with a silver mask, old funerary ornaments, and jewelry. Also from Homs is a silver ase variously dated between the 5th and 7th centuries, now in the ouvre.

The city underwent a long period of decadence after the Mongol vasion of 1260. It revived markedly from the middle of the 19th ntury and is today an important center for trade. Its severe and mber aspect is due to the material (gray basalt) used in almost all e buildings, which are mostly one story high, have no external rnamentation, and are separated by narrow tortuous lanes. Among

the main edifices are the Latin (Jesuit) church, the Greek Orthodox Church of the Forty Martyrs, and the Jāmi' al-Kabīr. In recent times the city has developed toward the west in the direction of the Orontes.

BIBLIOG. H. Seyrig, Le casque d'Emèse, Ann. Archéol. de Syrie, II, 1952, pp. 101–08; H. Seyrig, Antiquités de la nécropole d'Emèse, Syria, XXIX, 1952, pp. 204–50; XXX, 1953, pp. 12–24; W. J. Van Liere, Ager centuriatus of the Roman colonia of Emesa (Homs), Ann. Archéol. de Syrie, VIII–IX, 1958–59, pp. 55–58; EAA, s.v. Emesa; A. Al-'Ush, Les bois de l'ancien mausolée de Khalīd ibn al-Walīd à Hims, Ars Orient., V, 1965, pp. 111–39.

Jeble (Phoenician, Gabal; Gr., Γάβαλα; Rom., Gabala; Old Fr., Zibel). This ancient Phoenician town was founded by Arvad, and later became a Dorian colony. It has a Roman theater of large propor-tions (diam. ca. 300 ft.) whose structure is interesting, for it rises on a plain without making use of a hillside as is usual in that region. To the west of the city is a little port hewn out of the rock, most certainly of Phoenician origin but remodeled by the crusaders. To the north along the coast are numerous sepulchral grottoes with many niches and steps cut out of the rock. In the town stands a mosque, partially restored in modern times, that was built over the tomb of a Moslem saint (Sīdī Ibrāhīm ibn-Adham, who lived in the 8th century), which, in its turn, had been placed on the site of a church.

BIBLIOG. E. Renan, Mission de Phénicie, Paris, 1864, p. 111; Benzinger, RE, s.v. Gabala; E. Frézouls, Les théâtres romains de Syrie, Ann. Archéol. de Syrie, II, 1952, pp. 54–58.

Kadesh (Gr., Σκαβίωσα Λαοδίκεια, Λαοδίκεια πρός Λιβάνω; Rom., Laodicea ad Libanum; Ar., Tell Nebi Mend). Nearby took place the celebrated battle between the Hittites and Ramses II (ca. 1286 B.C.). From this site comes a stele, probably of the 3d millen-nium B.C., of a very schematic anthropomorphous shape (Damascus, Nat. Mus.). All that remains of the Roman period, during which the city was called Laodicea ad Libanum, is a few hardly distinguishable ruins.

BIBLIOG. M. Pézard, Qadesh, Mission archéologiques à Tell Nebi Mend, 1921–22, Paris, 1931.

Latakia (Gr., Λαοδίκεια ἡ πρὸς Θαλάσσῃ, Λαοδικεῖς οἱ Παράλιοι; Rom., Laodicea ad Mare; Ar., Ladhiqiya, Lattaqiya; Old Fr., La Liche). Founded by Seleucus I, Laodicea formed a tetrapolis together with Antioch, Seleucia Pieria, and Apamea. Damaged by earthquakes, it was restored by Justinian, who made it the chief town and metro-politan see of the new province of Theodorias. Traces have been preserved of the checkerboard plan of the streets, some of which were bordered by colonnades; there are also remains of a Roman tetrapylon, of a theater, and of the port installations with a light-house shown on coins of the Roman period. The necropolis stretches along the seacoast to the north of the city.

The old town, to the east, is medieval in its layout, with tortuous, narrow streets, which have recently been cut by wider and more regular arteries; the new town has developed to the north of the harbor along the seashore in accordance with modern criteria of architecture and city planning. Among the main buildings are the Latin, Maro-nite, and Greek Orthodox churches and the al-Siaha – al-Istiaf hotel. On the edge of the city there is a large public park. Of the old Church of St. Andrew and the powerful castles of the Crusaders, which dom-inated the harbor, no traces remain.

BIBLIOG. E. Renan, Mission de Phénicie, Paris, 1864, pp. 111–12; M. de Vogüé, Syrie centrale, architecture civile et religieuse, I, 1865, pp. 75–76; Honigmann, RE, s.v. Laodikeia; J. Sauvaget, Le plan de Laodicée-sur-Mer (note complémentaire), Institut française de Damas, B. d'Et. O., VI, 1936, pp. 51–52; H. Seyrig, Sur les ères de quelques villes de Syrie: Laodicée, Syria, XXVII, 1950, pp. 26–32; H. Seyrig, Le phare de Laodicée, Syria, XXIX, 1952, pp. 54–59; A. Giuliano, EAA, s.v. Laodicea al Mare.

Ma'arrat el-Nu'man. This Moslem center retains from the Ayyu-bid period the square minaret of the principal mosque (which was rebuilt in later times) and, by the same architect, the beautiful Shafite Madrasah (1199). From the Ottoman period there is a large khan (caravansary) with portal and foundation inscription.

Mari (Bab., Ma'er; Ar., Tell Hariri). Near Abu Kemal on the Eu-phrates. The seat of an extremely ancient Mesopotamian dynasty, Mari — this form of the name is Sumerian — was destroyed for the first time toward the middle of the 3d millennium; later, when it had become the capital of a powerful Semitic state, it was definitively annihilated by Hammurabi about 1700 B.C. Eight periods can be distinguished, from that of Jamdat Naṣr to that of the Seleucids;

they were revealed by the excavations directed by A. Parrot. Remains from the first period (Jamdat Naṣr) were discovered in the deepest layers of the temples of Ishtar and of Shamash; from the latter has come to light some gray pottery with incised decoration. The second period (pre-Sargonic or proto-dynastic, 27th–24th cent. B.C.) is evidenced by the early ziggurat of reddish brick and by the sanctuaries of Ishtar, Ninkhursag, Shamash, Ninnizaza, and Ishtarat, along with statues (especially remarkable are those of Ebih-il and Ur-Nanshe, now in the Louvre and the Damascus Nat. Mus. respectively), a mother-of-pearl mosaic, and stone vases (both in Damascus, Nat. Mus.). The third period (Sargonic, 24th–22d cent. B.C.) is difficult to identify, but to it are attributed certain temples beneath the esplanade of the ziggurat, several seals, and some bronzes. The fourth period (period of the Governors, 22d–21st cent. B.C.) is contemporaneous with the 3d dynasty of Ur and is documented mainly by works in the Temple of Ninkhursag.

The fifth period (period of the Kings, 21st–18th cent. B.C.) is the greatest of all: to it belong the reconstructed ziggurat; the temples of Ishtar, Ninkhursag, and Shamash in their ultimate form; the Temple of Dagan; and above all the palace (IX, FIG. 787), which in its last form dates back to King Zimrilim and was destroyed by Hammurabi. This palace, in which more than 20,000 cuneiform tablets were found (Louvre), is a magnificent example of Mesopotamian architecture in sun-dried brick; it spreads over a surface of about 6 acres and has 260 rooms: ceremonial halls decorated with frescoes (some now in the Louvre) showing royal investiture scenes and divine sacrifices, living rooms provided with water, quarters for the administrative services, schools for the scribes, archives, storerooms, workshops, etc. In the palace and temples many statues were found, the two most famous being that of a goddess with a flowing vase and that of Ishtup-ilum, King of Mari and founder of the Temple of Dagan (both Aleppo, Nat. Mus.); among other finds were seals (Damascus, Nat. Mus.), the bronze lions that guarded the Temple of Dagan (one is in the Louvre), and the votive deposit commemorating the foundation of this temple (Louvre). From the sixth period (Old Babylonian and Kassite, 17th–13th cent. B.C.) have been found traces only of poor dwellings set up over the ruins of the palace after its destruction by Hammurabi. The seventh period (Assyrian and Neo-Babylonian, 13th–6th cent. B.C.) has left some remains of burials in double-bell-shaped terra-cotta vessels, interred mainly in the ruins. The eighth and last period (Seleucid) has only recently been identified; it is attested by poorly furnished burials, scattered over the surface of the tell, and by some modest houses.

BIBLIOG. R. Dussaud, Topographie historique de la Syrie antique et médiévale, Paris, 1927, pp. 187–94; A. Parrot, Les fouilles de Mari, première campagne, hiver 1933–34, rapport préliminaire, Syria, XVI, 1935, pp. 1–28, 117–40; A. Parrot, Les fouilles de Mari, sixième campagne, automne 1938, Syria, XXI, 1940, pp. 1–2; A. Parrot, Mari, une ville perdue, Paris, 4th ed., 1948; A. Parrot, ed., Studia Mariana (Documenta et monumenta Orientis antiqui, IV), Leiden, 1950; A. Parrot, Les fouilles de Mari, septième campagne, hiver 1951–52, Syria, XXIX, 1952, pp. 183–203; A.

Parrot, La huitième campagne de fouilles de Mari, octobre-décembre 195? Ann. Archéol. de Syrie, II, 1952, pp. 137–48; A. Parrot, Mari, Paris, 195 A. Parrot, Les fouilles de Mari, Syria, XXXII, 1955, pp. 185–211; Missio archéologique de Mari: I, A. Parrot, Le temple d'Ishtar, Paris, 1956; I A. Parrot, Les Palais, Part 1, Architecture, Paris, 1958, Part 2, Peinture murales, Paris, 1958, Part 3, Documents et monuments, Paris, 1959; A Parrot, EAA, s.v.

Mishrife (Accadian, Qatna). An important political and commer cial center as early as the beginning of the 2d millennium B.C. To th Neo-Sumerian period (end of 3d millennium) belongs the temple o the goddess Ningal, together with a sacred lake and probably tw enclosures containing respectively a sacred tree trunk and some sacre stones (baetuli). The royal palace, of the Mitannian period (middl of the 2d millennium B.C.), has produced, among other things, frag ments of mural paintings. From Qatna come a collection of archives a basalt male head (Aleppo, Nat. Mus.), and the bronze statuette o a seated divinity (or prince, according to Frankfort, 1958) — one o the most interesting pieces of Syrian sculpture of the 2d millenniun for its workmanship and iconography (Louvre).

BIBLIOG. R. du Mesnil du Buisson, Les ruines d'El-Mishrifé au nord est de Homs (Emèse), Syria, VII, 1926, pp. 289–325, VIII, 1927, pp. 13 33; R. du Mesnil du Buisson, L'ancienne Qatna ou les ruines d'El-Mishrif au nord-est de Homs (Emèse), Deuxième campagne de fouilles (1927) Syria, VIII, 1927, p. 277–301, IX, 1928, pp. 6–24, 81–89; R. du Mesn du Buisson, Les ruines d'El-Mishrifë au nord-est de Homs (Emèse): Pre mière campagne de fouilles à Qatna (1924), Paris, 1927; R. du Mesnil d Buisson, Compte rendu de la IVe campagne de fouilles à Mishrifé-Qatna Syria, XI, 1930, pp. 146–63; R. du Mesnil du Buisson, Le site archéologiqu de Mishrifé-Qatna, Paris, 1935.

Neyrab (Aram, n r b). The site of a necropolis that has been date to the 7th and 6th centuries B.C. From here come two Aramaic fu nerary steles decorated with bas-reliefs representing the deceased an showing strong Assyrian influence (Louvre), a terra-cotta relief rep resenting a nude goddess with her hands on her breasts, and som Neo-Babylonian tablets. From these tablets and from the inscription on the steles it appears that here was once a sanctuary of the moon god Sahar.

BIBLIOG. B. Carrière and A. Barrois, Fouilles de l'école archéologiqu français de Jerusalem effectuées à Neirab du 24 septembre au 5 novembr 1926, Syria, VIII, 1927, pp. 126–142, 201–212.

Palmyra (Bab. Tadmur; Heb., Tadmor, Aram., t d m r; Gr. Παλμύρα; Ar., Tadmur). This is the largest and most spectacula group of ruins in all of Syria. The extraordinary wealth of monument reflects the prosperity that this city's happy position as a necessar stage for caravans traveling from the Euphrates valley to the Mediter ranean enabled it to enjoy between the 1st and 3d centuries of our er Its brilliant economic and architectural development preceded th

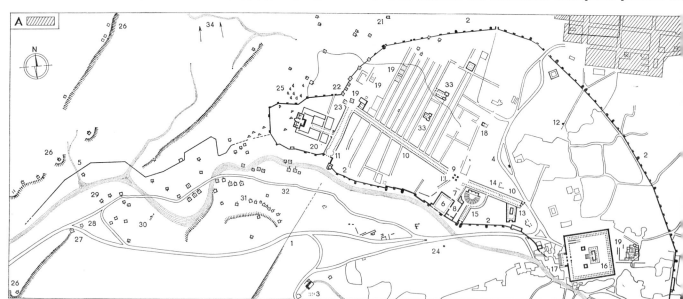

Palmyra, plan of the site. Key: (A) Modern village. Principal buildings of the ancient city: (1) Wall of the 1st or 2d century; (2) fortification wall completed by Justinian; (3) Efqa spring; (4) spring; (5) aqueduct; (6) agora; (7) senate house; (8) "seraglio"; (9) tetrapyle and transverse portico; (10 great colonnade; (11) transverse colonnade and oval open space; (12) votive column; (13) monumental arch; (14) Baths of Diocletian; (15) theater; (16 Temple of Bel; (17) propylaeum of the temple converted into a bastion; (18) cella of the Temple of Baal-shamin; (19) dwelling houses; (20) "Cam of Diocletian"; (21) House Tomb of Marōnā; (22) tower tombs reused as bastions; (23) portico of the Temple Tomb; (24) overturned votive colum and cemetery; (25) funerary grottoes; (26) tower tombs; (27) house tomb; (28) tower tomb; (29) Tower Tomb of Elahbel; (30) Hypogeum of Yarḥai (31) Tower Tomb of Jambliq; (32) house tomb; (33) Byzantine churches; (34) to the Arab castle (from J. Starcky, Palmyre, Paris, 1952, pl. 3)

eak of its political power, which is linked with the names of the prince denathus and his wife Zenobia, at first supporters and later rivals f Rome. Palmyra was destroyed by Aurelian in 273 and survived only s a fortress on the eastern limes of the Empire; its smaller surrounding all, built with reused material in the time of Diocletian, was later modeled by Justinian.

Inside the wall, the regular layout of the city and the principal ructures can still be recognized. Long sections of the colonnades that ned the main streets are still standing, as are many of the arches rected at the intersections. The square agora, surrounded by porti-oes, and a Roman theater of the Western type have been thoroughly xcavated. The Temple of Bel, the city's most important sanctuary, edicated in A.D. 32, stood in the middle of an artificial platform 245 ards square bounded by a high wall and porticoes. Almost equally ell preserved, the small Temple of Baal-shamin, erected in A.D. 31, was added to a more ancient monumental ensemble which com-rised several courts decorated with porticoes. Spread out around ne city are vast necropolises with their various types of collective urial structures, such as funerary towers, mausoleums, and hypo-eums, richly furnished with sculptures and often decorated with aintings.

A large museum has been built to house the finds made during xcavations.

BIBLIOG. R. Wood, The Ruins of Palmyra, otherwise Tedmor, in the esert, London, 1753; R. Wood, The Ruins of Palmyra and Balbec, London, 827; C. Watzinger, RE, s.v. Palmyra; H. Ingholt, Studier over palmy-nsk Skulptur, Copenhagen, 1928; T. Wiegand and D. Krencker, ed., almyra, Ergebnisse der Expeditionen von 1902 und 1917, 2 vol., Berlin, 932; H. Seyrig, Antiquités syriennes, Syria, 1934–58; O. I. Maenchen-elfen, from China to Palmyra, AB, XXV, 1943, pp. 358–62; H. Seyrig, almyra and the East, JRS, XL, 1950, pp. 1–7; J. Starcky, Palmyra, Guide rchéologique (Mélanges de l'Université Saint-Joseph, XXIV) Beirut, 941; H. Ingholt, Parthian Sculptures from Hatra: Orient and Hellas in Art nd Religion, Mem. of the Connecticut Acad. of Arts and Sciences, XII, 954; Palmyrene and Gandharian sculpture, an exhibition illustrating the ultural relations between the Parthian Empire and its neighbors, West and ast, Palmyra and Gandhara, Oct. 14 through Nov. 14, 1954 at the Yale niversity Art Gallery, New Haven, 1954; H. Ingholt, H. Seyrig, and J. tarcky, Recueil des tessères de Palmyre, Paris, 1955; P. Collart, Le sanctuaire e Baalshamin à Palmyre, fouilles Suisses 1954–55–56, rapport préliminaire, nn. Archéol. de Syrie, VII, 1957, pp. 67–90; K. Michałowski, Palmyre, uilles polonaises, 1959, Warsaw, The Hague, 1960; C. H. Kraeling, Color hotographs of the paintings in the tomb of the 3 brothers at Palmyra, nn. Archéol. de Syrie, XI–XIII, 1961–62, pp. 13–18 plus 42 figures on 16 lates; K. Michałowski, Fouilles polonaises à Palmyre, 1961, Ann. Archéol. e Syrie, XI–XII, 1961–62, pp. 63–82; C. Du Mesnil du Besson, De Sha-rafa dieu de Palmyre, à Baal Shamin, dieu de Hatra, aux IIᵉ et IIIᵉ siècles près J.-C. (Mélanges de l'Université Saint-Joseph, XXXVIII), Beirut, 962, pp. 143–160; R. du Mesnil du Buisson, Les tessères et les monnaies e Palmyre, inventaire des collections du Cabinet des Médailles de la Biblio-nèque Nationale, Paris, 1962; K. Michałowski, Fouilles 1960, Warsaw, 962; D. Schlumberger, Le prétendu camp de Dioclétien à Palmyre (Mé-nges de l'Université Saint-Joseph, XXXVIII), Beirut, 1962, pp. 79–97.

Qal'at Sim'an. Of this monastery complex, inside a perimeter all with towers, only impressive ruins remain. The basilica, which as probably built in the third quarter of the 5th century around the olumn of St. Simeon Stylites (d. 459), is the result of the fusion of a uilding on an octagonal plan with another on a cruciform plan. The ctagon consists of eight corner pillars with engaged columns, which ear great arches. The four arms that spread out from the octagon, ach divided into three aisles, are linked at the inner corners by apsid-oles; the eastern arm terminates in three apses flanked by prothesis nd diaconicon. The south entrance is preceded by a 6th-century arthex. The decorative sculpture, with traces of polychromy, is re-narkable. There are also remains of a baptistery, with adjoining ba-ilica, and monastic quarters.

BIBLIOG. M. de Vogüé, Syrie centrale: Architecture civile et religieuse, , Paris, 1865, pp. 141–52; H. C. Butler, American Archaeological expedi-on to Syria in 1899–1900, II, Architecture and other arts, New York, 1903, p. 18–294; H. C. Butler, Early Churches in Syria, Princeton, 1929, pp. 97–09; J. Mattern, À travers les villes mortes de Haute-Syrie: Promenades rchéologiques en 1928, 1929, 1931 (Mélanges de l'Université Saint-Joseph, VII), Beirut, 1933, pp. 117–135, 2d ed., 1944; G. Tchalenko, Villages an-ques de la Syrie du Nord, le massif du Bélus à l'époque romaine, 3 vols., aris, 1953–58.

Qalb Lauzeh. The basilica (late 5th or mid-6th cent.) has three isles separated by two rows of pillars that support great round arches. The projecting apse is decorated on the exterior with engaged columns nd Corinthian capitals. There is a narthex with three bays flanked y towers. Prothesis and diaconicon are included in the lateral aisles.

Bibliog. J. Lassus, Sanctuaires chrétiens de Syrie, Paris, 1947, pp. 75–6; G. Tchalenko, Villages antiques de la Syrie du Nord, le massif du Belus l'époque romaine, 3 vols, Paris, 1953–58.

Qanawat (Aram., Qanotha; Bib., Kenath; Gr., Κάναθα; Rom., Canatha, Kanatha). Situated in a picturesque setting of the Jebel ed-Druz region, Qanawat has a diversified group of Roman structures: the colonnades of several temples, a theater, a nymphaeum, some tombs, and, above all, the curious ensemble known as the "Seraglio." This last comprises columns belonging to a prostyle temple, as well as the portico, the atrium, and the hall of a large 4th-century basilica and the façade — with unusual decoration — of a barely more recent church.

BIBLIOG. M. de Vogüé, Syrie centrale: Architecture civile et religieuse, I, 1865, pp. 59–60; Moritz, RE, s.v. Kanatha; H. C. Butler, American Ar-chaeological expedition to Syria in 1899–1900, II, Architecture and other arts, New York, 1903, pp. 351–611; R. E. Brünnow and A. von Domaszewski, Die Provincia Arabia, III, Strasbourg, 1909, pp. 107–44; H. C. Butler, Princeton University Archaeological Expeditions to Syria in 1904–05 and 1909, II, Architecture, Section A, Southern Syria, Leiden, 1919, pp. 346–51; M. Dunand, Kanata et Κάναθα, Syria, XI, 1930, pp. 272–79; E. Frézouls, Les théâtres romains de Syrie, Ann. Archéol. de Syrie, II, 1952, pp. 61–64.

Qasr al-Hayr. This is the modern name ("the castle within the enclosure") designating two distinct archaeological complexes of the Syrian desert, the first (Qaṣr al-Hayr al-Gharbī, "the western") standing 45 miles by road to the southwest of Palmyra, the second (Qaṣr al-Hayr ash-Sharqī, "the eastern") about 75 miles by road to the northeast of the same city, near Sukhne. Since 1935 they have been partially excavated and can both be dated with certainty, thanks to inscriptions, to the time of the Ommiad caliph Hishām (724–43); they constitute important monuments of the most brilliant period of Arab dominion in Syria.

Qaṣr al-Hayr al-Gharbī (727) rises on a slight eminence where there had been a 6th-century Ghassanid monastery, some of whose elements were incorporated; it consisted of a rectangular enclosure with towers, a single monumental entrance, a central courtyard, and various apartments, baths, and service quarters between the courtyard and the outer wall — all according to the typical scheme of the Om-miad desert palaces. Of great historico-artistic importance are the vestiges of stucco ornamentation, consisting not only of geometric and floral elements but also of representations of living beings (e.g., dancing girls and a sovereign dressed in Persian fashion — perhaps the Caliph himself). Two large frescoes with various human figures reveal the same twofold Hellenistic and Sassanian influence. Both the paintings and the fragments of sculpture are exhibited in the Damascus National Museum, where many of the stucco lattices have been carefully re-stored.

Qaṣr al-Hayr ash-Sharqī (X, FIG. 751), which has been excavated only in part, was built two years later and consists of two groups of ruins. The first is the Caliph's palace, surrounded by the usual wall with towers; according to a plausible hypothesis, it is here and not at Sergiopolis that the Ruṣāfa of Hishām, the Caliph's favorite place of residence, should be located. Nearby but quite separate from the sov-ereign's residence is the fortified citadel (madīna), with a mosque whose three transverse aisles are divided by a central transept, as in the Great Mosque of Damascus.

BIBLIOG. D. Schlumberger, Les fouilles de Qasr El-Heir El-Gharbi (1936–38) Rapport préliminaire, Syria, XX, 1939, pp. 195–238, 324–73; D. Schlumberger, Deux fresques omeyyades, Syria, XXV, 1946, pp. 86–102.

Raqqa (Gr., Νικηφόριον, Καλλίνικον). This Moslem center on the Euphrates was originally founded by Alexander the Great. In 772 a new city was constructed here by the Abbasside caliph al-Manṣūr, founder of Baghdad, who called it Al Rafiqa. It was a fa-vorite summer residence of Hārūn al-Rashīd. Later, as the ancient town of Raqqa gradually fell into ruins, its name came to be applied to the new city. The modern town occupies only the southwestern corner of Al Rafiqa. The main archaeological remains are the city walls (built of unbaked brick) with round towers; the great mosque of al-Manṣūr, restored in the 12th century by Nūr ad-Dīn; the Qaṣr al-Salām (Palace of Peace) of al-Rashīd; and another palace, probably built by his son, the caliph al-Mu'taṣim. Many objects found in this locality are now in the Damascus National Mueseum. About 6 miles away, at Hiraqla (Heraclea), there is a circular complex with towers and four gates leading to an internal terraced construction. Many finds in glazed pottery of the characteristic local style (10th–13th cent.), have been made at Raqqa (Damascus, Nat. Mus.; Louvre; Vict. and Alb.; Met. Mus.; Washington, D.C., Freer Gall. of Art; etc.).

BIBLIOG. E. Herzfeld and F. Sarre, Archäologische Reise im Eufrat- und Tigrisgebiet, 4 vols., Berlin, 1911–20.

Rusafa (Bib., Rezeph; Gr., Ῥησάφα, Σεργιούπολις; Rom., Re-sapha, Sergiopolis). Located in a desert landscape south of the Eu-phrates, Rusafa is famous for its imposing ensemble of Christian structures, still well preserved as a result of their isolated location.

They evoke the memory of St. Sergius, who suffered martyrdom here about the year 305, and of the pilgrimages to his tomb. Inside a massive wall forming a rectangle, with its gates, towers, and sentry walk still almost intact, are the ruins of a large three-aisled basilica of the 5th or 6th century (IX, FIG. 87), of two other churches, and of some monumental cisterns.

BIBLIOG. H. Spanner and S. Guyer, Rusafa, die Wallfahrtsstadt des heiligen Sergios, Berlin, 1926; J. Kollwitz, Die Grabungen in Resafa, Herbst 1952, Ann. Archéol. de Syrie, IV-V, 1954-55, pp. 77-88; J. Kollwitz, W. Wirth and W. Karnapp, Die Grabungen in Resafa Herbst 1954 und 1956, Ann. Archéol. de Syrie, VIII-IX, 1958-59, pp. 21-54.

Sfira (Sefire). This small town probably corresponds to ancient Sipri. After the discovery of the torso of a statue representing an armed man, datable to about the middle of the 2d millennium B.C. (Aleppo, Nat. Mus.), a rapid exploration of the area was carried out, which led to the discovery of a great fortified gate and a circuit of massive walls with semicircular towers about 130 ft. apart. From the same locality come some important 8th-century Aramaic inscriptions containing the text of a treaty between the king of Arpad and the king of the Aramaic k t k.

BIBLIOG.: R. Dussaud, Torse de statuette de Sfiré, Syria, IX, 1928, pp. 170-71; A. Dupont-Sommer, Les inscriptions araméennes de Sfiré, Stèles I et II, Paris, 1958; A. Dupont-Sommer, Une inscription araméenne inédite de Sfiré, BMBeyrouth, XIII, 1956 (1958), pp. 23-41; C. Picard, Le rite magique des εἴδωλα de cire brûlés attesté sur trois stèles araméennes de Sfiré vers le milieu du VIIIᵉ siècle av. notre ère, RA, II, 1961, pp. 85-87.

Shagar Bazar (Chagar Bazar). This site can probably be identified as Shubat-Enlil. There is testimony of the existence of the ancient city from the 5th millennium to 1400 B.C. During the last centuries of its existence it passed under Assyrian and then Mitannian rule. Of the oldest period (Neolithic) there remain many terra-cotta figurines, which frequently represent the nude goddess or the bucranium; others were probably amulets (e.g., those in the form of a double ax). The city then passed through phases of Mesopotamian culture (Samarra and Tell Halaf) and, toward the beginning of the 2d millennium, became the center of diffusion for the so-called "Khabur ware." It was also a Hurrite center where horses were bred on a large scale; the horse is often represented in painted terra-cotta statuettes. From the Assyrian period there remain dwellings (with tombs under the pavement), a building used for archives, stables, and the so-called "house of the soothsayers."

BIBLIOG. M. E. L. Mallowan, The Excavations at Tall Chagar Bazar and an Archaeological Survey of the Habur Region, Iraq, III, 1936, pp. 1-86, IV, 1937, pp. 91-177; C. J. Gadd, Tablets from Chagar Bazar, 1936, Iraq, IV, 1937, pp. 78-185; M. E. L. Mallowan, The excavations at Tall Chagar Bazar and an Archaeological Survey of the Habur region, Second campaign, 1936, Iraq, IV, 1937, pp. 91-177; M. E. L. Mallowan, Excavations at Brak and Chagar Bazar, Syria, Iraq, IX, 1947, pp. 1-266; M. E. L. Mallowan, 25 years of Mesopotamian Discovery, 1932-56, London, 1956, pp. 12-23; C. Garbini, EAA, s.v. Chagar Bazar.

Shahba (Gr., Φιλιππούπολις; Rom., Philippopolis). Philippopolis was founded in the Jabel ed-Druz region by the emperor Philip the Arabian in the 3d century. The city was built according to the plan of a Roman camp. The gates of the quadrilateral surrounding wall, the flagged pavement of the cardo and the decumanus maximus, a theater, baths, and several other structures are still well preserved. Some large mosaics have been taken to the National Museum of Damascus.

BIBLIOG. E. Honigmann RE, s.v. Philippopolis; H. C. Butler, American Archaeological Expeditions to Syria in 1899-1900, II, Architecture and other arts, New York, 1903, pp. 376-96; R. E. Brünnow and A. von Domaszewski, Die Provincia Arabia, III, Strasbourg, 1909, pp. 145-79; H. C. Butler, Princeton University Archaeological Expeditions to Syria in 1904-05 and 1909, II, Architecture, Leiden, 1919, pp. 359-60; E. Frézouls, Les théâtres romains de Syrie, Ann. Archéol. de Syrie, II, 1952, pp. 64-96; E. Will, Une nouvelle mosaïque de Chahba Philippopolis, Ann. Archéol. de Syrie, III, 1953, pp. 27-48; P. Coupel and E. Frézouls, Le théâtre de Philippopolis en Arabie, Paris, 1956.

Si' (Gr., Σεῖα; Rom., Seia). In this Nabataean locality are the remains of a great cultual complex constructed around three successive courtyards, whose axis is slightly deviated toward the right. Each courtyard is flanked by terraces upon which stand minor temples, while monumental gates mark the passage from one court to another. At the farther end of the last court and surrounded by a colonnade stood the monumental temple of Baal-shamin, founded in 33 B.C. and constructed during the next two hundred years. Outside the sacred precincts there are Roman baths.

BIBLIOG. H. C. Butler, The Temple of Dūsharā at Si' in the Haur[Florilegium, ou Recueil de travaux d'érudition dédiés à Monsieur le Marq[Melchior de Vogüé à l'occasion du 80ᵉ anniversaire de sa naissance 18 oc[bre 1909, Paris, 1909, pp. 79-91; H. C. Butler, Princeton University Archa[logical Expeditions to Syria in 1904-05 and 1909, II, Architecture, Section Part 6, Leiden, 1916; G. Garbini, EAA, s.v. Seia.

Suweida (Gr., Σόαδα, Διονυσιάς; Rom., Soada, Dionysia[This city, founded by Nabataeans in the 1st century B.C. and und[Roman rule from the time of Trajan, was known from the 3d centu[as Dionysias. There are many remains of the Roman period, but th[have not yet been archaeologically explored: among the most importa[are a peripteral temple, a bridge over the Wadi Suweida, inscriptio[dedicated to Trajan and mentioning a nymphaeum, and a funera[monument dedicated to a woman named Hamrath. This last is co[posed of a quadrangular base with columns, above which rises a st[pyramid. From the same locality come numerous Nabataean sculptu[(especially noteworthy is a relief showing the Judgment of Par[now in the Louvre); some of these are in the National Museum Damascus and some in the small local museum.

BIBLIOG. R. E. Brünnow and A. von Domaszewski, Die Provin[Arabia, III, Strasbourg, 1909, pp. 88-102; M. Dunand, Rapport sur u[mission archéologique au Djebel Druze, Syria, VII, 1926, pp. 326-35;] Dunand, Mission archéologique au Djebel Druze: Le musée de Souei[inscriptions et monuments figurés, Paris, 1934; EAA, s.v. Dionysias.

Tartus (Gr., 'Αντάραδος; Rom., Antaradus, Tortosa; Old F[Tortose). This ancient colony of Arvad, rebuilt by Constantius in 346, underwent destruction and occupation many times. A power[fortress was erected (partly with archaeological materials) by the Te[plars in the 12th century and enlarged in the 13th. Inside its doub[row of walls, protected by two wide moats, is still to be seen part the medieval architectural complex, including the great hall, the chap[and the keep. The Cathedral of Our Lady of Tortosa with its Roma[esque and Gothic capitals was built in the 12th and 13th centur[over the original Byzantine shrine; it is now a museum.

Tell Brak. This locality of Neolithic origin was inhabited un[about 1400 B.C. In the oldest layers pottery of the Tell Halaf and ['Ubaid types has been found. About the beginning of the 3d m[lennium B.C. (period of Jamdat Nasr), the locality shows signs of clo[cultural relations with the Sumerian world; a temple, which was [built several times, has revealed numerous little stone idols of a qu[characteristic shape, from which it takes the name of the "Eye Ter[ple." Of the same period are some carved male heads that show[peculiar sensitivity that cannot be related to any Sumerian influenc[In the second half of the 3d millennium the city was conquered [the Accadian dynasty, and Naram-Sin built a great palace there. T[most interesting remains from the 2d millennium are vessels of t[Mitannian era, in the shape of human heads.

BIBLIOG. M. E. L. Mallowan, Excavations at Brak and Chagar Baz[Syria, Iraq, IX, 1947, pp. 1-266; C. Ziegler, Die Tempelterrasse von T[Brak, Mit. der Deutsch.-O. Gesellschaft, LXXXII, 1950, pp. 1-18; M. L. Mallowan, 25 Years of Mesopotamian Discovery, 1932-56, London, 19[pp. 24-38.

Tell Halaf (Accadian, Guzana; Bib., Gozan). In the oldest a[deepest layers of this site (4th millennium B.C.) a type of pottery h[been found with painted decoration consisting mainly of rather st[ized naturalistic motifs (animals and human figures), which has giv[the name "Tell Halaf" to a type of protohistoric culture. Much lat[at the beginning of the 1st millennium B.C., the locality bore the nar[of Guzana and was the capital of an Aramaic state (Bit Bakhya[in which the Neo-Hittite element was quite strong. To this peri[belongs the Palace of Kaparu (I, FIG. 879) — the typical and mc[famous example of a bît-hilani — with the architrave of its porti[supported by carved human figures; in the palace were also fou[numerous carved reliefs (Aleppo, Nat. Mus.; East Berlin, Vorde[asiatisches Mus.).

BIBLIOG. M. von Oppenheim, Der Tell Halaf, eine neue Kultur i[ältesten Mesopotamien, Leipzig, 1931; M. von Oppenheim, Tell Hal[4 vols., Berlin, 1943-62.

Tell Suqas. A coastal locality whose oldest settlement dat[back to the 6th millennium B.C. In the 2d millennium it entertain[close relations with Ugarit, attested by a tablet from Ugarit found [the spot. Later a colony of Greek merchants was established the[The buildings so far excavated belong to the 6th century B.C.; remar[able among them is a sanctuary near the southern harbor.

BIBLIOG. P. J. Riis, L'activité de la mission archéologique danoise s[la côte phénicienne en 1958, 1959, 1960, Ann. Archéol. de Syrie, VIII-I[1958-59, pp. 107-32, X, 1960, pp. 111-32, XI-XII, 1961-62, pp. 133-4[

ll Halaf, plan of the site. (1) City walls; (2) south gate; (3) walls of the citadel; (4) south gate of the citadel; (5) bastion of unbaked brick; (6) great
.rtyard; (7) Palace of Kaparu, the so-called "Temple Palace"; (8) large dwelling; (9) Assyrian house; (10) northeast palace; (11) Assyrian temple;
.) sanctuary (*from M. von Oppenheim, 1943, I*).

Til Barsip (Ar., Tell Ahmar). The first traces of settlement
te back to the 4th millennium B.C., as testified by pottery of the Tell
alaf and later of the al-'Ubaid style. There is a necropolis of the
l millennium. Dominated by the Hittites in the 2d millennium,
became the capital of the Aramaic state of Bit Adini at the beginning
the 1st. In 855 B.C. it was conquered by Shalmaneser III and became
provincial Assyrian capital (Kar-Shulmanasharidu, "Port of Shal-
aneser") with a palace and city walls, the latter having three gates
which at least one was flanked by lions. The most interesting
onuments of the city consist in a series of steles with reliefs repre-
nting divinities of the Syro-Anatolian type and frescoes from the
.ssyrian palace; the latter (Aleppo, Nat. Mus.), which belong to two
fferent periods (9th–8th and 7th cent.), generally reproduce the same
onography as appears on the reliefs of palaces in Assyria itself.

BIBLIOG. F. Thureau-Dangin and M. Dunand, Til-Barsip, Paris, 1936.

Ugarit (Ar., Ras Shamra). This locality was inhabited from the
ost ancient times, and, following the excavations conducted by C.
A. Schaeffer, at least five different periods can be distinguished
ter the early Neolithic (pre-ceramic). The first (5th millennium
C.) reveals pottery of a fairly archaic type; in the second (4th mil-
nnium), the pottery appears to be closely related to the Mesopo-
mian ware called al-'Ubaid; in the third (3d millennium), it is of the
anaanitic type. The period of greatest prosperity was the fourth,
om the 21st to the 14th century B.C. At that time, the city, in which
e Phoenician element was then definitely predominant, developed a
riving commerce with the main centers of civilization in the eastern
lediterranean — Egypt, Cyprus, and the Aegean, Cretan, and My-
naean areas; this was facilitated by the intense traffic of the harbor
.ευκός Λιμήν, mod. Minet el-Beida), from which it was easy to

reach the hinterland. It is from this period that the temples of Baal
and Dagon date. Ugarit's great economic prosperity was interrupted
in the middle of the 14th century B.C. by an earthquake accompanied
by a tidal wave and a great fire but still continued into the following
and last period of the city (14th–12th cent. B.C.), until it was finally
destroyed by the invasion of the Peoples of the Sea about 1180 B.C.

The royal palace (FIG. 874) belongs to the last two periods; it
is akin to those of Mari and Alalakh: around inner courts and gardens
stood the state rooms, the private apartments, the administrative and
diplomatic archives. In both periods, figural art was dominated by
eclecticism: Egyptian, Aegean, and Mesopotamian elements were
combined, superimposed, and sometimes, particularly in the case of
smaller objects, happily blended into subtle decorative compositions.
The ivories, goldwork, jewels, engraved stones, bronzes, and pottery
that have been found at Ugarit and Minet el-Beida, together with
the steles sculptured in relief, are nearly all conserved either in the
Louvre or in the National Museums of Damascus and Aleppo. In
the basement of the palace were five great burial chambers; the corbeled vaults that support the roofs of these and several other tombs
betray Aegean influence.

Situated at some distance to the east of the palace, the Temple
of Dagon contained two courts, in one of which was a massive stone
altar. Nearby, built around three sides of a courtyard, stood a library
which also served as the residence of the high priest and a school for
scribes.

Although outside the field of the figural arts, the fundamental part
played by Ugarit in the invention of the alphabet should not be overlooked; in the 15th and 14th centuries B.C. there was developed an
alphabetic form of writing, consisting of 30 cuneiform letters, in which
was set down a quantity of literature, mostly epic and mythological
poems.

BIBLIOG. C. F. A. Schaeffer, Les fouilles de Minet-El-Beida et de Ras Shamra, campagne du printemps, 1929, rapport sommaire, Syria, X, 1929, pp. 285–97, Note additionelle by René Dussaud, pp. 297–303; Mission de Ras-Shamra: C. F. A. Schaeffer, Ugaritica, I, Paris, 1939; Mission de Ras-Shamra, V: C. F. A. Schaeffer, Ugaritica, II, Paris, 1949; Mission de Ras-Shamra, IX: C. F. A. Schaeffer, Ugaritica, III, Paris, 1956; Mission de Ras-Shamra, XV: C. F. A. Schaeffer, Ugaritica, IV, Paris, 1962; C. F. A. Schaeffer, Première rapport sur la reprise des fouilles de Ras Shamra en Syrie, Ann. Archéol. de Syrie, I, 1951, pp. 5–18; C. F. A. Schaeffer, Les fondements pré- et proto- historique de Syrie, du néolitique précéramique au bronze ancien, Syria, XXXVIII, 1961, pp. 7–22, 221–42; C. F. A. Schaeffer, Nouvelles découvertes à Ras Shamra-Ugarit, CRAI, 1961 (1962), pp. 232–36, 299–300; C. F. A. Schaeffer, Résumé des résultats de la XXIIIᵉ campagne de fouilles à Ras Shamra-Ugarit, automne 1960, Ann. Archéol. de Syrie, XI–XII, 1961–62, pp. 187–96; M. Liverani, Storia di Ugarit, nell'età degli archivi politici, Rome, 1962; C. F. A. Schaeffer, Beauté et laideur à Ugarit, MPiot, LII, 1962, pp. 9–14.

Paul COLLART, Franceso GABRIELI, Francesco NEGRI ARNOLDI

Illustrations: 7 figs. in text.

SYRO-PALESTINIAN ART. Among the ancient art cultures of the Near East (see ASIA, WEST: ANCIENT ART), that of the Syro-Palestinian region displays an undeniable historical autonomy. While there is no denying the considerable cultural debt owed by Syria-Palestine to the major neighboring cultures, it is possible to identify some features of Syro-Palestinian art that are typical and autonomous with regard to the art of Egypt (see EGYPTIAN ART), of Mesopotamia (q.v.), and of Anatolia (see HITTITE ART).

SUMMARY. Prehistory (col. 867). Early Bronze Age (col. 868): *Architecture; Sculpture; Minor arts.* Middle and late Bronze Age (col. 872): *Architecture; Sculpture; Minor arts.* First millennium B.C. (col. 878): *Architecture; Sculpture; Minor arts.* Survivals and diffusion (col. 881).

PREHISTORY. From the 8th to the 4th millennium B.C. the Syro-Palestinian region, together with Mesopotamia, was in the vanguard of civilization (see MEDITERRANEAN PROTOHISTORY). It was precisely Syria and Palestine that witnessed the first signs of agricultural activity, the first urban settlements (Jericho and Ugarit rose in the Mesolithic period), and the first pottery. The discontinuity of the data available makes it impossible to identify either a coherent development or organically connected cultural areas and periods.

The earliest artistic manifestations of the region are probably represented by a few series of rock engravings — datable in all likelihood to the Mesolithic — discovered at Umm el-Qatafa (near Bethlehem) and at Kilwa in southeastern Jordan (XI, PL. 298). The engravings consist of animal representations which, by their arrangement in isolated figures (rather than superimposed), by the frequent rendering of only two of the quadrupeds' legs, and by the occasionally soft and wavy lines of the profiles, recall similar (though later) representations in the Sahara region. Also datable to the Mesolithic (Natufian) period are some bones carved in animal shapes, found in Palestine (see PREHISTORY, col. 616).

During the "prepottery" stage of the Neolithic (7th–6th millennium B.C.) there evolved at Jericho (IX, PL. 413) and Ugarit a type of defensive architecture of considerable dimensions, attaining a monumental character at Jericho in the large circular tower with a central passage. From Neolithic Jericho (6th–5th millennium) come the first manifestations of plastic art: the human skulls covered with fine clay and modeled so as to reconstruct the original features display, in the best specimens, a refined plastic sensitivity based only partly on the skull's bone structure (IX, col. 636 and PL. 414). The same talent for modeling is revealed also by some figures of unbaked clay: the modeling of the face in the best-known specimen (the head is completely flattened) is strikingly delicate, although the coarse addition of color intended to represent the beard and the hair reveals the primitive nature of the work (PL. 358). The last phase of the Neolithic saw the introduction of pottery and the diffusion of statuettes — among them a remarkable female figure in stone (Br. Mus.) from northern Syria, strongly recalling

those later brought to light at Hacılar (southwestern Anatoli To this phase, too, should probably be attributed the megalit monuments spread over the whole area but particularly r merous to the east of the river Jordan, as well as the rock e gravings of Demir Qapu (northeastern Syria): figures of anim and hunters are rendered here by pecking out the whole figu rather than just by an outline.

During the chalcolithic period from the middle of the ... millennium to approximately 3200 B.C. there are indications foreign trends that blended with local elements in Syria a Palestine. In the northern part of the country, and particula at Ugarit, the first pottery displays affinities to that of Cyp and Thessaly; later work appears related to the Mesopotam production of Tell Halaf — especially rich at Shagar Bazar and afterward to that of al'Ubaid (IX, PLS. 415, 416, FIG. 65 Tell esh-Sheikh (near Alalakh) provides an original producti only partly inspired by Mesopotamian models. The somewl complex manifestations of the architecture of this period c be seen from some specimens of cinerary urns in the form houses: the one from Hadera, painted and with a sloping ro reveals western influences; and one discovered at Azor displ a complex two-storied structure, with large windows even the façade. Isolated instances of seal impressions from the ch colithic period, with stylized bucranes, deer, and other anim have come to light in Palestine (Prausnitz, 1955); they rev a clear Mesopotamian origin, from the repertory of the T Halaf pottery. Toward the end of this period a culture emerg in the Palestinian region that displays its most original asp in the mural paintings of Teleilat Ghassul. Animals, demo geometric motifs, and possibly human figures that have co to light — albeit in fragments — from old and recent excavatic carried out on that site constitute an attestation unique of kind. The finds from Beersheba — among them some rema able bone figurines — belong to the last phase of this peri as may some metal objects discovered near the Dead Sea

EARLY BRONZE AGE. The 3d millennium B.C., which witnes the development of the early Bronze Age culture (3200–2 B.C.), constitutes Syria's protohistoric period; Mesopotam and, especially, Egyptian mentions provide indirect documen tion. At this point the cultural (and occasionally political) pr ence of Mesopotamia and Egypt began to make itself clea felt. This occurred more markedly — though not exclusively in the areas of direct contact with either of these regions; P estine was, besides, the route by which some Mesopotam influences reached Egypt. The early Bronze Age art cultu reached its peak between 2600 and 1300 B.C. (the establishm of many new Palestinian cities dates from this period), conte poraneously with the Mesopotamian protodynastic period a with the Egyptian Old Kingdom. While the general patt of the archaeological phases of this period is reasonably cle the same cannot be said of the artistic development, even thou the surviving monuments are more numerous than those of preceding period. The general view is therefore full of ga it can be stated, nevertheless, that, while relief sculpture and minor arts show some dependence on foreign models, architect and stone statuary display original aspects.

Architecture. The architectural remains of the early Bror Age, scarce though they be, provide an idea of both the typol ical richness and originality of building techniques of period. Little can be said about the palace of Alalakh X (2700–2350 B.C.) except for the presence of powerful br columns that reflect unquestionable contacts with Mesopotam but a temple belonging to the same level is unusual: the spa remains of this building — an interesting parallel to which a small clay model (Aleppo, Mus. Nat.) from Selemiya (Sa miyye, near Hama) — show a structure with a projecting e trance; inside this were a hearth and a staircase leading to actual sanctuary, which was placed on the prolongation of t main axis, raised by some 15 ft. This type of building has other parallels, except perhaps in some small Assyrian c models, if indeed these do not represent altars (Berlin, Sta Mus., Vorderasiatische Abteilung).

SYRO-PALESTINIAN ART

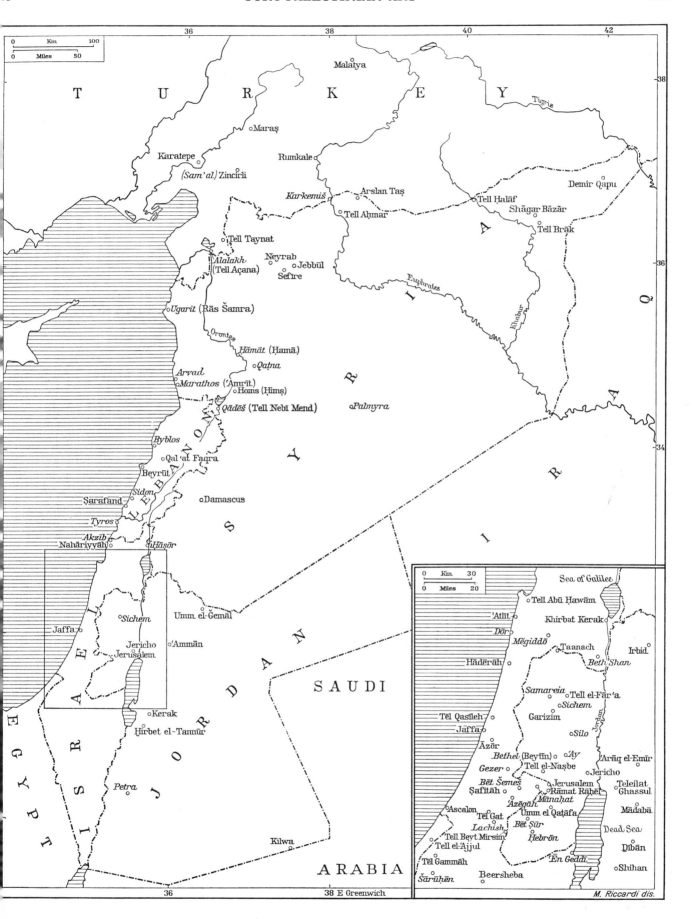

Principal archaeological centers and sites of the Syro-Palestinian area. (Broken lines indicate modern national boundaries.)

In the Palestinian region the most interesting remains are those of Tell Gat, Ai ('Ay; FIG. 871), and Megiddo. At Tell Gat, the building found at level VI, datable to the early Bronze Age rather than to the chalcolithic as suggested by S. Yeivin (1960), comprised a hall preceded by a trapezoidal courtyard with two rows of pillars along the walls facing the entrance, plus an isolated pillar to the right. The similarities of this building to that of Ai and to the later one of Megiddo XIX (elongated hall, internal pillars, entrance in one of the long sides) suggest

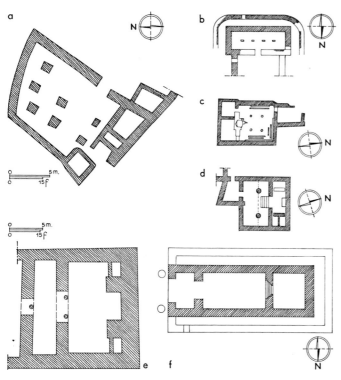

Plans of Syro-Palestinian temples. (a) Tell Gat, Level VI, early Bronze Age (from Oriens Antiquus, no. 1, 1962, p. 25); (b) Ai, about 2600 B.C. (from J. B. Pritchard, The Ancient Near East in Pictures, Princeton, 1954, p. 231); (c) Lachish, 14th–13th cent. B.C., and (d) Beth Shan, level VI, 12th cent. B.C. (from K. Galling, Biblisches Reallexikon, Tübingen, 1937, p. 514); (e) Alalakh, 13th cent. B.C. (from L. Woolley, Alalakh, Oxford, 1955, p. 83); (f) Jerusalem, Temple of Solomon, 10th cent. B.C. (from Galling, op. cit., p. 514).

that this also was a temple. The structure at Ai — built about the year 2600 — had a long rectangular hall with a central row of four pillars and with the entrance, preceded by a spacious rectangular forecourt, on one of the long sides. A second opening, in the right-hand corner of the same side, led to a narrow passage that skirted the hall on three sides. Finally, at Megiddo, there is a massive terracing wall dividing two wide platforms: on the lower was an extensive building with large rectangular rooms, the general plan of which, however, it has been impossible to reconstruct; there was in addition a sacred area, with a large stone altar (?) in the shape of a truncated cone, the top of which was reached by a series of steps. On the upper platform was a straight road flanked with houses.

Sculpture. Sculpture in the round is represented in the 3d millennium by some stone and metal pieces. Among the works in stone, a sort of basalt stele (28 in. high) from Tell Nebi Mend (Damascus, Nat. Mus.) is outstanding for its strict stylization and its adherence to an abstract vision; a roughhewn statue from Tell Brak, however, is quite grotesque (Br. Mus.). A head from Hama (Copenhagen, Nat. Mus.), in which an evident descriptive aim is frustrated by an equally evident poverty of expressive means, deserves some attention for its sense of volume, to be observed later in Hittite sculptures. Some bronze statuettes from Tell Jedeideh (Chicago, Univ., O. Inst.) reveal both a striking technical ability and that descriptive taste that characterizes

the most primitive handicrafts production. Some reliefs of th period can more easily be referred to specific art cultures. Th Mesopotamian model is evident in the iconography of tw steles from Jebelet el-Beida (M. von Oppenheim, Tell Hala London and New York, 1933, pls. 62–63) of extremely coars workmanship, and to a lesser extent — together with loc elements — in two steles from Rumkale (Louvre), where th workmanship is just as poor. (See also MESOPOTAMIA, col. 746

Minor arts. The manifestations of the minor arts are of less importance. Two small ivory bulls' heads from Jericho (Clev land, 1961) and Beth Yerah (mod. Khirbat Kerak; Bar-Ado 1962) are akin to Mesopotamian sculptures and show remarkab technical ability. In the field of glyptics (see GEMS AND GLYPTIC SEALS) there was a notable diffusion (initially going as far Egypt) of the Mesopotamian type of cylinder seal; one suc covered with hieroglyphs was discovered at Byblos (Beiru Mus. Nat.). The northern part of the country also retained th more ancient form, the stamp seal — examples have been foun at Tell esh-Sheikh — decorated with geometric and anim figures, the figural repertory depending largely on that of Me opotamia, with some stylistic anticipations of the glyptics the 2d millennium (Antioch, Archaeol. Mus.).

MIDDLE AND LATE BRONZE AGE. The Bronze Age cultu continued in Syria and Palestine through most of the 2d mi lennium B.C., divided from an archaeological point of view int two principal periods (middle Bronze Age, 2100–1550; lat Bronze Age, 1550–1200), during which the culture underwe no striking changes such as those that characterized the transitio from the early to the middle Bronze Age, and from the late Bronz to the Iron Age. From a political point of view, Palestine and th Phoenician cities lay within the sphere of more or less dire Egyptian domination, though enjoying a considerable measu of local autonomy; north-central Syria, after a few centuries division into states which were little more than cities and whic actively participated in Mesopotamian events, entered the Hi tite and Mitannian orbit with varying degrees of independenc while pursuing a policy of compromise with regard to Egyp In this context of continuous historical contacts there evolve a vast cultural koine, with numerous foreign motifs and livel local reactions. Greater originality is to be observed in nort central Syria during the period that witnessed more animate policies of independence and of aggrandizement, that is to sa at the time of the Amorite dynasties.

Architecture. The original character of the architectur of the 3d millennium was largely retained in the subsequer period. The outstanding structure is the great palace Yarimlim at Alalakh (18th cent. B.C.; FIG. 873), divided by spacious courtyard into two wings: the northern of an offici nature, with ample, regular rooms; the southern domestic, wit many small rooms around a private courtyard on the groun floor, while the upper floor comprises large rooms decorate with paintings and divided in part by wooden columns on ba salt bases. By the arrangement of the main reception room (a large hall, broader than long, through which was reached sort of anteroom separated from the audience chamber by monumental passage with four wooden columns), and by th use of basalt orthostats in the central courtyard and receptio rooms, the palace of Yarimlim anticipated the most character istic elements of the Syrian (and Assyrian) princely dwelling of the 1st millennium — the so-called hilani (see below) and th decoration on orthostats. Along more general lines, the palac can be related to the great princely structures of Beycesulta (IX, FIG. 651) and of Crete (I, col. 875; IV, FIG. 85; VII PL. 92; IX, FIG. 653).

In spite of notable economic prosperity, Palestine in th first half of the 2d millennium shows no structures comparab to that of Alalakh; the political subjection of the region to Egyp did not allow any monumental affirmations of the power exer cised by local governors or princelings. Architectural activity re sulted therefore in luxurious villas, which took up on a larg scale the plan of ordinary dwellings; examples have been foun

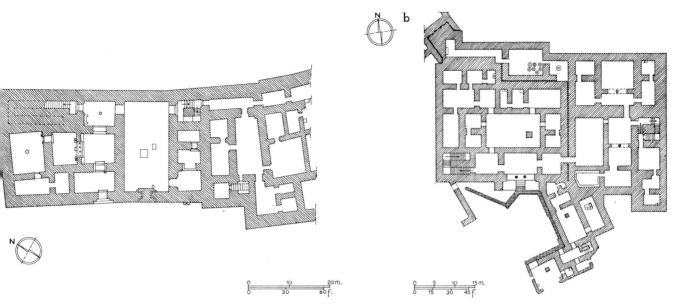

Alalakh, plans of the palaces. (*a*) Palace of Yarimlim; (*b*) Palace of Niqmepa (*from Frankfort, 1954, pp. 139, 146*).

Shechem (Sichem), Megiddo, Jericho, Bethel, Tell Beit irsim (FIG. 877), and Tell el-'Ajjul — the last-named being rtified. They were arranged around a spacious court usually iced in an eccentric position, on which opened more or less iple and regular rooms according to the importance of the iilding; in the center of the court stood a pillar that probably rved as support for a light roofing; the family rooms were on e upper floor. Typical of the middle Bronze Age are the forti- ation walls that rose all over the Syro-Palestinian region: un- e the more ancient ones, which were vertical, these have rather sloping outer face; the gateways have a nutcracker- aped ground plan with two or three narrowings. This type fortification, probably of Syrian origin — Alalakh, Ugarit, irchemish (Karkemiš), Qatna — spread subsequently in the ittite world and in Palestine [Shechem, Jericho, Lachish, Beit ır, Hazor (Ḥāṣōr), etc.].

In the field of religious architecture, various types of temple ere adopted. The three in Ugarit, built about the beginning the 2d millennium, all comprise a court with a central altar eceded by three steps; a pronaos leading to a wider cella ces the court. Of the two in Byblos (IX, FIG. 181), one com- ised two consecutive courts, of which the inner — slightly ised — contained the cella and some twenty obelisks of various mensions. The other, larger, temple was built about 2000 B.C. d survived until Roman times; it consisted of three consecutive lls, surrounded by a paved esplanade where were placed lossal statues of seated divinities and of rulers in the iconog- phy of the walking pharaoh. The court with the open-air :ar, common to Syrian temples, was perhaps due to a Semitic eminomadic) type of cult. In Palestine, the main lines of the eviously mentioned temple at Megiddo repeat the type of e 3d millennium. At Shechem, on the other hand, a new pe appeared, perhaps a simplification of the northern Syrian ie: its plan was rectangular and the cella was preceded by a all courtyard.

The most striking building of the late Bronze Age is the lace of Niqmepa at Alalakh (15th cent.; FIG. 873; PL. 357), here features from the palace of Yarimlim were taken up, arking a transition phase between the latter and the *hilani*. stepped portico led to the main entrance; the columns were ıly two in number; and the plan — which acquired greater eadth — became more definite. The palace was later enlarged the addition of several rooms on two sides. Similar to the lace of Niqmepa, although larger, is the approximately con- mporaneous one of Ugarit (FIG. 874); however, its many ctions were less organically arranged. The tradition of luxuri- s villas persisted in Palestine (Megiddo, Bethel, Taanach).

Greater variety is provided by religious buildings (FIG. 871): at Alalakh stood a temple contemporary with the palace of Niqmepa; its broad plan comprised three consecutive halls (like the one at Byblos) but lacked a courtyard. With various adaptations, this type of temple was retained at Alalakh until the end of the Bronze Age (during the Hittite domination the plan altered considerably, but it is not entirely clear); in time, a few pillars were added to the passages from one hall to the next. In Palestine, the temples of the late Bronze Age are fairly numerous. The successive adaptations of the one at La- chish show first the archaic type with a rectangular hall, central pillars, and the entrance in one of the long sides; then comes an almost square hall with pillars at the center, leading to a small cella placed eccentrically with respect to the main axis of the building. The plan of the Beth Shan temples is similar to that of the later ones at Lachish, which seems to imitate the Egyptian type of temple (the temples of Beth Shan were, in fact, built by Amenhotep III and Ramses II). The Syrian type with three consecutive halls, already anticipated in Palestine in the 17th century B.C. by the temple of Shechem, lasted into the late Bronze Age with a reconstruction, on a reduced scale, of the Shechem temple, itself, and with the temple of Hazor; in the latter, the columns placed at the sides of the entrance anticipated those of the Temple of Solomon and those to be

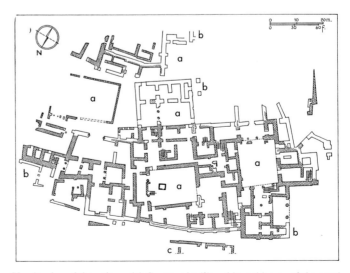

Ugarit, plan of the palace. (*a*) Courtyards; (*b*) archives; (*c*) area of the royal necropolis (*from Syria, XXXI, 1954, p. 17*).

found in the small Palestinian and Cypriote clay models of the 1st millennium. In the field of funerary architecture, the vaulted tombs at Ugarit, of Mycenaean inspiration, deserve mention.

Sculpture. The 2d-millennium stone sculpture in the round provides a rich and varied picture, in spite of its many gaps. It is interesting to note the total lack of connection, iconographic or stylistic, between this production and that of the 3d millennium: evidence, at least in the light of present knowledge, of the absence of a continuous artistic tradition. As in the case of the archaic sculpture of Tell Brak, there are works whose primitive coarseness precludes critical evaluation: this applies to some small idols from Alalakh, original in their iconography (AntJ, XXXVIII, 1948, pl. 7); to the so-called "colossus" of Byblos (Beirut, Nat. Mus.), a weighty and clumsy imitation of the type of the walking pharaoh; and to the two basalt figures from Hazor (PL. 364), only slightly more elaborate. But there are also works that reveal a high degree of artistic maturity, such as the so-called "head of Yarimlim" from Alalakh (I, PL. 520) and a head from Gabbula (mod. Jebbel). The former (18th century B.C.) displays a striking handling of masses in the modeling of the face, contrasting effectively with the linear rendering of the elaborately arranged hair, and a solid balance of volumes; it constitutes the most mature expression of a type of Syrian sculpture thoroughly independent of any Egyptian or Mesopotamian inspirations. The head from Gabbula (Louvre) is stylistically quite different: more solid in structure, and with the volume created by wide flat masses, the features have a terseness that is lacking in the head of Yarimlim. By their forceful originality, these two heads pose the problem of the existence of remarkable Syrian artistic trends whose precedents are unknown and whose rapid disappearance can be inferred. A formative period is implied in the very maturity of these works; they are the product of a school of which no traces are to be found subsequently. A small male head from Alalakh (ILN, 25 Oct. 1947, p. 471), approximately contemporaneous with that of Yarimlim, anticipates, or coarsely imitates, some of the latter's features. Again at Alalakh, a few centuries later, is found a work of some worth, the statue of King Idrimi (ca. 1400 B.C.; PL. 359): though not devoid of a certain monumentality of conception, it appears quite primitive both in technique and in style, oscillating between narrative taste and expressionist aim, between the monumental conception and the volumetric meagerness deriving from the frontal view. The other works from this period, though they complete the picture of the Syrian artistic culture and attest a fair level of craftsmanship, confirm the lack of coherent traditions. The torso of a statue from Sfira (Sefire), portraying a certain Aduniabiya (Aleppo, Nat. Mus.), comes within an Egyptian iconographic type, but it bears on the back an inscription in Middle Assyrian; this statue clearly evidences a descriptive interest. A head from Qatna (Aleppo, Nat. Mus.), in a rather poor state of preservation, shows a conscious emphasis on decoration in the treatment of the hair. Also worthy of mention are some high-relief lions, schematically rendered, from Alalakh (Antioch, Archaeol. Mus.) and from Hazor (PL. 364).

A cultural rather than artistic interest is elicited by the bronze sculpture; it is exemplified by a great number of small pieces but displays no work of true esthetic worth (PLS. 360, 361). The small Syrian bronzes, divided into typological classes and concentrated in certain production areas (Byblos, Ugarit, Palestine), usually display an iconography combining local and often Egyptian elements (more frequent in this field than in stone statuary), together with identifiable Anatolian influences. The local origin of this production is by now beyond dispute, but it is part of a wider pattern comprising Anatolia and — in part — Iran, countries with a considerable output of metalwork. On the artistic level there is a notable poverty of expression in this work, the product of a scarcely developed handicraft lacking artistic traditions, in spite of the fact that it lasted for over a thousand years (I, PL. 519; XI, PL. 129).

In the field of relief, the stele enjoyed in Syria in the 2d millennium a success that was to last until the Hellenistic period. It differed typologically from that of the 3d millennium, and

has a partial parallel only in a Sumerian stele representi Ur-Nina (sometimes called Ur-Nanshe), ruler of Lagash (2500 B.C.; I, PL. 502). The Syrian steles are flat, trapezoid rounded in the upper part, and rimmed. The most importa group comes from Ugarit: of these, one is decorated only w religious symbols and is akin to a stele from Hazor displayi two upraised arms (PL. 364); another four are with figures, revealing the presence of an Egyptian iconographic influenc which appears quite thoroughly assimilated. Stylistically spea ing, these steles are not uniform: the coarseness of the so-call "Stele of El," from Ugarit (XI, PL. 130, above, right), is contrast with the delicate sense of line displayed in the B with the thunderbolt (XI, PL. 130, left); a sense of volume anc balance of composition are to be found in the so-called "st of the pact" (Aleppo, Nat. Mus.), but the relief in that w the figure of a god wearing a tall headdress of Egyptian st (Syria, XII, 1931, pl. 8) is flat and unimpressive. Much grea importance is to be attributed to a relief from Beth Shan, whi does not display the usual typology (PL. 365). Two scenes, plac one above the other, represent a combat between a lion and dog: both subject and typology are quite unusual for the wh of West Asia, even though the animal figures have some parall in Syrian minor arts. In the case of two steles from Balu'ah a from Shihan respectively (PL. 365), there is some uncertainty to the dates: Albright (1949) suggests the end of the 3d mille nium, but the mid-2d seems more likely. Widely differing fro a stylistic point of view, they share the Egyptian origin of t iconography (the Anatolian elements attributed to the second a far from convincing). The elongated and stylized figures of t stele from Balu'ah are merely a local imitation of Egypti motifs. The stele from Shihan, where the Egyptian elemer are less evident, is remarkable for its strong feeling for modeli and for a certain preciosity, both indicative of expressive maturi this piece is probably somewhat earlier than the other. In concl sion may be mentioned the sarcophagus of Aḥīrām (IV, PL. 4 XI, PL. 130), variously dated to the end of the 2d millenniu the main bas-relief probably represents a funerary scene (ho age to the dead king enthroned like a god), the composition which recalls the triumphal scene recurring on an ivory pie from Megiddo and on a seal from Tell Abu Hawam, bo contemporaneous. Egyptian echoes are not lacking in the ic nography (the lion skin imitated on the lid of the sarcophagu and the winged sphinx that forms the sides of the throne), b it seems that this is a typically Syrian composition. Menti should also be made of some rough anthropoid terra-cotta s cophagi, Palestinian imitations of Egyptian models (PL. 36

Minor arts. Glyptics is one of the most original expressio of Syrian art in the 2d millennium. The 18th century B witnessed a sudden flowering of the art, probably related the region's active political participation in Mesopotamian even The type of the cylinder seal was retained, but the iconograph repertory was Babylonian only in part (PL. 366; XII, PL. 52 local motifs are amply represented (divinities and figures Syrian costume, decorative elements and religious symbols n connected with the Mesopotamian repertory), and Egypti motifs are not lacking, from the ankh (*crux ansata*) — oft used as a space filler — to divine figures, religious symbo and royal personages. In spite of the disparate origin of iconographic repertory, Syrian glyptics achieved a stylis uniformity and coherence that distinguish it from the contemp raneous and shoddier Mesopotamian production. Syrian ori inality, underestimated until recent years, manifested its mainly in the feeling for composition and in the plastic forc fulness of the figures. The earliest examples display an eff tively balanced division of the cylinder into zones defined for t most part by a plaited motif or by simple lines: in some cas a vertical iconographic element (such as the stylized Tree Life or the Pillar of Heaven) is used to give the scene an id center. These characteristics appear quite developed in the pr duction of northern Syria (Alalakh, Aleppo), where it h become possible to establish a chronological sequence on a stra graphic basis, proving the inconsistency of the previously appli chronology based on iconography (Moortgat-Correns, 1955).

To this more typically northern — though widespread — production is juxtaposed that of other no less strongly characterized centers: in the glyptics of Ugarit, for example, a linear taste prevails that has none of the plasticity of Alalakh; the figures are mostly placed in a row (as in Babylonian glyptics; at Ugarit, however, they appear in profile rather than frontally), and the presence of Egyptian iconographic motifs is more marked. Southern glyptics, less rigorous and more sensitive to foreign models (in Palestine, clear Cypriote influences can be observed), developed with a style of its own, especially in the second half of the millennium, when the vitality of the northern schools declined; the weakening in the forcefulness of composition was combined with a livelier ornamental taste, expressed on the one hand by the tendency to arabesques and on the other by the preference shown for animal figures, usually placed in rows but occasionally also in effectively distributed groups and often including landscape elements. Peculiar to Palestine is a rich glyptic production that avails itself of a typical Egyptian form: the scarab. The iconographic repertory of this production, sometimes known as "Hyksos," has revealed itself to be an autonomous creation — although it borrowed decorative motifs from Egypt — with local elements (costumes) and Aegean elements (for instance, the spiral meander).

FIG. 659, nos. 13 and 14); this was very widely produced in Syria and, at least in the early stages, clearly influenced by styles from the eastern Mediterranean. This appears in the presence of decorative elements common in those regions and largely adopted also in Syria, as for example spirals and stylized plant motifs. Moreover this painted pottery cannot be connected with the immediately preceding Khabur style. The pottery that appeared in Palestine toward the end of the 2d millennium and persisted for a few centuries reveals considerable Mycenaean contributions (accepted, however, with a certain provincial delay); since it is historically connected with the Philistines, it has been called "Philistine" pottery. Mention should be made, finally, of a large production of glazed vases in the shape of human or animal heads, discovered at Ugarit, Byblos, Jericho, and elsewhere.

Toreutics is not quantitatively much represented, but what little is known shows remarkable ability in this field (PL. 366). The most famous objects are a gold dish (XI, PL. 131) and a gold bowl (X, PL. 401) from Ugarit: on the first is represented a hunt from a chariot; the second bears groups of animals and a lion hunt. There are, in addition, a triangular bronze plaque from Tyre (Frankfort, 1954, fig. 69), with animals recalling those of the Ugarit bowl; and a semicircular gold

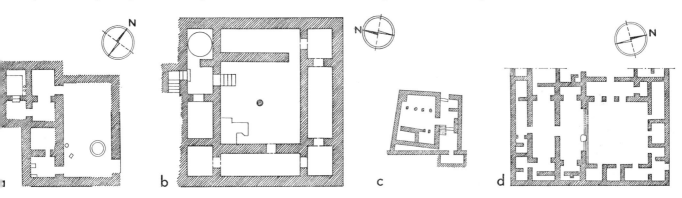

lans of Palestinian villas and dwellings. (*a*) Tell Beit Mirsim, ca. 1600 B.C.; (*b*) Mount Garizim, ca. 1600 B.C.; (*c*) Tell Beit Mirsim, ca 600. B.C.; (*d*) Lachish, Persian period, ca. 400 B.C. (*from Albright, 1949, pp. 91, 92, 141, 144*).

In the second half of the 2d millennium flowered another activity destined to enjoy a long period of success: ivorywork (see IVORY AND BONE CARVING). The region's close links with Egypt during the New Kingdom determined the rise of flourishing handicrafts schools. The technique and the iconographic repertory show evident Egyptian contributions: the plaques from Ugarit (Damascus, Nat. Mus.), the finds from Hazor, and a large part of those from Megiddo (Chicago, Univ., O. Inst.; Jerusalem, Palestine Archaeol. Mus.) and Lachish display numerous motifs of Egyptian provenance, from sphinxes to demoniac figures. However, with regard to Egypt, the same phenomenon occurred in ivorywork as had taken place for glyptics with respect to Mesopotamia: with an eclectic iconographic repertory, autonomous traditions evolved that produced stylistically uniform works. Among the most original creations are the small heads — human and animal — from Lachish (PL. 363) and from Megiddo, as well as a box and a panel from the latter site; the Megiddo panel represents a triumph that recalls the scene carved on the side of the sarcophagus of Aḥīrām. A strong Mycenaean influence (unless the piece was imported) can be perceived in a lid from the Port of Ugarit (mod. Minet el-Neida) bearing the figure of the Lady of the Beasts (VIII, PL. 237).

During the 2d millennium, painted pottery, which had practically disappeared at the beginning of protohistory, reappeared in the Near East. The first to stand out was a type of pottery known as "Khabur" — displaying analogies to the Iranian production — which spread throughout the Syro-Palestinian area, gradually acquiring local forms; its decorative motifs are mainly geometric. About the middle of the millennium it was replaced by the pottery called Mitannian or Nuzi (IX,

pectoral (Louvre) from Byblos, falcon-shaped in accordance with the Egyptian typology. The iconography of these subjects, especially at Ugarit, is largely indebted to Egyptian models, but the decoration skillfully blends motifs of various origins in the best Syrian handicrafts tradition.

FIRST MILLENNIUM B.C. The invasion by the "sea peoples" at the beginning of the 12th century B.C., which marked the transition from the Bronze to the Iron Age, caused a violent political and cultural disruption in the Syro-Palestinian region. It was the end of the Egyptian and Hittite political supremacy and opened the way to the formation of autonomous states: the Philistine Pentapolis, the Israelitic kingdom (later divided), the Phoenician, Aramaic, and neo-Hittite city-states. This situation was brought to an end, between the second half of the 8th century and the beginning of the 6th, first by the Assyrian conquest and then by the Babylonian. With the permanent loss of independence, the most typically Syro-Palestinian culture declines; in the field of art, after the 7th century, the survivals were more and more widely spaced. Between the 12th and the 7th century, therefore, there evolved an art culture whose characteristics were different for the most part from those of the whole preceding period. The disappearance of the Mitannian and Hittite states drew the cities of southeastern Anatolia into the Syrian political and cultural sphere, while the absence of Egypt favored a wider diffusion of the northern culture even in Palestine. Fruitful exchanges between the Syrian and the Anatolian (especially Hittite) traditions determined the rise of a new art — soon strengthened by an ever more marked Assyrian contribution — which manifested its highest originality in the *hilani*, in architectural relief, and in some colossal statues.

Though it is by now traditional to make a distinction in this production between an "Aramaic" and a "Syro-Hittite" art (both distinct from the "Phoenician"), such a distinction is without critical basis, founded as it is solely on a linguistic differentiation (and this not even wholly exact), but without any formal correspondence.

Architecture. During the first centuries of the 1st millennium secular architecture displayed various and often original solutions. The most typical creation of northern Syria was the *hilani* (Assyr., *bît-hilani*), the princely dwelling: the audience hall, broader than it was long (like the whole plan), preceded by a similar antechamber, and the porticoed entrance, raised on a few steps, constitute its distinctive elements. This type of structure, which represents the culmination of an evolution begun at Alalakh in the 2d millennium, came to be widely used also in eastern Anatolia and Upper Mesopotamia: the most characteristic example is that of Gozan (mod. Tell Halaf; I, FIG. 879). In Palestine, luxury dwellings abandoned the type with the eccentric courtyard in favor of the Assyrian model with a central courtyard. The establishment of the Israelite kingdom led, moreover, to the creation of a new type of palace; while almost nothing is known of the Solomonic palace of Jerusalem, some ruins have been found at Samaria (VIII, FIGS. 902, 932), Megiddo (PL. 357; VIII, FIG. 370), and Ramat Rahel that allow a reconstruction of princely dwellings. The plan is common to all of them: a large courtyard surrounded by a fortified wall, the parts of the building intended for habitation grouped in a corner of the courtyard itself. The eccentric position of the courtyard might suggest for these palaces a derivation from the villas of the 2d millennium. Typical of Palestinian architecture in this period are the fortified wall mentioned above; the architectural decoration with "proto-Aeolic" capitals (I, PL. 526) of northern origin (Phoenicia retained instead the bulbiform capitals of Egyptian origin); and the city gateways with nut-cracker-shaped plan, inherited from 2d-millennium northern Syria.

In the field of northern Syrian religious architecture the temple of Tell Taynat is remarkable: the elongated plan divided into three consecutive rooms and the two columns flanking the entrance parallel the temple erected for Solomon at Jerusalem by Phoenician workmen (FIG. 879; VIII, FIG. 901).

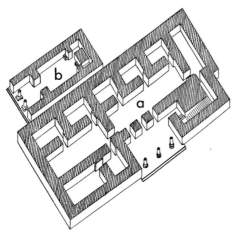

Tell Taynat, axonometric plan of the monumental complex. (*a*) Palace; (*b*) temple (*from AJA, XLI, 1937, p. 9*).

Sculpture. The most forceful expression of Syrian art in the 1st millennium is provided by sculpture, both in the round and, more particularly, in relief. The fact that by far the richer and more important production originated in the northern cities, in a cultural environment where the contribution of Hittite tradition was quite marked, is further support for the hypothesis that this art was simply "neo-Hittite" with, perhaps, some Aramaic contributions (see HITTITE ART). However, as rightly perceived by Frankfort (1954), a fully Hittite tradition can be cited for, at most, only the reliefs from Milid (mod. Ars-

lantepe, near Malatya; many of them in Ankara, Hittite Mus. for the rest, the Anatolian element constitutes only a part of th figural repertory. The Assyrian influence — which, howevei Frankfort tended to overestimate — appears quite strong, espe cially in the later production: the different ways in which th schools of the various towns reacted to the spreading of Assyr ian models reflects the existence of a local element at varyin stages of maturity.

At Carchemish (I, PL. 522; VII, PLS. 285–287), and to lesser extent at Sam'al (mod. Zinçirli; I, PL. 523), the art in fluenced by the Assyrians reached remarkably high level developing from an already mature stage of production. On th other hand, at Gozan and even more at Karatepe, the povert of expression evident in the local motifs continued in spite c foreign influence. Other areas do not add much to this pictur a relief from Aleppo (Nat. Mus.) and one from Damascu (Nat. Mus.) are isolated instances, the former with a subjec (two facing genii) that is closer to the Syro-Hittite repertor the latter with a sphinx, more in harmony with the souther tradition influenced by Egypt. Two statues in the round fror Amman (R. D. Barnett, Ann. Dept. Ant. Jordan, I, 1951 of rather squat proportions, show the existence of a culturall isolated provincial school.

The typology of the steles also continued and was to las until the Hellenistic period; their figural repertory inevitabl reflects the area where they weie produced (PL. 365): from th Syro-Hittite ones of Til Barsip (mod. Tell Ahmar) representin the god Teshub (VII, PL. 288); of Aleppo (Nat. Mus.), wit Melqart; of Marash, with figures of dead persons attending feast (Istanbul, Archaeol. Mus.); to the Assyrian-inspired on from Neyrab (I, PL. 525) and from Homs (Istanbul, Archaeo Mus.). The production of bronzes remained extremely primi tive, except when it imitated Egyptian figurines, and it was al ways, in any case, below what might be termed an "artistic level. (See also IV, PL. 450.)

Minor arts. The great development achieved during th first centuries of the 1st millennium B.C. by trade and by th colonizing activity of the Phoenicians constituted the mos favorable condition for an abundant production of the mino arts, in the field of luxury items for export. The greater pai of the art usually known as Phoenician comes within the spher (see PHOENICIAN-PUNIC ART), but this production does not ap pear to have been limited to the coastal towns; especially fo ivory, there seem to have been other production centers, in Syri proper and in Palestine.

While not a trace remains of the famous Phoenician fabric often mentioned by Greek sources, glyptic art is well represent ed. The cylinder seal of the Mesopotamian type almost disap peared in favor of the scarab or of the stamp seal; the Egyptia typology of the object obviously implied a wide adoption o that figural repertory which was nevertheless — as in all th minor production — blended with motifs of varied origin (XII PL. 524). Sphinxes and griffins, lions and goats, heraldic an suckling animals, Egyptian religious symbols and Mesopotamia demons, and scenes of worship represent the most commo motifs of this production, flanked in Judaea by that of the "royal seals bearing figures — stylized or not — of Egyptian scarab and falcons (see EMBLEMS AND INSIGNIA; JEWISH ART; VIII PL. 332).

The production of toreutics is particularly rich, especiall goblets and dishes (XI, PL. 131) of silver or bronze. Th richness of the Egyptian motifs, the hybridism of the figura repertory, the exclusively ornamental aim of the compositio are all elements that lead to consideration of this productio as Phoenician, although the pieces known were discovered i various regions from Etruria to Assyria and not in Phoenicia The fact that this toreutic tradition traces its origins back t the 2d millennium, both in the typology and in the figura repertory, and that there are objects, such as a few pieces fron Calah (mod. Nimrud; X, PL. 401), in which the Egyptian iconog raphy is less marked, favors the assumption that there wer various schools or production centers, as with ivory production (See also GOLD- AND SILVERWORK, col. 405.)

The most felicitous artistic expression achieved by Syro-
lestinian handicrafts is to be found in the production of ivory
jects (I, PLS. 510, 526; VIII, PLS. 237, 332; X, PL. 401; XII,
. 493). Side by side with a production that is quite closely
ated to the metalwork and glyptics by the profusion of Egyp-
n motifs — ivories of Haddatu (mod. Arslan Tash); Samaria;
yard group from Calah — a new and quite original production
s been brought to light that shows an iconographic repertory
much greater variety than that known previously (Loftus
oup from Calah and more recent finds in the same locality):
e themes used recall those of Syro-Hittite reliefs and reveal
unusual talent for composition. It has therefore been sug-
sted that this production be attributed to one or more Syrian
hools, similar to but independent of the strictly Phoenician
es (PLS. 362, 363).

SURVIVALS AND DIFFUSION. With the close of the 7th century
c., ancient Syro-Palestinian art practically came to an end.
he profound political transformation, soon followed by the
t more profound cultural transformation brought about by
e region's opening to Greek civilization, gave a new aspect
the artistic production, which, besides, remained quite lim-
d for a few centuries. In the period preceding the Hellen-
ation of the country, only the coastal towns show a fairly
h production. But an examination of the characteristics of
is production confirms the disappearance of Syrian art: apart
m some local iconographic survivals, the Phoenician works
the Persian period show the adoption of Egyptian motifs,
m architecture to relief, to a degree unknown previously.
he temples of 'Amrit and of Umm el-Ahmad, the torso from
repta (mod. Sarafand; Louvre), the steles of 'Amrit (Paris,
ll. De Clercq) and of Arvad (Louvre), the typology of the
thropoid sarcophagus (XI, PL. 132), give the full measure of
is last wave of Egyptian influence in Phoenicia.

Much less noticeable, but deeper-rooted and richer in
velopments, was the influence of the Mesopotamian tradition:
is found in a few examples chronologically rather late, well
the interior of Syria, but it was to condition, in the first
nturies of the Christian era, the development of Syrian art
an anti-Hellenistic direction. In the last pre-Christian
nturies, a few isolated motifs of Assyrian origin appeared in
ria: in the stepped pinnacle as a decorative motif (but perhaps
th an unrecognized religious significance) on small altars, in
e Maghāzil of 'Amrit (4th cent.), in the large altar of Qal'at
qra (1st cent. of our era), in the earliest Nabataean tombs
d cent. B.C.–1st cent. of our era; see ARABIAN PRE-ISLAMIC
T), and in the facing lions on the frieze of the palace of the
obiads at 'Araq el-Emir (2d cent. B.C.). Beside these Oriental
aditions, Greek culture prevailed from the 4th century B.C.
ward, albeit through some of its more peripheral expressions.

With the Hellenistic period, what remained of Syrian art
adually disappeared: all that survived were some fossils which
rmed the basis for certain distortions of Hellenistic models,
d which lasted, more or less transformed, in an interesting
t sterile autonomy. Such was the plan typical of Roman
mples in Syria: it repeats the archaic typology of the raised
lla preceded by a court. On the other hand the mere survival
some iconographic motifs is what one meets with, for instance,
a stele from Khaltan, of the 1st–2d century of our era, rep-
senting Hadad with elements of the northern Syrian repertory.

During its millennial evolution, Syro-Palestinian art made
s influence felt on the surrounding regions of the Near East,
addition to the diffusion of some of its motifs toward Cyprus,
rete, and the Aegean, within the framework of what might
e termed the artistic koine of the eastern Mediterranean. As
r Mesopotamia, iconographic motifs from Syria (figures of
ds and ornamental elements) were being adopted in the first
lf of the 2d millennium B.C., while at the beginning of the 1st
e hilani was widely imitated by the Assyrian rulers. As con-
rns Egypt, Syrian figures of gods were imported into that
untry in the 2d millennium B.C. and there more or less thor-
ghly adapted. An actual irradiation of Syro-Palestinian art
n be traced only in the one direction allowed by the history
this culture: Arabia, the last region of the Near East to enter

the historical sphere, and one which by its very geographic
position was in closer contact with Syria than with any other
cultural area. The presence of Syro-Palestinian culture in Arabia
is clearly perceivable from the 1st millennium B.C. onward:
the tomb reliefs and the sculptures of Dedan (mod. el-'Ula),
the Nabataean tombs of Hejra (mod. Mada'in Salih) — in fact,
all of Nabataean art — received impetus from Syria-Palestine,
in its Hellenistic aspect no less than in the more typically
Oriental one (see ARABIAN PRE-ISLAMIC ART). In southern Arabia,
at Marib, a bronze statue (I, PL. 330) has been connected with
the production of votive figures known to have been carried
on at 'Amrit; and, through a statue in the Suweida Museum,
clear Syrian echoes can be perceived even in the sculptures
discovered in 1959 at Hawelti Melazo in Ethiopia (Syria, XXXIX,
1962).

BIBLIOG. *General works*: G. Perrot and C. Chipiez, Histoire de l'art
dans l'antiquité, III, Paris, 1885 (Eng. trans., J. Gonino, 2 vols., London,
1890); J. Humann and O. Puchstein, Reisen in Kleinasien und Nordsyrien,
2 vols., Berlin, 1890; A. Moortgat, Die bildende Kunst des alten Orients
und die Bergvölker, Berlin, 1932; C. Watzinger, Denkmäler Palästinas, 2
vols., Leipzig, 1933–35; C. F. A. Schaeffer, Ugaritica, 4 vols., Paris, 1939–
62; N. Glueck, The Other Side of the Jordan, New Haven, 1945; N. Glueck,
The River Jordan, London, 1946; C. F. A. Schaeffer, Stratigraphie comparée
et chronologie de l'Asie occidentale, London, 1948; W. F. Albright, The
Archaeology of Palestine, Harmondsworth, 1949 (5th ed., 1960); A. Reifenberg, Ancient Hebrew Arts, New York, 1950; H. T. Bossert, Altsyrien,
Tübingen, 1951; H. Frankfort, The Art and Architecture of the Ancient
Orient, Harmondsworth, 1954, pp. 133–201; A. Jirku, Die Ausgrabungen
in Palästina und Syrien, Halle (Saale), 1956; R. D. Barnett, A Catalogue of
the Nimrud Ivories, London, 1957; H. G. Güterbock, Narration in Anatolian,
Syrian and Assyrian Art, AJA, LXI, 1957, pp. 62–71; A. Jirku, Die Welt
der Bibel, Stuttgart, 1957; N. Glueck, Rivers in the Desert, New York,
1959; G. L. Harding, The Antiquities of Jordan, London, 1959; K. M.
Kenyon, Archaeology in the Holy Land, New York, 1960; S. Yeivin, A De-
cade of Archaeology in Israel, 1948–58, Istanbul, 1960; J. A. H. Potratz,
Die Kunst des alten Orients, Stuttgart, 1961, pp. 296–328, 348–60; G. E.
Wright, The Archaeology of Palestine, The Bible and the Ancient Near
East, New York, 1961, pp. 73–112; E. Anati, Palestine before the Hebrews,
New York, 1963 (bibliog.); G. Garbini, EAA, s.v. Fenicia, arte.

Prehistory: H. Vincent, Canaan d'après l'exploration récente, Paris,
1907; M. Dunand, Remarques sur la céramique archaïque des pays cananéens,
Berytus, III, 1936, pp. 141–47; H. Rhotert, Transjordanien, Stuttgart,
1938; L. Woolley, On a Steatopygous Stone Figure from North Syria, Mél.
syriens offerts à R. Dussaud, Paris, 1939, pp. 135–37; M. Pervès, La pré-
histoire de la Syrie et du Liban, Syria, XXV, 1946–48, pp. 109–29; M. W.
Prausnitz, Earliest Palestinian Seal Impressions, Israel Exploration J., V,
1955, pp. 100–93; H. de Contenson, La céramique chalcolithique de Beersheba, Israel Exploration J., VI, 1956, pp. 163–79, 226–38; F. E. Zeuner,
Stone Age Exploration in Jordan, PEQ, LXXXIX, 1957, pp. 17–54; M.
Tallon, Monuments mégalithiques de Syrie et du Liban, Mél. Univ. St.-
Joseph, XXXV, 1958, pp. 221–34; J. Kaplan, The Neolithic Pottery of Palestine, BAmSOR, CLVI, 1959, pp. 15–22; M. Tallon, Tumulus et mé-
galithes du Hermel et de la Beqā' nord, Mél. Univ. St.-Joseph, XXXVI,
1959, pp. 89–111; H. de Contenson, Three Soundings in the Jordan Valley,
Ann. Dept. Ant. Jordan, IV–V, 1960, pp. 12–98; C. F. A. Schaeffer, Les fon-
dements pre- et protohistoriques de Syrie du Néolithique précéramique au
Bronze ancien, Syria, XXXVIII, 1961, pp. 7–22, 221–42.

Early, middle, and late Bronze Age: a. *General*: P. Montet, L'art phénicien au XVIIIe siècle avant J.-C. d'après les récentes trouvailles de Byblos, MPiot, XXVII, 1924, pp. 1–29; R. Dussaud, L'art syrien du IIe millénaire avant notre ère, Syria, VII, 1926, pp. 336–46; H. J. Kantor, The
Aegean and the Orient in the 2d Millennium B.C., Bloomington, Ind., 1947;
R. Dussaud, L'art phénicien du IIe millénaire, Paris, 1949; R. Amiran,
Syria and Cyprus in the Middle Bronze Age I, Eretz-Israel, V, 1958, pp. 25–
30 (in Hebrew); J. Leibovitch, The Art of Egypt and of the Hyksos, Eretz-
Israel, V, 1958, pp. 47–51 (in Hebrew); P. Matthiae, Ars Syra, Rome, 1962.
b. *Architecture*: M. Pillet, Le temple de Byblos, Syria, VIII, 1927, pp. 105–
12; A. Rowe, The Four Canaanite Temples of Beth-Shan, 2 vols., Philadelphia, 1930–40; M. V. S. Williams, Palestinian Temples, Iraq, XI, 1949,
pp. 77–89; H. Frankfort, The Origin of the Bīt Hilani, Iraq, XIV, 1952,
pp. 120–31; R. J. Bull, A Re-examination of the Schechem Temple, Biblical
Archaeologist, XXIII, 1960, pp. 110–19. c. *Sculpture*: R. Dussaud, Torse
de statuette de Sefiré, Syria, IX, 1928, pp. 170–71; S. Przeworski, Les figurines assises et le char divin, Syria, IX, 1928, pp. 274–77; G. Horsfield
and L. H. Vincent, Une stèle égypto-moabite au Balou'a, RBib, XLI, 1932,
pp. 417–44; L. Speelers, Deux figurines syro-hittites, Syrie, III, 1932, pp. 134–
40; E. Drioton, A propos de la stèle de Balou'a, RBib, XLII, 1933, pp. 353–
65; C. F. A. Schaeffer, La stèle de "Ba'al au foudre" de Ras Shamra, MPiot,
XXXIV, 1934, pp. 1–18; W. von Bissing, Sur un petit bronze appartenant
à l'art de l'Asie antérieure, Mél. Dussaud, Paris, 1939, pp. 751–54; L. Hennequin, Trois sarcophages anthropoïdes en poterie trouvés à Tell-Douwier
(Palestine), Mél. Dussaud, Paris, 1939, pp. 956–74; S. Przeworski, Les
reliefs de Roumkalé au Musée du Louvre, Mél. Dussaud, Paris, 1939, pp.
641–47; E. Porada, The Warrior with Plumed Helmet, Berytus, VII, 1942,
pp. 57–63; A. Parrot, Bronzes syriens, Syria, XXIX, 1952, pp. 44–53; H.
Seyrig, Statuettes trouvées dans les montagnes du Liban, Syria, XXX,
1953, pp. 24–50; O. Tufnell, The Shihan Warrior, Iraq, XV, 1953, pp. 161–

66; E. Sollberger, Statuettes de Syrie et du Liban, Mus. de Genève, XIII, 4, 1956, p. 2; D. P. Hansen, A Bronze in the Semitic Museum of Harvard University, BAmSOR, CXLVI, 1957, pp. 13-19; M. Haran, The Bas-Relief on the Sarcophagus of Ahiram King of Byblos, Israel Exploration J., VIII, 1958, pp. 56-65; A. Parrot, Figurines divines, Syria, XXXV, 1958, pp. 163-71; R. Giveon, King or God on the Sarcophagus of Ahiram, Israel Exploration J., IX, 1959, pp. 57-59; G. Garbini, The Phoenician "Goddess" in the Louvre, Orientalia, XXIX, 1960, pp. 323-28; G. M. A. Hanfmann, A Near Eastern Horseman, Syria, XXXVIII, 1961, pp. 243-55; O. Negbi, On Two Bronze Figurines with Plumed Helmet from the Louvre Collection, Israel Exploration J., XI, 1961, pp. 111-17. d. Glyptics: G. Contenau, La glyptique syro-hittite, Paris, 1922; A. Procopé-Walter, Ein Bindglied zwischen Rollsiegel und Hemiovoid (Skarabäoid), Arch. für Orientforschung, VI, 1930-31, pp. 165-75; H. Frankfort, Cylinder Seals, London, 1939, pp. 252-73, 288-91, J. Nougayrol, Cylindres-sceaux et empreintes de cylindres trouvés en Palestine, Paris, 1939; B. Parker, Cylinder Seals from Palestine, Iraq, XI, 1949, pp. 1-43; U. Moortgat-Correns, Neue Anhaltpunkte zur zeitlichen Ordnung syrischer Glyptik, Z. für Assyriologie, N.S., XVII, 1955, pp. 88-101; O. Tufnell, "Hyksos" Scarabs from Canaan, Anaolian S., VI, 1956, pp. 67-73; B. Buchanan, Further Observations on the Syrian Glyptic Style, J. Cuneiform S., XI, 1957, pp. 74-76; B. Buchanan, On the Seal Impressions on Some Old Babylonian Tablets, J. Cuneiform S., XI, 1957, pp. 45-52; W. Nagel and E. Strommenger, Alalaḫ und Siegelkunst, J. Cuneiform S., XII, 1958, pp. 109-23. e. Ivory: C. Decamps de Mertzenfeld, Les ivoires de Megiddo, Syria, XIX, 1938, pp. 345-54; R. D. Barnett, Phoenician and Syrian Ivory Carving, PEQ, LXXI, 1939, pp. 4-19; G. Loud, Megiddo Ivoreis, Chicago, 1939; H. J. Kantor, Syro-Palestinian Ivories, JNES, XV, 1956, pp. 153-74, 235; R. L. Cleveland, An Ivory Bull's Head from Ancient Jericho, BAmSOR, CLXIII, 1961, pp. 30-36; P. Bar-Adon, Another Ivory Bull's Head from Palestine, BAmSOR, CLXV, 1962, pp. 46-47. f. Ceramics: E. Saussey, La céramique philistine, Syria, V, 1924, pp. 169-85; L. H. Vincent, La peinture céramique palestinienne, Syria, V, 1924, pp. 81-107, 186-202, 294-315; J. G. Duncan, Corpus of Dated Palestinian Pottery, London, 1930; W. A. Heurtley, The Relationship between "Philistine" and Mycenaean Pottery, Q. Dept. Ant. in Palestine, IV, 1935, pp. 99-110; M. V. S. Williams, A Painted Pottery of the 2d Millennium from Southern Turkey and Northern Syria, Iraq, XV, 1953, pp. 57-68; V. R. Grace, The Canaanite Jar, The Aegean and the Near East, New York, 1956, pp. 80-109; B. Hrouda, Die bemalte Keramik des zweiten Jahrtausends in Nordmesopotamien und Nordsyrien, Berlin, 1957; N. Avigad, EAA, s.v. Filistea, ceramica; A. Dajani, Middle Bronze Age Pottery, Ann. Dept. Ant. Jordan, IV-V, 1960, pp. 99-113; J. L. Benson, A Problem in Orientalizing Cretan Birds: Mycenaean or Philistine Prototypes?, JNES, XX, 1961, pp. 73-84. g. Precious metals: H. J. Kantor, A "Syro-Hittite" Treasure in the Oriental Institute Museum, JNES, XVI, 1957, pp. 145-62.

First millennium: a. General: E. Unger, Hettitische und Aramäische Kunst, Arch. für Keilschriftforschung, I, 1923, pp. 78-82; W. F. Albright, Northeast-Mediterranean Dark Ages and the Early Iron Age Art of Syria, The Aegean and the Near East, New York, 1956, pp. 144-64; W. F. Albright, Was the Age of Solomon without Monumental Art?, Eretz-Israel, V, 1958, pp. 1*-9*; G. Garbini, Il problema dell'arte aramaica, RSO, XXXIV, 1959, pp. 141-47. b. Architecture: C. van Gelderen, Der Solomonische Palastbau, Arch. für Orientforschung, VI, 1930-31, pp. 100-06; H. Weidhaas, Der bīt ḫilāni, Z. für Assyriologie, XLV, 1939, pp. 108-68; A. Parrot, Le temple de Jérusalem, Neuchâtel, Paris, 1954 (Eng. trans., B. E. Hooke, New York, 1955); R. Naumann, Architektur Kleinasiens, Tübingen, 1955; R. B. K. Amiran and I. Dunayevsky, The Assyrian Open-Court Building and its Palestinian Derivatives, BAmSOR, CXLIX, 1958, pp. 25-32; F. Wachtsmuth, Was ist ein "Hilani", was ist ein "Bit ḫilani"?, ZMG, CVIII, 1958, pp. 66-73; Y. Aharoni, The Date of Casemate Walls in Judah and their Purpose, BAmSOR, CLIV, 1959, pp. 35-39; A. Ciasca, I capitelli a volute in Palestina, RSO, XXXVI, 1961, pp. 189-97. c. Sculpture: C. Clermont-Ganneau, La stèle phénicienne d'Amrith, Recueil d'archéologie orientale, IV, Paris, 1901, pp. 325-37; G. Contenau, Un bas-relief de la citadelle d'Alep, Rev. d'Assyriologie, XXVIII, 1931, pp. 108-10; F. Thureau-Dangin, Rev. d'Assyriologie, XXVIII, 1931, p. 199; M. Chéhab, Trois stèles trouvées en Phénicie, Berytus, I, 1934, pp. 44-46; M. Dunand, Stèle araméenne dédiée à Melqart, BMBeyrouth, III, 1939, pp. 65-76; M. Dunand, Les sculptures de la favissa du temple d'Amrith, BMBeyrouth, VII, 1944-45, pp. 99-107, VIII, 1946-48, pp. 81-107; Djafar Abd el-Kader, un orthostate du temple de Hadad à Damas, Syria, XXVI, 1949, pp. 191-95; E. Kukahn, Anthropoide Sarkophage in Beyrouth, Berlin, 1955; E. Sollberger, Un bas-relief phénicien, Mus. de Genève, XVII, 1960, pp. 5-6. d. Ivory: R. D. Barnett, The Nimrud Ivories and the Art of the Phoenicians, Iraq, II, 1935, pp. 179-210; J. G. and G. M. Crowfoot, Early Ivories from Samaria, London, 1938; C. Decamps de Mertzenfeld, Ivoires syriens, Mél. Dussaud, Paris, 1939, pp. 587-91; C. Decamps de Mertzenfeld, Inventaire commenté des ivoires phéniciens et apparentés, Paris, 1954; R. D. Barnett, A Catalogue of the Nimrud Ivories, London, 1957. e. Glyptics: K. Galling, Beschriftete Bildsiegel des ersten Jahrtausends v. Chr. aus Syrien und Palästina, Z. d. Palästina-Vereins, LXIV, 1941, pp. 121-202; A. Reifenberg, Ancient Hebrew Seals, London, 1950.

Influences: A. Alt, Verbreitung und Herkunft des syrischen Tempeltypus, Palästinajhb., XXXV, 1939, pp. 83-99; M. Avi-Yonah, Oriental Elements in the Art of Palestine in the Roman and Byzantine Period, Q. Dept. Ant. Palestine, X, 1940-44, pp. 105-51, XIII, 1947-49, pp. 128-65, XIV, 1950, pp. 49-80; O. Eissfeldt, Tempel und Kulte syrischer Städte in hellenistisch-römischer Zeit, Der Alte Orient, XL, 1941, pp. 1-160; M. Avi-Yonah, Oriental Art in Roman Palestine, Rome, 1961; G. Garbini, EAA, s.v., Nabatea, arte.

Giovanni GARBINI

Illustrations: PLS. 357-366; 6 figs. in text.

TABLE AND FOOD. The sum of the rules, custom and activities concerning the preparation and presentation foods has often been called the "art" of the table, since it in various ways acquire an esthetic quality. A table may spread artistically by combining the mere shapes and col of foods and table implements into esthetic patterns; a banq may be adorned with scenic effects, including elaborately scu tured or modeled foodstuffs and imaginative table decoratio and a banquet or feast may incorporate carefully studied ce monies and spectacles, which are sometimes even of ritual symbolic significance. In all these activities, the purpose clearly to give expression to artistic impulses and to create esthetic picture or scene; hence the art of the table may inde be considered to belong, if only marginally, to the esthe sphere of the visual arts, the more so in that during cert periods of history great artists devoted themselves to designing and preparing of banquets and feasts. This type artistic expression is obviously short-lived and "wasteful," the sense that its creation is immediately consumed, and this respect it is related to other ephemeral esthetic manifes tions, whether those of personal taste — costume, hair sty make-up — or those of collective life, such as games, parad theatrical spectacles, dances, and masquerades. But the art the table can also give rise, if only indirectly, to typical a lasting objects of artistic value in the instruments that it e ploys, that is, in cooking utensils, food receptacles, table f nishings, and the like (see CERAMICS; GOLD- AND SILVERWO HOUSEHOLD OBJECTS). Finally, the world of foodstuffs and ba quets, with its colorful, sensuous, sumptuous tones, has oft been an iconographic theme (see GENRE AND SECULAR SUBJEC STILL LIFE), and it is in this field that the ephemeral art of t table finds a lasting artistic reflection.

This article first treats the art of the table as an esthe phenomenon in itself, tracing its manifold expression throu history, and then presents its reflections in the representatio arts. The discussion concentrates on Europe, where the dev opment of the banquet and the feast was conspicuously involv with various artistic movements.

SUMMARY. Introductory critical analysis (col. 884). The foo stuffs (col. 885). Tableware and accessories (col. 887). The embellis ments of the banquet and the feast (col. 889). Table and food art (col. 891).

INTRODUCTORY CRITICAL ANALYSIS. The difficulty in evalua ing fully so complex and uneven a phenomenon as the art the table derives in the first place precisely from the transie elusive character of this esthetic manifestation, which makes hard to document, and secondly from the too strict distincti between major and minor arts and "pure" and "impure" ar which has long prevailed in critical methodology. On the oth hand, it is the very elusiveness and spontaneity of this art th appeals to the artistic spirit; this explains why its most significa manifestations have coincided with moments and environmer of particular artistic vitality and why great artists such Leonardo da Vinci, Buontalenti, Bernini, and Inigo Jones (qq. became interested in the preparation and staging of feasts a banquets.

It could be objected that the art of staging theatrical worl dances, masquerades, and so forth — being of a similarly epher eral nature — is subject to the same difficulties of evaluatic and yet has been the subject of organized studies. Such studi however, can rely on the stimulus of a literary text, on ampler graphic documentation in the form of sketches of co tumes and sets, and, finally, on the more stable nature of sta settings. But the esthetic value of a banquet created by Leonar was certainly not inferior to that of the performance of, sa Ariosto's Gli Suppositi, with sets by Raphael, in Castel Sant'A gelo in Rome, 1519; both spectacles were guided by disciplin staging, with true coups de théâtre and with carefully studi development. The action, which on the stage unfolded means of the individual characters, had as its protagonis during the banquet the courses themselves, with their herald and symbolic references, and included the studied effect of surprise "crescendo." Thus the esthetic alternation of the shapes and colors of the foodstuffs, the precious implements juxtaposed ingeniously with the shapes of the victuals, and the complex choreographic development in the presentation of the courses all blended to create a total stylistic and esthetic accomplishment.

Manifestations of this type are of hybrid nature; they rest simultaneously on formal values (the shapes of foodstuffs and decorations) and on the ephemeral pleasures of the eye (the spectacle) and of the palate. In this consists that "impurity" which has created, and still creates, a decisive obstacle to their inclusion in the history and the criticism of the visual arts, which in turn resulted in the almost total absence of technical treatises on the subject. The rare publications dealing with the preparation of the banquet (C. Messisbugo, 1549, and the anonymous *Epulario*, 1549) were, like those concerning pyrotechnics or scenography, generally rather arid and uncritical collections of practical rules.

THE FOODSTUFFS. At the basis of every gastronomic preparation can be recognized the desire to use the satisfaction of the eye as a psychological supplement to the sense of taste. The shape and color of the foodstuffs, whether left in their natural state or transformed into different shapes, are fundamental aids to this end.

Some types of food, such as fruit, whole animals or parts of them, or eggs, commonly retain their own pleasing shapes when used in a table spread; in such cases, deliberate esthetic effects are carried out on the level of the presentation only, that is, in the grouping of the pieces of food, in chromatic contrasts, in the "cut" (sliced meats, opened fruits), or in ornamental complements (sauces or vegetables). Other foodstuffs lend themselves readily to artificial shaping, for example, *pâtés*, breads (PL. 367; V, PL. 348; VII, PL. 355), puddings, cheeses, and the like. Although the problems of adoption, invention, and transmission of forms are rudimentary here, they are not unlike those encountered in the typology of other esthetically conceived objects of practical use, such as household utensils, tools, vessels and vases, toys, and similar items. The formal interest of these ephemeral manifestations may seem negligible; yet it has always been present in some way — more or less consciously — especially at the level of the primitive and popular cultures (see FOLK ART), where the esthetic sense manifested itself almost exclusively in products for everyday use.

Bread and pastry doughs are adaptable to any number of geometric forms — blocks, dice, spheres, hemispheres, or cones — and other shapes. The modeling process is similar to that of clay modeling or stuccowork, both in the shaping of the mass itself and in the application of ornamental trimmings, and even in the types of molds used. The relationship is so conspicuous as to justify the conjecture of an ancient close parallelism between the two crafts, even in the representational solutions (VII, PL. 355); the same can be said of the relation of twisted and braided doughs to the art of basketry. In other cases the shape or the decoration of the food product is determined to this day by the containers used for the mixtures; hence the truncated-cone shape, handed down through the millennia, of certain cakes or sweets, and the soft cheeses of many Mediterranean countries, which bear on their surface the imprint of the wicker mounting.

Obviously the shapes of dough products might also assume autonomous ornamental values; that is, the molds are deliberately shaped to enhance the esthetic appeal of the product. This gives free rein to the imagination of the creator, who can indulge his whims in complicated geometric or lobate forms, in heart-shaped, star-shaped, and other fanciful designs, and, finally, in the representation of fruits or edible animals — perhaps vaguely paralleling the use of small votive or funerary statuary as substitutes for the real objects or beings.

This leads into the consideration of "illusion" in gastronomic preparations. Antiquity, especially in the Hellenistic-Roman period, already knew this sense of the exciting surprise, of the trompe l'œil, which gave the banquet a double appeal — a hedonistic and an intellectual one — and tended to do violence to the nature of the foodstuffs with an ill-disguised contempt

for their humble material. Documentation of the Roman table and banquet comes not so much from culinary treatises — of which the only important one remaining is the *De re coquinaria* of the Roman imperial age, ascribed to Caelius Apicius — but comes, rather, from narrative and satirical literature, particularly from the episode of Trimalchio's dinner in the *Satyricon* of Petronius, as well as from illustrations and archaeological evidence like that found at Pompeii (PLS. 367, 370; VIII, PL. 232).

It is difficult to draw the line between art, artifice, and bad taste in the Roman and late-Roman feasts. The desire to create illusive effects must have often resulted in an overloaded ornamentation with violent chromatic contrasts, as for instance in the insertion of wafers, almonds, or colored sweetmeats to break the uniformity of the pastries and to create ornamental divisions. The effect was not unlike the decoration carried out on fresh stucco with glass pastes and shells that was typical of nymphaeums (cf. IX, PL. 395) and vaults, the mounted stones in jewelry, the preciosities of the *diatreta* glasses (VI, PL. 221), and so on. To this should be added the animals that were served in their original shape, reconstructed and stuffed, and the fish transformed into the shape of game or vice versa.

Such exuberant decoration, certainly familiar also to the societies and courts of the late-antique and Byzantine worlds, was destined to disappear with the coarse simplicity of barbarian cookery and with the monastic frugality of the Middle Ages. But in the late Gothic period and in the Renaissance a certain esthetic elaboration of forms returned. Products, such as bread, were given manifold shapes, sweets were decorated and colored, and cakes were studded with ornamental motifs made of colored sweetmeats or sugar "pearls," covered with gold and silver glazes, in accordance with a taste still found today in some typical regional cakes. Among the various guilds that had developed in the European countries, those of the confectioners and bakers assumed importance and prestige, and the artifice and ability of cooks were often displayed in monumental reproductions of figures and buildings on cakes and pies. Sweets tended once again to assume imitative shapes and new decorative forms and colors suggested by the large Renaissance table services of precious metals and stones (VI, PL. 269). Candied fruit, dough, colored sugar, and gold- and silver-glazed sweets were used to simulate fantasies of jewelry, from gem settings to cloisonné, from enamel to niello.

Completely new, however, was the appearance of compositions inspired by heraldic, legendary, mythological, fanciful, or satirical subjects in accordance with the courtly tastes of the period (PL. 371). Examples of this trend are the gastronomic inventions of the Florentines Giovan Francesco Rustici (1474–1554) and Andrea del Sarto (1486–1530) documented in Vasari's *Lives*. Rustici created a pie in the shape of a caldron with two figures, made of boiled capons molded into human shapes, representing Ulysses dipping his father into the vessel to rejuvenate him. Andrea made a church with a floor of colored jellies, and sausage columns with capitals of Parmesan cheese; at the center of the church was a lectern made of cold veal, bearing a book made of *lasagne* on which letters and musical notes were outlined with peppercorns; around the lectern was a choir of thrushes, with their beaks open, wearing surplices made of thin pig's caul.

The period of the Counter Reformation seems to have reacted to the scenographic artifice of the Renaissance banquet by a retreat toward physical reality or, here and there, toward the charm of rustic cooking. The almost sensual satisfaction of the eye in the rediscovered natural appearance of foods is reflected in the 17th-century still lifes of raw fish and game, red meats, or pulpy fruits (PLS. 202, 204, 205; V, PLS. 311, 313). Nevertheless, the banquet preparations of the courts continued in the spirit of contrived constructions imbued with allegory, in accordance with the tendencies of the baroque. Finally, in the 18th century, with the flowering of French gastronomy, a new rationalized and almost scientific orientation of culinary precepts became prevalent: foodstuffs were reduced to jellies, concentrates, *pâtés*, and the like and reconstructed in artificial shapes obtained by means of molds; the plasticity of the shapes was replaced by a subtlety of color schemes; certain juxtapositions and contrasts of main dish and side dishes gained importance and have remained canonical for the modern table, which has been progressively simplified.

TABLEWARE AND ACCESSORIES. The food receptacles, the table furnishing, and often the utensils used in preparing the food (PL. 368) can play as important a role as the foodstuffs themselves in the creation of the esthetic visual effects that heighten the pleasures of taste.

Since the earliest times and at all levels of civilization, kitchen implements and food vessels, from pottery to wineskins, gourds, baskets (I, PL. 203; II, PLS. 227, 232; VII, PLS. 311, 317) and recipients made of wood, stone, metal (I, PL. 215; III, PL. 274; VI, PL. 279; VII, PL. 311; VIII, PL. 44), or glass (VI, PL. 229; VII, PL. 316), have taken on special shapes according to their function (see also HOUSEHOLD OBJECTS). Such equipment comprises containers for storing, carrying, or preserving foodstuffs — from the pithoi of the ancient Cretans (PL. 106; IV, PL. 65) to the architectural structures of warehouses and silos; objects used in preparing, shaping, or cooking foods — from pestles and mortars to millstones, from butter molds to pastry cutters (PL. 368; V, PL. 348), from earthenware or metal braziers to ovens and stoves; and above all the serving dishes (VII, PL. 337) and, for liquids, jugs and bottles (III, PL. 274; VI, PLS. 218, 239), cups and glasses of various shapes (VI, PLS. 234, 235; VII, PLS. 325, 328; VIII, PL. 58). Also part of an esthetic table setting are the flatware in many different shapes and designs (V, PL. 343; VII, PLS. 324, 325); the table linen; table decorations such as centerpieces (PL. 374), candlesticks (VI, PLS. 252, 275, 279), or flower arrangements; and the furniture (q.v.) — serving tables, seats, and the dinner table itself (V, PLS. 449, 455; VIII, PL. 110).

In Greek pottery, certain typical shapes of vessels for the various uses of the banquet were fixed from the archaic age (II, PL. 38, last three): craters and amphoras for wine and hydrias for water; kylixes, kyathoi, and rhytons to drink from; and many others (III, FIG. 233). The vessels used by the Egyptians, the Etruscans, and the Romans for their banquets are amply documented in papyruses (PL. 370) and in wall paintings like the ones in the Etruscan tombs at Tarquinia (PL. 370; VI, PL. 55) and Orvieto (Golini Tomb I; now in Florence, Mus. Archaeol.) and the ones in Pompeii (PL. 370).

Throughout antiquity, as in the Oriental cultures and in the primitive world, the functional features of these objects were combined with ornamental elements that either were of a symbolic-ritual nature or were allusive to the foodstuffs; in the last connection might be mentioned the Cretan-Mycenaean painted pottery depicting marine fauna (IV, PL. 65), and the Italiote dishes with decorations of fish (PL. 369). In the silverwork and in the fine terra sigillata of the Roman period, however, ornamentation often used decorative and mythological motifs that were determined more by the widespread taste of the times. In some splendid silverware, such as that from the Boscoreale Treasure (VII, PLS. 216, 315), the functional shape was concealed by naturalistic plant or figural motifs in order to lessen the contrast between the stylized geometry of the container and its succulent contents of, say, olives or small fruits. It was perhaps a similar esthetic aim that in a much later period stimulated a Bernard Palissy to decorate his striking majolica with fish, crustaceans, reptiles, and other animals resting on beds of leaves (PL. 369; III, PL. 152).

The Middle Ages developed their own typical and ample banquet equipment. Medieval iconography reveals the use of temporary tables erected on trestles, of benches covered with cloths and cushions for the table guests, of separate serving tables, and of a seat of honor, sometimes surmounted by a canopy. The peculiar custom of setting up temporary dining facilities ennobled by precious materials and carpets was to spread to all the European courts and survive into the 16th century; one example of it is the famous banquet given in Rome by Agostino Chigi in 1518 in the stables of the Farnesina, where the walls and mangers were concealed by a long, gold-threaded carpet and the floor was covered with a silk gobelin. The implements used during the late medieval period testify

to the ornamental wealth of the banquets of the time: they are resplendent in the most imaginative combinations of ivory, gold, silver, rock crystal, jasper, and enamel, handled with meticulous workmanship of damascening, niello, or inlay.

With the Renaissance, table implements reached lofty heights of richness and elegance in shapes and in the use of precious materials. There were categories of precious objects of every type — candlesticks, bronze vessels, saltcellars (VI, PL. 141; VII, PLS. 320, 321) — whose design and execution were often entrusted to artists; an example is the well-known saltcellar of Francis I produced by Benvenuto Cellini (VI, PL. 269). In addition to objects of practical use, there were ornamental centerpieces and flowers, which, fresh during the warm season, were, according to Messisbugo's 16th-century description, "in winter artificial, of silk and of gold and of silver, to be placed, one to a setting, above the napkins." A new feeling for ancient and exotic cultures brought about a further enrichment of the table services. Greek, Roman, and Oriental receptacles of jasper, amethyst, sardonyx, or chalcedony were given elegant mountings of gold and silver (VI, PL. 267). It was the period of the Medici and Farnese table services, representatives of an art of entertaining that delighted in adding sophisticated allurement to the splendor of precious materials. With the development of the middle classes and the appearance of a well-to-do bourgeoisie, however, there was also a need to develop tableware that was less elaborate although still elegant; and such tableware found wide diffusion through a thriving ceramics industry. In the 17th century, thanks to changing European social conditions, the minor handicrafts expanded their market: objects of interior decoration and household items intended for the daily meal increased in number; and with chairs and stools made of walnut or upholstered in leather, with tables of various sizes and types — rectangular, oval, adjustable in size — a shape was gradually being given to that domestic room which was to become the characteristic bourgeois dining room of the 18th and 19th centuries.

Meanwhile, the use of pewter was spreading through northern Europe; the 18th century was to become the period of its greatest production, with an extraordinary variety of forms, sometimes determined by functional requirements (plates and trays, ewers and jugs, flatware) and sometimes responding to the demands of luxury or fashion, often by the addition of ornamental or figural decoration. Customs peculiar to various countries favored the development of specific household objects: thus the large consumption of beer in the Germanic countries encouraged the development of the typical tall, cylindrical pottery mug bearing figures, occasionally in relief, or ornamental writing, with lids often of pewter. Even the kitchen assumed a new and pleasing appearance, with its huge fireplaces fitted out with their iron accessories and the displays of molds and pots in soldered copper (VIII, PL. 91).

The development of cutlery was gradual and relatively late: the fork, an object of ostentatious elegance reserved for aristocratic tables since the end of the 16th century, in the 18th century became a necessary implement of widespread use. The picturesque confusion of the baroque table, with glasses and plates of different shapes and ornamentation, gradually gave way to a more uniform and orderly setting. For the aristocratic tables complete services of glasses, plates, cutlery, and table linen became the norm, and their habitual use determined those fixed and recurrent shapes from which were eventually to emerge the standard bourgeois table settings of the end of the 19th century and the beginning of the 20th. From this 19th-century standard also developed an elaborate array of fixed shapes for glassware of different uses in formal services — the water goblet, the wine glass, the liqueur glass — as well as for cutlery; the ornamentation, however, might vary widely, being drawn eclectically, in innumerable variants, from international rococo (q.v.), Empire, and neoclassic styles (q.v.).

At the beginning of the 20th century, Art Nouveau (q.v.) influenced the forms and ornamentation of table services, reaching an exceptional refinement with the work of Henri van de Velde (I, PL. 469; VI, PL. 278; VII, PLS. 325, 342). Through successive evolutionary stages, such work opened the way for

e mass production of these objects, freed from anonymity by
a ever-growing creative vigor in the field of industrial design
.v.), which balanced the functional aspect of the object (work
° the Bauhaus; see EUROPEAN MODERN MOVEMENTS) against the
thetic appeal (constantly insisted upon by Jacques Viénot in
s review *Esthétique Industrielle*). Among the nations most
volved in this search for new solutions have been — in addi-
on to France (the new shapes created by the goldsmiths of
.e Christofle workshop) — the Scandinavian countries (see
ANDINAVIAN ART) and the Netherlands, which have been par-
cularly outstanding in the production of glass (q.v.), especially
ystal, and of table services, cutlery, and table linens, as well
 dining furniture. New shapes of exceptional esthetic appeal
ere designed in glass (VI, PL. 239); the Swedes Nils Landberg
VIII, PL. 58) and Vicke Lindstrand and the Finns Saara Hopea
ad Timo Sarpaneva may be mentioned, among others, in this
onnection. Finally, by the 1960s Japan was exporting tableware
ad accessories of high esthetic standard, which assimilated the
rms of the international style even while retaining links with
s national traditions in its use of raw materials, its techniques,
ad — to some extent — its decorative style.

THE EMBELLISHMENTS OF THE BANQUET AND THE FEAST. As
ready mentioned, the complex esthetic structure of the classic
pe of banquet (PL. 373) resulted from the choreographic-
enographic order in the successive presentation of courses, in
ae movements of the servers — often regulated by meticulous
iles — and in the interpolation of elements of spectacle such
 music, mimes, and dances; these components were in most
ases symbolically linked either to the festive occasion (illus-
ious guests, anniversaries) or to the nature of the foods them-
lves (with historical, allegorical, or mythological references
onnected with hunting, pastoral life, or agriculture). In every
eriod and in every civilization, particularly in ancient classical
mes and the European Middle Ages, customs and scenic
attings of the banquet had their own esthetic definitions, how-
ver minimal; special treatment, however, must be given to
ae Renaissance world, which witnessed an increasingly intense
oncentration of those visual elements — psychological com-
lements to the sense of taste — that later, during the 17th cen-
iry, were to sort themselves into the various genres of opera,
allet, games, and masques as separate, independent forms of
atertainment.

Toward the end of the Middle Ages the rudimentary forms
f mimes and dances interspersed as intervals between courses
ready tended to articulate the entire banquet with a theme
ad a skillful scenic development, integrating the foods, the
ervice, and the guests themselves into a unified performance.
he first signs of this trend were perceivable at the papal court
 Avignon, in elaborate banquets like the one given by Pope
ohn XXII in 1324 for the wedding of a relative or the famous
ae given by Cardinal Annibale di Ceccano for Pope Clement VI
1 1343. For the latter, the hall was decked with tapestries and
irpets; four knights and twelve squires served the table, while
fty more squires formed a guard of honor. The nine courses,
ach comprising three dishes, were accompanied by concerts,
horeographic spectacles of an allegorical-heraldic nature, and
 tournament. Another impressive banquet was that presented
 Milan in 1368 by Galeazzo II Visconti on the occasion of
ae wedding of his daughter Violante to the Duke of Clarence,
on of Edward III of England. The 18 courses of the banquet
ere carried into the hall accompanied by wedding gifts, both
ourses and gifts having been chosen to present a common
oint of reference; for example, the roasted peacocks were ac-
ompanied by gifts of precious mantles embroidered with pearls,
nd the junkets and cheeses by a whole herd of oxen. But
ae banquet that defines the taste for spectacle that was to
ypify Renaissance feasts from then on is undoubtedly the one
ffered at Lille by Philip the Good, duke of Burgundy, in
454, which the chroniclers have handed down as the "banquet
f the pheasant." The tables were decked with colossal decora-
ons: a church; a pie in the shape of a tower on which stood
ae figures of 28 musicians and various mechanical puppets;
 sculptured representation of the castle of Lusignan, with the

moats full of orange syrup; two columns, to the first of which
the figure of a naked woman was tied, representing Constantinople, while the second bore a lion, the heraldic symbol of
the duke of Burgundy; finally, the form of a black giant represented the infidels, while the figure of an elephant bearing a
castle with the small figure of a woman in prayer was intended
as an allegory of the Church.

In the 16th century, there are some signs of a rational
measure which was inspired — at least in its intentions — by
antiquity and which kindled the interest in treatises on the
subject; the anonymous *Epulario* was widely circulated in innumerable reprints and was translated, and the cook at the duke's
court in Ferrara, Cristoforo Messisbugo, wrote his interesting
small work (1549) in which he described the banquets prepared
by him and listed all the banquet equipment necessary for the
princely table. In the light of the more reasonable approach,
a dinner like the one given by Galeazzo II Visconti in 1368
began to appear as an unbecoming grouping of repetitions. The
influence of the classical ideal made itself felt increasingly in
the scenographic displays. A 15th-century account (G. Perticari,
1843) tells of the banquet given at Pesaro in 1475 on the occasion of the wedding of Costanzo Sforza and Camilla of Aragon,
in which each course was introduced by a classical divinity or
by a nymph who presented the food in verse and addressed
praises to the newlyweds. The account shows a studied progression in the succession of the 12 courses that was undisturbed
by spectacular excesses or by cumbersome allegorical contrivances. (It is interesting to observe the greater concern with
cleanliness at that period; during the banquet, tablecloths and
plates were changed, and at the end of it, servants swept the
floor with myrtle brooms edged with gold.)   The chronicle of
Renaissance banquets is a rich one; every pretext for official
pomp gave rise to splendid festive displays that concluded with
opulent feasts, sometimes lasting as long as seven hours. Some
had distinguished settings, as, for instance, the one created by
Leonardo da Vinci in Milan in 1489 for the wedding of Gian
Galeazzo Sforza and Isabella of Aragon. Another typical Renaissance display of splendor was the banquet given by Pope
Alexander VI in 1501 on the occasion of the marriage of Lucrezia
Borgia to Alfonso I d'Este: 24 castles made of sugar were placed
on the table, and at the center of the banquet hall was a fountain
with 12 spouts from which poured different wines.

In some cases the mimed or danced intervals acquired such
distinction that, for instance, a banquet like that given by
Cardinal Girolamo Riario in Rome (1473) belongs more to the
history of classical ballet than to that of banquets. Nevertheless,
the aristocratic banquet tended, toward the end of the 16th century, to simplify its display and its esthetic elaboration. This
trend was encouraged by the Counter Reformation, which guided
customs toward a new penitential strictness. The newly acquired
social importance of the bourgeoisie, while it reduced the tone
of the aristocratic banquet, supplied the middle class, through
a broader diffusion of craft products, with more readily available means to elegance and taste (the *Epulario* itself clearly
represents a popularization of the aristocratic table in more
modest terms). Another factor in the decline of the great Renaissance banquet was the rise of opera, ballet, and other forms
of musical entertainment as independent genres, which deprived
the banquet of its typical character of complete entertainment.
Indeed, when Christina of Sweden arrived in Rome after her
abdication in 1654, instead of having her accept salutations in
verses from a nymph set atop a gigantic cake, it seemed more
appropriate to have her attend, after a normal banquet, a can-
tata staged in imitation of a gigantic cake, with concentric
circles of musicians and singers, topped by a group of *castrati*
dressed as allegorical or mythological characters.

When the separation of the element of spectacle from the
Renaissance banquet had been fully realized, what remained
was the natural daily act of victualing. While the bourgeois
table, even as it acquired a certain decorum and a disciplined
elegance, retained its typical tone of simplicity, the aristocratic
table tended to withdraw into a formal etiquette that, especially
at the French court, assumed the character of a ceremony: the
public dinner of the king of France was, in its demonstration

of strength and vitality, a ceremonial glorification of monarchical absolutism. It was on French soil that gastronomy attained a perfection that, assimilated to the standard of commercial food preparation (the public restaurant), was to be internationally diffused as the unquestioned norm of the official-banquet menu. It was, in fact, with the opening of the first public restaurant (Boulanger's in Paris, 1763) that the banquet and its esthetic achieved their latest (and still current) form. The choreographic element was reduced to the uniform of the waiter and to some of his typical movements (the way in which the wine is poured, a plate carried, or a dish served); and the esthetic conception of the table was limited to the color and the distribution of foods, tableware, and decoration. The culinary industry wrought basic changes also in public tastes, with the gradual disappearance of dishes adjusted to the individual palate. Perhaps the only positive element, representing an esthetic innovation derived from victualing, is the restaurant atmosphere or décor, which, from the initial 19th-century tendency to the monumental — large rooms, brightly illuminated and exuberantly decorated — inclines today to the intimate or the picturesque — low lights, rustic decorations, historical reconstructions, and the like.

TABLE AND FOOD IN ART. The realm of table and food — because of its colorfulness, sensuousness, and sumptuosity — has long been a source of inspiration for painting, although the treatment of the subject as well as the purpose of the representations has differed widely. Mythological, historical, religious, and other types of narration have sometimes offered a point of departure for the representation of a meal (VI, PL. 457; VIII, PL. 183; X, PL. 251; XII, PLS. 44, 77, 82, 93, 96, 365), from the depiction of an opulent court feast (XI, PL. 105) to the naturalistic portrayal of a simple peasant table. In other cases activities connected with the table, by assuming a ceremonial or symbolic significance (funerary or ritual banquet), inspired an extensive representational repertory, particularly in primitive cultures and in the ancient civilizations of the Mediterranean and the Near East. In Western culture the subject of the table and its food, after having been treated incidentally in medieval representations (VI, PLS. 198, 289) and in those of a considerable part of the Renaissance, often found independent expression within the genres of painting that came to the fore after the late Renaissance (cf. II, PLS. 182, 361; XIV, PL. 286) — especially in the still life (q.v.). Its character being generally alien to any narrative function, the still life gives a clearer measure of the importance of the esthetic quality inherent in the shapes and colors of the convivial display.

Among the most ancient iconographies concerning victualing, those revealed by Egyptian archaeological findings are of fundamental importance. The need of supplying the deceased with all that was necessary for the preservation of life after death led the Egyptians to provide their tombs — beginning with the time of the Old Kingdom — with representations of banquet scenes (PL. 370; IV, PLS. 334, 371; VII, PL. 358) and foodstuffs. The most customary scenes — painted or sculptured, in the round or in bas-relief — are those depicting the preparation of bread, from versions of a woman grinding wheat to the small models of the late Memphite period portraying bakers at work. In addition to these, there are scenes of the butchering of animals and the brewing of beer, as well as hunting, fishing, or harvesting scenes (IV, PLS. 335, 337). All these representations are excellent documentation of ancient Egyptian banquet customs and food preferences, for they portray in scrupulous detail the table and its victuals (IV, PLS. 362, 366, 371, 384; VI, PL. 54), endowing the subject with moral reality in keeping with an esthetic sensitivity that was later to be exemplified in the still life.

The iconography of the Etruscan world offers a similarly rich and varied documentation of banqueting, ranging from the reliefs of the small cippi from Chiusi to the frescoes of the tombs of Tarquinia (PL. 370; VI, PL. 55). Seldom, perhaps, has the daily act of eating resulted in so copious and unusual a representational glorification — albeit for clearly eschatological purposes (see ETRUSCO-ITALIC ART). It is generally on the table

itself and its equipment that these pictorial or sculptural image focus; from the initial human interest — the representation table guests (I, PL. 363; V, PL. 46) — there is a noticeable tren toward an increasingly detailed analysis of the table settir (Tomb of Orcus). Roman iconography related to the tab was less specific in its aims (PL. 370; VIII, PL. 232).

Subject matter inspired by the world of the table and foo is not encountered again in art until the late Middle Ages, in th miniatures of royal chronicles and religious texts (VI, PLS. 28 316; VIII, PL. 97; X, PL. 73), many of which depict Biblic scenes in contemporaneous settings. However, here it is n possible to speak of a specific influence exerted by the pi turesque, opulent, and colorful character of the feast on rep resentational art; rather, the art resulted from the need to illus trate a narration in detail. It is only in the 16th century, whic saw a new popularity of banqueting scenes in art, that, beyon the religious or historical pretext of the subject, one may discer the artist's satisfaction in dealing with a theme that is cor genial to him and in which he can express the ideal of mag nificence and elegance of his time. Even in some earlier 15th century examples, but predominantly in the painting of th second half of the 16th century and in the 17th century, th sacred subject matter, enriched by the particulars of a contem poraneous chronicle, skillfully masked the profane rendering striking examples are the many versions of such Biblical theme as the Marriage Feast at Cana (cf. PL. 372), Esther's banqu for Ahasuerus, Belshazzar's Feast, the feast in the house Levi (cf. XIV, PL. 348), and Christ at table with Mary an Martha (cf. PL. 198). Consequently, when in the course the 17th century the arts opened out to the interests of a huma and domestic reality, the sacred subject began to lose favo with artists and was replaced by themes of a prosaic actualit even in the case of a classicist such as Annibale Carracci (q.v. as in his Bean Eater (PL. 372); by the realistic scenes of everyda life of a Bernardo Strozzi, as in his La Cuoca (Genoa, Palazz Rosso); and by the even earlier realistic approach of a Vincenz Campi (PL. 198; VI, PL. 69). An extreme moral rigor wa assumed by the naturalism of Caravaggio (q.v.), in whic he raises the humble reality of the object to a poetic dignit nowhere better exemplified than in his Supper at Emmau (London, Nat. Gall.).

The still life, a logical outgrowth of the new orientation taste in the 17th century, is directly linked, in character an in choice of subjects, to the various experiences of 17th-centur life and sometimes to the baroque custom of the banquet. A early as the 16th century, the domestic environment of th dining room and the kitchen (V, PL. 294; VI, PL. 69) had becom a customary subject in the realism of northern European paint ing, a tendency that made its influence felt, in varying degrees in all European painting. The taste for domestic interiors for genre scenes with foods and drinks (V, PLS. 314, 31 VI, PL. 68), and for still lifes (VI, PL. 73), so typical of Flemis and Dutch art (q.v.; see also GENRE AND SECULAR SUBJECTS) found various interpretations in other traditions as well. I France they extended from the realism and the strong fol orientation of the Le Nain brothers (q.v.; IX, PL. 113) to the re fined compositions of Jean Baptiste Chardin (q.v.; PL. 207 III, PLS. 214–216); in Italy they embraced the innumerabl still lifes — from Caravaggio's Basket of Fruit (Milan, Pin Ambrosiana) to the works of Evaristo Baschenis (PL. 209 II, PL. 184) and Giovambattista Ruopolo (PL. 205) — as we as themes of domestic life and the rustic banquet, portraye especially by the Tuscans, such as Baldassare Franceschin ("Il Volterrano"; PL. 372; VI, PL. 70) and Jacopo Chiment (da Empoli), the Lombard painters, and the Roman Bamboc cianti (q.v.).

Piero M. CAPPONI

Still life and genre subjects continued to enjoy moderat favor in a variety of treatments during the 19th century, espe cially within the sphere of a narrative realism of romanti influence that reflected many aspects of contemporaneous cus tom (VI, PL. 77; XI, PL. 443). The contribution of Frencl art — from impressionism (q.v.) to Cézanne (q.v.; PL. 211; III

...s. 184, 185), to the Fauves and Picasso (qq.v.; IX, PL. 393) — ...ough continuing the tradition of still life, freed the represen-...tion of food or the table from narrative or environmental ...ntext and from its relation to the theme of eating or to con-...mporaneous customs. Interest is concentrated, rather, on the ...sential nature of the object and its poetic content, in a manner ...ttle different — except in stylistic treatment — from the ex-...ressive manner of Caravaggio in his *Basket of Fruit* or of ...hardin in some of his compositions. In the European and ...ternational tradition of the 20th century, whether objective ...r nonobjective, there is little connection between the table ...d still life other than the process of formal simplification ...at characterizes both, as exemplified in the poetic intimacy ...f Giorgio Morandi (PL. 211; IV, PL. 444; V, PL. 149), in the ...alism of Renato Guttuso (cf. XI, PL. 446), in the nonobjective ...pproach of Afro (Basaldella), or in other aspects of contemporary ...ternational art.

* *

BIBLIOG. Besides the sources and materials cited in the text and in ...e bibliographies of related articles, see: Epulario: quale tratta del modo ...i cucinare..., Venice, 1549 (Eng. trans., London, 1598); C. di Messi ...bugo (Messisbugo), Banchetti, compositioni di vivande, et apparecchio ...enerale..., 2 parts, Ferrara, 1549 (F. Bandini, ed., Venice, 1960); Le ...ouveau cuisinier royal et bourgeois, Paris, 1714; G. Perticari, Delle nozze ...i Costanzo Sforza con Camilla d'Aragona celebrate in Pesaro l'anno 1475, Pe-...ro, 1843; F. Zambrini, ed., Il libro di cucina del secolo XIV (Bib. univ. di Bo-...gna, cod. 158), Bologna, 1863; L. Nicolardot, Histoire de la table, Paris, 1868; ...I. J. L. Baudrillart, Histoire du luxe..., 4 vols., Paris, 1878–80; L. Gautier, ...a chavalerie, Paris, 1884 (2d ed., 1891; Eng. trans., H. Frith, London, ...891); O. Guerrini ("L. Stecchetti," pseud.), La tavola e la cucina nei secoli ...IV e XV, Florence, 1884; L. A. Gandini, Tavola, cantina e cucina della ...rte di Ferrara nel Quattrocento, 2d ed., Modena, 1889; E. Müntz, L'argent ...t le luxe à la cour pontificale d'Avignon, Rev. des questions historiques, ...XVI, 1899, pp. 5–44, 378–406; C. S. Gutkind, Das Buch der Tafelfreuden ...us allen Zeiten und Breiten gesammelt, Leipzig, 1929; G. de Batz, French ...uisines, AQ, IX, 1946, pp. 306–13; R. Levi Pisetzky, Banchetti, cene e ...erende, L'Illustrazione, ed., LXXIV, 1947, pp. 29–31; W. Fraenger, Aus ...ruegels Küche, Antiquariat, VII, 1951, pp. 81–84; Galerie Charpentier, ...e pain et le vin, Paris, 1954 (exhibition cat.); H. Thunoens, Mjödet genom ...derna, Daedalus, XXIV, 1954, pp. 47–72; Foire nationale des vins de ...rance, L'art et la table: Tapisseries et peintures du XVI⁸ siècle à nos ...urs, Mâcon, 1956 (exhibition cat.); L'arte e il convito, Milan, 1957 (exhibi-...on cat.); G. Berg, Om ostrom, Fataburen, 1957, pp. 15–28; G. Picard, ...a mosaïque des taureaux découverte à El-Djem, B. archéol., 1957, pp. 106–...3; M. T. Maugis, La gourmandise inspire les artistes, Jardin des arts, ...o, 1958, pp. 70–77; R. Pylkkanen, A History of Finland's Dining Habits, ...1us. News, XXXVIII, 2, 1959, pp. 32–35; G. and G. Blond, Histoire ...ittoresque de notre alimentation, Paris, 1960; M. Rohrlich, Brot: Ewiges ...Iotiv künstlerischen Schaffens, Detmold, 1960; S. de Marinis, La tipologia ...el banchetto nell'arte etrusca arcaica (S. archaeol., I), Rome, 1961; F. ...ournier, DA, s.v. cibaria; M. Pottier, DA, s.v. coquus.

Piero M. CAPPONI

Illustrations: PLS. 367–374.

TAGORE, ABANINDRANATH, GOGONENDRANATH, and RABIN-
-RANATH. The three Tagores (properly, Thakkur) have an im-
-ortant place in the artistic rebirth of India — particularly in
-espect to the evolution of modern Indian painting — and in
their country's contemporary culture (see ORIENTAL MODERN
MOVEMENTS). Their importance, moreover, is not limited to
the Republic of India but extends to the whole Indian subcon-
-inent; they have greatly influenced Pakistan and in lesser
measure Ceylon. These are three personalities of such prestige
that, in view of the historical period in which they were active
and within the framework of the contemporary political division,
they may truly be considered supranational figures.

Rabindranath (b. Calcutta, May 6, 1861; d. Santiniketan,
Bengal, 1941) is famous for his literary production, which was
awarded the Nobel prize in 1913. But he also has a far from
negligible place in the history of Indian art, thanks to his theories
on art and to his marginal activity as a painter, though these
were unrelated to the many schools and movements of modern
India. From the viewpoint of actual artistic production, how-
-ever, his two nephews, Gogonendranath and Abanindranath,
have a greater significance. His versatile intelligence and exten-
-sive culture make Gogonendranath (b. 1867; d. 1938) an in-
-teresting personality of the Indian renaissance. His paintings
are significant inasmuch as he attempted to adapt to Indian

style the esthetic phenomena and critical attitudes of the West
(especially in his partial adherence to cubism); above all, he
was an artist, an inquisitive artist, open to all kinds of inspiration, not lacking in originality, and with libertarian and social
inclinations.

His younger brother, Abanindranath (b. Jorasanko, Aug. 7,
1871; d. Dec. 5, 1951), was the first representative of modern
Indian painting after its disengagement from servility to Western
illusionistic techniques. Apart from his artistic work must also
be mentioned his activity as critic and theorist and as an animating influence, which constitutes his true greatness. Abanindranath owes his deep interest in the esthetic problems of Indian
art not only to his uncle's influence (exerted on the whole
Bengalese cultural community as well as on his family) but also
to E. B. Havell and in part to Ananda Kentish Coomaraswamy
(Kumarasvami). From Havell he gained the desire and the
means to formulate an esthetic evaluation of ancient Indian
works, considered apart from the symbolic and religious values
with which they are permeated. Conversely, Coomaraswamy's
research, with his severe but well-founded criticism of the
Western-influenced works of the Patna and Delhi schools and
particularly of Raja Ravivarman, showed Abanindranath the
importance of these traditional values and, even more, the importance of the philological method for the clarification of their
hidden meanings and of the sequence of doctrinal and formal
variations. From both men, as well as from his family and
cultural background, he acquired his love for Indian art and a
recognition of the potential world-wide importance of spreading
an objective and complete evaluation of Indian masterpieces.
Seeing in Indian tradition a great and inexhaustible esthetic
experience, he conceived a revival of this tradition that could
face the West with a renewal of India's creative power. Despite
his sensitivity and culture, however, he remained the slave of
an error that was almost unavoidable in his time — he measured
the esthetic value of Indian and, generally speaking, of Asiatic
works on the basis of the traditional tastes and values as well
as the innovations of the West.

Abanindranath began to study painting with Western masters: O. Ghilardi, an Italian, and Charles L. Palmer, an Englishman; but it was his meeting with Havell, in 1897, that brought
him to a decisive turning point. His previous works were
simple experiments revealing his search for a personal style and
a theoretical basis; the results were obviously immature and
often superficial works. Even the well-known portrait of his
famous uncle and the paintings that immediately followed his
personal discovery of the Rajput and Moghul miniatures (see
INDO-MOSLEM SCHOOLS; MOGHUL SCHOOL; RAJPUT SCHOOL) are of
limited value. His genius was chiefly literary, and remained
so even after the change brought about by Havell; Abanindranath was primarily an illustrator. The meeting with Havell
and his intensified interest in creative painting produced works
that were substantially narrative, such as *The Buddha and
Sujātā* (Calcutta, Indian Mus.) and *The Building of the Taj*
and *The Death of Shah Jahān* (both, Calcutta, Rabindra-Bharati).
Some of his works are, in effect, illustrations of classical works
of ancient India: *Summer* (Calcutta, Indian Mus.), for example,
is a composition that refers directly to Kālidāsa's short poem
"Ṛtusaṃhāra."

The contact with and study of Japanese techniques led
Abanindranath to discover their direct relationship to those
used in Iranian and Indian miniatures of the Moghul era and
determined a further evolution of his style, which became more
mature; this was also a result of the unquestionable success of
Japanese works in the West. Instinctively he felt that the Indo-
Iranian Moslem tradition, too, could coincide with the taste of
his times and, as a result, reveal its still vital significance. The
great diversity of origin, types, and styles separating the two
Asiatic productions, so distant in space and time, did not seem
to him sufficient to produce a difference in their success. But
such a difference was, after all, inevitable in view of the variations in historical knowledge and in existing "fashions" regarding Japanese art on one side and Indo-Moslem art on the other.
From this time on, in trying to draw technically closer to the
miniaturists, Abanindranath used water color and gouache

(PL. 376). The study of Orissa cultures gave his works, which were based essentially on color, a new plasticity. The cultural environment surrounding the strong personality of his uncle helped him to synthesize his personal experiences on a theoretical basis derived partly from the teachings of Okakura Kakuzō (Tenshin), who dreamed of an Asian cultural and political revival.

Thus was born the Bengal school, the first truly new and fertile artistic movement of modern India, which is responsible for the expressionistic approach of much recent Indian painting. Its followers include many well-known personalities influenced by the Tagore group. The school reflects not only the experiences of Abanindranath and his work as a vitalizing force but also the theoretical teachings of Rabindranath, often expressed in articles and lectures. The uncle is often engaged in veiled controversy with the nephew, as when he says: "Art is not a gorgeous sepulchre, immovably brooding over a lonely eternity of vanished years. It belongs to the procession of life, making constant adjustment with surprises"; and, more clearly: "Unfortunately there are those who believe it an advantage for a child to be able to borrow its grandparents' age and be spared the trouble and risk of growing, and think that it is a sign of wealthy respectability for an artist lazily to cultivate a monotonously easy success by means of some hoarded patrimony of tradition" (R. Tagore, The Meaning of Art, Visva-Bharati Q., IV, no. 1, April, 1926, pp. 12–13).

The theoretical foundation of the Bengal school, as conceived by Abanindranath on the basis of his experiences, linked the future advance of Indian painting to the tradition of the great Moghul Empire. This theory was based not only on the similarity of the Moghul miniatures to Japanese prints, and therefore to the Western taste of the late 19th century, but also on the desire to contrast the splendor of the Moghul Empire to the political decadence of India under British rule. The theory was in error in that it tied the future to a dead past (this caused further controversies and divisions within the school), but it contained the germ of a fruitful premise: the enormous value of non-Western traditions for the renewal of artistic taste, in delivering it — or at least helping it to deliver itself — from the weight and ties of Western traditions. It is undoubtedly for this reason that all modern art in India and Pakistan has been influenced by the Bengal school, though it later lost its creativity and was reduced to a meaningless academism — its task completed, it declined in a short time. Abanindranath decided to sever his relations with it and return to his brilliant works of illustration, such as the compositions forming the Thousand and One Nights series (Calcutta, Rabindra-Bharati). He finally abandoned the paint brush for the calmer skies of meditation, after having created The Last Voyage: whatever its disputable and certainly not too lofty esthetic value, its aim is to proclaim, with a sense of the tragic unknown to classical India, his profound disillusion.

Abanindranath can therefore be described as a man whose vivid intelligence was applied, for patriotic reasons, to an activity that was only partly congenial. The case of his brother, Gogonendranath (PL. 375), is somewhat different; the lively controversies aroused in connection with the work and personality of Abanindranath, often causing mistaken evaluations, distortions, and misunderstandings, are absent. Yet Gogonendranath, too, was a complex and fascinating personality. Artistically he was not influenced by the movements for the revival of traditional art, but he was deeply affected by the lessons of Japanese art, by both the work — which he studied directly, not merely through reproductions — and the theories of Okakura Kakuzō. His interest in Japanese painting led him to study the technique of painting on silk, and his experiments with gold backgrounds obviously derived from his diligent study of the works of Ogata Kōrin (q.v.). During the period preceding his full maturity, the best of his artistic work (most of it in Calcutta, Rabindra-Bharati) might be defined as inspired by a romantic realism through which he tried to express the yearning for freedom and the feeling of social injustice sensed so deeply in a country dominated by a foreign power (see his Power of Law, a work whose significance is clear). There were also occasional references to the legendary and mythological wor[l] of ancient India, as well as experiments in landscape painti[ng] and more complex studies, such as Pilgrim Beggars (X, PL. 41[?] a work interesting also for its handling of space. Here t[he] technique was obviously influenced by Japanese (and therefo[re] Chinese) art, but the style is quite personal.

Gogonendranath's inquisitiveness and profound cultu[re] brought him into contact with the Western world: cubis[m] attracted him by its treatment of form, but for many differe[nt] reasons rooted in his artistic training, he rejected its theoreti[cal] premises. Instead of considering the cubist structure as [a] unitary and symbolic transformation of a shattered and rea[s]sembled reality, he tried, more ingenuously, to see cubic stru[c]tures in reality itself as idealized by his imagination, superim[?] posing and inserting them at the crossing of planes and obtai[n]ing, thanks to his lively feeling for color, evocative and at tim[es] very pleasing effects. His imagination slid toward the borde[r] line of dreams, of nightmares, or of the fantastic, as a reflectio[n] perhaps, of the metaphysical structures of Giorgio de Chiri[co] (q.v.). The House of Mystery, the World of Dreams, and t[he] Mystical Knight are undoubtedly successful achievements wort[hy] of comparison with other, better known, Western masterpiec[es] Gogonendranath's organizing ability was apparent in his foun[d]ing, with his brother, of the Indian Society of Oriental A[rt] with the aim of achieving a cultural integration between Ind[ia] and England, although the Society later exerted a negati[ve] influence on Indian art, becoming a kind of conservati[ve] stronghold, much against the expectations of its founder.

The third personality of the Tagore family was Rabindrana[th] (PLS. 377, 378). His creative power was concentrated in h[is] prose, poetry, and philosophy; his chaotic and instinctive pain[t]ing is only their by-product, in the true sense of the wor[d]. The urge to paint, in fact, came to him late in life, as a resu[lt] of examining the corrections of his manuscripts and observi[ng] those casual forms which the pen, following thought, traced [on] paper, filling and completing, at first to obtain a clearer tex[t] and then to give a new and independent significance to the for[ms] themselves. He himself states: "When the scratches in m[y] manuscripts cried, like sinners, for salvation and assailed m[y] eyes with the ugliness of their irrelevance, I often took mo[re] time in rescuing them into a merciful finality of rhythm th[an] in carrying on what was my obvious task." On such a bas[is] it is obvious that the pictorial art of Rabindranath Tagore [is] isolated in the Indian world and is, as well, spontaneous an[d] linked to the subconscious. Only gradually do the creat[ed] images find connection with the memory of the outer wor[ld] and assume definite, often monstrous, forms, which in tu[rn] reveal a unique stylistic structure, in the masklike profiles, [in] the angular contours, in the geometric figures, as in the La[dy] with the Urn (several versions, Santini Ketan, Bengal, Rabindr[a] Sadana). The paintings of Rabindranath Tagore are few an[d] occasional, but in their indisputable originality they are relat[ed] to the creations of Wassily Kandinsky and Le Douanier Rou[s]seau (qq.v.), just as the common component linking them [is] the unconscious makes them comparable to other products [of] modern art (X, PLS. 106, 107).

For the painter himself, perhaps, his paintings were litt[le] more than a game, the instinctive need of a complex sou[l]. It is, however, the very geometric and formal originality of h[is] art that causes a problem; and undoubtedly it has not entere[d] into the esthetic evolution of modern India as a casual exerci[se] of one who is unquestionably a genius in other fields. On t[he] other hand, a character in one of Tagore's novels, who expec[ts] and demands from a new literary personality "creations, straig[ht] and sharp — like thorns, like arrows, like spear-heads . . . n[ot] self-complacent but aggressive; even if they be crude like [a] jute-mill or a Government secretariat," might be referring [to] the author himself and to his art, since the same charact[er] concludes: "Let us disenchant ourselves from the witchery [of] musical forms," which is a veiled allusion to the author's ow[n] poems. The later paintings of Rabindranath Tagore, whatev[er] value he himself attached to them, are an integral part of a[n] evolutionary process which led to a continuous surpassing [of] himself and which constituted his greatest significance.

BIBLIOG. J. Madsen, Abanindranath Tagore, Rupam, XIX–XX, 1924, p. 115–17; A. B., Abanindranath Tagore and the Renaissance of Indian Painting, Rūpa Lekhā, I, 1, 1929, pp. 41–48; G. Venkatachalam, Gogendra Nath Tagore, Rūpa Lekhā, 5, 1930, pp. 40–44; O. C. Gangoly, Gonendra Nath Tagore: The Great Indian Artist, Modern Rev., LXIII, 1938, pp. 327–29; ThB, s.v.; R. Chakravarty, Abanindranath Tagore: His Early Work, Calcutta, 1951; R. C. Chandra, Abanindranath Tagore, Calcutta, 1951; P. R. Ramachandra Rao, Modern Indian Painting, Madras, 1953; Chintamoni Kar, ed., Gogonendranath Tagore, Calcutta, 1957; N. C. Bhatcharyya, Paintings of Rabindranath Tagore, Rūpa Lekhā, XXVIII, 2, 1958, pp. 66–74; Vollmer, IV, 1958, p. 411; S. K. Nandi, Abanindranath Tagore's Concept of Aesthetic Universality, J. of Aesthetics, XVIII, 1959, p. 255–57; G. Tucci et al., Omaggio a Rabindranath Tagore, Rome, 1959 (at.); M. Rajanand, Painting of Rabindranath Tagore, Mārg, XIV, 2, 1961, p. 2–44; Rabindranath Tagore, Drawings and Paintings (Centenary 1851–1951), New Delhi, 1961.

Mario BUSSAGLI

Illustrations: PLS. 375–378.

TAMAYO, RUFINO.

Mexican painter (b. Oaxaca, 1899). One of the "big four" of Mexican art, Tamayo is fundamentally an easel painter and abstractionist, although he has also executed murals and revolutionary themes. His fellow painters Agustín Lazo and Roberto Montenegro introduced him to the folk art of Mexico and the avant-garde art of France soon after he completed a year of study in 1918 at the Academia de S. Carlos in Mexico City. At the precocious age of twenty-two Tamayo was appointed head of a department in the ethnographic section of the Museo Nacional de Antropologia, where he acquired an extensive knowledge of pre-Cortes artifacts. Out of this early background evolved the essential ingredients of his work: motifs from folklore and folk art, from pre-Columbian art, and from the school of Paris, leavened by a mystical expressionism (I, PL. 146). As early as 1926 — the date of his first exhibition — Tamayo had become the champion of a counter-Revolutionary minority opposed to the militant nationalism, reactionary esthetics, and Marxist ideology of the mural renascence. So well entrenched, however, were the muralists that after 1930 Tamayo began to orient his professional activities more and more toward New York.

As a whole, Tamayo's œuvre — something under two hundred canvases, a smaller number of prints and drawings, and some scattered murals — is narrow in range but rich. Certain themes predominate in his art (time — sun, moon, and stars; hunger — food scenes; terror and death — howling dogs, predatory birds, skulls, "Judas" figures), the mythopoeic character of which derives from his cultural heritage as a Mexican Indian. Tamayo has fleshed these powerful and violent concepts with a unique tissue of subtle, luminous colors; cyclically bright or muted, they register his moody response to external reality. Less personal are the forms he borrows and transposes from modern French sources. His later works indicate an increasing abandonment of mystical, cosmic space and an assertion of flat, textured surfaces.

MAJOR WORKS. a. Easel paintings: Women of Tehuantepec, 1939, Buffalo, N.Y., Albright-Knox Art Gall. – Women Reaching for the Moon, 1946, Cleveland, Mus. of Art. – Homage to the Indian Race, 1952, Palacio de Bellas Artes, Mexico City. – Venus in Her Bedroom, 1956, New York, Samuel Newhouse Coll. b. Murals: 1943, Northampton, Mass., Smith College, Hillyer Art Lib. – 1957, Paris, UNESCO headquarters.

BIBLIOG. X. Villaurrutia, Rufino Tamayo, Buenos Aires, 1951; P. Westheim, Tamayo: Una investigación estetica, Mexico City, 1957; O. Paz, Rufino Tamayo, Mexico City, 1959.

James B. LYNCH, Jr.

TANAGRA STATUETTES.

See ATTIC AND BOEOTIAN ART.

TAOISM.

This is the trend of thought that has affected most strongly the Chinese artistic civilization (see CHINESE ART). Because of its heterogeneous character, Taoism eludes rigorous definition, just as its very origin still escapes satisfactory historical reconstruction. As far back as the most ancient Taoist texts it is possible to encounter, alongside perceptions that are purely philosophical even though expressed in an idiom abounding in images, mythological elements that are partly original and partly derived from an already formed tradition. Subsequently, accepting and making its own certain practices of direct or remote shamanistic origin (see SHAMANISM), Taoism tended toward a pragmatic doctrine seeking to transform alchemically — according to special criteria and for particular purposes — natural and human reality; in this respect Taoism may also be considered one of the many magical conceptions of the world (see MAGIC). Having been enriched with a pantheon of historical or semihistorical deified figures and with a literature made up of imaginary stories in which the wondrous and the miraculous are the predominant elements, Taoism became for Chinese artists and craftsmen an inexhaustible source of inspiration from which they have continued to draw, as some productions of contemporary popular art testify. But it is above all the central idea of the Taoist conception — the harmonious union of man with the cosmos, to be effected by an integration with nature — that has had the consequences of greatest importance in the sphere of art, giving rise to the great Chinese landscape painting (see LANDSCAPE IN ART) and stimulating reflection on the artist's creative act and on the nature and value of his product (see ESTHETICS). Taoism also provided (and still provides) artists themselves with a point of departure for the formulation of their individual esthetic. Confucianism and Buddhism (qq.v.), initially not very sensitive to art as such, were forced by the rivalry of Taoism to take a deeper interest in this sphere of human activity and to devise a philosophy of art in the wake of the Taoist one.

SUMMARY. The tao (col. 898). Taoism in the Chou period (col. 899). Taoism and the crafts (col. 899). The concept of ch'i (col. 900). The Taoist pantheon and its reflection in art (col. 901). Taoism and the concept of art (col. 902).

THE TAO. The term "Taoism" is derived from the Chinese tao, meaning a road or a way. Specifically the word was used for major imperial highways that led to the metropolis or connected major centers. From this basic meaning there accrued to the word the sense of guidance and being guided, of the security that comes from riding or driving on a well-planned and well-laid-out road, thus avoiding the danger of being lost or worse, and the connotation of directedness and direction, since the road led toward a common goal or aim. Finally it came to have the meaning of commonly accepted conduct, since everyone would use this road who wanted to reach the desired goal.

In the terminology of Chinese philosophy the word "tao" was adapted and defined to serve special purposes in the conceptual system of almost all schools of philosophy. There is no doubt that differing usages by different schools were derived from one another and influenced one another, but it is a moot question which school used it first and in what specific meaning. It is a matter of record, however, that all early Confucianist writings, beginning with the Analects of Confucius, employed the term frequently. In the Analects it means a common or proper way of doing things, a pattern of behavior, more specifically one which is directed by the Confucianist virtues and which is supposed to become the natural, spontaneous way of acting for a good Confucianist. In late-Chou Confucianism (e.g., in the Hsün-tzŭ) "tao" does not necessarily denote a correct pattern of behavior but rather the pattern of behavior characteristic of a certain human type; thus there is the tao of the gentleman and the tao of the commoner. In later Confucianist terminology the stress is, however, on the proper way to act, and the connotation of guidance along the proper way is particularly emphasized, so that eventually "tao" came to mean the orthodox Confucianist tradition and to denote something like ethics, both in the sense of a transmitted and generally accepted ethical code and in the sense of an ethical pattern of behavior. Other connotations, however, have also been kept alive in the Confucianist tradition. When an early Confucianist classic defines the tao of higher education it means both the aim of higher education and the method by which this aim is achieved. The Confucianist school has not restricted the usage of the word to human aims and human behavior. The *wing* (commentaries) of the *I-ching* ("Book of Changes"), for instance, refer not only to the tao of man but also to the tao of heaven and the tao of earth, thus designating courses of events beyond human control, which, at least to a certain extent, dominate human fate.

Other schools of Chinese thought have subjected the term to different interpretations. For the Legalist school it was the immutable principle from which derived all relationships and events, particularly in the human sphere, a norm at times almost mechanistically understood. For the naturalist school it had a meaning that comes close to the Western concept of natural law. For the Politician and Strategist groups it meant the clue to the configuration of circumstances, taken dynamically, within which but also with which they worked.

TAOISM IN THE CHOU PERIOD. The term "tao" had its most interesting development in the school named from it: Taoism. The classic of this school, attributed to the philosopher Lao-tzu, is the *Tao-tê-ching* (variously dated 6th–3d cent. B.C.). In this book the Tao is conceived as transcending the rational and the pragmatic and is elevated to the metaphysical and even the mystical, although its manifestations pervade the rational and the pragmatic as well. Fundamentally beyond the grasp of the conscious human mind, the Tao is to be intuited rather than understood; because it is all-pervasive, it is only in consonance with it that existence and action can subsist. Against this foil temporal institutions and relationships become relative, they lose substance and essence. The character of this concept, which is observed in its working rather than in its being, owes much to the thought system of the *I-ching*. Other Taoist classics such as the *Lieh-tzŭ* (variously dated 5th cent. B.C.–3d cent. of our era) and the *Chuang-tzŭ* (3d cent. B.C.) elaborate on it in stories and fables whose images are the products of creative imagination and in part taken from traditional Chinese mythology and legend (see MYTH AND FABLE, cols. 491–92). With the help of these images a world conception is created in which human existence and human fate are stripped of their rational and pragmatic components. It is a world in which mystical relationships and magical powers play a great part, a world, however, given meaning and coherence by the all-pervading principle of the great Tao, which works spontaneously and on a level beyond human consciousness but which is occasionally rationalized into definable concepts such as "the great beginning" or personalized into the figure of a creator. In consonance with this power, which can be discerned mystically or by observation and experience, human existence, in the eyes of the Taoists, was assigned a much lower position in comparison to the postulates of other schools: it was an existence of sheer being.

TAOISM AND THE CRAFTS. The mythological pantheon of the Taoist classics was influenced by, and may to a degree have influenced, the content of traditional mythology; but even in preimperial China the process of the displacement of mythology from the high culture had progressed significantly. Mythology thus came to be more and more the domain of popular religions, faiths, and observances, where, in fact, it had always been strongest. This seems to have been particularly true for the beliefs and usages current in the craftsmen's guilds. In the surroundings of the smithy, the foundry, and the kiln, the workshops of the weavers, the builders, the wood carvers, and the stonecutters — that is to say, in all those contexts in which the mastery of a craft led to artistic creation — the images offered by traditional mythology and even specific mythologies had remained vibrantly alive. The affinity between the world view of Taoism and the religious moods prevailing in the crafts soon drew the two together. Taoist articulations benefited craft expression, and the crafts in turn enriched Taoism, so that eventually the applied arts were incorporated in the sector of Chinese life that was dominated by Taoism.

This marriage between Taoism and the crafts brought to Taoism a protoscientific knowledge of, and experience with, the products of nature that the craftsmen had mastered and th added a degree of concreteness to its nature concept and the concept of Tao itself. The specific way in which natu behaved, and was made to behave, in the workshops and the furnaces refined and gave direction to Taoist thinking co cerning the laws of nature. A more intimate knowledge these laws led to metarational and alchemical experimentati and speculation, to a search for the formula that would tran form baser metals into gold and for the essence that wou prolong human life and eventually make man immortal. The speculations were supported and elevated to a higher level generalization by the transformative (creative) aspects of t Tao and were influenced, too, by the basically asocial attitu of Taoism: serving individual, not social, aims, they took pla outside of, and at times in opposition to, the Confucianistica institutionalized mainstream of Chinese history. An exemplific tion of these trends may be seen in Liu An (d. 122 B.C.), prin of Huai-nan, who compiled a compendium of Taoist philosop and speculation, the *Huai-nan-tzŭ*, and was deeply involve like most rulers of his time, in alchemistic beliefs and practice

The world view expressed in craft products in turn gain cohesion, justification, and sophistication from these Taoist co nections. The mystical aspects of the Tao concept and Taoi mythology offered the craftsman an imaginative imagery tha even where it appears representational, depicts the essen behind appearance rather than appearance itself; the craftsm was not bound to shapes offered by the appearance of natu and the world of man or to the rationally functional. Th greater freedom broadened his range of expression to inclu the fantastic, in terms of both imagery of a nonrepresentation character currently accepted in the world of popular lore a mythology and imagery offered by his unconscious mind. E amples can be found in the phantasmagorical imagery of t lacquerers, stonecutters, and other artisans of the Han peri (II, PL. 31; III, PL. 232; XII, PL. 491), whose cosmos is po ulated by figures breathing the spirit of Taoist conceptions the world and the individual.

In addition to its enrichment by the crafts, Taoism w affected by regional religious and magicoreligious influenc (see MAGIC, cols. 390, 392). Certain parts of China were famo for their shamans and medicine men even in ancient time particularly the northeastern, central, and lower-Yangtze region Several contributions in the anthology *Ch'u-tzŭ*, especially th so-called "Nine Songs," testify to this influence. From thes influences Taoism absorbed shamanistic beliefs about cosm flights of the spirit, about mystical unions with deities, fr quently garbed in the form of beautiful young females, and th ensuing spiritual love-play (PL. 381), as well as much psycholo ical, psychosomatological, and even biological knowledge. Ide about the functions of the body and its different parts, pa ticularly the viscera and the pulse, and their links with th human soul or souls and about the independent character souls (or spirits) and their capacities made their way into e perimental and speculative Taoism from the world of th shaman and the medicine man.

THE CONCEPT OF *ch'i*. The Tao concept arrived at throug this expansion of interests and assumed responsibilities do not basically differ from the Tao concept propounded by th Taoist classics. Even when the world of Taoism had come t include biology and to an extent also the social order, the foc was always on the way in which the universe functioned. Th universe as such had vastly broadened; the original insight int its antithetical character had intimately familiarized the Taoi with the fact that it contained frightening aspects as well a pleasing ones and that it held in store defeat as well as rewar No value hierarchy was superimposed on these contrastin manifestations; the one was as valid as the other, the onl postulate being not to deviate from nature. Conscious effor toward an understanding of this universe expanded also, bu here too, the threshold was still recognized — blurred, to b sure, and not clearly defined — the region beyond which con scious efforts could not reach and apprehension was open onl to intuition and consonant empathy. Thus, although the Taois rely became actual anti-intellectuals, an all-embracing view the Tao yielded only to the innocence of the child or to the contemplation of the detached sage.

As the impulsion grew ever stronger to achieve not only a understanding of, or insight into, but also control over the creative force of the Tao, much use was made of the concept ch'i, a term designating first the breath and then also the vapor contained in breath. Early observations of the life-giving force of the breathing cycle and its rhythm added to the word 'i the further sense of pneumatic energy or, more generally, vital energy; concepts derived from the energetics of animate bodies, particularly human beings, were then extended to encompass the energetics of the spiritual and the artistically creative world. The workings of this vital force were conceived as being manifested in, or even carried by, another aspect of ch'i, the life-carrying vapor or vital fluid (see X, cols. 118–19). This aspect of the ch'i was at times almost materialistically understood as the essence of living matter or even as living matter itself. In search of this vital force or vital essence nature was explored; it was conceived, if the focus was on its dynamics, as partaking in this universal breathing process, or, if the focus was directed toward a specific moment in time and space, as being manifested in a specific atmosphere or mood. In the atmospheric or mood content of a given landscape at a given time of day or season of the year, or more specifically at a given historical moment, this vital essence could be grasped.

For the individual this desire to control and partake in the creativity of the Tao led to another application of the ch'i concept. It was believed that by exercises in the control of the breathing cycle the breath could be linked to and could exploit other sources of vital energy, particularly sexual energy, which in this way could be transformed into spiritual, creative, even magical power. These breathing exercises and the images connected with them resemble those of other civilizations. The strength and special character of the ch'i of an individual and the degree of control gained over it, either through these exercises or in a more spontaneous way, determined the degree and character of his individual creativity (in any of its senses). The specific creative force of an individual was, however, one with the created essence. Individual creativity and the atmospheric or mood content of the creation were frequently understood as merely different aspects of the same phenomenon. The Taoist thus could gain familiarity with, and sympathetic appreciation of, nature — not only its mechanical working but also the concentrated compactness of its momentary content — and could learn, furthermore, to see in his own creative vitality a consonant reflection of the process and the mood of nature. In this way an unobstructed interpenetration of man and the universe could be consummated.

THE TAOIST PANTHEON AND ITS REFLECTION IN ART. During the Chinese middle dynasties (7th–17th cent.) and later, Taoism operated on a variety of levels. There was, to begin with, the Taoist pantheon, bursting with deities, spirits, ghosts, demons, and immortals (PLS. 380, 382, 384, 385; IV, PL. 224; see also V, cols. 402–03). Anthropomorphic figures and, to a growing degree, deified historical or semihistorical personalities tended to predominate, superseding the prevalence of fantastic animals of the earlier period. Lao-tzu himself found an honored place here, as did many who were believed to have achieved immortality through spiritual or alchemical means. A sprinkling of female deities and fairies added charm to this assembly, among them the Mother Queen of the West, Hsi-wang-mu (see IV, col. 818), who became the object of several important cults; the fairy Ma Ku, whose mountain in Kiangsi (Chiang-hsi) Province produces a sweet and intoxicating wine and who gradually developed into a tutelary goddess of seafarers; and the fairies of rivers and lakes. Two legendary daughters of the legendary emperor Yao inhabited the Hsiang River in Hunan, and the fairies of other rivers in the north, such as the Lo in Honan (VIII, PL. 408), soon rivaled them in popularity. The Weaver located in the constellation Lyra, yearning for her yearly reunion with the Cowherd in the constellation Aquila across the Milky Way on the 7th day of the 7th moon, became

the tutelary deity of many female skills. The Taoist pantheon served and was invoked for all aspects of human and social life. Within the family the kitchen god vied with the Confucianistically revered ancestors, as did the couple of tutelary deities who watched over the conjugal bed. In rural parts there were rustic shrines in which traditional images of a male and a female divinity of the fruitful soil were happily united and represented as an elderly couple. All cities were protected by gods of the walls and moats, usually deifications of locally important historical characters (PL. 385). Temples of the god or gods of wealth were objects of pilgrimage for merchants and money-hungry people of all professions. On a national scale famous generals of the past such as Kuan-Yü (Kuan-ti; PL. 385) and Yüeh Fei were revered as gods of war, and the god of literature (IV, PL. 224), originally a somewhat pale Confucianist figure, eventually assumed powers much beyond what orthodoxy would permit.

Religious observances followed a yearly cycle. The most important were the New Year celebrations terminated by the colorful Lantern Festival on the 15th day of the 1st month. For a long time the 3d day of the 3d month was celebrated with considerable license as a spring festival. The 5th day of the 5th month, the Dragon-boat Festival, was celebrated in commemoration of a poet-official who committed suicide by drowning; and eventually the Harvest-moon Festival, the 15th day of the 8th month, became one of the major celebrations, observed, however, mainly within the family. Other religious observances centered around certain localities, particularly the Five Sacred Mountains, of which Mount T'ai in Shantung was the most revered and the frequent goal of even imperial pilgrimages. Taoist temples in the cities and villages or hidden in a mountain valley chosen for its natural beauty — frequently connected with monasteries or convents — became the sanctuaries in which the Taoist tradition was maintained and developed. The Taoist pantheon, with its wealth and color and festivals, became a rich source of inspiration for the pictorial as well as the literary arts.

The degree of acceptance of this variegated world ranged from a pristine credulity, expressed in popular beliefs and observances and in collections of tales of the marvelous, to a rather sophisticated, good-humored tolerance. The adept, however, lived in the web of Taoism on an entirely different level. An intense nature-consciousness was fostered by Taoist concepts and found perhaps its highest artistic expression in landscape painting, especially the mountain landscape (see LANDSCAPE IN ART, cols. 40–41). The Taoist on this level often chose to retire into solitude, perhaps to a hermitage; and experiences akin at times to the pastoral and at times responding to primordial images offered by the dynamics of nature provided the setting for basically mystical explorations. The search for immortality often led to an unfettered, independent spirit, and mystical descriptions of spiritual journeys beyond the trammels of the secular world were given shape in word pictures, paintings, sculpture, and miniature landscapes full of plasticity and color (PLS. 379, 383). A poetic genre, the "poetry of traveling immortals," was created for this purpose by the poets of the time, such as Chang Hua (232–300) and Kuo P'u (277–324), and poet-painters such as Ku K'ai-chih (q.v.) gave fanciful expression to their mystical experiences (VIII, PL. 408).

TAOISM AND THE CONCEPT OF ART. The prevalence of a Taoist approach even in non-Taoist speculation becomes obvious in art philosophy and art criticism. Both Confucianism and Buddhism (qq.v.), if taken strictly, assign only a limited value, and primarily a pragmatic one, to art, as giving dignified expression to concerns of a basically nonartistic nature; contrary strands within these two traditions were frequently considered peripheral or even bordering on the heterodox. The self-assertive force of art, however, was a phenomenon that even the Confucian and the Buddhist could not disregard. During the middle dynasties much thought was given to such problems as the nature of artistic creativity, of artistic expression, and of art evaluation. In all these fields Taoist concepts, or at least the Taoist understanding of certain concepts, were indispensable and were freely applied even by non-Taoists.

When, after a time, Confucianism and Buddhism began to contribute significantly to the understanding of art and to special styles of artistic expression, this was possible only because they had absorbed Taoist influences; even the undeniably profound contributions of the Ch'an Buddhist school in this field can be understood only in this way (see III, cols. 532–33).

Ts'ao P'i (187–226) in his essay on literature was already applying the Taoist *ch'i* concept of the continuum that comprises both the creativity of the individual artist and the mood and style of his product. The painter-poet Wang Wei the Elder (415–43), basically a Confucian, uses in his essay on landscape painting a thoroughly Taoist terminology (unfortunately his main work on art criticism, the *Hung-pao*, has been lost), and Tsung Ping (375–443), doctrinally a Buddhist, starts his essay on landscape painting with the statement that only one who embraces the Tao can respond harmoniously to nature. These two influential little essays must be understood as disclosures of the Taoist attitude toward, and experience of, the nature of both the creative artist and the world he expresses. And Chang Yen-yüan's *Li-tai ming-hua chi* (*A Record of the Famous Painters of All the Dynasties*; W. Acker, 1954, p. 61), finished in 847, starts out Confucianistically: "Now painting is a thing which perfects the civilizing teachings (of the Sages) and helps (to maintain) the social relationships," then goes on Taoistically: "It penetrates completely the divine permutations (of Nature) and fathoms recondite and subtle things," and finally synthesizes both schools: "It moves side by side with the Four Seasons. It proceeds from Nature itself and not from (human) invention."

This Taoistic pervasion of the high culture dominated by Confucianism is observable in all fields of human attitudes and actions. It became particularly strong in the arts, and it grew stronger the more the Confucian gentleman assumed responsibility for all human endeavor, including the arts. Taoism thus became a necessary determinant of the Confucian cultivated personality, once artistic expression such as poetry, calligraphy, and painting ceased to be considered the exclusive domain of the professional and became a natural and essential component of liberal (Confucian) education. This development found striking expression in Sung times when Su Shih (Su Tung-p'o, 1036–1101) boldly claimed painting as a field for the Confucian scholar-official, who, with this integration of arts into Confucianism, himself absorbed the typical stance of the artist, together with the artist's Taoist understanding of nature and of creativity. This Taoist posture is especially evident among the great painters of the Ch'ing period (1644–1912), in whose works both the craft and its object were transcended by the transformative power of the artist in creations that obeyed only their own laws; and in the theories of creativity of Wang Shih-chên (1634–1711), whose subtle sophistication illuminated anew the significance of spontaneity and of absorption in a frozen moment of nature or of history. Even in the 20th century, the Confucian philosopher and reformer K'ang Yu-wei revealed the same Taoist attitude at those times when he gave himself to creative work and to insights into the nature of creativity.

BIBLIOG. J. R. Ware, The Wei Shu and the Sui Shu on Taoism, JAOS, LIII, 1933, pp. 215–250, Corrigenda and Addenda, LIV, 1934, pp. 290–94; S. Jenyns, A Background to Chinese Painting, London, 1935, pp. 75–84; O. Sirén, The Chinese on the Art of Painting, Peiping, 1936; H. Maspero, Les procédés de "nourrir le principe vital" dans la religion Taoïste ancienne, JA, CCXXIX, 1937, pp. 177–252, 353–430; H. H. Dubs, Taoism, in H. F. MacNair, ed., China, Berkeley, Los Angeles, 1946, pp. 266–89; H. H. Dubs, The Beginnings of Alchemy, Isis, XXXVIII, 1947–48, pp. 62–86; H. Maspero, Mélanges posthumes sur les religions et l'histoire de la Chine, II, Le Taoïsme, Paris, 1950; W. R. B. Acker, Some T'ang and pre-T'ang texts on Chinese Painting, Leiden, 1954; H. G. Creel, What Is Taoism?, JAOS, LXXVI, 1956, pp. 139–52; H. Welch, The Parting of the Way, Lao Tzu and the Taoist Movement, Boston, 1957; M. Sullivan, The Birth of Landscape-painting in China, Berkeley, 1962; Chang Chung-Yuan, Creativity and Taoism, A Study of Chinese Philosophy, Art and Poetry, New York, 1963; Mai-Mai Sze, The Tao of Painting: A Study of the Ritual Disposition of Chinese Painting, with a translation of the Chieh Tzŭ Yüan Hua Chuan, or Mustard Seed Garden Manual of Painting, 1679–1701, New York, 1963; B. Gray, Great Taoist Painting, Oriental Art, N.S. 11, 1965, pp. 85–94.

Hellmut WILHELM

TAPA. The term "tapa," which is of Polynesian origi denotes a felted, paperlike fabric made from the beaten ba or inner bark of certain trees, principally members of th mulberry family. At its best this type of fabric, known general as bark cloth, is lightweight, flexible, absorbent, ar soft and pleasant to the touch, but it is neither strong n durable. As soon as woven fabrics are introduced into a socie bark cloth disappears. For this reason, almost none is bein made today. Bark cloth has been used in a variety of way It was used most often in clothing for utilitarian, prestige, ar ceremonial purposes. Frequently it was employed as beddin funeral wrappings, and architectural ornament. Sculptur objects, usually masks (q.v.), are less common, but they a very important esthetically. The making of bark cloth is tropical as well as a primitive art. With the exception of East Island and New Zealand, where little cloth was ever mad almost all the world production has been contained within global band bounded by 25 degrees latitude north and sou of the equator. The highest and most varied developme of the art is attributed to Polynesia, but beautiful exampl have been found also in Africa, the New World, Indonesi Micronesia, and Melanesia. Additional information pertainir to the production, decoration, and uses of tapa, or bark clot is included in Encyclopedia articles on the specific countrie culture areas, and geographical regions discussed below.

SUMMARY. *Central and South America. Africa. Indonesi culture area. Melanesia. Micronesia. Polynesia. Conclusion.*

Central and South America. Bark cloth of medium to po quality was made in Honduras, Nicaragua, Panama, Colombi Ecuador, Peru, Bolivia, Paraguay, Brazil, and British Guian Central Americans produced bark-cloth costumes and mask The Mosquito Indians of Honduras and Nicaragua used ba cloth with brown or red-brown bands of ever-changing painte designs. The remarkably imaginative patterns are crude. executed variations of geometric forms. Circles, triangle diamonds, dentates, and rosettes — often with hooklike a pendages — are common. Masks from the same area are made the form of a bag that covers the wearer's head and have simil motifs combined with painted faces. The Coclé of Panam made dance costumes of tapa, which they topped with de skulls covered with the same cloth. More recently, brillian colors such as yellow, green, and purple have been used, b earlier examples display a subdued brown and tan combinatic painted on whitish cloth. Rows of dentates and dots are th most common motifs in both cases.

The peoples of the Andean countries made very heterogeneou bark cloth. Sheets from Ecuador are bold, simple, and integrate in design. Brown and red-brown decorate tan cloth in banc of rough key forms or checkerboards. Peruvian tapa clot has very crude designs in black, brown, eggplant, and yello on either whitish or red-brown cloth. Some pieces have scatters and apparently unrelated motifs; some are a jumble of geometr designs; and a few have bold integrated patterns with draw outlines rather than painted forms like those of Ecuado Peruvians also produced some powerful masks covered wit red-brown bark cloth, decorated with areas of pitch, and som times accented with touches of white pigment. Most of thes masks have round faces, concentric circular eyes, and beaklik noses, with all the features made of raised ridges painted wit pitch. Bolivian bark cloth (PL. 389) is painted with whit blue, yellow, eggplant, dark red, and magenta on a whit background. Allover designs are composed of forms based o bilaterally and axially symmetrical rectangles. Meanders an hooklike shapes as well as brilliant colors give the cloth a strange Indonesian appearance.

Brazilian bark cloth is the largest in scale in the New Worl Along the upper Amazon large sheets of painted cloth we made. Black, brown, yellow, and French blue are used o sand-colored cloth to form circles, ellipses, diamonds, an drop shapes in a large, well-organized design that is bilateral and axially symmetrical. Indians of the Rio Negro area use bark cloth for huge dance masks that ended in fringed skir and cuffs that concealed the bodies of the wearers. A small stylized face, corresponding in position to that of the wearer, was painted on the mask, and the rest was covered with patterns of diamonds, triangles, dentates, and parallel lines in black, brown, and mustard on white.

Africa. Bark cloth varying in quality from fine to poor was produced in northern Ghana, Nigeria, the Congo region, Uganda, Tanganyika (now part of Tanzania), Northern Rhodesia, Nyasaland (now Malawi), and Madagascar (now the Malagasy Republic). In general the art was rather undeveloped, and many areas produced only undecorated cloth; but elsewhere the types of decoration show considerable variety. The Bushongo (Bakuba) had a unique method of sewing together small bits of tapa, alternating white and gray in simple, regular geometric patterns — most commonly triangles — which are usually bordered by several stripes; the neat stitches are of a contrasting red-brown. The Mangbetu used simple light-colored decorative stitching on otherwise plain dark-brown, blackish, or reddish sheets of dyed bark cloth. Similar cloth was made in Northern Rhodesia and Nyasaland. The Medje of the Mangbetu cluster also produced a cloth with distinctive hook designs (PL. 389). The natives of Uganda produced a red-brown cloth of fine quality and large size with a strong-ribbed watermark. It was decorated with black stamped, drawn, or painted patterns that are orderly, geometric, and usually linear in character. Most frequently, triangles filled with parallel lines or concentric circles are organized in repeated bands surrounded by a border composed of an arrangement of parallel lines. Neighboring Pygmies learned to imitate this type of cloth in crude form; they also used maroon, red, black, brown, and gray to achieve an unnaturally colorful simulation of animal spots and stripes. The Azande, too, made a crude variety of painted cloth with small, simple, repeated rosette patterns in dark gray on natural whitish tapa.

Indonesian culture area. Bark cloth, usually of fine quality, was produced in Ceylon, the Andaman Islands, the Nicobar Islands, the Malay Peninsula, Sumatra, Nias, Mentawai Island, Java, Ceram, Halmahera (the Moluccas), Celebes, Borneo, and the Philippines. Only the last three were important centers for decorated cloth. In the Philippines it was made with painted designs, decorative stitched patterns, and stripes of contrasting strips sewn together. Although almost every native group produced bark cloth, only a scanty amount has survived. In Borneo and Celebes cloth was made with appliquéd bands of contrasting colors combined with embroidery of cross-stitch, outline stitch, and other simple but imaginative forms. Some fine Dyak examples from Borneo display this same technique with the addition of appliquéd strips of dark-red painted designs that elaborate on triangles, dentates, diamonds, and squares. The Dyaks also used decorative stitching in allover designs that reinforced the cloth in a manner almost akin to woven fabrics. Celebes craftsmen used painted designs in black lacquer or gum that was sprinkled with bits of mica for a unique and glittering sequined effect. Linears, or multiple pens that look like bamboo forks, were used, as well as wood or bamboo stamps with simple circular, triangular, or rosette designs. Some cloth was perforated, and bits of mica were allowed to peep through the holes. Spangles, beads, fringe, and tinfoil were added to the surface of other pieces. Many painted patterns from Celebes appear to employ colors acquired through trade: magenta, green, cerise, purple, lilac, and blue. Black, yellow, brown, and indigo may have been native colors. The patterns, which are frequently bilaterally or axially symmetrical and contained within squares, consist of stylized birds, lizards, frogs, stars or rosettes, trees, leaves, centipedes, water buffaloes, and human figures, as well as geometric patterns. All the patterns are extremely complex, splintered, and kaleidoscopic and include hooklike shapes and teeth. Some appear to represent animal or human masks, which are disturbing and equally effective whether inverted or right side up.

Melanesia. Bark cloth of medium to poor quality was made in New Guinea, New Britain, the Admiralty Islands, New Hanover, New Ireland, the Solomon Islands, Santa Cruz, the New Hebrides, New Caledonia, and the Loyalty Islands, as well as in northern Queensland, Australia, and in Fiji, where cloth was made in Polynesian fashion. In the northern part of the former Netherlands New Guinea (now West Irian) totemic mortuary banners were painted with plant and animal forms. The plants are usually palms or other leafy trees drawn in stylized skeletal fashion and growing inward from a border that surrounds the entire square or rectangular field of design. The animals include birds, marine creatures, and lower vertebrates, all of which have a prickly appearance and a disturbing floating or swimming quality. Some animal outlines contain smaller animal forms, and others are decorated with painted curling shapes, spirals, undulating lines, and semicircles. Sometimes the painted designs exist in enlarged form and constitute the only decoration on a banner. Color is limited to red and black on tan.

Bark-cloth masks were made in the Sepik River, Huon Gulf-Tami Islands, and Papuan Gulf areas of New Guinea. The forms they assume are highly imaginative, powerful, and dramatic. Sepik River masks are enormous dome-shaped affairs that were designed to be supported above the heads of a whole group of wearers, while a long fringe of bast around the edge covered their bodies to the knees. The facial forms and painted designs on the masks are very similar to those of carved wooden types from the same area. The Huon-Tami *tago* masks of bark cloth are almost identical in general shape, specific features, and coloring to the carved wooden versions from the same region (IX, PL. 354).

A few sheets of bark cloth decorated in solid colors, plaids, or other designs with the same pigments as the masks were produced in the Papuan Gulf region, but the masks are far more important. Bark-cloth masks from the Papuan Gulf represent an independent art style that is most closely related to that of New Britain. Three types are the *hevehe*, the *eharo*, and the *kovave*. The *hevehe* masks are long ovals, somewhat pointed at the ends, which terminate in palmwood spires and range from 20 to 30 ft. in height. They represent sea or bush spirits inherited within clans. The face occupies the bottom third of the mask. The mouth is usually a carved snout with numerous sharp teeth, and rows of painted dentates in alternating red and black are a common addition. Eyes are concentric circles, frequently embellished with designs related to the specific spirits. Other designs, usually stylized plant and marine forms, as well as a forehead patch, generally fill the upper part of the masks. Dentates or parallel lines are most often employed as a border for the masks. If ears are used, they are wing or flap types that project from the sides. The masks, which are made of white bark cloth, have designs formed by cane embroidery painted in black, pink, rosy red, yellow, and gray. A second type, the *kovave* initiation mask, is usually shaped like a wine bottle. The *eharo* masks are similar in form; but, in addition to the tuft of bast at the top, concentric circular eyes, and diamond-shaped mouth with splinter teeth of the *kovave*, they may assume highly complex composite forms. Some have mouths and ears like those of the *hevehe* masks, and others have large complete heads or animals perched on top. All three types have a deep fringe of bast that hides the wearer's body.

In the Collingwood Bay area of New Guinea bark cloth was painted with black, brown, and rust designs. The design field is broken by groups of parallel lines or divided into rectangles of repeated pattern. The motifs include diamonds, triangles, crosses, chevrons, X's, and meanders. In the last type the twisting curves frequently contain a row of dots.

The Baining tribesmen of New Britain made a very similar bark cloth, except that the designs are far more varied, complex, and irregular. But here too masks are more important. Some masks are cylindrical and others conical (IX, PL. 358), but the best-known type is a grotesque animal or human head. It is roughly heart- or spade-shaped with huge concentric circular eyes and projecting lips, from which droops a long tonguelike appendage. The colors are red, black, and white on tan. Painted designs, usually dark lines with small white dots, form forehead patches, cheek patterns, and eye rings. A frequent motif found under the chin consists of alternating rows of black and red triangles. The backs of these masks are decorated with patterns like those on flat pieces of cloth. They were worn with a costume of leaves and bark. The Duk-duk society used tall, dark conical masks with a bold white pattern of concentric circular eyes and highly stylized features. A heavy fringe covered the wearer's body, and the mask was topped by a white tuft. A few of these masks have tiers of fringe and lack facial forms.

Bark cloth from the remainder of Melanesia is not plentiful, but it is varied, interesting, and often beautiful. The people of the Admiralty Islands produced bark-cloth dance aprons decorated with bands and fringe made of shells, seeds, and feathers. The designs were composed of diamonds or of clusters or rows of drops. The islanders of New Ireland made masks covered with bark cloth that are similar in style to carved wooden masks from the same area. Solomon Islands bark cloth is unique for the subtle French blue on powder blue color scheme of its bold painted designs. Santa Cruz bark cloth has drawn designs of fine black lines arranged in long zones of herringbones, rhombuses, diamonds, triangles, and crosshatching (PL. 390; in this example the black has now faded to blue). The natives of the New Hebrides Islands decorated their bark cloth with feathers, as well as with painted designs using stylized representations of rosettes, leaves, vines and trees arranged in allover patterns with heavy black outlines.

Micronesia. Though the Micronesians produced little bark cloth, the art was not unknown in the Caroline Islands, Uvéa (Wallis Islands), and Futuna. In the latter a stiff white cloth similar to inferior western Polynesian types was produced, but the decoration is purely Micronesian, an imitation of Micronesian and Indonesian mat patterns. Sometimes a red glaze was used with red, brown, and black paint. The surface of the cloth resembles graph paper. Some squares are filled, while others are left blank to simulate woven threads of contrasting colors. The borders of these pieces frequently contained larger and more complex motifs, including centipedes, cowrie shells, and abstract forms of Indonesian origin.

Polynesia. Bark cloth of fine quality was produced in Fiji, Samoa, Tonga, Niue, the Cook Islands, Tahiti, the Austral Islands, Rapa, the Tuamotu, the Marquesas Islands, Pitcairn Island, New Zealand, Easter Island, and Hawaii.

In Fiji, Tonga, and Samoa large white sheets were produced by pasting together a number of individual strips of cloth. The most typical form of decoration is a brownish-red design created by a rubbing process. The effect is that of a rather dense aggregation of slightly blurred parallel lines arranged in simple, regular geometric patterns — typically diamonds, crescents, triangles, bands, and herringbones (IX, PL. 458). Western Polynesians also produced a stiff dark-red, brown, or blackish glazed cloth, with or without an underpainted pattern. Rubbed designs were sometimes embellished with small quantities of glaze used for the purpose of singling out elements or adding new ones (PL. 388). In either case the worker used creative selection of a high esthetic order. Western Polynesian painted motifs are fairly homogeneous, but rosettes and designs of Melanesian and Indonesian origin are more typical of the Fiji Islands. Examples include mat patterns, swimming and crawling creatures, and trees, vines, and leaves (PL. 388). On the whole, Fijian tapa is darker and more dynamic and disturbing in design. Sharp, almost brittle stars with six or eight points placed sparingly on a white background, as well as small X's in the border, are common in many Fijian tapas (PL. 387). Tongan and Samoan tapa (PLS. 386–388) tends to be more regular and geometric in its organization of natural forms; and bright colors, such as yellow and powder blue, are more apt to relieve the red, brown, black, and white patterns.

Fringed ponchos were made in Niue, the Cook Islands, and Tahiti (PL. 388). Those from Niue are of stiff white cloth. They are decorated with drawn black geometric designs similar to those of western Polynesia, or with vines that suggest Indonesian influences, or with a combination of the two motifs. The Cook Islanders produced a distinctive type of poncho with perforated designs. Small angular holes form bands of geometric patterns, such as triangles and stars, as well as random designs. The cloth is a solid color, and the cutouts give it a pleasing lacy appearance. The Cook Islanders also made a great variety of decorated cloth. Typical of their production are a yellow and gray striped cloth; a design of very regular parallel lines that was probably printed with a roller (a device used also in Fiji); and a background of salmon-colored pigment that was painted with black and yellow in designs similar to the geometric type of western Polynesia.

The Austral Islanders lost the art of making bark cloth early. However, a fine piece in the Peabody Museum in Salem, Mass., has a bold rust, yellow, white, and black painted design of concentric circular motifs that reveals subtle and sophisticated variations on a simple theme.

The Tahitians produced an extremely fine cloth composed of strips that were felted together (PL. 388). It has a watermark of parallel ridges on each of the layers. Fringe, feathers, and rows of rosettes made of red and black seeds decorated some pieces. Perhaps the most distinctive pattern in Tahitian tapa is the leaf print, for which real fern or other leaves were used to make the impression in crimson on yellow. Together with painted geometric or amorphous patterns, the effect of the leaves is both colorful and delicate, as large areas of the cloth are left undecorated.

Easter Islanders employed fine seams to join irregular pieces of bark cloth into large sheets, which were dyed yellow or orange and may have been painted; but stuffed figures and headbands are the most important contributions from the area. The figures are stiff, with large modeled heads and thin arms and legs, and are covered with grotesque designs that suggest typical Polynesian tattooing or body painting. The headbands are padded and painted doughnut forms.

Hawaii is generally credited with the finest bark cloth in the world; this evaluation can be justified by the quality of execution, taste, and imagination. Hawaiian cloth, also, was felted together to form tremendous sheets. Here the watermark developed into simple geometric designs, which are sometimes related to the patterns that are printed or painted on the surface of the cloth. In some cases bits of bast of a contrasting color were beaten into the cloth to form flecks, and sometimes colors were daubed or sponged on the fabric to create a casual pattern. The most typical forms of Hawaiian tapa decoration, however, were achieved with the liner (PL. 390) and the stamp. The liner produced a great variety of results, such as stripes and complex plaids. Bamboo stamps were more common. They were carved with simple geometric patterns, usually parallel lines, dots, diamonds, squares, and herringbones. The long narrow stamps lent themselves particularly well to the repeat that formed stripes, bands, or borders. Most commonly black and rust were used for arrangements that left large areas of white background; occasionally larger and generally axially symmetrical stamped designs were used. Some of the most beautiful stamped patterns are small allover repeats of rosettes, leaf forms, or tiny geometric motifs. The color range in these patterns is unusually wide, including brown, cinnamon, rust, dark gray, yellow, red, black, and tan. The surface of the cloth is covered almost completely, and the central field of design is often surrounded by a border of linear stamped designs.

Conclusion. In every region the distinctive forms that bark cloth has assumed reflect the way of life and artistic preference of the native peoples. In areas with a strong tradition of painting or carving, identical motifs and color schemes are commonly found in bark-cloth decoration. Also, the degree of crudity or perfection in the cloth itself may be reflected in the quality of other products within a culture. For example, in areas where ceremonials are elaborate, frequent, or prolonged it is natural to find poor-quality cloth and a strong tradition of masks. It is, rather, in the many places where bark-cloth clothing has been used for prestige purposes that one finds

e fine quality, the enormously varied types of decoration,
.d the beautiful patterns that have elevated a simple fabric
the status of art.

BIBLIOG. J. Edge-Partington, An Album of the Weapons, Tools, Or-
ments, Articles of Dress of the Natives of the Pacific Islands, 3 vols., Man-
ester, 1890-98; W. T. Brigham, Ka Hana Kapa, Mem. of the Bernice
Bishop Mus. of Polynesian Ethn. and Nat. H., III, 1911; P. H. Buck,
moan Material Culture, B. of the Bernice P. Bishop Mus., LXXV, 1930;
C. Raven, Bark Cloth Making in the Central Celebes, Nat. H., J. of the
n. Mus. of Nat. H., XXXII, 4, July-Aug., 1932; K. Roth, The Manu-
:ture of Bark-cloth in Fiji, JRAI, 1934, pp. 289-303; A. Bühler and W.
umann, Bark Fabrics of the South Seas, Ciba Rev., XXXIII, May,
.o; E. Saccasyn-Della Santa, Tapas décorés de nos musées, Brussels, Mus.
.yaux d'Art et d'H., B., 3d ser., XII, Nov., 1940, pp. 121-32; F. E. Williams,
.e Drama of Orokolo, Oxford, 1940; W. Kaudern, Ethnographical Studies
Celebes, VI: Art in Central Celebes, Göteborg, 1944.

                                        JOAN T. BASTABLE

ustrations: PLS. 386-390.

TAPESTRY AND CARPETS. The term "tapestry,"
though it is loosely applied to many heavy, figured fabrics used
wall hangings and for furniture coverings, is properly re-
rved for a specific type of hand-woven fabric, usually of wool,
.d, by extension, is applied to machine-woven copies of this
pe in wool and other fabrics.

Although the technique of tapestry-weaving was known
the ancient East (see TEXTILES, EMBROIDERY, AND LACE),
was not developed in Europe until the Gothic period. The
rliest surviving European examples date from the 12th century,
.d from that time on tapestry production was continuous and
idespread throughout Europe, with major centers arising in
rance and the Low Countries. One of the most important was
rras, whose name popularly came to be used as a synonym for
:apestry."

The related art of carpet-weaving, which for the major
.urposes of this article will be considered the making by hand
` knotted pile fabrics into floor coverings, was most highly
.veloped in the Near East. Carpets are recorded as having
.en used in the ancient East and in the civilizations of classical
.ntiquity, but these were likely simply fabrics of heavier weight
.an normal, with no special characteristics, used as floor cov-
.ings; the knotting techniques peculiar to the Near Eastern
.untries produced the heavy, durable carpets popularly known
. "Oriental carpets." Only a few fragmentary examples of these
.ist from the period before the 14th century, although early
.ocuments (8th-14th cent.), especially those by the Arabian
.ographers, mention a widespread production of carpets in
.sia Minor and the Caucasus.

Although they never reached the high artistic level of the
.astern products, fine carpets were produced in Europe, espe-
.ally in France; and many of the European folk carpets, espe-
.ally those of Italy, Poland, Yugoslavia, and Spain, are inter-
.ting stylistically.

SUMMARY. I. TAPESTRY: Technique (col. 909). Romanesque
.eriod (col. 911): *Germany*; *Norway*. Gothic period (col. 913):
.rance; *Flanders*; *Germany and Switzerland*. The 15th and 16th
.nturies (col. 916): *Arras*; *Tournai*; *Brussels*; *Other Flemish and French
.anufacturing centers*; *Switzerland and Germany*; *Italy*; *Other countries*.
.he 17th century (col. 926): *Brussels*; *Other Flemish manufacturing
.nters*; *France*; *Italy*; *Other countries*. The 18th and 19th centuries
.ol. 931): *Brussels and Oudenarde*; *France*; *Germany*; *Italy*; *Russia*;
.pain; *England*. Contemporary trends (col. 936). II. CARPETS:
.echnique (col. 941). The earliest carpets (col. 942). The Middle
.ges (col. 942). Asia Minor (col. 943). The Caucasus (col. 947).
.urkistan (col. 948). Mameluke and Ottoman periods (col. 948).
.ersia (col. 951). India (col. 954). China (col. 955). Europe (col.
.55): *Spain*; *France*; *England*. Folk art (col. 957). Machine-made
.arpets (col. 958).

I. TAPESTRY. TECHNIQUE. In tapestry-weaving, the weft
.reads are passed through the warp threads first in one direction
.nd then in the other, winding around them and covering them
.ompletely. For this process two types of loom can be used,
.ne with a high warp and the other with a low. The first is a
.ertical loom, on which the warp threads are stretched between

two rollers known as cylinders (FIG. 910). The warp threads
(of linen, hemp, or worsted, rarely of silk) are divided by the
insertion of a rounded batten into two sets of odd and even
threads. The back set of threads is brought forward by pulling
by hand on the warp cords; these cords, one of which is looped
around each warp thread, are fastened to rounded staves hanging
horizontally, within convenient reach, about 1 ft. away from the
warp. The weft threads are wound onto wooden bobbins according to color and material (wool, silk, linen, sometimes silver

High-warp loom, Gobelins manufactory, 18th century.

or gold thread). The tapestry maker stands behind the loom,
with the wrong side of the tapestry toward him and the model
(cartoon) behind him. He must move to the front of the tapestry
or use a mirror to check the progress of the work, which proceeds from left to right as regards the design and from bottom
to top as regards the loom. The weft thread is passed first over
the back set of warp threads (half weft), then in the other direction over the front set, thus making a complete weft. As the
work gradually proceeds, the completed part is wound around the
lower cylinder, while the unwoven warp unwinds from the upper
cylinder. With the low-warp technique the warp is stretched
on a horizontal loom (FIG. 911); the warp cords are moved
by pedals, thus allowing more rapid progress, and the cartoon
is placed beneath the warp and reproduced in reverse. With
both techniques the cartoon is reproduced sideways on the loom,
so that when the tapestry is hung on the wrong side the warp
threads lie horizontally.

When the work is finished it is almost impossible to know
which method of weaving has been used except with the help
of a comparison with the cartoon, or by the presence of reversed
inscriptions, or some other peculiarity.

Both systems were already known and used in the earliest
works. In Brussels several very important series were woven
with the low-warp method; the *Acts of the Apostles*, for which
Raphael designed the cartoons (PL. 400); the *Conquest of Tunis*,

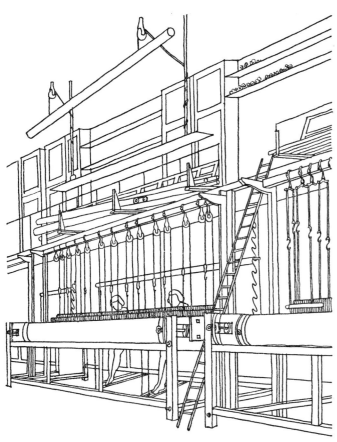

Low-warp loom, Gobelins manufactory, 18th century.

designed by Jan Vermeyen; and the *Life of St. Paul*, for which Pieter Coecke was the cartoonist. The low-warp technique did not therefore imply a lesser quality or value of the tapestries, except at the Manufacture des Gobelins, where low-warp tapestries were less highly esteemed. In the course of the centuries tapestry technique changed only in the details, such as the thickness of the stitch, the number of colors, and the fineness of the materials used.

ROMANESQUE PERIOD. *Germany*. The oldest surviving Occidental tapestry is the *Cloth of St. Gereon*, so named because it once belonged to the Church of St. Gereon in Cologne, where it hung in the choir. Fragments are preserved in Berlin (formerly in Kunstgewerbemus.), in Nürnberg (Germanisches National-Mus.), at Lyons (Mus. Historique des Tissus), and in London (Vict. and Alb. Mus.). The polemics as to this tapestry's origin [Oriental: Bock (1858), Karabaček (1883); Byzantine: Essenwein (1870); Western: Müntz (1883), Riegl (1893), Schmitz (1924), Kurth (1926)] have been brought to a close, as its Western origin has been confirmed by reference to numerous other works. Among these the most important is the Oriental series found in the tomb of Pepin the Short in the Church of St. Ursula, also in Cologne (Cologne, Schnütgen-Mus.). The two works contain the same motifs, namely, a bull surmounted by a griffin, between medallions. In the *Cloth of St. Gereon*, however, there appear, in the border and in the spaces between the roundels, ornaments that have exact counterparts in illuminated Romanesque codices such as the Freising and Altmünster gospel books (Munich, Staatsbib., cod. lat. 6204, 2939). It can therefore be assumed that the cloth was woven in Cologne, where the motifs of an ancient material were adapted to contemporary taste. The St. Gereon tapestry is woven of wool, with only seven colors and about 12–15 warp threads per inch. It displays all the technical characteristics of tapestry, although the medallions, which are equal in size and regularly spaced over the surface, testify to a spirit still closely allied to that of ordinary weaving. The work is generally attributed to the early 11th century.

The type of tapestry exemplified by the *Cloth of St. Gereon* seems to have had scant issue. The 12th- or early-13th-century tapestries of the Cathedral of Galberstadt are quite different. They are no longer purely ornamental, but are of a representative and narrative nature. They consist of two strips and a square cloth, which were made some time apart but probably originated in the same workshop. The oldest is a strip with the story of Abraham and the archangel Michael (PL. 391). It is woven of wool and linen, in a sharply linear style, without any plastic relief. It has been compared to other Romanesque production, notably to the miniature in the *Glossarium Salomonis* of 1153 (Munich, Staatsbib., Clm. 13002) and to the tomb figure, said to be that of Wittekind, in Enger (near Herford). However, it has not been possible to establish any precise interdependence. The tapestry has been variously attributed to the first third (Schmitz, 1924) and the last quarter of the 12th century (Göbel, 1923–34; Kurth, 1926). The later date is the more probable.

The second piece, *Christ among the Apostles*, was executed forty years later (Schmitz, 1924) or perhaps, as other scholars have suggested (Göbel, 1923–34; Kurth, 1926), only a decade or two later. The materials and certain technical peculiarities are identical in the two pieces; but the later one shows a stronger Byzantine influence, a greater freedom, and a livelier plastic sense. Numerous comparisons with Saxon works of art of the second half of the 12th century, especially illuminations, have been made by Kurth (1926), and it is evident that the strips were made in the same artistic climates. The presence of certain knotted stitches has suggested that the strips came from a workshop, probably a convent, in which both high- and low-warp looms were used. This would point, as an inevitable corollary, to an attribution to the workshop established by the abbess Agnes in the convent of Quedlinburg, where the great knotted rug illustrating the marriage of Mercury and Philology was woven. This work, finished in 1203, the year of the death of the Abbess, contains important analogies with the third Halberstadt tapestry, *Charlemagne among the Four Philosophers*. The latter is quite different from the strips. The peculiarity of the use of the vertical warp, characteristic of Coptic works, can be explained by the difficulty of weaving a cloth of a different shape on the same frame as that customarily used in weaving strips. The design has a model in such Carolingian manuscripts as the two Bibles of Charles the Bald (Paris, Bib. Nat., Ms. lat. 1, 2) and the Bible of San Paolo fuori le Mura in Rome. These show Christ among the Evangelists, which could suggest a possible symbolic intent in the tapestry — Charlemagne, in his capacity as founder of the diocese of Halberstadt, being likened to the figure of Christ. In this tapestry there is greater plasticity and softness of design and color, owing to the influence of classical art forms, which were spreading throughout Europe at the beginning of the 13th century. This influence is very apparent in the rug at Quedlinburg. Thus the attribution of *Charlemagne among the Four Philosophers* to the early 13th century (Göbel, 1923–34) seems quite plausible.

The weaving of tapestries does not seem to have been continued in Lower Saxony. No other tapestries woven in Germany in the 13th century have been preserved, while the few remaining 14th-century tapestries are of different provenance and are quite different in character.

Norway. Woven figured cloths are frequently described in the ancient Norse sagas. These cannot, however, be identified as tapestries with any certainty. Fragments dating from the mid-9th century have been found in Oseberg; but the most important example of early Norwegian tapestry art is the fragment of a bench cover from the church of Baldishoel (XII, PL. 415), which depicts the months of April and May ("Prilis" with beard and a long robe and "Ivis" dressed as an armored knight). The similarities that have often been pointed out between this cloth and the Bayeux tapestry are incontrovertible. In the Baldishoel tapestry, however, there is also evidence of the influence of French illuminations of the late 12th century or even earlier. The tapestry was certainly woven in Norway, as can be seen by comparison with later tapestries from the same locality that show a similar predilection for geometric ornamental motifs.

d the same tendency to cover the whole surface with a variety
designs. Because of its provincial origin, the Baldishoel tap-
try cannot be of earlier date than the early 12th century. That
estry-weaving was practiced in the 14th century is testified
the inventory of the church of Ylmheim (Jemheim), in the Di-
omatarium Norvegicum, but no examples have survived.

GOTHIC PERIOD. *France.* By the middle of the 13th century
estry production was quite flourishing in Paris. The *Esta-
ssement des mestiers de Paris* (1258) includes, in fact, the
uvriers de haute lice," to whom it forbids the weaving of
estry by artificial light, as well as prohibiting its practice by
men because it is "trop grevens." In 1308 Mahaut, Comtesse
Artois, commissioned tapestries in Paris, and her orders con-
ued in succeeding years. In 1315 she bought a cloth *a beste-
s* (with small animals), probably a tapestry with animals de-
cted against a millefleurs background. The hangings mentioned
documents of the early 14th century were, however, usually
corated with heraldic motifs.

The Paris tapestry industry reached the height of its splendor
the second half of the 14th century. Charles V of France
d his brothers, Louis d'Anjou, Jean, Duc de Berry, and Philip
e Bold, Duke of Burgundy, were prodigal patrons of the
risian ateliers. Three great merchants and master weavers
minated the scene: Nicolas Bataille (active ca. 1363–1400),
cques Dourdin (active ca. 1380–1407), and Pierre de Beau-
etz (active ca. 1383–1412). The documents relating to their
tivities are a source of information on the tastes and predi-
ctions of the purchasers. From Dourdin, the Duke of Burgundy
quired hangings with subjects from allegory (*Le Roman de
Rose*) and chivalry (story of Aubry the Burgundian) as well
pastoral and hunting scenes. Pierre de Beaumetz sold to
e duke cloths for which the themes were drawn from religion
e Credo) and mythology (story of Jason). Nicolas Bataille
pplied to Amadeus V of Savoy tapestries with heraldic motifs
lemish knots and eagles within geometric figures). He also
ld to the Duke of Burgundy tapestries of all sorts, among them
vers for mules and a caparison for the duke's favorite leopard.
taille's chief client, however, was Louis d'Anjou, for whom
wove *The Apocalypse* (PL. 393; VI, PL. 387; X, PL. 135),
hich, although only partially preserved, is one of the most
portant examples of Gothic tapestry work. It was designed
r the chapel in the Castle of Angers; there are records of ini-
al payments in 1377 to the weaver and the cartoonist (Jean
Bandol, also called Hennequin de Bruges). It is a recorded
ct that the cartoonist was inspired by an illuminated manuscript,
Apocalypse lent by Charles V to his brother. This has been
riously identified as a manuscript in the Bibliothèque Nationale
Paris or as one of several other manuscripts in the libraries
Cambrai, Metz, and Namur. The cartoonists of the 14th
ntury confined themselves to tracing the design and indicating
e colors. The models were usually enlarged by specialized
aftsmen, much liberty being left to the weaver. It would
pear, however, that the *Apocalypse* tapestries were executed
der the influence of a strong artistic personality — perhaps
at of Jean de Bandol — for, despite their size and the long
ne required for their weaving, they show an undeniable unity
style. In the seven hangings, each about 65½ ft. long, the
amed scenes succeeded each other, in two bands, with geometric
ecision and in an ordered rhythm that is accentuated by the
ternating red and turquoise of the backgrounds. The effect
these hangings is skillfully achieved with extremely simple
eans: a coarse stitch (about 12 warp threads per in.), a limited
d austere range of colors (barely over 20 in number), and
signs of great simplicity and linear clarity. The loose joins
tween the color sections give an impression of depth and create
subtle play of light and shadow.

Closely related to the *Apocalypse* tapestries is a fragment
owing the *Presentation in the Temple* (Brussels, Mus. Royaux
Art et d'Histoire), which was certainly part of a larger compo-
tion. It has been suggested, with convincing plausibility
urth, 1923; Thompson, 1930), that it may come from a *Life
the Virgin* woven in 1379 by Bataille for Louis d'Anjou.
Another important series is that of the *Nine Heroes* (PL.

392), a subject then much in vogue. These three tapestries,
which are partly fragmented, bear the arms of Jean, Duc de
Berry, but are not recorded in the inventory of that prince's
possessions and do not correspond to any of the many series on
the same subject recorded in other collections. Numerous affinities with the *Apocalypse* tapestries — in weaving, color, and
ornamental detail — suggest Bataille's authorship. It is difficult to make an attribution of the cartoons; Jean de Bandol and
André Beauneveu (q.v.) can be eliminated for stylistic reasons.
The composition of the *Nine Heroes* is much more complex
and spatially illusionistic than that of the *Apocalypse* tapestries.
For this reason the composition of the former is generally placed
at the end of the century (ca. 1390).

The production of the Parisian workshops came to a sudden
and tragic end; France, devastated by the Hundred Years' War,
lost (1418) its capital to the English. The workshops were closed
down and the weavers dispersed.

Flanders. Although the art of tapestry-weaving must have
been practiced in Arras in the 13th century, no documentation
is available before the following century. There is a contract
dating from 1313 in which Mahaut, Comtesse d'Artois, ordered
five hangings, probably with heraldic motifs, from Ysabiaus
Caurrée, the widow of Simon de Hallenes and the owner of a
workshop. Thereafter documents become more numerous and
attest to the great flowering of tapestry-weaving favored at first
by the constant orders of the countess Mahaut and of the French
court and then especially by those of the dukes of Burgundy.
Arras was an important manufacturing center, whose spinning
and weaving works were organized on an industrial scale.
The same became true for tapestries. Without a well-organized
production and without the use of the low-warp technique,
it would not have been possible to weave in so short a time
the enormous tapestries requested by the patrons. The great
Arras tapestry makers of the second half of the 14th century —
Vincent Boursette (d. 1376), Huart Walois (d. 1414), Jehan
Cosset (Gosset), Andreas de Mouchi (Monchy), Colart d'Auxy
(d'Ainsi, d'Inchy) — were not artisans but great entrepreneurs
and merchants belonging to the noble families of the city, whose
position was similar to that of Nicolas Bataille in Paris. The
tapestry industry in the two cities was in fact closely connected.
Arras manufacturers had warehouses in Paris; Jacques Dourdin,
the famous Parisian *tapissier*, was a citizen of Arras. Unfortunately no examples of the early Arras production have been preserved. Mentions of famous tapestry series have come down
to us in documents and inventories. Their subjects, as in Paris,
varied from sacred themes to legends of love (e.g., the *Royne
d'Islande* and *Ystoire du roi Artus* tapestries from the workshop
of Colart d'Auxy) and from the depiction of the prowess of
ancient heroes (e.g., the *History of Alexander* that Jehan Cosset
wove for Philip the Bold) to that of contemporaneous history
(e.g., the immense *Battle of Roosebeke* — approximately 220 ft.
long — which Philip the Bold commissioned in 1382 from Michel
Bernard and which he ordered Colart d'Auxy to cut into three
parts in 1402).

The only documented work of this period preserved from
Arras is the *St. Piat and St. Eleuthère* series, which the canon
Toussaint Prier commissioned from the atelier of Pierre Feré
and gave to the Cathedral of Tournai, where the four surviving
pieces still hang. An inscription (now lost) stated that the work
was finished in 1402. The surviving tapestries (which are long
but not high) do not represent the best of Arras production and
are moreover in a poor state of repair. The series is nevertheless
of great historical and documentary importance. The *Saga of
Jourdain de Blaye* (PL. 394) is a tapestry of the highest quality
showing certain characteristics of design and technique that are
a sure indication that the work can be attributed to an Arras
workshop (Kurth, 1923) and dated between the late 14th (Kurth,
1923) and the early 15th century (Göbel, 1923–34). In this work the spatial
definition is less precise and the narrative more closely knit
than in the French tapestries woven 20 years or so earlier, while
the technical and ornamental achievement can be considered
equal. The verses on the scrolls explaining the action are an
adaptation in the Picard dialect of a French 11th- or 12th-

century poem; certain details of the dialect confirm the attribution of the tapestry to Arras. The same attribution as regards place of origin and period can be made for the fragmentary *Offrande du coeur*, now in the Louvre. A tapestry which is remarkably similar to the *Jourdain de Blaye* fragment and which must therefore have been woven in Arras at about the same time is reproduced in the "Month of January" illumination of the *Très Riches Heures du Duc de Berry* (Chantilly, Mus. Condé, Ms. 65). The tapestry, which shows the exploits of Bègue de Belin, covers the entire wall at the end of the banqueting hall, extends around a corner to the side wall, thus hiding a door, and is raised above the hearth and partly covered by the canopy placed behind the duke. It is displayed with an aristocratic negligence that explains the rapid deterioration of such tapestries. But no other way of exhibiting tapestry could give so lively an illusion of penetration into a fantastic world — into a magic circle of beauty and splendor that implied a subtle connection with the select society privileged to enjoy such refinement.

Germany and Switzerland. In the German and Swiss production of the 14th century the technical development, the spiritual content, and the monumentality of the earlier Romanesque tapestries are absent. The patrons of the Romanesque period were probably powerful princes, whether ecclesiastics or feudal lords, but during the Gothic period they were nobles of lesser rank, rich burghers, and members of the middle clergy. Anyone who wanted a work of large proportions and rich materials turned to the French and Flemish manufacturers, who were the continuers of the monumental tradition of German Romanesque tapestry. The tapestries produced in Germany were not large: dossals, frontals, bench covers, and cushions were commissioned by churches and convents, which seldom made use of wall hangings. The latter were never found in domestic interiors, where, apart from serving as covers for benches, chair backs, and cushions, tapestries were used on tables and beds. The motifs were naturally suited to the tastes of the purchasers. They were no longer learned allegories or Biblical representations pondered in the studious atmosphere of monasteries that were at the same time lively cultural centers. These themes had been supplanted by readily intelligible stories whose abundant details were represented with great simplicity: sacred subjects for churches, scenes of daily life and popular fables and allegories for homes. The most common material was wool, often combined with linen. The colors were pure and bright and were distributed with a view to decorative rather than naturalistic effect. Within the framework of these common characteristics, which persisted in the tapestries of the 15th century, there were local variations (or rather regional variations, as there was no one dominant center), and production remained within the limits of a specialized craft. Many tapestries were in fact still woven in convents. The weaving was localized in three regions: the upper and middle Rhine areas and Franconia.

German and Swiss tapestries of the 14th century are rare. A small group comes from the Lake Constance region. It includes two strips — one a *Crucifixion* (PL. 395), the other depicting six saints (Nürnberg, Germanisches Nat.-Mus.) — as well as a fragment representing the Virgin (Saint Gallen, Iklé Coll.). The figures are linear and are set against a monochrome background dotted with stars. The generally accepted mid-century dating was established by comparison with the *Crucifixion* fresco in the sacristy of the Cathedral in Constance, which is dated 1348. The linear inflections, attitudes, and draperies reveal the influence of French models, interpreted by an artist who was certainly local. An example of Swiss tapestry-weaving is the frontal showing St. Maurice surrounded by medallions containing the symbols of the Evangelists and allegorical animals (Thun, Historisches Mus.), which was probably woven in the first half of the 14th century. The ornamental and allegorical motifs combine both popular and heraldic elements. Tapestries ornamented with medallions were common in the 14th century. Göbel (1923–34) attributes to the upper Rhine region a strip on which allegorical animals are enclosed in medallions and which he dates as more or less contemporaneous with the Thun frontal. The same kind of medallion composition is to be found in an embroidery cloth in the Wartburg Museum near Eisenac. *Tapis à compas* (medallion cloths) existed also in the collection of the courts of France and Burgundy. The ornamental idiom of all these works recalls the *Cloth of St. Gereon*, but the differences of period, style, and taste are too great for any relationship to be established in this connection.

To the middle Rhine region (more specifically, to Alsac can perhaps be assigned the so-called *Spielteppich* (Nürnber Germanisches Nat.-Mus.), a tapestry illustrating scenes fro feudal life. The style of dress represented and especially t affinity of the *Spielteppich* with the current International Goth style suggest that it was woven in the last 15 years of the 14 century. Its delicacy and refinement, which are rare in the usu Swiss and German products, have aroused considerable contr versy as to its origin. There is certainly a strong French influenc while any connection with the frescoes of the *Months* in t Castello del Buon Consiglio in Trent (VI, PL. 64), former suggested by Schmitz (1924), has been authoritatively eliminat by both Göbel (1923–34) and Kurth (1926). Nevertheless, th tapestry presents problems, for its very distinctiveness mak its attribution to any specific production center difficult. I Sigmaringen (castle mus.), Munich (Bayerisches Nationa mus.), and Regensburg (Rathaus) there are fragments of ta estries, woven in Alsace at the end of the century, that displ some of the same characteristics of manufacture as the *Spie teppich*, although they are completely different in style. Th depict *wilde Leute*: wild, hairy people engaged in everyd activities or in fantastic hunting and battle scenes. They a naïvely popular in spirit and predominantly ornamental character. This perhaps accounts for the widespread succe of the theme, which was to be amply elaborated in the Germa and Swiss production of the 15th century.

THE 15TH AND 16TH CENTURIES. Throughout the 15th centur the great production of tapestries continued in the French ar Flemish regions. They kept the form of wall hangings and the character as textiles, while varying, as is natural, in style. A in the 14th century, royalty, especially the French and Burgu dian, boasted enormous collections of tapestries which we constantly augmented because of their rapid deterioratio Wealthy clerics, feudal nobles, and the most affluent mechan also sought the luxury of possessing tapestries, which were us primarily as interior hangings, but also as decorations for feas and holidays, at peaceful assemblies, and in battle tents (witne the memorable booty of tapestries captured by the Swiss fro Charles the Bold when they defeated him on the battlefield Morat). Contemporaneous miniatures document such uses tapestries in the 15th century. The illustrations in the *Chroniq de Froissart* (1460–80, London, Br. Mus.) and in the *Toison d'C* (ca. 1480, Paris, Bib. Nat.), when compared with older exampl such as the "Month of January" in the *Très Riches Heur du Duc de Berry* (described above), show the prevailing tas for highly decorated and minutely ornamented works and co firm the predilection for rooms entirely hung with tapestrie The iconography offers nothing new except for an occasion subject such as that of the *Story of Gideon* tapestry (now los which alludes to the founding of the Order of the Gold Fleece. Myths, chivalrous and romantic adventures, most whose subjects were copies (in whole or in part) of existi models, didactic allegories — often extremely pedantic — a heraldic motifs persisted, along with continued interest in t chase, in pastoral scenes, and in millefleurs. Sacred subjec were common, but probably less so than would be imagin from the disproportionate number that have survived — b cause they were less frequently used. In Brussels, religious su jects predominated in the late 15th century; small altar cloth inspired by contemporary paintings are also still in existenc This tendency toward pictorial quality can also be seen in cert large tapestries, as in the *tapis d'or* from Brussels, but on t whole it is subordinated to a sense of the qualities inherent textiles.

In the 15th century, the art of tapestry-weaving was develop mainly in Arras and Tournai, which dominated the mark after the disappearance of the Parisian ateliers (owing to t

Hundred Years' War) and whose fortunes were directly tied to the splendid court of Burgundy. The tapestries from Arras and Tournai are rightly (though inexactly as far as period is concerned) called "Gothic," while those from early-16th-century Brussels belong to a different spiritual world.

Arras. In Arras, early in the 15th century (1402, according to an inscription now lost) but with 14th-century taste, was woven the *St. Piat and St. Eleuthère* series for the Cathedral of Tournai (see above). This is the only work to be documented with certainty. What makes it very difficult to assign later productions to Arras or Tournai is the fact that there were close continuous artistic and commercial relations between the two cities and that, moreover, the organization of the work was the same. It is therefore hard to find points of reference for a comparison on stylistic grounds, since no work from Tournai is certainly datable to the first half of the 15th century. The *History of St. Piat and St. Eleuthère* (Paris, Mus. de Cluny) and a fragment from the *Saga of Jourdain de Blaye* (PL. 394) serve at any rate as points of reference in the attribution to Arras of certain tapestries of the first decades of the century: the exquisite *Offrande du Coeur* (Paris, Mus. de Cluny); the five charming hangings showing scenes of feudal life (Paris, Mus. des Arts Décoratifs); and the gentle *Annunciation* in the Metropolitan Museum in New York, the small *Resurrection* in the Louvre, and the *Deposition* in the Victoria and Albert Museum, all Gothic in feeling. These tapestries do not date from later than the third decade of the century. Next to them can be placed the *Scenes from the Life of Christ* and the enormous *Crucifixion* in Saragossa (Mus. de Tapices de la Seo). The attribution of the latter to Arras is generally accepted. In fact, in its episodic discourse, in the soft flow of the composition can be recognized accents from the *History of St. Piat and St. Eleuthère,* while in the four large hunting scenes belonging to the Duke of Devonshire (Chatsworth House, Derbyshire) the various episodes are superimposed without any spatial sense. How distant are the structural rhythms and balanced intervals of 14th-century tapestries! The date of these works is generally accepted as being the 4th or 5th decade of the century but their attribution to Arras, and perhaps to the atelier of Jehan Walois (the chief weaver in that city), is still open to discussion (Göbel, 1953, for instance, does not concur). Even greater doubts surround the so-called *Baillee des Roses* (Met. Mus.), in whose background the colors of Charles VII are woven in alternating bands, as well as the *Bal des Sauvages* from Saumur (Notre-Dame-de-Nantilly). In neither case can Tournai be eliminated as the possible place of origin. Other tapestries of uncertain provenance can be more easily related to the known production of Tournai than to that of Arras.

Toward 1450 Arras began slowly to decline, while Tournai was gradually taking its place in the preferences of the dukes of Burgundy. If the vicissitudes of history after the death of Charles the Bold, culminating in the siege and sacks of Arras by Louis XI did not put an end to the manufacture of tapestries there, these factors at least accelerated its decline.

Tournai. By the 14th century, Tournai must already have had a fair production of tapestries, for in 1398 the industry was regulated by the city government. Production must have developed, much as in Arras, on an industrial scale and have been in the hands of a few great merchant-manufacturers.

The dukes of Burgundy do not seem to have commissioned tapestries from Tournai before 1446, the year in which Jehanne Pottequin, widow of Jehan Baubrée, undertook to furnish Philip the Good with a tapestry to complete a *chambre de verdure* executed by an important weaver from Arras, Willaume au Vaissel. Soon after, in 1449, the splendid *Story of Gideon* (eight tapestries destined for the chapter hall of the Order of the Golden Fleece) was commissioned by the same duke of two Tournai manufacturers, Robert Dary and Jehan de l'Ortye. The cartoons were by a painter from Arras, Baudoin du Bailleul, another clear proof of the relations which existed between the two cities. The series was completed in 1453 and was said to have been one of the most beautiful ever to have adorned a royal court. It

has been lost, however, as have the other works of Dary mentioned in contemporary documents. There do remain, however, certain examples of the production of the famous merchant-weaver Pasquier Grenier (d. 1493); two tapestries in the Galleria Doria Pamphili in Rome (PL. 397) were a part of the *Story of Alexander the Great* which, acquired for 5,000 gold pieces by Philip the Good in 1459, hung together with the *Story of Gideon* in the Hôtel d'Artois on the occasion of the entrance of Louis XI into Paris. There remain from a piece begun in 1454 (depicting the history of the Knight of the Swan) two tapestries now in Kraków (St. Katherine) and Vienna (Österreichisches Mus. für Angewandte Kunst). It is likely (but not certain) that fragments of the *History of the Sacrament* (Met. Mus.; Vict. and Alb.) are from a series donated by Grenier to the Church of St-Quentin in Tournai in 1475. With these tapestries as a point of reference, a large group of works can be assigned to Tournai and dated about 1450. These have not only superficial elements in common, such as the absence of borders, the use of explanatory verses in the dialect of Tournai, and so forth, but also very close stylistic affinities. The representation is all placed in the background, and the numerous episodes, which take place at different moments and in different places, are not presented chronologically, but merge and are superimposed in a kind of vertical projection. The composition is a fanciful mass of brightly colored areas enclosed in heavily drawn contours. A rigidly unified rhythm and a solemn grandeur are derived from this compactness. Never again perhaps was the monumental quality expressed so clearly and uncompromisingly in tapestry.

Not all scholars agree in ascribing to Tournai the *History of Clovis* (Reims, Mus. des Beaux-Arts), which in 1468 embellished the festivities at the marriage of Charles the Bold to Margaret of York. There has even been uncertainty as to the provenance of the *History of St. Peter* (Cluny, Mus.; Beauvais, Mus. and Cathedral; Boston, Mus. of Fine Arts), commissioned in 1460 by Guillaume de Hellande, Bishop of Beauvais, to celebrate the end of the Hundred Years' War, although its origin in Tournai seems to be confirmed by its probable derivation from the *toiles peintes* of the same subject made by Henri de Beaumetiel, after Robert Campin's cartoons, for the Chapel of St-Pierre in Tournai. There is no serious doubt, however, as to the tapestries in the Historisches Museum in Bern: an altar cloth showing the Adoration of the Magi, a millefleurs bearing the coat-of-arms of Charles the Bold, the *History of Julius Caesar* (a series which belonged to Louis of Luxembourg, d. 1475), the immense *Legend of Herkenbald* bearing the coat-of-arms of the Bishop of Lausanne, Georges de Saluces (d. 1461). This last was derived from the lost frescoes of Rogier van der Weyden in the Town Hall in Brussels (destroyed when the city was bombarded in 1659). But the model was very much reelaborated and adapted to the vivid stylization so typical of the Tournai tapestries. The Adoration of the Magi altar cloth also has a painting as a model, but does not succumb to pictorial softness. In the two large hangings depicting the Passion of Christ (PL. 399) the episodes, now solemn, now pathetic, now grotesque, unfold uninterruptedly and achieve a monumental unity. Perhaps the style of Tournai reached its height in the turbulent *Battle of Roncesvalles* (two fragments from one huge tapestry in Florence, the Bargello; and Brussels, Mus. Royaux d'Art et d'Histoire), with its fantastic twisting of limbs and weapons. In these pieces, although they were probably woven as late as 1460, the world of chivalry is still very much alive. Of a slightly later date are the tapestries depicting the history of Troy, the story of Hercules, and the story of Esther, as well as a rare example of a subject taken from contemporaneous history, the Portuguese conquest of Pastrana. Documents state that Grenier sold to Philip the Good a tapestry depicting the story of Esther in 1462 and, in 1472, one of the history of Troy, which was to be presented to Charles the Bold. None of the many surviving tapestries of the same subjects can be positively identified as these. It is known, however, that the series (Paris, Mus. des Gobelins; Brussels, Mus. Royaux d'Art et d'Histoire; priv. coll.) belonged to Charles of Bourbon and was woven between 1476 and 1488. In the Hercules tapestries the range of colors is a little more extended and occasionally more lively; the early stylization is still present, but it has become more elegant and ornamental, with a greater emphasis on detail. These variations do not, however, call for an attribution of the whole group to Brussels, as Göbel (1923–34) has suggested. Indeed, there is a technical reason for not making such an attribution, as the fairly large and irregular stitch (12–15 warp threads per in.) is in distinct contrast to the very regular and small stitch of the older Brussels works, as is also the coloration, which is here not fused, but applied in distinct areas. It is true, of course, that in the latter half of the century the Hapsburgs, who had succeeded to the throne of Burgundy, preferred the production of Brussels, and that Tournai suffered from this competition. In the first quarter of the 16th century, it still possessed very active workshops (that of Jehan, son of Pasquier Grenier, and of Arnold Poissonier); but after 1550, Tournai lapsed into secondary importance as a center of the industry.

After the edict of 1544, which imposed on all Flemish manufactures the adoption of distinctive trademarks for both the city and the weaver, Tournai took as its emblem a tower (see the *History of Abraham* in the civic museum).

Brussels. In Brussels, where earlier production of tapestries had been carried on in small ateliers for a long time (unlike the industrial systems of Arras and Tournai), the industry grew to major importance during the 6th and 7th decades of the 15th century. Even the earliest works display a technical perfection and a range of colors which was much more oriented toward painting than at Tournai. A whole group of altar cloths, among them an Annunciation, an Adoration of the Magi (Paris, Mus. des Gobelins), and a regal Virgin in Glory (Louvre), dated 1485, gracefully follows the painted models. For the first two the name of Vrancke van der Stock (or Stockt) has been suggested; for the Virgin, the "Maître des feuillages en broderie." In these tapestries even the frames and the triptych partitions have been reproduced. Late in the 15th century, the *tapis d'or* (so called because of the abundance and richness of gold thread used in the weaving) were inspired by polyptychs and wooden altarpieces. In them the various scenes are divided by small arches and columns, so that narrative continuity is sacrificed to a new sense of order. Precious materials are used with singularly decorative effect, as in the fine *History of the Virgin* (Madrid, Royal Palace) and in the *Glorification of Charles VIII* (Met. Mus.). Even when the divisions disappear and the tapestries are bordered with intricately twined flowers and fruits the composition maintains its balanced space and rhythmic intervals. The ideal of harmony is reflected in the figures as well. Their faces, much alike, occur almost as decorative motifs, and their costumes are richly decorated. The colors are delicate, and modeling is suggested, the turbulence of the 15th century has been softened by a more graceful narrative facility. The style of early-16th-century tapestries from Brussels is so unified as to indicate the inspiration of a single artist, probably Jan van Roome, court painter to Margaret of Austria and creator of the drawings for the *Communion of Herkenbald* (PL. 401). This tapestry is well documented: it was completed in 1513 for the Brotherhood of the Holy Sacrament in Louvain by one "Master Lyoen" (probably Léon de Smet) after a sketch by this same Jan van Roome, translated into a cartoon by a painter, one Philippe. The style of the *Communion of Herkenbald* is typical of scores of contemporary tapestries. In many of these, words of uncertain meaning have been found ("roem," "roam," "ron," etc.) and they have been interpreted as signatures. The use of "signatures" is confirmed by the *Discovery of the True Cross* (Brussels, Mus. Royaux d'Art et d'Histoire), which bears the name of Master Knoest. The word "Philiep" appears in the *Deposition* in Brussels (Mus. Royaux d'Art et d'Histoire); if this can be accepted as referring to the cartoonist of the Herkenbald tapestry, the artist shows himself, in this and in the related *Descent from the Cross* in the Palazzo Reale in Naples, as an interesting artist, relatively open to Renaissance influences, and with an evident leaning toward the style of painting.

In the early 16th century in Brussels large manufactories arose; among the most famous were those of Pieter van Aelst

and Pieter Pannemaker, furnishers to emperors (from Ma milian of Austria to Charles V), to kings, and to popes. Piet van Aelst was made responsible for the execution of the celebrate *Acts of the Apostles* tapestry, from cartoons by Raphael (P 400), and the lost *Putti at Play* by Giovanni da Udine. V Aelst executed in his workshop and signed his name to t traditional *Passion* in Trent (Cathedral) and Madrid (Roy Palace), dated 1507, and the *History of David* in the Castle Sigmaringen. Many other works have been ascribed to his ma ufacture, although without certain proof. Among these is t *History of Priam* (Piacenza, Collegio Alberoni), still permeat with the aura of courtly legend, and the grandiose *Glorificati of Charles VIII* (reassembled by the Met. Mus.), which perha was commissioned by Philip I the Handsome. The splend *History of David* (Paris, Mus. de Cluny); the noble *Last Supp* in Camaiore (PL. 402), dated 1516; and the tapestry supposed have been made for the throne of Emperor Charles V (Madri Royal Palace) have been attributed to the factory of Piet Pannemaker.

Conditions at that moment in history favored the diffusi of Brussels tapestries; Charles V, who had succeeded to the Bu gundian, Austrian, Castilian, and Aragonese thrones, seem to hold Europe in his hand, and the immense wealth of the Ame icas also flowed into his treasury. The circle of nobles a princes who desired luxurious tapestries was continually wi ening; thus the early functional use of tapestries was gradual supplanted by decorative and commemorative uses. Tapestri were in the early 16th century considered precious furnishing Van Aelst, for example, hastened to place those of the roy palace "en lieu seur . . . sans avoir adverty la Reyne" (in a sa place, without having notified the Queen) at the death of Phil the Handsome.

In the troubled times of the early 16th century, the sty of Jan van Roome may have been found delightful, but it w nevertheless archaic. Actually, it was difficult for the tapest medium to adapt itself to the new styles which were spreading the north from Italy. Not even the *Acts of the Apostles* (PL. 40 woven for the Sistine Chapel between 1515 and 1519 by V Aelst after cartoons by Raphael (seven of which are preserv in the Victoria and Albert Museum), succeeded in this; in t nine panels, Raphael had emphasized monumentality and t sense of mass and three-dimensionality without regard for th character of textile decoration which had until then been co sidered essential. The traditional esthetic principles were al disregarded in the more ornamental *Putti at Play*, woven 1520 from the cartoons of Giovanni da Udine, but the penetr tion of the new style in Brussels tapestries was slow. Not un late in the century did a Flemish artist, Bernard van Orle attempt the difficult reconciliation of the formal art of tapest and the new Renaissance style. In his early career Van Orl (1488–1541) still worked in the manner of Van Roome. In t tapestries executed from Van Roome's cartoons or inspired his work, deviations from the traditional method of compositi and the rendering of space are visible but limited (see the C maiore *Last Supper*, the Madrid Royal Palace *Le Chemin d'Ho neur*). In Van Orley's later works (*Hunts of Maximilian*, Louvi *Battle of Pavia*, Naples, Mus. di Capodimonte), on the contra there is a deliberate attempt to reconcile the new style wi the intrinsic qualities of tapestry. This program was difficu to carry out; and in fact Van Orley achieved only a compromis making use of tricks of perspective while leaning heavily on t anecdotal vein so characteristic of Flemish tapestries, but t results were only occasionally successful, as in the *History Jacob* (Uffizi).

Toward 1550, the Flemish artists who were influenced the Roman school began to follow Van Orley; Jan Vermey drew, between 1546 and 1548, the cartoons for the *Conqu of Tunis*, a commemorative hanging commissioned by Char V (Madrid, Royal Palace), and for the often-copied *Vertumn and Pomona* (PL. 405). Pieter Coecke was the brilliant and liv inventor of complex compositions (the *History of St. Pa* Vienna, Kunsthistorisches Mus.; the *Seven Deadly Sins*, Madri Royal Palace; and the *History of Romulus and Remus*, Bru sels, Mus. Royaux d'Art et d'Histoire), and Michiel Cox eated the *Story of Genesis* (*editio princeps* in Kraków, Wawel astle Mus.) in a cold style reminiscent of Raphael. Meanhile, Italian painters continued to furnish cartoons; Giulio omano's *Putti at Play* and the *History of Scipio* were often .d successfully repeated.

In 1528, a city ordinance required Brussels manufacturers mark their wares with a red sword between two B's (the itials of Brussels and Brabant). In addition to this mark, ch weaver was to sign his work with a personal mark. These onograms, only some of which have been identified, make it ossible to follow more easily the activities of the most important ctories (FIG. 921). Most famous and splendid among them as the workshop of Willem Pannemaker (active 1535–78), rnisher to both Philip II and Charles V, for whom, between 48 and 1554, he wove the *Conquest of Tunis*. Pannemaker terpreted the cartoons of the Roman-influenced Flemish tists, weaving the *Seven Deadly Sins* of Coecke, the *Apocalypse* Madrid, Royal Palace), and the *History of Jacob*, after Van Orley Jffizi; probably the work of Willem de Kempenere). Frans

Guebels, another great *tapissier*, was active 1540–90. Among the many works from his factory are the *Seven Virtues* and the *Months* in Vienna (Kunsthistorisches Mus.) and the *Triumph of the Gods* in Paris (Mobilier National). Some verdures bear his mark, though more often those of his successors, Jacques Guebels and Catherine van den Eynde, who kept the factory going until 1629.

The Leyniers family was already active in the first half of the 16th century; among them were Nicholas, who wove the *editio princeps* of the *Story of Genesis*, and his son Anton, who did several versions of the *History of Romulus and Remus*. Jan Gheteels probably wove the *Hunt of Maximilian* and the *Battle of Pavia*. But after this great period of activity in the last quarter of the century, wars and disorders caused a crisis in the production of Flanders.

The works of this period are mostly hunting scenes and verdures, which were hardly new subjects. The verdures took the place held during the Middle Ages by the millefleurs. In the middle of the 16th century, the verdures with large foliage were very much in vogue. Later pastoral scenes, hunts, and even

eavers' marks (left to right). Town marks: Bruges, Brussels, Delft, Oudenarde, Lille, Paris, Beauvais, Aubusson, Turin, Madrid, Florence, Mortlake. eavers' signatures and monograms: Jacques Neilson, Frans van den Hecke, Jan Raes, Jean Lefebvre I, François de La Planche, Michel Wauters, Martin eynbouts, Willem Pannemaker, Frans Spierincx; Frans Guebels, Nicolas Leyniers.

mythological subjects replaced them. In these tapestries, the horizon tends to be raised, so that the figures cover the whole field of the tapestry as in the earliest works. The colors, however, are dull, the designs feeble, the execution often poor. The lavish, delicately colored *Feasts of the Valois* (ca. 1575; cartoons attributed to François Quesnel and Antoine Caron; Uffizi) is the exception to the rule. In the wake of the interwoven floral designs in the manner of Van Roome, borders with festoons of bunches of fruit and others with ornate grotesques became popular. Toward 1600 allegorical figures appeared, hidden in the intricately interlaced leaves, spirals, and medallions. Finally, the style of the borders, like that of the figures, was to be completely re-created by Rubens in the baroque ideals.

Other Flemish and French manufacturing centers. Provincial 16th-century Flemish tapestries generally imitated the Brussels models. Among the numerous centers in which tapestries were woven, the town of Oudenarde enjoyed a certain reputation. Tapestry-weaving was an established industry there as early as the 15th century, but the surviving examples are mainly from the second half of the 16th century and are not generally of good quality. Verdures were favorite subjects, although there are examples of some of the usual historical themes such as the *Judgment of Paris* (PL. 405). These are rather archaic and provincial, but are not without a certain robustness of design. The city mark was a pair of spectacles.

Verdures of remarkable quality were woven at Enghien and Grammont. Bruges was also an active and fairly important center. Between 1502–06 the *tapissier* Jehan Sauvage (de Welde) wove there the *History of St. Anatole* (Paris, Mus. des Gobelins and Louvre). In the late 16th century the *Marriage of Gombaut and Macée* (Saint-Lô, Mus.), a folk subject, was variously repeated. The Bruges mark was an arm with a crowned gothic B.

Among the 15th- and early-16th-century tapestries is a large group of works from France whose exact origin is uncertain. Most impressive among them are the six panels of *The Lady with the Unicorn* (Paris, Mus. de Cluny), which bear the arms of the Le Viste family (gules on a bend azure, three crescents argent). The series is of exceptional quality, and the heraldic and courtly theme is expressed with absolute purity in magically poetic representations. Besides these should be mentioned the fragments of the *Famous Ladies* (Boston, Mus. of Fine Arts), which bear the arms of Cardinal Ferry de Clugny and which can be dated to the first years of the last decade of the 16th century; *The Lady with the Unicorn* cannot be much later if we accept the hypothesis (Crick-Kuntziger, 1954) that both these works come from the same cartoonist. A second group of tapestries includes the *Hunt of the Unicorn* (ca. 1499; New York, The Cloisters) and two millefleurs, one showing scenes of pastoral life (Met. Mus. and Paris, Mus. des Gobelins) and feudal life (Paris, Mus. de Cluny). They are generally of good quality and have many affinities with the production of Tournai of the late 15th century. A third group, of varying quality, is made up of religious subjects: the *Life of the Virgin* (Beaune, Cathedral), completed in 1500 from cartoons by Pierre Spicre of Dijon; and the *History of St. Rémy* and another *Life of the Virgin* (both, Reims, Mus. B.A.). Their origin is difficult to trace because of the lack of documents, but it has been suggested — though not completely convincingly — that these tapestries were the work of itinerant French weavers who set up their looms near the homes of the nobles who gave them commissions. The attribution of many of these works to Touraine or to the general region of the Loire (Göbel, 1923–34; Kurth, 1923; Schmitz, 1924) has not been proven, nor has the hypothesis (Ackermann, 1933) which denies the existence of a French provincial production. The spread of Renaissance taste, in any event, put an end to this kind of activity. When Francis I commissioned (ca. 1547) tapestries for the palace in Fontainebleau, they were patterned after the designs of Il Rosso and Francesco Primaticcio. Perhaps the *Story of Diana* (Château d'Anet; Rouen, Mus. B.A.; Met. Mus.), which bears the initials of Henry II and Diane de Poitiers, was also woven in Fontainebleau. However, the tapestry of Leonardo's *Last Supper*, offered in 1532 by Francis I to Clement VII (Vat.

Mus.) and often ascribed to Fontainebleau, is certainly of Br[us]sels manufacture. In 1551, Henry II established a factory [in] Paris at the Hôpital de la Trinité, where the orphans were tau[ght] the craft of tapestry-weaving. Here were woven the *Life [of] Christ* (1584–94) and the rather mediocre *History of St. Cris[pin] and St. Crispinian* (1634–35; Paris, Mus. des Gobelins).

Switzerland and Germany. In Switzerland and Germa[ny] the qualities that were to characterize the later products we[re] already well defined by the late 14th century. In the 15th cent[ury] small ateliers, a few of them in convents, continued to prod[uce] tapestries. Smaller sizes were preferred — dossers, bench c[ov]ers, altar frontals, table covers, cushion covers. Subjects we[re] drawn from popular sources: sacred and amorous legends, pr[ov]erbs, didactic and allegorical fables. The figural idiom [is] ingenuous and sometimes crude, but the stylization coupl[ed] with a certain spontaneity of color is often very effective.

Switzerland's most important weaving center was Bas[el]. Its production is amply documented in the local historical m[u]seum. Hunting scenes, the "garden of love" (*Minneteppich[e]*) and fabulous beasts (*Fabeltierteppiche*) were the most comm[on] themes, although other profane subjects such as that of the c[el]ebrated *Nine Heroes* (ca. 1460, Basel, Hist. Mus.) were al[so] produced; basically, however, the subject matter is of lit[tle] importance, as it serves merely as a decorative pretext.

Sacred subjects such as the Christ Child (ca. 1490) we[re] more numerous in the region around Freiburg and in t[he] north of Switzerland. Also, the theme of the *hortus conclus[us]*, sometimes interwoven with that of the mystic hunt of the u[ni]corn (Zurich, Schweizerisches Landesmus.; Berlin, Kais[er] Friedrich Mus.), was frequently interpreted with great stat[e]liness and was an especially popular theme all along the Rhi[ne] and in Alsace during the 15th century. The *History of Willi[am] of Orléans* (ca. 1410–20; Frankfurt am Main, Mus.) may ha[ve] been woven near Worms. The *Maiden in Search of Fai[th]* (Vict. and Alb.) was executed in a convent workshop in the regi[on] of the middle Rhine; it reappeared again in Hesse, in Swab[ia] and in Franconia. In Nürnberg religious subjects were prevale[nt] (e.g., the *Life of St. Sebaldus*, 1410; the *Life of St. Catheri[ne]* 1445; and the *Life of the Virgin*, 1480; all in the national museu[m] in that city). The nonmonumental character typical of Germ[an] weaving is reaffirmed in the *Passion* in the Bamberg Cathedr[al;] the nine episodes, inspired by the work of Martin Schongau[er] and Israel von Meckenem, are enclosed in as many compar[t]ments, thus precluding any unity of composition.

In the 16th century Swiss production declined greatl[y.] Some of the tapestries still in existence are from Basel, but mo[st] are from the area around Lucerne. It is evident that the art [of] tapestry did not survive the Gothic period in Switzerland. [In] Germany, on the contrary, tapestry received a new impetus fro[m] the immigration of religious exiles from Flanders. They intr[o]duced into Germany the styles of their homeland, while adop[t]ing at the same time certain local idioms. In the second ha[lf] of the 16th century many centers sprang up: Stuttgart, whe[re] Jakob de Carmes was active, Kassel, Frankenthal, Heidelber[g,] Cologne, Lüneburg, Torgau, Leipzig, Wesel, Wismar, and al[so] Dresden and Hamburg, where Joost I and II van Herse[lle] (Artsdael) were active. This production is interesting and vari[ed] in both technique and design.

Italy. In Italy, tapestries became fashionable relative[ly] late. In the 14th and 15th centuries, Italian nobles bought the[ir] large tapestries in the north, beyond the Alps. Itinerant craft[s]men attended to the necessary repairs and occasionally wo[ve] tapestries. It is known that a certain Jacquet d'Arras was activ[e] in Siena between 1447 and 1450, after which he moved to Rom[e.] Foreign weavers worked in Brescia, Todi, Perugia, Urbin[o,] and Modena. Rinaldo Duro worked between 1500–08 in Co[r]reggio and then from 1511–12 was to be found in Bologna. I[n] the 16th century, Vincenzo della Valle (van den Daele?) an[d] Albert of Brussels were to be found in Genoa and, later (1553–64) Dionys Martensz; in the same period Egidio da Castel[lo] and Pietro Bervet were active in Verona. In Venice, which w[as] the Italian center for the tapestry trade, foreign tapestry weave[rs]

ere intermittently busy; probably one of these wove, in the
st half of the century, the *Passion*, in S. Marco, which is
rthern in taste but shows complex influences which have been
ppily resolved into an artistic unity. Zanino di Pietro and Nic-
lo di Pietro have been suggested as authors of the cartoons.

About 1503, an Italian weaver, Benedetto da Milano, wove
Vigevano) for Gian Giacomo Trivulsio the *Months* (Milan,
us. del Castello Sforzesco) after cartoons inspired by the work
Bramantino. This is probably the oldest series to display
e Renaissance spirit so clearly. Antonio de Bazolo was active
Milan between 1533–37, and perhaps also wove, about mid-
ntury, the *History of John the Baptist* (Monza, Cath. Treas.)
om a painting by Bernardino Luini.

In Ferrara, which was very much influenced by northern
t, there were weavers from across the Alps as early as the 15th
ntury. Among these were Lieven Gillisz of Bruges (1467)
d Jehan Mille and Renauld Grue of Tournai (1463); in 1445
naud Boteram, more a merchant than a weaver, arrived in
aly from Brussels and established himself with the house of
te as well as with other noble Italian families. It is known
at Cosmè Tura furnished cartoons to the weavers and it is to
is early activity that the *Deposition* series (Cleve. Mus. of
rt; Munich, Lenbach Coll.) has been assigned. In 1536,
cole II d'Este established a tapestry factory which was di-
cted by Jan and Nicolaus Carcher (or Karcher) and Jan
st (Rostel, Rosto) from Brussels. The most surely documented
ries is the poignant and graceful *Metamorphoses* (Paris, Mus.
s Gobelins), which Jan Carcher wove in 1545 from models
Battista Dossi and cartoons by Camillo Filippo and Guglielmo
Malines. The *History of Hercules* (priv. coll.) was begun
1542 but was not completed until 1561. The *History of St.*
orge and St. Maurelius was woven between 1552 and 1553
r the Cathedral from models by Garofalo (B. Tisi), Camillo
lippo, and, for the borders, Luca d'Olanda. In 1539 Nicolaus
rcher left Ferrara for Mantua, while in 1545 Rost left for
orence. Jan Carcher remained, and was succeeded by his
n Luigi (Ludwig), who wove the *Life of the Virgin* for the
thedral in Como. With the death of Luigi in 1480, all activ-
y appears to have ceased. Whether several hangings woven
om about 1540–45 are Ferrarese or Mantuan is uncertain,
t the attribution to Ferrara is preferable both for the *Putti*
Play (Paris, Gulbenkian Coll.; Milan, Mus. Poldi Pezzoli),
hich exquisitely translates the design of Giulio Romano
to tapestry, and for the *History of Moses* (Milan, Cath. Treas.)
th its brilliant colors and magnificent design, and perhaps
r another *Putti at Play*, also in the Cathedral in Milan. In
antua *tapissiers* for whom Mantegna himself had furnished
rtoons had been active in the 15th century, and Nicolaus Car-
er was in the service of Federico Gonzaga there. Sometime
tween 1545–53 Carcher was called to Florence by Cosimo I,
ho commissioned him and Jan Rost to establish and direct
tapestry works. The contract for this transaction is dated
ct. 20, 1546. Cartoons were furnished by painters such as
ontormo, Francesco Salviati, and Bronzino, who quickly saw
tapestry a natural medium for their elegantly stylized designs.
he *History of Joseph* (Florence, Palazzo Vecchio) was begun
mediately, but Pontormo's sketches for the cartoons failed to
ease, and Bronzino finished the cartoons. Bronzino designed
her tapestries, including *Flora* (1553) and the *Resurrection* (ca.
52, Uffizi). Among the tapestries after cartoons by Salviati the
st is the small, agitated *Deposition* (Florence, Pitti, Mus. degli
rgenti). Bachiacca is responsible for the *Months* (1552–53,
ffizi), in which his great virtuosity is displayed in the tonal
finements and unusual color combinations, and also for the
mous *Grotesques* (ca. 1550, Uffizi), which strongly influenced
e subsequent development of tapestry. After 1553 Carcher
no longer mentioned as being in Florence. Rost, then very
d, ceased all activity in 1560. Later works show a deteriora-
n of quality, and gradually Florentine production dwindled
mediocrity. Giovanni Stradano's (Jan van der Straet) *Hunt*
ries (1567–68, Uffizi) was woven under the direction of Gio-
nni di Bastiano Sconditi and later of Benedetto di Michele
uilli; he also provided the model for the Florentine *Chronicles*
570–74; Florence, Accademia).

Other countries. As in Italy, so also in Spain the presence of
itinerant French and Flemish weavers is recorded as early as
the 14th century. In the 16th century, Joan Ferrer was active
in Barcelona, where he wove a *Life of Christ* (ca. 1561) for the
Chapter of Gerona, inspired by Flemish weavings. In Salamanca, the tapestry works of Pedro Gutiérrez had some importance. In 1578 he received an order from Queen Anna for some
small heraldic tapestries (*reposteros*). A small atelier belonging
to Gutiérrez was busy at repairs in Madrid. Velázquez portrayed
its interior in *Las Hilanderas* (II, PL. 193); after his death it
passed into the hands of Antonio Ceron. It should be mentioned,
however, that Philip II, writing to Cardinal Granvelle, affirmed
that anyone who had seen what was woven in Flanders would
not be satisfied with the Spanish product.

The departure of many weavers from Flanders as a result
of the religious wars led Hans Knieper to Elsinore, where, in
1581, he was commissioned by the Danish Crown to weave
the *Kings of Denmark* for Kronborg Castle (now, Copenhagen,
Nationalmus.).

Paul de Bücher turned to Sweden, where with Nils Eskilson,
a local weaver, he worked in the service of the Crown in various
royal residences: Kalmar, Stockholm, Svartsjö; together they
produced the series on the history of the kings of Sweden (Swedish Nat. Coll.) and a *David and Samuel*. De Bücher alone was
responsible for the *Apparition of Christ to the Virgin* (1554).

THE 17TH CENTURY. *Brussels.* At the beginning of the 17th
century, Brussels was still the most important center for the
production of tapestries. The taste for hunting scenes and verdures continued to prevail and was reflected in interpretations
of older models, for example, in the reworking of the *Vertumnus and Pomona* series (Brussels, Mus. Royaux d'Art et d'Histoire) by Martin Reynbouts (d. 1619), one of the most important
weavers of the period. The style of tapestries from Brussels
was completely revolutionized by Rubens (q.v.). His sketches
— done in oils as well as in the usual cartoon medium of tempera and then enlarged by his apprentices — show a desire
to restore to tapestries their preeminently monumental character.
To achieve this end he concentrated the compositional interest
in the foreground, where he placed large figures. The first
of the series that he designed, the *History of Decius Mus*, was
on the looms by 1618. Numerous sets exist (Madrid, Royal
Palace; Vienna, Kunsthist. Mus.; Brussels, Mus. Royaux d'Art
et d'Histoire; Mondovì, Bishop's Palace; and others), most
of which came from the ateliers of Jan Raes (active 1593–1649)
and Frans van den Hecke (active ca. 1614–65). The *History of
Decius Mus* was woven with a great variety of borders; in some
versions these were replaced by architectural forms by means of
which Rubens aimed at accentuating the structural unity of
his composition. To the same end he minimized the importance
of the backgrounds; for example, he used a uniform, draped
field for most of the allegorical processions of the *Triumph of
the Eucharist* series (PLS. 408, 409). The *editio princeps* of this
series, of which many sets exist (e.g., in Cologne Cathedral),
was woven, apparently in 1628, by Jan Raes for the Monasterio
de las Descalzas Reales in Madrid. The cartoons for these tapestries were commissioned from Rubens by the donor, the Arch-
duchess Isabella. Louis XIII commissioned the Rubens sketches for the *History of Constantine* (Philadelphia, Mus. of Art;
Paris, Mobilier Nat.) for the French tapestry ateliers, and
shortly afterward copies of the series were made in Brussels.
The date of the sketches for the *Achilles* series is a matter of
debate, some historians (e.g., Crick Kuntziger, 1934) maintaining that they may have been Rubens's last cartoons, inasmuch
as several versions of the series (Boston, Mus. of Fine Arts;
Santiago, Cathedral; Turin, Palazzo Reale and Palazzo Car-
gnano) include subjects which are based on cartoons by Jacob
Jordaens (q.v.) and which were apparently added after Rubens's
death. The Jordaens cartoons, although necessarily influenced
by the example of Rubens, show a much less rigorous unity
of action, with episodic digressions, elaborate settings, and a
taste for ornamentation. The tapestries designed by Jordaens
are extremely numerous. His cartoons for the series depicting
country life (complete set in Vienna, Kunsthist. Mus.), which

bears the mark of Conrade van der Bruggen (active 1622–69), probably date from the 1630s. Among his earliest cartoons are those for the *Ulysses* series, of which a set, bearing the mark of Geraert van der Strecken (Streecken; d. 1677), is partly in the Palazzo Reale in Turin and partly in the Palazzo del Quirinale. Tapestries of the *History of Charlemagne* series are rare; some panels signed by Jan Cordys and Mathias Roelants are in the Palazzo del Quirinale. More numerous are the tapestries of the *History of Alexander* (Turin, Palazzo Reale, with the initials of Jan Cordys). The series depicting equestrian exercises was designed by Jordaens before 1651; the set in Vienna (Kunsthist. Mus.) was woven by Heinrich Reydams (Rydams) and Evveraert Leyniers. Utilizing motifs from earlier compositions, Jordaens designed the cartoons for the *Proverbs* in 1644–47, of which the Vienna set (Kunsthist. Mus.), woven by Cordys, should be noted, as well as that in Tarragona (Mus. Diocesano). At this time the custom of inscribing the manufacturer's full name or initials was established, thus facilitating the identification of the workshop.

The series of cartoons by Justus van Egmont are brilliant and pleasingly theatrical. The *History of Aurelian and Zenobia* (ed. *princeps* completed 1665) was repeated several times by Gerard Peemans. The most complete set of this series is in the Palazzo Mansi in Lucca. Peemans also wove copies of Lebrun's *History of Alexander* (Vienna, Kunsthist. Mus.; Würzburg, fortress of Marienberg), a work that contributed greatly to the diffusion of French taste in Flanders, notably in Brussels, after 1650. A new style showing this French influence is visible in the pleasant *Months* (PL. 407), designed by Jan van der Hoecke. At the same time, a 16th-century series like the *History of Scipio* was still in great demand and was woven frequently in the manufactories of Geraert van der Strecken, Evveraert Leyniers, Jan van Leefdael, and Heinrich Reydams (a handsome version is in the Palazzo del Quirinale), while Jan Franz van den Hecke and Franz Raes repeated the Rubens series almost into the 18th century.

Toward 1700 Brussels began to suffer from the growing competition of the Manufacture des Gobelins, a state institution against which free commercial enterprises fought an unequal battle. Perhaps the fashion for tapestries modeled on paintings by Teniers (q.v.) or other genre painters was launched to counteract this difficult situation. These tapestries were immediately successful and were rapidly imitated by all the manufacturers. They opened the way for the copying of painting in tapestry, which became extremely fashionable and which could easily be achieved owing to the increasing fineness of stitch (20–23 warp threads per in.).

Other Flemish manufacturing centers. The same tendencies are discernible in other Flemish manufacturing centers such as Antwerp. This city was famous primarily as a center for the sale of tapestries and cartoons and had a flourishing tapestry industry after 1650. In 1687–88, the elaborate *History of St. Kilian* (Würzburg, Cathedral) was woven. The *Dido and Aeneas* series (Vienna, Kunsthist. Mus.; Cleve. Mus. of Art; Stockholm, Royal Palace), after cartoons by Giovanni Francesco Romanelli, was woven several times in the Wauters manufactory. At Oudenarde (ca. 1688) Jan Regelbrugghe wove the large *Calvary* in S. Maria Maggiore in Bergamo. In the 17th century Bruges manufacturers produced many fine tapestries displaying an unusual audacity and chromatic knowledge. Noteworthy are the *Months* (Vienna, Kunsthist. Mus.) and the *Seasons* (PL. 408), dated 1664, as well as the *Liberal Arts* woven after engravings by Cornelius Schut (Milan, Castello Sforzesco).

France. In the 17th century there was a revival of the tapestry industry in France that formed part of the royal plan to build up the power and status of the country. In 1607 Henry IV conceded important privileges to the Flemish weavers Marc de Comans and François de La Planche (van den Planken), who in 1601 had established a manufactory in Paris in the Faubourg Saint-Marcel. After the death of François de La Planche in 1627, the organization continued in existence until 1638. The *Artemis* series was the one most frequently woven

there (Paris, Mobilier Nat.; Minneapolis, Inst. of Arts; Tur Palazzo Chiablese, Palazzo Reale, Palazzo Madama). Design by Antoine Caron in honor of Catherine de Médicis, it w translated into cartoons by Henry Lerambert, who added seve subjects to it and adapted it to the glorification of Marie Médicis. In spite of its archaic and mannered idiom, this ries is remarkable for its dignity and decorative elegance. T *History of Coriolanus* (Paris, Mobilier Nat.) may have be inspired by models of Laurent Guyot, while the cartoons the pleasant *Diana* series (Vienna, Kunsthist. Mus.; Madr Royal Palace; Genoa, Palazzo Reale, etc.) were designed Toussaint Dubreuil. In 1622–23 the *petits patrons* of the *H* tory of Constantine arrived in Paris, commissioned from Rube by Louis XIII, and were interpreted in a severe style. 1633 Raphael de La Planche (van den Planken) moved to t Faubourg Saint-Germain, where he worked until 1667–68 replicas of the old series as well as on new themes (e.g., *Rinal and Armida*, after designs by Simon Vouet). The Comans fa ily remained in their original workshop, where they wov in addition to their previous subjects, the series of Old Test ment scenes (Paris, Louvre, Mobilier Nat., Mus. des Gobelin and the *Loves of the Gods* (Lisbon, Gulbenkian Coll.; M Mus.; Châteaudun Castle; Champchevrier Castle), both o signed by Vouet. The usual mark, in all these ateliers, was P and the royal fleur-de-lys (FIG. 921). Meanwhile, in 16c two French weavers, Maurice Dubourg (Dubout) and Gira Laurent, had installed an atelier in the Grande Galerie of t Louvre. Their production and that of their successors, whi continued until 1662, included the *History of St. Gervais a St. Protais* (Paris, Mus. Galliera, Mus. des Gobelins) aft cartoons by Philippe de Champaigne and others (ca. 1652–6 a *Psyche* series (Paris, Mobilier Nat.) after earlier models Michiel Coxie (Coxcie), and the above-mentioned *Old Test* ment series.

In 1662 Jean Baptiste Colbert, by order of Louis XIV, a quired the land and buildings in the Faubourg Saint-Marc that had once been the seat of the Gobelins and of other Pa sian dyers and were at that time occupied partially by the Coma workshop. To this nucleus were added all the existing Parisi tapestry ateliers. In 1667 the Manufacture Royale des Meub de la Couronne was instituted with letters patent. Until 16 the workers here included cabinetmakers, engravers, and go smiths. The Manufacture was rigidly organized, the state bei represented by a superintendent, while a director was in char of the artistic activity. Almost the entire production was de tined for the royal Garde Meuble. Initially there were thr ateliers using high-warp looms and two with low-warp loom The director was Charles Lebrun (q.v.). At first, existing ca toons were used, so that the *Acts of the Apostles* as well as su jects conceived by Lebrun for Nicolas Fouquet's manufacto in Maincy were repeated. In the earliest works, for examp the *Elements* (ed. *princeps*, 1664–69; Siena, Palazzo Pubblic Florence, Palazzo Pitti; Naples, Palazzo Reale) and the *Seasc* (ed. *princeps*, now lost, 1673), Lebrun showed a desire to combi a descriptive story told in great detail with unity of action. T thoughtful character of his work is apparent in the series of ta estries depicting children engaged in gardening (ed. *prince* 1685; Florence, Palazzo Pitti), an adaptation of a 16th-centu theme, and also in the three great series of the *History of Ale ander* (Vienna, Kunsthist. Mus.; Paris, Mobilier Nat.), the *L of the King* (Paris, Mobilier Nat.; Versailles, Palace; Vat. Mus and the *Royal Palaces* (PL. 410), which were started at clo intervals (in 1664, 1665, and 1668 respectively) and complet in 1680–81. Although the *History of Alexander* has recou to the old style, it is boldly composed. Flattery of the monarc which is merely suggested in this series, becomes patent in t *Life of the King*, which exalts the power and splendor of t Crown. The *Royal Palaces* is a newer subject. Here the pictor quality resulting from technical virtuosity is further accentuate The architectural frames, unlike those in Rubens's tapestri are meant to emphasize the "picture" quality of the centr landscapes. Numerous series woven under the direction Lebrun owe their inspiration to pictorial decorations, for examp the *Vatican Logge* (Paris, Mobilier Nat., Louvre; Uffizi), t llery of Saint-Cloud (Paris, Mobilier Nat., Palais de l'Elysée), d even the *Indies* (PL. 404; *ed. princeps* 1687-88, now lost), uich were taken from the exotic landscapes given to Louis XIV ˙ Maurice of Nassau. When Lebrun died in 1690 he was cceeded by Pierre Mignard. Financial difficulties caused the ısure of the manufactory in 1694, but it resumed its activity 1699.

In 1664, Louis XIV instituted a Manufacture Royale de apisserie at Beauvais under the direction of Louis Hinart. oduction consisted almost entirely of verdures. In 1684 e Fleming Philippe Behagle (d. 1705) was put in charge. he grotesques in the style of Jean Bérain that were woven this time forecast the ornamental taste of the 18th century. he *Conquests of Louis XIV* (ca. 1690; private coll.) by Jean ıptiste Martin, however, was still woven in the Lebrun anner.

In 1665 the workshops that had long been active at Aubusn were granted the title of Manufacture Royale de Tapisserie. heir production in the 17th and early 18th centuries was modt: verdures and an occasional rather crude figural tapestry. 1662 the workshops of Felletin also received the status of a ınufacture Royale. They produced mediocre figural tapestries well as the popular verdures.

A few works were created in Reims by the Flemish weaver aniel Pepersack, for example, a *Life of Christ*, woven for e Cathedral in 1633 and now in the Musée des Beaux-Arts. nother Reims weaver was Pierre Damour, who about 1650 ɔve in Paris a *Life of the Virgin* series (Strasbourg, Cathedral) ter models by Philippe de Champaigne. The De La Planchemans manufactory had a few looms active in Amiens, where enes from the Old Testament were woven (Paris, Mus. des obelins). In Maincy there developed a private manufactory r Fouquet, directed by Lebrun. Its activity (1658-61) was terrupted when Fouquet fell into disgrace and the equip-ent passed to the Manufacture Royale in Paris. The livelihood ˙ those manufacturers who were not in royal or princely serv-e was difficult, as tapestry was rarely a good industrial invest-ent. Even when princely munificence solved the financial oblem, the work was still fraught with difficulties.

Italy. In Italy the most important producer, the Medici ınufactory, did not maintain the high quality of the preceding ntury. Foreign weavers were called in — the Fleming Ber-ırd van Asselt and the French weaver Pierre Lefebvre (Le evere) — but the works produced were inferior. To be noted e the *Seasons* woven for the Palazzo Vecchio in Florence (1642-) in a decadent, mannerist style; the *History of Moses* (1651-); Germany, private coll.; Met. Mus.); and two Pietàs that e pictorial imitations. In 1673, the direction of the Medici orks was assumed by Giovanni Battista Termini, an able and ersatile artist. Under his supervision were woven the handsome legorical portieres for the Palazzo Pitti (1705), which prepared ιe way for the rivival of the Florentine manufactory in the 18th ntury.

The production of the workshop set up in Rome by Urban III's nephew Cardinal Francesco Barberini was of higher tistic quality. After meticulous preparation, weaving began 1627 under the direction of Jacopo della Riviera (d. 1639), ho was succeeded by his brother-in-law Gaspare Rocci ?ochi). After the death of Urban VIII in 1644, the Cardinal as forced to leave Rome (1646). Production ceased and was ot resumed until 1663, after which it continued until the Car-inal's death in 1679. In the first period numerous series were oven, among which the most notable are the continuation of the *listory of Constantine* given to the Cardinal by Louis XIII, vhich was woven after models by Pietro da Cortona (q.v.; .L. 407); the *Putti at Play* (1637-42; Rome, Mus. di Palazzo enezia), a free replica by Romanelli of the series, now lost, y Giovanni da Udine; the very baroque *Mysteries of the Life nd Death of Christ* (1643-56; New York, Cathedral of St. John ıe Divine) after designs by Pietro da Cortona (the *Crucifixion*) nd Romanelli. The *Scenes from the Life of Urban VIII* (Brussels, /lus. Royaux d'Art et d'Histoire) was woven in the second eriod.

Other countries. In the 17th century, as a result of various circumstances, ancient tapestry works gained prominence in towns that had little previous weaving tradition. In 1591 Frans Spierincx came to Delft from Antwerp. In his atelier was woven the *Destruction of the Invincible Armada*, once in the London House of Commons and now destroyed. In other surviving tapestries Spierincx interpreted with delicacy and fantasy the customary Flemish decorative formulas. His *Diana* series (Kent, Knole, Lord Sackville Coll.), *Orlando Furioso* (1602; PL. 406), and *History of Scipio* are unusually fine for the time. Weaving was continued after his death in 1630 for a decade by his sons Aert and Pieter. Karel van Mander (d. 1623) served as cartoon-ist for Spierincx from 1604-15. He then established his own manufactory, where the *History of Alexander* and the *History of Troy* (formerly Ferrara, Coll. G. Cavalieri; Jutland, Krabbe-schalm Castle) were produced. The atelier of Maximilian van der Gucht (d. 1689) was established about 1640 and produced, in 1648, the *Battle of Nieuport* (Brussels, Mus. Royaux d'Art et d'Histoire). The Delft weavers' mark was a striped shield between the letters H and D (FIG. 921). Tapestry manufactories also arose in Amsterdam, Middelburg, Leiden, Gouda, and Haarlem after the exodus of Protestant weavers from the southern provinces at the end of the 16th century. In the 17th century the *Story of Aeneas* (Stockholm, Royal Palace) was produced in Amsterdam and the *Dutch Victories* (formerly Abbey of Mid-delburg) was woven in Middelburg, in the De Maecht atelier.

In Sweden, Queen Ulrika Eleanora was the patron of a manufactory in Carlberg that produced a *Meleager* series (now lost) in the years 1688-95.

In 1604, a manufactory was established in Munich. Here, at the invitation of Maximilian I of Bavaria, Jean van der Biest of Brussels wove the *History of Otto of Wittelsbach* (ca. 1610), the *Months* (ca. 1613), and the *Seasons* (ca. 1614; all, Munich, Residenzmus.), after models by Pieter de Witte (known as Candid). Activity did not continue after 1615.

In England a private production of tapestries had been supported by William Sheldon in the preceding century. He put Richard Hickes (d. 1621) in charge of workshops in Bar-cheston and Weston, where heraldic and figural hangings were woven, as well as many copies of maps. A manufactory in the service of the Crown was established at Mortlake in 1620, under the direction of Sir Francis Crane. Among the *tapissiers* was Philipp de Maecht, who had formerly been active in Paris at the De La Planche-Comans ateliers. The work here began with replicas of early Brussels tapestries: the *Story of Vulcan* (*ed. princeps* 1620-22; London, Vict and Alb., St. James's Palace; Paris, Mobilier Nat.; Stockholm, Royal Palace; etc.), the *Months* (Genoa, Palazzo Municipale; London, Buckingham Palace, Royal Colls.; Melbury House, Earl of Ilchester Coll.), and the *Acts of the Apostles* (Vict. and Alb.; Paris, Mobilier Nat., Louvre; etc.). Seven of the cartoons for the latter were acquired in 1623 by Charles I. A fine new border was designed for the tapestries; it has frequently been attributed to Van Dyck, but it may be the work of Francis Cleyne, a cartoonist at Mortlake after 1624. Cleyne designed the *Hero and Leander* series (*ed. princeps* ca. 1630; Stockholm, Drottningholm Palace; Bratislava, Mu-nicipal Mus.; Derbyshire, Hardwick Hall; etc.) and the series known as the *Royal Horses* (*ed. princeps* 1625-35; Vict. and Alb.; Met. Mus.), both of which were often repeated. In 1636, Sir Francis Crane died. Shortly after, the Civil War broke out and Mortlake barely managed to continue production. At the time of the Restoration (1661) Sir Sackville Crowe made a vain effort to renew the glory of the manufactory, which finally, in 1667, passed into the hands of private entrepreneurs and was closed down about 1700. Meanwhile other workshops had arisen, started mostly by craftsmen who had been trained at Mortlake. It is not known whether the tapestry of the Battle of Solebay in Hampton Court Palace, which bears the name of Francis Poyntz (d. 1685), was woven at Mortlake or in a pri-vate workshop. In and around London the weavers of the Great Wardrobe were active in several workshops late in the century: first in the Savoy Palace, then in Hatton Garden, and finally on Great Queen Street in Soho.

Particular mention should be made of tapestry production

in Norway. Here the industry enjoyed a very old tradition, characterized by so marked a decorative stylization that it changed little through the years. In 16th- and 17th-century tapestries even the stimulus from the more advanced manufactories, such as those in Flanders and Germany, were assimilated and translated into rigidly geometric and highly ornamental forms. Noteworthy examples are the *Banquet of Herod* (1613; Oslo, Kunstindustrimus.) and *Solomon and the Queen of Sheba* (1659; Oslo, Norsk Folkemus.). A more indigenous style can be seen in the *Adoration of the Magi* (XII, PL. 416) and in the *Stags* (Oslo, Kunstindustrimus.), which come close to pure geometric ornamentation.

THE 18TH AND 19TH CENTURIES. *Brussels and Oudenarde.* The Brussels manufactories met with increasing difficulties in the 18th century. The market was more limited, and manufactories were arising everywhere in the service of princes capable of sustaining the costs. Furthermore, the demand was mainly for small ornamentation pieces, which could be produced by smaller manufactories. The vogue for genre scenes in the style of Teniers (PL. 412) was increasing. Brussels produced several successful series at the turn of the 17th century after cartoons by Ludwig van Schoor of Antwerp (*Seasons, Story of Perseus*). These were woven by various manufacturers, among them Josse (Jodocus) de Vos (active 1700–ca. 1725), who attained considerable fame for his productions. He was commissioned by the Crown of Austria to copy the *Conquest of Tunis* (Vienna, Kunsthist. Mus.), as well as the *Life of Christ* for the Cathedral of Valletta in Malta. He proved to be a delicate and sensitive interpreter in the *Pastor Fido* (Vienna, Kunsthist. Mus.), the *Mythological Divinities* (Turin, Palazzo Reale), and other series. The well-known Leyniers manufactory maintained a brisk production, which included the elegant mythological *Fables* designed in the French manner by Jan van Orley in collaboration with Augustin Coppens. Other works woven here were the *History of Telemachus*, the *Triumph of the Gods and Goddesses* (ed. princeps 1717; Ghent, Mus. B.A.), and the mannered *Military Scenes* by Hyacinth de La Pegna (1758; Vienna, Kunsthist. Mus.). The Van der Borcht manufactory, besides a large number of genre scenes, executed the *Life of Christ* for Bruges Cathedral from models by Van Orley, who was probably also the designer of the frequently repeated *History of Moses* (Vienna, Kunsthist. Mus.; Brussels, Mus. Royaux d'Art et d'Histoire). In 1785 the *Miracle of the Host* was woven for the collegiate Church of SS. Michel and Gudule in Brussels by Jacques van der Borcht from cartoons by Maximilian de Haese. At this time the Van der Borcht manufactory was the only remaining one of any importance in Brussels. It too was closed at the death of Jacques in 1794.

In the 18th century, Oudenarde's production increased notably in importance, especially that of verdures and animal tapestries, which were highly prized and sold far and wide. A very fine series is preserved in Brussels (Mus. Royaux d'Art et d'Histoire).

France. Both Brussels and Oudenarde were strongly influenced by French taste, which at this time was predominant throughout Europe. When the Gobelins works were reopened in 1699, they had two high-warp workshops and three employing low-warp methods. At first, production followed an easy course, with the completion, in 1701, of the *editio princeps* of the already partly woven *Triumph of the Gods* and the reweaving of tapestries produced in the period before suspension. Meanwhile, tapestry was rapidly being adapted to the tastes and necessities of the times. As the need for a unified composition was no longer felt and the action was no longer the focus of interest, tapestries became more purely ornamental. The nobility and rich bourgeoisie settled or stayed for increasingly long periods in Paris in small apartments whose decoration required delicate and pleasing tapestries that were not of monumental dimensions. Claude Audran III's portieres depicting the gods (1700; Paris, Mobilier Nat.; Stockholm, Royal Palace; Vat. Mus.; etc.) are elegant, as are his grotesque *Months* (1708–10; Paris, Mus. des Gobelins; Rome, Gall. Doria Pamphili).

The supreme example of this type of tapestry is, however, t[h]e *Don Quixote* series (PL. 411), which was immediately a gre[at] success. It was first woven in 1717 and was repeated througho[ut] the century, the settings and borders gradually changing a[nd] items from the 28 scenes designed by Charles Antoine Coyp[el] being variously selected. Illusionism, which creates the effe[ct] of a small painting hung on elegantly decorated damask, a ba[l]anced composition, continually enriched by innovations, and [an] episodic and discursive taste are the most outstanding characte[r]istics of this series. Its success was equaled only by that of t[he] melodramatic *History of Esther*, which was based on mode[ls] by Jean François de Troy (ed. princeps 1738–45; Paris, Mobili[er] Nat.; Château de Compiègne; Château de Fontainebleau; Uffi[zi] etc.). The success of Alexander-François Desportes's *Ne[w] Indies* (Vienna, Kunsthist. Mus.; Prague, Bishop's Palace; Berli[n,] Kunstgewerbe Mus. in Schloss Charlottenburg; Florence, P[a]lazzo Pitti) is more understandable. The artist drew the desig[ns] between 1737–41, reworking the cartoons of the old *Indies* [in] a more brilliant and colorful style. The great change in tas[te] can also be seen by comparing Lebrun's commemorative seri[es] with Charles Parrocel's *Turkish Embassy* (1731–37; Paris, M[o]bilier Nat.), where the subject is treated as an exotic curiosit[y,] or even more revealing is a comparison with the theatrical se[t]ting of Jean Baptiste Oudry's *Hunts of Louis XV* (1736–4[4;] Florence, Palazzo Pitti; Château de Compiègne), which is fu[ll] of tonal virtuosity and delicate landscape depiction. Oudry['s] influence at the Gobelins was considerable and caused t[he] manufactory to adopt a style that was more picturesque tha[n] pictorial. Later, François Boucher (q.v.) had a similar influen[ce] on artistic trends at the Gobelins, for which he designed t[he] cartoons for the central medallions in the *Mythological Scen[es]* (ed. princeps 1766–71; V, PL. 416). In these tapestries the se[t]tings are an elegant repetition of those designed for the *D[on] Quixote* series, a similar design being also in other series such [as] the *Fragments from Opera* (Louvre; Stockholm, Royal Palac[e]) and the *Scenes from Opera, Tragedy, and Comedy* (Stockhol[m,] Royal Palace). Boucher also painted the models for sever[al] tapestries depicting the loves of the gods (ed. princeps 1758–6[6;] XII, PL. 177). He insisted on absolute fidelity to the mode[ls,] which could by this time be reproduced in minute detail than[ks] to the skill of the weavers and to chemical innovations tha[t] permitted infinite pleasing, if not always permanent, variatio[ns] of color. Between Boucher and the Gobelins weavers there we[re] differences of opinion that give an idea of the difficulties bese[t]ting the tapestry industry at this time. Late in the centur[y] there were attempts to make tapestry a vehicle for historic[al] and didactic themes, but the results were all mediocre, f[or] example, the *History of Henry IV* after models by Franço[is] André Vincent (ed. princeps 1785–86; Naples, Palazzo Real[e;] Pau, Castle) and the *History of France* after models by variou[s] painters (Naples, Palazzo Reale; Rome, Palazzo del Quirinale[).] The minor works were more successful, some being purel[y] exercises in virtuosity, such as the portraits and copies of pain[t]ings, while others were purely functional, for example, th[e] exquisite upholstery fabrics.

During the Revolution, the Gobelins works, which had bee[n] nationalized, suffered somewhat from the political upheaval[s;] the only tapestries produced were those dedicated to patrioti[c] subjects. In the Napoleonic period production revived slightl[y.] The usual portraits were woven (for example, of the imperi[al] family) as well as copies of paintings (*Bonaparte Crossing th[e] Alps*, after Louis David), and Dubois designed an emblemati[c] series of portieres. The Restoration in no way altered the artisti[c] course of the manufactory. The historical scenes and copie[s] of ancient paintings that were woven at this time were muc[h] admired and prized by contemporaries. In 1864 the painte[r] Paul Baudry was commissioned to design an original series, th[e] *Five Senses*. Jules Chéret's *Seasons* and Jean Veber's *Fabl[es]* were woven at the turn of the century. Although artisticall[y] unsuccessful, they are an interesting attempt to adapt tapestr[y] to the language of contemporary art.

The other French manufactories followed more or less th[e] same course as the Gobelins. In Beauvais, after the death o[f] Behagle (1705) a difficult period began, during which, howeve[r,]

e first exotic and bizarre set of "Chinese tapestries" was pro-
uced (Louvre; Château de Compiègne; private colls.; etc.).
a 1726, Oudry was named painter to the manufactory, and in
734 he assumed its direction with Nicolas Besnier. Oudry
·oduced the cartoons for the *Country Amusements* in 1730,
ose for the *Molière Comedies* (Met. Mus.) in 1732, and the
esigns for the highly successful *Verdures fines* in 1736. The
eauvais manufactory was a private enterprise, which meant
aat it had to cater even more than the Gobelins to public taste.
udry was active in commissioning new cartoons. Charles
oseph Natoire's *Story of Don Quixote* (1735; Aix-en-Provence,
Ius. des Tapisseries) had scant success. Boucher, however,
esigned several series for Beauvais that met with great favor:
ae *Italian Revels*, the *Loves of the Gods* (Rome, Palazzo del
uirinale; Met. Mus.), the *Story of Psyche* (Turin, Palazzo Reale;
ome, Palazzo del Quirinale; Stockholm, Royal Palace), the
oble Pastoral (priv. coll.), and finally the second set of "Chinese
pestries" (PL. 413), which was repeated several times between
743 and 1775. Here the exoticism became picturesque and
aecdotal. After the death of Besnier (1753) and of Oudry
755), important tapestries were still produced, such as François
asanova's idyllic *Country Amusements* (1772; Paris, Palais de
Elysée), Jean Baptiste Le Prince's picturesque *Russian Games*
Paris, Mus. des Arts Décoratifs, Mus. Jacquemart-André,
Iobilier Nat.; Aix-en-Provence, Mus. des Tapisseries), and
an-Baptiste Huet's fanciful *Pastorals* (Pontoise, Hôtel de la
ous-Préfecture; Louvre). A somewhat different vogue was
augurated by Jean-Jacques Le Barbier in his classicizing *Four
uarters of the Globe* (1790; Vict. and Alb.). Beauvais was justly
mous for its upholsteries, which rivaled those of the Gobelins
. grace and elegance. After the Revolution and the Empire, the
aanufactory, which in 1794 had been taken over by the state,
onfined itself almost entirely to this type of production. The
eauvais mark was a letter B and the French fleur-de-lys
IG. 921).

The Aubusson manufactory could compete technically with
eauvais in the 18th century. It employed the painter Jean-
oseph Dumons in 1731 and Nicolas-Jacques Julliard in 1751,
a an effort to improve production. Series created for Beau-
ais such as Oudry's *Fables de La Fontaine* and Boucher's "Chiese tapestries" were repeated. The technique used was rather
mplified and summary, but this enhanced rather than reduced
ae picturesque and idyllic character of the models, lending them
kind of ingenuous charm. The Aubusson manufactory also
roduced upholstery fabrics, which were widely appreciated for
aeir fresh and lively color sense as well as for their relatively
aodest price. The Aubusson mark consisted of the initials
1.R.D., M.R.D.A., or M.R.D.B. (Manufacture Royale d'Au-
usson; FIG. 921).

In the early 18th century, at La Malgrange near Nancy,
ae *tapissier* Charles Mité (Mitté) wove the *Victories of Charles V
·* Lorraine (Vienna, Kunsthist. Mus.) and other works displaying
sure taste and skillful technique. In Lille, Jan de Melter, who
ame from Brussels, set up a manufactory, where his son-in-
w also worked and subsequently took over the directorship.
he manufactory specialized in tapestries with genre scenes in
ae style of Teniers, skillfully interpreted in a manner that was
aore Flemish than French.

Germany. Germany produced a large number of tapestries
1 the 18th century. In 1718, a colony of French *tapissiers*
ttled in Munich; their chief production was the *History of
ae Duchy of Bavaria* (ca. 1722; Munich, Residenzmus.). The
·rench weavers Jacques Santigny and Joseph Chédeville (d.
820) came to Munich in 1765 and 1769 respectively and di-
ected the weaving of various series, inspired by Gobelins tap-
stries. The pompous vivacity of the *Seasons* (1769; Munich,
Lesidenzmus.) was succeeded by the cold correctness of the
·tory of Achilles (1818; Munich, Residenzmus.), which still
ears the name of Chédeville. In Berlin, from the late 17th
entury to 1714, Pierre Mercier was active, weaving among
ther subjects the *History of the Great Elector*. His work was
ontinued by Jean Barraban, who in 1720 began to work in
ssociation with Charles Vigne (d. 1751). Barraban executed

several editions of a series of *Grotesque Inventions* in the manner
of Beauvais. Vigne remained active after the death of Barraban
and was responsible for the various editions of the *commedia
dell'arte* series [ca. 1745; Berlin, Kunstgewerbemus. (Schloss
Charlottenburg)] and the elegant *Story of Psyche* (ca. 1750;
Potsdam, Stadtschloss). Mercier had gone from Berlin to Dresden, where he produced the *History of Frederick Augustus* (Saxony, Moritzburg Castle). After Mercier's death in 1729, Jacques
Nermot continued his excellent production until about 1750. Tapestries were also produced in Schwabach, Erlangen, and Würzburg. The workers were for the most part French *emigrés*. In
Würzburg, Andreas Pirot executed the *Burlesques* (ca. 1740–45;
Würzburg, Veitshöchheim Castle); these are curious inventions
in which Venetian, or rather Tiepolesque, motifs are utilized.

Italy. During this period the tapestry industry was quite
productive also in Italy. In Florence, primarily owing to the
efforts of the *tapissier* Leonardo Bernini, production was of
excellent quality. The *Four Quarters of the Globe* (1715–30;
Florence, Mus. Bardini), The *Rape of Proserpine* (1733; Florence,
Mus. Archeol.), and the *Fall of Phaeton* (Florence, Mus. Archeol.),
after cartoons by Giovanni Sagrestani, Giuseppe Grisoni, and
Vincenzo Meucci respectively, achieve considerable decorative
elegance within the limits imposed by their close adherence
to the pictorialism of French works. With the extinction of the
Medici family at the death of Giovan Gastone in 1737, the
manufactory was closed down. The grand duke Francis Stephen
of Lorraine tried in vain to revive it between 1740 and 1744.
The mark of the manufactory was an F and a fleur-de-lys (FIG.
921). In Venice, Pietro Davanzo (d. 1771) and Antonio Dini
(d. 1769) were both active, the latter weaving works of small
dimensions. His daughters carried on his work until 1798.
At the turn of the century, the embroiderer Bernardino Bussoni
produced small tapestries, most of which reproduced painted
landscapes. In Rome, in the Ospizio di S. Michele a Ripa,
Pope Clement XI established a manufactory, which was directed
until 1717 by the painter Andrea Procaccini and the French
weaver Jean Simonet and thereafter until 1770 by the weaver
Pietro Ferloni. Woodland scenes were woven in the current
taste, although the largest production was of religious subjects,
most of which were copies of paintings. Papal portraits were
woven, and old series in the Vatican collections were reworked.
In 1770, Felice Cettomai became director; another Cettomai,
Filippo, wove curious little pictorial tapestries in the late 18th
century. From 1798–1823, the manufactory was inactive. In
1870 it was taken over by the Italian government and in 1926
was finally shut down.

In Turin, a low-warp workshop directed by Vittorio Demignot started to operate in 1731. The manufactory was given
official recognition by Charles Emmanuel III in 1737, when
Antonio Dini set up a high-warp workshop. Claudio Beaumont
provided the sketches for various series: the *History of Alexander*
(begun 1734; Turin, Palazzo Reale), the *History of Caesar*
(1741–50; Turin, Palazzo Reale), the *History of Cyrus* (1750–
56; Rome, Palazzo del Quirinale; Turin, Palazzo Reale, Mus.
Civico), and the *History of Hannibal* (four tapestries 1750–53,
one ca. 1760, and one 1778; Turin, Palazzo Reale). Beaumont
tried to preserve the monumentality of tapestry, using a heroic
form of expression that recalls the grand manner of Lebrun.
His effects in the larger tapestries were forced, but in those
where the field of action was more restricted he was usually
successful. The lesser works produced by the manufactory
closely reflected the various stylistic tendencies of the time;
examples are Pietro Antoniani's architectural subjects (1745–
48) and marine scenes (1749–51; Turin, Palazzo Reale; Rome,
Palazzo del Quirinale) and the rural scenes designed by Vittorio
Cignaroli and other artists (Monza, Villa Reale; Rome, Palazzo
del Quirinale, Palazzo Margherita). Vittorio Demignot (d. 1743)
was succeeded by his son Francesco and (1775) by Antonio
Bruno. In 1768 Francesco de Mura produced the sketches for
an *Aeneid* series, which had not yet been woven in 1799 when
the manufactory was closed. Between 1823 and 1832, during
a brief resumption of work, three new tapestries for the *History
of Alexander* series were woven after models by Laurent Pé-

cheux (Turin, Palazzo Reale, Mus. Civico; Rome, Palazzo del Quirinale). The mark of the manufactory was a letter and the shield of the house of Savoy.

More than any other, the tapestry manufactory in Naples, established by Charles III in 1737, was influenced in its production by the French style. The *Elements* (Naples, Palazzo Reale) for the Royal Palace in Caserta was woven here in 1746, as were other imitative works. In 1757, the tapestry maker Pietro Duranti took over the direction of the manufactory and began work the following year on the very large *Don Quixote* series (Rome, Palazzo del Quirinale). This was a copy of the Gobelin series, with only occasional variations in the central panels for some of which Giuseppe Bonito painted the cartoons. The work was completed in 1779. In 1783-86 the manufactory produced the *Story of Psyche* (Naples, Palazzo Reale), and in 1794-95 work began on the *Royal Apotheosis*. The influence of French taste is again apparent in the *History of Henry IV*, which, while differing in subject matter, is close in style to the Gobelin series of the same name. The manufactory ceased to operate in 1798.

Russia. The influence of French tapestry extended as far as Russia, where from 1716 on workers invited by Peter the Great and supervised by Behagle II and Pierre Camousse were active in St. Petersburg. After many difficulties, a series of grotesques was woven between 1733 and 1738. In 1745 the *Four Quarters of the Globe* (Moscow, Historical Mus.) was started. Besides these, portraits and other virtuoso items were woven. Production continued until 1859.

Spain. The Real Fábrica de Tapices y Alfombras in Madrid was of particular importance in the history of Spanish 18th-century tapestry production. The manufactory was instituted in 1720 by Philip V, who engaged a group of tapestry makers from Antwerp under the direction of Jacob van der Goten. Its first works were genre scenes in the style of Teniers (Madrid, Royal Palace), scenes from military life, and hunting scenes in the style of Wouwerman (1723-24; Madrid, Royal Palace). Van der Goten died in 1724, and was succeeded by his sons, who opened a workshop with high-warp looms on Calle de Santa Isabel in 1733 and continued the low-warp weaving in the original workshop. Andrea Procaccini designed the cartoons for the brilliant *Don Quixote* scenes (begun 1727; Madrid, Royal Palace). The *Four Seasons* (ca. 1756-59; Madrid, Royal Palace) is based on paintings by Jacopo Amigoni. The models for a group of Biblical scenes (Madrid, Royal Palace) were also Italian in origin: the *Story of Joseph* tapestries were woven after designs by Corrado Giaquinto and the *Story of Solomon* and the *Story of David* after models by Giaquinto and Luca Giordano, the paintings of these artists being adapted to cartoons for the use of the manufactory by José del Castillo. The weaving of these tapestries was begun about 1760. Meanwhile furniture coverings were also produced in the so-called "Pompeian" style, as well as the usual portraits and other virtuoso pieces. In 1762 Anton Raphael Mengs was appointed director of the manufactory. He commissioned cartoons from several painters, among them Francisco Bayeu, through whom Goya (q.v.) got his first commission (1776). From 1777-90 Goya executed no less than 43 large cartoons of genre scenes. The *Los Tapices* series (Madrid, Royal Palace) is based on these and cartoons by other artists illustrating similar subjects. In 1808 the French invaders destroyed the manufactory. After the Restoration there was a brief resumption of activity, tapestries being woven from 18th-century cartoons.

England. In the late 18th century, the workshops in Soho achieved greater importance. John Vanderbank (active 1689-1727) produced decorative *chinoiseries* on dark backgrounds. Later Paul Saunders specialized in landscapes and Joshua Morris in grotesques designed by a Frenchman, Adrian de Clermont.

In the 19th century there was a brief attempt to revive the art of tapestry-weaving in Windsor (1876). More important, however, was the manufactory established by William Morris at Merton Abbey, which produced, among other tapestries, the *Story of the Holy Grail* after models by Edward Burne-Jone. The attempt to revive the medieval tradition is evident this tapestry as well as in others woven at Merton Abbey. Wo. continued here until the 20th century.

CONTEMPORARY TRENDS. At the beginning of the 20 century the Gobelins and Beauvais works in France made tim attempts at a revival of tapestry-weaving. The private manufa tory of Marie Cuttoli commissioned models from Miró, Braqu Rouault, Picasso (qq.v.), and Jean Lurçat (1925-30). Aft this first experience as a cartoonist, Lurçat started to produ designs for the Aubusson manufactory. This collaborati started in 1933 and became increasingly close after 1938. these years Aubusson was the major center for the productic of tapestries in the modern manner, although the Gobelins wo Lurçat's *Illusions of Icarus* (Coll. of the Queen of the Netherland and the *Forest* in 1937-38. Around Lurçat there gradual gathered a whole group of artists — Marc Saint-Saëns, Vincer Guignebert, Jean Picart le Doux, Dom Robert — who design cartoons for the Aubusson workshops. A first exhibition their tapestries was held in Paris in 1944. The large exhibitic of French tapestry from the Middle Ages to modern time which was held in 1946 and also included tapestries designe by other artists, brought the movement to public and critic attention. The revival of tapestry as an architectural textile de oration was extremely successful. The group of artists wl promoted it formed, in 1947, the Association des Peintres Carto niers de Tapisserie. Another group of artists, including Lucie Coutaud, Maurice Brianchon, and Maurice Savin, headed tl Compagnie des Arts Français. Currently three centers are acti in France: the Gobelins, the Aubusson, and the Beauvais man factories. The Gobelins produced tapestries after models b Saint-Saëns (*Orpheus*, 1950), Picart le Doux (*Still Life*, 195 and Savin (the *Months*, 1948-51). Production at Beauvais i cluded a famous tapestry, *Polynesia* by Henri Matisse (q.v PL. 414), which is a play in balanced areas of color. At Aubusso private enterprises operating primarily in collaboration with tl Association des Peintres Cartonniers have executed a large num ber of tapestries. Of interest are Lurçat's *Liberty* (Paris, Mu d'Art Mod.), *Man*, and the *Midnight Sun* (PL. 414), whic has retained from the artist's youthful cubism a tenden toward a characteristic rhythmic fragmentation; Picart le Doux *Kleine Nachtmusik* and *Snow*, which are full of delicate lyricisr and the *Creation of Man* (Coll. of the Queen of the Netherland and *Autumn* (Paris, private coll.) by Dom Robert, who h preserved the exquisite delicacy of his early work as an illum nator. Another notable Aubusson work is the *Seasons* (193c 43; Paris, Mobilier Nat.), designed by an "independent," Marc Gromaire. A growing tendency toward nonobjectivism apparent in the tapestries after cartoons by Gilioli, Matégo Idoux, and others. Particularly interesting is Matégot's searc for textile values. Groups of painter-cartoonists, whose wo shows similar tendencies, have been formed in Belgium, Swi zerland, and Scotland.

The art of tapestry has also assumed a certain importan in Germany, where nonobjective themes are in the ascendan Noteworthy cartoonists are Fritz Winter, Franz Wahle, Ic Kerkovius, Fritz Landwehe, and Lotte Hofmann. The techniqu employed here, however, has frequently departed from trad tion, so that in some cases it is difficult to establish wheth the products should more properly be called tapestries, embro deries, or rugs intended as hangings.

Work has been revived in Italy both in small workshops an in larger manufactories. In Turin, Nervi, and Milan tapestri have been woven after cartoons by contemporary artists, parti ularly bearing in mind the textile and decorative requiremen of tapestry. Among these artists are Bruno Cassinari, Enri Prampolini, Alberto Magnelli, and Enrico Paolucci.

In Sweden, folk art provided examples of tapestries th were both austere and imaginative in their decorative stylizatio It is natural that these examples should have offered the insp ration for modern interpretations. In Poland, too, the stimul provided by popular models has been developed in compositio displaying a lively sense of the art of weaving.

BIBLIOG. *General*: A. Jubinal, Les anciennes tapisseries historiées, Paris, 338; A. Jubinal, Recherches sur l'usage et l'origine des tapisseries à per-nnages, Paris, 1840; F. Bock, Geschichte der liturgischen Gewänder des ittelalters, 3 vols., Bonn, 1856–71; J. Guiffrey, E. Müntz, and A. Pinchart, istoire générale de la tapisserie, 3 vols., Paris, 1878–85; E. Müntz, La ta-sserie, Paris, 1883 (Eng. trans., L. J. Davis, London, 1884); J. Guiffrey, istoire de la tapisserie depuis le moyen âge jusqu'à nos jours, Tours, 1886; . Riegl, Textilkunst (B. Bucher, ed., Geschichte der technischen Künste, I), Stuttgart, Berlin, Leipzig, 1893; J. Guiffrey, La tapisserie, Paris, 1904 ibliog.); G. B. Rossi, L'arte dell'arazzo, Milan, 1907; J. Guiffrey, Les pisseries du XIIe à la fin du XVIe siècle, Paris, 1911; G. L. Hunter, Tap-tries: Their Origin, History and Renaissance, New York, London, 1912; . Göbel, Wandteppiche, 3 vols. in 6, Leipzig, 1923–34; B. Kurth, Gotische ildteppiche aus Frankreich und Flandern, Munich, 1923; J. Demotte, La pisserie gothique, Paris, 1924; H. Schmitz, Bildteppiche, 3d ed., Berlin, 924; G. L. Hunter, The Practical Book of Tapestries, Philadelphia, London, 925; L. Guimbaud, La tapisserie de haute et basse lisse, Paris, 1928; E. anès, ed., La tapisserie gothique, Paris, 1928; G. Migeon, Les arts du tissu, l ed., Paris, 1929; W. G. Thomson, A History of Tapestry from the Earliest imes until the Present Day, 2d ed., London, 1930; H. C. Marillier, Hand-ok to the Teniers Tapestries, London, 1932; P. Ackerman, Tapestry: he Mirror of Civilization, New York, London, 1933; H. C. Candee, The apestry Book, New York, 1935; A. Lejard, ed., La tapisserie, Paris, 1942; . Göbel, Wandteppiche in den Niederländern, Leipzig, 1948; Artes textiles, hent, 1953 ff.; L. Mallè, Introduzione all'arazzo, Comm, IV, 1953, pp. 119–; G. W. Digby, European Tapestries and Carpets, in The Concise Ency-opaedia of Antiques, II, London, 1955, pp. 32–42; M. L. Plourin, Historia l Tapiz en Occidente, Barcelona, 1955; Marques des manufactures de pisseries, Connaissance des arts, 49, 1956, pp. 46–47; L. von Wilckens, extilien in Westeuropa: Literatur von 1945–61, ZfKg, XXIV, 1961, pp. 1–75; D. Heinz, Europäische Wandteppiche, I, Brunswick, 1963.

Germany and Switzerland: *a. General*: G. Stephani, Die textile Innende-ration des frühmittelalterlichen deutschen Hauses und die ältesten Sticker-en Pommerns, in Beiträge zur Geschichte und Altertumskunde Pommerns, ettin, 1898, pp. 124–76; J. Lessing, Wandteppiche und Decken des Mittel-ters in Deutschland, Berlin, 1910; B. Kurth, Die deutschen Bildteppiche s Mittelalters, 3 vols., Vienna, 1926; H. Göbel, Wandteppiche, III: Die rmanische und slavische Ländern, 2 vols., Berlin, 1933–34 (full bibliog.); . Steinbrucker, Von deutschen Bildteppichen, Karlsruhe, 1937; R. Jaques, eutsche Textilkunst, Krefeld, 1942; G. Townsend, A South German apestry, BMFA, LVI, 1958, pp. 5–17. *b. Cloth of St. Gereon*: F. Bock, as heilige Köln, Leipzig, 1858; A. Essenwein, Über ein Wollteppich der ımmlung der Gewebe im germanischen Museum, Anz. für Kunde der Vorzeit, XXV, 1870, cols. 33–35; A. Darcel, Exposition retrospective Lyon: Tapisseries, GBA, XVI, 1877, pp. 272–76; J. Karabaček, Die heodor Grafschen Funde in Ägypten, Vienna, 1883; O. von Falke, Kunst-schichte der Seideweberei, Berlin, 1915. *c. Halberstadt tapestries*: F. . H. Lucanus, Der Dom zu Halberstadt, Halberstadt, 1837; C. Elis, Wand-ppiche im Dom zu Halberstadt, Kirchenschmuck, II, 1858, pp. 44–45; . Soil de Moriamé, Tapisseries conservées à Quedlinbourg, Halberstadt, quelques autres villes du nord de l'Allemagne, Bruges, 1889; M. Creutz, us der Werkstatt des Rogerus, Z. für christliche K., XXII, 1909, cols. 7–70; M. Creutz, Die Anfänge des monumentalen Stils in Norddeutschland, ologne, 1910; V. C. Habicht, Der niedersächsische Kunstkreis, Hannover, 930; H. Appuhn, Der Karls-Teppich in Halberstadt, Aachener Kunst-ätter, XXIV–XXV, 1962–63, pp. 137–49. *d. Switzerland*: J. Stammler, ie Teppiche des Historischen Museum zu Thun, Bern, 1891; R. F. Burck-ırdt, Ein aus Bruchstücken ergänzter, gewirkter, oberrheinischer Wand-hang . . . , Jahresbericht des Historischen Mus. zu Basel, 1918, pp. 35–62; . F. Burckhardt, Gewirkte Bildteppiche des XV. und XVI. Jahrhunderts n Historischen Museum zu Basel, Leipzig, 1923; F. Gysin, Gotische Bild-ppiche der Schweiz, Basel, 1940 (Eng. trans., R. C. Allen, Swiss Medieval apestries, London, 1947); R. L. Wyss, Bildteppiche des 15. und 16. Jahr-ınderts, Bern, 1955; R. L. Wyss, Der Bubenbergteppich im Schweizer-chen Landesmuseum, ZfSAKg, XIX, 1959, pp. 53–59. *e. Constance pestries*: T. Hampe, Katalog der Gewebesammlung des germanischen useums, Nürnberg, 1892; Description d'une série de tapisseries gothiques partenant à M. Pierpont Morgan, Paris, 1911. *f. Alsace*: F. A. von Lehner, ürstlich Hohenzollernsches Museum zu Sigmaringen: Textilarbeiten, gmaringen, 1874; F. von der Leyen and A. Spamer, Die altdeutschen andteppiche im Regensburger Rathause, Regensburg, 1912; R. Bern-imer, The Wild Men in the Middle Ages, Cambridge, Mass., 1952. *g. ranconia*: Luitpold, Duke in Bavaria, Die frankische Bildwerkerei, 2 vols., unich, Florence, 1926.

France: *a. General*: J. Deville, Recueil de statuts et de documents latifs à la corporation des tapissiers de Paris, Paris, 1875; J. Guiffrey, es origines de la tapisserie de haute et basse lice à Paris, Mém. Soc. de l'h. Paris et de l'Ile-de-France, VIII, 1881, pp. 107–24; J. Guiffrey, Nicolas ataille, tapissier parisien du XIVe siècle: Sa vie, son œuvre, sa famille, ém. Soc. de l'h. de Paris et de l'Ile-de-France, X, 1884, pp. 268–317; J. uiffrey, ed., Inventaire des tapisseries de Charles VI vendues ou dispersées ır les Anglais, Paris, 1887; J. Marquet de Vasselot and R. A. Weigert, bliographie de la tapisserie, des tapis et de la broderie de France, Paris, 935, pp. 3–240; G. Bazin et al., La tapisserie française: Muraille et laine, ıris, 1946; A. Lejard, ed., French Tapestry, London, 1946; G. F. Wing-ld Digby, French Tapestries, London, New York, 1951; G. Fontaine, ed., razzi francesi dal Medioevo ad oggi, Rome, 1953 (cat.); I. Toesca, La mostra gli arazzi francesi a Roma, Paragone, IV, 41, 1953, pp. 62–64; M. Viale, ostra di arazzi francesi, BArte, XXXVIII, 1953, pp. 370–75; L. Lefran-is-Pillon, L'art du XIVe siècle en France, Paris, 1954; R. A. Weigert, La pisserie française, Paris, 1956; (Eng. trans., D. and M. King, London, 962) (bibliog.); F. A. Yates, The Valois Tapestries, London, 1959. *b. The Apocalypse tapestries*: X. Barbier de Montault, Les tapisseries du sacre d'Angers, Angers, 1863; L. Joannis, Les tapisseries de l'Apocalypse de la Cathédrale d'Angers, Angers, 1864; L. de Farcy, Notices archéologiques sur les tentures et les tapisseries de la Cathédrale d'Angers, Angers, 1875; L. de Farcy, Histoire et description des tapisseries de la Cathédrale d'Angers, Lille, 1889; C. Urseau, M. Aubert, and L. Deshairs, Les tapisseries d'Angers, Beaux-Arts, 1923, pp. 225–40; C. Urseau, Le Musee des tapisseries d'An-gers, Paris, 1930; M. R. James, The Apocalypse in Art, London, 1931; A. Lejard, Les tapisseries de l'Apocalypse de la Cathédrale d'Angers, Paris, 1942; L'Apocalypse: Tapisserien aus der Kathedrale von Angers, Basel, 1951 (cat.); R. Planchenault, Les tapisseries d'Angers, Paris, 1955; G. Schmidt, L'Apocalypse d'Angers, Œil, 60, 1959, pp. 60–66. *c. The Presentation at the Temple*: J. Destrée and P. van de Ven, Tapisseries des Musées Royaux du Cinquantenaire à Bruxelles, Brussels, 1910; M. Crick Kuntziger, Musées Royaux d'Art et d'Histoire à Bruxelles: Catalogue des Tapisseries, Brussels, 1956. *d. The Nine Heroes*: G. L. Hunter, Tapestries of Clarence H. Mackay, New York, 1925; J. J. Rorimer and M. B. Freeman, The Nine Heroes Tap-estries at the Cloisters, BMMA, N.S., VII, 1949, pp. 243–60. *e. Dame à la Licorne group*: A. F. Kendrick, Quelques remarques sur les tapisseries de la Dame à la Licorne au Musée de Cluny: Les ateliers de tapisserie en An-gleterre, Actes Cong. d'h. de l'art (1921), III, Paris, 1924, pp. 662–71; H. Martin, La dame à la licorne, MAF, LXXVII, 1924–27, pp. 137–68; L. de Varax, Les tapisseries du Cardinal de Clugny, Lyons, 1926; G. Townsend, Eight Fragments of 15th Century Tapestry, BMFA, XXVII, 1929, pp. 2–10; P. Ackerman, The Lady and the Unicorn, BM, LXVI, 1935, pp. 35–36; J. Marquet de Vasselot, Musée de Cluny: Les tapisseries dites de la Dame à la licorne, Paris, 1948; M. Crick Kuntziger, Un chef d'œuvre inconnu du Maître de la Dame à la licorne, Rev. belge d'achéol. et d'h. de l'art, XXIII, 1954, pp. 3–20. *f. Beauvais*: J. Badin, La manufacture de tapisseries de Beauvais, Paris, 1909; J. Ajalbert, Beauvais: La Manufacture nationale de tapisseries, Paris, 1927. *g. Gobelins*: A. L. Lacordaire, Notice historique sur les manufactures impériales de tapisseries des Gobelins de tapis et de tapis-series de Mobilier de la Couronne, 4th ed., Paris, 1859; A. Darcel, Les ma-nufactures nationales de tapisserie des Gobelins, Paris, 1885; E. Gerspach, Répertoire détaillé des Tapisseries des Gobelins, Paris, 1893; M. Fenaille, Etat général des tapisseries de la manufacture des Gobelins, 6 vols., Paris, 1903–23; J. Guiffrey, Les manufactures nationales de tapisseries: Les Go-belins et Beauvais, Paris, 1907; E. Dumontheir, Les tapisseries des Gobelins à l'époque napoléonienne, Renaissance de l'art, VI, 1923, pp. 234–43; M. Benisovich, The History of the Tenture des Indes, BM, LXXXIII, 1943, pp. 216–25; F. Dumont, Jean Bapiste Oudry, Connaissance des arts, 69, 1957, pp. 52–57; J. Niclausse, "Chasses Nouvelles" de Monsieur Oudry, GBA, XLIX, 1957, pp. 311–20; A. M. L. E. Erkelens, Vier Wandtapijten met Ovidius' Metamorphosen Manufacture des Gobelins, Atelier Jans-sen Lefebure, van vóór 1684, B. Rijksmuseum, VII, 1959, pp. 64–69; Les Gobelins (1662–1962): Trois siècles de tapisserie française, Nyon, 1962 (cat.). *h. Other examples*: J. Houdoy, Les tapisseries d'haute lisse: Histoire de la fabrication lilloise du XIVe au XVIIIe siècle, Lille, 1871; E. Müntz, Les fabriques de tapisseries de Nancy, Mém. Soc. archéol. Lorraine, XI, 1883, pp. 195–212; C. Pérathon, Essai de catalogue descriptif des anciennes tapisseries d'Aubusson et de Felletin, B. des Séances Soc. d'archéol. et d'h. du Limousin, XLI, 1894, pp. 488–542, XLII, 1894, pp. 392–457, LI, 1902, pp. 246–308; G. J. Phillips, Diane de Poitiers and Jean Cousin, BMMA, N.S., II, 1943, pp. 109–17; Artemisia Tapestries from the Barberini-Ffoul-ke Collection, B. Minneapolis Inst. of Arts, XXXVII, 1948, pp. 118–32; R. Pernoud, Les tapisseries de Daniel Pepersack et leurs cartons, GBA, XXXIV, 1948, pp. 33–38; A. S. Cavallo, The History of Coriolanus as Rep-resented in Tapestries, B. Brooklyn Mus., XVII, 1, 1955–56, pp. 5–22; J. Dautzenberg, Une tapisserie ancienne d'Aubusson d'après Etienne Jeaurat, B. Soc. de l'h. de l'art fr., 1958, pp. 89–90; C. Brisson, Une industrie oubliée: La manufacture royale de tapisseries d'Elbeuf, Rev. Soc. des savants de Haute Normandie, XXIV, 1961, pp. 23–55; D. G. Shepherd, Three Tapes-tries from Chaumont, B. Cleve. Mus. of Art, XLVIII, 1961, pp. 159–77.

Arras and Tournai: *a. General*: E. Van Drival, Les tapisseries d'Arras, Paris, 1864; E. Müntz, Les tapisseries d'Arras à la fin du XIVe siècle et au commencement du XVe siècle, Courrier de l'art, VI, 1886, p. 11; E. Soil de Moriamé, Les tapisseries de Tournai, Tournai, 1891; B. Prost, Inventaires mobiliers et extraits des comptes des ducs de Bourgogne de la maison de Valois, 1902; M. Morelowski, Der Krakauer Schwanenritterteppich, Kunst-hist. Jhb. der K. K. Zentralkommission, VI, sup. 1912, cols. 117–40; B. Kurth, Die Blütezeit der Bildwerkerkunst zu Tournai und des burgundischen Hofs, JhbKhSammlWien, XXXIV, 1918, pp. 53–110; P. Ackerman, The Ferrets and the Poissonniers, Art in Am., XIII, 1924–25, pp. 266–73; M. Crick Kuntziger, Les compléments de nos tapisseries gothiques, B. Mus. Royaux d'art et d'h., III, 1931, pp. 66–77, 104–13, 157–64, V, 1933, pp. 31–38; P. Rolland, M. Crick Kuntziger, and M. Morelowski, Le tapissier Pa-squier Grenier et l'église St. Quentin à Tournai, Rev. belge d'archéol. et d'h. de l'art, VI, 1936, pp. 203–21; M. Crick Kuntziger, Notes sur les tapis-series de l'Histoire d'Alexandre au Palais Doria, B. Inst. h. belge de Rome, XIX, 1938, pp. 119–32; M. Crick Kuntziger, La tenture tournaisienne de l'Histoire de Judith et d'Holopherne, B. Mus. Royaux d'Art et d'H., XII, 1940, pp. 26–34; J. Lestocquoy, Origine et décadence de la tapisserie à Arras, Rev. belge d'archéol. et d'h. de l'art, X, 1940, pp. 27–34; G. Janneau, Les tapisseries de Tournai, Arch. de l'art fr., N.S., XXII, 1950–57, pp. 33–38; L. Mallè, Considerazioni sui caratteri stilistici delle arazzerie di Arras e Tournai nel '400, Comm, IV, 1953, pp. 264–95; W. H. Forsyth, The Trojan War in Medieval Tapestries, BMMA, N.S., XIV, 1955–56, pp. 76–84; R. L. Wyss, Die Berner Caesarteppiche, Jhb. h. Mus. Bern, XXXV–XXXVI, 1955–56, pp. 103–232; W. Wells, The Seven Sacraments Tapestri: A New Discovery, BM, CI, 1959, pp. 97–105; B. Young, John Dynham and His Tapestry, BMMA, N.S., XX, 1962, pp. 308–16. *b. History of SS. Piat and Eleutherius*: E. Soil de Moriamé, Tapisseries du XVe siècle conser-vées à la Cathédrale de Tournai, leur fabrication à Arras en 1402, Tournai,

1883; A. Guesnon, Le bautelisseur Pierre Féré d'Arras, Rev. du Nord, I, 1910, pp. 201–15; M. Crick Kuntziger, Les plus anciennes tapisseries occidentales conservées en Belgique, Cah. de Belgique, III, 1930, pp. 177–84; Le siècle de Bourgogne, Brussels, 1951 (cat.). *c. History of Jourdain de Blaye*: V. Crescini, Frammento di una serie di arazzi nel Museo di Padova, Arch. storico dell'arte, II, 1889, pp. 415–20; A. Moschetti, Il Museo civico di Padova, Padua, 1938; M. and V. Viale, Arazzi e tappeti antichi, Turin, 1952 (cat.).

Brussels and Flanders: A. Wauters, Les tapisseries bruxelloises, Brussels, 1878; F. Donnet, Documents pour servir à l'histoire des ateliers de tapisserie de Bruselles, Audenarde, Anvers ... jusqu'à la fin du XVIIe siècle, Ann. Soc. royale d'archéol. de Bruxelles, XI, 1896, pp. 269–336; J. Destrée, Maître Philippe: auteur de cartons de tapisseries, Brussels, 1904; A. Wauters, Jean van Roome dit Jean de Bruxelles, Brussels, 1904; A. Thiery, Les tapisseries historiées de Jean van Roome dit Jean de Brussel, Louvain, 1907; M. Crick Kuntziger, Maître Knoest et les tapisseries "signées" des Musées Royaux, Liège, 1927; P. Ackerman, The Final Solution of Maître Philippe, Apollo, XIV, 1931, pp. 83–87; M. Crick Kuntziger, La tenture d'Achille d'après Rubens et les tapissiers Jean et F. Raes, N. Mus. Royaux d'Art et d'H., VI, 1934, pp. 2–12; M. Crick Kuntziger, Les marques et les tentures des Wauters, Rev. belge d'archéol. et d'h. de l'art, V, 1935, pp. 36–46; J. Denucé, Les tapisseries anversoises, Antwerp, 1936; M. Crick Kuntziger, De Vlaamse tapitweverij in de XIVe, XVe en XVIe eeuven, in S. Leurs, ed., Geschiedenis van de Vlaamse Kunst, I, Antwerp, 1936, pp. 482–510; M. Crick Kuntziger, Les cartons de Jordaens au Musée du Louvre, Ann. Soc. d'Archéol. de Bruxelles, XLII, 1938, pp. 135–46; A. Hullebroeck, Histoire de la tapisserie à Audenarde, Audenarde, 1938; M. Crick Kuntziger, Les arts décoratifs, in P. Fierens, ed., L'art in Belgique, Brussels, 1939, pp. 153–75, 339–62, 403–10; M. Crick Kuntziger, Recherches sur les tapisseries brugeoises des Arts Libéraux, Ann. Soc. d'Archéol. de Bruxelles, XLV, 1941, pp. 141–53; E. Tormo y Monzo, La Apoteosis eucarìstica de Rubens, AEArte, XV, 1942, pp. 291–315; E. Dahnens, Jan Van Roome, alias Van Brussel, Schilder, Gentse Bijdragen tot de Kunstgeschiedenis, XI, 1945–48, pp. 41–136; J. Ehrmann, Caron et les tapisseries de Florence, RArts, II, 1952, pp. 27–30; J. Duverger, Bijdragen tot de geschiedenis van de Oudenaardse tapijtkunst en tapijthandel, Artes textiles, I, 1953, pp. 38–64; M. Crick Kuntziger, La tenture de l'Histoire de Jacob d'après Bernard van Orley, Antwerp, 1954; J. J. Rorimer and M. Freeman, The Glorification of Charles VIII, BMMA, N.S., XII, 1954, pp. 281–301; E. A. Standen, The Twelve Ages of Man, BMMA, N.S., XII, 1954, pp. 241–48; J. Versyp, De geschiedenis van de tapijtkunst te Brugge, Brussels, 1954; M. Duverger, De externe geschiedenis van het Gentse tapijtwerersambacht, Artes textiles, II, 1955, pp. 53–104; A. Faria de Morais, Les tapisseries de Dom João de Castro, B. ét. portugaises et de l'Inst. fr. au Portugal, XIX, 1955–56, pp. 64–138; P. Verdier, The Tapestry of the Prodigal Son, J. Walters Art Gall., XVIII, 1955, pp. 9–58; R. A. d'Hulst, Jordaens and His Early Activities in the Field of Tapestry, AQ, XIX, 1956, pp. 236–54; S. Schneebalg-Perelman, "Le retouchage" dans la tapisserie bruxelloise ou les origines de l'édit impérial de 1544, Ann. Soc. Royale d'Archéol. de Bruxelles, L, 1956–61, pp. 191–210; J. R. Steppe, Vlaamse Wandtapijten in Spanije, Artes textiles, III, 1956, pp. 27–66; M. Ferrero Viale, Tapisseries rubéniennes et jordaenesques à Turin, Artes textiles, III, 1956, pp. 67–74; A. S. Cavallo, The Redemption of Man: A Christian Allegory in Tapestry, BMFA, LVI, 1958, pp. 147–58; E. A. Standen, The Shepherd's Sweet Lot, BMMA, N.S., XVII, 1958–59, pp. 226–34; A. Stemper, Der Prudentia-Teppich des Pfalzgrafen Ottheinrich im Kurpfälzischen Museum zu Heidelberg, Heidelberger Jhb., II, 1958, pp. 68–95; K. Vlaamse Acad. voor Wetenschappen ... van Belgie: Klasse d. schone kunsten, Het herfstij van de Vlaamse tapijtkunst (Int. colloquium), Brussels, 1959; F. A. Yates, The Valois Tapestries, London, 1959; M. Carlberg Le triomphe des vertus chrétiennes: Suite de huit tapisseries de Bruxelles du XVIe siècle, Rev. belge d'archéol. et d'h. de l'art, XXIX, 1960, pp. 3–36; E. Duverger, Jan, Jacques en Frans de Moor: Tapijtwevers en tapijthandelaars te Oudenarde, Antwerpen en Gent (1560 tot ca. 1680), Ghent, 1960; R. A. d'Hulst, Flämische Bildteppiche des 14. bis 18. Jahrundert, Brussels, 1961.

England: W. G. Thomson, Tapestry Weaving in England, New York, 1914; H. C. Marillier, History of the Merton Abbey Tapestry Works, London, 1927; E. A. B. Barnard and A. J. B. Wace, The Sheldon Tapestry Weavers and Their Work, Oxford, 1929; H. C. Marillier, English Tapestries of the 18th Century, London, 1930; A. K. Longfield, History of Tapestry-making in Ireland in the 17th and 18th Centuries, Royal Soc. of Ant. of Ireland, LXVIII, 1, 1938, pp. 91–105; G. Wingfield Digby, Late Mortlake Tapestries, Connoisseur, CXXXIV, 1954, pp. 239–45; G. Wingfield Digby, English Tapestries at Burlington House, BM, XCVII, 1955, pp. 388–91; M. Kay, French and Flemish Influences on English Tapestries, Proc. Huguenot Soc. of London, XIX, 1957, pp. 238–40; Y. Hackenbroch, English and Other Needlework, Tapestries and Textiles in the Irwin Untermeyer Collection, Cambridge, Mass., 1960; L. van Puyvelde, Vlaamse tapijtwevers in Engelland, Rev. belge d'archéol. et d'h. de l'art, XXX, 1961, pp. 199–208; H. C. Marillier, The Tapestries at Hampton Court Palace, 2d ed., London, 1962.

Italy: G. Campori, L'arazzeria estense, Modena, 1876; C. Conti, Ricerche storiche sull'arte degli arazzi in Firenze, Florence, 1876; G. M. Urbani di Gheltof, Degli arazzi in Venezia, Venice, 1878; C. Minieri Riccio, La real fabbrica degli arazzi della Città di Napoli, Naples, 1879; W. Braghirolli, Sulle manufatture di arazzi in Mantova, Mantua, 1881; E. d'Astier de la Vigerie, La fabrique royale de tapisserie de la ville de Naples, Paris, 1906; P. Gentili, Cenni storici sulle origini e vicende degli arazzi in Roma, Rome, 1915; M. Tinti, Francesco Bachiacca e i suoi arazzi, Dedalo, I, 1921, pp. 803–17; E. Possenti, La fabbrica degli arazzi di Torino, B. Soc. piemontese di archeol. e belle arti, VIII, 1924, pp. 1–11; P. Ackerman, Antichi arazzi gotici in San Marco a Venezia, Dedalo, VI, 1925, pp. 441–56; A. T luccini, L'arazzeria torinese, Dedalo, VII, 1926, pp. 101–31, 167–85; Göbel, Das Lebens Urbans VIII: Eine Teppichserie aus der Manufak des Kardinals Barberini, Cicerone, XXI, 1929, pp. 305–11; C. Vince Gli arazzi di Casa Trivulzio, Dedalo, X, 1929, pp. 45–60; G. Nicode Castello Sforzesco, Emporium, LXXXII, 1935, pp. 11–25; E. Posse L'arazzeria napoletana, BArte, XXIX, 1936, pp. 549–77; W. E. Su Documents Relating to the Trivulzio Tapestries, B. Needle and Bob Club of New York, XXVII, 1943, pp. 3–39; R. Longhi, Viatico per cin secoli di pittura veneziana, Florence, 1946; U. Barberini, Pietro da Cort e l'arazzeria Barberini, BArte, XXXV, 1950, pp. 43–51, 145–52; D. Shepherd, The Lamentation: A Tapestry Antependium Designed by (simo Tura, B. Cleve. Mus. of Art, XXXVIII, 1951, pp. 40–42; D. H kamp, Arazzi a soggetto profano su cartoni di Alessandro Allori, RA XXXI, 1956, pp. 105–55; R. Pallucchini, Nuove proposte per Niccolò Pietro, Arte veneta, X, 1956, pp. 37–55 at 51; A. S. Cavallo, Notes on Barberini Tapestry Manufactory at Rome, BMFA, LV, 1957, pp. 17– G. Townsend, Four Panels of Roman Baroque Tapestry, BMFA, I 1957, pp. 11–15; A. Santangelo, Tessuti d'arte italiani dal XII al XV secolo, Milan, 1959; M. Ferrero Viale, Arazzi italiani del Cinquecer Milan, 1961; A. M. Aguzzi and M. Baiardi, Appunti per una storia del tess d'arte barocca in Lombardia e in Piemonte, Arte lombarda, VII, 19 pp. 117–44; G. Cecchini, L'arazzeria senese, ASI, CXX, 1962, pp. 149–

Norway: H. Grosch, Gamle Norske Tæpper, Berlin, 1889; A. Ri Die Wirkerei und der textile Hausfleiss, Kunstgewerbeblatt, N.S.,I, 18 pp. 21–23; H. Grosch, Altnorwegische Bildteppiche, Berlin, 1901; H. Gros Gammel Norsk Vævkunst, 3 vols., Oslo, 1913–22; H. Dedekam, Bal sholtæppet, Oslo, 1918; H. Dedekam, Odins Træ et Stykke Billedv fra Osebergfundet, Kunst og Haandverk: Nordisk studier, Oslo, 19 pp. 56–75; H. Dedekam, "Perspektivet" paa Osebergdronningens tapisser Kunst og Kultur, VIII, 1920, pp. 145–77; H. Dedekam, Tapestry Weav in Norway, Am. Scandinavian Rev., XV, 1927, pp. 205–14; K. Mellb Billedvevningen i Norge under Renessansen, Oslo, 1932; B. Hougen, O bergfunnets billedvev, Viking, IV, 1940, pp. 85–124; H. Engelstad, Re Bunad, Tjeld: Middelalderens Billedtepper i Norge, Oslo, 1952; T. Kielland, Norsk billedvev, 1550–1800, 3 vols., Oslo, 1953–55; Art nor gien des Vikings au XVIIIe siècle, Brussels, 1954 (cat.); A. M. Franz Høylandteppet, Årbok Kong. Norske Videnskabers Selskab Mus., 19 pp. 87–103.

Netherlands: G. T. van Ysselsteyn, Geschiedenis der tapijtweveri in de Noordelijke Nederlanden, 2 vols., Leiden, 1936; E. Duverger, teratuuroverzicht betreffende de geschiedenis der textiele kunsten in Nederlanden (1958–59), Artes textiles, V, 1959–60, pp. 169–237.

Poland: J. Pagaczewski, Gobeliny polskie (Polish Gobelins), Krak 1929; T. Mańkowski, Polskie tkaniny i hafty XVI–XVIII wieku (Pol Textiles and Embroideries, 16th–18th cent.), Wrocław, 1954; M. Markiewi Z zagadnień polskiego tkactwa renesansowego (Polish Renaissance Gobelin S. renesansowe, III, 1963, pp. 483–520.

Spain: G. Cruzada Villaamil, Los tapices de Goya, Madrid, 1870; M. Monserrat, Los tapices de Zaragoza, Saragossa, 1917; E. Lafuente F rari, La tapicería en España, Madrid, 1943; V. de Sambricio, Tapices Goya, Madrid, 1946; V. de Sambricio, Tapices de José del Castillo, Go II, 7, 1955, pp. 22–28; V. Bernis, Tapicería hispano-musulmana: siglos X y XIV, AEArte, XXIX, 1956, pp. 95–115.

Modern: Besides those general works under specific geographic headir and the catalogues listed below, see: P. Courthion, Les tapisseries de J Lurçat, Art et décoration, II, 1929, pp. 51–54; P. Hirsch, Jean Lurçat la tapisserie, Lille, Paris, 1946; J. Lurçat, Tapisserie française, Paris, 19 (Eng. trans., B. Crocker, Designing Tapestry, London, 1950); M. Zah Les tapisseries de Jean Picart Le Doux, Mobilier et décoration, XXVI 1948, pp. 3–71; J. Cassou and G. Fontaine, Quatre années de tapisse française, Paris, 1949 (cat.); H. Gleizes, Tapisseries françaises, Paris, 19 (cat.); L. Degand, Un nouvel ensor de la tapisserie, XXe siècle, N.S., 1954, pp. 74–77; A. Heimendahl, Webkünstlerinnen der Gegenwart, I Kunstwerk, VIII, 1954–55, pp. 29–35; XT, Domus, 300, 1954, pp. 34– 45, 50–52, 65; R. Barotte, Dom Robert: Tapissier du Paradis terrest Plaisirs de France, XXII, 2, 1955, pp. 22–24; W. J. Strachan, Contempora Tapestries from France and Britain, Studio, CL, 1955, pp. 161–69; Fais le point de la tapisserie moderne, Connaissance des arts, 58, 1956, pp. 12 29; W. Volkaert, Wandtapijten van Emile Gilioli, Artes textiles, III, 19 pp. 119–22; D. Chevalier, Nouvelles tapisseries françaises, Graphis, 1957, pp. 244–49; G. Crook, Contemporary Tapestry: Styles and Techniqu Studio, CLIII, 1957, pp. 161–67; M. Damain, La tapisserie française et peintres cartonniers, Paris, 1957; Forme nuove in Italia, Rome, 1957; Neuwirth, Österreichische Bildteppichen von Heute, Alte und moder K., III, 3, 1958, pp. 26–30; D. B. van Dommelen, Decorative Wall Hangin Art with Fabric, New York, 1962.

Catalogues: X. Barbier de Montault, Inventaire descriptif des tapisser de haute lisse conservées à Rome, Arras, 1879; E. Ritter von Birk, Inven der in Besitze des Allerhöchsten Kaiserhauses befindlichen Niederländ Tapeten und Gobelins, JhbKhSammlWien, I, 1883, pp. 213–48, II, 188 pp. 167–220; C. Rigoni, Catalogo della R. Galleria degli arazzi, Ron Florence, 1884; J. Böttiger, Svenska Statens Samling af Wäfda Tapet 4 vols., Stockholm, 1895–98; J. Stammler, Der Paramentenschatz im histo schen Museum zu Bern, Bern, 1895; J. De Valencia, Tapices de la Coro de España, 2 vols., Madrid, 1903; J. Destrée and P. van de Ven, Tapisser des Musées Royaux du Cinquantenaire à Bruxelles, Brussels, 1910; Kumsch, Wandteppiche im Hause Krupp von Bohlen und Halbach, Dr

TAPESTRY AND CARPETS

len, 1913; A. Luzio, Gli arazzi del Gonzaga restituiti dall'Austria, Bergamo, 1919; E. Tormo y Monzo and P. Sánchez Cantón, Tapices de la Casa del Rey, Madrid, 1919; L. Baldass, Wiener Gobelinsammlung, Vienna, 1921; A. F. Kendrick, ed., Victoria and Albert Museum: Catalogue of Tapestries, London, 1924; A. Gomez Martìnez and B. Chillòn Sampedro, Los tapices de la Catedral de Zamora, Zamora, 1925; G. L. Hunter, Tapestries of Clarence H. Mackay, New York, 1925; J. Messelet and R. A. Weigert, Cinq siècles de tapisseries d'Aubusson, Paris, 1935; M. Gębarowicz and T. Mańkowski, Arasy Zygmunta Augusta (Tapestries of Sigismund Augustus), Kraków, 1937; J. Niclausse and G. Janneau, Le Musée des Gobelins, Paris, 1938; M. Crick Kuntziger, Les tapisseries de l'Hôtel de Ville de Bruxelles, Antwerp, 1944; P. Balle Huguet, Los tapices de la Catedral Primada de Tarragona, Tarragona, 1946; G. Bazin et al., La tapisserie française: Muraille et laine, Paris, 1946; La tapisserie française du moyen âge à nos jours, Paris, Brussels, 1946; J. J. Rorimer, Mediaeval Tapestries: A Picture Book, New York, 1947; J. J. Rorimer, The Museum Collection of Mediaeval Tapestries, BMMA, N.S., VI, 1947, pp. 91–98; J. Niclausse, Tapisseries et Tapis de la ville de Paris, Paris, 1949; C. Audran, ed., Dessins du National Museum du Stockholm, Paris, 1950; J. Lestocquoy, L'art du moyen âge en Artois, Arras, 1951; Le siècle de Bourgogne, Brussels, 1951; M. and V. Viale, Arazzi e tappeti antichi, Turin, 1952; G. Fontaine, ed., Arazzi francesi dal Medioevo ad oggi, Rome, 1953; Museum Boymans, Olieverfschetzen van Rubens, Rotterdam, 1953; F. Torralba Soriano, Los tapices de Zaragoza, Saragossa, 1953; J. Verzyp, Tapijtwerk in het Museum te Sint-Omers, Rev. belge d'archéol. et d'h. de l'art, XXII, 1953, pp. 153–74; M. Crick Kuntziger, Musées Royaux d'Art et d'Histoire à Bruxelles: Catalogue des Tapisseries, Brussels, 1956; J. Blažková, Wandteppiche aus tschechoslovakischen Sammlungen, Prague, 1957; Y. Hackenbroch, English and Other Needlework, Tapestries and Textiles in the Irwin Untermyer Collection, Cambridge, Mass., 1960; D. Heinz, Der Paramentenschatz der Stadtpfarrkirech in Linz, Vienna, Munich, 1962.

Mercedes FERRERO VIALE

II. CARPETS. TECHNIQUE. The characteristic feature of the knotted pile carpet consists in the knotting and fastening of short strands of material into a foundation weave in such a way as to form a dense layer — the pile — which covers the foundation completely on one side. The individual pile strands are wound around the taut warp threads and after each row is finished are firmly locked in by the weft, which, running at right angles to the warp, is carried across the entire width and tightly packed. Throughout the development of the technique in various regions many methods of stretching the warp were tried; these range from the simple wood constructions held by pegs to the large fixed looms at which many knotters could work together. The preferred material for knotted carpets was sheep's wool, although for certain luxury carpets silk was used and in certain regions goat's or camel's hair was used. The smooth quality of the cotton strand made it particularly suitable material and by far the most commonly used for the foundation weave. A silk warp or whole foundation is found in carpets requiring a particularly dense knotting. Threads wound with gold and silver, used to enrich the carpets, are not knotted but brocaded in so that they appear as a sort of sunken relief in the pile of the carpet. Depending on how the pile thread is tied around the warp, three kinds of knots can be distinguished. In the Turkish, or so-called "Ghiordes," knot the strand is laid across two (or more) warp threads on the front, the ends are drawn back and then toward the front again between the central warp threads. An empty space thus alternates with one filled by two (or more) strand ends. In the Persian, or so-called "Sehna," knot, the strand is laid under one warp thread and then wound around the next, so that each warp thread has a pile end hanging from it. This technique permits greater density in knotting. The third, and by far the rarest, form, the so-called "Spanish" knot, is worked around one warp thread, the pile ends issuing at each side of it. The next warp thread is then left free. The knots are staggered in the individual rows, so that in one the even, in another the uneven warp threads bear the knots. In all early fragments up to the 15th century the Turkish knot is found — in carpets from Asia Minor and the Caucasus as well as in those made in Europe. The Persian knot appears in Mamluke and Ottoman carpets as well as in Persian production. The density of the knotting varies extraordinarily from group to group and from one piece to another. As many as 800 knots to the square inch can be found in the oldest east Turkestan fragments and as few as 80 to the square inch in coarser examples.

For coloring the wool only dyes obtained from natural substances were used. Plants used included madder, indigo, turmeric, and cassia; cochineal was obtained from the kermes insect (coccus ilicis). The iron sulphate used to create the characteristically rich blacks was the only dye to deteriorate noticeably with age, frequently causing "falling out" of the black areas in old carpets. All the other natural dyes produced colors as durable and fade-resistant as they were beautiful. Synthetic dyes — the anilines — were introduced from Europe after the middle of the 19th century and quickly became popular because of their cheapness, but their brilliant colors, which seemed striking at first, soon lost their effectiveness and became positively muddy with age. They characterize the period of decline of the oriental carpet under European influence.

THE EARLIEST CARPETS. The origins and early history of the carpet are enveloped in darkness. The oldest carpet so far known is that found in 1949 by a Soviet expedition in an ice-bound grave in Pazyryk in the Altai. The piece (Leningrad, The Hermitage), preserved almost in its entirety (about 6 by 6½ ft.), has a central field with star rosettes in squares surrounded by a five-part border in whose bands appear rows of winged griffins, grazing elk, and men on horseback, stylistically related to the Achaemenid art of Persia. Since this carpet, which is attributed to the 5th–4th century B.C., shows a complete mastery and full artistic understanding of the technique, the origins must be presumed, to go back at least to the beginning of the 1st millennium B.C. This historically and artistically important work is isolated, however. The next finds, from the 3d and 6th centuries of our era, are small fragments with modest patterns brought to light by the expeditions of Mark Aurel Stein and the German Turfan expedition. The pieces found in Fostat, Noin-ula, and Dura-Europos (Syria) have carpetlike surfaces but are not knotted; they are nub or loop tapestries.

From the next six centuries not a single carpet has survived to document the continuation and development of the knotting technique. Written sources often mention carpets from the 8th century on but say nothing of techniques. They are therefore useless as evidence for knotting. The famous "springtime carpet" of Khusrau may well have been tapestry-woven or embroidered. The report that it bore countless precious stones and that large parts were worked in gold and silver is a strong evidence against its having been a pile carpet.

THE MIDDLE AGES. The oldest of the 12 carpets which were traced to the mosques of Konya and Beyşehir date from the middle of the 13th century (Istanbul, Mus. of Turkish and Islamic Art) and are probably of Seljuk origin. They are invaluable documents of medieval carpet art. Basically, their patterns, with simple geometric designs of tendrils, squares, and octagons that in staggered rows fill the entire interior area, display the essential features present throughout the subsequent development of the carpet art of Asia Minor. Seen as a whole, a steady line can be drawn from the East Turkestan fragments to these Seljuk works and on to the modern carpets of Asia Minor.

An essentially different design using animal motifs existed side by side with these. Information on the latter is furnished mostly by representations in European, particularly Italian, paintings from the late 13th century on. Only two extant fragments ("The Marby Rug," Stockholm, PL. 415; and Berlin) provide any evidence, apart from that in pictorial representations, of these "animal" carpets. In contrast to those of the geometric carpets, these patterns drew their essential inspiration from Western sources, even though they certainly came from Anatolia. While the arrangement of the fields in one-way rows recalls tiled floor decoration, the premises for the heraldic stylized animal designs are found in Byzantine fabrics.

Although the geometric patterns of the Konya type represent the main trend of the medieval carpet art, the post medieval developments betray the influence of animal decoration. Representations on Seljuk stone reliefs and Timurid miniatures provide important information on the further development of the severe designs with highly stylized plant motifs. Plait and knot patterns take on ever richer and more complicated arrangements in star, cross, and lattice shapes. The stiff, angular tracing of the lines gradually gives way to a more dynamic and flexible drawing in which the floral motifs, especially the intertwining

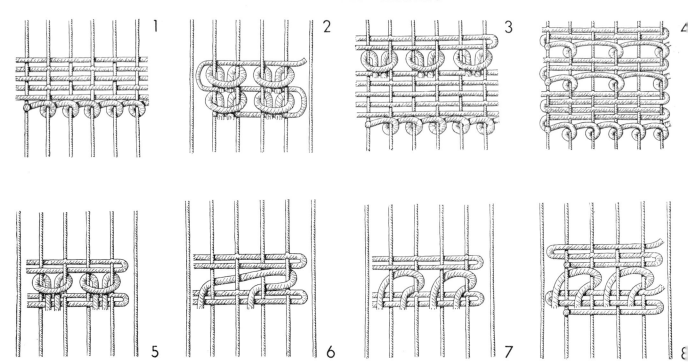

Examples of Oriental carpet weaves. (1) Kilim; (2 and 3) Turkish (Ghiordes) knotting; (4 and 5) Armenian knotting; (6) Afghan knotting; (7) Persian (Sehna) knotting; (8) Spanish knotting (*from Achdjian, 1949*).

arabesque tendrils, become increasingly important. Stemming from the antique, these floral motifs were among the most important motifs of Islamic surface decoration in all fields, and particularly in the Persian carpet, in the classic period, because its continually branching ramifications and curves could be adapted to any shape or surface and at the same time could fulfill the requirements of flat calligraphic linear development. These basic features of the form and pattern structure are common to all classes of carpets until the 15th century despite differences in detail. Particularly characteristic is the division of the inner area into regular repeated fields without a dominating motif; this permitted each pattern to be enlarged on all sides at will, giving the appearance of a section of a larger whole framed by the borders. Not until the second half of the 15th century was there a deviation from this principle in Egypt and Persia. At the same time the individual characteristics of the various groups began to be formalized, permitting the identification of individual patterns with particular regions. This differentiation of patterns occurred in the period during which the great national kingdoms were formed.

ASIA MINOR. In Anatolia and the Caucasus the medieval tradition lasted longest and in the purest form. The most uncharacteristic name of "Holbein" carpets has been given to a type (PL. 419) made in western Asia Minor, in the Ushak area. So called because they were used as background motifs in many of the paintings of Holbein and his school (VII, PLS. 304, 305), the "Holbein" patterns remained unaltered for almost two centuries, from the second half of the 15th century on. The earliest (and rarest) "Holbein" carpets clearly show the pattern arrangement of the medieval animal carpets, with octagons in squares or rectangles, the center forming a star. In later examples the pattern is on a smaller scale, with the stress laid on interlacing and extremely stylized scrollwork which both circumscribes and connects the octagonal motif of the inner field, The impression given by the most common type of "Holbein" carpet is determined by its arabesque forms alone, which cover the ground without stressing a division into fields, so that the way in which the pattern has been constructed is not easily recognizable, although clearly originating in superimposed and juxtaposed squares or octagons. The intermediate bands of the ground appear unified into crosses forming

a second pattern of equal importance. Thus the distinction between the ground and the superimposed fields is completely abolished and the pattern becomes a single surface, uniformly spreading out over the ground like a net. This impression is strengthened by the colors encountered in all carpets of this kind, owing to the sharp contrast between the light yellow scroll work and the glowing red ground. In patterns where the division into fields is more strongly emphasized, the fields are also differentiated by color contrasts. This drawing of the pattern into a single plane grew out of the desire for a stronger effect of flatness, evident also in the stylization of the plant motifs.

Contemporaneously, the Ushak carpets, named after the chief city of the district, were developed in the same province of western Asia Minor. Here too, various patterns can be distinguished, which, like the "Holbein" carpets, remained almost unchanged from the middle of the 16th to the end of the 17th century. The Ushaks have in common a characteristic deeply saturated coloring, predominantly dark blue and bright red, but the choice of forms for the patterns varied greatly. As in the "Holbein" carpets, a development from severe and angularly drawn forms to somewhat looser and broader ones can be observed. Staggered rows dominate the pattern arrangement, as in the medieval carpets of Anatolia. Most easily recognized are the star patterns (PL. 427), in which large eight-pointed stars regularly alternate with smaller star-shaped lozenges; slender vine scrolls fill the ground but contribute little to the over-all impression. Along the edges of the inner field the forms are often cut off by the borders, so that the whole appears as a detail of a continuous pattern, a concept basic to all these carpets. Even in the medallion Ushak carpet (PL. 420), whose main motif — a many-pointed medallion with pedants — as well as a general tendency to a freer drawing of the arabesque, is of northwest Persian origin, the dominating central motif is transformed into an endless continuum. This is most striking in very large pieces where an indication of the repeat is given on the narrow ends by the pendants and a small portion of the medallion. The secondary motif, in the form of a medallion or a star, appears not only as a quarter detail in the corner but also in approximatively two-thirds of its size as an element of almost equal importance. Another, much rarer type of carpet has a pattern in which many medallions in the shape of hexagons and stars, cut off by the border, are so close to each

her that the ground is nothing but a broad band which sepa-
tes the individual forms.

Various types of Ushak prayer rugs were also created.
nly one example (Berlin, Staat. Mus.) represents them in their
rly form, while from the period after the second half of the
th century a series of carpets has been preserved whose re-
tionship to this group is shown mainly by their deep colors
d by the drawing of the details. Often, the niche form, which
ces only one way, is doubled, thus resulting in a symmetrical
mposition whose center is marked by a small star, with only
small lantern to indicate the top. So-called "family" prayer
gs, which repeat the niches in rows in individual fields, first
pear in the 17th–18th century.

A group of pieces dating from the 16th–17th century,
hose color effect is determined by a bright white or light
llow ground, came from Asia Minor, but is not directly re-
ted to the Ushak carpets. The geometric, almost lozenge-

shaped leaves alternating in rows with rosettes and individual
flowers, thus resulting in starlike patterns, gave one group the
not entirely appropriate name of "bird rugs."

Not until the 17th century was a type developed which,
although originating in Anatolia, has many extant examples in
Transylvania (Siebenbürger), and is therefore called the "Siebenbürger" carpet. Like the corresponding Ushak prayer rugs
these all have the double niche form, but floral scrolls, departing
from the vaselike mosque lamps in the gables, fill the entire
inner field. Particularly characteristic is their border ornament
of elongated fields and eight-pointed stars. These motifs are
still present in later examples, in which the lamps are replaced
by blossoms or the inner pattern comes together in a lozenge-
shaped shield in the center. These designs have been continued
since the early 18th century in the so-called "Melas" carpets,
and the traditional pattern can be followed for a longer period
in the prayer rugs originating in Ladik. The rich subdivision

mbolic and decorative motifs of Oriental carpets. (1–7) Plant motifs: (1 and 2) pomegranate; (3) sunflower; (4) carnation; (5) palmettes, Kuba,
th century; (6) cypress; (7) variations of the Tree of Life. (8–29) Animal motifs: (8–10) camel; (11) dog; (12) dog, Shirvan, 18th century; (13) dragon;
4) running deer; (15) animal pelt, Sumak, 18th–19th century; (16–20) birds; (21) scorpion, Ghiordes, 17th–18th century; (22) tarantula, Shirvan, 18th cen-
ry; (23) scorpion, Kuba, late 16th century; (24) scorpion peculiar to carpets of central Asiatic nomads; (25) crab, Sumak, 18th–19th century;
6) stylized insect, Caucasian kilim, 18th–19th century. (27–45) Geometric motifs: (27–28) Turcoman Gül; (29) Afghan Gül; (30) star, Karabag, 1806;
1) star, Kuba, 18th century; (32) weaver's comb, Kirshehir, 17th–18th century; (33–34) weaver's comb and fork, Kuba, 17th–18th century; (35) "hand
Fatima," Bergamo, 18th century; (36–38) door-bolt key, Kuba, 17th–18th century; (39) poker, Kuba, 17th century; (40–41) Maltese cross and
osque lamp, Dagestan, 19th century; (42–45) Boteh, Persian (*from Achdjian, 1949*).

of the inner field with the three niches supported by columns seems to have been adapted from 16th-century Ottoman works. In the 18th century this motif was simplified or was completely omitted, leaving a relatively narrow field with a stepped gable. The characteristic transverse field above the niche, with pinnacles and upright tuliplike shapes, continues to be a feature of this type.

Many of the Asia Minor rugs, which were fully developed only in the 18th century, were also strongly influenced by the rich patterns of the Ottoman prayer rugs. The clearest examples of this inheritance are found in Ghiordes carpets. In the early pieces the niche, composed of sweeping arches, rests on columns. In the course of development, the architectural structure gradually lost its importance, hanging flower fillets replaced the columns, the gable became simpler and more severe, and the rhythmic floral scrolls gave way to close-pressed rows of flowers which, in their stylization, almost seem inscribed in rectangles. The breaking-up, which is to be generally observed, of the continuous vine pattern into individual motifs set next to each other in rows is most evident in Kula rugs from western Turkey, in many of which the border is subdivided into several narrow strips. A special type, the so-called "cemetery" Kula, has small landscapes on the ground of the niche.

Deviations from the main types and various influences, including European ones among the Kirshehirs, determine the manifold varieties of the Anatolian prayer rug. Each group has its own particular features, such as the steeply stepped gable of the Mudjur rug, or the geometric shapes representing a last tardy appearance of the medieval pattern structure in the examples from the Bergama (anc. Pergamum) region. The origin of the prayer rug, which was widely known and used in the 17th century, is obscure; specific data are lacking, for early pieces are very rare. Even 16th-century pieces are very few in number, perhaps owing to their continuous use. The particular purpose for which they were made explains the presence, to be found nowhere else in carpet designs, of an architectural form, the wall niche, which in the mosques shows the direction of Mecca, as well as forms such as the hanging lamps, the stylized footprints, and the lanterns on either side of the niche.

THE CAUCASUS. The relationship tomedieval carpets was just as strong in works from the region of the Caucasus as in Asia Minor, although the choice of forms was different. An extreme stylization, often leading to geometrization, marked the specific character of these carpets, and all the motifs, including those adopted particularly in the late period from outside sources, were subjected to this severe drawing. In contrast to the carpets of Asia Minor, animal motifs make their appearance — most frequently in the oldest examples, which date to the 15th century (such as that, in fragments since World War II, in Berlin, Staat. Mus.). In the course of development, which can be consistently followed up into the 18th century, the animal motif became rarer and was deformed and distorted until it became completely unrecognizable. The last to disappear in the 18th century was the dragon, to which these works owe their name of "dragon" carpets. The motifs here are not set in individual fields, but are integrated in an ascending lozenge chain whose direction is indicated by the standing palmettes. In direct correspondence to the animal representations, the over-all pattern of leaves is formed into broad bands, which with their indentations and hooks completely unify the pattern on its ground, which is generally red. The trend toward a severe, flat surface stylization, which approximated the natural forms to geometric figures, can be observed in the dragon carpets as well as in the pure floral patterns, although here motifs were often taken from Persian carpets. Particularly at the end of the classical period of carpetmaking, when a strong migration of patterns can be established, this transformation of foreign forms into the Caucasian mode of drawing is to be observed. Most indicative is the way in which forms borrowed from Persia lost their liveliness and naturalism, but retained the severity peculiar to the Caucasus, which, in its simplification, bestowed a certain grandeur upon all patterns. Just as logically the patterns were arranged into continuous rows, whether they were borrowed from the ascending

composition of the vase carpet, from the radial decoration of t northwest Persian animal carpet, or from the east Persi plant-stem pattern. The medallion arrangement seems to ha been adopted latest — at a time when the arts were declini also in the Caucasus — although much later than in Pers At the turn of the 18th century geometric decorative forms we still being borrowed from Bergama carpets and independent developed. At the end of the artistic development there occurr a return to a style similar to that of medieval carpets. The K zak (Armenia) carpets most clearly reveal its aftereffects, ev up to the present time, but the severe and geometricized sty zation also remained a characteristic of all other Caucasi works, such as the carpets from Lesghian, Daghestan, Kuba, ar related areas and manifested itself correspondingly in tapestr woven carpets with barely recognizable animal motifs. T strength of the Caucasian style manifested itself not only in t coherency with which the many foreign forms were adapted - resulting in a great wealth of variety that was controlled by basically uniform approach — but also in the influence whi it exercised on the bordering regions of northwest Persia.

TURKISTAN. Carpet fragments from the early centuries of t Christian era have been found in the eastern part of Turkista from where the Seljuks brought the art of knotting to the Wes The main influence seems to have been the early Anatoli carpets, within compositions of smaller geometric forms (guls In the arrangement and filling of these octagons, hectagon lozenges, and stars, which dominate the patterns, each grou offers particular variants which can be classified accordir to the tribes (Tekke, Khiras, Yomud) who created them. The form a large unified group, sometimes given the name of Bu khara, characterized by a deep, glowing red field with accen of blue, white, and, rarely, yellow. Floor carpets, small piec used as tent flaps, and carrying bags are commonly found these designs. In the pieces from Samarkand, Kashgar, Ya kand, and Khotan, Chinese influence is evident in both pattern and colors (blue, yellow, and ivory white).

MAMELUKE AND OTTOMAN PERIODS. Recent studies have i controvertibly indicated as of Egyptian provenance certai pieces which present a completely different solution of the basi principles of composition. Instead of the endless-patter relationship and the placing side by side of different forms (equal importance in regular alternation, in the carpets made Cairo in the 15th and first half of the 16th century (PL. 41 emphasis is placed on the center and many small forms are sub ordinate to a dominant motif occupying almost the entire inne field. The compositions were based on the particular size an form of the carpet instead of being composed of portions of continuous pattern. Even more than in the carpets of Asi Minor the dominant motifs are geometric — stars and polygon — into which rigorously stylized plant designs are incorporate The colors were rigidly prescribed: tones of light blue, yellow green, and raspberry red. The former designation of thes carpets as "Damascus" carpets has given way to the more ap propriate name of Mameluke carpet, since the type was develope during the period of the Mameluke domination of Egypt. Th art of ancient Egypt seems to have been an important influenc in the formation of the characteristic patterns of these carpet elements of the painting (small stars and polygons around central figure) can also be found in late Coptic tapestries. Th most important element of the plant decoration, a bush wit five small peltate leaves, can be traced to the papyrus moti of the Middle Kingdom.

At the beginning of the 16th century an effort was made t enrich and at the same time to make more flexible the stric form and color canons, thus permitting the appreciation o both the particular charm of the surface and the full array o the individual motifs in their various combinations. This i most beautifully shown in the only known example of a Mam eluke carpet with silk pile (Vienna, Österreichisches Mus für Angewandte Kunst). Although it is not yet possible to dis tinguish individual groups among the extant works as the pro duction of particular workshops, everything points to the con nporaneous existence in Cairo of a series of manufactories of rying importance and skill, so that for a while both stylistically ore advanced and more traditional works were being created multaneously. Nor did the conquest of Egypt by the Turks 1517 result in a decisive change of pattern, nor, even less, a decline of the Cairo manufactories; on the contrary, the for- ation and development of new carpet patterns with their char- teristic plant motifs, which are related most closely to Turkish ramics and textiles, took place in the most experienced work- ops of Cairo. This explains both the close similarity in techni- l execution of pieces differing greatly in pattern and the combi- tion of distinctly Turkish motifs with those of Mameluke igin, visible in a whole series of extant pieces (PL. 417). Yet ese two classes of patterns were so opposed to each other their basic concepts that the result was a mixture of disparate ements and not a gradual process of transformation, in the nse of a steady development. It therefore seems reasonable distinguish the new patterns which originated in the 16th ntury from those of the Mameluke period and to call them ttoman carpets. In them the whole wealth of Turkish plant namentation is unfolded, with its combination of strongly ylized and naturalistically drawn forms (predominantly rnations, tulips, and hyacinths). The arrangement consisted first of lozenges, then unobtrusive symmetrically drawn vines aced in the quarters of the field. Despite their marked indi- duality these Ottoman carpets were greatly influenced by rsian art. The symmetrically arranged vine system, especially, of Persian origin; and the frequent articulation of the inner ld, composed of a central medallion with quarter sections in e corners, seems to have been borrowed from northwest Persia. Of particular importance for the history of carpetmaking Turkey itself is a document of 1585 in which Sultan Murat

III sent for 11 carpetmakers and a given amount of material from Egypt. Although it cannot be definitely established whether a workshop was then set up in Istanbul or in Bursa, it seems probable that a group of works of particularly fine execution, which have in common a silk warp, the use of cotton for the white parts, and recurring motifs such as a twig with white rosette blossoms, can be related to this document.

Besides large floor carpets, many forms of prayer rugs were also developed during the Ottoman period. The one-way form of the inner field depended on its derivation from the prayer niche (mihrab; PL. 426). In the most beautiful and delicate ex- amples from the 16th century the entire niche ground is filled with rich floral ornamentation. The later Anatolian prayer rugs owe much to these 16th-century works. The relationship of the Mameluke carpets to a group that is often designated "checkerboard" carpets is less clear than that to the Ottoman carpets; here, forms from the severe Egyptian carpet patterns are combined with pronounced Anatolian characteristics. Their further development can be followed late into the 17th century. Octagons separated from each other by lozenges fill the field in the continuous relationship so characteristic of the patterns of Asia Minor, which also provides parallels for the border solutions; but the method of knotting, the vivid colors, the stressed border corners, and certain pattern motifs stem from the Mameluke carpets. These influences seem to have made their way to Anatolia from Egypt even before 1517; they de- veloped there for a long time, which explains how the central composition so characteristic of Mameluke carpets was replaced by the local Anatolian arrangement of rows. Apart from the Mameluke carpets, whose development stopped in the 16th century, none of the other classes mentioned displays a break with the medieval form. The limitation to the two-dimensional

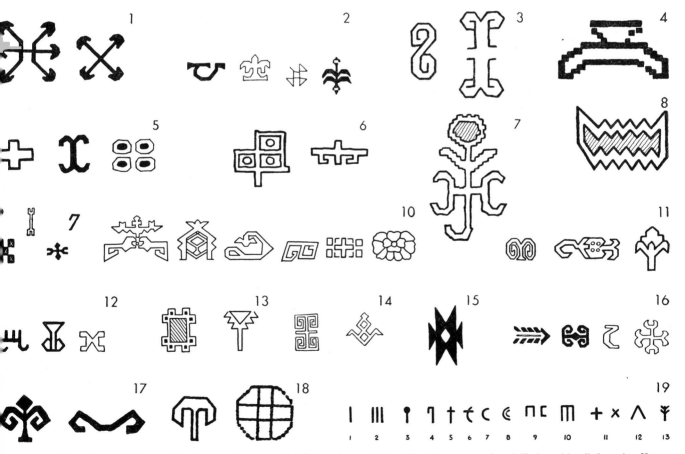

gnatures, tribal marks, and clan symbols from various areas. (1) Syria: clan symbols, 16th–17th century. (2–10) Turkey: (2) tribal marks, Konya, 5th–16th century; (3) clan symbols, Ushak, 16th–17th century; (4) tribal mark, Kirgiz, 17th-century Kuba; (5) three clan symbols, 17th-century shak; (6) tribal marks, Ushak, 17th–18th centuries; (7) initials of an individual or of a clan, Kirshehir, 17th–18th century; (8) serrated mark, known the "boat," Ghiordes, 17th–18th century; (9) clan symbols, 18th-century Kirman; (10) Turkish and Caucasian clan symbols. (11) Clan symbol, e-16th-century Kuba; (12) initials or signatures, 17th-century Kuba; (13) signatures or property marks, 18th-century Shirvan; (14) signatures or an symbols, 18th-century Kuba; (15) clan symbols, Caucasian kilim, 18th–19th century; (16) tribal or clan marks of Uzbek origin, Samarkand, d of the 17th century; (17) clan symbols of Turkish-Mongolian origin, Samarkand, 17th–18th century; (18) Uzbek clan symbols, Samarkand, 7th–18th century; (19) property or maker's marks used by nomads of the area between the Red Sea and the Persian Gulf (from Achdjian, 1949).

textile character and the strong bonds with tradition, however, contributed to the protection of the patterns from the corruption of design which was to become particularly evident in the period of the general decline of carpet weaving, and which was counteracted only where local traditions were strongest.

PERSIA. Persian carpets developed in a very different direction after the second half of the 15th century from that of the preceding period, which is documented by representations in miniatures. Of these there are sufficient to lead to the conclusion that patterns consisted of octagons, stars, crosses, and plaited bands, into which arabesques and plant motifs gradually found their way. In the second half of the 15th century, however, there was a clear break with medieval traditions and a completely new orientation arose in which the pattern forms were revolutionized. This was connected with the general blossoming of culture under the rule of the Safavid dynasty. In cities such as Ardebil, Tabriz, Kashan, and later Isfahan, large workshops were set up in all fields of art. They worked first and foremost for the court. The leading artists were the miniature painters, who also executed designs for various other mediums. Their influence on carpets design was great, and in certain individual cases was of decisive significance. This is most striking in the sudden change which took place in the important group of so-called "medallion" carpets, in which a large usually, star-shaped medallion occupied the center of the field, on the longitudinal axis of which two shield- or cartouche-shaped pendants were usually attached, thus causing the main motif to dominate the entire inner field. The quarter sections of similar medallions in the corners harmoniously closed the composition, without giving the impression of a continuation of the pattern beyond the border, which, treated as the frame of a strongly accentuated field, became more significant. Generally it was wider than in the rugs of Asia Minor, with strong color contrast and a balanced composition which provided logical corner solutions. This system first appeared in northwest Persian pieces, but also greatly influenced central and even southern Persia. Doubtless the illumination on ornamental pages and the rich bindings of books considerably stimulated the development of this kind of carpet pattern. It should, however, be noted that in 14th-century tiles this type of ornament had already been fully developed; this may also have been significant for carpet patterns. Representations of medallion carpets in Persian miniatures since the end of the 15th century, more or less, and the dates worked into two important extant carpets — 1539 (946 d.H.) on the so-called "Ardebil" carpet (Vict. and Alb.) and 1542/43 (949 d.H.) on the "hunting" carpet in Milan (Mus. Poldi Pezzoli) — testify that these patterns originated no later than the second half of the 15th century. Just as important as the adoption of a central composition planned for a given field was the multilayered appearance of the pattern. The medallion, whose decoration of floral scrolls around a central motif varied the composition of the inner field through its drawing and color, stands out as a distinct second layer from the pattern of the ground. This made possible the superimposition of several, at times completely traced-out, groups of shapes and even several tendril systems, in the ground pattern (PL. 422). A hitherto unthought-of wealth of forms was thus achieved in the pattern without impairing the strength or clarity of the drawing. In the ground alone as many as four layers may appear superimposed and side by side. Patterns in which the movement of the tendrils is drawn in a rather angular, stiff way are doubtless early. Gradually the linear execution became more rhythmical and rich and was often of calligraphic delicacy, as is to be seen in the "Ardebil" carpet, more than 34 feet long, from the shrine of Sheik Safī at Ardebil (PL. 423). The artistic center for this whole group was doubtless the court manufactory of Tabriz, but here, as in Cairo, several workshops existed side by side, as was also the case in other regions and cities of Persia, to which the various patterns can be attributed. This explains not only the countless variations of the basic types but also the simultaneous occurrence of stylistically more modern and somewhat more old-fashioned patterns. Characteristic individual forms and small differences in the technical execution permit closely related smaller groups

to be distinguished within the larger classes. With the admissi of animal representations into the designs the possibilities of t previously purely floral patterns were considerably enlarg and enriched. After representations of fauna, animal comb groups, which had been borrowed at quite an early period fro eastern Asian art, formed one of the favorite motifs (PL. 42 The influence of painters in the composition of carpets th grew in significance. The rigorous draftsmanlike discipline the Persian artists, which also protected painting from pure representative naturalism, offered suitable premises for t adoption of individual forms; but in those carpets which su ordinated the animal motifs not to a system of scrolls and te drils but to a freely composed landscape perspective the proble presented itself of transforming pictures conceived in terms volume into the strict two-dimensionality of the carpet. T spreading out of each individual form over the surface, a stro emphasis on outline instead of on volume, and the articulati of forms set over each other with only limited overlapping pr served the character of the surface without giving an illusi of space. The multilayered mode of drawing, as in the tend patterns, served here also to connect the individual motifs in a unified landscape. A corresponding method of transfer also shown in the carpets in which the loosening of the rigoro symmetry along the two axes of the ground and the introducti of the human figure brought them a step closer to painting, is best shown in the famous silk hunting carpet in Vienna (P 424). Undoubtedly the designer of this carpet was a painte yet the work displays the flat character necessary for a flo covering.

The silk luxury carpets with a distinctly courtly charact were created in Kashan, the important city of silk in centr Persia. Today very few examples are extant. There is a consi erably larger number of small silk rugs with purely floral patter dating from the second half of the 16th century and the ear 17th century. While in these the medallion system remain pure, except for variations, especially the appended shiel and cartouches, work of a completely free composition we also created in which the lack of symmetry and of repetitio enables them to be seen from top to bottom only, which enhanc their picturelike character and virtually excludes their use the floor. Stylistically related to the silk pile carpets of Kash with their figured patterns are the tapestry carpets, which we for the most part made early in the 17th century.

While in central Persia the medallion system became loos and was combined with free and rich background compositio in northwest Persia a change was also taking place. A numb of pieces from this area display a trend from the stressed centr composition back to the unending pattern relationship. Th the corner designs are exact quarter-segments of the central st with its pendants, or the central motif as a whole may be repeate several times and transformed into a sort of star-tile patter through the use of small connecting shapes (example in Londo Vict. and Alb.). From here it was only a step to the sma cartouches in marked star forms which, in connection with central medallion or by themselves, fill the ground. The simp aligning of cartouches of different shapes appeared in the 16t century side by side with the older decorative principle of th medallion system. This trend to continuous patterns as we as the often severe drawing of the north Persian carpets w undoubtedly also due to the proximity to the Caucasian region A more active relationship between Persian and Caucasia carpet patterns came to the fore, as has been indicated, in th 17th and 18th centuries, particularly in the strong restylizatio of Persian forms and their unification into a continuous surfac pattern.

The so-called "garden" carpets, whose inner field is divide into rectangular plots, appertain to the strictly drawn nort Persian patterns. The combination of the two different view of a garden is particularly interesting: the division of the plo by canals gives an aerial view, and the drawing of the individu trees, plants, or animals by contrast gives a side view.

The medallion system spread far into southern Persi where the unique so-called "Portuguese" carpets (PL. 428 an extraordinarily unified group, most likely came into bein hey owe their name to the representations of Europeans (perhaps Portuguese) in sailing ships which fill the corners of the inner field. The rest of the surface is entirely occupied by a serrated medallion without pendants which is so enlarged by concentric forms set off from each other by strong color that only the corner angles remain free. On the contrary, in the Herati carpets of eastern Persia, named after the main city of Herat, even though all of them were not produced there, no attempt is made to emphasize the center of the composition by means of a particular motif, although a scroll system departs from the center and is repeated symmetrically in the quarters of the field. The scroll issues from four large palmette blossoms set in a cross. As in the corresponding ground patterns of northwest Persian works, layers of alternately staggered and superimposed systems of floral scrolls determine the position and direction of all pattern forms. The earliest and at the same time richest examples (especially the pair, one in Vienna, Österreichisches Mus. für Angewandte Kunst, and one in New York, Met. Mus.) display animals and animal combat groups in a particularly lively type of drawing next to flowers and large palmettes. Many of the east Asian motifs which had spread through Persia, reappear here. Also unusual, there is in these works a fusion and intermingling of animal and plant forms: lion masks in flowers, animal heads in vines, reclining animals in the hearts of palmettes. Of this, the richest development of the east Persian pattern only a few examples from the 16th century have survived. Those carpets limited to the floral pattern form a large group, particularly from the 17th century; they show a progressive development and transformation in which the spirals and tendrils gradually lose meaning and extension, resulting in an impoverishment of the pattern, while the palmette blossoms and large sweeping lanceolate leaves come into the foreground and, after the middle of the 17th century, completely dominate the basic scrollwork. The sweeping, lively drawing, so characteristic of the early works, is complemented by warm, glowing colors, determined above all by the red of the ground in relation to other warm tones, in sharp contrast to the generally cooler and muted tones of northwest Persia (the patterns with dark arabesque leaf scrolls are more closely related to these). The Herati carpets influenced other classes far outside the boundaries of their native area, especially in India.

From the end of the 17th century on numerous transformations of east Persian plant patterns appear in Caucasian works. The so-called "vase" carpets present a unique relationship with the Caucasus which has not yet been clarified. They probably originated in southern Persia, with the center of production at Kirman. Here the Persian works apparently took over the principle of their pattern structure from the Caucasus, the influence therefore having been reciprocal. They are the only Persian carpets to possess a marked one-way lozenge pattern, a type fully developed in the Caucasus at least a century earlier. In any case, the transformation effected on the ground design by the three overlapping arabesque systems and large superimposed flowers which dominate the supporting scrolls is quite in keeping with the general character of Persian carpet art. The early examples of this class, which appeared in the 16th century, possess a repetitive, almost mathematically thought-out system, consisting of a design in which groups of 14 blossoms are used in such a way that eight are set on each lozenge-shaped vine scroll, and six large blossoms lie in each lozenge. These patterns do not stress the center of the field and are symmetrically repeated only along the longest axis of the carpet. The impression is determined by the large palmettes, or sometimes by single flower-filled vases to which the carpets owe their rather unsuitable name. As in all other types of Persian carpets, here, too, patterns of a rich and complicated structure, although clear and severe in line and form, belong to the first period. As in the last Persian examples, large lanceolate leaves also gradually became the leading motifs and crowded out the overlapping scrollwork. Parallel to the simplification of the pattern structure, which in the 17th century led to a simple alignment in rows, there became evident greater restlessness and movement in the individual forms, particularly in the contour design. In the group of carpet patterns which developed in the late 16th century,

most of the examples being of the 17th century, a slackening in strength and clarity is evident. These silk carpets, richly worked with gold and silver, are still often called "Polish" carpets, although it has long since been proven that they were not made in Poland, as was formerly thought, but in central Persia, the center being at Isfahan in the reign of Shah 'Abbās I, during the great artistic and cultural revival under this ruler. The pictorial charm of these carpets, with their bright colors and rich metallic effects, obviously caused them to be especially sought after in Europe, where they have survived in impressive numbers (PLS. 412, 429). In the adoption and varied adaptation both of forms and of compositional principles from other classes, these patterns clearly show that they belong to a late period. Medallion and simple vine decorations are to be found as well as continuous cartouche patterns. It is indicative that at times individual parts of the ground are set off by the use of a color that appears in other elements of the pattern, so that the clear separation of ground and superimposed decoration, rigorously observed in all carpets of the 16th century, here disappears. The direction in which they developed, already evident at the turn of the 16th century, was decisive for all 17th-century Persian carpets. Clarity, severity, and richness in the pattern structure often yielded to a restlessness and an overloading of the individual forms, as in the Herati patterns, the "vase" carpets, the picture-like compositions of central Persia, and the transformation of the medallion system in the "Portuguese" carpets mentioned above. Persian prayer rugs were also made in this period, but it is extremely difficult to identify the individual centers of production. In contrast to the carpets of Asia Minor, the prayer niche is often filled with floral patterns, while the upper parts, of the borders bear cartouches with proverbs from the Koran. A larger group (mostly in Istanbul, Topkapı Saray Mus.) originated in the 18th century and was probably made in Asia Minor after Persian models. The fact that they were related to painting and book art, and that the best workers were concentrated in the large court manufactories, caused carpet art to be more responsive to external conditions and to be often closely dependent on the economic prosperity of the country. The political upheavals at the beginning of the 18th century which led to the downfall of the Safavid dynasty were quickly followed by the collapse of the large court manufactories. Thus began a dispersal and exodus of the patterns, as well as a manifold transformation of complicated systems into simpler ones and a mixture of motifs of diverse provenance. In Persia the 18th century was thus in many respects already a period of decline and confusion. The Herati patterns and the northwest Persian medallion decoration in its various transformations prevailed longest. A few workshops in Kirman also seem to have continued production for a time. The two aforementioned forms of transformation of the classical pattern — on the one hand simplification and on the other an overloading of the single forms — manifested themselves diversely in each region.

Although the production of Persian carpets since the end of the 18th, century is on the whole merely an echo of the richness of the classical period, there were still numerous classes of carpets, generally named after the principal centers of production, based on creations of the classical period. This is especially true of the large city manufactories; the medallion system predominates in the Tabriz carpets, but often also in the silk Kashans and in the finely drawn pieces from Meshed, the capital of Khurasan province in northeastern Persia. Strongly naturalistic forms characterize the Kirman carpets, both in the purely floral patterns as well as in the picturelike compositions, which are quite common here. Of the continuous plant patterns, the Herati pattern is the most widespread and important, showing four large blossoms around a rosette, their stems framing the rosette in a lozenge. This, as well as the characteristic willow-tree motif, is frequently found on Isfahan carpets, which, however, often also reproduce richer floral scrolls and arabesque patterns in obedience to classical models.

INDIA. In India the art of knotting carpets was initiated and eagerly promoted by the Moghul emperors, so that in the 16th and 17th centuries large manufactories were created whose products are distinguished by an often surprising density and delicacy. Nevertheless, owing to the completely different conditions of climate, the art of knotting never attained great development, and in contrast to the Turkish and Iranian regions, India is of marginal importance in the field of the pile carpet. The most important artistic influences came from Persia, particularly eastern Persia; indeed, they were so strong that a whole category of carpets exists which is called "Indo-Persian." The Indian patterns are marked by their strong naturalistic transformation of the Persian models of flower and vine patterns. This is particularly evident in the asymmetrical freely drawn compositions full of animals and hunting scenes, which give the impression of paintings in pile (landscape carpet with birds, Vienna, Österreichisches Mus. für Angewandte Kunst). The earliest examples are from about 1500. In the later examples of pure plant patterns, which are more severely drawn, the influence of textile patterns with regularly repeated motifs can be felt. The color effect of the Indian carpets is mostly determined by a wine-red ground, to which other, also preferably warm, colors are added to produce a glowing effect.

CHINA. Although the finds in East Turkestan and references to 13th-century imperial pile-carpet workshops would seem to indicate an old tradition in the practice of this art, Chinese pile carpets have survived only from the Ch'ing dynasty (1644 on), with perhaps a few from the end of the previous (Ming) period. In contrast to carpets from the areas of Islamic culture, to which the Asia Minor production shows a relationship, the pure Chinese examples show freer, more restful drawing and quieter colors, often based on cool blues and sand yellow (PL. 430). Variations in the border meander and Taoist and Buddhist emblems in the central field constitute the most frequently used patterns. A special class is formed by the "post" or "column" carpets, composed so that when hung around a post the vertical edges coincide. In contrast to the floor carpets figural representations dominated here. A technical characteristic is the not infrequent sinking of the pattern contour in the pile. This may possibly indicate a relationship with appliqué felt carpets. The most important carpet-producing regions were the four northern provinces of Kansu, Shansi, Shensi, and Chilhi.

EUROPE. Not until modern times was the diffusion of the knotting technique of any consequence in Europe. The most important evidence of its having been known in medieval times is the famous pile carpet in Quedlinburg of about 1200. It is executed in a Spanish knot on a hemp warp and represents the wedding of Mercury and Philologia. Stylistically it is directly related to the late Romanesque painting of Lower Saxony.

Spain. Spain's close political and cultural bonds with Islam throughout the centuries resulted in the appearance of pile carpets earlier there than elsewhere in Europe. There is documentary evidence for carpets of Spanish origin in the 13th century, but only from the 15th century are there any great number of pieces known. Quite often the small continuous pattern of the inner field bears superimposed coats of arms or fields with Christian emblems marking the pieces as "grave" carpets. In the 16th century (PL. 418), next to works so closely related to Asia Minor carpets that they can be considered copies of Anatolian works, there appear patterns — vine decorations, pomegranate patterns, and grotesques — which owe their inspiration to contemporary textiles. The most important centers of production in the middle ages were Almería and Cuenca, and, up to the 17th century, Alcaraz. In the 18th century the Spanish carpet lost significance and artistic value. The so-called "Alpujarras" of the last two centuries are works of folk art in embroidery or loop work techniques.

France. The most important artistic development of the European pile carpet took place in the 17th and 18th centuries in France. Based on the Eastern technique, the intention from the very beginning was to create a floor covering of purely European character for furnishing rooms of state, in whose unified decoration the oriental carpet would have been out of place.

Jean Fortier and Pierre Dupont were the first who could boa mastery in this technique. The latter began his production Paris in 1606. Subsidized by Henry IV, Dupont was give an atelier in the Louvre, and his pupil Simon Lourdet was late given one in the Hospice de la Savonnerie at Chaillot. Th name of this former soap factory thus became the generic nam for French pile carpets, distinguishing them from the tapestr floor carpets called Aubusson after their most important plac of manufacture. Up into the last quarter of the 17th centur members of the Lourdet and Dupont families succeeded on another in the direction of these workshops. In 1672 Dupont manufactory was also transferred to the Savonnerie building where from 1687 on it continued alone. Savonnerie reached i peak in the second half of the 17th century, thanks to the larg commissions of the French court. At the beginning of the 18t century economic difficulties led to a considerable diminutio in production. The period of the Revolution represented a lo point, but commissions were again numerous in the period Napoleon's Empire. In 1826, for economic reasons, the work shops were transferred to the quarters of the Manufacture Na tionale des Gobelins, where they are still active.

The artistic character of the French carpet is determined b the principles of contemporary interior decoration, as well as b those of painting. The large number of carpets commissioned b Louis XIV, above all for the Great Gallery of the Louvre (P 433)), were designed by Charles Lebrun and his collaborato and pupils in harmony with the other furnishings of these room A strongly sculptural effect of the single forms, as well as imita tions of inset reliefs and pictures, testifies to the intention creating not a flat textile floor covering, but a complement t the interior decoration as a whole. In this respect it is partic ularly indicative that the large carpet compositions often cor respond to or even copy the ceiling decoration, but it is in smalle works that the direct relationship with painting is most eviden In the 18th century, purely pictorial projects, scenes, flowe pieces, and even portraits were transposed into pilework. Th Savonnerie carpets completely adhered to the stylistic transfor mation from the heavy forms of Lebrun to the lighter 18th-centur motifs, often interspersed with naturalistic flowers. The worl of classicizing form, with its rigorous drawing and antique moti was particularly well represented by works of the Napoleon era. Correspondingly the 19th-century revival of the rococ and Empire styles was clearly delineated in the French knotte carpets. Until recent times, next to the large floor carpets, th smaller rugs that exactly copy painted models and are, in effec pile "paintings" have continued to be sought after.

The marked individuality of the Savonnerie carpets, whos style was determined by the architectural decoration of th room and by painters, presents the sharpest possible contra to the carpets of Islamic production. Embodying the Europea conception and interpretation of the carpet, the Savonnerie considerably influenced European carpets as a whole.

England. The earliest English pile carpets date from th second half of the 16th century. A series of pieces with worked in dates indicates that both direct copies of Asia Minor carpet (differing only in their use of hemp or flax in the foundatio weave) and a purely European type were produced. The latte dominated in the 17th century; their scrollwork and flowe patterns show a special relationship to embroidery. But towar the end of the 17th century carpet-weaving came to a standsti in England and was revived only in the middle of the 18t century by French immigrants. The ateliers of Peter Parisc (lastly in Fulham) and Passavant (in Exeter; PL. 434) worke only for a short time in the mid-18th century. More significan and of longer duration were the workshops of Thomas Moor in Moorfields and, especially, those of Thomas Whitty in Ax minster (PL. 434).

Like the French Savonneries, the English carpets of th 18th century were often directly related to contemporary ar chitecture and its decoration. In Moorfields a series of carpe in the style of Robert Adams was produced, and some after hi designs, corresponding to the ceiling decorations (several i Osterley Park House, Middlesex; PL. 432). The rapid diffusio machine-made carpets in England in the first quarter of the [...]th century crowded out the hand-knotted works, so that [...]1835 the Axminster works closed down, and in the succeeding [...]rs virtually no knotted pile carpets were made. William [...]orris attempted to revive this craft. A series of carpets with [...]: characteristic Morris plant decoration, which was often [...]pired by older, particularly late Gothic, forms and patterns [...]s created in 1878 in Hammersmith, and then, from 1881 on, [...] Merton Abbey. As Morris and Co., the undertaking, in [...]ich carpets however play only a small part, has remained [...]ive up to the present time.

Dora HEINZ

FOLK ART. Only those countries in which industrialization [...]s been retarded are concerned with artisan folk weaving, [...]ich is now rare in Europe. Sporadic attempts to rescue the [...]ft from oblivion often have resulted in standardizing the [...]oduct and enervating the authentic local textile traditions. [...]rpets of good quality were still being produced in Greece, [...]the Balkan countries, and in isolated areas of northern Europe, [...]ain, southern and insular Italy, where folk artisan weaving [...] a family or local character remained of considerable im-[...]rtance up to the early 20th century. The production of real [...]rpets has always been limited however, in the peasant environ-[...]nt, in which primary importance is obviously given to the [...]oduction of saddles, covers, and textiles. Carpetmaking is a [...]ich more common phenomenon among the small rural middle [...]sses whose cultural products often adopt and elaborate on a [...]k level motifs and forms of the ruling culture. For this reason [...]rpets represent one of the classics of folk art in which the in-[...]ence on the great European and extra-European artistic [...]rrents was most felt.

It is probable that the early history of the European folk [...]rpet was represented by handmade pieces consisting of narrow [...]lticolored strips with small geometric decoration, which [...]uld be either the same or not in each band. Rugs of this [...]nd, of a more or less primitive execution, occur in areas less [...]posed to exterior influences. For example, the rugs of some [...]ions of Poland, Russia, Romania, Hungaria, and of such [...]all isolate Italian towns as Isnello (Sicily) and Altamura, [...]pulia) are designed in narrow horizontal and occasionally [...]rtical lozenges. In these, the most frequent ornamental motif [...] the lozenge and the colors are red, white, blue, and black. [...]ore evolved types are the rugs with wide varicolored bands [...]reece) or with broad decorative motifs of lozenges, stars, and [...]sses, to be found in some regions of Finland (Tavastland), [...]mania (Banat), and Yugoslavia (Slavonia) and in Sicily (Erice, [...]tralia).

Motifs of clearly Eastern origin are encountered in rugs [...] the Balkan countries, which were exposed to Turkish in-[...]ence. The extent to which Eastern weaving influenced Europe [...] displayed by the total difference between the carpets made [...] Muntenia, a less exposed region, and those made in Oltenia. [...]like the former, the latter consists of a rectangular central [...]ld with three or more borders. Stylized plant motifs, in which [...] occasional zoomorphic form stands out, are set in orderly [...]rangement both in the field and in the borders. Still better [...]amples for clarifiying the close relationship between Persian [...]gs and the Balkan folk products (and sometimes the Polish [...]d the Ukrainian) are the so-called "kilims" which are ele-[...]ntary copies of certain prayer rugs. The kilims of some Yugo-[...]vian regions (Bosnia) have a character of their own, with their [...]de geometric rhomboid or hexagonal decoration in unusual [...]es of brown, white, blue, and yellow.

Echoes of medieval and Renaissance art can be discerned [...]re or less clearly owing to the Eastern influences in carpets [...]m some areas of Finland, southern Norway, Spain, Sardinia, [...]bria, and the Abruzzi. In the rugs from these regions the [...]corative schemes are generally of plant and animal motifs. [...]range flowers and mythological animals such as the griffin, [...]: many-headed eagle, the unicorn, the siren, the centaur, [...]d the dragon, which are often enclosed in rectangles, alter-[...]te with more archaic symbolic motifs such as the tree of life [...]d the fountain of love. There is no lack, however, of more

realistic motifs such as the people on horseback, typical of Sar-dinian rugs, and the peacock, the dove, the stag, the rabbit, and the lion frequently seen in Spanish carpets. Colors vary from region to region.

Influences of more modern artistic currents are to be found in carpets with rich, more or less stylized floral decoration, the fashion for which seems to have spread from England to the rest of Europe in the 17th and 18th centuries. Carpets in which the ornamental repertory consists prevalently of naturalistic plant forms are or were made in England, France, Germany, Norway, Poland, Russia, Spain, and Italy. In the dyeing of artisan-made carpets commercial dyes are now of widespread use, but until the early years of the 20th century vegetable dyes were still common. Pale green was extracted from the leaves of the beech and ash, blue from indigo, yellow from saffron and turmeric, red from the marc of grapes, black from the lau-rel and from pomegranate rinds and iron sulphate boiled to-gether. The most common material for making folk carpets was and still is wool. Less commonly, cotton, pieces of cloth, raw silk, and straw were used.

While in Europe, horizontal looms were, with rare ex-ceptions, used for making carpets, in Africa the vertical hand loom is prevalent. The latter, which is more common in the central-southern regions and is used by the women even when the men use the horizontal loom (Tunisia), seems to be the older type. The horizontal foot loom, moreover, has only re-cently been introduced in some countries, such as Cameroun and Ghana. Here and in other bordering areas it was imported together with indigo dyeing and the so-called "plangi" tech-nique of dyeing by Mande tribes. In other African regions the foot loom is unknown and hand-weaving is customary in the making of mats and carpets, as among the Tebu of the Sahara. The carpets produced in the countries of Mediterranean Africa are sometimes composed of varicolored stripes. Here Asian influences, interpreted in a most original manner, have given this branch of craftsmanship a nobility unknown in the rest of the continent. The great development of the knotted pile carpet was, on the contrary, a powerful hindrance to the production of non-knotted carpets in Asia. In some areas far from the large centers of production and among primitive peoples there are still found carpets and mats similar in make and decoration to the African ones.

Antonino BUTTITTA

MACHINE-MADE CARPETS. The term "machine-made carpet" comprises all kinds of floor coverings which are not hand-knotted, but prepared on looms. Technically they may differ radically. Mats or strong smooth fabrics had long been in common use, but the development of the machine-woven car-pet as a substitute and competition for the hand-knotted carpet did not take place until the 18th century. Smooth surfaces were used on works in simple (but often double- and triple-woven) cloth which were primarily made in Wilton and Kidderminster in England from the first half of the 18th century on.

Other works which came into fashion in the first half of the 18th century are related to each other in their use of the technique of velvet-making; those usually called "Brussels" carpets have a closed looplike pile, while in the velvet carpets — often des-ignated Wilton carpets — the pile loops have been cut open, resulting in a softer, more even surface. This technique re-quires the invisible working into the foundation weave of most of the pile material, which considerably limits the number of colors. This was avoided in those carpets whose pile consisted of a warp specially printed with the pattern before weaving and which are often erroneously called "tapestry" carpets. In chenille carpets, on the contrary, it is the prepared chenille weft which completely covers the surface and correspondingly forms the decor. This method was originally designated "Patent Axminster." Yet another kind of machine carpet goes by the name "Axminster," although none of the type was ever pro-duced there. This has short, colored weft strands which are worked in according to the pattern to form an open velvetlike pile. In their effect these works came closest to that of the hand-knotted carpets. The most recent basically new technique in machine carpets was the invention of a knotting machine which fastened the prepared pile threads into the foundation weave with a Turkish knot. The nomenclature used to designate the various classes of carpets according to individual cities indicates only particular methods of production, but in no way their provenance. It can be justified only insofar as, for example, the so-called "Brussels" carpet was probably originally invented and made there, although it was brought into England before the middle of the 18th century.

The production and diffusion of machine-made carpets reached its peak in England in the second half of the 18th and in the 19th centuries. Toward the middle of the 19th century these had by far superseded the hand-knotted works; this was in great part due to the introduction in the 1820s of jute in large quantities as a much cheaper material for the foundation weave and particularly to the invention of the mechanical loom by J. M. Jacquard in 1805. Thus, in carpets as well as in textiles the tiring and slow work at the hand loom was replaced by the quicker and easier work at the Jacquard machine, which was already in use in 1825 in Kidderminster. About the middle of the 19th century, England inaugurated the use of steam as power for the machines.

In the age of general industrialization, machine carpet production on a large scale spread throughout all Europe. The techniques were so perfect that during the 19th century almost any pattern or model could be executed. Until about the middle of the last century carpets followed the general direction set by the hand-made products. As in the latter, the severely drawn classical patterns are to be found, followed by gay floral decorations related to the textile and embroidery patterns of the first half of the 19th century. Then the imitation and even direct copying of Oriental carpets stepped ever more into the foreground, and, together with contemporary designs, covers a considerable proportion of machine-made carpets even today.

BIBLIOG. *Oriental carpets*: *a. General*: 1. *Bibliographies*: R. M. Riefstahl, A Short Bibliography for the Student of Oriental and Western Hand-knotted Rugs and Carpets, New York, 1926; K. Erdmann, Bibliographie des Orientteppichs, in F. Sarre and H. Trenkwald, Altorientalische Teppiche, II, Leipzig, 1929, pp. 37–42; K. A. C. Creswell, A Bibliography of the Architecture, Arts and Crafts of Islam, Cairo, 1961, cols. 1139–1204. 2. *Studies*: V. J. Robinson, Eastern Carpets, 2 vols., London, 1882–93; J. Lessing, Orientalische Teppiche, Berlin, 1891; A. Riegl, Altorientalische Teppiche, Leipzig, 1891; W. Bode, Ein altpersischer Teppich im Besitz der Königlichen Museen zu Berlin, JhbPreussKSamml, XIII, 1892, pp. 26–49; W. Bode, Vorderasiatische Knüpfteppiche aus älterer Zeit, Leipzig, 1901; F. R. Martin, The Classification of Oriental Rugs, BM, VIII, 1905–06, pp. 35–37, 186–88, 332–37; H. Saladin and G. Migeon, Manuel d'art musulman, II, Paris, 1907, pp. 425–58; G. C. Birdwood, The Antiquity of Oriental Rugs, J. Royal Soc. of Arts, LVI, 1908, pp. 1041–59, 1064–74; F. R. Martin, A History of Oriental Carpets before 1800, Vienna, 1908; F. Sarre, Ancient Oriental Carpets, Leipzig, 1908; F. Sarre, Orientalische Teppiche, SbBerlin, 1908, pp. 32–35; C. Hopf, Die altorientalischen Teppiche: Eine Studie über ihre Schönheitswerte, Stuttgart, 1912; W. Bode and E. Kühnel, Vorderasiatische Knüpfteppiche aus alter Zeit, 2d ed., Leipzig, 1914 (4th ed., Brunswick, 1955; Eng. trans., Antique Rugs from the Near East, Brunswick, 1958; cf. K. Erdmann, Bibliotheca Orientalis, 1956, pp. 202–06; K. Erdmann, ZMG, N.S., XXXII, 1957, pp. 652–64; A. C. Weibel, Ars Orientalis, III, 1959, pp. 226–29); E. Kühnel, Die Entwicklung des Orientteppichs, Die Kunstwelt, III, 1914, pp. 441–60; R. Berliner, Probleme der orientalischen Teppichgeschichte, Kunst und Kunsthandwerk, XXIV, 1921, pp. 16–31; R. Biach, Bild und Teppich, Kunstwanderer, II, 1921, pp. 395–401; A. F. Kendrick and C. E. C. Tattersall, Hand-woven Carpets: Oriental and European, 2 vols., London, 1922; H. Glück and E. Diez, Die Kunst der Islam, Berlin, 1925, pp. 74–79, 561–67, abb., 373–93 (2d ed., 1931); F. Sarre and H. Trenkwald, Old Oriental Carpets, 2 vols., Leipzig, 1926–29 (Eng. trans., A. F. Kendrick; cf. A. U. Pope, AB, IX, 1926, pp. 164–72, XI, 1929, pp. 415–26); G. Migeon, Manuel d'art musulman, II, Paris, 1927, pp. 349–401; R. Koechlin and G. Migeon, Islamische Kunstwerke, Berlin, 1928, pls. 82–100; E. Kühnel, Die islamische Kunst, in A. Springer, Handbuch der Kg., VI, Leipzig, 1929, passim; M. S. Dimand, A Handbook of Mohammedan Decorative Arts, New York, 1930, pp. 231–79 (3d ed., 1958, pp. 279–323); A. F. Kendrick, Notes on Carpet Knotting and Weaving, London, 1930 (4th ed., C. E. C. Tattersall, London, 1939); W. H. Worrell, On Certain Arabic Terms for Rug, Ars Islamica, I, 1934, pp. 219–22, II, 1935, pp. 65–68; R. Ettinghausen, Kali, E. of Islam, Sup., Leiden, Paris, 1936, pp. 106–11; F. Mazzini, Tappeti orientali, Livorno, 1943; K. Erdmann, Zur Formenwelt des Orientteppichs, Forsch. und Fortschritte, XX, 1944, pp. 147–49; P. M. Campana, Il tappeto orientale, Milan, 1945; K. Erdmann, Musteranalyse: Ein neuer Weg zum Verständnis des Orientteppichs, Blick in die Wissenschaft, I, 1948, pp. 262–69; A. Achdjian, Un art fondamental: le tapis, Paris, 1949; H. Jacoby, ABC des echten Teppichs, Tübingen, 1949; H. M. Raphaelian, The Hidden Language of Symbols in Oriental Rugs, New York, 1953; K. Erdmann, Der orientalische Knüpfteppich: Versuch einer Darstellung seiner Geschichte, Tübingen, 1955
(2d ed., 1960; Eng. trans., C. G. Ellis, New York, 1960; cf. R. Ettinghaus
Oriens, XI, 1958, pp. 257–64); D. Heinz, Alte Orientteppiche, Darmsta
1956; Y. Brunhammer, Tapis d'Orient, Paris, 1957; O. Bernheimer, A
Teppiche des 16.–18. Jahrhundert der Firma L. Bernheimer, Muni
1959; R. de Calatchi, Tapis d'Orient, Jardin des arts, 61, 1959, pp. 10–
A. Ferrier, Initiation au décor rituel du tapis de prière, Connaissance
arts, 85, 1959, pp. 58–67; U. Schürmann, Sieben altorientalische Knü
teppiche, Weltkunst, XXIX, 20, 1959, pp. 38a–38d; H. Haack, Orien
Rugs, London, 1960; I. Schlosser, Der schöne Teppich in Orient und Ok
dent, Heidelberg, Munich, 1960; R. E. G. Macey, Oriental Prayer Ru
Leigh-on-Sea, 1961; K. Erdmann, Europa und der Orientteppich, Berl
Mainz, 1962; C. W. Jacobsen, Oriental Rugs, Tokyo, Rutland, Vt., 19
J. G. Lettenmair, Das grosse Orientteppichbuch, Munich, 1962. 3. *Exhi
tion catalogues*: A. von Scala et al., Wien, K. K. österreichisches Handelsmu
Katalog der Ausstellung orientalischer Teppiche, Vienna, 1891; A. Ri
and A. von Scala, eds., Orientalische Teppiche, Vienna, 1892–95; Wi
K. K. österreichisches Handelsmus., Teppicherzeugung im Orient, Vien
1895; F. R. Martin, Sammlungen aus dem Orient in der Kunst- und Industr
Ausstellung zu Stockholm, Stockholm, 1897; G. Migeon, Exposition des a
musulmans au Musée des arts décoratifs, Paris, 1903; C. Hopf, Die Teppic
des Orients: Zur Ausstellung altorientalischer Teppiche im Kunstgeschic
lichen Landesgewerbemuseum, Stuttgart, 1909; Ausstellung muhamme
anischer Kunst: Amtlicher Katalog, Munich, 1910, pp. 17–37 (cf. F. Sar
Die Teppiche, Kunst und Kunsthandwerk, XIII, 1910, pp. 469–86); W.
Valentiner, Catalogue of a Loan Exhibition of Early Oriental Rugs, N
York, 1910; W. R. Valentiner, The Exhibition of Rugs, BMMA, V, 19
pp. 221–22; C. Ruge, Die Ausstellung alter orientalischer Teppiche
Metropolitan Museum of Arts, New York, Kunst und Kunsthandwerk, XI
1911, pp. 205–18; F. Sarre and F. R. Martin, Die Austellunge von Meist
werken muhammedanischer Kunst in Munchen (1910), 1, 2, Muni
1912; K. Csány, S. Csermelyi and K. Layer, Erdélyitörök szönyegek kiá
tásának (Turco-Transylvanian Carpets at the Exposition), Budapest, 19
G. Migeon, Exposition de l'art musulman, Alexandria, 1925, pls. 56–
A. U. Pope, Catalogue of a Loan Exhibition of Early Oriental Carpe
Chicago, 1926; P. Ackerman, Rare Old Rugs and Textiles in the Internatio
Exhibition of Persian Art in London, Arts and Decoration, XXXIV, 19
pp. 40–41, 80; K. Erdmann, Persische Kunst in London, ZfbK, LX
1931–32, pp. 31–41; A. F. Kendrick, The Persian Exhibition, III: Textil
BM, LVII, 1931, pp. 15–21; Persian Art: An Illustrated Souvenir of t
International Exhibition of Persian Art at Burlington House, London, 19
Royal Academy of Arts, Catalogue of the International Exhibition of Persi
Art, London, 1931; C. E. C. Tattersall, Carpets and Textiles at the Persi
Exhibition, Apollo, XIII, 1931, pp. 82–89; K. Erdmann, Tappeti persia
Dedalo, XII, 1932, pp. 707–38; Turkische Kunst aus sieben Jahrhundert
Ausstellung, Vienna, 1932; G. Wiet, L'exposition d'art persan à Londr
Syria, XIII, 1932, pp. 196–200; G. Wiet, L'exposition persane de 19
Cairo, 1933; Basel, Gewerbemus., Der orientalische Teppich: Austellu
Basel, 1934; M. S. Dimand, A Guide to an Exhibition of Oriental Ru
and Textiles, New York, 1935; Kunstgewerbe-Mus., Austellung altorient
ischer Teppiche, Graz, 1936; P. Ackerman, Guide to the Exhibition of Persi
Art, New York, 1940; R. Ettinghausen, Six Thousand Years of Persi
Art, Ars Islamica, VII, 1940, pp. 106–17; Orientaliska Mattor, Stockhol
1946; Rijksmuseum, Catalogus van de Tentoonstelling van Oosterse Tap
ten, Amsterdam, 1946; C. F. Kelley, and M. O. Gentles, An Exhibition
Antique Oriental Rugs, Chicago, 1947; Catalogus van het Tentoonstelli
van Oosterse Tapijten, Delft, 1949; Catalogus van het Tentoonstelling v
Oosterse Tapijten, Groningen, 1949; K. Erdmann, Orientteppiche aus v
Jahrhunderten, Hamburg, 1950 (cf. K. Erdmann, O. Literaturz., XLVI
1953, cols. 197–205); K. Erdmann, Oosterse Tapijten 16e–19e eeuw, T
Hague, 1951; H. Jacoby, Ausstellung alter und antiker Teppiche des Orien
Stuttgart, 1951; M. and V. Viale, Arazzi e tappeti antichi (Exhibition, Tur
1948), Turin, 1952 (cf. K. Erdmann, Ars Orientalis, II, 1957, pp. 571–8
Musée des arts décoratifs, Splendeur de l'art turc, Paris, 1953, nos. 69
776; Orientalische Teppiche, Ausstellungskatalog Schloss Jegenstorf, 19
Ontario Museum, Oriental Rugs: The Kalman Collection Exhibition, T
ronto, 1958; Mus. für Kunst und Gewerbe, Kaukasische Teppiche, Hambu
1961 (cf. Weltkunst, XXXI, 15, 1961, p. 4); Museum für Kunsthandwe
Kaukasische Teppiche, Frankfurt am Main, 1962. 4. *Museum catalogu*
A. Riegl, Ältere orientalische Teppiche aus dem Besitz des Allerhöchst
Kaiserhauses, JhbKhSammlWien, XIII, 1892, pp. 267–331; R. Cox,
Musée historique des tissus de la Chambre de Commerce de Lyon, Lyo
1902, pp. 248–53; R. Cox, Sur quatre tapis du Musée historique des tiss
de Lyon, Rev. de l'art ancien et moderne, XXIX, 1911, pp. 289–98; F. Sar
Ein neues Museum muhammedanischer Kunst in Konstantinopel, Kch
XXV, 1914, cols. 522–26; A. F. Kendrick, Victoria and Albert Museu
Guide to the Collection of Carpets, London, 1915 (3d ed., 1931); F. Sar
Die orientalischen Teppiche aus dem ehemaligen Wiener Hofbesitz, Kun
wanderer, I, 1920, pp. 144–47; A. F. Kendrick and C. E. C. Tatters
Fine Carpets in the Victoria and Albert Museum, London, 1924; E. Kühn
Das Ewqâf-Museum in Kostantinopel, ZfbK, LVIII, 1924–25, pp. 41–
A. Lensi, Il Museo Bardini, Dedalo, X, 1929, pp. 69–98 at 92; S. Tr
Die Wiener Sammlung orientalischer Teppiche, ZfbK, LXIII, 1929–
pp. 247–56; Halil Edhem and G. Migeon, Les collections du Vieux Séra
Stamboul, Syria, XI, 1930, pp. 91–102; K. Erdmann, Bereicherungen d
Teppichsammlung, Berliner Museen, LIV, 1933, pp. 6–10; E. Kühn
Orientteppiche (Bilderhefte der islamischen Abteilung, 3), Berlin, 19
E. Kühnel, Die Sammlung türkischer und islamischer Kunst im Tschir
Köschk (Istanbul), Berlin, Leipzig, 1938; M. S. Dimand, Rugs of the N
East in the Metropolitan Museum, BMMA, XXXIV, 1939, pp. 90–
M. Aga-Oglu, Safawid Rugs and Textiles: The Collection of the Shri
of Imām 'Ali at al-Najaf, New York, 1941; K. Erdmann, Orientteppic
in deutschen Museen, ZMG, XCVI, 1942, pp. 392–417; K. Erdman
Teppicherwerbungen der Islamischen Abteilung, Berliner Museen, LXI
1943, pp. 5–17; Zakī Muḥammad Ḥasan, Moslem Art in the Fouad I U
versity Museum, Cairo, 1950, pls. 86–101; S. Troll, Altorientalische Te

iche: Museum für angewandte Kunst, Vienna, 1951; M. S. Dimand, Rugs the Altman Collection, BMMA, N.S., XIII, 1955, pp. 177–80; J. G. Lee, wo Bequests of Oriental Art: The J. L. Williams Memorial Collection Carpets, Phila. Mus. B., LI, 1955, pp. 15–17; A. H. von Briesen, The Iillion Dollar Carpets, Los Angeles Mus. Q., XIV, 1, 1957–58, pp. 74–75; . Erdmann, Orientteppiche im Besitz des Museums für Kunst und Geerbe, Festschrift für E. Meyer, Hamburg, 1957, pp. 28–31; Mohammed Iostafa, Neuerwerbungen des Museums für Islamische Kunst in Kairo, estschrift für E. Kühnel, Berlin, 1959, pp. 89–92; K. Erdmann, Teppiierwerbungen der Islamischen Abteilung 1956–61, Berliner Museen, .S., XII, 1962, pp. 40–49; D. Heinz, Die Sammlung altorientalischer eppiche im Österreichischen Museum für angewandte Kunst, Bustan, I, 1962, pp. 41–48. 5. *Catalogues of private collections*: A. Zeiss, Meine unstsammlung, Berlin, 1900, pls. 55–61; G. Migeon, La collection Kekian: Etoffes et tapis d'Orient et de Venise, Paris, 1908; J. K. Mumford, he Yerkes Collection of Oriental Carpets, London, New York, 1910; A. . Kendrick, Carpets at Boughton House, BM, XXV, 1914, pp. 73–79; . F. Kendrick, Guide to an Exhibition of Tapestries, Carpets, and Furniture ent by the Earl of Dalkeith, London, 1914; A. U. Pope, Catalogue of the Irs. Phoebe A. Hearst Loan Collection, San Francisco, 1917; F. Sarre, ie muhammedanische Kunst auf den Auktionen Engel-Gros und Townley, unstwanderer, I, 1920, pp. 470–72; J. Breck and F. Morris, The James . Ballard Collection of Oriental Rugs, New York, 1923; H. Jacoby, Eine ammlung orientalischer Teppiche, Berlin, 1923; J. A. MacLean and D. air, Catalogue of the Oriental Rugs in the Collection of J. F. Ballard, idianapolis, 1924 (full bibliog. of Eng. and Am. sources); American Art ssociation, The F. D. Gardiner Collection of Antique Oriental Rugs, ew York, 1926; E. Kühnel, Die Orientteppiche der Sammlung A. Cassirer, unst und Künstler, XXVIII, 1930, pp. 461–67; K. Erdmann, Katalog chefik Pascha, Berlin, 1931; Katalog der Austellung der Sammlung F. nd M. Sarre im Stadelschen Kunstinstitut, Frankfurt am Main, 1932, ssim; H. Wulff, A Collection of Oriental Carpets and Rugs Belonging to . Wulff, Copenhagen, 1934; M. S. Dimand, The Ballard Collection of riental Rugs in the City Art Museum of St. Louis, St. Louis, 1935; M. erner and J. Kinch, Antika Orientaliska Mattor i Sverige, Stockholm, 937; K. Erdmann, Die Teppichsammlung Pohlmann, Berlin, Pantheon, VII, 1944, pp. 129–36; F. Lewis, Oriental Rugs and Textiles: The Perez ollection, Leigh-on-Sea, 1953; E. Ganz-Ruedin, Tapis d'Orient, Berlin, 954; D. Heinz, Altorientische Teppiche in Fürstlichem Besitz (Schwarzenerg), Alte und moderne K., II, 7, 1957, pp. 27–29; M. H. Beattie, The urrell Collection of Oriental Rugs, O. Art, N.S., VII, 1961, pp. 162–69.

b. Early examples: A. Riegl, Ein orientalischer Teppich vom Jahre 202 und die ältesten orientalischen Teppiche, Berlin, 1895; A. Stein, Ancient hotan, 2 vols., Oxford, 1907; O. Jaeckel, Zur Urgeschichte der orientalischen eppiche, O. Arch., II, 2, 1911, pp. 167–72; A. Stein, Ruins of Desert athay, 2 vols., London, 1912; J. Strzygowski, Altai-Iran und Völkerwanerung, Leipzig, 1917; Aly Bahgat Bey and A. Gabriel, Fouilles d'Al Fouāṭ, Cairo, 1921; F. Sarre and T. Falkenberg, Ein frühes Knüpfteppichagment aus chinesisch Turkestan, Berliner Museen, XLII, 1921, pp. 110–4; A. Stein, Serindia, 4 vols., Oxford, 1921; P. Yetts, Discoveries of the ozlov Expedition, BM, XLVIII, 1926, pp. 168–85; M. S. Dimand, Egyptorabic Textiles: Recent Accessions, BMMA, XXII, 1927, pp. 275–79; . Stein, Innermost Asia, 4 vols., Oxford, 1928; M. S. Dimand, An Early ut-pile Rug from Egypt, Met. Mus. S., IV, 1933, pp. 151–62; R. M. Riefahl, Ein Knüpfteppich spätantiker Tradition aus Ägypten im Metropolitan Iuseum in New York, RM, XLVIII, 1933, pp. 127–52; Ali Ibrahim Pasha, arly Islamic Rugs of Egypt or Fostat Rugs, BIE, XVII, 1934–35, pp. 123–27; . J. Lamm, Cotton in Medieval Textiles of the Near East, Paris, 1937; . Fuhrmann, Der Gewebefund von Pilgramsdorf, C: Knüpfgewebe, Pr. ., XXX–XXXI, 1939–40, pp. 308–29; R. B. Serjeant, Material for a History Islamic Textiles up to the Mongol Conquest, Ars Islamica, IX, 1942, p. 54–92, X, 1943, pp. 71–104, XI–XII, 1946, pp. 98–145, XIII–XIV, 948, pp. 75–117, XV–XVI, 1951, pp. 29–85; C. J. Lamm, A Fragment of Early Carpet in Stockholm, Ars Islamica, XV–XVI, 1951, pp. 135–36; . D. Barnett, The World's Oldest Persian Carpet, ILN, CCXXIII, 1953, p. 69–71, CCXXVI, 1955, pp. 26–28; S. I. Rudenko, Kul'tura naseleniia ornogo Altaia v skifskoe vremia (Civilization of the High Altai Peoples in cythian Times), Moscow, Leningrad, 1953; H. Jacoby and K. Erdmann, eppich im ewigen Eis, Orion, IX, 1954, pp. 338–42; K. Erdmann, Zu einem natolischen Teppichframgent aus Fostat, Istanbuler Mitt., VI, 1955, p. 42–52; M. T. Picard Schmitter, Voici le plus vieux tapis du monde, tyle: Urbanisme, architecture, arts plastiques, I, 1961, pp. 76–86.

c. Medieval period: J. Lessing, Altorientalische Teppiche nach Bildern nd Originalen des XV. und XVI. Jahrhunderts, Berlin, 1877; F. Sarre, Iittelalterliche Knüpfteppiche kleinasiatischer und spanischer Herkunft, unst und Kunsthandwerk, X, 1907, pp. 503–25; F. Sarre, Erzeugnisse lamischer Kunst, II: Seldschukische Kleinkunst, Leipzig, 1909, pp. 49–4; J. Breck, Noch ein Beispiel für einen Drachen- und Phönix-Teppich, icerone, IV, 1912, pp. 133–35; G. Soulier, Les influences orientales dans peinture toscane, Paris, 1924, pp. 195–211; V. Sylwan, En orientalisk iatta, Fornwännen, XIX, 1924, pp. 106–19; K. Erdmann, Orientalische ierteppiche auf Bildern des XIV. und XV. Jahrhunderts, JhbPreussKamml, L, 1929, pp. 261–98; K. Erdmann, Zur Frage der ältesten orientalchen Teppiche, Cicerone, XXII, 1930, pp. 152–56; R. M. Riefstahl, rimitive Rugs of the "Konya" Type in the Mosque of Beyseehir, AB, III, 1931, pp. 177–220; E. de Lorey, Le tapis d'Avignon, GBA, VIII, 932, pp. 162–71; E. Cohn-Wiener, On the Origin of the Persian Carpet attern, Islamic Culture, XI, 1937, pp. 455–59; C. J. Lamm, The Marby ug and Some Fragments of Carpets Found in Egypt, Orientaliska Sällsarpets Arsbok, N.S., I, 1937, pp. 51–130; A. B. Thacher, 15th Century esign in a 19th Century Rug, AB, XXI, 1939, p. 401; K. Erdmann, Neue ierteppiche auf abendländischen Bildern des XIV. und XV. Jahrhunderts, hbPreussKSamml, LXIII, 1941, pp. 121–26; C. Schuster, Some Comparative Considerations about Western Asiatic Carpet Design, AAs, IX, 1946 pp. 68–92, 321–22; B. Scheunemann, Anatolische Teppiche auf abendländischen Gemälden (Diss.), Berlin, 1953; K. Erdmann, Der türkische Teppich des 15. Jahrhunderts, Istanbul, 1957; R. Ettinghausen, New Light on Early Animal Carpets, Festschrift für E. Kühnel, Berlin, 1959, pp. 93–116; A. Geijer, Orientaliska textilmönster, Konsthistorisk Tidskrift, XXVIII, 1959, pp. 1–12.

d. Asia Minor: F. Sarre, The Hittite Monument of Ivriz and a Carpet Design, BM, XIV, 1908–09, pp. 143–45; W. Kulczynski, Beiträge zur Kenntnis des orientalischen Gebetteppiche, Lemberg, 1914; H. Bell and R. M. Riefstahl, Special Loan Exhibition of Carpets and Other Textiles from Asia Minor, Philadelphia, 1919; C. E. C. Tattersall, A 17th Century Asia Minor Carpet and a Group of Rugs Akin to It, BM, XXVII, 1920, pp. 201–05; R. M. Riefstahl, Turkish "Bird" Rugs and Their Design, AB, VII, 1925, pp. 91–95; J. de Végh and C. Layer, Tapis turcs provenant des églises et collections de Transylvanie, Paris, 1925; M. S. Dimand, Dated Specimens of Mohammedan Art in the Metropolitan Museum, Met Mus. S., I, 1928–29, pp. 99–112; E. Kühnel, Ein neuerworbener Holbeinteppich, Berliner Museen, LI, 1930, pp. 140–45; E. Schmutzler, Altorientalische Teppiche in Siebenbürgen, Leipzig, 1933; K. Layer, Régi Kisázsiai szönyegek Kiállitása (Exhibition of Old Asia Minor Carpets), Budapest, 1935; K. Erdmann, Neuerwerbung der Islamischen Abteilung, Berliner Museen, LVII, 1937, pp. 36–37; K. Dirik, Eski ve yeni Türk halıcılığı ve Cihan Hall tiplerl Panaramasl (New and Old Turkish Art of Carpets and Panorama of Examples of Carpets of the World), Istanbul, 1938; K. Erdmann, Ein Teppichfragment des 15. Jahrunderts, Berliner Museen, LXI, 1940, pp. 47–50; Mohammed Mostafa, Turkish Prayer Rugs, Cairo, 1953; W. Hein, Türkische Mihrabteppiche, Alte und moderne Kunst, III, 1958, pp. 23–25; O. Aslanapa, Turkish Arts (trans. H. Kreider), Istanbul, 1959; M. Beattie, Antique Rugs at Hardwick Hall, O. Art, N.S., V, 1959, pp. 52–61; Y. Muller, Turetskii kovër XVI veka (A Turkish Carpet of the 16th Century), Soobshcheniia Gosudarstvennogo Ermitazha, XIX, 1960, pp. 44–47; J. Zick, Eine Gruppe Gebetsteppiche und ihre Datierung, Berliner Museen, N.S., XI, 1961, pp. 6–14; K. Erdmann, Weniger bekannte Uschak-Muster, Kunst des Orients, IV, 1963, pp. 78–97.

e. Caucasus: A. Sakisian, Les tapis arméniens, Rev. des ét. arméniens, I, 1920, pp. 121–27; A. U. Pope, The Myth of the Armenian Dragon Carpets, Jhb. der asiatischen K., XI, 1925, pp. 147–58; A. Sakisian, Les tapis à dragons et leur origine arménienne, Syria, IX, 1928, pp. 238–56; A. F. Kendrick, An Exhibition of Near East Carpets, BM, LV, 1929, pp. 15–16; A. U. Pope, Les tapis à dragons, Syria, X, 1929, pp. 181–82; A. Sakisian, Les tapis arméniens du XVe au XIXe siècle, Rev. de l'art ancien et moderne, LXIV, 1933, pp. 21–36; K. Erdmann, Later Caucasian Dragon Carpets, Apollo, XXII, 1935, pp. 21–25; A. Sakisian, Nouveaux documents sur les tapis arméniens, Syria, XVII, 1936, pp. 177–84; Z. Hofrichter, Armenische Teppiche, Vienna, 1937; M. S. Dimand, Loan of a Caucasian Rug, BMMA, XXXVI, 1941, pp. 185–87; M. Aga-Oglu, Dragon Rugs: A Loan Exhibition, Washington, 1948; V. S. Temurdzhian, Kovrodelie v Armenii (Carpetmaking in Armenia), Erevan, 1955; H. M. Raphaelian, Rugs of Armenia, New Rochelle, N.Y., 1960; U. Schürmann, Kaukasische Teppiche, Brunswick, 1961.

f. Central Asia: A. A. Bogoloubow, Tapis de l'Asia centrale faisant partie de la collection réunie par A. Bogoloubow (in Rus.), St. Petersburg, 1908; B. Laufer, Der Cyclus der zwölf Tiere auf einem altturkistanischen Teppiche, TP, X, 1909, pp. 71–75; J. Kuderna, Turkmenteppiche, O. Arch., II, 1911–12, pp. 11–16; A. Foelkersam, Ancient Central Asiatic Carpets (in Rus.), Starye Godi, June 1914, pp. 57–113, Oct.–Dec. 1915, pp. 17–40; H. Clark, Bokhara, Turkoman and Afghan Rugs, London, 1922; T. N. Goguel, Some Turcoman Carpets and Their Ornamentation, BM, L, 1927, pp. 251–54; G. Loukomsky, Les tapis transcaucasiens et transcaspiens, Rev. de l'art ancien et moderne, LI, 1927, pp. 223–36; A. von Le Coq, Die Teppiche der Karakirgisen, OAZ, N.S., V, 1929, pp. 15–17; A. B. Thacher, Turcoman Rugs, New York, 1940.

g. North Africa: P. Ricard, ed., Corpus des tapis marocains, 3 vols., Paris, 1923–27; L. Poinssot and J. Revault, Tapis tunisiens, 4 vols., Paris, 1950–57; L. Golvin, Les tapis algériens, Algiers, 1953.

h. Mameluke and Ottoman examples: F. Sarre, Die ägyptische Herkunft der sogenannten Damaskus-Teppiche, ZfbK, XXXII, 1921, pp. 75–82; F. Sarre and E. Flemming, Die ägyptischen Teppiche, Jhb. der asiatischen K., I, 1924, pp. 19–25; R. M. Riefstahl, Das Palmenmotiv auf einem ägyptischen Teppich der Ballard-Sammlung, Jhb. der asiatischen K., II, 1925, pp. 159–62; K. Erdmann, Some Observations on the So-called Damascus Rugs, Art in Am., XIX, 1930, pp. 3–22; K. Erdmann, Ägyptische Teppiche, Kunstwanderer, XII, 1931, pp. 196–200; A. Sakisian, L'inventaire des tapis de la Mosquée Yéni-Djami de Stamboul, Syria, XII, 1931, pp. 368–73; S. Troll, Damaskus-Teppiche, Ars Islamica, IV, 1937, pp. 201–31; S. Troll, Ein orientalischer Teppich aus kaiserlichem Besitz, JhbKhSammlWien, N.S., XI, 1937, pp. 221–42; K. Erdmann, Kairener Teppiche, Ars Islamica, V, 1938, pp. 179–286, VII, 1940, pp. 55–81; K. Erdmann, Kairo als Teppichzentrum, Forsch. und Fortschritte, XIV, 1938, pp. 207–10; Gamāl Muḥammad Meḥrez, Dos trozos de alfombras Mamluki conservadas en el Museo de Granada, Rev. Inst. egipcio de estudios islamicos en Madrid, II, 1954, pp. 174–99; B. Scheunemann, Das Papyrusmotiv auf ägyptischen Teppichen der Mamlukenzeit, K. des Orients, II, 1955, pp. 52–58; E. Kühnel and L. Bellinger, Cairene Rugs and Others Technically Related: 15th–17th Centuries, Washington, 1957 (cf. K. Erdmann, Oriens, XII, 1959, pp. 225–31); K. Erdmann, Weitere Beiträge zur Frage der Kairener Teppiche, Berliner Museen, N.S., IX, 1959, pp. 12–22; K. Erdmann, Neuere Untersuchungen zur Frage der Kairener Teppiche, Ars Orientalis, IV, 1961, pp. 65–105; C. G. Ellis, Gifts from Kashan to Cairo, Textile Mus.

J., I, 1962, pp. 33–46; J. Zick, Koptische Musterelemente und Mamlukische Knüpfteppiche, Jhb. der Hamburger Kunstsammlung, VII, 1962, pp. 93–109.

i. Persia: J. Karabacek, Die persische Nadelmalerei Susandschird, Leipzig, 1881; M. W. Conway, The Lesson of a Persian Carpet, Art J., 1891, pp. 371–73; W. Bode, Altorientalische Tierteppiche, Vienna, 1892; E. Stebbing, The Holy Carpet of the Mosque of Ardebil, London, 1893; A. Riegl, Zur Frage der "Polonenteppiche," Mitt K. K. österreichischen Mus. für K. und Industrie, N.S., V, 1894, pp. 225–30; W. Bode, Altpersische Knüpfteppiche, Berlin, 1904; F. Sarre, Ein persischer Baumteppich aus dem Beginn des 16. Jahrhunderts, Amtliche Berichte aus den Kunstsamml., XXX, 1908–09, cols. 146–49; J. Breck, A Polish Carpet, BMMA, V, 1910, pp. 170–71; F. Sarre, Ardebil, Berlin, 1910; W. R. Valentiner, The So-called Polish Rugs, BMMA, V, 1910, pp. 282–83; G. Migeon, Le tapis persan de la Cathédrale de Mantes au Musée du Louvre, Les mus. de France, II, 1912, pp. 96–97; M. W. Conway, A Persian Garden Carpet, BM, XXIII, 1913, pp. 95–96; R. Weinzetl, Über persische Teppiche, O. Archiv, III, 1913, pp. 65–84; R. M. Riefstahl, Oriental Carpets in American Collections: Three Silk Rugs in the Altmann Collection, Art in Am., IV, 1916, pp. 147–61; R. M. Riefstahl, The Pattern of Chinese Animals in a Landscape and Animal Rug in the William Morris Collection, Art in Am., V, 1917, pp. 231–40; A. Rava, I tappeti persiani della chiesa di San Marco, Dedalo, II, 1921, pp. 125–30; F. Sarre, Ein neuerworbener Gartenteppich, Berliner Museen, XLII, 1921, pp. 54–59; A. U. Pope, Polonaise Carpets, International Studio, LXXVI, 1922–23, pp. 535–49; M. S. Dimand, Medallion Carpets, AB, VI, 1924, pp. 82–84; H. Trenkwald, Die Technik des Jagdteppichs, Belvedere, VI, 1924, pp. 100–05; A. U. Pope, Research Methods in Muhammedan Art, AB, VIII, 1925, pp. 43–49; A. U. Pope, Datierte Seidenteppiche im Mausoleum von Kum in Persien, Kchr., XXXV, 1926, pp. 311–12; A. U. Pope, Un tappeto persiano del 1521 nel Museo Poldi-Pezzoli, Dedalo, VIII, 1927, pp. 82–108; K. Erdmann, Ein neuerworbener persischer Teppich, Berliner Museen, L, 1929, pp. 6–10; A. F. Kendrick, Garden Designs in Oriental Carpets, International Studio, XCIV, 1929, pp. 25–28; J. Breck, The Loan Exhibition of Persian Rugs of the so-called Polish Type, BMMA, XXV, 1930, pp. 146–48; M. S. Dimand, Loan Exhibition of Persian Rugs of the so-called Polish Type, New York, 1930 (cat.); A. F. Kendrick, Garden Carpets, Rupam, 41, 1930, pp. 14–16; A. U. Pope, An Introduction to Persian Art, London, 1930, pp. 118–43; A. Scrinzi, Un dono dello Schah Abbas il Grande al Doge di Venezia, Riv. di Venezia, IX, 1930, pp. 551–59; M. S. Dimand, A Persian Tapestry-woven Rug, BMMA, XXVI, 1931, pp. 294–96; K. Erdmann, Il tappeto con figure d'animali nel Museo Bardini a Firenze, Dedalo, XI, 1931, pp. 647–63; A. U. Pope, The Emperor's Carpet, B. Art Inst. of Chicago, XXV, 1931, pp. 61–63; F. Sarre, A "Portuguese" Carpet from Knole, BM, LVIII, 1931, pp. 214–19; F. Sarre, Zewi Hauptwerke persischer Teppichkunst, Pantheon, VII, 1931, pp. 24–31; K. Erdmann, Persische Wirkteppiche der Safawidenzeit, Pantheon, X, 1932, pp. 227–31; K. Erdmann, Tappeti persiani, Dedalo, XII, 1932, pp. 707–38; A. F. Kendrick, A Persian Carpet Belonging to Mr. F. W. Bruce, BM, LX, 1932, pp. 100–05; K. Erdmann, Ein wiedergefundener Teppich, Ars Islamica, I, 1934, pp. 121–27; V. Slomann, The Coronation Carpet of the King of Denmark, B. Am. Inst. for Persian Art and Archaeol., III, 1934, pp. 13–18; K. Erdmann, Zwei Medaillonteppiche in der Islamischen Abteilung, Berliner Museen, LVI, 1935, pp. 32–37; T. Mańkowski, Influence of Islamic Art in Poland, Ars Islamica, II, 1935, pp. 93–117; A. U. Pope, A Note on the Persian Origin of the So-called "Polonaise" Carpets, B. Am. Inst. for Persian Art and Archaeol., IV, 1935, pp. 28–29; A. Sakisian, Les tapis de Perse à la lumière des arts du livre, AAs, V, 1935, pp. 9–22; K. Layer, Régi perza szönyegek kiállitása (Exhibition of Old Persian Carpets), Budapest, 1936; T. Mańkowski, Note on the Cost of Kashan Carpets at the Beginning of the 17th Century, B. Am. Inst. for Persian Art and Archaeol., IV, 1936, pp. 152–53; T. Mańkowski, On Persian Rugs of the So-called Polish Type, Ars Islamica, IV, 1937, pp. 456–59; K. Erdmann, Ein persischer Wirkteppich der Safawidenzeit, Pantheon, XXI, 1938, pp. 62–66; K. Erdmann, The So-called "Polish Carpets," B. Am. Inst. for Persian Art and Archaeol., V, 1938, pp. 62–66; A. U. Pope, T. Mańkowski and H. Jacoby, SPA, III, pp. 2257–2465; M. S. Dimand, A Persian Garden Carpet in the Jaipur Museum, Ars Islamica, VII, 1940, pp. 93–96; K. Erdmann, The Art of Carpet Making, Ars Islamica, VIII, 1941, pp. 121–91; A. C. Weibel, Persian Silk Rugs of the So-called Polish Type, B. Art Inst. of Detroit, XXII, 1943, pp. 65–67; A. U. Pope, Masterpieces of Persian Art, New York, 1945, pp. 182–85; M. S. Dimand, A Gift of Persian Silk Rugs, BMMA, N.S., IX, 1951, pp. 142–44; A. C. Edwards, Persian Carpets, in A. J. Arberry, ed., The Legacy of Persia, Oxford, 1953, pp. 230–58; A. C. Edwards, The Persian Carpet, London, 1953; W. Hein, Der persische Inschriftenteppich im Österreichischen Museum, Alte und moderne K., III, 12, 1958, pp. 12–15; I. Schlosser, Ein Medaillonteppich aus der Blütenzeit der persischen Teppichkunst, Alte und moderne Kunst, III, 3, 1958, pp. 22–23; B. Scheunemann, Eine unbekannte Teppichgattung, K. des Orients, III, 1959, pp. 78–83; K. Erdmann, Die Kleinen Seidenteppiche Kaschans, Pantheon, XIX, 1961, pp. 159–63; K. Erdmann, Ein persischer Teppich im Museum für Kunst und Gewerbe, Jhb. der Hamburger Kunstsamml., VI, 1961, pp. 149–58; F. Heinz, Persische Teppiche, Alte und moderne Kunst, VII, 64–65, 1962, pp. 6–11.

j. India: A. F. Kendrick, Pile Carpet Belonging to the Worshipful Company of Girdlers of the City of London, Art Workers Q., III, 1904, pp. 97–99; T. A. Hendley, The Asian Carpets: 15th and 17th Century Designs from the Jaypur Palaces, London, 1905; F. H. Andrews, One Hundred Carpet Designs from Various Parts of India, JIAI, XI, 1906, pp. 1–10; H. Harris, Monograph on the Carpet Weaving Industry of Southern India, Madras, 1908; R. M. Riefstahl, An Indo-Isfahan Rug of the 16th Century, B. Art Inst. of Chicago, XX, 1926, pp. 48–49; A. C. Weibel, A Persian and an Indian Rug, B. Art Inst. of Detroit, X, 1929, pp. 95–97; M. Aga-Oglu, A Fragment of a Rare Indian Carpet, B. Art Inst. of Detroit, XIII, 1931, pp. 1–5; J. Irwin, Early Indian Carpets, Antiques, LXIX, 1956, pp. 154–57.

k. China: The Tiffany Studios Collection of Antique Chinese Rugs, New York, 1908; T. J. Larkin, A Collection of Antique Chinese Rugs, London, 1910; A. Hackmack, Der chinesische Teppich, Hamburg, 192 (Eng. trans., L. Arnold, Tientsin, 1924); W. C. Thomson, Chinese Carpets, Apollo, II, 1925, pp. 159–65; E. Kühnel, Mongolenteppiche, Cicerone, XX, 1928, pp. 461–64; G. B. Leitch, Chinese Rugs, New York, 1928; F. Sarre, Ein chinesischer Knüpfteppich der Ming-Zeit, OAZ, N.S., X, 1935, pp. 187–91; C. E. C. Tattersall, Carpets and Rugs from China, The Connoisseur, XCVII, 1936, pp. 76–83.

l. Modern examples: J. K. Mumford, Oriental Rugs, New York, 1900; W. D. Ellwanger, The Oriental Rug, New York, 1903; M. C. Ripley, The Oriental Rug Book, New York, 1904 (2d ed., 1936); R. B. Holt, Rugs, Oriental and Occidental: A Handbook for Ready Reference, 2d ed., Chicago, 1908; E. Dunn, Rugs in Their Native Lands, London, 1910; W. A. Hawley, Oriental Rugs: Antique and Modern, New York, London, 1913; G. G. Lewis, The Practical Book of Oriental Rugs, 5th ed., Philadelphia, 1920; R. von Oettingen and W. Grote-Hasenbalg, Meisterstücke orientalische Knüpfkunst, 2 vols., Berlin, 1921; W. Grote-Hasenbalg, Der Orientteppich Seine Geschichte und seine Kultur, Berlin, 1922; L. Arthur, Der echte Teppich, Vienna, 1926; R. Neugebauer and S. Troll, Handbuch der orientalischen Teppichkunde, 14th ed., Leipzig, 1930; J. Orendi, Das Gesamtwissen über antike und neue Teppiche des Orients, Vienna, 1930; H. Uhlemann, Geographie des Orientteppichs, Leipzig, 1930; A. U. Dilley, Oriental Rugs and Carpets, New York, London, 1931; C. E. C. Tattersall, The Carpets of Persia, London, 1931; W. Grote-Hasenbalg, Teppiche aus dem Orient, 2d ed., Leipzig, 1937 (Eng. trans., M. Brooke, Leipzig, 1939); M. Sterner, Orientens mattor och deras vård, Stockholm, 1944; P. Westermann, Aegte Taepper, Copenhagen, 1945; H. Jacoby, ABC der echten Teppichs, Tübingen, 1949; H. Hildebrand, Der persische Teppich und sein Heimat, Zurich, 1951; C. J. Delabère May, How to Identify Persian Rugs and Other Oriental Rugs, London, 1952; H. Jacoby, How to Know Oriental Carpets and Rugs, London, 1952; H. Ropers, Morgenländische Teppiche Ein Handbuch für Sammler und Liebhaber (ed. R. Dieke), 6th ed., Brunswick, 1953; S. Chabari, Le tapis persan, Geneva, Paris, 1957; U. Schürmann, Bilderbuch für Teppichsammler, Munich, 1960; J. Penry-Jones, Persian Women Pictures, Apollo, LXXIII, 1961, pp. 10–11; M. S. Dimand, Some Peasant and Oriental Rugs, Antiques, LXXXI, 1962, pp. 520–25; S. A. Milhofer, Das goldene Buch des Orientteppichs, Hannover, 1962.

European carpets: a. General: C. E. C. Tattersall, Handwoven Carpet Oriental and European, London, 1922; C. B. Faraday, European and American Carpets and Rugs, Grand Rapids, Mich., 1929; M. Matet, Tapi modernes, Paris, 1929; I. Schlosser, Der schöne Teppich in Orient und Okzident, Heidelberg, Munich, 1960.

b. Spain: W. G. Thomson, Hispano-Moresque Carpets, BM, XVII, 1910, pp. 100–11; A. van der Put, Some 15th Century Spanish Carpets, BM, XIX, 1911, pp. 344–50; F. Sarre, Some 15th Century Spanish Carpets, BM, XX, 1911, p. 46; O. S. Berberyan and W. G. Thomson, A Catalogue of Carpets of Spain and of the Orient in the Collection of Charles Deering, Esq., London, 1924; E. Kühnel, Maurische Kunst, Berlin, 1924, pls. 152–58; A. van der Put, A 15th Century Spanish Carpet, BM, XLV, 1924, pp. 119–20; D. Real, Tissus espagnols et portugais, Paris, 1925; A. F. Kendrick, Spanish Pile Carpets, Old Furniture, II, 1927, pp. 33–42; E. Kühnel, Maurische Teppiche aus Alcaraz, Pantheon, VI, 1930, pp. 416–20; F. Sarre and E. Flemming, A 14th Century Spanish "Synagogue" Carpet, BM, LVII, 1930, pp. 89–95; K. Erdmann, Eine unbeachtete Gruppe spanischer Knüpfteppiche des 15.–17. Jahrhunderts, Belvedere, XI, 1932, pp. 74–77; Fernandis Torrés, Esposición de alfombras antiguas españolas, Madrid, 1933 (cat.); J. Gimenez de Aguilar, Notas acerca de la antiqua fabricación de alfombras en Cuenca, Rev. española de Artes, II, 1933, pp. 367–70; J. Fernandis Torrés, Alfombras antiguas españolas, Madrid, 1941; F. L. May, The Single Warp Knot in Spanish Rugs, N. Hispanic, I, 1941, pp. 94–99; J. Fernandis Torrés, Alfombras moriscas "tipo Holbein," AEArte, XV, 1942, pp. 103–11; F. L. May, Hispano-Moresque, Rugs, N. Hispanic, V, 1945, pp. 30–69; E. Kühnel and L. Bellinger, Catalogue of Spanish Rugs 12th to 19th Century, Washington, 1953 (cf. K. Erdmann, Oriens, VII, 1954, pp. 119–22).

c. France: A. L. Lacordaire, Notice historique sur les manufactures impériales de tapisseries des Gobelins de tapis et de tapisseries de Mobilier de la Couronne, 4th ed., Paris, 1859; L. Braquenie and J. Magnac, La Manufacture de la Savonnerie du Quai de Chaillot, Paris, 1924; A. F. Kendrick, Savonnerie Carpets in the Mobilier National, International Studio, XCII, 1929, pp. 30–34; J. Marquet de Vasselot and R. A. Weigert, Bibliographie de la tapisserie, des tapis et de la broderie de France, Paris, 1935, pp. 243–54; J. Niclausse, La Savonnerie dans la tapisserie, Paris, 1947; J. Niclausse, Tapisseries et tapis de la Ville de Paris, Paris, 1948; Musée des Arts Décoratifs, Quatre siècles de tapis français: XVIIᵉ–XIXᵉ siècle, Paris, 1949 (cat.); Rare Carpet Exhibited in New York, Antiques, LXVIII, 1955, p. 482; E. Standen, A King's Carpet, BMMA, N.S., XIII, 1955, pp. 257–65; S. Faniel, ed., Le XVIIᵉ siècle français (Connaissance des arts, III), Paris, 1958, pp. 144–49; M. Jarry, Savonnerie Carpets at Waddesdon, BM, C, 1959, pp. 259–64; M. Jarry, Tapis Louis XIV du Mobilier National commandés à la "Savonnerie" pour la grande Galerie du Louvre, GBA, LXIX, 1962, pp. 65–80; O. Le Fuel, L'extravagante villa-musée de la belle Madame Ephrussi, Connaissance des arts, 121, 1962, pp. 74–83.

d. England: P. Parisot, An Account of the New Manufactory of Tapestry and of Carpets, London, 1753; T. Thomson, A Collection of Inventories of the Royal Wardrobe, Edinburgh, 1815; C. E. C. Tattersall, A History of British Carpets, London, 1934; E. Standen, A Light and Elegant Ornament, BMMA, N.S., XVI, 1958, pp. 204–07; M. J. Mayorcas, English Needlework Carpets: 16th to 19th Centuries, Leigh-on-Sea, 1963.

e. *Other European countries*: M. Dreger, Die Linzer Wollenzeug und eppichfabrik, Kunst und Kunsthandwerk, XX, 1917, pp. 289–369; U. Sirelius, The Hand-Woven Rugs of Finland, Helsinki, 1925; Finnische nüpfteppiche, Zurich, 1926 (cat.); B. Kurth, Die deutschen Bildteppich s Mittelalters, Vienna, 1926 (Quedlinburg tapestry, etc.; bibliog.); G. lszewski, Vieux tapis roumains, Cartea Romaneasca, Bucharest, 1926; , T. Sirelius, The ryijy-rugs of Finland (trans. A. Matson), Helsinki, 26; E. N. Woroniecki, Les tapis et les kilims polonais, GBA, XVI, 1927, . 248–57; A. Kuhn, Die polnische Kunst von 1800 bis zur Gegenwart, rlin, 1930; Städtlicher Schlossmuseum, Wandbehänge, Möbelbezüge und eppiche der kurpfälzischen Savonnerie Manufaktur, Mannheim, 1931 ibliog.); V. Sylwan, Svenska ryor, Stockholm, 1934; W. W. Kent, The ooked Rug, New York, 1937; Sardinische Teppiche, Zurich, 1938 (cat.); . Engelstad, Norske ryor, Oslo, 1942; E. H. Ries, American Rugs, Cleve-nd, New York, 1950; D. Heinz, Linzer Teppiche, Vienna, Munich, 1955; Geiger, Oriental Textiles in Scandinavian Versions, Aus der Welt der amischen Kunst: Festschrift für E. Kühnel, Berlin, 1959, pp. 323–35; G. Yakovleva, Russkie kovry (Russian Rugs), Moscow, 1959; D. N. oberman, Kovry Moldavii (Moldavian Rugs), Kishinev, 1960; Finnische eppiche, Linz, 1962 (cat.).

                                                        Dora HEINZ

Folk art: A. Sautier, Tappeti rustici italiani, Milan, 1922; H. T. Bossert, art populaire en Europe, Berlin, 1927; N. Iorga, L'arte popolare in Romania, ome, 1930; B. Aitken et al., Art populaire: Tr. artistiques et scientifiques Ier Cong. des arts populaires (Prague, 1928), II, Paris, 1931, pp. 78–95; Fernandis Torrés, Alfombras españolas, Madrid, 1934; K. Hahm, Ost-eussische Bauernteppiche, Jena, 1937; W. W. Kent and H. B. Braun, are Hooked Rugs, Springfield, Mass., 1941; H. T. Bossert, Ornamente r Volkskunst, Tübingen, 1949; R. Mrlian, Art populaire slovaque, Brati-va, 1954; E. Fél, T. Hofer, and K. K. Csilléry, Ungarische Bauernkunst, idapest, 1958; G. Focsa, Le musée du village à Bucarest, Bucharest, 1958; , S. Dimand, Peasant and Nomad Rugs of Asia, New York, 1961 (cat.); Stankov, Chiprovski kilimi (Chiprov Rugs), Sofia, 1963. See also various neral texts on ethnology as well as the works listed in the preceding section this bibliog. and in other bibliogs. on folk and primitive art.

                                                        * *

ustrations: PLS. 391–434; 6 figs. in text.

TECHNIQUES. Every artistic product presupposes a tech-ique, that is, a complex of manual and mechanical operations iat act upon the raw material to organize, shape, and mold according to specific artistic intentions. The present essay ialyzes the relationship between art and techniques used ac-ording to modern critical thinking; it describes techniques sed in the visual arts, beginning with the basic processes of roduction and extending to processes of execution inherent in ie creative process. Modern methods of studying the chemical id physical structures of works of art are examined from a istorical and critical point of view.

SUMMARY. I. General considerations (col. 965). II. Techniques production. Shaping processes (col. 969): *Stone; Wood; Clay; letal; Glass; Leather and hide.* Preparation and treatment of surfaces ol. 985): *Stone; Wood; Clay; Metal; Glass; Cloth.* Interweaving id interlacing (col. 998). Combining various materials (col. 1000). I. Techniques of representation. Realization of concepts (col. 1003): ainting; Sculpture.* Preliminary processes (col. 1006): *Painting; culpture.* Processes of execution (col. 1010): *Painting: a. Tempera; Oil; c. Fresco; d. Pastel; e. Water color; f. Gouache; g. Encaustic ainting; h. Engraving. Sculpture: a. Stone; b. Metal; c. Clay; Wood; e. Mixed materials. Other processes: a. Mosaics; b. Opus ctile and wood marquetry; c. Stained glass.* Terminal processes (col. 029): *Painting: a. Fresco; b. Oil; c. Water color, gouache, tempera, and astel; d. Gilding. Sculpture.* IV. Techniques of analysis (col. 1032).

I. GENERAL CONSIDERATIONS. Technique is a manual opera-on, with or without the help of instruments, performed upon ny sort of material with the intention of shaping an object ossessing value: the operation, intention, and value must all e present. The ideas of value and intention are interrelated nd imply a value placed upon the existing natural or raw iaterial, the desire to "improve" it through human action, and consequent increase in the value of the given material. Tech-ique is therefore the basis of all manmade phenomena intended o modify the natural environment and adapt it to the neces-ties of an increasingly complex social life. As a determining ictor in production, technique also includes the development f all such necessary instruments as tools and machines, as well s the advance preparation of materials in view of their more ffective exploitation. It is a specifically human characteristic o transform the environment; animals, on the contrary, adapt iemselves to it.

As a whole, the history of technique appears as a constant perfecting of preceding stages. There are, of course, static periods and periods of regression in certain sectors. These are usually due to the predominance of spiritual over material in-terests. Ideological premises may be established and developed in such periods, later promoting the birth and rapid progress of productive techniques, which sometimes occur through a radical transformation of the cultural terrain. For example, after the crisis of classical civilization (due largely to the spread of the Christian world view) there was a long pause in the progress of techniques. This was succeeded by a cycle of devel-opment caused precisely by the new ethical basis for human work introduced by Christianity and expressed in the great flowering of art and craftsmanship in the Romanesque and Gothic periods.

Because technical progress is inevitably rooted in the ethical and ideological conceptions of various periods of history, it does not always occur in the same manner. There is a kind of quantitative development consisting in the broadening and deepening of acquired experience. Sudden transformations also take place due to brilliant inventions that rapidly modify a process or group of processes, sometimes even the fundamental methodology of technical research. An invention may concern any phase of the productive process: choice and preliminary preparation of material; drawing up of the project; the struc-ture, power, and use of tools; and the order of operations. Often the invention occurs in esthetic or scientific research rather than the specifically technical field and is subsequently applied to the productive ends of technique. Whole operational cycles, for example, have been renewed by the application of thermal or electrical energy. At present a vast transformation is occurring with the spread of automation.

The history of productive techniques includes two main phases: artisan and industrial. The fact that the modern world is characterized by an industrial development so rapid and widespread as to provoke a profound crisis in artisan produc-tion does not imply that the two cycles are successive; they have, in fact, been long interrelated, and there is no precise dividing line between them. The technological method of the artisan, however, applies to objects produced individually or in a limited series, while the method of industry aims for mass production. In artisan technology the predominant aim has been qualitative; in industrial technology it has been quantitative. Only with the high development of mechanical methods in the modern world have industrial techniques proven capable of attaining qualitative values superior to those of artisan work-manship.

From the methodological point of view, in artisan produc-tion the actual operation rather than the planning phase is considered the principal factor in the determination of value; this very often reduces the preliminary planning to a mere experimental operational phase (sketch or model). In industrial production, however, where execution is essentially mechanical, the estimate of value and the solutions to problems take place during the planning phase. In artisan production progress is usually conditioned by experience, in industrial production by the systematic application of scientific methods. The progress of artisan techniques thus appears to be largely the develop-ment of a tradition, whereas the progress of industrial techniques is a constant succession of innovations and inventions.

Artistic techniques do not form a category apart and are no different from ordinary techniques of production in their institutions, structures, and procedures. A study of artistic tech-niques as a category can only be purely empirical, based on the fact that given techniques have at certain periods and in certain circumstances led to results of esthetic value. The lack or loss of such value, however, does not necessarily correspond to a phase of lesser development or decline in those particular productive techniques. Ceramics and textiles illustrate this point: their respective techniques have traditionally produced results of high esthetic value, but recently these same techniques have produced results of an almost exclusively economic charac-ter; but this in no way signifies that there has been a decline in technique or a pause in development.

While it is legitimate to state that artistic techniques are those whose final aim is the production of objects of esthetic value, it should be noted that in all periods esthetic quality is a component of the total value of the product and that it is to be found in a greater or lesser measure in all objects produced by men. Esthetic research may therefore be extended to nearly all the problems relating to the production of an object or limited to marginal aspects such as ornamentation. Since all objects have form, and since this form determines at least a part of the total value of the object, there can be no production technique that is not partially directed toward esthetic value or that cannot be also used to attain utilitarian value (assuming that the esthetic value cannot be separated from the structure and function of the object). While this point prevents the establishment of a special category for artistic techniques, it suggests that the artist, insofar as he is concerned with esthetic values, adopts a different attitude toward technique from that of the ordinary producer of material goods. Therefore, what actually constitutes an object of study for historians of artistic techniques is the behavior of the artist in using the common heritage of technical knowledge.

Since ancient times attempts have been made to isolate esthetic value — that is, to produce objects which could be evaluated only from an esthetic point of view. From this attempt is derived the distinction between major and minor arts or between pure and applied art. However, no theoretical basis has ever been established for this distinction. Even if it were accepted hypothetically, transposing the distinction to a technical level would prove impossible: no fundamental distinction can be established between the techniques of painting and the different techniques used in the mere application of color; or between the techniques of sculpture and the techniques of molding, carving, or casting used in normal production; or between the techniques of construction used in monumental architecture and those of ordinary construction. To maintain erroneously that techniques possess greater precision when their aim is the production of esthetic values only leads to the tautological conclusion that the attempt to isolate esthetic value aims at providing the productive techniques with standards of value. Furthermore, it can be maintained that works of "pure" art — so called because they are unrelated in form to functional objects in common use — have a religious, ceremonial, or decorative purpose and are therefore also utilitarian objects. Again, the hypothesis that pure art has its own techniques of representation beyond operational methods can be defended only with difficulty, for we must regard as creative or representational all those techniques which determine the form and ornamentation of an object.

The real point is that the quality of the artist's technical activity does not depend on accuracy and precision, which constitute the value of the normal production techniques; in other words, accuracy and precision can be referred to only in terms of the values realized in the image. Thus a seemingly incomplete process may be complete from the artistic point of view insofar as it crystallizes a quality that the slightest addition would only diminish or destroy. It is therefore erroneous to distinguish between artistic perfection and technical perfection, since the technique employed for the purposes of art is "perfect" when its aim is fully achieved. This freedom of the artist concerning methods and aims of productive techniques also appears in the continued use of outdated methods of production and in innovations lacking prior experimentation. Sculpture, for example, has preserved with only slight modification the most ancient procedures, whereas a far more rapid rhythm of innovation is apparent in painting and architecture.

The search for formal value must be considered an essential stage in the search for value as such. Thus it is readily understandable that the capacity to conceive forms, or new esthetic values, should determine innovations and thus contribute to the progress of technique, even outside the area of esthetics. Brunelleschi provides a good example. Requiring a new technique for the construction of a new form, the dome of S. Maria del Fiore (II, PL. 365), Brunelleschi conceived a true revolution in the field of building techniques.

Certain procedures have been adopted or rejected as pure artistic techniques quite independently of their survival progress as techniques of production. Like ceramics and weaving, which continued to progress as production technique while declining as artistic techniques, the goldsmith's technique after the Gothic period acquired new instruments and method of procedure but never again attained its former esthetic leve Similarly the Limoges enamels of the 16th century (IV, PL. 415 although technically more complex than those of the 12th century (IV, PLS. 406, 408), do not possess the value of the latte The tapestries of the 16th and 17th centuries, produced throug a technique far richer in materials and mechanical aids tha those of the 14th and 15th centuries, are quite obviously "applied art" by comparison. The development of glasswork, especially in the case of the great stained-glass windows, cam to an esthetic halt despite constant technical development glass production. In regard to wood carving, its artistic development has not kept pace with the advancement of mechanic processes. In most cases this esthetic falling off is due to the fact that any single technique first employed in a search for value is then transformed into a technique for application repetition, aimed primarily at diffusion and popularization. ceramics, enamels, and tapestries qualitative degeneration certainly due to the fact that painting has established its primac as pure art, and the most modern instrumental techniques a used for obtaining effects similar to those of painting — that i for the repetition of values already achieved.

It would be erroneous to assume an incompatibility of prin ciple between technical research on a scientific basis and esthet exploration, for the latter may well show a positive attitud toward scientific technique. For example, certain spatial solu tions of baroque architecture could not have been realized ha not the artist adopted technical processes made possible by th progress of mechanics. Further, modern architecture presup poses scientific knowledge of the properties of various materia such as cement and iron. Modern painting (e.g., impressionism exploits the infinite chromatic spectrum produced by the deve opment of chemical science and the industrial production colors. Painting based on the scientific analysis of light (e.g works of Seurat and the neoimpressionists) has attained artist results of a high order; and the color industry itself, in th production of new types of colors, has taken into account th effects obtained by painters through the combination of cer tain hues. Thus artistic techniques not only make use of bu sometimes alter techniques of production, insofar as the succeed as techniques for research in esthetic or visual value In the artistic sense, progress of technique in ceramics may b the achievement of translucency or luminosity. In glass it ma be a certain effect of light modulation or filtering. In textil progress may be represented by new relationships of color ornamental forms. In metalwork it may mean complete iden tification of the engraved or embossed image with the characte of the material. In this sense artistic technique is not fun damentally different from what is called style; it is identifie with the entire artistic process and not only with the manu operations indispensable to its achievement.

Any process for the preparation of material (e.g., polishin staining, hatching, dotting, modeling) as well as any plast process (e.g., building, modeling, carving) aims first at deter mining in a new manner the relationship between space an the material or object through effects of color, light, and shad and the reflection or refraction of light. Similarly all represen tational processes, while suggesting a new spatial dimensio through a representational image, substantially modify the orig nal spatial quality of the material.

The study of artistic techniques therefore leads, on an esthe ic level, to two main conclusions. (1) The visual or form value that inevitably belongs to any perceivable object has own structure; this structure may or may not coincide wit the mechanical or functional structure of the object itself an can be studied through the operational process that brings into being. The visual structure is, like mechanical or function structures, perfectible through the development of operation processes whose ultimate aim is esthetic value. The esthet value exists purely as such (i.e., as the exclusive determining factor in the existence of the object) in products possessing artistic value, and it exists as a more or less important component in products of normal economic production. (2) The relationship between artistic techniques and those used in normal production, insofar as they contribute to the formation of a common heritage of knowledge (although with varying ultimate aims), explains the importance that differing cultures have attributed to formal values; it is therefore the only legitimate basis for the sociological study of visual art in all its variety of forms and processes.

Giulio Carlo ARGAN

II. TECHNIQUES OF PRODUCTION. SHAPING PROCESSES. *Stone.* The most ancient evidence in the development of technique is connected with man's earliest need for tools for defense and obtaining food. Although the development of primitive tools probably had no esthetic motivations, it was nevertheless the source of the most elementary technique of roughhewing and therefore the source upon which more advanced cultures based sculptural representation. In processing stone for his earliest artifacts man employed various techniques.

With the hammerstone technique flakes were detached from a stone by the use of a hammer, thus giving the stone a rough form. The hammer itself was made of water-worn rock. Paleolithic man discovered that in order to detach a flake at the exact spot the striking angle must be about 120 degrees and the hammer should be aimed close to the edge of the stone.

The anvil technique detached larger flakes. The stone from which the flake was to be obtained was struck against an immobile stone. The angle was about the same as that used in the hammerstone technique. Large and small objects of this type were made during the Abbevillian phase of paleolithic culture.

With the cylinder-hammer technique thin flakes were detached from a stone. A more even surface was produced by means of a round-edged hammer made of a softer material (e.g., bone, a wooden branch, ca. 2 in. in diam., with bark removed). In this technique the full force of the blow is aimed at the edge of the stone.

The blade-flake technique, in use at the beginning of the Upper Paleolithic, produced long narrow flakes with parallel edges. First the block of flint, obsidian, or very fine-grained lava was broken in half so as to obtain an even striking surface. Another blow was then struck on a protuberance of the block in such a way that the section did not come off, and the block cracked transversely in the direction of the blow. After this preliminary process the block was further prepared for the removal of blade flakes. It was placed on one knee with the striking platform turned obliquely upward in the direction of the worker. Light blows were then struck with a hammerstone all along the edge, just above the spot where the block rested on the knee. At each blow the block was simultaneously tilted backward. Blows were directed at an angle of about 45° from the fractured surface (i.e., about 135° to the direction in which the flake was to be detached). The block was then made to revolve slowly on its own axis in order to detach a series of flakes (not the blade flakes) all along the circumference. Since these flakes were all detached in the same direction, the remaining block had a fluted form. It was then ready for the removal of the blade flakes. Each new blow was struck at the ridged intersection of two grooves produced by the removal of two of the earlier group of flakes in such a way that the ridge formed a central keel in the newly detached flake.

The techniques used for retouching (further processing of stone flake) are the same as those already described. The work was done with small hammerstones, which produced various results (e.g., step flaking and feather flaking), depending on the angle at which the blow was struck. Sometimes retouching benefited from a modification of the cylinder-hammer technique, using a piece of wood or bone no thicker than a finger. This method was employed throughout the Stone Age.

The anvil technique was also used, especially during the Upper Paleolithic period, for making burins or gravers. In this technique a rough point was formed at one end of a blade flake. This point was then lightly pressed against the edge of the anvil stone, with its sharp edge at a vertical angle to the anvil's surface. A sharp blow to the edge of the flake causes the point placed against the anvil to receive the rebound. If the point was placed at the proper angle, a long thin flake was detached from the upper edge of the blade. If the process was repeated on the opposite side, the intersection of the two surfaces resulting from the detachment of the two flakes at one end produced a burin of the *bec-de-flute* type.

In pressure flaking the pressure was brought to bear against a flake by another, thicker, flake fairly rectangular in shape, thus rapidly removing little flakes of stone from the edges. In order to turn a flat flake into an arrowhead or spearhead a special tool made of ivory, hard wood, or the incisor of a large rodent, such as a beaver, was placed against the part to be chipped off. With one push a flake was detached. A pressure-flaking tool could be tied to a wooden shaft resting on a man's chest while he held the stone in both hands. When the point of the utensil was placed against the stone, a forward thrust of the chest in the correct position detached a flat flake.

During the Neolithic age the working of hard rock was widespread. There developed techniques for polishing and grinding that required long processing with abrasive sand. In the same period the technique for boring holes was also developed and perfected. Probably hand and bow drills were used. For harder rock abrasive powders were also employed. Among the stone products for domestic use were jars and grindstones for cereals. In the manufacture of jars the external form was shaped with a chisel and the inside hollowed out with rough gouges. Both outside and inside were then finished with a rubbing process — abrasion and sometimes polishing — using gypsum, soapstone, alabaster, lava, consolidated ash, and other materials. The technique of perforation was developed, with repercussions on the manufacture of stone vases, which were then hollowed out by drills with flint bits; abrasives such as sand and emery were still used for finishing. To hollow out globular vessels a series of crescent-shaped flint bits of graduated sizes were used successively, depending on the progress of the operation. To obtain the required pressure several heavy stones were tied to the axis of the drill, a process that is depicted in a relief from a Saqqara tomb (2500 B.C.).

Wood. Almost nothing is known of paleolithic woodworking, which presumably experienced a parallel development to that of working stone. Most likely, the saw was not invented before the Neolithic period. Wood was probably split or cut with hatchets or crude knives. The material was broken in the direction of the grain, then treated across the grain with burin and chisel, and finally carefully smoothed with concave scrapers that were coarse precursors of the plane. Techniques improved with the fabrication of axes and large sharp chisels (end of the Mesolithic and the dawn of the Neolithic period), but only during the Neolithic did the mortise and tenon joint appear in its most primitive form. The tenon was laboriously carved, and the mortise (groove for the tenon) was hollowed out in the wood with a stone chisel. The discovery of copper and its use in toolmaking contributed greatly to the development of carpentry. Chisels, axes, adzes, bow drills with metal points, metal awls (for making small holes), saws (probably used with abrasives for harder woods), and other implements all made woodworking much simpler. The final touches were given by rubbing the wood with pieces of sandstone in different gradations of grain. The use of the lathe during the Paleolithic period cannot be documented with any certainty, although that instrument was undoubtedly employed after the 8th century B.C. However, some eastern Mediterranean wooden objects from the 2d millennium B.C. show surfaces that appear to have been turned with a lathe.

In the making of furniture, such as chests and coffers, there developed the system of gain jointing, of which several different types can be distinguished: tongue joints, miter joints, mortise and tenon joints, dovetail joints (the last in Egypt as early as the 4th dynasty, ca. 2690 B.C., possibly used earlier on ivory), scarf joints held firmly together with cramps (Middle Kingdom,

2400–1580 B.C.), bronze nails (chair in an 18th-dynasty tomb), and hardwood dowels for fixing vertical sections to their base, usually sawed off level with the external surface and always covered with plaster or paint (V, PL. 428).

In Egypt furniture parts were tied together with lashings of linen cord or rawhide; these were applied while damp and shrank as they dried (V, PL. 427). Sometimes thick bands of copper were used, as in sarcophagi. In order to enhance the ornamental character of the piece the dowels that secured the tenons to the mortises were occasionally left exposed (Egypt, New Kingdom; V, PL. 427) or were covered with gold, sometimes with elaborate granulation (furniture of Tutankhamen, 1350 B.C.; IV, PL. 391). To fix a smaller element to a larger section a tapered dowel was frequently made at the back of the object. The dowel was partially split lengthwise, and the two prongs were inserted into two drilled holes with a common orifice. In caskets and coffers wooden panels cut from the same trunk were used. The panels were fixed at the back by means of grooves, or they were drilled (their elements sometimes put together with mortised joints) and mortised to crosspieces. Woods used by the civilizations of Egypt and the Middle East before the spread of Greek and Roman culture were cypress, pine, Lebanon cedar, juniper, yew, and ebony (the most luxurious wood of Egypt). Woods of lesser value were grained and stained, mostly to imitate ebony. Ivory and ebony were closely associated, ivory being used for veneering and for inlay work (see INLAY).

The lathe probably came from the regions of the Middle East that were rich in wood. It spread slowly to the Greek zone and from there to the rest of the ancient world. By the late Hellenistic period the lathe had been introduced into Egypt and other parts of the Roman world. From the Mediterranean regions it then spread to northern Europe.

The instruments used for woodworking in the classical world differ from those of preceding eras in that they were made of iron rather than copper or bronze and were therefore more suitable to their function. A find of Assyrian tools from Thebes justifies the view that toward the 8th century B.C. iron tools were fully developed; almost every iron implement shows an advance over its copper prototype. In Roman times tools for woodworking included the scoop drill and the pump drill. Other novelties were the drawknife (undoubtedly in use before the Romans) and the plane. For cabinetwork the central Mediterranean regions supplied oak, maple, beech, yew, fir, and lime (PL. 455). The Romans of imperial times imported curly maple and bird's-eye maple from Germany and Central Europe, ebony from Corsica and Egypt, and cedar and terebinth from Syria and Africa. Other woods, all turned on a lathe, included ash, elm (for door frames and thresholds), cypress, lime, buckthorn sycamore, and olive. Because of its compact fiber, cedar was preferred for carving images of the deities and for making coffers, ceiling beams, and roofs. In the 3d and 2d centuries B.C. great skill was attained in the use of the lathe; highly elegant and bizarre forms were achieved, sometimes to the detriment of their practical use, as in furniture legs. Few pieces turned on the lathe have survived, but the influence of lathing can be seen in bronze objects.

In classical Roman times the systems of jointing continued to be used; thus dowels as well as tenon, tongue, and dovetail joints are found. Metal nails were left visible as ornamental elements. Various types of animal and vegetable glues were used as adhesives, especially for veneering, as was isinglass. Methods of curving wood by steaming had also been developed.

While woodworking in southern Europe was progressing with the aid of new processes and an extraordinarily rich assortment of tools, northern Europe was still at a neolithic stage; the ax, adze, and knife were used rather than the saw, chisel, and plane of the Roman craftsmen. This northern European technique was inherited in modified form by medieval craftsmanship. Thus the use of the screw in carpentry was forgotten, not to be revived until the 16th century. The plane did not come back into general use until the 13th century. Southern Europe, however, and especially Italy, preserved techniques that were more elaborate and varied (see UTENSILS AND TOOLS).

In the Middle Ages numerous techniques for furniture carving developed in Europe (V, PLS. 435–438). These range from carving in relief or in the round that was executed freehand with a chisel to various forms of low relief and engraving. Sunk carving was executed by removing the ground of the design; in some cases it was stippled with a special awl for greater contrast with the remaining parts. Simple dividing lines were incised on the surface with a gouge; this was often combined with other carving processes.

The semicircular point of the gouge was also used to make parallel grooves for simple but effective ornamentation that became typical of late Gothic wood-paneled rooms in Anglo-Saxon regions (e.g., Cardinal Wolsey's rooms, Hampton Court). Wood was also stamped with a steel punch to obtain such designs as circles or stars; this technique was used in combination with others. The set square and the compass, which were known in Roman times (archaeological finds at Pompeii), were used in the Middle Ages to draw the design for chip carving.

Clay. The most ancient technique for shaping clay jars probably consisted in hollowing out a ball of clay with a wooden stick or the valve of a shell and then exerting even pressure between thumb and index finger to obtain a uniform thickness in the walls (prehistoric examples in England, northwestern Europe, etc.). A less primitive method, used on all continents, was coiling. The clay was rolled into the shape of a long sausage and then coiled in a spiral, building upward; each coil was pressed and cemented by smearing to the one below. The material was usually set on a mat or some other support. In another process, the strip method, separate rings of sausage-shaped clay were used. Examples of both techniques appear in prehistoric England and neolithic northern Eurasia. A different method was used for making the base of the pot. If the base was to be rounded, the material was pressed into a mold—usually a shard sufficiently porous to absorb water from the damp clay. When the clay shrank it came clear of the mold. If the base of the pot was to be flat, the clay was pressed into a flat disk on a stone slab. The disk thus obtained was fused to the sides of the jar by finger pressure that raised the rim of the disk. A method of pottery making with liquid clay poured into molds has also been observed, but there are few examples of this (e.g., Palestine, Iron Age).

Except for the very earliest stages in the history of pottery making, clay jars were made of two or three parts luted together with liquid clay, or slip, applied after the sections had partially dried. In luting the points of contact are wet with a thin solution, and the parts are amalgamated by finger pressure, where possible. This process became necessary for the larger jars which had a tendency to sag under their own weight, or for vases with narrow necks, where the potter could not extend his arm inside the jar to work the lower portions. Pieces were made to join perfectly — a difficult procedure, since each separate part shrank as it dried. The Greek potters sometimes used porous terra-cotta molds that absorbed the water and thus made it easier to detach the molded clay.

Whatever the method, pottery making requires a rotating motion, which is facilitated if the pot is placed on a support. The earliest revolving supports were flat stones or shards. By the late Bronze Age the quality of certain clay objects suggests the use of a potter's wheel. In this technique the clay was placed, or "thrown," on a disk fixed at the top of a rotating vertical spindle; shape was given to the clay through the exploitation of energy produced by rotation (PL. 447). The technique of the potter's wheel included the manual processes of scraping and smoothing that were also used in the ancient technique of molding pots by hand. These processes were particularly useful for the lower part of the pot wall, which throwing tended to make too thick, and for the base, where the pot was separated from the wheel head by means of a string.

Preparation of the clay varies according to whether it is of the primary (not very pliable) or secondary (pliable) type. These clays must be mixed either with substances that considerably reduce the disadvantages due to shrinkage (e.g., fire clay, silica, graphite, coal dust, sawdust) or with substances that increase

he fusibility of the paste and cause vitrification, which makes
he clay watertight (e.g., natural alkaline silicas, carbon, and
me sulphate). In several periods the mixing of clay with water
nd other substances was accomplished by treading the materials
nderfoot, a practice that dates back to the 12th dynasty in
gypt. This ensured an even distribution of water and the
emoval of air bubbles.

Little is known of the techniques used in ancient times for
he purification of clay. In most cases it was probably washed
nd left to settle in a row of pools shaped like tubs, which
ere dug out on a slope. This was the method adopted in
he Middle Ages. The lowest pool contained the finer clay,
hich could subsequently be refined by passing it through
oth. Some primitive peoples (e.g., the Sindhi of India) beat
he clay dry and passed it through a sieve.

Before an object molded in damp clay could be scraped or
arved it had to be dried to a leather-hard stage at an even
emperature; the drying was made uniform over the entire
urface of the pot so as to prevent cracking. The object was
eady for further processing when its water content ranged
om 8 to 15 per cent. The most common system for reducing
orosity was burnishing, or smoothing, which consisted in
bbing with a smooth stone or other hard object to close the
urface pores. There are various systems of smoothing the
lay. A technique still used in China and Japan dates back to
rehistoric times: the surface to be smoothed is beaten with a
ooden paddle or bat while the object is supported from the
side by a convex wooden disk held in one hand. The final
noothing may be done with a wet cloth. Since the effective-
ess of burnishing depends on the fineness of the clay, the pot
ould be given a surface of the finest grain possible and
ipped in or brushed with slip. The most refined part of the
lay used in the molding process should be employed for this
urpose. If clay other than the type used in the molding is
nployed for the slip, its composition must be modified (e.g.,
y mixing with nonplastic substances) so that the contraction
f both pot and slip is identical; otherwise the slip detaches
self. After further drying, when the pot has reached the
hite-hard, or bone-dry, stage, and its uncombined-water con-
nt is 3 per cent, the pot is ready to be fired.

Firing can be done in a kiln or in an open fire with any
ind of fuel. The minimum firing temperatures vary from
50°C to 700°C. In the early days of pottery making the kiln
emperature rarely exceeded 1000°C and was frequently much
wer. The firing temperatures of ancient pottery are not
nown, except where experiments have been carried out on
olated pieces (e.g., fragment from the Iron Age, less than
00°C; pieces from Tell Beit Mirsim, 7th cent. B.C., less than
900°C; Mycenaean pottery, 1030°C). It is sometimes possible
 reconstruct ancient firing methods by observing modern
rimitive practices. One of the more elementary systems is
nat of filling the pots with hot peat ash and surrounding them
ith pieces of burning peat. Another practice is to pile the
ots in a hole in the ground with fuel underneath, in their
idst, and above. The most developed method is similar to
nat of charcoal burning: the fire is damped as far as possible,
nd vegetable material is piled atop the heap of pots and fuel.
iring may last three days. Assuming that a temperature of
50°–800°C can be attained with primitive methods, it is not
venly distributed, and many pots are spoiled for this reason.
he cooling process may require as long as seven days if frac-
ures are to be avoided.

By the Neolithic age a system had evolved for firing in
roper kilns, whose existence is demonstrated by a few rare
estiges (Olynthos, Macedonia). Egypt affords further proof of
his method in a painting from the 3d millennium B.C. Classical
reece inherited this more advanced technique of kiln firing,
hich guaranteed better preservation, heat distribution, and
ery high temperatures; this technique was then passed on to
he Romans, under whom kiln firing became the exclusive
ring practice.

From 700 B.C. onward the development of Greek ceramics
howed styles and shapes that varied according to the center
f production, but the technique remained essentially the same.

Vases were made of well-levigated clay on a wheel (or in a
mold for vases depicting human or animal heads; see below);
after firing, the clay took on a buff or pink hue. The pieces
were finished in black-brown glaze with additional touches of
red, white, or gold (see CERAMICS). Sedimentary or detrital
clay was used because of its high iron content, which often
imparted a red color on firing in ventilated kilns. White residual
clay, a material akin to kaolin (later important in making porcelain), was used by the Athenians only as a slip for white-
ground vases, although sometimes it may have been added to
red clay as an extra ingredient, as it is today. When the clay
had been cleansed through several successive washings and
then wedged, the shaping of the vase on the wheel began.
The smaller vases were made in one piece, the larger ones in
sections united at certain structural points (e.g., neck and body,
body and foot). To hide these junctures little bands of clay
were sometimes applied to the external surface of the vase.
Vases of more complex shape were put together piece by piece
following a drawn model, the measures carefully checked with
ruler and calipers. Once the vase had been thrown it was
detached from the wheel with a knife or string and left to dry
until it reached the leather-hard stage. Then it was again
placed on the wheel and finished with sharp-edged metal tools.
Cups and wide-mouthed vases were carefully smoothed on the
inside; then, when all signs of the work on the wheel had been
removed (probably in the same manner as today, with scrapers
and wet sponges), the handles were added, having been made
manually in a separate operation (III, PL. 135). The internal
surfaces of narrow-mouthed vases were not smoothed.

The use of molds was peculiar to vases in the shape of
human or animal heads (III, PL. 133; VII, PL. 9). For these
a terra-cotta mold in two pieces was used. The clay was pressed
inside each mold, and the two clay halves thus obtained were
joined with slip. The lip of the vase, which was generally
smooth, was separately prepared on the wheel and applied to
the part already made. The figure was then decorated with
paint or engraving. (Decoration on human heads appeared mostly
on the hair bands or on the neck in imitation of a necklace.)

In Hellenistic ceramics relief ornamentation gradually replaced painting. As has been observed, during the 4th century
B.C. in Attica there was a production of vases painted in tempera and decorated with barbotine relief, an ornamentation
obtained by spreading slip clay on the vase with a brush or a
holder and modeling it into lines, festoons, and figures of undefined contours. Most Hellenistic relief ornamentation, however, seems to have arisen in imitation of embossed metal ware
(III, PL. 138; VII, PL. 78). The reliefs were either molded
together with the vase itself or prepared separately and applied
to the dampened surface of the wheel-made vase and then
fixed with slip. This second method was used for the so-called
"Pergamene" ware (2d–1st cent. B.C.), whereas the first was
used in the fabrication of the so-called "Megarian" bowls
(3d cent. B.C.; II, PL. 59; VII, PL. 194). For the manufacture
of "Megarian" bowls two techniques were used: the wheel
and the stamping mold. The mold was shaped like a bowl
with thick walls and was made with a wheel. When it was
leather-hard the inner surface was worked upon with a stamp
so as to obtain an unbroken design. After firing, the mold
was fixed to the wheel, and inside it was placed a piece of clay;
the clay was spun over the inner surface of the mold. In this
way the bowl itself took shape. Pressure was exerted with the
fingers on this new inner surface according to the hollowness
of the form, thus producing reliefs on what was to become the
outer surface of the bowl. The resulting concavities in the new
inner surface were then filled with clay and smoothed out,
again by the wheel. When the bowl was removed from the
mold the last finishing touches were given to the ornamentation; finally the bowl was covered in a glaze that turned black
in a reducing fire.

In Italy the most ancient archaeological finds of ceramic
vessels are always known as impasto vases, in reference to the
coarse reddish material used and the primitive technique of
manual molding (distinguished from the later wheel molding).
Villanovan ceramics are also of the impasto type (III, PL. 124),

but they were sometimes produced partly by hand and partly by wheel. Most of the pieces date back to the 7th century B.C. and show signs of having been first roughly formed with the hands and then finished on the wheel. The clay, rich in iron oxide, was not purified; when fired it took on a blackish-brown or reddish color. Later developments and a perfecting of the impasto technique led, at the height of Etruscan culture, to bucchero ware (III, PL. 136; see ETRUSCO-ITALIC ART). Here the clay underwent a more meticulous purification process and acquired its characteristic shiny black color through various processes, including careful burnishing and firing in a completely reducing atmosphere. Even the oldest of these pieces were thrown with a wheel; frequently they have thin walls and incised or relief ornamentation. A fan-shaped ornamental motif (characteristic of the coastal southern zone from Cerveteri to Vulci) shows signs of having been executed with a little comb held firm at one edge and rotated. One type of relief ornamentation that often appears on the body and the handles of these vases (most frequently in the Chiusi area) was obtained by moving a carved roller over the soft clay so as to achieve a continuous stamped ornamental band. In bucchero ware the most ancient incised ornamentation of an Oriental character is later combined with this stamped ornamentation; however, in the examples from the 6th century B.C., which are of heavier workmanship and more complex form, the ornamentation appears to be in relief rather than engraved (V, PL. 33). The technique is practically the same as that of the "Megarian" ware, except that the complexity of bucchero ware shows that more than one mold was required. The foot was sometimes made with a wheel, sometimes with a mold. When there was no relief ornamentation the entire vase was shaped on the wheel; or the relief ornamentation was made separately and added on, especially when it was partly in the round. In the 3d and 2d centuries B.C. Etruscan pottery, like Greek pottery of the same period, imitates metal products. The relief portions were generally executed separately in molds and then applied to the vase in the leather-hard stage.

The technique of "Megarian" bowls led to a production of Roman pottery called terra sigillata, which began in the 1st century B.C. (III, PL. 138). The center of diffusion was Arezzo, from which the vases take the name Arretine ware (VII, PL. 216; XII, PL. 563; see below); the diffusion area later extended as far as Gaul. The terra sigillata models appear to have been the same as those of Hellenistic metal ware; the finish was executed with small wooden or metal instruments.

After the fall of the western Roman Empire large-scale production of wheel-made ceramics ceased in many parts of the northwestern provinces, where the barbarian traditions of handmade pottery became prevalent. In some regions, however, such as the Rhineland and parts of Gaul and Italy, the methods of the Roman ceramics industry continued to develop without interruption throughout the Middle Ages. In Britain, with the sole exception of Kent, the processes of wheel-made pottery fell into disuse between the 5th and 9th centuries, after which the technique was once again imported from the Rhineland. Most of the technical innovations that mark the late medieval ceramics industry had their first experimental phase in the 11th century under pressure of direct or indirect Eastern influences.

The Islamic world, which in turn was influenced by Chinese production, was of great importance in the ceramics field (III, PLS. 166, 246). In the 9th century T'ang stoneware and porcelain aroused a considerable renewal of interest in the Near East. At first, imitation of the Chinese products was open and blatant, but later original designs appeared. In the 12th century Persia became preeminent among the imitators of Chinese porcelain with a technical invention that concerned not only the outer glaze (as in the 9th century at Baghdad) but also the basic material. The Persian mixture was made of powdered quartz and glass and less than 10 per cent white peptized clay; however, it lacked malleability and ware made from it, although more durable than the tin-glazed ware, did not attain the fineness of the latter. Despite its high artistic quality, the Persian technique spread only to Egypt and scarcely influenced European ceramics.

Another Islamic influence on European production tech niques derived during the 15th century from Chinese blu and-white porcelain (III, PL. 170). The Chinese products th repeatedly influenced medieval European culture by way of th Near East were based on two substances: porcelain and ston ware. Porcelain consisted of kaolin (kao-ling), a fine white cla and petuntse (pai tun-tzŭ), a feldspathic mineral that vitrifi at a very high temperature (1250°–1350°C). The petuntse c mented the magma of the porcelain and thus became an in dispensable substance in porcelain production. Unique peculia ities of porcelain were its whiteness, translucence, and chara teristic metallic resonance. Production probably began in A. 700. Only a century later it reached the markets of the Ne East, especially Baghdad, where the first Islamic imitatio were made.

White stoneware has the same resonance and compactne as porcelain; it has neither its whiteness nor its translucenc Stoneware was obtained in the oldest pieces of the 4th centur by firing, at a very high temperature (ca. 1250°C), a fine plasti clay that became partly vitrified in the process, so that its har surface could be polished with emerylike quartz and hard stone Stoneware was imported into Egypt and Persia and imitate there. Independent of its diffusion in the East, stoneware wa widely distributed in the Rhineland from the Carolingian pe riod, reaching its greatest development in the 16th century From 1684 on, it was also widespread in England. The excelle quality of Carolingian Rhenish stoneware is probably due mo to the exceptional fineness and plasticity of the clay than the firing temperatures, which were undoubtedly low in th rudimentary kilns of the period.

A manual technique has been mentioned for making cla pots in rustic communities of post-Roman Europe. The metho used persisted in some Scandinavian cities up to the very en of the Viking period (9th cent. of our era) and until recentl in certain remote regions of northern Europe, such as norther Ireland. They consisted of the elementary hand-shaping of lump of clay; or the spiral superposition of ring-shaped rolls clay; or a crude process similar to turning, which was execute by revolving a tray manually. A 13th-century manuscript scen depicts a potter turning a wheel by pushing it with a stic this method obviously left only one hand free for shaping th vase. In the same period the use of the potter's wheel, whic had continued in certain highly developed provinces, once mo began to spread; various illustrated codices from the 13th t the 16th century contain pictures of kick wheels. In Englan there was no continuous tradition of the wheel after the disin tegration of the western Roman Empire. Reintroduced int East Anglia from the Rhineland about the 9th century, it sprea to the whole of Britain only in the 13th century. The mediev European wheel was used for vessels of all sizes. Rims vessels were usually reinforced through thicker modeling, whic was always obtained with a wheel. Complex vessels with ve narrow necks or pedestal bases were sometimes made in separat sections. After removal from the wheel these were luted t the main body of the vase while still damp; or the variou "biscuit" sections (i.e., pieces after a first firing) were joine together by a layer of glaze that melted in the second fir ing (Piccolpasso, 1934; PLS. 446, 447). Shallow vessels l platters and large bowls were molded by placing the clay o a convex mold situated on the wheel head. The mold gav its shape to the inside of the platter. For removing superfluou clay or for retouching while the piece was still on the whee templates or similar instruments were sometimes used. Th same system was employed in shaping the ring at the base dishes or in accentuating the narrow parts in order to increas the elegance of the shape. Other superficial finishing touche once the clay had reached the leather-hard stage, were com pleted on the wheel and not always with a mold; many profil (e.g., around the mouth of the vase) that at first sight appea to have been executed with instruments were in fact made b hand on a fast wheel.

The handles were generally made from thin strips of clay sometimes two or three twisted strips. The ornamental use animal figures on the handles betrays imitation of metal prod cts. (These flagons were typically Italian and were called *ronzo antico*.) Frequently the handles were attached to the body by luting and finger pressure while the material was still malleable. Even the finger mark was sometimes accentuated or ornamental purposes. The lips were formed by a simple pressure of the thumb and index finger on the rim, although the big "parrot-beak" spouts of French medieval pitchers were probably made separately and added to the vase, as were the handle and the rings at the base. Tubular spouts were made by perforating the vessel from the outside with a stick or from the inside with a finger and wrapping the projection with a layer of clay. The joins were obtained by pressing against the punctures. Mounting the handles and spouts was generally done before the vessel was removed from the wheel to avoid deformation under finger pressure. The bases, in imitation of metal products, were sometimes elaborately articulated, with feet shaped like feline paws. In Germany, especially in the stoneware production of the Rhenish ateliers, bases were graced with massive frills obtained by pinching and modeling a thick ridge of clay deliberately left at the bottom of the vessel.

Other ornamental motifs could be obtained in clay during the turning process, especially rim molding, body rilling, and tooled grooves. After the turning process was ended, and while the vessel was still on the wheel, which was rotated slowly, horizontal or vertical strips of pinched clay could be applied, as well as an impressed decoration of motifs obtained with cogged wheels, rouletting, comb marking, and scoring. After the vessel was removed from the wheel, further decoration could be applied by the addition of ornamental feet or by thumb pressure on the rim of the base. Other stamping methods included punches and little molds made of wood, bone, stone, or terra cotta (e.g., small face masks, rosettes). Decorative embellishment of the vessel after its removal from the wheel was widely practiced in Italy and France during the Middle Ages. In the 13th century this procedure spread to the Anglo-Saxon area, but it declined after the 14th century.

In Rome and in the Moslem world vessels were also made partly or entirely in molds. An original ornamental process appeared in 12th-century Persia, Mesopotamia, and Egypt, where ornamental interlacing was carved on the vessel while it was still in its leather-hard state. The drying process required special care; frequently the pieces were dried on shelves in sheds. Sometimes drying was obtained by means of special ovens. In western Europe pottery kilns were made on the same principle as those used in the Roman world, apart from a few experimental varieties. In northern Europe they were rather small, round or oval, and as a rule either horizontal or vertical. In Italy, by the end of the Middle Ages, rectangular brick kilns were used for the firing of more refined pottery. For peasant pottery, however, primitive methods such as open fires continued in use. Some medieval kilns were built so as to combine the functions of both the horizontal and the vertical type. To achieve more even heating the pots inside the kiln were separated by clay rings and piled upon each other or placed in saggers, which is still done today for firing fine porcelain.

One of the fundamental problems of pottery making in ancient times was the regulation of the firing temperature. As has been stated, the earlier processes of firing in kilns brought the object to a temperature of about 700°–800°C, while Roman terra sigillata was fired at much higher temperatures (ca. 1050–150°C). The highest temperatures attained were probably those of Rhenish stoneware production. In the areas of medieval western Europe where the kiln and the classical methods of firing continued, the temperatures used were those attained in Roman times, since both kilns and fuel (wood) were of the same type. During the actual firing a critical moment occurs when the temperature rises from 350°C to 500°C. At this point all the water has evaporated and the organic matter has burned. The gases released can easily damage the clay if generated too rapidly. Therefore, at 380°C attempts are made to slow down the temperature rise. Between 570°C and 600°C another process, the expansion of the silica, endangers the results of the firing. Above 600°C the temperature can be allowed to rise rapidly so

long as the kiln does not contain lead-glazed ware, in which holes can easily form.

The earliest potters were unable to watch, and therefore control, the inside of the kiln during the firing process. Even in the Middle Ages there are few indications that they had means of controlling the firing (as with the modern Seger cones). The Roman potters of Cologne, however, used shards during firing to verify the state of their lead-containing glazes.

Cooling was another extremely delicate process because of the shrinkage of silica at 573°C and the great likelihood of cracks. Once the maximum temperature was reached, the fire was damped down and the kiln sealed, allowing the pottery to cool gradually in a reducing atmosphere. This slow cooling could take over 24 hours and was essential to a satisfactory result. The process was particularly widespread during the Middle Ages. Throughout subsequent processes of drying and firing, clay shrinkage may be calculated at about $1/8$ to $1/6$ of the linear dimensions. See also CERAMICS for further discussion of ceramic techniques, various pastes, and porcelain techniques.

Metal. The earliest processing of native metals was executed by cutting, bending, and hammering with a stone hammer on a stone anvil. These techniques did not change when the metals were eventually extracted from the ore. An important discovery made by the first smiths was that metal hardens under continual hammering but can be softened and rendered less brittle by heat, without changing the hammered-in shape. This hammering and heating process is known as annealing. The technique of casting metal in a mold probably dates back to the El-'Ubaid–Uruk period (Mesopotamia, ca. 3500 B.C.). During the smelting process the ore was generally placed in crucibles of refractory clay or of mixed sand and clay in order to prevent the metal from coming into contact with the fuel.

Iron was already known in the ancient world (the Near East) by the 3d millennium, but because of its poor ductility it was rarely used at that time in artistic production. One of the regions in which the artistic working of iron first developed, at the end of the 2d millennium, was probably northeastern Persia. Meteoric iron was used; but it could not be processed in large quantities like bronze or copper, nor were there any high-temperature furnaces at that time. The earliest preserved objects were apparently executed with the same techniques utilized for stone.

Copper, which is fairly ductile, was hardened by hammering while the metal was cold. Many objects were apparently produced by alternating cycles of hammering and annealing, with a final hammering to obtain the required hardness. With the development of the casting technique, for which pure copper is inadequate, bronze came into prominence as the most widespread and characteristic copper alloy. It became preferable for the casting of objects in the round (PL. 443). From the first, bronze was an alloy of copper and tin, to which the occasional addition of other metals lent a particular color and consistency. The amount of tin usually varied from the 18 per cent of Pliny's *aes statuarium* (alloyed with 64 per cent copper and 18 per cent lead) to the minimum percentage of the Greek bronzes (e.g., horses of S. Marco, Venice, 4th–3d cent. B.C.: 3 per cent tin, ca. 91 per cent copper). For the Greeks there was no philological difference between copper and bronze, both of which went under the name of χαλκός. In Roman times six different mixtures of copper and tin were known: *aes statuarium, aes campanum, aes ollarium, aes Corinthium, aes deliacum,* and *aes aegineticum.*

In the oldest bronzes two basic casting techniques can be distinguished: open-mold casting, used for flat objects such as spearheads and only rarely for art objects, and closed-mold casting. The closed mold was composed of at least two corresponding parts to prevent if from breaking when the object was extracted. As technique progressed, molds in three or four parts were made. After casting, the bronze was carefully chased to remove roughness and unwanted marks left by the mold.

The simpler and more usual types of molds were made of clay that was thoroughly heated before casting; less frequently they were made of stone or metal. These were followed by molds with a core, usually made of baked clay, for producing hollow objects. The core was fixed to the base of the mold when the shape of the object permitted it, or it was kept equidistant from all sides of the mold by large spikes. These spikes were fixed to the core and incorporated in the casting. They were then cleansed with a chisel on the surface of the object. Sometimes, however, their presence is betrayed in the final product by a difference in the color of the metal. Porous clay was used for the mold so as to release air expanded by the heat of the molten metal being cast; the core was also provided with an air escape.

During the Shang period in China (see CHINESE ART) a bronze vessel of the *tsun* (wine vessel) type was made by the following procedure: a lump of clay was mixed with sand, powdered brick, and sawdust or bone dust to render the clay porous on firing. This mixture was the material for the core, and its shape corresponded to the concavity required in the vessel. Once the core was dry it was spread with a layer of wax of the thickness to be given the bronze. Projecting parts of the ornamentation were added in the wax itself, while the rest of the ornamentation was modeled. The mold, formed by applying successive coatings of clay to the oiled wax, was constructed in tiers, each consisting of several sections held together by wedge-shaped mortises. The mold parts were removed when they were sufficiently dry, and the wax was detached from the core. Any internal defects in the shape of the vessel could thus be easily rectified — a great advantage of piece molding. The parts, except for the wax, were then put together again around the core, and a thick layer of coarse molding material was spread over the entire mold except for the air vents and the channel to receive molten metal; this final layer kept all the parts together. The mold was left to dry slowly and then baked to the hardness of terra cotta; before it was cold the metal was poured into it. Sometimes (as in the case of Chinese caskets) the mold was directly shaped in clay over the original model and then removed, probably in separate parts that were later covered with wax before the core was made inside.

The cire-perdue, or lost-wax, process consists in casting the metal by means of a one-piece mold, from which the wax of the model is removed through melting. This technique was used in ancient times for work of the most delicate sort and, with slight variations, has remained in use to the present day. If the object to be cast is small the wax form can be solid; otherwise a core is required. The core may be prepared first; or the work may proceed from the outside in, beginning with the mold. In the former procedure, a wax model of the thickness and shape required of the final bronze object is constructed around the core. The mold is then constructed. In the latter procedure a complete one-piece mold is made in plaster or some flexible material (e.g., gelatin) into which is painted or poured a layer of wax of the thickness to be given the metal. Inside this, the core is then formed of clay and powdered brick (or other material) and provided with the necessary vents. When the core has solidified, the outer, temporary, mold is removed; a complete system of runners and vents is then constructed in wax rods, all in more or less the same direction, since each piece of melting wax must drain out of the mold. Once the runners and vents have been completed, a thin layer of clay is painted over the whole; successive layers are added, consisting of clay mixed with powdered brick (or other materials) to make the clay porous, until the mold is sufficiently thick. When necessary the mold is circled with wire. The external mold thus obtained is of one single piece and is placed in the oven for baking in such a position that the wax may escape. The metal is then cast, the mold is broken off, the runners and vents are cut away (these now cast in metal), and the rough surfaces are retouched with a chisel (chased). This system made it possible to avoid the markings left by the piece-molding process.

During the 3d millennium the technique of soldering developed. This gradually replaced the more rudimentary system of sewing thin plates of metal together with metallic wire or that of nailing and hammering them together. The oldest known gold or silver alloy for soldering was used in jewelry work in Ur about 2500 B.C. A good example of silver soldering is the Entemena vase from Telloh, Iraq (ca. 2800 B.C.; I, PL. 504). This technique, called hard-soldering, requires a temperature of 550°-900°C for the smelting of the alloy (which must always have a melting point lower than that of the metal to be joined) and the use of a flux, generally borax, to prevent oxidation of the metal surfaces to be soldered. Soft-soldering is used for joining on objects of lead or tin and requires a minimum temperature of 183°C with a flux of zinc chloride.

Another system, called "sweating," consists in covering the parts to be soldered with an appropriate alloy and raising the temperature of these areas so that the alloy melts. In "burning together," metal parts are joined without the use of an alloy, and a new piece is cast onto the object. The parts are made to fit tightly together, and a clay mold is formed over them, leaving a small area for the cast metal around the parts to be joined. The mold is given a funnel-shaped pour for the introduction of the metal and an outlet for the overflow. When the molten metal is poured in, its heat partially melts the two sections to be joined. Most of the metal runs out through the overflow outlet, but enough remains to make the joint strong. Superfluous metal is then removed.

Other alloys widely used in artistic production are pewter and brass. Pewter is composed of tin, lead, and antimony or copper; it was frequently used in the Middle Ages for liturgical or domestic furnishings. Brass, being comparatively nonmalleable and not easily corroded, was particularly useful for making scientific instruments (XII, PLS. 457-459). (For further discussion of the above-mentioned techniques in metal, see METALWORK.)

Glass. If alkalis (or alkaline salts), lime, and sand (silica) are melted together, there results a substance that is rigid and transparent but not crystalline. This is glass, upon analysis found to be a mixture of alkaline silicates (soda or potash) and alkaline earths (almost invariably lime oxide with alumina and magnesium oxide). Traces of barium monoxide sometimes appear among the alkaline-earth portions of glass. Glass first appeared about 4000 B.C. as a glaze for clay, for small stone objects, and for powdered quartz that was kneaded and baked (Egyptian faïence). As a molding material of independent conformation it was used about 2500 B.C. in Egypt and Mesopotamia for small freestanding objects. In these early applications, however, it is usually more accurate to speak of "frit" rather than "glass," the former term referring to partly fused but still unvitrified materials.

Glass is particularly sensitive to temperature changes. If cooled slowly, the material gradually becomes more viscous and then solidifies, remaining clear if it is composed of pure materials. But if glass is cooled rapidly, the silicates crystallize and the mixture becomes opaque and extremely brittle; this transformation is generally called devitrification. The ideal procedure would be a slow raising of the temperature in the crucibles and a slow cooling process during which the actual shaping operations can be carried out.

There is no established melting point. Soda glass gradually becomes similar to a fluid at about 1000° C, a temperature attainable with an ordinary charcoal fire. Potash glass, which is easily fusible, was largely produced in the West during the Middle Ages. Scrap glass was also added to the mixture of raw materials. Until the middle of the 19th century the production of glass involved two processes: (1) the calcination, or fritting, of the raw materials in a separate furnace or in a part of the melting furnace where the temperature is lower, thus producing the initial stages of reaction and eliminating some of the gases; (2) the actual melting, probably achieved at lower temperatures than those in use today. In Egypt during the 18th dynasty (ca. 1500-1300 B.C.) the temperature did not reach 1100° C and was therefore insufficient to expel the gas bubbles that cause so many old pieces of glass to be opalescent or opaque.

In ancient times the mixture of sodium and calcium silicate

which glass was composed was colored with small quantities metallic oxides. Cupric oxide and sometimes iron were added to produce light blue. Cobalt and perhaps a higher percentage of cupric oxide were added for a deeper blue; cobalt, used from the 18th dynasty on in Egypt and the Near East, was never found in ancient Western glass. Ferrous iron lent bottle-green color. Ferric iron produced transparent amber, and manganese oxide was added for purple or amethyst. A suspension of cuprous oxide produced a sealing-wax red; a high lead content brings this chemical mixture close to the red enamel on metalwork produced by the Celts and Romans and on work produced later in medieval Europe. White was obtained by a suspension of tin oxide or tiny bubbles of air; this appears occasionally in Egypt beginning with the 18th dynasty. Antimony compounds made an opaque yellow, and large quantities of iron or a mixture of copper and manganese produced black (in Egypt). Frequently the quality of the sand itself gave the glass a greenish color tending toward brown; although this was sometimes remedied by adding manganese dioxide (pyrolusite) to oxidize the iron and neutralize the color with its own slightly purple hue, it is doubtful that such an expedient was widely used in ancient times. Much ancient colorless glass (especially that of Alexandria) derived from the use of fine silver sands containing no iron.

The use of glass for receptacles was unknown to the Egyptians before 1500 B.C. The production of glass of many types and colors at such sites as Tell el'Amarna (VI, PL. 217) and Lisht dates from the middle of the 14th century B.C. At almost the same time glass receptacles spread in Mesopotamia. (Other evidence of this diffusion is found in Syria, Palestine, and Cyprus.) The typological and chronological parallelism in this diffusion makes it impossible to establish the place of origin of the most ancient pieces. Various methods of production were followed. The smaller and more simple objects were formed in clay molds as was contemporaneous Egyptian faïence. A frequently used technique was that of carving and grinding the cold glass as though it were stone. It is certain that designs on seals were made in this manner; probably there was a preliminary molding process, with the design incised and finished by a process similar to that adopted for jasper or porphyry. Simple glass receptacles were made by pressing the viscous glass into a clay mold or, possibly, by spreading it on a mold turned upside down. The basic procedure for making receptacles consisted in immersing a sand core wrapped in a cloth bag into a crucible of viscous glass-metal and subsequent modeling by rotation on a flat stone slab, or marver. The layer of glass covering the cloth and sand mold gradually cooled through contact with the stone, making it possible to obtain an even distribution of the material by rotation. Other ornamentation was then added to hide the points most difficult to mold, such as the base and the neck. This fundamental procedure remained in use so long that it became the exclusive method of receptacle production. Ornamentation usually consisted of plain or twisted glass threads or blobs of glass, occasionally differing in color from the body of the vase. Other ornamentation was obtained with a comb, possibly metal, with which the threads could be dented, thus giving the decoration a segmented or undulated appearance (IV, PL. 392). Sometimes the opaque glass added for ornamentation was marvered, producing a design of different color and transparency on the body of the vase. Chemical analysis of such glass reveals the presence of quartz sand, calcium carbonate (involuntarily included in the composition, since it was sometimes contained in sand), and either native sodium sesquicarbonate (natron) or plant ash.

In Egypt, glass was frequently used to imitate various stones such as lapis lazuli and red jasper. The cold-cut technique was practiced along with inlay technique and the framing of glass in metal as in the cloisonné technique. After the brilliant period at the end of the 2d millennium the history of glass becomes obscure. Few fragments other than necklace beads can be dated between 1100 B.C. and 750 B.C. Possibly the production of glass receptacles came to a complete halt, judging by the lack of archaeological evidence. By the 8th and 7th centuries B.C. the craft acquired renewed vigor, although its forms and centers of production were different. Generally they were Asiatic and were characterized by various features including the avoidance of color. These objects continued to be produced after the 7th century B.C.

At this time production of new forms for receptacles with sand cores began. It continued, with few changes in shape and ornamentation, until the end of the Hellenistic period. The mold technique also developed new methods exploiting the combination of glass of different colors. Alexandrian craftsmen and others experimented with processes for making mold-pressed ware with thin canes or rods of colored glass put together in different ways according to the ornamental intention. This method combines the mold and cold-carving techniques. Once the molding was finished and the glass had cooled, the receptacle was submitted to the necessary finishing touches such as wheel grinding and polishing, which revealed the colored pattern of the glass rods used in making the decoration; the effect was comparable to that of mosaics (particularly those which imitated colored mats) or multicolored woven cloth. Monochrome glass, also mold-pressed, was either rotary-polished, if it was plain, or fire-polished (i.e., reheated). The latter process was indispensable to the finishing of ribbed receptacles.

Blowing was the last fundamental glassmaking technique to be discovered, and its advent caused a decline of the ancient processes. The finishing treatment on cold glass, however, was retained — a procedure derived from the ancient system of cold cutting (earliest piece from Nimrud, ca. 720 B.C.). Blowing first appeared at the beginning of the 1st century B.C. in the Syrian centers, where glass was blown into a negative mold. The oldest known pieces made in Sidon and exported to Italy were created in this way. Developing simultaneously with mold blowing was the technique of free blowing, with results indicating great skill and the highest creative level. When the Eastern craftsmen later moved to Italy, local Roman production of blown glass began. A definite distinction was made in Roman times between the glass blowers (vitrarii: glassmakers) and the carvers and grinders (diatretarii). Under the Empire, glass production spread beyond the Alps to the Rhineland, Belgium, Britain, and the Rhone and Saône valleys. Spanish glass developed independently, preceding Roman production owing to the intense Syrian maritime traffic that particularly influenced the Iberian cultural area. During the entire period of Roman domination in the Mediterranean, frequent contacts with the Levant and the imigration of Eastern craftsmen to the West resulted in technical uniformity throughout the many local centers of glass-receptacle production. From this time on, no substantial modifications occurred in glassmaking techniques, other than the modern introduction of complex machinery for the mass production of objects for industrial use, such as bottles or light bulbs.

In contemporary artistic production glass blowing follows processes similar to those used by the ancient glassmakers in the East and West from Roman to medieval times. The viscous mass of sand and other materials, fused in refractory clay pans, is brought to a temperature of about 1200°C. Into this the craftsman introduces the extremity of his blowpipe (today usually a long iron tube) and draws upon the molten matter several times until the amount of glass required for the object is gathered at the bottom of his pipe. This "gather," or parison, is blown to the desired size and then rolled on a plane for a first shaping of the object. Blowing continues while the object is repeatedly twirled on the plane. Then the glass is heated again and the blowing repeated until the required size is attained. At this point the object is pressed, pinched with tweezers, and cut with special clippers, all of which provide the plastic and decorative characteristics that determine the esthetic nature of the final product. After this it is placed in a temperate oven for gradual cooling from 700°C down to air temperature.

After the end of Roman domination glass production continued in the Near East (VI, PL. 223) as well as in central and northern Europe (VI, PL. 222) — in Belgium and in Italy and the Rhineland, where, however, large-scale production of potash glass before the 9th century cannot be proven on the basis of analyses. Except for very brief interruptions, Italy passed from the manufactures of Aquileia in the late Empire to the Venetian glass of the 13th century, a production stimulated by contact with Eastern cultures during the Crusades. Norman production was also active in Italy during the Middle Ages, establishing important industries in Genoese territory. The two branches of Italian glassmaking, Venetian and Norman, mark the beginning of the modern glass industry in Europe in the 15th century (VI, PL. 228). Certain local products of northern Europe such as English crystal glass also derived from Italian processes.

In the East the Roman-Egyptian and Mesopotamian forms underwent innovations, such as faceting and relief work, although the Syrian blue-green blown glass continued to be produced until the 7th and 8th centuries of our era. By the 9th century many regions in the Near East began to produce colorless crystal glass decorated with engraving. In the 13th and 14th centuries Syria again came to the fore with an industry that employed remarkably refined processes, including enamel painting on colored or colorless glass (VI, PL. 227).

Only a few details are available concerning instruments used in glassmaking from ancient times to the Middle Ages. Apparently the furnaces were in three stories: fuel chamber, pot chamber, and annealing oven. The blowpipe was a thin iron rod, or pontil, that was applied hot to the partly formed glass object already on the stone marver. Other instruments employed were tweezers, scissors, various types of shears, and the reamer used for tooling. Some Roman molds are still extant, as well as various Arab clay molds dating from the Middle Ages; later, iron and copper molds became customary.

The decoration of glass was usually an essential part of its actual manufacturing — a secondary process carried out either when the glass was hot or when it had completely cooled. Casing, or layering, was prevalent in the Italian peninsula and in Mediterranean Egypt during the early Roman period. It was a difficult process, in which one or more glass layers were superimposed on the gather in such a way that the walls fitted together perfectly, without air bubbles or partial melting of one layer into another. In the most elaborate pieces the external layer was engraved like a cameo until it acquired the color of the layer underneath, which then became the ground for a design standing out in bas-relief — as, for example, in the Portland vase, with a mythological scene in white opaque glass on a blue ground (Br. Mus.; see also VI, PL. 219, X, PL. 276).

The technique of mosaic glass includes the entire series of processes employed for obtaining polychrome glass with designs, ranging from the molding and slicing of sections of fused glass rods or canes of various colors (resulting in tiny, generally floral, ornamental sections, or millefiori) to the fusion of sections of rods bound with spiral filaments forming a lacelike polychrome design. Other processes mix two or more pieces of colored glass to obtain a speckled or marblelike effect (VII, PL. 327). There is also a large category of mosaic glass obtained through the partial fusion and subsequent grinding of stripes or squares of different colors into a design that recalls a patchwork quilt; pieces of gilt glass were sometimes included. This last process was already in use for inlay work in Mesopotamia and Egypt in the 2d millennium B.C. and was widely used in Italy and Alexandria in the production of mosaic glass between 25 B.C. and A.D. 100.

In Roman and pre-Roman glassmaking almost all three-dimensional ornamental motifs were obtained by means of the wheel and by carving, even when the object had already been fashioned in a mold. For vessels in naturalistic shapes (e.g., animals, heads) blowing into a negative mold was employed, and the design was frequently finished by carving. Another method was the use of a simple mold with a corrugated pattern, the vessel receiving its definitive shape in a further blowing and rotating process; in this process the corrugations might be changed to twisted undulations. A variant of this procedure consists in first blowing into a patterned mold and then into a plain mold, thus obtaining a relief effect from both the inside and the outside of the vessel ("optic" blowing).

The first manifestation of an ornamentation known as "trailing" is found in Egypt on glass formed around a sand core (18th dynasty). The objects were decorated with ribbonlike strips of molten glass, some combed, that were trailed along the surface. The same technique is found on Syrian and Rhenish products (so-called "snake-thread" ware; Cologne, ca. A.D. 200) on the glass of the Franks and Merovingians, and on ancient Arabian glass. The most widespread applied decoration, although the most difficult, consisted of even and regular threads which were added while the vase was rotated at the extremity of the blowpipe. Blobs of glass, or prunts, were added by dropping them on the surface of the object, which was then heated once more until the drop expanded and partially fused into the wall of the vessel The color of the blob was different from that of the wall. In other instances the blobs were applied while viscous to the surface of the vase and left in relief, sometimes pinched like nipples. Sometimes they were marvered flush with the surface, producing an effect similar to inlay when the drops were of different color from the vessel wall.

Tooling was done with tweezers and reamers which were used to fashion parts of the vessel such as the rim, neck, and base. Reamers produced vertical ribbing and indentation, pinched nipples, and short ribbings.

Hollow cutting, relief cutting, and faceting are performed on the wheel, whose rotating motion is provided by a special lathe. Today the wheel is usually made of copper and spread with powdered carbide of silicate mixed with water. These techniques, in all periods (except for a brief interval in the West between the end of the Roman Empire and the late Middle Ages), have been an immediate and safe method of ornamentation in the finishing of glass objects. The graving technique is the same as drypoint or engraving on copper, and the results are often of the highest quality. Since ancient times it has been executed with sharp flint points or stones — more recently with diamond points. Graving is well adapted to the specific qualities of glass. (For more detailed information on glass techniques, see GLASS.)

Leather and hide. The processing of animal skins to make leather dates back to paleolithic times. Probably the first treatment to which skins were subjected was softening with grease or other substances. A step forward came with the removal of the hair, as evidenced by paleolithic skin scrapers made of bone. Egypt provides the earliest examples of artificially colored leather. Vegetable dyes were generally used: indigo for blue, pomegranate peel for yellow, brazilwood for brown, and an unidentified plant substance for green. Other dyeing materials used were archil or kermes, with alum as a mordant, as well as tannin with iron sulphate.

The molding of untreated hide (rawhide) to make vessels probably preceded discovery of the properties of fired clay. The system of molding damp rawhide or intestinal membrane over a core and then hardening them through drying is still used among the Tuaregs of the Sahara and certain tribes of the Sudan, Ethiopia, and northern India. These vessels are often decorated with color.

Another method of making skin vessels was to model leather that had been tanned with plant substances and then softened by wetting in a mold or on a core of hardened clay, wood, or damp sand. The vessel was then dried. If it was plunged momentarily into boiling water the relief became more resistant — a property of leather probably known in Mesolithic times. The technique was widely practiced in the Middle Ages and is still in use; the term *cuir bouilli* was, in fact, common by the 14th century.

A further method of ornamentation was the use of very hot metal instruments that darkened the leather at the point of contact. In the Middle Ages elaborately complex ornamentation was achieved by combining modeling with incising, engraving, and stamping with hot punches. Frequently molding was accomplished by pressing the damp leather on a wooden shape or by running a fluted wooden pommel over it for a simple decoration of parallel lines. The developing taste for bound books gave a strong impulse to the techniques of leather stamp g with carved metal punches (VII, PL. 331). Gold tooling, which was generally used for this purpose (VII, PL. 338), was applied by impressing gold leaf into the leather with a hot carved iron punch. The process originated in the East and developed markedly in Italy during the Quattrocento; through Venice it reached England in the reign of Henry VIII, and from the 16th century on it was widely used for the ornamentation of objects in common use (e.g., chairs, hangings). In the gold-tooling process used today the hide or leather surface to be decorated is smeared with egg white (occasionally mixed with vinegar, depending on the type of leather) and dried with a wad soaked in oil. Then the gold leaf is applied. The work is continued with a punch. Bits of gilt left over from the design made by the punch are removed with a cloth or sponge soaked in a solvent. Sometimes the punchwork is done before gilding, which is then applied within the prepared design.

In the 10th century of our era Theophilus described a process for gilding panels, wall hangings, and bookbindings that remained unchanged for many centuries. Extremely thin layers of silver or tin were used rather than gold leaf; these were fastened to the leather with egg white or shellac. Several coats of transparent yellow varnish were then applied, through which the metal acquired the color and richness of gold.

Relief-carved terrestrial and celestial wooden globes were covered with chamois that was rubbed with instruments of bone or smooth wood. Where the leather was pressed between the instrument and the carved reliefs, the leather surface was crushed; the design appearing behind these bruises stood out in a shiny brown against the more opaque biscuit-colored ground. In France, Flanders, Spain, and Holland, relief work was sometimes executed with large carved pieces of wood. This process allowed gilding and always preceded painting or varnishing. A superficial finishing in paint was a distinctive characteristic of leather mural panels. The relief design was painted partly in opaque colors and partly in colored varnish. High-relief panels were also made by a process resembling the *cuir bouilli* technique.

PREPARATION AND TREATMENT OF SURFACES. *Stone*. Marble without special surface preparation presents an opaque face, from which it is impossible to detect natural characteristics such as color, grain, and veining. Thus polishing processes on this stone have been constantly employed since the most ancient times (PLS. 435, 436). These processes range from the most primitive systems of "beating up" (rubbing two coarse slabs together) to the mechanical techniques of the modern marble industry.

Marble can be categorized as either white or colored. White marble is divided into the following types: (1) Carrara marble, which can be further subdivided into ordinary bluish clear-white marble and statuary marble of saccharoidal structure with a clear-white ground tending to yellow; (2) Parian marble (Greek; hard), which is very translucent, snow white and slightly bluish in color, frequently used in sculpture; (3) Pentelic marble (Greek; fine), which is yellowish white with flecks of mica that provide a brownish-gold patina when decomposed; it is saccharoidal in structure with a grain of varying size; and (4) Proconnesian marble, which is pure white with black veining.

Distinguished among the colored marbles (antique) are (1) cipolin (from Carystus), a greenish white or light greenish gray tending to yellow, with long undulating veins of mica; (2) Hymettian marble, in gray or bluish gray, with mica; (3) African marble (from Chios), which is spotted in many colors (e.g., dark red, green), showing gray cement and dark sections; (4) rosso antico (from Laconia), in dark red; (5) Tenasio (from Laconia), in dense black; (6) Numidian, in antique yellow, sometimes with red veining; (7) brocatel marble (from Spain), in gold yellow with spots of dark yellow or violet; and (8) *fior di pesco* (*marmor Molossium*, from Epirus), a peach-blossom color with darker gradations tending toward violet or, when lighter, to white.

Other kinds of marble include Medici breccia (heterogeneous, orange color with dark-violet cement); Portor (black with golden-yellow veins and knots; from Liguria); Portasanta (white and pink spots with dark-gray veins; in ancient times known as Cario); and Siena yellow (mixed yellows, or yellow with veinings, and a fine and compact grain).

Historically, these marbles have been put to different uses. Most of the colored marbles were employed in ornamental inlay work for architectural structures as well as in interior decoration and the enrichment of furnishings (II, PL. 313; VIII, PLS. 81, 82, 84). From historically documented periods there remain records of a technique in which colored marble was used in different ways for decorative work (e.g., *opus sectile*; VIII, PLS. 79,81); in architecture this work had the same function as frescoes. Colored marble was widely used, especially in Roman times, in various inlay techniques for the decoration of floors and walls. The industry of the Roman crustae (prepared inlay pieces) flourished for many centuries and declined only with the medieval derivatives of mosaics and the geometric porphyry paving known as *opus alexandrinum*. White marbles were widely used — the more common types in architecture (capitals, architraves, cornices, etc.) and the more desirable types, the so-called "statuary marbles" (Parian, Carrara, etc.), in sculpture. Marble has an extremely wide range of characteristics, based mainly on the finished aspect of the material, which can be polished, shined, and rendered translucent (see below).

Porphyry is a very compact and hard granitic stone composed of a great quantity of quartz crystals and colored elements, mostly green or red. In ancient times the types of porphyry most in use were red (dark red speckled with white) and green (diabase-porphyrite). Porphyry was widely used in Egyptian sculpture in the late-antique period and occasionally in minor sculpture of the late Renaissance and in baroque art (e.g., busts, medallions; IX, PL. 56; XII, PL. 488).

Alabaster (calcareous or Oriental) is a translucent variety of limestone, either fibrous in structure or showing concentric sections. It enjoyed long and constant use, from Egyptian facing and vases to Cycladic figurines, Cretan-Mycenaean vases, Phoenician balsam jars, Hellenistic statuettes, Etruscan sarcophagi, ornamental garden sculpture in Roman times, Renaissance inlay work, and contemporary craftsmanship (Volterra).

Other stones occasionally used in sculpture or architectural ornamentation were travertine (*lapis Tiburtinus*; VII, PL. 209), which is characteristic of the ornamental sculpture of 17th-century Roman churches, and peperino, a special kind of friable stone tuff preferred in late Renaissance garden sculpture for its dark-green color and tendency to deteriorate; because of these characteristics peperino readily harmonized with the surrounding trees and the idealized landscape of "ruins" that was one of the more ostentatious tendencies of mannerism (VIII, PL. 430). Travertine and peperino were given no superficial treatment before polishing, unlike marble and alabaster, whose surface holes were stopped up with cement.

Polish was obtained by the earlier process of simple abrasion, plus the use of grindstones and abrasives of increasingly fine grain, ranging from pumice to tin oxide. The ashes of kid bones were also used in the 18th century. Today mechanical polishers with sheet lead or oxalic acid produce a mirrorlike luster.

Wood. Wood surfaces are prepared or embellished by the following processes: facing, painting in oils or tempera, veneering, inlay work, and polishing (see INLAY; PAINTING). Polishing may be done with lacquer, shellac, alcohol, or wax (especially in the case of Renaissance walnut). To accentuate the color of the wood, water-soluble mordants are used before the actual polishing, which is done when the mordant is dry. The most ancient examples of wood surfaces treated with paint show that the same technique was used for sculpture and in the commercial production of furnishings; this technique was widely practiced in Egypt from the 5th dynasty on. In all cases the wood was primed with a thin layer of gypsum or whiting (calcium carbonate); if only one color was used, however, the color was applied directly to the wood (in Egypt).

Later, a type of glue appeared in this preparation, giving the gypsum layer greater compactness and resistance. The technique was customary in the preparation of painted wooden sarcophagi, in which brilliant pigments similar in appearance to enamel were sometimes applied directly to the wooden surface (sarcophagus of Djehuty-nekht; IV, PL. 351). Glue was never widely used, however, except in veneering. The Egyptians were particularly skilled in this technique, veneering ordinary wood with more precious wood; the system was that of ordinary inlay work, which was applied with an adhesive. Woods of various and contrasting colors were chosen, such as ebony and red woods, which were usually combined with ivory. The Mediterranean and, later, the Greco-Roman civilizations adopted the Egyptian veneering technique, for which they utilized yew, juniper, ebony, poplar, terebinth, boxwood, maple, holly, palm, alder, ilex, citron imported from Mauretania, and wood from both wild and cultivated olive trees. These veneers were used to cover the surfaces of furniture made of fig wood, willow, plane, cherry, elm, and ash.

Sometimes the common woods were painted (rather than veneered) in imitation of the graining in more precious woods such as terebinth, cedar, or maple. Painted imitation was also applied to more compact and desirable materials such as horn or tortoise shell. In Roman times great care was taken with finishing touches and the enhancement of the specific qualities of the wood such as color, grain, and compactness; smoothing was scrupulously carried out with the usual mineral abrasives as well as ray skin. Beeswax mixed with juniper or cedar oil provided a polishing agent. In the Middle Ages carved work was always finished with colored ornamentation and was very often gilded. For this a gypsum and glue preparation was first used, the thickness varying from the thinnest possible film to a fairly thick layer permitting plastic decoration independent of the processing of the wooden surface beneath. In Italy this technique involved the use of a light canvas stuck to the wood as a support for the gesso, thus preventing cracking and flaking in the superimposed layer. These preparations were, of course, intended as a ground for the paint or gilt with which the objects were finished.

During the Renaissance the custom of painting furniture declined, although painted stuccowork was reserved for certain categories of objects, such as marriage chests (cassoni) decorated with paste imitations of precious stones (IV, PL. 26). Renaissance wooden surfaces were generally finished with a light layer of transparent varnish (copal or lacquer). This system became prevalent in northern Europe as well, although the medieval tradition of painted wooden furniture persisted longer — in England up to Elizabethan times.

Clay. One type of surface preparation of terra-cotta products can be found on the so-called "impasto" vases of protohistoric tradition (see above). Although they were unglazed, these vases were carefully burnished with a wooden stick or smooth stone and thus acquired a certain sheen; however, they were apt to crack during the firing process. The application of color ultimately became the fundamental method of preparing a terra-cotta surface, the first examples of this technique appearing in the oldest terra-cotta products of Egypt, and Mesopotamia. Color was generally applied before firing when the clay had dried to the white-hard state. This limited the choice of color, since organic colors burn when exposed to heat. Only a few kinds of earth (sienna, umber, ocher) or mixtures of these with clay can withstand firing. It is important that absorption of the color by the porous clay surface should be even. If the brush is raised during color application, or if linear defects are corrected, staining will result.

In Egypt the oldest pottery was decorated with red ocher, blue frit, iron-oxide black, or varnish based on carbon. In Mesopotamia there are examples of ornamentation formed by incised lines filled with black, white, or red pigments. Pigments used for painted terra cotta were manganese-oxide black, animal black, and composites of blue and green copper or tin-antimony yellow.

An essential step in the technique of painted decoration in vase production is shown in a procedure developed in Greece and the Mediterranean coasts of Asia Minor. It was observed

that fired clay shows a range of hues depending on firing temperature and that different clays vary in their particular range. Thus there arose a system of pictorial ornamentation based exclusively on these processes.

In archaic Attic and classical ceramics ornamentation was executed before firing the leather-hard vase. Today it is customary to apply a glaze to the object after it has been fired (biscuit stage) and then to refire it; but Greek ceramics, except in a few rare cases, were probably fired only once. The black used for decoration was not glaze in the modern sense of the word, since it contained an insufficient percentage of alkali to cause fusion at a given temperature. It was rather a kind of liquid clay containing iron, similar to the composition of the vase itself, although peptized; that is, the heavier particles (quartz, feldspar, limestone) had been eliminated, and alkali had been added in amounts sufficient to provide considerable brilliance. Before ornamentation was begun the surface of the vase was covered with a thin protective wash (Lasur) composed of diluted and peptized clay; after firing, this produced a slightly shiny, reddish color.

In the more ancient black-figure ware, the design was executed in black against a red ground (II, PLS. 35, 36; V, PLS. 185, 186; VII, PLS. 20, 21). The details of the figures were then incised, which made the underlying red clay visible; finally the accessory red or white colors were added. In the later red-figure pottery (from ca. 530 B.C.) the preliminary sketch of the decoration was done with a fine metal point and is often clearly discernible (III, PL. 134; IV, PLS. 252, 253). The contours of the figures were traced with a thin line to which was added a wider stripe of color. Then the details within the red silhouette were added, and lastly the ground was completed in black. When necessary, more details were added in clay or color or incisions were made. Sometimes red ocher was applied, rubbed in such a manner as to penetrate into the clay to intensify the color. Some vases were painted entirely in black except for parts around the lip, handles, and foot.

In the 6th century B.C. the diffusion of white-ground ware began (II, PL. 48; III, PLS. 365, 366). This ware was obtained by the application of a slip of white clay on which decoration was painted in black. In some cases the design was limited to the contours and executed with diluted glaze or mat color. Although firing is normally considered a shaping technique, in Greek ceramics it had the function of a finishing process. Contributing to this was the quality of the coloring material (improperly called "varnish," although this term has been incorporated into the archaeological jargon); these attained their final color, indelibility, and brilliance from heat and oxidation during the firing. Further, the actual firing process was decisive. Once the ornamentation and drying were completed the vase could be fired. Three successive phases were necessary, characterized by alternate admission and limitation of air within the kiln. The first phase was oxidation, during which air was freely admitted. The second phase was reduction, during which the clay and glaze turned black. In the third and last phase, that of reoxidation, the clay turned red again, although the dense black glaze remained unchanged in color, partly melting in because of the small alkali content and thus acquiring the intended brilliance. At the same time the Lasur as well as the red retouching (red ocher mixed with peptized clay) were, like the terra cotta, sufficiently porous to reabsorb oxygen and thus regained their original color; however, the white color, made of peptized white clay and containing no iron, remained unaltered by firing in a reducing atmosphere.

In this procedure it is difficult to explain the system that made it possible for the more dense glazes (red applied in fairly thick coats) to avoid reduction and consequent blackening during the second phase of the firing. Possibly only the parts intended to be black were painted at first; the vase was then fired in the usual manner — first the oxidizing, then the reducing process; firing was then interrupted, and those parts that were to be red were painted; then a second firing occurred in an oxidizing atmosphere. The clumsiness of this procedure explains the comparative rarity of red-and-black ware (II, PL. 37). In exceptional cases, to obtain a special color effect, a very n second layer of glaze was probably spread over the parts eady painted and fired before submitting the vase to a third ng of less than usual intensity. With this technique it may ve been possible to obtain that brilliant red which is typical Greek ceramics and which is so important for its contrast ainst the black. Opinions vary, however, on the possibilities refiring the vases; although some authorities support the eory of a single firing, others suggest, by analogy with modern stems, that there were two or even three successive firings. two or three firings occurred the first would only be a general ocess preceding the application of color. For these procedures e temperature of the oven was raised no higher than 900°– o°C, which is less than that generally adopted today.

From the end of the 5th century B.C. on, during the Hel-istic era, new ornamental systems arose. One was plastic, ploying mold-made ornamental additions, which characterizes entire section of Greek vase production in the 4th century :. Another approach was pictorial and coincides with Attic oduction in the second half of the 5th century B.C. It tifies to the diffusion of tempera colors to represent cloth d other details. The colors used were red and yellow and, er, blue, purple, green, pink, and mauve. This technique s almost always executed on white-ground ware. It was ll practiced in late Hellenistic times, as is shown by the ces found on the border areas of Greek influence to the st and west (from Hadra near Alexandria to Canosa di glia [anc. Kanysion] in Apulia and Centuripe in Sicily). In llenistic times there was also a return to vases that were tirely black, on which polychrome ornamentation appeared at later stage (see GREEK ART, WESTERN; HELLENISTIC ART).

In Italy, from the Villanovan terra-cotta products to the ry earliest Etruscan bucchero production, various attempts re made to finish ceramics with black ornamentation, which s frequently obtained by a chemical process that profoundly nsformed the clay in the course of firing. The black color ay have resulted from the reduction of ferric oxide during ing (when ferrous components were present in the clay). t it may also have been produced either by impregnating e vase with oil and subjecting it to moderate heat in order carbonize the oil; or by causing particles of carbon to be posited throughout the material by throwing plant matter to the kiln at the end of firing; or by taking the vase out of e kiln and placing it while still hot among plant matter, ch as chaff.

The Etruscans produced certain types of painted ceramics pied from Corinthian, Ionic, and Attic models; however, they ver achieved the brilliant black of Attic ceramics — probably cause the superficial liquid clay was insufficiently peptized. red-figure pieces the figures were not always left in the lor of the underlying clay but were recolored with ocher or touched in red, still in imitation of the analogous Greek chnique. By the 3d and 2d centuries B.C. superficial surface eparation in imitation of metalware appeared in the form of vering; the object was probably covered with silver after the st firing.

Another glaze was provided by the Roman terra sigillata, which the Arretine ware imitated the oldest "Megarian" wls. The entire surface of the vase was covered by a uniform yer of glaze consisting of peptized clay of a very fine quality. turned a bright coral red after firing, unlike the glaze of the Megarian" bowls, which turned black. The ingredients of the rretine glaze were the same as those of the black glaze of orinthian, Chalcidean, and Attic vases, as well as those of agna Graecia. But, since the firing process was oxidizing, e Arretine ceramics acquired their characteristic red color. he technique of molding remained unchanged for centuries the production of terra sigillata. In vases with the light-hued rbotine ornamentation, however, the process of coloring in ack was in some cases maintained. Ceramics with a white ound ornamented with veinings imitating marble are typically oman. The ground was obtained with a very fine white slip, on which the ornamentation was then applied. Esthetically e most important examples of Roman production, apart from e Arretine vases, are those covered in a true glaze.

The oldest known art products showing vitrification are some pieces from steatite necklaces with a glazed coating that were found at Badari in Upper Egypt. Glazing on steatite continued during the dynastic period, but the glazing of quartz ceased after 2000 B.C.

The most frequent colors in Egyptian faïence were deep blue and green; other colors were occasionally used in glazing. Chemical examination of the glaze of certain faïence (A. Lucas, *Ancient Egyptian Materials and Industries*, London, 1948) has revealed the following percentages: silica, 95 per cent; alumina, oxide of iron, lime, and magnesia (in almost equal parts), 5 per cent. Another analysis of a later dark-blue faïence piece from the Fayum in Egypt gave silica, 75.5 per cent; potash, 10.7 per cent; soda, 5.6 per cent; lime, 3.8 per cent; copper oxide (for color), 1.8 per cent; and traces of the oxides of aluminum, iron, manganese, and magnesium. This glaze is similar in composition to ancient glass, although its lime content is lower and its silica content higher.

The present body of knowledge makes it impossible to tell whether Mesopotamian glazing (3000 B.C.) was an original invention or derived from Egyptian methods. Alkaline glazing was also practiced in India and in Crete (at the beginning of the 3d millennium B.C.), but never so widely as in Egypt. In Mesopotamia, preference was given to a lead glaze applied to a clay base, the recipe for which has been found on a cuneiform tablet of the 17th century B.C.: glass, 243 parts; lead, 40.1 parts; copper, 58.1 parts; saltpeter, 3.1 parts; and lime, 5 parts. This glaze is more vitreous and shiny, and it is usually thicker than alkaline glazes; but it also flakes more easily and can be made to adhere to the clay body only with difficulty. Other thinner and more adhesive varieties of lead glaze were developed in the late Hellenistic period and spread from the Levant across the Mediterranean to Europe. European centers of production developed, among them Saint-Rémy (Allier), France. These centers remained active throughout the Roman and Byzantine periods, producing pottery vessels, lamps, and other wares, mostly in yellow, brown, and green.

A distinction should be made between lead and alkaline glaze and frit glaze. The former is absolutely transparent, except when it is cooled too quickly or when errors in the gradation of the firing temperature are made in its manufacture. Frit, which is frequently mistaken for glass or faïence, gives the object an opaque surface that betrays a partial melting of the silica powder. The earliest finds that prove the existence of frit come from Egypt of the 18th dynasty and Mesopotamia during the same period; they are small objects such as seals and amulets (XII, PL. 524). The later process of mixing frit with clay of a particularly fine quality produced vessels that were mainly blue or green (Egypt). These vessels remained blue only if fired at a temperature of less than 685°C; at a higher temperature they became greenish because of fusion of the crystal structure. Powdered blue frit was also used as a pigment. In vessel production it was apparently not used later than the 2d millennium B.C., but it was still found in smaller objects toward the middle of the 1st millennium in the Mediterranean Basin. For pieces dating from the 19th dynasty chemical analysis generally reveals the following percentages: silica, 57 per cent; copper oxide, 18.5 per cent; lime, 13.8 per cent; soda, 7.6 per cent; and magnesium, iron, and aluminum oxides in smaller quantities. Glazing enjoyed another brief period of favor in the Ionian islands in the 6th century B.C.; it then penetrated to west-central Europe through the trans-Mediterranean export trade of the Phoenicians and through the Roman production of glazed vases.

The shapes and, to a certain extent, the ornamentation of these vases resembled those of the Arretine ware; but the glaze was true glaze in the modern sense in that it melts at a definite temperature. Blue (alkaline), green, yellow, and colorless lead glazes were used to great effect. The glaze was generally applied to the inside of the vase by pouring in such a way as to obtain a thin layer that isolated the porous terra cotta from liquids. The outer layer of glaze was thicker, however, and was applied by dipping. The outer surface was usually mat because of the relatively low temperature of firing (960°–1030° C). Only where the glaze vitrified did it become transparent and shiny. For firing the pieces were placed upon stilts — a method still in use today.

Generally, the application of vitreous glazes originated in the need to make terra-cotta vessels waterproof. But the very unevenness of the glazing often rendered it purely decorative, particularly in medieval production. The Romans used two kinds of vitreous glazes. Alkaline silicate glazes, whose composition resembles that of glass, were used in the eastern regions, but their use did not continue into the Middle Ages. Lead silicate glazes were widely used from Asia Minor to Britain and were the basis for most medieval glazing; they adhere to a ceramic surface better than alkaline silicate glazes and melt at a lower temperature. Glazing was generally used on both the inside and the outside of pottery, especially near the mouth.

Islamic ceramic technique continued the ancient processes and enriched them with new experiments (III, PLS. 140, 141). One of the most important inventions was a glaze that was made white and opaque with suspended particles of tin oxide. Baghdad was the most important center of production. In the 11th century the technique was imported to Cairo, where a great many ceramists had emigrated. During this period Persia stood in the vanguard of Near Eastern production. Tin-glazed pottery had an extraordinary development in Persia. The ornamental styles deriving from this ware had great influence in Europe, especially Spain and Italy, as the precursors of majolica and delftware (III, PL. 156). Although the fall of the Roman Empire produced no interruption in the Byzantine production of lead glazes their manufacture in Europe ceased until about the 10th century, when they reappeared in western Germany, the Rhineland, the Netherlands, and Britain (on pitchers in typical local shapes). The technique was probably reintroduced into Germany from the Byzantine area. Because of its geographic and cultural position between East and West, Byzantium automatically took on the function of a mediator in the field of glazing techniques and thus spread the knowledge to Europe. This diffusion should be divided into two phases. The first concerns west-central Europe primarily and centers on the strong Byzantine influences that acted upon Carolingian culture. The second phase came through Venice and renewed the use of lead glazing throughout the Italian peninsula in the 12th and 13th centuries; lead sulphide or lead oxide were mainly used. During the latter period the diffusion extended to all of Europe, including France and England.

The coloring and firing processes had meanwhile been modified. In Roman times a lead compound mixed with gum had been applied to the biscuit, which was then submitted to a second firing at about 900°–1000°C, the objects having been placed inside special pots with lids that acted as muffle kilns. However, some medieval products with lead glazing were probably fired only once, and the coating was applied to the vessel in its leather-hard phase. Most medieval glazed ceramics were fired in two distinct operations. It is not known what kind of kiln was used for the second firing, although the two operations may have been executed in the same kiln, which necessitated more than two separate firings.

Another characteristic production in Islamic ceramics was luster painting, which apparently derives from the work of painters on glass who were active in Egypt in the 7th and 8th centuries of our era (see FATIMID ART; ISLAM; V, PL. 253; IX, PL. 275; X, PL. 170). The technique spread throughout Mesopotamia about A.D. 830. At the end of the 10th century the best potters moved from Baghdad to the court of the Fatimids in Cairo, and from there the technique was brought to Spain in the 13th century (X, PL. 169). Metallic luster was obtained by combining silver oxide with sulphur (for yellow) and copper oxide (for the "luster"), which were sometimes mixed with fine ocher; refiring was then performed at a relatively low temperature (about 800°C) either in a reducing atmosphere in a muffle kiln or simply by piling up branches on the fire so as to produce thick smoke. In the course of firing the metals precipitated to the surface of the glaze, thus creating a bright patina. Where the coating was thick the patina resembled solid copper or silver; where the coating was thin the patina ranged from gradations of gold (golden luster) to a mother-of-pearl iridescence. In the 9th century in Mesopotamia this technique was used to give a metallic sheen to the various colors, but later it was limited to the greenish or brownish shades. Lusters similar to the Spanish-Moorish types of North Africa, Málaga, and Valencia began to be produced in Italy in the 16th century.

In the 14th century another process in the treatment of ceramic surfaces was developed in the Rhineland in the local production of stoneware. A great quantity of salt was thrown on the object in the kiln at an advanced stage of firing. The salt reacted with the minerals in the clay to produce a glazed surface. A reducing atmosphere made it possible to obtain a dark, mottled or blue-and-purple surface through two partial saltings of the stoneware (Cologne).

Apart from glazes, another material popular during the Middle Ages to decorate clay vessels was a semiliquid slip of fine plastic clay. It first served to unite the various parts of the vase in its leather-hard stage, especially to lute the spouts and handles to the body. There were two separate procedures: the vases receiving their first firing were placed underneath those which had already been painted (see the description by Piccolpasso, 1934) and were then replaced in the kiln for their second firing. A recipe for lead glazing given by Heraclius (De coloribus et artibus Romanorum, ca. A.D. 950) describes a composite of oil, glue, and baked and unbaked potter's earth applied to a previously baked vase; over this was spread boiled flour-and-water paste, and this in turn was immediately sprinkled with lead oxide. The vase was then fired "neither too strongly nor too slowly." This produced an even yellow glaze. Green was obtained by adding copper or brass filings, which oxidized with the lead in the course of firing. The widespread medieval production of jugs with yellow or orange glazing flecked with green shows the survival of Roman techniques of mixing copper filings with the lead before the glaze firing. In the Roman production of lead oxide glazing the use of copper produced a green color, whereas in the alkaline glazes of the Near East copper filings produced a beautiful shade of turquoise blue.

There was no red glazing in medieval Europe, save for the single case of Spanish ruby luster. Red enamel on metal was extremely common, however, in both East and West from the 3d century on; it was produced with red cuprous oxide suspended in lead silicate. Pale red glazing was obtained from suspended ferric oxide (iron rust); when dispersed through lead glaze it gives an intense yellow or orange, and under reducing conditions as ferrous oxide or the more fusible silicate, it produces a pale green. Iron in its ferrous state is the main element in the subtle varieties of green in medieval glazes. The palette of the northern European ceramists during the Middle Ages was at first limited to the yellow and orange of ferric iron and the green of ferrous iron and copper; olive green was obtained with copper plus a variable quantity of ferric iron.

It was customary to decorate the body of the vase with an opaque paint and applied clay stripes of colors contrasting with the ground under the uniform transparent glazing. The choice later became more extensive owing to the influence of products inspired by Islamic art that had been produced in southern Spain (III, PL. 142) and the eastern Mediterranean from the 10th century, in Italy from the 13th century, and in Flanders and England during the 16th century. These more advanced techniques used ferric oxide in several ways — for red or the various shades of yellow (when mixed with antimony). Blue was made with cobalt, and purple with manganese. Mixture of antimony and copper produced a brilliant light green or dark blue-green. Although cobalt blue had been known in the East for centuries, it was not used in Italy until the beginning of the 15th century. It spread through the Levant and Venice and was imported from Venice in the form of impure cobalt oxide (zaffer).

Although the artisans of the ancient empires had occasionally produced opaque glass and glazes with tin oxide suspended in lead silicate, this process was adopted on an extended scale only in the 9th century of our era by the Mesopotamian ceramists who made very successful imitations of the creamy porcelain imported from T'ang China. This procedure had the gre-

dvantage of preventing the paint, which was applied to the
repared mat surface, from running during the firing process.
aint that was directly applied to the surface of vases under
more fusible and flowing lead glaze tended to run. To avoid
iis disadvantage the Samarkand potters applied, under the
ommon lead glaze, pigments mixed with fine clay slip, sometimes
laced on a thin layer of the same slip (XII, PLS. 383–386).

Tin-containing glaze consisted of finely pulverized glass,
uartz, potash, tin, lead oxides, and a small percentage of salt.
fter its first firing the buff-colored vessel was immersed in a
quid suspension of this mixture and then dried on stilts.
'olors were applied with a brush. After drying, the surface
as extremely absorbent, demanding great dexterity of touch.
he second firing was then carried out, the decorated pots
eing placed above those which were still to be fired for the
rst time. Sometimes, in the case of finer objects, a third firing
as necessary to fix a thin layer of lead glaze (over the preceding
n glaze), which gave the glazed surface an extraordinary luster.
s these processes developed, Islamic ceramics in the 12th and
3th centuries attained results of the highest quality with a
aethod known as the "seven-color technique," the examples
f which are today known as *mīnā'ī* ware. In this chromatic
rnamentation alternating layers of glaze were applied over
nd under layers of paint, for its use as ornamentation:
x) application in a creamy consistency to obtain monochrome
r contrasting colored relief patterns (barbotine technique),
hich was widely used in the 16th-century Staffordshire potteries;
2) more diluted application, either with a brush or through
ipping (engobe; III, PLS. 139, 147), which was widely used
) give a fine, light-colored surface to ceramics made with the
aore common kinds of clay that could not be fired white.
n the Near East and in the West the latter practice was
timulated by the growing appreciation of Chinese porcelain
:om the 9th century onward. Used in the diluted application,
ngobe was considered a poor, superficial imitation of porcelain,
lthough it possessed some attractive qualities of its own.

The English ceramists greatly developed both these tech-
iques, executing ornamentation with liquid slip on dark grounds
r brown and black slip on light grounds, as well as applying
aolded ornaments to the piece. One of the main ornamental
ses of engobe was to provide a ground for sgraffito patterns
Piccolpasso, 1934). By incising the dipped coating of slip
he dark color of the underlying body was laid bare (III,
L. 147). The entire vase was then covered in transparent
2ad glaze. Sometimes colored pigments were applied along
he scratched lines, but they tended to run into the fusible
laze. This technique produced one of the most widespread
eramic styles of Islam and Byzantium and was later widely
ised in medieval Spain and Italy, and occasionally in France and
ingland (III, PLS. 139, 147). Tenth-century Persian imitations
if mottled Chinese stoneware also had sgraffito ornamentation.

The use of inlaid tiles for paving arose about 1200 in northern
'rance and then in the Netherlands and England, where the
•rocess was most widely adopted. The usual ornamentation
vas white on a dark ground. Clay tile was stamped with a
•unch that produced a hollow design, which was filled up with
. white clay used in the production of pipes. Before firing, the
ile was given a transparent lead glaze. A splendid example
•f this process of ornamentation is the floor of the Chapter
Iouse in Westminster Abbey in London (1253–59). A cheaper
ystem of production later made use of wooden punches already
:overed with thinned pipe clay. The results, however, were
1ever sufficiently successful to replace the more elaborate
nethods of inlaying.

The combination of relief designs with vivid chromatic
rnamentation (the seven colors of the *mīnā'ī* technique) is
)riental in origin and can be counted among the achievements
1f Islam in ceramic art. Incision was at first necessary to prevent
he different colored glazes from running into one another. By the
ı1th century the different sections were separated by lines of
1urple pigment mixed with grease, which disappeared during
iring; this technique was also adopted in Spain. Oriental
echniques for the production of ornamental tiles were widely
nd variously applied in Europe (see also CERAMICS).

Metal. Ever since antiquity metal has been submitted to
various surface treatments, apart from those finishing touches
with chisel or burin on the cast metal, which are necessary
because of the web, or drippings, that an annealed metal object
usually produces when being removed from the mold.

One of the most ancient methods of decorating metal was
repoussé work, which produced a relief design by means of
blows applied to the back surface of the object, which rested
on a yielding support of wood, lead, or pitch (V, PL. 184; IX,
PL. 501). When relief decoration was not desired, a simpler
process was adopted; the design was executed on the top surface
by hammering with a tracer, or small chisel with a blunt edge,
while the hot sheet of metal was fixed on a bed of pitch. In still
another technique, designs in very low relief (little more than
$1/_{16}$ in.) were obtained on a metal sheet fixed with flat-headed
nails on a smooth, compact wooden support. A flat-ended
punch of hardwood brought the metal close to its support.
When the design had been drawn with hammer and chisel,
as in the preceding technique, the ground of the relief was
pushed in with the punch. Occasionally the surface of the
relief design was lightly polished in order to make it more
prominent.

To obtain greater relief the metal was beaten with special
tools on its back surface in order to give the protuberances an
even thickness; this process required several annealings. The
technique of embossed work usually appears in combination
with that of chasing, which normally served to finish the relief
(I, PL. 509; VI, PL. 243; various gold figurines from the royal
tombs of Ur, before 2500 B.C.). A layer of melted pitch is
generally applied to the back of the surface to be chased and
then left to cool, functioning as a support. Chasing was always
performed on the front surface of the metal with metal chisels
of varying shapes.

For gold and silver personal ornaments (e.g., necklaces,
breastplates) a stamping technique was used to obtain the
exact duplication of a repeated ornamental motif. A unit of
the motif was carved on the end of a strong punch made of
iron bronze. The punch was driven into the cold lead to obtain
a mold. A thin leaf of gold or silver that had been properly
annealed was then impressed into the mold.

Another consisted in making the mold directly on the
punch by chiseling with very hard instruments. The effect
of this negative was tested in wax as the work proceeded. Then
a piece of thin sheet metal protected by a thick sheet of lead
was hammered on the punch mold.

There was no engraving on metal during the Bronze Age
because sufficiently hard and sharp utensils were not available.
The oldest example of metal engraving dates back to 859–825 B.C.
(inscriptions engraved on the bronze gates of Shalmaneser III
at Balawat). Engraving or incision can be performed with a
burin, which automatically removes superfluous metal while
producing a clear groove, or with a tracer or chasing tool, which
presses against the sides of the groove without removing any
of the metal (VI, PL. 249). The difference is easy to define
but very difficult to recognize in archaeological finds.

Skill attained in soldering techniques at the beginning of
the 3d millennium B.C. permitted the invention of new methods
of treating surfaces in the production of personal ornaments
from the more desirable metals. These methods utilized the
possibilities of cutting and melting gold into the most varied
shapes, such as disks, little knobs, simple or beaded wire,
lumps of all sizes, and granular ornamentation (Etruria, 7th
cent.; PL. 458; VI, PLS. 246, 247). The ornamentation obtained
by soldering together gold wires laid out in an ornamental
pattern on the smooth surface of an object is called filigree
(PL. 458; V, PLS. 59, 66–70, 74, 79, 80; see EUROPE, BARBARIAN).
Filigree ornamentation was frequently combined with little
metal disks, grains, or dome-shaped knobs, which were stamped
with a punch and then finished with a chisel and a file made
of abrasive stone (Sumeria and Egypt; V, PL. 244). To increase
the ornamental effect the wire could be twisted or undulated.

The wire for filigree was made in several ways: by cutting
a tiny strip of the edge of the gold sheet; by incising spirals
on a metal disk and finishing with a hammer; or by ordinary

stamping while the metal was hot. For geometric ornamentation the wire could be made into a succession of tiny beads by pressing it between two dies, a characteristic technique of late Egyptian goldsmiths' work. The wire was reduced to the proper size and then pushed through a groove between two dies, one above and one below. Since the wire was thicker than the groove it slightly raised the upper die, which was beaten with a hammer while the wire was made to turn slowly upon itself. When a section of wire had reached the desired shape it was pushed forward so that the next section could be introduced.

Another fundamental technique of ornamentation was the granulation obtained by soldering minute grains of gold upon a metallic surface. The extraordinary perfection of this technique, especially in the Etruscan pieces of Eastern inspiration, has suggested several hypotheses as to the exact procedure involved. The fused gold may have been passed through a sieve, allowing the drops to fall into water from a certain height to permit cooling; or a gold thread was cut into tiny segments, which were mixed with coal and then heated; or one end of the wire was melted down and the drops were collected. Coal was very likely used in a process fairly similar to that described by Cellini: "Take your gold or silver and melt it down. When it appears to be completely melted, throw it into a little vessel filled with crushed coal. It is in this manner that granules of all sorts are made."

Another difficult problem to solve concerns the process of soldering the wires and tiny grains to the metal surface of the object to be decorated. The existence of some soldering alloy has been suggested. In 1933 H. A. P. Littledale received a patent for a method of fastening the wires or grains in place with a copper compound mixed with glue. When heated, the glue carbonizes, the copper compound becomes copper oxide, and the carbon reduces the copper oxide to copper and disappears as carbon monoxide. The remaining copper is alloyed with some of the gold to produce a solder. This modern method, however, relies on the possibilities of modern chemistry; surely ancient peoples would have found it difficult to add an intermediate substance, such as an alloy, in the technique of granular ornamentation. In the earlier processes the grains could not be placed individually but were scattered over the surface, which had probably been spread beforehand with a kind of adhesive substance. Perhaps the grains were annealed with charcoal dust before being placed on the metal sheet; this would have made possible the formation of gold carbonate, which has a lower melting point than gold, thus obtaining from the surfaces of the grains the alloy necessary for soldering. Once the grains were distributed in the required design with the aid of an adhesive substance and a final scraping of smooth parts, the object could be submitted to heat; a partial fusion of the gold carbonate surface would be obtained at the points of contact of the grains, thus soldering them together and to the sheet of metal.

Throughout the history of technology there have been numerous processes for creating a patina — a surface film that forms on metals. In many cases the natural patina produced by atmospheric conditions has obscured or eliminated the one produced artificially by the craftsman; thus it is often impossible to reconstruct the most ancient processes. Apparently Greek bronzes had no artificial patina — only a superficial abrasion that favored the homogeneous formation of a natural patina. The artificial brown patina that characterizes Italian bronzes from the Renaissance onward was obtained by heating the metal with a blowtorch and dabbing it with a brush dipped in certain acids or salts, most frequently nitrates and chlorides. A patina can also be given while the metal is cold. Acids, depending on how they are chosen and administered, color the metal differently with types of apparently natural patina, either greenish or brown. In China and Japan solutions of common salt, sulphur, vinegar, copper salts, and so forth have been used to produce patinas of various colors (brown, red, purple, etc.).

Metals may be gilded chemically or mechanically (VI, PLS. 256, 267, 284, 285; VII, PLS. 320, 321; IX, PL. 407). *Plaqué* gilding is obtained by welding the gold leaf by means of heat and pressure; fire gilding by washing in gold and mercury and then heating; cold gilding by rubbing the object with very fin gold powder or by applying ashes from burned rags soaked i a solution of powdered gold and turpentine; gouache gildin by dipping the object in a solution based on sodium chlorid. Gilding today is generally performed with batteries (galvani gilding, or electroplating).

Another surface treatment for metal that gave it a mirrorlik finish was widespread in ancient times before the Roma invention of glass mirrors. The process consisted in thoroughl polishing the metal, to which a gold or silver leaf was sometime applied *allo spadaro*. Today the galvanic bath makes possibl many types of mirrors, whether by silver gilding of by an opera tion in which a layer of chromium is galvanized onto the met (see METALWORK).

Glass. Until Roman times painting on glass was not common process of ornamentation, despite the great antiquit of a few unusual examples (e.g., painted glass vase of Thut mosis III, ca. 1450 B.C.). The process was later characterize by a technique that remains in use with only slight modifications Painting was executed cold on the glass object with color obtained from fusible metal enamels, which today are use in solutions with essence of turpentine. It was only after second heating of the object at a temperature not exceedin 500°C that the painting acquired its definitive color, necessar solidity, and adherence to the glass surface. In some cases th ornamentation was applied with colors that do not seem t have been fired. In order to protect this fairly delicate decora tion a mat ground layer was superimposed in such a way tha the design was visible only through the glass on the side opposit the painted one. This type of glass painting temporarily fe into disuse in the West after the end of Roman civilization it continued in the Near East, and by the late Middle Age found new applications in European craftsmanship (VI, PL 228). In the Near East and in Fatimid Egypt, from the 8th t the 10th century, glass with a metallic luster was produced b an identical technique to that used in the lusterware of thi area. In Syria, between the 12th and 14th centuries, Aral artisans usually produced glass decorated with powdered frit which was applied to the vases and fired *in situ* (VI, PL. 227) The result was a true enamel ornamentation, far more brillian than that of the earlier Roman pieces.

As has been noted, mosaic glass made use of fragments o gilded glass insets for decoration. From the same period (2, B.C–A.D. 100) there is a glass group with elaborate gold-leaf flora motifs applied to the outer surface of a glass shell that was ther inserted into another glass receptacle and fixed by heating thus the ornamentation lay between two pieces of glass. In late pieces (3d and 4th cent. of our era) the gilding was applied t the inner surface of the outer shell of glass; then, before th inner shell of glass was inserted, gilding was covered on th back with a coloring, so that only the colored ground was visibl on the inside of the vessel. Gilding was rarely used in conjunc tion with just one layer of glass because of the lability of th glass; in such cases it was preferable to throw the powdere gold or minced gold leaf on the surface of the glass at moderatel hot temperatures. Later, in the ornamentation of Wester glass, surface gilding became frequent, but it was applied t glass that had been properly prepared by a thorough scratchin operation with a bone or ebony point; after this the gold wa fixed on the hot glass in a muffle kiln (VI, PLS. 220, 228, 229)

In Roman times, particularly in the later imperial era (2 and 3d cent.), the old polished or silvered mirrors were graduall replaced by glass pieces. A thin layer of melted lead-antimony-tir alloy was poured into glass that had been blown in the shap of a globe or cylinder. From such globes convex section could be cut and then mounted and used as mirrors. Ther was also the simpler method of backing a disk of specially cu blown glass with gold leaf, tin, or lead. In the Middle Age various combinations of metal alloys gave rise to mirrors wit amalgam sheeting, which was obtained by pouring the pures mercury onto a thin sheet of tin that had been smoothed ou on a completely flat stone slab. Placed upon this was a pan of glass totally free from any impurity or imperfection such bubbles or scratches. When the pane was pressed against the amalgam, it squeezed out the superfluous mercury and adhered perfectly to the tin sheet. The pane was kept in a vertical position for two or three weeks so that any residue of the mercury would run off; a protective layer of lacquer was then added to the back. This procedure was used from the Middle Ages to the 19th century, when it was replaced by the industrial silver-plating process. In this technique a thin covering of silver is placed on the glass by means of an ammonical solution of silver nitrate exposed to the action of appropriate reducing elements (see also GLASS).

Cloth. Ever since antiquity there have been two fundamental systems for coloring cloth. One is based on the use of wooden stamps. The other, probably an older method, depends on the use of organic substances applied to the thread either before or after weaving. By the 3d millennium dyeing was already known in Egypt and the Near East. Until the introduction of modern industrial methods the process made use of organic substances that were fixed in the cloth with special mordants. The first and most fundamental dyes used in ancient times were red, yellow, blue, purple, and black.

Red was obtained by drying and crushing the cochineal insect or by extracting the color from certain plants such as lichens (Roccella and Lecanora), madder (*Rubia tinctorum*), which was certainly known in Egypt, and henna (*Lausonia inermis*), found on an Egyptian statue of the Old Kingdom (ca. 2500 B.C.). Yellow was obtained from safflower (*Carthamus tinctorius*), curcuma, sumac (used for tanning and dyeing leather), and saffron (*Crocus sativus*), which was produced in Syria, Egypt, Cilicia (mod. Lesser Armenia, Turkey), and Crete. A yellow dye could also be extracted from pomegranate peel (ancient Mesopotamia, Egypt, and Palestine). Blue was extracted from indigo (*Indigofera tinctoria*), which has been found in Egyptian cloth dating from about 2500 B.C.; it came into common use about 300 B.C. Another source of blue was woad (*Isatis tinctoria*), which was well known in Egypt and Mesopotamia about 300 B.C.

The most highly prized dye of ancient times was purple, obtained from the mollusks Purpura and Murex (Mediterranean coast between Tyre and Haifa) and already known in 1500 B.C. It was produced by soaking and boiling a part of the organism in a 1 per cent salt solution for three days, during which period the liquid dwindled to $1/6$ its original volume. Black was taken from oak gall and myrtle. In Mesopotamia the natural black, brown, and white colors of wool were exploited; gray was produced by spinning black and white filaments together. Wool was frequently dyed with indigo and then dyed a second time with another color (e.g., madder, a substance that gives a purple hue).

Detergents were derived from the roots of *Saponaria officinalis* (soapwort) and asphodel. Natron (sodium carbonate, or washing soda) was also used. For fixing certain dyes on the cloth, the commonly used mordants were alum, copper salts, iron salts, and various types of organic matter. Different mordants produced different nuances in color.

The printing of cloth dates back to most ancient times. Probably India originated all the methods of printing cloth, although some scholars credit the Chinese. Pliny reports that the Egyptians were expert in printing cloth with different designs and colors by the application of mordants before the actual dyeing with natural substances (probably madder and indigo). It is difficult to say at what period this art was initiated in Europe. Judging by examples in London (Vict. and Alb.) printed cloth was probably known in Sicily in the 13th century. A fragment of cotton cloth from the 16th century may serve to prove that the art of printing cloth with brushes and wooden stamps was known in Italy at that time.

In hand printing, which is rarely practiced today, a relief pattern is engraved on blocks of hard wood, with one block for each color; the raised pattern is sometimes covered in felt so that it will hold more color. Pigmented stamping paste is spread on the blocks, or stamps, with a spatula, and the stamp is pressed vigorously against the stretched cloth so that almost all the color adheres to the cloth. This operation is repeated as often as necessary until the complete design in all its colors is obtained.

INTERWEAVING AND INTERLACING. In primitive cultures basket weaving preceded textile processes. There is iconographic evidence that the Sumerian civilization made ample use of basket weaving and probably some simple forms of wool weaving, using the wool similarly to plant fibers (i.e., without turning it into threads). Such interweaving was used for various purposes, from furnishings to clothing. In the Sumerian pastoral civilization sheepskin clothing was gradually replaced by rudimentary cloth.

The discovery of thread came in stages, from the twisting of fibers for increased strength to the development of plaiting for more solidity in proportion to fineness. Wool was undoubtedly the preferred material because of its strength and fineness, which made it possible to prepare thread to the length desired. Very likely the cradle of these experiments was a civilization between Mesopotamia and the Mediterranean Basin. There is a continuity between Sumerian basket weaving and the first Egyptian textiles that indicates a fundamental experience in the use of twisted thread, which became essential to all future textile processes.

A fundamental process in weaving is the technique of interweaving a series of parallel threads stretched on a special instrument with another series of threads that is passed by hand over and under the first series. The first series forms what is called the warp, which was at first either fixed to a tree or post or stretched out horizontally on the ground between two bars or beams. The wooden structure that serves to stretch the warp is called a loom. The thread that is passed through the warp, alternately over and under it, forms the weft. In order to expedite the threading operation a pointed instrument known as a spool, or shuttle, is used to pass the thread through the warp.

The elementary type of horizontal loom, which is a warp stretched between two beams set in the ground, is still in use among the nomads of the Near East. This particular device soon fell out of use in favor of the vertical loom, which first appeared in Egypt in the 2d millennium B.C. The Greeks used only the vertical loom, with the uppermost beam supported by two posts, and the warp was stretched by a series of metal weights attached to the ends of the threads like plumb lines. Weaving proceeded from the top downward. The beam could revolve, so that the cloth was rolled around it as the work proceeded, the working level thus remaining always the same.

The Roman loom was initially similar to the Greek model, but later the warp was stretched by wrapping it around a second beam at the base of the loom. A Virgil manuscript of the 4th century of our era (Vat. Lib., Cod. vat. lat. 3225) shows a loom of this type with a horizontal bar across the warp. This was probably a heddle rod, used to raise and lower warp threads in weaving. More likely the Roman loom had two heddles and a shed stick (to create a passageway through which the shuttle is thrown) as in the vertical loom used by the Greeks. Weaving proceeded from the bottom upward.

The Greek shuttle was a short rod around which the weft was wrapped; the Roman shuttle was sometimes made from hollow bone, but it is not certain how it was actually used. The weft threads were driven close together by a comb that could be used only if the work proceeded from the bottom upward.

The vertical loom with two beams, already in wide use in Egypt under the New Kingdom, is with slight modifications the same loom used today for carpet and tapestry weaving. With a system of two rotating beams it is possible to obtain a piece of cloth much longer than the distance between the beams; this is accomplished by unrolling the warp and rolling the cloth as the work proceeds. Modifications introduced in these ancient types of looms stemmed from the desire to facilitate the processes of distinguishing odd and even warp threads. It was then discovered that the warp threads could be attached to an instrument that would allow an easy and immediate separation of the threads, creating a shed for the passage of the weft. The various systems tried from time to time and the possibilities they suggested constitute a general history of the technical processes of textile art. The first instrument used for opening a shed for the thread of the weft was a dividing stick or sword; later, experiments were made with a string, which made it possible to lift the even threads alternately from both sides of the loom, thus opening up a second shed, or countershed.

The heddles, which make use of hand swivels on very tightly twisted linen cord, are suspended from two bars, one above and one below; by means of a balance these bars support and divide all the warp threads into even and odd heddles. They are made in such a way that they allow plain weave for cloth or, when the raising and lowering motion of the heddle is changed, a multiple-mesh weave that offers infinite possibilities for combinations according to the various alternations of the shed, which is opened to the shuttle by the movement of the heddles. This fundamental advancement in textile technique led to the classification of cloth into two main categories: plain and fancy.

An improvement of uncertain origin was the construction of the more complex horizontal loom. It appeared in Europe in the 13th century as an already perfected instrument, but it may have been known in the East some time before then. With this loom the warp was stretched horizontally between a warp beam at the back and another beam in front. A mechanism was introduced for the formation of the shed by means of pedal action, which allowed the weaver to work more comfortably, with both hands free for the actual weaving. A pedal, or treadle, is lowered during the weaving and the shuttle is thrown from hand to hand through the shed that has formed. The cloth is beaten in with the reed. Through the action of the other pedal the countershed is opened, once again the shuttle is passed through, and the warp is beaten into place. As the weaving proceeds the warp is unrolled from the warp beam by activating a lever, and the cloth is wrapped around the cloth beam. Only a plain weave can be obtained with this loom. With two more heddles and treadles, elementary designs such as twills and herringbones are possible. Thus the more heddles there are, the greater the possibilities of varying the designs in the cloth.

Plain cloth (tabby) can be divided into two types. The first is characterized by an equal number of threads in both warp and weft. The warp may dominate and almost completely cover the weft (warp-face weave), or the weft may conceal the warp (tapestry weave). (There are, of course, intermediate possibilities.) The second type of plain cloth is the canvas weave, in which two or more wefts cover two or more warps. Pattern weaving in plain cloth is entirely based on color. One type consists of equal plain-weave bands of different colors or of threads of different colors or textures on either warp or weft. Various combinations of these possibilities may be used — as, for example, in weaving checks. In the tapestry weave, small sections are covered with different colors. Vertical spaces or small openings are left along the line of contact of the various colors.

In motifs with "floats" some threads overlap others, on either the side of the warp or the weft. When the floats are on the weft side, the result is often called "brocading" (to be distinguished from "brocade"; see below).

The only double weave (also called "compound cloth") known in ancient times was a warp-face double weave with a motif on both sides of the cloth. Two groups of differently colored warps were placed one on top of the other; only one weft was necessary. Some threads of the lower warp were then pulled forward to replace other threads in the top warp; the latter were in turn pulled backward. The colors were made to alternate, and knots were tied between the sections of the cloth that would otherwise be separate.

There are several varieties of pile cloth. In the first, one or several threads are thrown together in the weft and at regular intervals pass around a little rod forming small loops; in the course of weaving, these loops form patterns, as in turkish

toweling. In Senna looping the weft passes around each alternate warp over a rod or a string to form a long loop, and then passes under the same warp again before passing around the next alternate one. The result is a plain-weave stripe that alternates with a pile stripe. In still another type of pile cloth, bunches of thread encircle two or more warps, their ends hanging in such a way as to create strips of pile between strips of plain weave.

Diagonal, or twill, weaving is obtained with only one warp and one weft. The weft passes over two or more, or under one or more, threads of the warp, instead of passing alternately over and under the contiguous threads as it does in plain weaving. The series of successive passages is transferred the distance of one thread to the right or the left so as to form a diagonal line. For the simplest diagonal pattern, at least three heddles are required (XIV, PLS. 6, 9, 17, 18).

In twined weaving the warp and the weft are interlaced: two weft threads are wound around one or more warp threads. This technique is similar to that used in matting or basketry.

In gauze weaving the threads of the warp are set in pairs and are so arranged that they can be twisted in a particular way; this positioning is fixed by the passage of the weft.

In the wrapped, or sumak, weave the weft thread is wound around the warps. On either side of a row of pattern wrapping there is generally a row of plain weave. The wrapping must always be done with the fingers. There are several varieties of sumak weave.

Some very ancient examples of these various techniques have been found. Plain weaving was practiced in Egypt in the 4th millennium B.C. At Deir el-Bahri some cloth fragments dating from the 11th dynasty (ca. 2160 B.C.) are made with the looped technique used in Turkey in the weaving of toweling. In ancient Peru (Chicama Valley) interesting combinations of twining and weaving were used for both clothing and certain household objects such as baskets. The tomb of Thutmosis I (Thebes, ca. 1405 B.C.) contained the oldest known example of tapestry weaving. The remarkably high technical level of Egyptian production is also documented by a painting (ca. 1580 B.C.) of a vertical loom with two beams; the same type of loom was still in use until recently in northern Africa.

The most complex expressions of these ancient techniques occurred between the 15th and 18th centuries of our era. This period saw the manufacture of brocades, velvets, damasks, and other fabrics. In brocades, which are fabrics in which both warp and weft threads are floated to produce ornamental effects, the threads may be uniformly or irregularly distributed; one weave or several may be employed. Additional warps and wefts are joined to the ordinary plain-weave process. The series of additional wefts may amount to three, each supported by a shuttle that runs through the entire width of the cloth. Supplementary wefts remain loose on the reverse side of the cloth and may be quite long, depending on the pattern. Silk mixed with gold or silver thread has also been used in brocade weaving. Damask and brocatel involve the additional weaving of patterns in relief (XIV, PLS. 8, 14); brocatel requires a ground of broad serge weft stretched diagonally from the meeting point of warp and weft.

Velvet is made with the loop technique in either warp velvet or weft velvet. Special grooved needles are placed in the loose loops. The groove is later used to guide a knife, which cuts the loops and divides the threads so that the nap surface is compact and homogeneous. Velvets were widely used from the 15th century on, woven in patterns and with additions of gold or silver, which were extremely beautiful. The process for manufacturing carpets is similar to that of warp velvet; like velvet the material can be cut or looped (the loops split or left whole), with or without needles; no needles are used in double patching (see BASKETRY). Further information on other techniques discussed above may be found in TAPESTRY AND CARPETS and TEXTILES, EMBROIDERY, AND LACE.

COMBINING VARIOUS MATERIALS. The most ancient and remarkable examples of the combination of different materials are generally characterized by the value of the materials chosen

ıe techniques became stabilized in the Roman *opus sectile* — a mposition of flat tesserae embedded or inlaid on a common ound (VIII, PLS. 79, 81). Among the ancient pieces from meria, important examples are the inlaid limestone frieze m al-'Ubaid, the mother-of-pearl inserts of the Mari panels, d, above all, the "Standard" of Ur (3d millennium B.C.), ıich has a mosaic ground consisting of large irregular fragments lapis lazuli and figures composed of shells, mother-of-pearl, d red limestone (Br. Mus.; VIII, PL. 77; IX, PL. 471). The ʒrior details of the inlaid figures are indicated by incised lines, ıich are occasionally filled in with a dark substance; this ʒates contrast and gives the design greater relief.

Also from a royal tomb at Ur comes the so-called "Ram ıught in a Thicket" (3d millennium B.C.; I, PL. 509), which modeled in the round and composed of gold, electrum, ıther-of-pearl, and lapis lazuli.

In western Asia, where these processes were developed ʒr, ivory was used as a supporting base. The techniques ıged from simple staining to the most elaborate systems of aying and embedding (PLS. 362, 363; X, PL. 401). Frequently ·le compartments were incised, leaving the contours in relief; ·o these compartments was then placed a colored paste based ıer on red or green copper frit or on a mixture of iron and ›per frit or glass (colored blue). The glass was inlaid while ld. In stone inlay work, analysis of a Phoenician ivory from mrud reveals that the lapis lazuli was fixed in the cavity means of a thin layer of calcium carbonate colored with wdered blue frit. In some cases inlay was executed without ʒ use of raised contours, with a technique called *tamlu* that ʒver became widespread because it was so difficult. When ›ry was joined to other materials, small joints were constructed, ısisting of a bottle-necked mortise and a tenon that was ıde separately and then fixed to the mortise with a pin. The ı was ivory rather than metal, to prevent staining or rusting. metimes glue and bitumen were used. These techniques ʒe employed particularly in Egypt, Syria, and Phoenicia.

In Egypt the combination of various materials achieved ⋅tinction in furniture and goldsmiths' work (IV, PLS. 343, ⋅, 391, 392, 407; VI, PL. 241). Gold-leaf dressing and inlay ›rk in gold, enamel, and semiprecious stones made use of a ⋅hnique dating back to the Sumerians, which was similar to ·isonné (see below). Small strips of metal were soldered ⋅tically onto a metallic surface, thus forming a network of ⋅tions on the support. Hard stones cut to the correct di- ⋅nsions were inserted in these sections and fixed with cement. certain cases the sections were filled with colored glass, ⋅ich was fused to the base of the metal support (generally ld, silver, copper, or bronze; in more recent times, iron). metimes chisels were used to produce the necessary cavities ⋅ the insertion of the inlay material (champlevé; see below).

Ivory carving, which was widely practiced in Assyria, derived ›m more ancient Sumerian processes that have already been ⋅ntioned. Rectangular engraved panels from Assyria were fixed the support with copper nails, a technique that was exported Greece in the 6th century B.C. Certain ivory statuettes of ʒ Minoan civilization in Crete present an interesting example the combination of ivory and bronze: on the heads, which ʒ joined to the bodies by mortise joints, there are locks of ⋅r made of braided bronze wire inserted into perforated holes. ʒe tools employed in these processes — small saws, drills, ⋅sels, and punches — were used for carving the ornamental ⋅gments that were to be embedded in the ground or for carving ʒ cavity required for the inlay work in the support. Probably ⋅imple kind of lathe was also used. Sometimes the ivory was ⋅t along a line of small holes drilled in the heads, rather than wed. Abrasives were used for smoothing the surface; in ›man times sharkskin was used. These processes for combining ⋅rious materials attained their most monumental achievement the creation of chryselephantine statues.

In Greco-Roman times a combination of materials in ⋅rniture, basically wood and bronze, was characteristic of the ⋅tire Mediterranean Basin (V, PLS. 429, 431). Inlay work ⋅s also frequently employed, ranging from very thinly sectioned ⋅rtoise shell to horn and ivory, both natural and colored.

Later, the objects were enriched by insertion of opaque colored-glass slabs or hard or semiprecious stones.

Inlay work may be executed either with solid materials (generally precious or hard stones) or with colored frit melted into the metallic cavity. The various processes are generally grouped under two headings — cloisonné and champlevé. In the former, the stone, glass, or enamel is inserted, cemented, or melted into cells bounded by thin metal strips or by wires welded vertically to the support; if there is no background the work is known as *plique-à-jour*. In champlevé the cavity that will contain the ornamentation is incised or chiseled on the metal ground. This process may be done during the actual casting.

The Greeks melted enamel on gold, confining it with fine gold wire. The oldest known examples of this technique are the cloisonné enamels from the Mycenaean tomb of Kuklia (Paphos) in Cyprus. These works anticipated by some 2,000 years the splendid flowering of Byzantine enamels (II, PLS. 482, 485, 486; IV, PLS. 405, 407). The Romans adopted both the champlevé and cloisonné techniques, especially in bronzework (IV, PL. 407). Later, the technique spread to the Roman provinces — particularly among the Saxons and Celts (mirrors and harnesses). The Greek and Roman traditions were never abandoned and exerted a decisive influence on Byzantine enamel-work. A fundamental piece in the *plique-à-jour* technique is the so-called "Cup of Khosrau" (6th–8th cent.; III, PL. 490, XII, PL. 395), made of engraved rock crystal and red and green stones set in gold. Among the oldest datable pieces of Byzantine cloisonné enamel is the reliquary of Justin II (6th cent.) in the Convent of Ste-Croix at Poitiers.

Another kind of inlay work that came into use in France in Merovingian times consists in simple linear designs obtained by hammering silver wire into chased grooves on the surface of an iron object. With this system certain surfaces can be covered in silver and gold; the cavity is prepared with parallel grooves cut by a tracer, and wires inserted into the contiguous grooves unite to form a single surface by means of a final hammering.

The beginning of the 13th century saw the diffusion in Persia, Arabia, and India of damascening, a polychrome incrustation obtained by using various metals. This technique produced the finest type of inlay work. The pattern was generally traced with a chasing tool on the surface to be decorated, though in some cases the design was stamped. The cavity was filled with sheets or wires of differently colored metals that were beaten while cold and frequently inserted on intermediate sheets of soft metal. The metal was pushed into the cells with a flat-edged thin punch (VI, PL. 281).

At the same time the niello process was becoming more widely known. Niello is obtained by filling grooves incised in metal with a special powdered amalgam made of silver, copper, and lead, which is then blackened with a sulphur mixture. The amalgam is poured onto the red-hot metal sheet containing the incised design, so that it melts and fills the hollows of the engraving. When the metal sheet has cooled off, the superfluous niello is scraped away, thus exposing the ornamentation. This can be extremely fine since the melted amalgam runs into the narrowest incisions in the metal. Niello was frequently used in combination with damascening (e.g., Sanctuary of S. Michele Arcangelo, Monte Sant'Angelo, Apulia, 1076). The color, hardness, and malleability of niello vary through the centuries according to the proportions of the metals used and the quantity of sulphur added for obtaining the required shades of black (steel blue, lead gray, coal black).

These techniques, whose greatest and most widespread use occurred during the 12th and 13th centuries, were not new in the history of the techniques of the Mediterranean civilizations. Metal incrustation work and damascening appear contemporaneously in Egypt and in the Cretan-Mycenaean world. Niello was also known in Egypt, but it was characterized by the use of an amalgam that was embedded in comparatively deep cavities. The Romans used niello only rarely (e.g., the Hildesheim Treasure), but in the Hellenistic world the combination of incrustation and niello lasted into the 2d century of our era. From Byzantine and medieval Italian damascening were derived the Renaissance techniques (VII, PL. 335); particularly remarkable were those of the Spanish and Milanese armorers (I, PLS. 447–450). Oriental damascening originated in Mesopotamia, where it derived directly from the Sassanian goldsmiths' work (XII, PLS. 396, 402–404, 407, 408); in most cases it was used in the decoration of metal vases with gold and silver damascening (mostly brass vases, called Mosul bronzes; III, PL. 7). Production spread in Persia in the 14th century and later reached the West through Venice (VII, PL. 313). India and Kashmir have a few rare examples of copper damascening that date from as late as the 17th and 18th centuries. A distinctive characteristic of this Oriental production was the practice of making a series of small holes along the contours of the pattern in order to fix the gold or silver leaf more firmly during the hammering process.

In the cloisonné and champlevé techniques the process of placing the glass paste in the cavities on the metal ground (PL. 458) is known as enameling. The glass material is colored by the addition of metal oxides as in glass technique. Once the pastes of different colors have been prepared, they are ground in a mortar under water and reduced to powder, which should be kept damp. On a base of gold, silver, copper, or bronze (in recent times, iron), this damp paste is pressed into the cells of the cloisonné or the cavities of the champlevé, and when it has dried it is submitted to heat until the fusion is complete. Fired enamel attains a very bright surface and a firm hold on the metal. After being fused, the surface is polished with pumice or charcoal powder. The oldest enamels were fused in open earthenware pots, which were either placed on their sides in a plant-charcoal oven or covered with a perforated metal bowl (as is recommended by the monk Theophilus in the *Schedula diversarum artium*, 10th cent.?).

The enamels were grouped according to the composition of the metal ground. In cloisonné small amounts of powdered glass are placed in each of the cells formed by thin metal strips or wires, upon which the enamel acquires a firm hold when melted (IV, PLS. 407, 408, 418, 419).

In champlevé work the enamel fills the cavity made in the metal by chiseling, engraving, stamping, or casting; the cavity is outlined by a raised portion of the metal. In *basse-taille* the pattern is engraved in bas-relief beneath the original level of the ground and is then covered with a layer of translucent enamel (IV, PL. 411). The pattern modeled beneath the surface remains visible through the enamel, and the depth variations of the relief show in the varying color intensity of the enamel. Incrusted enamels may enrich an irregular surface, decorate an object in cast metal, or cover the surface of a figure executed in sheet metal by a repoussé technique and a chisel.

The first attempts at painting enamels were made in Italy during the 16th century. The enamels were spread on a first layer of opaque blue enamel. Also in the 16th century a special technique was developed in France. After the pattern was traced on the surface of the metal, the enamel was spread with a spatula and brushes, either directly on the metal ground or on an intermediate layer of white enamel. At the end of the process a translucent enamel was spread over the whole. The various techniques can often be encountered together; for example, the famous Limoges enamels join flat sections in champlevé and relief sections in repoussé work (see ENAMELS; METAL-WORK).

III. TECHNIQUES OF REPRESENTATION. REALIZATION OF CONCEPTS. *Painting.* Many theories have been advanced regarding the ancient processes for the transcription of the pictorial image from its initial formulation to the completed work, but most frequently they have not gone beyond pure hypothesis. Nevertheless, in Egyptian painting an indication is provided by a find of smooth chips of limestone — called ostraca by extension of the later Greek usage, οστρακα — on which there can be seen actual sketches for designs, made with brushes and showing hesitations and corrections. These fragments appear sporadi-cally all through the course of Pharaonic civilization but are most highly concentrated in the period from the 18th to the

20th dynasty in the regions of Saqqara and western Theb (IV, PLS. 191, 200, 261; X, PL. 494). Many hypotheses ha been put forward on the use of these pictorial "notes." Ve probably they can be divided into two categories: worksh exercises and cartoons for the execution of frescoes. The sp radic presence of proportion squares on these Egyptian ostra is sufficient evidence of the existence of a technical process f the transposition, in scale, of a design onto a fresco, a techniq that is in every way similar to the one in use today. Asi from these limestone ostraca, proportion squares on papyr and wood were also used. As for preparations for wall paintir examinations of Egyptian ruins have shown that vertical ar horizontal lines (grids) and axes were brushed on in red pigme (IV, PL. 347). The frequent repetition of the same mod common to both sculpture and painting in Egypt, is obvio proof of the ostraca's didactic function.

The long and scrupulous training of skilled workers co tinued in the apprenticeship of the Greek ceramic painters, w achieved their extraordinary skill and lightness of touch on through long series of exercises — for example, the repeat drawing of the same anatomic contour — which gave the designs an easy flowing aspect (IV, PL. 263). In ceramic pain ing the initial sketch did not, except in rare cases, possess much the quality of a visual concept as that of a lineal gui copied from an already finished model. These models mu have been widely used and constituted the permanent pictor fund of a workshop; in the case of mural painting and mosai they were disseminated across Greece, Hellenistic Egypt, an later, over the whole of the Roman Empire, transmitted skilled workers specialized in the reproduction of the mo famous pictorial cycles. It is precisely because of the diffusi of these cartoons that the Hellenistic and Roman frescoes a remarkable for their peculiar iconographic unity. Even litera sources mention the custom of making preparatory drawin Pliny (*Natural History*, XXXV, 68) mentions the existence drawings on parchment by Parrhasios (q.v.) that were used the schools for a long time. It seems possible to recogni this type of drawing in certain eclectic Roman copies (perha connected with works by Zeuxis), such as the monochrom on marble from Herculaneum (Naples, Mus. Naz.; IV, PL. 26 XIV, PL. 453). What remains unclear in the case of the Hellenistic-Roman cartoons is the existence, or lack, of a pr cedure for transferring the design, according to scale, from small model to the wall by means of proportion squares from a second copy as large as the fresco (of the sort used fro medieval times onward for pouncing). In fact the Rom fresco, which bears no traces of a sinopia or pouncing, do show scratched linear marks that would be necessary for t transfer of the preparatory drawing — although it need n have been the same size as the fresco — to the actual plast

Only in the Middle Ages are there documents on the tec nical process of transcribing visual concepts. Between the 13 and 15th centuries this process of transcription and the techniq of modern fresco painting were laid down and defined (I PLS. 201, 266; IX, PLS. 119, 123). The artist fixed the fi composition in a series of sketches, then made his first measur ments on the designated wall. These measurements provid the necessary starting point for the fresco — that is, for t cartoon — through a transcription that frequently made use squaring. The cartoon in its most developed technical for was exactly the same size as the fresco and was mounted pasting together sheets of paper corresponding to the dimensio of the wall. In order to give the cartoon some firmness a rigidity diluted glue was spread over it. The drawing on t cartoon could be executed with pencil, pen, charcoal, or r pigment. It was shaded and included indications for the col (sometimes it was actually colored). Today it is customary draw the cartoon in charcoal and fix it with the fixatives us for pastels or with skimmed milk. After the application of t first layer of rough plaster, the cartoon, perforated with a spec pin along the main lines of the drawing, was placed upon t layer (in a proper state of humidity) and pounced with a fi cloth bag filled with charcoal powder which, by seeping throu the perforated lines, left a faint trace of the cartoon design the rough underlayer of plaster. These almost invisible lines were then reinforced by the artist either with color (sinopite; IV, PL. 266) or by incising the plaster with a nail or a piece of bone. In some cases, the painter "sought" the composition directly on the wall, drawing the contours with sinopite. The name "sinopia" given to the first transcription on plaster is derived from the material employed — sinopite, also called Armenian bole (although the two are not exactly alike); it is a red ocher, already known to the Greeks and Romans, which in ancient times was extracted in the environs of Sinope on the Black Sea. The material kept the name derived from its place of origin even though it was later found elsewhere. Its use was most widespread between the 13th and the 15th century in fresco painting, although it was present in mosaics as early as the 4th century B.C. Presumably the process was passed on to painting from mosaics. Cennino Cennini, in his *Libro dell'arte*, explains very clearly to what use it was put: "Take a little sinopite without tempera, and with a fine pointed brush proceed to mark out noses, eyes, the hair, and all the accents and outlines of the figures; and see to it that these figures are properly adjusted in all their dimensions, for these give you a chance to know and allow for the figures which you have to paint."

The sinopia was not the only means of transcription onto rough plaster; it was generally preceded by a number of processes that were absolutely indispensable, such as the partitioning of the space by snapping a string blackened with charcoal against the rough plaster to mark the "centers of the spaces"; a delineation of the figures and objects with charcoal; then the retouching of them with "a little ocher, without tempera but as thin as water"; and, finally, the execution of the detailed drawing with sinopite. In this system for transcribing a small design directly on the plastered wall the use of squaring appeared only later. A perfect example is the *Trinity* by Masaccio in Florence (IX, PL. 345), where the new process of squaring was applied for the first time only in the section of the fresco with the figure of the Madonna, while in the rest of the composition the medieval system continued to be employed (U. Procacci, *Sinopie e affreschi*, 1960). After completion of the transcription the cartoon was sometimes dismembered according to the foreseen "day's work"; often these fragments were resorted to after the last coat of plaster had been applied so as to determine (generally by scratching) certain essential internal lines in the section being worked on. This process is clearly recognizable in the Roman frescoes. Even today a second light pouncing on plaster is carried out; it tends to decrease any possibility of artistic initiative in the actual application of the colors.

In the case of book illustrations, both in ancient times and in the Middle Ages (IV, PL. 265), there was almost always a preparatory drawing, very often with written notes giving indications as to what colors to apply to each figure.

In the 15th century the invention and diffusion of paper in the West opened up new perspectives for the possibilities of directly noting pictorial ideas and for those forms of artistic formulation of concepts that require paper as an indispensable material support (engraving, lithograph, etching). Paper, made from cotton or linen rag or from hand-processed plant fibers, is of great importance as the grain and color facilitates sharp differentiation of the techniques of drawing (IV, PLS. 266, 276, 277). Charcoal very soon replaced graphite, with which it is difficult to cover large surfaces without incurring the disturbing effects of reflected light, while the impermanence of charcoal can be remedied by the use of fixatives with a water and milk or gum base. Another excellent technique for very precise and fine graphic effects is silver- or goldpoint, for which the paper must be prepared with China white (IX, PL. 119).

One of the most widespread techniques during the Renaissance and the 17th century was the sanguine drawing, in which natural red chalk was used either by itself (on colored paper) or in combination with black (II, PL. 280; IV, PLS. 271, 274). The light effects were obtained with rubber, the soft part of bread, or white lead. For chiaroscuro effects, aside from charcoal, bistre was also used (IV, PL. 269).

Another technique that has proved to be particularly well adapted to the sketchy and rapid transcription of ideas is that which makes use of inks and water colors (IV, PLS. 273, 277–279). For this purpose Rembrandt used bamboo sticks dipped in a walnut husk decoction of a very beautiful gold-brown color. Pens and brushes are used, the latter particularly for diluted China ink (sable brushes). Later, mechanical means came into use such as compasses, rulers, set squares, and curvilinear instruments for drawing; paper, leather, and cork stumps were used more and more frequently.

Sculpture. Certain archaeological finds lead to the supposition that small-scale models existed among the Assyrians. In the case of works in relief, fragments of small clay models have been preserved; as for sculpture in the round, it is thought that certain small sculptures of soft limestone may have served as models for works of monumental scale. Egyptian sculpture reveals great technical progress in the use of models (XIV, PL. 456). These were transferred by casting from the raw clay to plaster, which was stronger and more durable. It is interesting to observe that the process of reproducing models by casting them in plaster is practiced today only in conjunction with works of bronze or marble. The earliest evidence in Egypt of reproductions in plaster date back to the time of Akhenaten; but only in Hellenistic times did the practice become general, the favorite material always being clay, with or without a transfer to plaster. A distinction should be made, however, between models — which are in any case indispensable — for sculpture in bronze and those for sculpture in stone. It has been rightly observed that the increasingly frequent practice in marble sculpture of first transcribing the sculptural idea to a clay model was the result of the technological intervention of the methods of casting metal.

The model did not always have to be sculptured; in the case of the collective production of the craftsmen who worked under the direction of Phidias (q.v.), drawn models were used to help the collaborators in their work, particularly when bas-relief work did not make it difficult for the executant to interpret the model (friezes, metope). There are also documents on the models for the Mausoleum at Halikarnassos (PL. 41; III, PLS. 377, 378).

Thus two preliminary processes developed for sculpture — one the drawing, the other the model; the first, which fixes the initial conception of the sculptor, is sufficient only in specific circumstances for works executed in workshops, but it leaves (and this is clearly the case in Renaissance sculpture) the problems of volume and composition to the individual, private investigation of the craftsman. From the Renaissance on it became common to proceed from the first transcription to the final execution through an initial phase of drawing (mainly of details) and a second phase of sculptural reproduction in clay or wax. Wax was commonly used in the second half of the 16th century, while at the same time and in the following century small-scale terra-cotta models (II, PL. 276) became very important, especially for sculpture in marble. The models were sometimes the same size as the work itself, as in the case of nonmonumental works such as privately commissioned portrait busts (the Bernini portraits, II, PLS. 277, 278); but they were often only a small-scale guide for large works in stone (travertine, marble, etc.), the actual execution of which was not always carried out by the sculptor himself.

PRELIMINARY PROCESSES. *Painting.* It can hardly be said that there was any preparation of surfaces for painting during the Paleolithic period, but, rather, that a choice was made of natural walls, though a summary smoothing of the rock may sometimes have been necessary (XI, PLS. 258, 267, 268, 277, 278, 282); in some cases the very irregularity of the wall surface may have suggested some invention, so that instead of being an obstacle to the painter's imagination the technical difficulty may have furnished the pretext for more daring practical solutions that resulted in more complex esthetic achievements.

Only with the Egyptian, Mesopotamian, and Mediterranean cultures (Crete) was the use of a plaster coating introduced on a large scale. When this contained lime the technique of fresco painting was originated; however, in many cases the plaster merely served as a support for other types of painting. In Egypt, for instance, the thin layer of plaster applied on brick walls consisted of a preparation of gesso and glue adapted to the particular quality of the tempera used by the Egyptians (tempera dissolved with adhesives such as gelatine, glue, gum, or albumen in very liquid solutions). These processes were well known in the Cretan-Mycenaean world, but nothing is known of their reciprocal influences.

No other preparatory process is as important and as varied as that which is employed in fresco painting, considering the close connection between the plaster priming and the laying on of the colors. Since the work had to be done on wet plaster the painter had to divide the painting of the fresco over a certain number of days and could therefore spread the layer of plaster priming only as the work proceeded. With the passing of time, the plastering and the supporting wall underneath acquired greater solidity and thickness. The oldest Egyptian, Mesopotamian, and Cretan-Mycenaean remains show the presence of a very fine mixture of sand and lime or clay, sometimes with a coat of whitewash. The problem of the elasticity of the plastering brought about the practice of making two layers: the first a mixture of clay and chopped cow dung, horsehair, or straw; the second of gesso (I, PL. 366). In Mesopotamia clay plaster was also used, but more often a white lime mortar is found, sometimes mixed with ashes and applied in layers about $1/_8$ in. thick; this mortar later contained powdered brick, which increased its roughness (there are also traces of powdered brick in some Egyptian plaster). In other cases the brick walls were painted directly, sometimes even in silver and gold.

In Crete, in addition to the above process, wall painting was sometimes executed on damp pure lime plaster. In later times, this coat of plaster became less thick and was superimposed on a thicker gypsum ground. The colors were applied directly on the layer of damp lime.

In Etruria the preparatory layer for frescoes appears to have been extremely thin, sometimes nonexistent. In the Tomb of the Chariots in Tarquinia (I, PL. 368) analyses have shown that the preparation was composed of clay mixed with 1 per cent peat, as in some Oriental remains. Later, the plaster became smoother and thicker and was composed of sand and lime or of lime and chalk. Similar processes can be traced in India, where even in the 1st millennium of our era they were based on recipes contained in the Śilpaśāstras.

The technique for the preparation of the successive layers of undercoat and plaster, so accurately described by Vitruvius (q.v.), was first applied (judging from archaeological finds) in certain frescoes in Hellenistic tombs; it then spread to central Italy, where it is to be found, among other cases, in the Cardinal's tomb in Tarquinia. This process was to become the sole method used in the Roman world and in Renaissance and modern art. Vitruvius speaks of three successive layers, or undercoats, of rough paste, consisting of one part of slaked lime (at least a year old) and two parts of pozzuolana or sand (preferably of the river variety containing silicate and no iron), which were applied to a previously dampened wall. On these three layers, which were progressively thinner, another three layers of a mixture of lime, fine sand, and marble powder were applied, the thickness diminishing toward the surface. This is the plaster that Vitruvius advises to press with a trowel until the mortar no longer adheres to it. A special quality of Roman frescoes was, in fact, the extreme smoothness of the wall surface. The frescoes in the House of Livia on the Palatine correspond exactly to these precepts. It has been possible to discern the different days of work from the plaster on the back of detached frescoes. Against the risk of humidity, which is fatal to frescoes because of the inevitable efflorescence of saltpeter, Vitruvius and Pliny prescribe a process that was employed on a wall of the triclinium of the House of Livia on the Palatine, in the Villa of Livia at Prima Porta (VII, PL. 208), and in S. Maria Antiqua in the Roman Forum (II, PL. 445; XI, PL. 327); this was a mixture of lime, pozzuolana, tufa, and pieces of tile, which was placed between the wall and the first undercoat.

From the 2d century onward the process of plastering a wall was simplified, and the number of layers of plaster and undercoats was decreased until there was only one of each. This method remained in general use in medieval frescoes. The rough underlayer could be prepared by the painter's assistants, but the plastering itself, which is so closely linked with the daily rationing of the work, was often executed by the artist himself immediately before laying on the colors. In Renaissance and modern frescoes the dimensions of the layers, although they vary considerably from one technique to another, usually are about $2/_5$ in. in thickness for the undercoat and about $1/_4$ in. for the plaster. The outermost layer does not always present a perfectly smooth surface. Fra Pozzo (q.v.) preferred a granulous plaster for the vaults and cupolas because it gave a more luminous effect at a distance than the smoother type (II, PL. 172). Granulous plaster does, however, have great disadvantages, especially when it is applied to walls, for it collects dust. For this reason, in painting the vast surface of the Last Judgment in the Sistine Chapel, Michelangelo actually modified the incline of the wall itself by means of the undercoat, giving it a slight overhang (PL. 470; IV, PL. 179; IX, PLS. 533, 536).

Poplar, oak, and acacia were most commonly used for wooden supports. The natural resin of wood proved to be extremely harmful to paintings, and for this reason resinous wood was avoided. In Flanders the wood was even purified to make absolutely certain that no resin could form. Other dangers had to be safeguarded against: oak, after at least three years' seasoning, was left in running water long enough to free it from tannin. Cedar, teak, and dark walnut have been added to the list of woods commonly used in panel painting. Many devices for protecting the wood have been tried.

Of fundamental importance in the Middle Ages and the Renaissance were the methods of priming, which varied with the times mainly in relation to the different techniques in tempera (used in the Middle Ages until the end of the 15th century) and oils (X, PLS. 488, 490, 491). The priming that received the drawing or sketch for the painting became an integral part of the artistic work either because the shaded drawing (hatching) showing through the color actually guided the execution of the painting — as in the techniques that lasted until Giorgione (q.v.) made his experiments in color — or because the colored sketch acted as a ground. Theophilus and Cennino Cennini have provided interesting recipes for the priming of panels as a preparation for applying tempera. After the initial process of jointing the boards together with a kind of cement made of cheese mixed with lime, thin strips of canvas were applied to the joints (sometimes the whole board was covered with canvas, linen, or tanned leather). The surface was then covered with a layer of gesso mixed with glue or gelatine as a binding medium. A few days later, after the preparation had been smoothed, eight or more layers of gesso were applied with a bristled brush, and the surface was again smoothed by hand. Finally the panel was dried in the air and shade, and was worked over with flat scraper until the surface was as smooth as ivory.

Even more complicated was the preparation for oil painting described by Leonardo da Vinci ("The Practice of Painting," no. 628, The Literary Works of Leonardo da Vinci, J. P. Richter ed., London, 1939): "The panel should be cypress or pear or service-tree or walnut. You must coat it over with mastic and turpentine twice distilled and white, or if you like, lime, and put it in a frame so that it may expand and shrink according to its moisture and dryness. Then give it [a coat] of aqua vita in which you have dissolved arsenic or [corrosive] sublimate 2 or 3 times. Then apply boiled linseed oil in such a way that it may penetrate every part, and before it is cold rub it well with a cloth to dry it. Over this apply liquid varnish and white with a stick, then wash it with urine when it is dry. Then pounce and outline your drawing finely . . ." G. B. Armenini in his treatise De veri precetti della pittura (1587), and Vasari (q.v.) simplify the whole procedure in this manner: for "thin" painting, without oil, a simple layer of gesso is sufficient; oil on the other hand, require an adhesive made with varnish, cooked oil, Naples yellow, and white, which can evidently also

e used for priming the canvas. The preparation could also
e colored, sometimes with antique red or a reddish pigment
lat G. P. Lomazzo called "apisso" (*Trattato dell'arte della
pittura*, 1584).

The relationship between pictorial technique and the prep-
ration of the support also conditions the priming of the
anvas. It is said that the use of this support goes back to an
nvention by Margaritone d'Arezzo (ca. 1216 – ca. 1290); but,
a actual fact, Pliny, Juvenal, and Boethius speak of painting
n canvas, and the Fayum paintings (Egypt) are also canvas
aintings (X, PLS. 489, 492; XI, PL. 214; XII, PL. 197). More-
ver, in the Byzantine period canvas was commonly employed
n icons. Usually, the canvas was glued to a board and primed
ccording to a recipe given in detail in the *Painter's Manual
f Mt. Athos* (the *Hermeneia* by Dionysios of Fourna-Agrapha),
which consisted of an adhesive made of gypsum, soap, honey,
nd glue. The necessity of facilitating the transportation of
aintings led — already in the Byzantine world — to the ex-
edient of substituting the board with a wooden support in
he form of a stretcher. The diffusion of this process in the
estern world is entirely due to the Venetians. For it was in
enice that painting on canvas, which had hitherto been limited
o processional banners, found expression at the end of the
Quattrocento in the monumental canvases (*teleri*) of the Bellinis
nd Carpaccio. The Venetian painters altered the Byzantine
rocess, which by preparing the canvas in the same manner as
wood panel had made the canvas stiff and easily damageable;
he Venetians used a light and rather absorbent priming of
halk and glue (preceded by a size of sugar and starch glue).
The canvas was either linen or hemp. Silk gives poor results
ecause it cracks and disintegrates into dust under the action
f the oils (there is some uncertainty regarding the tradition
hat Guido Reni painted on silk). The risk of such damage
ed to an exaggerated use of plant glues, which when laid on
he canvas before the gesso priming caused many bumps and
letachment of the ground and the colors in the course of
ime. Even more dangerous are the more recent oil primings
hat dull the colors of the painting. Litharge, which has been
dopted in order to hasten the drying of the priming, also has
he disadvantage of making the surface granulous. In the
7th century grounds colored in red or brown were extensively
ised. With the passing of time these absorbed the half tones
nd reinforced the dark colors, thus destroying the balance of
he picture. New recipes were experimented with in France
t the end of the 18th century. Among others, priming with a
oney and wax base was used. Nevertheless, the thin chalk
nd glue preparation of the old Venetian canvases can still be
onsidered the best of all those which have been tried. The
rocedure followed for this preparation — still the most generally
dopted — is quite simple: the canvas is wetted and stretched
n stretchers with wedges at the corners to increase the perim-
ter and tauten the canvas; the borders are rounded off to pre-
ent cracking; a light coat of glue is applied, and the next day
gesso is spread over it, an operation that must be repeated a
ew hours later, but in the opposite direction; and before the
oat dries completely it is carefully scraped with a spatula.
Good results are obtained by mixing the gesso with milk into
paste that has the property of making the priming more
elastic. To protect the canvas against humidity the back is some-
imes spread with wax and resin, but this process often causes
slackening of the canvas.

Sculpture. In the case of stone sculpture it is not always
possible to make a clear and justifiable distinction between
he preliminary processes and the artistic execution. In ancient
imes, especially in Egypt and Greece, it was the artist
imself who had to choose and roughly shape the block of
narble in the quarry before it was transported to its emplace-
nent. All the preliminary work with hammer and chisel was
herefore an initial creative elaboration of the final image itself.
This was not the case with later works, which were generally
feeble repetitions of a famous subject, occasionally with eclectic
embellishments taken from other works. The use of models
nd the possibility of measuring the statue in the block by

means of pointing permitted the work of boasting to be left
entirely to minor craftsmen, who were often mere artisans,
completely devoid of creative talent but unerring technically.
The artistic process was therefore limited to the execution of
the main expressive element (generally the face), while to the
apprentices (who did impeccable work with the help of models
and methods of calculation and measurement) was left the
execution of the torso, draperies, and other details. In the
Middle Ages a return to the methods of direct execution can
be noted, often with results of high artistic quality; but during
the Renaissance and the following centuries the process varied
according to the temperament of the artist, the importance of
the work, or the role played by the workshop. It is not the
work following the chiseling process that marks the point of
direct intervention, nor that, more anonymous, of the passage
from the first rough shaping to the second (which is already
decisive for the expressive details). Statues entirely executed
by the artist from the very first chisel marks (e.g., Michelangelo's so-called "Slaves" or "Prisoners") alternate with works
in which direct intervention is reduced to the level of accurate
and helpful guidance (e.g., the figures of Leah and Rachel for
the tomb of Julius II by Michelangelo and Raffaele da Montelupo).

Far clearer is the preparatory process in certain large sculptures, which because of their size or of inlay work in various
materials required a supporting apparatus (armature) constructed
on principles entirely foreign to a sculptor; this step called for
the skill of an engineer, capable of constructing a wooden or
metal scaffolding suited to receive and sustain the facing of
carved sections (as in chryselephantine sculpture) or the welded
metallic elements of monumental sculpture (from the Colossus of
Rhodes to the Statue of Liberty by Frédéric Auguste Bartholdi).

PROCESSES OF EXECUTION. *Painting.* The simplest and oldest
technique is represented by designs executed with the finger
tip on a soft surface (clay of the Pech-Merle cave, France,
datable to the Upper Paleolithic age; PL. 105; XI, PL. 262).
The numerous remains of paleolithic painting allow one to
distinguish at least six different techniques: (1) dipping the
finger in paint like a brush; (2) painting with a stiff point
dipped in color, such as a pointed piece of wood, a quill (perhaps even a porcupine's spine), or a rough plant fiber for the
finer details; (3) daubing as seen in the many examples of
fully colored figures (in some cases the outline was drawn
first, and then the figure was filled in with color; in others
the color was laid on without preliminary outlining) that were
executed with the finger tips or sometimes, it seems, with a
pad of animal fur or moss dipped in color; (4) spray painting,
which was probably performed by spraying paint through the
lips; (5) dot or touch painting, in which sometimes only the
contours and sometimes entire figures were executed by means
of little dots, which were probably applied with a stick, to the
end of which was fixed a fur pad dipped in color; and (6) dry-
point technique, evidenced by finds of pointed crayons made
of soft coloring materials and charcoal, while the examination
of certain paintings justifies the opinion that such a technique
was practiced.

Among the pigments used in paleolithic painting, at least
in the examples known from the caves of Altamira and Lascaux
(XI, PLS. 258, 263–265, 267, 268, 277, 278, 281, 282), manganese
oxides and iron (for red and black), yellow carbonates of iron, and
soot can be recognized. These pigments, finely ground in a
mortar and mixed with an ingredient more watery than fatty,
were kept in hollow stones, bones, shells, or skulls. To these
pigments the Egyptians and the Mesopotamian cultures added
new ones, almost all of which were obtained by processing
mineral substances. The series is vast. Red was obtained
from red ocher (predynastic Egypt, Mesopotamia, Asia Minor,
Palestine), iron oxides, hematite, red ocherous clay, and red
lead (prepared by heating lead, lead dross, and white lead until
there formed a litharge, or lead oxide, which was then carefully
ground and reheated). Rose was prepared from red and white
pigments or other substances (sometimes shells reduced to
powder). Yellow was obtained mainly from ocher, limonite,

arsenic sulphide (Egypt from the 18th dynasty onward and Mesopotamia). Orange was made by mixing red and yellow ochers, yellow lead monoxide (predynastic Egypt), and basic lead antimonate (Babylon). Brown tints were taken from other natural ochers (Egypt), sometimes a mixture of ocher and gypsum, red on black pigments, hematite over black, and yellow ocher over hematite; green was prepared by powdering together malachite and chrysocolla or, sometimes, by blending blue frit with yellow ocher and verdigris (Egypt from the 6th dynasty and Mesopotamia); a green frit was obtained by melting together sand, alkali, and copper minerals and powdering before use. Blue came from powdered lapis lazuli, turquoise, and cobalt compounds; in 4th-dynasty Egypt a substitute for lapis lazuli, also known to the Assyrians, was produced by heating silica, malachite, calcium carbonate, and natron, and it was used in paints, glass, the manufacture of small objects, and glazes. Purple frit (Assyria) was obtained by blending sand, alkali, and copper salts, but it is not known whether it was ever used as a pigment. Gray tints resulted from a mixture of gypsum or of some yellowish light earth (ocher?) with lampblack or charcoal (Egypt). White pigments were prepared from calcium carbonate (chalk) and calcium sulphate (gypsum), ceruse, terra melia (a form of kaolin), and metallic mercury, called sublimate cinnabar (sometimes applied on the surface of metal statuettes). Black came from manganese dioxide (not proved with certainty), lampblack, bone black, charcoal, and bitumen (Mesopotamia). These colors were used for painting on plaster (Crete being particularly remarkable for its very wide range of pigments of various colors — red, white, black, yellow, dark red, orange, green, and blue; IV, PLS. 61, 62) and for painting on ceramics, stone, wood, ivory, cloth, metal, and semiprecious stones.

Glues were generally used as a vehicle for the colors. Examination of archaeological specimens has led to the recognition of the following types: casein, prepared from curdled milk; gum arabic, taken from the bark of the Arabian acacia (Egypt and Mesopotamia); grain starch (Egypt); gelatine and tragacanth; and egg white. To the water-soluble vehicles honey was sometimes added to make the gum arabic and the gelatine less brittle. From the previously mixed colors were made little cakes, which were pulverized by rubbing them against a stone and mixed with the vehicle and water.

Distinctions in the pictorial techniques are principally based on the quality of the solvents and binding media used at different times in the preparation of the colored pigments. A water solvent is adopted when the color is to be absorbed by the material of the support, as in fresco painting on plaster, or water-color painting on paper; in fresco painting the color is not fixed by its greater or lesser penetration into the porousness of the plaster, but by the formation of a film of calcium carbonate. Binding elements are used on grounds with little or no capacity for absorption and for less transparent effects in the color (see PAINTING).

The most ancient painting processes frequently used those binding media which are still required today in tempera or gouache. Ancient Egyptian painting, for example, presents substantial analogies with the gouache technique that reached its peak in the 18th century in France. The mineral, organic, and plant pigments were frequently amalgamated in ancient Egypt with tragacanth and honey before they were spread on the properly dampened support.

A brief analysis of the pigments is necessary for an examination of the various pictorial techniques (PL. 449).

Ceruse (white lead or silver white) is a basic lead carbonate made by soaking lumps of lead in acetic acid; when buried under tanner's bark or dung, the heat from the fermentation helped to form white lead (a Dutch process during the Middle Ages). It is described by Pliny, by Amplonius (De coloribus, naturalia exscripta et collecta, Erfurt, Stadtbib., Ms. Amplonius, Quarto 189), and by Cennino Cennini (Libro dell'arte) and appears in all painting on wood since the 13th century.

Zinc white (Chinese white, snow white), or zinc oxide, came into use about 1840.

Titanium white, or titanium oxide, has only recently come into use.

Genuine ultramarine (lapis lazuli) is a sodium-aluminum silicate (sodalite) found in a natural state (rocks). It was used by the Egyptians, Greeks, and Romans; Cennini considered it the noblest of colors and described the complex method of purifying it.

Blue copper pigments include Egyptian blue (double silicate of copper and calcium), which has been in use since Egyptian times and is mentioned by Vitruvius, and azurite (blue basic copper carbonate), called lapis Armenus by Pliny, which was frequently used by Titian.

Copper greens were used excessively from the 15th to the 17th century, after which they disappeared. In recipes of the 15th century they are mixed with lime and potassium plus ammoniac salt. On the subject of their peculiar impermanence Leonardo da Vinci points out in his Treatise on Painting that green made with copper, even when it is mixed with oil, loses its beauty if it is not immediately covered with varnish. It is this weakness that has prevented industrial production.

Cobalt blue, consisting of cobalt oxide and alumina, was first prepared by Louis Jacques Thénard in 1804 and is widely used in modern painting. It also exists in varieties known as cobalt ultramarine or Thénard blue.

Indigo is an Indian plant pigment used for tempera and cloth dyeing. It is mentioned by Pliny.

Smalt is made by grinding a blue potash glass that has been colored with cobalt. According to B. Neumann (Z. f. angewandte Chemie, XXXVIII, 1925, p. 863), this was the only blue used in painting in the Bronze Age. It was much used in Venice in the 15th century, when it was also combined with light blue and lapis lazuli. In addition to its appearance in mural painting (Leonardo used it in 1429 in the apartments of Lodovico Il More in the Castello Sforzesco in Milan), it was used also by Rubens in oil painting (through a now unknown formula he was able to dissolve it in essential oil and resin).

Artificial ultramarine is a combination of silica, alumina, soda, and sulphur that was discovered by J. B. Guimet in 1826.

Prussian blue, a compound of iron and cyanogen, was first made by Diesbach in about 1704.

Lazulite is an azure-blue hydrous phosphate of aluminum and magnesium. Amplonius's ancient formula used quicklime and strong wine, which were left in a warm place with horse manure for a month.

Malachite green is a basic copper carbonate that was known to the Greeks and Romans; other green pigments were prepared from terre verte (Verona green) or verdaccio, a green earth that was used, like all other types of earth, since prehistoric times. The 13th-century Italians used it as a substitute for bole in their silver-gilt grounds (III, PL. 321; IV, PLS. 283, 284, 289, 290); in the Renaissance it was used for fresco and oil painting.

Chrome yellow, a neutral lead chromate, was first produced industrially by L. N. Vauquelin in 1797.

Yellow earths (yellow ochers) consist of a native earth containing hydrated ferric oxide; they resist atmospheric action well and have been used from prehistoric times to contemporary painting; when heated they turn red (so-called "burnt ochers," although natural burnt ocher appears in volcanic regions).

Cadmium yellow is a sulphide of cadmium that was discovered in 1819 and first manufactured as a paint pigment in 1829.

Lakes are insoluble pigments obtained by the precipitation of coloring substances of animal or plant origin or coal tar with insoluble mineral substances (chalk, alum solutions, etc.). The tar solutions are quite recent, but some of the animal and plant solutions were known in ancient times. Among the natural lakes are Tyrian purple (extracted from the murex Brandaris and mentioned by Vitruvius and Pliny) and kermes (extracted from the cochineal insect and superseded by cochineal), known in the East as early as the 2d millennium B.C. One of the most important lakes, which was much used in Renaissance painting, was madder lake (laque de garance, extracted from the madder root, which Amplonius calls brasilium); it is now produced artificially. It ranges from dark red to pink, and its presence has been noted in Egyptian painting. In ancient times it was treated with opaque solutions that reduced the rilliance which has been characteristic of this pigment from the Middle Ages until today. Amplonius gives a recipe that sheds light on the medieval process [infusion, while cold, of grated roots and urine for three days, with successive additions of alum and whitestone (granulite), and final mixing and filtering operations].

Red earth colors (red ochers) were used even in prehistoric times and varied in shades according to the quantity and quality of the metal salts.

Cinnabar (vermilion), a mercuric sulphide, is mentioned by Theophrastus and Pliny as *minium*. Although it is found in a natural state, it has been artificially prepared since the Middle Ages. Once again, Amplonius gives a chemical recipe for the artificial fabrication of cinnabar. It must be used with great care in fresco painting because of its tendency to change in reaction to light.

Red lead (minium), an oxide of lead, is obtained by heating white lead in the presence of air. It was used by the Egyptians and frequently appears in Roman encaustic painting.

Brunino di Bergamo, a ferrous oxide used exclusively in fresco painting, is the *amatito* (hematite) or violet mentioned by Cennini. It was used extensively by Tiepolo in his wall paintings. In the form of a glutinous solution mixed with silicate of aluminum it is generally employed by gilders of nonmetallic objects as a ground preparation for gold (bole).

Bitumen (asphaltum), for which the oldest evidence of use appears in the Sumerian and Egyptian civilizations, is gradually disappearing in oil painting because it does not dry completely.

a. Tempera. This is a painting process in which the distinctive feature is the medium used as a vehicle. It can be divided into "fat" and "lean" tempera. Lean tempera generally requires, as a vehicle, either animal glue or organic adhesive substances, such as egg, milk, or fig latex. It is with these specific emulsions that some of the Fayum portraits were painted (X, PL. 492). Heraclius testifies to the use of the same procedure in the Middle Ages (colors ground in water with gum, glue, or egg), as do Cennini, Lomazzo, and others. Fat tempera, owing to the complexity of individual experiments, can almost be identified with the earliest paintings in oils. Even Vasari makes no distinction between the two processes, and he groups under the category of tempera all pastes (impasto), even oil and varnish. This has created many misunderstandings and doubts, involving even the manner of defining the techniques of the artist who, according to tradition, was the inventor of oil painting — Jan van Eyck (q.v.). According to E. Berger, Van Eyck used emulsions of oil and egg; according to others, his technique was based on an impasto of oils and hard resins. The passage from tempera to oils must certainly have occurred gradually, and in many cases the results were achieved by means of the mixed technique that was still an artistic heritage of the late 15th century and appears in tempera paintings on linen canvases by Mantegna and Botticelli (tempera mixed with resin-oil colors, or the latter superimposed on the tempera like a glaze). This glazing of the tempera with oil is possible on canvas; fat tempera, however, can be used only on wood and affords an extremely wide range of colors, permitting the use not only of colors soluble in watery solutions but also of lakes and of such pigments as can be dissolved only in oily solvents.

b. Oil. The oil technique is undoubtedly the one most widely used since the 15th century. Reports according to which the Van Eycks invented it and Antonello da Messina (q.v.) imported it into Italy have absolutely no historical foundation (besides, oil painting was already known to the Romans who painted shields and weapons using this technique). In actual fact, it would be more appropriate to speak of increasing experimentation with resin-oil impastos that Flemish artists carried out systematically (see FLEMISH AND DUTCH ART); eventually they came to use oily diluents almost exclusively. From the color itself, by increasing or reducing the quantity of the solvent, the Flemish painters obtained impastos that were either dense and thick, or liquid and transparent, with infinite possibilities for transparent glazes of body colors or, vice versa, body lights

on transparent shadows done with fluid colors. The diluent capacity of the oils and the rapidity with which they dried could be modified with essential oils or by adding volatile substances or resinous varnish. The mixture used by Van Eyck was light and fluid and dried easily. The colors were ground in linseed oil or nut oil, fused while hot with hard resins (amber and copal), and finally diluted with essential oils (oil of lavender, spike, or rosemary); the latter, owing to their varying degrees of rapidity in drying, made it possible to work slowly on nuances and to add fine, minute touches. The light-colored ground of the wood panel was used in many cases for the lights; nevertheless the "last touches of light," combining oil and varnish, were frequently applied with body colors, especially on the darker tones. The transparent pigments, such as lakes (mainly madder lake), were applied in successive layers of glazing in order to achieve a luminous reflection on the white ground; the result was extremely soft shading. These glazes were mixed with the varnish. The Venetian painters abandoned the Flemish habit of using hard resins, adopting instead soft resins, balsams, and essential oils. This made possible freer brushwork but also caused the chromatic effect to be more opaque. It is precisely to this exclusion of hard resins that the beginning of the technique of painting in oils on canvas is due; for hard resin, owing to its own rigidity, demanded a wooden support prepared with chalk and glue.

At this point in its development oil technique offered unlimited possibilities: retouching, subtle shading, the superimposition of transparent glazes or of liquid colors (bleeding as in water-color painting), and thick impasto applied with a spatula (as in encaustic painting). The brushes were made of fitchew, vair, squirrel, sable, or even of silk (Leonardo). A perfect example is Leonardo's technique. Apart from his manner of modulating the shadows on the basis of the principle of "values" (progressing, on one hand, from the shadows and the intermediate lights toward the darker shades and, on the other, toward the lighter tones), what was new in substance was the complete abandonment of the medieval chiaroscuro process (permeating Venetian painting) in favor of the structured painting that was to come into its own with Giorgione's and Titian's *camaïeu*. Leonardo achieved his transparencies (indispensable to his theory of light and shade) by means of thin coats of glazing with a diluent of nut oil, which allowed the light to penetrate the pigments to the very ground of the painting.

In Leonardo da Vinci's painting (q.v.), the ground is either in light colors (white, yellow, lake), in dark ones, or based on earths and black. Among the browns are burnt umber and a more transparent brown frequently used in Renaissance painting but not yet identified; the colors were based on ferrous oxide or manganese dioxide and were "encroaching," that is, they absorbed the superimposed colors. The lighter flesh tones were obtained with ceruse white, that had been treated so that it was completely purged of any acetate formation, following the method in use among the 15th-century masters; the surface shadows were done with earths mixed with lakes and made fluid with the usual cooked nut oil, camphor, or distilled juniper gum functioning as varnish to facilitate successive glazings.

The schools of Lombardy and Parma (VIII, PL. 196; XI, PLS. 45–50), from the time of Correggio, distinguished themselves by their use of Venetian turpentine, which made possible impastos producing nuances with transparency and fusion of color. The Venetians, for their part, inherited from Giorgione the new experience of sketching in body color on wood prepared with absorbent chalk and glue. Chromatic effects were obtained from the refraction of the color and not from its transparency. These sketches, done in lean color with vigorous strokes of the brush, were left to dry for months. The pigments were made into a paste and diluted first with purified oil and then with essential oils. In the final glazing a fatty varnish was used; some of them — thicker, more colored, and based on amber and copal dissolved in a fatty oil — had the disadvantage of drying more slowly; others, based on sandarac and bitumen, have, with time, caused partial blackening of the color. The study of the relationship between diluents and pigments led, at the end of the 16th century, to the most complicated and personal techniques: in one and the same picture — for example, in the works of Guercino (q.v.; II, PL. 197; III, PL. 311; VIII, PL. 218) — pure oil, oil with Greek pitch, and oils with other resins and gums were used. It was essential, in the interest of the good quality of a painting, that the underlying layers of body paint be as lean and as absorbent as possible (Reynolds, with his overdose of oils and resins in the underlying layers, caused his paintings to blacken and crack). New techniques were also introduced by Rubens, who combined the Flemish and Venetian processes by placing side by side transparent shadings (obtained by diluting and bleeding the colors as in water-color painting) and thick impasto lighting (spread with a hard brush and blended in afterward with light nuances and glazing).

From the 18th century on, the oil method became increasingly predominant. The diffusion of industrially manufactured colors in tubes (originally French) made possible easy and immediate painting — that "spontaneous" (so-called "action") painting which was cherished by mid-19th-century artists. The industrialization of color production has brought with it some serious disadvantages. To prevent the colors from drying in the tubes, the manufacturers exaggerate the quantity of oil (about a third more than necessary), also adding 20–30 per cent of wax, fats, tallow, and sperm oil. The excess oil causes the layers of paint to turn yellow, and the wax impedes the complete adhesion of successive layers, so dilution with benzine must therefore be resorted to. Nevertheless, the impastos and emulsions did profit from individual experiments, such as the use of resin and wax colors spread with a spatula (Van Gogh). Some processes originate in the accidental placing together of the most heterogeneous materials, depending solely on the impulse of the moment and lacking any technical concern for the resistance and durability of the work. In this manner one passes from oil colors with smalt, tempera, or synthetic varnish to the insertion of paper, sand, metal fragments, cloth, sawdust, wood, tin foil, glass, and cement (see MEDIA, COMPOSITE). Some contemporary artists do study technical problems with special care, superimposing innumerable layers of different substances.

c. Fresco. Fresco painting is executed on freshly spread, wet lime plaster (*buon fresco*, or true fresco); water is used as a vehicle for the pigments, the lime of the ground and the water combining to form a binding film of crystalline carbonate. *Fresco secco*, a method that uses a dry ground soaked with slaked lime before painting, has a very remote ancestry. It was practiced in the early civilizations of the Near East and in the zone of Cretan-Mycenaean influence. The proof that fresco painting and not some other process was used is shown by chemical analysis, which has revealed the presence of a film of carbonate over the painting (the residue of the evaporation of the water in the plaster at the time of painting). There is little information (most of it literary) concerning the practice of fresco painting in ancient Greece. Critical discussion of passages in the writings of Pausanias and Lucian has raised doubts about the technical process in the paintings of Polygnotos (q.v.) for the pynakotheke of the Propylaia in Athens, to the extent that they are now thought to have been panel paintings rather than wall paintings. But some fragments of painted plaster found in the Agora in Athens showed, when the color was analyzed, obvious traces of calcium carbonate (common to all fresco painting). In regard to the Etruscan civilization the frescoes in the tombs of Tarquinia, Vulci, Orvieto, Chiusi, and elsewhere provide much information (V, PLS. 32, 41, 42, 46, 52). Here, too, the characteristic film appears on the plaster.

Vitruvius and Pliny give specific details concerning the Roman processes (derived from the fresco technique of certain Hellenistic hypogeums). The specifically Roman quality consisted in the extreme smoothness of the paint layer (conditioned by the carefully smoothed and polished ground and by the presence in the ground of marble dust), on which the colors were spread with brushes, account being taken of those colors that can withstand lime (earths) and those that cannot and were therefore excluded (according to Pliny, the latter were purpuric,

indigo, cerulean, Melian white, arsenic trisulphide, Appian green and ceruse). The final process of varnishing with wax, almost always used in Roman frescoes, has caused divergences in opinion as to the quality of Roman fresco painting. According to some authorities it is practically nonexistent (since it is actually encaustic painting), while others, who point out that frequently the fresco was retouched after it had dried, instead consider it a process of *fresco secco*. Still others, basing their opinion on the results of analyses, have maintained that it is tempera painting with various solvents and adhesives and different processes of execution. The actual execution of the fresco was, of course, preceded by the grinding of the pigment with water — all of which were mineral (earths), except for plant and animal black — and by the normal processes of transcribing the ideas, which was done (as it still is today) by incising the fresh plaster with a point (a metal or bone stylet). There is no information about the quality of the brushes. (From the Renaissance on long pig's bristles or calf-hair brushes were used.) In some cases Roman fresco painting made use of colored grounds obtained by mixing the pigment with the last layer of plaster; tempera retouching appeared with increasing frequency in wall painting after the 4th century. The ancient processes of fresco painting remained almost unaltered throughout the Middle Ages and reached their culmination in the Renaissance. More important technical variations have occurred in the processes of transcription and preparation, while for the actual execution preference is given to highly fluid colors in an enormous variety of shades (thicker pastes are in disuse because they fall off with the seasonal alternation of heat and cold). Today the following colors are used in fresco painting: lime white, cadmium yellow, light ocher, golden ocher, vermilion (mercury sulphide) diluted with lime water for the various shades of pink, dark English red, Pozzuoli earth, Treviso earth, *caput mortuum* (iron oxide), burnt ochers, raw and burnt umbers, green from hydrated oxide of chromium and borax, cobalt green (cobalt oxide and zinc), Verona green, cobalt blue, ivory black, and vine black. The colors are tested on pieces of plaster or bricks because they change in the course of drying.

d. Pastel. The various pastels are obtained by preparing a paste with powdered pigments and water made slightly adhesive with substances that vary according to the shades and hardness required (usually a decoction of linseed or oatmeal, gum arabic, Marseilles soap, thin soapy water, etc.). This paste is molded and left to dry in the form of short cylinders, or pencils, of varying consistency — soft, semihard, and hard, the latter being specially treated with wax. Color gradations are obtained by adding white clay (Vicenza or Civita Castellana earth); for red Armenian bole is used and for the darker colors, iron-oxide black. The preparation is fairly complicated, for materials of different cohesion must be reduced to a common consistency.

Pastels, already in use in the 15th and 16th centuries, were mainly employed for coloring portraits sketched in a more "solid" technique (silverpoint or sanguine). Only Hans Holbein the Younger (q.v.) used them systematically in many of his works. In the 18th century, owing mainly to French artists, pastels developed as an autonomous artistic technique, but the difficulty of covering large surfaces always imposed limitations on the size of pastel paintings (III, PL. 216; X, PL. 497).

Execution is very simple. The color, when it comes into contact with the paper, adheres to it through friction without losing the opaque and absorbent quality of the paste. The shading is done with the fingers, which simplifies the blending of the tones and permits delicate gradations and fine modeling. The natural grease of the hand contributes to the adhesion of the chalk to the paper, and color effects can be infinitely varied through superimposition.

e. Water color. Water colors make use of colored pigments diluted in water and a binding medium, such as gum arabic. The colors must be inalterable under the effect of light; therefore, cadmium reds and yellows may be used, as well as blue, green, violet cobalts, ultramarine, chrome greens, all ochers and earths, ivory black, and Indian yellow. Each color requires a

fferent percentage of gum or, in some cases, additions of
)ney, glycerine, and sugar that make the colors more fluid.
. good adhesive is gum arabic, which can be mixed with cer-
in colors in its natural state and with others at a high tem-
erature. For the chromes (especially emerald green) dextrin
used to make them insoluble enough to be superimposed
ithout removing the preceding color with the brush. In works
larger size the drying of the colors is retarded with a tiny
)se of glycerine dissolved in water or with a solution of cal-
um chloride or tragacanth gum.

The pictorial process consists of painting dark on light.
he lighter tone (the equivalent of the "last lights" of oil
inting) is the support itself — that is, the paper. Once the
lor has been applied it can no longer be completely washed
vay, so the luminous quality of the lighter colors is threatened.
he tones when applied should always be a little more intense
an is necessary because they become paler and more trans-
arent as they dry. Water colors demand rapidity of execution
id sureness of touch because the colors dry quickly; retouching
impossible owing to the importance of the ground and the
itural transparency of the color. The fundamental masses of
e composition must be done with very watery and light
lors; when they are almost dry, the details are painted with
pointed brush and darker colors. Excellent results were ob-
ined with water colors having a base of sarcocolla (a gum
sin no longer in use), which could be dissolved in water or
cohol and gave the colors remarkable intensity; it is also
)ssible to use water-color glazes over gouache. Water colors
ere already known to the Egyptians in the 2d century B.C.
rom 250 B.C. there is evidence that water colors were used
China in painting on silk (see CHINESE ART). It was the
hinese, too, who, with the invention of paper, transferred the
chnique to this new and better support. Japan has also
rovided examples of water-color painting from the 13th cen-
iry. In the West this technique reemerged in the ornamenta-
on of medieval manuscripts and in the coloring of 15th-cen-
iry wood prints (see MINIATURES AND ILLUMINATIONS). Three
:nturies later the English landscape painters rediscovered, in
certain sense, the forgotten water-color technique, with which
urner (q.v.) attained particularly fine technical results (VI,
.s. 447, 450; XIV, PL. 222).

f. Gouache. The technique of painting with body colors is
illed gouache. A mixture of the same pigments as those in
ater colors with opaque white constitutes the more opaque
)uaches; in this mixture, the quantity of white determines the
ines of the colors. It is used on paper or dry plaster. Gouache
probably one of the oldest painting techniques; it was used
y the Egyptians and was a favorite with the French artists of
ie 18th century (Boucher, q.v.); today it is mainly used in
:age scenery, costumes, illustrations, and posters. In some
ises the techniques of gouache and water color were used
)gether (Dürer; IV, PL. 294). In both cases, sable, vair, swan,
nd fitchew brushes are used. In water-color painting camel-
air brushes of various sizes are particularly recommended.

g. Encaustic painting. Encaustic painting, which was already
racticed by the Greeks and Egyptians (X, PLS. 489, 495; XI,
.. 214; XII, PL. 197), as well as in the first centuries of the
hristian era, is often confused with ancient fresco painting
he latter was frequently given a final wax treatment, which
iade it seem like encaustic painting). Plutarch praises it for
ie splendor of its colors and its resistance to atmospheric
:tion. Pliny describes three different processes: (1) wax colors
pread on and smoothed with a spatula (*cestrum*); (2) painting
n ivory or wood by using a stylus to incise lines on a surface
iat had been saturated with paint; and (3) painting with a brush
nd wax colors liquified by heating. The colors and the wax
)uld also be diluted with essential oils (naphtha, turpentine),
r the wax could be saponified (made soluble with lye, since
ve contains sodium). These latter processes, carried out when
)ld, proved to be sensitive to humidity; fitchew brushes were
ised for them.

Encaustic painting has the advantage of offering a vast range
of colors of mineral and plant composition, most of which are
unstable. Wax serves to protect them, and they can be fixed
by placing them near braziers or other sources of heat.

In modern times various techniques of encaustic painting
have been tried in the hope of reviving the classical processes.
Mention should be made of the mixtures used by Aristide
Sartorio and the emulsions of Hilaire Hiler and Karl Zerbe.
Elena Schiavi obtained an excellent preparation by melting beeswax and sodium carbonate (Pliny's "natron") over a low flame
(saponification of the wax). The resulting colors are soluble in
water and can be used on wood, canvas, plaster, metal, and
glass. With this technique the use of very diluted colors with
a brush or of thick colors with a spatula is possible; it also
permits the superimposition of thick colors on previously colored
grounds and gives results comparable to those of Roman painting. For this reason Elena Schiavi considers her process to be
the one described by Pliny as "punic wax." (For additional
historical and technical information, see PAINTING.)

h. Engraving. The history of the techniques of engraving
on metal for printing appears to be very closely linked with
that of niello. In Italy the Florentine niello workers were in
the habit of testing the effect it would produce on a sheet of
metal before applying the niello. From these negative impressions on paper the idea of engraving copper plates for printing
could have been derived; however, since there exists no proof
to the contrary, it may have happened that the work of the
copper engravers suggested to the niello workers the process
of making direct proofs from a plate.

In the various techniques of engraving on metal certain
operations and materials recur. Preference is given to copper
plates prepared with a hammer and flattened and polished by
hand (PL. 453). The surface must be flat, shiny, and about
$1/16$ in. thick. For simpler or less important works zinc may
be used. An essential step in etching is that of cleaning the
plate, as the slightest trace of grease may cause the protective
varnish to became detached. The plate is therefore powdered
with finely ground whiting and rubbed in every direction with
gauze soaked in alcohol, caustic soda, chloroform, or sul-
phuric acid.

The plate must be protected by a varnish that either facilitates incising or prevents oxidation and the action of any chemical agents to which it may later be subjected. The most commonly used varnishes are solid, such as beeswax, asphalt (bitumen of Judea), and black varnish compressed into little loaves;
or the varnish can be liquid, prepared by dissolving bitumen
in turpentine. Good results are obtained by a process of varnishing while the plate is hot: a little black varnish wrapped
in silk (which filters and distributes it evenly) is allowed to
run over the heated plate. Then the plate itself is generally
smoked to obtain a brilliant black that increases the visibility
of the lines incised with the point. Retouching requires transparent varnish (made with most of the same ingredients as
solid varnish).

The most effective way of transferring a design to the plate
is to incise it in reverse on the chalk-dusted plate. The lines
are then filled with sanguine and pale pastels, and a sheet of
paper is placed on the varnished plate and passed through the
press. For more summary tracing oiled paper, tracing paper,
or transfer paper is placed on the copper plate. One or more
points that glide easily and are not too sharp can be used.

Mordants (acids) are required only in the case of engraving
with corrosive substances (etching, acquatint, etc.). There are
no precise rules regarding the length of time the plate is immersed
in the acid. The depth and quality of the lines can be varied
enormously by blocking out some of the lines with acid-resisting
varnish and by immersing the plate again and again in the
acid.

For printing, coloring materials ground in cooked oil (chalco-
graphic ink) and dampened paper with very little size are used.
The surface of the plate must be scrupulously cleaned of all
traces of varnish before being inked with a leather dabber.

Veiling is usually used to soften some of the lines of the
engraving; it consists of wiping the inked plate lightly with

gauze, so that the ink absorbed by the lines is partly distributed over the unengraved sections.

The burin, which is the most important instrument of engraving, consists of a steel shaft ending obliquely in a beak, or nose, at one end and in a wooden handle at the other. The shape of the burin facilitates the tracing of straight lines, but for curved lines the entire plate is rotated on a leather pad. The point of the burin enters the metal, and the grooves it traces are slightly triangular. The design is transferred to the plate (prepared in the same manner as for etching) by reversing it and tracing it with red tracing paper. The lines are then retouched with very light dry-point work, the varnish with which the plate had been prepared beforehand is removed, and work with the burin begins. Initially, a series of parallel signs, called hatching, were executed in order to obtain the maximum effect from the relationships of distance and thickness (see IV, col. 742). The crosshatching consisted in the crossing of the hatching at a more or less acute angle for the figures, and at right angles for the spaces. Only rarely were these marks crossed by others, termed double crosshatchings (IV, PL. 421). The "intersigns" were extremely fine lines interposed between two hatch marks for the enhancement of the values, while dots were placed at the center of the lozenges, or almonds, resulting from the crosshatching. Once the incising was finished, the burr (curls of metal raised by the burin) was removed with a scraper, and the abrasion was completed with willow charcoal or metal polish.

The processes of engraving on metal can be grouped into three categories: (1) direct manual action (dry point, mezzotint); (2) the action of corrosive substances (etching, acquatint, stipple engraving, soft-ground etching; (3) electric action (practiced in industrial production).

In dry point the design is done on a "bare" (unvarnished) plate of metal with a soft pencil or ink, then with a steel or diamond point. The burr is not completely removed and retains more ink, thus causing that peculiar pictorial irregularity of the lines that is so characteristic of dry point (see IV, col. 751; PL. 421). Because of the difficulty of manipulating the point the procedure is to incise very lightly in bands of almost touching lines rather than in one decisive stroke. In printing particular attention must be paid to the fact that the burr might curl over the lines under the pressure of the press. Owing to the extreme lability of the burr the plate is steeled, in other words given a galvanic bath that deposits a very fine layer of steel on the copper, permitting indefinite preservation of the plate. Steeling was executed for the first time by Luigi Calamatta (1802–69) in Paris; today it has been replaced by chromium plating. Steeling is also recommended during the making of the proofs. Excellent results are obtained by retouching with dry point on plates engraved by etching.

Mezzotint, a process invented by Ludwig von Siegen in 1642, became particularly widespread in England. The copper plate is prepared with a special steel comb, called a rocker, which incises the whole surface with a series of undulating lines (from top to bottom, right to left, and on two diagonals). After about twenty strokes the plate acquires a rough grain that provides a completely black impression. With special instruments the engraver scrapes and burnishes out the tiny indentations, always working from dark to light. The design is obtained by extracting the whites from the plate. The printing process is particularly difficult and steeling is indispensable. This technique was much used to reproduce oil paintings.

In etching (see IV, col. 753) the design is executed with a steel needle on a plate that has been covered with a thin layer of varnish (or wax). The plate is then subjected to a bath of nitric acid — a process called biting. So-called "Dutch mordant" can also be used, or even perchloride of iron. Biting has no effect on the metal protected by the varnish, but it does attack the metal along the incised lines and deepens its corrosive action in proportion to the length of the immersion of the plate (IV, PLS. 422, 429–444).

In aquatint (see IV, col. 755) the proof produces a design that has the quality of an ink water color — that is, it is devoid of any well-defined lines. Its application is limited, and aquatint is generally combined with etching. To obtain speci results a granular preparation of the plate is used. Positi grain is obtained by sprinkling the metal with a resinous powd (copal, mastic, colophony, etc.), which adheres under the actio of heat. The powdered grain, while protecting the plate, als appears as white spots in the parts covered with acid. Th negative grain consists of salt sprinkled over the fresh varnis When it has been washed in water the salt leaves, in the veil varnish, tiny holes that allow the acid to cut into the meta The acid is sometimes applied with a brush.

Stipple engraving (the punch-and-hammer method; see I col. 756) is a technique that uses minute dots (stipples) to buil the design. It is most commonly employed to reproduce drawin or paintings. Already known in the early 16th century, it w most widely used by Francesco Bartolozzi (1728–1815) and rare today.

Soft-ground etching is a technique using a softer formul for the ground: tallow is added in an amount equal to the ordinar etching ground. When placed on the plate the drawing execut ed on thin transparent paper is passed over with hard, sharpene pencils. One or more interposed pieces of tissue paper absor the ground under the pencil's pressure, thus uncovering th metal and exposing it to corrosion by the acid. In this proces the reproduction bears the mark of the pencil itself.

Any plate engraved by etching can be printed in such manner that the uninked incised line appears as white on blac (PL. 454). This process is used in the production of reli prints (engraving or etching in relief). The design is brushe on the metal with bitumen or soft varnish; a slow-acting aci is used for biting; and the lines then appear in white (in reli on a homogeneous dark ground. When the process is combine with that of aquatint the effect is greatly enhanced and the prin are devoid of any resemblance to woodcuts.

The origins of color prints can be found in the chiaroscur woodblocks of Ugo da Carpi (1480?–1520?), who started th technique (IV, PL. 428). Even before him engravings wer frequently retouched by hand coloring. The first color prin were printed with single plates. The later discovery of trichro matic printing concerns industrial and not artistic production

In xylography, or engraving on wood (IV, PLS. 421, 444 446–448), the wood (pear, apple, cherry, box, sycamore, an dogwood) is incised either with the grain or against the grair Engraving with the grain is older and results in simple linea contours in vivid contrasts of black and white, whereas mor recent woodcuts (cross grain) produce mainly the gray tone In any case the process consists of removing the wood from th sections that are to be white, while the lines of the design (i black) are left at the original level.

In engraving wood with the grain, the instrument used i a gouge, a little knife with a handle, with which the lines ar isolated by removing trenchlike chips along their edges. carpenter's gouge is used to empty the larger surfaces. Th drawing is generally transferred to the wood with a pencil an is then retraced in ink. To ascertain a clear idea of the resu the surface is colored with printing ink and the hewn-out part are whitened with chalk.

The burin is used for cross-grain wood engraving, for whic boxwood is preferred since it has almost no grain and is extreme compact. Because of the small size of the tree, the pieces c boxwood must be prepared by gluing (fitting) several segment together. The design is drawn in reverse on the block with pen or brush. The thickness of the lines is varied with a lozeng shaped burin. The gray parts are obtained with an instrumen that is similar to the rocker used in mezzotint.

The printing process may be done by hand because of th extreme simplicity of the operation: a gelatin or hide rolle picks up ink from a glass or zinc plate and transfers it to th block; the inked block is then pressed against the paper an after slight pressure, sufficient to cause adhesion of the pape the whole is turned upside down; and the back of the pape adhering to the wood is then passed over with burnisher. Th burnisher may be replaced by the press. In color wood print several wooden blocks are necessary, an operation of superimpo sition that requires high precision.

The various engraving techniques for printing were frequently applied in different combinations. As early as the 17th century there were used printing processes that combined copper engraving and wood blocks. Another frequent combination lithographic and metal engraving, and countless other combinations are known. (For historical information and other technical data on this subject, see ENGRAVINGS AND OTHER PRINT MEDIA.)

Sculpture. a. Stone. The earliest rudimentary processes for incising designs have been classified according to technique: (1) incised lines, which were executed mainly with the burin or with other tools made for the purpose; (2) pecked incision, which involved hammering the stone surface with a pointed stone, with the whole figure being hammered out in this manner in some cases, but only the contours in others (the elk engraved on a rock at Gjeithus, Norway); (3) smoothed contours, which instead of being engraved in the stone, were probably obtained by smoothing the stone with wood, sand, and water (the brown bear on a rock at Valle, Sweden); and (4) combined incising and painting, in which, once the contours had been engraved, a fat grease paint was applied with a brush (the so-called "Sorcerer" in Les Trois-Frères, Ariège, France; X, PL. 133).

In the early Upper Paleolithic period there developed primitive forms of bas-relief that were in some cases (generally the earliest) inspired by the natural lines and relief of the rock; these were probably executed with small burins. The first specimens of sculpture in the round are of the same period. In the case of the more ancient remains any distinctions made in the techniques of representation in reference to the materials used would unnecessarily subdivide a process that was extremely homogeneous (and remained so until the time when bronze was smelted and, as far as art production is concerned, even up to the modeling and firing of clay). Bone, which was already widely used in the Paleolithic era for the basic production of products (needles, arrowheads, necklace beads), was employed together with ivory and stag horn for small figures in the round that were made by a process similar to that of sculpture in limestone — that is, with burins, stone knives, scrapers, and sometimes little saws; there were no specialized techniques for specific materials. Only in the case of elephant or mammoth tusks (Paleolithic) was it found necessary to incise at a specific angle (transversally from the tusk) because of the course of the fibers and in order to obtain a clean incision and avoid the danger of flaking the ivory. Stag horn, on the contrary, is most compact and permits greater freedom of execution.

Owing to the importance of the sculpture of the Upper Paleolithic period the best-known examples will be listed here (see PREHISTORY). To the Aurignacian-Perigordian and Solutrean period belong the "Venus" statuettes from Savignano on the Panaro, which are made of serpentine rock, probably an alluvial fragment (XI, PL. 257); the steatite female statuettes of the Balzi Rossi; the limestone Willendorf "Venus," which is of great interest from the standpoint of technique for the burnishing executed with scrapers and the obvious use of the burin, and possibly even a drill, in the stylization of the hair (X, PL. 247); the bas-reliefs from Laussel, which are deeply hewn in the rock (XI, PLS. 254, 255); and the bas-reliefs of bisons from Le Fourneau du Diable. A very ancient specimen is the small female head in ivory, showing most precise workmanship, found at Brassempouy (XI, PL. 243); the incised checkerboard pattern on the head testifies to the use of stone knives and, perhaps, of small saws. Another beautiful piece, dating from the Magdalenian period, is the ivory horse from Saint-Germain-en-Laye (VIII, PL. 235); the animal's hair is very skillfully incised. Also from the Magdalenian period comes the abundant and valuable series of sculptures of reindeer horn, of which only the upper part of the horn is used so as to avoid the fragile porousness of the base (I, PL. 436). The natural ramifications of the horn frequently suggested to the artist bizarre and elegant figural designs.

In the Upper Paleolithic the primitive craftsman, having observed the properties of water when in contact with clay, mastered the technique of modeling, which in later times had such varied and complex uses. Modeling plastic material directly gives the artist greater and more immediate possibilities of carrying out his artistic conception. Two finds, especially, show a wealth of details: the first and more important is the herd of bisons at Le Tuc d'Audoubert in Ariège, France (XI, PL. 259); modeled in clay, mainly by hand, the details (eyes, manes, etc.) are finished with a wooden stick or possibly a pointed stone. The second group, found at Dolní Věstonice, in Moravia (XI, PL. 245), shows other interesting details: the figures, executed in the round, are made of clay mixed with powdered mammoth bone (to confer greater solidity on the paste). Naturally these sculptures are unbaked; only later, when copper smelting was practiced, did the technique of firing clay develop — a technique that greatly advanced the production of earthenware vessels.

In Egyptian sculpture, from the very earliest specimens, there can be observed a coordination and a reelaboration of all the previous experience of the cultures of the Mediterranean and the Middle East in Aëneolithic times. The process presents all the characteristics of a true technological synthesis disciplined by rigid rules and canons, as demonstrated in Julius H. Lange's studies on frontality, which prevailed in the depiction of the human figure, and in the canon pertaining to the proportions of the measurements established by Lepsius. These proportions were fixed by the craftsman on the block of stones before the actual execution of the work by means of a precise geometrical grid. The need for such a rigorous method of work was moreover closely related to the extreme hardness of the material used for these sculptures. Granite, red porphyry, and basalt require very careful, long, and patient workmanship and necessitate the use of well-sharpened chisels. The result is rigidity in the figural design, and the execution must of necessity be conducted along precise volumetric lines. Accordingly, sculpture in the round required previously drawn or sculptured models.

The technique of Greek classical sculpture can be seen almost exclusively through the study of the relatively few sculptures that retain their original surface or that, roughly carved and unfinished, afford the possibility of observing the various phases of elaboration and the nature of the instruments used. Any remarks in ancient literature concerning the execution of bas-reliefs and sculpture in the round are irrelevant, for they are at times made useless by the constant tendency of the authors to tell mere literary anecdotes; the actual texts produced by the craftsmen themselves — which are known to have existed — have all been lost.

In the case of the archaic period scholars are aided by the large unfinished sculptures in the marble quarries of Naxos, from which one can clearly discern some of the phases of the technical processes of Greek sculpture. In the first place it plainly appears that the first operation consisted in reducing the block by hammering to a form approximating that of the intended statue, according to measurements already established and previously marked on the block itself (Egyptian technique). Work was then carried out to a fairly advanced stage, so that when the sculpture was transported from the quarry to the place it was to occupy only the finishing touches remained to be executed. Sometimes, instead of specific measurements, an outline was engraved on the block with a chisel; this outline actually formed the outer edge of the rough draft (fragment of the rough draft of a horse from Sparta in the Br. Mus.).

In the case of sculpture in the round the work had to be executed on all sides at once by removing successive layers of marble in order to maintain the proportions of the rough draft and obtain the pre-established measurements of the finished sculpture. A bronze chisel, instead of the hammer used for the preliminary rough boasting done in the quarry, was employed for striking the marble perpendicularly (not obliquely as in present-day technique), thus removing layers $3/4$ in. to 1 in. thick. This process of boasting was performed with great force, and it was impossible, even after the finishing touches had been completed, to obtain the absolutely smooth surface that was necessary for the adhesion of the priming and the colors. Until at least the 5th century all sculptures were finished with color after careful smoothing with pumice (which did not, however, erase the traces of the perpendicular blows of the chisel and did not bring out the transparency of the marble, a superfluous measure as it was to be covered by a coat of paint). The chisel technique is attributed by some (C. Bluemel, *Greek Sculptors at Work*, London, 1955) to the Egyptians, who were accustomed to treating much harder materials than marble, such as diorite, granite, and basalt. This technique was probably transmitted by the Egyptians (or by the Mesopotamians) to the Greeks around the 7th century B.C. Sometimes this process of execution and temporary finishing with the chisel was supplemented by the use of the fine point (graving tool), especially in those parts where it was necessary to obtain a clear line of demarcation, both precise and continuous, such as in the outlines of the drapings, of the hair, and of the more delicate features of the face. The point had to be sufficiently fine to penetrate even the smallest interstices between the folds in order to create an openwork effect. Another instrument, which in the 5th century gradually replaced pumice for final smoothing, was the rasp, the use of which is established with certainty by the quality of the finished surfaces.

The development of sculpture in the round, no longer rigidly frontal but consisting in an autonomous and complex balance of spatial perspectives, created the necessity, from the 5th century on, for a preparatory model (of either wax or clay with an internal armature if the size required it). A model also became necessary because of the collective work called for by the great sculptural undertakings of the 5th century (the Parthenon, the temples in Olympia, etc.). The existence of drawn and plastic models produced by Phidias for his work squads during work on the Parthenon has been certified. The existence of these models has been proved by Tarentine archaeological finds (two casts from models: an enthroned goddess and a youth's torso) and by some Attic vase paintings.

An engraved gem, moreover, shows that for the establishment of the proportions in volume between the model and the final work a plumb line was used. For this purpose certain fixed points — bosses — of the original block were kept; they were generally at the extremities of the statue, the hair or the feet, and often clear traces remain of these bosses (usually not quite finished sections) on completed statues after they were installed (the pediment in Olympia). In more recent times the plumb line system led to the invention of a kind of diagram-grid, or frame, with which the depth of the sculpture, taken from the model, could be accurately calculated on the block (the measurements on the frame being the same). These measurements were marked by perpendicular rows of holes of varying depths. With the advent of mechanical calculation of a statue's proportions (PL. 437) the overall processing in successive layers became superfluous. In Hellenistic and Roman times work was carried out by sections; on unfinished sculptures, parts that had already been finished with the flat chisel can be seen beside others that were still in the initial phase of rough stone. The consequences of this technique were a total absence during execution of a general conception of the work as a whole and the loss, owing to the precision of mechanical checking, of that continuous and changeable flow of inspiration which led through innumerable stages to the final and irreplaceable version.

The technique of bas-relief corresponds in part to that of sculpture in the round. Here, too, one can observe a preliminary incising of the design, which was then carried out in successive deepenings of the ground between the figures, and the final finish — in the archaic period, quite summarily and mostly with the help of color — along the inner surfaces of the figures. Here, also, the instruments are the broad chisel — used perpendicularly — for the rough carving and the various finer chisels, including drills, for the finishing work. Characteristic of later Greek sculpture is another technique, which was first used in the 4th century, spread throughout the Hellenistic world, and penetrated into Roman culture — that of constructing a statue in separate pieces, sometimes even in different qualities of white marble. The origin of this procedure obviously lies in what had by then become the industrial production of statues: following the sculptor's model, the workshop carried out the figure in general, while the sculptor himself carved the "noble" parts, such as the face and the hands.

One of the oldest examples of this technique is the *Deme* from Knidos (III, PL. 380). Even more characteristic are certain Hellenistic works, such as the "Anzio Girl" (VII, PL. 15) in which the nude parts are carved out of a separate block Parian marble, which because of its finer crystalline gra creates a delicate tonal contrast with the clothed body. this technique it is clear that the esthetic tendencies whi marked the oldest chryselephantine sculpture also play a pa For it is no accident that Roman sculpture, probably by w of previous Hellenistic-Egyptian influences, developed a syste of joining pieces (with metal studs), even combining porphy and marble or different qualities of colored marble, sometim with inlay processes (the colossal seated goddess in Rome, Mu Naz. Romano).

The "messa a punti," or pointing, which was already ful developed from the Hellenistic period onward, has remaine throughout the Renaissance and to the present, the fundamen procedure for the transfer of the volumetric proportions fro the model to the block of stone. The plumb line also continu to be used; in the 15th and 16th centuries a wooden cage w set up with several plumb lines, which was superimposed the model and then on the stone, making it possible to establi the fundamental points of the sculpture with mathemati precision. The cage has now been replaced by a small cro in wood, which is placed at three points of the plaster mod (usually the most prominent points of the sculpture, whi are commonly called "capi punti"). On the cross is placed armature that can be moved in all directions, whose functi it is to find new points to be transferred to the block, fro which the surplus stone is removed with punches and chise This work of roughing out and boasting requires the use of mallet; the actual shaping by reducing the stone to a for from point to point, requires the use of chisels, which whe hit by the mallet create the graduated surfaces. The latter a then smoothed with a rasp and polished. The drill was rare used in classical times; after the Antonines, it was used excess in the 3d, 4th, and 5th centuries (also, in the East, the Byzantine sculpture that followed), but it was employ only in the final stages for the inner parts that the chisel cou not reach.

b. Metal. The technique of casting in a mold, with without a core, and the highly developed melted wax techniqu which has already been examined, were applied to both hous hold objects and sculpture in its true sense. In the earlie examples of monumental sculpture the Egyptians of the O Kingdom and the first Mesopotamian sculptors resorted figures of sheet metal. The oldest examples are the bull statu from El-'Ubaid (before 3000 B.C.) and the statue of Pepi from Hierakonpolis (about 2300 B.C.), all in copper. From t El-'Ubaid bulls it can be deduced that the metal sheets we fixed with nails to a wooden foundation covered with bitume The laminae, previously beaten over molds and annealed, we placed on the core when hot (after a final annealing) so th the bitumen could form a support for the lamina during t final chasing operation. This process of monumental sculptu in bronze, which was also adopted in Greek art, is called *sphy elaton* (IX, PL. 503). The technique of work on lamina in mold remained in use at the height of the classical period chryselephantine statues (see METALWORK).

In Egypt, Mesopotamia, and Palestine, toward the begi ning of the 1st millennium B.C., a technique was developed casting large-size bronze sculptures in the round. The mol were supported by burying them in the ground in front of t kiln, or they were even carved out of the ground itself (t mold of the large bronze basin of Solomon's temple in Jerus lem, ca. 950 B.C.; in specific cases the molds were provid with a core, which was kept in the correct position by mea of a supporting metal framework. It was precisely this inve tion of the core which made possible the casting of large inter ally hollow works and led to the flourishing of monumen sculpture in bronze. This, however, was still rare in the fi half of the 6th century, in spite of the activity (of which the is proof) of schools like those of Rhoikos and Theodoros amos, which literary tradition holds responsible for the "lost-ax" process of casting (actually, this was imported from Egypt). n the other hand, when the Persians, in 480, removed the oup of Tyrannicides (510 B.C.) by Antenor from the Agora Athens, they were impressed precisely by the rarity of monu-ental bronze sculpture executed by casting on a core.

The process employed for hollow casting is already recogniz-le in archaic examples, such as the fragment depicting hair om Chianciano (Florence, Mus. Arch.). The wax model was ade from a clay core. In Greece the core, which served as first sketch for the sculpture, was roughly modeled, and the ax covering it was worked on (in classical times) and modeled to the final state. Sometimes a cast was made of the finished ax before it was covered with clay so that the work could preserved in case the matrix broke at the moment of casting. he technique of wax casting is such that it does not allow y notable variants in different periods and cultures, and any riations that may occur are due more to local metallurgical chniques than to the process itself. In Greek sculpture the onze was always remarkably thick (a condition of the direct ork on the wax layer). The alloys vary not only according the imprecise and unreconstructible formula given by Strabo d Dioscorides of Anazarbus (Aegina alloy, Melian alloy, Corin-ian alloy, etc.) but also according to the technical tradition the workshop, in which the use of residue from previous stings constantly altered the quantitative relationship between e copper, tin, and lead. Toward the end of Hellenism the se of decorative sculpture of an industrial nature (bronzes for mphaeums and gardens, philosophers' herms, etc.) led to the mplification of the risky process of large-size casting. The ulptures were made in separate pieces, which were then sembled with small pins. The hair and the beard, for example, ere separately cast. Superficial uniformity was given to the eces by means of careful work with a burin. In some cases rls of hair were lightly incised on the neck with the burin, rolonging the molded ones on the added piece, thus hiding e marks of the welding of the two pieces. The eyelashes ere often mechanically cut from a metal sheet and inserted to the hollow eye orbit together with inlay of glass (the iris), etal (the pupil), and ivory (the cornea), with rather artificial sults (*Sappho* in the Mus. Naz., Naples).

In Roman times, depending on the requirements in each se, the late Hellenistic process was used as well as the clas-cal formula of lost-wax casting. Of special interest is the onze statue of Marcus Aurelius on the Capitoline hill in ome, which is composed of separate parts of large dimensions; analysis of the alloy gave the following percentages: 85.3180 er cent copper, 8.5470 per cent lead, and 5.8695 per cent zinc ut absolutely no tin). The only substantial technical modifica-on in the classical lost-wax process occurred in the Renais-nce. The function of the wax was transferred to some other aterial (clay, plaster, etc.), thus avoiding the risk of destroying e original in the actual process of casting; the mold permitted e casting of several replicas of the same work. Tradition has that Benvenuto Cellini was the inventor of this process and, fact, the artist did follow up the first small model with a rge one, from which he made the mold necessary for the ax. Naturally the finished product lost its character as an riginal work, since the wax itself was obtained by means of a atrix from the true original and was not directly executed y the artist. Consequently, there were two stages of execution: e first in clay, plaster, or some other material, which was sed, through a series of mechanical reproductions, for the ronze cast; the second was the final chasing — or, more pre-sely, the trimming — which, owing to the possibility of casting veral replicas of the same work, became the only distinguishing ature of the direct intervention of the artist on that particular ronze and on no other. Such is the case with a work like ernini's (q.v.) bust of Gregory XV, whose several replicas Paris (Mus. Jacquemart-André), Rome (Galleria Doria amphili), and Bologna (Mus. Civ.) have caused differences opinion among the critics as to which of these busts ears the mark of the artist's direct intervention in the final imming.

Lost-wax casting spread all over Europe with the migra-tions of Italian craftsmen at the end of the 16th century (begin-ning with Cellini himself). Particular interest in the Italian processes was shown by French craftsmen (PL. 442), who em-ployed a technique of casting with sand (that is, with a negative obtained through a mixture of sand and clay that was beaten against the model) and by Austrian artists, as evidenced by the monumental complex of the tomb of Maximilian in the Hofkirche, Innsbruck (VI, PL. 133), in which Ludovico and Giacomo del Duca also had a hand. Many other nations, such as Sweden and Russia, also welcomed the Italian artisans and employed them in making monumental works in bronze. The sculptor-caster ceased to exist at the end of the Renaissance. On the one hand, there is the artist who models (generally in clay) the work that is to be cast in bronze; on the other, there is the caster, who is often surprisingly skillful in the technical ability to retain in the bronze even the slightest manual traces of the creative artist. This division of labor, which grew more pronounced between the end of the 16th and the first half of the 17th century, created the independent figure of the caster, such as Ludovico del Duca or Giacomo Laurenziani, but weak-ened the artistic quality of bronze sculpture, so much so that even bronze works of the highest quality, like those modeled by Rodin (q.v.) and cast by Alexis Rudier, do not achieve that delicate relationship between the form and the material which characterizes, for example, the sculptures in bronze by Donatello or Verrocchio (IV, PLS. 242, 249, 250; XIV, PLS. 354, 355).

Contemporary casting techniques have remained essentially unchanged since the earliest attempts at metal casting. The lost-wax process is still the most commonly used method, although recent mechanical improvements have ensured a higher degree of success in the casting and a more faithful reproduction of the clay (or plaster) model (PL. 443). In the lost-wax process the clay model (or core) is covered with a wax coating, the thickness of which will correspond to the thickness of the metal when it is cast. Gates and vents are inserted to act as air vents, and the whole is covered with a rough outer layer of clay. This mold is heated in a kiln or oven, and the wax melts and runs out of the vents, leaving a hollow space. The mold is then cooled and buried in damp earth. Into it the liquid bronze alloy is poured from a crucible; after the bronze has cooled and hardened — forming the statue — the outer mold is broken away and the exposed statue is ready to receive its final polishing treatment.

c. Clay. For the techniques and history of ceramics, see the previous two sections (cols. 972 and 987), and the articles CERAMICS and SCULPTURE.

d. Wood. The methods of processing wood have never changed, whether for the decoration of furniture or for bas-relief. Perhaps the only distinction that can be made is that for some works, such as the doors of St. Catherine in Cairo, S. Sabina in Rome (IX, PL. 83), and S. Ambrogio in Milan, a model (probably drawn) undoubtedly existed, which served as a basis for the carving of the bas-reliefs. Other problems were posed by sculpture in the round, for one tree trunk does not afford the possibility of executing in one piece a sculpture of large size, especially in the case of the human figure if a minimum of movement is to be given to the limbs. In ancient Egyptian sculpture, as well as in the archaic Greek xoana, the process was to extract the body of the figure from the trunk by carving with a gouge, and then to join to it the more protruding ele-ments (arms, legs, etc.), with tenon and mortise in most cases. Naturally, the sculptor tried to avoid these joinings as much as possible, but in certain periods these became so necessary that the central trunk was reduced to a mere static support for the sculpture itself; for sculpture in wood did not produce a plastic style determined by the qualities inherent in the material itself but followed the model of marble, bronze, or stucco sculpture, according to the various stylistic demands of the different historical periods. This was the case with European wood sculpture in the 17th and 18th centuries, especially in the centers of rococo art (XII, PLS. 170, 171, 173). Sculptures were composed of innumerable added elements, from curls to limbs, from objects external to the group (animals, clouds, cherubs) to drapery, each element having been carved separately with great care, whereas the assembled statue received only a final polishing with abrasives. It is obvious that this kind of procedure required the use of a model (in the 17th and 18th centuries almost always of clay) and the very precise transference of measurements in scale (by the same methods used in stone sculpture); also necessary was a polychrome stucco surface dressing that would hide the ugly interruptions in the surface, which were all the more visible because of the different directions of the grain in the wood. The origins of Romanesque wooden sculpture in the round clearly testify to the dependence of wooden sculpture on other techniques; the crucifix at Mirabella Eclano in the Campania clearly shows its derivation from the embossed metal crucifixes of the Rhenish circle of Godefroid de Claire. Nevertheless, in the wooden sculpture of the Middle Ages a profound spiritual unity is recognizable, which was stimulated by the frequent technological exchanges between Catalonia, the Rhineland, the Tyrol, the Campania under Frederick II, Apulia, Provence, Aquitaine, Auvergne, and Lombardy (VI, PLS. 125, 129, 130; XII, PL. 490). Of course, the choice of wood varied according to local production and artistic demands. The sculptor attempted to protect his statue from splitting by paying particular attention to the quality of the grain and by studying on the model the forms that would require the fewest possible additions. The central pith was always removed from the trunk to decrease the wood's humidity and to hasten its seasoning. In figures that were intended to rest against a ground the hollowness is almost always visible. Only later, with sculpture in the round and the diverse processes of baroque wooden sculpture, was the hollow concealed with additions.

After the Middle Ages the technique of carving showed no great modifications (with the exclusion of the already mentioned technique of baroque sculpture in the round); however, it is important to note the artistic quality attained during the Renaissance owing to the activity of such great figures as Jacopo Della Quercia, Brunelleschi, and Donatello (qq.v.). Today, there is a tendency to return to wood carving, exploiting its surface qualities (grain, color) for new forms of expression.

e. Mixed materials. The techniques for processing precious or semiprecious materials (gold, lapis lazuli, ivory, etc.), such as those which are typical of the earliest Egyptian and Sumerian cultures (IV, PLS. 343, 361, 391; VI, PL. 244; XII, PL. 484), were primarily applicable to the production of works of art. The specific character of sculpture in various materials is inspired by the desire to give a permanent and unchangeable quality to the impermanent painted surface finish of archaic wooden and terra-cotta sculpture. Passing from the archaic Greek xoana (wooden figurines that could probably be taken apart and had stuccoed and polychromed hands and faces) to the acrolithic statues (with heads and hands of precious materials and bodies covered, like the xoana, with precious fabrics), one finds that in most cases the eyes were executed in minute inlay work of colored stones. The fabrics of the clothes were also replaced by materials that would not deteriorate and were, if possible, noble and in contrast with the light hues of the marble. The chryselephantine technique was an inevitable outcome of such an ideal: gold confers upon the modeling of the drapery the maximum of splendor and elegance, while ivory, even more than marble, renders the compact milky quality of flesh. The pieces of gold and ivory required a wooden support, upon which they were mounted by joining. The gold drapery folds were executed in separate pieces on clay matrices, a few specimens of which were recently discovered in Olympia. For working the ivory (cut into thin plaques) there existed a special category of craftsmen, the so-called "ivory softeners" (μαλακτηρες ελεφαντος), who gave to the plaques the contours necessary for the anatomic modeling of whatever part of the body they were applied to. Roman sculpture in different colored marbles is a modest version of these sculptures in mixed materials. An extraordinary example of the process of combining

precious materials in monumental sculpture is the famous stat of Serapis by Bryaxis mentioned in literary reports (Clement Alexandria), a copy of which is in the Greco-Roman Museu in Alexandria; this combination was achieved with an impas (obviously cold) of gold, silver, bronze, iron, lead, and t filings and crushed sapphires, rubies, emeralds, and topaze To this truly composite sculpture a blue surface finish w applied.

Other processes. Among the processes used in the executic of painting one must include those which, instead of employi liquid, fatty, or watery colors, use rigid fragments of colore substances such as marble, glass, and wood, deriving from the forms and polychrome effects through well-studied juxtapos tion and joining. Almost always, these artistic techniques requi a first transcription of the idea in the shape of a cartoon, whic functions as a guide (see MODELS; MEDIA, COMPOSITE).

a. Mosaics. The participation of skilled workers with wel defined tasks is indispensable in the case of mosaics. Th Justinian legislation (*Corpus juris civilis*) gives the names these categories of workers: *pictor imaginarius*, *pictor parietarii* and *musearius* (see VIII, col. 148). But these denominatio in no way clarify the exact technical contribution of each cat gory; on the contrary, they are easily subject to misunderstan ing. It is not known whether the subdivision of tasks followe the establishment of the pictorial idea from its general ideatic to the sinopia on the wall and to the composition of the piec of the mosaic, or whether there was a hierarchy established c the basis of each craftsman's individual capacity, one memb composing the human figure, another executing the rest, ar yet another preparing and choosing the pieces according to tl colors required by the *pictores*. The presence of a number participants in the mosaics of Ravenna (PL. 107; II, PLS. 44 446; IX, PL. 72; X, PLS. 179, 181, 190) has been ascertaine but it has been impossible to establish whether the artist wl drew the sinopia — by means of a procedure of preparation every way similar to that of fresco painting — also played a pa later in the actual positioning of the colored pieces. (For tl various techniques of mosaics and a historical survey, s MOSAICS.)

b. "Opus sectile" and wood marquetry. In certain perio the ornamental processes of marble intarsia of various colo and wood inlays acquired the importance of genuine art tec niques owing to the presence of a pictorial concept that guide the work. The techniques are those common to inlay wo and veneering. With the adoption of a great variety of mat rials — besides marble, mother-of-pearl, and glass, as in tl *opus sectile* in the Basilica of Junius Bassus in Rome (VII PL. 79; IX, PL. 70) — a practice that is reminiscent of ancie Near Eastern cultures, surprising chiaroscuro modulations a wonderful pictorial effects could be obtained in spite of tl rigidity of the materials.

Pictorial inlay in wood is executed with thin strips of woo of different colors, which are chosen and shaped according the color scheme indicated by the cartoon and fixed with gl to the wooden support (VIII, PLS. 77, 80, 83, 85-88, 90). Th inlay is then ready to be shaded with a hot iron. For heightene effects light woods (the spindle tree and boxwood) were use According to Vasari the process was carried to its highest poi of perfection by Fra Giovanni da Verona, who stained the woo with various boiled tinctures and oils (V, PL. 440).

c. Stained glass. The origins of medieval stained glass (q.v date from the end of the 10th century; the height of its develo ment was reached between the 12th and 15th centuries (PLS. 17 173). Cennini, in his lengthy description of the process execution (*Libro dell'arte*, chap. CLXXI), insisted on the ne for collaboration between the artist who provides the carto and the artisan who cuts the glass into the size and shape i dicated in the cartoon and then gives them the appropria chiaroscuro treatment. On the contrary, Theophilus, in l *Diversarum artium schedula*, wrote of a single executant, whi as certainly the case in Romanesque stained-glass windows. The cartoon is drawn, first with lead or tin, on a wooden board covered with a layer of moistened chalk (whitewash); the lines are then reinforced in red or black color, with letters marking the various color zones. The glass is then cut with a hot grozing iron or with a diamond point, which came into use after 1500. Once the edges have been smoothed (with a grozing iron), the details are painted on the glass (beards, eyes, noses, etc.) with a mixture of powdered glass, metallic oxide, and a gum substance known as grisaille. Highlights are added by scratching the glass through the pigment. The fragments of painted glass are fired in a special kiln at a low temperature. After firing the fragments are joined with lead strips that are soldered together.

The soldered parts naturally coincided with the main outlines given in the drawing; however, the iron framework used in mounting the window was completely independent. Various mixtures were used for painting on glass; Cennini even advised painting in oils (without firing) for the retouching of certain details. After the 14th century (PLS. 179, 180) the growing complexity of chromatic effects contributed to the weakening of the rigorous drawing in Romanesque windows, which were based on the application of panes of simple colors on a lead pattern of great purity. In the 17th and 18th centuries grisaille was used exclusively.

TERMINAL PROCESSES. *Painting.* In the varied and complex elaboration of the different pictorial techniques it is not always possible to separate the process of execution from the terminal process. Sometimes the quality of a technique can determine the finishing value of retouchings, but more often the execution passes through various stages — a succession of retouchings and glazings — in such a way that the function of a terminal process can be recognized only in those additions whose purpose is to protect the color.

a. Fresco. Among all painting techniques fresco painting, more than any other, requires a definite terminal process. Retouching can only be done with tempera after the painted plaster has dried. Many Roman frescoes appear to have been passed over with tempera treated in an emulsion containing adhesives. This custom became even more widespread after the decline of Roman civilization, for many late Byzantine and Romanesque wall paintings show, over a summary fresco painting, additions of details in tempera which are so glaring as to make the fresco itself seem little more than a mere preparation for the final retouching. In the late Middle Ages and the Renaissance retouching went through alternating phases: some practiced it in a very limited manner, while others made such excessive use of it that their works, rather than being retouched, may be said to have been executed in a mixed technique of *fresco* and *a secco* painting. To remedy the fragility of the tempera impastos, whose impermanence increased in proportion to their thickness, Anton Raphael Mengs, in the second half of the 18th century, experimented with a more durable kind of retouching. As a solvent for tempera he used skimmed milk mixed with aqua vitae. If the fresco is not to be directly exposed to the light, good results can also be obtained with a small percentage of honey dissolved in egg. It is not known whether it was this peculiar weakness of *a secco* retouching or the desire to give a wall the appearance of a marble surface that prompted the Romans to experiment with protecting their frescoes with a special wax preparation. If one takes into account the nature of the oldest Roman mural decoration (the painted "marble" of Style I) and the thorough smoothing of the last coating recommended by Vitruvius, the hypothesis of a protective wax as an imitation of marble becomes much more acceptable. However, nothing conclusive can be said in this respect so long as the available information concerning Hellenistic wall decoration (an essential predecessor of Roman fresco painting) remains in its present state of partial documentation. Wax varnishing (which so often leads to a confusion between fresco and encaustic painting) had evident similarities to the ganosis of Greek sculpture. When the fresco was dry, Pontic

wax, diluted with oil and very slightly warmed, was spread over the painted plaster. The heat from a cautery passed over the surface of the fresco at a certain distance was sufficient to cause the wax to penetrate the plaster. After cooling, the wall was polished with a linen cloth.

b. Oil. It would be a fundamental error to regard retouching and glazing in oil painting as a terminal process. In specific cases (Leonardo da Vinci) the whole pictorial execution consisted in a succession of superimposed glazes. Even in the case of varnishes — whose protective function is essentially terminal — prudence is advisable. Many pigments have a natural tendency to change color if they are not properly varnished. Consequently one may discover layers of varnish under a final glazing of color, so placed in order to protect a given pigment from atmospheric impurities or from contact with the glaze over it. The varnishes that cover the last layer of color in the painting differ in quality depending on the process, the period, or the particular technique adopted by an artist. The most ancient varnishes, which were used to fix tempera on wood, were made with egg albumen beaten to a froth with water and left to settle out. The later development of oil painting created the need for appropriate varnishes. Those in use from the end of the 15th century on were normally made with hard resins dissolved in hot oil and diluted with essential oils. Only later was there widespread use of oil varnishes consisting of amber or copal dissolved in fatty oils; those based on volatile oil, of even more recent adoption, are made of mastic and dammar dissolved in oil of turpentine or benzine. Oil varnishes were made to drip slowly and to be spread with the fingers. The natural warmth of the finger tips created the exact degree of fluidity required and resulted in a uniform and fine layer. Sometimes the varnish was mixed with a very small quantity of color. Account was taken, however, of the inherent tendency of varnishes to turn yellow when exposed to air; artificial aging was thus obtained.

c. Water color, gouache, tempera, and pastel. The need for protecting water colors presents greater problems, for fixatives generally spoil their delicate hues and cause them to turn yellow. In most cases the best that can be done is to keep the painting away from light and from contact with atmospheric conditions. At the end of the 17th century rapidly evaporating fixatives dissolved in alcohol were experimented with; these are still used today for this technique as well as for gouache, tempera, and pastel. They were imported by the Jesuits, who discovered them in China, where they were already well known. Another recipe was successfully used by Vibert, but he kept it secret. Almost all these recipes are known because among the French artists of the 18th century this pictorial technique was widely used. Maurice Quentin de Latour experimented all his life with new processes for fixatives, with varying success. Some complicated processes employ various forms of vaporization, either with a mixture of water, glue, and alcohol, or simply with hot water. The latter process has given doubtful results, for it changes pastels to such an extent that they resemble dull-colored gouaches. Generally, pastels become fixed by themselves without any aids, but in some cases it is useful to vaporize the reverse of the pastel with milk, water, and a highly diluted resin.

d. Gilding. Another terminal process that was typical of painting on wood and illumination in the period from the Middle Ages to the early Renaissance was gilding (IV, PLS. 283, 284, 289; X, PLS. 395, 396, 490), which had ancient precedents both in the Mediterranean basin (Egypt, Phoenicia, Greece, Rome; IV, PL. 378; XII, PL. 495) and in the eastern countries (China, Japan, India, Persia; X, PL. 501). The same methods usually characterize its wide range of application: from icons on a gold ground (II, PL. 451) and missal illuminations to the haloes in frescoes (X, PLS. 68, 83, 500). The thin leaves of gold required were prepared by goldbeaters and laid on a surface prepared with bole or a mordant. From a ducat beaten between two pieces of vellum a surface of about 22 sq. ft. of leaf could be obtained. Cennini (*Libro dell'arte*, chap. CXXXI) gives a recipe that deserves to be quoted: "Take the white of an egg in a very clean glazed porringer . . . and beat this white . . . until the whole porringer is full of a solid foam which looks like snow. Then take an ordinary drinking glass . . . not quite full of good clear water; and pour it over the white in the porringer. Let it stand and distil from evening to morning. Then grind the bole with this tempera, as long as ever you can. Take a soft sponge . . . and dip it in good clear water; . . .then rub lightly with this sponge, not too wet, wherever you want to gild. Then, with a good-sized minever brush, temper some of this bole, as thin as water for the first coat; and wherever you want to gild, and where you have damped down with the sponge, lay this bole all over, watching out for the breaks which the brush sometimes makes." The operation of painting with the bole must be repeated four times, constantly increasing the thickness of the bole solution. After the surface had been allowed to dry, it was smoothed and burnished with a dog's tooth and polished with a piece of linen cloth. Once the surface had been prepared with the bole, it was again dampened with water and egg white so that it would retain the gold leaf. The latter was applied with pincers, care being taken to make the gold adhere uniformly to the bole.

This recipe involves the classical process of applying a gold ground to wood, but the methods of gilding varied according to the support. On a wall, for example, a mordant made of cooked oil, turpentine, and yellow wax was spread while hot with a fine brush. On parchment there were diverse methods: one used cherry gum in vinegar with powdered gold; another was composed of gold, wine, gum, and gall, as described by Heraclius in *De coloribus et artibus romanorum* (Br. Mus., Sloane 1754; pub. in Eng. by M. Merrifield, *Ancient Practice of Painting*, 1849); in the anonymous *Libro dei colori* (Bologna, Bib. S. Salvatore, Ms. 165; pub. in Eng. by Merrifield, *Original Treatise Dating from the XII to the XVIII Century on the Art of Painting*, 2 vols., London, 1849) there is a recipe for egg white beaten with fig milk, gum arabic in powder, and a little saffron that was allowed to rest for a day before the gold leaf was applied.

"Mecca" gilding should also be mentioned. This was obtained by applying silver leaf and over it a transparent yellow varnish called "mecca." This ancient process was of Chinese origin; it was widely used in the medieval Byzantine period, and in Italy in the 17th and 18th centuries. In the 19th century certain bronze powders were put on the market under the name of purpurin; they were widely used for gilding, but the results were often poor because of the overly rapid oxidation of the metal.

In all periods gilding always required a terminal burnishing process. For this, animal teeth or carved and polished agates shaped like curved dogs' teeth and mounted on little wooden supports were used; Cennini also suggests topaz, garnets, sapphires, or emeralds. These burnishers had to be kept away from humidity and were warmed by rubbing against a woolen cloth.

Sculpture. Even in ancient Egypt (Old Kingdom) skilled workers had been confronted with the alternatives that are fundamental to the conditioning of the terminal processes of sculpture — that is, the various possibilities of qualifying the material through a polishing process or through concealment under a polychrome coat. The problem can be solved only by taking into account the material itself. In the case of a porous material, such as sandstone, a covering of gesso and paint is more appropriate than in the case of more compact, crystalline stones, such as granite and basalt (IV, PLS. 354, 377, 390; XII, PL. 488). On the other hand, the natural color, the grain, and the beauty of certain porphyries and granites automatically suggest a surface treatment that will not conceal them. Whereas sculpture in wood, sandstone, or limestone is treated with the same processes as those used in tempera on plaster, the more noble materials are treated with emery and abrasive powders.

The Greeks adopted both processes, but they reduced the thickness of the preparation, which as late as the height of the

classical period was found on such compact, crystalline wh marbles as Parian marble. This preparation, which has be discussed in relationship to the sculptures of Phidias on tl Parthenon (according to some it is a very fine layer of stucc while according to others it is a natural chalk incrustation th has been produced by meteorological influences), appears, ev on the most ancient pieces, to be a fine mixture of chalk and gl (XI, PLS. 125, 126). Be that as it may, from as early as tl 5th century on — if not from the end of the 6th — the ganos process started to spread, while the violent polychromy of tl archaic sculptures disappeared (especially the blue and re I, PLS. 337, 351, 361), being replaced by discreet coloring the hair, beards, pupils, lips, and cheeks. Ganosis, which w probably also applied to stuccoed marble, consisted of a mixtu of oil and wax, which when spread on marble gave it an adm rable golden patina.

Terra-cotta sculpture also required certain terminal processe On Etrusco-Italic sculpture of large dimensions, techniqu similar to those of vase painting were used; the surface of tl clay reached the desired color through firing (PL. 446).] Greek and Hellenistic statuettes, on the contrary, the actu coloring was done while cold (VII, PLS. 41, 61, 62). To tl white base (obtained by firing extremely fine white clay) we added unfired tempera pigments—generally blue, yellow, mauv and various shades of red. In some cases a few details of tl clothing were heightened with touches of gold. The same te minal coloring was also used in terra-cotta bas-reliefs.

In ancient Greek bronzes the whole surface was carefull worked over again when cold in order to scrape away the re idue of casting and uncover the metal (this is the opposite the modern practice of using an artificial patina). The wo was done with files and scrapers. The marks left by the chis (used to remove the casting web or more visible defects) we eliminated by filing, and any trace of the latter was remov by scrapers, which were used to clean the entire surface of tl sculpture. For the final luster abrasive powders were use the most common of which was that drawn from cuttlefish bon

Surface scraping of bronze was indispensable if the met was to be gilded. For the gilding of bronze both the Gree and the Romans employed the method known as *allo spadar* which is still considered the best. The statue, once it ha been scraped with the scraper and smoothed (not too mucl with abrasives, was smeared with mercury and then covere in gold leaf obtained by hammering gold laminae between tw pieces of vellum. Sometimes partial silver gilding was appli with the same method. Finally, Pliny reports a process f imitating gilding, and he mentions the use of thin leaves copper dyed with ox gall.

The complex terminal treatment for wooden sculpture e tends from surface polishing to stuccoing and painting by pro esses that varied according to the changes in stylistic requir ments. From the 15th to the end of the 18th century polychrom became a method of pictorial illusion that was very difficult execute. The statue was frequently covered with linen an gilded and varnished. Combinations of different materials we also used to increase the illusionistic effects (cloth, hair, gla eyes; XII, PL. 505), a fairly brief tendency that disappeare with the rise of a new plastic sense in the 19th century (no withstanding the existence of some "mixed media" sculptur experiments by the impressionists, among which the most in portant were found in the work of Degas; VII, PL. 434.)

Piero M. CAPPONI

IV. TECHNIQUES OF ANALYSIS. Data supplied by scientif research in the field of art is invaluable in historical and critic evaluation. In addition to providing comparative data an permitting the work of art and the method of its execution be placed in proper context, scientific techniques indica methods to follow in restoration and conservation (q.v.), reco the current conditions of art works, and aid in authenticatic (see FALSIFICATION AND FORGERY). The various physical, optica and chemical methods generally require specialized equipme and expert interpretation. They integrate but never replace tl ritic's intuitive judgment, providing proof only that an object is not what it purports to be.

The simple typological classification, description, and photographic documentation of the object is supplemented by a study of its technique of execution and internal structure. A brief listing of the principal means and their application follows. The binocular microscope with low- and high-power magnification (from 5× to 40×) is among the simplest scientific aids. It is used in conjunction with slanting or raking light, which throws into relief surface variations, and with a study of cross sections of lifted fragments and chemical reactions of particles.

X ray and special light photography (ultraviolet, infrared, sodium vapor) are of particular importance for studying painting. The X ray records a painting's densities, which vary according to pigment and age. They may also be used to discern the shape of metal objects covered by corrosion.

Ultraviolet rays cause the surface of a painting to fluoresce in specific patterns, depending upon the differences in age and the component properties of the paint. Its primary use is to disclose repainting and retouching. Since the fluorescence of certain varnishes may prevent examination of underlying layers, the varnish is often removed before submission to ultraviolet analysis. Infrared photography penetrates darkened varnish and thin layers of repainting and can show up the preparatory drawing, corrections, illegible writing, and so on.

For microchemical examination and stratographic sectioning minute samples are lifted from the work in question. To obtain a cross section the fragment is embedded in a liquid synthetic resin, subsequently hardened by a catalyst. The resulting transparent block is then cut, and the surface is flattened and polished. This method (PL. 450) may be applied to any kind of art object (paintings on canvas, wood, or walls, metal, ceramics, etc.). The cross sections are easy to interpret but furnish information only for the specific spot where the sample was lifted. The sections are also examined under ultraviolet rays and under polarized light. The latter is particularly useful in examining transparent sections. Whenever possible radiography and stratographic sectioning are used together.

The materials themselves can be analyzed chemically and physically. Traditional chemical analysis identifies simple elements or components present in the sample (qualitative analysis) and may also establish their quantity (quantitative analysis).

There are many more specialized methods that can be adopted in studying works of art. An enumeration of those which have proved their effectiveness in a given field must include diffraction of X rays, spectrography of emission, fluorescence of X rays, chromotography, spectrophotometry, mineralogical optical analysis, and determination of the point of fusion. Useful in the identification of the component materials of art objects are the diffraction of X rays and the resulting spectrum of diffraction (for crystalline substances) as well as X-ray fluorescence and the resulting spectrum of fluorescence (glass, glazes, and other inorganic matter).

Spectrography of emission is based on an examination of the visible radiations produced by atoms when submitted to the action of an electric beam. This method is especially effective in the identification of metal atoms and can be applied to the examination of the composition of alloys, products of corrosion, pigments, glass, glazes, and other elements.

Chromatography constitutes a rapid method of isolating and identifying substances in mixtures. The most frequently used is chromatography on paper, which has been applied to the study of the binding elements in layers of paint — an important problem, for upon it depends the determination of the techniques of various periods and schools (oil, tempera, etc.).

Infrared spectrophotometry (detection of the spectrum of absorption of the infrared radiations) has been used in studying organic molecules, such as wax, resins, and synthetic plastic materials.

Mineralogical optical analysis consists in the identification of the optical and crystallographic properties of crystalline substances by means of a mineralogical microscope. The method is particularly effective in the identification of transparent crystalline substances and is used for the analysis of pigments and products of corrosion of metals.

The establishment of the point of fusion is useful in analyzing organic binding elements, particularly wax. It is executed by observing, through a special microscope with a hot plate, the behavior of the gradually heated sample. Of particular interest for organic materials such as wood and cloth is the method for the approximate calculation of their age based on residual radioactivity due to the presence of carbon 14 in the material. Carbon 14 is contained in very small although relatively constant proportions in living tissues. Its quantity starts to diminish the moment the tissue dies. The speed at which carbon 14 decays is known, and measurement of the amount remaining gives an approximate date for the material in question (usually expressed as + or − a certain number of years, as in 1750 B.C. ± 250).

Observation of the crystal grain of metals brought to light by corrosive agents upon polished sections provides exact information regarding the processing methods and the thermic treatment to which the metal has been subjected as well as its state of internal preservation.

For the conservation of art works and as aids in estimating their age additional data on the external and internal environment is of great importance. Such data can be registered (particularly in museums) over a period of 12 months by special instruments (thermohygraphs, psychrometers, electrolythic hygrometers, etc.) that include the identification of the types of humidity (especially in the case of wall structures): humidity of capillarity, condensation, or infiltration. Equally important is the analysis of the atmosphere, which is done by means of a chemical analysis of gas. It should be remembered that the humidity, variations of temperature, and contamination due to industrial environments are among the main causes of the deterioration of monuments and wall paintings (see MUSEUMS AND COLLECTIONS; PRESERVATION OF ART WORKS).

The study of alterations due to biological causes (fungus, bacteria, insects, various parasites, etc.) requires still other types of research. Microbiological analysis ascertains the biological origin and kind of alteration (bacteria, fungus, algae, lichen, etc.) and provides the basis for the subsequent steps in conservation. If the deterioration is due to insects the advice of entomologists and parasitologists is required.

Analysis of the aging of materials, obviously of primary importance in the field of art conservation, is a relatively recent science. Research is based essentially on the registration of data concerning the behavior of materials that have aged in their natural context or through attempts to accelerate their aging by subjecting the materials to specific experimental conditions. The main experiments in accelerated aging, which may be useful in ascertaining the capacities of resistance of materials to be used in restoration, are those which measure resistance to biological agents, to alternating cycles of humidity and temperature, to conditions causing corrosion, to ultraviolet radiations, and to prolonged mechanical effects.

Evaluation of the aging of materials has been practiced by the more sagacious restorers of all periods along empirical lines (exposal to open air and to light, evaluation of older restoration, etc.). However, consideration of the damage done in the past by the frequent use of inadequate materials in the restoration of art works and the great number of new substances produced by modern industry induces present-day experts in conservation to be extremely prudent and to test their materials as much as possible.

Paolo MORA and Giorgio TORRACA

SOURCES. C. Plinius Secundus, Naturalis historia; Vitruvio, De architectura; Teofilo Monaco, Schedule diversarum artium; V. Biringuccio, De la pirotechnica, Venice, 1540; G. Agricola, De re metallica, Basel, 1556; J. Bassoni (J. Basson), Il theatro de gl'istrumenti e machine, Lyons, 1582; A. Ramelli, Le diverse et artificiose machine, Paris, 1588; F. Baldinucci, Vocabolario toscano dell'arte del disegno, Florence, 1681; C. Cennini, Il libro dell'arte, ed. and trans. D. V. Thompson, 2 vols., New Haven, London, 1932–33; C. Piccolpasso, The Three Books of the Potter's Art, London, 1934.

BIBLIOG. M. E. Chevreul, De la loi du contraste simultané des couleurs, 2 vols., Paris, 1839; G. Semper, Der Stil in den Technischen und Tektonischen Künsten, I, Frankfurt am Main, 1860, II, Munich, 1863; H. V.

Blümner, Technologie und Terminologie der Gewerbe und Künste bei Griechen und Römern, Leipzig, 1875–87; Technische Mit. f. Malerei, Munich, 1884–1941; E. Berger, Beiträge zur Entwicklungs-Geschichte del Maltechnik, Munich, 1912; H. Sachs, Lehrbuch der Maltechnik, Berlin, 1928; Tech. S. in the Field of the Fine Arts, I–IX, July, 1932–April, 1942; D. Thompson, The Materials of Medieval Painting, London, 1936; A. Burroughs, Art Criticism from a Laboratory, Boston, 1938; R. Mayer, The Artist's Handbook of Materials and Techniques, New York, 1940; A. P. Laurie, The Technique of the Great Painters, London, 1949; F. Klemm, Technik, eine Geschichte ihrer Probleme, Freiburg, Munich, 1954; C. Singer, E. J. Holmyard, and A. R. Hall, A History of Technology, 5 vols., Oxford, 1954; R. Gettens and B. Usilton, Abstracts of Technical Studies in Art and Archaeology, 1943–1952, Freer Gall. of Art, Occasional Pap., II, 2, Washington, D.C., 1955; Louvre, Laboratoire de recherches scientifiques, B., I, 1956 ff.; H. J. Plenderleith, The Conservation of Antiquities and Works of Art, Treatment, Repair, and Restoration, London, 1956; N. Clifford, Timber Identification for the Architect and Builder, London, 1957; K. Herberts, Die Maltechnichen, Düsseldorf, 1957; M. Hours-Miédan, A la découverte de la peinture par les méthodes physiques, Paris, 1957; P. Ducassé, Histoire des techniques, Paris, 1958; K. Herberts, The Complete Book of Artists' Techniques, New York, 1958; Brunsdon, The Technique of Etching and Engraving, New York, 1965. *Techniques of Analysis:* A. P. Laurie, The Pigments and Mediums of the Old Masters, London, 1914; A. Eibner, Entwicklung und Werkstoffe der Wandmalerei, Munich, 1926, p. 549; H. Hetterich, Über mikrochemische Bilduntersuchung, Mikrochemie, X, 1931, p. 27 ff.; F. E. Scheffer, L'examen chimique des tableaux, Mouseion, XIII–XIV, 1931, p. 94 ff.; A. M. De Wild, Naturwissenschaftliche Gemäldeuntersuchung, Munich, 1931; A. Eibner, L'examen microchimique des agglutinants, Mouseion, XX, 1932, p. 5 ff.; A. P. Laurie, Methods of Testing Minute Quantities of Materials from Pictures and Works of Art, The Analyst, LVIII, 1933, p. 468 ff.; A. Eibner, L'analyse chimique des couleurs, Mouseion, XXIX–XXX, 1935, p. 113 ff.; W. Ostwald, Microscopic Identification of Homogeneous Binding Mediums, Tech. Studies in the Field of Fine Arts, IV, 1936; S. Augusti, Applicazioni scientifiche moderne all'esame dei dipinti, Naples, 1936; E. M. Chamot, W. C. Mason, Handbook of Chemical Microscopy, New York, 1939 (2d ed.); R. J. Gettens, G. L. Stout, The Stage Microscope in the Routine Examination of Paintings, New York, 1947; S. Augusti, Alterazioni della composizione chimica dei colori nei dipinti murali, Naples, 1949; A. Schwankl, Welches Holz ist das?, Stuttgart, 1951; G. Cecchini, L'identificazione dei legnami, Milan, 1952; E. Stock, Analyse der Körperfarben, Stuttgart, 1953; F. I. G. Rawlins, Soft X-Rays in the Examination of Paintings, Studies in Conservation, I, 3, Apr. 1954, p. 135 ff.; C. F. Bridgman, S. Keck, H. F. Sherwood, The Radiography of Panel Paintings by Electron Emission, Studies in Conservation, II, 4, 1958, pp. 175–82; L. Looge, Stéréoradiographie, Studies in Conservation V, Apr. 1960, p. 85 ff.; J. Marette, Connaissance des primitifs par l'étude du bois, Paris, 1961; F. W. Jane, The Structure of Wood, London, 1962; H. Lougibson, The Photography of Infrared Luminescence, Medical and Biological Illustration, 1, 12, 1962, pp. 155–66, 2, 13, 1963, pp. 18–26, 3, 13, 1963, pp. 89–90; R. O. Woody, Jr., Painting with Synthetic Media, New York, 1965.

Illustrations: PLS. 435–458.

* *

TENIERS. A large family of Flemish painters of Antwerp, including the brothers Juliaen I (1572–1615) and David the Elder (1582–1649); the latter's four sons, David the Younger (1610–90; the most eminent of the family), Juliaen II (1616–1679), Theodor (1619–97), and Abraham (1629–70); and David the Younger's son David (1638–85).

Juliaen I, a painter of flowers and of religious and mythological subjects, became a free master in Antwerp in 1594 or 1595 and trained 11 apprentices, the most important being his younger brother David. After a period of instruction in his brother's workshop, David Teniers the Elder is thought to have gone to Italy and to have studied there under Adam Elsheimer and Peter Paul Rubens. In 1606 or 1607 he also became a free master in Antwerp. He seems to have been a dealer in pictures as well. Many of the numerous works listed in documents or formerly considered as his have been lost, and others, in the style of his son David the Younger, are no longer ascribed to him. Examples of his work are the *Transfiguration*, 1615, in Dendermonde (Termonde; Onze Lieve Vrouwekerk) and *The Seven Works of Mercy* in the Church of St. Paul in Antwerp. Of his four sons only David Teniers the Younger achieved notable success in his lifetime and a widespread fame and appreciation that have lasted through nearly three centuries.

After studying with his father, David the Younger began his career in Antwerp, where in 1632 or 1633 he became a free master of the painters' guild and later served as its dean. He married the daughter of Jan Brueghel the Elder, which brought him into contact with a large family devoted like his own to painting, and, more important, with the circle of Rubens. In 1651 he moved to Brussels, presumably invited by Archduke

Leopold William, who made him court painter and also keeper of his fine collection of works of art. David the Younger was extremely successful and bought an imposing country estate where he spent his summers. The great demand for his pictures forced him to intense production and to the employment of many helpers, which accounts for the lowered quality of some late works. His style at the beginning was based on that of Frans II Francken (cf. X, PL. 208); later he was much influenced by Adriaen Brouwer (q.v.; V, PL. 315; VI, PL. 73), developing an original style only after Brouwer's death in 1638. The work of David Teniers the Younger is fine in color, rich and luminous, his drawing exquisite; he had a great gift for bestowing individuality on his figures, and his series of paintings of monkeys — *Banquet of Monkeys*, *The Monkey Painter*, *The Monkey Sculptor* (all, Madrid, Prado), and others — reveal a nice satirical sense. He was one of the foremost masters of genre painting in 17th-century Flanders and portrayed a wide variety of ordinary people in everyday scenes and occupations (*Inn Scene*, The Hague, Mauritshuis; *Drinkers*, Antwerp, Mus. B. A.; *Villagers in Conversation*, Madrid, Prado). He also painted religious and mythological themes (*Temptation of St. Anthony*, versions in Antwerp, Mus. B. A.; Berlin, Staat. Mus.; Cologne, Wallraf-Richartz-Mus.; Madrid, Prado; *Neptune and Amphitrite*, Berlin, Staat. Mus.); contemporary historical scenes (*Panorama of Valenciennes* (Antwerp, Mus. B.A., painted in commemoration of the battle at that city in 1656); some portraits; and museum views, or "gallery pictures" (II, PL. 207; X, PL. 208), based on his knowledge of the archducal collection. He made small copies of the archduke's pictures and furnished designs for tapestries (e.g., *Dance of the Peasants*, Amsterdam, Rijksmus.) and for engravings.

David the Younger's son, also David, entered the painters' guild in Brussels in 1675, at the surprisingly mature age of thirty-seven, after a period of travel in Spain. Some of his altarpieces are in Belgian churches, and there is a *Holy Family* by him (Cologne, Wallraf-Richartz-Mus.) that was painted in 1684.

BIBLIOG. J. Smith, Catalogue Raisonné of the Most Eminent Dutch, Flemish, and French Painters, III, Anthony van Dyck and David Teniers, London, 1831; ThB, s.v.; H. Gerson and E. Hendrik ter Kuile, Art and Architecture in Belgium 1600 to 1800, Harmondsworth, 1960.

Margaretta M. SALINGER

TERBORCH, GERAERT (also GERARD TER BORCH). Dutch painter (b. Zwolle, 1617; d. Deventer, Dec. 8, 1681). Terborch undoubtedly began the study of art with his father, who practiced as a painter until 1621, when he accepted an office in the municipal treasury. The elder Terborch had spent a number of years in Rome in his youth and had brought back from his travels a collection of drawings, some by Italian artists. Young Geraert's earliest drawing is of a horse and rider (Amsterdam, Rijksmus.), dated 1625, when he was eight years old. In 1632 he appears to have made a stay in Amsterdam, the first of many visits and trips away from his small native town to centers in the Netherlands and elsewhere in Europe. In 1634 he studied under the landscape painter Pieter de Molijn in Haarlem, where he became a free master of the Guild of Saint Luke in the following year. In July of 1635 he was in London. During the years between 1636 and 1643 he seems to have traveled extensively, but the chroniclers' accounts of his journeys are vague and inconsistent. Like his father he visited Rome and Naples and possibly went also to Spain, where he is said to have painted a portrait of Philip IV and where he would certainly have come in contact with the famous court painter Velázquez. On his way back to Holland he probably stopped in France and also in Antwerp in Belgium, the city from which his mother came. He was home by 1640 and spent some time during the following five years working in Amsterdam.

Although Terborch went back to Holland at least once during the years 1645–48, most of his time during this period was spent in Münster in Germany, where delegates from all over Europe gathered in connection with the ratification of the famous treaty that made the United Provinces free and independent and ended eighty years of war. Terborch made portraits of members of the various delegations, many of them miniatures on copper or wood. He did one of the Spanish ambassador, the Count of Peñeranda (Rotterdam, Mus. Boymans-Van Beuningen); an equestrian portrait of the French ambassador Henri de Bourbon-Orléans (New-York Historical Soc.); and likenesses of a number of the Dutch delegates, of which two survive: those of Godard van Reede (Amsterdam, Rijksmus.) and Adriaen Clant (form. Paris, Coll. E. Warneck). His most important work of this time is a picture of the ceremony of the swearing of the oath ratifying the treaty, a group portrait (London, Nat. Gall.) known from a contemporary description to be an accurate record of the occasion. He included his self-portrait among the ministers.

After his return from Münster Terborch is heard of in Amsterdam, The Hague, and Kampen. From 1654 on, his life was bound up with Deventer, where he lived for the most part until his death 27 years later. He married there, became a citizen, acquired property, held honorary office in the city government, and painted a group portrait of the regents (Deventer, Stadhuis). Though he died in Deventer, he was buried in his native Zwolle.

Although Terborch studied with a landscape painter, he specialized exclusively in portraits and genre scenes (V, PL. 330; VI, PL. 74). The portraits, often small, are always distinguished by dignity, elegance, and a cool objectivity often regarded as evidence of the influence of Velázquez. His genre scenes owe something to the paintings of similar subjects by his Dutch contemporary Gabriel Metsu (q.v.) but surpass his in their exquisite refinement and delicacy of color and textures and in the very personal way they represent a quietly ordered and gracious way of life.

BIBLIOG. S. J. Gudlaugsson, Geraert ter Borch, The Hague, 1959-60; N. Maclaren, The Dutch School (Nat. Gall. Cat.), London, 1960; J. Rosenberg, S. Slive, and E. H. ter Kuile, Dutch Art and Architecture 1600 to 1800, London, 1966.

Margaretta M. SALINGER

TERBRUGGHEN (or TER BRUGGHEN), HENDRICK.

Dutch painter (b. in the province of Overijssel in Holland, probably near Deventer, 1587 or 1588; d. Utrecht, November, 1629). While Terbrugghen was still a young child, his family, probably Catholic, transferred to liberal Utrecht, presumably in 1591 when the Protestant Prince Maurice of Nassau subdued Deventer. He served an apprenticeship with Utrecht's chief artist, the mannerist Abraham Bloemaert. Far more influential, however, were the years he spent in Rome, 1603/1604–1614. At the beginning of his stay the center of artistic excitement was Caravaggio (q.v.), who lived in Rome until 1606. Terbrugghen must have come under the influence of this revolutionary young artist, whom he could well have known. In any case, when he returned to Utrecht via Milan, probably in the late summer or autumn of 1614, he brought with him a knowledge of the strong contrasts of light and dark, the diagonal compositions, and the realism, especially in genre subjects, that are characteristic of Caravaggio's Roman baroque style. Terbrugghen's *Calling of St. Matthew* in Le Havre (Mus. B.A.) is almost a direct copy, in reverse, of Caravaggio's famous picture in Rome (II, PL. 41). The decade in Rome revealed to Terbrugghen also the works of numerous other Italian artists, which, along with those of his compatriots and of the German artists Dürer and Grünewald (qq.v.), known through prints, combined to form his style.

The 15 years between the end of Terbrugghen's Italian sojourn and his death were spent in Utrecht. There he became a member of the Guild of St. Luke, married, and reared a family, including a devoted son Richard, who wrote a pamphlet to establish his father's claim to fame and in 1717 presented to the city of Deventer pictures of the Four Evangelists painted by his father (Deventer, Stadhuis).

Terbrugghen left no signed and dated picture earlier than 1620. The body of his work is small, comprising no more than 50 authentic pictures; 15 of these are in the United States.

His importance for the history of art is twofold. He was the earliest and one of the best of the northern followers of Caravaggio, whose impassioned Latin style he tempered and enriched by his experience of many other artists' works and by his own strong individuality. He was an impressive painter in his own right, worthy of the praise bestowed on him by Rubens, who on a visit to Utrecht in 1627 described him as the only real painter he had found in the Netherlands. In spite of the large number of jovial genre subjects to be found among his works, the reticent and sober temperament of Terbrugghen appears to have reached its fullest expression in such solemn and moving paintings as the *Crucifixion* (Met. Mus.) and the *St. Sebastian* (Oberlin, Ohio, Allen Memorial Art Museum), both painted about 1625.

BIBLIOG. B. Nicolson, Hendrick Terbrugghen, London, 1958; M. Maclaren, The Dutch School (Nat. Gall. Cat.), London, 1960; W. Stechow and L. J. Slatkes, Hendrick Terbrugghen in America (exhibition cat., Dayton Art Inst., and Baltimore Mus. of Art), 1965.

Margaretta M. SALINGER

TERROR AND THE MALIGN. The term "terror" is used here to indicate a particular aspect of religious art bound up with complex doctrinal considerations; in its simplest manifestations it confers terrifying attributes and forms on divinities who are not inherently malign. In these cases terror may be expressed as an assimilation of the divine (see DIVINITIES) to the demonic element (see DEMONOLOGY), since the terrifying form is assumed by the divinity to combat his adversaries on their own ground. In any case, it is an expression of the destructive power of the god, represented in forms that are a warning to the faithful as well as a clear expression of the divine supremacy in all spheres. Particularly widespread in Tantric Buddhism (see BUDDHISM), especially in the Tibetan and Mongolian iconography, the terrifying is also related to the ambivalent nature of particular divinities who may, at various times, assume a pacified aspect (corresponding to their beneficent nature) or a wrathful aspect (and therefore a terrifying one, corresponding to their destructive power). From another point of view the terrifying aspect of the god can be linked to the expression of divine wrath and punitive power and is thus part of the broader problem of good and evil within the perspectives of the divine *tremendum*. For this reason, features that are essentially terrifying — even though realized in forms opposed to the malign, or demonic — can be found in works of art that are inspired by a principle of marked differentiation between the divine and the forces of evil.

SUMMARY. Phenomenology of terror and the malign in art (col. 1038). The ambivalent divinity (col. 1043). The Buddhist repertory (col. 1044).

PHENOMENOLOGY OF TERROR AND THE MALIGN IN ART. The phenomenology of terror, which is relatively limited but varied, is made clear in many cases only with the help of texts. The purely malign, or demonic, element occurs seldom in the art of Buddhist Asia. Consequently, the aspects and attributes of the terrifying divinities correspond to those of the negative and destructive forces, with clear references to death, decay, and the powers of black magic (a prime example is the knot, the attribute of those divinities strongly gifted with magical paralyzing forces). The clearest exemplifications are found in the Buddhist iconography and iconology of India, Tibet, and Mongolia, but in reality the terrifying and the malign correspond to a complex of intuitions, feelings, and insights that have universal value. The assimilation of the divine to hostile demonic elements through the assumption, by the divinity itself, of a demonic form obviously presupposes an ambivalence of the divine. It also presupposes absolute dominion over all powers, including magical ones, which, in spite of the difficulty in distinguishing them from divine powers, especially in the Oriental world, are clearly attributed to the demonic forces alone. In this process there is evidently a psychological basis for the profound fear of the malign and demonic powers and for the belief that they can be eliminated by using the same means that the demonic powers themselves employ in performing their evil deeds. In practice, the normal power, so to speak, of the divinity proves ineffective; to the ingenuous eyes of the faithful believer, divine means are inadequate to ward off the destructive and chaotic elements that attack his equilibrium and his life. Such a conception (reduced here to extremely elementary terms) probably reacted not only with the religious imagination but also with the common, continuous, and doctrinally uncontrolled reflection on the images created by artists. This is a phenomenon that frequently recurs in the evolution of Buddhist iconography and doctrines as a continuous and profound interpenetration of the two kinds of activity: the imaginative and creative one of the artist and the speculative and exegetic one — both aimed at clarification and edification and eventually forming a special iconological aspect (see ICONOGRAPHY AND ICONOLOGY) that is usually neglected by scholars.

The presupposed ambivalence of the divine being, the accentuated protective power of the divinity itself, so clearly revealed in Buddhist thought, is reduced, in the evolution of Indian speculative thought, to an absolute unity wherein all values, even if opposed, converge, since it represents, in the most complex religious philosophy, the Absolute, the very manifestation of cosmic energy. In Hindu thought (see HINDUISM) this is demonstrated by the five activities (pañcakriyā) of Śiva Naṭarāja, Lord of the Dance (especially the first three): srṣṭi (creation, which is also expansion and development); sthiti (maintenance, equivalent to duration); saṃhāra (destruction, corresponding to reabsorption); tirobhāva ("hidden being," alluding to the fact that true being conceals itself behind masks and veils of illusory appearance, or maya); and anugraha (the acceptance of the believer, hence the appreciation by the god of the religious fervor of the faithful). Śiva, therefore, incarnates the opposing elements of the universe and of life so that he is both masculine and feminine, creator and destroyer, time and eternity. For this reason he is called Yamāntaka, vanquisher of Yama, the Lord of Death, and at the same time is himself the god of death, as are Kāla ("black one," and also Time) and Mahākāla ("Great Time," or Eternity; PL. 466). Unquestionably, Saivistic speculation is reflected in Buddhism (both Saivism and Buddhism pass through the particular analogous phase called Tantric, from tantra, meaning "book"), thus conditioning the phenomenon discussed here. Śiva, creator and destroyer, derives from Rudra, the Vedic god of mountains and storms, wrathful or placid, and in the eyes of the faithful he may appear as a kindly and creative divinity or a terrible and destructive one, since he contains within himself the extreme opposites, life and death.

But in Buddhist thought this ambivalence of the divine being, resolving itself in a coincidentia oppositorum, or union of opposites, assumes other subtleties and modulations. Received indirectly and placed in contact with a very different conception of the divine and the divinity, it nevertheless continues to express the essence of the universe and to be an expression of the all-pervading cosmic energy, but it contains new values that could be defined as apparent and symbolic. In addition to the fact that the concept of a supreme god, such as that nourished by the Hindu movements, is foreign to Buddhism and that in practice the gods figure as secondary, and not as essential, figures inferior to man and in a less privileged position in spite of their apparent power, it should not be forgotten that the aspect of the god, whatever it may be, is just as illusory for Buddhism as is the world of phenomena. This must be taken into consideration. There is much speculation and controversy concerning the aspect and the three bodies of the Buddha (trikāya): nirmāṇakāya (the "illusory body"), dharmakāya (the "body of the law," or essence of the universe), and saṃbhogakāya (the "body of bliss," essentially bound, in its genesis, to iconographic and representational data). This triune division is analogous to that of Docetism. The entire theoretical and iconographic evolution — passing from symbolic aniconism (see BUDDHIST PRIMITIVE SCHOOLS; IMAGES AND ICONOCLASM) to the figure of the Master assimilated to the supreme value of the Law (Dharma) preached by him and finally becoming split up into

the endless pantheon of late Buddhism — demonstrates t diversity of positions and assumptions that, in spite of the ma coincidences and interpenetrations, separates Buddhism fro Hinduism.

The introduction of terrifying images in the Tantric icono raphy seems to be almost in open contrast with the orthod belief, which, in confronting the problem, accepts them and ju tifies them only by considering them as symbolic values. Ho ever, this type of situation confirms the fact that such diviniti (almost always imagined, in the aspect reproduced by the artis with the help of esoteric meditative techniques) correspond psychological attitudes widespread among the faithful, like resurgence of ancient fears and archaic fantasies that imp more than a transformation, an involution of Buddhism. F this reason the terrifying aspect implies a protective value, whi is illusory to those with more open minds but is real to the mass of the faithful. And such a value can be overt, as in the ca of the lokapalas (world guardians) and generally of the defenso fidei, or latent (see below). The substantial ambivalence of t. Hindu divinities is replaced by a twofold aspect that does n affect the true essence of the entity represented, who remai unaltered (also because he is considered empty). Still, it shou be noted that these same divinities, with their monstrous fac many arms, macabre attributes, and agitated appearance, mo away from the human dimension and become nightmare fi ures. They are studied and created with the intention of acti in a direct and indirect way (through symbols of clear efficac upon the psyche of the faithful, even stirring the hidden dept of the unconscious. The contrast between the static, hiera images drawn from the Buddhist iconographic tradition and the semidemonic macabre figures, agitated by a bestial and monstro violence, can be explained not only by the interpenetration wi Hinduism (from which postures, such as those of the danc symbols, and details of composition are derived) and, throu this source, by the emergence of ancient intuitions and religio imaginings but also by the eruption in Buddhist thought, bo popular and otherwise, of elements connected with the wor of magic and with speculation concerning death and the herea ter; this speculation was set in motion on foundations as stran as they were free from every defined tradition.

Here it should be pointed out that the psychological effe of an image thus formed (whether conceived by an origin creative effort or by making use of accepted, and almost alwa macabre, symbolism) is obviously different, in the eyes of t believer, from that of the demonic figure, for the former, althou developing a sense of the tremendum and infandum, is reassuri and protective, whereas the latter is malign. Neverthele profound differences, truly inherent in the expressiveness of t image itself, are rarely observed between one and the oth type, since the terrifying figure is almost always limited expressing its own superiority through more or less compl symbols and, above all, through a very accentuated proportion symbolism. Apart from the dogmatic and interpretive subtl ties, it is evident that such a conception rests on a well-defin relationship between the divine and the demonic assumed the artist and, more than by the theologian, by a common an widespread need of the people. In such a relationship the cre tion of the terrifying image serves to insure protection and s curity, by making manifest its force, whereas in the demon portrayal, because of the very fact that it defines the demon appearance, its malignant power is limited and contained. Th curious and dangerous proximity of the terrifying and of t demonic aspect is not surprising, inspired as it is by the asce tained ambivalence of the ancient divinities, from Varuṇa Śiva. In fact, Indian thought has always tried to interpret th ambivalence either as the twofold aspect of a divine uni (Eliade, 1962, calls this "a divine unity-in-duality") or as essential coincidentia oppositorum, to use the language of Nich las of Cusa; but such an attitude is not exclusive to India.

The concept of the demonic fluctuates considerably, and would be impossible, for example, to adopt the same meanir for the demons of the Asian world as it is traditionally customa to attribute to the devil. He certainly is a demon, more less directly derived from the Hellenic Pan, but he gradual sumes the physiognomy of a radically evil being who cannot e to the idea of God, since he is the incarnation of the will posed to the divine will. Thus, for a long time, the idea of demption was to consist in freeing man from the devil's wer. On the other hand, the belief in demons not only reals anxiety before the horrible and the incomprehensible but, ove all, fear of a power that is indifferent to man's reason or s conduct. The demon is thus an expression of the irrational, ich nevertheless is always bound to the divine power in rious forms; if the devas of India are the gods, the daevas of an are the demons, and if the devas oppose themselves to the uras (demons), this does not alter the fact that their respective wers are complementary or that they even appear as different, ccessive phases of the same divine power. In the Tibetan dition concerning the stages following death (the intermediary istence), it is just this softened light of the deva (opposing, the ego of the deceased, that violent and less welcome one the First Principle) that leads the transmigrating individuality ck toward the phenomenal world, hindering it — also because an instinctive inclination of its own — from reaching nirvana. or is there any lack, especially in Buddhism, of famous exples of demons who perform good deeds or who even reach eir status as maleficent beings as a reward for good works. popular traditions outside of India, explicit indications can found hinting at a presumed brotherhood, or complementary aracter, of God and the demon. This is found not only in the nostic sects of the Bogomiles and the Ebionites, but winds in d out among the most varied peoples, from the southern Slavs the Yakuts. Eliade points out that in Iranian Zurvanism the vinities of good and evil are two brothers and, moreover, the align being is born before the divinity of good.

A particular case is that of the malign being of demonic aracter who becomes, in part, an attribute of the divinity d who with his strength increases the power of the divinity question. This is the case, within the sphere of influence of e Greek religion, of the gorgoneion (PL. 469), which retains e power of turning those who behold it to stone, and yet, hen placed on the aegis of the goddess Athena, becomes a cile weapon in the service of her will (PL. 468). Athena, godss of knowledge, remains a protective goddess, but she asmes in disguised form a special ambivalence that, at many ints, borders on the terrifying.

Basically all these speculations, which are more far-reaching an might normally be imagined, correspond to an almost conscious desire to penetrate the mystery of the existence of il and to explain — almost rationally, if this word can be used re — the imperfection of divine creation for which man, ecisely because of the presence of evil, must pay dearly. Later, the basis of a theological evolution (unnoticed by the faith-l, but clarified by modern exegesis), it was to be said that the tential equivalence of opposed elements could be realized only ithin a transcendental perspective that exists outside of time, hile, in the flow of life and phenomena, the continuous contrast tween good and evil remains an operative reality that calls man to face the problem of ethics and his own salvation. he idea of the power of terror therefore becomes particularly ear in the world of Indian thought, above all because the entire mplex of religious ideas and activities of India tends to underine the instinctive impression that human experience of the orld may be metaphysically valid. It is therefore understandable ow the resurgence of the most ancient traditional Indian backround of beliefs may have led, through the mediation of the nbivalent divinities (śānta, pacified, and kruddha, irritated), the iconographic scheme of the terrifying figures, responding a real psychological need in the faithful.

The Indian and Asian-Buddhist phenomenology constitutes e most important aspect of this problem, but it is one that is ssentially separate from almost all the other manifestations more r less connected with the terrifying power itself. The conception f the divinity in his relation to man always includes a sense of e tremendum, referring to the shock the believer experiences n finding himself face to face with the sacred. Such a sense is bviously all the more profound the more closely the divinity's wn essence is linked to the ethical and eschatological judgment

it expresses concerning the believer, whether with regard to his present life or, above all, his future one; it can therefore be related to the antinomy between good and evil through particular expressions that border, at least in some aspects, on the terrifying. In other words, where the reductio ad unum determines a vision of the world based on the coincidentia oppositorum, the phenomenology of the terrifying power becomes clear and apparent, expressed in the manner previously described; that is, as a setting on a level of the divine and the demonic, justified by the concept that any appearance, including the aspect of the divinity, is illusory. Where the antinomy between good and evil is irreducible, even if slight traces of a possible unity or similarity of the supernatural beings (divinity and demon) are perceptible, the expression of the two opposed concepts, and of the entities that animate them, come to be imagined on the basis of an unmistakable antithesis. Consequently there does not exist here — at least in the official line of thought — anything similar to the Buddhist concept of the terrifying.

But the opposition of the two concepts includes, as far as the divine power is concerned, the sense of the tremendum and that of the transcendant maiestas: two sentiments capable of profoundly shocking the spirit of the believer who finds himself in their presence, developing in him the terror before the sacred. The expression of art directed toward arousing such sentiments in the spectator often borders on the terrifying in a sufficiently obvious manner, even if it is constantly bound to the concept of divine justice (and punishment). As a result, some creations of the Western world, including imposing and famous works of art, may be considered as being close to the phenomenon under discussion. It must be kept in mind, however, that the imagination of the artist, who believes in the absolute incompatibility of good and evil, attempts to distinguish clearly between the two values, exalting their salient characteristics by all possible spiritual and technical means.

If the premises proposed here are valid, Michelangelo's Christ in Judgment (PL. 470) is obviously a terrifying image not only because of the violence of the gesture (the Mother herself is portrayed as terrified and grieved) but also because the gigantic power of the figure and composition is intended to obtain a shock effect. This does not alter the fact that Christ is shown in a supreme moment and in the guise of judge and that he remains the Saviour of mankind.

In countless other examples, when the divinity (or the expression of the divine power) is placed in direct contact with and confronts the forces of evil, which succumb to the deity, the artist's imagination attempts to clearly distinguish the divinity, conferring on it, in one way or another (as in the various interpretations of St. Michael the Archangel, e.g., XII, PLS. 37, 106), a superhuman power. This power is derived from the terror of the sacred and is meant to instill awe in the spectator, even though the figure has a human appearance, automatically opposed to the semibestial figure of the demon or, in other cases, to the images of the damned or of monsters (as in the legend of St. George, e.g., XI, PLS. 40, 421; XII, PL. 42). In this way the artist seeks an indescribable beauty, a superhuman vigor, a supernatural splendor, sometimes by means of symbols or iconographic conventions, at other times by an imaginative effort that affects the figure, the composition, the style.

This approach, which in Christian art is justified by the analogy between the divine and the human appearance (notwithstanding the inevitable difficulty of expressing the ineffable), is certainly more arduous and complex than the other and implies a totally different attempt on the artist's part, precisely because it presupposes the contrast, rather than the assimilation, as well as the direct or indirect sublimation of the human figure. Both approaches seek a common effect, at least partially, but by opposite means. Nor is it valid to refer to the divinity of justice and punishment, that terrible god of some religious movements, since among other things for the Western Christian school the dichotomy between divine and demonic connects the divine with a human appearance (and therefore with anthropomorphic forms) and the dichotomy must still be overcome although it remains essential. In any case, the body of examples in Western art, which is also bound, among other things, to the personality of the authors and to their religious sensitivities, is certainly more evanescent and less clearly expressible than that of Buddhist and Saivistic Oriental art, above all because it rests on subtleties and inconstant values. Nevertheless, it unmistakably evidences the correspondence of the terrifying to the religious sense of mankind.

THE AMBIVALENT DIVINITY. For the many and varied divinities who may assume a wrathful or appeased aspect and who have been defined as ambivalent, particularly the Indian ones, the typical example of the iconographic approach, directed at expressing this same ambivalence, is to be found in the images of the god Śiva and of his goddesses — Kālī (VII, PL. 229) or Durgā, Ambikā, Pārvatī, Umā, Vārāhī, Cāmuṇḍā (PL. 460), Gaurī, Haimavatī, Vindhyavāsinī — who, with him, form the cosmic couple. The iconographic fact is accompanied by iconological phenomena, but it is difficult to follow the concatenation because of the many gaps that it presents. On a seal from Mohenjo-daro (New Delhi, Nat. Mus.) is a figure that may represent a proto-Śiva as Paśupati (Lord of the Beasts). The first image of the god in a fully historical period appears, it seems, on a coin of the Śaka sovereign Maues (ca. 75 B.C.). Neither in this image nor in comparable ones on Kushan coins is there an attempt to express the terrifying power. But the four arms of the divinity that recur in some coin images of Huviṣka (mid-2d cent.) symbolically allude to the supreme power of the divinity, and the attribute of vajra (thunderbolt) indicates both the availability of the supreme weapon and the stormy character of the god — certainly connected with the cult of the mountains.

Instead, the three-headed image of Saozma Kala evidences a classical component in the archaic Saivite iconography, which is explainable but nevertheless unexpected, since it results from the juxtaposition of three Greek divinities (Herakles, Poseidon, and Zeus) already known in the local coins, whether those of the Greek sovereigns or the Śaka and Parthian ones (see COINS AND MEDALS). The image itself undoubtedly constitutes an iconological problem that, in its most simple aspect, gives evidence of an amalgam of foreign values adapted (also by way of intermediary interpretive modifications that do not damage the traditional physiognomy of the Greek divinities) to express the essential structure of another, extremely remote and complex divinity, whose characteristics, going through a formative process, slowly become specific in the final appearance. It is probable that the choice of the three Greek divinities carried an overtone of the tremendum traditionally emphasized in the structure of Zeus (recalling his wrath and power of domination), as well as in that of Poseidon. But it is certainly not possible to speak of terror, at least if the image is considered by Western eyes. Perhaps locally a reference to terror really did exist.

By contrast, with respect to the consort of Śiva, who is identified with various divinities in the highly composite religious milieu of the Kushan area, there already exists a dichotomy, revealed by the fact that she may appear in the guise of Umā (Ommo in the Greek script of the Iranian language used on the coins), as well as in that of Nanai (Nana or Nanaia, in the same inscriptions). This divinity is probably Semitic in nature (evidently borrowed) in which the terrible and warlike — if not outright negative — aspect is very strong and certainly prevalent, while in Umā the characteristics connected with fertility and fecundity are developed; these are also stressed by the attributes recurring in the images on the coins.

It seems, therefore, that the dichotomy manifests itself with greater clarity and precocity in the feminine component of the cosmic couple, precisely because she represents the very power of the god, his śakti, so to speak (IV, PL. 223). In this religious world, which is remarkably composite and dominated by a system of correlation in pairs, she is expressed either with an Indian form, iconographically adapted to foreign symbols, or with the borrowed form of an Irano-Semitic divinity, which was to reassume and personify, better than any other, the intuitions regarding the terrible and terrifying aspect of the goddess.

It is not surprising, therefore, if in another environment the Devīmāhātmya (chaps. 81–93 of the Mārkaṇḍeya Purāṇa) describes the goddess Durgā as the result of the combined wrath of all the gods, the personification of the supreme energy the universe, the only force capable of destroying the asu Mahiṣa — a demonic titan in buffalo form. And the image the goddess slaying the buffalo (in spite of the latter's transfo mations and the enormous power that had resisted both Viṣ and Śiva) is clearly and unquestionably a terrifying image, ev if demonic features do not occur in her stylistic and iconograph portrayal, as often happens, since it is preferable, in this speci theme, to exalt the marvelous beauty of her body — the bo of an indomitable warrior virgin — as conceived by Indian tas The relief at Mamallapuram, where the eight-armed godde sits astride a lion (IV, PL. 171), expresses the power of the a vancing goddess and the downfall of the asura and his forc by a compositional scheme. In later Rajput miniatures the go dess is depicted in her pacified aspect; she is mounted on a li and is preceded by the monstrous destructive force emanati from her, a force personified as a witch.

In the infinite variations of this iconographic theme the divine beauty is generally contrasted with the monstrosity, in various images, of the asura in buffalo form. However, the figu of the goddess, particularly in the many hypostases that form t Mātṛkā group, does at times assume monstrous aspects of a m lign type, with macabre touches either in the structure of t image, which becomes semiskeletal, or, above all, in its att butes. Such figures are related to Buddhist images, such as th of the red-colored, six-armed Vajracarcikā, whose hands a feet are clawed, and who dances on a corpse. On the other han Tantric Saivism contains images of Kālī trampling on Śiv a Śiva reduced to the state of a corpse (śava). Here, howeve a complex symbolism is substituted for the terrifying pow of the goddess. It is inspired by a scale of differing values th is intended to be the precise meaning of the cosmic structu and the essence of life. This is, therefore, far from the true ai proper concept of the terrifying power, even though, in appea ance, the distance is not pronounced.

As to Śiva, apart from the macabre attributes that bri him back to the concept of death and may be interpreted a kind of memento mori, it should not be forgotten that he also Yamāntaka (PL. 466), he who conquers the Lord of Dea either because he is supreme death or because he is life: thus ambivalence is confirmed. His monstrous creation, the kīr mukha ("face of glory") — that hungry being expressed by t god as a synthesis of his wrath in order to compel Rāhu to ree ter the order of the universe and who consumes himself un he remains only a head without a body — is a figure that slow becomes apotropaic and protective through an elaboration ideas that partakes, above all, of the popular influence on icono raphy and affects the religious ornamentation of vast are Perhaps the clearest expression, even if it is shot through wi popular beliefs, of Śiva's truly terrible aspect is found in t kīrtimukha, whereas elsewhere (especially in the Śiva who pe forms his cosmic dance) the indications and the macabre semidemonic structures allude solely to the ambivalence of t god and touch the truly terrifying only collaterally.

THE BUDDHIST REPERTORY. It is not possible in this artic to examine in detail the phenomenology of terror and the mali in the Buddhist world. The discussion is limited to exampl based on a partially empirical choice, of works that reflect t various problems. A particular aspect of terror and the mali in Buddhism is represented by the defensores fidei, among who Vajrapāṇi, the Buddha's companion, is the most important a one of the earliest (VI, PL. 15). In Gandharan art he assum almost grotesque aspects connected with his particular functio The genesis of this enigmatic divinity, carrier of the thunde bolt, the absolute weapon of the Heavenly world, is unknow Sometimes he appears in the aspect of Herakles; at other tim of Zeus, the hurler of thunderbolts. When he has the aspect Silenus (and therefore of a figure that is practically parademoni or when he assumes original physiognomies, curiously a strongly characterized, there exists, in the artist's intention, wish to arrive at a terrifying effect, which has been developed such a manner that uncertainty has arisen, among the fi scholars to take an interest in Gandharan art, concerning Vajrapāṇi's real nature.

In the late Tantric phase, as it appears in Tibetan texts and images, Vajrapāṇi (P'yag na rdo rje) wears blue clothes as prescribed by the *Sādhanamālā*, where he is called Nīlāmbara, and this may also be a reference to demonic powers (at least judging from the Central Asian iconography). Here it is used, however, in the apotropaic sense, so to speak, since Vajrapāṇi is the principal enemy of the demons, just as he is the protector of the nagas, or earth gods, against the Garuḍas, or threatening powers from the atmosphere. With his acolytes he forms four tetrads, characterized by the mudra of menace and by aggressive or macabre attributes which are fully described in the *bsTan agyur*, LXVIII, 225 (*Vajravidāraṇīnāmāsādhana*). This is illustrated, for example, in the fourth chapel of the first floor of the sKu abum (Kumbum) at Gyantse in Tibet.

The four sovereigns of the cardinal points developed along different lines, which, at least in some details, are rooted in the semiclassical iconography of the Hellenistic world. The physiognomic characterizations of these sovereigns, which are often grotesque, as is the case in those found in their Chinese and Japanese images, undoubtedly possess a terrifying power (PLS. 464, 467). Popular thought on the subject favors this gradual transformation, naturally adapting it to the taste of the various peoples who, through the expansion of Buddhism, came into contact with the four sovereigns.

As to the transformation and adaptation of some divinities who assume a terrifying form, there is no doubt that these phenomena follow the pattern of others that are iconographically similar but inspired by a different school of thought, such as those phenomena related to the ambivalence of the Hindu divinities. In Tibet, the continuous overwhelming presence of a world of terror, bound to the native religion, provokes the heightening of this phenomenon, with the respective transformation of the Mon bu putra (Skr., *putra*, the whole, in the Skr. of the liturgy = *yakṣa*) into protective deities of the Buddhist teachings. A typical example is provided by the cycle of the Mon bu putra in the temple of aBras k'ud (Dregun) at Samada in Tibet, studied by G. Tucci.

This cycle has ties with that of the protector of the Sa skya pa sect, Gur mgon, whose name signifies "protector of the cage." Since this term also indicates the skeleton, Gur mgon is he who helps man to destroy his corporal cage wherein ignorance holds him prisoner. A chthonian divinity, akin to Mahākāla, he is characterized by the *gaṇḍī*, the wooden spatula used to beat the hours in the monasteries (hence associated with Time), which was transformed into an instruemnt of punishment. The divinity is black, and is dressed in tiger skins, with a sword and skull full of blood in its hands, a crown of five skulls, and a necklace of mutilated heads dripping blood. His retinue consists of black dogs, black birds, jackals, black lamenting men, and Garuḍas; this retinue is connected with the *ḍākinī*, semidemonic female divinities.

In the cycle of Gur mgon, as well as in that of E ka dza ti (Skr., Ekajāṭā), a turquoise-colored female divinity of terrifying aspect, and in many other cycles, there is, in the Tibetan iconography, a curious reflection of what the texts teach. That is, entire groups of divinities, set in a structural pattern so as to form a kind of mandala (XIV, PL. 42), are linked, by means of other elements that serve as transitions from one figure to the other, to the mystic syllables upon which the evocation of these divinities depends. And since this evocative process is common to every type of divinity, it is quite clear that what is involved here are illusory figures, evoked by the power of meditation, but unreal in their essence. This is the reason that in these images, and particularly the terrifying ones, there is such a heavy emphasis on the macabre and horrifying details that serve to complete and complement the monstrous structure of the bodies. There are corpses that serve as vehicles, staring skulls, rotting bodies that are lacerated and reduced to a pulp, showers of flame, monstrous figures of Central Asian or Chinese origin. Just as the increase in the number of arms and the related attributes indicates the benevolent power of the protective divinities, so the increase of macabre characteristics and the deformity of the limbs (regulated by precise proportions in the graphic realization) serve to indicate the heightened combative power of the divinity itself against the forces of evil.

The terrifying images par excellence are not those examined above but others belonging to the cycle of Vajrabhairava (connected with Mañjuśrī; PLS. 459, 461; XIV, PL. 44), of Yama (XIV, PL. 39), and of Heruka (II, PL. 387; XIV, PL. 37). The examples chosen, however, take into account the fact that precisely in those divine forms that had a local origin and became absorbed or modified by Buddhism it is possible to observe a certain accentuation of the terrifying traits, with a greater liking for macabre details, even though, in the physical structure, the fact that some divinities of another type have a ferine head (e.g., a buffalo) seems to render them more monstrous. The structure itself derives from mystic hallucinations caused by the yoga technique (become a means of inspiration) and codified by the iconographic treatises that are so numerous in India and Tibet.

BIBLIOG. A. Grünwedel, Mythologie des Buddhismus in Tibet und der Mongolei, Leipzig, 1900; E. Valton, Les monstres dans l'art, Paris, 1905; J. G. Frazer, The Gorgon Head and Other Literary Pieces, London, 1927, pp. 3-34; G. Tucci, Indo-Tibetica, 4 vols. in 7, Rome, 1932-41; J. Masson, La réligion populaire dans le canon Bouddhique Pāli, Louvain, 1942; H. R. Zimmer, Myths and Symbols in Indian Art and Civilization, New York, 1946; G. Tucci, Tibetan Painted Scrolls, 2 vols. and portfolio of pls., Rome, 1949; J. N. Banerjea, The Development of Hindu Iconography, 2d ed. (rev. and enl.), Calcutta, 1956; B. Bhattacharyya, The Indian Buddhist Iconography, 2d ed. (rev. and enl.), Calcutta, 1958; E. S. Gifford, The Evil Eye, Studies in the Folklore of Vision, New York, 1958; C. Roy, Les arts fantastiques, Paris, 1960; M. Eliade, Méphistophéles et l'androgyne, Paris, 1962 (Eng. trans. J. M. Cohen, Mephistopheles and the Androgyne: Studies in Religious Myth and Symbol, London, New York, 1965); W. Kayser, Grotesque in Art and Literature, Bloomington, Ind., 1963.

Mario BUSSAGLI

Illustrations: PLS. 459-470.

PLATES

Pl. 1. Tsimshian statue of a shaman, British Columbia, Canada, 19th cent. Wood with fur, copper eyes, and dog's teeth; ht., 32 in. Paris, Musée de l'Homme.

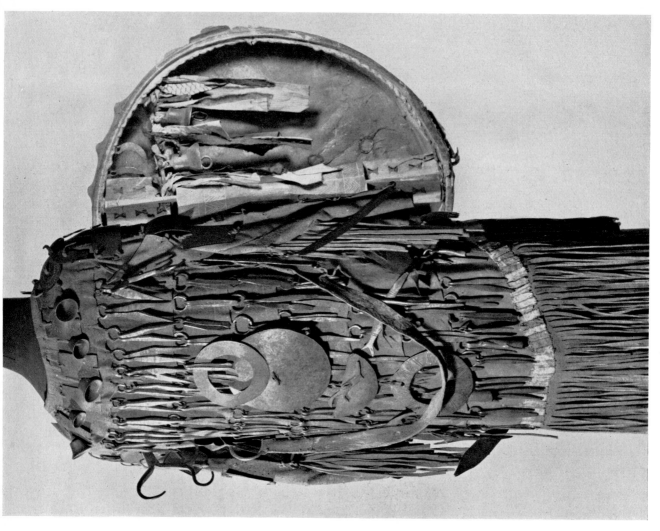

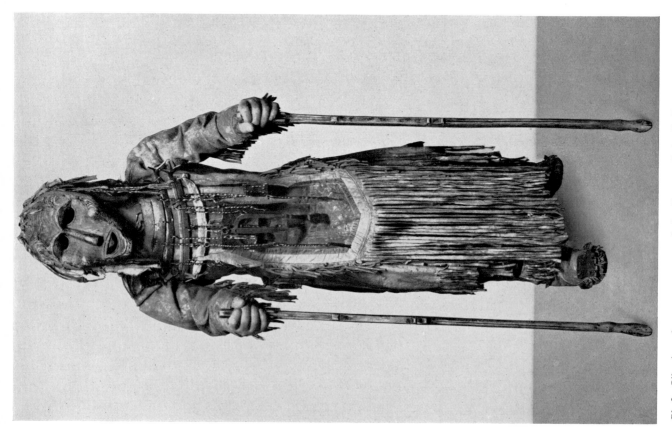

Pl. 2. Siberian shaman costumes. *Left*: Tungus, Lake Baikal area, collected 1861. Reindeer hide with iron attachments representing animal bones and spirits; wooden sticks in the form of reindeer legs. Copenhagen, Nationalmuseet. *Right*: Abakan Tartar, Minusinsk area. Skin with symbolic iron, copper, and brass attachments; skin drum.

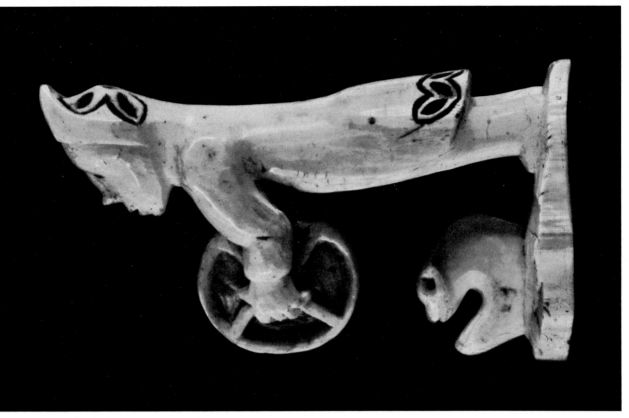

Pl. 3. *Left, above*: Tlingit dance or shaman's rattle in the form of a raven with frog and hawk, southeastern Alaska, collected before 1909. Painted wood, l., 14 in. Seattle, Thomas Burke Memorial Washington State Museum. *Below*: Haida and (*bottom*) Tsimshian healing instruments in the form of the double-headed serpent Sisiutl, British Columbia, Canada, collected before 1882. Bone with mother-of-pearl inlays. Berlin, Museum für Völkerkunde (both lost in World War II). *Right*: Koryak statuette, shaman beating a drum, with mythical animal, eastern Siberia. Walrus tusk with black paint, ht., 3 1/8 in. Leningrad, Ethnographical Museum.

Pl. 4. Ingalik mask, representing the *inua* (soul) of a salmon, lower Yukon, Alaska, collected before 1883. Wood with feathers. Berlin Museum für Völkerkunde (lost in World War II).

Pl. 5. Great Shrine of Ise, Mie prefecture, Japan, periodically reconstructed in traditional style since the 7th cent. *Above*: Aerial view of the Inner Shrine (Naikū), showing the 59th reconstruction (*at left*), 1954, adjoining the preceding one. *Below*: The main building.

Pl. 6. Great Shrine of Ise (cf. PL. 5), three principal buildings. *Above, left*: Main building, northwest view. *Right*: East treasure house. *Below*: West treasure house.

Pl. 7. Itsukushima Shrine, Hiroshima prefecture, Japan, 12th cent. (rebuilt 13th cent., later repaired), aerial view and detail.

Pl. 8. Itsukushima Shrine (cf. Pl. 7), detail of central buildings.

Pl. 9. Great Shrine of Izumo, Shimane prefecture, Japan, rebuilt 1744 and later, southwest view.

Pl. 10. Shinto divinity, 9th cent. Painted wood, ht., 33½ in. Kyoto, Matsunoo Jinja.

Pl. 11. Head of a Buddha image, from Nagara Paṭhama, Dvāravatī style, 6th–11th cent. Terra cotta, ht., 7⁷/₈ in. Bangkok, National
Museum.

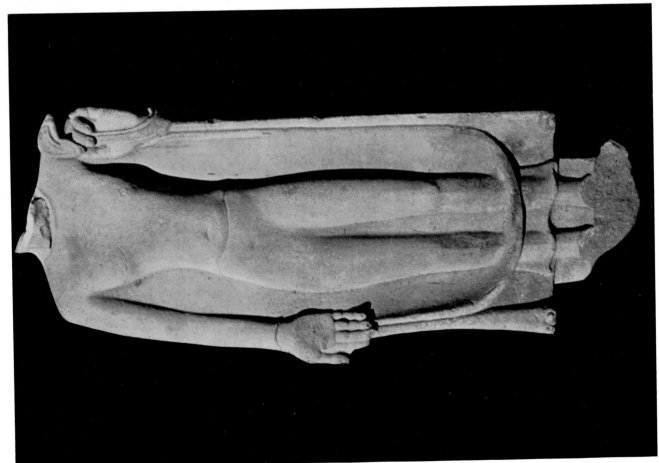

Pl. 12. *Left*: Standing Buddha, Dvāravatī style, 8th–10th cent. Stone, ht., 43¹/₄ in. Monkton, Md., Breezewood Foundation Coll. *Right*: Torso of a divinity, fragment, from the Pathamacetiya, Nagara Pathama, Dvāravatī style, 6th–11th cent. Stucco, ht., 19¹/₄ in. Bangkok, National Museum.

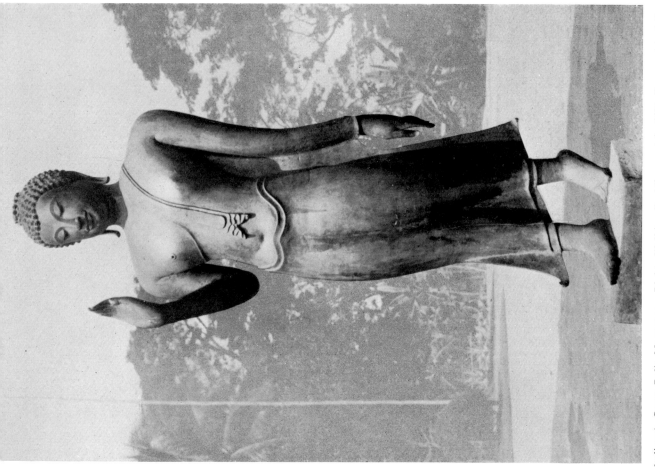

Pl. 13. *Left*: Walking Buddha, late 13th cent. (?), Stucco relief, ht., ca. 23 ft. Svargaloka (Chalieng), Great Relic Monastery. *Right*: Walking Buddha, cast in 1426. Bronze, ht., 6 ft., 1¼ in. Nan, Monastery.

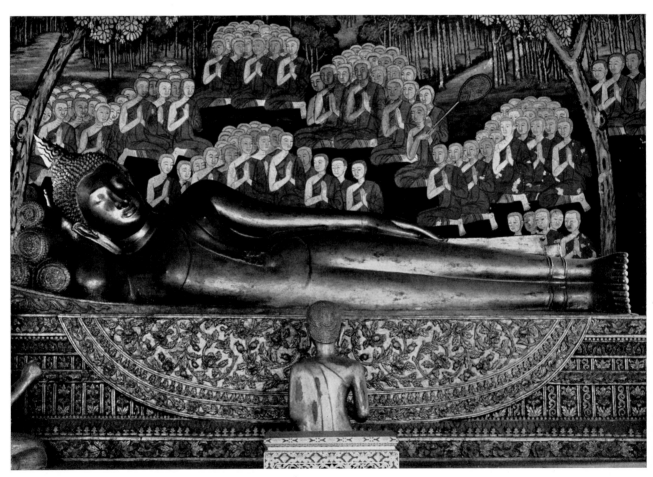

Pl. 14. *Above, left*: Standing Buddha, cast in 1541, late Sukhodaya or Ayudhyā style. Bronze, ht., 6 ft., 1⁵/₈ in. *Right*: Seated Buddha, 14th cent., Sukhodaya style. Bronze, ht., ca. 4 ft., 6 in. Both, Bangkok, Peñcamapabitra Monastery. *Below*: Reclining Buddha, 14th cent., Sukhodaya style. Bronze, l., 11 ft., 6 in. Bangkok, Monastery of the Excellent Abode (Pavaranivesa).

Pl. 15. Śiva, probably 14th cent., Sukhodaya style. Bronze, ht., ca. 5 ft. Bangkok, National Museum.

Pl. 16. *Above, left*: Svargaloka (Śrī Sajjanālaya), the "Elephant-Supported Stupa," 1285(?)–1292. *Right*: Svargaloka (Chalieng), Great Relic Monastery, mandapa, 15th cent.(?) and (*behind*) the *prāṅg*, second half of 14th cent.(?). *Below*: Sukhodaya, Great Relic Monastery, showing (*at center*) remains of vihara, 14th–15th cent.(?), and (*right*) main cetiya, first half of 14th cent.

Pl. 17. *Above*: Nagara Paṭhama, the Paṭhamacetiya, begun 1868, finished in 20th cent. (encasing an older monument).
Below: Bangkok, Jetavanārāma (commonly called "Monastery of the Bodhi Tree"), first half of 19th cent. with later restorations and additions.

Pl. 18. Bangkok, view of the Chapel Royal (so-called "Temple of the Emerald Buddha"), first half of 19th cent. with later restorations and additions.

Pl. 19. Sukhodaya, Great Relic Monastery, rebuilt 14th cent., detail of central shrine with stucco relief of the birth of the Buddha.

Pl. 20. Cetiya of the Mahābodhārāma, near Chieng Mai, 1455–ca. 1470.

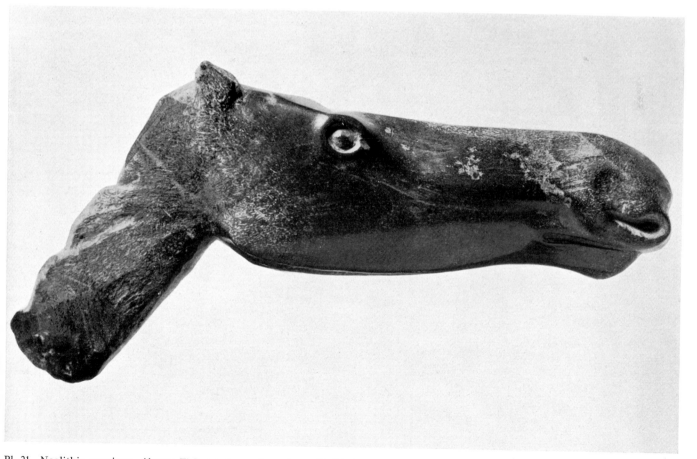

Pl. 21. Neolithic carvings. *Above*: Fish, used as a lure, from Verkholensk, Irkutsk, Baikal area. Stone, l., ca. 12 in. *Below*: Elk's head of the Shigir culture, found near Sverdlovsk, Ural area. Antler. Both, Leningrad, The Hermitage.

Pl. 22. Finds from the Gorbunovo peat bog, Tagil, Ural area, 2d millennium B.C. Wood. *Above, left*: Dipper with handle representing a goose. Ht., 4⁷/₈ in. *Right*: Head fragment of an idol. W., 4¹/₄ in. *Below*: Spoon with handle representing a swan. L., 4⁵/₈ in. All, Moscow, Historical Museum.

Pl. 23. Table legs, from Pazyryk, Barrow II, Altai area, ca. 4th–1st cent. B.C. (?). Wood. Leningrad, The Hermitage.

Pl. 24. *Above*: Wooden carvings, from Pazyryk, Altai area, ca. 4th–1st cent. B.C. (?). *Left*: Aquiline griffin head, from Barrow I. *Right*: Harness ornaments, from Barrow IV. *Below*: Finds from a barrow at Shibe, with animal-head ornament, Altai area, ca. 1st cent. B.C. Wood, with metal foil. All, Leningrad, The Hermitage.

Pl. 25. Portrait mask, from a barrow of the Tashtyk culture, near Saragash, Khakass, upper Yenisei area, ca. 1st cent. Clay. Leningrad, The Hermitage.

Pl. 26. *Above, left*: Nenets (Nentsian) female figurine, detail. Wood, ht., 12¼ in. *Right*: Buryat shaman's mask. Wood with sheepskin and metal, 13×8 in. Both, Leningrad, Ethnographical Museum of the Peoples of the U.S.S.R. *Below*: Udegei carved figure representing an anthropomorphic spirit, detail. Wood with fur. Khabarovsk, U.S.S.R., Museum.

Pl. 27. Nanai (Goldian) appliqué cloak. Lübeck, Germany, Museum für Völkerkunde (on loan to Hamburg).

Pl. 28. Yakut horse blanket. Fur mosaic, w., 23⅝ to 31½ in. Hamburg, Museum für Völkerkunde.

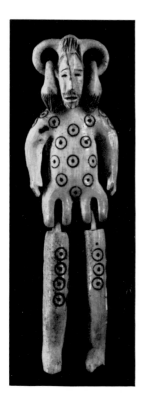

Pl. 29. *Above, left*: Koryak figurine with movable legs and movable pendants attached to the head-dress. Bone with incised circles painted black, ht., 5¹/₂ in. *Right*: Koryak carving of two men drinking vodka. Bone, ht., 2³/₈ in. Both, Leningrad, Ethnographical Museum of the Peoples of the U.S.S.R. *Below*: Yakut carvings of a hunter with spear and a dog. Bone. Property of the U.S.S.R.

Pl. 30. *Above*: Chukot (Chukchian) carving of a reindeer. Bone. Khabarovsk, U.S.S.R., Museum. *Below*:
Nivkhian (Gilyak) carving representing a bear spirit. Wood, l., 9⁷/₈ in. Leningrad, Ethnographical
Museum of the Peoples of the U.S.S.R.

Pl. 31. *Above, left*: Oirot (Oroch) container, with spiral decorations stained black. Incised birch bark and wood, ht., 9¹/₈ in. Vienna, Museum für Völkerkunde. *Right*: Ainu paddle for stirring rice or millet, from Hokkaido Island, Japan. Wood, l., 19³/₄ in. *Below, left*: Khant (Ostyak) container. Birch bark, ht., 7¹/₈ in. Last two, Paris, Musée de l'Homme. *Right*: Evenk harness piece. Incised mammoth bone, ht., 7¹/₄ in. Leningrad, Ethnographical Museum of the Peoples of the U.S.S.R.

Pl. 32. *Above, left*: Evenian woman's winter garment. Fur and hide with suede fringe, embroidered with glass beads; l., 32⅝ in. *Right*: Nanai (Goldian) woman's wedding robe of Chinese silk, detail of embroidery in raised satin stitch. *Below*: Tuvinian buckles. *Left*: Cast brass, 3×2¾ in. *Right*: Stamped white metal, 3⅛×2½ in. All, Leningrad, Ethnographical Museum of the Peoples of the U.S.S.R.

33. The Flagellation. Panel, 33 1/8 × 23 5/8 in. Milan, Brera.

Pl. 34. The Madonna and Child with saints and angels. Panel, 7 ft., 3 in. × 6 ft., 2³/₈ in. Perugia, Italy, Museo dell'Opera del Duomo.

Pl. 35. *Above*: The Conversion of St. Paul. Fresco. Loreto, Italy, Sanctuary of the Holy House, Sacristy of St. John. *Below*: Cycle of St. Benedict, scene with two monks breaking a rule of the Order. Fresco. Abbey of Monte Oliveto Maggiore, province of Siena, Italy.

Pl. 36. Frescoes of the Chapel of S. Brizio (Cappella Nuova). Orvieto, Italy, Cathedral. *Above*: The Resurrection of the Body. *Below, left*: Scene from the fifth canto of Dante's *Purgatorio*. *Right*: Empedocles.

Pl. 37. The Blessed, detail. Fresco. Orvieto, Italy, Cathedral, Chapel of S. Brizio (Cappella Nuova).

Pl. 38. Detail of the Madonna and Child with saints and angels, PL. 34.

Pl. 39. Istanbul, Mosque of Shah Zade, detail of interior.

Pl. 40. Istanbul, Mosque of Sultan Sulaymān, view from courtyard. (Cf. X, PLS. 444, 445.)

Pl. 41. *Above*: Heads from the Temple of Athena Alea at Tegea. *Left*: Herakles, from the west pediment. Marble, ht. of face, 6^1/$_2$ in. Piali (anc. Tegea), Greece, Museum. *Right*: Youth. Marble, ht. of face, 6^1/$_4$ in. Athens, National Museum. *Below*: Slab with Amazonomachy, from the frieze on the east face of the Mausoleum of Halikarnassos. Marble, ht., 2 ft., 11^3/$_8$ in. London, British Museum.

Pl. 42. Pothos, Roman copy. Marble; ht., excluding base, 5 ft., 11 in. Rome, Palazzo dei Conservatori, Museo Nuovo.

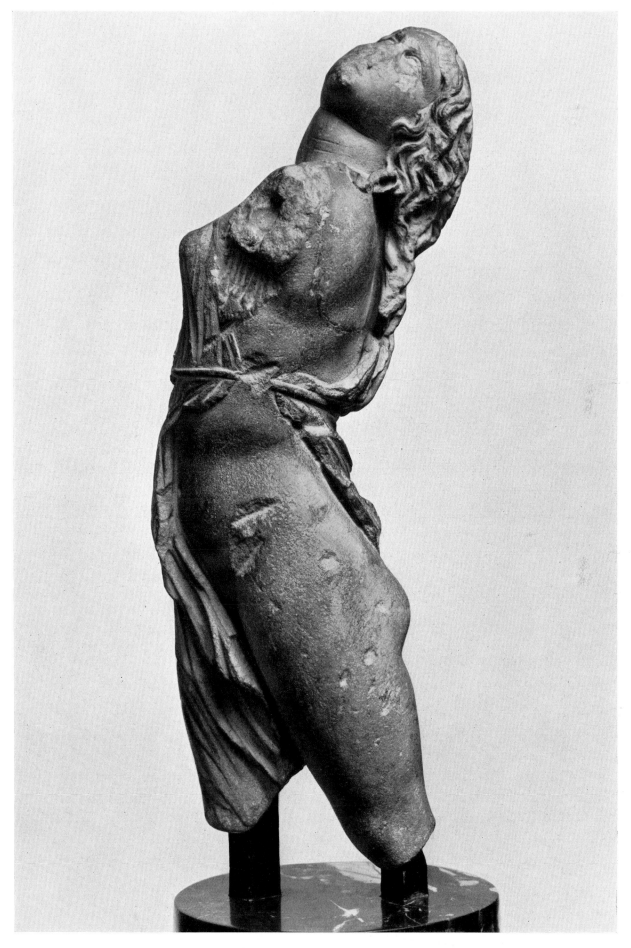

Pl. 43. Maenad, Roman copy. Marble, ht., ca. 18 in. Dresden, Albertinum, Skulpturensammlung.

Pl. 44. Meleager, Roman copy. Marble, ht., 6 ft., 10⅝ in. Rome, Vatican Museums.

Pl. 45. Bulgarian. *Above*: Preslav, ruins of the so-called "Church of Gold," late 9th–early 10th cent. *Below*: Madara, rock relief representing a horseman on the back of a lion, followed by a dog, ca. 8th cent.

Pl. 46. Bulgarian. *Above, left*: Panel of a sculptured frieze, from Preslav, 9th–10th cent. Marble. Kolarovgrad, Archaeological Museum. *Right*: Desislava, detail of the donor portrait of Sevastokrator Kaloyan, 1259. Fresco. Boyana, St. Panteleimon. *Below*: Mesembria, St. John of the Harbor, 13th–14th cent., southeast view.

Pl. 47. Serbian. *Above*: Sopočani, Church of the Trinity, south façade, third quarter of 13th cent., with 14th-cent. tower and portico at west end. *Below*: Studenica, Church of the Virgin, ca. 1183–90, with side chapels and narthex added 1230.

Pl. 48. Serbian. *Left, above*: Prizren, Church of Bogorodica Ljeviška, 1307–15. *Below*: Dečani, Monastery church, 1327–35. *Right*: Mileševa, Monastery church, ca. 1235.

Pl. 49. Serbian. *Left*: Studenica, Church of the Virgin (PL. 47), detail of portal. *Right*: Dečani, Monastery church (PL. 48), detail of triple window in the apse.

Pl. 50. Serbian. Ravanica, Monastery church, last quarter of 14th cent., apsidal view.

Pl. 51. Serbian. *Above, left*: Ravanica, Monastery church (PL. 50), stone decoration with griffins. *Right*: Kalenić, Monastery church, first quarter of 15th cent., double window on southeast side. *Below*: Manasija (Resava), Monastery, surrounded by its fortifications, 1407–18.

Pl. 52. Serbian. Simeon, detail of the Presentation in the Temple, 1164. Fresco. Nerezi, Monastery church.

Pl. 53. Serbian. *Above, left*: The Ascension, detail, 1037–40. Fresco. Ohrid, St. Sophia. *Right*: The Three Marys at the Tomb, detail, ca. 1235. Fresco. Mileševa, Monastery church. *Below*: The Nativity, detail, 1258–65. Fresco. Sopoćani, Church of the Trinity.

Pl. 54. Serbian. *Left, above:* The Birth of the Virgin, detail, ca. 1314. Fresco. Studenica, Church of Joachim and Anna. *Below:* St. Philip and the Eunuch, ca. 1335. Fresco. Dečani, Monastery church. *Right:* Prophet early 15th cent. Fresco. Manasija Monastery church

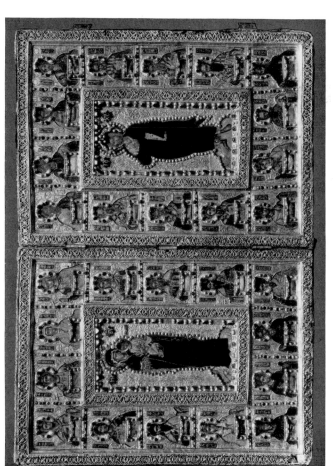

Pl. 55. Serbian. *Left, above*: The Archangel Michael destroying the Saracen fleet, 1341–49. Fresco. Lesnovo, Monastery church. *Below*: Icon with Christ and the Virgin and Child, Reliquary of Thomas Preljubovič, despot of Epirus, Serbian school, 14th cent. Panel, 15 1/8 × 21 5/8 in. Cuenca, Spain, Cathedral. *Right*: Iconostasis of the Monastery church of Kalenić, 15th cent.

Pl. 56. Russian. *Left*: Novgorod, Cathedral of St. Sophia, ca. 1045–50, apse. *Right*: Chernigov, Church of SS. Boris and Gleb, late 12th cent.

Pl. 57. Russian. *Left*: Vladimir, St. Demetrius, ca. 1193–97. *Right*: Chernigov, Church of Paraskeva-Pyatnitsa, late 12th–early 13th cent. (rebuilt after World War II)

Pl. 58. Russian. *Above, left*: Novgorod, St. Theodore Stratelates, ca. 1360–62. *Right*: Aloisio (Alevisio Novi), Cathedral of the Archangel Michael in the Kremlin, Moscow, façade, 1505–09. *Below*: Aristotele Fioravanti, Cathedral of the Dormition (or the Assumption) in the Kremlin, Moscow, 1475–79.

Pl. 59. Russian. Barma and Postnik, Cathedral of St. Basil the Blessed, Moscow, ca. 1554–60.

Pl. 60. Russian. *Above, left*: Y. Bukhvostov, Church of the Saviour at Ubory, 1694–97. *Right*: P. Potekhin, Church of the Trinity at Ostankino, near Moscow, 1668. *Below*: Moscow, Kremlin, the Redeemer Gate, 1491, with tower added by C. Galloway, 1625.

Pl. 61. Serbian. *Above*: Cain and Abel, 1340–50. Fresco. Dečani, Monastery church. *Below*: Michael and Eutychios, The Triumph of St. George, ca. 1318. Fresco. Staro Nagoričino, St. George.

Pl. 62. Serbian. The Communion of the Apostles, detail, 1407–18. Fresco. Manasija, Monastery church.

Pl. 63. Russian. Kizhi, cemetery, Church of the Transfiguration, 1714.

Pl. 64. Russian. *Left*: St. John Chrysostom, detail, 1043–46. Mosaic. Kiev, Cathedral of St. Sophia. *Right*: St. Helen, detail, 11th cent. Fresco. Novgorod, Cathedral of St. Sophia.

Pl. 65. Russian. The Communion of the Apostles, ca. 1108, detail of a mosaic from the Monastery of St. Michael. Kiev, Cathedral of St. Sophia.

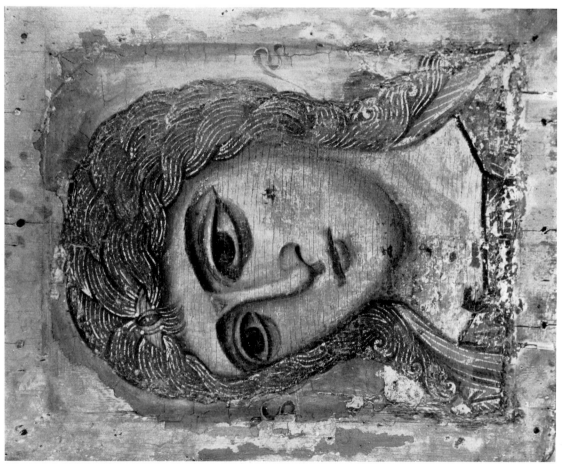

Pl. 66. Russian, School of Novgorod. *Left*: Icon with the head of an archangel, 12th cent. Panel, 19¹/₄×15¹/₄ in. Leningrad, Russian Museum. *Right*: St. George and the Dragon, ca. 1167. Fresco. Staraya Ladoga, Church of St. George.

Pl. 67. Russian. The Righteous Women, detail, late 12th cent. Fresco. Vladimir, St. Demetrius.

Pl. 68. Russian. *Above*: The Ascension, detail, second half of 14th cent. Fresco. Volotovo Pole, near Novgorod, Church of the Dormition. *Below, left*: A saint, detail, 1313. Fresco. Snetogorsk Monastery, near Pskov. *Right*: Theophanes the Greek, a stylite, detail, 1378. Fresco. Novgorod, Church of Our Saviour of the Transfiguration.

1. 69. Russian. *Above, left*: School of Novgorod, icon with SS. Florus and Laurus, last quarter of 15th cent. Panel. *Right*: School of Novgorod, icon, "Wisdom hath builded her house," ca. 1540. Panel. *Below*: S. Ushakov, Planting the Tree of the Russian Nation, detail of icon showing the Kremlin, Ivan I, and Czar Alexis I Mikhailovich, 1668. Panel; full size, $40^7/_8 \times 24^3/_8$ in. All, Moscow, Tretyakov Gallery.

Pl. 70. Russian. *Above*: Diadem with Deësis, from Kiev, 12th cent. Gold with enamel. Leningrad, Russian Museum. *Below*: *Pelen* "the cloth of Mary of Tver," with Veronica's veil at center, the Virgin, saints, and angels, ca. 1389. Silk and gold embroider Moscow, Historical Museum.

Pl. 71. Russian. School of Novgorod, The Virgin with saints, 15th cent. Panel. Moscow, Tretyakov Gallery.

Pl. 72. Russian. A. Rublëv, the Archangel Michael, ca. 1407. Panel, 5 ft., $^1/_2$ in. × 3 ft., 6$^1/_2$ in. Moscow, Tretyakov Gallery.

Pl. 73. Russian. *Above, left*: The Gospels of Ostromir, John the Evangelist dictating his Gospel to Prochorus, 1056–57. Illumination. Leningrad, State Library. *Right*: An evangelist, 15th cent. Carved bone. Leningrad, Russian Museum. *Below, left*: V. and F. Ivanov, *bratina* (loving cup), 1662. Bone in silver mounting with enamel and filigree. *Right*: Icon with the Annunciation, second half of 17th cent. Silver repoussé. Last two, Moscow, the Kremlin, Hall of Arms.

Pl. 74. Greek and Romanian. *Left*: Mount Athos, Greece, the Great Lavra, founded 962. *Above*: Refectory, 1512, with frescoes, ca. 1535. *Below*: General view of the monastery. *Right, above*: Arbore, Romania, Church of St. John, 1502. *Below*: Sucevita, Romania. Monastery, ca. 1582–85.

Pl. 75. Bosnian and Herzegovinian. *Left*: Bogomile tomb at Zgosča, 13th cent. Stone. *Right, above*: Tombs in the Bogomile cemetery at Radimlje, ca. 13th–15th cent. *Below*: So-called "Roman bridge," built by the Turks in Mostar, ca. 1566.

Pl. 76. Dalmatian. *Left*: Trogir (It., Traù), Cathedral of St. Lawrence, 13th cent. *Above*: Siren by Radovan, detail of decoration of the main portal, 1240. Stone. *Below*: Apse view. *Right*: Šibenik, Cathedral of St. James, 1431–ca. 1536. *Above*: Baptistery ceiling, detail. *Below*: Façade.

Pl. 77. Champmol, near Dijon, France, portal of the Chartreuse. (Cf. details, PL. 78; V, PL. 387.)

Pl. 78. Details of the portal of the Chartreuse (PL. 77). *Left*: John the Baptist and Philip the Bold, Duke of Burgundy, left jamb. *Right*: Margaret of Flanders, Duchess of Burgundy, and St. Catherine, right jamb.

Pl. 79. So-called "Well of Moses," originally the base of a calvary, courtyard of the Chartreuse, Champmol, near Dijon, France. Ht., 10½ ft. *Left*: View showing the prophets Daniel and Isaiah. *Right*: Jeremiah, Zechariah, and Daniel.

Pl. 80. *Above, left and right*: Weeping angels, details of the so-called "Well of Moses" (PL. 79). *Below*: Mourners, detail of the Tomb of Philip the Bold. Dijon, France, Musée des Beaux-Arts.

Pl. 81. Landscape, one of eight lake views, scroll (signed Shinsō, i.e Sōami). Ink and
faint color on paper. Kyoto, Daisenin.

Pl. 82. Attributed to Sōami, Landscape on sliding door, one of 20 panels. Ink and faint color on paper, 3 ft., 11 1/4 in. × 5 ft., 10 7/8 in. Kyoto, Daisenin.

Pl. 83. Scene of mourning, whole and detail, Pyandzhikent, Temple II, Wall B, 6th–8th cent. Wall painting (water-color copy).

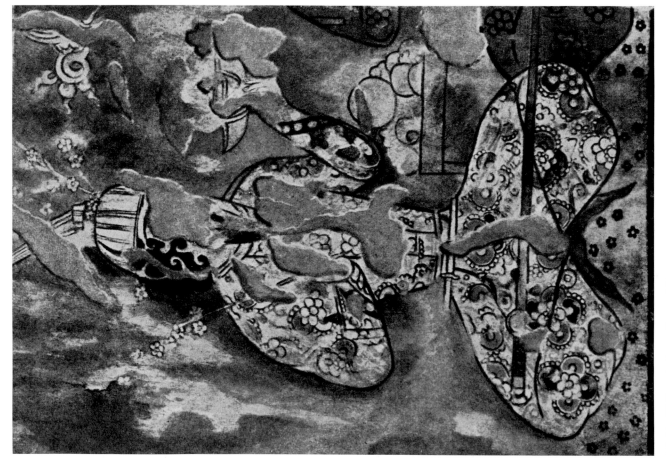

Pl. 84. Wall paintings, Pyandzhikent, 6th–8th cent. *Left*: Ritual feast, detail with male figure, Temple I. *Right*: Woman playing a harp, Sector VI, Room 1, south wall. (Both water-color copies.)

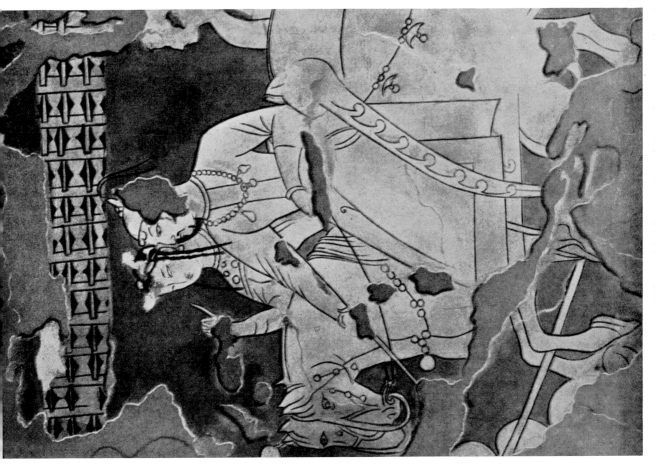

Pl. 85. Wall paintings, Pyandzhikent, 6th–8th cent. *Left*: Man and woman on horseback, Sector III, Room 17, west wall. *Right*: Banquet scene, detail, Sector VI, Room 1, west wall. (Both, water-color copies.)

Pl. 86. Wall paintings, Pyandzhikent, 6th–8th cent. *Above*: Warriors in combat, Sector VI, Room 1, south wall. *Below*: Fragment with prisoner and (*right*) detail of scene with men playing trick-track, Sector VI, Room 13, west wall. (All, water-color copies.)

Pl. 87. Fragmentary wall paintings, Pyandzhikent, Sector VI, Rooms 8 and 1, 6th–8th cent. (Water-color copies.)

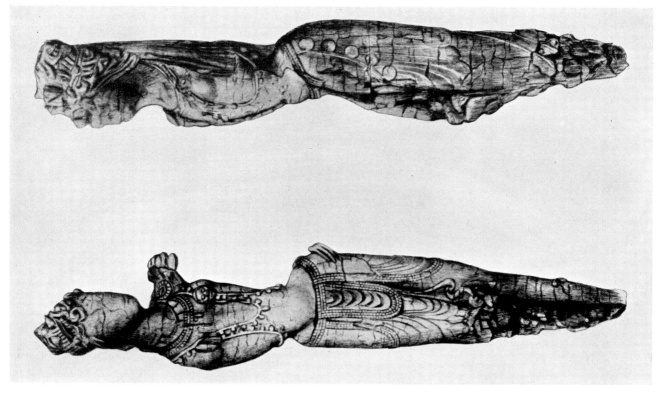

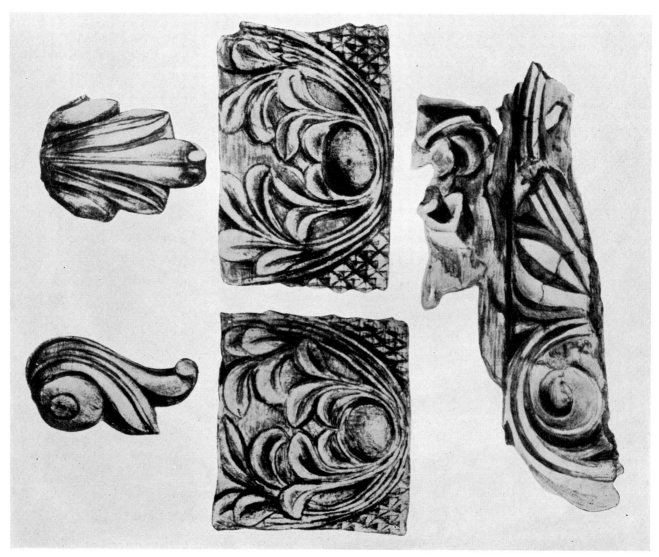

Pl. 88. Wood sculpture, Pyandzhikent, 6th–8th cent. *Left*: Drawings of decorative elements found on wooden fragments, Sector III, Room 47, Leningrad, The Hermitage. *Right*: Female figures, Sector III, Rooms 50 and 55.

Pl. 89. Scene with horse and rider, from Pyandzhikent, Sector VI, Room 41, 6th–8th cent. Wall painting. Leningrad, The Hermitage.

Pl. 90. Scene depicting two men playing trick-track, from Pyandzhikent, Sector VI, Room 13, 6th–8th cent. Wall painting. Leningrad. The Hermitage.

Pl. 91. Pre-Columbian statuette, from Venezuela. Painted pottery, ht., 6¹/₄ in. Paris, Musée de l'Homme.

Pl. 92. Pre-Columbian pottery from Marajó, Brazil. *Above, left*: Jar with incised geometric decoration. *Right*: Woman's pubic covering (*tanga*). *Below*: Painted bowl. All, Hamburg, Museum für Völkerkunde.

Pl. 93. Pre-Columbian Diaguita infant burial urn, in Santa María style, from northwest Argentina. Painted pottery, ht., 21 1/4 in. Rome, Museo Pigorini.

Pl. 94. Two-piece ceremonial costume, from the upper Amazon region. Bark cloth, feathers, seeds, shells, bird bones, and human hair; upper garment, 20¹/₈×29⁷/₈ in.; lower garment, 25⁵/₈×21⁵/₈ in. Rome, Museo Pigorini.

Pl. 95. Pre-Columbian "idol" of the Trombetas Valley culture, representing a man in the grasp of an animal, found at Sucurujú, on the Trombetas River, near Obidos, Amazonas, Brazil. Slate, ht., 6⅞ in. Göteborg, Sweden, Etnografiska Museet.

Pl. 96. Pre-Columbian pottery from northeastern Brazil. *Above*: Bottle with zoomorphic decoration, in Santarém style, from the Tapajóz River area, Pará. Ht., 7¹/₂ in. Philadelphia, University Museum. *Below, left*: Fragmentary figurine of a woman, from Santarém, Pará. Ht., 3¹/₈ in. *Right*: Effigy urn, from Monte Curú–Cunani River, Amapá Territory. Ht., 17⁷/₈ in. Last two, Belém, Museu Paraense Emilio Goeldi.

Pl. 97. Pre-Columbian Diaguita infant burial urn, in Santa María style, from northwest Argentina. Painted pottery, ht., 22 in. Rome, Museo Pigorini.

Pl. 98. Pre-Columbian Diaguita painted pottery, from northern Chile. *Above*: Bowl with anthropomorphic and geometric decoration. Diam., 3³/₈ in. *Below*: Handled cup (*puco*) with geometric decoration. Diam., 6¹/₂ in. Both, La Serena, Chile, Museo Arqueológico.

Pl. 99. Arawak bird sculpture, found in a cave on Spots Mt., Jamaica, British West Indies, in 1792. Wood. London, British Museum.

Pl. 100. *Above, left*: Galibí clubs, with incised human figures and geometric decoration, from French Guiana. Ironwood, l., 10⁵/₈ and 17³/₈ in. Paris, Musée de l'Homme. *Right*: Tapuya clubs, detail showing incised geometric decoration, from Brazil. Wood; full l., 4 ft., 2³/₄ in. and 4 ft., 4³/₈ in. Rome, Museo Pigorini. *Below*: Carajá stool in the form of a macaw, from Araguaia district, Brazil. Wood and feathers. Vienna, Museum für Völkerkunde.

Pl. 101. Carajá doll, from Bananal Island, central Brazil, collected 1947. Painted clay with banana-leaf loin-cloth; ht., 6³/₄ in. São Paulo, Museu Paulista.

Pl. 102. *Above*: Carajá doll, from Bananal Island, central Brazil, collected 1947. Painted clay, cotton, and wax (hair); ht., 5⁷/₈ in. São Paulo, Museu Paulista. *Below*: Cocama vessels with painted decoration, from eastern Peru, collected 1916–19. Pottery, ht., 7⁷/₈ and 6³/₄ in. Göteborg, Sweden, Etnografiska Museet.

Pl. 103. *Above, left*: Caduveo male and female figures, from the Paraguay–Brazil borderlands, ca. 1900. Wood with bead necklaces; ht., 9⁷/₈ and 10⁷/₈ in. *Right*: Payaguá anthropomorphic water vessel, upper Paraguay River, ca. 1900. Painted pottery with mother-of-pearl necklace; ht., 11 in. Both, Copenhagen, Nationalmuseet. *Below*: Carib vessel, from Surinam. Painted pottery, l., 9⁷/₈ in. Rome, Museo Pigorini.

Pl. 104. Caduveo painted and incised pottery, from the Paraguay–Brazil borderlands. *Above, left*: Vessel with scroll decoration. Ht. 11¼ in. *Right*: Food bowl. Diam., 18⅜ in. *Below*: Vessel in shape of a rooster. L., 11¾ in. All, Rome, Museo Pigorini.

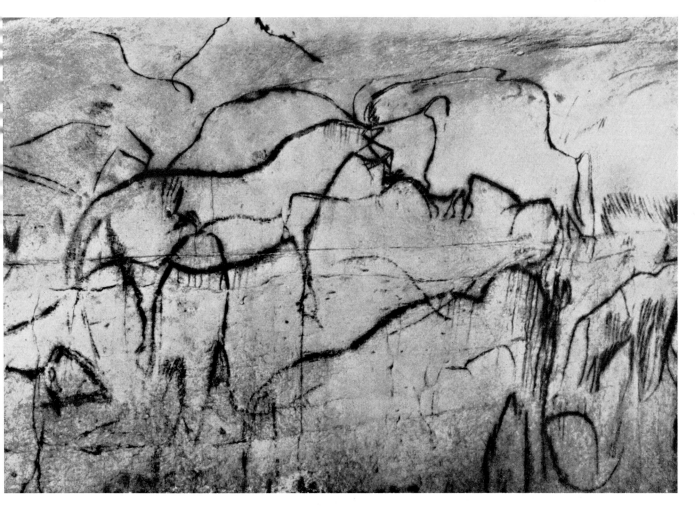

Pl. 105. Prehistoric animal figures, superimposed without regard to relationship in space. *Above*: Engraved pebble, from La Colombière, Ain, France. Lyons, University, Laboratoire de Géologie. *Below*: Detail of rock painting in the "Mammoth Chapel," Pech-Merle Cave, Lot, France.

Pl. 106. Continuous rhythmic design, conventionalized. *Above, left*: Neolithic vessel in Stentinello style, from Matrensa, Sicily, mid-4th millennium B.C. Ht., 7½ in. Syracuse, Sicily, Museo Archeologico. *Right*: Cretan pithos in Kamares style, from the palace of Phaistos, 19th–18th cent. B.C. Ht., 27⅛ in. Heraklion, Crete, Archaeological Museum. *Center*: Attic pyxis in Geometric style, detail. Ht. with lid, 7⅝ in. Athens, Museum of the Agora. *Below, left*: Askos, from Canosa, Apulia, Italy, 4th–3d cent. B.C. Naples, Museo Nazionale. *Right*: Exterior decorative detail of the Quṭb Minār, Delhi, begun 1199.

Pl. 107. Continuous rhythmic design, figural. *Above*: Architectural reliefs with rows of animals, from Hal Tarxien, Malta, second half of 3d millennium B.C. Limestone. Valletta, National Museum. *Center, left*: Late Geometric Attic bowl with dance scene, late 8th cent. B.C. Diam., 6¼ in. Athens, National Museum. *Right*: The Ascension, mosaic in the dome of St. Sophia, Salonika, Greece, 9th cent. *Below, left*: Marching warriors, from the palace of Tiglathpileser III at Arslan Tash, 8th cent. B.C. Basalt, ht., 35½ in. Istanbul, Archaeological Museums. *Right*: Procession of martyrs, detail, 6th cent. Mosaic. Ravenna, S. Apollinare Nuovo.

Pl. 108. Rhythm in architectural decoration. Athens, the Parthenon, west side of the cella, showing Doric frieze with alternation of metopes and triglyphs and Ionic frieze with continuous narration. 5th cent. B.C.

Pl. 109. Continuous narration. Rome, Trajan's Column, detail of base with beginning of the spiral frieze, A.D. 113.

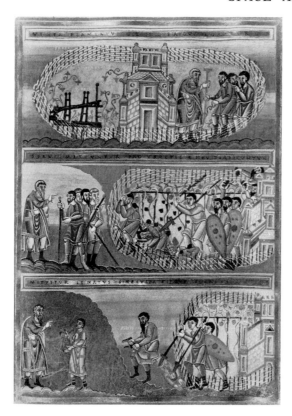

Pl. 110. Medieval narrative devices. *Above, left*: Episodes divided in registers. Codex Aureus Epternacensis, The Parable of the Vineyard, Echternach, ca. 1035–40. Illumination. Nürnberg, Germany, Germanisches National-Museum. *Right*: Simultaneous representation of episodes in unified composition. The Nativity, school of Novgorod, 15th–16th cent. Panel, 9^1/$_8$×7^1/$_2$ in. Moscow, Korin Coll. *Below*: Simultaneous representation of episodes within a continuous space. Scenes from the life of John the Baptist, 13th cent. Stone. Rouen, Cathedral, north portal of façade.

Pl. 111. Compression of successive events into a single scene. Sassanian plate, with hunting scene in relief, showing the king giving
chase and his kill, from Mazanderan, Iran, ca. 4th cent. Silver, diam., 9⁷/₈ in. Teheran, Archaeological Museum.

Pl. 112. Background without and with spatial articulation. *Left*: The Virgin adored by Admiral George of Antioch, ca. 1148. Mosaic. Palermo, the Martorana (S. Maria dell'Ammiraglio) *Right*: Giotto, "Noli me tangere," detail, ca. 1312. Fresco. Padua, Italy, Scrovegni Chapel

Pl. 113.   Perspective construction of space and implied space. *Left*: Filippo Lippi, The Annunciation, mid-15th cent. Panel, 5 ft., $1^3/8$ in. × 6 ft. Rome, Galleria Nazionale. *Right*: Rembrandt, The Holy Family, 1645. Canvas, $46^1/8 × 35^7/8$ in. Leningrad, The Hermitage.

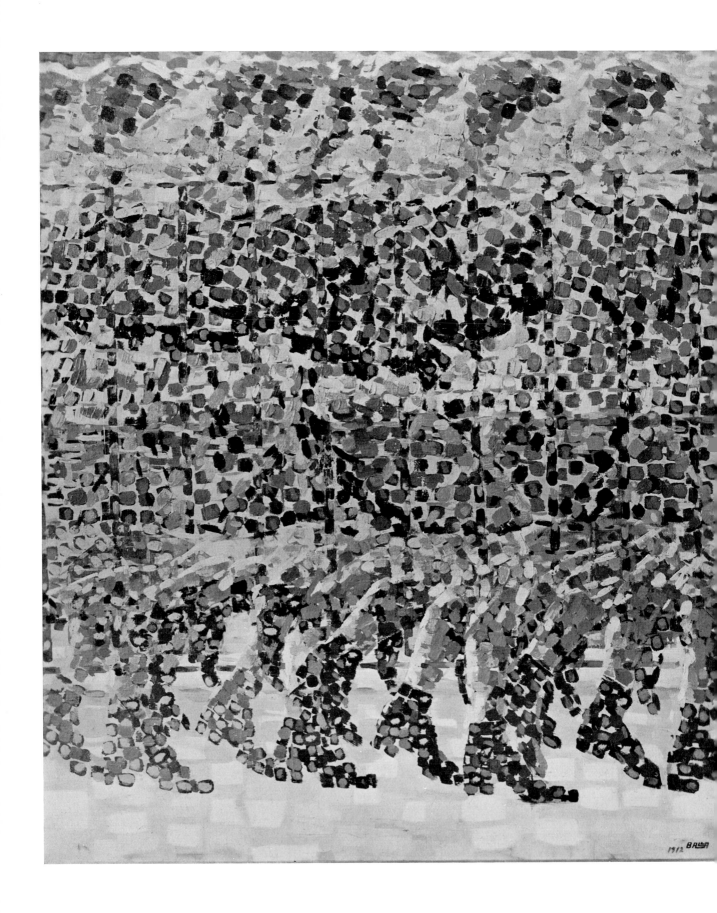

Pl. 114. Simultaneous view of successive movements; futurism. G. Balla, Girl Running on the Balcony, 1912. Canvas, 49¹/₄×49¹/₄ in Milan, Galleria d'Arte Moderna.

1. 115. Geometric analysis of form in space; cubism. J. Metzinger, study for the portrait of Apollinaire, 1909. Pencil drawing on pink paper, $16^{1}/_{2} \times 11^{3}/_{4}$ in. Paris, Musée d'Art Moderne.

Pl. 116. Photographic sequence of S. Ivo alla Sapienza, Rome, demonstrating duration of the "reading" of an architectural monument.

Pl. 117. Zamora, Spain, Cathedral, 1151–74, Puerta del Obispo.

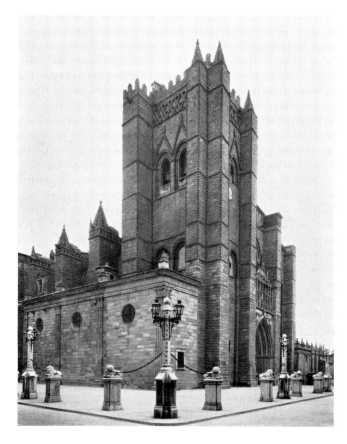

Pl. 118. *Above, left*: Rates, near Pòrto (Oporto), Portugal, S. Pedro, 12th cent. *Right*: Ávila, Spain, Cathedral, view showing tower and façade of 14th cent. *Below*: Ávila, aerial view with city wall, begun 1090, and Cathedral, 12th–14th cent.

Pl. 119. Spain. *Above*: Palma de Mallorca, Cathedral, begun early 14th cent. *Below, left*: Sigüenza, Guadalajara province, Cathedral, 12th–14th cent., crossing (restored). *Right*: Pamplona, Cathedral, nave, 1397–ca. 1525.

Pl. 120. Portugal. *Left, above*: Bragança (Braganza), Domus Municipalis, ca. 1200. *Below*: Batalha, Beira Litoral, Monastery of S. Maria da Victoria, begun ca. 1388, church. *Right*: Lisbon, Cathedral (begun mid-12th cent.), ambulatory, 14th cent.

Pl. 121. Spain. *Left*: Barcelona, aisle of the Reales Atarazanas (Royal Arsenal and Dockyard, now housing the Museo Marítimo), 14th cent. *Right*: Coca, Segovia province, the Castle, aerial view, 15th cent.

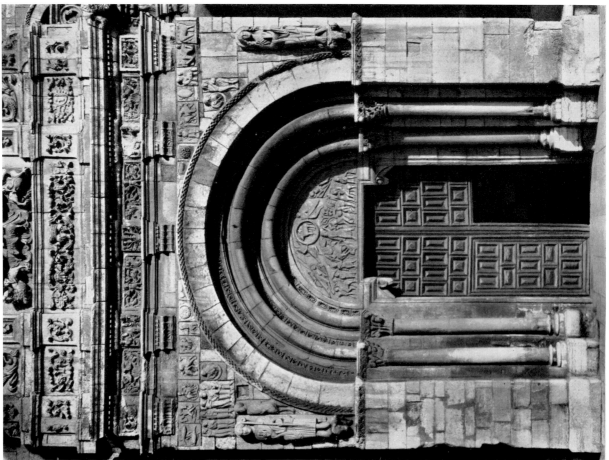

Pl. 122. Spain. *Left*: León, S. Isidoro, 11th–12th cent., main portal. *Right*: Toledo, Cathedral, begun 1227, Puerta de los Leones, 1452–65, with sculptures by A. de Egas (Egas Cueman) and J. Alemán (modern relief over door).

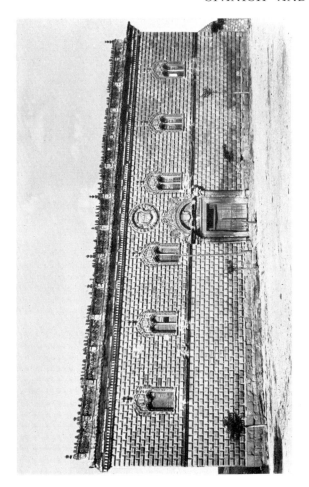

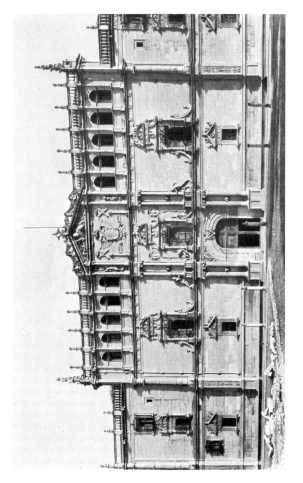

Pl. 123. Spain. *Left*: Seville, Cathedral, completed 1519, nave at crossing. *Right, above*: L. Vázquez, Medinaceli Palace, Cogolludo, Guadalajara province, 1492–95, façade. *Below*: R. Gil de Hontañón, façade of the University, Alcalá de Henares, near Madrid, ca. 1541–53.

Pl. 124. *Above*: Tomb of Doña Inés de Castro, mid-14th cent. Alcobaça, Portugal, Monastery of S. Maria, church. *Below, left*: Tomb of Chancellor Francés de Villaespesa (d. 1421) and his wife. Tudela, Navarra province, Spain, Cathedral. *Right*: Gil de Siloe and Diego de la Cruz, retable, 1496–99. Burgos, Spain, Monastery of Miraflores.

Pl. 125. The Virgin and Child, detail of frontal from Betesa, Lérida province, Spain, 13th cent. Panel. Barcelona, Museo de Bellas Artes de Cataluña.

Pl. 126. N. Gonçalves, portrait of Dom Henrique, detail of the "panel of the Infante," Polyptych of St. Vincent, second half of 15th cent. Panel, full ht., 6 ft., 9½ in. Lisbon, Museu Nacional de Arte Antiga.

Pl. 127. *Above, left*: Frontal of St. Margaret, detail, from a church near Torelló, north of Vich, Barcelona province, Spain, second half of 12th cent. Panel. Vich, Museo Episcopal. *Right*: The Nativity and the dream of Joseph, detail of lateral panel, Altar of St. Andrew, from Sagás, northwest of Vich, late 12th–13th cent. Panel. Solsona, Lérida province, Spain, Museo Diocesano. *Below, left*: A. Sanchez de Segovia, Isaiah and Daniel, 1262. Fresco. Salamanca, Spain, Old Cathedral, Chapel of St. Martin. *Right*: J. Serra, the Descent into Hell, detail of altarpiece, 1361. Panel. Saragossa, Spain, Museo Provincial.

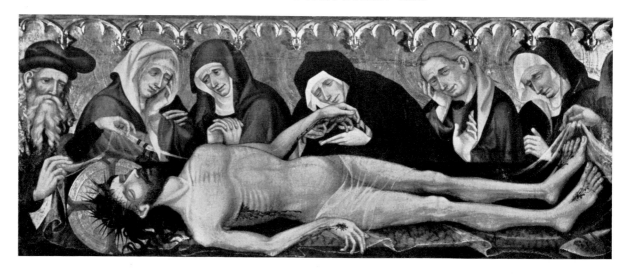

Pl. 128. *Above*: L. Borrassá, the Lamentation, detail of altarpiece, ca. 1410. Panel. Manresa, Barcelona province, Spain, S. María de la Seo. *Below*: L. Dalmau, Altarpiece of the Councilors, 1445. Panel, ht., 9 ft. Barcelona, Museo de Bellas Artes de Cataluña.

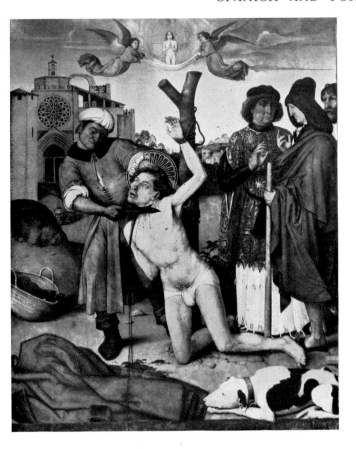

Pl. 129. *Above, left*: Anye Bru, Martyrdom of St. Cucuphas, 1504–07. Panel, 5 ft., 1³/₄ in. × 4 ft., 4 in. Barcelona, Museo de Bellas Artes de Cataluña. *Right*: J. Huguet, SS. Abdon and Sennen, 1460. Panel. Tarrasa, Barcelona province, Spain, S. María. *Below, left*: Fernando Gallego, The Flagellation, 1475–80. Panel. Salamanca, Spain, Museo Diocesano. *Right*: P. Berruguete (d. 1503?), St. Dominic presiding at an auto-da-fé. Panel, ca. 5×3 ft. Madrid, Prado.

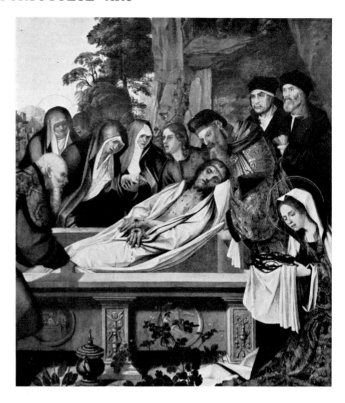

Pl. 130. *Above, left*: F. Henriques, The Pentecost, 1509–11. Panel, 8 ft., 1¹/₂ in. × 6 ft., 8 in. *Right*: C. de Figueiredo, The Entombment, ca. 1530. Panel, 5 ft., 11⁵/₈ in. × 5 ft., 1¹/₄ in. *Below*: G. Lopes (attrib.), The Virgin and Child with Angels, ca. 1536. Panel, 4 ft., 1¹/₄ in. × 5 ft., 5 in. All, Lisbon, Museu Nacional de Arte Antiga.

Pl. 131. *Above, left*: Diego de Siloe, Cathedral, Granada, Spain, begun 1528, interior. *Right*: J. de Herrera, church in El Escorial, near Madrid, 1575–82, façade, from the Patio de los Reyes. *Below, left*: J. de Nates, façade, Church of Nuestra Señora de las Angustias, Valladolid, Spain, 1597–1604. *Right*: F. Terzi, S. Vicente de Fora, Lisbon, begun 1582, façade.

Pl. 132. Spain. *Left*: F. Bautista (1594–1679), S. Isidro, Madrid, exterior view. *Right*: A. Cano, façade of Cathedral, Granada, 1667.

Pl. 133. Joaquín de Churriguera, Colegio de Calatrava, Salamanca, Spain, begun 1717, completed by A. de Churriguera.

Pl. 134. Spain. *Above, left*: P. de Ribera, hermitage of the Virgen del Puerto, Madrid, 1718. *Right*: F. de Casas y Novoa, main façade (Fachada del Obradoiro) of the Cathedral, Santiago de Compostela, 1738–49. *Below*: J. Bort y Miliá, façade of Cathedral, Murcia, begun ca. 1736.

Pl. 135. B. Bermejo, St. Dominic of Silos, 1474–77. Panel, 7 ft., 11 in. × 4 ft., 3 in. Madrid, Prado.

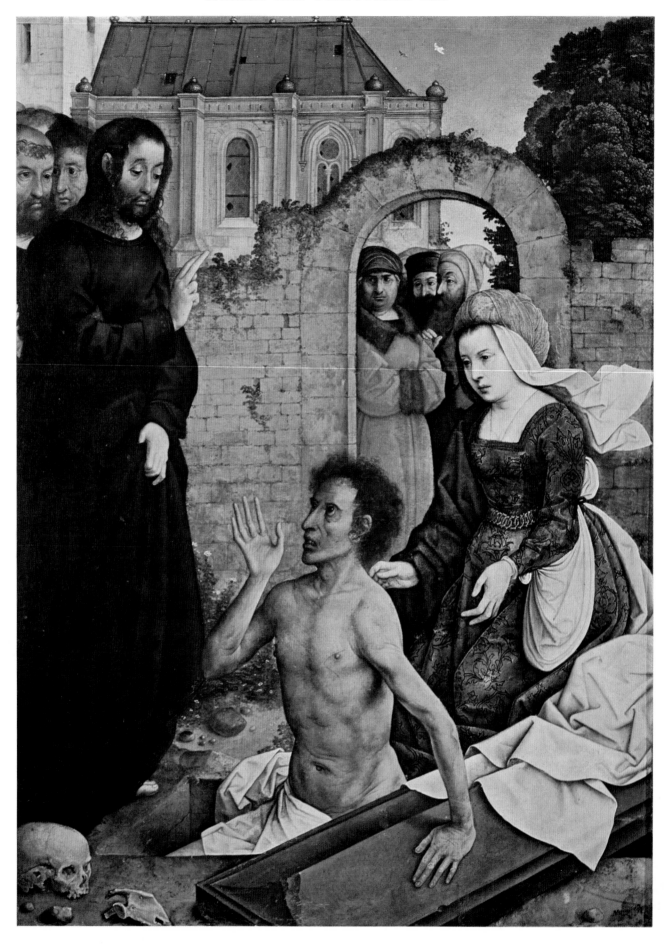

Pl. 136. Juan de Flandes, The Resurrection of Lazarus, ca. 1500. Panel, 43 1/4 × 33 1/8 in. Madrid, Prado.

Pl. 137. *Above, left*: H. Rovira y Brocandel, palace of Marqués de Dos Aguas, Valencia, Spain, remodeled 1740–44. (Cf. II, PL. 160). *Right*: J. F. Ludovice, University Library, Coimbra, Portugal, 1717–23, interior decoration by C. de Laprade. *Below*: M. Vicente de Oliveira, façade of the royal residence at Queluz, near Lisbon, 1747–52.

Pl. 138. L. de Figueroa (attrib.), S. Luis, Seville, Spain, 1699–1731.

Pl. 139. B. Ordóñez, the Adoration of the Magi, detail of altar, ca. 1514. Marble. Naples, Italy, S. Giovanni a Carbonara, Caracciolo Chapel.

Pl. 140. Diego de Siloe, the Virgin and Child, detail of choir stall, ca. 1530. Wood. Granada, Spain, S. Jerónimo.

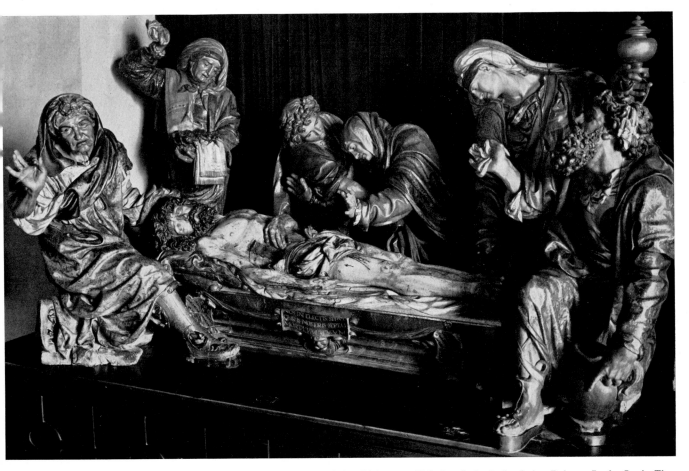

Pl. 141. Spain. *Above*: A. Berruguete, The Transfiguration, 1543–48. Alabaster. Toledo, Cathedral, choir. *Below*: J. de Juni, The Entombment, 1541–44. Polychromed wood. Valladolid, Museo Nacional de Escultura.

Pl. 142. Spain. Painted wood. *Above, left*: G. Fernández, St. Veronica, 1614. Ht., 5 ft., 9 in. Valladolid, Museo Nacional de Escultura. *Right*: A. Cano, statuette of the Immaculate Conception, 1655–56. Ht., 21^1/$_2$ in. Granada, Cathedral, sacristy. *Below, left*: A. Cano with P. de Mena, St. Anthony of Padua embracing the Christ Child, detail, 1653–57. Ht., 6 ft., 8 in. Granada, Palace of Charles V, Museo Provincial. *Right*: P. de Mena, Our Lady of Sorrows, 1673. Madrid, Descalzas Reales.

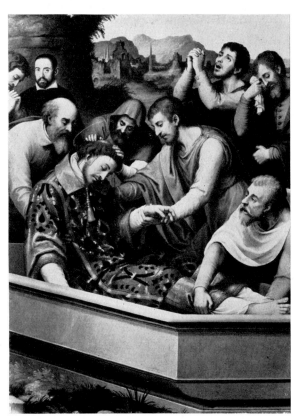

Pl. 143. *Above, left*: A. Fernández (d. ca. 1545), The Flagellation. Panel, $18^7/_8 \times 13^3/_4$ in. Madrid, Prado. *Right*: P. de Campaña (Kempener), The Deposition, 1547. Panel. Seville, Spain, Cathedral, sacristy. *Below, left*: P. Machuca, The Virgin and the Souls in Purgatory, 1517. Panel, 5 ft., $5^3/_4$ in. × 4 ft., 5 in. *Right*: Juan de Juanes (d. 1579), St. Stephen's Burial. Panel, 5 ft., 3 in. × 4 ft., $^1/_2$ in. Last two, Madrid, Prado.

Pl. 144. *Above*: F. Collantes, Ezekiel's Vision, 1630. Canvas, 5 ft., 9⁵/₈ in. × 6 ft., 8³/₄ in. Madrid, Prado. *Below*: J. de Pareja, The Baptism of Christ, ca. 1667. Canvas, 6 ft., 7 in. × 11 ft., 8 in. Huesca, Spain, Museo Provincial.

Pl. 145. L. de Morales (d. 1586), The Virgin and Child. Panel, 11 1/4 × 7 3/4 in. London, National Gallery.

Pl. 146. El Greco, The Feast in the House of Simon, ca. 1607 (?). Canvas, 4 ft., 8¼ in. × 3 ft., 3⅜ in. Chicago, Art Institute, J. Winterbotham Coll.

Pl. 147. *Above, left*: A. Cano, Miracle of the Well, 1638–52, episode from the life of St. Isidore. Canvas, 7 ft., 1 in. × 4 ft., 10¹/₂ in. Madrid, Prado. *Right*: F. de Herrera the Elder, St. Basil Dictating His Rule, 1639. Canvas, 8 ft., 2¹/₂ in. × 6 ft., 4³/₄ in. Paris, Louvre. *Below, left*: F. Ribalta (d. 1628), Christ Embracing St. Bernard. Canvas, 5 ft., 2¹/₄ in. × 3 ft., 8¹/₂ in. *Right*: M. Cerezo, St. Augustine, 1663. Canvas, 6 ft., 10 in. × 4 ft., 1¹/₂ in. Last two, Madrid, Prado.

Pl. 148. *Above*: L. Tristán, St. Monica, 1616, fragment of a dismembered altarpiece. Canvas, 16¹/₂×15³/₄ in. Madrid, Prado. *Below*: J. de Valdés Leal, "Finis Gloriae Mundi," 1660, detail. Seville, Spain, Hospital de la Caridad.

Pl. 149. *Above, left*: J. Carreño de Miranda, Mariana de Austria, 1669 (?). Canvas, 6 ft., 11 in. × 4 ft., 1 in. *Right*: J. B. M. del Mazo, The Infanta Margarita, 1666. Canvas, 6 ft., 10 in. × 4 ft., 10 in. Both, Madrid, Prado. *Below*: D. A. de Sequeira, St. Bruno Praying, ca. 1800. Canvas, 4 ft., 4 in. × 6 ft., 3¹/₂ in. Lisbon, Museu Nacional de Arte Antiga.

Pl. 150. D. Velázquez, The Infante Don Carlos, ca. 1626. Canvas, 6 ft., 10¹/₄ in. × 4 ft., 1¹/₄ in. Madrid, Prado.

Pl. 151. *Above*: J. Leonardo (ca. 1605–56), The Conquest of Brisach. Canvas, 10 ft. × 11 ft., 10 in.
Below: A. de Pereda (ca. 1608–78), The Relief of Genoa by the Marqués de Santa Cruz.
Canvas, 9 ft., 6 in. × 12 ft., 1¹/₂ in. Both, Madrid, Prado.

Pl. 152. Colonial manifestations. *Above*: Puebla, Mexico, S. Domingo, Rosario Chapel, completed 1690, interior of dome. *Below, left*: L. Rodríguez, Sagrario Metropolitano, Mexico City, 1749–68, façade. *Right*: Taxco, Mexico, SS. Sebastián and Prisca, completed 1758.

Pl. 153. Colonial manifestations. *Above, left*: Morelia, Mexico, Palacio de Gobierno (formerly Seminario de Valladolid), 1732–70, façade. *Right*: Guadalajara, Mexico, Nuestra Señora de Guadalupe, 17th cent. *Below*: Mexico City. *Left*: Fountain known as the Salto de Agua, completed 1779. *Right*: S. Domingo, reconstructed 18th cent. (dedicated 1736), exterior detail.

Pl. 154. Colonial manifestations. *Above, left*: Zacatecas, Mexico, Cathedral, dedicated 1752, detail of façade. *Right*: Retable, 18th cent. Gilded and painted wood, ht., 17 ft. Tepozotlán, Mexico, former Monastery. *Below, left*: A. F. Lisbôa (O Aleijadinho), Prophet, ca. 1800. Soapstone. Congonhas do Campo, Minas Gerais, Brazil, Bom Jesus de Matozinhos. (Cf. I, PL. 143.) *Right*: I. M. Barreda, Doña Juana María Romero, 1794. Canvas, 6 ft., 1⁵/₈ in. × 4 ft., 4³/₈ in. Mexico City, Museo Nacional de Historia.

Pl. 155. J. de Ribera, The Holy Family with St. Catherine, 1648. Canvas, 6 ft., 10¹/₂ in. × 5 ft., ³/₄ in. New York, Metropolitan Museum.

Pl. 156. B. E. Murillo (1617–82), The Pie Eater. Canvas, 48 5/8 × 40 1/8 in. Munich, Alte Pinakothek.

Pl. 157. The Crucifixion window, ca. 1165. Ht., over 26 ft. Poitiers, France, Cathedral.

Pl. 158. *Left*: Bishop Fulk, ca. 1190. Reims, France, St-Remi, choir. *Right, above*: The finding of St. Stephen's relics, ca. 1160. Châlons-sur-Marne, France, Cathedral, Cathedral of St-Etienne. *Below*: The Annunciation, ca. 1155, detail of window with the life of Christ. Chartres, France, Cathedral,

Pl. 159. The Assumption of the Virgin, ca. 1145. Le Mans, France, Cathedral.

Pl. 160. Moses and the burning bush, with a self-portrait of the artist (Master Gerlachus), reputedly from Arnstein, Germany, ca 1170–80. Frankfort on the Main, Städelsches Kunstinstitut.

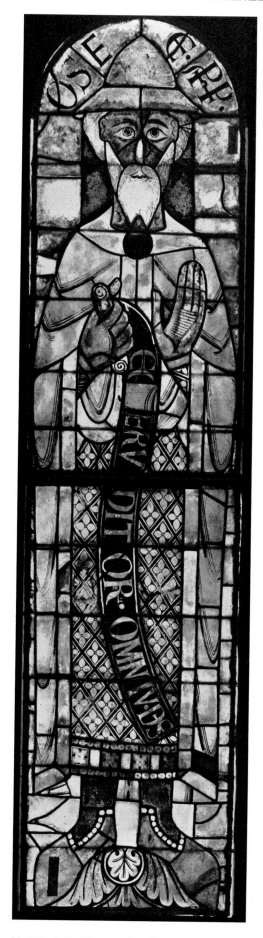

Pl. 161. *Left*: The prophet Hosea, ca. 1130. Augsburg, Germany, Cathedral. *Right*: The Magdalen, from Weitensfeld, Austria, ca. 1170. Ht., 15 in. Klagenfurt, Diocesan Museum.

Pl. 162. Chartres, France, Cathedral. *Left*: "Noli me tangere" and the Crucifixion, ca. 1155, detail of the Passion window, on the west side. *Right*: Scene of the battle between Roland and Ferragus, first half of 12th cent., detail of the Charlemagne window, in ambulatory of choir.

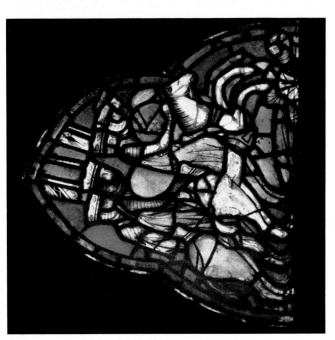

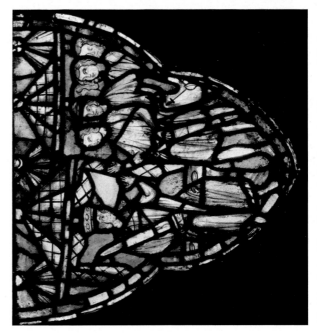

Pl. 163. *Left*: The flight of the Amorite kings and Joshua speaking to the people, ca. 1243-48. Ht., 28³/₄ and 29⁷/₈ in. Paris, Ste-Chapelle, fourth north window. *Right*: Scenes of the lives of SS. Gervasius and Protasius, ca. 1160, in a setting of ca. 1900 by the glazier Steinheil. Le Mans, France, Cathedral.

Pl. 164. *Above*: The Raising of Lazarus, ca. 1230. Diam., 28 in. Erfurt, Germany, Barfüsserkirche, east window of the choir. *Below*: Madonna and Child, ca. 1295–
1300. Assisi, Italy, S. Francesco, Upper Church, north transept.

Pl. 165. North rose, dedicated to the Virgin, and five lancets with St. Anne holding Mary, Melchizedek, David, Solomon, and Aaron, ca. 1230–35. Diam. of rose, 42 ft., 8 in. Chartres, France, Cathedral, transept.

Pl. 166. The Assumption of the Virgin, after a design attributed by some scholars to Duccio di Buoninsegna, ca. 1288. Siena, Italy, Cathedral, apse.

Pl. 167. *Above*: Life of St. Radegund, detail, late 13th–early 14th cent. Poitiers, France, Ste-Radegonde. *Below, left*: The Virgin and Child, part of a two-light window (with John the Baptist), 1333. W., 26³/₄ in. Evreux, France, Cathedral, choir. *Right*: Gamaliel revealing the location of St. Stephen's relics, ca. 1340. Rouen, France, St-Ouen.

Pl. 168. *Above*: The angel appearing to the shepherds, England, 14th cent. Diam., 11½ in. London, Victoria and Albert Museum. *Below*: Abraham entertaining the three angels (or the Feast of Ahasuerus?), detail, ca. 1320–30. Esslingen, Germany, Frauenkirche.

Pl. 169. Angel of the Annunciation, detail of the window of Jacques Cœur, ca. 1450. Bourges, France, Cathedral.

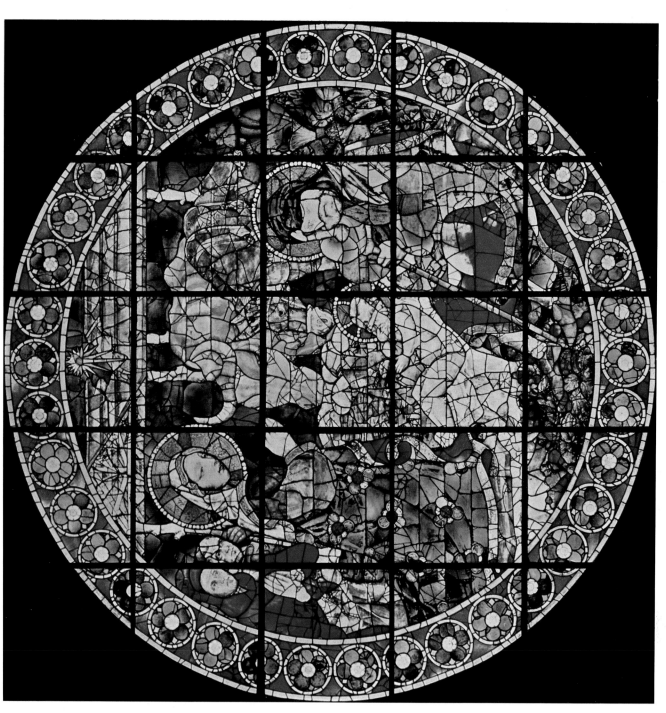

Pl. 170. The Nativity, designed by Paolo Uccello, executed by Angiolo Lippi, 1444, Florence Cathedral, oculus in the drum of the dome

Pl. 171. *Left:* Abraham entertaining the three angels, after a design attributed to L. Moser, ca. 1420-30. Ht., 26³/₈ in. Ulm, Germany, Cathedral, Besserer Chapel. *Right:* St. John the Evangelist, detail of the Schoonvorst window, 1387-98. Sichem, Netherlands, St-Eustache.

Pl. 172. *Left*: St. James with two members of the Trousseau family, detail of a window given by the family of the Duc de Berry, ca. 1414. Bourges, France. Cathedral. *Right*: Scenes from the legend of St. Catherine, attributed to H. Tiefenthal, ca. 1430. Sélestat.

Pl. 173. *Left*: The Flight into Egypt, detail of a panel from the New Testament window, designed by V. Foppa, executed by Antonio da Pandino (?), second half of 15th cent. Milan, Cathedral. *Right*: The Flight into Egypt, from the Castle of Issogne, Valle d'Aosta, Italy, 34⁵/₈×27¹/₈ in. Turin, Museo Civico.

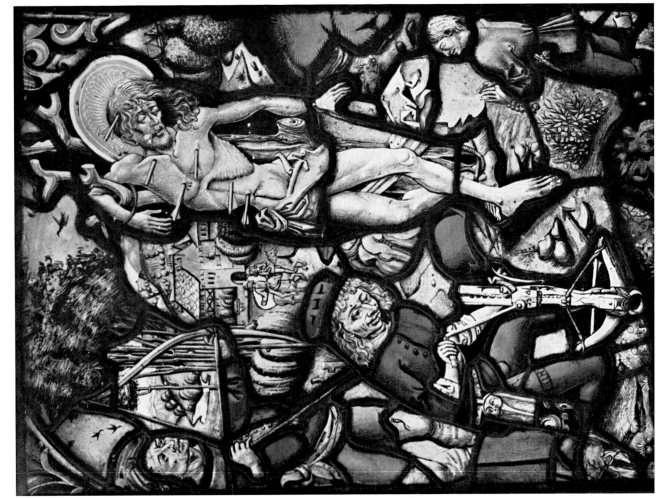

Pl. 174. *Left*: The martyrdom of St. Sebastian, after a design attributed to the Master of the Housebook. Middle Rhine, ca. 1480. Ht., 20⁷/₈ in. Stuttgart, Württem-bergisches Landesmuseum. *Right*: Lamentation, detail, France, ca. 1525. Montmorency, France, St-Martin.

Pl. 175. *Left:* Window with grotesques and the papal arms of Clement VII, ca. 1560. Florence, Biblioteca Laurenziana. *Right:* Panel with a family coat of arms, from Basel, 1590. Ht., 15 in. Basel, Kunstmuseum.

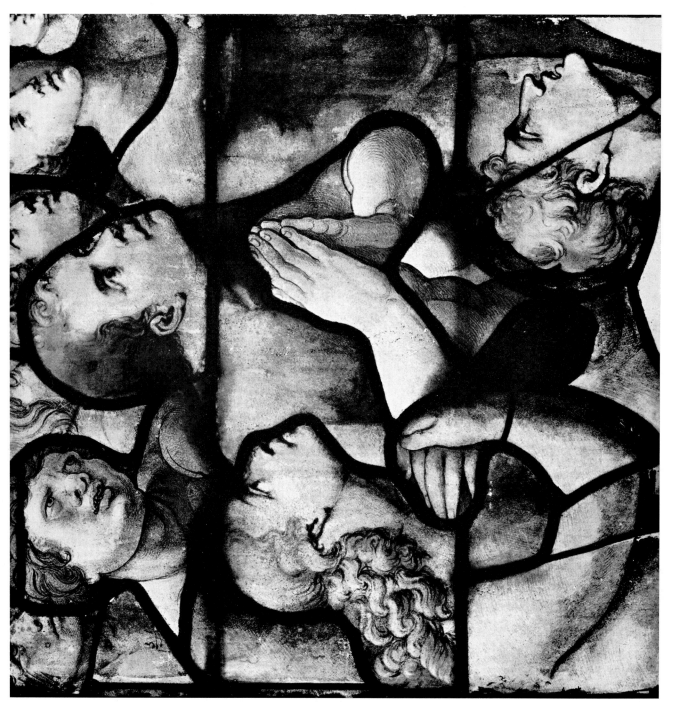

Pl. 176. The Last Judgment, detail, 1528. Brussels, SS. Michel and Gudule, window over the west portal.

Pl. 177. *Left*: The beheading of St. Faith, detail, by R. Buron, ca. 1535. Conques, Ste-Foy, choir. *Right*: The Annunciation, 1545. Gisors, France, St-Gervais-et-St-Protais.

Pl. 178. *Left*: Spring, designed by E.-S. Grasset, executed by the glazier Gaudin, 1894. Paris, Musée des Arts Décoratifs. *Right*: Maquette for the window Nuit de Noël, by H. Matisse, 1952. Gouache on cut and pasted paper, ht., 10 ft., 7 in. New York, Museum of Modern Art.

Pl. 179. The money-changers driven from the temple and Christ with the woman taken in adultery, by Guglielmo de Marcillat, ca. 1524. Arezzo, Italy, Cathedral, south side.

Pl. 180. The capture of Leonhard Thurneysser at the Battle of Summershausen and the arms of Archbishop Gebhard of Cologne, by C. Murer of Zurich, 1579. Ht., 25¹/₄ in. Basel, Kunstmuseum.

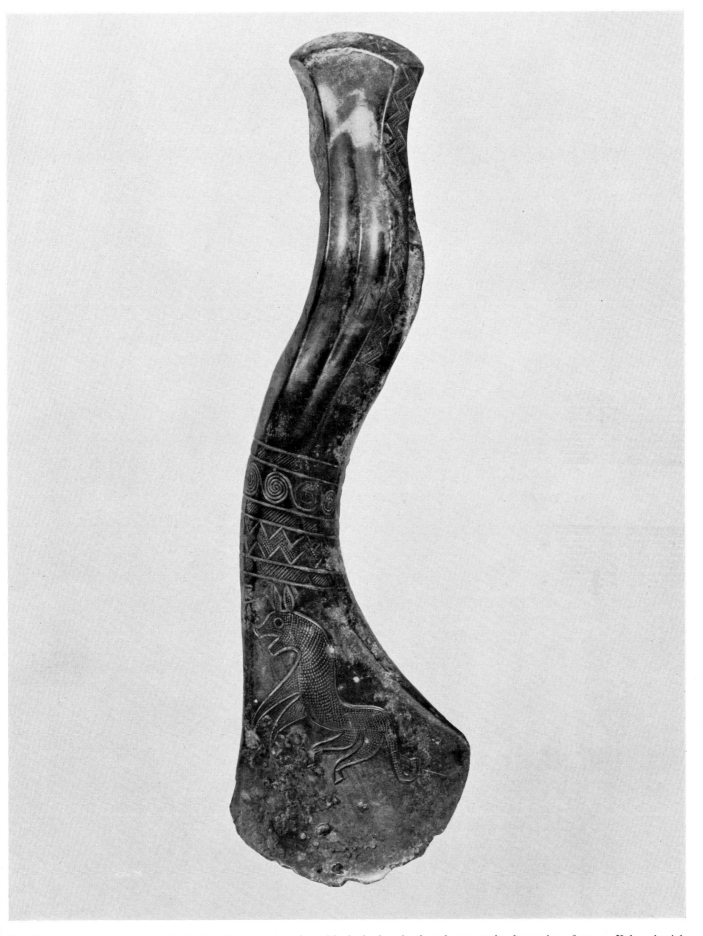

Pl. 181. Caucasian, ca. first half of 1st millennium B.C. Ax with incised animal and geometric decoration, from a Koban burial. Bronze, l., 7¹/₈ in. Saint-Germain-en-Laye, France, Musée des Antiquités Nationales.

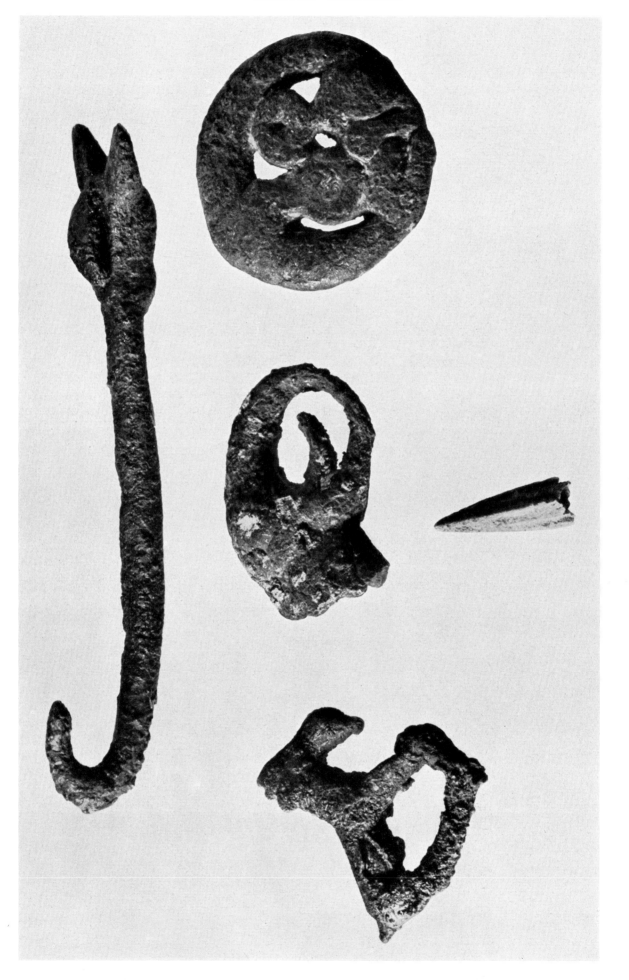

Pl. 182. Caucasian, ca. first half of 1st millennium B.C. Belt hook, ornaments, and weapon point. Bronze, l. of belt hook, 4³/₈ in. Vienna, Museum für Völkerkunde.

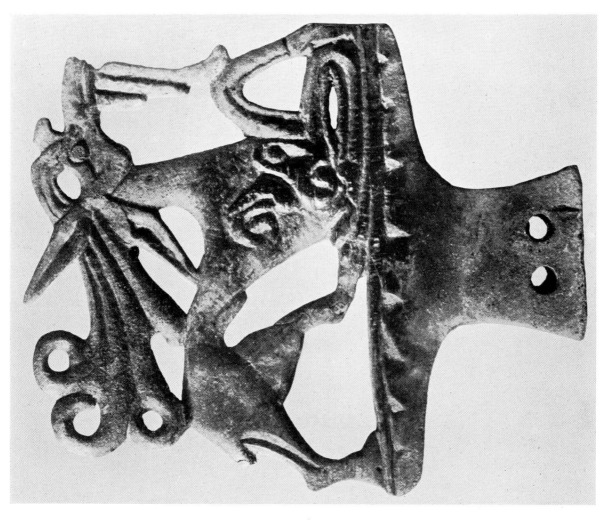

Pl. 183. Scythian. *Left*: Finial (standard top or chariot ornament ?), from Barrow II near Ulski, Kuban district. Bronze, ht., ca. 11 in. *Right*: Finial, from a barrow in the Dnieper area. Bronze. Both, Leningrad, The Hermitage.

Pl. 184. Ordos. *Above*: Goat, two pendants, ring surmounted by an onager (?), and S-shaped appliqué terminating in feline heads. Bronze, ht., 1⁵/₈ in. except appliqué, ⁵/₈ in. *Below*: Deer. Bronze, ht., 4³/₄ in. All, Paris, Musée Cernuschi.

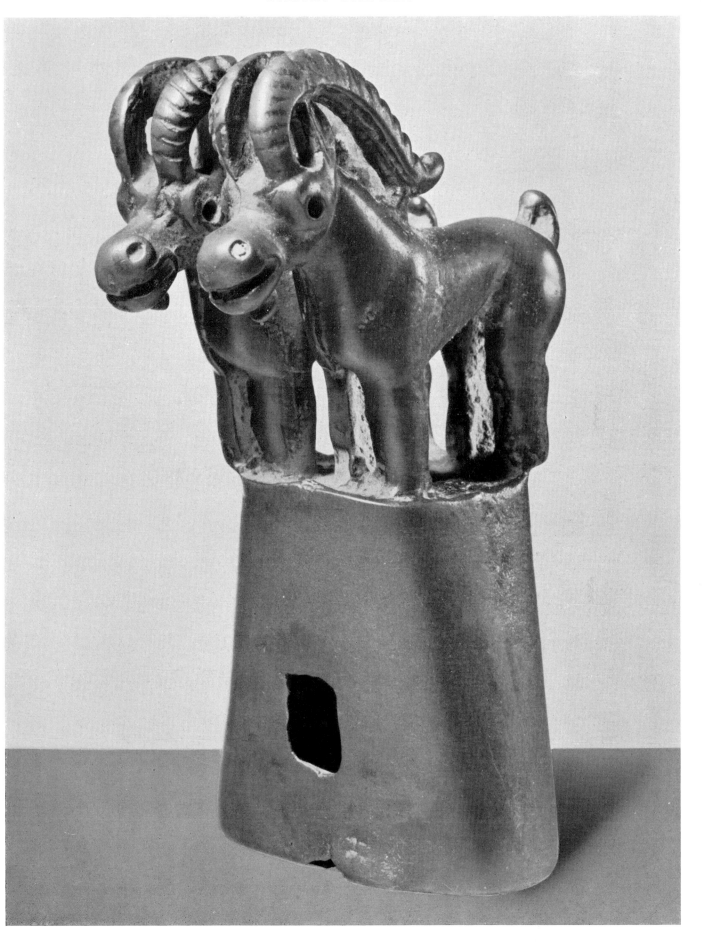

Pl. 185. Ordos. Pole top. Bronze with turquoise incrustation, ht., 4¹/₂ in. Stockholm, Museum of Far Eastern Antiquities.

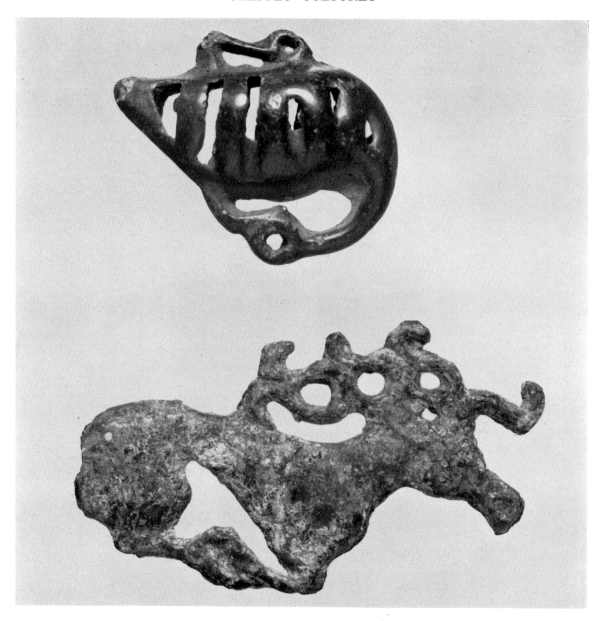

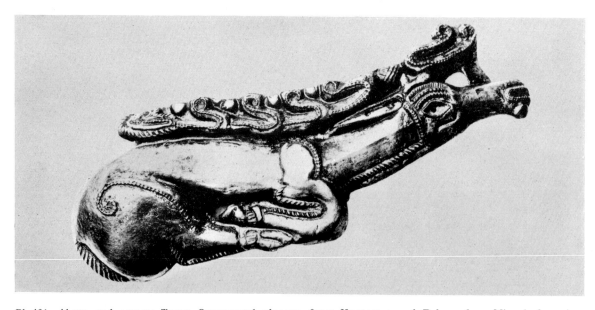

Pl. 186. *Above and center*: Tagar. Ornamental plaques, from Kaptereva and Beloyarskoe, Minusinsk region. Bronze, l., 2 and 3¹/₈ in. Helsinki, Kansallismuseo. *Below*: Scythian. Stag, centerpiece of a shield (?), from Tápiószentmárton, Hungary. Gold (eye and ear originally inlaid). Budapest, National Museum.

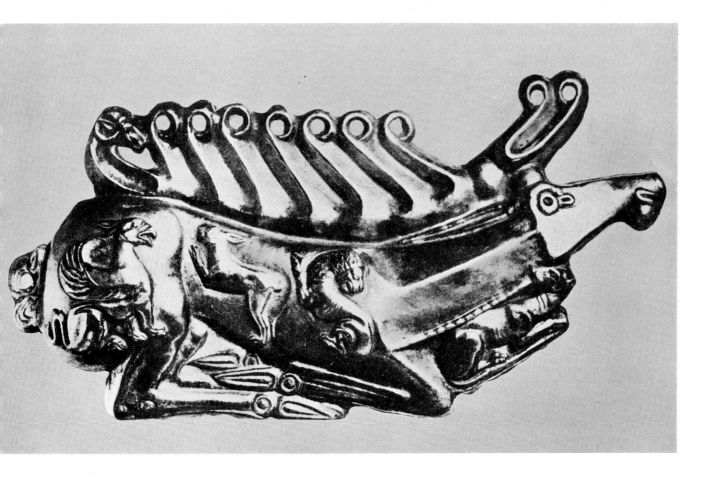

Pl. 187. *Above*: Scytho-Siberian. Plaque with animals, from the Altai region (?). Gold. *Below*: Greco-Scythian. Stag, inscribed in Greek, from Kul Oba, Crimea. Gold, l., ca. 12 in. Both, Leningrad, The Hermitage.

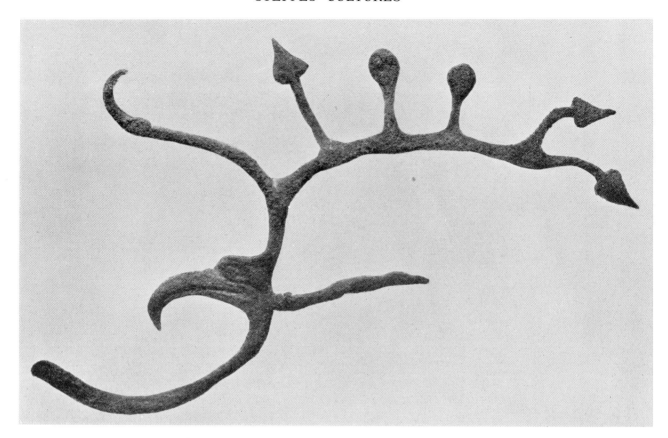

Pl. 188. Pazyryk. *Above*: Ornament with bird head, from Barrow IV. Hide, l., 5⁷/₈ in. *Below, left*: Head of a deer in the jaws of a wolf, harness ornament, from Barrow IV. Wood, l., 4 in. *Right*: Head of a deer in the beak of a griffin, from Barrow II. Horn and hide, ht., ca. 8 in. All, Leningrad, The Hermitage.

Pl. 189. Pazyryk. Head of a deer in the beak of a griffin, from Barrow II. Wood and hide, ht., 10⅝ in. Leningrad, The Hermitage.

Pl. 190. *Above*: Pazyryk. Pile carpet, detail, from Barrow V. Wool; ht., of horseman, ca. 6¹/₂ in. (full size, 6 ft., 2³/₄ in. × 6 ft., 6³/₄ in.). Leningrad, The Hermitage. *Below*: Hunnish. Woven carpet with quilting and appliqué, detail with yak fighting a lion dragon, from Noin-ula, Mongolia. Leningrad, Ethnographical Museum of the Peoples of the U.S.S.R.

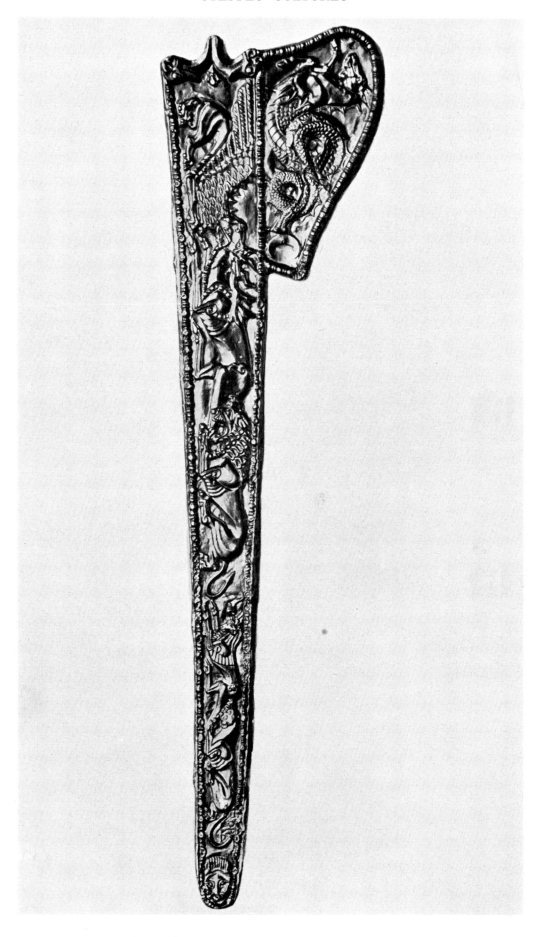

Pl. 191. Greco-Scythian. Gold casing on a sword sheath, inscribed in Greek, from Kul Oba, Crimea.
L., ca. 27 in. Leningrad, The Hermitage. (Photograph from an electrotype.)

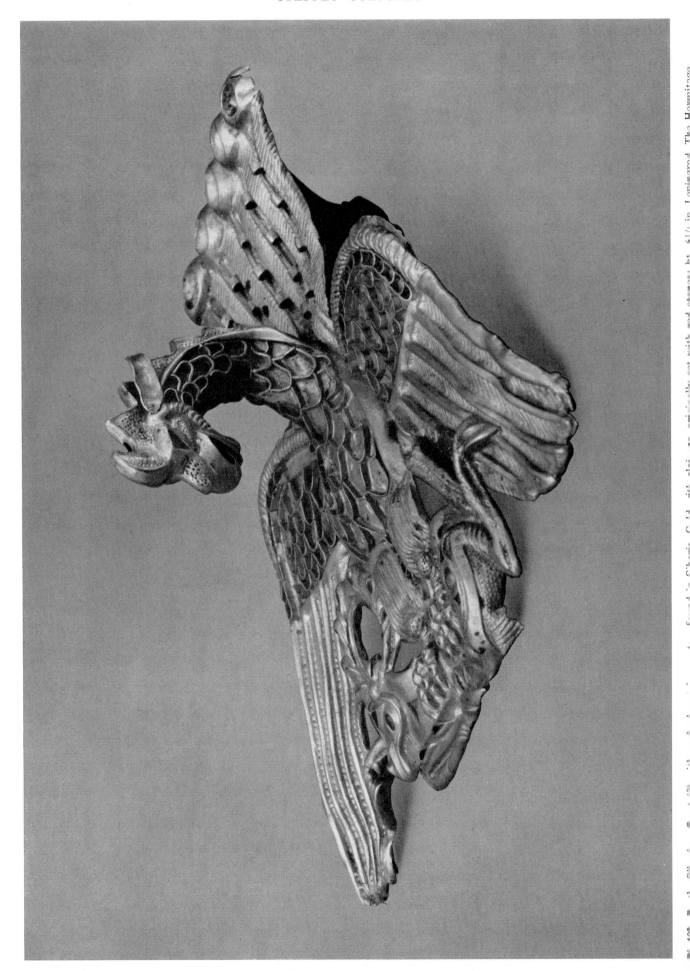

Pl. 193. Composition with fish and shellfish, from Pompeii, 1st cent. Wall painting, $17^{3}/_{4} \times 16^{1}/_{8}$ in. Naples, Museo Nazionale.

Pl. 194. Composition with fruit and game, from Pompeii, 1st cent. Wall painting, 15³/₈ × 15 in. Naples, Museo Nazionale.

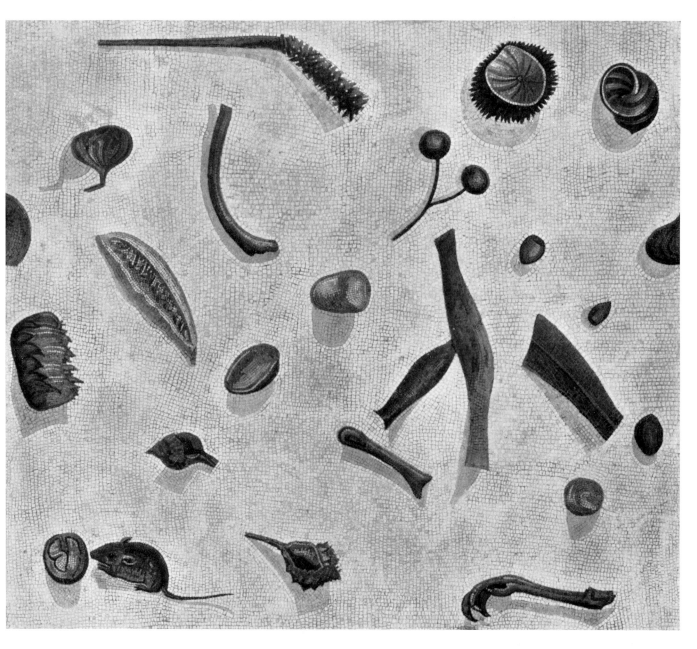

Pl. 195. *Above*: Festoon with mask, flowers, and fruit, detail, from Pompeii, House of the Faun, 2d cent. B.C. Mosaic (probably after a painting of the 3d cent. B.C.). Naples, Museo Nazionale. *Below*: Herakleitos, Unswept Room (asarotum), Rome, 2d cent., fragment. Mosaic (after a Hellenistic original by Sosos of Pergamon). Rome, Vatican Museums.

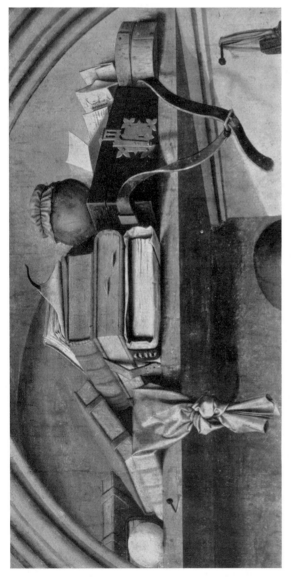

Pl. 196. *Left, above:* Master of the Aix Annunciation, Jeremiah panel of the Annunciation, detail, 1445. Panel; full size, 5 ft. × 2 ft., 10 in. Brussels, Musées Royaux des Beaux-Arts. *Below:* Colantonio, St. Jerome Extracting a Thorn from the Lion's Paw, detail, mid-15th cent. Panel; full size, 4 ft., 1¼ in. × 4 ft. 11 in. Naples, Museo di Capodimonte. *Right:* V. Dalle Vacche (Vincenzo da Verona), books and scientific and musical instruments, from Padua, S. Benedetto, 16th cent. Wood inlay. Paris, Louvre,

Pl. 197. *Left*: H. Memling (ca. 1440–94), Still Life, symbolizing attributes of the Virgin Mary (painted on back of portrait of a young man). Panel, 11³/₄ × 8¹/₂ in. Lugano, Switzerland, Thyssen-Bornemisza Coll. *Right*: J. Brueghel the Elder (1568–1625), Vase with Flowers. Panel, 44¹/₂ × 33⁷/₈ in. Amsterdam, Rijksmuseum.

Pl. 198. *Above*: P. Aertsen, Christ in the House of Mary and Martha, 1553. Panel, 4 ft., 1½ in. × 6 ft., 6¾ in. Rotterdam, Museum Boymans-Van Beuningen. *Below*: V. Campi (1536–91), Fish Vender. Canvas, 4 ft., 9 in. × 7 ft. Milan, Brera.

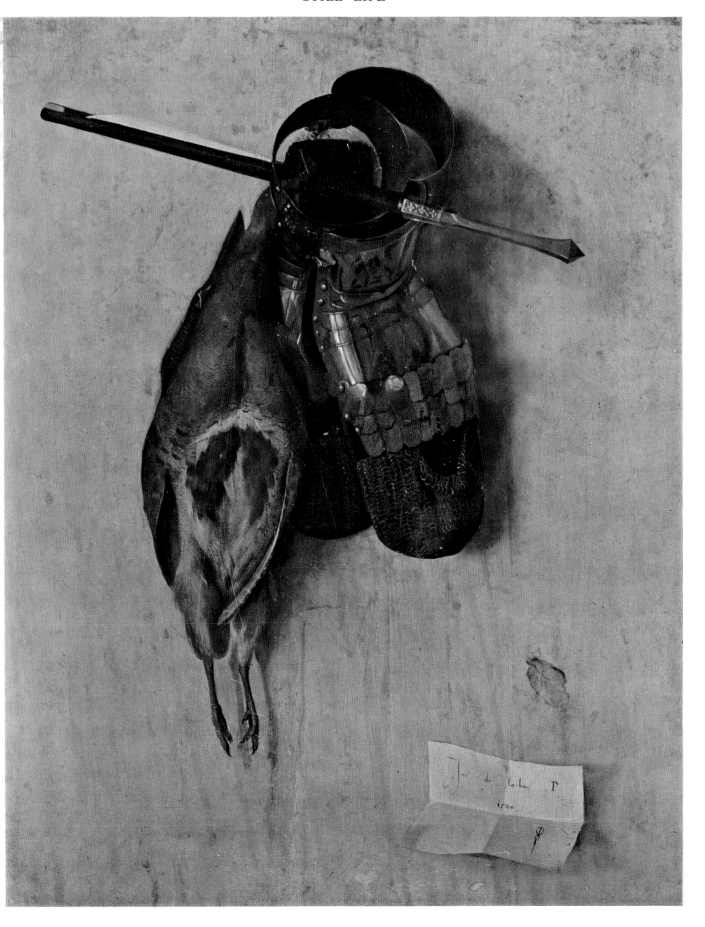

Pl. 199. Jacopo de' Barbari, Still Life, with partridge and iron gauntlets, 1504. Panel, 19^1/$_4$×16^1/$_2$ in. Munich, Alte Pinakothek.

Pl. 200. T. Salini (1575–1625), Still Life with Figure, detail. Canvas; full size, 2 ft., 6³/₄ in. × 4 ft., 5 in. Rome, private coll.

Pl. 201. *Left, above*: Baugin, Books and Papers by Candlelight, 1630. Panel, 18 1/2 × 25 5/8 in. Rome, Galleria Spada. *Center*: F. de Zurbarán (1598–1664), Still Life. Canvas, 18 1/8 × 33 1/8 in. *Below*: L. Melendez, Still Life, 1772. Canvas, 16 1/2 × 24 3/8 in. Last two, Madrid, Prado. *Right, above*: L. Susi, Still Life, 1619. Panel, 13 3/4 × 18 5/8 in. St. Louis, City Art Museum. *Center*: J. van der Hamen, Still Life, 1622. Canvas, 20 1/2 × 34 5/8 in. *Below*: J. de Arellano, Flowers and Landscape, 1652. Canvas, 22 7/8 × 28 3/4 in. Last two, Madrid, Prado.

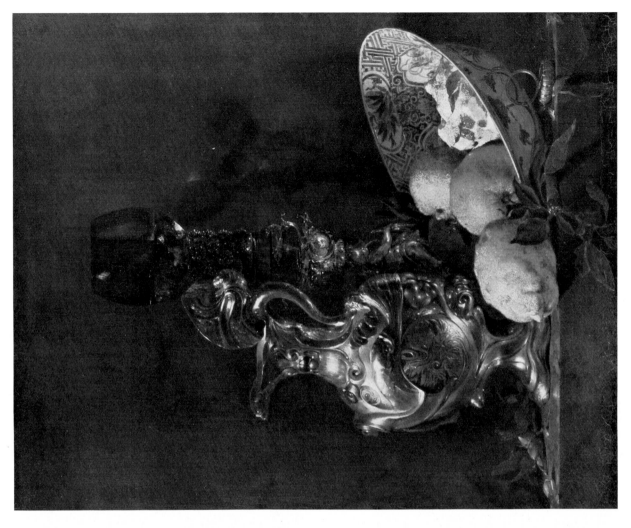

Pl. 202. *Left, above:* W. Claesz. Heda, Still Life, 1634. Panel, 16⁷/₈×22¹/₂ in. Rotterdam, Museum Boymans-Van Beuningen. *Below:* A. van Beyeren (ca. 1620–90), Still Life with Crab. Panel, 17³/₄×24³/₈ in. Munich, Alte Pinakothek. *Right:* W. Kalf (1622–93), Still Life. Canvas, 28×24³/₈ in. Amsterdam, Rijksmuseum

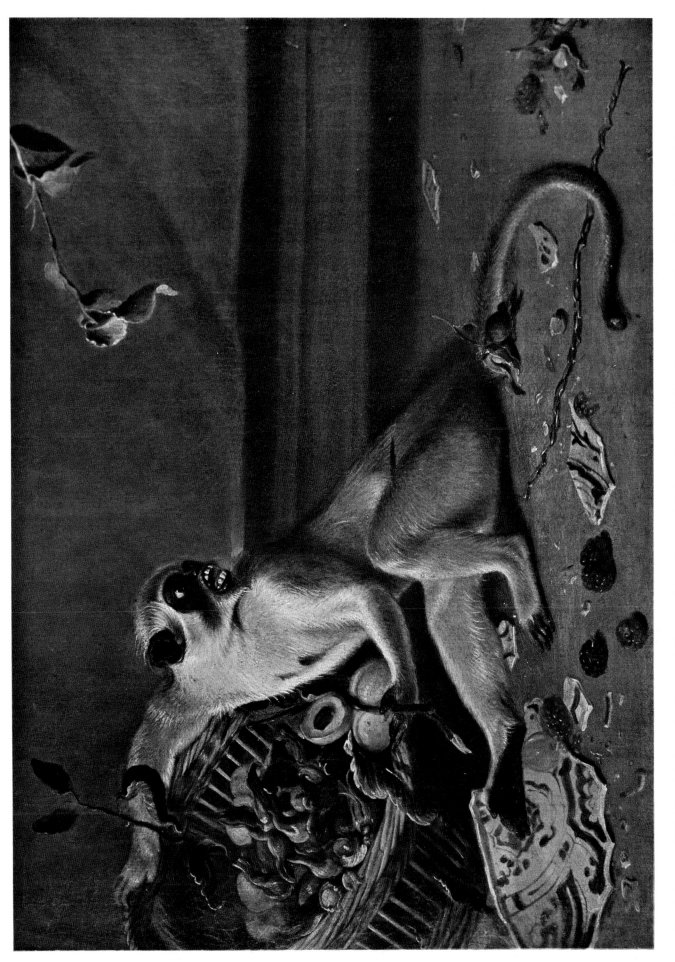

Pl. 203. F. Snyders (1579–1657), Still Life with Fruit and Flowers, detail. Canvas; full size, 5 ft., 5 in. × 7 ft., 7³/₄ in. Antwerp, Musée Royal des Beaux-Arts.

Pl. 204. G. Recco (1634-95), Still Life with Fish. Canvas, 3 ft., 3³/₈ in. × 4 ft., 6 in. Naples, Museo Nazionale di S. Martino.

PL. 205. *Left, above*: J. Fyt (1611–61), Still Life with Dog and Cat. Canvas, 30¹/₄×44¹/₈ in. Madrid, Prado. *Below*: G. B. Ruopolo (1620–85), Fish and Shellfish. Canvas, 3 ft., 3³/₈ in. × 4 ft., 1⁵/₈ in. Stockholm, Nationalmuseum. *Right, above*: P. Porpora (1617–ca. 1673), Still Life. Canvas, 14¹/₈×25⁵/₈ in. Naples, Museo di Capodimonte. *Below*: A. Brueghel (1631–1720), Still Life with Fruit. Canvas, 3 ft., 1 in. × 4 ft., 4³/₈ in. Rome, Galleria Nazionale.

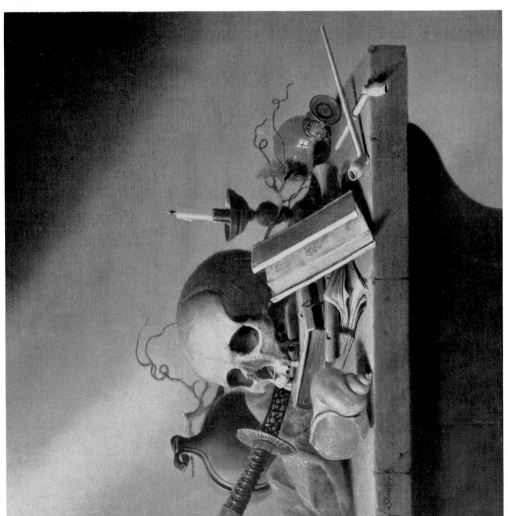

Pl. 206. *Left*: Harmen van Steenwyck, Vanitas, 17th cent. Panel, 14⁵/₈×15 in. Leiden, Stedelijk Museum "De Lakenhal." *Right*: W. Vaillant, Board with Letters, 1658. Canvas, 20¹/₈×15³/₄ in. Dresden, Gemäldegalerie.

Pl. 207. *Left*: A. Belvedere (ca. 1652–1732), Flowers. Canvas. Sorrento, Museo Correale di Terranova. *Right, above*: F. Desportes (1661–1743), Still Life. Canvas, 35⁷/₈×46¹/₂ in. Stockholm, Nationalmuseum. *Below*: J.-B.-S. Chardin, Still Life, ca. 1760–65. Canvas, 19×22⁷/₈ in. Washington, D.C., National Gallery.

Pl. 208. *Left, above*: F. Goya, The Plucked Turkey. Canvas, 17³/₄×24³/₈ in. Munich, Alte Pinakothek. *Below*: E. Delacroix, Still Life, 1826. Canvas, 31¹/₂×39³/₈ in. *Right*: E. Manet, Vase with Flowers: Peonies, ca. 1864. Canvas, 35⁷/₈×27¹/₈ in. Last two, Paris, Louvre.

Pl. 209. E. Baschenis (1617–77), Still Life with Musical Instruments. Canvas, 34¼×45¼ in. Bergamo, Italy, Galleria dell'Accademia Carrara.

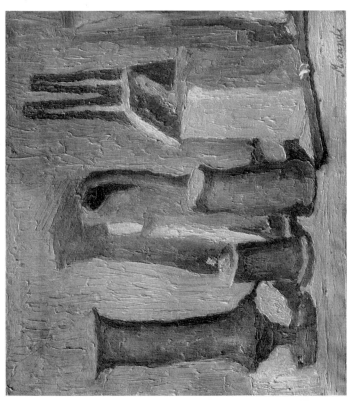

Pl. 211. *Left*: P. A. Renoir, Spring Bouquet, 1866. Canvas, 41¹/₂×31¹/₂ in. Cambridge, Mass., Fogg Art Museum. *Right, above*: P. Cézanne, Onions and Bottle, 1895–1900. Canvas, 26×31⁷/₈ in. Paris, Louvre. *Below*: G. Morandi, Still Life. Canvas. Rome, Coll. Albonetti.

Pl. 212. *Above*: Wang Yüan, A Branch of Wild Camellia, China, Yüan period. Color on silk. Tokyo, K. Magoshi Coll. *Below, left*: Plate, Damascus school, 16th cent. Ceramic. Paris, Musée Guimet. *Right*: Plate, Nabeshima ware, Japan, Edo period. Porcelain. Tokyo, Shiobara Coll.

Pl. 213. The archangel Raphael and the young Tobias. Wood, ht., 38¹/₄ and 33¹/₄ in. Nürnberg, Germany, Germanisches National-
Museum.

Pl. 214. Christ on the Mount of Olives. Sandstone with traces of paint, 5 ft., 1³/₈ in. × 4 ft., 6 in. Kraków, Poland, National Museum.

Pl. 215. Elementary building methods. *Above*: Pygmy beehive hut thatched with leaves, Ituri region, Congo. *Below*: Alpine log cabin, Bellamonte, Trentino region, Italy.

Pl. 216. Stone walling. *Above, left*: Upright megaliths, Dolmen type Kerhan, Saint-Philibert, Morbihan, France, late 3d–early 2d millennium B.C. *Right*: Polygonal masonry, Cyclopean walls of Norba, Italy, 6th–4th cent. B.C. *Below*: Ashlar masonry. *Left*: Limestone facing in even courses over a stone core, pyramid of King Zoser, Saqqara, Egypt, 3d dynasty. *Right*: *Opus quadratum*, Roman aqueduct known as the "Pont du Gard" (V, PL. 474), near Nîmes, France, Augustan period.

Pl. 217. *Above and below, left*: Roman walling. *Above, left*: *Opus incertum*, stone (with brick bonding), Sanctuary of Fortuna Primigenia (VII, PL. 199), Palestrina, Italy, late 2d–early 1st cent. B.C. *Right*: *Opus reticulatum*, brick, house in Ostia Antica, Italy, 2d cent. *Below, left*: *Opus latericium*, brick, vestibule of the Imperial Palace on the Palatine, Rome, 1st cent. *Right*: Byzantine stone and ornamental brick masonry, Panagia Parigoritissa, Arta, Greece, 1282–89.

Pl. 218. Development of skeletal construction and curtain walls. *Above, left*: Choir of the Cathedral, Aachen, Germany, begun 1355 (glass, modern). *Right*: Wainwright Building (I, PL. 86), St. Louis, Mo., by Adler & Sullivan, 1890–91. *Below, left*: The Seiryōden of the Imperial Palace, Kyoto, Japan, rebuilt (1854) on original lines of 794. *Right*: Fagus factory (V, PL. 103), Alfeld an der Leine, Germany, by W. Gropius and A. Meyer, 1911–14.

Pl. 219. Post-and-lintel construction. *Above*: Dolmen of Kergavat, Plouharnel, Morbihan, France, late 3d–early 2d millennium B.C. *Below, left*: Corridor in the southern temple at Mnajdra, Malta, second half of 3d millennium B.C. *Right*: The so-called "Temple of Concordia," Agrigento (anc. Akragas), Sicily, mid-5th cent. B.C.

Pl. 220. Arches. *Above, left*: Parabolic corbeled arch of massive dressed stone blocks, Royal Gate of Hattushash (mod. Bogazköy), Turkey, 14th–13th cent. B.C. (Cf. reconstruction, VII, FIG. 569.) *Right*: Arch built in the Servian Wall, Rome, republican period, now enclosed in Palazzo Antonelli. *Below, left*: Segmental arch of the Roman propylaea near the Temple of Apollo in Cyrene, Libya, 2d cent. or later. *Right*: Semicircular arches supported by ancient columns with Corinthian capitals, S. Sabina, Rome, first half of 5th cent.

Pl. 221. Arches. *Above, left*: Semicircular and pointed arches, Sant'Angelo in Formis, near Capua, Italy, ca. 1073. *Right*: Cusped pointed arches with bar tracery, Loggia, 1267, of the Palazzo Papale, Viterbo, Italy. *Below, left*: Round horseshoe and scalloped arches, mihrab built by Ḥakam II, 961, in the Great Mosque, Córdoba, Spain. *Right*: Ogee arches, courtyard of the Mosque of Emir Sultan, Bursa, Turkey, 1804–05.

Pl. 222. Vaulting. *Above, left*: Corbeled ("false") vault, passageway of a nuraghe, Santu Antine, Torralba, Sardinia, 8th–6th cent. B.C. *Right*: Barrel vaulting over stairway to the middle terrace of the gymnasium, Pergamon, Hellenistic period. *Below*: Cross vaulting, main hall of Trajan's Marketplace, Rome, by Apollodoros of Damascus, early 2d cent.

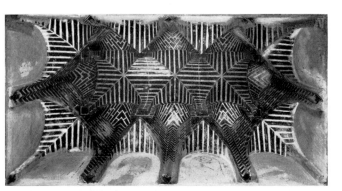

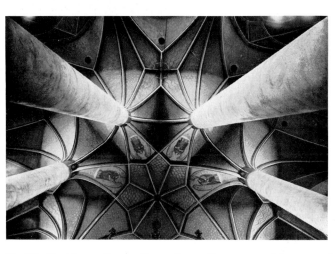

Pl. 223. Vaulting. *Above*: Cross-rib vaults supported by central piers, chapter house of the Cistercian Abbey (12th–13th cent.), Fontenay, France. *Left, center*: Vault painted to imitate brick, Torre de las Infantas, ca. 1445–61, the Alhambra, Granada, Spain. *Below*: Lierne (star or stellar) vault, St. Martin (begun 1421), Amberg, Germany. *Right*: Coffered barrel vault, vestibule of the sacristy (XII, PL. 6), 1489–92, Sto Spirito, Florence.

Pl. 224. Domes. *Above*: Corbeled beehive domes. *Left*: So-called "Treasury (or Tomb) of Klytemnestra," Mycenae, Greece, 15th cent. B.C. *Right*: Royal tumulus, Kerch, U.S.S.R., 4th cent. B.C. (Cf. diagram, VI, FIG. 854.) *Below, left*: Hemispherical dome with oculus, concrete bonded with brick, Pantheon, Rome, ca. A.D. 118–28. *Right*: Dome with ten brick ribs on decagonal base, so-called "Temple of Minerva Medica" (IX, PL. 37), Rome, second half of 3d cent.

Pl. 225. Domical structures. *Above, left*: Groined vaulting and squinches, choir and transept of the Cathedral, formerly Stiftskirche St. Georg, Limburg an der Lahn, Germany, 13th cent. *Right*: Central dome, semidomes, and cupolas, New Mosque (Yeni Cami), Istanbul, 1597–1663. *Below, left*: Dome on pendentives, S. Maria delle Carceri, Prato, Italy, by Giuliano da Sangallo, 1484–95. *Right*: Dome on drum, with lantern, S. Agnese in Agone, Rome, by F. Borromini, ca. 1657.

Pl. 226. Roofs. *Above, left*: Model of a gabled temple roof with terra-cotta tiling, from a stele, necropolis of Gela, Sicily, 5th cent. B.C. Limestone. Syracuse, Sicily, Museo Archeologico. *Right*: Gambrel roof with upswept eaves, throne hall of Kyungbok Palace, Seoul, rebuilt ca. 1867. *Below, left*: Gothic gabled roofs, view of houses, church, and castle at Marburg, Germany. *Right*: Roof of the royal chapel, ca. 1700, by J. Hardouin Mansart, Palace of Versailles.

Pl. 227. Ceilings and roof interiors. *Left, above:* Roof trusses, Cathedral of Chiusi, Italy, 12th cent. *Right, above:* Diaphragm arches supporting wooden framework, fortress at Montefiascone, Italy, ca. 1363. *Below:* Coffered wood ceiling, 16th cent., of Aquileia, Italy. *Below:* Carinate ceiling, 1348. Cathedral (11th cent.) (restored late 19th cent.). S. Maria in Aracoeli (13th cent.), Rome.

Pl. 228. *Above, left*: Stone flying buttresses, built after 14th-century plans, south transept of the Cathedral of Cologne (13th–19th cent.). *Right*: Cast- and wrought-iron framework, Bibliothèque Ste-Geneviève, Paris, by H. Labrouste, 1843–50. *Below*: Ferro-vitreous construction. *Left*: Roof of the central pavilion, Botanical Gardens, Sheffield, England, attributed to J. Paxton, ca. 1836. *Right*: Hall of Machines at the Paris Exhibition of 1889, by F. Dutert, architect, and Contamin, engineer.

Pl. 229. Construction with reinforced concrete. *Above, left*: Jahrhunderthalle, Breslau, Germany, by M. Berg, ca. 1912. *Right*: Housing unit (*unité d'habitation*), Marseilles, France, by Le Corbusier, completed 1952. *Below, left*: Yale Hockey Rink, New Haven, Conn., by Eero Saarinen, completed 1958. *Right*: Airport terminal, Washington, D.C., by Eero Saarinen, shown under construction, 1963.

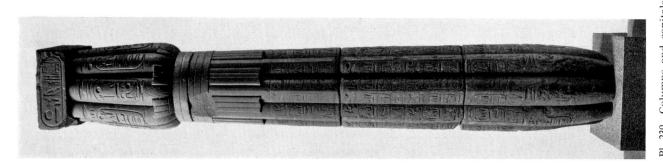

Pl. 230. Columns and capitals. *Two at left*: Egyptian columns (cf. IV, FIG. 682). *Left*: Bundled papyrus, probably from Memphis, 1450 B.C. London, British Museum. *Second from left*: Palmiform and campaniform, interior of the porch, 122 B.C., Temple of Horus, Edfu. *Above, center*: Hathor capital, with lotus capital surmounted by a Hathor head and a naos, from Larnaca (anc. Kition), Cyprus, ca. 500 B.C. Paris, Louvre. *Right*: Aeolic capital, from Neandria, Aeolis, Asia Minor, 7th cent. (?). Istanbul, Archaeological Museum. *Below*: Etruscan capital of Aeolic type, Tomb of the Capitals, Cerveteri (anc. Caere), Italy, 6th cent. B.C.

Pl. 231. Columns and capitals. *Left, above:* Achaemenid capital with bull protomas, from the Palace of Artaxerxes II, Susa, Iran, late 5th–4th cent. B.C. Paris, Louvre. *Below:* Achaemenid column, the Apadana, Persepolis, late 6th–early 5th cent. B.C. *Center, above:* Rock-cut column, Cave I, Ajanta, Bombay, India, ca. 600. *Below:* Bracket capitals in temple corridor, Rameshwaram, Madras, India, 17th–18th cent. *Right:* Japanese wooden bracket clusters, Kondō of the Tōshōdaiji, Nara, late 8th cent.

Pl. 232. Engaged columns. *Left*: Ionic columns on the so-called "Tomb of Theron," Agrigento, Sicily, Hellenistic-Roman period. *Right*: Doric or Tuscan, Ionic, and Corinthian orders on the Colosseum, Rome, Flavian period.

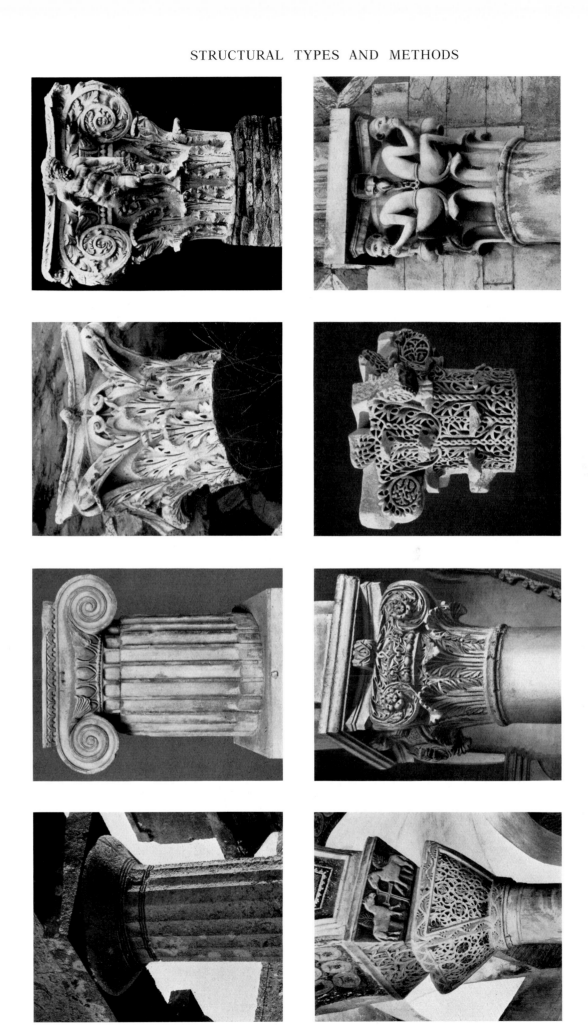

Pl. 233. Capitals. *Above, left*: Greek Doric, Temple of Aphaia, Aegina, ca. 500 B.C. *Center, left*: Greek Ionic, from Magnesia-on-the-Meander, Turkey, late 3d cent. B.C. Istanbul, Archaeological Museums. *Center, right*: Roman Corinthian, Arch of Trajan, Leptis Magna, Libya, A.D. 110–11. *Right*: Roman composite figural, Baths of Caracalla, Rome, ca. 3d cent. *Below, left*: Byzantine, with impost block, S. Vitale, Ravenna, mid-6th cent. *Center, left*: Composite, Cathedral of Massa Marittima, Italy, 13th–14th cent. *Center, right*: Moorish Corinthian, Medina az-Zahra, near Córdoba, Spain, ca. 953–56. *Right*: Romanesque figural, Campanile of Pisa, 1174–75.

Pl. 234. Columns and capitals. *Above, left*: Gothic clustered columns, Abbey of Fossanova, Italy, chapter room, mid-13th cent. *Right*: Renaissance composite columns, fluted and engaged. Palazzo Bevilacqua, Verona, detail of façade, by M. Sanmicheli, 1530. *Below*: Baroque columns with twisted and spiral-fluted shaft. Palazzo S. Marzano (later, Turati, Carpano), Turin, ca. 1684–86.

Pl. 235. Openings. *Above, left*: Door with cavetto cornice, Ptolemaic temple, Deir el-Medineh, Egypt. *Right*: Trapezoidal doorways and molding, Tomb of the Cornice, Cerveteri (anc. Caere), Italy, ca. 6th cent. B.C. *Below, left*: False door with double leaves and engaged columns, so-called "Tomb of the Christian Woman" (I, PL. 18), Tipasa, near Cherchel, Algeria, ca. early 1st cent. (?). *Right*: Three-tiered city gate with openings of aedicula type and engaged pilasters, Porta dei Borsari, Verona, Italy, 1st–3d cent.

Pl. 236. Arcading and windows. *Above, left*: Romanesque arcading, apse of the Cathedral, Speyer, Germany, 11th–12th cent. *Right*: Gothic window with cusped arch, unglazed tile, remains of the Casa dei Panigarola, Milan, 14th–early 15th cent. *Below, left*: Renaissance windows, portico, and decoration (1510–20) on a renovated Gothic structure, Hôtel Gouin, Tours, France. *Right*: Indo-Islamic domed half-oriel windows filled with perforated screens, Hawā Mahal, Jaipur, Rajasthan, India, ca. 1728.

Pl. 237. Windows. *Left*: Renaissance. *Above*: Window of Palazzo Ducale, Urbino, Italy, second half of 15th cent. *Below*: Balcony window, Palazzo Cocconi (Del Pecora), Montepulciano, Italy, attributed to Antonio da Sangallo the Elder, first half of 16th cent. *Right*: Baroque. *Above*: Window of Palazzo dei Padri delle Missioni, Florence, by B. Radi, 17th cent. *Below*: Dormer window of palace, Der Grosse Garten, Dresden, by J. G. Starck, 1679–83

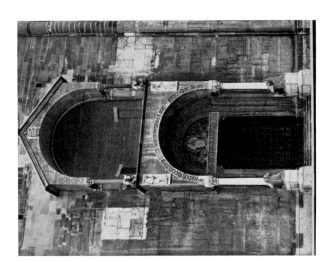

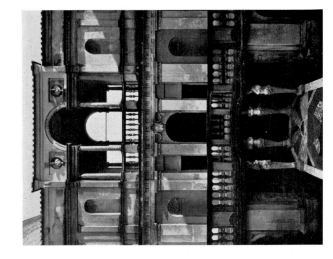

Pl. 238. Portals and balconies. *Above, left*: Main portal of the Cathedral, Piacenza, Italy, 1122–1233. *Center*: The Foscari Arch, 15th cent., by A. Rizzo and B. Bon, Doges' Palace, Venice. *Right*: Entrance of the Palazzo della Gherardesca, Florence, ca. first quarter of 16th cent. *Below, left*: Loggia, by B. Ammanati, Nymphaeum of the Villa Giulia (1550–55), Rome. *Center*: Loggia del Capitanio, detail of XI, pl. 35, by A. Palladio, Vicenza, Italy, 1571. *Right*: Portal, ca. 1734, by G. Valvassori, Palazzo Doria (facade on the Corso), Rome.

Pl. 239. Interior architectural furnishings. *Left:* Ambo of the Cathedral, Bitonto, Italy, 1229. *Right, above:* Mantelpiece, after 1474, Palazzo Ducale, Urbino, Italy. *Below:* Mantelpiece with marble and oak carving, designed by L. Blondeel, 1528, executed by G. de Beaugrant and others, courtroom of the Palais de Justice, Bruges.

Pl. 240. Stairs. *Left, above*: Steps leading to the cella, Temple of Apollo, Pompeii, ca. early 1st cent. B.C. (restored A.D. 1st cent.). *Below*: External staircase on pensile arch, Casa Poscia, Viterbo, Italy, probably early 14th cent. *Right, above*: The Hieroglyphic Stairway, Copán, Honduras, classic Maya period. *Below*: Stairway of the Mimalaungkyaung, Pagan, Burma, 1174.

Pl. 241. Stairs. *Left, above*: Scroll-like flight of steps, 1574, by B. Buontalenti, S. Stefano (formerly in Sta Trinita), Florence. *Below*: Escalier du Fer à Cheval, 1634, by Jean A. Ducerceau the Elder, Pavillon Central, Château at Fontainebleau. *Right*: Main staircase, ca. 1745, by G. B. Sacchetti, Royal Palace, Madrid.

Pl. 242. Structures "without internal space." *Left, above:* The pyramids of kings Cheops, Chephren, and Mycerinus, Giza, Egypt, 4th dynasty. *Below:* Etruscan tumulus, Cerveteri (anc. Caere), Italy, 7th cent. B.C. *Right, above:* The ziggurat of Ur-Nammu, restored remains, Ur, Iraq, late 3d millennium B.C. (Cf. I, FIG. 867.) *Below:* Pyramid of the Moon, Teotihuacán, Mexico, Teotihuacán II phase.

Pl. 243. Structures "without internal space." *Left, above*: Stupa No. 2, Sanchi, Madhya Pradesh, India, 2d cent. B.C. *Below*: The Shwesandaw stupa, Pagan, Burma, 11th cent. *Right, above*: The trophaeum of Augustus, La Turbie, France, 7–6 B.C. *Below*: Commemorative arch, Medinaceli, Spain, Roman period.

Pl. 244. Types evolved on a simple circular plan. *Above*: Thatched beehive dwellings (shown finished and unfinished at right), pile village on Camorta, Nicobar Islands. *Center, left*: Malo wattling hut with thatched roof, southwest Ethiopia. *Right*: Trullo of dry-stone masonry, Apulia, Italy. *Below, left*: Peripteral round temple (dedicated to Portunus?), Rome, Forum Boarium, 1st cent. B.C. (?). *Right*: The Rotonda, or Old Cathedral, Brescia, Italy, early 12th cent.

Pl. 245. Types evolved on a simple rectangular plan. *Above*: Maori house with ornamental carving, Tokanganui-a-Noho, Aotea Harbor, New Zealand. *Center, left*: Toba Batak house with boat-shaped roof, Sumatra. *Right*: Slate-roofed house for cheese making, mountain area near Laguiole, Aveyron, France. *Below, left*: Entrance hall of Nijō castle, Kyoto, Japan, 1602–22. *Right*: Roman temple known as Maison Carrée, Nîmes (anc. Nemausus), France, ca. late 1st cent. B.C.

Pl. 246. Multiple stories. *Above, left*: House of Diana, with balconied upper story (ruined), Ostia Antica, Italy, 2d cent. *Right*: Himeji castle, Hyogo prefecture, Japan, ca. 1580–1600. *Center, left*: Houses on Neustadt market place, Landshut, Germany, 14th–15th cent. *Right*: Palazzo Gondi, Florence, by Giuliano da Sangallo, begun 1490. *Below*: Skyscrapers seen from Lincoln Park, Chicago, 20th cent.

Pl. 247. Dwellings in relation to open air. *Above, left*: Atrium of the House of the Silver Wedding, Pompeii, mainly of the 1st cent. *Right*: Arches opening onto the great court of Azem Palace, Damascus, Syria, 18th cent. *Center*: Façade and surrounding gardens of Villa Cordellina, Montecchio Maggiore, Italy, by G. Massari, 18th cent. (Cf. VIII, PL. 442.) *Below*: Home of James Dinwiddie, Lafayette, Calif., featuring extensive use of glass, by J. E. Dinwiddie, 1948.

Pl. 248. Fortification. *Above, left*: Brick wall of the Ishtar Gate, Babylon, 6th cent. B.C. (Cf. reconstruction, IX, Pl. 494.) *Right*: Moat with piers of the drawbridge, Euryelos castle, Syracuse, Sicily, ca. 4th cent. B.C. *Below, left*: Porta S. Paolo (anc. Porta Ostiensis), in the Aurelian walls (3d cent.), Rome, showing exterior construction of later date. *Right*: Citadel of Bam, Iran, built of unbaked brick, Islamic period.

Pl. 249. Fortification. *Left*: The Garisenda and Asinelli towers, Bologna, Italy, ca. 1109–19. *Right, above*: The Castle of the Counts (Gravensteen), Ghent, Belgium, mainly 12th cent. (restored). *Below*: Castle at Ostia, Italy, by B. Pontelli or Giuliano da Sangallo, begun 1483.

Pl. 250. Public buildings. *Above, left*: Ekklesiasterion (assembly hall), Priene, Turkey, ca. late 3d cent. B.C. *Right*: Tabularium (record office) on the Capitoline, Rome, completed 78 B.C. (with modern superstructure). *Below*: Curia (senate building) in the Forum, Rome, reconstructed under Diocletian, early 4th cent. (restored).

Pl. 251. Public buildings. *Above, left*: Palazzo dei Priori, Volterra, Italy, 1208–54 (top of tower added, 1846). *Right*: Town Hall, Oudenaarde, Belgium, built by H. van Pede, 1526–36. *Below*: Palais-Bourbon (Chambre des Députés), Paris, redesigned under Napoleon with porch by B. Poyet of ca. 1806–08.

Pl. 252. Sanctuaries and temples. *Above, left*: Megalithic sanctuary, Stonehenge, England, first half of 2d millennium B.C. *Right*: Mortuary temple of Queen Hatshepsut, Deir el-Bahri, Egypt, 18th dynasty. *Below, left*: So-called "Temple of Neptune," Paestum, Italy, ca. 450 B.C. *Right*: Temple of Fortuna Virilis, Forum Boarium, Rome, ca. mid-1st cent. B.C.

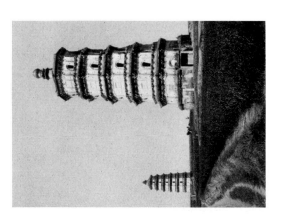

Pl. 253. Temples and pagodas. *Above, left:* Temple I, atop pyramid, Tikal, Petén, Guatemala, classic Maya period. *Center:* Keśava temple, Somnathpur, Mysore, India, second half of 13th cent. *Right:* Wat Arun (Temple of the Dawn), near Bangkok, second half of 18th cent. *Below, left:* Pair of pagodas, Tsinkiang (Ch'üan-chou), Fukien, China, brick construction of mid-12th cent., encased in stone, mid-13th cent. *Center:* Model of the Ch'i-nien-tien (Hall of the Annual Prayers), Peking, late Ch'ing period. *Right:* Daibutsuden (Hall of the Great Buddha), Tōdaiji, Nara, Japan, Edo period.

Pl. 254. Edifices with longitudinal plan. *Above, left*: The Basilica at Poreč, Yugoslavia, 6th cent. *Right*: St. Kastor, Koblenz, Germany, mainly 12th–13th cent. *Below, left*: Aerial view of the Cathedral, Orléans, France, 13th–17th cent. *Right*: Benedictine church, Ottobeuren, Germany, 1736–66 (longitudinal foundations with central space under domed

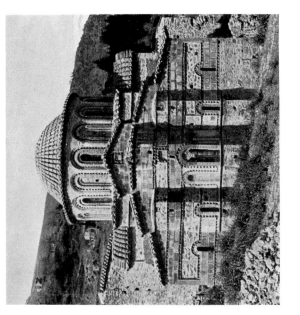

Pl. 255. Edifices with central plan. *Above, left*: Baptistery of the Orthodox, Ravenna, Italy, 5th cent. *Center*: Church of SS. Theodore, Mistra, Greece, 1291. *Right*: Selimiye mosque, Konya, Turkey, 16th cent. *Below, left*: The Radcliffe Camera (Library), Oxford, England, by J. Gibbs, 1737–49. *Center*: Church of the Ascension, Kolomenskoe, U.S.S.R., 1532. *Right*: Chapel, 1954–55, by J. H. Moya, Gimnasio Moderno, Bogotá, Colombia.

Pl. 256. Theaters and arenas. *Above, left*: Supposed theater area of the second palace, Phaistos, Crete, 1700–1400 B.C. (Cf. IV, PL. 53.) *Right*: Ball Court, Tula, Hidalgo state, Mexico, Toltec culture. *Below*: Amphitheaters. *Left*: Segesta, Sicily, Hellenistic period. *Right*: Pompeii, first half of 1st cent. B.C.

Pl. 257. Arenas. *Left, above*: Stadium, Epidauros, Greece, 5th cent. B.C. *Below*: Circus of Maxentius, Rome, early 4th cent. *Right*: Olympic Stadium, Rome, ca. 1954–55.

Pl. 258. Theaters and auditoriums. *Above, left:* Teatro Farnese, Parma, Italy, by G. B. Aleotti, 1618 (photographed prior to war damage). *Right:* Residenztheater, Munich, by F. de Cuvilliés, 1751–53 (rebuilt after World War II). *Below, left:* Teatro San Carlo, Naples, by G. A. Medrano and A. Carasale, 1737, remodeled by A. Niccolini, first half of 19th

Pl. 259. Libraries. *Left*: Convento di S. Marco, Florence, library by Michelozzo, 15th cent. *Right, above*: *Salone* of the Biblioteca Casanatense, Rome, second half of 17th cent. (shelving, 18th cent.; cf. VIII, Pl. 106). *Below*: Municipal Library, Vyborg (formerly Viipuri), U.S.S.R., by A. Aalto, 1927–35.

Pl. 260. Hospitals and schools. *Left, above*: Hospital of Sto Spirito in Sassia, Rome, engraving (17th cent.) of the main ward. *Center*: Hospital in Swindon, England, by P. Powell and J. H. Moya, mid-20th cent., view across the raised terrace. *Below*: School in Copenhagen, by A. Jacobsen, 1952. *Right, above*: Christ Church College, Oxford, England, the Great Quadrangle (Tom Quad) with Wolsey's gateway, begun 1525, and Tom Tower, completed by C. Wren, 1682. *Center*: Hollis Hall, collegiate dormitory of Harvard University, Cambridge, Mass., 1736. *Below*: Courtyard of Gonville and Caius College, Cambridge, England, by L. Martin and C. St. J. Wilson, 1962.

Pl. 261. *Above*: Monastery, the Certosa of Galluzzo, near Florence, founded 14th cent. *Below*: Hotels, mid-20th cent. *Left*: The Dover Stage, Dover, England, by L. Erdi. *Right*: Motel, Kalabaka, Greece, by A. Konstantinidis.

Pl. 262. Commercial buildings. *Above, left:* Thermopolium (tavern), Via di Diana, Ostia Antica, Italy, 2d cent. *Right:* View of the Halles Centrales (market), Paris, third quarter of 19th cent. *Below, left:* Shopping area with arcades and pedestrian court, St. Andrew's St., Cambridge, England, by Hughes & Bicknell, mid-20th cent. *Right:* Department store and office building on Sergel Square, Stockholm, by S. Ancker, B. Gate, and S. Lindegren, mid-20th cent.

Pl. 263. Industrial and scientific buildings. *Above, left*: Sunila cellulose factory, near Kotka, Finland, by A. Aalto, 1936–39. *Right*: Rubber factory at Brynmawr, South Wales, by Architects' Co-Partnership (engineer Ove Arup), 1949. *Below, left*: Saipal bakery at Lourenço Marques, Mozambique, by A. Guedes, completed 1954. *Right*: Nuclear science buildings, Sidney, Australia, by Bunning & Madden, showing (*left to right*) lecture theater, studies block, canteen.

Pl. 264. Constructions designed to utilize water. *Left, above*: Baths of Caracalla, Rome, view with the calidarium in the foreground, early 3d cent. *Center*: Nymphaeum beside pool, early 18th cent. (?), garden of the Villa Reale of Marlia, near Lucca, Italy. *Below*: The Cisternone, a reservoir with Doric portico, Leghorn, by P. Poccianti, 1829–42. *Right, above*: The Fountain of the Bees in Piazza Barberini, Rome, by G. L. Bernini, 1644. *Below*: Concrete water tower, Örebro, Sweden, by L. Reinius and associate, mid-20th cent.

Pl. 265. Aqueducts and bridges. *Left, above*: Roman aqueduct, so-called "Puente de las Ferreras," Tarragona, Spain, restored 10th cent. *Center*: Roman bridge over the Tagus River, Alcántara, Cáceres, Spain, ca. A.D. 105–06. *Below*: Ponte della Maddalena ("Ponte del Diavolo") over the Serchio River, at Borgo a Mozzano, near Lucca, Italy, 14th cent. *Right, above*: Ponte Sta Trinita, Florence, rebuilt by B. Ammanati, 1570 (photographed before destruction, 1944; rebuilt). Stone. *Center*: Bridge over the River Severn, near Coalbrookdale, Shropshire, England, by T. F. Pritchard, A. Darby, and J. Wilkinson, 1777–79. Cast iron. *Below*: Bridge over the Rhine at Tavanasa, Switzerland, by R. Maillart, 1905 (destroyed by landslide, 1927). Reinforced concrete.

Pl. 266. Transportation facilities. *Above*: Main railway station, Stuttgart, Germany, by P. Bonatz with F. E. Scholer, 1913–27. *Left, center*: Service area on the Hamburg-Hanover Autobahn, Germany, mid-20th cent. *Below*: So-called "Oasis" with overbridge restaurant, one of a series on the tollway system near Chicago, mid-20th cent. *Right*: Two views of Leonardo da Vinci Airport at Fiumicino, near Rome, by R. Morandi and associates, opened January, 1961.

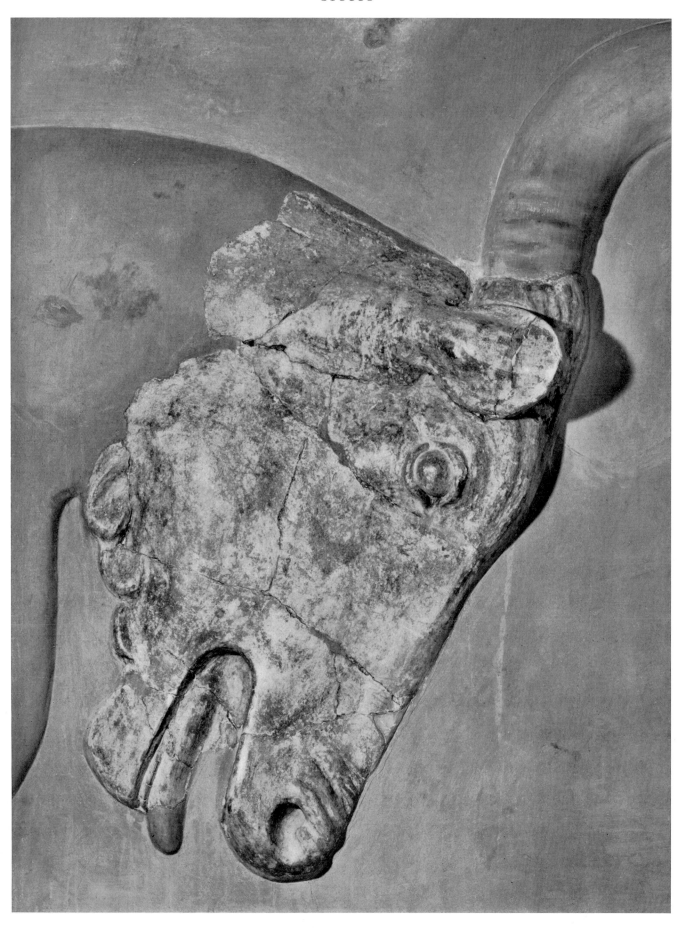

Pl. 267. Bull's head, detail of painted relief, second palatial period (1700–1400 B.C.). Knossos, Crete, Palace.

Pl. 268. *Above*: Etruscan painted tomb decoration, with utensils, arms, and mythological figures, 3d cent. B.C. Cerveteri, Italy, Tomb of the Reliefs. *Below*: Xunantunich (Benque Viejo), British Honduras, Structure A6-2d, decorated bands on east façade, showing deity mask, hieroglyphs, and human figures, central lowlands Maya, late classic period, probably 9th cent.

Pl. 269. Rome, subterranean Basilica di Porta Maggiore, view of the nave showing decoration of vault and apse, mid-1st cent. (See X, PL. 246.)

Pl. 270. *Above*: Landscape with figures, from the House of the Farnesina, Rome, Augustan period (31 B.C.–A.D. 14). Rome, Museo Nazionale Romano. *Below*: Pompeii, ca. 1st cent. *Left*: Stabian Baths, detail of vault decoration. *Right*: House of the Silver Wedding, niche dedicated to Hercules.

Pl. 271. *Above*: Priam begging the body of Hector from Achilles, portion of Homeric frieze in the shrine to Venus and Diana, House of the Cryptoporticus, Pompeii, ca. 1st cent. *Below*: The story of Sappho, mid-1st cent, detail of PL. 269.

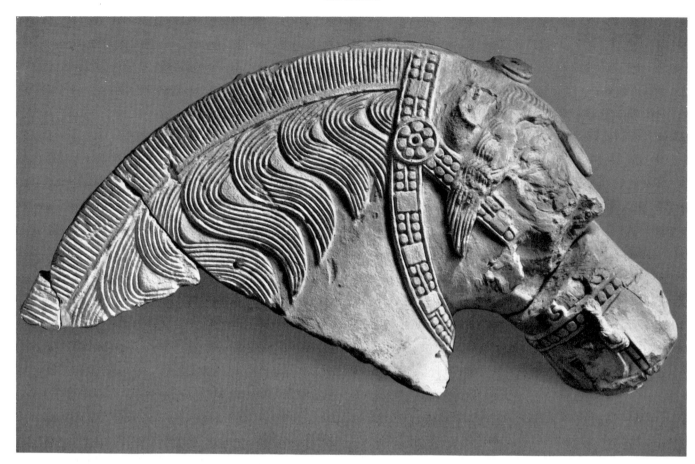

Pl. 272. *Above*: Horse's head, from Nizamabad, Iran, Sassanian period. Low relief with traces of color; l., 29 in. Berlin, Staatliche Museen. *Below, left*: Head of a man, from Gandhara, India, 3d–4th cent. New Delhi, National Museum of India. *Right*: Head of a goddess, from Tumshuk, Sinkiang province, China, 7th cent. Ht., 5⁷/₈ in. Paris, Musée Guimet.

Pl. 273. Ravenna, Italy. *Above*: Baptistery of the Orthodox, polychromed reliefs of saints in niches, mid-5th cent. *Below*: S. Vitale, decoration of arches, 6th cent.

Pl. 274. Figures of saints and architectural decoration (cf. XI, PL. 324), of disputed date. Cividale del Friuli, Italy, S. Maria in Valle ("Tempietto").

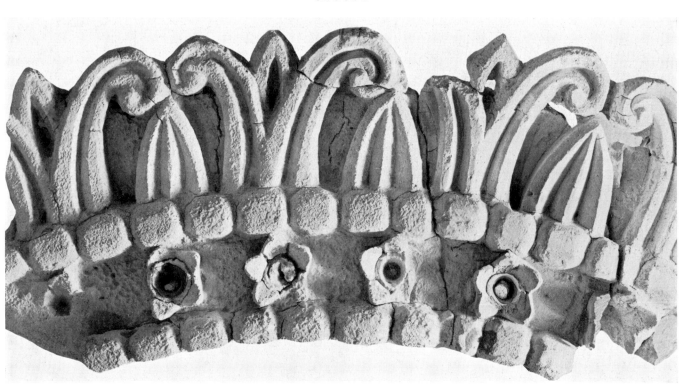

Pl. 275. *Above*: Fragment of decoration with lily motif, 8th cent. (?). Brescia, Italy, S. Salvatore. *Below*: Angel and ornamental bands, detail of a pendentive, ca. 1165–70. Münster, Graubünden, Switzerland, Chapel of St. Ulrich.

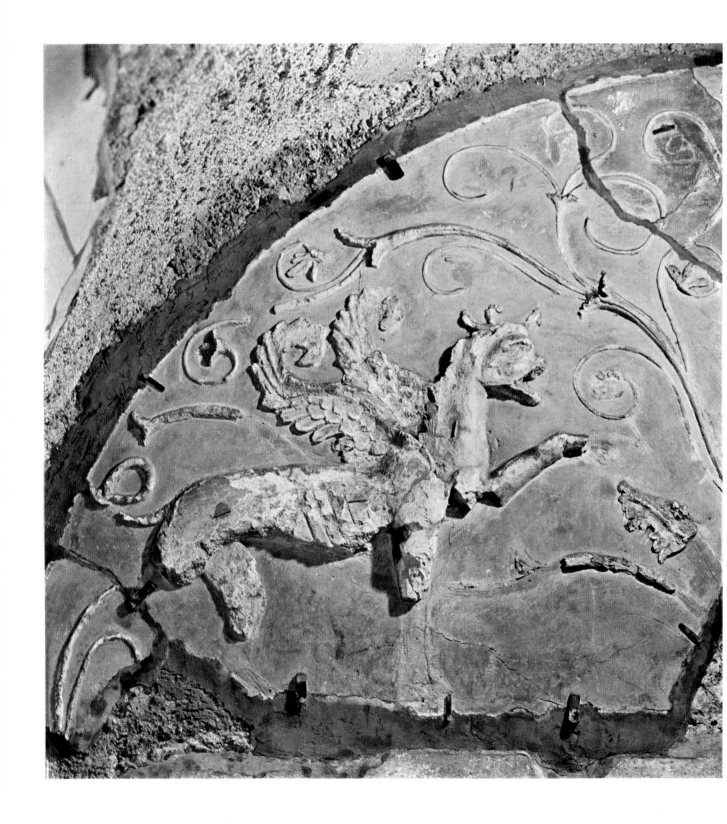

Pl. 276. Rome, House of the Griffins on the Palatine hill, detail of painted and stuccoed lunette in the Room of the Griffins, 2d cent. B.C.

Pl. 277. Cordova, Spain, Mosque (begun 785), detail of decoration of the cupola preceding the mihrab.

Pl. 278. *Above*: Saint venerated by two women, detail of ciborium in S. Ambrogio, Milan, of disputed date. *Below, left*: Christ, detail of the "Noli me tangere" on the Holy Sepulcher in St. Cyriakus, Gernrode, Germany, 1000–1120. *Right*: A saint, detail of north choir screen in St. Michael, Hildesheim, Germany, late 12th cent.

Pl. 279. Tuscan *cassoni*. Stucco decoration over wood. *Above*: A marriage procession, early 15th cent. London, Victoria and Albert Museum. *Below*: Mythological motifs, ca. 1475. Rome, Museo di Palazzo Venezia.

Pl. 280. P. Ligorio, vault decoration in the Casino of Pius IV, 1558–62. Rome, Vatican Gardens.

FIGGO CUPIDO E A SEGUIR
BELVE ATTENDO
CHE NON SI VINCE AMOR
SE NON FUGGENDO

DO LEGGE AI FLUTTI,
E M UBBIDISCE IL MARE
MA LONTANO DAL CIEL
PENA E IL REGNARE.

Pl. 281. *Left:* F. Primaticcio and assistants, sacrificial scene, detail of decoration in the Gallery of Francis I, ca. 1533–44. Fontainebleau, Château. (Cf. XII, pl. 100.) *Right:* A. Vittoria, Neptune and Diana, detail of decoration in the grotto of Villa Barbaro, Maser, near Treviso, Italy, second half of 16th cent. (Cf. VIII, pl. 434.)

Pl. 282. A. Vittoria, vault decoration of the Scala d'Oro, detail, second half of 16th cent. Venice, Doges' Palace.

Pl. 283. Rome, ceiling decorations after designs by C. Maderno. *Above, left*: G. B. Ricci, M. Ferabosco, and others, portico of St. Peter's, detail, ca. 1619. *Right*: M. Ferabosco and others, Cappella Paolina in Palazzo del Quirinale, detail, 1615–17. *Below*: D. Maggi, stairway in Palazzo Mattei, detail, ca. 1618.

Pl. 284. *Left*: C. Mariani, St. Jerome, ca. 1600. Rome, S. Bernardo alle Terme. *Right*: C. Rusconi, Justice, 1686. Rome, S. Ignazio.

Pl. 285. Giulio Romano and Giovanni da Udine, decoration in the loggia of Villa Madama, Rome, 1520–23. (Cf. XII, pl. 51.)

Pl. 286. *Above*: G. L. Bernini, detail of decoration in the dome of S. Maria dell'Assunzione, Ariccia, Italy, 1662–64. *Below*: F. Borromini, detail of ceiling decoration over aisle in St. John Lateran, Rome, mid-17th cent.

Pl. 287. G. B. Cambi (called "Bombarda"), after designs by Palladio (?), allegorical ceiling decoration of the Sala delle Quattro
Porte, detail, in the Doges' Palace, Venice, after 1574.

Pl. 288. G. Mazzoni (attrib.), decoration in the Corridor of the Stuccoes, Palazzo Spada, Rome, mid-16th cent.

Pl. 289. *Above*: A. Raggi, decorative panel with putti, 17th cent. Rome, Church of the Gesù. *Below*: G. Serpotta, allegorical figures, putti, and a scene of the mysteries of the rosary, 1686–1718. Palermo, Sicily, Oratory of S. Zita.

Pl. 290. G. B. Barberini (d. 1666), detail of wall and vault in S. Cecilia, Como, Italy.

Pl. 291. Granada, Sacristy of the Cartuja, detail of interior decoration, ca. 1742–47.

Pl. 292. *Above*: Alcove in Palazzo Barbarigo at S. Maria del Giglio, Venice, 18th cent. *Below, left*: Ceiling of the Hall, Clandon Park, near Guildford, Surrey, second quarter of 18th cent. (Copyright, *Country Life*.) *Right*: Wall decoration, by J. B. Zimmermann, Schäftlarn Abbey church, Bavaria, Germany, detail behind the main altar (altar of wood, with figures slightly over life-size), mid-18th cent.

Pl. 293. J. Christian, The Baptism of Christ, 1768. Ht., 7 ft., 10½ in. Ottobeuren, Germany, Abbey church.

Pl. 294. Stoneleigh Abbey, Kenilworth, Warwickshire, England, detail of the saloon, 18th cent. (Copyright, *Country Life*.)

Pl. 295. G. B. Piranesi, detail of ceiling decoration, S. Maria del Priorato, Rome, ca. 1765.

Pl. 296. R. Adam, the library of Kenwood House, London, 1768. (Copyright, *Country Life.*)

Pl. 297. E. Q. Asam, detail of decoration in the Abbey church, Osterhofen, Germany, ca. 1735–40.

Pl. 298. F. Aprile, scenes from the Passion of Christ, second half of 17th cent. Rome, S. Giovanni dei Fiorentini, Chapel of the Crucifix.

Pl. 299. Sanga, Bandiagara, Mali, Dogon house and granary.

Pl. 300. *Above*: Circle of Bandiagara, Mali, Dogon palace. *Below*: Logone area, Chad, Musgu dwellings and preparation of mud for repairing them.

Pl. 301. Dogon granary shutter, from Mali. Wood, ht., 14⁵/₈ in. Paris, Musée de l'Homme.

Pl. 302. Dogon wood carving, from Mali. *Above*: Trough for ritual family meal. L., 5 ft., 6⁷/₈ in. Paris, Musée de l'Homme. *Below*: Lock, from Bandiagara, collected ca. 1931. L., 18¹/₈ in. Copenhagen, Nationalmuseet.

Pl. 303. Dogon mask representing a black monkey, from Mali. Wood, ht., 13³/₄ in. Paris, Musée de l'Homme.

Pl. 304. *Above, left*: Senufo "firespitter" helmet mask (*waniougo*), from the Ivory Coast. Wood, ht., 36¼ in. Paris, Musée de l'Homme. *Right*: Senufo face mask (*kpélié*), from the Ivory Coast. Wood, ht., 12¼ in. Rome, Museo Pigorini. *Below*: Dogon masks from Bandiagara, Mali. Wood and fiber. *Left*: A foreigner, ht., 41⅜ in. *Right*: Yasigine, the only woman admitted into the *Awa* mask societies, ht., 4 ft., 7⅛ in. Both, Paris, Musée de l'Homme.

Pl. 305. Bambara ancestor figure, collected 1908. Wood, ht., 22 in. Vienna, Museum für Völkerkunde.

Pl. 306. *Above*: Dogon wood sculpture, from Mali. *Left*: Male figure, ht., 23³/₄ in. Brussels, private coll. *Right*: Female figure, ht., 20¹/₈ in. Berlin, Museum für Völkerkunde. *Below*: Senufo female figures bearing containers, from the Ivory Coast. Wood. *Left*: Abidjan, Ivory Coast, Museum. *Right*: Ht., 20⁷/₈ in. Rome, Museo Pigorini.

Pl. 307. Bambara boys' secret society mask (*N'tomo*) surmounted by an antelope, from Ségou region, Mali, collected 1905. Wood, ht., 29 1/8 in. Paris, Musée de l'Homme.

Pl. 308. Senufo carved bird, crowning element of central pole above the roof of a chief's hut, northern Ivory Coast (?). Wood, ht., 13³/₈ in. Rome, Museo Pigorini.

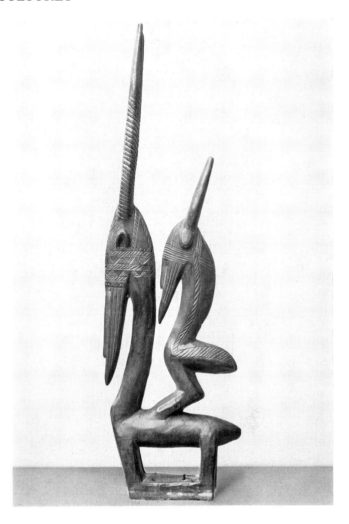

Pl. 309. *Above, left*: Bobo statuette of a crane, from Upper Volta. Painted wood, ht., 21 5/8 in. Brussels, private coll. *Right and below*: Bambara antelope headpieces (*tji wara*), from Mali. *Right*: Wood. London, British Museum. *Below*: Painted wood, metal eyes; l., 5 ft., 7 in. New York, Brooklyn Museum.

Pl. 310. *Above*: Dogon exhibition urns with sculptured lids, from Mali. Wood. *Left*: Paris, Musée de l'Homme. *Right*:
Ht., 23¼ in. Berlin, Museum für Völkerkunde. *Below, left*: Senufo female figure carrying a covered jar,
from Fanterila, collected 1931–32. Wood, ht., 20⅞ in. Copenhagen, Nationalmuseet. *Right*: Headrest supported by ancestor figures, from western Sudan. Wood, ht., 6¼ in. Vienna, Museum für Völkerkunde.

Pl. 311. Jukun stool with female figures, from Wukari, Nigeria. Wood, ht., 22 1/2 in. Berlin, Museum für Völkerkunde.

Pl. 312. Female figurine with leather charm pouches attached at the waist, probably belonging to the Jebba-Tada group of bronzes, 15th cent. (?), collected among the Nupe in Bida, Nigeria. Bronze, ht., 12¹/₄ in. London, British Museum.

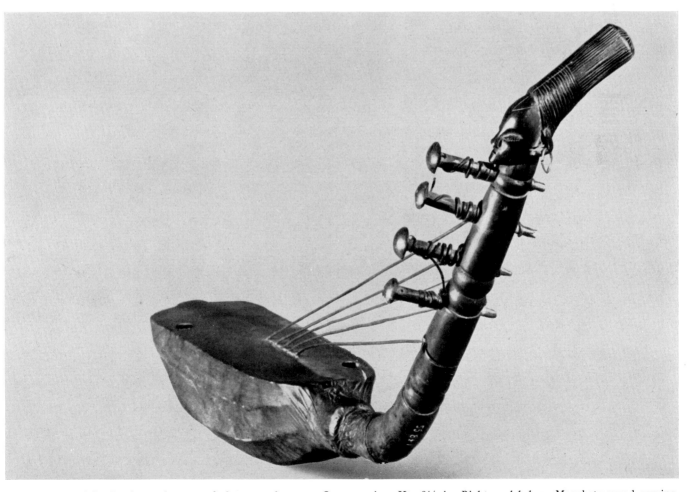

Pl. 313. *Above, left*: Zande earthen vessel, from northeastern Congo region. Ht., 9¹/₂ in. *Right, and below*: Mangbetu wood carving, from northeastern Congo region. *Right*: Pipe bowl. Ht., 3¹/₈ in. *Below*: Arched harp with carved human head. L., 25³/₄ in. All, Tervueren, Belgium, Musée Royal de l'Afrique Centrale.

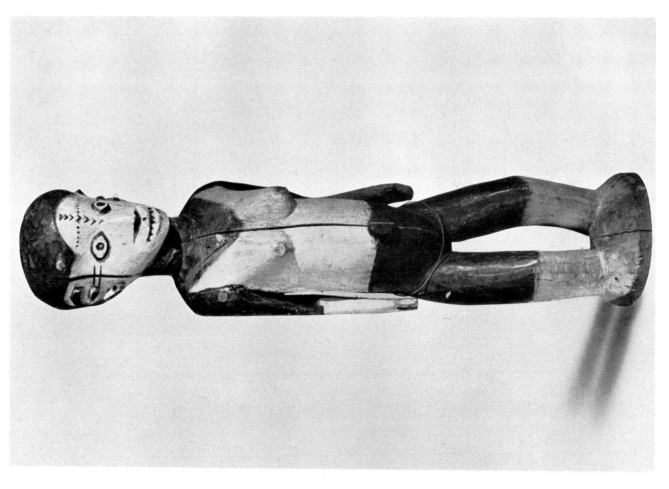

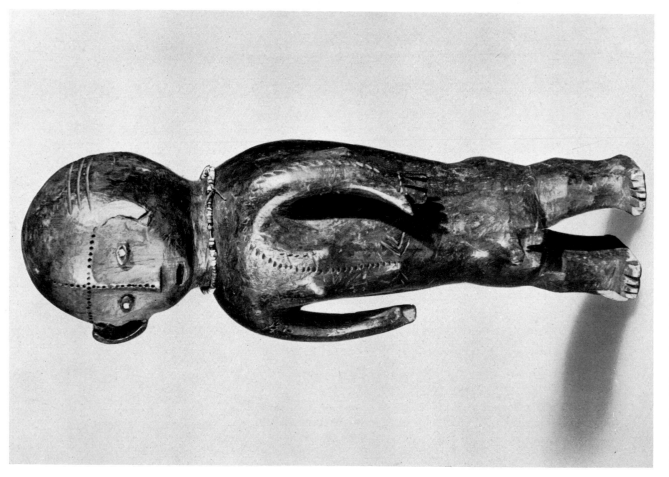

Pl. 314. *Left*: Ngbaka figurine, from northwestern Congo region. Wood, ht., 4 in. *Right*: Mbanza fetish figure, from northwestern Congo region. Wood, ht., 22¹/₈ in. Both, Tervueren, Musée Royal de l'Afrique Centrale.

Pl. 315. Mangbetu slit drum decorated with human figures, from northeastern Congo region, collected 1930. Wood, ht., 21½ in. Florence, Museo Nazionale di Antropologia e Etnologia.

Pl. 316. *Above, left*: Piti effigy jar, from eastern Nigeria, collected 1935. Pottery, ht., 16 1/2 in. Copenhagen, National-museet. *Right*: Southern Zande box surmounted by a carved human head, 19th cent. Bark and wood, ht., 21 1/8 in. *Below, left*: Mangbetu effigy jar, from Uele area, Congo. Pottery, ht., 9 3/8 in. Last two, Tervueren, Belgium, Musée Royal de l'Afrique Centrale. *Right*: Nupe vessel with lid, decorated with modeled birds, from Nigeria. Painted pottery, ht., 12 1/2 in. Oxford, England, Pitt Rivers Museum.

Pl. 317. J. Arp, Forest, 1917. Painted wood, 12$^1/_2$×8$^1/_4$ in. London, Roland Penrose Coll.

Pl. 318. A. Masson, Ibdes in Aragon, 1935. Canvas, 23⁵/₈ × 36³/₈ in. London, Tate Gallery.

Pl. 319. *Left*: M. Duchamp, Le passage de la Vierge à la Mariée, 1912. Canvas, 23³/₈×21¹/₄ in. New York, Museum of Modern Art. *Right*: F. Picabia, Three Seated Nudes. Drawing with gouache. Formerly, Amsterdam, Regnault Coll.

Pl. 320. *Above*: A. Masson, Battle of Fishes, 1927. Oil, sand, and pencil on canvas, 14¹/₄×28³/₄ in. New York, Museum of Modern Art. *Below*: M. Ernst, The Great Forest, 1927. Canvas, 3 ft., 9 in. × 4 ft., 9¹/₂ in. Basel, Kunstmuseum.

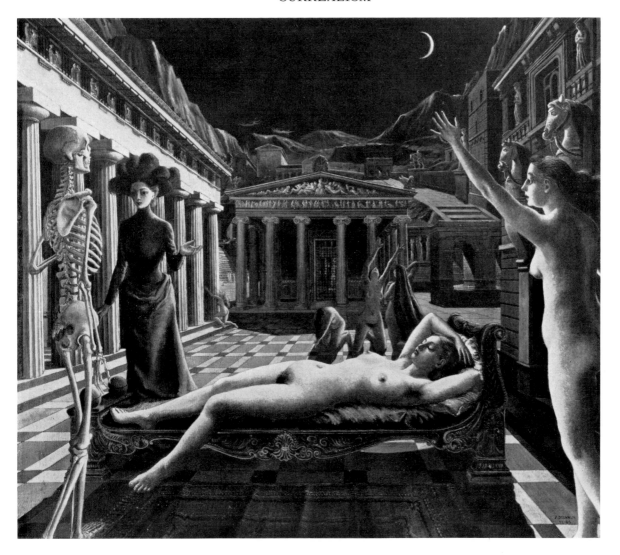

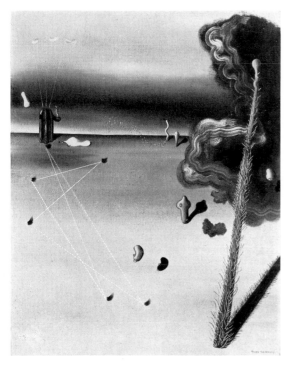

Pl. 321. *Above*: P. Delvaux, Venus Asleep, 1944. Canvas, 5 ft., 8 in. × 6 ft., 6³/₈ in. London, Tate Gallery. *Below, left*:
Y. Tanguy, Mama, Papa is Wounded!, 1927. Canvas, 36¹/₄×28³/₄ in. New York, Museum of Modern Art. *Right*:
Y. Tanguy, The Rapidity of Sleep, 1945. Canvas, 50×40 in. Chicago, Art Institute, J. Winterbotham Coll.

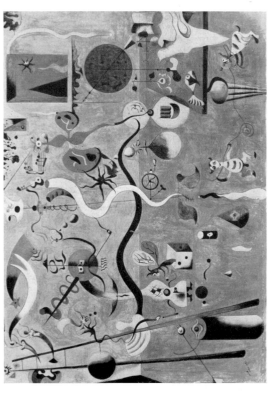

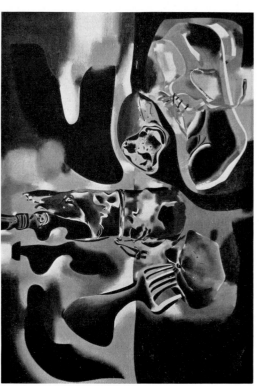

Pl. 322. *Left, above*: J. Miró, Carnival of Harlequin, 1924-25. Canvas, 26 × 36⅝ in. Buffalo, N. Y., Albright-Knox Art Gallery. *Below*: J. Miró, Still Life with an Old Shoe, 1937. New Canaan, Conn., James Thrall Soby Coll. *Right*: G. Sutherland, Thorn Trees, 1945. Oil on cardboard, 42³/₄ × 39³/₄ in. Buffalo, N. Y., Albright-Knox Art Gallery.

Pl. 323. H. Moore, Crowd Looking at a Tied-up Object, 1942. Water color, 16×22 in. Saltwood Castle, Kent, England, Sir Kenneth Clark Coll.

Pl. 324. *Left*: F. Bacon, Figure in a Landscape, 1946. Canvas, 57×50½ in. London, Tate Gallery. *Right*: F. Hundertwasser, Le Bateau Babel-Les 16 Fleuves Sont Arrivés, 1958. Mixed media on canvas, 58×37 in. Paris, Coll. H. Kamer.

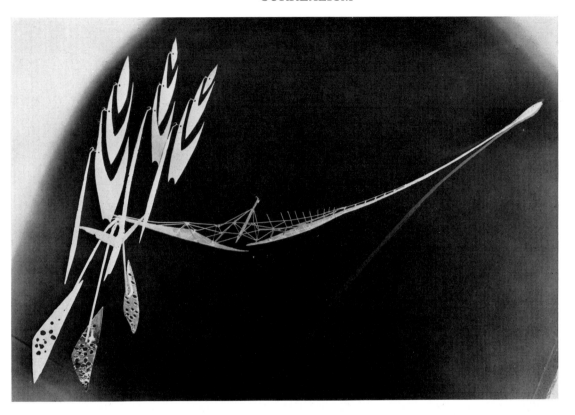

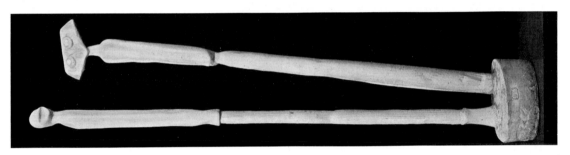

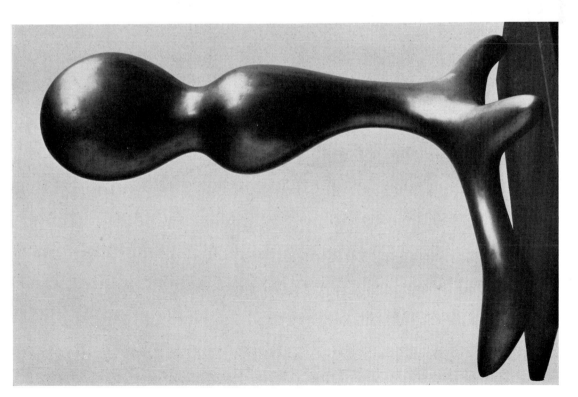

Pl. 325. *Left*: J. Arp, Alou aux griffes, 1942. Bronze, 23×10×17 in. Venice, Galleria Internazionale d'Arte Moderna. *Center*: M. Ernst, Lunar Asparagus, 1935. Plaster, height, 5 ft., 5¼ in. New York, Museum of Modern Art. *Right*: L. Chadwick, Dragonfly, 1951. Iron mobile, length, 9 ft., 8 in. London, Tate Gallery.

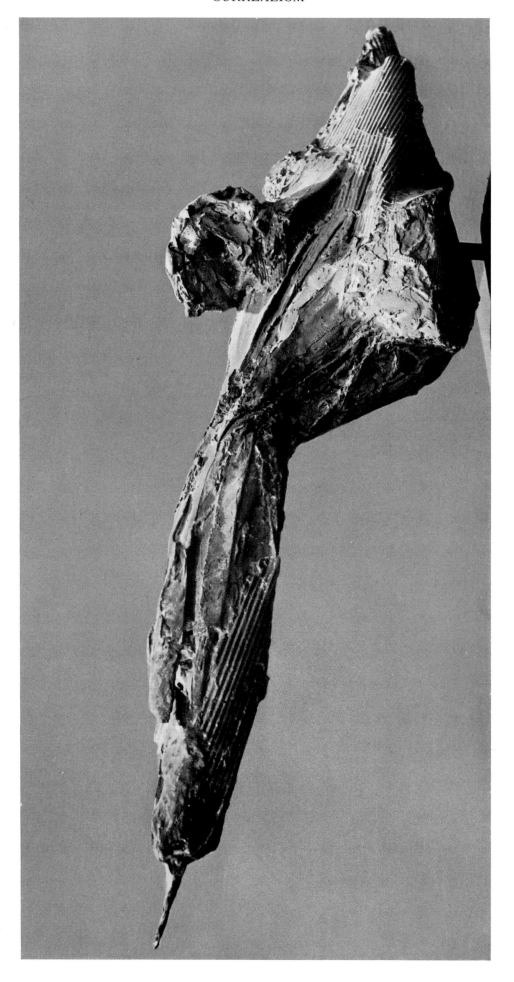

Pl. 326. J. Delahaye, Cavalier II, 1956. Bronze, 5 ft, 5 in. × 1 ft, 7³/₄ in. Paris, Coll. Daniel Cordier and Sweden, private coll.

Pl. 327. J. Miró, The Bullfight, 1945. Canvas, 3 ft., 9 in. × 4 ft., 8³/₄ in. Paris, Musée National d'Art Moderne.

Pl. 328. S. Dali, The Sacrament of the Last Supper, 1955. Canvas, 5 ft, 5⅝ in. × 8 ft, 9⅛ in. Washington, D.C., National Gallery, Chester Dale Coll.

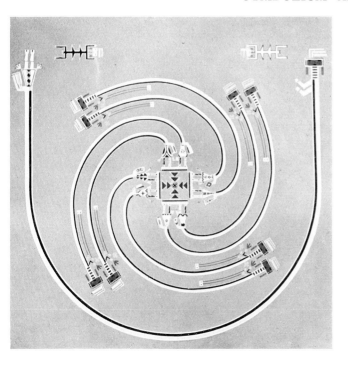

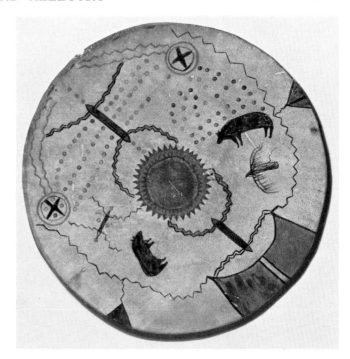

Pl. 329. *Above, left*: Navaho sand painting for the Night Chant or Yebechai ceremony with water symbol and triangular moisture clouds in a square (the four directions), four pairs of Whirling Rainbow People surrounded (protected) by the Rainbow Goddess, and (*at top*) two guards or Messenger Flies. Copy in casein paint, ht., 8 ft. Santa Fe, N. M., Museum of Navajo Ceremonial Art. *Right*: Navaho shield with central sun symbol, two bears (Chiefs of the Mountains), an eagle (Chief of the Sky), zigzag lightning, two directional symbols, and map of an encampment, from Peach Springs, Ariz. Painted deerskin, diam., ca. 20¹/₂ in. Oxford, England, Pitt Rivers Museum. *Below, left*: Bambara *tji wara* representing the antelope, headpiece of a mask for agrarian rites. Wood, ht., 31¹/₂ in. Zurich, Coll. E. Leuzinger. *Right*: Ekoi bifront mask headpiece (Sky and Earth) bearing a female deity, southern Nigeria. Antelope hide over wood. Hamburg, Museum für Völkerkunde.

Pl. 330. Egypt. *Above*: Winged sun disk as a symbol of Horus, on a lintel from Meroë, ca. 300 B.C. Sandstone, 8⅝×27½ in. Copenhagen, Ny Carlsberg Glyptotek. *Below*: Amulets and tomb models. *Left to right, from top*: *Tyet* (protection); plaque with female divinities; *wedjat*, eye of Horus (soundness, completion); *ankh* (life, prosperity); *djed*, pillar (stability); model headrest; *wedjat*. Faïence. Florence, Museo Archeologico (sporadic finds, 24th–25th dynasty); New York, Metropolitan Museum (*ankh* from the tomb of Thutmose IV, 18th dynasty).

Pl. 331. *Above, left*: Horus and Seth twining papyrus and lily (heraldic plants of the two Egypts) around the hieroglyph "to unite,"
with the name of the king and benediction symbols, detail of the throne of Sesostris I, from Lisht, early 12th dynasty. Limestone. Cairo, Egyptian Museum. *Right*: Babylonian *kudurru* with emblems of deities invoked to protect the boundary, 12th
cent. B.C. Black limestone, ht., 13³/₄ in. London, British Museum. *Below*: Old Babylonian relief depicting the prowess of the
culture hero (slaying of Humbaba by Enkidu and Gilgamesh?). Terra cotta, 3¹/₄×5¹/₂ in. Berlin, Staatliche Museen.

Pl. 332. Teotihuacán rain god, pre-Columbian period. *Above*: Symbolic representation on a crenelated architectural ornament. Basalt with traces of red paint, 4 ft., 11½ in. × 4 ft., 9⅛ in. Teotihuacán, Mexico, Museum. *Below*: Geometric stone head on the Temple of Quetzalcoatl (X, PL. 6).

Pl. 333. Buddhist symbolism. Sanchi, Madhya Pradesh, India, Stupa II (*above*) and the Great Stupa, 2d–1st cent. B.C.
Above: The Wheel of the Law with worshipers, symbolizing the First Preaching, pilaster of east entrance. *Below, left*: Trisula (trident, denoting the Buddha, Law, and Order), wheel, and "jar of fortune" with lotus, shown (*at left*) on a detail of the north gate. *Right*: The Buddha, symbolized by two trees, descending from the Heaven of the Thirty-three Gods, panel of north gate.

Pl. 334. Japanese Taizōkai (womb world) mandara, central detail showing the Buddha seated in the eight-petaled lotus (heart of the universe, flower of purity) surrounded by buddhas, bodhisattvas, etc., late 9th–10th cent. (?). Color on silk; full size, 6 ft. × 5 ft., 4 in. Kyoto, Tōji.

Pl. 335. Emblems of cities and states. *Above*: Coins. *Left*: Sybaris, silver stater with bull, 6th cent. B.C. *Center*: Athens, silver tetra-drachma with Athena's owl and an olive twig (for the sacred tree on the Acropolis?), 490–480 B.C. Both, Paris, Cabinet des Médailles. *Right*: Roman republic, gold coin with eagle on a thunderbolt, ca. 187–155 B.C. Rome, Museo Nazionale Romano. *Below*: She-wolf, emblem of Rome, early 5th cent. B.C. (twins added, before 1509). Bronze, i., 44⁷/₈ in. Rome, Palazzo dei Conservatori.

Pl. 336. Atlas supporting the world ring carved with signs of the zodiac and (behind his head) Phosphoros and Hesperos with torches and star (central figure of Jupiter enthroned not original), late 2d cent. Marble. Rome, Torlonia Coll.

Pl. 337. Personification. *Left, above*: Rain (Jupiter Pluvius) in a battle scene, detail of relief on the Column of Marcus Aurelius, Rome, last quarter of 2d cent. Marble. *Below*: Sun (Sol Invictus) on his chariot, rising from the ocean (Oceanus), with the torchbearing Lucifer before him, medallion on the Arch of Constantine, Rome, ca. 312–15. Marble. (Cf. counterpart with Moon, IX, PL. 54.) *Right*: Autumn bearing fruit, from the Constantinian villa at Daphne-Harbie, Antioch, Turkey, ca. 4th cent. Mosaic. Paris, Louvre. (Cf. Summer and Spring, IX, PL. 73.)

Pl. 338. Personification. *Above, left*: Fortune with cornucopia and the tiller resting on the world globe, found in Ostia, Roman copy of a Greek original of 4th cent. B.C. (tiller and globe, Roman additions). Marble, ht., 7 ft., 3 in. Rome, Vatican Museums. *Right*: Victory with palm, wings, and wreath, late 3d cent. Marble. Florence, Boboli Gardens. *Below*: The Nile with 16 putti (signifying the cubits of the Nile flood) and symbols of fruitfulness, from the sanctuary of Isis and Serapis in Rome, Roman adaptation of a Hellenistic original. Marble, l., 10 ft., 2 in. Rome, Vatican Museums.

Pl. 339. Personification. *Above, left*: Representations of Etruscan *populi*: (*left to right*) seafaring hero with helm (Vetulonians), enthroned goddess (Vulcians), and the hero-priest Tarchon (Tarquinians), on a relief from Caere (mod. Cerveteri, Italy), Roman imperial period. Marble. Rome, Lateran Museums. *Right*: Two of the Roman provinces, reliefs from the Temple of Divus Hadrian, dedicated A.D. 145, Rome. Marble; ht. of panel, 5 ft., 9 in. Rome, Palazzo dei Conservatori. *Below*: Female figure symbolizing the region of the hunt (Africa or Arabia?), with elephant-tusk cornucopia, tigress, elephant, phoenix, and a cult tree, mosaic in the corridor of the Great Hunt, Roman villa at Casale, near Piazza Armerina, Sicily, 4th cent.

Pl. 340. *Left*: Mosaic alluding to human transience: skull, with level (inexorable justice), butterfly (the soul), and wheel (Nemesis, Fortune), flanked by draped lance and pedum (cessation of earthly activities), from Pompeii, 1st cent. Ht., 18½ in. Naples, Museo Nazionale. *Right*: The phoenix as a sacred bird identified with the sun, from the House of the Phoenix, Daphne-Harbie, Antioch, Turkey, 5th cent. Mosaic; ht. of bird, 6 ft., 5 in. Paris, Louvre.

Pl. 341. Christian symbols. *Above, left, and center:* Fish with loaves (Christ and the Eucharist) and anchor (the Cross, salvation), wall paintings in the catacombs of Callixtus (*left*) and Pamphilus (*center*), Rome, ca. 3d cent. *Right:* Peacock (the Resurrection), sculptured slab, 12th cent. (?), found at Constantinople. Stone, $30^3/_4 \times 46^3/_4$ in. Istanbul, Archaeological Museums. *Below, left:* The Lamb of God, northern Italy (?), second half of 5th cent. Silver set with garnets on an ivory diptych; full ht, $14^3/_4$ in. Milan, Cathedral Treasury. *Center:* Pelican piercing its breast to feed its young (the Eucharist), detail of altar cloth, Milan, ca. 1450. Milan, Museo Poldi Pezzoli. *Right:* Doves around the emblem of Christ, detail of altar cloth, Florence, 1449. San Gimignano, Italy, Museo di Arte Sacra.

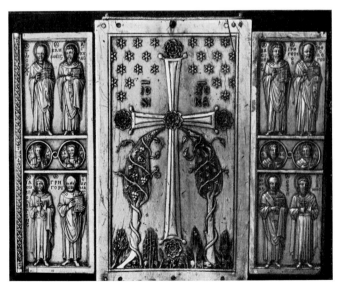

Pl. 342. Christian symbolism. *Left*: Paradise, with Adam and animals, adaptation (or copy?) of the theme of Orpheus, from the vicinity of Mainz, late 4th cent. Ivory, ht., 11⁵/₈ in. Florence, Museo Nazionale. *Right, above*: Sheep (believers) adoring the Cross with the letters alpha and omega (representing Christ), the Felix sarcophagus, early 8th cent. Marble. Ravenna, S. Apollinare in Classe. *Center*: Medallions with the symbols of the Four Evangelists, on the altar frontal of Sigwald, ca. 762–86. Marble. Cividale del Friuli, Italy, Cathedral. *Below*: Cross appearing in the Garden of Paradise, with the inscription "Jesus Christ Conquers," verso of the central panel of the Harbaville triptych (on the wings, saints), Constantinople, ca. mid-10th cent. Ht., 9¹/₂ in. Ivory. Paris, Louvre.

Pl. 343. Christian symbolism. *Above*: Mater Ecclesia, illumination of an Exultet from Montecassino, Italy, late 11th cent. Rome, Vatican Library (Cod. Barb. lat. 592, fol. 1). *Below, left*: The Victory of Christianity over Paganism, Venetian school, ca. 1400. Panel, 37³/₈×31¹/₈ in. Stuttgart, Staatsgalerie. *Right*: Pacino di Buonaguida (active ca. 1303–20), The Tree of the Cross, with scenes of the life of Christ in medallions on the branches. Panel, 8 ft., 1¹/₂ in. × 4 ft., 11¹/₂ in. Florence, Accademia.

Pl. 344. *Above*: Master of the Assisi Vault (Maestro delle Vele), the mystic marriage of St. Francis to Poverty, first half of 14th cent. Fresco. Assisi, Italy, S. Francesco, Lower Church. *Below*: Andrea da Firenze, St. Thomas Aquinas enthroned between the Doctors of the Old and New Testaments, with personifications of the Virtues, Sciences, and Liberal Arts, ca. 1365. Fresco. Florence, S. Maria Novella, Spanish Chapel.

Pl. 345. *Above*: The Holy Lamb with angels, Virtues and Vices, Wise and Foolish Virgins, and signs of the zodiac with labors of the months, 12th cent., St-Pierre-de-la-Tour, Aulnay-de-Saintonge, France. *Below, left*: Labors of the months, detail, Pieve di S. Maria, Arezzo, Italy, 13th cent. *Right*: Giovanni Pisano, holy-water stoup with the Theological and Cardinal Virtues. Marble. Pistoia, Italy, S. Giovanni Fuorcivitas.

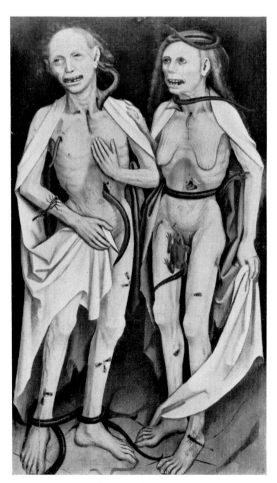 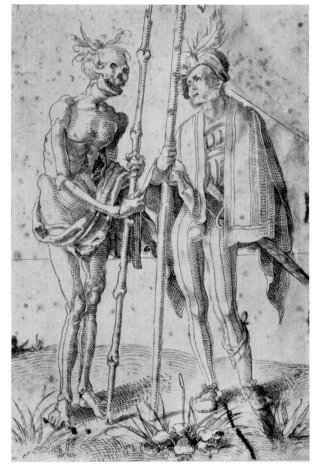

Pl. 346. Death. *Above*: The Triumph of Death, fresco series with iconography from Petrarch, detail with the three living and the three dead (corpses in various stages of decomposition), Sienese school, late 14th cent. Subiaco, Italy, Sacro Speco. *Below, left*: Les Amants Trépassés, by an unknown artist on the back of a panel by M. Schongauer, 1469 (?). Panel, 25¹/₂ × 15³/₄ in. Strasbourg, Musée des Beaux-Arts (*en dépôt*, Musée de l'Œuvre Notre-Dame). *Right*: H. Baldung-Grien, Death and the Lansquenet, 1503. Pen drawing, 11 × 7³/₄ in. Modena, Italy, Galleria Estense.

Pl. 347. *Above, left*: Divisions of the Empire offering tribute to Otto III, detail of illumination in the Gospel Book of Otto III, Reichenau school, ca. 1000. Munich, Bayerische Staatsbibliothek (Clm. 4453, fol. 23 v). *Above, right, and below*: Board covers (*tavolette*) of public account books, Siena, Italy. *Above, right*: Benvenuto di Giovanni, the Commune's finances in time of peace and war, *tavoletta di Gabella* (Collector's office), 1468. Ht., 21 in. *Below, left*: Il Vecchietta (attrib.), the coronation of Pope Pius II, Siena between two chimeras, and heraldic devices, *tavoletta di Biccherna* (Treasury), 1460. Ht., 23 in. *Right*: Sano di Pietro, Wisdom emanating from God, *tavoletta di Gabella*, 1471. Ht., 22½ in. Last three, Siena, Archivio di Stato.

Pl. 348. *Above, left*: Hope on her palace, holding out cords to the towers of earthly power, virtue, God, health and life, and love, illumination in *Documenti d'Amore* by Francesco da Barberino, 1309–13. Rome, Vatican Library (Cod. Barb. lat. 4076, fol. 66). *Right*: The Garden of Love, in a Lombardian *De Sphaera*, 15th cent. Illumination. Modena, Italy, Biblioteca Estense (Cod. lat. 209, fol. 10r). *Below*: The Triumph of Love, showing Aristotle ridden by Phyllis and Samson and Delilah, *desco da parto* (cf. XII, PL. 566), Florence, mid-15th cent. Panel, diam. 24¼ in. London, National Gallery.

Pl. 349. Love. *Above*: Master of René of Anjou, Heart, overcome by the black knight at the perilous bridge, is saved from the water by Hope (cf. V, PL. 385), from *Le livre du Cœur d'Amour épris*, ca. 1457. Illumination. Vienna, Nationalbibliothek (Cod. 2597, fol. 21v). *Below, left*: Bartolommeo Veneto (?), Lovers looking into a mirror, with flower in glass, allusive to vanity and the transience of love, verso of a portrait, first half of 16th cent. Panel, 23½×17¾ in. *Right*: G. Baglione (1571–1644), Sacred and Profane Love. Canvas, ca. 6×4 ft. Last two, Berlin, Staatliche Museen.

Pl. 350. Time. *Above*: N. Poussin (1594–1665), A Dance to the Music of Time, with personifications of Pleasure, Fame, Wealth, and Poverty. Canvas, 32½×41½ in. London, Wallace Coll. *Below*: S. Vouet, Time Vanquished by Hope, Love, and Beauty, 1627. Canvas, 42⅛×56 in. Madrid, Prado.

Pl. 351. *Above*: A. Mantegna (1431–1506), Allegory of Calumny, based on descriptions of a painting by Apelles: Calumny, crowned, dragging Innocence by the hair and attended by Deception and Envy, is introduced to a judge attended by Suspicion and Ignorance; at right, Penitence and Truth. Pen and brown ink with touches of white, $8^{1}/_{2} \times 15$ in. London, British Museum. *Below, left*: P. Veronese, Merit Crowned by Glory, ca. 1561. Fresco. Maser, near Treviso, Italy, Villa Barbaro (now Volpi), Sala dell'Olimpo. *Right*: S. Vouet, Allegory of the Human Soul, personified by Intellect, Memory, and Will, ca. 1625. Canvas, 5 ft., $10^{1}/_{2}$ in. × 4 ft., $8^{3}/_{4}$ in. Rome, Palazzo dei Conservatori.

Pl. 352. *Above, left*: Jan Brueghel the Elder, Sight, with a woman contemplating a painting of the Healing of the Blind, 1617, one of the series on the Five Senses. (Cf. V, Pl. 298.) Canvas, 25⁵/₈×42⁷/₈ in. Madrid, Prado. *Below*: L. Giordano (1632–1705), Africa. Canvas. Naples, Palazzo Reale. *Right*: A. Corradini, Modesty, 1751. Marble. Naples, S. Maria della Pietà dei Sangro.

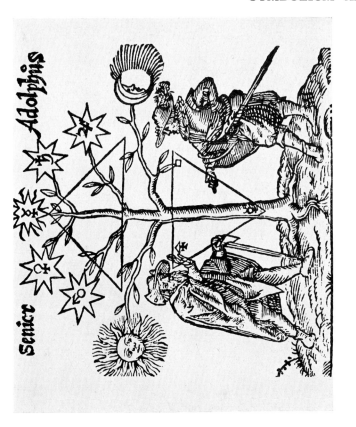

Pl. 353. Occult symbolism. *Left:* Frontispiece of *Kabbala denudata*, I, by C. Knorr von Rosenroth, Sulzbach, 1677, showing Wisdom walking toward the Palace of Secrets beneath a sephiric symbol. *Right, above:* Illustration in *Azoth*, a treatise on alchemy by Basilius Valentinus (ed. and trans. J. Laigneau), Paris, 1659. *Below:* Masonic diploma, Italy, 19th cent. Formerly, Milan, Museo del Risorgimento e Raccolte Storiche. (Destroyed in 1943.)

Pl. 354. The arts. *Left, above*: S. Botticelli, Lorenzo Tornabuoni presented to the Seven Liberal Arts, ca. 1486. Detached fresco. Paris, Louvre. *Below*: L. Seitz, scene symbolizing unison between Pagan Art and Christian Art, the latter being crowned, against a background of ancient monuments and churches of Rome, 1883-87. Fresco. Rome, Vatican Museums, Galleria dei Candelabri. *Right*: M. Rosselli (1578-1651), The Fine Arts. Canvas, 8 ft. × 5 ft., 7 in. Rome, Galleria Colonna.

Pl. 355. *Left, above*: Leonardo da Vinci, Church and Empire, depicting a boat (the Church) with a wolf (the Papacy) pointing the compass at an eagle on the globe (the Emperor, or world dominion), ca. 1510. Drawing in red chalk, 6³/₄×11 in. Windsor, England, Royal Colls. *Below*: G. Vasari, Paul III receiving the homage of the nations, 1546. Fresco. Rome, Palazzo della Cancelleria. *Right*: J. Tintoretto, Jupiter proclaiming Venice Queen of the Adriatic, 1577-78. Canvas. Venice, Doges' Palace.

Pl. 356. G. Guglielmi, The Blessings of Peace, symbolized by the flourishing of the arts and sciences, agriculture, and commerce, 1760–62. Fresco. Vienna, Schönbrunn Castle.

Pl. 357. *Above*: Alalakh (Tell Atchana), Syria, Palace of Niqmepa, entrance from the forecourt, 15th cent. B.C. *Below*: Megiddo, Israel, Solomonic stables, with hitching posts and mangers, 1000–800 B.C.

Pl. 358. Head, from Jericho, Neolithic period. Painted clay with shell eyes, ht., 8⁵/₈ in. Jerusalem, Jordan, Palestine Archaeological Museum.

Pl. 359. King Idri-mi, from Alalakh, Syria, ca. 15th cent. B.C. Dolomite and magnesite, ht., 41 in. London, British Museum.

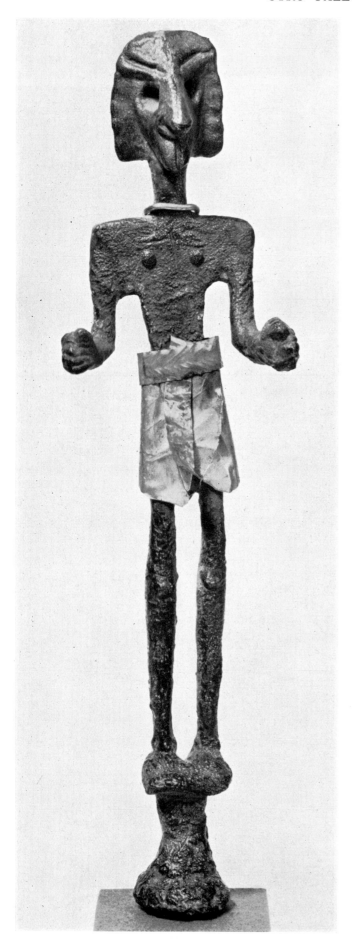 

Pl. 360. *Left*: Statuette of a god, from Ugarit (Ras Shamra), Syria, early 2d millennium B.C. Silver and sheet gold, ht., 11 in. *Right*: Female divinity, from Beirut (?), 2d millennium B.C. Bronze, ht., 6¹/₂ in. Both, Paris, Louvre.

Pl. 361. Statuette of a god (Resheph?), from Minet el-Beida, Syria, 15th–14th cent. B.C. Bronze and silver with sheet-gold crown and gold armlet; ht., 7 in. Paris, Louvre.

Pl. 362. Phoenician female head, found at Nimrud in Assyria, 9th–8th cent. B.C. Colored ivory, ht., 6½ in. Baghdad, Iraq Museum.

Pl. 363. Ivories, 9th–8th cent. B.C. (except *above, left*). *Above, left*: Head, inlay for furniture (?) in Egyptian-Syrian style, from Lachish (Tell ed-Duweir), Israel, late Bronze Age. Ht., ca. 2 in. Jerusalem, Jordan, Palestine Archaeological Museum. *Middle*: Fragment of a box, from Hazor. Ht., 2¹/₂ in. Ayelet-Hashachar, Israel, Hazor Museum. *Right*: Infant Horus on a lotus blossom, plaque, originally with insets and gold foil, from Samaria. Ht., ca. 2¹/₂ in. Jerusalem, Palestine Archaeological Museum. *Center, left*: Stag, with encrusted eye and traces of gold, from Arslan Tash, Syria. L., ca. 5 in. Paris, Louvre. *Right*: Lion grappling with bull, from Samaria, 1⁵/₈×4¹/₂ in. *Below, left*: Plaque with stylized palm, from Samaria. Ht., 3³/₄ in. Last two, Jerusalem, Palestine Archaeological Museum. *Middle*: Plaque with Egyptian motif, from Arslan Tash. W., 3 in. *Right*: Figure of a Syrian prince (?), from Arslan Tash. Ht., 7 in. Last two, Paris, Louvre.

Pl. 364. *Above and below, left and right*: Elements of a Canaanite shrine, from Hazor, second half of 2d millennium B.C. Basalt. Ayelet-Hashachar, Israel, Hazor Museum. *Above*: Orthostat with crouching lion. Ht., 13 in. *Below, left*: Statue of the male deity. Ht., 15³/₄ in. *Right*: Stele. Ht., 18 in. *Below, center*: Anthropoid sarcophagus, from Beth Shan, Israel, second half of 2d millennium B.C. Pottery, ht., 6 ft., 1 in. Jerusalem, Jordan, Palestine Archaeological Museum.

Pl. 365. *Above*: Basalt reliefs, Bronze Age. *Left*: Warrior, from Rujm el-'Abd, near Shihan, Jordan. Ht., 3 ft., 4¹/₂ in. Paris, Louvre.
Right: Divinities and a suppliant, from Balu'ah, Jordan. Ht., 6 ft. Amman, Jordan, Archaeological Museum. *Below, left*:
Orthostat with scenes of combat between lion and dog, from northern Syria (?), found at Beth Shan, Israel, probably 14th
cent. B.C. Stone, ht., ca. 3 ft. Jerusalem, Jordan, Palestine Archaeological Museum. *Right*: Stele with warrior, from Arslan
Tash, Syria, 9th–8th cent. B.C. Stone, ht., 4 ft., 9 in. Istanbul, Archaeological Museums.

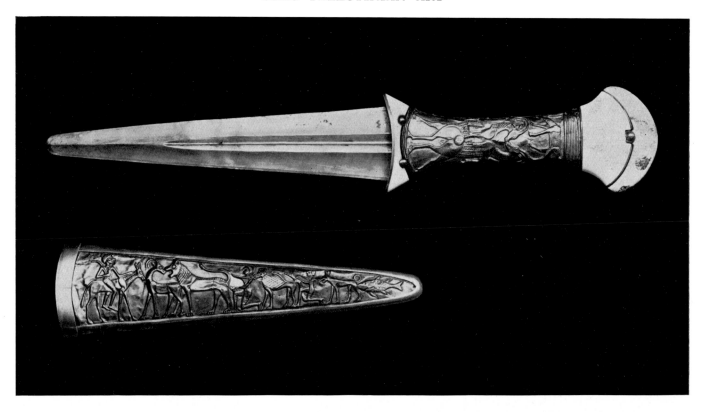

Pl. 366. *Above*: Dagger, from Byblos, Lebanon, ca. first half of 2d millennium B.C. Hilt and sheath of embossed and engraved gold, l., 13³/₄ in. Beirut, National Museum. (Restored.) *Center, left*: Canaanite "mother goddess" plaques, from Tell el-Ajjul, Israel, ca. 1500 B.C. Sheet gold, l., ca. 3¹/₈ in. *Below, left*: Syrian seal impression, mid-2d millennium B.C. Last two, Oxford, Ashmolean Museum. *Right*: Shrine model, from Beth Shan, Israel, 11th cent. B.C. Pottery, ht., 19³/₄ in. Philadephia, University Museum.

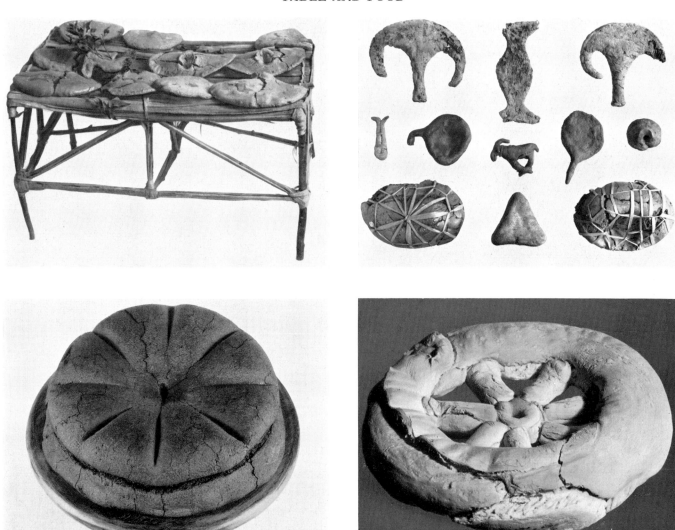

Pl. 367. *Above*: Bread from the tomb of Kha, Thebes, 18th dynasty: loaves on a cane table (*left*), fan and animal shapes, and loaves tied with palm leaves. Turin, Museo Egizio. *Center, left*: Bread from Pompeii, carbonized after the eruption of Vesuvius, A.D. 79. Naples, Museo Nazionale. *Right*: Wheel-shaped bread from Calabria, Italy. Rome, Museo delle Arti e Tradizioni Popolari. *Below*: Traditional Christmas bread of unleavened dough, Czechoslovakia. Basel, Schweizerisches Museum für Volkskunde.

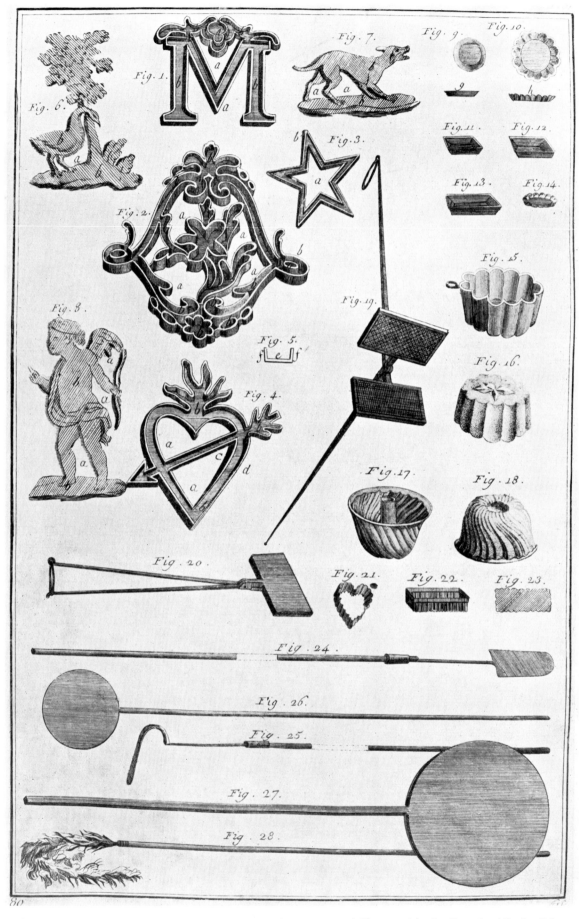

Pl. 368. Utensils (molds, baking pans, waffle irons, peels, cutters, etc.) illustrated in the *Encyclopédie des Sciences, des Arts, et des Métiers* (reproduced from the Lucca edition, 1758–76, Tome VIII, 1773, *Planches pour L'Encyclopédie des Sciences, des Arts Libéraux, et des Arts Méchaniques*).

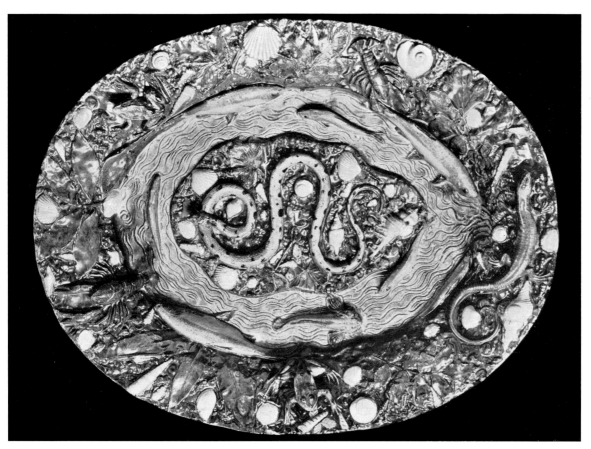

Pl. 369. *Above*: Patera decorated with fish, Apulian or Campanian style, Italy, 4th cent. B.C. Terra cotta, diam., 7⁷/₈ in. Rome, Museo di Villa Giulia. *Below*: B. Palissy, platter in *style rustique*, second half of 16th cent. Majolica. Paris, Louvre.

Pl. 370. *Above*: Offering table, detail of the Papyrus of Queen Netchemet, Egypt, 21st dynasty, ca. 1050 B.C. London, British Museum.
Below, left: Banquet scene, detail of Etruscan wall painting, Tomb of the Shields, Tarquinia, Italy, 3d–2d cent. B.C. *Right*:
Table with silverware, wall painting from Pompeii, 1st cent. Naples, Museo Nazionale.

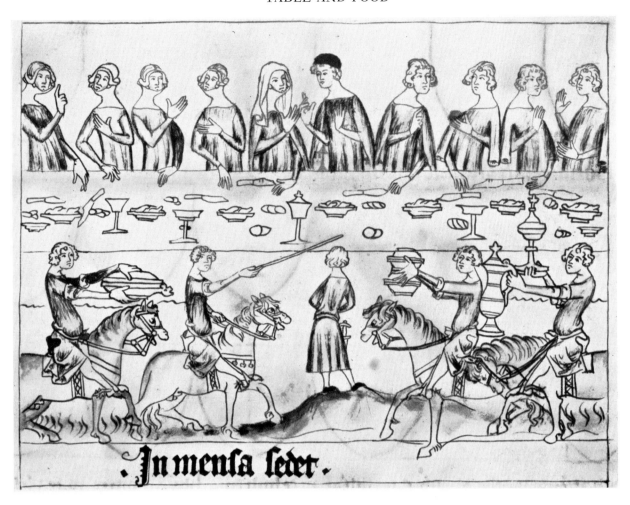

Pl. 371. *Above*: Open-air banquet with servingmen on horseback, given by Archbishop Balduin in Trier, June 2, 1308, from the Codex Balduineus, 14th cent. Pen and wash drawing. Koblenz, Germany, Staatsarchiv. *Below*: Banquet table, Düsseldorf, 1585, with decorations (probably of sugar or wax) in the form of coats of arms and a castle with surroundings, from D. Graminäus, *Festberichte*, Cologne, 1587. Engraving.

Pl. 372. *Left, above:* L. tom Ring the Younger, kitchen scene, The Marriage at Cana, 1562. Canvas. Formerly, Berlin, Kaiser Friedrich Museum (destroyed). *Below:* Annibale Carracci, The Bean Eater, ca. 1585. Canvas, 22½×26¾ in. Rome, Galleria Colonna. *Right:* B. Franceschini ("Volterrano"), men at table, detail of A Joke on the Country Parson Arlotto (VI, Pl. 70), 17th cent. Tempera on canvas. Florence, Uffizi.

Pl. 373. *Left, above*: Banquet in the Castle of Rivoli, near Turin, for the birthday of Madama Reale, showing one of four rooms decorated for the successive courses, illustration from the dedicatory volume, *Il dono del Re de l'Alpi*, 1645, by T. Borgonio. Turin, Biblioteca Nazionale (Ris. V. q. 60). *Below*: Wedding feast of Prince Anthony of Saxony and Princess Caroline of Savoy, 1781, by J. G. B. Theil. Colored engraving by C. G. Geyser. Turin, Museo Civico. *Right*: Banquet in Casa Nani, Venice, 1755. Canvas, 4 ft., 3¹⁄₈ in. × 3 ft., 2¹⁄₄ in. Venice, Museo Correr.

Pl. 374. Centerpiece in the form of a Temple of Love, after a model by J. J. Kändler, ca. 1750. Painted Meissen porcelain in 114 separate pieces, ht., 45⅝ in. Frankfort on the Main, Germany, Museum für Kunsthandwerk.

Pl. 375. Gogonendranath Tagore, The Well. Water color, 12¹/₂×9¹/₈ in. Trivandrum, Kerala, India, Sri Chitra Art Gallery.

Pl. 376. Abanindranath Tagore, Alone. Water color, 11×9 in. Trivandrum, Kerala, India, Sri Chitra Art Gallery.

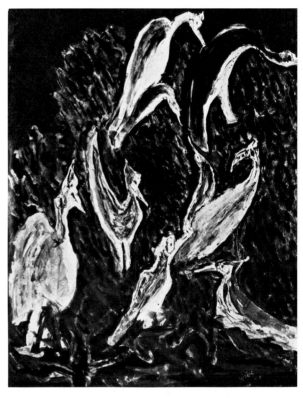

Pl. 377. Rabindranath Tagore. *Above, left*: The Bird. Water color, 8¹/₈×7 in. Trivandrum, Kerala, India, Sri Chitra Art Gallery. *Right*: Figures of Birds. Water color, 21¹/₂×16⁷/₈ in. *Below*: Composition. Water color, 5×9³/₄ in. Last two, Santiniketan, India, Visva-Bharati Rabindra-Sadana.

Pl. 378. Rabindranath Tagore, Male figure. Water color, 14×7¹/₄ in. Santiniketan, India, Visva-Bharati Rabindra-Sadana.

Pl. 379. Censer with lid representing the Island of the Immortals, China, Han dynasty (206 B.C.–A.D. 221). Bronze, ht., 7¹/₄ in. London, Victoria and Albert Museum.

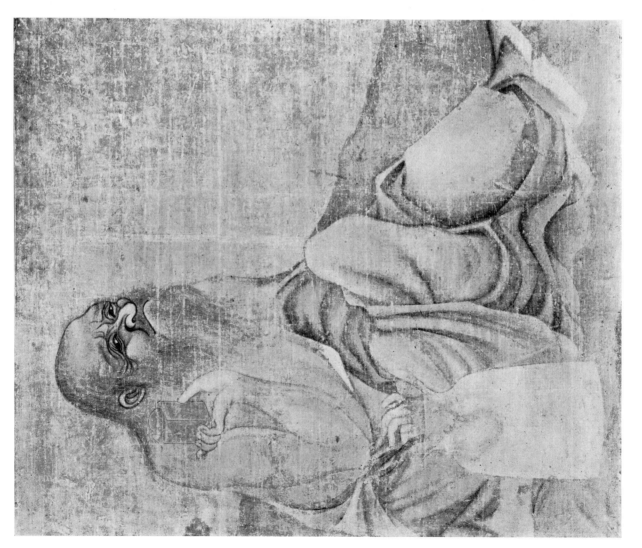

Pl. 380. *Left*: A Taoist Immortal, Yüan period (1260–1368). Ink and color on paper, 42×36¹/₂ in. Stockholm, Östasiatiska Museet. *Right*: Liu Chün, Three Immortals Dancing around a Toad, early 16th cent. Ink and color on silk, 52¹/₂×33 in. Boston, Museum of Fine Arts.

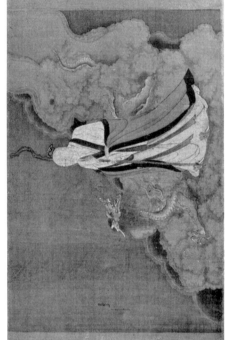

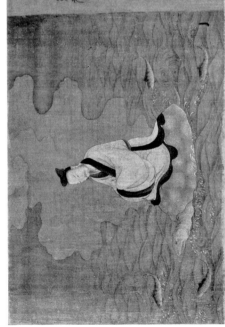

Pl. 381. Chang Wu, The Nine Songs of Ch'ü Yüan, details of a hand scroll, 14th cent. Ink and color on silk, ht., 9³/₄ in. (full l., ca. 20 ft.). Boston, Museum of Fine Arts.

Pl. 382. Ch'ên Hung-shou (1599–1652), Lady and the God of Longevity. Ink and slight color on paper, 6 ft., 3 in. × 3 ft., 5¹/₄ in. London, British Museum.

Pl. 383. Li Kung-lin (d. 1106), Realms of the Immortals, detail of hand scroll. Ink on paper; full size, 1 ft., 4½ in. × 31 ft., 1 in. Washington, D.C., Freer Gallery of Art. (Cf. IX, pl. 136.)

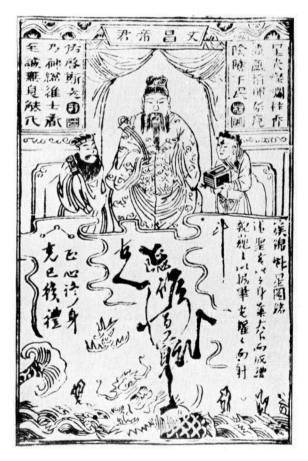

Pl. 384. The popular Taoist pantheon in prints of the Ch'ing period (1644–1912). *Above, left*: The Jade August One, Yü-huang, and his court. *Right*: The god of alchemy (figure at right). *Below, left*: The Great Emperor of Letters, Wên-ch'ang Ti-chün, with attendants and (below) K'uei Hsing, another divinity of literature. *Right*: The Three Agents (of heaven, earth, and water).

Pl. 385. The popular Taoist pantheon in prints of the Ch'ing period (1644–1912). *Above, left*: The goddess of lightning and the gods of rain and wind. *Right*: The Lady Horse-head. *Below, left*: A soul examined by the god of walls and moats before Kuan-ti, a war divinity. *Right*: The Transcendent Official pursuing a fox demon.

Pl. 386. Painted tapa with cobweb and flower designs, from Samoa, collected 1882. Full size, 6 ft., 8³/₄ in. × 4 ft., 5¹/₂ in.
Copenhagen, Nationalmuseet.

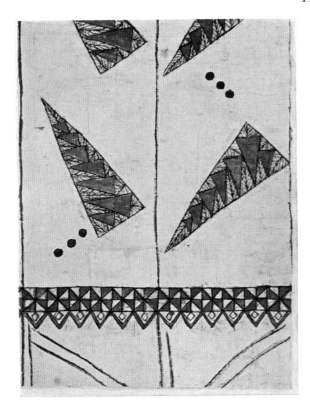

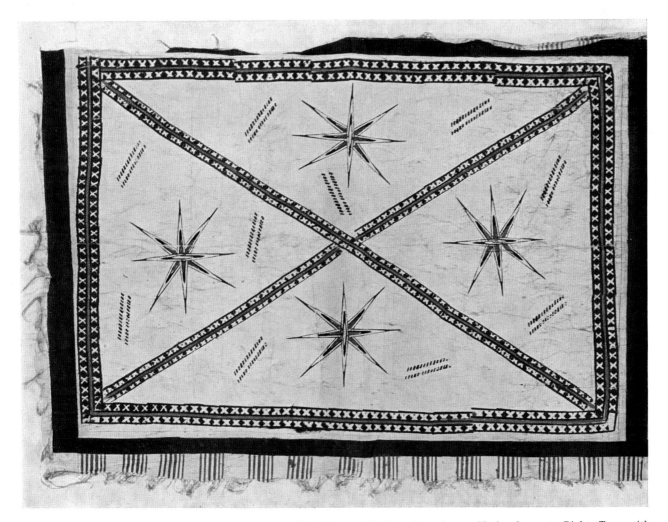

Pl. 387. *Above, left*: Tapa, from the Tonga Islands. Full size, ca. 16×5 ft. Copenhagen, Nationalmuseet. *Right*: Tapa with mat patterns, from the Fiji Islands (shown rolled). Full ht., ca. 32 in. Cambridge, England, University Museum of Archaeology and Ethnology. *Below*: Tapa, from the Fiji Islands, collected 1875. Ht., ca. 29¹/₂ in. Copenhagen, Nationalmuseet.

Pl. 388. *Above, left*: Painted tapa, from the Fiji Islands, collected ca. 1900. Salem, Mass., Peabody Museum. *Center*: Tapa printed by the rubbing process, with overpainting, from Samoa. *Right*: Tapa with mat patterns resembling Indonesian prototypes, from the Fiji Islands. *Below, left*: Painted tapa, from the Fiji Islands. *Center*: Fringed shirt, from Tahiti. *Right*: Tapa overpainted on a rubbed design (now faded), from Samoa. Last five, Hamburg, Museum für Völkerkunde.

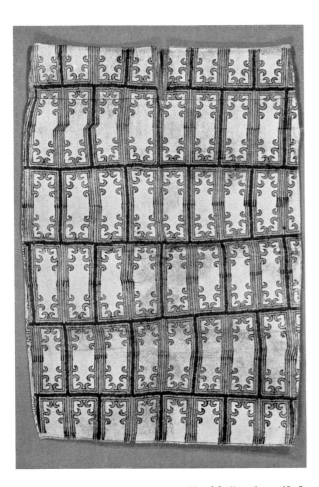 

Pl. 389. *Above*: Mortuary banner (?) with lizard motif, from Collingwood Bay, New Guinea. Full size, 2 ft., 1 in. × 3 ft., 10 in. London, British Museum. *Below, left*: Poncho, from southeast Bolivia, acquired 1925. Full size, 3 ft., 9½ in. × 2 ft., 8½ in. Oxford, Pitt Rivers Museum. *Right*: Medje tapa, from the Uele area, Congo, collected 1928. Full size, 4 ft., 8½ in. × 4 ft., 4 in. Tervueren, Belgium, Musée Royal de l'Afrique Centrale.

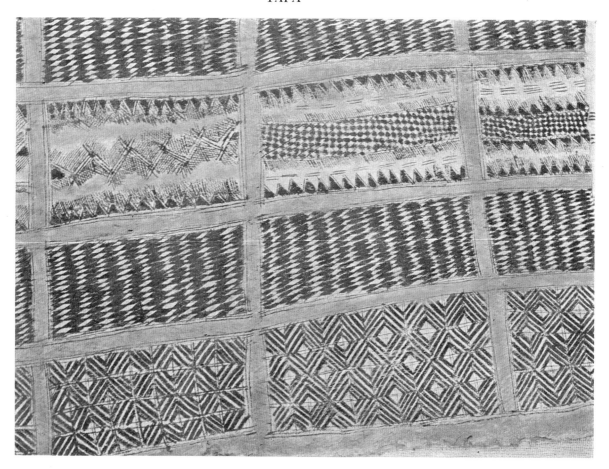

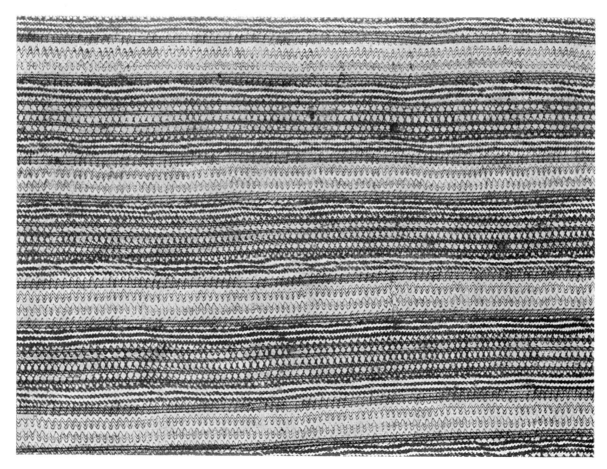

Pl. 390. *Above*: Painted tapa with mat patterns, from the Santa Cruz Islands. *Below*: Tapa printed with the liner, from the Hawaiian Islands. Both, Hamburg, Museum für Völkerkunde.

Pl. 391. Abraham entertaining the three angels, detail showing Sarah handing bread and drink to Abraham, Lower Saxony, probably
third quarter of 12th cent. Wool and linen, ht., ca. 4 ft. Halberstadt, Germany, Cathedral, choir.

Pl. 392. The Nine Heroes Tapestries, detail with Joshua and King David, workshop of N. Bataille (attrib.), Paris, ca. 1385–90. Wool, original ht., ca. 16 ft. New York, Metropolitan Museum, The Cloisters.

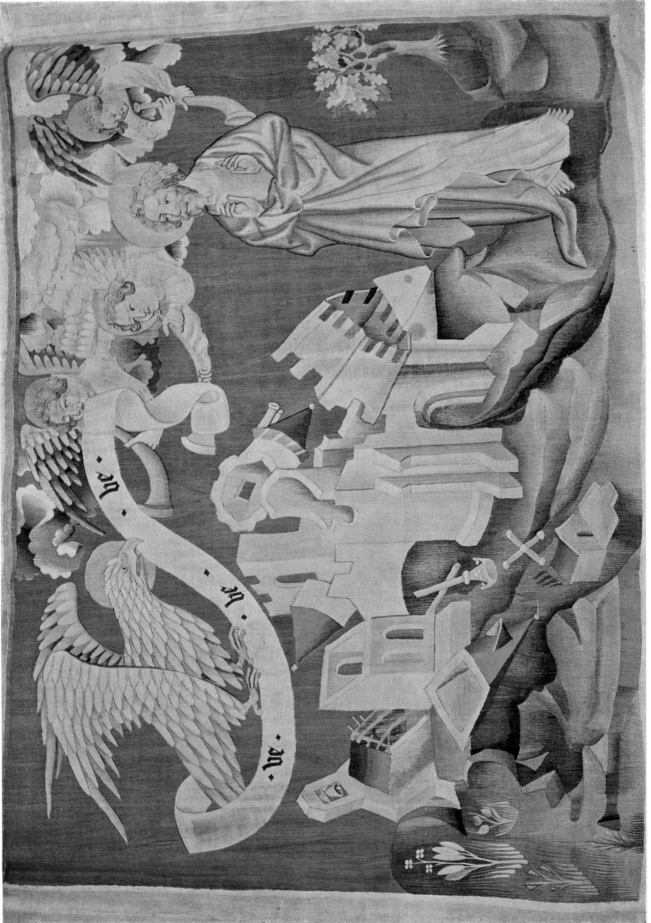

Pl. 393. The Apocalypse, detail with the Fall of Jericho, by J. de Bandol (Hennequin de Bruges) and N. Bataille, Paris, ca. 1381. Size of scene, ca. 6½×10 ft. Angers, France, Musée des Tapisseries.

Pl. 394. Saga of Jourdain de Blaye, detail, Arras, ca. 1400. Wool, full size, 10 ft., 9 in. × 12 ft., 6 in. Padua, Italy, Museo Civico.

Pl. 395. *Above*: *Minneteppich*, with lovers and fabulous beasts, Basel, ca. 1480. Wool, 3 ft., 9 in. × 8 ft., 5 in. Basel, Historisches Museum. *Below*: Christ on the Cross, with the Madonna and saints, environs of Lake Constance, ca. 1350. Wool, ht., ca. 29 in. New York, Metropolitan Museum.

Pl. 396. Crucifixion, detail, Arras, ca. 1420–30. Wool and gold thread, full ht., 13 ft., 7 in. Saragossa, Spain, Cathedral, Museo de Tapices.

Pl. 397. Story of Alexander the Great, detail, workshop of P. Grenier, Tournai, mid-15th cent. Wool, silk, gold and silver threads; full size, 13 ft., 7 in. × 32 ft., 4 in. Rome, Galleria Doria Pamphili.

Pl. 398. *Millefleurs. Left*: The Sense of Taste, detail, from the Lady with the Unicorn series, Loire region, ca. 1490–1500. Paris, Musée de Cluny. *Right*: Heraldic tapestry with the coat of arms of Charles the Bold, detail, Tournai, 1450–70. Wool, silk, gold and silver threads; full size, 10 ft. × 22 ft. 6 in. Bern, Historisches Museum.

Pl. 399. The Passion, detail with the Last Supper, Tournai, ca. 1460. Full size, 13 ft., 8 in. × 26 ft., 11 in. Rome, Vatican Museums.

Pl. 400. Christ giving the keys to St. Peter, detail, from the Acts of the Apostles series, cartoons by Raphael, woven by P. van Aelst, Brussels, ca. 1515–19. Wool and silk. Rome, Vatican Museums.

Pl. 401. The Communion of Herkenbald, detail, after a sketch by J. van Roome, Brussels, 1513. Brussels, Musées Royaux d'Art et d'Histoire.

Pl. 402. The Last Supper, workshop of P. Pannemaker (attrib.), Brussels, 1516. Wool and silk, 12 ft., 1½ in. × 19 ft., 7 in. Camaiore, Italy, Museo d'Arte Sacra.

Pl. 403. Panel with grotesques, cartoon by F. Ubertini (known as Bachiacca), executed by the workshop of N. Karcher, Florence, ca. 1550. Wool, silk, gold and silver threads. Florence, Uffizi.

Pl. 404. Indian on Horseback, after a painting by A. van der Eeckhout, Gobelins, 1687–88. Wool, 15 ft., 5 in. × 11 ft., 10 in. Paris, Mobilier National.

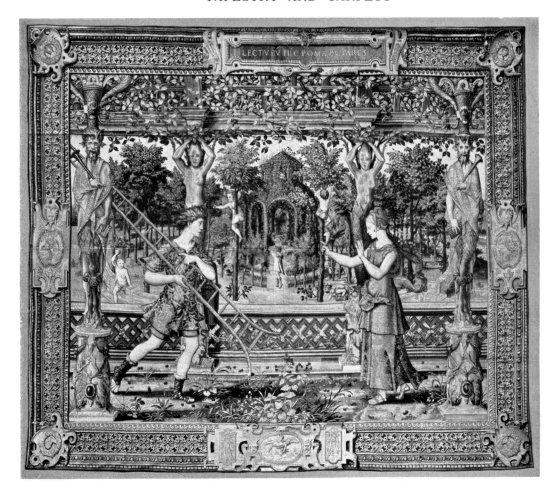

Pl. 405. *Above*: Vertumnus and Pomona, from a cartoon by J. C. Vermeyen, Brussels, mid-16th cent. Wool and metallic threads, 13 ft., 11¹/₂ in. × 16 ft., 5 in. Vienna, Kunsthistorisches Museum. *Below*: Judgment of Paris,
Oudenaarde (Flanders), second half of 16th cent. Turin, Coll. G. Agnelli.

Pl. 406. Episode from *Orlando Furioso*, woven by F. Spierincx, Delft, 1602. Wool and silk, full size, ca. 9×14 ft. Milan, Museo Poldi Pezzoli.

Pl. 407. *Above*: The Campaign against Licinius, cartoon after a design by Pietro da Cortona, ca. 1634. Tempera on paper attached to canvas, 10 ft., 7½ in. × 19 ft., 7¼ in. Florence, Coll. Corsini. *Below*: July and August, after a design by J. van der Hoecke, Brussels, ca. 1650. Vienna, Kunsthistorisches Museum.

Pl. 408. *Left*: The Vintage (Autumn), Bruges, 1664. Wool and silk, 13 ft., 6 in. × 13 ft., 9 in. Brussels, Musées Royaux d'Art et d'Histoire. *Right*: Gathering the Manna, detail, from the Triumph of the Eucharist series, designed by P. P. Rubens, woven by J. Raes, Brussels, commissioned ca. 1625-30. Wool and silk. Madrid, Descalzas Reales.

Pl. 409. The Triumph of the Eucharist over Idolatry, from the Triumph of the Eucharist series, designed by P. P. Rubens, woven by J. Raes, Brussels, commissioned ca. 1625–30. Wool and silk, 16 ft., 2 in. × 24 ft., 7 in. Madrid, Descalzas Reales.

Pl. 410. The Château of Chambord (September), from the Royal Palaces series (also known as "The Months"), designed by C. Lebrun, Gobelins (first series woven 1668–81), fifth repetition, 1776–82. Property of the Mobilier National, Paris; presently in the French Embassy, Rome.

Pl. 411. Don Antonio's Ball, from the Don Quixote series, centerpiece designed by C. A. Coypel and woven under M. Audran, border designed by C. Audran III, Gobelins, 1746–48. Wool and silk, 12 ft., 3 in. × 16 ft., 9 in. Turin, Palazzo Reale.

Pl. 412. *Left, above:* Kermis, detail, in the style of D. Teniers, Brussels, 18th cent. Wool and silk, full size, 10 ft. × 10 ft., 8¹/₂ in. *Below:* The Aviary, cartoon after F. Boucher, probably woven by J. P. Picon, Aubusson, second half of 18th cent. Wool and silk, 9 ft., 10 in. × 10 ft., 8 in. Both, Brussels, Musées Royaux d'Art et d'Histoire. *Right:* Juggler dancing a toy bear, cartoon by V. A. Cignaroli, woven by F. Demignot, Turin, ca. 1763-65. Wool and silk, 12 ft., 3¹/₂ in. × 9 ft., 8 in. Turin, Museo Civico.

Pl. 413. The Chinese Fair, detail, from the "Chinese Tapestries," after designs by F. Boucher, Beauvais, mid-18th cent. Turin, Palazzo Reale.

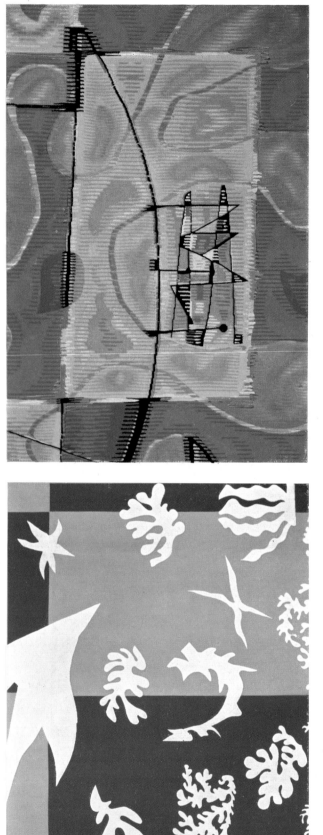

Pl. 414. Contemporary French tapestries. *Above, left:* Polynesia, detail showing the sea, cartoon by H. Matisse, Beauvais, 1946. Wool and linen, full size, 6 ft, 5 in. × 10 ft, 4 in. *Right:* The Sailing of the Ships, detail, cartoon by G. Singier, Beauvais, 1951. Wool, full size, ca. 9×7 ft. Both, Paris, Mobilier National. *Below, left:* Cocks, detail, cartoon by J. Lurçat, Aubusson, 1946. Full size, 8 ft, 2 in. × 9 ft, 7 in. *Right:* The Midnight Sun, cartoon by J. Lurçat, Aubusson, 1952. Full size, 5 ft, 4 in. × 9 ft, 7 in. Last two, property of the artist.

Pl. 415. "The Marby rug," from Anatolia or Caucasia, 14th–15th cent., found in Marby, Jämtland, Sweden. Wool with knotted pile, 5 ft., 3³/4 in. × 3 ft., 5 in. Stockholm, Statens Historiska Museum.

Pl. 416. Mameluke rug, from Egypt, ca. 1500. Wool, 6 ft., 2 in. × 4 ft., 3 1/2 in. Berlin, Staatliche Museen.

Pl. 417. Cairene rugs, used as table covers (?), Egypt, 16th cent. Wool. *Above*: W., 8 ft., 4 in., including flaps. London, Victoria and Albert Museum. *Below*: W., 7 ft., 11½ in. Washington, D.C., Corcoran Gallery of Art, W. A. Clark Coll.

Pl. 418. Medallion carpet, from Spain, late 16th cent. Wool, 14 ft., 11 1/2 in. × 6 ft., 10 in. London, Victoria and Albert Museum.

Pl. 419. Canvas-work rug with motifs related to those of the so-called "Holbein rugs" of western Anatolia, from Schaffhausen, Switzerland, 1533. Wool embroidery, 6 ft. × 4 ft., 6³/₈ in. Zurich, Schweizerisches Landesmuseum.

Pl. 420. Medallion Ushak rug, from western Anatolia, 16th cent. Wool, 7 ft., 5½ in. × 13 ft., 5 in. London, Victoria and Albert Museum.

Pl. 421. *Left*: Tapestry carpet bearing the arms of Sigismund III (Vasa) of Poland, from Kashan, Iran, ca. 1601. Silk, with gold and silver thread; 8 ft, 2½ in. × 4 ft, 6 in. Munich, Residenzmuseum. *Right*: Carpet with arms of the Kretkowski and Güldensztern families, from Poland, ca. 1665 (?). Wool. Munich, Bayerisches Nationalmuseum.

Pl. 422. Medallion and arabesque carpet, from northwest Iran (Tabriz?), first third of 16th cent. Wool, 26 ft., 6 in. × 13 ft., 7 in. New York, Metropolitan Museum.

Pl. 423. Medallion Tabriz rug, from the shrine of Sheik Ṣafī at Ardebil, Iran, 1539–40. Wool pile and silk, 34 ft., 6 in. × 17 ft., 6 in. London, Victoria and Albert Museum.

Pl. 424. *Left*: Great hunting carpet, designed by Sultan Muḥammad (?), detail, from Kashan, Iran, ca. mid-16th cent. Silk enriched with metal threads; full size, 22 ft., 4 in. × 10 ft., 6 in. Vienna, Österreichisches Museum für Angewandte Kunst. *Right*: Carpet with scenes from Persian romances, from Kerman (?), Iran, late 16th cent. Silk, 12 ft., 3¹/₂ in. × 8 ft., 10¹/₄ in. Paris, Musée des Arts Décoratifs.

Pl. 425. Multiple medallion and animal carpet, detail, from Tabriz, Iran, early 16th cent. Wool pile and silk; full size, 18 ft. × 9 ft, 10 in. London, Victoria and Albert Museum.

Pl. 426. Prayer rug, from Istanbul or Bursa, 1610. Wool pile and silk, ca. 6 × 4 ft. Berlin, Staatliche Museen.

Pl. 427. Star Ushak carpet, from western Anatolia, 17th cent. Wool, 7 ft., 10½ in. × 4 ft., 8 in. Berlin, Staatliche Museen.

Pl. 428. Persian carpet of so-called "Portuguese" type, 17th cent. Wool pile on cotton, w., 12 ft., 2¹/₂ in. Vienna, Österreichisches Museum für Angewandte Kunst.

Pl. 429. Border motif of a Persian carpet, probably from Isfahan, ca. 1600. Silk enriched with silver and gilded-silver threads; full size, 4 ft., 7 in. × 7 ft., ¹/₂ in. (motif ca. actual size). Venice, Museo Marciano.

Pl. 430. Chinese carpet, detail with central medallion, Ch'ing dynasty, 18th cent. Wool. Rome, Coll. Taliani De Marchio.

Pl. 431. Loom-woven carpet of folk production, detail, from Pescocostanzo, Italy, 18th cent. Wool; full size, ca. 10×5 ft. Rome, Museo Nazionale delle Arti e Tradizioni Popolari.

Pl. 432. Carpet, detail, designed by R. Adam, ca. 1775, for Osterley Park House, Middlesex, England, executed by T. Moore, Moor-fields, London (*in situ*, VIII, PL. 110). Full size, 17 ft., 3 in. × 14 ft., 10 in.

Pl. 433. Royal Savonnerie carpet, one of a group ordered by Louis XIV for the Great Gallery of the
Louvre, late 17th cent. Wool, 29$^{1}/_{2}$×16 ft. New York, Metropolitan Museum.

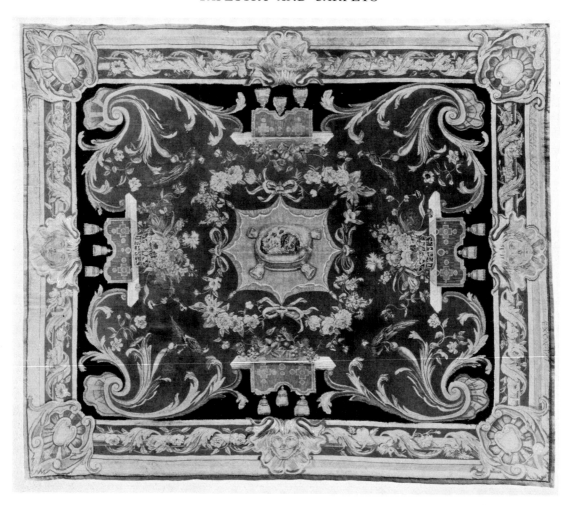

Pl. 434. *Above*: Carpet made by Passavant at Exeter, England, 1757. Wool, 14 ft., 9 in. × 18 ft. London, Victoria and Albert Museum. *Below*: English carpet, probably Axminster, 1780–90. Wool and flax, 16×23 ft. (border missing). New York, Metropolitan Museum.

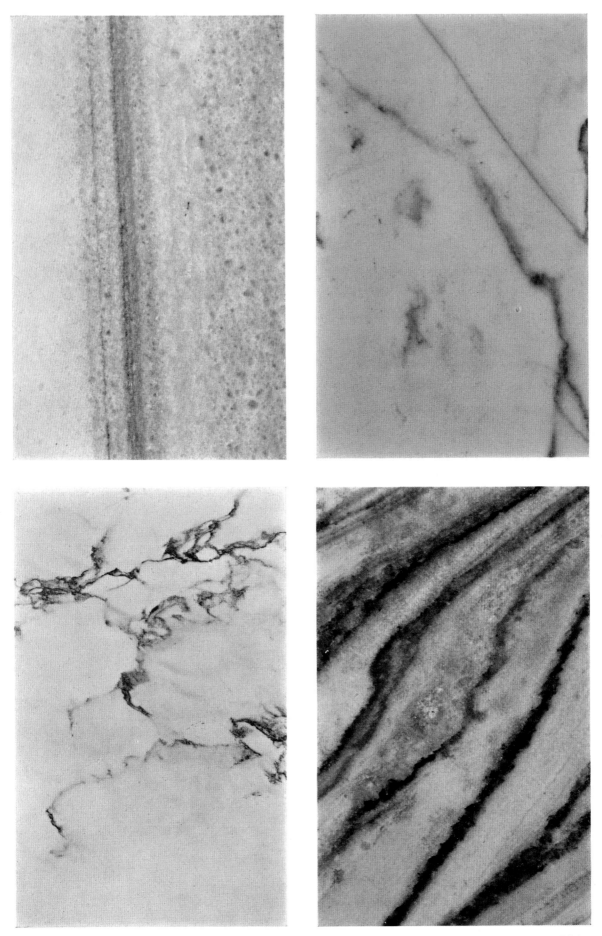

Pl. 435. Varieties of marble. *Above, left*: Pentelic. *Right*: Giallo antico, Algerian. *Below, left*: Paonazzetto. *Right*: Cipolin.

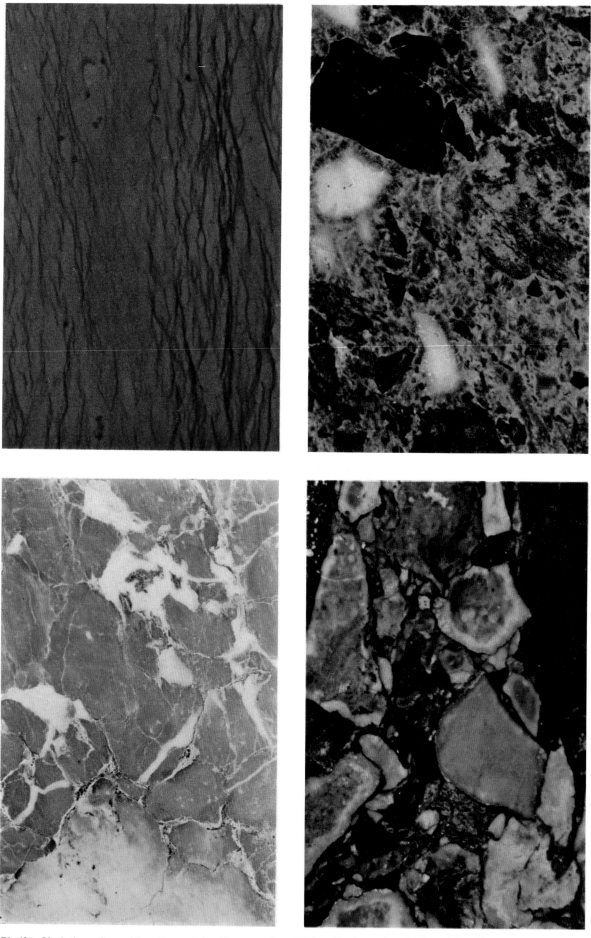

Pl. 436. Varieties of marble. *Above, left*: Rosso antico. *Right*: Verde antico. *Below, left*: Fior di pesco. *Right*: Breccia.

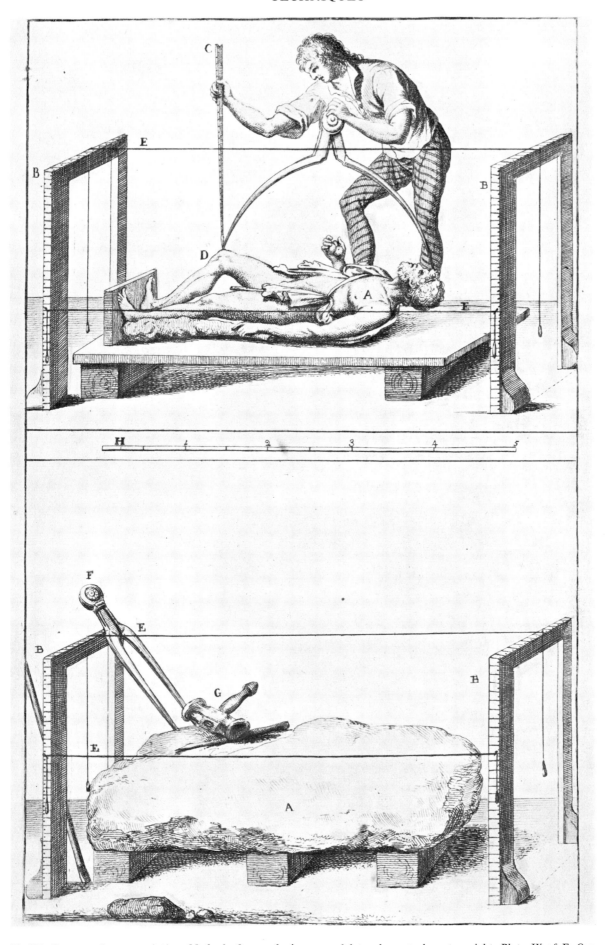

Pl. 437. Stone sculpture, pointing. Method of reproducing a model too large to be set upright, Plate IX of F. Carradori, *Istruzione elementare per gli studiosi della scultura*, Florence, 1802.

Pl. 438. Stone sculpture, showing various chisel marks in rough and smooth areas. Michelangelo, the Medici Virgin, detail, ca. 1521–31. Florence, S. Lorenzo, New Sacristy.

Pl. 439. Stone sculpture. *Above, left*: Flat relief with engraved details. Syro-Hittite orthostat showing an archer, from the palace of Kaparu, Tell Halaf, Syria, 9th–8th cent. B.C. Basalt, 22½ × 13¾ in. Paris, Louvre. *Right*: High relief showing drill work in hair and fleece and strong undercutting. Early Christian sarcophagus with the Good Shepherd, detail, Rome, 4th cent. Marble. Rome, Palazzo dei Conservatori. *Below*: Sculpture highly polished. A. Canova, Pauline Borghese, detail, 1805–ca. 1807. Marble. Rome, Galleria Borghese.

Pl. 440. Stone sculpture, hoists and scaffolding. Pieces of sculpture to be restored and the equipment needed for such an operation, Plate XIII of F. Carradori, *Istruzione elementare per gli studiosi della scultura*, Florence, 1802.

Pl. 441. Wood sculpture, with rear view showing hollowed-out trunk and joined parts. The Virgin and Child, Tuscan (?), 13th cent. Polychrome painting (partly original) and silver gilding (rings and Child's crown, later additions); ht., 5 ft. Castelnuovo dell'Abate, near Montalcino, Italy, Abbey church of S. Antimo.

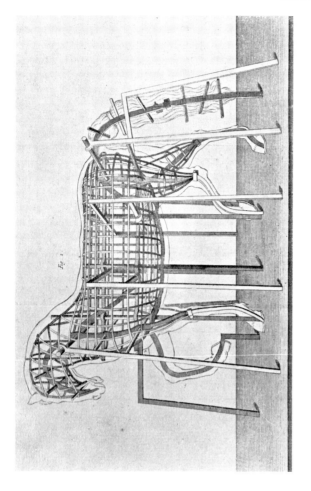

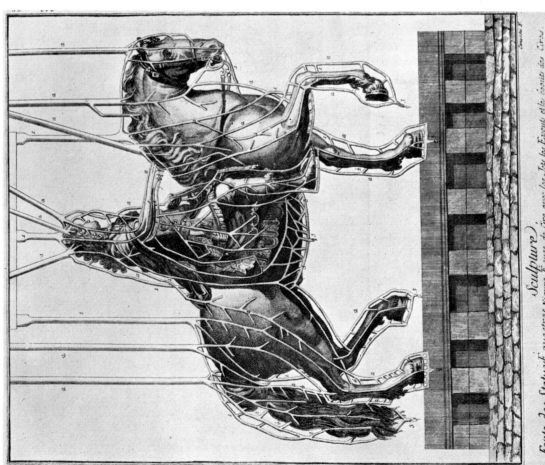

Fonte des Statues Equestres, Figure Equas de Cire, avec les Jets, les Events et le Egouts des Cires

Sculpture).

Pl. 442. Bronze, preparation of an equestrian figure for casting. Illustrations in the *Encyclopédie des Sciences, des Arts, et des Métiers*, 18th cent.: *Above, right*: Iron armature of the horse with supporting struts for the rider. *Left*: Figure modeled in wax, with gates and vents applied. *Below, right*: Cross section of the whole embedded in brickbats and (*far right*) covered with foundry earth reinforced by iron bindings. [Reproduced from the Lucca edition, Plates III, IV, V (234, 236, 237), Tome VIII, 1773, *Planches pour L'Encyclopédie des Sciences, des Arts Libéraux, et des Arts Méchaniques.*]

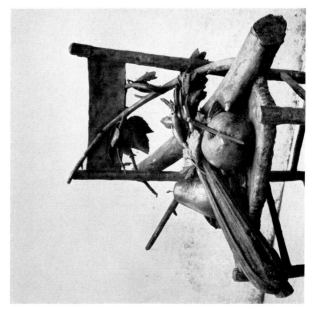

Pl. 443. Bronze, stages of a work by G. Manzù, Il Trofeo della Pace, 1962. *Left to right, above:* Support and initial section of the brass armature (for chair seat); elements modeled in plaster; wax coating, partially applied. *Below:* Addition of chair frame coated with plaster; the piece ready for casting with connecting bridges; the finished work, detail. Rome, private coll.

Pl. 444. Bronze sculpture, 13th cent. or earlier, showing deterioration and repairs. *Above* and *below, right*: Griffin, with wings replaced in 1284 and later restorations. *Below, left*: Lion, detail. Both, Perugia, Italy, Palazzo dei Priori, north façade.

Pl. 445. Bronze with silver inlay, showing patina and effects of corrosion after cleaning, Roman couch, from Amiternum, Italy, 1st–2d cent., details of end rest. Rome, Palazzo dei Conservatori.

Pl. 446. Pottery, stages in firing and glazing. *Above, left*: Unfired. *Right*: In the biscuit stage. *Below, left*: With glaze applied, ready for the second firing. *Right*: The finished piece, (Courtesy of the ceramist N. Caruso.)

Pl. 447. Ceramists at work. *Above*: Corinthian plaques showing (*left*) a potter shaping the vessel with a tool while turning the wheel and (*right*) a potter at the kiln. Both, Paris, Louvre (drawings from Rayet-Collignon, *Histoire de la Céramique grecque*, Paris, 1888). *Below, left*: Illustration of the third book, on the manner of painting, from a manuscript of C. Piccolpasso, *Li tre libri dell'arte del vasaio*, ca. 1556–59, fol. 57 v. (Pub. Rome, 1857; Pesaro, 1879; Eng. and Ital. ed., *The Three Books of the Potter's Art*, Victoria and Albert Mus., London, 1934.) *Right*: Potter at a modern wheel, shaping the lip of a bowl. Photograph by O. Savio.

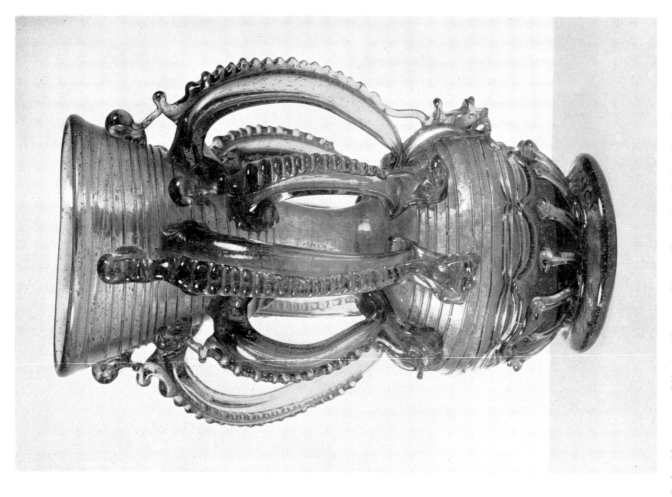

Pl. 448. *Left*: Pottery sculpture, showing hair shaped with a stick. Head from Taranto, Italy, 4th cent. B.C. Life-size. Taranto, Museo Nazionale. *Right*: Glass, blown, with raised threading and applied crested handles. Vase from Andalusia, Spain, 16th–17th cent. London, Victoria and Albert Museum.

Pl. 449. *Above*: Powdered pigments. *Left to right*: White, cadmium yellow, yellow ocher, vermilion, burnt umber, ultramarine, black. *Below*: Prepared oil colors, shown full-strength and (lower portion) mixed with white lead, exemplifying manufacturers' specimens applied to canvas and photographed for reproduction in printed charts.

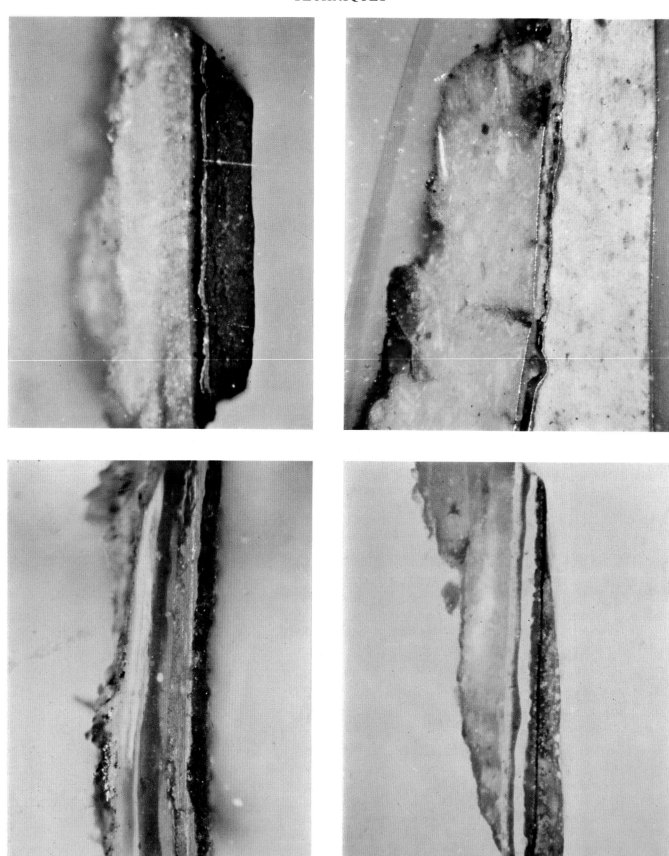

Pl. 450. Analysis of layers of paintings prior to restoration (cross sections of lifted fragments, magnification ca. 1:120). *Above, left* (layers from left to right): Ground, pigment, varnish, three layers of repainting. Madonna del Bosco, 14th cent. Sassari, Sardinia, Cathedral. *Right*: Ground, bole, gold, gesso, bole, gold. Madonna di S. Luca, prior to 13th cent. Rome, Convento di S. Maria del Rosario. *Below, left*: Two coats of ground, pigment, dirt, two layers of repainting, dirt. Madonna della Clemenza, 8th cent. (?). Rome, S. Maria in Trastevere. *Right*: Ground, four layers of pigment, varnish, stucco, repainting. St. Anthony, Umbrian school, 16th cent. San Marino, S. Francesco. (Photographs, Istituto Centrale del Restauro, Rome.)

Pl. 451. Painting, showing various stages of completion. Detail of the "Manchester Madonna," style of Michelangelo, first half of 16th cent.: blocking in of main design in opaque gray wash (background at top); light gray wash over gesso (above head); underpainting in various tones of gray with hatching in the manner of a pen-and-ink drawing and shadows in black (mantle, intended to be finished in blue); outlines engraved in unhardened paint or ground (neckline and shoulder at right); hair, probably unfinished; flesh areas, in finished state. Panel; full size, 41¹/₂×30¹/₄ in. London, National Gallery.

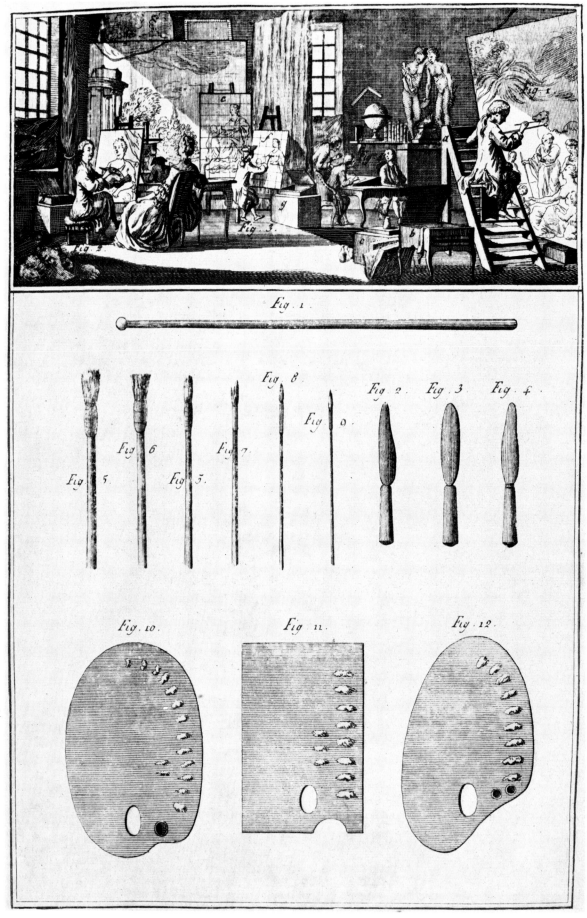

Pl. 452. Various types of painters and their tools. Illustration in the *Encyclopédie des Sciences, des Arts, et des Métiers*, 18th cent. *Above*: Portrait painting, copying with a grid, miniature and historical painting. *Below*: Maulstick, brushes, knives, palettes. [From the Lucca edition, Plate I (137), Tome VIII, 1773.]

Pl. 453. Painters (*above*) and engravers (*below*) at work, after drawings by J. van der Straet (Johannes Stradanus), ca. 1550, engraved by T. Galle (from the series "Nova Reperta" by H. Collaert and T. Galle, first half of 17th cent.).

Pl. 454. Etching. G. B. Piranesi, Parti di Ampio Magnifico Porto..., from *Opere varie di architettura, prospettive, grotteschi*, 1750. *Above*: The etched copperplate. *Below*: A print. Rome, Calcografia Nazionale.

Pl. 455. Varieties of wood, varnished samples exemplifiying range of color and variations in grain. *Left to right, above*: Oak; mahogany. *Center*: Brazilian rosewood (palisander); *Afrormosia elata*, a so-called "teak" from West Africa. *Below*: Walnut; Slavonian ash. (For examples of pictorial use see V, PLS. 434, 440, 454.)

Pl. 456. Pietra dura. *Left to right, above*: Agate; amethyst; lapis lazuli. *Second row*: Jasper; chalcedony. *Third row*: Coralline limestone; brecciated jasper. *Below*: Corsican jasper; malachite.

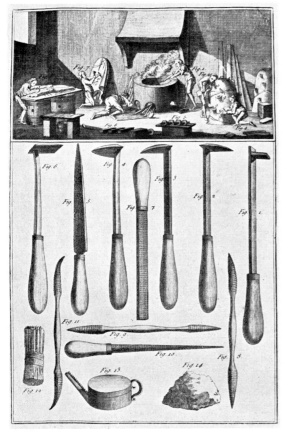

Pl. 457. Metalwork. *Above*: Cretan mold for a placque, from Sitia, 1700–1400 B.C., shown with a plaster impression. Schist, 3¹/₂×8⁵/₈ in. Heraklion, Crete, Archaeological Museum. *Below*: Lead foundry with tools (*left*) and goldsmith's workshop with examples (*right*). Illustrations in the *Encyclopédie des Sciences, des Arts, et des Métiers*. (Reproduced from the Lucca edition, Tome VIII, 1773.)

Pl. 458. Jewelry. *Above*: Repoussé and granulation. Etruscan ornament with human heads, lion, chimera, and sphinxes, from the Barberini Tomb, Palestrina, Italy, 7th cent. B.C. Sheet gold. Rome, Museo di Villa Giulia. *Below, left*: Cloisonné. Visigothic buckles, from Spain, ca. 6th cent. Bronze with vitreous paste and stones. Barcelona, Museo Arqueológico. *Right*: Filigree. Barbarian brooch, from Senise, Italy, 7th cent. Gold with turquoise enamel, diam., 3¹/₂ in. Naples, Museo Nazionale.

Pl. 459. Image of Kālabhairava, one of the Bhairavas ("the Fearful"), Katmandu, Nepal, 18th cent. Stone.

Pl. 460. The goddess Cāmuṇḍā, from Dinajpur, Pakistan, 11th cent. Black basalt, ht., 23 in. Rajshahi, Pakistan, Varendra Research Society Museum.

Pl. 461. Tanka with rDo rje aٜjigs byed, terrifying manifestation of Mañjuśrī, Tibet, 18th cent. Rome, Museo Nazionale d'Arte
      Orientale.

Pl. 462. Tanka with rTa mgrin yab yum (Skr., Hayagrīva) as a manifestation of Padmasaṃbhava, Tibet, 18th cent. Without borders, 24³/₄×16¹/₂ in. Rome, Museo Nazionale d'Arte Orientale.

Pl. 463. Tanka with rDo rje k'yuṅ (Skr., Vajragaruḍa), Tibet, 18th cent. Rome, Museo Nazionale d'Arte Orientale.

Pl. 464. Buddhist divinity, painting on a pillar in the Tahōtō, Ishiyamadera, Shiga prefecture, Japan, late 12th cent. (?).

Pl. 465. Kwihyŏng, shown in a stylized landscape, from Puyo, Korea, 7th cent. Gray earthenware tile, 11¼×11⅛ in. Seoul, National Museum of Korea.

Pl. 466. *Left*: gŚiṅ rje gśed (Skr., Yamāntaka), a manifestation of Mañjuśrī as the Destroyer of the Lord of Death, Tibet, 18th cent. Gilded bronze, ht., 7¹/₈ in. Prague, National Gallery. *Right*: mGon po p'yag drug pa (the Black or Blue Mahākāla), Tibet, 18th cent. or earlier. Gilded bronze, ht., 17¹/₈ in. Prague, Náprestek Museum.

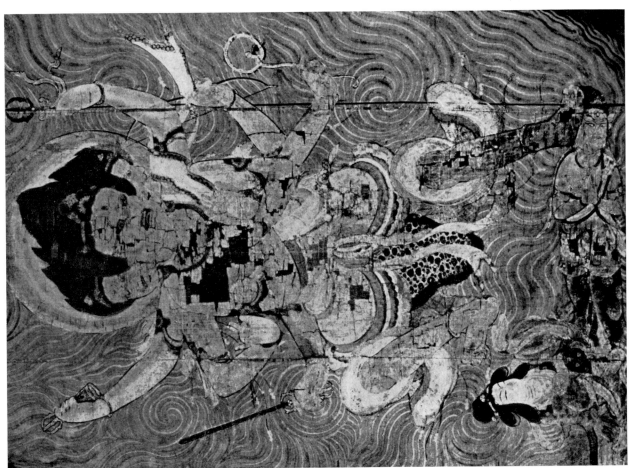

Pl. 467. *Left*: Gōsanze, one of the Five Great Kings (Godai Myōō), Japan, ca. 1100. Color on silk, 4 ft., 11 in. × 4 ft., 2 in. Kyoto, Tōji. *Right*: Zōchō, one of the Shitennō (Four Heavenly Kings), Japan, 12th cent. Ink and slight color on silk, 4 ft., 5 in. × 3 ft., 1½ in. Nara, Kōfukuji.

Pl. 468. Douris (attrib.), Athena, shown wearing the aegis with gorgoneion, and Jason disgorged by the Colchian dragon, detail of the interior of a kylix, 490–470 B.C. Terra cotta, diam. of kylix, 11³/₄ in. Rome, Vatican Museums.

Pl. 469. B. Cellini, Perseus with the head of Medusa, mid-16th cent. Bronze. Florence, Loggia della Signoria.

Pl. 470. Michelangelo, Christ in Judgment, detail of the Last Judgment, 1535–41. Rome, Vatican, Sistine Chapel, west wall.